P9-DOG-546

FRONT PAGE HISTORY OF THE WORLD WARS

I WANT YOU FOR U.S. ARMY

NEAREST RECRUITING STATION

FRONT PAGE HISTORY OF THE WORLD WARS

as reported by

The New York Times

Edited by
Arto DeMirjian, Jr.
and
Eve Nelson

ARNO PRESS

NEW YORK • 1976

A Note to the Reader

Original copies of *The New York Times* were not available to the publisher. This volume, therefore, was created from 35mm microfilm.

Library of Congress Cataloging in Publication Data

Main entry under title:

Front page history of the World Wars as reported
by the New York times.

1. European War, 1914-1918–Sources.
2. World War, 1939-1945–Sources. I. DeMirjian, Arto. II. Nelson, Eve, 1952- III. New York times.
D505.F93 940.3 76-7428
ISBN 0-405-06674-0

Manufactured in the United States of America

2 3 4 5 6 7 8 9 10

WORLD WAR ONE

"All the News That's Fit to Print."

The New York Times.

THE WEATHER
Local showers today; Tuesday, fair; fresh, shifting winds, becoming northwest.
For full weather report see Page 17.

VOL. LXIII...NO. 20,610. NEW YORK, MONDAY, JUNE 29, 1914.—EIGHTEEN PAGES. ONE CENT In Greater New York, Jersey City and Newark. | TWO CENTS

CALIFORNIA GOES ON ROCKS IN FOG

Tory Island, Off Northwest Irish Coast, Scene of Mishap to Anchor Liner.

IN NO IMMEDIATE DANGER

Bows Badly Stove In and Ship Taking Water Through Two Holes in Hold.

PASSENGERS STILL ABOARD

Ship Carries 1,000 Persons—Rescue Vessels, Called by Wireless, Standing By Throughout Night.

Special Cable to THE NEW YORK TIMES.

LONDON, June 28.—The Anchor liner California, with more than 1,000 persons aboard, has gone ashore on Tory Island, off the northern coast of Ireland. The destroyer Swift, the fastest and largest vessel of her class in the world, and other vessels have gone to her assistance in response to wireless calls for aid.

The ship is said to be in no immediate danger.

LONDONDERRY, June 28.—In a thick fog and rain which rendered Tory Island invisible from the mainland, the Anchor Line steamer California, bound from New York for Glasgow, went ashore tonight on the rocks off that island. Wireless calls for help brought speedy assistance from a number of small gunboats and torpedo boats which were patrolling the Northwest Irish Coast for gun runners in connection with the Ulster movement.

The latest news received here is that the California is stuck fast on the rocks, but is in no immediate danger. She struck with such force that the lower part of her bows was badly stove in, and she is making water through two holes in her forehold and second hold.

The steamer, which has on board 121 saloon and more than 300 second cabin passengers, lies in five fathoms of water forward and seven fathoms aft.

The passengers and crew are still on board. There was no panic when she struck the rocks.

Several steamers, including one liner, and the gunboats are standing by, and other vessels are expected to arrive at the scene during the night.

LONDON, June 28.—Capt. Coverley of the California late tonight sent out this wireless dispatch:

"Ran ashore in fog about half mile from the lighthouse. Di dnot hear foghorn. Sea quiet. Three men-of-war and steamer Cassandra standing by to transfer passengers."

CARRIED 841 PASSENGERS.

Place Where California Struck Ten Miles Out of Her Course.

The California sailed from New York at noon on Saturday, June 20, for Glasgow via Moville with 116 first-class, 350 second-class, and 375 third-class passengers. She signaled Malin Head yesterday afternoon, and should have been off Moville about 8 o'clock. Tory Island is more than ten miles out of her course.

The California carries a crew of 240 officers and men, and was commanded by J. A. Coverley, one of the most experienced Captains in the Anchor Line service. This was his second voyage on the California after having been twelve years on the Calabria in the New York-Mediterranean service, and more recently in command of the liner Elysia in the Indian service of the Anchor Line.

The California is the second largest vessel of the Anchor Line in the New York trade, and was built at Glasgow by D. & W. Henderson Bros. in 1907. She is 470 feet long, with a beam of 58 feet 2 inches and a depth of hold of 23 feet 6 inches. She is a twin-screw steamer, with an average speed of 15 knots.

The Captains and other officers of the Anchor Line are accustomed to fog around the coasts of Scotland and Ireland and always keep a man on the lookout on the foc'sle head, as well as in the crow's nest, and the officers are on double watches nearing the land, which means that there are three on the bridge all the time in addition to the commander, who comes up and stays while the fog lasts.

The stormy, rocky coast of the North of Ireland is looked upon by mariners as the most dangerous part of the British Isles, and steamers proceed very cautiously when entering or leaving Lough Foyle, where the small calling port of Moville is situated.

This is the third steamship within two weeks that has gone ashore during a fog in those waters. The hospital ship Maine was wrecked on the west coast of Scotland. Her patients and crew were taken off in small boats. She became a total wreck. The liner Buelow of the North German Lloyd on her way up the English Channel to Bremen from China went ashore near Portland. She landed passengers and cargo.

The fog was also responsible for three collisions, beginning with the one between the Empress of Ireland and the Storstad in the St. Lawrence River, in which 1,019 lives were lost. Another took place in the English Channel off Portsmouth between the North German Lloyd liner Kaiser Wilhelm II. and the Johnston Line steamer Incemore, and 300 miles east of Sandy Hook on June 3 a collision occurred between the American liner New York and the Hamburg-American steamer Pretoria.

Capt. Kinnard of the Cameronia, a sister ship of the California in the Anchor Line service, was found last night on board his ship, which is laid up for overhauling at Robbins's Dry Dock in the Erie Basin.

"The California was a good, strong ship," he said, "and unless she is badly on the reef there will be hope of getting her off safely. At Tory Island

Continued on Page 2.

STAYS IN AIR 21 HOURS.

Berlin Aviator's Feat Held to be a World's Record.

BERLIN, June 28.—Herr Landmann, an aviator, today concluded a non-stop flight of 21 hours 49 minutes.

It is asserted that this flight constitutes a world record.

DEWEY IN CANAL PARADE.

Will Be Invited to Make Trip Aboard His Old Flagship Olympia.

Special to The New York Times.

WASHINGTON, June 28.—Admiral George Dewey may take his old flagship, the Olympia, through the Panama Canal next March in the naval parade. Rear Admiral Clark, retired, has been ordered to take command of his old ship, the Oregon, for the occasion, and Secretary Daniels said this afternoon that he had decided to invite Admiral Dewey to take part. If the Admiral does not feel like making the journey via the canal, he may go overland to San Francisco and go aboard the Olympia upon the arrival of the pageant fleet there.

The President and Secretary Daniels will make addresses upon the arrival of the fleet at the exposition city. It is likely that Admiral Dewey and Admiral Clark also will speak. The entire brigade of midshipmen will be taken to San Francisco for the occasion. This will probably take the place of their annual cruise.

The Oregon and the Olympia will be moored at a specially constructed wharf and will be on exhibition throughout the entire exposition. Behind them will be anchored seven typical modern naval ships—a dreadnought of the New York or Oklahoma type, a battleship of the Connecticut or Minnesota type, an armored cruiser of the Tennessee or Montana type, one of the three scout cruisers, a destroyer, a submarine, and a collier, each of the latest build. In addition, the entire Atlantic Fleet will remain throughout nearly the whole of the exposition.

Neither Admiral Dewey nor Rear Admiral Clark has been aboard his ship since relinquishing their commands shortly after the close of the Spanish-American war.

A NEW GAME FOR BROADWAY.

But Auto Owners Hope Trundling Stolen Tires Won't Become Popular.

Harry E. Sullivan with his brother and two women rode up to Shanley's Restaurant, in West Forty-third Street, last evening in a limousine auto with a new white tire strapped like a life preserver to the back. Two men who had the appearance of chauffeurs came down the street after the owners of the auto entered the restaurant. With businesslike briskness they unbuckled the new white tire and trundled it down the street. The taxicab starter at Shanley's scratched his head. Then he spoke to Patrolman Louis Fick.

"They did it so natural," he explained, "that I didn't think to bother them."

The patrolman jumped into an auto and started in pursuit of the tire. By its tread-prints on the damp pavement he followed it down to Ninth Avenue, up to Forty-fourth Street, around the corner, and there the artful dodgers foiled him by rolling it into the street where its trail was lost in a maze of tire tracks. The tire was worth $75.

"If it's as easy as that," said Mr. Sullivan when he heard of his loss, "rolling rubber hoops in Broadway is apt to become a popular pastime. The first rule of the game is: 'A rolling tire must gather no moss.'"

SCORES BRYAN AND TREATY.

Francis B. Loomis Calls Colombian Agreement "Stupendous Blunder."

Special to The New York Times.

SAN FRANCISCO, June 28.—Bryan's proposed treaty between the United States and Colombia is vicious as to motives and purpose, says Francis B. Loomis, former Assistant Secretary of State. In a statement here tonight Mr. Loomis said:

"Bryan's Colombian treaty is a covert attempt to loot the United States Treasury by lobbyists and political brigands, into whose hands the Secretary of State is playing.

"Bryan and the President are trying to besmirch and discredit the achievement of the previous Administration, which made the canal a reality.

"The treaty is one of the most stupendous blunders made by Bryan, who is running wild with his 'world peace' theories. The United States owes Colombia nothing, either by treaty or otherwise.

"Mr. Bryan's contention that the people of Latin America feel aggrieved because we refuse to permit the Colombian troops to cross the Isthmus for the purpose of engaging in bloody encounters, and closing the lines of transit is not supported by ascertainable facts. The truth is the important Governments of South America such as Argentina, Brazil, and Chile care nothing about Colombia, and they deplore her misdeeds as much as we do."

STATE'S TOLL OF ACCIDENTS

Automobiles Killed Nearly Half as Many as Railroads in April.

Special to The New York Times.

ALBANY, June 28.—There were nearly half as many deaths in New York State from automobile accidents during April as there were from railroad accidents. This is shown in the vital statistics issued by the State Department of Health for April. The deaths resulting from railroad accidents numbered 58, from automobiles 25, from street cars 15, and other vehicles 20. Landslides killed 12 individuals, and 3 others died from injuries inflicted by animals. There were 128 suicides during the month and 35 homicides.

The other external causes of death ran the total up to 735 for the month.

$120,000 FOR SHACKLETON.

Sir James Caird's Gift for His Antarctic Expedition.

Special Cable to THE NEW YORK TIMES.

LONDON, June 28.—Sir James Key Caird, the millionaire jute manufacturer of Dundee, has given $120,000 toward the expenses of the Shackleton antarctic expedition.

Sir James made the gift after Sir Ernest Shackleton had personally explained to him the programme which he hoped to carry out.

Sir Ernest says the gift puts the expedition on a sound basis, and there is now no fear that it will not start well equipped.

FEDERALS DESERT AGUASCALIENTES

Next Big Town South of Zacatecas Is Evacuated by Huerta's Forces.

CARRANZA-HUERTA DEAL?

American, Reaching Vera Cruz, Reports Parleys Are On in Mexican Capital.

ENVOYS TOLD OF REBEL NOTE

Says He Must Consult His Associates—Answer Is Regarded as Favorable.

ZACATECAS, June 27, via EL PASO, June 28.—Aguascalientes, capital of the States of the same name, has been evacuated by the Federals, according to information reaching Gen. Villa's headquarters today.

Owing to this, his plan of campaign has been changed, and the troops of the division are returning to Torreon.

Part of the division left last night. The rest will leave for the north today. Gen. Villa will follow his troops during the day. Last Wednesday it was announced that the Villa troops would be taken toward Aguas Calientes overland.

Late reports show that the losses of the Federals here were much greater than at first supposed. The number of prisoners taken by Villa's troops exceed 4,300. The number of killed was close to that figure.

The latest casualty report of the Constitutionalists was over 700 dead and 1,100 wounded, but these figures are not complete.

Special to The New York Times.

EL PASO, June 28.—A message was received today stating that 2,000 Federals, fleeing from Zacatecas toward San Luis Potosi, had been overtaken by Gen. Benavide, head of the Zaragoza brigade, and had been decisively defeated at Salinas, a point about midway between Zacatecas and San Luis Potosi. Four hundred Federals were killed or wounded, according to the message.

CARRANZA-HUERTA DEAL?

Report of Peace Negotiations Comes from Mexico City.

VERA CRUZ, June 28.—Secret peace negotiations between Gen. Carranza and President Huerta have been in progress in the capital, according to Antonio Magnon, an American who arrived from Mexico City today. Mr. Magnon said it was positively known that representatives from Carranza had been in the capital for several days in conference with President Huerta, but that the details of the discussions had been kept secret.

It was thought in the capital that a peace agreement between Huerta and Carranza based upon Huerta resignation, was certain to come soon, Carranza having been forced to make some concessions because of his disagreements with Gen. Villa and Gen. Angeles.

It is reported in Mexico City that supporters of Villa and Carranza have been fighting near Monterey.

Mr. Magnon said also that President Huerta's volunteer forces at San Luis Potosi, including all the noted chieftains, such as Gen. Pasquale Orozco and Gen. Antonio Rojas, had refused to cooperate further with the regular army or to withdraw toward the capital, but would fight the Constitutionalists in that region. The volunteer leaders, most of whom are veterans of the three years' border warfare, and all frontiersmen, and, according to Mr. Magnon, say that the Federal recruits are hopeless as soldiers and only hamper the actions of the veteran volunteers.

Gen. Joaquin Maass, Federal commander at San Lois Potosi, went to the capital last Friday to confer with President Huerta, Mr. Magnon said, and was still there when Magnon left Saturday. Mr. Magnon said Gen. Maass, whom he had known for years, confirmed the reported action of the volunteers.

The Federals are fortifying Aguascalientes against a Constitutionalist advance, but it is understood in the capital that Gen. Villa plans to direct his next blow against Queretaro, cutting both the National and Central Railways and compelling the abandonment by the Federal forces of much territory in order to prevent themselves from being cut off from the capital.

Mr. Magnon said that he learned at Soledad that the Federals were gathering railway equipment for the narrow gauge Inter-Oceanic Railroad and preparing for the withdrawal of Gen. Rubio Navarrete and his entire force, now stationed at the San Francisco railroad bridge, guarding it against a possible American advance.

Gen. Garcia Pena, according to Mr. Magnon, is still at Soledad, but there are many indications that the Federal forces before Vera Cruz are being rapidly reduced, and that only a thin fringe of rural guards will be left to maintain the outposts. Mr. Magnon said it was generally believed in the capital that the refusal of the volunteers to take orders from the regular officers would be a severe blow to President Huerta, as they were his most trustworthy troops.

MEDIATING POWERS VEXED?

Rumor That They Resent Mexico's Delay in Thanking Them.

Special Cable to THE NEW YORK TIMES.

MEXICO CITY, June 28.—It is rumored here that the mediating powers are somewhat offended by Mexico's delay in thanking them for their good offices, and also that they consider Gen. Huerta's recent statement to THE NEW YORK TIMES rather impolitic. It is pointed out that, whatever the fate of the peace arrangements may be, the

Continued on Page 5.

Propose Pan-American Memorial to Columbus

A splendid tomb topped by a great light is proposed to be erected in Santo Domingo, in the Caribbean Sea, by subscriptions from peoples of all lands. See

NEXT SUNDAY'S TIMES.

OUR GUNS FIRE ON SANTO DOMINGO

Few Shots from the Machias Stop Bombardment of Puerto Plata by President Bordas.

WARNED BY CAPT. RUSSELL

Told Not to Endanger Foreigners in Attack on Rebels There—Refugees Taken Off by Our Boats.

Special to The New York Times.

WASHINGTON, June 28.—Following general instructions from the Navy Department to protect the lives and property of Americans and foreigners in Santo Domingo, the little American gunboat Machias on Friday afternoon entered the inner harbor of Puerto Plata, and with a few shots from her main battery silenced a battery of President Bordas's forces that was bombarding the town.

The bombardment was in violation of emphatic orders from Capt. Russell, commanding the American squadron, that the attack on the city, which is in the hands of rebels, be conducted in such a way as not to imperil the lives of foreigners.

Capt. Russell is in personal command of the first line battleship South Carolina, that was detached from service at Vera Cruz when conditions in Santo Domingo became threatening. His dispatch to the department, which, like all dispatches from Santo Domingo, took two days to come, makes no mention of casualties. His dispatch follows:

PUERTO PLATA, June 26, 1914.

This afternoon, about 5:30, when the Bordas artillery ashore fired shells into the city of Puerto Plata, the Machias anchored in the inner harbor and with some shots from her main battery stopped the artillery fire into the city, after which there was no further firing. We have the situation well in hand, and no additional vessels, either United States or foreign, will be needed to prevent the bombardment of Puerto Plata. The prompt stopping of the artillery fire into the city this afternoon will have a very reassuring effect upon the Americans and other foreigners in the city, who have recently displayed great anxiety about their protection and safety.

At 8:30 P. M. Friday the revenue cutter Algonquin took on board forty-two persons for passage to San Juan, thirty-three being Porto Ricans and nine Americans, ten men, thirteen women, and nineteen children, and then steamed for San Juan. The Clyde Line steamer Seminole, from Norfolk en route to Santo Domingo City, arrived at 3 P. M. Friday, and after delivering mail took away from Puerto Plata four persons—one French, two Spanish, and one Chinaman. The Clyde Line steamer Algonquin, en route to New York, arrived at 7 P. M. Friday and took away from Puerto Plata twenty-four persons—five Americans, thirteen British, three French, and three Cubans. These passengers were put on board the three vessels named by the South Carolina boats. RUSSELL.

The Navy Department today was emphatic that Capt. Russell's summary enforcement of his orders indicated no change in policy, and that the silencing of President Bordas's battery did not mean that American intervention on a wider scale would be undertaken. The orders had been emphatic, and the attacking forces seemed to think they could be disregarded with impunity. The United States has never indicated its sympathies as to the contending forces, though as under the treaty it was responsible for the Custom House at Puerto Plata, its obligation in this instance was clearly not to encourage attack by the Government's troops.

The Machias is a gunboat of 1,177 tons, 204 feet in length, and with 32 feet beam. Her main battery consists of eight guns of about 4-inch calibre and four smaller guns. She was formerly used by the Naval Militia of Connecticut.

Secretary of the Navy Daniels said the other day that there was no intention to send more ships to the island, and Friday's incident is not thought to have changed his mind on that score.

$500,000 FIRE AT DOVER, N. J.

Incendiaries Destroy Richardson & Boynton Stove Plant.

DOVER, N. J., June 28.—All of the plant of the Richardson & Boynton Company, except the shipping department building, was destroyed by fire today. The firm manufactured stoves and ranges, and its plant, which was Dover's largest industry, covered thirty acres of ground. The loss is $500,000, partly covered by insurance. The works, which ordinarily employ 1,100 men, were shut down three weeks ago for repairs.

Charles Helfer, a night watchman, says he made the rounds of the works at 6:30 A. M. and found everything all right. At 7:30 o'clock he saw smoke coming from the trimming shop. Men who were in the street say they saw flames in three or four different places at the same time.

Dover's two steamers and an auto chemical engine and truck manned by the Volunteer Fire Department responded to the general alarm. All the buildings were frame except the shipping building, which is built of concrete. The water pressure was inadequate, and the flames spread rapidly to the casting and cleaning shop, the mounting, boiler, patent filing, drill and patternmakers' shops, each in a separate building. Three Lackawanna Railroad box cars in the yard near the shipping building were burned. All the finished stock on hand was in the shipping building. The firemen concentrated their efforts to save that building.

For an hour or two there was fear the flames might spread to the town. The firemen successfully defended the nearest buildings.

Incendiarism is suspected. Secretary and Treasurer W. L. R. Lynd, who is also Mayor of Dover, said he couldn't account for the fire. There was no fire in any building of the plant, and the engines had been cold since the shutdown. It is recalled that a threatening letter was sent to Mayor Lynd demanding he should prevent the delivery of the Slattery anti-Catholic lectures. He declined to interfere, and the lectures were delivered on May 15 and 16 last.

The plant will be rebuilt at once. At noon a gang of laborers was put to removing the débris. The company has offices in New York.

HEIR TO AUSTRIA'S THRONE IS SLAIN WITH HIS WIFE BY A BOSNIAN YOUTH TO AVENGE SEIZURE OF HIS COUNTRY

Francis Ferdinand Shot During State Visit to Sarajevo.

TWO ATTACKS IN A DAY

Archduke Saves His Life First Time by Knocking Aside a Bomb Hurled at Auto.

SLAIN IN SECOND ATTEMPT

Lad Dashes at Car as the Royal Couple Return from Town Hall and Kills Both of Them.

LAID TO A SERVIAN PLOT

Heir Warned Not to Go to Bosnia, Where Populace Met Him with Servian Flags.

AGED EMPEROR IS STRICKEN

Shock of Tragedy Prostrates Francis Joseph—Young Assassin Proud of His Crime.

Archduke Francis Ferdinand and his Consort the Duchess of Hohenberg

Slain by Assassin's Bullets.

Special Cable to THE NEW YORK TIMES.

SARAJEVO, Bosnia, June 28, (By courtesy of the Vienna Neue Freie Presse.)—Archduke Francis Ferdinand, heir to the throne of Austria-Hungary, and his wife, the Duchess of Hohenberg, were shot and killed by a Bosnian student here today. The fatal shooting was the second attempt upon the lives of the couple during the day, and is believed to have been the result of a political conspiracy.

This morning, as Archduke Francis Ferdinand and the Duchess were driving to a reception at the Town Hall a bomb was thrown at their motor car. The Archduke pushed it off with his arm.

The bomb did not explode until after the Archduke's car had passed on, and the occupants of the next car, Count von Boos-Waldeck and Col. Morizzi, the Archduke's aide de camp, were slightly injured. Among the spectators, six persons were more or less seriously hurt.

The author of the attempt at assassination was a compositor named Gabrinovics, who comes from Trebinje.

After the attempt upon his life the Archduke ordered his car to halt, and after he found out what had happened he drove to the Town Hall, where the Town Councillors, with the Mayor at their head, awaited him. The Mayor was about to begin his address of welcome, when the Archduke interrupted him angrily, saying:

"Herr Burgermeister, it is perfectly outrageous! We have come to Sarajevo on a visit and have had a bomb thrown at us."

The Archduke paused a moment, and then said: "Now you may go on."

Thereupon the Mayor delivered his address and the Archduke made a suitable reply.

The public by this time had heard of the bomb attempt, and burst into the hall with loud cries of "Zivio!" the Slav word for "hurrah."

After going around the Town Hall, which took half an hour, the Archduke started for the Garrison Hospital to visit Col. Morizzi, who had been taken there after the outrage.

As the Archduke reached the corner of Rudolf Street two pistol shots were fired in quick succession by an individual who called himself Gavrio Princip. The first shot struck the Duchess in the abdomen, while the second hit the Archduke in the neck and pierced the jugular vein. The Duchess became unconscious immediately and fell across the knees of her husband. The Archduke also lost consciousness in a few seconds.

The motor car in which they were seated drove straight to the Konak, where an army Surgeon rendered first aid, but in vain. Neither the Archduke nor the Duchess gave any sign of life, and the head of the hospital could only certify they were both dead.

The authors of both attacks upon the Archduke are born Bosnians. Gabrinovics is a compositor, and worked for a few weeks in the Government printing works at Belgrade. He returned to Sarajevo a Servian chauvinist, and made no concealment of his sympathies with the King of Servia. Both he and the actual murderer of the Archduke and the Duchess expressed themselves to the police in the most cynical fashion about their crimes.

ARCHDUKE IGNORED WARNING.

Servian Minister Feared Trouble if Heir Went to Bosnia.

Special Cable to THE NEW YORK TIMES. [Dispatch to The London Daily Mail.]

VIENNA, June 28.—When the news of the assassination of the Archduke Francis Ferdinand and the Duchess was broken to the aged Emperor Francis Joseph he said: "Horrible, horrible! No sorrow is spared me."

The Emperor, who yesterday left here for Ischl, his favorite Summer resort, amid acclamations of the people, will return to Vienna at once, in spite of the hardships of the journey in the terrible heat.

The Archduke, who was created head of the army, went to Bosnia to represent the Emperor at the grand manoeuvres there. This was the first time the Archduke had paid an official visit to Bosnia. The Emperor visited the provinces immediately after their annexation, in 1908, and the manner in which he mixed freely with the people was much criticised at the time, as those in his party were always afraid lest some Slav or Mohammedan fanatic might attempt the monarch's life. The Emperor's popularity, however, saved him from all danger of this kind.

Before the Archduke went to Bosnia last Wednesday the Servian Minister here expressed doubt as to the wisdom of the journey, saying the country was in a very turbulent condition and the Servian part of the population might organise a demonstration against the Archduke. The Minister said if the Archduke went himself he certainly ought to leave his wife at home, because Bosnia was no place for a woman in its present disturbed state.

The Minister's word proved correct. The people of Sarajevo welcomed the Archduke with a display of Servian flags, and the authorities had some difficulty in removing them before the Archduke made his state entry into the city yesterday, after the conclusion of the manoeuvres. In these manoeuvres were the famous Fifteenth and Sixteenth Army Corps, which were stationed on the frontier throughout the recent Balkan war, and they carried out the evolutions before the Archduke.

Greeted with Cheers.

The details of the tragedy, as received in Vienna, were as follows: The Archduke was driving in a motor car toward the Town Hall in Sarajevo, with the Duchess of Hohenberg by his side. A large crowd assembled to watch them go by. The Archduke, raising his hand to his military cap, acknowledged the cheers, while the Duchess was smiling and bowing, her pretty face framed by her blonde hair.

Suddenly the Archduke's sharp eye caught sight of a bomb hurling through the air. His first thought was for his wife, and he threw up his arm in time to catch the bomb, which thus was turned aside from its course and fell on the pavement and exploded. The Archduke's motor car hastened on its way, its occupants unharmed, but the two Adjutants who were seated in the next motor car were injured by splinters from the bomb. Several persons on the pavement were very seriously hurt by the explosion of the bomb, which was thrown by a young man named Tabrinovitch, (Gabrinovics,) who is a typist from Trebenje, in Herzegovina, and is of Servian nationality. He was arrested some twenty minutes later.

The Archduke and his wife left the Town Hall, intending to visit those who had been injured by the bomb, when a schoolboy 19 years old, named Prinzip, who came from Grahovo, fired a shot at the Archduke's head. The boy fired from the shelter of a projecting house.

Wore Bullet-Proof Coat.

The boy must have been carefully instructed in his part, for it was a well-guarded secret that the Archduke always wore a coat of silk strands which were woven obliquely, so that no weapon or bullet could pierce it. I once saw a strip of this fabric used for a motor-car tire, and it was puncture-proof. This new invention enabled the Archduke to brave attempts on his life, but his head naturally was uncovered.

The Duchess was shot in the body. The boy fired several times, but only two shots took effect. The Archduke and his wife were carried to the Konak, or palace, in a dying condition.

Later details show that the assassin darted forth from his hiding place behind a house and actually got on the motor car in which the Archduke and his wife were sitting. He took close aim first at the Archduke, and then at the Duchess. The fact that no one stopped him, and that he was allowed to perpetrate the dastardly act indicate that the conspiracy was carefully planned and that the Archduke fell a victim to a political plot. The aspiration of the Servian population in Bosnia to join with Servia and form a great Servian kingdom is well known. No doubt today's assassination was regarded as a means of forwarding this plan.

Break News to Children.

The Archduke's children are at Glumex, in Bohemia, and relatives already have left Vienna to break the news to them. The Duke of Cumberland motored to Ischl immediately upon receipt of the news and was received by the Emperor, who will arrive in Vienna at 6 o'clock tomorrow. The bodies of the Archduke and his wife will not be brought to Vienna until tomorrow a week.

The Archduke Charles Francis Joseph, the new heir to the throne, is at Reichenau, near Vienna, with his wife, Princess Zita of Parma, and their little son and daughter. He is expected in Vienna tonight.

When the first news of the assassination became known in Vienna, early this afternoon, crowds collected in solemn silence and discussed the report, which was not credited at first. Every one connected with the press was stormed by crowds asking whether confirmation had been received, and on hearing the truth they said, "How awful!" and then dispersed, to go about their ordinary business or pleasure. The newspapers are getting out extra editions, and the whole city talks of nothing else.

New Heir Popular.

The Archduke Charles Francis Joseph, who is now heir to the throne, always has enjoyed great popularity. He was trained for the throne from the first, although he was kept somewhat in the background, being sent to country garrisons. He was not allowed to undertake to act as the representative of the Duchy of Vienna to as great an extent as the Viennese would have wished. This, however, did not detract from his popularity, while the Princess Zita, his wife, won all hearts before she married the heir to the throne, and the birth of a son two years ago completed her popularity, if, indeed, anything was lacking.

General opinion here connects the assassins with the Servian faction, and it is feared that it will lead to serious complications with that unruly kingdom, and may have far-reaching results. The future of the empire is a subject of general discussion. It is felt that the Servians have been treated too leniently, and some hard words are being said about the present foreign policy.

All the public buildings are draped in long black streamers and the flags are all at half-mast.

BRAVERY OF ARCHDUKE.

Gave First Aid to Those Wounded by the Bomb.

SARAJEVO, Bosnia, June 28.—Archduke Francis Ferdinand, heir to the Austro-Hungarian throne, and the Duchess of Hohenberg, his morganatic wife, were shot dead in the main street of the Bosnian capital by a student today while they were making an apparently triumphant progress through the city on their annual visit to the annexed provinces of Bosnia and Herzegovina.

The Archduke was hit full in the face and the Duchess was shot through the abdomen and throat. Their wounds proved fatal within a few minutes after they reached the palace, whence they were hurried with all speed.

Those responsible for the assassination took care that it would prove effective, as there were two assailants, the first armed with a bomb and the other with a revolver. The bomb was thrown at the royal automobile as it was proceeding to the Town Hall, where a reception was to be held, but the Archduke saw the deadly missile coming and warded it off with his arm. It fell outside the car and exploded, slightly wounding two aids de camp in a second car, and half a dozen spectators. It was on the return of the procession that the tragedy was added to the long list of those that have darkened the pages of the recent history of the Hapsburgs.

As the royal automobile reached a prominent point in the route to the palace, an eighth grade student, Gavrio Prinsip, sprang out of the crowd and poured a fusillade of bullets from an automatic pistol at the Archduke and the Duchess. Both fell mortally wounded.

Prinsip and a fellow-conspirator, a compositor from Trebinje, Nedeljo Gabrinovics, barely escaped lynching by the infuriated spectators and were finally seized by the police, who afforded them protection. Both men are natives of the annexed province of Herzegovina.

Wards Off the Bomb.

The first attempt against the Archduke occurred just outside the Girls' High School. The Archduke's car had restarted after a brief pause for an inspection of the building, when Gabrinovics hurled the bomb. This was so successfully warded off by the Archduke that it fell directly beneath the following car, the occupants of which, Count von Boos-Waldeck and Col. Merizzo, were struck by splinters of iron.

Archduke Francis Ferdinand stopped his car, and after making inquiries as to the injuries of his aids and lending what aid he could, continued his journey to the Town Hall. There the Mayor began the customary address, but the Archduke sharply interrupted and snapped out, "Herr Burgomeister, we have come here to pay you a visit and bombs have been thrown at us. This is altogether an amazing indignity."

After a pause, the Archduke said: "Now you may speak."

On leaving the hall the Archduke and his wife announced their intention of visiting the wounded members of their suite at the hospital on their way back to the palace. They were actually bound on their mission of mercy when, at the corner of Rudolf Street and Franz Josef Street, Prinsip opened his deadly fusillade.

A bullet struck the Archduke in the face. The Duchess was wounded in the abdomen and another bullet struck her in the throat, severing an artery. She fell unconscious across her husband's knees. At the same moment the Archduke sank to the floor of the car.

Plunges Into River.

After his unsuccessful attempt to blow up the imperial visitors Gabrinovics sprang into the River Miljachka in an effort to escape, but witnesses plunged after him and seized him.

A few yards from the scene of the shooting an unexploded bomb was found.

"All the News That's Fit to Print."

The New York Times.

THE WEATHER
Fair today and Thursday; fresh north and northeast winds.
☞For full weather report see Page 15.

VOL. LXIII...NO. 20,640. NEW YORK, WEDNESDAY, JULY 29, 1914.—EIGHTEEN PAGES. ONE CENT In Greater New York, Jersey City and Newark. Elsewhere TWO CENTS.

AUSTRIA FORMALLY DECLARES WAR ON SERVIA; RUSSIA THREATENS, ALREADY MOVING TROOPS; PEACE OF EUROPE NOW IN KAISER'S HANDS

MME. CAILLAUX FREED BY JURY

Wild Tumult in Court After the Verdict—Mobs in Streets Display Anger.

'MURDERESS!' CRIES CROWD

Spectacle of Opposing Counsel Embracing Calms the Uproar for a Moment.

MME. CAILLAUX RECEIVES

Attired in an Evening Gown, Is Congratulated by Her Friends — Says Labori Obtained Acquittal.

Special Cable to THE NEW YORK TIMES.

PARIS, July 28.—The jury in the trial of Mme. Henriette Caillaux, wife of the ex-Premier and ex-Minister of Finance, tonight acquitted her of the charge of murdering, on March 16, Gaston Calmette, editor of the Figaro.

The jury had been out for fifty minutes. Although no one expected a severe sentence, the verdict for the moment stunned all in the courtroom except a crowd in the extreme rear, which apparently had a premonition of what was going to happen and was prepared to voice its emotions in loud cheers.

M. Caillaux evidently had a similar vision, for exactly at the moment when the jury left the court room to go through the form of meditating and deliberating its verdict the large 'aillaux limousine, stocked with pil- 's, rugs, and attendants, drew aside he entrance to the prisoners' exit he Conciergerie.

the time the angry crowd left rt room and a mob of several d in the street had realized ad happened, the released ad signed the book at the rie and had been safely vay.

on of gendarmes surrounded prison and the Palais de adjoining it from early evening, but the crowd broke the ranks nd a wild fight ensued.

Mobs Shout "Assassin!"

The boulevards until a late hour were filled with mobs numbering thousands, yelling "Assassin!" and "Down with Caillaux!" The crowds were finally dispersed by dragoons.

There was pandemonium in the courtroom from the time the jury went out until the guards cleared it half an hour after the verdict was returned. It was impossible for anybody to sit, see, or hear. Free fights occurred all over the place, even within the rail marking the space reserved for the court officials. When the jury returned the noise reached the climax, Judges and guards trying to produce order.

It was several minutes before the foreman of the jury could be heard. After the verdict Mme. Caillaux, who had been lying back in her chair, threw her arms about her counsel, Maitre Labori. M. Caillaux was not in court, but was in his car outside.

The demonstrations in the courtroom were chiefly against the verdict, there being "boos" and hisses and cries of "Assassin!" Finally there was a round of cheers for Maitre Labori and another for Maitre Chenu, counsel for The Figaro, who smiled grimly as the verdict was read.

The day's session was devoted to the summing-up speeches of the barristers. There were few incidents, except at the beginning, when the crowd, which was bigger than on any preceding day, became unruly.

At a critical moment of Maitre Chenu's speech—just as he began to describe the scene of the shooting—Mme. Caillaux had another fainting spell, and was carried from the prisoners' inclosure.

There were many arrests of boulevard demonstrators tonight. The trouble would probably have been more serious had not the war situation attracted the greater attention.

Prisoner Falls on Labori's Neck.

PARIS, July 28.—Mme. Caillaux was acquitted after a trial lasting nine days.

The announcement of the jury's verdict was followed by the wildest tumult.

Mme. Caillaux tottered and fell on the neck of her counsel, Fernand Labori, and embraced him. Her hair was undone and fell over her shoulders. Her hat dropped to the floor. The spectators stood up on desks and chairs. "Caillaux!" "Labori!" and cries of "Caillaux! Assassin!" merged into one.

The din was deafening. Several groups of barristers came to blows, and Republican Guards, in an endeavor to separate them, joined in the mêlée. The spectacle of Maitre Labori and Maitre Chêne, the latter counsel for the Calmette family, embracing each other, calmed the tumult for a moment, but it was redoubled when they left the building with Mme. Caillaux.

Failing to make himself heard, the presiding Judge, followed by the other lges, marched out of the room. The vocates took complete possession of e court, and some of them mounted ie Judges' desks and harangued the rowd. The guards then cleared a porion of the court, and, comparative quiet eing re-established, Presiding Judge Albanel returned and read the judgment, rdering the release of Mme. Caillaux.

Much shaken with emotion, Mme. Caillaux departed by the witnesses' door, the guards making a lane through the crowd. She covered her face with her hands as if to shield herself from the furious cries of "murderess!" by way of a number of narrow corridors and back staircases, reaching a small side door in the Palace of Justice, where an automobile was waiting, and she drove off unobserved.

M. Caillaux left the building by the main entrance on the arm of his devoted friend, Deputy Pascal Ceccaldi, amid mingled cheers and hoots.

Thus ended the most sensational trial that the Paris courts have had to deal with in years. Each day provided its dramatic thrill, and although the verdict has been pronounced the ultimate outcome cannot be foretold.

The session of the court today was devoted to speeches by counsel. Mme. Caillaux had come into the prisoner's dock pale and worn, and she collapsed in the course of the address of Maitre Chene, who denounced her bitterly.

Prosecutor's Speech Mild.

The speech of the Procurator General, Jules Herbaux, was unusually mild in tone. To the jurors he said: "Your duty, as the defenders of the interests of society, requires you to find a verdict of guilty, but no one expects you to be pitiless."

Maitre Labori, who came last, delivered a masterpiece of passionate eloquence. He concluded amid tempestuous applause:

"My wish is that Mme. Caillaux shall leave here acquitted, and that the press shall be purified. Let us keep our anger for our enemies abroad. Let us leave this court resolute and united to face the perils which threaten us!"

Mme. Caillaux had been becoming visibly weaker as the sitting continued today, and appeared unconscious of what was taking place in court. A hot-water bottle was placed beneath her feet and a cushion at her back soon after she entered the court.

Meanwhile Maitre Edward Seligman, one of the attorneys representing the family of the murdered editor, continued his address. He said:

"The sons of Gaston Calmette asked us to bring them to this court to seek justice. We refused to do so, but do not forget, gentlemen of the jury, with what anguish the orphans await your verdict. You have heard witness after witness speak in praise of the late M. Calmette. There has been only one discordant note, and that came from M. Caillaux. What connection with the case has the fortune of the murdered man? How many millions must a man have in order to permit his being assassinated with complete impunity?"

Following Maitre Seligman came Maitre Chenu, and his cutting analysis of the actions of Mme. Caillaux on the day of the tragedy was too much for the prisoner. She collapsed and fell in a heap on the floor of the prisoners' enclosure.

At the moment Mme. Caillaux swooned Maitre Chenu was saying:

"I will speak of nothing except the assassination of M. Calmette. I will ask the accused whether, when she spoke of her love for her daughter, she thought of the two children of M. Calmette, whose pictures never left him. I shall not attempt to go into the biography of Mme. Caillaux. She is a cool, sensible woman, without emotion or pity. She has tears only for herself. She worked with tenacity to break up her lover's home. You see the result—the mistress triumphed over the lawful spouse. They are bound up in each other—in their happiness, in their hopes, even in their murder plans.

"M. Caillaux is a man of inordinate and limitless ambition, whose power rests on his own audacity and on the fear he inspires.

"M. Caillaux omitted to tell his wife of the assurances given by President Poincaré that Calmette was incapable of printing private letters. They did not fear that. What they feared was the publication of the report by Victor Fabre on the Rochette swindle.

"The husband's violent words at the lunch table decided the wife to substitute herself for him, and she prepared the assassination with as much calm as a society woman fitting in calls between two tea parties."

"Down With Caillaux!"

Demonstrations against the Caillaux verdict occurred in several places tonight. In the Boulevards excited crowds discussing the merits of the case, grew to large proportions, and when the jury's verdict became known there were shouts of derision and cries of "Down with Caillaux!"

In one section the mob became so disorderly that mounted Republican Guards were hastily summoned to assist the police in quelling the disturbances. A large number of police and rioters were injured, and many arrests were made.

Maurice and Jean Rostand, sons of the dramatist, were among those taken into custody.

The Figaro office was also the scene of a demonstration.

After dining at home with her husband and a few friends Mme. Caillaux attired in a handsome evening gown, received a number of intimate acquaintances.

"It is Maitre Labori," she said, "to whom I owe the good fortune to be finally free. He pleaded today with all his fine talent, and I am profoundly grateful to him."

Press Condemns the Verdict.

Special Cable to THE NEW YORK TIMES.

PARIS, Wednesday, July 29.—The acquittal of Mme. Caillaux rouses scanty but hostile comment. The Eclair says: "When the news was published yesterday Paris growled." Echo de Paris says: "The country will attribute the result to the baneful influence of politics."

The Figaro says: "It is the most enormous scandal of our epoch and covers the radical republic with mud and blood. It is an abominable parody of justice. Mme. Caillaux has torn an acquittal from a dazed jury, a terrified Government, and sold Judges."

The Matin gives an account of the incidents following the acquittal and refrains from comment, as does The Journal.

STORY OF THE CRIME.

Shooting Due to Calmette's Newspaper Campaign Against Caillaux.

The Caillaux case, the most celebrated French trial since the Dreyfus case, began on the evening of March 16, when Gaston Calmette, editor of The Figaro, was shot in his office by Mme. Henriette Caillaux, wife of Joseph Caillaux, ex-Premier and Minister of Finance in Premier Doumergue's Cabinet. He died a few hours later. The shooting was the consequence of a vigorous newspaper campaign carried on by Calmette against Caillaux.

Caillaux is an excellent financier and campaign manager. He was Premier in 1911, holding office during the Morocco crisis, and resigning in January, 1912, on account of popular dissatisfaction at the settlement made with Germany at that time.

Calmette's attacks charged, among other things, that Caillaux had used his influence to delay the trial of the swindler, Henri Rochette, in 1908, so as to give him time to escape to Mexico, and that as Minister of Finance he had promised to certain claimants against the Government $1,200,000 on condition that they subscribe 80 per cent. of that sum to the Radical campaign fund. It is said that Calmette had various letters in his possession charging that Caillaux was a tool of Germany in the Morocco crisis, which he had not yet published at the time of his death.

WARBURG IS WON, HITCHCOCK THINKS

Expects Nominee for the Reserve Board to Appear Before Committee.

SECRET CONFERENCE HERE

Banker Is Made to Understand There Is No Discrimination Against Him.

TECHNICAL POINT EXPLAINED

Charles R. Crane Called to White House, Presumably to Get Offer of Jones's Place.

Senator Gilbert M. Hitchcock of Nebraska, who has been acting as Chairman of the Banking and Currency Committee during the absence of Senator Owen in Europe, had an unofficial conference in this city last night with Paul M. Warburg in which he urged on Mr. Warburg that he should appear before the committee, which has under consideration his nomination for membership in the Federal Reserve Board.

Senator Hitchcock was found at the Pennsylvania Station just as he was leaving for Washington at midnight. He seemed greatly pleased with the result of his conversation with Mr. Warburg, and said he saw no reason now why Mr. Warburg should not consent to appear before the committee.

"Did Mr. Warburg say whether or not he would do so?" Senator Hitchcock was asked.

"No," the Senator replied, "but he seemed to understand after our talk just how the committee felt toward him, and that there had been no discrimination against him, and he indicated in every way that he would be willing to appear. I believe Mr. Warburg's attitude has been changed by the explanation I have been able to make to him. I think it has been made clear to him that it is the wish of President Wilson that he should understand that no desire to discriminate against him was intended."

Senator Hitchcock had been down to Southampton, L. I., to visit his family and stopped over in the city a few hours on his way to Washington. He would not say where the interview was held.

No Discrimination Intended.

"I think Mr. Warburg's attitude," he said, "was due to the feeling that there was some discrimination in the committee against him, but generally a committee always has the privilege of inviting before it for investigation men who are nominated to Judgeships and other high offices. This is due only to a desire on the part of the Senate to acquaint itself fully with these men and what they have done.

"Personally I know that Mr. Warburg is an important man in the business and financial world, and has been connected with big things, but he has been in this country only a comparatively short time, and it is to inform itself further of his achievements that the committee has invited him before it. I think the Senate feels the same way toward Mr. Warburg as the committee feels.

"The reason Mr. Warburg felt that he had been discriminated against was probably because three of the five nominees for members of the Federal Reserve Board were readily confirmed. Two of these were officials in Washington, and there was little that could be asked of them that was not already known in official life in Washington. The third man was W. P. G. Harding of Birmingham, Ala. He wrote out for the committee a complete history of his life, and this was sufficient for its purposes."

SUGGEST A. BARTON HEPBURN.

Administration Still Hopeful of Warburg's Confirmation.

Special to The New York Times.

WASHINGTON, July 28.—While the Administration is hopeful that Paul M. Warburg will appear before the Senate Committee on Banking and Currency to testify in regard to his appointment on the Federal Reserve Board, nothing definite has been heard from Mr. Warburg on the subject.

While the impression prevails that Mr. Warburg would be confirmed if he found it consistent with his dignity to accept the committee's invitation to appear, his continued refusal has resulted in the suggestion of others to take his place. A. Barton Hepburn of the Chase National Bank of New York was the most prominently mentioned today, though there is nothing official indicating that serious consideration has been given to any candidate other than Mr. Warburg.

Senators of the Committee on Banking and Currency were mildly shocked today to learn that Chairman Owen favored for the place his lifelong friend, the Rev. Dr. J. M. T. Johnston, a retired minister now in the banking business in Kansas City. At Mr. Owen's request Dr. Johnston appeared before the committee last Summer in support of the Owen-Glass Currency bill. Much of the anecdotal part of his testimony has been stricken from the committee's record. Quickly wearying of the academic topic assigned to him, the Rev. Dr. Johnston branched out into stories of an intimate domesticity that were received in silent astonishment by his mixed audience.

C. R. CRANE CALLED BY WILSON

Chicago Capitalist May Be Offered Jones's Place.

Special to The New York Times.

CHICAGO, July 28.—Charles R. Crane, who is about to retire from the Presidency of the Crane Company, has been invited to Washington by President Wilson.

The action of the President is taken to mean that Mr. Crane will be offered the place on the Federal Reserve Board made vacant by the withdrawal of the nomination of Thomas D. Jones.

According to the intimate friends of Mr. Crane, he is not disposed to undertake the duties of a member of the Federal Reserve Board, since they would tie him to Washington. Should the President persuade him, however, to take the position, it is declared he undoubtedly would be of service in the organization and administration of the new banking and currency systems, as his long business experience would be invaluable in this connection.

President Wilson is to see Mr. Crane at the White House tomorrow.

Notice Sent to the Powers of the Opening of Hostilities.

SERVIAN VESSELS SEIZED

Sharp Fighting Begins Along the River Drina on the Bosnian Frontier.

COUNTER INVASION PLAN

Montenegrin and Serb Armies to Invade Bosnia and Start a Rebellion There.

GREY'S PEACE PLAN FAILS

Kaiser Declines to Join in Conference to Exert Pressure on Austrian Ally.

BUT REPLY IS CONCILIATORY

And London Still Has Faith That His Influence Will Avert General Conflict.

Special Cable to THE NEW YORK TIMES.

LONDON, Wednesday, July 29.—Austria-Hungary declared war on Servia yesterday. The declaration was made at noon to the Servian Government by means of an open telegram. The Austro-Hungarian forces followed up the declaration by seizing two Servian vessels at Orsova, on the Danube, together with a number of boats.

The question whether the Austro-Servian war can be localized and a European Armageddon can be avoided now depends, so far as anything can depend on one man, upon Emperor William.

THE NEW YORK TIMES correspondent referred yesterday to the hopes of the British Foreign Office that the Kaiser's personal influence would be exercised for peace. Now that Germany has refused to accept Sir Edward Grey's suggestion of an ambassadorial conference and Austria has declared war on Servia, the only hope of avoiding that greater conflict, which the whole world apprehends, lies in the conversations that are proceeding directly between Vienna and St. Petersburg, and particularly the turn which can be given them by the German monarch.

The Kaiser's Role.

THE TIMES correspondent is informed on the best authority that great hopes are based on Emperor William's influence in this direction. This information is reflected in The Times editorial this morning, which says:

"There is reason to believe that in the most exalted quarter of Germany the maintenance of European peace is warmly and honestly desired. The pressure from all manner of influential personages and groups is doubtless being exerted to overcome the pacific leanings of the Emperor. It may tax his powers of resistance severely, but in foreign affairs he is the undoubted master and he has often shown that he has a will and judgment of his own. We still hope with some confidence that they will be exerted on the side of that peace which it has often been his honorable boast he helped to keep for six and twenty years.

"Our Paris correspondent repeats that grounds exist for the belief that Germany has already given a better proof of her wish for peace than is known to France."

In London Germany's reply to Sir Edward Grey's proposal is not looked upon as a diplomatic rebuff. The tone of the reply was conciliatory, and Prince Lichnowsky, the German Ambassador here, explained that Germany, while most anxious to co-operate with Great Britain in the attempt to find a settlement, was unable to accept the rôle of a mediator so far as the Austro-Servian dispute was concerned, as she must eschew anything calculated to create the impression that she was not in entire harmony with her Austrian ally. The German Ambassador particularly insisted on the weight which Germany attaches to co-operation with Great Britain with a view to localizing the conflict.

The conversations at St. Petersburg between Count Szapary, the Austrian Ambassador, and Premier Sazonoff, are understood to be proceeding on a tone which gives good hope that it will be found possible to prevent the conflagration spreading beyond the present limits.

Up to a late hour this morning no definite confirmation had been received here of the various reports that Russia had begun a general mobilization.

Statements that the army corps in the west and southwest of Russia were being brought up to their war strength were accepted without hesitation as part of the precautionary measures which every country in Europe, big or small, with the exception of Spain, Portugal, and Switzerland, considered necessary. The news of the issue of orders for a general mobilization of Russian forces would mean that a great European conflict would be precipitated.

May Strike First at France.

Berlin dispatches state that Germany has made it quite clear in St. Petersburg that even "a partial mobilization" will be answered immediately by the mobilization of the German Army, which, according to one dispatch, "nothing could then hold back."

This is in accordance with what is known of the German war policy. The German General Staff does not contemplate simultaneous campaigns on a great scale against both France and Russia. France can mobilize nearly as quickly as herself. Russia takes some weeks to mobilize and more weeks to move her armies from mobilization centres to the frontier.

Germany's safety lies in taking advantage of the slowness of Russian mobilization. She will content herself with a comparatively slight screen of troops along her Eastern frontier to hold back the Russians and will launch all her striking force against the French lines of defense, hoping to pierce them and break the back of the French armies before Russia is ready to act.

The next few hours is likely to show whether Germany thinks the extensive military movements which are taking place along the Russian side of the German-Austrian frontiers constitutes a partial mobilization.

In this connection extreme importance attaches to the statement made in a special dispatch to THE NEW YORK TIMES from St. Petersburg that Russia will declare a general mobilization if Austria occupies Belgrade.

A military expert who is acquainted with the European situation said, when shown the dispatch, that he hoped the correspondent's forecast was incorrect, for such a step would precipitate an Armageddon, as Germany could not afford to throw away the advantage which the slowness of Russian mobilization, the chief weakness of the Dual Alliance, gave her, and would immediately strike at France.

Probable Plans of Opposing Armies.

The Servians are reported to have formed a division in the Sanjak of Novi Bazar and to be concentrating strong forces on the River Lim, which runs through the Sanjak. Montenegrin troops are stated to be in close contact with the Servian forces.

The object of these movements, according to The London Times, is apparently to threaten Herzegovina and Bosnia, where the nature of the ground is favorable for guerrilla operations.

Rumors of fighting on the Drina River that forms the frontier between Bosnia and Servia, were circulated in Vienna and Berlin. Part of the Austro-Hungarian forces is expected to advance across the Drina in the direction of Kraguoyevatz. The Servian forces, on the other hand, are expected to cross into Bosnian territory with the object of raising an insurrection among the Bosnian Serbs.

It is stated on Austrian authority that the object of Austria-Hungary is to crush and disarm Servia and, in particular, capture the Servian artillery and compel Servia to reduce her army in future to inoffensive proportions.

Austria-Hungary also is determined to sieze Mount Lovtchen, a Montenegrin stronghold, which commands the important naval base of Bocche di Cattaro, despite the opposition which Italy is expected to offer to this proceeding.

Three Italian training ships now on a visit to the Clyde have been recalled.

Austrian naval concentration has been ordered at Fiume.

Black Sea Lights Out.

The Russian authorities have ordered all lights along the Russian Black Sea coast extinguished, with the exception of the Chersonesf Lighthouse near Sebastopol harbor. Sebastopol itself is open only to Russian warships.

Russia has ordered the mobilization of fourteen army corps in the neighborhood of the Austrian frontier, but these orders are understood to be merely preparatory, not final. In diplomatic circles it is stated that Germany will not reply to this partial mobilization unless a Russian army is mobilized also in the north.

Two French Cabinet councils were held yesterday. No mobilization order has been issued, but considerable military preparations are being made. All officers and men on leave have been recalled to the colors. The French Socialists have issued a manifesto calling upon the Government to use its influence in Russia in favor of peace.

Military preparations are proceeding in Holland and Belgium, with the view of maintaining the neutrality of those countries against an attack by the great powers.

Hungarian Diet Enthusiastic.

Great enthusiasm prevailed in the Hungarian Chamber when Count Tiza, the Prime Minister, announced the outbreak of war and declared the situation demanded a deed of arms, not words. Count Apponyi, leader of the Opposition, supported the Premier. The Parliament was prorogued by royal decree.

Patriotic demonstrations took place in St. Petersburg, the crowds cheering the friendly embassies and legations, including those of Great Britain and Servia.

The Times St. Petersburg correspondent reports the growth of pessimism in official circles. News of the Austro-Hungarian occupation of Belgrade would inflame public feeling. Russian statesmen are convinced that England alone can save the situation, and that Sir Edward Grey's proposals by no means exhaust all his possibilities of persuasion.

Captured Passengers Detained.

BELGRADE, July 28, (by Indirect Route.)—The Servian steamers Deligrad and Morava were seized today at Orsova, on the Danube, by Austrians. The Servian colors were hauled down and the Austrian flag hoisted. The passengers were detained.

Many Servian families have left the capital for the country districts in spite of the advice of the authorities, while there has been a great exodus of Austrians and Hungarians from Belgrade and other parts of Servia.

Perfect order prevails in the capital, the police duties having been undertaken by a corps of volunteers composed of students.

Military preparations are being carried out with feverish activity. The troops have been concentrated in fortified positions. The headquarters of the army has been established at Kragouyevatz, but in the event of necessity will be transferred to Krushevatz, ninety miles southeast of Belgrade.

Two Army Corps at the Border.

BERLIN, July 28.—Reports from the Austrian border today state that the transport of the Eighth and Ninth Austrian Army Corps from Bohemia toward the Servian frontier began yesterday, and that there was no other traffic on the Bohemian railroads except troop trains. The two army corps in Bohemia consist of thirty-two battalions of infantry with a large number of quick-firing machine guns, six regiments of cavalry, two regiments of field artillery, and two regiments of the Army Service Corps.

An unconfirmed dispatch from Gumbinnen, Eastern Prussia, to the Taegliche Rundschau, today says Russia has occupied Wirballen, Russian Poland, with a force of engineers, cavalry, artillery, and two regiments of infantry while Russian guards have been placed along all roads on the frontier. The dispatch adds that a squadron of German Uhlans has advanced to Eydtkuhnen on the Russian frontier.

AUSTRIA MAY PAUSE.

Suggestion in Paris That She May Take Some Territory and Wait.

PARIS, July 28.—According to what is believed to be responsible opinion, there remains the possibility that when Austria has occupied some Servian territory she will in a day or two announce her intention not to proceed further, but to hold what she has taken until Servia gives competent guarantees that she will observe Austria's wishes. Russia would not then be likely to intervene, it is argued, except diplomatically, and negotiations appear to be going on at the present time between Austria and Russia.

On the announcement of war tonight Paris became animated. There were patriotic demonstrations in the capital and many other cities throughout the republic, but there were also demonstrations against the war.

A large number of noted French aviators, led by Roland Garros, in a letter to the Minister of War, have offered their services.

Maurice Barres, member of the Chamber of Deputies and President of the League of Patriots, has issued a call for a big demonstration on the arrival at Paris of President Poincaré to signify affirmation of the Triple Entente and readiness for the service of France.

Text of Austria-Hungary's Declaration of War.

VIENNA, July 28.—Austria-Hungary's declaration of war against Servia was gazetted here late this afternoon. The text is as follows:

"The Royal Government of Servia not having replied in a satisfactory manner to the note remitted to it by the Austro-Hungarian Minister in Belgrade on July 23, 1914, the Imperial and Royal Government finds itself compelled to proceed itself to safeguard its rights and interests and to have recourse for this purpose to force of arms.

"Austria-Hungary considers itself, therefore, from this moment in a state of war with Servia.

(Signed) "COUNT BERCHTOLD,
"Minister of Foreign Affairs of Austria-Hungary."

Russia Announces Its Wish to Remain at Peace Yet Is Determined to Guard Its Interests.

ST. PETERSBURG, July 28.—The Russian Government tonight issued the following official communication:

"Numerous patriotic demonstrations of the last few days in St. Petersburg and other cities prove that the firm pacific policy of Russia finds a sympathetic echo among all classes of the population.

"The Government hopes, nevertheless, that the expression of feeling of the people will not be tinged with enmity against the powers with whom Russia is at peace, and with whom she wishes to remain at peace.

"While the Government gathers strength from this wave of popular feeling and expects its subjects to retain their reticence and tranquillity, it rests confidently on the guardianship of the dignity and the interests of Russia."

CZAR'S FORCES MASS ON EASTERN BORDER

His Capital Expects War and Counts Confidently on England's Aid.

MOBILIZATION ORDER READY

German Official Says Its Issue Would Mean Launching of Kaiser's Army.

Special Cable to THE NEW YORK TIMES.

ST. PETERSBURG, July 28.—With the actual opening of the war the localization of the conflict becomes impossible. Even if Austria-Hungary goes no further than the occupation of Belgrade by the troops thrown across the Save at Semlin, Russia will declare a general mobilization.

Already rapid mobilization is proceeding in the west and southwest, virtually from the German frontier to the Black Sea.

The gravity of the situation is reflected in the diplomatic movements in this capital. The Emperor today gave audience to both the Foreign Minister and the War Minister.

A strong opinion prevails here that in the event of the outbreak of a general European war England would actively support Russia and France, her co-partners in the Triple Entente.

ST. PETERSBURG, July 28.—The fact that Austria had declared war became known here late this evening.

Thousands of persons then gathered, and, cheering wildly, marched through the main streets to the British and French Embassies, where there were scenes of enthusiasm.

Mounted police eventually scattered the crowds, without great disorder.

Says Germany Will Strike Hard.

BERLIN, July 28.—No confirmation had been received up to a late hour this evening by the German Foreign Office or the Russian Embassy of the mobilization of army corps in Russia reported in dispatches to London.

A German official said flatly that any Russian mobilization against Austria, partially or otherwise, meant war. German mobilization orders would then, he said, immediately be issued, and when these once had been sent there would be no possibility of recalling them or of Germany resting on her arms while negotiations continued, as the strategic necessities of war on her two fronts would force Germany to strike immediately and hard.

The opinion was expressed tonight in well-informed Russian circles, however, that partial mobilization of Russian troops along the Austrian frontier was quite probable as an answer to the Austrian declaration of war on Servia.

Servian officials here appeared to think that such a step could be undertaken without evoking a German counter mobilization.

PEACE CONGRESS PROTEST.

Meeting Place to be Changed from Vienna to Berne.

BRUSSELS, Belgium, July 28.—The International Peace Association, at the request of the American delegates now here, has called a meeting for next Friday.

As a protest against the warlike action of Austria the association has decided to change the meeting place of the Universal Peace Congress in September from Vienna to Berne.

Austrian Emperor to Take Command at Vienna Headquarters.

WAR FEVER AT CAPITAL

Crowds Cheer Outbreak of Hostilities and Demonstrate at Friendly Embassies.

OUTBREAK OF FOOD RIOTS

Prices Soar as Hostilities Are Declared and the Government Steps In to Regulate Them.

MANIFESTO FROM EMPEROR

Forced to Grasp the Sword, He Says, to Defend the Honor of His Monarchy.

FRANCE FEARS A GREAT WAR

Army Moves to the Frontier—Belief in Paris That Russia Will Not Desert Servia.

Special Cable to THE NEW YORK TIMES.

VIENNA, July 28.—Upon the issue of the formal declaration of war against Servia today Emperor Franz Josef gave orders for the removal of the Summer Court from Ischl to the capital. His entourage tried to persuade him that Vienna air would not suit him, but the aged Emperor replied:

"I do not want the air of Vienna. I want the atmosphere of headquarters."

The opening of the war has caused the imposition of all kinds of restrictions upon public business. All the railways, of course, are under military control, and the telegraphs are being reserved entirely for the servi e of the State.

The hope is still entertained here that the war will be confined to Austria-Hungary and Servia. The report that Russia and France have intervened in Vienna is incorrect. In official circles here it is maintaine that any action by those powers m be supported by the third party t Triple Entente, namely, Great P It is known that Great Brita and France do not want a European war. Peace among the great powers or war among the great powers must depend on the action of St. Petersburg.

At the Foreign Office here it is freely stated that now that war has begun Austria-Hungary will be bound to no more conditions such as she propounded prior to the outbreak of hostilities.

Food Prices Up in Vienna.

There was an abnormal rise in the price of provisions today, which caused great indignation on the part of the public, who flocked to the markets to lay in stores in anticipation of a possible scarcity. Vegetables in many cases trebled in price. Feeling ran so high that in many instances stallkeepers in the markets were mobbed or assaulted, and the police had to be called out to restore order. The authorities declare that the sudden increase in the prices of provisions and vegetables is totally unwarranted.

A permanent committee appointed to deal with the question of provisioning the country, sat today to discuss th regulation of prices in order to p vent the public being cheated. similar meeting with the same obj also was held in the Diet.

It was officialy asserted that th was no reason for apprehension wi regard to the food suply, and that was needless for citizens to start t accumulation of stores of provisions. The only effect of such procedure, it was added, would be to still further raise prices.

Official arrangements have been made to take care of families of reservists called to the colors. In the event of a reservist being killed or reported missing an allowance of about 25 cents per day for each adult and 12 1-2 cents a day for children will be continued for six months.

The Declaration of War.

By The Associated Press.

VIENNA, July 28.—It is with a feeling of intense relief that the people in the dual monarchy look forward to the war with Servia, which for several days has seemed to be inevitable, and

"All the News That's Fit to Print."

The New York Times.

THE WEATHER
Partly cloudy today; Friday, fair; moderate to fresh north winds.
For full weather report see Page 17.

VOL. LXIII...NO. 20,641. NEW YORK, THURSDAY, JULY 30, 1914.—EIGHTEEN PAGES. ONE CENT In Greater New York, Jersey City and Newark. | Elsewhere TWO CENTS.

RUSSIA EXPECTS WAR, MOBILIZES 1,200,000 MEN; CZAR ALSO SUMMONS RESERVISTS TO THE COLORS; BELGRADE BOMBARDED AND OCCUPIED BY AUSTRIA; KAISER IN COUNCIL ON NAVAL PREPARATIONS

WILSON REASSURES N. Y. CONGRESSMEN

Won't Oppose Tammany Men Who Support His Administration, He Tells Delegation.

BUT VISITORS ARE DAZED

Can't Exactly Make Out President's Intentions, Especially as to Patronage—Malone Not Mentioned.

Special to The New York Times.

WASHINGTON, July 29.—Thirteen of the twenty Democratic Congressmen from New York City went to the White House this afternoon to find out who was who and what was what in New York politics. They had worked themselves up to a high state of indignation, but the indignation apparently oozed out before they reached the Executive offices, where the President received them. Tonight the New Yorkers are wondering what happened, anyway.

The New York City Congressmen went to the White House primarily to ascertain if Dudley Field Malone, Collector of Customs for the Port of New York, had any authority for giving the impression that President Wilson was opposed to the Tammany men in the House of Representatives. Mr. Malone's name was not mentioned at the White House conference.

There had been feeling among the Congressmen against William G. McAdoo, Secretary of the Treasury, who is the President's son-in-law, and at [illegible] there was talk of complaining [illegible] to Mr. Wilson about Mr. McAdoo's attitude toward organisation [illegible] in his State—New York. At [illegible]rence Mr. McAdoo's name was [illegible]oned.

[illegible]teen New Yorkers swore themselves to secrecy as to what occurred [illegible] their conversation with the [illegible], but one of them unbosomed [illegible] enough tonight to remark that the White House visit reminded him of the King of France and his 40,000 men, who, it will be remembered, marched up the hill and then marched down again. Some of the thirteen are accusing the delegation, themselves included, of a lack of courage in stating their case to the President.

The five New York Congressmen who did most of the talking told the President that certain unnamed Federal of[illegible] in New York, who had been [illegible] by Mr. Wilson, had done [illegible] possible to make it difficult [illegible] New York City Congressmen to [illegible] renominations. These office[illegible], they said, had given the im[illegible] to the public that they had [illegible] from the White House to oppose [illegible] Congressmen.

[illegible] President showed himself to be a [illegible]ner. When it came his time to [illegible]thing, he told the New York[illegible] he regarded the situation with [illegible] they were concerned in two [illegible] that of a State contest and that [illegible] contest involving national issues. He said that Democratic Congressmen from New York who had supported the Administration and its policies had nothing to fear from him. The Administration, he declared, would not put any [illegible] in the way of their desire to obtain renomination. And to this the President added that any appointee of his who sought to put out the impression that the Administration was opposing the efforts of the New York Democratic Congressmen to obtain renomination was acting without authority.

After the conference the following statement, supposed to have been prepared by the President, was given out at the White House:

The conference was taken up by a very full and frank expression of opinion about the political situation in New York and the prospects of the party there in the Congressional elections. The conference was welcomed by the President. No plans were discussed. It was understood to be a conference for information. The conference was characterised by a spirit of cordiality on both sides.

The thirteen members of the New York City delegation who visited the White House were Frank E. Wilson, Harry H. Dale, James P. Maher, John J. Fitzgerald, Daniel J. Griffin, James H. O'Brien, and Herman A. Metz of Brooklyn; Daniel J. Riordan, Michael F. Conroy, John F. Carew, Thomas G. Patten, and Henry Bruckner of Manhattan, and Joseph A. Goulden of the Bronx. Those who were not present were Henry M. Goldfogle, George W. Loft, Jefferson M. Levy, Peter J. Dooling, Jacob A. Cantor, and Henry George, Jr., of Manhattan, and Denis O'Leary of Queens.

Mr. George and Mr. Loft are in Europe. Mr. Levy and Mr. Cantor did not attend because they were not in sympathy with the purpose of the visit. Mr. Dooling, who intended to accompany his fellow-members to the White House, was obliged to go to New York. Members of the delegation said that Messrs. Goldfogle and O'Leary had started for the White House, and that it was not known what had become of them.

After the White House conference some of the New York Congressmen indicated that action by the White House in the near future would determine how they stood with the President. This was taken to mean that if the President in filling Federal appointments in New York did not select pronounced anti-Tammany men his disposition toward the New [illegible] Congressmen of his party [illegible] be regarded as favorable.

[illegible] of the New Yorkers found a fly [illegible] ointment of Executive non-inter[illegible]. They were satisfied with what [illegible] President told them, so far as it [illegible] were disappointed that he [illegible] prefer to announce publicly that [illegible]tions of anti-Tammany Demo[illegible]ing nomination to Congress [illegible] had the Administration in[illegible] were unauthorized. Such an [illegible]ent, they thought, would put a quietus on the activities of Collector Malone and other leaders of the independent movement in the Democratic Party.

The New Yorkers told the President that conditions in the Democratic Party in New York City were becoming [illegible] and that only united effort [illegible] produce party victory. They de[illegible] that there was a feeling against [illegible] Administration through the creation [illegible] impression that it had discrimi[illegible] against the metropolis. The New [illegible] did not particularise, but it [illegible] known afterward that what [illegible] in mind was dissatisfaction [illegible] action of the Organization [illegible] of the Federal reserve bank[illegible] in failing to include Connec[illegible] Northern New Jersey in the [illegible] Federal Reserve District.

[illegible] President told the Congressmen [illegible] was not conscious of having [illegible] discrimination against New [illegible] certainly did not intend to [illegible]. He declared that in the [illegible] York political situation the thing [illegible] in mind was not men, but the [illegible] of Democratic principles, and [illegible] would be actuated by that idea.

EUROPE'S CRISIS
By Dr. ALBERT BUSHNELL HART.
The noted Harvard Professor of History visited Servia and Austria after the Balkan war and prophesied the present trouble. Read his article
IN NEXT SUNDAY'S TIMES.

TOURISTS HELD UP IN THE YELLOWSTONE

Two Lone Bandits Collect $3,000 from a Line of Park Stages.

HELD THEM UP ONE BY ONE

Many Easterners Among Those Compelled to Disgorge—Robbers Take Only Cash.

Special to The New York Times.

MAMMOTH HOT SPRINGS, Wyo., July 29.—One hundred and sixty-five persons, many of them tourists from Eastern cities, were held up in Yellowstone National Park this morning by two bandits and relieved of cash which aggregated about $3,000. The robbers refrained from taking any jewels. They made their escape.

The hold-up occurred about 10 o'clock near Shoshone Point, between Old Faithful Inn and the Thumb Lunch Station. The 165 tourists were traveling through the park on thirty-five stage coaches owned by the Yellowstone Park Transportation Company, the Yellowstone Western Stage Company, the Wylie Camping Company, and the Shaw & Powell Camping Company.

As each of the thirty-five coaches reached the point of the holdup, a lone highwayman, about 5 feet 8 inches in height and armed with a Winchester rifle, compelled the passengers to descend from the vehicle and deposit their money in a sack which the robbers had prepared for the purpose. The chief highwayman politely informed the astonished passengers that he required "cash only."

The second highwayman had taken up a position a short distance down the trail, preventing the coaches from retreating to Old Faithful Inn to give the alarm.

Driver Frazier of the Yellowstone Western Stage Company, with Lieut. R. B. Paddock and a party in a coach somewhat behind the thirty-five others, on coming to the top of Shoshone Point, saw in the road below all the stages lined up and being robbed. Frazier turned and made a lively retreat to Old Faithful, where he reported the hold-up to Col. Brett, Superintendent of the Park.

Following is a partial list of the passengers robbed:

Mrs. S. P. Kidder, Madison, Wis.; Martin Rutkowski and wife, Milwaukee; Frank Bole, Davenport, Iowa; Russell Bole, Davenport, Iowa; Mrs. H. J. Baldwin, Joplin, Mo.; Mrs. H. L. Cawley, Kansas City; Carolin J. Williams, Carolyn Shepherd, Stayner Richards and Mrs. Richards, and Mr. and Mrs. C. C. Neslen, all of Salt Lake City.

One man in the party reported to have had $1,000 discreetly dropped a fifty-cent piece in the extended sack and got away in safety with the rest of his money.

Some of the passengers who had cameras and who had somewhat regained their nerve asked for leave to take pictures of the hold-up. The bandits agreed and several passengers took photographs.

After an hour's delay the bandits consented to the coaches proceeding, and Thumb Lunch Station was reached about an hour later, none of the 165 passengers having suffered any physical injury. The robbers had cut the wires to the Yellowstone Park Hotel before starting the hold-up, and some time elapsed before an alarm could be given.

Col. Brett has a large force of men pursuing the robbers, who are reported to be heading toward the Jackson Hole country in Wyoming. The transportation companies offered rewards aggregating $500 for the capture of the highwaymen.

Passengers on the stage said the one man who did the actual work of robbing held up each stage as it passed the canyon by pointing a gun at the driver.

The highwaymen had the advantage because Government regulations prevent any person except those with permits from carrying arms in the park.

FALLS UNDER WILD HORSE.

Policeman Hurt Mortally in Stopping Runaway Near the Waldorf.

Shortly after 11 o'clock last night persons in Broadway were thrilled by the sight of a runaway horse galloping down the street with a pair of shafts and part of the whiffletree banging at his heels, while behind came half a dozen automobiles, headed by one which carried on its running board a policeman blowing his whistle to warn traffic. The horse had bolted at Fifty-first Street and had broken loose from the victoria to which it was harnessed.

The chase continued down Broadway and at Thirty-fourth Street the policeman, George Doerr of the West Forty-seventh Street Station, got near enough to the horse to reach for its bridle. He missed and frightened the animal out of its course into Thirty-fourth Street. Near the Waldorf Doerr made another attempt, and this time caught the bridle. Before he could bring the animal to a stop, however, it had veered toward the sidewalk and plunged into a six-foot excavation in front of the hotel. Doerr landed underneath.

A block and fall was rigged and the horse was pulled out. Then they got Doerr. He was unconscious and was taken to Bellevue Hospital. On his arrival there it was found he had serious internal injuries and his recovery was considered doubtful.

Latest Shipping News.

BY MARCONI WIRELESS—SS Adriatic, (White Star Line,) Liverpool to New York, was 784 miles east of Sandy Hook at 2:33 P. M.; due 31st, afternoon.

SS Michigan, (Phoenix Line,) Antwerp to New York, was 780 miles east of Sandy Hook at 2:30 P. M.; due Aug. 1, afternoon.

St. Petersburg Convinced Political Miracle Only Can Avert War.

CZAR WOULD HEAD ARMY

Grand Duke Nicholas and War Minister Soukhomlinoff Seconds in Command.

PRAYERS FOR SERB VICTORY

Sacred Ikon Presented for King Peter's Forces—Great Patriotic Demonstrations.

BALTIC LIGHTS OUT NOW

Warsaw Arsenal Reported Blown Up — Bombs in Post Office — Revolution Rumor Denied.

New York Times-London Chronicle Special Cable Dispatch.

ST. PETERSBURG, July 29.—This evening Russia's intervention in the Austro-Servian conflict appears to be imminent. Certainly, after the receipt of the news of the bombardment of Belgrade I was so informed at the Foreign Office.

Russia even now will take steps to stay Austria's mobilization, being pushed forward actively, and an official announcement has been issued that a general mobilization will be Russia's reply to Austria's action.

The Vienna theory that the war is a mere punitive expedition is not admitted by Russia. The utmost admitted is that if Austria retires immediately there may still be room for diplomatic efforts.

Measures have been taken on the Baltic and at Sebastopol for the preparation of two fleets and there has been hurried promotion of officers.

Gradual transfer of the control of the railways to the War Office is proceeding.

These and other stirring events all indicate that the decisive moment is approaching.

A fateful manifesto expected tonight had not been forthcoming to the time of wiring.

Nothing could be more warlike than the official and popular attitude just now, and yet I found moderate people who still hold that the possibility of peace remains if Austria will but evacuate Belgrade immediately after its occupation.

Many people here eagerly grasp at the hope that the British fleet will intervene by a demonstration or otherwise to help Russia to bring pressure to bear on the Middle Empire.

Russia Believes the Die Is Cast.

By The Associated Press.

ST. PETERSBURG, July 29.—In Russian eyes the die is cast. Only a political miracle can avert war.

Russia does not swerve from her determination to support Servia, and partial mobilization has been ordered. There is every indication that the whole vast military machinery of Russia will soon be set in motion.

Should, as is understood, Emperor Nicholas become generalissimo of the forces an immense wave of enthusiasm will sweep over Russia.

The political parties have sunk their differences. The general attitude is not "jingoistic," but one of resolute confidence in the justice of the country's cause, and readiness to make all sacrifices.

The proposal attributed to Austria to discuss terms when Belgrade has been occupied is regarded as impossible. It is pointed out that before the opening of hostilities Russia proposed to Austria a direct exchange of views which Austria rejected.

[The foregoing paragraphs were passed by the censor without revision—a fact which is considered highly significant.]

Czar's Seconds in Command.

It is considered probable that Emperor Nicholas will become the Generalissimo of the Russian forces, his seconds in command being his second cousin, Grand Duke Nicholas Nicholaievitch, and Gen. Soukhomlinoff, the Minister of War.

The cadets of the naval school were promoted today to the rank of officers. In addressing them, the Emperor said:

"I have given orders that you should be incorporated in the navy in view of the serious events through which Russia is passing. During your service as officers, do not forget what I say to you—trust in God and have faith in the glory and greatness of our mighty country."

By orders of the Emperor, the enforcement of the legislative resolution restricting the acquisition of real estate by companies and also restricting the inclusion of Jews on Boards of Directors has been temporarily suspended.

The Maritime Bureau has announced the closing of additional lights, both in the Baltic and Black Seas.

In Yalta and the surrounding districts in the Crimea a state of reinforced protection or a modified form of martial law has been proclaimed.

Great Patriotic Demonstrations.

A great patriotic demonstration took place on the Nevsky Prospect this afternoon. A procession was formed and with banners flying marched to the Servian Legation, where there were speeches, singing, and cheering. Thence the procession moved to the French and British Embassies, where similar scenes of enthusiasm were indulged in. The German and Austrian Embassies were guarded on all sides by strong detachments of police, and nobody was allowed to stop on the adjacent footpaths.

At the Kauzan Cathedral a special service was held and prayers were offered for victory to the Slav arms. The cathedral was thronged, and the officiating priest, after the ceremony, presented to the Servian Minister a fac simile of the ikon of the Holy Virgin of Kazan for the Servian Army. The Minister handed the ikon to officers who are starting for the front tonight.

A monster demonstration in favor of Servia was held at Moscow.

At Odessa processions marched through the streets bearing the portraits of Emperor Nicholas and the Kings of Servia and Montenegro, and cheering for Servia, France, and Great Britain.

A confident feeling prevails here of Great Britain's support. Germany's attitude is regarded as incomprehensible, except on the assumption that she is anxious for a trial of strength at the present moment.

FRANCIS JOSEPH TO CZAR.

Personal Letter Expected to Have Important Influence on the Crisis.

ST. PETERSBURG, July 29.—The Novoe Vremya says that the Austrian Emperor has addressed a personal letter to Emperor Nicholas which is likely to have an important influence on the crisis.

VIENNA, July 29.—Germany and Italy today continued their efforts to localise the war declared yesterday by their ally, Austria-Hungary, against Servia, and the efforts of all the European diplomats are being directed toward the same object.

The Russian Ambassador conferred with Count Leopold von Berchtold, Austro-Hungarian Foreign Minister, but it is understood the interview was only for the purpose of obtaining information.

Nothing whatever is known here of the reported intention of Russia to make a declaration of neutrality in case Austria-Hungary should renounce the idea of territorial expansion at the expense of the Balkan State.

When the British Ambassador here called on Count von Berchtold yesterday to submit the mediation proposal put forward by Sir Edward Grey, the British Foreign Secretary, he was informed that the good intentions of Great Britain were appreciated, but that war had been declared already.

The war spirit is increasing hourly. The streets of Vienna tonight were crowded with enthusiastic processions, singind and hurrahing, and traffic in the leading thoroughfares was almost brought to a standstill. The patriotic demonstrations today surpassed in extent and fervor anything witnessed within memory.

The City Council, at a special war session today, voted large sums to start relief funds for the families of the soldiers at the front and for Red Cross purposes.

Czar Summons Immense Number of Reservists; His Ukase Sweeps Empire for Additional Soldiers

ST. PETERSBURG, July 29.—An Imperial ukase, issued by the Emperor tonight, calls to the colors an immense number of reservists. The men called out are:

First—All the reservists of twenty-three whole governments and of seventy-one districts in fourteen other governments.

Second—Part of the reservists of nine districts of four governments.

Third—The naval reservists in sixty-four districts of twelve Russian governments and one Finnish government.

Fourth—The time-expired Cossacks of the territories of Don, Kuban, Terek, Astrakhan, Orenburg and Ural.

Fifth—A corresponding number of reservist officers of the medical and veterinary services, in addition to needful horses, wagons and transport services in the governments and districts thus mobilized.

WAR CHEERS GREET POINCARE.

Great Crowd Welcome the President on His Return from Russia.

Special Cable to THE NEW YORK TIMES.

PARIS, July 29.—President Poincaré returned to Paris this afternoon from Russia, accompanied by Premier Viviani.

The President's homecoming was made the occasion of a great patriotic demonstration. Hundreds of thousands of Parisians lined the streets from the Gare du Nord to the Elysée and shouted, "Vive Poincaré!" "Vive l'Armée!" "Viva France!" "Vive l'Alliance!"

The demonstration was the more significant on account of its spontaneity, for it was not known until late this morning at what hour the President would arrive.

A detachment of mounted guards went to the station to act as M. Poincaré's escort. The men were loudly cheered by the crowd. When the Presidential train arrived there was an impressive silence for a few moments. Then, as M. Poincaré came into view, a great cry of "Vive La France!" arose. Heads were bared, handkerchiefs were waved, and bouquets were thrown from balconies.

Many notable persons were in the crowd, including Edmond Rostand, who shouted with enthusiastic fervor, "Vive la France!"

After the Presidential procession formed the demonstrators lined up and marched behind the escort of mounted guards, singing the "Marseillaise," while along the route people marching on the pavement took up the refrain.

President Poincaré landed at 9 o'clock at Dunkirk, where several political notabilities awaited him. A huge crowd there gave him a rousing welcome. A wireless telegram from the battleship France announced that a German torpedo boat passed within a mile of the French warship carrying the President, and gave him a salute of twenty-one guns, to which the Jean Bart responded.

M. Poincaré presided this afternoon at an important Cabinet Council. This evening the President had several interviews with leading politicians, including ex-Ministers of Foreign Affairs Ribot, Pichon, and Delcassé. Premier Viviani received several Ambassadors.

Although the general impression in Paris is more pessimistic today, the population remains self-reliant and there is no fear of a panic. The boulevards and principal streets today displayed considerable animation, everybody discussing the latest events and the possibility of forthcoming mobilization.

At the Bank of France and leading Paris banks large crowds have gathered to draw out money. There has been in the last few days a rush for gold everywhere. At many Paris shops gold in change for bank notes is given only to customers buying more than ten francs' worth of goods.

The prospect of mobilization has led to a considerable number of orders to military tailors' shops. One of these has received 1,500 orders from reserve officers for new uniforms.

The army authorities are taking the necessary precautions on the Eastern frontier. Six army corps are fully ready to move.

On all the railway lines from Paris to the Eastern frontier the tunnels and bridges are being guarded by soldiers.

All aeroplane factories are guarded by soldiers and orders have been issued to aeroplane manufacturers prohibiting them from delivering aeroplanes to private customers.

It is generally expected that the next move of the Government will be to recall to the colors the contingent of men who completed their period of active military service last year, which would mean an addition of 200,000 to the present strength of the army.

Heavy Bombardment of Belgrade Failed to Provoke Response.

MANY BUILDINGS DAMAGED

Two Banks Hit and a Banker Wounded—Protest Lodged at German Legation.

SEMLIN BRIDGE BLOWN UP

Big Gun Duel at Vichnitza—Serbs in Dual Monarchy Held as War Prisoners.

TWO ARMIES OF INVASION

Gen. Von Hoetzendorf, in Chief Command, to Attack Servia and Gen. Ermoly, Montenegro.

Austria Occupies Belgrade

LONDON, Thursday, July 30.—A Vienna dispatch to the Exchange Telegraph Company says:

After a heavy bombardment by the Danube gunboats, Belgrade was occupied by the Austrian troops Wednesday.

By MARTIN H. DONOHUE.

New York Times-London Chronicle Special Cable Dispatch.

SEMLIN, Hungary, July 29.—The Austrians began hostilities this morning by bombarding Belgrade.

Three monitors took up their positions at the confluence of the Danube and the Save, but close to shore, and opened fire. The monitors' guns were directed on the Belgrade barracks, and no pains were taken to avoid hitting the public buildings, some of which were seen, even from here, to be damaged. The Servians made no reply to the Austrian gunfire, but have destroyed the railway bridge between Semlin and Belgrade. The bombardment was bloodless, so far as the imperial forces were concerned.

Banks Damaged. Banker Wounded.

Special Cable to THE NEW YORK TIMES.

ATHENS, July 29.—The Servian Legation has received the following telegram from Nish, dated July 29:

"During the night Belgrade was bombarded. Shells fell in various quarters of the town, causing great damage. Several fell on the Franco-Servian and the Androvitch banks. M. Androvitch, of the banking firm, was wounded. Both banks have lodged a protest at the German Legation.

"An artillery duel is proceeding at Vichnitza, about 3½ miles down the river from Belgrade."

LONDON, Thursday, July 30.—It is stated in connection with the blowing up of the railway bridge across the River Save by Servians, that the Austrians have another bridge in sections on their side of the river, which they can put up in a few days.

Dispatches from Servian points yesterday indicated that the Bosnian frontier was looked upon as the most likely point of attack of the Austrian troops, and thither the soldiers of King Peter were being hurried in great numbers.

Strong forces were dispatched to the fortified towns of Valyevo and Uzhitza, on the frontier, and to Svilajnatz, in the eastern part of the country, while strong divisions of volunteers reinforced by regulars were gathering along the River Drina, near Losnitz.

The Montenegrin soldiery, evidently preparing to support their brother Serbs, have also concentrated along the Bosnian frontier. A brigade with a mountain battery was stationed near Priboj, where the women were busy building earthworks.

Servian and Austrian aviators at the same time were flying along the frontiers, trying to locate the positions of the opposing forces.

VIENNA, July 29.—The Servians at 1:30 o'clock this morning blew up the bridge spanning the River Save between the Austrian town of Semlin and Belgrade. The Austrian infantry and artillery stationed at Semlin, in conjunction with monitors on the Danube, fired on the Servian positions beyond the bridge. The Servians retreated after a short engagement, with trifling losses.

The shells wrought havoc in the exposed part of the city, damaging the King's Palace, the fortification walls, and the barracks and other buildings.

A small detachment of pioneers, in co-operation with the customs officers, yesterday captured two Servian steamers laden with ammunition and arms. The pioneers and revenue guards, after a short, sharp encounter, overcame the Servian crews and took possession of the vessels and their dangerous cargoes. The captured ships were towed away by one of the Danube steamers.

Emperor to Go to Budapest.

Emperor Francis Joseph will return to Vienna from Ischl tomorrow and may then go to Budapest in order to be near the scene of action. Popular enthusiasm is growing since the Emperor's manifesto, and patriotic demonstrations are being held all over the country. Runs on the savings banks are diminishing.

All Servians liable to military service residing in Austria-Hungary are being arrested and handed over to the military as prisoners of war.

Special Cable to THE NEW YORK TIMES.

BERLIN, July 29.—The Berliner Tageblatt learns that the Austrian plan of campaign consists of operations by two great armies under the general command of Gen. Baron von Hoetzendorf, Chief of General Staff. The larger army, under the command of Field Marshal Potiorek, is to carry out the invasion of Servia, while the smaller army, commanded by Cavalry Gen. Ermoly, will attack Montenegro.

KAISER AND CZAR CONFER.

Cabinet Meeting Follows Naval Council of War at Potsdam.

Special Cable to THE NEW YORK TIMES.

BERLIN, Thursday, July 30.—The Kaiser last evening held a naval council of war, which was attended by Admiral von Tirpitz, Minister of Marine; Prince Henry of Prussia, Admiral Commanding in Chief; Admiral von Pohl, Chief of the Admiralty General Staff, and Vice Admiral von Mueller, Chief of the Imperial Naval Cabinet.

This meeting was followed by a council of the Cabinet, which lasted for some time.

No announcement of what occurred at either meeting was made.

The Crown Prince also was in conference with the Kaiser today, the interview lasting three hours.

Imperial Messages Exchanged.

After a day of what financiers called "almost intolerable anxiety" Berlin learned officially late in the afternoon that an exchange of telegrams regarding the international situation was in progress between the Kaiser and the Czar.

It appears that the Czar dispatched a telegram to the Kaiser, which crossed a message which the German Emperor had just sent to Emperor Nicholas. No details of the communications passing between the two monarchs have been disclosed, but the fact that they are in progress has created an unmistakably favorable impression.

The German Foreign Office simultaneously authorized the statement that "more peaceable sentiments now prevail in Russia."

The North German Gazette, on the strength of this alleged circumstance, said:

"The amicable tone of the official Russian communiqué of July 28 evokes a lively echo in Berlin. The German Imperial Government shares the wish for the maintenance of peaceful relations. It hopes the German people, by continuing to conduct itself with moderation and quiet, will support the Government's endeavors."

Anxiety Over Russian Movements.

The Lokal Anzeiger, obviously on Foreign Office inspiration, published the following:

"The pretended conciliatory aspect of the Russian policy is in grave contrast to the restless, comprehensive military dispositions of the Czar's army on the German frontier. As long as these continue there can hardly be any question of the relaxation of the political tension. It can only be hoped that the Czar will also give some tangible proof of his peaceable inclinations by ordering the immediate cessation of the conspicuous concentration of troops in the western regions of the empire."

The German high seas fleet, which was in the midst of its Summer battle practice in Norwegian and Danish waters when the crisis broke out, returned to its home stations yesterday, the North Sea squadrons anchoring at Wilhelmshaven and the Baltic divisions at Kiel.

All the Powers Massing Great Armies in Fear of Possible Conflict.

CZAR CALLS 16 CORPS

France Is Gathering Her Forces—Persistent Report That Germany Has Begun Mobilization.

FIRST BRITISH FLEET SAILS

Under Sealed Orders, but an Official Statement Says the Step Is Only Precautionary.

KAISER MEETS WAR CHIEFS

Gathering Follows Reported Exchange of Messages with the Russian Monarch.

Special Cable to THE NEW YORK TIMES.

LONDON, Thursday, July 30.—Premier Asquith's simple announcement to the House of Commons yesterday that the European situation, growing out of the Austro-Russian crisis, was one of extreme gravity, summarizes the present position of affairs.

The exchange of views that was proceeding between the Russian Foreign Minister, Sazonoff, and the Austro-Hungarian Ambassador in St. Petersburg, Szapáry, have ceased. On the other hand, German diplomacy is believed to be trying to re-establish relations between St. Petersburg and Vienna. The result of these efforts is not known.

An exchange of telegrams is alleged to have taken place between the German and Russian Emperors.

Rumors of an impending mobilization of the German Army are circulating in several Continental capitals, but these rumors are not yet confirmed.

The hostilities between Austria and Servia, which, according to one report, have resulted in setting Belgrade afire, shrink into insignificance before the military preparations which are reported to be in progress in every part of Europe. In most countries these are described as precautionary measures, but they are upon a scale never before known in history.

The news of Russia's partial mobilization, given in the St. Petersburg dispatch to THE NEW YORK TIMES yesterday, is confirmed. In diplomatic circles Russia is understood to have informed Germany that only the southern and southwestern corps of the Russian Army are mobilizing. These sixteen corps at their war strength represent 1,200,000 men. In the event of war the Czar, it is [illegible] will take the field as the Com[illegible] in Chief.

The Russian mobilization, according to St. Petersburg, affects only the Austrian, not the German [illegible] and does not imply war between Russia and Austria.

Says Russia Spoiled Peace [illegible]

The Frankfurter Zeitung, [illegible] Berlin telegrams are frequently inspired, asserts that the Russian mobilization has prejudiced the diplomatic negotiations "perhaps fatally."

According to The London Times this morning, direct diplomatic intercourse between Austria-Hungary and Russia was suspended yesterday. This suspension indicates the growing tension of the situation. Since October, 1908, when diplomatic intercourse was interrupted between Russia and Austria-Hungary after the annexation by the latter of Bosnia and Herzegovina, there have been several periods of such silence.

In the Spring of 1909 and again in the Winter of 1912-13 large bodies of Russian and Austro-Hungarian troops faced each other for months on either side of the Russo-Galician frontier. On the latter occasion the ominous silence between Vienna and St. Petersburg was broken only by the action of Emperor Francis Joseph in dispatching Prince Gottfried von Hohenlohe-Langenburg to the Russian Court on a special mission.

The gravity of the present situation lies less in the breaking off of the exchange of [illegible] than in the fact

"All the News That's Fit to Print."

The New York Times.

THE WEATHER
Partly cloudy today and tomorrow; moderate northeast winds.
For full weather report see Page 17.

VOL. LXIII...NO. 20,642. NEW YORK, FRIDAY, JULY 31, 1914.—EIGHTEEN PAGES. ONE CENT In Greater New York, Jersey City and Newark. | Elsewhere TWO CENTS.

KAISER CALLS ON RUSSIA TO HALT WITHIN 24 HOURS; IF SHE REFUSES GERMANY, TOO, WILL MOBILIZE; ENGLAND AND FRANCE READY, BUT HOPE FOR PEACE; AUSTRIANS DRIVE SERVIANS BACK FROM BELGRADE

BANKERS HERE CONFER ON WAR

Closing of Stock Exchange Not Necessary, Meeting at Morgan Offices Decides.

NO SCARCITY OF BUYERS

New York Stands Up Well When Big Foreign Liquidation Crumbles Prices.

1,296,000 SHARES ARE SOLD

Trading Machinery Unaffected by Biggest Day Since Oct. 27, 1907—Call Money 6 Per Cent.

War's Effect On Our Markets

Stock sales yesterday, 1,298,000 shares.
Extreme declines, 20¼ points in General Motors, 17⅛ in Reading.
Average decline, 4.65 points.
Sales of bonds, $4,476,000.
Wheat up to $1.02 a bushel.
Corn up 3 cents a bushel.
Cotton down $4 a bale.
Gold engaged for export $9,000,000.
Total gold engagements for the week, $37,280,000.
Insurance on gold shipments, $10,000 per $1,000,000, a new high level.

Some of the most important bankers in the financial district were summoned late yesterday afternoon to a significant meeting at the offices of J. P. Morgan & Co. It was at the behest of the late J. P. Morgan that similar meetings were held in the Morgan home during the 1907 crisis.

The late financier's son presided at yesterday's meeting, which was attended by Henry P. Davison of the Morgan firm, A. Barton Hepburn, Chairman of the Chase National Bank; Francis L. Hine, President of the First National Bank; Benjamin Strong, Jr., Vice President of the Bankers Trust Company; Charles H. Sabin, Vice President of the Guaranty Trust Company; Henry G. S. Noble, President of the New York Stock Exchange, and W. C. Van Antwerp, a member of the Board of Governors of the Exchange. The bankers were in session for about three hours, the two Stock Exchange representatives entering when the meeting was nearly over.

When the conference broke up it was stated that it had been called primarily for an exchange of views and the comparison of cables received by the various bankers. It was informal, and not designed to take action. Apparently all of the conferees were convinced that the situation did not call for the closing of the New York Stock Exchange. One of the biggest bankers, who spoke for the others, after asking that his name not be used, said:

"We think the Exchange should not be closed on account of the heavy European liquidation so long as there are [illegible] in the market willing to take [illegible]rities. That is my belief, and [illegible]ate that none of the banking [illegible] represented here today favored [illegible] under present conditions. So [illegible] there are buyers there is a mar[illegible] London, as you are aware, the [illegible]e has been nominally open, but [illegible]ve been no buyers, and hence [illegible]al list of quotations.

"Those conditions do not exist here. We have had today a very active market and plenty of purchasers. The question of closing shop must only be considered when there are no buyers."

Another banker at yesterday's meeting said that he would regard a decision to close this Exchange, the only open market in the world today, as deplorable. He said that the cash reserves in this country were sufficient to handle all the securities dumped here without having recourse to emergency currency.

"It is not a question of currency anyway," said this man, "but of credit."

On leaving the meeting bankers said that no conferences were to be held last night, and that they were so little worried that they were dispersing to go out of New York. Mr. Morgan returned to a yachting party from which he had been summoned, and Mr. Davison left for his Summer home on Long Island.

One of the bankers said that the last advices, received in the course of the conference, were of a more encouraging nature, and if borne out meant the end of serious trouble.

Notwithstanding the general reluctance of bankers and local brokers to have the Exchange closed, it was learned last night that pressure to this end was being brought to bear by many members of the Exchange owing to the difficulty of protecting margined accounts for customers who have got out of reach of the wires, or who are unable to get money here to protect themselves. Out-of-town houses were being heard from in strong terms urging President Noble to close the Exchange. A number of telegrams to be forwarded to Mr. Noble at Great Neck were coming over private wires last evening.

In some quarters it was believed that yesterday's conference implied an agreement among bankers to come to the support of the market today if it threatens to get out of hand.

OUR STOCKS CRUMBLE

But Exchange Stands Strain Well—Heavy Foreign Liquidation.

Prices of most of the leading stocks crumbled on the New York Stock Exchange yesterday in a collapse the like of which has not been seen since October, 1907. On sales of 1,298,000 shares—the biggest day's business since Oct. 27, 1907—standard dividend payers tumbled to new low levels. So great was the decline following the report that the German Government had sent an ultimatum to Russia that a movement looking to the closing of the Stock Exchange gained headway notwithstanding assurances from members of the Governing Board that no such action would be taken.

After a series of informal conferences between brokers, and after advising with leading bankers, it seemed certain last night that the Exchange would open at the usual time this morning, no matter what the nature of the war news. There is little question but that the Sock Exchange will be guided in this matter by the big banking institutions, and the heads of several of these said yesterday that the situation did not warrant closing the New York Exchange.

Those who were in favor of closing the Stock Exchange said it was foolish to allow a panic in Europe to wipe out values in this country. Brokers and bankers looked at the question from another angle. The banks are carrying large amounts of stock as collateral for loans, and if there was no open market for these issues it would be impossible to tell what loans were secured. If the Exchange closed a big market on the Curb would be established at once for securities on a cash basis, as the Clearing House facilities would not be open to outside brokers.

Exchange Stands Strain Well.

Yesterday's tremendous liquidation, due to the fact that many of the principal Exchanges of Europe were closed, was taken care of by New York in an orderly manner, even when the weakness in prices was most pronounced. There was no trouble with the sheets of any of the brokers at the Exchange Clearing House, and the air was entirely free from rumors of financial troubles. There has been no breakdown in the machinery of stock trading at this centre, and unless matters grow much worse it is not likely that the authorities will vote to close.

Call money advanced to 6 per cent., where it closed, but a few loans were taken care of at 4½ per cent. In the money crowd it was agreed early in the day that it would be better to mark the rate up to 6 per cent. and attempt to keep it from going higher than to have sudden fluctuations. The National City Bank was a big lender at 6 per cent., and there was no trouble in supplying all the funds wanted.

At no time yesterday did the conditions on the floor of the Exchange equal those panicky days in 1907. Looking down with the big crowd of out-of-town visitors in the Exchange gallery, it did not seem possible that on the floor below stocks were breaking in some instances more than a point between sales. The floor presented a lively appearance, but there was very little excitement. The brokers were all engaged in executing orders in which they had no personal interest, which may account for the lack of tension. In 1907 the traders trying to scalp profits between transactions made a frenzied market. The business done this week has been almost entirely for account of outside buyers and sellers. The brokers on the floor have maintained for the most part an impartial attitude.

Stocks Closed at Low Price.

Unlike the previous markets, stocks closed yesterday about at the low price of the day, owing to the fact that the most alarming news came out in the final hour. So wide were the breaks in many issues that many houses served notice on their customers that they would accept no margin accounts unless they were protected heavily.

Yesterday's market was full of surprises. Some of the biggest declines were explained on the ground that there was practically no short interest in these issues to cushion the drop. That was the case in Reading, which fell 16 points, although it is one of the most valued stocks on the list. On the other hand, Steel, with its $500,000,000 of stock outstanding, usually the most volatile of the speculative issues, resisted every attempt to force a rout, and gave ground only moderately on sales totaling a quarter of a million shares—in itself a good day's business.

General Motors, which sold up to 99 two months ago on reports of big earnings, went down yesterday to a fraction below 55. General Motors preferred, which sold at 95 earlier in the Summer, lost 10 points between two successive sales, and touched 70 yesterday. Intrinsic values and rates of dividend were lost sight of in the mad scramble abroad to realize on everything that could be converted into cash.

Some of the heads of brokerage firms were worried yesterday because they could not get hold of customers who were in the wilds of this country or in Europe. Accounts that seemed protected beyond any possible danger brought a loss to brokers yesterday, and they faced the dilemma of selling out and losing a customer's friendship, or of advancing money of their own at the risk of increasing this loss.

Transactions in Leading Stocks.

This table shows how the slump yesterday weakened the market:

Sales.		Last Sale Yesterday.	Yesterday's Net Loss.	Total Decline on War Scare.
94,500	Amalgamated Cop.	49½	9	20¾
14,700	A., T. & S. F.	89⅝	4	10⅝
16,100	Balt. & Ohio	72	3⅝	8⅝
14,800	Brooklyn R. T.	79½	7½	11
43,800	Canadian Pacific	157½	8⅝	27½
4,400	Ches. & Ohio	41½	2⅝	4⅝
10,200	C., M. & St. P.	85¼	7	12½
13,800	Chino Copper	32	4⅛	8
22,200	Erie	20½	2⅝	5
13,400	Great Northern pf.	114	3⅛	8¼
19,800	Lehigh Valley	121	9⅛	13⅝
16,000	N. Y. Central	77	6⅝	8⅝
6,000	N. Y., N. H. & H.	51	2	2
17,800	Northern Pacific	97	6⅞	12⅛
18,200	Pennsylvania	106	2½	4⅝
129,100	Reading	140	14½	22½
68,000	Southern Pacific	84⅞	6⅞	11⅝
14,200	Southern Ry.	17½	1½	4⅝
132,000	Union Pacific	112½	6½	14⅛
270,700	United States Steel	57⅞	4⅞	9⅞
22,100	Utah Copper	46	7	10⅝
7,600	West. E. & M.	65½	8½	12⅛

Brokers Work All Night.

The heavy declines of the last few days have brought in thousands of buyers who have held aloof from the stock market for years. As a result the odd-lot business has reached unprecedented proportions and the machinery of clearing transactions was run late into the night.

One big house which does not seek this class of business but accepts it as do most other houses more as a matter of accommodation bought 13,000 shares for buyers, taking less than 100 shares each yesterday, and sold but 4,000. The odd-lot dealers on the Exchange, who have twelve and fourteen brokers on the floor, were almost swamped by the demands made on them by other houses.

Two of these firms had clerks at work throughout the whole night. Wall Street, which has been suffering from dry rot for three years, hardly knew itself last night with nearly every brokerage office illuminated and all of the employes at work settling up the day's transactions. In a small chop house, the business of which is usually over at 3 o'clock in the afternoon, sixty men were getting dinner last night preparatory to returning to their desks.

The Stock Exchange Luncheon Club, on the seventh floor of the Exchange Building, and the principal lunch clubs in the big office structures were deserted at noon yesterday and were crowded to the limit of their capacity after the close of the market. It was impossible to get into communication with some of the houses having numerous trunk telephone lines yesterday. In the old days, when million-share sessions were not uncommon, there were much larger forces on hand to take care of the business, and the rush of the last four days has pushed the decimated staffs to their limit.

Kaiser's Blunt Questions to the Czar Extreme Expedient to Avert War.

SENDS PEACEMAKER, TOO

Czarina's Brother, Grand Duke of Hesse, at St. Petersburg to Urge Peace.

CALL TO ARMS PREPARED

Would Add 2,000,000 Men to the Army and 80,000 to the Naval Forces.

AUSTRIA TO ATTACK RUSSIA?

Report That She Will Force the Issue by a Declaration of War Today.

Special Cable to THE NEW YORK TIMES.

BERLIN, July 30.—"Peace or mobilization within twenty-four hours," that, according to high authority, is the German Government's summary of the situation tonight.

The Kaiser's Government, as a last extreme move on behalf of peace, launched today a peremptory demand upon St. Petersburg for an unqualified explanation of Russia's "menacing mobilization" on the German and Austrian frontiers. Russia has been given to understand that unless these movements are abandoned forthwith Germany will respond in kind.

Little hope is cherished in Berlin that Germany's demand will be complied with. Indeed, a report which has just reached here that Russia's reserves in twenty-three districts have been called up seems like a defiant answer to Berlin's representations. In fact, hope that peace can be maintained has been all but abandoned.

Although Germany does not say she will declare war if Russia's military preparations are not canceled, and only threatens to retaliate with a counter demonstration, no secret is made of the fact that a counter-demonstration would be tantamount to war.

Mobilization a Mere Formality.

The fiction is still propagated by the Foreign Office, the War Office, and the Admiralty that no mobilization in any sense of the word has so far taken place, but when it does come it will turn out to be a mere formality. Germany at this hour is as ready to take the field as she will be when the ominous red placards formally gazetting the fact are posted on the public hoardings.

Late this afternoon the officials of the embassy of a certain great power applied to a wholesale provision firm for ten barrels of flour. They were informed that no such order could possibly be filled as everything already had been commandeered for the army and the navy.

Mobilization, it is understood, will call out all reserves for the years extending back to 1908, or the so-called "active reserve." This would mean in the case of the navy roundly 80,000 men and in the case of the army 2,000,000 men.

Decision at Wednesday's Council.

Germany's momentous decision to take a strong stand at St. Petersburg today was made at the New Palace, at Potsdam, last night at a council of war.

The council lasted far into the night. It was presided over by the Emperor in his capacity of Supreme War Lord, and included the Chancellor, the Foreign Secretary, the Minister of Marine, the Chief of the General Staff of the Army and the Chief of the Admiralty Staff, and a number of other distinguished military, naval, and civilian personages. Admiral Prince Henry of Prussia, fresh from England, also was present, as well as the Crown Prince, who, in accordance with Prussian traditions, will lead one of the German armies.

Gen. von Falkenhayn, the Minister of War, informed the conference that, while complete Russian mobilization, in a technical sense, had not taken place, the dispositions at the St. Petersburg War Office were of such an unmistakable character that Germany could only consider them as formal preliminaries to actual mobilization.

The conference came to the conclusion, after hearing satisfying reports from Gen. von Falkenhayn and Gen. von Moltke, Chief of the General Staff, as to the state of Germany's own preparedness, that the moment had arrived to launch a pointed question at St. Petersburg in regard to the significance of Russia's measures. It was decided that while Russia's reply to Germany's inquiry was pending Germany must not delay taking preliminary counter-precautions.

It was determined, according to the Government-controlled Lokal Anzeiger, that Russia must finally be given to understand that Berlin was no longer inclined to view with indifference the "continuous rattling of the Russian sabre in Germany's face." Germany has come to the conclusion that only the plainest speaking on her part can perhaps, at the eleventh hour, still preserve Europe from Armageddon.

"We believe," says The Lokal Anzeiger, "that the next twenty-four hours will bring forth decisions of enormous importance."

The Lokal Anzeiger this afternoon caused a sensation by publishing an extra announcing that the "entire German Army and Navy had been ordered to mobilize." People stood discussing the news excitedly on the streets. Twenty minutes later, however, another extra of the same paper appeared with the following strange announcement:

"Through a gross misdemeanor an extra edition of the Lokal Anzeiger was circulated this afternoon with the information that Germany had determined to mobilize. We herewith state that this news was incorrect."

One explanation of this incident is that the Lokal Anzeiger, wanting when the hour arrived to be first in the field with the news, printed an "emergency" extra edition and that carriers and others who for several days had been drilled in "smartness" overreached themselves and obtained possession of the extra before being authorized to take it from the Lokal Anzeiger's premises.

Panic at Saarbrucken.

There was an extraordinary war panic today at Saarbrucken, Alsace. The populace indulged in mad competition to buy up the available supplies of provisions. Shops of all kinds were stormed and there was a run on the savings bank. Potatoes, flour, salt, sugar, and tinned vegetables soared to unprecedented prices, and paper money was frequently refused.

All bridges in that region are guarded by troops, and trains bound for France are carefully inspected.

The Town Council of Breslau held a secret session today to discuss ways and means of provisioning the city in case of war with Russia.

Two motor cars, said to belong to Grand Duke Orloff and Grand Duke Nicholas of Russia, were seized at Saarlouis. The cars contained a typewriter, a field writing desk, and several field chairs. Two chauffeurs and a servant were detained. They appear to have been bound for Paris.

Three Questions Put to Russia.

By The Associated Press.

BERLIN, Friday, July 31.—In diplomatic quarters here it is stated that the note dispatched to Russia yesterday morning giving that power twenty-four hours to explain her intentions with regard to mobilization asked three questions—the object of the mobilization, whether it was directed against Austria-Hungary, and whether Russia was willing to order a stoppage of the mobilization.

Grand Duke Ernst of Hesse, brother of Empress Elizabeth Feodorovna of Russia, was sent by Emperor William to St. Petersburg today in a last endeavor to arrange for peace.

Major Gen. Erich von Falkenhayn, Minister of War, and Lieut. Gen. Count Helmuth von Moltke, Chief of the German General Staff, had a long conference today with Dr. von Bethmann-Hollweg, the Imperial Chancellor; Prince Henry of Prussia, the Emperor's brother, and several of the Imperial Ministers who assembled at the Chancellor's palace.

Rumors were current afterward that a call had been issued for a session of the Federal Council, which is composed of representatives of the States of Germany, and that the First German Army Corps, with headquarters at Koenigsberg, had been mobilized.

State railroad employes armed with carbines and ball cartridges were placed on duty today at all the railroad bridges and culverts throughout Germany.

It is known that no steps have been taken toward the mobilization of the German Navy. The battle squadrons are concentrated at Kiel and Wilhelmshaven and are still on a normal footing, while none of the reserve ships has been manned, according to the Admiralty. Everything, however, is in instant readiness for bringing the navy up to war strength should the call come.

WAR FERVOR IN RUSSIA.

Sailing of the British Squadron Causes Much Enthusiasm.

NEW YORK TIMES-London Chronicle Special Cable Dispatch.

ST. PETERSBURG, July 30.—War fever seized on St. Petersburg immediately after the announcement of the mobilization, and increased almost to delirium on the receipt of the news of the sailing of the British squadron from Portland.

Business is half suspended, the activities of the streets being confined to cheering, reading the newspapers, and talking of the prospects of war.

To all appearances, war would be popular in St. Petersburg.

I am asked to deny that an order for partial mobilization is intended merely as a reply to the Austria declaration of war. As a matter of fact, the mobilization is absolute, and the general reservists in the northern districts are also being summoned to arms.

No bills are being discounted, in view of the closing of the Bourse. Cash payments on Government securities have been suspended.

Measures are being taken to conciliate dissatisfied elements of the population. The order prohibiting the participation of Jews in joint stock companies has been temporarily rescinded.

It is anticipated that private shipping firms will unite to help in the defense of the Baltic coasts in case of a Russo-German war. The sailors of both fleets are to be in readiness by tomorrow.

The sailing of the English squadron is interpreted as aiming at the localization of the conflict to Austria, Servia, and Russia.

ST. PETERSBURG, July 30.—The streets of the Russian capital are overflowing again tonight with enthusiastic subjects of the Emperor, and patriotic demonstrations continue without cessation.

The British and French Embassies and the Servian Legation are surrounded by crowds of cheering Russians, who apparently have been stirred to a high degree of patriotism by the war spirit which prevails everywhere and the report that the Emperor, in case of hostilities, is to take command.

This feeling has extended also to the distant workmen's sections of the city.

GREAT ACTIVITY IN WARSAW.

Troops Going to Strategic Points—Railways Taken Over.

NEW YORK TIMES-London Chronicle Special Cable Dispatch.

WARSAW, July 30.—By well-informed persons here the situation is regarded as most serious, although the town in general is as quiet as usual.

With a view to averting financial panic and a complete dearth of gold the committee of the Stock Exchange has wired the Finance Ministry for assistance. The State Bank has refused to discount local bills. The bank is under the control of the military authorities, who, of course, have also taken over the railways.

All freight traffic is suspended. No passengers are allowed to leave Warsaw or any part of Russian Poland for Austria.

No demonstrations have been made and the laboring classes who have just returned to work after the recent general strike are well in hand. Citizens who were on holidays are hurrying back home before all communications are closed.

All officers and men have returned from their Summer quarters, and troops are being rapidly dispatched to strategic points.

Government gold and State papers are coming into Warsaw under strong convoys from all the Polish provincial cities. From here the treasure and documents are to be forwarded to St. Petersburg and Moscow.

There are rumors that general mobilization will be announced tonight.

I cannot say that people here are in favor of war. The financial and industrial crisis, caused by the attitude of the State Bank, and the militarization of the public services, has been the means of arousing much disquiet among middle-class civilians. An enormous amount of loans are being called in by the banks.

The opinion has been everywhere expressed that troops would be called up all over the country. Up to now, however, we find that Poland and Lithuania have been excepted.

The prospect of war comes very near home to some Polish families. In many cases some members of the family have been called up by Austria, while others have to serve under the colors of Russia.

TO DECLARE WAR ON RUSSIA.

Austria Will Act Today, According to St. Petersburg.

LONDON, Friday, July 31.—A dispatch from St. Petersburg to Reuter's Telegram Company, says it is believed in St. Petersburg that Austria will declare war against Russia today.

The dispatch adds that if this should be the case it is understood that Emperor Nicholas will go to Moscow to deliver a pronunciamento in the Uspensky Cathedral.

MARTIAL LAW AT RIGA.

Steamers Have to Get Special Permission to Pass In or Out.

RIGA, July 30.—Martial law was proclaimed today over Bolderaa and the mouth of the River Düna and its vicinity.

Steamers have to obtain special permission to pass in and out.

The field of submarine mines outside the entrance to the harbor is to be completed tonight.

London Fears the Great Conflict Is About to Begin.

DEFENSIVE MEASURES TAKEN

Portsmouth and Dover Harbors Closed, Coast Guards Stationed.

BRITAIN MAY BE DRAWN IN

Unionist Journals Take Ground That England Must Fight if Germany Attacks France.

AWAIT RUSSIA'S RESPONSE

Report That She Has Already Stated She Cannot Halt Mobilization Orders.

Special Cable to THE NEW YORK TIMES.

LONDON, Friday, July 31.—"On the Brink of War" is the headline with which The Times this morning sums up the situation, in which there seems to be but one gleam of hope that Europe will be preserved from the greatest catastrophe in history.

In practically all quarters last night THE NEW YORK TIMES correspondent found the belief prevalent that the beginning of an Armageddon was only a matter of hours. There was one noteworthy exception—the London head of one of the great financial establishments of the world, who informed THE TIMES correspondent that he had received advices which indicated that there still remained a strong likelihood of Germany and Russia coming to an understanding, which would set a limit to Russian mobilization that would be accepted by Germany and would obviate the necessity from the Berlin point of view of German mobilization.

In conjunction with this optimistic statement reports come from Berlin that the Grand Duke of Hesse has left on a special train for St. Petersburg in order to hand to the Czar a personal communication from Emperor William.

It is also stated that the German Government yesterday made a final effort for peace by notes addressed to St. Petersburg, Paris, and other capitals. Should the replies to these be unsatisfactory, Germany, it is added, will mobilize her armies at once.

A Berlin dispatch, received here late last night, gives another and alarming version of possibly the same action. This said that the German Government had addressed a request to Russia for an explanation of the mobilization and asking whether Russia was willing to order a cessation of mobilization. This was accompanied, it was stated, by a request that the Russian Government reply as speedily as possible.

One German paper speaks of a "twenty-four hours' ultimatum."

Reported Refusal by Sazonoff.

A report has also reached London that the Russian Foreign Minister, Sergius Sazonoff, has already replied to the German note by stating that the mobilization has been ordered and cannot be canceled.

The measures taken, though extensive, can not be called a mobilization, for neither the army nor the navy can be mobilized in the strictest sense of the word without a royal proclamation. Nevertheless, the British military and naval machinery, created in the last ten years, provides, says a London paper, "so thorough a groundwork for the process of mobilizing of not only the fighting forces but also other services of the State on which in time of war those forces would have to rely for defense of these islands and the dominions oversea, that the preparations brought last night without commotion or excitement to a culminating point when it could be said we are ready, whatever may occur." The Times, on the other hand, says that the Government has incurred a grave responsibility by delaying the orders for a general mobilization.

Premier Asquith and Sir Edward Grey, the Foreign Secretary, discussing the crisis in the House of Commons yesterday, spoke in terms of the gravest apprehension.

The House was hushed in impressive silence as the Premier said that the issues of peace or war were hanging in the balance, and with them the risk of a catastrophe of which it was impossible to measure either the dimensions or the effects. Mr. Asquith appealed for a truce of domestic politics in the face of the national emergency, and Mr. Bonar-Law followed with the declaration that, whatever the domestic differences of the British might be, "they will not prevent us presenting a united front in the councils of the world."

England Preparing in Earnest.

Information reaching THE TIMES correspondent from trustworthy sources indicates that Great Britain is making every preparation for war. Various announcements have been made from the Admiralty and the War Office that the measures which are being taken are merely "precautionary," but the extent of these can be estimated from the fact that English newspapers have been officially requested to publish no news of naval or military movements.

The Times says this morning:

"Naval and military measures of a precautionary defensive character are being carried out quietly and calmly throughout the British Empire. The actual steps taken it would be unpatriotic to mention, but the reports which reach us from places as wide apart as the North of Scotland and the Channel Islands indicate the thoroughness of these preparations.

"This knowledge should have a reassuring effect on the public mind. Not only at home are many necessary things being done to safeguard British interests, but from the outward marches of the empire, the dominion and the dependencies, the same note of precaution is struck.

"It would be highly improper to do otherwise than maintain a discreet silence about the disposition of ships, the activity in the dockyards, the movements of coast guards and soldiers, or the work of replenishing the stores of munitions of war."

All the English papers loyally refrain from printing any news of this kind. Here are some facts that betray no important secrets.

The naval boom across Portsmouth Harbor was put down at 11 o'clock last night. Dover Harbor has been cleared of all shipping, and the cross-Channel steamers will not be able to use it today and will have to go to Folkestone.

Troops for Queenborough and other east coast ports have been dispatched from Shorncliffe camp.

Woolwich Arsenal is guarded by a strongly increased force.

The patrols around the eastern and southern coasts were strengthened.

Part of the troops quartered in Ireland have been ordered to Aldershot and the garrison at Falmouth has been increased.

The Admiralty is offering generous prices for all the available stocks of coal in Cardiff.

Even the metropolitan police are being called into requisition. Men on annual leave have been recalled, and those about to get leave have had it stopped.

Say England Must Fight.

The question whether Great Britain will be drawn into a Continental war is being hotly debated. Whether she will or not future developments alone can show. The best information obtainable was given in these dispatches last week, and nothing has occurred since to make the statement less likely to prove a correct prediction.

The press is divided into two camps. One argues that England's duty and interest will require this country to take its stand with France and Russia. The Times and The Daily Mail this morning print special articles on the subject. One says:

"The full gravity of the European situation cannot be appreciated unless it is clearly and definitely understood that in the event of the outbreak of a general conflagration this country cannot, in its own vital interest, afford to stand out.

"There is no question of Great Britain espousing the cause of Servia, no question of Great Britain blindly following the lead of France and Russia, her friends in the Triple Entente.

"In the event of a European conflagration Austria-Hungary and Germany on the one side and Russia and France on the other will not fight about the merits of the Austro-Servian conflict.

"The balance of power in Europe will be the stake.

"In other words, the control of the European continent and the whole security of the British Empire depend on the maintenance of the balance of power."

Other Unionist papers like The Telegraph and The Morning Post take the same view, though they do not express it so flatly as Lord Northcliffe's papers.

Liberal papers like The Chronicle and The Daily News argue that no treaty obligation binds Great Britain to take an active part in war, and quote Mr. Asquith's statement to that effect on March 24, 1914. Many things have happened since then, and the facts in regard to this particular aspect of the situation are that if a general war involving the two triple combinations of powers breaks out, England will play an active part in it.

Austria Hurls 500,000 Men in Four Divisions at Servia.

DANUBE AND SAVE CROSSED

March Southward on the Road to Nish Begun, Following Capture of Belgrade.

BIG BATTLE IN BOSNIA

Servians Reported to Have Been Defeated There, with Loss of 800 Men.

MONTENEGRINS IN CATTARO

Occupy Dalmatian Seaport Covered by Their Guns on Mount Lovtchen—Greece Ready to Mobilize.

LONDON, Friday, July 31.—A Semlin dispatch to The Standard says:

"The Austrians crossed the Danube thirty miles to the east of Belgrade and the Save ten miles to the south. Belgrade has been captured and is now occupied by Austrian troops, and the force which invaded Servia at Semendria is advancing along the road which leads to Palanka, and ultimately to Nish.

"The occupation of Belgrade was carried out without serious difficulty. The invading troops crossed the river partly by means of the remnants of the railway bridge, which was blown up by the Servians, and partly by a pontoon bridge constructed under its cover, and approached the Servian capital from the south. The attacking forces advanced by a steep hill, driving the Servians before them. The Servians retreated, partly along the road leading to Groca and partly toward Popovatz. The losses on both sides appeared to have been comparatively light.

"The invasion of Servia at Semendria was a much more difficult task. The Austrians built a pontoon bridge under the cover of darkness from an island in the middle of the Danube, where the channel narrows to 200 yards and the current is swift. The construction of the bridge was a hazardous operation. The work was perceived from the Servian shore and the Servians opened fire. The attacking forces were aided by artillery and infantry along the south shore of the island, and succeeded in completing the bridge, over which they passed."

British Legation Struck.

A dispatch from another source says the ancient Fortress of Belgrade was reduced by the Austrian artillery, which caused only slight damage to other parts of the Servian capital. The British Legation was struck by an Austrian shell.

An Athens dispatch to The Daily Telegraph says it is reported from Corfu that the Russian warship Terets in port there has received news by wireless that Belgrade was occupied by the Austrians after heavy fighting, and that 200 Austrians and 100 Servians were killed.

Earlier telegrams received by the Servian Legation yesterday announced that the Austrians attempting to cross the Danube twenty miles east of Belgrade, presumably near Semendria, were repulsed, and that a big artillery engagement was in progress; also that the Servian troops successfully resisted the Austrian advance at Losnitza, to the west of Belgrade.

The Austro-Hungarian invaders followed the valley of the River Morava and first encountered a body of Servian troops at Semendria, on the Servian side of the Danube, southeast of Belgrade. The Servians held their ground until nightfall and then retired. Both Austrians and Servians suffered heavy losses, several hundred soldiers being killed in the engagement.

Austrian Check at Losnitza.

On the western side of Servia an Austrian column came into contact with a Servian force at Losnitza, which offered a stubborn defense and held the fort there until dark, inflicting heavy losses on the Austrians.

Unconfirmed reports reached here

The forces of the Czar, well-equipped and well-officered, display their artillery.

Wide World Photos

Russian reservists, on their way to active duty, are accompanied by their families.

"All the News That's Fit to Print."

The New York Times.

THE WEATHER
Generally fair today and Monday; gentle to moderate south winds.
For full weather report see PAGE 8, SPORTS SECTION.

VOL. LXIII...NO. 20,644. .... NEW YORK, SUNDAY, AUGUST 2, 1914.—88 PAGES, In Seven Parts, Including Picture and Rotogravure Section, Real Estate Directory, and Review of Books. PRICE FIVE CENTS.

GERMANY DECLARES WAR ON RUSSIA, FIRST SHOTS ARE FIRED; FRANCE IS MOBILIZING AND MAY BE DRAWN IN TOMORROW; PLANS TO RESCUE THE 100,000 AMERICANS NOW IN EUROPE

Transports for Refugees Being Considered by State Department.

MAY CHARTER VESSELS

Appropriation Will Probably Be Asked from Congress to Rescue Stranded Americans.

MIGHT SEND OVER GOLD

To Relieve Those Unable to Get Cash on Paper or to Obtain Passage.

FEW WARSHIPS NOW THERE

Consuls Being Confronted with Many Urgent Calls for Assistance.

ANXIOUS INQUIRIES POUR IN

Washington Can Only Reply That Our Representatives Are Instructed to Give All Possible Aid.

WASHINGTON, Aug. 1.—The Administration has under consideration the sending of army and navy transports to bring American refugees back from Europe, and a special request to Congress for an appropriation is expected to be made.

The President and Mr. Bryan discussed several plans, but will not make a final decision until tomorrow, when they will confer again and get the opinion of the bankers who usually serve the State Department abroad in normal times.

If necessary the Washington Government is prepared to send American vessels abroad with gold for the relief of Americans. Immediately after the conference with the President Mr. Bryan cabled all consulates, legations and embassies to spare no pains in caring for Americans who remain in the war zones, and to give every facility to those who wished to leave.

State Department officials admitted that a most serious problem was confronting them in the plight of Americans abroad. They estimated that at least 100,000, and possibly as many as 300,000, were scattered throughout Europe. The disorganization of European exchange has made it practically impossible to cash checks or letters of credit. American consulates, legations and embassies are devoid of funds for the emergency which has suddenly confronted them. They are being besieged on all sides with requests for financial assistance.

With the cancellation by several steamship lines of their sailings many Americans find themselves unable to get passage on the overcrowded boats of American register. American warships would be of little use, as they have hardly any capacity for passengers. Naval officers have suggested that the Government could charter immediately some of the big ocean liners of foreign register to bring Americans home.

By special arrangement, officials believe the American Government could obtain the use of foreign ships, securing exemption from seizure if used only for transportation of Americans.

The only American warships in European waters are the little gunboat Scorpion, station ship at Constantinople, and the battleship Maine at Villefranche, with Annapolis midshipmen and the officers and crew of the battleship Idaho taken over at that port by the Greek Government. The Maine will leave Villefranche today for Annapolis.

A special appropriation would be required to charter steamships to bring Americans home. Congress always has acted promptly in such emergencies, and is expected to do so again.

Many applications were received at the State Department from persons in the United States desirous of having American Consuls investigate and report upon the safety of their friends and relatives in Europe. The State Department is returning the uniform answer that under their general instructions the Consuls will look after and report the case of any Americans in distress in their respective districts, and consequently that no special instructions are needed.

ENGLAND HESITATES WHAT COURSE TO TAKE

Grey Wants to Throw the Weight of Great Navy at Once in Favor of Russia and France.

Special Cable to THE NEW YORK TIMES.

LONDON, Sunday, Aug. 2.—Great Britain's rôle in the European war now begun is now a great question. THE TIMES correspondent learns on good authority that the Cabinet is practically divided into equal parts on the question whether to take immediate action or await developments in the hope of remaining outside of the struggle.

Sir Edward Grey, according to this information, heads the party which believes that it is England's duty and interest to throw the weight of her navy at once into the scales on behalf of France and Russia.

Lloyd George leads the other faction, which believes that this country can with honor and advantage hold itself outside and not engage in a European conflict.

One statement, which is given for what it is worth, is that the Chancellor of the Exchequer thinks that England and the United States can together intervene at a propitious moment in such fashion as to reduce to some extent the horrors of a Continental Armageddon. In passing it may be mentioned that the wildest reports have been current on all aspects of the situation for a week past. THE TIMES correspondent refrained from chronicling them because the actual facts of the situation require no sensational embroidery.

Cabinet to Meet Tonight.

A special meeting of the Cabinet has been summoned for the unprecedented hour of 11 o'clock tonight. Most of the Ministers are remaining in town till then, and none is going out of reach. Some hope to get a day's golfing as a respite.

The Cabinet Council sat for two and a half hours yesterday. Sir Edward Grey left in the middle of the proceedings for the Foreign Office.

With reference to the Cabinet's position, The Observer this morning says:

"France and Germany have cast the die on their frontiers. Before nightfall, or even before these lines see the light may be fired in the western and decisive theatre of war the first shots of a tremendous struggle that will decide the destinies of the Old World for generations. The first great actions may decide the final issue, first in the West and then in the Near East.

"If after the lamentable wavering of last week we hesitate one day more we shall be too late to influence an arbitrament which indirectly but surely will decide our own fate no less than that of France. Our hours are numbered. If the Ministry decides today to desert France, then they will strike us out of the list of nations that any power can trust."

Fleet Ready for a Blow.

It is said that the Cabinet is likely to reach a decision tonight. One factor that will probably influence the decision is the total absence of indications of any of that anti-German sentiment which has been a feature of the spurious agitation of recent years. In the event of the Cabinet deciding upon war, speculation is rife as to what the fleet will do first.

The First Home Fleet, which sailed under sealed orders, is believed to be off the coast of Holland or in the neighborhood of Denmark. A high official of the Admiralty said to THE TIMES correspondent tonight:

"It is idle to speculate. Only three men in England know what its orders are."

Thanks to the recent Spithead review by the King, Great Britain's navy is practically ready for war, and a proclamation of mobilization would only really affect the second line. Its ability to strike a sudden, serious blow is not doubted in England, and, as is evident from the orders given to German liners, the blow is apprehended in Germany.

The Admiralty is, of course, in wireless touch with the commanding officers, and to prevent any possibility of interference with the radio communications stringent instructions have been issued that all amateur or private wireless systems must be stopped.

Poincare Orders Mobilization, Telling France It Is Not War Yet

PARIS, Aug. 1.—President Poincaré and the members of the Cabinet today issued the following joint proclamation to the French nation:

For some days the States of Europe have been considerably aggravated, and, notwithstanding the efforts of diplomacy, the horizon has darkened. At the present hour a greater part of the nations have mobilized their forces. Even the countries protected by neutrality conventions have deemed it their duty to take this measure as a precaution.

The powers whose constitutional or military legislation differs from ours have, without issuing a decree of mobilization, begun and carried on preparations which, in reality, are equivalent to mobilization, and are but the anticipated execution of it.

France, who always has affirmed her desire for peace, who on many a tragic day has given to Europe counsels of moderation and a living example of decorum, and who has multiplied her efforts to maintain the peace of the world, has now prepared herself for all eventualities, and has taken from henceforth her first indispensable dispositions for the safeguarding of her territory.

But our legislation does not permit the completion of these preparations without a decree of mobilization. Conscious of its high responsibility, and feeling that it would fail in its sacred duty if it did not take this measure, the Government has signed the decree.

Mobilization is not war. Under the present circumstances it would appear, on the contrary, to be the best means of assuring peace with honor.

Strong in its ardent desire of arriving at a peaceful solution of this crisis, the Government under cover of these essential precautions will continue its diplomatic efforts, and still hopes to succeed. It counts upon the coolness of the people not to give itself up to unjustified emotion. It counts upon the patriotism of every Frenchman, and it knows that there is not a single one who is not ready to do his duty at this hour.

There are no longer any parties. There is an eternal France—a France peaceful and resolute. There is a fatherland of peace and justice, all united in calm vigilance and dignity.

France Orders Mobilization After Germany Asks Her Intentions.

DELCASSE WAR MINISTER

Germany's Old Enemy Heads Army Organization — Once Nearly Caused Conflict.

CLEMENCEAU IN CABINET

President and Cabinet Issue a Manifesto to French Nation.

PLAIN WORDS TO GERMANY

"You Are Mobilizing; We Know It," Says Prime Minister to German Envoy.

ORDERS TO FOREIGNERS

Americans May Stay on Getting Permits—Austrians and Germans Liable to Arrest.

PARIS, Aug. 1.—An official decree orders a general mobilization of the French Army, beginning tomorrow.

The mobilization, according to the official decree, is to be completed at 11:59 o'clock Sunday night.

The wildest enthusiasm was manifested on the Paris boulevards when the news of the order became known. Bodies of men, formed into regular companies in ranks ten deep, paraded the streets, waving the Tricolor and other national emblems and cheering and singing the "Marseillaise" and the "Internationale," at the same time throwing their hats in the air.

Here and there the cry, "On to Berlin!" was raised.

On the sidewalks were many weeping women and children. All the stores and cafés were deserted.

Relations Not Yet Severed.

The decree of mobilization of the French Army, which was followed by a proclamation by the President and the Cabinet to the nation, has, however, not terminated diplomatic relations between France and Germany. Conversations between the powers, notably between Russia and Austria and between France and Germany, continued this evening.

Up to a late hour tonight, it was stated, the German Ambassador was still in Paris.

A rumor in circulation here tonight was to the effect that there were some waverers in the Cabinet yesterday on the question of ordering the mobilization, but that the views of those who asserted that it would be suicidal to allow Germany to put France to further expense with regard to war preparations without actual mobilization prevailed.

The course of diplomatic events since yesterday afternoon can be stated briefly as follows:

Baron von Schön, the German Ambassador to France, called on the French Premier, René Viviani, at 7 o'clock last evening and formally notified him that Germany had addressed an ultimatum to Russia, desiring to know by noon today whether the St. Petersburg Government would discontinue the mobilization of the Russian Army.

Baron von Schön was directed by his Government to ask what were the intentions of France should Russia's reply to Germany be a refusal to demobilize.

The German Government fixed "before 1 P. M. today" as the period within which France must answer. Baron von Schön called at the French Foreign Office at 11:40 A. M. to receive France's reply. Premier Viviani made an earnest appeal to the German Ambassador, asking if Germany could not yet do something to avert war.

The Baron promised to communicate with Berlin and to return to the Foreign Office at 4 P. M., which he did.

"You Are Mobilizing. We Know It."

In the course of their second interview today Premier Viviani said to the German Ambassador:

"You are mobilizing. We know it."

Baron von Schön did not reply, and M. Viviani continued:

"This attitude of your Government has dictated ours. We were compelled to take precautions similar to yours. Our peaceful intentions remain unchanged. We wish peace, and the best proof we can give you of this is that at the present moment the French Parliament has not been convoked. Under our constitution we should be compelled to convoke it if our intentions were not peaceful."

Baron von Schön said: "But frontier incidents are unfortunately to be feared."

Premier Viviani replied:

"How can you suppose such things? Our troops are five miles from the frontier. We are, in fact, exposed to the violation of our frontier, and there is not another power in the world which would have consented to do such a thing."

This refers to the withdrawal of the French troops from the immediate frontier.

The Premier proceeded to point out that the German troops were at the very foot of the frontier posts, and said he concluded from this that if incidents occurred they could only be provoked by the German military forces.

The German reply was submitted to a French Cabinet Council, which, within a few minutes afterward, ordered a general mobilization of the French Army.

The date of the mobilization was set for tomorrow, but it really begins immediately. The men are called out in classes at intervals of days, according to the year in which they entered the army. Precise instructions are always in the possession of every man, so that he may know what to do when a general mobilization is posted.

Reservists Obey Instantly.

The response to the order of mobilization was instant, and the stations of all the railways, particularly those leading to the eastward, were crowded tonight with departing reservists. Many women accompanied the men until close to the stations, where, the women softly crying, farewells were said.

The Russian Ambassador, M. Iswolsky, called on Premier Viviani at 11 o'clock tonight and informed him that Germany had declared war on Russia.

Nothing is known among the general public as to what is going on behind the screen which fell along the German frontier at about 4 o'clock yesterday afternoon.

Arrangements were made last night by Myron T. Herrick, the American Ambassador, acting under instructions from Washington, to take over the affairs of the German Embassy, while Alexander H. Thackara, the American Consul General, is to look after the affairs of the German Consulate.

All foreigners may leave Paris or France before the end of the first day of mobilization by train, but not by automobile. Those deciding to leave France may do so by certain trains, the time tables of which are posted on the walls of Paris tonight, or by sea.

American citizens or British subjects may remain in France, except in the regions on the eastern frontier and near certain fortresses, provided they make declarations to the police and obtain special permits.

No foreigner will be permitted to leave France after the first day of mobilization without a passport signed by a Prefect. Americans, Englishmen, and other foreigners may remain in Paris by obtaining special permits from the police.

Delcasse War Minister.

LONDON, Aug. 1.—A Paris dispatch to the Central News by indirect route reports that Premier Viviani has made changes in the Cabinet.

Théophile Delcassé becomes Minister of War, and Georges Clemenceau, the ex-Premier, joins the Ministry.

M. Delcassé is one of the bitterest enemies of Germany among French statesmen. He nearly caused a war with that country in 1905.

Cabinet Council in Session Till 4 A. M.

PARIS, Sunday, Aug. 2. The Council of Ministers, which held a late night session to discuss the European situation, adjourned shortly after 4 o'clock this morning. It will continue its discussion of the situation this afternoon. No announcement of the result of the deliberations has been given out.

KAISER SIGNS ORDER MOBILIZING HIS ARMY

"Let Your Hearts Beat for God and Your Fists on the Enemy," Cries Chancellor.

BERLIN, Aug. 1.—Emperor William, at 5:15 o'clock this evening, signed an order mobilizing the German Army.

A semi-official statement says that the threatening danger of war necessitates that military measures be taken for the protection of the German frontier and railway lines. Restrictions, therefore, on the postal, telegraph, and railway services are inevitable, owing to the requirements of the military authorities.

It was officially announced that the time limit of the German ultimatum to Russia expired at noon.

An official communication published in the North German Gazette says the Russian Emperor on July 29 telegraphed to Emperor William urgently requesting him to help in averting the misfortune of a European war and to try to restrain his ally Austria-Hungary from going too far.

Emperor William replied that he would willingly take up the task of mediator, and accordingly diplomatic action was initiated in Vienna.

While this was in progress the news that Russia was mobilizing arrived in Berlin, and Emperor William telegraphed to the Emperor of Russia that his rôle as mediator was by this endangered, if not made impossible.

The communication adds that a decision was to have been taken in Vienna today in regard to the mediation proposals in which Great Britain had joined Germany, but that meanwhile Russia had ordered the full mobilization of her forces. Upon this Emperor William addressed a last telegram to Emperor Nicholas emphatically declaring that his own responsibility for the safety of the German Empire had forced him to take defensive measures.

War Speech by Chancellor.

The German Imperial Chancellor, Dr. von Bethmann-Hollweg, addressed a huge procession of demonstrators today from the window of his official residence, making a stirring speech, in which he said:

"At this serious hour in order to give expression to your feelings for your Fatherland you have come to the house of Bismarck, who with Emperor William the Great and Field Marshal von Moltke welded the German Empire for us.

"We wished to go on living in peace in the empire which we have developed in forty-four years of peaceful labor.

"The whole work of Emperor William has been devoted to the maintenance of peace. To the last hour he has worked for peace in Europe, and he is still working for it. Should all his efforts prove vain and should the sword be forced into our hands we will take the field with a clear conscience in the knowledge that we did not seek war. We shall then wage war for our existence and for the national honor to the last drop of our blood.

"In the gravity of this hour I remind you of the words of Prince Frederick Charles to the men of Brandenburg:

"'Let your hearts beat for God and your fists on the enemy.'"

Enthusiastic cheers and the singing of the national anthem greeted the close of the Imperial Chancellor's speech.

Germany's War Challenge Delivered to Russia at 7:30 Last Evening

EMBASSY THEN DEPARTS

Enrollment of Reservists Begun Throughout the Czar's Vast Empire.

STIRRING SCENES ATTEND IT

Hardly a Family but Loses a Protector, Yet They Take the Call Submissively.

FRANCE HAS TILL MONDAY

Reply to Germany Due Then, but Issue May Be Forced Earlier.

ITALY REMAINS NEUTRAL

Triple Alliance Obligations Not Touched, She Says—Feared a Revolution.

LUXEMBURG INVADED.

Germans Seize a Neutral State Between Them and Paris.

LONDON, Aug. 2.—The Germans have invaded the Duchy of Luxemburg. They seized the Government offices and telephones. The news reached here in a Reuter telephone message from Brussels at 4 A. M. New York time.

Luxemburg is a neutral State southward of Brussels, with its borders on Germany and France. A straight line drawn between Berlin and Paris would pass through the heart of the Duchy of Luxemburg.

Special Cable to THE NEW YORK TIMES.

LONDON, Sunday, Aug. 2.—The news that Germany had declared war against Russia reached London from St. Petersburg late last evening, only half an hour after a Central News dispatch from Paris had raised the hopes of all by the statement that Germany had extended for forty-eight hours, that is, until Monday noon, the period in which Russia and France could reply to the German ultimatums.

The first of these ultimatums was one demanding that Russia cease the mobilization of her army in twelve hours.

The second was a note presented by Baron von Schoen, the German Ambassador in Paris, to Foreign Minister Viviani calling upon France to inform Germany whether in the event of the outbreak of war between Germany and Russia, France would remain neutral.

These notes were regarded as diplomatic skirmishing, designed to cover the hard fact that Germany was bending all her energies to the delivery of the first blow, which might affect the whole course of the war, now officially begun.

In the history of modern warfare an official declaration of war is either accompanied or preceded by an actual stroke of war.

In London this morning it is believed Germany would not officially declare war upon Russia unless her plans for a rapid attack had been entirely completed. Where or how the first blow will be struck is a matter of the widest speculation.

France Next to Be Involved.

France's reply to the German request as to the former's attitude in case Germany engaged in war with Russia is stated to have proved unsatisfactory to Berlin. It was bound to be. Germany could count confidently on it being so. Therefore, according to speculation in London this morning, the eventual news is likely to show that Germany has taken an unsatisfactory reply from France for granted, and while declaring war on Russia has struck or has made her chief preparations to strike at France. This, of course, is pure speculation, and THE NEW YORK TIMES correspondent mentions it for what it is worth.

The established facts, bearing on the crisis in yesterday's developments, are important to note. The first is that the effort made by King George to bring influence to bear on the Czar in favor of peace failed of effect.

The terms of the King's telegram are guarded as the strictest secret. All information THE TIMES correspondent could obtain was that the message was of a highly personal and confidential nature. It followed an interview with Premier Asquith at 2 o'clock yesterday morning.

Italy Feared a Revolution.

The second development was a confirmation of the report that Italy would remain neutral as long as she was assured that her interests were not menaced.

From an official source THE TIMES correspondent learns that the Italian Government was practically forced to this decision by the apprehension that the taking up of arms on behalf of Austria in a quarrel, precipitated by the hereditary enemy of Italy, would have caused an immediate revolution in Italy.

Italy's abstention is a serious blow to the Triple Alliance and may yet prove an important factor in determining, if not the issue of peace or war, at least the duration of the conflict.

One of the ways suggested to prevent the outbreak of war was that Italy and Great Britain should combine and declare themselves on the side of France and Russia. The suggestion utterly disregarded the treaty by which Italy was bound to the Triple Alliance, but it was given some color of vraisemblance by the fact that the British and Italian Ambassadors in various capitals have been working together in a manner which indicated that the Italian Government preferred any peaceable solution of the war to the treaties which bound her to Germany and Austria.

The third important development of the night was the news that the French Government had issued orders for general mobilization.

This came a few hours after the severance of telephonic communications between London and Paris. The French Government informed the British authorities that the telephone was cut for ordinary communication in order to prevent any leakage of news.

Up to 2 o'clock this morning practically no news beyond the announcement of the mobilization had been received here from Paris.

The fullest confirmation of the general mobilization was obtained in London by the issue of a notice to the French Embassy here. This called upon all Frenchmen liable to military service to return to France within twenty-four hours. The news speedily became known in Soho, the French quarter of London, and this morning bands of enthusiastic Frenchmen paraded through Leicester Square.

The almost complete severance of telegraphic and telephonic communication with Paris was shown by the fact that a London paper which had made most elaborate arrangements to obtain a special wire, under a guarantee that nothing in the nature of leakage of military secrets could possibly occur, had not received a word out of Paris up to 3 o'clock this morning.

Telephonic and telegraphic communications with the Continent were generally interrupted.

GERMANY'S DECLARATION

Served by the Retiring Ambassador as Russian Enrollment Begins.

ST. PETERSBURG, Aug. 1.—The German Ambassador, in the name of his Government, sent a declaration of war to the Russian Minister of Foreign Affairs at 7:30 o'clock this evening. Count von Pourtales and the entire staff of the German Embassy then left St. Petersburg.

Martial law has been proclaimed in the capital and its suburbs.

Announcement of the declaration of war was made to the people two hours after it had been received. The city immediately presented a spectacle of extraordinary animation. The Nevsky Prospect and all the leading thoroughfares are filled with war-frenzied people marching in processions, carrying portraits of the Emperor, with flags waving and torches blazing. From time to time there is an outburst of cheering, followed by singing.

Speakers fired with patriotic fervor harangue the crowds. In front of the Kazan Cathedral each procession halts and a sudden hush falls over the processionists, then the strains of the national anthem, sung in perfect harmony by a section of the procession, are heard, and the crowds listen silently with bared heads. On the conclusion of the hymn the procession moves forward and the demonstrations are resumed with greater ardor.

Enrollment of the reservists started at a hundred centres in St. Petersburg at 6 o'clock this morning and was accompanied by stirring scenes. Crowds of women and children accompanied their husbands and fathers to the assembling stations, while priests everywhere blessed the reservists as they marched through the streets singing hymns.

The Municipal Council of Warsaw has voted 1,000,000 roubles (about $500,000) for the Red Cross service of Russia and friendly powers.

The Fateful Red Posters.

Special Cable to THE NEW YORK TIMES.

ST. PETERSBURG, Aug. 1.—All attention is now concentrated on the mobilization of the troops. During the night bills were posted in all parts of the city summoning the whole of the reservists to the colors, and the population awoke to read the startling news on posters printed in red.

Women wept, but the men took it for the most part quietly and seriously, in sad submissiveness.

"I don't care for my life," said one peasant to me, "but I am sorry for the children."

Such expressions are frequent on all hands. Hardly a house, hardly a family

Chronology of Yesterday's Fateful Events

12 Midnight—Germany demands that Russia cease mobilization and gives a twelve-hour limit.

2 A. M.—King George of England, after an audience with Premier Asquith, telegraphs to the Czar, making a strong appeal for peace.

12 Noon—The time limit of Germany's ultimatum to Russia expires.

5:15 P. M.—Emperor William signs an order for the mobilization of the German Army.

7:30 P. M.—The German Ambassador at St. Petersburg delivers to the Russian Government a declaration of war in the name of Germany and leaves St. Petersburg.

First Shots Fired in the Russo-German War.

BERLIN, Aug. 1.—A German patrol near Prostken was fired on this afternoon by a Russian frontier patrol. The Germans returned the fire. There were no losses.

Prostken is a village of 2,300 inhabitants, in East Prussia. It is situated about two and one-half miles west of the international boundary line, on the Konigsberg & Lyck Railroad. The nearest Russian village is Grajevo, about three miles across the international boundary.

Kaiser Forgives Enemies, Prays for Victory.

BERLIN, Aug. 2.—The Emperor again spoke from a window of the Castle tonight to a crowd of 50,000 beneath, who cheered and sang patriotic songs until he appeared. He said:

"I thank you for the love and loyalty shown me. When I enter upon a fight let all party strife cease. We are German brothers and nothing else. All parties have attacked me in times of peace. I forgive them with all my heart. I hope and wish that the good German sword will emerge victorious in the right."

The speech was thrice interrupted by vociferous cheering. At its conclusion the Kaiser bowed in all directions, retiring amid a frenzied demonstration.

The Imperial Chancellor also addressed the assembly, saying:

"All stand as one man for our Emperor, whatever our opinions or our creeds. I am sure that all the young German men are ready to shed their blood for the fame and greatness of Germany. We can only trust in God, Who hitherto has always given us victory."

An imperial decree convokes the Reichstag on Aug. 4.

Czar Nicholas II of Russia

Emperor Francis Joseph of Austria

Kaiser Wilhelm II.

Mid-Week Pictorial

Ambassador Bakmeteff (center) and the Russian War Mission.

"All the News That's Fit to Print."

The New York Times.

THE WEATHER
Fair today and tomorrow; gentle northeast winds, becoming southeast tomorrow.
For full weather report see Page 15.

VOL. LXIII...NO. 20,646. NEW YORK, TUESDAY, AUGUST 4, 1914.—EIGHTEEN PAGES. ONE CENT In Greater New York, Jersey City and Newark. | Elsewhere TWO CENTS.

ENGLAND WILL PROTECT FRENCH COAST AND DEFEND BELGIUM; GERMANY RECALLS ENVOY; HESITATES AT FRENCH FRONTIER; HER ARMY SEIZES RUSSIAN TOWNS, NAVY WINS A VICTORY; GERMAN LINER SLIPS OUT OF NEW YORK IN WAR PAINT

Invading Germans Seize Three Border Cities of Russia

WITH ONLY A SKIRMISH

Czestochowa, Bendzin, and Kaliez, Having 90,000 Population, Fall Into Foes' Hands.

KAISER'S FLEET WINS FIGHT

By Capturing Aland Islands from Russian Fleet, Germany Menaces St. Petersburg.

CLASHES ON FRENCH BORDER

But Chief Danger to Republic Now Lies in a German Dash Across Belgian Territory.

THOUGH BRUSSELS OBJECTS

France Promises to Guard Belgian Neutrality, Now Menaced by Great Army of Germans.

BERLIN, Aug. 3.—German troops began the invasion of Russia today, and now occupy the cities of Czestochowa, Bendzin, and Kaliez, all in Russian Poland.

Czestochowa was taken by German border troops from Lublinitz, Silesia, after a short skirmish with Russians.

The force which took Kaliez consisted of the first battalion of the 155th Infantry, with a machine gun company, accompanied by the First Regiment of German Uhlans, known as the Emperor Alexander III. of Russia Uhlans. The infantry made a rapid advance from Ostrowo, in Prussian Poland.

ALLENSTEIN, East Prussia, Aug. 3.—The fighting on the Russian frontier was confined to small engagements between cavalry outposts until 6 o'clock last evening. Then an attack was made by Russian invaders on Johannisburg, which is occupied by a squadron of the Eleventh Pomeranian Dragoons.

The railroad from Johannisburg to Lyok, on the Russian frontier, has been cut, and also the light railroad running to Diottowen.

The losses of the Russian troops are believed to have numbered about twenty men, while the Germans have not lost any killed, although several have been slightly wounded.

Of the three cities in Russia occupied by German troops, Czestochowa, with about 50,000 inhabitants, is on the River Waethe, near the frontier. Bendzin, a coal and zinc mining centre, has a population of slightly over 20,000. Kaliez, the capital of the province of the same name, is the most westerly city in Russian Poland. It has about 20,000 population.

GERMAN RAIDS INTO FRANCE.

Patrols Attack Joncherey—Rumored French Attempt Through Holland.

LONDON, Tuesday, Aug. 4.—German cavalry yesterday raided the French frontier near the fortress of Belfort and attemped to commandeer horses, according to dispatches from Paris.

German patrols also twice attacked Joncherey, near Belfort.

BERLIN, Aug. 3.—An official communication regarding alleged acts of hostility by France against Germany was published here tonight. It said:

"The German troops have hitherto obeyed the orders given by the German commanders not to cross the French frontier. French troops, on the contrary, have made several attacks on our frontier posts since yesterday, without any declaration of war having been made.

"The French have crossed the frontier at several places in spite of the fact that the French Government a few days ago informed us that it would not infringe on the unoccupied zone of six miles from the frontier, and since last night companies of French troops have been in the occupation of a number of German villages.

"French Army aeronauts have been flying over Baden and Bavaria yesterday and today, throwing bombs, and have violated Belgian neutrality by flying over Belgian territory into the province of the Rhine in an effort to destroy our railways.

"In this way France has opened the attack upon us and has established a state of war which has compelled the German Empire to take defensive measures for the security of its territory.

"French soldiers crossed the frontier Saturday night at Laschlucht, a small village in the Vosges Mountains. Shots were fired on the German post, but no damage was done."

A dispatch from Coblenz, Germany, says:

"A party of eighty French officers, dressed in Prussian uniforms, attempted yesterday to cross the German frontier in automobiles near Walbeck, on the Dutch frontier, to the west of Geldern. The attempt was unsuccessful."

United Russia Will Rise Against Insolent Foe, Says Emperor Nicholas, Calling His People to War

ST. PETERSBURG, Aug. 3.—Emperor Nicholas issued a manifesto today in which he outlined the events leading up to the declaration of war by Germany, and said that "Russians will rise like one man and will repulse the insolent attack of the enemy."

The manifesto reads as follows:

"By the grace of God, we, Nicholas II., Emperor and Autocrat of all the Russias, King of Poland, and Grand Duke of Finland, &c., to all our faithful subjects make known that Russia, related by faith and blood to the Slav peoples and faithful to her historical traditions, has never regarded their fates with indifference.

"But the fraternal sentiments of the Russian people for the Slavs have been awakened with perfect unanimity and extraordinary force in these last few days, when Austria-Hungary knowingly addressed to Servia claims inacceptable for an independent State

"Having paid no attention to the pacific and conciliatory reply of the Servian Government, and having rejected the benevolent intervention of Russia, Austria-Hungary made haste to proceed to an armed attack, and began to bombard Belgrade, an open place.

"Forced by the situation thus created to take necessary measures of precaution, we ordered the army and the navy put on a war footing, at the same time using every endeavor to obtain a peaceful solution. Pourparlers were begun amid friendly relations with Germany and her ally, Austria, for the blood and the property of our subjects were dear to us.

"Contrary to our hopes in our good neighborly relations of long date, and disregarding our assurances that the mobilization measures taken were in pursuance of no object hostile to her, Germany demanded their immediate cessation. Being rebuffed in this demand, Germany suddenly declared war on Russia.

"Today it is not only the protection of a country related to us and unjustly attacked that must be accorded, but we must safeguard the honor, the dignity, and the integrity of Russia and her position among the great powers.

"We believe unshakably that all our faithful subjects will rise with unanimity and devotion for the defense of Russian soil; that internal discord will be forgotten in this threatening hour; that the unity of the Emperor with his people will become still more close, and that Russia, rising like one man, will repulse the insolent attack of the enemy.

"With a profound faith in the justice of our work, and with a humble hope in omnipotent Providence in prayer, we call God's blessing on holy Russia and her valiant troops. NICHOLAS."

HOLLAND INVADED?

Antwerp So Reports, Though Germany Had Promised Hands Off.

BRUSSELS, Aug. 3.—The Burgomaster of Antwerp announced tonight that the Germans had invaded Limburg, Holland, and that the Province had been placed under martial law.

Limburg has a population of nearly a quarter of a million.

LONDON, Aug. 3.—A report was current tonight that Holland has been invaded through the Province of Limburg.

The people of the Dutch Kingdom, resolved to go to the extremity, are said to be opening the dikes and flooding the country, which would make the passage of an army imposible.

THE HAGUE, Aug. 3.—The German Minister has given the Government positive assurances that Germany will respect the neutrality of the Netherlands, provided it is strictly observed.

The President of the Council of Ministers, in a speech, announced that the Queen and the Ministers were in perfect accord, and that the country was ready and determined to maintain neutrality at all costs.

ANTWERP IN STATE OF SIEGE.

Populace Calm in Face of Reported German Invasion.

New York Times-London Chronicle Special Cable Dispatch.

ANTWERP, Aug. 3.—All telephonic and telegraphic communication with the interior has been stopped except for war purposes, and all messages are censored.

There is no confirmation of the reported engagement between French and German forces at Nancy.

The report of the occupation by German troops of the Duchy of Luxemburg and of their crossing the frontier of Belgium were received here in an agony of suspense but with unflinching courage and calm.

A wave of relief passed over the city at nightfall when it was learned that a report that Germans had crossed the frontier near Vise was due to a telephonic error.

The late evening bulletins were all on the hopeful side.

In every public place notices have been posted, signed by the Burgomaster, declaring Antwerp in a stage of siege and appealing to his fellow-citizens to preserve order.

CZAR'S FLEET BEATEN; HIS CAPITAL MENACED

Reported Capture of Aland Islands Would Give Germany Entrance to Finland Also.

Special Cable to THE NEW YORK TIMES.

LONDON, Tuesday, Aug. 4.—Reports come from Stockholm that a German fleet engaged a Russian fleet Sunday off the Aland Islands and drove them in flight into the Gulf of Finland.

This, with the report of a Russian-German naval engagement at Libau, is regarded in some quarters as conveying the news of a great German victory, probably the bottling up and perhaps the crippling of the Russian fleet.

With the occupation of the Aland Islands Germany gets possession of a safe, high road into Finland and a naval and military base from which to operate against St. Petersburg itself. Within the shelter of those islands a fleet might lie in perfect security and would command the entrance to the Gulf of Finland, the sea route to St. Petersburg, and the Russian naval stations of Reval and Cronstadt.

Strategically the islands have always been considered the outer defense of St. Petersburg. In 1907-8 Russia was anxious to fortify them, but was prevented by the powers, Great Britain among them.

When the islands were transferred from Sweden to Russia in 1809 there was a clause in the treaty forbidding Russia to erect fortifications. The powers held Russia down to this provision, largely because Russia was suspected of designs on Sweden.

Sweden's attitude is also to be considered. The Swedish King and nation have been suffering from a bad Russian scare, and probably with good reason. The recent crisis and the general elections were on this issue of a Russian menace, powerful campaigns of agitation being run in Sweden for an alliance with Germany against Russia. One of the leaders of this agitation is Dr. Sven Hedin. It is at least possible that Sweden will take the advantage afforded her by Germany of removing the Russian peril once and for all. The population of Finland is Swedish.

TRONDHJEM, Norway, Aug. 3.—Four battleships were seen passing Hammerfest, traveling eastward.

STOCKHOLM, Aug. 3.—A battle was fought yesterday between the German and Russian fleets off the Aland Islands and resulted in the Russians being driven back.

The Russian war vessels took refuge in the Gulf of Finland, where they still remained today.

COPENHAGEN, Aug. 4.—A Russian warship is aground at the Aland Islands. It is said to be the Andrei Pervosvannyi, a battleship of 17,400 tons, laid down in 1903.

NOVOROSSIYSK, Russia, Aug. 3.—The Russian authorities today seized the German steamer Atlas and ordered the crew to disembark. They sent vessels in pursuit of a German steamer which left port yesterday.

ST. PETERSBURG, Aug. 3.—A dispatch from Libau says a German cruiser on Sunday bombarded the town. The cruiser fired twenty shells, one of which struck the naval hospital. Slight damage was done, and no one was killed or wounded. The cruiser then departed.

Kronprinz Wilhelm Sails With Cargo of Coal and War Stores.

TO AID KAISER'S CRUISERS

Dresden, Strassburg, and Karlsruhe to be Replenished from Liner.

BURNS ONLY LEGAL LIGHTS

Turns South Outside the Hook, Which Shows She's Not Bound for Europe.

RAISES NEUTRALITY POINT

Authorities Doubt if United States Is Chargeable with More Than Neglect.

FEAR CABLES ARE IN DANGER

German Cruiser Reported to be Grappling for Sea Lines Near Here—Rumor Discredited.

The North German Lloyd liner Kronprinz Wilhelm sailed unexpectedly from Hoboken at 7:30 last night.

Officials of the North German Lloyd Line said that she had sailed for a German port under hurry orders from the Kaiser's Government, to be used for military purposes.

The fact that she took aboard 2,000 tons more coal than she would need to cross the Atlantic besides hundreds of tons of sea stores such as are not carried by passenger boats led to reports, which were later confirmed in a measure, that she was going to sea to transfer supplies and fuel to the German cruisers Dresden, Strasburg, and Karlsruhe. These cruisers have been reported, ever since the war scare began, to be dodging British warships and seeking an opportunity to replenish stores.

Not Heading for Europe.

The Captain of the Ward liner Seguranca, which arrived at Quarantine last night from Santiago, Cuba, reported that he had passed the Kronprinz Wilhelm outside the Ambrose Channel Lightship. He said that only the running lights, that is, the masthead, port, and starboard lights, were burning. The liner, he said, was steering southward, instead of northeastward, which is the usual course for steamships bound for Europe.

The Kronprinz Wilhelm also carried on her forward deck a big wooden packing case which might very well cover a naval gun, mounted for use. An official of the line said it was an extra crank shaft, but those who saw the big box said it did not look like the covering of such a piece of machinery.

The departure of the Wilhelm, it was feared in some quarters, might involve the United States in a neutrality controversy, but authorities agreed that gross negligence or collusion would have to be shown; also that the ship carried war materials.

The Wilhelm arrived here last Wednesday from Bremen and was scheduled to sail with mails and passengers at 1 A. M. today for Plymouth, Cherbourg, and Bremen. When the order was received from Europe last Friday the agents of the North German Lloyd Steamship Company canceled the sailings of their steamers indefinitely, and the Kronprinz Wilhelm was supposed to be laid up with the Princess Irene, Barbarossa, Friedrich der Grosse, Grosser Kuerfuerst, and the George Washington, which arrived yesterday.

Heavy Cargo of Coal.

Since Friday morning it was noted that the Kronprinz Wilhelm was busy taking on coal from lighters stretched along her full length. Yesterday, in addition to the coal, a quantity of sea provisions, including salt pork, salt beef, and hardtack in barrels, potatoes, barley, split peas, and other dry stores, were being put aboard in large quantities.

The interest of the longshoremen on the adjoining piers was concentrated on a curiously shaped wooden case on the forward deck that was between fifteen and twenty feet long and constructed in the form of a maltese cross, which strongly suggested that it might inclose a naval gun. The case was firmly secured to the stanchions on either side of the deck. When officials of the North German Lloyd were asked what

Continued on Page 2.

GERMAN AMBASSADOR DEPARTS FROM PARIS

Leaves Interests in Our Charge—French Envoy Ordered to Quit Berlin.

Special Cable to THE NEW YORK TIMES.

PARIS, Aug. 3.—Baron von Schön, the German Ambassador, left Paris between 10 and 11 tonight. A special train was waiting at a little loop-line station in the West of Paris to take the Ambassador and his staff with their luggage.

Two hours before the Ambassador's departure the American Consul took possession of the German Embassy, which will be under the protection of the United States during the war. No hostile demonstration took place.

The French Government immediately instructed the French Ambassador in Berlin, Jules Cambon, to apply for his passports and leave Berlin at once.

GERMANY HALTS AT FRENCH FRONTIER

Only a Few Men Cross, Apparently to Provoke the Declaration She Hesitates to Make.

Special Cable to THE NEW YORK TIMES.

PARIS, Tuesday, Aug. 4.—As far as is known, the German invasion of France is so far of no great military significance. It consists of stray incursions of German cavalry reconnoitering along the frontier and in the frontier zone, which, with a view to avoiding frontier incidents, by order of the Government, have not been occupied by French troops.

It is possible, however, that the incursions reported near Cirey and Longwy, on the Luxemburg frontier, are an attempt to provoke a French declaration of war.

The German occupation of Luxemburg and the invasion in force on that route have long been foreseen by the French military authorities. The construction of German camps at Essenborn and Wasserlisch and the extension of the German strategic railway lines were plain indications of what was to be expected in the event of trouble between the countries.

Up to noon today no news of any real fighting between French and Germans had been received. No further frontier incidents have been reported.

ENGLAND BOUND TO FIGHT.

That Is the View of All the London Newspapers.

LONDON, Aug. 4.—All the morning papers, even those representing the peace party, are unanimous in support of the Government's view that England is bound to fight on behalf of France and in defense of Belgian and Dutch neutrality.

AEROPLANES FLY OVER PARIS

Flotillas of Two to Five Start Out Toward the East.

PARIS, Aug. 3.—Numerous aeroplanes from the French aviation centres in the west and south moved swiftly over Paris today in flotillas of twos, threes, and fives toward the east.

Strings of horses requisitioned from private stables were to be seen going toward the freight yards of the Eastern Railway.

DIRIGIBLES SPY BELGIUM.

French Minister Reports German Airships Flying Over Country.

BRUSSELS, Aug. 3.—The French Minister has informed the Belgian Government that three German dirigibles were observed tonight flying toward Brussels, having invaded Belgian territory.

GERMANS CHASE FOOD SHIP.

Try to Catch Craft Bound for Vladivostok.

Special Cable to THE NEW YORK TIMES.

LONDON, Tuesday, Aug. 4.—A dispatch to The Daily Mail from Tien-Tsin says:

"The Norwegian steamer Tungas, chartered by an American firm, left for Vladivostok Friday night. The Germans sent a ship to chase her. Her cargo consists of foodstuffs for the Russian troops."

Britain Only Waits for German Ships to Fire on France.

PLEDGED TO GUARD COAST

Fleet Attack in Channel England's Signal to Strike, Grey Tells Commons.

WILD CHEERS GREET HIM

Reads Belgium's Appeal for Protection and Says England's Interests Are at Stake.

POINTS TO HOLLAND'S PERIL

Navy, Regulars, Reserves, and Territorials All Fully Prepared for Conflict.

CHANGES IN THE CABINET

John Burns, Opposed to War, Retires—Kitchener May Take War Portfolio.

Special Cable to THE NEW YORK TIMES.

LONDON, Tuesday, Aug. 4.—All England is in martial array, and she is ready to strike the moment the German fleet fires upon the Channel coast of France.

This policy of determination to defend the French coast was announced by Sir Edward Grey in a speech to the House of Commons yesterday, and was greeted with the wildest applause.

The Foreign Minister said the French fleet was in the Mediterranean and her northern coasts defenseless.

"If a foreign fleet engaged in war against France should come down and battle against those defenseless coasts we could not stand aside," he exclaimed.

Sir Edward read the appeal of the King of the Belgians for diplomatic intervention to safeguard the integrity of that country, and asserted that if the integrity of Belgium were destroyed that of Holland also would be lost.

As a result of the policy announced, John Burns, President of the Local Government Board, resigned from the Cabinet owing to his inability to agree. Mr. Burns was once a member of the council of the Workmen's Peace Society.

It is announced as practically certain this morning that Lord Kitchener will take charge of the War Office.

Commons in Memorable Session.

The sitting of the House of Commons will rank among the most memorable in history. Sir Edward Grey's speech was characterized by suppressed fire and unadorned simplicity. It rang with accents of sincerity and vibrated with high patriotic feeling. The House never listened to a speech more effective in its purpose. That purpose was to prove that British neutrality, in the face of the present conflict in Europe, was impossible unless Great Britain was prepared to forfeit her own self-respect and the world's confidence. Honor, duty, and interest required British intervention, the Minister said.

Sir Edward spoke without bitterness, but the impression he conveyed was that Germany was a wanton disturber of European peace. He made no allusion to Russia.

The most striking feature in the attitude of Sir Edward Grey's audience was the enthusiasm of the Irish Nationalists. The Liberal benches seemed sombrely acquiescent.

Irish Applaud Grey.

The most applause came from the Conservatives, while the Irishmen acclaimed Sir Edward Grey's determination to stand by France with resounding enthusiasm. William Redmond and Dr. Lynch, the latter of whom fought against Great Britain in the Boer war and was condemned for treason, waved their handkerchiefs vehemently while they applauded. The old links of historical association of Celtic feeling explained the warm sympathy of the Irishmen for France.

One of the most dramatic scenes of the day was the intervention of John Redmond. For the first time in many years the Irish leader associated himself heart and soul with the feelings of the average Englishmen in the face

King Albert's Appeal to King George; Asks England to Protect Belgium

LONDON, Aug. 3.—King Albert of Belgium sent this telegram to King George today:

"Remembering the numerous proofs of your Majesty's friendship and that of your predecessor, of the friendly attitude of England in 1870, and the proof of the friendship which she has just given us again, I make a supreme appeal to the diplomatic intervention of your Majesty's Government to safeguard the integrity of Belgium."

of the great national emergency. Mr. Redmond spoke briefly, but with an eloquence that thrilled the House. Now, in these times of trial and danger for Great Britain, he said, the Irish people turned to the British democracy with anxiety and sympathy. He recalled how in 1776, at the moment of dire peril for England, 100,000 Irish volunteers leaped to arms.

"Today," he said, "there are in Ireland two large bodies of volunteers. I say to the Government they may tomorrow with safety withdraw every one of their troops from Ireland, and the coasts of Ireland will be defended from foreign invasion by her armed sons. In this matter the armed Catholics of the South will gladly join arms with the armed Protestants of the North."

Clinches Home Rule.

Cheers, wherein Liberals, Tories, and Nationalists participated with equal warmth, proclaimed their delight at this vibrant speech, so eloquent and timely. The battle for home rule is already won. Redmond's little gem of oratory made the assurance of its early triumph doubly sure. That England's danger is Ireland's opportunity is now true in quite a new sense.

It was noticeable that Mr. Asquith warmly cheered the Nationalist leader.

Sir Edward Grey, in his speech, made a pointed allusion to Ireland when he spoke of it as the one bright spot in the picture. He stressed this in order that it might be understood abroad that Ireland would not weaken England's arm in this momentous crisis.

Government Free to Decide.

Sir Edward Grey spoke seventy-five minutes, and the House of Commons listened with an absorption that was almost painful in its tension. After a recital of the course of European affairs since 1906 he said that in the present crisis "we have perfect freedom to decide." The Government was free, he said, consequently Parliament was free. The present crisis had not originated in any question affecting France, he asserted, but in a dispute between Austria and Servia.

"France is involved in this war simply because she has undertaken to fulfill an obligation of honor," said he. "Great Britain is under no such obligations of honor, but for years she has had a friendship with France. Whether that friendship involves obligations, let every man look into his own heart and feelings and construe the obligations for himself."

Sir Edward did not disguise his own feelings. He spoke of France with an emotion for which his audience was quite unprepared from a man of his apparently cold and passionless nature. He pointed out that the French fleet was in the Mediterranean. The northern and western coasts of France are absolutely unprotected by French ships, he said, because the French Government confidently relied on the friendship of the British Government.

Then came a passage which stirred the House to its very depths and made every man who listened tingle with emotion. "If a foreign fleet came down the English Channel and bombarded and battered the unprotected coasts of France," he exclaimed, "we could not stand aside with our arms folded." Tremendous cheering and applause broke afresh when he added, "And I believe that to be the feeling of this country."

Italy as a Key.

He asked the House to consider the possible consequences of a European conflagration. Italy is neutral, he said.

Here there were Radical cheers. "Yes," said the speaker, turning to the benches whence the cheers had come, "Italy is neutral because she regards this as an aggressive war."

Loud applause followed this.

"But suppose," he went on, "Italy departs from her attitude of neutrality. She might depart from it at a moment when the keeping open of the trade routes of the Mediterranean might be vital to us. A negative attitude by us at this moment would expose Great Britain to most appalling risks. France is entitled to know, and know at once, whether or not in event of an attack on her northern and western coasts she may depend on Great Britain for support.

Therefore, Sir Edward said, on Sunday afternoon he gave written assurance to the French Ambassador that if the German fleet came into the Channel or through the North Sea to undertake operations against the French coast or French shipping the British fleet would give all the protection within its power.

Questions German Assurances.

This was not a declaration of war, Sir Edward carefully added.

He said that yesterday afternoon he received from the German Government assurance that if Great Britain would pledge itself to neutrality the German fleet would not attack the northern coasts of France.

"I only heard that shortly before I came into the House," said Sir Edward, "but it is far too narrow an engagement."

He next turned to the question of the neutrality of Belgium.

"If the independence of Belgium goes, the independence of Holland follows," he said. If France were beaten to her knees, which, assuredly he did not anticipate, and if Belgium, Holland, and Denmark fell under the same domination, then assuredly in Gladstone's words the world would see an unmeasured aggrandizement of a single power.

In conclusion Sir Edward said that, though no final decision to resort to force had been reached, Great Britain stood ready. The efficiency and readiness of the navy and army were never at a higher mark.

"Never have we been more justified in reposing confidence in the power of the navy to defend our commerce and shores. Suffering and misery will follow in the train of war, yes, but no neutrality will protect us from that. The situation has developed with such startling rapidity that the British people does not realize all that is involved, but when it does realize the issues at stake and the magnitude of the danger in Western Europe, then, I am confident, the Government will be supported by the determination, courage, resolution, and endurance of the whole country."

England Will Be Involved.

Sir Edward Grey's speech must be taken in conjunction with the orders for the mobilization of the British Army, which, it is officially announced, will be given by Royal proclamation today. The reserves will be called out, and the territorial forces be embodied.

No doubt exists that Sir Edward's exposition of the situation means that England will be involved. Sir Edward laid two contingencies necessitating British action—one a raid on the French coasts by German ships, the other the invasion of Belgium by German troops.

Germany's designs of a naval attack on the French North Coast is problematical, but her plans in regard to Belgium are clearly indicated by the ultimatum addressed to the Belgian Government on Sunday evening.

The ultimatum gave Belgium twelve hours to reply, and it required Belgium to facilitate the movements of German troops through her territory. This demand was a flagrant breach of the Treaty of London of 1839, whereby the powers guaranteed the neutrality of Belgium. The King of the Belgians appealed to King George for aid.

According to The Daily Mail, in its ultimatum to Belgium, Germany went further than was indicated in Sir Edward Grey's statement. The paper learns that Germany demanded from Belgium an attitude of friendly neutrality, which should extend to the passage of German troops through Belgian territory, promising in return to maintain, on the conclusion of peace, the independence of the Kingdom of Belgium and its possessions, and threatening, in the event of refusal, to treat Belgium as an enemy.

The Belgian Government replied that a violation of Belgian neutrality would be a flagrant violation of the rights of nations and that to accept such a demand as that presented by Germany would mean the sacrifice of the honor of the nation, which was conscious of its duty. The Government, it was added, was firmly resolved to repel aggression by all the means in its power.

Pay Homage to the King.

The King and Queen stood on a balcony at Buckingham Palace last night

BRITAIN · NEEDS
YOU · AT · ONCE
PUBLISHED BY THE PARLIAMENTARY RECRUITING COMMITTEE, LONDON POSTER No 108
PRINTED BY SPOTTISWOODE & Co LTD LONDON E.C.

Muddy, tired Belgian soldiers prepare for a new attack on German trenches.

"All the News That's Fit to Print."

The New York Times.

THE WEATHER
Fair today; unsettled, warmer Friday; gentle to moderate south winds.
For full weather report see Page 14.

VOL. LXIII...NO. 20,648. .... NEW YORK, THURSDAY, AUGUST 6, 1914.—EIGHTEEN PAGES. ONE CENT In Greater New York, Jersey City and Newark. | Elsewhere, TWO CENTS.

BELGIANS DEFEAT GERMANS, KILL OR WOUND 3,500 MEN; BRITISH THIRD FLOTILLA HAS A BATTLE IN THE NORTH SEA; RUSSIANS DRIVE OUT THE GERMANS AND ENTER PRUSSIA; GERMANY SAID TO HAVE SENT AN ULTIMATUM TO ITALY

Kitchener Goes Into British Cabinet as War Secretary.

MEETS POPULAR ACCLAIM

Appointment of Famous Soldier Regarded as Excellent Move for England.

MORLEY AND BURNS OUT

Premier Asquith Announces Their Resignations in Speech of Regret.

FOOD PRICES ADVANCING

People Urged Not to Hoard Gold and Assured That There Is No Cause for Panic.

ISSUE SMALL GOLD NOTES

Bankers and Government Officials Soon to Announce New Plan of Finances.

Special Cable to THE NEW YORK TIMES.

LONDON, Aug. 5.—The war situation has already brought a break in the British Cabinet, and there is said to be a divergence of opinion among the members as to the advisability of sending an expeditionary force to the aid of Belgium and France.

A popular stroke on the part of the Government was announced today in the appointment of Lord Kitchener as Secretary of State for war. Earl Beauchamp succeeds Viscount Morley as President of the Council, and Walter Runciman takes the place of John Burns as President of the Local Government Board.

Premier Asquith announced in the House of Commons the resignations of Viscount Morley, John Burns, and C. P. Trevelyan. The Premier said he had accepted the resignations with great regret. Viscount Morley had long desired to shake off the burden of ministerial office, and it was natural that a man of his pacific views and political antecedents should desire to have no part in the responsibility of a great war. Tributes to Viscount Morley as a man of the most sincere convictions and patriotism were paid even by the most vehement partisans of war. He is the last of the old Gladstonian veterans, and his departure from the Cabinet marks the end of that era. Mr. Trevelyan resigned because he had always opposed any Continental entanglements on the part of England.

David Lloyd George, Chancellor of the Exchequer, announced in the House of Commons various measures to deal with the financial situation. The limited moratorium already proclaimed has brought immediate relief, but the bankers and merchants, who again conferred at the Treasury this afternoon, think a more extended moratorium may be necessary—extended, that is not in time, but in scope—to relieve other debtors by giving them a month's grace. The Chancellor will indicate the nature of the extension on Thursday.

Issue Gold Notes.

The Chancellor's statement next confirmed the points of an earlier dispatch in reference to banknotes. About £3,000,000 ($15,000,000) worth of £1 and 10 shilling notes will be available on Friday morning, and afterward will be issued at the rate of £5,000,000 a day until the supply is adequate for the situation, now so well in hand.

The Bank of England intends reducing the Bank rate from 10 per cent. to 6 per cent. on Friday. As the Bank rate is the index of financial health, its reduction to 6 per cent. in the week when the country has embarked on a great war supplies a remarkable proof of the elasticity and efficiency of the banking and currency systems.

Mr. Lloyd George told the House that while it was necessary to suspend the Bank charter it was not necessary to suspend specie payments, as there was an ample sufficiency of gold in the country for all normal requirements, but on no account ought

Continued on Page 2.

Russia Anxious to Aid Our Refugees, The Czar's Foreign Office Tells The Times

By Cable to the Editor of THE NEW YORK TIMES.

ST. PETERSBURG, Aug. 5.—In reply to your cable of Aug 3, I am anxious to say that the Imperial Russian Government is ready to sanction any measure that the United States Government would undertake to aid the removal of American citizens from Russia as long as such measure is not antagonistic to the military interests of the Empire.

A. NERATOW,
Assistant Minister Foreign Affairs.

RUSSIAN DIPLOMATS ASSAULTED IN BERLIN

German Embassy in St. Petersburg Wrecked and Furniture Burned By a Mob.

ST. PETERSBURG, (via London,) Aug. 5.—The Russian Ambassador in Berlin, M. de Sverbeew, and his staff are reported to have been subjected to much abuse after the declaration of war. Some of the members of the Ambassadorial suite, including Princess Belosselsky, who was Miss Susie Whittier of Boston, and First Secretary of Embassy Charovitski are alleged actually to have been struck by persons in the crowd which followed their motorcars to the railroad station when they were leaving Berlin.

According to an eyewitness the Embassy was surrounded, and when the Ambassador, who was escorted by mounted police, departed for the station in an automobile the people howled abuse at him and the police had the greatest difficulty in protecting him and the members of his staff. Friends of the Ambassador, who followed him in motor cars, also are said to have been forced to run a gantlet of hostile Germans.

The crowd followed the cars, abusing the occupants, throwing stones, spitting in the faces of the embasy staff, and striking both men and women with sticks and umbrellas, it is said. M. Charovitski received a blow on the head which cut open the scalp. He is said to be under medical treatment in Copenhagen. Princess Belosselsky was hit on the back and shoulder by an old, well-dressed man, and other persons in the crowd spat at her. The other members of the party are declared to have been similarly treated.

The children were placed in the bottom of the automobiles in order to protect them.

The German Embassy here was wrecked and a bonfire made of the furniture and pictures by a mob today. The people were angered by the reports of what they deemed to be an indignity shown to the Dowager Empress Maria Feodorowna by being stopped in Berlin on her arrival from London on her way to St. Petersburg and compelled by the German authorities to go to Copenhagen.

An entrance was forced by the crowd through the windows. Most of the rooms were wrecked and the furniture pitched into the streets. A number of students and workmen climbed to the roof and tore the gold eagle from the top of the flagstaff. They then ran up the Russian flag.

A piece of massive statuary depicting a group of horses led by men was hacked to pieces with axes and the débris hurled into the canal. A bonfire then was made of the contents of the embassy and an attempt was made to put a torch to the building, but mounted police routed the rioters.

Another crowd later tried to repeat the performance at the Austrian Embassy, but that building was too strongly guarded.

The body of a Russian footman is alleged by the authorities to have been found in the German Embassy. The man had been shot in the head and stabbed and had been dead for some days.

MARTIAL LAW IN HOLLAND.

Dutch Prepare, Though Germans Have Not Crossed the Border.

THE HAGUE, Aug. 5.—Martial law has been declared in all parts of Holland.

It is officially announced that up to the present time the Germans have not violated the Dutch frontier.

AVIATORS DUEL IN MIDAIR

Engage in Revolver Fight, Manoeuvring for Position.

LONDON, Thursday, Aug. 6.—The Standard's correspondent at Liege sends a story of a duel between a Belgian aviator named Fornau and a German airman.

The two exchanged revolver shots while manoeuvring for the top position. Finally both planed to the ground.

LONDON, Aug. 6.—The Daily Mail's correspondent at Brussels reports that a German aeroplane, flying at a height of 1,500 feet, was brought down by a shot which also wounded the pilot.

A Zeppelin airship, manned by Germans, was struck by the fire from a Belgian fort and fell near Herve.

RUSSIAN PATROLS RAID EAST PRUSSIA

Drive German Invading Forces Before Them and Begin a Counter Invasion.

WARSAW, Russian Poland, Aug 5 (via London.)—Russian frontier patrols driving the enemy's cavalry before them have crossed the East Prussian frontier at Lyk and Biala, and penetrated ten miles into German territory.

The Russians captured and burned the German railway stations at Borjemin and Biala and cut communications from Lyk to Johannesburg, the enemy falling back all along the front, burning villages as they retired.

ST. PETERSBURG, Aug. 5.—Russian troops have established contact with the enemy along the greater part of the Russo-German frontier in northeastern Prussia.

FRENCH REPULSE GERMANS.

Two Border Encounters Result Adversely for Invaders.

PARIS, Aug. 5.—German cavalry and infantry are crossing the French frontier everywhere in reconnoitering parties, according to a statement issued by the Minister of War, who adds:

"A squadron of German dragoons bore down on Villers-la-Montagne, in the Department of Meurthe-et-Moselle, but was repulsed by French riflemen.

"A regiment of German cavalry advanced as far as Morfontaine, in the same Department, but fell back before a body of French infantry.

"The French mobilization is proceeding with the greatest order. Most of the reservists have already joined. An excellent spirit prevails in Alsace."

Dispatches say that a German officer was taken prisoner when the French infantry repulsed a party of German cavalry at Morfontaine.

The customs and telegraph offices at Homecourt and Joeuf in Meurthe-et-Moselle have been sacked by German infantry.

An official announcement says that seventeen Alsacians, while endeavoring to cross into France, were captured by the Germans and summarily shot.

Santos Dumont, the aviator, has offered his services to the French Government.

The one-armed General, Paul Pau, who fought in the war of 1870, has been placed in command of one of the French armies.

It is stated that the Germans in Alsace are shooting persons suspected of giving information to the French. The Mayor of Saal, Bavaria, is said to have been shot for having tried to smuggle into France the news of proclamation of martial law by Germany.

A German cavalry patrol has been routed by French cavalry on the Swiss frontier. Three Germans were killed and two taken prisoners. The remainder fled into Switzerland, where they were disarmed by Federal troops.

SERVIAN FLAG UP IN AUSTRIA

But Austrian Attempts to Cross the Save Have Failed.

BELGRADE, Aug. 5.—The Austrian attempt on Monday to cross the river Save at Avala, nine miles from Belgrade and Obrenovac, sixteen miles to the southwest, failed. The Servian volunteers crossed the river, and hoisted the Servian flag at Delarme.

Servian officials expressed the opinion that the passage of the Austrian troops through Servian territory has become impossible.

Belgrade Bombarded Again.

BELGRADE, (via London,) Aug. 6.—The Austrians renewed the bombardment of this city today. They seriously damaged the royal palace, the national theatre, the British Legation, and many private houses.

The Servians did not reply to the fire. Three persons were killed and many injured.

28 Wounded Brought Back to Harwich of Whom 22 Are Germans.

200 PRISONERS COMING IN

Little Cruiser Amphion, Flagship of Flotilla, Has Batteries Slightly Damaged.

MINE LAYER DESTROYED

Small German Coast Steamer Fitted as Auxiliary Sunk by the Amphion.

ALLIES SEIZE MANY PRIZES

Czar's Warships Round Up German Merchant Shipping Trapped in the Black Sea.

HAULS IN BRITISH PORTS

Steamer Crews, Mostly Naval Reservists, Are Prisoners of War—French Make Captures, Too.

Special Cable to THE NEW YORK TIMES.

HARWICH, Aug. 5.—The third flotilla left this port for the open sea at daybreak this morning and went into action almost immediately.

Heavy gun firing was heard at intervals throughout the day, and this evening the cruiser Vigo, anchored off Harwich pier, received a wireless message to be ready to receive 200 prisoners. The authorities were also requested to prepare to receive wounded who were being brought in by a torpedo boat.

Later the flotilla returned to port, little the worse for the encounter. The light cruiser Amphion, flagship of the flotilla, had her batteries slightly damaged.

Twenty-eight wounded were brought ashore and taken to the Shotley Naval establishment, opposite Harwich. Of the wounded twenty-two were Germans and six English.

As the flotilla steamed out of the harbor at daybreak the crews of the vessels still to go lined up and heartily cheered their comrades. Soon afterward a Hook of Holland boat, crammed with passengers, mostly Americans, and an Antwerp boat, equally crowded, passed the flotilla. The passengers realized the significance of the departure and cheered lustily. They received hearty response from the sailors.

During the day there were alarming rumors that the houses between Harwich and Walton would be blown down tonigh as being in the line of fire from the shore batteries.

Big Battle Yet to Come.

Special Cable to THE NEW YORK TIMES.

LONDON, Thursday, Aug. 6.—A naval battle of importance off Harwich is unlikely. The German high seas fleet would be unwise to issue forth to give general action. Two hundred prisoners is a small number and can represent no more than the crew of a small cruiser.

The belief in London this morning is that a German mine-layer was captured after a short engagement. There are likely to be many encounters of this character.

What probably happened in the North Sea is that German torpedo boats and submarines were making raids upon the British blockading fleet. Similarly, British torpedo boats and submarines are darting in past Helgoland to do what damage they can to the sheltered German high seas fleet. British mine layers must string the approaches to the Elbe, while German vessels will be attempting to sweep up the mines sowed by these ships.

All this mosquito work on both sides means constant engagements, and a steady stream of wounded and prisoners may be expected at British eastern ports, but this is merely incidental to naval warfare.

By The Associated Press.

LONDON, Aug. 5.—It is officially announced that the British cruiser Amphion has sunk the small German coasting steamer Königin Luise, which had been fitted out for mine laying.

A message from Guernsey, Channel Islands, says that a French gunboat, towing a large German steamer, anchored in the roadstead under the guns of the castle.

Later it was learned that the captured vessel was the steamer Poro, belonging to the Oldenburg-Portuguese Steamship Company. She is a vessel of 1,800 tons and plies between Hamburg and Portuguese ports.

Several German steamers anchored at Hull have been taken over by the British authorities as prizes. The crews, made up mostly of naval reservists, were made prisoners of war.

A British warship seized the German bark Perkeo, which left New York July 18 for Hamburg.

Two German steamers have been seized in the North Sea.

LONDON, Thursday, Aug. 6.—A dispatch to The Times from St. Petersburg says that ten German steamers with coal and timber were seized at Archangel.

The Koenigin Luise, which was sunk by the British cruiser Amphion, was a passenger ship of 2,000 tons register, which for several years had been in service from Hamburg to Summer resorts on the German coast.

The Amphion is a cruiser of 3,400 tons.

The Perkeo, seized by a British warship at Hull, flew the German flag for the first time less than a month ago. From the time she was built, in 1901, until a day or so before she sailed from New York last month, she was a British vessel, her name being the Brilliant. The Perkeo was a vessel of 3,000 tons burden.

CATCH KAISER'S SHIPS IN TRAP

English and French Fleets Help Capture Goeben and Breslau.

NEW YORK TIMES-London Chronicle Special Cable Dispatch.

PARIS, Aug. 5.—After they had bombarded the Algerian towns of Bona and Philippeville, the German cruisers Goeben and Breslau and the gunboat Panther were caught like rats in a trap.

The British fleet awaited them to the east and west and part of the French fleet left Toulon in pursuit.

The French detachment overtook the German vessels, captured the Goeben and Breslau and sank the Panther.

BERLIN, Aug. 5, (via London.)—German warships have destroyed some fortified towns and places for the embarkation of French troops on the coast of Algeria.

The battle cruiser Goeben was one of Germany's finest ships of her type. She is a sister of the Moltke, which visited New York two years ago. She is one of the swiftest cruisers in the world. She has made as high as 28.6 knots an hour. Her armament consists of ten 11-inch guns, mounted in turrets fore and aft, the turrets being so arranged that all the guns can be fired in a single broadside. Her secondary battery consists of twelve 9.5-inch guns, and twelve 3.4-inch guns. With a tonnage of 22,640 she was the seventh largest ship in the German Navy. She was manned by a crew of 1,013 officers and men.

The Breslau is a cruiser of the protected class as distinguished from the semi-armored types. She displaces 4,500 tons, and carries in her main battery twelve 4.1-inch guns.

GERMANS BOMBARD SVEABORG

Squadron Sails Into Gulf of Finland and Opens Fire.

LONDON, Aug. 6.—The Daily Mail publishes a dispatch from Copenhagen stating that a German squadron is bombarding Sveaborg, Finland.

ST. PETERSBURG, Aug. 5.—A German fleet of nineteen ships was sighted yesterday near the east coast of the Baltic Sea, between Memel and Libau.

Russian warships in the Black Sea have captured many German merchantmen.

TORPEDO BOAT BLOWS UP.

Thirty Men Lost by Destruction of German Craft.

NEW YORK TIMES-London Chronicle Special Cable Dispatch.

COPENHAGEN, Aug. 5.—A private telegram from Gedser this evening to the newspapers state that a German torpedo boat exploded and sank in the Baltic Sea two miles off of Gedser, and thirty men were drowned.

Men on the Danish lightship at Gedser reef, near by, on witnessing the accident, which occurred at 10 o'clock this morning, signaled to shore for help. A motor boat was sent out and returned with confirmation of the news.

Severe Check to German Arms in the First Belgian Fight.

BATTLE LASTS FOR HOURS

Victors Afterward Fall Upon Detached German Forces and Annihilate Them.

800 WOUNDED FOES IN LIEGE

Belgian Aviators Show Their Mettle—Forts Resist Heavy German Fire.

GERMAN PRINCE IS COMING

Reported Near Liege with 30,000 Fresh Troops, Ready to Attack Today.

FRENCH ARMY RUSHING UP

Force Has Already Effected Junction with Belgians—English Army Expected.

Crown Prince Bringing Aid; German Loss So Far, 3,500

Special Cable to THE NEW YORK TIMES.

AMSTERDAM, Thursday, Aug. 6, 3 A. M.—The German Crown Prince is hourly expected before Liege at the head of 30,000 fresh troops. The Germans now have crossed the river by means of pontoon bridges, developing the attack on Liege.

In yesterday's battle 3,500 Germans were killed or wounded.

The Postmaster of Vise met his death like a hero. The Germans ordered him to send telegrams to assist them. He refused and was shot.

BRUSSELS, (via Paris,) Aug. 6, 1:38 A. M.—Several thousand dead and wounded is the toll paid by the German Army of the Meuse for its attack on Liege in an attempt to force its way to the French frontier.

The Belgians made a heroic defense, repulsing the Germans after heavy and continuous firing. The assailants were unable to renew the assault.

The Belgians delivered a vigorous counter-attack on Germans who had passed the forts, killing all of them.

Eight hundred wounded Germans are being transferred to Liege, where they will be cared for.

The fortified position in and around Liege had to support yesterday the general shock of the German attack.

The forts afforded admirable resistance to the German shells. Evegnee Fort, which was in action all day, was absolutely unharmed.

The Belgian aviators proved themselves every whit as good as the Germans.

One Belgian squadron attacked and drove back six German squadrons.

The War Office announces that after fierce fighting in the environs of Liege the situation is excellent so far as the Belgians are concerned.

"The Germans," the announcement says, "were driven back by a heroic attack made by a Belgian mixed brigade, which had already earned for itself the highest honors. No German who passed the fort survived."

Another official bulletin says:

"The Belgian losses are trifling compared with those of the Germans."

LONDON, Thursday, Aug. 6.—A dispatch to The Exchange Telegraph from Brussels says that the Belgian War Office issued the following statement:

"The Second Corps of the German Army made an advance attack over the Vesdre River into the Province of Liege. A counter attack by Belgians was brilliantly successful and the enemy was forced back over the Dutch frontier. The victorious Belgian troops did not follow up their success into Dutch territory."

85,000 Engaged in Battle.

New York Times-London Chronicle Special Cable Dispatch.

BRUSSELS, Aug. 5.—In the hostilities between Liege and Vise, 45,000 Germans were repulsed by 40,000 Belgians.

At 4 o'clock this afternoon the Germans, who had been trying to storm the Liege forts, were repulsed everywhere. The attack on the forts was not renewed.

The King and his staff have left for the front in motor cars amid scenes of great excitement.

Great Heroism of Belgians.

Special Cable to THE NEW YORK TIMES.

LONDON, Thursday, Aug. 6.—A Brussels Daily Mail dispatch, dated Wednesday, 5:30 P. M., says:

"The Ministry of War made the following announcement at 4:40 o'clock tonight:

"'The Germans suffered disaster before Liege today. After a desperate struggle, displaying superb heroism, the Belgian Army victoriously repulsed all the German attacks.

"'The Belgian victory was greatly assured by a heroic counter attack by a brigade of Belgians which veritably proved itself glorious. Not a single German who penetrated into the line of forts escaped alive.

"'A soldier of the Fourteenth Regiment of Belgian Infantry threw himself alone among Germans who were pursuing his comrades and killed four Germans.

"'The Belgian aeroplanes were infinitely superior to the German.

"'They have experienced no accidents, while a German aeroplane has fallen near Argenteau. Besides this the Germans fired by mistake on a German aeroplane, which they brought down.

"'The Germans were forced to violate Dutch neutrality.

"'Some German cavalry regiments who were on the left (Belgian) bank of the Meuse suffered severely by fire from Fort Liers.'"

Belgians Make Strong Resistance.

NEW YORK TIMES-London Chronicle Special Cable Dispatch.

BRUSSELS, Aug. 5.—Verviers was occupied by German troops last night, and they advanced as far as Trooz, about eight miles from Liege.

The first engagement took place near Fouron le Comte. A German cavalry reconnoissance was stopped by the Twelfth Belgian line regiment, assisted by a force from Fort Barchon. Twenty-five Germans were made prisoners.

Another party of German cavalry came up the right bank of the Meuse toward the bridge at Vise, which was blown up by the Belgians.

A Belgian monoplane rendered great service and escaped safely from the fire from the German shells.

Hundreds of motor cars left Brussels this morning for the front to look after the wounded. They were loudly cheered as they passed along the boulevards.

A German aviator was flying over Liege when a Belgian aviator attacked him and cut up his aeroplane.

A boy scout at Liege, named Niston, caught first two German spies.

The Minister of War reports that under trying circumstances the Belgian soldiers are showing the finest examples of bravery and discipline.

Invaders Moved On Three Lines.

BRUSSELS, Aug. 5.—The German troops crossed the Belgian frontier at three points—at Dalhem, seven miles north of Liege, and at Francorchamps and Stavelot, both about twenty-five miles southeast of Liege.

The Tenth German Army Corps operated along the northern line, and, finding unexpected resistance, is reported to have moved further northward and invaded Dutch territory at Tillburg, crossing the Meuse at Eysden.

Another dispatch says the German troops in that district tried to cross the River Meuse on a pontoon bridge, but a broadside from batteries of the forts destroyed the bridge as soon as it was completed. Later the invaders succeeded in crossing the river near Maestricht, also in Dutch territory.

In addition to the Tenth Corps, Belgian scouts located two other corps, the Seventh, 40,000 strong, at Verviers, and the Sixth Army Corps in another locality, not named. The total force of 100,000 men apparently had Liege as the chief objective point.

Prompt destruction of bridges by the Belgian troops checked the advance of the Germans.

The capture of the frontier town of Vise, says a Liege dispatch, was affected by German troops after an engagement lasting several hours. It is stated that the victors set fire to the town, killing those of the population who resisted them. The town of Argenteau is also in flames.

Platoon of Cavalry Wiped Out.

Le Peuple says that in the fighting near Vise a platoon of Prussian cavalry was almost annihilated by the enfilading fire of the Belgians from a building on the bank of the river. The Prussians in revenge, the newspaper says, fired on civilians.

At Flemalle, near Argenteau, a Belgian force surprised a body of Prussians and killed 70 out of 10 officers and 80 men. The Belgian losses were 2 officers killed and 10 men wounded.

A German officer taken prisoner by the Belgians said he was amazed at the resistance offered to the German advance. The Germans had been given to understand at Berlin that they would not be opposed in Belgium.

The Official Gazette announced that the entire Seventh and Tenth German Army Corps had invaded the Province of Liege and had reached the vicinity

German Ultimatum to Italy Is Reported; Italy About to Declare War on Austria?

LONDON, Thursday, Aug. 6.—It is reported that Germany has sent an ultimatum to Italy. The report lacks official confirmation but is regarded here as not improbable.

There have been rumors that Italy, owing to the strong antagonism existing between Austrians and Italians, was likely to break away from the Triple Alliance and declare herself on the side of England.

LONDON, Thursday, Aug. 6.—The Telegraph in a late edition today says it is believed in diplomatic circles that Italy is on the eve of declaring war on Austria. Italy's alliance with Austria was never popular with Italians. The two peoples, in their aims and aspirations as regards Asiatic affairs and the Balkans, are notoriously irreconcilable, says The Telegraph.

Lusitania Fleeing Before German Cruisers, Says Wireless Message Picked Up at Portland

Special to The New York Times.

PORTLAND, Me., Aug. 5.—The Cunard liner Lusitania, according to an intercepted message picked up here by an amateur, is being pursued by two German cruisers and is heading back for Portland or Boston at full speed.

A later dispatch from a British cruiser said that she was on her way to render any possible assistance and advised the Lusitania to continue at top speed to the nearest port.

It is believed that the pursuing German cruisers are the same ones which have been reported to be cruising about off this coast for the last two days.

Tonight, far out to sea, searchlights are flashing beams of light across the heavens, but their source has not yet been determined.

Herman Winter, Assistant General Manager of the Cunard Line, said last night that he knew nothing of the pursuit of the Lusitania or of any orders for her to return.

"All the News That's Fit to Print."

The New York Times.

THE WEATHER

Local thunder showers, somewhat cooler, late today and probably Tuesday; moderate south winds today.

For full weather report see Page 16.

VOL. LXIII...NO. 20,652. .... NEW YORK, MONDAY, AUGUST 10, 1914.—TWELVE PAGES. ONE CENT In Greater New York, Jersey City and Newark. { Elsewhere TWO CENTS.

FRENCH ARE DRIVING THE GERMANS BACK IN ALSACE; AUSTRIANS GO TO AID KAISER THERE; GERMANS IN LIEGE, BUT FORTS ARE UNTAKEN; FRENCH AND BRITISH NEAR; GERMANS IN A NAVAL FIGHT, LOSE A SUBMARINE

VICTORY IN ALSACE STIRS ALL FRANCE

Calmly Exultant in the Prospect of Revenge After Forty-four Years of Waiting.

SEE LOST PROVINCES REWON

Gen. Joffre's Dash to Muelhausen Hailed as "Dawning of Glory in the Eastern Sky."

GRATITUDE TO BELGIUM

The Academy Sends Messages of Cheer to the "Little People with Mighty Souls."

Special Cable to THE NEW YORK TIMES.

PARIS, Aug. 9.—In Alsace the French Army is keeping the anniversary of the battle of Wissembourg, the first big engagement of the Franco-Prussian war. After forty-four years, today France is taking her revenge.

Although official news from the front comes slowly—indicating that the French Government knows its business this time—there is every reason to suppose that the German Army, already smashed in its initial plan of attack through Belgium, has suffered far greater reverses on the French frontier, which is all the more wonderful when one remembers that only a week ago the general mobilization began.

The Paris populace received the news of the first victory of their own troops with the same sang-froid that has characterized them since the first suspicion that the war typhoon was likely to burst. Newsboys ran along the boulevards shouting "Good news!" but Frenchmen and Frenchwomen seized the papers, read, and only smiled the same smile of perfect confidence, which, at such utter variance with the national attitude during four decades, has in a week been written in history.

It is certain that every citizen of the Republic has had one fact instilled into his very soul—that when "the next time" came to cross swords with Germany there would be no defensive tactics, but at the very start a straight lunge into the enemy's heart. Frenchmen tonight see already the German Empire tottering to its fall, but they are keeping quiet about it. They know many more props must go in addition to the two so quickly kicked away before the military giant that has awed the world comes crashing down.

Found Germans' Weak Spot.

That their military strategists, after many years of contemplation, have discovered the weak place in Germany's splendid frontier defense seems certain. While the Germans, evidently deluded into a belief in Belgian meekness, if not support, counted on delivering a vital attack through the Meuse Valley, afterward making a flank attack on the main French Army on the eastern frontier, the French discovered the heretofore unheard-of valley of the River Ill, through which to project a like campaign against the Emperor's legions further north along the frontier, where the strongest fortresses are situated. The speed which the French have attained in these brilliant first successes—already driving the enemy beyond Mülhausen toward the defenses fronting Colmar and the Rhine—gives every indication that the far-famed organization and morale of the Germans is already broken.

A famous military strategist, talking to me some months ago in London, after witnessing both the French and the German army manoeuvres, the latter as the guest of the Kaiser, discussed the then remote possibilities of a conflict, basing his deductions on the temperament of the two armies. He declared: "If the Germans lose at the start, they are finished." Now his listeners believe him. He continued:

"In times of peace there is nothing in the world like the German Army. Its manoeuvres are the acme of perfection, but in war, mark my word, the brainwork of the French Army, both individual and collective, will be brilliant in comparison. The Germans will obey orders, but they know nothing beyond that. The French will obey equally well, but at the same time have a definite idea of the whole plan of campaign—with the central idea instilled in boyhood, namely, the siege of Berlin. The German Army is a wonderful machine, but if a cog

Continued on Page 3.

TESTING GERMAN LINE TO UNCOVER PLANS

France's Aim to Find Where Big Blow Is Coming—May Be Through Belfort.

Special Cable to THE NEW YORK TIMES.

LONDON, Monday, Aug. 10.—The German reverses in Belgium and Alsace may have an incalculable effect upon the morale of all the armies engaged in the fighting, but exaggeration of their military importance must be avoided.

It was a matter of great importance for the Germans to confirm that impression of invincibility which for forty-four years has shadowed Europe like a cloud. They were to strike a stunning blow, and in so doing would stick at nothing. They appear to have failed at Liege, as the fortress has made a magnificent stand. The Germans may have entered the town, but the forts have held out, and they must be reduced or the Germans must cover them by leaving a large force there.

The German military mind evidently failed to realize either the strength of the formidable defenses raised by Gen. Brialmont or to anticipate the resistance which would be raised by their violation of the neutrality of Belgium.

Namur is an even more formidable position than Liege, owing partly to the topography, which enabled the engineers to give commanding positions to its guns. It is encircled by forts, the guns of which command the intervals between them.

Huy, which lies between Liege and Namur, is also a fortress, but of lesser importance.

None of the places on the Meuse can compare with Antwerp, which has a double ring of forts and is regarded as impregnable.

A strong light will be thrown upon the use of fortresses in war by the events in Belgium.

The French have made a bold advance through the gap of Belfort into Alsace where they appear to have been received with very natural joy. They have occupeid Mülhausen on the Rhine. This is disconcerting to the Germans and is possibly the opening of hostilities in this sphere of the war and many prelude decisive events.

Mülhausen is the Manchester of Germany. The fighting was not of great importance and the French have not advanced far into Alsace.

Neubrisach, north of Mülhausen, is a fortified place, and commands the approach up the Rhine to Strassburg, a strongly fortified city. The Germeans have an immense reserve of men, so it is impossible to forecast the course of operations. It is worth recalling the fact that at Saarbruck, in 1870, the late Prince Imperial received his baptism of fire in a success which was the prelude to a series of unexampled disasters. Neither the French Army nor the German is what it was in those days.

In regard to the fighting both around Liege and in Alsace it is necessary to bear in mind that these operations are only preliminary encounters to the real shock of great battles, which, as pointed out some days ago, cannot well begin before Aug. 16.

In Alsace probably only a couple of brigades were engaged, one on each side. The French advance was only a reconnoissance in force, designed to test the strength of the enemy in front of Belfort. Possibly the French commanders were also influenced by the knowledge the effect of a re-occupation of part of Alsace would have upon patriotic sentiment. This, of course, is a side issue.

The problem before the French General Staff is to determine where the German concentration is taking place and where the chief offensive stroke is likely to be made.

Three routes are available, through Nancy, through Belgium, and through Belfort. Undoubtedly the German plan will be to utilize all three, but which will be their main line of attack? It looks as if the operations around Liege were designed to distract French attention from other avenues of German approach, but the occupation of Vic and Moyenvic last week showed that the French were feeling the German strength before Nancy, and the penetration of Alsace means that they are feeling the strength of the enemy before Belfort.

The Swiss telegram, reporting that Austrian troops are near Basle, indicates that the Belfort route is likely to be the chief line of German advance.

The presence of Austrians in this theatre of war shows that Austria realizes as well as Germany the vital necessity of swiftly crushing France before the Russian mobilization is completed.

A Brussels dispatch says reports received by the Belgian Minister of War reveal that the Germans showed the same want of dash at Mülhausen as at Liege. When their officers were killed the men became helpless, and fled like sheep, seeming to have no stomach for fighting.

The report that the civil population fired on the Germans, the dispatch says, is false, and was spread by them to justify reprisals.

German Forces in Alsace Fall Back Upon Neu Breisach.

RETREAT CALLED A ROUT

Alsatian Populace Welcomes Gen. Joffre with Frenzied Joy—French Losses 'Not Excessive.'

MARTIAL LAW PROCLAIMED

Germans Threaten Summary Death to French Sympathizers—May Have Lost Colmar.

AUSTRIA SENDS 40,000 MEN

France Demands an Explanation of Their Presence Near Basle, Where Battle Is Expected.

Special Cable to THE NEW YORK TIMES.

PARIS, Aug. 9.—The French arms have triumphed in the first fighting in Alsace, although the report that they have followed up their capture of Altkirch and Mülhausen by taking Colmar, lacks confirmation.

Altkirch was taken by a French brigade on Friday night. The German brigade which was intrenched there, after offering some resistance, took flight under cover of darkness, pursued by a regiment of French dragoons.

The French cavalry advanced on Saturday morning along the railway across the low country, and at 5 o'clock arrived at Mülhausen, a large industrial town, which was unfortified, and captured it in less than an hour.

The only important military fact developed by this engagement is that with equal numbers the Germans are unable to sustain a French bayonet charge; but the occupation of Alsace will have a great moral influence.

The Germans retired from Mülhausen upon Neu Breisach, fourteen miles to the north, first firing a great number of the Mülhausen buildings, notably provision shops and fodder stores. They also burned the forest of Hard, near Colmar.

The Alsatians, who have been terrorized by the German military authorities, welcomed the French with open arms.

French Report of Victory.

PARIS, Aug. 9.—French military authorities, while recognizing that the occupation of Altkirch and Mülhausen by the French troops is not of high strategical importance, are of the opinion that the successful advance of the French Army far across the German frontier will have considerable moral effect.

It is also unofficially reported that Colmar, further to the north, with its 30,000 inhabitants, has fallen into the hands of the French.

None of these three places was strongly fortified, and all of them lie outside the line of real German defense, being regarded as outposts of the strongly fortified cities. Their German garrisons were numerically fairly strong, but it was understood that in case of attack they would merely endeavor to hinder the French advance before falling back upon their supports.

Neu Breisach, to which they are said to have retired, lies to the east of Colmar, and is strongly fortified, while Strassburg, situated some distance to the north, is the centre of a great aggregation of German troops, is strongly fortified, and is supposed to be prepared for a long siege.

French Losses "Not Excessive."

Official reports of the fighting between the French and German troops state that the French losses were "not excessive," while those of the Germans are declared by the French to have been "very serious."

Before retiring from Mülhausen the German troops are said to have set fire to numerous buildings in that city, especially the warehouses where food and forage were stored, and the forest of Hard, near Colmar, is said to have been razed.

The French Minister of War gives the following official account of the occupation of Mülhausen by the French on Saturday:

"During the march from Altkirch the French forces passed the abandoned earthworks and defenses of Mülhausen. The populace came out from the town and in a frenzy of delight welcomed the French troops. The cavalry, galloping through the streets, pursued the German rearguard. The French established themselves north of Mülhausen.

"Rout is the only word with which to describe the German retreat. The French losses were not excessive when the result is considered. The occupation of Mülhausen, the great industrial and intellectual centre of Alsace, will reverberate through Europe.

"The Germans retired in the direction of Neu Breisach. The whole of Alsace will rise against them and aggravate their position."

War Minister Thanks Gen. Joffre.

The Minister of War sent a congratulatory telegram to Gen. Joffre, saying:

"This initial success will have a moral effect in bringing profound satisfaction to the nation. I thank you in the name of the Government."

It was nightfall on Friday when the advance guard of the French brigade approached Altkirch, says the official statement. The city was well defended and occupied by a German brigade. The French began the assault with ardor, a regiment of infantry distinguishing itself in a furious charge, soon after which the Germans retired in disorder.

A regiment of French cavalry followed the enemy, pursuing them in the direction of Wallheim and Tugolschen, inflicting serious losses upon them. A French Colonel and seven of his men were wounded.

Alsatians Cheer the French.

Darkness permitted the Germans to conceal themselves, and the troops of France entered the city amid the cheers of the people. All the windows of the houses were thrown open, veterans of 1870 embraced the French soldiers, and a great shout resounded.

At dawn of day the advance guard resumed its march. The cavalry failed to find the German patrols, and the march of the entire brigade on Mülhausen was begun.

In the afternoon of Saturday the scouts found that numerous and important defenses protecting the city had been abandoned, and in less than half an hour later the French, loudly cheering the tri-color, occupied Mülhaused. Later it was learned that the Germans had retired in the direction of Neu Breisach.

Gen. Joffre, commander in chief of the French forces, issued the following proclamation at Mülhausen:

"After forty-four years of sorrowful waiting French soldiers once more tread the soil of your noble country. They are pioneers in a great work of revenge. For them what emotion it calls forth and what pride to complete the work which they have made at the sacrifice of their lives!

"The French nation unanimously urges them on, and in the folds of their flag are inscribed the magic words, 'Right and Liberty.' Long live Alsace! Long live France!"

Martial Law in Alsace.

Martial law had been proclaimed in Alsace, and it is said that the Germans announced that any person suspected of sympathizing with the French would be executed without delay.

All the wireless stations in France and Algeria were today closed by the Government, except in cases where special authorization had been given or where they were used for military purposes.

Joseph Caillaux, former Premier, has joined the French Army, and has been attached to the Treasury Department as Inspector of Finances.

Colmar Reported Taken by French.

LONDON, Monday, Aug. 10, 3:50 A. M.—The Paris correspondent of The Chronicle says it is reported that the French, after winning another great battle, which was fought between Mülhausen and Colmar, occupied the latter place.

The Paris correspondent of The Standard in a dispatch describes in detail the French attack upon Mülhausen. Simultaneously with the advance from Belfort, other forces went forward from Delle, crossing the frontier in an easterly direction. Another force proceeded to Huningen, opposite Basle, Switzerland, executing a wide turning movement against Mülhausen.

All the attacks were preceded by aeroplane scouting, and were aided by cavalry and artillery.

Belgian Estimates Unofficial.

LONDON, Aug. 9.—It is understood that the Belgian Minister of War's announcement regarding the loss of 80,000 killed and wounded by the Germans and 15,000 by the French in the battle at Altkirch, Alsace, was based on unofficial reports of the fighting reaching the Belgian Ministry of War.

The Daily Mail's Rome correspondent says that, according to dispatches from Basle, the Germans have evacuated Sankt Ludwig in Alsace, four miles to the northwest of Basle, and that a battle is imminent on the Franco-Swiss frontier.

30,000 AUSTRIANS ARRIVE.

Reported at Basle to Give Aid to Kaiser's Army in Alsace.

LONDON, Aug. 10, 6:10 A. M.—The Rome correspondent of the Exchange Telegraph Company forwards a dispatch from Basle, Switzerland, saying that the Austrian troops have arrived there, coming by the way of Constance. They comprise 30,000 men of the Fourteenth Corps, under command of the Grand Duke of Tuscany, which were withdrawn from Tyrol to prevent them being sent against the Servians.

They will reinforce the German troops encamped at Istein, where the Germans are massing on the hills and in the fortifications, following the French success in Alsace.

Reinforcements in 48 Trains.

Special Cable to THE NEW YORK TIMES.

PARIS, Aug. 9.—The correspondent of the Echo de Paris at Rome says that reinforcements sent by Austria to the German troops in Alsace arrived today at Leopoldshöhe, Baden, in forty-eight trains, and that other Austrian regiments are advancing through Bavaria and Würtemberg.

The French Ministry of Foreign Affairs has asked the Austrian Government what it means by this movement. Apparently, Austria is co-operating with Germany by dispatching Tyrolean and Bosnian troops to Alsace.

Sending Slavs to Fight French.

PARIS, Aug. 9.—Reports of the arrival of an Austrian army corps on the Swiss frontier near Basle were the object of close attention by the French military authorities today. It was said that several more Austrian army corps were being organized in the Tyrol, whence they would later be sent toward the French frontier.

It was reported today that Austria was sending her Fifteenth Army Corps across Germany to the French frontier. This corps is composed principally of Slav subjects, who, it is thought, may not be dependable in an action against Russia.

40,000 Austrians Near Basle.

LONDON, Aug. 9.—A dispatch to The Times from Berne says that 40,000 Austrian troops have concentrated near Basle and that German and French troops also are near the Swiss frontier, so that a big battle may occur at any moment.

ROME, (via London,) Aug. 9.—Forty-eight trainloads of Austrian troops from the Tyrol arrived today at Leopoldshöhe, in Baden, to the northwest of Basel, Switzerland. They were on their way to Alsace to assist the Germans.

Kaiser Off to the Front to Take Command; Paris Believes This Is Signal for Big Battle

LONDON, Aug. 9.—A dispatch from Rome to The Daily Mail says that a report is current that Emperor William has left Berlin in a motor car for the Alsatian frontier.

A dispatch to the Exchange Telegraph Company from Rome says that, on the contrary, Emperor William has arrived at Aix-la-Chapelle to join his army.

PARIS, Aug. 9.—The military critic of the Journal des Debats considers the report from Rome that Emperor William has left Berlin to join the general staff of the German Army on the Alsatian frontier shows that the Germans are ready to engage the French in great force, and that a general engagement is impending.

British Beat Off German Submarines, Sinking One

LONDON, Monday, Aug. 10, 1:30 A. M.—The Admiralty has announced that one of the cruiser squadrons of the main fleet was attacked yesterday by German submarines. None of the British ships was damaged. One German submarine boat was sunk.

No details are given as to the place at which the fight occurred.

The submarine sunk by the British fleet was the U 15, which was built in 1912 and displaced 300 tons. She carried a crew of twelve men.

Allies Effect Junction in Belgium to Fight Germany.

FRENCH FORCES IN FRONT

Have Cleared Foes from Region South of Liege and Pushed Back Their Outer Lines.

GERMAN ADVANCE HALTS

Artillery Attack on Forts Stops—Kaiser's Forces Said to be Short of Food.

CAPTURE OF LIEGE DENIED

Belgian War Minister Answers Report—Berlin Insists City Is in German Hands.

French Close to Liege, Force Germans Back

BRUSSELS, Aug. 9, via London, Monday, Aug. 10, 1 A. M.—The following statement has been issued by the Belgian General Staff:

"The position of the German troops has hardly changed since Saturday.

"Their advanced detachments are retreating under the irresistible pressure of the French troops, who are in considerable force in all the country south of the Meuse, which was cleared of German troops.

"The enemy's offensive movement has been completely stopped. The French and Belgian troops will take the offensive simultaneously in accordance with concerted plans."

By MARTIN H. DONOHOE.

Special Correspondent of THE NEW YORK TIMES and London Daily Chronicle.

Special Cable to THE NEW YORK TIMES.

BRUSSELS, Aug. 9.—Everything goes well at Liege. Though it is still invested, it is holding out heroically against the wave of German invasion which has shattered itself against the forts held by the brave Third Division and the Fifteenth mixed brigade, commanded by Gen. Leman.

The initial loss sustained by the German invaders is the most serious encountered by any army in modern times. Confident of their strength, the Seventh, Ninth, and Tenth Corps, comprising the Third German Army, was thrown in full strength against the Liege defenses, only to recoil broken and shattered.

Everything points to the German losses being unusually severe. The reverse has only made the enemy's commander reckless, so he is determined to capture the fortress and city at all costs.

The forts at Evegnee and Fleron to the east and Boncelles at the extreme south bore the brunt of the repeated attacks.

Especially was this the case at Fort Boncelles, because the ground here was more favorable for an attack. Dense masses of the Prussian infantry hurled themselves against the forts, but not a single Prussian ever established himself within a fort.

The attack in mass and flinging of immense bodies of men against a selected position is a pet theory of the German General Staff. It has been tried and failed lamentably, thanks chiefly to the undaunted courage of a mere handful of Belgian defenders.

The great Prussian assault on Fort Boncelles ended in a terrible slaughter, the storming infantry melting away before the machine guns of the defenders. It reminded one of the early days of the Port Arthur siege when the valiant Nogi sacrificed thousands of lives in the vain attempt to storm the Russian fortress.

The morale of the Prussians was entirely broken toward the end of the general attack. The men, despite the threats and exhortations of the surviving officers, would no longer return to face the Belgian fire.

The casualties amongst the German officers seem to have been considerable, and this has added to the general demoralization.

The attackers also ran short of rifle ammunition. On the dead and wounded Germans the Belgians found empty cartridge cases.

Some of the German wounded begged piteously for food and water, declaring that they had had no food for two days.

One of the prisoners said that the German Army had been rushed to the front without waiting for supplies.

This furnishes abundant proof that the German Army was not ready and that the supply department hopelessly collapsed under the strain.

Once more German Imperial impulsiveness has outrun discretion with disastrous consequences for the Prussian Army autocrat, who foolishly counted on the twin weapons of terror and surprise to overcome Belgian resistance.

How Marchand Saved Gen. Leman.

In these moments of glorious military doings, Belgian joy is tinctured with sorrow for its many heroic sons who have fallen with their faces to the foe. Among the many who nobly yielded up their lives at the sacred call of duty there is one whose name is on all Belgian lips and imperishably enshrined in all Belgian hearts.

That is Commandant Marchand, who bravely fell saving Gen. Leman, Commandant of Liege, from assassination by one of those detestable ruses of war which is not now associated with the military methods of so-called civilized people. A party of German officers entered Liege in an armored motor car, clad in new service uniforms easily mistaken for English. In fact, many spectators, mistaking their nationality and mission, cried "Vive les Anglais!"

The officers drove to the Commander's headquarters and, hurriedly descending from the car, asked for Gen. Leman. Some Belgian officers, who also were deceived, gave the intruders a polite reception. Marchand arrived at this moment and, suspecting treachery, called out, "They are not English, they are Germans; beware!"

In another moment the brave officer had closed the door leading to Gen. Leman's office and paid for the act with his life, for immediately he was shot dead. But the gallant officer's death was speedily avenged by his infuriated comrades, who, maddened at the dastardly violation of the rules of civilized warfare, spared not, but slew.

German Invasion Long Planned.

It is clear that the war against France and the preliminary raid into Belgium had been planned for some time. An interesting proof of this is furnished by an incident at Liege. During the bombardment a house in the city itself was set afire by a German shell and completely destroyed. While exploring the ruins the firemen discovered a partially consumed stock of German military rifles of the latest pattern and also quantities of rifle ammunition. The place had been a veritable German arsenal.

The arms unquestionably were intended for the use of German soldiers. It had been arranged that in the event of partial success they should surreptitiously slip into Liege, clad as civilians, and, seizing the store of hidden arms, turn them against the citizens.

In the absence of their elders on actual military service spy hunting has been pursued by the Belgian boy scouts with considerable success at Brussels and Namur. Four German suspects were arrested last night.

Trophies from the stricken field, chiefly Prussian helmets and Hussars' busbies, rifles, and swords, have been brought by motor cars from Liege to the War Office here today and exhibited in the streets to frantically cheering crowds.

The correspondent of La Derniere Heure contrived to get into Liege yesterday. After remaining a few hours he succeeded in returning to Brussels. He saw a number of German infantry and cavalry, and large numbers of their dead and wounded lying in the square in front of the Hotel de Ville.

The invaders themselves, as well as their horses, appear to be thoroughly exhausted.

Few citizens have left Liege. Others are wisely keeping within bounds, fearing German reprisals.

LIEGE INVESTED, FORTS SAFE.

Germans and Belgians Both Right, from Their Points of View.

Special Cable to THE NEW YORK TIMES.

BRUSSELS, Aug. 9.—Liege City has been invested by the Germans passing between the fortifications, but no forts have been taken. The situation is good.

INDEPENDANCE BELGE.

Special Cable to THE NEW YORK TIMES.

BRUSSELS, Aug. 9.—"Tout va bien" (All goes well) was the answer to a question at the Ministry of War today. There were smiles on the face of my informant, and his general bearing went to confirm the information.

Liege is invested and all communication with it is cut off, but the forts are still intact and can hold out for months.

The intermittent bombardment by the Germans continues, but the character of the firing seems to show that the Germans are short of ammunition.

The Belgian field forces continue to receive reinforcements and are now well supplied with everything in the shape of material. Their morale is excellent, the events of the past week having filled the soldiers with buoyant confidence.

A large part of Belgian Luxemburg is now cleared of Germans. The French and Belgian cavalry are acting together and doing splendid work in this direction.

Tells of Occupation of Liege.

Special Cable to THE NEW YORK TIMES.

LONDON, Monday, Aug. 10.—The Daily News has a dispatch from Brussels, describing the "peaceable occupation" of the city of Liege by the Germans on Friday night and Saturday morning. The seeming contradiction in the dispatches about the situation at Liege lies in two ways of looking at the same thing. The Germans report the capture of Liege, which is true in so far that some of their forces have managed to steal through the line of forts and occupy the town itself. On the other hand, the forts are reported not to have been taken, and to be quite as capable of inflicting damage as ever; but, of course, their defenders do not wish to destroy the town itself in order to dislodge the Germans there. It is from this point of view that the Belgians deny the "capture" of Liege, which in their eyes involves not only the occupation of the town but the reduction of the forts.

The description of the occupation by The Daily News's Brussels correspondent follows:

"Entry into the town was effected through the interval between Forts

Governor and Bishop of Liege Held as Hostages; German Threat to Wipe Out Civilian Foes

Special Cable to THE NEW YORK TIMES.

AMSTERDAM, Aug. 9.—Both the Governor of the Province of Liege and the Bishop of Liege are held as hostages by the Germans, who say they will be put to death if the Belgian forts continue to fire.

Refugees say that when they left Liege the inhabitants were firing at the Germans from the windows. All who were caught after doing this were instantly shot.

German Warning of Reprisals

BERLIN, (via London,) Aug. 9.—A semi-official statement, published here, accuses Belgian civilians in the vicinity of Liege of having participated in the fighting against the Germans.

It says that doctors, attending the wounded, were fired on from ambuscades, and that the population on the French frontier opposite Metz fired from an ambuscade upon German patrols.

The statement continues:

"Possibly these facts are due to the mixture of the nationalities in the industrial districts, but it is also possible that France and Belgium are preparing to engage in a franc tireur war against our troops.

"If this is proved by further incidents, our adversaries themselves will be responsible if war with inexorable strength is extended to the guilty populations. The German troops are accustomed to fight only against the armed power of a hostile State, and cannot be blamed if, in self-defense, they should adopt exceptional measures."

National Archives

The Germans' revolutionary 420-mm. howitzer was responsible for the destruction of the fortifications around Liège.

"All the News That's Fit to Print."

The New York Times.

THE WEATHER

Fair today and Friday; gentle to moderate shifting winds.

☞ For full weather report see Page 13.

VOL. LXIII...NO. 20,655. NEW YORK, THURSDAY, AUGUST 13, 1914.—SIXTEEN PAGES. ONE CENT In Greater New York, Jersey City and Newark. | Elsewhere TWO CENTS.

BELGIAN LEFT WING WINS AS GREAT BATTLE BEGINS; ALLIED ARMIES DRAWN UP BEFORE KAISER'S MILLION MEN; GERMANS ADMIT HEAVY LOSSES ON RUSSIAN FRONTIER; FIRST THOUSAND REFUGEES HOME, PENNILESS BUT GLAD

Homecomers Sing Gayly As the Philadelphia Brings Them In.

SILK CLAD IN STEERAGE

And Women, 16 to a Cabin, Took Turns in Sharing the Berths.

SHIP GUIDED PAST MINES

Halted by Torpedo Boats Outside Queenstown Harbor and by a Cruiser Here.

WARM WELCOME AT PIER

Relief Committee Formed Aboard Cares for the Penniless—Criticisms of Ambassador Page.

The Philadelphia of the American Line, carrying the first American refugees to leave Europe after hostilities began, arrived at Pier 59, North River, at Eighteenth Street, at 10:20 o'clock last night, with 703 cabin passengers and 369 steerage. Of those in the steerage 198 were American citizens, many of whom under ordinary conditions traveled in the first cabins of the best transatlantic ships, but they were glad to get to America under any conditions. Ordinarily the Philadelphia accommodates about 450 passengers, so even those possessing cabin tickets were crowded beyond any idea of comfort.

As the ship proceeded up the river 2,500 persons who had procured pier passes and 300 more outside the gates set up a great cheer, which was answered by the Philadelphia's passengers, every one of whom was lined as close as possible to the rail. The ship's band struck up "The Star-Spangled Banner," and the throngs on land and water joined in singing the anthem. As the ship docked there was another outburst of cheering that lasted for several minutes.

The Philadelphia left Southampton at 11:20 o'clock in the morning a week ago yesterday and stopped at Queenstown, which she left at 3:45 o'clock last Thursday afternoon. She was escorted out of Southampton by a British torpedo boat and immediately the harbor was closed to commerce, thus making the Philadelphia the last ship to leave that port.

Stopped by Torpedo Boats.

After the torpedo boat escort had left the Philadelphia, Capt. Arthur R. Mills, her commander, said last night, two French torpedo boats and four submarines hailed her. One of the torpedo boats attempted to get alongside while the Philadelphia was in motion, but was unable to make the steamship's speed. The torpedo boat Captain gave orders for the Philadelphia to stop and Capt. Mills hove to. Inquiries and answers were exchanged with Capt. Mills until the Frenchman was assured of the Philadelphia's destination, nationality, and cargo.

"As soon as he knew who we were," said Capt. Mills, "the French officer shouted through his megaphone, 'Passez, Monsieur,' and we went on our way."

By an arrangement of private signals the Philadelphia was admitted to the Port of Queenstown. She was challenged repeatedly going both in and out by British and French torpedo boats, Capt. Mills said.

As the Philadelphia neared Sandy Hook the British cruiser Suffolk hailed her to inquire what her colors were. Capt. Mills immediately stopped the Philadelphia and waited for the cruiser to steam alongside. The English officer was assured of the nationality of the liner and wished the Americans a safe entry into port as his cruiser backed away.

After the Philadelphia had been out a few days this Marconigram reached her:

"Advise passengers that a relief committee has been organized to assist those in need of actual financial help when they reach home. Try to ascertain how many passengers need such help."

Relief Committee Found.

Before the wireless was received a relief committee had been organized on the ship and had found that fifteen of the passengers were in actual need of help. All were taken in charge by the ship's committee after the Philadelphia had docked. The committee was composed of:

Charles Plankinton of Milwaukee, Chairman; Martin Vogel, Assistant United States Treasurer at New York; William H. Porter of J. P. Morgan & Co., Thomas F. Gilroy, son of the late Mayor Gilroy of New York; Leroy W.

Continued on Page 3.

JAPAN IS CUT OFF FROM EUROPE BY CABLE

Has Been Ready to Join England in War—Significant Conference in St. Petersburg.

TOKIO, Thursday, Aug. 13.—Telegraphic communication between Japan and Europe is interrupted.

Japan has been reported for a week as ready to join England and her allies in the European war, and the last reports from Tokio were that 43,000 troops were already on board transports.

LONDON, Thursday, Aug. 13, 4:40 A. M.—The St. Petersburg correspondent of The Times says that much interest has been excited by the conferences recently held between the Japanese Ambassador, Baron Molono, and the Russian Foreign Minister, M. Sazonoff.

GERARD LEAVES BERLIN SUDDENLY FOR HOLLAND

Amsterdam Learns That Ambassador Is Coming—Rumor of His Retirement.

Special Cable to THE NEW YORK TIMES.

LONDON, Thursday, Aug. 13, 4:10 A. M.—An Amsterdam message received here this morning quotes the Vaz Dias agency of Amsterdam for a report to the effect that James W. Gerard, the American Ambassador at Berlin, is leaving the German capital at 12:40 o'clock this morning by special train for the frontier. It is added that the Ambassador will make his way to Holland.

The Morning Post's Amsterdam correspondent says the American Ambassador at Berlin has left the German capital for Amsterdam, and will cross the German frontier tonight.

Special to The New York Times.

WASHINGTON, Aug. 12.—It was learned here tonight that John W. Garrett of Maryland, the American Minister to the Argentine Republic, who is now on his way to Europe on the United States armored cruiser North Carolina, would not return to his post in Buenos Aires. Coupled with this information was an unconfirmed report that James W. Gerard of New York, the American Ambassador at Berlin, might retire from the diplomatic service, and that it was not improbable that he would be succeeded by Mr. Garrett.

As far as THE TIMES correspondent can ascertain there is no foundation for the report concerning Ambassador Gerard, other than an untraceable bit of gossip that Mr. Gerard is not enamored of a diplomatic life. This rumor does not accord with anything that has reached official circles. As far as Mr. Garrett is concerned, however, there is foundation for the statement that he will not resume his diplomatic duties at Buenos Aires. It is understood that he will go to Berlin and assist Ambassador Gerard in the heavy duties that have been imposed upon him by the European war.

OFFER BELGIUM BRIBE TO LET HER ARMY PASS

Germany Tries to Negotiate Even After the Battles at Liege.

Special Cable to THE NEW YORK TIMES.

PARIS, Thursday, Aug. 13.—The special correspondent of The Temps at Brussels sends an article showing how much justification existed for the German hopes that Belgium would not resist and also how much France owed to the Belgian King and his chief Minister, Baron Broqueville. The article concludes with this more interesting news:

"Even now, after war has been waged, Germany has not ceased to make overtures to Belgium through the medium of Holland, asking leave to traverse the Meuse valley peaceably, promising in return not only integrity, but also considerable increase of Belgian territory."

King Albert and his Ministers refused even to listen to the suggestion. The article says:

"The fact is the Belgian mobilization was at first not well received on account of a feeling that Germany would not infringe on Belgian independence.

"Moreover, as one Belgian said, 'We thought it madness to resist Germany, who would only make a mouthful of us.'

"But the heroic defense of Liege electrified us. In an instant we realized our mistake. Today we bless Baron Broqueville and can never show how deeply grateful we are.

"All who opposed military service have rushed to the colors."

German Attempt to Recapture Eydtkuhnen Is Unsuccessful.

AEROPLANES AT FRONTIER

Official Admissions of Losses by Berlin an Indication of Important Engagements.

AUSTRIANS DEFEATED ALSO

Cavalry Brigade Said to Have Been Wiped Out by Artillery and Cossacks.

SVEABORG EXPECTS ATTACK

Population of Finland Fortress and of Helsingfors Ordered by Commander to Leave.

ST. PETERSBURG, (via London,) Aug. 12, 11:45 P. M.—An attempt by the Germans to re-occupy Eydtkuhnen, East Prussia, one of the points to which Russian troops were dispatched early in the war, has failed.

The Germans, consisting of a detachment of infantry with artillery, were repulsed with loss.

It is announced officially that German aeroplanes have been carrying out extensive manoeuvres along the Russian frontier, but have done no damage.

LONDON, Thursday, Aug. 13, 2 A. M.—A Berlin dispatch to The Daily Telegraph says the German Staff admits heavy losses on the Russian frontier.

A St. Petersburg dispatch to The Daily Mail says it is reported in the newspapers there that Germany has formed twenty-five reserve divisions, each of 20,000 men and six batteries, with thirty-one reserve cavalry regiments, which will constitute the main part of the German forces on the Russian frontier.

LONDON, Aug. 12.—The Russian commander of the fortress of Sveaborg, Finland, has ordered all the inhabitants of that place and Helsingfors to leave.

A battle or a bombardment is believed to be imminent.

AUSTRIAN CAVALRY WIPED OUT

Whole Brigade Said to Have Been Annihilated on Russian Border.

LONDON, Aug. 12.—A dispatch from Rome to The Central News says the Corriere d'Italia publishes a telegram from the frontier stating that an Austrian cavalry brigade has been exterminated on the Austro-Russian frontier.

The Austrian cavalrymen are said to have attacked the Cossacks, who were accompanied by artillery. They were unable to hold their own, and tried to get back across the frontier, but rain had fallen and men and horses were caught in the marshy ground and shot down until not a man remained alive.

PARIS, Aug. 12.—A dispatch from St. Petersburg to the Matin says:

"The Austrians have received a check on the Dniester River. Four regiments of Austrian infantry and eight regiments of Uhlans were routed. The approaching big battle will probably be a decisive one."

ST. PETERSBURG, via London, Thursday, Aug. 13, 2:50 A. M.—The Austrian troops on the Russian frontier have been placed under the command of a German General.

The news is confirmed that certain divisions of Austrian forces, comprising Tyrolean Czechs regiments, have been transported to French territory.

BOMBARD FRENCH TOWN.

German Shells Kill and Wound Residents of Pont-a-Mousson.

PARIS, Aug. 12.—The bombardment by the Germans of Pont-a-Mousson, in the Department of Muerthe and Moselle, about twenty miles northwest of Nancy, began yesterday morning.

A hundred shells of large calibre fell in the town, killing or wounding a number of the inhabitants and demolishing buildings.

BRITAIN AND AUSTRIA ON VERGE OF WAR

Ambassador to Leave England Today and a Declaration Is Expected at Any Time.

LONDON, Aug. 12.—A declaration of war between Great Britain and Austria-Hungary is expected at any moment. The significant announcement was made tonight that the Ambassador from Austria would leave England tomorrow.

The Ambassador, Count A. Mensdorff-Pouilly-Dietrichstein, has been in England for eighteen years and served as Secretary and Minister before becoming Ambassador. He is a close friend of the British royal family.

Austrian Envoy to Italy Resigns.

VIENNA, (via London,) Aug. 12.—The Austro-Hungarian Ambassador to Italy, Kajetan Merey de Kapos-Mere, has resigned his post on the ground of ill-health. Baron Karl von Macchio, Departmental Chief at the Austro-Hungarian Foreign Office, has been appointed to succeed him temporarily.

CRUISER GOEBEN SOLD TO TURKEY?

Report Credited in London—Turks Angry With Britain for Keeping Dreadnought.

Special Cable to THE NEW YORK TIMES.

LONDON, Aug. 12.—Chief among the items issued by the Press Bureau of the British War Office today was the information regarding the Atlantic situation, ignorance regarding which caused much uneasiness among many Americans who are about to return home.

It is reported that Turkey has bought the German cruiser Goeben, and if it is true, which is regarded as likely, it will render the Mediterranean clear for France and England at present. But the aggressive attitude of Turkey, with a large army mobilized in Thrace and under the command of a German General, points to possible further dangers. Also must be remembered the navy of Austria-Hungary, with which France is at war.

By The Associated Press.

LONDON, Aug. 12.—The Daily Mail says it understands that Turkey has assured the British Government that the German cruisers Goeben and Breslau, which are now in the Dardanelles, will be disarmed, but that there is reason to believe Turkey has purchased the two vessels and intends to put them in commission.

"If Turkey intends to enter the war as Germany's ally, or to pay off her old scores against Greece," says The Daily Mail, "she must be warned that in either case retribution will be swift and certain.

"It appears that Germany offered to sell the Goeben to Turkey some time ago, but that the deal fell through because Turkey stipulated that the vessel should be handed over with her crew."

Special Cable to THE NEW YORK TIMES.

CONSTANTINOPLE, Aug. 12.—The Tanin, the Young Turk organ, expresses considerable indignation at the taking over by Great Britain of the Turkish dreadnought Sultan Osman I. while being built in England.

It is stated that possession of it was taken only half an hour before the time fixed for hoisting the Ottoman flag over the vessel.

HOW IT IS DONE.

Putting Through the News with a Little Help from the Censor.

Special Cable to THE NEW YORK TIMES.

LONDON, Aug. 12.—Additional facts regarding the loss of the Amphion have been obtained from members of the crew who arrived at Devonport. The mine was struck about 6:30 in the morning.

SHOOT FRENCH WOUNDED.

Germans Also Wear Uniforms of Dead Belgians, It Is Charged.

PARIS, Aug. 12, 11:58 P. M.—The following official statement was issued tonight:

"A wounded French cavalryman at Mezières declares he saw a German cavalryman shoot a wounded Frenchman. He says he heard five or six other shots and saved himself by feigning death.

"The Germans are wearing uniforms taken from Belgians killed in battle."

To Strike England at Sea While Land Battle Is On, Germany's Plan, According to London Times Critic

Special Cable to THE NEW YORK TIMES.

LONDON, Thursday, Aug. 13.—Col. Repington, the London Times military expert, says:

"We are on the eve of a great struggle on the Meuse. Surrounded as she is by powerful enemies, a great victory is very necessary for Germany at this moment. Will she strike by sea when she strikes by land? This is the only blow open to Germany which can do us mortal hurt if it succeeds. The chances are against success, and with every day of the war the last chances become less, because our land forces are daily growing in numbers and solidity.

"We must regard the problem through German eyes, and however much we may disbelieve in the German solution, we must be prepared for a stroke which would accord with the German soldiers' theories of war."

Atlantic Safe, But No Reassurance as to North Sea, Where, Admiralty Says, Germans Have Spread Mines

LONDON, Aug. 12.—The British Admiralty has sent out cruisers which will ply the Atlantic to protect trade routes. The French Government also has sent out warships to search for German cruisers known to be in the Atlantic.

"The enemy's ships," says the official Admiralty report, "will be hunted continuously, and although some time may elapse before they are run down, they will be kept too busy to do much mischief.

"A number of fast merchant vessels, fitted and armed at British arsenals, also are patrolling the routes and keeping them clear of German commerce raiders. With every day that passes British control of trade routes, especially those of the Atlantic, becomes stronger.

"In the North Sea, where the Germans have scattered mines indiscriminately, and where the most formidable operations of the naval war are proceeding, the Admiralty can give no reassurance."

Huge Army of Germans Moves on Brussels and Battle Opens.

BIG CAVALRY FORCE LEADS

Belgians the Victors in First Encounter of the Greatest Conflict in History.

CLASHES ON 200-MILE LINE

Invaders Are Armed with 4,000 Field Guns and 1,200 Rapid-Fire Guns.

LIEGE FORTS UNDER FIRE

Fierce Attack Renewed by Germans—City's Garrison Again Takes the Offensive.

Belgians' Left Wing Drives Back Germans

Special Cable to THE NEW YORK TIMES

LONDON, Thursday, Aug. 13—A Brussels dispatch received this morning says:

"The Belgians have routed the Germans in a fierce encounter between the Belgian left wing and massed German cavalry, infantry and artillery.

"The Belgians displayed wonderful control under the fierce fire, and their victory has aroused the liveliest enthusiasm along the whole line of the allied troops."

Special Cable to THE NEW YORK TIMES

LONDON, Thursday, Aug. 13.—The first encounters in the greatest battle in history seem to be taking place along nearly the whole front of 200 miles.

The German concentration along the Liege-Luxemburg-Metz line now seems to be complete and fifteen army corps with two Austrian corps are in Belgium or within striking distance of the French frontier.

The total strength of this force is estimated at 1,000,000 men with 700,000 infantry, 50,000 cavalry, 4,000 field guns and howitzers, and 1,200 machine guns. This is about double the strength of the force which von Moltke had at his disposal in 1870.

Before a decisive success is obtained there will be a several days' battle, probably the bloodiest of all time.

Allies or French troops are in contact with the Germans on almost the whole line.

Such news as has been received here confirms the view that the main German advance will be through central and Southern Belgium and Luxemburg.

Private advices received in London last night from Belgium intimated that a German attack upon Brussels and the capture of the city were regarded there as imminent.

The residents of Brussels themselves have shown no signs of panic, having full confidence in the ability of their army to hold off the German attack, which is not expected by them to develop in great force, owing to the necessity of the Germans pushing forward every available man to the French frontier.

The private messages which reached London, however, spoke with expectation of a German occupation of Brussels.

An Englishwoman and well-known writer who arrived in Belgium yesterday with a mission to report events from a woman's point of view for a London paper was brusquely sent back to the seashore by the chief correspondent of the paper, who said it was the height of folly for any Englishwoman not forced to be in Belgium to venture there.

English correspondents are likely to be regarded as spies by Germans and summarily shot.

Special Cable to THE NEW YORK TIMES.

PARIS, Aug. 12.—It is thought here that the first big battle of the war has begun near Tirlemont, Belgium, and that it is the intention of the Germans to try a stroke at Louvain and Brussels.

First Fight in Open Country.

BRUSSELS, Thursday, Aug. 13, (via London.)—The first battle between Germans and Belgians in the open country is reported in the following official communication:

"After having passed the night (Tuesday) in the position they had reached after their retreat yesterday, the Germans this morning advanced in force toward a point in our dispositions which they thought was not held.

"Our staff, however, was alert and informed by cavalry reconnoissances was able to give the necessary orders with the result that the enemy found their advance checked. An engagement took place in which our troops were successful. Ten thousand men took part in the fight.

"This was the first action of our troops in open country and their conduct is a good augury for the future. Apart from this the situation to all appearances has undergone no change.

"As regards our allies, the plan, arranged beforehand, is being followed out exactly according to programme."

A regiment of dragoons, coming from the direction of Liege, who attempted to surprise the Belgians at Aineffe, in the Province of Liege, were driven off leaving 153 dead and 102 prisoners.

A fight of importance took place yesterday near Tirlemont, where a thousand German cavalry with quick-firing guns mounted on horses attacked a regiment of Belgian lancers. The latter retired owing to numerical inferiority. The Belgians lost two officers and a small number of men in killed and wounded.

Where the Battle Is Raging.

LONDON, Thursday, Aug. 13.—The Admiralty and War Office Information Bureau issues the following:

"An engagement is in progress northwest of Hasselt in the Province of Limburg between a Belgian cavalry division, supported by a brigade of infantry, and the German Second Cavalry Division, 2,500 strong, supported by a battalion of infantry and twelve pieces of artillery.

"The German Fourth Cavalry Division is reported moving toward Jodoigne, in the Brabant province of Belgium.

"No German infantry is known to be on the left bank of the Meuse except the above-mentioned battalion.

"The Germans are entrenching at Vise.

"The Liege forts are holding out. The Germans are constructing batteries north of Liege preparatory to a siege. Heavy guns have been heard already.

"The Germans are constructing a railway between Vise and Homburg, parallel with the frontier of Dutch Limburg. They are also entrenching themselves in Liege.

"Huy, Marche, and Houffalize are points held by German cavalry. Columns of German cavalry are moving eastward toward the valley of the Ourthe.

"The French retreat from Mülhausen was well carried out. The proportion of opposing forces was four Germans to each Frenchman. The German field artillery proved far inferior to that of the French."

A previous statement said:

"Of the twenty-six German army corps, the bulk has been located, and it is evident that the mass of German troops is concentrated between Liege and Luxemburg.

"The number of German troops known to be on the western side of that country proves that in the eastern theatre of war the Russo-German frontier, so far as Germany is concerned, is comparatively lightly guarded, unless by reservists."

The Telegraph's military correspondent at Paris says of the position of the German force stretched across Belgian Luxemburg and Namur Province:

"The German right flank rests on the Meuse near Huy. Three army corps with supporting cavalry are established on the left bank. This army threatens to attack Brussels or invade France in the direction of Mons, in the Belgian province of Hainaut."

Cavalry Screen German Advance.

BRUSSELS, Aug. 12, (via Paris.)—The German Army has moved north of Liege and is advancing into the heart of Belgium.

It is difficult to determine its objective. There is a screen of German cavalry in extraordinary force along the whole front of the allied armies.

The French cavalry is actively engaged in sharp fighting.

Both the German and allied armies are feeling their way. A new German corps is investing Liege.

Belgian and French troops have effected a junction south of Brussels.

On the report that operations on an extensive scale were imminent, a correspondent by permission of the War Board of Control made a circuit along 20 miles of the Belgian front, visiting the extreme advance and talking with the officers and men.

The impression of the correspondent was that no heavy fighting was likely in Belgian Limburg, where the Germans had little or no infantry. By the opposition, offered by the Belgian troops at Liege, the Germans lost precious time, which was profitably employed by the French and British in concentrating masses at convenient points.

The allied forces have been so disposed as to be supported by a fortified position at many of the chief points, but little or nothing has been done around Brussels, and it is thought that Brussels is being used as a bait to attract the Germans.

It is certain that vast preparations have been made by the allies, now spread out for battle, and they are likely to move quickly when the hour comes to strike.

Belgian aviators made flights today as far as the German frontier.

Baron Zuylen de Nyvelt was shot by a sentry today while riding in an automobile along the Namur-Liege road.

Berlin Reports the Capture of 1500 French Troops in Alsace.

SAYS FRENCH ARE EXPELLED

Paris, However, Maintains That the Strategic Position in Alsace Remains Excellent.

ADMITS PARTIAL RETREAT

But Announces That More French Troops Are Being Sent Into the Province.

FIGHTING ALONG FRONTIER

War Office Says French Have the Advantage in Unimportant Cavalry Engagements.

BERLIN, (via London,) Thursday, Aug. 13.—The German troops near Mülhausen have captured ten French officers, 500 men, four guns, ten wagons, and many rifles.

According to the report, German territory has been cleared of the French. It is also stated that at Lagarde the German troops made more than 1,000 prisoners, about one-sixth of the two defeated French regiments.

Special Cable to THE NEW YORK TIMES.

PARIS, Aug. 12.—There is no news from the eastern frontier, except of outpost skirmishes. The public may expect to hear of the abandonment of small districts here and there all along the front of 300 kilometers, (186 miles.)

Explains Muelhausen Retreat.

By The Associated Press.

PARIS, Aug. 12, 3:15 P. M.—The following official announcement has just been issued by the French War Department:

"Up to the present hour no encounters between the German and French forces, except those of outposts, have taken place.

"The occupation of Mülhausen was effected by a French brigade of infantry in order to destroy the German intelligence centre in operation in that town. That having been accomplished, the brigade was withdrawn, as the General in command considered the position too perilous.

"The French brigade was followed by the entire Fourteenth German Army Corps and a division of the Fifteenth Army Corps, which were halted by our principal lines.

"Our strategical situation remains, as before, excellent."

The Minister of War explains that the engagements on the Franco-German frontier are no more than outpost skirmishes.

"The best denial that can be given to the report that the French lost 20,000 men at Altkirch," says the Minister, "is that the total effective French troops did not reach that number."

It is further explained that the advance of the French infantry on Mülhausen was to cut the centre of German communication, and it is added that this movement was successfully carried out.

The communication concludes:

"We are placing in Upper Alsace a considerable number of troops."

French Cavalry Superior.

LONDON, Aug. 12.—A dispatch from the French Foreign Minister received here says:

"Small, unimportant engagements have occurred along the whole line where the French and German Armies are facing each other, from Belfort, opposite the southernmost part of Alsace, to Liege, in Belgium. In these encounters the French cavalry has always maintained its superiority over the German mounted troops, while our artillery has been splendidly served.

"Our troops have kept the crests and passes of the Vosges Mountains, and they dominate the heights of Alsace.

"A line between Thann (22 miles southwest of Colmar, Alsace) and Altkirch (the first position occupied by the French Army after its invasion of Alsace) is held by our armies. This line runs slightly to the rear of Mülhausen.

"The French Government indignantly denies that there was any violation of German territory by the

Wide World Photos

German Infantry with machine guns attack Russian positions at the Vistula River.

Mid-Week Pictorial

French Infantry in action behind a natural breastwork in Belgium.

"All the News That's Fit to Print."

The New York Times.

THE WEATHER

Generally fair today and Tuesday; gentle to moderate shifting winds.

For full weather report see Page 9.

VOL. LXIII...NO. 20,659. NEW YORK, MONDAY, AUGUST 17, 1914.—TWELVE PAGES. ONE CENT In Greater New York, Jersey City and Newark. | Elsewhere TWO CENTS.

JAPAN GIVES GERMANY A WEEK TO QUIT THE FAR EAST; TWO AUSTRIAN WARSHIPS SUNK BY FRENCH FLEET; GERMANS SHIFT BELGIAN ATTACK TO THE SOUTH

CZAR SETS POLES WILD WITH JOY

They See in Promise of Autonomy Realization of the Dreams of 142 Years.

MASTER COUP, FRENCH SAY

Resuscitation of Ancient Kingdom Would Be Great Barrier Against Pan-Germanism.

MOVEMENT MAY SPREAD

Slavs in Galicia and Bohemia and Holstein Danes, They Think, Will Break Away.

By G. H. PERRIS.

NEW YORK TIMES-London Chronicle War Service.

Special Cable to THE NEW YORK TIMES.

PARIS, Aug. 16.—The greatest news of many a day and of many a year is that of the Czar's appeal to the Poles of Austria and Germany and his promise to set up a new Poland enjoying complete autonomy, with freedom of language and religion.

The student of history will recognize the tremendous irony of this proclamation by the descendant of Catherine the Great at the cost of the descendant of her ally in the dismemberment of 1772, Frederick the Great.

I can myself testify that even among the most patriotic of Poles the hope of recovering their national independence was the faintest and most visionary. Those who believed that this European war would spring upon the world many sensational surprises find here their first justification. The reconstruction of the map of Europe has begun. Expectations that were impossible yesterday are today defined so clearly that nothing can extinguish them.

Probably it is as true today as formerly that an absolutely independent Poland could not exist between three empires which have previously amputated it, but constituted in the terms of the imperial proclamation, under Russian suzerainty, its position and the numbers of its population will inevitably favor liberal development, and this will react upon the condition of the whole of the Russian lands.

War has always for Russia presented such dramatic necessities as this. The Crimean War led to the emancipation of the serfs and the Japanese war to the establishment of the beginning of parliamentary institutions. It was inevitable when the Russian advance upon Austria and Germany began that the Polish populations from the Baltic to the Carpathians should receive some such dramatic inducement to choose their destiny.

They are not all in the same case. The Poles in East Prussia have been subjected for twenty years to a brutal systematic campaign which, however, has not succeeded either in destroying their social unity or driving them from the land. In Galicia they have been more fortunate and therefore more loyal. But in Austria, Russia, and Germany alike a word has been spoken that cannot be recalled and will set millions of hearts beating and millions of feet atramp. It is one of the great masterstrokes of history, and no man can say where and when its reverberations will cease.

Unspeakable joy reigns this evening in the Polish colony in Paris. Family groups gathered to celebrate the good news, while many pious Polish women went to their mission church to offer up prayers of thanksgiving. Mgr. Leon Postawka, the veteran prelate, who is at the head of the Polish mission, was overcome by emotion when the glad tidings was shown to him in print by a correspondent. He exclaimed:

"Magnificent! Sublime! I am overwhelmed with joy. For so many years we have prayed and hoped for this news, and now that it has come it dazes us. I am no longer a young man, but I preached this morning to our young people and urged them to go forward in the French fighting line against Germany's barbarians. They needed little urging, and have all volunteered with the same deliberate calm that imbued me when, forty-four years ago this very day, I volunteered for France myself against the same enemy.

"Our Lord is with the weak and oppressed, and it is His voice that dictated to Emperor Nicholas the manifesto just issued to the Polish Nation."

The aged ecclesiastic's friend Dr. Joseph Landau, a Pole, who served in the French Army, said:

"We have from infancy dreamed and hoped for the restoration of Poland. Our hearts today are filled with joy and with gratitude toward God and the Czar. By its exalted language and self-evident sincerity the proclamation of the Grand Duke Nicholas has intensified our happiness. Many of us, although men, have wept today, but our tears were of joy. Our hearts are so overfilled

Continued on Page 2.

The Day's War Situation

Japan sends an ultimatum to Germany, demanding the withdrawal of her armed ships from Far Eastern waters and the turning over to Japan of Kiau-chau, the German concession in China, which Japan promises to restore to China. An answer is demanded by noon of Sunday, Aug. 23. Japan acts under the clause of her agreement of alliance with England, providing for the preservation of peace and protection of general interests in the Far East.

A naval battle is reported to have occurred in the Adriatic, in which a French fleet sank two Austrian warships.

The French force again takes the offensive along the line from Luneville to Saarburg on the road to Strassburg, capturing several small towns.

A renewal of the fighting in Alsace at Mulhausen is reported, the French attempting to retake the city.

French and German forces are in touch near Dinant, in the valley of the Meuse. Here the French claim victory over the German invaders.

There is a lull in the fighting at Liege and to the north of the city on the road to Brussels.

Military observers believe that the opening of the big battle along the 248-mile front from Holland to Switzerland cannot long be delayed.

Victories on the Austro-Servian and Austro-Russian frontiers are claimed by both sides.

Poles all over the world welcome the Czar's promise of autonomy.

The United States armored cruisers Tennessee and North Carolina arrived yesterday evening at Falmouth with a supply of gold for Americans stranded abroad.

ITALY IN A FERMENT; ACTIVITY ON FRONTIER

Martial Law on Austrian Side —Italians Await News of Austrian Fleet's Defeat.

Special Cable to THE NEW YORK TIMES.

ROME, Aug. 16. (Dispatch to The London Standard.)—Since England has been at war with Austria the old traditions and feelings which united Italy and Great Britain have been revived and intensified. England now is as popular as when she refused to receive Mazzini and other exiles and when she did receive Garibaldi as a hero.

All here look toward London, impatient to know developments in the activities of the British squadron in the Adriatic, understanding that the fate of that sea has now been entrusted to the Anglo-French fleets.

Excitement over the war, already acute, is becoming a frenzy. The authorities are making an effort to prevent manifestations. As illustrating the situation, it is reported that the police have proclaimed a new gospel, to the effect that "one is forbidden to think against the Government."

Little is known concerning the Austrian fleet, but it is believed that, fearing the superiority of the Anglo-French ships, it has retired to the Northern Adriatic, under the protection of the guns of Pola.

By The Associated Press.

ROME, Aug. 16.—The Giornale d'Italia, commenting today on the approaching struggle in the Adriatic Sea between the Anglo-French and Austrian war vessels, says:

"It seems impossible there should be a naval fight in those waters without the participation of the descendants of the great Venetian republic."

The newspaper adds that "the names of the ships likely to be engaged show which civilizations are confronting each other. Austrian vessels bear the names of Tegethoff and Radetsky, who personified the worst tyranny of Austria over the Italians, while four of the French vessels bear the names Voltaire, Danton, Mirabeau, and Diderot."

It is announced that navigation in the Northern Adriatic Sea is dangerous because of the mines strewn by the Austrians as a defense against a possible Anglo-French naval attack.

TROOPS ON ITALIAN BORDER.

Martial Law Proclaimed in Five Austrian Districts There.

Special Cable to THE NEW YORK TIMES.

LONDON, Monday, Aug. 17.—A dispatch to The Daily Mail from Venice says:

"Martial law was declared today in Carinthia, Carniola, Trieste, Istria, and Gorse (Austrian districts near the Italian frontier) by the General commanding the army corps at Gratz.

"There is a considerable movement of troops on both sides of the frontier. Searchlights were playing along the frontier as we passed."

THE POPE ILL IN BED.

Has Gouty Catarrh—Depressed by the European War.

Special Cable to THE NEW YORK TIMES.

ROME, Aug. 16.—Pope Pius is ill mentally as well as physically. The war has been the greatest shock the Pontiff has ever had, coming when he is enfeebled by age and by the intense heat of a Roman Summer.

He is suffering from gouty catarrh, with a rise in temperature, and has been ordered to bed by his physician.

Ever since the war began the aged Pope has slept only fitfully, dreaming of the conflict at night and discussing it by day.

No real anxiety is at present felt about his condition, but if there is a continuation of the intense heat it may become worse. He said this morning: "I shall not cease to implore God to put a stop to this inhuman butchery."

Clash with French Near Dinant Prelude of a Big Movement.

UP MEUSE RIVER VALLEY

Threatened Blow to the North Toward Brussels Withheld by Kaiser's Forces.

FRENCH STRONGLY POSTED

Germans Expected to Hurl Four Corps Against Them, While Holding Liege with Another.

By THOMAS NAYLOR.

NEW YORK TIMES-London Chronicle War Service.

Special Cable to THE NEW YORK TIMES.

BRUSSELS, Aug. 16.—The War Office issued a communication this afternoon which seems to indicate that the Germans are no longer pressing forward their ttack on the main Belgian Army. No large masses of German troops are to be seen, and at no point on the long Belgian line have any conflicts with the enemy taken place today.

This, taken in connection with the fighting at Dinant yesterday, would seem to indicate that the main German attack will be in the valley of the Meuse.

Further news arrived this morning of the fight at Dinant. The French took the offensive and attacked the Germans, who attempted a flanking movement.

At one time the French force was in danger, but they stood their ground with all the bravery shown by French armies since Rocroi. Enormous losses were inflicted upon the Germans, who were driven back.

The action yesterday was the culmination of a series of outpost engagements, which had been going on for two days, and in which the advantage always rested with the French.

The Germans attempted to cross the Meuse between Yvoir and Anseremme from a plateau near Bouxignes.

The German columns could be seen winding along the valley toward Dinant, and there is every sign that a big battle will take place in that region before many hours are over.

The French, who are strongly posted, hold a splendid defensive position with their artillery and machine guns.

Anything like their tactics and strategy is entirely wanting in the German dispositions, for they blunder into strongly entrenched positions and are butchered wholesale.

Special Cable to THE NEW YORK TIMES.

BRUSSELS, Aug. 16, (dispatch to The London Daily News.)—This afternoon's news was reassuring. I learn from an official source that the situation has not changed, and that the Belgian Army has not been able to discover any German concentration in front of it, and is at no point in direct contact with their forces.

Four German Corps to Attack.

Special Cable to THE NEW YORK TIMES.

BRUSSELS, Aug. 16, (Dispatch to The London Morning Post.)—There is news this morning that the French have pushed back a strong reconnaissance attack, south of Namur, toward Dinant. The Germans were driven toward the fort of Dave with a loss.

It is calculated that four German army corps will be engaged in the attack, with a fifth investing Liege and holding the lines.

The mitrailleuses are proving very effective on both sides. The Belgian mitrailleuses are drawn into action by dogs, which on the battlefield show complete coolness.

FRENCH PURSUE FOR 9 MILES

Artillery Fight Across the Town of Dinart for Hours.

Special Cable to THE NEW YORK TIMES.

LONDON, Monday, Aug. 17.—The correspondent of The London Times at Namur sends this dispatch under date of Saturday:

"From 6 o'clock this morning till 6 this evening and even later there has been a great battle between the French and the Germans on the Meuse.

"In the afternoon I had the good fortune to witness it by the side of the French troops at a distance of two to three kilometers, at a spot where, thanks to the conformation of the hills, it was possible all the time to follow the manoeuvres of the troops, and above all of the artillery.

"By 6 P. M., when I had to leave the field of battle to travel to Brussels and send off my dispatch, the French Army had driven back the Germans about fifteen kilometers (nine miles) to the south, and were pursuing them all the time.

"The battle was divided into two parts, the first part occupying the day up to 2 P. M., and the second half the rest of the afternoon.

"It began, as I have just said, in the morning at about 6 o'clock. At that time the Germans had taken possession of the part of the town which is on the left side of the Meuse. At the same time a regiment of French infantry, advancing from the south to the north, occupied the other side of the town—that is to say, the right bank.

"After that for some hours there were skirmishes between the two forces. The first part of the fight was spent in these operations. In the afternoon from about 2 o'clock it was principally an artillery engagement.

"The French infantry withdrew into the woods on this side of the Meuse and the artillery took charge of the battle.

"Between 3 and 6 o'clock, after the German cavalry, which had occupied the part furthest away, had been driven out, the guns of the two armies fired on each other across the town.

"It was always the Germans who were retiring along the hills to the south of the town and always the French who, little by little, moved forward their batteries, of which there were six. These batteries were deployed in the wheat fields to the west of the town. At the same time there were bigger French guns, hidden either in the side or behind the woods to the right, toward the southwest, and further from the town.

"Gradually the French drove the Germans southward, probably along the road to Han-sur-Lesse, pursuing all the time with infantry and chasseurs. To all appearances the French made better practice than the Germans."

French Fleet Sinks Two Austrian Battleships, Wrecks Another in Adriatic Sea Fight.

LONDON, Aug. 17.—6:40 A. M.—A dispatch to Reuter's Telegram Company from Nish, Servia, under date of Sunday, says:

"A naval battle between French and Austrian warships began off Budua, Austria, in the Adriatic at 9 o'clock this morning. The French squadron coming from the southwest attacked the Austrian warships.

"Two Austrian ironclads were sunk, one was set on fire and a fourth fled northward toward Cattaro.

"The fight lasted over an hour."

GERMANS WIPE OUT VISE, A BELGIAN TOWN

Men Made Prisoners, Women Driven to Holland—Charge Firing From Houses.

Special Cable to THE NEW YORK TIMES.

ROTTERDAM, Aug. 16, (Dispatch to The London Daily News.)—Vise, which ten days ago was a flourishing market town, with nearly 4,000 inhabitants, was razed to the ground today by German troops. Hardly one stone now remains upon another.

According to the story of a German officer, the townsfolk, who up till then had been friendly, opened fire on the military at 11 o'clock last night, killing an officer, a Sergeant, and four men, and wounding six. The soldiers immediately entered the houses, which they set on fire, after turning the inhabitants out, without regard to age, sex, or rank.

The men were marched to the railway station, where they were kept until morning surrounded by a military guard. This afternoon they were taken to Aix-la-Chapelle as prisoners of war. The women were all told they must leave by 4 o'clock today and at 6:30 o'clock this evening they reached Maastricht with their children.

Few have any more possessions than the clothes in which they stand, and they are pictures of utter despair. The poor creatures are being cared for by the Dutch and have been housed in the schools.

KAISER OFF TO THE FRONT?

Again Reported on His Way to Join the Army in the Field.

TOKIO, Aug. 17.—A Reuter dispatch from Paris says a message received there from Berlin announces that the German Emperor this morning started fo Mainz with the General Staff.

LONDON, Aug. 17.—An Amsterdam dispatch to The Central News says Berlin reports that the German Emperor has left for the front.

FRENCH DRIVE BACK GERMANS IN BELGIUM

Republic's Troops Still Pressing on in Alsace—Capture 1,000 More Prisoners.

PARIS, Aug. 16.—The following official statement was issued tonight:

"A forward movement developed today all along the front from Rechicourt (Rixengen), in Lorraine, eleven miles southwest of Saarburg, to Sainte Marie Aux Mines. We carried the latter and advanced into the region of St. Blaise.

The French troops, that occupied Donon Saturday, continued to advance, their progress being especially rapid in the Schirmeck Valley. We have taken 1,000 prisoners, in addition to 500 on Friday. Large quantities of equipment were abandoned by the Germans. We have also captured Thels. We pushed as far as Lorquin Height, capturing a convoy belonging to a cavalry division consisting of nineteen automobiles and lorries.

"The Germans attacked Dinant Saturday. Their force consisted of a guard division and the First Cavalry Division, supported by several battalions of infantry and machine gun companies. When these forces appeared on the left bank the French attacked with great vigor and dash. The Germans soon gave way and recrossed the Meuse in great disorder. Many who failed to reach the bridge slipped down the steep bank and fell into the swiftly flowing river and were drowned.

"Profiting by the disorder, the French light cavalry regiment followed over the river and pursued the Germans for many miles. This regiment put to flight and drove before it greatly superior forces of German cavalry.

"The Russian mobilization has been carried out with remarkable rapidity. The army is now ready to assume the offensive, which soon will make itself felt. Already in Galicia Russian cavalry has crossed the frontier, driving back the Austrians. Further east an Austrian detachment, which penetrated south of Tranopol, has been defeated.

"Troops are marching on Germany. The Germans made superhuman efforts last year to strengthen the fortresses on the Vistula, Gaudens, and Thorn. Nevertheless, their situation is insecure. They have been obliged to call up all kinds of reserves to back the five army corps, and it is doubtful whether these forces will be able to resist the Russian attack as long as the Germans hoped."

Story of Frontier Fighting.

Another official statement says of the operations on the frontier, where the French troops advanced in great force Friday and Saturday in the direction of Strassburg:

"The French have succeeded in driving further back the Bavarian corps, which had already retreated, near Cirey.

"Germans taken prisoners after the battles at Mangienne and Billom declared that the French force demoralized them. A number of Poles captured asserted that they sought to be taken. Some of the Germans declared the war absurd and said that it had been opposed in numerous cities.

"All the prisoners complained of being badly fed."

Another official statement gives this report of the previous fighting near the frontier:

"Further details of the fighting around Blamont and Cirey-sur-Vezouze in the French Department of Muerthe-et-Moselle show that the Germans were strongly intrenched behind earthworks near Blamont when on Friday evening the French division began their attack.

"The German outposts repulsed the French, who at daybreak the following day resumed the offensive, supported by artillery, and succeeded during the afternoon in taking Blamont and Cirey.

Again Attacking Muelhausen.

Special Cable to THE NEW YORK TIMES.

LONDON, Aug. 16.—The Daily Mail correspondent at Delmont, Switzerland, near the German and French frontiers, in a dispatch dated Sunday, 11 A. M., says:

"Fighting has begun again in Upper Alsace, between Belfort and Altkirch. The sound of gunfire continues to be heard near the frontier. I have heard here that the French force which retired from Mülhausen has been reinforced and has renewed the attack."

Japan Notifies Germany She Must Give Up Kiau-chau at Once.

AND WITHDRAW SHIPS

Necessary, She Says, to Remove All Cause of Disturbance in the Far East.

ONE WEEK FOR A REPLY

Cites Alliance with England—Tells United States Neutral Interests Will Be Guarded.

TOKIO, Aug. 16.—Japan sent an ultimatum to Germany Saturday night at 8 o'clock, demanding the withdrawal of German warships from the Orient and the evacuation of Kiau-chau and giving Germany until Sunday, Aug. 23, to comply with the demand. Otherwise, the ultimatum asserts, Japan will take action.

The general expectation here is that the ultimatum will be followed by war.

Takaaki Kato, the Japanese Foreign Minister, simultaneously with the dispatch of the ultimatum, conferred with George W. Guthrie, the American Ambassador, and made to him a broad statement calculated to assure the United States that American interests in the Far East would be safeguarded and the integrity of China upheld.

Owing to doubts whether communications with Berlin were assured, Japan in order to insure the arrival of the ultimatum forwarded it to Berlin by six channels, including Washington, London, and Stockholm. The Government also notified Count von Rex, German Ambassador to Japan, and likewise retarded the time limit for a reply until Aug. 23.

Germany Storing Provisions.

Inspired utterances express regret at the inability to maintain neutrality, but say that Great Britain, the ally of Japan, is compelled to defend herself against the aggressions of Germany. Moreover, it is pointed out that Germany is making preparations day and night at Kiau-chau, where it is storing provisions, while its warships are scouring the seas of Eastern Asia to the great detriment of commerce, and that its converted cruisers are seizing English merchant vessels. Such actions, it is argued, are directly calculated to disturb the peace of Eastern Asia, and, accordingly, after full and frank communication with Britain, Japan has found herself compelled to send an ultimatum to Germany.

Count Okuma, the Japanese Premier, today invited the peers, the newspaper men, and the leading business men of Tokio to come to his office at noon, at 4 o'clock, and at 6 o'clock in the afternoon, respectively, when he made known to them the terms of the ultimatum and announced that he would give out the negotiations in connection with the alliance. The Japanese War Office also summoned all newspaper men at 1 o'clock this afternoon, in order that they might receive instructions in regard to the publication of news in the event of a state of war coming into force.

Ministers Counsel Calmness.

The text of the ultimatum created a profound impression, although it had been predicted that Japan was making ready to precipitate war. Count Okuma and Takaaki Kato, in addressing the merchants, members of Parliament and others, counseled a calm attitude. They insisted that Japan had no ambition for territorial aggrandizement.

In reply to a question propounded by a merchant the Foreign Minister unequivocaly denied reports that the United States had interfered in any way in the situation and he added, the United States was not likely to. He said the American Government would be fully informed as to the Japanese position.

Kiau-chau, from which Japan has demanded the withdrawal of Germany, is a town on the peninsula of Shantung, China, leased, with adjoining territory, by Germany in 1898, and soon afterward made a protectorate. The German territory has an area of about 200 square miles. Germany also controls an extended waterfront. Tsing-tau, the seaport in the territory controlled by Germany, is strongly fortified.

CHINA IS HOPEFUL.

Proposal to Restore Territory Is Regarded with Favor.

PEKING, Aug. 16.—Copies of the Japanese ultimatum to Germany were handed to the Chinese Government and the foreign legations today.

As it is not considered likely that Germany will comply with the Japanese demands, preparations are proceeding for a campaign by force of arms. Three British regiments in China have received instructions to hold themselves in readiness for transportation.

The statement in the Japanese ultimatum that Japan proposed to return Tsing-tau, the seaport of the territory controlled by Germany, to China is regarded hopefully by Chinese officials. The Chinese Foreign Board announced tonight that China realized she could not forcibly prevent transgression of her territory. She is, however, strengthening her forces at Tsinan, with the view only to regulating Chinese affairs. A protest will be lodged if the allies land troops beyond the fifty-kilometer limit allowed to German troops for maneuvres.

According to Japanese figures, the German troops at Tsing-tau number 3,500. There are several hundred reservists at the various treaty ports. It is not known where the German fleet has gone. It left port about ten days ago with colliers.

Japan's Ultimatum Demanding That Germany Quit the Far East and Surrender Kiau-chau

TOKIO, Aug. 16.—This is the ultimatum sent to Germany by Japan:

"We consider it highly important and necessary in the present situation to take measures to remove the causes of all disturbances of the peace in the Far East, and to safeguard the general interests as contemplated by the agreement of alliance between Japan and Great Britain.

"In order to secure a firm and enduring peace in Eastern Asia, the establishment of which is the aim of the said agreement, the Imperial Japanese Government sincerely believes it to be its duty to give the advice to the Imperial German Government to carry out the following two propositions:

"First—To withdraw immediately from Japanese and Chinese waters German men-of-war and armed vessels of all kinds, and to disarm at once those which cannot be so withdrawn.

"Second—To deliver on a date not later than Sept. 15 to the Imperial Japanese authorities, without condition or compensation, the entire leased territory of Kiau-chau, with a view to the eventual restoration of the same to China.

"The Imperial Japanese Government announces at the same time that in the event of it not receiving by noon on Aug. 23, 1914, an answer from the Imperial German Government, signifying its unconditional acceptance of the above advice offered by the Imperial Japanese Government, Japan will be compelled to take such action as she may deem necessary to meet the situation."

JAPAN NOTIFIES BRYAN.

Mikado's Envoy Says Neutral Interests Will Be Guarded in Far East.

Special to The New York Times.

WASHINGTON, Aug. 16.—The Administration received its first official news of Japan's ultimatum to Germany tonight when the Japanese Ambassador, Vicount Chinda, delivered it to Secretary Bryan in the form of a written announcement. At the same time the Ambassador communicated Japan's assurance to this Government that she would use the utmost effort to safeguard the interests of all nations not immediately concerned in the operations in the Far East.

After the Ambassador's call it became known that the United States Government had determined not to be drawn into the controversy between Japan and Germany in any way. It is said that this Government considers satisfactory the promise of Japan to restore the territory of Kiau-chau to China eventually.

Ambassador Chinda and Mr. Bryan conferred at the home of the Secretary of State. With the substance of the ultimatum to Germany the Japanese Ambassador presented the communication from the Foreign Office at Tokio, and added a strong statement concerning Japan's purposes of maintaining the territorial integrity of the Chinese Republic by restoring to her the territory of Kiau-chau.

While the statement made no direct reference to the United States, it gave assurance that the interests of all powers interested in maintaining the territorial status quo in the Far East would be protected to the utmost.

It developed as a result of the conference that Japan had no assurance up to the present time that its ultimatum had been delivered to Germany, owing to the cable difficulties with that country. In order to make certain of its delivery, a copy of the ultimatum will be communicated to Berlin through the channels of the American Government.

To many of the best-informed persons in Washington, Japan's warlike attitude toward Germany came as a surprise. There had been conflicting advices of an official character, and some officials chose to believe that Japan had no intention of becoming involved in the European struggle. Although officials here are maintaining an attitude of profound circumspection, there is no gainsaying the fact that the new development in the war situation is causing some uneasiness.

Ambassador Chinda called on Secretary Bryan yesterday and when the news of the ultimatum came this morning it was believed in some quarters that the Ambassador had requested this Government to take charge of Japanese interests in Germany should occasion arise.

Sure Proof of Friendliness.

This request, if it was made, contains a grain of comfort to the United States for the reason that a Government would not entrust to a neutral power the care of its citizens and their property rights in the territory of a nation with which it was at war unless the friendliest feeling existed between the neutral nation and the Government to whose interests it would attend. Such a request emphasized friendly feelings between Governments.

It has been admitted by officials, although in a guarded way, that the State Department had under consideration the matter of taking up with Japan and the nations concerned in the European conflict the matter of neutralizing the territory in China controlled by foreign Governments. But the State Department has never acknowledged that it had made any representations on the subject to Japan. After Ambassador Chinda's first call Secretary Bryan declined to say anything about the purpose of the Ambassador's business, and he would not discuss the report that the neutralization scheme had been the occasion for exchanges between the Japanese and American Governments. However, the neutralization suggestion is now a matter of the past. The ultimatum of the Japanese Government disposes of it effectually.

The Administration has sought to maintain the friendliest relations with Japan. Its attitude with regard to the protest of Japan over the alien land law enacted by the California Legislature showed that it had no sympathy with the course of the Pacific Coast State. But the Japanese Government insisted that the matter was one that involved violation of treaty obligations, and that it must be adjusted on that basis. The negotiations have rested there for weeks, and nothing has appeared recently to indicate that they were to be resumed with any prospect of reaching an agreement.

Cause for Uneasiness.

The unsatisfactory condition of these negotiations has been a cause of some uneasiness in Washington, but there has been nothing to show that the controversy over the California land question was likely to get beyond the scope of diplomacy. As the matter stands now it would not afford any real cause for a demand by the radical element in Japan that the Tokio Government take advantage of its attitude toward Germany to insist that the United States settle the land question forthwith. The Japanese Government has shown a firm, but not unfriendly purpose in conducting the negotiations over the land question, and officials here believe that they have reason to hope that the jingo party in Japan will not be strong enough to force strained relations between two nations that have stood together on many occasions in recent years.

It should be understood that discussion of Japan's course in the Orient, so far as it might affect the United States, has been largely academic. Nothing has ever been brought forward to show that, aside from the irritation caused in Japan over the discrimination against Japanese in the Pacific Coast States, there has been any cause for a disturbance of the good relations that have existed between the two Governments. It is true that Congressman Richmond Pearson Hobson and a few others have insisted that a conflict between the United States and Japan was inevitable, but the Government's policy in the Far East has been of a disinterested character, and Japan has had every assurance, through the attitude of the Washington Administrations for the last fifteen years, that she had nothing to fear from the United States. The friendliness of the United States was emphasized prior to the Japanese-Russian war, when this Government stood shoulder to shoulder with Great Britain and Japan in the effort to preserve the territorial and administrative entity of China.

Fear Japan's Jingoes.

There has been much discussion in Washington in the last few days over the possibility of Japan's becoming a party to the European war. Some persons professed to believe that the military spirit might gain such ascendency in the Empire that there would be a demand that the operations of the Japanese Fleet be extended to include the capture of German Samoa, which would make Japan a next-door neighbor of the United States and give her a site for a coaling or naval station in the South Pacific. There was some apprehension that the jingo element might insist that now was the time to demand that the United States adjust the California land question in accordance with the Japanese proposals.

But these things have not been supported by any comment from those in authority, and there has been an evident disposition on the part of officials to preserve a "correct" attitude and to discourage any suggestions that

"All the News That's Fit to Print."

The New York Times.

THE WEATHER

Unsettled, probably showers and cooler today; partly cloudy Friday; gentle to moderate winds.

For full weather report see Page 17.

VOL. LXIII...NO. 20,662. NEW YORK, THURSDAY, AUGUST 20, 1914.—EIGHTEEN PAGES. ONE CENT In Greater New York, Jersey City and Newark. | Elsewhere TWO CENTS.

POPE PIUS X. DIES AT 1:20 THIS MORNING; END HASTENED BY THE EUROPEAN WAR

His Deathbed Call to the World to Pray for Peace.

SUDDEN RELAPSE YESTERDAY

Heroic Treatment Revived Him Briefly from an Attack of Bronchitis.

HAD REIGNED 11 YEARS

Funeral Will Take Place in Nine Days—Conclave Will Follow It.

ROME, Thursday, Aug. 20.—Pope Pius X. died at 1:20 o'clock this morning. He had been ill for several days, but alarming symptoms did not develop until yesterday morning.

Throughout the day Doctors Marchiafava and Amici devoted their utmost energies to stimulating their patient and keeping him alive. The Cardinals were notified of the Pope's grave condition, and some of them who entered the sick room describe the impressive and heart-rending scenes, especially when the Pontiff, rousing himself from time to time, spoke. Once he said:

"In ancient times the Pope by a word might have stayed the slaughter, but now he is impotent."

The Scene at the Deathbed.

Extreme unction was administered by Mgr. Zampini, Sacristan to the Pope, amid a most touching scene. The sisters of the Pope and his niece were overcome with grief. Cardinal Merry del Val, the Papal Secretary of State, knelt by the side of the bed, where other Cardinals joined him, the members of the household intoning prayers.

The dying Pope in a moment of lucidity said:

"Now I begin to think, as the end is approaching, that the Almighty in His inexhaustible goodness wishes to spare me the horrors Europe is undergoing."

In another lucid moment the Pope whispered:

"Now I am forced to see the spectacle of my own children, even those who yesterday worked here with me, leave for the war, abandon the cassock and cowl for the soldier's uniform. Yesterday, although they were of different nationalities, they were here studying, in sympathetic companionship; now in different fields they are armed against each other, ready to take each other's lives.

Yesterday was one of the most anxious days in the history of the Papacy. The whole world knew that the Pope was indisposed, but it was supposed that he was suffering from his usual ailment, the gout. Up to noon even the members of the household were unaware of the seriousness of the developments. Almost without warning came word that the Pontiff was at death's door.

Pontiff in Agony All Day.

All day his agony continued. At times he revived and was able to say a few words, but hope of saving him was finally abandoned. Several times throughout the city and at the Apostolic Palace the rumor spread that the Pope had passed away, only to be denied later.

In the presence of Cardinal Merry del Val, Cardinals Ferrata, Cagiano and Bisleti, and the two sisters of the Pope, a bulletin on the condition of the Pontiff was posted early in the afternoon on the bronze door of the Vatican, where the Swiss guards stood on watch. A great crowd outside gazed with grief-stricken faces up at the Pope's chamber on the second floor, where the windows were closed with shades.

Delay in issuing a bulletin last night caused suspicion that the end had come, while the withdrawal of the Noble Guard from before the door of the sick chamber, on the other hand, caused a rumor that the Pope was better, as the guard is supposed to maintain watch over the person of the Pontiff, without pause, until either death ensues or he is out of danger. It was learned that the guard was withdrawn because of overfatigue.

Nobles and citizens, wishing to hear the latest word from the bedside, gathered in groups in the streets near the Vatican. Some of them shed tears, and there were whispered stories of the goodness of the Pope and the piety of his sisters.

Prayers were said by thousands, and the bells of the churches sounded when the Sacrament was exposed upon all the altars.

When the Court learned of the Pope's condition there was the deep-

Continued on Page 6.

THE LATE POPE PIUS X.

Exhortation to the World to Pray For Peace, The Last Official Message of Pope Pius X.

ROME, Aug. 19.—The last conscious act of Pope Pius X. was to address the following exhortation to the whole world:

At this moment, when nearly the whole of Europe is being dragged into the vortex of a most terrible war, with its present dangers and miseries and the consequences to follow, the very thought of which must strike every one with grief and horror, we whose care is the life and welfare of so many citizens and peoples cannot but be deeply moved and our heart wrung with the bitterest sorrow.

And in the midst of this universal confusion and peril we feel and know that both Fatherly love and the Apostolic ministry demand of us that we should with all earnestness turn the thoughts of Christendom thither "whence cometh help"—to Christ, the Prince of Peace, and the most powerful mediator between God and man.

We charge, therefore, the Catholics of the whole world to approach the throne of Grace and Mercy, each and all of them, and more especially the clergy, whose duty furthermore it will be to make in every parish, as their Bishops shall direct, public supplication so that the merciful God may, as it were, be wearied with the prayers of His children and speedily remove the evil causes of war, giving to them who rule to think the thoughts of peace and not of affliction.

From the palace of the Vatican, the second day of August, 1914.

PIUS X.,
Pontifex Maximus.

GERMANY TO REJECT JAPAN'S DEMANDS

Mikado's Envoy Preparing to Leave Berlin and Police Guard the Embassy.

LONDON, Aug. 20.—The Rotterdam correspondent of The Times says he has learned from official sources in Berlin that Germany will reject the Japanese ultimatum.

COPENHAGEN, Aug. 19, (via London)—A dispatch received here from Berlin says:

"The Japanese Ambassador's departure from Berlin is approaching. The police are guarding the embassy. The Japanese college is empty. All Japanese students in German universities have left. The Vossische Zeitung says, commenting on Japan's ultimatum to Germany, 'One more declaration of war cannot frighten Germany, and Japan's action is without any importance.'"

GERMANS ADMIT 8,500 LOST.

Dead 1,500 and Wounded 7,000, According to the Cologne Gazette.

ROTTERDAM, Aug. 19, (via London.)—The casualty list of the German Army, published in The Cologne Gazette, gives in detail the losses of the Germans, up to yesterday. They total about 1,500 dead and 7,000 wounded. The list as printed gives the name of each person killed or injured.

According to another German newspaper the German fleet, not now blockading Russian ports, is at Kiel and in Heligoland.

About 2,000,000 Germans are now in the field, but mobilization continues. The railroads in the west are carrying nothing but soldiers and supplies.

Many Austrian troops are on their way to France, according to this newspaper.

German Gunboat Disarmed in China

LONDON, Aug. 19.—The Central News publishes a dispatch from Rome saying that the German gunboat Vaterland has been forced to disarm at Nanking, China. The Vaterland is 164 feet long and has a displacement of 166 tons.

MASSACRE AT PRAGUE AFTER CZECH RISING

Austrian Soldiers Accused of Committing Terrible Atrocities After Recapturing the City.

Special Cable to THE NEW YORK TIMES.

LONDON, Thursday, Aug. 20.—A dispatch to The Daily Mail from St. Petersburg says:

"The Novoe Vremya's Kieff correspondent states that the Czech residents have received letters from relatives and friends in Bohemia, in which it is stated that Czech and Polish troops shot down their officers, shouting, 'Down with William! Down with Austria!' and 'Long Live Russia!'

"Prague for a whole day was in the hands of the mutineers. Next day the Austrians, reinforced, re-entered the city and there were fearful reprisals. Women and children were shot down and every Czech caught in the street was killed. The River Moldava, it is declared, ran red with Czech blood. The finest monuments in the city were destroyed. The Austrians pillaged the shops and assaulted women.

"These shocking cruelties called forth a new uprising two days later, which was followed by fresh reprisals. The Russian Consul, M. Zhukovsky, si believed to have been executed."

FIGHTING NEAR ALTKIRCH.

Large Bodies of Troops Seen from Swiss Town.

Special Cable to THE NEW YORK TIMES.

LONDON, Thursday, Aug. 20.—A Daily Mail dispatch from Delemont, Switzerland, under date of Wednesday, says:

"Sound of gunfire in Alsace was again heard yesterday morning. Skirmishes are taking place near Altkirch and it seems as if battle was imminent. Large bodies of troops have been seen in Upper Alsace, moving northward.

"The French hold the passes and crests of the Vosges mountains. They seem to have the trump cards.

"A man who was at Altkirch when the French advance guard entered, says that a woman threw a bomb into a group of French officers, who were holding a consultation in the principal street.

"Paris motor omnibuses have passed through the French frontier town of Delle."

Paris Prepares for All Eventualities; Third Reserve Army Raised, Food Stored

Special Cable to THE NEW YORK TIMES.

PARIS, Aug. 19 [dispatch to The London Morning Post.]—Paris continues to make preparations for all eventualities. It is the base for the third line of defense, and the third army of reservists is being mobilized round the city.

Great supplies of provisions and materials are being centralized in Paris. The race courses of Long Champs and Auteuil provide accommodations for thousands of cattle. Parts of the Bois de Boulogne and the Park of St. Cloud were yesterday inclosed for this purpose, the latter space containing 27,000 oxen.

Preparations are being made to convert the pretty little city parks of Monceau and the Buttes Chaumont for the same purpose, and in a few days they will be sheep pens, the former housing about 20,000 head.

U. S. WILL BUY SHIPS TO MOVE THE CROPS

A Government-Owned Line Decided Upon to Meet the War Emergency.

Special to The New York Times.

WASHINGTON, Aug. 19.—At a conference held at the White House today the President, the Secretary of the Treasury, and Congress leaders reached the conclusion that it was necessary for the Government to purchase merchant vessels and operate them in order to carry abroad the enormous quantities of American grain and other products that are ready or soon will be ready for export. A proposal was adopted which provided for the formation of a corporation controlled by the Government to undertake the management of the Government-owned ocean transportation service.

In addition, approval was given to the proposal to establish Government war risk insurance of commercial cargoes, supplementing the present commercial insurance, and bills to carry out this purpose later were introduced in both houses of Congress.

In just what way the money necessary to buy ships will be obtained was not determined definitely.. One proposal under consideration is that Congress be asked to appropriate $25,000,000 immediately for the purchase of vessels available. Another is that the Secretary of the Treasury shall offer Panama Canal bonds to the amount of $25,000,000 or $30,000,000 and apply the subscription money to the purchase of merchant vessels. It is likely that some definite action will be taken tomorrow.

Those concerned in the matter have not reached the point where they have decided on the vessels that may be purchased by the Government. It was said authoritatively tonight that it was too early to say whether the Government would endeavor to acquire steamships of the North German Lloyd and Hamburg-American lines that have been put out of business by the European war. American ships only might be bought, it was explained.

This uncertainty means that the Government will not buy foreign vessels that fly the flags of nations now at war unless it has received assurances from the warring Governments that the proposed transfers will be respected. It is obvious that if a ship owned by the United States Government were taken as a prize by the war vessel of a foreign power, a cause for critical international trouble, to say the least, would exist. Furthermore, the question is raised as to the rights of the United States, under the terms of President Wilson's declaration of strict neutrality between the nations now at war, to carry grain and foodstuffs to one or another of the belligerents.

South American Trade First.

Such questions, of course, require serious consideration, but it is understood that, pending their settlement, such ships as would be bought by the Government immediately would be used in carrying wheat to South America. If ships now of American register were purchased by the Government the problem would be solved easily. Such ships could carry grain to such neutral countries as Holland, Italy, Spain, Sweden, Norway, and Denmark, as well as to all the countries of South America. But there are very few available ships of American register.

The conference at the White House at which this momentous decision was reached was attended, in addition to President Wilson and Secretary McAdoo, by Senator Clarke of Arkansas, Chairman of the Committee on Commerce; Senator Simmons of North Carolina, Chairman of the Committee on Finance; Representative Underwood of Alabama, Chairman of the Ways and Means Committee, and Representative Alexander of Missouri, Chairman of the Committee on Merchant Marine and Fisheries. The following statement was issued by Joseph Tumulty, secretary to the President:

The conference was about the development and safeguarding of the merchant marine, and every aspect of the question was gone over. It was recognized that the present emergency called for prompt action to relieve a situation which can be relieved if action is promptly taken. It was agreed that a bill should be introduced in Congress providing for the insurance of war risks by the Government.

In addition to the agreement of opinion as to the insurance bill, there was an extensive discussion of the best means of immediately providing ships to carry goods now waiting for their markets. Several plans were proposed and it was finally agreed that a bill should be drawn and introduced at a very early date, which should provide for the purchase of an adequate number of ships by the Government and their operation through a corporation controlled by the Government, as in the case of the Panama Railroad Company, which now operates ships, as well as the railroad itself, and which is controlled by the Government.

One of the main objects behind the decision to urge legislation for Government ownership of merchant vessels is the upbuilding of the American merchant marine, although the bill to be introduced will be an emergency measure,

Continued on Page 4.

GERMAN WIRELESS RUNNING ILLEGALLY

Tuckerton Station Has no License and Can be Confiscated—Bryan Sends Notice.

The Chamber of German-American Commerce at 11 Broadway yesterday received a message from Secretary of State Bryan in which he announced that the Goldschmidt wireless station on Hickory Island, near Tuckerton, N. J., was operating without a Federal license. Under the laws governing wireless stations the infringement may mean the forfeiture of the plant and apparatus to the Government in addition to the imposition of a fine of $500 on the owners of the station.

The Tuckerton station communicated with the German cruisers Dresden and Karlsruhe, which were operating off the North Atlantic Coast. It was because of these operations at Tuckerton and the Telefunken station at Sayville, L. I., that President Wilson issued his order forbidding the use of wireless stations for the sending or receiving of code and cipher messages or of plain messages of an unneutral nature. Lieut. C. B. Platt, U. S. N., has been on duty as censor at Tuckerton. Whether or not the station will be closed now as a result of being unlicensed was not known here last night.

Several German-American organizations and the German Embassy have filed complaints in Washington against the censorship on the ground that it constitutes a discrimination against Germany and in favor of Great Britain, France, and their allies.

That the station was being operated without a lincense never entered anybody's mind, and it was not until that information was conveyed by Secretary Bryan yesterday that the fact became known. He simply said he had been advised by the Department of Commerce that no license permitting the operation of the station had been issued by the Department of Commerce.

The discovery that the station was operating without a license was said to have been made by Colville Barclay, Chargé d'Affaires of the British Embassy in Washington, who used the fact as his principal argument against the relaxation of the censorship.

Disputed German Protest.

When Mr. Barclay made his protest the Chamber of German-American Commerce immediately wired Mr. Bryan disputing him and calling attention to the fact that President Wilson and Kaiser Wilhelm had exchanged greetings through the station at Tuckerton on June 20. It was in reply to that telegram that Secretary Bryan wired the Chamber as follows yesterday:

Department of State,
Washington, D. C., Aug. 18, 1914.
Chamber of German-American Commerce, Inc., 11 Broadway, New York:
Your telegram Aug. 16 relative date of establishment Tuckerton wireless station department is advised that no license for operation this station has been issued by Department of Commerce under act of Aug. 13, 1912. W. J. BRYAN, Secretary.

In reply the Chamber of German-American Commerce sent this telegram to Secretary Bryan:

New York City, Aug. 19, 1914.
To Hon. William J. Bryan, Department of State, Washington, D. C.:
Tuckerton station formally opened by exchange of messages between President Wilson and Kaiser Wilhelm on June 20. Station has been operating with permission and full knowledge of Department of Commerce since early part of May, this year. No license is required for receiving messages over wireless. Sending license, as Government Radio Bureau knows, has not been applied for as yet on account of questions of inner organization.
CHAMBER OF GERMAN-AMERICAN COMMERCE, INC.

Section 1 of the law deals directly with the question at issue. It states:

"That a person, company, or corporation within the jurisdiction of the United States shall not use or operate any apparatus for radio communication as a means of commercial intercourse among the several States, or with foreign nations, or upon any vessel of the United States engaged in interstate or foreign commerce, or for the transmission of radiograms or signals the effect of which extends beyond the jurisdiction of the State or Territory in which the same are made * * * except under and in accordance with a license, revocable for cause, in that behalf granted by the Secretary of Commerce upon application therefor.

* * * Any person, company, or corporation that shall use or operate any apparatus for radio communication in violation of this section or knowingly aid or abet another person, company, or corporation in so doing, shall be deemed guilty of a misdemeanor, and on conviction thereof shall be punished by a fine not exceeding $500 and the apparatus or device so unlawfully used and operated may be adjudged forfeited to the United States."

The law states that every such license as referred to above shall be issued only to citizens of the United States, or Porto Rico, or to a company incorporated under the laws of some State or Territory of the United States or Porto Rico.

Power to Close Stations.

That President Wilson was entirely within the law when he took over the supervision of the wireless stations on the American coast is shown by the law which states that "every such license shall provide that the President of the United States in time of war or public peril or disaster may close any station for radio communication and the removal therefrom of all radio apparatus, or may authorize the use or control of any such station or apparatus by any department of the Government upon just compensation to the owners."

BIG ARMIES IN BATTLE NEAR WATERLOO; ALLIES FALL BACK, MAY QUIT BRUSSELS

Heavy German Pressure Forces the Allies to Withdraw.

READY FOR FINAL STRUGGLE

Hot Fighting on Tuesday Followed by Continued Advance by Germans Yesterday.

BRUSSELS AWAITS CAPTURE

Streets Barricaded, but It Cannot Resist Much—May Be Cut Off from Antwerp.

Special Cable to THE NEW YORK TIMES.

BRUSSELS, Aug. 19.—It was the turn of the Germans today to move forward. The enemy appeared in considerable force at several points on our front and pressed in overwhelming numbers.

The allies gave ground slowly, evacuating advanced positions, which were occupied as the result of yesterday's great cavalry drive.

The Germans fired several shells into Tirlemont without doing any damage, and the allies have now narrowed the front, occupied in a new defensive position, close to the capital.

The next move on the part of the invader is eagerly awaited.

Louvain is occupied.

We are now faced by a large army, and the next twenty-four hours should witness important developments.

BELGIAN LINES FORCED BACK.

Germans Compel Retirement of Advanced Troops of Enemy.

Special Cable to THE NEW YORK TIMES.

BRUSSELS, Aug. 19, (Dispatch to the London Daily News)—The Germans showed signs of pushing forward in force against the center of the Belgian position yesterday. The cavalry division and cyclist corps, which had been holding the advanced troops of the Kaiser in check, has fallen back on the main force.

The Brussels papers were invited to recall all their correspondents near the troops. One of the last to come was the representative of La Derniere Heure, from whose account of yesterday's operations the following is taken:

"At this moment the new advance of the Germans toward the interior of Belgium is preparing. Before the overwhelming weight of numbers the Belgian cavalry withdrew in good order.

"Our advanced troops were commissioned to hold the enemy as long as possible before falling back to our second line in intrenched position, made strong as it possibly can be to meet the German attack. A complete line exists, covering the approach to Louvain, Brussels and Antwerp.

"Yesterday's fighting started at 3.30 A. M. At dawn a German aeroplane flew low over our front. First one volley was fired at it, and then a second. The machine caught fire in the air and fell in the German lines.

Battle on Seven-Mile Front.

"After several feints the attack developed about 6 o'clock. Strong forces of cavalry and infantry, supported by artillery and machine guns, poured down on the village. It was no mere skirmishing this time.

"A furious battle was soon raging along a seven-mile front, the points of attack being on the north of the line and on the south.

"The enemy tried to push through. They were opposed by a determined resistance. The cavalry dismounted and occupied trenches and bravely withstood the hail of fire for two hours. While the Belgian cavalry were acting as infantry behind earthworks, a party of German cavalry got in behind them and shot their horses.

"Inch by inch the ground was fought. Numbers of Germans were killed in their relentless move forward. The Belgian defenders suffered rather serious loss in their stubborn defense.

"At Berdingen the resistance was equally praiseworthy. In a trench where seven cavalrymen were making a great fight, Lieut. Count Wolfgang Dursel was struck by a bullet in the head and fell. His companions pressed around him.

"'I have got my account,' he said. 'You leave me. Do your duty.'

"He breathed his last a little later.

"When their retreat was ordered each Belgian cavalryman did his best to help the comrades whose horses had perished in the raid.

"At this point two Belgian squadrons, totaling about 240 men, showing great bravery, were holding 2,000 Germans. In spite of their superior numbers the Germans could claim no distinct advantage, but after two hours' resistance the Belgian retreat was sounded.

"When our cavalry retired the Germans advanced in great numbers and occupied Diest. They wrecked the railway station and bombarded the town. The terrifed inhabitants fled from it by the only route that remained open, and soon a struggling mass was rushing across the open country in search of a place of safety.

"The inhabitants of Tirlemont fared better. Seeing the inevitable approaching, three trainloads of refugees were hurriedly gotten away. As the last train left German shells were flying over the town, and several houses were in flames."

Following the announcement that the seat of Government and the royal family had moved to Antwerp, there was a large exodus of people from Brussels yesterday, particularly for the coast.

French Report Further Advance Into Lorraine; Admit Germans Have Recaptured One Village

PARIS, Aug. 19, 10:55 P. M.—The following official statement was given out tonight:

"Latest advices are to the effect that the French Army has reached Morhange (Morchingen) in Alsace-Lorraine, 19 miles southeast of Metz. Our advance was very rapid in the afternoon beyond the River Seille, especially the central part of our line. At the end of the day we reached Delme, on one side, and Morhange on the other.

"There is little change in the situation in Upper Alsace. We continue to advance in the Vosges. The Germans have retaken the village of Ville, where we had an outpost. Our troops on the Seille have occupied Chateau Salins and Dieuze, but face well fortified and strongly held positions. Our progress at first was necessarily slow.

"Our cavalry has had a successful encounter with the Germans at Florenville, Belgium. Very large German forces, it is announced, are crossing the Meuse between Liege and Namur.

"One of the French Brigadiers has asked the Commander-in-Chief to make public the following fact: A French Hussar, made prisoner, was dragged by German soldiers into an Alsatian village and his throat was cut before the villagers, who testify to the deed."

FRENCH TAKE THE OFFENSIVE

Battle Ground Picked on Which the Battle Will Take Place.

Special Cable to THE NEW YORK TIMES.

BRUSSELS, Aug. 19, (Dispatch to the London Daily News.)—The news reaches me by eye-witnesses from the front, Genappe, Wavre, and Gembloux, which for the present are forbidden ground to journalists, that the French are assuming the aggressive and hunting the Uhlans out of the woods back across the road between Namur and Brussels.

Further, from a good source, I have news that the French Generals have chosen their battle grounds and have the Germans now in such a position that they cannot avoid fighting a battle in which two-thirds of their northern force must be engaged if it is to face the body of the French, which has been rolled up into Belgium.

This battle will decide the fate of Brussels, if that is not already decided, by giving it as a bait to Germany. It will also in large measure decide the fate of the war on this northern side, perhaps of the whole. The temptation to say more is considerable. What I have said is permissible, for the French have already shown their hand.

Things are being made very difficult for us now in the way of getting even stale news, but I managed a hurried run late in the afternoon today toward the eastern line to reassure myself that things were quite as I had expected.

Heavy Pressure Is On.

It is a curiously subtle thing, this question of attack and defense. I could feel the difference in the atmosphere at the different points where they have touched the line, and there is not the slightest doubt from what I saw that the pressure is slowly turning against the invaders. There is real ground to hope that in a week or so they will be on the defensive and fighting for their lives.

The carnage will be awful. The German officers (such is the statement one of them made in a Belgian paper) have sworn not to return unless victorious, and to any one who knows the unbending stuff, heroic or brutal, just as you view it, of Prussian officers, it is quite certain that they will keep their oath.

Down at Dinant and Namur the battle is likely to be worse in the sense that it will be a rushing lance-to-lance and bayonet-to-bayonet affair up and down the steep hills by the Meuse, but at the battlefield which the French have chosen their artillery will get full play, and unless the Germans abandon their usual massed formation the slaughter will be terrible.

Wherever the English are, too, there will be a lot of cut and thrust work as well as good marksmanship.

Brussels, Nervous, Expects Capture.

Brussels is very nervous this evening, and there seems to be reason for it. All the official statements as to the situation are reassuring, but so they have been every day.

Brussels' nerves are taut. Notices posted in the streets tonight that any-one with arms in his possession should deposit them with the police, as otherwise he was liable to be shot by any invaders, attracted the crowds all the evening. Their distribution seemed significant, as did the departure yesterday of the royal family and Ministers of State to Antwerp.

Significant, too, are the barricades and intrenchments, now put all round the city, especially to the south and east.

Bruxelloise are sadly reconciled. If their beautiful city must be sacrificed in the great game the powers are playing, why, then, it is only on a level with the usual rôle of Belgium in which Fontenoy, Jemappes, Fleurus, Ligny, Neerwinden, Waterloo, and a score of other great battles have been fought.

BELGIANS ADMIT FALLING BACK

But Say German Delay Has Made for Defenders' Advantage.

LONDON, Thursday, Aug. 20.—A Havas dispatch from Brussels gives this official communication concerning the present state of the field operations in Belgium:

"After having lost much time and a great number of men, besides important war material, the Prussian right wing has succeeded in gaining on both banks of the Meuse the ground to bring them into contact with the allies' armies.

"The German troops on the north bank of the Meuse comprise sections of different army corps, whose efforts have been directed toward the capture of Liege and who are now disengaged. There are also bodies of cavalry, thanks to which the Germans have been able to make considerable disturbance and extend themselves north and south.

"On the south the allied Belgian and French armies have been able to repulse them but on the north on the contrary they have had a free fi[eld] and could penetrate in small bodies far into the country.

"In a word, the Germans have taken a number of our positions, but have wasted fifteen days in arriving at this result, which is greatly to the honor of our army. It is not a question of single battle evolutions or captures of certain parts of the country or of towns. These matters are secondary in regard to the object assigned our troops in the general dispositions. This aim cannot be resolved and the most penetrating minds will be unable to discover it owing to the necessarily vague particulars furnished concerning the operations."

"Fighting is proceeding on the whole front, extending from Basle, Switzerland, to Diest, Belgium, and in these numerous contacts the more the opposing armies approach each other and the nearer come the deciding battles, the more one must expect to hear of an advantage on this side and of yielding on that.

"In operations so vast and with those engaged using modern arms, too great attention must not be paid to the operations in our immediate vicinity. Au evolution, ordered in a particular previously determined aim are not necessarily a retreat. The engagements of the last few days have had the result of rendering our adversaries very circumspect. The delay of the enemy's advance had the greatest advantage for our general plan of operation.

"There is no need for us to play into the hands of the Germans. That is the motive of the movement now being carried out. Far from being beaten, we are making arrangements for beating the enemy under the best possible conditions.

"The public should in this matter place full confidence in the commander of the army and remain calm and trustful of the outcome of the struggle, not doubtful. Meanwhile the newspapers should abstain from mentioning the movements of troops. Secrecy is essential to the success of our operations."

Another Havas dispatch from Brussels, sent in a very vague form, leads to the belief that the Germans made a surprise advance close to the Belgian positions defending Brussels. They encamped for the night, but a Belgian aviator discovered their position and revealed it to headquarters in time. Cavalry was hurrie

Wide World Photos

Allied soldiers protect themselves from the cold in a trench in Belgium.

National Archives

German Infantrymen advancing in France.

"All the News That's Fit to Print."

The New York Times.

THE WEATHER

Thunder showers today; probably fair tomorrow; moderate shifting winds.

For full weather report see Page 15.

VOL. LXIII...NO. 20,668. NEW YORK, FRIDAY, AUGUST 21, 1914.—SIXTEEN PAGES. ONE CENT In Greater New York, Jersey City and Newark. { Elsewhere TWO CENTS.

GERMAN CAVALRY FORCE CAPTURES BRUSSELS; BELGIAN ARMY RETIRES TO DEFEND ANTWERP; FRENCH WIN IN ALSACE, CHECKED IN LORRAINE

DEATH OF POPE MAY AID PEACE

Conclave Likely to Seek United States Assistance to End the European War.

SISTER OF PIUS X. DEAD

Succumbs to Shock Caused by Pontiff's Loss—With Him When He Died.

FORBADE "SPANISH VETO"

The Pope, Though Elected Owing to It, Recently Made Its Further Employment Impossible.

LONDON, Friday, Aug. 21.—The death of Pope Pius will be made the occasion for another effort to restore peace.

It is stated that when the Conclave meets in Rome to elect a new Pope it will send an appeal to the warring nations for peace and will ask the United States to aid it in bringing about the cessation of hostilities.

Special Cable to THE NEW YORK TIMES.

ROME, Aug. 20.—The shock caused by her brother's death resulted in the death tonight of the late Pope's aged sister Anna.

All the accounts of the last moments of Pope Pius X. agree in one respect—that the European war not only hastened his death, but remained in his memeory till his last conscious moment.

The Camerlengo (Chamberlain) of the Holy See, Cardinal Della Volpe, who was hastily summoned from Imola yesterday when it was realized that the Pope was dying, is in charge of the affairs of the Vatican during the interregnum. In his capable hands all is proceeding smoothly.

Pope's Body Embalmed.

In the death chamber a profound calm reigns. The body of the Pope was embalmed today. It is clothed in plain white vestments and lies on a bier. Huge lighted candles are at the head and feet. The body is continually watched by Noble Guards, immobile as statues, while a continuous unbroken chant rises from the Penitentiaries, who are Franciscan monks.

The stillness is broken only by the soft footsteps and muffled sobs of those few who are permitted to view the body.

The Pope died after a period of great agony. The cause was a complication of diseases—gout, nephritis, bronchitis, and depression. When it was known that the end was near the Pope's two sisters and his niece were admitted. The members of the household also gathered to take leave of their beloved master. The actual passing away was peaceful.

Tomb in St. Peter's.

In St. Peter's there is being prepared a temporary resting place for the dead Pontiff. A new niche is necessary, as Pius's predecessor still occupies the usual niche where the Popes lie until definitely sepulchred.

Pope Leo XIII.'s tomb in St. John Lateran has been ready for years, but the Vatican authorities never considered it safe to carry the body across the city.

Pope Pius, instead, will be buried in he crypt of the Basilica of St. Peter's when a simple tomb is finished.

A Possible Interregnum.

Special Cable to THE NEW YORK TIMES.

MILAN, Aug. 20.—The Catholic world is seemingly on the eve of one of the most remarkable Conclaves in its history. Will it be necessary to proclaim an interregnum till the dove of peace again hovers over Europe, or will the belligerent Governments, intimately interested in the election of a new Pope, grant every facility for foreign Cardinals desirous of journeying to Rome?

The Vatican is already sounding the great powers relative to their dispositions in this matter. It is certain, owing to the neutrality of Italy in the European conflict, that the Italian Government, as on the occasions of the deaths of Pius IX. and Leo XIII., will exert itself to the utmost to guarantee the perfect liberty of the Conclavists. Nor is there any desire among the Cardinals to hold the Conclave away from Rome, than which city, as recent history proves, no fitter or freer meeting place could be found.

Ten days must elapse from the Pope's death before the Cardinals can meet. The war has utterly upset earlier forecasts as to what is going to happen when the Sacred College enters upon its extraordinary session, but, whatever political struggle may be waged inside the Conclave consequent on the European upheaval, it is certain that the recent decretals of Pius X., which have been incorporated into the Canon Law code, not only inflict excommunication upon any Cardinal attempting to proclaim or promote the veto of any secular sovereign, but also annul absolutely the validity of the election of any Pope nominated in like conditions.

The principal trend of opinion in

Continued on Page 5.

BRITISHER DEFIES CRUISER DRESDEN

The Hostilius' Skipper Wouldn't Sign Pledge Not to Fight Even to Save His Ship.

Special Cable to THE NEW YORK TIMES.

HAVANA, Aug. 20.—The British steamer Hostilius, which arrived here today from Buenos Aires, reports that the German cruiser Dresden captured her about 700 miles off Cienfuegos.

The Dresden tried to compel the Captain to sign a document swearing that he would not take up arms against Germany in the present war. The Captain refused. He told the Dresden's commander that he could make any disposition of the ship he was minded to, but that he (her Captain) would sign no document, even to save her from being sunk. The ship was finally released.

The Hostilius reports that the Lynton Grange, another Britisher similarly captured, did sign the document.

The Hostilius, a 3,325-ton steamer, was built in 1900, and is owned by the British and South American Steam Navigation Company. The Lynton Grange is a 4,252-ton steamer, built in 1912, and owned by the Houlder Line, Ltd.

RUSSIAN LEGIONS IN GENERAL ADVANCE

Two Important Positions in Prussia Taken—First German Division Forced Back.

Special Cable to THE NEW YORK TIMES.

PARIS, Aug. 20. (Dispatch to The London Standard.)—Encouraging telegrams tell of the forward movement of the Russian colossus a fortnight sooner than was expected.

An official communiqué issued by the General Staff at St. Petersburg says that several columns have crossed the frontier and assumed the offensive "along the whole line."

In East Prussia the latest news is that the Russians have already occupied Gumbinnen and Lyk, two very important positions, and forced the first German division to fall back.

What the Russian advance will be like is sketched by a Russian diplomatist in Paris, who said:

"When we are ready we shall pour 400,000 men across the frontier, and the next week another 400,000, and continue to do so as long as is necessary."

Complete harmony and agreement exist between the British, French, and Russian staffs.

ST. PETERSBURG, (via London,) Aug. 20.—A body of Russian troops, according to an official communication given out today, has occupied Gumbinnen, twenty miles from the Russian frontier of East Prussia, capturing at the same time twelve German guns and a large number of prisoners.

LONDON, Friday, Aug. 21.—A St. Petersburg dispatch to The Daily Mail says The Novoe Vremya published an account of the fighting at Eydtkuhnen, East Prussia, by an eyewitness, who says:

"The fighting here seemed to prove that the German Army's military qualities did not justify its reputation. The men in the skirmish huddled together, making an excellent target for our fire.

"The German cavalry avoided ours, retreating when the Russians advanced for the charge. The German infantry likewise retired before our bayonet charges.

"The Neuvo Vremya comments on Japan's ultimatum as follows:

"'The enemies of our enemies are our friends. The cry of the yellow peril is not justified. The yellow peril race, even as the white race, rises against German violence.'"

A dispatch to Reuter's Telegram Company from St. Petersburg quotes a communication issued by the Russian General Staff covering the operations of the army from Aug. 15 to Aug. 19, in which successes are claimed for the Russian arms in skirmishes on both the Austrian and German frontiers.

"Austrian cavalry which entered Russian Poland at Kielce, Rijbniza, and other points," says the communication, "was driven back with great casualties, while Austrian infantry which attacked Krasnik was defeated and lost heavily. The Russians took 250 prisoners. On the Prussian border the Russians took the offensive near Windballen, captured Lyk, and took eight German guns and two quickfirers."

Count von Benckendorff, the Russian Ambassador in London, has received a telegram which states that his youngest son, Count Peter von Benckendorff, was slightly wounded in the shoulder while fighting with the Russian forces on the German eastern frontier. He is now in a hospital at Vilna.

Special Cable to THE NEW YORK TIMES.

LONDON, Friday, Aug. 21.—A dispatch to The Daily Telegraph from St. Petersburg says that explosive bullets are reported to have been discovered among the ammunition captured from the Austrians by the Russians during the fighting at Sokal.

HOLD KIAU-CHAU, IS KAISER'S ORDER

London Hears Germany Will Defend Her Chinese Stronghold to the Last.

FEAR FOR DUTCH COLONIES

Berlin Press Asserts Japan Has Long Planned to Drive Germans from Far East.

CHINA SEEKS OUR AID

Asks United States to Consider Taking Over Kiau-chau as Temporary Expedient.

Special Cable to THE NEW YORK TIMES.

ROTTERDAM, Aug. 20 (Dispatch to The London Daily News).—A semi-official message from Berlin says that every preparation is being made at Kiau-chau for resistance to Japan.

By The Associated Press.

LONDON, Aug. 20.—According to information received in official circles here this evening Emperor William has ordered that resistance be made to the last to Japan's attempts to oust Germany from Kiau-chau.

A dispatch to The Express from The Hague says:

"Japan's ultimatum to Germany has been the cause of some grave thinking on the part of many Dutchmen, who wonder whether there is likely to be any danger to the Dutch colonies in the event of a great shuffle of Asiatic possessions."

German Press Expects Refusal.

BERLIN, (via Copenhagen and London,) Aug. 20.—The Japanese ultimatum has been the subject of much comment by the German press.

The Norddeutscher Allgemeine Zeitung believes that Germany will reply with a polite yet definite refusal.

Count Ernst von Reventlow, the naval expert, publishes an article in The Tages Zeitung, showing that Japan's policy has been prepared for a long time. He recounts how M. Sugimura, the former Japanese Ambassador at Berlin, who was friendly toward the Germans and always had directed his efforts toward a rapprochement between Germany and Japan, at the time of his departure from Berlin had said to Count von Reventlow that he had been suddenly ordered to return from Berlin when on leave.

The Ambassador had added this significant remark: "I will go and I will never return to Berlin."

TOKIO, Japan, Aug. 20.—Confirmation has been received here of the arrival in Berlin of the Japanese ultimatum. No hostility is shown to Germans here.

Japan Explains to United States.

WASHINGTON, Aug. 20.—Interference by German cruisers with the shipping of Japan's ally, Great Britain, the seizure of Japanese goods on German ships and the consequent injury to Japan's trade are the principal reasons set forth by Japan in explanation of the ultimatum delivered to Germany last Sunday. Cable dispatches contained a brief outline of the Japanese grievances, but it was not until today that the full text of the statement issued by the Japanese Foreign Office bearing upon this subject became available. This document said:

"From the beginning of hostilities between England and Germany the latter has been bending all her energies to strengthening all the fortifications at Kiau-chau, even to the extent of enforcing labor by means of the Chinese coolies. Meanwhile, the Government's squadrons stationed in the Far East have been making incessant appearances in Chinese waters, making Kiau-chau their base, and, in co-operation with German converted cruisers, threatening and interfering with British shipping and commerce, thereby jeopardizing and injuring to a considerable extent the commercial interests in general of Great Britain.

Trade Demoralized.

"In the meantime the above action on the part of Germany has not failed to greatly demoralize the trade interests of Japan by obstructing and disturbing her shipping routes and commerce. In fact, the whole eastern commercial world has been thrown into a state of utmost uneasiness. Some of the Japanese merchant vessels have been detained, and all of the Japanese import and export cargoes on board German merchant vessels have been requisitioned.

"It is clear that unless Germany has a strong base at Kiau-chau the conditions such as above outlined could never have been produced. It is this position of Kiau-chau that is solely responsible for it all; it is the strongest weapon in the hands of Germany so far as the Far East is concerned.

"The history of the seizure of the place by Germany and her conduct preceding and including her intervention, in conjunction with Russia and France, after the Chino-Japanese war show that it is absolutely necessary to eliminate such possession completely if Japan is to restore immediately complete peace in the Far East in accordance with the terms of the Anglo-Japanese alliance. If Japan is to look far enough into the future and adopt measures to insure an abiding peace in Eastern Asia she must realize that a strong military base in the hands of a hostile militant power right in the heart of the country cannot in itself fail to be a menacing factor."

CHINA SEEKS OUR HELP.

Would Have United States Take Over Kiau-chau Temporarily.

PEKING, China, Aug. 20.—China today inquired of the United States what its attitude would be toward the cession by Germany to the United

Continued on Page 3.

French Reoccupy Muelhausen, Driving Germans Out with the Bayonet.

OTHER GAINS IN ALSACE

Germans' Position Weakened by the Loss of Gebweiler and Morhange.

CHECK FRENCH IN LORRAINE

Advancing Prussians Intrench Themselves Before Briey, with Support from Metz.

PARIS, Aug. 20.—The reoccupation of Mülhausen, Alsace, by French troops is announced officially here today.

The recapture of the town was preceded today by a very severe battle, during which the French troops took one of the suburbs at the point of the bayonet. They also took as the result of their victory six German cannon and six ammunition wagons.

The official note says the situation in the Vosges Mountains is unchanged. In Upper Alsace the French have occupied Gebweiler, 14 miles southwest of Colmar.

The official announcement continues:

"Our troops have met with brilliant successes in Alsace, especially between Mülhausen and Altkirch.

"In Lorraine, the day was less fortunate for us. Our advanced troops found themselves faced by exceptionally strong positions. They were forced by a counter attack to fall back in a body, which is solidly established on the Seille, and along the canal from the Marne to the Rhine."

The situation in the Duchy of Luxemburg and in Belgium is unchanged.

German Losses Heavy.

LONDON, Friday, Aug. 21.—A dispatch to the Havas Agency from Belfort, by way of Paris, says:

"The battles around Mülhausen have been particularly bloody for the Germans who, knowing the French would spare as much as possible the Alsatians and their property, hid themselves in houses protected by the Red Cross, whence they fired upon the French.

"The French directed a violent rifle and artillery fire upon their assailants, causing veritable carnage. Every German leaving the houses was shot down.

"A battery of six guns, with their caissons filled with ammunition, was captured from the Germans. They were taken to Belfort, where crowds of curious people gathered to see them. Eighteen other guns captured today are expected to reach Belfort tomorrow, together with 600 prisoners."

VALUE OF FRENCH VICTORIES.

Paris Believes German Position in Alsace Now Dangerous.

By G. H. PERRIS,

NEW YORK TIMES-London Daily Chronicle War Service.

Special Cable to THE NEW YORK TIMES.

PARIS, Aug. 20.—Rumors that there has been prolonged and severe fighting in southern Alsace are to some extent confirmed this afternoon by an official dispatch saying that Mülhausen has been reoccupied by the French after a stiff action, in the course of which six cannon and six artillery wagons were captured. Again a French bayonet charge proved irresistible.

German Position Endangered.

Though the Germans have held out so long, and must therefore be in strong force, their position in southern Alsace is becoming somewhat dangerous. It is true that the French have lost the village of Ville, at the head of one of the branch lines of railway leading from the Vosges Mountains to Shlestadt, but by way of compensation they have taken Gebweiler, a textile manufacturing town of 14,000 inhabitants and the largest industrial centre in Alsace after Mülhausen.

With the French fixed at Gebweiler, Cerney, Thann, and Mülhausen, there would seem to be no safe German position west of the Rhine and south of Colmar. The old village of Morhange, which has just been occupied, has been made in recent years a considerable German garrison town, covering the important strategic railway centre of Benestroff, whence forces could be thrown by several lines upon the frontier. Large barracks and magazines overlook the dull country, much cut up by lakes and streams. Château Salins and Delme, otherwise less important and detached places, have recently been connected by a strategic railway.

The most advanced of the positions that have been captured was just such a little inferno as that described by Lieut. Bilse in "Aus einer kleinen Garnison." Many of the old French population had emigrated, and the remainder were very restive under their German masters.

Looking still further north, a slow German advance is reported in the region of Longwy and Briey. The Temps says that the Germans have intrenched themselves before Briey, with support from the garrison of Metz.

Positions Deemed Impregnable.

Special Cable to THE NEW YORK TIMES.

PARIS, Aug. 20 (Dispatch to The London Standard).—All French and German military writers have concurred hitherto in considering the country about Mülhausen as almost impregnable, and it will be interesting to learn how the French success was achieved. The public scarcely recognizes the importance of the feat, which reflects immense credit on the staff which conceived it and the gallantry of the troops in executing it.

Far from seeking to exaggerate victories, the Government notices are sober, almost to excess, in reporting doings at the front.

As for the army in Belgium, nobody has any idea, even approximately, of the disposition of the French, British and Belgian forces.

French Victory Near Luneville.

LONDON, Aug. 20.—A dispatch to The Times from Paris says that the first point at which the Germans crossed the French frontier was at Cirey-sur-Vesouse. Since then there has been continued fighting in that region until a day or two ago when it ended in the victorious advance of the French forces, who inflicted a decisive defeat on the enemy and drove them back across the frontier east of Lunéville.

The correspondent says that the laconic reports of the French Minister of War give little idea of the desperate struggle that occured around the handful of villages scattered along the French border. Point after point was taken and retaken by one side or the other.

He gives the following story of the fighting at the village of Badonviller, as told by the villagers:

"The village was occupied by a battalion of chasseurs as a covering force and was prepared for defense by numerous trenches. The battle began on Aug. 10. The Germans bombarded the village compelling the chasseurs to evacuate it. The latter retired on Celles and afterward took up a position on Donan Ridge.

"After nightfall the Germans increased the bombardment and the inhabitants sought refuge in cellars as a continuous rain of shells kept wrecking the houses and setting them afire. It was a terrible sight. Women fell on their knees and prayed, while children cried piteously.

"The chasseurs retired defending every house, foot by foot, and making the Germans feel their fire. The sun rose on a village in ruins. It had been under bombardment fifteen hours. When the Germans entered they fired first on all the windows and down loopholes into the cellars. No corner was spared."

Special Cable to THE NEW YORK TIMES.

ROTTERDAM, Aug. 20 (Dispatch to the London Daily News).—A private message from Berlin states that forty-eight trains were required to convey the Austrian troops for use against France to Leopoldshöhe, near Basle, and that eight Austrian regiments also proceeded to Baden, via Constance.

WATCH SKY FOR MESSAGES.

British Public Told to be on Lookout for Aeroplane Notes.

LONDON, Aug. 20.—Aeroplanes now are playing the part in war which formerly only carrier pigeons could perform, and seem to have greater possibilities than pigeons.

An official notification issued tonight to the people of England requests them to be watchful for messages dropped from aeroplanes, describes the peculiar wrappings which will inclose messages and instructs the finders to forward them immediately to the addresses they bear.

French aeroplanes scattered messages to the inhabitants of Alsace in the early days of the war, and the Russians adopted the same method for announcing the proclamation of Emperor Nicholas to the Poles.

BAYONETS WITH TEETH.

Germans Said to be Using a Terrible Weapon.

Special Cable to THE NEW YORK TIMES.

LONDON, Friday, Aug. 21.—The Daily Mail's Brussels correspondent telegraphs:

"The Germans are using a bayonet with teeth on it, which slips in easily but tears the flesh to pieces in the process of withdrawal.

"On the other hand, the Prussian bullet, by reason of its extreme pointedness, is saving the Red Cross much work. Extractions have been reduced 25 per cent., the bullet passing clean through more often than not."

Belgians Withdraw as the German Host Advances.

HEADQUARTERS GIVEN UP

Abandonment of Louvain Leaves the Capital an Easy Prey for the Invaders.

ENTER WITHOUT RESISTANCE

Belgians Hint Their Retirement Fits Into the Big Campaign Plan of the Allies.

PARIS, Aug. 20, 11 P. M.—The German cavalry have occupied Brussels. This official announcement was made tonight.

Strong columns are following up this movement.

The Belgian Army is retiring on Antwerp without having been engaged by the Germans.

The official statement says:

"In conformity with a prearranged plan, the Belgian field army retreated to the intrenched camp of Antwerp, after brilliantly fulfilling their duty.

"Antwerp has a double role. It is a formidable intrenched camp, fortified on most modern lines, and is the base from which the Belgian army can threaten the German flank and co-operate effectively with the allies.

"The Antwerp defenses consist of three fortifications, whose power of resistance can be heightened by flooding a large area around all the works. Antwerp is fully equipped with the most perfect appliances.

"To besiege the fortress the Germans would have to detach imposing forces and a large siege train. This they are not likely to do. If they do not, they will be obliged to cover themselves against the operations of the Belgian Army, which is intact, thanks to the skilful retreat and augmented by the Antwerp garrison.

Liege Forts Holding Out.

It is to e added that the Liege forts still hold out. Those at Namur have not yet been attacked. They are as strong as the forts at Liege and have been considerably strengthened in the last two weeks.

"From this it would seem that the advancing German armies are caught between the positions of Namur and Antwerp, a distance from each other of thirty-five miles, as the crow flies.

"The German situation is, then, a difficult one, since they lack the chief postulates of a plan of march through Belgium. Namely, free passage of the Meuse, a route by Liege and Namur, and inaction on the part of the Belgian Army."

No Resistance Offered by City.

NEW YORK TIMES-London Daily Chronicle War Service.

Special Cable to THE NEW YORK TIMES.

GHENT, Aug. 20.—The Prussian cavalry this morning were very active along the whole front of the allies. Small bodies of Uhlans have been close around Brussels and also in the neighborhood of Malines, (thirteen miles northeast of Brussels.) My information does not enable me to say whether Malines is still occupied by the Belgians.

A German aeroplane flew over Brussels this morning and was seen at Ghent.

Just as I was leaving Brussels for the coast today [the censor has here evidently elided the words, "the German cavalry entered Brussels."] They met with no resistance, in accordance with instructions of the Belgian authorities. They were, however, coldly received. The streets were deserted and some brave persons manifested their grief by draping the national flag with black.

ANTWERP IS MAKING READY.

Houses Destroyed That Would Shelter Foe—Flood Gates Open.

NEW YORK TIMES-London Daily Chronicle War Service.

Special Cable to THE NEW YORK TIMES.

AMSTERDAM, Aug. 20.—A correspondent, who left Antwerp this afternoon and made his way over the Dutch frontier, telephones late tonight from Rosendaal that Antwerp is being put in a stage of defense. The woods are cut down over a wide area and the villas are being destroyed outside of the town so as to afford no shelter to the Germans. New earthworks are to be seen everywhere in the fields and part of the country of the fortification line has been flooded.

A party of French staff officers who arrived today were loudly cheered.

Two fast steamers from the Dover-Ostend route lie in the Scheldt to take away the Queen and royal family and Court if the Germans enter the town.

Great herds of cattle have been driven in from the country and are now in the parks, and everything is being done to provision the town.

The Chamber is to meet in the Flemish Opera House and the Senate in the Dutch Theatre.

LOUVAIN SLIMLY DEFENDED.

Only 3,000 Belgians Left There to Check the German Advance.

Special Cable to THE NEW YORK TIMES.

BRUSSELS, Aug. 20, (Dispatch to The London Daily News).—Today the Germans occupied Louvain, which was until this morning the headquarters of the Belgian army, and to-morrow they may be in Brussels.

The first hint I got of what was afoot was on returning from Antwerp early in the afternoon. At a crossroads below the railway line I met a whole company of Belgian infantry and artillery marching away from Louvain. They were moving in perfect order except for the dust. The men had not been in action.

Earlier in the day I had noticed an enormous number of loaded motor cars, and it had been whispered that the army headquarters would be transferred immediately.

On my return to Brussels I hurried out toward Louvain. Soon I met many indications of what had happened.

A force of about 3,000 men, or perhaps more, had been left in the trenches to meet the enemy and cover the retreat. With these the Germans, who had advanced by three roads from Diest, Tirlemont, and Hamme-Mille, on the Eghezee road, had a sharp encounter. The Belgians fought stubbornly, and by all accounts their losses were far smaller, as they have been in each encounter, than those of the assailants.

They beat the Germans back at all points in the first attack, and could have held the position, a wounded man told me, against an even greater number for much longer, but in the lull following the attack they drew back quietly. They were well upon their way when the Uhlans rode into the town.

There is a story among the refugees that Louvain has been fired, but that seems hardly likely. At all events, from a distance of about two miles I saw no trace of burning of any extent.

Pitiful Crowds of Refugees.

At this point I was stopped by an enormous crowd of refugees flocking along the Brussels road on foot and in vehicles and by Red Cross cars. The sight was pitiful—of all these people leaving their homes.

By far the greater number were women with young children, whose fathers were at the front. Some were old men and women, driven out by fear begotten by the stories, which have been circulated freely, of German atrocities. These, in fact, have of late been the only items of news that seemed to go uncensored, and it would have been far better if they had been blue-pencilled with the rest.

One woman with two children told me how the Uhlans made their supper of children if they could not get enough to eat, and old men recounted an ancient tale, as old as war itself, of how they roasted people head down over a slow fire.

Fear and ignorance had seized the mob. As I was going out a peasant fired his double-barreled gun at my car, mistaking my fishing hat for a German helmet, and blew the tail lamp to pieces. For fear his indiscretion should lead him into far worse trouble I stopped the car, got the gun from him, and broke it across the breech, for undoubtedly the German soldiers will retaliate upon any civilians who use arms. It is devoutly to be hoped that the notices in the streets of Brussels, telling every one to give up arms to the police, have been obeyed, otherwise there will be serious trouble.

Brussels is now curiously quiet, though big crowds are gathering around the railroad stations to watch the wounded passing through. I do not think the panic will be great here.

In Antwerp in the morning there were hundreds of fugitives near the station who came in from Turnhout, Herenthals, and other places where there had been some fighting, and these were for the most part being sent back by train to their homes, where they are likely to take as little hurt as in the city. None of the many that I spoke to had even seen the German troops, but it is easy to find an excuse for women left alone with children.

Drove Her Sheep Before Her.

A gendarme told me of one old woman who arrived last evening at the barricades, driving six sheep. She did not want the Germans to have them, she explained, and had brought them with her. She was quite willing that the Belgian soldiers should have them if they would keep her safe. Perhaps, she added, the Queen and the Princes might need some of her mutton. Antwerp, however, has good stores of food to last a siege, and the Princes, whom I saw this morning walking through the streets with their tutors, are hardly likely to be in need.

Of the defense of Antwerp it is not necessary to speak. They are as nearly impregnable as any can be, and the force, defending them is the strongest in the country, not even excepting Namur.

In a train just leaving Brussels are about 300 wounded Belgian soldiers, going to Ghent to large hospitals which are being mostly run by Belgian and French nurses.

German Officers Are Targets.

Details of the fighting are difficult to get, for no soldier ever knows what happens outside of his own experience; but the field guns seem to have done deadly work on the advancing Germany infantry, and the policy of shooting at officers was kept up, as at Liege.

As I went to Antwerp early this morning a great German monoplane, with curved wings and fan-shaped tail, followed the railway lines, keeping exact pace with the express train, from outside Brussels till we were half way on our journey. It flew about 3,000 or 4,000 feet up, and every now and then passed through the clouds; but watchful eyes were in it, and if the Germans did not know when they attacked Louvain what the result would be, the Belgians must have concealed their movements very closely. The monoplane was at the time fifteen or twenty miles inside the Belgian lines, and passed directly across the line taken in the afternoon by the retreating troops.

Nearly all the English except residents and the Red Cross contingent, have left Brussels, and the rest will probably follow in the morning. From one of the Red Cross nurses I got this message just before I left:

"Tell them in England that we are cheery and anticipate no danger. Our work is far too useful to the Germans, as well as to the Belgians, for any harm to come to us."

BELGIAN PEASANTS' PANIC.

Abandoned by Their Army, Without Notice, to the Mercy of Germans.

Special Cable to THE NEW YORK TIMES.

BRUSSELS, Aug. 20 (Dispatch to The London Daily News).—We are still waiting, and far too little news is given out. Our nerves are beginning to feel the blank, because rumor fills it too readily.

It should have been a quiet day—a quiet wandering through a picturesque lane well behind the supposed fighting lines of the armies—but, as officially stated, the Germans have occupied the line from Diest to Tirlemont, and cavalry were using this stretch of open country, which seems to have been designed for them, pushing in all directions.

So we came down to a town which a short time ago was filled with troops, but is now empty save for the uneasy crowds at the corners and the shifting swarm at the Mayor's office.

We passed cheerfully out on the big shaded road, confident of a good passage. The feeling changed in that odd way it does in the most peaceful scenery. With a rush down the road came a cyclist wearing a tweed cap. Behind him, 300 yards off, from be-

French Airship Hit by Ninety-seven Bullets In Daring Flight to Drop Bombs in Germany

LONDON, Aug. 20.—Adolphe Pegoud, the noted French aviator, has returned to Paris from the war zone to get a new aeroplane. According to a Paris dispatch to the Exchange Telegraph Company, the wings of Pegoud's old machine were riddled by ninety-seven bullets and two shells when he made a flight of 186 miles into German territory with a military observer.

Pegoud could not say just where he had been except that he recrossed the Rhine and blew up by means of bombs two German convoys.

Capt. Finck, a military aviator, Pegoud said, had destroyed a hangar near Metz and wrecked a Zeppelin, and also destroyed three aeroplanes which were in the hangar.

"All the News That's Fit to Print."

The New York Times.

THE WEATHER
Generally fair Sunday, preceded by showers; Monday, fair; moderate shifting winds, becoming west.
For full weather report see Page 13.

VOL. LXIII...NO. 20,672. ... NEW YORK, SUNDAY, AUGUST 30, 1914.—88 PAGES, In Seven Parts, Including Picture and Rotogravure Section, Real Estate Directory, and Review of Books. PRICE FIVE CENTS.

FRENCH RIGHT WINS, BUT THEIR LEFT IS TURNED, AND PARIS ORDERS HOUSES DOWN FOR SIEGE; GERMAN FORCE WITHDRAWN TO MEET RUSSIANS

FLEET VICTORY THRILLS ENGLAND

Details of Heligoland Fight Show It Was One of the Most Daring in Navy's History.

GERMAN SHIPS SURPRISED

Traversing Mine Field in Fog, British Were Upon Them Before They Knew of Peril.

SAILORS SAY 11 SHIPS SANK

German Report Admits the Loss of Four Ships—Fought Superior Force.

The German Account of the Sea Battle

COPENHAGEN, Aug. 30 (via London), 6:35 A. M.—A dispatch to the Wolff Bureau from Berlin says:

Yesterday forenoon during partly foggy weather several small British cruisers and two flotillas comprising about forty destroyers appeared in the North Sea northwest of Heligoland.

A desperate isolated engagement ensued between them and our small forces. Small German cruisers steamed westward, and on account of the short distance came into contact with several large English cruisers.

Thus the cruiser Ariadne was attacked at short range by two large cruisers of the Lion class and sunk after a glorious fight. The majority of the crew, numbering 250, were saved.

The destroyer N 87 was bombarded by a small cruiser and ten destroyers and sunk. She went down firing her guns. Her Captain, who was Squadron Commander, was killed.

The small cruisers Coeln and Mainz are missing, and, according to Reuter dispatches, were sunk after an engagement with superior forces.

Of their crews eight officers and ninety-one men appear to have been saved by British warships.

Special Cable to THE NEW YORK TIMES.

HARWICH, England, Aug. 29 (Dispatch to The London Evening News).—Thrilling stories of the naval engagement off Heligoland yesterday were told by the men on board the cruiser Fearless and the destroyers which arrived here today. The engagement lasted about eight hours, during which time a mist hung over the fleets. The fighting is described as sharp and terrible, and the British losses seem to have been miraculously light. Of the destroyers only one presents any signs of having taken part in a battle.

Although the official report said only five German vessels were sunk in the battle, the crews of the destroyers say there were at least eleven.

A non-commissioned officer of the Fearless, which in the thick of battle picked up many German wounded, said:

"The whole operation took place in a thick haze. When we opened fire there was not a single searchlight playing upon us. The Germans all seemed to be asleep. The action was very hot while it lasted. We must have done a lot of damage."

Pick Up Survivors.

The Fearless picked up more than twenty survivors, including several who were badly wounded. Twelve died on the way to Harwich and were buried at sea. Two destroyers brought about fifty German wounded. The Fearless came between 2 and 3 o'clock this morning. She convoyed about thirty Germans to Lord Tredegar's Red Cross yacht, which is being utilized as a hospital ship.

All morning the arrival of the destroyers was watched by a large crowd on the pier, and many rousing cheers were given for the British sailors. All the tugboats hoisted the Red Cross flag and assisted in the removal of the wounded to the pier. The men were carried on stretchers by the boys of the hospital bearers' corps, clad in white duck overalls. They were grouped on the end of the pier, and worked in parties of four. At one time I counted fifteen groups maknig their way up the hillside.

Several of the wounded were badly injured about the head. One German who was being lifted from the tug to the pier made an effort to thank his rescuers by signs. The officers in charge of the arrangements for the removal of the wounded repeatedly exhorted the bearers to go carefully, and the German wounded were handled with the same care as the British wounded. The work of transferring the injured from the destroyers to the hospital was very slow, and was still proceeding this afternoon.

Shells Swept Decks.

British sailors, who boarded the Mainz after she was put out of action, said the effect of the British gunfire was terrible. The masts were shot away and the turrets were battered in. The decks were a mass of wreckage,

Continued on Page 3.

ITALY WITH 800,000 MAY JOIN THE ALLIES

Swiss Papers Learn of Country-Wide Preparations for War—French Frontier Vacated.

Special Cable to THE NEW YORK TIMES.

GENEVA, Aug. 25, (Dispatch to The London Standard.)—Several Swiss papers publish telegrams from Rome, Milan, and Turin from their correspondents stating that Italy is arming to join the Triple Entente. I give textually a telegram received today by the Gazette de Lausanne, one of the most serious Swiss papers, from Novara:

"Troops are passing incessantly, coming from Liguria and Piedmont, their destination being Udine. The French frontier has been entirely vacated.

"The Italian soldiers are full of strength and joy to 'chasser l'Autrichien.'

"In Venetia and on the frontier there are 800,000 men. Within the next eight days the Italian Army will enter the field."

It should be added that since the Anglo-French fleet entered the Adriatic the effect on the Italian people has been so great that it may force the hands of the King and Government to take decisive measures, even if they wish to remain neutral.

GENEVA, Sunday, Aug. 23, via Paris, Aug. 29, (Delayed in Transmission.)—There is much talk on the Swiss side of the Italian border of Italy's reported preparations to join with England and France against Germany and Austria.

Italians in Switzerland have been called to the colors, and it is reported here that the Italian fleet has been concentrated at a certain port on the Adriatic preparatory to joining the British and the French squadrons before Trieste.

A ZEPPELIN CAUGHT BY RUSSIAN GUNS

Eight Soldiers With Quick-Firers and Explosives Harassed Polish Border.

LONDON, Aug. 29.—A Reuter dispatch from St. Petersburg says that a Zeppelin dirigible which bombarded the railway station at Miawa, just over the border of Russian Poland, was brought down by Russian fire.

There were eight soldiers in the car, with quickfirers and explosives.

EXCHANGE OF ORDERS BETWEEN EMPERORS

Francis Joseph Decorates William for Victories—Receives "Pour le Merite."

LONDON, Aug. 29.—According to Berlin official dispatches received by Marconi wireless, the Austrian Emperor, in a telegram to the German Emperor, says:

"The splendid victories gained by the German armies under your command over your powerful enemies are due to your iron will. You have sharpened and swung the mighty sword. To the laurels which adorn you as victor I should like to add the highest military honor which it is in my power to confer by asking you to accept the Grand Cross of Maria Theresa.

"Knowing how highly you and your army value the achievements of Gen. von Moltke, I bestow upon him the Commander's Cross of the Maria Theresa Order."

The German Emperor has bestowed upon the Austrian Emperor the Order "Pour le Merite" and upon Gen. Baron Conrad von Hotzendorf the Iron Cross of the First and Second Class.

GERMAN SAILORS GOING TO AID TURKEY?

800 with Officers Reported Passing Through Bulgaria—May Aim at Moslem Revolt in India.

LONDON, Aug. 29.—The correspondent of the Reuter Telegram Company at Athens says:

"According to a semi-official statement, news has been received from a trustworthy source in Constantinople that 800 German officers and sailors as well as a quantity of ammunition passed through Bulgaria Friday in a special train on their way to Constantinople."

ROME, Aug. 29 (Dispatch to The London Daily Mail).—The situation is becoming much more serious throughout the whole Balkan peninsula. All the Balkan States are getting ready to take part in the European conflict.

If Germany and Austria are trying to induce Turkey to enter the war against the Allies, they may possibly be doing so on the theory that a declaration of war by the Sultan, who is the head of the Mohammedan religion, would embarrass England by tending to incite revolt among her Moslem subjects in England, and embarrass France by stirring up the Moslem tribesmen against her African colonies.

Should Italy enter the war on the side of the Entente, a war of Turkey against Italy would also tend to embarrass her in her newly acquired African colony in Tripoli.

Turkey herself could do little harm to the Allies in Europe, as, if she declared war, she would be likely to be attacked by Greece, which is friendly to the Entente.

CZAR'S TROOPS AT KOENIGSBERG

Russians and Germans Both Report Big Victories in East Prussia.

RUSH CHECKED, SAYS BERLIN

Victorious Everywhere and Germans Are in Retreat, St. Petersburg Avers.

AUSTRIANS PRESSED BACK

Regiment Cut Up and Flag Captured, but Vienna Asserts That Tide Has Turned.

PARIS, Aug. 29.—The French War Office gave out the following official statement this afternoon:

"The Russian Army has completely invested Königsberg and occupied Allenstein, both in East Prussia. The Germans continue to retreat."

LONDON, Sunday, Aug. 30.—The Russian advance in East Prussia, according to a dispatch to The London Times from St. Petersburg, gave rise to three days of prolonged and stubborn engagements in the vicinity of Soldau, Allenstein, and Bischoffsburg, where the Germans had concentrated the army corps which retreated from Gumbinnen and some fresh troops. Allenstein has been successfully occupied by the Russians.

The German losses were particularly heavy at Meuhlen, between Osterode and Nordenburg, and their troops are in full retreat.

On the Galician front the fighting had on Wednesday assumed the character of general engagements, developing in the southern districts of Lublin and in Eastern Galicia on the roads to Lemberg. The front of the battle extended for 200 miles. At first the fighting was more of the character of attack and counter-attack, but gradually the Austrians were compelled to assume the defensive.

Took a Regiment's Colors.

A Russian foot regiment, in a hand-to-hand fight with the Eleventh Hungarian Reserves, captured their colors and nearly annihilated the enemy.

The Austrians on Friday made a bold bid for the offensive by trying to seize the left flank of the Russian position in Poland, with the obvious intention of relieving the pressure on the German forces in Northeastern Prussia.

Two or three army corps advanced as far as Kielce, where they encountered a strong Russian force. A pitched battle was fought, and resulted in the overthrow of the invaders, who suffered heavy losses. It was here that the Eleventh Hungarian Reserves met their fate.

Operations in Eastern Galicia, according to the dispatch, are developing fast and the Russian net is drawing around Lemberg. The German Allenstein army is in full retreat toward Elbing and Marienburg.

"The reported capture of Königsberg is not confirmed," says The Times correspondent, "but I have the best of authority for stating that Königsberg is completely surrounded."

Among the arrivals in London from the Continent today was H. Silverstone of Johnstown, Penn., who left Königsberg two weeks ago. He said that when war was declared the German police visited every house where Russians resided and rounded up a large number of them, including women and children. The Russians were taken to the palace yard, where they were held for three days and subjected to many hardships. They were forced to sleep on the bare ground and had scanty food.

A Copenhagen dispatch to the Exchange Telegraph Company says that the Captain of the German steamer Derkid, which has arrived from Danzig, told of a terrible panic there owing to the fear of the Russian invasion. He said the inhabitants were in a desperate condition and that there had been fierce rioting. Foreigners and their possessions, he said, were ruthlessly misused.

Germans Lose Heavily.

WASHINGTON, Aug. 29.—The British Embassy today received from the London Foreign Office the following dispatch on Russian operations in Prussia:

"East Prussia is being rapidly overrun by the Russian Army, and a great part of this region is already in Russian hands. The German forces, consisting of three army corps and several divisions, have been repeatedly defeated and have lost heavily in men and guns."

Russian troops are only thirty kilometers from Lemberg, and the Servian Army headquarters has moved forward to Zalievo, according to official dispatches today to the French Embassy.

Col. Golejewski, Military Attaché to the Russian Embassy, received yesterday the following cable message from the General Staff at St. Petersburg:

"The Russian troops are approach-

Continued on Page 2.

GERMAN CORPS IS SHIFTED

Troops Being Sent in 160 Trains Northeast Through Belgium.

NEEDED NOW IN PRUSSIA

Sudden Movement of Large Force Taken to Mean Step to Check Russians.

FEW ARE LEFT AT BRUSSELS

German Garrison Only 2,000—Art Treasures to be Seized if War Levy Is Not Paid.

Special Cable to THE NEW YORK TIMES.

ANTWERP, Aug. 29, (Dispatch to The London Daily Mail.)—It is thought that as a result of the bad news from Eastern Prussia the Germans are recalling troops from the French frontiers. All yesterday and during last night 160 German trains, conveying an army corps, with its transport, crossed Belgium from southwest to northeast.

This morning Brussels was practically destitute of German troops. Only 2,000 men remained.

LONDON, Aug. 29.—One hundred and sixty railroad trains loaded with German troops passed through Belgium last night from the southwest toward the northeast, according to a Reuter dispatch from Antwerp.

This, it is added, indicates that the Germans are sending troops back on account of the Russian advance. The German force at Brussels has been reduced to a minimum.

These 160 trains, the dispatch continues, are transporting one army corps, with full equipment, and it would appear that the rapid advance of the Russians is compelling the Germans to withdraw troops from the line of the Meuse."

An official announcement issued at Antwerp says:

"It is confirmed that numerous trains on Friday last transported German troops from the Courtrai region in an easterly direction. The retirement of the German troops is strongly increasing. The enemy has abandoned the country north of the line including Merchtem, Vilvorde, Aerschot, Huyst-Op-Den-Berg, Tremmelom, and Haeght. The province of Antwerp and part of Limburg are free of the enemy. The general position is regarded with confidence."

A dispatch to The Evening News from Copenhagen says:

"Ordinary railroad transportation in Germany has been suspended for the present, because the railroads are engaged in carrying troops from the west front to the hard-pressed east front."

Despite these two reports, many here think that it is not likely that the Germans will make any great demands upon the western army until the big battle in Northern France, in which there seems to have been a lull, has been definitely decided.

TO LOSE ART OR $40,000,000.

American Says Brussels Treasures Are in Danger of Seizure.

Special Cable to THE NEW YORK TIMES.

LONDON, Aug. 29.—"The Germans will force Brussels to pay an indemnity of $40,000,000, or they will sack the city." This is the assertion made by James R. Evans, an American who arrived this morning from Brussels, having left that city on Thursday night on his way to England via Ostend.

Mr. Evans confirms the reports that the Germans intend to seize works of art and other treasures unless the Belgians meet their demands. He says that the Belgians have contributed only about one-eighth of the sum demanded, and say that they are unable to pay the balance.

"The Germans," he said, "intend to make the Belgians pay an indemnity to them equal to the amounts loaned to Belgium by England and France, and a large part of it will of course be levied upon Brussels."

Mr. Evans had been in Brussels for four weeks, and brought out with him letters to Consul General Skinner from Consul General Watts in Brussels. He said that there were only about 400 German soldiers in Brussels, all the others having been withdrawn to the fighting line toward the south or toward Antwerp.

Fear-Inspiring Proclamations.

"Although few troops have been left in Brussels," he said, "the city is practically under the government of German officials, and by means of hair-raising proclamations the people have been scared into submission. These proclamations are posted in conspicuous places all over the city. One of the latest of these is to the effect that the most drastic measures will be taken if the telegraph wires connecting the German positions are cut again, as they were a few days ago. Some suspect the Germans themselves of cutting the wires, to give them an excuse for frightening the populace with another death-breathing proclamation.

"The Germans have been circumspect in Brussels. I was informed from a reliable source that two soldiers were shot by the order of Major Gen. Jarowski, the commandant, when he heard that they had insulted young girls. Gen. Jarowski was formerly Military Attaché of the German Embassy at St. Petersburg.

"As the result of protests made to him by the Burgomaster, a proclamation was issued that for eight days there would be no more requisitioning of foodstuffs and that during that time all things would be paid for. For a while after the German occupation of Brussels a serious situation arose because the whole milk supply had been commandeered. This entailed suffering among infants and invalids, while some suffering was caused by the commandeering of other food staples. These hardships at last resulted in the Burgomaster's protest.

"At present all the cafés in Brussels are closed at 9 P. M. No liquors are sold, but there is no objection to the sale of beer. This, however, is not the German variety, for as soon as Belgium was invaded the Belgians stopped selling it with a few exceptions, and the places which sold it were demolished by the populace.

"It is true that the Germans are trying to live off the country, saving their own food supply. It is almost impossible to learn anything about their movements, for the soldiers received strict injunctions before entering Brussels to engage in no conversations with civilians and to divulge to no one the army's plans of action. However, it is known that the greater portion of the troops coming through Brussels, which numbered fully 300,000, went south. The rest form the investing force gathering before Antwerp and stretching back from that place almost to Brussels. There is no doubt that the Germans intend to get hold of Antwerp, which accounts for the formidable array of siege guns which has been taken in that direction. The Germans planned to take Ostend and get control of the wireless outfit there. All panic in that place disappeared when the English marines appeared.

Expect to Reach Paris in 5 Days.

"All the Germans seemed to feel that they would reach Paris in five days, the officers telling the men that such would be the case. No one has a word to say about the navy."

Mr. Evans was able to get near the scene of fighting between Belgians and Germans, fifteen miles from Brussels, but it was unexpected.

"I was near Eppeghem," he said, "when I heard shooting, and went toward it. I soon found I was getting near, for I almost fell over the bodies of several Germans in the grass. A German officer cautioned me not to go any further, and I didn't. I met a German Red Cross doctor who had been attending the Belgian wounded. While he was doing so shrapnel from the Belgian guns fell among the wounded, killing most of them."

Mr. Evans has been for three years in the Belgian Congo, which he left last April. He is now on his way home to Butte, Mon. He says the Belgians have plenty of native troops in the Congo, and that the Germans have a powerful force in the Cameroons, but it is improbable that they will attack the English possessions to the north.

BIG GUNS AS AID TO GOD.

Will Help Him Make a Right Decision, Said a Hanover Clergyman.

ROME, Aug. 29.—The practical way in which the Germans view the war is well illustrated by a story told here today by A. R. Miller of Louisville, Ky.

"A certain Protestant clergyman of Hanover," said Mr. Miller, "presiding over a large congregation on the morning following mobilization, said among other things:

"'We are now face to face with a peculiar situation. No doubt the Russians, French, and English will pray God to give them victory, but there is but one God, and since He is just and impartial and they are also His children, we, in order to win, must work as well as pray. We must fight harder than the others. God may not always side with big guns, but big guns will certainly help Him make a right decision.'"

FRENCH VICTORY AT GUISE

Right Wing of Big Army Wins, But the Left Suffers Defeat.

GERMANS MOVE ON LA FERE

Their Cannonading Heard at Amiens—Stories of Their Great Losses Confirmed.

PARIS PREPARES FOR SIEGE

Houses Obstructing Forts' Fire Are Ordered Destroyed--Allies Evacuate Boulogne.

Paris, Sunday, Aug. 30, 12:59 A. M.—This announcement was made by the War Office this morning:

"In Lorraine our forces have advanced. We occupy a line along Mortagne (possibly Montagne) and our right wing is pushing forward.

"There is no news from the Meuse.

"A violent battle occurred yesterday (Saturday) in the region of Lannoy, near Lille, (and also near) Signy L'Abbaye, and Chateau Poicien, but the results have not been decisive, and the attack will be resumed tomorrow.

"Four French army corps engaged in a violent battle on the left wing.

"The right wing of these four corps, taking the offensive, drove back on Guise the Tenth German Corps and the Guard, both suffering considerable losses.

"Our left was less fortunate. The German forces are advancing in the direction of La Fere," (a town in Aisne, fourteen miles northwest of Laon, and a fortress of the second class.)

Official announcement is also made that the Military Governor of Paris has ordered all residents of the zone within action of the city's defending forts to evacuate an ddestroy their houses within four days from today, (Sunday.)

This brief dispatch chronicles three different battles in the crucial war area of Northern France, aside from the fighting in Lorraine, in which the French troops seem to be winning some success.

One of these is proceeding near Lannoy a little northeast of Lille and close to the Belgian frontier.

A second battle is in progress fifty miles south of Lille, close to La Fere, a fortified place in the second line of French defenses. A dispatch from Berlin tells of the defeat of a British force at St. Quentin in that region. Paris now recounts a success at Guise, twenty-five miles to the northeast of St. Quentin, but admits that the left wing of the same army (comprising four corps, or at least 160,000 men,) has been beaten back and that the Germans are marching on La Fere.

With its right wing at Guise and its left wing pushed back toward La Fere, this French army will be fronting to the northwest, and there is apparent danger that the Allies' line will be broken to the southward, if, indeed, the Germans with their strong turning movement have not already forced their way through there or to the westward.

The third battle, mentioned in the French War Office dispatch, is being fought forty miles to the east of Guise, at Signy l'Abbaye and Château Porcien. These are small places on the road from Rheims to Rocroi, Belgium, and are about ten miles apart.

ALLIES ARE REINFORCED.

Germans Attacking Vigorously and Paris Not Too Confident.

PARIS, Sunday, Aug. 30.—Yesterday was a long and anxious day in Paris. As the War Office had nothing to issue, the pessimists began to show themselves, and everybody asked what is going on in the north.

As far as could be learned, the French troops appeared to be intact, except for the losses inevitable in a week's heavy fighting over a vast front.

Every day had seen reinforcements moving up to aid the troops engaged on the Belgian frontier. The French, operating along the interior lines, were able to shift an army corps from one part of the front to another swiftly, and it is stated that the Allies are probably in a stronger position now than last Sunday.

Train service between Paris and Boulogne was suspended yesterday until further notice. When the announcement was made in the afternoon it was supposed here that the step was taken because the allied armies were about to engage the Germans on or near the railroad line running into Boulogne.

Apparently the Germans, owing to the increasing pressure of Russia, are throwing themselves against the intrenched positions of the Allies, and are suffering very severely. They are still hopeful of being able to break through the lines in Northern France.

Reports Boulogne Evacuated.

LONDON, Aug. 29.—A Central News dispatch says that Boulogne has been evacuated by the allied troops.

A Paris dispatch says that Americans, coming from Paris to England, are being sent by way of Dieppe, while English travelers are being routed by way of Havre.

Berlin Tells of British Defeat.

BERLIN, Aug. 29.—No news was received here today concerning the situation on the French frontier beyond a special dispatch to the Tages-Zeitung saying that the British defeat at St. Quentin was complete.

The British loss was heavy, it is said, and the routed British soldiers were forced to accept battle by the German cavalry, who were in masses on their line of retreat.

FIRING NEAR AMIENS.

Heard There Yesterday—How the British Fought at Mons.

Special Cable to THE NEW YORK TIMES.

LONDON, Sunday, Aug. 30.—An Amiens dispatch to The London Times, dated Saturday, gives a connected account of the fighting in Northern France. It says:

"First let it be said our honor is bright. Among all the straggling units seen, the flotsam and jetsam, of the fiercest fight in history, I saw fear in no man's face. It was not an army of hunted men, nor in all the plain tales of officers, non-commissioned officers and men did a single story of the white feather reach me.

"No one could answer for every man, but every British regiment and every battery of which any one had knowledge has done its duty, and never has duty been more terrible.

"Since Monday morning last the German advance has been one of almost incredible rapidity. The British force engaged in a terrible fight which may be called the action of Mons. Although it covered a big front on Sunday, the German attack was withstood to the utmost limit. A whole division was flung into the fight at the end of a long march, and had not even time to dig trenches.

"The French supporters who were expected do not seem to have been in touch, although whether they were many hours late I cannot say. Further to the right the French, after a long day's gallant fighting, broke. Namur fell, and Gen. Joffre was forced to order a retreat along the whole line. The Germans, fulfilling one of the best of all precepts in war, never gave the retreating army one single moment's rest.

"Pursuit was immediate, relentless, and unresting. Aeroplanes, Zeppelins, armored motors, and cavalry were loosed and served at once to harass retiring columns and to keep the German staff fully informed of the movements of the allied forces.

"The British force fell back. Desperate fighting took place southward continually. The army fought its way desperately, with many stands, but was forced backward by the sheer unconquerable numbers of the enemy, who were prepared to throw away three or four men for the life of every British soldier.

"Tonight I write to the sound of guns. All the afternoon the guns were going on the eastern roads. A German aeroplane flew over us this morning and was brought crashing down. A Royal Engineer chauffeur told me that the axle of his car was broken and he had to abandon it. He had no more than left it when it was blown up.

"Losses are great. I have seen broken bits of many regiments. Let me repeat that there was no failure in discipline, no panic, no throwing up of the sponge. Every one's temper is sweet; nerves do not show.

"A group of men, it may be a dozen less or more, arrives under command of whoever is entitled to command it. Men are worn with marching and ought to be weak with hunger, for of course no commissariat could cope with such a case; but they are steady and cheerful, and wherever they arrive make straight for the proper authority to report themselves and seek news of their regiment. Apparently every division was in action.

German Losses "Colossal."

"Certain things about the fighting seem clear. One is the colossal character of the German losses. I confess that when I read daily in the official bulletins in Paris of how much greater the German losses were than those of the Allies I was not much impressed. Much contemplation of Eastern warfare, where each side claims to have annihilated the other, has made me over-skeptical in such matters, but three days among the combatants has convinced me of the truth of the story in this case.

"It is clear that although the French General Staff knew that their eastern frontier defenses had been so perfected as to forc Germany to turn to the flanks to find a weak spot, and although they knew also that not for nothing did Germany antagonize England and outrage international opinion by violating the neutrality of Belgium, nevertheless they underestimated the force of the German blow through Belgium. All estimates of the number of the German army corps in Belgium will need revision, and behind the screen in Alsace and Lorraine there were probably far fewer than was supposed, else perhaps Mülhausen would not have had to be retaken twice.

"The German commanders in the north advance their men as if they had an inexhaustible supply. Of the bravery of the men it is not necessary to speak. They advance in deep sections so slightly extended as to be almost in close order, with little regard for cover, rushing forward as soon as their own artillery has opened fire.

Mowing Down German Ranks.

"On our position our artillery mows long lanes down the centres of sec-

Summary of War News

The left flank of the main French Army has been reinforced, and the War Office announces that four army corps met and defeated a German corps and the guard, driving them back on Guise, twenty-five miles northeast of St. Quentin. It is admitted, however, that the left flank of the force was repulsed, probably at St. Quentin, where the Germans report a British defeat. The Germans are marching on La Fere, one of the forts in the second line of French defenses. La Fere is eighty miles from Paris.

The Military Governor of Paris has ordered all residents of the zone within the line of fire of the city's defending forts to abandon their homes and destroy them before next Thursday.

The War Office announces that there was desperate fighting near Lille all day Saturday, without decisive result, and that the engagement will be resumed today.

German Army Headquarters in Berlin announces that Gen. von Hindenburg, after a three-day battle near Gilgenburg and Ortelsburg, defeated the Russian Army proceeding from the River Narew, which consisted of five army corps and three divisions.

It is also reported that five Russian army corps have been defeated by the Austrians and Germans south of Allenstein, where the Russians were reported on Friday.

Austria's War Office says that the Austrian troops are pursuing the Russians from Krosnik, and that another Austrian Army has invaded Russia and has occupied Zamose, in Russian Poland. The regions to the west, north, and southwest of Lemberg, Galicia, are being held, and the Austrian forces have advanced to the Dniester River against a strong invading force.

On the other hand, St. Petersburg says that the Russian Army is drawing a net around Lemberg and is making ready for a great battle with the Austrian forces, which have been reinforced by the Germans.

The French War Office says that the Russian Army has completely invested Koenigsberg and has occupied Allenstein.

England's Foreign Office announces that East Prussia is being rapidly overrun by the Russian Army, and that the German Army, consisting of three army corps and several divisions, have been repeatedly defeated, losing heavily in men and guns.

The first detachment of Canada's expeditionary force, consisting of 1,000 men of the Princess Patricia Light Infantry, has left for the front on board the White Star liner Megantic.

Field Marshal Lord Roberts says that Great Britain may require hundreds of thousands of men for the present conflict.

The Japanese have again drawn fire from the Kaio-Chau fortifications, when a shell was thrown at a small landing party at Cape Jaeschke. No damage was done.

Belgian peasants search through the ruins of their homes.

"All the News That's Fit to Print."

The New York Times.

THE WEATHER
Fair Monday; Tuesday, fair, warmer; moderate shifting winds, becoming south.
For full weather report see Page 11.

VOL. LXIII...NO. 20,673. .... NEW YORK, MONDAY, AUGUST 31, 1914.—TWELVE PAGES. ONE CENT In Greater New York, Jersey City and Newark. { Elsewhere TWO CENTS.

BLOWING UP HOUSES OUTSIDE PARIS FORTS; GERMAN AEROPLANE DROPS BOMBS ON CITY; FRENCH LEFT AGAIN DRIVEN BACK BY GERMANS; BRITISH LOSS, 6,000; LINES ARE REINFORCED

BRITISH LOST 29 IN NAVAL BATTLE

Two Officers and 27 Men Killed and 40 Wounded—870 Germans Known to Have Died.

FIVE GERMAN SHIPS SUNK

Official British Statement Says That German Officers Were Seen Shooting Their Men.

THE LAUREL'S GREAT FIGHT

She Led the Attacking British Destroyers and Met a Rain of Fire.

Special Cable to THE NEW YORK TIMES.

LONDON, Aug. 30.—It is officially announced that the British losses in the naval battle off Heligoland were two officers and twenty-seven men killed and forty wounded. The official statement also says that of the 1,200 men composing the crews of the German warships sunk in the action only 330 survived, and that five German vessels are known to have been sunk.

The Laurel's Brave Fight.

The most striking experience in the battle was that of the destroyer Laurel, which led the division of four destroyers sent ahead by the British fleet to lure the Germans out.

When the destroyer division, led by the Laurel, turned about to face the oncoming German destroyers it not only found itself unsupported by the cruisers, but saw coming out of the haze the light cruisers of the enemy.

Nothing daunted, the division opened fire. The Laurel, which was in an inside berth, had for some time to face the fire of one cruiser and two destroyers. The men engaged made light of the German marksmanship, declaring that they ought to have been sent speedily to the bottom. The first shell which hit the Laurel found its way to the engine room, killing four men. The second struck the forward gun, jamming the charge which was just about to be fired and killing three men.

Her Commander Wounded.

The third shell to strike her wounded Commander Frank Rose seriously in the left leg, but though urged by his men to go below, he shifted his weight on to the other leg and continued to issue his orders as though nothing had happened.

All this time the Laurel was making it desperately uncomfortable for the two destroyers with which she was engaged, one of which shortly afterward went to the bottom, and giving as good as she was getting from the cruiser as well.

A piece of the fourth shell struck the commander on the sound leg and brought him down on the bridge, but he still declined to give way, though his signal man insisted on tearing off his trousers to prevent his wounds from being poisoned. He continued to fight his ship until he lost consciousness, just after he had learned that they had managed to extract the charge from the damaged gun.

As he lay unconscious on the bridge one of the petty officers fastened tenderly a lifebelt round him, for by this time only three rounds of ammunition remained, and though the British cruisers had appeared on the scene it appeared impossible that the Laurel could live much longer in the fire to which she was exposed.

A final shell struck her amidships, enveloping her in a dense cloud of dust and smoke, and all on board were certain that she was going to the bottom. That last shell, however, was to prove her salvation, for a dense cloud hung to her as she lay helpless on the water, and though it was split in all directions by the enemy's projectiles, not one succeeded in finding her. In the heart of it there was not the slightest flurry, though even the satisfaction of fighting had been taken from them.

"Good-bye, old man," said a bluejacket, bleeding to death on the forecastle, to his mate, stretched on the deck beside him.

"My time is up, too," replied the other, calmly, reaching out a hand to him, and with that handclasp they died.

Official Account of the Battle.

The official announcement says: "A light-armored cruiser played the principal part. This vessel flew the pennant of the Commodore commanding the flotillas of the First Fleet. The principle of the operation was a scouting movement by a strong force of destroyers to cut off the Germans' light craft from home and engage them at leisure in the open sea. The line of destroyers was first attacked by two German cruisers and was sharply engaged for twenty-five minutes at a range of about 3,000 yards, with the result that the British light cruiser sustained some damage and some casualties. But she drove off the two German cruisers, one of which she seriously injured with her 6-inch guns. Later in the morning she engaged at intervals two other German vessels that were encountered in the

Continued on Page 4.

BRITISH SEIZE APIA IN SOUTH SEA RAID

Germany's Capital City in Samoan Islands Surrenders to New Zealand Expedition.

Special Cable to THE NEW YORK TIMES.

LONDON, Aug. 30.—The Secretary of State for the Colonies received a cable dispatch today from the Governor of New Zealand saying that Apia, in German Samoa, surrendered at 10 o'clock yesterday morning to an expeditionary force sent by the Government of New Zealand.

WASHINGTON, Aug. 30.—Diplomatists here believe the United States would have little to fear in the transfer of Apia from German to British sovereignty, provided the surrender of the port should result in permanent British occupancy.

If sovereignty is to change, it is argued, the United States would prefer that Great Britain and not her ally, Japan, should have control of the islands.

Germany's Samoan Islands have been considered for strategical purposes the most valuable of her possessions in the Pacific. She acquired them by a treaty signed at Washington in 1899, which guaranteed equality of commerce to Great Britain, Germany, and the United States, but divided possession of the islands between the United States and Germany. The most valuable island obtained by the United States was Tutuila, the strategic key to the group, which has at Pago Pago a splendid landlocked harbor and a naval and coaling station.

Apia, seized by the British, the capital of the group, has several churches, numerous fine houses, and is the seat of the training college of the London Missionary Society. Robert Louis Stevenson made his home on Upolu for the last years of his life and is buried there on one of the mountains. Apia became world known in March, 1889, when a hurricane swept over the harbor, wrecking several American and German warships.

GERMAN MINE SINKS GERMAN TRAWLER

Gerda Was Warning Off Neutral Vessels When She Herself Struck.

LONDON, Monday, Aug. 31.—The German armed trawler Gerda of Hamburg was blown up Saturday by striking a German mine off Langeland, a Danish island in the Great Belt.

The Gerda was acting as a guardship, for the purpose of warning neutral ships off the mines. She was about to warn off the Danish schooner Capella when she herself struck.

WASHINGTON, Aug. 30.—Great Britain has laid no mines up to this time, according to a memorandum forwarded to the State Department today by the British Embassy here, denying a published report that an Iceland trawler had been sunk by an English mine. The memorandum follows:

"His Majesty's Government has learned that on or about Aug. 26 an Iceland trawler is reported to have struck a mine twenty-five miles off the Tyne, and sunk, and at least one foreign newspaper has stated that the mine was English. Although the German action in laying mines has forced the Admiralty to reserve to themselves the right to do likewise, the statement already made by his Majesty's Government, that no British mines have been laid, remains absolutely true to this moment. The mines off the Tyne were laid thirty miles to seaward, not as part of any definite military operation, nor by German ships of war, but by German trawlers, of which a considerable number appear to have been engaged in this work. The number of one such trawler actually seen to be doing this was A. E. 24 Emden.

DUE IN PARIS WEDNESDAY.

German Press Have Faith Troops Will Be There on Schedule Time.

Special Cable to THE NEW YORK TIMES.

COPENHAGEN, Aug. 30, (Dispatch to The London Times.)—The German press confidently assert that the official prediction that the troops will be in Paris by Sept. 2 (Wednesday) will be fulfilled.

The Kaiser and several exalted officers are selling their English and Russian orders for the benefit of the Red Cross Fund.

PUT GERMAN DEAD AT 60,000

Paris Estimates Are 130,000 Wounded or Prisoners.

Special Cable to THE NEW YORK TIMES.

PARIS, Aug. 30, (Dispatch to The London Daily News.)—It is estimated in Paris that since the outbreak of hostilities the Germans have lost 60,000 killed and 130,000 wounded or prisoners. Their casualties are six times greater than the combined losses of the Allies.

A wounded Frenchman at Rouen, describing the fighting at Charleroi, said:

"We were aided by Senegalese sharpshooters, who kept whole regiments of Germans at bay. They are as black as devils, and when the Germans see them, with their fiery eyes blazing from their inky faces, they take to their heels like rabbits."

WANTS JAPANESE IN FRANCE.

Ex-Minister Pichon Asks Why They Should Not Fight There.

PARIS, Aug. 30.—Stephen Pichon, former Minister of Foreign Affairs, in an article in the Petit Journal, asks why the Japanese Army should not participate in the war in Europe. He says he is convinced that all that is required is an agreement between London, St. Petersburg, and Paris to enable several hundred thousand Japanese to be sent to France. Concluding the article, he says:

"I need not add that we should hasten."

HAVE KONIGSBERG, RUSSIANS HEAR

Big Vistula Forts of Thorn and Graudenz Besieged and Heavily Bombarded.

DANZIG POPULATION FLEES

Through Railroad Now from St. Petersburg to Insterburg on Russian Gauge.

DISASTERS TO AUSTRIANS

Division Cut Up, Whole Regiments Surrendered, It Is Said — 3,000 Men Captured Near Lemberg.

LONDON, Monday, Aug. 31.—The Daily Chronicle's St. Petersburg correspondent sends the unofficial report that the Russian forces, hotly pursuing the German Army, succeeded during the general confusion in entering the City of Königsberg, East Prussia, on the heels of the enemy and obtaining command of the town and fortress.

Special Cable to THE NEW YORK TIMES.

LONDON, Monday, Aug. 31.—A dispatch to the Exchange Telegraph Company from St. Petersburg says:

"It is announced officially that in Eastern Prussia the Russian troops have attacked the garrisons in the fortresses of Thorn and Graudenz with a large number of siege guns. The Russian offensive continues along the whole front.

"Fierce fighting on the Austrian front continues. The Austrian forces concentrated in Kielce are proceeding along the right bank of the Vistula, in order to take part in a battle to the east of Lemberg, where the Russians took 3,000 prisoners.

"Near to the town of Podgayzy (Podhayce?) the enemy lost 3,000 men, four cannon, and a large number of caissons. In the region to the north of Tomacher (Tomaszow?) 1,000 prisoners were taken. East of Tomacher the Fifteenth Hungarian Division was defeated and entire regiments surrendered. In other regions fierce fighting continues. In the direction of Lublin, where the enemy has concentrated his principal forces, a serious battle is taking place.

A dispatch to Reuter's Telegram Company from St. Petersburg gives the following official story:

"Fresh troops have appeared on the Prussian frontier and are taking the offensive in some places. The battle continues all along the Austrian frontier.

"To the south of Lublin (Southeast Russian Poland) the Russians have assumed the offensive and are marching through a district incumbered by the bodies of Austrian soldiers which the enemy had been unable to remove.

"Although some regiments already have been in action for more than a week, the combat is being carried on with unabated fury. The fighting near Tomacheff has been of a particularly stubborn character. The Russians have captured many caissons, guns, and quick-firers and one flag.

"Near Lemberg, Galicia, after heavy fighting, the Russians seized the line to Kamionka, Gliniany, Przemyslany, and Brzukovitze, all in Galicia."

The Observer's St. Petersburg correspondent wires:

"The German railways in East Prussia have been relaid on the Russian gauge and there is now through communication between St. Petersburg and Insterburg.

"A thousand Austrian prisoners have reached Kiev, and about 800 Germans have been brought to Moscow.

"Several captured batteries of field guns have been brought to Vilna, Kiev, and Moscow, while others, especially Maxims, have been turned over to regiments at the front for use against their former owners."

The Daily Chronicle's St. Petersburg correspondent, wiring yesterday, says:

"The only official news from the Russian front today is that the Russian advance is continuing and that the garrisons of Graudenz and Thorn are taking part in the fighting with heavy artillery.

"This probably means that the garrisons have come out to reinforce the Twentieth Army Corps that has been in retreat for some days past.

"The Grand Duke Nicholas, Commander in Chief, has issued an order announcing that members of the Volunteer Corps from Galicia, the so-called 'Falcons,' will be treated by Russian troops not as combatants but as francs-tireurs, more particularly in view of the fact that they use explosive bullets.

"A large number of German soldiers who have been taken prisoners are Poles. They declare that the Poles of Posen probably will go over in a body to the Russians as their deliverers.

Panic now reigns in Danzig, the population of which is fleeing to Berlin, according to a dispatch to The Daily Mail.

Special Cable to THE NEW YORK TIMES.

ST. PETERSBURG, Aug. 30, (Dispatch to The London Daily Mail.)—It is suspected that the Austrian Army in Galicia is still non-existent, it being scattered all over Bosnia, Slavonia, Bohemia, and the Servian and Italian frontiers suppressing riots and

Continued on Page 2.

BOMBARDS PARIS FROM AIR

German Lieutenant Drops Five Bombs, Wounds Two Women.

LEAVES MANIFESTOES, TOO

"German Army at the Gates; You Can Do Nothing but Surrender," They Read.

CITY PREPARING FOR SIEGE

Cattle Gathered and Storehouses Filled—People Sobered by Crisis, but Not Downcast.

Blowing Up Houses So Forts Can Fire

Special Cable to THE NEW YORK TIMES.

PARIS, Aug. 30, [Dispatch to London Daily Mail.]—Thousands of houses, shops, and factories are being blown up to clear the field of fire for the Paris forts. The sound is faint, because it is sixty or eighty miles distant. I hear it coming from the Valley of the Oise.

LONDON, Aug. 30.—A Paris dispatch to the Exchange Telegraph Company says:

"A German aviator flew over Paris this afternon and dropped five bombs, which fell in the most populous quarter of the city. In one case two women were wounded.

"One bomb fell in front of the shop of a baker and wine merchant at the corner of Rue Albouy and Rue des Vinaigriers; two fell on Quai de Valmy, one of which did not explode and the other struck the walls of the Night Refuge behind St. Martin's Hospital. Two others were dropped in the Rue des Callettes and Rue Marcin, neither of which exploded."

"The aviator, who signed himself Lieut. von Heidsen, dropped manifestoes on which was written:

"'The German Army is at the gates of Paris; you can do nothing but surrender.'"

The territory over which a German aeroplane flew yesterday afternoon, dropping bombs, is in the northeastern part of Paris, and scarcely a mile from the heart of the city. In the district are the big military hospital, the Hospital St. Louis, St. Lazare Prison for women, the Church of St. Laurent, which dates from the sixteenth century; the North Railway station, the magnificent Church of St. Vincent de Paul, the Lariboisière Hospital, one of the largest in Paris; several colleges and several theatres.

Count Johann Heinrich von Bernstorff, the German Ambassador to the United States said yesterday afternoon that he had received no confirmation from his home Government that a German aviator had flown over Paris and dropped bombs. He reiterated in this connection what he had previously said with regard to the Zeppelin raid over Antwerp, namely, that if Paris had been attacked from the air he was certain that the assault was directed against the fortifications, and not against the city in general.

Count von Bernstorff said he really could not countenance the idea that his countrymen would drop bombs on places occupied by women and children. Such an action, he added, would be against all the traditions of the German Army.

Aeroplanes Fail in Belfort Attack.

BASLE, Switzerland, Aug. 30, (via Paris.)—Two German aeroplanes made an unsuccessful attempt early today to destroy with bombs the dirigible balloon hangar at Belfort, France, which is 35 miles northwest of here.

PARIS POPULACE SOBERED.

Realizes a National Crisis, but Maintains Its Calmness.

Special Cable to THE NEW YORK TIMES.

PARIS, Aug. 30.—This day marks the realization, sudden but final, on the part of everybody, even down to the children, that the nation must fight for her existence and that the fate of her capital hangs in the balance.

The Temps thus solemnly states the situation, after the issuing of the official communiqué that the class of 1914 and all classes of the active reserves, even the oldest of the territorial army, are called to the colors:

"We are at the hour when every Frenchman, without distinction of state or age, must contribute in all possible measure, according to the efficacy of his individual or collective energies, to the defense of the country. No one is absolved from the obligation of this national duty. There is a place for every one in the battle engaged in for saving our country and safeguarding our civilization."

The Temps's military correspondent sums up the news from the front slightly more cheerfully. He says:

"We are passing through difficult moments, certainly, but nothing in the events is of a nature to discourage us."

An argument to offset alarmist reports was furnished me yesterday by an eminent military strategist, who carefully outlined, from the information contained in official communiqués, and also from knowledge derived through diplomatic channels, the exact status of the opposing armies. He argued that merely because the Allies were now back on the line from the River Somme to the Vosges, the likelihood of the speedy investment of Paris was a possibility quite as remote as though the original defensive line in Belgium had held, and the British troops forming the extreme left flank had not been steadily pushed back.

His reasons for saying so are that the French Army, now spread out in a convex curve, forms what strategists call "an interior line," behind which are uninterrupted railway lines for the quick transfer of troops. The Germans, on the other hand, are on the exterior line, which makes it necessary for them to spread their troops over a much greater space, with a hostile country behind them. The German right is thus furthest from its base of supplies.

One thing, however, which is clearly shown by the situation is that the Germans "got the jump" on the Allies by pounding through Belgium in force before the French early advance in Alsace had accomplished its object of bringing the German legions down from the north to act on the defensive. If the Allies do not succeed in this effort it is altogether likely that a great battle will occur to the north of Paris.

To say that the population was surprised by yesterday's announcement that the Allies' line is held from the River Somme to the Vosges is to put the situation mildly. As a matter of fact, the majority of Parisians at first misread the communiqué to mean the River Sambre, in Belgium, where the line originally formed. Careful official methods merely eliminated the recital of all happenings between the Sambre and the Somme. The similarity in name undoubtedly had much to do with quelling apprehension.

An official communiqué yesterday illustrated the situation. First it told of the deaths of six officers nine days ago, then confirmed the news that three German cruisers had been destroyed, which was issued in England the day before, and continued by announcing the Russian advance on Königsberg (now ancient history) and recounting how a German cyclist corps was completely routed. The War Office at the same time made a gift to the journalists of the fifteenth number of the newspaper for the Army Bulletin, which gave an exhaustive summary of the week's news, a story of how Paul Déroulède joined the army in 1870, and advice for curing blistered feet, as well as a proclamation concerning a victory, signed by all the members of the new Cabinet.

Parisians Keep Up Their Courage.

This also sums up the attitude of the populace; for, although every one's nerves are drawn as taut as a bowstring, the city is entirely calm. Even the passing of a German aeroplane overhead and the dropping of bombs failed to disturb the silent crowds sitting at the cafés or the throngs of soldiers standing at every corner discussing the situation.

The Bonnet Rouge, commenting on the aeroplane incident, says:

"Parisians, it is the salute of the barbarians to the city. Courage! Confidence! The salute will be returned."

L'Intransigeant is especially scornful. It predicts that the German advance will fall on account of starvation, pointing out the fact that all the live stock has been driven out of the invaded country, and that cattle are now browsing by thousands in the Paris parks or the plains to the southward.

The Temps speaks placidly but firmly concerning Turkish activity: "The Ottoman Government throws off the mask; it is getting ready to enter action against Greece, and, as one thing follows another, to take part in the European war in the German camp. Turkey forgets that Russia does not need all her millions in Germany. The traditional day-by-day politics of Turkey does not see tomorrow. This time her débacle will be definite."

Big American Rush Today.

There is every indication of a big American scramble tomorrow, when the boats via Havre and Dieppe resume their schedules for England. No large exodus of Parisians is likely to occur, as all the citizens view the future with equanimity and pin their faith on Gen. Gallieni and the army under him for the defense of the city.

Continued on Page 3.

ALLIES' FLANK PUSHED BACK

Paris Admits German Pressure Proved Too Severe.

ROAD TO PARIS STILL HELD

One German Corps Reported Wiped Out, Perhaps by Pau's Army Fresh from Alsace.

FIGHTING IS PERSISTENT

Republic's Forces on the Left Engaged--British After Heavy Losses Ready for Battle.

PARIS, Aug. 30, 11:30 P. M.—An official statement issued by the War Office tonight said:

"The passage of the German right wing has obliged us to yield ground on the left."

"The situation generally remains the same as this morning. After a lull, the battle has been resumed in the Vosges and Lorraine.

"On the Meuse at Sassaye, near Dun, a hostile regiment of infantry, endeavoring to cross the river, was almost annihilated."

Gen. Lacroix, former Commander in Chief of the army, takes a hopeful view of the situation, saying:

"The Germans continue their turning movement on the right. We have replied by assuming the offensive at Novion Porcien, and at Guise. The result is indecisive in the first direction, but our attack will be resumed.

According to La Liberté, the Germans have penetrated a short distance further on the River Somme.

The British, in conjunction with the French left, have resumed a vigorous offensive.

Further west the French troops are said to have checked the enemy's advance guard.

At the other extremity of the line on the Meuse the French are offering a strong and successful resistance, which extends along nearly the whole front.

La Liberté says:

"Our offensive succeeded on our right, but was checked on our left. The Germans gained ground toward La Fere, as announced. At any rate, we hold firm and even under attack—a sure sign of the confidence of our army."

Gen. Pau, recently commander of the Alsace invading force, but since recalled to aid the Allies in Northern France, was in Paris today for a brief visit to the Minister of War. He will return to the front very soon.

The Ministry of War announces that it has been decided to call out the class of 1914, which will give at least 200,000 additional troops, and also to call out the active reserve and the eldest classes of the territorial reserve.

Reports German Corps 'Wiped Out.'

Special Cable to THE NEW YORK TIMES.

LONDON, Monday, Aug. 31.—A Dieppe dispatch to The Daily Mail says:

"It is announced officially at the sub-prefecture at Dieppe that a German Army corps has been 'wiped out' by Gen. Pau's troops."

There is no confirmation of this at the official press bureau.

KITCHENER TELLS OF BATTLE.

British Losses 6,000, but Troops Have Been Reinforced.

Special Cable to THE NEW YORK TIMES

LONDON, Aug. 30.—Lord Kitchener issued the following statement tonight through the official press bureau:

"Although official dispatches from Sir John French on recent battles have not yet been received, it is possible now to state in general outline what the British share in the recent operations has been.

"There has, in effect, been a four days' battle, on the 23d, 24th, 25th, and 26th of August. During the whole of this period the British troops in conformity with the general movement of the French armies, were occupied in resisting and attacking the German advance and in withdrawing to new lines of defense.

"The battle began at Mons on Sunday. During this day and part of the night the German attack, which was stubbornly pressed and repeated, was completely checked on the British front.

"On Monday, the 24th, the Germans made a vigorous effort in superior numbers to prevent the safe withdrawal of the British Army and to drive it into the fortress at Maubeuge. This effort was frustrated by the steadiness and skill with which the British retirement was conducted, and, as on the previous day, very heavy losses, far in excess of anything suffered by us, were inflicted upon the enemy, who in dense formation and enormous masses marched forward again and yet again to storm the British lines.

"The British retirement proceeded on the 25th, (Tuesday,) with continuous fighting, though not on the scale of the previous two days, and by the night of the 25th the British Army occupied the line of Cambrai-Landrecies-Le Cateau.

"It had been intended to resume the retirement at daybreak on the 26th, (Wednesday,) but the Germans' attack, in which no less than five corps were engaged, was so close and fierce that it was not possible to carry out this intention until afternoon.

"The battle on this day was of a most severe and desperate character. The troops offered a superb and most stubborn resistance to tremendous odds, and at length extricated themselves in good order, though with serious losses. No guns were taken by the enemy except those the horses of which were all killed or which were shattered by high explosive shells.

British Losses 5,000 to 6,000.

"Sir John French estimates that during the whole of these operations from the 23d to the 26th, inclusive, his losses amount to 5,000 or 6,000 men.

"The losses suffered by the Germans are out of all proportion to those which we suffered. In Landrecies alone on the 26th, as an instance, a German infantry brigade advanced in the closest order into a narrow street, which they completely filled. Our machine guns were brought to bear on this target from the end of the town.

"The head of the column was swept away. A frightful panic ensued, and it is estimated that no less than 800 to 900 dead and wounded Germans were lying in this street alone.

"Another incident, which may be chosen from many like it, was a charge of a German Guard cavalry division upon the British Twelfth Infantry Brigade, when the German cavalrymen were thrown back, with great loss and in absolute disorder.

"These are notable examples of what has taken place over practically the whole front during these engagements, and the Germans have been made to pay an extreme price for every forward march they have made.

"Since the 26th, apart from cavalry fighting, the British Army has not been molested. It has rested and refitted after its exertions and glorious achievements.

Fresh Guns and Men Received.

"Reinforcements amounting to double the loss sustained have already joined, every gun has been replaced, and the army is now ready to take part in the next great encounter with undiminished strength and undaunted spirit.

"Today the news is again favorable. The British have not been engaged, but the French armies, acting vigorously on their right and left, have for the time being brought the German attack to a standstill.

"Sir John French also reports that on the 28th the Fifth British Cavalry Brigade, under Gen. Chetwode, fought a brilliant action with the German cavalry, in the course of which the Twelfth Lancers and the Royal Scots Greys routed the enemy and speared large numbers in flight.

"It must be remembered throughout that these operations in France, vast though they are, are only one wing of the whole field of battle.

"The strategic position of ourselves and our allies is such that, whereas a decisive victory to our arms in France would probably be fatal to the enemy, the continuance of resistance by the Anglo-French armies upon such a scale as to keep in the closest grip with the enemy's best troops can, if prolonged, lead only to one conclusion."

Summary of War News

Blowing up of the houses outside the Paris forts to permit a clear range for the defending forts has begun.

A German aeroplane flew over Paris yesterday and dropped several bombs, wounding two women.

The French War Office announces that the advance of the German right wing has caused the French left to yield ground again.

France has called out the 1914 reserves, the young men, and boys.

Lord Kitchener announces that the British losses were between 5,000 and 6,000 in four days of fighting, beginning a week ago yesterday, against superior numbers of Germans, on whom the British inflicted heavy losses. He adds that reinforcements amounting to double the losses sustained have already joined, every gun has been replaced, and the army is now ready to take part in the next great encounter with undiminished strength and undaunted spirit.

The Czar's forces have advanced in East Prussia to the German lines at the Vistula and are bombarding Thorn and Graudenz. As they advance the Russians are changing the railway lines to their gauge.

Russians and Austrians are in battle in Poland, where the Czar's troops are said to have won a big victory. Near Lemberg, in Austrian Galicia, they have also won, capturing many men and guns.

British losses in the naval battle in the North Sea, where the Germans were defeated, were 29 dead and 40 wounded.

Japanese troops have been landed at several points on the coast near Kiao-Chau.

Apia, Germany's capital city in the Samoan Islands, has surrendered to a British force from New Zealand.

Canada's expeditionary force has disembarked at Quebec, where it will await the arrival of a transport to convey it to the front.

German reports say that Turkey is preparing to enter the war against England and Russia.

VIVID NARRATIVE OF GREAT RETREAT

Immense Slaughter of Germans as the French Retire---Panic in Unprotected Northern France.

By PHILIP GIBBS.

NEW YORK TIMES-London Daily Chronicle War Service.

Special Cable to THE NEW YORK TIMES.

NEAR AMIENS, Aug. 30.—Looking back on all I have seen during the last few days, I find it difficult to piece together the various incidents and impressions and to make one picture. It all seems to me now like a jigsaw puzzle of suffering and fear and courage and death—a litter of odd, disconnected scraps of human agony and of some big grim scheme which, if one could only get the clue, would give a meaning, I suppose, to all these tears of women and children, to all these hurried movements of soldiers and people, to the death carts trailing back from unknown places, and to the great, dark fear that has enveloped all the tract of country in Northwest France through which I have been traveling, driven like one of its victims from place to place. Out of all this welter of individual suffering and from all the fog of mystery which has enshrouded them until now, when the truth may be told, certain big facts with a clear and simple issue will emerge and give one courage.

The French Army and our English troops are now holding good positions in a much stronger and closer line and stemming the tide of the German hordes rolling up to Paris. Gen. Pau, the hero of this war, after his swift return from the Eastern front, where he repaired the deadly check at Mülhausen, has dealt a smashing blow at a Geman Army corps which was striking to the heart of France.

Paris is still safe for the time being, with a great army of allied forces, French, English, and Belgians, drawn across the country as a barrier which surely wil not be broken by the enemy. Nothing that has happened gives cause for that despair which has taken hold of people whose fears have exaggerated the facts, frightful enough when taken separately, but not giving any proof that resistance is impossible against the amazing onslaught of the German legions.

I have been into the war zone and seen during the last five days men who are now holding the lines of defense. I have been among their dead and wounded, and have talked with soldiers marching fresh to the front. I have seen the horrid mess which is cleared up after the battle and the grim picture of retreat, but nothing that I have seen or heard from either British or French leads me to believe that our army has been smashed or the Allies demoralized.

British Held Line in Retreat.

It is impossible to estimate our own losses. Our wounded are being brought back into Havre and Rouen, and undoubtedly there are large numbers of them. But, putting them at the highest, it is clear to me, from all information gained during the last five days, that there has been no overwhelming disaster, and that in the terrible actions fought on the four days from the 23d to the 27th, and afterward in the further retirement from the line of Cambrai and Le Cateau, swinging southward and eastward upon St. Quentin, our main

"All the News That's Fit to Print."

The New York Times.

THE WEATHER

Fair, somewhat cooler today; fair tomorrow; moderate west winds.

☞For full weather report see Page 23.

VOL. LXIII...NO. 20,677. NEW YORK, FRIDAY, SEPTEMBER 4, 1914.—SIXTEEN PAGES. ONE CENT In Greater New York, Jersey City and Newark. { Elsewhere TWO CENTS.

GERMANS PRESS ON, FORTY MILES FROM PARIS; TAKE LA FERE AND AMIENS, ATTACK LAON NEXT; PARIS CALM IN FACE OF APPROACHING SIEGE

DELLA CHIESA ELECTED POPE; IS BENEDICT XV.

Sacred College, After Three Days' Conclave, Chooses the Archbishop of Bologna.

[illegible] CARDINALS TOO LATE

[illegible] and O'Connell Arrive in Rome Just After the Election.

POPE IS 60 YEARS OLD

Is of Noble Birth and Was Made a [illegible] Only Four [illegible] Ago.

[illegible] DIPLOMATIST

The Eur[illegible] War Believed to Have [illegible] the Card[illegible] Choice.

[illegible] GREAT THRONG

[illegible] St. Peter's and Is [illegible] that He is a [illegible] of America.

[illegible], Sept. 3.—The Sacred College of Cardinals today elected Cardinal [illegible] della Chiesa, Archbishop of Bologna, Supreme Pontiff to succeed the late Pope Pius X. His coronation as Benedict XV. will take place next Sunday.

Immediately after his election the Pontiff said he could not imagine how his frail being was capable of enduring the weight of enormous responsibility thrown upon his shoulders, especially at a moment when almost all the countries of [illegible] when the wounds inflicted upon humanity were also inflicted on the Church, and when countless victims of the war were being cut down.

The war, he said, had armed faithful against faithful, priest against priest, while the Bishops of each country offered prayers for the success of the armies of their own nations. But victory for one side meant slaughter to the other, the destruction of children equally dear to the heart of the Pontiff.

The Conclave of the Sacred College had been in session since the evening of last Monday, and the final vote was not taken until 11 o'clock this morning.

When the name of Cardinal della Chiesa was cried out by the Cardinals' scrutineers as having received the prescribed two-thirds vote there was much excitement among the members of the Conclave.

Then followed the traditional formula, the Cardinal being asked whether he accepted the election. Amid breathless silence he answered in the affirmative, but his reply, owing to his profound emotion, was scarcely audible. Immediately all the Cardinals, except della Chiesa, removed the canopies from above their stalls, this being the tangible sign that the leadership of the Church had passed from them to the newly elected Pope.

Mgr. Boggiani, Secretary of the Conclave, with the Master of Ceremonies, the Dean of the Cardinals, and other high church dignitaries, then bowed before the chair where Cardinal della Chiesa was seated.

Chooses Name of Benedict XV.

In answer to a question put by the Dean of the Cardinals, the new Pope said he desired to take the name of Benedict XV.

Mgr. Boggiani, assisted by the other officials, recorded the act of election and the acceptance. The Pontiff was then clothed in a flowing white robe, red slippers, and high stock with a broad red cravat. Cardinal della Volpe, the Chamberlain of the Holy See, placed over his shoulders a red stole embroidered with gold. The Pope then mounted the throne to receive the homage of the Cardinals.

The Cardinals first kissed the feet and then the hands of the Pontiff, who administered the accolade and pronounced the benediction. Cardinal della Volpe placed upon the Pontiff's finger the Fisherman's Ring, which the Pope returned to Mgr. Damico to have engraved with his name.

The Pontiff proceeded from the Sistine Chapel to the Basilica of St. Peter's, where he gave a benediction. He then returned to the Sistine Chapel, where a second act of homage by the Cardinals was accorded to him. The Cardinals surrounded him and addressed their greetings to him in Latin.

When the Pope was asked to present himself before the people for the first benediction he turned to Cardinal Merry del Val, the Papal Secretary of State, and said:

"I hope I shall have strength to overcome my emotion."

The News Outside the Conclave.

Prince Chigi-Albani, one of the Assistants to the Throne in the Pope's household, was notified at 11:15 A. M. that Cardinal della Chiesa had been elected Pope. Five minutes later Mgr. Misciatelli, Sub-Prefect of the Sacred Palaces and Governor of the Conclave, received a communication from the new Pope asking that the gratings of the Basilica of St. Peter be opened, because he purposed in a short time to issue his proclamation.

At the same hour the Master of Ceremonies

Continued on Page 2.

BRITISH CASUALTIES NOW TOTAL 10,399

Latest Report Adds 18 Officers and 62 Men Killed—78 Officers and 312 Men Wounded.

LONDON, Sept. 3.—The official press bureau has issued a further statement of British casualties as follows:

Killed, 18 officers and 62 other ranks.

Wounded, 78 officers and 312 other ranks.

Missing, 89 officers and 4,672 other ranks.

The official bureau explains that the missing mentioned in the list of casualties are men not accounted for and include unwounded prisoners and stragglers as well as men killed and wounded.

As regards the "other ranks" it is announced that 2,682 men are returned as having been sent back to their base as unfit, and that a large proportion of these should be included in the number shown as missing in this and the previous return from general headquarters.

In the report of casualties received tonight the names of the officers were given. Only their next of kin have been informed and the names will be published as soon as possible. No names of the men in the other ranks have yet been received, but several wounded already have been brought home.

With the list reported yesterday, this makes the total British casualties 10,399, divided as follows:

Killed, 98 officers and 189 men.
Wounded, 135 officers and 941 men.
Missing, 181 officers and 8,855 men.

GERMAN AIRMAN AIMS BOMB AT TRANSPORT

British Troops in Seine Have Narrow Escape—Missile Hit Their Tug.

Special Cable to THE NEW YORK TIMES.

LONDON, Sept. 3.—Dr. G. T. Stewart, ex-Superintendent of Bellevue Hospital in New York City, who has arrived here from Paris, reports that he learned at Rouen on Tuesday that a German aeroplane had dropped a bomb in the Seine there aimed at a transport bearing British troops.

The bomb missed the transport, but struck a tug towing the troopship, putting the tug out of commission.

DROPS BOMBS IN BELFORT.

German Aviator Said to Have Violated Swiss Neutrality by Flight.

BELFORT, France, Sept. 2—(Delayed.)—A German aeroplane last night dropped several bombs here. The missiles made much noise, but did no damage.

The aviator, to avoid the fire of the Belfort forts, made a detour over Swiss territory. Also, he came from the south, instead of direct from Alsace, and it is declared here that this act apparently constitutes a violation of the neutrality of Switzerland.

WIED QUITS ALBANIA IN FLIGHT TO ITALY

In New Bombardment of Durazzo by Insurgents Shells Fell Near Royal Palace.

DURAZZO, Albania, (by way of Paris,) Sept. 3.—Prince William of Wied quit his new kingdom this morning, taking passage for Venice on the Italian steamer Misurala.

ROME, Sept. 2.—News received from Durazzo, Albania, says that the insurgents have again bombarded the town. Two projectiles fell near the Royal Palace, which is still guarded by Italian sailors.

William of Wied, a member of one of the historic mediatised houses of Germany, whose wife, the Princess Sophie, came of an old Rumanian family, was selected by the powers of Europe to be the ruler of Albania when it was decided to make that country autonomous after the Balkan war had freed it from Turkish rule.

It was reported that he had serious misgivings when the offer was made to him, but on Feb. 9 of this year he accepted the newly created crown of Albania and made a round of ceremonious visits to the rulers of Great Britain, Austria, and Italy. On March 8 he arrived at Durazzo, which he made his capital, on a handsome steam yacht hired from the Borden Harrimans.

Ever since that date William of Wied has been in trouble. He found the Epirotes in rebellion and refused to lead an army against them on the ground that he could not trust the loyalty of his own followers.

Essad Pasha, the War Minister, and the strong man in Albania, who was suspected of wishing to make himself King, requested permission to lead the Albanians against the Epirotes, who in April invaded Albania, captured 250 Albanian Mohammedans at Hormova, crucified them in a church, and burned the church. His request was refused. On May 18 Essad Pasha resigned as Minister of War, and 5,000 of his supporters attacked the capital.

Foreign warships landed detachments, which marched to the relief of the new King. Essad Pasha was captured and deported to Naples. The rebellion, however, continued, and Prince William and his family fled from the city and took refuge on an Italian cruiser, but subsequently landed again at Durazzo. A few weeks ago his family left the country.

RUSSIAN ARMY NOW IN BELGIUM?

72,000 Troops Transported from Archangel via England, According to Report.

NEW COUP AGAINST AUSTRIA

Plan of Invasion by Way of the Danube Believed to be in Preparation.

SERVIA TO STRIKE AGAIN

Boys and Old Men Called Out to Reinforce Serbo - Montenegrin Forces for Advance of Conquest.

A Russian army of 72,000 men, transported from Archangel, the most northern part of Russia, was landed at Aberdeen, on the east coast of Scotland, on the night of Aug. 27, according to officers and passengers of the Cunard liner Mauretania, which reached New York yesterday.

From Aberdeen the troops, it is said, were conveyed on special trains to Harwich, Grimsby, and Dover, where transports were waiting to convey them to Ostend.

Every precaution was taken by the military authorities to keep the transportation of the foreign soldiers through England from becoming known, and the service on the East Coast railway lines was suspended during the seventeen hours the troop trains were on the journey.

It was believed that the Russians would be joined at Ostend by 2,000 British marines, who were waiting there to receive them, and that these combined forces would co-operate with the Belgian Army at Antwerp.

The journey from Archangel to Aberdeen occupied three days.

Transportation of troops from Archangel would be a relatively easy task at this time of the year, as the harbor usually is free of ice from July to September. A few weeks ago a party of American tourists blocked in Russia by the declaration of war chartered a steamer at Archangel and were taken to Bergen, Norway, whence they were able to reach England by ordinary steamer.

Naturally the greatest secrecy would be observed in transporting troops from Russia to aid the sorely pressed Allies in France. Nothing in all probability could be learned of such an expedition's progress through the Arctic Ocean and down to Scotland. This, it was pointed out, would be more feasible than carrying the troops direct through the North Sea to Belgium.

Moreover, the transports engaged in the work, spared the long trip down the North Sea, could return for further reinforcements from Russia's great store of soldiers while the first expedition was being rushed overland to the east and south coasts of England and conveyed across the Channel by the immense fleet of vessels assembled at the British ports for moving troops to the Continent.

RUSSIA AIDING SERVIA.

May Invade Austria with Servians by Way of the Danube.

LONDON, Friday, Sept. 4.—A dispatch to the Central News Bureau from Copenhagen says that a message received at Berlin reports the receipt of advices from Austrian Army headquarters stating that Russia is transporting ammunition continuously by way of the Danube to Servia. At the mouth of the Danube extensive measures are being taken preparatory to the dispatch of Russian troops to Servia.

The Petrograd (St. Petersburg) correspondent of The Morning Post wires:

"The Russian Commander in Chief on the Austrian front apparently plans to drive in strongly with one army from the east, starting from the Russian provinces adjoining Rumania, and in the meantime merely aims to restrain the Austrian advances into the Polish provinces, thus keeping Austria on the alert along the line of 200 to 300 miles."

A dispatch to The Star yesterday from Athens says:

"The Servians are sending as many troops as possible to reinforce those already at the River Drina. There is no truth in the report that the Austrians are withdrawing troops from the Servian frontier and sending them to meet the Russians. On the contrary, Austria is sending more men against Servia, to prevent the Servians entering Bosnia."

Special Cable to THE NEW YORK TIMES.

ROME, Sept. 3, (Dispatch to The London Standard.)—Dispatches received here from Belgrade say that throughout Servia and Montenegro boundless enthusiasm has been excited by the victories of the Servian and Montenegrin armies; so, if they are inactive, it is only because they are

Continued on Page 3.

PARIS KEEPS UP COURAGE

Accommodates Itself Calmly to Regulations of Gen. Gallieni.

MILITARY PASSES REQUIRED

None May Leave or Enter at Night Without Them—Several Gates Closed.

MANY DESERT THE CAPITAL

Some to Seek Refuge in the West, Others to Follow the Government to Bordeaux.

BORDEAUX, Sept. 3.—President Poincaré and the members of the French Cabinet, who arrived here last night and were greeted by immense and cheering crowds, have established headquarters for the Government.

President Poincaré has taken a residence in the Prefecture. The Ministry of War is located in one of the buildings of the University of Bordeaux. Offices for the other Ministries have been found in various public buildings.

Trains from Paris are arriving every half hour, bringing the members of the foreign embassies and legations and numerous functionaries of the State.

None of the newspapers had mentioned the decision of the Government to come here, and yet every one in the city appeared to know what was happening and the very hour at which the party from Paris might be expected.

The hotels, boarding houses, and private homes are overcrowded with the new arrivals, who, including officials of various grades, number probably 5,000.

Paris Calm as Deputies Depart.

PARIS, Sept. 3.—Two trains reserved for the Presidents and the members of the Senate and the Chamber of Deputies, left the city for Bordeaux this afternoon. Fifteen Judges of the Court of Cassation will also be transferred to the provisional capital of France.

Following the example of the American Ambassador, the Swiss Minister, M. Lardy, has decided to remain in Paris.

The city again today showed its remarkable adaptability to circumstances. Though all allusions to such a contingency had been strictly forbidden in the newspapers, that the seat of government would be transferred to Bordeaux was an open secret several days ago among journalists and public officials and in military circles. Among these persons the effect of the announcement had been largely discounted. The public, after its first surprise, is viewing the situation with composure, and tonight there seems to be a better feeling all around.

Military secrets are being so well guarded that all reference to them is largely speculation, but it is a reasonable supposition that Gen. Joffre prefers to accept a decisive battle against the Germans in front of the forts and the intrenched camp of Paris.

No Airship Attack.

Parisians were disappointed today; no German aeroplane flew over the city. Crowds gathered in the Place de la Concorde, the Place de la Bourse, the Place de l'Etoile, and the Quai de Quartières from 4 o'clock in the afternoon until 7 to watch for aeroplanes, but none came.

Several French machines patrolled the sky, ready to engage the enemy.

Many of the people of Paris have been astonished that the French aviators have not given chase to hostile machines flying over the city. It is explained, however, that only a plunging fire is effective against aeroplanes, and that over a city a machine gun attack causes risk to more lives from bullets that miss the mark than are endangered by bombs.

The plan now is for the French machines which are on patrol duty to pursue the German aviator into the open country and have the argument out there.

Temps Predicts Allies' Success.

The Temps this evening printed another article in which it predicted final success for the Allies. The newspaper's reasons for its optimism are contained in the following résumé of the situation:

Diminution of pressure by the enemy on the extreme left of the Allies' line, absolute inactivity in the centre, and the progress of the French troops in Lorraine and on the right bank of the canal which passes a few miles north of Lunéville, in the Department of Muerthe and Moselle.

These circumstances are taken by the Temps as evidence that the enemy has been hard hit and is suffering from losses in men and lack of supplies.

The Liberté quotes an English officer who arrived here this morning from Pierrefitte, twenty-eight miles southeast of Pau, as saying he was wounded in a fierce battle near Compiègne, in which the Germans were driven back several times with heavy losses. He said that the moment he was wounded by a shell the French and English offensive was successful over a front of several miles, the Germans retreating toward the left.

A large number of families left the city for the west today, taking with them household necessities. These refugees from the capital have been forced to make very long detours, since the railroads are incumbered with military trains. The railroad lines out of Paris to the north have virtually ceased running trains, owing to fears of possible raids by German cavalry.

Gallieni Issues a Proclamation.

Gen. Gallieni, commander of the army defending the city, today issued the following proclamation to the inhabitants of Paris:

"The members of the Government of the Republic have left Paris in order to give a new impetus to the defense of the nation. I have been ordered to defend Paris against the invader. This order I will fulfill to the end. "GALLIENI.

"Military Governor of Paris, Commanding the Army of Paris."

It was announced today that the Paris Bourse, which was closed yesterday, would remain closed indefinitely. The closing quotations will be regarded as official.

The Government will issue a proclamation tomorrow transferring the Bank of France from Paris to Bordeaux.

The Temps announces its intention to follow the Government to Bordeaux and issue the paper from that city.

Beginning tonight no persons may leave or enter Paris between 8 o'clock in the evening and 5 o'clock in the morning without a military pass. Automobiles may enter freely during the day, but may not leave without permits. Pedestrians are permitted to pass without challenge through certain gates, while other gates are closed. Gardeners bringing fresh vegetables to the city are admitted at half hour intervals during the night.

Walter Burley Griffin, the American artist, returned today from Nantes. He observed along a beautiful road from Paris to Orléans an almost unbroken procession of automobiles loaded with Parisians and their baggage. About every 150 yards was a disabled machine. He says that it appeared as though all the taxicabs in Paris were going southward.

Exodus from Paris Fills Tours.

TOURS, (via Paris,) Sept. 3.—Tours is crowded to overflowing with travelers bound for Bordeaux. All the hotels are full, and some of the landlords are asking as much as forty francs ($8) for a single room. Many automobilists are sleeping in their cars because of the lack of accommodations in the hotels.

An uninterrupted procession of conveyances of all kinds is passing through this city, and many Paris taxicabs, with cans of gasoline attached, are seen everywhere. In fact, the city is much more animated than Paris.

The military element is but little in evidence. Here and there some officers and soldiers are seen, but these generally have their arms in slings or show other evidences of having been wounded in the fighting in the north.

TO GUARD HUMAN INTERESTS.

One of Ambassador Herrick's Reasons for Staying in Paris.

PARIS, Sept. 3.—The American Ambassador, Myron T. Herrick, has decided to remain in Paris, and this course has been warmly commended by the Ministry of Foreign Affairs because the representative of the most powerful neutral Government will be able, should the occasion arise, to serve the French as well as his own people.

Mr. Herrick's reasons for remaining are, in substance, that he can better look after the several thousand Americans who stay in Paris. They are principally permanent residents in business or persons of moderate means unable to leave conveniently. He also feels that he can better protect American business interests, among them several American banks and banking agencies with deposits of Americans. These would have transferred their

Continued on Page 2.

FORTRESS OF ALLIES FALLS

La Fere Taken by Germans Saturday, Amiens the Next Day.

SOUTHWARD RUSH KEEPS ON

Huge Forces of Invaders Move Down the Oise Valley to Attack Laon and Rheims.

ALLIES GIVE UP COMPIEGNE

Whole Left Wing Swung Back Again Under Enemy's Assaults —Paris in Real Danger.

LONDON, Friday, Sept. 4.—Revelations of recent serious losses of positions by the left wing of the allied forces in Northern France are contained in belated dispatches reaching the London newspapers. These show the critical state of the campaign, with some of the invaders within forty miles of Paris.

The fortress of La Fere, part of the strong defensive line of the Allies, was captured by the Kaiser's force Saturday after a fierce combat.

Amiens, an important city to the northwest of La Frere, was abandoned without a fight on Sunday.

Germans were expected to occupy Compiegne, far to the south, as early as Tuesday.

The invaders are now reported to be moving in force upon Laon and Rheims, which are the last interior fortified positions held by the Allies outside of the Paris defenses.

An undated dispatch from France to The Times says:

"The Valley of the Somme has been abandoned. La Fere has been taken after a bloody combat. We were obliged to retire Saturday evening.

"The right wing of the Germans," says the correspondent, "is too far advanced, and there is a chance that it will be cut and caught between two fires if the British should be found in force.

"Our centre is resting well, and the right wing of our army appears to be taking the offensive."

A dispatch from Amiens to The Daily Mail, dated Tuesday, says that the Germans have taken possession of that city, after three days' fighting.

The success of the Germans at Moreuil made the capture of Amiens certain, says the correspondent, and the entry was not contested. He goes on:

"It was 7 o'clock Sunday evening when a party of Uhlans entered Amiens by the Rue Jules Barny. After a brief reconnoissance they retired to the German main body at Camon.

"A half hour later they returned, accompanied by an envoy bearing a white flag. The latter interviewed Mayor Figuet at the Town Hall. After an hour's discussion the Mayor appeared in front of the Town Hall with trumpeters and officially announced the surrender of the city. He urged that the citizens make no disturbance.

"Later the Mayor and the municipal councilors drove out in carriages to pay a formal visit to the German commander, who told them that they would be held personally responsible with their lives for the good conduct of the citizens.

"The Germans, thereupon, went to the Town Hall, where they hauled down the French flag and hoisted the German colors. The German troops began entering the city about midday Monday, singing as they came 'Die Wacht am Rhein' and 'Deutschland über Alles.'

"No time was wasted, however, as the orders were to move swiftly out on the high road to Paris. Only a few men were left to guard the city. The only casualties in connection with the German occupation were those of a chauffeur, who was shot at the city gates because he did not stop quickly enough at the order of the sentry and that of a local sausage maker, who got into a war of words with some troopers over the price of his wares.

"When the Germans entered Amiens the French retired to Picquigny, (eight miles northwest of Amiens,) blowing up both bridges over the Somme."

Germans Win, Attacking in Fog.

The Paris correspondent of The Mail sends this dispatch, which has been much delayed:

"I have just returned from Compiegne. The English have left the town. The bridges over the Oise were blown up this (Monday) morning. The Germans were expected here hourly.

"One important section of the battle, which drove back the Allies' left, was fought at Bapaume on Thursday and Friday. On Friday morning the Germans brought up many machine guns in a dense fog, and in a six hours' engagement the French suffered severely.

"A British force unexpectedly arrived and occupied the French position and allowed the weary French to retire. Then, though hard pressed, the British continued to fight a magnificent rear-guard action."

Summary of War News

Capture by the Germans on Saturday of La Fere, a fortress on the Allies' left wing in Northern France, and evacuation of the important city of Amiens, on Sunday, are announced in belated dispatches to London. The Anglo-French wing has now been driven back below Compiegne, and part of the German advanced forces are probably less than forty miles from the heart of Paris.

Bordeaux is now the official capital of France. President Poincaré and his Cabinet are installed in temporary administration quarters.

Paris is being deserted by many of the inhabitants, but the great bulk of the people are awaiting events with calmness.

A report comes from England that 72,000 Russian soldiers have been sent from Archangel through the White Sea and the Arctic, and down to Aberdeen, Scotland, thence by train to Dover and Harwich, and from there in British transports to Ostend, to join the army of the Allies.

Austrian Army headquarters has informed Berlin that Russia is transporting ammunition continuously to Servia by way of the Danube. News comes from St. Petersburg that the Russian Commander in Chief apparently plans to invade Austria with a new army operating by way of the Danube.

Servia and Montenegro are in a fever of martial enthusiasm. Boys and old men have been called out to swell the army for the conquest of Bosnia, Herzegovina and Dalmatia.

Japan has occupied seven islands near Kiao-Chau and is still landing troops within marching distance of the German fortifications, in the face of continued protests by China. The Japanese landing party is now estimated at 60,000, and 24,000 more are on their way.

The German Governor and his staff in Samoa have been made prisoners of war by the British and sent to the Fiji Islands.

Turkey will probably make her first declaration of war against Russia, and is said to be delaying the announcement in order to complete her military preparations.

LAON AND RHEIMS NEXT.

Germans Advancing Along Oise Valley to Attack Fortresses.

New York Times-London Daily Chronicle War Service.

Special Cable to THE NEW YORK TIMES.

ROUEN, Sept. 2.—I have just come from Paris, where I learned that there had been an engagement between Germans and Allies reaching even so far south as the Compiegne district, and that a strong party of Uhlans had been observed near Beauvais.

The Germans are advancing along the Oise Valley and are now making a determined effort to invest Laon and Rheims. Should these great fortresses fall, there will be nothing between them and the outer ring of forts around Paris except the retiring French Army, and it is just possible that there will be a battle within a few miles of greater Paris.

Paris itself was in an unusually jumpy state when I left it yesterday. The dropping of bombs from aeroplanes over the city, despite the powerful night searchlights and the vigilance of the aviation corps, stationed a few miles outside the city, exercised a tremendous effect on the impressionable Parisians. The railway stations are crowded with people, flocking to Brittany, the South of France, and Spain.

When I left St. Lazare station at 3 A. M. there were many travelers sleeping on the platforms so as to be in time to obtain seats in trains that left at 7 or 8 o'clock.

One of the many surprises of the war is the comparative failure of aircraft for offensive purposes. While several aeroplanes and at least one airship have been destroyed, not much damage has been done by bombs from the air.

A Belgian force with a number of machine guns drawn by the famous dogs marched out of town at midday yesterday.

As at Paris, there is a general rush to the south. Others are coming in from the coast. There have been several exciting scenes at the small station, and two or three times the platform barriers have been broken down. For every train there are twice as many passengers as seats.

WAR OFFICE NON COMMITTAL.

No Mention of La Fere in French Official Report.

PARIS, Sept. 3.—In an official statement issued today the War Office says:

"There has been no contact with the German forces in the region of Compiegne and Senlis since yesterday.

"Precautions have been taken to stop any offensive movement of the enemy.

"Measures have also been taken to provide for the pursuit of German aeroplanes, especially those of the armored type, which will be prevented from flying over Paris.

"The situation in the northeast is the same as yesterday."

GERMANS [illegible] WEDGES.

Mass Attacks [illegible] Irresistible, but Allies Contest Fiercely.

Special Cable to THE NEW YORK TIMES.

GOURNAY-EN-BRAY, France, Sept. 2, (Dispatch to The London Daily News.)—Roughly speaking, the Germans are massed wedge-shaped and the Allies contain them in lines running approximately northeast and northwest. I am not sure about the eastern line, but it appears to be sound and on the offensive.

As to the western line I could say a great deal from what I saw on my return journey from Paris today. The joys of a journey which one really wishes to finish in good time are lessened by the sight of cannon poking through the shrubberies and soldiers prone in the grass, very still and on the watch for something beyond you which appears to be quite close.

Let us see what seems to have happened since my dispatch from Amiens appeared last Monday. On that day the staff of the famous General commanding the extreme left wing of the [illegible] (censored by censor.) Down from the [illegible] the Germans seemed to be advancing in great force. On the other wing Gen. Pau had fine success near Guise, where he handled severely the Tenth Corps and the Imperial Guard in a fight running throughout Saturday and Sunday last. I was informed that he caught them and "smashed them into the Oise."

On Monday they were forced to retreat with heavy losses, but in the centre and left centre the [illegible] (the British were in this affair) were not so successful. The concentration of Germans was, no doubt, against these points. There was great fighting last Sunday.

Allies Remain Confident.

But, knowing this and more than all this, I am not very much alarmed any more than are the French and British officers and men I spoke to in my unpleasant journey close to the fighting line. They know that they are only at the beginning, that the French and British lines are [illegible], and that the men who have been working hard and skillfully to stem the awful German torrent are quite confident that success will ultimately be theirs.

Huge masses of obedient men the German commanders fling, regardless of loss of life, into the fierce and desperate effort to burst through quickly to Paris. Though such masses necessarily force back opposition, the opposition meets them resolutely, calmly, and with intelligence and military science.

When the history of this war is written it will be seen that fully as wonderful as was the German advance (the Germans are staking everything on immediate success) was the retirement of the allied forces.

It is hardly possible to understand how such masses of men and guns, (it is believed that nearly all the German Army is in France,) continually pushing along, should not overwhelm everything human, however well armed and skillfully handled, which stood before them. Well, it has not overwhelmed the Allies. It is perhaps incredible, but it is true.

It looks to me, from all the evidence I could gather, that if the Germans have the weight the Allies certainly have the ready aid and science. These, with the reinforcements of troops, will eventually win.

I arrived at this little railway junction today at noon, after a trip to Paris and back. Here I was told that on Monday French cavalry were seen on the hills to the south and southwest, and that fighting had been going on to the east, 10 kilometers away.

Found French Army Awaiting Foe.

From all I heard of the progress of the German advance up to Saturday I judged that it would be unwise to visit the little town. On the road I found as peaceful a countryside as though it had never heard of the war. A sight of the [illegible] cathedral, apart from the [illegible], was restful enough. There was [illegible] uncanny, [illegible] silent [illegible]

"All the News That's Fit to Print."

The New York Times.

THE WEATHER
Fair Sunday; Monday cloudy, probably late showers; fresh east winds.
For full weather report see Page 5, Sports Section.

VOL. LXIII...NO. 20,686. .... NEW YORK, SUNDAY, SEPTEMBER 13, 1914.—92 PAGES, In Seven Parts, Including Picture and Rotogravure Section, Real Estate Directory, and Review of Books. PRICE FIVE CENTS.

WHOLE GERMAN LINE RETIRES, HOTLY PURSUED; ALLIES WIN FIRST PHASE OF THE GREAT BATTLE; WILSON SOUNDS THE KAISER ON PEACE TERMS

RUSSIA STRIKES AGAIN IN GALICIA

Austrians Reported to Have Lost 130,000 Men in the Second Great Battle.

90,000 PRISONERS TAKEN

Two Austrian Army Corps Surrounded and Their Surrender Is Expected.

GERMAN ATTACK CHECKED

Importance of Retreat from East Prussia Denied in Petrograd—New Stand at Border.

LONDON, Sept. 12.—Another important Russian victory in Galicia is reported. A Central News dispatch from Rome says:

"A telegram received here by The Messaggero from Petrograd states that the second battle in Gaiicia resulted even more satisfactorily to the Russians than the first. The losses of the Austrians are estimated at 130,000, of whom 90,000 are prisoners."

New York Times-London Chronicle Special Cable Dispatch.
Special Cable to The New York Times.

PETROGRAD, Sept. 12.—Two Austrian armies are surrounded and 60,000 prisoners have been taken, including 500 officers, from another. Surrender of both armies is impending.

The Germans are again moving troops from east to west.

ROME, (via Paris,) Sept. 12.—News from the Austrian frontier says that the Austrian army in Galicia is demoralized and that the efforts of the officers to restore confidence are in vain. It is added that the Austrian soldiers are in a panic and are fleeing for safety.

PARIS, Sept. 12.—A dispatch to the Havas Agency from Petrograd says it is officially announced that Russian troops, in pursuit of retreating Austrians, are approaching the River San.

Another dispatch from the same source says:

"Russian successes are reported everywhere in the theatre of operations. Notwithstanding the brilliant efforts of the Hungarian cavalry and the ability of the Austrians to entrench themselves in a clever manner, the Russians have completely crushed the bulk of the opposing armies and are occupying more territory every day.

"The Russian artillery was so effective at the bombardment of Nikolaieff, south of Lemberg, that the Austrian guns were silenced the first day, whereupon the Austrians began their evacuation without awaiting an assault. Russian airmen signaled the Austrian retreat, and the Russian artillery and cavalry gallantly dashed around, cutting them off and inflicting enormous losses."

Germans Too Late.

Another Havas Agency dispatch from Petrograd says that the Austrian left wing near Tomaszow was surrounded in a triangle formed by the Vistula River and a tributary of the San. The wing was crushed before the arrival of the Germans, who came by forced marches to the aid of the Austrians. Poor and inadequate bridges delayed the Germans and made the defeat of their allies inevitable.

The Russians followed up this victory by pursuing the retreating Austrians twenty miles and taking up positions in the fortified localities of Opole and Tourobine. The Russians suffered heavy casualties in taking Tomaszow.

The Germans lost heavily when they were repulsed in the vicinity of Myschinez and Chorzele in Russian Poland, (Province of Plock,) on the frontier of Prussia.

PETROGRAD, (via London,) Sept. 12.—The Warsaw correspondent of Novoe Vremya gives an account of the fighting beyond Lublin, Russian Poland. His dispatch follows:

"The Russians were compelled to take several lines of fortifications step by step, ejecting the Austrians from the trenches. I rode along twenty miles of abandoned trenches, and saw many guns and much equipment which had been thrown away by the Austrians. Taking up a position near our artillery, I watched the progress of the fight.

Surrender in Retreat.

"The enemy was deluged with a hail of shrapnel, alternating with gunfire, and his line of retreat was marked by burning and deserted villages. Along the roads in the direction of Lublin were marching Austrian prisoners, who were surrendering in companies and battalions.

"For six hours I watched the battle. The artillery fire was maintained in the distance above a wood, shrapnel bursting and white clouds rising over the horizon. Suddenly from the wood appeared a black mass, which, on growing clearer, was seen to be an Austrian battalion, which fled out and surrendered. At night the thunder

Continued on Page 3.

Summary of War News.

British and French official reports declare that after six days of fighting the whole front of the German Army as far east as Verdun and Nancy is in retreat, abandoning guns and stores in large quantities.

The British report the capture of 6,000 prisoners and 15 guns, while the French are credited with the capture of 160 guns.

Berlin reports to the German Embassy in Washington contain no news of the battle in France.

Washington discloses that the Kaiser has had under consideration for several days an informal inquiry by President Wilson as to whether he is willing to discuss terms of peace, and England and France, through our Ambassadors, have also been approached. The inquiry followed a meeting here between James Speyer, Oscar Straus, and Count von Bernstorff, the German Ambassador.

The Belgians have defeated a German force at Cortenberg, between Louvain and Brussels, according to a news dispatch from Antwerp. A German Army corps was completely cut up and the Belgians took many prisoners. The Belgians now assert that the German Army in Belgium has been cut in two.

The Russians have defeated the Austrians in a second great battle in Galicia, according to news dispatches from Petrograd. Austria's loss is 130,000 men in killed, wounded, and prisoners. Other advices from the Russian capital state that the German advance in East Prussia has been checked.

The British Admiralty announces that the British Pacific Fleet has occupied Herbertshöhe, the seat of the Government of the German Bismarck Archipelago and the Solomon Islands. The Germans surrendered unconditionally.

The Italian Government has again been approached by representatives of Germany and Austria, who have urged the Italians to abandon their neutrality. The action taken by Italy, these representatives urged, would decide the war one way or the other.

GERMAN LOSSES PUT NOW AT 19,168

Ratio of Dead Extremely High—Time Which the List Covers Is Not Made Public.

ROTTERDAM, (via London,) Sept. 13, 5:40 A. M.—A dispatch from Berlin says that the total losses sustained by the Germans, including the twenty-first casualty list, which has just been published, are given as 6,535 dead, 8,391 seriously wounded, and 4,242 slightly wounded.

The number of officers killed and wounded was extremely high. The ratio of wounded to the dead was about two to one, which is also extreme. The usual rate is five to one.

It is not known to what date the list extends.

CONSTANCE, (via Paris,) Sept. 13, 1:48 A. M.—The headquarters of the 114th German Infantry are in mourning, as practically the entire regiment has been destroyed. Many pitiful scenes are enacted when the women come to examine the posted list of the dead.

The war loan is causing anxiety to German financiers, as it will force the hands of the bankers, while the attitude of the people is somewhat uncertain, in view of the imminent disastrous retreat of the German Army in France.

GERMAN REPORT TELLS OF 218,410 PRISONERS

Amsterdam Hears Amazing Figures as to the Capture of Allies and Belgians.

New York Times-London Daily Chronicle War Service.
Special Cable to The New York Times.

AMSTERDAM, Sept. 12.—An official Berlin message claims that the prisoners of war in Germany number:

British, 160 officers, 7,350 men.
French, 1,630 officers, 86,000 men.
Russian, 1,830 officers, 91,000 men.
Belgian, 440 officers, 30,000 men.

This is a total of 218,410.

The captives include two commanding Generals of the French Army, two commanding and thirteen other Generals of lesser rank of the Russian Army, and the Belgian commandant at Liége.

A Prague newspaper says that Servian women and children are helping fight the Austrians. A twelve-year-old girl who is lying wounded in the Neusatz hospital boasts of throwing sixteen hand grenades at her country's enemies.

FRENCH AVIATORS KILL GERMAN BOMB-HURLERS

Pursue the Enemy's Aeroplane Fifteen Miles and Bring It to the Ground.

PARIS, Sept. 12.—News has just been received here of an aerial battle near Troyes. A German aeroplane threw several bombs into the city, and a French machine arose and gave chase. After a pursuit of fifteen miles the French aeroplane overtook the German aircraft near Piney, where an engagement ensued.

The French machine soon secured the advantage in position. Immediately afterward the German aeroplane was precipitated to earth, and the two officers on board were killed.

BELGIANS DIVIDE GERMAN FORCES

Victory at Cortenberg Cuts Off Army Operating Against Antwerp.

THREE PROVINCES CLEARED

No Germans Now in Antwerp, Limburg, or Flanders—Their Losses Heavy.

GERMAN RELIEF FORCE HELD

Sortie from Antwerp Kept One Army Corps from Reinforcing von Kluck.

New York Times-London Daily Chronicle War Service.
Special Cable to The New York Times.

OSTEND, Sept. 12.—The Provinces of Antwerp, Limburg, and Flanders have been entirely cleared of Germans. There is a strong offensive movement in the direction of the south by the Belgian forces that have been guarding Antwerp.

The Flandre Libérale of Ghent issues the following statement:

"We learn from excellent sources that the German army which intended to attack Antwerp has been cut off between Brussels and Louvain by the Belgian army."

Special Cable to The New York Times.

LONDON, Sept. 12.—An Antwerp dispatch to The Observer says:

"The offensive action by the Belgian Army against the German observation army near Antwerp still continues with great dash and success. The action is becoming far more extended. The Belgian heavy six-inch field guns are doing effective work. It was fortunate that the Government Committee, just before the outbreak of the war, had decided in favor of this French type of weapon. Under its fire the German troops of the Landsturm and the Austrian forces become demoralized.

"The invaders are slowly retiring in the direction of Brussels. Belgian advance guards on protected motor cars with quick-firers have already reached the gates of Louvain, scattering bands of Uhlans on the way."

LONDON, Sept. 12.—The Belgian Legation announced today that the Belgian Army had again taken the offensive, which was being pushed satisfactorily. An extended sortie was made from Antwerp on Sept. 10, and the Germans everywhere were forced to retire. Malines and Aerschot were retaken.

At the legation it was also said that Belgians had destroyed the railway between Louvain and Tirlemont, thus cutting off the German communications between Brussels and Liège.

The Antwerp correspondent of the Exchange Telegraph Company in a dispatch dated Saturday says:

"Fierce fighting continued today southeast of Antwerp. To the left our division was obliged to give way before the enemy's offensive. In the centre and on the right wing we made good progress. The battle will be resumed tomorrow, when it is hoped that the Belgians will recover the ground which was lost on the left wing."

An Ostend dispatch to the Exchange Telegraph Company says:

"The Belgian troops have just gained an important success at Cortenberg, between Louvain and Brussels, cutting up a German corps and taking a number of prisoners. The line toward Liège has been occupied by the Belgians.

"The Belgian victory at Cortenberg is very important, as the Germany army occupying Belgium has been cut into two sections as a result of it. The victory was due in great part to artillery of heavy calibre, which was used for the first time there."

A German force of about 10,000 men spent Friday night in the neighborhood of Desselghem and Waereghem, between Ghent and Courtrai, according to a Reuter dispatch from Ostend. About 8 o'clock Saturday morning they set out to march in a southwesterly direction, sending out numerous patrols in every direction. A force of 400 Uhlans proceeded toward Dixmude and Furnes and toward the French frontier.

A dispatch to the Central News from Amsterdam says:

"According to a Ghent dispatch, the Belgian Government, having opposed the delivery of the army necessaries requisitioned by the Germans, a Belgian force has again occupied Ghent. The necessaries, which had already been prepared, were not delivered."

The Antwerp correspondent of the Daily Telegraph sends the following:

"A courier brings news of fighting at Hofstade, near Malines. King Albert motored out and participated in the general engagement, which is apparently going well.

"The German artillery figured considerably, but the Belgian infantry, well supported by guns, gradually forced the Germans back."

New York Times-London Daily Chronicle War Service.
Special Cable to The New York Times.

AMSTERDAM, Sept. 12.—The Belgian troops, which have moved out of Antwerp, have resumed the offensive with brilliant success, so that today the Provinces of Antwerp and Limburg are entirely, and East Flanders almost entirely, cleared of Germans. This has not been effected without heavy fighting.

Continued on Page 4.

PEACE MOVE BY PRESIDENT

Emperor Perhaps Ready to Discuss Terms, Wilson Learns--Allies Sounded.

NO MAKESHIFT FOR BRITAIN

Terms Must Be Such as to End Permanently Menace of War in Europe, Says Grey.

INVADERS MUST WITHDRAW

Is France's Stipulation—Allies Unite in Demanding Compensation for Belgium.

WASHINGTON, Sept. 12.—Emperor William has had under consideration for several days, it was learned tonight, an informal inquiry from the United States Government as to whether Germany desires to discuss terms of peace with her foes. Up to a late hour no reply had come. On its tenor when it does arrive depends to some extent whether the informal peace movement, inaugurated a week ago tonight, can be pursued further with Great Britain, France, and Russia.

The inquiry was not a formal one, such as President Wilson's original tender of good offices, but an effort of an official character to determine whether Germany's reported willingness to talk peace was based on fact.

The chronology of the peace movement was revealed tonight after a canvass of officials, diplomatists, and others directly concerned. The story of the seven days of peace talk, as told by some of the principals, is substantially as follows:

Saturday, Sept. 5.—Count von Bernstorff, the German Ambassador, dined with James Speyer, the banker, at the latter's residence in New York. Oscar S. Straus, American member of The Hague Tribunal and former Cabinet officer, was present. During the evening, as the conversation turned to the subject of peace in Europe, the German Ambassador said that, while he had no advices from his Government since leaving Berlin, he recalled a conversation with the Imperial Chancellor there in which the latter said he believed the Emperor would be willing to discuss measures of peace through mediation. Previous to the Ambassador's conversation with the Chancellor, Emperor William had acknowledged President Wilson's tender of good offices, but had been noncommittal as to its acceptance.

Mr. Straus immediately asked the German Ambassador for permission to repeat the conversation to Secretary Bryan at Washington. Count von Bernstorff gave his consent.

Negotiations Through Gerard.

Sunday, Sept. 6.—Mr. Straus arrived in Washington and went to the home of Secretary Bryan, where they secretly conferred. The Secretary communicated later with President Wilson. It was decided to get the German Ambassador's consent to report the incident to Ambassador Gerard for discussion with the German Foreign Office. In the meantime Mr. Straus was advised to talk the situation over with the British and French Ambassadors here. He saw each of these Ambassadors that day.

Monday, Sept. 7.—The German Ambassador reached Washington and conferred privately with Mr. Bryan. As a result of the conference the Secretary cabled Ambassador Gerard to convey to Emperor William an inquiry from the American Government as to whether he desired to confirm the statement reported to have been made by him to the Imperial Chancellor and repeated by the Chancellor to Count von Bernstorff in private conversation. Copies of the message to Ambassador Gerard were sent by Secretary Bryan to Ambassador Page at London and Ambassador Herrick at Paris.

Meanwhile Mr. Straus had talked with the British and French Ambassadors, both of whom said they could make no definite statement without instructions, as they had heard nothing from their Governments on the subject of peace. They were acquainted by Mr. Straus with what had occurred at the dinner in New York. Both the French and British Ambassadors reported the incident unofficially to their respective Foreign Offices.

Tuesday, Sept. 8.—Secretary Bryan told the British Ambassador, Sir Cecil Spring-Rice, what had occurred in detail and learned that the Ambassador had made inquiries of his Government to learn its attitude toward peace.

Wednesday, Sept. 9.—Sir Edward Grey discussed with Ambassador Page the inquiry which the latter had received from Secretary Bryan. On the same day Sir Edward Grey cabled the British Ambassador that, as Great Britain, France, and Russia had in the preceding week agreed not to make peace without common consent, the position of the Triple Entente was unanimous on the question of terms. Sir Edward said that what the powers wanted was no temporary truce, but a permanent peace in Europe, so that the world could be insured against the sudden outbreak of war after Germany had recouped herself.

The British Foreign Secretary, moreover, declared that England from the first had tried to avoid war and wanted peace, but that before the subject could be considered seriously definite terms would have to be submitted. Great Britain, Sir Edward pointed out, would insist that Belgium be fully compensated by Germany for her losses. This information was communicated to Secretary Bryan by the British Ambassador.

Must Drive Invaders Out First.

Thursday, Sept. 10.—The French Ambassador called on Secretary Bryan, and, it is understood, discussed the point of view of France. Ambassador Herrick coincidentally reported the earnest wish of France that there might be peace, but pointed out that until the French had driven the invaders from their territory and Belgium had been compensated terms of peace could not be negotiated.

During the afternoon Ambassador Page's report of his conversation with Sir Edward Grey also reached the White House. Great Britain, according to Ambassador Page, was determined to make no peace until German militarism had been crushed, because of its danger to the world's civilization. On the same day came personal messages from Emperor William and President Poincaré of France concerning the use of dumdum bullets.

Friday, Sept. 11.—President Wilson and Secretary Byran conferred on the situation and, it is understood, determined to await the reply of the German Emperor to the inquiry sent on the previous Monday before acknowledging the two personal messages from Emperor William and President Poincaré. Should the Emperor's reply be a favorable one, the President may take advantage of the messages addressed to him to express a hope that the atrocities complained of may be ended through the making of peace.

Among diplomatists friendly to the Allies the view was expressed tonight that, while the efforts to make peace seemingly had failed, a sudden turn of events might at any moment change the situation. It was pointed out that if the retreat of the German Army continued, so that it was forced to the border of France, and that if Austria's reverses were prolonged, President Wilson's personal influence in Great Britain and France might be brought to bear to obtain a definite statement of peace terms.

These same diplomatists said that one version of Emperor William's views on peace that had reached them was that he had declared at the outbreak of the war that he would be ready to make peace within a month. This view, it was said, he held because of his confidence in the ability of his army to take Paris in that period. To German bankers, too, it was said by these same diplomatists, this assurance had been given, and they had approved the entry of Germany into the war because they believed the country's finances could be handled through a moratorium of a month's duration. It would not be surprising, it was suggested, if further efforts to make peace were stimulated by German bankers.

SPAIN AS A MEDIATOR.

Buenos Aires Paper Says King Has Offered His Services.

Special Cable to The New York Times.

BUENOS AIRES, Sept. 12.—The newspaper La Nacion announces that it has heard from reliable sources that the King of Spain has offered the services of his Government on behalf of mediation of the war in Europe.

THE PLACID ACADEMICIANS.

Preparing New Dictionary, They Reach "Exodus" at Right Moment.

LONDON, Sept. 13, 2:35 A. M.—A Paris dispatch to the Reuter's Telegram Company says that undisturbed by the turmoil of war, the French Academicians continue their labors on the dictionaries.

A few days ago they were discussing, appropriately, the word "Exode."

REPORT KAISER'S SONS DEAD

Crown Prince and Two Next in Line Killed, Belgians Hear.

Special Cable to The New York Times.

ANTWERP, Sept. 12 (Dispatch to The London Observer.)—News has reached the authorities that the Kaiser's second son, Prince Eitel Friedrich, has been killed in action and although the message is not yet officially confirmed, there is reason to believe it is true.

The fifth son, Prince Joachim, who was injured earlier in the week, is reported to be in a grave condition.

LONDON, Sunday, Sept. 13.—An Ostend dispatch to the Reuter Telegram Company says:

"Crown Prince Frederick William and Prince Adelbert of Prussia, the Emperor's third son, and Prince Carl of Württemberg are reported to have died in a hospital at Brussels."

Prince Adelbert, the Kaiser's third son, is a Lieutenant in the German Navy and was last reported assigned to the Köln. Many reports have been circulated that the Crown Prince had been wounded, but all these were denied later.

GERMANS RETIRE IN HASTE

Collapse of Their Right Wing Affects Line to Verdun and Nancy.

LOSE MANY MEN AND GUNS

Big Stores of German Ammunition Also Fall Into Hands of Pursuing Allies.

LUNEVILLE IS RECAPTURED

London Sees in Growing Success Proof of Fatal Error by Kaiser's Strategists.

PARIS, Sept. 12, 11:30 P. M.—An official statement issued tonight says:

"Notwithstanding the fatigues occasioned by five days of incessant fighting, our troops are vigorously pursuing the enemy, which is in general retreat.

"This retreat appears to have been more rapid than the advance. This has been so precipitate at certain points that our troops have gathered up at the general quarters, notably at Montmirail, charts, documents, and personal papers abandoned by the enemy, and also packages of letters which had been received or were ready to be forwarded.

"In the district of Fromentieres the enemy abandoned several batteries of mortars and a number of caissons of ammunition.

A later bulletin said:

"First—On our left wing the general retreat of the Germans continues before the French and British forces, who have reached the lower courses of the Aisne.

"Second—Likewise in the centre the German armies are retreating. We have crossed the Marne between Epernay and Vitry-le-François. On our right wing the enemy has in like manner begun today a retiring movement, abandoning the region around Nancy. We have reoccupied Lunéville."

An official bulletin, given out in the afternoon, said:

"On our left wing the Germans have begun a general retreating movement between the Oise and the Marne. Yesterday their front lay between Soissons, Braine, and Fismes and the mountain of Rheims.

"Their cavalry seems to be exhausted. The Anglo-French forces, which pursued them, encountered on Sept. 11 only feeble resistance.

"At the centre on our right wing the Germans have evacuated Vitry-le-François, where they had fortified themselves, and also the valley of the Saulx River. Attacked at Sermaize and at Revigny, they abandoned a large quantity of war material.

"The German forces which have been occupying the Argonne region have begun to give way. They are retreating to the north through the Forest of Bellenon.

"In Lorraine we have made slight progress. We occupy the eastern boundary of the Forest of Champenoux, Rehainvillers, and Gerbenviller.

"The Germans have evacuated St. Die.

"In Belgium the Belgian Army is acting vigorously against the German troops, who are before the fortifications of Antwerp.

"In the Servian field of operations, the Servians have occupied Semlin, Austria."

LONDON, Sunday, Sept. 13.—A Reuter dispatch from Paris says that the French occupied Soisons, Department of Alsace, at 6 o'clock last evening.

ALLIES IN ACTIVE PURSUIT.

Four Days of Successful Advance Described by British War Office

LONDON, Sept. 12, 11:25 P. M.—The official Press Bureau gave out this statement today:

"A summary, necessarily incomplete, may be attempted of the operations of the British expeditionary force and the French Army during the last four days:

"On Sept. 6 the southward advance of the German right reached the extreme point at Coulommiers and Provins, cavalry patrols having penetrated even as far south as Nogent-sur-Seine.

"This movement was covered by a large flanking force, west of the line of the River Ourcq, watching the outer Paris defenses and any allied force that came from them.

"The southward movement of the enemy left his right wing in a dangerous position, as he had evacuated the Creil-Senlis-Compiègne region through which his advance had been pushed.

"The Allies attacked this exposed wing, both in front and on the flank. On Sept. 8 the covering force was assailed by a French Army, based upon the Paris defenses, and brought to action on the line between Nanteuil-le-Haudouin and Meaux.

"The main portion of the enemy's right wing was attacked frontally by the British Army, which had been transferred from the north to the east of Paris, and by a French corps, advancing alongside it on a line between Crécy, Coulommiers, and Sezanne.

"The combined operations have up to the present been completely successful. The German outer flank was forced back as far as the line of the Ourcq River. There it made a strong defense and executed several vigorous counter-attacks, but was unable to beat off the pressure of the French advance.

"The main body of the enemy's right wing vainly endeavored to defend the line of the Grand Morin River, and then that of the Petit Morin. Pressed back over both of these rivers and threatened on its right, owing to the defeat of the covering force by the allied left, the German right wing retreated over the Marne on Sept. 10.

"The British Army, with a portion of the French forces on its left, crossed this river below Chateau Thierry—a movement which obliged the enemy's forces west of the Ourcq, already assailed by the French corps forming the extreme left of the Allies, to give way and retreat northeastward in the direction of Soissons.

"Since Sept. 10 the whole of the German right wing has fallen back in considerable disorder, closely followed by the French and British troops.

"Six thousand prisoners and fifteen guns were captured on the 10th and 11th, and the enemy is reported to be continuing his retirement rapidly over the Aisne, evacuating the Soissons region.

British Cavalry at Fismes.

"The British cavalry is reported today to be at Fismes, not far from Rheims.

"While the German right wing has thus been driven back and thrown into disorder, the French armies further to the east have been strongly engaged with the German centre, which had been pushed forward as far as Vitry-le-François.

"Between Sept. 8 and 10 our Allies were unable to make much impression west of Vitry. On the 11th, however, this portion of the German Army began to give way, and, under the impulse of the French troops, eventually abandoned Vitry-le-François, where the enemy's line of battle was forming a salient.

"Between the upper Marne and the Meuse the French troops are following up the enemy and driving a portion of his forces northward toward the Argonne Forest country.

"The Third French Army reports today that it has captured the entire artillery of a hostile army corps—a capture which probably represents about 160 guns.

"The enemy, thus in retreat along the whole line west of the Meuse, has suffered gravely in morale, besides encountering heavy losses in personnel and material."

The Press Bureau gave out this statement in the afternoon:

"Our troops have crossed the River Ourcq and are moving this morning in rapid pursuit of the enemy.

"Two hundred prisoners were captured. The cavalry of the Allies were between Soissons and Fusine last night.

"The enemy are retreating north of Vitry-le-François.

"The Third French Army has captured all the artillery of one German Army Corps.

"Our aeroplanes report that the enemy's retreat is very rapid."

GERMAN AMMUNITION TAKEN.

Capture of 150 Bargeloads May Explain Right Wing's Retreat.

PARIS, Sept. 12.—One hundred and fifty canal barges loaded with ammunition, which had been hidden under a covering of coal, have been captured by the French in the River Oise. This may explain the German shortage of ammunition in some parts of the fighting line, although the military critics refuse to believe that a fighting machine such as the German Army, with an open country at its back, while advancing, could be allowed to run short as a whole.

The military writers, especially the critic of the Journal des Débats, although appreciating fully the German reverse along the line from Paris to Verdun and applauding the splendid feat of arms of the French and British troops, caution the public against a too rapid assumption that the invaders are beating a disorderly retreat.

It is pointed out that a great army such as the Germans pushed into France still possesses considerable power of resistance to pursuers, even after such a reverse, and that owing to its enormous numbers, it may assume a counter-offensive at any moment.

Special Cable to The New York Times.

PARIS, Sept. 12, (Dispatch to The London Daily News.)—Evidence accumulates on every side that the Germans on the Marne during the last few days have been very short of ammunition. At the close of a hot engagement two Germans who were taken prisoners confessed that they had not been able to fire a shot for hours, and that all the men in their regiment were in the same predicament for two days. They said strict orders had been given to all the men in that army corps to be very careful of their ammunition.

Meagre German Report of Battle in France; No Definite News, But Its Severity Admitted

BERLIN, (via Copenhagen and London,) Sept. 13, 2:41 A. M.—The evening papers, although without definite news from France, print with the permission of the censor articles indicating that the fighting near Paris has been severe. They say that the battle is of an indecisive nature and may last for some time before it is finally decided. It is added that the battle line probably stretches from Nanteuil, northeast of Paris, over Meaux and Sezanne to Vitry-le-Francois. The British Army is opposing Gen. von Kluck and the French are attacking an extended front from Coulommiers to Vitry. Part of the troops are veterans, the others are fresh troops.

The Lokal Anzeiger says: "Our troops, now battling for the fruits of former victories, will risk everything to inflict a destructive defeat on the Allies in an open battle."

The Tageblatt says: "The victory is not likely to rest with one side immediately. Before victory can come to either side the fortunes of war will frequently change, and defeats must be expected."

The newspapers warn the people against placing credence in foreign reports. The Tageblatt prominently displays an apparently inspired denial of foreign reports in regard to the German situation near Paris. Various rumors concerning the fate of Verdun are in circulation, but there is no trustworthy information.

THREATEN TO SPLIT WHOLE GERMAN FORCE

Allies Pursue Two of Kaiser's Armies One Way, Two Another—They Fail to Form Junction.

Special Cable to The New York Times.

PARIS, Sept. 12.—The Eclair's comment on the military situation gives a clear idea of the results already achieved in the campaign. It says:

"Gen. Joffre has been successful in one of the hardest problems in military science, a change from a prolonged defensive to the offensive.

"He was forced to meet the attack of five German armies, totalling nearly a million men, advancing south in parallel columns.

"The result of the struggle to date shows that two of these armies, commanded, respectively, by Gen. von Kluck and Gen. von Bülow, are retreating hastily toward Soissons and Compiègne, while the third, the Saxon, with the fourth, under the Grand Duke of Württemberg, have been hurled violently away from the two former, with which they tried to establish contact by means of the Prussian Guard. They are now retreating northeast, in almost the opposite direction to the line followed by von Kluck and von Bülow.

"As a consequence, a fissure in the German dispositions opens by way of Epernay, Rheims, and Rethel before the Allies, who now menace the flank of the enemy if they persist in remaining before Mailly and Vitry-le-François.

"The announcement in the latest bulletin of a German rétirement between Sezanne and Revigny shows that the enemy realize the danger and have begun a general retreat."

Joffree Nearly Caught von Kluck.

PARIS, Sept. 12.—Apparently the only persons outside of the Allies' military authorities who knew the whereabouts of the French forces at the beginning of the great battle of the Marne were the Germans, who learned of it none too soon, and their diversion from Paris, heretofore attributed to fear of the city's defense works, was a manoeuvre to escape a desperate situation.

The Germans penetrated France in five armies, with at least 800,000 men. The plan was for a swift direct attack on Paris by Gen. von Kluck, while the armies of Gen. von Bülow, the Grand Duke of Württemberg, the Prince of Saxony, and the Crown Prince dealt with the other armies of the Allies.

The audacious commander of the German right wing, surprised by the resistance of the Allies at Guise and Compiègne, was rendered cautious and must have discovered the presence of the Army of Paris on his flank. He showed his resourcefulness by a sharp

Library of Congress

British gun crew prepares to fire a round on the Western Front.

Library of Congress

French machine gunners in 1914.

"All the News That's Fit to Print."

The New York Times.

THE WEATHER
Showers this afternoon or tonight and probably tomorrow; gentle to moderate south winds.
☞For full weather report see Page 11.

VOL. LXIV...NO. 20,712 . . . NEW YORK, FRIDAY, OCTOBER 9, 1914.—SIXTEEN PAGES. ONE CENT In Greater New York, Jersey City and Newark. | Elsewhere TWO CENTS.

ENVOYS NOW LOOK FOR SHORTER WAR

Believe That Defeated Austria-Hungary Soon Will Come to Terms with Russia.

GERMANY THEN ENCIRCLED

Length of Front to be Defended Would Render Further Resistance Impossible.

RUSSIANS NOW NEAR THORN

Forcing Germans Back on Border—Fortification at Przemysl Captured, Forts' Surrender Demanded.

Special Cable to THE NEW YORK TIMES.

LONDON, Friday, Oct. 9.—A belief that the war will be far shorter than the present situation indicates is gradually gaining ground in diplomatic circles here. The Secretary of the embassy of one of the involved powers has made a large wager that the war will be over within three months, and he is known as a careful bettor, not anxious to lose his money.

This optimistic feeling seems to be reflected in the American Embassy, though nobody there will make prophecies about the conflict's duration.

It is understood that this cheerful change from the deepest pessimism is inspired by information from Petrograd and Vienna concerning the Russian programme in Austria-Hungary. Through diplomatic channels the word has reached London that the Russian invasion of Hungary means moving on Vienna from the south, and there is little indication that the resistance by the Hungarians will be very bitter, as already there are signs that the Hungarian leaders are seeking understanding about the future with Russia.

Once in Vienna, the Russians are expected to have little trouble in coming to terms with Austria, for the Aus[illegible] already have complained about [illegible] of German support, and if Russ[illegible] treats them fairly, they will probably decide—so diplomats here believe—that the game of encouraging the Kaiser's world empire schemes is not worth the candle. In that case Austria and Hungary would be considered as separate nations, which certainly would appeal to the Hungarians.

Austria's armies are so badly shattered now that further resistance is doubtful in any case if Vienna falls. The capitulation of Austria would mean the complete investment of the German Empire, and even the Kaiser could not hope to hold the foe at bay long on such a huge front.

ROME, Oct. 8.—A dispatch received here from Petrograd says there have been sanguinary fights between German and Austrian prisoners, who accuse each other's Generals of responsibility for Russian victories.

GERMAN ATTACKS FAIL.

Russians Repulse East Prussian Army—Capture Biala in Galicia.

PETROGRAD, Oct. 8.—An official communication from General Headquarters says:

"The fighting on the East Prussian frontier continued on Oct. 7 with the same ferocity. In spite of German reinforcements all their attacks in the region of Wirballen (Russian Poland) and Philipoff have been repulsed with great losses. By a night assault the Russian troops have captured the village of Kamenka, near Bakalargewo.

"In the forest of Massalstchizna, west of Ratchka, our troops in a night attack surrounded a German detachment, which was partly exterminated, the others being dispersed, abandoning their rapid firers.

"Russian troops have also captured the town of Biala, (in Galicia, 43 miles west-southwest of Cracow.) In other regions there is nothing of importance to record.

"In the attack against the Przemysl garrison conditions are in our favor, our troops capturing by assault a strong fortification, constituting one of the principal positions."

ROME, Oct. 8.—A dispatch from Russian headquarters says that the intimation has been given to the Austrians holding the town of Przemysl, Galicia, that they will be permitted to surrender with military honors, but that if they refuse no quarter will be given to them.

A dispatch to the Tribuna from Petrograd says the Russians have driven the Germans from Wloclawek, (Russian Poland, thirty-five miles southeast of Thorn, East Prussia,) and have fortified themselves within a few miles of the fortress of Thorn. The German left wing in Poland is said to have been partly enveloped.

PANIC IN HUNGARY.

Refugees, Fleeing from Cossacks, Reach Budapest—Austrian Defeats.

Special Cable to THE NEW YORK TIMES.

MILAN, Oct. 8, (Dispatch to The London Morning Post.)—According to news received by the Corriere della Sera from Vienna, the Russian invasion of Hungary has caused a panic among the inhabitants.

Two thousand five hundred refugees from Maramaros-Sziget have arrived at Budapest in a destitute condition. The last train left Maramaros-Szigeth Thurs-

Continued on Page 3.

Summary of War News

Antwerp is holding out under a fierce fire from the German siege guns and bombardment by Zeppelins. King Albert has left the city with a part of his army, and is presumably marching toward Ghent. The German force, said to comprise five army corps, has crossed the Nethe River, and has broken its way through the first line of forts which defend the city. Thousands of refugees are crowding into Holland, and many more have reached England.

A censored news dispatch from Amsterdam states that a large force, apparently British, has been brought up with heavy artillery, to assist the Belgians in the defense of the city.

The French War Office announces that the situation is stationary, notwithstanding several violent engagements, notably in the region of Roye. The report issued earlier in the day stated that the Germans had been driven back in the fighting north of Arras, and also drew back on the centre between Verdun and St. Mihiel.

German Army Headquarters reports that the engagements on the right wing of the German army in France have not led to any decision. The attacks of the French in the Argonne and from the northeast front of Verdun, have been repulsed. In the eastern theatre of war, it is stated that the Russian attack on the Government of Suwalki has been repulsed, the Russians losing 2,700 prisoners and many machine guns.

The Russian General Staff announces that one of the principal positions at Przemysl has been captured. The German army, heavily reinforced, attacked Wirballen and Philipoff, in Russian Poland, but was repulsed with heavy losses.

German aeroplanes which flew over the suburbs of Paris yesterday dropped several bombs, one of which injured three persons.

The Canadian expeditionary force arrived at Southampton yesterday.

The Japanese War Office announces that the fire of the German fortifications at Tsing-tau is slackening.

GERMAN DROPS BOMBS ON PARIS; THREE HURT

Two Are Thrown, But One Does No Damage — Troops Ordered Not to Fire.

PARIS, Oct. 8.—A German aeroplane flying over Paris and the suburbs of Aubervilliers and Saint Denis at 9 o'clock this morning dropped two bombs, one of which wounded three persons. The other did no harm.

Hostile aircraft have usually avoided Paris and its vicinity early in the day because of the dangerous atmospheric currents then present. The French troops stationed in the city and suburbs have been commanded not to fire upon the aeroplanes because of the incidental danger to the public from falling bullets.

1,000 SPORTSMEN HAVE NOW ENLISTED

Titled Men in the Unique British Battalion—A Woman Financing It.

Special Cable to THE NEW YORK TIMES.

LONDON, Oct. 8. Recruiting for the famous Sportsman's Battalion is proceeding apace, the enrollment to date totaling about 1,000.

It is in many ways a unique corps. It is raised and financed by Mrs. Cunliff Owen and is in all probability the only battalion of any of the great modern armies to be brought into being by a woman. It is certainly the only battalion in the British forces in which the age limit has been specially extended by the authorities. The recruiting posters read: "The Sportsman's Battalion is a corps for gentlemen up to forty-five years of age." Payment by a recruit for his equipment is optional. The training and equipment are what are required by an ordinary infantry company.

Among the distinguished men already enrolled as privates are Sir Norman Pringle, Bart.; Sir William Wallace; Sir Robert Newman, Bart., and two sons of peers who have not yet passed the medical examination.

The percentage of rejection among the applicants is a low record for recruiting in the campaign. Up to date it is less than 5 per cent.

GERMAN SCHOOLBOYS ENROLLED FOR ARMY

States Organizing Two Reserve Lines Including Lads Only 14 Years Old.

Special Cable to THE NEW YORK TIMES.

BERLIN, Oct. 5 (By Indirect Route to The London Daily Standard)—Several States of the German Empire are taking vigorous steps to organize the boys who have not yet reached the age of enlistment, which is nineteen, for military service. The Prussian Minister of Education has issued a decree authorizing the headmasters of elementary and secondary State schools to take necessary measures in conjunction with military authorities to raise a reserve army consisting of boys between the ages of sixteen and nineteen.

Boys between sixteen and nineteen will be available for active service in the field when they have been trained. Boys between the ages of fourteen and sixteen are to receive special military drill to enable them to become active soldiers the moment they attain the age of sixteen.

In Berlin itself several regiments of lads between sixteen and twenty already have been formed and similar reports come from many provincial towns.

GERMANS CLAIM GAINS IN FRANCE

No Decisive Action on Flanks, but French Repulsed in Centre.

FRONTAL ATTACKS COSTLY

Berlin Reports That Heavy Losses Have Caused Direct Assaults to be Deferred.

RUSSIAN ADVANCE CHECKED

Capture of 7,500 Prisoners in Suwalki and Poland Officially Announced.

LONDON, Oct. 8.—A Berlin dispatch to the Reuter Telegram Company contains an official statement given out at general headquarters in Berlin on the evening of Oct. 7. It follows:

The engagements on the right wing in France have not led to any decision. The attacks of the French in the Argonne and from the northeast front of Verdun have been repulsed.

Off Antwerp the attack has crossed a section of the River Nèthe.

The attacks of the Russians on the Government of Suwalki have been repulsed, the Russians losing 2,700 prisoners and nine machine guns.

In Poland, in minor, successful engagements west of Ivangorod, we captured 4,800 prisoners.

Defer Costly Frontal Attacks.

BERLIN, Oct. 5, (via London, Oct. 8.)—According to the latest dispatch reaching here from ——(name deleted by censor, but probably some place in France) frontal attacks have proved so costly in lives to both sides that they have been deferred. The antagonists are awaiting the results of flanking movements which promise greater effect with fewer casualties.

The German soldiers on the centre of the line (in France) live in their trenches. The only warm meal they get is served in the night. It is impossible to kindle a fire in the daytime as the smoke would divulge their position. Otherwise the men live on cold victuals, fruits, and beets.

Dissolves Anti-Polish Union.

BERLIN, Oct. 8.—(By wireless to Sayville, L. I.)—According to news given out officially today in the German capital, the splendid and loyal conduct of the Polish soldiers in the German Army has made possible the dissolution of the German Anti-Polish Union.

A great part of the German Army under Gen. von Hindenburg has effected a junction with the Austrians on the Vistula River at Ivangorod, in Russian Poland, where the Russians are concentrating on the right bank of the river.

Only a small portion of von Hindenburg's army remains near Suwalki; these troops succeeded in preventing the Russian advance in the direction of East Prussia, and this in spite of the numerical superiority of the enemy.

Copies of The London Times received here express amazement at the German foolhardiness in taking the offensive in four war arenas at the same time.

Reports received here from the Netherlands say the situation of Antwerp is most critical. The people of the city are depressed, and fear that their water supply will be cut off. The Belgian Government is moving to Ostend.

Deny Suwalki Advance.

WASHINGTON, Oct. 8.—The German Embassy today received the following wireless from Berlin:

"Official headquarters says that the report of an advance of Russian forces across the Niemen River in the district of Suwalki, Russia, is a lie. The battle took place near Augustowo, where the Germans on Oct. 1 and 2 completely defeated two Russian army corps, took 3,500 unwounded prisoners and twenty guns, of which one was a heavy battery gun, and a number of machine guns. (Here part of the message was lost in transmission).

"On Oct. 4, German troops threw a brigade of Russian rifle guards from a fortified position between Opatow and Ostrowiec, in Russian Poland, and took 3,000 prisoners and numerous guns and machine guns. On Oct. 5, the Germans attacked near Rudow two and one-half Russian cavalry divisions and parts of the Ivangorod reserve and drove the Russians back on Ivangorod.

"Elsewhere (along the Russian front) the movement of German troops, for strategical reasons, has caused a lull in the fighting.

"In France, we are gaining ground slowly but surely, and the situation continues favorable. The battle front of the right wing has been extended until it is north of Arras where our vanguard came in touch with the enemy's cavalry and the same west of Lille."

Editor and Diplomat Decorated.

BERLIN, (via London,) Oct. 8.—Major Gen. Augustus Zelman, commander of the Second Bavarian Field Artillery, was killed in action on Sept. 26. The fact has just become known here.

Two new Knights of the Order of the Iron Cross have been created. One is

Continued on Page 2.

ANTWERP BOMBARDED FROM LAND AND SKY; KING AND PART OF THE ARMY MOVE OUT; CITY STILL HELD; ALLIES PRESSING NORTHWARD

TERRIFIC FIRE POURED IN

Germans Move Up to Second Line of Defense and Shell Antwerp.

ZEPPELINS SLAY AND BURN

Fleet Drops Bombs on Houses and Forts, Killing a Score and Setting Fires.

PLAN A VIGOROUS DEFENSE

British Force May Be Aiding Belgians—Thousands More Flee to Holland and England.

LONDON, Oct. 8.—Having broken through the outer forts of Antwerp, the Germans are now bombarding the city and the second line of defenses. At the same time Zeppelins have appeared over the city dropping bombs, which are reported to have caused many deaths and added to the terror of the people, thousands of whom are fleeing from the city.

News has reached Bordeaux that King Albert, at the head of a part of the Belgian Army, marched out of Antwerp today. Such a move had been predicted to prevent the bottling up of the forces or capture if the city falls. A sufficient number of troops to man the fortifications has been left.

The bombardment of Antwerp has been so violent that the houses at Rosendaal, a Netherlands town more than twenty miles distant, have been visibly shaken, according to a telegram from that town to the Central News by way of Amsterdam.

Some wounded civilians have arrived at Rosendaal, and the Dutch Government has ordered all trains to proceed to that place to be held in readiness to transport the refugees and injured. Thousands of refugees have already arrived.

Throughout the entire night, the message adds, a red glare illuminated the sky.

Shells Near the Cathedral.

The correspondent of The Star at Ghent says:

"Antwerp was subjected to a furious bombardment throughout last night. Shells from the German sixteen-inch guns were falling early this morning in the Place Verte, close to the cathedral."

The attack on Antwerp began at midnight Wednesday, according to an official dispatch received in Amsterdam from Berlin, after Gen. Hans H. von Beseler, commander of the siege army at Antwerp, had notified the authorities of Antwerp, through the representatives of neutral States, that bombardment was about to open.

Zeppelins Kill a Score.

From Antwerp, under date of Wednesday, this report is received:

"The condition of panic among the people was increased today by the appearance at 11 o'clock this morning and at 3 o'clock this afternoon of German aircraft, which dropped bombs, destroying seven houses and killing a score of people.

"On account of the Zeppelins' successful attack, the large avenue leading to the railroad station quickly became black with a struggling mass of people eager to escape from the city. Seized with an unreasoning, terrible fear of a bombardment or of a charge of German cavalry, the people are transporting invalids, cripples, and even the occupants of lunatic asylums.

"The situation, however, quickly changed again. While at 2 o'clock even grown-up men were weeping with terror and were fighting for places around the railway station, at 6 o'clock everybody was again certain that the forces would be able to hold out against the Germans and even throw them back across the River Nèthe, while everybody was telling his neighbor how far superior the —— guns were to the German heavy artillery.

"The people remaining in the city tonight are taking to the cellars, prepared to hear the first German shell in the morning.

"The Belgian Ministers are trying to reach Ostend through Flanders and via Holland.

"The Belgian Army is marching into the city, tired out, leaving the guarding of the forts for the night to fresh —— troops."

[The blanks denote words cut out by the censor. They may relate to forces and guns sent to Antwerp by Great Britain.]

During Wednesday night no fewer than six Zeppelins flew over Antwerp, dropping bombs in all directions, the Central News correspondent at Amsterdam says. The extent of the damage done is not known, but one of the bombs damaged the Palace of Justice.

ANTWERP'S DEFENSES—INNER FORTS NOW ATTACKED

The arrows show the courses of attack on the city open to the Germans, the outer forts, from Waelhem on the south to Broechem on the east, having been reduced. The Berlin official statement says the assault has begun on the south, at Waelhem and Wavre. On the west the defenses hold, the Germans having been checked in the attempt to cross the Scheldt below the city.

Reuter's Amsterdam correspondent says that Zeppelin airships cruising above the fortifications of Antwerp dropped bombs on some oil tanks at Hoboken, which caught fire. To prevent a general conflagration, the other tanks were hastily drained.

Close to City, Says Berlin.

An official dispatch received here tonight from Berlin by the Marconi Wireless Telegraph Company says:

"It is reported from Dutch sources that fierce fighting occurred yesterday in the Nèthe district, (Province of Antwerp.)

"The Germans approached in a northerly direction from Forts de Wavre and de Waelhem and commenced a bombardment of Antwerp from these positions.

"Early in the morning the shrapnel shells already had caused great damage in many places, showing that the investing force is close to the city.

"The whole of the Belgian field army has been concentrated in the district between Antwerp, Lierre, (nine miles to the southeast of the city,) and the River Scheldt, in which area fighting is proceeding."

Both sides confirm the report that the Germans have succeeded in crossing the River Nèthe, but the trenches along the River Scheldt are still holding out against their determined attacks.

According to a message from Baarle-Nassau, the Netherlands, to the Nieuw Rotterdamsche Courant, the Germans occupied Turnhout, twenty-five miles east-northeast of Antwerp, this morning, presumably to join the attack on Antwerp from the east.

Thousands of fugitives have arrived at the Baarle-Nassau station. A train coming from the Dutch frontier was fired upon by the Germans, who destroyed the locomotive.

ANTWERP DEFENDERS IN VIOLENT BATTLE

Germans Cross Rivers at Enormous Cost—City Makes Ready for Attack.

Special Cable to THE NEW YORK TIMES.

LONDON, Oct. 8.—Delayed dispatches from Antwerp give an impressive picture of how the fighting there has progressed. The Chronicle's correspondent, telegraphing on Wednesday, says:

"The situation here is developing in a dramatic fashion. At 7:30 o'clock this morning the commander of the German troops besieging the city sent an officer carrying a white flag to inform the town authorities that the besiegers were going to begin the bombardment of the city at 9:30 A. M. The news of this intention naturally spread like wildfire, and there was an immediate rush of civilians from the place. Some of the fugitives traveled to Ostend, but many made for the Dutch frontier. The commandant of the city issued a notice that anybody who wished to leave the city could do so freely, but added: 'It must be distinctly understood that while Antwerp is being besieged no authorization whatever will be given to any one to return to the city.'

"At midday the seat of Government was transferred from Antwerp to Ostend. This eventuality had been provided for. In fact, I have received reliable news that they departed yesterday at 1 o'clock. I have no official confirmation of this, however, and I send the news under every reserve.

"Despite the exodus of so many people, however, there is an air of quiet confidence that the Germans will never capture the city. Numbers of forts are still holding out with great stubbornness, and the threatened bombardment is considered a desperate manoeuvre to try to force these to capitulate in order to save the city itself from damage. If so the Germans will have a rude awakening, for the city will be defended to the uttermost.

"Despite the fact that numbers hastily left today, the city is still full of people, the ordinary population having been added to during the last few weeks by many who have fled here for safety from the more eastern towns which the Germans have destroyed by bombardment.

"It is generally hoped and believed that the Belgian Army will be fully capable of repelling any attempt of the Germans to break through the present line of defenses. Every effort is being made to strengthen the defenses and reinforce the army now holding the Germans at bay. The military commandant of Antwerp has issued an appeal to young men of the city in the interest of the national defense. He says: 'It is absolutely necessary that our army be reinforced. In these circumstances I make a patriotic appeal to all young men between the ages of 18 and 30. Young men, your country has need of you. Reply to my appeal. Do not let your country be exposed to the mercy of the invader. Do not remain inactive. Those who enlist will be trained in that part of the country which is not invaded by the enemy.'

Churches Hang Out Flags.

"For some days past flags with red and white diagonal stripes have flown from the tops of several churches and other buildings. Those floating from the Cathedral and tower of St. Jacques are particularly conspicuous. These flags indicate that the buildings serve no military end, and it is hoped they will therefore not be singled out for destruction. It is stated, indeed, that the Germans have declared they will endeavor to spare as much as possible the churches and other important buildings not used as lookouts or upon which mitrailleuses are not mounted.

"Yesterday evening shortly before dark a Zeppelin was reported to be coming over the city and all lights were immediately put out. The Zeppelin did not appear, but all lights now go out at dusk and all shops close at 6 P. M.

"There are rumors to the effect that the Iron Cross and 25,000 marks ($6,125) have been offered by the Kaiser to the first man to enter Antwerp.

A Combat of Artillery.

"For some days now the fighting before Antwerp has been practically a tremendous combat of artillery and, of course, the victory may be secured by the side with the heaviest guns, but one always has to consider the man behind the gun, and the Belgians are fighting with the heroism that has now made them famous throughout Europe. For twenty-four hours the German army has scarcely made any advance, though if their 42-centimeter guns are now in position they are certainly near enough to carry out their threat and bombard the town.

"The Germans have fiercely bombarded the village of Linth. The Belgians held it until it was in flames and then evacuated the place.

"Yesterday the Belgians found two of the German batteries and very quickly put them out of action.

"In the east, at Lierre, the position remains unchanged for the moment, but the heavy German artillery fire in this quarter is telling. On the other hand some progress by the Belgians is reported at Rumpst and Hewndouck, southwest of Antwerp, where the Belgian field guns caused the German retirement a kilometer or two behind the Nèthe.

"The Germans are placing mitrailleuses and guns on every high building commanding the line of the River Nèthe, although they protested against a similar act on the part of the Belgians. The latter are replying by blowing up every high building on the line on which they believe the Germans will advance.

"Le Matin announces that at the point of the bayonet the Belgians yesterday silenced two German batteries.

Excellent work has been done by the Belgian aviators in surveying German positions despite the fact that the wind has been very high during the last two days. Volleys of German shrapnel greet their appearance, but no casualties have been reported.

"Near Termonde the Germans still fight desperately to cross the Scheldt. The latest news is that they have not yet succeeded in doing so.

Need Road to Ghent.

"It is of the utmost importance to the Belgians that they keep the line open between Antwerp and Ghent. The Germans are pressing forward on the east. It is now known they have succeeded in crossing the river Nèthe. On the east they were only held at bay by the desperate efforts of the Belgians. This offensive movement, however, has cost the Germans, it is said, at least 20,000 men.

"On the south, that is in the region of Contich, Boom, and Willebroeck, the German attack appears to have been brought to a standstill. I motored yesterday along the main road as far as Waerloos, eighteen kilometers from Antwerp, and I believe it would have been safe to have proceeded further. The Belgian battery on my right was pouring shells into Malines, but there was no response from the German artillery. On my left, in the direction of Lierre, there was a sound of very heavy firing, indicating a forward German movement.

"The Germans were making desperate efforts to break the line between Duffel and Lierre, but every time they tried to cross the river they were literally mown down by the Belgian mitrailleuses.

"In some parts hand to hand encounters with bayonets have been the order of the day, and it is on these occasions that the bravery of Belgians has been principally demonstrated. If result depended on the heroism of the Belgians it would be an easy triumph. Time and again during the attacks on the outer line of forts the defenders waited unmoved in the trenches while a terrible rain of shells fell around and among them.

"One may wonder why the attack on Antwerp has been so long delayed. It is not so much due, it seems, to the length of time the Germans have taken in bringing up their big siege guns as to the fact that the German lines of communication were threatened by Belgian raids. Their own food supplies remain very plentiful."

Later on Wednesday night the same correspondent reported the German forces as near as Broechem, within seven miles of the city. He added:

"East of Duffel the Germans were fifteen times repulsed by the deadly fire of the Belgian mitrailleuses, and on each occasion their losses could be counted by hundreds. At Waelhem the country has been flooded to check the invaders' advance."

BELGIAN LINE STRONG SOUTH OF THE CITY

Visit on Wednesday Found Defenders Repulsing Germans Who Moved Eastward.

Special Cable to THE NEW YORK TIMES.

LONDON, Oct. 8.—Sir Alfred Sharp, at St. Nicholas, near Antwerp, sends the following dispatch to The Chronicle under Wednesday's date:

"I visited today the western portion

Continued on Page 2.

ALLIES GAIN NEAR ARRAS

Push Germans Back in Battle North of the Town.

FIERCE FIGHTING AT ROYE

Germans Still in Force There, While French Hold Recaptured Positions.

FAR-FLUNG CAVALRY LINE

Opposing Forces Now Reach Nearly to the Coast of the North Sea.

PARIS, Oct. 8, 11:36 P. M.—The official communiqué issued by the French War Office tonight says:

On the whole, the situation is stationary, the positions occupied remaining the same, notwithstanding several violent engagements, notably in the region of Roye.

Following is the official announcement made in Paris this afternoon:

First—On our left wing, in the region of the Department of Nord, the enemy has made progress at no point. At certain points he has moved back, particularly to the north of Arras, where the fighting is developing under conditions favorable for us. The operations of the opposing forces of cavalry are developing at the present time almost as far as the seacoast on the north.

Between the Somme and the Oise, in the vicinity of Roye, the enemy is still in force, but we have retaken the major part of the positions we were obliged to give up.

To the north of the Aisne the numerical strength of the German troops seems to have diminished.

Second—On the centre, between Rheims and the Meuse, there is nothing to report. On the heights of the Meuse, between Verdun and St. Mihiel, the enemy has drawn back to the north of Hatton-Chatel. He still holds St. Mihiel and some positions to the north of St. Mihiel on the right bank of the Meuse.

In the Woevre district the violent attacks delivered by the enemy to the west of Aprémont have failed.

On our right wing, Lorraine and the Vosges, there has been no change.

In Russia, along the front of East Prussia, the Russian offensive continues. Very spirited fighting is taking place on the frontier to the west of Suwalki.

15,000 GERMANS NEAR LILLE.

Cavalry and Artillery Force Cuts Railway Lines About Ypres.

Special Cable to THE NEW YORK TIMES.

OSTEND, Oct. 7 (Dispatch to The London Daily Express)—Some 15,000 Germans, chiefly cavalry and artillery, coming from Mons and Enghien, have passed through Mouscron, Roubaix and Tourcoing. They camped at Mont Salluin and sent patrols of Uhlans to Menin and Ypres, where they cut the railway lines.

Most of the masterpieces in the museum at Lille, including the famous wax head by Leonardo da Vinci, have been removed to a place of safety.

It appears clear that this new German force is operating to protect the retreat of the right wing, for yesterday large bodies of tired German troops, retiring from France, crossed the Belgian frontier and passed through Tournai.

LONDON, Oct. 8.—The Daily Mail's Ostend correspondent telegraphs that on Tuesday German troops were being transferred through Belgium to strengthen the attack on the Allies' left. The tide of battle, says the correspondent, rolls fiercely in from Arras to Lens and beyond.

Douai, which was attacked by the Germans fifteen days ago, was captured on Thursday last. The inhabitants were treated with severity on the pretext that civilians had fired on German troops from their houses, some forty of which were burned. All the small villages in the vicinity were utterly destroyed.

A dispatch to the Exchange Telegraph Company from Ostend, filed on Tuesday, but delayed in transmission, says:

"Fierce fighting has taken place for two days around Lille, where the French troops came into contact with the enemy, who sustained heavy losses. The German batteries fired on the station, the prefecture, and other buildings.

"In the fierce fighting the Germans

"All the News That's Fit to Print."

The New York Times.

THE WEATHER

Local Showers today; unsettled Sunday.

For full weather report see Page 13.

VOL. LXIV...NO. 20,713. ... NEW YORK, SATURDAY, OCTOBER 10, 1914.—EIGHTEEN PAGES. ONE CENT In Greater New York, Jersey City and Newark. { Elsewhere TWO CENTS.

LONDON HEARS THAT ANTWERP HAS FALLEN; CITY AFLAME UNDER RAIN OF GERMAN SHELLS; FRENCH CAPTURE 1,600 GERMANS NEAR ROYE

BRAVES CAPTURE FIRST GAME, 7-1; BENDER ROUTED

Boston Wins Easy Victory Over Athletics in Opening World's Series Contest.

RUDOLPH TAMES MACKMEN

Indian Hurler Driven from Box for the First Time in Blue-Ribbon Event.

GOWDY STARS AT THE BAT

Maranville Also Helps Drive in Runs—To Investigate Police Ticket Graft Scandal.

20,562 AT SHIBE PARK

Athletics Were Outclassed, Says Evers—Stallings Punches Annoyer—Speculators Reap Harvest.

Special to The New York Times.

PHILADELPHIA, Oct. 9.—Baseball calculation and reasoning went all topsy turvy at Shibe Park on this fair Indian Summer afternoon, and the victory-inspired Boston Braves, in the first game of the world's series, savagely swept the great Athletic team aside and drove from the box one of the greatest pitchers of all time, the veteran Chippewa, Chief Bender. When the game was over the Mackmen were crushed under the wreckage of a humiliating defeat by 7 to 1.

As Mack's valiant slabman was slipping into oblivion a new pitching star arose to take his place in the history of the National pastime—Dick Rudolph of the Bronx, New York.

Worn and battered through the strife the most sensational spurt ever made a major league ball club, this Bronx ...ith, smiling pleasantly and looking as ...sh as if he had just come back from a ...mmer vacation, showed the Mackian ...iggers the most mysterious pitching ...ey have ever faced. It was a tantalizing combination of a deceptive slow ... and a barrel-hoop out curve which ...apudently refused to kiss the Athletics' bats.

Intoxicated with joy the Royal Rooters of Boston, led by Former Mayor "Honey Fitz," who is known on dinner menus as the "Hon. John F. Fitzgerald," say there is nothing to it now. They say the spell of the Athletics' greatness has been broken and the world's calico will next season wave on Beacon Hill.

Philadelphia partisans, on the other hand, say the Mackmen are only slumbering, and that now the Athletics will wake from their lethargy and tame the Braves as they did the Cubs and the Giants. At the restaurants, theatres, and on the street corners here tonight nothing else is talked of except the Boston Braves.

Passing of Chief Bender.

There was real sadness about the passing of Chief Bender. In the sixth inning, when the battering of the Braves caused his exit, the imposing figure of the redman stalked slowly to the bench and a hush fell over the big crowd which jammed every corner of the park. Not a sound was heard except the hornet-like buzz of the hundreds of telegraph instruments which were ticking the tidings of the Indian's downfall to bulletin boards in every corner of the country.

For the first time in a world's series Bender was yanked from his post of duty on the firing line, called to the bench because the sturdy right arm had failed, that sinewed arm which had carried the wonderful ball club of Connie Mack to the heights of victory. Formerly the delivered ball had gone from his hand like a shot; now it floated over so slowly that when it reached the batter it had assumed the size of a toy balloon.

Sharing the plaudits of the Bostonese tonight with Rudolph is Hank Gowdy, the lean, lank, redheaded catcher from Texas. Clumsy he may appear and awkward, but he measured up to his task this afternoon and set the pace in slugging which brought about the fall of the Athletic machine. A great fellow is Gowdy, with his batting average of 1,000. Look at it—a triple, a double, a single, and a base on balls out of four times up!

Gowdy's right-hand man in the run getting was Walter Maranville, who before this spectacle is over promises to be the most sensational shortstopper the game has seen. When Gowdy got on the bases, Maranville, following him at the bat, spanked out the hits which sent Hank's long legs ambling over the plate. What fielding Maranville had to do was done with smoothness and grace. The "Rabbit" plays ball just as if he were run by an electric motor —he's not human.

20,562 In Shibe Park.

All the powers in baseball were in the big throng that saw the game. The official attendance figures were 20,562, but 10,000 others watched the contest from the bleachers built on surrounding housetops. These houseowners reaped a harvest that will buy the winter's coal, charging as much as a dollar in some cases for a place. The police tried to put a stop to the deadhead delegations, but it seems that in this

Continued on Page 8

Summary of War News

The bombardment of Antwerp by the heavy German artillery continues. The city is on fire at several points and many civilians are reported killed.

A report reached London early this morning that the city had fallen, but it lacked official confirmation.

Another fort, south of Antwerp, has been taken, Berlin says, and the attack on the inner fort line has begun, it is stated.

King Albert has been slightly wounded, according to a report in Berlin. A news dispatch from Amsterdam, on the other hand, says that the King of the Belgians has reached the Dutch frontier with his army.

The French War Office announces a lively engagement in the region of Roye, where, in the last two days, the French forces have captured 1,600 prisoners. The cavalry forces are still operating in the vicinity of Lille and the fighting near Arras is very violent.

German Army Headquarters reports progress near St. Mihiel and the Argonnes.

The Russian General Staff announces that the Russian forces have again invaded East Prussia and captured Lyck, after a two-day battle. A news dispatch from Petrograd states that the city of Przemysl is on fire and on the point of capitulation, but this is denied by the Austrians, who assert that the forts still hold out, and that the Russian advance in Galicia has been halted.

British aeroplanes have made another raid on the Zeppelin hangars at Dusseldorf, where some damage by bombs was done.

A news dispatch from Petrograd states that the relations between Russia and Turkey have become very strained. It is semi-officially announced that Turkish troops have attacked Cossacks on the Turco-Persian frontier.

The Japanese have mounted their heavy siege guns on Prince Henry Mountain, which overlooks the forts at Tsing-tau, and are about to begin the bombardment of the fortifications.

RUSSIA AND TURKEY DRIFTING TOWARD WAR

Situation on Turco-Persian Frontier Threatening—Kurds Attack Cossacks.

Special Cable to THE NEW YORK TIMES.

PETROGRAD, Oct. 9 (Dispatch to the London Daily Telegraph).—It is semi-officially stated that the situation on the Turco-Persian frontier must be regarded as threatening. Kurds disguised as Redifs (Turkish second line troops) have been attacking Cossacks in that region.

The relations between Russia and Turkey have become very strained.

ATHENS, Oct. 9.—Col. von Geck has arrived at Damascus and has taken over the direction of the General Staff of the Syrian troops and is also recruiting Bedouins.

Special Cable to THE NEW YORK TIMES.

LONDON, Oct. 9.—The London Standard's Petrograd correspondent writes:

"The organ of the Russian War Office states that the Turks are busy making preparations for war in Asia Minor, especially in the vicinity of Batoum and Erzerum. Caucasians are so accustomed to the idea of hostilities between Russia and Turkey that the rumors of the last few days cause very little excitement.

"Last spring Armenian merchants expressed most decided opinions with regard to the Turks being under the influence of the Germans. They were gradually assuming a most provocative attitude toward Russian subjects, while in the bazaars an energetic propaganda was carried on with the object of inciting the people against Russia. It was represented that Russia, after taking the whole of northern Persia, now wished to annex Turkish Armenia.

"In Trebizond, Keresun Bairut, Erzerum and Hasan Kales German officers were constantly found busily inspecting the forts and garrisons.

"As soon as Germany declared war Turkey hastily mobilized, concentrating her forces on the Asiatic frontier of the Caucasus. The mobilization, however, was not a success. Many reservists employed in the Crimea and in Caucasia either returned to the colors with exceeding reluctance or endeavored to escape service.

"According to the native inhabitants Turco-German officials have been busy traveling in Asia Minor as emissaries for the Young Turks and have succeeded in convincing the fanatical people that Russia intends to take the Dardanelles as well as Turkish Armenia."

It is stated that the forces of Turkey are in a most wretched condition. There is no unity among the officers, who are continually quarreling with one another. The Government, however, is busy distributing spare rifles and cartridges.

WASHINGTON, Oct. 9.—Efforts to be made by Great Britain, France, and Russia to open the Dardanelles, as announced in a declaration credited to the Russian Foreign Minister, were said at the Russian Embassy here today to have only a commercial and not a warlike purpose. The great hindrance to commerce caused by Turkey's action in closing this channel into the Black Sea was pointed to by Embassy officials as making the proposed step necessary.

FRANCE LOSES TWO SHIPS.

Torpedo Boats in Collision in Mediterranean—Crews Saved.

LONDON, Saturday, Oct. 10, 1:50 A. M.—A Reuter dispatch from Toulon says that two French torpedo boats, Nos. 338 and 347, were in collision yesterday (Friday) morning off Porquerolles, one of the Hyères Islands, in the Mediterranean, and sank.

The crews of both vessels were saved, but the salvage of the ships will be impossible.

ARMY GAINING ON LEFT FLANK, BERLIN REPORTS

General Staff Claims Some Progress Made Near St. Mihiel and the Argonnes.

PUSHING ANTWERP ATTACK

Announces Fall of Fort Breendonk and Assault on Inner Line of Fortifications.

VIEWS ON WILSON MESSAGE

Favorable Comment by German Press on President's Reply to the Kaiser.

LONDON, Oct. 9.—An official statement of the German General Staff, given out at Berlin last evening, is contained in a Reuter dispatch from Amsterdam. It says:

"From the western scene of war no facts of decisive importance can be mentioned. Small progress has been made near St. Mihiel and in the Argonnes.

"Before Antwerp Fort Breendonk (south of Antwerp) has been taken, and the attack on the inner fort line has begun therewith.

"The bombardment of the quarter of the town lying behind was begun after the declaration of the commander of the stronghold that he took the responsibility.

"The airship hall at Düsseldorf has been hit by a bomb, thrown by a hostile aviator. The roof of the hall was pierced and the cover of an airship in the hall was demolished.

"In the east the Russian column is marching from Lomza (Russian Poland) and has reached Lyck, (in East Prussia just beyond the frontier.)"

BERLIN, Oct. 8, (via London, Oct. 9.)—It is officially announced that the Germans continue to make progress at Antwerp, and that they are already over the flooded area along the river Nèthe.

A writer in the Militair Wochenblatt, however, warned the people last night against an excessive optimism regarding Antwerp, as the garrison of the fortress there is still able to continue a desperate resistance.

The newspapers are reprinting President Wilson's reply of Sept. 16 to Emperor William's communication, in which he reported the finding of dumdum bullets at Longwy and protested against the way in which the war was being waged by Germany's opponents. President Wilson's reply in effect was that it was unwise to express a final judgment on the dumdum protest, and expressed the opinion that an accounting would come at the war's conclusion, when the nations would assemble to make a settlement.

The newspaper comment on this reply is most friendly, and is to the effect that any other answer could not be expected.

The Tageszeitung says in this connection:

"We have a clear conscience from the viewpoint of justice and humanity in this war, and can look the world in the face without fear. We, however, do not need to regard the public opinion of the world. In the last instance the German people, united with the Emperor, are alone competent to decide the correctness of Germany's course."

Crop reports for October show that potatoes, sugar beets, clover, and alfalfa are middling to good. Autumn planting is making good progress, despite the earlier drought.

BRITISH AIRSHIP RAID DESTROYS A ZEPPELIN

Successful Dash to the Hangar at Dusseldorf—British Aeroplanes Lost.

LONDON, Oct. 9.—The following official statement was issued tonight in regard to an attack by a British air squadron on a German airship shed at Düsseldorf:

The Secretary of the Admiralty announces that Squadron Commander Grey reports that, as authorized, he carried out, with Lieut. R. L. G. Marix and Lieut. S. V. Sippe, a successful attack on a Düsseldorf airship shed. Lieut. Marix's bombs, dropped from a height of 500 feet, hit the shed, went through the roof, and destroyed a Zeppelin.

Flames were observed 500 feet high, the result of the igniting of the gas of an airship.

All three officers are safe, but their aeroplanes have been lost.

Special Cable to THE NEW YORK TIMES.

AMSTERDAM, Oct. 9.—The Germans admit that damage was done by an aeroplane which visited the district around Düsseldorf and Cologne this week. A Cologne message says:

"A hostile aeroplane was seen over the airship sheds at Pivkendorff on Thursday. On being fired at it disappeared in the direction of the gas works at Ehrenfeld, where a bomb was dropped. Then it flew over the southern bridge to Fort Deckstein, and afterward went west.

"At Düsseldorf an aeroplane, presumably the same, damaged the Zeppelin airship shed and an airship."

DESTRUCTION IN ANTWERP

Fire Spreads in Several Quarters and Many Non-Combatants Fall.

TERROR GRIPS THE PEOPLE

City Streets and Avenues of Escape Choked with Refugees —Rest Hide in Cellars.

FORTS FIGHT DESPERATELY

Zeppelin Said to Have Been Brought Down—Some Public Buildings Struck by Shells.

Special Cable to THE NEW YORK TIMES.

LONDON, Saturday, Oct. 10.—The Morning Post says:

"We are informed on good authority that Antwerp has fallen.

"The news will be received with the profoundest regret by all who have watched the heroic defense that has been maintained by the Belgian Army.

"The foregoing has been submitted to the Press Bureau, which permits its publication but gives no confirmation.

"The regrettable news was conveyed last night by a representative of The Morning Post to Count de la Laing, the Belgian Minister, who was naturally much perturbed. He had not heard of the occurrence up to midnight, and had no official confirmation of it."

The Daily Chronicle publishes the following:

"The Germans have entered Antwerp. The inhabitants are quite calm. Most of those who desired to leave the city did so before the bombardment commenced.

"This message has been submitted to the official censor, who has no objection to publication, but adds that 'the Press Bureau gives no confirmation of this news.'"

Desperate Fighting Reported.

Special Cable to THE NEW YORK TIMES.

ROTTERDAM, Oct. 9, (Dispatch to The London Daily News.)—The defenders of Antwerp are now fighting behind the second line of forts and are determined to resist to the last. The bombardment of the city goes on. Fire in the city is said to have reached tremendous proportions, and desperate fighting is proceeding.

It is confidently reported to me by a man who watched the bombardment of Antwerp from a distance that at 4:30 o'clock on Thursday afternoon he saw the guns of the forts concentrate their fire on one particular spot in the air; a number of shells burst together, and almost at the same moment he saw a large, cigar-shaped body fall to earth. He has seen several Zeppelins in peace time, and is confident that the falling object was a Zeppelin. Bystanders, he says, were similarly confident.

Last night was a terrible one for the people of Antwerp, for the shells were literally rained on the town, and many civilians were killed and wounded before they could take shelter in cellars.

The special correspondent of the Nieuwe Rotterdamsche Courant, who left Antwerp this morning, relates that the first shrapnel fell on the town at 9 o'clock, and almost immediately fire broke out, especially in the neighborhood of the South Station. At Berchem, a southern suburb, grave damage was done.

During the whole night projectiles literally rained on the town, sometimes at the rate of more than twenty a minute. In the neighborhood of the station many houses were absolutely destroyed, while the Hippodrome has been burned to the ground. The Law Courts and Museum have been damaged.

Severe fighting is still proceeding outside the town, and many wounded were being brought from the fighting line. Belgian troops which had been fighting to the west of the Scheldt were repulsed by the Germans. They crossed the river and came into town.

Night of Terror in the City.

Special Cable to THE NEW YORK TIMES.

LONDON, Saturday, Oct. 10.—The Daily News correspondent at Ghent, wiring on Thursday night, says:

"This morning shells were falling thickly in Antwerp in the neighborhood of the Place Verte. An officer whom I just met states that the bombardment of the cathedral had begun when he left the city. Fire had broken out in many places, and whole streets had been reduced to ruins. The Germans are using their sixteen-inch howitzers with terrible effect on the inner ring of forts, but the guns of smaller calibre probably are being employed for the destruction of the city itself.

"At 11 o'clock last night a Zeppelin dropped a bomb on the Law Courts. The airship was subjected to a terrific fire and was certainly hit, but under cover of the diversion fresh guns were got into position.

"At 11:30 o'clock shells began to fall thickly upon the southern side of the city, and by 1 A. M. a wide area was under fire. The population became terrified. The scene was awful, the total darkness being only relieved here and there by flames of burning buildings and the flash of exploding shells. Thousands fled as soon as daylight came, and the roads to the west became hopelessly congested.

"The bombardment has continued all day, but the spirit of the people is unbroken. The Burgomaster has declared his fixed intention of supporting the military in resisting to the last."

The First Shell.

A dispatch to The Chronicle from Antwerp, dated Thursday, says:

"Exactly at midnight the bombardment of the town began. I was awakened from my sleep by the whirl of a shell, and ten seconds after a crash resounded. It had evidently found its mark in the direction of Berchem. I went out into the street and listened. A German shell again landed in the town in the same direction as the first.

"People darted out of houses, and then, on the sound of firing, darted back again into cellars. Others rushed in mad haste to cross the bridge over the Scheldt, and so get to St. Nicolas. In my hotel all the women have taken refuge in the cellar. There are only seven of us upstairs.

"Thursday, 5 A. M.—Firing continues very close. I am informed now that the bombardment to which I have referred failed actually to reach the town by a few hundred yards. We have all been turned out of our beds by the proprietor, who has fled, leaving us in charge. There is a report that this firing all night has been a vigorous offensive action assumed by the Belgians.

"Thursday, 6 A. M.—The night has passed without any incident. I have witnessed most extraordinary scenes down by the Quai Jordaens, where two boats are leaving for Ostend. There is room for 800 on each of these boats, and about 10,000 are waiting to embark. Desperate pleas are being urged by those who wish to leave. Panic reigns and the crowd sways to and fro, shouting hoarsely."

Scheldt Ablaze with Oil.

Another Chronicle correspondent at Antwerp wrote on Thursday at 4 P. M.:

"The bombardment of Antwerp has now been proceeding without cessation for sixteen hours. It began practically at midnight on Wednesday. As a result of the enemy's terrific fire, all the oil tanks along the river bank are ablaze, and blazing oil, flowing down the stream, is threatening the pontoon bridge.

"Practically the whole of Berchem, the southern suburb of Antwerp, has been destroyed or is in flames, and houses are burning all over town since the early hours of the morning. A continuous torrent of fugitives has been making its way over the pontoon bridge. Such boats as remain in the stream are now packed with the fleeing population, and along either bank is a straggling line of these unfortunate folk, making their way northward, carrying such of their household goods as they have been able to snatch up in a few moments.

"Up to the present, I believe, none of the public buildings has been hit. They are all flying The Hague Convention flag, but nevertheless shells have dropped in close proximity to the cathedral. This I know, because I am sitting in the Place Verte, and one projectile, which I judged to be a six-inch shell, a few minutes ago struck a café on the other side of the square, which now is in flames. The Germans are also making every attempt to destroy the pontoon bridge. The cathedral tower is in direct line of fire. [Here a portion of the message has been deleted by censor.]"

King Leaves Antwerp.

From Amsterdam The Chronicle receives the following dispatch, dated Thursday:

"The departure of the King of the Belgians for Selzaete is described in the Handlsblad. There was a great crowd of refugees on the bank of the Scheldt. Suddenly loud cries of 'Long live the King and Queen!' were given, and the people saw in their midst a gray motor car containing the royal pair. For a moment all forgot their sorrows and anxieties in the hearty cheers. The crowd was so dense that the motor had to be brought to a standstill until the police had cleared a way. Then some one cried 'Au revoir,' and there was more cheering, and for a moment the King's gravity relaxed into a smile of gratification. Then the motor crossed the military pontoon bridge to the west side of the Scheldt, where the royal train had been kept standing ready in the station. It had been struck by a shell and damaged, but fortunately no one was near.

"No trains are running from Ghent in a northerly or an easterly direction.

"The Germans have advanced to Neerpelt and Achel, near the Dutch frontier. All inhabitants in the district have fled."

The Daily Mail receives the following from Ostend, dated Thursday:

"Eleven Antwerp forts, presumably all belonging to the outer line of defense, have been put out of action by German shells. According to the latest advices the situation shows a distinct improvement. The troops have made a very successful sortie which resulted in the capture of 3,000 Germans and forced the Germans to abandon their guns at Linth and recross the Nèthe.

"This intelligence has naturally created hope that the gallant defenders may yet hold out till the Allies are able to raise the siege."

Latest News Bulletins From Antwerp Showed City Aflame and Many Civilians Killed

Special Cable to THE NEW YORK TIMES.
Dispatch to The London Daily Chronicle.

ROSENDAAL, Oct. 9.—With the full force of their big guns, including 16½-inch howitzers, the Germans today are continuing the bombardment of Antwerp and the inner line of forts. Incendiary shells, which the Germans are pouring into the place, are having their effect, and the city is now burning at several points. Fire brigades are restricting the area of the outbreaks.

Many civilians have been killed by falling shells. Practically the town has now been deserted except for the Belgian troops.

Report That Bombardment Has Slackened.

LONDON, Saturday, Oct. 10.—The Daily Mail's Ostend correspondent, telegraphing late on Friday, says:

"Stubborn fighting is proceeding before the Antwerp fortifications. Four assaults have been repulsed at No. 4 Fort, at Vieux Dieu. The bombardment of the town appears to be somewhat diminishing in intensity."

OUR CONSUL TELLS OF ANTWERP HORROR

Flees From City With Family After One Night Under German Shells.

Special Cable to THE NEW YORK TIMES.

GHENT, Oct. 9, (Dispatch to The London Daily Chronicle.)—Henry W. Diederich, United States Consul at Antwerp, escaped with his family from the city yesterday by motor car. The following is his account of the bombardment:

"For days we heard the sound of heavy gun fire, and were told of the fall, one after another, of the outer forts. It soon became apparent that nothing could avail against the great German cannon, and in conjunction with other neutrals we endeavored to mediate with the Germans to spare at any rate some of the most valuable buildings of world-wide interest, but the negotiations failed to lead to a successful result.

"I had intended to remain in Antwerp throughout the bombardment which we saw was inevitable. I was told to clear out of the city as its destruction was inevitable, but I did not realize until almost too late the horror which was coming.

"At 11 o'clock at night we were going to bed when we were roused by frightful noises in the air reminding us of the previous visits of the Zeppelins. Soon we realized that the bombardment had commenced, and then I had the most horrible experience of my whole life. I went with my family to the basement, and we crouched there all night, shells falling every few minutes. They came with a dreadful whistling sound followed by a thunderclap and the collapse of some buildings.

"Opposite the Consulate is the Home for Old Folk. The front was torn out by a shell. Some of the débris scattered over my house and the rest fell on a two-story building, crumpling it up entirely and setting it on fire. After this another shell blew out the facade of a house lower down our street.

"As dawn came we were wearied out, and my family having utterly collapsed from fright and strain, we decided to endeavor to leave the city. I succeeded in communicating with my chauffeur and got my car, but did not know where to go, being left with nothing but what we had on, and being exposed every moment to exploding shells.

"With my wife, daughter, two servants and a refugee's child I crossed the pontoon bridge over the Scheldt. It took us four hours to do this, the street being a seething mass of every kind of vehicle and a dense crowd of fugitives. The scene was indescribably dreadful, everybody being moved by the same desire to get away from the awful horror.

"From Antwerp to Ghent the roads are a mass of fleeing humanity. As we left we saw vast volumes of smoke arising from Antwerp from burning buildings and blazing petroleum tanks. Instead of two hours to Ghent it took us three, owing to the traffic. One of the German big guns situated near Vilvorde and a number of comparatively smaller guns have joined in the bombardment."

LONDON, Oct. 9.—The American Embassy in London has been very anxious to hear from Consul General Henry W. Diederich and Vice Consul Harry T. Sherman of the American Consulate at Antwerp.

Hugh S. Gibson, Secretary of the American Legation at Brussels, and

Continued on Page 2.

ATTACK ON BRITAIN AFTER ANTWERP'S FALL

Germans Said to Plan Cross-Channel Operations—Navy to Get Busy Under von Tirpitz.

ROME, (via Paris.) Oct. 9.—The war against Great Britain, according to German newspapers received here, will commence at the end of October, after Antwerp has fallen. Belgium then will become the base of operations against Great Britain, the newspapers say.

They add that Admiral von Tirpitz, the Minister of the Navy, who is now at General Headquarters with Emperor William, has announced that he will go aboard the flagship of the German fleet and direct the operations of the navy.

Since it became evident on Oct. 2 that the Germans intended seriously to invest Antwerp with three army corps three explanations have been put forward by military critics:

1. That the reduction of the military capital of Belgium as a base for Belgian operations against German lines of communication into France was necessary in order to make use elsewhere of the large bodies of troops protecting these lines.

2. That with Antwerp in the hands of the Germans the city could be used as a base for Zeppelins to attack the English coast towns and particularly London.

3. That Antwerp could be used as a station for warships from which they could not only attack England's eastern coast towns, but also harm English commerce on the North Sea, which supplies the British Isles with most of their food products.

Antwerp is 180 miles from London, and it would be physically possible to operate Zeppelins with London as the objective. In fact, London has feared a Zeppelin attack for some time, and has protected herself against it. The lighting of the streets is reduced at night, and strong searchlights sweep the heavens over the Thames, several hydroplanes are ready to attack the invaders, and stations on the Channel keep watch night and day. Incidentally, Lloyds is insuring against Zeppelin attacks. Military experts, however, doubt that the Germans would trouble to set up a Zeppelin base in hostile territory at Antwerp when they already have established bases at Dusseldorf, barely an hour's sail distant (by air), and on Heligoland.

Antwerp, 180 miles from London, however, is less than 100 miles from the English Coast. The present Zeppelin station and their distances from the English Coast are as follows:

Heligoland (possibly inactive), about	400 miles
Emden, about	400 miles
Hamburg, about	450 miles
Düsseldorf (badly damaged Wednesday), about	300 miles
Cologne, about	300 miles
Bremen, about	410 miles

The idea of Antwerp as a naval base is open to two objections: the lack of ships and the fact that if German ships could escape from the German North Sea coast, before they could take up their position at Antwerp, they would be obliged to navigate the neutral waters of Holland. That is, they could not reach Antwerp without sailing through the Scheldt for fifty miles and thus violate Dutch neutrality. If Holland objected, as Belgium did, the forts at the mouth of the Scheldt would probably give as good account of themselves as did Liège and Namur.

LONDON LIGHTS LOWER.

New Police Warning to Hide the City from German Airships.

Special Cable to THE NEW YORK TIMES.

LONDON, Oct. 9.—London is becoming constantly darker with the carrying out of police orders directing the lowering of all lights in the city in order to disguise localities from hostile aircraft.

New instructions were issued tonight to warn the people that burning bright lights endangers their section of the city as well as the community generally. The number of lights is now reduced to those necessary for traffic.

ALLIES WIN SHARP FIGHT

Encounter Around Roye One of Many Along the Left Wing.

CAVALRY BATTLES GO ON

Large Forces of Mounted Men on Each Side North of Lille.

ARTILLERY DUEL ON MEUSE

Germans in Force Are Reported at Points West of Lille and South of Ostend.

PARIS, Oct. 9, 11:09 P. M.—This bulletin was issued by the War Office this evening:

There is nothing new to report except that there has been a lively engagement in the region of Roye, where in the last two days we have captured 1,600 prisoners.

This official announcement was given out in the afternoon:

The general situation has undergone no change.

On our left wing the two opposing bodies of cavalry are still operating to the north of Lille and La Bassée, and the battle continues along the line marked by the regions of Lens, Arras, Bray-sur-Somme, Chaulnes, Roye, and Lassigny.

On the centre of the Oise and on the Meuse only actions of minor importance have been reported.

On our right, in the Woevre district, there has been an artillery contest along the entire front.

In Lorraine, in the Vosges, and in Alsace there has been no change.

In Bosnia, Montenegrin troops have continued their advance in the direction of Serajevo as far as the fortified line, which protects the city at a distance from it of eight kilometers.

Report Allies' Line Is in Belgium.

LONDON, Oct. 9.—It is reported tonight that the long battle line in France has finally passed the frontier, and now reaches into Belgium.

The Allies hope to extend their lines to Antwerp, and thus force an opening for the garrison of the fortress.

Much of the success of the Allies' campaign may depend upon the length of the siege of Antwerp. Every day the Belgians hold out is reckoned by military strategists here as a day gained by the Allies. The strategists argue that if the fortress is captured or capitulates, a German army of 125,000 men will be sent to the assistance of Gen. von Kluck, and that their number will tell.

GERMAN ADVANCE HALTED.

Allies' Lines Hold Against Terrific Assault of Left Wing.

ON THE BATTLE FRONT, Oct. 9, (via Paris.)—The sharp, offensive movement of the Germans on the western wing of the Allies at the Belgian frontier has evidently failed in its object of bending or breaking the French and British line.

The long extension of the battle line, which has now gone beyond the four rivers, the Scarpe, Somme, Oise, and Aisne, was initiated by the Allies in an endeavor to find a solution of the problem of ousting the Germans from their strong position in Northeastern France.

In these positions the Germans had been besieged nearly a month, since the conclusion of the bloody battle of the Marne, a frontal attack being regarded as inexpedient by the Allies. The present front is within about 68 miles of Antwerp, where the Belgians have offered such heroic resistance to the bombardment of the heavy German artillery.

Toward the centre of the Allies' line the severest fighting continued today at Roye, where the Allies took a large number of prisoners. Rheims again was subjected to a short bombardment.

In other parts of the centre the opposing forces remain constantly alert. The cannonade has diminished in intensity and the Allied troops, occupying the trenches, are becoming thoroughly accustomed to the situation. Many of them spend the intervals between the spells of the rifle firing reading newspapers to their comrades beneath the bomb-proof shelters.

The allied artillerymen seem indefatigable, replying with vigor whenever a cannon opens fire. The men throw themselves on the ground when they

Mid-Week Pictorial

Belgian soldiers defend an approach to Antwerp.

"All the News That's Fit to Print."

The New York Times.

THE WEATHER
Fair today and tomorrow, not much change in temperature; moderate west winds.
For full weather report see Page 11.

VOL. LXIV...NO. 20,733. NEW YORK, FRIDAY, OCTOBER 30, 1914.—SIXTEEN PAGES. ONE CENT In Greater New York, Jersey City and Newark. | Elsewhere TWO CENTS.

TURKEY BEGINS WAR ON RUSSIA; WARSHIPS SHELL BLACK SEA PORTS; DEADLOCK ON LINES IN BELGIUM

ALLIES PLACING BIG WAR ORDERS

Factories, Meat Packers, and Arms Plants Here Turning Out Army Supplies.

BRITAIN BUYS 30,000 HORSES

New England Concerns Turning Out 2,200,000 Pairs of Boots and Shoes for Troops.

RECORD BARLEY CROP SOLD

California Exports Huge Shipments of Grain, Fruit and Fish—Gary Predicts Better Times.

Special to The New York Times.

BOSTON, Mass., Oct. 29.—New England manufacturers of shoes have already booksd orders for 2,200,000 pairs for export to the European belligerents. Negotiations are under way for further orders, but some manufacturers hesitate because the profit is hard to calculate.

France, which has already placed large orders, desires hob-nailed boots for her soldiers. These must be made by hand, and it is a question as to how expensive the hob-nailing process will be. One manufacturer has installed special machinery for this purpose.

The W. H. McElwain Company, which received an order for 200,000 pairs for France last week, has had the order increased to 300,000 pairs. It is debating whether to increase its facilities and accept an order for 1,000,000 pairs of boots. The Endicott-Johnson Company is making 500,000 pairs of boots for Greece.

There is a corresponding boom in leather. One company, with an annual turnover of $12,000,000, is running its factories day and night at 125 per cent. capacity. Before the war it was running at 40 per cent. capacity. Most of the leather is for England, and is to be made into boots there for the army. So far England has bought no boots in the United States, but is expected to place orders soon. Its demand for leather has put up the price 4 to 6 cents a foot.

BUY 20,000 MORE HORSES.

Missouri and Illinois to Furnish Mounts for the Allies.

ST. LOUIS, Oct. 29.—Twenty thousand additional head of horses are to be purchased in Missouri and southern Illinois by agents of the British, French, and Russian Governments, according to reports in livestock circles here today. It is said that the agents of the various Governments have been instructed to make the purchases.

A uniform price of $270 is being paid for each horse.

The French agents, also, have bought 100,000 barrels of flour and great quantities of other provisions here; and orders have been placed with local shoe factories for thousands of pairs of shoes.

The German Government is said to be offering $600 to $800 a head for horses delivered in Germany.

MILLIONS FOR CHICAGO.

Packers Have Enough War Orders to Run for a Year.

CHICAGO, Oct. 29.—War orders for clothing, trucks, harness, tinned meats, and the like in the Chicago and neighboring markets amount to between $7,000,000 and $8,000,000, and purchasing agents of the British and French Governments are still buying. England has $3,000,000 gold in a local bank to be used for purchases. The meat packers have enough European orders on hand to keep them running full time for a year.

The opposing Governments have agents watching the purchases of each other in this market. They begin by apparently sincere correspondence about prices and quantities, but their queries invariably lead to details of transport. With this information their warships are kept on the lookout for shipments to hostile Governments.

$1,500,000 ORDER FOR LATHES.

Arms Companies Also Busy Making Army Supplies.

Special to The New York Times.

HARTFORD, Conn., Oct. 29.—Within the last two weeks 1,700 machine lathes of moderate capacity, such as 12 to 14 inches, have been shipped to Europe. One thousand more of these lathes are required, the whole to cost $1,500,000. The order will exhaust the present stock of such lathes in the United States. The Colt, the Smith & Wesson, the Remington & Union metallic cartridge plants are working overtime on machine guns, pistols, and ammunition, and these eventually find their way to Europe, though the manufacturers deal only with their regular American agents.

CALIFORNIA DOING WELL.

Record Exports of Barley, Canned Fruits, and Salmon.

SAN FRANCISCO, Oct. 29.—The effect of the war upon Pacific Coast staples is shown in a tabulation prepared here today by the Chamber of Commerce.

Barley this year was a bumper crop. The exports from this port for the last three months reached the unprecedented total of 3,785,452 quintals, as against 332,891 for the corresponding period in 1913.

For canned fruits the figures are 780,-093 cases this year, against 523,039 in

Continued on Page 4.

MADISON AVE. CAR KILLS W. B. SHEARDOWN

Woman Companion Succors Standard Milling Official Until Ambulance Arrives.

Ward B. Sheardown of 644 Madison Avenue, Second Vice President of the Standard Milling Company, 49 Wall Street, started across Madison Avenue yesterday afternoon in front of the car barns at Thirty-second Street. He was escorting a woman, and in assisting her stepped so close to the tracks that a northbound car struck him. The woman escaped injury.

Mr. Sheardown was knocked senseless. He was carried into the car barns, where his companion ministered to him until Dr. Taylor arrived from Bellevue Hospital. He found that Mr. Sheardown had a fractured skull and internal injuries, and hurried him to the hospital, where he died early in the evening.

The woman tried to ride in the ambulance, and when she was not permitted to do so followed to the hospital, where she left two telephone numbers, asking that she be notified of any change in Mr. Sheardown's condition. The hospital authorities refused to make these public.

Three men, one of whom said he was a physician, called also at the hospital, but were told that Mr. Sheardown had succumbed. They left without giving their names. Mr. Sheardown was 55 years old and was single.

DOUBTS OUR PATRIOTISM.

Real Thing Only in Middle West, Admiral Stockton Thinks.

Special to The New York Times.

WASHINGTON, Oct. 29.—Rear Admiral Charles Herbert Stockton, President of George Washington University, in presenting diplomas to twelve students at the Fall convocation today, said that the efforts now being put forward by the contending powers of Europe afforded a lesson in patriotism that Americans might well take to heart. The Admiral pointedly asked the question whether Americans would be willing to make such sacrifices, and his answer was less than a weak affirmative.

"Have we its equal in this country?" asked Admiral Stockton. "I doubt it. If it is to be found any place, it is in the Middle West. And that is because it is built on a love of community. I believe that the maximum of patriotism in the United States is to be found in the States of the Middle West, and the minimum in the City of Washington. When something arises that requires action, the Middle West says: 'What shall we do?' In Washington we say, 'What shall Congress do?' But I can see signs of a better civic spirit arising.

"Let me impress upon you a few of the great virtues of several of the countries engaged in the war. Take the marvelous efficiency, military and civil, that is shown by Germany. It is a thoroughness that goes to the bottom. Consider the charm that is presented by France, both in literature and general culture. Its clarity, its beauty, bring you within the realm of imagination. And what is life without imagination? Why, without imagination, even the daily war news you read in the papers means very little—a touch of brilliancy, perhaps; but with imagination present then all war's sorrow and horror is brought home.

"Do not be simply a professional man. Be an active member of society in its broader phases. What you do, do with the thoroughness of the Germans, accompany it with the charm of the French, and the patriotism of the middle-class Russians."

100,000 STEEL MEN IDLE.

Figures for Pittsburgh District — Conditions Worse in Nearby West.

Special to The New York Times.

PITTSBURGH, Oct. 29.—After investigation The Gazette-Times declares that in the Pittsburgh industrial district there are 100,000 mill workers idle, a ratio larger than for many years. The average activity of the steel plants is placed at less than 40 per cent. while in the immediate adjoining districts of the Middle West the depression has reduced operations to between 25 and 30 per cent.

The Carnegie Steel Company has just blown out the last of its Isabella blast furnaces, and the stacks of the same company at Sharpsburg are idle. The company now has twenty-six furnaces operating out of a total of fifty-nine, the lowest number on the active list for many years. Other big plants, such as the Independent Jones & Laughlin Company, are operating at even less capacity.

In the Connellsville coke region actual operations are only at 40 per cent. of capacity. The Frick Coke Company this week blew out 1,200 ovens.

The same authority reports the outlook in the steel trade as dismal in the extreme. The export business developing as a result of the European war promises the only considerable business in sight for iron and steel manufacturers. Up to the present export orders have materially assisted many plants.

NO WORD FROM CUNARDERS

But Lusitania and Franconia Are Expected to Dock Today.

The agents of the Cunard Line stated last night that no message had been received from the Captains of the Lusitania and Franconia before the office closed at 6 o'clock. The company was notified that the Nantucket Lightship wireless apparatus was out of commission, which may account for the lack of news regarding the movements of the ships.

The Lusitania is expected to be at her pier about 8:30 A. M. today and the Franconia about noon. Both vessels are from Liverpool. The Cedric of the White Star Line from Liverpool is expected to arrive about 11 A. M.

CROWN PRINCE WOUNDED?

Kaiser's Heir Reported Injured While Leading Attack on Verdun.

ROME, Friday, Oct. 30.—It is reported here that the German Crown Prince has been wounded while leading an attack on Verdun.

This is the second or third time that reports have come that the Kaiser's eldest son had been wounded.

FRANCE BORROWS $10,000,000 HERE

National City Bank Will Provide Warring Republic with Cash on Treasury Notes.

ALL TO BE SPENT HERE

No Public Offering of Notes Will Be Made, Thus Avoiding Neutrality Issues.

FIRST LOAN TO BELLIGERENT

Germany Likely to Reopen Negotiations for American Funds—$3,000,000 to Norway.

The French Government has arranged for a loan of $10,000,000 in the United States to help carry on the war. The money is to be provided by the National City Bank of New York, which will accept 6 per cent. Treasury notes running for nine months. No public offering of the notes will be made.

Emphasis was laid on the fact that these notes are not to be sold to investors when bankers were asked last night for an expression of opinion on the question of neutrality involved. In frowning upon an earlier proposal for a French loan, the State Department disclaimed reliance upon any legal prohibition, but stated that a public offering of securities of a belligerent country might easily lead to rivalry that would cause bad feeling.

Another objection interposed by the State Department to the earlier proposal was that it would lead to large gold exports, to the embarrassment of this country's financial position. It is not expected that any money will go to France out of the proceeds of the notes just sold. The money is being advanced on the understanding that it is to be spent in the United States, presumably for munitions of war and foodstuffs, which are going out in increasing volume.

As a national bank cannot loan more than 10 per cent. of its capital and surplus to a single borrower, $4,000,000 or $5,000,000 of the $10,000,000 will be taken by other banks. J. P. Morgan & Co., who carried the question of neutrality to Washington, in the early part of the war, were consulted in regard to this loan, but are to have no part in it.

First Loan to Belligerent.

This is the first loan made to any of the belligerents by bankers in this country. In the early part of August, immediately following the outbreak of hostilities, J. P. Morgan & Co. arranged for an interchange of credits with the Bank of France, under the terms of which $12,000,000 was placed at the disposal of the French Ambassador here in return for a like amount transferred to Morgan, Harjes & Co. in Paris. It was promised that the French Government would not call for gold under this agreement, but would use its credit to pay for supplies purchased here. The credit obtained in Paris by the Morgan house there was used to relieve the scarcity of funds to satisfy American letters of credit and other needs.

The original arrangement was subsequently enlarged to $16,000,000 and a few weeks later the French Government approached J. P. Morgan & Co. in an effort to float a loan of $50,000,000. The bankers took the matter up with Secretary Bryan, who made it plain that this Government would not countenance advances to any of the belligerents, whereupon negotiations were dropped.

Government Modifies Stand.

Two weeks ago the State Department modified its stand by saying that American bankers, collectively or individually, were free to make loans to the European nations. It was made clear, however, that where such transactions were submitted to the President for his opinion he would not favor them. It was said that the President would not take cognizance of loans that were made without consulting him.

"This loan is not a violation of the sentiments expressed by the Washington authorities," said a banker, who took part in the negotiations leading to the loan just placed. "It amounts to the establishment here of a credit to the French Government. It is a banking, rather than an investment matter. Any belligerent nation has the undoubted right to get funds here to pay for obligations incurred in this country. The same thing is done in times of peace; we have often arranged for a credit abroad under a similar arrangement."

The National City Bank has also loaned $3,000,000 to Norway. As that country is neutral, no question could be raised as to the bankers' right to furnish the money. Switzerland attempted to borrow money here a few weeks ago, but did not succeed in obtaining funds.

In the light of the French loan, interest was reawakened last night in efforts made some days ago by the German Government to float a loan here. Inquiries made on behalf of Berlin were discontinued at the suggestion that it was deemed unwise to loan to any of the belligerents, but it now appears likely that negotiations will be reopened.

GERMAN SUBMARINE SUNK.

Craft That Attacked British Battleship Sent to the Bottom.

LONDON, Friday, Oct. 30.—The Daily Mail correspondent "on the Allies' left wing" reports that a German submarine boat, which attacked the British battleship Venerable off the Belgian coast, has been sunk.

$500,000,000 MORE ON BRITISH WAR BILL

$435,000,000 Spent Already—New List of Casualties Out Contains 88 Officers.

LONDON, Friday, Oct. 30.—It is announced that when Parliament reassembles on Nov. 11 Premier Asquith will move a vote for another $500,000,000 on account of the war.

A similar amount was voted in August, of which $435,000,000 is already gone.

A new British casualty list, dated Oct. 24 and Oct. 27, issued last night, gives the names of twenty-three officers killed, forty-eight wounded, and seventeen missing.

Among the killed are Capt. the Hon. Charles Henry Stanley Monck of the Coldstream Guards, heir of Viscount Monck, and Lieut. Col. W. L. Loring of the Royal Warwickshire Regiment.

In the list of wounded appear the names of Major Lord Esme Charles Gordon-Lennox of the Scots Guards, second son of the Duke of Richmond; Lieut. Col. G. [illegible] T. Fielding of the Coldstream Guards, Brevet Lieut. Col. C. G. Stewart of the Royal Field Artillery, and Lieut. Col. Hugh Davie White-Thomson of the Royal Horse Artillery.

19 WOMEN KILLED BY AEROPLANE BOMB

Dropped from a German Machine—Fell in a Group in French Market Place.

Special Cable to THE NEW YORK TIMES.

LONDON, Friday, Oct. 30.—A Daily Mail correspondent telegraphs from the "North of France," under date of Thursday:

"Two German aeroplanes flew over yesterday and dropped two bombs at Bethune. The first did not explode, but the second fell among a group of women in the market place, nineteen being killed and forty injured."

Another Daily Mail correspondent telegraphs that he was walking near the Dunkirk Town Hall on Wednesday when two bombs were dropped by a Taube and fell within fifty yards. One woman and a child of 10 years were killed. Seven or eight French aeroplanes chased the Taube with an unknown result.

GIANT SUBMARINES TESTED BY GERMANS

Said to be Four Times the Size of Existing Craft—Can Cruise For Forty Days.

Special Cable to THE NEW YORK TIMES.

LONDON, Oct. 29.—The Daily Mail's Copenhagen correspondent says it is reported from Hamburg that two giant submarines are making trial trips at the mouth of the Elbe.

They are said to be four times the size of any existing submarines and to be able to keep at sea for forty days without having to replenish or even join mother ships.

At the outbreak of the war Germany was credited with having thirty submarines, of which twenty-four were kept in commission during 1913.

The latest known series, beginning with U 21, are 213 feet long, with a beam of 20 feet, and have three torpedo tubes and two guns mounted forward. Details of these vessels are not obtainable owing to the secrecy that shrouded their construction, but it is known that they have a surface speed of 17 knots and an under-water speed of about 12. Their average cruising speed will not exceed 10 knots, and this gives them a cruising range of about 1,000 miles under their own fuel. They can remain submerged about ten hours.

KING URGES BELGIANS TO DRIVE OUT INVADERS

Greater Disasters Will Follow if Country Is Not Freed, He Tells the People.

LONDON, Oct. 29.—The Exchange Telegraph's Amsterdam correspondent sends the following proclamation issued by King Albert to the Belgian troops:

"Our towns have been burned and our houses destroyed, and there is mourning over the whole country. But more terrible disasters will follow if we do not free the country of the invaders.

"That is your imperative duty, and it is a duty you can fulfill with the assistance of our allies."

CANADIAN BORDER TALKING OF INVASION

Fear That Germans and Austrians Living in the United States May Attempt It.

Special to The New York Times.

OTTAWA, Ontario, Oct. 29.—Reports have reached here of a feeling of nervousness at certain places along the international border over the supposed danger of an invasion by Germans and Austrians living across the line.

Such fears are declared to be unnecessary because the Government is fully cognizant of conditions along the border, and in addition there will be from now until the end of the war a force of approximately 40,000 men mobilized and under arms in different parts of the country. These include about 10,000 on guard duty and home defense, and 30,000 in training for overseas service. This whole body would be an effective protection against any possible raid.

The Militia Department has also been informed of a factory at St. John, on the Isle of Orleans, controlled by Germans, who are said to have a branch factory at Port Arthur. They make cement blocks, and it is suggested that these places have been secretly established for purposes of attack like those found near Paris and London. The factory site on the Isle of Orleans commands the river leading to Quebec.

CRIMEAN TOWN ATTACKED

The Breslau Bombards Theodosia—Goeben Sinks Two Ships.

NOVOROSSYSK SHELLED, TOO

Another Report Says the Hamidieh Only Demanded Caucasian Town's Surrender.

TENTH NATION IN CONFLICT

Tokio Announces Turkey's War on Russia—Allies Threaten, if Egypt Is Invaded.

TOKIO, Friday, Oct. 30, 11:15 A. M. —The Russian Embassy here announces that Turkey has opened war on Russia.

Turkey is the tenth nation to enter the war. The other nine in the order of their beginning hostilities are: Austria, Servia, Germany, Russia, France, Montenegro, Belgium, Great Britain, and Japan.

Special Cable to THE NEW YORK TIMES.

PETROGRAD, Oct. 29, (Dispatch to The London Times.)—Turkey has begun hostilities by bombarding peaceful seacoast towns. Messages just received at Petrograd announce the simultaneous appearance this morning of the cruiser Breslau off Theodosia, Caucasia, and the cruiser Hamidieh off Novorossysk.

The German-Turkish warships shelled these unfortified places.

THEODOSIA, Crimea, via Petrograd, Oct. 29.—From 9:30 to 10:30 o'clock this morning a Turkish cruiser with three funnels bombarded the railway station and city, damaging the Cathedral, the Greek Church, a pier, and some sheds.

One soldier was wounded.

A branch of the Russian Bank of Foreign Commerce was set on fire.

At the conclusion of the bombardment the cruiser departed in a southerly direction.

NOVOROSSYSK, Caucasia, via Petrograd, Oct. 29.—The Turkish cruiser Hamidieh, which arrived here today, demanded the surrender of the city and the Government properties, threatening in case of refusal to bombard the town.

The Turkish Consul and other officials were arrested.

The cruiser withdrew.

INVASION OF EGYPT MEANS WAR BY ALLIES

Grand Vizier Warned, If Turks Cross the Frontier, the Triple Entente Will Fight.

CONSTANTINOPLE, (via London,) Friday, Oct. 30.—In anticipation of the possible invasion of Egyptian territory, British Ambassador Mallett, acting under instructions from his Government, has plainly informed the Grand Vizier that if the Turks cross the frontier it would mean war with the powers of the Triple Entente.

It is understood that the embassies of the allied powers, fearing a rupture, have already made the necessary arrangements for the departure of the diplomatic representatives.

GOEBEN SINKS TWO VESSELS.

Torpedoes the Yalta and Kazbek—Many Lost with Latter.

LONDON, Thursday, Oct. 30.—A Petrograd dispatch to Reuter's Telegram Company says:

"A dispatch from Kertch, a seaport in the Crimea, reports that near Takol Lighthouse the Russian steamer Yalta, from the Caucasus, was sunk by a torpedo launched by the Turkish cruiser Goeben. The crew and passengers were saved.

"The steamer Kazbek, which went to the rescue, was struck by two torpedoes and sank. Many persons aboard were drowned."

ALLIES READY FOR TURKEY.

Greece, Too, Is Fully Prepared, The London Times Asserts.

Special Cable to THE NEW YORK TIMES.

LONDON, Friday, Oct. 30.—The Times's war editorial says:

"The Allies are quite ready for Turkey and have been ready for her for a long time. All preparations for a

Continued on Page 4.

Summary of War News.

The Russian Embassy in Tokio announced this morning that Turkey had begun war on Russia. A Turkish cruiser yesterday bombarded Theodosia, in the Crimea, inflicting considerable damage. The Turkish cruiser Hamidieh appeared off Novorossysk, in the Caucasus, and demanded the surrender of the city, but departed without firing.

The French War Office announced the capture of German trenches in the region between the Aisne and the Argonne, and the repulse of all German attacks. A Bordeaux dispatch received in Washington told of the dislodging of some German outposts along the frontier between Moselle and the Vosges.

The German General Headquarters gave out a statement to the effect that the Germans were slowly gaining ground south of Nieuport and making good progress west of Lille. It also reported the repulse of French attacks southwest of Verdun and the occupation of the main French position.

Petrograd advices say that the main German armies in Poland have been widely separated and are in full retreat. On the East Prussian frontier both sides claim success.

The German cruiser Emden, flying the Japanese flag, entered the Harbor of Penang in the Straits Settlements and sank the Russian cruiser Jemtchug and a French destroyer.

The agent of the American Committee for Belgian Relief sends word to London that he fears the hungry Belgians, in desperation, may attack the authorities in some of the towns, which would be followed, he says, by great loss of life.

PEACE OVERTURES MADE TO FRANCE

German Suggestion That if She Quit Now She Might Get Metz and More—Quick Refusal.

Special Cable to THE NEW YORK TIMES.

LONDON, Friday, Oct. 30.—G. H. Perris, Paris correspondent of The Daily Chronicle, describes in a dispatch to his paper an alleged German attempt to make peace with France at the expense of the other Allies. His dispatch says:

"For combined audacity and trickiness, nothing within my knowledge equals the attempt which the Kaiser's advisers and agents have made during the last few days to separate France from her allies and enable the German Government, while posing before the outer world and its own people as earnestly desirous for peace, to pursue the war with hopes of success.

"Information has been conveyed to certain influential Frenchmen, who were expected to act as intermediaries, that the German Imperial Government recognizes the splendid showing made by the French armies; that it has never regarded France as its principal enemy in this struggle, and that it is ready to make peace on terms not merely honorable but generous to the republic. These terms would include the transfer to France of Metz and the neighboring portion of Lorraine, and perhaps a part of Alsace.

"I need say nothing of the spellbound astonishment with which this proposition—conveyed, it is true, not through official, but through commercial and financial channels, yet with apparent authority—was listened to. No Frenchman can now for a moment ignore the horrible injuries the war is working—it is even easier for false than for true prophets of peace to play upon this note—but neither can any responsible Frenchman ignore for a moment the fact of the multiple alliance and all it stands for in the present and future. What about Servia? What about Russia? What about England? Above all, what about the martyrland, Belgium?

"I am informed that before these questions the would-be negotiators fell to vague shrugging of dubious shoulders, but opined that Germany would have to require at least an enclave on the Scheldt—in other words, Antwerp and Northern Belgium.

"As to the other three powers, they could look after themselves; but here was an opportunity for France, an arrangement which she could not hope to better, even if, with her friends, at a frightful cost, she was able to carry the war to a victorious issue.

"I believe that, with all the bitter suffering that lies heavy on this land, no public man dare openly favor, and probably not one would privately entertain, a bargain which would be universally regarded as treachery to France, as well as betrayal of her friends. It is not even a question of loyalty to a written promise, to the 'scrap of paper' in which the Allies undertook at the outset of the war not to conclude peace separately. Despite the suspicions which the old-fashioned diplomacy, of a time now dead and gone, has brought upon itself, the peoples of England and France believe deeply in honoring the promises made for them; but they are bound together now by the tie of the blood of a common sacrifice, necessarily stronger than any such scruple or the instrument in which it is expressed.

"There never was, or could be, a moment's hesitation as to the answer France would make to such a proposition, and if that were the whole question it would not be worth while for me to invite the inevitable dementi from Berlin. But, to say nothing now of a future, possibly distant, in which genuine peace negotiations will have to take place, there is an immediate reason why this piece of Prussian diplomacy should be made public.

"The Allies cannot afford to leave Count von Bernstorff, Dr. Dernburg, and Prof. Münsterberg any new text from which they can attempt to mislead American opinion. Intelligence, interest, and even lack of interest combine in the United States to produce a vague feeling that the war should be brought to an end somehow, anyhow. It is a sentiment altogether creditable to a great humane and neutral power

Continued on Page 2.

PRINCE LOUIS RESIGNS AS FIRST SEA LORD

Gives Way to Clamor Over German Spies and Leaves High Naval Office in England.

Special Cable to THE NEW YORK TIMES.

LONDON, Friday, Oct. 30.—Prince Louis of Battenberg, who for many weeks has been the target of all sorts of innuendo, has resigned as First Sea Lord.

The King has appointed Prince Louis a member of the Privy Council.

LONDON, Friday, Oct. 30.—Announcement of Prince Louis' resignation was made last night in the Court Circular, which recorded that the Prince had been received in audience by the King on relinquishing his appointment.

The Admiralty has issued the following correspondence between Prince Louis and Winston Spencer Churchill, First Lord of the Admiralty. Prince Louis in a letter to Mr. Churchill, dated Oct. 28, said:

> Dear Mr. Churchill—I have lately been driven to the painful conclusion that at this juncture my birth and parentage have the effect of impairing in some respects my usefulness on the Board of the Admiralty. In these circumstances I feel it to be my duty as a loyal subject of His Majesty to resign my office of First Sea Lord, hoping thereby to facilitate the task of the Administration of the great service to which I have devoted my life and to ease the burden laid on his Majesty's ministers. I am yours very truly,
>
> LOUIS OF BATTENBERG, Admiral.

Mr. Churchill under date of Oct. 29 replied to Prince Louis as follows:

> My Dear Prince Louis: This is no ordinary war, but a struggle between nations for life or death. It raises passions between the races of a most terrible kind. It effaces the old landmarks and frontiers of our civilization.
>
> I cannot further oppose the wish you have during the last few weeks expressed to me to be released from the burden of responsibility which you have borne thus far with so much honor and success.
>
> The anxieties and toils which rest upon the naval administration of our country are, in themselves, enough to try a man's spirit, and when to them are added the ineradicable difficulties of which you speak I could not at this juncture, in fairness, ask you to support them.
>
> The navy of today, and still more the navy of tomorrow bears the imprint of your work. The enormous impending influx of capital ships, the score of 30-knot cruisers, the destroyers and submarines, unequaled in modern construction, which are coming now to hand, are the results of labors which we have had in common and in which the Board of Admiralty owes so much to your aid.
>
> The first step which secured the timely concentration of the fleet was taken by you. I must express publicly my deep indebtedness to you and the pain I feel at the severance of our three years of official association.
>
> In all circumstances you are right in your decision. The spirit in which you have acted is the same in which Prince Maurice of Battenberg has given his life to our cause, and in which your gallant son is now serving in the fleet.
>
> I beg you to accept my profound respect and that of our colleagues on the board. I remain yours very sincerely, WINSTON S. CHURCHILL.

The Times says it understands that Baron Fisher, Admiral of the fleet, will succeed Prince Louis as First Lord of the Admiralty.

LONDON PRESS REGRETFUL.

Pay Tribute to the Prince as a Naval Officer.

Special Cable to THE NEW YORK TIMES.

LONDON, Oct. 29.—Commenting on the resignation of Prince Louis of Battenberg, The London Daily News says this morning:

"He is an officer whose talents are recognized throughout the navy, and there is as little reason to imagine that any failures on his part caused his retirement as there is to imagine that his distinguished connections were responsible for his appointment. His withdrawal is a very real loss to the navy, and we are afraid that the circumstances which are probably responsible for it are not creditable to our press or to our public life.

"Certain journals have been disputing Prince Louis's fitness for the post of First Sea Lord on the ground that he was born in Austria. Prince Louis, as a sensitive man as well as a brave and skillful officer, has thought fit to offer himself as a sacrifice to this silly and cowardly campaign.

"It must be presumed that he persisted in doing so, for on no other hypothesis could acceptance by the Government of his resignation be defended. The yellow press in its exploitation of the vulgarest of fears and passions, has

Continued on Page 2.

BATTLE AT A STANDSTILL

Both Sides Claim Advantages in Northern Operations.

ALLIES GAIN NEAR OSTEND

Carry Two Villages by Bayonet Charges — Bavarians Surrender Without Fighting.

GERMANS TAKE TRENCHES

Announce Successes to the West of Lille and to the Southwest of Verdun.

PARIS, Oct. 29.—The capture by the Allies of German positions between the Aisne and the Argonne and the repulse of German attacks were announced in this afternoon's bulletin of the French War Office.

An official communication, issued tonight, said:

> There is no important news to report, according to the latest information received.

The text of the afternoon communication follows:

> During the day of yesterday we made progress at several points along the line of battle, but particularly around Ypres and to the south of Arras.
>
> There is nothing new on the front between Nieuport and Dixmude.
>
> Between the Aisne and the Argonne we took possession of some trenches occupied by the enemy, and not one of the partial attacks undertaken by the Germans resulted successfully.
>
> We advanced also in the forest of Aprémont.

Berlin Reports Successes.

BERLIN, Oct. 29, (via Amsterdam and London.)—The German General Headquarters this morning gave out this report concerning the situation in France and Belgium:

> Our attacks to the south of Nieuport are slowly gaining ground. At Ypres the battle is unchanged.
>
> To the west of Lille our troops are making good progress. Several fortified positions of the enemy have been taken. Sixteen British officers and 300 men, as well as four cannon, have been captured.
>
> French counter attacks everywhere have been repulsed. A French battery, stationed before the Cathedral of Rheims, and artillery observers, posted on the steeple of the Cathedral, have been bombarded.
>
> In the Argonne region the enemy was chased from several trenches and some machine guns captured.
>
> To the southwest of Verdun severe French attacks have been repulsed. In counter attacks our troops succeeded in breaking through the French lines to the main position of the enemy, which was occupied. The French suffered terrible losses.
>
> To the east of the Moselle all the attempts of the enemy have been repulsed.

LONDON, Oct. 29.—This dispatch from Berlin has been received by the Marconi Wireless Company:

"It is reported that the Germans are bringing heavy batteries to the Belgian coast to enable them to control the entrance to the Scheldt and to the North Sea between the Sandbanks and the coast. The British ships will be obliged, therefore, to pass on the high sea."

BRITISH FLEET LOSES 10 KILLED OFF BELGIUM

Vessels Received Only Slight Damage, Admiralty Reports—Shore Guns Silenced.

LONDON, Oct. 29.—The Secretary of the Admiralty makes the following announcement:

"The British naval flotilla continues to support the Allies' left, and, since the morning of Oct. 27, the fire of 12-inch guns has been brought to bear upon the German positions and batteries.

"Reports received from shore testify to the effect and accuracy of the fire and to its galling character. The flank is thus thoroughly maintained.

"Yesterday and the day before the enemy brought up heavy guns and replied vigorously to the fire of Admiral Hood's ships. The vessels received only trifling structural damage. Today the opposition from shore has practically

Wide World Photos

Turkish soldiers march through the streets of Constantinople as they prepare to fight the Allies.

"All the News That's Fit to Print."

The New York Times.

THE WEATHER
Fair, colder today; fair tomorrow; strong northwest winds on the coast diminishing.
For full weather report see Page 16.

VOL. LXIV...NO. 20,751. .... NEW YORK, TUESDAY, NOVEMBER 17, 1914.—TWENTY PAGES. ONE CENT In Greater New York, Jersey City and Newark. { Elsewhere TWO CENTS.

GERMANS WIN BIG VICTORY IN POLAND; RUSSIAN ATTACK SETS CRACOW AFIRE; SNOW AND FLOOD HALT BELGIAN FIGHT

RESERVE BANKS START BUSINESS IN TWELVE CITIES

Begin Receiving Reserve Deposits and Applications for Rediscounts.

$99,611,670 PAID IN HERE

Of This $78,213,740 Is in Gold—270 Banks in This State Still to Remit.

$21,000,000 FROM CITY BANK

Makes First and Largest Deposit—$5,000,000 in Excess of Requirements.

ONE $2,200,000 REDISCOUNT

None Reported from Other Districts, but Several Applications Received.

The twelve Federal Reserve Banks established by the new banking and currency law were opened yesterday. The only business undertaken by them at the start was to receive the reserve deposits of the member banks and applications for rediscounts. No actual rediscounts were reported in any district save that of New York. Here one transaction was made, amounting to $2,200,000.

In several of the districts payments on account of reserves were small because notices were not sent out until yesterday, and the only deposits made were volunteered by some of the members in advance of such notification.

In those districts, like New York, where large sums were received, the total yesterday will be considerably swelled when the banks outside of the cities where the Reserve Banks are located have had time to ship their money.

Only estimates could be obtained last night of the amounts paid in at the eleven Reserve Banks in other centres. These, with actual figures for this city, showed the following results:

District.	Deposits.	Discounts.
1. Boston	Not Reported	None
2. New York	$99,611,670	$2,200,000
3. Philadelphia	5,000,000	None
4. Cleveland	5,000,000	None
5. Richmond	Not Reported	Not Reported
6. Atlanta	1,000,000	None
7. Chicago	Not Reported	Not Reported
8. St. Louis	1,500,000	None
9. Minneapolis	880,000	Not Reported
10. Kansas City	500,000	None
11. Dallas	1,500,000	None
12. San Francisco	1,250,000	None

$99,611,670 Paid In Here.

The amount paid in to the Federal Reserve Bank of New York yesterday was $99,611,670, of which $78,213,740 was in gold, gold certificates, and Clearing House deposit certificates representing gold or gold certificates.

These payments were made by 210 of the 480 member banks, including all of those in the central reserve city of New York, which does not include Brooklyn and outlying districts. These city banks, numbering 33, furnished the lion's share of the payments, but the aggregate will be increased largely when the payments of the other 270 member banks are received. The Reserve Bank already had $3,321,910 in gold paid on account of subscriptions to its capital stock, so that its total gold holdings at the end of the day were $81,535,650.

There were only three applications for rediscount yesterday, of which one, amounting to $2,200,000, was granted. The others, for comparatively small amounts, were not acted on. The name of the bank obtaining the first discount was not given out, but Governor Strong, in a statement made on Saturday, said that the Chemical National Bank of this city had asked the privilege of being the first to show in this way its desire to support the operations and use the facilities of the new banking system.

Some payments for expenses have been made by the Federal Reserve Bank, but, leaving these out of account, its position at the close of business yesterday, based on the figures given above, might be represented in tabular form in this way:

ASSETS.	
Gold and gold certificates	$81,535,650.32
Other cash	21,397,930.10
Discounts	2,200,000.00
Total	$105,133,580.32
LIABILITIES.	
Capital	$3,321,910.22
Deposits	101,811,670.10
Total	$105,133,580.32

The payments were received at three places. For convenience it had been arranged that eleven of the largest banks in this city should make theirs at the Clearing House, where R. U. Giles, acting assistant cashier of the Reserve Bank, with a dozen assistants drawn from the expert forces of a number of the member banks, was ready to receive the certificates, count them and give receipts for them.

The exact time for payment by each of the banks had been arranged in advance, so that they were disposed of one at a time and were handled with expedition. All had been received and counted before closing time came at 3 o'clock. The payments at this point totaled $58,843,000, of which $43,383,000 was in gold or its representatives.

City Bank Makes First Payment.

The first payemnt, as well as the largest, was made at the Clearing House by the National City Bank. To fulfill its reserve deposit requirements of 7 per cent. of its deposits it turned in $16,000,000, and by way of excess or optional deposit it added $5,000,000, making a total payment of $21,000,000. The National City got the first receipt issued to the depositing banks and consented to its reproduction in THE TIMES.

The National Bank of Commerce turned in $9,000,000, which was $500,000 in excess of its requirements. The Chase [illegible]

Continued on Page 6.

MR. HERRICK TO RETURN.

Ambassador Sharp to Present His Credentials on Dec. 1.

WASHINGTON, Nov. 16.—William G. Sharp will present his credentials as American Ambassador to France to President Poincaré on Dec. 1, and take over the office held by ex-Gov. Myron T. Herrick of Ohio.

Mr. Sharp was nominated and confirmed several weeks ago, and has been waiting in Paris some time. The outbreak of the war added greatly to the onerousness of the duties of Mr. Herrick. Mr. Sharp's home is at Elyria, Ohio. He was a Representative in Congress at the time of his nomination. The transfer of the office was left to the convenience of the two men. Mr. Herrick probably will return to the United States.

RECABLES TIMES DISPATCH.

London Morning Post Praises Its Account of German Headquarters.

Special Cable to THE NEW YORK TIMES.

LONDON, Nov. 16.—The Morning Post's Washington correspondent has cabled to his newspaper a column summary of the dispatch from THE NEW YORK TIMES staff correspondent at German Great Headquarters, printed in last Sunday's TIMES and giving an account of the life there. The Post correspondent describes the dispatch as the best account that has yet appeared in any American newspaper of the daily doings at that important point.

FELL INTO TREASON TRAP.

Three Held for Trying to Smuggle Austrians Out of Canada.

NIAGARA FALLS, Ont., Nov. 16.—Joseph Snyder and his two sons, Richard and Arthur, are under arrest at the Forty-fourth Regiment Armory charged with high treason in attempting to take Austrian reservists across the border to the American side. They are liable to the death penalty. The Snyders have been under surveillance for some time and are said to have been caught in a trap.

Forty dollars was offered to them to land four Austrians on the American side. The money was paid, it is alleged, and four men posing as Austrians were brought to them. A squad of militiamen surrounded the party and imprisoned the Snyders in the armory. The case is in the hands of the military authorities.

NEW WIRELESS DETECTOR.

Navy Device Ferrets Out a Secret Station in Florida.

WASHINGTON, Nov. 16.—Using a newly devised apparatus for the detection of wireless stations, navy experts are working close on the trail of persons suspected of surreptitiously communicating with belligerent vessels in the Atlantic Ocean.

So far evidence has been obtained implicating some persons in Florida, but the Maine woods' mystery remains unsolved. Within a few days, however, the detection of all these secret stations is regarded as inevitable.

The new instruments were perfected by American naval officers.

MAKING 100,000 RIFLES.

Winchester Company Also Turning Out 100,000,000 Cartridges.

Special to The New York Times.

HARTFORD, Conn., Nov. 16.—The New Haven factory of the Winchester Repeating Arms Company is being operated night and day with more than 5,000 hands employed in the day shift and half that number at nights. They are turning out war material. The company is putting up new buildings to cost $500,000 and the construction work is being pushed twenty-four hours a day.

It is reported that the company has an order for 100,000 army rifles, and is under contract to complete 300 rifles every working day for six months. These guns are said to be similar to the standard rifles used in the French Army.

Officials of the company have been questioned as to the destination of the arms and of a recent order for 100,000,000 cartridges, but all they would say was that they were "ordered by a missionary from South America who dropped into the factory a few days ago while he was on a vacation."

EIFFEL GIBES WITH NAUEN.

French and German Operators Send Wireless Taunts.

Special Cable to THE NEW YORK TIMES.

PARIS, Nov. 15, (Dispatch to The London Times.)—There has been an amusing little interchange of wireless messages between the German station at Nauen and the Eiffel Tower.

Finding that their messages were tapped by the French, the German operators sent the following message in German to the Eiffel Tower:

"Where did you cause our plan to fail? Where did you thrust our armies back? The news is improbable and scanty, Eiffel Tower, and is not very honest."

The Frenchmen replied:

"Oh, German Army, have you forgotten that Paris expected you for luncheon on Sedan Day? Where have you dawdled?"

The messages were sent in the form of rude verse.

COLD SNAP HAS ARRIVED.

It Is Expected Thermometer Will Go Below Freezing Today.

The cold wave predicted by the Weather Bureau began yesterday morning, after the end of the heavy warm rains. At 8 o'clock yesterday morning the thermometer registered 60 degrees. By noon it was down to 52, by 9 P. M. to 42, and by 11 P. M. to 38. It was expected to go below freezing this morning, and perhaps as low as 25 degrees on Wednesday. The cold wave will be even more severe in the Middle West, where a general drop of thirty degrees is expected. The alleviating feature is that it is not likely to last very long; today and tomorrow will be sharp and blustery, but the wind will go down as the temperature begins to come back up.

The rains are over for the time being, driven away before the northwest gale. The humidity was 98 per cent. at 8 A. M. yesterday and 40 at 8 P. M. Between 3 and 9 o'clock yesterday morning the barometer went up from 29.54 to [illegible]

CARRANZA AGREES TO YIELD POWER

Wires Gutierrez Accepting Him as President, So Washington Is Notified.

VILLA CONSENTS TO RETIRE

Will Quit Mexico and Travel in United States—Conflicting Reports Disturb Washington.

GUTIERREZ OUTLINES PLANS

Promises Reign of Justice and Asks Evacuation of Vera Cruz in Telegram to Wilson.

Special to The New York Times.

WASHINGTON, Nov. 16.—The United States Government was advised today that Venustiano Carranza had agreed to retire from office as the executive head of the Mexican Government in favor of Eulalio Gutierrez, who was chosen Provisional President of the Republic by the convention of the Mexican factions held at Aguascalientes.

Official information of Gen. Carranza's agreement to retire came to the State Department from Mr. Canova, its agent at Aguascalientes, who telegraphed:

"Everything has been satisfactorily arranged. Carranza has telegraphed Gutierrez his willingness to retire."

The State Department gave out the following late tonight:

"A dispatch from Consul Silliman, dated this forenoon at Mexico City and received by the State Department tonight, reports negotiations are still pending. We do not know whether this conflicts with the report we received from Aguascalientes this afternoon or whether Canova (American Consular representative) who is there, has later information."

President Wilson received a long telegraphic message from Gen. Gutierrez in which he announced that he had assumed office as Provisional President and soon would set up his Government in Mexico City.

Information has been received here that as part of the pending settlement of political affairs in Mexico Gen. Carranza and Gen. Francisco Villa have agreed to leave the country. No official confirmation of the advices to this effect are obtainable from the State Department, but that is no reason for doubting that they have been received. The story goes that Carranza made the stipulation that his retirement from the head of the Government should be contingent on the departure of Villa from Mexico, and that if Villa left his native land Carranza also would go into voluntary exile. Persons supposed to be acquainted with Carranza's purposes said tonight that he contemplated a tour of the United States, and that he had promised to visit his friend, Richard Cole of Los Angeles.

Secretary Bryan showed that he was happy when he announced this afternoon that Carranza had agreed to surrender control of Mexican affairs to Gutierrez. Mr. Bryan said that peace had been re-established.

In his message to President Wilson President Gutierrez did not ask for recognition from the United States, but it is taken for granted here that within a short time after Gutierrez assumes the reins of government in the national capital formal recognition of the new administration will be accorded by President Wilson. The original American proposals to Carranza immediately after he took charge of the Government at Mexico City embodied a promise to grant recognition to the Central American authority if Carranza complied with certain conditions. These conditions now apparently are about to be met.

President Gutierrez's message to President Wilson follows:

Gutierrez States His Case.

The republic has undergone in the last few years a terrible crisis in which the democratic ideals of government and the yearnings of the people for justice and economical improvement have triumphed and been vindicated. The last civil strife ended with the overthrow of Gen. Huerta's dictatorship, and since the Constitutionalist forces occupied the capital of the republic, Señor Carranza assuming charge of the executive power ad interim, it was thought, on account of the prevailing disagreement, that the best way to establish a Government acceptable to all, was to hold a national convention, where all the militant factions attached to the revolution of principles that has just triumphed should be represented.

After several conferences between the various chiefs, it was agreed to designate the City of Aguascalientes as the meeting place, and on Oct. 10 last the Military Convention of Aguascalientes met, with representatives of all the revolutionist elements present. Subsequently the said assembly declared itself to be the sovereign power of the republic, as being the representatives of the people in arms that had fought to reconstitute the nationality.

In virtue thereof the convention proceeded to elect the Provisional President of the republic, and I was designated by a majority of the votes to hold the office. In so proceeding the convention has given expression to the purposes of the revolution and endeavored to demonstrate that no government can subsist in Mexico unless it emanates from the will of the people. For the time of dictatorships, born of violence and personal ambitions, has passed forever.

In the same democratic form and voicing the sentiment of the revolutionary and reforming majority, the convention is continuing its work in formulating the programme of Government which my provisional Administration must comply with and the reforms which are to be brought forward to accomplish the ends of the revolutionary movement. It will also appoint the day on which elections will be held to designate the constitutional powers of the republic.

In the meanwhile, and while my provisional Presidency lasts, I will strive to adopt the policy of the Government to the needs of the country, respect the legitimate rights of the nationals, set up the reforms that the revolution demands, and scrupulously guarantee the life and property of the foreigners who have come under the protection of our hospitality and laws, to co-operate with us in the aggran- [illegible]

Continued on Page 5.

BUSY CENSOR SLASHES EVEN LORD'S PRAYER

Paris Writer's Attempt at Ridicule Results in Amusing Literary Hash.

Special Cable to THE NEW YORK TIMES.

PARIS, Nov. 16.—As threats and entreaties have proved equally vain against the censorship, the Temps tonight attacks it with ridicule, which is regarded as the deadliest weapon in the Parisian armory.

Pierre Mille, one of the best-known contributors, writes a column article, beginning:

"Regarding the origin of the convulsion which is shaking Europe, together with the least known diplomatic secrets and the most concealed strategic projects, I am going to make some most important revelations."

Before he can reveal anything here, however, the censor intervenes with a four-line cut. He continues:

"It will be remembered that Napoleon once cried before the Pyramids—" Here is another slash.)

The writer goes on:

"But we do not need the support of history or the remembrance of the victories won by Jeanne d'Arc at (name excised) or at Valmy by (another obliteration.) One fact I will add" (Here follows a ten-line cut.)

He continues:

"His undaunted attitude at" (This time ten lines more disappear.

The article proceeds:

"She cried in a trembling voice: 'O, daughter, cruel'—(the woman's speech is all excised save the words "The devourers fight among themselves," although the passage appears to be taken from nothing more modern or harmful than a famous tragedy.)

The writer makes a last effort:

"The adversary's position was now very serious. Throwing himself upon his knees, he cried: 'Our Father, which art—' (Even of the Lord's prayer the censor allows only this beginning and the final "amen.")

The Temps says in a postscript:

"We regret the slashing which the censor finds it necessary to inflict, but despite it our contributor asserts that the article can still be understood."

HEARS THAT AUSTRIA IS TO SEEK PEACE

Rumor in Petrograd—Her Army Loss Put at 903,126—Finest Regiments Wiped Out.

Special Cable to THE NEW YORK TIMES.

LONDON, Tuesday, Nov. 17.—The Daily Telegraph has this dispatch from Athens, dated Sunday:

"Diplomatic intelligence from Petrograd states that information has reached that capital that Austria is contemplating asking for terms of peace independently of Germany."

Special Cable to THE NEW YORK TIMES.

LONDON, Tuesday, Nov. 17.—The Morning Post publishes the text of a letter received by the London correspondent of a Budapest paper from a friend in Hamburg, in which the writer comments bitterly on the way in which the Austrian public is kept ignorant of the appalling losses among the Austrian troops.

The writer, who himself had copied figures from a report shown to him by an official in the Honved Ministry, says the Austrian losses in the campaign against Servia up to Nov. 1 reached a total of 148,598 officers and men, being almost one-third of the whole army originally sent to that region. In Galicia they reached the total of 752,756 and in East Hungary, 1,772. Thus Austrians lost during the first three months of the war a little over 900,000 officers and men, which is something like 27 per cent. of the whole army engaged.

The writer says one of the reasons why, in his opinion, the Government refrains from the publication of statistics for the present is that the most popular Hungarian regiments, the Magyar Hussars, and the First, Seventh, and Sixteenth Cavalry, were almost completely annihilated in France and Belgium.

"Never a word was published officially as to their being sent to reinforce the Uhlans in the west," says the writer. "There were rumors about it, but not even letters reached the people of the Hussars in Hungary. I understand these have been kept back in order that uneasiness should not arise.

"I shouldn't wonder if it had created not merely uneasiness but rebellion, for people here hold that as long as Hungary is seriously threatened and is being invaded, even by the Servians, as was the case, we can't afford to have even our Honved regiments in Belgium for Germany's sake."

MORE TITLED ENGLISH KILLED AND WOUNDED

Baron Dunleath's Heir Dead—Irish Guards Heavy Sufferers—Latest List Totals 69.

LONDON, Nov. 16.—A casualty list dated Nov. 8, issued here tonight, gives the names of twenty officers killed, thirty-four wounded, and fifteen missing. In this list the Irish Guards are heavy sufferers.

Capt. the Hon. A. E. S. Mulholland of the Irish Guards, eldest son of Baron Dunleath, is among the dead. His widow is a daughter of the Earl of Strafford.

In the list of the wounded appear the names of Lieut. Col. Lord Ardee of the Irish Guards, who married Lady Aileen Wyndham-Quin, daughter of the Earl of Dunraven; Lieut. the Earl of Kingston of the Irish Guards; Lieut. Sir George Duckworth-King of the Grenadier Guards; Lieut. Col. A. Martyn of the Royal West Kent Regiment; Capt. the Hon. Thomas E. Vesey of the Irish Guards, son of Viscount De Vesci, and Lieut. the Hon. Harold R. L. G. Alexander of the Irish Guards, brother of the Earl of Caledon.

GEN. FITZCLARENCE KILLED.

Relative of the Earl of Munster Falls in Battle.

LONDON, Tuesday, Nov. 17.—Announcement is made that Brig. Gen. Charles Fitzclarence of the Irish Guards [illegible]

23,000 RUSSIANS TAKEN

Several Army Corps, Hurled Back, Forced to Abandon Some Guns.

KAISER REVEALS DANGER

German Public Informed at Last That the Czar's Hosts Are at the Frontiers.

RETREAT A GLORIOUS FEAT

Fatherland's Troops as Proud of It as the British Are of Their Withdrawal from Mons.

BERLIN, Nov. 16, (by Wireless Telegraph to London.)—This official communication was given out this afternoon:

The fighting in the east continues. Yesterday our troops operating in East Prussia repulsed the enemy in the region south of Stallupoenen. Troops from West Prussia successfully resisted the advance of Russian forces at Soldau and after a successful battle at Lipno drove them back in the direction of Plock.

Strong Russian forces are advancing along the right bank of the Vistula River. In this fighting we made 500 prisoners and captured ten machine guns up to yesterday.

A decision has been arrived at in the battle which has been going on for the last few days in continuation of our successes at Wloziawsk, in Russian Poland, on the Vistula, thirty miles northwest of Plock, where several Russian army corps in opposition to us were driven back beyond Kutno. According to the present reports we made 23,000 prisoners and captured over twenty machine guns, as well as some cannon, the number of which has not yet been ascertained.

Included in the information given to the press today in official quarters is the following:

Prince Dolgoroukoff, in an article appearing in the Russky Wufdomosty, published in Moscow, demands vainly the liberation of Russian Jews from special legislation.

People Told of Russian Danger.

BERLIN, (via London,) Nov. 16.—Germany again is under the sign of the Russian danger to quote the astrological metaphor frequently used by the Germans.

The combined German and Austrian armies, which by a well-timed and well-executed change in front and with timely reinforcements were able to sweep through Poland to the line of the Vistula and threaten Warsaw and Ivangorod, were in turn outflanked by the masses of Russians, and have fallen back to their own frontiers. The timid inhabitants of the border regions are leaving their homes for the interior.

The professional pessimists draw long faces and a certain amount of disquietude is being manifested in civilian circles in Berlin. There are many indications, however, that the retirement before Warsaw is not that of a beaten army, but of one which, realizing that it had failed in its object of a surprise campaign, promptly changed its strategic plan and retreated. Predictions are hazardous, but the great news of the next fortnight may come when the armies facing one another meet on Poland's Wintery fields.

The common report is that Gen. von Hindenburg is ready to accept or give battle on the new ground he has chosen. The eighth army intrusted with the defense of East Prussia again has a new commander. It originally was commanded by Gens. von Prittwitz and Gaffon and passed into the hands of Gen. von Hindenburg and Chief of Staff von Ludendorff. The new commander is Gen. von Bülow, one of a family of military brothers of high rank.

The retirement from Warsaw resembles in many respects that from the environs of Paris in September, the Germans in both cases assuming the great risk of running out of ammunition and supply trains, and exposing their flank and rear, hoping to smash a supposed demoralized army. They had hoped, in the Warsaw campaign, like Stonewall Jackson at Chancellorsville, to catch the enemy's right wing napping and roll up that portion of it west of the Vistula and press across the river and capture Warsaw. Holding strong the line from East Prussia on the north to Galicia on the south, they expected to be able to stand off Russia and devote their principal attention to the western campaign.

That is why, it is said, Gen. von Hindenburg in September transferred his headquarters from East Prussia to Breslau, in Silesia, acting in concert with the Austrian commanders' change of front against the Russians invading Western Galicia from the north.

The Russians were on the alert, however, and quickly retired to the safe side of the Vistula. The only important [illegible]

Continued on Page 3.

Summary of War News.

The French War Office announces that artillery duels comprised all the fighting from the Yser Canal to Dixmude yesterday, and that fresh inundations had extended the flooded area south of that town.

The Germans report that three small British warships, which have been assisting the allied land forces in Belgium, have been disabled by German shells. The storm along the battle front caused a slackening in the fighting yesterday.

A news dispatch from Rome says that the City of Cracow is burning, and that the inhabitants are fleeing.

Berlin states that the Russian advance in East Prussia has been checked after a battle south of Stallupoenen. The Russian forces advancing from Soldau are also said to have been defeated and driven back toward Plock. Another strong Russian army is said to be advancing along the right bank of the Vistula River. In Russian Poland, the Russians have been driven back to Kutno, after the German success at Wloziawsk, where, "according to present reports," 23,000 prisoners have been taken.

The Austrians report that the garrison at Przemysl made a successful sortie from the invested fortress, defeating a strong Russian column.

Berlin reports that the Khedive of Egypt, who is now in Constantinople, is preparing to lead an anti-British force to Egypt.

The Pope yesterday issued a strong appeal for peace, attributing the war to the lack of mutual love among men, contempt for authority, injustice on the part of one class against another, and the consideration of material welfare as the sole object of human activity.

The House of Commons yesterday, after listening to an appeal from Premier Asquith, voted an additional credit for war purposes of $1,125,000,000, and a call for 1,000,000 more men. The Premier told the House that the war was costing England nearly $5,000,000 a day.

CRACOW BESIEGED, SAID TO BE BURNING

Sortie from Przemysl Fortress Repulsed With Heavy Loss by Russian Artillery and Cavalry.

ROME, Nov. 16.—A special dispatch from Petrograd to the Giornale d'Italia says that the overwhelming advance of the Russians toward Cracow is overcoming all obstacles, both the difficulties of the passes and the desperate resistance of the Austrians. Cracow is entirely besieged on the northeast.

A sortie from Przemysl has been repulsed by Russian artillery and cavalry, which inflicted severe losses on the Austrians.

According to a dispatch from Venice to the same newspaper, Cracow is burning and its inhabitants are in flight.

Special Cable to THE NEW YORK TIMES.

LONDON, Tuesday, Nov. 17.—According to the Rome correspondent of The London Morning Post, news has reached Venice that part of Cracow is ablaze.

Cracow is invested on the north, and is expected to fall immediately. The inhabitants are in flight.

The Russian forces have made a very rapid advance and reached Cracow sooner than expected. For the Russians the fall of Cracow means the key to the industrial districts of Silesia, striking a vital economic blow at Germany.

WALES GOES TO FRONT TO BE STAFF OFFICER

Prince, With Consent of King and Lord Kitchener, Joins Army in France.

Special Cable to THE NEW YORK TIMES.

LONDON, Tuesday, Nov. 17.—The Prince of Wales has gone to the front. He crossed the Channel yesterday, and had a magnificent reception at the hands of the troops of the Allies who saw him disembark. A train filled with wounded soldiers was alongside the quay, and when the news became known that the Prince had joined the active forces there was tremendous enthusiasm. Several of the injured men were held up to the windows of the carriages to see him, and he shook hands with some and spoke to others. The Prince was in khaki, and seemed very fit and in excellent spirits.

When the war began the Prince of Wales, then attached to the First Grenadier Guards, was exceptionally keen on the route marches and other features of a soldier's training. He was full of enthusiasm and confident that he would get his chance of going on active service, but his hope was not at first realized, for when his regiment was ordered to the front he was transferred to other duties.

The young Prince did his best to move the authorities, and even made a personal call on Lord Kitchener at the War Office, but the Secretary for War was adamant. He pointed out to his Royal Highness that he had not served his full course of military training, and that until this had been done no exception could be made even in favor of the heir to the throne. Although disappointed by this rebuff, the Prince went about his duties with sustained enthusiasm, and no doubt has been winning powerful influence to his side.

The Prince of course is a mere boy; he was only 20 years old last June. When at Oxford the Prince was in the university officers' training corps and took his gruelling with the rest. He marched to camp under a blazing sun and bivouacked by the roadside in a blanket with his jacket and shirt-collar wide open and his cuffs rolled back. He was unrecognizable among the khaki-clad cadets, striding along the dusty roads from Mytchett camp to Bramshill House.

The Chronicle says this morning:

"The last Prince of Wales to leave this country on a warlike expedition to French soil was the Black Prince, who won the great victory of Poictiers in his second foray into France in 1356. It is true that Henry V. was the Captain of Calais in 1410, when he was Prince of Wales, but it is not recorded that he took part in either of the two English expeditions of his father's reign. [illegible]

SHELL-TORN GLASGOW REACHES RIO JANEIRO

British Cruiser, Which Survived Pacific Battle, Shows Marks of the Fray.

RIO JANEIRO, Nov. 16.—The British cruiser Glasgow, which was one of the vessels engaged in the fight with the German squadron off the coast of Chile Nov. 1, arrived here today. The damage caused by the German shell fire is plainly visible on the cruiser.

The British Admiralty's statement on the sea fight off Chile said the Glasgow was engaged by both the Leipzig and Dresden of the German squadron while the Gneisenau and Scharnhorst were fighting the Good Hope and the Monmouth. It added, however, that the Glasgow was not extensively damaged and suffered few casualties.

After the battle the Glasgow, accompanied by the transport Otranto, sailed south and passed through the Straits of Magellen to the Atlantic Ocean.

VALPARAISO, Chile, Nov. 16.—The Chilean hospital ship Valdivia, which has been searching for possible survivors of the British cruisers lost in the engagement with the German squadron off the Chilean coast on Nov. 1, arrived today at Talcahuana and reported that her search had been entirely without success. She found nothing in the way of wreckage or boats from the British vessels.

VICTORIA CROSSES FOR NINE BRAVE MEN

England Rewards Rank and File for Daring Deeds—Haig Promoted.

LONDON, Nov. 16.—The Victoria Cross has been conferred on British officers and non-commissioned officers as follows:

Capt. Francisco Grenfell of the Ninth Lancers for aiding and saving the guns of the British in Belgium on Aug. 24; Capt. Douglas Reynolds of the artillery, who was wounded in a similar exploit; Capt. Theodore Wright of the Engineers, who was mortally wounded while rescuing a wounded man; Surgeon Harry Sherwood Ranken for attending men under fire after he had received wounds from which he died; Lieut. Maurice Dease and four non-commissioned officers.

Lieut. Gen. Sir Douglas Haig has been promoted to the rank of General for distinguished service in the field.

Field Marshal Sir John French, in his dispatch to the British War Office of Sept. 7 describing the famous retreat from Mons, credited Sir Douglas Haig with having extricated his corps from a difficult position on Aug. 25 at Landrecies. The Commander in Chief wrote of the incident:

"I sent urgent messages to the commander of the two French reserve divisions on my right to come up to the assistance of the First Corps, which they eventually did. Partly owing to this assistance, but mainly to the skillful manner in which Sir Douglas Haig extricated his corps from an exceptionally difficult position in the darkness of the night, they were able at dawn to resume their march south toward Wassigny on Guise."

MINE CAST UP BY SEA KILLS 7 IN HOLLAND

Explodes Under Examination and Three Naval Officers Are Among the Slain.

LONDON, Nov. 16.—A mine washed ashore near Westkapelle, Holland, exploded today while being examined, killing three naval officers, one civilian and three sailors. This information was contained in an announcement made by the Dutch Ministry of Marine and sent by cable from Amsterdam to Reuter's Telegram Company.

Several mines had been taken to pieces [illegible]

WESTERN FIGHTERS SUFFER

New Inundations by Belgians Drive Germans from Trenches.

SOME GUNS ARE ABANDONED

Isolated Attacks of Germans Beaten Back and a Regiment Destroyed.

ARGONNE FIGHTS RENEWED

Berlin Reports Important Successes Gained Over the French in That Region.

PARIS, Nov. 16.—New inundations, probably caused by the Belgians, and most inclement weather, in which fog and rain turned to heavy snow, have seriously checked the war operations in Belgium and northern France. The roar of cannon was less violent and the troops scarcely came in contact with each other.

It is believed here that the new inundations put many of the German guns out of action, while they also prevented the movement of troops.

It is almost impossible to gain an accurate insight into the prodigious action over the 300-mile Franco-Belgian front, at the ends of which the fighting has been extremely severe in the last three weeks.

The continuous night marches and attacks made by the Germans, which have been met by counter-attacks from the Allies near Dixmude and Ypres, are said to have resulted in a considerable thrusting back of the Germans.

A near-by coal basin in North France, which is partly occupied by the Germans, has been the scene of heavy fighting. The long lines of small houses belonging to the miners form a capital shelter for the infantry, who are frequently engaged in a hand-to-hand conflict.

These combats of cold steel have seen the British infantry engaged against the Prussian Guards, and, according to descriptions of the fighting from the front, the encounters were terrific. The Prussians fought four deep—the front rank lying down, the second rank kneeling, and the third rank standing erect. The British fire, it is said, caused awful slaughter, and finally, when the British charged with the bayonet before the Germans could bring their machine guns into action, hundreds of men fell.

The semi-siege operations along the remainder of the line find both sides apparently immobile. But the Allies continue daily in their work of sapping and approaching the German positions, and there is said to be a possibility of a general assault at any moment.

Heavy falls of snow in the Vosges Mountains, lasting over twenty-four hours, have made the movement of artillery there most difficult, and fighting is almost at a standstill.

Reports from the front tell how a regiment of French hussars near Ypres stuffed uniforms with straw and attached them to wounded horses. These they drove into the German lines. While the Germans were firing at the dummies on horseback, the hussars charged their flank, it is said, and took a large number of prisoners.

Fighters Suffer Amid Snow.

SLUIS, Holland, Nov. 16, (via The Hague and London.)—The battle front on the Yser is unchanged. The weather is most unfavorable, the fog turning into a heavy wet snow. Existence in the trenches is almost unbearable. Since yesterday there has been an almost complete cessation of operations on both sides.

Word comes from Ypres that while the town has suffered severely from fire, the thirteenth century guildhouse has not been damaged.

A stream of German wounded continues to come from the front.

The people in Flanders are kept in ignorance of the fighting that is taking place around them.

FLOODS SOUTH OF DIXMUDE.

Isolated German Attacks Repulsed, According to Paris.

PARIS, Nov. 16, 10:39 P. M.—After announcing in the afternoon that artillery duels comprised all the fighting yesterday along the Yser Canal to Dixmude, and that fresh inundations had extended the flooded area south of that town, the War Office stated tonight that "the situation is without modification."

The afternoon bulletin was as follows:

"In the day yesterday, along the Yser Canal, from Nieuport to the country up the river from Dixmude, the fighting was limited to artillery exchanges.

The country having been further inundated, the submerged territory now stretches to the south of Dix- [illegible]

Mid-Week Pictorial

Polish Infantry of the German Army in East Prussia firing from rifle pits.

United Press International

Russians, awaiting removal to a prison camp, are guarded by Germans.

Mid-Week Pictorial

Belgians in armored cars on their way to the Flanders front.

"All the News That's Fit to Print."

The New York Times.

THE WEATHER
Fair, warmer today; fair, colder Friday; south, shifting to west winds.
☞For full weather report see page 18.

VOL. LXIV...NO. 20,753. .... NEW YORK, THURSDAY, NOVEMBER 19, 1914.—EIGHTEEN PAGES. ONE CENT In Greater New York, Jersey City and Newark. | Elsewhere, TWO CENTS.

TROOPS RUSHED TO STOP VILLA; CAPITAL MOVED

Transferred to Orizaba, as Villa, Nearing Queretaro, Takes Big Towns.

HOPES OF PEACE VANISH

Washington is Informed That a Clash of Arms Now Appears to be Inevitable.

CARRANZA GENERALS LOYAL

Gutierrez Reported a Prisoner of Villa—Mexicans Stop American Papers at Texas Border.

Special Cable to THE NEW YORK TIMES.

MEXICO CITY, Nov. 18.—Gen. Obregon, who yesterday assumed complete control of the capital, said today:

"I consider useless anything except armed force, though we must await the return of the commission headed by Iglesias Calderon to see what results it has accomplished. Meantime, let us prepare for the struggle.

"I am proud to say that fortunately the Army of the Northwest, which I command, is prepared to enter the contest in defense of the principles for which the Mexican people have been fighting during the last four years. I have shipped all my artillery, and my troops can be mobilized at the first order. Yesterday two trains with artillery departed for San Juan del Rio, State of Queretaro."

Gen. Obregon condemns the futility of conventions and discussions and adds:

"In the midst of these absurdities, the result of personal ambitions, we do not think of protesting against the presence of invading troops on our soil and against the lowering of our sacred ensign to make place for the Stars and Stripes. Not only do we not protest, but for our greater shame there have been protests against the evacuation of Vera Cruz which have come from Villa through his representative, Llorente."

The Government of Gen. Carranza has now moved to Orizaba, and Mexico City, for the first time since the days of the French intervention, ceases to be the seat of Federal powers.

In moving to Orizaba Gen. Carranza is following in the footsteps of Juarez, who, during the Wars of Reform and the French intervention, established his capital at different points in national territory according to the exigencies of the campaign. At Orizaba Gen. Carranza will command the Mexican Railway between Mexico City and Vera Cruz, and when Vera Cruz is turned over to his forces he will control the chief port and route for exports and imports and would thus have an important advantage over any hostile power established at Mexico City.

Members of the diplomatic corps say they see no reason, at any rate for the present, why they should go to Orizaba. They point out that the Carranza Government is unrecognized by any foreign power, and therefore it is their business to treat with any de facto authority established in this city.

Villa Takes Important Towns.

EL PASO, Nov. 18.—Telegraphic reports from Leon tonight said that the Villa forces had occupied Irapuato and Guanajuato without firing a single shot. Six thousand men of the Carranza garrison at Irapuato surrendered unconditionally, it was declared.

All American newspapers were prohibited from entry into Mexico by an order from Gen. Villa put into effect today along the border. Even persons crossing the international border at this port were relieved of newspapers they carried by the Villa inspectors. No explanation was given for the order.

The Villa troops were reported tonight as pressing south against the Carranza forces after the taking several days ago of Leon. From Carranza officials came reports of preparations to meet the Northerners. The Carranza adherents expressed themselves as confident in view of the loyalty to the First Chief of Gen. Pablo Gonzales and Gen. Alvaro Obregon, chief of the division of the Northwest.

WASHINGTON IS WARNED.

Agents in Mexico Report War Moves of Rival Factions.

WASHINGTON, Nov. 18.—Gen. Francisco Villa, in command of the troops under the control of the Mexican convention at Aguascalientes, is marching on Mexico City. His army took Leon, the first important railroad centre south of Aguascalientes, without firing a shot.

The forces of Gen. Pablo Gonzales, loyal to Carranza, are gathered at Queretaro and Irapuato, where the first important clash in the hostilities between Carranza and Villa will probably occur.

These facts were reported in official messages received today from George C. Carothers, American Consular Agent, accompanying Gen. Villa. Mr. Carothers said that Gen. Villa was well equipped for the march.

From American Consul Silliman came a dispatch saying conditions were far more serious in Mexico City than they had been since the parleys for peace began. He regards actual hostilities as inevitable, though some of the Generals are still trying to patch up the differences that have arisen.

Gen. Carranza, according to Mr. Silliman and Leon Canova, Special Commissioner at Aguascalientes, has declared that he had been misunderstood; that he never intended to deliver the executive power except to Gen. Pablo Gonzales or some other man of his own selection, and in whom he had entire confidence. Although there has been no definite advices, it was believed by officials tonight that Gen. Gutierrez, chosen Provisional President by the convention at Aguascalientes, had ordered a general attack on Carranza garrisons. Gutierrez controls practically all of the northern half of Mexico, and Gen. Villa's advance guard is within 200 miles of the Mexican capital.

One column of convention forces is endeavoring to cut off the forces of Gen. Jesus Carranza at Puerto Mexico from communication with Mexico City

Continued on Page 3.

ALL OHIO PLANNING WELCOME TO HERRICK

Queen Mary Thanks the Ambassador and His Wife, Who Sail for Home Nov. 28.

Special to The New York Times.

CLEVELAND, Nov. 18.—Plans for a big reception for Myron T. Herrick, Ambassador to France, on his return from Paris early in December, became State-wide today.

It is now expected that all the larger cities will take part in the celebration. Detailed plans will be arranged and sub-committees appointed on Thursday at a luncheon meeting of fifteen prominent citizens invited by Fred H. Caley, Secretary of the Cleveland Automobile Club.

Members of the General Committee appointed to make preliminary plans for the Herrick reception are enthusiastic over the idea. Mayor Baker will probably be appointed Chairman of the General Committee and Chairman of the Committee on Arrangements. It is planned to appoint Senator Theodore E. Burton Chairman of the Reception Committee and to make the address of welcome.

Plans discussed Wednesday contemplate a big parade. The Engineers Battalion, Troop A, Battery A, the Fifth Regiment, the Ninth Battalion of Naval Reserves, the Cleveland Grays, and other uniformed organizations will march as a guard of honor.

The reception will probably be held in the afternoon of the day of the Herricks' arrival, at either the Grays' or the Central Armory, and a dinner will be given at night. It is planned to have Senator Atlee Pomerene, Senator-elect Warren G. Harding, Gov. Cox, Gov.-elect Frank G. Willis, and other State officials present.

PARIS, Nov. 18.—Myron T. Herrick, the American Ambassador, who is to be relieved of his duties late this month by William G. Sharp, has engaged passage for the United States on the steamer Rochambeau, which will sail on Nov. 28.

Mr. Herrick and his wife have received invitations from persons distinguished in public life in France and England to visit them before leaving Europe, but they have declined because they consider that this is not the time for social visits.

Queen Mary has written Mrs. Herrick a personal letter, expressing appreciation for what she and other American women have done for the British wounded in Paris.

Sir Edward Grey, the British Foreign Minister, has written Mr. Herrick in the same vein, and David Lloyd George, the Chancellor of the Exchequer of Great Britain, has sent a letter of thanks to Mr. Herrick "in behalf of the British Government" for his services to British subjects.

The departure of Mr. and Mrs. Herrick will, at their desire, be as quiet as possible. There will be no farewell banquets or any other demonstrations because, as the Ambassador says, these days in France are extremely tense and sad.

Mr. Sharp will go to Bordeaux in a few days to present his credentials to President Poincaré.

"WILD MAN" WAS ONLY ILL.

Dread of Rodriguez Turned to Pity When He Told His Story.

Special to The New York Times.

PORT JEFFERSON, L. I., Nov. 18.—Women and girls of this place, who had been frightened frequently in the last few months by the appearance in deserted stretches of road near the town of a "wild man," learned with relief today that Constable Harry Gover had caught the man. Their fears changed to sympathy when they learned the "wild man's" story, and his capture probably will result in his getting assistance.

He said his name was Juan Rodriguez, and that he had come from Monterey, Mexico, ten years ago. He was sent to a hospital in New York some time ago, and eight months back was discharged as cured. It was Spring then and he walked out into the country looking for work.

His strength had been sapped by his long illness, he said, and at last he found himself too weak to work. Then he took to the woods, subsisting on what he could beg at first and then, as his clothes became mere tatters and his appearance began to frighten strangers, on what he could find in the woods.

He said he had never accosted a woman or a girl, though he realized many had seen him and had run, and he said he had frequently spent the night in trees while he listened to farmers beating the woods around him for traces of him after their wives or daughters had seen the "wild man."

He was fed and decent clothes were given to him, and tomorrow he will have a hearing before Justice of the Peace Jacob Dreyer.

TAMING ROCKEFELLER DEER

Pets at Pocantico Becoming as Sociable as Their Master.

Special to The New York Times.

TARRYTOWN, N. Y., Nov. 18.—John D. Rockefeller's deer are becoming as neighborly as their owner at Pocantico Hills. Every morning six or more of them follow the mail man to the Post Office and to the railroad station, where he goes on Mr. Rockefeller's business.

The deer roam about the street unmolested, and often allow people to pet them. Mr. Rockefeller delights in seeing them on his estate.

HELD FOR ELECTION FRAUD.

Eighteen Men Arrested in Indiana on Government's Complaint.

INDIANAPOLIS, Ind., Nov. 18.—Eighteen men were arrested in Terre Haute today, on charges of conspiracy to defraud the United States Government in the recent election for United States Senator and Congressmen. They were brought to Indianapolis late this afternoon by United States Marshals and arraigned before the United States Commissioner, who held them in $2,500 bond each for the Federal Grand Jury.

They are lodged in jail, while counsel are arranging the bonds.

HEADS CANAL ZONE TROOPS.

Brig. Gen. Edwards Ordered to That Post by War Department.

WASHINGTON, Nov. 18.—Brig. Gen. Clarence R. Edwards, commanding the First Hawiian Brigade, is to be succeeded by Brig. Gen. John P. Wisser, now commanding the Pacific Coast Artillery District.

Gen. Edwards is ordered to command on the Canal Zone.

WILL DIG SUBWAYS, BUT FIGHT ALIEN ACT

Contractors Decide to Obey the Law, but Doubt if They Can Hire Enough Citizens.

90 PER CENT. NOW FOREIGN

Public Service Lawyers Plan Test Case—Mayor Would Put City's Idle to Work.

Forty subway contracting firms were represented last night at a meeting at the Engineers' Club in West Fortieth Street, at which the situation which has arisen through the sudden enforcement of the provision of the labor law forbidding the employment of alien labor on public work was discussed.

They decided to continue, if possible, work on the subways without breaking the law, but at the same time they expressed the opinion that the law was unconstitutional, and that a test should be made as quickly as possible.

At the end of the meeting this statement was given out by C. A. Crane, Secretary of the General Contractors' Association:

> The General Contractors' Association, at its meeting tonight, declared the intention of its members to comply with the law of the State in every particular. At the same time it desires to call public attention to the extreme difficulty of constructing the vast public works now under way and at the same time excluding all alien labor.
>
> It is believed that the alien labor law is not constitutional and is in violation of treaties with other countries. Steps will be taken as speedily as possible to submit the question to the courts.

The F. L. Cranford Company, the Degnon Contracting Company, the Holbrook, Cabot & Rollins Corporation, the United States Realty and Improvement Company, the Flinn-O'Rourke Company, and the Foundation Company were appointed a committee to consider the best method by which to carry a test case through the highest court.

Ninety Per Cent. of Labor Alien.

When the possibility of carrying on the subway work without alien labor was discussed with the contractors last night they were not sure it could be done. It is estimated that of the unskilled labor employed on subway contracts 90 per cent. of it is alien, and that even among the skilled laborers, who in the main belong to unions, 50 per cent. have never become citizens. All the contractors would say was that they would make out as best they could, and would not close down if they could help it.

Mayor Mitchel offered a suggestion yesterday. He thought use might be made of the many city laborers for whom there is no work in Winter. He said:

> I have no sympathy with any attempt to stop subway work, but I agree with the labor unions that native laborers should be employed in preference to aliens on public works. I don't want to inject myself into the situation, as it is the Public Service Commission which has to deal with such matters. But I should like to see the men not needed in the city departments receive jobs on these big contracts. They have long been residents of this city, and it is natural that we should care for them before others.

The Mayor was referring to the city employes, who have either been dropped or put on part time. Thus, in the Dock Department, 750 men were kept on until Jan. 1 on reduced hours, by a special appropriation of $150,000 in the budget for 1915 for the purpose.

Hope for Early Test of Law.

The contractors felt last night that much depended upon the attitude of the Public Service Commission and the labor leaders. It is in the power of either to force the situation, the commission by refusing to issue vouchers, and the labor leaders by causing the arrest of any contractor who employs aliens. If they will hold off, the contractors believe a test case can be decided and the matter cleared up.

Chairman McCall, speaking yesterday at a luncheon of the North Side Board of Trade, told of a man who said he could hire 5,000 qualified subway laborers a day, but who came back and admitted he could find only 100. He added:

> The situation is embarrassing, as American citizens cannot be found for the work. The commission is in a dilemma, but it will not be moved by threats or otherwise.
>
> I hope the situation will be cleared up, and that there will be no delay in the work, but I want to make it plain that the use of alien labor will be stopped. The commission has no choice. It must either annul an offender's contract or be itself liable as a party to the offense for prosecution for misdemeanor.

John Gill of the Bricklayers' Union, who first brought up the alien question, gave out a statement last night, in which he condemned the employment of aliens on the subways as a scandal, and accused certain contractors with political influence of deliberately underbidding contractors who were willing to comply with the law. Speaking of the suggestion that a test case be brought by the Public Service Commission, he said:

"It seems to me that such a step would be inconsistent with the duty of all public officials to enforce not only the letter but the spirit of the law."

He then attacked the contention of the contractors that they could not get citizen labor, and asserted that it was merely a matter of wages, and that an advertisement offering jobs at $2.50 a day would bring far more labor than was needed.

Civil Action Quicker.

Counsel for the Public Service Commission were trying yesterday to devise a method for testing the law speedily. It is likely that they will prefer civil to criminal proceedings, for it would be possible to take a civil suit to the Court of Appeals for argument by next month, whereas the criminal process would be much slower.

It is also realized that the commission must be careful in annulling contracts in view of the doubt as to the constitutionality of the act. If it were declared void the contractors who had lost their contracts would have claims against the city for lost profits. There is about $90,000,000 worth of work to be done under present contracts, and the contractors might claim 20 per cent. or $18,000,000.

Other expenses resulting from the stoppage of the subway construction would arise from the damage, which would undoubtedly occur to the half completed work as soon as the men were taken off.

The rush of subway laborers to get the protection of naturalization papers continued yesterday. Both at the New York and Bronx County bureaus the clerks were overwhelmed with Italian applicants.

KIPLING'S TRIBUTE TO LORD ROBERTS

Reproaches England for Refusing to Hear His 'Pleading in the Market Place.'

Special Cable to THE NEW YORK TIMES.

LONDON, Thursday, Nov. 19.—The Daily Telegraph publishes the following poem, by Rudyard Kipling:

LORD ROBERTS.

[Copyright, 1914, by Rudyard Kipling.]

He passed in the very battle-smoke
Of the war he had descried.
Three hundred miles of cannon spoke
When the Master Gunner died.

He passed to the very sound of the guns,
But before his eye grew dim
He had seen the faces of the sons
Whose sires had served with him.

He had touched their sword-hilts and greeted each
With the old, sure word of praise;
And there was virtue in touch and speech,
As it had been in old days.

So he dismissed them and took his rest,
And the steadfast spirit went forth
Between the adoring East and West
And the tireless guns in the North.

Clean, simple, valiant, well-beloved,
Flawless in faith and fame;
Whom neither ease nor honors moved
A hairsbreadth from his aim.

Never again the war-wise face,
The weighed and urgent word
That pleaded in the market-place—
Pleaded and was not heard!

Yet from his life a new life springs
Through all the hosts to come;
And glory is the least of things
That follow this man home.

JAPAN TO EVACUATE ISLANDS IN PACIFIC

England Agrees to Take Over Marshall and Other German Colonies Until War Ends.

Special Cable to THE NEW YORK TIMES.

SYDNEY, Nov. 18, (Dispatch to The London Morning Post.)—The following official statement was issued by Mr. Pearce today:

"The Japanese Government has intimated to the British Government that it is ready to hand over the Marshall and other German islands in the Pacific, which are temporarily occupied by the Japanese, to an Australian force. The British Government has informed the Japanese Government of its intention to act accordingly. A special Australian force will be dispatched to the islands and will remain in occupation until the termination of the war, when the matter of the ultimate disposal of the islands will be a question for consideration by the allied powers.

"As the Federal Government will have the responsibility for the occupation of islands it is necessary that not only the military occupation, but such matters as trade, food supply, and postal and commercial affairs be investigated and organized. Commander Pethebridge will accompany the force to make the necessary arrangements."

TREBLE THE CAPITAL OF KRUPP WORKS

War Causes Directors to Expand—12 Per Cent. Dividend—Family Takes New Stock.

BERLIN, Nov. 18, (Via The Hague and London.)—The capital of the Krupp Company, which manufactures Germany's big guns and other war material, is to be increased from 70,000,000 to 250,000,000 marks, (about $60,000,000,) according to proposals of the Directors submitted to a general meeting of the company at Essen on Nov. 12. The increase was justified, it was stated, by the demands of war and by earlier enlargements of the works, purchases of coal fields, and so forth, which locked up considerable capital. The new stock issue will as usual be taken by the Krupp family. A part of the new capital will be paid in on Dec. 31.

The Directors proposed a dividend of 12 per cent., as against the 14 declared in the previous year. The Directors also voted 3,000,000 marks toward the relief of the families of soldier employes, 2,000,000 to the Employes' Furlough Fund, and 1,000,000 to the Pension Fund.

KAISER INFORMS SON OF MOSLEM HOLY WAR

Says the Sheikh-ul-Islam Has Issued a Proclamation to the Whole Islamic World.

Special Cable to THE NEW YORK TIMES.

AMSTERDAM, Nov. 18, (Dispatch to The London Times.)—The German press says the Kaiser has sent the following telegram to the Crown Prince:

> To His Imperial Highness the German Crown Prince:
>
> The Sheikh-ul-Islam has established a fetwa according to which every Mussulman must, as a religious duty, fight to the uttermost against England, Russia, and France, the oppressors of Islam.
>
> This fetwa will be distributed throughout the entire Mohammedan world, and is now proclaimed to pilgrims in Mecca.
>
> This means a holy war for the whole Islamic world.
>
> WILHELM.

The Sheikh-ul-Islam is the nominal supreme spiritual head of the Mohammedan world and has great powers apart from his spiritual office.

It is doubtful if a large proportion of the Mohammedans will obey such an edict, even if it has been issued. The Aga Khan, the spiritual head of a large section of the Moslems in India, has told them to remain loyal to Great Britain.

PORTE MUST EXPLAIN SHOTS AT OUR FLAG

Our Ambassador Directed to Inquire About Firing on Tennessee's Launch.

CAPT. DECKER CONFIRMS IT

Alarm Expressed About Consul's Safety—Cruisers Withdrawn, Pending Inquiry.

Special to The New York Times.

WASHINGTON, Nov. 18.—The United States Government today directed Henry Morgenthau, Ambassador at Constantinople, to ask the Ottoman Government for an explanation of the action of the Turkish land forces in firing at a launch from the cruiser Tennessee in the harbor at Smyrna. The incident was confirmed by a report from Capt. B. C. Decker of the Tennessee today.

By direction of President Wilson Secretary Daniels cabled to the commanders of the Tennessee and the North Carolina to do nothing that might embarrass this Government and to await further instructions from Washington. The messages to the commanders were sent by every available route to make certain their prompt delivery.

The Navy Department announced the messages to the two commanders in this statement:

> Secretary Daniels sent a message to the Captains of the Tennessee and North Carolina, both of which are in the Mediterranean, to take no action which could involve this Government without specific instructions from the Navy Department.

While officials of the Navy Department still hope that further details may explain the incident as of minor importance, they were worried today over a sentence in the official report saying that the American Consul at Smyrna was anxious for the fate of the Consulate. This sentence was a part of the report which said that a launch from the Tennessee had been fired at as it proceeded from Vourlah across the bay to Smyrna.

Another serious aspect is put upon the situation by the fact that at the request of the American Ambassador, who first suggested that the Tennessee go to Vourlah, the Tennessee has left Vourlah, withdrawing altogether from Turkish waters, and is now lying in the harbor of Chios, capital of the island of the same name, which since the Balkan war has been under the dominion of Greece.

The Navy Department's official statement on the subject, which largely embodies the text of the report of Capt. Decker of the Tennessee, is as follows:

> Capt. B. C. Decker, in command of the Tennessee, wired Secretary Daniels this morning that while proceeding from Vourlah to Smyrna to make official calls the boat was fired at. Consul anxious for safety of Consulate. Tennessee proceeded to and left Vourlah at request of Ambassador, and is now anchored in the harbor of Scio, (Chios,) from which Capt. Decker's telegram was sent. Secretary Daniels wired for fuller information.

Daniels Is Anxious.

Mr. Daniels remained late at the department today in the hope of news that would clear up points left uncovered by Capt. Decker's report and show that there was no intentional act of hostility against the American flag committed by Turkish officials. His hope is that it will be learned that Smyrna, without the knowledge of this Government, had been declared a closed port on account of Turkey's entrance into the European war, and that when the Tennessee's launch tried to enter a shot was simply fired over the launch's bow. The language of Capt. Decker's report, however, which says that the boat was "fired at," hardly lends itself to this interpretation.

The State Department has heard nothing from Ambassador Morgenthau on the subject. It was explained today that the last dispatch from Mr. Morgenthau was dated Nov. 12 and had just been received, and if there was the same tardiness of communication it would be Nov. 24 before a further report would be received from him. Acting Secretary of State Lansing today cabled Mr. Morgenthau for a full report on the incident.

The deepest interest existed today as to whether the American Consul's alarm for the safety of his Consulate arose prior to the firing at the Tennessee's launch or after it. If before, that might explain Capt. Decker's trip in the launch to Smyrna, although his report gave "official calls" as the explanation. If his anxiety arose after the incident his alarm would suggest the very serious thought that the firing was intentional, and that either the Turkish officials later threatened steps against the Consulate, or, what would seem more likely, that a mob beyond control of the authorities had become threatening. It does not seem, however, that in a strongly fortified city, garrisoned, it is understood, by 25,000 men, a mob could make much headway without the sympathy of the military.

An unexplained phase of the references to the part played in the incident by Mr. Morgenthau and Consul General Horton is that, according to both the State and Navy Departments, there has been nothing recently to suggest any particular need for the presence of an American warship at Smyrna. Mr. Lansing said this afternoon that several months ago there were rumors of trouble there, but that was before the war began. Naturally, since the war in Turkey has assumed some of the aspects of a "holy war" there is uneasiness as to outbreaks against Christians of all nationalities, although there has been no reason to localize the uneasiness as to Smyrna.

Even before Turkey entered the war this uneasiness gave rise to an incident that takes on the appearance of greater importance now than it did at the time. That was the incident that culminated in the retirement from his post of Rustem Bey, the newly appointed Turkish Ambassador at Washington. Rustem Bey sought to answer American publications about the danger of atrocities in Turkey by publicly calling attention to American lynchings and suggesting that his people were as civilized as the Americans.

Received Prompt Rebuke.

His utterances received a severe rebuke from the American Government in the form of a letter from Secretary Bryan asking him to refrain from further disparaging comment on the country to which he was accredited. Rustem

Continued on Page 2.

BIG GUNS IN DUEL ON FLANDERS FRONT; FRENCH IN A MINE TRAP NEAR ST. MIHIEL

Summary of War News.

Violent cannonading marked the day along the battle front in France, according to the French War Office bulletin. Zouaves, after a fierce bayonet encounter, won a forest near Bixschoote, which had been contested several days. Near St. Mihiel, on the eastern front, the Germans blew up the west part of Chauvoncourt, which the French occupied the day before.

German Army Headquarters reports that the fighting in West Flanders continues and the situation remains unchanged. Successful attacks, it is stated, continue in the Argonne Forest, while French sorties south of Verdun were repulsed. An attack by the Allies near St. Mihiel, originally successful, broke down, and the French were compelled to surrender some of their positions southeast of Cirey.

The Russian General Staff announces that the advance guards between the Vistula and the Warth have been driven back in the direction of Bzoure. The Germans, it is said, gained a footing in the region of Lenczyca and Orloff. In East Prussia the Russians continue their advance, and fighting is going on near Gumbinnen and Wagerburg.

Berlin reports, in connection with the fighting in the eastern theatre, that new battles have developed in the Lodz region in Russian Poland, but no decision has been reached. In East Prussia, it is stated, the Russians have been forced to retreat from Soldau toward Mlawa.

A German squadron on Tuesday bombarded the Russian Baltic port of Libau according to an official statement from Petrograd. On the same day the Russian Black Sea fleet, which had been cruising off Trebizond, bombarded that town.

The British supply ship Crown of Galicia is reported sunk by the German fleet off the coast of Chile.

Ambassador Morgenthau has been directed by Washington to ask the Sultan to explain the firing of shots at the launch of the cruiser Tennessee by Turkish forts at Smyrna. Secretary Daniels has requested the commanders of the Tennessee and the North Carolina to take no action that might embarrass the United States. The Tennessee has withdrawn to Chios.

A dispatch from Sydney reports the Japanese Government offered to turn over to Australia the German island possessions seized by Japan since the war began. The British Government has accepted the offer.

GERMANS SHELL LIBAU SETTING FIRE TO CITY

Petrograd Reports Bombardment in Baltic—Russians Attack in Black Sea.

PETROGRAD, Nov. 18.—The following statement was issued this evening by the General Staff of the Russian Navy:

> On the morning of Nov. 17 a German squadron of two cruisers, ten torpedo boats, and several other steamers appeared before Libau. The Germans bombarded the city and harbor, setting on fire several buildings.
>
> The same day, very early, the Russian Black Sea fleet, which had been cruising off Trebizond, steamed close to the town and bombarded the harbor and barracks and set on fire buildings along the coast.
>
> No Turkish ships were sighted off the coast.

LONDON, Thursday, Nov. 19.—"German cruisers and torpedo boat destroyers bombarded the naval harbor here Tuesday for over four hours," says The Daily Mail's Libau correspondent. "Several factories were damaged and a petroleum reservoir was shelled and destroyed by fire. The railroad station and some houses in the poorer parts of the town also suffered.

"The Germans sank several small cargo steamers at the entrance to the harbor.

"Five persons were killed by shells, including a woman, and over thirty persons were wounded."

On Aug. 8, eight days after Germany declared war on Russia, the port of Libau was bombarded by a German squadron, and several merchant vessels were sunk at their moorings. The port is one of the chief points of departure for the Russian export trade on the Baltic, particularly with the United Kingdom and Scandinavia. It is 142 miles southwest of Riga, is a favorite watering place in Summer, and has a population of about 75,000.

TURKS' ACT MAY FORCE RUMANIA INTO WAR

Destroyers Said to Have Entered Sulina Arm of Danube, Protected by Treaty.

By Marconi Transatlantic Wireless Telegraph to The New York Times.

PETROGRAD, Saturday, Nov. 14, (Dispatch to The London Morning Post.)—Three Turkish destroyers have appeared before Sulina and are reported actually to have entered the Sulina arm of the Danube delta with the object of getting into communication with representatives of Austria and Germany, or possibly merely as a protest against the governance of the Danube delta.

The Sulina arm of the delta, with other mouths of the Danube, is under the public law of Europe, and protected by a series of treaties from 1856 down to that of London of 1883.

Rumania, as a result of this action, has the question put broadly on whether she will take sides with Germany and her ally Turkey, or whether she will maintain her own rights and support the [illegible] the law of Europe. In the latter case these Turkish warships, attempting to utilize the protected waterway running through Rumanian territory as a base for warlike activity against Russia, will be disarmed and interned.

Rumania's action in this matter is being closely watched.

The Sulina Channel is the middle channel of the three estuarine arms of the Danube, traversing the Dobrudje region of Rumania. It is fifty miles long, its width is barely 100 yards, and its depth varies from fifteen to sixty feet.

The channel is used by vessels of great draft in navigating the Danube. At its mouth is Sulina, a free port built upon piles with a population of about 6,000.

BRITISH SUPPLY SHIP SUNK IN THE PACIFIC

Valparaiso Hears Crown of Galicia Was Destroyed by the German Fleet.

VALPARAISO, Chile, Nov. 18.—There are persistent rumors here that the British supply ship Crown of Galicia has been attacked by German cruisers and sunk. It is not known whether the vessel was sunk by her own crew or by the Germans.

The crew of the steamer, it is said, was saved and will be landed at Valparaiso by the steamer Rhakotis of the Kosmos Line.

The Crown of Galicia was a steamer of 4,821 tons. She was built in 1906 and belonged to the Crown Steamship Company.

In a special dispatch to THE NEW YORK TIMES from Valparaiso on Nov. 9 it was announced that the Crown of Galicia had arrived at that port with British war materials, and that the German cruisers were awaiting her outside the harbor.

FLEETS IN BATTLE IN THE BALTIC SEA?

Copenhagen Gets a Report of Heavy Cannonading Which Lasted for Many Hours.

Special Cable to THE NEW YORK TIMES.

COPENHAGEN, Nov. 18, (Dispatch to The London Daily News.)—A Baltic naval engagement is reported from Visby, on the Island of Gothland.

Yesterday afternoon very heavy cannonading was heard on the north and west coast, and it is believed to have been a battle between German ships and the Russian fleet, which left Helsingfors two days ago.

The firing was apparently of heavy guns and then of broadsides. It lasted for an hour uninterruptedly, and then, after an interval of fifteen minutes, it started again and lasted till late last night.

The Swedish ferry services were stopped during the engagement.

The Island of Gothland is approximately 100 miles northwest of Libau. It would be entirely possible for the German squadron, which Petrograd reports shelling Libau Tuesday morning, to reach Gothland some time in the afternoon. As it consisted of only two cruisers and ten torpedo boats it would hardly risk a conflict with the Russian Baltic fleet, which was reported to have left Helsingfors earlier in the week. This consists of several cruisers and some pre-dreadnoughts.

If a heavy engagement has taken place off Gothland, as reported in the special cable from Copenhagen, it is more likely that the Russians have met another and more powerful squadron of the Kaiser's naval forces in the Baltic.

EMDEN RIDDLED BY SHELLS.

Her Rudder and All Her Funnels Shot Away by the Sydney.

LONDON, Nov. 18.—A dispatch from Melbourne, Australia, to Reuter's Telegram Company contains part of the report which Capt. John Glossop, of the Australian cruiser Sydney, made regarding the fight in which the German cruiser Emden was destroyed. It says:

"The Emden's firing soon failed when the Sydney began to hit the mark. The Emden's rudder was destroyed early in the fight, her speed suffering greatly in consequence.

"Her next loss was the number one funnel, then the foremast, and this was followed by the number two funnel. Finally the number three funnel fell."

LILLE TAKEN BY BRITISH?

English Motorist Brings Story of Its Evacuation by the Germans.

Special Cable to THE NEW YORK TIMES.

PARIS, Nov. 18, (Dispatch to The London Daily Express.)—News has reached Paris that the Germans have evacuated Lille, and that the town is now occupied by British forces.

This statement is made on the authority of an Englishman who motored into Paris today. He said that when he left Douai that town also was about to be entered by the Allies.

Allowed to Win Village Which the Germans Then Blew Up.

DEADLOCK STILL IN BELGIUM

Both Sides Hold Their Ground in Muddy Trenches Around Ypres.

GERMANS GAIN NEAR CIREY

Berlin Reports the Taking by Storm of Chateau Chatillon and Neighboring Defenses.

PARIS, Nov. 18.—The following official bulletin was issued tonight:

> The day has been marked by a very violent and almost uninterrupted cannonade on our front in the north.
>
> In the region of St. Mihiel the Germans have blown up the west part of Chauvoncourt, which they had mined.
>
> There is nothing to report from other parts of the front.

The text of the afternoon communication was:

> The day of yesterday, Nov. 17, passed much as did the day before. There were numerous artillery exchanges and some isolated attacks on the part of the enemy's infantry, all of which were repulsed.
>
> From the North Sea to the Lys the front was subjected to a fairly active bombardment, particularly at Nieuport and to the east and to the south of Ypres.
>
> Near Bixschoote the Zouaves, charging with the bayonet, brilliantly took possession of a forest which had been disputed between the enemy and ourselves for three days.
>
> To the south of Ypres an offensive movement on the part of the enemy's infantry was repulsed by our troops. The English army also maintained its front.
>
> From Arras to the Oise there is nothing new to report.
>
> In the region of Craonne our artillery on several occasions secured the advantage over the batteries of the enemy.
>
> The bombardment of Rheims has continued. From Rheims to the Argonne there is nothing new to report.
>
> In the region of St. Mihiel, in spite of counter-attacks by the Germans, we have retained in our possession the western part of the village of Chauvoncourt.
>
> In Alsace the Landwehr battalions sent into the region of Ste. Marie-aux-Mines have had to be taken out for the reason that they lost one-half of their effective strength.

British Gain 500 Yards.

LONDON, Nov. 18.—The Official Information Bureau today gave out a statement as follows:

> Our third division was subjected yesterday to a heavy attack, first from artillery and then from infantry, the brunt of both falling upon two battalions of the division. These were shelled out of their trenches, but they recovered after a brilliant counter-attack which drove the enemy back in disorder for some 300 yards.
>
> During the day an attack was made also on a brigade of the second division. In this the enemy were repulsed with heavy loss.

Berlin Reports Argonne Successes.

BERLIN, (via London,) Nov. 18.—An official communication issued today by the German General Headquarters says:

> Fighting in West Flanders continues, and the situation on the whole remains unchanged.
>
> In the forest of Argonne our attacks continue successfully. French sorties to the south of Verdun were repulsed.
>
> An attack was made against our forces which had moved forward on the western bank of the River Meuse near St. Mihiel, and, although it was originally successful for the enemy, it broke down completely later on.
>
> Our attack to the southeast of Cirey compelled the French to surrender some of their positions. The Château Châtillon was stormed and taken by our troops.

MAY BATTLE AGAIN ON WATERLOO FIELD

Germans Said to Have Constructed Concrete Trenches for a Winter Campaign.

Special Cable to THE NEW YORK TIMES.

NORTHERN FRANCE, Nov. 18, (Dispatch to The London Daily Chronicle.)—A stinging hail storm swept the trenches in France and Belgium yesterday and covered them and the men imprisoned there with a white layer of icy cold dampness.

At the time, which was toward midday, the heavy guns thundered from their concealed emplacements from Nieuport to La Bassée, and, since the German offensive was again due, the allied forces had to lie prone and wait. They waited patiently and bravely, although they were cold to the marrow, and their clothes wet and sticking to their skins, their boots clogged with heavy mud, their feet soaked by the constant drip from their overcoats.

They await the next German offensive

"All the News That's Fit to Print."

The New York Times.

THE WEATHER

Local snow or rain today; partly cloudy Thursday; moderate west winds, becoming variable.

For full weather report see Page 17.

VOL. LXIV...NO. 20,815. NEW YORK, WEDNESDAY, JANUARY 20, 1915.—EIGHTEEN PAGES. ONE CENT In Greater New York, Jersey City and Newark. { Elsewhere TWO CENTS.

ZEPPELINS KILL 5 IN RAID ON ENGLAND; ONE BROUGHT DOWN BY WARSHIP'S GUNS; BOMBS FALL AT NIGHT ON SIX TOWNS; KING'S SANDRINGHAM HOME A TARGET

VILLA PLANNING A NEW REPUBLIC

Recent Moves Indicate He Will Join Maderos and Angeles in a Northern Government.

TO SURRENDER MEXICO CITY

Carranza General Approaching from the East and Great Uncertainty Prevails There.

RAILWAY OFFICES SHIFTED

Villa Calls Gutierrez a Traitor and Says He Took $5,000,000 When He Fled from the Capital.

Special to The New York Times.

WASHINGTON, Jan. 19.—Gen. Francisco Villa is believed in well-informed circles in Washington to be contemplating the evacuation of Mexico City, the withdrawel of his forces toward Torreon, and the establishment of an independent government or republic in Northern Mexico.

Official dispatches received by the State Department strengthen this impression and indicate that Villa, supported mainly by Gen. Felipe Angeles and the Maderos, may set up such a government in the north, giving it the color of authority by asserting that it is done under the name of the so-called convention.

Villa has not entered Mexico City in the present crisis. He started for the capital from Aguascalientes when he learned of the flight of Provisional President Gutierrez, but halted at Queretaro, and is giving orders to his agents in the capital from that point. There have been reports in Mexico City that Villa was coming there, but the belief is growing that he, will return to the North instead of taking chances on being cooped up in the capital.

Official advices to the State Department said today that Villa was preparing to evacuate the capital. He has given orders to the general offices of the National Railways Company of Mexico to move north. The railways have been operated by Villa as military lines. The various departments of the National Railways spent yesterday packing up records and furniture which are to be taken into the North with Villa when he gives orders for the evacuation of the capital.

While Villa is preparing for the contingency of the capture of the capital by Gen. Obregon's forces and arranging for withdrawal toward the north, Gen. Angeles, who has for some time been Villa's real choice for the Presidency, is handling the situation in the north from Monterey as a base. On Friday, just before the flight of Gen. Gutierrez from the capital, Gen. Angeles entered Monterey with the Maderos and delivered a significant speech to the people. He made a strong plea for the support of all the religious elements of the country, and declared in favor of religious toleration. The Angeles speech is interpreted by some as a keynote speech for the Provisional Presidency of the proposed Villa Government in the North.

Extent of the Villa Territory.

These and other developments today are regarded as strengthening the theory that it is Villa's intention to establish a new republic in the North which would include everything north of a line drawn from aMtamoras at the mouth of the Rio Grande River, through onterey, Torreon, and Durango to the Pacific oCast. The new Villa Government, it is believed, would take over the States of Sonora, Sinaloa, Chihuahua, Durango, Coahuila, and the northern ends of Nuevo Leon and Tamaulipas. It is generally admitted here that if Villa, Angeles, and the Maderos should mass their troops in this region it would be difficult for the Carrancistas or any other element to dislodge them without a most difficult campaign.

Gen. Obregon, the leading commander of the Carrancista forces, is now preparing to capture the Mexican capital, and expects to be in control there very soon. The fact that the Villa Provisional Government forces are moving records because they are uncertain of thir ability to dfend the capital, is interpreted as a forerunner of the evacuation of Mexico City and its capture by the forces of Gen. Obregon.

Forces acting under the directions of Gen. Obregon and the Constitutionalists are now in control of the region westward from Guadalajara to the Pacific Coast. Guadalajara is expected to fall any day, if it has not already been evacuated by the convention forces, as the Constitutionalist claim. The capture of Guadalajara and the occupation of Mexico City by the forces of Gen. Obregon would render precarious the position of detached convention units.

After the withdrwal of the Provisional Government forces and the establishment of Villa's republic in the north, it is believed to be Villa's plan to count upon the possibility of dissension among the Carranacistas and to attack them in an effort to retake the capital at the first favorable moment. Should the Carrancistas be able to strengthen their Government in Mexico City it would develop into a contest between the Villistas and the Carrancistas, and between the north and south.

Uncertainty in the Capitol.

The State Department's announcement of the situation in Mexico City today, said:

"The department is in receipt of a dispatch, dated Jan. 18, 3 P. M., from Mexico City, with reference to the general political situation. The dispatch states that the city is quiet, but there is much uncertainty as to what turn affairs may take in the near future. It has been widely published in Mexico City that Villa is on his way there with a large force.

"On the other hand, there are reports that he will not come further south than Queretaro, where he now is.

"The general offices of the National

Continued on Page 4.

THE MORGAN ESTATE TO BE REAPPRAISED

Both the Heirs and the State are said to be Dissatisfied With the Marx Figures.

The appraisal of the contents of the three homes of the late J. Pierpont Morgan, made by Samuel Marks for the State Controller, probably will be thrown out and the work done all over again. Exclusive of the books and manuscripts, the value of the contents of the house at 219 Madison Avenue was said to be $1,000,914, of the library furnishings $253,745, of the house at Highland Falls $82,000, and of Camp Uncas $8,903. It has been known for some time that this appraisal was not at all satisfactory.

Efforts to discover yesterday just what the dissatisfaction was based upon were not successful, but John W. Hutchinson, Jr., special attorney for the State in the Morgan appraisal, said:

"In a day or two I shall go over the matter with Controller Travis, and some decision will then be arrived at. By Friday or Saturday I hope to have a statement ready, telling in detail just what will be done. The appraisal already made has cost the State and the estate $7,500 each, a total of $15,000. It would be unfair to subject the people and the estate to another heavy charge without good reason. I can say, however, that the chances are now that a new appraisal will be made, and that it will be undertaken without any regard to the work of Mr. Marx."

Asked if he thought the Marx appraisal too small, Mr. Hutchinson replied:

"The new appraisal may make the figures larger or it may make them smaller. That is not the point. The idea is to procure an absolutely accurate appraisal. Neither the executors of the estate nor the Controller has any other interest in the matter. We want the work to be done properly."

Mr. Hutchinson said that his idea was to procure the assistance of the best experts in the various articles to be appraised. He was sure, he said, that the cost of the work would be small in comparison with the amount received by Mr. Marx. It came out during the talk with Mr. Hutchinson and other connected with the Controller's office that the first bill presented by Mr. Marx was for $40,000, and that such vigorous objection was made to it that it was gradually reduced until $15,000 was agreed upon.

"The rare objects of art collected by Mr. Morgan," said Mr. Hutchinson, "are just what they are represented to be. There are no bogus articles among them. Added to their great value is another value due to the fact that Mr. Morgan gathered them. This fact guarantees that they are genuine."

SPY HINT IN ROEBLING FIRE.

Plant Was Making Chains, Supposed to be for French Army Use.

Special to The New York Times.

TRENTON, N. J., Jan. 19.—There is at least suspicion in the mind of Charles G. Roebling, President of the John A. Roebling's Sons Company, that a foreign spy may have started the fire that did $1,500,000 damage last night to the plant and destroyed fifteen houses near by.

"It might have been a foreign spy," said Mr. Roebling today. "Possibly some one might have lighted a cigar carelessly, or some one might have done it deliberately, for there is a bad element in town. I don't know a thing about it, but we may be able to trace the origin later on."

In one of the larger buildings destroyed, the company was making 15,000 sets of trace chains, supposed to be intended ultimately for French army use. Mr. Roebling admitted today that the chains were being made. He said the order came through the company's Pittsburgh branch, but that he was not sure for whom they were intended. No plans have been made for rebuilding.

$162,687 TO AID PATRICK.

Amount Spent for Lawyer Condemned for Rice Murder Revealed.

Special to The New York Times.

DENVER, Colo., Jan. 19.—It cost John T. Milliken of St. Louis and others $162,687.16 to aid Albert T. Patrick, who served many years in Sing Sing as the slayer of William Marsh Rich, and was finally pardoned by Gov. ix. This statement was made on the witness stand here today by Milliken in reply to charges brought against him in a suit by Leonidas Hill of New York, to have an accounting of all funds raised by members of the Patrick family and others for the man's defence.

Hill said he contributed $4,200 cash to the Patrick fund, and that other relatives, including Patrick's mother, gave all they could. Hill and Milliken married sisters of Patrick. When he had no more money, Hill testified, he gave Milliken 20,000 shares of Milliken Oil Company stock on which to raise money. He said Milliken had never returned the stock and had never rendered an accounting.

Milliken, in denying Hill's charges, said that, of the $162,687.16 spent in behalf of Patrick, only about $28,000 had been paid by other members of the family.

FAVORS NATIONAL GUARD.

Gov. Blease's Successor Declares for Strong State Militia.

COLUMBIA, S. C., Jan. 19.—Richard I. Manning, who was inaugurated Governor of South Carolina today, declares in his address that he "favored a strong, well-maintained, well-disciplined National Guard." The South Carolina militia was disbanded by Gov. Blease before he retired last week.

Gov. Manning recommended the appointment of a legislative commission to investigate working conditions and to prepare a workingman's compensation act, urged repeal of the State income tax law, and recommended an amendment of the child labor law to raise the age limit from 12 to 14 years.

EXPLOSION ON WARSHIP.

Five Men Injured in Accident on Submarine Tender Fulton.

BOSTON, Jan. 19.—An explosion occurred today in an oil-burning boiler on the new submarine tender Fulton at the Charlestown Navy Yard, injuring five men. William Flaherty, a first-class fireman, was burned about the head and body. His condition was said to be critical. Frank H. Eaton, also a fireman, suffered serious burns, but will probably recover. Seaman Kingston, Mead, and Coulter were injured less severely.

The Fulton served as a repair ship for all submarines on the Atlantic Coast. She has been in commission only about two months, having been turned over to the Government by her builders in November. She is commanded by Lieut. Seymour C. Holliday.

1 KILLED, 20 SHOT BY STRIKE GUARDS

Deputies Drive Off Laborers at the Liebig Fertilizer Works in Carteret, N. J.

GRAND JURY TO TAKE ACTION

Witnesses Call Attack on Men Seeking Strikebreakers in Train Unprovoked.

PROTECTED BY SEARCHLIGHT

Plant Threatened at Night by Angry Crowd—Wives in Parade Appeal to Mayor.

The brilliant white "eye" of a searchlight, mounted on the Liebig Fertilizer Works at Carteret, N. J., swept the swampy ground surrounding this plant and that of the Williams & Clark Fertilizing Company, abotu a mile away, last night with the regularity of a pendulum, and now and thn disclosed groups of me, more than 700 persons all told.

The men were strikers formerly employed at the two plants, and they shook fists at the beam of light and muttered threats of what they would do to repay a tragedy of yesterday morning, when one striker was shot dead and more than a score were injured by bullets fired by Deputy Sheriffs employed by the fertilizer companies as guards.

Many of the crowd had relatives, all had friends, among the wounded. They asserted many men were injured whose names did not appear on the official lists made up at hospitals in Elizabeth, because they had crawled away or been helped off by friends. The official lists showed one dead, four on the point of death, seven still unable to leave the hospital, and seven more who were treated and sent home.

THE DEAD.

ALESANDRO, DESEDERIO, Chrome, N. J., 28 years old, shot in the leg and back; died at 3 o'clock in Alexian Brothers Hospital, Elizabeth.

THE INJURED.

BIBICK, PAUL, Chrome, N. J., 40 years old, married; two bullets in left leg and one in left hand.

COCHANTO, ANTON, Carteret, N. J., 32 years old; shot in back of neck; may die.

CUBILO, FRANK, Chrome; shot in leg; treated in hospital and went home.

DODD, STEPHEN, Cateret, 12 years old; buckshot in legs and thighs.

ERDA, STEFAN, Cateret, 14 years old, married; ten buckshot in right leg and three in left.

FURTY, JOSEPH, Chrome, 19 years old, single; two shots in left hip.

GONHOS, ANDREW, Chrome, 35, shot in left leg, treated in hospital and went home.

GOBARISKY, JOHN, Chrome, 50, married; four shots in right leg; condition serious.

HECTA, STANISLAUS, Chrome, 28, three shots in body; treated in hospital and went home.

KONIVUSKY, MICHAEL, Chrome, 29, shot in left hip.

KORINVCO, JACOB, Carteret, shot in right foot.

MUSIKA, JOHN, Carteret, 31, married; six shots in right leg; may die.

PATTY, CARMAN, Chrome, 38, married; shot in left arm and abdomen; may die.

PODNER, GEORGE, Carteret; shot in hand; treated in hospital and went home.

ROBB, CHARLES, Chrome; shot in thigh; treated in hospital and went home.

SAVETSKY, JOHN, Carteret, 28; buckshot wounds in body; may die.

TRIOTHER, LAUTO, Chrome; shot in thigh; treated in hospital and went home.

YANOS, CARLO, Carteret; shot in chest and thigh; treated in hospital and went home.

Cochanto and Savetsky were in the General Hospital in Elizabeth last night. The other wounded, except those who went home after being treated, were in the Alexian Brothers Hospital, in Elizabeth.

Grand Jury to Act.

There were conflicting reports of how the trouble started, but the witnesses examined by Prosecutor W. Edwin Florance of Middlesex County at an inquiry in the Borough Hall at Chrome in the afternoon were all in accord except the Deputy Sheriffs. Policemen and citizens joined the strikers in their declaration that the attack was unprovoked. The deputies asserted the strikers had fired the first shots. Mr. Florance adjourned the meeting after hearing fifty witnesses. He said he already had sufficient evidence to submit to the Grand Jury in New Brunswick this week.

Several men said they had seen three boats loaded with Deputies put out from the Williams & Clark works immediately after the shooting and cross Staten Island Sound to Staten Island, where they disappeared. A. R. Roosman, Superintendent of the plant, denied that a single guard had left.

The Prosecutor was told in effect that the employes of the two fertilizer plants, together with those employed by Armour & Co. and the Consumers' Fertilizer Company, near by, struck on Jan. 4 for a return to the $2 a day wage scale, which was cut to $1.60 last October, when Leonard Frasina, an organizer of the American Federation of Labor, unionized all four plants. The Consumers' Company immediately met the demand, and its men went to work. Liebig and Williams & Clark are part of the American Agricultural Company, and the Armour Company has a working agreement with them, it was testified. They held out.

Piled Ties on Tracks.

The strikers yesterday heard that strikebreakers were to be imported into the Liebig and Williams & Clark plants, and between 300 and 400 of them gathered outside the Liebig plant shortly before 7 o'clock in the morning. The first train from Elizabethport over the Sound Shore Branch of the Central Railroad of New Jersey reached the Liebig station, about half way between the towns of Carteret and Chrome, at 6:57 o'clock.

The strikers heaped ties on the tracks and surrounded the train when it halted. Chief of Police Henry Harrington of Roosevelt had been warned of the hold-up and was on the train. He assured the strikers that there were no strikebreakers aboard and suggested that if they would remove the ties and permit the train to proceed unmolested, the train crew probably would allow them to pass through the cars and convince themselves there were no strikebreakers there. The strikers moved the ties at once, a committee passed through the train, and it was allowed to proceed.

But in the last four days 100 deputy sheriffs had bee nstationed in the Liebig

Continued on Page 6.

RUSSIAN TRENCHES ALMOST TOUCH FOE'S

Impregnable Line in Poland Against Which Germans Hurl Themselves in Vain.

INCESSANT HAIL OF SHELLS

Czar's Officers Calmly Bide Time to Resume the Offensive and Are Confident of Victory.

By PERCEVAL GIBBON.

Special Cable to THE NEW YORK TIMES.

ZYRDOW, Poland, Received in London Jan. 19.—There is a spot above the river which must not be indicated too explicitly, but whose name signifies in Russian the place of tombs. It is thus christened by the troops who camp in a great forest which shadows the whole position. It is a point at which the new German plan of thrusting toward the railway instead of as hitherto toward the road has produced fighting of more than Homeric quality.

The Russians, who never misjudge the value of ground, were established here in well-made trenches, with the shelter of the forest at their backs for reserves and supports. Upon this iron front the Germans spent themselves in fruitless attacks, incurring crippling losses. It was only after repeated and disastrous failure of these tactics that they began a diffent method of approach.

Here, as everywhere else, they have a large amount of artillery, and under incessant shell fire they proceeded to sap their way toward the Russian trenches. Incidentally they expended shells enough to last an army through the whole of a small war, and where formerly six acres of rtees projected from the main forest there are now no trees at all.

The parapet of their trench is only thirty-five paces from the Russian parapet, and the men crouching behind their shelter can hear the voices of their enemies. None dare lift head or hand to even the loopholes on the breastworks, since the worst shot in the world can send bullet after bullet through any loophole at that distance. The Russians are able to throw hand grenades, with which their trenches are supplied, clear into the German trenches, which the German shelling has had to cease since their own men are in equal danger from any shell aimed at the Russian treches.

I rode down through the forest in an effort to reach one of the trenches two nights ago, passing from the pale shine of the snow upon the bare fields to sheer darkness. I found the staff establishtd in a spacious dugout some 400 yards behind the actual first line. Here, as always, was a straw-padded, candle-lit interior, with an orderly waiting, with telephone to ear, and all those rough-and-ready contrivances by which men live who have death for ever at their elbow. Here, too, their faces, disguised by weeks of beard and grimed with the smirch of war, were burly Russian officers, those adequate and quietly confident men who are the strength and inspiration of the Russian Army.

In all that gloom, where all life was balanced on a hair, one thing was steadfast and cordial, and that was the unshaken assurance of these cheerful, expert fighting men in their power to hold the Germans and presently to resume the offensive, to which each one of them looks forward, and advance at least toward the frontier of Germany. None underestimates the enemy. They criticise him in a spirit of absolute professional impartiality, admiring quite frankly the organization and courage of the German infantry, but condemning the artillery and pooh-hooing the cavalry.

Yesterday morning the Germans renewed their bombardment of the positions at Radziwilow, where the fine Russian trench is practically impregnable, and has already cost them huge losses in their attempts to assault it.

I had an illustration of their lack of system in artillery fire while returning along the rear of this position. Their shells sailed up across the woods to the south of the railway, bursting on an empty stretch of frields about a thousand yards away, and turned seven or eight hundred acres of virgin snow into an infero of smoke and torn earth, but no single shell fell nearer than a thousand yards to any living soul.

During the last day or two I have seen a change in the nature of the fighting on this front. The German proceedure has no longer its old character of desperate decision but has become more desultory and their pressure flickers up and down the line as though in a panic of effort to find some point at which the defence is weak.

I learn here from prisoners that the Germans lately have been celebrating victories. Berlin and other cities are said to be gay with flags and Gen. von Hindenburg has been acclaimed as a national hero. I can only keep my eyes on the small portion of the long front limited by Sochaczew on the north and Mszczonow on the south, but in regard to this region I can offer my personal testimony that at no point have the Germans gained anything in nature of a success nor made any attack which has not been immensely more costly in lives to them than to the Russians.

AUSTRIANS SEIZED AT SEA.

Steamer Rotterdam Held Up by French Destroyer and Searched.

Officers of the Holland-American liner Rotterdam, which reached Quarantine last night from Naples with 254 first and 673 second cabin passengers and mails, reported that the ship was stopped in the Gulf of Lyons by a French destroyer.

All the passengers passports were examined and two Austrians, who were traveling in the second cabin, were taken off. After a two hours delay the Rotterdam proceeded to Gibraltar and passed through the Straits without being stopped by the British, who had evidently been notified by the French authorities that the passenger list was alright.

Among the passengers was Mrs. Charles Arthur Moore of Greenwich, Conn., bringing back the body of her husband, who died on the Rotterdam a few days after the liner left New York on her eastward trip.

CARDINAL MERCIER REFUTES GERMANS

His Liberty Was Restrained, He Says in Letter to Priests Secretly Circulated.

SOLDIERS INVADED HIS HOME

Not Allowed to Visit His Bishops—'Your and My Rights Violated,' He Says—Germans Had Denied This.

LONDON, Jan. 19.—The Amsterdam correspondent of Reuter's Telegram Company telegraphs that Cardinal Mercier has made a formal protest against his treatment at the hands of the German authorities in Belgium. The Cardinal has published his protest in the form of a letter, dated Jan. 10, and has sent copies to all priests in his diocese. The letter follows:

"Without doubt you have seen the communication from the German Government of Brussels, as published in the daily papers, and in which it is declared 'that Cardinal Mercier, Archbishop of Malines, is in no wise hindered in the exercise of his episcopal work.' The facts show how far this report is from the truth.

"On the evening of the 1st of January and on the next day soldiers forced their entry into the vicarage, seizing my pastoral letter, and, contrary to my episcopal order, they prohibited reading of the letter before congregations, threatening the severest punishment, which would have been inflicted on vicars or parishes. My own dignity they did not spare.

"On the 2d of January, early in the morning, at 6 o'clock, I received an order to appear on that same morning before the Governor General to answer for my letter to the priests and parishioners. The next day I was forbidden to attend the service at the Cathedral at Antwerp. Finally, I was not allowed to move about freely to visit other Bishops in Belgium.

"Your and my own rights are thus violated. As a citizen of Belgium, as a pastor, and as a member of the Holy Congregation of Cardinals, I strongly protest against it. However others may interpret it, this experience has proved that my pastoral letter has caused no danger of a rebellion. On the contrary, it has been instrumental in calming minds and appeasing them.

"I congratulate you that you have done your duty."

According to the Amsterdam Tijd the letter of the Cardinal was distributed secretly by special couriers to all parishes throughout the See of Malines.

FRENCH RUSH ONWARD TO CUT OFF ST. MIHIEL

Another German Field Works Taken in Advance Near Alsace Frontier.

LONDON, Jan. 19.—A further advance has been made by the French troops operating northwest of Pont-a-Mousson in the effort to cut the lines of communication between St. Mihiel on the Meuse and the fortress of Metz.

Another field work in the forest of La Prêtre has been won from the Germans, according to the official Paris bulletin, which states that the French troops now ocupy over a quarter mile of the trenches of the invaders in this vicinity.

This success follows up the gains reported yesterday, and military men ascribe considerable importance to the operations in this region. In conjunction with the continued French pressure on the German lines west of Perthes, the French attacks near Pont-a-Monsson will if successful balk the German offensive against Verdun, around which troops have been drawn in a half circle ever since their invasion of France assumed definite form.

Little activity is being shown at other points on the battle front. The weather conditions have been so severe in Flanders, where there have been heavy falls of snow, that the fighting has been confined almost entirely to artillery engagements.

The Germans have failed to follow up their success in the region of Soissons. The Kaiser's troops are remaining inactive beyond the River Aisne, and the only activity in this vicinity in the last twenty-four hours has been the bombardment of St. Paul.

GEN. VON OMPTEDA SLAIN.

Killed at the Head of His Corps in the Western Theatre of War.

AMSTERDAM, Wednesday, Jan. 20, (via London.)—Lieut. Gen. Freiherr von Ompteda of the German Army has been killed in the western arena of the war at the head of his corps.

Baron or Freiherr Ludwig von Ompteda was born in Hanover in 1855 and was educated at the Lüneburg Military School. In 1847 he became a Lieutenant of infantry, after having been Battalion Adjutant and Regimental Adjutant he was made a Major General in 1909 and a Lieutenant General in 1912.

He lectured on military subjects and was well known as an organizer and supply expert.

GERMANY NEEDS LABORERS.

Advertising in Switzerland, but Won't Accept Italians.

Special Cable to THE NEW YORK TIMES.

BERNE, Jan. 19. (Dispatch to The London Morning Post.)—Germany's lack o fskilled labor is becoming so serious that she is advertising in Switzerland for all categories of metal workers. Those who accept a contract for a year will have their travelling expenses paid.

No Italians, however, are being accepted.

One of the Raiders Wrecked By Fire of Warship, London Hears

LONDON, Jan. 20, 2:15 A. M.—A Zeppelin has been brought down at Hunstanton, a few miles north of Sandringham, according to a dispatch from King's Lynn to the Central News.

The dispatch adds that the Zeppelin was brought down by the fire of a warship.

CANNOT CRUSH US, SAYS FALKENHAYN

Coolly Confident, the Kaiser's Field Chief Says Germany Can Fight on Indefinitely.

SCOFFS AT BRITISH EMBARGO

Food and War Materials Ample—Plenty of Men to Fight for Honor to the Last Ditch.

GENERAL FIELD HEADQUARTERS OF THE GERMAN ARMIES IN FRANCE, Jan. 16, (via London, Jan. 19.)—"More of such offensive," (referring to the present operations of the Allies,) "can only be welcome to us.

"The British are good fighters, but an army without the necessary officers and non-commissioned officers is scarcely an army.

"We are fully prepared for any attempt at a landing in Belgium; the sooner it comes the better."

These are some of the statements, full of quiet optimism, of Lieut. Gen. Erich von Falkenhayn, the Gov'er[illegible] Minister of War and Chief of Staff of German armies in the field, who today received an Associated Press man in the first interview given to any correspondent.

The General talked frankly of the present military situation and the prospects of the war, which, it is evident, he does not expect will be a short one.

Gen. von Falkenhayn is the man responsible under the Emperor for the strategy in the war. He is a young man, as commanders go, the youngest of any of the leaders of the European armies, and has a tremendous capacity for hard work necessary for the control of the great apparatus of Germany's forces.

From dawn until late at night he is at his desk in an old French Government building which houses the German General Staff, and an unbroken stream of officers, with reports and plans, calling for his decision, flows all day long in and out of the little, square conference room, with its table loaded with maps.

He performs the dual functions of Minister of War and Chief of the General Staff, and has little time for exercise or recreation. He sleeps at headquarters with his hand, as it were, on the throttle of the big machine, yet his slender figure is as erect and his manner almost as elastic and vigorous as the day when he flashed into public notice with his defense of the German Army in the Zabern debates in the Reichstag.

Germany Defending Herself.

"This is not a war of aggression," said Gen. von Falkenhayn, taking up the causes of the war; "not a war brought about by a 'military caste or military party' in Germany, but one of self-defense. As a soldier I cannot, of course, talk on the political aspects or the causes of the war, but can speak from a military standpoint.

"It was forced upon us by the Russian mobilization, in the face of which we could do nothing else but arm ourselves. Russia had been advised and warned by his Majesty through our Ambassador that if she mobilized we must, in self-defense, order a general mobilization and take the steps necessary to protect our national existence. Russia, nevertheless, went ahead with its mobilization, while continuing diplomatic negotiations.

"If a man comes into your room for a discussion with gun drawn, you can scarcely be expected to wait for him to cock and level it at you before reaching for your own to defend your life.

"Our present situation is excellent. We have no cause to complain. We have carried the war into the enemy's country on both fronts; we are still there, after five months of war. Our present lines are very strong; the advantage is all on our side thus far.

"If our first advance against Paris," said the General in response to a question, "had succeeded fully and in all respects it would have been reckoned as a most brilliant achievement. As it stands, it is an admirable one. I can say so freely because I had nothing to do with the conception of the plan of campaign. But one cannot expect to carry on war without some checks, and when we fell back we swung over to the present line of action, in which we have been thoroughly successful.

Success in Holding Flanders.

"It is wrong to interpret the operations in Flanders as an attempt on our part to reach Calais and outflank the allied armies. On the contrary, that phase of the campaign is the result of an attempt on the part of the French and British to force their way north, to separate us from the sea and envelop our right flank and rear, relieve Antwerp, and oblige us to retire from Belgium.

"Their plan was the failure, our counter-stroke the success, of the operations in Flanders. They have not outflanked us, and we are still there."

"What is your view of the widely heralded general offensive of Kitchener's new army?" he was asked.

"The offensive," replied the German Chief of Staff, "was to begin, according to Gen. Joffre's order, on Dec. 17. So far we have no reason to be dissatisfied with its results. We have not only held our lines successfully, but have even gained ground. More of such offensive can only be welcome to us.

"As to Kitchener's army, the British are good fighters, and I have all respect for them, but an army without necessary officers and non-commissioned officers is scarcely an army, according to present-day standards. They may send them over to attack us, but I think we are strong enough to beat them and drive them back with bloody heads.

Ready for Landing of Foe.

"The proposed landing in Belgium? We are fully prepared for an attempt in this direction; the sooner it comes the better."

There was nothing of the boastful in Gen. von Falkenhayn's manner. These statements were made instead in a quiet tone and with confidence in the preparedness of the German Army and its ability to meet the situation.

"What effect upon the German conduct of the war," Gen. von Falkenhayn was asked, "has the British blockade and contraband policy exercised?"

"Practically none at all," he replied. "Of food we have enough. Have you observed any scarcity in Germany? We may have to husband certain things and be sparing with our wheat consumption, but our 'war bread' (referring to bread made from rye, potato meal, and wheat flour) is as tasty and nutritious as the regular wheat bread.

"The problem of feeding the civil populations of Belgium, Poland, and the occupied parts of France, particularly such cities as Lille or Lodz, presents some difficulties, but for ourselves we have enough.

"As for the embargo on copper—(here Gen. von Falkenhayn laughed) "We have no copper underground, it is true, but above ground we have more than enough for all military needs. If our regular supplies become exhausted, we need only draw on the enormous quantities of manufactured copper already in Germany. In our cables for transmitting high-tension electricity, for instance, we have a two years' supply.

"British interference with copper shipments, it seems to me, is a heavy blow for America, but for us it is nothing." (Gen. von Falkenhayn used the vigorous South German expression for "utter indifference.")

Can Fight Indefinitely.

"How long do you think the war may last, or can last—Lord Kitchener's three years?"

"It can last," said the German Chief of Staff, picking out that particular part of the question, "indefinitely for us. I see nothing that can force us to stop fighting.

"Food and materials? We are amply supplied. Our strategic position is god. Human material? Do you know that the recruits of the 1915 class are to be called to the colors? October 1, 1915, is the normal date. I was occupying myself with this question yesterday. Does that look as if there was any lack of soldiers? We have more troops in Berlin today than in peace times. They still need training, however. No men are sent to the front without adequate preparation.

"Enthusiasm? You have been at the front and know that there is no slackening in the zeal of the men for their task. No; we can go on indefinitely.

"And if in this war, in which Kalmucks, Kamschatkans, Turcomans, Senegal negroes, Indians, and what-not have been brought in to maintain in the white man's Europe the so-called balance of power; if in this war to crush a nation whose offense is that through industry and hard work it has prospered and is prosperous, we should go down, we shall go down with honor, fighting to the last ditch and the last man."

"And how far does Germany wish to carry this war, your Excellency? Until the other side is completely crushed?"

"Until they are so defeated that the possibility of a repetition of this unprovoked attack upon us is completely eliminated," he said earnestly.

Doubts Italy's Entrance Into War.

"What about the new clouds on the horizon—Italy and Rumania?"

"Those are questions you should address to the Imperial Chancellor or the Foreign Secretary."

"But under certain contingencies they might become questions of interest to the Chief of the General Staff."

"Out of the question," was the emphatic reply. "I cannot believe that these two States, which have been united to us for twenty years by ties of alliance, should suddenly array themselves in the ranks of our enemies. I consider that utterly impossible."

GERMAN PAPERS SUSPEND.

Dr. Dietz Says That 1,000 Have Ceased Publication Since the War.

Special Cable to THE NEW YORK TIMES.

COPENHAGEN, Jan. 19. (Dispatch to The London Daily Chronicle.)—Speaking in Berlin, at a meeting of the German Lyceum Club, Dr. Alexander Dietz, Director of the Wolff Agency, said that 1,000 German papers, 120 of them political ones, have been forced to cease publication owing to the war.

Royal Family Had Left for London Before the Raiders Came.

YARMOUTH SUFFERS MOST

Buildings Torn Apart and Four Residents Killed as Aircraft Sweep Over City.

GERMANS USE SEARCHLIGHT

Flashes Seen and Whirr of the Motors Heard, but Darkness Hides Enemy from View.

TRAVELED OVER 400 MILES

Seen in Early Morning as They Left the German Base to Cross the North Sea.

LONDON, Wednesday, Jan. 20.—Under cover of darkness, several German aircraft, presumably all Zeppelins, raided the County of Norfolk, on the east coast of England, last night.

One of the Zeppelins was brought down near Hunstanston, a little watering place north of Sandringham, the seat of the royal palace, in the western part of the county. The Central News dispatch which reports this adds that the Zeppelin was brought down by the fire of a warship.

Besides dropping bombs close to Sandringham Palace, without doing any great damage, the German airmen attacked the seaport of Yarmouth, Cromer, a watering place forty miles northwest of Yarmouth, and Sheringham, in the same neighborhood; Beeston, and King's Lynn, ninety miles west of Yarmouth and near the Wash.

If the German raiders hoped to blow up the royal residence while the King and Queen were in it, they missed their mark, for King George and Queen Mary, with their family, who had been staying at Sandringham, returned to London yesterday morning to resume their residence in Buckingham Palace.

Five Known Dead

Only scattering reports have reached here from the towns that were bombarded, but it is known that at least five persons have been killed, four in Yarmouth and one in King's Lynn.

The damage done to property by the bombs was apparently small except at Yarmouth, but the noise of the terrific explosions caused a panic in several places. In Yarmouth the people, in their fright, rushed pellmell out of the houses.

The raiding Zeppelins apparently flew across the North eSa during the day, timing their arrival so as to attack without any alarm being given.

A Copenhagen dispatch to a London morning paper reported increased activity among the German air fleet, and told of a huge Zeppelin being seen yesterday morning close to the southern border of Denmark.

Three German airships, according to a dispatch from Amsterdam, passed over the Island of Ameland, in the North eSa, at 2:30 o'clock yesterday afternoon. They were flying in a westerly direction, according to advices received from Nes, the principal town of the island.

The Attack on Yarmouth.

Six hours later, or about 8:30 o'clock in the evening, an aircraft appeared over Yarmouth, which is 190 miles across the sea from Ameland.

It was dark at the time of the attack, and it was impossible, therefore, to see the aircraft, which some believe was an aeroplane, and not a Zeppelin.

The whirring of the propellers and noise of the engine first attracted attention to the arrival of the Germans. It was evident that the machine carried a searchlight, as flashes of light could occasionally be seen coming from it.

Scarcely had the noise of the engine been heard in the city than there came the sound of explosions, as the raiders hurled their bombs. From five to seven of these were thrown, and

"All the News That's Fit to Print."

The New York Times.

EXTRA 5:30 A. M.

Weather Today and Sunday: Fair.

VOL. LXIV...NO. 20,923. NEW YORK, SATURDAY, MAY 8, 1915.—TWENTY-FOUR PAGES. ONE CENT In Greater New York, Jersey City and Newark. | Elsewhere TWO CENTS.

LUSITANIA SUNK BY A SUBMARINE, PROBABLY 1,260 DEAD; TWICE TORPEDOED OFF IRISH COAST; SINKS IN 15 MINUTES; CAPT. TURNER SAVED, FROHMAN AND VANDERBILT MISSING; WASHINGTON BELIEVES THAT A GRAVE CRISIS IS AT HAND

SHOCKS THE PRESIDENT

Washington Deeply Stirred by the Loss of American Lives.

BULLETINS AT WHITE HOUSE

Wilson Reads Them Closely, but Is Silent on the Nation's Course.

HINTS OF CONGRESS CALL

Loss of Lusitania Recalls Firm Tone of Our First Warning to Germany.

CAPITAL FULL OF RUMORS

Reports That Liner Was to be Sunk Were Heard Before Actual News Came.

Special to The New York Times.

WASHINGTON, May 7. — Never since that April day, three years ago, when word came that the Titanic had gone down, has Washington been so stirred as it is tonight over the sinking of the Lusitania. The early reports told that there had been no loss of life, but the relief that these advices caused gave way to the greatest concern late this evening when it became known that there had been many deaths. Although they are profoundly reticent, officials realize that this tragedy, involving the loss of American citizens, is likely to bring about a crisis in the international relations of the United States.

It is pointed out that the sinking of the Lusitania is the outcome of a series of incidents that have been the cause of concern to this Government in its endeavor to maintain a strictly neutral position in the great European war.

Nation's Course in Doubt.

It is impossible to say tonight what effect the loss of American lives on the Lusitania will have on the Government. Judged from the little that can be learned it is a safe prediction that President Wilson will endeavor to ascertain all the facts, including evidence as to whether a German submarine was responsible for the sinking of the vessel, before proceeding to determine the course to be pursued. The news that many lives had been sacrificed, probably as many as a thousand, was given to him at the White House about 10 o'clock this morning, but no word came from him as to what effect this intelligence had on him.

The State Department tonight sent instructions to the American Embassy in London to send the names of any Americans who might have been killed or injured in the disaster. A bulletin from THE TIMES, saying probably 1,000 lives had been lost, was sent to the White House as soon as received and laid before President Wilson. The news that two torpedoes had been fired into the Lusitania by a submarine and that the Lusitania sank fifteen minutes afterward was also sent to the White House, but reached there after the President had gone to bed. The President retired about 11 o'clock.

On account of the many inquiries it had received from friends and relatives of passengers on the Lusitania and the intense public interest in the tragedy, orders were given tonight to the telegraphers and cipher clerks in charge of the telegraph office in the State Department to remain at their posts all night. They also had instructions to make public any messages bringing official details regarding the Lusitania's passengers. Usually the telegraph office closes at midnight.

Rumors of Congress Session.

There were reports this evening that Congress would be called in extra session, but these were not justified and the most that can be said is that while the Government is greatly concerned over the situation, it has shown no inclination toward excitement or taking hasty action.

Senator W. J. Stone, Chairman of the Committee on Foreign Relations, said tonight:

"I cannot comment on a supposed

Continued on Page 4.

The Lost Cunard Steamship Lusitania

X Where the First Torpedo Struck. XX Where the Second Torpedo Struck.

Cunard Office Here Besieged for News; Fate of 1,918 on Lusitania Long in Doubt

Nothing Heard from the Well-Known Passengers on Board—Story of Disaster Long Unconfirmed While Anxious Crowds Seek Details.

Official news of the sinking of the Lusitania yesterday reached New York in fragmentary reports, and several hours elapsed between the first unverified rumor of the disaster and the cable messages that told at night of the saving of some of the passengers and gave meagre details of the most sensational incident of its kind in the war.

The early accounts that indicated all on board had been saved reassured hundreds of friends and relatives of passengers. Later, it was made known that lives had been lost and probably many persons had been injured

Among the prominent passengers rescued was George A. Kessler. The list of those of whom no word was received included A. G. Vanderbilt, Charles Frohman, Charles Klein, Justus Miles Forman, and Elbert Hubbard, besides persons widely known in society.

A cablegram sent to Farley Hopkins of The Yale News staff at New Haven, by his father, who was aboard the Lusitania, stated that the vessel was sunk, not beached, that three hundred persons had been already landed, and that the rest in small boats were making for shore. The message reached New York at 8:15 o'clock and was signed "Lee Higginson & Co., London."

Word of the safety of Charles E. Lauriat, Jr., of Boston, Mass., a member of the firm of Charles E. Lauriat & Co., booksellers, who was a first-cabin passenger, reached relatives there in a cablegram early this morning. The message, dated at Queenstown, 2:40 A. M. Read simply:

> Charles E. Lauriat, Jr., safe and well.

For more than half a century it was the boast of the Cunard Line that it never had lost a life. The regon was sunk in collision near Fire Island in 1886, but no lives were lost until five passengers were swept off the Campania's forward deck by a wave on Oct. 5, 1905. The sinking of the Lusitania is the first big disaster the Cunard Line has had.

Message to Cunard Office.

The first word of the sinking of the Lusitania received here reached the local offices of the Cunard Line, 21 State Street, at 11:41 o'clock yesterday morning, but was not made public until late in the afternoon. The message, which was sent from the head office in Liverpool, read:

> The Lusitania, we regret to advise, an unconfirmed report states to have been torpedoed by a submarine at 2 P. M., Friday, ten miles from Kinsale, and sunk at 2:30. There is no news as to the safety of passengers or crew.

Following this dispatch there was a message which had been picked up by the wireless station at Land's End, evidently a distress call from the liner, which said:

> Come at once. Big list. Position ten miles west Kinsale.

A third dispatch from Queenstown stated:

> All available craft in harbor dispatched to assist. Weather here beautifully fine. Wind southeast, light.

By 3 o'clock in the afternoon the news of the sinking of the Lusitania had been spread in the city and the Cunard offices were besieged by relatives and friends of the passengers on board. Owing to the alterations in and additions to the passenger list on sailing day, last Saturday, it took some time to get the correct figures, which were finally given out as 290 first, 601 second, and 362 third class passengers. Of the cabin passengers thirty-six had been transferred fro mthe Cameronia on Saturday morning. This delayed the Lusitania's departure from 10 o'clock to 12:28.

1,918 Persons on Board.

The officers and crew numbered 665 men instead of the usual complement of 950, on account of fewer men being carried in the engineers' and stewards' departments. Thus there were in all 1,918 persons on board.

The Cunard agents told all inquirers that they would give out the messages as fast as they were received and had no intention of keeping back the news from the public. Several bulletins were received from the Liverpool office, but few of them contained any definite statements and they were cancelled, in some instances, within an hour. One received at 4 P. M. read:

> Motor fishing boats towing two boats filled with passengers, probably fifty. Tug Stormcock making Kinsale. Some passengers on board. Many rescue vessels are now apparently making Queenstown.

The first dispatch stating positively that the Lusitania had sunk reached the Cunard office at 5 P. M. It read:

> Old Head Kinsale Station reports about twenty boats, all belonging to Lusitania, are in vicinity where sunk. About fifteen boats are making for the spot to resume.

An unconfirmed report was received late in the afternoon that all the passengers and crew had been saved in small boats and rafts. This information was given out to the people waiting in the Cunard office, and many of them went home. It was estimated that fully 500 inquiries were received by telephone and telegraph in the afternoon from relatives and friends of passengers on board. Long-distance calls were received from St. Louis, Atlanta, Montreal, and Toronto.

The next bulletin made public at the Cunard office was the following:

> Liverpool, May 7.
> 1:51 P. M., (New York Time.)
> Following received by Admiralty, Galley Head, 4:25 P. M.: Several boats, apparently survivors, southeast nine miles. Greek steamer proceeding to assist.

The next bulletin was:

> Liverpool, May 7.
> 2:33 P. M., (New York Time.)
> Queenstown wires Old Head: Large steamer just arrived in vicinity, apparently sending assistance. Tugs, patrols, &c.,

Continued on Page 3.

List of Saved Includes Capt. Turner; Vanderbilt and Frohman Reported Lost

LONDON, Saturday, May 8, 5:30 A. M.—The Press Bureau has received from the British Admiralty at Queenstown a report that all the torpedo boats and tugs and armed trawlers, except the Heron, which went out from Queenstown to the relief of the Lusitania have returned.

These vessels have landed 595 survivors and forty dead. Fifty-two more survivors are reported aboard a steamer, while eleven others and five bodies have been landed at Kinsale, making the total number of survivors 658, besides forty-five dead. The numbers will be verified later, and it is considered possible Kinsale fishing boats may have rescued a few more.

Among the survivors is the Captain of the Lusitania, William T. Turner. Some of the survivors at Queenstown say that Alfred Gwynne Vanderbilt was drowned. Every effort to find Mr. Vanderbilt and Charles Frohman, the theatrical manager, among the survivors has failed.

The Central News says that the number of the Lusitania's passengers who died of injuries while being taken to Queenstown will reach 100.

QUEENSTOWN Saturday, May 8, 4:45 A. M.—The list of the Lusitania's survivors, as far as compiled, follows:

TURNER, Captain.
MATHEWS, A. T., Montreal.
ABRAMOWITZ, S.
LANE, G. B.
MEYERS, W. G. E.
TRIMMINS, J. T.
WITHERBEE, Mrs. A. F.
MACKWORTH, Lady.
ADAMS, Mrs. HENRY, Boston.
RANKIN, ROBERT, New York.
SHARP, SAMUEL.
BYRNE, M. B., New York.
DAVIS, EMILY.
WALKER, ANNIE.
HOUSNELL, E.
CROSS, A. B.
YOUNG, PHILIP, Montreal.
VASSAR, W. A. F., London.
STEELE, GEORGE.
CROSLEY, CYRUS.
PARKER, JAMES.
COLEBROOK, the Rev. R.
MORRIS, H. C. S.
FISH, Mrs., and two children.
MARTIN, Miss R.
GAUTLETT, F. J., New York.
MAYCOCK, Miss MAY.
HENDERSON, VIOLET.
MARDERUD, UNO.
LEVIN, THOMAS D.
THOMAS, D. A., Cardiff, Wales.
EVANS, T. J. M.
CLARKE, A. R.
BURGESS, W. G.
CHARLES, J. H., and daughter, Toronto.
LONEY, Miss, New York.
HERRIS, JOHN.
HOLLAND, Miss.
BRANDELL, Miss JOSEPHINE, New York.
PERRY, F. K. A.
GRAB, O. H.
MOSLEY, G. G., New York.
BROOKS, J H., New York.
JEFFRY, A. M.
CAIRNS, M.
HAMMOND, O. H., New York.
MANLEY, A.
NEATH, H.
NORTH, Miss.
WINTER, Miss.
WINTER, Miss.
DUGUID, GEORGE.
MOORE, DANIEL.
McCONNELL, JOHN W., Memphis, Tenn.
SHARPE, Miss.
CONNER, Miss.
DALY, H. M.
CLIFFE, PATRICK.
BOHAN, JAMES, Toronto.
CROSLEY, Mrs. CYRUS.
BRETHERTON, Mrs. CYRIL H., and two children, Los Angeles, Cal.
HOPKINS, A. L., New York.
LASSETTER, Mrs. H. B., of Sydney, Australia, wife of General Lassetter.
LASSETTER, Master P.
LAURIAT, CHARLES E., Jr., Boston, Mass.
PAYNTER, Miss IRENE, Liverpool, England.

KINSALE, Ireland, May 8.—Eleven survivors of the Lusitania have been landed here, together with the bodies of five persons who were dead. Among the survivors are:

SMITH, J. RESTON, New York.
BOTTOMLEY, FREDERICK.
BOYLE, N. L.
HOTCHKISS, CHARLES.
HARRIMAN, CORNELIUS.
LIVERMORE, VERNAR.
SULLIVAN, Mrs. F.

Consul's List of Saved.

WASHINGTON, May 8.—Consul Lauriat at Queenstown sends this report:

"Total saved of all nationalities, 700. The following are American survivors of Lusitania. Other names will follow:

CRAB, O. S.
PEARL, Major and Mrs., and two children.
SMITH, Mrs. JESSIE TAFT.
HARDWICK, CHARLES C.
EARL, STUART D.
PEARL, AMY.
STANLEY, Mrs.
LINES, L. B.
HILL, C. T.
RANKIN, ROBERT.
LONEY, Miss.
DOHERTY, Mrs. WILLIAM and infant.
PHILLIPS, THOMAS.
McADAMS, WILLIAM.
HOUGHTON, J. H.
SWEENEY, JOHN M.
HAMMOND, OADEN H.
BROOKS, J. H.
JEFFRY, CHARLES T.
LUND, Mrs. C. H.
SHEPPERDSON, ARTHUR.
MOORE, Dr. D. V.
BERNARD, CLINTON.
LIGHT, HERBERT.
LINNSON, J., Jr.
WILLIAMS, EDITH.
LEARY, JAMES J.
SLIDELL, THOMAS.
WOLFENDEN, Mrs. JOHN.
HOLLAND, Mrs. NINA.
MESH, Mrs. THOMAS.
KESSLER, GEORGE A.
McMURRAY, L.
KAY, ROBERT.
LOCKHART, R. R.
CANNON, OWEN.
HARRIS, DURIGHT C.
JUDSON, FRED S.
COLLIS, ED M.
WRIGHT, R. C.
GAUNTLET, F. J.
KNOX, S. N.
O'DONNELL, PATRICK.

Saw the Submarine 100 Yards Off and Watched Torpedo as It Struck Ship

Ernest Cowper, a Toronto Newspaper Man, Describes Attack, Seen from Ship's Rail—Poison Gas Used in Torpedoes, Say Other Passengers.

Queenstown, Saturday, May 8, 3:18 A. M.

A sharp lookout for submarines was kept aboard the Lusitania as she approached the Irish coast, according to Ernest Cowper, a Toronto newspaper man, who was among the survivors landed at Queenstown.

He said that after the ship was torpedoed there was no panic among the crew, but that they went about the work of getting passengers into the boats in a prompt and efficient manner.

"As we neared the coast of Ireland," said Mr. Cowper, "we all joined in the lookout, for a possible attack by a submarine was the sole topic of conversation.

"I was chatting with a friend at the rail about 2 o'clock when suddenly I caught a glimpse of the conning tower of a submarine about a thousand yards distant. I immediately called my friend's attention to it. Immediately we both saw the track of a torpedo followed almost instantly by an explosion. Portions of splintered hull were sent flying into the air, and then another torpedo struck. The ship began to list to starboard.

"The crew at once proceeded to get the passengers into boats in an orderly, prompt, and efficient manner. Miss Helen Smith appealed to me to save her. I placed her in a boat and saw her safely away. I got into one of the last boats to leave.

"Some of the boats could not be launched as the vessel was sinking. There was a large number of women and children in the second cabin. Forty of the children were less than a year old."

Poison Fumes from Torpedoes.

From interviews with passengers it appears that when the torpedoes burst they sent forth suffocating fumes which had their effect on the passengers, causing some of them to lose consciousness.

Two stokers, Byrne and Hussey of Liverpool, gave a few details. They said the submarine gave no notice and fired two torpedoes, one hitting No. 1 stoke hole and the second the engine room. The first torpedo was discharged at 2 o'clock. In twenty-five minutes the great liner disappeared.

Signals have been received at Queenstown that an armed trawler, believed to be the Heron, and two fishing trawlers are bringing in 100 more bodies.

The Cunard Line agent states that the total number of persons aboard the Lusitania was 2,160.

Loss of the Lusitania Fills London With Horror and Utter Amazement

Special Cable to THE NEW YORK TIMES.

LONDON, Saturday, May 8.—Stupefaction is the word which best describes the first impression created by the news of the sinking of the Lusitania. People seemed unable to realize that at this stage of the world's progress such a deed could be committed as an act of war.

"I have no words for it," said Lord Rosebery, and everywhere one found the same sentiment repeated.

It was some hours between the time

Continued on Page 3.

SOME DEAD TAKEN ASHORE

Several Hundred Survivors at Queenstown and Kinsale.

STEWARD TELLS OF DISASTER

One Torpedo Crashes Into the Doomed Liner's Bow, Another Into the Engine Room.

SHIP LISTS OVER TO PORT

Makes It Impossible to Lower Many Boats, So Hundreds Must Have Gone Down.

ATTACKED IN BROAD DAY

Passengers at Luncheon—Warning Had Been Given by Germans Before the Ship Left New York.

Only 650 Were Saved, Few Cabin Passengers

QUEENSTOWN, Saturday, May 8, 4:28 A. M.—Survivors of the Lusitania who have arrived here estimate that only about 650 of those aboard the steamer were saved, and say only a small proportion of those rescued were saloon passengers.

Official Confirmation.

WASHINGTON, May 8.—A dispatch to the State Department early today from American Consul Lauriet at Queenstown stated that the total number of survivors of the Lusitania was about 700.

LONDON, Saturday, May 8.—The Cunard liner Lusitania, which sailed out of New York last Saturday with 1,918 souls aboard, lies at the bottom of the ocean off the Irish coast.

She was sunk by a German submarine, which sent two torpedoes crashing into her side at 2:30 o'clock yesterday afternoon while the passengers, seemingly confident that the great, swift vessel could elude the German underwater craft, were having luncheon.

The great inrush of water caused the liner to list heavily to port, so that she could not launch many of her lifeboats.

About 1,260 of those on board the great ship, including many Americans, apparently went down with her, as a statement issued late this morning by the Admiralty says the total number of survivors is only 658.

There were 1,253 passengers on board the steamship, including 200 who were transferred to her from the steamer Cameronia. The Americans totaled 188. The crew numbered 665.

It is believed that only a few first class passengers were saved as they thought the ship would remain afloat, and made little effort to escape.

There appears to be a large proportion of the ship's crew among the survivors landed at Queenstown. Only a few offi-

"All the News That's Fit to Print."

The New York Times.

THE WEATHER
Fair today and Tuesday; diminishing northwest winds.
For weather report see next to last page.

VOL. LXIV...NO. 20,989. NEW YORK, MONDAY, MAY 24, 1915.—EIGHTEEN PAGES. ONE CENT In Greater New York, Jersey City and Newark. | Elsewhere TWO CENTS.

EDISON INVENTS PHONE RECORDER

Has a New Device to Fix Words of Both Speakers for Future Reference.

RESULT OF 37 YEARS' WORK

Sees Great Possibilities in Use for Making Quick Business Contracts.

SAVE MILLIONS OF LETTERS

Will Also Take Down Message for an Absent Person and Hold It Till He Returns.

Special to The New York Times.

WEST ORANGE, N. J., May 23.—Thomas A. Edison today announced the perfection of the telescribe, a combination of the telephone and phonograph; a long distance dictating machine that doubles back.

It will give to both parties to a telephone conversation, although a thousand miles apart, each a phonographic record of what both have said.

Mr. Edison regards its commercial possibilities almost unlimited, for he believes it will do away with millions of letters a year in the making of business agreements. The phonograph makes voices easily recognizable, and Mr. Edison is confident that telescribe records will be as eloquent arguments for good faith on the part of business men as signed letters.

Mr. Edison has experimented with the Telescribe between his Orange plant and his offices in various parts of America, and so confident is he of its success that a large number of the machines are now being built. It was in the June, 1878, issue of the North American Review that Mr. Edison predicted a machine that would record telephone conversations. He has been working on it ever since.

The mechanics of the Telescribe are not complicated. It is used with the ordinary telephone, but with two receivers. One is fitted to the arm of dictating phonograph; the [illegible] is used in the ordinary manner. A record of what both persons say is made [illegible] of the line. A [illegible] what the record says and copies are interchanged for confirmation. That concludes a business arrangement which might in ordinary practice take a dozen letters and weeks of time.

Will Take Message for You.

"The telephone is used a million times an hour," said Mr. Edison today, "showing that science has provided the telephone for the most rapid transmission of intelligence. But with the Telescribe we will now be able to put our exact spoken words into writing." He also pointed out that in cases of messages of great importance where the person wanted was not at the moment available, any one could press a button and take the message on the phonograph, to be read at leisure by the person for whom it was intended.

The Telescribe may also be used as a long-distance dictograph, and a machine on its principle could be used for taking court proceedings, though that would call for great development as the ordinary phonographic record can take only 1,500 words.

William H. Meadowcroft, one of Mr. Edison's Lieutenants, said tonight that there was no danger of the Telescribe putting many stenographers out of work. "You see," he explained, "someone has to write out the record, but of course the Telescribe means fewer letters in the future."

An Earlier Device.

Mr. Edison's Telescribe is not the first invention for its purpose. In 1900 Valdemar Poulsen, a Danish inventor, contrived the telegraphone for the reproduction of conversations at a distance. Its principle was the retention of magnetic impressions by a copper wire. The length of wire for an ordinary conversation was about three and a half miles. Each impression on a fraction of the wire represented a sound, and when the machine was reversed the talk was reproduced. William J. Burns, the detective, gave its prominence in 1912, when he reproduced a conversation by the President of the Common Council of Detroit in which the official was alleged to have offered to sell his vote. It was used to record the debates of the Medical Congress in Boston in 1912. Speeches by President Roosevelt were several times reproduced by the telegraphone.

'FOR PRESIDENT, W. A. SMITH'

The Michigan Senator Announces His Candidacy for 1916.

Special to The New York Times.

GRAND RAPIDS, Mich., May 23.—United States Senator William Alden Smith of this city will be a candidate for the Republican Presidential nomination in 1916. His candidacy will be formally announced tomorrow through a double-page article in his paper, The Grand Rapids Herald.

Arthur H. Vandenburg, editor of The Herald and writer of the article, had this to say in making the announcement:

"I make this statement advisedly. Michigan will undoubtedly ask the National Convention to nominate United States Senator William Alden Smith for President. A Michigan organization has been formed to promote this end. Many a home critic would be surprised to peep at the voluntary offers of support which have already come to this organization from the Atlantic to the Pacific. The movement is one of the most formidable in contemporary American politics. Time will demonstrate the truth of this declaration. Whatever the final outcome—and I am not assuming here to write as a prophet—Michigan influence and Michigan power in the convention of 1916 will probably be greater than it has ever been before, and certainly greater than at any time, with the possible exception of the convention of 1876."

FISHER OUT FOR GOOD, A SUCCESSOR SOUGHT

Sir Henry Jackson May Become First Sea Lord—Lansdowne to Aid Grey.

LONDON, Monday, May 24.—The new British Cabinet, according to The Times, will have as members both Lord Curzon of Kedleston, former Viceroy of India, and Sir Edward Carson, the Ulster leader. The newspaper also states that the acceptance of office by Lord Lansdowne was due to the urgent necessity of giving relief to Sir Edward Grey at the Foreign Office.

Lord Lansdowne was Foreign Secretary in the last Unionist Administration, and as Sir Edward Grey is troubled with an affection of the eyes which compels him to take an occasional holiday in the country, it was necessary to find a qualified substitute to act during respites from the superhuman strain that has been placed on Sir Edward's shoulders since the outbreak of the war.

It is believed that the distribution of the portfolios in the fighting departments is still undecided and that they are giving Premier Asquith much trouble. It seems to be certain that Admiral Lord Fisher, who has gone into the country, will not return to the Admiralty, and it is rumored that he will be succeeded as First Sea Lord by Admiral Sir Henry Bradwardine Jackson, former Chief of the war staff, but who is best known in connection with the introduction and development of wireless telegraphy in the navy.

There seems still to be a likelihood that David Lloyd George, Chancellor of the Exchequer, will go to the War Office as a sort of Minister for Munitions. The Daily Mail, backed by The Times, still demands that some kind of a national service be organized, and urges that a supply of the proper ammunition is the most urgent need of the day.

GREEK KING WORSE AFTER AN OPERATION

Pleurisy Attack Arouses Apprehension and Berlin Specialist Is Summoned in Haste.

ATHENS, May 23.—King Constantine of Greece, who is ill with pleurisy, became more feverish after undergoing an operation yesterday, his temperature increasing to 103.2.

PARIS, May 23.—A Havas Agency dispatch from Athens says that after a conference of the Greek Cabinet Ministers with the doctor treating King Constantine, it was decided to telegraph to Berlin for a specialist. The King's fever increased yesterday, and an urgent operation was considered necessary. Premier Gounaris has given up his contemplated voyage to Saloniki.

A dispatch from Athens to the Intransigeant says that Professor Friedrich Kraus of Berlin, who is familiar with the King's condition, having treated him in Berlin, has been requested [illegible] Greek [illegible]

[illegible] of the King [illegible] caused grave anxiety in Athens. Crown Prince George is at his father's bedside. Dispatches from Athens comment on the fact that the Prince, who is 25 years old, is very close to ex-Premier Venizelos, who resigned the Premiership last March because King Constantine did not approve of his warlike policy, and is very friendly to the Triple Entente.

LONDON, May 23.—A message from Athens to Reuter's Telegram Company says that Professor Kraus of Berlin, who has been summoned to the Greek capital for a consultation regarding the illness of King Constantine, will travel through Vienna, Bucharest, and Dedeaghatch, where the Greek destroyer Panther will await him. The Greek Government has requested the authorities of the countries through which the professor will pass to extend every facility in order to accelerate his journey.

This morning's bulletin of the King's condition was posted on the street corners and on the newspaper bulletin boards in Athens, and attracted crowds. The King's illness engrosses the attention of all circles in Athens, where it has aroused sympathy and apprehension.

SUBMARINE ATTACKS BELGIAN RELIEF SHIP

Torpedo Fired at the Comeric Passed Thirty Yards from the Vessel.

LONDON, Monday, May 24.—The steamer Comeric, one of the Belgian Relief Commission vessels bound for Rotterdam, narrowly escaped a torpedo near North Hinder lightship last Thursday.

The second mate of the steamer says he saw a German torpedo fired at the Comeric and that it passed thirty yards from the ship. The submarine which fired the torpedo, according to the mate, disappeared and the Comeric was not attacked again.

THREAT TO BLOW UP A BAYONNE FACTORY

Electric Launch Company Said to Be Making Fifty Fast Patrol Boats for England.

Detectives from the Bayonne Police Headquarters were sent yesterday afternoon to guard the big plant of the Electric Launch Company on Newark Bay, according to statements made at headquarters, in consequence of an anonymous threatening letter received by the company. While the police refuse to give out the contents of this letter, it is understood that its purport was a threat to blow up the plant unless the company should cease giving aid to the Allies. A request for protection was sent immediately afterward, it is said, to Detective Captain Griffin, who ordered two men to watch the plant until the company should supply its own guards.

While the company officials refuse to discuss the matter, persistent rumors are current that the Electric Launch Company has a contract to build for the British Government fifty 70-foot high-speed motor launches to be used on patrol duty and especially to look out for submarines.

E. B. Conrad, General Superintendent of the plant, could not be found yesterday. It was said he was out of town. Other officials of the company in Bayonne refused to discuss the matter, but admitted the company had a contract to build thirty life-saving boats for the United States Government.

SAYS PRUSSIANS KILLED SAXONS

British Eyewitness Describes Slaughter of a Battalion That Tried to Surrender.

WHITE FLAG WAS SHOWN

Then German Cannon Are Said to Have Annihilated the Unarmed Detachment.

ENGLISH THREE-MILE GAIN

Captured Positions Extend from Richebourg l'Avoue to Festubert, North of La Bassee.

LONDON, May 23.—The British eyewitness at the Army Headquarters in France explains in a descriptive account dated May 21 that the British action during the first part of the week consisted almost entirely in consolidating and expanding the ground gained in the attack of last Sunday to the north of La Bassée. This was successfully accomplished.

In the attack on May 17, he says, the Germans, who had retained their hold on the ground between the salients won by the British to the south of Richebourg l'Avoué and north of Festubert, pressed on three sides and subjected to cross-fire and continuous bombardment, reached the limit of their endurance, and more than 300 surrendered. The British, having thus joined hands, pressed the Germans still further to the eastward, forcing them out of one post after the other. Entire groups gave themselves up.

The British official describes the scene mentioned in the official report at the time of German artillery fire being directed on their own men who were offering to surrender near Cour de la Boue farm.

"Desperate fighting," says the narrative, "was going on in front of this farm when the remains of a battalion of Saxons which, it appears, had been hastily brought down from further north, was thrown into the fight. Having decided to surrender en bloc, they advanced toward our line. Not knowing what the movement of the mass of men implied, our infantry poured a hail of bullets into them, whereupon the survivors, some hundreds strong, halted, threw down their rifles and held up their hands. One of their number waved a white rag tied to a stick.

[illegible]

"Our guns continued to fire from the rear, and whether our infantry who by this time had had some experience in the treachery of the enemy, would have paid any attention to these signals is uncertain, but the matter was taken out of their hands, for as soon as the Prussian infantry on the north of this point realized what their Saxon comrades were trying to do, they opened a rapid fire from the flank, enfilading the mass.

"It appears also that the news of what was happening must have been telephoned to the German artillery further east, which also probably was Prussian, since its guns suddenly opened on the Saxon infantry, and under this combined fire most of the latter were very soon accounted for.

"Among the many scenes of the war there probably has been no more strange spectacle than the masses of gray-coated soldiers, standing out in the open with hands raised and amid dead and dying, being butchered by their comrades before the eyes of British infantry.

"The fact that the victims of this slaughter were Saxons was a source of regret to us, since Saxons always have proved more chivalrous and less brutal than either Prussians or Bavarians. In fact, they are cleaner fighters in every way.

"While we were pressing forward on the section between our two original points of penetration, our troops on the right in front of Festubert were making good progress southward along the German trenches. The Germans were soon cleared out of this quarter up to a short distance south of Festubert, where they made a strong resistance and checked our further lateral progress.

"The fighting here was made up of a series of isolated desperate hand-to-hand combats with the bayonet and hand grenade, and since the Germans were at many points outflanked and enfiladed, their losses were very heavy. For in the narrow trenches there often was no room to escape, and the only alternatives were death or surrender.

"In some places the trenches presented a horrible sight, being heaped with German corpses, many of whom had been blown to pieces by our bombardment. On the extreme right the Germans were pressed back along their communication trenches in such large numbers that they occasionally formed an excellent mark for the machine guns in our own line to the north of Givenchy, which were able to do great execution at certain points.

"At nightfall the situation roughly was as follows: We held a continuous line, embracing the whole German original front trenches, from south of Festubert to Richebourg L'Avoué, [a distance of about three miles,] and in many places possession of the whole series of hostile intrenchments, with the exception of a few supporting points and machine gun posts in the rear of the zone in advance of our new front line. Also we were in occupation of various points from which the enemy had been dislodged.

"Thus the second day of the action ended in the attainment of very substantial results by us. Not only had our new front been to a great extent straightened out and our two forces connected up, but the gain of ground extended laterally further to the south."

A German Trick Discovered.

The eyewitness then explains how a party of sixty Germans, "dressed in khaki, taken from the dead," advanced toward the British trenches, one of their number calling out in excellent English: "Don't shoot! We are Grenadier Guards!" When an officer walked toward them, the eyewitness says, he was fired upon, and thereupon his men opened fire and charged with bayonet. Some of the Germans stood and fought to the last, but most of them turned and tried to escape, but all of them were killed.

The narrative says further progress was made by the British Wednesday and Thursday, but that then the weather interfered with the fighting, and the men were set to work to strengthen the positions they had won.

"Our losses," the writer says, "though not light, have not been so severe as previous fighting of this character entailed."

The eyewitness repeats a British officer's charge that British dead and wounded whom it had been impossible to bring in, were set on fire by incendiary bullets fired from the German trenches.

SUBMARINE OIL BASES DISCOVERED BY ALLIES

British Said to Have Laid Traps Around German Petrol Stations in War Zone.

LONDON, May 14. (Correspondence of The Associated Press.)—Rumors from Copenhagen that German naval authorities admit the loss of seventeen submarines since the opening of the war are generally believed here. In fact, many English officials are inclined to believe the German submarine losses are considerably greater than seventeen. One report has placed the number at thirty-four.

Ever since the capture of the two German submarines whose crews were made prisoners by the English, it has been generally believed in England that many captures were being made which the Admiralty did not care to make public. Wire nets placed by the Admiralty in waters where German submarines may lie in wait for ships are supposed to have made possible many captures.

These nets are much like woven wire fencing, except that their meshes are much coarser. By means of wooden blocks the nets are kept submerged at about the depth submarines are likely to move. When the submarines strike the nets their fins and propellers become entangled in the wire and they are forced to rise to the surface.

When a submarine hits a net an electrical connection flashes a signal to some naval base, thus making it possible for naval craft to rush to the disabled submarine before it can disentangle itself.

The British and French Navies have located many of the oil tanks planted by the Germans to supply petrol to the submarines, and nets are reported to have been placed near these supply stations. Rumors have been circulated that in some cases the English have diluted the petrol in the supply tanks and mixed it with chemicals which would ruin submarine engines if they attempted to use it.

Petrol supply tanks are reported to have been located on the coast of the Orkney Islands, along the north and west coast of Ireland, and in the Bay of Biscay.

The news that the British have not made public the total number of German submarines believed to have been lost since the war zone order went into effect, tallies in many respects with a story told by an officer of the Atlantic Fleet during the visit of the fleet to New York. He said that in a letter written by an officer of the British Navy to a friend in the Atlantic Fleet the British officer said that several German submarines had been "netted" by the British.

The identity of the American officer to whom the letter was written was not disclosed by the officer who told the story. It was said that the British officer in his letter mentioned two or three specific instances in which German submarines had been captured, news of which has been withheld by the British Admiralty.

BRITISH SUBMARINE SINKS 4 TURKISH SHIPS

Paris Hears One Transport Sent Down in Dardanelles Was Loaded With Men.

LONDON, May 23.—A more detailed account has been received by the Admiralty of the recent operations in the Dardanelles of the British submarine E-14, the crew of which was rewarded several days ago.

The report says that on her passage into the Sea of Marmora the E-14 sank a Turkish gunboat of the Berk-I-Satvet class; in the Sea of Marmora she sank a transport on April 29, a gunboat on May 3, and a large transport, full of troops, on May 10. On May 13 the E-14 compelled a small steamer to run aground. The return journey of the submarine was made on May 18.

"The Admiral of the Dardanelles," says the Admiralty statement, "says it is impossible to do full justice to this great achievement, and that the King's appreciation and reward for this service have, throughout the Allied fleet, given universal satisfaction."

Lieutenant Commander Edward Boyle of the E-14 received the Victoria Cross for the work of the submarine against the Turks. The distinguished service cross was given to Lieutenant Edward Stanley and Acting Lieutenant Reginald Lawrence, and the distinguished service medal to every member of the crew of the submarine.

ALLIES TO PUNISH TURKS WHO MURDER

Notify Porte That Government Heads Must Answer for Armenian Massacres.

LONDON, May 23.—A joint official statement by Great Britain, France, and Russia, issued tonight, says:

"For the past month Kurds and the Turkish population of Armenia have been engaged in massacring Armenians with the connivance and help of the Ottoman authorities. Such massacres took place about the middle of April at Erzerum, Dertshau, Moush, Zeitun, and in all Cilicia.

"The inhabitants of about a hundred villages near Van were all assassinated. In the town itself the Armenian quarter is besieged by Kurds. At the same time the Ottoman Government at Constantinople is raging against the inoffensive Armenian population.

"In the face of these fresh crimes committed by Turkey, the allied Governments announce publicly to the Sublime Porte that they will hold all members of the Government, as well as such of their agents as are implicated, personally responsible for such massacres."

MASSACRES BY WHOLESALE.

Turks and Kurds Have Killed Thousands Since the War Began.

One of the first sparks fanned into flame in the East by the European War was that of the old hatred between the Armenian Christians in Asiatic Turkey and Persia and the Mohammedan Turks and Kurds.

By the middle of February reports of the slaughter of Armenians began to come to America, and the days of 1895-6, when to be an Armenian Christian was to be in constant danger, were recalled.

ITALY DECLARES WAR UPON AUSTRIA; GERMANY WITHDRAWS HER ENVOY; ITALIAN CHASSEURS EXPEL INVADERS

CLASH NEAR ALPINE PASS

Patrol Force Which Entered Italy Driven Back Across the Border.

800,000 TEUTONS MASSED

German General Staff May Conduct the Operations and Attempt a Crushing Blow.

KAISER'S OFFICERS AT TRENT

Italian Army, Intrenched, Awaits with Enthusiasm Order to Attack Foe.

KING TO GO TO THE FRONT

Princes Rush to Join Army as Privates—Mayor of Rome and Three Sons with Colors.

ROME, May 23.—A clash, which is generally regarded here to be the first skirmish of the war, occurred today between Italian and Austrian troops at Forcellini di Montozzo, in the pass between Pont di Legno and Pejo. An Austrian patrol crossed the frontier, but was attacked by Italian Alpine chasseurs and driven back over the border.

When the first great blow will be struck cannot be foretold, but after many months of preparation, the army, which has been greatly strengthened, [illegible] task may be set them. Exceedingly strong forces are in position all along the Austro-Italian frontier, on the Austrian side of which feverish preparations have been going on the last few days to make the fortifications as strong as possible and to clear the way for effective artillery action.

800,000 Teuton Troops Ready.

About 800,000 Bavarians and Hungarians have already been concentrated along or near the border, Austria insuring commissariat service for them.

Although Field Marshal Baron Conrad von Hoetzendorf, Chief of Staff of the Austrian Army, had prepared for many years for this conflict, the belief is held here that the campaign will be conducted by the German General Staff, which, it is said, has planned a strong offensive movement in the hope of breaking the Italian lines and forcing their way into Italian territory. Should such an attempt fail, the Austrians and Germans would then have to resort to defensive measures against a certain invasion.

The Austrian defenses are particularly strong and have been constructed everywhere, even along the Dalmatian coast, which is already protected by fixed and floating mines and guarded by a dozen submarines, carrying German officers and sailors.

The Austrian fleet is centred at Pola, with only a few torpedo boats and destroyers at Cattaro and Spalato. Other Austrian warships are in the Dalmatian Archipelago, on the northeast coast of the Adriatic Sea. Naval men here do not consider it likely that the Austrian fleet will leave Pola unless forced by an Italian attack.

Call to Colors Causes Sensation.

Great gitation was caused throughout Rome yesterday when all the street corners were placarded with manifestos calling to arms all men born in the years 1876 to 1895.

Although the measure had been expected at any moment for the last fortnight, a crowd of persons gathered at each corner to read the manifesto. The crowds were so great that in some points in the centre of the city traffic was interrupted.

Advices from Udine say that the last men called to the colors in that vicinity were ordered to bring with them not only shoes, but food for three days.

Priests Ask Leave to Enlist.

Special Cable to THE NEW YORK TIMES.

LONDON, Monday, May 24.—The Rome correspondent of The Daily News says:

"A decree has been issued indicating Italy's intention to seize all Austro-German steamers taking refuge in Italian ports since the outbreak of war.

"The Pope has ordered the hospices of Santa Marta, an annex of the Vatican, and seven seminaries and colleges, including the German South American colleges, to be placed at the disposal of the Red Cross organization

Continued on Page 2.

Text of the Formal Declaration of War Presented by Italy to Austria-Hungary

VIENNA, May 23, (via Amsterdam and London, May 24.)—The Duke of Avarna, Italian Ambassador to Austria, presented this afternoon to Baron von Burian, the Austro-Hungarian Foreign Minister, the following declaration of war:

Vienna, May 23, 1915.

Conformably with the orders of His Majesty the King, His august Sovereign, the undersigned Ambassador of Italy has the honor to deliver to His Excellency, the Foreign Minister of Austria-Hungary, the following communication:

"Declaration has been made, as from the fourth of this month, to the Imperial and Royal Government of the grave motives for which Italy, confident in her good right, proclaimed annulled and henceforth without effect her treaty of alliance with Austria-Hungary, which was violated by the Imperial and Royal Government, and resumed her liberty of action in this respect.

"The Government of the King, firmly resolved to provide by all means at its disposal for safeguarding Italian rights and interests, cannot fail in its duty to take against every existing and future menace measures which events impose upon it for the fulfillment of national aspirations.

"His Majesty the King declares that he considers himself from tomorrow in a state of war with Austria-Hungary."

The undersigned has the honor to make known at the same time to His Excellency, the Foreign Minister, that passports will be placed this very day at the disposal of the Imperial and Royal Ambassador at Rome, and he will be obliged to His Excellency if he will kindly have his passports handed to him.

AVARNA.

11 NATIONS NOW INVOLVED IN WAR

Washington Expects Rumania, Bulgaria, and Greece Soon to Join the Allies.

TRADE PROBLEMS CREATED

Switzerland, Now Isolated, Must Look to Italy for Means to Get in Supplies.

Special to The New York Times.

WASHINGTON, May 23.—Official confirmation of the declaration of war by Italy against Austro-Hungary had not reached Washington tonight, but the press dispatches on the subject and other developments today greatly interested officials and diplomats. As soon as authoritative confirmation comes from either side that the fromal declaration of war has been issued President Wilson will add another to his already long list of proclamations of neutrality. In this new proclamation the United States Government will go on record as a neutral as between Italy and the dual monarchy.

In diplomatic circles here it is predicted that Rumania, Bulgaria, and Greece soon will enter the war, following the lead of Italy, and that they will all go on the side of the Allies in the order named. It has been the belief in well-informed diplomatic circles for two months that the entry of Greece into the war awaited the attitude of Italy. Now that the Italians are in the conflict and will figure in the general peace conference that will be held after the war for remaking the map of Europe, it is argued that the Greeks cannot now long remain out in view of the reckoning that will be had when hostilities cease regarding the new status to be established in the Near East.

The statement was made here tonight that the Bulgarians could not afford to remain out of the war or to enter it except on the side of the Allies with Serbia and Italy already on that side and Romania and Greece as prospective participants joined with them. It was furthermore pointed out that the situation had now so shaped itself that Bulgaria, taking advantage of the Italian declaration and the prospect of the participation of Roumania, would feel justified in joining the Allies and going against Turkey in an attempt to take Adrianople—the goal of the Bulgarians in the Balkan war.

There are now eleven nations engaged in war or involved in declarations of war since Aug. 1 last. They are Great Britain, France, Russia, Belgium, Germany, Austria-Hungary, Japan, Turkey, Serbia, Italy, and Montenegro. With Roumania, Bulgaria, and Greece entered, the total number of involved nations would be increased to fourteen.

One of the subjects on which information is awaited with much interest here is the attitude of Italy toward the naval operations of the Allies, whether Italy will subscribe to the order-in-council making impossible all commercial intercourse with Germany and Austria through the Mediterranean and whether the same rigid rules as to contraband will be enforced by the Italian fleet as by the Anglo-French fleet.

The situation of Switzerland is likely to be a cause of much concern, for should the same rules as to ultimate destination of cargoes be put into effect with respect to shipments consigned for transshipment through Italian ports, as imposed by the Allies, the little republic, isolated in the centre of Europe without a sea outlet, may suffer seriously. Already there has been much difficulty in getting supplies to Switzerland, and it is believed Switzerland will press hard for arrangements with the French and Italian Governments to obtain products, giving guarantees against re-exportation.

The cutting off of commerce to Germany and Austria through the Mediterranean, it is thought in allied quarters here, will soon be seriously felt by the central powers, and may even compel

Continued on Page 2.

4-POWER ENTENTE AS ALLIANCE DIES

Italy Joins Great Britain, France, and Russia in a New Compact.

FORMAL ACTION IS TAKEN

Terms of Italy's Participation in the War Signed and Sealed as Teuton Envoys Depart.

Special Cable to THE NEW YORK TIMES.

ROME, May 22, (Dispatch to The London Daily Chronicle.)—Baron Sonnino, the Foreign Minister, this afternoon received the German Ambassador, Prince von Bülow. The latter did not stay long. His visit was practically one of formal leave taking.

What actually took place at the final interview is not stated, but when the Kaiser's emissary came downstairs from the Foreign Office he looked pale and excited and seemed to have lost his habitual calm look of confidence. As he turned into the Via Venti Settembre he was swinging his walking stick and muttering to himself. He entered a covered automobile at a short distance from the Consulate and drove toward the German Embassy.

Baron von Macchio, the Austrian Ambassador, also paid a hurried farewell visit to Signor Sonnino. The colloquy between the Italian Foreign Minister and the Vienna envoy was even briefer than that with Prince von Bülow. The departing Austrian barely stayed five minutes. On leaving, he hurried away, absent mindedly carrying his hat in his hand until he reached the foot of the great staircase giving access to the Minister's office.

Signor Sonnino then received the British, French, and Russian Ambassadors. As a result of this official interview, I am able to state that the hitherto existing Triple Entente has from today become the Quadruple Entente. This first official meeting between the representatives of the newly born alliance was most cordial. The basis of Italy's active co-operation, economic, naval, and military, was settled, signed, and sealed. Due notice of Italy's action will be given to neutral powers. From today Italy is with her new allies whole-heartedly, with her national soul, her national sword, and her national purse.

HATE FOE "UNUTTERABLY."

Austrians Furious at What Is Called Italy's Treacherous Surprise Attack.

AMSTERDAM, May 23.—The Frankfurter Zeitung today prints a telegram received from Vienna saying:

"The exasperation and contempt which Italy's treacherous surprise attack and her hypocritical justification arouse here (Vienna) are quite indescribable.

"Neither Serbia nor Russia, despite a long and costly war, is hated. Italy, however, or rather those Italian would-be politicians and business men who offer violence to the majority of peaceful Italian people, are so unutterably hated with the most profound honesty that this war can be terrible."

BARS WAR CORRESPONDENTS.

Italy to Adopt Press Bureau System of Britain and France.

TURIN, Italy, May 23.—Commander in Chief Cadorna, Premier Salandra, and Foreign Minister Sonnino have agreed, says the Stampa, that no war correspondents shall be allowed with the Italian Army.

The Italian Press Bureau is to operate in the same manner as do those in France and Great Britain.

TEUTON ENVOYS TAKE LEAVE

Von Macchio Receives Passports; Von Buelow to Go With Him.

ENVOYS TO POPE GO ALSO

Italian Ambassador to Austria Gets Word to Withdraw from Vienna.

WHOLE NATION REJOICING

Rome Ablaze with Flags and Great Crowds Parade to National Airs of the Allies.

30,000 ITALIANS PRISONERS

Detained in Germany and Austria, Although Enemy Nationals Are Allowed to Leave Italy.

ROME, May 23.—Italy is at war with Austria-Hungary. Official announcement of the declaration of hostilities was made by the Government last night at 8:15 o'clock, simultaneously with the issuance of an order for general mobilization. The state of war begins tomorrow.

Passports were handed to Baron von Macchio, Austro-Hungarian Ambassador to Italy, at 3:30 o'clock this afternoon, and he will leave tonight or tomorrow morning.

Three special trains have been held in readiness, one for Baron von Macchio, one for Prince von Buelow, and the Prussian Envoy to the Holy See, and the third for the Bavarian Envoy to the Quirinal and the Vatican.

The Italian Ambassador at Vienna, the Duke of Avarna, has been recalled.

Enthusiastic Throughout the Country.

Although drastic action has been looked for momentarily, Italians of all classes were electrified by the swiftly moving events. Reports from all towns in Italy say that the decree of mobilization was received everywhere with the greatest enthusiasm. Processions and demonstrations were held in all towns, the people acclaiming the King and wishing victory for the country.

In some places portraits of the King and Queen were carried triumphantly through the streets by crowds singing the national airs and war songs popular with their grandfathers and fathers who fought in 1848, 1859, 1860 and 1866, or who climbed the scaffolds to meet the Austrian executioners.

In Rome early this morning great crowds gathered around the Quirinal to await the ministers who called on the King for the purpose of discussing the situation and signing decrees. When Premier Salandra and Signor Sonnino, the Foreign Minister, left the palace the people cheered them enthusiastically. The troops changing guards at the Royal Palace were the object of a stirring manifestation amid "Vivas" for the army and for war.

General Zuppeli, Minister of War, and Vice Admiral Viale, Minister of Marine, remained with the King for a considerable time after the others left, and later they had a conference with Lieut. Gen. Cadorna, Chief of Staff, and Vice Admiral Phaon di Revel, Chief of the Naval Staff.

From Germany come reports that considerable resentment is felt in official circles there against what is alleged to be the obstinacy of the Austrian diplomacy responsible for the failure of the negotiations with Italy initiatew by Prince von Bülow, the German Ambassador. The suggestion had even been made that Austria should be left alone to fight Italy, but pledges taken by the German General Staff and by the German Emperor personally with Emperor Francis Joseph resulted in the triumph of those advocating Austro-German solidarity, even in a new war against Italy.

According tot the Giornale d'Italia, the problem concerning the diplomats accredited to the Vatican has been solved satisfactorily. The Austrian and German diplomats, ignoring the situation in Italy, will depart, as though they were merelytaking their Summer vacations before the regular time. It had been urged by some that the Italian Government move energetically with respect to these diplomatic representatives, and by others that the Vatican resist any effort to force them to withdraw. But these extreme measures failed, and thus the Law of Guarantees remains untouched.

Alarming reports have been received

Mid-Week Pictorial

A charge by Italian Infantry.

Mid-Week Pictorial

Italian Infantry taking cover in front of the Austrian trenches.

"All the News That's Fit to Print."

The New York Times.

THE WEATHER
Fair today; showers tomorrow; variable winds, becoming light southwest.
For full weather report see Page 17.

VOL. LXIV...NO. 20,957. .... NEW YORK, FRIDAY, JUNE 11, 1915.—TWENTY-FOUR PAGES. ONE CENT In Greater New York, Jersey City and Newark. | Elsewhere TWO CENTS.

PRESIDENT WILSON TELLS GERMANY THAT SHE HAS NO RIGHT EVEN TO ENDANGER LIFE ON SHIPS UNARMED, UNWARNED; 'ON THIS PRINCIPLE THE UNITED STATES MUST STAND'; AGAIN ASKS ASSURANCES THAT SUCH ATTACKS SHALL CEASE

BERLIN SHOWS ANXIETY

Puzzled Over Bryan, and Deeply Concerned to Avoid a Break.

WANTS NO WAR WITH US

Dreads the Effect of a Rupture Especially in Stiffening the Resistance of Russia.

WOULD NOT MODIFY SEA WAR

Unless the Ends for Which Submarines Are Used Can Be Attained Diplomatically.

PRESS GROWS MILDER

No Longer Attacking America—Awaiting Publication of Note, Which Has Arrived.

The Note Reaches Berlin; Gerard Sees von Jagow

BERLIN, June 10, (via London, Friday, June 11.)—The first sections of the American note to Germany arrived in Berlin late this afternoon, and the other sections began coming in early in the evening. The note will be deciphered and presented to Gottlieb von Jagow, the German Foreign Secretary, tomorrow.

In the afternoon James W. Gerard, the American Ambassador, called on Herr von Jagow and was closeted with him for over half an hour.

From a Staff Correspondent.
Special Cable to THE NEW YORK TIMES.

BERLIN, June 10, (via The Hague.)—Mr. Bryan's resignation as Secretary of State was a bolt from the blue and the biggest political sensation here since Italy's declaration of war. Official optimism, which had mounted with each day's delay, is now reduced, and in official circles there is an ill-concealed state of worry and anxiety.

Leading statesmen whom I interviewed yesterday were too nonplussed to express an opinion. They were still puzzled today and uncertain whether Bryan's resignation was for better or worse. Therefore, they were unwilling to express any opinion because they will have none until they are in possesion of more facts.

A high official of the Foreign Office today threw up his hands and said: "We are pursuing a policy of watchful waiting—waiting for the note."

To understand the puzzled Germans' feelings Americans must remember that few Germans are initiated into the mysteries of American politics and American character. The fact is the Germans have consistently "roasted" Bryan as pro-British and Germany's worst enemy. Scanty cables from America, via England, now indicate that Bryan is the man of peace and virtually Germany's best friend, and Germans are staggered by the denouement.

A leading German statesman, discussing the controversy with the United States, has just said to me helplessly:

"What can I say before I see the text of the note? I don't know what to think, but I sincerely hope for a peaceful solution. Americans should take into account that submarine warfare is merely a measure of reprisal forced upon us; that all we want is that England be forced to discontinue violating international law."

I got the impression that German high officials are still unable to grasp the obvious conclusions from Mr. Bryan's resignation. They are clearly worried because they are unable to take in the meaning of its consequences, but are still unwilling to believe that it portends increased tension of German-American relations, and absolutely scout the idea that the breaking point is approaching. They still cling to the hope that a satisfactory and mutually honorable modus vivendi can be arrived at diplomatically if both sides keep their heads.

Certain facts must be emphasized now: First, that, while the German people are greatly embittered toward America, owing to the ammunition shipments, the Government does not want war with America under any circumstances, and earnestly desires to avoid a diplomatic rupture if it is humanly possible. Official circles fully realize the gravity of the consequences of such a rupture, particularly in Germany's complete isolation and the tremendous moral sup-

Continued on Page 2.

President Wilson's Answer to Germany's Note

The Secretary of State ad Interim to the American Ambassador at Berlin:

DEPARTMENT OF STATE
WASHINGTON, JUNE 9, 1915

You are instructed to deliver textually the following note to the Minister of Foreign Affairs:

In compliance with your Excellency's request I did not fail to transmit to my Government, immediately upon their receipt, your note of May 28 in reply to my note of May 15, and your supplementary note of June 1, setting forth the conclusions, so far as reached, by the Imperial German Government concerning the attacks on the American steamers Cushing and Gulflight. I am now instructed by my Government to communicate the following in reply:

The Government of the United States notes with gratification the full recognition by the Imperial German Government, in discussing the cases of the Cushing and the Gulflight, of the principle of the freedom of all parts of the open sea to neutral ships, and the frank willingness of the Imperial German Government to acknowledge and meet its liability where the fact of attack upon neutral "ships which have not been guilty of any hostile act" by German air craft or vessels of war is satisfactorily established, and the Government of the United States will in due course lay before the Imperial German Government, as it requests, full information concerning the attack on the steamer Cushing.

With regard to the sinking of the steamer Falaba, by which an American citizen lost his life, the Government of the United States is surprised to find the Imperial German Government contending that an effort on the part of a merchantman to escape capture and secure assistance alters the obligation of the officer seeking to make the capture in respect of the safety of the lives of those on board the merchantman, although the vessel has ceased her attempt to escape when torpedoed. These are not new circumstances. They have been in the minds of statesmen and of international jurists throughout the development of naval warfare, and the Government of the United States does not understand that they have ever been held to alter the principles of humanity upon which it has insisted. Nothing but actual forcible resistance or continued efforts to escape by flight when ordered to stop for the purpose of visit, on the part of the merchantman, has ever been held to forfeit the lives of her passengers or crew. The Government of the United States, however, does not understand that the Imperial German Government is seeking in this case to relieve itself of liability, but only intends to set forth the circumstances which led the Commander of the submarine to allow himself to be hurried into the course which he took.

Your Excellency's note, in discussing the loss of American lives resulting from the sinking of the steamship Lusitania, adverts at some length to certain information which the Imperial German Government has received with regard to the character and outfit of that vessel, and your Excellency expresses the fear that this information may not have been brought to the attention of the United States. It is stated that the Lusitania was undoubtedly equipped with masked guns, supplied with trained gunners and special ammunition, transporting troops from Canada, carrying a cargo not permitted under the laws of the United States to a vessel also carrying passengers, and serving, in virtual effect, as an auxiliary to the naval forces of Great Britain.

Fortunately these are matters concerning which the Government of the United States is in a position to give the Imperial German Government official information. Of the facts alleged in your Excellency's note, if true, the Government of the United States would have been bound to take official cognizance in performing its recognized duty as a neutral Power and in enforcing its national laws. It was its duty to see to it that the Lusitania was not armed for offensive action, that she was not serving as a transport, that she did not carry a cargo prohibited by the statutes of the United States, and that, if in fact she was a naval vessel of Great Britain, she should not receive clearance as a merchantman; and it performed that duty and enforced its statutes with scrupulous vigilance through its regularly constituted officials. It is able, therefore, to assure the Imperial German Government that it has been misinformed. If the Imperial Government should deem itself to be in possession of convincing evidence that the officials of the Government of the United States did not perform these duties with thoroughness, the Government of the United States sincerely hopes that it will submit that evidence for consideration.

Whatever may be the contentions of the Imperial German Government regarding the carriage of contraband of war on board the Lusitania, or regarding the explosion of that material by the torpedo, it need only be said that in the view of this Government these contentions are irrelevant to the question of the legality of the methods used by the German naval authorities in sinking the vessel.

But the sinking of passenger ships involves principles of humanity which throw into the background any special circumstances of detail that may be thought to affect the cases; principles which lift it, as the Imperial German Government will no doubt be quick to recognize and acknowledge, out of the class of ordinary subjects of diplomatic discussion or of international controversy. Whatever be the other facts regarding the Lusitania, the principal fact is that a great steamer, primarily and chiefly a conveyance for passengers, and carrying more than a thousand souls who had no part or lot in the conduct of the war, was torpedoed and sunk without so much as a challenge or a warning, and that men, women, and children were sent to their death in circumstances unparalleled in modern warfare. The fact that more than 100 American citizens were among those who perished made it the duty of the Government of the United States to speak of these things, and once more, with solemn emphasis, to call the attention of the Imperial German Government to the grave responsibility which the Government of the United States conceives that it has incurred in this tragic occurrence, and to the indisputable principle upon which that responsibility rests.

The Government of the United States is contending for something much greater than mere rights of property or privileges of commerce. It is contending for nothing less high and sacred than the rights of humanity, which every Government honors itself in respecting, and which no Government is justified in resigning on behalf of those under its care and authority. Only her actual resistance to capture, or refusal to stop when ordered to do so for the purpose of visit, could have afforded the Commander of the submarine any justification for so much as putting the lives of those on board the ship in jeopardy. This principle the Government of the United States understands the explicit instructions issued on Aug. 3, 1914, by the Imperial German Admiralty to its Commanders at sea to have recognized and embodied, as do the naval codes of all other nations, and upon it every traveler and seaman had a right to depend. It is upon this principle of humanity, as well as upon the law founded upon this principle, that the United States must stand.

The Government of the United States is happy to observe that your Excellency's note closes with the intimation that the Imperial German Government is willing, now as before, to accept the good offices of the United States in an attempt to come to an understanding with the Government of Great Britain by which the character and conditions of war upon the sea may be changed. The Government of the United States would consider it a privilege thus to serve its friends and the world. It stands ready at any time to convey to either Government any intimation or suggestion the other may be willing to have it convey, and cordially invites the Imperial German Government to make use of its services in this way at its convenience. The whole world is concerned in anything that may bring about even a partial accommodation of interests or in any way mitigate the terrors of the present distressing conflict.

In the meantime, whatever arrangement may happily be made between the parties to the war, and whatever may, in the opinion of the Imperial German Government, have been the provocation or the circumstantial justification for the past acts of its Commanders at sea, the Government of the United States confidently looks to see the justice and humanity of the Government of Germany vindicated in all cases where Americans have been wronged or their rights as neutrals invaded.

The Government of the United States, therefore, very earnestly and very solemnly renews the representations of its note transmitted to the Imperial German Government on the 15th of May, and relies in these representations upon the principles of humanity, the universally recognized understandings of international law, and the ancient friendship of the German nation.

The Government of the United States cannot admit that the proclamation of a war zone from which neutral ships have been warned to keep away may be made to operate as in any degree an abbreviation of the rights either of American shipmasters or of American citizens bound on lawful errands as passengers on merchant ships of belligerent nationality. It does not understand the Imperial German Government to question those rights. It understands it also to accept as established beyond question the principle that the lives of noncombatants cannot lawfully or rightfully be put in jeopardy by the capture or destruction of an unresisting merchantman, and to recognize the obligation to take sufficient precaution to ascertain whether a suspected merchantman is in fact of belligerent nationality or is in fact carrying contraband of war under a neutral flag. The Government of the United States deems it reasonable to expect that the Imperial German Government will adopt the measures necessary to put these principles into practice in respect of the safeguarding of American lives and American ships, and asks for assurances that this will be done.

ROBERT LANSING,
Secretary of State ad Interim.

Bryan Explains His Idea of "The Real Issue"—For Persuasion, Not Firmness or Force

WASHINGTON, June 10.—William Jennings Bryan, in an appeal "to the American people," put on the wires tonight eleven minutes after President Wilson's note to Germany, asks them to hear him before they pass sentence upon his laying down the portfolio of Secretary of State in the midst of international stress.

Interpreting the new American note to Germany, which he refused to sign, as conforming to the "old system" of firmness based on potential force, and characterizing himself as a champion of the new system of persuasion instead of force, and as "an humble follower of the Prince of Peace," he pleads for the United States to lead the world "out of the black night of war."

Mr. Bryan tomorrow will issue another statement, an appeal, he says, to "German-Americans." With that he says he will rest his case.

Mr. Bryan's statement, headed "The Real Issue," follows:

An Appeal for Judgment.

To the American people:

You now have before you the text of the note to Germany—the note which it would have been my official duty to sign had I remained Secretary of State. I ask you to sit in judgment upon my decision to resign rather than to share responsibility for it.

I am sure you will credit me with honorable motives, but that is not enough. Good intentions could not atone for a mistake at such a time, on such a subject, and under such circumstances. If your verdict is against me, I ask no mercy; I desire none if I have acted unwisely.

A man in public life must act according to his conscience, but, however conscientiously he acts, he must be prepared to accept without complaint any condemnation which his own errors may bring upon him; he must be willing to bear any deserved punishment, from ostracism to execution. But hear me before you pass sentence.

The President and I agree in purpose; we desire a peaceful solution of the dispute which has arisen between the United States and Germany. We not only desire it, but, with equal fervor, we pray for it; but we differ irreconcilably as to the means of securing it.

If it were merely a personal difference, it would be a matter of little moment, for all the presumptions are on his side—the presumptions that go with power and authority. He is your President, I am a private citizen without office or title—but one of the one hundred million of inhabitants.

But the real issue is not between persons, it is between systems, and I rely for vindication wholly upon the strength of the position taken.

Force Versus Persuasion.

Among the influences which Governments employ in dealing with each other there are two which are pre-eminent and antagonistic—force and persuasion. Force speaks with firmness and acts through the ultimatum; persuasion employs argument, courts investigation, and depends upon negotiation. Force represents the old system—the system that must pass away; persuasion represents the new system—the system that has been growing, all too slowly, it is true, but growing for 1,900 years. In the old system war is the chief cornerstone—war, which at its best is little better than war at its worst; the new system contemplates an universal brotherhood established through the uplifting power of example.

If I correctly interpret the note to Germany, it conforms to the standards of the old system rather than to the rules of the new, and I cheerfully admit that it is abundantly supported by precedents—precedents written in characters of blood upon almost every page of human history. Austria furnishes the most recent precedent; it was Austria's firmness that dictated the ultimatum against Serbia, which set the world at war.

Every ruler now participating in this unparalleled conflict has proclaimed his desire for peace and denied responsibility for the war, and it is only charitable that we should credit all of them with good faith. They desired peace, but they sought it according to the rules of the old system. They believed that firmness would give the best assurance of the maintenance of peace, and, faithfully following precedent, they went so near the fire that they were, one after another, sucked into the contest.

Never So Frightful as Now.

Never before have the frightful follies of this fatal system been so clearly revealed as now. The most civilized and enlightened—aye, the most Christian—of the nations of Europe are grappling with each other as if in a death struggle. They are sacrificing the best and bravest of their sons on the battlefield; they are converting their gardens into cemeteries and their homes into houses of mourning; they are taxing the wealth of today and laying a burden of debt on the toil of the future; they have filled the air with thunderbolts more deadly than those of Jove, and they have multiplied the perils of the deep.

Adding fresh fuel to the flame of hate, they have daily devised new horrors, until one side is endeavoring to drown noncombatant men, women, and children at sea, while the other side seeks to starve noncombatant men, women, and children on land. And they are so absorbed in alternate retaliations and in competitive cruelties that they seem, for the time being, blind to the rights of neutrals and deaf to the appeals of humanity. A tree is known by its fruit. The war in Europe is the ripened fruit of the old system.

This is what firmness, supported by force, has done in the Old World; shall we invite it to cross the Atlantic? Already the jingoes of our own country have caught the rabies from the dogs of war; shall the opponents of organized slaughter be silent while the disease spreads?

Would Prolong Negotiations.

As an humble follower of the Prince of Peace, as a devoted believer in the prophecy that "they that take the sword shall perish with the sword," I beg to be counted among those who earnestly urge the adoption of a course in this matter which will leave no doubt of our Government's willingness to continue negotiations with Germany until an amicable understanding is reached, or at least until, the stress of war over, we can appeal from Philip drunk with carnage to Philip sobered by the memories of an historic friendship and by a recollection of the innumerable ties of kinship that bind the Fatherland to the United States.

Some nation must lead the world out of the black night of war into the light of that day when "swords shall be beaten into plowshares." Why not make that honor ours? Some day—why not now?—the nations will learn that enduring peace cannot be built upon fear—that good-will does not grow upon the stalk of violence. Some day the nations will place their trust in love, the weapon for which there is no shield; in love, that suffereth long and is kind; in love, that is not easily provoked, that beareth all things, believeth all things, hopeth all things, endureth all things; in love, which, though despised as weakness by the worshippers of Mars, abideth when all else fails.

W. J. BRYAN.

FOR HUMANITY'S RIGHTS

'Which No Government Would Be Justified in Abandoning.'

LUSITANIA WAS NOT ARMED

Our Own Official Reports Cited, and Germany Invited to Disprove Them if She Can.

AS TO ENGLAND'S ATTITUDE

This Government Is Always Glad to Serve Its Friends by Facilitating Communication.

POLITE, PACIFIC, BUT FIRM

Dismisses Germany's Contentions as Irrelevancies, but Is Even More Conciliatory in Tone Than the Note Bryan Signed.

Special to The New York Times.

WASHINGTON, June 10.—President Wilson's note to Germany regarding the sinking of the Lusitania, which was made public this evening, "very earnestly and very solemnly renews the representations of its (his) note transmitted to the Imperial German Government on the 15th of May, and relies in these representations upon the principles of humanity, the universally recognized understandings of international law, and the ancient friendship of the German Nation."

What is regarded here as the mandatory part of the note is summarized in the last sentence, in which the American Government "asks for assurances" that Germany "will adopt the measures necessary to put into practice in respect to the safeguarding of American lives and American ships" the principle that the lives of non-combatants cannot be placed in jeopardy in the destruction of unresisting merchantmen, and "the obligation to take sufficient precaution to ascertain whether a suspected merchantman is in fact of belligerent nationalty, or is in fact carrying contraband of war under a neutral flag."

The flat request in Mr. Wilson's note today for "assurances" from Germany that the acts complained of shall cease is viewed in Washington as being measurably stronger than any passage in his first note on this subject. In the earlier note the President asked for "just, prompt, and enlightened action in this vital matter," and he further invited the German Government to disavow the acts of its submarine commanders. But the request for "assurances" is regarded here as meaning not only that Germany must in fact stop the illegal practices, which might be accomplished inconspicuously, without any obvious surrender, but asks that assurances shall officially be conveyed to the United States of a radical change in its submarine policy.

Other Features Milder.

In every other respect the note made public today is regarded as noticeably milder than the earlier communication, which Mr. Bryan signed. Today's note is not viewed in any respect as an ultimatum. It is in itself a polite discussion of the incidents that have already occurred, and it invites evidence, if Germany has any, in contradiction of our own official reports, on at least one phase of the most serious of those incidents arising from the destruction of the Lusitania—the question whether the ship was armed and whether it violated American laws regarding dangerous cargoes on passenger vessels. It is pointed out here that there is no reference in today's note to a "prompt" reply, and there is no demand for the cessation of the submarine warfare pending the receipt of the assurances asked for.

From the German point of view, it is said, the most promising feature of the note is the President's statement that "the Government of the United States would consider it a privilege to serve its friends and the world" by again submitting proposals to either Great Britain or Germany regarding the lifting of the British blockade and the consequent termination of Germany's submarine attacks. Germany has all along contended that the British blockade was the reason and justification for the submarine

"All the News That's Fit to Print."

The New York Times.

THE WEATHER
Partly cloudy today and Friday; warmer Friday; moderate west winds.
For full weather report see Page 16.

VOL. LXIV...NO. 20,970. NEW YORK, THURSDAY, JUNE 24, 1915.—TWENTY PAGES. ONE CENT In Greater New York, Jersey City and Newark. [illegible]

LEMBERG TAKEN BY AUSTRO-GERMANS; LLOYD GEORGE GIVES BRITISH LABOR SEVEN DAYS TO MAN WAR WORKSHOPS

THAW TRIAL GIVES DOUBLE SURPRISE

State Declines to be Limited by Prisoner's Short Direct Examination.

TO USE HIM AS ITS WITNESS

That Will Enable Deputy Attorney General to Go Into Slayer's Life History.

ATTACKED AS DEGENERATE

Cook, Bitter in Opening, Defends Stanford White's Memory—Stanchfield Attacks Alienists.

Harry K. Thaw was on the witness stand for twenty minutes yesterday at the jury trial of his sanity before Justice Hendrick in the Supreme Court. His hope that he would be immediately cross-examined and have the ordeal over at this time was shattered when Deputy Attorney General Cook announced that he had no questions to ask. He said he would call Thaw later as a witness for the State.

Mr. Cook made it known that at that time he would, through his examination of Thaw, endeavor to lay before the jury all of the facts in connection with Thaw's life "from the day of his birth until the present time."

The direct examination by Mr. Stanchfield, chief of counsel for Thaw, who called him as the first witness in his own behalf yesterday, was confined almost exclusively to his escape from Matteawan and subsequent events. He did not question Thaw at all about the killing of Stanford White or of his life prior to the murder. Then he turned the witness over to Mr. Cook, but the Deputy Attorney General, with a smile, shook his head. He made it known that he wanted Thaw as one of the late witnesses, not as the first, so that his appearance under examination would be fresh in the minds of the jurymen when they retired to deliberate.

Counsel Springs A Surprise.

It was a dramatic moment in a day that had interesting situations. Thaw had leaned forward in the chair, his mind alert, ready to answer whatever questions Mr. Cook might ask. He had been cool and self-possessed during his brief examination by Mr. Stanchfield and was apparently ready for the struggle of wits. When he found that his examination was not to go on he looked about the court room with roving eyes which expressed his surprise.

The situation surprised the spectators in the courtroom, and there was a buzz of voices which was quieted quickly. Then Mr. Stanchfield called his next witness, John D. Blackburn, one of the jurymen who voted to free Thaw of the charge of conspiracy last March. Blackburn said he thought Thaw was sane. He was followed by others, including a member of the jury at Thaw's second trial for Mr. White's murder. Tombs chaplains, newspaper men, and others who expressed the same belief. At the afternoon session the Thaw lawyers piled up a great mass of testimony of this character which the State was unable to break down very successfully on cross-examination. While the day held its disappointment for Thaw, there was much which plainly encouraged him.

A touch of the sensational was given to the proceedings at the opening of the morning session when Mr. Stanchfield for Thaw and Mr. Cook for the State delivered their opening addresses. Mr. Cook, beginning in a quiet, even voice, soon let himself loose in a torrent of denunciation of the way Thaw had lived and his alleged degeneracy at the time of the murder.

Defends White's Memory.

"I don't care what Jerome said," he asserted, referring to the former District Attorney's reference to White at the second murder trial which had been read by Mr. Stanchfield. "I think the shame of attacking Stanford White, one of the most eminent of architects, whose name was known all over the world, has gone far enough without one word being said in his own defense. It is a shame and a disgrace to the honesty and decency of the American people to longer make a beast out of White when the only evidence is the testimony of Evelyn Nesbit Thaw, which was produced so that Thaw 'might hide behind her skirts.'"

While Mr. Cook bitterly attacked him, Thaw sat most of the time with his head bowed. Frequently he whispered to one of his lawyers, and at one allusion, which he evidently thought extravagant, he smiled nervously.

Mr. Stanchfield, in opening, reminded the jurymen that the murder of Stanford White had taken place nearly ten years ago. While the unwritten law was not Thaw's plea at the time, he said, he wanted to refer to it, and then he described the circumstances of the killing of White, and told of Evelyn Thaw's story of her treatment at White's hands, of Thaw's marriage to her despite that story, and of the word Thaw had received later that White had told May McKenzie that he intended to win Evelyn Thaw away from him again.

"At that time," said Mr. Stanchfield, "Thaw was a man of convivial habits, not the sobered, chastened man you see now—chastened by discipline and growing years. Thaw is now 44 years old."

Mr. Stanchfield referred to the Thaw of today as a broad-minded, philosophical, and educated gentleman. Then he read from the address made by William T. Jerome to the jury in the second murder trial, in which Jerome said that he believed that the revelations concerning White made by Evelyn Thaw were true. He wanted that picture to rest in the minds of the jurymen, he said, for it was the picture drawn by the prosecuting attorney.

Next Mr. Stanchfield asked what evidence there was that Thaw was insane. He read from the record of the commission appointed by Justice Fitzgerald at the first murder trial, which found Thaw sane, and from the record of the Federal Commission appointed in New Hampshire in December, 1913, which found him sane. He said he could call all of the members of the jury at Thaw's second trial for murder and that they would testify that they be-

Continued on Page 4.

DYNAMITE AT HOME OF ANDREW CARNEGIE

Watchman Finds Three Sticks at the Iron Master's Mansion in Fifth Avenue.

George Malone, a Holmes patrolman, on duty outside the home of Andrew Carnegie at Ninety-third Street and Fifth Avenue, found three sticks of dynamite outside the iron master's house at 11 o'clock last night and carried them to the East Eighty-eighth Street Station, where he turned them over to the lieutenant.

Pieces of Chinese punk were attached to the sticks.

Malone said he had no idea how they had come where he found them. He had seen no one pass and there was no one in the neighborhood when he stumbled upon the explosive.

The police were not inclined to believe that the sticks were placed there with any intent to injure Mr. Carnegie. The latter is in Bar Harbor now, and they argued that any one anxious to do him an injury certainly would keep sufficiently well posted on his movements to know that he was not even in the city.

At the time of the attempt to dynamite St. Patrick's Cathedral, however, the police recalled that threats were made by the dynamiters that they would demolish not only the churches but the palaces of the wealthy along Fifth Avenue, naming those of Mr. Carnegie and the Rockefellers, father and son. Detectives set out at once on the theory that the dynamite last night might have been placed by members of the same gang, and Owen Egan, head of the Bureau of Explosives, took up the case.

AN EMDEN OFFICER ESCAPES TO MANILA

Flees Singapore During Mutiny and After Four Months' Wandering Reaches Manila

Special Cable to THE NEW YORK TIMES.

MANILA, June 23.—Lieutenant Lauterbach, an officer of the German sea raider Emden, which was sunk by the Australian cruiser Sydney off Los Cocos Island on Nov. 9, escaped from Singapore during the mutiny of the native troops there the middle of last February, and, accompanied by Adolph Schoenberg, a German business man who was interned by the British, after a remarkable experience arrived in this city today.

Lieutenant Lauterbach and his companion managed to seize a small sailing craft during the uprising at Singapore and cross the Strait of Malacca to Sumatra, a distance of about seventy-five miles. From Sumatra they proceeded to Java, and then crossed the Java Sea to Dutch Borneo.

In northern Borneo the daring pair obtained a native sailing vessel in which they voyaged north through a terrible monsoon toward the southernmost point of the island of Mindanao in the Philippines, which they finally reached after fearful hardships.

Here they chartered a sailboat and followed the western coast of Mindanao north to Malabang, from which military port they made their way fifty miles overland, via Camp Keithley, to Iligan Bay, where they caught a steamer for Manila, and their troubles were over.

AMERICANS IGNORE BRITISH PASSPORT RULES

Page Reports Many Reaching England Without Proper Papers—Blames Steamship Companies.

Special to The New York Times.

WASHINGTON, June 23.—Complaint has been made to the State Department by Ambassador Page, at London, that many Americans continue to arrive at English ports without passports or other satisfactory documents of identification such as are required by the British regulations. The Ambassador also complains that the fault lies almost entirely with the steamship companies, who, he asserts, continue to sell tickets to Americans unprovided with the necessary documents, despite the State Department's warnings.

The State Department tonight made public this excerpt from the dispatch of Ambassador Page:

"Notwithstanding the warning which the department has conveyed to steamship agencies, I regret to report that there is no improvement in respect of the arrival of Americans from the United States. The Consul at Liverpool informs the Embassy that they continue to arrive in increasing numbers, with no means of identification, and that the aliens' officers at that port, who at first showed a disposition to treat as leniently as possible infractions of the regulations which were due to ignorance, have now been obliged to deal more severely with such persons.

"Much inconvenience and delay are caused to travelers as a result of the aliens' officers at the port having to refer such cases to the Home Office in London before permission to land and proceed to their destination can be given to persons without passports, and the result would appear to lie, almost entirely, with steamship companies who sell tickets to Americans unprovided with the necessary documents."

Two months ago the State Department announced that it had received a telegram from Consul General Skinner at London, reporting that after April 25 no alien should enter or leave the United Kingdom without a passport or document of identification bearing a photograph of the holder. The Bureau of Citizenship, which is charged with the issuance of passports and which has been very much overworked, receives many telegrams and telephone calls regarding passports for persons who are on the eve of leaving this country for Europe. These persons are shocked to learn that it is necessary for every person desiring a passport to make a sworn application before a clerk of a court and send it to the State Department with duplicate unmounted photographs, one attached to the application and the other to be attached to the passport by the Department.

Passports are now absolutely necessary for entrance into most European countries. The State Department has frequently issued the caution that if all Americans who expect to travel abroad will only take time by the forelock and submit proper applications within a reasonable period before sailing, they will save themselves much worry and inconvenience.

CLASH OVER PLAN TO CURB WALL ST.

Proposed Exchange Incorporation Starts Controversy Before Albany Convention Committee.

UNTERMYER FIGHTS FOR IT

Calls Boosting of Rock Island a Swindle and Urges State Control.

MILBURN DEFENDS BOARD

Asserts Regulation Is Unnecessary and That Incorporation Would Cause Divided Responsibility.

Special to The New York Times.

ALBANY, June 23.—There was a heated discussion at a hearing today before the Committee on Corporations of the Constitutional Convention in proposals requiring incorporation of the Stock Exchange and providing for closer supervision by the State of the operations of the Exchange and similar bodies. The proposals were introduced by Israel T. Deyo of Broome County. Samuel Untermyer and John G. Milburn joined issue over the suggested amendments, Mr. Untermyer urging their adoption by the Convention.

In an effort to prove that the legislation placed on the statute books in the Sulzer Administration to prevent wash sales and manipulation of securities did not accomplish those purposes, Mr. Untermyer reviewed some recent Stock Exchange history in connection with the booming of Rock Island stock, engineered, according to Mr. Untermyer, by Daniel G. Reid and ex-Judge Moore. Mr. Untermyer denounced the Sulzer Stock Exchange legislation as a "blind and a fraud."

"Manipulation of the objectionable kind is going on every day, despite the measures to which I have referred (the Sulzer bills)," said Mr. Untermyer. "A striking illustration has been afforded through disclosures made in connection with a recent attempt to boost Rock Island stock. On March 29 the shares sold on the Stock Exchange at $18. On that day Reid and Moore decided to put the road in the hands of a receiver. The receivership papers were actually prepared, but were not filed until April 20. Between those dates, with these papers in existence the stock was run up from $18 to $39. In this period 1,000,000 shares were dealt in. On April 20, the day the receiver was appointed, 240,000 shares were sold, mostly at the high figure.

Colossal Swindle, Untermyer Says.

"It was one of the most colossal, one of the most transparent swindles ever perpetrated on the public and it was perpetrated by a company that had done the same thing over and over again. The public is being swindled day by day, hour by hour, by just that kind of methods and there is no way of holding anybody responsible. And yet, you protest against gambling, bookmaking, and lottery selling and put prohibitions in the Constitution against such practices and propose to let this sort of thing go on."

Mr. Milburn held that the Legislature was empowered as the Constitution stood at present to protect the public against dishonest or unfair practices on the Stock Exchange and there was no need of writing into the Constitution any provision for the incorporation of the Stock Exchange or for a closer supervision of stock market practices.

"How about the Rock Island?" asked Mr. Untermyer.

"Ah, that's it," said Mr. Milburn. "Mr. Untermyer happens to be allied with one of the fighting parties in the Rock Island. You have listened to a statement from one of the counsel in this Rock Island imbroglio."

"But if what Mr. Untermyer said is true, green-goods swindlers and wire tappers are saints compared with the gentlemen on the Stock Exchange," suggested Peter Donovan of the Bronx, a Democratic member of the committee. "The report of the Hughes Committee in this State which investigated the Stock Exchange and its practices and of the Pujo Committee, which made its report to Congress, seem to bear out the claim made by Mr. Untermyer that the Stock Exchange should be incorporated and subjected to closer control."

"The Pujo Committee," exclaimed Mr. Milburn, "was a most remarkable body. My friend Untermyer was not merely counsel for the committee—he was its king. Mr. Untermyer ran that committee to suit himself, and he produced what witnesses he desired to produce and no other."

"I produced all the officers of your Stock Exchange," interrupted Mr. Untermyer. Mr. Milburn ignored this and assailed the report of the committee.

"When the report was handed in," he continued, "we found that the committee had arrogated to itself rather an extraordinary degree of license in dealing with facts. The hand from which the report came was the hand of the Pujo Committee, but the voice was the voice of Samuel."

"It was signed by all the members," said Mr. Untermyer. "Why do you find fault with the report for calling a spade a spade?"

"That committee would have signed anything you wrote," Mr. Milburn rejoined, "and if all the things that you called spades had been spades it would have been all right, but there were so many things you called spades which were not spades at all."

Urges Exchange Regulation.

In beginning his argument Mr. Untermyer said that all the committees that had investigated the question had reached the conclusion that there was need of Government regulation of the Stock Exchange and similar bodies. It was also evident, Mr. Untermyer said, "that it should be done through the Constitution."

"There is no use of our blinking the fact," Mr. Untermyer continued. "There are institutions in our State which have attained such astounding power and influence that they cannot be reached by the Legislature. The Stock Exchange, through the men behind it, is one of these. It is run as a private club above and beyond the law."

The lawless spirit of the Stock Exchange was illustrated, Mr. Untermyer asserted, by the fact that a member convicted before the Board of Governors of fraudulent dealings was suspended for thirty to sixty days. A member convicted of splitting commissions was suspended for four to six years. Another illustration of "that lawless spirit," Mr. Untermyer said, was afforded when the New York Stock Ex-

Continued on Page 4.

LANSING NOW HEADS WILSON'S CABINET

President Appoints the Former Counselor Secretary of State to Succeed Bryan.

GIVES UP HIS OLD POST

Cone Johnson or Chandler Anderson May Be Promoted to Counselorship in Department.

Special to The New York Times.

WASHINGTON, June 23.—Announcement was made at the White House this evening that Robert Lansing of Watertown, N. Y., had been appointed Secretary of State. The announcement was contained in this statement:

> The President before leaving this evening for a brief rest in New Hampshire announced that he had offered the post of Secretary of State to Robert Lansing, the present counselor of the Department of State, and that Mr. Lansing had accepted the appointment.

Mr. Bryan's resignation was tendered formally to President Wilson on June 8, and took effect on the following day, just two weeks ago. Since then Mr. Lansing has exercised the duties of Secretary of State ad interim, under the designation of the President. With his new appointment he will vacate the post of counselor of the State Department. Who will be chosen for this place, which has become of great importance, has not been disclosed.

Cone Johnson of Texas, the present Solicitor of the State Department, and Chandler Anderson of the District of Columbia, who has been helping Mr. Lansing in determining the course of the Government in the delicate questions that have arisen on account of the war in Europe, are mentioned in connection with filling the vacancy. Mr. Johnson is a personal friend of ex-Secretary Bryan, and was Mr. Bryan's personal selection for the Solicitorship. Mr. Anderson has been counselor of the department, and has made a reputation as an authority on international law.

The appointment of Mr. Lansing to the Cabinet was no surprise. From the day that Mr. Bryan resigned he had been regarded as having the best chance of all those mentioned for the portfolio.

Mr. Lansing had come to be looked upon not only as an authority in matters affecting the laws and practices of nations, but had shown himself to be a man of courage and initiative. The President and the members of the Cabinet have formed a high opinion of his abilities.

The President is understood to have abandoned early in his consideration of the problem of choosing a Secretary of State the suggestion that the office should go to a man of great prominence in the Democratic Party. This course, it was pointed out, would be in accordance with practice. While the names of Richard Olney of Massachusetts, who was Secretary of State in the second Administration of President Cleveland, and John Bassett Moore of New York, who was Counselor of the State Department for the first year of the Wilson Administration, were brought forward it was apparent very soon after the retirement of Mr. Bryan that Mr. Wilson would confine his selection to some man connected with the Government.

The choice narrowed down to Mr. Lansing, Lindley M. Garrison, the Secretary of War, and Franklin K. Lane, the Secretary of the Interior.

The only objection to the appointment of either Mr. Garrison or Mr. Lane was that each had done so well in his own executive department that it would be a mistake to transfer him. An army officer expressed the high opinion held for Mr. Garrison's abilities when he said that it would cause a riot in the army if there was a change in the office of Secretary of War. The President's great admiration for the ability and judgment of Mr. Lane was no secret in official circles, and it was generally understood that he regarded the Secretary of the Interior as measuring up to the requirements of a Secretary of State.

It was understood early today that the President would announce the appointment of a Secretary of State before he started for New Hampshire on a midnight train, and no doubt was felt that Mr. Lansing was his selection. Mr. Lansing was with the President for a considerable time today, and it was said afterward that they had gone over a number of matters connected with the business of the State Department. When Mr. Lansing left the Executive Office Building after his interview with the President several persons there offered their congratulations, but he smilingly declined to receive them. Tonight after the formal announcement from the White House Mr. Lansing went out to dinner.

In the two weeks that President Wilson will be away from Washington Secretary Lansing will be the senior officer of the Government on duty here. It will be mainly through him that matters of great importance will be communicated to the President at Cornish.

The promotion of subordinate officers of the State Department to the office of Secretary of State is unusual, but not unprecedented. Robert Bacon of New York was appointed Secretary of State to succeed Elihu Root when Mr. Bacon was holding the post of Assistant Secretary in the State Department, but that was at the very close of the Roosevelt Administration. He served only thirty-six days. William R. Day of Ohio, now an Associate Justice of the United States Supreme Court, was Assistant Secretary of State when he was appointed Secretary of State in April, 1898, at the beginning of the Spanish War, to succeed John Sherman of Ohio. He served until the following September. John Hay of Ohio was Assistant Secretary of State, but retired from the office more than seventeen years before he was appointed Secretary of State by President McKinley. According to the official register of the Department of State these are the only cases of the promotion of an Assistant Secretary or other State Department official to the post of Secretary of State.

WARNING IN THE COMMONS

Labor Leaders Called On to Make Their Promises Good.

COMPULSION IF THEY FAIL

Strikes and Lockouts Barred by Munitions Bill, Which Passes First Reading in Commons.

THOMAS'S MISSION HERE

Welsh "Coal King" Not to Supersede the Morgan Firm, but to Co-operate with It.

LONDON, June 23.—David Lloyd George, the Minister of Munitions, has given British labor seven days in which to make good the promise of its leaders that men will rally to the factories in sufficient numbers to produce a maximum supply of munitions of war.

This was the most striking statement in the new Minister's speech in the House of Commons today in the course of outlying the munitions measure, which is designed to control not only the output, but the men responsible for it.

The first of the seven allotted days will begin tomorrow, and with its dawning will be launched a great campaign to recruit the workers.

Adequate Supply or Conscription.

"I had a fresh discussion with the trade union leaders," said Mr. Lloyd George in his speech, "and told them if an adequate supply of labor could not be secured compulsion was 'nevitable. The union representatives answered: 'Give us a chance to supply the men needed in seven days. If we cannot get them we will admit that our case is considerably weakened.'

"The seven days will begin tomorrow," continued Lloyd George, "and advertisements will appear in all the papers The Union representatives have engaged 180 town halls as recruiting offices, and the assistance of every one has been invited."

There will be no age limit for the men enrolled. They will not wear uniforms, but will have to give their full time to the work, and they will receive a certificate attesting that they are working for King and country.

The Munitions bill makes strikes and lockouts illegal, provides for compulsory arbitration, limits the profits of employers, creates a voluntary army of workmen pledged to go wherever they are wanted, and contains other provisions which will give the Minister full powers to carry out the plans he has devised to develop the production of munitions.

David Thomas's Mission.

After emphasizing the absolute necessity of vast supplies of guns and ammunition, which he described as the great essential of victory, the Minister announced that he had sent David Thomas, managing director of great colliery companies in South Wales, and known as the "British Coal King," to represent the munitions department in the United States and Canada. Respecting this appointment the Minister said:

"In consequence of the great importance of the American and Canadian markets and the numerous offers to provide munitions, it is very desirable that we have some one over there. Accordingly, we have sent a very able business man, Mr. D. A. Thomas, who will be given the * * * fullest responsibilities for the discharge of his important duties There is not the slightest idea of superseding our existing agencies. They have worked admirably, and have saved us many millions. Mr. Thomas will co-operate with the Messrs. Morgan with a view to expediting supplies."

Independent of Kitchener.

The Minister, in winding up the debate on the bill, said he would hold himself responsible for the supply of ammunition at the front and would make himself thoroughly acquainted with what was going on there.

This was in answer to Sir Arthur Markham, Liberal, who said that if Mr. Lloyd George was not going to be independent of the War Office, by which he meant Lord Kitchener, his scheme was foredoomed to failure.

Mr. Lloyd George, continuing, said he was sure that Lord Kitchener would agree that the Minister of Munitions should have a free hand. He hoped that the bill would be printed by Friday, when the members could read it, and they would see that it satisfactorily disposed of most of the criticisms.

The bill passed its first reading. It will receive its second reading Monday.

Assails German "Trickery."

Speaking of German preparation, the Minister said:—

"Germany has been piling up material. Until she was ready she was friendly with everybody. During the Balkan crisis none could have been more modest or unpretentious. She had a

Continued on Page 2.

British Cruiser Roxburgh Is Torpedoed But Suffers Little Damage and Reaches Port

LONDON, June 23.—An official communication issued by the Admiralty tonight says:

> The British cruiser Roxburgh was struck by a torpedo in the North Sea Sunday last. The damage sustained was not serious and the cruiser was able to proceed under her own steam. There were na casualties.

The Roxburgh is a vessel of 10,850 tons, and is 450 feet long. Her complement in peace times was 665 men. The cruiser was built in 1904, and has a speed of about 21 knots.

The last preceding attack of German war vessels on British war vessels in the North Sea was on May 8, when the British destroyer Maori was sunk off Zeebrugge. The Maori struck a mine, and the British torpedo boat destroyer Crusader went to rescue her crew, but was driven off by the German shore batteries. German destroyers later captured the boats of the Maori and the Crusader, containing seven officers and eighty-eight men.

In the early months of the war the North Sea was the field of operation of German submarines. Here, on Sept. 22, 1914, the submarine U-9 sank the British armored cruisers the Hogue, the Cressy, and the Aboukir, and on Oct. 15 the old armored cruiser Hawke. The gunboat Niger was torpedoed by a German submarine on Nov. 11 and the auxiliary cruiser Bayana on March 11.

FRENCH CHARGE ROUTS THE TURKS

Strong Attack by the Allies Wins a Commanding Point at the Dardanelles.

STRUGGLE IS DESPERATE

Moslems Are Reported to Have Suffered Heavy Losses in Their Retreat.

PARIS, June 23.—This official report on operations in the Dardanelles was issued by the War Office tonight:

> The expeditionary corps in the Orient yesterday attacked the Turkish lines on two-thirds of the front. After an artillery preparation the infantry sallied from the trenches with superb spirit. Our left, in a single bound, carried two lines of the enemy's trenches and these they held, notwithstanding violent and numerous counter-attacks.
>
> To the right, on more difficult ground, the struggle continued throughout the day on the ruins of the Turkish works, which had been razed by the artillery. The enemy, bringing up fresh troops, without cessation, had succeeded in retaking these intrenchments when a battalion of the Foreign Legion and a battalion of Zouaves, in a bayonet assault, carried the position in 10 minutes. This brilliant charge decided the issue and finished for the day the efforts of the Turks to regain the ground lost.
>
> In a counter-offensive on our right this morning the enemy was cut to pieces without having achieved any gain.
>
> Summing up, the day ended with success along the whole line, despite the desperate nature of the struggle. We took some prisoners, among whom were several officers.
>
> The battleship St. Louis has effectively bombarded the batteries on the Asiatic side.
>
> At our left the British army gave us efficacious support. Everything goes to confirm that the enemy's losses were very heavy.
>
> The important point is that we have occupied the ground, which commands the head of the ravine of Kereves Dere, which the Turks had defended with the utmost determination for several months, using all their resources to hold it.

CABINET OFFICERS HOLD SECRET MEETING

Deep Mystery Surrounds Conference in Lansing's Office—Hints of Neutrality Move.

Special to The New York Times.

WASHINGTON, June 23.—A mysterious conference which gave rise to much speculation, and is believed to involve some matter of importance in connection with the maintenance of American neutrality, was held at the State Department late this afternoon. Those participating in the conference were Secretary Lansing, Josephus Daniels, Secretary of the Navy; William C. Redfield, Secretary of Commerce, and Eugene T. Chamberlain, Commissioner of Navigation.

Secretary Lansing would not disclose the nature of the conference. The others who participated refused point blank to indicate its nature or to divulge the slightest detail.

The most persistent belief here tonight was that the conference had some bearing on the relation of the use of radio stations to the question of American neutrality. This assumption is based on the fact that the Navy Department, which was represented in the conference by Secretary Daniels, had charge of the censorship over radiograms and the fact that the Bureau of Navigation is the particular branch of the Government which enforces laws regarding radio communication.

Another interesting bit of speculation was that the conference may have related to the enforcement of the passenger act and other Federal laws relative to the shipment of ammunition or explosives in steamers bound for Europe. But it was pointed out that it was hardly likely that the navy would have any function to exercise in that connection unless it should be necessary to halt steamers trying to violate the statutes.

Whatever the basis for the conference, the extreme reticence of those participating in it led to the belief that it was a matter of deep importance.

WESTERN FIGHTING FAVORS GERMANS

Take a Hill in Alsace and Also Trenches on the Meuse Heights.

FRENCH WIN VOSGES TOWN

And Tell of Further Progress Against German Lines [illegible].

LONDON, June 23.—In the relatively unimportant engagements on the western front today—chiefly infantry attacks and counter-attacks—the Germans appear to have a slight advantage.

The most violent fighting was on the heights of the Meuse, centring upon the Calonne trench, where the French at first lost their gains of yesterday and later in the day partly retrieved their losses. They took two trenches near Leintrey, in Lorraine, but yesterday lost a hill in the Ban-de-Sapt region of the Vosges, of which they recaptured a part.

Germany has again bombarded Dunkirk at long range.

The following official communication was issued by the War Office in Paris tonight:

> In the region to the north of Arras nothing was reported today except several infantry actions. To the north of Souchez we made slight progress and repulsed a German counter-attack. The cannonade has not ceased in the sector between Angres and Ecurie.
>
> Near Berry-au-Bac, at Hill 108, we exploded a mine which caused an excavation measuring thirty-five meters in diameter and very seriously damaged the German trenches.
>
> In Champagne, on the Perthes-Beauséjour front, an action by means of mines occurred, with a violent cannonade.
>
> On the heights of the Meuse, at the Calonne trench, the enemy this morning delivered a violent counter-attack which enabled him to retake his former second line. In the course of the afternoon a new German attack was started. It was immediately checked. Taking, in our turn, the offensive, we regained a foothold in the second line of the enemy.
>
> In the outskirts of Le Prêtre Forest the enemy bombarded in a particularly intense fashion our positions in the "Quart-en-Réserve."
>
> In Lorraine we have occupied two works near Leintrey. We took some prisoners, among them three officers.
>
> In the Vosges storms and a thick fog prevailed.

Following is the French official afternoon report:

> In the region to the north of Arras bombardments have been continued on both sides, and lasted throughout the entire night. The Germans furthermore endeavored to deliver new counter-attacks, one near the Neuville cemetery, and the other in the direction of the Labyrinth. Each was completely repulsed.
>
> To the west of the Argonne, not far from the road running from Binarville to Vienne-le-Château, the fighting is going on in the German trenches, hand grenades being used. On the remainder of the front in the Argonne the Germans have expended a vast amount of ammunition, but without delivering any infantry attack.
>
> On the heights of the Meuse, at Calonne, we yesterday evening reconquered a further section of the second German line.
>
> In Lorraine yesterday saw fresh counter-attacks against the positions which we have taken near Leintrey. They were repulsed, and we retained all our gains, at the same time making some prisoners.
>
> In the Vosges, at Fontenelle, in the region of Ban-de-Sapt, the enemy yesterday evening, after having thrown nearly 4,000 shells in a few hours against one of our works, advanced along a front of 200 yards and succeeded in gaining a footing. At the same time an attack upon neighboring trenches was delivered. This German offensive was immediately checked by a French counter-attack led with great brilliancy. We captured almost all the lost ground. The enemy was successful in maintaining his position only at the extremity of our work. We took 142 prisoners, including three officers.
>
> In the region of the Fecht River we have occupied Sondernach, and we have pushed our lines along the slopes to the east of this village.

Berlin makes this report of the day's operations:

> We subjected the fortress of Dunkirk and the troop concentration camps of the enemy near the villages of Bergues, Hondschoote, Furnes, and Cassel to our fire. From Givenchy,

Continued on Page 3.

GERMAN WEDGE DRIVEN FAR

Berlin Believes That the Russian Forces Are Split in Twain.

LEMBERG ARMY OUT INTACT

Retreats on New Front with Artillery and Stores—Losses in Prisoners Few.

KAISERS TO MEET IN CAPITAL

Victory Causes Jubilation in Germany and Austria—Russian People Roused.

LONDON, Thursday, June 24.—The Russians have lost Lemberg. They occupied the Galician capital on Sept. 3 last, only six weeks after Austria had declared war against Serbia, and had held it continuously until Tuesday, when the combined Austro-German forces compelled them to retreat from the city, which is only sixty odd miles due west from the nearest point of the Russian frontier.

Whether the fall of Lemberg means that the Russian army operating south of it in Southeast Galicia is effectively cut off from the army to the north, stretching across Poland to the Baltic, cannot yet be said. The newspapers of both Vienna and Berlin say this is the case and that the Russian arms have received a blow from which they cannot recover.

If the stroke proves as crushing as the Teutons predict, its effect, military observers here say, soon should be felt in the transfer of vast German forces to the West, where for days they have been hard pressed by the French.

Up to midnight last night Petrograd had not conceded the fall of Lemberg. Previous dispatches from the Russian capital, however, related details of what purported to be the systematic withdrawal of the Russians from the town, and if these details prove correct it is believed in military circles here that when the count is taken of the Austro-German booty it will be not large, for, as was the case at Przemysl, the Russians are said to have worked hard to move everything of military value.

Foes Admire Russians' Retreat.

Telegrams received from Vienna concerning the capture of Lemberg and recounting the celebration of the populace in Vienna over the victory add that the Austrian correspondents with the Teutonic armies pay tribute to the magnificent rear guard action fought by the Russians, who are declared to have retreated in good order, leaving behind few prisoners and even removing the Russian documents from the city, which, since the Russians occupied it, has been called by them Lvov.

One telegram from Vienna says that Emperor William and Emperor Francis Joseph purpose to meet soon in the recaptured Galician capital for "fitting ceremonies to mark the end of Russia's dominance in Galicia."

The news of the fall of Lemberg was known on the Continent on Tuesday, but it did not reach London until late yesterday afternoon, when bulletins arrived almost simultaneously by wireless from Berlin and Vienna by way of Amsterdam. The British press had been expecting such a development and there was no more than passing comment on it, though it drove home, according to military observers, the fact how ample must have been the Austro-German ammunition supply to accomplish the feat.

Berlin and Vienna are reported to be filled with joy over the victory of their forces. Archduke Frederick of Austria, Commander in Chief of the Austrian forces, and General August von Mackensen of the German Army both have been made Field Marshals of the Prussian Army in recognition of their services in the Galician campaign.

On the River Dniester, south of Lemberg, the battle is still raging.

Emperor Nicholas left Petrograd for the front yesterday, according to Reuter's Petrograd correspondent.

Austrian Version of Victory.

The following official version of the operations around Lemberg was issued yesterday by the Vienna War Office:

> The northwest and west fronts of Lemberg, on the line of Zolkiew to Mikolaiow, were strongly occupied by Russian defensive forces. Tuesday at 5 o'clock in the forenoon the Vienna Landwehr stormed the Rzesna works, on the road from Janow to Lemberg, from the northwest. At the same time our troops advanced across the heights east of the Mlynewka Rivulet and stormed several bulwarks before Lysa Gora Heights.
>
> During the forenoon, while advancing further in the direction of the town, the remaining works, northwest and west of the fronts, were captured after sanguinary fighting. In this fighting the Russian front again was broken, and the enemy, who suffered heavy losses, again was forced to retreat.
>
> Our troops, pursuing the enemy across the heights east and northeast of the town, crossed south of the Lemberg road to Mikolaiow.
>
> Amid demonstrations of joy by the population General von Boehm-Ermolli entered the town of Lemberg at 4 o'clock in the afternoon with the troops of the Second Army.
>
> Near Zolkiew and Rawa Ruska the Russians are retreating. Isolated Russian attacks on the Tanew River have been repulsed.
>
> Last night the enemy began a further retreat between the [illegible] Rivers and in [illegible]

Mid-Week Pictorial

Russian Infantry and Cavalry in full retreat.

"All the News That's Fit to Print."

The New York Times.

THE WEATHER
Fair today, partly cloudy tomorrow; moderate west to northwest winds, becoming variable.
For full weather report see Page 17.

VOL. LXIV...NO. 21,027. NEW YORK, FRIDAY, AUGUST 20, 1915.—TWENTY PAGES. ONE CENT In Greater New York, Jersey City and Newark. | Elsewhere TWO CENTS.

WHITE STAR LINER ARABIC, TORPEDOED WITHOUT WARNING WITH 26 AMERICANS ABOARD, SINKS IN ELEVEN MINUTES; 391 SAVED, SOME INJURED; TWO AMERICANS AMONG 32 MISSING

SHOCKS PRESIDENT WILSON

Arabic Disaster Gravely Viewed in All Circles at Washington.

IS IT BERLIN'S ANSWER?

Attack Regarded in Some Quarters as "Deliberately Unfriendly" Reply to America.

LANSING AWAITS THE FACTS

Administration Guardedly Silent —Hints of a Diplomatic Break with Germany.

Special to The New York Times.

WASHINGTON, Aug. 19.—The State Department received a cable dispatch late tonight from Lewis C. Thompson, Vice and Deputy Consul of the United States at Queenstown, in which he said that survivors of the Arabic said the ship was torpedoed without warning and sank in eleven minutes. Mr. Thompson said that no authentic information had been obtained at the time his dispatch was sent "as to whether any or how many were lost." He gave a list of sixteen American survivors.

The statement in the Vice Consul's message that survivors declared that the Arabic was sunk without warning lent the gravest aspect to the incident because of the effect it may have on relations between Germany and the United States.

The question in the minds of Government officials tonight is: Was the sinking of the Arabic Germany's answer to the last American note concerning the Lusitania? If it was, this Government faces another crisis in its dealings with Germany. But officials were not willing to say tonight whether in the attack the German Government proceeded on the principle that actions speak louder than words and wished it to be understood that the German submarine warfare against unarmed merchant vessels was to continue without observance of the requirement upon which President Wilson has insisted —that passengers and crew shall have ample time to escape to places of safety before the vessel is torpedoed.

First News from Consul.

Vice Consul Thompson had sent a message earlier in the day informing the State Department that the Arabic had been sunk sixty miles from Queenstown and that survivors were being brought to that place. He gave no details, however, and department officials waited anxiously for a full report. After the receipt of Mr. Thompson's second message, in which he said that survivors declared that the Arabic was sunk without warning, the views of responsible officials as to the possible consequences of the act of the German submarine could not be obtained.

On the basis of the Vice Consul's first message high officers of the Administration declined to comment on the Arabic incident. "Nothing to say," was all that came from Secretary Lansing's office.

The White House was silent, but President Wilson's concern was indicated by the fact that he canceled an engagement to play golf and called Secretary Lansing on the telephone to ascertain what information the State Department had with regard to the sinking of the White Star liner.

Awaits All the Facts.

The position of the Administration is that no determination as to the course it will take can be reached until full reports of the circumstances attending the loss of the Arabic have been received. It was realized immediately after the first news of the sinking reached here that the affair might bring to a head the already strained relations between Germany and the United States and for that reason officials became extra cautious in answering questions on the subject.

If all the American passengers on the Arabic escaped with their lives, it does not change the application of the principles which this Government has laid down with reference to Germany's submarine warfare. The fact that the lives of American citizens were endangered through the German submarine's refusal to observe the well-established rule that non-combatants on merchant vessels must have an opportunity to reach places

Continued on Page 2.

President Wilson's Warning to Germany

"The very value which this Government sets upon the long and unbroken friendship between the people and Government of the United States and the people and Government of the German nation impels it to press very solemnly upon the Imperial German Government the necessity for a scrupulous observance of neutral rights in this critical matter. Friendship itself prompts it to say to the Imperial Government that repetition by the commanders of German naval vessels of acts in contravention of those rights must be regarded by the Government of the United States, when they affect American citizens, as deliberately unfriendly."—*From the American note to Germany, sent on July 21.*

LONDON PRESS ASKS WHAT WE WILL DO

Fate of Americans the First Inquiry When News of Arabic Disaster Reaches England.

Special Cable to THE NEW YORK TIMES.

LONDON, Aug. 19.—The news of the torpedoing of the steamer Arabic reached London between 5 and 6 o'clock this evening and created a sensation only secondary to the sinking of the Lusitania. The first point upon which attention centred was whether there were American passengers aboard.

At the offices of the White Star Line it was definitely announced that there were twenty-two Americans on the passenger list. It was added that there were possibly more, but this could not be stated definitely, as it is a rule of the company that booking clerks shall not press clients to give their American addresses. Consequently it occasionally happens that American passengers are simply entered on the books as registered at a London hotel.

The next point of inquiry was whether any American passengers had lost their lives. The White Star officials expressed their belief that late news would show that all the passengers had been saved, and pending definite information on the point declined to give any particulars as to the identity of the passengers on the ground that possibly unnecessary anxiety would be caused their relatives and friends.

Look for a Crisis.

Further information which the evening brought forth tended to confirm the belief that no American lives had been lost. This had the effect of removing the early idea that the sinking of the Arabic might set America aflame and precipitate an immediate breach in German-American relations. None the less, it is believed here that the incident is bound to bring about new developments in the already strained situation. President Wilson's second note to Germany is quoted as a clear indication that the United States cannot tolerate the torpedoing of a passenger ship carrying Americans in circumstances under which the Arabic was sunk. The principles laid down by the President that "the high seas are free and that the character and cargo of a merchantman must first be ascertained before she can be lawfully seized or destroyed, and that the lives of non-combatants may in no case be put in jeopardy unless the vessel resists or seeks to escape after she has been summoned to submit to examination," are held here on the information so far available, to have been clearly violated in the case of the Arabic.

Await Our Answer.

Comments in the London papers show special interest as to what the United States will do about the attack.

The Daily Chronicle says:

"We await with interest the action which the American Government will take in the face of this new challenge to peaceful seaborne traffic."

The Daily News says: "It is a definite challenge to neutrals, and it does not stand alone. The seizing of the Norwegian mails, which aroused great and natural indignation in Norway, is merely another illustration on a smaller scale of the entirely unlimited rights which Germany is arrogating to herself over all neutral commerce.

"The defense put forward is, as in the case of Belgium, simply Germany's necessities. As in the case of Belgium, it is an entirely false defense, even on its very slender merits. It is now certain that the defense of Germany in no sense required the invasion of Belgium, and it is equally certain that the balance of sea power against her is in no degree redressed by her submarine outrages.

"But the doctrine itself is one which, if pushed to its practical conclusions, the neutral world cannot afford to tolerate. No State has the right to set its own convenience above the elementary rights of all the rest of the world. The theory may provoke nothing but protests, but if an attempt is made to enforce it, and to enforce it as Germany is doing, with a total disregard to human life and human feelings, the ultimate result can only be to proclaim

Continued on Page 3.

THE TORPEDOED WHITE STAR LINER ARABIC.
X shows where the torpedo struck, which sent her to the bottom in eleven minutes.

Two Americans Unaccounted For on Lists of the Arabic's Saved

Mrs. Josephine L. Bruguiere of New York and Edmund Woods Were First Reported Rescued, But Revision of List Puts Their Safety in Doubt.

A revised list of survivors, compiled from cable reports received from Liverpool early this morning, indicated that Mrs. Josephine Bruguière of New York and Edmund Woods were still unaccounted for among the American passengers. They were mentioned as having been saved in previous reports.

At 3 o'clock this morning the agents of the White Star Line said that, including the third-cabin list, 161 passengers of the Arabic had been accounted for, leaving twenty of the listed passengers still missing to complete the total of 181, as sent from Liverpool.

Besides Mrs. Bruguière and Woods, they said they had received no confirmation that James Houlihan, cabin, and Thomas Elmore, steerage, had been rescued, as stated in advices to Washington. The others were six cabin and ten third-class passengers.

The foreigners now missing, according to the lists received here, are as follows:

CABIN.

MARY ENGLISH.
PATRICK FITZGERALD.
ELLEN MILIA.
L. L. MEILLIER.
Miss MARIE MILLS.
Mrs. W. G. RANDALL.
Mrs. TATTERSALL.
Miss Irene TATTERSALL.
WILLIAM BULLIHANT.
Mrs. JOHN H. NEAVE.

THIRD CLASS.

Mrs. L. HERMANS.
MARY HARRINGTON.
THOMAS McMAHON.
MARY RADINGTON.
CORNELIUS SULLIVAN.
FLORENCE THOMAS.

The names of rescued Americans contained in these lists were as follows:

AMERICANS.
CABIN.

Mr. and Mrs. FRED BURGESS.
Master BRUGUIERE.
Mr. and Mrs. JAMES CALMON.
Mr. and Mrs. P. W. A. COLLINS.
Mr. and Mrs. DELLAH COVINGTON.
JOHN F. A. DAY.
The Rev. Dr. E. A. McALLISTER.
CHRISTOPHER McTAMMEY.
LEOPOLD P. MOORE.
A. HULME NEBEKER.
JOHN DOLAN.
CLAUDE ROODE.
JAMES M. ROWLEY.
W. E. RAMSDELL.
Miss F. E. SHRIMPTON.

Reports from Washington state that Vice Consul Thompson has cabled of the safety of these other Americans:

CABIN.

JAMES H. OULIHAN.

THIRD CLASS.

JOHN OLSEN.
THOMAS ELMORE.

Private cables from Liverpool reported the safety of the following:

THIRD CLASS.

WILLIAM HUGHES.
J. KELLETT.

It is possible that some Americans boarded the liner as she was about to sail and were carried in the list given out by the White Star Line as of other nationalities.

OTHER NATIONALITIES.

The first list as given out here by the White Star Line accounted for the following passengers of other nationalities:

CABIN PASSENGERS.

Mrs. FLORENCE C. ALLISON.
JAMES BARNES.
ROBERT BOND.
Mr. and Mrs. JAMES CLAMON.
Miss ETHEL M. CHADWICK.
Miss CATHERINE CHRISTIE.
ISAAC CORRAK, Jr.
Miss BRIDGET CUFFE.
WILLIAM CUMMINS.
Mrs. MARIE DALTON.
JOHN DEIGHTON.
Miss ROY DUNCAN.
Miss EVELYN EATON.
Mrs. RUTH GODDARD.
AUBREY GUALTER.
A. P. HILLER.
ALBERT INGAM.
Mrs. JOHN B. KELK.
Master JOHN W. KELK.
Misses DOROTHY, VIOLET and OLIVE KELK.
CHARLES KFESSER.
Miss ISABELLA G. LOHR.
FREDERICK LARKIN.
SAM MEADOWCROFT.
Miss BRIDGET MILLS.
Major G. L. MONEY.
CYRIL MONEY.
Misses MABEL and EDITH MONEY.
JOHN H. NEAVE.
Miss TERESA O'FARRELL.
JOHN OLSCHEWSKI.
Miss BESSIE PORTER.
C. W. PRINGLE.
W. J. RANDALL.
Miss E. M. RANDALL.
JOE ROBINSON.
Miss S. D. ROSSALL.
Mrs. E. SMITH.
JOHN STEWART.
ALFRED STILL.
Miss GLADYS TATTERSALL.
FRANK TATTERSALL.
Miss BERTHA TATTERSALL.
Rev. AUGUSTINE WALDNER.

Later another list of cabin passengers saved was issued as follows:

R. A. BURNS.
Miss G. A. CARNE.
STELLA CAROL and HUSBAND.
Miss M. CHRISTOPHERSEN.
JOHN CRITCHLEY.
S COX.
A. J. CORLSON.
Miss L. G. DAY.
C. J. DENNEHY.
K. DOUGLAS.
Miss E. DUNLOP.
Mrs. DAVEY.
Mrs. M. E. EATON.
Miss MARY FEENEY.
Mr. and Mrs. W. NEGUS.
J. PEARSON.
Mrs. A. E. PHILLIPS.
Master W. D. PHILLIPS.
Master S. M. PHILLIPS.
Miss G. PHILLIPS.
Miss A. M. PHILLIPS.
Miss R. PHILLIPS.

Among the survivors of the crew, it was stated, were the Captain, all the deck officers, all the engineers, except London, the doctor; the Purser, assistant Purser, Chief Steward, Second Steward, Chief Third Class Steward, and Chief Stoker.

Cable advices late at night from London gave the name of John F. A. Day as among the American survivors of the Arabic.

A third list gave these additional names of rescued:

A. E. PHILIP.
F. PRYCE.
C. E. ROSS.
Miss M. ROSS.
Mrs. and Miss TEWKSBURY.
J. USHER.
Mrs. A. M. F. VAN SCHELLE.
Mrs. BEATRICE WHITE.
W. L. ADAMS.
Miss V. H. ALDERSON.
W. BATHURST.
J. C. BOLAND.
Miss M. E. BOLAND.
Miss M. M. BOUDET.
M. BRADLEY.

A fourth list of the survivors of other nationalities was as follows:

Miss A. HYDE.
HARVEY JUDD.
Miss IVY JUDD.
A. LAWADSKY.
G. W. LYONS.
DENNIS McCULL.
A. M. MORTON.
Mrs. J. GILLANDER.
Master W. N. GILLANDER.
Mrs M. GREAVES.
Miss MARGARET GREAVES.
Miss M. HARRISON.
Mrs. S. HILL and infant.
Mrs. M. C. PRESCOTT-HELLER.
JOSEPH DE LORIMER.
Mrs. GABRIEL CANTOR.
W. MASON.

Survivors of Third Class.

The following list of steerage survivors was given out:

KATE CONNORS.
ANNE MOONEY.
SARAH E. SALT.
FRANK SALT.
MONA SALT.
FLORENCE SALT.
LIZZIE MAHONEY.
MARY HAYES.
ROSE WEBER.
KATE FALVEY.
DELIA QUINN.
JOHN MORRISSEY.
JOHN KENNEDY.
MARTIN FLANAGAN.
ELIZABETH WILLOUGHBY.
JOHN SULLIVAN.
JOHN KESSEN.
FRANCIS CARRAGHER.
HUGH HANLEY.
MARTIN LOGAN.
MARTIN LOFTUS.
REUBEN LISS.
WILLIAM DUCKERS.
EUGENE KILDUFF.
DENIS FALVEY.
THOMAS HAYES.
GEORGE LYONS.
JOSEPH WALDRON.
JAMES MANNION.
NAT MOORE.
Mrs. LOUISA FARMER.
Mrs. FRANCES REA.
Miss VALDERSON.
Miss AMY JONES.
MARGUERITE MULQUEEN.
JOHN DIGHTON.
Mrs. KELLETT.
DOMINICK MORRIE.
JOHN TUMULTY.
CHARLES HOWE.
JOHN DOHERTY.
PETER PUGAL.
JAMES WALDRON.
TIMOTHY HAYES.
JENNIE MANGAN.

Survivors in Pitiable Plight; Women in Boats in Night Clothes

Many in Their Berths When Torpedo Struck the Ship—All Owe Their Lives to Gallantry of Arabic's Crew.

QUEENSTOWN, Friday, Aug. 20.—The landing here yesterday evening of the survivors of the White Star Line steamer Arabic was a striking scene. All of them were scantily clothed, and none of them had hat or head covering of any kind.

A large number of the survivors were suffering from injuries to their heads and other wounds or from shock, and the effects of being forced to take to open boats scantily clothed.

Many of the women were in their berths when the liner was torpedoed and ran to the deck in their night clothing. These were provided with blankets when they were taken from boats and rafts by the crews of the rescue ships. A number of those saved were picked out of the water and arrived here in their sea-soaked clothing. The people of Queenstown gave them every possible attention and provided fresh outfits for many of them. There were some pathetic scenes of grief over the loss of the members of some of the families on board the liner.

A. Hulme Nebeker of Logan, Utah, who when he arrived here had on only a bathrobe, said that the crew worked splendidly under Captain Finch's direction in the short ten minutes which they had to get the passengers into the boats, and but for the discipline maintained and the excellent work of the rescuing tug officers at least 200 persons would have been lost. The submarine, according to Mr. Nebeker, was seen before it launched the torpedo, but there was not time enough to escape it.

The American Vice Consul here assisted the local authorities in aiding the survivors.

Captain Finch, who is suffering from injuries to his leg, said last night that he did not see the submarine, but distinctly observed the torpedo approaching the ship.

"It was then impossible to escape it," the Captain said. "We had only eight minutes to get the boats away and save all on board."

George L. Money of Stratford, Ontario, who, with his daughter and brother, was returning home on the Arabic, said the passengers in large numbers were enjoying the beautiful weather about decks after breakfast. Their attention had just been attracted to the steamer Dunsley, the boats of which were being launched.

[The censor here evidently has deleted the facts concerning the Dunsley.]

The Arabic, Mr. Money added, was making toward the Dunsley when the streak of a torpedo fired from a submarine lying in the wake of the Dunsley was seen making for the Arabic. There were cries of alarm and all hands made for lifebelts and the lifeboats.

"Fortunately," continued Mr. Money, "all precautions had been taken, the lifebelts being in readiness on deck and the boats in position for launching. The torpedo struck the ship and there was a terrible explosion. The ship began to settle immediately and sunk in a few minutes. It was marvelous how so many boats were got afloat. It spoke well for the discipline of the crew. I was an hour and a half swimming."

A member of the crew of the Arabic said when the steamer was struck she was going at sixteen knots for the Dunsley. When the torpedo struck a part of the ship was borne away, and he saw the bodies of coal trimmers and of five engineers whose watch was below blown to pieces and into the sea.

Although the steamer was torpedoed in the forenoon, it was 8 o'clock in the afternoon before the survivors were picked up by the Primrose and Mongolian. On board these boats all the rescued received the best of care and attention.

Charles Pringle of the Motor Company, Limited, of Toronto, said that most of the passengers on board the Arabic were Canadians. Discussing the work of rescue, Mr. Pringle said:

"It was really marvelous that so many persons were saved. All the lifeboats were crowded when they were launched, and some persons were thrown into the water. There were some very panicky scenes, but the crew kept cool heads and rescued most of those struggling in the water. The floating rafts did good service, several passengers clinging to them for a considerable time.

"One woman, the mother of three children, had an arm broken and became separated from her children when the boats were lowered. She did not know of their fate until she met them at the landing place. It was an affecting scene as she clasped them to her breast."

The Assistant Purser of the Arabic said:

"The torpedo hit near the engine room and the boilers of the steamer exploded. This accounts for the rapidity of her sinking.

"The Captain was the last man to leave the ship. The boats were rowed about for four and a half hours before they were picked up."

ROWED FOR 4½ HOURS, SAYS ACTOR DOUGLAS

He Noted No Panic or Accident Among the Arabic's Passengers.

Special Cable to THE NEW YORK TIMES.

LONDON, Friday, Aug. 20.—Kenneth Douglas, an actor, who was one of the Arabic survivors, has telegraphed from Queenstown to The Daily Mail as follows:

"We were struck by the torpedo at 9:28 A. M. All the passengers saved were got away in boats in twelve minutes. The boats had been lowered for any emergency. We rowed about for four and a half hours until we were picked up by a ship. I am feeling quite all right. There was no panic, and there was no accident of any kind. We in the boats were picked up by two ships."

SAYS ONE AMERICAN IS LOST.

Six Other Passengers and 25 of Crew, According to Liverpool.

Special Cable to THE NEW YORK TIMES.

LIVERPOOL, Friday, Aug. 20, (Dispatch to The London Daily Mail.)—I have just been officially informed that of the thirty-two persons on the Arabic not accounted for twenty-five were members of the crew, the other seven being passengers. A message just received states that at least one of the missing is an American.

The passengers were made up of the following nationalities: British, 145; Americans 26; French, 3; German, 1; Belgian, 1; Russian, 3; Swiss, 1; Spanish, 1. The German is the Rev. Augustine Waldner, who was traveling with a Home Office permit.

The majority of the crew come from Liverpool, and there is a crowd of women outside the White Star offices waiting for news.

Latest Shipping News.

Arrived: SS Ryndam, at Falmouth, Aug. 19.

Ship's Whole Side Blown Out; Many Survivors Injured

Special Cable to THE NEW YORK TIMES.

QUEENSTOWN, Aug. 19, (Dispatch to The London Daily News.)—Three hundred and seventy persons who were rescued from the Arabic were landed at Queenstown at 6 o'clock this evening. A large number of them were badly injured. The ship sank in six minutes, according to some survivors, almost the whole of one side being torn out of her.

Several of those who were injured were engaged in watching another ship which was being torpedoed when their own vessel was struck.

The survivors were four hours in the ship's boats before they were rescued.

CAPTAIN PRAISES WORK OF THE CREW

Engineers and Firemen Sacrificed Their Lives to Execute Orders from the Bridge.

QUEENSTOWN, Friday, Aug. 20.—Captain Finch of the Arabic has given The Associated Press a detailed account of the loss of the liner.

"We were forty-seven miles south of Galley Head at 9:30 o'clock yesterday morning," he said, "when I perceived the steamer Dunsley in difficulty. Going toward her, I observed a torpedo coming for my ship, but could not discern a submarine. The torpedo struck 100 feet from the stern, making terrible havoc of the hull. The vessel began to settle immediately, and sank in about eight minutes.

"My order from the bridge about getting the boats launched was promptly obeyed. Two boats capsized. We had taken every precaution while in the danger zone. There were plenty of lifebelts on deck, and the boats were ready for immediate launching. The officers and crew all behaved excellently and did everything possible in the circumstances, getting people into the boats and picking up those in the sea.

"I was the last to leave, taking the plunge into the sea as the ship was going down. After being in the water some time I got aboard a raft, to which I also assisted two men and women."

Captain Finch paid special tribute to the heroic conduct of several engineers and firemen who remained at their posts to the last and sacrificed their lives to execute orders from the bridge. Among those lost was the Captain's nephew.

The Arabic's commander spoke appreciatively of the kind treatment received by passengers and crew aboard rescuing vessels, and likewise of the arrangements made for their comfort at Queenstown. His chief regret was that he was not able to save the lives of every one on board.

"If I had been given a little more time by the submarine," he said regretfully, "I am satisfied I could have saved everybody."

Sang "Tipperary" to Cheer Women.

Special Cable to THE NEW YORK TIMES.

QUEENSTOWN, Aug. 9.—Stella Carol, a professional singer, gave an interesting description of the scenes on the Arabic. She got quietly into the boat, which reached the water safely. She saw the Captain dive off as the ship went down, and said he was a hero all through. Five women were in the boat she was in and twenty-nine men. The women became much distressed after a time, and she sang "Tipperary" to cheer them up. She also took a hand at rowing the boat.

Miss Carol was on the east coast of England on Sunday night during an air raid, and now thinks she has had enough of the Germans.

REPORTS EXPLOSION KILLED SOME ON BOARD

Assistant Purser Says the Torpedo Blew Up Arabic's Boilers.

Special Cable to THE NEW YORK TIMES.

QUEENSTOWN, Aug. 19. (Dispatch to The London Daily Mail.)—B. Curry, assistant purser of the Arabic, said of his experience:

"The ship was struck at 9:40 and she sank at 9:53. The torpedo hit near the engine room and her boilers exploded.

"Not the slightest warning was given. Most of the passengers had just finished their breakfast, but some of them were still in their cabins.

"There was nothing approaching a panic, and the passengers were got into the boats smoothly.

"The Captain was the last man to leave the vessel. The ship went down very quickly. It was the most wonderful sight I have ever seen."

James Barnes, a passenger, said:

"The first we knew that anything was wrong was the sound of an explosion. The Arabic must have been struck in a vital part, for she sank almost immediately.

"Everything on board went wonderfully smoothly, and there was no trouble in getting the passengers into the boats. I saw a few people in the water, and I cannot be sure if they were saved."

It is reported here that some persons were killed on board by the explosion.

WOMAN NEW YORKER LOST?

U-Boat Emerged and Fired Torpedo Without Slightest Warning.

PASSENGERS SAW PERIL

Watching Attack on Another Vessel When Fatal Bolt Struck the Arabic.

BOATS QUICKLY LAUNCHED

But Many Persons, Including a Woman, Were Hurled Into Sea —Maimed Reach Queenstown.

LONDON, Friday, Aug. 20.—The big White Star Line steamer Arabic, formerly a favorite ship of the Liverpool-Boston service, but which on her present trip was on the way to New York, was torpedoed and sunk by a German submarine at 9:15 o'clock yesterday morning southeast of Fastnet.

The steamer, according to a statement of the White Star Line, was attacked without warning and went down in ten minutes. Of the 423 persons on board—181 passengers and 242 members of the crew—32 are missing and are believed to have perished.

Most of those who have not been accounted for belong to the crew. Only six of the passengers are reported missing.

Whether any of those not accounted for are Americans has not yet been determined, but there were only twenty-six citizens of the United States on board, twenty-two being in the second cabin and four in the steerage. The Arabic carried no first-class passengers, having lately been turned into a two-class liner.

Survivors at Queenstown.

The survivors, who left the steamer in the ship's boats and were picked up later by passing vessels, arrived in Queenstown tonight. They are being accommodated by the White Star Line in hotels and boarding houses in the little town which so short a time ago cared for the survivors and the dead of the Lusitania.

Details of the sinking of the Arabic are lacking, but that the loss of life was not greater was doubtless due to the fact that the weather was fine and that steamers plying the German submarine zone now keep their boats swung out and are otherwise prepared for emergencies.

The torpedo that sunk the Arabic struck her on the starboard side 100 feet from her stern. The vessel had left Liverpool Wednesday afternoon and taken a southerly course, well off the Irish coast, doubtless with a view of avoiding the submarines which frequent the waters nearer the shore.

When some fifty miles west of where the Lusitania was sunk in May the German submarine came to the surface and launched a torpedo.

The marksmanship of the Germans, as in the case of the Lusitania, was deadly accurate, and like the Lusitania, the big liner quickly settled and soon disappeared from view.

Some of the survivors, according to reports received here, say that they had just witnessed the torpedoing of a British steamer, presumably the Dunsley, and that this had caused great alarm on board the Arabic.

In their fright the passengers had rushed for life preservers, and had barely adjusted them when the German submarine turned its torpedo against the Arabic's side.

Passengers Fall Into Sea.

Ten life boats and a number of life rafts were quickly got over the side of the steamer, and into these a large number of the passengers and members of the crew scrambled.

Many of the passengers, however, fell into the water, but they got hold of the rafts and clung to them and later were rescued. One woman who fell into the sea screamed pitifully for help. The weather and tidal conditions being favorable, two sailors swam to her assistance and succeeded in lifting her upon a raft.

Among those who were rescued were Captain William Finch, commander of the Arabic, all the deck officers, the chief engineer, the surgeon, the purser, the assistant purser, the chief steward, and the third-class steward. Third Engineer Lugon is among the missing.

One of the passengers on board was Kenneth Douglas, a well-known English actor. Mr. Douglas was on the Lusitania when she was sent to the

"All the News That's Fit to Print."

The New York Times.

THE WEATHER
Sunday rain; Monday fair; moderate to fresh south to southwest winds.
For full weather report see Page 6 9.

VOL. LXIV...NO. 21,029. NEW YORK, SUNDAY, AUGUST 22, 1915.—90 PAGES, In Seven Parts, Including Picture and Rotogravure Section and Review of Books. PRICE FIVE CENTS.

ITALY, FLEET AND ARMY WAITING, DECLARES WAR ON TURKEY; FRENCH ARMY IS NOW READY TO BEGIN A GREAT OFFENSIVE; ARABIC NOT CONVOYED AND GOT NO WARNING, PAGE CABLES; PRESIDENT GIVES BERLIN CHANCE TO EXPLAIN BEFORE ACTING

COTTON NOW CONTRABAND

Britain Issues Formal Declaration, in Which France Joins.

TRADE RELIEF PROMISED

Government Will Adopt Some Measure Temporarily to Ameliorate Expected Depression.

SITUATION LITTLE CHANGED

New Order Carries Out Purpose of Blockade Without Ambiguity, Lord Milner Explains.

LONDON, Aug. 21.—Cotton has been declared absolute contraband of war by Great Britain, according to a statement issued by the Foreign Office this afternoon. The statement declares that the Government proposes to initiate measures to relieve depression which might temporarily disturb the cotton market because of the contraband order. The announcement reads:

His Majesty's Government have declared cotton absolute contraband. While the circumstances might have justified such action at an earlier period, his Majesty's Government are glad to think that the local conditions of American interests likely to be affected are more favorable for such a step than they were a year ago, and, moreover, his Majesty's Government contemplate initiation of measures to relieve as far as possible any abnormal depression which might temporarily disturb market conditions.

PARIS, Aug. 21.—The Foreign Office announces that the Journale Official tomorrow morning will contain an announcement by the French and British Governments declaring cotton absolute contraband of war.

JUSTIFIES MAKING COTTON CONTRABAND

Essential to Munitions, Lord Milner Points Out—Why Decision Was Delayed.

Special Cable to THE NEW YORK TIMES.

LONDON, Aug. 21.—Lord Milner today gave to THE NEW YORK TIMES correspondent an interview which may be regarded as an authoritative exposition of the British attitude on the question of cotton as contraband and as an informative supplement, coincident with the declaration on the subject issued by The Foreign Office.

"You ask me," said Lord Milner, "whether the declaration of cotton as contraband is justifiable. I am not a lawyer, but I should have thought it was quite clear that any belligerent nowadays was entitled to declare cotton contraband. Lists of contraband articles vary necessarily with every war, but the broad principle is clear enough. Anything may be declared contraband which is esential to a belligerent for the continuance of the war. It is quite true that considerable doubt has existed, until this war, as to whether cotton comes within this category. But the present war has shown that the successful conduct of military operations requires an enormous consumption of munitions of all kinds, and since cotton is the basis of almost all propulsive explosives in actual use, vast quantities of cotton have to be employed and are in fact indispensable to a belligerent. In short, cotton is now just as as essential a part of munitions of war as were in the old days, the component parts of gunpowder or the raw materials from which ships or cannon were made."

"Why, then, was cotton not declared contraband long ago?" Lord Milner was asked.

"That question is one which only a member of the Government can fully answer," he replied. "I do not suppose it was realized by the Government or their advisers in the early months of the war that a vast demand for cotton for military purposes would arise, and it is obvious that no Government would wish to take a step so restrictive of neutral rights as a declaration that cotton was contraband unless they were satisfied that the military necessities compelled them to do so. The British Government have all along been most anxious not to strain their belligerent rights. In particular they have been anxious to avoid friction with the United States. In this respect I think they have truly interpreted the feelings of the nation.

Value American Sympathy.

"Sentiment and policy alike cause us to desire most earnestly that the relations between our country and yours

Continued on Page 4.

British Royal Proclamation Declaring Cotton Contraband

LONDON, Aug. 21.—The British declaration making cotton contraband is effective from today. A royal proclamation on the subject was published in a supplement of The London Gazette tonight. After a brief preamble, the proclamation says:

Now, therefore, we do hereby declare, by and with the advice of our Privy Council, that, during the continuance of the war, or until we do give further public notice, the following articles will be treated as absolutely contraband, in addition to those set out in our royal proclamation aforementioned: Raw cotton, cotton linters, cotton waste, and cotton yarn.

And we do hereby further declare that this our royal proclamation shall take effect from the date of its publication in The London Gazette.

The proclamation was signed yesterday by King George.

KAISER REJOICES IN 'SUBLIME DAY'

"I Humbly Thank God," He Telegraphs Chancellor on Fall of Novo Georgievsk.

LAUDS GENERAL AND MEN

Calls It "One of the Finest Feats of Arms Ever Accomplished by Any Army."

LONDON, Aug. 21.—A message expressing deep gratification over the capture of Novo Georgievsk and paying high tribute to the courage of German troops has been telegraphed by Emperor William to Dr. von Bethmann-Hollweg, the German Imperial Chancellor, according to the Norddeutsche Allgemeine Zeitung of Berlin, says a Reuter dispatch from Amsterdam. The Emperor's message as given by the newspaper follows:

"Thanks to God's gracious assistance, the tried bravery of the conqueror of Antwerp, General von Beseler, the heroic courage of our brilliant troops, and the excellent German and Austro-Hungarian siege artillery, the strongest and most modern Russian fortress, Novo Georgievsk, is in our hands.

"Deeply moved, I have just expressed my thanks to my brave troops, whose spirit was splendid. It is one of the finest feats of arms ever accomplished by any army. It was a sublime day, for which I humbly thank God. The booty in Kovno has increased to 600 guns."

The Chancellor replied to the Emperor with the following message:

"Full of gratitude to God, the entire people rejoice over the heroic deeds of the army, and, knowing our cause is just, look to the future with entire confidence. The unanimous resolution of the Reichstag shows the entire people are firmly united behind our brilliant army. Thousands last evening sang songs of triumph and 'Now Let Us All Thank God' before the Palace."

RUSSIA SUSPENDS LAW AGAINST JEWS

Refugees Allowed to Settle in Cities of Empire Except Petrograd and Moscow.

PETROGRAD, Aug. 21, (via London.) Owing to the occupation by the Germans of a great part of the pale of Jewish settlements and the inclusion of the remainder in the sphere of military operations, the condition of the Jews is critical. Five hundred thousand Jewish residents have been deported and probably greater numbers have taken refuge in the interior provinces, where they have no legal rights.

Prince Cherbatoff, the Minister of the Interior, brought the question of their status before the Council of the Empire, and that body has decided temporarily to permit Jews to settle in the cities of the empire with the exception of those of Moscow and Petrograd and the suburban residences of Emperor Nicholas.

LONDON, Aug. 21.—Reuter's correspondent at Petrograd telegraphs that the newspapers there announce that an order will shortly be issued abolishing during the war Jewish residential restrictions in regard to towns, with the exception of Petrograd and Moscow.

FRENCH EAGER TO BEGIN

Times Correspondent Hints at Advance 'Before Leaves Are Red.'

SEES THREE BATTLE POINTS

Visits Sections of the Front Which Were Previously Barred to Journalists.

TELLS OF GERMAN SURPRISE

They Found French Had Taken Forest of Parroy in the Night Without Firing a Shot.

From a Staff Correspondent.

Special Cable to THE NEW YORK TIMES.

PARIS, Aug. 21.—With an officer of the General Staff—the same who accompanied me on prevous trips to the front—I have just visited three points on the French battle line, heretofore barred to correspondents.

I waited for this trip in preference to the privilege of describing rides in aeroplanes or visits to famous generals or similar "stunts," in order that I might obtain the closest view of the French army accorded to anybody.

For weeks there have been "reliable" rumors concerning the "German plan when the Russian campaign is over." We have been regaled with details of just how and where Germany intended to hurl new millions of men and shells. There have been disturbing whispers. In fact, Paris has been so crazy with misinformation that the idea has scarcely occurred to any one that perhaps the army's higher command might have an entirely commendable plan of its own for the ultimate victory of the French arms.

This is not to be an account of fighting, such as the spectacle of the Battle of the Labyrinth permitted me to describe. Of all the war I have seen, this trip seemed the least like war.

When I rode through the majestic pine forests between the mountain peaks of the Vosges there was not a sound to disturb tranquility of thought, although armies were secreted there, watching. When I walked through the meadows of Lorraine I could scarcely believe there was anything but peace in all the world, although several times observers informed the party that we were unnecessarily exposing ourselves to German artillery.

But artillery did not breathe a sound those beautiful afternoons. When, from observatory posts on the lofty ranges in the north I looked down upon the dense and tranquil woods, I knew them full of hidden troops and cannon. Afterward I saw them close, but it was like the quaint forest life of old story books—these Summer encampments.

Men Playing and Bathing.

Everybody was happy. Men played quoits and ninepins or fished and bathed in the streams, and slept at night on pine boughs in funny little houses of rough bark or mud. Perhaps it was the pines and balsam that proved so delusive, but one could not realize that only a few yards further on were the trenches where sentries never slept. On this peaceful excursion I did not get shot at once, I did not experience a single thrill of danger; yet, if my Captain censor would only permit me to tell all I know that I did not know before, I believe I would be able to thrill my readers to their souls—for I saw several things that made a greater impression on me than anything I had ever before seen.

But my Captain censor will not permit me to tell it all. That is, he will not permit it to the degree that might be called satisfactorily specific.

In addition to covering a great portion of the lines in the Vosges and Lorraine, my trip included the Grand Couronne de Nancy from end to end. This is a natural fortification of high hills half circling the city North and East. Five years after the Franco-Prussian war France wanted to build forts there for the defense of Nancy. The Germans declared that such action would be a casus belli, and beaten France desisted. In the light of the present day uselessness of forts against heavy artillery, she never ceases to be thankful that she did not build them, for, with the place left open to army operations, it was there that General Castelnau threw back Prince Rupprecht of Bavaria at the time of the Battle of the Marne.

Other points where I was the first correspondent allowed since the war began are a portion of the Forest of Champenoux, near Badonviller, and the Forest of Parroy, lying east of the Grand Couronne just on and off the Franco-German frontier.

Stalked Each Other Like Indians.

This latter forest until a few weeks ago was a no-man's land, rival trench lines extending along both sides, a distance of several miles separating them. Patrols of both armies enjoyed themselves constantly, riding through the dense brush, stalking each other in Indian fashion for a pot shot. It became a game which grew in intensity to such an extent that one morning the French General of that particular army said words equivalent to: "I have had enough of this sort of thing."

His orders were executed under cover of the darkness a few mornings later. The Germans rubbed their eyes in astonishment at finding new trenches just a few yards in advance of them. The French had taken the Forest of Parroy without firing a shot.

In the trenches of Champenoux Forest I had the unique experience of being in a section where the Germans had been active with the use of poisonous gases. Although there was not even a rifle shot to disturb us, these trenches were fully equipped with preventive paraphernalia in case gases were used. Every soldier in the trenches wore goggles and a mask. Also there were large tubs of water at intervals.

Everywhere on the trip I was impressed as never before with the impregnability of the French positions. The French trenches are all on slopes looking down. In some places they are only forty yards from the Germans, but, carefully squinting through loopholes in the observation posts, I could see barbed wire entanglements so thick that a kitten could not crawl between them.

Mustn't Discuss Offensive.

The soldiers were more cheerful than ever before, the officers more buoyant, more eager for the "general offensive," signs of which I also sought. But regarding this matter of a general offensive my lips are sealed by my Captain censor.

By the way, I wish I could give his name, but he only says, when I ask permission: "I am nobody. In the French Army it is not the custom of officers to be advertised." But if I had permission, I am sure my readers would be quite as interested as when correspondents with the German Army are permitted to mention the names of certain officers accompanying them to the battlefields.

But I do know, and I hope to be permitted to say, that the words "general offensive" are not a mere idle phrase. * * *

Several paragraphs inserted here have been entirely deleted by my censor, who has already seen this copy, and I can only conclude by saying that the French Army, from the soldiers in troop trains to those in the trenches, is steadfast for its "higher command" to the very last man.

The Kaiser said a year ago that he would beat France "before the leaves fall from the trees." Perhaps the French reply may now come before the leaves are red.

Spain Makes Protest Against Submarines

MADRID, Aug. 21, (via Paris.)—The Spanish Government has protested to Germany against the torpedoing of two Spanish steamers, the Peria Castilio and the Isidoro, in the North Sea.

The German Ambassador at Madrid has writen a private letter to the Foreign Minister expressing regret.

The Spanish steamer Isidoro was sunk by a German submarine between Aug. 14 and 18. It is not known whether there was any loss of life.

The records of the recent activity of the German submarines contain no reference to the Peria Castilio.

FRENCH ARE DOMINANT IN ARTILLERY DUELS

Their Shells Wreck German Ammunition Depots in Alsace—Rheims Bombarded.

LONDON, Aug. 21.—Violent artillery combats were fought last night and today at many points along the western

Continued on Page 3.

NEW FOE FOR THE MOSLEMS

Rome Resents Turkey's Aid to Libyans and Detention of Citizens.

REPORT BULGARIA MENACING

She Is Said to be Massing 150,000 Troops on Her Turkish Frontier.

RUMANIA ALSO TO MOBILIZE

Bucharest Says Steps Will Be Taken This Week—In Close Touch with Other States.

LONDON, Sunday, Aug. 22.—Italy has declared war against Turkey, according to a Steffani News Agency dispatch from Rome.

This announcement receives confirmation in an official telegram from Constantinople received in Amsterdam and transmitted to The Central News with the added information that the Marquis di Garroni, the Italian Ambassador at Constantinople, presented the declaration yesterday and demanded his passports.

The reasons given in the note for Italy's declaration of war were the support of Turkey of the revolt in Libya and the prevention of the departure of Italian residents from Syria.

A Reuter dispatch from Constantinople, via Berlin and Amsterdam, says that the Ambassador has left the Turkish capital.

The Italian Government, says another dispatch from Rome, has telegraphed to all its representatives abroad a circular setting forth the questions at issue between Italy and Turkey. The circular closes with these words:

"In view of these obvious infractions of categorical promises made by the Ottoman Government, and following upon our ultimatum of Aug. 3, provoked by evasions of the Ottoman Government, particularly with regard to the free departure of Italian subjects from Asia Minor, the Italian Government has sent instructions to its Ambassador at Constantinople to declare war upon Turkey."

Dispatches from Italy three days ago told of the mobilization of a squadron of fast cruisers at Taranto, ready for action against Turkey, and of the concentration of five army corps (200,000 men) in Apulia, under orders to prepare for departure to an unknown destination.

150,000 BULGARS MASS ON TURKISH FRONTIER

Ottomans Strengthen Fortifications in Thrace—Rumania About to Mobilize.

NAPLES, Aug. 21, (via Paris.)—A dispatch to the Mattino from Saloniki says that Bulgaria has concentrated 150,000 troops on the Turkish frontier.

LONDON, Aug. 21.—Telegrams from the Balkan capitals state that Turco-Bulgarian relations have reached the breaking point, and that Turkey is strengthening her fortifications in Thrace because of the fear of a Bulgarian invasion.

No open breach between the Bulgars and Turks is likely, however, until Bulgaria learns whether the Serbian Parliament, which has been in secret session for three days, is willing to cede Macedonia to her.

Recent news dispatches from Sofia have agreed that Bulgaria is satisfied with the territorial concessions offered her by the Entente powers as the price of her aid in the war and is only awaiting the consent of Serbia and Greece to these terms before acting.

Rumania Preparing for Action.

GENEVA, Aug. 21.—The Bucharest correspondent of The Tribune sends the following:

"Between Nish and Bucharest constant telegrams are passing.

"It is believed that Rumania will

Continued on Page 3.

"Time for Words Has Passed," Says Roosevelt, He Declares It Not Enough to Dismiss Bernstorff

OYSTER BAY, N. Y., Aug. 21.—Ex-President Theodore Roosevelt issued this statement tonight:

I see it is suggested in the papers that the German answer to our last note—that is, the sinking of the Arabic by a German submarine and the consequent murder of certain American citizens—will be adequately met by the Administration dismissing Bernstorff and severing diplomatic relations with Germany. I earnestly hope the Administraton will not take this view, for to do so would be a fresh sacrifice of American honor and interest.

The President's note to Germany in February last was an excellent note, if only it had been lived up to. But every subsequent note has represented nothing but weakness and timidity on our side, and the sinking of the Lusitania and of the Arabic, the attacks on the Gulflight and the Falaba, and all the similar incidents that have occurred, represent the arrogant answers which this weakness has inspired. Germany will care nothing for the mere severance of diplomatic relations.

The time for words on the part of this nation has long passed, and it is inconceivable to American citizens, who claim to be inheritors of the traditions of Washington and Lincoln, that our governmental representatives shall not see that the time for deeds has come.

What has just occurred is a fresh and lamentable proof of the unwisdom of our people in not having insisted upon the beginning of active military preparedness thirteen months ago.

6 WARSHIPS LOST IN BALTIC FIGHTS

British Submarine Sinks a German Cruiser—Others Smaller Craft.

2 RUSSIAN GUNBOATS SUNK

Germans Admit Loss of Two and Damage of One Torpedo Boat by Mines.

LONDON, Aug. 21.—According to official statements issued tonight in London and Berlin, a British submarine has sunk a German cruiser in the Baltic, while the Germans lost two torpedo boats and the Russians three small warships in the fighting in the Gulf of Riga. A third German torpedo boat was damaged and taken into port.

The official Russian statement follows:

During the fighting in the Gulf of Riga Wednesday, Thursday, and Friday, the enemy's losses were not less than two torpedo boats.

A British submarine successfully torpedoed a German cruiser in the Baltic Sea.

The Russian vessels, which were sunk, were the gunboats Sivutch and Koreets, and a torpedo boat. The German ships sunk or put out of commission were all torpedo boats. One damaged German boat was escorted to port.

A statement from the German Admiralty concerning the battle reads as follows:

Our Baltic naval forces penetrated the Gulf of Riga after mine sweepers had swept the mine field and net obstructions. In the outpost engagements which developed a Russian torpedoboat of the Emir Pucharskii class was destroyed, and other torpedoboats, among them the Novik, and one large vessel, were severely damaged while retreating.

On the evening of the 19th in Moon Sound the Russian gunboats Sivutch and Koreets were sunk by artillery fire and torpedoboats, after brave resistance. Forty members of the crew, including two officers, some severely wounded, were rescued by our torpedoboats.

Three of our torpedoboats were damaged by mines. One sank, one was run ashore, and one was escorted to port.

Our loss of life was small.

PETROGRAD, Aug. 21, (via London.)—The newspaper Russky Invalid states that the chief units of the Russian Baltic fleet are not in the Gulf of Riga, which a German fleet has entered and engaged the Russian naval defenders. The Gulf of Riga, the newspaper declares, is defended by mines and small warships.

The Sivutch and Koreets were sister ships of 875 tons displacement. They were 218 feet long and 36 feet beam. They were armed with two 4.7-inch guns and four 3-inch guns. Their normal complement was 140 men each.

For nearly a fortnight a powerful German squadron was engaged in an attempt to force an entrance into the Gulf of Riga for the purpose of assisting the German army which occupies the western coast of the Gulf. The Russians asserted that they repelled on Aug. 8 an attack delivered by nine German battleships, twelve cruisers, and a large number of destroyers, but the Germans asserted this was not a general attack, but merely a reconnoissance. Later the Russians announced that their warships had been drawn in closer on account of the superiority of the German squadron, and an official communication received last night from Petrograd said that a German fleet had penetrated the Gulf and engaged the Russian vessels.

The character of the vessels sunk bears out a statement from Petrograd that the chief units of the Russian Baltic fleet were not in the Gulf of Riga, which was defended by mines and small warships.

GERMANS TO STRIKE NORTH.

Naval Attack Foreshadows New Offensive—Bielsk Captured.

LONDON, Aug. 21.—The naval activity in the Gulf of Riga, where the Russians apparently have only small craft, foreshadows, it is thought, another big Ger-

Continued on Page 4.

GERMANS SLAY 14 HELPLESS SAILORS

Torpedo Boat Attacks Stranded British Submarine in Danish Waters and Shoots Crew.

DANES GO TO THE RESCUE

Warn Germans Away, but They Return with Reinforcements—All Scandinavia Aroused.

LONDON, Aug. 21.—Details of the sinking of the British submarine E-13, the loss of which was reported yesterday, were told in an announcement from the Admiralty today.

The report says that while the submarine was aground German war craft entered the neutral area and destroyed her. When her crew abandoned her and the sailors were struggling in the water, according to the report, the Germans fired upon them with machine guns and shrapnel. Fourteen are said to have been killed.

The Danish and Swedish newspapers bitterly denounce the attack as an unwarranted encroachment on Danish neutrality.

The British Admiralty report is as follows:

"A report has been received from Lieut. Commander Layton, commanding the E-13, whose grounding on the Danish island of Saltholm was published yesterday. The Lieutenant Commander reports that the submarine grounded in the early morning of Aug. 19. All efforts to refloat her failed.

"At 5 o'clock a Danish torpedo boat appeared on the scene and informed the E-13 that she would be allowed twenty four hours to get off. At the same time a German torpedo boat arrived and remained close to the submarine until two more Danish torpedo boats came up, when she withdrew.

"At 9 o'clock, while the three Danish torpedo boats were anchored close to the submarine, two German torpedo boats approached from the south. When about half a mile away one of these hoisted a commercial flag signal, but before the commanding officer of the E-13 had time to read it the German destroyer fired a torpedo at her from a distance of about 300 yards. The torpedo exploded on hitting the bottom close to her.

"At the same moment the German destroyer fired with all her guns, and Lieut. Commander Layton, seeing that his submarine was on fire fore and aft and unable to defend herself owing to her being aground, gave orders for the crew to abandon her. While the men were in the water they were fired upon by machine guns and with shrapnel.

"One of the Danish torpedo boats immediately lowered her boat and steamed between the submarine and the German destroyers, who, therefore, had to cease fire and withdraw."

Danish Press Aroused.

The Copenhagen correspondent of Reuter's Telegram Company sends the following regarding the sinking of the British submarine:

The destruction of the British submarine E-13 in Danish territory by German destroyers, under circumstances which placed the shipwrecked craft under Danish protection, has aroused widespread indignation, which finds expression in the Danish newspapers. It is urged that there can be no explanation or plausible excuse for the deliberate violation of Danish territory, as a German torpedo boat had thoroughly investigated the locality before returning with the others to attack the defenseless crew. The Vortland says:

"There can be no question that the German commander was aware he was violating Danish neutrality. The incident is simply in accordance with Ger-

Continued on Page 3.

PAGE SENDS ARABIC REPORT

Cables Affidavits of Americans That Liner Was Not Warned.

VESSEL HAD NO ESCORT

Admiralty Statement and Captain's Story Bear Out Tales of the Survivors.

WILSON MOVES CAUTIOUSLY

Will Give Germany a Chance to Explain—Open Talk of Diplomatic Break.

Berlin Silent on the Arabic, Press Under Tight Curb

BERLIN, Aug. 21, (via London, Aug. 22, 1:35 A. M.)—No statement is obtainable in official quarters regarding the sinking of the steamer Arabic. The tendency, however, seems to be to consider the question without excitement.

The press thus far has avoided comment of any nature.

This dispatch contains the only reference to the Arabic obtainable from Berlin Saturday.

Special Cable to THE NEW YORK TIMES.

LONDON, Aug. 21.—Ambassador Page cabled a report to Washington today giving the details of the sinking of the Arabic, and making the point that from statements communicated to him the submarine fired its torpedo without giving the slightest warning. That is the Ambassador's official report, based upon all the information available.

The Ambassador talked with James Colman, an American citizen, who had been living in London for some years and had sold his property here in the last few months, so as to return to America. He was aboard the Arabic. Mr. Colman called at the Embassy to assure Mr. Page that the torpedo was fired without the slightest chance being given to the passengers to save their lives.

"The first any one knew of the torpedo," he said, "was while some were looking at the steamer Dunsley foundering a little distance away. Suddenly the cry went up that a torpedo was coming toward us. Captain Finch was zigzagging his vessel, for evidently he had already spotted the submarine, and was trying to avoid it. Before any one of us fully realized it, crash came the torpedo into the ship, almost knocking the ship over, it seemed. The Germans did not fire any shot across the bow of the Arabic to stop her, and did not make any effort to ascertain if there were Americans aboard. It was simply a cold-blooded attack with utter disregard of the consequences.

"Every American on the ship to whom I have since talked agrees that the Germans apparently were determined to kill every one."

Sends Other Affidavits.

Ambassador Page cabled Mr. Colman's statement to Washington with others communicated to him from the Consul at Queenstown, who interviewed all the American survivors. All were intensely indignant at Germany's flagrant disregard of the warning in President Wilson's latest note to Germany. Ambassador Page also cabled the official statement of the Admiralty that the Arabic was not convoyed by British or any other war craft.

The Admiralty report and the affidavits cabled by Ambassador Page are held to show that the Arabic was not convoyed. The Admiralty statement is also backed up by affidavits made by several English passengers who were on the Arabic. Ambassador Page cabled the affidavits of four American passengers taken at Queenstown. Officials, too, also state positively that reports from America that the Arabic attempted to ram the submarine are untrue. The facts as developed by the Admiralty investigation and supplemented by reports to Ambassador Page show that the submarine was not seen by any one

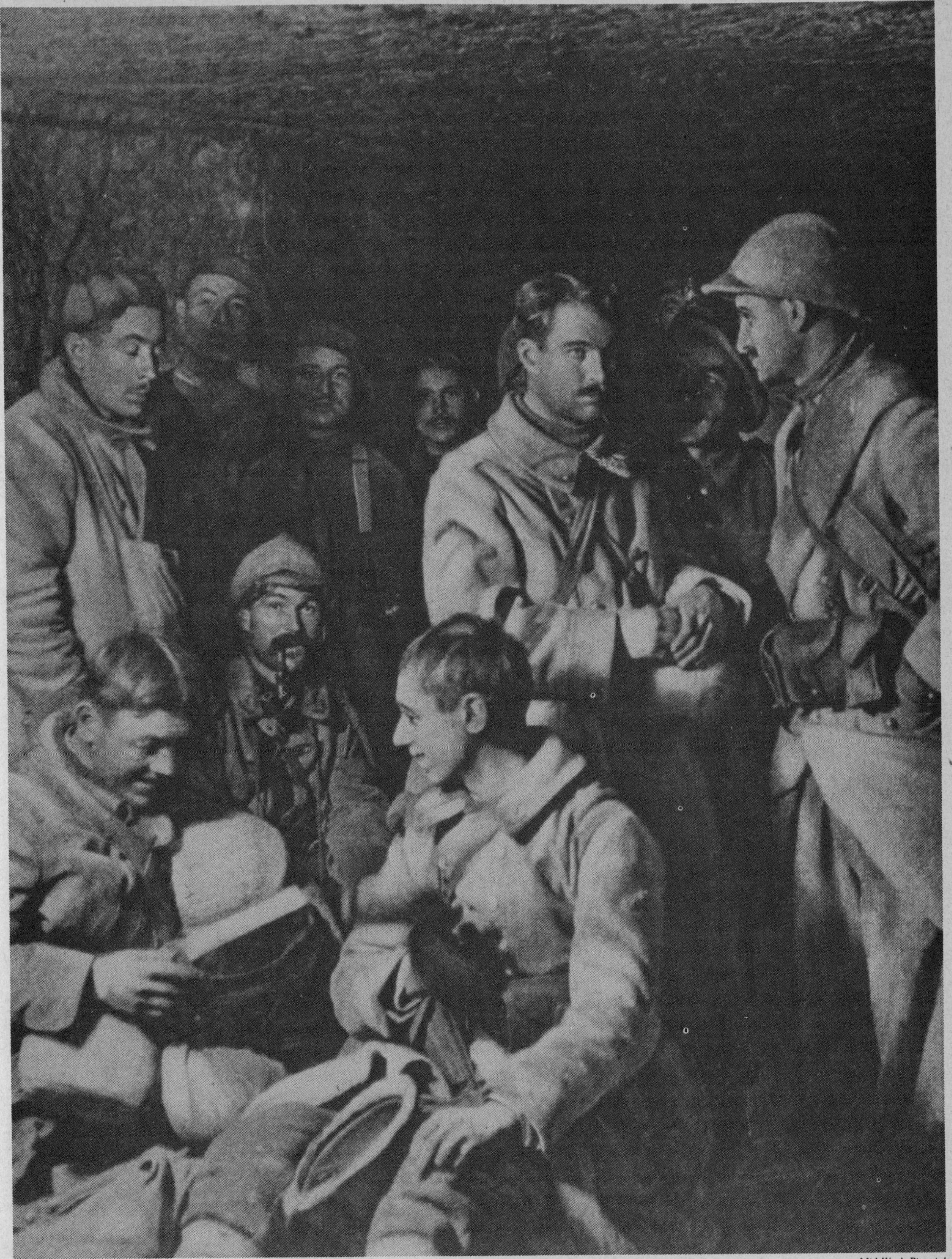

Mid-Week Pictorial

French Infantry in the fortress of Malmaison.

"All the News That's Fit to Print."

The New York Times.

THE WEATHER
Fair and colder Monday; probably fair Tuesday; northwest gales diminishing.
For full weather report see Page 18

VOL. LXV...NO. 21,065. NEW YORK, MONDAY, SEPTEMBER 27, 1915.—EIGHTEEN PAGES. ONE CENT In Greater New York, Jersey City and Newark. | Elsewhere TWO CENTS.

ALLIES' DELEGATES GO WEST ON LOAN

Terms All Agreed Upon, They Will Confer with Bankers of West and South.

START FOR CHICAGO TODAY

War News Pleases Them and May Prove Helpful by Widening Syndicate Support.

5-YEAR BONDS TO BE ISSUED

$500,000,000 of These at 5% to be Convertible Into Ten or Fifteen Year Bonds at 4½%.

An agreement among New York bankers to co-operate with the Anglo-French Financial Commission in the raising of $500,000,000 for the stabilization of the foreign exchange market was reached at conferences held on Saturday and yesterday afternoon, and today four members of the commission, accompanied by one of the partners of J. P. Morgan & Co., will leave for Chicago.

The Western trip was decided upon for the purpose of bringing bankers throughout the Middle West into accord with the position taken by leading New York financiers. George M. Reynolds, President of the Continental and Commercial Bank; J. B. Forgan, head of the First National; J. Ogden Armour, and other influential Chicago capitalists have been lukewarm toward the proposals made for a big commercial credit, and the visit of the Commissioners is expected to give the negotiations a national character.

The commission does not expect to go further West than Chicago, but bankers from St. Louis, Kansas City, Omaha, St. Paul and other centres have been asked to meet the members there to go over the points brought out at the conferences in this city, and it is believed that objections which they have raised can be overcome by a frank discussion with the commission.

Lord Reading, chairman of the commission, and Basil B. Blackett will be of the party which leaves this afternoon, and it is expected that the other two members will be Sir Henry Babington Smith and Earnest Mallet. The Morgan firm will be represented by either Henry P. Davison or Thomas W. Lamont. Sir Edward Holden had expected to make the trip, but it appeared likely last night that he would remain in New York with one of the two representatives of the French Government.

Terms of the Loan.

There was another important meeting of Morgan partners and several other New York bankers yesterday afternoon, at which some of the Commissioners were present. It was decided that while the success of the proposed loan has been practically assured by the support already enlisted, bankers at other important centres who have not had an opportunity to make their views known should be consulted before the final details are decided upon. If these men are won over, the loan will be announced in a few days along the lines already outlined. These are:

The provision of $500,000,000 to be deposited with banks in this country and to be expended exclusively for commercial purchases.

Great Britain and France to issue five-year 5 per cent. notes, payable in dollars at New York, these notes to be a joint obligation on the two Governments having priority as to principal and interest over all other Government debts.

The notes to be convertible, at the option of the holder, into 4½ per cent. fifteen or twenty year bonds at maturity.

The notes to be sold to a huge syndicate of banks, firms, and individuals, probably at 97½, with the understanding that they shall be offered to investors at about 99.

Russia's needs for credit here to be taken care of in other ways, and none of the money provided by this loan to be used for that country's account.

The Commissioners made this statement regarding the purpose of their Western trip:

We have spent much of our time since our arrival in studying conditions in this country, and have conferred with many bankers and business men. We are now desirous of meeting some of the leading men of affairs from other great centres, and for that purpose, the Chairman and some other members of the mission will start tomorrow for Chicago.

We have been greatly pleased with the active and cordial desire for cooperation shown by diverse interests throughout the country, and we feel confident that an arrangement will be effected for the attainment of the common ends sought, namely, to preserve and maintain international trade between the United States of America, on the one hand, and Great Britain and France, upon the other, by the removal of the impediments which arise from instability in the rate of exchange.

Both the bankers who have been at work on the arrangements for bringing out the largest security issue ever floated in one operation in this country and the members of the Anglo-French Commission were highly pleased with the war news yesterday. It was said that the beginning of the long-planned general offensive movement on the part of the Allies could not have been better timed for the influence which it had upon sentiment affecting the bond offering. It has been argued that while the credit of the two nations could not be questioned, even if their ultimate defeat were conceded, the flotation of the $500,-

Continued on Page 2.

OUR FORCES ATTACKED BY HAITIAN REBELS

Forty Natives Killed and Ten of Our Marines Wounded—Haitians Had Refused to Disarm.

CAPE HAITIEN, Sept. 26.—In an attack by Haitian rebels on an American force, about two miles from Cape Haitien, forty Haitians were killed. Ten Americans were wounded.

The rebels have refused to disarm, and the Americans are marching on Haut du Cap, in the plain of the north.

Special to The New York Times.

WASHINGTON, Sept. 26.—The Navy Department tonight was without confirmation of the report of another clash between American marines and Haitians at Cape Haitien today, in which forty Haitians were killed and ten Americans wounded. Admiral Caperton's report of the fight is expected at any time.

Word reached Washington today that the committee of the Haitian Parliament that had been considering the protectorate treaty would report tomorrow or next day. It is confidently expected that the report will be favorable and that ratification will follow in short order.

The executive authorities in Haiti have already signed the treaty, and pending its acceptance by Parliament its more important provisions have been put into practical operation by the American naval forces around Haiti under a sort of modus vivendi.

American officials are already in charge of the Haitian Custom Houses, and American marines, some on foot and some mounted, are operating in the interior.

BLAKE WINS RELEASE FROM AMERICAN POST

Ambassador Sharp Persuades Ambulance Committee Not to Hinder Surgeon's Work.

Special Cable to THE NEW YORK TIMES.

PARIS, Sept. 26.—The American Ambulance versus Dr. Blake controversy over the latter's resignation to accept the post as chief surgeon of the British hospital at Ris Orangis was settled today in favor of Dr. Blake by the intervention of the American Ambassador. However, even this powerful influence did not prevent a big fight in the Executive Committee, during which several members offered their resignations before the Ambulance climbed down from its position.

The battle has raged ever since Dr. Blake's ultimatum of last Thursday, when asked to reconsider his resignation, in which he gave the only terms acceptable to him to remain. The committee then discovered that the War Ministry first desired the acceptance of his resignation by the hospital before officially confirming him in his new position. It was then decided to hold up the acceptance even though Dr. Blake quit his services with them.

Dr. Blake, who had received a cable from Robert Bacon, then called on Ambassador Sharp, who asked Laurence Benet of the Ambulance Committee to see that a letter of acceptance was written. Several members of the committee went over to the Blake cause, declaring the American institution would be split in two if they prevented another hospital from obtaining the services of so able a surgeon just because he desired to leave them. The remainder of the committee then saw the light and decided to give a letter provided the offered committee resignations be withdrawn, and also that Dr. Blake take no members of the hospital with him.

WIRELESS TOWER FALLS IN FRONT OF EXPRESS

Locomotive of Fast B. & M. Train Derailed When Tufts College Structure Is Blown on Track.

MEDFORD, Mass., Sept. 26.—The new wireless telegraph tower at Tufts College, 204 feet in height, was blown over during a gale today, and fell a few feet in front of an express train from Concord, N. H., on the Boston & Maine Railroad. The locomotive was derailed when it plunged into the steel framework, but no one was injured.

Passengers in a trolley car also had a narrow escape. The car was approaching the tower when the motorman, glancing upward, saw it swaying, and brought the car to a standstill within 100 feet of the falling steel. A group of sightseers standing near the cement base of the tower jumped back in time to escape being struck.

All of the electric wires in the neighborhood were torn down, several poles were broken, and two large trees were uprooted. Electric and steam traffic was held up for several hours until the wreckage could be removed. The breaking of a temporary guy wire as the structure swayed in the wind is believed to have led to the accident.

REPORT THAT YAQUIS BURNED 60 PERSONS

Dispatches from Sonora Tell of Terrible Death of Women and Children in Hay Car.

SAN DIEGO, Sept. 26.—Eighty passengers on a Southern Pacific Mexican train were thrown into a car containing hay and the car set on fire by a band of Yaqui Indians on Friday, near Torres, Sonora, according to wireless advices received here today from Hermosillo, via Guaymas.

Only twenty passengers have been accounted for thus far, the others having been burned to death.

The Indians, according to the report, numbered about sixty, and were deserters from one of the Mexican factional armies. They first derailed the train, which was running from Campo Verde to Torres, after which they placed the passengers, most of whom were women and children, in the hay car, and applied the torch. So far as is known no Americans were on the train.

Torres is a small town, about seventy miles north of Guaymas, and a junction point of the railroad, a spur line running into the mining district.

HALT CITY TRAFFIC TO TEST SUBWAYS

Police Close Many Streets as Experts Investigate the New Excavations.

TWO INQUIRIES UNDER WAY

Mayor Appoints Committee and Service Board Gets Men from Other Cities.

ACCIDENT REPORTS PENDING

One Victim of Broadway Collapse in Critical Condition—Changes in Street Car Routes.

Where Cars Will Run Today, and Where They Will Not

Frank Hedley, Vice President and General Manager of the New York Railways Company, issued the following statement at midnight:

In the morning the Eighth Street and Fourteenth Street crosstown lines will be running as usual.

It is expected that the shoring that we have ordered at Thirty-fourth Street and Broadway will be completed by 8 o'clock. When it is in place the cars will be in operation for through traffic across Thirty-fourth Street, and will permit of the completion of through traffic up and down Sixth Avenue.

The Broadway cars cannot be operated immediately north or south of Thirty-eighth Street on account of the cave-in.

North of the cave-in the Broadway cars will run north from Forty-third Street.

It is expected that the Twenty-third Street Crosstown line will be in operation by 10 A. M.

The Seventh Avenue line will be operated only north of Thirty-third Street for possibly a week or more.

Two separate investigations into the safety of streets over the new subway excavations began yesterday, following the collapsing of Broadway at Thirty-eighth Street on Saturday evening, when a woman was killed and three men were injured, and a similar accident in Seventh Avenue, between Twenty-third and Twenty-fifth Streets, where seven persons were killed and eighty-five injured on Wednesday.

Mayor Mitchel appointed a committee of twelve engineers to conduct an inquiry in co-operation with him and other city officials, with Commissioner of Accounts Wallstein in general charge. The Public Service Commission, already equipped with a formidable array of construction experts, sent for other engineers from Boston, Philadelphia, and San Francisco to examine the cut and cover work here, report on its safeness, and recommend means to prevent further disaster.

City Officials Apprehensive.

The nervousness of city officials over the entire subway situation was shown by the activity late in the afternoon when a six-inch water pipe burst in the excavation of the Seventh Avenue subway at Rector and Greenwich Streets. The water flowed down a grade into a hollow underneath a pumping station and was pumped out quickly.

It was decided after examination that no supports had been undermined, and that there was no danger of a cave-in. But as soon as the report of another misfortune in the subway had been received there was a hasty exodus of officials, and presently there gathered at the scene Police Commissioner Woods, Chief Inspector Max Schmittberger, Public Service Commissioner William Hayward, Secretary Travis H. Whitney of the Public Service Commission, the commission's principal subway engineer, Robert Ridgway; Deputy Police Commissioner Lawrence Dunham, and Frank Hedley, Vice President and General Manager of the Interboro Rapid Transit Company. The damage done here was only slight and traffic soon was resumed.

Downtown Traffic Tied Up.

Meantime, the Police Department enforced widespread restrictions of traffic that tied up vehicular transportation in the heart of the city. With the light travel of Sunday, these regulations did not fall so heavily on the public as they may today when tens of thousands of workers must ride to their places of business. Also, shuttle services relieved the situation.

The Twenty-third and Thirty-fourth Street crosstown lines and the Sixth Avenue were the principal arteries affected. It is expected that they will be running this morning, as will the Eighth Street and Fourteenth Street crosstowns. Traffic on Broadway, between Thirty-third and Thirty-ninth Street, and on Seventh Avenue below Thirty-third Street, will continue to be held up.

Parties of engineers under the direction of the Public Service Commission and the Mayor were at work all day examining the roofed streets over the excavations. The Mayors' committee made an inspection of all the unfinished subway construction work which is being conducted by the United States Realty and Improvement Corporation, the builder of the sections where both of last week's accidents occurred, and today it will examine all of the subway construction throughout the city where there are roofed excavations in which

Continued on Page 4.

Austria Is Calling Out Reserves of Eighteen

ZURICH, Switzerland, Sept. 26.—The Austrian eighteen-year-old landsturm class has been ordered to join the army on Oct. 15, according to a dispatch from Vienna. Other classes, including the ages of 19, 20, 24, and from 38 to 43, will be summoned to the colors the middle of November.

The oldest classes, from 43 to 50 years, will be called out at the end of November.

OPERA SINGER SHOT; HER FIANCE A SUICIDE

Girl Was to Have Opened Tonight in Victor Herbert's "Princess Pat" at the Cort.

ROMANCE BEGAN ON STAGE

Young Man, in Tears an Hour Before, Had Lamented Sweetheart's Waning Love.

As he passed the music conservatory of Mme. Alice Andres Parker, 240 West Seventy-second Street, at 11 o'clock last night, Policeman Koenig of the West Sixty-eighth Street Station heard four revolver shots, raced up the steps, and of Mme. Parker, who admitted him, demanded where the shooting had been.

"Why, it must be outside," replied Mme. Parker. "We didn't hear it."

"It was in your top floor," responded the policeman, and he led the way to the top story front room. The door was locked. Koenig burst it open. Those behind Koenig saw that the body of Miss Pearl Palmer, a light opera singer, who was to have opened tonight at the Cort Theatre, playing the second lead in Victor Herbert's "Princess Pat," lay on the floor near the bed.

Beside her lay Herbert Heckler, also a singer in light opera. Both were wounded in the head, where two bullets had struck each. The girl was conscious, and tried to speak as the policeman and the others entered, but before she could utter a word she lost consciousness.

Dr. Robert Rose of 363 West End Avenue was paying a call at the house and was in the parlor, on the ground floor. A shout brought him running upstairs, and one glance at Miss Palmer caused him to exclaim:

"She's dying. Hurry her to a hospital."

Then he bent over Heckler, and rose in a moment with the announcement, "He is dead."

An ambulance was called from the Polyclinic Hospital, and the girl was hurried to that institution. She is in a critical condition, and it is feared there is little hope of her recovery.

Mme. Parker and others in the conservatory who had known both the young man and the young woman for years were almost prostrated by the tragedy, but several of them said they had feared something would happen because of Heckler's infatuation for the girl and his growing belief that she was losing her love for him, although they were engaged to be married.

They met three years ago while playing in the same company, and a year later announced their engagement. Why they had not married before this no one seemed to know, unless they were ambitious and were progressing in their profession so that neither was willing to abandon chances for further success.

Miss Palmer had sung last week in Philadelphia and reached Mme. Parker's home yesterday afternoon. The conservatory was recently taken over by the Aborns to become the Aborn Classes for Operatic Training, but Mme. Parker was still in charge, and she gave Miss Palmer her old room on the top floor.

Heckler, who is said to be the son of a wealthy jeweler of Chicago, apparently had not been singing this Summer, for he had been in the city for a month, and presently was to have taken a position as teacher in the Aborn school, it was said. He called at the house last evening, apparently as soon as he learned that Miss Palmer had returned to town, and Mme. Parker directed him to the girl's room.

Heckler had lived in the house himself on former occasions and was well known to Mme. Parker. She told him that Miss Palmer had complained of nervousness over tonight's opening, and Heckler, making some sympathetic remark, passed on up to her room, greeting W. W. Houston, a music teacher of 21 West Thirtieth Street, and also a caller at the house, as he passed through the parlor.

Presently he came downstairs again and asked Mr. Houston to accompany him to a near-by hotel, where he could buy a bottle of ale.

"Miss Palmer doesn't feel well," he explained, "and I thought the ale would do her good if taken just before she retired."

Houston accompanied him, and they walked to Broadway and Seventy-second Street, where they got the ale and started back. As they neared the house Heckler complained:

"Something's the matter. I'm losing Pearl's love. She isn't the same as she was. She is very successful and ambitious, and I think she's forgetting me in her pride in her work. If I can't have her love I don't want to live."

Then, to the amazement of Houston, he burst into tears. Houston tried to calm him, and by the time they reached the house had so pacified him that he was able to pass on up to Miss Palmer's room without exciting the comment of others.

The room on the top floor is three stories above the parlor floor, so that ordinary sounds do not carry so far, but Mme. Parker, Mr. Houston, and the others did hear Miss Palmer laugh once, and they recalled afterward that it was a laugh in which there was no joy, no humor. It sounded harsh, scornful, cynical, as though the girl were amused at Heckler's protestations.

Then they heard the voices of both, and knew they must be raised for the sound to have reached to the lower floor, but still none went upstairs, for neither Heckler nor Miss Palmer was of the sort who might be expected to give way to a quarrel. And then came several screams.

It was found that Heckler had fired two bullets into Miss Palmer's head and two in his own. The first bullet had grazed the top of the girl's scalp and from the position of her body she apparently had tried to reach the door and escape when Heckler fired the second time. This bullet entered below her left ear and lodged in the brain.

To shoot himself Heckler had put the weapon to his own temple and it was disclosed how close he must have stood to his victim when his body was found stretched so close to her on the floor that they touched.

Heckler was 27 years old and Miss Palmer was two years younger. It was said at the conservatory last night that her family was supposed to be named Foster and to live at 220 East Seventy-seventh Street.

Mme. Parker said afterward that Heckler had been taking vocal instruction from her for the last three months and had been such a hard worker that she wouldn't be surprised if his labors had turned his brain. She seemed to think this might have made him imagine a coldness on the part of his fiancée.

ALLIES ATTACK FROM SEA TO VERDUN; SMASH 20 MILES OF GERMAN FRONT; 20,000 PRISONERS, MANY GUNS TAKEN

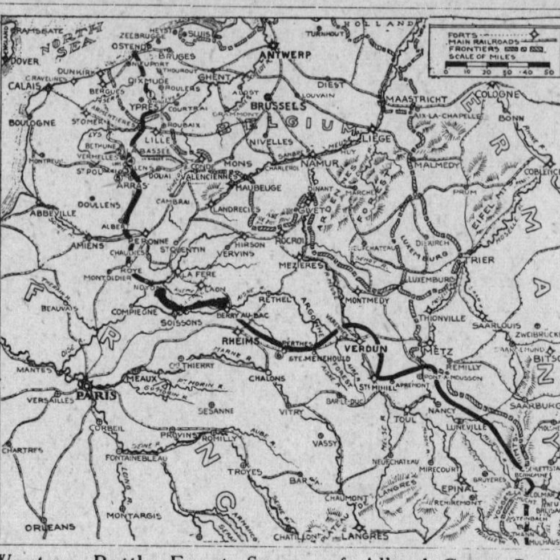

Western Battle Front, Scene of Allies' Great Drive

1. Hooge, the northern limit of the British attack.

2. Here the British captured five miles of trenches.

3. The British capture of Hill 70, a mile from Lens, threatens the German occupation of that town.

4. Loos, captured by the British, is about twelve miles from Lille, the most important city of Northern France held by the Germans.

5. Souchez, after months of fighting, now entirely in French hands.

6. Perthes, middle of the Champagne line, along which the French captured fifteen miles of trenches.

Greatest Advances Made in Champagne and North of Arras.

SOUCHEZ AND LOOS TAKEN

British Capture of the Latter Threatens the Germans' Possession of Lens.

A 70-HOUR BOMBARDMENT

It Preceded French Assaults Which Won 15 Miles of Trenches Near Perthes.

33 FIELD GUNS CAPTURED

Booty of the Allies Includes Many Machine Guns and Much Other War Material.

GERMANS ADMIT REVERSES

Report Evacuation of Loos and Champagne Positions — Rushing Reinforcements Through Belgium.

LONDON, Sept. 26.—The great allied offensive in the west began yesterday was successfully continued today. Tonight the net result is the taking of more than 20,000 unwounded German prisoners, the occupation of twenty miles of German trenches, (the German lines having been penetrated at some points to a depth of two and one-half miles,) and the capture of upward of thirty field guns, besides other war material.

The attack which resulted in the French and British victories began Saturday morning. For several weeks there has been an almost incessant bombardment with big guns, which late last week increased in intensity, particularly in the sectors where the infantry attacks took place.

The French, who have the most important gain to their credit, directed their chief onset against the German lines around Perthes, Beausejour, and Suippes, in Champagne, where in December they made a considerable gain of ground. Saturday's attack, however, backed by a tremendous artillery fire, gave them possession of more territory than they had retaken from the Germans since the latter dug themselves in after the battle of the Marne.

According to the French account the Germans in Champagne were driven out of their trenches over a front of fifteen miles, varying in depth from two-thirds of a mile to two and a half miles. The French in this engagement captured more than 12,000 prisoners, and apparently the advantage is being pressed still further.

Weakens German Argonne Positions.

The importance of this gain lies in the fact that every yard of ground taken in this region weakens the German position around Verdun, from which the Germans might be compelled to retire should the French succeed in making any further advance.

The French also have regained, first the cemetery and then the whole town of Souchez and trenches east of the Labyrinth in the Arras district, which was the scene of much heavy fighting earlier in the year. This battle was fought in co-operation with the British, who attacked on either side of La Bassée Canal. The attack to the south of the canal, Field Marshal Sir John French reports, was a complete success. Trenches on a five-mile front were taken at this point, the victors penetrating the German lines 4,000 yards.

This push forward gives the British possession of the road from Lens to La Bassée, which was used by the Germans for moving troops and supplies north and south, and threatens to outflank the German troops holding the town of Lens.

British Only Twelve Miles from Lille.

Hill No. 70, one of the positions taken on the road, is less than a mile directly north of Lens, with Hulluch, which also fell into the hands of the British, is at the end of the road near La Bassée. It is only twelve miles from Hulluch to Lille, the cheif city of Northern France.

North of the canal the British, although they fought all day yesterday, were unable to hold the ground gained and had to fall back to the trenches which they had left in the morning. The attack, however, accomplished one purpose, as, according to Sir John French, German reserves were sent to check this move, this giving the British south of the canal an opportunity to consolidate their new positions unmolested.

A somewhat similar manoeuvre took place to the north and south of the Menin Road, east of Ypres, and the results were the same. North of the road the British were unable to hold the ground taken, while to the south they

ENTENTE ARMY TO AID GREECE

Saloniki to be the Base for Operations in the Event of Balkan War.

BULGARIA NOW HEDGING

Assures Powers Mobilization Is Purely Defensive—Germans Keenly Disappointed.

LONDON, Monday, Sept. 27.—While the intentions of Bulgaria continue to be surrounded with considerable mystery it is clear that should that vacillating Balkan power venture to attack Serbia she will immediately find herself arrayed also against the army of Greece and in all likelihood that of Rumania, aided by a formidable force of British and French troops. Advices from Athens intimate that this aid has been offered to Greece by Great Britain and France, and that in the event of hostilities Saloniki will be used as a base by the Entente expeditionary corps.

Meanwhile Bulgaria, which had been definitely placed on the side of Germany and Austria as the result of recent news from Sofia, is showing every disposition to "hedge." She confirmed officially yesterday to the Governments of the Entente powers the semi-official statement published on Saturday that her mobilization had been ordered in the national interests and that it had not the slightest aggressive character.

The Bulgarian Premier, M. Radoslavoff, in an interview with the Sofia correspondent of the Berlin Tageblatt, reiterated this statement, but it is noteworthy that, while he said the measure was not directed against Greece or Rumania, he omitted Serbia.

In Germany keen disappointment and not a little uneasiness is felt at the turn of affairs. It had been confidently expected that Bulgaria would enter the war on the side of the Central Empires as soon as her mobilization was completed.

King Constantine and the Greek Premier, M. Venizelos, apparently have entirely composed the differences which led to their separation when the Premier early in the war wanted to join the Allies against Turkey. The cheering of the Greek populace gathered in front of the office of the British Minister, Sir Francis E. H. Elliot, was a significant incident in Saturday's crisis, says the correspondent at Athens of Reuter's Telegram Company. Although Greece still feels the effects of the late Balkan war, the correspondent adds, all shades of opinion support the mobilization of the Greek army as the only possible course which the Hellenic Government could take.

The whole matter may yet be smoothed over, as Bulgaria is continuing her negotiations with the Entente powers, the Bulgarian Minister at Petrograd having had a long conference with the Russian Foreign Minister, M. Sazonoff, while the Ministers at other capitals insist that the Bulgarians would not fight against their old friends, Great Britain and Russia.

On the other hand, the Austro-German offensive against Serbia, which seems to

Continued on Page 3.

SAY AUSTRIANS SET FIRE ON SANT' ANNA

Two Jumped Overboard, Officers Report, and Three Are Under Arrest.

NAPLES, Sept. 26, (via Paris.)—The commander and officers of the Fabre Line steamership Sant' Anna, which has arrived here from New York after having put in at the Azores with fire in her cargo, asserts that they have collected undisputable evidence that the fire was set by five Austrian passengers who gave false names when they boarded the vessel.

Three of these passengers, it is asserted, have been arrested, while the two others threw themselves overboard and disappeared.

The Sant' Anna sailed from South Brooklyn on Sept. 7 for Naples and Marseilles with 1,764 passengers, who were mostly Italian reservists.

A message was received at the State Department in Washington on Sept. 17 from Walter H. Schultz, the United States Consul at St. Michaels, saying that eighteen fuses had been discovered on the orlop deck of No. 2 hold, where the baggage was stowed, and several explosions had been heard by the crew of the steamship before the fire started. After transferring to the Ancona 695 passengers, who occupied the steerage forward and had been driven out by smoke and water, the Sant' Anna proceeded to Naples.

Since the fire broke out on the Sant' Anna the Fabre Line has adopted the plan of the other transatlantic lines out of New York of having all baggage searched before it is placed on board ship.

The passenger agents of all transatlantic lines out of this port operating under neutral flags will not accept any male German, Austrian or Hungarian passengers on their steamships unless they have safe conduct passes from the Allies.

FOG SAVED THE CYMRIC WITH BIG WAR CARGO

Crew of the White Star Liner Thinks Submarine Mistook the Hesperian for Her.

Members of the crew of the White Star liner Cymric, which arrived yesterday from Liverpool, said that when the vessel sailed from New York on Aug. 27 she had 17,000 tons of cargo, the largest shipment of ammunition made since the war began. In addition to hundreds of cases of rifle and revolver cartridges, the Cymric carried a large number of empty shells to be filled at Woolwich Arsenal, England. The cargo was stowed up to the hatches and staggered the longshoremen in Liverpool when the hatches were taken off. Some of the empty shells weighed 185 pounds.

German submarines were on the lookout for the Cymric off the coast of Ireland and the North of Scotland, because word had been sent from New York of the ammunition she had on board, the sailors said, but they missed her in the fog. One hundred miles west of Fastnet the liner was met by a cruiser and two torpedo boat destroyers to escort her into port.

The crew of the Cymric all believe that the Allan liner Hesperian was torpedoed by mistake for their ship, because the vessels were of very similar design. Captain F. E. Beadnell and the officers of the liner were noncommittal regarding the ammunition carried on the last eastward voyage, but admitted that the liner was escorted into Liverpool by a cruiser and two torpedo boat destroyers.

The Captain said that while the Cymric was in Liverpool he went to Belfast and brought the Olympic round to Southampton. She is being converted into a hospital ship for the Dardanelles.

DVINSK BATTLE GROWS IN FURY

Germans Making Desperate Efforts to Capture the Russian Fortress.

SEEK TO SPLIT TWO ARMIES

Austrians Say Ivanoff's Fierce Drive to Break Their Front in Volhynia Has Failed.

LONDON, Monday, Sept. 27.—Some of the fiercest fighting of the campaign is in progress on the Russian front. The Germans continue their furious attacks in an effort to drive the Russians out of Dvinsk and separate the Czar's forces there from the army which retreated so successfully from Vilna, while in Volhynia and Galicia the Russians continue to harass the Austro-Germans who had designs on Kiev, from which town they are now further away than they were a few weeks ago.

General Ivanoff apparently is determined to hold back the Austro-Germans, and his efforts are meeting with a considerable measure of success. The fortress triangle, which includes Dubno, Rovno, and Lutsk, is almost entirely in the possession of the Russians.

In Galicia the Austrians have been driven back across the rivers which run parallel to the border.

Russians Face 2,600,000 Men.

Special Cable to THE NEW YORK TIMES.

PETROGRAD, Sept. 26, (Dispatch to The London Daily News.)—The military expert of the Russky Invalid estimates that there are 130 Austro-German divisions, comprising 2,600,000 men, over the 1,000-mile front from Riga to the Rumanian frontier. The distribution is as follows: Sector of Riga, Dvinsk, and Svenziany, 12 divisions, 7 infantry, 5 cavalry; sector of Svenziany, Vilna, and Orani, 15 divisions, 12 infantry, 3 cavalry; sector of Orani, Slonim, and Pinsk, 47 divisions, 45 infantry, 2 cavalry; sector of Pinsk, Dubno, Brody, Tarnipol, and Novo Selizy, 54 divisions, 44 infantry, 10 cavalry.

There is a marked ascendancy in cavalry in Below's and Eichhorn's armies, which are used to break through and cut off the railways and get to the rear o the Russian forces. The cavalry succeeded on the Vilna-Dvinsk and Lida-Polozk lines, but the infantry failed in its task, causing the general operations to be frustrated.

The fighting in the Dvinsk region is growing fierce and more stubborn. With every step forward the enemy is losing heavily. Experts of the staff say latterly they have noticed the enemy are greatly reinforcing at Dvinsk, and evidently accumulating considerable forces, with the object of breaking the Russian front and separating the Dvinsk from the Molodechno groups.

Such a plan necessitates a widening of the scope of main operations. Experts on the staff do not believe the enemy is aiming at Petrograd or Kiev.

Continued on Page 2.

"All the News That's Fit to Print."

The New York Times.

THE WEATHER
Fair Monday and Tuesday; warmer; moderate north winds.
For full weather report see Page 12.

VOL. LXV...NO. 21,093. .... NEW YORK, MONDAY, OCTOBER 25, 1915.—EIGHTEEN PAGES. ONE CENT In Greater New York, Jersey City and Newark. | Elsewhere TWO CENTS.

LAST AIR RAID COST 150 TO 300 LIVES IN LONDON

Americans Back from England Put Zeppelin Death Roll Far Above First Figures.

THREE ATTACKS ON OCT. 13

Raiders Plainly Seen 3,000 Feet Up in a Clear Sky, Eyewitnesses Say.

ALDWYCH SUFFERED MOST

Scrap of Shell Hit Tribune Office and Correspondent Narrowly Escaped Death.

The American liner St. Paul arrived yesterday from Liverpool with the first eyewitnesses of the Zeppelin raid over London on Oct. 13. All accounts agreed that the night was clear, that the Zeppelins could be seen plainly when the searchlights shone on them, and that there was no cloud of steam emitted by the airships to hide them from view.

The shells from the anti-aircraft guns fell short of the Zeppelins, it was said, and caused great destruction of property. According to those who timed the visit of the raid, it occupied only seven minutes altogether. There were three to five Zeppelins coming from the city from the northeast, but the squadron split up before reaching the outskirts, and the units took different routes afterward. To show their contempt for the British anti-aircraft guns the Germans returned to London twice on the night of Oct. 13 and got away without receiving serious injury from shells.

Among those who gave graphic descriptions of the raid were Thomas Evarts Adams, Frederick W. Whitridge, and Mrs. Langtry. Several of those who were aboard the St. Paul said the death roll had been far underestimated in the cabled reports reaching New York. They gave various estimates of the number of dead from 150 to 300.

Folkestone Attacked.

The most complete account of the raid was supplied to THE TIMES by a passenger, who did not wish his name used, as follows:

"As far as can be made out there were five Zeppelins engaged in the raid, which ranged from Folkestone on the South coast to Hertford, the county town of Hertfordshire on the north, and as far west of London as Guildford. So far as London itself is concerned, four bombs were dropped in the neighborhood of Aldwych, another fell at the top of Cancery Lane, close by Holborn Viaduct Tube station, and others were dropped in the neighborhood of the Minories.

"The chief damage in London was around the Aldwych. One bomb dropped fifty yards away from the Waldorf Hotel in the middle of the road. The New York Tribune office is at 43 Aldwych, next door to the Waldorf Hotel. Its windows were all smashed, and a piece of shell two inches square drove right through the office, knocking off the stone coping of the window, tearing a hole through a thick curtain, and making a cavity as big as one's fist in the wall opposite. This was just about twenty minutes past 9, and only one man, Mr. Kerney, was present at the time. How he escaped was a marvel, for his chair was just in the line taken by the piece of shell, which, had he been sitting in his chair, would have caught him just about neck high. The probability is that he heard the noise of one of the other bombs dropped in the neighborhood and jumped out of his chair before the bomb fell in the Aldwych. All that he remembered afterward was falling down stairs with the office boy.

"Another bomb dropped by one of the doors of the Waldorf Theatre; another fell close by in Wellington Street, not more than twenty yards away from the Lyceum Theatre. Here it was that the greatest number of casualties in this part of London was caused, several people being killed in a public house in Wellington Street, just beyond The Morning Post offices, which had a great number of their windows blown out. A gas main in Wellington Street was shattered and the gas took fire, the flame continuing until about 9 o'clock the following morning. Throughout the darkness of the night the scene was an extraordinary one, the blaze from the gas main luridly illuminating the surroundings. There were cordons of police holding back the spectators, who numbered thousands.

Strand Theatre Shattered.

"Considerable damage was also done to the Strand and Gaiety Theatres by another bomb, which fell close by one of the side entrances of the former building. That side of the theatre was severely shattered and inside the concussion brought down part of the ceiling. Most of the windows of the Gaiety Theatre opposite were shattered. The dance scene in "The Scarlet Pimpernel" was in progress at the Strand Theatre when the first crash of the bomb was heard. A moment or so later parts of the roof fell in, crashing down into the auditorium itself. A number of people were injured and at least one killed.

"At first there was some panic, which was increased as several hysterical persons began calling out 'fire.' These, however, were promptly silenced by those around them, and almost instantly Mr. Fred Terry appeared on the stage, only dimly discernible through the dense crowds of dust. He success-

Continued on Page 2.

BRITISH SUBMARINE SINKS GERMAN CRUISER

Warship of the Prinz Adalbert Class Sent to Bottom in Baltic Near Libau.

PETROGRAD, Oct. 24, (via London.)—A British submarine operating near Libau attacked and sunk a German cruiser of the Prinz Adalbert class, according to official announcement made tonight.

A semi-official statement refers to the cruiser that was sunk simply as the Prinz Adalbert. According to this statement, the cruiser was sunk near Libau by a clever manoeuvre of the British submarine. The cruiser, it is said, formed part of a squadron and was probably charged with a special mission.

The vessel destroyed in the Baltic may have been one of these three German ships.

The Prinz Adalbert, an armored cruiser of 8,858 tons displacement, 393 feet in length, 65 feet beam and 24 feet depth. She was built at Kiel in 1903, had a speed of 20.5 knots, and carried a complement of 504 men.

The Prinz Heinrich, an armored cruiser of 8,750 tons, 396 feet in length, sixty-four feet beam, and twenty-five feet in depth. She was built at Kiel in 1902, had a speed of twenty knots, and carried a complement of 528 men.

The Roon, an armored cruiser of 9,350 tons, 403 feet in length, 65 feet beam, and 24 feet depth. She was built at Kiel in 1905, had a speed of 21.17 knots, and carried a complement of 638 men. The Roon was badly damaged in the battle with a Russian squadron last July. The Russian report said her guns were silenced and that she was set on fire.

Two other vessels of this class have been sunk. They were the Friedrich Karl, sunk by a mine in December, 1914, and the Yorck, sunk by a German mine in the Jahde, Nov. 3, 1914.

10,000 LED TO ENLIST BY MISS CAVELL'S FATE

Execution of Nurse a Powerful Stimulus to Recruiting in Great Britain.

Special Cable to THE NEW YORK TIMES.

LONDON, Oct. 24.—The execution by the Germans of Edith Cavell in Brussels is proving as effective an appeal for recruits as the statement issued last week by King George, according to many trained observers.

The Daily News says this morning:

"There is little doubt but that the German court which sentenced Edith Cavell to death has been responsible already for adding 10,000 men to the strength of the British Army.

"Recruiting Sergeants are unanimous in saying that Miss Cavell's heroic end has made an irresistible appeal to those men who needed some strong emotional stimulus before taking up arms, that stimulus which in the early days of the war was supplied by the overrunning of Belgium and the retreat of the British Army from Mons."

MAILED FIST HEAVIER ON BELGIAN TOWNS

New Military Governor of Brussels Is Reported Terrorizing the Inhabitants.

Special Cable to THE NEW YORK TIMES.

ROTTERDAM, Oct. 24, (Dispatch to The London Daily News.)—I hear on good authority that since the appointment a few weeks ago of a Prussian cavalry officer as the new Military Governor life in Brussels has been unbearable, the most oppressive regulations have been instituted, and large numbers of people arrested.

The principle of the mailed fist has also spread to Antwerp, where between twenty and thirty persons have already been sentenced to long terms of imprisonment and transported to Germany.

In the villages the same process has been carried out. Lokeren, Rotselaer, and Eltichoe have each been fined 5,000 marks ($1,250) because their authorities had not discovered in the three places a total of sixteen pigeons.

In this connection a remarkable description of the reign of terror in Brussels is contributed to the Nieuwe Rotterdamsche Courant by its Brussels correspondent—and the message is all the more extraordinary because it passed the German censorship.

"For some days past," it says, "the walls here have been covered with placards in such superfluity as has not been seen for a long time. Not only the quantity but the tone and contents of the notices prove that something has altered. What it is precisely is difficult to describe. Perhaps I can indicate it by saying that the iron fist will make itself felt.

"On Oct. 12 there was an order for the surrender of all men who during the war had belonged to the enemy's army and might be hidden here. Not only must the men themselves report, but everybody who knew of their presence was commanded, under threats of heavy punishment, to disclose their knowledge.

"Now the inhabitants are threatened that on the renewal of the visit of the Allies' fliers they will have German soldiers billeted upon them. To the uninitiated the logical connection may not be immediately grasped. It is this: The enemy's fliers have repeatedly chosen as targets buildings in which it was known German troops assembled. It is presumed that the population has made known these buildings to the Allies; therefore the population is held responsible, and, in order that they may be watched more narrowly, soldiers will be quartered in their houses if the fliers come again."

Special Cable to THE NEW YORK TIMES.

AMSTERDAM, Oct. 24, (Dispatch to The London Morning Post.)—According to the Echo Belge, a rumor is current that 7,000 Belgians, aged from seventeen to thirty-five years, have been removed from Brussels to Germany.

The Journal at first had no confirmation of this report, but at the moment of going to press received this message:

"Last Wednesday it was announced in Brussels that all Belgians of military age had to report themselves at the Commandant's office within forty-eight hours, and that those who did not appear would incur the penalty of execution."

At midnight the Echo Belge received the following:

"The rumor that a large number of young Belgians are going to Germany is confirmed in many quarters, but the exact number is not known. It appears that 1,500 men reported themselves on the first day. They were accompanied by relatives, but these were removed by force by the German soldiers. It is said that these 1,500 have already been taken to Germany."

GERMAN OFFICIAL DEFENDS KILLING OF EDITH CAVELL

Regrettable, Says Dr. Zimmermann, but the Safety of the Army Required It.

WAS A TIME FOR STERNNESS

"In War," He Goes On, "One Must Be Prepared to Seal One's Patriotism with Blood."

MILDER POLICY CONSIDERED

But, If Adopted, He Insists, It Will be No Admission of Harshness in Suspended Sentences.

> ### *Kaiser Summons Officials to Report on Edith Cavell*
>
> Special Cable to The New York Times.
>
> AMSTERDAM, Oct. 24, (Dispatch to The London Daily Express.)—It is said in Brussels that Governor General von Bissing and Civil Governor von der Lancken have been called to the imperial headquarters to report on Miss Edith Cavell's death.

From a Staff Correspondent.

Special Cable to THE NEW YORK TIMES.

BERLIN, Oct. 24.—Moved by foreign denunciations of the execution of Miss Edith Cavell, out of which he says Germany's enemies are making capital, Dr. Alfred F. M. Zimmermann, Under Secretary for Foreign Affairs, has granted an interview in which he defends the action of the German authorities in Belgium as necessary to insure the security of the German armies, but intimates that leniency may be shown the other prisoners who have been convicted for offenses similar to those of the British nurse.

Says the Killing Was Necessary.

"It was a pity," said Dr. Zimmermann, "that Miss Cavell had to be executed, but it was necessary. She was judged justly. We hope it will not be necessary to have any more executions.

"I see from the English and American press that the shootin of an Englishwoman and the condemnation of several other women in Brussels for treason has caused a sensation, and capital against us is being made out of the fact. It is undoubtedly a terrible thing that the woman has been executed; but consider what would happen to a State, particularly in war, if it left crimes aimed at the safety of its armies to go unpunished because committed by women. No criminal code in the world—least of all the laws of war—makes such a distinction; and the feminine sex has but one preference, according to legal usages, namely, that women in a delicate condition may not be executed. Otherwise man and woman are equal before the law, and only the degree of guilt makes a difference in the sentence for the crime and its consequences.

"I have before me the court's verdict in the Cavell case, and can assure you that it was gone into with the utmost thoroughness, and was investigated and cleared up to the smallest details. The result was so convincing, and the circumstances were so clear, that no war court in the world could have given any other verdict, for it was not concerned with a single emotional deed of one person, but a well-thought-out plot, with many far-reaching ramifications, which for nine months succeeded in doing valuable service to our enemies to the great detriment of our armies. Countless Belgian, French, and English soldiers are again fighting in the ranks of the Allies who owe their escape to the activities of the band now found guilty, whose head was the Cavell woman. Only the utmost sternness could do away with such activities under the very nose of our authorities, and a Government which in such case does not resort to the sternest measures sins against its most elementary duties toward the safety of its own army.

"All those convicted were thoroughly aware of the nature of their acts. The court particularly weighed this point with care, letting off several of the accused because they were in doubt as to whether they knew that their actions were punishable. Those condemned knew what they were doing, for numerous public proclamations had pointed out the fact that aiding enemies' armies was punishable with death.

"I know that the motives of the condemned were not base; that they acted from patriotism; but in war one must be prepared to seal one's patriotism with blood whether one faces the enemy in battle or otherwise in the interest of one's cause does deeds which justly bring after them the death penalty. Among our Russian prisoners are several young girls who fought against us in soldiers' uniforms. Had one of these girls fallen no one would have accused us of barbarity against women. Why now, when another woman has met the death to which she knowingly exposed herself, as did her comrades in battle?

"There are moments in the life of nations where consideration for the existence of the individual is a crime against all. Such a moment was here. It was necessary once for all to put an end to the activity of our enemies, regardless of their motives; therefore the death penalty was executed so as to frighten off all those who, counting on preferential treatment for their sex, take part in undertakings punishable by

Continued on Page 3.

RUMANIA EXPECTED TO JOIN THE ALLIES

Rome Hears Agreement Is Being Reached Between Government and Opposition.

Special Cable to THE NEW YORK TIMES.

LONDON, Monday, Oct. 25.—The Rome correspondent of The Daily Mail sends this message:

"Telegrams from Bucharest state that Rumania is on the eve of taking grave decisions.

"Agreement is on the point of being arrived at between the Government and Opposition in favor of intervention on the side of the Allies."

LONDON, Monday, Oct. 25.—A Cabinet crisis in Rumania is imminent, according to a dispatch to The Daily News from Rome, owing to the resignation of several of the Ministers who oppose Rumania's intervention in the war.

GEN. DIMITRIEFF SEEKS TO OVERTURN FERDINAND

News of Russia's Declaration of War Kept From the Bulgarian People.

Special Cable to THE NEW YORK TIMES.

[The Cologne Gazette Dispatches.]

SOFIA, Oct. 23.—The Bulgarian General in the Russian service, Radko Dimitrieff, who is in Rumania, is endeavoring to get into contact with fellow partisans in Bulgaria with a view of instigating a revolution with the aid of the army, as in former years. The Bulgarian Government is well informed regarding this effort and has taken the necessary preventive measures. Dimitrieff was last seen in Kalagat, across from Vidin.

Should the campaign continue to progress favorably there is no prospects of success for his scheme, as the Bulgarians are unanimously bent on the acquisition of Macedonia.

The newspaper, Mir, supporting the Ussen party interests, says:

"Besides England and France, Italy also has declared war against us. It is believed Russia will not join in this shameful action of her allies. These allies, during a period of fifteen months, have not been able to beat Germany and Austria; thus they are now bombarding the shores of Bulgaria on the Aegean Sea without at all aiding their spoiled protégé, Serbia, and without injuring either us or the Germans."

Most other Bulgarian papers declare that in the bombardment of the Bulgarian shore hardly a single one of the large shells fired had any more effect than the destruction of a few cottages.

COUNTS COST OF WAR AT $45,000,000,000

Banker Shearson, Back from England, Assumes Struggle Will Last 18 Months Longer.

Edward Shearson, head of Shearson, Hammill & Co., bankers, of 71 Broadway, returned yesterday from London on the American liner St. Paul. He had been away since June. He spent most of the time at Ascot, near Windsor.

"The financial conditions are very serious in England," said Mr. Shearson, "graver, I fear, than the London financiers realize. The taxation to meet the cost of the war will be the greatest that any nation has had to bear in the history of the world. By officials in the Government service and men of affairs in England I was told that the war certainly would last another eighteen months. Taking this as a basis for a rough estimate, formed from the expenditure up to date, it will cost the belligerent nations about $45,000,000,000 for the destruction of property, waste, and labor in this war.

"England has done wonderful work, work that never has been equaled before. She has 3,000,000 trained soldiers, perfectly equipped for war, at the present time, and her navy is invincible. There are 1,000,000 British troops in France, 350,000 in the Dardanelles, and 1,650,000 in Great Britain awaiting orders to proceed to the front."

IRISHMEN FLEE HERE; FEAR CONSCRIPTION

The St. Paul, From Liverpool, Arrives With 250—Several Passengers Are Detained.

The American liner St. Paul arrived here yesterday afternoon from Liverpool with 145 first, 331 second, and 331 third class passengers, among whom were 250 young Irishmen leaving their country to avoid the expected conscription. Several passengers in the cabin were detained by the Immigration Inspectors and sent to Ellis Island for further examination before a special Board of Inquiry.

Among them was Emilio Veraga, a young Peruvian who came over to live with his aunt, Mrs. Juana de Sanders, whose home is at 108 West Seventy-eighth Street. He lacks four days of being 16 years old, which brings him under the immigration law. He was accompanied on the liner by Norbetta Condore, a Peruvian Indian girl 8 years old, who would have been sent to the Immigration Bureau, too, but his aunt came to the pier for her and the Inspector allowed her to land.

Emilio Vergara told the officials that he had left Peru with his aunt Juana two and a half years ago, and had been to school in England. His uncle, who was an American, had died in Peru, and his aunt had sent for him because she was afraid of the Zeppelins in England. The little girl, he said, came from Cuzco, 11,000 feet up in the Andes, where it is always cold, and had been adopted by his uncle years ago, when he was constructing a railroad there. She had gone to London with him and had been staying at a French convent in Golden Square, Soho.

The Rev. J. A. Johnson, Bishop of the African Methodist Church from the Zambesi to Cape Town, was another passenger. He is on his way home to Philadelphia. He said the war had changed conditions in Africa so much that his return home was almost a necessity.

FLEET'S SHELLS WIPE OUT 1,000 BULGAR SOLDIERS

Crowded Barracks Hit at Dedeaghatch—Enormous Damage to the Port.

ALLIES MAY LAND AT LAGOS

French and Serbians Capture Village Near Strumnitza—Bulgars Take Uskub.

DANUBE IS CROSSED AGAIN

Austro-German Army in New Invasion Alongside the Frontier of Rumania.

> ### *King Would Die With Serbs Rather than Survive Conquest*
>
> Special Cable to THE NEW YORK TIMES.
>
> ROME, Oct. 24, (Dispatch to The London Daily Telegraph.)—Telegrams from a German source state that the King of Serbia has issued the following proclamation:
>
> "Age has taken my arms from me. I, who was elected your King, have no longer force to guide my armies to the war in defense of the Fatherland. I am but a feeble old man who can do nothing but bless Serbia's soldiers, citizens, women, and children. But I swear to you if a new invasion shall bring upon us the shame of being conquered I shall not survive the ruin, but I, too, shall die with the country."
>
> King Peter of Serbia is 71 years old.

LONDON, Monday, Oct. 25.—The bombardment of Dedeaghatch caused the death of ten civilians and over a thousand soldiers, and there also were a large number of soldiers wounded, says a dispatch to the Exchange Telegraph Company from Athens.

A large proportion of the military casualties, the correspondent adds, were in the barracks which housed the Fortieth Bulgarian Regiment. The barracks was crowded with soldiers, who were preparing for their meal when the bombardment was opened at 1 o'clock with accurately aimed shells, which demolished the barracks, burying the occupants in the ruins.

Troops engaged in digging trenches around the town also suffered very heavy losses.

Fires caused by the exploding shells destroyed the railway station and surrounding buildings, doing enormous damage. It is stated that the entire loss from the bombardment, which lasted four hours, will be several million pounds.

The correspondent says the bombardment was directed by aeroplanes, which flew over the town throughout the afternoon. Twenty warships participated. The Bulgarians are now engaged in preparing defense works on the surrounding mountains.

Porto Lagos was fiercely bombarded by eight warships Thursday and again on Friday.

Uskub Taken by Bulgarians.

It is understood that the Allies plan to make a landing on the Bulgarian coast at Porto Lagos.

The Bulgarians, according to their official report issued yesterday, have reached Uskub, an important junction on the Saloniki-Nish Railway, and have thus placed themselves across the route by which the Allies' reinforcements for the Serbs would travel.

An official announcement issued at Nish on Saturday by the Serbian General Headquarters Staff confirmed reports that the Bulgarians had occupied Kumanovo, on the Nish railroad, about twelve miles northeast of Uskub, and Veles, on the Vardar River, about twenty-five miles southeast of Uskub.

A dispatch to The Times from Athens dated Saturday, however, says:

"A telegram from General Sarrail, Commander in Chief of the French army in the Orient, says the Bulgarians have occupied only a portion of the town of Veles. They are on the left bank of the Varder, which runs through the town. French troops stopped the Bulgarian attack, and the Serbians retired to the hills on the right bank, which they are fortifying. Bulgarian official communication speaks of bad weather having interrupted their progress."

French on Bulgar Soil.

It is announced officially to the French War Office that the French troops operating with the Serbians have captured the village of Rabrovo, on Bulgarian soil nine miles south of Strumnitza.

The Austro-Germans in the north have begun a more vigorous offensive, and have crossed the Danube near Orsova, close to the Rumanian frontier. This brings much nearer the linking up of the armies of the Germanic allies and those of Bulgaria and the opening of the way through Bulgaria to Constantinople. Success, however, is not being achieved without heavy losses, as the Serbian veterans, well intrenched in their mountains, are offering stubborn resistance and are making the invaders pay a big price for every mile of country invaded.

Without the active co-operation of Greece and Rumania, however, the Allies, it is feared here, will not be able to do much for some weeks.

Official Reports of Fighting.

The German official report of the latest operations, issued by the Berlin War Office yesterday, says:

East of Lucavica the army of General von Koevers, of Field Marshal von Mackensen's group, drove the Serbians back in a westerly direc-

Continued on Page 4.

ARREST GERMAN FOREIGN OFFICE MAN HERE AS A SPY WITH EXPLOSIVES TO BLOW UP SHIPS LEAVING NEW YORK

> ### *Explosions Said to Have Been Set by Spies on Ships and in Powder Plants Making Munitions*
>
> ON STEAMSHIPS.
>
> | Sailed | Sailed |
> |---|---|
> | March 6—Touraine. | May 8—Bankdale. |
> | April 27—The Devon City. | July 9—Minnehaha. |
> | April 29—The Lord Erne. | July 24—Craigside. |
> | April 29—Cressington Court. | Sept. 8—Athinai. |
> | May 1—Sandland. | Sept. 13—Sant' Anna. |
> | May 1—Lord Downshire. | Dynamite found on Arabic on Aug. 4. |
> | May 2—Kirkoswold. | |
> | May 8—Strathtay. | |
>
> IN THE MUNITION PLANTS.
>
> April 1—Equitable powder plant, Alton, Ill.
> March 5—Du Pont plant, Haskell, N. J.
> April 4—Caps for shells exploded in Pompton Lakes, N. J., freight depot.
> May 10—Du Pont plant, Carney's Point, N. J.
> May 15—Two explosions same place.
> May 25—Explosion same place.
> July 15—Central Railroad grain elevator, Weehawken.
> Aug. 11—Westinghouse Electric plant, Turtle Creek, Penn.
> Aug. 29—Dupont plant, Wilmington, Del.

BOMB FACTORY IN HIS ROOM

Prisoner, an Officer in the Kaiser's Army, Carried Map of Harbor.

MECHANIC AID ALSO TAKEN

Kept High-Power Automobile and Motor Boat, Always Ready for Fast Service.

A NEW INFERNAL MACHINE

Telescope Device Found in Lodgings, with Supply of Most Powerful Explosive.

The attempt by two Germans to buy ten pounds of picric acid, the chemical which enters into the composition of most high explosives, from a New York firm a few weeks ago resulted yesterday afternoon in the arrest in a wood near Grantwood, N. J., of Robert Fay and Walter Scholz, who are locked up in the Weehawken police station on the charge of conspiracy.

Fay, according to papers found in the apartments which the two men shared at 27 Fifth Street, Weehawken, is a Lieutenant in the German Army. It is said that he took part in the battle of the Marne, and came to the United States last April.

Other documents found in his rooms indicate a connection, according to the Federal Secret Service men and the New York and New Jersey detectives who made the arrest, with the German Foreign Office. What this connection was no one would say last night, but it is intimated that there can be no doubt that he had close relations with Wilhelmstrasse.

Fay is 34 years old and a man of culture and refinement. He speaks English fluently and possesses a striking personality. Scholz is 27 and a mechanic, who has been in this country two years. It is said that he represented himself as Fay's brother-in-law.

Held for Conspiracy.

The two men are held on the charge of conspiracy, and will be arraigned this morning before Recorder Rander in Weehawken. But it is understood that they are believed to have been connected with a recent explosion in a West Shore Railroad elevator in Weehawken, and it is intimated by the detectives that there is reason for connecting them with the series of explosions in ammunition factories, of bomb explosions on board steamers carrying supplies to the anti-German coalition in Europe, which has been a feature of the American export trade in munitions for the last few months.

In the men's rooms, and in a compartment in a West Hoboken storage warehouse which it is said they rented, were found explosives of the highest power, together, according to the police story, with mines fitted out with apparatus for attaching them to the sterns of ships.

The apprehension of the two men began with the activity of Acting Detective Captain Thomas Tunney, in charge of the dynamite squad at New York Police Headquarters, who was ordered by Commissioner Woods some time ago to devote his energies to hunting down the men who have been concerned in the placing of bombs on merchant ships.

Tunney and his men thereupon started a careful scrutiny of every place in Manhattan where high explosives are manufactured, stored, or sold, and every man who came or went, who bought or sold anything, was carefully looked over and investigated. It was some time ago that the two Germans who tried to make the purchase of picric acid came under Tunney's observation. His men followed them when they left the place where they had tried to buy the explosives, followed them across the river into New Jersey, and up to the apartment house in Fifth Street, Weehawken.

Secret Service Joins Work.

For some time after that New York and New Jersey detectives kept a watch on the two. It was discovered, according to the police, that they were in the habit of taking a trolley car to a lonely spot near Grantwood, there to make experiments with explosives, small quantities of which they took with them. After the police had found this out Chief William J. Flynn of the Federal Secret Service was notified, and he sent up two of his men, James Bush and James E. Savage, to take part in the investigation.

Yesterday afternoon Captain Tunney, Detective Lieutenant Barnets, and several of his men, accompanied by Fifth Deputy Police Commissioner Guy H. Scull and Inspector of Combustibles Healy, crossed over to Jersey and were joined by Bush and Savage, Detective Lyons of Weehawken, and Detective Lieutenant Charles Gillman of Union Hill.

The two men who had been under surveillance left the apartment in Fifth Street about the middle of the afternoon, carrying something with them in a suitcase. They got on a car to Grantwood and one of the detectives took the same car and went along with them.

The others followed in an automobile,

DRIVE SERBIANS BACK IN MOUNTAINS

Gen. Gallwitz's Army, Marching Knee-Deep in Mud, Makes Important Gains.

WOMEN DIE IN TRENCHES

Defenders, Unable to Withstand Withering Fire, Shelled Out of Position After Position.

BY WILHELM CONRAD GOMOLL.

Special Cable to THE NEW YORK TIMES.

[The Cologne Gazette Dispatches.]

HEADQUARTERS OF THE ARMY OF GENERAL VON GALLWITZ IN SERBIA, Oct. 23.—During the last two days our forces have made highly successful attacks and succeeded in quickening their rapid advance into the Morova valley.

In spite of bad roads, converted by recent rains into muddy slime, into which the troops sank to their knees at every step, the advance on both sides of the Morova valley continued until we had obtained complete command of the valley. As the troops gained ground through the adjacent hilly country lying to the east up to the Miawa valley the front was extended in the direction toward Palanka and Terowatz, with the result of securing an unexpected gain of territory.

In spite of the Serbian resistance our troops were everywhere successful. The central group of the army of General Gallwitz has opened the gate to the south still further. Our positions were advanced north and west toward the mountain district of Ranovac.

It appears that the Serbians sought to make a new stand there with furious energy, with the intention of stopping our further progress.

The mountains at this point are higher and more inaccessible. The right wing of General Gallwitz's army, however, is pushing on irresistibly toward the south from Selevac. It is based on the troops of General Koevess, now vigorously fighting for possession of the Ralja valley, where the advancing forces of the Serbians also fell back. By means of heavy artillery and infantry fire their line was driven back nearly ten kilometers.

The storming of the heights of Slatina during the fighting stands as a wonderful feat of arms, the troops taking this position, lying nearly 300 meters high, after the artillery had poured a rain of shells upon it. They forced their way at the point of the bayonet into the Serbian trenches on the surrounding heights, and also succeded in winning ground on the Kolubara.

The roads of the Morova valley, like those leading from the Pobonawley highlands, are the chief lines of communication leading to Kraguyevac, which for centuries was the centre of Turkish military power.

Fought for Hill Tops, Step by Step.

HEADQUARTERS OF THE ARMY OF GENERAL VON GALLWITZ IN SERBIA, Oct. 22.—Fighting has been renewed in the mountainous country southeast of Posarevec, between the Pek and Miawa Rivers. After the centre of the army of General von Gallwitz in the valley of the Morava had advanced over the Poljana to Wlaschki Dol and taken this place, the left wing pressed on with a strong force between Wlaschki Dol and the little town of Raschkanre, on the Miawa. The advance went forward through a country commanded by many high summits, whose heights range from 200 to 300 meters. They were strongly fortified by the Serbians.

The struggle to gain possession of the hilltops was fought step by step, for the defensive positions of the enemy were

Continued on Page 3.

ITALIANS FORCING FOE TO SHIFT MEN

Austrians Said to be Obliged Now to Call Troops from Some Other Front.

DRIVEN FROM SECOND LINE

General Offensive Continues to Gain—1,000 More Austrian Prisoners Taken on Isonzo.

Special Cable to THE NEW YORK TIMES.

MILAN, Oct. 24, (Dispatch to The London Daily News.)—Magnificent success is attending the offensive that is being pushed along the whole front. The Austrian losses have been very heavy. Preparation for the offensive by three days of artillery fire was most destructive, both to the trenches and the men in them, particularly in the group of Austrian defenses protecting the Col di Lana.

Until the Italian offensive is completed it is impossible to gauge its importance on the future campaign, but it already is evident that the Austrians, almost along the entire length of the front, have been driven from the second line of defenses, which for four months they have been engaged in fortifying. Many of these positions I had the opportunity of observing when visiting the front at the invitation of the Italian Government. The natural difficulties they presented were reinforced by every defensive device known to soldiers. The success of the Italian moves confirms the high estimate my colleagues and I myself made of the value of the Italian Army from the point of view of command, equipment, and, above all, efficiency of soldier as a fighting unit.

It is significant that the Italian advance is of a nature to prevent the Austrians from taking advantage of strategic routes and moving troops from place to place in support of threatened positions and to fill gaps, which are numerous, because, in addition to the heavy losses in killed and wounded in two days, the Austrians' loss in prisoners totals 3,500.

Austria will now be forced to draw upon troops in one of her other fighting fronts or further deplete the watching force kept near the Rumanian frontier.

Italians Take 1,000 Prisoners.

ROME, Oct. 24, (via Paris.)—The official statement issued today from Italian General Headquarters reads as follows:

A new and brilliant success has marked our offensive in the Ledro Valley. Our troops penetrated, on the 22d, into Bezzeca Basin, occupied the village and the heights dominating it to the north on the two sides of the Concei Valley.

In upper Cordevole our troops are closing their grip on the difficult defenses of the Col di Lana. Two more field forts were stormed and twenty-five prisoners taken.

In the Rienz Valley, on the night of the 23d, the enemy attempted to attack our positions at a point where the Popena debouches, but was repulsed.

In the Fella Valley fresh actions, turning in our favor, were fought near Pontafel and Leopoldskirchen.

In the Monte Nero zone we completed the occupation of the crest southeast of Mrzli, and repulsed two violent enemy attacks on our Vodil positions. On Monte Sabotino and on Podgora Height, in the Gorizia zone, our troops have taken several trenches by assault.

On the Carso the troops fought all day yesterday, both sides showing great determination. Our infantry, undismayed by the deadly effects of the enemy's artillery, advanced impetuously several times to the conquest of the enemy's positions, which, previous to that, had been plowed up by the accurate and effective shelling of our batteries. Our adversary opened a violent and rapid fire from numerous masked field and machine guns, and launched fresh columns in a counterattack.

Important positions were several times stormed, then lost, and restormed, but at evening our troops held securely the ground won on the left wing, east of Peteano, and in the centre, toward Marcottini.

We took 1,083 prisoners, sixteen of whom were officers, together with three machine guns and other war material. This booty marks the success of our arms during a hard day's fighting along the Isonzo front.

"All the News That's Fit to Print."

The New York Times.

THE WEATHER
Fair Sunday and Monday; moderate northwest to north winds.
For full weather report see Page 23.

VOL. LXV...NO. 21,106. ... NEW YORK, SUNDAY, NOVEMBER 7, 1915.—104 PAGES, In Seven Parts, Including Picture and Rotogravure Section and Review of Books. PRICE FIVE CENTS.

12 BURN TO DEATH IN FACTORY AS 200 FIGHT ON THREE FLOORS TO REACH SINGLE FIRE ESCAPE

36 INJURED, 15 MISSING

Blaze Starts in Elevator Shaft and Cuts Off Stairs at Every Landing.

GIRLS LEAP FROM WINDOWS

Women Burn Like Torches on Red-Hot Grill That Had Been the Fire Escape.

EIGHT DIE ON ONE PLATFORM

Owners of Williamsburg Building Held Without Bail for Ignoring Fire Orders.

Where a big double factory building that rose five stories from the street stood yesterday at 281 and 283 North Sixth Street, Williamsburg, there appeared last night, illumined by the rays of three Fire Department searchlights, a heap of débris, surmounted by the shell of what had been the walls.

In the ruins firemen and policemen dug for the bodies of men and women who were missed after flames had swept through the place yesterday afternoon, after men had fought girls to reach the single fire escape that last night hung, still hot, down the front of the building, and after there had been an accounting of the building's inmates that showed twelve persons killed and thirty-six injured.

As in the case of the Triangle Shirt Waist fire, when the girls threw themselves from windows, so yesterday many of the injured received their hurts when, driven by the flames, they sprang from window ledges and the fire escape.

The dead were found in the building and on the fire escape, which almost at once had become a huge grill on which the unfortunates were roasted to death. Eleven had been identified last night. One of fifteen reported as missing one may be found later in the single charred body of a girl resting in the Kings County Hospital Morgue, but the diggers last night worked with the assurance that some time they must come on the bodies of other victims. Here are lists of those found so far and of those sent to hospitals:

THE DEAD.

BERGER, HENRY, 45, 14 Rutgers Place, Manhattan; identified in the Morgue.
BRICKER, SOLOMON, 1,775 Prospect Place; identified by John Ginsburg.
BROOK, CECILIA, 19, 463 Rodney Street.
DOTTY, IRENE, 19, 181 Holt Street.
GOLDMAN, ROSE, 16, 244 Wallabout Street; identified by John Ginsburg.
GOLDSTEIN, LENA, 20, 339 South Second Street.
GRASS, JENNIE, 21, 356 South First Street.
NAPOLITANO, MARIE, 21, 210 New Jersey Avenue.
ROSSMAN, BERTHA, 15, 275 North Sixth Street.
SKANDEE, GEORGE, 185 Ten Eyck Street.
WALLACK, A., 326 Bristol Street; died in the Williamsburg Hospital.
ONE UNIDENTIFIED WOMAN, body in the Morgue at the Kings County Hospital.

THE INJURED.

In St. Catharine's Hospital.

DOBSKY, WILLIAM, 41 Stagg Street.
GELLIA, JENNY, 26 Monitor Street.
KATZ, GUSSIE, 469 Marcy Avenue.
SHESTER, ESTHER, 617 Metropolitan Avenue.
SKYOK, AGNES, 40 Ten Eyck Street.

In Cumberland Street Hospital.

LISTER, BELLA, 348 Bristol Street.
SCHMEXELLA, STELLA, 21, 68 Eckford Street.
STASERENES, ANTON, 20 Hope Street.

In Greenpoint Hospital.

COHEN, LENA, address unknown.
GRACE, EDNA, 27, 103 Freeman Street.

In Eastern District Hospital.

ASTRYKAS, MARCELLA, 24, 90 North Sixth Street.
GREENBERG, MORRIS, Metropolitan Avenue and North Sixth Street; may die.
HARTMAN, CHARLES, 32, 458 New Jersey Avenue.
LONESTAN, LOUIS, 48, 162 Riverdale Avenue.
LUNOVICS, FRANCES, 25, 230 Gill Street, Hicksville, L. I.
WARNACHS, GEORGE, 39, 164 Holt Street.

In Williamsburg Hospital.

ARMAN, JOHN, 26, 65 Ten Eyck Street; injuries mortal.
BERMAN, IKE, 41, 175 Hopkins Street.
BOKRASS, JOSEPH, 23, 241 Broome Street, Manhattan; injuries mortal.
BUSH, JOSEPH, 49, 105 South 4th Street.
KRISCUINAS, A., 28, 233 Berry Street.
LASK, HELEN, 21, 22 Garden Street.
MENIK, HYMAN, 32, 134 Boerum Street; injuries mortal.
MORASKY, JOHN, 40, 407 Rodney Street.
NELLANCO, CRECENI, 22, 57 Columbia Street.
POLSKI, WILLIAM, 30, 100 Ten Eyck Street.
RAVINAS, JOHN, 23, 573 Lorimer Street.
SHUEBERS, SELIG, 40, 93 Bedford Avenue.
ANDRUZEVIZE, JOHN, 20, 146 North Third Street.
BERGER, ANNIE, 18, 51 Cannon Street, Manhattan.
BERGER, MARIE, 17, 51 Cannon Street, Manhattan.
BRADSKY, ROSE, 64 Moore Street.
LUONIDO, LOUIS, 23, 4 Meuger Street.
SAVOULA, EVA, 22, 350 South Second Street.
SILVERMAN, LOUIS, 31, 175 Madison Street.
SILVERMAN, ROSE, 17, 64 Tompkins Avenue.

Owners of Building Arrested.

That the State Labor Department, by precautionary orders for fireproofing, endeavored as long as three months ago to forestall just the tragedy that occurred was a fact developed when Coroner Ernest C. Wagner held an immediate inquiry, in conjunction with Assistant District Attorneys Reuben Wilson and Louis Goldstein, in the assembly room of Public School 143, only half a block away, at Havemeyer and North Sixth Streets. As a result, the Coroner ordered the arrest of Edward L. Dia-

Continued on Page 19.

State Labor Department Had Ordered Owners of Burned Factory to Fireproof the Stairs

The law which the owners of the burned Williamsburg factory building, in which twelve persons perished yesterday, are charged with violating is Article 2 of Section 79 of Chapter 31 of the State Labor law as amended in 1913, and reads:

All interior stairways serving as required means of exit in buildings more than four stories in height, and the landings, platforms, and passageways connected therewith, shall be inclosed on all sides by partitions of fire-resisting material extending continuously to the basement. Where the stairway extends to the top floor of the building such partitions shall extend for three feet above the roof. All openings in such partitions shall be provided with self-closing doors constructed of fire-resisting materials, except where such openings are in the exterior wall of the building. All such partitions and the doors provided for the openings therein shall be constructed in such manner as the Industrial Board may prescribe by its rules and regulations.

Fire Commissioner Adamson said last night that the State Labor Department had charge of the enforcement of this law, which was added to the Code on the recommendation of the State Factory Investigating Commission, which was created after the agitation caused by the Triangle Shirtwaist Company fire. It was the State Labor Department that issued the order to the Diamonds to fireproof the factory stairs.

ITALIAN CONSULATE SHAKEN BY A BOMB

Explosion Occurs Just After the Consul General Enters Office —Many Windows Broken.

POLICE FAIL TO FIND CLUE

Dynamite May Have Been Intended, They Think, for Count G. Fara Forni's Room.

For the third time within a year an attempt was made yesterday to blew up the offices of the Italian Consulate at 226 Lafayette Street. A dynamite bomb was set off near the street entrance to the building a few minutes after Count G. Fara Forni, the Consul General, had gone to his office on the third floor.

A dozen windows were broken on the side of the structure nearest the explosion, but greater damage was caused to the shops and tenement apartments in the four buildings immediately to the south of the Consulate, at 218, 220, 222, and 224 Lafayette Street. No one was injured, although there were many persons near the explosion.

The concussion was heard and felt at Police Headquarters, two blocks distant. Fifty detectives, headed by Captains Deevy and Tunney, Deputy Commissioners Dunham and Scull, and Sergeant Barnitz of the bomb squad, followed by the reserves from the Mulberry and Elizabeth Street Stations were at the place in a few minutes, but they could not find anything to show what form of an explosive had been used. Not a scrap of metal or anything like the piece of a bomb was to be found.

Two patrolmen, Otto F. Bruns and Thomas Mulhall, and two traffic policemen were within fifty feet of the explosion, but they saw no one run away after the explosion or any one near the spot where it took place before it occurred. In the hallway leading to the elevator of the Consulate building was Policeman Joseph Caravette, who had been detailed there as a special guard since the Consul had been registering the Italian reservists. He saw the explosion, but knew no more about it than the others.

The explosion occurred on the pavement, about two feet from the curb, midway between the entrance of the Consulate building and the Italian bank of A. Alvino & Son, on the street floor of 224 Lafayette Street. While the shock destroyed the plate glass in the shop and every one of the forty windows in the two tenements next the Consulate, and broke many of the windows in the two houses to the south of them, it left scarcely a mark on the pavement. Only a little of the filling around one or two of the paving blocks was forced out. The bomb was placed at a point where the Consul usually leaves his automobile in front of the building, it was said. Yesterday, however, he went to his office by the subway a few minutes after 10 o'clock, and the explosion occurred at 10:30.

The detectives believe that the explosive was in the form of a fuse-cap dynamite bomb, and was intended to be placed in the Consul's office, but was exploded prematurely. According to this theory, the man with the bomb was not aware that the Consulate was guarded by a policeman, and as he saw the officer in the hallway behind the street door, he dropped the lighted bomb in the gutter and escaped in the street crowd a moment before the explosion.

Count Forni and his assistants said there had been no recent trouble at the office which could account for any such attack. The detectives made inquiries among the tenants of the two shattered tenements, where twenty families live, and were convinced by them that the explosive had not been thrown from one of the windows or the roof of either building.

Mrs. Carmelia Nuzzio of Sterling, N. J., who was visiting her mother, Mrs. P. Sparandera, and was sitting in her rooms on the fourth floor of the house at 222 Lafayette Street, told the police she had seen a man place something in the street just before the explosion. His back was toward her, and she said she could not give a description of him.

Several pieces of torn paper scattered at the edge of the sidewalk were picked up by Captain Deevy. One was part of a draft representing $25,000, bearing the name of "E. S. Seevey, 3,002 C Street, Santiago, Cal." On the reverse side was this memorandum written in ink, "Prince George, 14 East Twenty-eighth Street."

This name and address will be investigated, but they are not regarded by the police as of much importance. They supposed the paper was part of the rubbish of the Italian Savings Bank at the corner of Lafayette and Spring Streets, which is situated on the first floor of the Consulate building. The paper, it was suggested, had been thrown out of its receptacle by the explosion.

One of the frightened tenants, all of whom fled to the street, told the police that the bomb might have been intended for John J. Soldo, proprietor of a grocery store at 222 Lafayette Street, the entire front of which was demolished. Soldo's daughter, Bessie, had been married a week ago. It was said, and as her father drove away another suitor a few days before the wedding the bomb might have been meant to avenge this action. The young woman, her husband, and her father, however, denied this statement.

FAY'S BLACK BOX UNDER SUSPICION

He Carried It When He and Scholz Were Arrested at the Navy Yard in Washington.

BUT IT WAS NOT EXAMINED

Authorities Seek Evidence of a Conspiracy in Attempt to Enter Machine Shops.

Special to The New York Times.

WASHINGTON, Nov. 6.—Robert Fay, who is said to be a Lieutenant in the German Army, and Walter Scholz, alleged to be his confederate in bomb plots under investigation in New York, were arrested in the Washington Navy Yard in September. The two men tried to enter the yard in the morning with a crowd of workmen, but were held up by a sentinel. By the time they tried another entrance an order had been passed for their admission, and they were permitted to walk in.

Before they could reach the machine shops, however, they were halted, taken before the commandant and compelled to leave the yard. They had with them a black box, but the yard authorities did not ascertain what it contained.

Various attempts have been made to damage the American naval equipment. An attempt was made to dynamite the dry dock in Philadelphia, it is said, and another to blow up the cruiser Prairie, and mysterious fires broke out on the battleship Oklahoma.

The Department of Justice was informed today that Sergeant Frank E. Jackson of the Marine Corps, on duty at the navy yard here, and a civilian employe had positively identified Fay and Scholz in New York. The department is considering the advisability of pressing for indictments. It is not known positively, however, whether evidence before the New York Grand Jury will support a charge of conspiracy.

Tried to Enter Munition Works.

A man who said he was Joseph W. Stahl of Woodland Avenue, Cleveland, Ohio, was committed to the Hudson County Jail in Newark yesterday by Justice Branegan of Harrison, while the police investigate him. He tried to get into the Crucible Steel Works in Harrison yesterday morning, and, rebuffed at one gate, he tried at another. The plant is engaged in munition work. The prisoner could not account for his desire to get into the plant, and it was said he denounced the United States for allowing ammunition and supplies to be made for the Allies.

AEROPLANE LAUNCHED FROM MOVING WARSHIP

Navy Perfects Catapult and Tests It Successfully Aboard the North Carolina.

Special to The New York Times.

WASHINGTON, Nov. 6.—Franklin D. Roosevelt, Assistant Secretary of the Navy, announced tonight that the aeroplane launching device that had been under test at the aeronautic station at Pensacola for some time had finally been installed on the cruiser North Carolina, and that on Friday an aeroplane was successfully launched from this device while the North Carolina was under way.

It was the first time an aeroplane ever had been launched from a ship under way, and represented the culmination of a series of experiments which started in 1912. The launching device, or catapult, was first suggested and tried out by Captain W. I. Chambers, U. S. N., who was then in charge of aviation. The first device was made and tested at the Washington Navy Yard, but was purely experimental and rather crudely built, simply to demonstrate the principle.

Two successful flights were made from this launching device. A new and improved device was constructed and shipped to the aeronautic station at Pensacola, where it was installed on a barge and put through a complete series of tests before being placed aboard the North Carolina. Several successful flights by different aviators were made. The flight from the North Carolina was made in navy aeroplane AB-2, with Lieutenant Commander H. C. Mustin as pilot.

The launching device is in the form of a car propelled along a track, the aeroplane being secured to the car until it reaches the end of the track. When the car stops the aeroplane is released and proceeds under its own power in flight. The aeroplane is landed on the car, fastened in place, and the motor started. The aviator takes his place in the aeroplane, and when all is ready the car is propelled along the track at a gradually increasing speed up to about fifty miles an hour, when the car is brought to a standstill and the aeroplane released.

German Submarines Sink Four Ships in Mediterranean

ALGIERS, Nov. 6, (via Paris.)—The steamship Sidi Ferruch was sunk yesterday forty miles off this port by a German submarine. The steamer's crew of twenty-eight men arrived today at Algiers. The Sidi Ferruch carried no passengers.

PARIS, Nov. 6.—The Strait of Gibraltar again has been passed by German submarines, which on Thursday sank two French and one Italian steamships. The crew of one vessel is missing.

The following statement was made by the Marine Ministry today:

"The enemy's submarines, coming from the Atlantic, passed through the Strait of Gibraltar on the night of Nov. 2. They sank on Nov. 4 the French ship Dahra, off Arzeu, Algeria, and the French ship Calvados and the Italian ship Ionio, near Cape Ivi.

"The crews of the Dahra and Ionio were saved. There is no news from the crew of the Calvados."

REFUSES TO BRING 900 IRISHMEN HERE

Cunard Line Acts After Rioting at Liverpool and Threats of a Strike.

200 SAIL FROM GLASGOW

London Paper Demands Inquiry as to Who Is Paying Passage of These Men of Military Age.

LIVERPOOL, Nov. 6.—Nine hundred Irishmen who intended to sail for New York today on the Cunard Line steamship Saxonia were prevented by the steamship company from taking passage. The company declined to permit them to sail after there had been several stormy encounters with street crowds, which took the view that able-bodied men should not be permitted to evade liability to military service in this manner.

The arrival of the Irishmen in Liverpool drew a crowd outside the steamship offices. Two of the Irishmen were knocked down by women. Others were set upon and decorated with white feathers.

Ignoring cries of "Cowards! Traitors!" and refusing to listen to the appeals of recruiting sergeants, the Irishmen marched to the dock. When they arrived there the Saxonia's firemen, witnessing the street encounters and catching the spirit of the crowd, informed the steamship company that they would not leave with the Saxonia if the Irishmen were permitted to sail.

The company, after a brief meeting, upheld the firemen and refused permission to sail to all British of military age. It was stated in addition that the same course would be followed in future on all Cunard liners, and that it was hoped other lines would follow the same procedure.

Five of the detained men afterward enlisted.

GLASGOW, Nov. 6.—About 200 Irishmen, eligible for military service, sailed today by the Anchor Line steamer California for New York.

The most strenuous efforts of seven recruiting Sergeants, who were authorized to promise a refund of their fares to those who enlisted, resulted in the enlistment of only two men.

The public were not allowed on the quay and there was no demonstration.

LONDON, Nov. 6.—Daily increasing crowds of youths of military age are besieging the passport department of the Foreign Office, seeking permits which they hope will enable them to escape the conscription they anticipate and fear. Most of them apparently have discovered relatives in America and elsewhere whom they are obliged to visit.

The rush has been so great since Lord Derby's recruiting scheme was promulgated that in the last three days more than 300 applicants of military age have been put back while the authorities decide how to deal with the situation.

The Saturday Review, referring to the crowds of Irish emigrants, demands a strict inquiry as to where the money comes from to pay the fares of these men, who are of the poorer classes, and the additional $50 which each must have on landing in America.

KING PICKS SKOULOUDIS FOR GREEK PREMIER

But Members of the Former Zaimis Cabinet Will Remain in Office.

LONDON, Sunday, Nov. 7.—A Reuter dispatch from Athens says:

"The King has charged M. Skouloudis with the formation of a Cabinet.

"The ex-Ministers are to retain office, M. Skouloudis taking the portfolio of Foreign Affairs."

A previous dispatch from Athens, which reached Paris, stated that the newspapers insisted that King Constantine had definitely accepted the resignation of the Zaimis Cabinet.

Other Athens advices stated that Parliament would be dissolved by King Constantine, and M. Zaimis would probably reconsider his determination not to retain the office of Prime Minister in the interval which must elapse before a general election would be called, according to the opinions expressed in authoritative quarters.

The M. Skouloudis, mentioned in the Reuter dispatch is probably Stephanos Skouloudis, Minister of Foreign Affairs in the Cabinet of M. Rhallis in 1897. On behalf of Greece, he signed the peace treaty made in 1913 between the allied Balkan States and Turkey in the London Peace Conference. As Minister of Foreign Affairs in the Rhallis Cabinet, he was able to mitigate greatly the terms of peace which were imposed on Greece by the victorious Turks after the war of 1897.

KITCHENER OFF TO AID IN BALKANS; RETAINS POST AS WAR SECRETARY; NISH CAPTURED BY THE BULGARS

KITCHENER RUMORS SPREAD

Government Strongly Denies That He Is Out of the Cabinet.

FITTED FOR THIS TASK

Has Knowledge of the East—May Go On to Egypt to Study Its Defenses.

LONDON PAPER SUPPRESSED

The Globe Seized for Insisting That War Secretary Had Offered His Resignation.

LONDON, Nov. 6.—Earl Kitchener, the British War Secretary, has gone to the eastern theatre of war at the request of his colleagues, apparently to study the situation in that now critical field of conflict.

Disturbing rumors concerning the departure of Kitchener from the country and stories that he had resigned from the Cabinet, or was about to do so, filled London all day. To settle these reports two official statements were issued during the day and another tonight, the latter stating in behalf of the Cabinet that the War Secretary's journey was being made at the express wish of his colleagues.

This official statemnet was issued early in the day.

"Earl Kitchener, at the request of his colleagues, has left England for a short visit to the eastern theatre of war."

At night this additional bulletin was issued:

"The statement that Earl Kitchener has resigned his post as Secretary of State for War has already been authoritatively denied. It is equally untrue to suggest that Earl Kitchener has tendered his resignation or that his visit to the King had any relation to any such subject, or that his visit to the Eastern theatre of war in any way betokens that such resignation is contemplated.

"On the contrary, this visit is undertaken by him in discharge of his duty as Secretary of State for War, which duty he has no intention of abandoning."

May Visit Egypt and Gallipoli.

The announcement that Lord Kitchener was to visit the East did not come as a surprise in well-informed circles. It was generally believed when it became known he was about to undertake a mission that the Balkans would be his destination, for there is no man in the British Empire better equipped with a knowledge of near Eastern affairs, military and political, than he.

It is thought that his activities will not be confined to this theatre of the war, however, but that he will visit Egypt to inspect the defenses of the Suez Canal against a possible German or Turkish attack, Mesopotamia, where the British expedition is doing bigger things than was expected of it, and is now nearing Bagdad, and the Dardanelles, where steps are being taken to push the operations to a conclusion.

Besides this, it is understood that his duties will include efforts to co-ordinate the work of the general staffs of the Allied Armies.

It is thought impossible for Premier Asquith to hold both offices of Prime Minister and Minister of War for any length of time. The Earl of Derby, Director of Recruiting, has been mentioned as a possible incumbent during Earl Kitchener's absence.

When the vote of credit is introduced by the Premier in the House of Commons on Wednesday there will be full opportunity for debate and for the extraction of such information as the Government is then in a position to furnish.

The Globe Seized; Resignation Denied.

The London Globe, which has been bitter in its attacks on the conduct of the war and which announced yesterday that Kitchener had resigned, was seized and suppressed by the police today. In today's issue it stuck to its guns and again asserted that Kitchener has resigned because of "manoeuvres and machinations" of politicians. It added that King George had refused to accept his resignation.

This reiteration brought forth another authorized categorical statement to the contrary, as follows:

"Not only is it untrue that Earl Kitchener has resigned, but it is equally untrue that his Lordship ever tendered his resignation to the King."

This action against The Globe is the first action of the kind taken by the authorities since the outbreak of the war against a daily paper in the United Kingdom. Some weekly papers, both in England and in Ireland, including The Labor Leader, were similarly treated some time ago, but The Labor Leader, after a secret trial of the case, was allowed to resume publication.

Linked with Joffre's Visit.

Comment in the morning newspapers indicated a belief in some quarters that the sudden development regarding Earl Kitchener related to the visit of General Joffre, the French Commander in Chief, to London recently. In this connection The Weekly Nation made an interesting revelation.

"General Joffre's visit," it says, "has been one of the personal sensations of the war. Our politicians expected to

Continued on Page 2.

Kitchener Took Trip at Colleagues' Request, The Cabinet Announces After Asquith Sees King

LONDON, Nov. 6.—"Lord Kitchener, at the request of his colleagues, has left England for a short visit to the eastern theatre of war."

This announcement, made this evening after a Cabinet council, (an unusual meeting for Saturday,) and a long audience which Premier Asquith had with the King, set at rest the rumors which were current as to the War Secretary's present intentions.

SAYS ENGLAND IS DOING HER DUTY

J. L. Garvin Defends Her Conduct of the War Against Roosevelt's Criticisms.

VAST LOANS TO HER ALLIES

$2,000,000,000 Placed at Their Disposal—1,000,000 Men for France, Munitions for Russia.

Special Cable to THE NEW YORK TIMES.

LONDON, Nov. 6.—In an interview dictated to THE NEW YORK TIMES correspondent J. L. Garvin, editor of The Observer, vigorously defends England against Colonel Theodore Roosevelt's criticism of her conduct of the war. While he wishes it to be understood that he is a warm personal friend and admirer of the Colonel Mr. Garvin explains that he is forced to take direct issue with him.

"The trouble is," he says, "that Colonel Roosevelt has failed to give England credit for her real achievements in a war that started with fearful odds in favor of Germany. I wish the Colonel would come over here and see this war and the part England is playing from this viewpoint. I am sure if he did he would change his mind about things that from the viewpoint in America may seem all wrong. I do not mean that we have not made some mistakes; but there are many things that, when seen in the light of Great Britain's relation to the Allies and all the other circumstances involved, give a different aspect."

Mr. Garvin, after reading Colonel Roosevelt's criticism, reprinted from The Metropolitan Magazine, from a copy of THE NEW YORK TIMES, started his reply by the observation that it was unfair to accuse Great Britain of not taking the war seriously, and also of not doing her part, as France and Russia had done theirs.

"No country in the history of the world," he said with emphasis, "has in its essence taken up its duties in the present crisis more seriously than England and more nobly discharged them. Without a show of boasting, proclamation, advertisement or display of our deep feelings, we have gone on with the war, fighting the bitterest struggle of our existence.

"Tempting Offers" to Join Germany.

"To look at the essence of the matter, we were not prepared for war because we didn't want war. As all the world knows, the most tempting offers and suggestions came to England before the war to desert her allies, and there is not the smallest doubt that at any time within the last fifteen years we could have formed arrangements with Germany that would have been very profitable to ourselves if we would have joined in a war of conquest against France or South America. There is no doubt that after the Spanish-American War and at the time of Queen Victoria's Diamond Jubilee Germany feared the ascendency in the world of the English-speaking peoples who at that time had become knit together by ties of intimacy and cordiality that had never existed before. Germany was looking abroad for colonies where she could plant her own power overseas. She wanted to dominate South America. England not for a moment considered joining Germany.

"In this war our arrangement with our allies is clear, and faithfully have we carried out our part. At first it was thought that it would be sufficient for us to hold our sea power; but as a duty apart from that we offered to go to the aid of France with what I might call the spearhead of a small but disciplined array, an expeditionary force of 150,000 men. Let us see how we have discharged that duty. We have come to the aid of France with not 150,000, but 1,000,000 men. We have spread our men along the western front and supported our French allies with a force that is nearly ten times greater than that originally offered. We are ready to do ten times more—yes, twenty times more—than we bargained to do. In all the history of the world that example of support to an ally has never been equaled.

"As to Belgium, we unfortunately could not save Antwerp, as our forces were too small; but through our navy we succeeded in landing sufficient men in Belgium to march on to Ghent, in great peril though they were, so that we joined King Albert's troops and

Continued on Page 2.

RUSSIANS CAPTURE 8,500 IN GALICIA

Surprise Attack Demoralizes Gen. von Linsingen's Austrian Forces on the Stripa.

STRIKE AGAIN NEAR DVINSK

But Berlin Reports 6,000 Prisoners Taken and Attacks in North Repulsed.

PETROGRAD, Nov. 6, via London, Sunday, Nov. 7.—The official communication issued tonight reports the capture by the Russians of 8,500 prisoners as the result of a surprise attack near the village of Semikovitze (Sienikowce) on the Stripa River.

The text of the statement follows:

West of Riga, near the village of Uchine, we repulsed several attacks.

German counterattacks continue south of Lake Sventon. Further south, as far as the Pripet region, there is no change.

According to supplementary reports we took twenty-two officers and 712 men prisoners and captured seven machine guns and two guns in the fight near the village of Kostioukhova, west of Rafalovka. We repulsed enemy attacks in the direction of the village of Budki, driving him back in disorder to his trenches.

The period of extremely desperate fighting in the region of the village of Semikovitze and on the western shore of Lake Ischkuve has now ended. Swift frontal surprise attacks undertaken some days ago, including the crossing of the River Stripa near the village of Semikovitze, justified all our expectations. We took over 8,500 men prisoners besides capturing a number, not yet determined, of officers and machine guns. Our valiant troops had to overcome the greatest difficulties while sending the enormous number of Austrian and German prisoners to the rear and across the River Stripa and Lake Ischkuve.

BERLIN, Nov. 6, (by Wireless to Sayville, N. Y.)—The Austro-German forces in Galicia are said by the War Office today to have won a further victory over the Russians in the fighting along the Stripa River. The Russians were thrown back to their old positions on the east bank of the river. The official report follows:

Army group of Field Marshal von Hindenburg: The Russians repeated their attempts to break through our lines near Dvinsk, with the same bad results.

Army group of Prince Leopold of Bavaria: The situation remains unchanged.

Army group of General von Linsingen: Further Russian positions were captured northeast of Budka. At Sienikowce quiet reigns. The enemy has been driven back into his old positions on the eastern bank of the Stripa River. In the now completed battles the Russians have lost in prisoners fifty officers and about 6,000 men.

VIENNA, (via London,) Nov. 6.—The Austrian War Office today gave out the following statement:

Yesterday the Russians made two strong attacks southeast of Wisniawczyk against our Stripa front, (in Eastern Galicia.) His attacking columns collapsed under our fire, sustaining heavy losses. Finally the Russians retired here and east of Burkanow and Bieniawa to their main positions. We have captured fifty officers and 6,000 men in battles around Sienikowce.

On the lower Styr our attacks made slow progress.

WITH THE RUSSIAN HEADQUARTERS STAFF

Business-like Routine of the Czar and His Military Advisers.

PETROGRAD, Nov. 6, (via London.)—In a white two-story building in a town of perhaps 40,000, but resembling more nearly an overgrown village than a city, is stationed the staff which directs the defense of Russia against her enemies. The Director in Chief is the Czar, and to this forlorn town from the Imperial Palace of Tsarskoe Selo he has banished himself for the time being, in order that he may live in daily touch with the affairs of his armies in the field, advise with the officers and supervise the conduct of the war.

Although many hours' journey by train from the nearest battle line, the Emperor and his staff are in almost instant communication by telegraph with all points along the thousand-mile front, and nothing of importance occurs that is not immediately flashed to this controlling centre. It is in this building, which was formerly used for local Government purposes, that the daily official communications to the world are written.

The Chief of Staff, General Michael Alexieff, is a modest man, about 60 years of age, who shuns self-glorifi-

Continued on Page 2.

SERBS' WAR CAPITAL FALLS

Bulgarian Army Marches Into Nish But Gets Little Booty.

TEUTONS ALSO SWEEP ON

Form Junction with Main Bulgar Force and Quick Advance Is Looked For.

ALLIES RUSHING UP TROOPS

Those Already in the Field Defeat the Bulgars in the South.

LONDON, Sunday, Nov. 7.—Bulgarian troops have occupied Nish, the Serbian war capital, which gives them complete control of the railway from Prahovo, on the Danube, and thus opens a through route for the central powers to Sofia and Constantinople.

In addition to this Teutonic success, which caused the more gloom in London yesterday because of the coincidence with the disturbing rumors about Lord Kitchener, the main Bulgarian and German armies have effected a junction at Krivivir, northwest of Nish.

As a result of the union of forces the campaign against Serbia, which has been somewhat slower than expected, will probably move at a faster pace. In fact, the invasion of King Peter's domain is already gathering more headway. Official reports from Berlin and Vienna indicate that all the invading forces are making progress against Serbia's resistance, except in the south, near the Greek frontier.

In that region, however, according to reports coming from the German Legation at Athens and also from Serbian sources, the British, French, and Serbians, who are evidently in superior force, have inflicted a severe defeat on the Bulgarians at Izvor, ten miles west of the Vardar River, and at the entrance to Babuna pass, where the French left wing joins the right of the Serbian southern army. The Bulgars are reported to be retreating toward Veles. British cavalry and French infantry are said to be engaged in this battle.

Allies Rushing Up Troops.

More allied troops are being sent from Saloniki to the scene of the fighting, in the hope that they will be able, by the capture of Veles, to compel the Bulgarians, who advanced west of Uskub and Veles, to retire and clear the Saloniki-Mitrovitza railway so that assistance can be sent to the Serbs' northern army.

All assistance that reaches the Serbians must apparently be sent by the British and French, for, despite the defeat of the Zaimis Government and the triumph of Venizelos in the Greek Chamber, there is no evidence yet that Greece intends to change her policy of "benevolent neutrality" and join the war on the side of the Allies.

Meanwhile Rumania, like Greece, is remaining neutral in the face of agitation in favor of intervention to aid the Allies.

No news is forthcoming concerning the Russian expedition, which was reported early in the week to have been massed on the Rumanian frontier. Russian attacks are, however, preventing the Austro-Germans from dispatching any additional troops from her front to the Balkans.

There is evidence of renewed allied activity on the Gallipoli Peninsula, and the impression prevails here that another big attempt will be made to open the straits before the German ammunition reaches the Turks.

The Petit Parisian's correspondent at Saloniki takes a cheerful view of the situation in the south. He cables under date of Friday:

"The Serbian situation has improved in the view of the British and French staffs at Saloniki. British troops, in splendid form, now have taken their place in the first line.

"The Serbians are still holding on at Prilip, according to a wireless message. The Bulgarians subjected the French at Krivolak to an intense bombardment for forty-eight hours. The net result was one man wounded.

"Fresh troops left today for the Serbian front as well as convoys of arms, munitions, and provisions."

Teuton Report of Successes.

The official bulletin issued in Berlin says:

In the valley of the Western Morava fighting goes on. To the southeast of Cacak the town of Kraljevo has been taken. The enemy is being pursued to the east of Kraljevo, and Etubal has been reached.

The Zupanyevac sector has been crossed. In the valley of the Morava our troops pressed on after the enemy as far as Obrez-Sikirice.

By means of a clever stroke our troops took possession of Varvarin during the night. More than 3,000 Serbians were taken prisoners.

At Krivivir a connection between the fighting German and Bulgarian main forces has been established.

The army of General Boyadjieff (Bulgarian) has defeated its opponents near Lukovo and near Sokobanya. More than 500 prisoners were taken and six cannon were captured.

After battles which lasted three days the fortified capital of Nish was captured yesterday afternoon, notwithstanding the stubborn resistance of the Serbians. During battles, in th

"All the News That's Fit to Print."

The New York Times.

THE WEATHER
Fair today and Thursday; moderate northwest winds.
For full weather report see Page 19.

VOL. LXV...NO. 21,109. ... NEW YORK, WEDNESDAY, NOVEMBER 10, 1915.—TWENTY-TWO PAGES. ONE CENT In Greater New York, Jersey City and Newark. | Elsewhere TWO CENTS.

AUSTRIAN SUBMARINE SINKS ANCONA; 270 SAVED, 312 MISSING FROM LINER BOUND FOR NEW YORK FROM NAPLES

Italian-American Liner Ancona, Torpedoed in Mediterranean.

ARRESTED, CHARGE PLOT FOR AUSTRIA

Alexander and Hector Gondos, Editors, of Bridgeport, in a Police Trap Here.

ACCUSE JULIUS PIRNITZER

Banker Says They Asked $2,000 to Suppress Story He Was Agent of Teutons.

LINKED WITH THE FAY BAND

Trust Company Head Financed Them, Brothers Allege—He Denies Charge Vehemently.

After an examination which already had lasted for several hours, Deputy Police Commissioner Guy Scull and Inspector Faurot were still busy early this morning at Police Headquarters questioning Alexander and Hector Gondos, who are said to be powers in Austrian affairs in this country, and conferring with Julius Pirnitzer, President of the Transatlantic Trust Company of 67 William Street, who had caused their arrest, charging that they conspired to extort $2,000 from him.

The Gondos brothers admitted they had been prepared to publish in their newspapers, The Bridgeport, a Hungarian daily, and The Bridgeport Daily News, a publication in English, offices of which are in Bridgeport, Conn., stories that the Transatlantic Trust Company was agent here of the central powers abroad, and that through it "Lieutenant" Robert Fay and other plotters had obtained the funds to carry on their work; that Mr. Pirnitzer was a foreign agent and head of an information service which had attracted the attention of the United States Secret Service, which already had seized the books of the company.

Denounced by Pirnitzer.

Mr. Pirnitzer, who was beside himself with apprehension over the results of these assertions, denounced them vehemently as malicious lies. There was not a word of truth in them, he said; they were the work of jealous bankers whose business on the east side had been injured by the activity of his company. He had no affiliation with any foreign Government, and his company did only a plain banking business, he asserted.

"The good name of a bank is like the good name of a woman," he cried. "A thing once said, no matter how false, is remembered always."

In statements which were taken down by an official stenographer, the Gondos brothers coolly admitted that Mr. Pirnitzer was correct in saying they had been employed by an association of bankers to wage a crusade against the Transatlantic Trust Company, but they denied that the charges they had meant to publish were without foundation in fact.

So positive were they in their statements that Inspector Faurot, who first had conducted their examination alone, hurried away in his automobile to return shortly before midnight with Commissioner Scull, who has had charge of the work of the police in connection with the case of Fay and the other German plotters now under Federal indictment.

Although Commissioner Scull declined to make public the statements of either Alexander Gondos or his brother, it was learned that Alexander had told the police he was well acquainted with Mr. Pirnitzer, having known him for fourteen or fifteen years. He said the banker had been in the Austrian Consular Service for many years and had served in Johannesburg, South Africa; Tien Tsin, Saloniki, and other posts before returning to Budapesth about four years ago. At that time the Hungarian Diet appropriated 8,000,000 kronen, Gondos was reported as saying, to establish a Government bank with two branches in Austria-Hungary and one in this country. Mr. Pirnitzer was selected at a salary of $20,000 a year and under contract for ten years to manage the branch here, and, according to the report of Gondos's statement, this was the Transatlantic Trust Company, which Mr. Pirnitzer organized.

Mr. Pirnitzer did not learn of Gondos's statement, but he denied indignantly that his company was subsidized by the Austrian Government.

Mr. Scull said at 12:30 o'clock this morning:

"The statements made by the Gondos brothers are startling, to say the least, and if they are true, a point we are now trying to establish, they will have a very important bearing on the investigation into German plots which this department now has in hand."

Take Arrest Lightly.

The Gondos brothers took their arrest lightly once they reached Police Headquarters and decided to talk freely. They seemed to be of the opinion that they could turn their arrest to their own account. They did not offer to deny the charge that they had tried to get $2,000 from Mr. Pirnitzer, but seemed to consider themselves perfectly justified in having attempted what they evidently deemed only an ordinary piece of business.

The brothers had been approached by the association of bankers, they said, with the proposal to manage a campaign against the trust company by publishing and syndicating articles. For this they were to be paid, and it occurred to them that Mr. Pirnitzer might be willing to pay a higher price to have the campaign abandoned. Hector Gondos, who is an engineer with a doctor's degree, called on Mr. Pirnitzer in his office on Monday, outlined quite frankly the campaign they had been asked to start, and suggested they would be willing to drop it.

Mr. Pirnitzer made an appointment for both brothers for yesterday at 5 o'clock, and notified District Attorney Perkins. Mr. Perkins told Inspector Faurot, and

Continued on Page 4.

PRUSSIAN CASUALTIES NOW TOTAL 2,099,454

Losses in Last Three and a Half Months Put at 503,190—Ten New Lists Published.

Special Cable to THE NEW YORK TIMES.

ROTTERDAM, Nov. 9, (Dispatch to The London Daily News.)—Ten more Prussian casualty lists have been published covering the period from Oct. 22 to Nov. 2, inclusive. In this period the Prussian losses amounted to 78,376, or roughly 21,000 more than in the previous ten lists published.

The Nieuwe Rotterdamsche Courant suggests that the increase in casualties justifies the supposition that these lists are losses suffered during the great allied offensive. The paper adds that the total Prussian losses alone now amount to 2,099,454. In addition 230 Bavarian, 28 Saxon, and 283 Württemberg lists have been published, along with 55 naval lists.

The Courant further publishes a table giving the Prussian losses since the middle of July, from which it is seen that Prussia alone has in the last three and a half months lost 503,190 men from all causes.

RUSSIA SEES SIGNS OF EASTERN TROUBLE

Preparations Are Making to Meet Possible Consequences of German Plotting.

Special Cable to THE NEW YORK TIMES.

PETROGRAD, Nov. 9, (Dispatch to The London Morning Post.)—The reorganization and extensive changes which are now being introduced into certain branches of the Russian Army plainly indicate that the Russians contemplate a prolonged struggle. They are making preparations which will be progressively effective, if the war should last five years more.

As Germany is obviously expanding her last energies in an endeavor to stir up the whole Musselman Orient, Russia probably foresees the necessity for increased strength with which to clear up possibly formidable struggles in the world, which the Germans, even after defeat, will leave as a heritage behind them.

BRITAIN PREPARING TO ENFORCE ECONOMY

Sumptuary Laws Foreshadowed by Asquith, Answering Complaint in Commons Against Luxury.

LONDON, Nov. 9.—That the Government has under consideration the passage of sumptuary laws to insure the strictest domestic economy was the information given to Charles Bathurst, Unionist member for Wiltshire, by Premier Asquith in the House of Commons today. The Premier added that he would be glad to receive any suggestions concerning such legislation.

Mr. Bathurst had asked the Premier whether, "in view of the serious state of the nation's finances and of the thoughtless extravagance and unnecessary luxury still being indulged in by many persons to the annoyance of their neighbors, the Premier would consider the advisability of passing drastic sumptuary laws which would insure the strictest domestic economy, and put all classes upon a footing during the war of greater equality in their mode of living."

BRITAIN TAKES STEPS TO LIMIT EMIGRATION

Rush of Able-bodied Men Abroad to Be Halted by Passport Regulation.

LONDON, Nov. 9.—The British Government today took its first definite steps toward preventing emigration of able-bodied British subjects, who in considerable numbers are suspected of using this means of evading military service.

A regulation was issued by the Home Office requiring subjects of the United Kingdom 19 years old or more, and contemplating emigration, to apply at the Foreign Office for passports. If the passports are refused, they must hand to the officers supervising the embarkation the reply of the Foreign Office to their passport application, together with their birth certificates, with photographs attached.

Since the refusal of the Cunard Company to carry abroad British subjects eligible for military service last Saturday the Anchor Line and the White Star Line have adopted an identical course. Other lines are expected to follow with similar action.

OIL LADEN STEAMER IS AFIRE AT SEA

Crew of Italian Ship Has Been Taken Off—Was Bound for Buenos Aires.

GALVESTON, Texas, Nov. 9.—An Italian ship, loaded with oil from Port Arthur, Texas, for Buenos Aires, is on fire at sea sixty-five miles east of Sabine Bar, and has been abandoned, according to wireless advices received here tonight from the steamer Gulfstream, which is standing by.

The crew of the burning vessel has been taken off by the tug Russell. The fire was reported in No. 3 hold and the name of the ship was not given.

The Gulfstream reported that she was unable to get close enough to the burning vessel to make out her name, but shipping men here expressed the belief that the abandoned steamer is the Levietta, bound for Buenos Aires, because the Levietta and the Gulfstream from Port Arthur left at about the same time today. The two steamers, the Gulfstream bound for Bayonne, would have been in the locality tonight from where the steamer was reported abandoned.

The Levietta carried a crew of twenty-five and Captain R. Rico is master of the vessel. She is a steamer of 1,700 tons, owned by Darrost Brothers of Genoa, Italy, and was built in 1899 at Sestri, Italy. Her cargo today consisted of 81,400 cases of oil and 40,000 cases of gasoline.

ROB SHIP AT SEA OF $100,000 GEMS

Rochambeau's Coin Room Entered and Box of Precious Stones Opened.

ONLY RICHEST GOODS TAKEN

Pearls Rolling About on Deck Give Purser His First Clue to the Strange Theft.

SHIPPED TO JEWELERS HERE

Rumored That Members of Liner's Crew Were Taken Back to France in Irons.

A strange robbery, involving the loss of pearls valued at nearly $100,000, shipped to this port on the French Line steamship Rochambeau, arriving here on Election Day, became known yesterday.

The pearls, some of them of unusual size, with two packages of cut diamonds and some strings of imitation pearls, were forwarded from Paris in charge of a representative of the American Express Company, who at Bordeaux turned the consignment over to the ship's purser. The goods were inclosed in a strong wooden box about six inches square. Inside the box were the various lots, packed in white papers similar to those used for holding medicine powders.

The box was put by the purser into the Rochambeau's coin room, access to which was supposed to be restricted to the purser and his assistant. According to the story told yesterday, the theft was discovered a day or two before the steamer arrived in port, when a number of loose pearls were found scattered on one of the decks. No passenger was found to have lost them, and the purser thought of the box in the strong room.

The Pearls Missing.

The inspection showed that the box had been opened and pearls to the value of $96,306 extracted. For some reason not understood by the steamship men, two packages of diamonds valued at $1,500 were left untouched, as were the strings of imitation pearls.

Captain Juham made a searching inquiry but the result could not be ascertained. Customs officials and others in a position to know were uncommunicative yesterday.

Charles Crane, Foreign Import Manager of the American Express Company, when asked about the robbery, said he must decline to discuss the case.

One report was that one or more members of the crew were connected with the theft, and that they were held in irons to be taken back to France for trial. So far as could be learned, the police here made no arrest in connection with the robbery.

That the search was thorough was evident from the fact that the box containing the remainder of the gems was not turned over to the customs officials until last Saturday, a few hours before the Rochambeau sailed. It was delivered to Acting Deputy Collector Harry Fellows at the Appraiser's Stores by Superintendent Wolf of the French Line, who reported the theft.

Although no invoices accompanied the importation, the box was sent at once to William B. Treadwell, the Government's gem expert, who made an examination of its contents. After comparison with a bill of lading presumably in the possession of the express company, Mr. Treadwell found that all of the genuine pearls were missing.

Coming to New York Firms.

Special Deputy Appraiser George W. Wolf refused to talk, but it was learned that the American Express Company was acting as forwarder for Lebolt & Co., 534 Fifth Avenue; Dreicer & Co., 560 Fifth Avenue; Milton L. Ernst, 88 Gold Street, and The Sun Company, forwarders, of Pier 45, North River.

The Lebolt and Dreicer consignments were all of genuine pearls, their losses being complete, according to reliable report, although of the two Lebolt & Co. was the heavier loser. One of the Dreicer pearls was said to have a value of $6,980, being of unusual size and shape. It was found that the loss to the Sun Company amounted to $10,301, the balance of its consignment being intact. None of the imitation pearls belonging to Mr. Ernst was missing.

Customs officials declared that the robbery was the first of its kind in many years. The pearls were insured for their full value with Lloyds of London, besides a bonus of 10 per cent. carried by the same policies.

ROCHAMBEAU FIRE OUT AND VESSEL PROCEEDS

Captain of French Liner Sends Word He Is On His Way to Bordeaux.

The fire which started in the coal bunker of the French liner Rochambeau Monday afternoon, forty-eight hours after she sailed for Bordeaux with 421 passengers on board, has been extinguished, and the steamer is now proceeding on her voyage.

Word of this was received early yesterday by the agents of the French Line in a wireless message from Captain Junam, reading:

Have succeeded in extinguishing the fire and am proceeding to Bordeaux. All well on board.

Paul Faguet, General Agent of the line, said yesterday that he expected a full report would be made to the company when the Rochambeau reached her destination.

Agents of the Fabre Line, which has had several fires start on steamers chartered to carry war munitions, have taken every precaution possible to prevent the cargoes being tampered with while they are in transit on the lighters. They employ eighteen private detectives to watch the longshoremen, and the shippers have their own detectives on the lighters. In spite of all these precautions shippers admit that it is wellnigh impossible to prevent bombs being placed in sugar bags or among coal.

Berlin Reports the Removal of Brand Whitlock's Aide

LONDON, Wednesday, Nov. 10.—Reuter's Amsterdam correspondent sends the following:

"A telegram received here from Berlin says that M. Deleval, Counsellor of the American Legation at Brussels, who made a report to Brand Whitlock, the American Minister, concerning the efforts that were made to save Miss Edith Cavell from being executed by the Germans in Brussels, has been removed from his office."

SAYS DUMBA TRICKED CITY AND RED CROSS

Substituted Contraband Dispatches for Anti-Tetanus Serum, Providence Journal Says.

BOX CONTENTS CHANGED

Work Alleged to Have Been Done in Austrian Consulate Here, with von Nuber's Connivance.

Special to The New York Times.

PROVIDENCE, R. I., Nov. 9.—The Providence Journal will say tomorrow morning:

"A plot by which the American Red Cross was tricked by Ambassador Dumba and Consul General von Nuber into becoming a party to the sending of military information, in violation of the neutrality laws, was revealed after an investigation made in New York yesterday by The Providence Journal.

"As a result of this plot, three wooden cases, supposed to contain anti-tetanus serum, but really filled with hundreds of incriminating documents, were taken aboard the steamer Rotterdam when she sailed on June 1, and, by reason of certificates furnished by the Health Department of the City of New York and the receiving station of the American Red Cross in that city, were successfully carried to their destination, which was the Foreign Office in Vienna.

"An employe of the Austro-Hungarian Consulate in New York, Anton Wedl, was used by the Ambassador and the Consul General in carrying out this scheme. After delivering to Albert W. Staub the three packages which really contained the serum described, as packed by the New York Health Department, the packages were switched. They were out of the possession of the Red Cross three days before the Rotterdam sailed and during that time were in the office of the Consul General at 24 State Street.

"At some time in that period, according to a statement made yesterday to The Journal by an ex-employe of Consul General von Nuber, the packages were emptied of their contents and great numbers of letters, reports, plans of fortifications, and receipted bills showing expenditures in bringing about strikes in munitions plants and the subsidizing of many newspapers were put in the boxes.

How Boxes Were Obtained.

Before the shipment could be made the plotters got the three cases into their own possession on a pretext of having found means to rush delivery by sending the serum as personal baggage of two passengers on the steamship Rotterdam, which was to sail from New York on June 1.

"Three days before the Rotterdam was to sail the Consul sent a man with a horse-drawn cab to take the three cases to the steamer. He took them to the Consulate, where at their leisure the schemers made their shift and planted their illicit information in the anti-toxin boxes.

"The plotters induced Albert W. Staub, superintendent of the Red Cross station at the Bush Terminal, to provide two letters on the official paper certifying that the cases sent to the Rotterdam contained only tetanus antitoxin serum forwarded by the American Red Cross to the Austrian Red Cross at Vienna, to be used for medical purposes.

"To guard against suspicion, the letters named two passengers on the Rotterdam, Consular Agent Anton Wedl and Mrs. Charles S. Hurd, as the ones intrusted with the delivery of the serum. Two of the cases were to be sent in the care of Wedl and the third in care of Mrs. Hurd."

The Journal prints all the correspondence with relation to the transaction, both from the Consul General's office and the Red Cross, and then gives the following statement from Albert W. Staub, Superintendent of the American Red Cross station at Bush Terminal, Brooklyn.

"I never would have written the letters stating that the three cases of hospital supplies to be taken on the Rotterdam by Mr. Wedl and Mrs. Hurd contained tetanus anti-toxin if I had not received from the headquarters of the Health Department of the City of New York an official declaration as to the contents of the cases, and I must confess that at the time I never had the remotest idea of the loophole it afforded—innocently on the part of the Board of Health for the Austro-Hungarian Consulate to trick the Red Cross in such a way. I can see clearly enough now that I placed myself in a bad position.

"I did not examine the contents of the cases while they were here, although it is our custom to repack and to make a detailed list of all articles in cases shipped by us. This is necessary in order to obtain the permit required for us to send our hospital supplies through to Germany or Austria.

"But in this exceptional instance the three cases came to me officially certified by the Board of Health of the City of New York as containing 54,780 cubic centimeters of tetanus anti-toxin serum. There surely was no reason to think of an irregularity on the part of the Board of Health. The loophole was afforded after the cases were taken away from here to be carried to the steamship Rotterdam.

A Donation from Von Nuber.

"We had received the three-case consignment of serum on May 12, and understood it to be a donation from Consul General von Nuber. It came to us as if they wanted us to ship it to the Austrian Red Cross at Vienna. It was placed in the store room to be shipped when we had other supplies to send to Austria.

"Then came the request from the Austro-Hungarian Consulate asking me to turn the three cases over to a man who would be sent from the Consulate to take them to the steamer Rooterdam.

Continued on Page 3.

SURE TO WIN WAR, ASQUITH ASSERTS

Premier, at Lord Mayor's Banquet, Voices Allies' Stern Will to Emancipate Europe.

TIDE OF WAR NEAR TURN

Enemy's Successes at Limit, Balfour Declares—Bulgaria's Greed and Fear.

LONDON, Nov. 9.—"We are right and we are sure to win," Premier Asquith declared tonight, speaking at the banquet given in the Guild Hall in celebration of the inauguration today of Sir Charles Cheers Wakefield as Lord Mayor of London.

"We shall not falter nor pause," said the Prime Minister, "until we have secured for the smaller States of Europe their charter of independence and for Europe itself final emancipation from a reign of force."

Mr. Asquith said Lord Kitchener had gone to the Near East to look over the ground at close quarters and would shortly return.

That the tide of the enemy's successes had reached its limit and that the ebb was at hand was asserted by the First Lord of the Admiralty, Arthur J. Balfour. Other speakers were the French Ambassador, Paul Cambon; the Secretary for Home Affairs, Sir John A. Simon; the Lord Chief Justice, Baron Reading, and the Attorney General, Sir Frederick E. Smith.

The Attorney General spoke of the American note and said it contained legal contentions which he hoped the bar of England would be able to contradict.

A Feast Under War's Shadow.

One difference between the function tonight and those of other years was to be observed in the curtailment of the customary sumptuous menu, one more appropriate to war economy taking its place. Many of the guests were in military uniform.

Premier Asquith, his wife, and daughter were cheered when they entered the hall, and cheers were also given for the Serbian Minister, the French and Italian Ambassadors, and the Russian Grand Duke Michael. The High Commissioner of New Zealand, the Hon. William Thomas Mackenzie, brought his son, who was blinded while serving in the Dardanelles, and the young soldier received an ovation. The Earl of Derby, Director of Recruiting, was warmly received, as was the Belgian Minister.

When the toast, "The King," was given the assembly rose and sang the national anthem, something never done before at a Lord Mayor's banquet.

Sir John A. Simon, Secretary for Home Affairs, responding to the toast, "Our Allies," said that the alliance would become stronger with the duration of the war.

The Two Sides of the War.

Paul Cambon, the French Ambassador, said: "Although the number of our enemies may have increased since last year, the number of our friends has been augmented. I am happy to see today our Italian colleagues."

Describing the war, he said: "On the one side are tranquil courage, faith in an ideal of justice and liberty and the will to employ only legitimate means of defense. On the other, thoughts of lucre, forgetfulness of all the principles of humanity, the destruction of an open town, the taking of innocent lives, a sort of perverse joy in the accomplishment of evil, and a plan, pursued with childish disregard of scruple, to dominate the world by terror."

He made reference to the execution of Miss Edith Cavell, saying: "Quite recently we saw a German military tribunal sentence a noble woman to death for the crime of generosity and a German officer indulge in the pleasure, though not compelled to do so, of executing the sentence himself by murdering this defenseless victim."

The Ambassador concluded: "When the hour strikes for the enemy to realize that all his schemes for world domination have broken down, we shall see him a prey to a moral depression which will

Continued on Page 2.

LARGE BRITISH FORCES ARE LANDED IN SERBIA

And Decisive Move Is Near—Berlin Reports 300,000 Allies Are There.

Special Cable to THE NEW YORK TIMES.

SALONIKI, Nov. 9, (Dispatch to The London Daily Telegraph.)—There are good grounds for hoping that the misfortunes of the Serbians have ended and that the tide which has been running against them has reached its high-water mark and that what is left of their sorely tried country will be saved from invasion.

Large British forces have arrived and more are expected.

The Allies will soon be in a position to take a decisive offensive.

LONDON, Wednesday, Nov. 10.—Newspapers of Berlin, as quoted by the correspondent at Copenhagen of the Exchange Telegraph Company, say that the Allies already have landed 300,000 men at Saloniki.

In spite of this, however, every hour adds to the peril of the Serbian armies, which are fighting desperately to hold back the Austro-Germans pressing them from the north and the Bulgarians, invading their country from the east, until the assistance their allies are sending can reach them.

The Bulgarians have extended their grip on the Belgrade-Saloniki Railway north and south of Nish, and have occupied Leskovac, south of the captured capital, and Aleksinac, to the north. At the latter point they are in close touch with the German Army, which, after occupying Krusevac, extended its left wing as far as Gyunis, on the left bank of the Bulgar Morava.

The Austro-Germans, advancing southward, are making progress except in the west, where they are being held by the Montenegrins. The invading forces are now reaching the most difficult part of Serbia, the mountainous region, where the natives, knowing every hill and gully, can offer the strongest resistance. The Austrians and Germans, however, are plentifully supplied with mountain guns, with which they expect to drive the defenders from their fastnesses.

Allies Clear Railroad to Veles.

In the south the ever-growing strength of the French and British forces is beginning to tell. They are carrying on an energetic offensive against the Bulgars, have managed to keep the railway clear as far as Veles, and are barring the Bulgars' route to Monastir.

A Paris Havas dispatch from Athens filed on Monday says the French have reached Gradsko on the railroad from Krivolak to Veles. A Bulgarian attack against Krivolak, with heavy forces of infantry and artillery, is reported to have been repulsed, after which the French occupied the village of Komental.

On the Anglo-French front, northwest of Guevgeli, the advance of the Allies continues, and the Bulgarians now occupy only the village of Ourmandi in Serbian territory.

A dispatch from Rome tends to confirm the recent reports that Italy will send troops to Albania to aid the Serbs. It states that a semi-official note has been issued which says that while Italy did not participate in the recent expedition of the Allies to assist Serbia she has found a better way to oppose the Austro-German-Bulgarian attack upon Serbia.

This way, the note says, was opened by the Bulgarians themselves, when they threatened to invade Albania to reach the Adriatic, a design so dangerous to Italy's interest that, "the mere threat must oblige Italy to take appropriate measures to frustrate it immediatedly."

A Bucharest dispatch by way of Geneva says that 60,000 Albanians are preparing to attack the Serbians in the rear at Monastir and Prisrend.

Official Reports of Operations.

The text of yesterday's German official statement concerning the operations follows:

South of Kraljevo and southwest of Krusevac the enemy has been driven out of his rear-guard positions. Our troops are continuing the advance. The heights near Gyunis, on the left bank of the Morava, were stormed.

The booty taken at Krusevac was increased to about 50 cannon, including 10 heavy pieces. The number of prisoners was increased to 7,000.

The army (Bulgarian) of General Boyadjieff on the evening of Nov. 7 had reached the Morava at a point northwest of Aleksinac, which is to the northwest of Nish. Southwest of Nish, in conjunction with other Bul-

Continued on Page 2.

PLEDGES GREECE'S FAITH TO ALLIES

New Premier Urges France Not to be Influenced by Malicious Reports.

CHAMBER TO BE DISSOLVED

Bulgaria Warns Greece She Considers Landing of Allies a Breach of Neutrality.

PARIS, Nov. 9.—The French Government received today from Premier Skouloudis, head of the new Greek Cabinet, formal assurance of "our neutrality, with the character of sincerest benevolence toward the entente powers."

The communication was in the form of a telegram from the Greek Premier to Athos Romanos, Greek Minister at Paris, which the Minister delivered to Jules Cambon, General Secretary of the Foreign Ministry. The telegram follows:

"Athens, Nov. 9.—Please give to the President of the Council the most formal assurance on my part of our firm resolution to continue our neutrality, with the character of the sincerest benevolence toward the entente powers.

"Please add that the new Cabinet accepts as its own the declarations of former Premier Zaimis regarding the friendly attitude of the Royal Government as to the allied troops at Saloniki. It is too conscious of the real interests of the country and of what it owes to the powers which are protecting Greece to swerve from this line of conduct. It hopes that the friendly feelings of these powers for Greece will not for a moment be influenced by malicious and misleading news purposely circulated with the main object of changing the good relations that exist between the entente and Greece."

The Greek Government is reported to have appealed to the Allies for further financial assistance. A dispatch from Athens to the Havas News Agency says that the Government desires to obtain an additional advance of 40,000,000 francs, ($8,000,000,) and that this request is being considered sympathetically.

The Temps prints a dispatch from Saloniki in which Premier Radoslavoff of Bulgaria is quoted by the Sofia correspondent of the Pesti-Hirlap of Budapest, Hungary, as declaring:

"The Grecian Government now has been warned that it cannot hold the Bulgarian Government responsible for the consequences of its future attitude."

This notification, according to the correspondent, followed representations made by the Premier to M. Naoum, Greek Minister to Bulgaria.

Premier Radoslavoff, the correspondent declares, regards the facilities accorded for the disembarkment of allied troops at Saloniki as incompatible with Greek neutrality, and has informed Minister Naoum to this effect.

WASHINGTON, Nov. 9.—The Foreign Office at Athens cabled the Greek Legation here today that "the new Cabinet intends to put through the same policies in foreign politics as were maintained by the late Cabinet."

SEES RUIN TO GREECE IN DISSOLUTION NOW

Venizelos Supporters Calls Decree Unconstitutional—Two-thirds of Voters in Army.

Special Cable to THE NEW YORK TIMES.

LONDON, Wednesday, Nov. 10.—A decree dissolving the Greek Chamber will be published today, says a dispatch from Athens to The Daily Chronicle.

The Athens correspondent of The Daily News wires under yesterday's date:

"The expedient of a dissolution of the Chamber was characterized by a supporter of former Premier Venizelos in an interview with me today as unconstitutional. He considered, having regard to the foreign situation, that a general election would mean the ruin of the country. The result, he maintained, could not be representative of the people's wishes, as two-thirds of the electorate would be unable to vote because they were serving with the colors."

At a meeting of his party yesterday former Premier Venizelos, according to

Continued on Page 4.

LOST IN MEDITERRANEAN

She Is Believed to Have Left Italian Por Only Yesterday

SURVIVORS AT BIZERTA

They Report That the Undersea Craft That Sunk Steamer Was a Large One.

SOME VICTIMS WOUNDED

Agent of the Line Thinks It Likely Some Americans Were Aboard the Vessel.

ROME, Nov. 9, (via Paris.)—The Italian liner Ancona, bound from Naples to New York, has been sunk by a large submarine, flying the Austrian colors.

She carried 422 passengers and 160 men were in the crew.

Two hundred and seventy survivors, some of them wounded, have been landed at Bizerta.

The Ancona sailed from New York for Naples on Oct. 17. She had on board 1,245 Italian reservists and a general cargo. She arrived at Naples on Oct. 29, and was due to sail from Naples for New York yesterday.

William Hartfield of the firm of Hartfield, Solari & Co., 1 State Street, agents for the Italia Societa Navigazione a Vapore of Naples, which owned the Ancona, said last night:

"The Ancona has accommodation for forty-eight first-class passengers, and usually has a few Americans on the westward voyage to New York and Philadelphia. She is commanded by Captain Massardo, who is a very skillful navigator and a careful man.

"I understood she was to have left Naples today but had not received any cablegram from the head office. I will send a dispatch at once and ask if there were any Americans on the passenger list."

Mr. Hartfield characterized the sinking of the Ancona as "an unnecessary crime" and "absolute murder."

Most of the Ancona's passenger list, Mr. Hartfield went on, had been made up hitherto of women and children. He believed she carried a large number of women and children on her present voyage.

The Ancona, he added, carried a crew of 160 men, all of them being Italians.

At no time, he said, did the Ancona carry guns or munitions of war, because it was against the rules of the company to carry war munitions on the same vessels with passengers.

One Explanation of Austrian Flag.

Shipping men recalled last night that Italy and Germany had not declared war on each other, and it was suggested that if a German submarine was responsible for sinking the Ancona the raising of the Austrian flag was very easily explained.

The Ancona was built in Belfast in 1908. She was a twin-screw steamer of 8,210 gross tonnage, 482 feet long, and with a beam of 58 feet.

The Ancona has been in the Italian Line service six years, and without her cargo was valued at more than $1,000,000. She played a prominent part in the rescue of passengers from the burning Fabre liner Sant' Anna in mid-Atlantic in September last, coming to the Sant' Anna's aid and taking off more than 600 passengers. The Sant' Anna succeeded in checking the fire and proceeded to the Azores without further assistance.

For several months before Italy's entrance into the war the Ancona was engaged in carrying home Italian reservists from this country and supplies for the Italian Government. On one of her trips from New York to Naples late in August last year the Ancona was stopped by the British at Gibraltar and twenty-four Germans and one Austrian were taken off the ship.

Bizerta, where her survivors were landed, is a French naval station on the north coast of Africa, about thirty-five miles northwest of Tunis.

Since the beginning of October Captains and officers of incoming steamers have reported sighting submarines in the Mediterranean and usually off the African coast.

The Lamport & Holt steamer Voltaire sighted a big submarine off Tunis on her way to New York from Genoa, according to her officers, just after daybreak. Apparently the commander must have mistaken the steamer for a cruiser on account of her gray-painted funnel and hull and dived under the surface about two miles off on the port bow. When the Voltaire reached Gibraltar the officers heard that a French and a British steamer had been torpedoed on the same day that they sighted the submarine off Tunis.

They said that the German and Austrian submarines kept over to the African Coast, to be out of the way of the

"All the News That's Fit to Print."

The New York Times.

THE WEATHER
Snow or rain today; partly cloudy tomorrow; fresh southeast winds, shifting to northwest.
For full weather report see Page 21.

VOL. LXV...NO. 21,142. ... NEW YORK, MONDAY, DECEMBER 13, 1915.—TWENTY-TWO PAGES. ONE CENT In Greater New York, Jersey City and Newark. | Elsewhere, TWO CENTS.

PRESIDENT DEMANDS ANCONA DISAVOWAL AND REPARATION, ALSO PUNISHMENT OF THE GUILTY SUBMARINE COMMANDER, IN NOTE REQUIRING THAT AUSTRIA'S COMPLIANCE BE PROMPT

President Wilson's Note to Austria on the Ancona Sinking

DEPARTMENT OF STATE
WASHINGTON, DEC. 6, 1915

The Secretary of State to Ambassador Penfield:

Please deliver a note to the Minister of Foreign Affairs, textually as follows:

Reliable information obtained from American and other survivors who were passengers on the steamship Ancona shows that on Nov. 7 a submarine flying the Austro-Hungarian flag fired a solid shot toward the steamship, that thereupon the Ancona attempted to escape, but, being overhauled by the submarine, she stopped, that after a brief period and before the crew and passengers were all able to take to the boats the submarine fired a number of shells at the vessel and finally torpedoed and sank her while there were yet many persons on board, and that by gunfire and foundering of the vessel a large number of persons lost their lives or were seriously injured, among whom were citizens of the United States.

The public statement of the Austro-Hungarian Admiralty has been brought to the attention of the Government of the United States and received careful consideration. This statement substantially confirms the principal declaration of the survivors, as it admits that the Ancona, after being shelled, was torpedoed and sunk while persons were still on board.

The Austro-Hungarian Government has been advised, through the correspondence which has passed between the United States and Germany, of the attitude of the Government of the United States as to the use of submarines in attacking vessels of commerce, and the acquiescence of Germany in that attitude, yet with full knowledge on the part of the Austro-Hungarian Government of the views of the Government of the United States as expressed in no uncertain terms to the ally of Austria-Hungary, the commander of the submarine which attacked the Ancona failed to put in a place of safety the crew and passengers of the vessel which they purposed to destroy because, it is presumed, of the impossibility of taking it into port as a prize of war.

The Government of the United States considers that the commander violated the principles of international law and of humanity by shelling and torpedoing the Ancona before the persons on board had been put in a place of safety or even given sufficient time to leave the vessel. The conduct of the commander can only be characterized as wanton slaughter of defenseless noncombatants, since at the time when the vessel was shelled and torpedoed she was not, it appears, resisting or attempting to escape, and no other reason is sufficient to excuse such an attack, not even the possibility of rescue.

The Government of the United States is forced, therefore, to conclude either that the commander of the submarine acted in violation of his instructions or that the Imperial and Royal Government failed to issue instructions to the commanders of its submarines in accordance with the law of nations and the principles of humanity. The Government of the United States is unwilling to believe the latter alternative and to credit the Austro-Hungarian Government with an intention to permit its submarines to destroy the lives of helpless men, women and children. It prefers to believe that the commander of the submarine committed this outrage without authority and contrary to the general or special instructions which he had received.

As the good relations of the two countries must rest upon a common regard for law and humanity, the Government of the United States cannot be expected to do otherwise than to demand that the Imperial and Royal Government denounce the sinking of the Ancona as an illegal and indefensible act; that the officer who perpetrated the deed be punished, and that reparation by the payment of an indemnity be made for the citizens of the United States who were killed or injured by the attack on the vessel.

The Government of the United States expects that the Austro-Hungarian Government, appreciating the gravity of the case, will accede to its demand promptly, and it rests this expectation on the belief that the Austro-Hungarian Government will not sanction or defend an act which is condemned by the world as inhumane and barbarous, which is abhorrent to all civilized nations, and which has caused the death of innocent American citizens.

LANSING.

CAN'T FIND THE SUBMARINE

That Is Given as Austria's Reason for Not Answering Our Inquiry.

MAY HAVE BEEN DESTROYED

Berlin Paper Defends Act of the Commander as Due to the Ship Trying to Escape.

OUR GERMAN PRESS CRITICAL

One Renewal of Suggestion That President Warn Americans to Keep Off Belligerent Ships.

VIENNA, Dec. 11, (via London, Dec. 12.)—The reason for Austria's delay in replying to the American Government's inquiry for details in the Ancona case, The Associated Press correspondent learns from a well-informed source, is that it has been found impossible thus far to get into communication with the submarine involved, although every effort has been made to do so.

Ambassador Penfield submitted the American communication on Nov. 18, and received assurances that the desired information would be obtained as soon as possible. Up to the present, however, nothing is known as to the movements of the submarine, which is a large one, with a wide radius of action. It is considered possible that the submarine has met with misfortune.

Since the submarine commander's first report on the sinking of the Ancona already had been published, it was necessary, it is asserted here, to submit to the commander the allegations of the Ancona's crew and passengers before the questions asked by the United States could be answered. It now appears that a supplementary report issued on the case contained details supplied by the submarine commander in his first report, and was not based upon any second communication from him.

BERLIN, Dec. 12, (via London.)—Commenting upon the United States note to Austria concerning the sinking of the Ancona, the Morgen Post says:

"If the report is correct, President Wilson is endeavoring to create utterly new maritime law, for, according to existing law, upon which America, indeed, based her attitude, it was permissible to fire at a ship which disregarded a demand to stop and attempted to flee, irrespective of whether or not passengers were aboard. In such a case the Captain of the fleeing ship assumes the responsibility for the welfare of his passengers."

GERMAN PRESS VIEWS ON NOTE TO AUSTRIA

Ridder Hopes for Arbitration, Saying President Wilson's Demands Are Unjust.

Comments on the Ancona note by German newspapers in the United States follow. Bernard Ridder, in the New Yorker Staats-Zeitung, expresses the hope that Austria-Hungary will ask for arbitration, and says:

"President Wilson's Ancona note is his first concise and statesmanlike document, and, if his premises were unassailable, he would find the whole nation solidly behind him.

"Unfortunately President Wilson rests his demands on an erroneous assumption. Brushing aside the Declaration of London of 1907 and that of Paris of 1856, both of which were concluded to guide nations over disputed ground, he bases his demands on the law of nations as it existed before the Declaration of Paris. Of this law, however, the nations of Europe—and inferentially also the United States, for Lincoln wished to sign it—spoke as is stated in the preamble of the Declaration.

"If the Austro-Hungarian submarine commander had spared the Ancona, Austria-Hungary claims, the steamer would have carried on her return trip death for the Austrian soldiers. American lives must be held sacred everywhere, but not at the cost of making unjust demands on other nations, and so long as the President's interpretation of the law of nations is not proved to be correct, however pleasant it may be to all of us, his peremptory demands on Austria-Hungary cannot be called just. American honor, like Caesar's wife, should be above suspicion. This

Continued on Page 3.

BRITISH RALLY TO NATION'S CALL

Rush of Recruits Surpasses All Hopes and Makes Conscription Unnecessary.

TOTAL ABOUT 4,000,000

Whole Staffs of Mercantile Houses Take Oath Together—Bank Clerks in a Body.

Special Cable to THE NEW YORK TIMES.

LONDON, Monday, Dec. 13.—While no official computation was forthcoming last night on the recruiting accomplished under Lord Derby's scheme, outside estimates agree that the number of men responding to the call for volunteers approximates 4,000,000. This, I was informed by a recruiting official, must be taken only as an unofficial estimate, as the actual figures are held secret until Lord Derby's report reaches Premier Asquith's hands.

The rush of recruits during the last two weeks has been so great as far to exceed the rosiest expectations of Lord Derby and his aids. A considerable proportion of those offering themselves failed to meet the medical requirements.

I am assured that Lord Derby is immensely elated over the outcome of his gigantic effort, and that it is now likely that conscription will be avoided. If the number as finally revealed falls slightly below the mark, it is more than likely, I am told, that more men will be obtained by another call without resorting to conscription.

While the voluntary recruiting was supposed to end Saturday night, the War Office officials, by giving another day to accommodate the crowds that were unable to get themselves attested, owing to the rush in the last hours, made it possible Sunday for many thousands more to enlist throughout Britain. All day the recruiting stations in London and elsewhere were at work putting down the names of men who carried away with them Saturday only slips showing that they had offered themselves, but had been unable to get their attestation slips fully filled out.

Further grace will be allowed until Wednesday night for others to do the same.

Lord Derby was out of town yesterday, catching his breath after his recruiting efforts.

Last Monday the recruiting tide began to flow full and strong. Day by day it increased in volume, until on Friday it became a great flood. Men of all ranks and conditions in life came forward. Clerks from the great banks marched to the stations in a body; the orchestra of one theatre volunteered as one man between the acts, and whole staffs from mercantile houses took the oath together.

Although a great number of the royal servants at Windsor enlisted long ago in compliance with the King's wishes, all eligibles in the royal service are now attested and have been placed in their respective groups.

All the big provincial cities witnessed

Continued on Page 3.

DROPS CENSORSHIP IN FOREIGN OFFICE

British Editors to Be Responsible for the International News They Print.

LONDON, Dec. 12.—The following official statement was made public tonight:

"Sir Edward Grey has arranged that from Dec. 20, 1915, censorship by the Press Bureau on behalf of the Foreign Office shall be suspended. This will not mean a change in the provisions of the Defense of the Realm acts or of regulations made thereunder. They will be binding, as heretofore, but the responsibility of seeing that they are complied with as regards the publication in any newspaper or by any news agency of matter relating to foreign affairs will rest upon the directors of that newspaper or news agency.

"As regards matter telegraphed from this country, the responsibility will rest with the senders of telegrams. The censorship of press telegrams from one foreign country to another over British cables will remain unaltered, since the senders of such telegrams are not within British jurisdiction, and cannot be proceeded against under the Defense of the Realm acts.

"Nothing in this announcement affects the existing arrangements for the censorship of naval or military matter, to which wholly different considerations apply, nor the censorship of other matters, save so far as they relate to foreign affairs."

REPORT BRITISH LOSS OF THREE BATTALIONS

Turks Say That They Surrendered on the Retreat from Bagdad.

BERLIN, Dec. 12, (by Wireless to Sayville, N. Y.)—"According to private advices from Constantinople," says the Overseas News Agency today, "three British battalions of the army that retreated down the Tigris from the City of Bagdad were surrounded by Turkish troops near Kut-el-Amara and surrendered.

"It is expected that the British will retreat southward from Kut-el-Amara in the near future, as their posts to the rear are in danger of being cut off."

PETROGRAD, Dec. 12, (via London.)—The Germans in Persia are seeking to divert the attention of the Russian Army of the Caucasus, according to the Russky Invalid, and cause it to scatter its force over a large front in order to allow the Turks to throw a part of their troops into the Mesopotamian campaign to save Bagdad.

CONSTANTINOPLE, Monday, Dec. 13, (via London.)—The Turkish War Office has issued the following official communication:

On the Irak front our troops, by energetic attacks, captured the advanced enemy positions near Kut-el-Amara and repulsed the enemy to his main position. The enemy's loss in this fighting was over 700 men, while ours has not yet reached 200 dead and wounded.

KAISER PRESIDES AT FIELD WAR COUNCIL

With Hindenburg and Mackensen He Confers With Turks and Bulgars.

LONDON, Monday, Dec. 13.—An important war council, over which the German Emperor is presiding, is now taking place at German Headquarters on the eastern front, according to a Copenhagen dispatch to The Daily Mail.

Among those at the council are General von Falkenhayn, Chief of Staff; Field Marshal von Hindenburg, Field Marshal von Mackensen, and members of the Turkish and Bulgarian General Staffs.

Berlin Disavows Rintelen's Plots in Official Order to Bernstorff

Notifies Ambassador That German Agent, Accused of Financing Strikes and Mexican Revolution, Had No Instructions to Violate Our Laws.

WASHINGTON, Dec. 12.—Count von Bernstorff, the German Ambassador, announced today that he had been authorized by his Government "to disavow" Captain Franz von Rintelen, and declared that he had no instructions to commit acts which were in violation of the laws of the United States. The Ambassador will convey this information to the State Department.

It was said at the Embassy that when Rintelen was in America he acted solely in the capacity of a purchasing agent for private interests.

Rintelen, a German agent, now a prisoner in the Tower of London, has been charged with coming to this country armed with a large corruption fund to incite strikers in munition factories. He also has been accused of being concerned in attempts to set up a counter-revolution in Mexico, and in the financing of the organization known as Labor's National Peace Council.

Rintelen, who is said to be a friend of Emperor William, was apprehended by British authorities at Falmouth while attempting to return to Germany.

Rintelen's Activities Here.

Captain Franz von Rintelen, who was said to have ranked next to the Ambassador among German officials in this country, was captured by the British when he was traveling from this country on the Noordam on the way back to Germany.

At the time of his capture he was under suspicion of having shipped supplies to Germany by way of Sweden, but agents of the Department of Justice, in investigating his stay in this city, found that he had spent enormous sums of money. Various plots have since been charged against him by witnesses before the Federal Grand Jury. One of these was an alleged effort to stir up a new Mexican revolution in order to force this country to intervene and commandeer munitions now being manufactured for the Allies. Another was a plot to spend large sums of money through Labor's National Peace Council to cause strikes in munitions factories and in other industries where they would be harmful to the Allies.

Rintelen has been reported shot as a spy, but word received recently by Government officials in this city is that he is alive in the Tower of London. It was reported from England at one time that the German Government had made great efforts to procure his exchange, and had even offered twenty imprisoned British officers for his release. Extended reports to the German Government on his activities here were said to have been captured by the British.

After he left here he was indicted by the Federal Grand Jury under the names of von Rintelen, Fred Hansen, Miller, Müller, and Edward V. Gasche. He arrived here at about the same time that Huerta, the former Mexican dictator, came to this country from Barcelona.

Had $30,000,000.

The money at Rintelen's disposal is said to have been almost unlimited. After one of his principal aides had told men connected with the Department of Justice of Rintelen's activities here, an investigation of the various sources of his income made it appear that he had more than $30,000,000 to his credit here. One item of $500,000 deposited with the Transatlantic Trust Company at 67 William Street has been traced until the disposition of practically every cent of it is known to agents of the Department of Justice.

According to various witnesses Rintelen considered both Huerta and Felix Diaz as leaders of the counter-revolution. It was said that 10,000 rifles of modern pattern had been offered to Huerta. Rintelen's efforts, successful and unsuccessful, to purchase rifles and other munitions in this country have been traced by Government officials. These were at first believed to be for Germany, but abundant evidence came later to show that they were intended for use in Mexico.

At the same time that he was working for the Mexican revolution, Captain von Rintelen was busy directing the plot to "purchase strikes" as United States District Attorney Marshall phrased it. One of the first men that he met in this connection, according to evidence brought out in the investigation now being made of Labor's National Peace Council, was David Lamar, "the Wolf of Wall Street," who is alleged to have received a fund of between $250,000 and $300,000, which was intended for certain labor leaders.

Captain von Rintelen was also accused of being implicated in the passport frauds. When he was taken off the Noordam he was traveling with a fraudulent Swiss passport. It was charged that, after a discovery made by Carranzista officials had ended the project to start a counter-revolution in Mexico, von Rintelen and his associates sought to send all their agents out of this country with false passports, some to attempt to get to Germany and others to act as spies in countries of the Allies.

Captain von Rintelen came to this country first in 1905 to study banking and economics. His ostensible purpose was to found a branch of the Bank of Berlin in this country. The following year he went to South America and Mexico for banking interests in Germany. He was well known in this city and formerly was a resident member of the New York Yacht Club.

LAYS RECALL TO POLITICS.

Von Reventlow, with Others, Impugns Motives of Americans.

BERLIN, Dec. 12, (via London.)—Count von Reventlow in the Tages Zeitung, commenting on the recall of the German naval and military attachés at Washington, declares he finds it impossible to believe that the request that they be recalled was not due to political reasons. He knows of no case, he says, in which the recall of both military and naval attachés was demanded simultaneously. In addition, he comments, is the fact that the recalls were demanded after a long campaign "of the British press and of the American press, which takes sides with the enemies of Germany."

Count von Reventlow quotes a Washington dispatch referring to the danger of a severance of relations between Austria and the United States, and says he does not know how highly Austria estimates the danger of a severance, and is curious to learn what position it will take. He quotes with approval the remarks of the Lokal Anzeiger concerning the saving of lives of passengers of the Ancona, and declares that the United States demands a submarine shall not fire when a ship flees after

Continued on Page 3.

AMERICANS ESCAPE SAFELY FROM GIEVGELI

Mme. Grouitch Reaches Saloniki With 38 Orphans—Why Allies Are Retreating.

By RICHARD HARDING DAVIS.

Special Cable to THE NEW YORK TIMES.

SALONIKI, Dec. 11.—There seems to be no longer any doubt that Gievgeli was evacuated early Friday by the French and Serbian forces. The Serbian inhabitants had already fled. On account of the bombardment even the Bulgarian residents moved out. The Director of the Post Office, who arrived here this morning by horseback, says he was the last to leave the city, which was being bombarded.

He says shells set fire to the former American Hospital operated by Dr. James Donnelly, and which, after his death, was taken over by the French for the French and Serbian wounded, all of whom were safely removed. The railroad station also was destroyed.

Mme. Mabel Grouitch, the Serbian-American in charge of the Frothingham unit, with her assistant, Elva Reed La Grane of Oregon, left Gievgeli on the 9th, bringing safely here in a freight car thirty-eight Serbian orphans. These women are doing splendid work. The orphanage, which is supported by Mr. Frothingham of Baltimore, was originally at Nish. When driven from there the staff took refuge at Gievgeli. When your correspondent visited Gievgeli last week these women were managing restaurants, with the profits of which they supported the orphans. Lady Scott's unit of five nurses, who are Scotch, also escaped safely. No Americans or English remain in Gievgeli.

Refugees are now crowding into Saloniki on mattresses in carts, carrying their pitiful possessions in kerchiefs and baskets. It is a picture of this war that has been made familiar, but that these refugees are forerunners of a Bulgarian advance upon Saloniki does not follow. But Gievgeli is so near the border that if the Bulgarians mean to halt there or fight on Greek soil the next few hours should decide.

It is now possible to give in more detail an explanation of the withdrawal of the French and British to their second line of defense. To understand this withdrawal find on the map Krivolak, the former French advanced position, and follow the railroad and River Vardar southeast to Gradec, the present first French line.

The cause of this retreat is the inability to hold Monastir and their withdrawal west leaving a gap in the former line of the Serbians, French and British. The enemy is now south and west of the French, and their left flank is exposed.

On Dec. 3, finding the advanced position at Krivolak threatened by four divisions—100,000 men—General Sarrail began the withdrawal, sending south by rail without loss all ammunition and stores. He destroyed the tunnel at Krivolak and all the bridges across the Vardar and on his left at the Cerna River. The fighting was heavy at Prevedo and Biserence, but the French losses were small. He

Continued on Page 4.

IRISH SAVE ARMY FROM BULGARIANS

Three Regiments Cover Retreat to Greek Border Against Overwhelming Odds.

GREECE YIELDS TO ALLIES

But Teutons and Turks May Follow Them Across Her Border—Bulgarians Barred.

LONDON, Monday, Dec. 13.—The Anglo-French troops who last week began their retirement from their advanced positions in Southern Serbia are now approaching, if they have not crossed, the Greek frontier, and the attitude Greece will adopt becomes more and more important.

Greece will not demobilize, but will withdraw all her troops from Saloniki except one division, according to The Times Paris correspondent. This, the correspondent adds, is the result of the negotiations at Athens, and the Entente Allies have decided to prosecute the Saloniki enterprise vigorously. What will happen and just what Greece will do if the Teutons cross the frontiers remain a matter of doubt. It is not believed that the Bulgarians will be permitted to cross, whatever their German allies may do.

Some of the questions which are seriously occupying the Greek Government have to do with the use of the railways, which are needed for the Greek troops, and the damage that might be done to them with the object of impeding Bulgarian pursuit, should the Sofia Government decide that the British and French are to be followed into Greek territory.

The Greek Government has good evidence of the effective manner in which the French engineers destroy railways in the work done along the line north of the Greek frontier. So well was this accomplished that the Bulgarians were greatly delayed, having to use roads covered with snow, with the result that the French escaped almost unscathed.

British Retreat More Difficult.

The British, who had advanced further from the railway to the northeast of Lake Doiran, had a much more difficult feat to accomplish when retirement was decided on, and suffered more heavily. They were faced by greatly superior forces, and, according to an official report issued last night, their successful withdrawal to a position extending from Lake Doiran to the Vardar Valley was largely due to the gallantry of three Irish regiments. The report says:

After sustaining violent attacks delivered by the enemy in overwhelming numbers, the tenth division succeeded, with the help of reinforcements, in retiring to a strong position from Lake Doiran westward toward the Valley of the Vardar in conjunction with our allies.

The division is reported to have fought well against very heavy odds, and it was largely due to the gallantry of the troops, especially the Munster Fusiliers, the Dublin Fusiliers, and the Connaught Rangers, that the withdrawal was successfully accomplished.

Owing to the mountainous nature of

Continued on Page 4.

THREATENS GOOD RELATIONS

Government Said to Be Prepared for a Diplomatic Break.

NO LOOPHOLE FOR PARLEYS

Vienna's Contention That Ancona Was Trying to Escape Is Brushed Aside.

ACT 'A WANTON SLAUGHTER'

"Illegal and Indefensible," "Condemned by World as Inhumane and Barbarous."

Special to The New York Times.

WASHINGTON, Dec. 12.—Apparently leaving no loophole for compromise or discussion, the United States Government has called upon the Government of Austria-Hungary for prompt compliance with a demand for disavowal and reparation on account of the sinking of the Italian-American liner Ancona by an Austro-Hungarian submarine, and the punishment of the submarine's commander. The text of the formal diplomatic communication containing the demand was made public by the State Department today.

The demand follows a statement informing Austria-Hungary that "the good relations of the two countries must rest upon a common regard for law and humanity." The note arraigns the shelling and torpedoing of the liner as "inhumane," "barbarous," and a "wanton slaughter" of "helpless men, women, and children."

Not in any of the diplomatic notes of this Government to Germany concerning the Lusitania was such direct and menacing language used. As a consequence of this communication, which bears all the marks of being an ultimatum, the gravest danger threatens the continuance of relations between the Governments of Austria-Hungary and the United States.

"Ultimatum" is the term used by some officials in describing the substance of the American position. Generally in Administration circles the view appears to prevail that President Wilson and Secretary Lansing have burned all bridges behind them, and are prepared to take extreme measures to showing their resentment if the Vienna Government declines to comply with the demands made. In diplomacy "demand" is about the strongest word that can be used, and it is used twice in the Ancona note.

Must Accede Within a Week.

The course the United States will pursue is understood to have been determined upon. A reasonable time will be given Austria-Hungary in which to reply to the communication before further action is taken. The word "prompt" as used in the note is understood to mean that Austria-Hungary must accede to the demand of the United States within a week, at the most. If the demand is not complied with, immediate severance of diplomatic relations is regarded as certain.

The Administration has been sensitive over the criticism, heard most frequently during the critical period of the Lusitania negotiations, that all the action of the Government in dealing with Germany's destruction of merchant vessels, with the loss of innocent lives, was confined to writing diplomatic notes. With particular reference to this criticism, it is declared by officials that the note on the Ancona case means exactly what it says, and that the country should be prepared for a break in the relations between Washington and Vienna if the Austro-Hungarian Government does not promptly accede to the demand to "denounce the sinking of the Ancona as an illegal and indefensible act, that the officer who perpetrated the deed be punished, and that reparation by the payment of an indemnity be made for the citizens of the United States who were killed or injured by the attack on the vessel."

The manner in which the American note dismisses the Austrian contention that the Ancona sought to escape removes that phase of the incident from the field of discussion. A point-blank refusal to accept the Austrian view seems to be a correct construction of the American position. Judged by what is being said in a guarded way by officials here, the Austro-Hungarian Government must either accept or reject what is demanded by the United States. There is no half-way point

"All the News That's Fit to Print."

The New York Times.

THE WEATHER
Fair and colder Monday; probably fair Tuesday; northwest gales diminishing.
For full weather report see Page 14.

VOL. LXV...NO. 21,065. ... NEW YORK, MONDAY, SEPTEMBER 27, 1915.—EIGHTEEN PAGES. ONE CENT In Greater New York, Jersey City and Newark. | Elsewhere TWO CENTS.

HALT CITY TRAFFIC TO TEST SUBWAYS

Police Close Many Streets as Experts Investigate the New Excavations.

TWO INQUIRIES UNDER WAY

Mayor Appoints Committee and Service Board Gets Men from Other Cities.

ACCIDENT REPORTS PENDING

One Victim of Broadway Collapse in Critical Condition—Changes in Street Car Routes.

Where Cars Will Run Today, and Where They Will Not

Frank Hedley, Vice President and General Manager of the New York Railways Company, issued the following statement at midnight:

In the morning the Eighth Street and Fourteenth Street crosstown lines will be running as usual.

It is expected that the shoring that we have ordered at Thirty-fourth Street and Broadway will be completed by 8 o'clock. When it is in place the cars will be in operation for through traffic across Thirty-fourth Street, and will permit of the completion of through traffic up and down Sixth Avenue.

The Broadway cars cannot be operated immediately north or south of Thirty-eighth Street on account of the cave-in.

North of the cave-in the Broadway cars will run north from Forty-third Street.

It is expected that the Twenty-third Street Crosstown line will be in operation by 10 A. M.

The Seventh Avenue line will be operated only north of Thirty-third Street for possibly a week or more.

Two separate investigations into the safety of streets over the new subway excavations began yesterday, following the collapsing of Broadway at Thirty-eighth Street on Saturday evening, when a woman was killed and three men were injured, and a similar accident in Seventh Avenue, between Twenty-third and Twenty-fifth Streets, where seven persons were killed and eighty-five injured on Wednesday.

Mayor Mitchel appointed a committee of twelve engineers to conduct an inquiry in co-operation with him and other city officials, with Commissioner of Accounts Wallstein in general charge. The Public Service Commission, already equipped with a formidable array of construction experts, sent for other engineers from Boston, Philadelphia, and San Francisco to examine the cut and cover work here, report on its safeness, and recommend means to prevent further disaster.

City Officials Apprehensive.

The nervousness of city officials over the entire subway situation was shown by the activity late in the afternoon when a six-inch water pipe burst in the excavation of the Seventh Avenue subway at Rector and Greenwich Streets. The water flowed down a grade into a hollow underneath a pumping station and was pumped out quickly.

It was decided after examination that no supports had been undermined, and that there was no danger of a cave-in. But as soon as the report of another misfortune in the subway had been received there was a hasty exodus of officials, and presently there gathered at the scene Police Commissioner Woods, Chief Inspector Max Schmittberger, Public Service Commissioner William Hayward, Secretary Travis H. Whitney of the Public Service Commission, the commission's principal subway engineer, Robert Ridgway; Deputy Police Commissioner Lawrence Dunham, and Frank Hedley, Vice President and General Manager of the Interboro Rapid Transit Company. The damage done here was only slight and traffic soon was resumed.

Downtown Traffic Tied Up.

Meantime, the Police Department enforced widespread restrictions of traffic that tied up vehicular transportation in the heart of the city. With the light travel of Sunday, these regulations did not fall so heavily on the public as they may today when tens of thousands of workers must ride to their places of business. Also, shuttle services relieved the situation.

The Twenty-third and Thirty-fourth Street crosstown lines and the Sixth Avenue were the principal arteries affected. It is expected that they will be running this morning, as will the Eighth Street and Fourteenth Street crosstowns. Traffic on Broadway, between Thirty-third and Thirty-ninth Street, and on Seventh Avenue below Thirty-third Street, will continue to be held up.

Parties of engineers under the direction of the Public Service Commission and the Mayor were at work all day examining the roofed streets over the excavations. The Mayors' committee made an inspection of all the unfinished subway construction work which is being conducted by the United States Realty and Improvement Corporation, the builder of the sections where both of last week's accidents occurred, and today it will examine all of the subway construction throughout the city where there are roofed excavations in which

Continued on Page 4.

OUR FORCES ATTACKED BY HAITIAN REBELS

Forty Natives Killed and Ten of Our Marines Wounded—Haitians Had Refused to Disarm.

CAPE HAITIEN, Sept. 26.—In an attack by Haitian rebels on an American force, about two miles from Cape Haitien, forty Haitians were killed. Ten Americans were wounded.

The rebels have refused to disarm, and the Americans are marching on Haut du Cap, in the plain of the north.

Special to The New York Times.

WASHINGTON, Sept. 26.—The Navy Department tonight was without confirmation of the report of another clash between American marines and Haitians at Cape Haitien today, in which forty Haitians were killed and ten Americans wounded. Admiral Caperton's report of the fight is expected at any time.

Word reached Washington today that the committee of the Haitian Parliament that had been considering the protectorate treaty would report tomorrow or next day. It is confidently expected that the report will be favorable and that ratification will follow in short order.

The executive authorities in Haiti have already signed the treaty, and pending its acceptance by Parliament its more important provisions have been put into practical operation by the American naval forces around Haiti under a sort of modus vivendi.

American officials are already in charge of the Haitian Custom Houses, and American marines, some on foot and some mounted, are operating in the interior.

BLAKE WINS RELEASE FROM AMERICAN POST

Ambassador Sharp Persuades Ambulance Committee Not to Hinder Surgeon's Work.

Special Cable to THE NEW YORK TIMES.

PARIS, Sept. 26.—The American Ambulance versus Dr. Blake controversy over the latter's resignation to accept the post as chief surgeon of the British hospital at Ris Orangis was settled today in favor of Dr. Blake by the intervention of the American Ambassador. However, even this powerful influence did not prevent a big fight in the Executive Committee, during which several members offered their resignations before the Ambulance climbed down from its position.

The battle has raged ever since Dr. Blake's ultimatum of last Thursday, when asked to reconsider his resignation, in which he gave the only terms acceptable to him to remain. The committee then discovered that the War Ministry first desired the acceptance of his resignation by the hospital before officially confirming him in his new position. It was then decided to hold up the acceptance even though Dr. Blake quit his services with them.

Dr. Blake, who had received a cable from Robert Bacon, then called on Ambassador Sharp, who asked Laurence Benet of the Ambulance Committee to see that a letter of acceptance was written. Several members of the committee went over to the Blake cause, declaring the American institution would be split in two if they prevented another hospital from obtaining the services of so able a surgeon just because he desired to leave them. The remainder of the committee then saw the light and decided to give a letter provided the offered committee resignations be withdrawn, and also that Dr. Blake take no members of the hospital with him.

WIRELESS TOWER FALLS IN FRONT OF EXPRESS

Locomotive of Fast B. & M. Train Derailed When Tufts College Structure Is Blown on Track.

MEDFORD, Mass., Sept. 26.—The new wireless telegraph tower at Tufts College, 304 feet in height, was blown over during a gale today, and fell a few feet in front of an express train from Concord, N. H., on the Boston & Maine Railroad. The locomotive was derailed when it plunged into the steel framework, but no one was injured.

Passengers in a trolley car also had a narrow escape. The car was approaching the tower when the motorman, glancing upward, saw it swaying, and brought the car to a standstill within 100 feet of the falling steel. A group of sightseers standing near the cement base of the tower jumped back in time to escape being struck.

All of the electric wires in the neighborhood were torn down, several poles were broken, and two large trees were uprooted. Electric and steam traffic was held up for several hours until the wreckage could be removed. The breaking of a temporary guy wire as the structure swayed in the wind is believed to have led to the accident.

REPORT THAT YAQUIS BURNED 60 PERSONS

Dispatches from Sonora Tell of Terrible Death of Women and Children in Hay Car.

SAN DIEGO, Sept. 26.—Eighty passengers on a Southern Pacific Mexican train were thrown into a car containing hay and the car set on fire by a band of Yaqui Indians on Friday, near Torres, Sonora, according to wireless advices received here today from Hermosillo, via Guaymas.

Only twenty passengers have been accounted for thus far, the others having been burned to death.

The Indians, according to the report, numbered about sixty, and were deserters from one of the Mexican factional armies. They first derailed the train, which was running from Campo Verde to Torres, after which they placed the passengers, most of whom were women and children, in the hay car, and applied the torch. So far as is known no Americans were on the train.

Torres is a small town, about seventy miles north of Guaymas, and a junction point of the railroad, a spur line running into the mining district.

ALLIES' DELEGATES GO WEST ON LOAN

Terms All Agreed Upon, They Will Confer with Bankers of West and South.

START FOR CHICAGO TODAY

War News Pleases Them and May Prove Helpful by Widening Syndicate Support.

5-YEAR BONDS TO BE ISSUED

$500,000,000 of These at 5% to be Convertible Into Ten or Fifteen Year Bonds at 4½%.

An agreement among New York bankers to co-operate with the Anglo-French Financial Commission in the raising of $500,000,000 for the stabilization of the foreign exchange market was reached at conferences held on Saturday and yesterday afternoon, and today four members of the commission, accompanied by one of the partners of J. P. Morgan & Co., will leave for Chicago.

The Western trip was decided upon for the purpose of bringing bankers throughout the Middle West into accord with the position taken by leading New York financiers. George M. Reynolds, President of the Continental and Commercial Bank; J. B. Forgan, head of the First National; J. Ogden Armour, and other influential Chicago capitalists have been lukewarm toward the proposals made for a big commercial credit, and the visit of the Commissioners is expected to give the negotiations a national character.

Will Not Go West of Chicago.

The commission does not expect to go further West than Chicago, but bankers from St. Louis, Kansas City, Omaha, St. Paul and other centres have been asked to meet the members there to go over the points brought out at the conferences in this city, and it is believed that objections which they have raised can be overcome by a frank discussion with the commission.

Lord Reading, chairman of the commission, and Basil B. Blackett will be of the party which leaves this afternoon, and it is expected that the other two members will be Sir Henry Babington Smith and Earnest Mallet. The Morgan firm will be represented by either Henry P. Davison or Thomas W. Lamont. Sir Edward Holden had expected to make the trip, but it appeared likely last night that he would remain in New York with one of the two representatives of the French Government.

Terms of the Loan.

There was another important meeting of Morgan partners and several other New York bankers yesterday afternoon, at which some of the Commissioners were present. It was decided that while the success of the proposed loan has been practically assured by the support already enlisted, bankers at other important centres who have not had an opportunity to make their views known should be consulted before the final details are decided upon. If these men are won over, the loan will be announced in a few days along the lines already outlined. These are:

The provision of $500,000,000 to be deposited with banks in this country and to be expended exclusively for commercial purchases.

Great Britain and France to issue five-year 5 per cent. notes, payable in dollars at New York, these notes to be a joint obligation on the two Governments having priority as to principal and interest over all other Government debts.

The notes to be convertible, at the option of the holder, into 4½ per cent. fifteen or twenty year bonds at maturity.

The notes to be sold to a huge syndicate of banks, firms, and individuals, probably at 97½, with the understanding that they shall be offered to investors at about 99.

Russia's needs for credit here to be taken care of in other ways, and none of the money provided by this loan to be used for that country's account.

The Commissioners made this statement regarding the purpose of their Western trip:

We have spent much of our time since our arrival in studying conditions in this country, and have conferred with many bankers and business men. We are now desirous of meeting some of the leading men of affairs from other great centres, and for that purpose, the Chairman and some other members of the mission will start tomorrow for Chicago.

We have been greatly pleased with the active and cordial desire for co-operation shown by diverse interests throughout the country, and we feel confident that an arrangement will be effected for the attainment of the common ends sought, namely, to preserve and maintain international trade between the United States of America, on the one hand, and Great Britain and France, upon the other, by the removal of the impediments which arise from instability in the rate of exchange.

War News Pleases Delegates.

Both the bankers who have been at work on the arrangements for bringing out the largest security issue ever floated in one operation in this country and the members of the Anglo-French Commission were highly pleased with the war news yesterday. It was said that the beginning of the long-planned general offensive movement on the part of the Allies could not have been better timed for the influence which it had upon sentiment affecting the bond offering. It has been argued that while the credit of the two nations could not be questioned, even if their ultimate defeat were conceded, the flotation of the $500,-

Continued on Page 2.

Austria Is Calling Out Reserves of Eighteen

ZURICH, Switzerland, Sept. 26.—The Austrian eighteen-year-old landsturm class has been ordered to join the army on Oct. 15, according to a dispatch from Vienna. Other classes, including the ages of 19, 20, 24, and from 38 to 45, will be summoned to the colors the middle of November.

The oldest classes, from 43 to 50 years, will be called out at the end of November.

SLAYS OPERA SINGER; HER FIANCE A SUICIDE

Girl Was to Have Opened Tonight in Victor Herbert's "Princess Pat" at the Cort.

ROMANCE BEGAN ON STAGE

Young Man, in Tears an Hour Before, Had Lamented Sweetheart's Waning Love.

As he passed the music conservatory of Mme. Alice Andres Parker, 240 West Seventy-second Street, at 11 o'clock last night, Policeman Koenig of the West Sixty-eighth Street Station heard four revolver shots, raced up the steps, demanding of Mme. Parker, who admitted him, where the shooting had been.

"Why, it must be outside," replied Mme. Parker. "We didn't hear it."

"It was in your top floor," responded the policeman, and he led the way to the top story front room. The door was locked. Koenig burst it open. Those behind Koenig saw that the body of Miss Pearl Palmer, a light opera singer, who was to have opened tonight at the Cort Theatre, playing the second lead in Victor Herbert's "Princess Pat," lay on the floor near the bed.

Beside her lay Herbert Heckler, also a singer in light opera. Both were wounded in the head, where two bullets had struck each. The girl was conscious, and tried to speak as the policeman and the others entered, but before she could utter a word she lost consciousness.

Dr. Robert Rose of 363 West End Avenue was paying a call at the house and was in the parlor, on the ground floor. A shout brought him running upstairs, and one glance at Miss Palmer caused him to exclaim:

"She's dying. Hurry her to a hospital."

Then he bent over Heckler, and rose a moment with the announcement, "He is dead." An ambulance was called from the [illegible] Hospital, and the girl was hurried to that institution, where she died early this morning.

Mme. Parker and others in the conservatory who had known both the young man and the young woman for years were almost prostrated by the tragedy, but several of them said they had feared something would happen because of Heckler's infatuation for the girl and his growing belief that she was losing her love for him, although they were engaged to be married.

They met three years ago while playing in the same company, and a year later announced their engagement. Why they had not married before this no one seemed to know, unless they were ambitious and were progressing in their profession so that neither was willing to abandon chances for further success.

Miss Palmer had sung last week in Philadelphia and reached Mme. Parker's home yesterday afternoon. The conservatory was recently taken over by the Aborns to become the Aborn Classes for Operatic Training, but Mme. Parker was still in charge, and she gave Miss Palmer her old room on the top floor.

Heckler, who is said to be the son of a wealthy jeweler of Chicago, apparently had not been singing this Summer, for he had been in the city for a month, and presently was to have taken a position as teacher in the Aborn school, it was said. He called at the house last evening, apparently as soon as he learned that Miss Palmer had returned to town, and Mme. Parker directed him to the girl's room.

Heckler had lived in the house himself on former occasions and was well known to Mme. Parker. She told him that Miss Palmer had complained of nervousness over tonight's opening, and Heckler, making some sympathetic remark, passed on up to her room, greeting W. W. Houston, a music teacher of 21 West Thirtieth Street, and also a caller at the house, as he passed through the parlor.

Presently he came downstairs again and asked Mr. Houston to accompany him to a near-by hotel, where he could buy a bottle of ale.

"Miss Palmer doesn't feel well," he explained, "and I thought the ale would do her good if taken just before she retired."

Houston accompanied him, and they walked to Broadway and Seventy-second Street, where they got the ale and started back. As they neared the house Heckler complained:

"Something's the matter. I'm losing Pearl's love. She isn't the same as she was. She is very successful and ambitious, and I think she's forgetting me in her pride in her work. If I can't have her love I don't want to live."

Then, to the amazement of Houston, he burst into tears. Houston tried to calm him, and by the time they reached the house had so pacified him that he was able to pass on up to Miss Palmer's room without exciting the comment of others.

The room on the top floor is three stories above the parlor floor, so that ordinary sounds do not carry so far, but Mme. Parker, Mr. Houston, and the others did hear Miss Palmer laugh once, and they recalled afterward that it was a laugh in which there was no joy, no humor. It sounded harsh, scornful, cynical, as though the girl were amused at Heckler's protestations.

Then they heard the voices of both, and knew they must be raised for the sound to have reached to the lower floor, but still none went upstairs, for neither Heckler nor Miss Palmer was of the sort who might be expected to give way to a quarrel. And then came several screams.

It was found that Heckler had fired two bullets into Miss Palmer's head and two in his own. The first bullet had grazed the top of the girl's scalp and from the position of her body she apparently had tried to reach the door and escape when Heckler fired the second time. This bullet entered below her left ear and lodged in the brain.

To shoot himself Heckler had put the weapon to his own temple and it was disclosed how close he must have stood to his victim when his body was found stretched so close to her on the floor that they touched.

Heckler was 27 years old and Miss Palmer was two years younger. It was said at the conservatory last night that her family was supposed to be named Foster and to live at 236 East Seventy-seventh Street.

Mme. Parker said afterward that Heckler had been taking vocal instruction from her for the last three months and had been such a hard worker that she wouldn't be surprised if his labors had turned his brain. She seemed to think this might have made him imagine a coldness on the part of his fiancée.

ALLIES ATTACK FROM SEA TO VERDUN; SMASH 20 MILES OF GERMAN FRONT; 20,000 PRISONERS, MANY GUNS TAKEN

Greatest Advances Made in Champagne and North of Arras.

SOUCHEZ AND LOOS TAKEN

British Capture of the Latter Threatens the Germans' Possession of Lens.

A 70-HOUR BOMBARDMENT

It Preceded French Assaults Which Won 15 Miles of Trenches Near Perthes.

33 FIELD GUNS CAPTURED

Booty of the Allies Includes Many Machine Guns and Much Other War Material.

GERMANS ADMIT REVERSES

Report Evacuation of Loos and Champagne Positions — Rushing Reinforcements Through Belgium.

LONDON, Sept. 26.—The great allied offensive in the west began yesterday was successfully continued today. Tonight the net result is the taking of more than 20,000 unwounded German prisoners, the occupation of twenty miles of German trenches (the German lines having been penetrated at some points to a depth of two and one-half miles) and the capture of upward of thirty field guns, [illegible] other war material.

The attack which resulted in the French and British victories began Saturday morning. For several weeks there has been an almost incessant bombardment with big guns, which late last week increased in intensity, particularly in the sectors where the infantry attacks took place.

The French, who have the most important gain to their credit, directed their chief onset against the German lines around Perthes, Beausejour, and Suippes, in Champagne, where in December they made a considerable gain of ground. Saturday's attack, however, backed by a tremendous artillery fire, gave them possession of more territory than they had retaken from the Germans since the latter dug themselves in after the battle of the Marne.

According to the French account the Germans in Champagne were driven out of their trenches over a front of fifteen miles, varying in depth from two-thirds of a mile to two and a half miles. The French in this engagement captured more than 12,000 prisoners, and apparently the advantage is being pressed still further.

Weakens German Argonne Positions.

The importance of this gain lies in the fact that every yard of ground taken in this region weakens the German position around Verdun, from which the Germans might be compelled to retire should the French succeed in making any further advance.

The French also have regained, first the cemetery and then the whole town of Souchez and trenches east of the Labyrinth in the Arras district, which was the scene of much heavy fighting earlier in the year. This battle was fought in co-operation with the British, who attacked on either side of La Bassée Canal. The attack to the south of the canal, Field Marshal Sir John French reports, was a complete success. Trenches on a five-mile front were taken at this point, the victors penetrating the German lines 4,000 yards.

This push forward gives the British possession of the road from Lens to La Bassée, which was used by the Germans for moving troops and supplies north and south, and threatens to outflank the German troops holding the town of Lens.

British Only Twelve Miles from Lille.

Hill No. 70, one of the positions taken on the road, is less than a mile directly north of Lens, with Hulluch, which also fell into the hands of the British, is at the end of the road near La Bassée. It is only twelve miles from Hulluch to Lille, the cheif city of Northern France.

North of the canal the British, although they fought all day yesterday, were unable to hold the ground gained and had to fall back to the trenches which they had left in the morning. The attack, however, accomplished one purpose, as, according to Sir John French, German reserves were sent to check this move, this giving the British south of the canal an opportunity to consolidate their new positions unmolested.

A somewhat similar manoeuvre took place to the north and south of the Menin Road, east of Ypres, and the results were the same. North of the road the British were unable to hold the ground taken, while to the south they

Western Battle Front, Scene of Allies' Great Drive

1. Hooge, the northern limit of the British attack.
2. Here the British captured five miles of trenches.
3. The British capture of Hill 70, a mile from Lens, threatens the German occupation of that town.
4. Loos, captured by the British, is about twelve miles from Lille, the most important city of Northern France held by the Germans.
5. Souchez, after months of fighting, now entirely in French hands.
6. Perthes, middle of the Champagne line, along which the French captured fifteen miles of trenches.

ENTENTE ARMY TO AID GREECE

Saloniki to be the Base for Operations in the Event of Balkan War.

BULGARIA NOW HEDGING

Assures Powers Mobilization Is Purely Defensive—Germans Keenly Disappointed.

LONDON, Monday, Sept. 27.—While the intentions of Bulgaria continue to be surrounded with considerable mystery it is clear that should that vacillating Balkan power venture to attack Serbia she will immediately find herself arrayed also against the army of Greece and in all likelihood that of Rumania, aided by a formidable force of British and French troops. Advices from Athens intimate that this aid has been offered to Greece by Great Britain and France, and that in the event of hostilities Saloniki will be used as a base by the Entente expeditionary corps.

Meanwhile Bulgaria, which had been definitely placed on the side of Germany and Austria as the result of recent news from Sofia, is showing every disposition to "hedge." She confirmed officially yesterday to the Governments of the Entente powers the semi-official statement published on Saturday that her mobilization had been ordered in the national interests and that it had not the slightest aggressive character.

The Bulgarian Premier, M. Radoslavoff, in an interview with the Sofia correspondent of the Berlin Tageblatt, reiterated this statement, but it is noteworthy that, while he said the measure was not directed against Greece or Rumania, he omitted Serbia.

In Germany keen disappointment and not a little uneasiness is felt at the turn of affairs. It had been confidently expected that Bulgaria would enter the war on the side of the Central Empires as soon as her mobilization was completed.

King Constantine and the Greek Premier, M. Venizelos, apparently have entirely composed the differences which led to their separation when the Premier early in the war wanted to join the Allies against Turkey. The cheering of the Greek populace gathered in front of the office of the British Minister, Sir Francis E. H. Elliot, was a significant incident in Saturday's crisis, says the correspondent at Athens of Reuter's Telegram Company. Although Greece still feels the effects of the late Balkan war, the correspondent adds, all shades of opinion support the mobilization of the Greek army as the only possible course which the Hellenic Government could take.

The whole matter may yet be smoothed over, as Bulgaria is continuing her negotiations with the Entente powers, the Bulgarian Minister at Petrograd having had a long conference with the Russian Foreign Minister, M. Sazonoff, while the Ministers at other capitals insist that the Bulgarians would not fight against their old friends, Great Britain and Russia.

On the other hand, the Austro-German offensive against Serbia, which seems to

Continued on Page 3.

SAY AUSTRIANS SET FIRE ON SANT' ANNA

Two Jumped Overboard, Officers Report, and Three Are Under Arrest.

NAPLES, Sept. 26, (via Paris.)—The commander and officers of the Fabre Line steamship Sant' Anna, which has arrived here from New York after having put in at the Azores with fire in her cargo, assert that they have collected undisputable evidence that the fire was set by five Austrian passengers who gave false names when they boarded the vessel.

Three of these passengers, it is asserted, have been arrested, while the two others threw themselves overboard and disappeared.

The Sant' Anna sailed from South Brooklyn on Sept. 7 for Naples and Marseilles with 1,764 passengers, who were mostly Italian reservists.

A message was received at the State Department in Washington on Sept. 17 from Walter H. Schultz, the United States Consul at St. Michaels, saying that eighteen fuses had been discovered on the orlop deck of No. 2 hold, where the baggage was stowed, and several explosions had been heard by the crew of the steamship before the fire started. After transferring to the Ancona 805 passengers, who occupied the steerage forward and had been driven out by smoke and water, the Sant' Anna proceeded to Naples.

Since the fire broke out on the Sant' Anna the Fabre Line has adopted the plan of the other transatlantic lines out of New York of having all baggage searched before it is placed on board ship.

The passenger agents of all transatlantic lines out of this port operating under neutral flags will not accept any male German, Austrian or Hungarian passengers on their steamships unless they have safe conduct passes from the Allies.

FOG SAVED THE CYMRIC WITH BIG WAR CARGO

Crew of the White Star Liner Thinks Submarine Mistook the Hesperian for Her.

Members of the crew of the White Star liner Cymric, which arrived yesterday from Liverpool, said that when the vessel sailed from New York on Aug. 27 she had 17,000 tons of cargo, the largest shipment of ammunition made since the war began. In addition to hundreds of cases of rifle and revolver cartridges, the Cymric carried a large number of empty shells to be filled at Woolwich Arsenal, England. The cargo was stowed up to the hatches and staggered the longshoremen in Liverpool when the hatches were taken off. Some of the empty shells weighed 185 pounds.

German submarines were on the lookout for the Cymric off the coast of Ireland and the North of Scotland, because word had been sent from New York of the ammunition she had on board, the sailors said, but they missed her in the fog. One hundred miles west of Fastnet the liner was met by a cruiser and two torpedo boat destroyers to escort her into port.

The crew of the Cymric all believe that the Allan liner Hesperian was torpedoed by mistake for their ship, because the vessels were of very similar design. Captain F. E. Beadnell and the officers of the liner were noncommittal regarding the ammunition carried on the last eastward voyage, but admitted that the liner was escorted into Liverpool by a cruiser and two torpedo boat destroyers.

The Captain said that while the Cymric was in Liverpool he went to Belfast and brought the Olympic round to Southampton. She is being converted into a hospital ship for the Dardanelles.

GERMANS CEASE DVINSK ATTACKS

Heavy Fighting in Russia Taken Up on the Front East of Vilna and Lida.

RUSSIANS CARRY POSITIONS

Capture Prisoners and Guns—Austrians Repulse All Attacks Near Galician Border.

LONDON, Monday, Sept. 27.—After their desperate attacks before Dvinsk, which were repulsed by the Russians, the Germans have transferred their principal activity to the front east of Vilna and Lida. The German official report does not mention the Dvinsk front, and Petrograd tells of driving the Germans from one position there.

According to last night's Petrograd report the Russians are doing much more than holding their own. They have repulsed many attacks, have carried several villages, and taken a number of prisoners and guns. The Berlin report claims insignificant advances.

South of the Pripet to Galicia the Russians have failed to carry on their successes of last week. The Austrians have repulsed attacks near the border of Galicia, and the Petrograd report has nothing to note in this theatre.

Russians Face 2,000,000 Men.

Special Cable to THE NEW YORK TIMES.

PETROGRAD, Sept. 26. (Dispatch to The London Daily News.)—The military expert of the Russky Invalid estimates that there are 130 Austro-German divisions, comprising 2,000,000 men, over the 1,000-mile front from Riga to the Rumanian frontier. The distribution is as follows: Sector of Riga, Dvinsk, and Svenziany, 12 divisions, 7 infantry, 5 cavalry; sector of Svenziany, Vilna, and Orani, 15 divisions, 12 infantry, 3 cavalry; sector of Orani, Slonim, and Pinsk, 47 divisions, 45 infantry, 2 cavalry; sector of Pinsk, Dubno, Brody, Tarnipol, and Novo Selizy, 54 divisions, 44 infantry, 10 cavalry.

There is a marked ascendancy in cavalry in Belows's and Eichhorn's armies, which are used to break through and cut off the railways and get to the rear of the Russian forces. The cavalry succeeded on the Vilna-Dvinsk and Lida-Polozk lines, but the infantry failed in its task, causing the general operations to be frustrated.

The fighting in the Dvinsk region is growing fierce and more stubborn. With every step forward the enemy is losing heavily. Experts of the staff say, latterly they have noticed the enemy are greatly reinforcing at Dvinsk, and evidently accumulating considerable forces, with the object of breaking the Russian front and separating the Dvinsk from the Molodechno groups.

Such a plan necessitates a widening of the scope of main operations. Experts on the staff do not believe the enemy is aiming at Petrograd or Kiev.

Continued on Page 2.

"All the News That's Fit to Print."

The New York Times.

THE WEATHER
Fair today, partly cloudy tomorrow; not much change in temperature; light variable winds.
For full weather report see Page 17.

VOL. LXV...NO. 21,160. NEW YORK, FRIDAY, DECEMBER 31, 1915.—EIGHTEEN PAGES. ONE CENT In Greater New York, Jersey City and Newark. | Elsewhere, TWO CENTS.

AUSTRIA REPLIES THAT SHE HAS PUNISHED U-BOAT CAPTAIN FOR NOT TAKING ACCOUNT OF THE PANIC ON THE ANCONA; 'SACRED LAWS OF HUMANITY MUST HAVE WEIGHT IN WAR'

Austria's Reply to Our Second Ancona Note

LONDON, Dec. 31.—4 A. M.—The Austrian reply to the second American note on the Ancona states that the Commander of the Austrian submarine has been punished for not sufficiently taking account of the panic aboard the Ancona, which rendered disembarkation more difficult.

The Austrian reply is forwarded to Reuter's Telegram Company from Vienna by way of Amsterdam, as follows:

VIENNA, Dec. 29.

In reply to the second American Ancona note, the Austro-Hungarian Government fully agrees with the Washington Cabinet that the sacred laws of humanity should be taken into account also in war, and emphasizes that it, in the course of this war, has given numerous proofs of the most humane feelings.

The Austro-Hungarian Government, too, can positively concur in the principle that enemy private vessels, so far as they do not flee or offer resistance, shall not be destroyed before the persons aboard are secured.

The assurance that the United States Government attaches value to the maintenance of the existing good relations between Austria-Hungary and the United States is warmly reciprocated by the Austro-Hungarian Government, which now, as heretofore, is anxious to render these relations still more cordial.

[The Austro-Hungarian Government then communicates the results of the inquiry into the sinking of the Ancona, which was recently concluded.]

The inquiry showed that the Commander of the submarine from a great distance, in the first instance, fired a warning shot on the steamer, sighted at 11:40 o'clock in the forenoon, which he at first believed to be a transport steamer, at the same time giving a signal for the vessel to stop.

As the steamer failed to stop, and tried to escape, the submarine gave chase and fired sixteen shells at the steamer, of which three were observed to hit. The steamer only stopped after the third hit, whereupon the Commander ceased firing.

Already during the flight, it is declared, when at full speed, the steamer dropped several boats filled with people, which at once capsized. After the steamer stopped the Commander of the submarine observed that six boats were fully manned, and they speedily rowed away from the steamer.

Approaching nearer, the Commander of the submarine saw that a great panic prevailed aboard the steamer and that he had before him the passenger vessel Ancona, on account of which he gave those aboard more time than was necessary to leave the vessel in lifeboats.

At least ten lifeboats were still aboard, which would have more than sufficed to rescue the persons still on the vessel, but as no other preparations were made to hoist out the boats the Commander decided, after the expiration of forty-five minutes, to torpedo the vessel in such a manner that it ought to remain afloat for a still longer time, in order to leave sufficient opportunity for the people still aboard to be rescued.

BRITISH REINFORCE SALONIKI LINES BY NEW LANDING

Put Men Ashore 60 Miles East, While French Take Greek Isle to Guard Suez.

TEUTONS FALLING BACK?

Rome Reports Austro-Germans Retiring in Macedonia to Meet Russian Menace.

CZAR'S CAMPAIGN GROWING

And London Hears That When Bukovina Has Been Won Back Rumania Will Join Allies.

LONDON, Friday, Dec. 31.—Two new landings have been made by the allied forces in the Near East, one by the British, sixty miles east of Saloniki, to guard the right flank of the long defense line around the Allies' Balkan base, and the other by the French on an island off the Asia Minor coast, whence a stroke can be delivered at the communications of any Teuton-Turkish force, operating against Egypt.

Almost coincident with news of these moves, which evidence the manifest purpose of the Allies to give real resistance to any further advances of the Central powers in the Near East, comes a report from Rome that the Germans and Austrians have begun a general withdrawal along the entire front in Macedonia, owing, it is asserted, to the strong Russian advance in Bessarabia.

The landing of British troops was made at Orphanos, a small Greek port on the gulf of the same name. The men were transferred from Saloniki, evidently with the intention of checking any possibility of a hostile advance on the great Greek port from the east or northeast.

The French landing was also on Greek soil, the island of Castelorizo, not far from the important Turkish seaport of Adalia.

An athens dispatch says that the French aim to occupy Adalia. A railway runs north.

While the report of an Austro-German retirement from the Macedonia, which comes in a dispatch to the Exchange Telegraph, quoting a message from Saloniki, is not confirmed from any quarter, the impression is general in the entente capitals that the Russian campaign in Bessarabia, which was designed to put pressure on the Central Powers to check the operations in the Balkans, is of a serious character and, proceeding in the face of unfavorable weather conditions, is likely to have an important bearing on the whole war situation.

Austrians Tell of Hard Fighting.

The official Austrian reports, telling of attacks by dense masses of Russian troops, indicate that an important battle is under way. The fighting centres at a point near Toporoutz, a small town just within the border of Northern Bukowina, but a simultaneous attack is being made along an extended front, reaching from the Pruth to a position north of the Dniester, a distance of about forty miles.

The official bulletin, issued by the Vienna War Office yesterday, has this to say:

The battles in East Galicia are increasing in extent and violence. The enemy yesterday directed attacks not only against the Bessarabian front, but also against our positions to the east of the lower Middle Stripa his advance failed, due mostly to the fire of our batteries. Where the storming columns endeavored to penetrate our positions they collapsed under the fire of artillery or machine guns.

When attacked at the bridgehead of Burkanow the enemy left 800 dead or wounded. Three officers and 870 men surrendered. The total number of prisoners taken yesterday in East Galicia was 1,200.

On the Ikwa-Putilowka front there were local artillery battles. On Kormyn Brook, a tributary of the Styr, the Austro-Hungarian troops repulsed several Russian attacks.

Expect Speedy and Big Results.

From Petrograd comes this dispatch concerning the significance of the fighting south of the Pripet:

"The German and Russian official bulletins regarding the operations south of the Pripet River laconically declare that the battles are proceeding. The importance of the engagements seems to be considered by the Russian military critics as great.

"The General Staff commentaries lay stress on the difference between these struggles and the last notable collisions between the Russians and Teutons before the period of calm. The battles of Czartorysk, Novo Alexinieff, and elsewhere between the Pripet River and the Carpathian Mountains were sporadic and designed only to correct positions on different parts of the line before the cessation of strategic movements on account of the approach of Winter.

"It is agreed now that a struggle is proceeding on the entire southwest line, and that apparently it is equally ardent everywhere. It is intimated that both sides are aiming at the accomplishment of exceedingly important tasks. The Russians and Teutons are equally alert, each side here and there taking the initiative.

"The expectation here is that the outcome of this gigantic, but still obscure,

Continued on Page 2.

LURING TEUTONS ON TO SALONIKI

French Generals Who Fought Before Paris Use Same Tactics in Greece.

ALLIES HOLD STRONG LINES

And Intend to Stick, if Only to Repay Russia's Tannenburg Sacrifice.

By RICHARD HARDING DAVIS.
Special Cable to THE NEW YORK TIMES.

PARIS, Dec. 30.—The same team that, to put it politely, drew the enemy after them to the gates of Paris, have been drawing the same enemy after them to Saloniki. That they will throw him back from Saloniki, as they threw him back from Paris, is assured.

General Sarrail, who was one of those who commanded in front of Paris, commands the Allies in Greece, and General Castelnau, who also commanded at the battle of the Marne and is now Chief of Staff of General Joffre, has just visited Saloniki. He was sent to "go, look, and see." He reports that the position, now held by the Allies, is impregnable.

The perimeter, held by the Allies, is fifty miles in length and stretches from the Vardar River on the west to the Gulf of Orplanos on the east. There are three lines of defence. To assist the first two on the east are Lakes Beshik and Langaza and on the west is the Vardar River. Should the enemy penetrate the first lines they will be confronted ten miles from Saloniki by a natural barrier of hills. Should they surmount these hills the allied warships in the harbor can sweep them off those hills as a firehose rips the shingles off a roof.

The man who pretends to understand the situation in Saloniki is of the same mental calibre as one who understands a system for beating the game at Monte Carlo. But there are certain rumors as to what the situation may become that can be eliminated. First, Greece will not turn against the Allies. Second, the Allies will not withdraw from Saloniki. They now are agreed that it is better to resist and attack or stand a siege, even if they lose 200,000 men, than to withdraw without a fight.

Easy Field for Spies to Work.

The present Government here believes that had the Government it overthrew in October sent troops to aid the Serbian Army four months ago this war would have been made shorter by six months. The present Government is now determined. Apart from resisting the expected advance of the German-Austrian-Bulgarian forces the presence of 200,000 men at Saloniki will hold Rumania from any aggressive movement on Russia.

To aid the Allies Russia at Tannenberg made a sacrifice and lost 200,000 men. The French now feel bound in honor to see by keeping the armies at Saloniki that Russia is not threatened. As a member of the Government said to me today: "There is no western line or eastern line. The line of the Allies is wherever a German attacks. France went to the Balkans to help Serbia. She went too late, which is not the fault of the present Government. But there remains to keep the Germans from Egypt and to keep Rumania from an attack upon the flank of Russia. The Allies are in Saloniki until this war is ended."

In Saloniki I saw many evidences that

Continued on Page 2.

THESSALONIKI OFFICERS ASK AID, IGNORE CAPTAIN

Wireless Message Received at Navy Yard Said Master Would Not Accept Assistance.

There is a disagreement among the officers of the Greek steamship Thessaloniki, which is drifting helplessly at sea with 300 passengers aboard. This was disclosed yesterday when it became known that a wireless message had been received at the Navy Yard asking for assistance, signed by Chief Officer Orloff and three other deck officers, against the wishes of Captain Goulandis. The message was sent by way of Siasconsett, and was received at 12:30 A. M. Wednesday, Dec. 29, and forwarded by the operator at the Navy Yard to Captain Francis M. Dunwoody, in charge of the coastguard service at this port.

Captain Dunwoody said yesterday that the wireless message received by him last Wednesday morning which caused him to dispatch the Seneca to search for the Thessaloniki was signed by Chief Officer Orloff and three other deck officers. It was addressed to the navy yard via Siasconsett and asked for a ship to be sent to help the Thessaloniki, as she was in a serious condition, and the Captain did not want to accept assistance. On receipt of this message Captain Dunwoody got in touch with Captain F. A. Levis of the Seneca, anchored off Tompkinsville, and she sailed at 3:20 o'clock on Wednesday morning, but was not able to steam very fast on account of the weather.

Steamship managers and marine Superintendents in New York who were asked last night for an expression of opinion on the action taken by the four officers of the Thessaloniki in sending the message to the navy yard said that they had never heard of a similar case. They agreed that it was an act that under some conditions might be insubordination, or even mutiny, and that the officers of the Greek steamer must have had some very good, urgent reasons for them to adopt such an unusual course. The Captain is regarded as the master of the ship and is held responsible, the marine Superintendents said, for the lives of all on board. They asserted that the owners or agents of the Thessaloniki should make a strict investigation into the circumstances concerning the action of the officers when the vessel reachest port.

Managers of Line Give Views.

When John Galanos, one of the managers of the National Steam Navigation Company of Greece, was informed that Captain Dunwoody had received a wireless message signed by the deck officers of the Thessaloniki, who had sent it because the Captain had declined assistance, he replied that he had not heard of such a thing, and that it might be better to wait until the steamer arrived and hear Captain Goulandis's story. When the suggestion was made that the Captain had declined assistance and risked the lives of all those on board rather than pay salvage, he seemed pained and surprised at the idea, and said that the Captain was the best judge as to the ability of his ship to make port.

The Thessaloniki was coming slowly, and might be here tomorrow, Mr. Galanos added, and neither he nor his brother, N. A. Galanos, the senior member of the firm, felt any alarm about the safety of the ship.

The latest message from the Thessaloniki, picked up at 6 P. M. yesterday gave her position as 160 miles southeast of Nantucket, making her 353 miles from Sandy Hook. According to a message received during the afternoon at the office of the National Steam and Navigation Company of Greece, the steamship Thessaloniki is progressing toward this port at a speed of four knots, when the weather is fine. The dispatch reads: "On account of small damage, we come with lessened speed. Engineers assure us there is no cause for alarm. Because of strong winds our speed is only four miles an hour. When weather improves speed will be six or seven miles."

It was estimated that the disabled steamer with 300 passengers on board was about 150 miles east of Sandy Hook when the Captain sent off the wireless message at noon, and should arrive in Quarantine late tomorrow of the weather remains fine. Up till a late hour last night no word had been received from Captain F. A. Levis of the United States coastguard cutter Seneca of his having reached the Thessaloniki.

German Order Maroons Americans in Austria; Must Have Birth Certificates with Passports

Special to The New York Times.

WASHINGTON, Dec. 30.—Americans in Vienna desirous of leaving there are unable to do so because the German Consulate in that capital is refusing to visé or countersign American passports for travel in Germany unless the bearers present certificates of birth or naturalization. This makes it practically impossible for Americans to return home from Austria by way of Germany and Holland.

Notification of this action was conveyed to the State Department today in a dispatch from Frederic C. Penfield, Ambassador at Vienna. The dispatch was sent from Vienna to Berne, Switzerland, from which point it was forwarded by Pleasant A. Stovall, American Minister, as follows:

Vienna, Dec. 28, 1915.
Secretary of State, Washington:
German Consulate at Vienna refuses to visé American passports for travel in the German Empire unless bearers present certificates of birth or naturalization. Americans here not possessing these documents are consequently being detained. Have presented matter to German Embassy, with request for modification of present regulations to enable American citizens to return to their homes, and informed the embassy at Berlin, requesting their good offices in presenting the matter to the German authorities. The above regulations practically exclude from Germany bona fide American-born and naturalized citizens, bearers of American passports but not the required additional documents, and will tend to work hardships and delay, making it practically impossible for such persons to embark from Holland. PENFIELD.

The grounds upon which Germany is refusing to permit passports to be viséed without the production of birth or naturalization certificates are not understood here. One theory is that Germany is seeking to gain detailed information regarding the antecedents of persons carrying American passports. Another theory is that the more stringent German requirements are intended as a retaliation against the restrictions imposed by Great Britain and the other allied powers upon persons of German, Austrian, or Turkish origin traveling with American or other passports.

Since last July the French Government has been discouraging all attempts on the part of naturalized Americans of German or Austrian origin to obtain passports, and has been refusing to visé them. This has applied to Americans of German origin desirous of going to Paris to inspect the fashions as buyers.

Ambassador Gerard on Dec. 22 notified Secretary Lansing that new regulations for viséing passports for use in Germany had been adopted, the pertinent parts applicable to American citizens being that a new visé of a passport by a German diplomatic or Consular officer would be required for each separate entry into Germany, that to obtain the visé the bearer of the passport must apply in person to the German diplomatic or Consular officer; that the bearer must present two photographs, similar to the ones on his passport, for the files of the German diplomatic or Consular officer, and that a visé would not be granted unless the journey seemed to be necessary and the necessity shown by the bearer.

Furthermore, in the report received from Ambassador Gerard last week it was pointed out that "applicants for the visé of German diplomatic or consular officers are required to present their certificates of naturalization or birth certificates."

It was under authority of this new regulation that the German Consulate in Vienna refused to visé American passports.

Secretary Lansing today issued this warning to Americans going to Germany.

"The department is advised by the American Embassy at Vienna that Americans holding passports are required, in order to have them viséd for use in Germany, to present their birth certificates, if they are American citizens by nativity, or their naturalization certificates, if they are of foreign birth. It is, therefore, recommended that Americans going to Germany carry their birth certificates or naturalization certificates with them."

WHITMAN DECIDES TO OUST OSBORNE

Governor Writes Letter of Resignation, but Warden Refuses to Sign It.

KIRCHWEY WILL SUCCEED

Ignoring Advice of His Lawyers and Friends, Sing Sing Reformer is Storm Centre at Albany.

Special to The New York Times.

ALBANY, Dec. 30.—After Warden Thomas Mott Osborne of Sing Sing tonight refused the advice of counsel, friends, and the Governor and rejected the demand of Superintendent of Prisons John B. Riley that he resign, at least temporarily, Governor Whitman came out of a conference at the Executive Mansion and told waiting newspaper men that Dr. George W. Kirchwey, former dean of the Columbia Law School, would be Warden of Sing Sing in a day or two.

Superintendent Riley sat in the lobby of the Ten Eyck Hotel tonight for hours waiting for the Governor's word to remove Osborne. In the meanwhile Mr. Osborne sat in a room at the Hotel Hampton and defied everything and everybody, having not one word to say except that he would never resign.

The Sing Sing fight took a sensational turn when Governor Whitman, who had been trying to shield Osborne, prepared a graceful letter of resignation for him to sign. The Warden scorned it. The Governor delayed a dinner at the Executive Mansion at which ex-Judge and

Continued on Page 3.

BUCHANAN AWAITS ARREST AT CAPITAL

Plot Warrants Not Yet Served, but Accused Man Probably Will Be Arraigned Today.

LONG FIGHT IS EXPECTED

Congressman Rainey Declares His Colleague Is Entitled to Immunity and Will Test It.

Special to The New York Times.

WASHINGTON, Dec. 30.—So far no arrests of members of Labor's Peace Council in conection with pro-German plots have occurred in this city. Representative Buchanan of Illinois, formerly President of the organization, waited in his office at the Capitol all day for the appearance of the United States Marshal. The other defendants, ex-Congressman Fowler of Illinois, general counsel for Labor's Peace Council, and H. B. Martin and Herman Schultheis, the militant members of the council, also waited to be arrested, but the ceremony did not take place.

This evening it was arranged between Henry E. Davis, counsel for Fowler, Martin, and Schultheis, and Assistant District Attorney Archer that tomorrow morning at 10 o'clock the indictments found against these men would be proffered to Anson Taylor, United States Commissioner, and bench warrants will be asked for their arrest. By agreement the defendants will voluntarily appear at the appointed time and furnish bail.

Under the usual precedure Commissioner Taylor will grant a hearing probably next week. The bench warrants

Continued on Page 3.

ROUT AUSTRIAN FLEET, SINKING TWO VESSELS

Allied Squadrons Surprise Foe in Raid on Durazzo—Italians Now Occupy the City.

LONDON, Dec. 30.—Dispatches from Rome and Paris announce that in a sea engagement off Durazzo, in the Adriatic, yesterday, an Austrian squadron was routed with the loss of two destroyers.

The following official communication was issued in Rome today.

"Yesterday morning an enemy scout ship and five destroyers appeared off Durazzo in order to bombard the place. They did insignificant damage and then were attacked by Italian and allied ships cruising in the neighborhood. The Austrian torpedo boat destroyers Triglav and Lika were sunk. Survivors from the Lika were taken prisoners.

"An enemy aeroplane was shot down by one of our destroyers.

"All of our ships returned to port undamaged."

The French Marine Department gave out the following report of the engagement:

"An Austrian naval division, having come out from Cattaro for the purpose of bombarding Durazzo, certain squadrons of the Allies went forth to give battle. The Austrian torpedo boat destroyer Lika encountered a mine and was blown up. The destroyer Triglav, of the same type, was destroyed by the fire from the ships of the Allies. The remaining warships of the enemy were pursued and fled in the direction of their base."

There have been several previous encounters of lesser importance than the one now reported in connection with Austrian attempts to interrupt the transportation of Italian troops to Albania and of supplies for the Serbian forces which have retreated to that country. Several supply ships have been sunk by Austrian warships.

The destroyers Liska and Triglav were sister ships built in 1913. They were 266 feet long, of 787 tons displacement. Each was equipped with two 3.9-inch guns, six eleven-pounders, and two torpedo tubes.

ITALIANS OCCUPY DURAZZO.

German Consul and His Staff Flee from Albanian Port.

GENEVA, Dec. 30.—It is reported here on good authority that Italian troops have occupied the Albanian seaport of Durazzo.

This report apparently is corroborated by the fact that the German Consul at Durazzo, the members of his staff, and fifty other Germans passed through Bellinzona, Switzerland, yesterday, on their way to Berlin.

Durazzo and Avlona are the principal Albanian ports. Avlona was occupied by the Italians several months ago, before Italy entered the war. Durazzo is on a peninsula in the Adriatic Sea, forty miles south of the Montenegrin border. There have been previous reports of Italian activity there, principally in connection with the landing of supplies for the Serbian Army.

FIRE IN DU PONT PLANT.

300 Workmen Imperilled by Incendiary Blaze in Wisconsin.

APPLETON, Wis., Dec. 30.—Three hundred workmen at the du Pont Powder Company's plant at Barksdale were imperilled last Tuesday night by a fire of incendiary origin, according to District Attorney Catlin, who returned from that place yesterday.

Effort was made to keep the fire a secret, according to Mr. Catlin. Workmen shut off the blazing section from another part of the building where a great quantity of nitroglycerin was stored. The pecuniary loss was small.

Deny U-Boat's Loss in Baltic.

BERLIN, Dec. 30, (by Wireless to Sayville.)—"The report from Bucharest, sent out by a British news agency, that a German submarine had been lost in the Baltic, is declared by competent German authorities to be an invention," the Overseas News Agency announced today.

PLAN COMPULSION FOR WARTIME ONLY

Conscriptionists Hope to Carry Their Point Without a Break in the Cabinet.

LABOR CONGRESS CALLED

Leaders Are Reticent, but There Are Hints of Support for the Asquith-Derby Measure.

LONDON, Friday, Dec. 31.—An audience which Premier Asquith had with the King yesterday gave rise to reports of actual Cabinet resignations. It is stated, however, on the best of authority that this was not the case, and that Mr. Asquith saw the King with reference to the general situation and the New Year's honors.

It is reported that the Draft Committee of the Cabinet, which is said to include Sir John A. Simon, engaged in preparing the proposed bill, has rejected two or three drafts already, but has now virtually settled on the method, which will be to make the Derby scheme statutory and only for the duration of the war. The men who have not attested will be ordered to enroll themselves within a given period of a fortnight or three weeks.

It is said that the Government is confident of its ability to pass the bill through all stages in a fortnight—that is, several days before Parliament would die a natural death but for the bill prolonging its life. This bill has still to runt the gantlet of its final stages, and if obstructive tactics should be adopted with regard to the compulsory recruiting measure, it might still be possible for the Ministers to resort a general election as an exit from a defficult situation.

Hope of Averting Resignations.

This, however, is not regarded as probable. In fact, the feeling in political quarters is more confident than ever that the crisis will entail no resignations of importance. The fact that the King returned to Sandringham last night seems to confirm this view.

A special Trades Congress, to which all societies affiliated with the labor movement are invited to send representatives, will be convened in London Jan. 6 to consider the Government's bill for the compulsory enlistment of single men, which Premier Asquith will introduce in the House of Commons next Wednesday.

The calling of the congress is the result of a protracted conference of the Parliamentary Committee of the Trades Union Congress, the Executive Committee of the Labor Party, and the Management Committee of the General Federation of Trades Unions, held yesterday under the Presidency of Arthur Henderson, President of the Board of Education.

An official report of the conference says:

"The national situation arising out of the Government's proposal with regard to the compulsory enlistment of single men was very fully discussed. It was agreed that the importance of the issue involved is so serious that any decision on behalf of the trades union and labor movement could only be reached by a national conference of representatives of the entire movement."

This recommendation was subsequently discussed with the Parliamentary Labor Party and received its full concurrence. One reason for the recommendation, the official report on the con-

Continued on Page 2.

TONE OF NOTE CONCILIATORY

Says Liners Should Not Be Torpedoed Unless They Fly or Resist.

REPORTS ON INQUIRY MADE

Tells How Submarine Chased Steamer and Compelled Her to Stop.

NOTE 3,000 WORDS LONG

Ambassador Notifies State Department Text Will Be Forwarded Promptly.

Special to The New York Times.

WASHINGTON, Dec. 30.—The reply of the Austro-Hungarian Government to the second American note on the Ancona case is en route to Washington. A cablegram from Frederic C. Penfield, the American Ambassador at Vienna, was received at the State Department this afternoon informing Secretary of State Lansing that the Austrian answer was delieved to Ambassador Penfeld at Vienna yesterday.

In making this announcement Secretary Lansing said that the message from the Ambassador gave no forecast of the note, but merely said that the reply had been delivered, that it was about 3,000 word long, and that it would be forwarded to Washington as soon as it could be translated and enciphered.

The message from Ambassador Penfield reached the State Department at 2:45 o'clock, and bore evidence of having been relayed from Vienna via Berne, Switzerland, in twenty-four hours. Up to midnight tonight the text of the note had not begun to come into the State Department telegraph offices.

Experience has demonstrated that long cipher messages require not less than two days for transmission to Washington from Vienna. The text of the note is not expected to reach the State Department before tomorrow, and possibly not until Saturday.

Secretary Lansing maintained his custom today of not commenting on the Austrian situation. Not until he has had opportunity to consider carefully the Austrian response and confer with the President will the Secretary of State authorize any announcement indicating the effect the communication from Austria may have on the present acute situation between the two nations.

Germany never has acquiesced in the correctness of the principles of international law insisted upon by the United States. The crisis between Germany and the United States was avoided merely by the assurances given by the Berlin Government that "liners will not be sunk by our submarines without warning and without safety of the lives of noncombatants, provided that the liners do not try to escape or offer resistance."

This guarantee was accompanied by rigid instructions to the German submarine commanders, which were observed, except in the Arabic case, where the German submarine commander attacked the Arabic because he "was convinced that the Arabic intended to ram the submarine." It is true that there was disavowal by Berlin on the attack on the Arabic, but this disavowal was made because—as stated in Count von Bernstorff's note of Oct. 5 to Secretary Lansing—Germany was "prompted by the desire to reach a satisfactory agreement with regard to the Arabic incident," and in order to do so the Berlin Government agreed to accept the affidavits made by the British officers of the Arabic, according to which the Arabic did not ntend to ram the submarine.

But, aside from issuing instructions, giving guarantees and observing its pledge, the Berlin Government has not admitted the correctness of the principles of international law upon which the United States has been insisting. As was pointed out here in responsible quarters today, Germany did not admit that the Teutonic submarine warfare on merchant vessels was wrong, but justified them as reprisals.

Baron Zwidlinek, Chargé of the Austro-Hungarian Embassy, called upon Counsellor Polk at the State Department today. At the conclusion of the conference neither would comment on the subject discussed beyond saying that it had to do with a "routine matter." The counselor is handling for the State Department the protest made by Baron Zwiedinek against a statement issued in the name of the Department of Justice referring to the activities of Dr. von Nuber, Austro-Hungarian Consul General at New York.

JEALOUS OF NAVAL HONORS.

Lecaze Compares Ciotat Attack with German Touchiness at Hague.

PARIS, Dec. 30.—Admiral Lecaze, the Minister of Marine, referring in the Chamber of Deputies yesterday to the sinking of the French steamer Ville de la Ciotat by a submarine in the Mediterranean with a loss of eighty lives, told of an incident at The Hague Conference of 1907 growing out of a question as to the humanity of German naval officers.

"I had the honor to represent the French Navy at the conference," said Admiral Lecaze, "and remember the dramatic sitting at which Baron Marschall von Bieberstein, Germany's chief dele-

"All the News That's Fit to Print."

The New York Times.

THE WEATHER
Rain Sunday; Monday colder, probably fair; fresh south winds, becoming northwest and strong by Monday.
For full weather report see Page 22.

VOL. LXV...NO. 21,162. ... NEW YORK, SUNDAY, JANUARY 2, 1916.—124 PAGES, In Eight Parts. PRICE FIVE CENTS

WARN AMERICANS NOT TO SAIL ON THE LAFAYETTE?

Messages Sent to Passengers Like That Sent to Frohman Before His Ill-Fated Voyage.

LUSITANIA CAUTION ECHOED

Unsigned Note to Prominent Men Said to Have Foretold Cunarder's Fate.

NEW LINER STARTS TODAY

French Steamer Arrived Here from Bordeaux on Maiden Voyage Last November.

By RICHARD HARDING DAVIS.
Special Cable to THE NEW YORK TIMES.

PARIS, Jan. 1.—Many Americans are sailing tomorrow on the passenger steamer Lafayette. The most prominent among them have received telegrams expressing good wishes for the New Year and letters the same as those sent to the manager of the Empire Theatre when he sailed from New York.

Charles Frohman, head of the Empire Theatre, was one of the ill-fated passengers on the steamship Lusitania when she sailed on May 1, 1915, to be torpedoed and sunk by a German submarine off the coast of Ireland on the afternoon of May 7.

On the morning of the ship's departure the newspapers published the famous advertisement of the German Embassy warning American travelers not to sail on British vessels, and on the pier just before the vessel sailed there were many reports that passengers, including Alfred Vanderbilt, Mr. Frohman, and others, had received telegrams and letters warning them specifically that it would not be safe to sail on the Lusitania. Mr. Frohman, it was reported, had received at his office the day before an undated anonymous note, delivered by messenger, saying that it would not be safe to sail on the Lusitania.

Gustave Frohman said last night that he did not know his brother Charles had received such a message until after the Lusitania sailed.

"I heard afterward that he had received a message from a man in Washington," Mr. Frohman said, "but I do not remember his name. I know that he received what might be called an official warning not to sail, and that it was similar to that received by Mr. Vanderbilt. Of course, Mr. Frohman received a number of messages and telegrams from those connected with the Frohman enterprises asking him not to sail on the Lusitania."

The message received by Alfred Vanderbilt, according to reports published at the time, read: "Have it on definite authority that the Lusitania is to be torpedoed. You had better cancel passage immediately."

THE NEW YORK TIMES on May 9 published the following paragraph:

> Mr. Frohman sailed on the Lusitania against the advice of his associates. All of the members of his executive staff did their utmost to dissuade him from embarking on an English ship, and so real was their fear that telegrams were sent to Maude Adams and his favorite stars on tour asking them to wire their pleas for him to take another boat. But he had crossed on the big ship many times, he had made up his mind to sail at that particular time, and nothing could avail to make him alter his plans.

On the other hand, the officials of the Cunard Line twice denied that any of the Lusitania's passengers had received warning messages, the last denial being made on May 8.

As having possibly some bearing on the meaning of Mr. Davis's dispatch from Paris, it may be stated that THE TIMES has knowledge of an intending passenger on the Lafayette who canceled his passage a few days ago, and notified his friends in America that he was going to England to sail on an English vessel. He was anxious to reach New York as quickly as possible, and had no particular business to call him to England.

The warning advertisement published by the German Embassy on the morning of the Lusitania's sailing read:

> Travelers intending to embark on the Atlantic voyage are reminded that a state of war exists between Germany and her allies and Great Britain and her allies; that the zone of war includes the waters adjacent to the British Isles; that, in accordance with formal notice given by the Imperial German Government, vessels flying the flag of Great Britain or of any of her allies are liable to destruction in those waters, and that travelers sailing in the war zone on ships of Great Britain or her allies do so at their own risk.

Despite this advertisement the Lusitania left port with 1,388 passengers, the greatest number to embark on the eastward voyage last year. On the morning she sailed many of the passengers professed to be amused at the German Embassy's advertisement and others expressed surprise that Count von

Continued on Page 2.

AIR RAIDERS AIMED AT ALLIES' WARSHIPS

Seizure of the Teuton Consuls at Saloniki a Natural Reprisal.

Special Cable to THE NEW YORK TIMES.
By RICHARD HARDING DAVIS.

PARIS, Jan. 1.—The raid of Bulgarian and German aeroplanes over Saloniki reported in the French bulletin does not necessarily mean that an attack by troops will follow. London and Paris were raided by air craft, but no troops have yet reached those cities.

Nor is it probable that the raid was for the purpose of observation. There is no need to send a man conspicuously in an aeroplane to count the warships in the harbor when an inconspicuous man on the wharf has for weeks been furnishing more accurate information, and when Saloniki is full of spies who are able to communicate with Doiran, Gevgheli, and Monastir.

An observer 2,000 yards in the air would be unable to tell the Central Powers anything of which they are not already informed. Their agents are on the quays, streets, and roads leading to and beyond the military camps, and even at work building roads in the camps.

The object of the raid was more likely for moral effect or to throw bombs on transports and warships. The bomb reported dropped upon a battalion of Greek soldiers was probably launched by mistake, owing to the Greek uniform being of khaki colored cloth similar to the British at a distance.

It is evident that the French squadron of air craft were taken by surprise, and that if the raiders return they will receive a warmer welcome, as during the Serbian campaign the French aeroplanes showed splendid efficiency and furnished valuable information. This was accomplished under most unfavorable conditions of snow, fog, and treacherous cross currents above valleys and over a terrain barren of landing places.

In arresting and removing the Consuls of the enemy in reprisal for the raid, General Sarrail followed the only possible course. The consulates have been the headquarters of army and navy officers of the Central Powers, Turkey and Bulgaria, besides furnishing a clearing house for all the spies.

Saloniki is supposed to be neutral territory, but the presence of foreign Consuls at the base of two armies has been a most serious menace. Their enforced departure will add to the responsibilities of the American Consul in looking after their interests. Our Government is represented in Saloniki by John E. Kehl, long in the service and most admirably fitted to meet the present crisis. He has been a resident of Saloniki for the last four years, during which his experience as Consul during the Italo-Turkish war, the two Balkan wars, and the present one has trained him to meet any emergency that may now arise.

When the Greeks captured Saloniki Consul Kehl was one of those sent out to meet King Constantine and arrange that the city should not be bombarded.

The position of a Consul in Saloniki, owing to the former ex-territorial privileges and right to conduct trials and sentence to death, gives the post peculiar authority. In importance it outranks many [illegible] The consulates [illegible] in an imposing building, surrounded by gardens and trees, facing the harbor on Reine Olga Street, and guarded by a staff of uniformed kavass.

Before I left Saloniki the Consuls of the Central Powers had already sent their families to Athens and were arranging with Consul Kehl to take over their archives.

(Copyright, 1916, by Richard Harding Davis.)

AUSTRIAN U-BOATS SINK FOOD SHIPS

Montenengro Complains of Scarcity Due to the Enemy's Activity.

PARIS, Jan. 1.—The Montenegrin Consul General in Paris has received this official statement from Cettinje, dated Thursday:

"The provisioning of Montenegro is becoming absolutely impossible, the situation being more difficult daily.

"Austrian submarines are attacking sailing vessels and steamers on our coast and those on the Albanian coast.

"Yesterday a Montenegrin sailing vessel laden with food was sunk at Dulcigno.

"Today a steamer carrying 2,000 tons of provisions met a similar fate off San Giovanni di Medua."

SUSPEND INDIA LEAGUE MEETING AFTER RIOTING

Session in Bombay Is Summarily Ended Because of Demonstrations.

LONDON, Sunday, Jan. 2.—A Reuter dispatch from Bombay, dated Saturday, says:

"Today's session of the Moslem League was suspended after noisy demonstrations."

A dispatch from Bombay on Monday told of the opening of the annual Indian National Congress with 10,000 delegates in attendance. The meeting was notable for the loyal utterances of the speakers, the President, Sir Satyendra Sinhha, asserting that millions of persons in India were waiting to serve Great Britain.

BALTIC BRINGS $35,000,000.

Said to be the Biggest Shipment to This Port Since War Began.

The White Star liner Baltic arrived yesterday from Liverpool bringing $35,000,000 in gold consigned to New York banks. This was said to be the largest gold shipment brought to this port by any steamer since the war began.

Because yesterday was a holiday and today Sunday, the $35,000,000 will be kept on board the Baltic under guard until tomorrow morning, when it will be landed and taken away from the pier. In addition to the regular watchmen employed by the White Star Line, twelve private detectives were sent to the pier at the foot of West Nineteenth Street to be on duty four at a time to see that no thieves got on the ship. A watch is also kept on the pier opposite to see that no motor launches approach the vessel from the river. The specie will go to J. P. Morgan & Co., the Guarantee Trust Co., Irving National Bank and National City Bank.

ALLIES EXPECT TO WIN THE WAR BEFORE '16 ENDS

Unabated Confidence in the Greetings Exchanged at Opening of the Year.

POINCARE IS SANGUINE

'We Shall Not Become Wearied,' He Tells the French Armies.

LAUDS BRAVERY OF TROOPS

And Declares Fervidly: "You Will Win!"—Entente Rulers Pledge Their Faith.

PARIS, Dec. 31, (Delayed.)—"Nineteen hundred and sixteen will be our year of victory," says President Poincaré in a message to "the officers and soldiers of France," which was distributed along the whole front tonight. The message, which is one of great simplicity, expresses the confidence of the entire nation in its defenders. The letter follows:

"Like you, my noble friends, I have read with emotion in the Army Bulletin, messages addressed to you on the eve of the New Year by the Mayors of our large cities. The same language is used by all these French cities, and it is easy today to draw from these numerous expressions the unanimous sentiment of the country.

"Everywhere you have seen maintained without effort this sacred union spontaneously established seventeen months ago under the menace of the enemy. Why would not the civil population follow the example of agreement and harmony which you give it? In the trenches and on the battlefields you hardly think of considering your personal opinions.

"Civil discord does not disturb the fraternity of arms, which, with its common perils and identical duties, binds one and all. You have your eyes fixed on an ideal which constantly diverts your attention from secondary objects, and you know that your patriotic mission cannot be performed by others.

"While you are thus sacrificing everything to the salvation of the nation, is it not natural that those Frenchmen whose age, health, or duties prevent them from meeting at your side the fatigue and perils of war work should at least repel harmful suggestions of hatred and conserve jealously the public peace?

"The Mayors of France have spoken of some of the charitable works resulting from the successful joining of hearts. Most of these institutions are destined to aid you, your aged parents, your children, your wounded or imprisoned brothers. In cities furthest from the front your condition thus remains constantly present in all minds and concentrates, as is well in view of the tragic realities of the time, the thoughts of those who might be inclined to forget.

"The mourning which has darkened the home of so many families, moreover, imposes on those who have been less severely afflicted the pious obligation of meditation and gravity. All the French people feel the same affliction, and there is not one who does not listen with respect to the stern lesson of the day—a lesson of courage, of patience, of will, of calm, of confidence, and of serenity.

The Problem Before France.

"Everywhere it is the same—a determined resolution to hold fast, to endure, and to vanquish. Every one knows the stakes of the war are great and that the outcome concerns not only our dignity, but our life. Shall we tomorrow be the vassals of a foreign empire? Shall our industries, our commerce, our agriculture, be placed forever under the influence of a power which openly flatters itself on aspiring to universal domination, or shall we safeguard our economic independence and national autonomy? This is a terrible problem, which admits of no half-way solution. Any peace which came to us with suspicious form and equivocal purpose would bring us only dishonor, ruin, and servitude. The free and pure genius of our race, our most venerated traditions, the ideas which are dearest to us, the interests of our citizens, the fortunes of our country, the soul of the nation, everything which has been left by our ancestors and all that we ourselves own, would be the prey of Germanic brutality.

"Who then would, by impatience or lassitude, thus sell to Germany the past and future of France? Yes, certainly, the war is long. It is rigorous and it is bloody, but how much future suffering are we spared by our present suffering? No French person desired this war. All the governments since 1871 have endeavored to avoid such a war. Now that it has been declared against us in spite of ourselves, we must carry it on with our faithful allies until we have gained victory, the annihilation of German militarism, and the entire reconstitution of France. To permit ourselves to falter even momentarily, would be to be ungrateful to our dead and to betray posterity.

"We must persevere obstinately in the will to win. Is it not the surest means of bringing about victory?

We Shall Not Become Wearied.

"In the war which we are carrying on so valiantly in France, Belgium, and the East, the part played by implements of destruction has become of essential importance, and it is the imperious duty of the Government to furnish you constantly with the most powerful weapons and an abundance of munitions. But moral power is the foremost consideration for final success. The bravest soldiers will not necessarily be that which has had the heaviest losses or has endured the most misery. It will be the one which becomes wearied first. We shall not become wearied.

"France is confident because you are your officers say: 'Never at any time have we had a finer army. Never have men been better trained, more brave, more heroic, than ours.' Wherever I

Continued on Page 3.

LINER PERSIA TORPEDOED; HUNDREDS PERISH; THREE AMERICANS, ONE A CONSUL, ON BOARD; WASHINGTON SEES A NEW CRISIS THREATENED

ATTACK SHOCKS CAPITAL

Strikingly Similar to That on Arabic After Lusitania Disaster.

U-BOAT PROBABLY AUSTRIAN

Situation Is Complicated by Vienna's Compliance with Our Ancona Demands.

OFFICIAL REPORT AWAITED

Comment Withheld Pending Details as to Whether Liner Was Fleeing or Resisting.

President Silent on Persia Till Facts Are Learned

HOT SPRINGS, Jan. 1.—Information regarding the situation with Austria was forwarded to the President by Secretary Lansing today, but its nature was not disclosed. Mr. Wilson would not comment on the possible effect of the sinking of the liner Persia, saying he could not form any opinion until he had more complete information.

Special to The New York Times.

WASHINGTON, Jan. 1.—Washington was shocked by the news that the P. and O. liner Persia had been torpedoed in the Mediterranean with a large loss of life. The attack was made just when hopes were highest here that the second note from the Austro-Hungarian Government not only would avoid a diplomatic rupture over the sinking of the Ancona but also would pave the way for a settlement of the submarine warfare controversy with Germany. This attack overlaps the Ancona issue with startling similarity to the manner in which the attack on the Arabic was thrust into the controversy over the Lusitania.

Washington officials are reserving judgment on the sinking of the Persia in view of the fact that when the details are known they may involve no new complications. Until detailed facts are obtained it will be impossible to gauge the diplomatic significance of the attack.

If the Persia was attacked without warning the fact undoubtedly would precipitate a real crisis; if torpedoed while attempting to escape the gravity of the situation would be reduced from a diplomatic standpoint, for it has not been the contention of this Government that liners are entitled to any immunity while attempting to escape or if they offer resistance. It is possible that the attack on the Persia was made by a submarine that had been out of touch with the Austrian Admiralty and which might not have been advised of the manner in which the Austrian Government had dealt with the submarine commander who attacked the Ancona, or had not received any new Admiralty instructions growing out of that case.

Lack of Harmony Suggested.

Still another suggestion heard here today was that perhaps the Austro-Hungarian Admiralty had not issued any new instructions on the basis of the Ancona settlement and that lack of harmony of opinion might exist between the Austro-Hungarian Admiralty and the Foreign Office, just as there was a clash of views in Germany between the Foreign Office and Grand Admiral von Tirpitz, head of the Admiralty, over the concessions made by Germany to the United States in the dispute over submarine warfare.

In this connection, it was pointed out tonight, no new instructions seemed to be called for under the position taken by Austria, the submarine commander who sank the Ancona being punished for infraction of existing instructions.

If the Persia was not trying to escape, and if she was not resisting the submarine, it is the expectation of the Washington Government that the Vienna Government or the Berlin Government, as the case may be, will immediately and in very convincing manner repudiate the attack and explain the circumstances.

Cabled press accounts of the attack on the Persia were widely circulated in Washington today and cast depression over the New Year's Day celebrations in official circles. The fact of the attack was confirmed in cablegrams from Robert G. Skinner, the American Consul General at Lon-

Continued on Page 3.

THE P. & O. LINER PERSIA
And Robert N. McNeely, American Consul at Aden, Who Was Aboard When She Was Torpedoed

The Persia Torpedoed Without Warning, Says Consul Skinner; Bases This Statement on Secret Information Reaching London

Special Cable to THE NEW YORK TIMES.

LONDON, Jan. 1.—When word reached Consul General Skinner today that the P. & O. liner Persia had been sunk off Crete with Americans aboard, he immediately stirred himself to ascertain if any American lives had been lost. Up to a late hour tonight Mr. Skinner had received no word, and it is not known in London whether any Americans were drowned.

Three Americans, according to Mr. Skinner's information, boarded the Persia when she left London on Dec. 18. They were Robert N. McNeely, who was going to Aden, a British possession in Arabia on the Indian Ocean, to become American Consul; Charles Hastings Grant, a commercial traveling man of Boston, and E. N. Rose, a lad of 17, who was on his way from Denver, Col., to study in a school in Spain. Consul General Skinner said tonight:

"Information coming to me here, that I take as authentic, indicates that the Persia was sunk by a torpedo and that no warning was given. While I cannot divulge the source of my information, I have every reason to believe it to be an undoubted fact that it was a torpedo that sank the ship. I am getting all the information I can for Washington, but I must wait for a full report until I hear from the Consul at Alexandria or other sources as to the exact facts.

"I have no doubt that Mr. McNeely and Mr. Grant were on the Persia when she was torpedoed. Mr. McNeely came to London on the steamer Ryndam with me on my return from Washington, arriving here on Dec. 8. He had just been appointed to the post at Aden before leaving Washington, and was full of eagerness to get on the job. It was his first appointment in the Consular service. He is a young fellow, and brimful of life. On arriving at London Mr. McNeely told me that he expected to sail within a few days for Marseilles, and after a few days' visit go on to Aden. But he stayed longer than he expected in London and booked on the Persia instead. I saw him nearly every day of his stay here, and he was elated over getting down to work at Aden."

The Times correspondent is informed that Mr. McNeely was engaged to marry an American girl, who intended to join him later at Aden. Mr. Grant reached London on Dec. 14, staying at the Saint Ermines Hotel until he sailed on the Persia.

GERMANY PLEASED BY AUSTRIA'S NOTE

Believes Good Relations Assured—Berlin's Efforts to Prevent a Break Confirmed.

OFFICIAL LID ON COMMENT

Government Wants No Press Outbreak Over Vienna's Allusion to Munitions Shipments.

From a Staff Correspondent.
Special Cable to THE NEW YORK TIMES.

BERLIN, Jan. 1.—With popular interest and expectation riveted on Saloniki and Egypt, the second Austrian note to the United States Government on the Ancona affair caused not even a mild sensation here. In high political circles, where it is now believed the ghost of a break with America has been laid for all time, satisfaction over the favorable turn of events is mingled with just the least touch of relief, for, while a conciliatory reply had been expected as a result of the very friendly tone of the second American note, there was no telling, up to the last moment, what the Austrians, who are running their own foreign affairs, might do.

How determined the German Government is to take no chances of having good relations with America strained again is indicated by the fact that so far practically all the important Berlin papers, morning and evening, have refrained from all comment, with the exception of Count Reventlow in the Tageszeitung, who says plaintively:

"The Austrian note practically gives in to all the American demands, particularly on the two main points, punishment of the submarine commander and reparation. We are prevented from commenting editorially on it in a manner consistent with our interpretation and judgment of it."

The reason for the political censorship lid on note comment is not because its very conciliatory spirit would receive harsh condemnation from the German press, which, with the exception of a few

Continued on Page 3.

FORD AT QUARANTINE; LANDS THIS MORNING

Arrives on the Bergensfjord and Is to be Taken Off on a Private Tug.

The steamer Bergensfjord of the Norwegian-American Line, with Henry Ford, the peace advocate, on board, arrived in Quarantine at 1:15 o'clock this morning and anchored until daylight.

After the passengers and crew had been passed by the Health Officer of the Port, Mr. Ford would be transferred to a private tug about 7:30 o'clock this morning, it was said.

Mr. Ford's wife and his son, Edsal Ford, arrived here yesterday afternoon, accompanied by several friends, to await his coming. It is expected the party will leave for Detroit this afternoon.

Many Members to Leave Party.

COPENHAGEN, Jan. 1, (via London.)—About one-third of the members of the Ford peace expedition, the majority of whom are students, will leave the party at Copenhagen. The remaining members of the expedition, about 100 Americans, are going to The Hague.

The reason assigned for the students' action is that it was thought undesirable for them to take the risk of a voyage through the North Sea.

The expedition has obtained information that it will possibly take six days more time than is usually required for the voyage to The Hague, on account of the ship being required to move only in the daytime. Members of the expedition express a desire to reach The Hague, as they are unable to obtain publicity or hold meetings in Copenhagen.

Mayor Lindhagen of Stockholm has arrived in Copenhagen and joined the party.

The Danish friends of the Ford expedition gave the delegates a reception tonight at the Old Glyptothek. The Rev. Jenkin Lloyd Jones of Chicago and Judge Ben B. Lindsey of Denver spoke. The proceedings were private.

ENGLAND SWEPT BY STORM.

Houses Unroofed and Trees and Wires Are Blown Down.

LONDON, Jan. 1.—Another storm of great severity swept over parts of England today, doing much damage. At Liverpool large shop windows were broken. Monmouthshire suffered extensively. Houses were unroofed and trees and wires blown down.

It is feared coastwise shipping suffered heavily.

Continued on Page 3.

AMERICANS ON TORPEDOED LINER

Robert N. McNeely Was on the Way to Aden as United States Consul.

BROTHER ACCOMPANIED HIM

C. H. Grant Going Out as Oil Manager—E. A. Rose, a Boy Heir, Probably Escaped.

Special to The New York Times.

WASHINGTON, Jan. 1.—Robert N. McNeely, American Consul at Aden, who was on board the torpedoed liner Persia, was born in Waxhau, N. C., and his home is at Monroe in that State. He is 32 years old. Mr. McNeely was graduated from the University of North Carolina. From 1901 until 1903 he taught school; after that he served as a mail carrier until 1905. Later he practiced law at Monroe, of which place he was City Clerk and Town Treasurer in 1907 and 1908. He was then for two years a member of the lower branch of the North Carolina Legislature, and at the latest legislative session he was a State Senator.

Mr. McNeely took the examination for appointment to the United States Consular Service on Jan. 25, 1915, and was appointed a Consul of the eighth class on Oct. 18, 1915. He was one of a class of newly appointed Consuls who had spent the greater part of last year in the State Department at Washington undergoing instructions. He was appointed American Consul at Aden, and sailed from New York on Nov. 27 for England on the Holland liner Ryndam as a fellow-passenger with Consul General Skinner, who was returning to London. Mr. McNeely remained in London until Dec. 18, when he sailed on the Persia.

The post to which he was being sent as Consul, Aden, was considered important at this time. Aden is at the southwestern tip of Arabia, on the Gulf of Aden, near the Strait of Bab-el-Mandeb, at the southern entrance to the Red Sea. Aden is a British garrison town and a military observation centre for the Red

Continued on Page 3.

SHIP IS SUNK OFF CRETE

British P. & O. Steamer Was on Her Way from London to Bombay.

ONLY FOUR BOATS GOT AWAY

160 Passengers and Crew of 250 to 300 Aboard, Most of Whom Perished.

DOUBT AS TO WARNING

Consul Skinner Strives to Get Facts and Names of Americans Who May Be Lost.

LONDON, Jan. 1.—The British passenger steamer Persia, bound from London for Bombay, was torpedoed and sunk off the Island of Crete in the Mediterranean, on Thursday, and it is believed that several hundred persons, some of whom were Americans, perished.

It is known that the majority of the passengers and crew were lost. Only four boats got clear of the liner before she sank. These boats were picked up by a steamer bound for Alexandria, and the survivors were expected there this morning.

Robert McNeely, American Consul at Aden, was a passenger on the Persia. Members of the Consul's family say that his brother was with him.

Two other American passengers are known to have been on the vessel when she left London. Charles H. Grant of 49 Federal Street, Boston, was on his way to Bombay. Edward Rose, a schoolboy, was on the ship from Denver to Gibraltar. Rose probably landed at Gibraltar and was not on board the boat at the time she was sunk.

160 Passengers Aboard.

Sixty-one first-class passengers and eighty-three second-cabin passengers, including eight children, boarded the steamship at London, according to information obtained at the Peninsular & Oriental Line, owners of the liner. At Marseilles thirty-five of the first class and thirty-two of the second cabin boarded the vessel.

The company estimates that after deducting the number of passengers leaving the ship at her various ports of call about 160 passengers were aboard when the vessel was sunk.

A Lloyd's dispatch says that most of the passengers and men of the Persia were lost.

A message from the Admiralty to the Peninsular & Oriental Company makes the definite announcement that the Persia was torpedoed. The disaster occurred at 1 o'clock on Thursday afternoon. The company does not know whether the vessel received a warning or not.

Cable communication with the East is so slow that details of the disaster are not expected to arrive for a day or two. A majority of the Persia's passengers were British, bound for India, including many women.

Lord Montagu was on the passenger list. He was proceeding to India to assume the post of Inspector of Mechanical Transport Vehicles. He appeared in the list of New Year honors, receiving the order of the Star of India for services in connection with the war. He was well known in America. He was prominent in athletics and has traveled extensively, visiting the United States, Japan, China, India, and Egypt. He was a war correspondent in Rhodesia during the Matabele war. He was interested in railway and transport problems.

Crew of More Than 250.

The crew of the Persia numbered between 250 and 300 men. They were nearly all Lascars. There was not much cargo aboard the Persia, but she was carrying very heavy mail.

The four boats which got away from the sinking vessel were capable of carrying 60 persons each, but it is not known if the boats were full.

Every effort is being made by Consul General Skinner to get some information about Robert McNeely, the American Consul at Aden, and the two other Americans known to be on the passenger list. The British Admiralty informed Mr. Skinner it had no information with regard to the fate of individual passengers. Mr. Skinner sent a cablegram to the American Consulate at Alexandria, requesting the Consul to ascertain the

Mid-Week Pictorial

The ruins of a once beautiful forest in the Verdun sector.

"All the News That's Fit to Print."

The New York Times.

THE WEATHER
Fair Monday and probably Tuesday; rising temperature Tuesday; strong west winds, diminishing.
For full weather report see Page 17.

VOL. LXV...NO. 21,219. ... NEW YORK, MONDAY, FEBRUARY 28, 1916.—EIGHTEEN PAGES. ONE CENT In Greater New York, Jersey City and Newark. | Elsewhere, TWO CENTS.

GERMAN GUNS BLOW UP VERDUN FORTS; FOUR SHOTS DESTROYED DOUAUMONT; SINGLE SHOT LEVELS A SECOND FORT

BERLIN STANDS BY NEW SEA ORDER; TELLS OF ATTACKS

Instructs von Bernstorff That Pledges Hold, but Don't Include Armed Ships.

ALSO ASKS FOR WARNING

Believes Americans Should Not Take Passage on Armed Belligerent Vessels.

CHARGE BRITISH VIOLATION

Germany Declares England Has Not Kept Faith with Us with Regard to Armed Liners.

Special to The New York Times.

WASHINGTON, Feb. 27.—Count von Bernstorff, the German Ambassador, today received a long cipher communication from the German Foreign Office conveying instructions for his guidance in further confidential negotiations with Secretary Lansing over the German submarine campaign in the future, as now involved in the consideration of the Lusitania case.

Here are the basic elements of his instructions:

First—Germany will stand by the assurances she has previously given to the United States with respect to the future conduct of submarine warfare.

Second—Germany does not regard its newly proclaimed policy of sinking armed merchant vessels on sight after Feb. 29 as having nullified the assurances previously given.

Third—Germany's interpretation of the assurances previously given that ships will not be attacked without warning is applicable only to unarmed merchant ships, and not as being broad enough to cover belligerent merchant vessels armed for defense, and which may use their armaments offensively against German submarines.

Fourth—Germany regards the Lusitania case as embracing only the question of that Government's attitude toward unarmed merchantmen and not as involving the question of the treatment of armed merchant ships.

Fifth—Germany does not offer to suspend her proposed campaign of submarine attack without warning against armed merchantmen, and inferentially the campaign is to become effective on Tuesday, as planned.

Sixth—Germany calls attention to the assurances given by the British Ambassador the first month of the war to the effect that guns on British merchantmen will never fire unless such vessels are fired upon first, and contends that these assurances have been violated by British armed ships, and by secret instructions issued by the British Government, and in support of this contention Germany offers what she regards as evidence enumerating vessels that have used their guns offensively against German submarines and also copies of the alleged secret instructions to British merchant vessels.

Seventh—Germany is willing to discuss with the United States the question of when defensive armament may be regarded as having become offensive.

Eighth—Meanwhile Germany urges that Americans be warned not to travel on armed enemy merchantmen.

Await Secret Papers.

The instructions to the German Ambassador are supplemented by several exhibits, which are being sent to him in installments, naming the British and French merchantmen alleged by Germany to have used their guns offensively, and embracing the text of the alleged British secret instructions and supplementary orders to merchant ships regarding the use of their armament.

These exhibits have not been received in their entirety by the Ambassador. They are expected to reach this embassy by Tuesday. The understanding tonight was that the Ambassador would, within the next two days, ask the Secretary of State for an appointment for a conference, at which he will be ready to renew the diplomatic discussion of the matter in the light of his new instructions.

In some respects the instructions to the Ambassador were disappointing. It was expected that the German Government would adopt Count Bernstorff's suggestion that it take the position that the assurances previously given were intended to be applicable only to unarmed merchant vessels, but it was more than a disappointment to learn that the German Government made no offer to suspend or postpone putting into effect the orders already issued for submarine attacks without warning on armed enemy merchant ships after Feb. 29.

Attacks to Begin.

It is understood that submarines, under the orders thus issued, have already been sent out by the German Admiralty, and that it would probably be impossible to reach most of these U-boats until they return to their home ports. Should any of these submarines sink an armed merchant vessel without warning, and thereby cause the loss of American lives, a serious crisis in the relations between the two Governments will be caused.

The Administration is hoping that the instructions given to the German submarine commanders are such as to avert a contingency of that kind. In Teutonic Embassy circles it is intimated that, pending further negotiations over the question of what is to be regarded as constituting defensive and what offen-

Continued on Page 2.

Germany Unlikely to Change; Some U-Boats Already at Sea

BERLIN, Feb. 27, (via London, Monday, Feb. 28.)—No authoritative announcement is available here concerning the report that Germany will postpone the putting into effect of her announced intention to sink armed merchantmen without warning. The matter is said to be still under advisement.

AMSTERDAM, Feb. 27, (via London, Monday, Feb. 28.)—According to the North German Gazette, all reports that the German authorities would deviate from their plans with regard to the sinking of armed enemy merchantmen are unfounded.

"An energetic conduct of our submarine war according to the principles laid down in the memorandum will begin at the stated time," says the newspaper, which is the semi-official German organ.

WASHINGTON, Feb. 27.—Confidential advices received from Berlin state that German and Austrian submarine commanders already have their new orders, and that from midnight Tuesday they will be authorized to sink without warning all armed merchant ships of the enemies of Germany. It was said also that many of the submarine commanders probably had left their bases on voyages, and that even should the United States request the postponing of the opening of the campaign it would be impossible to get word to many of the submarines.

WILSON WOULD NOT GIVE ALL FOR PEACE

Ought to Keep Out of War, but Not by Abandoning Humanity and Justice.

HIS GRIDIRON CLUB SPEECH

Answers Clamor in Congress to Warn Americans Off Armed Ships—True Valor.

Special to The New York Times.

WASHINGTON, Feb. 27.—In a short speech delivered just before the conclusion of the Gridiron Club dinner here last night President Wilson discussed the duty of the United States in connection with the war in Europe, and inferentially answered some of his critics. He made what was taken to be a reply to the element in Congress which attempted last week to force him to modify his attitude in dealing with Germany in the armed ship issue by saying bluntly that he preferred to know what the people throughout the country were thinking rather than what was being said in Congressional cloakrooms. He made what amounted to an answer to the allegation that his course in the German submarine issue was actuated by political expediency, declaring that America should keep out of the war at the sacrifice of everything except humanity and justice.

It was a peace speech with a ring in it. It was an intimate talk, not intended for publication. One of the two rules of the Gridiron Club is that "reporters are never present" to record the speeches of guests, an inducement to freedom of language of which most of those who have addressed this organization of Washington newspaper correspondents have taken advantage. The President's speech created such an impression, however, that arrangements were made today for its publication. In giving out copies of the speech to the press tonight the White House attached to it this note:

"So many requests from those attending the dinner that the President's address be published have been received at the White House that both the President and the Gridiron Club have consented to its publication."

President Wilson was cheered wildly when he concluded his remarks at the dinner; the club members and their guests were on their feet waving napkins and cheering. So prolonged was the demonstration that twice the President felt constrained to rise and bow his acknowledgments. The greatest outburst of approval in the course of the speech came when the President declared that "America ought to keep out of the war" at the sacrifice of everything except her sense of humanity and justice, upon which the history and character of the country were founded.

The President's address follows:

Principle, Not Expediency.

I have very little to say tonight, except to express my warm appreciation of the invariable courtesy of this club, and of the reception you have so generously accorded me. I find that I am seldom tempted to say anything nowadays unless somebody starts something, and tonight nobody has started anything.

Your talk, Mr. Toastmaster, has been a great deal about candidacy for the Presidency. It is not a new feeling on my part, but one which I entertain with a greater intensity than formerly, that a man who seeks the Presidency of the United States for anything that it will bring to him is an audacious fool. The responsibilities of the office ought to sober a man even before he approaches it. One of the difficulties of the office seldom appreciated, I dare say, is that it is very difficult to think while so many people are talking, and particularly while so many people are talking in a way that obscures counsel, and is entirely off the point.

The point in national affairs, gentlemen, never lies along the lines of expediency. It always rests in the field of principle. The United States was not founded upon any principle of expediency; it was founded upon a profound principle of human liberty and of humanity, and whenever it bases its policy upon any other foundations than those it builds on the sand and not upon solid rock.

It seems to me that the most enlightening thing a man can do is suggested by something which the Vice President said tonight. He complained that he found men, who, when their attention was called to the signs of Spring, did not see the blue heaven, did not see the movement of the free clouds, did not think of the great spaces of the quiet continent, but

Continued on Page 2.

THE MALOJA SUNK BY MINE, 40 DEAD, IN SIGHT OF DOVER

Thousands on Shore Watch the P. & O. Liner Turn Turtle and Go to Bottom.

CHILDREN ON DECK KILLED

Officers Refuse to Take to the Boats, but Stand at Their Posts to the Last.

RESCUING TANKER BLOWN UP

The Empress of Fort William Is Destroyed — 147 Lives Lost, Estimate in London.

DOVER, Feb. 27.—The steamship Maloja, a 12,431 ton vessel belonging to the Peninsular & Oriental Line, struck a mine and sank within half an hour two miles off Dover today. More than forty persons were drowned or killed.

The Maloja left Tilbury only yesterday for Bombay with mails, 119 passengers of all classes, and a crew numbering about 200, most of them Lascars. Other passengers were to join the ship at Marseilles.

The steamer had just passed Admiralty Pier at Dover, and was opposite Shakespeare Cliff, when an explosion shook her from end to end. She listed immediately to port. High seas were running, and the Captain, realizing that great damage had been done to the after part of his vessel, tried to run her ashore, but the engine room was swamped and the ship became unmanageable.

The plight of the vessel was observed and dozens of craft went at full speed to her rescue. One of them, the British tanker Empress of Fort William, of 2,181 tons, struck another mine and sank nearby.

Boats Had Been Swung Out.

Aboard the Maloja everything possible was done to get the passengers and crew off. All the boats had been swung out before she struck, as a precaution against accident, and all the persons aboard had sufficient time to put on lifebelts, instruction in the use of which had been given the previous evening.

Boat after boat and a number of rafts were sent away, but several persons leaped into the water and were picked up by the surrounding craft. It was at first thought that all had been saved, but later bodies were washed ashore and their number was gradually added to during the day.

Owing to the fact that Dover is under strict military law, it was possible to obtain only meagre details from those rescued. The Captain said that both passengers and crew behaved splendidly.

The passengers were for the most part British officials in the Indian Service, the most prominent being Judge Oldfield of the Indian High Court.

Only one of the crew of the Empress of Fort William was drowned.

Children Playing on Deck.

It was about 10:30 in the morning that the disaster occurred. The Maloja was steaming down the channel, children playing on the deck and most of the passengers carrying lifebelts in their hands. Suddenly a terrific explosion blew in the side of the second saloon, and twenty minutes later the Maloja sank.

Just before she went to the bottom the vessel turned turtle and for a few seconds the keel was visible above the surface. According to eyewitnesses there was a second explosion, and while under water the vessel righted herself, the masts became visible and then she went down.

The captain and officers stuck by the ship to the last. Though all of them were saved, not one left the ship in the boats. They were all picked out of the water.

The Captain from the bridge directed the lowering of the boats, and called on everybody to keep calm, and everybody kept calm wonderfully, for the scene immediately after the explosion was one sufficiently terrifying to cause a panic. Several children were blown to pieces, and the deck was covered with wreckage and wounded, but there was no sign of a panic.

Only a few boats could be lowered, and the heavy sea made the rescue work difficult. The majority of those saved were on rafts, of which the ship carried a large number. Most of the women and children lost their lives owing to the fact that one boat already in the water drifted under another, which was being lowered, and capsized.

Captain Sticks to His Post.

The Captain remained on the bridge until thrown into the water by the last lurch of the ship.

Up to midnight the bodies landed from the Maloja include eighteen men, eleven women and four children, in addition to eleven Lascars. Among the dead is Mrs. McLeod, wife of General McLeod.

The Peninsular & Oriental Line has issued the following statement:

The Peninsular & Oriental Line regrets to state that at 10:30 o'clock Sunday morning, when the steamer Maloja was midway between Dover and Folkstone, she was struck by a mine, the after part of the ship being blown up.

There was a high sea running at the time. The captain tried to beach her, but was unsuccessful. The vessel sank in about half an hour.

There were 119 passengers on board, of which a large number were rescued from the water and from the ship's boats by torpedo boats and other craft, and landed at Dover, where they were attended by the hospital ship St. Davids. It is believed that almost all of the passengers were saved.

The Captain reports that all of the passengers and members of the crew behaved splendidly.

Thousands of residents of Dover witnessed the rescue work from shore. Many actually saw the blowing up of the ship, while almost the entire population reached the water front before the vessel went down.

Market Hall was converted into a morgue, where the police laid out the bodies of the dead on improvised biers for identification today. Several deaths occurred on board rescuing vessels, the victims suffering from exhaustion and exposure. Captain C. Irving was in command of the Maloja.

Captain Shepherd of the Empress said that the sinking of the Maloja bore a remarkable resemblance to the familiar picture of the sinking of the German cruiser Blücher, with her keel nearly showing and swarms of people clinging to her sides. Captain Shepherd photographed the ship as she was sinking.

Continued on Page 2.

TWO MORE VILLAGES TAKEN

German Reports Tell of the Sweep Onward After the Fall of Douaumont.

TROOPS FIGHTING FIERCELY

Burning with the Flame of Patriotism That Inspired Them in 1914, Says One Observer.

WORK OF THE HEAVY GUNS

Second Fort Blew Up After Douaumont Under Deadly Fire of German Artillery.

By KARL ROHNER.

Berlin Lokal Anzeiger Dispatches.

Special Cable to THE NEW YORK TIMES.

GERMAN GREAT HEADQUARTERS, Feb. 26.—Again a fresh wave of attacks has engulfed the whole row of enemy positions on a broad front and brought them into our possession. The high hill which yesterday, when I was permitted to visit the great battlefield, still lay under preparatory fire, has been taken by us, and, in addition to this strongly fortified position southwest of Louvemont, the village itself and a group of fortifications to the east have fallen into our hands.

The brilliant feat of our Brandenburgers in the splendid storming of Fort Douaumont was preceded by the no less glorious work of our artillery. The armored fortress of Douaumont lay since Thursday in ruins. Four shots of our heavy guns had been fired against it, and every one of these shots scored a bullseye on the distant target. Explosions in the interior of that proud bulwark followed the hits.

Douaumont was not only the strongest corner fort in the chain around Verdun. Situated on a high, steep hill, it was at the same time a symbol of impregnability.

Now not only Douaumont but Dieppe and Fromezey to the east have fallen to us. Likewise further south and southeast our successes here are making themselves felt. The resistance of the enemy in the Woevre district has collapsed, and our troops have pressed after the enemy to Marcheville, south on the old Roman road to Metz, Dieppe, and Paris.

In these days I have seen men who have been in the fierce Verdun fighting whose eyes have flashed as in those August days of 1914. The flame that then burned in every German burns in every single soldier here to whom it is given to sacrifice himself for our future in this powerful driving advance.

Second Fort Blown Up.

The Berlin Tageblatt Dispatches.

Special Cable to THE NEW YORK TIMES.

GERMAN GREAT HEADQUARTERS, BEFORE VERDUN, Feb. 26.—The giant block of cement and steel armorplate that was Douaumont lies in ruins. A second fort not far off blew up, just as did Fort Loncin at Liége, as the result of a single large calibred shell crashing through to the ammunition magazine.

The organization of the attack on the north front of Verdun was a masterpiece in itself. Preparations of vast extent had first to be carried out in complete concealment from the enemy if the fight against the invincible fortress was to succeed.

To the great distance over which heavy artillery had to be brought without using railways were superadded the great difficulties resulting from continuous bad weather and the consequent condition of roads. Hundreds of men had first to build good roads.

Another of the difficulties was the proper laying of the beds on which the great guns rest, and on whose firmness depends in the first line the accuracy of our heavy gun fire. How unbelievably accurate was their fire is now known.

Yesterday there was hardly any firing of importance to be heard from the forts. On the other hand, prisoners said that the effect of our artillery was indescribably frightful; nobody could hold out long against it.

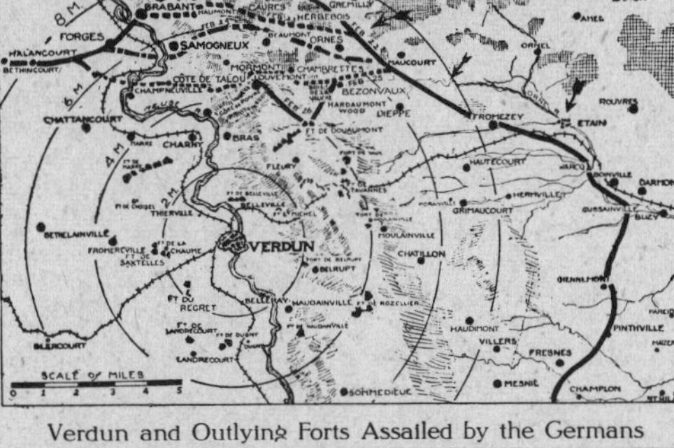

Verdun and Outlying Forts Assailed by the Germans

Verdun Victory Hinges Now on Ammunition; French Rush Men and Guns to Threatened Front

Special Cable to THE NEW YORK TIMES.

PARIS, Feb. 27, (Dispatch to The London Daily Mail.)—Wounded soldiers who have reached Paris say that the carnage among the Germans has been simply terrible. At many places the German dead formed huge dams across the ravines, impeding the water on its downward course to the Meuse. Every now and then one of these dams gives way, and the reddened stream swirls on again, carrying with it hundreds of corpses.

During the week of battle the French have not been idle, and along the eastern railway line have been rushing troops and munition trains night and day. The French Generals realize that victory in the present battle will go to the army which makes the best use of its artillery, and so battery after battery of light and heavy guns since Monday has been sent up to the Argonne and Meuse Heights.

The French hitherto have regarded their artillery offensive of last September in the Champagne as the greatest effort of the war, but the present battle upset all the calculations of the staffs and the consumption of shells of every calibre has greatly exceeded all estimates. The French have plentiful supplies, however, and if the battle ends for lack of munitions that lack will be on the German and not on the French side.

French Rushing Reinforcements to Verdun

OTTAWA, Feb. 27.—British lines in Belgium and France are being extended to replace French troops who are being rushed to the Verdun region to take part in the fighting "which has settled down to a terrific slaughter," according to advices received here from the battle front.

Approximately twenty army divisions (400,000 men) have been thrown into the battle by the Germans, while the French troops number fifteen divisions, cable messages say.

Early Days of the Battle.

By DR. MAX OSBORN.

Berlin Vossische Zeitung Dispatches.

Special Cable to THE NEW YORK TIMES.

GERMAN HEADQUARTERS, NEAR VERDUN, Feb. 25.—The victorious fighting on the Meuse north of Verdun yesterday resulted in further successes of great importance. I had an opportunity this noon from several high points in the firing line of surveying the mighty battlefield over which the thunder of cannon rolled in assaulting. The whole terrain east of the river, where our advance began a few days ago, consists of a chain of wooded ranges of hills. In the Valley of the Meuse lies the village of Consevoye, which formed the right wing of our attacking line. From Consevoye our front ran over Flabas and Ville-devant-Chaumont to Azannes up to last Sunday.

On this whole front sector on the 21st at 8:30 in the morning, our artillery opened a murderous fire. Thanks to the splendid activity of our fliers the enemy aeroplanes were prevented from forcing their way into the air zone behind our front. Thereby the enemy's observations were prevented. Till late in the afternoon our fire raged with increasing fury against the indescribably strong positions of the enemy, crushing trenches, tearing wire entanglements to shreds and barring all approach from the south. At 5 in the afternoon we advanced first in the centre of the sector south of Flabas, toward Haumont Wood, north of the hamlet of Haumont. The whole section of woods had been converted into one colossal wilderness by weaving barbed wire from tree to tree; but our powerful artillery had ripped apart this impenetrable net, and so our infantry could get possession of the woods with slight losses. By 8 in the evening it was firmly in our hands, likewise the strongest redoubt of the wood region—the so-called star position—fell into our hands.

Our troops had plunged through so far that the French body of troops that still sat in the ravine northwest of the Haumont woods found itself threatened from the rear, and was forced next morning to withdraw from its position with heavy losses.

Simultaneously on the 21st an attack was launched further east, against Caures woods, north of Beaumont and between Haumont and Herbebois.

The following day, the 22d, the same game of clock-like co-operation between artillery and infantry was repeated. The batteries placed their fire further south on the next positions of the enemy. Again at 5 in the afternoon the storm was launched, and after half an hour brought Haumont into German hands, while simultaneously further east Caures wood was completely traversed.

The movement continued further, shifting in a southwesterly direction. Now the objective was the so-called Brabant position of the French in the hamlet of Brabant-sur-Meuse. The mortars and howitzers spat death and destruction against these strong field fortifications, and on the 23d, the Brabant position and the village had been taken.

You must see for yourself the bare ridge that runs south from Consenvoye to Brabant to realize what it means to capture such terrain by storm; but even further rushed the irresistible tide, always with methodical alternation of drumfire and assault.

On the 23d the ravine between Haumont and Samogneux, as well as the village of Samogneux itself, and Herbebois, to the east, fell; then, on the 24th, the important Hill 344, east of Samogneux, one of the enemy's strongest bulwarks; then, in the evening, the so-called Cotelettes Mill. In the evening Beaumont, too, fell into our hands.

The driving power, endurance, and discipline of our troops in all these fights was incomparable. Commanders and officers never tire of giving praise and recognition of their performance. Our losses, happily, were not very great.

BERLIN IS FLYING FLAGS

News of the Fall of Verdun's First Fort Stirs Enthusiasm.

From a Staff Correspondent.

Special Cable to THE NEW YORK TIMES.

BERLIN, Feb. 27.—Flags are beginning to appear in celebration of the news of the fall of the first fort at Verdun; and not even the fall of Warsaw or of any of the great Russian fortresses has evoked such intense, quiet, restrained rejoicing as this first breach of the French line.

The German public is still in the dark as to whether it really marks the beginning of the long-expected great offensive, or is a great demonstration to cloak another elsewhere, and German military experts are observing the utmost reticence in discussing the event. All emphasize their special satisfaction that the "Iron Guard of Brandenburg" is heading the drive. The conquerors of Douaumont are the infantry regiments of the Grand Duke Friedrich Franz II. of Mecklenburg-Schwerin, and the reigning Prince has started for the front to congratulate the victorious troops whose nominal chief he is.

The Berlin Gazette's military critic writes:

"A new and splendid success has crowned our previous attacks against Verdun more quickly than had been expected. The German attack on the fortress has led to a decisive success, and once again Germans have shown themselves masters in attacking fortresses. The hardest step in conquering a fortress is the first break through the circle of outer forts. Therefore, success at this point is, as a rule, of decisive import. Reviewing the fortress war in the east and west, it appears that in the case of all the French and Russian fortresses attacked by us the storming of the first permanent outer forts has been the hardest part of the whole attack."

FIERCE FIGHTING ON SLOPES

Those of Douaumont Strewn With Dead Bodies of Germans.

CHAMPNEUVILLE IS TAKEN

Village West of the Fort Falls—Talou Ridge Untenable for Either Side.

15,000 FRENCH PRISONERS

Berlin Celebrates the Taking of Fort Douaumont, Decking Buildings with Flags.

LONDON, Feb. 27.—Today's fighting in the Verdun region has been most intense around the armored fort of Douaumont, for the possession of which French and Germans are desperately contending. Apparently the Germans yesterday succeeded in throwing a force into this position and have maintained themselves there despite repeated counterattacks, of which the Berlin report mentions five. The capture of Champneuville and the Côte de Talou (both to the west of Fort Douaumont) and of the fortified wood of Hardaumont, to the east, is reported from Berlin. [illegible] Paris asserts that the French still hold Hardaumont and that the Talou ridge is so swept by artillery fire as to be untenable for neither side.

The official statement from Berlin says:

On the heights to the right of the Meuse the French attempted by attacks, repeated five times with fresh troops, to reconquer the armored fortress of Douaumont. They were repulsed with sanguinary losses.

To the west of the fort our troops have taken Champneuville, the Côte de Talou, and have advanced as far as Nave on the southern border of the wood northeast of Bras.

To the east of the fort we took by storm the extended fortified works of Hardaumont.

In the Woevre plain vigorous fighting is taking place on the German frontier, the battles extending as far as the Côte Lorraine.

According to information at present in hand the number of unwounded prisoners amounts to nearly 15,000.

In Flanders our aeroplane squadrons repeated their attacks on the camp of the enemy troops.

A bomb attack on Metz by enemy aviators resulted in the injury or death of eight civilians and several soldiers. Several houses were damaged.

In the neighborhood of the fortress a French aeroplane was brought down in an aerial battle and by the bombardment of the anti-aircraft guns. The occupants of the machine included two Captains, who were captured.

On various portions of the front there were intense artillery and mine battles.

South of Ypres a British attack was repulsed.

The official communication issued in Paris tonight reads as follows:

In the region to the north of Verdun, following the violent actions of the preceding days, there has been some abatement in the efforts of the enemy in the course of the day, except between the height of Douaumont and the plateau to the north of the village of Vaux, where a strong attack carried out against our positions was repulsed.

To the east and west of the position of Douaumont, the slopes of which are covered with German bodies, our troops are pressing closely the enemy detachments which were able to gain a foothold there, and which are maintaining themselves with difficulty.

According to the latest reports, the Côte de Talou, rendered untenable as well for us as for the enemy by the bombardment of the artillery of both sides, is not occupied by any of the adversary forces.

In the Woevre the enemy has come in contact with our advance posts in the direction of Blanzée and Moranville, where their efforts to debouch toward Hill 255 failed.

Between Soissons and Rheims destructive firing has been carried out on the enemy works in front of Venizel and to the east of Troyon.

In the Vosges there was an artillery

"All the News That's Fit to Print."

The New York Times.

THE WEATHER
Increasing cloudiness, probably snow today; snow tomorrow; not much change in temperature; moderate variable winds.
For full weather report see Page 15.

VOL. LXV...NO. 21,220. .... NEW YORK, TUESDAY, FEBRUARY 29, 1916.—TWENTY PAGES. ONE CENT In Greater New York, Jersey City and Newark. | Elsewhere TWO CENTS.

GERMAN DRIVE AT VERDUN CHECKED; BATTLE STILL RAGES AT DOUAUMONT WHERE KAISER'S FORCE IS HEMMED IN

WON'T SINK SHIPS ON SIGHT UNLESS ARMING IS PROVED

Memorandum Presented by von Bernstorff Renews Pledges Affecting U-Boat Warfare.

PROOF IS NOT DEFINED

But Ambassador Believes It Will Be Use of Guns by Merchantmen When Challenged.

STATE DEPARTMENT'S VIEW

Does Not Contend That Americans Are Immune on Vessels Ordered to Fire Offensively.

Special to The New York Times.

WASHINGTON, Feb. 28.—"No enemy merchantman is to be torpedoed without warning unless the presence of armament on board such vessel is proved."

This assurance on behalf of the German Government was given to the United States Government today in a memorandum presented by Count von Bernstorff, the German Ambassador, based on the confidential cipher instructions received by him yesterday from the Berlin Foreign Office. Moreover, Count von Bernstorff is believed to have intimated that the "proof" of the existence of such guns would lie in their use in resistance. Baron Zwiedinek, Chargé d'Affaires of the Austro-Hungarian Embassy, called on Mr. Lansing after the departure of the German Ambassador from the State Department and announced that the Vienna Government's views were identical with those submitted by Count von Bernstorff. Thus the Central Powers stand together on the submarine issue as affected by the new Austro-German policy of sinking armed belligerent merchantmen without warning, to become effective at midnight tomorrow.

The German Government's response to the inquiries submitted on behalf of the United States Government through Count von Bernstorff is that the Berlin Government intends to live up to all of the assurances previously given in its pledges to the United States, and that, according to Germany's interpretation of these pledges, they are not to be modified by the new German campaign against armed enemy merchantmen.

The memorandum presented by the German Ambassador makes it plain that the German Government takes the position that its prior pledges were not to be construed as broad enough to entitle armed enemy merchantmen to warning before being torpedoed. In carrying out this policy, however, Secretary Lansing was notified, "no enemy merchantman is to be torpedoed without warning unless the presence of armament on board such vessel is proved." This is understood to be substantially the wording of this portion of the German memorandum.

The memorandum is silent regarding the manner in which the German submarine commanders are to obtain proof as to the presence of armament on board enemy merchantmen, but it is understood that Count von Bernstorff informed the Secretary of State that it was his opinion that German submarine commanders would regard the actual use of the guns on such merchantmen as the proof for which they must look before carrying out their instructions to sink armed belligerent merchantmen without warning.

Use of a Gun the Proof.

Upon what the German Ambassador based this opinion could not be ascertained, but the impression is strong that the Ambassador's confidential instructions from his Government vested him with authority to make such a statement. At any rate, if this is the correct interpretation to be placed upon the orders given to German submarine commanders the situation will take on a somewhat different complexion from that given to it by the official perusal of the German and Austrian memoranda to the neutral powers, which have been regarded as susceptible of no other construction than that it was the purpose of the Central Powers to inaugurate an indiscriminate campaign of sinking armed belligerent merchant men without warning and on sight.

In view of this impression, the memorandum presented by the German Ambassador, as well as the Ambassador's interpretation of it, came as something of a surprise to high officials. Under this construction it would appear to be the German contention, on the one hand, that armed enemy merchantmen—particularly those of Great Britain—have lost their immunity from attack without warning because they are regarded as being offensively armed, but that, on the other hand, at least in the opening stages of the new campaign against armed merchantmen due for inauguration tomorrow night, German submarine commanders must have proof of the presence of guns on board enemy merchant ships before attacking them, and this proof must take the particular form of actual use of the guns of the merchantmen. If such should be the practice, the liner in effect would be attacked not because it was armed but because it resisted.

The German Ambassador said tonight that he regarded as authentic a cabled news dispatch from Berlin, via Amsterdam, printed here late this afternoon, which asserted that submarine commanders in their new campaign would act under these instructions:

"They will not torpedo every ship encountered, trusting to prove later that it is armed. They will not violate in-

Continued on Page 2.

Reported Move for Peace By Turkey and Bulgaria

Special Cable to THE NEW YORK TIMES.

ATHENS, Feb. 28 (Dispatch to The London Daily Chronicle.)—It is stated that both the Turks and Bulgarians are asking for an understanding with the Entente. The only thing they request is that they be permitted to retain their position and integrity.

The Turks, perceiving the danger to Asia Minor from the Russian advance do not consider their existence safe nor do they expect any decisive help from Germany.

The highest Bulgarian military circles are greatly in fear of the extension of the existing frontier and do not hide the fact that although they may be at Monastir and in Albania their capital runs the risk of falling into the enemies' hands.

PANIC UNDER RIVER IN STALLED CARS

Switch at Brooklyn Terminus Fails to Work in Time, Causing Big Tieup.

WOMEN FAINT FROM FEAR

Crowded Ten-Coach Train Stopped by Emergency Brakes, Averting a Collision.

When, at 6 o'clock last evening, a ten-coach subway train bound from Manhattan to Brooklyn, and jammed to the doors with passengers, failed to take the proper switch upon reaching the Atlantic Avenue station, an interruption in service resulted that caused many women to faint on other equally heavily loaded trains that were stalled for more than fifteen minutes in the tube under the East River.

More than a dozen subway trains were brought to a standstill between the Bowling Green and Borough Hall stations, and over an hour and twenty minutes elapsed before normal running schedules were restored.

The excitement at the Atlantic Avenue station, and among some of the passengers of the stalled trains who in some way learned the details, was intensified by the narrow escape of the ten-coach train, which was stopped only just in time to escape crashing into another train that was taking on passengers at the station for Manhattan.

The motorman was forced to apply the emergency brakes, and many persons were thrown in struggling heaps against the forward ends of the cars.

The accident happened just as the ten-coach train, coming from Bronx Park, reached the station. As the Atlantic Avenue station is the terminus in Brooklyn of the Interborough system, provision is made for switching trains around the platform and back to Manhattan. One of these trains, partly filled with passengers, was standing on the rails to the right of the station as the ten-coach, Bronx Park train approached, and the switchman on the platform attempted to send the incoming train to the rails on the left.

Switch Fails to Work in Time.

The switch for some reason failed to work until after the forward wheels of the first car had entered on the rails on which the other train stood, and less than six feet of space was left between the two when the motorman was finally able to lock the wheels with the emergency brakes.

The switch having slipped into its proper place immediately after the front wheels of the Bronx Park train had passed over it, the train could not be backed without derailing the first car and it was stalled at a point where there was no egress for the passengers save through the front and side doors of the first car which, fortunately, had progressed far enough to come alongside the platform.

Some of the frightened passengers were forced to walk the whole length of the train to reach these exit, but all were able to escape without injury. It took about twenty minutes, however, to empty all the coaches.

There was some delay in sending word back along the line that the Atlantic Avenue Station trains were stalled, and meanwhile other trains, also heavily crowded, entered the tube under the river, and were forced to stop there.

One of the passengers on one of these trains was Miss Ida Striffer, 21 years old, a stenographer, of 536 Dean Street, Brooklyn. She became hysterical with fright as the minutes elapsed and the train failed to move, and she finally fainted. Several other women, alarmed at the girl's plight, also fainted.

Girl Faints Amid Excitement.

When this train finally was able to make its way to the Borough Hall Station Miss Striffer was revived by Dr. Herring of the Brooklyn Hospital and sent to her home. He also treated several other women who refused to give their names and who took surface cars home as soon as they were able to make their way out of the crowded station. No one, as far as could be learned, was injured. The guards walked through the cars and attempted to calm the passengers by telling them they were in no danger.

The subway tie-up caused a great deal of inconvenience and confusion also at the subway stations between Brooklyn Bridge and Bowling Green, in Manhattan. When the Interborough officials finally became convinced that the interruption in service was to be a lengthy one persons waiting on the platforms were notified that no trains were being run to Brooklyn, and a majority sought the street and took surface and elevated cars for their homes. Several policemen assisted the special subway policemen and guards to relieve the congestion at Brooklyn Bridge. Trains were operated for a time as far south as Bowling Green, but the number of these was reduced because of the necessity of switching them at South Ferry.

At 7:19 o'clock a wrecking crew, sent to the Atlantic Avenue station, succeeded in hoisting the first car of the Bronx Park train back on the proper rails, but it was 7:30 before anything like normal service was restored.

THOMPSON TO GET EXTENSION OF TIME AT LEAST TO JULY 1

Speaker Sweet Will Not Oppose It if Committee Reports Its Expenditures.

GILLESPIE TO SHOW BOOKS

New Subpoenas on Interborough and B. R. T. Call for Details of Stock Issues.

ASK FOR LIST OF BONUSES

Hearing on the Whitney and Hervey Appointments Goes Over for a Week.

Special to The New York Times.

ALBANY, Feb. 28.—At a conference of the Republican Senators after tonight's session, at which Senator Thompson attended and defined the plans and purposes of his committee, it was agreed that the time of the Thompson committee should be extended until July 1.

After the conference Senator Thompson said that the date had been fixed over his protest and announced that he would put in a resolution tomorrow providing for an extension of the committee's time until Jan. 10, 1917. The result is not in doubt, however. Twenty-four Republican Senators voted for the July 1 limit and only six to extend the time until Jan. 1.

It is understood that Senator Thompson told the conference that he wanted the additional time for the purpose of pursuing to the end his investigation of the circumstances surrounding the letting of the contracts for the dual systems, and that the committee did not intend taking up any new leads.

"It has been suggested," said the Senator, "that the committee ought not to carry its investigation into the campaign months. There is some force to this suggestion. It might place the committee under suspicion of 'fat frying' from public service corporations for campaign purposes."

"It has been suggested," Senator Thompson was told, "that with immunity from your committee after July 1 pledged the corporations affected might be even more likely to come up with contributions."

"There is something in that, too," he admitted. "However, I am not willing to become a stalking horse in any move to 'shake down' public service corporations for campaign purposes."

Speaker Sweet of the Assembly, when asked what the lower house would do with regard to the Thompson resolution, said:

"I am not opposed to an extension of time for the Thompson Committee, but I believe the interests of the people demand that Senator Thompson file a tentative report of the expenditures of his committee, so that they may know the condition of the committee's finances."

"That is fair enough," said Senator Thompson, when told of the Speaker's statement. "He will have such a report. I have asked Controller Travis to give me a man to go over the committee's accounts and prepare such a report. That work will begin tomorrow."

Senator Thompson said he still remained firm in his opposition to the confirmation of Travis H. Whitney and Charles S. Hervey, whose nominations for vacancies on the Public Service Commission for the First District Governor Whitman sent to the Senate three weeks ago and which have been held up since in the Senate Finance Committee pending a hearing. The hearing had been fixed for tomorrow at the request of Senator Thompson and Senator Robert R. Lawson of Kings, another member of the Thompson Committee who is opposed to the confirmation of Messrs. Whitney and Hervey.

Late tonight Senator Henry M. Sage, Chairman of the Senate Finance Committee, announced that owing to the absence of many Democratic Senators on account of the Democratic State Convention the hearing would go over for a week.

GILLESPIE TO PRODUCE BOOKS.

New Subpoenas Issued for More Interborough Records.

Dissatisfied with the records furnished so far by the Interborough and the Brooklyn Rapid Transit Company, the Thompson Legislative Committee, through its counsel, Frank Moss, yesterday issued new subpoenas on both companies that are more far-reaching than any previous demands. Full information about stock and bond issues, how they are carried on the books of the companies and what funds have been expended are demanded. From these detailed records the committee expects to learn all about the dual subway contracts.

Some of the subjects covered by the subpoenas which contain fifteen specifications are: The authorized issue of capital stock of both companies, the amount of preferred and common and for what issued and when and to whom; the amount of bond issues; all assets and liabilities of the companies; all cash bonuses paid to any one for special services of any kind and full particulars about any stock bonuses.

Continuing his refusal to give up the books and papers of his concern asked for by Senator Thompson, T. H. Gillespie, son of the head of T. A. Gillespie & Co., declared yesterday that the books contained no evidence of a "yellow dog" or a "slush" fund. Paul D. Cravath of counsel for the company said the subpoena duces tecum did not

Continued on Page 5.

Italy May Declare War On Germany This Week

LONDON, Tuesday, Feb. 29.—Great interest is being displayed here in the possibility of a declaration of war on Germany by Italy when the Italian Parliament opens. At the date of adjournment in December it was stated that Parliament would be convened March 1.

According to Rome dispatches the Italian Government has not yet decided whether it will yield to the popular demand for a war with Germany. The Italian newspapers assert that the Italian Cabinet council yesterday voted to make a declaration on the subject in Parliament only if the Government was pressed to do so.

BOLD MAIL ROBBERS GET BIG BOOTY HERE

Value of 4 Registered Pouches Taken Estimated Even as High as $1,000,000.

WASHINGTON DENIES THEFT

But Bags Are Missing and a Widespread Search Is Being Made for Them.

Four pouches of registered mail, containing 20 packages from Baltimore and Washington, together with part of a shipment of currency from the Treasury in Washington to banks in this city, and variously estimated to be worth between $200,000 and $1,000,000, disappeared from a locked United States mail truck on the Jersey Central ferryboat Wilkes-Barre, about 4:30 Saturday morning between Jersey City and the Liberty Street dock, Manhattan, and Federal agents arare proceeding on the theory that they were stolen.

William E. Cochran, Inspector in charge of the New York division of the postal service, said the loss would have been increased hundreds of thousands of dollars if the thieves had not overlooked two bags, one containing more currency from the Treasury.

Two United States mail motor trucks met the 3:52 A. M. Baltimore & Ohio train at the station in New Jersey Saturday to carry the mail to the Post Office Building at Thirty-third Street and Eighth Avenue. Thirty bags of first-class mail, together with the six registered pouches, were thrown into the iron-meshed cage of the first truck. The doors were locked with the regulation lock placed on all mail wagons and pouches.

According to the Inspectors none but clerks on the railway mail cars and a few employes in the Post Offices have keys to fit these locks.

Guards Left Their Posts.

It was a cold morning and the drivers and guards of the two trucks violated the rules, according to the Inspectors, and left their wagons to go into the warm cabin.

Although only the few passengers who left the train in New Jersey were on the ferry, the Inspectors are puzzled to understand how the robbers—if they were on the ferry—managed to unlock the door and take the four pouches, unnoticed by any one. Whether they took the bags off at the ferry entrance or dropped them into a boat dragged at the ferry's side the Inspectors are unable to surmise, although the railroad's ferrymaster said that it would have been almost impossible for them to drop bags into boats without attracting attention. They admit that it would be equally difficult for them to carry the distinctively marked mail pouches past the ferry entrance and escape all eyes.

Not until the truck had reached the Post Office Building was the loss discovered. There were no marks on any part of the wire screen or the gate to indicate that the robbers had used force to break into the cage. It is believed they either had found a key or that they had been able to get one from a Government employe to make a duplicate.

Estimates of the Loss.

Chief Cochran said a thorough search was being pursued by post Office Inspectors, and that they did not intend to ask the aid of other departments or of the police.

Inspectors said should a check prove that bags from the Treasury Department had been stolen the sum would probably be larger than any other postal robbery known. In 1911 it was said pouches containing $500,000 in drafts and checks had been stolen in Thalman, Ga.; in the same year three pouches valued at $50,000 were taken from a ferry plying between San Francisco and Oakland, and in 1913 two men stole a pearl necklace valued at $650,000 from the post between Paris and London.

Baltimore Joins in Hunt.

Special to The New York Times.

BALTIMORE, Feb. 28.—New York Post Office Inspectors tonight came to Baltimore to seek a possible clue to the perpetrators of the robbery of mail pouches in New York early Saturday morning, which resulted, it is believed here, in the loss of several hundred thousand dollars in currency, bonds, and negotiable papers. It is said the mail contained large sums consigned to New York banks and brokerage houses by local banking institutions and brokers. One missing package from a local banking house contained $4,750 in currency and bonds.

The local Post Office inspectors are working on the case. Letters to all of the senders of registered letters or packages on that mail were sent out with a request that they call at the Post Office here tomorrow and estimate their value.

Washington Denies Serious Robbery.

Special to The New York Times.

WASHINGTON, Feb. 28.—It was denied at the Post Office Department tonight that any serious loss had occurred in the miscarriage of four mail pouches on the Jersey Central ferryboat last Saturday morning. As such accidents happen not infrequently in various parts of the country, the department had not been informed of the matter until late today. Chief Inspector Koons at once started an inquiry, with the result that he established the fact that the report of a large financial loss was probably exaggerated.

After ascertaining the sources of the mail and the points of transfer and the amount carried, Chief Inspector Koons called up Inspector Cochran at New York and conferred with him over the telephone with the result that a prompt denial was made of the report that a robbery had been committed.

INFANTRY AGAIN A FACTOR

Paris Sees Vital War Lessons in the Verdun Combat.

TRENCHES ARE "SCRAPPED"

And the Old-Fashioned Pitched Battle Takes the Place of Deadlock.

TWO MILES OF SLAUGHTER

Greatest Battle of War Now Concentrated Within Two Narrow Fronts.

Special Cable to THE NEW YORK TIMES.

PARIS, Feb. 28.—The French counterstroke at Verdun may mark the battle raging there as the beginning of the end of the war on the western front, according to military authorities here, reading between the lines of tonight's official bulletin.

That trenches have literally been scrapped and the long-drawn field fortress deadlock displaced by an old-fashioned pitched battle is the great lesson of the German attempt to take Verdun. But in teaching it there are good reasons to believe, according to the view here, that Germany may have signed her own death warrant.

What has been already indicated in the Champagne battle is now clearly proved by the German cannonade at Verdun: That under the concentrated fire of hundreds of great howitzers hurling shells weighing from one-half to three-quarters of a ton, even the strongest trenches are smashed into a defenseless chaos, and the mitrailleuse emplacements, which have previously rendered the heroism of infantry fruitless, are blasted into nothingness.

Foot soldiers have become once more, as throughout history, the decisive factor of warfare. Torn to pieces by shells, their front ranks melting under the cannonade, the waves of German soldiers nevertheless flowed incessantly over their comrades' bodies until at last General Joffre unleashed his waiting legions and man fought man as of old.

Two facts stand out clearly from the week's orgy of slaughter. The first is that German artillery cannot silence French, and the second is that if sacrifices are ignored and reserves are sufficient, infantry can advance despite the artillery and because of the practical obliteration of the mitrailleuses, may only be checked by infantry.

A Lesson for Allies.

Should Germany win five Verduns she cannot, it is held here, escape defeat, now that the Allies have learned that bloody lesson. Sooner or later the allied workshops will deliver the needed quantity of guns and munitions and the allied army will attain sufficient numerical superiority. Then will come a series of these blasting attacks, terribly expensive, but culminating inevitably, according to opinion here, in Germany's downfall. In the last resort only her infantry can save her, but her infantry has been wasted like sand from the banks of the Marne to the Riga swamps.

While the previous great battles of the war have been fought on fronts of thirty, fifty, or a hundred miles, what makes the Verdun struggle so appalling is it final concentration from a twenty-five-mile front into two short sections, each barely a mile across. The first is on the French left, and stretches from Champneuville to Côte du Poivre. The second is one the right and comprises the Douaumont spur, which is being attacked from the north and east simultaneously.

In the first section the German efforts were vain. The Kaiser's troops, directly they debouched from the ravine toward the crest, were swept away by a terrific fire from the French batteries across the Meuse, aided by mitrailleuses, which were comparatively sheltered from the German artillery.

Against Fort de Douaumont they succeeded on Saturday morning, but what they conquered and announced to the world was not a fort like the forts of Liége or Brest-Litovsk. It was armored and cemented, perhaps, as are the shelters in the Labyrinth or on Tahure Hill, but the frowning battlements and huge fixed cannon gave place six months ago to modern style rabbit-warren defenses.

The German capture, announced seven hours earlier than the usual bulletin for the Swiss afternoon papers, was just a strong position, not, as they indicated, the cornerstone of the Verdun defenses. And as a strong position it was recaptured in the afternoon by the French infantry.

Even had the counterattack failed, the German gain was far from all-important. Behind Douaumont spur are Forts Thiaumont, Damloup, Belleville, Souville, and St. Michel, the guns of which sweep the centre plateau, here bare of the woods that afforded some shelter in the attack on Fort de Douaumont.

French Soldier Pictures the Fight for Douaumont; German Charge at One Point Blocked by Own Dead

Special Cable to THE NEW YORK TIMES.

PARIS, Feb. 28.—A wounded Colonial infantryman who reached Paris this morning gives THE NEW YORK TIMES correspondent a picture of the taking and retaking of Fort de Douaumont at Verdun.

"The German cannonade had leveled the parapets and trenches until the position looked like a newly plowed field," he said. "It seemed as if every gun in the world was concentrated upon that one point. The noise was far greater than in the battle of Champagne.

"Some Boche infantry were creeping up a narrow ravine on the right front, others were crawling through the wood directly before the position. Suddenly they surged forward in a gray mass from both quarters at once. There must have been 5,000 in the ravine and perhaps 20,000 from the wood. As the former reached the plateau a single shell burst right among them, flinging pieces in all directions. The front was enveloped in a storm of shells, fragments of men, and lumps of earth.

"Through the smoke one could see them advancing, heads down, as if sheltering themselves from rain. Soon the ravine head was choked with bodies. Others tried to clamber over and kept rolling down the hillside. The heaps of dead gave us a more effective barricade than our own intrenchments. They simply could not pass.

"But in front, where the slaughter was even greater, they came on incessantly.

"Truly, they are brave, those Boches. I would never have believed that human beings could face such a terrific fire. Yet they knew it was certain death, for the wounded were stifled under corpses or torn in pieces by fresh shells.

"Wave after wave advanced. At last they reached the spot where our fortifications had been on the spur of the hill, and began piling up bodies to protect them from our fire. Douaumont was theirs, but at ghastly cost.

"Further back our hearts were burning. Were the Germans to be allowed to consolidate their victory? For three days they had kept us idle while the gunners did all the work. Since we retook Caures wood they held us, saying it was a useless sacrifice.

"We watched our shells concentrate upon Douaumont, tearing the German defenses into fragments. Our hearts beat fast. Surely we should attack soon.

"At last our turn came. I took part in the Champagne charge, but it was nothing like this. We were mad. Nothing could have stopped us. Despite the German fire, which perhaps was hampered by the fear of hitting their own men on the spur, we hurled ourselves at them with the bayonet among the shell holes and ruined emplacements.

"This was real war as I had never seen it. For a moment it was furious and equal. Then came another blue-clad wave and another. We hurled them back, screaming, over the hillside. It was a battle without quarter. We only captured corpses.

"They had had enough. Fort de Douaumont was French once more.

"As we lay there, panting and too exhausted to cheer, I suddenly found that my thigh was bleeding from a deep stab. My boot was already full of blood, but I had not noticed it."

SWEPT GERMANS INTO THE RAVINE

French Counterattacks to Win Plateau Proved Resistless.

Special Cable to THE NEW YORK TIMES.

PARIS, Feb. 28.—The heart of the defense of Verdun on Friday morning still lay on the knot of hills between Beaumont and Louvemont.

In the afternoon under a heavy snowfall and before a series of mass attacks, repeated with a violence which French officers declare to be without precedent, the advanced French lines were drawn back to the broad slopes of Côte du Poivre, Hill 378 and Hill 347, the right of which is covered by the Bois de la Vauche.

Here the further waves of assault were successfully repulsed, but in the course of Saturday the French right had to be further withdrawn, Hill 378 and Vauche Hill being abandoned in favor of the higher and broader position of Douaumont, immediately to the south.

The line then lay strong and level from Talou Ridge, (Côte de Talou,) behind Champneuville, due eastward over the crest of Côte du Poivre to Douaumont Plateau. It had been withdrawn rather less than four miles in the course of six days' fighting of unexampled severity.

The Germans are no nearer breaking the French Army today than they were a week ago, but because the economizing of effectives is a French military principle, never more respected than under General Joffre, and because it is evident common sense in a grand action to fight on your strongest ground, they have won four miles of French salient by sacrifices which, when they are known, will send a shiver of horror through the German nation.

The abandonment of the French segment lying beyond the hills in the flats of the Woevre is rather different. The French Staff decided upon the movement on Friday night without any special pressure from the Germans. It is not difficult to one who knows the region to divine their motives. Always marshy in Winter, the clay on the plain would be like a sponge under Friday's sheet of snow. Moreover, the trenches here facing eastward would be under a rear and flank fire from the new German positions on the hills, while if only the northern portion on the crescent were given up the remainder would be a protrusion difficult to defend. Hence, doubtless, the withdrawal to the foot of the hills. So far from being forced, it was fully twelve hours before the German watchers discovered that the positions had been evacuated.

Throughout Saturday the combat continued with undiminished intensity between Champneuville and Douaumont, and even with increased desperation on the right. I well remember the ground about Fort de Douaumont. When General Sarrail laid down the present scheme of defense the old fort, with its stone glacis, moat, and bridge, was dismantled. The ridge was seamed with intrenchments, which have since been multiplied, and the slopes spread with horrible networks of barbed wire at every critical point.

The momentary capture of such a position is far from being an altogether discouraging piece of news for the Allies. The recapture of the position proves, if that were needed, that the French poilus at the end of nine days of mortal trial are as strong as any Brandenburgers the Kaiser can hurl at them.

The ways of approach to Douaumont are narrow, being limited to a defile between Hill 378 and the Vauche wood, with a few hill tracks coming over the spur of the Louvemont hills on the northwest.

The Germans were swept back into these approaches by the French assault of Saturday afternoon, and the plateau, thus cleared, is now, it is believed, securely held.

These events, it is needless to say, are being followed with breathless interest. There is, of course, anxiety, both private and public, but no failing of the confidence that has borne the republic through so many sufferings and will yet, it is believed, carry it through victory to a stable peace.

GERMANS PAY TRIBUTE TO VERDUN DEFENSES

But Say They Have Been Proved Unable to Withstand Heavy Artillery.

AMSTERDAM, Tuesday Feb. 29, (via London.)—Accounts of the fighting at Verdun in German newspapers received here pay high tribute to the cunning of the defense works constructed by the French, explaining that prolonged use of the heaviest German artillery was necessary before the German infantry could come into the open.

Several of the correspondents dwell upon the comparative smallness of the German losses. Accounts of the fall of Douaumont lay emphasis on it as further proof of the inefficiency of forts against heavy artillery.

FIGHTING HAND TO HAND

Crucial Struggle Going On in the Centre of Battle Front.

FRENCH WIN BACK REDOUBT

And Still Hold Village Before Fort in Spite of Terrific German Attacks.

GERMAN RIGHT PRESSES ON

Teuton Forces in the Champagne, by a Sudden Stroke, Win a Mile of Trenches.

PARIS, Feb. 28.—Strong attacks are being pressed by the Germans to the north of Verdun today, but according to the official communications issued by the War Office the French lines are holding firm.

Counterattacks are being made by the French in the region around Fort Douaumont, and the Germans are said to have been driven out of a redoubt, west of the main works, in a hand-to-hand encounter.

The fortress itself apparently is still held by the Germans, but is "closely encircled" according to the War Office. In the village of Douaumont, a few hundred yards from the fort, there was a furious struggle last night, but the War Office announces that German attempts to capture the village resulted in failure.

Artillery fire continues with great intensity here, but on the west of the Meuse there has been a slackening of the bombardment.

An extension of the German offensive along the front to the east and southeast is indicated by the official bulletins. The afternoon statement reports a futile German attack against Manheulles, ten miles southeast of Verdun, which apparently indicates a German advance in that quarter. The night report chronicles two attacks on Fresnes in the same region. Both are said to have been failures.

Outside of the vitally important struggle at Verdun the most noteworthy feature of the official reports is the admission of loss of ground in Champagne. Here the Germans were able to occupy outer French trenches and also a supporting trench.

Fighting Hand to Hand.

The night bulletin of the War Office is as follows:

In the Argonne our heavy batteries and field guns shelled the roads of access of the enemy, particularly in the region of the Cheppy wood. This morning at Hill 285 we exploded a mine, the crater of which we occupied.

In the region to the north of Verdun artillery activity on both sides is still very spirited, except in the sector to the west of the Meuse, where an abatement of the enemy bombardment is reported.

The Germans during the course of the day attempted several partial attacks, which were driven back by our fire and our counterattack.

To the west of Fort Douaumont particularly our troops have engaged in hand-to-hand encounters with the adversary, who was ejected from a small redoubt, where he had succeeded in installing himself.

In the Woevre two attacks against Fresnes completely failed.

In Lorraine our artillery has displayed marked activity in the sectors of Reillon, Domebre, and Badonviller.

The afternoon bulletin of the French War Office reads:

In Belgium our batteries have bombarded German organizations located opposite Steenstrate.

In Champagne, in the region of the Navarin Farm, to the north of Souain, the enemy was successful by a surprise attack in occupying certain trenches of our advance line; they also took a supporting trench.

In the region to the north of Verdun the bombardment has continued with intensity, particularly in the central sectors and on our right. There has been no further attack on the Côte du Poivre.

Furious Assaults on Douaumont.

Yesterday evening German forces made several attempts to occupy the village of Douaumont. Their efforts were broken by the resistance of our troops, who withstood the most furious assaults.

There is no change in the situation at the Fort of Douaumont, which still remains closely encircled.

The fighting is less spirited on the plateaus to the north of the village of Vaux.

In the Woevre district the enemy yesterday evening and last night assumed an attitude of greater activity. The railroad station at Eix, captured and recaptured several times by the attacks and counterattacks of the two opposing forces, now remains in our possession.

All the attacks against Hill No. 255 to the southeast of Eix, were futile, failing to dislodge our troops.

Further to the south a German attack against Manheulles resulted in complete failure. Our artillery is combat-

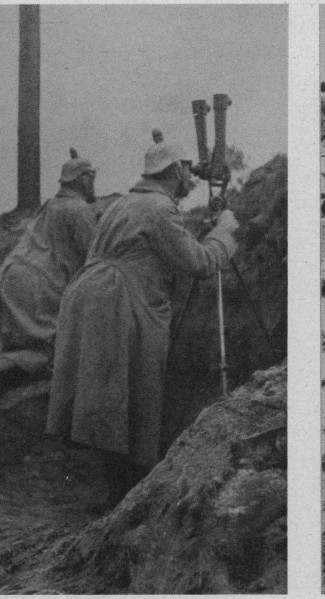

German artillery observers.

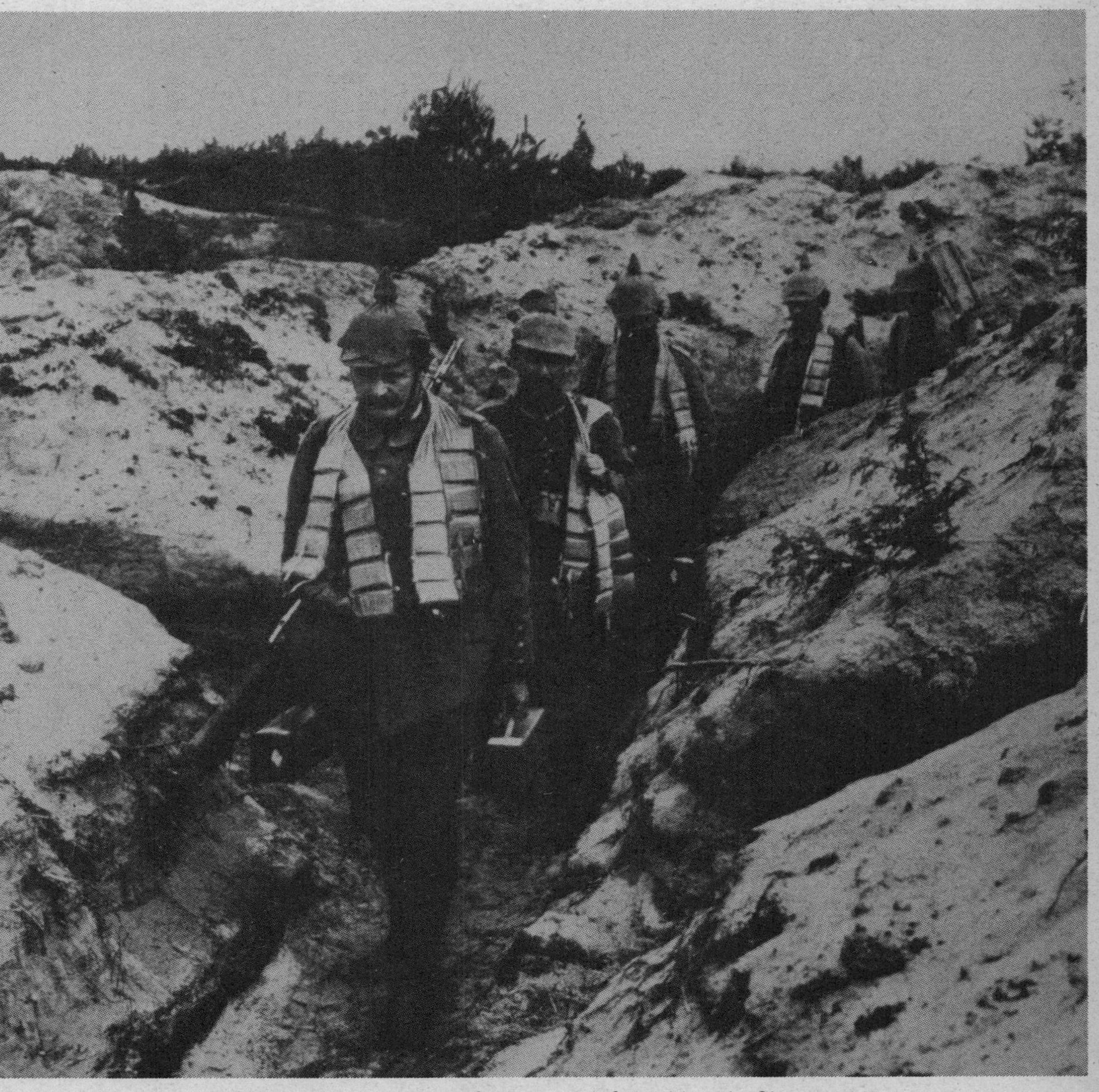

German soldiers carrying a fresh supply of munitions in Champagne.

"All the News That's Fit to Print."

The New York Times.

THE WEATHER
Partly cloudy Thursday and Friday; rising temperature; moderate variable winds.
For full weather report see Page 23.

VOL. LXV...NO. 21,271. ... NEW YORK, THURSDAY, APRIL 20, 1916.—TWENTY-FOUR PAGES. ONE CENT In Greater New York, Jersey City and Newark. | Elsewhere, TWO CENTS.

PRESIDENT ADDRESSES CONGRESS AND NOTIFIES GERMANY THAT SUBMARINE WARFARE ON MERCHANTMEN MUST STOP OR WE SHALL BE COMPELLED TO SEVER RELATIONS WITH HER

BERNSTORFF ADVISES BERLIN

That We Mean What We Say and that Something Be Done Quickly.

HE SUGGESTS A NEW PLAN

Urges a Declaration as Broad as That Made to Cover Mediterranean Operations.

BERLIN PRESS IN THE DARK

Still Urging That Germany Cannot Yield or Compromise on the U-Boat War.

WASHINGTON, April 19.—Count von Bernstorff, the German Ambassador, sent to Berlin tonight a long dispatch, interpreting the situation in Washington and making certain recommendations. He is understood to have advised his Government that he believed the United States meant just what it said in its submarine note and that something would have to be done quickly if friendly relations were to continue.

The Ambassador himself, having read the address of the President and the note, said:

"I can make no comment either upon the address or upon the communication which has been sent to my Government."

He was authoritatively described, however, as having advised the Berlin Foreign Office in the message sent tonight that he believed at least some such declaration as that made regarding the conduct of submarine warfare in the Mediterranean Sea should be issued immediately to cover all submarine operations.

The Mediterranean declaration was handed to Secretary Lansing on Jan. 7. It contained assurances, much broader in their scope than those given to cover the activities of submarines in the war zone around the British Isles, where Germany has contended from the first that she was engaged in a campaign of retaliation for the British blockade.

The assurances were to the effect that only a cruiser warfare would be conducted against enemy merchant shipping, and that noncombatant ships of every character, freight as well as passenger carrying, would receive proper warning and have safety for their passengers and crews. The assurances, which have been given for the war zone around the British Isles, covered only "liners."

The declaration of Jan. 7 also promised that German submarine commanders who failed to obey the assurances given would be punished and that reparation would be made for death or injury to American citizens. German commanders operating in the Mediterranean, it was stated in the declaration, which was issued after the steamship Persia had gone down, had particular instructions to exclude such measures of reprisal as were applied in the war zone around the British Isles.

It is expected that Count von Bernstorff will confer with Secretary Lansing tomorrow. The Secretary informed him today that he was ready to discuss the matter at his convenience. Since the inception of the present situation Count von Bernstorff has made two attempts to discuss the situation with the Secretary. On each occasion he was informed, however, that he would have an opportunity later. The time of the proposed conference had not been definitely fixed tonight.

While the Ambassador tonight appeared more perturbed than at any time since the beginning of the submarine controversy, he was said to feel that his Government would go to every possible length to prevent the severance of diplomatic relations.

Persons in close touch with affairs at the Embassy quoted him as saying:

"I believe that some way will be found satisfactorily to meet the position of the United States."

NO INKLING YET IN BERLIN.

German Papers Know, However, von Jagow's Reply Is Unsatisfactory.

From a Staff Correspondent.
Special Cable to THE NEW YORK TIMES.

BERLIN, April 19.—Although it is known to a limited circle here that President Wilson was to address Congress today on the submarine question, nothing of what is contained in the address has yet arrived as this dispatch is sent.

Commenting on the general situation, the Frankfurter Zeitung says:

"Against all the expectations in Germany, the last von Jagow note did little to clear up the pending conflicts. The positive statement of the German Admiralty that the Sussex was not attacked from the German side ended the case for us, but the Americans are not satisfied with the explanation.

"We may remark in passing that the excitement in a few German papers over 'the inquisition' which the American Government is instituting into the activities of the German submarines appears

Continued on Page 2.

President Wilson's Address to Congress

Spoken before both Houses, in joint session, at Washington, April 19, 1916.

Gentlemen of the Congress:

A situation has arisen in the foreign relations of the country of which it is my plain duty to inform you very frankly.

It will be recalled that in February, 1915, the Imperial German Government announced its intention to treat the waters surrounding Great Britain and Ireland as embraced within the seat of war, and to destroy all merchant ships owned by its enemies that might be found within any part of that portion of the high seas, and that it warned all vessels, of neutral as well as of belligerent ownership, to keep out of the waters it had thus proscribed, or else enter them at their peril. The Government of the United States earnestly protested. It took the position that such a policy could not be pursued without the practical certainty of gross and palpable violations of the law of nations, particularly if submarine craft were to be employed as its instruments, inasmuch as the rules prescribed by that law, rules founded upon principles of humanity and established for the protection of the lives of noncombatants at sea, could not in the nature of the case be observed by such vessels. It based its protest on the ground that persons of neutral nationality and vessels of neutral ownership would be exposed to extreme and intolerable risks, and that no right to close any part of the high seas against their use or to expose them to such risks could lawfully be asserted by any belligerent Government. The law of nations in these matters, upon which the Government of the United States based its protest, is not of recent origin or founded upon merely arbitrary principles set up by convention. It is based, on the contrary, upon manifest and imperative principles of humanity, and has long been established with the approval and by the express assent of all civilized nations.

Notwithstanding the earnest protest of our Government, the Imperial German Government at once proceeded to carry out the policy it had announced. It expressed the hope that the dangers involved, at any rate the dangers to neutral vessels, would be reduced to a minimum by the instructions which it had issued to its submarine commanders, and assured the Government of the United States that it would take every possible precaution both to respect the rights of neutrals and to safeguard the lives of noncombatants.

What has actually happened in the year which has since elapsed has shown that those hopes were not justified, those assurances insusceptible of being fulfilled. In pursuance of the policy of submarine warfare against the commerce of its adversaries, thus announced and entered upon by the Imperial German Government, despite the solemn protest of this Government, the commanders of German undersea vessels have attacked merchant ships with greater and greater activity, not only upon the high seas surrounding Great Britain and Ireland but wherever they could encounter them, in a way that has grown more and more ruthless, more and more indiscriminate as the months have gone by, less and less observant of restraints of any kind, and have delivered their attacks without compunction against vessels of every nationality and bound upon every sort of errand. Vessels of neutral ownership, even vessels of neutral ownership bound from neutral port to neutral port, have been destroyed along with vessels of belligerent ownership in constantly increasing numbers. Sometimes the merchantman attacked has been warned and summoned to surrender before being fired on or torpedoed; sometimes passengers or crews have been vouchsafed the poor security of being allowed to take to the ship's boats before she was sent to the bottom. But again and again no warning has been given, no escape even to the ship's boats allowed to those on board. What this Government foresaw must happen has happened. Tragedy has followed tragedy on the seas in such fashion, with such attendant circumstances, as to make it grossly evident that warfare of such a sort, if warfare it be, cannot be carried on without the most palpable violation of the dictates alike of right and of humanity. Whatever the disposition and intention of the Imperial German Government, it has manifestly proved impossible for it to keep such methods of attack upon the commerce of its enemies within the bounds set by either the reason or the heart of mankind.

In February of the present year the Imperial German Government informed this Government and the other neutral Governments of the world that it had reason to believe that the Government of Great Britain had armed all merchant vessels of British ownership and had given them secret orders to attack any submarine of the enemy they might encounter upon the seas, and that the Imperial German Government felt justified in the circumstances in treating all armed merchantmen of belligerent ownership as auxiliary vessels of war, which it would have the right to destroy without warning. The law of nations has long recognized the right of merchantmen to carry arms for protection and to use them to repel attack, though to use them in such circumstances, at their own risks; but the Imperial German Government claimed the right to set these understandings aside in circumstances which it deemed extraordinary. Even the terms in which it announced its purpose thus still further to relax the restraints it had previously professed its willingness and desire to put upon the operations of its submarines carried the plain implication that at least vessels which were not armed would still be exempt from destruction without warning and that personal safety would be accorded their passengers and crews; but, even that limitation, if it was ever practicable to observe it, has in fact constituted no check at all upon the destruction of ships of every sort.

Again and again the Imperial German Government has given this Government its solemn assurances that at least passenger ships would not be thus dealt with, and yet it has again and again permitted its undersea commanders to disregard those assurances with entire immunity. Great liners like the Lusitania and the Arabic, and mere ferryboats like the Sussex, have been attacked without a moment's warning, sometimes before they had even become aware that they were in the presence of an armed vessel of the enemy, and the lives of noncombatants, passengers and crew, have been sacrificed wholesale in a manner which the Government of the United States cannot but regard as wanton and without the slightest color of justification. No limit of any kind has, in fact, been set to the indiscriminate pursuit and destruction of merchantmen of all kinds and nationalities within the waters, constantly extending in area, where these operations have been carried on; and the roll of Americans who have lost their lives on ships thus attacked and destroyed has grown month by month, until the ominous toll has mounted into the hundreds.

One of the latest and most shocking instances of this method of warfare was that of the destruction of the French cross-Channel steamer Sussex. It must stand forth, as the sinking of the steamer Lusitania did, as so singularly tragical and unjustifiable as to constitute a truly terrible example of the inhumanity of submarine warfare as the commanders of German vessels have for the past twelve months been conducting it. If this instance stood alone some explanation, some disavowal by the German Government, some evidence of criminal mistake or willful disobedience on the part of the commander of the vessel that fired the torpedo might be sought or entertained, but unhappily it does not stand alone. Recent events make the conclusion inevitable that it is only one instance, even though it be one of the most extreme and distressing instances, of the spirit and method of warfare which the Imperial German Government has mistakenly adopted and which from the first exposed that Government to the reproach of thrusting all neutral rights aside in pursuit of its immediate objects.

The Government of the United States has been very patient. At every stage of this distressing experience of tragedy after tragedy in which its own citizens were involved it has sought to be restrained from any extreme course of action or of protest by a thoughtful consideration of the extraordinary circumstances of this unprecedented war; and actuated in all that it said or did by the sentiments of genuine friendship which the people of the United States have always entertained and continue to entertain toward the German nation. It has of course accepted the successive explanations and assurances of the Imperial German Government as given in entire sincerity and good faith and has hoped, even against hope, that it would prove to be possible for the German Government so to order and control the acts of its naval commanders as to square its policy with the principles of humanity as embodied in the law of nations. It has been willing to wait until the significance of the facts became absolutely unmistakable and susceptible of but one interpretation.

That point has now unhappily been reached. The facts are susceptible of but one interpretation The Imperial German Government has been unable to put any limits or restraints upon its warfare against either freight or passenger ships. It has therefore become painfully evident that the position which this Government took at the very outset is inevitable, namely, that the use of submarines for the destruction of an enemy's commerce is of necessity, because of the very character of the vessels employed and the very methods of attack which their employment of course involves, incompatible with the principles of humanity, the long-established and incontrovertible rights of neutrals, and the sacred immunities of noncombatants.

I have deemed it my duty, therefore, to say to the Imperial German Government that if it is still its purpose to prosecute relentless and indiscriminate warfare against vessels of commerce by the use of submarines, notwithstanding the now demonstrated impossibility of conducting that warfare in accordance with what the Government of the United States must consider the sacred and indisputable rules of international law and the universally recognized dictates of humanity, the Government of the United States is at last forced to the conclusion that there is but one course it can pursue and that unless the Imperial German Government should now immediately declare and effect an abandonment of its present methods of warfare against passenger and freight carrying vessels, this Government can have no choice but to sever diplomatic relations with the Government of the German Empire altogether.

This decision I have arrived at with the keenest regret; the possibility of the action contemplated I am sure all thoughtful Americans will look forward to with unaffected reluctance. But we cannot forget that we are in some sort and by the force of circumstances the responsible spokesmen of the rights of humanity, and that we cannot remain silent while those rights seem in process of being swept utterly away in the maelstrom of this terrible war. We owe it to a due regard for our own rights as a nation, to our sense of duty as a representative of the rights of neutrals the world over, and to a just conception of the rights of mankind to take this stand now with the utmost solemnity and firmness.

I have taken it, and taken it in the confidence that it will meet with your approval and support. All sober-minded men must unite in hoping that the Imperial German Government, which has in other circumstances stood as the champion of all that we are now contending for in the interest of humanity, may recognize the justice of our demands and meet them in the spirit in which they are made.

Text of the American Note to Germany

DEPARTMENT OF STATE
WASHINGTON, APRIL 18, 1916

The Secretary of State to Ambassador Gerard:

You are instructed to deliver to the Secretary of Foreign Affairs a communication reading as follows:

I did not fail to transmit immediately, by telegraph, to my Government Your Excellency's note of the 10th instant in regard to certain attacks by German submarines, and particularly in regard to the disastrous explosion which on March 24, last, wrecked the French steamship Sussex in the English Channel. I have now the honor to deliver, under instructions from my Government, the following reply to Your Excellency:

Information now in the possession of the Government of the United States fully establishes the facts in the case of the Sussex, and the inferences which my Government has drawn from that information it regards as confirmed by the circumstances set forth in Your Excellency's note of the 10th instant. On the 24th of March, 1916, at about 2:50 o'clock in the afternoon, the unarmed steamer Sussex, with 325 or more passengers on board, among whom were a number of American citizens, was torpedoed while crossing from Folkestone to Dieppe. The Sussex had never been armed; was a vessel known to be habitually used only for the conveyance of passengers across the English Channel; and was not following the route taken by troopships or supply ships. About eighty of her passengers, noncombatants of all ages and sexes, including citizens of the United States, were killed or injured.

A careful, detailed and scrupulously impartial investigation by naval and military officers of the United States has conclusively established the fact that the Sussex was torpedoed without warning or summons to surrender, and that the torpedo by which she was struck was of German manufacture. In the view of the Government of the United States these facts from the first made the conclusion that the torpedo was fired by a German submarine unavoidable. It now considers that conclusion substantiated by the statements of your Excellency's note. A full statement of the facts upon which the Government of the United States has based its conclusion is inclosed.

The Government of the United States, after having given careful consideration to the note of the Imperial Government of the 10th of April, regrets to state that the impression made upon it by the statements and proposals contained in that note is that the Imperial Government has failed to appreciate the gravity of the situation which has resulted, not alone from the attack on the Sussex, but from the whole method and character of submarine warfare as disclosed by the unrestrained practice of the commanders of German undersea craft during the past twelvemonth and more in the indiscriminate destruction of merchant vessels of all sorts, nationalities, and destinations. If the sinking of the Sussex had been an isolated case the Government of the United States might find it possible to hope that the officer who was responsible for that act had willfully violated his orders or had been criminally negligent in taking none of the precautions they prescribed, and that the ends of justice might be satisfied by imposing upon him an adequate punishment, coupled with a formal disavowal of the act and payment of a suitable indemnity by the Imperial Government. But, though the attack upon the Sussex was manifestly indefensible and caused a loss of life so tragical as to make it stand forth as one of the most terrible examples of the inhumanity of submarine warfare as the commanders of German vessels are conducting it, it unhappily does not stand alone.

On the contrary, the Government of the United States is forced by recent events to conclude that it is only one instance, even though one of the most extreme and most distressing instances, of the deliberate method and spirit of indiscriminate destruction of merchant vessels of all sorts, nationalities, and destinations which have become more and more unmistakable as the activity of German undersea vessels of war has in recent months been quickened and extended.

The Imperial Government will recall that when, in February, 1915, it announced its intention of treating the waters surrounding Great Britain and Ireland as embraced within the seat of war and of destroying all merchant ships owned by its enemies that might be found within that zone of danger, and warned all vessels, neutral as well as belligerent, to keep out of the waters thus proscribed or to enter them at their peril, the Government of the United States earnestly protested. It took the position that such a policy could not be pursued without constant gross and palpable violations of the accepted law of nations, particularly if submarine craft were to be employed as its instruments, inasmuch as the rules prescribed by that law, rules founded on the principles of humanity and established for the protection of the lives of noncombatants at sea, could not in the nature of the case be observed by such vessels. It based its protest on the ground that persons of neutral nationality and vessels of neutral ownership would be exposed to extreme and intolerable risks, and that no right to close any part of the high seas could lawfully be asserted by the Imperial Government in the circumstances then existing. The law of nations in these matters, upon which the Government of the United States based that protest, is not of recent origin or founded upon merely arbitrary principles set up by convention. It is based, on the contrary, upon manifest principles of humanity and has long been established with the approval and by the express assent of all civilized nations.

The Imperial Government, notwithstanding, persisted in carrying out the policy announced, expressing the hope that the dangers involved, at any rate to neutral vessels, would be reduced to a minimum by the instructions which it had issued to the commanders of its submarines, and assuring the Government of the United States that it would take every possible precaution both to respect the rights of neutrals and to safeguard the lives of noncombatants.

In pursuance of this policy of submarine warfare against the commerce of its adversaries, thus announced and thus entered upon in despite of the solemn protest of the Government of the United States, the commanders of the Imperial Government's undersea vessels have carried on practices of such ruthless destruction, which have made it more and more evident as the months have gone by that the Imperial Government has found it impracticable to put any such restraints upon them as it had hoped and promised to put. Again and again the Imperial Government has given its solemn assurances to the Government of the United States that at least passenger ships would not be thus dealt with, and yet it has repeatedly permitted its undersea commanders to disregard those assurances with entire impunity. As recently as February last it gave notice that it would regard all armed merchantmen owned by its enemies as part of the armed naval forces of its adversaries and deal with them as with men-of-war, thus, at least by implication, pledging itself to give warning to vessels which were not armed and to accord security of life to their passengers and crews; but even this limitation their submarine commanders have recklessly ignored.

Vessels of neutral ownership, even vessels of neutral ownership bound from neutral port to neutral port, have been destroyed, along with vessels of belligerent ownership, in constantly increasing numbers. Sometimes the merchantmen attacked have been warned and summoned to surrender before being fired on or torpedoed; sometimes their passengers and crews have been vouchsafed the poor security of being allowed to take to the ship's boats before the ship was sent to the bottom. But again and again no warning has been given, no escape even to the ship's boats allowed to those on board. Great liners like the Lusitania and Arabic, and mere passenger boats like the Sussex, have been attacked without a moment's warning, often before they have even become aware that they were in the presence of an armed ship of the enemy, and the lives of noncombatants, passengers and crew, have been destroyed wholesale and in a manner which the Government of the United States cannot but regard as wanton and without the slightest color of justification. No limit of any kind has, in fact, been set to their indiscriminate pursuit and destruction of merchantmen of all kinds and nationalities within the waters which the Imperial Government has chosen to designate as lying within the seat of war. The roll of Americans who have lost their lives upon ships thus attacked and destroyed has grown month by month until the ominous toll has mounted into the hundreds.

The Government of the United States has been very patient. At every stage of this distressing experience of tragedy after tragedy it has sought to be governed by the most thoughtful consideration of the extraordinary circumstances of an unprecedented war and to be guided by sentiments of very genuine friendship for the people and Government of Germany. It has accepted the successive explanations and assurances of the Imperial Government as, of course, given in entire sincerity and good faith, and has hoped, even against hope, that it would prove to be possible for the Imperial Government so to order and control the acts of its naval commanders as to square its policy with the recognized principles of humanity as embodied in the law of nations. It has made every allowance for unprecedented conditions and has been willing to wait until the facts became unmistakable and were susceptible of only one interpretation.

It now owes it to a just regard for its own rights to say to the Imperial Government that that time has come. It has become painfully evident to it that the position which it took at the very outset is inevitable, namely, the use of submarines for the destruction of an enemy's commerce, is, of necessity, because of the very character of the vessels employed and the very methods of attack which their employment of course involves, utterly incompatible with the principles of humanity, the long-established and incontrovertible rights of neutrals, and the sacred immunities of noncombatants.

If it is still the purpose of the Imperial Government to prosecute relentless and indiscriminate warfare against vessels of commerce by the use of submarines, without regard to what the Government of the United States must consider the sacred and indisputable rules of international law and the universally recognized dictates of humanity, the Government of the United States is at last forced to the conclusion that there is but one course it can pursue. Unless the Imperial Government should now immediately declare and effect an abandonment of its present methods of submarine warfare against passenger and freight-carrying vessels, the Government of the United States can have no choice but to sever diplomatic relations with the German Empire altogether. This action the Government of the United States contemplates with the greatest reluctance, but feels constrained to take in behalf of humanity and the rights of neutral nations.

LANSING.

The appendix, "A statement of facts" regarding the torpedoing of the Sussex by a German submarine in violation of Germany's pledge, is printed in full on Page 2 of THE TIMES.

VIEWED AS AN ULTIMATUM

Wilson Says He Is at Last Forced to Conclusion There Is But One Course.

SPEAKS FOR ALL NEUTRALS

Declares We Are the Responsible Spokesmen of the Rights of Humanity.

SOLEMN SCENE IN CONGRESS

President Delivers Message in Grave and Measured Tones—Cheers Greet Him at Close.

Special to The New York Times.

WASHINGTON, April 19. Before a joint session of the Senate and House, President Wilson this afternoon, speaking in behalf of the rights of the United States and its citizens and the rights of humanity in general, announced that he had notified Germany that "unless the Imperial Government should now immediately declare and effect an abandonment of its present methods of submarine warfare against passenger and freight-carrying vessels, the Government of the United States can have no choice but to sever diplomatic relations with the German Empire altogether."

It was explained later at the State Department that immediately did not mean as late as two weeks hence, and that an answer to the American note, which was forwarded yesterday, was expected before Sunday.

The President's address to Congress and his note to Germany are paraphrases of each other, whole passages being identical. The President's quiet manner before Congress was made ominous by the known fact that his indictment of Germany had been communicated to the German Government. For in spite of the forced reserve of the President's manner and his expressions in both documents, they constitute the severest arraignment of a great power disclosed by the history of recent years.

The feeling of both the executive and legislative branches of the Government is that the severance of relations with Germany is now inevitable, although the hope and apparently the belief, at both ends of the avenue is that war will not follow. The note to Germany demands the immediate abandonment of the "present methods of conducting submarine warfare." But throughout the note and the President's address runs the inference, bluntly stated at the close of the note, that the use of submarines for destroying commerce is "of necessity utterly incompatible with the principles of humanity, the long-established and incontrovertible rights of neutrals, and the sacred immunities of noncombatants."

Must Stop Submarines Altogether.

This general statement and the demand upon the German Government must be construed together. It was explained by the State Department this afternoon that Germany must abandon not only her present methods of submarine warfare, but that warfare itself, as now directed against commerce, before any discussion of the possible use of submarines against commerce would be permitted. There are cases in which a submarine may properly and effectively be used against merchantmen, as where a merchantman is overhauled in fair weather near shore, but after a year of German failure to conduct submarine warfare within those limitations, the United States is determined that the whole submarine warfare against commerce be stopped in sign of good faith, before discussions are resumed.

It is over this point that the break with Germany is expected to come. Germany is expected to repeat what she said many times, that this warfare will be continued according to international law, but that she cannot surrender the arm altogether. This ordinarily, if believed, would be satisfactory to the United States. But, after a year of violations of such assurances, the American Government is determined that the warfare shall end altogether before it enters into a discussion of the terms under which it may be permitted. Germany is not expected to agree to this, and the sinking of a single merchantman by a German submarine in the meantime would, in all probability, be taken as the final signal for a rupture.

Guilty of Bad Faith.

Through both note and speech runs the plain implication, and in one place is the plain statement, that Germany has been guilty not only of atrocities on, of bad faith toward the United States. In the speech the German allegations regarding the Sussex are utterly ignored with the direct statement that the ship, unarmed and unwarned, was torpedoed by a German submarine. In the note the American Government says that the German allegations merely confirm other unquestionable evidence that the ship

"All the News That's Fit to Print."

The New York Times.

THE WEATHER
Local showers today; Sunday fair; strong south, shifting to west, winds.
For full weather report see Page 21.

VOL. LXV...NO. 21,315. NEW YORK, SATURDAY, JUNE 3, 1916.—TWENTY-TWO PAGES. ONE CENT In Greater New York, Jersey City and Newark. | Elsewhere, TWO CENTS.

25 WARSHIPS WITH 7500 MEN LOST IN BATTLE OFF DENMARK; BRITISH FLEET HAS 14 VESSELS SUNK AND THE GERMANS 11; GERMANY ACCLAIMS IT A VICTORY, BUT ENGLAND IS CALM

MAY ALTER OUR NAVY PLAN

Loss of Battle Cruisers Interests Experts at Washington.

FIVE IN THE NEW PROGRAM

American Officers Have Been Strong Defenders of This Type of Ship.

PEARY'S VIEW UNCHANGED

Speculation at Capital as to the Effect Battle Will Have on Peace Talk.

Special to The New York Times.

WASHINGTON, June 2.—Keenest interest was shown in naval, diplomatic, and official circles generally tonight here over the result of the battle in the North Sea between the British and German fleets. Among naval officers particularly the story of the engagement is eagerly looked for, in view of the fact that three modern battle-cruisers are admitted to have been lost by the British.

Already there is speculation as to the effect the result of the sea fight will have on the new building program of the United States Navy. The Naval Appropriation bill was passed by the House of Representatives today. It now goes to the Senate for consideration. The bill authorizes the construction of no battleships, but does call for the building of five battle cruisers, each costing approximately $20,000,000.

There are now no battle cruisers in the United States Navy, but naval strategists and experts are strongly in favor of the introduction of this type of vessel. They have been insisting that up to date the greatest naval lesson taught by the war in Europe was the value of the battle cruisers with which the British won the fight off the Falkland Islands. Unofficial accounts received here today are regarded by naval experts as too meagre and indefinite to show anything one way or the other regarding the value of the battle cruisers in the battle just fought.

Navy Officers Silent.

While it appears to be almost the universal opinion in expert circles here that the British navy has sustained a severe defeat that will seriously affect its prestige and spirit, the information thus far received regarding the battle does not give enough facts and circumstances to enable experts to form any effective opinion as to the value of battle cruisers, and whether the destruction of the vessels is to be regarded as a warning against th construction of vessels of this type for the United States navy. The experts want to know whether these vessels were sunk by gun-fire, torpedoes, mines, or Zeppelin attacks; whether they were sunk near or far from the coast, and the exact circumstances of the battle.

So far as facts were covered by press dispatches received here tonight navy officers, unwilling to talk for publication, are not inclined to the opinion that the loss of the British battle cruisers should be regarded as upsetting their arguments in favor of the construction of these vessels, which are intended primarily for service on the high seas where battles can be fought between vessels of extended radius of action.

Peary's Views Unchanged.

Rear Admiral Robert E. Peary, U. S. N., retired, when asked for his opinion regarding battle cruisers, prepared the following statement for THE NEW YORK TIMES:

"Replying to THE TIMES request, the reports of the naval battle in the Skagerack in no way change my conviction, already expressed in recent communications to THE TIMES, that the battle cruiser is the best naval type for the United States. Contracted waters, such as this battle occurred in, are especially advantageous for mines, torpedo boats, and submarines, and particularly disadvantageous for the large, swift battle cruisers.

"The instant lesson of the battle is that we should lose no time in naval preparedness. Every ship that is added to our building program this year may be worth two added next year."

Politically and diplomatically the result of the sea fight is destined to have important results. There is speculation here as to whether it will accentuate the movement in favor of peace, and also as to its effect on neutral public opinion.

The State Department received no report on the battle tonight and the Navy Department insisted that it had not heard from its naval attaché's office in London on the subject. It was not known in Government circles whether an American naval attaché was on board one of the battle cruisers of the British force during the battle, although there was such a rumor.

The British Embassy had no comment to make on the battle. It received tonight a dispatch from the British Foreign Office giving the same information as that contained in the Admiralty announcement issued in London today and cabled to this country in press dispatches. The Embassy was without information as to the personnel of officers in command of the British vessels.

The German Embassy here is closed. Ambassador von Bernstorff and the Embassy staff are established at Rye.

Estimated Losses of Ships, Men and Money in the Most Destructive of Naval Battles

Loss of life, British, (estimated)	4,800
Loss of life, German, (estimated)	2,000 to 2,750
Number of vessels lost, British	14
Number of vessels lost, German, (estimated)	10 or 11
Tonnage lost, British	115,000
Tonnage lost, German, (estimated)	27,000 to 51,000
Loss in money value, British	$115,000,000
Loss in money value, German	$27,000,000 to $51,000,000

In the destruction of the Russian Admiral Rojestvensky's fleet in the war with Japan, in 1905, twenty-one ships were sunk and 4,000 lives were lost.

Danish Seamen Saw 45 German Ships and 19 British Warcraft in Battle

According to an Eyewitness the Kaiser's Warships Were Retiring Before Foe—Another Account Says Germans Chased Foe First, Then Withdrew as More British Vessels Came Up.

Special Cable to THE NEW YORK TIMES.

COPENHAGEN, June 2, (Dispatch to The London Daily Mail.)—The steamer Naesborg, from Sunderland with coal, arrived today. The officers state that the German fleet in the North Sea battle consisted of forty-five ships of different kinds, among which they noticed several of the largest type.

The British fleet consisted of eleven vessels, which steamed southward at full speed after the German fleet. Later on eight British ships appeared from the north, firing heavily.

Many sailing ships were seen passing through the firing line. The weather was clear and the sea smooth.

The German fleet retired in a southwesterly direction uninterrupted, and heavy firing was heard from both sides until midnight.

A Zeppelin crossed directly over the Naesborg, the crew of which say the concussion of the shell explosions were felt on board their ships as if their legs were being violently beaten with sticks.

LONDON, Saturday, June 3.—The Captain of the steamer Naesborg is quoted in a Copenhagen dispatch as giving this account of the sea fight:

"When the Naesborg was ninety-five miles west of Cape Hanstholm, on the northwest coast of Jutland, a few small British warships appeared, pursued by the German fleet. Suddenly the British warships turned and steamed westward, violently shelled. In a few minutes a large number of British dreadnought cruisers appeared from the north and west.

"The British then began attacking the German ships, which were reinforced by a large number of ships from the south along the west coast of Jutland. A violent fight began. The sky seemed filled with smoke and the sea was in a state of uproar. Shells fell around my steamer, although we were several miles away.

"During the fight the cannonading was so violent that our crew could not stand on deck. We saw several large warships sunk, but I am unable to say whether they were British or German.

"At last the German fleet withdrew southward, pursued by the British, while several more British warships appeared, coming from the westward. The German fleet was divided into two parts, one of which escaped. The fate of the other fleet I do not know."

Another Copenhagen dispatch tells this story, which may be another account from the Naesborg:

"According to the Politiken, a Danish steamer arrived today (Thursday) at Friedrichshaven which had witnessed a battle in the North Sea.

"The steamer reports that yesterday (Wednesday) afternoon, when 120 miles off Hanstholm, it was stopped by two British torpedo boats to have its papers examined.

"At the same moment a large German fleet appeared, and the British warships immediately prepared for action. The German fleet, which approached at full speed, consisted of five large modern dreadnoughts, eight cruisers, and twenty torpedo boats and destroyers.

"Suddenly the Germans began firing, and several hundred shells splashed around the torpedo boats, without, however, hitting them. The British ships went westward, pursued by the German fleet.

"At 5 o'clock the cannonade was renewed, and continued until 9 o'clock in the evening.

"Two Zeppelins were seen going at full speed northward to the scene of the battle."

Fought Fifty Miles from Shore

YMUIDEN, Holland, via London, Saturday, June 3.—A description of the naval battle off Jutland was given today by Captain Thomas Punt of the British trawler John Brown, which was taking soundings in the vicinity. He said:

"The battle began at 4:15 P. M. Wednesday and lasted until 11 o'clock at night. It extended over an area reaching from longitude 56.8, latitude 6.25 to longitude 55.50, latitude 5.50. (These measurements place the scene of the battle about fifty miles due west of the Horn, running northward to the Little Fisher Bank.)

"At 2 o'clock on Wednesday afternoon I saw a great fleet of fifty ships of different kinds, apparently German, cruising from the southeast to the northeast. Two hours later another great fleet, evidently British, appeared suddenly from the northeast and obviously attempted to cut off the retreat of the Germans. The weather was misty, making it difficult to distinguish the outlines of the ships.

"At 4:15 P. M. the first gun shot came from about two miles away. Fifteen minutes later there were more shots, and in a few moments there was constant and heavy firing. Many sailing ships passed through the firing line.

"The British ships did not seem to be of as heavy tonnage as the Germans. They were reinforced by larger vessels, which I observed to come up as it was getting darker. The German fleet then began to retire, and as they were withdrawing I saw two big columns of smoke, evidently some vessels which had been badly hit. The next moment I observed two large vessels, one of either fleet, burning.

"The British fleet pursued the German to longitude 56.40 and latitude 5.50, when it noticed two torpedo destroyers and three submarines dashing toward it at full speed, apparently heralding further reinforcements for the Germans. The British ships then drew off."

VOTE $270,000,000 TO BUILD UP NAVY

House Defeats Minority Report for Larger Program by a Majority of Only Six.

Special to The New York Times.

WASHINGTON, June 2.—Before passing the Naval Appropriation bill today the House came within six votes of adopting the "big navy" program of the Republican members of the Committee on Naval Affairs.

By a vote of 189 to 183 a motion to recommit the bill and include the Republican minority's building plan was defeated. After this final stand by the minority, practically the entire House membership voted for the naval budget on final passage, the vote being 355 to 4. Those voting against it were Browning, New Jersey, and Graham, Pennsylvania, Republicans; Randall, California, Prohibitionist, and London, New York, Socialist.

So close was the vote on the motion to recommit that a recapitulation was ordered before the result was announced.

Continued on Page 5.

MOST COSTLY FIGHT IN NAVAL HISTORY

Tonnage of the Ships and Value of the Material Lost Off Denmark Was Never Equaled.

In tonnage of ships and treasure lost, and possibly in the number of lives lost, when compared with the naval units sunk, the battle at the entrance of the Skagerak, off the coast of Denmark, will be regarded as the greatest sea battle of all time.

Until this engagement the British genuine naval losses, excluding troops sunk on transports, had amounted in round numbers, including war craft of all sorts, to 300,000 tons, 7,000 lives, and $300,000,000 in naval property, and the German 200,000 tons, 4,000 lives, and $250,000,000 in naval property. While the entire loss to the Allies was represented by 375,000 tons, 8,000 lives, and $375,000,000 in naval property, and the Central Empires and Turkey respectively

Continued on Page 2.

BERLIN CLAIMS VICTORY

Reports Sinking Nine Vessels Besides Many Destroyers.

LOST A NEW CRUISER

Weisbaden, Pommern, and Frauenlob the Only Large Vessels Admitted Sunk.

FIGHT LASTED ALL NIGHT

Admiralty Reports Main Portions of High Sea Fleet Safe in Home Ports.

Loss Admitted by Germans

Battleship.
Pommern.
Cruisers.
Wiesbaden.
Frauenlob.
Several torpedo boats.

Berlin Statement of British Loss

Battleships.
Warspite (sunk.)
Marlborough, "hit by torpedo."
Battle Cruisers.
Queen Mary.
Indefatigable.
Cruisers.
Two armored cruisers of Achilles type.
One small cruiser.
Destroyers.
"Flagships" Turbulent, Nestor, and Alcastar.
"Large number of torpedo boat destroyers."
Submarine.
One.

BERLIN, June 2, (via London.)—Germany's high sea fleet met the main part of the British fleet in battle in the northeastern section of the North Sea on May 31.

In the heavy engagement which followed the German fleet, according to a report issued by the German Admiralty, sank the British battleship Warspite, the British battle cruisers Queen Mary and Indefatigable, two armored cruisers, believed to be of the Achilles type, and a large number of warships of smaller tonnage. Several other British battleships are reported to have been damaged, including the battleship Marlborough, which was struck by a torpedo.

The German losses are announced as the battleship Pommern, sunk by a torpedo; the cruiser Wiesbaden, sent to the bottom by gunfire; the protected cruiser Frauenlob, reported missing, and several torpedo boats, which did not return to port.

BERLIN, June 2, (by Wireless to Sayville.)—The German Admiralty announced today that the German high sea fleet on May 31 had encountered a British fighting fleet. The engagement which developed, the Admiralty says, was favorable to the Germans. The battle continued all night.

The German Admiralty announces that the large British battleship Warspite, the battle cruisers Queen Mary and Indefatigable, and two armored cruisers were destroyed.

It is also reported that a small British cruiser, a number of torpedo-boat destroyers, and torpedo boats were sunk.

The German Admiralty statement adds that by observation it was established that a large number of British battleships suffered damage from the fire of the German battleships and the attacks of the torpedo-boat flotilla.

The Admiralty statement also declares that the British battleship Marlborough was hit by a torpedo, this being confirmed by the prisoners rescued. Several of the German ships rescued parts of the crews of the British ships which were sunk, they including, it is said, two men from the Indefatigable, the only survivors from that ship.

Torpedo Sank the Pommern.

On the German side the small cruiser Wiesbaden was sunk by gunfire and the Pommern was sent to the bottom by a torpedo. The fate of the Frauenlob is not known, and some torpedo boats did not return. The German high sea fleet, the statement adds, returned to port on June 1. The text of the German Admiralty report, which is dated June 1, says:

During an enterprise directed to the northward our high sea fleet on May 31 encountered the main part of the English fighting fleet, which was con-

Continued on Page 3.

Official Reports of the Battle in the North Sea Given Out by British and German Naval Officials

The official accounts of the North Sea battle, as issued by the British and German Admiralties, are as follows, the statement given out in Berlin being dated Thursday and those made public in London being dated Friday:

German Admiralty Report.

During an enterprise directed to the northward our high sea fleet on May 31 encountered the main part of the English fighting fleet, which was considerably superior to our forces.

During the afternoon, between Skagerak and Horn Riff, a heavy engagement developed, which was successful to us, and which continued during the whole night.

In this engagement, so far as known up to the present, there were destroyed by us the large battleship Warspite, the battle-cruisers Queen Mary and Indefatigable, two armored cruisers, apparently of the Achilles type; one small cruiser, the new flagships of destroyer squadrons, the Turbulent, Nestor, and Alcaster, a large number of torpedo-boat destroyers, and one submarine.

By observation, which was free and clear of objects, it was stated that a large number of English battleships suffered damage from our ships and the attacks of our torpedo-boat flotilla during the day engagement and throughout the night. Among others, the large battleship Marlborough was hit by a torpedo. This was confirmed by prisoners.

Several of our ships rescued parts of the crews of the sunken English ships, among them being two and the only survivors of the Indefatigable.

On our side the small cruiser Weisbaden, by hostile gunfire during the day engagement, and his Majesty's ship Pommern, during the night, as the result of a torpedo, were sunk.

The fate of his Majesty's ship Frauenlob, which is missing, and of some torpedo boats, which have not returned yet, is unknown.

The high sea fleet returned today (Thursday) into our port.

British Admiralty Reports.

On the afternoon of Wednesday, the 31st of May, a naval engagement took place off the coast of Jutland.

The British ships on which the brunt of the fighting fell were the battle-cruiser fleet and some cruisers and light cruisers, supported by four fast battleships. Among these the losses were heavy.

The German battle-fleet, aided by low visibility, avoided a prolonged action with our main forces. As soon as these appeared on the scene the enemy returned to port, though not before receiving severe damage from our battleships.

The battle-cruisers Queen Mary, Indefatigable, and Invincible, and the cruisers Defence and Black Prince were sunk.

The Warrior was disabled, and after being towed for some time had to be abandoned by her crew.

It is also known that the destroyers Tipperary, Turbulent, Fortune, Sparrowhawk, and Ardent were lost, and six others are not yet accounted for.

No British battleships or light cruisers were sunk.

The enemy's losses were serious. At least one battle cruiser was destroyed and one was severely damaged. One battleship is reported to have been sunk by our destroyers.

During the night attack two light cruisers were disabled and probably sunk.

The exact number of enemy destroyers disposed of during the action cannot be ascertained with any certainty, but must have been large.

Later this further statement was issued:

Since the foregoing communication was issued a further report has been received from the Commander-in-Chief of the Grand Fleet stating that it has now been ascertained that our total losses in destroyers amount to eight boats in all.

The Commander-in-Chief also reports that it is now possible to form a closer estimate of the losses and the damage sustained by the enemy fleet.

One dreadnought battleship of the Kaiser class was blown up in an attack by British destroyers and another dreadnought battleship of the Kaiser class is believed to have been sunk by gunfire. Of three German battle cruisers, two of which are believed were the Derfflinger and the Lützow, one was blown up, another was heavily engaged by our battle fleet and was seen to be disabled and stopping, and the third was observed to be seriously damaged.

One German light cruiser and six German destroyers were sunk, and at least two more German light cruisers were seen to be disabled. Further repeated hits were observed on three other German battleships that were engaged.

Finally, a German submarine was rammed and sunk.

GERMANY HAILS FLEET AS VICTOR

Britain's Sea Supremacy Shattered, Is Verdict of Some Berlin Naval Writers.

NEWS ELECTRIFIES PUBLIC

Battle Is Expected to Have a Far-Reaching Moral Effect—Navy Thanked in Reichstag.

From a Staff Correspondent.
Special Cable to THE NEW YORK TIMES.

BERLIN, June 2.—The reported victory of the German High Sea Fleet in the greatest naval battle of the war has electrified even the Germans, who have long been accustomed to digesting good news soberly. The report even temporarily eclipsed the news of the restrictive meat ordinances in popular interest, which is saying a great deal nowadays. Berlin is flag decked and the school children are to have a holiday.

The satisfaction over the reported crushing defeat administered to the British Grand Fleet is particularly intense, because the dreadnought at last has been engaged in open battle. It is pointed out here that the sinking of the battleship Warspite, the battle cruisers Queen Mary and Indefatigable, and two armored cruisers of the Achilles class, cost the British Navy a loss of more than 100,000 tons, whereas the only big German unit lost, the Pommern, was less than 14,000 tons.

The Reichstag session was the scene of a great patriotic demonstration when President Dr. Kaempf announced "a great naval victory" on opening the day's business. He said: "While further details are still lacking it is obvious that our young navy has achieved a great and beautiful success. To be sure, we, too, have losses to regret, but those of the enemy are many times greater. Above all, it has been demonstrated that our fleet is able to stand against the much stronger English fleet and win a victory for which we owe the heartiest thanks to our whole navy."

All the Reichstag members arose and cheered with the exception of Leader Haase and his colleagues of the extreme Socialist wing. The Socialists were overwhelmed with cries of "Shame!"

In a statement to the Reichstag Rear Admiral Heddinghaus, Director of the Admiralty, gave the particulars of the battle. He said the entire German high sea fleet and the greater part of the English fighting fleet, including

Continued on Page 2.

Kaiser to Inspect Fleet That Fought the British

LONDON, June 2.—Emperor William is expected at Wilhelmshaven tomorrow to inspect the German fleet on its return from the North Sea battle, says the Exchange Telegraph's Amsterdam correspondent quoting a telegram received in Amsterdam from Berlin.

SIX ZEPPELINS JOINED IN THE SEA COMBAT

One Said to Have Been Hit Several Times—Kaiser Urged the German Venture.

LONDON, Saturday, June 3.—Six Zeppelins participated in the naval engagement off the coast of Jutland Wednesday, according to a dispatch from Copenhagen to The Daily Mail.

One of the dirigibles, the L-24, was hit several times and badly damaged, the report says, but she was able to reach the Schleswig coast after a narrow escape. Several of her men were wounded, and all her supplies had to be thrown overboard.

A dispatch from the same source said it is generally stated in Berlin that the activity of the German fleet was due to the energetic demands of Emperor William to his brother, Admiral Prince Henry of Prussia, Commander in Chief of the Navy, and Admiral von Capelle, Minister of the Navy, on the Emperor's visit last week to Wilhelmshaven.

VICE ADMIRAL SCHEER LED THE GERMAN FLEET

New Chief Placed in Permanent Command of High Sea Force Only a Few Days Ago.

From a Staff Correspondent.
Special Cable to THE NEW YORK TIMES.

BERLIN, June 2.—Immediately on hearing the news of the naval battle in the North Sea, Marine Minister von Capelle left Berlin for Wilhelmshaven.

The victor of Skagerak, the Chief of the German High Sea Fleet, is Vice Admiral Reinhard Scheer, who assumed temporary command of the fleet when the late Admiral von Pohl was forced to resign on account of illness.

Vice Admiral Scheer's appointment was made permanent only a few days ago.

Special to The New York Times.

WASHINGTON, June 2.—Vice Admiral Reinhardt Scheer is considered one of the most capable tacticians in the German navy, and is regarded as a man not only of forcefulness, but also of ideas. He was for a long time employed as Director of the General Marine Department at the Admiralty, and has held command in the active service as Chief of Staff of the High Sea Fleet, and as commander of a battle squadron.

LONDON IS EAGER FOR MORE DETAILS

Keen Speculation on the Way Fight Started and the Cause of the Big Losses.

BEATTY POSSIBLY THERE

One Writer Thinks British Ships Were Surprised in Some Important Enterprise.

Special Cable to THE NEW YORK TIMES.

LONDON, Saturday, June 3.—Commenting on the sea fight off Jutland, The Daily Chronicle's naval correspondent says this morning:

"We must assume that some enterprise was in hand by the British fleet.

"Possibly the grand fleet was making a sweep through the North Sea, but of that there is no evidence. More probably there was a desire to test the German position.

"We can hardly suppose that the battle cruiser and other squadrons were intending to enter the Baltic.

"The battle cruiser squadron, which suffered heavily and which the press bureau describes as a fleet, bore the brunt of the fighting with some cruisers. The light cruisers would be the Black Prince and Warrior of the Duke of Edinburgh class and the Defence of the Minotaur class, all three of which have been sunk. They were supporting four fast battleships.

"The German official mentions the Marlborough of the Queen Elizabeth class as having been injured by a torpedo. All these ships were evidently acting in concert.

"The force engaged included battleships of modern class, doubtless dreadnoughts, battle cruisers, other cruisers, light cruisers, destroyers and, according to the German statement, submarines.

"It is no light thing to lose that noble battle cruiser, the Queen Mary, and two other battle cruisers of the Invincible class, the Invincible herself, which was in the Falklands Isles battle, and the Indefatigable.

"We do not know, but it is possible that Sir David Beatty was in command with his flag on the Lion, though that ship is not mentioned. He is an officer of great experience and tried service, but presumably his senior officer would have his flag on one of the battleships.

"We have, happily, according to the official statement, lost no battleship, but six vessels are unaccounted for. Presumably these are destroyers additional to the list of those which are officially stated to have been lost. The Tipperary, which has gone down, was a new flotilla leader of 1,850 tons, and doubtless it was her flotilla that was engaged.

"We do not know by what agency

Continued on Page 2.

FIRST NEWS SHOCKED BRITISH

But Later Bulletin Telling Foe's Loss Was More Assuring.

MOURN SIX BIG SHIPS GONE

Loss of Life Believed to be Heavy, but the Censor Withholds Unofficial Accounts.

FEW FACTS OF FIGHT KNOWN

Combat Began Wednesday Afternoon and Lasted Into Night—Six Zeppelins Took Part.

Loss Admitted by British

Battle Cruisers.
Queen Mary.
Indefatigable.
Invincible.
Cruisers.
Defence.
Black Prince.
Warrior.
Destroyers.
Tipperary.
Turbulent.
Fortune.
Sparrowhawk.
Ardent.
Three others.

London Statement of Foe's Loss

Battleships.
One battleship of Kaiser class blown up.
Another of same class sunk.
Battle Cruisers.
Derfflinger or Lützow, blown up.
Another "disabled."
Another "seriously damaged."
Cruisers.
One "light" cruiser sunk.
Two others disabled.
Destroyers.
Six sunk.
Submarine.
One rammed and sunk.

LONDON, June 2.—Picking its way from its base in the Kiel Canal the German high sea fleet on Wednesday afternoon emerged into the North Sea and off the coast of Jutland, engaged a British fleet throughout the afternoon and night in what probably was the greatest naval battle in the world's history so far as tonnage engaged and tonnage destroyed was concerned.

When the battle ended Great Britain had lost the battle cruisers Queen Mary, Indefatigable, and Invincible, the cruisers Defense, Black Prince, and Warrior, and eight torpedo-boat destroyers, while the German battleship Pommern had been sent to the bottom by a torpedo and the cruiser Wiesbaden sunk by the British gunfire. In addition several German torpedo craft were missing and the small cruiser Frauenlob had last been seen badly listed and was believed to have gone to the bottom. These losses have all been admitted by Great Britain and Germany.

Aside from Great Britain's conceded losses, Germany claims that the British battleship Warspite, sister ship of the Queen Elizabeth, and one of the largest and most powerful ships afloat, had been sunk; that the battleship Marlborough, a vessel of 25,000 tons, had been hit by a torpedo, and a submarine had been destroyed. Great Britain also added to Germany's acknowledged losses with the claim that one dreadnought of the German Kaiser class—vessels of 24,700 tons, and carrying a complement of 1,088 men—had been attacked and destroyed by British torpedo craft; that another battleship of the same class was believed to have been sunk by gunfire; that one battle cruiser had been blown up, and two others damaged, and that a submarine also had been sent to the bottom.

Great Britain's admitted loss in tonnage was 114,810 for the six battle cruisers and cruisers. That of Germany, including the tonnage of the Wiesbaden, supposed to be of the Breslau class, (4,550 tons,) was 20,262. Adding the tonnage of the six destroyers and one submarine which the British say they sank, the figures would approximate 27,000. If, as the British allege, they also sank a dreadnought of the Kaiser class, the total German tonnage destroyed was 51,000.

The tonnage of the capital ships sunk by the Japanese in their fight with the Russians in the battle of Tsushima in May, 1905, aggregated 93,000. Twenty-one Russian craft

"All the News That's Fit to Print."

The New York Times.

THE WEATHER
Showers today and probably Thursday; fresh southeast winds.
For full weather report see Page 23.

VOL. LXV...NO. 21,319. • • • • NEW YORK, WEDNESDAY, JUNE 7, 1916.—TWENTY-FOUR PAGES. ONE CENT In Greater New York, Jersey City and Newark. | Elsewhere, TWO CENTS.

HUGHES MOVEMENT GAINS STRENGTH WITH NO DARK HORSE YET IN SIGHT; DICKERING WITH MOOSE FRUITLESS

CAN'T DELIVER CONVENTION

Penrose Tells Perkins that Delegates Will Handle Matters This Time.

OYSTER BAY GETS REPORTS

And Roosevelt Will Shape Final Moose Action—Impatient Progressives Pacified.

CONVENTION MEETS TODAY

Talk of Hughes's Nomination Saturday on Third Ballot—His Supporters Avoid Dickering.

Special to The New York Times.

CHICAGO, June 6.—With no alternative to the nomination of Justice Hughes as the Republican candidate for President, except agreement on a dark horse, agreement on a dark horse looks less probable tonight than at any time. No favorite son can defeat Hughes, and neither can Root nor Roosevelt. No dark horse can stampede the convention, for this convention cannot be stampeded by anybody. But a dark horse sprung as the result of compromise on the ground that he can win could be nominated. The trouble is that there is no prospect of such an agreement; and while the effort to make one stumbles along, the Hughes movement canters evenly and plainly along toward the goal to be reached in the convention, which will assemble tomorrow for the first day's session.

The names of General Leonard Wood and Senator Lodge were brought forward today in the conferences as a counter-proposition to such names as those of Senator Harding of Ohio and others who quite certainly would not do. Nobody can be a dark horse who does not quite suit the Progressives.

Roosevelt Directs Conferences.

Colonel Roosevelt is directing the harmony conferences in person. The radical Progressives, who are so suspicious that Perkins is making a mess of things, will be vastly enlightened when they learn that the Republican leaders who have been going into Perkins's room at the Blackstone to confer wih him have really been talking, voice to voice if not face to face, with the Colonel himself. They have been talking with him over Perkins's own telephone, and it is almost the only way they can get into communication with him, for Perkins and a few others are the only persons in Chicago whose telephones can be connected with the Colonel's, no matter how much other persons may request the telephone company to make the connection.

Senator Lodge talked with the Colonel over Perkins's telephone last night and again today, and other Republican leaders have done the same thing today and tonight. The Colonel is in command; he is in command of the Progressives and is fast taking command of the Republicans. The platform is his now; if Hughes is nominated probably it will be because an agreement has been reached with the Colonel about the problem of Hughes's silence; if any other man is nominated it will be a dark horse stamped with the approval of Oyster Bay and not one of those favorite sons who are anathema to him. The absent figure is the whole show.

Senator Borah of Idaho was in conference tonight with George W. Perkins and afterward talked with Colonel Roosevelt at Oyster Bay over the telephone. He seemed satisfied after these conferences that in the end harmony would be brought about. It is significant that after these talks with Perkins and the Colonel Borah was as strongly for Hughes as ever. He is going to release the Idaho and Wyoming delegations from their support of himself, which means an addition to the Hughes column.

Senator Borah is one leader who is in favor of suspending negotiations with the Progressives.

Would Now Ignore Moose.

"What we must do now," said Mr. Borah, "is to proceed just as we would have done had there never been a third party. The traditions of our historical party demand it. Harmony is to be desired, but we cannot be expected to descend to bartering our dignity and independence.

"I believe that ultimately we shall have harmony. If we go ahead and name the candidate that our free delegates think is best fitted to carry the burden of the campaign peace will come. We will make a good platform, one with which no fault can be found by any faction of the party, and we will draw to our support many voters who left us four years ago."

With Hughes as the nominee and with a sanely progressive platform, the Senator said he thought Progressive Republicans would flock to the Republican banner. He even thought it possible the Progressives might later withdraw their third ticket, if they put one in the field, should the attitude of the nominee of the Republican Party satisfy their demands respecting campaign issues.

At present both Republicans and Progressives are making the most of the differences between them, but a distinguished leader and participant in the conferences said tonight that this was merely playing the game, and that when the showdown came the insuperable obstacles would be found not to be insuperable after all.

"I don't doubt that we can nominate a candidate who can win," said Senator William Alden Smith of Michigan to THE NEW YORK TIMES correspondent tonight. "But what shall it profit us to elect and lose the Senate? The Senate can block the President. And, even allowing the utmost that we can expect, we will have no easy job avoiding a tie in the Senate. We must make a nomination which will give us the Senate as well as the Presidency."

Senator Smith's point bears heavily on

Continued on Page 3.

Line-Up of the Delegations at Chicago On Eve of the Republican Convention

STATES.	Hughes	Roosevelt	Root	Fairbanks	Weeks	Burton	Cummins	Scattering
Alabama	6	3	..	3	..	4	..	..
Alaska	..	..	..	..	..	..	..	2
Arizona	1	..	..	..	..	4	..	1
Arkansas	5	..	6	..	..	..	..	4
California	8	..	7	..	..	4	7	..
Colorado	..	7	4	1	..	..	..	..
Connecticut	5	2	5	1	1	..	..	..
Delaware	..	..	..	..	..	..	..	6
District of Columbia	..	..	..	..	..	..	..	2
Florida	3	1	..	..	..	..	..	4
Georgia	..	..	..	..	..	..	..	17
Hawaii	..	..	..	..	..	..	..	2
Idaho	8	..	..	..	..	..	..	..
Illinois	..	2	..	..	..	..	..	56
Indiana	..	..	..	30	..	..	..	..
Iowa	..	..	..	..	..	..	26	..
Kansas	10	..	..	..	..	..	..	10
Kentucky	11	..	..	14	..	..	..	1
Louisiana	..	..	3	3	..	3	..	3
Maine	8	2	..	..	2	..	..	..
Maryland	3	3	1	..	8	..	..	1
Massachusetts	..	4	..	..	27	..	..	5
Michigan	..	..	..	..	..	..	..	30
Minnesota	..	..	..	..	..	..	24	..
Mississippi	5	4	..	..	..	..	..	3
Missouri	..	..	..	..	..	..	..	36
Montana	..	..	..	..	..	..	8	..
Nebraska	..	..	..	..	..	..	14	2
Nevada	4	2	..	..	..	..	..	..
New Hampshire	..	..	..	..	..	..	..	8
New Jersey	15	2	4	..	2	..	..	5
New Mexico	2	3	1	..	..	..	..	..
New York	43	2	40	..	..	..	..	2
North Carolina	6	10	..	..	..	2	..	3
North Dakota	..	..	..	..	..	..	..	10
Ohio	..	..	..	..	..	48	..	..
Oklahoma	6	5	2	..	6	..	..	1
Pennsylvania	2	6	..	..	..	..	..	68
Philippines	..	..	..	..	..	..	..	2
Porto Rico	..	..	..	..	..	..	..	2
Rhode Island	10	..	..	..	..	..	..	..
South Carolina	4	..	..	..	..	..	..	7
South Dakota	..	..	..	..	..	..	10	..
Tennessee	19	..	..	..	1	..	..	1
Texas	4	2	5	11	5	5	..	1
Utah	..	..	..	..	..	..	..	8
Vermont	8	..	..	..	..	..	..	..
Virginia	7	..	4	2	2	..	..	..
Washington	..	..	..	..	..	..	..	14
West Virginia	15	..	..	..	..	..	..	1
Wisconsin	..	..	..	..	..	..	..	20
Wyoming	6	..	..	..	..	..	..	..
Total	224	60	82	65	54	70	89	339

These votes are assured to the various candidates on the first ballot, according to a poll made last night. However, Chicago dispatches indicate that the leading candidates will receive even more than these. The Oregon figures were not obtainable.

Among the other candidates who will poll votes on the first ballot are Sherman, who will get Illinois's 56 votes; La Follette, 26 from Wisconsin and 10 from North Dakota; Knox, 40 from Pennsylvania; Brumbaugh, 19 from Pennsylvania; du Pont, 6 from Delaware and 4 other scattered votes, and Ford, who will get Michigan's 30 votes and 8 others.

HUGHES IN LEAD WITH 224 VOTES

Poll Shows His Strength on the First aBllot, with Probable Rush to Him Later.

QUICK DECISION EXPECTED

Choice of Jurist on the Second Count Possible—Favorites' Booms Threatened.

Special to The New York Times.

CHICAGO, June 6.—That there had been shifts in the plans of the State delegations for their voting on the first ballot in the Republican Convention was shown today when correspondents of THE NEW YORK TIMES visited the headquarters of all the fifty-three delegations.

The canvass indicated positively that Justice Charles E. Hughes would lead at the start, and that after the first ballot there would be a rush to his standard, causing his nomination for the Presidency possibly on the second, almost certainly on the third or fourth, ballot.

It is impossible to give exact tabulation of how the vote will be recorded. Many of the delegates have not made known their intentions and are awaiting the result of the secret conferences of the leaders.

The following forecast of the result of the first ballot is as close as anybody can make it late tonight:

Hughes	224	La Follette	36
Fairbanks	86	Knox	40
Weeks	82	Brumbaugh	19
Root	90	McCall	5
Cummins	91	Du Pont	10
Burton	72	Taft	1
Roosevelt	62	Doubtful and scattering	79
Ford	32		
Sherman	56		
Total			985

These figures are given without regard to late rumors that one or more favorite son booms are collapsing. In the event of such an occurrence before the balloting begins, the favorites' pledged votes would be scattered, but it is assumed that the changes would merely hasten the final outcome in favor of Hughes, unless some unforseen alignment should smash all predictions by ushering in a dark horse.

On the second ballot, when the avalanche toward Hughes begins, there will be a few other shifts, including a considerable block of votes to Colonel Roosevelt, among whose supporters are several scores pledged to vote at first for favorite sons.

Following are the facts gathered at the delegations' headquarters, some of which had caucuses lasting until late tonight:

Arkansas.

The Arkansas delegation, consisting of fifteen uninstructed delegates, at its caucus today re-elected the National Committeeman, H. L. Remmell, to both that office and the Chairmanship of the delegation and elected John I. Worthington to be a member of the Committee on Resolutions and M. A. Eisley as a member of the Committee on Rules. The delegation was not polled as to Presidential preferences, but it was said that it probably would give Hughes five on the first ballot, Root

Continued on Page 4.

COLONEL TO STAY IN RACE TO FINISH

No Sign of Compromise at Oyster Bay in Fight for Republican Nomination.

THIRD TICKET SIGNS GROW

Roosevelt Almost Certain to Run if Reactionary Is Named—No Order About Hughes.

Special to The New York Times.

OYSTER BAY, June 6.—Colonel Theodore Roosevelt is in the fight to a finish to win the Republican nomination for the Presidency. There was no talk of a compromise at Sagamore Hill today by reason of the address by Justice Hughes to the pupils of the National Cathedral School at Washington, D. C., and the Colonel offered no comment on the speech.

Colonel Roosevelt made the direct statement tonight that he had not sent a message to his leaders in Chicago stating unequivocally that he would head a third ticket in the event of the nomination of Hughes. Such a report, according to dispatches received here by the correspondents, had been circulated in Chicago. The Colonel was satisfied to stand pat regarding a third ticket, but it can be said that indications are that the danger of a third ticket is steadily increasing. In fact, it is almost a foregone conclusion that there will be such a ticket, headed by the Colonel, if Harding, Root, Burton, or any Old Guard representative of that type is nominated by the Republicans.

The situation has not been so tense for days. The Colonel meets assertions by Progressive leaders in Chicago that there will surely be a third ticket if the Republicans do not nominate him with the statement that he has not said he was for or against any candidate, but he has not denied these assertions flatly.

Reports reaching Colonel Roosevelt by telephone from his leaders in Chicago today were more favorable than at any time since the clans gathered, and this fact has served to arouse to even a higher pitch the Colonel's fighting spirit.

The proposition that he declare definitely now that he will run on a third ticket if the Republican Convention refuses to accept him has not been put to him flatly by his leaders in Chicago. If they declare that he will run on such a ticket they are doing it because they believe they know which way the wind is blowing and not because the Colonel has made the flat statement.

It would appear, at least at the present, that the Colonel has not arrived at the point where he would positively accept any candidate who has been put forward. There will have to be some radical and unexpected change in the situation as it affects any of these candidates to have the Colonel fall in with a movement to call off his Progressives.

It is a situation charged with dynamite, with the Colonel holding the match which would light the fuse, and no one can foretell at this moment just what the outcome will be.

The most definite statement that can be made at this time is that the Colonel is in a very determined frame of mind, and is listening to the reports of what his workers in Chicago are doing with

Continued on Page 6.

Lansing Questions Gerard About Alleged Peace Talk

Special to The New York Times.

WASHINGTON, June 6.—Secretary Lansing, who has again returned to his desk in the State Department, admitted today, in response to direct interrogation, that an inquiry has been sent to James W. Gerard, the American Ambassador at Berlin, asking him whether he was responsible for two alleged interviews cabled from Berlin crediting the Ambassador with having made certain statements in regard to peace.

In one of these alleged talks Mr. Gerard is credited with having said that nothing could shake his confidence that peace was on its way; that President Wilson had much greater freedom of action now to deal with the immense world problem of peace, that neutrals were as much interested in bringing about peace as the belligerents, and that the American Government was under an obligation to its citizens to do everything to serve the cause of peace.

25,480 AUSTRIANS CAPTIVES OF CZAR

Petrograd Regards Great Drive as Beginning of the Long-Awaited Offensive.

SWIFT ADVANCE EXPECTED

Austrian Correspondents Tell of Countless Waves of Russian Infantry Moving Into Battle.

PETROGRAD, June 6.—The sudden blow struck by the Russians along the entire Galician front of 275 miles from the Pripet to Rumania, which so far has resulted in the capture of 480 officers, over 25,000 men, 27 cannon, and half a hundred machine guns, is, in the unanimous opinion of the military critics here, a brilliant beginning of the long-awaited Russian offensive. The condition of the roads is now perfect, and with a plentiful supply of ammunition the Russian advance is expected to develop swiftly.

The movement derives significance from the fact that it is not an isolated attack against any one portion of the Austrian lines, but a carefully co-ordinated movement embracing the whole front. The movement is under the leadership of General Brussiloff, who conducted the brilliant campaign in the Carpathians in 1914, and who is generally conceded to be one of the best strategists of the Russian staff.

The forces opposing the Russian advance are estimated at forty Austrian infantry divisions and from ten to fifteen Austrian cavalry divisions, assisted by at the most two divisions of Germans. This brings the total Teutonic forces operating on this front up to 600,000 men.

No details of the Russian attacks are yet at hand, but it was preceded as usual by a vigorous artillery bombardment, after which the Russians moved forward along the whole line, capturing first-line Austrian positions. The initiative belongs entirely to the Russians, and the Austrians, evidently taken by surprise, fell back without being able to start a counteroffensive.

Aside from its military and strategic importance for this front, the Russian movement undoubtedly will have a powerful effect upon the military situation elsewhere, decreasing Austrian pressure on the Italian front from the necessity of bringing reinforcements to this theatre, while it also is expected to influence the situation in the Balkans.

A War Office communication today make the following brief announcement:

On the front from the Pripet River to the Rumanian frontier we continued to developed successes. Thus far we have taken as prisoners 480 officers and over 25,000 men and captured 27 guns and over 50 machine guns.

Of the operations on the rest of the battle line in Russia the communication says:

In the region of Dvinsk and north of the Poniewesch Railway a German offensive was repulsed by our fire. South of Smorgon Sunday night the Germans attempted to capture one of our advance trenches, but our machine gun fire and a counterattack compelled them to return to their trenches.

AMSTERDAM, June 6.—Dispatches from Vienna report that a violent battle has been raging during the last twenty-four hours on the Russian front along a sweep of 300 kilometers. (about 200 miles.) The correspondents describe countless waves of Russian infantry being sent into the battle.

General Brussiloff, who is believed to be in command of the Russian forces on this front, seems, according to the advices, to be following the tactics pursued by the Russians in the Carpathians, making attacks in mass, in an effort to break through the hostile lines.

DUMA CHEERS ADVANCE.

Austro-German Front Weakened for Attacks on Verdun and Italy.

Special Cable to THE NEW YORK TIMES.

PETROGRAD, June 6.—The news of the beginning of General Brussiloff's offensive on the southwestern front was greeted in the Duma yesterday with ringing cheers. The general feeling is one of hopeful anticipation.

The moment chosen is singularly opportune. The Central Powers have thrown all the emphasis of their offensive to the West. The Germans engaged at Verdun had left their section of the Russian front heavily fortified and were with their allies boasting that, with the help of their artillery and machine guns, they would be able to hold the Russians behind their forests of barbed wire. The Austrians were engaged on the Italian campaign and had left on the Russian southwestern front forces not exceeding 700,000, supported by not more than two German divisions.

The long spell of warm weather having dried up the roads, the Russians have not now to contend with those serious transport difficulties that hampered the advance in December. The swamps behind them during the Winter were made passable by the construction of a remarkable network of timber roadways. The whole technical organization of General Brussiloff's armies has made amazing progress. The men are in splendid form, and their accumulation of energy is such that for some time the whole front has been restlessly waiting for the command to advance.

KITCHENER AND STAFF PERISH AT SEA; LOST ON CRUISER, PERHAPS TORPEDOED; ENGLAND SUSPECTS SPIES OF THE DEED

INTERN ALIENS, BRITISH CRY

London Newspapers Sure Germans Knew of War Chief's Plans

AND SANK THE HAMPSHIRE

Stock Exchange Applauds a Member Who Calls for Quick Action to Curb Foes.

TRIBUTES TO KITCHENER

Northcliffe Papers, Once Earl's Opponents, Join in the Chorus of Praise.

New Orkney Restrictions Strengthen Talk of Spies

LONDON, Wednesday, June 7.—In connection with suggestions that information of Earl Kitchener's movements may have been conveyed to the Germans by spies, it is interesting to note that the official Gazette last night contained an order placing new restrictions on passengers landing at ports in the Orkney Islands.

Henceforth no person may land at such ports without specific permission of the military authorities at Kirkwall.

Special Cable to THE NEW YORK TIMES.

LONDON, Wednesday, June 7.—In connection with its comment on the death of Earl Kitchener The Daily Mail makes this statement this morning:

"Earl Kitchener's intention to go to Russia was known to a great many people in London on Thursday. It ought not to have been so known. The news of it may have reached the enemy.

"The public mind has been quick to associate his death with the work of spies.

"We have every sympathy with the demand which comes to us from many parts of the country that all alien enemies who are still at large, and especially those in high places, should be interned at once."

The Daily Mail says that many members of the Liverpool Cotton Exchange have sent messages to the newspaper, demanding that the Government intern all enemy aliens, whether they are naturalized or not.

Several newspapers this morning refer to an exciting scene which took place at the close of the Stock Exchange session yesterday. Referring to the loss of Kitchener and his staff a member cried:

"This is the work of German spies. Will you gentlemen tolerate any longer the presence of German-born members in your midst?"

His words were received with a burst of applause.

LONDON, Wednesday, June 7.—Commenting on the disaster to the Hampshire, carrying Lord Kitchener, The Morning Post says this morning:

"Circumstances point at espionage or treachery, and the country will suspect this the more owing to the singular freedom still allowed to enemy subjects in Great Britain."

The morning newspapers give up their editorial space to black-bordered eulogies of Earl Kitchener. Chief interest attaches to the tributes of the papers of Lord Northcliffe, which, after hailing Earl Kitchener in the early days of the war as the only man for the War Office, turned on him a year ago with bitter denunciations as being an over-rated man who had had no experience except in little Asiatic border campaigns.

Today, however, The Daily Mail and The Times sound no discordant note in the chorus of praise of the fallen leader. The Daily Mail says:

"So ends, with distressing suddenness, a career of romantic distinction which had assumed extraordinary significance in the estimation of his countrymen."

The Times says: "It was his doggedness in doing his work that won him popular trust, because it was akin to the people's own temperament. He had none of the gifts by which politicians win favor. He was no orator, he did not court the multitude, and he had few friends. It was in strange loneliness that he trod the path of duty with stern and unwavering purpose."

The Daily Express says:

"Without Earl Kitchener it is probable that we would have lost the war months ago."

Touching on the question of a successor to Earl Kitchener, The Morning Post thinks it would be a mistake to choose David Lloyd George, and urges that Lord Milner is the only suitable man on the horizon.

LONDON HUSHED BY SUDDEN NEWS

City's Life Seemed Almost to Stop When Kitchener's Death First Became Known.

Special Cable to THE NEW YORK TIMES.

LONDON, Wednesday, June 7.—The scene in the streets when the newspapers appeared yesterday afternoon with the first public announcement of the loss of the cruiser Hampshire with Lord Kichener on board was one not to be forgotten.

What most impressed the observer was the deep and poignant emotion aroused by the news, the sudden hush as it were, which this tragic passing away of a great soldier caused and which seemed for the moment almost to arrest the busy life of the great city.

Only on one other occasion since the war began has any news so gripped the public mind and seemed so completely to stay for a time the roaring tide of the streets. The first occasion was last Friday, when the first Admiralty announcement of the North Sea battle was made.

Count Benckendorff, the Russian Ambassador, paid this tribute to Kitchener:

"Russia's grief will be deepened when she learns that he met his tragic fate on a journey to Russia, which he undertook at the Emperor's invitation. Russia has thus been deprived of the opportunity of paying to the late Field Marshal a high tribute to his great achievements in the war, which have been followed in Russia with keen admiration."

A dispatch to The Times from Edinburgh says that the people in Edinburgh who know the Orkney Islands hold out no hope that any one who sailed in the Hampshire may be saved. The precise locality in which the disaster occurred is not yet stated. All that is known is that it was west of the Orkneys, apparently in sight of shore.

The western coast of the islands presents to the Atlantic an inhospitable front of high, rugged cliffs, the haunts of millions of sea birds, backed by ridges of hills which for the most part are desolate. No surprise is expressed in Edinburgh that the search of such a shore from the sea could be completed before the search from inland, and Jellicoe's fear that the search from land must also be hopeless is shared by all there.

Earl Kitchener of Khartum

"The terms on which I am serving are the same as those under which some of the finest portions of our manhood, now so willingly stepping forward to join the colors, are engaging. That is to say, my term of office is for the duration of the war, or for three years if the war should last longer than that. It has been asked why this period has been limited. It is because, if this disastrous war be prolonged—and no one can foretell for a certainty its duration—after three years of war, others will take our places and see this matter through."—From Earl Kitchener's speech in the House of Lords on his appointment as Secretary for War, August 25, 1914.

ALL FRANCE MOURNS FOR LORD KITCHENER

Was the Most Admired of the British Generals—Briand Sends Condolences to Asquith.

PARIS, June 7.—The tragic end of Earl Kitchener caused a deep and sorrowful impression throughout France, where he was better known and more admired than any other British General. The fact that Kitchener fought for France in 1870 was ever present in the French mind and went far to obliterate any lingering resentment over the Fashoda incident.

Quite recently Kitchener met Brig. Gen. Marchand, with whom he had clashed in 1898 in the village of Fashoda, Sudan, for the first time since the incident. It was during one of Kitchener's trips to the French front, and the two men exchanged cordial handclasps, in which all the old bitternesses were sunk.

The disappearance of an organizing genius of the first rank is deplored in military circles, where Earl Kitchener's qualities always were fully appreciated, but it was pointed out yesterday that however cruel his loss to the Allied cause and to the British people, his great work, so soundly conceived and carried out, would survive him. The newspapers print long reviews of Earl Kitchener's career and express sympathy with England in her mourning.

Premier Briand in telegraphing the condolences of the French Government to Premier Asquith, said:

"All France will regret from the bottom of her heart the loss of the great Chief who caused a magnificent army to spring from British soil. My country will never forget that the brave and efficient organizer, whose premature end it now mourns with the British people, fought in the ranks of the French army forty-six years ago."

When the war started Kitchener was regarded by the French as the greatest of British Generals, and it was hoped that he would be sent to command the British Army in France. When he was called to the portfolio of War Minister, the French press frankly accused their allies of having made a mistake. Ynez Guyot, former Minister of Public Works, was first to reassure them. He wrote:

"Let us consider the effort of the English: to create an army in all its departments. To assemble the men, lodge and clothe them; to give them rifles, cannon, and ammunition; to instruct and train them; to select officers who are to command them, and the officers of the General Staff who are to direct them, and to find a sufficient number of non-commissioned officers; to create the proper departments in the rear of the army, the transportation service, the hospitals, the ambulance and all in gigantic proportions, and in a few months—all these things form a work absolutely unequaled in the history of former wars. To this great work the name of one man will be forever attached—a great organizer, one of the greatest, Lord Kitchener. It is he who has prepared the men who are fighting. His service is greater than it would be on the field."

Last November Lord Kitchener went to look over the lines at Gallipoli and Saloniki—he had several times visited the British Army in Flanders—and stopped off a few hours in Paris. He went directly to the Quai d'Orsay, where he found the Prime Minister, M. Briand; the new Minister of War, the late General Gallieni, and the Generalissimo Joffre waiting for him. There was also a young officer who had been sent from the Minister of Public Instruction to act as interpreter.

"But for whom?" inquired M. Briand.

"For my Lord Kitchener."

Everybody laughed, and General Gallieni said:

"Go back and tell them that M. Kitchener could give them lessons in French."

On his retirement in 1868, Kitchener's father, Colonel Henry Kitchener, with his second wife, went to live in Dinan, France. Young Kitchener, then 20 years of age, visited them there in 1870, the year in which the Franco-Prussian war broke out. At Dinan everybody, says M. Théophile Janvrais, the historian of the place, speaks of Lord Kitchener as "the General." It was to M. Janvrais that Kitchener's stepmother, who still lives at Dinan, told how her son had come to enter the French Army. She said:

"He had come to spend three months with us, for he had just been graduated from Woolwich and had his commission. He was enthusiastic for the French and wanted to help them. But the Colonel, his father, remonstrated, fearing that he would lose his commission in the British Army. With a French friend, however, he went to Paris and enrolled.

"I remember very little of what he did—only this: At Laval he went up in a balloon with some officers to observe the enemy. In this way he received an attack of pleurisy which has bothered him ever since. And it brought an end to his campaigning for France, for he was in bed until it was all over, at the siege of Paris."

WAR CHIEF GOING TO RUSSIA

Vessel Sinks at Night Off the Orkneys—Probably None Saved.

LONDON APPALLED BY NEWS

Crowds Snatch at Evening Papers Containing Jellicoe's Brief Account of Sinking.

WAR COUNCIL HAS SESSION

Earl's Work in Raising Huge Armies for This War Called Supreme Achievement.

King George in Army Order Praises Kitchener's Work

LONDON, June 6.—By the King's command this order has been issued to the army:

The King has learned with profound regret of the disaster whereby the Secretary of State for War has lost his life while proceeding on a special mission to the Emperor of Russia.

Field Marshal Lord Kitchener gave forty-eight years of distinguished service to the State, and it is largely due to his administrative genius and unwearying energy that the country has been able to create and place in the field the armies which today are upholding the traditional glories of our empire.

Lord Kitchener will be mourned by the army as a great soldier, who, under conditions of unexampled difficulty, rendered supreme and devoted service both to the army and the State.

His Majesty the King commands that the officers of the army shall wear mourning with their uniforms for the period of one week. Officers are to wear crepe on the left arm of uniform and of greatcoats.

LONDON, Wednesday, June 7.—Bound for Russia on an important military errand, Earl Kitchener, the British War Secretary, and his staff were lost off the West Orkney Islands Monday night by the sinking of the cruiser Hampshire.

Whether the warship struck a mine or was torpedoed by a submarine is not known, according to Admiral Sir John Jellicoe, Commander in Chief of the Grand Fleet, whose brief official report to the Admiralty gives the only published facts about the catastrophe which by its suddenness has stunned the entire people of Great Britain.

The Hampshire went down about 8 o'clock, according to Jellicoe. Four boats were seen to leave the vessel, but a heavy sea was running and the Admiral thinks the chance of any on board having been saved is small. Only a capsized boat, and a few bodies have been picked up.

Earl Kitchener was going to Russia at the request of the Russian Government. He intended to land at Archangel and visit Petrograd, and probably go to the Russian front. His mission had chiefly to do with the supply of munitions for Russia, but an official statement issued last evening said that he was to have discussed important military and financial questions with Emperor Nicholas. The Earl expected to be back in London for the reopening of Parliament on June 20.

Accompanying Earl Kitchener as his staff were Hugh James O'Beirne, former counselor of the British Embassy at Petrograd; O. A. Fitzgerald, Kitchener's private military secretary; Brig. Gen. Ellershaw, and Sir Frederick Donaldson. Several minor army officers were also on the Hampshire.

News a Shock to the Public.

The circumstances under which the news of the loss of the Hampshire with Earl Kitchener came out did not soften the blow to the public, to whom it was a profound shock, even greater than that which was sustained last week when the newspapers gave the Admiralty statement of the British losses in the North Sea fight, with virtually no intimation that there was any compensation in the way of German losses.

The nation was depressed and grieved at the news of General Townshend's surrender at Kut-el-Amara, but not before has it been saddened as yesterday. The official news of Earl Kitchener's death was the greater surprise, because few knew that he had left England.

The message from Admiral Jellicoe to the Admiralty, giving the bare facts of the sinking of the Hampshire, reached the Admiralty about 11 o'clock in the morning. It read as folows, apparently being sent this morning:

I have to report with deep regret that his Majesty's ship Hampshire, Captain Herbert J. Savill, R. N., with Lord Kitchener and his staff on board, was sunk last night at about 8 o'clock, to the west of the Orkneys, either by a mine or a torpedo.

Four boats were seen by observers on shore to leave the ship. The wind was north-northwest and heavy seas were running. Patrol vessels and destroyers at once proceeded to the spot and a party was sent along the coast to search, but only some bodies and a capsized boat have been found up to the present.

As the whole shore has been searched

"All the News That's Fit to Print."

The New York Times.

THE WEATHER
Showers Monday; partly cloudy Tuesday; moderate northeast to southeast winds.
For full weather report see Page 17.

VOL. LXV...NO. 21,352. . . . NEW YORK, MONDAY, JULY 10, 1916.—EIGHTEEN PAGES. ONE CENT In Greater New York, Jersey City and Newark. | Elsewhere, TWO CENTS.

GERMAN U-BOAT REACHES BALTIMORE, HAVING CROSSED ATLANTIC IN 16 DAYS; HAS LETTER FROM KAISER TO WILSON

FRENCH SWEEP REACHES SOMME WEST OF PERONNE

Advance on Front of 2½ Miles Captures Biaches, with 300 Prisoners.

BRITISH GAIN AT OVILLERS

Announce Steady Progress in Heavy Fighting—Stop Violent Counterattacks.

BERLIN ADMITS SOME LOSS

French Took 9,500 Prisoners and 76 Cannon in the First Week of Their Drive.

3,012,637 German Casualties In Lists to the End of June

LONDON, July 9.—German casualties from the beginning of the war to the end of June, as computed from official German lists, are given as 3,012,637 in an official statement made public here today. This announcement follows:

German casualties, reported in German official casualty lists, exclusive of corrections, in the month of June, follow: Died of wounds and sickness, 18,585; prisoners and missing, 6,279; wounded, 68,187; total, 88,051.

These, added to those reported in previous months and including corrections reported in June, 1916, bring the totals reported in German official lists since the beginning of the war to: Died of wounds and sickness, 767,237; prisoners and missing, 242,673; wounded, 1,812,687; total, 3,012,637.

These figures include all German nationalities—Prussians, Bavarians, Saxons, and Württembergers. They do not include naval casualties or casualties of colonial troops. They are not an estimate by the British authorities, but merely casualties announced in German official lists.

LONDON, Monday, July 10.—French troops south of the Somme swept forward yesterday on a front of four kilometers, (two and one-half miles,) penetrating German positions to a depth of one to two kilometers (five-eighths to one and one-fourth miles) and capturing the village of Biaches, lying just across the Somme from Peronne and within a mile of that city, which is the first French objective in this sector. Three hundred German prisoners were captured.

North of the Somme the British report steady progress in stubborn fighting. In two reports yesterday the War Office announced that the British were extending their grip on Ovillers. It is here that the struggle has been most violent, reducing the site of the former village to a mass of ruined trenches and shell holes. "In another sector," the afternoon British statement says, a group of defended buildings was captured.

On the British right, in and near the Bois des Trones, north of Hardecourt, the Germans yesterday delivered two violent counterattacks against the positions recently won from them. The British succeeded in stopping these assaults, the night bulletin says.

The Berlin statement received here yesterday admits that the Allies penetrated ...

...

Last night between the Ancre and the Somme the fighting was considerably less violent than during the last two days. We made further progress in the neighborhood of Ovillers, and in another sector captured a group of defended buildings.

The Germans made no further at-

Continued on Page 4.

German Aeroplanes Drop Bombs on English Coast

LONDON, Monday, July 10.—Hostile aeroplanes have dropped bombs on the English coast, but so far as is known did no damage. An official statement issued this morning says:

"Shortly before midnight Sunday enemy aeroplanes visited the southeast coast of England. From the information available about five bombs were dropped. No damage is reported so far. Anti-aircraft guns engaged the raiding machines. No further details have been received."

A German aeroplane, apparently on a scouting mission, had appeared over the English coast previously, but was driven off and dropped no bombs. The Official Press Bureau gave out the following account of the incident: "An aeroplane crossed the Kent coast Sunday morning. Anti-aircraft guns fired on the aeroplane, which turned seaward, chased by British machines. It was not overtaken. No bombs were dropped."

RUSSIANS SMASH GERMAN FRONT

Take 3 Towns After Advance of 15 Miles and Cross Stokhod River.

ONLY 22 MILES FROM KOVEL

German Retreat Precipitate and Whole Line May Go—Delatyn, in Galicia, Captured.

LONDON, July 9.—The Russian forces in their attacks on the Teutonic line are going from success to success. Not only General Letchitsky, in the south, where his army has now occupied the railroad junction at Delatyn, west of Kolomea, thus cutting off General von Bothmer from his supply base, but General Brusiloff, in the north, is making advances on both sides of the Kovel Railway toward the Stokhod River.

Tonight's Russian communication reports the German forces in this region retiring in great disorder and adds that the Russians have occupied Gulevitchi and Kachova, which are about 22 miles to the east of Kovel. According to a Reuter dispatch from Petrograd they have crossed the Stokhod River at Ugli, which is approximately half way between the railways running to Kovel from Sarny and Rovno, at the point of the '7 formed by the river turning sharply from southwest to northeast. The dispatch adds that inasmuch as the Austro-German forces defending Kovel are chiefly concentrated along these lines, the Russian move in the centre threatens both groups.

Germany's possession of Baranovichi and Kovel are essential if she is to retain her hold over the invaded parts of Poland and Lithuania, but it is thought likely that it is only a matter of a few days before the Russians will be in possession of Kovel, which would compel von Linsingen's retirement from the Lutsk salient.

German official and unofficial dispatches indicate that anxiety over the Russian advance is greater than over the Anglo-French offensive, which the military critics contend will not interfere with the operations against Verdun. Major Moraht and other critics express surprise at the extent and persistence of the Russian offensive and the endless resources of ammunition.

It is reported from Rome that at a recent council of German and Austrian Marshals, von Hindenburg asserted that it would be impossible to attempt a new offensive on a large scale without reinforcements of at least a quarter of a million men.

The Rumanian Government, according to a Berne dispatch, has declined an invitation from the German and Austrian Governments to participate in a conference of the Danube powers.

Brusiloff's Brilliant Move.

PETROGRAD, July 9.—The right wing of General Brusiloff's armies, by brilliant manoeuvres between the Stokhod and Styr Rivers, north of Lutsk, have succeeded, it is declared, in completely ...

...

eral Letchitsky's army took prisoners 674 officers and 30,875 soldiers, and captured 18 cannon, 160 machine guns, and 14 caissons.

There was nothing important on the remainder of this front.

An earlier official statement read as follows:

Our offensive on the lower Stokhod

Continued on Page 3.

MAYOR MOBILIZES CITY'S EMPLOYES IN PARALYSIS WAR

Heads of Departments Meet Him for Orders at the Bar Association.

SUNDAY SCHOOLS CLOSE

At Many Which Hold Sessions Children Are Examined by Doctors and Nurses.

THE DAY'S DEATH TOTAL 20

Number of New Cases for the Five Borough 91, with 225 Deaths and 983 Cases to Date in City.

Day's Record of the Disease in City.

Borough	Deaths	New Cases
Brooklyn	14	69
Manhattan	4	6
Queens	1	8
Richmond	1	3
Bronx	..	5
Total	20	91
Total of cases to date		983
Total of deaths to date		225

Those who could help in the war against infantile paralysis by refraining from doing things, yesterday to a large extent refrained, and those who could help by going out and doing things, to a large extent went out and did. Thousands of persons, especially children, following the Health Commissioner's warnings against crowds and congregations, stayed away from church, Sunday school, and outings of all kinds, and the heads of the city departments, who ordinarily would have enjoyed a holiday, assembled at the Bar Association to discuss definite plans for curbing the disease.

Health Commissioner Emerson and his assistants were at "field work" nearly all day, inspecting homes and hospitals and superintending health work. Street Cleaning Commissioner Fetherston toured the city in an automobile to inspect conditions of the streets. The police, reinforced by members of the Home Defense League, were diligent in enforcing the sanitary regulations.

Mayor Mitchel presided at the Bar Association meeting, and those present were the Commissioners or acting Commissioners of the Health, Street Cleaning, Police, Water Supply, and Tenement House Departments, each of whom agreed to do his part in the campaign, with the Health Department directing the work.

Apportionment of Work.

Tenement House Commissioner Murphy said he would send agents to see that all buildings in the department's jurisdiction were kept in sanitary condition. Street Cleaning Commissioner Fetherston obligated himself to keep all pavements washed clean, and to have 180 gangs of men working day and night, if the Department of Water Supply could furnish 4,000,000 gallons of water daily. Commissioner Williams said he would supply that quantity of water.

The Department of Charities sent word that it would furnish supplies, ambulances, hospital beds, nurses, and doctors. The Fire Department offered hose and anything else needed from its resources. The Department of Licenses, it was announced, would continue to bar children from places of amusement. Acting Police Commissioner Godley said the ...

...

streets shall be taken, in so far as the City Government has the power to enforce the action.

Accumulations of refuse containing garbage in the public streets at various

Continued on Page 18.

Mexico Arranges to Hold Conferences in America

MEXICO CITY, July 9.—The preliminary arrangements for a conference of the representatives of the United States and Mexico to be held in some city in the United States have been completed, it is learned from a trustworthy source, and it is believed that by Tuesday the Mexican Ambassador Designate at Washington, Eliseo Arredondo, will advise the State Department at Washington of the details of the plans for peace parleys. These, it is understood, will be held without delay.

COLONEL OFFERS ARMY TO NATION

Letter to War Department Proposes That He Lead as a Major General.

NOTABLE MEN FOR OFFICERS

Admiral Winslow, Stimson, Bacon, Bullock, Groome, and Dr. Derby to Fill High Posts.

Colonel Theodore Roosevelt has made a formal offer to the Government in Washington of a division of volunteer troops to be assembled at the call to arms for a war with Mexico. This was learned by THE TIMES yesterday on high authority.

The Colonel's offer was made in a letter to the Secretary of War, and though its contents remain a carefully guarded secret, both in Washington and Oyster Bay, it is said by men close to Mr. Roosevelt that the letter gives every detail of the organization of the force which the Colonel hopes he will be authorized to lead.

If his application is allowed—and the Secretary of War, it is said has told friends of Colonel Roosevelt that it undoubtedly will be—then on a call for volunteers the Colonel will become a Major General and will be in command of more than 20,000 soldiers, each of whom might almost be said to have been chosen personally by Colonel Roosevelt himself.

In the letter which brings his division to the official notice of the War Department the Colonel tells what he has already done, what he is doing now, and what he intends to do if they get the chance to serve. He has applied for a detail of regular officers, naming the men he wants, some of them the best-known soldiers in the army.

Lumberjacks and Lawyers.

Among the civilians he has designated for command under himself are men from every walk of life, from the lumberjack and cowpuncher to the lawyer and wealthy Wall Street man.

Rear Admiral Cameron McRae Winslow, who retires on July 29 from com...

...

In arming his men the Colonel will try to achieve efficiency with weapons quickly learned. It is said that when he was asked by one of his prospective officers if he thought of arming his cavalry with lances and sabres he replied:

"Lances and sabres? Never! I

Continued on Page 6.

BOAT AND ERRAND A PUZZLE

Officials in Washington Prepare to Determine Deutschland's Status.

LEGAL QUESTIONS RAISED

If the Craft Is a Merchantman New Problems Will Be Set in International Law.

ENVOY MAY BE ABOARD

Lively Interest Shown in His Personality and His Errand Here.

Special to The New York Times.

WASHINGTON, July 9.—Another of the perplexing questions of international law growing out of the war in Europe will be presented to the United States Government by the arrival at Baltimore tomorrow morning of the German submarine Deutschland, which entered Chesapeake Bay this morning.

When the Deutschland reaches Baltimore the State Department will be called upon to determine whether the first undersea craft to make the transatlantic voyage shall be treated as a merchant vessel or as a belligerent warship.

If the submarine is held to be a merchant vessel engaged in peaceful commerce, (and this is the prevalent view,) it will receive all the rights and prerogatives of any other belligerent merchant vessel in an American port, free to come and go as it pleases, and at its own risk of incurring damage from enemy vessels outside the entrance to American territorial waters.

But if the decision of the State Department is that this submarine entered American waters as a belligerent warship, the so-called "twenty-four hour rule" will be applied, and the Deutschland will be governed by the rules of international law that this Government invoked in the cases of the Kronprinz Eitel Friedrich and the Prinz Friedrich Wilhelm.

Mr. Polk, the Acting Secretary of State, refused tonight to comment on the probable attitude of the United States Government in the Deutschland case, on the ground that it would soon have to be considered officially by the ...

...

Diplomats May Be Aboard.

Unofficial information reaching Washington is that the submarine also carried half a dozen passengers. There is considerable speculation as to their identity. One of the current assumptions here tonight was that the German Gov-

Continued on Page 3.

Germans Insist U-Boat Carries No Arms and Was Built Solely for the Merchant Service

Special to The New York Times.

BALTIMORE, Md., July 9.—This much can be authoritatively told about the Deutschland: She belongs to the Ocean Rhoderei of Bremen, a corporation formed to attempt the sub-surface crossing of the Atlantic, the possibility of which Germany has been boasting for some time. She was built to carry cargo, mails, and official dispatches, and her agents here assert that she carries no arms whatever.

Special to The New York Times.

WASHINGTON, July 9.—The statement was made tonight in a well-informed German quarter that the submarine Deutschland was sent to this country not as a naval vessel, but as a merchant submarine by the North German Lloyd Company, and that its commanding officer was not an officer on the active list of the German Navy, but a merchant Captain who was formerly in command of the German steamship Neckar.

LAKE THREATENS TO LIBEL CRAFT

Inventor Suspects Devices Are Infringed, but Hails New Era in Shipping.

WILL INSPECT HER TODAY

Krupps Copied His Designs, He Charges, When He Sought Patent Rights.

Special to The New York Times.

BRIDGEPORT, Conn., July 9.—Simon Lake, inventor of the even-keel type of submarine, and Treasurer of the Lake Torpedo Boat Company, announced tonight that he, F. B. Whitney, his chief counsel, and Mercer D. Blondell, a patent attorney, would go to Baltimore tomorrow and inspect the German submarine Deutschland.

"If it has any of my devices on it, and I have every reason to believe it has," Mr. Lake said, "I will libel the German boat."

That the day of the commercial submarine has arrived, and that nations would now build two types of submarines, one for commercial use and the other for warfare, was another statement by Mr. Lake. "The possibilities of undersea commerce are great," he said. "For twenty-five years I have been urging commercial submarines, but no one seemed to think such an idea practical. Submarines can be built that will carry cargoes of 5,000 tons.

"While I have no patent rights in Germany on my devices, I control my patents in the United States. If they are used here without my consent I can bring legal action. This does not mean, of course, that the submarine will have to stay in the United States. If the officers can furnish a satisfactory bond I can't have the submarine held here.

"When I was in Germany in 1904 and in 1905 negotiating with the Krupps and the German Government to buy my submarine and trying to show them its ...

...

private one of the North German Lloyd Steamship Company.

He said he did not know what cargo was aboard, whether or not regular trips would be made, or whether or not the submarine carried a message for President Wilson. His only information concerning the craft, he said, was received from newspapers and from friends who also had read the newspapers.

HINTS AT REGULAR UNDERSEA SERVICE

North German Lloyd Agent Thinks Other Submarines Will Cross the Atlantic.

HAS FAITH IN COMMANDER

Consignee of the Deutschland Believes Skipper Can Elude His Foes.

Special to The New York Times.

BALTIMORE, July 9.—Henry G. Hilken, senior member of the firm of A. Schumacher & Co., local agents of the North German Lloyd Company, consignees of the cargo aboard the German submarine Deutschland, expressed his elation today over the feat of sending a submarine across the Atlantic. He told how such a singular idea was conceived some eight months ago in Bremen, and how step by step the project was furthered, and intimated that it was not beyond the range of possibility for the German Government to reconstruct numerous other submarines so as to permit their entrance into neutral ports as merchantmen.

On one point only Mr. Hilken appeared a bit skeptical. That was in regard to the possibility of the submarine's getting safely out of the Chesapeake Bay after taking on a cargo for Germany.

"Do you think there will be any trouble?" he was asked.

"That's what I don't know," he replied. Then came a twinkle in his eyes. "A German commander entered the Capes successfully, didn't he? Well, trust to him to get out again."

Mr. Hilkin explained that the idea of such a trade project was conceived during the later part of last year by Alfred Lohmann, son of a former Director General of the North German Lloyd.

"It was in Bremen," said Mr. Hilken, "that the idea first took life. Germany is as sorely in need of certain commodities as this country, and unprecedented action had to be taken. Then Mr. Lohmann struck upon the idea of reconstructing a submarine, that is, dismounting its guns and providing space ...

...

cessful carrying out of the plan."

He was asked if he had been skeptical when the plan was first suggested.

"Well, no," he said. "The truth is we weren't approached until the first constructive stages had been passed. But even if we had known of its inception, I wouldn't have been skeptical. Not a bit, because it was a plan furthered by Germans and their plans usually go through without a hitch."

DODGES ALLIES' CRUISERS

Runs Past Warship Patrols at Cape Henry and Gets Into Port.

VALUABLE CARGO ABOARD

With Dyes and Chemicals, She Gains Port at Night and Will Dock Today.

GERMAN AGENTS ELATED

Special Berth Prepared for Vessel Where She Can Be Safe from Inspection.

Special to The New York Times.

BALTIMORE, July 9.—The German supersubmersible Deutschland, the announced arrival of which inside the Virginia capes at 1:45 o'clock this morning aroused intense interest here, dropped anchor at 10:15 o'clock tonight in Baltimore harbor, just off Quarantine. She stopped just in the lee of the interned North German Lloyd steamer Necker. Beside her anchored the tug Thomas F. Timmins, which had convoyed her from the Virginia capes. The end of the journey of more than 4,000 miles came in an electrical storm which every now and then etched out the lines of the strange looking craft with startling clearness.

Thus ended the half-humorous discussion of weeks here about the coming of the submarine. The Deutschland, it is said, carries a cargo of dyestuffs, some mail, and a message from the Kaiser to President Wilson. Henry G. Hilken, senior partner in A. Schumacher & Co., American agents for the ship, said he thought the cargo of dyestuffs would not exceed 500 tons. He knew nothing regarding the report that the Deutschland also carried mail.

A yacht met the Deutschland and her convoy off Sandy Point about 8 o'clock tonight and attempted to range alongside.

"Hello, Deutschland!" the newspaper men shouted.

"Hello! What do you want? Who ...

...

of dyes and mail, also a messenger, who has a special message from Emperor William to the President.

Three hours after her arrival, convoyed by the tug Thomas F. Timmins and piloted by Captain Fred Cocke, of the Virginia Pilots' Association, the giant submersible began the voyage up

United Press International

Austrian officers captured by Russians.

"All the News That's Fit to Print."

The New York Times.

THE WEATHER
Fair today and Sunday, warmer Sunday; moderate east to southeast winds.
For full weather report see Page 15.

VOL. LXV...NO. 21,371. ... NEW YORK, SATURDAY, JULY 29, 1916.—SIXTEEN PAGES. ONE CENT In Greater New York, Jersey City and Newark. | Elsewhere, TWO CENTS.

RUSSIANS TAKE BRODY, MENACE LEMBERG; BREAK THE GERMAN LINE IN VOLHYNIA; BRITISH WIN LONG-CONTESTED GROUND

STATE APPRAISES MORGAN RICHES AT $78,149,024

Value of Late Financier's Interest in Two Great Banking Firms Put at $29,875,847.

THE FIGURES A SURPRISE

Total Estate $25,000,000 Less Than Estimates Made Soon After Banker's Death.

MANY MORE WEALTHY MEN

Collections of Books and Art Objects Constituted Nearly One-third of the Whole.

The transfer tax appraisal of the estate of J. Pierpont Morgan, who died on March 31, 1913, will be filed today by Deputy State Controller Boardman and will show that the gross estate left by Mr. Morgan is valued at $78,149,024, or more than $25,000,000 less than he was supposed to have had.

The report, which was signed yesterday by Appraiser John J. Lyons, fixes the value of Mr. Morgan's interest in J. P. Morgan & Co. of New York and Drexel & Co. of Philadelphia at $29,875,847. The appraiser states specifically that this interest includes Mr. Morgan's share in the good will of J. P. Morgan & Co., "at its fair market value as of the date of the decedent's death." The valuation of Mr. Morgan's interest in his firm was accepted by John W. Hutchinson, Jr., special counsel for the State Controller, as the result of the following stipulation:

"It is hereby stipulated between the parties hereto that John W. Hutchinson, Jr., Esq., the attorney for the Comptroller herein, has personally examined the books and records of the firm of J. P. Morgan & Co. and has ascertained that the same show that the interest of said decedent and of his estate in the firm of J. P. Morgan & Co. was the sum of $29,875,847.77, as stated in the affidavit of John Pierpont Morgan, verified the 22d day of May, 1916, and the affidavit of William Pierson Hamilton, verified the 14th day of June, 1916, and heretofore filed herein, and that the interest of said decedent and of his estate in the firm of Drexel, Morgan & Co. (in liquidation) was the sum of $13,580, as stated in the affidavit of John Pierpont Morgan verified on the 22d day of May, 1916, and heretofore filed herein.

Debts to the Bank.

"It is further stipulated that said John W. Hutchinson, Jr., has ascertained by personal inspection of the said books and records that the same show that at the time of his death said decedent was indebted to the said firm of J. P. Morgan & Co. in an account known as "Account No. 4" in the sum of $1,497,772.00, and in a special account in the further sum of $2,102,291.36, as stated in an affidavit of John Pierpont Morgan verified on the 13th day of June, 1916, and heretofore filed herein."

The affidavit submitted by the Morgan estate as to the decedent's interest in the firm was made by William Pierson Hamilton, one of the executors, in which he said:

"William Pierson Hamilton, being duly sworn, says that he is one of the executors of the last will and testament of J. Pierpont Morgan, deceased, who died on the 31st day of March, 1913, and that said decedent and deponent were on said 31st day of March, 1913, members of the firm of J. P. Morgan & Co., bankers, doing business at No. 23 Wall Street, New York City; that deponent had personal charge and custody of the books of said firm in which were kept the partnership accounts of all of the members of said firm; that it appears by said books that the value of the interest of said decedent at the time of his death, and of his estate in the said firm, amounted to the sum of $29,875,847.77, and that the sum of $29,875,847.77 has been or will be paid to the executors of the estate of said testator, or upon their order and by them received in full payment and satisfaction of the interest of said testator and of his estate in the said firm, and that no other or additional sum was or is payable, or has been or will be paid to said executors, or to any other person, by reason of the interest of said testator or of his estate in said firm."

Many Richer Men.

On the basis of the report signed by Appraiser Lyons, Mr. Morgan, who was believed to be one of the richest men, if not the richest man in the United States, because of his financial activities, was worth less than many other wealthy men whose estates have been passed upon by the tax appraisers. It is much less than the estate of John Jacob Astor, who had $85,311,228, and his net estate does not equal that of Anthony N. Brady, who left $77,042,443. The estate of John S. Kennedy, also a banker, but who was little known compared with Mr. Morgan, amounted to $67,137,735. The E. H. Harriman estate was $58,000,000.

Mr. Morgan's securities were appraised at more than $18,000,000, but the list of stocks and bonds attached to the report shows that more than $7,000,000 par value of stocks and half a million dollars in bonds were worthless. Mr. Morgan's net estate was $68,384,680, to which was added a trust fund of $1,115,052, set aside for his wife by his father, Junius S. Morgan, in 1887, which made the total property bequeathed by Mr. Morgan $69,499,732. Of this amount the bequests to his son John Pierpont Morgan, aggregated $63,684,918.

Mr. Morgan's debts were $7,226,538.

Continued on Page 4.

British Patrol Boat Sunk by Submarine

BERLIN, July 28, (via Sayville.)—In a naval battle between several German submarines and three British patrol boats off the coast of Scotland one of the British vessels was sunk, according to a report received by the Dutch newspaper Handelsblad and telegraphed to the Overseas News Agency. The dispatch continues:

"The patrol boats were the Nellie Nutten, Onward, and Eva. The Nellie Nutten was sunk. Three members of her crew were killed and the remaining eleven were rescued by a Dutch fishing boat and landed in a Scotch harbor. Three of the eleven men rescued later died in consequence of their wounds. The other two patrol boats are supposed to have been lost with the whole of their crews."

LONDON, July 28.—A German submarine has raided a British fleet of herring fishing boats. Eight of the vessels were sunk. The crews were landed today at the North Sea port of Tynemouth.

POLICE OUST THUGS FROM STRIKE ZONE

Gangsters Turned Back and Railway Company Warned Not to Employ Them.

RIOTING STILL GOES ON

Strikers in Bronx Stone Cars and Attempt to Drive Off All Strikebreakers.

The discovery that gangsters and members of notorious east side organizations were being employed in the strike on the lines of the Union Railway Company caused Police Commissioner Wood yesterday to send every policeman available for strike duty to the Bronx.

Seven members of Jack Sirrocco's band were met by Deputy Police Commissioner Lord and Captain Andrew Wines of the Bronx Detective Branch as they were crossing the Fordham Bridge at 207th Street and ordered to leave the neighborhood. The gangsters were crossing the bridge in an automobile, apparently bent for one of the barns of the Union Railway Company, when they were discovered. They insisted that they had been employed by the company to act as guards, but were not permitted to cross the bridge.

Mr. Lord and Captain Wines later called on the officials of the Union Railway Company, and warned them that they would not be permitted to employ as guards men who belonged to any of the gangs of the city. No evidence was obtained that men of this calibre were in the service of the carmen's union, but Mr. Lord and Captain Wines, nevertheless, went to all the halls engaged by the strikers, and informed the leaders not to enlist the services of any one whose presence might tend to add to the violence in the Bronx.

"The Police Department is determined to eliminate gangsters and men of evil reputations from the strike situation," said Mr. Lord. "Men who might start trouble and are known as having that kind of reputation must go out of the Bronx and stay out. We have notified the agency through whom the seven men were engaged by the Union Railway Company that such characters will not be tolerated."

Edward A. Maher, Jr., Vice President of the Union Railway Company, told reporters that the company relied on the agency with which it did business to send only men who were fit for the work.

More Cars Running.

The Union Railway Company was able to run more of its cars yesterday than on any day since the strike began, but shut down its service completely again from 9 P. M. until this morning, as a precautionary measure. At one time 87 of the 120 cars running out of the West Farms barn were in operation. One hundred and fifty cars are generally sent out during the day from the Kingsbridge barn, and of these ninety-one were running, Mr. Maher said.

The vigilance of the police kept down the number of outbreaks, but many arrests were made, and many of the strikebreakers suffered severely at the hands of mobs.

The Amalgamated Association of Street and Electric Railway Employes of America made every effort, in the meanwhile, to extend the strike to the lines of the Third Avenue Railway Company. A mass meeting of the employes of that road has been called for this afternoon, at which time they are expected to strike.

William D. Mahon, International President of the carmen's association, said last night at the general headquarters of the union at the Continental Hotel, Broadway and Forty-first Street, that the organization of the union at Boston had pledged all of its available funds to the support of the strike in this city. He added that representatives of the employes of the Brooklyn Rapid Transit Company and of the transit lines on Staten Island had called on the officials of the union and had asked to be organized.

The conductors and motormen of the City Island Railroad, a small line which runs cars from Bartow Station of the New Haven Railroad to Belden Point, went on strike just before the afternoon rush hour. The road operates twelve cars, which generally accommodate about 2,000 commuters. Persons living at City Island and at Tent City in the Pelham Bay Park section had to engage buses and taxicabs to reach their homes.

Abraham Meyers of 2,050 Third Avenue, one of the men injured in the collision at West Farms Square on Thursday night, in which the motorman of a car was killed, died at Fordham Hospital last night. Meyers had both of his legs crushed when the car crashed into a subway pillar. He had been engaged by the railway company as a strikebreaker.

There was a report last night that the New York Railways Company had decided to increase the pay of some of its motormen and conductors who have been in service for five years or more.

Blames Strikers for Wreck.

Edward A. Maher, Jr., Assistant Vice President and General Manager of the Union Railway, said he was convinced that the accident at Tremont Avenue and Boston Road on Thursday night in

Continued on Page 7.

REPLY TO MEXICO AGREES TO PARLEY OVER ALL POINTS

American Note Accepts Plan of Joint Commission to Adjust Differences.

ENLARGES BODY'S POWERS

Conferees Will Take Up Every Matter That Has Menaced Friendly Relations.

CARRANZA ASSENT ASSURED

Each Nation to Name Three Representatives — May Meet on New Jersey Coast.

Special to The New York Times.

WASHINGTON, July 28.—An agreement for an adjustment of the differences between the United States and Mexico through the offices of an international joint commission was reached today. The commission will have broad powers that will enable it to take into consideration every matter that has served to imperil the friendly relations between the two countries. The basic principle of the understanding reached is the prevention of war, but beyond that the commissioners will endeavor to effect an agreement that will provide for a permanent settlement of the troubles that have so frequently brought the two nations to the verge of hostilities.

Frank L. Polk, the Acting Secretary of State, handed to Eliseo Arredondo, the Ambassador Designate of Mexico, late this afternoon, a formal note in which the Mexican proposal for the appointment of a joint commission is accepted by President Wilson. The text of the note follows:

July 28, 1916.

Sir:—I have the honor to acknowledge the receipt of your communication of July 12th last, in which you transcribe a note addressed to my Government by the Secretary of Foreign Relations of your Government, and to request that you will be good enough to transmit to him the following reply:

"Mr. Secretary:

"I have the honor to acknowledge receipt of your Excellency's note transmitted under date of July 12th by Lic. Eliseo Arredondo, your Government's confidential agent in Washington, informing me that your Excellency has received instructions from the Citizen First Chief of the Constitutionalist Army charged with the executive power of the Union to propose that each of our Governments name three commissioners, who shall hold conferences at some place to be mutally agreed upon and decide forthwith the question relating to the evacuation of the American forces now in Mexico, and to draw up and conclude a protocol or agreement regarding the reciprocal crossing of the frontier by the forces of both countries, also to determine the origin of the incursions to date, in order to fix the responsibility therefor and definitely to settle the difficulties now pending or those which may arise between the two countries on account of the same or a similar reason; all of which shall be subject to the approval of both Governments.

Spirit of Frank Cordiality.

"In reply I have the honor to state that I have laid your Excellency's note before the President and have received his instructions to inform your Excellency that the Government of the United States is disposed to accept the proposal of the Mexican Government in the same spirit of frank cordiality in which it is made. This Government believes, and suggests, however, that the powers of the proposed commission should be enlarged so that, if happily a solution satisfactory to both Governments of the question set forth in your Excellency's communication may be reached, the commission may also consider such other matters the friendly arrangement of which would tend to improve the relations of the two countries; it being understood that such recommendations as the commission may make shall not be binding upon the respective Governments until formally accepted by them.

"Should this proposal be accepted by your Excellency's Government, I have the honor to state that this Government will proceed immediately to appoint its commissioners, and fix, after consultation with your Excellency's Government, the time and place and other details of the proposed conferences.

"Accept, Mr. Secretary, the assurances of my highest consideration.

"FRANK L. POLK,
"Acting Secretary of State."

I am, Sir, Yours very sincerely,
FRANK L. POLK.

While the language of the note gives the impression that agreement on the commission plan will not be reached until the Carranza Government has considered the American proposal it is understood that assent has been assured in advance through the frequent conferences between Acting Secretary Polk and Ambassador Designate Arredondo. A formal acceptance of the American proposal is expected to be furnished promptly by the Carranza Government.

No time will be lost in appointing the commissioners, three from each Government. They will meet with the least possible delay at some place to be agreed on. It had been suggested that the joint commission hold its sessions at Niagara Falls, Ontario, where the A B C Mediation conference on Mexican affairs took place in 1914, but it has been determined that no necessity exists for the commission to conduct the suggestions outside the United States. A Summer resort, probably one of those along the New Jersey coast that have Long Branch for their centre, will be chosen.

The State Department will insist that the meeting be held in the United States, as the question is not one of mediation which would require a neutral setting.

It is the purpose of President Wilson, according to statements in official circles, to appoint as the American representatives on the commission three men of the highest standing. No disclosure has been made of the names of those likely to be chosen, but it has been suggested that the President consider Chief Justice White and Associate Justice Brandeis of the United States Supreme Court, Major Gen. George W. Goethals, the builder of the Panama Canal, and Frederick W. Lehman of St. Louis, who was a member of the Niagara Falls conference.

Original Scope Enlarged.

Delay in reaching an agreement for the appointment of a joint commission has been due mainly to the apparent

Continued on Page 3.

King of Denmark Escapes Drowning

LONDON, July 28.—King Christian of Denmark had a narrow escape from drowning this afternoon through the capsizing of a boat which he was sailing near Aarhus, says a Reuter dispatch from Copenhagen.

The King went out alone in a small sailboat and a sudden puff of wind capsized the craft, throwing the King into the water.

The King swam to the overturned craft, and, pulling himself upon it, sat astride the keel, where his plight was observed from the shore. Boats immediately hastened to his assistance and rescued him, none the worse for his immersion.

LLOYD GEORGE STILL HOPES FOR IRELAND

Has Not Despaired of an Eventual Solution of the Problem, He Asserts.

WORKS ON FOR HOME RULE

Believes Nationalists Made a Serious Mistake in Not Accepting Offer Made to Them.

LONDON, July 28.—"I don't despair about an eventual solution of the Irish problem, in spite of the recent failure to reach an agreement between the Nationalists and the Unionists," said David Lloyd George today.

He was replying to a request from The Associated Press for his views on the breakdown of the negotiations for putting the Irish Home Rule act into effect immediately.

"We achieved at least one thing that had never hitherto been accomplished," continued the British War Secretary. "We brought the representatives of the Irish Nationalists and the Ulster Unionists to the point of shaking hands, instead of shaking fists, at each other."

Mr. Lloyd George, acting as the chosen arbitrator in the century-old Irish controversy, had succeeded in so far mollifying the opposing factions that he had brought them within measurable distance of reaching an agreement. Then, Mr. Lloyd George said, in a tone of regret, fate intervened, as it had so often done before in Irish affairs, and at the last moment a breach occurred.

The Secretary for War, however, is still full of optimism regarding the Irish difficulty. He feels about this problem as about everything else he undertakes—that a solution can be reached, and it is his intention to strive on until he is successful. In reply to a question whether the Nationalists were justified in refusing the proposed settlement, he said:

"Never has a better offer been made by all the British parties together. The only new stipulation inserted was one concerning the British, and not the Irish Parliament. The moment the demand was put forward by the Unionists that Ireland should be represented at Westminster only in proportion to her population, except when the question of the Irish settlement was under consideration, it had to be conceded.

Ulster Exclusion Imperative.

"It is true," Mr. Lloyd George continued, "that the Home Rule act is on the statute book, but only with the pledge that before it becomes operative an amending bill is to be passed dealing with the exclusion of Ulster."

The Secretary said the main principles of the settlement remained, namely, the immediate creation of an Irish Parliament, exclusion for the present for the part of Ireland which is unwilling to participate in the Home Rule measure, and consideration of the whole question of the future of the Irish Government by an imperial conference at the close of the war.

The correspondent found Mr. Lloyd George at the War Office in the room and seated in the chair so long occupied by Lord Kitchener. All around him hung maps showing the positions of the British troops and their recent gains on the front in France. Through the windows the buildings of the Admiralty were visible directly opposite, and all about were evidences that one was at the very nerve centre of the war. Callers on important matters connected with the war leave the Minister scarcely a moment of leisure. He starts work at a very early hour in the morning and continues his labors until evening without respite.

Mr. Lloyd George does not follow the example of Lord Kitchener in working late, because he finds himself at his best in the morning. His boyhood training in the country accustomed him to early hours, and he retains this habit, as he also does the habit of enjoying the open air. He finds, in fact, that he must go into the country to sleep, and he therefore travels nearly every evening to his cottage at Walton Heath. It is to his liking of the open-air life that Mr. Lloyd George attributes his remarkable health. He is almost the only Cabinet Minister who has retained his physical fitness unimpaired since the beginning the war.

Although the Secretary is almost overwhelmed with work in his new department, he consented to give a short talk to The Associated Press concerning his efforts to bring about a solution of the Irish question, about which his knowledge is very deep. He said that naturally he was somewhat saddened by the ill-success of his attempt to bring the Irish parties completely together.

Always Favored Home Rule.

"I have always been an ardent Home Ruler during my political career, and still remain one," Mr. Lloyd George said. "In my opinion a nation which can and does produce such soldiers as the Irish troops who are now fighting by the side of their fellow-Britons from all over the empire with a valor almost indescribable, and which gives us such intellects in all branches of life, can and must rule itself."

In answer to a question as to how the breach in the Irish negotiations came about Mr. Lloyd George said:

"There were two points on which there was disagreement at the end of the negotiations. One dealt with the means by which the exclusion of the six Ulster counties was to continue or to be brought to an end. This, to my view, although I believe Mr. Redmond differs on that point, was less a matter of substance than of words. The Nationalists agreed it was impossible that the Ulster counties should be coerced into an Irish Parliament. It was understood that when they were willing to come in no one would seek to keep them out. Their exclusion for the present would not have affected in the slightest degree the full powers given to the Nationalist part of Ireland under the Home Rule act. The question of their coming in voluntarily afterward

Continued on Page 3.

ALL OF LONGUEVAL TAKEN

Last of Brandenburgers Expelled from Delville Wood Near Village.

PROGRESS MADE EASIER

London Expects Forward Movement of Offensive Will Be Greatly Facilitated.

GERMANS ATTACK IN VOSGES

Penetrate Advanced Trenches, but Are Driven Out by Bayonet Charges.

Workers and Soldiers Exchange Congratulations

Special Cable to THE NEW YORK TIMES.

LONDON, July 28.—The following telegrams have passed between the management of the Committee of the General Federation of Trade Unions and Sir Douglas Haig:

The management of the Committee of the General Federation of Trade Unions, representing over a million British workers, sends sincere congratulations to you, to your staff and to your heroic soldiers on the successes achieved since July 1. Also wishes speedy recovery of wounded and expresses deepest sympathy with relatives of those who died in defense of honor and civilization.

APPLETON, Secretary.

This is General Haig's reply:

To the Secretary of the Federation:

Your inspiring message has appealed to us all. On behalf of my staff, the army in France, and myself, I beg to express to the members of the General Federation of Trade Unions our warmest thanks for their kindness in congratulating the British Army in France on its success. All ranks realise how much this success is due to the patriotism, self-denial and whole-hearted co-operation of their brother workers at home.

DOUGLAS HAIG.

LONDON, July 28.—Tonight's official report of the British War Office shows that the British are continuing their successful progress. The whole of Longueval is now in their hands as well as Delville Wood, from which they drove the Fifth Brandenburg Division.

The final capture of Delville Wood is very gratifying to the British people. It was first taken on July 17, but was afterward abandoned. For many days the wood and the village of Longueval have been the scene of some of the heaviest fighting of the whole campaign.

The possession of this wood and of Longueval is expected to facilitate greatly the further progress of the Franco-British forces.

An attack by the Germans against French positions south of Sainte Marie Pass, in the Vosges, resulted in their gaining a lodgment in the advanced French trenches, according to the official statement given out in Paris tonight. The statement adds, however, that later the Germans were driven out with the bayonet.

Progress for the French on the right bank of the Meuse is reported.

Russians reconnoitring at Auberive, in the Champagne, the French official statement issued this afternoon says, penetrated the German trenches and cleared them with hand grenades. The Russians took some prisoners.

A German attempt to attack near Lihons, north of Chaulnes, was arrested by French infantry fire.

The Berlin report says strong British attacks against the German positions in Foureaux, or High Wood, in the Somme region, broke down yesterday under the German fire.

The official statement given out tonight by the British War Office says:

Continuing their success of yesterday our troops have captured the last enemy strongholds in Longueval, together with a number of prisoners.

In the vicinity of Pozières hand-to-hand fighting has continued throughout the day. Elsewhere on the battle front there was considerable artillery activity by both sides.

Two hostile aeroplanes were destroyed by one of our aerial patrols in the neighborhood of Bapaume yesterday.

Brandenburgers Expelled.

The British official statement of this afternoon follows:

After severe fighting we have driven the Fifth Brandenburg Division from their remaining positions in Delville Wood, capturing three officers and 158 men.

The whole wood now is in our hands and two German counterattacks have been beaten off with heavy loss to the enemy.

We made further progress in Longueval Village and near Pozières, and in

Continued on Page 2.

German Airships in New Raid on England; Bombs Are Dropped on Northeast Coast

LONDON, Saturday, July 29, 3:03 A. M. — German airships raided the east coast of England early this morning, according to an official statement just issued.

"The number of raiders," says the statement, "has not yet been established. The reports as to the raiders crossing the coast come from Yorkshire and Lincolnshire. Bombs were dropped, but details are lacking."

Both Yorkshire and Lincolnshire are on the East Coast of England and have, particularly the former, been the scene of Zeppelin raids. Yorkshire extends from the River Tee to the Humber estuary and contains the great manufacturing towns of Leeds, Sheffield, Bradford, and Halifax, together with the historic city of York and the fishing town of Hull.

Lincolnshire's coast, from the Wash to the Humber embraces Grimsby, Lincoln with its cathedral, Grantham, Gainsborough, and Boston.

Hull is understood to be a cruiser and minesweep base.

GERMANS EXECUTE BRITISH SKIPPER

Shoot Capt. Fryatt of the Brussels for "Attempting to Ram a Submarine."

ENGLAND IS INDIGNANT

Asks Gerard for Details—Washington Fears U-Boat War May Be Renewed.

BERLIN, July 28, (by Wireless to Sayville.)—Captain Charles Fryatt of the Great Eastern Railway steamship Brussels, which vessel was captured by German destroyers last month and taken into Zeebrugge, has been executed by shooting after trial before a German naval court-martial. The death sentence was passed upon Captain Fryatt because of his alleged action in attempting previously to ram a German submarine.

Testimony was presented at the court-martial to show that while Captain Fryatt did not belong to the armed forces he had attempted on March 28, 1915, while near the Maas Lightship, to ram the German submarine U-33. Captain Fryatt and the first officer and the first engineer of the Brussels received from the British Admiralty gold watches for "brave conduct," and were mentioned in the House of Commons.

The submarine U-33, according to the official account of the trial, had signaled to the British steamer to show her flag and to stop, but Captain Fryatt did not heed the signal, and, it is alleged, turned at high speed toward the submarine, which escaped only by diving immediately several yards below the surface.

Captain Fryatt, the official statement says, admitted that he had followed the instructions of the British Admiralty. Sentence was confirmed and the Captain was executed and shot for a "franc-tireur crime against armed German sea forces." The trial was held at Bruges yesterday.

When captured by German torpedo boats on June 24, Captain Fryatt was piloting the steamship Brussels from Rotterdam to Tilbury. Several German warships dashed out of the naval base at Zeebrugge and escorted the Brussels to the Belgian harbor. On board the Brussels was an unusually large number of Belgian women and children refugees, and she carried an all-British crew of forty-four men. Included in the cargo were forty tons of margarine and quantities of fish, butter, and meat.

Dutch newspapers said it was generally believed that the capture of the Brussels was brought about by a passenger who said he was an American but who was believed to be a German. This man remained on deck throughout the voyage, and was said to have made signals with lights, with the result that the German warships steamed up and halted the vessel.

BRITAIN WANTS DETAILS.

Asks American Ambassador to Report on Capt. Fryatt's Execution.

LONDON, July 28.—News of the execution of Captain Fryatt of the British steamer Brussels caused a painful impression at the British Foreign Office. Under the instructions of Viscount Grey, the Foreign Secretary, a note was dispatched immediately to the American Embassy requesting that James W. Gerard, the American Ambassador at Berlin, procure complete details of the affair.

The first intimation of the trial of Captain Fryatt was called to the attention of the Foreign Office by press reports on July 18, to the effect that he was to be tried as the result of finding on him a watch containing an inscription reciting his efforts to ram a German submarine.

From inquiries made of the owners of the steamship Wrexham, which Captain Fryatt commanded when the alleged incident took place, the Foreign Office learned the Captain had with him when captured neither a watch nor a letter to the effect that he had attempted to ram a submarine. Therefore, officials here state, the charge must have been based on press reports.

The German official account received here of the execution concludes with these words:

"One of the many franc-tireur actions of English merchant shipping against our war vessels has thus found late but merited expiation."

"Worse Than Cavell Case."

Discussing the case with The Associated Press, Baron Newton, Under Secretary for Foreign Affairs, who during the conversation was summoned to Foreign Secretary Grey's office for a conference on the subject, said:

"On the face of the details of the

Continued on Page 3.

A 'TAME' DAY ON THE STOKHOD

Correspondents in German Line Treated to Shrapnel Shower by the Russians.

CEMETERY NO SAFE PLACE

Gully Filled with Mud and Water Made Into Outer Trench by Cheerful Soldiers.

By CYRIL BROWN,
Staff Correspondent of The New York Times.
Special Cable to THE NEW YORK TIMES.

SWIDNIKI, ON THE STOKHOD FRONT, Volhynia, July 25, (by Courier to Berlin, July 26.)—The fighting at this crucial point of the Stokhod line, while voted reasonably hot by an amateur, was characterized as comparatively tame now by professionals.

As typical of the sharp intermittent fighting here, we were about to leave "Dead Man Bastion" when the lookout reported signs of Russian life stirring in a distant house beyond the railroad bridgehead. From a signal tower the Front Captain telephoned a sharp command to rearward, and presently a giant calibre German mine catapulted by a minewerfer, came hurling overhead and burst ten feet from the house with the disproportionately terrific detonation peculiar to "battle mines." But sharp-eyed Russian observers, too, had spotted the correspondents' bobbing heads, and Russian artillery began peppering away with shrapnel.

Heavy Battery Gets Busy.

It took no further orders for the German heavy battery instantly to open fire in reprisal, shelling with methodical slowness and correcting each shot, which irritated the Russians, who directed their fire on the little cemetery of Swidniki, which we had picked provisionally as probably the safest retreat. Instead, we ran for individual holes. The fact that my seat proved on examination to be a case of hand grenades failed to add enchantment to the scene.

After half an hour the worst of the artillery squall blew over and we resumed our intensive study of the Stokhod front, enjoying the quaint sensation of a hundred-yard sprint over open country, with young Linsingen setting the pace, then promenading for an hour through a mud and water filled gully, which the good-natured Teuton soldiers still engaged in digging and building it out optimistically called a trench. It was a brand new advanced position which these patient exponents of superpreparedness were pushing ahead of the old first line of defense that ran 500 yards behind us. Then Uncle Linsingen's boy asked if I wanted to go still further out to a nearby woodpatch, where a German and a Russian patrol were playing hide and seek. The Front Captain said, cheerfully philosophizing: "I am at your disposal as long as you want, but in your own interest I suggest moving rearward. Your principal duty, after all, isn't to get shot dead, is it?"

I made the fastest recorded time by the shortest route back to division headquarters, only stopping to note that the Germans had several successive defensive lines, and more building, which perhaps explained why the dashing young cavalry General commanding the Blood and Iron Division wasn't worrying about a resumption of the Russian offensive.

Says Russians Can't Get By.

I wasted time asking him what would be the effect on the whole of Linsingen's line if the Russians should succeed in forcing the Stokhod here. He looked puzzled, then said: "They can't get by me. They can't force the Stokhod, ausgeschlossen." And he refused to admit even the faint possibility for the sake of argument. But then he explained why ausgeschlossen:

"The Stokhod is from fifteen to fifty feet wide on my sector of the front and only waist deep. The Russians have web hands and feet. They're like ducks, not a bit afraid of the water. It can't stop them. They can easily cross the Stokhod, but then they have to go over six or eight hundred yards of swampy meadow, though not in masses, for the Russians can neither throw themselves down nor intrench, and while we lay a barrier fire behind them and shrapnel on them our machine guns mow them down from the front and flanks. The Russian masses that storm across the Stokhod fall into the fire trap from which few miraculously escape.

"The Russians tried their amazing Cossack tactics on me once, but only once, undertaking a cavalry charge against my machine guns over the meadows at Liniewska, but they all faded away under artillery fire before the machine guns had a chance to get busy. A cavalry attack under such conditions is heroic, but nevertheless madness. No other nation would have done it. The Russians as a rule don't repeat

Continued on Page 2.

RUSSIANS PURSUING FOES

Take 9,000 Germans With 2 Generals and 46 Guns West of Lutsk.

DRIVE AUSTRIANS SOUTH

Communications of Whole Teuton Front Imperiled by Swift Advance.

BIG BATTLE IN LITHUANIA

Berlin Reports Leopold Attacked in Baranovitchi Region and Issue in Doubt.

70,000 Turks in Hungary; Aged Emperor at Budapest

LONDON, Saturday, July 29.—A Turkish army, estimated at 70,000 strong, is now concentrated on the Hungarian plains for the defense of Hungary, says a dispatch to the Exchange Telegraph Company from Lausanne, Switzerland.

The dispatch adds that the Austrian Emperor has gone to Budapest, where intense excitement prevails.

PETROGRAD, July 28.—The Russians, having driven the Austro-German forces from the line of the Rivers Slonevka and Boldurovka, have occupied Brody, the important Teuton base in Northeast Galicia, on the railroad from Dubno to Lemberg, and only fifty-eight miles from the Galician capital. In Volhynia the Czar's army has broken through the entire first line of the Teuton allies west of Lutsk, where they captured more than 9,000 prisoners, including 2 Generals, and 46 guns, and are following up their success.

Following is the text of the official report issued tonight by the War Office announcing these victories:

West of Lutsk, (Volhynia,) we took the offensive, and broke through the whole first line of the enemy, inflicting severe losses. Our troops are now advancing and the cavalry is pursuing the fleeing enemy.

In this district we captured 46 guns, including 6 mortars and 6 machine guns, and 30 officers, including 2 Generals and 2 commanders of regiments, and over 9,000 men.

In the valley of the Rivers Slonevka and Boldurovka, (Northeast Galicia,) the enemy has been defeated along the whole line, and is now being pursued in the direction of Brody. Explosions were heard in Brody, and fires were observed. Dense columns of goods trains were seen moving from there.

Later.—At 6:30 o'clock Friday morning Brody was captured by our troops. The number of prisoners and the amount of booty captured are not yet known.

Another official statement issued earlier in the day follows:

In the district of Krevo an enemy aeroplane was hit by our artillery fire. It fell within the enemy lines.

In the districts northeast and southeast of Baranovitchi there were artillery duels and encounters between advance guards. We made small advances at some points.

In the region of the River Slonevka and the River Boldurovka our advance continues successfully.

Berlin Reports Big Battles Raging.

BERLIN, July 28, (by Wireless to Sayville.)—Attacks by two Russian army corps on German positions east of Gorodische, in the Baranovitchi region were delivered yesterday, but failed to gain ground, the War Office announced today. The battle is still in progress.

The Russians have resumed their attack southeast of Vladimir-Volynski in Southern Volhynia and succeeded in penetrating General von Linsingen's lines northeast of Sviniusky, but are being vigorously counterattacked by the Germans.

BERLIN, July 28, (via London.)—The German War Office today issued the following report of the operations in the Russian theatre of war:

Army Group of Field Marshal von Hindenburg: The situation generally is unchanged.

Army Group of Prince Leopold of Bavaria: The Russians have renewed their attacks in this region. Since yesterday afternoon they have attacked six times in vain with two army corps on the front of Skrobova and Vygoda, to the east of Gorodische. Further attacks are in progress. The attacking waves of two divisions ebbed back and forth several times before our Shara positions to the northwest of Liachovichy. The losses of the enemy were the heaviest.

Army Group of General von Linsingen: Russian attacks northeast of Sviniusky at first gained ground. Counterattacks are in progress.

Austro-Hungarian troops near Postomyty repulsed the Russians from their advanced positions.

VIENNA, July 28, (via London.)—An official statement given out by the Austro-Hungarian War Office today says:

Russian War Theatre.—On the upper part of the Czarny Czeremosz River several Russian attacks failed.

In the region north of Brody the enemy continued yesterday during the

Continued on Page 2.

"All the News That's Fit to Print."

The New York Times.

THE WEATHER
Generally fair Monday and Tuesday; moderate temperature; light northwest winds.
For full weather report see Page 17.

VOL. LXV...NO. 21,401. NEW YORK, MONDAY, AUGUST 28, 1916.—EIGHTEEN PAGES. ONE CENT In Greater New York, Jersey City and Newark. | Elsewhere, TWO CENTS.

UNION CHAIRMEN QUIT CAPITAL AS WILSON PLANS AGAINST STRIKE; WON'T STOP CITY FOOD TRAINS

HINTS OF FEDERAL SEIZURE

President Confers With Secretary Lane and Senator Newlands.

MAY ADDRESS CONGRESS

Railway Heads Expect to Present Their Refusal of Peace Terms This Morning.

8-HOUR DAY FINAL HITCH

Brotherhoods Ready to Bargain on Other Demands—"Strike Don'ts" Sent to Workers.

Special to The New York Times.

WASHINGTON, Aug. 27.—The 640 railway brotherhood Chairmen left Washington today with conditional strike orders in their pockets. The Presidents of the four brotherhoods remained, and will send to the Chairmen on or about Sept. 1 the word that will mean peace or industrial war.

It seems tonight that the only thing that can prevent the strike is acceptance by the railroads of President Wilson's plan of settlement.

Meanwhile President Wilson, realizing the critical situation, took means to ascertain what legislative or executive action might be possible to keep the country from suffering if a strike should come. As a result of a conference at the White House this afternoon it is believed that serious consideration is being given to the question of "keeping open the avenues of transportation," it was expressed tonight, through Governmental supervision or control of train service, but no authoritative statement to that effect has been made. The impression that the President is taking the precaution to learn in advance whether he would be justified in adopting drastic measures to prevent a complete tie-up of train service was gained from what was said after the conference.

Wilson May Address Congress.

After the President had made a trip to the Senate office building in the rain tonight, and had sent a policeman to call Senator Kern of Indiana from his committee room for a conference, Senator Kern refused to deny that the President contemplated addressing Congress in joint session on the railway crisis.

Senator Kern talked with the President for ten minutes in the hall of the office building, and then they walked upstairs to the President's room, after a janitor had been found to turn on the lights. The conference ended, the President left without consulting other Democratic leaders.

"I cannot discuss the subject of the President's visit," said Senator Kern, "further than to say that it concerned the railroad situation. If the negotiations to settle the strike fail, Congress must endeavor to solve the difficulty." Asked if arrangements for the President to address a joint session of Congress had been made, he would not deny that such a joint session in the immediate future was in contemplation. It may be called for Tuesday, when a quorum of the House has been summoned to reach Washington.

Brotherhood Chairmen Depart.

Senator Newlands, after a conference with the President today, said:

"In event of a strike the most serious immediate problem will be that of keeping the railroads in operation, and determining how far the Federal Government should go to prevent demoralization of business and complete stagnation of commerce. A strike of the dimensions of that now threatened would be civil war. It is idle to ignore the fact that such a strike could not be won without force. It would be necessary for the Government to use force and to resort to the military and every other agency at its disposal to offset violence and keep the roads open. How far the Government should go in the matter of forcing operation of the roads is a serious problem for Congress to consider."

The brotherhood Chairmen sent word to the White House last night that they would leave today, and at 3 o'clock this afternoon, after a continuous five-hour meeting, they went from their hall to the National Hotel, received more than $25,000 expense money, paid their bills, and took trains for home.

At the Chairmen's meeting a resolution was adopted giving the four brotherhood Presidents power to accept anything except recession from the eight-hour day demand. Since the eight-hour day is the one thing the railroads have refused, there might seem little chance of much bargaining.

Before they left the Chairmen received bundles of strike instructions, to be distributed to local Chairmen on the various roads. In addition, each received a sealed envelope containing a code, to be opened upon the receipt of a code message from the four Presi-

Continued on Page 3.

Wilson May Address Congress in Joint Session In a Last Effort to Avert Great Railway Strike

By The Associated Press.

WASHINGTON, Aug. 27.—Plans for a joint session of the Senate and House, possibly on Tuesday next, to hear President Wilson ask for legislation to prevent the threatened nation-wide railroad strike were discussed tonight by the President with Senator Kern, the Democratic leader, when it seemed virtually certain that a break between the railroads and their employes must follow final conferences at the White House tomorrow.

Possibilities of legislation were talked over by the President with Senator Newlands, Chairman of the Interstate Commerce Committee, and Secretary Lane during the day, and tonight the President made a quiet trip to the Senate office building to find Senator Kern attending a meeting of the Finance Committee.

Since last night the belief has been growing that negotiations between the railroad executives and representatives of the men would end without an agreement. Whether the plans considered by President Wilson and his advisers at the Capitol will be carried out depends upon tomorrow's developments, but it is understood that if all efforts fail to bring the employers and their men together the President will go before Congress and ask that it deal with the situation, even if that necessitates indefinitely prolonging the present session.

After the President's unprecedented Sunday night visit the meeting of the Finance Committee Democrats was turned from the task of polishing up the Revenue bill to discussion of the prospects before Congress of legislation relating to the railroad crisis.

Of course, all adjournment plans have been forgotten., said Senator Simmons. I think the first things Congress should do in event of failure of negotiations tomorrow is to enact some legislation to prevent an actual break between the railroads and the men. How this may be done I do not know, but I believe definite plans along this line are already being considered.

Several Senators asserted that Congress could prevent the strike, and some went so far as to say that it must prevent it, and would, but they added that public discussion about the method of accomplishing this result should await an actual break in pending negotiations.

REA SAYS ROADS CANNOT YIELD

Better to Face Strike Than Surrender, Pennsylvania President Asserts.

COST WOULD BE TOO GREAT

Railways Confident Their Action Will Be Indorsed by the Country at Large.

Special to The New York Times.

WASHINGTON, D. C., Aug. 27.—Samuel Rea, President of the Pennsylvania Railroad, who came to Washington from the Pacific Coast when he learned that the strike crisis was acute, announced tonight that the railroads were ready to face a strike and all its consequences rather than accept President Wilson's plan of settlement. On behalf of the railroad Presidents Mr. Rea made the following statement:

"For the managements of the railways to yield to the demands and threats of the labor organizations, and to accept President Wilson's proposal, would be to destroy at one blow the principle of arbitration as the paramount and recognized method of settling labor disputes. The threatened strike would be postponed, it is true, but we would have no assurance that it would be permanently prevented. Except that the principle of eight-hour day would be considered, the issues of the very controversy now pending would be left unsettled, while the future of the railways would indeed be rendered dark and uncertain.

"These, in brief, are the reasons why the heads of the railways, with a full appreciation of the solemn and weighty responsibility resting on them, as well as of their duty to the public and to their shareholders, have been forced to the conclusion that it is better to face the alternative of a strike than to surrender.

"Let any man who questions the soundness of this conclusion consider, in the light of their history of the last ten years, the position in which the carriers now find themselves.

"The great labor movements culminating in the present one began a decade ago, almost simultaneously with the adoption of effective regulation. From that time the managements have been in a desparate struggle to prevent net revenue from being so impaired as to destroy the credit of the railways and completely stop their development. After the first large increases in wages, appeal was made to the Interstate Commerce Commission for advances in rates, which the commission in 1911 denied. Even in the face of this railway managers were undaunted and in good faith applied all their energy and ability to increasing efficiency. Never in the history of any industry was more hard, conscientious, able and successful work done to increase efficiency than has been done on the railways of this country during the last ten years.

"What has been the result? The labor movement has continued, and one arbitration board after another has awarded advances in wages. In spite of increased efficiency the companies could not stand the strain, and in 1914 again appealed to the Interstate Commerce Commission. This time the commission decided that their earnings were not adequate, and granted some advances in rates, but before this relief was accorded there were more miles of railway in the hands of receivers than ever before, and new construction had reached the lowest ebb since the civil war.

"This period of profound depression has been followed by a year of comparative prosperity in the railway busi-

Continued on Page 3.

STRIKE CRISIS MAY HOLD UP CONGRESS

Leaders Fear the Railroad Situation Will Spoil Plan for Adjournment This Week.

UNDERWOOD FIGHTS ON

Alabaman Determined to Oppose Tariff on Dyes—Other Revenue Contests.

WASHINGTON, Aug. 27.—Plans for adjournment of Congress next Friday are not maturing as rapidly or as certainly as leaders had contemplated. The crisis in the railroad situation is the principal obstacle encountered at the eleventh hour, and no one tonight would predict what might happen or when the long and arduous session would end.

Plans for adjournment were in progress yesterday when President Wilson visited the Capitol to talk over legislation which the threatened railroad strike might demand. This disturbed all calculations, and leaders are going ahead on the assumption that Congress may adjourn when it completes the legislative program now before it unless railroad legislation develops in the meantime to alter the situation.

The Senate has begun the final drive on the Revenue bill, and will continue consideration of amendments tomorrow, with some of the Democrats who are opposed to various features of the bill proposing amendments. Senator Underwood, whose revolt against the income tax provisions was defeated yesterday, will make another protest against the proposed increased tariffs on dyestuffs. He intends to fight to the last on the ground that it is undemocratic. Senator Phelan of California wants amendments to the wine tax, and Senator Overman of North Carolina will lead a revolt against the proposal to tax manufacturers of materials entering into munitions of war. He will propose to exempt all agricultural products from this tax, his amendment being designed to prevent taxation of cotton, which enters into explosives.

When amendments have been disposed of, the Senate will lay aside the Revenue bill long enough to pass the General Deficiency Appropriation bill as soon as it comes from the House on Tuesday or Wednesday. With the last of the appropriations out of the way and conference reports completed, Administration leaders hope to pass the Revenue bill, to defeat motions that will be made to take up the Corrupt Practices and Immigration bills, and then to adjourn. Senator Owen will struggle to the end for action on Corrupt Practices.

House leaders are going ahead with the completion of their program. The House will meet on Tuesday and act on the Deficiency Appropriation bill. It will follow this with action on the amended Shipping bill, which has been held up because of the lack of a quorum.

TWO HURT IN AUTOS' CRASH.

Woman and Brooklyn Man Injured. Driver Is Arrested.

Special to The New York Times.

GREENWICH, Conn., Aug. 27.—A small touring car, owned and driven by Mrs. E. W. Smith, proprietress of a Summer hotel in Sound Beach, was struck by another car, owned by Laurence Moran, a jitney driver, at Mianus, on the Boston Post Road, early today. Otto Frank of Brooklyn, who was riding in Mrs. Smith's car, suffered a broken left leg and severe cuts and bruises. He was taken to the Stamford Hospital.

Mrs. Smith suffered a number of cuts and bruises. There were two other persons in the car whose names were not learned.

Moran was arrested and directed to appear in court Tuesday on a charge of reckless driving.

Berlin Insists the Bremen is Going to Baltimore

BERLIN, Aug. 27, (by Wireless to Sayville.)—According to the Cologne Gazette, as quoted by the Overseas News Agency, the German merchant submarine Bremen is now on her way to the United States with a cargo of dyes.

BERLIN, Aug. 27, (via London.)—The Tageblatt today prints an interview had in Cologne with Director Lohmann of the company owning the submarine Bremen, in which he says the Bremen is already on her way to Baltimore, and that trade by means of a submarine fleet will soon be increased materially.

All the recent indications here have been that the Bremen, when she arrived, would put in at New London.

WM. A. BRADY HURT IN MOTOR ACCIDENT

Jules E. Goodman and John Turk Also Injured as Manager's Car Breaks Down.

TAKEN TO JERSEY HOSPITAL

Mishap Occurs After the First Production in Plainfield of "The Man Who Came Back."

PLAINFIELD, N. J., Aug. 27.—William A. Brady, theatrical producer of Manhattan; Jules Eckert Goodman, author of "The Man Who Came Back," and John Turk, business manager for Mr. Brady, were badly injured shortly before midnight last night in an automobile accident near Dunellen. All three are in the Muhlenberg Hospital here, recovering from injuries and shock.

Mr. Brady came here last night to witness the opening performance of "The Man Who Came Back" at the Plainfield Theatre. With him were Mr. Goodman and Mr. Turk. They remained in the theatre until the close of the show, and then made preparations to start for Wilmington, Del., where the play is to have another tryout tomorrow night.

The three men got into Mr. Brady's large auto, driven by his chauffeur, and everything went well until the party was near Dunellen. Then the rear axle broke and a wheel came off, causing the car to skid to one side of the road. The three men, riding in the rear seat of the motor, were hurled out and thrown into a ditch.

They were rushed to the Muhlenberg Hospital here early this morning. It was said at the hospital tonight that all three were badly bruised, but would be able to leave for New York tomorrow.

TWO KILLED IN RACE AS 11 CARS PILE UP

Peacock's Machine, Leading in 100-Mile Contest at Kalamazoo, Skids, Blocking Track.

KALAMAZOO, Mich., Aug. 27.—Two men were killed and eight others injured, one of them fatally, when eleven of fourteen automobiles piled up at the first turn during the 100-mile race at Recreation Park here today.

The dead are:

ARNOLD, MARION, mechanician, Chicago; decapitated.
PEACOCK, JACK, driver, Brooklyn; both hips broken and head crushed; died in hospital.

Probably fatally injured:

MARQUETTE, F. E., Kalamazoo, mechanician for Peacock; head injured and left leg broken in three places; unconscious.

The others injured are:

DOWNS, HAROLD W., Kalamazoo, driver; cut about face and head.
NEWTON, ROY, Kalamazoo, mechanician for Downs; cuts on face and head.
BALL, THOMAS, Coldwater, Mich., driver; back injured.
BAILEY, GUY L., Coldwater, mechanician for Ball; face and back injured.
ALEXANDER, JIMMY, Sioux City, Iowa, mechanician; badly bruised.
BURT, ANDY, driver, Chicago; badly bruised.
HENNING, OTTO, driver, Chicago; minor injuries.

Peacock's car, leading in the race, skidded and struck the fence at the first turn. It was overturned and thrown squarely across the track. Before track attendants could signal the other drivers, ten of the machines going at a terrific clip plowed into the overturned car. Five of them were completely demolished.

The car driven by Andy Burt, whose mechanician, Marion Arnold, was killed, was the first to strike that of Peacock. Nine others came into the wreckage a moment later.

At the same park in 1911, Lee Oldfield's racing car plowed through the fence and killed eight persons.

AUTO FALLS IN RIVER; 4 KILLED, 4 INJURED

Family Party on Way to Attend a Funeral Goes Over Bank Near Covington, Penn.

WELLSBORO, Penn., Aug. 27.—Two men and two children were killed and four other persons were injured late last night when an automobile occupied by Earl Sherman and his family of Endicott, N. Y., went over an embankment into the Tioga River near Covington, Penn. The dead are Earl Sherman, 35 years, Captain of Fire Police, Endicott; neck broken; Frank Perry, chauffeur, 22, drowned; two daughters of Sherman, 2½ years and 5 months old, both drowned.

Injured, Mrs. Caroline Becker, Mrs. Sherman, and two men whose names were not learned.

The family was on its way to Lorenton, Penn., to attend the funeral of Mrs. Sherman's mother. Heavy rains had fallen and a dense fog had arisen over the river. Perry was unable to make a curve on the down grade on the slippery road, and the car went over a twelve-foot embankment and turned bottom side up. It took twelve men to raise the car from the bodies beneath it.

ITALY DECLARES WAR ON GERMANY; ROME EXPECTS RUMANIA TO FOLLOW; BULGARS IN KAVALA SHELLED FROM SEA

FORTS TAKEN FROM GREEKS

Three British Warships Promptly Begin Bombardment of Invaders.

BULGARS ENTER ALBANIA

Are Also Near Mouth of the Struma in Advance Along East Bank of River.

SERBS REPEL ATTACKS

Russian Seaplanes Drop Bombs on Varna and Foe's Aircraft Attack Czar's Squadron.

LONDON, Aug. 27.—Hostilities are growing on the Saloniki front. The Paris War Office in its official communiqué tonight says that violent fighting between Bulgarian and Serbian troops continues on the Macedonian front, in the region of Lake, Ostrovo, where Serbian counterattacks have pushed back the Bulgarians.

On the extreme of this, the left wing of the Entente Army, Bulgarians have invaded Albania and occupied the town of Malik, ten miles west of the Greek border, according to advices from Berlin, which also announce that the Bulgarians on the right wing, marching down the Struma along the east bank, have almost reached the mouth of that river.

Further to the east all but one of the forts about the Greek Port of Kavala have now been occupied by the Bulgarians, and two British monitors and a cruiser are bombarding the positions seized.

"Despite German assurances to Greece that Seres, Dhama, and Kavala would not be occupied by the Bulgars," says Reuter's Saloniki correspondent, "an order sent last Tuesday to the commander of the forts at Kavala said if the Bulgars advanced the forts were to be handed over to them. Friday the Bulgars entered the town and took possession of the forts. British warships in the harbor then opened fire on the forts, but details of the results of the fighting are not permitted to be sent."

Terrible Panic in Kavala.

"The effect of the Bulgarian occupation of Doxato, the scene of alleged atrocities of which the Greeks accused the Bulgars in the last war, is prodigious.

"Kavala is the theatre of amazing scenes of disorder. Thousands of refugees are pouring into this port from the hinterland and crowding the steep, narrow streets until they are impassable.

"The streets are littered with every kind of household goods, flung away by the owners, fleeing before the advancing Bulgarians as before the plague.

"These goods were abandoned by the fugitives upon their discovery that means of escape from the city by sea transport were inadequate. Small boats, dangerously overloaded with women and children, are rowing aimlessly about the harbor, their occupants seeking asylum aboard any vessel regardless of its destination or the price of passage. A thorough panic prevails."

Activity is reported on the Black Sea coast of Bulgaria, where Russian seaplanes have dropped bombs on Varna and Bulgarian seaplanes have attacked a Russian squadron ten miles off that port.

Following is the French official report of the operations:

On the Struma front our artillery has continued to bombard enemy organizations. A Bulgarian battalion was caught by our fire. There was an intermittent cannonade between Lake Doiran and Majadagh.

West of the Vardar the Bulgarians renewed their attempts against Vetrinik and northwest of Kukuruz. Five successive attacks, conducted with extreme violence, were shattered by the Serbian artillery fire.

In the region of Lake Ostrovo desperate fighting continues, particularly west and northwest of the lake, where several Bulgarian attacks were driven back by counterattacks of the Serbian infantry.

Friday two British monitors and a cruiser bombarded the forts at Kavala which had been occupied, with one exception, by Bulgarians.

Berlin Reports Bulgar Successes.

BERLIN, Aug. 27, (via London.)—"Bulgarian forces which are advancing on the eastern bank of the Struma (in northeastern Greece) are approaching the mouth of the river," the War Office announced today.

BERLIN, Aug. 27, (by wireless to Sayville.)—Bulgarian forces are invading Albania, and have occupied the town of Malik, ten miles west of the Greek border, an official statement issued yesterday at Sofia reports. Occupation of the territory in northeastern Greece continues, and further Bulgarian detachments have reached the Aegean Sea. The repulse of a Serbian attack in the Moglenica Valley, on the western part of the front, also is announced. The statement follows:

Our right wing continues to march on. A detachment advancing south from Ochrida Lake reached and cap-

Continued on Page 2.

Allies Tell Greece They Won't Defend Thessaly and Ask What the Athens Government Intends

LONDON, Monday, Aug. 28.—A delayed dispatch from Athens says that the French and British Ministers on Thursday evening asked Premier Zaimis how far the Greek Government proposed to countenance the Bulgarian advance without resistance, pointing out that it would be of no military interest to the Entente Powers to defend Central Thessaly from invasion, as Saloniki was supplied from the sea and could not be cut off by land.

"The embarrassment of the Greek Government," continues the dispatch, "grows hourly in the face of popular resentment against the Bulgarian invasion. The Venizelist organs criticise the inaction of the Government, the Cretan declaring that the hour has come for action similar to that taken in 1909.

"M. Pachitch, former Serbian Premier, has arrived here on his way to Saloniki."

Greek People Stirred by Bulgar Invasion.

Special Cable to The New York Times.

LONDON, Monday, Aug. 28.—The Daily Chronicle prints the following dispatch from Athens, dated there Aug. 24:

"Popular interest regarding the situation arising out of the Bulgar invasion of Greece increases with the approach of Sunday, the day on which a great demonstration of protest will be held here. The papers devote long articles to the situation. The Patris, a journal always well informed, makes the following interesting statement, which may be regarded as diplomatically inspired:

"'Recent events in Greece have given rise to a new exchange of views between the Entente Powers. As to the decisions that may be reached as a result we are not yet in a position to know, but what we can affirm is that the diplomacy of the Entente is recasting its views on Greece and examining whether the conditions imposed by the note of June 21 are sufficient to meet the altered conditions created by the Bulgar invasion. A decision will shortly be reached.'

"I would emphasize the importance of this statement. Here signs are everywhere that the descent of the Bulgars on Hellenic soil had a great effect on the popular mind, and especially has affected the belief of those who, by persuasion or by other means, had been induced to place their faith in a pro-German policy as best suited for the country.

"After a considerable period of absence from the Greek capital, the main impression gathered on my return here is that the mass of Greek people, despite everything, are Ententists. I believe Sunday's demonstration will set this forth in a manner that will show, as the greater section of the press here says, that the culminating point has been reached, from which, with careful handling and diplomacy, the Greek people will attain their proper place in the world struggle. The Bulgar invasion has undoubtedly opened the people's eyes."

BRITISH SMASH AHEAD ON SOMME

They Capture a 200-Yard Front North of Bazentin and Push Nearer to Ginchy.

BAD WEATHER PREVAILS

Germans Again Attack at St. Mihiel Salient and in Lorraine, but Are Repulsed.

LONDON, Aug. 27.—Bad weather today hindered the fighting north of the Somme, but the British last evening captured a further 200 yards of a German trench north of Bazentin-le-Petit, which village is situated about four miles southeast of Thiepval. In this sector the British are almost at the outskirts of Martinpuich. Tonight the War Office reports that General Haig has gained ground northwest of Ginchy, which lies directly east of Bazentin.

The French official report today emphasizes the continuation of German attacks on the southern line of the St. Mihiel salient, as well as clashes of reconnoitring patrols in Lorraine. The Germans also made three attacks on the French positions in the Vaux-de-Chapitre Wood, northeast of Verdun. All these attacks were repulsed.

The British communication issued this afternoon reads as follows:

In the successful attacks reported in the communiqués of Friday seven more machine guns were captured than originally reported.

Yesterday evening we took a further 200 yards of a German trench north of Bazentin-le-Petit, capturing one machine gun.

During the night the enemy's artillery fire has been active between the Somme and the Ancre. The enemy also shelled the neighborhood of Bethune during the night, and our heavy artillery retaliated on railway stations and barracks used by the enemy.

Near Hill 60 the enemy exploded a mine, which caused no damage. There is nothing to report from the rest of the front.

British Gain Near Ginchy.

The following official communication was issued this evening:

During the last twenty-four hours bad weather to some extent has interfered with our operations. We have, however, gained ground northwest of Ginchy.

In the afternoon there was considerable artillery activity by both sides, the enemy fire being directed against our support trenches, and more especially toward the north of Longueval. Our guns blew up some of the enemy's bomb stores.

Between Neuve Chapelle and Armentières we exploded mines. The enemy blew up two small mines southwest of Auchy and south of the Ypres salient. There were no casualties in either case.

Four German officers and fifty-five men of other ranks were captured south of the Ancre last night and this morning.

The French afternoon statement follows:

On the Somme front the night was comparatively calm. Persistent bad weather interfered with operations.

On the right bank of the Meuse (Ver-

Continued on Page 2.

RUSSIANS TAKE HUNGARIAN HILL

Capture More Positions Along the Frontier in the Carpathian Mountains.

CHECKED AT DVINA RIVER

Germans Stop Attempts of the Czar's Forces to Cross—Bombard Trenches Along Stokhod.

PETROGRAD, Aug. 27.—Russian troops in the Carpathians, whose advance through the mountains toward Hungary has been held up recently, are again moving forward near the Hungarian border. The War Office announced today the capture of positions three miles northeast of Koverla Mountain, on the frontier. The statement follows:

Enemy airships flew over our positions on the Dreswiaty Lake and dropped bombs, killing a Chaplain, Father Joakim Sedletski, while he was fulfilling his pastoral duties.

On the River Stokhod, in the region of the village of Tobol, the enemy opened fierce artillery fire on our crossings. Here the gallant regimental commander Colonel Mykov was killed.

In the Carpathians, in the region of Koverla Mountain, (on the frontier, ten miles southeast of Korosmezo,) our troops drove the enemy out of his positions on Hill 1,129, three miles northeast of Koverla Mountain, and occupied this height. In this operation we captured 3 officers, 175 men, and 4 machine guns. Our advance continues.

BERLIN, Aug. 27, (via London.)—After a long period of comparative inactivity over the northern end of the eastern front, the Russians last night opened an attack on the Dvina, attempting to cross the river at two points. These efforts were made near Lennewaden, forty miles southeast of Riga, and Friedrichstadt, ten miles further up the river. Today's official report says these efforts failed. The statement follows:

Front of Field Marshal von Hindenburg: On the Dvina front repeated attempts by the Russians to cross the river in boats east of Friedrichstadt and near Lennewaden were frustrated.

Southeast of Kiselin, in Volhynia, twenty-five miles southeast of Kovel, small German detachments penetrated as far as the enemy's third line, and after destroying trenches returned to their own positions, in accordance with their plans, bringing with them 128 prisoners and three machine guns.

Front of Archduke Charles Francis: Apart from patrol engagements north of the Dniester, in which we were successful, there were no events of importance.

OPEN WAY WITH ANCHORS.

Russians Use Them to Tear Up German Wire Entanglements.

PETROGRAD, Aug. 27.—An exploit which is of unusual character, even under present conditions of war, is singled out for especial mention in the official announcement from the War Office today.

"In the region of Shmarden Farm (near Riga) gallant detachments of Lettish battalions broke through the first line of the enemy's entanglements at two points," the statement says. "Fastening an anchor at each of these points, they pulled up with a winch the intervening entanglements, together with all the posts, for a distance of thirty paces.

"The enemy opened fire on our Lettish troops without result."

BUCHAREST NEAR TO ACTION

Crown Council Today May Put Rumania On Side of the Allies.

NEW COMMANDER FOR ARMY

Gen. Averescu, Who Favors Entente, Chosen—Bratiano Bent on Ending Neutrality.

OUTLOOK WORRIES AUSTRIA

Hungary's Plea for Coalition Cabinet Is Rejected and a Serious Political Crisis Impends.

Special Cable to The New York Times.

ROME, Aug. 27.—Italy issued today a declaration of war on Germany. This move caused general satisfaction here, as it at last put an end to an intolerable situation.

In political circles this formal action by Italy is declared to be in strict conjunction with the entrance of Rumania into the war.

She promised to join the war over a year ago when Italy entered, but found it impossible, under the circumstances at that time.

Political leaders now confidently expect a declaration of war by the Bucharest Government.

It is felt here that Germany in the past has not been without pretext for breaking definitely with Italy, as, for instance, when Italy signed the pact of London. It is believed that Germany's patience with Italy was not only to protect her great interests in this country, but to deceive the German people still further. Germany on her side has continually protested that she has never done anything incompatible with her situation as an enemy of Italy, yet not declaring war on her.

Germany has denied that any of her soldiers were sent to fight Italy on her northern or northeastern frontiers. Unofficial reports have told of the presence of German troops there, but these reports have never been confirmed. It is said, however, that the Italian Government now has possession of proof of these and other acts by the Germans, including the torpedoing of Italian steamers on the high seas.

BERLIN, Aug. 27, (by Wireless to Sayville.)—The following official announcement was made here today:

The Italian Government has declared through the Swiss Government that it considers itself, from Aug. 28, at war with Germany.

Crown Council Called in Rumania.

LONDON, Aug. 27.—The Rumanian Crown Council, which had been convened for 10 o'clock Monday morning, has been postponed until 5 o'clock in the afternoon, a Bucharest dispatch received in Amsterdam says.

According to another Bucharest dispatch, the King of Rumania has convened a conference of representatives of all the political parties, former Premiers, former Presidents of the Legislative Chambers, Ministers, and Government representatives, with the idea of ascertaining the views of all sections of public opinion on the present situation.

Special Cable to The New York Times.

LONDON, Monday, Aug. 28.—The Bucharest correspondent of The London Times sends the following, dated Aug. 21:

"General Averescu (former Minister of War and in the councils of the Headquarters Staff one of the chief advocates of intervention) is stated in military circles to have been selected for chief command of the army.

"The German Minister, who on Wednesday had another audience of the King, is reported to have delivered to his Majesty an autograph letter from the Kaiser."

A Budapest dispatch to The Morning Post, dated Aug. 20, quotes the Bucharest correspondent of Nepzava as saying, under date of the previous day:

"The general opinion expressed by the Bucharest press of all political shades is that a decision of the Cabinet is at hand. The Bina, a pro-German organ, says that, in spite of the fact that nothing of the nature expected by Premier Bratiano has happened on the European fronts and that the Entente Powers have achieved no prominent successes, the Rumanian Premier finds it fit and timely to abandon neutrality. Neither the Allies in the west nor Russia or Italy, it goes on, can boast of any great measure of success, 'yet the Rumanian Cabinet is feverishly preparing for war.'

"According to another Rumanian

"All the News That's Fit to Print."

The New York Times.

THE WEATHER
Fair, continued cool today; tomorrow, fair; light west to southwest winds.
For full weather report see Page 1

VOL. LXV...NO. 21,402. ... NEW YORK, TUESDAY, AUGUST 29, 1916.—TWENTY PAGES. ONE CENT In Greater New York, Jersey City and Newark. | Elsewhere, TWO CENTS.

RAILWAY STRIKE ORDER ISSUED; WILSON TO ASK CONGRESS FOR ARBITRATION AND 8-HOUR LAWS

UNION SECRET BETRAYED

Sealed Mandate Calling for Walkout on Sept. 4 Is Opened.

RAILROADS TO END PARLEYS

Presidents to Quit Capital Tomorrow if Unions' Order Stands.

STILL HOPE FOR PEACE

Though Brotherhood Heads Tell President Notice to Members Can't Be Recalled.

Special to The New York Times.

WASHINGTON, Aug. 28.—After conferences that promised to keep him from his bed till dawn President Wilson announced tonight that he would go before Congress tomorrow or Wednesday to ask for legislation to stop the impending strike on the railroads of this country.

At 3 o'clock this afternoon the railroad Presidents told Mr. Wilson that a strike had been called for Sept. 4, and that it was imperative that they get away from Washington. The President asked that he have confirmation of the calling of the strike, expressing incredulity that the brotherhoods could have taken such a step while he was trying to get the eight-hour day for them.

When he returned from the Capitol after a two and a half hours' conference with Senate leaders he found awaiting him at the White House a copy of the strike order which 640 Chairmen of the unions last night took to their members on every railroad in the United States.

At once he sent for A. B. Garretson, President of the conductors; W. S. Stone, Grand Chief of the engineers; W. S. Carter, President of the firemen, and W. G. Lee, President of the trainmen, and demanded that they cancel the order. To his surprise the four told him it was not in their power.

The President then notified the railroad executives of the development and they held a hurried meeting. Many were in favor of leaving Washington at once to prepare to fight the strike, but it was decided to remain here until tomorrow, when President Wilson is expected to address a joint session of Congress in a supreme effort to avert the disaster.

The strike order was dated Aug. 14, and it was charged tonight by the railroad executives that the union heads had decided at that time on the strike and allowed the negotiations here to continue while they perfected arrangements for the strike they intended to call all the while.

Still Hope for Settlement.

On the surface a nation-wide railroad strike was nearer tonight than it had ever been. Nevertheless confidence was expressed in official quarters that the steps under contemplation would have the effect of preventing the walkout. The President, realizing the disaster which would come to the country if the railroads are tied up, was said to be determined to prevent a strike at any cost. In his conferences with the executives he strongly urged that they change their hitherto unyielding attitude, and when he saw the employes he declared that all suggestions from the executives should be given most careful consideration.

Both the executive and legislative branches of the National Government have dropped practically all other business in a supreme effort to avert the strike. President Wilson spent the day in conferences at the Capitol and White House with Administration leaders in Congress. Here is the legislation the President wants:

A bill providing for the eight-hour day on interstate commerce carriers.

A bill instructing the Interstate Commerce Commission to investigate the working of the eight-hour day and to decide what increase in rates would be needed to recompense the railroads.

A bill creating an industrial commission similar to that in Canada which would have the power to suspend all strike activities until it made an investigation.

Bore Sealed Strike Orders.

Not all the 640 brotherhood Chairmen who left Washington last night for their posts knew that in sealed envelopes in their pockets was an order for a strike on Sept. 4. That fact was supposed to be known only to the four heads of the brotherhoods. The sealed envelopes were not to be opened until the receipt of a code word on Sept. 1. One of the envelopes was obtained today, and it was found to contain an official order declaring a strike effective Sept. 4 at 7 A. M. While the orders were not signed, there was a blank space for them to be signed by the General Committee. Their date of Aug. 14 marks the first day, two weeks ago, that the President met the brotherhood leaders and the railroad managers and sustains the assertion frequently made by the labor men that they were all ready to strike when the President intervened.

Labor Day was agreed upon as the time for the tentative strike order to become operative, it was said today, after careful consideration of several dates. It was chosen finally because of the belief that a demonstration by the 2,000,000 or more union men who would march in Labor Day parades in behalf

Continued on Page 4.

Union Strike Order Can't Be Rescinded, Leaders' Answer to President's Appeal

Special to The New York Times.

WASHINGTON, Aug. 28.—President Wilson called the brotherhood heads to the White House tonight and asked them if they had issued a secret strike order, a copy of which he had obtained, calling a strike for 7 o'clock A. M. Labor Day. They acknowledged that the order had been issued. The President said he was shocked and surprised and appealed to the brotherhood heads to have the order rescinded. They told him that the order was beyond recall and that the strike was inevitable.

The President took the foregoing action after he had conferred in the afternoon with a committee of railroad Presidents, who told him of the secret action taken by the unions. Leaving the White House, the railroad Presidents issued this statement:

> At a conference at the White House today at 2:30 P. M., between the President and the Committee of Eight of the railroad Presidents, a suggestion was laid before the President in the nature of a proposition for progress toward a solution of the questions at issue, and this was left with him for his consideration.
>
> The committee expects to see the President in the near future, but before leaving the committee pointed out to him that if the reports that the date for declaring the strike had been fixed for Sept. 4 were true, it would force an early conclusion of the negotiations and compel the Presidents to return to their properties to prepare for the issue.

News that copies of the strike order were in the hands of the railway Presidents occasioned no surprise among the brotherhoods. After it became known yesterday that they suspected three of their number of acting as spies for the railroad heads, they said frankly that they expected the strike order soon would be in their employers' hands.

"There was one traitor among the twelve Disciples," one of the brotherhood heads said, "and our average appears to be higher than that."

Every effort was made to keep the call of the union leaders at the White House secret. When they left they all declined to discuss their conference.

WALL ST. HOPEFUL OF RAILWAY PEACE

Brief Sag in the Stock Market Yesterday, but Recovery Comes Speedily.

EXPECT UNIONS TO GIVE IN

Houses in Closest Touch with Washington Get Optimistic Reports on Situation.

For the first time yesterday the accumulation of unfavorable news from Washington on the differences between the railroad executives and the brotherhoods served to unsettle security prices. The market had a good opening, but began to sag as the tickers reported a growing belief at the capital of the possibility of a strike.

The downward movement had not gained much headway when banks and brokerage houses, which heretofore have always kept closely in touch with developments at Washington, received reassuring advices. Their effect was immediately noted by a fresh wave of buying. Traders on the floor of the Exchange were generally bearish on the situation, but the recovery in prices forced many of them to cover positions on the short side taken earlier in the day, and the close, while irregular, was such as to indicate little fear of a break.

One man who sent a representative to Washington to watch the trend of negotiations received a dispatch shortly after noon yesterday to the effect that the pressure of public opinion, converging on the White House, was beginning to make itself felt. The correspondent reported that, in his opinion, the brotherhoods were going to agree to arbitration on the best terms they could make.

A member of the Stock Exchange, who is recognized as an authority on railway economics, was of the opinion that rigid adherence to the principle of arbitration would be construed as bullish by most holders of railroad securities. Certainly, he said, no railroad security would be benefited by surrender to a demand for payment of ten hours' wages for eight hours' work and the consequent chance of obtaining less than eight hours' real work from employes loafing on their runs so that a rate and a half might be charged for overtime. Moreover, the grant of the demand for an eight-hour day to 400,000 employes would certainly be followed by demands from the others of the 2,300,000 were the railroads to accept the proposition that an eight-hour day is a basic principle.

That railroad stocks might sell off in the event of a strike he was willing to admit, but he did not think that professionals would sell them heavily or the reason that there has been no top-heavy speculation in the rails, and he expected actual liquidation from none except excessively timid holders. Such selling, in his opinion, would be more than offset by the confidence inspired in investors by rigid adherence to principle.

The stock market has persistently disbelieved nearly everything printed about the railway labor controversy. Timid customers, after reading all of the morning papers, have come downtown for several days in the expectation of seeing a very bad market, but they have not yet discovered any serious liquidation inspired by the fear of a strike.

One big operator is reported to have bought 50,000 shares of stock yesterday after getting a message that the brotherhoods were going to submit to arbitration after holding off till the last minute to make as much capital as possible out of their surrender.

TO END UNIONS' EXEMPTION.

House Leader Thinks Strike Would Cause Clayton Law Change.

Special to The New York Times.

WASHINGTON, Aug. 28.—A railroad strike that cripples the traffic of the country is likely to be followed by an agitation in Congress for the repeal of that section of the Clayton anti-trust law which exempts labor unions from the operation of the Sherman act. This was the prediction today of a House Democratic leader who is watching developments in the strike situation.

SECRET ORDERS FIX STRIKE FOR SEPT. 4

Sealed Envelopes Handed to Brotherhood Chairmen as They Leave Capital.

INSTRUCTIONS TO MEMBERS

Obedience to Law and No Violence Are Counseled in Official Statement.

Special to The New York Times.

WASHINGTON, Aug. 28.—Here is a copy of the secret strike order handed in sealed envelopes to the 640 brotherhood Chairmen who left Washington today. In addition to this order, secret instructions were issued to the members for their guidance in the event of a strike. The strike order reads:

> Brotherhood of Locomotive Engineers.
> Brotherhood of Locomotive Firemen and Enginemen.
> Order of Railway Conductors.
> Brotherhood of Railway Trainmen.
> Aug. 14, 1916.
>
> *To all local Chairmen, members, and others employed in classes of service represented by the B. of L. E., B. of L. F. & E., O. R. C., and B. R. T.:*
>
> Sirs and Brothers: This is to advise that a vote of the employes in train and engine service on the eight-hour day and time and one-half for overtime proposition was overwhelmingly in favor of a strike.
>
> Notwithstanding this your representatives have been unable to effect a satisfactory settlement, and a strike under the laws of the respective organizations becomes effective Sept. 4, 1916, at 7 A. M.
>
> Impart this information so that those interested will understand that they are to promptly obey.
>
> Fraternally yours,
>
> .... General Chairman,
> .... R. R.

The instructions, which counsel obedience to the law in the event of a strike, and define the duties of members and their local Chairmen, follow:

> Brotherhood of Locomotive Engineers.
> Brotherhood of Locomotive Firemen and Enginemen.
> Order of Railway Conductors.
> Brotherhood of Railway Trainmen.
>
> *Sirs and Brothers:*
>
> In connection with the strike you will observe the following instructions:
>
> DUTIES OF MEMBERS.
>
> 1. No man in road service involved in the strike will perform any service after the hour set to strike, unless he has already begun his trip and has actually left the terminal. If the train has left the terminal he will complete the trip and deliver the engine and train at the end of the run, or tie-up point, if tied up under the law, after which he will perform no further service until the close of the strike. Men in other than road service will leave the service at the appointed time.
>
> So far as your legal right to strike is concerned, there is no difference between a mail train and a freight train. You have identically the same right to refuse to perform service on a mail train as you have to refuse to perform service on a freight train.
>
> 2. All men on strike will keep away from the companies' property, except such men as are designated certain duties to be performed by authority of the organization.
>
> 3. Every man should understand that the laws of the land must be obeyed. Acts of violence of any nature will not be tolerated by the organizations.
>
> 4. The local representatives will arrange for a hall for meeting purposes at all terminals, using one of their own lodge rooms if available. Immediately after the strike becomes effective all men will assemble at the hall secured for meeting purposes. When thus assembled an organization will be perfected by the election of a Chairman, Vice Chairman, and Secretary. No person will be permitted to be present in the meeting hall other than those who are on strike except by permission of the assembly.
>
> 5. The Secretary will arrange a roll call (alphabetically) with each organization on a separate sheet. Roll will be called twice daily, morning and afternoon. The names of the non-members will be kept separate on the roll from the names of those who are members of the organizations. All strikers will be required to answer the roll call, and also to be in the halls, where halls are provided, during the day at all times, unless excused by committee action or by Chairman of

Continued on Page 4.

Mexicans Expect Pershing To Withdraw by Sept. 15

Special Cable to THE NEW YORK TIMES.

MEXICO CITY, Aug. 28.—Chihuahua City reports that the American punitive expedition is preparing for general withdrawal from Mexico were received here today with great enthusiasm. Officials believe that in view of General Funston's recommendation that the troops retire, the withdrawal undoubtedly will be promptly agreed to at the first conference of the joint commission. It is expected all the troops will have retired before Sept. 15, the anniversary of Mexican independence.

A high Government official stated this afternoon that when the American expedition retired the greatest cloud on the Mexican horizon would be eliminated and General Carranza would be able to devote his efforts to the re-establishment of constitutional government.

It is reported that Carranza and other high members of the Government will leave for Dolores Hidalgo, Guanajuato, early in September to celebrate the anniversary of independence at the same spot where the priest, Miguel Hidalgo, ringing the bell of a village church, proclaimed Mexican freedom.

SAN ANTONIO, Texas, Aug. 28.—General Pershing has withdrawn the Thirteenth Cavalry from El Valle to Colonia Dublan, Department Headquarters announced today. General Funston said the move was designed to facilitate the supplying of forage for the organization and had no significance. El Valle is the advance base of the expedition, and is about fifty miles southeast of Colonia Dublan.

OYSTER BAY REVOLTS OVER POLIOMYELITIS

Townsmen Blame the "Corruption of Men and Microbes" by Rockefeller Millions.

THEY SEIZE TOWN MEETING

And Resolve "Medico-Politico Barbarism" Must Cease Despite All Incentive.

Special to The New York Times.

OYSTER BAY, Aug. 28.—The corruption of men and microbes by the millions of John D. Rockefeller and Andrew Carnegie, and the gullibility of Col. Theodore Roosevelt are responsible for the "chaosless hysteria and the needless hardships of the alleged infantile paralysis epidemic," according to townsmen of Oyster Bay who met today in tumultuous assembly and adopted resolutions expressing their angry opinions.

The meeting began with a session of the Town Board, at which Dr. W. E. Caldwell of the State laboratory at Roslyn, and Dr. William J. Burns, Health Officer of Oyster Bay, appeared to give information concerning the epidemic. The doctors had difficulty in sticking to their subjects because of interruptions by irate fathers who wanted to know why their children had been snatched away to the isolation hospital when they were not suffering from infantile paralysis. The citizens seemed to be especially incensed because of the health regulation permitting the forcible removal of children to the hospital, and a recent incident when it took the authority and strength of four deputy sheriffs and two physicians to get a child from its father to the hospital was emphasized as an especially flagrant offense against the freedom of the community.

Drs. Caldwell and Burns finally left the meeting in the hands of Joseph Steinert, Chairman of the Town Board, who was powerless to preserve order, and left himself within a short time, followed immediately by the members of the board.

Then the townsmen took charge of the meeting. They elected Colonel Henry M. Bennett Chairman, and appointed a committee to draw up resolutions representing the opinion of those present. The resolutions were adopted, and will be presented to the Town Board when it comes back to its hall, with the demand that the regulation governing the removal of children to hospitals without the consent of parents, except in cases where the parents are unable to provide proper care, be repealed.

The resolutions began by asserting that the community, "through the intriguing and propaganda of certain so-called medical and scientific men," had been gradually led from a quiet, peaceful, and law-abiding condition to "a state of excitability, frenzy, and even terror of a mysterious bug, germ, or miasma," which is supposed to float up from backyards or from the atmosphere, "but which exists solely in the minds of a paid coterie of public servants whose business is to find such things to further the sale of their nostrums." Then came this clause in the preamble:

"Through the inspiration and incentive which a great endowment offers to most ambitious men, Mr. John D. Rockefeller and Mr. Carnegie, actuated by a desire to return a small measure of good for the millions which they have extorted from the common people, have seen fit to set aside from their unearned increment a stupendous fund which no microbe, germ, bacillus, or even an honorable physician could overlook."

The succeeding clause dealt with the activities of guards in turning back persons attempting to enter the town with children, and said that this "merely causes the community to be advertised as unhealthy, unclean, unsanitary, and teeming with the germs of polio, which will soon be understood as money-o."

The resolutions further insisted that "both profane and modern history are replete with the medico-politico barbarism of which we are now receiving a sample, as any one who knows the history of quarantine must understand and acknowledge." This quarantine, added the resolutions, "is being perpetrated upon the community for private gain and newspaper notoriety." Having thus stated their reasons the townsmen of Oyster Bay declared:

"Therefore, be it resolved that it is the sense of this committee that the credulity of the public has been preyed upon sufficiently long in this neighborhood; that the business interests are sufficiently paralyzed; that frenzy and terror have been sufficiently propagated; that it is high time for a return to common sense, the discharge of the medical maniacs, the resumption of local business, the recall and restoring to confidence of our easily scared Summer residents, and the application of common horse sense to the so-called epidemic with which we, as well as other communities, have been afflicted."

The meeting adjourned with applause of the resolutions.

RUMANIA IN WAR, ATTACKS AUSTRIA; GERMANY DECLARES WAR IN ANSWER; EUROPE EXPECTS GREECE TO FIGHT

ALLIES SEE VICTORY NEARER

Entry of Rumania Into War Is Expected to Shorten Conflict.

HER DIPLOMACY PRAISED

Her King, It Is Argued, Held the Country Neutral Until the Proper Time.

BULGARIA THOUGHT DOOMED

London, Paris, and Petrograd Rejoice Loudly Over Coming of Another Ally.

Special Cable to THE NEW YORK TIMES.

LONDON, Aug. 28.—The entry of Rumania into the war following upon Italy's declaration of war against Germany is popularly regarded here as the clearest indication that the fortunes of the Teutonic powers are ebbing.

The fullest confidence has been felt in well-informed quarters for some time past in the imminence of the present developments, and the prediction has been frequently made of late that once the harvest had been gathered Rumania would openly cast in her lot with the Entente Powers. It is essential to point out that such views have never received any open official sanction, and even now official quarters here preserve the utmost reticence, even to the point of declaring that no confirmation of today's reports have been received by the British Foreign Office. The events, however, are completely borne out by the view held for some time past in well-informed unofficial quarters, where the varying news as to Rumania's attitude issued from Germany has been received with quiet unconcern.

A Rome dispatch today describes the dramatic scene when the King of Rumania received the German Minister at Bucharest. The Minister, with tears in his eyes, implored the King to continue to maintain neutrality, declaring a Hohenzollern should not make war on a Hohenzollern. The King replied he was simply the King of Rumania and must follow the national will.

King Ferdinand's Diplomacy.

Whether the incident in question is true or of the ben trovato variety, the view is put forward that Ferdinand in policy is entirely and deliberately Rumanian. His diplomacy is described as based upon that most skillful and astute of royal diplomats, the late King Carol, who possessed as few men have done the whole art of balancing and using forces, one against the other, which is the function of diplomacy. It has been said that the late King Carol had a steady pro-German tendency, although in fact such a tendency would be very hard to trace. Of his successor, at least, no such accusation can be made. King Ferdinand has aimed steadily at the realization of Rumanian national hopes and the achievement of Rumanian national unity, but his policy has been one of insurance and calculation. During the long and critical months since his accession to the throne he had two main considerations before him: (1) the provision of his army with heavy artillery equipment that modern war has proved necessary, and, (2) the withholding of any decision until the most favorable moment had arrived. Both from military and political points of view these two considerations have been necessarily interdependent. Rumania was to enter the war, militarily equipped to take her due part and politically assured of the fruits of victory. Both aims have now been achieved.

The Military Situation.

In this connection it is worth recalling that often at the earlier stages it had been advanced that Rumania was not in a position to enter the war because of the inadequacy of military supplies. Particularly, it was said, her heavy armament would not last out two weeks of modern warfare. It will be interesting later to see how the deficiency has been met.

The effect of the Rumanian action on the whole Balkan situation can be gauged by the coolness with which the allied command at Saloniki has taken the Bulgarian extension to Kavala. Observers here regard the recent developments in that neighborhood as clear proof of the superiority attained by the Allies in a political and military sense. The extension of the Bulgarian front began when Berlin was assuring the world that Rumania was "safe." In order to carry out the plan for the occupation of Greek territory east of the Saloniki line, Bulgaria is understood to have drawn upon her troops along the Danube frontier, a proceeding which observers here suggest must have rejoiced the hearts of the Entente strategists who were aware of the blow that Rumania had in contemplation.

As yet Rumania is not announced at war with Bulgaria, and if the latter's northern frontier is weakened in its defenses, it is suggested there is even the possibility of a declaration of war by Rumania upon Bulgaria becoming unnecessary to complete the latter's downfall. Recollections of the part played by Rumania in the last Balkan war give some plausibility to this theory, which takes into account the recent re-

Continued on Page 3.

Pro-Russian Riots Are Raging in Bulgaria; German Troops Are Called to Suppress Them

Special Cable to THE NEW YORK TIMES.

LONDON, Tuesday, Aug. 29.—A dispatch to The London Times from Bucharest, dated Sunday, says:

"According to trustworthy news received by the Journal Epoca, the situation in Bulgaria is very critical. During the last few days pro-Russian demonstrations have taken place at Philippopolis, Yamboli, and Stara Zagora, and the Government was compelled to call upon the German division to crush them. The population attacked the soldiers, who fired, killing and injuring a great number of rioters.

"It seems that the situation of the Radoslavoff Cabinet is very critical."

Another dispatch to The Times from the Rumanian capital, bearing date of Saturday, says:

"Bulgarian deserters who have arrived in Rumania declare that the spirit of the Bulgarian troops is very low, on account of their not receiving pay for six months and insufficient food. All their movements have been made on foot, whereas the Austro-Germans are well fed, regularly paid, and all their movements are made by train.

"According to trustworthy information, Bulgarian troops are continually being moved toward the south in order to meet General Sarrail's offensive."

RUMANIA'S STEP SHOCK TO GERMANS

People Are Calm in Face of What They Admit Is Bad News from the Balkans.

RESULTS WIDELY DISCUSSED

Military Leaders, It Is Said, Have Discounted the Action of King Ferdinand.

From a Staff Correspondent.

Special Cable to THE NEW YORK TIMES.

BERLIN, Aug. 28.—Italy's declaration of war on Germany created little interest in Berlin. The fact became known late yesterday afternoon, being published along with the official bulletin, causing no demonstrations and practically no comment. I found a lack of interest amounting to apathy among the thousands of hero-worshippers massed about the Hindenburg colossus opposite the Reichstag, celebrating the second anniversary of the battle of Tannenberg.

These happy thousands did not know what only insiders were aware of, that Italy's declaration of war was only a prelude to Rumania's declaration of war on Austria.

The report of Rumania's declaration of war on Austria, a short sentence but fraught with the gravest import for the German people of any news item of the year, reached Berlin at 2 o'clock this morning, and without the slightest added details or editorial comment was made known to the public through the morning papers. Then the apathy of last evening vanished.

Little else but the possible consequences of Rumania's entry into the struggle is being talked about this morning. The German people have swallowed and are digesting this bad news with their usual uncanny calm and unemotional quiet, but it is undeniably a severe shock to even the stoic fatalism of the Germans, the shock of reaction being accentuated by the fact that the public here hoped and believed to the very last moment that Rumania would once more balk at plunging into the world war, that Premier Bratiano would again hesitate and procrastinate to avoid taking the fateful step, that King Ferdinand and a large part of the Rumanian Army were at heart pro-German, and that apart from all this, Rumania would be kept out of war by the magic of Hindenburg's name, by fear of Mackensen and his victorious veterans and by the fact that the Bulgarians were burning to make a second Serbia of Rumania and settle the score, which has been standing since the last Balkan war.

In well-informed military circles the entry of Rumania had long been discounted and prepared for. Adequate measures had been taken in time by the general staffs of the Teutonic allies against the increasing certainty of Rumania's joining the conflict. The undiminished confidence of German military men is reflected in the feeling that Rumania's entry will not involve results unfavorable in a military way to the Central Powers and Bulgaria, but that on the contrary the Balkans may now be completely and for all time "cleaned up."

FOOD PROBLEM UNAFFECTED.

Germany's Excellent Crops, It Is Said, Will Obviate a Shortage.

BERLIN, Aug. 28, (via London.)—Semi-official statements today expressed the belief that the influence of Rumania's entry into the war on Germany's food problem would not be considerable. The grain contracts for the 1915 crop have been largely filled, it is said, and the loss on imports of the 1916 crop will not be severely felt, in view of Germany's excellent home crop. Imports of Rumanian grain of all kinds had been placed at 1,400,000 tons, whereas the German crops are now estimated to be 3,000,000 tons above those of 1915, excluding the occupied territories.

Owing to the doubtful attitude of the Rumanian Government, the authorities in charge of Germany's food supplies completed some time ago their plans for feeding the population for the next twelve months without the assistance of Rumania. It is even announced that the bread ration will soon be increased. The authorities are planning an economic policy by which a goodly surplus will be saved from the 1916 crops for a possible shortage in the 1917 crop. Among other things it has been decided to use no grain in the making of brandy, and the grain consumption of breweries has been reduced to below half the normal.

Notwithstanding the growing indications of Rumania's warlike plans, Ger-

Continued on Page 3.

GREEK ARMY CHIEF OFF FOR SALONIKI

Will Meet Allied Generals There, and Says He Can Be "Advocate" of Entente.

SERBS DRIVE THE BULGARS

Are Pushing Back the Foe in West—British Silence Guns on Doiran Front.

ATHENS, Saturday, Aug. 27, (via London.)—General Constantine Moschopoulos, the new Chief of Staff, expressed to The Associated Press yesterday the hope that his eleven months' close association with the allied forces during his command of the Greek troops at Saloniki, the cordial relations between himself and General Sarrail and the British Generals, and his personal knowledge of the difficulties of the problems confronting the Entente Allies in Macedonia, would serve to strengthen the good relations between Greece and the allied powers and dispel any misunderstanding which had previously arisen.

"I think I can be a precious advocate of the Entente," he said.

General Moschopoulos will go to Saloniki on Sunday [last] and will remain there several days. He will confer with the French Commander in Chief before returning to take up his duties here.

Satisfaction with the appointment is widespread. It is generally felt that it will bring to an end much that the Allies found unsatisfactory in the direction of the Greek Army.

Venizelos Addresses Huge Crowd.

Fifty thousand Greeks joined in a demonstration before the residence of Venizelos, the former Premier, today, and cheered him with boundless enthusiasm when he proposed that they send a committee to King Constantine to urge him to support the present Government and prepare the army for "a possible rupture of existing conditions." Addressing the multitude, Venizelos said:

"Last week I summoned you to a demonstration to show you what to do. Now I exhort you to send a committee before the King and to say to him:

"'Your Majesty, you were the victim of persons who persuaded you there would be a German victory, and you thought you could violate the Constitution. The people do not approve of these facts. The reservists telegraph you that they are ready to follow you, because they think you always will remain neutral.

"'Elections are necessary, but you must not use you influence politically because the results would be destructive. The present Government is absolutely necessary. The Premier (Alexander Zaimis) is an excellent man. You should give the Government full political authority. You must now show the Entente Powers most benevolent neutrality and exercise the army in preparation for a possible rupture of existing conditions. The Liberal Party is confident as regards your position.'"

In concluding Venizelos declared, "I think our desire will be favorably accepted, otherwise I will do my best."

SERBIAN DRIVE MAKES PROGRESS

Bulgars Are Driven Back Near Vetrenik and Repulsed in Ostrovo Region.

LONDON, Aug. 28.—Serbian forces operating in Macedonia west of the Vardar River have made considerable progress near Vetrenik, and in the Ostrovo region have repulsed three attacks, with heavy losses to the Bulgarians, according to the official statement given out tonight by the French War Office, which says:

> From the Struma to the region of Ljumnica there was an artillery duel. East of the Cerna the Serbians, pressing their vigorous offensive, have made considerable progress near Vetrenik. On the road from Banica to Ostrovo three Bulgarian attacks against Serbian positions, delivered after intense artillery preparation, were repulsed with heavy losses. Artillery fighting continued violently in this sector.
>
> The Bulgarians have occupied different localities abandoned by the Greeks west of Kavala. British monitors have bombarded enemy forces at the mouth of the Struma.

Contrary to statements made in the Bulgarian official communication for the 28th, Serbian troops, far from having suffered a defeat in the region

Continued on Page 3.

RUMANIANS ENTER PASSES

Army Begins the Invasion of Transylvania in Two Directions.

HOPES TO SHORTEN WAR

Also to Realize National Ideal, Vienna Is Told in Declaration of Hostilities.

TWO CITIES ARE MENACED

Hermannstadt and Kronstadt the Immediate Objectives of King Ferdinand's Forces.

All Rumania's Army Moving; Germany Shifting Troops

Special Cable to THE NEW YORK TIMES.

LAUSANNE, Switzerland, Aug. 28. (Dispatch to The London Daily News.)—I learn from a high diplomatic source in Berne that almost the entire Rumanian Army is moving rapidly.

The Swiss frontier is closed.

The closing of the Swiss frontier obviously indicates that movements of German troops are in progress to meet the new situation, created by the entry of Rumania into the war.

LONDON, Tuesday, Aug. 29.—Rumania has declared war against Austria-Hungary, Germany has retaliated by declaring war against Rumania, and fighting has already begun on the frontier of Transylvania.

The note declaring that Rumania, from 9 o'clock Sunday evening, considered herself in a state of war with Austria-Hungary was presented to the Austro-Hungarian Foreign Minister last night by the Rumanian Minister at Vienna, who personally visited the Ministry of Foreign Affairs.

The note was a lengthy document, in which Rumania set forth her grievances. The Paris newspaper La Liberté has received a summary as telegraphed from Geneva. According to this the persecution of Rumanians by Austro-Hungarian officials is alleged, and it is charged that agreements which existed between Rumania and the former members of the Triple Alliance have been broken in letter and spirit from the time Germany and Austria entered the war. Italy, the declaration says, was obliged to detach herself from Austria and Germany.

Motives for Declaring War.

In conclusion, the communication sets forth as follows the motives in compelling Rumania to enter the war:

First—The Rumanian population in Austrian territories is exposed to the hazards of war and of invasion.

Second—Rumania believes that by intervening she can shorten the world war.

Third—Rumania places herself on the side of those Powers which she believes can assist her most efficaciously in realizing her national ideal.

An official statement issued in Berlin and forwarded by Reuter's correspondent at Amsterdam says:

> After Rumania, as already reported, disgracefully broke treaties concluded with Austria-Hungary and Germany she declared war yesterday against our ally.
>
> The Imperial German Minister to Rumania has received instructions to request his passports and to declare to the Rumanian Government that Germany now likewise considers herself at war with Rumania.

Rumania's decision to enter the war was reached at a meeting of the Crown Council held Sunday morning at the Controceni Palace, Bucharest. King Ferdinand presided, and the session was prolonged over a period of several hours. The Council consists of nineteen members, of which number it is believed that four to six opposed intervention.

Besides conferring with the council, with whom the final decision rested, King Ferdinand had conferences with the leaders of all Rumanian political parties, including those favorable to intervention in the great war and those who had been the strongest supporters of Rumania continuing her neutrality.

The Rumanian military officials had discussed for some days what probably would be the first step taken when war was declared and had dismissed all alien employes many of whom were Germans. An especially large number of Germans were employed in the technical services.

General Averescu, former Minister of War, will have, it is said, chief command of the Rumanian Army.

The Bucharest newspaper, Adeverul, commenting on the council meeting, said:

> At last the decisive hour has struck. Events have dictated to the Government intervention and the realization of Rumania's national claims. The King, in view of the recent events, like the late King Carlos, convoked the Crown Council. The politicians when they

"All the News That's Fit to Print."

The New York Times.

THE WEATHER
Fair, somewhat warmer Monday; overcast, warmer Tuesday; moderate south winds.
For full weather report see Page 13.

VOL. LXV...NO. 21,408. ... NEW YORK, MONDAY, SEPTEMBER 4, 1916.—FOURTEEN PAGES. ONE CENT In Greater New York, Jersey City and Newark. | Elsewhere, TWO CENTS.

PRESIDENT SIGNS 8-HOUR BILL IN HIS PRIVATE CAR

Will Affix His Signature Again on Tuesday to Clinch Question of Legality.

ALL CEREMONY IS AVOIDED

Mrs. Wilson Sees Him Make Adamson Measure a Law and Engineer Toots a Whistle.

UNION HEADS QUIT CAPITAL

Four Pens Used to Sign the Bill Will Go to the Railway Brotherhoods Leaders.

Special to The New York Times.

WASHINGTON, Sept. 3.—Seated in his private car, the "Federal" at the Union Station, President Wilson signed the railroad eight-hour bill at 9:11 o'clock this morning, thereby consummating the successful effort of the Government to avert a national railroad strike, which had been set for 7 o'clock tomorrow morning.

The only persons who saw the signing of the measure were Mrs. Wilson, her brother, John R. Bolling, Rudolph Forster, the White House Executive clerk, and a group of trainmen in their overalls, who paused in their work and looked through the car window. An engineer, passing in a yard engine, celebrated the occasion with several prolonged blasts of his whistle.

The President used four pens to write across the bill "Approved, 3 September, 1916, Woodrow Wilson." The pens, one for each syllable of his name, will be presented to the four heads of the railway brotherhoods. To meet any question of the legality of the act being signed on Sunday, the President will sign it again when he returns to Washington on Tuesday.

The President's train reached Union Station at 7:10 o'clock this morning from Long Branch, N. J., where he delivered his speech of acceptance yesterday. It had been supposed at the White House that the President would go there to sign the measure, but he decided to have it brought to his car, and at 9 o'clock Mr. Forster reached the station with the bill passed in a memorable forty-eight hours by Congress. After signing it the President went for an automobile ride with Mrs. Wilson, returning to his car in time to leave at 9:30 o'clock for Hodgenville, Ky.

Railway Heads Leave Capital.

The signing of the eight-hour bill by President Wilson was the fulfillment of his promise to the brotherhoods through Secretary of Labor W. B. Wilson to prevail upon the labor leaders to issue the strike recall order last night, in order that there might be no doubt of its delivery by 7 o'clock tomorrow morning.

Wearing no boastful air, but proud of their achievement, the brotherhood heads today closed their offices in Washington, which they established three weeks ago, and most of them left the capital tonight.

Elisha Lee, Chairman of the National Conference Committee of the Railways, who led the opposition of the railroads to accepting the eight-hour day voluntarily, left Washington with his attachés at 11 o'clock this morning for Philadelphia. He was the last of the railroad executives to go. He took with him copies of the eight-hour law, which will be laid before the railway attorneys on Tuesday, to get their opinions as to its constitutionality.

The eight-hour law settlement, as made by Congress, puts on the railroads a heavier burden than they would have sustained through an acceptance of the terms offered by President Wilson, which they rejected. The President's plan would have applied only to engineers, firemen, conductors, and trainmen on freight trains. The bill as passed prescribes the eight-hour day for all employes on trains engaged in interstate commerce. This means, of course, that the Government has prescribed the eight-hour day for passenger as well as freight workers.

Other Railway Workers Benefit.

It means also, according to the labor chiefs, that the army of negro trainmen in the South, excluded from the negotiations for the eight-hour day as conducted by the brotherhoods, are also included. They also say that telegraphers and switchmen will be benefited. Furthermore, while the negotiations between the four brotherhoods and the Conference Committee of managers were conducted on behalf of 125 railway systems, the eight-hour law applies as well to the seventy-five systems engaged in interstate commerce which were not represented by the Conference Committee. These seventy-five roads constitute, it is estimated, one-fifth of the total railway mileage of the country. All in all, the labor leaders are very much pleased with what Congress gave them.

"I have always considered the Sabbath as one of the best days of the week," said A. B. Garretson, leader of the labor chiefs, when asked how he felt now that the bill was signed.

Mr. Garretson gave the assurance that there was no danger of a strike in the near future over the application of the Adamson law. He said that if the law was not obeyed the brotherhoods would bring action in the Federal courts against the railroads, instead of resorting to another strike threat. He pointed out that the strike vote under which the brotherhoods have been operating in their negotiations since Aug. 6 is now ineffective. Mr. Garretson said that he and the

Continued on Page 3.

Five Merchant Steamers Are Sunk by Submarines

LONDON, Sept. 3.—Lloyd's shipping agency today reported that the following British steamships had been sunk: The Duart, 3,108 tons, unarmed; the Strathallan, 4,404 tons, unarmed; the Kelvinia, 3,140 tons, unarmed, crew and passengers saved; the Mascotte, 1,007 tons, of Leith.

A dispatch to Reuter's Telegram Company from Amsterdam says the Dutch steamer Zeerarend has been torpedoed. The crew was saved.

The Zeerarend was 147 feet long and of 462 tons gross. She was built in 1913, and was owned at Rotterdam.

UNION WILL PRESS INTERBORO DEMAND

Committee of Subway and Elevated Employes to Meet Hedley Tomorrow.

A STRIKE MAY BE ORDERED

Men Denounce as a "Sharp Trick" the Efforts to Get Individual Wage Contracts.

Final arrangements for their conference with Frank Hedley, General Manager of the Interborough Rapid Transit Company, tomorrow morning on the demands made by the union, which may cause a strike of service employes on the subway and elevated lines, were made last night by members of the Amalgamated Association of Street and Electric Railway Employes.

The subject of chief importance to be discussed at the conference is a proposed contract, copies of which were circulated by the company among its employes last week, asking them to sign an agreement "as individuals" to work for the company for two years under a new scale of pay that went into effect yesterday, and which gave them advances aggregating about $1,250,000 annually.

Members of the Amalgamated Association, composing the Interborough Rapid Transit Company Committee, asserted again at a meeting at the Continental Hotel last night that this contract would not be accepted by the union, notwithstanding it had already been signed by many of the employes, and that a refusal by the company to rescind it probably would result in a strike.

The meeting with Mr. Hedley is arranged for 11 o'clock tomorrow at his office, at 165 Broadway. Mr. Hedley will remind the union delegates that the contract circulated among the men for "individual" signature was not a violation of the agreement by which the surface car strikes were settled on Aug. 7, because the Interborough Rapid Transit Company was not a party to the negotiations leading up to that arrangement. Nor did it participate in any of the conferences and investigations presided over by Mayor Mitchel and Chairman Oscar S. Straus of the Public Service Commission before and after the recent strikes were settled.

The only companies involved in these deliberations were the New York Railways Company, the Third Avenue Railroad Company and its subsidiaries, the Second Avenue Railroad Company, the New York & Queens County Railroad Company, and the Richmond Light & Railway Company, on all of which lines the union had called strikes because of refusals to arbitrate with organized employes.

The Interborough Rapid Transit Company contends that since it has had no dealings with any union and has signed no agreement with employes affiliated with any labor organization, it had a perfect right to enter into any arrangement with its workers which is acceptable to both sides and which is considered legal and just.

Opposition to the contract by the union grows out of its contention that the contract circulated by the company is a violation of the right of its employes to organize and is an attempt to defeat the efforts of the labor organization to win for the men the improvement in their conditions of employment to which the labor organization feels they are entitled. The labor leaders do not consider that the contract is binding on the men who accepted it, because, it is said, most of them signed it without knowing what they were doing and because all of them felt they would jeopardize their positions by refusing to do so.

"You can very well see," said one of the labor leaders last night, "that this contract seeks to deprive the employes of the Interborough of the opportunity of winning the same concessions that we are now striving to get for the New York Railways Company men. Moreover, it is a violation of good faith in the company's dealings with its employes, since they forced them to do something that was detrimental to their interests. The Amalgamated Association of Street and Electric Railway Employes has a right to object, as a majority of the service employes of the company are members of the union.

"Were we to permit the company to do this thing our union would be bound hand and foot and our efforts to perfect an organization would be defeated. It was not fair for the company to circulate this contract, too, because its organized employes had made certain demands upon it which cannot be discussed if the men are already bound down by a contract. It is a piece of sharp practice, and the union certainly does not intend to tolerate it.

"The Interborough Rapid Transit Committee of organized employes has full power to call a strike if such action seems necessary, and its members are determined not to permit Mr. Hedley to get away with this effort to coerce the men into accepting a contract that robs them of many of their rights. I do not know if a strike on the subway and elevated lines will be called, but I probably will know after the conference with Mr. Hedley on Tuesday morning."

ROBBERS MURDER LAWYER IN AUTO AT VAN CORTLANDT

Dwight Dilworth of Montclair, N. J., Shot Dead as He Resists Two Highwaymen.

WOMAN WITH HIM UNHURT

Men Spring from Bushes as Motor Stalls and Open Fire Crying "Hands Up!"

POLICE SURROUND THE PARK

Search With Flashlights, and Hold Three Suspects—Three Bullets in Lawyer's Body.

Two men stepped out of the bushes in a lonely wooded spot in Van Cortlandt Park last night and shot to death Dwight Dilworth, a lawyer, of Montclair, N. J., when he tried to jump from his automobile and resist their command of "Hands up!"

The highwaymen fled after the shooting, and at midnight, an hour after the murder, the police with electric flashlights were searching every foot of the park.

Miss Mary McNiff of 102 West Seventy-fifth Street, a stenographer, who was riding with Dilworth, fainted when the lawyer with three bullets in his body fell lifeless into the seat from which he tried to spring upon his assailants. She became hysterical, and when she regained consciousness the investigation which Coroner William J. Flynn of the Bronx started at once into the murder was delayed because of her inability to give coherent answers to questions asked her in the Kingsbridge Police Station.

The murder occurred on the Golf Link Road, 400 feet from Mosholu Parkway, and in a neighborhood where there have been frequent hold-ups during the Summer. The police believe that the motor of Dilworth's car stalled and that the men hiding in the bushes for just such an opportunity, took advantage of the consequent stop to dash for their victim. They learned that the car had halted before the attack was made.

Fail to Get Lawyer's Valuables.

No doubt was entertained by the authorities that robbery was the motive but the pair, frightened by the noise of their own shots, made off into the bushes without trying to seize either the diamond ring on Mr. Dilworth's finger or the roll of bills in his pocket.

Mr. Dilworth lived at 36 North Fullerton Avenue in Montclair and had an office at 15 Broad Street, in New York. From the first excited account of the killing that the police were able to extract from his companion, they learned that in response to the highwaymen's order of "hands up," Dilworth, a well built man of 40, cried "I won't," and attempted to spring to the ground toward his assailants.

Whether one pistol was fired at him or more is not known, but in less than a second he had fallen back dead in his seat, with one bullet in his chin and two in his chest.

The shots and the screams of Miss McNiff brought Patrolman Crook of the Kingsbridge Police Station, rapping and blowing for assistance as he ran. By the time the patrolman reached the car and a few passing motorists had halted at the spot, Miss McNiff had fainted, and there remained only the mute evidence of the standing car and the dead man in the seat to tell what had happened.

Dr. Hennelly of Kingsbridge Hospital examined Dilworth, who had been lifted to the roadside, wrote "Dead on arrival" in his case book, and ordered that the Coroner be notified.

Woman Companion Prostrated.

Crook then took Miss McNiff to the Kingsbridge Station so that she might tell what had occurred. Meantime the reserves were guarding every entrance to the park, while others of their number beat up every wooded place in the effort to find the highwaymen. The only description they were able to get from Miss McNiff after Dr. Hennelly had revived her was that they were of medium height and wore caps pulled down over their eyes.

Early this morning the police arrested three suspects whom they found roaming in various parts of the park. They were examined by Deputy Police Commissioner Guy Scull, Assistant District Attorney Quigley of the Bronx, and Inspector Cray, in charge of the Detective Bureau. Miss McNiff was unable to identify any of them.

When she became calmer Miss McNiff told the police she had known the lawyer about a year, during which time he had been counsel for her family. He invited her for a ride about 6 o'clock last night. They rode northward to the city line, stopped for dinner, and were returning when the car stopped. An instant later the robbers appeared.

Captain McKeon of the Kingsbridge Precinct was soon joined by Acting Captain Wines of the Bronx Detective Bureau and a squad of men who began an all-night hunt for the murderers.

At 102 West Seventy-fifth Street it was said last night that Miss McNiff was 38 years old, that she had lived there with a family named Corwin for the last three years, and that she was employed by a perfumery concern at 225 Fifth Avenue. According to the City Directory, the Nudak Company, dealer in fruit extracts, is located at that address on Fifth Avenue.

Special to The New York Times.

MONTCLAIR, N. J., Monday, Sept. 4.—Dwight Dilworth's home in Montclair was closed and dark early this morning. A neighbor said that Dilworth had a wife and one child, a young boy. Mrs. Dilworth, he said, had gone to visit her family at 3,101 East Thirtieth Street, Kansas City, Mo., two weeks ago and had taken the boy with her. The neighbor said Dilworth had been taking his breakfasts at his (the neighbor's) home. Recently, he added, Dilworth, in talking of his experiences, and then little dreaming of his approaching tragic end, had related how his father was murdered by thieves some years ago.

The neighbor said Dilworth was in prosperous circumstances, stood well in the town, and was thought to have had a good law practice in Manhattan.

French Airmen Attack Ten Places Around Metz

PARIS, Sept. 3.—Wholesale raids by air squadrons on stations and depots in the vicinity of Metz are reported in the day report of the French War Office. The bulletin reads:

"One of our airmen brought down a German aeroplane which fell close to Dieppe, northeast of Verdun. On the Somme front four more German aeroplanes were badly hit in encounters and descended abruptly in their own lines.

"Our bombing air squadrons carried out numerous operations yesterday with excellent results. Our squadrons twice visited the railway station of Metz-Sablons and threw altogether eighty-six shells of 120 calibre on the buildings and railway tracks. The damage observed was considerable.

"Sixty shells of 120 millimeter calibre also were dropped on military establishments north of Metz. Our aeroplanes bombed the station of Maizières-les-Metz, Conflans, Sedan, and Audun-le-Roman, as well as the cantonment and depots at Ham, Mesle, Guiscard, Athis, Manchy, and Lagache. In all 210 bombs were dropped in these places.

"A large number burst on the targets and outbreaks of fire at many places were observed."

SHACKLETON SAVES POLAR EXPEDITION

He Arrives Safely with 22 Men at Punta Arenas from Elephant Island.

"ALL WELL," HIS MESSAGE

Ice-Locked Explorers Had to Subsist on Half Rations as Leader Met Delays.

Special Cable to THE NEW YORK TIMES.

LONDON, Monday, Sept. 4.—Lieutenant Sir Ernest Shackleton has saved the men of his Antarctic expedition who were marooned on Elephant Island. A message in which this news is conveyed is published by The Chronicle this morning and reads:

"Punta Arenas, Sept. 3.—All saved; all well. Shackleton."

PUNTA ARENAS, Chile, Sept. 3.—Lieutenant Sir Ernest H. Shackleton has rescued the members of his antarctic expedition who were marooned on Elephant Island. Lieutenant Shackleton returned here today with his men safe and well on board the rescue ship Yelcho.

Fourth Attempt to Rescue Men.

This was the fourth attempt made by Sir Ernest Shackleton to rescue the twenty-two men who had been marooned on Elephant Island since April 24. The other attempts, made during June and July, failed on account of unfavorable ice conditions.

He started on this last and successful voyage on Aug. 26. It was feared that this would also be a failure, and the British Government on July 21 announced that the Discovery, the vessel of the Company of Adventurers of England Trading Into Hudson Bay, would be placed at Sir Ernest's disposal as soon as the ship could be refitted and be sent out to Punta Arenas.

The explorer, however, felt that he did not dare wait for the Discovery, because the men on Elephant Island were left with only five weeks' rations and two seals. He estimated that these would last for ten weeks at half rations and that they might be able to kill penguins, but of this there was no certainty. The rescued men were members of the crew of the Endurance, in which Sir Ernest sailed from Buenos Aires on Oct. 26, 1914, to cross the antarctic continent, reaching the south pole, and for mapping that land. Much of this work was accomplished, including the discovery of 200 miles of new coast line, the making of a complete hydrographic survey of Weddell sea, the elimination of South Greenland, and the taking of many important observations and cinema records.

The Endurance encountered almost impassable ice from the time she entered the antarctic regions, and on Oct. 27 was practically torn to pieces. The party was forced to abandon the ship, and the wreck of the Endurance sank on Nov. 20. For the next two months the party drifted north in three boats that were seaworthy. With them were the dog teams, five of which were shot for food during January. They crossed the antarctic circle during this month, with their tents worn out, and a shortage of fuel. On April 13 Sir Ernest decided that the only salvation was to run for Elephant Island, and two days later they reached the north end of that land.

Breaking Ice Stopped Effort.

Progress had been hampered by the breaking ice and by the time the Elephant Island camp was made, Sir Ernest realized that it would be impossible to bring the party out and with five volunteers he started for South Georgia, 750 miles away, on April 24, to organize a rescue expedition. He reached South Georgia on May 20, 1916, and Port Stanley, in the Falkland Islands, a day later. All during this voyage the little party met most unfavorable conditions and suffered privations, many times facing death.

On May 26 Sir Ernest made his first attempt to rescue the men on Elephant Island. He set out in an eighty-ton unprotected whaler, commanded by Captain Thom, but was forced to turn back to the Falkland Islands because he "found the ice too formidable for the vessel," according to his own account. On June 18 he again started for the island in a steam trawler lent by the Uruguayan Government, and again the ice stopped him. The third attempt was made in a seventy-ton wooden schooner lent by the British in Chile, and once more the ice prevented his reaching Elephant Island.

Following is the list of the men who had been left on Elephant Island: Frank Wild, commander of the party and second in command; James Wordie, geologist; George Marston, artist; Clark, biologist; Leonard H. Hussey, meteorologist; R. W. James, physicist and magnetician; F. Hurley, cinematographer; Dr. Macklin, surgeon; Dr. Milroy, surgeon; Captain Orde Lees, storekeeper; Hudson, navigating officer; Dickinson, chief engineer; Kerr, second engineer; Greenstreet, chief officer, and Bakewell, Blackborn, Chewham, Green, Holness, Howe, McLeod, and Stevenson, seamen.

ALLIES SMASH GERMAN SOMME FRONT, TAKE 3 TOWNS, OVER 2000 MEN, 62 GUNS; GREEK KING SWITCHES TO ENTENTE

ALL GREEK PARTIES UNITED

Allies Demand Control of Posts and Telegraphs and Expulsion of Teutons.

GERMAN MINISTER FLEES

Baron Schenck and 30 Men with Grenades Barricade Themselves in His House.

FLEET BLOWS UP U-BOAT

Traps Undersea Craft at Phaleron—May Establish Army-Navy Base at Piraeus.

Text of New Allied Demands on the Greek Government

LONDON, Monday, Sept. 4—Following is the text of the note presented to the Greek Government on Saturday night by the Ministers of France and England:

By order of their governments, the undersigned Ministers of France and Great Britain have the honor to bring the following communication to the attention of the Greek Government:

First—The two Allied Governments having from a sure source learned that their enemies receive information in divers ways, and, notably through the agency of the Greek telegraphs, demand the control of the posts and telegraphs, including the wireless system.

Second—Enemy agents employed in corruption and espionage must immediately leave Greece not to return until the conclusion of hostilities.

Third—Necessary measures have been taken against such Greek subjects as rendered themselves guilty of complicity in the abovementioned corruption and espionage.

Special Cable to THE NEW YORK TIMES.

ATHENS, Sept. 3, (Dispatch to The London Times.)—I learn from a reliable source that King Constantine has declared to the Entente Ministers that after Rumania's participation in the war he is disposed to reconsider Greek policy.

Special Cable to THE NEW YORK TIMES.

ATHENS, Sept. 3, (Dispatch to The London Daily Chronicle.)—After an eventful day the political situation is moving toward a satisfactory solution. Both sides may be said to have come to a tacit agreement to give their support to the Zaimis Cabinet, which will therefore cease to be an interregnum Cabinet and become a political Cabinet, enjoying the full confidence of the Crown and complete support of the Venizelist party.

I understand the King has expressed his belief in the expediency of Greece now leaving her neutrality. Venizelos, on the other hand, equally approves this solution, and, desiring the welfare of his country before place and power, will efface himself when he sees the realization of the policy for which he has fought so long.

Anglo-French Note to Greece.

A joint note was handed to the Government last evening by the British and French Ministers. It says that the enemies of the Entente are informed in divers ways, and especially by the Greek telegraph, of the Allies' movements. The Allies demand control of the posts and telegraphs, including the wireless; that the enemy agents of corruption and espionage leave Greece immediately and not return there until the close of hostilities, and that necessary measures be taken against such Greek subjects as have rendered themselves culpable as accomplices of this corruption and espionage.

It may be taken that the note will be accepted in its entirety and that we may look for the entry before long of Greece into the war on the side of the Allies.

Diplomats and politicians had a very busy day on Friday. Premier Zaimis at first received the Minister for War, General Calaris, and later M. Streit, former Minister of Foreign Affairs. About 11 A. M. Sir Francis Elliott motored to Dekelia Sir Francis Elliott motored to Dekelia and had a long audience with the King. Premier Zaimis in the afternoon received the French Minister, M. Guilleman, who called a second time toward 6 o'clock, accompanied by the English Minister. The diplomatic representatives informed the Premier of the coming presentation of the note from the Entente Powers, the contents of which were outlined subsequently in extra editions of the Greek papers, and caused a panic among the Teutons and their henchmen here.

German Minister Flees.

Count Mirbach, the German Minister, left in a motor car at 9 o'clock last

Continued on Page 2.

Bulgar-Teuton Army Invades Rumania; Carries War Across the Dobrudja Border

BERLIN, Sept. 3, (via London.)—German and Bulgarian troops have crossed the Dobrudja frontier, in southeastern Rumania, between the Danube and the Black Sea, the German official statement today says. The statement follows:

Balkan Theatre—The Dobrudja border between the Danube and the Black Sea has been crossed by German and Bulgarian troops. The Rumanian frontier guards were thrown back with losses.

On the Macedonian front there was nothing of importance to report.

An official statement from Austrian Army Headquarters under yesterday's date tells of fighting in Albania. It says:

Southeastern War Theatre—To the west of Avlona an Italian automobile detachment advanced beyond the Voyusa. It was attacked in the front and on the flank and was repulsed, after two days' fighting.

In the Lower Danube our Danube flotilla sank a Rumanian gunboat.

Skirmishing Continues on the Saloniki Front

PARIS, Sept. 3.—The War Office communication today concerning the operations on the Saloniki front is appended:

On the Struma front and in the Lake Doiran zone some rather violent artillery actions were reported. Patrols carried out numerous reconnoissances on the left bank of the Struma. Northeast of Kukuruz a Bulgarian attack near Zborsko was repulsed by the fire of Serbian infantry. The enemy sustained heavy loss.

There is nothing to report from the Lake Ostrovo region.

London Millions Saw Zeppelin Fall; Second Is Reported Hit by Shell

Night Crowds Rushed Into Streets, Cheered and Sang National Anthem, as Raider Burst, Riddled by Shells from Enfield Gun Factory—Thirteen Craft in Raid—Two Persons Killed.

Special Cable to THE NEW YORK TIMES.

LONLON, Sept. 3.—Thirteen Zeppelins constituted the raiding squadron that visited England last night, but only three of them got near the outskirts of London, and one of these was shot down about fifteen miles north of the city.

There are reports, however, that another one was hit and, disabled, drifted out to sea. A correspondent on the east coast says that when the searchlights found their objective, the anti-aircraft guns got to work and soon succeeded in driving one Zeppelin seawards. Three hours later this Zeppelin made a futile attempt to get inland. In the full glare of a powerful searchlight the raider was distinctly seen.

"It was kept in full view, and the guns made a grand practice," says this observer, "their shells bursting all about the Zeppelin. The raider was evidently hit, for after some minutes it became perfectly perpendicular, and in that apparently crippled and helpless plight it drifted away slowly over the North Sea and was lost to sight."

The casualties officially reported are two dead and eleven persons injured by the many bombs dropped by the raiders.

The following account by an eyewitness of the bringing down of the Zeppelin was given to THE NEW YORK TIMES correspondent by Sir Charles Inigo Thomas, former Secretary to the Admiralty:

"I was awakened about 2:30 o'clock by the information that gunfiring was going on. Looking from my windows, I saw the flashes of the guns in all directions. In a certain direction particularly there was a great display of searchlights, but the weather was foggy and nothing was very distinct. Suddenly about 2:15 o'clock there appeared a glow in the sky which gradually increased in intensity until it became something like a great star. This rapidly increased in size until it clearly assumed the shape of a Zeppelin. The whole looked like a mass of molten metal such as one sees falling out of a furnace pipe. The outline which at first was horizontal, gradually turned and became almost perpendicular, at the same time falling earthward. As it fell it seemed to shrink in size, until the last I saw of it was a sort of stream of deep-red fire. The first appearance of flame was noticeably of a yellow tint. I have said gradually, but of course the whole descent from the time the starlike centre appeared took no more than a minute, or perhaps a minute and a half."

Like a Bar of Steel in Sky.

Another eyewitness of the destruction of the Zeppelin writes: "When the guns opened fire, the Zeppelin already had been centred in a ball of light created by the myriad arms of pale light which shot up suddenly from the darkness. The Zeppelin was at a great height, so great, indeed, that it seemed just like a bar of polished steel about the thickness of an engine piston rod. There it remained apparently motionless and undecided which way to go while the guns peppered it without cessation.

"Shells burst around it, in front and behind, above and below, and it made a turn as if to go in the direction of the coast, but a shell burst ominously near its nose and caused it to swing around in the opposite direction. Its tail dipped and it made a move to ascend still higher, when a shell burst directly over it. Another descent was necessary, and three shells burst simultaneously below, behind, and in front of it. It seemed impossible for it to go north, south, east, or west, and there it remained for a second or two helpless, with shells bursting all around it.

"Then away up there in the centre of the ball of light something happened. It seemed as if a black shadow passed between our vision and the brilliant light. In the sky when we looked again the airship had gone. Firing ceased and the searchlights, splitting their focussed rays, shot backward and forward across the firmament, but the Zeppelin was gone. Under cover of a cloud of smoke she had made a wild dash upward beyond the ray of light and through the ring of bursting shells.

"Suddenly, away further to the north, a ball of fire in the sky riveted our attention. The ball spread in size, and there was a great explosion. The whole of London, north, south, east, and west, was illuminated by the one flash. The dome of St. Paul's and the towers at Westminster, hitherto obscured, stood out with remarkable clearness, and for a brief second it looked as if a panorama of the whole of London had been thrown upon a screen in a darkened hall.

"There was no need now to speculate as to the fate of the invader. Persons who came out into the streets raised cheer after cheer and sang the national anthem. The burning Zeppelin could now be seen falling nose downward to the earth like a huge blazing cauldron from which poured a spray of sparks."

Wreck Almost Fell on Them.

A Daily Chronicle dispatch from Cuffley says the Zeppelin brought down here this morning fell headlong, a blazing mass, with a tearing sound in a meadow midway on the road from Potters Bar to Enfield. This is the story of her bringing down told by reliable witnesses who were almost underneath the falling airship, who indeed most narrowly escaped destruction with her:

"We first heard the Zeppelin over us about 1 o'clock this morning," said Mr. Grey of Cuffley Hill Farm. "She remained overhead for about twenty minutes, then went away southward over Enfield. It was very foggy, and, as the ship was not illumined by searchlights, we couldn't see her, but we heard the sound of the engines die away in that direction. Ten minutes or a quarter of an hour later we heard gunfire and the sound of bombs dropping. Then we again heard the Zeppelin overhead. All that we could see at the time was a deep and general glow in the air. We thought the Zeppelin had dropped star shells. Then we looked up and saw the ship above us like a huge incandescent mantle with an orange centre of flame.

"Almost immediately one end of her dipped and the orange centre extended till she seemed all on fire. Then the Zeppelin, now in a vertical position, fell headlong. She dropped with a terrible tearing sound and struck the ground with a crash that could be heard for miles around. The wreckage burned for hours, lighting up the whole countryside. Every few minutes came a popping from her machine-gun ammunition.

"A policeman was the first on the scene. Then came a few villagers and myself and soon afterward a corps of special constables from Goff's Oak. We did our best with buckets of water from the pond near by and an old hose to put out the flames and rescue some of the bodies we saw entangled in that blazing wreck. Curiously enough at first we did not know whether she was one of our own airships or a Zeppelin, she made such a comparatively small patch on the ground for the reason, of course, that she struck nose on. Then we came across half of a propeller with a charred body mixed up with the wheel and immediately behind that two other bodies. On one of them we found a piece of cloth with some German buttons on it and nearby some German cartridges and a German cap. Then, for the first time, we knew it was a Zeppelin.

"About 4 A. M. parties of military arrived and took charge. From that time to 7 A. M. altogether eighteen bodies were taken out of the débris, together with some more or less damaged machine guns."

Song "God Save the King."

Describing the scene which followed the destruction of the raider a suburban correspondent says: "As soon as it was realized that it was a Zeppelin in flames there was pandemonium. Everyone was shouting, hands were being clapped, steamers were using their sirens incessantly, and a few railway engines that were about were cock-a-doodling with steam whistles until the uproar resembled nothing so much as the advent of a new year in the shipping area.

"Gradually the glowing mass was lost behind the outlines of houses, but the sky for some time was lit up brilliantly. Then we talked excitedly, we wrung each other's hands and acted like children, till suddenly, in sweet contralto tones, were heard the opening bars of the national anthem, and there we stood, men, women, and children, singing 'God Save the King,' while the

Continued on Page 2.

BIG STROKE NORTH OF CLERY

Germans Are Swept Out of Positions On a 6½-Mile Front.

COMBLES IS NOW MENACED

French Reach Outskirts of Town Besides Taking Village of Forest—British in Ginchy.

GUILLEMONT ALSO IS WON

At Some Points the Allied Advance Penetrates Foe's Lines Three-fourths of a Mile.

LONDON, Sept. 3.—In a severe stroke delivered by British and French troops on the Somme today, the German front for a distance of six and one-half miles, from Ginchy to Cléry, was smashed. Three towns were occupied by the Allies, Guillemont by the British, who also won a hold on Ginchy, and Forest and Cléry by the French. Two thousand prisoners were captured by Joffre's troops and "several hundred" by Haig's forces. The French night report chronicles the seizure of twelve cannon and fifty machine guns in the sector of Forest alone.

The wide assault on the German positions was made at midday and was carried out with great dash. At some points the Allies swept over trenches and strong positions to a depth of over three-fourths of a mile. The French troops in their advance reached the outskirts of Combles, which is also menaced by the British drive from the north.

The night bulletin of the French War Office, telling of the success, reads:

North of the Somme, after artillery preparation, French infantry, in conjunction with the British Army, attacked shortly before midday the German positions on a front of about six kilometers, (three and three-quarters miles,) reaching from the region north of Maurepas to the river, with remarkable dash, against which the resistance of the enemy was useless for the moment.

Our troops swept away large enemy forces and carried all their objectives. The villages of Forest, east of Maurepas, and Cléry-sur-Somme are entirely in our possession.

North of Forest we have taken all the German trenches along the road from Forest to Combles, as far as the outskirts of Combles. Between Forest and Clery-Sur-Somme we also carried all the enemy positions, and crossed at numerous points the road connecting these two places.

German counterattacks with heavy forces, launched against our conquered positions south of Forest, broke down under the fire of our batteries, and the enemy retired in disorder, leaving numerous dead.

Up to the present the number of unwounded prisoners in our hands exceeds 2,000, while the captured war material includes twelve cannon, taken in the single sector of Forrest, and fifty machine guns.

On the right bank of the Meuse, (Verdun sector,) the Germans made since this morning a series of violent attacks on our positions at Vaux and Chapitre. Repulsed several times along the whole front with heavy losses, the enemy had succeeded at the end of the afternoon in setting foot in one salient of our line, where the combat is continuing bitterly.

Shortly after beginning this action we attacked the German positions east of the village of Fleury. Our troops carried several trenches and powerfully organized works. Another attack was made by us northwest of the village of Fleury and enabled us to occupy a part of the crest from the village to Thiaumont work. In the course of these attacks we made 300 prisoners.

British Take Part of Ginchy.

The British War Office statement reads:

In co-operation with the French on our immediate right we attacked the enemy Sunday at several points. We captured part of Ginchy and the whole of Guillemont. Our front now runs some 500 yards east of Guillemont from Ginchy to near Falfemont Farm.

On the east side of Ququet Farm we also gained ground. We captured several hundred prisoners.

Between our right and the Somme the French made substantial progress, capturing a considerable number of prisoners. The fighting continues.

Aircraft did useful work, co-operating with the artillery and infantry. The enemy's aeroplanes, which made desperate attempts to interfere, were unsuccessfully engaged in many aerial fights and driven off with the loss of three machines destroyed and at least four others damaged, while we lost three.

The day bulletin of the British War Office reads:

Last night generally was quiet. Fighting was in progress this morning near Mouquet Farm, south of Thiep-

Wide World Photos

German troops at the battle of the Somme.

Wide World Photos

A British soldier examines the ruins of a French village church at the Somme front.

"All the News That's Fit to Print."

The New York Times.

THE WEATHER
Partly cloudy Monday; not quite so warm; fair Tuesday, cooler; moderate west and northwest winds.
For full weather report see Page 21.

VOL. LXVI...NO. 21,443. NEW YORK, MONDAY, OCTOBER 9, 1916.—TWENTY-TWO PAGES. ONE CENT In Greater New York, Jersey City and Newark. | Elsewhere, TWO CENTS.

GERMAN SUBMARINES SINK 6 TO 9 SHIPS OFF NANTUCKET; ONE A LINER WITH MANY AMERICANS, BUT ALL ARE SAVED; WASHINGTON SEES GRAVE PERIL IN RAIDS OFF OUR COAST

BRITISH PROTEST EXPECTED

Point Raised That U-Boat Attacks Constitute a Virtual Blockade.

ALL REGULAR, SAY GERMANS

Their Embassy Holds That the Pledges Given to President Are Not Violated.

STATE DEPARTMENT SILENT

New U-Boat Activities Aimed at Munitions Trade, Says Definite Report.

Special to The New York Times.

WASHINGTON, Oct. 8.—A new and serious problem, the outcome of which cannot be forecast, confronts the United States Government as a result of the attacks on merchant shipping by a German war submarine off the New England Coast. For the present the policy the Government will adopt is problematical. But it is admitted that questions of a most delicate nature have been presented by the sinking of merchant vessels a few miles from our shores by a belligerent undersea craft within a short time after she had left an American port.

News came to Washington recently from a source in which reliance was placed that the German Government had decided to send submarines to waters adjacent to the American coast for the purpose of sinking merchant vessels engaged in carrying munitions and other supplies to Germany's enemies. That this information had been received here became known in connection with the arrival of the U-53 at Newport. It assumed a new importance then. According to this information a number of German submarines are to engage in the work. The main object of the German Government is to break up the shipment of war munitions between the United States and British and French ports, according to those who learned in advance of the German plan.

It is already well established that the British Government will protest against the action of the United States naval authorities at Newport in permitting the U-53 to put to sea. While this Government has not agreed that submarines should be treated differently from other vessels of war, it was emphasized in communications from the State Department to the British Embassy that the United States regarded it as in violation of good international usage for the British Government to permit its patrolling warships to hold up and examine merchant vessels off the Port of New York. As a result of the American attitude in this connection the British Government modified the instructions to the commanders of its patrol vessels in these waters. A question somewhat similar has arisen in the U-53 case.

The possibility of international complications relates both to Germany and Great Britain. Two important questions—both arising out of the use of the submarine in actual warfare—are involved. One has been brought forward, and will be brought forward again, by the contention of the British Government that all submarines of a belligerent, whether commercial or military, should be interned when they enter neutral waters. The other question is the right of a belligerent submarine to bring the great war near to the shores of the United States and many thousand miles from the real scene of actual conflict.

Were the Rules Observed?

In some quarters in Washington tonight the belief prevails that this question may assume a great importance, approaching that of the U-boat controversy which nearly produced a break in the relations between Germany and the United States. But outside of this aspect of the problem there is another phase which has assumed considerable proportions in the minds of officials. This is whether the German submarine or submarines that attacked merchant vessels near the shores of the United States observed the rules governing U-boat warfare laid down by President Wilson, to which the German Government agreed to adhere and upon which the United States insists upon a scrupulous observance.

In other words, has the U-53 initiated a revival of relentless U-boat warfare, without adherence to the rule of warning demanded by the United States of Germany and agreed to by the German Government after a long and delicate controversy that appeared at one time to bring the two nations to the verge of war. This rule was that merchant ships, even those that flew belligerent flags, should not be sunk without warning or without affording opportunity for the passengers and crew to

Continued on Page 2.

Our Last Warning to Germany On Her Submarine Warfare

From President Wilson's notice to Germany that submarine warfare on merchantmen must be kept within the law, April 18, 1916:

Vessels of neutral ownership, even vessels of neutral ownership bound from neutral port to neutral port, have been destroyed, along with vessels of belligerent ownership, in constantly increasing numbers. Sometimes the merchantmen attacked have been warned and summoned to surrender before being fired on or torpedoed; sometimes their passengers and crews have been vouchsafed the poor security of being allowed to take to the ship's boats before the ship was sent to the bottom. But again and again no warning has been given * * * and the lives of noncombatants, passengers and crew, have been destroyed wholesale and in a manner which the Government of the United States cannot but regard as wanton and without the slightest color of justification.

The Government of the United States has been very patient. * * * It has become painfully evident to it that the position which it took at the very outset is inevitable, namely, the use of submarines for the destruction of an enemy's commerce, is, of necessity, because of the very character of the vessels employed and the very methods of attack which their employment of course involves, utterly incompatible with the principles of humanity, the long-established and incontrovertible rights of neutrals, and the sacred immunities of noncombatants.

If it is still the purpose of the Imperial Government to prosecute relentless and indiscriminate warfare against vessels of commerce by the use of submarines, without regard to what the Government of the United States must consider the sacred and indisputable rules of international law and the universally recognized dictates of humanity, the Government of the United States is at last forced to the conclusion that there is but one course it can pursue.

BRITISH WARSHIPS ARRIVE ON SCENE

Three Cruisers Reached Nantucket Lightship at 2:40 This Morning.

OTHER VESSELS ON WAY

Warnings Flashed to Merchant Craft That May Be in Danger from U-Boats.

NANTUCKET, Mass., Monday, Oct. 9—2:50 A. M.—Three British cruisers arrived off Nantucket Island at 2:40 o'clock this morning.

Radio messages in code were constantly exchanged by the vessels.

Other cruisers of the allied naval forces were expected in the same waters soon.

BOSTON, Oct. 8.—During the day no word came from the British and French patrol vessels which have been watching the Atlantic Coast, from which vessels of the Allies with munitions of war have daily set out. It was reported, however, that British cruisers and patrol boats were already hurrying from Halifax.

The British Consul said he had no information as to the present whereabouts of British patrol boats, although he assumed that these vessels had been notified by wireless that the U-53 was a few miles off the coast.

Many rumors were afloat today, including one that a fleet of German submarines was off the coast. Another had it that the Germans had established a submarine base on the Canadian coast. Another speculation was that supply ships were co-operating with the U-53. Those who held to the latter opinion pointed out that the submarine, after ostensibly crossing the Atlantic unassisted, arrived at Newport fully provisioned for three months, and not requiring fuel or so much as a jug of water.

Special to The New York Times.

NORFOLK, Va., Oct. 8.—It is reported that the British cruisers Essex and Cumberland, in the vicinity of Currituck Inlet, proceeded northward immediately on receipt of news of the arrival of the German submarine at Newport. The French cruiser Corida and two Britishers of the Falmouth type, doing duty further north, are also reported to have disappeared. A converted cruiser whose identity has never been determined, guarding the Cape Henry entrance to the bay for weeks, can no longer be seen. They have seemingly scattered.

The news of the presence of the submarine off the New England coast was transmitted to the warships off the Virginia and Carolina coast, with instructions to notify all merchant ships already at sea. They are reported to have immediately scattered in the performance of this mission. They are expected to haunt the lanes of travel to convoy ships beyond the danger zone at present known.

The German Submarine U-53 at anchor in Newport Harbor saturday

Officers and crew of the U53 lined up against her turret

Photos © by O.W. Waterman

Map showing location of Nantucket Lightship near which the U53 attacked British shipping yesterday

International Marine Holds in Port Ships Which Carry British Flag

First to Cancel Sailings, But General Tie-up Is Expected Marine Insurance Agents Will Meet Today to Discuss Higher Rates.

The sinking of British steamships yesterday off Nantucket Lightship by the German submarine U-53 will result in a tie up of British shipping in American ports, according to steamship agents who were questioned yesterday. The International Merchantile Marine has already acted. No British ships of that line will leave Atlantic ports pending further orders.

As soon as he had confirmed the reports of the sinking of the West Point, Strathdene, Stephano, and Kingston, P. A. S. Franklin, Vice President and General Manager of the International Mercantile Marine, sent telegrams to the agents in Boston, Baltimore, Philadelphia, Portland, and Montreal, ordering all steamships of the company, under the British flag, to be kept in their respective ports until further instructions were received. The order issued by Mr. Franklin stops all sailings of the White Star, Atlantic Transport, Leyland, Dominion, and Red Star Lines from American ports and the White Star-Dominion Lines sailing from Montreal and Quebec.

This order will not interfere with the sailing of the American Line steamships or any of the company's vessels under the American flag.

Marine insurance agents said yesterday it was probable that orders would be received today from London and Liverpool canceling sailings of all British steamships from American ports until further notice. They said that Mr. Franklin was the only shipping official who had the power to act on his own responsibility without waiting to consult the head offices abroad.

The question of increasing the rates on insurance would be considered today, at a meeting of the New York Fire and Marine Underwriters.

An official of the Cunard Line said that no changes would be made in the sailing dates of the steamships of the company from this side until instructions were received from the head office in Liverpool. All the Cunard vessels, he said, were armed with four-inch rapid fire guns, similar to those on the Alaunia, which sailed on Saturday for London. Thus far the German submarines, he said, had avoided steamships carrying guns.

One of the officials of the French Line said the French vessels would sail as usual. The liners were all armed with 3½-inch guns, he said, and the cargo boats carried 3-inch rapid-fire guns. Orders to change sailing dates, he said, would have to come from the head office in Paris.

Officials of the Italian lines appeared to share the opinion of the Cunard agents, that as their vessels were armed with two 3-inch guns aft they could take care of themselves in case of submarine attack. The Dante Alighieri, which sailed yesterday for Genoa, carried many passengers. Her Captain will go south toward Bermuda instead of taking the northerly course for Gibraltar by Nantucket.

Panic Seizes Boston Shippers.

BOSTON, Oct. 8.—Something like a panic seized the minds of shippers in this city and at other points along the coast, when the first reports of the activities of the U-53 were received from the radio station. Anxious inquiries were received at the newspaper offices from seemingly almost everyone who had a friend on the water or owned a share of stock in a merchant ship.

The British freighter, Isle of Lewes, carrying food products and other supplies intended for war purposes, sailed early in the morning for Manchester, notwithstanding knowledge of the U-53's visit to Newport.

The Great City, another British freighter, deferred her sailing with a cargo of steel and horses consigned to the French Government at St. Nazaire, but her agents said it was because of slow loading rather than any fear of danger.

Line Suspends Baltimore Sailings.

Special to The New York Times.

BALTIMORE, Oct. 8.—Furness, Withy & Co., to which the steamship West Point belonged, one of the four British shipping concerns here, announced a temporary suspension of sailings in consequence of the sinking of the steamship. A. E. Sidebotham, Baltimore agent of the company, has cabled to the Liverpool office of the company for instructions. There are no vessels in port now belonging to the company, but twelve steamships for which the company is agent are on the way here to load for cargoes. They will not be ordered to return to the ports from which they are coming, but on arrival here will be held pending further orders.

The agent of the Terminal Shipping Company said today that he was not worried about German submarines, while the agents of the Atlantic Transport Line did not see any use of having their ships now en route here return to their home ports as there they are in danger from any number of submarines, while on this side there was only one that they had any knowledge of.

Ships Sail from Norfolk.

Special to The New York Times.

NORFOLK, Va., Oct. 8.—News of the submarine peril, although immediately transmitted to merchant ships in the harbor and to shipping agents, failed to check sailings today. Three English and two French merchantmen carrying cargoes of foodstuffs, horses, &c., sailed in the past twenty-four hours for European ports.

When the full details of the U-53's ex-

Continued on Page 3.

President Silent on U-Boat Raids Pending Receipt of Navy Reports

Government Officials Try to Get Full Information Quickly—Von Bernstorff to See President Wilson at Shadow Lawn Today.

Special to The New York Times.

LONG BRANCH, N. J., Oct. 8.—No statement was given out either at Shadow Lawn or at the White House executive office tonight on the sinking of British and neutral ships off the New England coast by the German submarine U-53.

Joseph P. Tumulty, secretary to the President, said that no official reports of the submarine activities had been received, and that until the President got full information from the Navy Department he would make no comment. The Secretary was interested in press reports, and said the Navy Department probably would send full details as soon as they could be gathered.

Government officials were plainly worried over the situation, and made efforts to get all information obtainable, as quickly as possible. The questions for them centred around whether any Americans had been lost and whether the vessels were warned in accordance with international law. It was stated that a very thorough investigation would be made, but that no hasty action would be taken.

Today's events have given new importance to the President's conference set for tomorrow afternoon with Count von Bernstorff. The German Ambassador made the engagement nearly a week ago with the object, it was announced at the time, of discussing the Polish relief question. He was understood to be bringing to Mr. Wilson the German Emperor's reply to the President's personal note on that subject sent last Summer.

It is said here that the coming of the U-53, with the new problems which may arise through her bringing the U-boat warfare close to Americans waters, cannot fail to inject some discussion of the submarine question into the conference, even if complete reports show that the United States is in no way officially involved.

It will be the first time in months that the Ambassador has seen the President. Count von Bernstorff is to reach Shadow Lawn at 2 o'clock.

Jules Jusserand, the French Ambassador, will come to Shadow Lawn on Tuesday for a conference with Mr. Wilson. His appointment, like that of the German envoy, was made to give him an opportunity to discuss Polish relief personally with the President, and it is supposed that he conveys President Poincare's reply to Mr. Wilson's solicitations on behalf of the war sufferers in Poland.

Mr. Wilson has an engagement tomorrow to see Judge William L. Chambers, Commissioner of the Federal Board of Mediation and Conciliation, which handled the recently threatened nation-wide railroad strike up to the point where the President intervened. It was understood that the investigation of the railway eight-hour law about to be started by the board named last week by the President would be discussed.

William F. McCombs, Democratic nominee for Senator from New York, will take luncheon with the President on Tuesday. They will take up New York State politics, including arrangements for the President to deliver two speeches in that State.

Mr. Wilson spent most of today quietly at Shadow Lawn, but this afternoon he took an automobile ride. He is to leave on Wednesday for Indianapolis, where he will make two speeches on Thursday. "Pennsylvania Day" will be celebrated here Saturday. Mr. Wilson will deliver an address to a large delegation of Pennsylvanians.

There was a report in New York last night that Count von Bernstorff, German Ambassador, would be here overnight on his way to call on President Wilson at Shadow Lawn, but at midnight nothing had been heard of his arrival. Several of his friends here said they believed that news of the submarine's activities off the coast had caused him at the last moment to change his plans and to delay his departure from Washington until this morning.

NAMES OF AMERICANS WHO WERE SET ADRIFT

30 Were Aboard the Stephano When She Was Attacked by the Submarine.

Special to The New York Times.

HALIFAX, N. S., Oct. 8.—Following is list of first and second cabin passengers on the S. S. Stephano:

First Cabin.

William Bierschenck, German-American; J. Sanchez, R. Fernandez, F. Anqua, F. Fernandez, Spanish; J. Johansen, Norwegian; Mrs. E. Ricksen, Newfoundland.

Following are Americans:

J. E. Evans, W. C. Ellis, W. J. Levison, J. Stewart, C. Bostwick, F. Bostwick, E. Saxon, M. Harris, H. F. Graham, J. L. Taylor, G. Hurlburt, H. Hurlburt, H. L. Barnum, R. B. Ludy, N. Huffman, F. Jennings, C. Evans, S. Evans, C. F. Ulrich, S. Wilson, J. Wilson, J. O. Andrew, M. Curtis, L. Howley, V. F. Burke, M. Kennedy, M. Cutler, P. Fitzpatrick, G. Gregory, -- Kennedy.

Following belong to Newfoundland:

E. A. Butler, H. Trambelt, M. Driscoll, P. Haley, G. McGrath, J. O. Marsh, H. Rowe, Mrs. E. Rickson.

Following were from Newfoundland:

C. Leate, E. M. Kain, L. Leate, V. Squires, M. Gosse, A. Lawlor, A. Hickey, R. Kain, J. Kain, F. O'Toole, M. Brown, G. Felth m, M. Doyle, A. Carew, C. Carew, K. Ludridgan, C. Engles, S. L. Shephard, M. Griffin, A. Norris, A. Conway, M. Casch, F. Perry, C. Gushin, N. Gushin, J. Fenner, — Saunders, M. Clouter, M. C. Clouter, W. H. Clouter, E. Gushin.

Following are Canadians:

R. E. Tough, Miss Sylvia Carew.

Teuton Diplomats Pleased; One Calls This 'Cruiser Warfare'

WASHINGTON, Oct. 8.—News of the sinking of many ships today drew expressions of satisfaction from the ranking Teutonic diplomats. The German Embassy, however, still maintained that it was without prior knowledge whatsoever regarding the visit of the U-53 or her mission in American waters. The dispatch sent to Count von Bernstorff by Lieut. Capt. Hans Rose arrived today, but was said to have contained no information of importance. Neither did it inclose any official communication from the German Government.

The dispatch was brief, being written in German upon one sheet of paper. Captain Rose opened by reporting his arrival, adding that he entered Newport to show his ship to the American Navy, knowing that many ships were gathered there. The communication closed with the statement that he thought he might secure some supplies, should they be offered to him, and requested the embassy to pay any bills.

The embassy appeared to be disappointed because the commander of the submarine failed to give more information regarding himself, his vessel, and his intentions.

A diplomat of rank attached to one of the embassies of the Central Powers, who, in accordance with the general practice, declined to permit the use of his name, said:

"The U-53 and other German submarines, if there are others operating with her, are conducting what is known in international law as cruiser warfare. I can assure you the promises given by Germany to the United States will be strictly lived up to. The U-53 is engaged in doing to commerce of the Allies just what the British tried to do to the Deutschland when she left America. It is a plain case of what sometimes is known as commerce raiding. It is being done by submarines, that is all. Warfare such as that which has been conducted in the Mediterranean has been brought across the Atlantic. It should be easy to destroy more of the overseas commerce of the Allies, which is principally with America, near to where it originates."

SIX OF OUR SHIPS SEE STEPHANO SUNK

Destroyers Watch While Passengers and Crew Are Taken Off and Valves Opened.

THREE SHOTS FOR WARNING

Late Report Says Nine Ships Fell Victims of Three Submarines Altogether.

Special to The New York Times.

NEWPORT, R. I., Monday, Oct. 9, 3 A. M.—The destroyer Ericsson came into the harbor at 1:30 A. M., with survivors from the Stephano on board. Ten minutes later the Drayton came in. Both had averaged over 30 knots out to Nantucket Shoals and back. None of the survivors have landed yet.

The survivors aboard them were huddled in the cabin and came out on deck as soon as they slowed down to anchor. A woman with a baby in her arms on the Ericsson was outlined on deck by a light placed at the companionway.

The Captain of the West Point was taken from the Drayton to the cruiser Birmingham in a launch, but he refused to make any statement to Admirals Knight and Gleaves before reporting to the company owning his ship.

The executive officer of the Drayton said that the Captain of the Nantucket Light vessel sent a wireless message that he had seen three German submarines operating on the Shoals, and that nine steamships all told had been sunk.

The first survivors from the liner Stephano who came ashore tonight stated emphatically that she was not torpedoed and not attacked without warning. They also brought the news that as far as is known not a life has been lost.

There were six destroyers on the scene when the Stephano was stopped and United States naval vessels were thus put in position of umpiring the hold-up.

The passengers on the Stephano said they were hailed by the Ericsson and asked how many Americans were aboard.

Charles T. Evans of 203 West Walnut Lane, Germantown, a wealthy Philadelphian past middle age, was on the Stephano with his wife, returning from a trip to St. Anthony, Newfoundland. Mr. Evans said three shots were fired by a white-hulled submarine, probably the U-53, across the Stephano's bow. The liner came to a stop and orders

Continued on Page 2.

POSSIBLY THREE U-BOATS

Swift Harvest of Victims Follows the Visit of U-53 to Newport.

4 BRITISH, 2 NEUTRAL SHIPS

Red Cross Liner Stephano Is Torpedoed After the Passengers Take to Boats.

U.S. WARSHIPS GO TO RESCUE

Seventeen Destroyers Rushed from Newport—Crew of One British Ship Missing.

Nine Vessels Reported Sunk By Three German Submarines

NEWPORT, R. I., Monday, Oct. 9.—3 A. M.—It was reported without confirmation early this morning that three submarines were operating off the coast and that a total of nine vessels had been sunk by them.

The executive officer of the destroyer Drayton, which has just returned to port, says the Captain of the Nantucket Lightship wirelessed that the total number of vessels destroyed was nine.

The Captain of the lightship also said that three submarines were at work.

BOSTON, Oct. 8.—The submarine arm of the Imperial German Navy ravaged shipping off the eastern coast of the United States today.

Four British, one Dutch, and one Norwegian steamer were sent to the bottom or left crippled derelicts off Nantucket Shoals.

Tonight under the light of the hunters' moon the destroyer flotilla of the United States Atlantic Fleet was picking up passengers and crews of the destroyed vessels and bringing them into Newport, R. I. So far as known, there was no loss of life, although at a late hour the crew of the British steamer Kingston had not been accounted for.

According to a very definite report tonight two submarines were concerned in the work this afternoon. The Newport Naval Station has received a wireless from the Captain of the lightship, stating that he recognized two submarines at work.

A submarine held up the American steamer Kansan, bound from New York for Genoa with steel for the Italian Government, but later, on establishing her identity, allowed the American to proceed. The Kansan came into Boston Harbor late tonight for her usual call here.

This submarine is believed to be the U-53, which paid a call to Newport yesterday and disappeared at sunset.

Day's Work of Havoc.

The record of submarine warring, as brought to land by wireless dispatches, follows:

THE STRATHDENE, British freighter, torpedoed and sunk off Nantucket. Crew taken aboard Nantucket Shoals Lightship and later removed to Newport by torpedo boat destroyers. The vessel left New York yesterday for Bordeaux, and was attacked at 6 A. M.

THE WEST POINT, British freighter, torpedoed and sunk off Nantucket. Crew abandoned the ship in small boats after a warning shot from the submarine's gun. Officers and men were taken aboard a destroyer. The vessel was attacked at 10:45 A. M. She was bound from London for Newport News.

THE STEPHANO, British passenger liner, plying regularly between New York, Halifax and St. John's, Newfoundland, sunk by opening valves when southeast of Nantucket, while bound for New York. Passengers and crew, numbering about 140, were picked up by the destroyer Balch and transferred to the destroyer Jenkins. The attack was at 4:30 P. M.

THE KINGSTON, British freighter, torpedoed and sunk southeast of Nantucket. Crew missing and destroyer searching for them. This vessel is not accounted for in maritime registers, and may be the Kingstonian. The attack was at 6 P. M.

THE BLOOMERSDIJK, Dutch freighter, torpedoed and sunk south of Nantucket. Crew taken aboard a destroyer. The steamer was bound from New York for Rotterdam, having sailed last night.

THE CHRISTIAN KNUDSEN, Norwegian freighter, torpedoed and sunk near where the Bloomersdijk went

Continued on Page 2.

"All the News That's Fit to Print."

The New York Times.

VOL. LXVI...NO. 21,444. ... NEW YORK, TUESDAY, OCTOBER 10, 1916.—TWENTY-FOUR PAGES. ONE CENT In Greater New York, Jersey City and Newark. | Elsewhere, TWO CENTS.

THE WEATHER
Fair, cooler today; tomorrow fair; fresh northwest to north winds.
For full weather report see Page 23.

U-BOAT SENT SIX SHIPS DOWN, ALL ABOARD SAVED; SUPPLY BOAT BELIEVED TO BE WITH THE RAIDER; WILSON INSISTS GERMAN PLEDGES MUST BE KEPT

HUGHES ROUSES GREAT CROWD ON U-BOAT ISSUE

Refers to Lusitania and Pledges Protection to Americans on Land and Sea.

TAKES BLACKLIST STAND

Won't Tolerate That or Any Improper Interference with Our Property or Mails.

EXPLAINS DANBURY CASE

Decision Solely on the Law—Big Philadelphia and Newark Meetings.

Special to The New York Times.

PHILADELPHIA, Penn., Oct. 9.—For the first time in his fight for the Presidency, since his speech of acceptance, Charles E. Hughes tonight brought forward the sinking of the Lusitania by a German submarine as a campaign issue, pointing out that as a result of the sinking the "lives of American men, American women and American children were ruthlessly destroyed." He followed this with the declaration that "we propose to protect American lives on land and sea."

Coming at a time when German submarines were sinking ships off the coast of the United States, the statement stirred up much speculation. It was greeted with enthusiastic applause. It was obvious that it had served to emphasize in the minds of his auditors the fact that Germany had carried its U-boat warfare to the shores of this country.

Mr. Hughes, in a statement issued earlier in the day at Newark, had let it be known that he would not discuss the danger of complications because of the U-boat exploits, as he did not wish to embarrass the Administration in dealing with current events. He did not mention tonight the newest phase of the international relations between this country and Germany.

The nominee was in fine form, and was stirred to his best efforts by a great crowd, which filled the huge Metropolitan Opera House to overflowing. He made his reference to the Lusitania part of a comprehensive declaration of his belief as to what should be the attitude of the Government of this country in upholding the rights of its citizens.

With the Lusitania out of the way, he turned to the alleged wrongdoings of England and other allied countries in their attitude toward the United States.

Will Protect American Trade.

"I do not put life and property on the same footing," he said, and later added:

"We do not propose to tolerate any improper interference with American property, with American mails, or with legitimate commercial intercourse. No American who is exercising only American rights shall be put on any blacklist by any foreign nation."

Mr. Hughes did not mention England or France, but he made his meaning plain. Then came this declaration:

"I repeat in Philadelphia what I said in Milwaukee: We have no intrigues, no unstated purposes, no covert understandings or arrangements. We stand four-square to the world, representing the United States and its interests, and its interests alone, first, last and all the time."

The crowd, which earlier in the evening had started a long demonstration at the mention of the name of Roosevelt by President Riddell of the Union League Club, who presided, accorded Mr. Hughes the most enthusiastic applause of the night when he struck out for the maintenance of American rights.

Mr. Hughes made his declaration of Americanism an answer to the assertion of President Wilson that the Republican Party stood for a war policy. That assertion, he said, was simply an effort of the Administration to escape deserved condemnation.

In addition, Mr Hughes, for the first time, answered the charge that as a Justice of the United States Supreme Court he had personally dealt a blow at organized labor in the Danbury Hat case decision, a charge which has been frequently laid at his door during his campaign tours—tossed at him here and there in labor centres in insulting, derisive tones.

This climax of the night came while Mr. Hughes was midway in his declaration about Americanism and the protection of American lives, property, and commerce. A man in the gallery shouted "How about the Danbury hatters' case?"

There were hisses and shouts of "Put him out."

"Now, my friend," said Mr. Hughes, "I will tell you all about that case as soon as I get through with this part of my statement."

When he came to answer it a few minutes later there was another disturbance in the gallery, and cries of "Make him stand up" were heard.

"Oh, no, no, do not embarrass him," said Mr. Hughes. Then with a firm voice and emphatic gestures the candidate took up the case.

Explains Danbury Decision.

"The question related to the Danbury hatters' case," he said, "a case decided by the Supreme Court of the United States, of which I was a member. The decision was a unanimous one; and, as that statement implies, I concurred in it. I did my duty as a Judge, enforcing the laws of the land.

"Now, what was this case? There was a manufacturer who said that he suffered in his business through what is known as a secondary boycott; that there was an association of workingmen who, through their officers, had destroyed his business. He brought a suit in the Federal Court to recover treble damages under the Sherman anti-trust act.

"The first question presented was whether, on his own statement, he had made out a case. That went to the Supreme Court of the United States long

Continued on Page 24.

Japan Is Pressing Demands on China

PEKING, Oct. 9.—The Chinese press expresses alarm at the insistent manner in which Japan is pressing the demands made in consequence of the recent clash between Chinese and Japanese troops at Chenchiatung, Manchuria. The newspapers express the fear that the new Japanese Cabinet will adopt an aggressive attitude.

Baron Hayashi, the Japanese Minister, visited the Foreign Office today and discussed with Chen Chin Tao, Chinese Minister of Finance, the Chenchiatung demands. Baron Hayashi emphasized Japan's demand for police rights in Inner and Southern Manchuria and in Eastern and Inner Mongolia.

Chen Chin Tao gave no definite reply, saying that action by the Cabinet was necessary.

OSBORNE, RESIGNING, ATTACKS GOVERNOR

Sing Sing Warden Asserts That Whitman Acquiesced in the Charges Against Him.

REFORMS BLOCKED, HE SAYS

Tells Supt. Carter Recent Orders Have Made It Impossible to Run the Prison Properly.

Thomas Mott Osborne has resigned as Warden of Sing Sing Prison, to take effect Oct. 16. In his letter of resignation, which was made public here last night, the Warden charged Governor Whitman with "acquiescence in the shameful attacks made upon me in Westchester County," and asserted that the Governor "broke every promise he ever made to me, both before and after he took office."

The direct cause of Mr. Osborne's decision not to continue as head of Sing Sing was the recent order issued by James M. Carter, Superintendent of Prisons, restricting "lifers" and men serving long terms to the prison walls. The order, according to Mr. Osborne, meant that fifty-four of the eighty-four trusties employed at responsible tasks outside of the prison must give up their work.

Superintendent Carter, according to Warden Osborne's letter of resignation, which was addressed to the prison Superintendent, had never given the Mutual Welfare League system "a fair and full trial." "Your recent orders," he continued, "issued to the press before they even reached the Warden—thus giving no time to object, to correct, or to modify—are such as to make good administration in any institution impossible. They aim to discredit any administration of the prison and the operation of the Mutual Welfare League."

Resigned First by Telegram.

The Warden's letter followed a telegram of resignation sent to Superintendent Carter, which was made public in Buffalo yesterday morning. Mr. Osborne declined to discuss his action early in the day. Later he motored to New York and went to the University Club, where he wrote the letter of resignation and arranged to have it given out at the Hotel Belmont by Martin Loonin, Employment Agent of the Mutual Welfare League. He returned early last night to Sing Sing, where he said that he would continue as Warden until his successor was appointed, if he was asked to do so. Superintendent Carter said that nothing had been decided as to a new Warden.

In his letter of resignation, Mr. Osborne says:

"When I returned to Sing Sing last July it was with the distinct assurance that the Wardens of the State prisons were to be permitted full control of the details of the respective institutions under their charge, without being subjected to the annoying and mischievous interference, to say nothing of the scandalous persecution, that made good administration at Sing Sing impossible under your predecessor. It was also clearly understood that the Mutual Welfare League system would have what it never yet had—a fair and full trial.

"I regret to say that you have not kept faith, you have forbidden that the public shall have full knowledge of what is going on in their own penal institutions, yet this very secrecy which you enforce is the very thing that made possible the graft and brutality of the old system, and still makes possible a continuance of graft and brutality in one of the State prisons under your own charge. Escapes and prison delinquencies which have always existed under the old system, but have been materially reduced under the new, are made your excuse for spreading abroad doubt and distrust of the Mutual Welfare League and even for the actual destruction of its activities."

Resents Restrictions on Prisoners.

Referring to the restriction of "lifers" to the prison walls, Warden Osborne charges that the order disorganized his office, taking away clerks from the Controller's office, the package and visiting rooms, and the administrative force of the Highway Department.

"It is the latest of a series of orders aiming to discredit my administration of the prison and the operation of the Mutual Welfare League," the letter continues.

"What other interpretation can be placed upon your order of Sept. 20, in which you write:

"'I have now come to the definite conclusion that either the new ideas are not workable or that lax methods are employed in their development.'

"You have reached the definite conclusion without sufficient knowledge either of the working of the league in Sing Sing Prison or any real study of its results. You made the short and hurried visit here during Dean Kirchwey's Wardenship. You have spent part of one day here since my return—three visits in your seven and a half months of office.

Says Whitman Wants Old System.

"I appreciate the difficulty and the embarrassment of your position. I credit you with the desire and intention, when you became Superintendent, to conduct your office with fairness and common sense, but the reactionary forces about you have been too strong. The Governor who appointed you is

Continued on Page 21.

BIG PROBLEMS FOR WILSON

Washington Impressed by Perils to Us in War Off Our Coast.

MIGHT ATTACK OUR SHIPS

Another Complication Seen in Reports of a Submarine Base in Maine.

WATCH U-BOAT'S CONDUCT

Question Already Raised as to Halting of Stephano and Putting Passengers in Boats.

Special to The New York Times.

WASHINGTON, Oct. 9.—On President Wilson has been placed the responsibility of determining what course the Government shall pursue with reference to the action of Germany in bringing the European war close to the shores of the United States. The seriousness with which the President looks upon the situation is plain from his action in summoning Secretary Lansing to Long Branch for a conference tomorrow.

The activities of the German submarine, or submarines, off Nantucket have made a deep impression in Government circles, and have raised the question whether the United States will be justified, for its own protection and for the future, in permitting belligerent submarine activity at the very doors of the nation.

Evidence has reached here that the U-boat is accompanied by a tender, presumably loaded with torpedoes, fuel, and other supplies, and there is a strong intimation that officials suspect that a German submarine base has been established within American waters. The Department of Justice has had cause to suspect that surveys were being made on islands near the Maine coast with a view to the location of German submarine bases there.

The British and French Embassies in Washington have for some time been making requests of the State Department to be informed of the prospective arrival and departure of United States submarines at places along the coast where British and French patrol squadrons are being maintained, the object of the requests being to obviate the danger that American submarines would be attacked by the allied cruisers in the belief that they were German.

This fact became known today in connection with the activities of the raider off Nantucket. It assumes considerable importance at this time, since it shows that the British and French Governments had reason to believe that German submarines would visit American waters and were on the lookout for them. Beyond that, however, the matter takes on a new phase in the danger that it brings, since the arrival of a German submarine near the coast of the United States, to naval vessels of this Government.

The action of Germany in sending a submarine on a mission of war to this side of the Atlantic has thus jeopardized warships of the United States, a neutral nation. With British, French, and German vessels of war near the coast, American submarines are not free, without grave danger, to carry on the practice cruises in which they are actively engaged.

Whether the President, in giving consideration to the new turn in the U-boat issue, will study the effect on international relations of the danger to American submarines, and perhaps to other American warships and innocent merchant vessels through the British patrol warships, can only be surmised. It is said, however, that the President may be impressed, as officials here have been, by the feeling that as long as British, French, and German vessels of war remain in waters adjacent to the shores of the United States, the maintenance of friendly relations between this Government and these belligerents will be jeopardized.

Many Perplexing Questions.

The problems before President Wilson in connection with the coming of a German submarine or submarines to western Atlantic waters may be stated as follows:

Has the United States a right to object to having the European war brought close to its shores, 3,000 miles from the nearest scene of actual conflict?

Are German submarines operating from bases on American territory or within American territorial waters?

Did the U-53 enter Newport harbor to obtain military information, such as whether the German merchant submarine Bremen has reached this country or what merchant vessels carrying supplies to the Allies had just departed or were about to depart from American ports?

Has a virtual blockade of American ports been established by the U-boat activity?

Does the danger to American warships of attack by British and French cruisers and German submarines in these waters justify the President in demanding that the British and French patrol of the Atlantic coast be discontinued, and that German submarines be withdrawn from near the coast of the United States?

With reference to this last question, it is pointed out that the U-53 might easily mistake an American warship for a British or French warship and torpedo her. Officials think it likely that the U-53 will make an attempt to sink one or more of the warships of the British and French patrol squadron along the Atlantic Coast.

The theory is that such an attack would be made at night, as the submarine could hardly escape if she encountered a British or French warship in broad daylight. That the danger of error is very great has been demonstrated forcibly by the frequent requests made to the State Department by the British and French Embassies in Washington that advance notice be given to the allied patrol ships whenever any American submarine is about to depart from or enter places which the allied vessels are guarding.

Comment on Allies' "Inactivity."

Some critical comment was heard here today, based on an understanding that the British and French patrol vessels had made no move to overhaul the U-53. It is known here that three ships of the allied patrol squadron were off the Virginia Capes Saturday night. By that time, according to what was said today, these vessels must have known that the U-53 had put into Newport. So it was contended that the patrol ships were showing lack of initiative by remaining off the Virginia Capes while the German submarine was preparing to play havoc with shipping carrying munitions of war to England and France.

The questions enumerated above are all outside of those involved in Germany's pledges to conduct submarine warfare in accordance with international practice. Until the facts are obtained, officials say, it will be impossible for the Government to determine its course. These facts, it is explained, must include the following points:

By compelling crews and passengers, including American women and children, to take to small boats in the open sea, was the U-boat violating pledges to make certain that persons on merchant ships sunk by German submarines would not be jeopardized through being left to the mercy of the sea at a considerable distance from the nearest land?

Was proper warning and time for passengers and crew to disembark given in all cases of vessels sunk by the German submarine?

Was the rule of visit and search followed in each instance by the submarine?

After reading the newspaper accounts of the exploits of U-53 yesterday off Nantucket Shoals Lightship, officials who discussed the matter today were of the opinion that U-53 had not violated the pledges the German Government had given to the United States.

It was conceded, however, that possible ground for complaint on the part of this Government was given in the case of the Stephano. This ship, while sailing under British colors, was bound for a United States port, and could not be regarded as engaged in carrying contraband of war.

It is not questioned that the German submarine had the right to make a prize of the Stephano and send her to a port with a prize crew or convoy her there. But it is pointed out that the German submarine took grave chances of violating its Government's pledges to the United States by sinking a vessel not engaged in contraband trade, when the lives of American women and children were jeopardized by compelling them to take to small boats in the open ocean.

Lansing Challenged Allies' Plea.

The memorandum of the British Government, sent on behalf of the Entente Allies to neutral powers, urging them to bar belligerent submarines from neutral waters, the text of which was cabled from London tonight, was dated Aug. 21. In this statement the Entente Allies took the ground that submarines were outside the application of the laws of nations because they could escape control and observation by submerging and because it was impossible to identify them, whether neutral or belligerent, combatant or noncombatant.

In a reply to the memorandum Secretary Lansing held that the characteristics of each submersible must govern the case. Concerning the contention of the Allies that it was difficult for warships to distinguish between armed and merchant submarines, Mr. Lansing, it is said, replied that it was equally difficult to distinguish between sailing merchant vessels, some of which may have masked batteries.

The position of the United States is that submarine boats are to be classified as super-marine boats, the facts in each case determining whether the submarine is entitled to treatment as an armed submarine or a commercial submarine. In practice this is what has been done respecting the only belligerent submarines that have entered American ports since the war began—the Deutschland and the U-53. The Deutschland was treated as a commercial submarine and allowed to depart at will. The U-53 was regarded as a naval submarine and treated as such.

Advices to some diplomats here have stated that Norway, Sweden, and Spain have forbidden their harbors to merchant submarines as being "indistinguishable" from war craft. This would indicate that they subscribe to the doctrine laid down by the Entente Allies which has been challenged by the American Government.

A story was circulated here today that Secretary Daniels had informed President Wilson that the official reports to the Navy Department showed that the U-53 had not violated any of Germany's pledges to the United States with respect to the conduct of submarine warfare. This was untrue. Secretary Daniels confined his communications to the President to the reports from Rear Admiral Knight, telling of the work done by the United States destroyers in rescuing the persons who were forced to take to small boats when the ships upon which they were employed or were traveling were sunk by the German submarine. Like Secretary Lansing, Mr. Daniels declined to comment for publication on the situation caused by the

Continued on Page 3.

Norway Hears the Bremen Is On Its Way to Africa

Special Cable to THE NEW YORK TIMES.

COPENHAGEN, Denmark, Oct. 9.—The evening paper of the Norwegian town of Bergen states today that, according to communications from a man well known in German naval circles, the German submarine Bremen was not bound for America, but for some East African harbor.

The paper also states that the value of the Deutschland's cargo brought from America was 8,000,000 reichsmarks.

WILSON SUMMONS LANSING

Secretary and President to Confer Today on New U-Boat Problem.

HAS TALK WITH BERNSTORFF

Tells Him Berlin Must Keep Its Promises and Makes Similar Public Announcement.

CAREFUL WATCH TO BE KEPT

All Official Reports So Far Indicate No Violation of Law by German Craft.

Special to The New York Times.

LONG BRANCH, N. J., Oct. 9.—Secretary Lansing is coming to Shadow Lawn tomorrow to take dinner with the President and remain all night. The announcement was made this evening by Secretary Tumulty.

No reason for the sudden engagement was given, but it is assumed that the President wishes to talk over in full with the Secretary the problems raised by the spectacular raid of the German submarine or submarines on the commerce off the coast of New England

Aside from the possible implications in the invitation to Secretary Lansing, there is no indication here tonight that the Administration regards the activities of the German submarines as producing anything like a crisis in the relations between the United States and Germany. The danger, it is felt, lies in the future, with the complications which may arise with the continuance of commerce raiding near the American coast. It is fully realized that these may include, most serious of all, the loss of American life through a submarine commander's mistake.

All advices which have so far reached the President from official sources tend to show that the German submarines have scrupulously adhered to the pledges given by the Berlin Government. In this connection President Wilson issued this statement today:

> The Government will of course first inform itself of all the facts that there may be no mistake or doubt as far as they are concerned, and the country may rest assured that the German Government will be held to complete fulfillment of its promises to the Government of the United States.
>
> I have no right now to question their willingness to fulfill them.

The President is believed to hold that nothing has yet been done to make him doubt German fulfillment of the pledges given. Nevertheless, the work of the submarines will be carefully watched. Secretary Daniels made several reports to the President today, and further information will be sent to Mr. Wilson as rapidly as it is obtained by United States vessels in the neighborhood of the German raiders.

Bernstorff's Visit Encouraging.

The visit of Count von Bernstorff, the German Ambassador, to the President this afternoon, has served on the whole to give officials further confidence about German intentions. Although the German envoy skillfully parried all leading questions as to the subjects he discussed with the President, he left a general impression that there was no serious cloud on the international horizon. He seemed in excellent humor when he left.

It is understood that Mr. Wilson made it clear to the envoy that, while the American Government had no intention of interfering with the legitimate activities of submarines, it would insist on the strict observance of the pledges given previously by the German Government.

The Ambassador reached Shadow Lawn at 2 o'clock, and stayed fifteen minutes, leaving for New York almost immediately. To reporters, who waited for him at the east entrance, he said that he would have to refer all questions about the conference to the White House.

To a question as to how he regarded the present submarine situation, aside from his talk with the President, the Ambassador said that he knew nothing of it except what he had seen in the papers. He went on:

"I am sure there will be no violation of German pledges about submarine warfare. The German Government has promised that, and the German Government always keeps its promises, everywhere."

He denied that he had any previous knowledge of the coming of the U-53, and said that the letter, left at Newport to be sent to him, contained nothing but a report from the submarine commander, saying that he had come and gone. Some one remarked that the submarine had evidently crossed the Atlantic with a different purpose than the mere delivery of that message.

"Well," said the Count with a smile, "you'd better see the British Embassy about that."

The Ambassador said that he had delivered to the President the German Emperor's reply to Mr. Wilson's personal note regarding Polish relief. He was asked if he had mentioned peace in

Continued on Page 2.

Wilson Will Hold Germany to U-Boat Pledges; Hughes Silent to Avoid Embarrassing the Government

LONG BRANCH, N. J., Oct. 9.—President Wilson issued the following statement to the American people today just previous to receiving a call from Count von Bernstorff, the German Ambassador:

> The Government will, of course, first inform itself as to all the facts, that there may be no doubt or mistakes as far as they are concerned, and the country may rest assured that the German Government will be held to the complete fulfillment of its promises to the Government of the United States.
>
> I have no right now to question their willingness to fulfill them.

This statement in regard to the sinking of allied merchantmen by a German submarine was given out yesterday by Charles E. Hughes at the Ebert Treat Hotel, Newark, N. J.:

Mr. Hughes was asked for his views in respect to the present submarine situation. He refused to discuss it. He said he was not in control of the official agencies and was not in receipt of official information.

He said, further, that he did not desire to embarrass the Administration in dealing with any current matter as to which the Administration had the sole responsibility.

Allies Urged Neutrals to Bar Belligerent Submarines.

LONDON, Oct. 9.—The text of the memorandum recently sent by the Allies to neutral Governments respecting the admission of belligerent submarines into neutral waters or ports is as follows:

> In view of the development of submarine navigation and by reason of acts which in the present circumstances may be unfortunately expected from enemy submarines, the allied Governments consider it necessary, in order not only to safeguard their belligerent rights and liberty of commercial navigation, but to avoid risks of dispute, to urge neutral Governments to take effective measures, if they have not already done so, with a view to preventing belligerent submarine vessels, whatever the purpose to which they are put, from making use of neutral waters, roadsteads, and ports.
>
> In the case of submarine vessels, the application of the principles of the law of nations is affected by special and novel conditions: First, by the fact that these vessels can navigate and remain at sea submerged, and can thus escape all control and observation; second, by the fact that it is impossible to identify them and establish their national character, whether neutral or belligerent, combatant or noncombatant, and to remove the capacity for harm inherent in the nature of such vessels.
>
> It may further be said that any place which provides a submarine warship far from its base with an opportunity for rest and replenishment of its supplies thereby furnishes such addition to its powers that the place becomes in fact, through the advantages which its gives, a base of naval operations.
>
> In view of the state of affairs thus existing, the allied Governments are of the opinion that submarine vessels should be excluded from the benefit of the rules hitherto recognized by the law of nations regarding the admission of vessels of war or merchant vessels into neutral waters, roadsteads, or ports, and their sojourn in them. Any belligerent submarine entering a neutral port should be detained there.
>
> The allied Governments take this opportunity to point out to the neutral powers the grave danger incurred by neutral submarines in the navigation of regions frequented by belligerent submarines.

BRITISH OFFICIALS SILENT ON U-BOATS

Decline to Embarrass This Government by Discussing New Submarine Problems.

PRESS SEES US FLOUTED

One Paper Suggests That Mexican Submarines Might Bar Our Access to England.

Special Cable to THE NEW YORK TIMES.

LONDON, Oct. 9.—British officials today maintained an attitude of firm refusal to discuss the exploits of German submarines off the American coast. It was explained to THE NEW YORK TIMES representative at the Foreign Office that the Government wished to avoid the slightest word that might appear to project itself into a situation that was one for the American Government alone. No hint was allowed to escape as to whether the British Government believed that there had been any violation of international law by Germany when the U-53 entered Newport Harbor, or in any incident pertaining to the sinking of nine ships off Nantucket.

The Government here has cabled to Sir Cecil Spring-Rice for detailed information on the whole episode, and that is as far as it has gone. For the present—at least so THE NEW YORK TIMES correspondent is informed at the Foreign Office—no comment will be forthcoming.

A semi-official opinion expressed to the correspondent as to underlying motives of the Germans' sudden campaign was that they might be trying to establish a blockade of American ports against commerce to and from allied countries, but the correspondent's interlocutor said that in attempting to carry out any such policy Germany would undoubtedly get herself into trouble with the Government at Washington.

Another semi-official comment was that Germany might simply wish to impress Americans by a display off their own shores, implying a warning to them to keep themselves out of the submarine broil if Germany should decide to renew ruthless warfare in British waters.

No definite reports from the commanders of the allied vessels in American waters are at hand to show exactly what submarines were engaged in the attacks, but it is reported that the U-53 was one of the squadron, while it is rumored that there were two others, one of them the U-61. Many persons believe that the U-53 has a base somewhere on the American coast or in a ship lying off it.

Intense interest is manifested in London today over the submarine's exploits, the newspapers playing them up on their first pages with big headlines. Crowds

Continued on Page 3.

INCOMING LINERS CHANGE COURSES

Frederick VIII., with Gerard on Board, and the Cameronia Running Off Regular Lane.

ONE SAILING CANCELED

Pierce Liner for Italy Stays in Port—Believe U-Boat Has Latest Shipping Information.

The seriousness with which transatlantic companies viewed the sinking of vessels by the U-53 was shown last night when wireless messages were received from the Anchor liner Cameronia and the Scandinavian-American ship Frederick VIII. that indicated that they were proceeding to this port well off their customary courses. Both steamers have heavy passenger lists and among those on board the latter vessel are Ambassador Gerard and his wife.

That the commander of the German submarine U-53, operating off Nantucket, has the latest information concerning the movements of transatlantic shipping to and from New York, Boston, Philadelphia, and Norfolk, was the opinion expressed by many shipping men. In this opinion an official of one of the allied governments in New York concurred.

"When the U-53 put into Newport on Saturday," said that official, "her commander undoubtedly received complete schedules of shipping to and from the Atlantic seaboard of this country. That, in my opinion, was the real reason for his unexpected visit to Newport."

Despite the uneasiness in local shipping circles the sailing of only one transatlantic steamship was canceled yesterday. That was the Pierce liner San Guglielmo, which was to have sailed for Italy yesterday morning. No other cancellations were announced during the day. At the offices of the various lines it was said that there was no reason at present to anticipate any disruption of the regular schedules as a result of German submarine activities in American waters.

"For two years," said one steamship man, "we have been going through worse than this in the North Sea and in the Mediterranean and I don't think we will give in at this late date when they try to transfer their operations to this side."

Big Liners Nearing Port.

The Espagne of the French Line was expected to pass Nantucket some time last night or this morning. This ship has among her passengers Mme. Sarah Bernhardt.

At the offices of the French Line it was said that the company had no present intention of canceling the sailing of any of the ships of that line

Continued on Page 4.

SUBMARINE DISAPPEARS

Navy Searchers Find 216 Survivors from Wrecks and End Hunt.

SUPPLY SHIP BESIDE U-BOAT

Stephano's Captain and Men of Destroyers Declare They Saw Both Craft.

PROBABLY BUT ONE RAIDER

Newport Officers Indignant at Useless Attacks, but See Nothing Illeg'l.

Special to The New York Times.

NEWPORT, R. I., Oct. 9.—Two hundred and sixteen passengers and seamen from six steamships sunk by the German submarine raider U-53 off the New England coast yesterday were landed here today, every one of them uninjured.

On the Birmingham, flagship of the torpedo flotilla, it was announced late tonight, by authority of Rear Admiral Gleaves, that the search for the survivors was completed and that all destroyers engaged in the hunt had been recalled.

The crew of the sunken Kingston was bound for New York, it was made known, on a Greek steamer, the name of which was confused in wireless transmission. A previous report to the flagship that two of the Kingston's crew were on a destroyer and were being brought back to Newport was erroneous.

Abandonment of further search was interpreted here as meaning that the Navy Department had rejected an early report that nine steamers were torpedoed, and instead was satisfied that every soul on every ship attacked was accounted for.

Six Ships Sunk.

A list of the ships sunk by the U-53, with the approximate times of the attacks, follows:

Strathgena, British freighter, 7 A. M.
Christian Knudsen, Norwegian freighter, 9 A. M.
West Point, British freighter, 11:10 A. M.
Stephano, British passenger liner, 3:50 P. M.
Kingston, British freighter, 6 P. M.
Bloommersdijk Dutch freighter, 6:10 P. M.

Rear Admiral Albert Gleaves, commanding the torpedo boat destroyer flotilla which did such remarkably rapid rescue work yesterday, said tonight that the reports of all his officers agreed that to the best of their observation one raider only was concerned. This boat presumably was the German U-53, which called at Newport Saturday afternoon to mail a letter to Ambassador Bernstorff, and then put to sea without taking on an ounce of supplies, although she was seventeen days from her base, according to the statement of her officers.

Where Next? the Question.

A day's sober reflection on the shifting of the scene of Germany's submarine activities to the verge of American waters, partly because of the fact that the day has brought but vague and disquieting answers to many suddenly serious problems, has wrought the whole Atlantic seaboard to a pitch of tense expectancy.

Wherever there were ships and men who travel on them there was tonight uneasy attempt to answer these two questions: "Where next?" and "When?" For though the U-53 and whatever accomplices in destruction she may have had vanished as quietly and as battlingly as they came, no one qualified to hazard an opinion believed the raids of Sunday were only a sudden, spectacular demonstration of Germany's long reach under the sea, designed to strike terror in some quarters and produce elation in others.

There were not many tangible facts tonight on which to base the prevailing apprehension which gave rise to early rumors (that so far had proved false) of "another ship sunk," but there was at least one that was more than pertinent. Captain Clifton Smith of the British passenger liner Stephano, who told a clear and connected story of the adventure, insisted that when he first encountered the submarine she was lying alongside a large vessel which he felt sure must have been a supply ship. "She could hardly have been anything else," he asserted. Several passengers from the Stephano corroborated his report.

Significance of Mother Ship.

Because of the location of the United States Navy's torpedo station on Goat's Island here, expert knowledge of underwater craft and their possibilities is to be had on every hand, and the opinion was unanimous that the presence of a mother ship meant, first, that the submarine or submarines had come to stay, and, second, that so long as a convenient floating base was at their command the submersibles could lurk in these waters just as long as they choose.

Admiral Gleaves admitted this afternoon that he had heard of the presence of the mother ship, but said he had no official corroboration which would justify him in affirming its presence.

That the Administration was giving grave consideration to reports that the U-boat was convoyed by a mother ship

"All the News That's Fit to Print."

The New York Times.

THE WEATHER
Overcast today; Sunday fair; slight temperature changes; west winds.
For full weather report see Page 19.

VOL. LXVI...NO. 21,483. NEW YORK, SATURDAY, NOVEMBER 18, 1916.—TWENTY PAGES. ONE CENT In Greater New York, Jersey City and Newark. | Elsewhere, TWO CENTS.

WILSON'S VERDICT TODAY TO SETTLE MEXICAN DEADLOCK

Secretary Lane Will Consult the President to Obtain His Final Orders.

CRISIS EXPECTED MONDAY

Question of Continuing Negotiations of Commission May Be Decided Then.

CABRERA STILL OBDURATE

Carranza's Chairman Reported to Insist on Points Derogatory to United States.

Special to The New York Times.

ATLANTIC CITY, N. J., Nov. 17.—President Wilson will be asked to say the final word in the Mexican situation tomorrow by Secretary of the Interior Lane of the American-Mexican Joint Commission. Secretary Lane leaves for Washington tomorrow morning and will have a long conference with the President. It is expected here that he will return on Monday with full powers to bring the delicate situation which has obtained since the first part of the week to a final crisis, which will determine the action the United States is to take toward Mexico.

The Commission adjourned this afternoon without having arrived at any agreement and was in reality as far from reaching such an agreement as it was when it convened three months ago. Luis Cabrera refused to be convinced of the sincerity of the American Commissioners or their Government and insisted on proposals which were considered by the Americans to be derogatory to the honor and vital interests of the United States. Efforts on the part of his colleagues and on the part of the American section to bring him to what they considered a reasonable point of view were without avail.

It was learned today that two memoranda had been submitted to Washington and to Mexico City "some time ago," but that up to the present the Mexican Commissioners professed to be without any word from the First Chief on the questions submitted to him. This delay has evoked no explanation from the Mexican Commissioners and the Americans are beginning to tire of the situation.

Two Drafts of Protocols.

The two memoranda are rough drafts of protocols which will be signed by the Commission if agreement is arrived at. They are not alternative plans, but embody subjects which are so different that it has been thought best to take them up in separate documents, in order to facilitate action upon them and reference to them in the future. One of them refers to the plan for border control which has been evolved, while the other deals with matters which are considered as having a direct bearing on the international situation, but which are not of such vital interest and relate more to the protection of property rights than to the safety of the lives of Americans.

It was stated authoritatively tonight that no action had been taken by the Commission which would warrant the Commissioners in submitting to their Governments anything not essentially tentative. In view of the statement made early in the week that a settlement might be expected at any moment, it was considered that the Commission had gone backward rather than forward in the last two days. Such a situation is not expected to continue for any great length of time.

The American Commissioners so far have abstained from putting the situation to the Mexicans in the nature of a choice between two definite plans, but unless there is a change in Mr. Cabrera's attitude next Monday it is expected they will do so with the full authorization of the President as to what the alternatives are to be. The plans as suggested by the American Commissioners and approved by Mr. Bonillas and Mr Pani will be submitted as one of the alternatives, and it only remains with the President to decide what the other course of action shall be.

Persons here who are in close touch with the President are authority for the statement that he will leave the matter absolutely in the hands of the Commissioners, and will give them plenary powers so far as he has a right to do so. Should such be the case, the other alternative may be expected to be drastic and final.

Cabrera's Plan Shelved.

Authoritative information tonight was that the proposals which were advanced by Mr. Cabrera on Monday as a substitute for the plan already agreed on by the American Commissioners and Mr. Bonillas and Mr. Pani had not received further consideration. The understanding here is that Mr. Cabrera has not been able to force a consideration of this because of the attitude of his colleagues and that therefore he has prevented action of the other plan pending some word from his Government.

Mr. Cabrera left for New York tonight to confer with representatives of American mining interests in Mexico regarding Carranza taxation decrees. He has stated that it was probable some changes would be made in these decrees, and it is believed that these changes will be along lines which have been outlined by the mining men as equitable.

The Mexican Commission tonight issued a copy of a telegram received from the Mexican Consul in El Paso. It stated that General Trevino, commander of the Carranza troops in the State of Chihuahua, was to take the field against Villa. This is a contradiction of reports previously printed that General Murgia was to succeed General Trevino at Chihuahua. The telegram follows:

"Chihuahua headquarters reports

Continued on Page 4.

Flies 435 Miles in Raid On Munich, Lands in Italy

PARIS, Nov. 17.—In retaliation for the bombardment of Amiens, says the War Office, a French aviator, Captain de Beauchamp, flew from the French lines to Munich today, where he threw several bombs on the railway station. On his return trip he crossed over the Alps, alighting near Venice. The distance covered in the flight was 435 miles. The feat is announced by the War Office in the following statement:

"The aviator, Captain de Beauchamp, started this morning at 8 o'clock in the direction of Munich, where he arrived at noon. He dropped several bombs on the station in retaliation for the bombing of the open city of Amiens a few days ago. Captain de Beauchamp then landed at Santa Dona di Piave, in Italy, twenty kilometers north of Venice after having crossed the Alps. The Captain thus covered a distance of 700 kilometers, (approximately 435 miles.)"

MUNICH, Nov. 17, (via Amsterdam and London.)—An official statement issued here today says:

"An enemy airman appeared over Munich at 1 o'clock this afternoon and dropped seven bombs, causing only slight material damage and no casualties. He disappeared westward."

FEAR NO RAIL STRIKE AS SUITS PILE UP

Washington Officials Predict Hasty Action by the Unions Would Cause Legislation.

HAVE NO TEST CASE PICKED

The Department of Justice Will Let Lower Courts Thrash Out the Facts.

Special to The New York Times.

WASHINGTON, Nov. 17.—Department of Justice officials apparently do not take seriously the renewed threats of a great railroad strike as an outcome of the injunction suits which are being brought by the railroads of the country against the Adamson eight-hour law.

Officials said today that there would be no strike and that the employes knew this as well as any one. A strike while the constitutionality of the Adamson law was before the courts, they said, would so prejudice the cause of the employes that there would be little time lost in passing a law in line with President Wilson's recommendations for legislation to prevent strikes.

Whether this would be the Canadian Disputes act, or something similar, was not indicated, but it was confidently predicted that a law to fit the situation could be passed very promptly. The whole situation, it was pointed out, had been clarified by the re-election of President Wilson.

It was asserted at the Department of Justice today that the purpose was to meet the action of the railroads in all the cases brought, but as it might happen that no two cases would develop the same set of facts, the only course that could be pursued was to await the trial of cases as they came on in the courts below. The Attorney General desires to take a case to the Supreme Court that will cover all the questions in dispute and have them all passed on in one decision.

An official of the department said today that no one in the department had any idea whatever as to which of the many cases would be brought to trial first, or which might be the case to be taken to the Supreme Court. The attitude of the department, it was said, was to wait and see how events shape themselves. An appeal would be taken by the Government in the particular case which seemed best to embody all the questions at issue.

Dr. Max O. Lorenz, assistant statistician of the Interstate Commerce Commission, has been appointed Secretary of the commission which will investigate the operation of the eight-hour law. Major Gen. Goethals, the Chairman of the commission, went to New York today to arrange for a preliminary meeting there next Thursday. Rooms in the New York custom house probably will be assigned to the commission.

ADAMSON PROMISES RELIEF FOR THE ROADS

Discusses Railway Problems at Washington Conference—Says Congress Will Act Promptly.

Special to The New York Times.

WASHINGTON, Nov. 17.—The National Council of the United States Chamber of Commerce opened a conference here today for the discussion of the railroad situation. This meeting is looked upon as extremely important in its bearing on the affairs of the railroads, as it will develop the general sentiment of business men from all parts of the country.

In addressing the council, Representative W. C. Adamson of Georgia, Chairman of the House Committee on Interstate and Foreign Commerce, and a member of the joint committee of investigation, said that Congress would act promptly in giving legislative relief and that it would not be in the direction of Government ownership.

"Government ownership would mean the subjugation of the Government to the railroads," said Mr. Adamson. "If the roads are capitalized at $25,000,000,000, bonds would be issued to buy the roads, and the only people who could take up those bonds would be the present holders of the railroad securities of the country. In the end the Government would not own the railroads, but the present owners would still own them and then we would have the most powerful oligarchy ever seen on the face of the earth."

Charles R. Van Hise, President of the

Continued on Page 3.

FIVE MEN DROWN AS DEUTSCHLAND CRASHES INTO TUG

Submarine, in Dash to Sea, Sinks Convoying Craft, with Loss of Entire Crew.

FREIGHTER BADLY DAMAGED

Forced to Return to New London for Repairs—May Be Delayed Two Weeks.

TIDE CAUSES COLLISION

Passage at Race Rock Scene of Disaster—Hinsch Saved from Sea After Wreck.

Special to The New York Times.

NEW LONDON, Conn., Nov. 17.—The German submersible freighter, Deutschland, an hour after leaving her pier here this morning on her second trip back to Bremerhaven, rammed and sank the tug T. A. Scott, Jr., which was convoying her out to sea, drowning five persons aboard the tug and injuring herself so badly that she had to return to this port for repairs that will delay her sailing a week or more.

Of those aboard the tug, Captain Hans F. Hinsch, of the North German Lloyd liner Neckar, who had been in charge of the practical end of the submarine enterprise, alone was saved. The others died without so much as a chance to leave their stations of duty.

The men who lost their lives in the collision were:

Captain John Gurney, William A. Caton, engineer; Edward Stone, fireman; Clarence B. Davison, cook, and Eugene Duzant, deckhand, of the tug T. A. Scott, Jr. All except Duzant lived in New London. He is believed to have made his home in Pawtucket, R. I. Gurney and Caton were married and had children. The others were single.

Blame for the accident has not been fixed as yet, but in advance of official findings the facts indicate that the submarine was running too close to the tug, that the latter was halted when she turned in the Race and met the full force of the flood tide, and the larger vessel, its momentum unchecked by the powerful adverse current, chiseled its keen cutwater through the port side of the tug's bow, slicing it in two before Captain Paul Koenig of the submarine could even realize what was happening.

Federal Inquiry On.

Steamboat inspectors of the Department of Commerce undertook late this afternoon a preliminary inquiry into the tragedy. Under the law it was conducted in secret to form the basis for a public hearing within the next few days.

Rumors which reached New York that the accident was due to the two tugs which accompanied the Deutschland, and that vessel itself not carrying proper running lights, were proved to be entirely unfounded. The three ships carried the regulation signals when reporters observed their departure early this morning, and they still showed them when the collision occurred about twelve miles from the State pier.

The findings of the investigation would be of importance in case of admiralty litigation, but the Eastern Forwarding Company, American agents of the submarine, already has notified the T. A. Scott Company, to whom the tug belonged, that all damage would be settled.

The Deutschland's unexpected departure early this morning and her even more startling return gave rise to a flock of wild rumors that kept this little seaport highly excited. Chief among these was a story that a German war submarine with a gun mounted on her deck was observed off Fisher's Island while the Deutschland was proceeding thither. There was an attempt to make Commander Yates Stirling of the United States Naval Submarine Flotilla in these waters responsible for the report. Commander Stirling, however, declared tonight that his investigation had established beyond doubt that the submarine observed belonged to the United States Navy and was proceeding westward on a ninety-hour test cruise.

How the Accident Occurred.

Preceded by the tug Scott and followed, a mile or more astern, by the tug Cassie, the Deutschland was making ten knots when the trio neared Race Rock, off the end of Fisher's Island in Long Island Sound. The tug swung to port to make the passage between the rock and the island, when the full force of the flood tide brought her to a dead standstill for the few seconds it would have taken her to regain her momentum against the opposing flow of the water which runs swiftly through the narrow gut.

The Deutschland, not yet arrived at the point where she, too, would have ported her helm, slid dead ahead and an instant later she sliced straight through the bow of the tug.

Captain Hinsch stood on the deck of the tug, behind the pilot house, a megaphone in his hand and keeping a sharp lookout for intruders. Suddenly the submarine struck the tug and the latter went to the bottom in three hundred and fifty feet of water, carrying her crew of five men with her. Hinsch jumped into the water, but the others had no chance.

Oddly, the veteran Captain of liners could not swim. Again and again he sank, but each time the buoyancy of his heavy clothing brought him to the surface. There he would tread water until gravity once more pulled him below.

The Deutschland had whistled a warning and backed away. Captain Koenig and two of his crew were on deck when the crash came, but none of them was jarred enough to be thrown off his feet. The Cassie, crowding her engines to the utmost, came racing to the rescue, lowering her small boat as she reached the spot where the Deutschland was sweeping the sea with her searchlight. The sea was calm and the moon gave light enough to make small objects visible. Albert Mix, Assistant Superintendent of the Scott Company, a local wrecking concern, leaned out of the boat, while those manning it fought hard to keep it still in the sea. Mix flung a life preserver and Hinsch grabbed feebly and just managed to close his hand over it. An instant later, half drowned, he had been lifted

Continued on Page 2.

Norwegian Mail Ship Is Sunk by U-Boat But the Passengers and Crew Are Saved

CHRISTIANIA, (via London,) Nov. 17.—The Norwegian passenger and mail steamer Vega of Bergen, a vessel of 1,203 tons, was sunk yesterday by a German submarine. Sixteen passengers and the crew of thirty-two men, who put off in five boats, were saved by the motor ship Columbia and landed at Stavenger in the evening.

The registered mail on board the Vega was saved by the mail clerk. Most of the baggage of the passengers also was saved.

LONDON, Nov. 17.—Lloyds shipping agency announced today that the Italian steamer San Giovanni, supposed to be a vessel of 1,200 tons, and the Greek steamers Styliani Bebis, 3,003 tons, and Ioanmis, 3,828 tons, have been sunk by a German submarine.

The agency also announced that the Danish steamer Therese, of 1,332 tons, and the British steamer Trevarrack, of 2,098 tons, have also been sunk.

The Norwegian steamship Torridal has also been sunk, according to an announcement made by Lloyds. It was also reported that the British steamship F. Mattarazzo had been abandoned by her crew.

The F. Mattarazzo, of 2,823 tons, was formerly the Ennisbrook. She was 317 feet long, 46 feet beam, and 21 feet deep. The vessel was built at Sunderland in 1906, and owned by the F. Mattarazzo Steamship Company, Ltd., of London.

Available shipping records do not contain the name of the Norwegian steamship Torridal. There is, however, a Torsdal, of 3,620 tons gross. This vessel was built at Newcastle in 1894, and owned at Tonsberg, Norway.

AUSTRIA CONCERNED OVER U-BOAT WAR

Burian, on Visit to Berlin, Said to Have Discussed Possibility of a Break with Us.

HEAR OF WARNING BY WILSON

Rumor in Europe That His Patience Is Nearly Exhausted—Washington Denies Direct Message.

LONDON, Nov. 17.—The visit of Baron Burian, the Austro-Hungarian Foreign Minister, to Berlin is stated to have been in connection with a conference with Dr. von Bethmann Hollweg, the German Imperial Chancellor, regarding the relations of the two empires with the United States, according to a dispatch under a Berne date given out today by the Wireless Press.

The question under discussion, says the dispatch, was whether the submarine campaign should be continued in its present form, with the possibility of a rupture of relations with Washington, or whether it should be modified.

"During the last few days," adds the dispatch, "the German Government has received a plain verbal warning that President Wilson's patience was on the verge of exhaustion."

Special to The New York Times.

WASHINGTON, Nov. 17.—A flat denial of the statement from Berne that a verbal warning had been given to Germany that President Wilson's patience in connection with the renewal of U-boat warfare was on the verge of exhaustion was made tonight by an official in a position to speak with authority.

"I do not know who could have given such a warning," he said. "Certainly this Government did not give it."

For some reason a rather easier feeling exists in official circles over the situation created by the activity of German submarines. While officials do not profess to have new information it is evident that today, judged from what they said, they were not as much concerned over the prospect of a violation of the German pledges. The comment of officials may have been intended to allay agitation. It was apparent that the impression desired to be conveyed was that this Government was not doubting Germany's good faith.

By The Associated Press.

WASHINGTON, Nov. 17.—The reported visit of Baron Burian, the Austro-Hungarian Foreign Minister, to Chancellor von Bethmann Hollweg at Berlin for a full discussion of submarine warfare and its effect on the United States aroused interest here, but could not be confirmed from official dispatches.

Some officials fear that the Teutonic powers may at any moment launch a starvation campaign against England which could not fail to involve the United States.

Secretary Lansing today, however, authorized the statement that as yet "there is absolutely no truth in the reports that the department has information that definite decision has been reached to launch a ruthless German submarine campaign."

Five serious cases are now pending, the sinking of the British steamer Marina, without warning and with the loss of six American lives; the sinking of the British liner Arabia, also apparently by a torpedo and without warning; the shelling of the boats of survivors of the British steamer Rowanmore, which had fled, and the sinking of the American steamers Lanao and Columbian for carrying contraband. Investigation is being made in all cases, but has not yet been completed.

SCOUTS ZIMMERMANN'S PLEA.

British Press View of Germany's Defense of U-Boat Warfare.

Special Cable to THE NEW YORK TIMES.

LONDON, Nov. 17.—Commenting on THE NEW YORK TIMES Berlin correspondent's interview with Herr Zimmermann, the German Under Secretary of Foreign Affairs, which was cabled to this morning's papers, The Westminster Gazette says:

"We do not wonder that this is taken as confirming the fears of Washington that a new submarine crisis is at hand. Herr Zimmermann is impudent enough to claim that Germany is conducting cruiser warfare, waged by means of submarines acting in punctilious compliance with the rules of international law applying to a cruiser war. We should have a much better opinion of our enemy if he stopped this absurd pretense that he is playing the game according to the rules. It only adds insult to injury. It would be far better to admit the breaking of all rules and to plead that necessity knows no law. Even so, the plea would not be a convincing one, but it would at least not be hypocritical."

ARMED SHIP IS DETAINED.

Norfolk Authorities Refuse Clearance Papers to Italian Vessel.

NORFOLK, Va., Nov. 17.—Pending instructions from the Treasury Department, local customs officials announced today that they would refuse clearance papers to the Italian steamer Coltano, which arrived in the Roads this morning from Genoa, in ballast, for Philadelphia. The steamer has a 57-millimeter gun mounted on her poop deck. The commander claims that the gun is for defensive purposes only, and that no naval or military gunners are aboard.

In all other cases of armed merchantmen Federal officials have permitted the vessels to clear upon assurances that their arms would be used only for defensive purposes.

ROB MRS. HARRIMAN OF $65,000 GEMS

Thieves Are Sought Who Took $50,000 Necklace and Other Jewels from Safe.

DETECTIVES LACK A CLUE

Fifth Avenue Home of Railroad Man's Widow Scene of Mysterious Theft.

Mrs. E. H. Harriman has employed private detectives and enlisted the confidential services of the regular police department in the hope of recovering a diamond and ruby necklace with a pendant, valued at $50,000, and a pair of pearl earrings worth $15,000, which disappeared from a safe built into the wall of her home at Fifth Avenue and Sixty-ninth Street. Though Mrs. Harriman discovered her loss last week and detectives have been at work ever since, it was learned last night that not one of them has got trace of the missing jewels or has been able, even, to advance a theory that seems reasonable as to how they left the safe.

This safe is one in which Mrs. Harriman has been accustomed to keep a large variety of jewels. It is said that she has worn only a few pieces since her daughter, Mrs. Charles Carey Rumsey, was robbed of jewels worth $120,000 at Narragansett Pier, R. I., in 1913. But on the opening night of the opera she decided to wear the necklace and unlocked her safe. Other jewels were there, but the necklace and the earrings were gone.

Mrs. Harriman was puzzled and dismayed, but she said nothing to any one and went on to the opera, after having made a search about the house which convinced her that the jewels had not been mislaid. On her return from the opera she got in touch with a representative of Police Commissioner Woods and made known her loss. It is said she insisted that no suspicion attached to any of her household.

Detectives have sent to every pawnshop in the city a description of the missing gems, and it has been ascertained that none of them has been offered for pawn here.

SEES WILSON VICTORY AS LIGHT TO WORLD

English Editor Says President's Task Is to Make Force Grind Wheels of Peace.

LONDON, Saturday, Nov. 18.—"When Europe emerges from the present struggle the balance of the hemispheres will have been fundamentally changed in favor of the Western, and the United States will have an authority in the affairs of the world which it never had before and which, even if it had had, its historic policy would not have permitted it to exercise."

This statement is contained in a feature article in The Daily News, written by Alfred G. Gardiner, editor of the newspaper, who, in emphasizing the indebtedness of the Entente Allies to the United States in the matter of munitions, says:

"We rejoice in the election of the most sagacious statesman American politics has thrown up since Lincoln. If we had reason to be thankful that Mr. Wilson was elected in 1912, there is still more reason to be thankful that he was re-elected in 1916. It is the one indisputable gleam of light in the dark future that lies before the world.

"He cannot eliminate force, but it is in his power and the power of the American nation to make force grind the wheels of peace instead of the wheels of war. This will not be welcomed by the militarists of any country, it will be treated as a mere day dream by those who believe war an indestructible character of human society. But it will have the passionate support of the common people of all lands, and it is the only hope of democracy winning an enduring victory over despotism."

LONDON, Nov. 17.—The Nation, which is an advocate of a moderate peace, describes the German Chancellor's recent speech as a "break in the clouds." The newspaper suggests that it offers the United States an opportunity to talk to Europe as follows:

"The war has not been concluded, but your statesmen are beginning to be talkative. Your ideas do not appear quite incompatible, for you all seem to want peace and wish to base it on justice and a scheme of common organization and counsel. Can I help clarify them? Can I take you a step beyond? Your representatives assert that they did not want the war, and that they have a common notion of how they wish to live together after the war. Can I help find out for you whether the security you all seek has been advanced by your various definitions of it?"

The Nation then adds:

"We could not resent such an attitude, and if, as we believe, peace should be moderate as regards the future organization of States, we should have one substantial reason for welcoming it. For it is clear that force alone cannot determine such a change in State relationship. It must be the issue of good-will."

VIENNA, Nov. 16, (via London, Nov. 17.)—News dispatches reporting that President Wilson is furthering a plan to bring about peace among the belligerents are received with keenest interest by the leading newspapers here. Editorials point out that the least that could result from President Wilson's reported action would be to show the world who is interested in the continuation of the strife, and generally manifest warm support of the proposal.

GERMANY TO DEPORT 300,000 BELGIANS; NATION IS WILD WITH GRIEF AND TERROR; ALLIES PLAN STRONG COUNTERSTROKE

Poles Must Join Kaiser's Army Even by Force Or Grant of Separate Kingdom Will Be Revoked

LONDON, Nov. 17.—The Wireless Press today gave out the following, under date of Berne:

"Before the Main Committee of the Reichstag on Nov. 9 Chancellor von Bethmann Hollweg stated that Germany's promise to create a new Kingdom of Poland was only conditional, being dependent on the success of the plan to raise a Polish army which would fight for Germany. If the number of Poles enlisting voluntarily should be insufficient, Germany would introduce compulsion, and if the Poles resisted or if the projected Polish army proved unsatisfactory to the General Staff, the Emperor would annul his promise to create a new kingdom.

"The Chancellor made this statement in reply to Conservatives and National Liberals, who denounced the policy of creating a Polish Kingdom."

AMSTERDAM, Nov. 17, (via London.)—The Berlin Germania announces that a Vice Regent will be appointed immediately for Poland. This dignitary will hold office until a King is formally elected.

GIVE NEW RIGHTS TO POLISH JEWS

Germans Announce Formation of a Complete Religious Organization.

TO HAVE SUPREME COUNCIL

Berlin Stipulates That Poland Shall Never Again Be Under Russian Rule.

From a Staff Correspondent.
By Wireless to THE NEW YORK TIMES.

BERLIN, Nov. 17, (via Sayville.)—Baron von Burian returned to Vienna last night after conferences with Chancellor von Bethmann Hollweg and Foreign Minister von Jagow which are understood to have been concerned almost exclusively with the still unsettled details regarding the constitution of the new Kingdom of Poland.

Meanwhile General von Beseler, Governor General at Warsaw, has taken another highly important step along the promised lines of giving Polish Jews liberal and just treatment, which may be interpreted as official recognition of the civil equality of the Jews with the other constituents of the population of Poland.

An ordinance made public yesterday in Warsaw by von Besseler provides for the first time for the creation of an organization of the heretofore unorganized and unrecognized Jewish religious communities. The organization is to embrace the whole general Government of Warsaw. The Jewish communities are to be united into district communities, each with a governing council elected by the heads of the Jewish communities and to which the State further appoints three members. At the head of the entire organization, which is created on a purely religious basis, is the Supreme Council, composed of fourteen Jewish laymen and seven rabbis, four laymen and two rabbis being the appointment of the Government of the State and the rest elected by the district councils.

The Polish communities, the district communities, and the Supreme Council will have the rights and status of corporations, the Jewish religion thereby being full recognition in the eyes of the law in Poland as in other kuratur States. Rabbis in the future will be required to have a writing and speaking knowledge of the Polish language.

Russia's protest to neutral powers against the proclamation of the independent kingdom of Poland is considered in diplomatic circles here to be a feeble and hopeless effort, not to be taken seriously, to counteract the moral effect of this action on the part of the Central Powers. Now, as before, the view taken here in official quarters is that independence is the unalterable fait accompli, and that one of Germany's principal peace conditions will be that Poland must never again be under the Russian yoke.

Benefits as Berlin Sees Them.

BERLIN, Nov. 17, (by Wireless to Sayville.)—"Under Russian rule the Jews in Poland, as in all Russia, lived almost without a religious organization," says the Overseas News Agency in describing the new order, issued by General von Beseler, organizing a Jewish religious body. "The hostility of the Russian authorities against the Jews found expression in well-known laws and in uninterrupted persecutions and oppressions of the Jewish community, as well as in the fact that a religious body to which 14 per cent. of the population of Poland belongs was deprived of all uniform organization. Only the formation of organizations of isolated parishes was allowed, and the union of parishes into a larger organization was forbidden.

"By the present order of the Governor General the members of the Jewish Church are reorganized as a religious body according to public right. Local Jewish communities in the counties, according to the new order, are united to county organizations.

"The local communities will be administered through a board elected by the citizens of the Jewish parish under majority rule. This board will have four members in addition to the rabbi. For the large local communities a special organization has been provided. They will be under the rule of an assembly of parish delegates, which will have parliamentary functions, and of an administrative council, which will have administrative functions. The election of parish delegates will be according to the proportional system, and in two sections. Each section will elect the same number of delegates. People without a school education, those who have attended a special trade or agricultural school and Jewish citizens who, on account of their knowledge of Jewish literature, have received the title of rabbi, will vote in the first section. All other classes will vote in the second section. The parish delegates also will have a part in the administrative council.

Will Have Religious Freedom.

"The formation of associations for divine service will be allowed in every

Continued on Page 2.

ENTENTE LEADERS CONFER IN PARIS

Purpose to Take Vigorous Measures to Offset Teuton Mobilizing of Belgians and Poles.

WILL BE PARTLY ECONOMIC

Conferees Send Message to Russian Premier, Applauding Protest Concerning Poland.

Special Cable to THE NEW YORK TIMES.

PARIS, Nov. 17.—The German mobilization of the civil populations of Belgium and Poland is likely to bring a swift reply from the Allies. From information obtained in high official circles I can affirm that the Allies' council now assembled here is discussing measures to be adopted as a counterstroke to the German effort. These will be twofold—first military and secondly economic Premier Asquith is conferring with M. Briand on the diplomatic situation, Lloyd George and Albert Thomas are discussing the munitions question, while the chiefs of the allied armies are daily debating the military situation.

I understand that economic measures have already been outlined, and probably an identical program will be adopted by each allied Government. The allied council probably will continue its conferences for several days.

PARIS, Wednesday, Nov. 15, (Delayed.)—Aristide Briand, the French Premier; Herbert H. Asquith, Prime Minister of Great Britain; David Lloyd George, British Secretary for War, and other representatives of the Entente Allied Governments held a conference today. Later the British officials and Paolo Sarcano, the Italian Minister of the Treasury, were the guests of President Poincaré.

At the close of the conference M. Briand and Mr. Asquith sent the following joint telegram to Boris V. Sturmer, the Russian Prime Minister:

"We have learned with the liveliest satisfaction of the declaration published Nov. 14 in the Russian press, by which the Imperial Government, taking note of the fresh violation of the law of nations and of international conventions committed by Germany and Austria-Hungary, protests against their pretension of creating a new State out of territory momentarily occupied by them and of raising an army among the population of those regions.

"We rejoice to see that, foiling the machinations of our enemies and throwing clear light on the illusory character of their promises, Russia, having since the beginning of the war given the peoples inhabitating all Polish lands assurances conformable to their secular hopes, now solemnly renews the unchangeable decision announced more than two years ago in the name of his Majesty, the Emperor, to realize their autonomy.

"We are deeply gratified by the generous initiative taken by the Government of his Majesty, the Emperor of Russia, in favor of a people to whom we are bound by ancient sympathies, and who, reuniting, will constitute a primordial element in the future stability of Europe. We are happy to associate ourselves with the views which the Imperial Government intends to realize for the benefit of the noble Polish people."

OATH FOR NEW POLISH ARMY.

Volunteers Must Swear Allegiance to Kaiser as Their Chief.

From a Staff Correspondent.
By Wireless to THE NEW YORK TIMES.

BERLIN, Nov. 17, (via Sayville.)—The working out of details of the organization of the new Polish volunteer army is progressing rapidly and satisfactorily. Following the settlement of questions of uniforms and the kinds of formations to be set up, as well as the higher and highest commands, which for the duration of the war will be in German hands, the nature of the "flag oath," which Polish volunteers will swear, has been determined. Polish soldiers will swear, by the Polish national colors, loyalty to "their Polish fatherland, to the German Kaiser as commander-in-chief in this war, and to the monarchs of both Central Powers as guarantors of the Polish State." This is believed to cover all contingencies, while satisfying both Polish and Austrian sensibilities.

BELGIAN VICTIMS DEFIANT

Sing Patriotic Songs As Packed in Cattle Trucks They Go To Exile.

30,000 ALREADY TAKEN

Despairing Women Throw Themselves Before Trains and Are Removed by Force.

TOURNAI OBJECTS, IS FINED

Representatives of Neutrals Are Appealed To for Aid to End the Deportations.

Germany Acknowledges Our Representations

Special to The New York Times.

WASHINGTON, Nov. 17.—Acknowledgment of the informal representations made by the United States regarding the deportation of Belgian civilians into Germany has been received by Secretary Lansing from the German Government, which indicated through the Chargé in Berlin that it will later make a detailed statement of its position.

Secretary Lansing stated today that he had not seen the communication which Mr. Havenith, the Belgian Minister, said he had delivered to the State Department, asking the active intervention of the United States to stop deportations of Belgians.

LONDON, Nov. 17.—Thirty thousand Belgians already have been deported to Germany, according to information received here through official channels.

Reports from the same sources say that the Germans plan to take some 300,000, judging from the order issued in a number of cities for all males over seventeen to report for inspection.

The Municipal Council of Tournai has formally declined to accede to the German demand, the reports say, protesting that hitherto it had acquiesced in all the German orders. General Hopffer thereupon imposed a fine of 200,000 marks, it is added, for the refusal of the Council to furnish a list of male inhabitants, with a further fine of 20,000 marks daily as long as the Council refused to give the list.

A circumstantial report from the Mons district says that the entire male population over seventeen years was summoned to report at German Headquarters at 8 o'clock on the morning of Oct. 26.

The priests, professors, teachers, local officials, members of the Food Committee, and the physically defective were dismissed, but, it is added, 1,200 men, composing 20 per cent. of the eligible males, both employed and unemployed, were selected and immediately placed on cattle trucks and started for Germany. Being ignorant of the purpose of the summons the men had assembled without clothing for traveling and without food. Relatives, who hurried to the station with food and clothing were not permitted access to the men, the reports add.

Tournai Council's Resolution.

The resolution of the Municipal Council at Tournai concerning the request by the German authorities for a list of workmen, says the Council decides to preserve its negative attitude, and adds the following:

"The City of Tournai is prepared to submit without resistance to all the exigencies authorized by the laws and customs of war. Its sincerity cannot be doubted, as it has shown perfect composure and has avoided any active hostility during the period of over two years that it has had to endure the present occupation, to billet the troops and feed them. The city has thus clearly shown that it is not animated by an undue spirit of bravado.

"But at the same time the Municipal Council could not furnish weapons against their own children, fully conscious that natural law and international law, which is derived from it, forbids them to do so.

"In his proclamation of Sept. 2, 1914, the Governor General of Belgium made this statement: 'I am not asking any one to renounce his patriotic feeling.' The city of Tournai remains confident in this statement, which must be considered as expressing the feeling of his Imperial Majesty, the German Emperor, in whose name the Governor General was speaking. Consequently, in following the call of honor and patriotism, the city remains faithful to a primary duty of which a higher German officer cannot fail to realize the nobleness.

"The members of the Municipal Council are confident that the loyalty and frankness of this attitude will help to avoid all misunderstandings between themselves and the German Army."

Reply of Military Chiefs.

The above resolution was dated Oct. 20. Under date of Oct. 23, Major Gen. Hopffer replied as follows:

"The fact that the municipality allows itself by the decision of the Town Coun

Mid-Week Pictorial

German troops evacuating Liège, Belgium.

British field gunners on their way to the front.

"All the News That's Fit to Print."

The New York Times.

THE WEATHER
Fair today; Thursday increasingly cloudy, warmer; east winds.
For full weather report see Page 23.

VOL. LXVI...NO. 21,487. NEW YORK, WEDNESDAY, NOVEMBER 22, 1916.—TWENTY-FOUR PAGES. ONE CENT In Greater New York, Jersey City and Newark. | Elsewhere, TWO CENTS.

EMPEROR FRANCIS JOSEPH IS DEAD AFTER 68 YEARS ON AUSTRIA'S THRONE; CARL FRANCIS JOSEPH IS NOW EMPEROR

The Late Emperor Francis Joseph.

AGED RULER STRONG TO END

Refused to Obey Orders of Physicians and Gave Audiences Daily.

WAS UP ALL DAY MONDAY

But Is Reported to Have Received the Last Sacraments on Saturday.

REIGN FULL OF TROUBLE

His Death Amid War He Precipitated One of Many Hapsburg Tragedies.

LONDON, Wednesday, Nov. 22.—Emperor Francis Joseph died last night at 9 o'clock at Schönbrunn Castle, according to a Reuter dispatch from Vienna, by way of Amsterdam.

He had been suffering for some time from lung trouble, which a few days ago became acute.

A Geneva dispatch forwarded to Reuter's by way of Amsterdam yesterday quoted the Katolische Zeitung as saying the sacrament was administered on Saturday.

The Emperor retained his extraordinary vigor to the end, and his disinclination to obey the orders of his physician caused them the greatest anxiety. He insisted on giving audiences daily, and on Sunday conferred with Premier von Koerber for an hour, according to Vienna advices. He was out of bed all day Monday, it is stated, and in the evening received several visitors.

The first intimation received here that his health was again the subject of solicitation was contained in a dispatch dated Nov. 12, emanating from a Vienna news agency, which reported that the Emperor had been suffering for some days from a slight catarrhal affection.

Subsequent reports from various sources, more or less conflicting, represented that his condition was becoming worse, but none indicated that his illness threatened to reach a critical state until the following bulletin was issued in Vienna early last evening:

"The seat of the inflamation in the right lung, established yesterday, has increased. The patient's temperature early this morning was 38.1 reaumur, at 2 o'clock 39.5, and this evening 39.6. Breathing had accelerated to 30 respirations a minute. Appetite small and vitality visibly lowered."

What gave credence to the suspicion that his condition was much graver than the official bulletins indicated was the report, which still lacks official confirmation, that it had been decided to associate the heir to the throne Archduke Carl Francis, in the government of the country and that he was to assume the position on Dec. 2, on the sixty-eighth anniversary of the Emperor's ascension to the throne.

Telegraphing from Amsterdam the Central News correspondent says:

"Vienna reports that although the death of the Emperor had been expected, the news, which was printed in special editions of the newspapers, made a deep impression on the public. A special Cabinet meeting was held. The heir to the throne, Archduke Charles Francis, has been for some time in Vienna.

"A meeting of the Hungarian Cabinet has been called at Budapest. Premier Tisza will afterward come to Vienna."

London Prints Special Editions.

Special Cable to THE NEW YORK TIMES.

LONDON, Wednesday, Nov. 22.—News of the death of the Austrian Emperor last evening at Schoenbrunn Castle was received in London too late to catch the ordinary editions of the papers, so no editorial opinion is available as to the probable affect, if any, it will have on the course of the war or on the Austrian people.

The Daily Mail in a late special edition publishes a short obituary in which it says:

"Emperor Francis Joseph had been politically defunct for two years. In the present war he played a very insignificant part and it is exceedingly doubtful whether had he been in vigorous health he would ever have consented to become the passive agent of a German plot.

"The initial disasters which befell Austria weighed heavily upon him. The loss of Galicia in the Autumn of 1914 he felt as a crushing blow. From then onwards Germany assumed virtual control of the dominions of the once proud Hapsburg. A reign which began with the abdication of his weak predecessor ended in his own virtual abdication in favor of Emperor William.

"From first to last his reign has been marked by domestic misfortunes and tragedies which recall the fearful doom of the House of Atreus. It has also been politically unfortunate. It opened with civil war and disaster, it witnessed the loss of his Italian provinces and provinces ruled [illegible]

POPE PREPARES NEW PEACE PLEA AS FINAL EFFORT

Pontiff's Allocution on Dec. 4 Will Avoid Polish and Belgian Questions.

HARDEN ARRAIGNS TEUTONS

Calls Their Talk of Ending War Insincere Unless Their Aims Are Changed.

LONDON'S VIEW OF 'COSMOS'

Any Move to End the War Now Vehemently Denounced—Don't Believe President Will Try.

Special Cable to THE NEW YORK TIMES.

ROME, Nov. 21.—The Pope is working daily with Cardinal Gasparri on an allocution which he will deliver in a secret consistory on Dec. 4. This allocution will be one of the most important documents issued by the Papacy since the beginning of the war. The Pope consulted on the subject also Cardinals Delai, Falconio, Vannutelli, and Serafini.

The allocution will show, it is said, the perfect impartiality of the Holy See, which desired altogether to prevent the war, but, having failed, used all means at its disposal to shorten the conflict, meanwhile making arrangements to alleviate the sufferings caused by the war without any distinction of nationality or creed of the belligerents. The allocution, it is reported, will make another desperate appeal in favor of peace, inviting the faithful throughout the world to continue their prayers with that as the object.

The discussion with the Cardinals dealt with the extent of the allocution, whether to include passages concerning the autonomy of Poland, the deportation of Belgians, and efforts made toward the conclusion of peace by several neutral States, especially by President Wilson and King Alfonso, but so far it seems the opinion prevailed not to enter into particulars for fear of compromising the supreme interests.

According to the Vatican reports, among the innumerable messages of greeting received by the Pope today on the occasion of his birthday this year, those wishing success for his action in favor of peace are almost three times as numerous as last year.

INSINCERE, SAYS HARDEN.

Urges Germans to Put Government Into People's Hands.

Special Cable to THE NEW YORK TIMES.

LONDON, Wednesday, Nov. 22.—The Amsterdam correspondent of The London Times writes that in a new article in Die Zukunft Maximilian Harden condemns German efforts to provoke peace discussion as insincere and useless.

He argues that for Germany to say "we do not want annexation," but to reject the independence of every State is meaningless, because annexation nowadays is possible in forms not covered by the ordinarily accepted meaning of the word, and under the appearance of independence a State may, nevertheless, be handed over to the power of its stronger neighbor. Moreover, the statement that Germany fears no tribunal of inquiry does not mean that Germany is willing to submit her case to an impartial jury for trial of all causes of the war.

Harden urges Germany to understand the real objects of the Entente and say that they are the first to bring Germany into line with the political system of Western Europe and to end what the Entente powers certainly consider to be a survival in Germany of bellicose feudalism; secondly, to introduce into Germany parliamentary government, so that the people shall really have something to say in the policy of the country; thirdly, the establishment as the central idea of German preparations of the determination to keep the peace and not, as hitherto, the determination to be ready for war; fourthly, to restrict armaments in proportion to population, and fifthly, to establish real international arbitration based upon such guarantees as will insure the punishment of the rebellious.

Harden indicates that an offer to endeavor to fulfill these conditions would find a fruitful response before Christmas. Meanwhile he prides himself that the German preparations for a Spring campaign are following the lines which he recommended "immediately after the disaster of the Marne and Kitchener's sober three-year prophecy."

LONDON'S COMMENTS ON 'COSMOS' ARTICLES

Called "A New Peace Kite"—Asquith's Guildhall Declaration Still Stands.

Special Cable to THE NEW YORK TIMES.

LONDON, Nov. 21.—A summary of the first "Cosmos" article in THE NEW YORK TIMES was published in this morning's Times and Daily Mail. The subject is not mentioned in any other morning paper.

The Times displays a dispatch from its Washington correspondent, giving the summary prominently under the headings, "The Peace Kite, No Allied Breeze to Carry It—New York Suggestions." The headlines are followed by an italicised paragraph saying:

"In courtesy to THE NEW YORK TIMES and in recognition of the natural desire for peace entertained by a respectable body of opinion in the United States, we publish the following dispatch. The British reply is still contained in Premier Asquith's Guild Hall declaration: 'We shall never sheathe the sword, which we have not lightly drawn, until Belgium recovers in full measure all and more than all that she has sacrificed, until France is adequately secured against the menace of aggression, until the rights of the smaller nationalities of Europe are placed upon an unassailable foundation, and until the military domination of Prussia is wholly and finally destroyed.'"

The London Times's Washington correspondent in the course of his dispatch says:

"There can be no doubt, as already indicated in this correspondence, that the drawn war theory is gaining ground here. The theory is not based upon any

Continued on Page 4.

REPORTS 8 SHIPS SUNK BY U-BOAT IN CHANNEL

But British Admiralty Denies German Statement That French Warship Was Destroyed.

BERLIN, Nov. 21, (via London.)—A German submarine sank, in the English Channel, Nov. 14, a French guard vessel and seven merchantmen, one of them a Norwegian, according to an official communication issued today. The communication says:

One of our submarines in the English Channel on the 14th sank a French guard vessel, apparently a torpedo-boat destroyer of the Arc or Sabre class, and besides six enemy merchantmen. The same U-boat sank the Norwegian steamer Ullvang, which was carrying war material for the French Government.

LONDON, Nov. 21.—This communication was issued by the British Admiralty tonight in connection with the Berlin report of the sinking of a French guard vessel:

"The British Admiralty states on authority of the French Ministry of Marine that no French war vessel was sunk on the 14th in the English Channel."

GERMAN AUTHORITIES UNCIVIL TO U. S. CONSUL

D. I. Murphy Reports Discourtesy to Himself and Wife at Warnemuende.

AMSTERDAM, Nov. 21, (via London.)—Dominic I. Murphy, American Consul General at Sofia, Bulgaria, reached here today after a journey through Germany from Stockholm, whither he went recently with his wife to visit their daughter.

Despite the fact that Mr. Murphy had a special pass from the German Legation at The Hague, it is stated that the German authorities at Warnemunde treated the couple with incivility on their way to Stockholm and again on their return, notwithstanding the intervention of Dr. Maurice F. Egan, the American Minister to Denmark, and also of the German Minister to Stockholm, who had assured Mr. Murphy that the treatment accorded him and his wife would not be repeated.

Mr. Murphy will leave here for Sofia on Wednesday.

ALL ON SIBIRIA SAVED FROM GOODWIN SANDS

Fifty-three Persons Rescued by English Lifeboat After Twenty-four Hours of Peril.

DOVER, England, Nov. 21.—The passengers and crew—fifty-three in all—of the American steamer Sibiria, stranded on the Goodwin Sands, were landed at Deal today by the Kingsdown lifeboat.

They had a distressing experience during the twenty-four hours they were on the steamer awaiting assistance, in momentary peril of the vessel being engulfed in the treacherous quicksands.

Fruitless efforts were made yesterday by lifeboats from neighboring stations to rescue the passengers. Several men of the lifeboat crews were injured and the boats narrowly escaped destruction.

The Sibiria is still aground.

A violent southeasterly gale drove the ship on the sands, near the spot where the Italian steamship Val Salice, whose crew was rescued yesterday, grounded. Attempts were made all day yesterday by the Deal and Ramsgate lifeboats to rescue those on the Sibiria who were huddled together on the bridge. Two lifeboats were driven back badly damaged.

Last evening volunteers were called for to man the South Downs boat, the only one remaining intact. A British patrol boat towed the lifeboat as near as possible to the Sibiria. The searchlights of the patrol boat were fixed on the stranded ship, showing that all but the bridge had disappeared. While trying to get alongside the steamship the lifeboat was thrown on its side by the heavy sea and filled with water, but righted itself. The fight continued until the rescue was effected.

The lifeboat was again taken in tow by the patrol boat, which brought her to the Downs.

ARCHANGEL EXPLOSION KILLED 341; HURT 667

Large Number of Victims Explained by Fact That Blowup Occurred at Dinner Hour.

PETROGRAD, Nov. 21, (via London.)—It is announced officially that 341 persons have been killed and 667 wounded by an explosion at Bakaritza. The statement follows:

"According to supplementary information, the number of persons killed by the explosion at Bakaritza was found, after clearing the debris of masonry, to be 341, while the number of persons injured, according to reports received from hospitals, amounts to 49 officers and officials, 43 soldiers, 131 civilians, and 25 women. Of the crews of British merchant ships, 27 were killed and 25 injured.

"The large number of victims is explained by the fact that the explosion occurred during the dinner hour, when the men were resting in huts wrecked by the explosion."

LONDON, Nov. 21.—A Reuter's dispatch from Petrograd says it is authoritatively announced that only two vessels were destroyed in the recent explosion in the harbor of Bakaritza, near Archangel. These were the British steamer Baron Driesen and the British coal steamer Earl of Forfar, moored beside the Baron Driesen. Russian authorities make a categorical denial of the German report that seven munition-laden ships were destroyed, and the Russian Admiralty declares that the German report, attributing the first explosion on board the Baron Driesen to a submarine, is absurd, adding that German submarines cannot possibly penetrate to Bakaritza harbor.

BERLIN, Nov. 21, (by Wireless to Sayville.)—Reports received from Swedish sources say that at least twenty steamers caught fire in the recent series of explosions near Archangel and were forced to stay in the harbor until it was ice-bound, says the Overseas News Agency. According to these reports it is estimated that ammunition valued at 80,000,000 rubles, ($40,000,000;) 20,000 bales of cotton belonging to the Moscow Association of Cotton Mills, and 15,000,000 rubles, ($7,500,000,) worth of rubber were burned. A new automobile train, for Petrograd and Moscow, is reported to have been partly destroyed.

U. S. STEEL RAISES WAGES $28,000,000 FOR 260,000 MEN

Grants to Employes Third Rise of Year, Making Total Advance 33%.

$9 A MONTH MORE TO ALL

Action Announced by Chairman Gary Is Taken to Meet High Cost of Living.

CLERICAL FORCES TO SHARE

New Scale Effective on Dec. 15—Other Steel Concerns Likely to Follow Suit.

To meet the increased cost of living the United States Steel Corporation decided yesterday to increase the wages of its employes at steel-works and blast furnaces 10 per cent., with a proportionate advance in case of workers in the mines and transportation companies. This is the third increase made this year for a total of 33 per cent. over the wages in force Jan. 1. After the weekly meeting of the Finance Committee, Chairman E. H. Gary issued this statement:

"Ordinarily the question of wages would not come up for consideration or decision at this time of the year, but in consequence of the abnormal conditions now existing it has been decided to increase the wage rates of our iron and steel companies about 10 per cent., to take effect Dec. 15. As to other departments, increases will be equitably proportioned.

"The clerical forces in the various offices of subsidiary companies are expected to share in the upturn." [illegible]

[illegible]

In this table is presented the monthly record of employes and payroll for the first half of this year and the average number of employes and total payroll in the five preceding years:

1916.	Employes.	Payroll.
January	252,540	$17,982,366
February	250,195	19,400,000
March	251,043	21,101,125
April	244,430	19,850,415
May	258,713	23,312,153
June	256,268	22,975,408
Total wages for 6 months	....	$124,759,205

Wages for Last Five Years.

Year	Employes	Payroll
1915	191,126	$176,800,864
1914	179,353	162,379,000
1913	228,906	207,206,176
1912	221,025	189,351,001
1911	196,888	161,419,031

It is expected that the Republic Iron and Steel Company, the Lackawanna, the Cambria, and other big producers of iron and steel will put the same advance into operation. They followed the lead of the Steel Corporation when the other increases were voted last January and April.

While wages have advanced 33 per cent., the prices for steel products have risen this year from 200 to 600 per cent.

In voting the two previous wage increases, the Finance Committee of the Steel Corporation considered as one factor the rising cost of living throughout the country. Presumably the same item had influence in yesterday's action.

PITTSBURGH, Nov. 21.—The increase in wages announced by the United States Steel Corporation affects five corporations and approximately 75,000 men in the Pittsburgh district, according to officials of the Carnegie Steel Company. The corporations are the Carnegie Steel Company, the National Tube Company, the American Bridge Company, the American Sheet and Tin-plate Company, and the American Steel and Wire Company. By the increase ordinary laborers will be paid a minimum wage of 27½ cents an hour. Local independent steel manufacturers indicated tonight that a similar increase in wages would be granted their employes.

40,000 MILL HANDS GET WAGE INCREASE

American Woolen Company and Arlington Mills Grant a 10 Per Cent. Advance.

BOSTON, Nov. 21.—A 10 per cent. wage increase in all the mills of the American Woolen Company, which employs 35,000 hands in New England and New York State, was announced at the headquarters of the company here tonight. At the same time the Arlington Mills, whose big cotton plant at Lawrence employs 5,000 hands, announced "a higher scale of wages," the amount of which was not specified. It was believed that the new scale would be similar to that made public last night by the Cotton Manufacturers' Association of New Bedford, granting their 33,000 employes a 10 per cent. raise.

Franklin W. H. Hobbs, President of the Arlington Mills, in announcing the new scale of his company, said:

"The increase is in accordance with the policy of the corporation to adapt its scale of wage to improved conditions of business, and keep it at least on a parity with the best wage scale among its competitors in New England."

ADAMS, Mass., Nov. 21.—Wage increases of 10 per cent., effective Dec. 4, were announced today by several cotton mills in this vicinity. Notices to this effect were posted by William B. Plunkett, who controls four mills in this town: W. C. Plunkett & Sons, Greylock Manufacturing Company, with mills at Greylock, Williamstown, and North Pownal, Vt., and the Hoosac Cotton Company of North Adams.

Several thousand operatives are affected. The promised increase will be the third of the calendar year, making the total advance 25 per cent.

Submarine Deutschland Sails in Daylight; Has $2,000,000 Cargo; Crowds View Start

Special to The New York Times.

NEW LONDON, Conn., Nov. 21.—The German merchant submarine Deutschland left here suddenly at 2:30 o'clock this afternoon, and when last seen was far beyond Race Rock Light on her way to Bremerhaven.

On her previous return voyage, the submersible stole away from Baltimore under the cover of night, but today, for some inscrutable reason, Captain Paul Koenig took his vessel out in sunshiny mid-afternoon when any allied warship on watch could discern the low craft.

The boldness of Koenig's second venture is generally accounted for by the fact that once out of the Thames River and past Race Rock Light, there was deep water on all sides, so that an enemy cruiser apparently had slight chance to get him. When he passed out the Virginia Capes on his first trip back to Germany his emerging point was to some extent localized.

The tug Alert and the steam fishing vessel Frank E. Beckwith, chartered by the T. A. Scott Company, convoyed the submarine as far as the light. Both of them kept astern of her, making a repetition of the fatal accident of last Friday morning, when she sank a tug, causing the drowning of five of the crew, impossible. On the deck of the Beckwith, huge megaphone in hand, stood Captain Frederick Hinsch, shore superintendent for the Eastern Forwarding Company, the American agents for the Deutschland's owners.

Though the manifest of the ship's cargo has not been made public, it is fairly well established that she carries nearly a thousand tons of crude rubber, nickel, crude tin, and "iron alloy," estimated to be worth $2,000,000. She also has seven pouches filled with mail, brought here by members of the German Embassy at Washington.

The Deutschland apparently was ready to sail late last night or early this morning, but for some unknown reason plans were changed. Two tugs had steam up all night ready to act as convoys, but finally they were dismissed at 2:30 o'clock this morning. During the forenoon there was unusual activity on the State pier and on board the Willehad, the submersible's mother ship.

The Alert and the Frank Beckwith went up the harbor to the pier at 2 o'clock. Fifteen minutes later the steel net guarding the pocket was hauled up and the pontoon bearing a fence fifteen feet high was pulled to one side. When the Deutschland was ready to start the waterfront was lined with spectators, housetops were crowded, and there was a rush for ferryboats and small craft.

The great whaleback poked her stern out into the river, her convoy keeping respectful distance. Then she swung her nose slowly down stream, turning almost in her own length, and slid away. The ferryboat Governor Winthrop stopped to give her passengers a good look, several tugs edged near, the decks of a couple of Government transports became alive with watchers, and from the side of the United States naval cruiser Columbia a small launch loaded with officers shot out into the river.

In the conning tower of the submarine were Captain Koenig and Chief Officer Kraohl, while the twenty-seven others of her ship's company posed about her clean, cleared decks. She carried no pilot. Her telescoped masts were snug in their grooves in the deck floor, her wireless aerials had not been strung up, and it was evident it needed but the command "diving stations" and the touch of a lever or two to send her quickly below the surface.

So artfully had the Deutschland been repainted that she blended amazingly with her surroundings. The whole of her had been colored a wave green at least as far as the water line, and she melted into sky and sea at a startlingly short distance.

The submarine rounded Race Rock at 3:45 o'clock and headed for the sea, apparently intending to pass east of Block Island not far from No Man's Land off Martha's Vineyard. Before dark she was beyond the three-mile limit and there was activity about her decks that indicated that her masts were about to be raised, her wireless strung, and her running lights illuminated, unless she decided to submerge.

RUSH 8-HOUR CASE AS LABOR PREPARES

Government Attorney Springs a Surprise by Forcing Action at Kansas City.

EXPECT DECISION TODAY

Industrial Armies Practically Join Forces at Baltimore Convention—Gompers Warns Men of Wealth.

Special to The New York Times.

WASHINGTON, Nov. 21.—There was swift manoeuvring today by all concerned in the fight on the Adamson eight-hour law.

In speeches made before the Federation of Labor convention in Baltimore by the chiefs of the four railway brotherhoods and Samuel Gompers, President of the federation, sentiments were expressed which are regarded here as confirming the impression produced by events of the last few days that the greatest battle between capital and labor is imminent.

United effort on the part of organized labor in the country to obtain a universal eight-hour day seems to be the certain outcome of the working agreement reached here on Sunday between the brotherhoods and the Federation of Labor and of the statements made in the convention today by the leaders of both bodies.

The Government forces sprang a surprise in Kansas City today when they urged haste in the injunction proceedings against the eight-hour law brought by the receivers of the Missouri, Oklahoma & Gulf Railroad. Judge Hook, it is intimated, may hand down a decision today. In Kansas City it is believed that this will be the test case on which the law will get before the Supreme Court.

Confer with Attorney General.

The interest of the Government in the railroads in getting a quick decision from the Supreme Court was shown tonight by a conference at the Department of Justice, in which the participants were Attorney General Gregory, Solicitor General Davis, and representatives of the New York Central, the Pennsylvania, and the Chicago, Burlington & Quincy Railroads. The conference was entirely informal, and afterward the Attorney General said that no conclusions were reached and no recommendations made.

It is understood, however, that the test case matter was discussed, and there were hints that the Missouri, Oklahoma & Gulf case might not be the one finally selected for advancement to the Supreme Court, despite the statements of the Government's counsel. Indeed, Department of Justice officials caused some confusion tonight by saying that no decision to expedite any of the pending cases had been reached. Mr. Gregory said that no one knew which of the cases would be selected. In view of the fact that the Government has employed a special attorney and has sent two officers of the Department of Justice to appear on Thursday at Kansas City in the hearing of the suit filed there by the Union Pacific and Santa Fé it had all along been supposed that the Government would be inclined to agree that this case should afford the test.

President to Renew Recommendations.

Because of the renewed seriousness of the dispute over the Adamson act, President Wilson has made recommendations for railroad legislation the principal part of his next address to Congress, which he completed late today. These recommendations, it became known definitely tonight, will be practically the same as those made to Congress last August when the Adamson bill was enacted. The question was discussed at today's Cabinet meeting.

It was learned today that the President has been strongly but vainly urged to recommend to Congress legislation authorizing the Interstate Commerce Commission to fix wages paid on railroads. In addition to the proposals made last Summer for enlargement of the commission, enforced investigation of disputes before strikes or lockouts, and authorization to the commission to consider wages in fixing freight rates, the President is understood to have de-

Continued on Page 5.

MEXICANS SHOCKED AT FINAL PROPOSAL

Cabrera Especially Perturbed Over the American Terms of Settlement.

DEFINITE ACTION DELAYED

Right to Pursue Raiders Over Border and Conditional Troop Recall Outlined.

Special to The New York Times.

ATLANTIC CITY, N. J., Nov. 21.—The American members of the joint commission today laid before the Mexican section a memorandum embodying the final proposals of the United States for settlement of the international difficulties arising out of the frequent raids along the border. The memorandum contained also suggestions for decided reforms in the internal affairs of the southern republic which, in the minds of the Commissioners, are calculated to make the recurrence of difficulties less likely.

Everything indicated tonight that the proposals of the American section and the manner in which they were presented took the Mexicans completely by surprise, and they had not yet recovered their composure tonight. Mr. Pani and Mr. Bonillas seemed less perturbed than Mr. Cabrera, who for the first time since the commission convened lost his presence of mind, if not his temper. He left for Philadelphia tonight in something very much resembling a fit of offended pride.

Hope that the Mexican question might be settled within the next few days vanished when Dr. John R. Mott of the American section left for Cleveland, Ohio, to attend a Y. M. C. A. convention, with the intention of being away until Thursday night. It was stated officially that his absence would not stop the work of the commission, as his colleagues were fully conversant with his attitude and opinions, and would be able to deal with anything which might come up in the way of questions from the Mexican side. It was evident, however, that no definite action was expected until he returned.

Cabrera Angry at Press.

Mr. Cabrera sent Mr. Rojo, Secretary of the Mexican section, from the Mexican offices to tell reporters that he already had left for Philadelphia. His appearance in the hall a few minutes later did not surprise the newspaper men, who promptly asked for some statement on the developments of the day. He refused to talk, and left hurriedly, with a few caustic remarks about newspapers.

The American Commissioners at the morning session presented a partial memorandum covering the question of the withdrawal of the American expeditionary column from Mexico. The commission expressed its willingness to recommend the withdrawal at the end of ninety days provided the absence of revolutionary activity in the territory now occupied by the column and contiguous to the international line showed that this could be done with safety. It is known that the Mexicans have objected to this on the ground that they did not consider it a fair test of the ability of the Mexican Government to handle the situation in the north.

The question of a border patrol was dismissed with a reiteration of existing international usage, which leaves each nation to protect its own territory. It is understood that the United States maintained its right to send the present expeditionary column into Mexico and reserved the right to repeat the operation without limitation should occasion demand.

Several efforts have been made by the Mexicans to obtain from their associates a statement that the expeditionary column had no right to be in Mexico and that there would be no repetition of this method of procedure except in accord with such stipulations as might be agreed upon by the Commissioners.

Counterproposals Made.

The morning session adjourned to enable the Mexican Commissioners to recover from the shock and to talk over the new proposal among themselves. Mr. Cabrera was violent in his insistence that a demand be made for material changes in this plan before it was discussed, but his colleagues were finally successful in persuading him to

Continued on Page 6.

VON JAGOW GIVES UP HIS PORTFOLIO

Kaiser's Foreign Minister Resigns, Giving Continued Illness as the Reason.

POST FOR ZIMMERMANN

Under Secretary Likely to Succeed His Former Chief—Advocate of War on Armed Ships.

AMSTERDAM, Nov. 21, (via London.)—Gottlieb von Jagow, the German Minister of Foreign Affairs, has resigned, according to a Berlin dispatch. The condition of his health is given as the cause of his resignation.

Dr. Alfred Zimmermann, Under Secretary of Foreign Affairs, the dispatch adds, probably will succeed Herr von Jagow.

The Tageblatt prints a rumor that Herr von Jagow will become Ambassador at Vienna.

Herr von Jagow, the retiring Imperial Secretary of Foreign Affairs, and Herr Zimmermann, the Under Secretary of State, who may succeed him, figured large in the British and German White Papers, published for the first time by THE NEW YORK TIMES in the Fall of 1914. Since then the former has signed most of the notes sent to Washington in regard to the U-boat controversy.

It also fell to his lot to conduct the negotiations with Sir Edward Goschen, the British Ambassador, which terminated in Great Britain's declaration of war. Von Jagow was known to have worked hard for a British-German alliance.

Although von Jagow bears no title his family has been noble since the eleventh century. He was Ambassador at Rome when he was made Secretary of State in January, 1914.

Herr Zimmermann saw Sir Edward Goschen after the memorable interview with the Imperial Chancellor, Dr. von Bethmann Hollweg, in which the latter had characterized the Belgian neutrality treaty as "a scrap of paper," and it was he who said that Germany's failure to reply to the British ultimatum was, "in fact, a declaration of war."

Herr Zimmermann, aside from explaining to American interviewers many times that Germany's U-boat campaign was conducted within the law, has been chiefly occupied with the cases of Sweden and Norway—particularly with the latter, which forbade U-boats to provision at her ports so long as her ships were sunk. Zimmermann, however, has always contended that armed merchant vessels should be treated as warships.

CAUGHT U-53 MESSAGE SENT TO BERNSTORFF

Captain Angelo Sturlese of the Italian liner Dante Alighieri, which arrived yesterday from Genoa, told of an interesting wireless message he had picked up on the eastward voyage, which was sent by Commandant Hans Rose of the submarine U-53 to the German Ambassador. The Captain said that he left New York on Sunday, Oct. 8, about four hours after the West Point had been sunk off Nantucket Lightship, and took a zigzag course southward.

"At two o'clock on Monday morning," Captain Sturlese continued, "the chief operator picked up a message from the U-53, calling Siasconsett Station. No answer was received, and after repeating it three times the German submarine flashed this message broadcast in the hope that it would be picked up by some friendly ship and forwarded to Washington:

"Count von Bernstorff, German Ambassador, Washington:
"Have sunk several merchant steamships today. Am looking for nine more vessels. "COMMANDANT U-53."

Captain Sturlese said that he zigzagged for five days after leaving New York, but did not see or hear anything more of any German submarine.

CRAIOVA TAKEN BY FALKENHAYN

Swift Success of Teutons Puts Rumanian Army in Wallachia in a Critical Position.

ORSOVA NOW IN DANGER

London Also Fears That Mackensen May Join Forces with Invaders Across the Danube.

LONDON, Nov. 22.—The occupation of the Rumanian town of Craiova was reported by the German Official Headquarters bulletin last night.

This has not yet been confirmed from the Entente side, but the fact that no Rumanian official report has been issued since Sunday leaves little reason to doubt its correctness.

The official reports from both German and Russian Headquarters the last two days had prepared the public for this news of the success of the Central Powers' thrust at Rumania, but it had been hoped that Russia, which was known to be sending reinforcements into Rumania as fast as possible, might be in time to avert the blow. According to information in Rumanian quarters in London, the Entente Allies had made provisions so that the huge stores of grain in Craiova should not fall into enemy hands.

Craiova is in the centre of a great grain district on the edge of the Wallachian Plain, and is an important railway junction. Its possession by the Central Powers cuts the railway communications of the Rumanian armies holding the Orsova region to the west. As the lines from Targujiulu, south of the Vulcan Pass, and from the Danube frontier, opposite Vidin, pass through Craiova, the position of the Rumanian forces in Orsova is now extremely critical, and they may be compelled to evacuate the Orsova region, the holding of which has up to the present barred the Teutonic Allies from the use of the Danube.

The swiftness with which von Falkenhayn struck his blow has caused surprise here, as today's Russian official communication reports the Rumanian retreat as having only reached Filliash, about twenty miles northwest of Craiova.

Some anxiety is felt that nothing has been heard of the German Field Marshal von Mackensen's operations in Dobrudja for some time, and it is suggested that his recent retreat may have been a deliberate move to conceal the assemblage of big forces for a possible crossing of the Danube opposite to where General von Falkenhayn is fighting, in which case he might be expected to be heard of at Nikipoli or further west at Ranova.

The London morning papers show no disposition to underestimate the gravity of the situation in Rumania.

The Daily Chronicle says:

"More alarming than the fall of Craiova is the speed with which it was reached and captured. This points to an out-manoeuvring of the western Rumanian defensive under which the latter temporarily and locally has suffered complete collapse. It is scarcely likely that the Allies can prevent the southwestern corner of Wallachia from passing under German control."

The Daily News says:

"It seems certain that Western Wallachia is lost for the time being. Orsova, if garrisoned, may hold out for a long time, but the fate of isolated fortresses when attacked with modern artillery has not been encouraging in this war. Fortunately the chances of assistance from Field Marshal von Mackensen have been diminished by the fall of Monastir, and the allied activities thereabout must prove the greatest embarrassment to the enemy, already hard pressed for men."

A Petrograd dispatch to The Daily News says:

"The German advance at the worst only allow him to occupy a narrow strip of Western Rumania. An advance

Continued on Page 3.

"All the News That's Fit to Print."

The New York Times.

THE WEATHER
Fair today; Friday rain, warmer; west winds, diminishing.
For full weather report see Page 23.

VOL. LXVI...NO. 21,502. .... NEW YORK, THURSDAY, DECEMBER 7, 1916.—TWENTY-FOUR PAGES. ONE CENT In Greater New York, Jersey City and Newark. | Elsewhere, TWO CENTS.

LLOYD GEORGE TO BE BRITISH PREMIER; TEUTON HOSTS OCCUPY BUCHAREST; JOFFRE'S RETIREMENT CONSIDERED

BRYAN WARNS PARTY IT MUST BACK PROHIBITION

Tells Democrats They Won Without Aid of Liquor Interests and Their Course Is Clear.

300 HAIL HIM AT BANQUET

He Advocates Direct Election of President as an Imperative Reform.

FAVORS WAR REFERENDUM

Condemns Exclusive Federal Control of the Railroads as a Peril to the Government.

Special to The New York Times.

WASHINGTON, Dec. 6.—W. J. Bryan, at a dinner given in his honor tonight at the Hotel Lafayette by more than three hundred Democrats, many of them of national prominence, formally advocated the adoption of prohibition as a national issue by the Democratic Party.

"The Democratic Party is the party of the people," Mr. Bryan said, "and the home is the people's citadel. The fight against the saloon is a fight for the home and for humanity. The Democratic Party, therefore, cannot hesitate to choose the home against the greatest enemy that has arisen to menace it."

The dinner was a remarkable tribute to Mr. Bryan. President Wilson, who was unable to be present, sent a letter to be read by the toastmaster. The President wrote:

"Will you not be kind enough to convey my very cordial greetings to Mr. Bryan and to those who are assembled to do him honor at the dinner on Wednesday evening? In the recent campaign no one rendered more unselfish service than Mr. Bryan, and I am happy to know that this dinner expresses the genuine admiration of all Democrats for him. May I not by this means convey to him my warmest congratulations and best wishes for his continued health and happiness?"

It was an old-time Democratic love feast. And it was a "dry" banquet, notwithstanding the fact that the price was $5 a plate.

In the course of his speech, which was vigorously applauded, besides advocating the prohibition issue, Mr. Bryan expressed opposition to exclusive Federal control of railroads, and to an increase in the military and naval forces of the country. He said he believed the Federal amendment establishing woman suffrage would eventually come, and urged an easier method of amending the Constitution. He also suggested the establishment of a "national bulletin" to acquaint the voters with the public questions, especially at election time, suggesting that it might be printed in a space reserved by the Government in the newspapers in return for mailing privileges.

"An effort is now being made by the railroads to secure legislation, and if necessary, a constitutional amendment depriving the States of all regulative power over them, and giving to Congress exclusive control over railroad regulation," said Mr. Bryan. "This is the most far-reaching change that has been proposed since the organization of our Government—and which, if made, would involve incalculable harm. It would do more than that. It would practically obliterate State lines and lead to a centralization which would threaten the very existence of our dual form of Government."

After expressing his opposition to militarism, especially in the form of universal military service, Mr. Bryan spoke of the clumsiness of the Electoral College, saying that the unpopularity of one elector might change the result in a close contest, and advocated some method for the direct election of the President. He suggested having the votes cast by Congressional districts rather than by States.

"Another reform for which it seems to me we are now ready is a change in the Constitution making it more easily amendable," he said. "I venture to suggest that the rule of the people would be made more secure by a constitutional amendment permitting a change in our organic law when a majority of both houses in two successive Congresses submit an amendment, and that amendment is ratified by a majority of the States, provided the amendment also receives a majority of all the votes cast on that proposition in all the States."

Mr. Bryan departed from the prepared text of his speech to advocate a referendum on proposed declarations of war.

"The experience through which Europe is passing," he said, "suggests the adoption of a constitutional amendment providing for a referendum on any declaration of war, except when the country is actually invaded. This will not only be a safeguard to us, but it will be an example to the nations of Europe, where the right to declare war is vested in the executive instead of with the legislative body as here."

"I have saved for the last," he continued, "the reform which will involve the fiercest contest, and which will, when accomplished, bring the largest benefit, namely, abolition of the saloon. I did not expect until within four years to live to see the time when it would be an acute national question. But owing to causes which no one could foresee the issue has been precipitated upon us and must be met. The injurious effect of alcohol upon the system has been known for ages, but three impulses have recently added to the momentum with which the cause moves forward. Science, religion, and war have joined forces against King Alcohol. Twenty-three States have already prohibited the open saloon—two-thirds of them having adopted this policy within the last four years. More than half of the people of the country now live in dry territory, and the reform sweeps on from the West and South to the Northeast with increasing velocity and momentum.

"The Democratic Party, having won without the aid of the wet cities, and having received the support of nearly all the prohibition States, and the States where women vote, is released from any obligation to the liquor traffic. It is free to take the moral side of this great moral issue, and I have no doubt that it will live up to its opportunities and obligations."

Spanish Ship Sinks in Storm; 100 of Her Crew Are Drowned

MADRID, Spain, Dec. 6. (via Paris.)—One hundred men of the crew of the Spanish steamship Pio IX., from New Orleans for Barcelona, were drowned by the sinking of the vessel in a storm when 200 miles off the Canary Islands. Twenty-two of the crew were saved.

The Pio IX., laden with cotton, carried no passengers. The steamship Buenos Aires, which was in the vicinity, was able to give but slight assistance on account of the high sea.

NO WAGE BONUSES FOR BROTHERHOODS

Not a Member Will Share in Santa Fe's $2,750,000 Rise to Employes.

FOR UNORGANIZED LABOR

Road's Decision Based on Fact That Adamson Law Benefits Union Men Alone.

Not a dollar of the $2,750,000 Christmas present to employes of the Atchison, Topeka & Santa Fé Railroad—10 per cent. bonuses, to meet the high cost of living, just announced by the road—will go to the members of the four railway brotherhoods. This means that those employes affected by the Adamson eight-hour law, which the roads so bitterly fought, are entirely excluded.

This was disclosed by a careful reading of President Ripley's statement announcing the wage rise, one short clause of which bars the brotherhoods from participation. That clause says bonuses will be paid to employes "whose compensation is not paid according to present or former contract schedules."

The brotherhoods and railroads have wage contracts on all lines. D. L. Gallup, Controller of the Santa Fé, was asked last night to comment on the action of the road in excluding organized labor from its Christmas present. He said:

"It's a recognition of unorganized labor."

Hugh Frayne, general organizer of the American Federation of Labor, was asked what he thought of it.

"It's just a sop to the poor unorganized fellow who can't help himself to make him believe he is as well off as the union man," he said. "It's an old trick of capital."

The Santa Fe's action was a general subject of conversation about railroad offices yesterday, where it was recalled that it was President Ripley who first announced that the Adamson eight-hour law would be attacked in the courts. It was generally agreed that the brotherhoods were excluded because the operation of the Adamson law would give its members substantial increases which the other workers would not get. Even if the Adamson law is declared unconstitutional, it is pretty well assured now that the railroads stand ready to effect a compromise which will give the members of the four big unions a substantial increase in pay.

30,000 WORKERS MAY GET 10 PER CENT. RISE

Garment Manufacturers Consider Advance, Hear Co-Operation Pleas.

The Union-Made Garment Manufacturers probably will grant an increase of 10 per cent. in wages to their more than 30,000 employes as the result of negotiations now going on between a committee of the manufacturers and representatives of the United Garment Workers of America. The manufacturers are holding a convention at the Hotel Astor, and are expected to consider the question of wages tomorrow.

The association includes more than 100 manufacturers from all parts of the United States, and has been a pioneer in the adoption of an eight-hour day, put into effect several years ago by members of the association.

The members and officers of the union were guests of Sweet, Orr & Co. at a banquet at the Hotel Astor last night, at which the keynote of speeches was the desirability of co-operation between labor and capital.

Edward N. Hurley, Chairman of the Federal Trade Commission, in an address, emphasized the necessity of co-operation both as between laborers and as between manufacturers and between the two classes.

T. A. Rickert, President of the United Garment Workers, expressed the hope that the increase considered by the manufacturers and the union might be brought up in the convention, and that it might be treated in a spirit of equity.

Mr. Hurley, at the outset of his speech, referred to the necessity of co-operation between labor and capital.

"This spirit of co-operation which you manifest by gathering here tonight is abroad in the land," he said. "It pervades all classes and kinds of people. Laboring men are co-operating in unions for the furthering of their common ends. Business men are co-operating among themselves, particularly in trade associations, for the purpose of standardizing their products and processes; of removing unfair practices from their industries; of improving the quality of their products; of establishing more healthful conditions in their factories; of increasing the sales of American goods in foreign markets, and, above all, of laying a sound, intelligent foundation for industry by improving their cost-accounting methods.

"I am in favor of co-operation among laboring men and I am in favor of co-operation among business men. But I am opposed to co-operation among business men which resorts to price-fixing, and I am opposed to co-operation among laboring men which resorts to violence. I have urged upon business men the importance of sound and adequate cost accounting methods in our factories. It will seem a far cry to laboring men to appeal to them in behalf of sound cost accounting methods.

"Labor as well as capital has an interest in the integrity of industry. If the wheels of industry do not move, labor does not work. We are talking a great deal nowadays about industrial preparedness. This preparedness, if it is to be sound, must be based on intelligence, and we cannot have intelligence in industry unless we have sound cost accounting methods. Such differences as do arise between labor and capital

Continued on Page 5.

FOOD COST INQUIRY UNDER PRESIDENT TO SWEEP NATION

Every Agency of Government to be Put to Work in Effort to Solve Problem.

OFFENDERS TO BE PUNISHED

Exchanges in New York, Chicago, and Several Other Cities Face Investigation.

COAL SITUATION INCLUDED

Commissioner Dillon Appeals to the President for Support of Remedial Measures.

WASHINGTON, Dec. 6.—The Federal investigation of the high cost of living began today to take definite form, with indications that it would be one of the most comprehensive ever undertaken, and would extend to every part of the United States. Not only is a sweeping inquiry into the causes of the soaring cost of foodstuffs contemplated, but the recent pinch in the coal supply and its resultant price advances probably will be made the subject of broad investigation.

From President Wilson down, officials began to cope in earnest with the problems presented by the situation. The President took under consideration preliminary reports, which, with others to come, will form the basis for recommendations he may make to Congress.

A dozen speeches on the subject were made in the House. Several resolutions proposing inquiries were introduced and referred without discussion, most of them going to the Interstate and Foreign Commerce Committee, of which Representative Adamson, who is opposed to export embargoes, is the Chairman.

Department of Justice officials held all-day conferences with members of the Federal Trade Commission, and District Attorney Anderson of Boston, in charge of the department's investigation, came here to formulate a definite plan of conducting the nation-wide inquiry. About fifty picked men of the department's Bureau of Investigation were reported to be at work throughout the country gathering data which will determine the Attorney General's course of action.

Inquiry in New York.

The Interstate Commerce Commission probably will be called on to aid by furnishing data relative to shipments of foodstuffs, and Mr. Anderson will confer with Commission officials. In New York or Chicago or both, Grand Jury investigations of the reasons for rising prices are said to be still under consideration.

With the program still in process of formation, there were increasing indications that officials were considering the situation from three angles, namely:

1.—Determination of the actual causes of the rapid rise in foodstuffs and coal, whether it is due to natural economic laws, to the unwarranted action of individual dealers and producers in advancing prices, or whether there exists agreements among groups of dealers or producers to boost prices.

2.—Vigorous prosecution of persons or firms, if any, who, by violation of existing laws, in making agreements to raise prices or otherwise, have contributed to the upward trend of prices.

3.—Enactment of legislation to remedy the present situation and to prevent its recurrence.

The situation is in the first of these stages, so far as the Department of Justice is concerned. With its investigators already at work, department officials called on the Federal Trade Commission for co-operation and the Commission promised all data which it already may have, and further aid in obtaining information which can be acquired without adding materially to the burden imposed on the commission by other pending inquiries.

Exchanges Under Fire.

In addition department officials are understood to be considering the advisability of investigating such organizations as the Chicago Board of Trade, the Chicago Butter and Egg Exchange, the Elgin Board of Trade and the New York Produce, Sugar and Coffee exchanges, with a view of ascertaining by what practices the market values of certain foodstuffs dealt in by the bodies are determined. An inquiry into the amount of foodstuffs held in all the cold storage establishments of the country and possibly the volume of grain stored in elevators also is said to be under consideration.

Complaints have reached the department that coal prices were advanced recently because, in large measure, of the activities of certain independent dealers, not heretofore in the business, who are reported to have contracted with the chief coal companies for virtually their entire unsold output for the Winter. It was charged that these dealers, scenting fat profits, tried to corner the available supply and thus forced up prices.

These and other complaints under investigation will be considered with a view to prosecution, if warranted, under Federal laws, which require that the supplies in question must have been in or for interstate commerce.

DILLON WRITES TO PRESIDENT.

Asks Mr. Wilson's Support in Campaign for Markets.

State Food and Market Commissioner Dillon in an open letter to President Wilson asks his support for the campaign for public markets and slaughterhouses and Government control of market quotations. Only when these agencies are controlled by the Government will the law of supply and demand be the true regulator of prices, Mr. Dillon contends. After a review of the results of his investigation of the methods of commission men and food exchanges, he says:

"The Federal Government, I understand, is now spending something in the neighborhood of $25,000,000, largely for

Continued on Page 8.

26 Women Die In Explosion In British Munitions Plant

LONDON, Dec. 6.—Twenty-six women were killed and about thirty injured by an explosion in a munitions factory last night, according to an official announcement.

It is added that the effect of the accident upon the munitions output will be negligible.

PLEDGE TO ALLIES RENEWED BY ITALY

Premier Reiterates Unshakable Resolve to Fight—Peace Motion Is Defeated.

TERROR REIGNS IN ATHENS

French and British Colonists Flock to Piraeus, Where They Embark on Ships.

ROME, Dec. 5.—The Allies do not desire to force Greece into war, nor do they support any anti-dynastic movement in Greece, asserted Premier Boselli in his report on the war delivered before the Chamber of Deputies today. Premier Boselli reiterated the unshakable determination of Italy to maintain the war with her allies and employ all her energies until the restoration of Belgium, Serbia, and Montenegro was accomplished. He termed this "the noble and essential object of the war." At the close of his speech he sent a message of greeting to "our valorous Latin sister, Rumania," trusting for her final success.

The Premier's speech was very long, and in it he recapitulated the whole history of Italy's participation in the war and enumerated the reasons which induced King Victor to enter into the struggle. The Premier declared that victory would insure the equilibrium on the Eastern Mediterranean, which he termed one of the chief foundations of Italian policy. He said that Avlona would be Italy's strategic post on the Adriatic, from which would radiate her future commercial expansion in the Balkans.

A motion introduced by the Socialists, urging peace, was defeated by a vote of 343 to 47. Premier Boselli asked the rejection of the motion to emphasize the country's opposition to peace while the country was pledged with its allies not to end the war until victory was attained.

HOUSES IN ATHENS LOOTED BY SOLDIERS

Streets Are Barricaded and Venizelists Seized, Beaten and Killed.

PARIS, Dec. 6.—The entire French Colony left Athens yesterday, a Havas dispatch from Athens says. The foreign colonies now fill all the hotels of Piraeus, and many have embarked on the vessels in the harbor.

"Athens is apparently calm," the dispatch continues, "but the population is much impressed by the exodus of the foreigners and in a great state of anxiety. Arrests of supporters of former Premier Venizelos and searches of their residences continue, while the Venizelist organs no longer appear.

"Barriers have been raised in the streets and are guarded by Royalist regular troops augmented by voluntary enrollments of reservists. The Entente Ministers have been looking after the departure of their nationals."

LONDON, Dec. 6.—Official telegrams show that Athens is quiet, at least temporarily. Steps are being taken to insure the safety of the British colony, part of whose members have gone to Piraeus. A steamship is being held in readiness to remove the others should it become necessary.

The Foreign Office has issued a statement to the effect that there is reason to believe that press messages do not give an accurate picture of the actual situation at Athens, both because the Royalists have succeeded in regaining control of the cable and press censorships, and because the allied press correspondents in Athens are living under threats of personal violence, in common with all those suspected of Venizelist leanings. The Foreign Office adds:

"There is unfortunately reason to believe that very grave acts of violence have been committed by Royalist forces and the mob."

Dispatches received by the Foreign Office state that the looting of Venizelos's own house was conducted by Greek regulars under command of superior officers, including one General, who wore prominent decorations. The Royalists asserted that shots were fired from the house, but the British authorities deny that there is the slightest evidence to support this charge.

After the house was sacked and the articles removed, including the former Premier's personal clothing, ten Cretans lodging there were imprisoned. Their subsequent fate is unknown.

Royalists then attacked the house of M. Kalopthakis, translator for the American Legation. He took refuge in the American Legation, where the Minister is protecting him. But the house occupied by his sister and servants has been besieged for two days.

Another prominent Venizelist was shot down in cold blood, while Dr. Rendel, a British diplomat, whose house was attacked, says he saw another prominent man, named Descall, repeatedly clubbed with rifles in the hands of regulars and kicked in the body until he fell unconscious. Mr. Rendel also reports that while he was in jail he saw a number of Venizelists kicked and clubbed.

In a dispatch dated yesterday Reuter's Saloniki correspondent says:

"Piraeus is occupied by detachments of allied troops. The railway service between Athens and Piraeus is not interrupted, but the telegraph and telephone lines have been cut by Royalists.

"The Provisional Government has received news of great excesses at Larissa, where all the shops were closed as the result of pillaging. Bands of Reservists marched through the town shouting 'Death to the Venizelists.' The people are declared to be panic-stricken. Similar scenes took place at Trikkala and Volo."

FRENCH ARMY CHIEF MAY GO

Nivelle, Now Commander at Verdun, Suggested to Succeed Him.

PETAIN FIRST PROPOSED

But He Is Said to Have Demanded Larger Control Than France Alone Could Grant.

CRISIS BEFORE DEPUTIES

Washington Hears Secret Sessions in Paris Are the Scene of a Momentous Debate.

Special to The New York Times.

WASHINGTON, D. C., Dec. 6.—That part of official Washington, inclusive of the foreign diplomatic body which follows with close attention the trend of events in Europe, is on the tiptoe of expectation over the prospect of momentous changes in the administration of the great war by the Entente Allies. The feeling of expectancy has been emphasized by bits of information that have drifted into Washington from European capitals indicating substantial basis for the guarded press comment from London and Paris concerning dissatisfaction over the conduct of the struggle with the Central Powers.

Beyond what is printed in the newspapers, little is known here as to the ins and outs of the reported Cabinet crisis in Great Britain. For many reasons, however, there is a disposition to credit suggestions that a new deal is impending in the Government of hostile operations by both England and France. What is known most definitely applies particularly to French conduct of the war.

The secret sessions of the French Chamber of Deputies now being held are expected to develop important changes, of which a hint has already been heard on this side of the Atlantic. It is known here that one of the chief questions the Chamber has been considering is the reorganization of the French high command and that this may include the retirement of General Joffre.

Dispatches from Paris, published in the newspapers, are already speaking of "considerable alterations at the front," of "steps taken and to be taken in reorganizing the high command," and of the "organization of an inter-allied command," all implying that General Joffre is to quit his present post.

That the great French commander is about to retire from active service in the field will come as a surprise to most people. But the considerations that have led to the understood decision to relieve him are regarded as paramount in the present circumstances. It is felt that General Joffre has done his work. He has organized a superb defense and made the French Army an instrument that is capable of bringing victory to the Allied arms under a younger and more active man. Joffre is 64.

When the decision was reached that General Joffre should relinquish his command General Petain, Commander of the French forces in the notable successful resistance of the German attempt to take Verdun, was picked as Joffre's successor. Difficulties arose, however, over accomplishing the contemplated change. It is understood that the proposal to Petrain was that he should command, personally and directly, all the allied forces in France—French, British, and Belgian.

Petain's rise in rank and fame has been remarkable. At the beginning of the war he was only a Colonel of infantry. When things were going badly at Verdun, Joffre took Petain out of the reserve army and appointed him commander of the forces defending that sector. He is a modest man, with marked objection to being advertised, and little has been heard of him in this country. But in the French Army he is looked upon as a wonderful soldier and some of those who know him have predicted that he would prove to be the superman who would eventually lead the French forces to victory.

After some discussion, however, General Petain, it is understood, has declined the flattering proposal of those who determine matters of policy in France. The whole story affecting his attitude has not reached this country, but enough is known to indicate that Petain's declination was due to a belief on his part that, in order to achieve victory, he must be invested with greater authority than it was proposed to give him.

How much power he demanded is not made clear. It may have been the supreme command of all the allied armies in their several fields of activity. Or it may have been that Petain felt that to gain the end he sought—victory for the allied cause—he should have not only command of the armies in France, but control over the resources of the nation. Perhaps, it is suggested, Petain may have insisted that all armies and all resources should be placed in his charge by the allied Governments. At any rate, the negotiations ended in his elimination, for the present, from the choice for supreme command.

In the consideration given to the important changes proposed, the matter of retaining General Joffre in some important capacity had not been overlooked. It was proposed to transfer him to an important post, perhaps in a military advisory capacity, or to the civil establishment, quite likely as Minister of War. But the old soldier is believed to have vetoed the suggestion. As this phase of the matter is interpreted here, Joffre is supposed to have become aware of the intention to remove him. It has therefore obviously become necessary to put somebody in his place at once. He can now retire as a popular hero, honored and respected by his countrymen and famous throughout the world as one of the great strategists of modern times.

Failing Petain, various French Generals who have shown ability in the great war have been suggested in con-

Continued on Page 4.

Kaiser Tells His Empress Bucharest's Fall Is a Success on the Road to Complete Victory

AMSTERDAM, Thursday, Dec. 7, (via London.)—According to a Berlin official statement, Emperor William has sent the following telegram to Empress Augusta Victoria:

Bucharest has been taken. What a magnificent success on the road to complete victory has been gained with God's help!

By sudden strokes our incomparable troops, side by side of our brave allies, have beaten the enemy wherever he offered resistance. Their well-tried commander has guided them.

May God further vouchsafe His help!

[Signed.] WILLIAM.

Rumanians Have Lost Bucharest; Second Army in Peril of Capture

Teutons Are Closing In from North and South on Lines of Retreat—Defenders Demoralized by Foe's Swift Advance—Russian Drive Gains Northeast of Kronstadt.

LONDON, Dec. 6.—The fall of Bucharest and Ploechti is announced in the German official communication tonight. It has not been confirmed from other sources, but the position revealed by the previous German and Russian communiqués left little hope that the Rumanian capital could be saved.

No official Rumanian statements have been received in London since Sunday, but the Russian official reports today recorded the steady retirement of the Rumanians before the victorious Teuton forces. The rapidity of the advance of the Central Powers seems to show that no attempt was made to defend the capital, and the actions fought have probably been only of a delaying nature.

The fall of Ploechti, perhaps, is of even greater importance than that of Bucharest. Ploechti is a railway junction and the centre of the great oil district of Prahova Valley. Unless the Rumanians have been able to destroy or disable the oil wells, machinery, and stores of oil the Germans will get a much-needed prize. Moreover, in the Prahova Valley they are on the line of retreat of a portion of the Rumanian second army.

It is believed that the Rumanians will be compelled to retire until they can secure a shorter line between the Carpathians and the lower Danube, which will be within easier reach of Russian reinforcements.

A wireless dispatch from Berne says: "The Frankfurter Zeitung warns Germans against expecting double rations as a result of the invasion of Rumania. It says the Russo-Rumanians may save their harvests and granaries, which are situated mainly on the lower Danube, in territory which has not been invaded."

Commander Locker Lampson, who has been in three actions on the Dobrudja front with British naval armored cars, has been wounded, says Reuter's Petrograd correspondent. The dispatch adds that six British petty officers are missing, but that none of the cars has been lost.

German Announcement of Victory.

BERLIN, Dec. 6, (By Wireless to Sayville.)—Bucharest, the capital of Rumania, has been captured, it was officially announced today. Ploechti, the important railway junction town, thirty-six miles northwest of Bucharest, also has been taken.

Russian troops again attacked yesterday in the Carpathian forest, north of Tartar Pass, and on the Ludova, but these new assaults brought them no success. In the Trotus Valley, (northeast of Kronstadt,) however, they made a strong attack and succeeded in reaching the German second positions. North of Oituz Pass a Russian point of support was captured.

These last operations are reported in the following statement, which preceded the brief announcement of the fall of Bucharest and Ploechti:

Front of Archduke Joseph: The Russians attacked in the wooded Carpathians, north of Tartar Pass, and four times on the Ludova. These new sacrifices of men brought the enemy no success.

The number of prisoners taken in the engagements on the Verchdebry, which were favorable for us has increased to 275 men and the booty to five machine guns and four mine throwers.

In the Trotus Valley strong pressure by the Russians against our most advanced line was parried in a prepared second position situated nearby in the rear.

North of Oituz Pass a Russian point of support was captured. Our losses were small. Sixty prisoners remained in the hands of the German attacking forces.

In the Bazska Valley, southwest of the basin of Kezdi Vasarhely, a raid carried out by German and Austro-Hungarian troops, brought a considerable section of a Rumanian position, with two officers and more than eighty of the rank and file and much accumulated ammunition into our possession.

Army Group of Field Marshal von Mackensen: The Ninth Army, advancing victoriously, is approaching, fighting its way forward, the Bucharest-Ploechti-Campina railroad. Under the influence of this movement the enemy evacuated his positions north of Sinaia, which town was captured by the Austro-Hungarian groups after an attack in the evening.

The Danube Army cleared the towns on the south bank of the Argechu still occupied by the Rumanians and is advancing toward Bucharest.

On the Danube Russian attacks from the east were repulsed.

German and Austro-Hungarian troops under Colonel von Szive are pursuing in Southwestern Wallachia Rumanian forces which are retreating in utter confusion. Our troops forced the enemy on the Alt to accept battle. The enemy, whose way has been blocked on the east bank of the river, lost yesterday 26 officers and 1,600 men in prisoners and four cannon. In addition to this number, more than 4,400 other Rumanians were taken prisoner on Dec. 5.

On the railroad northwest of Bucharest considerable stores of wheat bought by the British Government and labeled as such by signs fell into our hands.

On the front in Dobrudja there was calm.

CONSTANTINOPLE, Dec. 5, (via London, Dec. 6.)—An official communication issued today says:

Our troops are participating in the battle north of the Danube (Rumania). Have captured 3,600 men and sixty officers and three batteries of field guns.

Russian Report of Operations.

PETROGRAD, Dec. 6.—Concerning the operations on the Carpathian and Rumanian front, the War Office today issued the following:

In the wooded Carpathians we occupied a height three versts west of Jablonitza, but in consequence of the enemy's violent artillery fire we were compelled to leave.

On the Transylvanian frontier, in the valleys of the rivers Trotus, Sulta, Tchebiniash, Uzul, and Dos Dostiana, engagements are continuing.

In Wallachia the attacks have continued. The enemy was successful in the direction of Tergovistea and Ploechti and in the region of Dokaneshti, on the railway from Titu to Bucharest, where, in consequence of the piercing of their front, the Rumanians were compelled to retire.

In other sections the enemy attacks were beaten back.

ADVANCE INCREDIBLY SWIFT.

Demoralized Rumanians Unable to Stand Against Invaders.

WITH THE GERMAN ARMIES BEFORE BUCHAREST, Dec. 4, (by Courier to Hermannstadt and Wireless via Sayville, Dec. 6.)—The armies of Field Marshal von Mackensen and General von Falkenhayn after a campaign, the rapidity of which has been almost unparalleled in military history, have swept through half of Rumania, have crushed the resistance of the Rumanians at one strong point after another, and now, having driven the Russo-Rumanian forces beyond Bucharest, both to the north and the south of the capital, are clamping their tentacles on the Rumanian city from three sides.

The Germans with the aid of Austro-Hungarians, Bulgarians and Turks have battered their way through Western Rumania to their present concentric position around Bucharest within a wonderfully short time. They have breasted the natural fortifications of the Transylvanian Mountains and the Danube River and have beaten their way through the strongest kind of scientific defenses obviously prepared long in advance. They have thrown the Rumanian army numbering hundreds of thousands of men back in such disorder that even apparently impregnable positions such as those along the Rivers Alt and Argechu could not be held more than a few hours.

Bridges Over the Argechu Intact.

The line of the Argechu River, with its flooded, dashing torrent 300 yards to a quarter of a mile forming a natural defense, appeared to be so strong that the Germans themselves expected this last line of defense before Bucharest would require time and a hard effort to force. But the river was crossed both to the north and to the south of the city almost without breaking the stride of the advancing armies. The Rumanians left the bridges across the stream to the north of the city intact.

The advance of the Teutonic forces has been so rapid that the military staffs have been forced to change their bases at intervals of only a few days to keep up with the troops, and to lay plans for settling in towns not yet captured. A trip of 1,000 miles by automobile in this region, just completed by The Associated Press correspondent, showed how difficult it was to move as quickly as the invading forces.

The journey began at Livazeny, just within the Hungarian frontier, with Craiova as the first objective. Before the Transylvanian passes had been traversed Craiova had been captured. Bombardment of Slavina began the day after Craiova was reached. This bombardment was watched for a time from Piatra, across the Alt River from Slavina. The Germans believed the Rumanians would be able to hold for some time the almost impregnable heights along the river, and the correspondent left to watch other features of the advance, but it was necessary to return at top speed to reach Slavina twenty-four hours after its evacuation and forty-eight hours after witnessing the cannonading.

The next objective was Karakulu, but it had fallen, together with Slatina, by the time the correspondent could arrive, and even the headquarters troops were moving. Hastening northward toward Tanetesti, one of the seemingly innumerable divisions of General von Falkenhayn was found to have passed already east of the line on which the Rumanians late in November attempted to make a stand, only to lose 1,000 prisoners and scores of guns.

Field Marshal von Mackensen's troops, which crossed the Danube, had come in touch with General von Falkenhayn's forces between Rochi de Vede and Alexandria, southwest of Bucharest, before the correspondent could swing southward again, meeting everywhere the premature report that Bucharest had fallen.

The advance, which often has averaged twenty or more miles a day, has been possible mainly for two reasons. First, is the seeming demoralization and lack of leadership of the Rumanians, evidenced by the capture of entire staffs and large-sized units, with many guns and much material, by insignificant German detachments, which often amounted only to cavalry patrols. Second, is the amazing offensive speed of the Germans, which was indicated by the fact that the correspondent frequently met close behind the front, pressing forward, troops which had been seen but a few days previously miles behind in the Transylvanian passes.

Rumanian Moves Amazed Foe.

PITECHI, Rumania, Dec. 2, (via Berlin and Wireless to Sayville, Dec. 6.)—In another desperate attempt to

Continued on Page 4.

ALL PARTIES IN CABINET

Bonar Law and Derby Likely to Play Big Role in the New Ministry.

KING STRIVES FOR HARMONY

Confers with Leaders at Palace, but Bonar Law Refuses to Take the Helm.

LABORITES HOLD ALOOF

Look on the New Premier as an Enemy—Nationalists Also Withhold Support.

LONDON, Thursday, Dec. 7.—David Lloyd George, having overthrown the Asquith Cabinet, will become Prime Minister himself.

The new Government will be coalition, similar to the old one, but probably without the same measure of harmonious support which attended the formation of the first coalition Government, because its birth has created additional factional differences.

The official announcement, as made in the Court circular last night, read:

The King gave a further audience this evening to Mr. Bonar Law, who intimated that he was unable to form an administration. Thereupon the King summoned Mr. Lloyd George, who, at his Majesty's request, undertook to endeavor to form an administration.

This result emerged from another day of active and hurried party conferences, and a day of intense suspense and interest throughout the country.

There was a prospect yesterday afternoon that the personal offices of the King might solve the situation, and many thought that the Asquith régime might be continued. The King called the party leaders to Buckingham Palace and conferred with them for more than an hour.

Mr. Asquith and Mr. Lloyd George of the Liberals, Mr. Bonar Law and Mr. Balfour of the Unionists, and Mr. Henderson of the Labor Party, were with the sovereign. It is many years since a British ruler assembled the representatives of the different factions face to face when they had shown themselves unable to settle their differences. But no such serious crisis had arisen before to require such action by the King.

Whatever passed in the conference is held secret, but the inference that the King tried to arrange a reconciliation appears a most natural one. The five statesmen departed separately, at 4:30 o'clock, four in their motor cars, and the workingmen's spokesman afoot.

According to persons who saw Mr. Asquith, he presented a worn and grave appearance. The war has left unmistakable marks upon his vigorous frame and features, but yesterday there was something more—a tinge of weariness, physical, as well as mental. Usually reserved and singularly unemotional, he betrayed signs of the strain in the very gesture with which he flung himself well back out of public sight in the corner of his motor car.

After Mr. Asquith returned to his official residence, he was visited by several of his colleagues in the late Government. Mr. Lloyd George was also in consultation with some of his supporters.

Afterward the King gave an audience to Mr. Bonar Law, who declined to undertake the formation of a new Ministry, and then to Mr. Lloyd George, who accepted the responsibility, as every one expected he would if the opportunity came to him.

The official announcement at night that Mr. Lloyd George had undertaken the task, with the co-operation of Mr. Bonar Law, was a notification that the new Government would be coalition. Any party Government would be impossible because neither the Unionists nor the Liberals have a majority in the House of Commons; either one must obtain the support of the Irish Nationalists or the Laborites to command a majority.

The Nationalists have refused to participate in the Government until home rule becomes established. The Laborites are sworn enemies to Mr. Lloyd George because they resent his accusations that the workingmen have put their personal interests above the national interests at times during the war.

That the Laborites are not likely to support a Lloyd George administration was further indicated at a meeting yesterday of the Parliamentary Committee of the trades unions, which adopted a resolution unanimously expressing profound regret "that certain statesmen, influenced by the press campaign, have, in the hour of the nation's crisis, entirely failed to observe loyalty and self-sacrifice, which they repeatedly urged upon the workmen during the war."

The resolution continues:

"Further, we earnestly hope that the present unseemly quarrel among those intrusted with great responsibilities shall immediately cease, and so set a better example to the workers."

Bonar Law, Sir Edward Carson, and the Earl of Derby probably will act under Mr. Lloyd George, as they supported his ultimatum to Premier Asquith regarding the formation of a smaller war council.

What New Government Means.

The country awaits the rising of the curtain on the next act of this historical and remarkable crisis with an expectancy which never surrounded the beginning of any previous Government. The Lloyd George Ministry means the direction of the war by a Dictatorship in the form of an Inner Council of the Cabinet and means the scrapping of

"All the News That's Fit to Print."

The New York Times.

THE WEATHER
Fair, colder, diminishing west winds today; Thursday fair, cold.
For full weather report see Page 23.

VOL. LXVI...NO. 21,508. NEW YORK, WEDNESDAY, DECEMBER 13, 1916.—TWENTY-FOUR PAGES. ONE CENT In Greater New York, Jersey City and Newark. | Elsewhere, TWO CENTS.

GERMANY AND HER ALLIES OFFER TO NEGOTIATE FOR PEACE; NO TERMS NAMED IN NOTES TO NEUTRALS AND THE POPE; LONDON SKEPTICAL, BUT WILL CONSIDER THE PROPOSALS

ALLIES MUST FIRST CONSULT

Members of Entente Pledged to Agree Before Accepting Terms.

CALL IT A POLITICAL MOVE

"No Peace Possible on Assumption Germany Is Victorious," Say Many.

DERBY'S VIEWS RECALLED

His Promise of Due Consideration of German Proposals Is Government's Attitude.

Special Cable to THE NEW YORK TIMES.

LONDON, Wednesday, Dec. 13.—Germany's peace proposals will be considered by the Allies. This does not necessarily mean that what would properly be described as peace negotiations will be opened. Between such overtures as Chancellor von Bethmann Hollweg made in the note issued to the belligerent Governments in Berlin through the intermediary of American and other neutral diplomatic channels and the sitting of a peace conference at Washington or Madrid or The Hague there is a considerable distance.

The German Chancellor speaks of "the proposal which the four allied powers will bring to the negotiations." This is an assumption that actual peace negotiations will follow. It is a natural assumption from the German point of view. But the Entente Powers have to acquiesce before such a stage can be reached. They have to be in agreement that the conditions, both actual and probable, justify their entering into any arguments other than the arguments of war, which Germany began.

Von Bethmann Hollweg's advances cannot be rejected out of hand. A brutal refusal even to consider the possibility of arriving at terms of peace cannot be the position taken by by the Entente powers. Under the terms of agreement arranged by Lord, then Sir Edward Grey, in the early months of the war between Great Britain, France, and Russia and later adhered to by Italy and Japan, there can be no separate negotiations for peace. Equally, a reply to Germany's present proposals must be a joint response arrived at after consultation between all the Allies.

It is impossible to say definitely what will be the nature of that joint reply, seeing that there has not yet been time for any exchange of views between the Entente Cabinets. There exists, however, a very clear-cut impression that the German proposals will encounter a good deal of skeptical investigation. Peace is no less the desire of the allied Governments than it is of Germany. On what terms can peace be attained is the question.

Reports from Washington suggest some belief that the basic idea in the German mind is a return to the status quo ante. This is too vague for practical purposes. It is thought probable that further information may be requested.

Lord Derby's reply to the query put to him by THE NEW YORK TIMES correspondent in regard to the Cosmos articles probably gives the clearest indication of what will be the atttitude of the British Government in the face of von Bethmann Hollweg's proposals. Lord Derby said:

"Any peace proposal that came from Germany would be met by the Allies with all the consideration it deserved."

What consideration the present proposals deserve is the question which the Entente Cabinets have to determine. Further information must be available before that question can be answered. How far is Germany willing to go to ensure lasting peace? A peace which should evade the main issue for which the Allies are fighting is unthinkable. That main issue is the destruction of the military domination of Prussia. Can that consummation be reached without the disarmament of the German military machine? Once disarmament were agreed upon, the grounds upon which a lasting peace could be negotiated would become possible with the Constitution of such a league of nations as the League to Enforce Peace has in view. What reason is there to believe that Germany is prepared to abandon the system which enables the Chancellor to speak of mighty successes? There lies the reason for scepticism with which von Bethmann Hollweg's proposals are regarded here.

There was tendency in some quarters to regard Bethmann Hollwegs proposals as designed for the double purpose of first obtaining kudos for Germany in the eyes of the neutral world and particularly America and secondly, encouraging the German people to support the strain from which all evidence shows them to be suffering severely. Reference to the stores obtained from Rumania and the defence of their existence are grounds upon which this view is based.

While they may be trust in the deductions, it is suggested in other

Continued on Page 3.

Text of the Teutonic Notes to the Neutral Powers and the Pope

To the Neutral Powers.

BERLIN, Dec. 12.—Following is the text of the note addressed by Germany and her allies to the neutral powers for transmission to the Entente Allies:

"The most terrific war experienced in history has been raging for the last two years and a half over a large part of the world—a catastrophe which thousands of years of common civilization was unable to prevent and which injures the most precious achievements of humanity.

"Our aims are not to shatter nor annihilate our adversaries. In spite of our consciousness of our military and economic strength and our readiness to continue the war (which has been forced upon us) to the bitter end, if necessary; at the same time, prompted by the desire to avoid further bloodshed and make an end to the atrocities of war, the four allied powers propose to enter forthwith into peace negotiations.

"The propositions which they bring forward for such negotiations, and which have for their object a guarantee of the existence, of the honor and liberty of evolution for their nations, are, according to their firm belief, an appropriate basis for the establishment of a lasting peace.

"The four allied powers have been obliged to take up arms to defend justice and the liberty of national evolution. The glorious deeds of our armies have in no way altered their purpose. We always maintained the firm belief that our own rights and justified claims in no way control the rights of these nations.

"The spiritual and material progress which were the pride of Europe at the beginning of the twentieth century are threatened with ruin. Germany and her allies, Austria-Hungary, Bulgaria, and Turkey, gave proof of their unconquerable strength in this struggle. They gained gigantic advantages over adversaries superior in number and war material. Our lines stand unshaken against ever-repeated attempts made by armies.

"The last attack in the Balkans has been rapidly and victoriously overcome. The most recent events have demonstrated that further continuance of the war will not result in breaking the resistance of our forces, and the whole situation with regard to our troops justifies our expectation of further successes.

"If, in spite of this offer of peace and reconciliation, the struggle should go on, the four allied powers are resolved to continue to a victorious end, but they disclaim responsibility for this before humanity and history. The Imperial Government, through the good offices of your Excellency, asks the Government of [here is inserted the name of the neutral power addressed in each instance] to bring this communication to the knowledge of the Government of [here are inserted the names of the belligerents.]"

To the Vatican.

BERLIN, Dec. 12.—The note of the German Government, as presented by Dr. von Muhlberg, German Minister to the Vatican, to Cardinal Gasparri, Papal Secretary of State, reads as follows:

"According to instructions received, I have the honor to send to your Eminence a copy of the declaration of the Imperial Government today, which by the good offices of the powers instrusted with the protection of German interests in the countries with which the German Empire is in a state of war, transmits to these States, and in which the Imperial Government declares itself ready to enter into peace negotiations. The Austro-Hungarian, Turkish, and Bulgarian Governments also have sent similar notes.

"The reasons which prompted Germany and her allies to take this step are manifest. For two years and a half a terrible war has been devastating the European Continent. Unlimited treasures of civilization have been destroyed. Extensive areas have been soaked with blood. Millions of brave soldiers have fallen in battle and millions have returned home as invalids. Grief and sorrow fill almost every house.

"Not only upon the belligerent nations, but also upon neutrals, the destructive consequences of the gigantic struggle weigh heavily. Trade and commerce, carefully built up in years of peace, have been depressed. The best forces of the nation have been withdrawn from the production of useful objects. Europe, which formerly was devoted to the propagation of religion and civilization, which was trying to find solutions for social problems, and was the home of science and art and all peaceful labor, now resembles an immense war camp, in which the achievements and works of many decades are doomed to annihilation.

"Germany is carrying on a war of defense against her enemies, which aim at her destruction. She fights to assure the integrity of her frontiers and the liberty of the German nation, for the right which she claims to develop freely her intellectual and economic energies in peaceful competition and on an equal footing with other nations. All the efforts of their enemies are unable to shatter the heroic armies of the (Teutonic) allies, which protect the frontiers of their countries, strengthened by the certainty that the enemy shall never pierce the iron wall.

"Those fighting on the front know that they are supported by the whole nation, which is inspired by love for its country and is ready for the greatest sacrifices and determined to defend to the last extremity the inherited treasure of intellectual and economic work and the social organization and sacred soil of the country.

"Certain of our own strength, but realizing Europe's sad future if the war continues; seized with pity in the face of the unspeakable misery of humanity, the German Empire, in accord with her allies, solemnly repeats what the Chancellor already has declared, a year ago, that Germany is ready to give peace to the world by setting before the whole world the question whether or not it is possible to find a basis for an understanding.

"Since the first day of the Pontifical reign his Holiness the Pope has unswervingly demonstrated, in the most generous fashion, his solicitude for the innumerable victims of this war. He has alleviated the sufferings and ameliorated the fate of thousands of men injured by this catastrophe. Inspired by the exalted ideas of his ministry, his Holiness has seized every opportunity in the interests of humanity to end so sanguinary a war.

"The Imperial Government is firmly confident that the initiative of the four powers will find friendly welcome on the part of his Holiness, and that the work of peace can count upon the precious support of the Holy See."

Austria's Separate Statement.

LONDON, Dec. 12.—An official Austrian statement, referring to the peace offer, says:

"When in the Summer of 1914 the patience of Austria-Hungary was exhausted by a series of systematically continued and ever increasing provocations and menaces, and the monarchy, after almost fifty years of unbroken peace, found itself compelled to draw the sword, this weighty decision was animated neither by aggressive purposes nor by designs of conquest, but solely by the bitter necessity of self-defense, to defend its existence and safeguard itself for the future against similar treacherous plots of hostile neighbors.

"That was the task and aim of the monarchy in the present war. In combination with its allies, well tried in loyal comradeship in arms, the Austro-Hungarian Army and Fleet, fighting, bleeding, but also assailing and conquering, gained such successes that they frustrated the intentions of the enemy. The quadruple alliance not only has won an immense series of victories, but also holds in its power extensive hostile territories. Unbroken is its strength, as our latest treacherous enemy has just experienced.

"Can our enemies hope to conquer or shatter this alliance of powers? They will never succeed in breaking it by blockade and starvation measures. Their war aims, to the attainment of which they have come no nearer in the third year of the war, will in the future be proved to have been completely unattainable. Useless and unavailing, therefore, is the prosecution of the fighting on the part of the enemy.

"The powers of the Quadruple Alliance, on the other hand, have effectively pursued their aims, namely, defence against attacks on their existence and integrity, which were planned in concert long since, and the achievement of real guarantees, and they will never allow themselves to be deprived of the basis of their existence, which they have secured by advantages won.

"The continuation of the murderous war, in which the enemy can destroy much, but cannot—as the Quadruple Alliance is firmly confident—alter fate, is ever more seen to be an aimless destruction of human lives and property, an act of inhumanity justified by no necessity and a crime against civilization.

"This conviction, and the hope that similar views may also be begun to be entertained in the enemy camp, has caused the idea to ripen in the Vienna Cabinet—in full agreement with the Governments of the allied [Teutonic] powers—of making a candid and loyal endeavor to come to a discussion with their enemies for the purpose of paving a way for peace.

"The Governments of Austria-Hungary, Germany, Turkey, and Bulgaria have addressed today identical notes to the diplomatic representatives in the capitals concerned who are intrusted with the promotion of enemy nationals, expressing an inclination to enter into peace negotiations and requesting them to transmit this overture to enemy States. This step was simultaneously brought to the knowledge of the representatives of the Holy See in a special note, and the active interest of the Pope for this offer of peace was solicited. Likewise the accredited representatives of the remaining neutral States in the four capitals were acquainted with this proceeding for the purpose of informing their Governments.

"Austria and her allies by this step have given new and decisive proof of their love of peace. It is now for their enemies to make known their views before the world.

"Whatever the result of its proposal may be, no responsibility can fall on the Quadruple Alliance, even before the judgment seat of its own peoples, if it is eventually obliged to continue the war."

THE CHANCELLOR'S SPEECH

Tells Reichstag Germany and Her Allies Are Unconquerable.

BUT ARE READY FOR PEACE

Disclaims Any Aim to Shatter or Annihilate Their Adversaries.

THRONG CHEERS HIS WORDS

Floor and Galleries Packed, While Huge Crowds Surround Building.

BERLIN, Dec. 12, (by Wireless to Sayville.)—Proposals by Germany and her allies to the Entente Powers to enter into peace negotiations were announced in the Reichstag today by Chancellor von Bethmann Hollweg in the course of a speech, during which he read an identical note submitted through the United States, Spain, and Switzerland.

Earlier in the day the Chancellor had received the representatives of these countries, which are protecting German interests in hostile countries, and had handed the note to them with the request that they bring it to the knowledge of the hostile countries.

In the note the four Central powers propose to enter forthwith on peace negotiations. The propositions, which they bring forth for such negotiations, are, according to their firm belief, appropriate for the establishment of a lasting peace.

The Governments at Vienna, Constantinople, and Sofia transmitted identical notes and also communicated with the Holy See and all other neutral powers."

Practically all the Members of Parliament answered the unexpected summons. The crowded House and thronged galleries listened in attentive silence when the Chancellor rose for his speech. The Chancellor first outlined the extraordinary political situation and then, insisting upon the achievements of the Central Powers, made the announcement which possibly may be the turning point in the war which for more than two years held the world under its spell.

Diplomats Hear Speech.

The galleries and the royal box were crowded when the Chancellor began speaking. All the Ambassadors and Ministers of foreign Governments were in the diplomatic box. The American Chargé d'Affaires, Joseph C. Grew, and Mrs. Grew were among those present, as were the Ministers of Argentina, Brazil, Chile, and the other States of Central and South America.

The Reichstag building was surrounded by a great crowd, and the adjoining streets were thronged. The people were intensely interested, and the Imperial Chancellor, on his arrival, was cordially greeted in the usual fashion.

The Chancellor began his speech in a clear, loud, ringing voice. His first utterances were greeted with applause on all sides, and at frequent points in his speech the assembly assented in demonstrative fashion. Later, however, when he touched upon the question of policy, differences of opinion made themselves felt, the applause coming mainly from the Catholic Centre and the Left. At the conclusion of his address a majority of the House applauded and the galleries joined in the handclapping.

The Chancellor said:

"The Reichstag had been adjourned for a long period, but fortunately it was left to the discretion of the President as to the day of the next meeting. This discretion was caused by the hope that soon happy events in the field would be recorded, a hope fulfilled quicker, almost, than expected. I shall be brief, for actions speak for themselves."

The Chancellor said Rumania had entered the war in order to roll up the German positions in the east and those of Germany's allies. At the same time the grand offensive on the Somme had as its object to pierce the German western front, and the renewed Italian attacks were intended to paralyze Austria-Hungary.

"The situation was serious," said the Chancellor. "But with God's help our troops shaped conditions so as to give us security which not only is complete, but still more so than ever before. The western front stands. Not only does it stand, but in spite of the Rumanian campaign it is fitted out with larger reserves of men and material than it had been formerly. The most effective precautions have been taken against all Italian diversions. And while on the Somme and on the Carso the drum-fire resounded while the Russians launched troops against the eastern frontier of Transylvania, Field Marshall von Hindenburg captured the whole of western Wallachia and the hostile capital of Bucharest, leading with unparalleled genius the troops that in competition with all the allies made possible what hitherto was considered impossible.

Vast Supplies Seized.

"And Hindenburg does not rest. Military operations progress. By strokes of

WILSON PONDERS METHOD OF ACTION

Hint That He May Transmit Note with a Recommendation for Consideration.

BERLIN'S TERMS FORECAST

Believed to Include Evacuation of Belgium and France if German Colonies Are Restored.

Special to The New York Times.

WASHINGTON, Dec. 12.—Official Washington received with mixed feelings the news from Berlin that Germany and her partners in the war had asked the United States and other neutral Governments to propose a discussion of peace terms to the Entente Allies. As far as the Administration is concerned, judgment as to the meaning and effect of this move is suspended until the official text of the German offer has been received here; but it was said in an informed quarter that President Wilson was giving earnest consideration to the method he should follow in presenting the proposal to Great Britain and the other allied nations.

This intimation gave rise to the impression that the President, in presenting the German communication to the Entente Powers, might go much further than necessity required—that is, he might not merely content himself with transmitting Germany's proposal to the Entente without comment, but might accompany it with a note in which he would point out to Great Britain, France, Russia, Italy, and the other Governments allied with them, that the United States was deeply interested in the German effort for peace and requested those to whom the communication was addressed to give it their most careful consideration.

It was explained, however, that the President had seen only press accounts of Chancellor von Bethmann Hollweg's speech in the Reichstag and had no knowledge of the extent and character of the proposal which he announced. In these circumstances, it was said, the President could not be expected to have any definite views as to what his course should be, and the American people therefore must wait until the offer had been formally brought to the attention of this Government before any indication of the President's purpose could be given.

May Act Only "As Messenger Boy."

But among certain influential members of the Administration whose views would have great weight in the determination of the policy to be pursued by the President, a very strong opinion prevailed that this Government could take no other course than to serve as the mere intermediary for the transmission of the peace proposal of the Central Powers to the Governments of their enemies. As expressed in one quarter, the part which the United States would perform would be merely that of a "messenger boy" with no responsibility and no authority in connection with the offer.

There would be no impropriety on the part of the United States in transmitting the peace offer of Germany, Austria-Hungary, Turkey, and Bulgaria. All communication between the British and German Governments, for example, is now conducted by the United States, which would be following the line of that service in transmitting the peace overtures.

At a brief session of the Cabinet this afternoon Germany's move for peace was discussed, but it was said afterward

Continued on Page 2.

Possible Terms of Peace As Heard in Washington

Special to The New York Times.

WASHINGTON, Dec. 12.—While the text of the Teutonic note did not contain the terms on which the Central Powers would make peace, it was said in well-informed Teutonic circles here that they were expected to contain substantially these provisions:

The restoration of Belgium and the evacuation by Germany of all French territory in return for the restoration to Germany of her colonies.

The establishment of Poland and Lithuania as separate kingdoms, or a separate kingdom.

The restoration to Bulgaria of all territory lost in the second Balkan war and the retention of Constantinople by Turkey.

The retention of part of Serbia by Austria as a portion of the Austro-Hungarian Empire.

Another version intimated that Germany might be willing to leave the settlement of the Balkan question to the peace conference.

France Names War Council of Five; Nivelle Put in Command of Army

General Lyautey, Governor of Morocco, Becomes New War Minister—Joffre to Head Allied War Board With Title of Marshal.

PARIS, Dec. 12.—Coincident with the announcement tonight of the formation of the new Cabinet, containing a special War Council of five members, it was officially stated that General Nivellé, commander of the French troops at Verdun, had been appointed Commander in Chief of the armies of the north and northeast.

The official announcement of this appointment says it is the first step toward the reorganization of the higher command. It is suggested that General Joffre may be appointed to head the Military Council of the Allies, retaining the title of Commander in Chief and receiving the rank of Marshal.

The new Cabinet is as follows:

Members of the War Council.

Premier and Foreign Minister—ARISTIDE BRIAND.

Minister of Finance—ALEXANDRE RIBOT.

Minister of War—General HUBERT LYAUTEY.

Minister of Marine—Rear Admiral LACAZE.

Minister of National Manufactures, including Munitions and Transport—ALBERT THOMAS.

Other Members of the Cabinet.

Minister of Public Instruction—PAUL PAINLEVE.

Minister of the Interior—LOUIS J. MALVY.

Minister of Commerce and Agriculture—ETIENNE CLEMENTEL.

Minister of National Subsistence and Labor—M. HERRIOT.

Minister of the Colonies—GASTON DOUMERGUE.

Minister of Justice and Public Works—RENE VIVIANI.

Three Under Secretaries will also be members of the Cabinet under M. Thomas, namely M. Loucheur, for Munitions; Albert Claveille, for Transportation, and Justin Godart, for Sanitary Service.

General Lyautey, the new Minister of War, has been Governor of Morocco for the last five years. M. Herriot is Mayor of the City of Lyons, where he has done remarkable work in organizing the city's war and charity activities.

Premier Briand, speaking to a group of reporters last night, said:

"There is nothing absolutely positive as yet, but you can announce that the new Government will in all probability appear in the Chamber of Deputies Wednesday."

Some of the Deputies are not satisfied with the plan of a concentrated Ministry and desire to condense Parliament. Deputy Georges Bonnefous has introduced a bill for the creation of a Parliamentary Committee of National Defense, which will continue for the duration of the war. This committee would consist of thirty delegates elected by the Deputies and forty elected by the Senate. The committee would meet weekly to consider information relative to the military, diplomatic, and economic conduct of the war as communicated by the Government. The Chamber and the Senate would hold a brief session not more than once a month in which to transact necessary business and ratify the decisions of the committee.

The members of the new Cabinet after having been presented to President Poincaré held their first meeting, which lasted until midnight. They decided to appear in the Chamber tomorrow and in the Senate on Thursday.

FRANCE'S ABLEST MEN IN NEW WAR COUNCIL

Stephane Lauzanne Gives Particular Praise to Briand and Lyautey.

Stéphane Lauzanne, formerly editor in chief of Le Matin of Paris, one of the newspapers, which have advocated the bringing about of just such a reorganization in France as has now been accomplished by Premier Briand, said last night that Premier Briand had selected as his associates in the new French War Council four of the ablest and most far-seeing men in all France. The new War Council, Mr. Lauzanne added, would work hand in hand with the British War Council. Briand and Lloyd George, he said, were men of the same type and both possessed of great driving power—"as much alike as two fingers on the same hand."

Mr. Lauzanne, who is at the Hotel Vanderbilt, commented as follows on the members of the new War Council:

"First of all, there is Premier Briand. Everybody knows about him, and so I won't discuss his achievements. I may say, though, that we in France consider Briand perhaps the ablest of all our public men. All France trusts Briand. Did you ever stop to consider the remarkable physical resemblance of Briand and to Lloyd George? Look at the pictures of the two men and you will note a resemblance almost as striking as that of the Czar to King George. And Briand and Lloyd George have the same ideas and the same convictions as to

Continued on Page 4.

Kaiser Notifies His Army of Germany's Peace Move

LONDON, Dec. 12.—A Central News dispatch from Amsterdam says it is anounced officially in Berlin that Emperor William has notified his commanding Generals of Germany's peace offer, and has informed them it is still uncertain whether the offer will be accepted. Until that uncertainty is ended, the message says, they are to fight on. The message is quoted as follows:

"Soldiers: In agreement with the sovereigns of my allies, and with the consciousness of victory, I have made an offer of peace to the enemy. Whether it will be accepted is still uncertain. Until that moment arrives you will fight on."

BERLIN, Dec. 12.—Emperor William's order to his Commanding Generals was addressed also to "my navy, which in the common fight has loyally and effectively staked all its strength."

KAISER DRAFTED THE NOTE.

Majority of Deputies Knew Nothing Before the Announcement.

Special Cable to THE NEW YORK TIMES.

LONDON, Wednesday, Dec. 13.—The Daily Telegraph's Rotterdam correspondent says:

"I understand the notes were handed to the Ambassadors of neutral States last evening. This was done in the name of the Kaiser by the Chancellor, who returned from Field Headquarters on Saturday. The note was drafted personally by the Kaiser after a conference at Army Headquarters with King Ludwig of Bavaria, von Bethmann Hollweg, the Minister President of Bavaria, and Foreign Secretary Zimmerman.

"The leaders of political parties in the Reichstag were not let into the secret until this morning, when they were received by the Foreign Secretary. The majority of the Reichstag Deputies were in the dark until the last moment."

PEACE OFFER TO BELGIUM.

Said to Have Involved Co-operation With Teutons, or Destruction.

LONDON, Wednesday, Dec. 13.—The Daily Telegraph today prints prominently the following:

"We have received information from an unimpeachable source that the Central Powers recently offered peace to Belgium on the following terms: 'The Belgians are invited to insist upon immediate peace. In return for this their country will be restored to them, its independence guaranteed, and financial assistance given for its economic rehabilitation.'

"In the event of these terms being refused the intimation has been given to Belgium that her very existence—her monuments, her public buildings, and even her towns—is threatened."

BERLIN READY FOR A DEATH GRAPPLE

In Case the Entente Allies Reject or Ignore the Peace Proposals Now Made.

INTENT ON OUR OPINION

Most Fervent Hopes Are Expressed That Peace Move Will Bring Results.

By CYRIL BROWN

Special Cable to THE NEW YORK TIMES.

BERLIN, Dec. 12.—The Chancellor's Reichstag speech and the peace note are certain to absorb public interest in Germany for several days to the exclusion of everything else. Nothing, however, will be looked for with more eagerness than the reception of the note by Germany's enemies and the impression it will create in America.

Will the hand, extended by Germany, be grasped or scorned by the Entente? is a question people are asking and are eagerly awaiting answer.

It would be thought most unfortunate here were Germanys formal announcement of a willingness to make peace be interpreted in America or among the Allies as a move dictated by desperation or even a sign of weakening. The Chancellor took particular pains in his speech to emphasize amid rousing cheers that Germany, as well as her allies, were determined to fight on to a finish, if forced to do so, and that in this event the military situation could be expected to turn still further to the advantage of the Central Powers, as "Hindenburg never rests." Therein he sounded a popular keynote of "a determination to fight on, though ready to make peace."

Should Germany's declaration of a readiness to enter into peace negotiations meet with a negative answer or no answer at all, it is certain that Germany will not again take the initiative to bring about peace and a deathblow will

Continued on Page 2.

"All the News That's Fit to Print."

The New York Times.

THE WEATHER
Fair, not so cold today; Thursday cloudy; light, variable winds.
For full weather report see Page 21.

VOL. LXVI...NO. 21,515. NEW YORK, WEDNESDAY, DECEMBER 20, 1916.—TWENTY-TWO PAGES. ONE CENT In Greater New York, Jersey City and Newark. | Elsewhere, TWO CENTS.

LLOYD GEORGE DEMANDS FOR ALLIES COMPLETE RESTITUTION, FULL REPARATION, EFFECTUAL GUARANTEES FOR FUTURE—SURER GUARANTEES THAN THOSE GERMANY 'SO LIGHTLY BROKE'

SOME HOPE AT CAPITAL

Washington Believes Lloyd George Has Not Closed Door to Peace.

TEUTONS ARE OPTIMISTIC

Bernstorff Believes There Will Be at Least One More Exchange of Notes.

WANT TERMS KEPT SEÇRET

Circles Close to German Embassy Doubt if an Open Discussion Would Avail.

Special to The New York Times.

WASHINGTON, Dec. 19.—The speech of David Lloyd George, the British Prime Minister, today has not closed the door to peace in Europe, in the opinion of a considerable contingent of persons here, who are hopeful that the offer of Germany and her allies to discuss means of ending the war will not result in failure. Some officials of the Government believe that the Prime Minister has made a very clever diplomatic move in giving the Central Powers an opportunity to state the terms upon which they will enter into negotiations with their enemies.

Count von Bernstorff, the German Ambassador, is among the optimistic ones. "I expect at least one more exchange of notes," he said this evening. "It looks to me as if it is not finished."

But the belief in a favorable outcome of the German effort is by no means unanimous. Many interested men have failed to find in the printed extracts of the Prime Minister's speech any ground for expecting a continuance of diplomatic exchanges. Lloyd George's statement of the agreement of Great Britain with the practical rejection of the peace proffer by France and Russia was considered to be deeply significant. One of those who finds little encouragement for a peace agreement in the speech of Mr. Lloyd George is Representative Hal D. Flood of Virginia, Chairman of the House Committee on Foreign Affairs.

"It does not appear to me," he said, "that there is anything very definite concerning peace in the day's developments. While those who desire peace may see something in the British attitude, it would appear that there is considerable doubt of a peace agreement at any time soon. I do not care to comment in detail after a hurried reading of Mr. Lloyd George's speech."

Door Not Entirely Closed.

A more hopeful view was taken by Representative Henry A. Cooper of Wisconsin, the ranking Republican member of the Committee on Foreign Affairs. "While it is true that no definite progress has been made, there is yet a chance for peace negotiations that may end successfully," he said. "The door is not entirely closed by the British attitude and there is a possibility yet that a way out may be found. The situation is somewhat encouraging."

It was to Count von Bernstorff that most of those interested went for guidance when they read the extracts from the British Prime Minister's speech in the afternoon papers. But the German Ambassador did not care to say more than he is quoted as saying in this dispatch. He evidently regarded the situation as too delicate to justify comment and contented himself with uttering the one note of optimism. But in diplomatic circles where the German view of pending questions is understood and reflected, everything that was said bore out the impression that the feeling there was decidedly optimistic, although it was admitted that Lloyd George's statements were not entirely clear as to the British position on the peace offer.

There is reason to believe from what is said in the circles mentioned that the Central Powers are not inclined to disclose the terms upon which they will be willing to negotiate a peace treaty until their negotiators are face to face with the peace envoys of the Entente Allies across the council table. Germany's great effort—conceding that Germany will dominate the course of her partners—is to get the statesmen of all the belligerent nations in one room and let them attempt to work out a solution of the momentous problem. For this reason it is believed that the answer of the Central Powers to the formal response which the Entente Governments will send will be a suggestion that Germany will be glad to disclose her views as to a proper adjustment of the issues of the war whenever peace commissioners of Great Britain, France, Russia, and Italy meet peace commissioners of Germany, Austria-Hungary, Turkey and Bulgaria.

The statements made by Mr. Lloyd George today do not lend much encouragement to the hope that Great Britain will consent to this. The inference from the remarks of the Prime Minister was that before she entered into a discussion of peace Great Britain, at least, must have from her enemies an ex-

Continued on Page 2.

Replies of Other Allies to Germany's Proposals Indicated by Statements of Leaders and Czar's Council

PARIS, Dec. 19.—Premier Briand announced in the Senate today that the Entente Allies would send a concerted reply tomorrow making known "to the Central Powers that it is impossible to take their request for peace seriously."

The Premier's statement follows:

"No one is duped by Germany's manoeuvre. Tomorrow a concerted reply will make known to the Central Empires that it is impossible to take their request for peace seriously. The Central Empires are at bay. Their request for peace is a last bluff that Germany wishes to try. She would like, also, to exonerate herself by making believe that the war was imposed upon her, but the war had been decided upon by her forty years ago. It was in the blood of the Germans, who felt certain they would conquer."

M. Briand recalled Dr. von Bethmann Hollweg's speech, in which he said Germany was compelled to violate the neutrality of Luxemburg and Belgium, and added:

"Germany will bear before the ages the responsibility of having unchained this war."

Proposal Lacks Sincerity, Italy's View

ROME, Dec. 18, (via Paris, Dec. 19.)—Addressing the Chamber of Deputies today on the subject of the peace overtures from Berlin, Baron Sonnino, the Foreign Minister, said:

"I do not desire to use exaggerated language, but the accent of boastfulness and the lack of sincerity which characterize the preamble to the enemy's note certainly inspire no belief that these mysterious peace conditions which the Central Empires announce they have the intention of exposing later on, with the object of guaranteeing the existence, honor, and free development of their peoples, do constitute an answer to the postulates we have laid down."

Czar's Advisers Urge a Flat Refusal

LONDON, Dec. 19.—A Reuter dispatch from Petrograd says that the Council of the Empire adopted today an order of the day identical with that adopted by the Duma, declaring its members unanimously in favor of refusing, in the present conditions, to enter into any peace negotiations with Germany.

PREMIER'S SPEECH UPSETS WALL ST.

Most Extraordinary Session Since German Peace Proposal Was Made.

RUMORS OF MANIPULATION

U. S. Steel Common Advances, Drops Violently, and Closes with Loss of One Point.

In some respects yesterday's stock market was the most extraordinary session which has developed since the peace proposal of the Central Powers was made. The Street was treated to the unusual spectacle of United States Steel common swinging upward 3½ points, then violently downward 6½ points, with a closing price only 1 point under the last quotation the day before. Even more radical fluctuations occurred in International Mercantile Marine preferred, United States Industrial Alcohol, and others of the less active list. The total sales for the day were 1,725,551 shares.

Preceding the receipt of extracts from Premier Lloyd George's address to Parliament the market moved strongly forward, gains over Monday's final quotations extending from 2 to more than 6 points. While traders implied in their observations of the morning that much would depend upon the attitude of Great Britain toward peace, in the half hour after the first dispatch appeared on the news tickers, indicating that the British Government would stand firm on the position previously taken by Russia and France, stocks did not move much either way.

Before 1:30 o'clock the Street knew the substance of Lloyd George's remarks and security prices were firm. About this time a heavy selling movement developed, with Steel the most prominent pressure point, and for the next forty minutes prices were slaughtered right and left. Steel appeared on the tape in blocks of thousands of shares. Industrial Alcohol, Utah Copper, Central Leather and several others were thrown overboard by weak holders, and active short selling aided the general rout. Then selling slackened almost as suddenly as it began, and a strong recovery occurred nearly everywhere before the close.

Much Gossip Heard on Floor.

The bearish demonstration was exceptional enough to arouse a great deal of gossip on the floor of the Stock Exchange. In the opinion of conservative members the collapse of prices had far less connection with Mr. Lloyd George's address, and the prospects it held for a continuance of the war, than with the operations of a number of powerful speculators. The public, according to these observers, had little to do with the day's business on either the buying or selling side, as the result of general advice by brokers to customers to be light with their committments until the situation had cleared.

According to the floor gossip several big operators began to buy Steel, Marine, and the war stocks on the break of last week, and kept it up until yesterday afternoon. Then, the stories had it, other speculators, deciding that prices had risen enough to be vulnerable to short sales, put out long lines of short stock in a hurry and broke the market down. The clique of buyers, seeing their profits melting away, thereupon sold their stock in great blocks in order to save what they could from the wreck.

Among the traders mentioned prominently in the rumors on the Exchange was Burton S. Castles, who has long been known as a successful operator in cotton. Mr. Castles is a member of the Stock Exhcange, but seldom appears there. He was reported as a heavy buyer when prices looked their worst last week, and the rumors were yesterday

Continued on Page 3.

SEES GERMAN TRAP IN PEACE OFFERS

Foreign Minister Sonnino Says Italy and Her Allies Will Not Be Taken in It.

PLEDGES UNITY OF POLICY

Deputies Cheer the Declaration and Shelve Resolutions Dealing with Berlin's Offer.

Special Cable to THE NEW YORK TIMES.

ROME, Dec. 19.—Almost continuous applause greeted Foreign Minister Sonnino's speech on the German peace proposals in the Italian Parliament yesterday, in which he substantially repeated the statement made before the French Deputies by Premier Briand. Expressing his belief that the overtures made by Berlin were intended as a trap for the Allies, he predicted that they would not fall into it, and solemnly reaffirmed the unshakable solidarity of the Entente Powers, which, he said, would soon be made evident in the identical reply which would be sent to the Central Empires and their allies.

ROME, Monday, Dec. 18, (via Paris, Dec. 19.)—Baron Sonnino, the Foreign Minister, said in the Chamber of Deputies today that several resolutions which had been introduced in the Chamber in regard to the peace proposals of the Central Powers seemed to be based on the supposition that the Government had or would have concrete and precise indications as to the basis on which negotiations would be opened.

"As I said on the day before yesterday, this supposition does not correspond with the facts," he continued. "There is no sign of conditions or bases for negotiations in the enemy's note. I possess no information in regard to eventual conditions of peace beyond the note from the enemy which I read in the Chamber.

"Should propositions be made subsequently we should consider what to do, but it would be neither practical nor proper to discuss that question today. Moreover, it should be understood clearly that no one of the Entente Allies could take into consideration any condition whatever which by hypothesis might be eventually offered to him under separate form. In the public interest and out of respect to the Allied Governments, I cannot communicate to you anything whatever as to the substance of the answer we shall give to the note of the four enemy powers. The answer will be published as soon as it is drawn up.

"We all wish peace, and lasting peace. But we consider a lasting peace to be a careful settlement whose duration depends not on the solidarity, but on an exact balance among the states, based on respect for the principle of nationality, rules laid down in the laws of nations, and reasons of humanity and civilization.

"If we were in the presence of genuine proposals, with bases of a nature to satisfy the general postulates of civilization and justice which I have just mentioned, none would reject them abruptly. But there is nothing to show even faintly that this is the case, and there are many reasons for believing the contrary.

"I do not desire to use exaggerated language, but the accent of boastfulness

Continued on Page 3.

THRILLING SCENE IN HOUSE

Hall Caine Pictures the Tension as Lloyd George Rises to Speak.

KNEW WORLD WAS LISTENING

Premier's Swiftness of Wit and Power of Scorching Ridicule in Full Play.

ASQUITH WARMLY RECEIVED

Gets a Tumultuous Welcome as He Takes His Seat with the Opposition.

By HALL CAINE.

Special Cable to THE NEW YORK TIMES.

LONDON, Dec. 19.—A great and memorable scene! Even if the heavy duty and solemn responsibility, before God and humanity, of replying to the braggadocio of Germany's so-called offer of peace had not fallen on the new Prime Minister as the first official act of his Premiership, today's sitting of Parliament would have been almost without parallel in Parliamentary annals. I doubt if any of us yet know how far it will go. It may be the signal for the beginning of a new order which will completely alter the character of Parliament.

Meantime one thing is certain: if there is any remaining doubt in neutral nations that on the moral issues of the war the soul of our empire is on fire, if there is any lingering hope among our enemies that internal dissensions have weakened our will to win, today's scene must have dispersed such delusions; and if I am asked to say what it means, what its lesson and its message are, I answer in the language of the streets: "Get on with the war!"

The theatre of the event added little to its impressiveness. It must be admitted that as a mise-en-scène of a historic spectacle the British House of Commons is almost contemptible. One has usually to fill it with ghosts in order to make it effective—to see visions of Gladstone with his fiery eyes; Disraeli, with his apparently slumberous eyes; the shaggy head of Carlyle looking down from the gallery at the peepshow. Yet even as a spectacle today's event was not without its interest. Everybody was there. The galleries were full of peers, publicists, soldiers, and sailors. So crowded was the floor of the House that many of the members of Parliament, including one of the Ministers, the Labor Minister, had to find seats upstairs.

We had been led to expect sensational changes in the aspect of the House itself. Hardly anything of the kind was visible. With a few exceptions the members of the various parties were as far as was compatible with personal comfort in their accustomed places. A suggestion by the Speaker that, in obedience to the traditions of the House, the parties who act together should sit together met with a cool reception. One's first sight of the House gave the impression that Liberals and Unionists were sitting, if not side by side, at least in the same section. Why shouldn't they? There is no party question in Great Britain now.

Signs of Personal Feeling.

Some signs of personal feeling there certainly were. All the leading Ministers of the late administration, with one most notable exception, were on the front bench of the Opposition, none having taken office in the new Government. Why? Some had not been asked, others had declined. There was an uneasy feeling that the late Prime Minister had not been fairly treated; that both he and his oldest and most honored lieutenants had been the victims of a system of organized attack, which, though not countenanced by their former colleagues, had certainly not been condemned by them, and an attack conducted without scruple by what Mr. Asquith called omniscient amateurs and irresponsible slingers of mud, on the principle of bludgeoning a man's reputation morning and night in an arena he could not enter to defend it. There was also a suspicion of the deliberate betrayal by a hostile press of a Cabinet secret which, if faithfully kept, might have warded off a crisis which was dishonoring at home and dangerous abroad.

On the other hand, there was indignation at the insinuation of treachery on the part of a man on whose brows shame would be ashamed to sit; repudiation of the charge of organized conspiracy as so much organized hypocrisy; contempt of the notion that the betrayal of a Cabinet secret could ever do mischief without worse mischief being behind it—witness the betrayal of the Corn Law secret and the unnecessary resignation of Sir Robert Peel—and, finally, passionate conviction that the interests of the nation at a time of tragic urgency had been sacrificed to sloth and indecision, and that loyalty to party and fidelity to friends, however precious they might be, were as dust and ashes in the balance against the national welfare.

It was the old pathetic human story over again—the story of Essex and Bacon, of Burke and Fox—but today it was all kept under. On the surface there was nothing but unanimity of purpose on both sides of the House—how best to get on with the war.

Tumultuous Welcome for Asquith.

Mr. Asquith came in toward the close of question time, and had a tumultuous welcome. The fallen Minister—if I may so call him—was obviously moved by his reception as he passed to his place in the middle of the front opposition bench, between Mr. Samuel and Mr. McKenna. He bore himself with fortitude, composure, and even a certain cheerfulness; but I thought it was easy to see that, notwithstanding his subsequent protest, he had gone through a good deal. The last days had told on him. He is, as most of us know, a man of proud and perhaps shy reserve, schooled in self-restraint, yet with a deep well of feeling and an immense capacity for silent suffering.

He has known, as he said today in a moving passage, the full bitterness of suffering, both in public and private life. In the midst of the heaviest responsibilities that can rest on mortal man he suffered the most terrible loss that can befall a father—the loss of a brilliant son. None can know what that means except those who have gone through it.

Premier's Anomalous Position.

Look at Mr. Lloyd George in relation to the nation. It is a familiar fact that the Prime Minister is a person who has no legal existence. Lord Greville said that the title was an odious one; Lord North would never allow himself to be called by it. The House of Lords narrowly escaped condemning it as contrary to the spirit of the Constitution. We have the authority of Gladstone for saying that eight Ministers of the Crown have the right of precedence over the Prime Minister, though King Edward changed this by giving the Prime Minister the first place in the social order by royal warrant—next after the two Archbishops and the Lord Chancellor. It is a curious fact, which casts a sinister light on the events of the last fortnight, that the only right the Prime Minister appears to possess is the courtesy right of supervising the army and navy; and yet there remains the strange paradox that, while there is no such Minister as the Prime Minister, he is not only the first, but practically the sole, Minister of the Crown.

Lloyd George "Practically Dictator."

A French writer points out that the British race at almost every epoch have been dominated not by abstract ideas, but by the image of a man—some brave, assiduous citizen, who has embodied the virtues it likes best. At our general elections we select our man; the King sends for him and he becomes supreme. In the present case the country, without an election, has selected Lloyd George, and, with the King's consent, Mr. George has nominated so brilliant a company of Ministers that they may risk the proverbial fate of a Ministry of all the talents, but he has reserved to himself almost complete control over the one subject which matters.

Now, the members of his War Committee also are his nominees; they are his advisers. Two of them are without portfolios, and only one is in any degree under the control of Parliament. Therefore the new Prime Minister is practically dictator—dictator by the will of the people. Perhaps no subject of the British Crown has ever before occupied a position of so much power. Pitt's position at the end of the reign of George II. was not so powerful as that of Mr. Lloyd George at the beginning of the reign of George V., although in the middle of the war with France the great Commoner demanded control of the war and foreign offices and the leadership of the House of Commons, while our new Prime Minister has relinquished all of these.

The nation—our nation, the cradle of representative government—has voluntarily surrendered nearly all its powers for the time being to the brilliant, impetuous, adventurous spirit to whom it has committed the control of its destinies. Why? Because in these dark hours of national danger, when all our happiness, all our hopes, all our fortunes, all our lives, are in peril, the nation believes he is the one man capa-

Continued on Page 3.

No Faltering Till Victory, Lloyd George Cables Borden

Special to The New York Times.

OTTAWA, Ont., Dec. 19.—Sir Robert Borden has received the following cable from David Lloyd George on his accession to the Premiership:

"On taking up the high office with which his Majesty has charged me I send to you on behalf of the people of the Old Country a message to our brothers beyond the seas. There is no faltering in our determination that the sacrifices which we and you have made and have still to make shall not be in vain, and that the fight which we are waging together for humanity and civilization shall be fought to a triumphant issue. We realize that we shall still need every man that we can put in the field, every pound that rigid private and public economy can provide, and every effort which a united people can put forth to help in this heavy task of our soliders and sailors.

"The splendid contributions to the common cause already made by the Dominion give me sure confidence that their determination is no less high than ours, and that, however long the path to final victory, we shall tread it side by side."

FULL TEXT OF THE SPEECH

Premier Says the Swashbuckling in Europe's Streets Must End.

DAMAGES MUST BE EXACTED

And It Must Be Now, So That No Such Grim Inheritance Shall Be Left to "Our Children."

ALLIES TO REPLY QUICKLY

Declarations Made by France and Russia Approved in Speech That Stirs Commons.

David Lloyd George.

Special Cable to The New York Times.

LONDON, Tuesday, Dec. 19, 5:40 P. M.—David Lloyd George, Prime Minister, rose in the House of Commons at 4:10 o'clock this afternoon and said:

I shall have to claim the indulgence of the House in making the few observations that I have to make in moving the second reading of the Bill.

I appear before the House of Commons today with the most terrible responsibility that can fall upon the shoulders of any living man. As the chief Minister of the Crown, and in the midst of the most stupendous war in which this country ever has been engaged, a war upon which its destinies depend, the responsibilities which rest upon the Government have been accentuated by the declaration of the German Chancellor, and I propose to deal with that at once.

The statement made by him in the German Reichstag has been followed by a note presented to us by the United States Minister, without any note or comment. The answer which is given by the Government will be given in full accord with all our various allies. Already there has been an interchange of views, not upon the note itself, because it has only recently arrived, but upon the spirit which propelled the note. The note is only a paraphrase of the speech, so that the subject matter of the note itself has been discussed informally with the allies, and I am glad to be able to say that we arrived separately at identical conclusions.

I am very glad that the first answer was given to the German Chancellor by France and by Russia. They have unquestionably the right to give the first answer. The enemy is still on their soil and their sacrifices have been greater. The answer they have given has already appeared in all the papers, and I stand here today on behalf of the Government to give a clear and definite support to the statement they have already made. And here let me say that any man or set of men who wantonly and without sufficient cause prolongs a terrible conflict like this has on his soul a crime that oceans could not cleanse; on the other hand, a man or set of men who from a sense of war weariness abandoned the struggle without achieving the high purpose for which we entered upon it would be guilty of the most ghastly poltroonery ever perpetrated by any statesman.

Quotes Lincoln's Words.

I should like to quote the well-known words of Abraham Lincoln under similar conditions:

> We accepted the war for an object, a worthy object. The war will end when that object is attained. Under God I hope it will never end until that time.

Are we to achieve that object by accepting the invitations of the German Chancellor? That is the only question we have to put to ourselves.

There has been some talk about the proposals of peace. What are those proposals? There are none. To enter, on the invitation of Germany, proclaiming herself victorious, without any knowledge of the proposals she intends to make, into a conference, is putting our heads into a noose with the rope end in the hands of the Germans.

This country is not altogether without experience in these matters. It is not the first time we have fought a great military despotism, which was overshadowing Europe, and it will not be the first time we shall help to overthrow it. We have an uncomfortable historical memory of these things. We can recall how one of the greatest of these despots, having a purpose to serve in the organization of his nefarious scheme, appeared in the garb of the angel of peace. He usually appeared under two conditions—when he wished for time to assimilate conquest and reorganize for fresh advances; or, secondly, when his subjects showed symptoms of fatigue and war weariness. The appeal was always made in the name of humanity. He demanded an end of bloodshed, at which he professed himself to be horrified, but for which he himself was mainly responsible. Our ancestors were taken in and bitterly did they and Europe rue it. The time was devoted to reorganizing his forces for a deadlier attack than ever upon the liberties of Europe.

Stands by Asquith's Terms.

Examples of the kind cause us to regard this note with a considerable measure of reminiscent disquiet. We feel we ought to know before we give favorable consideration to such an invitation that Germany is prepared to accede to the only terms on which it is possible for peace to be obtained and maintained in Europe.

What are these terms? They have been repeatedly stated by all the leading statesmen of the Allies. All I can do is to quote what the leader of the House, Mr. Bonar Law, said last week when he made practically the same statement of terms as those put forward by Mr. Asquith—"restitution, reparation, guarantees against repetition."

So that there shall be no mistakes, (and it is important that there should be no mistake in a matter of the life and death of millions,) let me say complete restitution, full reparation and effectual guarantees.

Did the German Chancellor use a single phrase that would indicate that he was prepared to accept such terms? Was there a hint of restitution? Was there any suggestion of reparation? Was there any indication of any security for the future, that this outrage on civilization would not again be perpetrated at the first profitable opportunity?

The very substance and style of the speech constituted a denial of peace on the only terms on which peace is possible. He is not even conscious now that Germany has committed an offense against the rights of free nations. Listen to this quotation: "Not for an instant had they, (the Central Powers,) swerved from the conviction that a respect for the rights of free nations is in any degree incompatible with their own rights and legitimate interests." When did they discover that? Where was the respect for the rights of other nations in Belgium?

That, it is said, was for self-defense. Menaced, I suppose, by the overwhelming army of Belgium, the Germans were intimidated into invading Belgium, burning Belgian cities and villages, massacring thousands of inhabitants, old and young, carrying survivors into bondage—yea, carrying them into slavery at the very moment when the note was being written about the "unswerving conviction of the respect for the rights of other nations."

What guarantee is there that these terrors will not be repeated in the future? That if we enter into a treaty of peace, we shall put an end to Prussian militarism? If there is to be no reckoning for these atrocities by land and sea, are we to grasp the hand which perpetrated them without any reparation being made?

We have to exact damages. We have begun; already it has cost us much. We must exact it now, so as not to leave such a grim inheritance for our children.

Criticises Speech and Note.

Much as we all long for peace, deeply as we are horrified at the war, their note and speech give small encouragement to hope for an honorable and lasting peace. What hope is given in that speech? The whole root and cause of this bitterness—the arrogant spirit of the Prussian military caste—will it not be as dominant as ever if we patch up a peace now?

The very speech resounds with the boast of the Prussian military triumph; the very appeal for peace was delivered ostentatiously from the triumphal chariot of Prussian militarism.

We must keep a steadfast eye on the purpose for which we entered the war. Otherwise the great sacrifices we are making will be all in vain. The German note states that for the defense of their existence and for the freedom of national development, the Central Powers were constrained to take up arms. Such phrases cannot but deceive those who listen to them. They are intended to deceive the German nation into supporting the designs of the Prussian military caste.

Who ever wished to put an end to their national existence or to the freedom of their national development? We welcomed their development so long as it was on behalf of peace. The greater their development in that direction, the greater would humanity be enriched by that development.

That was not our design and it is not our purpose now. The Allies entered into this war to defend Europe against the aggression of Prussian military domination and they must insist that the end is a most complete and effective guarantee against the possibility of that caste ever again disturbing the peace of Europe.

Prussia, since she got into the hands of that caste, has been a bad neighbor—arrogant, threatening, bullying, shifting boundaries at her will, taking one fair field after another from weaker neighbors and adding them to her own dominions, ostentatiously pil-

"All the News That's Fit to Print."

The New York Times.

THE WEATHER
Snow or rain today; Friday colder, probably fair; shifting winds.
For full weather report see Page 19.

VOL. LXVI...NO. 21,516. NEW YORK, THURSDAY, DECEMBER 21, 1916.—TWENTY PAGES. ONE CENT In Greater New York, Jersey City and Newark. | Elsewhere, TWO CENTS.

PRESIDENT WILSON CALLS UPON ALL THE WARRING NATIONS TO STATE THE TERMS UPON WHICH THE WAR MAY BE ENDED; OUR INTERESTS, SERIOUSLY AFFECTED, MUST BE SAFEGUARDED

[illegible] HAILED IN CONGRESS

[illegible]icans and Democrats Alike Laud President's Peace Step.

[illegible] WELCOME SURPRISE

[illegible] Received in House, and [illegible] Think It Will Hasten the War's End.

[illegible] TIMELY, SAYS STONE

[illegible] of Foreign Relations [illegible] Believes the Notes Will Bring Results.

Special to The New York Times.

WASHINGTON, Dec. 20.—Senator [illegible] Missouri, Chairman of the [illegible] on Foreign Relations, unre[illegible] approves the President's move [illegible] the views of the belligerents [illegible].

"[illegible] most timely proffer," said the [illegible], "and I believe and hope [illegible] the beginning of the end. It [illegible] the question of continuing the [illegible] on the belligerents, and I [illegible] hope it will lead to negotia[illegible] and peace.

"[illegible] all events I trust that it will [illegible] result desired by the Presi[illegible] all peace-loving people. The [illegible] for the sending of the [illegible] is particularly [illegible], [illegible] in thinking of [illegible] Good Will to Men,' and I hope the spirit of Christmas will enter into the hearts of the belligerent nations. The President is to be heartily com[illegible] for his courage, and to be con[illegible] on having seized the logical [illegible] to urge the substitution of [illegible] for the carnage of the battle [illegible]."

[illegible] news of the transmission of the [illegible]'s message reached the Senate [illegible] this afternoon to permit gen[illegible] on the timeliness and [illegible] effect of the move. The Re[illegible] who were asked their opinion [illegible] refused to make any com[illegible] until they had had an opportunity [illegible] the messages more fully. [illegible] the few Democratic Senators [illegible] be reached at the Capitol, the [illegible] feeling seemed to be that the [illegible] was the best judge of the [illegible] of the move.

[illegible] would express any opinion for [illegible] about it, saying they were [illegible] willing to trust the President's [illegible] in the matter. It seemed to [illegible] felt, however, that the [illegible] would not have changed his [illegible] about interfering in the Euro[illegible] struggle unless he had received [illegible] evidence that such a move would [illegible] to all the belligerents at [illegible].

Caused Rejoicing in House.

The President's action caused general satisfaction and rejoicing in the House of Representatives. House members [illegible] heard of it through a representa[illegible] of The Times, who informed Mr. Kitchin, the majority leader, and mem[illegible] of the Foreign Affairs Committee of the President's action.

As soon as the news was conveyed to him Mr. Kitchin circulated among members of the lower body and transmitted the peace tidings. On every hand there were expressions of "fine," "a great move," and "good news."

These expressions came from both Republicans and Democrats and there was widespread commendation of the [illegible] that the time had arrived for a peace conference and a cessation of [illegible].

[illegible] the warring powers would ac[illegible] the President's suggestion in the [illegible] in which it was sent was the [illegible] opinion in the lower chamber. While no one could make a prediction of early peace, the consensus was that Mr. Wilson had acted wisely, courage[illegible] and opportunely.

Speaker Champ Clark expressed the hope several days ago that the Presi[illegible], following the overtures of Germany, would step in and offer the aid of the United States in bringing about a peace conference. When told of the President's action today, the Speaker [illegible]:

"I am exceedingly gratified that the President has taken this action. It will [illegible] in the re-establishment of peace. As I have said, the President has a [illegible] opportunity of service, and he is to be congratulated that he has com[illegible] with the belligerent powers [illegible] an end of the war."

[illegible] Republican Applause.

[illegible] Henry A. Cooper, rank[illegible] member of the Foreign Affairs Committee, made a gesture of [illegible] approval when informed of Mr. [illegible].

"[illegible]!" he exclaimed. "The [illegible] himself by [illegible] taken the initia[illegible] [illegible]

President Wilson's Note to the Belligerent Nations

The Secretary of State to the American Ambassadors at the Capitals of the Belligerent Powers:

DEPARTMENT OF STATE,
WASHINGTON, D. C., Dec. 18, 1916.

The President directs me to send you the following communication to be presented immediately to the Minister of Foreign Affairs of the Government to which you are accredited:

The President of the United States has instructed me to suggest to the [here is inserted a designation of the Government addressed] a course of action with regard to the present war, which he hopes that the Government will take under consideration as suggested in the most friendly spirit, and as coming not only from a friend but also as coming from the representative of a neutral nation whose interests have been most seriously affected by the war and whose concern for its early conclusion arises out of a manifest necessity to determine how best to safeguard those interests if the war is to continue.

[The third paragraph of the note as sent to the four Central Powers—Germany, Austria-Hungary, Turkey, and Bulgaria—is as follows:]

The suggestion which I am instructed to make the President has long had it in mind to offer. He is somewhat embarrassed to offer it at this particular time, because it may now seem to have been prompted by a desire to play a part in connection with the recent overtures of the Central Powers. It has, in fact, been in no way suggested by them in its origin, and the President would have delayed offering it until those overtures had been independently answered but for the fact that it also concerns the question of peace and may best be considered in connection with other proposals which have the same end in view. The President can only beg that his suggestion be considered entirely on its own merits and as if it had been made in other circumstances.

[The third paragraph of the note as sent to the ten Entente Allies—Great Britain, France, Italy, Japan, Russia, Belgium, Montenegro, Portugal, Rumania, and Serbia—is as follows:]

The suggestion which I am instructed to make the President has long had it in mind to offer. He is somewhat embarrassed to offer it at this particular time, because it may now seem to have been prompted by the recent overtures of the Central Powers. It is, in fact, in no way associated with them in its origin, and the President would have delayed offering it until those overtures had been answered but for the fact that it also concerns the question of peace and may best be considered in connection with other proposals which have the same end in view. The President can only beg that his suggestion be considered entirely on its own merits and as if it had been made in other circumstances.

[Thenceforward the note proceeds identically to all the powers, as follows:]

The President suggests that an early occasion be sought to call out from all the nations now at war such an avowal of their respective views as to the terms upon which the war might be concluded and the arrangements which would be deemed satisfactory as a guaranty against its renewal or the kindling of any similar conflict in the future as would make it possible frankly to compare them. He is indifferent as to the means taken to accomplish this. He would be happy himself to serve, or even to take the initiative in its accomplishment, in any way that might prove acceptable, but he has no desire to determine the method or the instrumentality. One way will be as acceptable to him as another, if only the great object he has in mind be attained.

He takes the liberty of calling attention to the fact that the objects, which the statesmen of the belligerents on both sides have in mind in this war, are virtually the same, as stated in general terms to their own people and to the world. Each side desires to make the rights and privileges of weak peoples and small States as secure against aggression or denial in the future as the rights and privileges of the great and powerful States now at war. Each wishes itself to be made secure in the future, along with all other nations and peoples, against the recurrence of wars like this and against aggression or selfish interference of any kind. Each would be jealous of the formation of any more rival leagues to preserve an uncertain balance of power amid multiplying suspicions; but each is ready to consider the formation of a league of nations to insure peace and justice throughout the world. Before that final step can be taken, however, each deems it necessary first to settle the issues of the present war upon terms which will certainly safeguard the independence, the territorial integrity, and the political and commercial freedom of the nations involved.

In the measures to be taken to secure the future peace of the world the people and Government of the United States are as vitally and as directly interested as the Governments now at war. Their interest, moreover, in the means to be adopted to relieve the smaller and weaker peoples of the world of the peril of wrong and violence is as quick and ardent as that of any other people or Government. They stand ready, and even eager, to co-operate in the accomplishment of these ends, when the war is over, with every influence and resource at their command. But the war must first be concluded. The terms upon which it is to be concluded they are not at liberty to suggest; but the President does feel that it is his right and his duty to point out their intimate interest in its conclusion, lest it should presently be too late to accomplish the greater things which lie beyond its conclusion, lest the situation of neutral nations, now exceedingly hard to endure, be rendered altogether intolerable, and lest, more than all, an injury be done civilization itself which can never be atoned for or repaired.

The President therefore feels altogether justified in suggesting an immediate opportunity for a comparison of views as to the terms which must precede those ultimate arrangements for the peace of the world, which all desire and in which the neutral nations as well as those at war are ready to play their full responsible part. If the contest must continue to proceed toward undefined ends by slow attrition until the one group of belligerents or the other is exhausted; if million after million of human lives must continue to be offered up until on the one side or the other there are no more to offer; if resentments must be kindled that can never cool and despairs engendered from which there can be no recovery, hopes of peace and of the willing concert of free peoples will be rendered vain and idle.

The life of the entire world has been profoundly affected. Every part of the great family of mankind has felt the burden and terror of this unprecedented contest of arms. No nation in the civilized world can be said in truth to stand outside its influence or to be safe against its disturbing effects. And yet the concrete objects for which it is being waged have never been definitively stated.

The leaders of the several belligerents have, as has been said, stated those objects in general terms. But, stated in general terms, they seem the same on both sides. Never yet have the authoritative spokesmen of either side avowed the precise objects which would, if attained, satisfy them and their people that the war had been fought out. The world has been left to conjecture what definitive results, what actual exchange of guaranties, what political or territorial changes or readjustments, what stage of military success, even, would bring the war to an end.

It may be that peace is nearer than we know; that the terms which the belligerents on the one side and on the other would deem it necessary to insist upon are not so irreconcilable as some have feared; that an interchange of views would clear the way at least for conference and make the permanent concord of the nations a hope of the immediate future, a concert of nations immediately practicable.

The President is not proposing peace; he is not even offering mediation. He is merely proposing that soundings be taken in order that we may learn, the neutral nations with the belligerent, how near the haven of peace may be for which all mankind longs with an intense and increasing longing. He believes that the spirit in which he speaks and the objects which he seeks will be understood by all concerned, and he confidently hopes for a response which will bring a new light into the affairs of the world.

LANSING.

[Copies of the above will be delivered to all neutral Governments for their information.]

STOCKS FALL AGAIN ON PEACE EFFORTS

Prices Break Violently with Heavy Liquidation in Industrials.

ADVANCE NEWS OF NOTE

Wall Street Knew Before Market Closed That President Was Addressing Belligerents.

The hurried liquidation of a large volume of speculative accounts in stocks, coupled with determined selling from professional sources, caused another sharp decline in the market yesterday.

The destructive influences behind values were cumulative. Bear drives followed one another in quick succession in the afternoon, assisted by various rumors regarding new developments in the peace plan. The most abrupt dip of the day followed the publication of a Washington dispatch, stating that hope was entertained in Administration circles that a way would yet be found to get the belligerents together for a conference. The nervousness of persons with market commitments on the long side was heightened by a report that President Wilson had already dispatched a note to the various nations offering the services of this country in an effort to work out acceptable peace terms. A report to this effect was printed on one of the Wall Street news tickers between 2 and 3 o'clock. It was during that hour that prices were weakest. The President's note, however, was not sent to the newspapers until 8 o'clock in the evening, and was not to be released for publication until after midnight.

The Street appeared to be more impressed than before that possibilities of negotiations between the Allies and the Teutonic Powers were to be considered as a market factor for some time to come. The readjustment expected to come with peace was an anxious subject of conversation in brokerage houses, and lent not a little to the success attained by the professionals in overturning quotations.

The trend of sentiment in the Street indicated that Premier Lloyd George's address to Parliament possessed, in the fuller reading of the newspapers, a more disturbing element for holders of stocks than was contained in Tuesday's brief dispatches. The International Mercantile Marine issues crumpled up on the information that a proposal to put all British shipping under Government supervision was being considered. Traders interpreted this as evidence that earnings of the big combination would be seriously affected, as most of the ships carry the English flag. Opening 2 points under Wednesday's closing figure, Marine preferred was hammered all day long, the brief rallies being merely signals for the bears to smash it again. The preferred dropped 16 points and the common 6 points, and at 80 the former stood 2 points under the total of accumulated dividends, in regard to which owners of the shares had long maintained fond hopes.

The retreat amounted to a rout in International Mercantile Marine, Steel, Central Leather, Crucible Steel, and several more of the recently popular issues, their losses for the day running from 4 to more than 14 points. Bethlehem Steel slumped 72 points in sales of no more than 800 shares. Bearish influences gathered force as the session progressed, and the close found gloom thick in commission houses, where a fortnight ago the prospects of greater and greater profits were bright for the bull side.

Steel Lower Than in Big Break.

Steel was pounded lower than it went in the big break of last Friday, under sales amounting to 423,000 shares, but the fate of this leading industrial was no worse than that of a large number of other issues. Whenever one of the war stocks looked as though it might display some degree of resiliency there was always somebody ready to hit it on the head. Again it was the industrials to suffer almost alone, as "good" buying was reported in Union Pacific and companion rails, and the list of carriers were affected only slightly. The day's turnover aggregated 1,018,600 shares.

In the accompanying table comparison is made with the lowest levels of last Friday, showing that the rails mentioned did not go through the minimum of that panicky day:

	Yest'y Low.	Low Dec. 15.	Yest'y Net Loss.
Anaconda	[illegible]	[illegible]	[illegible]
American Can	[illegible]	[illegible]	[illegible]
Baldwin Locomotive	[illegible]	[illegible]	[illegible]
Bethlehem Steel	600	[illegible]	[illegible]
Central Leather	[illegible]	[illegible]	[illegible]
Crucible Steel	[illegible]	[illegible]	[illegible]
Lackawanna Steel	[illegible]	[illegible]	[illegible]
Marine preferred	[illegible]	[illegible]	[illegible]
New York Central	[illegible]	[illegible]	[illegible]
Reading	[illegible]	[illegible]	[illegible]
Republic Iron & Steel	[illegible]	75	[illegible]
Union Pacific	146¼	143¼	[illegible]
U. S. Ind. Alcohol	106	104	[illegible]
U. S. Steel	[illegible]	[illegible]	[illegible]
Utah Copper	[illegible]	[illegible]	[illegible]

*Gain.

The same uncertainty over developments of the immediate future was reflected in dealings in the grain and cotton markets. Cotton started from $1.25 to $1.50 under the preceding night's closing levels, later moved upward part of the distance lost, and finally reacted sharply again. Wheat opened down and afterward shot forward 5 cents a bushel in the futures market. Uncertainty was the dominant note of all the markets when the business day ended, with the bears monopolizing what cheer there was discernible in speculative circles.

BRITAIN TO RUSH REPLY TO GERMANY

London Hears the Note, Now Nearly Framed, Will Be Sent by Saturday.

LIKELY TO LEAVE DOOR OPEN

Manchester Guardian Says Sentiment for Effort to End War Grows in the Army.

LONDON, Thursday, Dec. 21.—There is a strong probability that Great Britain's note in reply to the German peace proposal will be made before Christmas. This was the opinion in well-informed Government circles last night, where it is also believed the reply will be brief and likely will follow the lines of Mr. Lloyd George's maiden speech as Prime Minister in so far as it will leave the door open for Germany to make concrete peace proposals.

Great Britain's official reply to Germany, as prominent officials preferred to term it, will be dispatched simultaneously with that of her allies. Ever since the German note was handed to the Foreign Office by the American Ambassador it has been the subject of discussions between Premier Lloyd George and his Cabinet Council, which meets daily. The note and the nature of the reply also have been discussed with Great Britain's allies, and it is said that these conversations have progressed so rapidly that preliminary drafts have already been made.

It would, therefore, not be surprising if the Allies' replies were ready by the end of the week. Especially, it is said, would this be true in the case of Great Britain's note, which the Prime Minister is declared to be anxious to dispatch without delay.

When the terms of the note are definitely agreed upon and the document is signed by Lord Robert Cecil, who is Acting Foreign Secretary in the absence of Mr. Balfour, it may be handed to Ambassador Page with the request that he forward it to the State Department at Washington for transmission to Germany. This is said to be the most likely method, inasmuch as the United States represents the Allies' interests in Germany. It is just possible, however, that Great Britain may decide to dispatch the reply direct to the British Ambassador at Washington, with instructions to turn it over to the State Department.

MANY IN BRITAIN FOR PEACE.

Sentiment Strong in the Army, Says The Manchester Guardian.

Special Cable to The New York Times.

LONDON, Dec. 20.—It is recognized here as in America that "Lloyd George has not shut the door on peace with that resounding bang for which some of his less well-balanced supporters in the press were listening," to quote the words of The Manchester Guardian.

There is a reference in the same paper to a matter which for some time has been the subject of considerable private discussion, although for obvious reasons it has not been publicly ventilated in the press. The Guardian says:

"There is in this, as in all the countries at war, a great volume of opinion, too little vocal, unfortunately, in favor of a serious effort on the part of European statesmen to put an end to the carnage which is destroying a whole generation of young men who are not in a mood to fight on blindly, killing and being killed for the sake of fighting. They are fighting for a peace based on the reign of justice and law. This they will have, but they want none of the trappings of military glory. They know the cost of these in human blood and misery too well.

"This growing volume of opinion every Government in Europe must carry and to carry it must prove itself determined to neglect no opportunity of getting at the mind of the opponent. If the armies themselves could speak, this volume of opinion would be revealed as even greater and more set than it is in the homes for which those armies, one and all, are longing. These are the conditions of mind out of which peace must eventually come, and Lloyd George may yet prove himself on an immeasurably vaster field a master hand at reconciliation, that we in this country so well know him to be in our domestic strife."

Great Britain has set her teeth and will fight on, if fight she must, to attain the objects outlined by Lloyd George and his predecessor in office. But her citizen army is more than willing to lay down the weapons of war and take up the spade and plowshare and pon and other implements of peace if the war can be ended honorably and a secure peace won by negotiation.

In all the speeches yesterday there was not one word about the destruction of Germany except in way of negation. Lord Curzon, whose speech in the House of Lords was in some respects the most remarkable utterance of the day, eliciting high praise from every quarter, and being described by Lord Chaplin, who, as Henry Chaplin, had fifty years' experience of British oratory, as the best speech he ever heard, said:

"We are not fighting to destroy Germany. Such an idea never entered into the mind of any thinking human being in this country."

In the minds of many Englishmen, who know a good deal about the deeper and hidden currents that flow beneath the surface appearance of the war, one of the most important lessons to be learned from yesterday's debates was conveyed in references by Lloyd George and Asquith to "unity of action by the Allies." Readers of The New York Times have read what Lloyd George said on this question in full.

When the full story of the recent crisis comes to be told it will be found that one of the chief underlying reasons

Continued on Page 4.

MEDIATION TALK IN SCANDINAVIA

Berlin Gets Dutch Report of a Serious Peace Movement in the North.

HOLLAND ASKED TO JOIN

German Press Declines to Take Lloyd George's Speech Very Seriously.

BERLIN, Dec. 20, (by Wireless to Sayville.)—A peace movement is being considered by Norway, Sweden, Denmark, and Switzerland, in which they wish the co-operation of Holland, according to Deputy Schaper of the Dutch Parliament, as quoted in a dispatch to the Overseas News Agency from Rotterdam. The news agency says:

"According to telegrams from Rotterdam, Deputy Schaper of the Dutch Parliament, in a speech made at Dalfsel, announced that Switzerland and the Scandinavian countries were inclined to act as peace mediators, and that they wish the co-operation of Holland. Deputy Schaper advocated greater activity by Holland along this line."

DERIDES "REPARATION" TALK.

Berlin Paper Scoffs—Cologne Gazette Won't Take George Seriously.

AMSTERDAM, Dec. 20.—Commenting on Premier Lloyd George's speech, the Tägliche Rundschau of Berlin says:

"Reparation could be demanded by England only if Germany had declared war on England, if we were to blame for the war, if we had committed crimes against international law, and if we had been defeated."

The Lokal-Anzeiger takes the viewpoint that Mr. Lloyd George's remarks about reparation are of no value, inasmuch as nothing has been said thus far about peace conditions. This newspaper continues:

"If Lloyd George means to postpone satisfying Europe's desire for peace until the time when the Entente is successful in conquering Germany's armies and those of her allies, then the whole of Europe, as well as Lloyd George, knows full well that this announcement means eternal war, unless it is in the power of the German command to bring it to an earlier termination than Lloyd George supposes."

The Tageblatt says it prefers to await the promised reply of the Entente, adding:

"For the present it appears that the gulf is very great between Lloyd George's standpoint and that described from the German side as the basis for peace."

The following is from the Socialist newspaper Vorwärts:

"Lloyd George says that whoever wantonly prolongs the war will have a crime upon his soul. Do not these words imply strong self-condemnation if England rejects the negotiations offered by the Central Powers?"

The Cologne Gazette says:

"The language of the British Prime Minister must not be taken too seriously. We are taught this by some reflections on English peace conclusions in the past, such as that in which she lost the United States and the peace of Amiens in 1802. There is a limit where the blindest obstinacy finds itself confronted with the impossible, and this limit is being brought nearer and nearer by our submarines. Another possible contingency compelling England to make peace would be the secession of one of her allies."

GERMANS SENTENCE 20 BELGIANS TO DIE

11 Shot, 44 in Penal Servitude 64 Ordered Deported—Citizens Slain on Somme.

AMSTERDAM, Dec. 20, (via London.)—Of twenty Belgians who had been sentenced to death by a German court-martial at Hasselt, eleven were shot last Saturday, says the Maastricht les Nouvelles. Forty-four other persons were sentenced to various terms of penal servitude and sixty-four others ordered deported to Germany.

The newspaper adds that another court-martial was begun to hear the cases of 192 Belgians who were charged with espionage.

The frontier correspondent of the Amsterdam Telegraaf asserts that many citizens of Ghent who were deported to the Somme front were killed or very seriously wounded recently in a fight by French machine guns. The correspondent adds that a thousand men from Ghent are compelled to work on that front, and that 4,000 more are about to be sent there.

Les Nouvelles says a large number of young people from villages in the Belgian Province of Luxemburg have been deported from the Commune of Virton, among them children between the ages of 12 and 15 years. The correspondent adds that a large number of workmen were deported on Friday and Saturday from the Grand Duchy of Luxemburg, and that at Aix-la-Chapelle 800 Belgians are reported to be imprisoned.

DUTCH PRESS HOPEFUL.

Thinks Lloyd George Left Way Open for Peace Negotiations.

AMSTERDAM, Dec. 20.—The Socialist paper Het-Volk says with reference to Mr. Lloyd George's speech:

"The elements which could lead to negotiations are not lacking."

The Catholic Tijd is also hopeful that "Mr. Lloyd George's speech still leaves Germany the possibility of a reply." [illegible]

NOTES PREPARED ON MONDAY

And Forwarded to Belligerents and Neutrals Tuesday Morning.

IF THE WAR GOES ON

"It May Presently Be Too Late to Accomplish the Greater Things Which Lie Beyond."

FOR A PERMANENT CONCORD

In Which the United States Would Co-operate—Bernstorff Prohpesies a Conference.

Special to The New York Times.

WASHINGTON, Dec. 20.—President Wilson has called on all the belligerent [illegible] to state the terms which might serve as a basis for the restoration of peace.

The texts of the communications sent by the President's direction to each group of combatants were made public tonight, and created a sensation throughout official Washington, particularly in the European diplomatic [illegible].

"Now I am perfectly convinced there will be a conference," said Count von Bernstorff, the German Ambassador, when he learned the details of President Wilson's undertaking.

While the notes say that the President "would be happy himself to serve or even to take the initiative" to bring a statement of terms from the belligerents, they also assert that "the President is not proposing peace; he is not even offering mediation."

"He is merely proposing," [illegible] Secretary Lansing, whose name [illegible] signed to the notes, "that soundings [illegible] taken in order that we may learn, the neutral nations with the belligerent, how near the haven of peace may be [illegible] which all mankind longs with an intense and increasing longing."

There are two notes, one addressed to the Entente Governments and their smaller allies and the other to the Central Power group, led by Germany. Identical language is used in the communications except in one paragraph, where the changes are not material, except to the extent that the note to the Teutonic allies gives assurance to them that the President's course is not "prompted by a desire to play a part in connection with the recent overtures of the Central Powers."

Antedate Lloyd George's Speech.

Each note bears date of Monday, indicating that the communications were prepared before Mr. Lloyd George, the British Prime Minister, delivered his response in the House of Commons to the German peace offer. All were [illegible] on Tuesday morning.

The sensation created by the announcement of the President's action was accentuated by the general understanding that it had been determined by the President to take no hand in the [illegible] movement to end the war. Late Friday afternoon, following a meeting of the Cabinet, The New York Times correspondent was told by one of the highest officials that it had been decided that the German peace offer would be forwarded to the Entente Governments without comment from this Government. It was explained that this action was definite, but it was desirable that the press should not say that the Government had determined to take no part in the peace movement because the President was anxious that the impression should not be created that the United States had closed the door to participation in any effort to end the war. Circumstances might arise in the future, it was explained, that would make it desirable for this Government to [illegible] a peace movement.

The announcement this evening that President Wilson had addressed communications to all the belligerents calling upon them for "such an avowal of their respective views as to the terms upon which the war might be concluded" caused astonishment among those who had gained the impression that the United States would make no move toward peace at this time.

Action Long Contemplated.

What produced the apparent change of purpose on the part of the Government? According to an explanation obtained tonight from a thoroughly informed official, there was no change. The President, it was said, had had in mind [illegible] weeks the idea of taking the action embodied in the notes sent on Monday and made public tonight. His hesitation in the matter, it was explained, was due to uncertainty as to when would be a propitious time to transmit the communications.

The decision to forward the [illegible] peace offer without [illegible] application, it was [illegible] of the United States [illegible] day. That, it [illegible]

"All the News That's Fit to Print."

The New York Times.

THE WEATHER
Fair, cold today; Saturday probably snow, warmer; northwest winds.
For full weather report see Page 21.

VOL. LXVI...NO. 21,588. NEW YORK, FRIDAY, JANUARY 12, 1917.—TWENTY-TWO PAGES. ONE CENT In Greater New York, Jersey City and Newark. | Elsewhere, TWO CENTS.

TERRITORIES OVERRUN, EVEN IN THE PAST, TO BE RESTORED; EXPULSION OF THE TURK AND REORGANIZATION OF EUROPE; THESE, WITH INDEMNITIES, ARE THE ALLIES' TERMS OF PEACE

EXPLODING SHELLS RAIN FOUR HOURS; $5,000,000 LOSS

Last of Great Consignment to Russia Blows Up in Kingsland, N. J.

1,400 WORKERS ESCAPE

Projectiles Bombard the Countryside and Hundreds Flee in Terror to Frozen Marshes.

NO HINT OF A PLOT

Fire Believed to Have Started from a Spark — Falling Shell Wrecks an Auto.

Fire in the ammunition plant of the Canadian Car and Foundry Company, near Kingsland, N. J., yesterday afternoon destroyed the factory, with a loss estimated at $5,000,000, forced the evacuation of a large part of the town of Kingsland, making 1,000 people homeless for the time, and furnished a spectacle more magnificent than the munitions fire on Black Tom Island last September.

For four hours Northern New Jersey, New York City, Westchester, and the western end of Long Island listened to a bombardment that approximated the sound of a great battle—a bombardment in which probably half a million three-inch high explosive shells were discharged. Yet so far as the police and hospitals of all that section have been able to learn, not a single life was lost.

The reason for this is chiefly to be found in the fact that the shells, which were being loaded for the Russian Government, were not to be equipped with detonating fuses until they reached Russia. As fast as they were filled with trinitrotoluol they were set aside, point upward, in cases, like bottles. Consequently, as the flames reached each case of shells and exploded the propelling charges, the projectiles shot high into the air—oftentimes several hundred feet, but descending without the fuse, which alone could explode the charge, their fall was only that of so much metal. Even so, the fact that not one of the thousands of people in the neighborhood was hurt, so far as can be learned, was due principally to the prompt police measures in clearing out the houses in the endangered districts nearby.

Start an Investigation.

Kingsland, Rutherford and other places near by were filled last night with refugees, who had fled from their homes in the vicinity of the plant. A dozen persons were arrested at Kingsland on charges of larceny, and orders were issued by Sheriff Courter of Bergen County to the guards sent out by him in all directions to shoot looters.

The fire was still smouldering late last night in the ruins. Shells exploded almost continuously until 7:30 o'clock, but after that hour the detonations were intermittent.

Thomas J. Huckin, County Prosecutor, and his assistants began last night an investigation to fix responsibility for the disaster. It was said at the offices of the Canadian Car and Foundry Company that their inquiry had not been completed, and that no statement would be issued until today.

Captain William N. Offley of the United States Department of Justice, said he should not order an investigation into the cause of the explosion unless he received an intimation that it had been caused by some unlawful act. He will send a representative from his department over to Kingsland today to inquire into the circumstances.

Finishing $100,000,000 Contract.

The plant lies in the Jersey meadows, seven miles west of the Hudson and about a mile east of the edge of the hill on which lie the twin towns of Kingsland and Lyndhurst. The company was just finishing a contract of nearly $100,000,000 for the Russian Government, which had kept its plant busy for two y[illegible].

Thirty-[illegible] one and two story frame buildings, [illegible] with corrugated iron, had been erected in the meadows alongside the Lackawanna tracks, and three shifts of 1,400 workmen each, mostly negroes, were employed in filling the explosives purchased from powder companies into the shell cases, some of which were bought from the Bethlehem Steel Company and others manufactured by the Canadian Car and Foundry Company elsewhere. The contract was within two weeks of completion, and one of the shifts was laid off night before last. At work in the plant when the fire broke out were the 1,400 workmen, a considerable number of office employes, and 200 or 300 guards in olive-drab uniform, who have been patrolling the factory ever since its erection.

It was twenty minutes of four when a blaze broke out in the room in building No. 30, where ten or twelve men were at work cleaning the brass cases of the shells with denatured alcohol before the process of filling was begun. Somehow, from somewhere, a spark fell into a tub of the alcohol and set it

Continued on Page 4.

London Estimates Casualties of Germans at 4,010,160

LONDON, Jan. 11.—The total German casualties since the beginning of the war were placed at 4,010,160 in an official summary issued by the British Government today, which reads:

"A summary of the German casualties reported in official German casualty lists published during December gives a total of 89,291, which, added to those previously reported, brings the total German casualties to 4,010,160. The naval and colonial casualties are excluded."

THAW CUTS THROAT BUT WILL RECOVER

Tries to Die in a Philadelphia House Where, as 'Mr. West,' He Hid from New York Police.

DEBAUCH PRECEDED HIS ACT

Under Arrest in Hospital, He Will Be Brought Here to Face Charge of Whipping Boy.

Special to The New York Times.

PHILADELPHIA, Jan. 11.—Harry K. Thaw, slayer of Stanford White, added attempted suicide to his escapades today. Hunted down by detectives with a New York warrant that charged him with whipping Fred Gump, Jr., the nineteen-year-old schoolboy, and depressed by the effects of heavy drinking, he slashed his left wrist and throat with a razor this morning in a room where he was hiding in a little two-story brick boarding house run by Mrs. Elizabeth Tacot at 5,260 Walnut Street, West Philadelphia.

Thaw's wounds, while severe enough to make it probable that he actually attempted to end his life and was not simply courting sympathy because of the new ordeal he faced, will not cause death unless unexpected complications arise. He was taken to St. Mary's Hospital in the Kensington section, seven miles from the house. There several bichloride of mercury tablets were found in one of his pockets, but there was nothing in his condition shortly before midnight to indicate that he had swallowed any of them. He was very weak from loss of blood and was unable to make a statement. He is under arrest in the hospital, not on a charge of attempted suicide, but on the New York whipping charges.

With his attempt upon his life it developed that Thaw had been brooding over the suicide of Bernard W. Lewis, the young Pittsburgher who shot himself in Atlantic City when hunted down by the police, who wanted him in connection with the murder of Mrs. Grace Roberts in her apartment here. He had discussed the case with several persons, the last conversation being with Mrs. Jacot as late as 2 o'clock this morning. He had told her he thought Lewis was not guilty and had been "hounded into suicide."

Police May Have Been Deceived.

This latest spectacular act of Thaw's, the climax of a series of lesser escapades which have marked his life since he was adjudged sane in July, 1915, followed a clever game of hide-and-seek with the police of New York and Philadelphia which has been going on since 4 o'clock Tuesday morning. At that time Thaw was apparently warned by telephone that a warrant for his arrest had been sent from New York, and that his capture was imminent.

In this contest of wits the police believe Thaw got aid from Oliver C. Browler of Cincinnati, now under arrest here, and operatives of the O'Farrell Detective Agency of New York. It is even probable that some one took steps to deceive the police about Thaw's whereabouts at different times since his indictment by having it reported that he was in one place when he was miles away.

Samuel G. Maloney of the detective agency notified Captain of Detectives Tate this morning that Thaw was in the house in West Philadelphia. He strolled into the Chief's office and asked if Thaw was wanted, and supplemented this by the assertion that he was prepared to put the police on his trail. At the same time he gave the information that Thaw had wounded himself, he did not know how seriously.

Indications tonight were that Thaw would have to remain in the hospital for several days before it is possible to remove him to New York to face the charges in the indictment. His mother has been notified and is expected here soon.

Thaw is at present under the direct medical care of Dr. Ellwood J. Kirby, Medical Superintendent of St. Mary's Hospital, who has taken a kindly interest in his affairs for years. Thaw was taken to this hospital, so many miles further from the West Philadelphia house than other hospitals, at his own request. He has a large room on the second floor, and every possible comfort has been provided for him. Six detectives, however, were detailed by Chief Tate to keep a constant watch on him. Two of them always are in his room.

Turned from Philadelphia Hotel.

Thaw's actions in Philadelphia during the forty-eight hours preceding his disappearance caused no little comment among the frequenters of cafés and hotels. He was "hitting a pace," to quote one observer, drinking heavily and entering into gay night parties with several men friends. Early Tuesday morn-

Continued on Page 22.

LLOYD GEORGE SPEAKS AGAIN

Full Text of Guildhall Address Predicting Victory in "Next Few Months."

ASKS FOR A BIG LOAN

Reminds Hearers That the Conflict is "a War of Equipment" and Cites Rumania's Plight.

FIGHTING FOR A REAL PEACE

It Must Be Founded "on the Rock of Vindicated Justice" —Pleads for Self-Denial.

Special Cable to THE NEW YORK TIMES.

LONDON, Jan. 11.—In a forty-five-minute speech at this afternoon's meeting at the Guildhall to launch the new British loan, Premier Lloyd George said that the Allies, having received from the Central Powers, not a peace offer but "a trap baited with fine words," could not be charged with having rejected peace terms; that they demanded a real peace, and, after the Rome conference, were satisfied that, though its achievement might be difficult, defeat was impossible. With the financial backing which the Government sought from the projected loan, he said the armies of the Entente would "cleave a road to victory" in the next few months. The Premier's speech, which was enthusiastically received, was as follows:

"My Lord Mayor, my Lords, Ladies, and Gentlemen: The Chancellor of the Exchequer in his extremely lucid and impressive speech has placed before you the business side of this proposal, and I think you will agree with me, after hearing his explanation of his scheme, that he has offered for subscription a loan which possesses all the essential ingredients of an attractive investment. They are the most generous terms that the Government can offer without injury to the taxpayer. I agree that the Chancellor was right in offering such liberal terms because it is important that we should secure a big loan now, not merely in order to enable us to finance the war effectively, but as a demonstration of the continued resolve of this country to prosecute the war; [loud cheers;] and it is upon that aspect of the question that I should like to say a few words.

"The German Kaiser a few days ago sent a message to his people that the Allies had rejected his peace offers. He did so in order to drug those whom he could no longer dragoon. [Laughter and cheers.] Where are those offers? We have asked for them; we have never seen them. We were not offered terms; we were offered a trap baited with fair words. They tempted us once, but the lion has his eyes open. [Loud cheers.] We have rejected no terms that we have ever seen. Of course, it would suit them to have peace at the present moment on their terms. We all want peace; but when we get it it must be a real peace. [Cheers.]

War Better Than a Prussian Peace.

"The allied powers separately and in council together have come to the same conclusion. [Cheers.] Knowing well what war means, knowing especially what this war means in suffering, in burdens, in horrors, they have still decided that even war is better than peace at the Prussian price of domination over Europe. We made it clear in our reply to Germany; we made it still clearer in our reply to the United States.

"Before we attempt to rebuild the Temple of Peace we must see now that the foundations are solid. They were built before upon the shifting sands of Prussian faith; henceforth, when the time for rebuilding comes, it must be on the rock of vindicated justice. [Applause.]

"I have just returned from a council of war of the four great allied countries upon whose shoulders most of this terrible war falls. I cannot give you its conclusions; [laughter;] they might be information to the enemy. [Renewed laughter.] There were no delusions a to the magnitude of our task; neither were there any doubts about the results.

"Victory Difficult, Defeat Impossible."

"I think I can say what was the feeling of every man there. It was one of the most businesslike conferences I ever attended. We faced the whole situation, probed it thoroughly, and looked its difficulties in the face, and made arrangements to deal with them. [Laughter and applause.] We separated feeling more confident than ever. [Renewed applause.] All felt that if victory were difficult, defeat was impossible. [Applause.] There was no flinching, no wavering, no faint-heartedness, no infirmity of purpose.

"There was a grim resolution at all costs that we must achieve the high aim with which we accepted the challenge of the Prussian military caste and rid Europe and the world forever of her men-

Continued on Page 3.

Mercier Says Belgians Want Peace with Victory

PARIS, Jan. 11.—Cardinal Mercier, in a private letter printed in La Croix, the official church organ, declares that if the truth were known about Belgium neutral nations would not confine themselves to words. The Belgian Cardinal declares that Belgium is now suffering as never before. He writes:

"We are all prisoners here, but if the neutrals knew of the treatment inflicted on us, I do not believe that they would confine themselves to verbal remonstrances. If they did, we should have to despair of fraternal charity and humanity."

The Cardinal adds, in a postscript, that although the Belgians are depressed, they are by no means discouraged and few want peace without victory.

WAR AIMS WON, GERMANY ASSERTS

Tells Neutrals She Fought for Liberty and Existence, and These Are Obtained.

ISSUES INDEPENDENT NOTE

Assails Entente Powers as Seeking Conquest and Blocking Road to Peace.

BERLIN, Jan. 11, (by Wireless to Sayville.)—Germany today handed to the neutral Governments a note concerning the reply of the Entente to the German peace proposals, the Overseas News Agency announces.

It is first stated, says the news agency announcement, that the German Government has received the reply of the Entente to the note of Dec. 12 containing a proposition to enter at once into peace negotiations. The note then continues:

"Our adversaries declined this proposition, giving as the reason that it is a proposition without sincerity and without importance. The form in which they clothe their communication excludes an answer to them, but the Imperial Government considers it important to point out to the Governments of neutral powers its opinion regarding the situation.

"The Central Powers have no reason to enter into any discussion regarding the origin of the world war. History will judge upon whom the immense guilt of the war shall fall. History's verdict will as little pass over the encircling policy of England, the revengeful policy of France, and the endeavor of Russia to gain Constantinople as over the instigation of the Serbian assassination in Sarayevo and the complete mobilization of Russia, which meant war against Germany.

"Germany and her allies, who had to take up arms for defense of their liberty and their existence, consider this, their aim of war, as obtained.

"On the other hand, the hostile powers always went further away from the realization of their plans, which, according to the declarations of their responsible statesmen, were, among others, directed toward the conquest of Alsace-Lorraine and several Prussian provinces, the humiliation and diminution of the Austro-Hungarian monarchy, the partition of Turkey, and the mutilation of Bulgaria. In the face of such war aims, the demand for restitution, reparation, and guarantee in the mouth of our adversaries produces a surprising effect.

Resents Insincerity Charge.

"Our adversaries call the proposal of the four allied (Teutonic) powers a war manoeuvre. Germany and her allies must protest in the most energetic fashion against such a characterization of their motives, which were frankly explained. They were persuaded that a peace which was just and acceptable to all the belligerents was possible; that it could be brought about by an immediate spoken exchange of views, and that therefore the responsibility for further bloodshed could not be taken. Their readiness was affirmed without reservation to make known their peace conditions when negotiations were entered into, which refutes every doubt as to their sincerity.

"Our adversaries, who had it in their hands to examine the proposition as to its contents, neither attempted an examination nor made counter-proposals. Instead, they declared that peace was impossible so long as the re-establishment of violated rights and liberties, the recognition of the principle of nationalities, and the free existence of small States were not guaranteed.

"The sincerity which our adversary denies to the proposals of the four allied powers will not be conceded by the world to these demands, if the world holds before its eyes the fate of the Irish people, the destruction of the liberty and independence of the Boer Republic, the subjugation of Northern Africa by England, France, and Italy, the suppression of Russian alien nations, and also the violation of Greece, which is without precedent in history.

Accuses Foes of Lawlessness.

"Against the pretended violations of the laws of nations by the four allies, (Teutonic,) those powers are not entitled to complain, which from the beginning of the war trampled on justice and tore to pieces the treaties upon which it is built. England already during the first weeks of the war had repudiated the London Declaration, the content of which had been recognized by its own delegates as a valid law of nations, and in the further course of the war violated in the most severe fashion also the Paris Declaration, so that, by

Continued on Page 2.

Text of Allies' Reply to Wilson

Ambassador Sharp to the Secretary of State:
(Telegram No. 1,806.)

AMERICAN EMBASSY,
Paris, Jan. 10, 1917.

The following is the translation of the French note:

The allied Governments have received the note which was delivered to them in the name of the Government of the United States on the 19th of December, 1916. They have studied it with the care imposed upon them both by the exact realization which they have of the gravity of the hour and by the sincere friendship which attaches them to the American people.

In a general way they wish to declare that they pay tribute to the elevation of the sentiment with which the American note is inspired and that they associate themselves, with all their hopes, with the project for the creation of a league of nations to insure peace and justice throughout the world. They recognize all the advantages for the cause of humanity and civilization which the institution of international agreements, destined to avoid violent conflicts between nations would prevent—agreements which must imply the sanctions necessary to insure their execution, and thus to prevent an apparent security from only facilitating new aggressions.

But a discussion of future arrangements destined to insure an enduring peace presupposes a satisfactory settlement of the actual conflict. The Allies have as profound a desire as the Government of the United States to terminate as soon as possible a war for which the Central Empires are responsible and which inflicts such cruel sufferings upon humanity. But they believe that it is impossible at the present moment to attain a peace which will assure them reparation, restitution, and such guarantees to which they are entitled by the aggression for which the responsibility rests with the Central Powers, and of which the principle itself tended to ruin the security of Europe—a peace which would, on the other hand, permit the establishment of the future of European nations on a solid basis. The allied nations are conscious that they are not fighting for selfish interests, but, above all, to safeguard the independence of peoples, of right, and of humanity.

The Allies are fully aware of the losses and suffering which the war causes to neutrals as well as to belligerents, and they deplore them, but they do not hold themselves responsible for them, having in no way either willed or provoked this war; and they strive to reduce these damages in the measure compatible with the inexorable exigencies of their defense against the violence and the wiles of the enemy.

It is with satisfaction, therefore, that they take note of the declaration that the American communication is in nowise associated in its origin with that of the Central Powers transmitted on the 18th of December by the Government of the United States. They did not doubt, moreover, the resolution of that Government to avoid even the appearance of a support, even moral, of the authors responsible for the war.

The allied Governments believe that they must protest in the most friendly but in the most specific manner against the assimilation, established in the American note, between the two groups of belligerents; this assimilation, based upon public declarations by the Central Powers, is in direct opposition to the evidence, both as regards responsibility for the past and as concerns guarantees for the future; President Wilson, in mentioning it, certainly had no intention of associating himself with it.

If there is a historical fact established at the present date, it is the willful aggression of Germany and Austria-Hungary to insure their hegemony over Europe and their economic domination over the world. Germany proved by her declaration of war, by the immediate violation of Belgium and Luxemburg, and by her manner of conducting the war her simulating contempt for all principles of humanity and all respect for small States. As the conflict developed, the attitude of the Central Powers and their allies has been a continual defiance of humanity and civilization.

Is it necessary to recall the horrors which accompanied the invasion of Belgium and of Serbia, the atrocious régime imposed upon the invaded countries, the massacre of hundreds of thousands of inoffensive Armenians, the barbarities perpetrated against the populations of Syria, the raids of Zeppelins on open towns, the destruction by submarines of passenger steamers and of merchantmen even under neutral flags, the cruel treatment inflicted upon prisoners of war, the juridical murders of Miss Cavell, of Captain Fryatt, the deportation and the reduction to slavery of civil populations, et cetera? The execution of such a series of crimes, perpetrated without any regard for universal reprobation, fully explains to President Wilson the protest of the Allies.

They consider that the note which they sent to the United States in reply to the German note will be a response to the questions put by the American Government, and, according to the exact words of the latter, "constitute a public declaration as to the conditions upon which the war could be terminated."

President Wilson desires more: he desires that the belligerent powers openly affirm the objects which they seek by continuing the war; the Allies experience no difficulty in replying to this request. Their objects in the war are well known; they have been formulated on many occasions by the chiefs of their divers Governments. Their objects will not be made known in detail with all the equitable compensation and indemnities for damages suffered until the hour of negotiations. But the civilized world knows that they imply, in all necessity and in the first instance, the restoration of Belgium, of Serbia, and of Montenegro, and the indemnities which are due them; the evacuation of the invaded territories of France, of Russia, and of Rumania, with just reparation; the reorganization of Europe, guaranteed by a stable régime and founded as much upon respect of nationalities and full security and liberty of economic development, which all nations, great or small, possess, as upon territorial conventions and international agreements, suitable to guarantee territorial and maritime frontiers against unjustified attacks; the restitution of provinces or territories wrested in the past from the Allies by force or against the will of their populations; the liberation of Italians, of Slavs, of Rumanians, and of Tcheco-Slovaques from foreign domination; the enfranchisement of populations subject to the bloody tyranny of the Turks; the expulsion from Europe of the Ottoman Empire, decidedly alien to Western civilization. The intentions of his Majesty, the Emperor of Russia, regarding Poland have been clearly indicated in the proclamation which he has just addressed to his armies.

It goes without saying that if the Allies wish to liberate Europe from the brutal covetousness of Prussian militarism it never has been their design, as has been alleged, to encompass the extermination of the German peoples and their political disappearance. That which they desire above all is to insure a peace upon the principles of liberty and justice, upon the inviolable fidelity to international obligations with which the Government of the United States has never ceased to be inspired.

United in the pursuit of this supreme object, the Allies are determined, individually and collectively, to act with all their power and to consent to all sacrifices to bring to a victorious close a conflict upon which, they are convinced, not only their own safety and prosperity depend, but also the future of civilization itself. SHARP.

Belgium's Separate Reply to the President.

Ambassador Sharp to the Secretary of State:
(Telegram.)

AMERICAN EMBASSY,
Paris, Jan. 10, 1917.

Copy of Belgian note as follows:

The Government of the King, which has associated itself with the answer handed by the President of the French Council to the American Ambassador on behalf of all, is particularly desirous of paying tribute to the sentiment of humanity which prompted the President of the United States to send his note to the belligerent powers, and it highly esteems the friendship expressed for Belgium through his kindly intermediation. It desires as much as Mr. Woodrow Wilson to see the present war ended as early as possible.

But the President seems to believe that the statesmen of the two opposing camps pursue the same object of war. The example of Belgium unfortunately demonstrates that this is in no wise the fact. Belgium has never, like the Central Powers, aimed at conquest. The barbarous fashion in which the German Government has treated, and is still treating, the Belgian nation does not permit the supposition that Germany will preoccupy herself with guaranteeing in the future the rights of the weak nations, which she has not ceased to trample under foot since the war, let loose by her, began to desolate Europe.

On the other hand, the Government of the King has noted with pleasure and with confidence the assurances that the United States is impatient to co-operate in the measures which will be taken after the conclusion of peace to protect and guarantee the small nations against violence and oppression.

Previous to the German ultimatum, Belgium only aspired to live upon good terms with all her neighbors. She practiced with scrupulous loyalty toward each one of them the duties imposed by her neutrality. In the same manner she has been rewarded by Germany for the confidence she placed in her, through which, from one day to the other, without any plausible reason, her neutrality was violated, and the Chancellor of the Empire, when announcing to the Reichstag this violation of right and of treaties, was obliged to recognise the iniquity of such an act and predetermine that it would be repaired.

But the Germans, after the occupation of Belgian territory, have displayed no better observance of the rules of international law or the stipulations of The Hague Convention. They have, by taxation as heavy as it is arbitrary, drained the resources of the country; they have intentionally ruined its industries, destroyed whole cities, put to death and imprisoned a considerable number of inhabitants. Even now, while they are loudly proclaiming their desire to put an end to the horrors of war, they increase the rigors of the occupation by deporting into servitude Belgian workers by the thousands.

If there is a country which has the right to say that it has taken up arms to defend its existence, it is assuredly Belgium. Compelled to fight or to submit to shame, she passionately desires that an end be brought to the unprecedented sufferings of her population. But she could only accept a peace which would assure her, as well as equitable reparation, security and guarantees for the future.

The American people, since the beginning of the war, has manifested for the oppressed Belgian nation most ardent sympathy. It is an American committee, the Commission for Relief in Belgium, which, in close union with the Government of the King and the National Committee, displays an untiring devotion and marvelous activity in revictualing Belgium. The Government of the King is happy to avail itself of this opportunity to express its profound gratitude to the Commission for Relief as well as to the generous Americans eager to relieve the misery of the Belgian population. Finally, nowhere more than in the United States have the abductions and deportations of Belgian civilians provoked such a spontaneous movement of protestation and indignant reproof.

These facts, entirely to the honor of the American Nation, allow the Government of the King to entertain the legitimate hope that at the time of the definitive settlement of this long war the voice of the Entente Powers will find in the United States a unanimous echo to claim in favor of the Belgian nation, innocent victim of German ambition and covetousness, the rank and the place which its irreproachable past, the valor of its soldiers, its fidelity to honor, and its remarkable faculties for work assign to it among the civilized nations. SHARP.

NO AIM TO CRUSH GERMANY

Frank and Friendly Tone of Reply to President Pleases Capital.

WILSON'S COURSE IN DOUBT

But Unofficial Washington Thinks the Document Closes Door to Peace at Present.

BERLIN LIKELY TO ANSWER

One Forecast Says Teutons' Terms Will Be Made Known, Insuring Continuance of War.

Special to The New York Times.

WASHINGTON, Jan. 11.—The State Department this evening gave out for publication the reply of the Entente Governments to President Wilson's note of Dec. 18, addressed to the belligerent nations, in which he suggested that they state the objects for which they were fighting and indicate the terms upon which they would be willing to undertake an adjustment of the war.

Unlike the Central Powers group, the Entente Allies do not stand on the technicality that the President merely suggested that a modus be provided for ascertaining what the President desires. Instead they outline their terms and show in general a disposition to respond frankly and specifically to the request of the President. The reply expressly states that the Allies will not make known their war objects in detail until "the hour of negotiation," but it adds that these objects "imply in all necessity in the first instance" certain terms. These may be summarized as follows:

- Restoration of Belgium, Serbia, Montenegro, with indemnities.
- Evacuation of invaded territories of France, Russia, and Rumania, with reparation.
- Reorganization of Europe under guarantees to insure to all nations respect and liberty of development.
- Restitution of territories wrested in the past from the Allies by force or against people's will.
- Liberation of Italians, Slavs, Rumanians, and Tcheco-Slovaks from foreign domination.
- Enfranchisement of populations subject to the Turks.
- Expulsion from Europe of the Ottoman Empire.

To these terms the Allies add that Russia has already clearly indicated her intentions toward Poland, and that if the Allies wish to free Europe from Prussian militarism, it has never been their design to "encompass the extermination of the German people and their political disappearance."

Frankness Pleases Officials.

On account of the frankness of the Entente reply it has created an excellent impression in high official quarters, where the Allies' attitude is construed as a hopeful sign for further exchanges between the belligerents and the United States. It should be understood, however, that this sentiment is not to be taken as an expression of the Administration view. There is no Administration view so far. That depends on the interpretation placed by President Wilson on the Entente reply. It should be understood also that opinion in official circles is not unanimous as to the meaning and effect of the Entente note. While officials were cautious in expressing themselves, no doubt is felt that some of them agree with a rather general unofficial view that the Allies have closed the door to peace at this time.

This unofficial view is shared at the German Embassy, where the answer of the Entente is, if expressions heard there this evening represent the real feeling, a real disappointment. But the Embassy finds a grain of comfort in the thought that the Entente's attitude will arouse the allies of Germany and make them more than ever determined to fight to a finish. The German idea is that while the people of Germany may take note of the assurance of the Entente that "it has never been their design to encompass the extermination of the German peoples and their political disappearance," the nations allied with Germany will find in the note the expression of a purpose to cause their territorial and political disintegration, and this will impel them to fight harder.

As to whether the Entente rejection of the peace offer of the Central Powers will cause Germany to undertake reprisals with her submarine craft, the flat statement was made in German circles that Germany would live up to her pledges given to the United State[s] in the Sussex case. At the same time [it] was pointed out that Germany has rea[son] to believe that Great Britain w[as] arming merchant vessels for offensi[ve] action, and this might cause the Berlin Government to take its own measures to meet such a situation. The German Government, it was said, had never denied the principle asserted by the United States that merchant vessels had the right to arm for defensive purposes and, in fact, had no [illegible]

"All the News That's Fit to Print."

The New York Times.

THE WEATHER
Rain Thursday; fair, cold wave by night Friday.
For full weather report see Page 21.

VOL. LXVI...NO. 21,558. NEW YORK, THURSDAY, FEBRUARY 1, 1917.—TWENTY-TWO PAGES. ONE CENT In Greater New York, Jersey City and Newark. | Elsewhere, TWO CENTS.

GERMANY BEGINS RUTHLESS SEA WARFARE; DRAWS 'BARRED ZONES' AROUND THE ALLIES; CRISIS CONFRONTS THE UNITED STATES

THIS PORT CLOSED

Collector Malone Stops All Outgoing Ships at Narrows.

GERMAN SHIPS SEARCHED

No Evidence of Unusual Activity on Vessels at Hoboken.

GUARD SET ON THIS SIDE

Police Ordered Out at Midnight to Keep Watch Over Ships Off 130th Street.

ANXIOUS FOR SHIPS AT SEA

Shipping Men in This and Other Ports Fear for Them in Blockade.

[illegible] Off to Washington

Colonel E. M. House left hurriedly for Washington on the Pennsylvania Railroad at 12:30 o'clock this morning. He entered the station through a private stairway and secluded himself in the car before the train was opened to the general traveling public.

The Port of New York was sealed tight last night by order of Dudley Field Malone, Collector of the Port. Vessels of every description, including tugboats, were turned back at Quarantine by the torpedo boat stationed there to maintain the neutrality of the United States.

The purpose of Mr. Malone's order remained a mystery upon which he declined to throw any light. He has full authority to act upon his own initiative in case of emergency, as he is held responsible for enforcing neutrality.

Even naval officers are under orders to take instructions from Mr. Malone in all matters affecting the neutrality of New York.

Rumors that the crews of the German ships interned at Hoboken would attempt to scuttle the vessels and destroy the machinery in the event of war, sprang up everywhere last evening as soon as the German note was made public. Collector Malone called up Chief of Police Patrick Hayes of Hoboken, who was attending the annual patrolmen's ball, and the Chief, with half a dozen plain-clothes men, left the dance and hurried down to the piers to reinforce the eleven men of the Neutrality Squad on guard there. Deputy Collector George F. Lamb was present.

A thorough search made by the neutrality guards under Roundsman Miles disclosed no evidence of any preparations to justify the rumors. The Hamburg-American and North German Lloyd liners have been tied up at the piers for two years and a half, during which time there has been no opportunity to dredge out the slips, so it was said that they were practically lying in the mud, and that scuttling them would be rather pointless.

As to the possibility of an attempt to escape from the harbor, it was said that none of the ships had enough coal to last for more than a single day's steaming, at the end of which period they must inevitably be captured, even if they could pass the destroyers on guard at the Narrows. The Vaterland has more coal than any of the others, but in her case it was said that most of the officers of the interned liners have been living on board of her and that the coal was needed to get up steam for heating and lighting.

Watch Put on German Ships Here.

At midnight Police Inspector Thomas Ryan of the Sixth Inspection District, including the district between 110th Street and Spuyten Duyvil and West of Fifth Avenue, received orders to keep in reserve all men who were about to go off duty at that hour. Twenty

Continued on Page 2.

Text of Germany's Note to the United States

Washington, D. C., Jan. 31, 1917.

Mr. Secretary of State:

Your Excellency was good enough to transmit to the Imperial Government a copy of the message which the President of the United States of America addressed to the Senate on the 22d inst. The Imperial Government has given it the earnest consideration which the President's statements deserve, inspired, as they are, by a deep sentiment of responsibility.

It is highly gratifying to the Imperial Government to ascertain that the main tendencies of this important statement correspond largely to the desires and principles professed by Germany. These principles especially include self-government and equality of rights for all nations. Germany would be sincerely glad if in recognition of this principle countries like Ireland and India, which do not enjoy the benefits of political independence, should now obtain their freedom.

The German people also repudiate all alliances which serve to force the countries into a competition for might and to involve them in a net of selfish intrigues. On the other hand, Germany will gladly co-operate in all efforts to prevent future wars.

The freedom of the seas, being a preliminary condition of the free existence of nations and the peaceful intercourse between them, as well as the open-door for the commerce of all nations, has always formed part of the leading principles of Germany's political program. All the more the Imperial Government regrets that the attitude of her enemies, who are so entirely opposed to peace, makes it impossible for the world at present to bring about the realization of these lofty ideals.

Germany and her allies were ready to enter now into a discussion of peace, and had set down as basis the guarantee of existence, honor, and free development of their peoples. Their aims, as has been expressly stated in the note of Dec. 12, 1916, were not directed toward the destruction or annihilation of their enemies and were, according to their conviction, perfectly compatible with the rights of the other nations. As to Belgium, for which such warm and cordial sympathy is felt in the United States, the Chancellor had declared only a few weeks previously that its annexation had never formed part of Germany's intentions. The peace to be signed with Belgium was to provide for such conditions in that country, with which Germany desires to maintain friendly neighborly relations, that Belgium should not be used again by Germany's enemies for the purpose of instigating continuous hostile intrigues. Such precautionary measures are all the more necessary, as Germany's enemies have repeatedly stated, not only in speeches delivered by their leading men, but also in the statutes of the Economical Conference in Paris, that it is their intention not to treat Germany as an equal, even after peace has been restored, but to continue their hostile attitude, and especially to wage a systematical economic war against her.

The attempt of the four allied powers to bring about peace has failed, owing to the lust of conquest of their enemies, who desired to dictate the conditions of peace. Under the pretense of following the principle of nationality, our enemies have disclosed their real aims in this way, viz.: To dismember and dishonor Germany, Austria-Hungary, Turkey, and Bulgaria. To the wish of reconciliation they oppose the will of destruction. They desire a fight to the bitter end.

A new situation has thus been created which forces Germany to new decisions. Since two years and a half England is using her naval power for a criminal attempt to force Germany into submission by starvation. In brutal contempt of international law, the group of powers led by England does not only curtail the legitimate trade of their opponents, but they also, by ruthless pressure, compel neutral countries either to altogether forego every trade not agreeable to the Entente Powers or to limit it according to their arbitrary decrees.

The American Government knows the steps which have been taken to cause England and her Allies to return to the rules of international law and to respect the freedom of the seas. The English Government, however, insists upon continuing its war of starvation, which does not at all affect the military power of its opponents, but compels women and children, the sick and the aged, to suffer for their country pains and privations which endanger the vitality of the nation. Thus British tyranny mercilessly increases the sufferings of the world, indifferent to the laws of humanity, indifferent to the protests of the neutrals whom they severely harm, indifferent even to the silent longing for peace among England's own allies. Each day of the terrible struggle causes new destruction, new sufferings. Each day shortening the war will, on both sides, preserve the lives of thousands of brave soldiers and be a benefit to mankind.

The Imperial Government could not justify before its own conscience, before the German people and before history the neglect of any means destined to bring about the end of the war. Like the President of the United States, the Imperial Government had hoped to reach this goal by negotiations. After the attempts to come to an understanding with the Entente Powers have been answered by the latter with the announcement of an intensified continuation of the war, the Imperial Government—in order to serve the welfare of mankind in a higher sense and not to wrong its own people—is now compelled to continue the fight for existence, again forced upon it, with the full employment of all the weapons which are at its disposal.

Sincerely trusting that the people and the Government of the United States will understand the motives for this decision and its necessity, the Imperial Government hopes that the United States may view the new situation from the lofty heights of impartiality, and assist, on their part, to prevent further misery and unavoidable sacrifice of human life.

Enclosing two memoranda regarding the details of the contemplated military measures at sea, I remain, etc.,

J. BERNSTORFF.

Text of the Annex to German Note, Outlining Barred Zones and Prescribing Conditions for American Vessels

WASHINGTON, Jan. 31.—Following is the text of the annex to the German note presented to the State Department by Count von Bernstorff:

MEMORANDUM.

"From Feb. 1, 1917, sea traffic will be stopped with every available weapon and without further notice in the following blockade zones ["barred zones," according to a version received via Sayville] around Great Britain, [illegible]

[The Sayville version says: "In the North Sea, the district around England and France, which is limited by a line twenty nautical miles."]

"The zone is confined by a line at a distance of twenty sea miles along the Dutch coast to Terschelling Fireship; the degree [meridian?] of longitude from Terschelling Fireship to Udsire; a line from there across the point 62 degrees north, 0 degrees longitude, to 62 degrees north, 5 degrees west; further to a point three sea miles south of the southern point of the Faroe Islands; from there across a point 62 degrees north, 10 degrees west, to 61 degrees north, 15 degrees west; then 57 degrees north, 20 degrees west, to 47 degrees north, 20 degrees west; further, to 43 degrees north, 15 degrees west; then along the degree [parallel?] of latitude 43 degrees north to twenty sea miles from Cape Finisterre, and at a distance of twenty sea miles along the north coast of Spain to the French boundary.

"In the South—The Mediterranean:

[illegible] to 38 degrees 20 minutes north and 6 degrees east; also north and west of a zone sixty sea miles wide along the North African Coast, beginning at 2 degrees longitude west. For the connection of this sea-zone with Greece there is provided a zone of a width of twenty sea miles north and east of the following line: 38 degrees north and 6 degrees east to 38 degrees north and 10 degrees west, to 37 degrees north and 11 degrees 30 minutes east, to 34 degrees north and 22 degrees 30 minutes east.

"From there leads a zone twenty sea miles wide, west of 22 degrees 30 minutes eastern longitude, into Greek territorial waters.

"Neutral ships navigating these blockade zones do so at their own risk. Although care has been taken that neutral ships which are on their way toward ports of the blockade zones on Feb. 1, 1917, and have come in the vicinity of the latter, will be spared during a sufficiently long period, it is strongly advised to warn them with all available means in order to cause their return.

"Neutral ships which on Feb. 1 are in ports of the [illegible]

"The instructions given to the Commanders of German submarines provide for a sufficiently long period during which the safety of passengers on unarmed enemy passenger ships is guaranteed.

"Americans en route to the blockade zone on enemy freight steamers are not endangered, as the enemy shipping firms can prevent such ships in time from entering the zone.

"Sailing of regular American passenger steamers may continue undisturbed after Feb. 1, 1917, if

(A) The port of destination is Falmouth.

(B) Sailing to or coming from that port course is taken via the Scilly Islands and a point 50 degrees north, 20 degrees west.

["Along this route," says the Sayville version, "no German mines will be laid."]

(C) The steamers are marked in the following way, which must not be allowed to other vessels in American ports: On ship's hull and superstructure three vertical stripes one meter wide, each to be painted alternately white and [illegible] should show a large flag checkered white and red, and the stern the American national flag. Care should be taken that, during dark, national flag and painted marks are easily recognizable from a distance, and that the boats are well lighted throughout.

(D) One steamer a week sails in each direction with arrival at Falmouth on Sunday and departure from Falmouth on Wednesday.

(E) United States Government guarantees that no contraband (according to German contraband list) is carried by those steamers.

["Two copies of maps on which the barred zones are outlined are added," says the version received via Sayville.]

BRITAIN TO MEET GERMAN MENACE

Fleet of 4,000 Vessels Ready to Chase U-Boats and Protect Merchant Ships.

PORTS WILL BE KEPT OPEN

Liverpool and Bordeaux to be Especially Protected — Fore and Aft Guns for All Vessels.

Great Britain and her allies are prepared to meet Germany's moves in her submarine campaign, it was authoritatively asserted in shipping circles last night. The Entente Powers were convinced weeks ago that ruthless warfare with undersea boats would be decreed sooner or later and have known for ten days that the decision had been reached, it was said.

The ports of Liverpool and Bordeaux will be kept open at all hazards, British steamship representatives asserted, even if it becomes necessary to convoy every merchant ship which crosses the Atlantic. The first step to be taken by the British Admiralty, which virtually controls the merchant fleets of the Allies, will be to arm every ship with guns fore and aft for defensive purposes, it was predicted.

To meet the emergency the British Government has been assembling for months, it was said, a large fleet of small, fast cruisers to be used as "submarine chasers." This type of war craft has proved very effective against undersea boats, well informed shipping men declared. Agents of British lines declared the Admiralty now has a fleet of 4,000 vessels available to keep the sea lanes clear of raiders and submarines and to act as convoys.

There are said to be hundreds of patrol boats and mine sweepers, independent of torpedo boat destroyers, which are on the lookout to convoy liners and freighters when they arrive in the danger zone bound for French or British

Continued on Page 3.

"Barred Zones" and "Safety Lanes" Outlined in Germany's Note.

Surrounding the British Isles and bordering the coasts of France, Belgium, and Holland is a "barred zone" (indicated by black areas on the map) twenty nautical miles wide. The boundaries of a secondary "barred zone," shutting off the British Isles and running as far south as Cape Finisterre, on the northwestern coast of Spain, are indicated by a heavy black line. This zone is pierced by the route to Falmouth, as laid down for one American ship a week in the annex to the German note.

In the Mediterranean the safety zone leading to Greek territorial waters is indicated by the white areas shown in the map of that sea. The territorial waters of France, Italy, and the British possessions in the Mediterranean are apparently included in the barred zones.

CHANCELLOR TELLS GERMAN DECISION

He Outlines to Reichstag Committee Measures for Defense by Land and Sea.

AGREED ON AT CONFERENCE

Results of Headquarters Discussion Quickly Told to German Leaders.

BERLIN, Jan. 31, (via London.)—The Imperial Chancellor, Dr. von Bethmann Hollweg, is to make a statement on foreign affairs and the military situation this afternoon to the Ways and Means Committee of the Reichstag. According to the newspapers, the Chancellor will make important declarations regarding "the decisions of the Government," and will explain the grounds upon which these decisions are based.

BERLIN, Jan. 31, (by Wireless to Sayville.)—In its announcement today reporting the result of the recent conference at German Great Headquarters, the Overseas News Agency says:

"Chancellor von Bethmann Hollweg and Foreign Secretary Zimmermann have returned from Great Headquarters, where the planned offensive of the Entente was discussed at the meetings, and a unanimous agreement regarding all measures of defense was formulated. The Central Powers calmly await coming events, conscious of their own power."

LONDON, Jan. 31.—Chancellor von Bethmann Hollweg and Foreign Secretary Zimmermann have returned to Berlin from headquarters at the front, where a complete agreement on measures to be taken by Germany on land and water was reached, according to a Berlin telegram transmitted by Reuter's Amsterdam correspondent.

Kaiser Predicts "Hard Times."

AMSTERDAM, Jan. 31, (via London.)—The Reichsanzeiger publishes an Imperial rescript conveying the German Emperor's thanks for birthday congratulations extended to him. It says:

"From these numerous manifestations there ring out with the overwhelming force of unanimity indignation at the contemptuous rejection of our peace

Continued on Page 2.

A SHIP A WEEK FOR US

To and From Falmouth on a Prescribed Route.

BECOMES EFFECTIVE TODAY

Bernstorff Delivers a Note Which Ends Germany's Pledges to Us.

BECAUSE OF PEACE FAILURE

The Kaiser Now Proposes to Employ All Means of Sea Warfare at His Command.

CAPITAL TAKES GRAVE VIEW

President Studies Note Alone—Break Predicted in Some Quarters.

President Amazed by News; Spends Evening Studying Note

WASHINGTON, Jan. 31.—When The Associated Press dispatches telling of the German note began arriving at the White House today President Wilson was in his office talking with a friend. Secretary Tumulty hurried to him with the news. The President could not believe it until he was assured that the information was contained in a formal note already before the State Department.

The President went to bed at 11 o'clock after spending the evening alone in his study with a copy of the German note. This apparently disposed of suggestions that some action might be taken before morning.

The President saw no callers, but is understood to have used the telephone freely.

As far as could be learned, no plans have been laid for him to go before Congress, as he did to announce the sending of the Sussex note threatening to break off diplomatic relations.

Special to The New York Times.

WASHINGTON, Jan. 31.—The United States Government tonight faces its greatest international crisis since the Lusitania was sunk. With full knowledge that her action almost certainly means a break with America, Germany announced to this Government today that she intended to abandon the pledges she gave last year to observe the rules of international law in the conduct of her submarine warfare against merchant shipping. How a break can be avoided, observers here are unable to see. The gravity of the situation cannot be exaggerated.

Beginning at midnight tonight the German U-boats will sink without warning any merchant vessel, neutral as well as enemy, entering a prescribed zone that extends from north of the British Isles around into the Mediterranean to include even the waters of Greece.

That is the sum and substance of Germany's communication to this Government today, delivered to Secretary Lansing in Washington by Count von Bernstorff, the Kaiser's Ambassador, and to Ambassador Gerard, in Berlin, by the Imperial Foreign Office.

Recalls Final Warning.

The United States Government is on record as determined to break diplomatic relations with Germany if pledges concerning submarine warfare are not observed in letter and in spirit. Today's notification of the Imperial Government brings the United States to the point where it must decide whether it intends to make good the following warning to Germany, contained in a note of April 18, 1916:

"Unless the Imperial Government should now immediately declare and effect an abandonment of its present methods of submarine warfare against passenger and freight-carrying vessels the Government of the United States can have no choice but to sever diplomatic relations with the German Empire altogether. This action the Government of the United States contem-

"All the News That's Fit to Print."

The New York Times.

THE WEATHER
Fair, warmer today; fair, colder Monday.
For full weather report see Page 19.

VOL. LXVI...NO. 21,561. NEW YORK, SUNDAY, FEBRUARY 4, 1917.—98 PAGES, In Eight Parts, including Picture and Rotogravure Section and Review of Books. PRICE FIVE CENTS.

RELATIONS WITH GERMANY ARE BROKEN OFF; AMERICAN SHIP HOUSATONIC SUNK, CREW SAFE; MILITIA CALLED OUT; GERMAN SHIPS SEIZED

STATE FORCES READY TODAY

Mobilization of Land and Naval Units Starts at Once.

GUARDS DOUBLED AT FORTS

Police Posted on Bridges and Home Defense League Ordered to Prepare for Duty.

GOVERNORS ISLAND BUSY

Corporation Employes to Protect Plants—German Meeting Places Listed.

All of the National Guard of New York State not on duty elsewhere and all three battalions of the Naval Militia of New York were ordered immediately into service last night. The order calling the armed forces of the State to the colors was issued by Governor Whitman, at the request of Mayor Mitchel, after a conference at the Hotel St. Regis between the Governor, the Mayor, Adjt. Gen. Louis W. Stotesbury, Major Gen. John F. O'Ryan, commanding the National Guard Division of New York, and Commodore Robert P. Forshew, in command of the naval militia. It is expected that the mobilization will be completed some time today.

The guardsmen and naval militiamen will be used as reinforcements to the police forces of the various cities of the State in guarding waterworks, particularly the great watersheds upon which New York and other cities depend for their water supply; Federal, State, and municipal buildings, factories, and other plants engaged in the production of munitions; bridges, arsenals, armories, and other structures and places against which plots might be directed.

Mayor Shows Need of Guard.

Governor Whitman arrived from Albany shortly after 7 o'clock last night, and on his arrival at the St. Regis was met by the Mayor, General O'Ryan, Commodore Forshew, and Adjt. Gen. Stotesbury. They immediately went into conference, and Mayor Mitchel handed to Governor Whitman the following official communication:

Whereas, Diplomatic relations between the United States and the Imperial German Government have been broken off, and there have been during the past year or more various acts of violence directed against property within the City of New York, or in the immediate vicinity, which acts constituted breaches of the peace, and were committed for the apparent purposes of embarrassing one or more of the belligerents engaged in the war in Europe; and

Whereas, There exists in the opinion of the undersigned imminent danger of the commission of similar acts of violence and breaches of the peace against property and public utilities in the City of New York; and

Whereas, The affect of such acts if committed may be of disastrous proportions and consequence to the lives and welfare of the residents of the City of New York; and

Whereas, the civil authorities of the City of New York have not for the present sufficient and adequate forces at their disposal to properly and adequately guard against the commission of such acts,

I do, therefore, pursuant to Section 115 of the military law of the State of New York, request that your Excellency order out such detachments of the National Guard and Naval Militia as may be necessary for the purpose of aiding the civil authorities in the maintenance of law and order until such time as such authorities may provide adequately against the commission of such acts of violence and breaches of the peace.

JOHN PURROY MITCHEL,
Mayor of the City of New York.

After the conference General O'Ryan and Adj. Gen. Stotesbury hurried to the armory of the First Field Artillery, Sixty-eighth Street and Broadway, where the order calling the guard into active service was drawn up and telegraphed to the commanding officers of the various units in all parts of the State. Commodore Forshew issued his orders from Naval Militia Headquarters at 2 Rector Street.

"Orders Carried Out," Says O'Ryan.

None of the officers would give out any detailed information concerning the mobilization. Governor Whitman said he would remain in New York today and would keep in touch with the progress of the mobilization, which is expected to be completed by noon at the latest.

"All that I have to say now," the Governor replied, "is that everybody is standing loyally behind the President."

General O'Ryan refused to discuss the mobilization.

"I am not in a position to talk now," he said, "and for the present, at least, a censorship has been established so far as the actual carrying into effect of the Governor's order is concerned. It would not be proper to divulge the number of men affected by the mobilization order,

Continued on Page 9.

Navy Department to Take Charge of All Shipping

Special to The New York Times.

WASHINGTON, Feb. 3.—Sailings of vessels, American merchant ships in particular, from American ports are now out of the hands of the State Department, and have become a military matter. It was broadly intimated today that ships flying the American flag would not leave port until they received permission from the Navy Department, and that their movements at sea would be under the guidance, if not under the direction, of the Navy Department, by wireless.

THE ST. LOUIS HELD; MAY MOUNT GUNS

Convoy or Six Rapid-Firers to Protect American Liner on Voyage to Europe.

SAILING TOMORROW LIKELY

Adriatic Leaves for the War Zone with 44 Passengers—Others to Depart.

Announcement was made at 8 o'clock last night by P. A. S. Franklin, President of the International Mercantile Marine Company, that the American liner St. Louis would not sail for Liverpool until noon tomorrow. This followed a conference between the representatives of the company and the State Department in Washington, and ended the uncertainty that had existed since noon on Saturday, when the departure of the liner was first postponed.

While nothing official was said on the subject it was learned on good authority that the St. Louis's detention until noon tomorrow was due to the fact that the State and Navy Departments had not come to any decision regarding the protection to be given to the liner on her voyage across to Liverpool and back to New York.

It was pointed out by an official of the Government that there were two kinds of protection suitable for the emergency. One is to have the St. Louis convoyed by two fast cruisers, and the other is to have her equipped with quick-firing guns for her own defense in case of attack. It is believed that the latter method will be adopted, in which case the liner will have to carry gun crews to handle the armament, as the seamen she has on board are not qualified navy men.

Special Plates for Guns.

The St. Louis has plates on her decks which were specially strengthened for the mounting of six four-inch guns—two forward on either side of the bow, two abaft the bridge on the upper deck, and two at the stern.

If the Navy Department decides the question today, it is understood that a tug from the navy yard with the guns, 300 rounds of ammunition, and armorers will be sent to the American Line pier at West Twenty-second Street to fit her out for the voyage, so that she will be ready to sail at noon tomorrow.

Including several Russians who had transferred their booking from the Hellig Olav on Friday, the St. Louis had 184 passengers on her list at noon yesterday, comprising 75 first-class, 69 second-class, and 40 third-class.

It was decided by Mr. Franklin at 10 o'clock in the morning that the American liner should be detained until noon today, as there was a shortage of coal, and no answer had been received from the State Department at Washington as to the sailing. Passengers were notified by telephone not to go down to the pier, and the majority

Continued on Page 7.

TEUTON SHIPS ARE SEIZED

Federal Officials Take Over Vessels Held in Our Ports.

DISPOSSESS APPAM'S CREW

Two German Auxiliary Cruisers Also Are Among Those Now in Custody.

LINER HAD BEEN CRIPPLED

Kronprinzessin Cecile Is Found Useless—Austrian Ship Here Is Damaged.

Special to The New York Times.

WASHINGTON, Feb. 3.—Secretary Daniels this afternoon sent instructions to naval officers in command of the various navy yards to take such steps as were necessary for the safety of any German warships interned. In response to this order word reached Washington tonight that the crews of the interned German auxiliary cruisers Kronprinz Wilhelm and the Prinz Eitel Friedrich, both at Philadelphia, had been removed from those vessels and placed in isolation barracks.

Lieutenant Hans Berg and his German prize crew were removed from the liner Appam at Newport News, Va., by coast guard cutters under direction of a United States Marshal. The ship is in the custody of the Federal Court pending appeal to the United States Supreme Court from a decision awarding her to her English owners. Lieutenant Berg had been allowed to retain possession of the vessel under bond given by the German Government.

A Federal Marshal removed the Captain an crew of the North German Lloyd liner Kronprinzessin Cecilie at Boston and took possession of her. The action was a civil proceeding.

Two German and three Austrian steamers which had taken refuge at New Orleans were placed under guard. American military authorities took possession of four German ships in Cristobal harbor, Panama.

Kronprinzessin Cecilie Damaged.

BOSTON, Feb. 3.—United States Marshal Mitchell tonight took physical possession of the North German Lloyd liner Kronprinzessin Cecilie, which has been nominally in his custody since the litigation instituted against the owners by the National City Bank of New York.

The Kronprinzessin Cecilie was found to be crippled beyond possibility of early usefulness, according to an official who assisted in the seizure. The liner's boilers were said to have been cleared of all water, the fires were burning at top capacity, and countless valves in the engine room had been mutilated, transferred or removed entirely, this official asserted.

Captain Charles A. Polack and the skeleton crew of 112 men, who have made the ship their home for more than two years, were put ashore and housed for the time being at the Immigration Bureau. The German engineers, firemen, and others whose services have been required to keep the ship in condition, were replaced by American citizens and fifty men of the city police force were put on board.

This action followed notice to the marshal by attorneys for the National City Bank and the Guarantee Trust Company of New York that they would hold him liable for any damage to the

Continued on Page 3.

Col. Roosevelt Squarely With the President

Special to The New York Times.

OYSTER BAY, N. Y., Feb. 3.—Colonel Theodore Roosevelt pledged himself tonight in support of President Wilson in upholding the honor of the United States, and offered his own and the services of his four sons to the country in case hostilities are not averted.

Plans for a volunteer army division, to be commanded by the Colonel, which his friends have worked on since the sinking of the Lusitania, again have jumped to the fore, and the Colonel tonight said he had asked the War Department for permission to raise such a body of troops.

"Of course, I shall in every way support the President in all that he does to uphold the honor of the United States and to safeguard the lives of American citizens," he said. "Yesterday I wrote to the War Department asking permission to raise a division if war is declared and there is a call for volunteers. In such event I and my four sons will go."

BERNSTORFF WAS NOT SURPRISED

But on Receiving Passports Did Not Hide His Concern Over Failure of His Efforts.

HAS NO SAFE CONDUCT YET

Details of Arrangements for His Departure Not Settled—His Wife an American.

Special to The New York Times.

WASHINGTON, Feb. 3.—Count von Bernstorff, who had been Ambassador from Germany to the United States since Dec. 30, 1908, received his passports promptly on the stroke of 2 o'clock this afternoon. These were broad enough to cover the German Ambassador, his family and all the members of the embassy suite, but no communication was delivered to the Ambassador to the effect that he would receive safe conduct from this country to Germany. This is a detail that will have to be arranged later.

The passports were delivered by Lester H. Woolsey, an Assistant Solicitor for the State Department, who is attached in a confidential capacity to the office of Secretary Lansing. Mr. Woolsey also delivered to the Ambassador the text of a note from Secretary Lansing, which was worded so as to embrace the main portions of the text of the President's address to the Senate. The note handed to Count von Bernstorff did not, however, embrace that part of the President's speech which declared that this Government did not desire any "hostile conflict" with Germany, and that only actual overt acts on the latter's part could make the President believe that Germany intended to disregard its long friendship with this country.

Demanded by "Dignity and Honor."

The note begins as follows:

"*The Secretary of State to the German Ambassador:*

"Department of State, Feb. 3, 1917.

"Excellency: In acknowledging the note, with accompanying memoranda, which you delivered into my hands on the afternoon of Jan. 31, and which announced the purpose of your Government as to the future conduct of submarine warfare, I would direct your attention to the following statements appearing in the correspondence which has passed between the Government of the United States and the Imperial German Government in regard to submarine warfare."

Then follow the quotations used by the President in addressing Congress, including the citations from the memorandum accompanying the German note of Jan. 31, giving notice of unrestricted naval warfare.

"In view of this declaration," concludes the State Department note, "which withdraws suddenly and without prior intimation the solemn assurance given in the Imperial Government's note of May 4, 1916, this Government has no alternative consistent with the dignity and honor of the United States but to take the course which it explicitly announced in its note of April 18, 1916, it would take in the event that the Imperial Government did not declare and effect an abandonment of the methods of submarine warfare then employed, and to which the Imperial Government now purpose again to resort.

"The President has, therefore, directed me to announce to your Excellency that all diplomatic relations between the United States and the German Empire are severed, and that the American Ambassador at Berlin will be immediately withdrawn, and in accordance with such

Continued on Page 5.

FIRST SINKING REPORTED

London Hears No Warning Was Given Housatonic Off Scilly Islands.

25 AMERICANS ON BOARD

Armed British Steamer Picks Up the Officers and Crew of the Vessel.

NEWS STIRS WASHINGTON

But if U-Boat Took Precautions Attack Will Not Be Adequate Cause for Action.

LONDON, Feb. 3.—The American steamer Housatonic was sunk this noon by a German submarine near the Scilly Islands.

All the officers and crew were saved by a British armed steamer.

The rumor is current that the Housatonic was sunk without warning.

WASHINGTON, Feb. 3.—News of the sinking of the Housatonic caused a sensation here, but State Department officials pointed out that it would depend upon the circumstances whether the incident would affect the present situation.

The ship was carrying contraband, and if she was destroyed after proper warning had been given and provision made for the safety of her crew, or while she was trying to escape, the United States would only have a claim for damages, as in the Frye case.

The first effect of the incident in official quarters was to direct attention anew to the President's declaration in his address to Congress today that, if American ships and lives were sacrificed "in needless contravention of the just and reasonable understandings of international law," he would again go before Congress for authority to "use any means that may be necessary for the protection of our seamen and our people."

FORMERLY GERMAN OWNED.

Housatonic Was Sold to Americans by Hamburg-American Line.

The steamship Housatonic was formerly the Georgia of the Hamburg-American Line. She was sold by the latter company on April 16, 1915, for $85,000 to the Housatonic Steamship Corporation, of which Edward F. Geer of 21 State Street is the manager. This company was organized in this State for the express purpose of buying German ships under the law permitting ships of foreign build to be transferred to American registry. The other incorporators of the corporation were George F. Allison, Frank Southard, Edward Sandford, and Henry M. Hewitt. Sandford is a lawyer who has represented the Hamburg-American Line, and defended Karl Buenz, Director of that concern, when tried and convicted in 1915 on a charge of falsifying manfests and sending ships out of this harbor with cargoes intended to supply German warships.

After buying the Housatonic the corporation found that the Hamburg-American Line, which was under the control of the German Government, had reversed its policy of selling ships, in consequence of the decision of the German Government to forego the ready money to be obtained by such sales rather than add to the active merchant marine of the world and indirectly to strengthen the Allies.

The British Government refused to sanction the addition of German ships to the world's supply of operating tonnage because of the presumption that such sales were made with strings attached to them and that the owners of such former German ships would try to operate them in the interests of Germany.

Two other Hamburg-American Line ships which were sold before the German Government reversed its decision were the Dacia and the Alexandria. The Dacia was sold to Edward N. Breitung, and during its brief career was under the suspicion of having the mission of causing legal entanglements between the United States and the Allies. It sailed from New York with a cargo of cotton, bound for Germany, before the British blockade had been made stringent and while there was a question as to whether cotton could be considered contraband. The Dacia was captured by a French cruiser, taken to a French port, and held to be a lawful prize.

The Alexandria, which was transferred

Continued on Page 4.

Text of President Wilson's Address

WASHINGTON, Feb. 3.—The President's address to the joint session of Congress today was as follows:

GENTLEMEN OF THE CONGRESS:

The Imperial German Government on the 31st day of January announced to this Government and to the Governments of the other neutral nations that on and after the 1st day of February, the present month, it would adopt a policy with regard to the use of submarines against all shipping seeking to pass through certain designated areas of the high seas, to which it is clearly my duty to call your attention.

Let me remind the Congress that on the 18th of April last, in view of the sinking on the 24th of March of the cross-Channel steamship Sussex by a German submarine without summons or warning, and the consequent loss of the lives of several citizens of the United States who were passengers aboard her, this Government addressed a note to the Imperial German Government, in which it made the following declaration:

If it is still the purpose of the Imperial German Government to prosecute relentless and indiscriminate warfare against vessels of commerce by the use of submarines without regard to what the Government of the United States must consider the sacred and indisputable rules of international law and the universally recognized dictates of humanity, the Government of the United States is at last forced to the conclusion that there is but one course it can pursue. Unless the Imperial Government should now immediately declare and effect an abandonment of its present methods of submarine warfare against passenger and freight carrying vessels, the Government of the United States can have no choice but to sever diplomatic relations with the German Empire altogether.

In reply to this declaration the Imperial German Government gave this Government the following assurance:

The German Government is prepared to do its utmost to confine the operations of war for the rest of its duration to the fighting forces of the belligerents, thereby also insuring the freedom of the seas, a principle upon which the German Government believes now, as before, to be in agreement with the Government of the United States.

Th German Government, guided by this idea, notifies the Government of the United States that the German naval forces have received the following orders: In accordance with the general principles of visit and search and destruction of merchant vessels recognized by international law, such vessels, both within and without the area declared a naval war zone, shall not be sunk without warning and without saving human lives, unless these ships attempt to escape or offer resistance.

But [it added] neutrals cannot expect that Germany, forced to fight for her existence, shall, for the sake of neutral interest, restrict the use of an effective weapon if her enemy is permitted to continue to apply at will methods of warfare violating the rules of international law. Such a demand would be incompatible with the character of neutrality, and the German Government is convinced that the Government of the United States does not think of making such a demand, knowing that the Government of the United States has repeatedly declared that it is determined to restore the principle of the freedom of the seas, from whatever quarter it has been violated.

To this the Government of the United States replied on the 8th of May, accepting, of course, the assurance given, but adding:

The Government of the United States feels it necessary to state that it takes it for granted that the Imperial German Government does not intend to imply that the maintenance of its newly announced policy is in any way contingent upon the course or result of diplomatic negotiations between the Government of the United States and any other belligerent Government, notwithstanding the fact that certain passages in the Imperial Government's note of the 4th inst. might appear to be susceptible of that construction. In order, however, to avoid any misunderstanding, the Government of the United States notifies the Imperial Government that it cannot for a moment entertain, much less discuss, a suggestion that respect by German naval authorities for the rights of citizens of the United States upon the high seas should in any way or in the slightest degree be made contingent upon the conduct of any other Government, affecting the rights of neutrals and noncombatants. Responsibility in such matters is single, not joint, absolute, not relative.

To this note of the 8th of May the Imperial German Government made no reply.

On the 31st of January, the Wednesday of the present week, the German Ambassador handed to the Secretary of State, along with a formal note, a memorandum which contained the following statement:

The Imperial Government therefore does not doubt that the Government of the United States will understand the situation thus forced upon Germany by the Entente Allies' brutal methods of war and by their determination to destroy the Central Powers, and that the Government of the United States will further realize that the now openly disclosed intention of the Entente Allies gives back to Germany the freedom of action which she reserved in her note addressed to the Government of the United States on May 4, 1916.

Under these circumstances, Germany will meet the illegal measures of her enemies by forcibly preventing, after Feb. 1, 1917, in a zone around Great Britain, France, Italy, and in the Eastern Mediterranean, all navigation, that of neutrals included, from and to England and from and to France, &c. All ships met within the zone will be sunk.

I think that you will agree with me that, in view of this declaration, which suddenly and without prior intimation of any kind deliberately withdraws the solemn assurance given in the Imperial Governments' note of the 4th of May, 1916, this Government has no alternative consistent with the dignity and honor of the United States but to take the course which, in its note of the 18th of April, 1916, it announced that it would take in the event that the German Government did not declare and effect an abandonment of the methods of submarine warfare which it was then employing and to which it now purposes again to resort.

I have therefore directed the Secretary of State to announce to his Excellency the German Ambassador that all diplomatic relations between the United States and the German Empire are severed and that the American Ambassador at Berlin will immediately be withdrawn; and, in accordance with this decision, to hand to his Excellency his passports.

Notwithstanding this unexpected action of the German Government, this sudden and deplorable renunciation of its assurances, given this Government at one of the most critical moments of tension in the relations of the two Governments, I refuse to believe that it is the intention of the German authorities to do in fact what they have warned us they will feel at liberty to do. I cannot bring myself to believe that they will indeed pay no regard to the ancient friendship between their people and our own or to the solemn obligations which have been exchanged between them, and destroy American ships and take the lives of American citizens in the willful prosecution of the ruthless naval program they have announced their intention to adopt. Only actual overt acts on their part can make me believe it even now.

If this inveterate confidence on my part in the sobriety and prudent foresight of their purpose should unhappily prove unfounded; if American ships and American lives should in fact be sacrificed by their naval commanders in heedless contravention of the just and reasonable understandings of international law and the obvious dictates of humanity, I shall take the liberty of coming again before the Congress to ask that authority be given me to use any means that may be necessary for the protection of our seamen and our people in the prosecution of their peaceful and legitimate errands on the high seas. I can do nothing less. I take it for granted that all neutral Governments will take the same course.

We do not desire any hostile conflict with the Imperial German Government. We are the sincere friends of the German people, and earnestly desire to remain at peace with the Government which speaks for them. We shall not believe that they are hostile to us unless and until we are obliged to believe it; and we purpose nothing more than the reasonable defense of the undoubted rights of our people. We wish to serve no selfish ends. We seek merely to stand true alike in thought and in action to the immemorial principles of our people which I have sought to express in my address to the Senate only two weeks ago—seek merely to vindicate our right to liberty and justice and an unmolested life. These are the bases of peace, not war. God grant that we may not be challenged to defend them by acts of willful injustice on the part of the Government of Germany!

BREAK WITH AUSTRIA, TOO

Notice of Her Blockade Arrives as President Is Speaking.

EXPECTS NEUTRAL SUPPORT

President Expresses Belief That They Will Follow America's Course.

STILL HOPES AGAINST WAR

Mr. Wilson Unable to Believe That Germany Means to Carry Out Threat.

Special to The New York Times.

WASHINGTON, Feb. 3.—Diplomatic relations between Germany and the United States were severed today. It was President Wilson's answer to the German notice that any merchant vessel which entered prescribed areas would be sunk without warning. Count von Bernstorff, the Kaiser's Ambassador, has received his passports; in other words, he has been dismissed by this Government. James W. Gerard, the American Ambassador at Berlin, has been ordered to return home with his staff.

President Wilson made the sensational answer in a momentous address delivered before the two houses of Congress assembled in joint session this afternoon. Congress appears to be unanimous in a determination to stand by the President in whatever measures he takes. Party lines have been obliterated in the general desire to support the Administration in dealing with a critical situation that most observers expect to result in the entrance of the United States into the European conflict.

War has not been declared. The President in his address said: "We do not desire any hostile conflict with the German Government." But preparations for war are being made. Navy yards have been closed to the public. For the present private shipbuilding concerns and other plants engaged in Government work will take their own precautionary measures. Private shipbuilders have offered, to place their establishments under the control of the Government, and a provision authorizing the Secretary of the Navy to do this will be offered by the Naval Committee in the House on Monday.

German merchant ships at American ports are being closely guarded, and some have been seized. Our war vessels are said to have received precautionary orders. Army arsenals have been told to guard against danger. Public buildings here and elsewhere are being guarded also.

Break with Austria, Too.

Diplomatic relations with Austria-Hungary are to be severed also. This was made certain by the receipt by the State Department today of a note from the Vienna Government containing notice of adherence to the German submarine blockade policy. President Wilson did not know this when he went to the Capitol. Count Tarnowski von Tarnow, the newly accredited Ambassador of Austria-Hungary, who had reached the United States on Thursday, went to the State Department today to arrange for his formal presentation to President Wilson. Word was brought to him that Secretary Lansing would be unable to receive him. Hardly had the Ambassador gone when the department received a cable message from Frederic C. Penfield, the American Ambassador at Vienna, giving the text of the Austro-Hungarian adherence to the German war zone order. As Count Tarnowski has not been formally received by this Government he may not be dismissed in the same way as Count von Bernstorff was, but he will be invited to leave the country, with the members of his suite and embassy staff. Ambassador Penfield and his embassy staff will be ordered home. If war results it will be war not only with Germany but with Austria-Hungary and Turkey as well, and possibly with Bulgaria.

Demands Release of Americans.

Taking it for granted that war is inevitable, speculation is being indulged in here as to how soon the clash will come. That it will come soon is a general opinion tonight. A German submarine is reported to have sunk the American freight steamer Housatonic. Word came officially today that Germany was holding as prisoners of war sixty-odd American citizens taken from merchant ships by a German raider. This Government has demanded their release immediately. If Germany refuses—and this is expected—the President may ask Congress to authorize him to take measures of reprisal. He will certainly do so if Germany does not spare American merchantmen entering the forbidden areas.

An important aspect of the situation

Attempt to Scuttle Destroyer Jacob Jones At Philadelphia; Petty Officer Put In Irons

PHILADELPHIA, Feb. 3.—An attempt was made today to scuttle the United States torpedo boat destroyer Jacob Jones by opening several of her sea cocks at the Philadelphia Navy Yard, according to unofficial but reliable reports. Officials at the yard refused to confirm or deny the reports, pointing out that upon instructions from Washington a strict censorship had been placed upon all activities at the navy yards throughout the country.

An officer of the Jacob Jones, it was said, found that the ship was listing heavily to port as she was being towed from her anchorage in the Delaware River to a dock, and all persons aboard were detained and questioned. The chief machinist's mate, whose identity was not disclosed, was arrested and placed in irons in the brig of one of the battleships. Whether the prisoner is a German sympathizer or a fanatic is not known.

More than two feet of water were in the hold of the Jacob Jones when it was discovered that her sea cocks had been opened. They were quickly closed, and two Government tugs assisted in warping the destroyer into her dock.

Do you believe in preparedness now? Much work must yet be done. Join National Security League, 31 Pine Street. Memberships, $1 to $250.—Advt.

"All the News That's Fit to Print."

The New York Times.

THE WEATHER
Probably snow, colder by tonight; Friday fair, much colder.
For full weather report see Page 21.

VOL. LXVI...NO. 21,565. NEW YORK, THURSDAY, FEBRUARY 8, 1917.—TWENTY-TWO PAGES. ONE CENT In Greater New York, Jersey City and Newark. | Elsewhere, TWO CENTS.

LINER CALIFORNIA SUNK WITHOUT WARNING, MANY MISSING; GERARD AND ALL AMERICANS IN GERMANY HELD AS HOSTAGES; NO CONVOYS GRANTED, AMERICAN LINE CANCELS SAILINGS

SENATE INDORSES WILSON

Break With Germany Approved, 78 to 5, After Five-hour Debate.

PARTY LINES DISAPPEAR

Lodge Calls Upon Republicans to Stand Firmly Behind the President.

CHAIRMAN STONE CRITICISED

His Resolution of Indorsement Called Ill-Timed—Not Asked For by Wilson.

Special to The New York Times.

WASHINGTON, Feb. 7.—By a vote of 78 to 5 the Senate today formally indorsed the President's action in severing diplomatic relations with Germany. The vote was taken on a resolution introduced by Senator Stone, Chairman of the Committee on Foreign Relations. Two Democrats, Kirby of Arkansas and Vardaman of Mississippi joined with three Republicans, Gronna of North Dakota, La Follette of Wisconsin, and Works of California, in opposing the resolution.

In spite of the overwhelming indorsement given to the President on the final and basic question when the vote was reached, there were many divisions of sentiment, and Senator Stone's request early in the day for consideration of his resolution precipitated a stirring debate, which continued for five hours. Three of the Senators who finally voted against the resolution, Kirby, Vardaman, and Works, vigorously attacked the President's course. Senator Kirby declared that to vote for the Stone resolution would be equivalent to voting for a preliminary declaration of war on Germany, while Senators Works and Vardaman asserted that Americans should waive their rights to travel in the submarine danger zone. Senator Works virtually attempted to justify the German course as forced by military necessity.

President's Course Defended.

These attacks brought speeches from nineteen Senators warmly defending the President's course. The movement for the adoption of the resolution was led jointly by Senator Stone and Senator Lodge of Massachusetts, ranking Republican member of the Foreign Relations Committee, and in ordinary times one of the President's bitterest critics. Senator Lodge took the ground that on such a question party lines should vanish, and Congress should stand squarely behind the President.

While this was obviously the prevailing sentiment in the chamber, several Senators who voted for the resolution deprecated the action of Senator Stone in bringing it before the House, declaring that it was not proper for the Senate to take action at this time, as the President did not need action by the Senate to sustain him; that it served to emphasize differences of opinion which might better have been kept hidden; and that it tended to commit the Senate in advance to a declaration of war should the President find it necessary to come before Congress again in case of an overt act by Germany.

Senator Stone, who is understood to have felt that the President should have waited for an overt act before breaking off relations, devoted his speech requesting the passage of the resolution almost entirely to showing that the President was wholly within his constitutional rights in acting as he did. Senator Stone was asked by Senator Underwood if the resolution was introduced because the Administration wished it passed. Mr. Stone replied that he had brought it up without consultation with the President or any other executive official because he thought it "would be an advisable thing for the Senate officially to say that it approves the action of the President."

Calls Resolution Ill-advised.

"If the President desired in this emergency, action by the Senate to sustain his course," Senator Underwood replied, "I would give it unhesitatingly and without criticism of any kind, but if it has not been the desire of the President, and if he has not felt it is necessary to sustain his course by this resolution I think it has been very ill-advised and very ill-timed on the part of the Senator from Missouri."

Senator Underwood, however, declared that he would vote for the resolution, because he felt that a failure to do so might be misinterpreted abroad; but he did not wish his vote to be regarded as committing him in any way should the question of declaring war come before the Senate. He praised the President highly for having kept the nation out of war up to this time.

Senators Jones and Townsend took a similar position on the question of the timeliness of the resolution, while Senator Norris asserted that before the resolution was indorsed the President should lay before the Senate all the

Continued on Page 3.

Allies Resolved to End War This Summer, Hodge Says

LONDON, Feb. 7.—Addressing a meeting in London tonight, John Hodge, Minister of Labor, said he thought he was giving away no secret in saying that at the recent conference between representatives of the Entente Allies the determination had been arrived at to terminate the war by the end of Summer.

NEUTRAL NATIONS SEND PROTESTS

Spain, Brazil, Argentina, and Cuba Refuse to Consent to U-Boat Blockade.

MADRID NOTE MADE PUBLIC

Alfonso's Government Firm in Its Stand Against Illegality of Berlin's New Decree.

MADRID, Feb. 7.—The Spanish Government's reply to Germany's submarine war zone note, which was handed to the German Ambassador yesterday, is a firm and dignified protest against it. The note will be made public as soon as the Central Powers have knowledge of its contents.

It declares that Germany's decision to close completely certain sea routes is outside the legal principles of international life. It adds that if Germany hopes to have Spain's help to avoid more loss of life it must be understood that Spain, while ready at the proper time to lend the initiative in support of the establishment of peace, cannot accept the legality of exceptional methods of war.

The text of the reply follows:

"His Majesty's Government has attentively examined the note which your Serene Highness was good enough to remit to me the 31st of January, in which is set forth the German Government's resolute intention to interrupt as from the following day all sea traffic, without further notice, and by no matter what arm, around Great Britain, France, Italy and in the eastern Mediterranean.

"I must say that the note caused a very painful impression on the Spanish Government. The attitude of strict neutrality which Spain adopted from the beginning and has maintained with loyalty and unshakable firmness gives her the right to expect that the lives of her subjects engaged in sea trade should not be placed in such grave peril. It also gives her the right to expect that that trade should not be troubled nor diminished by such an increase in the extent of the zones in which the Imperial Government insists that, in order to attain its ends, it must use all weapons and suppress all limitations which it has hitherto imposed upon its methods of naval warfare.

"Even before the Imperial Government had set aside these restrictions his Majesty's Government had protested, holding them insufficient to comply with the prescriptions of national maritime law. But the methods of war, announced by Germany, are being carried to such an unexpected and unprecedented extreme that the Spanish Government, considering its rights and the requirements of its neutrality, must with still more reason protest calmly but firmly to the Imperial Government and must make at the same time the necessary reserves, imposed by the legitimate presumption of ineluctable responsibility, which the Imperial Government assumes, principally in view of the loss of life which its attitude may cause.

"Pretended Right of Destination."

"His Majesty's Government bases its protest on the fact that the decision to close completely the road to certain seas by substituting for the indisputable right of capture in certain cases a pretended right of destruction in all cases is outside the legal principles of international life. Above all and beyond all it considers that the extension, in the form announced, of this pretended right of destruction to the lives of noncombatants and the subjects of neutral nations such as Spain is contrary to the principles observed by all nations even in moments of the greatest violence.

"If the German Government, as it says, expects that the Spanish people and Government will not close their ears to the reasons which have caused its decision, and hopes that they will co-operate to avoid further calamities and sacrifices of human life, it will also understand that the Spanish Government, while disposed to lend at the proper time its initiative and support to everything that could contribute to the advent of a peace, more and more wished for, cannot admit the legality of exceptional methods of warfare. These methods, indeed, notwithstanding Spain's rights as a neutral and her scrupulous fulfilment of the duties incumbent on her as such, make more difficult and even stop altogether her sea trade, compromising her economic life and threatening with grave dangers the lives of her subjects.

"His Majesty's Government, supported more firmly than ever by the justice of its position, does not doubt that the Imperial Government, inspired by the sentiments of friendship which unite the two countries, will find, not-

Continued on Page 3.

SHIPS CAN ARM THEMSELVES

Washington Concedes Right of Liners to Take Steps to Meet Attack.

MESSAGE TO AMERICAN LINE

Says Government 'Cannot Give Advice to Private Persons' as to Whether Ships Should Sail.

HEAVY FOREIGN MAIL HELD

Ryndam Is Recalled to New York When Only 12 Hours From Falmouth, England.

After five days of waiting and uncertainty, P. A. S. Franklin, President of the International Mercantile Marine Company, announced last night that the sailing dates of the American Line steamships St. Louis and St. Paul, now in the Port of New York, had been indefinitely postponed. This decision was reached by the Directors of the company at the offices, 9 Broadway, after the receipt of a message by long-distance telephone from the Secretary of State at Washington, which read:

The Government cannot give advice to private persons as to whether their merchant vessels should sail on a voyage to European ports by which they would be compelled to pass through the waters delineated in the declaration issued by the German Government on Jan. 31, 1917.

It, however, asserts that the rights of American vessels to traverse all parts of the high seas are the same now as they were prior to the issuance of the German declaration, and that a neutral merchant vessel may, if its owners believe that it is liable to be unlawfully attacked, take any measures to prevent or resist such attacks.

Consider Arming of Ships.

The American Line officials said last night that they had now taken under consideration whether to sail their steamships without protection or to provide guns, if they can be obtained, and gunners on their own account.

Mr. Franklin explained that the official message received from the State Department was in reply to the request made by the management of the American Line, asking if the Government would give any protection to the steamships carrying the United States mails, and whether it was advisable for them to go to sea under present war conditions.

A statement was received from Washington early yesterday that the Government would not provide any convoy for American ships bound through the war zone. On receipt of this information the American Line telegraphed to its agents all over the United States and Canada as follows:

Present situation makes it necessary to consider the sailing dates of American Line steamships, and until this is settled please stop booking passengers of all classes. Please tell all applicants for passage that the White Star Line has regular sailings, and that their ships are accorded protection by the British Government when they are in the territorial waters of the British Isles.

British Consulate's Warning.

On account of the dangerous conditions on the Atlantic the British Consulate advised all "women and children" to refrain from going abroad unless through dire necessity.

The crew of the St. Louis, numbering about 390, are still standing by the ship, and will be paid off when the American Line officials have decided definitely whether they will send the liner across to Liverpool armed, as permissible under the message received from the State Department.

One of the officials at the United States Shipping Commissioner's office said that the crew had signed articles for a commercial voyage carrying the United States mails from New York to Liverpool and back to New York. If the country should go to war with Germany then the circumstances would be different and if the vessel should carry guns it was probable that fresh articles would be drawn and signed. Under the new Seamen's act, members of the crew of an American ship may leave just before the sailing hour if a substitute can be found and on twenty-four hours' notice at any other time.

The St. Louis has now 5,000 sacks of mail on board and 3,300 tons of general cargo, including frozen meat, fruit, and provisions, which is to remain there for the present unless the Postmaster General decides to send the mails on the White Star liner Cedric, which sails for Liverpool Saturday or Sunday.

Mail Held Since Jan. 27.

No mail has been sent from New York to Liverpool since the departure of the American liner Philadelphia on Jan. 27. In addition to the 5,000 sacks on board the St. Louis, it is understood that another 2,000 sacks are waiting at the Post Office. The officials of the Ameri-

Continued on Page 3.

German Dynamite Factory Explodes; 200 Killed

AMSTERDAM, Feb. 7, (via London.)—According to Les Nouvelles of Maestricht, Holland, a dynamite factory at Schlebusch, near Cologne, was blown up on Jan. 27, causing the death of 200 persons, mostly women.

An explosion last Thursday on the railway between Aix-la-Chapelle and Louvain, this newspaper reports, caused the death or injury of 26 Belgian workmen.

SEND GERMAN GOLD TO SOUTH AMERICA

Berlin's Faith in Latin-American Neutrality Seen in Transfers from New York.

$2,000,000 TO BUENOS AIRES

May Also Serve to Help Quick Resumption of German Foreign Trade After the War Ends.

It was learned in quarters of high authority yesterday that large balances of German banks here, some on deposit in trust companies, had been transferred quietly but rapidly from this city since the new submarine campaign was announced. A significant factor in these transfers is that, while a part of the bank balances have been sent to Berlin, there has been a heavy movement to neutral countries, chiefly in South America.

The heavy remittances to South America for German account are considered of great significance in quarters where the opinion of Berlin bankers is known. They indicate, the bankers here assert, that, while German financial leaders are persuaded that the United States may finally come into a state of war with Germany, this country's action will not be supported by certain of the South American nations, and, therefore, funds lodged in those countries will be safe, whatever may develop here.

Rumors that gold was being sent to South America for German banks were denied in responsible quarters, although it was said that the volume of remittances in exchange had worked to stimulate gold exports. Yesterday between $700,000 and $1,000,000 in gold was withdrawn from the Sub-Treasury for shipment to the Argentina, and the total of such transfers this month is more than $2,000,000. Exchange on Buenos Aires has long been at a stiff premium, making remittances in gold cheaper than in exchange and local bankers have sought to make their payments in the Argentine in gold as rapidly as shipments have been made possible through the sailing of American steamers. The expansion of the demand for exchange, in sending German balances south, has helped to increase the premium and therefore quickened the export of gold.

The process of removing German funds to other countries has by no means been confined to New York. Bank deposits have been drawn down in practically all the larger cities of the country, according to a prominent foreign exchange banker, many millions of dollars having gone this week.

In so far as the Berlin exchange market has reflected the movement of funds, transfers actually made to Germany have been moderate compared to the flow elsewhere. The first pronounced strength displayed by reichsmark quotations in several weeks occurred yesterday, when concentrated buying orders caused the cable rate to shoot forward more than 3 cents to the four marks. From a rate of 67⅛ cents the quotation moved up to 70½ cents before noon. The rise from Tuesday's final price was more than 4 cents. It was reported that two orders, one calling for 450,000 marks and the other for about 325,000 marks, appeared and found the supply light.

The confidence with which the German banks have sent funds to South America has persuaded many financiers here that this may have a strategic import as regards commercial transactions after the war ends. A big accumulation of funds would enable Germany to forward rapidly purchases of goods for importation without making recourse to the credit market necessary. South American merchants have been accustomed for years to finance their transactions, both buying and selling, through London, and of more recent years through New York. It may be that German interests, fearing that the end of hostilities might find them without financial connections in either of these centres, for some time at least, desire to be strongly intrenched with actual funds in the Southern markets.

TEUTONS WITHDRAW MONEY.

Large Amount of Savings Taken Out of Boston Postal Savings Banks.

BOSTON, Feb. 7.—The withdrawal since Monday of large sums of money from postal savings banks here by Austrians, Germans, and Poles was reported today by Post Office officials. The total deposits in the postal savings banks in this city are approximately $2,500,000, most of which is in branches in the foreign section.

MIDLAND, Penn., Feb. 7. About 1,000 Austrian coal miners drew their savings from two banks here yesterday, following a report that the severance of diplomatic relations with Austria would mean confiscation of their money by the United States. American depositors paid no attention to the flurry among foreigners when informed of the nature of the report.

GERARD SENDS WORD TO EGAN

Minister to Denmark Told That Americans Cannot Leave.

ENVOY CANNOT USE CODE

Berlin Wants Assurance of Safety of Bernstorff and the German Crews Here.

WASHINGTON IS STIRRED

Inclined to Question Report of Such Radical Action by Berlin Government.

Special Cable to THE NEW YORK TIMES.

COPENHAGEN, Feb. 7.—I am authorized by the American Legation to say that Minister Egan today received several sensational dispatches from Ambassador Gerard.

The latter telegraphs that the German authorities will not permit Americans to leave Germany at present. He says that he, his staff, and all American Consular officials will be detained until the fate of Count von Bernstorff and the German crews from the captured German ships in America has been decided.

The German authorities are denying Mr. Gerard the right to telegraph in code. All correspondence with the Copenhagen Legation is now in plain English.

Ambassador Gerard advised Minister Egan that the sailors captured on the Yarrowdale will be detained on the same grounds as the other Americans.

Confirmation from Berlin.

Special Cable to THE NEW YORK TIMES.

BERLIN, Feb. 7, (via London, Feb. 8, 5:40 A. M.)—Ambassador Gerard is still without instructions from the Foreign Office as to his departure. These seem to be withheld until arrangements regarding Count von Bernstorff's repatriation are concluded.

BERLIN, Feb. 6, (via London, Feb. 7.)—The Foreign Office thus far has received no definite information in regard to the former German Ambassador at Washington, Count von Bernstorff, which probably must arrive before the details of Ambassador Gerard's departure can be decided.

Mr. Gerard has not yet received his passports, and does not know definitely when he will depart, although he has decided upon the route via Switzerland.

The rush of Americans seeking passports and information at the American Embassy lessened considerably today, and at the closing hour most of the work had been completed by the officials and employes.

REPORT STIRS WASHINGTON.

But Capital Hopes It Is Not True—Detention a Serious Matter.

Special to The New York Times.

WASHINGTON, Feb. 7.—Press dispatches from Berlin, dated yesterday, and received in this country late tonight, have given a very sensational turn to the situation produced by the breaking of relations between the United States and Germany. These dispatches, read in the light of messages received previously, indicate that James W. Gerard, Ambassador to Germany and the members of his staff are being detained by the German Government as hostages to insure fair treatment of Count von Bernstorff, the German Ambassador to the United States, and the members of his suite.

Any such action by the German Government would give great offense to the United States and might result in a declaration of war by this Government if Germany did not immediately comply with a demand to relieve the American Ambassador and those under his protection from restriction of this character.

A report came to this country from Copenhagen yesterday that Ambassador Gerard would not be permitted to leave Berlin until definite information concerning the status of Count von Bernstorff had been received by the German Government. Tonight THE NEW YORK TIMES received a dispatch from its correspondent in Copenhagen saying he was authorized by the American Legation there to say that Minister Egan

Continued on Page 3.

---

14 Vessels, of 29,997 Tonnage, Sunk Yesterday, Brings Total Tonnage Since Feb. 1 Up To 116,341

The destruction of shipping in the war zone since the announcement of the German blockade order, to take effect Feb. 1, was raised to 115,219 tons by the sinkings announced yesterday. The results attained to date follow:

Reported Sunk Yesterday.

Ships.	Tonnage.	Ships.	Tonnage.
California, British....	8,662	Ferruccio, Italian....	2,192
Crown Point, British.	5,218	Lorton, Peruvian.....	1,419
Azul, British........	3,074	Saxon Briton, British.	1,337
St. Ninian, British...	3,026	Macarena, Spanish	1,122
Corsican Prince, British	2,776	Vistra, British.......	1,021
		2 trawlers, British...	100
		2 fishing boats, British	50

Total reported sunk yesterday......................29,997
Previously reported sunk......................86,344

Total tonnage sunk since Feb. 1......................116,341

Summary of Ships Sunk Since Feb. 1.

American	Other Neutrals	British	Other Belligerents
1	21	32	5

BRITISH CONFIDENT U-BOATS WILL FAIL

Admiralty Official Says "We Knew It Was Coming and Prepared for It."

HINTS OF NEW MEASURES

Eight Vessels Fired at in One Day Escaped Without Damage, He Declares.

Special Cable to THE NEW YORK TIMES.

LONDON, Feb. 7.—Notwithstanding the heavy losses of shipping reported today, expert opinion regarding the submarine menace remains firm that the German hopes of starving out Great Britain are vain.

Admiral von Cappelle's statistics, published in the Lokal-Anzeiger, are alarming on their face value, and it is, not denied even by the most optimistic that considerable reduction in the country's overseas supplies may be brought about by submarine agencies. The Germans assert that British shipping to the extent of 400,000 tons was sunk during December last and at the rate of destruction recorded in today's announcements, which show twenty-two ships aggregating 54,000 tons sent to the bottom, the 6,750,000 tons which von Cappelle calculates is all that Great Britain can utilize for bringing supplies into the country would be seriously reduced by the end of January next. It is pointed out, however, that the announcements made today do not mean that this toll of ships sunk is a criterion of what submarines can do. Some of the vessels were sunk several days ago.

Sir Norman Hill, Secretary of the Liverpool Steamship Owners' Association, says that from the beginning of the war the Germans never in any single month sank more than 1 per cent. of British ocean-going tonnage, half of 1 per cent. having been the average, and he does not believe that the present submarine menace is on the whole seriously aggravated. It is further pointed out that the best antidote to any nervousness about the unrestricted campaign is provided by the new scheme for the insurance of British ships, which shows the new rates fixed by underwriters and brokers in consultation with the Government to be well below those hitherto quoted for neutral vessels carrying essential cargoes. The high rates charged for the insurance of neutral ships, prejudiced arrangements for the use of as large a quantity of neutral tonnage as possible, and the lower figure will bring more vessels into the freight market. Incidentally, The Westminster Gazette remarks that it will show the world that those in authority do not believe Germany will be able to carry out her fiercest threats.

This confidence is particularly marked at the British Admiralty. An official who was questioned by THE NEW YORK TIMES correspondent today about the unrestricted submarine campaign said:

"It is on. They are sinking everything they can."

He went on to say that although the Germans had sent out all the submarines they could, the British Admiralty had long been expecting the present campaign and the Germans had met with "some surprises."

"From the evidence we have had of German submarine activity there is no doubt in the world that the Germans are out to sink every craft afloat if they can." The official continued: "That means that sooner or later they are going to torpedo a ship with Americans aboard, perhaps an American ship itself. The Germans gave a warning months ago that they were going to try to starve Great Britain. They boasted that they could sink enough ships to starve us within a few weeks' time. They started on Feb. 1 with all the submarines they could send out. The British Navy was not asleep, however, and I can say that we have met their attack in a way quite satisfactory to us. It means that we have done just what we expected" was the reply.

"If Germans thought they would sink every ship in sight they made a miscalculation. As evidence of what they have failed to do I might say that at least eight British merchantmen, at

Continued on Page 6.

SHELLED EAVESTONE WITHOUT WARNING

Attack Made in the Open Sea 100 Miles from Land, Survivors Say.

CREW ENTERED TWO BOATS

Guns Turned on These When Two Ship's Lengths Away, Killing Wallace and Five.

Special Cable to THE NEW YORK TIMES.

LONDON, Thursday, Feb. 8.—The Daily News says this morning:

"Survivors of the crew of the Eavestone who arrived yesterday, stated that there was no justification whatever for the submarine firing on them as everybody had left the ship. They were a hundred miles from land in the open sea for nine hours in tempestuous weather.

"A message from Queenstown says that the survivors stated that without warning the submarine commenced to fire shells at them. The crew of the Eavestone then got two boats over the ship's side into the water and succeeded in getting away from the vessel, which had been terribly damaged by shell fire.

"They were only two ships' lengths away when the guns of the submarine were turned on to the two boats, killing Richard Wallace of Baltimore and five others."

LONDON, Feb. 7.—Ambassador Page today forwarded to Wesley Frost, the American Consul at Cork, instructions from Washington to obtain affidavits from the members of the crew of the British steamship Eavestone for transmission to the State Department. The American Embassy here has been advised that the survivors have been landed on the Irish coast.

The steamship Eavestone, according to an official report, was sunk by a German submarine, which shelled the boats as they were leaving the sinking steamer, killing the Captain and three seamen, one of whom was Richard Wallace, an American negro, of Baltimore.

Fourteen Vessels Reported Sunk.

LONDON, Feb. 7.—Several lives were reported lost in connection with the sinking of thirteen more ships announced by Lloyd's Shipping Agency today. The fatalities occurred on the British steamers Corsican Prince and the Saxon-Briton. Seventeen members of the former's crew are still missing and two of the latter's crew were killed by shellfire from a German submarine.

Of the vessels destroyed today Britain was again the greatest sufferer in the matter of tonnage, the eleven vessels sunk under her flag having a total tonnage of 25,264. Only one neutral ship was listed among the new victims of the U-boats, that being a Peruvian vessel. The other ship destroyed was owned by Italians. The vessels announced as lost were:

The California, British; the Crown Point, British; the Azul, British; the St. Ninian, British; Corsican Prince, British; Ferruccio, Italian; Lorton, Peruvian; the Saxon-Briton, British; the Vistra, British, and two British trawlers and two British fishing boats.

The Corsican Prince was sunk this morning and part of her crew was landed. The Captain and fourteen others from the Saxon-Briton also have been landed. Twelve survivors from the Azul were rescued by a sailing vessel. Whether there was any loss of life on this vessel is unknown at the present time.

The Peruvian sailing vessel Lorton, while on a voyage from Callao, Peru, was sunk by a German submarine on Monday inside Spanish territorial waters, according to a British official announcement, which says:

"The Peruvian sailing vessel Lorton, on a passage from Callao, was sunk by

Continued on Page 3.

AMERICAN, IN CREW, SAVED

Two Women and Several Children Among Missing; One Known Death.

TWO TORPEDOES HIT SHIP

Fired Without Warning from a Distance of 300 Yards, the Captain Asserts.

MAY BE THE 'OVERT ACT'

News Creates Great Excitement in Washington—Wilson Will Move Cautiously.

Special to The New York Times.

WASHINGTON, Feb. 7.—The State Department was officially notified tonight by Wesley Frost, American Consul at Queenstown, that the British steamer California of the Anchor Line had been sunk without warning off the coast of Ireland with 200 persons on board. Some of the passengers and crew, he reported, were still missing, including two women and several children.

There was at least one American survivor—John A. Lee of Montgomery, Ala., thought to have been a member of the crew, and who is reported by Consul Frost as having been saved.

Consul Frost's first message regarding the loss of the California reached the State Department late this afternoon, and was given out in paraphrase as follows:

"Anchor Line California has been sunk, bound for Glasgow, presumably from New York. Two hundred persons on board. One death, thirty hospital cases. Survivors reached here late tonight."

The State Department made public tonight additional information received from Consul Frost. This information is understood to have been received in a second message from the Consul, and declared that the California went down immediately, after having been fired at with two torpedoes, and that it was torpedoed without warning.

The text of Consul Frost's message containing this information was not given out by the State Department, but this paraphrase of the Frost message was issued:

"Consul Wesley G. Frost, at Queenstown, cabled the State Department tonight that the British liner California had been torpedoed without warning off the Irish coast, and that one American, known to have been on board, was saved. Some of the passengers and crew still were missing, including two women and several children.

"The Captain of the ship was quoted as saying the submarine did not hail or give any warning before firing two torpedoes from a distance of 300 yards. The American survivor was John A. Lee of Montgomery, Ala., who was supposed to have been a member of the crew."

The statement in Consul Frost's message that the California was sunk without warning at a distance of 300 yards, that women and children are missing, and that at least one American was on board, gives the California case a most grave aspect in the present crisis, and if this information is fully confirmed the cast may be regarded by the President as the overt act which he told Congress he was unready to believe Germany intended to commit.

Whether any Americans were or were not killed, complete proof that the vessel was attacked without warning without regard for the lives of men, women, and children on board, will present the gravest possible situation in the present crisis, as the mere presence of a single American on board means that an American life was jeopardized by an attack that is officially reported to have been without warning.

Consul Frost says that the Captain of the California is quoted as saying the submarine did not hail or give warning, but fired two torpedoes. Whether or not the Consul has been able to confirm the Captain's statement from other sources is not disclosed, but it is a fact that the announcement authorized by the State Department tonight, based on Consul Frost's dispatch, says without qualification or reservation the Consul reported that the vessel had been torpedoed without warning.

The mere fact that one American survivor was saved does not alter the issue as laid down in the various notes to Germany during the past two years, in which it has been steadily insisted upon, that the lives of Americans on any peaceful merchant steamers should not be "jeopardized" by unwarranted attacks.

If the steamer was attacked without warning and without affording safety for human lives, and lost no immunity through attempting to escape or through resistance while Americans were on board, the issue is as serious as if those Americans had been killed.

That an Am[illegible]

"All the News That's Fit to Print."

The New York Times.

THE WEATHER
Cloudy, colder today; Thursday snow or rain; wind northeast.
For full weather report see Page 19.

VOL. LXVI...NO. 21,585. NEW YORK, WEDNESDAY, FEBRUARY 28, 1917.—TWENTY PAGES. ONE CENT In Greater New York, Jersey City and Newark. | Elsewhere, TWO CENTS.

PRESIDENT FINDS THE LACONIA'S SINKING AN 'OVERT ACT'; AWAITS FULL POWER FROM CONGRESS BEFORE TAKING ACTION; BILL REFRAMED AND STRENGTHENED FOR THE SENATE

GERMANY IS "GOING AHEAD"

Chancellor Regrets Break Over U-Boats, but Can't Alter His Policy.

OUR NEUTRALITY ONE-SIDED

Evidenced by "Submission" to British Restrictions, While We Refuse to Accept Germany's.

DENIES BREAKING PLEDGES

Tells Reichstag Assurances to Us Were Conditional on England's Adherence to Law.

BERLIN, Feb 27, (by Wireless to Sayville.)—Chancellor von Bethmann Hollweg's address to the Reichstag, postponed from last week, was delivered today. The Chancellor said, in part:

"While our soldiers on the front stand in the drumfire of the trenches, and our submarines, defying death, hasten through the seas, while we at home have no other—absolutely no other—task but to produce cannon, ammunition, and food, and to distribute victuals with justice; in the midst of this struggle for life and for the future of our empire, intensified to the extreme, there is only one necessity of the day which dominates all questions of policy, both foreign and domestic—to fight and gain victory."

Turning to the establishment of the barred zones around England, France, and Italy, and to the answers received from neutrals to the communication made by the Central Powers, the Chancellor said:

"We by no means underestimate the difficulties caused to neutral shipping, and we therefore try to alleviate them as much as possible. For this purpose we made an attempt to supply raw materials, such as coal and iron, needed by them, to neutral States within the boundaries of our sea forces. But we also know that all these difficulties, after all, are caused only by England's tyranny of the seas. We will and shall break this enslavement of the all non-English trade. We meet half way all wishes of neutrals that can be complied with. But in the endeavor to do so we never can go beyond the limits imposed upon us by the irrevocable decision to reach the aim of the establishment of the barred zone.

Sure Neutrals Will Thank Germany.

"I am sure that later the moment will come when neutrals themselves will thank us for our firmness, for the freedom of the seas which we gain by fighting is of advantage to them also.

"As is generally known, we did not declare a blockade, but merely established definite barred zones within which every ship has to count on immediate attack. That isolated ships escape danger is therefore self-evident. But that does not change total success. This success we shall be able to obtain partly by sinkings, partly by discouraging neutral shipping, which already has happened in the widest sense.

"Thanks to the incomparable bravery of our submarines, we are fully willing to await with full confidence further developments, which will be on the increase."

American Break "Unprecedented."

Discussing the attitude of neutrals toward the intensified submarine campaign, Dr. von Bethmann Hollweg said:

"One step further than that taken by European neutrals has been taken, (as is known,) by the United States of America. President Wilson, after receiving our note of Jan. 31, brusquely broke off relations with us. No authentic communication about the reasons which were given for his step reached me. The former United States Ambassador here in Berlin communicated only by spoken words to the State Secretary of the Foreign Office of breaking off relations, and asked for his passports. This form of breaking off relations between great nations living in peace is probably without precedent in history.

"All official documents being lacking, I am forced to rely upon doubtful sources—that is, upon the Reuter office's version of the contents of the message sent by President Wilson on Feb. 3 to Congress. In this version the President is reported to have said that our note of Jan. 31 suddenly and without previous indication intentionally withdrew the solemn promises made in the note of May, 1916. To the United States Government, therefore, no choice compatible with dignity and honor was left other than the way which had been announced in her note of April 20, 1916, covering the case if Germany should not want to give up her submarine method.

"If these arguments are correctly reported by Reuter, then I must decidedly protest against them. For more than a century friendly relations between us and America have been carefully promoted. We honored them—as Bismarck once put it—as an heirloom from Freder-

Continued on Page 4.

Reports Austria's Answer Will Be Made Tomorrow.

BERNE, Feb. 27, (via Paris.)—The American Legation here today was unofficially informed that Austria-Hungary's reply to the American note concerning the submarine situation would probably be given to Ambassador Penfield in Vienna Thursday.

The information received by the legation contained no hint as to the probable tenor of the reply.

AMERICANS READY TO LEAVE AUSTRIA

Penfield Completes Arrangements for All Diplomatic and Consular Agents to Depart.

BELIEVES BREAK IMMINENT

Spain to Take Over Our Interests—Ambassador Awaits Reply to His Aide-Memoire.

WASHINGTON, Feb. 27.—Complete arrangements for the withdrawal of American diplomatic and consular officers from Austria-Hungary have been made by Ambassador Penfield on instructions from the State Department. It was learned today that the Ambassador had been directed to take this step, the belief at the department being that a break in relations is inevitable. The Spanish Government has been asked to take over American interests, and plans have been made to expedite the withdrawal of all Americans if the break occurs.

The last report from Ambassador Penfield, a brief cable received after these instructions were sent, suggested a slight possibility that Austria's reply to this Government's aide-mémoire, asking a definition of her attitude in the submarine situation, might be favorable. No real hope was raised here, however, and no change in instructions followed.

Pending a reply to the aide-mémoire, the Austrian situation will remain in the same indefinite stage which has characterized it since the day of the rupture with Germany, when a note similar though not identical to Germany's submarine proclamation, was received from Ambassador Penfield. Then the aide-mémoire was sent asking for an exact definition of Austria's intentions, because of the difference between American relations with that country and those with Germany.

The State Department recently notified the Austrian Embassy here that Count Tarnow Tarnowski, the new Austrian Ambassador, who landed at New York the day the German proclamation was received, could not present his credentials to President Wilson until the issue between the two countries was cleared up.

The feeling prevails here that while both this country and Austria are seeking to avoid a break Germany is determined that her ally shall support to the greatest degree possible the submarine campaign. The withdrawal of the American Diplomatic and Consular Corps from Austria will not present as difficult a problem as in the case of Germany. The embassy force at Vienna is smaller, and there are only about twelve Consuls in the Dual Empire. Latest official reports indicate that while there are several hundred Austro-Americans there, there are fewer than fifty native Americans who would return to the United States in case of a break.

Penfield Hopeful, Says Berlin.

BERLIN, Feb. 27, (by Wireless to Sayville.)—"According to a telegram received here from Vienna," says the Overseas Agency, "Frederic C. Penfield, the American Ambassador, in a conversation expressed optimistic views concerning the relations between the United States and Austria-Hungary. He declared himself to be a friend of Austria, and said he was working hard in order to maintain friendly relations between the two countries. As to the probable result he was hopeful.

"The Ambassador spoke in the highest terms of the Austro-Hungarian Foreign Minister, Count Czernin, and finally asserted that he did not expect there would be a change in the relations between Germany and United States as they now stand."

BRYAN OPPOSES POWER SOUGHT BY PRESIDENT

Announces That He Will Go To Washington To Have the Request Refused.

JACKSONVILLE, Fla., Feb. 27. W. J. Bryan, in a statement issued here today, announced he was opposed to granting powers to the President such as Mr. Wilson requested of Congress yesterday. He announced he would go immediately to Washington and use his influence to have the request declined.

After reading President Wilson's address to Congress, Mr. Bryan canceled five speaking engagements in Florida and has since been in communication by telegraph with Congressional friends in Washington.

"Whatever power is conferred upon the President should, I think," said Mr. Bryan, "be so limited as not to constitute a surrender of the power of Congress."

Mr. Bryan said he had the greatest faith in the President's high purpose, but he was of the opinion that it would be unwise to delegate to the President the authority asked for "no matter how much confidence we have in the executive."

SENATORS AGREE ON GRANT

Foreign Relations Committee Reports Bill to Arm Ships.

WITH $100,000,000 CREDIT

Widened Scope of Measure Believed to Meet All the Demands of President.

LA FOLLETTE HOLDS IT UP

Action Is Expected Tomorrow and Cloture Rule May Put It Through House.

Special to The New York Times.

WASHINGTON, Feb. 27.—After many hours of discussion and with four dissenting votes, the Senate Committee on Foreign Relations this afternoon agreed on an amended draft of the bill prepared under President Wilson's direction to put into effect the proposals of his address to Congress yesterday.

The committee's amendments, while affirmatively unimportant, generally tended to strengthen the bill, while all amendments proposed with a view to curtailing the powers to be given to the President were voted down as fast as they were presented.

All of the committee's amendments related to the question of arming merchantmen. The first of these would permit shipowners as well as the President to arm American vessels and would give shipowners and ship crews full authority to protect themselves against unlawful attacks. The second amendment strikes from the bill the possible implication that the time for arming ships has not yet come, as set forth in the original measure permitting the President to arm these vessels "should it in his judgment become necessary for him to so do." The only other important amendment permits the defensive armament referred to, but expressly declares that these defensive guns may be placed "fore and aft."

Three Democratic Dissenters.

The importance of the vote in committee favoring the amended measure lies in the fact that three of the four opponents are Democrats—Senator Stone of Missouri, Chairman of the committee; Senator O'Gorman of New York, and Senator Hitchcock of Nebraska. The one Republican opponent is Senator Smith of Michigan. But a scrutiny of the Democratic names listed in opposition removes surprise and to a large degree diminishes the importance of their attitudes. Mr. Stone, although a loyal supporter of the Administration, has never favored strong measures against Germany. Mr. O'Gorman's sympathies have been interpreted as strongly anti-British. Mr. Hitchcock has been so uniformly pacifistic that his critics class him as pro-German.

The bill as finally agreed on in committee carries to the full the blanket grant of power to the President contained in the original measure. In its present form Mr Lodge of Massachusetts, the ranking Republican of the committee, said this afternoon that he could support it with pleasure.

That makes it almost certain that the bill when it is brought into the Senate tomorrow night or Thursday morning will encounter no concerted Republican opposition. Nor is Mr. Stone expected to oppose the bill's enactment. He said this afternoon that he would state his objections on the floor of the Senate, and that is expected to be the extent of his defection. In fact, this afternoon Mr. Stone labored conscientiously to expedite the bill's progress when he presented it in the Senate under instructions from his committee.

But an incident then suggested that the measure may have a stormy course before it passes the upper house. Mr. La Follette of Wisconsin, a Republican and perhaps the most violently pacifist critic of the Administration, objected to the formal reading of the bill in hopes of delaying it one day. This is taken to mean that the filibuster which Mr. La Follette already planned against the increases in the Naval bill would be extended to the bill agreed on today. When questioned directly on this point tonight, however, Mr. La Follette refused to commit himself further than to say that he would study the bill carefully.

Friends of the President's bill said today that they did not believe its failure to obtain enactment before March 4 would induce him to call an extra session. They point to his statement in his address yesterday that he believed he had the powers he asked Congress formally to ratify, and they express the belief that should circumstances arise calling, in the President's judgment, for the exercise of those powers, he would proceed without Congressional sanction, except as to the specific grant of a credit

Continued on Page 3.

Berlin Told 200 Were Killed in Paris Munitions Explosion

BERLIN, Feb. 27, (By Wireless to Sayville.)—The Frankfurter Zeitung says it has received from a private source in France, by way of Switzerland, a report that more than 200 persons were killed and 700 wounded by an explosion of ammunition depots on Feb. 2.

According to this report, more than 80,000 tons of ammunition were destroyed.

BERLIN DETAINING AMERICAN SEAMEN

Reports Infection in Yarrowdale Captives' Camp and Says They Are in Quarantine.

INDIGNATION AT CAPITAL

Washington Resents New Reason and Sends Another Inquiry Through Spanish Embassy.

BERLIN, Feb. 26, (by Wireless to Sayville, Feb. 27.)—The release of the American prisoners brought to Germany on the Yarrowdale, although ordered some time ago, says the Overseas News Agency, cannot be carried out for the moment, as an infectious disease has been discovered at the place of their residence.

As the outbreak of the malady necessitates a quarantine measure affecting the number of persons about to leave Germany, the Overseas Agency states that the delay in the departure of the Americans is in the interests of neutral countries. The hope is expressed that the quarantine will be of short duration.

The American citizens, it is announced, are safe and well.

WASHINGTON, Feb. 27.—Germany's procrastination in complying with repeated American demands for the release of the Yarrowdale prisoners is bringing the controversy to a stage of extreme gravity.

Accounted from the first perhaps the most serious difficulty between the two countries aside from the submarine issue itself, the case of the American sailors taken to Germany aboard the Yarrowdale, has been a source of growing concern and indignation among officials, some of whom now are convinced that Germany's intention is nothing more nor less than to hold the American seamen as hostages pending a decision as to peace or war. Such an act would be regarded here as not only a flagrant violation of international law and treaty rights, but an open insult to the dignity and good faith of the United States. While the Administration has been inclined to subordinate all collateral issues to the paramount principles involved in the submarine campaign, the plight of these seamen has forced itself steadily forward as one of the most important factors in the whole German crisis.

First word that the American seamen were not to be held longer as prisoners came in a dispatch from Ambassador Gerard at the time relations between the United States and Germany were broken off. Later it was learned that the German assurances of purpose to let the men go had not been carried out. This caused the State Department to forward a vigorous protest through the Spanish Government. Afterward a news dispatch said the men were about to be released.

When it was found that this was untrue a second protest was sent. The apparent answer to that was a notice received yesterday through Ambassador Willard at Madrid that the prisoners had been released on Feb. 16. This information was based on a statement by the Berlin Foreign Office to Señor Polo y Bernabe, Spanish Ambassador at Berlin.

GERMAN TOLD GERARD NOT TO GO FROM SPAIN

Washington Reports No Mention of Possible Danger Has Been Made by Former Envoy.

Special Cable to THE NEW YORK TIMES.

CORUNNA, Feb. 27. (Dispatch to The London Times.)—The members of the United States Embassy lately in Berlin in the confidence of former Ambassador Gerard are embarking here for America not without anxiety. Mr. Gerard was earnestly warned before he left Berlin by a high German friend, who always is well informed, not to risk the voyage from Spain. Mr. Gerard is hated by the German Navy, which believes that for a year and a half he stood between it and its prey.

The weather is delightfully fine.

LONDON, Wednesday, Feb. 28.—The Daily Mail's Corunna correspondent, referring to the embarkation yesterday of Mr. Gerard and his party for the United States, says:

"All the town turned out to watch the grand embarkation, which possibly is destined to become historical. The embarkation was the largest seen here in many years, as, in addition to the Americans, the Infante Isabel is carrying 1,750 Spanish emigrants to Cuba."

WASHINGTON, Feb. 27.—Reports that ex-Ambassador Gerard had been advised in an informal way by a high German official in Berlin not to sail for the United States in the way he had planned caused surprise among State Department officials, who thought Mr. Gerard would certainly have forwarded information of that sort, if received. The only instructions sent him were in reply to his query as to what to do in case of war, and advised that he hold to his original plans unless otherwise ordered.

The details of the former Ambassador's plans, including the vessel, the date and the port, were communicated to Berlin through the Spanish Ambassador. No safe conduct could be requested because the two countries are not at war. The ship is a neutral vessel, and the route does not traverse the prohibited zones.

LACONIA CASE "CLEAR CUT"

President and Advisers View It as Violation of Sussex Pledge.

FURTHER INQUIRY NEEDLESS

Next Step in Meeting the Situation Rests with Congress, Officials Hold.

WILSON READY FOR ACTION

May Arm Ships Anyway, Even if Congress Does Not at Once Grant Express Authority.

Special to The New York Times.

WASHINGTON, Feb. 27.—The sinking of the Cunarder Laconia by a German submarine 150 miles off the Irish coast, without warning, at night in rough seas, and with the loss of American lives, is regarded by President Wilson and his advisers as a clear-cut case of violation of the pledge which the German Government gave to the United States after the Lusitania and Sussex cases. From very high authority the statement was obtained tonight that the "Laconia case is clear-cut."

The Laconia case constitutes the overt act which the President has indicated would be a first step toward compelling a more vigorous policy in dealing with Germany. No further facts are needed by this Government, and no inquiry is necessary to establish the facts of the case. That was acknowledged officially today, but for the present the situation rests with Congress, whose attitude is to determine the measure of resentment to be shown by the Government over Germany's paralysis of American trade and the killing of two American citizens.

Until Congress acts on President Wilson's recommendations that he be vested with broad powers to protect American ships and lives from German aggression the President will take no action in regard to the sinking of the Laconia.

Congress Prepares to Act.

The chances are excellent that Congress will pass a bill carrying out in practically complete form the recommendation for protection made by the President in his address before the two houses of Congress yesterday. The Senate Committee on Foreign Relations this afternoon finished its consideration of the bill proposed by the Administration and made few important changes in it. The House Committee on Foreign Affairs found plenty of opposition in its membership to the President's proposals, and was obliged to postpone further consideration of the measure until tomorrow. From present appearances an effort will be made to pass the bill in the House before adjournment tomorrow night and the Senate will begin its consideration on Thursday.

After a conference had taken place early this morning between President Wilson and Secretary Lansing, it was acknowledged in authoritative quarters that the sinking of the Laconia presented a clear-cut case of violation of international law and constituted an overt act. Later in the day a regular meeting of the Cabinet was held, but nothing that occurred there seems to have changed the international situation. The President is understood to be of the opinion that instead of again going to Congress, this time to ask that the sinking of the Laconia be construed as an act of war, the better plan is to wait until Congress has granted the authority to him to protect American ships and American lives on the seas, and use that power in a way that will make Germany realize that the United States means business. It is contended that this course is in strict accordance with the program outlined by the President in his address to Congress on Feb. 3 when he announced that he had directed that diplomatic relations with Germany be severed.

Ready for War on U-Boats.

The President's plans, while not officially disclosed, are understood to contemplate arming all American merchant ships and sending them out under instructions to sink any German submarine that may attack or attempt to attack them. Whether United States naval vessels are to be employed in convoying merchantmen flying the American flag has not been made known and perhaps has not been determined. But the impression was conveyed this evening in circles where the purposes of the Administration are understood that the President will be ready to use to the utmost the authority granted to him by Congress, and will employ every means within the power of the Government to resist German attack on Amer-

Continued on Page 3.

Text of Senate Bill to Authorize the Arming of Ships and Provide $100,000,000 Defense Credit

WASHINGTON, Feb. 27.—The text of the bill drafted by the Senate Foreign Relations Committee to carry out President Wilson's policy of armed neutrality is as follows:

Be it enacted by the Senate and House of Representatives of the United States of America, in Congress assembled:

That the commanders and crews of all merchant vessels of the United States and bearing the registry of the United States are hereby authorized to arm and defend such vessels against unlawful attacks, and the President of the United States is hereby authorized and empowered to supply such vessels with defensive arms, fore and aft, and also with the necessary ammunition and means of making use of them; and that he be, and is hereby, authorized and empowered to employ such other instrumentalities and methods as may in his judgment and discretion seem necessary and adequate to protect such vessels and the citizens of the United States in their lawful and peaceful pursuits on the high seas.

The sum of $100,000,000 is hereby appropriated, to be expended by the President of the United States for the purpose of carrying into effect the foregoing provisions, the said sum to be available until the first day of January, 1918.

For the purpose of meeting the expenditures herein authorized, the Secretary of the Treasury, under the direction of the President, is hereby authorized to borrow on the credit of the United States and to issue therefor bonds of the United States not exceeding in the aggregate $100,000,000, said bonds to be in such form and subject to such terms and conditions as the Secretary of the Treasury may prescribe and to bear interest at a rate not exceeding 3 per centum per annum; Provided that such bonds shall be sold at not less than par, shall not carry the circulation privilege, and that all citizens of the United States shall be given an equal opportunity to subscribe therefor, but no commission shall be allowed or paid thereon; that both principal and interest shall be payable in United States gold coin of the present standard of value, and be exempt from all taxation and duties of the United States as well as from taxation in any form of all State, municipal, or local authorities; that any bonds issued hereunder may, under such conditions as the Secretary of the Treasury may prescribe, be convertible into bonds bearing a higher rate of interest than 3 per centum per annum, if any bonds shall be issued by the United States at a higher rate than 3 per centum per annum by virtue of any act passed on or before Dec. 31, 1918.

In order to pay the necessary expenses connected with the said issue of bonds, or any conversions thereof, a sum not exceeding one-fifth of 1 per centum of the amount of bonds herein authorized to be issued, or which may be converted, is hereby appropriated, out of any money in the Treasury not otherwise appropriated, to be expended as the Secretary of the Treasury may direct.

The President is authorized to transfer so much of the amount herein appropriated as he may deem necessary, not exceeding $25,000,000, to the Bureau of War Risk Insurance, created by act of Congress, approved Sept. 2, 1914, for the purpose of insuring vessels, their freight, passage moneys, and cargoes against loss or damage by the present risks of war.

WON'T GUARANTEE CRUISERS' SAFETY

Germany Refuses to Give Assurance That Relief Ships Will Not Be Attacked.

REQUEST MADE TO TURKEY

State Department Did Not Wish to Send Vessels to Syria Without Promise.

Special to The New York Times.

WASHINGTON, Feb. 27.—Germany has refused to guarantee the safety of the United States naval vessels Des Moines and Caesar, which are now at Alexandria, Egypt, if sent to Asia Minor laden with supplies destined for the destitute Syrians and Armenians. It was expected that when they had performed this mission of mercy the warships would bring out of Turkey about 1,000 Americans now assembled at Beirut.

A few days ago the United States Government informed the Turkish in effect that it desired assurances from Germany that the cruiser Des Moines and the collier Caesar would not be molested if they were authorized to proceed to Jaffa, where they were to unload their relief supplies, thence to Beirut, to take on board the American refugees. It was learned from an unquestioned diplomatic authority tonight that Germany had replied to the inquiries of the Turkish Government, asserting that it could not guarantee the safety of the Des Moines and Caesar from either submarine attacks or from mines, but that it had instructed its submarine commanders not to attack those vessels.

It was also stated that Turkey would not promise to furnish pilots for the American naval vessels if they entered Turkish waters, but would deal with the situation as it might exist after its waters had been entered. The Government has assurances from the Turkish Foreign Office and from the Sultan himself that the Sublime Porte desires to maintain its present friendly relations with America, but whether the Turkish military authorities and the German commanders in Turkey sympathize with the attitude of the Turkish civil officials is not known here. It is apprehended that there might be among the Turkish military authorities in Syria individuals in high command who would not hesitate to cause embarrassments if the opportunity offered.

It could not be learned tonight whether, in the absence of definite assurances from Germany that the Des Moines and the Caesar would not be attacked, those vessels would be authorized to proceed on their long-interrupted mission. It is believed that the decision will be reached by President Wilson himself in full appreciation of the dangers surrounding a voyage through the Mediterranean Sea of American naval ships. It is not doubted that an attack upon them or either of them would constitute, not "an overt act," but an act of war. That a decision must be made, however, is clear, unless the Administration elects to run no risks at all and permits the two vessels to be confined to the harbor of Alexandria or directs them to return to American waters via the Suez Canal, and thence eastward through the Pacific Ocean.

HOY SENDS APPEAL TO THE PRESIDENT

American, Who Lost Mother and Sister, Asks: "What Will America Do?"

AGED FATHER PROSTRATED

Young Man, in London, Warned His Mother Five Times to Postpone Sailing.

Special Cable to THE NEW YORK TIMES.

LONDON, Feb. 27.—"As an American whose mother and sister were drowned in the torpedoing of the Laconia, I feel I have a right to ask President Wilson, 'What is America going to do?'" Austin Hoy said today. "If this was not the overt act for which the President was waiting, then I don't know what to call it."

Mr. Hoy, who is head of the Sullivan Machinery Company of London and Chicago and a resident of Putney, a London suburb, discussed with a NEW YORK TIMES correspondent the death of his mother, Mrs. Mary Hoy, and his sister, Miss Elizabeth Hoy, after the report of their death in an open boat off the Irish coast had been confirmed by the Cunard Steamship Company. All yesterday, after the news was received here of the sinking of the Laconia, Mr. Hoy, who is 36 years old, had hoped that they would be among the survivors. He was just leaving his home at Putney, where with his father, a retired manufacturer, 75 years old, he had been awaiting word from Queenstown, when a telegraph message came giving the dreaded information of the double tragedy.

Fears for Father's Life.

Dr. Albert Harris Hoy, the father, who had been in poor health, swooned on hearing the news, and his son said tonight that he feared the tragedy would have a fatal result in the aged man's case.

"I am going to telegraph President Wilson asking him as an American citizen that the death of my mother and sister be avenged," said young Mr. Hoy.

As he spoke the young man's eyes filled with tears.

"I feel I'm entitled to do that," he continued. "I cannot rest until something is done about it. If America goes into war on account of the sinking of the Laconia I want to be the first American to enlist in the army.

"If we don't go in, I intend to join the British or French Army and go to the front to do what I can to avenge myself and my father. What else could I do? Our home is broken up because of the murderous work of the German submarine. Any man with a drop of red blood in his veins, I think, would do the same as I am going to do."

Mr. Hoy said that his father, who had lived in Chicago for years, had been a surgeon in the Federal Army in the civil war, enlisting with the Nineteenth Wisconsin Regiment. Mrs. Hoy, who was 65 years old, and her daughter, who was 30, were on their way home from a trip to Chicago on which they started from here last November.

The elder Mr. Hoy, with his wife and daughter, took up a home in England some five years ago after Austin Hoy had established himself in the machinery manufacturing business in London. The family home was at 461 North State Street, Chicago, and a branch of the Sullivan Machinery Company is at 122

Continued on Page 2.

SURVIVORS LANDED SINGING

Chant "Rule, Britannia," and Cheer on Reaching Queenstown.

MRS. HARRIS AIDED CAPTAIN

Wife of American Army Officer Was Last Woman to Leave Sinking Cunarder.

MANY TALKED WITH U-BOAT

Germans Sought Liner's Captain—Scoffed at Survivors' Peril—12 Probably Lost.

Special Cable to THE NEW YORK TIMES.

LONDON, Wednesday, Feb. 28.—A Queenstown dispatch to The Evening News says that just before 11 o'clock Monday evening the rescue ship, with the survivors of the torpedoed Cunarder Laconia on board, came into port jubilant with melody led by the women, of whom there were a hundred forward, with their hair hanging loose over their shoulders and with inflated lifebelts fixed around them.

The whole crowd sang "Rule, Britannia," and then cheered and cheered again for the Captain and officers of the sloop which had picked them up.

The first to step ashore was an American, Mrs. Harris, wife on an American Army officer, and the last woman to leave the liner as it was sinking. She stuck bravely by Captain Irvine until he had to force her into a boat which had been intended for himself.

The last dinner of the voyage was over and some of the women had already turned in and were actually in bed. In the smokeroom men were playing auction bridge. Half a dozen children were romping in the saloon. The Laconia was showing no lights and keeping a sharp lookout.

No Sign of Submarine.

Immediately following a glimpse of uninterrupted moonlight at about 9:15 o'clock the first torpedo crashed into the liner, hitting her well aft. There was no sign of the attacker and nobody even saw the sharkfin wake of the torpedo on its journey. The ship shivered under the blow. Everybody felt it and knew what had happened, but there was not the slightest panic on board.

Captain Irvine instantly ordered the turning on of every light in the ship, and in half a dozen seconds the vessel was ablaze with electricity. The familiar boat drill, practiced zealously every day by all on board, was repeated all over again as if it were a drill and no more. All the boats, fully equipped and provisioned, were swung out. As the ship began to settle down, the women and children were taken off first, and the rest of the passengers followed.

A quarter of an hour after the ship had been struck she had listed heavily to starboard. Then, as the watertight bulkheads on the port side began to fill, she slowly righted herself and lay on an even keel once more.

The Laconia was sinking, but so slowly that the murderous U-boat, watching near by, bobbed up again close alongside and let fly another torpedo. Far amidships it crashed into the engine room, and that was the end of the Laconia. Within an hour of the first shot she sank, and Captain Irvine, the wireless operator, and several officers were swimming about in the moonlight.

Liner Sank by Moonlight.

All the boats were well out of range of the maelstrom as she went down. Round about in the flickering moonlight the little fleet of lifeboats lay rocking on the swell, their passengers watching her last struggles, every soul silent and tense with emotion.

Boat 15 was standing by with women passengers of the second class on board and a full complement of sixty persons all told. Suddenly, right under her bows, rose the submarine once more, as a long cloak of cloud trailed across the moon and darkened the sea.

"We could only see the beast dimly," said one of the women, "but it was a huge black shape, dwarfing us and drenching us as it rose. We could make out two guns on board, and big guns they were, too.

"Standing by, on the platform by the periscope, were two or three men, and one of them, who said he was commander, spoke to us in a very soft voice. His English was quite good, but guttural.

"'What is the name of your ship, her tonnage and her cargo?' he said.

"Somebody near me said: 'Don't tell the murderer anything; let's just sing "Rule, Britannia," at him and defy him to do his worst.' But the steward in charge of the boat wisely said, 'No, we had better not do that. We are entirely in his hands, and the best thing to do is to answer his questions.' Then he sang out:

"'I want to tell you, first, that we

"All the News That's Fit to Print."

The New York Times.

THE WEATHER
Probably snow or rain today and Friday; wind northeast.
For full weather report see Page 21.

VOL. LXVI...NO. 21,586. NEW YORK, THURSDAY, MARCH 1, 1917.—TWENTY-TWO PAGES. ONE CENT In Greater New York. | TWO CENTS New England and Middle States. | THREE CENTS Elsewhere.

GERMANY SEEKS AN ALLIANCE AGAINST US; ASKS JAPAN AND MEXICO TO JOIN HER; FULL TEXT OF HER PROPOSAL MADE PUBLIC

CONGRESS TO BACK WILSON

Laconia Tragedy Adds Strength to President's Support.

MODIFIED BILL IN HOUSE

But Leaders Predict That Senate's Armed Neutrality Measure Will Prevail.

THINK PUBLIC IS AROUSED

Detention of Five Consuls in Germany Increases Crisis—New Demand on Turkey.

President Insists on Passage of Senate Armed Ship Bill

Special to The New York Times.

WASHINGTON, Feb. 28.—The statement was authorized by the White House tonight that President Wilson would insist on the passage of the Senate bill giving him power to arm and protect merchant ship[illegible]

WASHINGTON, Feb. 28.—Opposition in Congress to granting authority to President Wilson to protect American [illegible] and lives at sea began [illegible] [illegible] Administration leaders [illegible] predicted action within another twenty-four hours.

There were indications that many of the Republicans of the Senate who, though favoring the steps proposed, insist that Congress should be called in extra session, would vote for the measure requested by the President when the roll was called. The chief, if not the only, reason for uncertainty was found in the attitude of Senator La Follette, who has given indications of preparing for a single-handed filibuster in the closing hours of the session.

Details of the destruction of the Cunard liner Laconia, published in the morning papers and telling of the suffering and death of an American mother and daughter among the passengers, had its effect during the day. Members of the House and Senate, whose communications had come largely from pacifists, began receiving telegrams from their constituents calling for vigorous action by the Government.

The House Foreign Affairs Committee early in the day reported out the Flood bill, authorizing the President to arm American ships, with amendments eliminating the provision for the use of "other instrumentalities," and adding a prohibition against the insurance of munition ships by the Government War Risk Bureau. A special rule to expedite passage of the measure was introduced by Chairman Flood of the Foreign Affairs Committee, who said he probably would press it tomorrow. It would provide for a vote not later than 4 o'clock P. M.

Hope in Senate Bill.

The Administration plan is to have the Senate substitute for the House measure the bill reported by the Senate Committee and based upon a memorandum prepared by the President. In the form of a conference report the leaders anticipate no difficulty in having the House pass promptly the substitute.

President Wilson probably will pay particular attention to the German crisis in his second inaugural address next Monday. He has not begun work on it yet, and has put off its preparation pending further developments in the foreign situation.

An aggravating incident was added to the German situation today by the receipt of word from Germany that four American Consuls were being held there because a German Consul on his way from the United States to Ecuador had been delayed in Cuba. A statement of the facts, with a request for immediate release of the Americans, was cabled tonight.

Announcement was made at the State Department that instructions had been sent to Ambassador Elkus at Constantinople to report definitely and immediately whether Turkey would guarantee, not only for herself, but for her allies, the safety of the American cruiser Des Moines and the naval collier Caesar in taking relief supplies into Syria and bring out the 1,000 or so marooned Americans there. Ambassador Elkus, having sent a rather ambiguous promise from the Turkish authorities, was told to say that unless definite and specific guarantees were

Continued on Page 4.

No Ships Sunk Yesterday; 456,817 Tons Lost in February

No new sinkings by German submarines were reported yesterday. A record of the tonnage sunk in the German blockade zone during the whole month of February, compiled from British Admiralty figures and reports received from other sources, follows:

NUMBER OF SHIPS SUNK:

American.	Other Neutrals.	British.	Other Belligerents.
2	51	110	20

TOTAL TONNAGE DESTROYED.

American.	Other Neutrals.	British.	Other Belligerents.
3,322	93,019	316,204	44,272

Grand total: (Feb. 1-28,) 456,817 tons.

WILSON GIVES OUT APPEAL FROM HOY

American Whose Mother and Sister Died on the Laconia Asks That They Be Avenged.

OFFERS SERVICES TO NATION

Young, Nephew of Mrs. Hoy, Appeals to Wilson, Lansing, Wadsworth, and Chandler.

WASHINGTON, Feb. 28.—President Wilson has given out for publication the following cablegram which he received from Austin Y. Hoy, whose mother and sister died in a lifeboat after the Laconia was torpedoed by a German submarine:

"I am an American citizen, representing the Sullivan Machinery Company of Chicago, living abroad, not as an expatriate, but for the promotion of American trade. I love the flag, believing in its significance. My beloved mother and sister, passengers on the Laconia, have been foully murdered on the high seas.

As an American citizen outraged and as such fully within my rights and as an American son and brother bereaved, I call upon my Government to preserve its citizens' self-respect and save others of my countrymen from such deep grief as I now feel. I am of military age, able to fight. If my country can use me against these brutal assassins, I am at its call.

If it stultifies my manhood and my nation's by remaining passive under outrage, I shall seek a man's chance under another flag.

George A. Young of this city, nephew of Mrs. Mary Elizabeth Hoy, who, with her daughter, lost her life on the Laconia, made public yesterday letters he wrote to President Wilson, Secretary Lansing, Senator Wadsworth of New York and Representative Walter M. Chandler of New York.

To the President, Mr. Young wrote:

"I am advised by cable this morning that my aunt, Mrs. Mary Elizabeth Hoy, and my cousin, Miss Elizabeth Hoy, both American born and American citizens, lost their lives as a result of the torpedoing on Sunday of the Cunard liner Laconia.

I am, myself, American born and an American citizen. My father and I are the nearest male relatives in this country of Mrs. and Miss Hoy. Mrs. Hoy, her husband, and her daughter have spent most of their time of late years in London with Mrs. Hoy's only son, Austin Y. Hoy, who is European manager for the Sullivan Machinery Company, an American corporation.

Now, Sir, you will perhaps pardon me if in this moment of distress I speak somewhat strongly. My aunt and cousin are dead, and nothing that can be done by you or the American nation can return them to life. But is it not time, Sir, that you, as leader of this nation, assume your duty of leadership, stop talking, and take some definite action to prevent the recurrence of such a disaster?"

With a similar introduction, Mr. Young's letter to Secretary Lansing read:

You will perhaps pardon me if in this moment of distress I ask you if it is not time that the great American Nation, in the government of which you have an important part, should take some definite action other than windy words to prevent the repetition of an occurrence such as that related above? Inevitably, the longer such action is postponed the greater, it seems to me, will be the penalty which must be paid by the American people.

I appreciate fully the responsibility which weighs upon you and the other members of the Administration and the difficulties under which you labor as a result of the apparent differences of opinion among the American people. But this is, it seems to me, a time for leadership to assert itself, and that leadership should be of a much stronger and more definite character than any which has been displayed

Continued on Page 3.

Zimmermann Says Again Neutral Ships Will Be Sunk; Escape of the Orleans Only an Instance of Luck

Special Cable to THE NEW YORK TIMES.

BERLIN, Feb. 28, (via London.)—The report of the safe arrival of the freighter Orleans at Bordeaux did not cause much surprise here, as it was known that there were heavy fogs along the course most likely to be selected by the American vessel, which would naturally render the operations of the U-boats extremely difficult.

The fact that the Orleans, despite her speed, took nearly three weeks for the passage is regarded here as sufficient evidence that her course must have been roundabout and zigzaggy, it being assumed that she was not any too anxious to meet a U-boat.

"One swallow does not make a Summer," is the comment of the newspapers, who say it would be a mistake if the Americans supposed the U-boats had received orders to let American ships pass unmolested. No such orders have been given, according to the Berlin papers, who leave no doubt about it by quoting Foreign Secretary Zimmermann, who in an interview with a Spanish newspaper man recently took occasion to make the following unmistakable statement:

"We make absolutely no distinction in sinking neutrals' ships within the war zone. Our determination is unshakable, since that is the only way to finish the war the coming Summer, in which desire we all share."

This, it is held, can be interpreted in no other way than that American ships, like those of all other neutrals, must comply with the U-boat rulings or take the consequences.

The sinking of the Laconia, a much larger ship than the Orleans, which crossed the danger zone at about the same time, is regarded as proof that even in propitious circumstances, such as foggy weather, it is difficult to escape the U-boats.

"As a casus belli, the Orleans was a failure," says the Zeitung am Mittag, and it would seem as if the people here were rather glad it was.

Says It's Only Luck That No American Ship Has Been Sunk

AMSTERDAM, Feb. 28, (via London.)—Referring to President Wilson's statement to Congress in asking for power to arm American ships that the overt act had not yet occurred, the Cologne Volks-Zeitung says:

"It is only due to a lucky accident that American ships have not been sent to the bottom, and unless American ships avoid the danger zone the overt act is bound to come. There is no doubt that the arming of American merchantmen will mean a fight between submarines and American vessels, which necessarily will produce a state of war."

BERLIN TO REPLACE SEVEN DUTCH SHIPS

Offers Freighters for Vessels Sunk, but Holland Must Buy Them After War.

MOTIVE BEHIND SINKINGS

Hint in Washington That Berlin Ordered Destruction of Ships to Settle Holland's Policy.

THE HAGUE, Feb. 28, (via London.)—The German Government has offered to replace the seven Dutch merchantmen which were torpedoed off the English Coast last week with German freighters until the end of the war, on condition that Holland purchase them afterwards.

LONDON, Feb. 28.—At the Dutch Legation it was said today there was no confirmation of the report published earlier in the week that the Dutch steamship Bandoenig, Eemland, and Zaendijk were still afloat. On the contrary the latest information received by the Dutch officials led to the belief that the vessels had been lost. A search for the steamships proved unavailing.

Special to The New York Times.

WASHINGTON, Feb. 28.—Information received here today has suggested that Germany ordered the destruction of the seven Dutch steamers torpedoed off Falmouth Thursday in order to force the Dutch Government to show its attitude toward the Central Powers. Germany is not blind to the possibilities of danger, contained in the entrance of Holland into the war, with the opportunity it would offer to the Allies to throw an army behind the main German line of defense. Knowing that resentment against her treatment of Dutch shipping was already high, she thought, by her stroke of last week, it is suggested, to force the Netherlands Government to express itself in a way which would commit it definitely to a course of action.

In doing it, it is pointed out, Germany took advantage of certain weaknesses in Holland's immediate military situation. The dykes are frozen and cannot be cut down with the necessary promptness and thoroughness to flood the country. Germany would therefore have an open passage across the country, as the Dutch Army of 300,000 men, while adequately trained and equipped, could not expect to resist successfully the force which Germany could throw into Holland without the dykes as an auxiliary defense.

By attempting to force the Netherlands to show its hand at this time, therefore, the impression has been created in some quarters here that Germany was attempting to force its small neighbor into a subservient attitude when Holland was not in position to assert its rights.

Although the entrance into the war of The Netherlands might result in a second Belgium, and the Dutch Government has made it plain that only wanton aggression would force it into open hostilities, Germany is by no means unaware of the damage which might result from Holland's enmity, whether expressed in actual war or in commercial destruction. Besides the enlargement of the front which she would have to defend, Holland might also harm Germany without entering the war by putting an embargo on commerce between The Netherlands and Germany, thus cutting off one of Germany's principal sources of food supply.

In addition to these considerations, it was pointed out, there are a large number of interned Belgian and British soldiers in Holland, who would be reorganized into fighting units, should Holland break with Germany and decide to resist German attacks and who would be utilized immediately in operations with the Dutch Army.

GERMANY HOLDS FIVE U. S. CONSULS

Held Because a Teuton Was Detained in Cuba—Their Release Now Asked.

RITTER UNDER SUSPICION

Officials Think Swiss Legation Leaked on Detaining of Consuls and Yarrowdale Note.

WASHINGTON, Feb. 28.—Immediate release of five American Consuls being detained in Germany was asked in a note sent the Berlin Government tonight by the United States.

The request was made in a communication replying to a note received from Germany earlier in the day in which it was announced that the American officials would be allowed to travel to new posts in Europe when the Berlin Government had been officially informed that German Consuls in this country ordered to South America and Central America had been permitted to proceed.

The action of Germany was based upon circumstances which, through no fault of this Government, detained Consul Mueller at Havana, Cuba, when he was on his way from Atlanta to his new post at Quito, Ecuador. The United States in its reply made it clear that the departure from this country of German consular officials had not been interfered with and that this Government could not control the movements of German Consuls in Cuba or other foreign territory.

In all, five American consular officers are being held in Germany. Mueller was Acting Consul, representing Germany at Atlanta, when the break in diplomatic relations occurred. After his arrival in Havana he notified Berlin that he had been "detained." It is assumed that the German Government misconstrued his message and concluded that he meant to convey the impression that he was being "held" through some fault of the United States.

"Leak" Displeases Washington.

The facts that five American Consular officers were being held in Germany, pending the satisfaction of the German official mind as to the status of Mueller, and that notes had been delivered to the State Department regarding the Mueller case, were made public here late this afternoon and caused vexation and displeasure at the State Department, where the impression was created that the Swiss Legation in Washington was responsible for the "leak."

Dr. Paul Ritter, the Swiss Minister, is now representing the interests of Germany in Washington. From what could be gathered in official circles today, the State Department would be displeased to learn that Dr. Ritter or any one connected with his legation had been indiscreet enough to disclose for publication the contents of messages passing between the United States and German Governments with the Swiss Government acting as intermediary.

When confirmation of the reported detention of the five Americans was sought at the State Department a high official refused to deny or affirm the story until he could be assured of the source of the information on which the report was based. It was made plain that the State Department had not disclosed anything regarding the case, and the question was even asked in State Department circles whether this story had emanated from the Swiss Legation.

Dr. Ritter's position was described as simply that of a "messenger" be-

Continued on Page 3.

JAPAN CALLS IT MONSTROUS

Embassy Issues Statement Scouting Germany's Proposal.

RELATIONS WITH US CLOSER

Tokio Gratified by Abandonment of Exclusion Bills in Oregon and Idaho.

FLOOD SURE OF CONGRESS

Representative Says Revelation Will Insure Backing of President for Defense Preparation.

Special to The New York Times.

WASHINGTON, Thursday, March 1.—At the Japanese Embassy at an early hour this morning, when THE TIMES correspondent sought information about the German appeal to Mexico and Japan to enter into an alliance with Germany against the United States, the idea that Japan would enter such an alliance was declared to be absolutely impossible and monstrous. One of the highest officials of the embassy, after briefly considering the matter, gave to THE TIMES the following:

STATEMENT BY THE JAPANESE EMBASSY.

"This story is quite unexpected. It is a very monstrous story. It is an impossible story, and an outrageous story. It is the first knowledge that the embassy has had that any such proposal was made. If such a proposal has been made by Germany we have no knowledge that it ever reached the Japanese Government. But if such a proposal were made, it is one that could not be entertained by the Japanese Government, as it is an absolutely impossible proposal. Japan is not only in honor bound to her allies in the Entente, but could not entertain the idea of entering into any such alliance at the expense of the United States."

THE NEW YORK TIMES correspondent feels justified in stating that the United States Government has been for some time in the possession of information concerning the communication of Foreign Minister Zimmermann to the German Minister in Mexico.

Any suggestion that Japan would for a moment entertain a proposition that would mean an abandonment of her conflict with Germany in alliance with Great Britain and the other members of the Entente was scouted as ridiculous in well-informed American quarters this morning.

In this connection it may be of interest to state that THE NEW YORK TIMES correspondent had occasion a few days ago to make inquiry in the proper circles concerning a report that Japan was seeking an arrangement with the United States that would border closely on an alliance.

The information obtained from a source that could be regarded as authoritative was that while it was not true that any such arrangement was in course of consideration there was no doubt that the Japanese Government had a much more cordial regard for the United States on account of several recent occurrences that proved to Japan that the Washington Government was sincerely anxious to live up to its obligations to the Japanese.

An instance of the attitude of the United States that had caused Japan to feel most kindly toward this Government was the action of the Wilson Administration in seeking to have the Legislatures of Oregon and Idaho abandon restrictive legislation aimed at Japanese subjects in those States. There have been other instances here lately indicating that Japan was becoming convinced that her suspicion of American friendship was based on erroneous ideas.

Reports have been in circulation for some time that Japan was seeking an arrangement with the Mexican Government which would give her an advantage in a contemplated war against the United States. These rumors have been persistent. The latest phase of them was that Francisco Villa was preparing to start for Japan, and that when he returned he would bring news that would make every Mexican throw up his hat and cheer. The State Department

Continued on Page 2.

Text of Germany's Proposal to Form an Alliance With Mexico and Japan Against the United States

[Supplied by the Associated Press as an authentic copy of the German Foreign Minister's note to the German Minister in Mexico.]

BERLIN, Jan. 19, 1917.

On the 1st of February we intend to begin submarine warfare unrestricted. In spite of this, it is our intention to endeavor to keep neutral the United States of America.

If this attempt is not successful, we propose an alliance on the following basis with Mexico: That we shall make war together and together make peace. We shall give general financial support, and it is understood that Mexico is to reconquer the lost territory in New Mexico, Texas, and Arizona. The details are left to you for settlement.

You are instructed to inform the President of Mexico of the above in the greatest confidence as soon as it is certain that there will be an outbreak of war with the United States, and suggest that the President of Mexico, on his own initiative, should communicate with Japan suggesting adherence at once to this plan. At the same time, offer to mediate between Germany and Japan.

Please call to the attention of the President of Mexico that the employment of ruthless submarine warfare now promises to compel England to make peace in a few months.

ZIMMERMANN.

FILIBUSTER FOR EXTRA SESSION

Senate Republicans Force Interminable Roll Calls on Amendments to Revenue Bill.

BILL PASSED, 47 TO 33

La Follette Consents to Taking Up Armed Ship Bill Friday, and Senate Recesses.

Special to The New York Times.

WASHINGTON, Thursday, March 1.—Senate Republicans last evening began in earnest a filibuster that seemed the result of a fixed determination to force an extra session. Democratic leaders now practically despair of preventing an extra session, though still bending every effort to beat down the Republican dilatory tactics.

The filibuster began when voting was in order on the Revenue bill. Under the unanimous consent agreement, after 8 o'clock speeches could not be made, but the proceedings were prolonged by formal roll calls on an indefinite number of amendments.

The revenue bill, designed to raise \$350,000,000 through special taxes and bond issues, was passed by the Senate at 12:10 A. M. by a strict party vote, 47 to 33.

The filibuster was continued until about 1:30 A. M., when the Senate adjourned until 10 A. M.

Immediately after the vote on the Revenue bill Senator Stone, at 12:15 A. M., moved to adjourn until 12:30 A. M. so as to clear the legislative situation for consideration of the Armed Neutrality bill. Senator Penrose countered with a motion to adjourn to 10:30 A. M. That and another by Senator La Follette were beaten.

Then a motion to adjourn until 12:55 A. M. was carried 60 to 9. There were protests in the Republican ranks against the tactics of their leaders, and Senators Borah and Fall told their colleagues they were tired of seeing time wasted and wanted the Senate to get down to business.

Senator La Follette began a single-handed filibuster against the Armed Neutrality bill when the Senate reconvened at 12:55 A. M. after a recess of ten minutes.

Armed Ship Bill Advanced.

Senator Stone, Chairman of the Foreign Relations Committee, sought unanimous consent to dispense with parliamentary formalities in order to get formally before the Senate the armed neutrality measure reported by the committee, which would authorize the President to arm American ships and employ "other instrumentalities" to protect American life and rights on the sea.

Prompt objection came from Senator La Follette, who insisted upon consuming time reading the journal of previous days, over the vigorous objection of Senators Fall and Poindexter, Republicans.

Finally the Wisconsin Senator was induced to withdraw his objection on condition that there should be no attempt to pass the bill before Friday. When Democratic leaders agreed to this the committee presented the bill with a favorable report, and Senator Stone asked that it lay over until Friday.

Then the Senate adjourned until 10 A. M., the majority abandoning plans for taking up the Naval Appropriation bill.

There was no indication as to what would be the attitude of Senator La Follette when the Revenue bill came before the Senate for action. The Democrats are taking it for granted that he will oppose it, but hope he will not undertake to force an extra session by a persistent filibuster.

It was considered significant that during the closing debate on the Revenue bill there were protests from the Republican ranks against the tactics of their leaders. Senators Fall and Borah told their colleagues they were tired of dilatory tactics, that, while they believed there was business requiring an

Continued on Page 3.

PACIFISTS PRESS VIEWS ON WILSON

Bryan, Jane Addams, and Others in Two Groups Confer with the President.

FEAR DECLARATION OF WAR

Approve Executive's Grasp of the Siuation—Bryan Wants Sea Restrictions.

Special to The New York Times.

WASHINGTON, Feb. 28.—William J. Bryan with other pacifists invaded Washington today to bring their influence to bear on the President and Congress to avert war with Germany. Mr. Bryan hurried here from Miami, Fla., last night.

Two groups, the first including Jane Addams, Professor Emily Balch, Joseph Cannon, and William I. Hull, and the second Amos Pinchot, Max Eastman, Paul Kellogg, and Lillian Wald, had conferences with the President this afternoon, both lasting more than an hour. Although none of the eight would discuss their conversations with the President in detail, they said they were impressed with the grasp of the situation the President showed, and that he had assured them he would use his best efforts, as he had in the past, to keep this country out of war if possible.

Mr. Bryan, after conferring in the morning with the leaders of the Emergency Peace Federation, went to the Capitol, where he talked with the members of Congress who are particularly friendly to his peace policies. Although he insisted that he believed the bills now pending before Congress to give the President power to deal with the German crisis should be phrased so as to leave no doubt that Congress was not in any sense declaring war, he would not say that he disapproved of the proposal to give the President added powers in the present emergency.

Asked to commit himself definitely on this point, he said he preferred not to give any one advice on the subject, as his attitude would depend altogether on the phraseology with which the bill was worded when finally approved by Congress.

Mr. Bryan insisted that particular emphasis should be laid on the part of the President's address to Congress in which he said he was not proposing war or measures which must lead to war.

"I am sure that in that the President correctly interpreted the hope of the people," Mr. Bryan said. "The people desire peace, but we have a war element in the country who are doing all in their power to manufacture war sentiment."

He contended that Americans should be prevented from traveling on armed ships, and also that passengers should not be allowed to travel on ships carrying munitions. He called attention in this connection to a dispatch in a New York paper of Feb. 24 saying that the British authorities at Halifax had taken off a number of women and children from a transatlantic steamer under a regulation forbidding them to travel on the ocean during the continuance of the present unrestricted submarine blockade while three American women who were on the same ship were allowed to remain.

"Is it possible," Mr. Bryan said, "that any one will say that our Government is less careful about its people than is the British Government? I believe that American citizens should be restrained from traveling on belligerent ships at a time like this. The Captain of a belligerent ship forfeits every life aboard if he tries to escape when warned to stop.

"Life is more important than merchandise and the first duty of those in charge of a passenger ship is to guard the lives of the passengers. A ship Captain cannot give to his passengers the care and protection to which they are entitled if his thoughts are on a contraband cargo.

"The President in his message said: 'I am not now proposing or contemplating war or any steps that might lead to it.' This statement is so plain that no one ought to suppose for an instant that the President desires Congress to surrender its exclusive right to decide whether the country should go to war and when it should go to war."

WASHINGTON EXPOSES PLOT

Our Government Has Zimmermann's Note of Jan. 19.

BIG PROMISES TO MEXICO

Conquest of Texas, New Mexico, and Arizona Held Out as a Lure to Her.

BERNSTORFF CHIEF AGENT

German Embassy in Washington Head Centre of All Intrigues in This Hemisphere.

[The following dispatch was sent out by The Associated Press last night with the statement that its contents had been fully authenticated.]

WASHINGTON, Feb. 28.—The Associated Press is enabled to reveal that Germany, in planning unrestricted submarine warfare and counting its consequences, proposed an alliance with Mexico and Japan to make war on the United States if this country should not remain neutral.

Japan, through Mexican mediation, was to be urged to abandon her allies and join in the attack on the United States.

Mexico, for her reward, was to receive general financial support from Germany, reconquer Texas, New Mexico, and Arizona—lost provinces—and share in the victorious peace terms Germany contemplated.

Details were left to German Minister von Eckhardt in Mexico City, who by instructions signed by German Foreign Minister Zimmermann at Berlin, Jan. 19, 1917, was directed to propose the alliance with Mexico to General Carranza and suggest that Mexico seek to bring Japan into the plot.

These instructions were transmitted to von Eckhardt through Count von Bernstorff, former German Ambassador here, now on his way home to Germany under a safe conduct obtained from his enemies by the country against which he was plotting war.

Germany pictured to Mexico, by broad intimation, England and the Entente Allies defeated, Germany and her allies trumphant and in world domination by the instrument of unrestricted submarine warfare.

A copy of Foreign Secretary Zimmermann's instructions to von Eckhardt, sent through von Bernstorff, [printed in adjoining columns on this page of THE TIMES] is in the possession of the United States Government.

Document in President's Hands.

This document has been in the hands of the Government since President Wilson broke off diplomatic relations with Germany. It has been kept secret while the President has been asking Congress for full authority to deal with Germany, and while Congress has been hesitating. It was in the President's hands while Chancellor von Bethmann Hollweg was declaring that the United States had placed an interpretation on the submarine declaration "never intended by Germany" and that Germany had promoted and honored friendly relations with the United States "as an heirloom from Frederick the Great."

Of itself, if there were no other, it is considered a sufficient answer to the German Chancellor's plaint that the United States "brusquely" broke off relations without giving "authentic" reasons for its action.

The document supplies the missing link to many separate chains of circumstances which, until now, have seemed to lead to no definite point. It sheds new light upon the frequently reported but indefinable movements of the Mexican Government to couple its situation with the friction between the United States and Japan.

It adds another chapter to the celebrated report of Jules Cambon, French Ambassador in Berlin before the war, of Germany's worldwide plans for stirring strife on every continent where they might aid her in the struggle for world domination which she dreamed was close at hand.

Climax to Bernstorff's Intrigues.

It adds a climax to the operations of Count von Bernstorff and the German

"All the News That's Fit to Print."

The New York Times.

THE WEATHER
Fair today; tomorrow rain or snow; moderate northwesterly winds.
For full weather report see Page 19.

VOL. LXVI...NO. 21,601. NEW YORK, FRIDAY, MARCH 16, 1917.—TWENTY PAGES. ONE CENT In Greater New York. | TWO CENTS New England and Middle States. | THREE CENTS Elsewhere.

REVOLUTION IN RUSSIA; CZAR ABDICATES; MICHAEL MADE REGENT, EMPRESS IN HIDING; PRO-GERMAN MINISTERS REPORTED SLAIN

RAILWAY STRIKE ORDERED TO BEGIN TOMORROW NIGHT

Managers and Heads of Brotherhoods End Final Conference, Both Defiant.

WILSON NOW THE ONLY HOPE

President Seems to Have No Authority, but May Make Appeal to Patriotism.

FIVE DAYS' GRACE FOR MILK

Travelers to Have Time to Get Home—Appeals for the Public's Approval.

The eight-hour fight between the 250 railroads of the United States and the 400,000 trainmen has placed the country again face to face with a nation-wide railway strike.

The National Conference Committee of the Railways yesterday defied the ultimatum of the four brotherhoods that the eight-hour day should be put into effect at once, and the labor chiefs formally served notice that their strike order stood and that a progressive strike program would begin tomorrow night at 7 o'clock. Freight alone will be affected at the start.

As was the case last Fall, when the railroads and the unions broke off diplomatic relations, the only hope of averting a strike lies with President Wilson, and both the managers and the brotherhood leaders remained in New York overnight in the expectation that Mr. Wilson would take a hand in the situation. However, it is a moot question what steps the Government could take to prevent paralysis of transportation facilities and consequent weakening of the nation's resources in the international crisis. The general opinion among officials in Washington last night seemed to be that the President could do little beyond appealing to the patriotism of both sides. A provision to empower him to take over the roads in such an emergency was among the Administration recommendations for railway legislation which failed at the last session of Congress.

Daniel Willard, President of the Baltimore & Ohio, and a member of the National Defense Council, who has been watching the strike developments in New York for the last three days, left late yesterday afternoon for Washington.

Last August after the two sides broke, President Wilson sent the members of the United States Board of Mediation and Conciliation to New York to bring the two sides together. The board failed, and when a strike order was about to be issued, the President sent his Secretary, Joseph P. Tumulty, to New York, with a request that the managers and the labor leaders come to the White House. It was after he kept the two sides in Washington all during the month of August that the Adamson law was passed after a call for a national strike, effective Sept. 4, had been issued. Both sides as represented here now are in readiness to go to Washington.

Monday is decision day for the Supreme Court, and if it should hand down a decision on the Adamson law then it might lead to a renewal of conferences between the two sides regardless of the strike situation. The railroad managers have all along expressed the opinion that the law would be held invalid. The haste of the brotherhoods in forcing the issue has caused the managers to believe that the labor leaders also think the law will be thrown out. While the brotherhood heads say the action of the court one way or the other will not affect their demands, the railroad managers believe that the invalidating of the Adamson law would give them an advantage.

The word of the deadlock here yesterday was flashed to all parts of the country last night, and notices of embargoes and strike preparations were put out by nearly all of the railroads. Appeals to the patriotism of the men were made by many roads. President Wilson was among the first to get notice of the break.

Joseph Hartigan, City Commissioner of Weights and Measures, was quick to appeal to the brotherhoods to permit the movement of food trains into this city. In reply to his plea he received this letter, signed by the chiefs of the four organizations:

"Every indication now seems to warrant the statement that the freight train, engine, and yard employes on certain railways entering this city will peaceably withdraw from service at 7 P. M., Saturday, March 17, and that the employes on other lines will continue in service for several days thereafter, making it possible, in our opinion, to furnish this city food and fuel supplies for several days after the strike becomes effective.

"We regret exceedingly the necessity

Continued on Page 20.

Government Heads Hold a Mysterious Conference

Special to The New York Times.

WASHINGTON, March 15.—A conference surrounded with much mystery took place late this afternoon in the office of the Secretary of State. In addition to Secretary Lansing, it was attended by Mr. Baker, the Secretary of War; Mr. Gregory, the Attorney General; Mr. Daniels, the Secretary of the Navy; Mr. Polk, the Counsellor of the State Department, and Mr. Woolsey, personal legal adviser to the Secretary of State.

After the conference it was said by one of those who attended it that no particular subject had been discussed. It had been devoted, he indicated, to many questions that naturally came up for discussion at this critical period in the international relations of the United States. Elsewhere, however, the impression was given that the conference was called to consider matters of rather pressing importance.

FRYATT'S FATE FOR OUR GUNNERS

German Threat to Put to Death Crews of Any Armed American Ships They Capture.

WARNING IN MUNICH PAPER

Assumes That President "Realizes Fate to Which He Is Subjecting His Artillerymen."

BERNE, Switzerland, March 15, (via Paris.)—The crews of armed American merchantmen who venture to fire upon German submarines before a state of war exists between Germany and the United States, must expect to meet the fate of Captain Fryatt, warns the Munich Neueste Nachrichten, a copy of which has reached Berne, in commenting on the announcement of the State Department that American merchantmen will be armed.

"We assume," the newspaper says, "that President Wilson realizes the fate to which he is subjecting his artillerymen. According to the German prize laws it is unneutral support of the enemy if a neutral ship takes part in hostilities. If such a ship opposes the Prize Court then it must be treated as an enemy ship. The prize rules specify as to the crews of such ships. If, without being attached to the forces of the enemy, they take part in hostilities or make forcible resistance, they may be treated according to the usages of war.

"If President Wilson, knowing these provisions of International law, proceeds to arm American merchantmen, he must assume responsibility for the eventuality that American seamen will meet the fate of Captain Fryatt."

The Captain Fryatt referred to in the foregoing dispatch was Captain Charles Fryatt of the Great Eastern Railway steamer Brussels. He was tried before a German naval court-martial in July, 1916, and sentenced to death, on a charge that he had attempted to ram the German submarine U-33. The sentence of the court-martial was executed.

STONE ASKS FOR LIST OF AMERICAN SHIPS

Senate Adopts His Resolution, Which Causes Much Speculation in Washington.

Special to The New York Times.

WASHINGTON, March 15.—Senator Stone of Missouri caused some comment at the Capitol today by introducing a resolution directing the Secretary of Commerce to give the Senate a full list of sea-going vessels applying for American registry between Jan. 1, 1916, and March 15, 1917; the name and character of such vessels before and after registration, the names of the ships' owners, and the precise date of application for registry and date of receiving it. The resolution was read and adopted without discussion, and Secretary Redfield will forward the information tomorrow.

There was a good deal of speculation as to why Mr. Stone, Chairman of the Committee on Foreign Relations, should want this information made public. One suggestion was that he might think that some belligerent nation was permitting its ships to be registered in the United States, so that through the later torpedoing of these ships by German submarines the United States might be drawn into the war. It was suggested that if Mr. Stone wanted the information for his own use, he could have got it by telephoning the Department of Commerce.

Mr. Stone showed no desire to explain his resolution and seemed prepared to rebuff questioners. He said that his resolution spoke for itself. When asked if the changes in the ownership of the Algonquin had prompted his resolution, the Senator said that he would not be interviewed.

LONDON HAILS REVOLUTION

Expected Czar's Overthrow and Sees Brighter Prospects for the Allies.

THINK THE COUP DECISIVE

Well-Informed Observers Believe the Patriotic War Party Has Made Its Control Secure.

FEAR NO SEPARATE PEACE

With Weak Ruler Deposed and Pro-German Advisers Ousted, They Predict New Victories.

Special Cable to THE NEW YORK TIMES.

LONDON, Friday, March 16.—It is the belief in well-informed circles here that the Provisional Government which has been set up in Russia by the military party will be able to keep the upper hand in maintaining a policy that means the uninterruptedly vigorous prosecution of the war to a victorious end.

The overthrow of the Czar was expected, and observers here are confident that the Grand Duke as regent will have the solid support of the war party, while they are equally sure of the elimination of any element with a pro-German taint.

An Anti-German Uprising.

As the situation is explained to THE NEW YORK TIMES correspondent, the revolution simply means that German sympathizers within the Russian Government have been overthrown, and that no chance remains for a separate peace being secretly arranged with Germany. This, it is felt, is the real basis of the revolution that has worked such a sudden change in Russian politics.

This revolution, which has been on the verge of boiling over for months, reached its crisis three days ago, when the military leaders, with the Duma behind them, started outbreaks in Petrograd and Moscow. It is evident from the way in which the uprising was conducted, says THE NEW YORK TIMES correspondent's informant, that it had been carefully planned and skillfully executed.

"After it got under way," he says, "there was no hesitation of movement until the members of the military party were masters of the situation. The details of what occurred in Petrograd and Moscow are lacking, but enough is known to show that they have been in a fever of sanguinary revolution for the last three days.

"Dashes of troops against the headquarters of the pro-German leaders, with the capture of Protopopoff and Stürmer as prisoners of war, were conspicuous features of the revolution. The houses of German sympathizers were burned in both cities, and the occupants either taken captive or forced to flee.

"Now that the military party is in control the situation is said to be settling down, with every prospect that the aim of the Revolutionists will be accomplished."

In fact, the situation was described last night as being "entirely satisfactory."

For months, said the informant of THE NEW YORK TIMES correspondent, Great Britain had been expecting an outcome of the Russian political crisis that would mean the solid intrenchment of the war party and the downfall of those seeking a separate peace with Germany. Now it may be confidently expected that Russia will play her part in the war with even greater vigor than before.

German-Born Czarina Blamed.

The Daily Chronicle in its leading article says:

"From a very early period the German-born Czarina and the clique of pro-German reactionaries whom her influence made powerful with the Czar were bent on ending the war prematurely in the interests of reaction. The Ministers set up under these auspices have for over two years acted in defiance of public opinion. Their policy was not obscure; they hampered the army in respect of munitions, disorganized the country in respect of its distributive services, brought about artificial famine in a land which is one of the world's chief food producers, and themselves, through police agents, tried to stir up abortive revolts in order that they might plead military failure and internal revolution as a reason for withdrawing from the war.

"The people foiled them for long by magnificent and much enduring patriotism. When the Government left the army without munitions the local authorities—the zemstvos and unions of towns—stepped in and organized their

Continued on Page 2.

Duma Appeals to the Army for Unity Against Foe; Gives Pledge of No Weakening or Suspension of War

LONDON, March 15.—The Reuter correspondent at Petrograd telegraphs under date of yesterday:

"The Military Committee of the Duma has asked all the officers not yet employed by the committee to undertake the organization of the soldiers who joined the people, and help guard the capital. The committee issued a statement, pointing out that at the present moment, when facing an enemy who wished to take advantage of the temporary weakness of the country, it was absolutely necessary to make every effort to maintain the power of the army. It added that the blood of the Russians who had died during the two and a half years of war pledged the people to do this.

"The President of the Duma sent telegrams to the commanders of the Baltic and Black Sea fleets, to the chiefs of the armies on the northern, southwestern, western, Rumanian, and Caucasus fronts, and to the Chief of the General Staff, requesting that the army and navy preserve absolute calm, and to be sure that the struggle against the foreign enemy was not suspended or weakened even for a single moment. The telegram sent these commanders added:

> As hitherto, the army and navy must continue firmly and valiantly to defend the country, and while the Provisional Committee is aided by the military element in the capital and with the moral support of the people in restoring calm and regular activity, each officer, soldier, and sailor should fulfill his duty.

"The officers of the Petrograd garrison at a general meeting unanimously agreed to recognize the authority of the Executive Committee of the Duma until the formation of a permanent Government.

"An imperial bodyguard regiment rode into Petrograd today. It is estimated that there are now 60,000 troops in the capital."

People in Revolt Burn and Slay in Streets of Russia's Capital

Fashionable Hotel Riddled by Machine Guns When Pro-German Shoots at Crowd—Count Fredericks's Home Set on Fire and Family Ill-Treated—General de Knorring Shot.

Stuermer and Protopopoff Reported Assassinated

Special Cable to THE NEW YORK TIMES.

LONDON, Friday, March 16.—The Exchange Telegraph's Copenhagen correspondent sends the following:

"A telegram to the Extrabladet reports that the Russian Consul in Haparanda states that the pro-German ex-Prime Minister, Boris Stürmer, and Minister of Home Affairs Protopopoff have been murdered."

Special Cable to THE NEW YORK TIMES.

LONDON, Friday, March 16.—Belated dispatches from Petrograd, giving details of the revolution in Russia, are arriving here. A dispatch to The Morning Post, dated Wednesday, says:

"Every weapon save only heavy artillery has been freely used in Petrograd streets for four days past, and today there is still considerable firing at various points at intervals. Rifles, revolvers, machine guns, and armored motors—all have been used and are still in use.

"The military hotel, formerly the Astoria Hotel, which lodged exclusively officers from the front, their wives and families, with the majority of officers present here as representatives of the Allies, was subjected to a heavy fusillade from machine guns on armored motors, entirely as the result of what was represented as provocation on the part of a pro-German resident, who fired upon the people from the windows.

General's Daughter Wounded.

"The daughter of the Russian General Prince Tumanoff, who is now commanding a cavalry division at the front, was severely wounded in the neck, and her rooms were ruined by the fusillade. A mob of armed men—soldiers, sailors, and civilians—thoroughly searched the Astoria, and disarmed all the Russian officers, but showed marked consideration for the allied officers.

"Similar scenes have been enacted throughout Petrograd, while in the transpontine regions occupied by the factory population, heavy fighting has been in progress for days, until the alleged excessive cruelty of the police caused the Cossacks and soldiery to espouse the side of the people.

"The ease with which the whole of the capital fell into the hands of the revolutionaries very greatly mitigated the bloodshed inevitable in civil tumults, but the butcher's bill is undoubtedly heavy enough."

Supplementing this by a telegram dated Thursday the same correspondent says:

"Precisely one week ago peaceful street demonstrations, at first largely composed of women and children, were made in protest against the inadequate supply of black bread. The police, unable to cope with the movement, which they felt bound to crush by the usual police methods, called in the aid of the Cossacks.

"The workmen, who had held aloof from the overt demonstrations as organized bodies and who were at first represented only by the younger, irresponsible workingmen, were enraged at the rough treatment by the police of their women and children and were encouraged by the obvious reluctance of the Cossacks and soldiery generally to back up the police oppression. Finally the Cossacks turned on the police, who fled before them, and there was a pandemonium of irregular shooting.

"Matters were not improved by the setting at liberty of political prisoners and criminals and the burning of prisons. On the whole, however, the bloodshed, compared with the magnitude of the achievement, has been infinitesimal. Regiment after regiment, brought in from outside the capital, promptly joined their comrades on the side of the people, and when a special body of lifeguards known as the Imperial Convoy also came in it felt that the old régime had fallen indeed.

Rowdy Element Breaks Loose.

"In the meantime the red revolutionary parties were preaching anarchy in all its forms, and the rowdy elements of the population of the great city were busy indulging their professional instincts.

"Happily the worst incentive to violence—alcohol in all its forms—was almost unprocurable, and the disciplined sense of the soldiery, who now formed the majority, was against excesses which disgraced what was now felt to be the great cause of national freedom.

"M. Rodzianko, at the head of the Duma Committee, soon issued commonsense orders for the disarming of civilians and for the checking of red revolutionary manifestations. The soldiers and people themselves put a stop to the looting. Throughout the city a careful search was made for stores of foodstuffs, which were promptly put on sale. The results warrant the belief that unscrupulous profiteering on an incredible scale had long been prevalent.

"At the present moment a careful search is being made for higher military officers and other functionaries, who are being induced to accept the new conditions and carry on their public duties or undergo arrest. The secret police, that scourge of the Russian nation whose service is despised by all, and which has been for a generation past the refuge for defaulters and detected miscreants of all other public services receive no mercy, but the ordinary police are being merely put under arrest.

Police Stations Destroyed.

The Petrograd correspondent of The Daily Chronicle sent the following, bearing Wednesday's date:

"In Moscow, Kiev, and Kharkoff the troops have signified adherence to the new movement, and in Moscow the police have surrendered of their own accord. The Department of Police in Petrograd has been rifled and the building of the secret police, that hotbed of political intrigue, has been burned, and all police stations in town looted and their contents burned or scattered.

"The ordinary and political police, in some cases, were killed. In other cases, they were dragged from their hiding places and lodged in dark cells in the fortress of St. Peter and St. Paul, where so many have suffered martyrdom for Russian freedom. The political prisoners, victims of the old régime, have been freed from the jails, and many are now taking part in the reorganization of the Government."

Count Fredericks's Home Burned.

LONDON, Friday, March 16.—The Times Petrograd correspondent describes the sacking of the residence of Count Fredericks, Minister of the Imperial Court and Aide de Camp to the Emperor, as one of the most deplorable incidents of the revolt.

Count Fredericks's house was set on fire. His aged wife was carried out fainting. His daughter, who is frail, rushed out, carrying her favorite dog. The girl was ill-treated by the drunken mob, and the dog was killed. Both women eventually were taken to a place of safety.

Count Fredericks is now in attendance upon former Emperor Nicholas.

General de Knorring was ordered to report to the Duma, but refused to comply with the summons. On the contrary, he armed himself and the janitor

Continued on Page 2.

ARMY JOINS WITH THE DUMA

Three Days of Conflict Follow Food Riots in Capital.

POPULACE TAKE UP ARMS

But End Comes Suddenly When Troops Guarding Old Ministers Surrender.

CZAR FINDS CAPITAL GONE

Returns from Front After Receiving Warning from Duma and Gives Up His Throne.

Empress Reported Under Guard or Hiding From Angry People

Special Cable to THE NEW YORK TIMES.

PETROGRAD, March 14. (Dispatch to The London Daily Chronicle.)—The Empress of Russia has been placed under guard.

LONDON, March 15.—According to information received here the Russian people have been most distrustful during recent events of the personal influence of Empress Alexandra. She was supposed to exercise the greatest influence over Emperor Nicholas.

It is stated that her whereabouts is not known, but it is believed she is in seclusion, fearing the populace.

The Empress Alexandra before her marriage to the Emperor of Russia in 1894 was the German Princess Alix of Hesse-Darmstadt.

PETROGRAD, March 15.—Emperor Nicholas of Russia has abdicated, and Grand Duke Michael Alexandrovitch, his younger brother, has been named as Regent.

The Russian Ministry, charged with corruption and incompetence, has been swept out of office. One Minister, Alexander Protopopoff, the head of the Interior Department, is reported to have been killed, and the other Ministers, as well as the President of the Imperial Council, are under arrest.

A new national Cabinet is announced, with Prince Lvoff as President of the Council and Premier, and the other offices held by the men who are close to the Russian people.

Petrograd has been the scene of one of the most remarkable risings in history, beginning with minor food riots and labor strikes last week Thursday. The people's cry for food reached the hearts of the soldiers, and one by one the regiments rebelled, until finally those troops which had for a time stood loyal to the Government gathered up their arms and marched into the ranks of the revolutionists.

Duma President Leading Figure.

Michael V. Rodzianko, President of the Duma, was the leading figure among the Deputies, who unanimously decided to oppose the imperial order, issued last week, for a dissolution of the House. They continued their sessions, and M. Rodzianko informed the Emperor, then at the front, that the hour had struck when the will of the people must prevail.

Even the Imperial Council realized the gravity of the situation, and added its appeal to that of the Duma that the Emperor should take steps to give the people a policy and government in accordance with their desires and in order that there should be no interference with carrying on the war to a victorious ending.

The Emperor hastened back to the capital, only to find that the revolution had been successful and that a new Government was in control.

The Empress, who, it is alleged, has been influential in the councils opposed to the wishes of the people, is reported to have fled or to be in hiding.

Although considerable fighting took place, it is not believed that the casualties are large. One report says that they do not exceed 500.

A few defenders of the old régime put up a last feeble defense last night from the roofs of the wrecked Astoria Military Hotel and St. Isaac's Cathedral, facing on two sides of the same square.

The city is now quiet and perfect order prevails. So far as is known, no foreigners were injured.

The Imperial Palace at Tsarskoe-Selo is said to have been in a state of siege, but thus far no firing has been reported between the guards defending the palace and the revolutionists and troops.

According to one report the Emperor expected trouble to follow from his decree dissolving the Duma, and so warned the residents of Tsarskoe-Selo to arrange to remain in the suburb for an indefinite period.

Began From Strikes a Week Ago.

The most phenomenal feature of the revolution was the swift and orderly transition whereby the control of the city passed from the régime of the old Government into the hands of its opponents.

The visible signs of revolution began on Thursday, March 8. Strikes were declared in several big munitions factories as a protest against the shortage of bread. Men and women gathered and marched through the streets, most of them in an orderly fashion. A few bread shops were broken into in that section of the city beyond the Neva, and several minor clashes between strikers and police occurred.

Squads of mounted troops appeared, but during Thursday and Friday the utmost friendliness seemed to exist between the troops and the people.

This early period of the uprising bore the character of a mock revolution, staged for an immense audience. Cossacks, charging down the street, did so in a half-hearted fashion, plainly without malice or intent to harm the crowds, which they playfully dispersed. The troops exchanged good-natured raillery with the working men and women, and as they rode were cheered by the populace.

Long lines of soldiers stationed in dramatic attitudes across Nevsky Prospect, with their guns pointed at an imaginary foe, appeared to be taking part in a realistic tableau. Machine guns, firing rounds of blank cartridges, seemed only to add another realistic touch to a tremendous theatric production which was using the whole city as a stage.

On Saturday, however, apparently without provocation, the troops were ordered to fire on people marching in Nevsky Prospect. The troops refused to fire, and the police, replacing them, fired rifles and machine guns.

Then came a clash between troops and police, which continued in desultory fashion throughout Saturday night and Sunday. The Nevsky Prospect was cleared of traffic by the police and notices were posted by the commander of the Petrograd military district warning the people that any attempt to congregate would be met by force.

Until Sunday evening, however, there was no intimation that the affair would grow to the proportions of a revolution. The first serious outbreak came at 5 o'clock, when the men of the Volyn Regiment shot their officers and revolted when they received an order to fire upon striking workingmen in one of the factory districts.

Another regiment detailed against the mutineers also joined the revolt. The news spread rapidly to the other barracks and four more regiments went over. Some of the revolting troops marched to the St. Peter and St. Paul Fortress on the left bank of the Neva, and after a brief skirmish with the garrison took possession of it.

Dissension spread among the troops, who did not understand why they should be compelled to take violent measures against fellow-citizens whose chief offense was that they were hungry and were asking the Government to supply bread. Several regiments deserted. A pitched battle began between the troops who stood with the Government and those who, refusing to obey orders, had mutinied, and even slain their officers.

A long night fight took place between the mutinous regiments and the police at the end of St. Catharine Canal, immediately in front of the historic church built over the spot where Alexander II. was killed by a bomb. The police finally fled to the rooftops all over the city and were seen no more in the streets during the entire term of the fighting.

Turning Point in Revolution.

Still, on Monday morning the Government troops appeared to control all the principal squares of the city. Then came a period when it was impossible to distinguish one side from the other. There was no definite line between the factions. The turning point appeared to come about 3 o'clock in the afternoon. For two hours the opposing regiments passively confronted each other along the wide Liteiny Prospect in almost complete silence.

From time to time emissaries from the revolutionary side rode to the opposing ranks and exhorted them to join the side of the people. For a while the result seemed to hang in the balance. The troops appeared irresolute, awaiting

Leading Figures in Russian Revolution.

Czar Nicholas II who has Abdicated. Czarevitch Alexis 12 Yrs old who will succeed to the Throne.

Grand Duke Michael Alexandrovitch who has been named Regent. Michael Rodzianko, Head of the Revolution and the Temporary Government.

Prince Lvoff Heads Cabinet; Milukoff Foreign Minister

PETROGRAD, via London, Friday, March 16.—The members of the new National Cabinet are announced as follows:

Premier, President of the Council, and Minister of the Interior—Prince Georges E. Lvoff.

Foreign Minister—Professor Paul N. Milukoff.

Minister of Public Instruction—Professor Manuiloff of Moscow University.

Minister of War and Navy, ad Interim—A. J. Guchkoff, formerly President of the Duma.

Minister of Agriculture—M. Ichingareff, Deputy from Petrograd.

Minister of Finance—M. Tereschtenko, Deputy from Kiev.

Minister of Justice — Deputy Kerenski of Saratoff.

Minister of Communications—N. V. Nekrasoff, Vice President of the Duma.

Controller of State—M. Godneff, Deputy from Kazan.

"All the News That's Fit to Print."

The New York Times.

THE WEATHER
Rain by tonight; wind south; Sunday rain, strong northwesterly winds
[illegible]

VOL. LXVI...NO. 21,602. NEW YORK, SATURDAY, MARCH 17, 1917.—TWENTY PAGES. ONE CENT In Greater New York. | TWO CENTS New England and Middle States. | THREE CENTS Elsewhere.

THE ROMANOFF DYNASTY ENDED IN RUSSIA; CZAR'S ABDICATION FOLLOWED BY MICHAEL'S; CONSTITUTIONAL ASSEMBLY TO BE CONVOKED

WILSON APPEALS TO PATRIOTISM TO AVERT STRIKE

Sends Lane, Wilson, Willard, and Gompers of Defense Council Here to Mediate.

NIGHT MEETING FRUITLESS

Committee Asserts Government Has No Plan to Take Over Roads.

EMBARGOES TIGHTENED UP

President Leaves Sickbed to Attend Cabinet Meeting—Gompers Not at First Conference.

The Council of National Defense, at the instance of President Wilson and the Cabinet, last night stepped into the breach between the railroads and the four brotherhoods, and in the name of patriotism appealed to both sides to avert the nation-wide transportation strike called to begin at 7 o'clock tonight. It was the most important action taken by the Council since it was formed recently to mobilize the defense resources of the United States.

President Wilson, after a Cabinet meeting and a session of the Council in Washington, named this committee to make an appeal to the railroads and to the brotherhoods: Secretary of the Interior Lane, Secretary of Labor Wilson, Samuel Gompers, President of the American Federation of Labor, and Daniel Willard, President of the Baltimore & Ohio Railroad—all members of the Council or of the advisory council thereof.

Mr. Willard reached New York at 6:30 o'clock to make appointments for peace parleys. Mr. Lane came at 9 o'clock and went at once to the Hotel Biltmore, where he began a conference with the four brotherhood leaders—W. S. Stone of the Engineers, W. S. Carter of the Firemen, L. E. Sheppard, President of the Conductors, and W. G. Lee, President of the Trainmen. Mr. Wilson arrived at 10:30 o'clock, and it was said Mr. Gompers would be here later in the night.

At midnight no intimation had come from the unions that they had receded in any way from their stand, and it seemed probable that the conference would last until dawn. Mr. Gompers had not then arrived, but the other conferrees had no doubt that he would put in an appearance in due course. He was not in Washington when the others left there. Officials of the American Federation of Labor explained that he had been keeping in touch with the brotherhood leaders from a point near New York and could be counted on to attend the proceedings.

Joint Conference Begins.

Shortly after 1 o'clock this morning the railroad managers were called into the conference jointly with the brotherhood representatives. Although no announcement was made, it was assumed that this joint resumption of negotiations seemed to presage possible peace, but this view was altered when, thirty minutes later, the union men walked out. They said they had no statement to make. At 3:45 o'clock this morning the conference adjourned, and Mr. Wilson announced that there was no statement to give out. The conference will be resumed with the brotherhoods at 9:30 o'clock this morning, and with the railroad officials at 11.

It was reported authoritatively that a majority of the managers were considering proposing to the brotherhoods that they accept the terms of the switchmen's award which would give the men nine hours' pay for eight hours' work. The Adamson law provides ten hours' pay for eight hours' work.

The opinion was expressed last night that Mr. Gompers might find himself in an embarrassing situation. The brotherhoods are not affiliated with the American Federation of Labor. They had with the federation a working agreement in the eight-hour fight, but the belief has been exercised that Mr. Gompers does not approve of their pushing the issue at this critical time.

Mr. Lane explained that he had no instructions from the President to threaten that the Federal Government would take over the railroads and operate them in the event the strike started, adding that he "had no club," and had come merely to appeal to the patriotism of the men.

Both the labor leaders and the railroad managers had received late in the afternoon a plea from the White House, in which the President asked them to forget their differences for the time being, and not to call a strike which would further embarrass the Government, already deeply concerned in international complications.

The first thing Secretary Lane did when he met the labor chiefs was to present to them the following letter, signed by Secretary of War Baker, as Chairman of the Council of National Defense:

"At a meeting of the Council of

Continued on Page 4.

President Wilson's Plea for Railway Peace Based on Country's Need and War Danger

Special to The New York Times.

WASHINGTON, March 16.—This is President Wilson's personal appeal to the representatives of the contending factions in the railroad controversy:

"I deem it my duty and right to appeal to you in this time of national peril to open again the questions at issue between the railroads and their operatives with a view to accommodation or settlement.

"With my approval a committee of the Council of National Defense is about to seek a conference with you with that end in view.

"A general interruption of the railway traffic of the country at this time would entail a danger to the nation against which I have the right to enter my most solemn and earnest protest.

"It is now the duty of every patriotic man to bring matters of this sort to immediate accommodation. The safety of the country against manifest perils affecting its own peace and the peace of the whole world makes accommodation absolutely imperative and seems to me to render any other choice or action inconceivable."

The President's message was sent to Elisha Lee, Chairman of the Conference Committee of Railroad Managers; L. E. Sheppard, acting head of the Conductors; W. G. Lee, head of the Trainmen; W. S. Stone, Grand Chief of the Engineers, and W. S. Carter, President of the Firemen and Enginemen.

STRIKE EMBARGOES GROW TIGHTER

New York Central Notifies All Shippers That No Freight Will Be Received.

NEW HAVEN LESS DRASTIC

Pennsylvania Will Haul Food and Government Freight—Pullman Service May Stop.

Practically all of the big railroads, including the New York Central, New Haven, and Pennsylvania, with terminal facilities in New York City or New Jersey, which bring the food and other freight vital to the existence of the city's population, issued the expected embargo orders, more or less drastic, yesterday, because of the threatened strike. In most instances the orders became effective last night. The New Haven announced that all sleeping and dining car service would be discontinued, beginning tonight.

The Pennsylvania announced that, for the present, an effort would be made to continue the movement of live stock, food for human and animal consumption, shipments consigned to officers of the United States Government, fuel and supplies for use of the Pennsylvania and affiliated lines, and news print paper, but that these shipments would be accepted only subject to delay, loss, and damage. The New Haven left milk off the restricted list, and added the warning that passenger service might be cut and the limited trains taken off.

The New York Central was the first great Eastern system to take the step, and this order was sent to all agents on its 12,000 miles of line:

> Please notify all shippers that, effective at once, we cannot accept freight from them until further notice.

The New York, New Haven & Hartford followed with an embargo order which read:

> Beginning 6 P. M. Saturday, provided the prospective strike order of the four brotherhoods of train and engine men becomes effective, the passenger and freight service of the New York, New Haven & Hartford Railroad Company will be subject to serious delay and curtailment.
>
> The passenger service is threatened by the calling out of the yard men in Grand Central and other terminals Saturday evening, in connection with the discontinuance of service on other lines. Yard service is an important factor in controlling operation of passenger trains.
>
> All freight and much express are being placed under embargo and the prospects for the continued handling of both are indefinite.
>
> The company will make every endeavor to operate such trains as it can. Patrons are advised of the probable entire suspension of yard and freight train service, curtailment of passenger service, involving a more or less number of trains on such schedules as it may be practicable to establish, and the probable discontinuance of limited trains.
>
> The New York, New Haven & Hartford Railroad Company and the Central New England Railway Company have issued the following freight and express embargoes:
>
> Effective at 5 P. M. this date these companies will not accept freight of any kind, except milk, for points on or via these lines. This includes freight in transit.
>
> No express will be received through the Grand Central Terminal after 4 P. M., and from or via other points after 10 P. M. Saturday, March 17.

The embargo order of the Pennsylvania Railroad read:

> Effective close of business Friday, March 16, on account of threatened strike, Pennsylvania Railroad, Philadelphia, Baltimore & Washington Railroad, and West Jersey & Seashore Railroad, embargo all freight of all kinds from all points for all destinations, except livestock and foodstuffs for human and animal consumption, (domestic,) shipments consigned to officers of the United States Government, fuel, and supplies for use of Pennsylvania Railroad and affiliated lines, and news print paper.
>
> All freight as above described which may be in transit will not be accepted from the New York, Philadelphia & Norfolk Railroad, the Cumberland Valley Railroad, Cornwall & Lebanon Railroad, the Susquehanna, Bloomsburg & Berwick Railroad, the Pennsylvania Lines West of Pittsburgh, or other connecting lines at any junction point after date and hour above named, regardless of date on which shipment was accepted, as indicated by date on billing.
>
> All bills of lading issued on and after strike March 17, 1917, and until further notice, must bear the following notations:
>
> "This shipment accepted subject to delay, loss, and damage account of threatened strike."

Representatives of the Pennsylvania said the management thought the pre-

Continued on Page 4.

SINISTER HAND SEEN IN STRIKE

Calvin of Union Pacific Fears Brotherhood Heads Don't Speak for Men.

BIG AID TO OUR ENEMIES

Congestion After Walkout Would Block Movement of Troop and Munition Trains for Weeks.

OMAHA, Neb., March 16.—E. E. Calvin, President of the Union Pacific Railroad, issued this statement today:

"In connection with the threat of a general railroad strike at this time the question arises, Is some power shrewder and more astute than the brotherhood leaders back of the plan to precipitate a transportation tieup at this time, and establish in this country a condition, which, to the minds of our enemies in Europe, may seem like a revolt against our Government? I am in hearty sympathy with Elisha Lee, Chairman of the National Conference Committee of the Railways, when he calls attention to the fact that the serious international situation should cause every citizen to put every thought of personal right or desire second to his duty to his country.

"In a letter addressed to President Wilson some days ago the brotherhood leaders gave assurance that, in case of war, they would render every possible assistance to the Government. They have overlooked the fact that, in many ways, a railroad strike in this country would be worth more to our enemies than the winning of many battles, for the reason that it would paralyze and stagnate all our resources, and even if the strike be called off, should war be declared, the strike tieup would have resulted in such a congestion of freight in the terminals and on the sidings that weeks, and probably months, would be required to get this congestion cleaned up before the railroads would be in normal running condition again. This would mean that the movement of troops would be seriously interfered with and the movement of commissary supplies and munitions so seriously interrupted as to give our enemies a tremendous advantage.

"A day or two ago an officer of our navy said: 'A tieup of the railroads for even two days would be a serious blow to the national welfare at this critical time. We must keep the fleet fully coaled and equipped with other supplies.'

"Moreover, we are rushing construction work in the navy, and a two days' tieup of transportation of the materials urgently needed might mean a two months' delay in the emergency work we have undertaken. The rank and file of the railroad brotherhoods have waited for ten weeks for the decision of the United States Supreme Court as to the constitutionality of the Adamson law, a decision which may be handed down almost any day.

"In accordance with our agreement, the Union Pacific, in common with the other railroads of the country, kept separate time records since Jan. 1, scrupulously recording the increased pay that would be due to their employes in case the Adamson law was upheld. Further, the strike vote taken by the men was for a specific time and purpose, and in the minds of many of the brotherhood men to make use of the strike vote taken last Summer to call a strike at this time would be illegal.

"When we are on the verge of a decision respecting the legality of the Adamson law, and when we stand face to face with the probability of a war which will tax all our energy, it seems to me that in speaking of the plans of the brotherhood leaders to tie up the transportation industry of the country the people are justified in using a stronger term than ill-advised. To me it seems incredible that the rank and file of brotherhood members would respond to a strike call which must have the universal condemnation of the patriotic citizens of this country.

"It is impossible to believe that the brotherhood leaders, who have heretofore shown real generalship, will lead those who trust in them upon such a fool's errand."

PLEDGE OF REFORM RINGS IN GERMANY; JUNKERS ASSAILED

Bethmann Hollweg's Speech Accepted as Heralding a New Era in the Empire.

PARTY TRUCE IN DANGER

Chancellor Moved to Action by Demands of Socialists in Prussian Diet.

U-BOAT WAR DENOUNCED

London Believes Reform Promises Are the Result of Russian Revolt.

Special Cable to THE NEW YORK TIMES.

BERLIN, March 15, (via London, March 16.)—Chancellor von Bethmann Hollweg's speech before the Prussian Diet yesterday afternoon, which is regarded as the greatest speech that has come from the lips of a German statesman since Bismarck's day, is the subject of comment in every corner of the empire today.

There was every evidence that the Chancellor had not prepared his speech, and that he merely walked into the House, found the subject of debate and the moment opportune and delivered it. In fact, he said he had had no thought in the morning that he would address the House in the afternoon.

The immediate cause of the eruption which brought about the speech is so insignificant that Americans will have difficulty in understanding how it could ever acquire such importance. But one must remember that for months now the Left, and to some extent Centrists, have lost no opportunity of making it clear to the Right in no unmistakable terms that privileges would have to be curtailed after this war, and that they would insist on thorough reforms, and that only the truce that they swore to keep prevented them from beginning these reforms at once.

The Conservatives listened with ever-increasing wrath and suddenly surprised the Left and Centre with a bill in the lower Prussian House intended to make the inheritance laws of the landocracy still more formidable than they had been. This was regarded as a breach of the truce, and hot words were exchanged over it that should have shown clearly to the Conservatives that the people would not stand for any more privileges.

About a week ago the upper house of the Diet, in the course of its routine work, passed upon and rejected a bill granting to members of the lower house the usual daily allowance and free fare on the railways. The principal Conservative speaker, Yorck von Wartenburg, on this occasion left no doubt that the Conservatives were only using this very unimportant bill as a vehicle to let the other parties know just where the Conservatives stood—namely, exactly in the same spot where they left off the day the great catastrophe broke over the world.

Indignation Even in Prussia.

There was the greatest indignation not only in Prussia, but in the whole of Germany, and the leaders of all parties decided that it must be made clear to the Prussian landocracy that this is the twentieth century.

There was an enormous crowd in the galleries of the House when yesterday's session began. These crowds expected to hear plain speech, and they heard it, first from Dr. Porsch of the Centrist Party, who ridiculed Yorck von Wartenburg as the custodian of antiquity, then from Fredberg, the National Liberal, who not only threw down the gauntlet and said his party would no longer keep the truce but wanted electoral reforms at once.

Dr. Pachnicke of the Progressive Party followed with similar demands, and while he spoke of the Chancellor who had promised them so much and who might afterward be prevented by circumstances from fulfilling his promises, Bethmann Hollweg entered the chamber. He listened quietly to Pachnicke's censure, and when the latter had finished he began his great speech.

"Woe to the statesman who cannot read the signs of the times!" When the Chancellor thundered this variation of the threat by a Conservative orator, it was as though he had cast a spell upon the sentiments of all the parties that only a few minutes before had clashed in violent discord. Everybody present, even the crowds in the galleries, felt as though they had suddenly realized the turning point of a new epoch.

The Chancellor continued:

"Woe to the statesman who believes that after this catastrophe, such as the world has never seen before—a catastrophe whose scope contemporaries and those directly engaged in it cannot possibly measure—woe to him if he believes he can start again from where he left off before the catastrophe. It he should try to put new wine into old bottles—woe to that statesman!"

The Chancellor said he had had no thought in the morning that he would appear at the Chamber. He evidently had not prepared for any speech. Sometimes he stopped to find the right ex-

Continued on Page 3.

WIDE REFORMS PLANNED

Universal Suffrage and Full Political Amnesty Are the Bases.

CROWDS CHEER PROMISE

Duma Committee and Workingmen Busy Planning for a Constituent Assembly.

FOOD PRICES FALL RAPIDLY

Calm Restored in Petrograd, but Partisans of Old Regime Are Still Being Arrested.

LONDON, Saturday, March 17.—Universal suffrage in elections to be held for members of a new constituent Assembly and full political amnesty will be features of the new régime in Russia, according to dispatches from Petrograd. In fact, Deputy Kerenski, the new Minister of Justice, who is a Socialist, accepted the portfolio on the stipulations that there should be absolute freedom of speech and of the press, and full political amnesty, and that the Assembly should be convoked.

Addressing an assemblage of thousands of soldiers and civilians from the gallery of the lobby of the Duma, M. Kerenski, says a Reuter dispatch from Petrograd, dated yesterday, announced that the Provisional Government took office by virtue of an agreement with workingmen's and soldiers' delegates. The council of these delegates approved the agreement by several hundred votes to 15. The first act of the new Government, M. Kerenski stated, was the immediate publication of a decree of full amnesty. Continuing, the Minister said:

"Our comrades of the second and fourth Dumas, who were banished illegally to the tundras of Siberia, will be released forthwith. In my jurisdiction are all the Premiers and Ministers of the old régime. They will answer before the law for all crimes against the people."

"Show them no mercy," many voices in the crowd exclaimed.

"Comrades," M. Kerenski replied, "regenerated Russia will not have recourse to the shameful methods utilized by the old régime. Without trial none will be condemned. All prisoners will be tried in open court.

"Comrades, soldiers, citizens, all measures taken by the new Government will be published. Soldiers, I ask you to co-operate. Free Russia is now born, and none will succeed in wresting liberty from the hands of the people. Do not listen to the promptings of the agents of the old régime. Listen to your officers. Long live free Russia!"

The speech was greeted by a storm of cheering.

The labor leader, Chkueidse, addressing the officers and soldiers, paid a glowing tribute to the soldiers and workingmen who had participated in accomplishing the revolution. He recounted the recent provocative efforts by the secret police in publishing proclamations regarding the murders of officers by soldiers. He exhorted the soldiers to regard their officers as citizens who had helped raise the revolutionary flag and as brothers in the great cause of Russian liberty.

Subsequently officers, soldiers, and workingmen carried M. Chkueidse on their shoulders through a cheering throng of soldiers and civilians.

Apparently the new Provisional Government is proceeding promptly to organize itself on a stable basis, to reconstitute the Governmental departments, and prepare steps for the vigorous carrying on of the war. There is no sign of serious hindrance to the completion of the work of this extraordinarily swift and successful revolution.

Former Premiers Golitzine and Goremykin have been placed in the Fortress of St. Peter and St. Paul, as have Generals Soukhomlinoff and Beliaeff, former Ministers of War; A. B. Protopopoff, former Minister of the Interior; J. G. Chtcheglovitoff and M. Makaroff, former Ministers of Justice, and M. Malakoff and General Kurloff, former Chiefs of Police. Other prominent persons under arrest are being detained temporarily in the Duma Building.

It is announced that there will be no further trials for political offenses, and that the Government has opened the bar to Jewish lawyers, who have been excluded heretofore.

At a conference of the members of the Duma Executive Committee and delegates representing the workmen, which lasted until 5 o'clock this morning, says a dispatch from Petrograd, an agreement was reached concerning the transitional period before the election of a constituent assembly. The executives insisted in the interests of the war on

Continued on Page 2.

New Russian Government Asks People's Support; States Its Policy as Freedom and Suffrage for All

LONDON, March 16.—The Provisional Government in Russia has issued an appeal to the people, according to a Reuter dispatch from Petrograd. The document begins:

"Citizens.—The Executive Committee of the Duma, with the aid and support of the garrison of the capital and its inhabitants, has succeeded in triumphing over the obnoxious forces of the old régime in such a manner that we are able to proceed to a more stable organization of the executive power, with men whose past political activity assures them the country's confidence."

The names of the members of the new Government are then given and the appeal continues:

"The new Cabinet will base its policy on the following principles:

First.—An immediate general amnesty for all political and religious offenses, including terrorist acts and military and agrarian offenses.

Second.—Liberty of speech and of the press; freedom for alliances, unions, and strikes, with the extension of these liberties to military officials within the limits admitted by military requirements.

Third.—Abolition of all social, religious, and national restrictions.

Fourth.—To proceed forthwith to the preparation and convocation of a constitutional Assembly, based on universal suffrage, which will establish a governmental régime.

Fifth.—The substitution of the police by a national militia, with chiefs to be elected and responsible to the Government.

Sixth.—Communal elections to be based on universal suffrage.

Seventh.—The troops which participated in the revolutionary movement will not be disarmed, but will remain in Petrograd.

Eighth.—While maintaining strict military discipline for troops on active service, it is desirable to abrogate for soldiers all restrictions in the enjoyment of social rights accorded other citizens.

"The Provisional Government desires to add that it has no intention to profit by the circumstances of the war to delay the realization of the measures of reform above mentioned."

DUKE NICHOLAS AGAIN HEADS ARMY

The Czar Turns Over Supreme Command to His Uncle, Whom He Deposed.

GENERAL AT THE CAPITAL

With Alexieff, Chief of Staff, He Urged Emperor to Take Only Step to Save Russia.

Golitzin a Suicide?

Special Cable to THE NEW YORK TIMES.

COPENHAGEN, March 17.—A leading Swedish paper, the Social Demokraten, tells that the former Russian Premier, Prince Golitzin, has committed suicide.

LONDON, Saturday, March 17.—A Reuter dispatch from Petrograd says that prior to his abdication the Emperor transferred the supreme command of the Russian armies to the Grand Duke Nicholas, his uncle. The latter has reached Petrograd.

A previous dispatch from Petrograd said that the Grand Duke had telegraphed President Rodzianko of the Duma that, in accord with General Alexieff, Chief of Staff, he had asked the Emperor, in order to save Russia and bring the war to a successful end, to take the only step possible in the present fateful circumstances.

Special Cable to THE NEW YORK TIMES.

COPENHAGEN, March 16.—The Dagens Nyheder states that Russian officials and officers incline to believe that the Grand Duke Nicholas has the confidence of the revolutionists, and that he will get dictatorial authority over the army until conditions are settled.

When the war in Europe began and the Grand Duke Nicholas was appointed Commander in Chief of the Russian armies in the southwest, he came to this distinction partly through inheritance, partly through his intimacy with the Czar, and partly on account of his past service and the affection the mujic soldier had for him. Among the officers he was not popular; he was too hard a worker.

The Grand Duke is 61 years of age and his father, likewise named Nicholas, commanded the Russian forces in the Turkish war of 1877. With his father the young Nicholas, then 21, served with distinction at Plevna, Lovcha, and the Shipka Pass, receiving the decoration of the Cross of St. George.

From 1879 till 1914 the Grand Duke was closely identified with the Russian Army and, at the same time, made himself familiar with most of the other armies of Europe.

At the beginning of the present war he was in command of the Petrograd military district. As Commander in Chief his first invasion of East and West Prussia and Galicia was the carrying out of a plan long before laid. The subsequent retreat, with half-starved soldiers, lacking effective artillery, frequently without rifle ammunition when the rear guard had to use bayonets against machine guns, and over a front of nearly 1,000 miles, and without losing through surrender a single compact army unit, was one of the greatest strategic feats in history.

The retreat began in April, 1915, and six months later the Grand Duke safely brought his armies into prepared works. While military authorities all over the world were praising him, he was suddenly sent to the Caucasus to command the army there, while the Czar had himself proclaimed Commander in Chief of the armies of Russia.

In the Caucasus, with supplies and

Continued on Page 2.

RUSSIANS HERE AID NEW CAUSE

Form a Committee to Take Over Functions of Embassy and Consulates in America.

ASK FIRST FOR AUTHORITY

Overthrow of the Government Causes Wild Joy Among the Jews of the East Side.

Believing that the Russian democracy has come to stay, a number of the leading members of the Russian-American colony in New York held a meeting yesterday and planned to co-operate with the new Government even to the extent of taking over the functions of the embassy, consulates, and heads of various munition departments.

The meeting was held in the office of Professor N. G. Kouznetsoff in the Longacre Building, and an executive committee was formed consisting of Professor Kouznetzoff, who is a member of the Faculty of the Petrograd Military Institution; Ivan Narodny, author and journalist; Ivan Okuntsoff, editor of the Russky Golos, published in this city, and Joseph Dalinda, a correspondent of several Russian newspapers.

According to the announcement made yesterday, this committee, an unofficial and self-appointed body, intends to take over ultimately all the Russian Government offices in the United States and Canada. To accomplish this sweeping change in Russian officialdom on this side of the ocean the committee will get into immediate communication with the members of the provisional Government. Until official sanction has been obtained the committee intends to offer its services to the new régime as an advisory board.

"The Executive Russian Committee of America," reads the official announcement, "is of the opinion that the present newly established form of the Government is merely a stepping stone to the United States of Russia, which is bound to come soon after the end of the war. It makes no difference whether the nominal ruler will be Michael or Grand Duke Nicholas, as the real power will remain in the hands of the Cabinet that will be appointed jointly by the Duma and Council of the Empire. It is even very likely that the Council of the Empire will be abolished. The main question of the new Government is to unite all the nation under the present régime till the end of the war and fight the enemy with all the full vigor.

"This will mean a new era for Russia, new life and new events. The present Russian Cabinet will work hand in hand with England and France. The Czar will remain like the King of England, a decorative figure of the country. The real constitution will be drafted after the war, which may resemble the Constitution of the United States. All the political refuges will get amnesty, all the exiles will be given full freedom.

"The revolution and political change of Russia will not affect the economic and financial life of the country in the least. On the contrary, Russia will be now richer than she ever was, stronger than she ever was, and the world will be surprised by the tremendous reforms that will now take place."

While Russian Liberals and refugees in New York regard the overturning of the Cabinet as the beginning of a new era, the more conservative element is reluctant to concede a complete victory for Russian democracy. Opinions were expressed in several quarters yesterday to the effect that the present upheaval is nothing more than a purely "political coup d'état" without any popular significance whatever. It was pointed out that the best evidence of this fact consists in the retention of the Romanoff family in power. No "revolutionary" program, it was said, could tolerate the continuance of the present dynasty, either through Nicholas II. or any member of his family. The Constitution of the new Cabinet was also believed by several prominent Russians here to be an

Continued on Page 2.

GAVE UP SON'S RIGHTS, TOO

Czar Yielded at Midnight Thursday; Grand Duke Michael Yesterday.

DUMA IS NOW IN CONTROL

Executive Committee Acting with Cabinet It Chose After the Revolution.

NATION BACK OF CHANGE

New Ministers Assume Their Duties and Are Starting Preparations to Push the War.

PETROGRAD, Friday, March 16, 5 P. M., (via London, Saturday, March 17.)—Emperor Nicholas abdicated at midnight last night on behalf of himself and the heir apparent, Grand Duke Alexis, in favor of Grand Duke Michael Alexanderovitch.

At 2:30 o'clock this afternoon Grand Duke Michael himself abdicated, thus bringing the Romanoff dynasty to an end.

The Government, pending a meeting of the Constitutional Assembly, is vested in the Executive Committee of the Duma and the newly-chosen Council of Ministers.

A manifesto to this effect was issued by the Duma Committee today and it will be telegraphed to the General Army Headquarters this evening.

Unless improbable events occur, Russia has today become a republic.

The outcome depends on how the manifesto of the new Government is received by the 6,000,000 soldiers at the front.

Except for the unqualified rejection of the throne by the Czar Nicholas II.'s only brother, the Grand Duke Michael, the Romanoff-Holstein dynasty might be preserved by any number of Czar Nicholas's kinsmen. But the title of Autocrat, since the days of the first Michael Romanoff, in 1613, may only be conferred by a Romanoff. As the Czar chooses no successor after the Grand Duke Michael, and the Grand Duke names no successor at all, the dynasty ends as a reigning house unless a new Government places it upon the throne. Even so, the Romanoffs might decline to recognize the authority of such a Government, as they assert that their right to reign and rule is entirely independent of the will of the people.

The house of Romanoff is descended from Andrei Romanoff, who is said to have gone to Moscow from Prussia in the fourteenth century. Michael Feodorovitch Romanoff was the first of the family to ascend the throne. This was in 1613, when he was 17 years old. He died in 1645. The direct male line of the Romanoffs terminated in 1730 and the female line in 1762, when the Holstein-Gottorp branch came into power and has since ruled.

Milukoff's Plan That Failed.

Special Cable to THE NEW YORK TIMES.

PETROGRAD, March 16, (Dispatch to The London Daily News.)—Professor Milukoff announced the list of new Ministers in a speech in Catherine Hall of the Duma, and was finally carried out on the shoulders of the enthusiastic crowd. His speech was often interrupted by questions, and he was repeatedly asked for the program. He said:

"I can already tell you the most important points. [A voice, "the dynasty?"] You ask about the dynasty. I know beforehand that my answer will not please all of you, but I give it. The old despot, who brought Russia to the edge of disaster, will voluntarily abdicate or be deposed. (Applause.)

"The Government will pass to a Regent, the Grand Duke Michael Alexandrovitch [continuous row and applause] and the heir Alexis the Czarevitch [yells—"but that is the old dynasty"]

"Yes, gentlemen, that is the old dynasty, which perhaps you do not like and which perhaps I dislike myself.

"We propose a parliamentary constitutional monarchy. Perhaps others have different views, but if we stop to discuss, instead of instantly deciding, Russia will find herself in a state of civil war and the destroyed régime will be broken."

Order Growing Out of Chaos.

PETROGRAD, March 16, (via London.)—Russia today appeared to be in a fair way toward solving the greatest problem with which any nation, per-

"All the News That's Fit to Print."

The New York Times.

THE WEATHER
Fair today and Tuesday; northwest winds, becoming variable.
For full weather report see Page 17

VOL. LXVI...NO. 21,604. NEW YORK, MONDAY, MARCH 19, 1917.—EIGHTEEN PAGES. ONE CENT In Greater New York. | TWO CENTS New England and Middle States. | THREE CENTS Elsewhere.

THREE AMERICAN SHIPS SUNK, ONE UNWARNED, 22 MEN MISSING; U-BOATS REFUSE AID; MILITIA DEMOBILIZATION IS STOPPED AND RAILROAD STRIKE ABANDONED ON PRESIDENT'S ORDER

RUSSIA TO FIGHT BESIDE HER ALLIES TILL WAR IS WON

Army, Fleet, and Church for New Regime, and Red Flag Replaces National Colors.

IMPERIAL CHILDREN ARE ILL

"I Am Only a Sister of Charity," Empress Tells Soldiers as She Forbids Bloodshed.

CZAR'S PORTRAIT BANISHED

Exile of Rasputin's Slayers Ended—Grand Duke Nicholas Calls on Caucasian Army to Fight On.

Nicholas Romanoff Retires to His Estates in Crimea

PETROGRAD, March 18, (via London, Monday, March 19.)—Nicholas Romanoff, as the former Emperor is now designated, left with his staff today for his personal estates at Livadia, on the south coast of the Crimea.

PETROGRAD, March 18.—With the final cementing of the elements concerned in the construction of the new Government upon the ruins of the old, the new Cabinet Ministers, relieved of the heavy grind of the endless conferences of the last few days in which they suffered many anxious hours, have assumed the posts to which they were assigned. Professor Paul N. Milukoff spent yesterday at the Foreign Office. In the afternoon he received the diplomatic representatives of the Allies, after which he entered upon a long Cabinet conference.

One of the first acts of the Minister was to send a series of cable messages to the Russian diplomats abroad to the effect that Russia was united in the desire to fight out the war with the Allies, the determination to continue the conflict until the victory is achieved being stronger than ever. Following is the text of his message:

"The news transmitted by the Petrograd Telegraphic Agency (the semi-official Russian news bureau) already has acquainted you with the events of the last few days and the fall of the old political régime in Russia, which collapsed lamentably in the face of popular indignation provoked by its carelessness, its abuses, and its criminal lack of foresight. The unanimity of resentment which the order of things now at an end had aroused among all healthy elements of the nation has considerably facilitated the crisis. All these elements having rallied with enthusiasm to the noble flag of revolution, and the army having lent them its speedy and effective support, the national movement obtained decisive victory within eight days.

"This rapidity of realization happily made it possible to reduce the number of victims to a figure unprecedentedly small in the annals of upheavals of such extent and importance.

"By an act dated from Pskov March 15, Emperor Nicholas renounced the throne for himself and the hereditary Grand Duke Alexis Nikolaievitch in favor of Grand Duke Michael Alexandrovitch. In reply to a notification which was made to him of this act, Grand Duke Michael Alexandrovitch, by an act dated Petrograd, March 16, in his turn renounced assumption of supreme power until the time when a constituent assembly, created on the basis of universal suffrage, should have established a form of government and new fundamental laws of Russia. By this same act Alexandrovitch invited the citizens of Russia, pending a definite manifestation of the national will, to submit to the authority of the Provisional Government constituted on the initiative of the State, which holds full power. The composition of the Provisional Government and its political program have been published and transmitted to foreign countries.

Responsibility Fully Realized.

"This Government, which assumes power at the moment of the greatest external and internal crisis which Russia has known in the course of her history, is fully conscious of the immense responsibility it incurs. It will apply itself first to repairing the overwhelming errors bequeathed to it by the past, to insuring order and tranquillity in the country, and, finally, to preparing the conditions necessary in order that the sovereign will of the nation may be freely pronounced as to its future lot.

"In the domain of foreign policy the Cabinet, in which I am charged with the portfolio of the Ministry of Foreign Affairs, will remain mindful of the international engagements entered into by the fallen régime, and will honor Russia's word. We shall carefully cul-

Continued on Page 2.

Milukoff's Announcement to the World That Russia, True to Her Allies, Will Fight Till War Is Won

PETROGRAD, March 18.—A message sent by Foreign Minister Milukoff to the Russian diplomats abroad explains the revolution and its purposes and instructs these envoys to make known to the Governments to which they are accredited Russia's unalterable resolve to carry on the war, in conjunction with her allies, to a completely victorious conclusion. On this point the message says:

Russia did not will the war which has been drenching the world with blood for nearly three years. But, victim of premeditated aggression prepared long ago, she will continue, as in the past, to struggle against the spirit of conquest of a predatory race which has aimed at establishing an intolerable hegemony over its neighbors and subjecting Europe of the twentieth century to the shame of domination by Prussian militarism. Faithful to the pact which unites her indissolubly to her glorious allies, Russia is resolved, like them, to assure the world at all costs of an era of peace among the nations, on the basis of stable national organization guaranteeing respect for right and justice. She will fight by their side against the common enemy until the end, without cessation and without faltering.

The Government of which I form a part will devote all its energy to preparation of victory and will apply itself to the task of repairing as quickly as possible the errors of the past, which hitherto have paralyzed the aspirations and the self-sacrifice of the Russian people. I am firmly convinced that the marvelous enthusiasm which today animates the whole nation will multiply its strength in time and hasten the hour of the final triumph of a regenerated Russia and her valiant allies.

I beg you to communicate to the Minister of Foreign Affairs [of the country to which the diplomat addressed is accredited] the contents of the present telegram.

Germans Retire on 85-Mile Line: Abandon Peronne and Noyon

British and French Cavalry Pursuing Teuton Rearguards—Allied Advance Extends from Arras to Soissons, to Depth of Twelve Miles, Recapturing Over Sixty Villages.

LONDON, March 18.—The German retirement in France, which continued yesterday at three separate points, spread today over a front of approximately eighty-five miles, from south of Arras on the north to Soissons on the Aisne. The important towns of Péronne, Chaulnes, Nesle, and Noyon were evacuated, together with scores of villages, some of them only slightly damaged as the result of military operations.

The advancing British and French troops, keeping in close touch with the German rearguard, have pushed forward to a depth of from ten to twelve miles. Allied cavalry rode into Nesle, northeast of Roge, at almost the same time.

The occupation of Noyon, one the Oise River, and the nearest point to Paris held by the Germans, removes the famous Noyon elbow or salient, from which some military men here expected the Germans to launch another drive on Paris.

The text of the British statement reads as follows:

We have occupied Nesle, Chaulnes, and Péronne.

Pressing back the enemy's rearguard, we advanced several miles during the past twenty-four hours to a depth up to ten miles in places on a front of approximately forty-five miles, from south of Chaulnes to the neighborhood of Arras.

During this period, in addition to the towns above mentioned, we gained possession of over sixty villages.

Two enemy raiding parties reached our trenches in the night northeast of the Vermelles area.

The text of the French night statement follows:

From the Avre to the Aisne on a front of more than sixty kilometers the advance of our troops continued during the course of the day. North of the Avre our cavalry this morning entered Nesle, and we immediately sent out patrols in the direction of the Somme. There were several engagements with enemy rearguard detachments, who resisted feebly. The inhabitants of Nesle acclaimed our troops.

Northeast of Lassigny we have up to the present advanced more than twenty kilometers in the direction of Ham.

Further to the south our light cavalry detachments, moving along the Valley of the Oise, occupied Noyon about 10 o'clock this morning.

Between the Oise and Soissons (Aisne sector) the entire German first line, as well as the villages of Carlepont, Morsain, Nouvron, and Vingre, fell into our hands. We have gained a foothold on the northern plateau of Soissons and occupied Crouy.

The French afternoon statement follows:

Between the Avre and the Oise our troops made important progress during the night. All the ground between our old lines and the Rove-Noyon road, from Damery as far as the Lagny height, is now in our hands.

There were rather spirited engagements with portions of the enemy rearguard, which terminated to our advantage, and did not impede our progress. The pursuit continues north of the Noyon road.

A dispatch from British Headquarters tonight in France says:

"So rapid became the pursuit of the Germans retreating in the Ancre and Somme sectors today that the British cavalry came into play after restless months of waiting. It has been a wonderful sight to see the cavalry squadrons moving toward the front for several days past. They have included some of the crack English regiments, looking very grim and businesslike in steel shrapnel helmets and equipped with gas masks.

"The fine drying weather of the last three days has helped the pursuit, which in some places has reached solid ground that has been little damaged by shellfire.

According to French military critics it is difficult to say where the Germans propose to establish a stable defense. The retreat of modern armies, encumbered with great supplies of material, can be effected only with extreme slowness, which permits an active and resolute adversary to maintain contact unceasingly.

The victorious entry of the French into Roye on the heels of the retiring Germans was marked by stirring incidents, in which 800 liberated citizens participated, regardless of danger. The inhabitants threw themselves in front of the arriving French soldiers, all shouting as they did so, "Vive la France!" Women hugged them, while old people grasped their hands. Tears were in the eyes of all, when suddenly a twelve-year-old boy began singing the "Marseillaise," which was taken up instantly by the population. Onrushing waves of soldiers joined in, and it was to the strains of the national anthem that the French outposts left Roye, pressing the retreating Germans.

BERLIN, March 18, (by Wireless to Sayville.)—Systematic retirement of the German troops between Arras and the Oise, on the French front, is announced by the War Office today. Péronne, Noyon, Bapaume, Roye, and several other towns have been abandoned by the Germans. The statement follows:

Between La Bassée Canal and the Scarpe River there was lively fighting. Near Loos German reconnoitring detachments brought eighteen prisoners from the British lines.

On both sides of Arras hostile reconnoitring detachments in strength of one battalion advanced against our positions, and were for the most part repulsed by our fire. Near Roclincourt and Tilley enemy forces which had entered our positions were defeated in a hand-to-hand fight and left a number of prisoners in our hands.

Between Arras and the Oise the British and French, in a strip of land systematically abandoned by us, occupied our former positions and several towns, among which are Bapaume, Péronne, Roye, and Noyon. Our protecting troops inflicted considerable losses on the enemy and then gave way, as had been ordered.

In a supplementary official report issued tonight it is announced that "in the strip of land between Arras and the Aisne, voluntarily evacuated by us, only in some places are our protecting groups in fighting touch with the hostile cavalry and infantry."

RETREATING GERMANS BURNING EVERYTHING

Whole Countryside Behind Their Armies Aflame—Wells Poisoned With Arsenic.

By PHILIP GIBBS.

Special Cable to THE NEW YORK TIMES.

WAR CORRESPONDENTS' HEADQUARTERS, March 18, (Dispatch to The London Daily Chronicle.)—Today British troops entered Péronne. Standing alone, that statement would be sensational enough. The French fought for Péronne desperately through more than two years of war, and now it is the luck of British troops to enter it after a short action with the German rear guards.

But the news does not stand alone. The whole of the old German line south of Arras, strong as one vast fortress, built by the labor of millions, dug and tunneled and cemented and timbered, with thousands of machine guns and redoubts, with an immense maze of trenches protected by forests of barbed wire, had slipped away as though by a landslip and the Germans are in rapid retreat to new lines many miles away. As they go they are laying fire and waste to the countryside northeast of Bapaume into which the British went yesterday.

East of Péronne scores of villages are burning. One of them, larger than a village, the town of Athies, is a flam-

Continued on Page 4.

WILSON'S MANDATE HEEDED

Sinking of Ships Determines Him, and Conferees Accept

THE RAILROADS CAPITULATE

Agree to Any Terms the Mediators May Arrange with the Brotherhoods.

EIGHT-HOUR DAY THE BASIS

Deadlock of 50 Hours Ended—Lansing Had Planned to Come Here Today.

The Conference Committee of Railroad Managers early this morning authorized President Wilson's mediators to make whatever arrangements were necessary with the railroad brotherhoods to call off the threatened strike. This action followed within half an hour of the announcement that President Wilson, in consequence of the sinking of three American ships by German submarines, had resolved that there must be no railroad strike.

Secretary of the Interior Lane issued this statement at 2:30 o'clock this morning:

"Regardless of the decision of the Supreme Court on the Adamson law the basic eight-hour day will go into effect.

"The details are being worked upon by a joint committee, which will have its negotiations completed by noon."

He then gave out the following letter from the railway managers:

March 19, 1917.

Hon. Franklin K. Lane, Hon. William B. Wilson, Mr. Daniel Willard, Mr. Samuel Gompers, Committee of the Council of National Defense:

Gentlemen—In the national crisis precipitated by events of which we learned this afternoon, the National Conference Committee of the Railways joins with you in the conviction that neither at home nor abroad should there be fear or hope that the efficient operation of the railways of the country will be hampered or impaired.

Therefore, you are authorized to assure the nation that there will be no strike, and as a basis for such assurance we hereby authorize the Committee of the Council of National Defense to grant to employes who were about to strike whatever adjustment your committee deems necessary to guarantee the uninterrupted and efficient operation of the railways as an indispensable arm of national defense.

Yours very truly,

THE NATIONAL CONFERENCE COMMITTEE OF THE RAILWAYS.
By ELISHA LEE, Chairman.

Secretary Lane and the other members of the committee shook hands with the managers, who left fifteen minutes after the letter had been given out. Immediately Secretary Lane sent for the four brotherhood leaders, who, after half an hour's conference, agreed to accept the railroad peace offer, and began at once sending word to Chicago, St. Louis, Pittsburgh, and Baltimore, and local Chairmen that a satisfactory settlement had been reached.

So far as the eight-hour question itself was concerned, disregarding the patriotism involved in the situation, the settlement marks a victory for the brotherhoods; it means that they get just what President Wilson proposed as a settlement last August. It marks the end of the fight for the eight-hour day, which resulted twice in the United States being placed within two hours of a nationwide tieup of transportation.

The railroads estimate that the settlement will cost them $50,000,000 a year. It is also agreed that the eight-hour day goes into effect as of Jan. 1, and the 400,000 brotherhood members will thereby get $13,000,000, which stands to their credit as what they would have received had the law been in operation since Jan. 1.

Secretary Lane, Secretary Wilson, Mr. Willard, and Mr. Gompers, the mediators, will remain in New York until the peace pact is formally ratified today by both sides signing it. This is expected to take place some time this afternoon.

Secretary Lane was in communication with the White House about midnight. Approximately the same time it was said in Washington that President Wilson had determined to balk the railroad strike at any cost. It is known that Secretary Lane impressed upon both sides the gravity of the international situation that was precipitated by the sinking of the three American ships, but it was said by representatives of both the managers and the labor leaders that they had received no word from President Wilson directly.

The settlement was reached within thirty minutes after the receipt of news from Washington that President Wilson, in view of the increasing gravity in the international situation as created by the sinking of three American vessels by U-boats yesterday, had determined that there should be no strike at any hazard.

This news was received at 12:15 o'clock and copies of the dispatch were rushed to the Hotel Biltmore, where for more than fifty hours the representatives of both sides in the controversy had been in futile conference. As late as midnight the only hope held out for averting a strike and consequent paralysis of the country's transportation system was the belief held in some quarters that the Supreme Court would today hand down its decision on the constitutionality of the Adamson law.

All day neither side had yielded a point, the union heads insisting that they should have the eight-hour day and its emoluments regardless of whether the Supreme Court held the law constitutional. All hope of peace seemed far off when word of the President's decision came, then the railroad managers quickly drafted their proposal, which was immediately submitted to the mediators and a little later to the union leaders. However, both sides were still in conference at 1:30 this morning, but in the meantime announcement had been made that there would be no strike.

President's Stand Made Known.

The Washington dispatch of The Associated Press telling Mr. Wilson's determination that there should be no strike read as follows:

WASHINGTON, March 18.—President Wilson, in view of the added seriousness given to the foreign situation by the sinking of three American ships by German submarines, became determined today that the threatened nation-wide railroad strike must be prevented at all hazards.

What further steps to avert the strike he will take if the mediatory efforts of members of the Council of National Defense in New York fail were not disclosed, if they had been decided upon.

The President was hopeful tonight that the railroad managers and the representatives of the brotherhoods would reach an agreement on their own account as a patriotic duty, and thus make unnecessary any further move on his part.

Before the beginning of the negotiations now in progress the heads of the brotherhoods sent the President a message assuring him that in case the United States became involved in war they would stand by the Government.

The Administration takes the view that the time for making good this promise has now practically come. Regardless of whether the Supreme Court hands down a decision in the Adamson eight-hour law case tomorrow, Government officials think an immediate settlement must be reached.

Interest turned intensely today upon tomorrow's opinions in the Supreme Court. Anticipation that the court might then announce its long-awaited decision upon the constitutionality of the Adamson law was, however, without other than pure speculative basis.

Before last night's sudden settlement was reached it was reported that Secretary of State Lansing would come to New York today in connection with the railroad strike situation. It was presumed that if he came it would be to lay before both sides the gravity of the international situation.

At 11 o'clock last night Secretary of the Interior Franklin K. Lane dictated this statement after concluding a conference with the railway managers:

"We have been negotiating all day. There has been no joint meeting. We have made various propositions to both sides. There has been no change in the situation."

Brotherhoods Stood Firm.

The brotherhoods had steadfastly refused to grant another delay, sticking to the declaration they made Saturday, when they agreed to postpone the strike for forty-eight hours from Saturday at 7 P. M.

After the making and the rejection of many propositions, the situation at midnight was this:

The railroads agree to put the Adamson law into effect if it is upheld on a basis accepted by the brotherhoods.

The brotherhoods insist that if the law is held invalid, the railroads shall give them the same concessions as if it were upheld.

The railroads declare that if the law is held invalid, they will do no more than agree to an arbitration of the whole controversy by any body the President may select.

Among the propositions made to the railroads and the labor chiefs by the committee were: Postpone all action until the international crisis is past; submit the whole controversy to arbitration if the law is thrown out; postpone the strike until the Supreme Court acts; let the railroads give the brotherhoods a modification of the provisions of the Adamson law. These propositions were all rejected by one side or the other.

The members of the committee, Secretary Lane, Secretary of Labor Wilson, Daniel Willard, and Samuel Gompers, urged upon both sides the peril of the international crisis brought on by the sinking of three American ships yesterday. They told the men that a strike at such a time would so incense the people that the next Congress would be forced by public opinion to pass laws curtailing the power of the unions to tie up transportation. They warned the railroads

Continued on Page 18.

Berlin Puts U-Boat Toll at 781,500 Tons in February, With 368 Merchantmen Sunk

By Wireless to THE NEW YORK TIMES.

BERLIN, March 18, (via Tuckerton.)—The results of the first month of intensified U-boat war seem to have satisfied the most optimistic expectations of the Germans, since the total of nearly 800,000 tons of merchant shipping destroyed represent a full month's work. In the first place, the intensified operations only began on Feb. 4, and even after that date a grace was observed by the U-boats on various routes by an agreement with several neutral nations to permit certain belated vessels to get safely home, from which circumstance English shipping also derived some advantage.

It is estimated that if the U-boats had not been thus handicapped and had been working a full month they would have passed the million mark. In addition to the above described disadvantages, the weather was very unfavorable to operations a part of the time, and last, but not least, the short hours of daylight must be reckoned with in arriving at a correct judgment of the first month's results. The figure named indicates by no means the total effectiveness of the new operations, since for their purposes every ton remaining unemployed in neutral or hostile ports for fear of meeting the U-boats counts as much as the tonnage actually sunk.

German naval circles here are very enthusiastic regarding the U-boats' success.

BERLIN, Friday, March 16, (by Wireless to Sayville, March 18.)—Merchant ships of an aggregate gross tonnage of 781,500 were destroyed in February as a result of the war measures of the Central Powers, the Admiralty announced today. The statement says:

"In February 368 merchant ships of an aggregate gross tonnage of 781,500 were lost by the war measures of the Central Powers. Among them were 292 hostile ships, with an aggregate gross tonnage of 644,000 and 76 neutral ships of an aggregate gross tonnage of 137,500. Among the neutral ships sixty-one were sunk by submarines, which is 16.5 per cent. of the total in February, as compared with 29 per cent., the average of neutral losses in the last four months."

There is a wide disparity between the official German figures of the destruction of shipping in February, the first month of unrestricted submarine warfare, and the figures given out in England. It was said authoritatively in London on March 3, that in February German submarines sent to the bottom, in round numbers, 490,000 tons of shipping. No mention was made of ships destroyed by mines.

HOLD GUARD UNITS IN FEDERAL ARMY

Government Suddenly Changes Its Plans to Muster Out All Militiamen.

55,000 STILL ON DUTY

New York Troops, Washington Hears, Are Among Those Retained by Secret Orders.

Special to The New York Times.

WASHINGTON, March 18.—There were strong intimations tonight that recent events had effected a quick change in the War Department's plans for immediately mustering the remaining units of the National Guard out of the Federal service. Whether this change has to do with Germany or with the threatened railroad strike is unknown. There are still about 55,000 National Guardsmen in the Federal service, and some of them at least, it now appears, will be held for the time being.

Some time ago orders were issued for all National Guard troops on the Mexican border to entrain for their home rendezvous not later than March 21. It was then expected that they would all be ready for muster out by April 1. Up to yesterday afternoon no orders had left the War Department changing the previous orders for muster out. But it is known that something has happened since then changing the prospective status of National Guardsmen still on the Federal muster rolls.

Since the German situation became more acute, the War Department has been working night and day to perfect its machinery and bring the available fighting forces up to a high standard of efficiency. The announcement made on Friday, that preliminary mobilization instructions had been sent to the Adjutant Generals of all the States, showed that the department was preparing for a quick response by the National Guard if developments justified recalling it to service. It is almost physically impossible, however, that any orders in regard to postponing muster-out should have been sent from Washington since news was received late this afternoon of the sinking of the three American ships.

It was explained here that Commanding Generals of military departments could on their own initiative postpone mustering out if emergencies in their departments justified. A strike might be such an emergency, it was said. Reports have been received that the mustering out of National Guard units in New York and North Carolina has been postponed. Both these States are in the Department of the East, under the command of Major Gen. Leonard Wood, with headquarters at Governors Island, New York.

Whatever orders have been issued were issued secretly, and there is no disposition now to permit publicity of details. When Secretary of War Baker was questioned on the subject to-

Continued on Page 2.

EXPECT ACTION BY WILSON TODAY

President May Call Congress to Meet at Once or Declare a State of War Exists.

NO DOUBT OF OVERT ACTS

Officials, Though Cautious, Are Convinced That Germany Is Challenging War.

Special to The New York Times.

WASHINGTON, March 18.—Technically the sinking of three American merchant vessels by German submarines has not changed the international situation; actually these sinkings have given a more critical turn to it and paved the way for the initiation of a state of war between Germany and the United States.

Whether the Government regards the sinking of the three ships as the overt act which President Wilson mentioned in addressing Congress as cause for taking more drastic measures than a break in diplomatic relations is not being disclosed tonight. It is doubtful if it has been determined. The President, as far as known, has not consulted with any of his advisers, and there have been no conferences between members of the Cabinet. But officials who have been aware all along of the attitude of the President expressed the opinion this evening that the situation was "grave" and cautiously indicated that the overt act had been committed.

What is meant by the statement that technically the sinkings have not changed the status of the international situation is that they are merely repetitions of other offenses by German U-boats since relations between the two countries were broken off and President Wilson served notice that he would be obliged to adopt other measures if Germany carried out her declared intention of resorting to sinking merchant vessels on sight.

President May Act at Once.

After it was evident that German submarines were engaged in relentless warfare against merchant craft, President Wilson again appeared before Congress and asked for authority to arm American merchant vessels. Up to that time two American merchant ships had been sunk by submarines without warning, but no lives had been lost, and the indications were that the Germans had intended to give those on board a chance to escape. They had not been so careful of merchant vessels flying other flags, however. Then came the sinking of the American ship Algonquin, a clear case of sinking without warning. No action was taken by the Administration, although opinion was general that the overt act had been committed, and the understanding was that the answer of the Government would be to arm American merchant vessels and meet the submarine menace in that way in the hope that it would prove effective.

But the sinking of three American vessels, two of them perhaps without warning, has aggravated the situation, and it is not doubted in official circles tonight that the President will take steps tomorrow morning to meet the new status.

The importance of these cases is regarded as resting in the fact that they seem to demonstrate that the German Government has no intention of abandoning its relentless U-boat policy. In addition, the deliberate sinking of American vessels without warning, after the return of Count von Bern-

Continued on Page 2.

PATROL PICKS UP SURVIVORS

City of Memphis Crew Is Abandoned at Sea In Five Open Boats

VIGILANCIA SAW NO U-BOAT

29 of Her 43 Men Landed at Scilly Islands After She Is Torpedoed Unawares.

TANKER ILLINOIS ALSO LOST

Oil Ship and City of Memphis Were Returning to United States in Ballast.

LONDON, March 18.—The sinking of the American steamships City of Memphis, Illinois, and Vigilancia by German submarines was announced today. Fourteen men from the Vigilancia are missing, as are twenty-four men from the City of Memphis. The crew of the Illinois was landed safely.

[Later advices which were received by the State Department at Washington said that of the fifty-seven men on the City of Memphis fifteen had landed at Schull and thirty-four were on an Admiralty vessel, which was searching for the eight others.]

The City of Memphis, which left Cardiff Friday in ballast for New York, was sunk Saturday. When she left port the steamship had the Stars and Stripes painted on both sides. She encountered a submarine about 5 o'clock Saturday evening. The German commander ordered the Captain of the steamer to leave his ship within fifteen minutes.

The entire crew entered five boats, and the submarine then fired a torpedo which struck the vessel on the starboard side, tearing a great hole through which the sea poured. The steamer settled down quickly and foundered within a few minutes.

Three Boat Crews Picked Up.

In the night the boats became separated, and at 4 o'clock Sunday morning three boat crews were picked up by a patrol vessel and landed. These boats contained thirty-three men, mostly Americans. All of the officers were Americans. The officers believe that the other boats will be rescued.

Third Engineer Thompson of the City of Memphis, in an interview with the Central News, said that the submarine fired a warning shot for the steamer to slow down, and subsequently signaled for her to stop and for the crew to abandon the ship. Ten or eleven shells were fired at the vessel, which began to sink. Then followed a terrific explosion which caused the vessel to tremble all over, and within twenty minutes she sank, stern first. The crew suffered a great deal from exposure during the night.

Thompson said the ship was on charter to discharge her cargo at Havre. From Havre she went to Cardiff, and the skipper, knowing he was in the danger zone, kept the flag, which was yards in length, flying at the masthead. Nobody seems to have expected an attack.

Captain Borum briefly consulted with the officers after the Germans ordered him by megaphone to leave the ship because it was intended to sink her, said Thompson. All agreed that there was no alternative. After describing the sinking of the steamer, Thompson continued:

"When the ship had been destroyed the German commander steamed to our boat and asked for the Captain, but none of our lads answered him. He then went from boat to boat until he found Captain Borum, who briefly conversed with him. I do not know what was said.

Flarelights Bring Rescuers.

"The weather was not too bad, but there were heavy swells. We kept the boats together, and during the evening we rowed together toward the coast. The night closed with a biting wind, and some of our young chaps were very sick. Our flarelights were seen between 3 and 4 o'clock in the morning by the patrol vessels, which rescued two boats' crews. The other two had become separated. We lost everything we possessed."

The following American officers are known to have been landed: Chief Officer C. G. Laird, Chief Engineer W. I. Percy, Assistant Engineer F. Bevill, Third Engineer W. M. Thompson, Third Officer M. Dierland, Wireless Operators J. Welch and P. J. Donahue, and Electrician Phillips.

[The statements that the steamer, City of Memphis was sunk by gunfire, also that she was torpedoed, apparently are cleared up by the statements of Third Engineer Thompson that she was first shelled and was sinking when "a terrific explosion, which caused the vessel to tremble all over," occurred. This seemingly would indicate that the steamer was torpedoed after she had been shelled.]

The Vigilancia was torpedoed without warning. The submarine did not appear. The Captain, First and Second Mates, First, Second, and Third Engineers, and twenty-three men of the crew have been landed at the Scilly Isl-

U. S. Navy

American tanker S. S. Illinois fired upon, stopped and sunk by a German submarine in the English Channel, March 18, 1917.

"All the News That's Fit to Print."

The New York Times.

THE WEATHER
Fair, colder today; tomorrow warmer, probably rain; wind northwest.
For full weather report see Page 73.

VOL. LXVI...NO. 21,619. NEW YORK, TUESDAY, APRIL 3, 1917.—TWENTY-FOUR PAGES. ONE CENT In New York City. | TWO CENTS New England and Middle States. | THREE CENTS Elsewhere.

PRESIDENT CALLS FOR WAR DECLARATION, STRONGER NAVY, NEW ARMY OF 500,000 MEN, FULL CO-OPERATION WITH GERMANY'S FOES

ARMED AMERICAN STEAMSHIP SUNK; 11 MEN MISSING

The Aztec Is First Gun-Bearing Vessel Under Our Flag to be Torpedoed.

SURPRISE ATTACK AT NIGHT

12 Navy Men and Their Chief Among 17 Survivors Picked Up by a Patrol.

11 IN A LIFEBOAT THAT SANK

Liner St. Paul, with Cannon, Reaches British Port in Safety—Had 61 Passengers.

PARIS, April 2.—The American steamer Aztec has been sunk by a submarine near an island off Brest. Some of the crew were rescued and are being brought into Brest. A number of the men are missing, and little hope is held that they can be saved, as the steamer was torpedoed at night while a heavy sea was running.

A French patrol picked up nineteen of the crew of the Aztec. Twenty-eight men are reported missing.

William Graves Sharp, the American Ambassador, was informed this afternoon by the French Government of the torpedoing of the Aztec and immediately cabled the State Department at Washington.

Representatives of the American Government will proceed to Brest to take the depositions of survivors of the disaster.

Bluejackets and Officer Saved.

WASHINGTON, April 2.—French Admiralty dispatches to the French Embassy here tonight announcing the sinking without warning of the first armed American merchantman, the freighter Aztec, by a German submarine, said apparently Lieutenant W. F. Gresham and twelve American bluejackets, constituting the armed guard of the vessel, had been saved, but that eleven of the crew were reported missing.

The Admiralty report said the Aztec, bound from New York to Havre, was torpedoed without warning yesterday off Ouessant. The torpedo struck squarely amidships, emitting a powerful gas and putting the wireless out of commission. The guard with the Captain and three other members of the crew in the second boat to put off apparently were picked up by the French patrol boat Sirrius after three hours. Eleven men are thought to have been drowned when the first boat to put off was smashed. The third boat, containing the second officer and eighteen men, is not directly accounted for, but the fact that only eleven are reported missing leads to the belief that it must have been picked up.

The Navy Department tonight gave out the names of the navy members on the Aztec as follows:

Officer in charge—Lieutenant William F. Gresham of Tennessee.

Crew—John I. Eopolucci, boatswain's mate; mother, Annie M. Eopolucci, 649 I Street, Southeast, Washington.

Jacob J. Hilfiker, electrician; father, Jake Hilfiker, 2,206 Preston Street, Baltimore, Md.

Thomas E. Dillon, Quartermaster; father, Thomas I. Dillon, 78 Boyd Avenue, Jersey City, N. J.

William H. Douglas, coxswain; mother, Sarah D. Douglas, 1,459 South Second Street, Terre Haute, Ind.

Adolph Hendrickson, coxswain; father, Charles Hendrickson, 3,034 Eleventh Avenue, Minneapolis, Minn.

Samuel Earl Israel, seaman; mother, Annie Israel, Kellerman, Ala.

Clarence H. Kelley, Quartermaster; mother, Margaret Kelley, 434 South Broad Street, Trenton, N. J.

Joseph Kiewinsky, seaman; father, John Kiewinsky, Rural Free Delivery, Route 3, Box 40, Newburg, W. Va.

William F. Rominger, gunner's mate; brother, Donnie Rominger, Elizabethton, Tenn.

Joseph A. Rucker, seaman; guardian, Joseph W. Rucker, Roanoke, Ala.

Clarence W. Whitney, Quartermaster; father, James H. Whitney, Front and Broadway, Cincinnati, Ohio.

All the naval crew were taken from the United States dispatch boat Dolphin at Washington to be placed on the Aztec.

Officials tonight said the disaster would not affect the policy of arming ships, which would be continued in the most efficient manner possible.

First Armed American Ship Sunk.

The American steamship Aztec, the third armed merchant vessel to sail from

Continued on Page 24.

Text of the President's Address

Gentlemen of the Congress:

I have called the Congress into extraordinary session because there are serious, very serious, choices of policy to be made, and made immediately, which it was neither right nor constitutionally permissible that I should assume the responsibility of making.

On the 3d of February last I officially laid before you the extraordinary announcement of the Imperial German Government that on and after the first day of February it was its purpose to put aside all restraints of law or of humanity and use its submarines to sink every vessel that sought to approach either the ports of Great Britain and Ireland or the western coasts of Europe or any of the ports controlled by the enemies of Germany within the Mediterranean. That had seemed to be the object of the German submarine warfare earlier in the war, but since April of last year the Imperial Government had somewhat restrained the commanders of its undersea craft, in conformity with its promise, then given to us, that passenger boats should not be sunk and that due warning would be given to all other vessels which its submarines might seek to destroy, when no resistance was offered or escape attempted, and care taken that their crews were given at least a fair chance to save their lives in their open boats. The precautions taken were meagre and haphazard enough, as was proved in distressing instance after instance in the progress of the cruel and unmanly business, but a certain degree of restraint was observed.

The new policy has swept every restriction aside. Vessels of every kind, whatever their flag, their character, their cargo, their destination, their errand, have been ruthlessly sent to the bottom without warning and without thought of help or mercy for those on board, the vessels of friendly neutrals along with those of belligerents. Even hospital ships and ships carrying relief to the sorely bereaved and stricken people of Belgium, though the latter were provided with safe conduct through the proscribed areas by the German Government itself and were distinguished by unmistakable marks of identity, have been sunk with the same reckless lack of compassion or of principle.

I was for a little while unable to believe that such things would in fact be done by any Government that had hitherto subscribed to humane practices of civilized nations. International law had its origin in the attempt to set up some law which would be respected and observed upon the seas, where no nation has right of dominion and where lay the free highways of the world. By painful stage after stage has that law been built up, with meagre enough results, indeed, after all was accomplished that could be accomplished, but always with a clear view, at least, of what the heart and conscience of mankind demanded.

This minimum of right the German Government has swept aside, under the plea of retaliation and necessity and because it had no weapons which it could use at sea except these, which it is impossible to employ, as it is employing them, without throwing to the wind all scruples of humanity or of respect for the understandings that were supposed to underlie the intercourse of the world.

I am not now thinking of the loss of property involved, immense and serious as that is, but only of the wanton and wholesale destruction of the lives of noncombatants, men, women, and children, engaged in pursuits which have always, even in the darkest periods of modern history, been deemed innocent and legitimate. Property can be paid for; the lives of peaceful and innocent people cannot be. The present German submarine warfare against commerce is a warfare against mankind.

It is a war against all nations. American ships have been sunk, American lives taken, in ways which it has stirred us very deeply to learn of, but the ships and people of other neutral and friendly nations have been sunk and overwhelmed in the waters in the same way. There has been no discrimination.

The challenge is to all mankind. Each nation must decide for itself how it will meet it. The choice we make for ourselves must be made with a moderation of counsel and a temperateness of judgment befitting our character and our motives as a nation. We must put excited feeling away. Our motive will not be revenge or the victorious assertion of the physical might of the nation, but only the vindication of right, of human right, of which we are only a single champion.

When I addressed the Congress on the 26th of February last I thought that it would suffice to assert our neutral rights with arms, our right to use the seas against unlawful interference, our right to keep our people safe against unlawful violence. But armed neutrality, it now appears, is impracticable. Because submarines are in effect outlaws, when used as the German submarines have been used against merchant shipping, it is impossible to defend ships against their attacks as the law of nations has assumed that merchantmen would defend themselves against privateers or cruisers, visible craft giving chase upon the open sea. It is common prudence in such circumstances, grim necessity indeed, to endeavor to destroy them before they have shown their own intention. They must be dealt with upon sight, if dealt with at all.

The German Government denies the right of neutrals to use arms at all within the areas of the sea which it has proscribed, even in the defense of rights which no modern publicist has ever before questioned their right to defend. The intimation is conveyed that the armed guards which we have placed on our merchant ships will be treated as beyond the pale of law and subject to be dealt with as pirates would be. Armed neutrality is ineffectual enough at best; in such circumstances and in the face of such pretensions it is worse than ineffectual; it is likely only to produce what it was meant to prevent; it is practically certain to draw us into the war without either the rights or the effectiveness of belligerents. There is one choice we cannot make, we are incapable of making; we will not choose the path of submission and suffer the most sacred rights of our nation and our people to be ignored or violated. The wrongs against which we now array ourselves are no common wrongs; they cut to the very roots of human life.

With a profound sense of the solemn and even tragical character of the step I am taking and of the grave responsibilities which it involves, but in unhesitating obedience to what I deem my constitutional duty, I advise that the Congress declare the recent course of the Imperial German Government to be in fact nothing less than war against the Government and people of the United States; that it formally accept the status of belligerent which has thus been thrust upon it; and that it take immediate steps not only to put the country in a more thorough state of defense, but also to exert all its power and employ all its resources to bring the Government of the German Empire to terms and end the war.

What this will involve is clear. It will involve the utmost practicable co-operation in counsel and action with the Governments now at war with Germany, and, as incident to that, the extension to those Governments of the most liberal financial credits, in order that our resources may so far as possible be added to theirs.

It will involve the organization and mobilization of all the material resources of the country to supply the materials of war and serve the incidental needs of the nation in the most abundant and yet the most economical and efficient way possible.

It will involve the immediate full equipment of the navy in all respects, but particularly in supplying it with the best means of dealing with the enemy's submarines.

It will involve the immediate addition to the armed forces of the United States, already provided for by law in case of war, of at least 500,000 men, who should, in my opinion, be chosen upon the principle of universal liability to service, and also the authorization of subsequent additional increments of equal force so soon as they may be needed and can be handled in training.

It will involve also, of course, the granting of adequate credits to the Government, sustained, I hope, so far as they can equitably be sustained by the present generation, by well conceived taxation.

I say sustained so far as may be equitable by taxation, because it seems to me that it would be most unwise to base the credits, which will now be necessary, entirely on money borrowed. It is our duty, I most respectfully urge, to protect our people, so far as we may, against the very serious hardships and evils which would be likely to arise out of the inflation which would be produced by vast loans.

In carrying out the measures by which these things are to be accomplished we should keep constantly in mind the wisdom of interfering as little as possible in our own preparation and in the equipment of our own military forces with the duty—for it will be a very practical duty—of supplying the nations already at war with Germany with the materials which they can obtain only from us or by our assistance. They are in the field and we should help them in every way to be effective there.

I shall take the liberty of suggesting, through the several executive departments of the Government, for the consideration of your committees, measures for the accomplishment of the several objects I have mentioned. I hope that it will be your pleasure to deal with them as having been framed after very careful thought by the branch of the Government upon whom the responsibility of conducting the war and safeguarding the nation will most directly fall.

While we do these things, these deeply momentous things, let us be very clear, and make very clear to all the world, what our motives and our objects are. My own thought has not been driven from its habitual and normal course by the unhappy events of the last two months, and I do not believe that the thought of the nation had been altered or clouded by them. I have exactly the same things in mind now that I had in mind when I addressed the Senate on the 22d of January last; the same that I had in mind when I addressed the Congress on the 3d of February and on the 26th of February. Our object now, as then, is to vindicate the principles of peace and justice in the life of the world as against selfish and autocratic power, and to set up among the really free and self-governed peoples of the world such a concert of purpose and of action as will henceforth insure the observance of those principles.

Neutrality is no longer feasible or desirable where the peace of the world is involved and the freedom of its peoples, and the menace to that peace and freedom lies in the existence of autocratic Governments, backed by organized force which is controlled wholly by their will, not by the will of their people. We have seen the last of neutrality in such circumstances. We are at the beginning of an age in which it will be insisted that the same standards of conduct and of responsibility for wrong done shall be observed among nations and their Governments that are observed among the individual citizens of civilized States.

We have no quarrel with the German people. We have no feeling toward them but one of sympathy and friendship. It was not upon their impulse that their Government acted in entering this war. It was not with their previous knowledge or approval. It was a war determined upon as wars used to be determined upon in the old, unhappy days, when peoples were nowhere consulted by their rulers and wars were provoked and waged in the interest of dynasties or of little groups of ambitious men who were accustomed to use their fellow men as pawns and tools.

Self-governed nations do not fill their neighbor States with spies or set the course of intrigue to bring about some critical posture of affairs which will give them an opportunity to strike and make conquest. Such designs can be successfully worked out only under cover and where no one has the right to ask questions. Cunningly contrived plans of deception or aggression, carried, it may be, from generation to generation, can be worked out and kept from the light only within the privacy of courts or behind the carefully guarded confidences of a narrow and privileged class. They are happily impossible where public opinion commands and insists upon full information concerning all the nation's affairs.

A steadfast concert for peace can never be maintained except by a partnership of democratic nations. No autocratic Government could be trusted to keep faith within it or observe its covenants. It must be a league of honor, a partnership of opinion. Intrigue would eat its vitals away; the plottings of inner circles who could plan what they would and render account to no one would be a corruption seated at its very heart. Only free peoples can hold their purpose and their honor steady to a common end and prefer the interests of mankind to any narrow interest of their own.

Does not every American feel that assurance has been added to our hope for the future peace of the world by the wonderful and heartening things that have been happening within the last few weeks in Russia? Russia was known by those who knew her best to have been always in fact democratic at heart in all the vital habits of her thought, in all the intimate relationships of her people that spoke their natural instinct, their habitual attitude toward life. The autocracy that crowned the summit of her political structure, long as it had stood and terrible as was the reality of its power, was not in fact Russian in origin, character, or purpose; and now it has been shaken off and the great, generous Russian people have been added, in all their naive majesty and might, to the forces that are fighting for freedom in the world, for justice, and for peace. Here is a fit partner for a League of Honor.

One of the things that has served to convince us that the Prussian autocracy was not and could never be our friend is that from the very outset of the present war it has filled our unsuspecting communities, and even our offices of government, with spies and set criminal intrigues everywhere afoot against our national unity of counsel, our peace within and without, our industries and our commerce. Indeed, it is now evident that its spies were here even before the war began; and it is unhappily not a matter of conjecture, but a fact proved in our courts of justice, that the intrigues which have more than once come perilously near to disturbing the peace and dislocating the industries of the country, have been carried on at the instigation, with the support, and even under the personal direction of official agents of the Imperial Government, accredited to the Government of the United States.

Even in checking these things and trying to extirpate them we have sought to put the most generous interpretation possible upon them because we knew that their source lay, not in any hostile feeling or purpose of the German people toward us, (who were, no doubt, as ignorant of them as we ourselves were,) but only in the selfish designs of a Government that did what it pleased and told its people nothing. But they have played their part in serving to convince us at last that that Government entertains no real friendship for us, and means to act against our peace and security at its convenience. That it means to stir up enemies against us at our very doors the intercepted note to the German Minister at Mexico City is eloquent evidence.

We are accepting this challenge of hostile purpose because we know that in such a Government, following such methods, we can never have a friend; and that in the presence of its organized power, always lying in wait to accomplish we know not what purpose, can be no assured security for the democratic Governments of the world. We are now about to accept the gauge of battle with this natural foe to liberty and shall, if necessary, spend the whole force of the nation to check and nullify its pretensions and its power. We are glad, now that we see the facts with no veil of false pretense about them, to fight thus for the ultimate peace of the world and for the liberation of its peoples, the German peoples included; for the rights of nations, great and small, and the privilege of men everywhere to choose their way of life and of obedience.

The world must be made safe for democracy. Its peace must be planted upon the tested foundations of political liberty. We have no selfish ends to serve. We desire no conquest, no dominion. We seek no indemnities for ourselves, no material compensation for the sacrifices we shall freely make. We are but one of the champions of the rights of mankind. We shall be satisfied when those rights have been made as secure as the faith and the freedom of nations can make them.

Just because we fight without rancor and without selfish object, seeking nothing for ourselves but what we shall wish to share with all free peoples, we shall, I feel confident, conduct our operations as belligerents without passion and ourselves observe with proud punctilio the principles of right and of fair play we profess to be fighting for.

I have said nothing of the Governments allied with the Imperial Government of Germany because they have not made war upon us or challenged us to defend our right and our honor. The Austro-Hungarian Government has, indeed, avowed its unqualified indorsement and acceptance of the reckless and lawless submarine warfare, adopted now without disguise by the Imperial German Government, and it has therefore not been possible for this Government to receive Count Tarnowski, the Ambassador recently accredited to this Government by the Imperial and Royal Government of Austria-Hungary; but that Government has not actually engaged in warfare against citizens of the United States on the seas, and I take the liberty, for the present at least, of postponing a discussion of our relations with the authorities at Vienna. We enter this war only where we are clearly forced into it because there are no other means of defending our right.

It will be all the easier for us to conduct ourselves as belligerents in a high spirit of right and fairness because we act without animus, not with enmity toward a people or with the desire to bring any injury or disadvantage upon them, but only in armed opposition to an irresponsible Government which has thrown aside all considerations of humanity and of right and is running amuck.

We are, let me say again, the sincere friends of the German people, and shall desire nothing so much as the early re-establishment of intimate relations of mutual advantage between us, however hard it may be for them for the time being to believe that this is spoken from our hearts. We have borne with their present Government through all these bitter months because of that friendship, exercising a patience and forbearance which would otherwise have been impossible.

We shall happily still have an opportunity to prove that friendship in our daily attitude and actions toward the millions of men and women of German birth and native sympathy who live among us and share our life, and we shall be proud to prove it toward all, who are in fact loyal to their neighbors and to the Government in the hour of test. They are most of them as true and loyal Americans as if they had never known any other fealty or allegiance. They will be prompt to stand with us in rebuking and restraining the few who may be of a different mind and purpose. If there should be disloyalty, it will be dealt with with a firm hand of stern repression; but, if it lifts its head at all, it will lift it only here and there and without countenance except from a lawless and malignant few.

It is a distressing and oppressive duty, gentlemen of the Congress, which I have performed in thus addressing you. There are, it may be, many months of fiery trial and sacrifice ahead of us. It is a fearful thing to lead this great, peaceful people into war, into the most terrible and disastrous of all wars, civilization itself seeming to be in the balance.

But the right is more precious than peace, and we shall fight for the things which we have always carried nearest our hearts—for democracy, for the right of those who submit to authority to have a voice in their own Governments, for the rights and liberties of small nations, for a universal dominion of right by such a concert of free peoples as shall bring peace and safety to all nations and make the world itself at last free.

To such a task we can dedicate our lives and our fortunes, everything that we are and everything that we have, with the pride of those who know that the day has come when America is privileged to spend her blood and her might for the principles that gave her birth and happiness and the peace which she has treasured.

God helping her, she can do no other.

The War Resolution Now Before Congress

This resolution was introduced in the House of Representatives last night by Representative Flood, Chairman of the Foreign Affairs Committee, immediately after the President's address:

JOINT RESOLUTION, Declaring that a State of War Exists Between the Imperial German Government and the Government and People of the United States and Making Provision to Prosecute the Same.

Whereas, The recent acts of the Imperial German Government are acts of war against the Government and people of the United States:

Resolved, By the Senate and House of Representatives of the United States of America in Congress assembled, that the state of war between the United States and the Imperial German Government which has thus been thrust upon the United States is hereby formally declared; and

That the President be, and he is hereby, authorized and directed to take immediate steps not only to put the country in a thorough state of defense but also to exert all of its power and employ all of its resources to carry on war against the Imperial German Government and to bring the conflict to a successful termination.

MUST EXERT ALL OUR POWER

To Bring a "Government That Is Running Amuck to Terms."

WANTS LIBERAL CREDITS

And Universal Service, for "the World Must Be Made Safe for Democracy."

A TUMULTUOUS GREETING

Congress Adjourns After "State of War" Resolution Is Introduced—Acts Today.

Special to The New York Times.

WASHINGTON, April 2.—At 8:38 o'clock tonight the United States virtually made its entrance into the war. At that hour President Wilson appeared before a joint session of the Senate and House and invited it to consider the fact that Germany had been making war upon us and to take action in recognition of that fact in accordance with his recommendations, which included universal military service, the raising of an army of 500,000 men, and co-operation with the Allies in all ways that will help most effectively to defeat Germany.

Resolutions recognizing and declaring the state of war were immediately introduced in the House and Senate by Representative Flood and Senator Martin, both of the President's birth-State, Virginia, and they are the strongest declarations of war that the United States has ever made in any war in which it has been engaged since it became a nation. They are the Administration resolutions drawn up after conference with the President, and in language approved and probably dictated by him, and they will come before the two Foreign Affairs Committees at meetings which will be held tomorrow morning and will be reported at the earliest practical moment.

Unreservedly With the Allies.

Before an audience that cheered him as he has never been cheered in the Capitol in his life the President cast in the lot of America unreservedly with the Allies and declared for a war that must not end until the issue between autocracy and democracy has been fought out. He recited our injuries at Germany's hands, but he did not rest our cause on those; he went on from that point to range us with the Allies as a factor in an irrepressible conflict between the autocrat and the people. He showed that peace was impossible for the democracies of the world while this power remained on earth. "The world," he said, "must be made safe for democracy."

We had learned that the German autocracy could never be a friend of this country; she had been our enemy while nominally our friend, and even before the war of 1914 broke out. He called on us to take our stand with the democracies in this irrepressible conflict, with before our eyes "the wonderful and heartening events that have been happening in the last few weeks in Russia." He reaffirmed his hope for peace and for freedom, and looked to the war now forced upon us to bring these about; for, he said, a world compact for peace "can never be maintained except by a concert of the democracies of the world."

The objects for which we fight, he said, are democracy, the right of those who submit to authority to have a voice in their own government, the right and liberties of small nations, the universal dominion of right, the concert of free peoples to bring peace and safety to all nations, and to make the world free. These have always been our ideals, and to accomplish them, we accept the war Germany has made upon us. In fighting it we must not only raise an army and increase the navy, but must aid the Allies in all ways, financial and other, and so order our own preparations as not to interfere with the supply of munitions they are getting from us.

Trouble-making Pacifists Barred.

The President delivered this speech before an audience that had been carefully sifted. All day Washington had been in the hands of belligerent pacifists, truculent in manner, and determined to break into the Capitol. They tried to take possession of the Capitol steps, up which the President must go when he entered, and met the same fate that Coxey's rioters fell in with twenty-three years ago at the hands of the police, who dispersed them.

A handful of them fell upon Senator Lodge and assaulted him. Others en-

"All the News That's Fit to Print."

The New York Times.

THE WEATHER
Rain tonight and Friday; moderate temperature; southeasterly winds.
For full weather report see Page 23.

VOL. LXVI...NO. 21,621. NEW YORK, THURSDAY, APRIL 5, 1917.—TWENTY-FOUR PAGES. ONE CENT In New York City. | TWO CENTS New England and Middle States. | THREE CENTS Elsewhere.

SENATE, 82 TO 6, ADOPTS WAR DECLARATION; ITS OPPONENTS SCORED; HOUSE ACTS TODAY; BERLIN FEARS OUR INFLUENCE ON RUSSIA

SENATE INDORSES WAGNER, ENDING MITCHEL INQUIRY

Adopts Resolution of Confidence at an All-Night Secret Conference.

NO CENSURE OF MITCHEL

Mayor Is Cross-Examined on the Rockaway Fortification Measures.

HE MEANT NO ATTACK

Explains That His Reference to the "Gentleman from Prussia" Was in the Nature of a Retort to Wagner.

Special to The New York Times.

ALBANY, Thursday, April 5.—The contempt proceedings against John Purroy Mitchel, Mayor of New York City, before the Senate came to a close at 2 o'clock this morning when resolutions expressing confidence in Senator Robert F. Wagner were brought in.

The resolutions were adopted at an executive session which had been in progress since 9 o'clock last night.

An attempt was made to pass a resolution mildly censuring Mayor Mitchel, but this failed.

When the Senate met in the evening it was after a day during which Mayor Mitchel had been subjected to an exceptionally severe cross-examination at the hands of Samuel Untermyer, chief counsel for Senator Wagner. The Mayor occupied the witness chair practically the entire day. The sole respite was when Colonel Frederick V. Abbot of the Corps of Engineers of the United States Army was summoned as a witness for Mayor Mitchel in order to afford him an opportunity to return to duty immediately in response to an urgent call from the War Department.

The Senate went into session at 9 o'clock in the evening. Senator Charles D. Newton of Geneseo, Chairman of the Board of Managers appointed to supervise the contempt proceedings, at once moved that an executive session be ordered and that the Senate, in order to save the time that would be necessary to clear the Senate chamber and galleries, which were packed to suffocation, withdraw into the Senate Finance Committee room.

Untermyer Cross-Examines Mitchel.

Samuel Untermyer, chief counsel for Senator Wagner, took up the cross-examination of Mayor Mitchel the moment the Senate was called to order yesterday morning. The early part of the testimony dealt with the circumstances under which the interview attacking Senator Wagner had been given to the newspapers by the Mayor.

Mr. Untermyer then took up the record of Senate proceedings on March 22—the day of the interview—and read the speeches by Senator Brown and Senator Wagner indicating that after conferences of the Republican and Democratic members of the Senate, an agreement had been reached that it would be better to obtain the land needed for the Rockaway Point fortifications through condemnation proceedings than through exercise of the option obtained by the Federal Government from the Rockaway Pacific Corporation, contingent on a conveyance of some land by the city to the company. Senator Brown, in the statement which was read, set forth that General W. W. Wotherspoon, State Superintendent of Public Works and a member of the Military Condemnation Commission, had assured the Republican Senators that the incidental delay would not interfere with the development of the Rockaway defenses, and that it would not be difficult to avoid any substantial consequential damages.

Mayor Mitchel, in reply to questions from Mr. Untermyer, said that he had learned of this action after his statement had been made, possibly on the next day.

"Do I understand that on March 23 you did not know that the majority of the Senate in conference and the minority in conference had both agreed that the course of wisdom and patriotism was to take this property by condemnation and not under the agreement?" asked Mr. Untermyer.

"I did not say that," said the Mayor. "If you leave out the words 'wisdom and patriotism' I know that fact."

A moment later the Mayor admitted that he had learned of the condemnation proceedings on the evening of March 22, the day of his interview, from Senator Charles F. Murphy of Kings. Both were guests at a dinner

Continued on Page 11.

Austria to Break with Us If We Join War on Kaiser

Vienna, April 3, (via London, Thursday, April 5.)—It appears certain that Austria-Hungary will sever diplomatic relations with the United States if Congress declares that a state of war exists between America and Germany.

The Government has placed a special car at the disposal of Ambassador Penfield, who will probably leave Vienna on Thursday. Before leaving Ambassador Penfield will be received by Emperor Charles. The Ambassador will travel by way of Switzerland.

RUSSIAN ATTACHE STRANGELY SHOT

Michael Borzatovsky, Wounded, Is Found in a Room in Baltimore Country Club.

ACCIDENT, FRIENDS INSIST

Police Suspect Spy Attacked Diplomat Who Came from Petrograd Recently.

Special to The New York Times.

BALTIMORE, April 4.—Suffering from a dangerous gunshot wound in his chest about which he remains stubbornly silent, Michael Borzatovsky, Commercial Attaché of the Russian Embassy in Washington, is in a critical condition in the Church Home and Infirmary. He was shot about 4 o'clock this morning in his bedroom at the Baltimore Country Club, where he was a guest.

Two theories are entertained regarding the affair, which the members of the Baltimore Country Club have done their best to shroud in mystery. The friends of the attaché in Baltimore declare the wound was self-inflicted accidentally while he was removing a revolver from his clothes.

The police have been told the wound was inflicted from a gun and not from a revolver. They find it hard to reconcile the fact that the man said good-bye to his friends at 11 o'clock Tuesday evening, and that the shot was fired after 3 o'clock in the morning, with the statement from club members that the shooting occurred when Mr. Borzatovsky was undressing to go to bed. They are following clues which lead them to believe he was the victim of a shot from a German spy, bent on assassination.

[illegible] to the latter theory by the report that Borzatovsky, who came to America within the last two weeks, was returning from a conference with the Russian Ambassador at Washington with an important message for the new Government in his home land.

It was only with the utmost difficulty that detectives and police got any information regarding the shooting, and in a number of instances the information was absolutely incorrect and designed deliberately to lead the inquirers off the track.

On the person of the Russian diplomat was a large sum of money, but detectives scout the theory that robbery was the motive, if, as is confidently believed in many quarters, the wound was not self-inflicted. They believe that interests here inimical both to the Russian and the United States Governments regarded it as extremely dangerous for Brozatovsky to return to Russia, and resorted to desperate means to prevent him from getting there.

Borzatovsky came to the United States from Petrograd eight days ago and went immediately to Washington, where he had business for his Government with his embassy. Some years ago, in Petrograd, he had made the acquaintance of E. Griswold Thelin of Roland Park, who is the Baltimore manager of the Prudential Insurance Company, and also of other Baltimoreans at that time in the Russian capital. On his return journey he decided to visit these persons, and Mr. Thelin arranged for him to remain at the Baltimore Country Club, where he arrived on Saturday last.

Entertainments were given in his honor, and there was a particularly brilliant dinner party on Tuesday evening. Present there at the table were some of the most active and influential members of the club, in addition to Mr. Thelin and other Baltimore friends of the visitor. The party dispersed after 11 o'clock, and the departing guests left Borzatovsky apparently in fine spirits.

George S. Jackson, President of the Baltimore Country Club, said that two bellboys had told him Mr. Borzatovsky remained for possibly two hours, or even longer, in the green room writing letters. Soon afterward he retired to his room and later attendants hearing a shot went to the room. They found Borzatovsky with a serious wound in his chest. He was conscious and calm. He asked that Mr. Thelin be called. Mr. Thelin summoned Dr. R. V. Norment, and in the physician's automobile the wounded man was hurried to the Church Home and Infirmary.

Mr. Thelin informed the doctor there had been an accident. Mr. Borzatovsky said he had been partly undressed; that some whim prompted him to examine his service revolver, the gift of a friend; that quite unaccountably it had exploded.

Had Mysterious Bundle.

SAN FRANCISCO, April 4.—Michael Borzakovsky arrived in San Francisco recently on the Korean Maru on an unexplained mission to the United States. A red, sealed bundle, closely guarded by two Russian detectives, gave an air of mystery to the Russian agent's trip. Borzakovsky was the guest during a few days' stay here of A. M. Wyvodseff, the Russian Consul-General.

WASHINGTON, April 4.—Michael Borzatovsky, who was found shot at the Baltimore Country Club today, was a commercial messenger for the Russian Government, but had no connection with the Russian Embassy here, and was not a Count, embassy officials said tonight. They added that they understood he had shot himself accidentally while handling a pistol.

AUSTRIA TO PROPOSE PEACE

Charles to Make Statement to World on Behalf of Teutonic Allies.

OPPOSES PRUSSIAN JINGOES

Pressure Brought to Bear on Reactionaries Who Demand Territorial Aggrandizement.

PEOPLE STIRRED BY RUSSIA

But Dual Monarchy May Be Compelled by Germany to Break with United States.

Special Cable to THE NEW YORK TIMES.

THE HAGUE, April 4.—The Frankfort Gazette's Vienna correspondent sends his paper a long telegram declaring that there never was in Austria a party "like the Prussian Conservatives" who sympathized with the Czar's absolutism. He says: "It needs direct warnings of saner individuals to prevent the bulk of the population of Austria-Hungary from making untimely demonstrations in favor of the new Russia."

The correspondent then says Germany should note very carefully Count Czernin's insistence on the fact that Austria is not after annexations, and continues:

"Germany also can therefore hardly desire to make peace dependent on the possibility of annexing territory. But if certain German parties should attempt this they must be absolutely clear that such efforts would find no echo in Austria-Hungary."

This is the plainest possible indication that pressure is being put by Austria on German reactionaries.

The Vossische Zeitung states there is slight possibility that the Entente countries would be unanimous in the wish to confer with the Central Powers, but that a separate peace with Russia would be more conducive to German interests.

"Since the revolution Russia is much occupied with interior affairs," it says, "and a large part, if not a majority, of the Russian people want peace, in spite of what is said in England. The Chancellor has made it quite clear that Germany is ready for a peace with Russia which would be honorable for both sides."

LONDON, Thursday, April 5.—What The Evening News correspondent at The Hague terms an obviously inspired telegram from Vienna to the Frankfurter Zeitung says:

"Germany cannot possibly wish to make peace dependent on the possibility of annexation. If certain German parties should still attempt this it must be made clear that such efforts would find no support in Austria-Hungary."

The telegram describes the Austrian terms simply as a "guarantee for integrity and possibility of existence—that is, in relation to Serbia and Rumania."

The newspaper makes further quotations from President Wilson's denunciation of the German Government and demand that there be no peace with the Hohenzollerns.

A dispatch from The Hague to the Exchange Telegraph Company says that Austria-Hungary will break diplomatic relations with the United States as the result of strong German pressure.

At the conference attended by Emperor William and Emperor Charles and the Ministers and Generals of the Central Powers, the correspondent says, the chief subject dealt with was the American situation.

The conference is also said to have received important declarations from Count Czernin von Chudenitz, the Austro-Hungarian Foreign Minister, on the possibility of an early peace. The Emperor of Austria intends, it is added, to make a statement to the world shortly to that effect in the name of the Central Powers.

The Westminster Gazette says the conferees "can hardly fail to notice that the overthrow of their system and the clearance from the world of war lords and war makers is more than ever projected into the foreground as the primary object of the Allies. That is the central theme of President Wilson's address to Congress and the main purpose for which the Western democracy enters the war."

The Pall Mall Gazette says that President Wilson "indicates quite clearly his determination to make no treaty with perverts for whom treaties have no meaning," and adds that all of the allied nations are in line with his resolution.

BERLIN, April 2, (by Wireless to Sayville, April 4.)—Premier Radoslavoff of Bulgaria endorsed in the Bulgarian

Continued on Page 3.

Popular Celebration in France to Mark Our Entry Into War

PARIS, April 4.—A great national demonstration to mark the entry of the United States into the European war was proposed today to the French Government.

It was suggested that the demonstration should be of a popular character, in order to enable the French people to participate in it.

PUTS GREAT HOPES IN AMERICAN AID

British Public Watches Developments in Congress with Intense Interest.

COMMISSION TO SAIL SOON

Westminster Gazette Says It Will Discuss the Scope of Our Co-operation with Allies.

LONDON, April 4.—The British nation tonight is awaiting with the same intense interest as the American people the decision of Congress, whose proceedings are fully reported in the English press. This is not because any doubt exists here as to what the result of the vote in the American Congress will be, but because the nation is anxious to have a formal official expression of its sentiments of satisfaction at America's entry into the struggle on the side of the Allies cross the Atlantic from Parliament, which will adjourn tomorrow for the Eastern recess, and there is a general desire that Congress arrive at its decision in time to allow this to be done before the House of Commons rises.

Pending the decision of Congress, the Ministers and responsible officials in London hesitate to make any public expression of their ideas and sentiments on American co-operation with the Allies.

The present mood of the British public is perplexed. On the one hand, it has daily evidence from the western front of the splendid success of the Allies' continuing advance; on the other hand, the War Office is constantly insisting upon the urgency of providing more men for the front, and the Ministers are imposing increasing food restrictions, warning the country that still greater sacrifices than any yet endured will be needed.

There were two instances of this today. General Robertson, Chief of the Imperial Staff, at Army Headquarters, declared that the Germans were now stronger by a million men than at any time before, and that the struggle would entail heavy sacrifices and greater determination. Winston Spencer Churchill in the House of Commons, in the course of a discussion of the air service, referred to America's entry into the war as "God-granted aid to struggling Christendom," and declared that but for this aid no prudent man could have said that the issue of the war was settled.

Never since the victory of the Marne had the position been more serious, added Mr. Churchill, and even with America in the struggle a most oppressive situation lay before the nation, and the most vehement efforts were needed. The most terrible months of the war were coming, and it would only be by the highest wisdom, utmost daring, and truest comradeship that the Allies could come safely through.

Faced by the gloomy predictions, the people, who only a few weeks ago were inclined to belittle any practical assistance the United States could render, even if she came into the war, have now a tendency to go to the other extreme and hope for everything from American co-operation. While it is recognized that the greatest aid possible in the immediate future would be from the American Navy and in the realm of finance and supplies, keen curiosity is displayed as to the line co-operation with the new ally will take.

The Westminster Gazette says that a commission will soon be sent to the United States to decide the scope of this co-operation.

Ambassador Page had another prolonged conference with A. J. Balfour, Secretary for Foreign Affairs, today, and the American Naval Attaché was in close communication with Admiralty officials on the naval co-operation. All reports of American war preparedness were read with eagerness and satisfaction.

An interesting phase of the situation is the renewed peace talk and, although Premier Lloyd George questioned in the House of Commons today about these rumors, said he was not aware of any peace terms being suggested by the Central Governments, there is a very general belief that the reports from Vienna and in inspired German papers of renewed peace tentatives are

Continued on Page 3.

MAY BLOCK SEPARATE PEACE

America's Stand a Menace to German Negotiations with Duma Government.

COMMENT OF GERMAN PRESS

Can't Understand Reason for War, but Will Face Eleventh Enemy Bravely.

WISH FOR A BRYAN TREATY

Plan 'Foolishly Rejected' Would Have Held Us Off for a Year, Tageblatt Says.

Special Cable to THE NEW YORK TIMES.

BERLIN, April 4, (via The Hague.)—Reports of yesterday's proceedings in the American Congress, scant as they are, leave no doubt in the minds of the German people and Government that President Wilson will have his way in everything, and that their eleventh enemy is about to make his appearance in the theatre of war.

Nobody is excited here, but nobody is underestimating the effect of America's entrance into the war against Germany. In military circles it is considered that the immediate effect on the various fighting fronts will not be considerable. In political circles what is most feared is that America's action may influence the present rulers of Russia to a degree that they will resist the temptation to accept the peace offered by Germany. The masses of the German people are utterly at a loss to understand this war with a nation 4,000 miles away, with whom they have no quarrel whatever. The news from America arrived so late that most of the afternoon papers abstained from lengthy comment, contenting themselves with explaining to their readers the workings of the Washington Government machinery. But the Tageblatt states the German position very lucidly as follows:

Sees the Hand of England.

"In his last speech the Chancellor prepared us for the fact that there was no chance of continuing on peaceful terms with the United States. If the English press pretended that it was just this speech that had knocked the bottom out of the barrel, this is only another of those tricks which have had such fatal success with American public opinion. The English press also hoped to minimize thereby the Chancellor's declaration that the German people would go into this war without hatred or enmity, but would be sure to bear patiently this new burden.

"Are the American people in a like condition of mind? It is difficult to answer this question.

"It is a foregone conclusion that Congress will grant all of President Wilson's demands made in his message. He had little trouble to overcome the opposition which was raised against him in the last Congressional session. Of the few Senators who resolutely carried out the operations of obstruction against his policy very few are left, if English sources have informed us correctly. They gave way under the pressure of public opinion even in some of the Western States, where that Zimmermann letter seems to have had some effect after all.

"Since then there has been a feverish war propaganda. Meanwhile the Bryan pacifists did their best to avoid the worst. But it was quite clear that when once the war fever caught Madison Square there would be no stopping this hysterical wave.

"Hatred? Enmity? We know nothing about it. The emotions dictating to Congress its action and which were nourished by President Wilson and his partisans were of another kind. They were nothing but anger over supposed violations of American rights. Despite all efforts to enlighten him President Wilson clung tenaciously to his original view, and he still upholds it with surprising acuteness.

"In order not to disavow his pretended pacifism, Mr. Wilson now seeks to avoid an American declaration of war against Germany. That is why he insists on a fiction, as though Germany by her U-boat war had been guilty of a warlike action, necessary now, for America has recognized the existence of a state of war.

Wish for a Bryan Treaty.

"We realize now what a big mistake it was that German policy saw fit to refuse to conclude the Bryan peace treaty such as England and other powers entered into with the United States. If such a contract existed today the United States would be compelled to submit even the gravest differences to a court or arbitration before breaking relations. This would mean gaining at least a year. It is not at all impossible that President Wilson in his embarrassment would have taken that course to

Continued on Page 5.

Text of War Resolution Adopted by Senate and the Detailed Vote Upon Its Passage

WASHINGTON, April 4.—Following is the text of the resolution declaring war upon the Imperial German Government, which was adopted by the Senate tonight:

> *Whereas*, The Imperial German Government has committed repeated acts of war against the Government and the people of the United States of America; therefore, be it
>
> *Resolved*, by the Senate and House of Representatives of the United States of America in Congress assembled, That the state of war between the United States and the Imperial German Government, which has thus been thrust upon the United States, is hereby formally declared; and
>
> That the President be, and he is hereby, authorized and directed to employ the entire naval and military forces of the United States and the resources of the Government to carry on war against the Imperial German Government; and to bring the conflict to a successful termination all the resources of the country are hereby pledged by the Congress of the United States.

The detailed vote of the Senate on the declaration of war was as follows:

FOR THE RESOLUTION—82

Democrats—43.

ASHURST,	JAMES,	OWEN,	SIMMONS
BECKHAM,	JOHNSON, (S. D.)	PHELAN,	SMITH, (Ariz.)
BROUSSARD,	JONES, (N. M.)	PITTMAN,	SMITH, (Ga.)
CHAMBERLAIN,	KENDRICK,	POMERENE,	SMITH, (S. C.)
CULBERSON,	KING,	RANSDELL,	SWANSON,
FLETCHER,	KIRBY,	REED,	THOMPSON,
GERRY,	LEWIS,	ROBINSON,	TRAMMELL,
HARDWICK,	McKELLAR,	SAULSBURY,	UNDERWOOD,
HITCHCOCK,	MARTIN,	SHAFROTH,	WALSH,
HUGHES,	MEYERS,	SHEPPARD,	WILLIAMS.
HUSTING,	OVERMAN,	SHIELDS,	

Republicans—39.

BORAH,	FRANCE,	LODGE,	SMOOT,
BRADY,	FRELINGHUYSEN	McCUMBER,	STERLING,
BRANDEGEE,	GALLINGER,	McLEAN,	SUTHERLAND,
CALDER,	HALE,	NELSON,	TOWNSEND,
COLT,	HARDING,	NEW,	WADSWORTH,
CUMMINS,	JOHNSON, (Cal.)	PAGE,	WARREN,
CURTIS,	JONES, (Wash.)	PENROSE,	WATSON,
DILLINGHAM,	KELLOGG,	POINDEXTER,	WEEKS,
FALL,	KENYON,	SHERMAN,	WOLCOTT.
FERNALD,	KNOX,	SMITH, (Mich.)	

AGAINST THE RESOLUTION—6.

Democrats—3.

LANE,	STONE,	VARDAMAN.

Republicans—3.

GRONNA,	LA FOLLETTE,	NORRIS.

Eight Senators were absent, but all would have voted for the resolution. They were, Bankhead, Gore, Hollis, Newlands, Smith, (Maryland;) Thomas and Tillman, Democrats; Goff, Republican.

ARMY CALL READY FOR 500,000 MEN

War Department Has Universal Service Plan Worked Out and Waits on Congress.

BACKED BY GENERAL STAFF

Selective Conscription Scheme to be Submitted When War Resolution Passes.

Special to The New York Times.

WASHINGTON, April 4.—The plan of selective conscription, under which the first increment of 500,000 men is to be obtained under the universal military service plan of raising an army for the war with Germany, will be presented to Congress by the War Department as soon as that body adopts the war resolution.

In his address to Congress the President said that the entrance of the United States into the war would "involve the immediate addition to the armed forces of the United States already provided for by law in case of war at elast 500,000 men, who should, in my opinion, be chosen on the principle of universal liability to service, and also the authorization of subsequent additional increments of equal force as soon as they may be needed and can be handled in training."

The War Department has a well-worked-out plan, representing the views of the General Staff and Army War College, as to how this army may be raised and the machinery for registering and enrolling the various increments of 500,000 men.

But the plan has been carefully guarded, and Secretary Baker said today that the War Department's recommendations would not be made public until after they had been sent to Congress. While the department has a plan, Secretary Baker asserted today that the initiative with respect to the raising of an army rested with Congress, and that the Administration would carry out the will of that body as embraced in the legislation to be enacted.

In view of the President's recommendation in favor of universal liability to service, and the sentiment throughout the country in favor of universal military service, it is now assumed in Administration circles that the legislation soon to be enacted by Congress will be based on that principle.

In raising the first increment of 500,000 only young men of certain designated ages are to be called to the colors. These will include mainly unmarried men 18 to 19 years of age, but may include men up to 23. The age limits to be recommended by the War Department to Congress were not disclosed at the department today.

The unmarried males from 18 to 24 years of age in the United States at the beginning of the present year are estimated to have been as follows:

Between 18 and 19 years....	1,981,298
Between 20 and 24 years....	3,775,376
Total, 18 to 24 years....	5,756,674

These figures are based on the 1910 census plus a 10 per cent. increase suggested by the Census Bureau as approximately correct for the period 1910-1916. It is not to be assumed that all these unmarried men would be called to the colors or that they are all without dependents. In addition to exemptions in favor of married men, and others with dependents, there will also be exemptions in favor of men needed in war in-

Continued on Page 3.

HOUSE WILL PASS RESOLUTION TODAY

Continuous Session Will Be Held from 10 A. M. Until Declaration Is Adopted.

COMMITTEE FOR IT, 17 TO 2

Both Sides File Reports, the Majority Reviewing the Wrongs Suffered at Germany's Hands.

Special to The New York Times.

WASHINGTON, April 4.—The war resolution, in the form reported to the Senate by the Foreign Relations Committee, was reported today by the House Committee on Foreign Affairs, and will be the order of business in the lower body of Congress tomorrow. Chairman Flood obtained unanimous consent agreement that the House should meet at 10 A. M. and proceed immediately to consider the resolution. No time limit was fixed, but there was a tacit understanding that the resolution will be passed by night.

Announcement was made tonight by Representative Fred A. Britten, Republican of Illinois, a member of the Naval Affairs Committee, that he would offer this amendment tomorrow to the war resolution:

> Provided, however, that no part of the military forces of the United States shall be ordered to go land duty in any part of Europe, Asia, or Africa until so directed by act of Congress.

Unless such an amendment is included in the war resolution Mr. Britten will oppose its passage. Mr. Britten has not evinced pacifist tendencies before, but has been one of the radical preparedness advocates.

"The resolution, authorizing the President to employ the entire naval and military forces of the United States to carry on war against the Imperial German Government is nothing more nor less than a complete declaration of war," said Mr. Britten. "I do not believe the great masses of our people are in favor of such a resolution, and I am certain they are opposed to the use of our military in the bloody trench warfare which has already annihilated the flower of the youth of the most civilized countries on earth.

"It is not yet too late diplomatically to consider the differences between Germany and ourselves, and I am sure a sincere effort in this direction would prove more valuable and creditable to the country than a declaration of war."

Two members of the Foreign Affairs Committee, Representative Cooper of Wisconsin, ranking Republican, and Representative Shackelford, a Democrat, of Missouri, voted against a favorable report on the resolution. Seventeen votes were cast in its favor.

Representative Cooper contended in the committee that the English blockade was responsible for the present conditions, and the United States should not single out Germany for a declaration of war.

Both majority and minority reports were filed from the committee. The majority report, filed by Chairman Flood, arraigns the German Govern-

Continued on Page 3.

KEEN DEBATE FOR 13 HOURS

La Follette Scourged by Williams as Pro-German and Anti-American.

'TREASON' CRY AT NORRIS

Nebraska Senator Denounced for Hinting That Commercialism Prompted Nation's Course.

OPPONENTS 'WILLFUL MEN'

Three from Each Party—La Follette, in 4-Hour Speech, Assailed Great Britain.

President at Theatre Is Cheered by Audience

WASHINGTON, April 4.—President Wilson, attending a theatre tonight after working most of the day on war plans, was greeted with enthusiastic cheers. The orchestra played "The Star-Spangled Banner," and as the President was recognized the audience rose for a tumultuous demonstration.

Special to The New York Times.

WASHINGTON, April 4.—At 11 minutes past 11 o'clock tonight, the Senate, in the presence of a great throng on the floor and in the galleries, passed the resolution declaring a state of war between the United States and the German Government, and pledging all the resources of the United States for the successful prosecution of the war.

While the recorded vote was 82 to 6, the Senate's true alignment on the question of war is 90 to 6, as the absent Senators all favored the resolution. The House is expected to pass an identical resolution tomorrow by a still more overwhelming vote.

The six Senators opposing the declaration were equally divided between the two parties. They were La Follette of Wisconsin, Gronna of North Dakota, and Norris of Nebraska, Republicans; and Stone of Missouri, Lane of Oregon, and Vardaman of Mississippi, Democrats. All were members of the group of "willful men" whom President Wilson denounced.

Of the other six opponents of armed neutrality at the last session Senators Cummins, Kenyon, and Kirby voted for the resolution tonight. Senators O'Gorman, Clapp, and Works have retired to private life.

The vote came after thirteen hours of debate, that had lasted continuously since 10 o'clock in the morning.

Awed by the Occasion.

The passage of the resolution was marked by no outburst from the galleries. On the floor the Senators themselves were unusually grave and quiet. Many of them answered to their names in voices that quivered with emotion.

As the last name was called, and the Clerk announced the vote, there was hardly a murmur of applause. The great crowd was awed by the solemnity of the occasion and sobered by the speeches they had heard.

The resolution was adopted in the form approved by the Committee on Foreign Relations. Only one effort was made to change the committee's draft. That was in a substitute offered by Senator McCumber of North Dakota, in which the United States would simply proclaim certain principles of international law, with the warning that war would be made on any country violating them. Mr. McCumber cast the only vote for the substitute.

Throughout the long hours of discussion only five speeches were made against the resolution, and all efforts in opposition to it ceased with the conclusion of Mr. La Follette's four-hour attack on the President and defense of Germany's course. The remaining hours of the session were consumed by brief statements from Senators, one after the other, telling why they regarded war as necessary, how they had gradually come to change from advocates of peace to believers that war was essential to the safety and honor of the nation.

Last Stand of Germany's Apologists.

Today's debate, slow-moving as much of it was, postponing for weary hour after weary hour the declaration for which the country waited, was in itself the culmination of almost three years of intermittent discussion.

That long discussion had the same subject on the part of most Senators as today's debate, resentment of German outrages of every sort, murders on the high seas, affronts to Americans in Germany, and gross violation of American hospitality by the Imperial representatives in the United States. During these three years, as was again the case today, there was a bi-partisan minority defending the acts of Germany, extenuating her offenses, and doing everything to hold the United States back from vigorous assertion of her rights.

Both these aspects were summed up in the speeches today, and both aspects seemed to lead to the end of today's debate—a solemn declaration of war against the house of Hohenzollern. For the subject matter of discussion has been increased from month to month by new German outrages, while the defenders of Germany in the Senate have presented a constantly dwindling front. The vote tonight, which every recent event insured would be overwhelming, might be regarded as the point of intersection of these two converging lines of change.

The loss of American sympathy for Germany was never more evident than it was in today's proceedings in the Senate. Senator Stone of Missouri, Chair-

"All the News That's Fit to Print."

The New York Times.

THE WEATHER
Clearing today; tomorrow probably fair; southwest gales.
For full weather report see Page 21.

VOL. LXVI...NO. 21,622. NEW YORK, FRIDAY, APRIL 6, 1917.—TWENTY-TWO PAGES. ONE CENT In New York City. | TWO CENTS New England and Middle States. | THREE CENTS Elsewhere.

HOUSE, AT 3:12 A.M., VOTES FOR WAR, 373 TO 50; $3,000,000,000 ASKED FOR ARMY OF 1,000,000; NATION'S GIGANTIC RESOURCES MOBILIZED

HUGE BUDGET FOR WAR

$3,401,000,000 Needed for the Army and Navy at Once.

ESTIMATES GO TO CAPITOL

Taxation and a $3,500,000,000 Bond Issue Considered as a Means of Getting Funds.

MAY RAISE INCOME LEVIES

Fixed Price of 3½ for Bonds Considered—Daniels Explains the Navy's Plans.

Special to The New York Times.

WASHINGTON, April 5.—Three billion four hundred and one million dollars is needed immediately to place the United States on a proper war footing and to meet the first expenses of actual operations in the war with the German Government. This fact was disclosed when William G. McAdoo, as Secretary of the Treasury, today sent to the Capitol the first of the estimates from the various executive departments of the Government based on "military necessity." These estimates call for the appropriation of $3,401,865,684.87, of which the sum of $3,400,932,484.87 is for the army and navy alone, while the rest is for use by other departments as collateral war expenditures.

This total of $3,400,932,484 will enable the Government to raise, organize, equip and officer an army of 1,000,000 men during the next year, but will not pay for the employment of that force beyond June 30, 1918; it will enable the navy to raise its enlisted strength of 150,000 men and the Marine Corps to increase its enlisted personnel to 30,000 men, in addition to certain active operations in the war.

The total of $3,400,932,484 is also in addition to the sum of $517,273,802 already provided for the navy's use during the next fiscal year by the Naval act of March 4, 1917, and the sum of $246,000,000 carried by the Army Appropriation bill which passed the House yesterday under a suspension of the rules.

Hastening War Measures.

Great strides toward getting the fighting forces of the United States ready for the war were taken by the various branches of the Government today. These included:

First—Secretary of War Baker conferred at the Capitol with Chairman Chamberlain of the Senate Military Committee regarding the wishes of the President for authority to raise not less than 1,000,000 men, including the expansion of the regulars and guard forces during the coming year, and the raising of a force of approximately an additional 1,000,000 men next year.

Second—The Administration bill providing for the creation of this new army was sent to the Capitol with its provisions for raising two separate forces of 500,000 men each, to be composed of men between the ages of 18 and 25, to be obtained by a selective draft system.

Third — Chairman Fitzgerald and members of the House Appropriations Committee began consideration of the stupendous war budget within ten minutes after it had been received by the House of Representatives.

Fourth—Senator Simmons of North Carolina, Chairman of the Senate Finance Committee, conferred with House leaders regarding plans to meet the financial demands for preparedness by a bond issue of $3,500,000,000, bearing interest at not exceeding 3½ per cent.

Fifth—Members of the House Naval and Military Affairs Committees conferred on proposals that a lump sum of $3,500,000,000 be placed in the hands of the President to spend on the army and navy as he deems necessary, thereby abandoning the ordinary policy of making specific appropriations in separate bills and making the details public.

Although the needs of the army and navy were not given in detail, the estimates submitted today by Secretary McAdoo, acting for the other departments of the Government, show that they cover all phases of the needs of the Government from doubling the number of men in the navy and marine corps and to quadrupling the number of men in the present regular army and National Guard force to providing extra watchmen for the State, War, and Navy Building.

McAdoo's Detailed Estimates.

These are the important recommendations made by Secretary McAdoo in his estimates to prepare the United States for entry into the war with the German Government:

First—To make an army of 1,000,000 men ready for war both in personnel and material within a year—$2,932,537,933.

Second — To increase the enlisted strength of the navy from its present authorized emergency strength of 87,000 men to full war strength of 150,000 men, and to increase the Marine Corps from present authorized emergency strength of 17,500 men to full war strength of 30,000 men—$175,855,761.87.

Third. Extraordinary expenditures on materials for the naval establishment, including guns, ships, and

Continued on Page 2.

American Men in Belgium May Be Interned in Germany

LONDON, April 5. A dispatch to the Exchange Telegraph from The Hague says:

"A frontier correspondent asserts that he understands General von Bissing, the German Governor General in Belgium, intends to order the internment of all Americans between the ages of 17 and 45 living in Belgium.

"The correspondent adds that they will be sent to Western Germany, probably to Aix-la-Chapelle."

FIVE GERMAN SHIPS AT BOSTON SEIZED

Crews Dispossessed Early This Morning On Port Collector's Order.

600 GUARD. LINERS HERE

Malone's Neutrality Squad On Watch and He Waits Up All Night.

BOSTON, Friday, April 6. — Five German steamships, which have been in refuge at this port, were ordered seized, and their crews dispossessed, by Collector of the Port Edmund Billings early this morning. The vessels taken over are the Amerika and Cincinnati, passenger ships, and the Wittekind, Köln, and Oekenfels, freight steamers.

Malone Waits Up All Night.

Anticipating the passage by Congress of a declaration of war by this country against Germany, Dudley Field Malone, Collector of the Port of New York, prepared to remain in his office all night. He has upward of 600 special guards about the German ships now in this port, the bulk of them in Hoboken, where are the greatest of the German vessels, and on which are 1,200 men and 350 officers. At midnight Mr. Malone said, "I am waiting," and authorized the statement that the heavy guards had been sent out.

It was evident that the guards were vigilant to prevent possible destruction of the vessels.

German officers and sailors aboard the interned liners in Hoboken, including the great Vaterland, were calm and ready for whatever might be demanded of them. Some officers thought the ships would be seized, others that, as German property, they would be held inviolate by this Government. Over the fact that the machinery of all of the ships has been damaged so that none now are navigable, there was unconcealed satisfaction.

Government tugs aided yesterday in moving the Maia and the German sailing vessel Indra, which have been at anchor near Staten Island since the beginning of the war, across the bay to an anchorage near the City Dock at Brooklyn. The Portonia, which was moved from an anchorage in the bay to Brady's Dock, Staten Island, on Wednesday, was also moved yesterday across the bay to an anchorage near the Brooklyn shore. The idea of the movement was to concentrate separated ships in the event of action by the Government.

The Teuton ships at this port are:

German.

Name and Dock.	Tonnage.
President Grant, Hoboken	18,072
President Lincoln, Hoboken	18,168
Vaterland, Hoboken	54,282
Nassovia, Hoboken	3,902
Armenia, Hoboken	5,541
Bohemia, Hoboken	8,414
Pisa, Hoboken	4,967
Pennsylvania, Hoboken	13,333
Harburg, Hoboken	4,472
Magdeburg, Hoboken	4,497
Adamsturm, Hoboken	5,000
Matador, (sailing,) Hoboken	1,168
George Washington, Hoboken	25,570
Kaiser Wilhelm II., Hoboken	19,360
Friedrich der Grosse, Hoboken	10,771
Prinzess Irene, Hoboken	10,893
Grosser Kurfurst, Hoboken	13,102
Barbarossa, Hoboken	10,984
Hamburg, 135th Street	10,531
Koenig Wilhelm II., 135th Street	9,410
Allemania, 135th Street	4,680
Prinz Eitel Friedrich, 135th Street	4,650
Prinz Joachim, 135th Street	4,760
Portonia, Stapleton	2,778
Maia, Stapleton	2,555
Clara Mennig, Stapleton	1,685
Indra, (sailing,) Stapleton	1,770

Austrian.

Name and Dock.	Tonnage.
Dora, Brooklyn	7,037
Ida, Brooklyn	4,730
Martha Washington, Stapleton	8,312
Himalaia, Newark Bay	4,948

Malone Confers at Washington.

WASHINGTON, April 5. — Collector Dudley Field Malone, who has general supervision over the war-bound German merchant ships in New York harbor, conferred with Secretary McAdoo today, and it was understood that the question of taking possession of the vessels was under consideration. Secretary Wilson, who would have jurisdiction over the crews of the ships under the immigration law, conferred with Secretary McAdoo last night.

A final decision as to whether the ships shall be taken over had not been reached today, and depends upon the final interpretation by the Government upon the Prussian-American Treaty of 1828, which, the American Government contends, has already been violated in several respects by Germany. The formal abrogation of the treaty has been considered.

In case the ships are taken, it is believed that they will first be turned over to the Shipping Board for repairs to their machinery, which was damaged when diplomatic relations were broken off.

DETAILS OF THE ARMY BILL

Universal Service Embodied in Measure Presented to Congress.

SELECTIVE DRAFT AT ONCE

Regulars and Militia to be Put On a War Footing and 500,000 Others Called.

MEN 19 TO 25 MUST ENROLL

President Authorized to Enlist 500,000 More When Needed —Want Military Graduates.

Special to The New York Times.

WASHINGTON, April 5.—A bill embracing the War Department's recommendations for temporarily increasing the military establishment of the United States for use in the existing emergency was submitted to Senator Chamberlain, Chairman of the Senate Committee on Military Affairs, and to Chairman Dent of the House Military Committee today by Secretary Baker.

The bill provides for the raising of the regular army to full war strength, the drafting of the National Guard into the Federal service and raising it to war strength, and the enlistment of 1,000,000 additional men by selective drafting. Under the terms of the bill it is estimated that authority is granted to the President to raise and maintain an army of 1,727,846 men, including regulars, National Guardsmen, and those to be drafted under the principle of universal military service. This force would be made up about as follows:

Regular army, including five increments of increase, provided for by the National Defense act of June 3, 1916, when raised to full war strength—287,846 men.

National Guard, when raised to full war strength—440,000 men.

Additional force of men to be chosen by selective drafting—500,000.

Second additional force of men to be chosen by selective drafting—500,000.

Total—1,726,846.

Million Men This Year.

It is not the present intention of the Administration to raise and equip a force of more than 1,000,000 during the next twelve months. This is about all that could be brought together and properly trained with our present military facilities during the first year. If the bill is adopted the Government would begin raising the regular army to full war strength, would draft the National Guard ino Federal service and begin raising its units to maximum war strength, and then raise the balance by selective drafting.

The enlisted men to bring the regular army and the National Guard up to war strength are to be raised by voluntary enlistment, but if the President decides that they cannot beso raised he may resor to selective draft. All other forces provided for by the bill which the War Department sent to the Capitol today are to be "raised and maintained by selective draft exclusively."

The bill submitted today is intended to serve only the needs of the Government during the present emergency and is not a permanent plan for the increase of the army. In voicing his indorsement of the principle of universal military service the President has adopted that method of obtaining soldiers only for the purposes of the present war. What is to happen after the war is over is considered another matter from the immediate and practical needs of the Government at the present time.

The selective draft, under the terms of the bill, will take in men between the ages of 19 and 25, which means that all males between these ages will have to present themselves for registration under penalty of imprisonment for failure to do so. The drafting is to be determined in proportion to the population of the various States, or at the ratio of about 1,100 for each Congressional district. Credit is to be given to each State and Congressional district for its quota of men furnished to the regular army or National Guard forces.

The act is not to be construed to compel the service of those whose creeds forbid participation in war.

The President is also authorized by the bill to exclude or discharge from the draft the following: Custom House clerks, persons in the United States mail service, workmen in Government armories, arsenals, and navy yards; mariners actually employed in American sea service, pilots, persons engaged in munition and military industries, those with dependents, and those physically or morally unfit.

To Train an Army of Officers.

In drafting its program the General Staff recognized the fact that the United States must start at the beginning and train first an army of 100,000 officers and noncommissioned officers to undertake the training of the thousands of youths who will enter

Continued on Page 3.

German Warships Seize Ship That Helped Save U-Boat

COPENHAGEN, April 5, (via London.)—The Tidens Tegen's Trondhjem correspondent sends a story of the capture by the Germans and taking into port of the Norwegian steamer Nanna, after the Nanna had endeavored to tow a helpless submarine in the North Sea to a German port. The steamer was taken to Hamburg by German torpedo boats and is being held there.

According to the story, the Nanna agreed to tow the helpless submarine, but the towline broke off the west coast of Jutland. The submarine thereupon signaled for assistance and eight German torpedo boats appeared. The crew of the Nanna was ordered below and the torpedo boats took the steamer, together with the submarine, to Cuxhaven.

The Germans, so the story goes, refused the request of the Norwegians to be piloted back through the minefield. Instead the Nanna was taken to Hamburg, where she is still detained, despite persistent efforts by the Norwegian authorities to obtain her release.

AMERICAN SHIP SUNK; CREW SAVED

Unarmed Missourian, Returning in Ballast, Is Destroyed in the Mediterranean.

REPORT 5 OTHER SHIPS LOST

Two of Them Belgian Relief Vessels with Valuable Cargoes —Americans on Board Others.

WASHINGTON, April 5.—The sinking without warning of the unarmed American steamer Missourian, which left Genoa April 4, with thirty-two Americans among her crew of fifty-three, was reported to the State Department today by Consul Wilbur at Genoa. The crew was saved. The Consul's dispatch, which was undated, follows:

"Unarmed American steamer Missourian, 4,981 net tonnage, Master William Lyons, built at Sparrows Point, owner American Hawaiian Steamship Company, fifty three crew all told, including master and officers, thirty-two American citizens, balance various nationalities, according to records this office sailing from Genoa, April 4, in ballast, bound for the United States, sunk without warning, according telegram just received from master, as follows: 'Dated Porto Mauridio, 5th. Sunk without warning, crew saved, leave for Genoa, 7 o'clock P. M., April 5. (Signed) Lyons.' As soon as master and crew arrive will prepare and transmit full report."

The American steamship Missourian, owned by the American-Hawaiian Steamship Company and chartered by the France and Canada Steamship Company, left this port on March 8 for Genoa. The ship was unarmed and carried a general cargo. The Missourian was a vessel of 7,914 tons gross, and was built at Sparrows Point, Md., in 1904. She was first named the Missouri. For many years she was engaged in the New York-Panama trade, and was transferred to the Atlantic trade after the beginning of the European war. She was for a time in the service of the United States Government, having been taken over as a transport shortly after General Funston was sent to Vera Cruz in 1914.

AMERICANS ON 2 SHIPS SUNK.

Saved from British and Norwegian Freighters Destroyed by U-Boats.

WASHINGTON, April 5.—Destruction of two more vessels, one British and one Norwegian, with Americans on board, was reported to the State Department today by Consul Lathrop at Cardiff. The Norwegian steamer Sandvikgoole was sunk by a submarine believed to have been German, while the British steamer Lincolnshire was sunk without any submarine being seen. Crews of both vessels were in small boats for two hours, in dangerous positions, before being rescued. Consul Lathrop's reports follow.

"Frank Kragle, American fireman on the Norwegian unarmed steamer Sandvikgoole, England to Gothenburg, cargo iron and iron ore, reports vessel sunk by submarine, believed German, about noon, March 27, five miles off Aberdeen. Warned, sank fifteen minutes after crew left. Weather clear and cold, sea rough, wind high; no vessel in sight; no passengers, crew rescued after two hours by British mine sweeper; landed Aberdeen; no casualties.

"Felix Morris, colored American Seaman on British unarmed steamer Lincolnshire, New York to France, reports vessel torpedoed without warning afternoon March 29, fourteen miles off Irish coast. Vessel sank six minutes after crew left. Weather clear, very cold; sea moderate; wind fresh; no vessel in sight; no passengers, submarine unseen;

Continued on Page 2.

32,000 PLANTS OFFERED

No Nation Ever Had Such Enormous Resources for Waging War.

TWO YEARS OF PREPARATION

Summary of What Has Been Achieved in Naval, Military, and Industrial Fields.

OUR NAVY READY FOR ACTION

Army Waits on Congress—Extraordinary Work by the Council of Defense.

WASHINGTON, April 5.—Actual and potential resources which, all told, probably never have been equaled by those of any other nation in the history of the world, are brought into the great war under the American flag.

Into the balance against Germany are thrown a navy in strength and efficiency among the foremost afloat, an army comparatively small but highly efficient, backed by a citizenry of upward of 20,000,000 capable of military duty, industrial resources incomparably the greatest in the world, already mobilized for public service, and the moral force of more than 100,000,000 Americans awakened to their country's peril and united behind their President with a patriotic fervor reincarnating the spirit of '76.

Although much remains to be done, officials believe the nation's destinies are secure now, no matter how stubborn or prolonged the pressure of German militarism or how wide the scope of German intrigue. The slowly maturing preparedness sentiment has borne fruit in military, naval, and industrial measures which already have put the United States on a defense basis not even hoped for two years ago. What more it will do, the President believes, can be measured only by what the Administration finds will be necessary.

The navy, always the first line of defense, has cleared its decks of antiquated incumbrances, has added new units modernized to meet the German tactics, and through the patriotic co-operation of ship and material makers is hurrying to completion other mighty fighting craft that will be the last word in power and efficiency. Authorized but ten days ago to recruit to the full war strength of 87,000 men, the navy already has almost attained the total. To provide additional officers a class of midshipmen has been graduated three months ahead of its time. A newly organized coast patrol of submarine chasers is on duty, and hundreds of small craft to augment it are under construction.

Army Waits on Congress.

Army preparations are less complete because of the uncertainty over what Congress will authorize for that branch of the service. The regulars, numbering nearly 120,000 and trained and equipped in a way which their officers believe matches, unit for unit, the boasted efficiency of Germany's best, are ready to respond overnight to whatever call may come. The National Guard, 150,000 strong and hardened by months of service at the border, already has many units in active service for police duty throughout the country and can be fully mobilized on short notice. Without additional authorization by Congress the regulars and guardsmen could be recruited to a combined strength of 700,000, and detailed plans for whatever larger army may be authorized have been prepared, and great quantities of equipment for it purchased.

Industrial preparations, thanks to lessons of the war and the patriotic attitude of industry, have produced a great, compact scheme of national resources with almost unlimited possibilities. The Council of National Defense, in daily conferences with the nation's leading financial, commercial, scientific, and labor chiefs, not only has worked out a definite and detailed industrial mobilization plan, but has secured the indorsement and pledges of the men who can put it into effect at a moment's notice, bringing to the aid of the military arms of the service the full resources of the richest nation, organized with characteristic Yankee skill and business thoroughness.

For military reasons only a small part of the details of these preparations has been permitted to reach the public. It is known, however, that for many months the Government has considered war more than a possibility, and has strained every resource to make ready. In the tense waiting period since relations were broken, the President, while hoping fervently that hostilities could be avoided, has kept the whole machinery of the Government in motion day and night to prepare against eventualities. To any close observer at the capital it now is apparent that Germany again has misjudged if she thought to find the United States hopelessly impotent and unprepared.

Shipyards in Nation's Service.

The Navy Department, in order to complete in record time the enormous

Continued on Page 4.

List of Fifty Members of House of Representatives Who Voted Against the Adoption of War Resolution

WASHINGTON, Friday, April 6.—The fifty Representatives who voted against the war resolution were:

ALMON, BACON, BRITTEN, BROWNE, BURNETT, CARY, CHURCH, CONNOLLY, (Kan.) COOPER, (Wis.) DAVIDSON, DAVIS, DECKER, DILL, DILLON, DOMINICK, ESCH, FREAR, FULLER, (Ill.) HAUGEN, HAYES, HENSLEY, HILLIARD, HULL, (Iowa,) MISS RANKIN, REAVIS, ROBERTS, RODENBURG, SHACKLEFORD, SHERWOOD, SLOAN, STAFFORD, VAN DYKE, VOIGT, WHEELER, WOODS, (Iowa,) IGOE, JOHNSON, (S. D.) KEATING, KING, KINKAID, KITCHIN, KNUTSON, LA FOLLETTE, LITTLE, LONDON, LUNDSEN, McLEMORE, MASON, NELSON, RANDALL.

GERMANY GARBLES WILSON'S ADDRESS

Nothing About Mexican Intrigue or Spies Allowed to Reach the Public.

PRESS FURIOUS AT WILSON

His Distinction Between German Government and People Called False.

COPENHAGEN, April 5, (via London.)—The German public up to the present time has had no opportunity to hear the full story of the reasons leading up to the entry of the United States into the war, as only condensed and expurgated versions of President Wilson's message appeared in German newspapers yesterday under headings indicating that this was practically the complete text. This in part is apparently due to the fact that the first version of the speech telegraphed from England to neutral countries on the Continent on Tuesday were sharply condensed, whole sections having been eliminated, particularly from the latter part of the message.

President Wilson's reference to the attempt to embroil Mexico against the United States is deemed improper reading for Germans, nor are they allowed to hear President Wilson's reasons for the conviction that the autocratic German Government has not only no friendship for America, but is ready at any opportunity to plot against its security.

The reference to dynastic wars, too, is twisted into a shape which has aroused indignant comment from every German newspaper.

The full text of the message was received in Copenhagen only today. It reads almost like another document as compared with the earlier version. The first part of the two versions is substantially the same, except for condensations and omission of non-essential matter. The second part has been cut wholesale. The President's reasoning on the inadvisability of armed neutrality is given completely; no reference is made to the proposed financing of the Allies, and the paragraphs relating to Russia are dismissed in two sentences. Only the briefest summary is made in the German papers of the concluding paragraphs of the message.

But a comparison of this tabloid version as received in Denmark with that published in Berlin shows that the German censors' pencils had been vigorously employed to strike out references to the conduct of German agents, which constitutes one of the main items of President Wilson's indictment of the autocratic German Government.

Says Democracy Has Failed.

Special Cable to THE NEW YORK TIMES.

BERLIN, April 5, (via London.)—Regarding President Wilson's declaration that American hostility was not directed against the German people, but against the German Government, the Lokal-Anzeiger says it is the acme of hypocrisy to say that an autocratic Government provoked the war against the will of the German people.

"It is impossible," says the Lokal-Anzeiger, "that the ruler of a nation who has at his disposal the reports of his Ambassador and numerous other sources of information regarding the events of the early part of August, 1914, in Berlin, should really believe that this war was not begun with the assent of the German people. If he ever read the report of the Reichstag session of Aug. 4 he must know that his contention is untrue. If he upholds it, despite his better knowledge, he only does it to prove by an untruth his untenable theory of the only true and gratifying democracy, and his whole cardboard house of artificial evidence miserably collapses by which he seeks to prove to Congress the justification and honesty of his policy and the noble spirit of his attitude.

"The history of the war has proved the actual contrary to Wilson's contention. Those nations whose fate is determined by parliamentary representation have become tools without a will in the hands of small groups of vainglorious men and have been degraded to mere pawns on the chessboard of political intrigue. It is also true that the foreign policy of parliamentary government States remains the secret of a few men, just as it does in monarchical States. We cannot presume that this well-known fact, the truth of which is acknowledged by the radical press of all countries, should have remained

Continued on Page 3.

FRANCE AROUSED BY OUR DECISION

Members of Both Chambers Cheer for America — Many Cities Adopt Resolutions.

POINCARE CABLES WILSON

Deputies Suggest Offering Us the Port of Brest as a Naval Base.

PARIS, April 5.—This was America's day in France. Extraordinary scenes of enthusiasm over the United States's entry into the war were witnessed in both houses of Parliament, while municipal councils met in cities throughout the Republic and adopted resolutions acclaiming the United States.

In Paris the American flag was seen everywhere. The appearance of the Stars and Stripes in different parts of the city multiplied rapidly as the day advanced, and soon the available supply was exhausted. Such was the demand for newspapers that the evening editions giving the vote of the United States Senate on the war resolution were quickly exhausted. The crowded subway cars were more animated than at any time since the war began, while knots of soldiers and civilians in front of all cafes and at all street corners discussed the great event with manifest satisfaction.

The sentiment in Paris and throughout the country is epitomized by President Poincaré in the following cablegram he sent today to President Wilson:

At the moment when, under the generous inspiration of yourself, the great American Republic, faithful to its ideals and its traditions, is coming forward to defend with the force of arms the cause of justice and of liberty, the people of France are filled with the deepest feelings of brotherly appreciation.

Permit me again to convey to you, Mr. President, in this solemn and grave hour, an assurance of the same sentiments of which I recently gave you evidence, sentiments which, under the present circumstances, have grown in depth and warmth.

I am confident that I voice the thought of all France in expressing to you and to the American nation the joy and the pride which we feel today as our hearts once again beat in unison with yours.

This war would not have reached its final import had not the United States been led by the enemy himself to take part in it. To every impartial spirit it will be apparent, in the future more than ever in the past, that German imperialism, which desired, prepared, and declared this war, had conceived the mad dream of establishing its hegemony throughout the world. It has succeeded only in bringing about a revolt of the conscience of humanity.

In never-to-be-forgotten language you have made yourself, before the universe, the eloquent interpreter of outraged laws and a menaced civilization.

Honor to you, Mr. President, and to your noble country. I beg you to believe in my devoted friendship.

RAYMOND POINCARE.

Brest to Be American Port.

The first war measure to be taken in connection with the expected entrance of the United States into the war, which was introduced in the Chamber today, provides for an agreement with the United States, if necessary, for the use of the Port of Brest by American naval forces. The measure provides generally for the utilization of the port to the best interests of the national defense.

Not since the historic session of Aug. 4, 1914, has there been a parallel to the scenes in Parliament. Alexandre Ribot, the venerable Premier, arose immediately after the Chamber came to order and began an address in solemn and impressive tones to the silent assemblage which filled every part of the House. The Deputies listened with unbroken attention until the first mention of the United States. Then they broke out in applause. At first it was a decorous clapping of hands, and then the whole House spontaneously arose, cheering for the United States and President Wilson.

The American Ambassador, William G. Sharp, was in the diplomatic gallery. The Deputies turned toward him and the demonstration continued. The Am-

Continued on Page 6.

DEBATE LASTED 16½ HOURS

One Hundred Speeches Were Made—Miss Rankin, Sobbing, Votes No.

ALL AMENDMENTS BEATEN

Resolution Will Take Effect This Afternoon with the President's Signature.

KITCHIN WITH PACIFISTS

Accession of the Floor Leader Added Others to the Anti-War Faction.

Special to The New York Times.

WASHINGTON, Friday, April 6.—At 3:12 o'clock this morning the House of Representatives by the overwhelming vote of 373 to 50 adopted the resolution that meant war between the Government and the people of the United States and the Imperial German Government.

War will formally begin this afternoon when President Wilson will approve the resolution which was passed by the Senate Wednesday night and was approved by the House this morning without the crossing of a "t" or the dotting of an "i."

The House presented an impressive spectacle as the roll call proceeded on the adoption of the war resolution. Nearly every member was in his seat.

The galleries were crowded for the most part by men and women who had sat there all the evening, some of them since 10 o'clock yesterday morning when the House met. Some of the men and women were in evening dress. Men and women who were in the diplomatic box had come directly from dinner parties.

There were crowds also in the corridors outside the galleries, seeking a chance for a peep at the events inside.

Usually when the roll of the House is called there is much confusion, and it is often difficult to hear the responses of the Representatives as their names are droned by the reading clerk.

But there was a marked difference this morning. The House, which had been full of levity at times during the long debate, felt the solemnity of the moment. No sound disturbed the proceedings. Every member's answer came distinctly and was heard by the throng that listened almost breathlessly to the "Ayes" and "Noes" that followed the calling of the roll.

Miss Rankin Votes "No."

Miss Jeanette Rankin, the woman Representative from Montana, had been absent from the House most of the evening, but took her accustomed place while the roll call was in progress. When her name was called she sat silent. "Miss Rankin," repeated the clerk. Still no answer. The clerk went on with his droning, and floor and galleries buzzed.

On the second roll call Miss Rankin's name was again called. She sat silent as before. The eyes of the galleries were turned on her. For a moment there was breathless silence. Then Miss Rankin rose. In a voice that broke a bit but could be heard all over the still chamber she said:

"I want to stand by my country, but I cannot vote for war. I vote no." The "No" was scarcely audible.

And the maiden speech of the first woman Congressman ended in a sob. She was deeply moved and big tears were in her eyes.

It was a sympathetic House, however, and although most of the persons there were plainly in favor of the war resolution, a wave of applause swept through floor and gallery.

When the roll call had been completed and a slip containing the count handed to Speaker Clark the latter's gavel came down with a bang. The House became quiet instantly.

"On this motion," said the Speaker "the Ayes are 373 and the Noes are 50."

The cheers that followed drowned the Speaker's announcement that the resolution had been adopted. Then the floors and galleries cleared, Representatives and spectators knowing that war had again come to the United States.

The Senate adjourned Wednesday night, to meet again at noon today. As the resolution must be returned to the Senate, while that body is in session President Wilson will not receive the historical document for signature until this afternoon. From the moment of his approval war will be on.

The Early Morning Scenes.

At 1:20 o'clock this morning, when Representative Kelly of Pennsylvania began to express his views, the tally list showed that he was the eightieth member to address the House on the war resolution.

At that hour the galleries were crowded, women forming a majority of the spectators. All through the evening

"All the News That's Fit to Print."

The New York Times.

THE WEATHER
Fair today and tomorrow, rising temperature; wind northwest.
For full weather report see Page 21.

VOL. LXVI...NO. 21,626. NEW YORK, TUESDAY, APRIL 10, 1917.—TWENTY-TWO PAGES. ONE CENT In New York City. | TWO CENTS New England and Middle States. | THREE CENTS Elsewhere.

BRITISH BEGIN THE GREAT DRIVE, TAKE 6,000 PRISONERS; PLANS TO DISCUSS WITH ALLIES OUR SHARE IN THE CONFLICT; CONSCRIPTION FEATURE OF ARMY BILL MEETS OPPOSITION

WAR BY AUSTRIA MAY FOLLOW OUR SEIZURE OF SHIPS

American Embassy Staff and Consuls Recalled—Safe Conduct for Austrians Here.

SPAIN WILL ACT FOR US

Break with Turkey and Bulgaria Expected—Lansing Reviews Parleys with Vienna.

SHIPS TAKEN TOTAL 14

Most of Them Damaged, but the Big Martha Washington is Intact—Crews Interned.

Special to The New York Times.

WASHINGTON, D. C., April 9.—The Government of Austria-Hungary has severed diplomatic relations with the Government of the United States.

Baron Erich Zwiedinek, who has been Chargé d'Affaires of the Austrian Embassy ever since the recall of Dr. Dumba, former Ambassador, called at the State Department today and demanded passports for himself, all his embassy staff, including Ambassador-designate Tarnowski, and all Austrian Consular officers in the United States and its possessions. He delivered to the State Department a brief note which was not made public, but which made it plain that Austria-Hungary was breaking relations with the United States because the latter Government had declared the existence of a state of war with the German Government, to which the Vienna Government is joined by a war alliance.

Almost simultaneously with the action of Baron Zwiedinek in demanding his passports word reached the State Department in a dispatch from Minister Stovall at Berne that the dual monarchy had broken diplomatic relations with the United States yesterday.

The diplomatic break does not necessarily and of itself involve the two nations in hostilities, but it is everywhere accepted in diplomatic and political Washington that it is a prelude toward a declaration by Austria of the existence of a state of war, especially as all Austrian vessels in American ports have been seized. The policy of the Washington Government will be to await the expected declaration or some overt act by the Vienna Government or its agents.

It is true that the United States Government has declined to receive Count Tarnowski, but this objection was based on the fact that the Austrian note of Jan. 31, 1917, declared almost the same submarine danger zone that was declared by Germany. This note was received on the same day that Count Tarnowski arrived in Washington. It was explained to him that this Government could not possibly receive an Ambassador from Austria and at the same time dismiss the German Ambassador unless the Austro-Hungarian Government could recede from the position taken in its submarine note.

Seizure of Austrian Ships.

As soon as the announcement of the break was received by the Administration orders were given for taking possession of the Austrian merchant vessels that have been self-interned in this country. Secretary Lansing said tonight that this was done as a precautionary measure. Secretary McAdoo made formal announcement of the action taken by the Government, as follows:

"For the purpose of protecting the vessels from further injury and until a decision can be reached as to their proper disposition, customs guards have been placed on board all Austrian merchant vessels anchored in the ports of the United States. The officers and crews have been taken into custody by the Department of Labor pending a determination of their status."

The status of these vessels will depend on whether a state of war comes into existence.

At the request of the United States Government, the Spanish Government has taken over American interests in Vienna, while the Swiss Government has taken over the interests of Italy, France, and Rumania, and Spain has taken over those of England and Japan, which since the entry of those nations into the war had been handled by the United States Government. W. A. F. Ekengren, the Swedish Minister to the United States, has at the request of the Vienna Government taken over its interests in this country.

The break of relations interferes with the good work the United States was doing in prison camps in Austria, as well for Austrians in the prison camps of the Entente armies. It relieves the United States of the responsibility for looking after the treatment of nearly 2,000,000 war prisoners, of whom about 1,380,000 were in Russia and the rest in France. The United States was also looking after the treatment of Italians and Rumanians who were prisoners of war in Austrian camps.

The United States Government has asked for safe conduct from the Entente Allies for Count Tarnowsky, Baron Zwiedinek, and the various Austrian diplomatic and Consular officers when

Continued on Page 3.

British Destroying U-Boats at Rate of One a Day

The British have been destroying U-boats at the average rate of one a day since Feb. 1, and latterly at an even higher rate, according to information brought to New York yesterday by persons returning from Europe, who said they had the authority of naval officers and officials high in the Admiralty for the figures. In the month following the declaration of unrestricted submarine warfare British ships sank thirty-two submarines. Since then, it is said, the average number destroyed a week has been between seven and fifteen, with the number running as high as twenty-three in the week.

British naval officers assert their methods in fighting the submarine are being improved constantly. The small motor boat, known as the "submarine chaser," following in the wake of destroyers dragging cables or chains between them, has sunk most of the U-boats with a new explosive bomb, effective within a circumference of 200 yards. Airplanes are used also, while the practice of equipping merchant ships with guns forward, as well as aft, has caused the destruction of several U-boats.

British officer say the Germans profess to be turning out a submarine a day, but they do not see how submarines, manned by competent crews, can be sent to sea at this rate.

BOND ISSUE BILL WILL BE RUSHED

Measure Authorizing $5,000,000,000 Expected to Reach House on Thursday.

TIME IS RIPE, MORGAN SAYS

Banker Predicts Success of the Issue to Secreary McAdoo—House to Prevent War Waste.

Special to The New York Times.

WASHINGTON, April 9.—War legislation began to assume definite form in the House today with the announcement that the bill authorizing a bond issue of $5,000,000,000 would be presented on Thursday, and the development that the Appropriations Committee, assuming by general consent certain of the supply powers of other committees, is to become the "War Budget Committee" of the lower body.

Simultaneously it developed in the House debate that, while the leaders of that body are willing to give the Administration every dollar needed for war purposes, detailed estimates must be submitted by the executive branch of the Government, "and there is to be no destruction of our fiscal system because we are at war."

That the Appropriations Committee and the House intend to keep a tight hold on the nation's purse strings was disclosed when the General Deficiency Appropriation bill, carrying a Senate amendment putting $100,000,000 at the disposal of the President for national defense, was sent to conference. Leaders on both sides of the aisle said that lump sum appropriations would not be appropriated "blindly," and the legislative branch of the Government would insist upon estimates more in detail than those submitted recently by Secretary McAdoo when he requested war appropriations of more than $3,400,000,000.

Representatives Sherley of Kentucky and Garner of Texas assured the House that detailed estimates would be forthcoming.

"I hope we will not be obliged to abolish real democracy at home in protecting democracy throughout the world," said Mr. Mann, the Republican floor leader, in offering a temporary objection to sending the General Deficiency bill to conference. Mr. Mann said the House should ascertain for what purpose the $100,000,000 lump sum appropriation inserted by the Senate without investigation was to be used.

"I do not believe the time has come," said Chairman Fitzgerald of the Appropriations Committee, "when we should be governed by the most absolute autocracy the world has ever known. I am in favor of giving the Administration every dollar it needs, but I will not act blindly, and I am not willing to destroy the fiscal system of this Government. I want to give every dollar necessary, but I am not in favor of appropriating money to be expended indefinitely."

Mr. Garner said he had discussed appropriations with executive officers, and had been assured that explanatory estimates would be submitted for every dollar requested. Mr. Sherley, a Democratic member of the Appropriations Committee, said that he was not in favor of Congress relinquishing any of

Continued on Page 2.

CONGRESS AGAIN SHOWS A LEANING TO VOLUNTEERS

Anxious to Give Wilson the Forces He Asks, but Many Are Against Any Draft.

HOUSE COMMITTEE HOSTILE

Chairman Dent, Summoned to Conference by the President, Departs Unconvinced.

COMPROMISE TALKED OF

Some Favor Limited Test of a Volunteer Call—Senator Nelson Speaks Against Conscription.

Special to The New York Times.

WASHINGTON, April 9.—The Administration learned today that strong opposition existed in the House of Representatives to the conscription feature of the Army bill. President Wilson called to the White House Representative Dent, Chairman of the Committee on Military Affairs, and an hour's conference developed a sharp difference in views.

The President made it clear to Chairman Dent that he believed the safety of the nation rested on the action of Congress in this regard. He will make a similar exposition of the military situation tomorrow to Representative Anthony of Kansas, who has led the opposition to the draft plan among Republican members of the committee.

Secretary Baker found today among the members of the Military Committee decided opposition to the proposed Army bill. Not only is Chairman Dent opposed to the selective draft, as provided in the bill, but most of the committee are said to be against it.

That only about half a dozen of the twenty-one members of the committee were in favor of conscription was asserted today. Representatives Kahn, Crago, and Tilson, Republicans, and Olney and Caldwell, Democrats, are regarded as steadfast advocates of the conscription plan. All other members may not be against the bill, but apparently they will support conscription only as a last resort.

Chairman Dent is said to have told President Wilson that anti-conscription sentiment in the committee was strong, and that even if a Conscription bill was brought into the House there was doubt of its approval. He said that he and many other members of the House believed the volunteer system would suffice to raise an army. President Wilson did not share in this optimism.

Mr. Dent intimated that some form of compromise legislation might come out of the committee. He suggested that the legislation reported be for a temporary period, that is for the duration of the war, if anything approaching conscription was to be in the bill. He said today that he did not expect to report any measure for a week.

Mr. Dent added:

"There is no question on the part of any one as to giving the President all the men and money needed to carry on the war. The only controversy is as to the means of doing so."

There is some talk that because of Chairman Dent's attitude some other member of the House Committee may present the Administration bill if it is reported, as officials hope it will be, substantially in the form in which it was drawn.

Secretary Baker told the committee again today that the volunteer system would not meet the present emergency. He made little headway toward obtaining the acceptance of his views, it is said.

Secretary Baker is said to have urged the committee to report the bill as drawn because, for one thing, it would show Germany the earnestness of this country in entering the war. The psychological effect of a conscription measure, the Secretary feels, would be very great.

The Secretary has endeavored to impress the committee with the Government's desire not to raise a heterogeneous army. It is seeking by selective draft to raise an army of active equally-aged men, who can take an aggressive part in warfare after training. The volunteer system, under which there would be a less systematic mobilization, is regarded as unfit for the present emergency.

Promotion for Guard Officers.

Mr. Baker approved a suggestion that instead of authorizing two increments of selective draft forces, 500,000 to an increment, the bill should authorize the President to call as many such increments from time to time as he deemed necessary to prosecute the war.

Mr. Baker said the only provision of the bill, which would militate against the continuance of National Guard units

Continued on Page 2.

Brazil's Break May Come Today; Won't Hear Envoy

RIO DE JANERIO, April 9.—An early rupture of relations between Brazil and Germany is expected, by tomorrow morning at the latest.

The break depends solely on the formality of the reception of the official report from the Legation in Paris on the sinking of the Brazilian steamer Parana by a German submarine, for which an urgent request was sent today by Dr. Lauro Muller, the Foreign Minister.

The break probably will be followed by the seizure of German ships in Brazil. (Forty-six German ships are known to be in Brazilian ports.)

Dr. Muller today refused to receive the German Minister. He then gave urgent orders that a steamer in Rio Janeiro be made ready at once for a mission abroad. Later he conferred with the War Minister and the Chief of Staff.

It is reported in political circles that President Braz intends to issue an urgent call for a special session of Congress.

A Epoca reports that the Brazilian fleet has concentrated in the neighborhood of the island of Fernando de Noronha, 125 miles east of Cape San Roque.

A Noite says that the Minister of Marine has received a report from the commander of the destroyer Alajoas at Desterro that he had intercepted several mysterious wireless messages sent from an unknown station. The commander also reported that he had noticed light signals flashing in the neighborhood of the Desterro forts, contrary to the military regulations governing the forts.

NEW BERLIN MOVE TO WIN RUSSIANS

Socialist Leaders, with Government Sanction, Start on Mission for Separate Peace.

EASTERN OFFENSIVE HALTED

Copenhagen Hears It Has Been Suspended While Parleys with 'Comrades' Are Proceeding.

COPENHAGEN, April 9, (via London.)—In the midst of the interest in America's own preparations for participation in the war and impending German and allied offensives in the west, it would be wise not to lose sight of the fact that the Germans, particularly the Socialists, are working industriously toward peace with Russia and have not lost hope of success, despite the discouraging pronunciamentos of a war to a victorious end coming from Petrograd.

It is announced in Berlin that the Socialist leader, Philipp Scheidemann, head of the majority Socialists in the Reichstag and a politician close to the Chancellor, has left Germany on "a mission." The nature of this mission is not specified, but there is reason to assume that, as a well-known Russo-German Socialist, known by the pen name of "Parvus," also came abroad just after the conference of the majority Socialists which was called to consider the possibilities of the Russian situation, Herr Scheidemann's mission involves an attempt to open communications with the Russian Socialists and Social Revolutionists of the extreme school, who favor an immediate peace.

It is said that the German Government has given its support to the endeavors by an assurance that no general offensive on the Russian front will be undertaken for the time being, in order not to interfere with attempts at fraternization, the army leaders probably considering that the recent drive against the Stokhod bridgehead had only a local bearing.

The Socialist and other German newspapers appear to be much encouraged through reports from Russia of peace sentiments in the Council of Workmen's and Soldiers' Deputies and of troubles between that body and the organs of the Provisional Government and the Duma Executive Committee. The Socialist effort is said to be in line with directions given out before the convocation of the historic session of the American Congress, namely, to try first for a general peace, and then, if that effort should prove a failure, owing to the attitude of the Western Powers, to concentrate efforts on a separate peace with Russia.

The peace advocates are reported to have been preparing to make overtures to the United States to undertake mediation on favorable terms when President Wilson's sharp message and the unresponsive attitude of the Western Powers to the peace discussions of Count Czernin, the Austro-Hungarian Foreign Minister, and the Norddeutsche Allgemeine Zeitung showed the futility of the effort. Vorwärts, in line with the original directions, pledged in yesterday's leading editorial article the most vigorous patriotic support of the Socialists to the Government in the struggle with the United States.

Count von Reventlow in yesterday's Tageszeitung, devotes an article to the Dardanelles problem in the light of the Russian Socialist declaration that the annexation of Constantinople or of territorial acquisitions at the Dardanelles is beyond the purview of their plans. He says there is no reason now why a peace perfectly satisfactory to Russia, Germany, Austria-Hungary, and Turkey cannot be arranged by Turkey assuring to Russia the widest use of the straits.

FULL ALLIANCE UNLIKELY

But America Will Have a 'Gentlemen's Agreement' With Entente.

NAVAL CO-OPERATION FIRST

Financial Aid Goes with This, but Political Support Will Be Carefully Considered.

'SEPARATE PEACE' A PUZZLE

Question of Joining Allies' Compact Hinges on Exact Statement of Their Objects.

Special to The New York Times.

WASHINGTON, April 9.—There are indications of closer arrangements between the United States and the Governments of the Entente Allies for the purpose of bringing the war against the German Government to a victorious ending, but no formal action has yet been taken to lay the foundation for official agreements. It is too soon to make statements as to any compacts into which the United States may enter with the Allies, but it is believed that there will be nothing approaching an alliance within the ordinary meaning of that term.

The allied Governments have shown great delicacy in their attitude toward the United States in the new situation created by the entrance of this country into the conflict. They have made no definite approaches to the Washington Government regarding arrangements that will insure concert of plan and action between all the nations which seek to bring the German autocracy to an end. But it is expected that exchanges will be begun soon.

An indication of the closer communion between this Government and the Allies has been given in the more frequent calls of diplomatic representatives of the Entente powers at the State Department. This afternoon Mr. Jusserand, the French Ambassador, and Sir Cecil Spring-Rice, the British Ambassador, saw Secretary Lansing.

The chances are that the United States will enter into a gentleman's agreement with the Entente Allies, which will be assurance that the Entente may count on the United States to do its part in co-operation with them in a military and economic way to bring down the German Government in defeat. Several members of the Cabinet are in sympathy with the plan of having a complete arrangement to insure harmony of program and action, but for the present there appears to be a disposition not to agitate the subject. It is probable that the Entente Governments realize this, and are willing to let the United States Government take its time in determining what is the best course to follow to insure co-operation.

In denying today a report that he was in consultation yesterday with Naval Attachés of the Entente Governments, Secretary Daniels said that he did not care to make any statement other than that there would be co-operation between the United States and the Governments of the Entente in operations against the common foe. His remark is regarded as confirming the understanding that in military and naval ways the United States will go to the limit of its capacity in helping Great Britain, France, Russia, Italy, and Japan vanquish the German Government.

Representatives of the United States are already in touch informally with the Entente Governments, with a view to obtaining an idea of what is expected of this Government in fighting the war. A foundation for business arrangements that will expedite the shipment of supplies and transportation of troops is also being laid unofficially.

The real exchanges between the United States and the Entente Governments have not been begun, however, and will not be, it is understood, until all parties have had an opportunity to give mature consideration to the proposed plans of co-operation. At the same time, it is not going too far to say that there would be general surprise if it were made known how much progress had been made in the direction of reaching an understanding designed to prove to the advantage of all the anti-German forces.

Naval and Money Aid First.

The military and naval situation, as far as it affects the United States, is comparatively easy of adjustment. For the present the United States will confine its assistance to naval co-operation, with the extension of financial help to the Entente Powers.

The political aspect of the new relations into which this Government has entered with the other nations engaged in fighting the German Government presents problems that must be handled with the greatest care, however. Officials who were approached today with reference to this phase of the matter indicated that they were not prepared to discuss it.

One opinion, held in well-informed quarters, is that the Entente Governments will not seek to obtain from the United States a treaty agreement similar to those into which they have entered among themselves not to make a separate or premature peace with Germany and her allies. It is recognized in European Chancelleries, it is thought here, that the United States occupies a special position and is bound by tradition and principles which would

Continued on Page 2.

Scene of the New British Offensive.

The British, opening a tremendous offensive against the strong positions protecting the northern point of the Hindenburg line, broke through on a front of twelve miles, from Givenchy to Henin, advancing to a depth of from two to three miles. The extent of the advance is shown above.

Great Battle East of Arras Begins With Scenes of Infernal Splendor

Attack, Following a Week's Bombardment, Threatens to Turn Hindenburg Line—British Gunfire Twenty Times Stronger Than the Germans'.

By PHILIP GIBBS.

Special Cable to The New York Times.

WAR CORRESPONDENTS' HEADQUARTERS, April 9, (Dispatch to The London Daily Chronicle.)—Today at dawn the British armies began a great battle which, if fate has any kindness for the world, may be the beginning of the last great battles of the war. The British troops attacked on a wide front between Lens and St. Quentin, including Vimy Ridge, that great, grim hill which dominates the plain of Douai and the coal fields of Lens and the German positions around Arras. In spite of bad fortune in weather, at the beginning of the day so bad that there was no visibility for the airmen, and the men had to struggle forward in a heavy rainstorm, the first attacks have been successful, and the enemy has lost much ground, falling back in retreat to strong rearguard lines, where he is now fighting desperately. The line of attack covers a front of some twelve miles southward from Givenchy en Gohelle, and is a sledgehammer blow, threatening to break the northern end of the Hindenburg line, already menaced around St. Quentin.

As soon as the enemy was forced to retreat from the country east of Bapaume and Péronne in order to escape a decisive blow on that line he hurried up divisions and guns northward to counter a British attack there while he prepared a new line of defense known as the Hindenburg line. The southern part of the Hindenburg line, which joins it, is known as the Siegfried position, after the great hero of old German mythology. He hoped to escape there before the new British attack was ready, but they have been too quick for him, and his own plans were frustrated.

A Terrific Bombardment.

So today began another titanic conflict which the world will hold its breath to watch because of all that hangs upon it. I have seen the fury of this beginning and all the sky on fire with it, the most tragic and frightful sight that men have ever seen, with infernal splendor beyond words. The bombardment which went before the infantry assault lasted several days, and reached a great height yesterday. When coming from the south I saw it for the first time. Those of us who knew what would happen today—the beginning of another series of battles, greater perhaps than the struggle of the Somme—found ourselves yesterday filled with tense, restless emotion. Some of us smiled with a kind of tragic irony because it was Easter Sunday. In the little village behind the battle lines the bells of the French churches were ringing gladly because the Lord had risen, and on the altar steps priests were reciting splendid words of faith—"Resurrexi et adhuc te cum sum, Alleluia."

The earth was glad yesterday. For the first time this year the sun had a touch of warmth in it—although patches of snow still stayed white under the shelter of banks—and the sky was blue and the light glinted on wet tree trunks and in furrows of new plowed earth.

"As I went up the road to the battle lines I passed a battalion of British troops, who are fighting today, standing in a hollow square with bowed heads while the Chaplain conducted the Easter service. It was Easter Sunday, but no truce of God. I went to a field outside Arras and looked into the ruins of the cathedral city. The cathedral itself stood clear in the sunlight, with a deep black shadow where its roof and aisles had been. Beyond was a ragged pinnacle of stone, once the glorious town hall, and the French barracks and all the broken streets going out to the Cambrai road. It was hell in Arras, though Easter Sunday. The enemy was flinging high explosives into the city, and clouds of shrapnel burst above, black and green. All around the country, too, his shells were exploding in a scattered aimless way.

From the British side there was a great bombardment all along Vimy Ridge, above Neuville St. Vaast and sweeping around St. Nicholas and Blangy, two suburbs of Arras, and then southwest of the city on the ridge above the road to Cambrai. It was one continuous roar of death, and all the batteries were firing steadily. I watched the shells burst, and some of them were monsters, rising in great, lingering clouds above the German lines.

There was one figure in this landscape of war who made some officers about me laugh. He was a French plowman who upholds the traditions of war. Zola saw him in 1870. I have seen him on the edge of another battlefield, and here he was again, driving a pair of sturdy horses and his plow across the sloping field, not a furlong away from a village where German shells were raising a rosy cloud of brick dust. So he gave praise to the Lord on Easter morning and prepared for the harvests which shall be gathered after the war.

Scenes Behind the Front.

All behind the front of battle there was great traffic. All that modern warfare means in organization and in preparation for the enormous operation was here in movement. I had just come from the British outpost lines down south, from the silence of that great desert which the enemy has left in the wake of his retreat east of Bapaume and Péronne, and from that open warfare with village fighting, where small bodies of British infantry and cavalry have been clearing the countryside of rearguard posts. Here round about Arras was concentration for the old form of battle, the attack upon intrenched positions, fortified hills, and great natural fortresses defended by masses as before the battles of the Somme.

For miles on the way in front were great camps, great stores, and restless activity. Everywhere supply columns of food for men and guns moved forward in an endless tide. Transport mules passed in long trails, field batteries went up to add to the mass of metal ready to pour fire upon the German lines. It was a vast circus of the world's great war, and everything that belongs to the machinery of killing streamed on and on, columns of ambulances for the rescue, for that other side of the business, came in procession followed by an army of stretcher bearers, more than I have ever seen before, marching cheerily as though in a pageant. In some of the ambulances were army nurses, and the men marching on the roads waved their hands to them and they laughed and waved back. There were greetings which made one's heart go soft awhile. In the fields by the roadside men were resting, lying on the wet earth between two spells of long march, or encamped in rest, the same kind of men whom I saw on July 1 of last year, some of them the same men—clean shaven, gray-eyed, so young and so splendid to see. Some of them sat between their stacked rifles writing letters home, and the tide of traffic passed them and flowed on to the edge of the battlefields where today they are fighting.

The Opening of the Battle.

I went up in the darkness, long before light broke today, to see the opening of the battle. The roads were quiet until I drew near to Arras, and then onward there was the traffic of marching men going up to the fighting lines.

In the darkness there were hundreds of little red lights, the glow of cigarette ends. Outside one camp a battalion was marching away, and on the bank above them the band was playing them out with fifes and drums. On each side of me as I passed by the men were densely massed, and they were whistling and singing and calling out jests and gibes, wonderful lads that they are. Away before them were the fires of death to which they were going very steadily, with a tune on their lips, carrying rifles

Continued on Page 2.

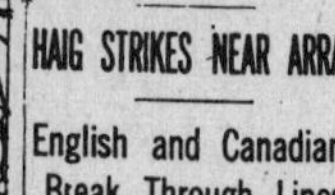

HAIG STRIKES NEAR ARRAS

English and Canadians Break Through Lines on 12-Mile Front.

SEIZE FAMOUS VIMY RIDGE

Villages and Fortified Points Captured to Depth of Two to Three Miles.

"TANKS" LEAD THE ADVANCE

British Also Push Forward Toward Cambrai and North of St. Quentin.

LONDON, April 9.—The British troops launched a terrific offensive today on a twelve-mile front north and south of Arras, penetrating the German positions to a depth of from two to three miles. Many important fortified points were captured, including the famous Vimy Ridge.

Nearly 6,000 prisoners, mostly Bavarians, Württembergers, and Hamburgers, have been taken so far, and they continue to pour into the receiving stations. Large numbers of guns, trench mortars, and other war material have been captured. The advance continues, the British having blasted their way clear through the German front and rearward positions.

The line of advance extends from Givenchy en Gohelle, southwest of Lens, to the village of Henin, on the Cojeul River, southeast of Arras. The attack began at 5:30 this morning, after a terrible night of artillery fire. For the last week the British guns have been bombarding the German lines in this sector without cessation, but last night's bombardment outdid even the terrific bombardments that preceded the Somme offensive last year.

The honor of capturing Vimy Ridge, where the French lost thousands of men last year in an attempt to hold this dominating height, fell to the Canadians. This ridge protects the French coal fields lying to the eastward. Once before the British gained the crest of this ridge, but, under a tremendous concentration of German guns, they were compelled to give it up. All Winter long Canadians have held a footing on the ridge, with the German lines looking down on them. All the fighting today was against dominating positions on high ground, some of which had been held by the Germans for two years and were lavishly hemmed with wide belts of some of the toughest and longest-pronged barbed wire which has been seen in the war.

Along the greater part of the front, says Reuter's correspondent at the front, the advance of the infantry was strenuously opposed. Near Arras the Germans offered determined resistance and a large pocket of the Germans was reported to be still holding out at midday, although entirely surrounded.

The famous redoubt named "The Harp," only a little less formidable than the noted "Labyrinth," was captured with virtually the whole battalion defending it. Several "tanks" were seen climbing Telegraph Hill, which commands "The Harp," and probably had much to do with the surrender of this position. Here three German battalion commanders were captured.

Along the railway running through to the valley of the Scarpe the British made good progress, while upon the Lens branch of the line they captured Maison Blanche Wood.

Battle Begins at Daybreak.

The early British report, which is timed 11:25 A. M., is as follows:

We attacked at 5:30 o'clock this morning on a wide front from south of Arras to south of Lens. Our troops have everywhere penetrated the enemy's lines and are making satisfactory progress at all points.

In the direction of Cambrai we stormed the villages of Hermies and Boursies and have penetrated into Havrincourt Wood.

"In the direction of St. Quentin we captured Fresnoy le Petit and advanced our line southeast of Le Verguier.

No estimate of the prisoners taken can yet be given, but considerable numbers are reported captured.

The text of the statement issued this evening reads:

The operations continue to be carried out successfully in accordance with the plan. Our troops have everywhere stormed the enemy defenses from Henin-sur-Cojeul to the southern outskirts of Givenchy-en-Gohelle to a depth of from two to three miles, and our advance continues.

The enemy's forward defenses on this front, including Vimy Ridge, which was carried by the Canadian troops, were captured early in the morning. These defenses comprise a network of trenches and fortified localities—Neuville, Vitasse, Telegraph Hill, Tilloy Les Mofflaines, Observation Ridge, St. Laurent-Blangy, Les Tilleuls, and La Folie Farm.

Subsequently our troops moved forward and captured the enemy's rearward defenses, including, in addition

Mid-Week Pictorial

Battlefield scene near Arras. A battery of the British Royal Field Artillery take up positions closer to the enemy. In the foreground, Infantrymen advance to take possession of the trenches.

"All the News That's Fit to Print."

The New York Times.

THE WEATHER
Overcast, probably showers tonight and Monday; cool; wind east.
For full weather report see Page 19.

VOL. LXVI...NO. 21,645. NEW YORK, SUNDAY, APRIL 29, 1917.—98 PAGES, In Eight Parts, Including Picture and Rotogravure Section and Review of Books. FIVE CENTS In Greater New York | Elsewhere SEVEN CENTS

CONGRESS PASSES DRAFT BILL: HOUSE, 397 TO 24; SENATE, 81 TO 8; COMMAND OF ENTIRE FRONT IN FRANCE OFFERED TO PETAIN; GROWING DEMAND IN MEXICO FOR A STAND WITH UNITED STATES

200 IN CONGRESS ASK LLOYD GEORGE TO FREE IRELAND

Representatives Sign Petition Which Is Cabled to the British Premier.

CITE WILSON'S PRINCIPLES

Settlement of Question Urged to Add to America's Enthusiasm in War.

ULSTER BLOCKS PROGRESS

Insistence on Her Method of Conducting a Referendum Hampers Lloyd George.

Special to The New York Times.

WASHINGTON, D. C., April 28.—Nearly two hundred members of the House tonight signed and dispatched a cablegram to David Lloyd George, asking that England "shall now settle the Irish problem."

The first signature on the American plea for Irish independence was that of Speaker Champ Clark. Representative Claude Kitchin, the Democratic floor leader; Representative John J. Fitzgerald of New York, Representative Williamson of Georgia, Representative Irvin L. Lenroot of Wisconsin, and Representative Julius Kahn of California were among the House leaders signing the cablegram.

Democrats and Republicans alike signed the cable petition. The movement originated today at a conference attended by Mr. Fitzgerald, Mr. Gallivan of Massachusetts, Mr. Griffen, and Mr. Carew of New York, and several other members of Celtic sympathies. The cablegram read:

The Right Hon. David Lloyd George, M. P., London, England.

You are quoted as saying that "the settlement of the Irish question is essential for the peace of the world and for a speedy victory in the war."

May we, members of the American Congress, suggest that nothing will add more to the enthusiasm of America in this war than a settlement now of the Irish problem.

We believe that all Americans will be deeply stirred and their enthusiastic effort enlisted if the British Empire will now settle this problem in accordance with the principles announced by President Wilson in his address to Congress asking it to declare war on autocracy for the world-wide safety of democracy and of small nationalities.

The Representatives who signed the cablegram were:

Adamson, Georgia; Ayres, Kansas.

Black, Texas; Bruckner, New York; Byrnes, South Carolina; Brumbaugh, Ohio.

Caldwell, New York; Campbell, Kansas; Carter, Massachusetts; Chandler, New York; Clark, Florida; Coady, Maryland; Carew, New York; Collier, Mississippi; Clark, Missouri; Costello, Pennsylvania.

Dale, New York; Decker, Missouri; Dempsey, New York; Denison, Illinois; De Walt, Pennsylvania; Dooling, New York; Doolittle, Kansas; Dupre, Louisiana; Dyer, Missouri.

Eagan, New Jersey; Eagle, Texas; Emerson, Ohio.

Farr, Pennsylvania; Fitzgerald, New York; Fess, Ohio; Fisher, Tennessee; Flynn, New York; Fuller, Massachusetts.

Gallagher, Illinois; Gard, Ohio; Gallivan, Massachusetts; Garland, Pennsylvania; Glynn, Connecticut; Griffin, New York.

Hammill, New Jersey; Hardy, Texas; Heaton, Pennsylvania; Heflin, Alabama; Hensley, Missouri; Hilliard, Colorado; Holland, Virginia; Houston, Tennessee; Howard, Georgia; Hulburt, New York; Humphreys, Mississippi.

Igoe, Missouri.

Keating, Colorado; Kehoe, Florida; Kitchin, North Carolina; Kennedy, Rhode Island.

Lenroot, Wisconsin; Linthicum, Maryland; London, New York; Lonergan, Connecticut; Lunn, New York.

McAndrews, Illinois; McCormick, Illinois; McKeown, Oklahoma; McLaughlin, Pennsylvania; McLemore, Texas; Madden, Illinois; Maher, New York; Martin, Illinois; Mason, Illinois; Meeker, Missouri; Mondell, Wyoming; Montague, Virginia; Morin, Pennsylvania.

Norton, North Dakota.

O'Shaughnessy, Rhode Island; Overmyer, Ohio.

Park, Georgia; Parker, New York; Phelan, Massachusetts.

Randall, California; Riordan, New York; Rodenberg, Illinois; Rouse, Kentucky; Rowe, New York.

Sabath, Illinois; Scully, New Jersey; Sims, Tennessee; Smith, New York; Snyder, New York; Sullivan, New York; Tague, Massachusetts; Timberlake, Colorado; Tinkham, Massachusetts.

Van Dyke, Minnesota; Vare, Pennsylvania; Walsh, Massachusetts; Ward, New York; Watson, Pennsylvania; Webb, North Carolina; Wilson, Illinois; Green, Massachusetts; Haskell, New York; Laguardia, New York; Doremus, Michigan; Britten, Illinois; Templeton, Pennsylvania; Mott, New York; Bacharach, New Jersey; Scott, Pennsylvania; Rowland, Pennsylvania; Clark, Pennsylvania; Kiess, Pennsylvania; Darrow,

Continued on Page 4.

Geneva Hears Greek King Will Abdicate on May 6

GENEVA, April 28, (via Paris.)—The Journal de Geneve, discussing the recent meeting of allied Ministers at St. Jean de Maurienne, believes that affairs in Greece will shortly take a new turn, which is already foreshadowed by the recent outspoken tone of the French press.

The same paper refers to a rumor, according to which Constantine is contemplating abdicating in favor of his son on May 6, which is the name day of his late father and also of the present heir to the throne.

BRITISH ADVANCE AGAIN ON SCARPE

Capture German Positions on Two-Mile Front in War's Bitterest Fighting.

CANADIANS TAKE VILLAGE

Enemy Sacrifices Large Numbers of Men in a Vain Attempt to Halt Attackers.

LONDON, April 28.—The British began a new attack north of the Scarpe (northeast of Arras) this morning, the fighting extending over a front of several miles. At the end of the day General Haig's troops had captured German positions over a front of more than two miles north, and south of the village of Arleux and including that village. Arleux is about nine miles due west of Douai. The British also pushed forward northeast of Gavrelle, in the direction of Oppy, and on the western slopes of what is known as Greenland Hill, between Gavrelle and Roeux. South of the Scarpe the British gained ground north of Monchy.

The British attacks today met with greater opposition than any yet encountered. Many violent counterattacks were launched by the Germans with large forces, but they were all repulsed with heavy losses, although at times the fighting was hand to hand.

The battle still continues tonight at some points of the line. Several hundred prisoners have already been taken.

General Haig's early statement said:

Early this morning we attacked on a front of several miles north of the Scarpe, meeting considerable opposition, but making good progress.

The statement issued this evening follows:

Severe fighting, in which our troops have had the advantage, took place throughout the day from the Scarpe River to the Acheville-Vimy Road. We captured Arleux-en-Gohelle and enemy positions on a front of over two miles north and south of the village.

Our troops also progressed northeast of Gavrelle and the western slopes of Greenland Hill, between Gavrelle and Roeux. South of the river we have gained ground north of Monchy-le-Preux.

The enemy again delivered many violent counterattacks with considerable forces and suffered heavily from our artillery and machine gunfire. In the neighborhood of Roeux and Oppy heavy fighting is continuing. Several hundred prisoners were captured by us during the day.

Three German airplanes were felled yesterday in air fighting and a fourth was shot down by our anti-aircraft guns. One hostile observation balloon also was destroyed. Three of our airplanes are missing.

The German advanced positions north of the Scarpe contained many disconnected defenses of great natural strength, the extent of which could be determined only by the test of attacks. In fact, the situation in the past week had become reminiscent of the late Autumn fighting in the Somme Valley, when every shell crater became a potential machine-gun trap. One great distinction, however, is that the British are now spared the pestilential mud, which made progress quite impossible in the Fall.

A dispatch tonight from British headquarters says:

"There was more desperate fighting along the British front today, and the Germans, evidently spurred on by the declarations from Field Marshal von Hindenburg that they must hold their present positions at all costs, are making a resistance more stubborn than any heretofore encountered. At various points captured in the first onward rush by the British the Germans have been ordered into counterattacks with a reckless disregard for loss of life.

German Ranks Shattered.

"The battle was still in progress late today and it was possible near Oppy to see at one time no less than five gray waves of Germans blindly facing the British fire in an attempt to retake their lost positions. Heavy shells broke upon them in a great explosive torrent, and where each shell burst great gaps were cut in the ranks of the oncoming men. Those who penetrated the British barrage from the larger calibred guns were met by field guns and mown down under continuous sprays of machine gun bullets.

"Under this galling fire the attack utterly broke down. In some places there was ferocious hand-to-hand fighting. The British got in well with the bayonet, but there was one bit of fighting in which even bayonets were forgotten, and the men went at each other's throats and eyes. Many Germans went to their death from blows from rifle butts.

"At times the fighting was wholly obscured by great clouds of dust, the muddy battlefields of ten days ago having entirely disappeared. The dust raised by the barrage fire [illegible] an approaching storm. Shrapnel bullets were pelting the dry earth like so many leaden drops of rain, and great mushrooms of dust seemed to spring from the earth everywhere.

"The attack began with the coming of [illegible]

Continued on Page 3.

TO BUILD A SHIP EVERY 10 DAYS TO FEED THE ALLIES

A Thousand Men to be Set to Work Tomorrow on a Plant Near City.

EACH TO BEAR 5,000 TONS

First Will Be Ready in a Few Months and Others Will Follow with a Rush.

ALL TO BE STANDARDIZED

Wood Alone Used for Construction of Hull—Cost of Each Will Be About $350,000.

The United States Government awarded yesterday to the Foundation Company of this city a contract for building an indefinite number of wooden ships, part of the fleet which is to "bridge" the seas carrying food, munitions, and supplies to our allies. Tomorrow more than 1,000 men will be put to work building the plant near this city, which, when it is running at maximum capacity, will be able to turn out one ship ready for service every ten days. The plant will occupy 55 acres, with 1,500 feet of water frontage.

Everything has been in readiness for some time for the signing of the contract, it is said, and the builders, the material makers, and the transportation companies have worked out a scheme of co-operation. The result will be, it is said, that the work will begin as though at the firing of a starting gun. The right of way on all railroads will be given to the materials needed for the work.

The land on which the plant will spring up was leased to the Government and the Foundation Company for a nominal sum by Joseph P. Day, the real estate man, of this city. The plant will be up and the ways ready for the laying of the keels of the first ten ships by the end of May. When it is working at top speed 3,000 men will be employed working in day and night shifts. Franklin Remington, President of the company, said the plant would be under the supervision of the Government and under Government guard.

The first vessel will be the pattern for the others, and this will take longer in building than the rest. Standardization will be the secret of speed in construction, and the plans worked out by the Government experts call for the standardization of every part of the vessel. While ten are under construction on the ways manufacturers in other parts of the country will be turning out piece after piece, all ready to be fitted together, just as portable houses are now built. The pattern ship, according to present plans, will be ready to take the water within ninety days after the keel is laid and will be ready to take on cargo about a month and a half later.

While this is going on nine others will be approaching completion, and the keel of the eleventh laid down as the first leaves the ways. As one vessel will be completed every ten days, according to present estimates, it means that by the time the pattern ship is ready for service nine others will be almost ready to go into commission.

It was roughly estimated by President Remington that the cost of each vessel would be $350,000. He anticipated no trouble in getting either material for construction or the engines. In the present plant of the foundation company are many carpenters, calkers, and others capable of shipbuilding, for the company already maintains a shipbuilding plant in which it has constructed its own fleet of small craft.

The wooden vessels will be of 3,000 gross tons each and have a cargo carrying capacity of about 5,000 tons. They will be 290 feet long, 46 feet beam, and have a draft of 17 feet. They will be equipped with reciprocal engines and, it is estimated, will have a speed of sixteen knots an hour.

"We have only just closed the contract," said President Remington, "and for that reason I cannot go into its terms. The company is not only going to build ships for the Atlantic trade, but we are also investigating facilities on the Pacific Coast, for the Government is figuring on putting up another plant there. We have timber already for present needs and the railroads will bring in material just as fast as we need it."

Mr. Remington was asked whether green timber would be used in the construction, and he replied that green timber, it had been shown, could be employed in shipbuilding. In this connection it is figured that a million and a quarter feet of timber will be required for each boat. This will be sawed up on the plant, where great mills are to be a feature of the work.

"We are not going ahead in the dark," continued Mr. Remington. "The plans have been very intelligently laid out down to the very smallest detail, and nothing has been left to chance. Ships are to be manufactured just as are automobiles and other articles that are standardized, and in order to carry out this plan the vessels will have straight sides and flat decks."

"Are they to be armed?" he was asked.

"The question of arming them is uncertain," he replied. "It is a matter for the Government to decide. I believe that they will be built capable of mounting guns, but of that matter I am not authorized to speak."

The building of wooden ships capable of bearing the strain of rough weather on the Atlantic, and still be of sufficient size to carry considerable cargo, has been the subject of dispute among shipping men, but the designers of the wooden craft are sure they will be able to do effective service. The plans have been carefully gone over by the Government architects, and are said to meet the approval of Major Gen. Goethals.

It is believed, moreover, by those who are to build the fleet that the problem [illegible] standardization of parts and the simplification of construction [illegible] as skilled as were the ship carpenters of the olden day.

Continued on Page 5.

Spain Makes A New Protest Over U-Boat Attack on Ship

MADRID, April 28, (via Paris.)—Premier Prieto has announced that he has received official confirmation of an attack by a German submarine on the Spanish steamer Triana, and has addressed a strong protest to Germany.

Details of the incident show that a few minutes after a shell had been fired at the Triana, the commander of the submarine boarded the ship and offered excuses, insisting that he only fired after the steamer had ignored a blank shot. The Captain of the Triana, in a sworn statement, before the Cadiz port authorities, affirms that neither he nor his crew heard any shot until the ship was struck by a shell. The Triana was going at reduced speed at the time, he says, and the Spanish colors were flying conspicuously.

El Imparcial comments indignantly on the attack, occurring as it does at a moment when negotiations are proceeding between Spain and Germany on the subject of similar aggressions. The Triana is a small steamer of 745 tons, exclusively engaged in the coasting trade. She was bound from Gijon to Cadiz when attacked.

AMERICANS LED CHINA TO BREAK

Washington Not Pleased with Efforts of Dr. Reinsch, Who Headed "Flying Wedge."

TWO AUSTRALIANS HELPED

And Leaders of the Young China Party Were Induced to Threaten Revolt.

Special to The New York Times.

WASHINGTON, April 28.—Recent reports that the United States Government was displeased with the excessive activity on the part of Dr. Paul S. Reinsch, Minister to China, in connection with the desire of President Wilson to have other neutral nations follow the example of this country in breaking off relations with the German Government, appear to be explained by an article published in The Saturday Evening Post of this week, which states that a group of Americans and Australians, headed by Dr. Reinsch, formed what is called a "flying wedge" and induced the President of the Chinese Republic to sever diplomatic intercourse with the autocracy at Berlin.

The article gains credence here because the writer is Samuel G. Blythe, whose reputation for reliability is of the best. Mr. Blythe, who returned recently from China, is well acquainted with the questions of which the article treats and had superior means of obtaining information as to the events he chronicles.

When the Chinese President hesitated to break off relations, mainly because he thought Germany would win the war, some of those who had taken part in the effort to bring China's moral influence to bear against the continuance of Prussianism went so far as to induce some young Chinese Generals to threaten to revolt with their troops; but Mr. Blythe does not include Minister Reinsch in this movement. The threat, apparently, was successful, for the Chinese Government broke off relations with the German Empire.

Officials who were questioned today were reticent concerning the revelations made by Mr. Blythe, but there is a suspicion that, anxious as President Wilson was that China, as well as other neutral nations, should follow his suggestion that they sever diplomatic intercourse with Germany, he felt it necessary to take exception to the course of Mr. Reinsch. That the latter was rebuked for his activity in the matter is not stated, but in ordinary times such activity on the part of a diplomatic representative would probably result in positive action by the Washington Government. Since the war with Germany was begun, however, all has been forgiven.

After the break in relations between the United States and Germany, Mr. Blythe says, Mr. Reinsch received word from the State Department of the event, together with a copy of the note, sent to all neutrals inviting them to join in the action, which the note said "would make for the peace of the world." To Dr. Reinsch and to five other Americans and two Australians this course seemed the best for China and the world, and they determined to see that China followed this course.

In the American group, besides Dr. Reinsch, according to Mr. Blythe, were Dr. John C. Ferguson of Newton, Mass.; Roy S. Anderson, a man versed in Chinese politics; Charles Stevenson Smith, and Mr. Blythe himself, and two Australians, Dr. G. E. Morrison, political adviser to the President of China, and W. H. Donald, editor of The Far Eastern Review. Others joined the movement later, but these seven constituted the "flying wedge" which began the work.

Admiral Tsai Ting-Kan, Naval Aid to the President, who was educated in the United States, was called into conference and agreed that it was advisable to break off relations. It was determined that he and Dr. Morrison should [illegible]

"I am a student of this war," he said, "and I am a soldier. I see no way [illegible]

Continued on Page 3.

BIGGER POWERS THAN NIVELLE'S FOR GEN. PETAIN

Washington Hears French, British, and Belgian Armies Will Be Under Him.

HE HAS NOT YET ACCEPTED

But the Post Was Offered, Following Paris Criticism of the New Offensive.

WOULD ACT INDEPENDENTLY

New Commander's Direction Likely to be Free from War Council's Decisions.

Special to The New York Times.

WASHINGTON, April 28.—Criticisms in Paris newspapers of the manner in which the great offensive against the Germans on the western front is being conducted tend to confirm the understanding in certain circles here that a change in the supreme command of the forces opposed to the Germans on the western front—the French front—is under consideration.

The man whose selection for this great work is being discussed—to whom, indeed, it is known that the post has been offered—is General Petain, who was proposed for the high command of the French forces at the time that Marshal Joffre retired from active duty in the field, but who refused then, mainly, it is understood, because he could not be assured that he would have supreme charge of the entire forces opposed to Germany in Western Europe, those of Great Britain as well as of France, and probably the Italian forces in addition. It must be stated that this information does not come from the French Commission now in Washington, whose members profess entire ignorance of the contemplated change.

It is not understood that the appointment of General Pétain to the supreme command of the allied armies in France and perhaps in the whole of Western Europe will mean necessarily that General Nivelle will give up the high command of the French forces, the place in which he succeeded Marshal Joffre. Should Pétain accept command of all the allied armies, Nivelle could be left in his present position just as General Haig would be still the commander of the British forces, although subordinate to General Pétain.

General Nivelle, who was chosen to succeed General Joffre, was second in command to Pétain. It was at Pétain's suggestion, however, that Nivelle was chosen. He was highly commended by Pétain, who was willing to retain his own subordinate position rather than take Joffre's place in order to maintain a principle.

That principle was that the situation required that all the forces on the western front should be commanded by one man. He adhered to the contention that the British forces should not merely co-operate with the French but that both French and British forces should receive their orders from one supreme commander.

It was said at the time that General Pétain believed that this principle should be extended so that the commander of the forces on the western front should have command of the Italian forces. He maintained that in order to insure success to a supreme commander such as he desired to see appointed the man chosen should be left free from supervision by any war council sitting in Paris.

The French Government was unable to view these considerations in the light in which they were presented by General Pétain, and as a consequence General Nivelle was named as Marshal Joffre's successor, but with command only of the French armies. Since then General Pétain has retained his subordinate rank.

The freedom with which the French newspapers are commenting in a critical way on the effort to drive back the Germans on the western front is taken as an indication of the Government's willingness to prepare the people for another change in the command of the French forces.

In this connection it has been suggested that the French War Council or a joint war council of all the allied nations whose troops are engaged on the western front should sit at a point nearer the battle line than Paris.

An intimation of the way feeling is running in France concerning the big drive in which the French and British troops are engaged is given by the statement of a member of the Chamber of Deputies that better progress would be made on the western front if the allied troops there were under a supreme command.

At that time THE NEW YORK TIMES announced exclusively in a Washington dispatch that Marshal Joffre was to retire and that General Nivelle probably [illegible]

Continued on Page 3.

Falling Off in Recruiting for Regular Army; Only 8,521 Enlisted in Five Days Last Week

Special to The New York Times.

WASHINGTON, April 28.—Army recruiting shows a falling off that is commencing to occasion considerable concern in army circles. Yesterday a total of 1,099 men were enlisted, less than half the number enlisted last Monday. The figures for the week have been:

Monday, April 23	2,268
Tuesday, April 24	1,995
Wednesday, April 25	1,654
Thursday, April 26	1,375
Friday, April 27	1,099
Total	8,521

On April 1 the army needed 183,898 men to raise it to war strength of 287,000 men. Since that date an aggregate of 30,286 men has been obtained. The State of Pennsylvania led yesterday with 108 recruits. New York ranked second with a contribution of 82 men. Illinois, which for several weeks led daily, was third yesterday with 71 men.

Not a recruit was obtained for the army yesterday from Delaware, the District of Columbia, New Hampshire, North Carolina, and Vermont. Maryland and New Mexico each gave 1 army recruit yesterday, Idaho 3, Arizona 5, Montana 9, Rhode Island 2, Virginia 5, and Louisiana 5.

Mexico to Take Her Stand With Us; Movement for a Break With Germany

May Even Join in the War—Business Interests Act, Recognizing That Our Help Is Essential—Guatemala Breaks With Germany.

Special to The New York Times.

MONTEREY, Mexico, April 28.—Mexico probably will break off relations with the Central Powers within a few weeks and declare an alliance with the Entente Powers. Mexico's example will be followed by one other Central American power, possibly by Guatemala, also. [The breaking of relations by Guatemala was announced yesterday.]

The attitude of the various Government officials plainly shows that they have received orders from higher up. Some of the hot-headed officials who lately were loudest in their anti-American talk have developed a friendly feeling for the Americans. As one General expressed himself to the correspondent:

"We must be friends now, as we Mexicans will fight with you Americans instead of against you."

In the northern cities which are near the border there is a strong movement afoot among the business men and the rich farmers to force action. Many of the prominent business men are writing letters to the recently elected Senators and Congressmen demanding that they take action at once. While there are a number of Senators who are known to be pro-German yet there are enough others who realize the danger that Mexico is in. It is expected that when this matter is presented before the Senate it will cause a stormy session, but the motion will pass with a large majority.

The German influence with the Mexican people in the northern part of the republic has been very much overestimated, as the majority of thinking men see the danger and are tired of revolutions and trouble. Business men want peace and an opportunity to work.

While the majority of Mexicans do not love the United States, yet they well understand that they must have the friendship of Uncle Sam to avoid ruin. As one of the largest business men in Monterey stated to the correspondent this morning:

"We do not love the Americans, as we blame them for the Villa trouble, which is the only obstacle that prevents Mexico from getting on her feet. If the United States would not allow Villa to get ammunition Mexico would be at peace within three months. We cannot believe that the United States are our friends until we see that they are willing to assist us. We do not love your people, yet we realize that we must have your co-operation. When you Americans know us better and we know the American people better, then Mexico and the United States will be close friends. Help us and you will not find us ungrateful."

With a lift from the United States Mexico will in a few years become a rich, self-sustaining nation.

GUATEMALA BREAKS RELATIONS WITH BERLIN

Offers Us the Use of Her Ports and Railways for Common Defense.

GUATEMALA CITY, April 28.—The National Assembly today approved the decree issued by President Cabrera severing diplomatic relations between this country and Germany. Later passports were delivered to Dr. Lehmann, the German Minister, who received eight days' notice to leave the country. Dr. Manuel Arroyo, the Guatemalan Minister to Germany, has been recalled by cable.

A wireless plant has been discovered on a German plantation here. The exequaturs of German Consuls have been canceled.

There are extensive German interests in Guatemala, including the electric plant in this city.

Special to The New York Times.

WASHINGTON, April 28.—Guatemala has broken diplomatic relations with Germany and handed passports to the German Minister, Dr. Lehmann, who was one of the leading figures in the spoiled plot to stir up a series of revolutions in Central America with a view to diverting the attention of the United States from the war with Germany. An effort will be made to obtain safe conduct for Dr. Lehmann by way of the United States to Germany, just as has been done in the case of the German diplomatic and Consular officials in Cuba and China, who are to sail for Germany on the steamer Ryndam on May 4.

Official notification of the action of the Guatemalan Government was communicated to Secretary Lansing by Jaquin Mendez, the Guatemalan Minister to the United States. Official word reaching Washington from Guatemala City is to the effect that the ground upon which Estrada Cabrera, President of Guatemala, and his Government have broken relations with Germany has been their desire to stand with the United States Government in its contest for the supremacy of democracy and the preservation of international law.

The action of Guatemala is considered very important, since the relations between that country and Mexico have been strained, and the step now taken by Guatemala is expected to have an impressive influence in Mexico.

The communication in which Mr. Lansing was notified of Guatemala's action was delivered by that country's Minister as follows:

Mr. Secretary of State:

I have just received the following cable from the Minister for Foreign Affairs of Guatemala:

Minister Mendez, Legation of Guatemala, Washington:

The Government of Guatemala today broke off relations with the German Empire, handing his passports to Minister Lehmann and canceling the exequatur of the German Consul accredited to Guatemala. Advise the American Government.

TOLEDO H.

In communicating the action of my Government to your Excellency, I take pleasure in reiterating that Guatemala from the first has adhered to and supported the attitude of the United States in the defense of the rights of nations, the liberty of the seas, and of international justice, and that it has always considered itself in unity with your great nation in the lofty principles which it has so wisely proclaimed for the good of humanity.

Therefore, Guatemala takes the greatest pleasure in offering to the United States of America her territorial waters, her ports, and railways for use in common defense, as also all elements which may be available for the same purpose.

I avail myself of this opportunity to reiterate to your Excellency the assurances of my highest consideration and respect.

JOAQUIN MENDEZ.

Minister Mendez issued a statement tonight saying the Guatemalan Government's decision to break relations was taken "on account of the plots of the Germans against the safety and the independence, not only of Guatemala, but of the whole of Central America, and through solidarity with the principles of the rights of peoples, the freedom of the seas, and universal justice.

Mexico Notified of the Action.

Special Cable to THE NEW YORK TIMES.

MEXICO CITY, April 28.—Guatemala has officially notified Mexico of her rupture of relations with Germany. It is expected that large numbers of Germans will leave that republic for Mexico. The towns of Quezaltenango and Huehuetenango, centres of the coffee districts, are entirely controlled by Germans, who also dominate the northwestern part of the country from Guatemala City to the Mexican border. The coffee plantations, hide trade, and general mercantile business in the republic are backed by German capital, and 90 per cent. of the coffee shipments are consigned to the Reichsbank. The leading business firms of Guatemala City and other towns are also owned by Germans.

In view of the numerous German population of Guatemala and President Cabrera's reported declaration of martial law before the break in relations, it is believed here that the Germans had attempted to arouse internal disturbances.

It is expected that Honduras will follow the example of Guatemala, as it is well known in Central America that President Cabrera directs the political action of the neighboring republic.

Expect Spain to Declare War.

Special Cable to THE NEW YORK TIMES.

MEXICO CITY, April 28.—Among Spaniards here there is an expectation that Spain will declare war in the next few days. The Government has instructed the local authorities to prevent [illegible] of ill-will toward foreign powers.

ENLISTED PAY IS DOUBLED

Big Majorities in Both Houses Against the Volunteer System.

SENATE FOR ROOSEVELT

Accepts Amendment House Rejected—Conflicts Must Be Settled in Conference.

AT ODDS ON AGE LIMITS

House Sticks to Provision Fixing 21 to 40, While Senate Accepts 21 to 27.

Special to The New York Times.

WASHINGTON, Sunday, April 29.—Both houses of Congress late last night passed the Army bill embodying the Administration's plan for selective draft. The vote in the Senate was 81 to 8; in the House it was 397 to 24. Differences between the two houses will be adjusted in conference this week.

The final vote in the House preceded by a few minutes the final vote in the Senate. The vote followed a decisive defeat of the pro-volunteer forces in both houses. The Kahn amendment, striking from the bill authorization for the calling out of volunteers, was adopted in the House by 313 to 109. A great demonstration was staged in the House as the Administration victory was announced. The Senate voted against the volunteer plan, 69 to 18.

The Senate took the final vote on the stroke of 11. Five Democrats and three Republicans voted against the bill. The Democrats were Gore, Hardwick, Kirby, Thomas, and Trammell; the Republicans, Borah, Gronna, and LaFollette. Senator Vardaman of Mississippi, Democrat, who is opposed to the measure, asked to be excused from voting, and the Senate permitted it.

After the vote was announced the Senate recessed for thirty minutes to learn the action the House had taken, in order to refer the bill to conference. Several amendments were not considered because of lack of time before the hour agreed upon for a vote. One amendment made by Senator LaFollette, proposing a substitute for the entire bill, was ruled out by the Vice President. Mr. LaFollette responded with the remark that it would be a long time before his consent could be secured to another agreement.

When the Senate reconvened the House bill was formally referred to the Committee on Military Affairs, which reported back the Senate bill as a substitute. The bill then went to the calendar for action Monday.

House Members Who Voted "No."

The twenty-four members of the House who stood out to the last against passage of the bill were:

Democrats—Burnett, Alabama; Church, California; Clark, Florida; Claypool, Ohio; Crosser, Ohio; Dill, Washington; Dominick, South Carolina; Gordon, Ohio; Hilliard, Colorado; Huddleston, Alabama; Keating, Colorado; Sears, Florida; Sherwood, Ohio; Sisson, Mississippi.

Republicans—Bacon, Michigan; Hayes, California; King, Illinois; La Follette, Washington; Lundeen, Minnesota; Mason, Illinois; Nolan, California; Powers, Kentucky.

Prohibitionist—Randall, California.

Socialist—London, New York.

Voting present—Hollingsworth, Ohio.

Majority Leader Kitchin voted against the Kahn conscription amendment, but voted aye on final passage of the bill. Chairman Dent of the Military Affairs Committee, who led the anti-conscription fight during a week of debate, likewise voted for the bill on final passage. Speaker Clark voted against the Kahn selective draft amendment, but for the bill on final passage. Miss Jeanette Rankin of Montana followed a similar course.

Spirited debate, continuing for almost twelve hours, and the offering of scores of amendments, most of which failed, signalized the final day of the discussion which began in the House last Monday.

An amendment written into the bill in the House was one authorizing the President to include in the exempted classes persons "engaged in agriculture." Farmers had not been specifically mentioned in the exemption clause which authorized the President to use in part or exempt entirely from military service those engaged in pursuits needful in the maintenance of the military forces of the United States.

The House twice recorded itself overwhelmingly in opposition to the volunteer system. In committee of the whole the lower body voted, 279 to 98, for the Kahn amendment eliminating all reference to volunteers and authorizing only the selective draft. The roll call vote was even more decisive—313 to 109.

The Senators voting for the volunteer plan were:

Democrats—Gore, Hardwick, Kirby, McKellar, Reed, Thomas, Trammell, and Vardaman—8.

Republicans—Borah, Cummins, Curtis, Fall, Gallinger, Gronna, Johnson, California; La Follette, Norris, Sherman—10.

Enlisted Pay Raised.

Both Senate and House adopted amendments just before the final roll-calls which would greatly increase the pay of enlisted men during the war. The House provision would make their pay $30 a month, and that approved by the Senate would fix it at $[illegible]. The present pay is $15. Chairman Fitzgerald of the [illegible]

"All the News That's Fit to Print."

The New York Times.

THE WEATHER
Fair, cool today and Sunday; moderate north winds.
For full weather report see Page 19.

VOL. LXVI...NO. 21,658. NEW YORK, SATURDAY, MAY 12, 1917.—TWENTY PAGES. ONE CENT In Greater New York. | TWO CENTS New England and Middle States. | THREE CENTS Elsewhere

BALFOUR AND VIVIANI WELCOME US AS ALLY IN THE WAR FOR CIVILIZTAION; STIR DINERS TO WILDEST ENTHUSIASM

RUSSIAN COUNCIL MOVES FOR WORLD PEACE CONFERENCE

Delegates' Committee to Appeal to All Nations, Hoping to End the War This Summer.

BACKS STOCKHOLM MEETING

Will Send Delegates There—Others to Visit Neutral and Allied Countries to Press Peace.

CHIEF CALL TO SOCIALISTS

But All Parties Agreeing with Appeal Will Be Welcome at the Proposed Gathering.

PETROGRAD, May 10, (via London, May 11.)—An appeal to the peoples of the world in behalf of the calling of a peace conference in a neutral country will be published immediately by the Council of Soldiers' and Workmen's Delegates, according to a resolution adopted at a meeting yesterday of the Executive Committee of the Council.

The committee also decided to send a delegation to establish relations with the Socialist delegates at Stockholm and to have delegates visit neutral and allied countries to further the peace movement.

It was further decided to call a conference of the Socialist Internationale and invite thereto representatives of all parties, agreeing with the council's appeal.

The resolutions, adopted by the Executive Committee, included:

First—To convoke a conference of the Socialist Internationale.

Second—To invite to the conference representatives of all parties and fractions of the international proletariat agreeing with the Council of Soldiers' and Workmen's Delegates' appeal to the peoples of the world.

Third—To form a special commission of representatives of the Executive Committee and one representative of each of the Socialist parties to organize the conference and arrange a program.

Fourth—To publish immediately an appeal to the peoples of the world and a special appeal to the Socialists in allied countries for the convocation of a peace conference.

Fifth—To send a delegation of the Executive Committee to neutral and allied countries and establish contact with the Socialist delegates at Stockholm.

Sixth—The peace conference is to take place in a neutral country.

Seventh—The committee, recognizing as a necessary condition that free passage be accorded to all parties and fractions without distinction, requests that all parties in said countries demand from their Governments free passage for their delegates.

Skobeleff, who moved the report of the Executive Committee of the Council concerning the Socialist conference at Stockholm, said that for the sake of restoring the Internationale and stopping the war he was willing to meet not only Scheidemann but the devil and his grandmother.

The tone adopted by Russian Socialist pacifists is illustrated by Gorky's Novaia Zhizn, which asserts that even if the British and French Socialists refuse to participate in the conference, the Russian Socialists will. The paper adds that in acting otherwise Socialists would violate their direct duty and betray the covenant and traditions of the Internationale.

HOPES FOR PEACE IN SUMMER.

Russian Council's Plans as Reported by Danish Editor.

Special Cable to THE NEW YORK TIMES.

COPENHAGEN, May 11.—The Social Demokraten publishes a telegram from its editor, Borgbjerg, from Haparanda, Sweden, in which he reports upon his peace journey to Petrograd.

He tells how he reached the Russian capital on April 27 and was welcomed by the Workmen's and Soldiers' Council. On following days he had conversations with Chiedse, Skobeleff, and Kerensky, all leaders in the Council. He goes on:

"After the political crisis of May 3 and 4 my appeal to the Russians for participation in the International Socialist Peace Conference was read in the Workmen's and Soldiers' Council. I had received information before my departure from Denmark about the program, on the basis of which the German Socialist Majority and trade unions would participate in the conference.

"On May 8 the Council resumed discussion and voted unanimously to approve the idea of a peace conference.

"In order to obtain support from all countries and factions of the labor movement the Council, which includes all factions, will take charge of the matter and send out invitations. French and English Socialists are certainly expected to come.

"The Council will send a delegation to Stockholm in order to make all the necessary arrangements. It is hopeil that the Peace Conference will be held June 1, and it is expected that it will lead to general peace this Summer."

BERLIN, May 11, (via London.)—Socialists here disclaim all knowledge of authorization or instruction of the Danish Socialist, Borgbjerg, to carry peace proposals to the Russian Socialists. They explain his outline of terms as a volun-

Continued on Page 9.

Fight for Roosevelt's Division to be Carried Back to Congress

Special to The New York Times.

WASHINGTON, May 11.—Notice was given in the House today that an effort would be made tomorrow to reject the conference report on the Army Draft bill because of the elimination of the amendment permitting Theodore Roosevelt to organize a division of volunteers for service in France.

Anxiety was evident among Administration supporters in the House late today over the prospect of a defeat of the conference report. Supporters of the Roosevelt amendment claimed to have made a poll of State delegations which showed the vote would be close and probably against adoption of the report in its present form.

Colonel Roosevelt telegraphed to Senator Harding and Representative Gardner today saying he did not desire to see the Army Draft bill held up because of a fight over his offer to lead an expeditionary force to France. Nevertheless Mr. Gardner will insist on a "showdown" on the Roosevelt issue, and Senator Harding said if the House overturned the conference report the approval of the Roosevelt amendment by both Houses probably would follow quickly.

Representative Lunn of New York, a member of the House Military Affairs Committee, telegraphed to Colonel Roosevelt last night suggesting that he withdraw his offer and not delay final approval of the Army bill. The ex-President replied today as follows:

"Have telegraphed Harding and Gardner, whom please see. Incidentally I would like to point out that if my offer had been accepted when made expeditionary force could have sailed for France tomorrow."

Representative Lenroot of Wisconsin was tentatively selected by the "Roosevelt group" in the House today to make the principal speech tomorrow on the conference report. Others who will insist upon the inclusion of the Roosevelt amendment include Representatives Gardner, Anthony of Kansas, and McCormick of Illinois. Mr. Anthony, one of the House conferees on the Army bill, refused to sign the conference report because of the elimination of the Roosevelt amendment.

Representative Hulbert of New York introduced a bill today to authorize the acceptance of the "Roosevelt volunteers" as a part of the National Guard of the District of Columbia. The District Guard, he said, was a national force, and Colonel Roosevelt could command a division affiliated with the District of Columbia Guard.

With the selective draft feature written into the Army bill, it was said today that a number of Democrats in the House who were opposed to the original Roosevelt amendment were now ready to support it. The situation was such that Administration leaders worked all afternoon enlisting support for the adoption of the conference report.

Announcing that the conference report would take precedence in the House tomorrow, Chairman Dent of the Military Committee attempted today to get an agreement for debate not exceeding two hours. Representative Gardner objected and there was no agreement. Mr. Dent will endeavor to move the previous question on the report after limited debate tomorrow.

"Everybody knows what the fight will be about tomorrow," said Mr. Gardner. "We should have more than two hours to discuss this Roosevelt amendment."

"This is the time for action, not talk. The Army bill has been held up long enough and the country has waited long enough," interjected Representative Sherley of Kentucky.

"Yes, the country has waited three years for preparedness," retored Mr. Gardner. "I don's suppose a few hours will hurt."

DEFENDS TAX BILL AS FORCED BY WAR

Fordney Sees "Some Injustices," but Pledges His Support.

SENATE HEARINGS BEGIN

Emphatic Protests Made by Business Interests—Opposition to Excess Profits Impost.

Special to The New York Times.

WASHINGTON, May 11.—Contending that posterity should bear a large part of the cost of the war with Germany, Representative Joseph W. Fordney, ranking Republican of the Ways and Means Committee, told the House today that he would vote for the $1,800,000,000 war taxation bill, although it satisfied no member of the committee and contained some injustices. Like Representative Kitchin, the Democratic leader, Mr. Fordney said that the committee made no attempt to defend the bill except as a war measure and because "we need the money." He warned the House, however, that there should not be excessive taxation of the present generation and that the taxpayers of thirty or forty years hence should pay much of the war cost. The present war, Mr. Fordney said, was for the peace of the world in the future and the burden ought to be distributed equitably among this and succeeding generations.

During a discussion of the proposed increases in postage on second-class mail matter, Mr. Fordney said that the Ways and Means Committee would offer a committee amendment providing that the salaries of Postmasters should not be increased during the war.

This amendment was drawn at the suggestion of Representative Bland of Indiana, after conferences with officials of the Post Office Department.

The necessity for such an amendment, it was explained, lay in the fact that the salaries of fourth class Postmasters were based on the cancellation receipts of the small Post Office, while the salaries of first, second, and third class Postmasters are based on office receipts. With increased letter, postal card, and second-class mail rates, it was pointed out, salaries would be increased automatically.

In the case of fourth class Postmasters their compensation is to remain on the basis of existing postage rates; that is, by computing each letter and postcard stamped at two and one cents, respectively.

After the conclusion of Mr. Fordney's speech the House debate on the Revenue bill began to lag. There were less than forty members in attendance in the latter part of the afternoon, and the speeches became more or less perfunctory and for home consumption. It is probable that the general debate will be concluded tomorrow afternoon and the bill will be taken up for reading by sections on Monday.

Fordney Analyzes the Bill.

"I am glad to say there was no partisan feeling in the Ways and Means Committee in preparing this bill," said Mr. Fordney in his formal speech. "No man on the committee was satisfied with everything that went into the bill. There are some injustices in the bill, no doubt. The answer to the whole thing is that we must have the money.

"I am going to enter my objections to some of the items in this bill, but I am going to vote for the bill when the time comes. At the time of the civil war there were some 31,000,000 people in this country, two thirds of whom were north of the Mason and Dixon's Line. The entire cost to those 21,000,000 north of that line was $6,-190,000,000, not including money contributed by the various States.

"At this session of Congress we are appropriating from direct taxation and the proceeds of bonds more money than the entire civil war cost the people of the North. It is my opinion that we are making a mistake by imposing upon the people at this time such a large portion of the expense.

Continued on Page 13.

ABOLISH TRADING IN MAY WHEAT

Chicago Board Members Decide on This After Conferences with Government Officials.

PRICE SHOOTS UP TO $3.25

Trading in July and September Wheat Is Not Affected by the Change.

Special to The New York Times.

CHICAGO, May 11.—All trading in May wheat on the Chicago market was discontinued by an unprecedented action taken by directors of the Board of Trade tonight after nearly three hours of discussion. Trading in wheat for delivery in July and September will not be restricted.

All existing contracts in May wheat will be adjusted by delivery of the cash article or by a settling price to be determined by a committee consisting of James A. Patten and the ex-presidents of the board, A. Stamford White, and Hiram N. Sager, who were appointed by President J. P. Griffin.

The action of the Board, while not interfering with the freedom of contract on the part of either individuals or the Government, compels those requiring wheat for immediate consumption to make purchases from farmers and grain dealers rather than through the medium of a contract for future delivery on the floor of the exchange.

The amount of wheat on this market was said to be 180,000 bushels on Saturday and that probably the amount now here was short of those figures.

The decision to call a halt in deals in May wheat futures came as the price had touched $3.25 a bushel, although the close was at but $3.18, an advance of 3 cents for the day. Cash wheat sold to millers at $3.30 to $3.40 a bushel. It compares with $1.29 for May on April 2, since that time the price having jumped 10 to 15 cents a day, the greatest upturn in the history of the trade.

The decision came as a climax to a series of events which, despite refusal of officials to discuss them, are known to have had the closest connection and relative significance. These events were:

United States District Attorney Charles F. Clyne and Special Assistant Attorney Robert W. Childs held an extended conference at the Chicago Club Thursday afternoon with A. G. Anderson, Vice Chairman of the British Royal Food Commission, and Herbert T. Robson, Purchasing Agent for the British Government in the United States.

More than 40 of the most prominent operators on the Chicago Board responded to a call from Mr. Clyne and Mr. Childs this morning and conferred with them regarding the situation.

Mr. Anderson and Mr. Robson held a second conference with the Federal prosecutors this afternoon simultaneously with the Board of Trade Directors' meeting, which resulted in the prohibition of further trading in May futures.

So precarious and delicate was the general situation that the Federal lawyers refused to discuss the matter in any way. Even when the action of the Board Directors was made known, no Government representative of authority could be induced to make a statement. Among those who participated in the conference in Mr. Clyne's office were J. C. F. Merrill, Secretary of the board; John R. Mauff and John J. Stream, Vice Presidents, and Henry H. Dennis and J. Herbert Ware.

The condition of the wheat market, aside from the general investigation of the food situation under way before the April Grand Jury, is known to have had close attention of the Government for several weeks. The continued rise in price and the condition of the market, from the standpoint of future deliveries, had been viewed with growing alarm.

Just what led to the conference with Mr. Anderson and Mr. Robson is a mat-

Continued on Page 20.

PLAN ONE BOARD TO BUY SUPPLIES FOR THE ALLIES

Government Intends to Make Our Billions Loaned Efficient to the Last Cent.

McADOO CONSULTS ENVOYS

Great Britain, France, and Italy Ready, It Is Asserted, to Enter the Agreement.

MAY CHANGE OUR SYSTEM

Government Officials to Control Food, Munitions, and Transportation May Be Named.

Special to The New York Times.

WASHINGTON, May 11.—A program for the reorganization of the whole economic conduct of the war, which will involve the other allied countries as well as the United States, is under consideration by President Wilson and his Cabinet. It contemplates the concentration of authority over the purchase in this country and shipment of war supplies to Europe for all the Allied nations in one commission to consist of business men of the highest standing.

The contemplated radical change of method is intended also to prevent demoralization of food prices in the United States which the Administration fears will be the outcome of present conditions unless a sharp check is applied.

It is believed that as a result of the consideration thus far given to the subject by the Cabinet, which held a meeting this afternoon, the President also will find means to create three executive offices which will administer Food Control, Munitions Control, and Transportation Control.

The Directors of the Departments of Food, Munitions, and Transportation will not have places in the Cabinet, but to all intents and purposes will rank with Cabinet officers. Some differences of opinion exist among the President's advisers as to whether it will be necessary for him to obtain the authority of Congress to appoint these officials. It is contended by members of the Cabinet that the President can create the new departments and make the appointments of their chiefs by an Executive order.

The problem of transportation probably will involve carrying to Europe the army which the United States is raising to send to the front. It is too early yet to make any positive statement with reference to names in connection with the appointment of heads of the contemplated new offices or the purchasing commission, but it is surmised that Daniel Willard, President of the Baltimore & Ohio Railroad, would be placed in charge of transportation, Bernard M. Baruch in charge of munitions, and Herbert C. Hoover in charge of food control. Mr. Willard and Mr. Baruch are members of the Advisory Commission of the Council of National Defense. Mr. Hoover recently returned to this country from Europe, where he had charge of the Belgian relief work. He is in Washington, having been summoned here for consultation with the President concerning food conservation measures.

The practical decision to undertake the proposed radical change of method is in part the outcome of the discussions that have taken place here between officials of the United States Government and members of the British and French War Missions now in this country.

Secretary McAdoo is to draw up the proposed agreement regarding the purchasing commission. He already has held a number of conferences with foreign envoys on the subject. Great Britain, France, and Italy, it is understood, have signified their desire to enter such an agreement, and other Entente Governments are likely to assume the same attitude.

The discussion of the proposed agreement has reached a stage where the chief beneficiaries of the huge American loan have agreed that it would be to the interest of all concerned to eliminate absolutely competition among themselves for American products, and have signified their readiness to pledge themselves to so do. The agreement, when drafted, would have for its aim the attainment of maximum efficiency, both for the Allies and the American Government for every dollar spent in this country for war purposes.

Wide Scope of the Plan.

The commission, when created, would have the widest purchasing powers ever intrusted to any one body in the history of the world. It virtually would be a purchasing agency without parallel. It would eliminate entirely competitive bidding among the Allies and this Government for American products and would seek to insure 100 cents' worth of value for every dollar spent.

By its creation domestic conditions prevalent in this country for the last two decades, under which the big producer gradually by combinations and normal growth assumed the dominance in all markets, with thousands of customers abiding by the price he fixed, would be almost completely reversed. Not the producer, but the buyer would be the dominant factor, for there would be but one buyer for the belligerent nations, and through him all producers in all lines would have to market their wares.

The plan involves no fixing of prices, however. The first efforts will be confined to a program eliminating competitive bidding for the foodstuffs, steel, munitions, clothing, and countless other articles which America alone can supply to the Allies.

To Keep Prices Down.

Were there no check upon the efforts of the Allies to satisfy individual requirements in this country it is realized that their united demands would send

Continued on Page 20.

BRITISH ENVOY'S ARRIVAL

Thousands Fill the Streets to Greet Balfour Mission.

RECEPTION AT CITY HALL

Balfour Holds Out as Reward for America the Glory of Defending Civilization.

SPEAKS IN SOLEMN PHRASE

Choate Recalls Aid Given by Chief Guest Against Germany in Our War with Spain.

The Right Hon. Arthur James Balfour, British Secretary of State for Foreign Affairs, was greeted yesterday by New York on his arrival in the city with other members of the British commission, not as a stranger but as a friend and counselor, come to aid America in a common cause. Landing where the last British soldier left the city in 1783, riding up Broadway between buildings once more flying the Union Jack, and lined with crowds that cheered him as they had cheered the Marshal of France and the Vice President of the French Council of Ministers two days before, he was received at the City Hall as America's old friend.

The Mayor's Committee and guests, assembled in the Aldermanic Chamber of the City Hall, cheered again and again when Mr. Choate referred to Balfour's friendly support of America in 1898, and when Mr. Balfour declared that America would share the trials of the Allies, share their sacrifices and share their triumph.

Around City Hall Park the arrangements for the reception of the British party were the same as those made for the French on Wednesday. Again the Seventh Regiment Band at one end of the plaza, and the band of the Veteran Corps of Artillery at the other, alternated in playing patriotic and military airs while the crowd was waiting for the arrival of the city's guests. Again the lawns across from the entrance to the building were filled with school girls, and the pyramidal structure behind was covered by ranks of Boy Scouts. Again the Old Guard and the officers of Veteran Corps of Artillery in full uniform, with the rank and file of the latter organization in khaki, received the soldiers, sailors, and statesmen of the British mission.

It was a better day for color and spectacle than Wednesday; the sun shone, albeit half-heartedly, and the weather was warm enough to make waiting in the streets something less than a severe hardship. And the colors of the crowd before the City Hall yesterday were effective enough. The deep blue bunting that covered the pyramid and the background wall around it was fronted by the khaki of Boy Scouts, flecked with their colored scarfs. In front the bright green of the Spring grass peeped out here and there, but most of the area was covered with the groups of schoolgirls—2,000 of them—all clad in white middy blouses and dark blue skirts with red hair ribbons; nearly all of them dark-haired, and practically every one carrying some sort of a flag. The Stars and Stripes the French and Italian tricolors, the Union Jack, and the green flag and golden harp of Ireland were all seen in nearly every school unit, together with the orange, white, and blue of the city, and many school or society banners.

Union Jack in Motion.

One boy behind the groups of girls carried a huge Union Jack which he waved vigorously above the crowd as the British delegation entered and left the City Hall. The white groups of girls gave place in the centre to a colmn of Boy Scouts drawn up in front of the pyramid, and these were fronted by the blue-clad band of Public School 21, which with a Boy Scout fife, drum, and bugle corps filled in the intervals when the two adult bands were not playing.

The ravages of fire and weather—for the heavy wind of Thursday night had blown down part of the blue-covered structure opposite the entrance—had been for the most part repaired before the commission arrived. Workmen laboring all night had cleared out wagon loads of débris from the fire which damaged the City Hall on the previous afternoon; the charred timbers and shattered plaster had been carted off, the pools of water through the building had been dried up, furniture and pictures had been restored to their places, and blotches on the walls had been covered with tarpaulins, covered in their turn with bunting. Only the gutted and blackened cupola remained as evidence of the fire of the day before; a cupola, naturally, without its flagstaff, but topped by a small American flag, which had been run up on a halyard the lower end of which was fastened on the roof. It was of necessity a small flag, and in curious contrast to the big banners of Britain and France, the State and the city, which flew from the staffs on the front of the building.

Again City Hall Park was kept clear by police under Inspector Dwyer, while the crowds gathered in immovable masses along Broadway and Park Row and Nassau Street. Again the cornices of the old Post Office were lined with men standing where the view was good, and again the windows of the blocks of skyscrapers on the east and of the Woolworth Building to the southwest were alive with eagerly gazing office

Continued on Page 2.

Copyright Underwood & Underwood, N. Y.

Right Hon. Arthur J. Balfour and Joseph H. Choate.

'Splendid, Wonderful' Says Joffre Admiring the West Point Cadets

"I Have Been Happy," He Adds After a Day of No Speeches and No Ceremony, but Just Soldiers Together Talking Shop.

West Point was taken by Marshal Joffre yesterday afternoon, and Marshal Joffre was captured by West Point. The Marshal passed most of the afternoon on the historic reservation, and in the course of those few hours he saw America's wonderful corps of cadets at their very best; he had a simple luncheon with officers of the regular army, every one of them a West Point graduate, most of whom speak French; he motored through the beautiful wooded highlands behind the point, and when it was all over he said that so long as he might live his afternoon at West Point would be one of the dearest and most cherished memories of his long life.

"I have not had in these last three years," Marshal Joffre said to Colonel John Biddle, Corps of Engineers, U. S. A., Superintendent of the Academy, "very many opportunities to enjoy myself and be happy, but today here at beautiful West Point I have been happy."

The Marshal of France seemed as carefree as a schoolboy and was proud of his West Point allies. There was no possible doubt about that. He went to West Point hoping to be received by his American comrades as just another soldier. He hoped that there would be no elaborate repast with set speeches and much formality. He hoped to see the famous corps of cadets at its best. All these hopes were gratified.

"He has been so happy that it's a pity he has to go so soon," said one of Marshal Joffre's staff officers.

As for the 600 cadets who manoeuvred on the plain for Joffre and who were later inspected by him, after which they passed in review as only West Pointers can, it may be said on authority that Marshal Joffre considers them the finest drilled, most efficient, smartest appearing young officers—that's what the Marshal of France called them—he has ever seen. Some time today an autograph letter from the great French commander will be delivered to Colonel Biddle. In that letter, said Lieutenant de Tessan, Marshal Joffre's personal aid, the Marshal will transmit a message to the West Point Cadets and it will be, said the Lieutenant, "a tribute that will come from the heart." The letter, and this can be said officially, too, will be made a permanent record of the United States Government and will be embodied in a general order which will be read to the corps.

Black Troop Escort.

A finer day than yesterday could not have been asked for a trip to West Point. All morning the whole reservation was on tip-toes, so to speak, in anticipation of the coming of the highest ranking field commander in the world. Other great soldiers from foreign lands, among them England's great Kitchener, have been officially received at West Point and have reviewed the West Point Corps, but never before had the corps been reviewed by a Marshal of France. There were no decorations, and West Point was as it is on every other day in the year, just West Point and nothing more.

At 12:45 the special train bearing the victor of the Marne arrived at the little valley station at the foot of the hill on the crest of which rises the great headquarters building. Drawn up to receive him were the black troopers of the regular army, who are stationed at West Point. Colonel Biddle, Lieut. Col. Guy V. Henry, the Commandant of Cadets; Major C. C. Carter, the Adjutant, and Colonel C. De W. Wilcox, who is the best French linguist in the army, stood on the platform. Wilcox had been detailed to act as the Marshal's aid, and later the Marshal said that in all France he doubted if there was a man who spoke French more fluently than does Colonel Wilcox.

The troopers, every one of them a veteran of the Ninth or Tenth regular cavalry, swung into position just ahead of the leading automobile in which rode Marshal Joffre, Colonel Biddle, Colonel Wilcox, Lieutenant de Tessan, and Lieut. Col. Fabry, the "blue devil of France." The other members of the Marshal's staff were escorted by Colonel Henry, Major Carter, Captain Creswell Garlington, Captain George M. Russell, First Lieutenant Parker C. Kalloch, and First Lieutenant Carl S. Bradford.

As the head of the cavalry column appeared over the crest of the hill a battery of field artillery, stationed near the Battle Monument, began thundering out the Marshal's salute of seventeen guns. The entire Corps of Cadets was in parade formation and in single file, the line of gray coated cadets forming a great semi-circle which extended from the old to the new barracks building. The West Point band was massed on the plain in front of the barracks, and it was the "Marseillaise" that Marshal Joffre heard as he reviewed for the first time the young Americans, perhaps 200 of whom may be fighting for France in France before another year rolls around.

"It is splendid, wonderful," Marshal Joffre exclaimed, as he looked into the faces of that long line of cadets.

For a brief moment the Marshal stopped at the historic residence which has been the home of West Point Superintendents from the days of Robert E. Lee to the present. There he was presented to Mrs. Biddle, and after that he had his first big treat, the army luncheon in the officers' mess hall in the club building, which stands on the cliff just south of Cullum Hall.

All Talked His Own French.

The Marshal reached the mess hall at 1 o'clock, and there awaiting him were the tactical and academic staffs of the Academy. Every arm of the service was represented and the Marshal was immediately at home. Lieutenant de Tessan stood by, expecting to be called into service as an interpreter, and then came another happy surprise for practically every officer present could converse with Joffre in his native tongue.

Colonel Henry, son of the late Major Gen. Guy Henry, who won fame at Santiago, is himself a graduate of the famous French cavalry school at Saumur, and Colonel Wilcox has spent so much of his time in France that he knows the country almost as well as he does his own. Colonel Biddle is another fine French speaker, and so it was all down the line—Joffre had at last found a place in America where he could talk freely to brother officers in arms who understood him, who venerated him, and who were determined to make his afternoon at West Point a memorable incident in his career.

Here are some of the officers who sat with Joffre at that long table in the mess hall: Major Ulysses S. Grant, Colonel Robert E. Lee Michie, Lieut. Col. Henry A. Shaw, Lieut. Col. Edward J. Timberlake, Major George H. Estes, Colonel G. J. Fiebeger, Colonel William B. Gordon, Colonel Charles P. Echols, Colonel Wirt Robinson, Lieut. Col. Edward M. Markham, Lieut. Col. Edward A. Kreger, Lieut. Col. Edwin R. Stuart, Lieut. Col. Lucius H. Holt, Captain Adna R. Chaffee, Captain George R. Goethals, and several scores from the various staffs and departments.

In the mess hall the meals are served on a single long table that reaches almost the length of the room. Everybody sits close and every meal is a family gathering. The waiters are Filipinos, who are as noiseless as they are efficient, and the meals are all army cooked. At this table, and to this kind of meal, Joffre and his staff sat down. The Marshal was at the right of Colonel Biddle, who was at the head of the table, and opposite him sat Colonel Fabry, the Marshal's chief of staff.

Joffre Just Talks Shop.

The Marshal and his hosts remained at the table for more than an hour and a half. There was not a speech, unless a little heart to heart deliverance, in which Joffre talked "shop" to men who understood, can be called a speech. What the Marshal said was not given out, but whatever it was it made a deep impression, and the way it was received was most gratifying to the gray-haired French officer. There was four toasts, one to President Wilson, another to President Poincaré, a third to the armies of France, and the fourth to the regular army of the United States and West Point.

When the French officers and West

Continued on Page 3.

CITY LEADERS THE HOSTS

Call to Do Our Utmost in the War Loudly Cheered.

CRIES OF "LET TEDDY GO!"

Balfour Says the Very Heart of Civilization Is Trembling in the Balance.

VIVIANI ROUSES THE THRONG

Asserts German Kultur Is All Very Well Until Crossed; Then It Is Like a Beast.

A gathering distinguished as even New York has rarely seen before, more than 1,000 of the leaders of the city's public life, business, art, finance, science, and education, gathered at the Waldorf-Astoria last night at the dinner given by the Mayor's Committee to the British and French commissions. At the high table sat with the Mayor and the leading members of the visiting missions two ex-Presidents of the United States, the Governor of New York, the junior United States Senator, and a group of the most prominent men of the city. On the floor were two former Presidential candidates, Charles E. Hughes and Alton B. Parker, great financiers and business men, and the officers and civilians lower in rank of the British and French commissions.

The diners did more than cheer the Mayor's official welcome and the responses of the visitors; they threw their whole enthusiasm into repeated cheers whenever the demand was voiced for immediate and active prosecution of the war, for the sending of American troops as quickly as possible to assist those of Great Britain and France.

Great Applause for Colonel.

When the guests of honor filed in two by two to take their places at the high table the order of march became somewhat disturbed, and Colonel Roosevelt came in almost at the tail of the procession. When the crowd saw him the cheers for Joffre, Viviani, and Balfour, which had rung out as the leaders of the visiting commissions made their way to their seats, rang out again for the Colonel. The crowd had more excuse for cheering when the Colonel shook hands with Marshal Joffre, who sat beside him; and it was with difficulty that it was finally stilled.

Every time the Colonel moved after that somebody cheered him. While the dinner was going on he slipped out for a few minutes to talk to the members of the University of California Ambulance Unit, sailing for France, who were dining in another room in the hotel; and there were cheers from a few devotees as he left his seat and as he returned to it.

When the Mayor in enumerating the list of distinguished guests for the visitors mentioned "two ex-Presidents of the United States," there were clamorous cries of "Teddy! Teddy!" from all parts of the hall. The cries continued long and vigorously and toward the end were mingled with cheers for Taft.

And again the diners had a chance to exercise their lungs for their favorite when Mr. Choate, calling for immediate and vigorous aid to the Allies, cried: "Let Teddy go!"

During most of the dinner the Colonel and Marshal Joffre were engaged in a voluble conversation in French, and those on the floor who speculated as to the subject did not have to guess many times to find an answer that satisfied them.

Cheers for General Wood, Too.

Of other Americans the one who received most applause was Major Gen. Leonard Wood, who, when mentioned by Mayor Mitchel in his Who's Who of the high table, was cheered enthusiastically by all the diners. General J. Franklin Bell, U. S. A., who succeeded General Wood in command of the Department of the East, was absent.

The dinner was arranged by a committee headed by Fire Commissioner Robert Adamson, which had the painful duty of turning down thousands of requests for seats from persons who applied too late. It was held in the grand ballroom, where in 1902 another dinner, which at the time was believed by many people to be the beginning of a new era in American affairs, was given for Prince Henry of Prussia. But the dinner on that occasion was far more sumptuous. Last night, because the committee wanted to give an example of the economies rendered desirable by war conditions, there was a simple menu of five courses, most of them characteristically American—the simplest ever served at a great public function in the history of the Waldorf.

The diners began with cherrystone clams. Then came pepper pot [illegible], Delaware planked shad, cucumber [illegible], squab chicken roasted with sweet potatoes, strawberry ice cream and petits

Mid-Week Pictorial

Major Gen. John J. Pershing (right), Commander in Chief of the American expeditionary force on the western front.

"All the News That's Fit to Print."

The New York Times.

THE WEATHER
Generally fair today and Sunday; moderate west to variable winds.
For full weather report see Page 19.

VOL. LXVI...NO. 21,665. NEW YORK, SATURDAY, MAY 19, 1917.—TWENTY PAGES. ONE CENT In Greater New York. | TWO CENTS Elsewhere N. Y. State, N. J., Conn. | THREE CENTS Other States.

PRESIDENT CALLS THE NATION TO ARMS; DRAFT BILL SIGNED; REGISTRATION ON JUNE 5; REGULARS UNDER PERSHING TO GO TO FRANCE

A Proclamation by the President of the United States

Executive Mansion, Washington, D. C., May 18, 1917.

Whereas, Congress has enacted and the President has on the 18th day of May, one thousand nine hundred and seventeen, approved a law, which contains the following provisions:

SECTION 5.—That all male persons between the ages of 21 and 30, both inclusive, shall be subject to registration in accordance with regulations to be prescribed by the President: And upon proclamation by the President or other public notice given by him or by his direction stating the time and place of such registration, it shall be the duty of all persons of the designated ages, except officers and enlisted men of the regular army, the navy, and the National Guard and Naval Militia while in the service of the United States, to present themselves for and submit to registration under the provisions of this act: And every such person shall be deemed to have notice of the requirements of this act upon the publication of said proclamation or other notice as aforesaid, given by the President or by his direction: And any person who shall willfully fail or refuse to present himself for registration or to submit thereto as herein provided, shall be guilty of a misdemeanor and shall, upon conviction in the District Court of the United States having jurisdiction thereof, be punished by imprisonment for not more than one year, and shall thereupon be duly registered; provided that in the call of the docket precedence shall be given, in courts trying the same, to the trial of criminal proceedings under this act; provided, further, that persons shall be subject to registration as herein provided, who shall have attained their twenty-first birthday and who shall not have attained their thirty-first birthday on or before the day set for the registration; and all persons so registered shall be and remain subject to draft into the forces hereby authorized unless excepted or excused therefrom as in this act provided; provided further, that in the case of temporary absence from actual place of legal residence of any person liable to registration as provided herein, such registration may be made by mail under regulations to be prescribed by the President.

SECTION 6.—That the President is hereby authorized to utilize the service of any or all departments and any or all officers or agents of the United States and of the several States, territories, and the District of Columbia and subdivisions thereof in the execution of this act, and all officers and agents of the United States and of the several States, territories, and subdivisions thereof, and of the District of Columbia; and all persons designated or appointed under regulations prescribed by the President, whether such appointments are made by the President himself or by the Governor or other officer of any State or territory to perform any duty in the execution of this act, are hereby required to perform such duty as the President shall order or direct, and all such officers and agents and persons so designated or appointed shall hereby have full authority for all acts done by them in the execution of this act by the direction of the President. Correspondence in the execution of this act may be carried in penalty envelopes, bearing the frank of the War Department. Any person charged, as herein provided, with the duty of carrying into effect any of the provisions of this act or the regulations made or directions given thereunder who shall fail or neglect to perform such duty, and any person charged with such duty or having and exercising any authority under said act, regulations, or directions, who shall knowingly make or be a party to the making of any false or incorrect registration, physical examination, exemption, enlistment, enrollment, or muster, and any person who shall make or be a party to the making of any false statement or certificate as to the fitness or liability of himself or any other person for service under the provisions of this act, or regulations made by the President thereunder, or otherwise evades or aids another to evade the requirements of this act or of said regulations, or who, in any manner, shall fail or neglect fully to perform any duty required of him in the execution of this act, shall, if not subject to military law, be guilty of a misdemeanor, and upon conviction in the District Court of the United States, having jurisdiction thereof, be punished by imprisonment for not more than one year, or, if subject to military law, shall be tried by court-martial and suffer such punishment as a court-martial may direct.

Now, Therefore, I, Woodrow Wilson, President of the United States, do call upon the Governor of each of the several States and Territories, the Board of Commissioners of the District of Columbia, and all officers and agents of the several States and Territories, of the District of Columbia, and of the counties and municipalities therein, to perform certain duties in the execution of the foregoing law, which duties will be communicated to them directly in regulations of even date herewith.

And I do further proclaim and give notice to all persons subject to registration in the several States and in the District of Columbia in accordance with the above law, that the time and place of such registration shall be between 7 A. M. and 7 P. M. on the fifth day of June, 1917, at the registration place in the precinct wherein they have their permanent homes. Those who shall have attained their twenty-first birthday and who shall not have attained their thirty-first birthday on or before the day here named are required to register, excepting only officers and enlisted men of the regular army, the navy, the Marine Corps, and the National Guard and Naval Militia, while in the service of the United States, and officers in the Officers' Reserve Corps and enlisted men in the Enlisted Reserve Corps while in active service. In the territories of Alaska, Hawaii, and Porto Rico a day for registration will be named in a later proclamation.

And I do charge those who through sickness shall be unable to present themselves for registration that they apply on or before the day of registration to the County Clerk of the County where they may be for instructions as to how they may be registered by agent. Those who expect to be absent on the day named from the counties in which they have their permanent homes may register by mail, but their mailed registration cards must reach the places in which they have their permanent homes by the day named herein. They should apply as soon as practicable to the County Clerk of the county wherein they may be for instructions as to how they may accomplish their registration by mail. In case such persons as, through sickness or absence, may be unable to present themselves personally for registration shall be sojourning in cities of over 30,000 population, they shall apply to the City Clerk of the city wherein they may be sojourning rather than to the Clerk of the County. The Clerks of counties and of cities of over 30,000 population in which numerous applications from the sick and from non-residents are expected are authorized to establish such agencies and to employ and deputize such clerical force as may be necessary to accommodate these applications.

The Power against which we are arrayed has sought to impose its will upon the world by force. To this end it has increased armament until it has changed the face of war. In the sense in which we have been wont to think of armies, there are no armies in this struggle, there are entire nations armed. Thus, the men who remain to till the soil and man the factories are no less a part of the army that is France than the men beneath the battle flags. It must be so with us. It is not an army that we must shape and train for war; it is a nation.

To this end our people must draw close in one compact front against a common foe. But this cannot be if each man pursues a private purpose. All must pursue one purpose. The nation needs all men; but it needs each man, not in the field that will most pleasure him, but in the endeavor that will best serve the common good. Thus, though a sharpshooter pleases to operate a trip-hammer for the forging of great guns and an expert machinist desires to march with the flag, the nation is being served only when the sharpshooter marches and the machinist remains at his levers.

The whole nation must be a team, in which each man shall play the part for which he is best fitted. To this end, Congress has provided that the nation shall be organized for war by selection; that each man shall be classified for service in the place to which it shall best serve the general good to call him.

The significance of this cannot be overstated. It is a new thing in our history and a landmark in our progress. It is a new manner of accepting and vitalizing our duty to give ourselves with thoughtful devotion to the common purpose of us all. It is in no sense a conscription of the unwilling; it is, rather, selection from a nation which has volunteered in mass. It is no more a choosing of those who shall march with the colors than it is a selection of those who shall serve an equally necessary and devoted purpose in the industries that lie behind the battle line.

The day here named is the time upon which all shall present themselves for assignment to their tasks. It is for that reason destined to be remembered as one of the most conspicuous moments in our history. It is nothing less than the day upon which the manhood of the country shall step forward in one solid rank in defense of the ideals to which this nation is consecrated. It is important to those ideals no less than to the pride of this generation in manifesting its devotion to them, that there be no gaps in the ranks.

It is essential that the day be approached in thoughtful apprehension of its significance, and that we accord to it the honor and the meaning that it deserves. Our industrial need prescribes that it be not made a technical holiday, but the stern sacrifice that is before us urges that it be carried in all our hearts as a great day of patriotic devotion and obligation, when the duty shall lie upon every man, whether he is himself to be registered or not, to see to it that the name of every male person of the designated ages is written on these lists of honor.

In Witness Whereof, I have hereunto set my hand and caused the seal of the United States to be affixed. Done at the City of Washington this 18th day of May in the year of our Lord one thousand nine hundred and seventeen, and of the independence of the United States of America the one hundred and forty-first.

WOODROW WILSON.

By the President:
ROBERT LANSING, Secretary of State.

WILL NOT SEND ROOSEVELT

Wilson Not to Avail Himself of Volunteer Authority at Present.

COMMENDS THE COLONEL

But Declares the Business at Hand Is Scientific and for Trained Men Only.

SAYS RESPONSIBILITY IS HIS

Sending of Pershing Division Believed to be in Direct Response to France's Call.

Special to The New York Times.

WASHINGTON, May 18.—Announcement was made at the War Department tonight by Secretary Baker that an expeditionary force of approximately one division of regular troops, under Major General John J. Pershing had been ordered to proceed to France on as early date as practicable. General Pershing and his staff will precede the troops to the fighting area.

Shortly before this announcement came from Secretary Baker, the White House gave to the press a statement from President Wilson in which he said that he would not avail himself, "at any rate at the present stage of the war," of the authority conferred by the Military Selective Draft act, which he had just approved, to organize volunteer divisions.

While referring in complimentary terms to Colonel Roosevelt's public service and gallantry, the President made it plain that he was entirely out of sympathy with the Roosevelt proposal that volunteers be sent to France without delay.

"Politically, too," said the President, "it would no doubt have a very fine effect and make a profound impression," but he added that "the business now at hand is undramatic, practical, and of scientific directness and precision." The President indicated that he did not regard Colonel Roosevelt as a military expert. He also stressed the point that upon the Executive rested the responsibility for the successful conduct of the war, and that he intended to be influenced by considerations along that line and let everything else wait.

It is apparent from President Wilson's statement that his present state of mind is strongly opposed to sending Colonel Roosevelt or any volunteer force to France.

The official announcement that an expeditionary force of regular troops would be sent to France "at as early date as possible" was handed to newspaper men at the War Department by Major Douglas MacArthur of the General Staff at 9:30 o'clock with the injunctions that it was not to be published through extra editions or otherwise until 10 o'clock. The statement containing this important announcement follows:

"The President has directed an expeditionary force of approximately one division of regular troops under command of Major Gen. John J. Pershing to proceed to France at as early a date as practicable. General Pershing and staff will precede the troops abroad. It is requested that no details or speculations with regard to the mobilization of this command, dates of departure, composition, or other items, be carried by the press, other than the official bulletins given out by the War Department relating thereto."

The President's Statement.

The President's statement regarding Colonel Roosevelt follows:

"I shall not avail myself, at any rate at the present stage of the war, of the authorization conferred by the act to organize volunteer divisions. To do so would seriously interfere with the carrying out of the chief and most immediately important purpose contemplated by this legislation, the prompt creation and early use of an effective army, and would contribute practically nothing to the effective strength of the armies now engaged against Germany.

"I understand that the section of this act which authorizes the creation of volunteer divisions in addition to the draft was added with a view to providing an independent command for Mr. Roosevelt and giving the military authority an opportunity to use his fine vigor and enthusiasm in recruiting forces now at the Western front.

"It would be very agreeable to me to pay Mr. Roosevelt this compliment and the Allies the compliment of sending to their aid one of our most distinguished public men, an ex-President who has

Continued on Page 2.

PLANS FOR NATIONAL ARMY

First Draft of 500,000 Men to be Divided Into Sixteen Divisions.

MILITIA SIMILARLY PLACED

Arrangement of Concentration Camps Will Be Near Home Regions of Units.

CALLS OUT NATIONAL GUARD

Entire Force to Mobilize and Recruit to War Strength, Beginning on July 15.

Special to The New York Times.

WASHINGTON, May 18.—President Wilson, tonight at 10 o'clock, issued his proclamation fixing June 5 as the day on which registration is to take place for the national army of 500,000 men to be drafted under authority of the Draft bill, which he signed tonight. On this date all men in the country between the ages of 21 and 30 years, inclusive, will be required to present themselves for registration. Those away from home will register by mail, according to the terms of the proclamation. The registration date for Hawaii, Alaska, and Porto Rico will be announced later.

The President's proclamation sets forth in detail the plans for registration and was telegraphed tonight by the War Department to all parts of the country official posting and publication. It is so as to have the widest publicity by expected that the registration will occupy about five days. After that those entitled to exemption will be excluded from the draft. About 10,000,000 men between 21 and 30, inclusive, are expected to be registered. After the registration and exemptions have been completed, those declared to be eligible for drafting will have their names placed in jury wheels and 500,000 will be drafted for Federal service in the formation of the new national army.

Plans for the formation of the new army have been completed. It will be divided into sixteen divisions, each to consist of 28,000 men. They will be mobilized in sixteen concentration camps, the names of which soon will be announced. The draft army will be officially known as the National Army, in contradistinction to the regular army and the National Guard army. These National Army divisions will be numbered consecutively from one to sixteen.

New York and Pennsylvania will furnish enough men in the draft to form three National Army divisions, exclusive of what they will furnish for the regular army and the National Guard army. New York and Pennsylvania will each furnish about a division and a half for the National Army. The only other State to furnish as much as a division for the National Army will be Illinois. Seven Pacific Coast States, where the population is not so dense, will furnish the sixteenth National Army division.

Distribution of Divisions.

The distribution of the divisions, according to the States that will form them, will be as follows:

First—Massachusetts, Maine, Connecticut, Rhode Island, Vermont, and New Hampshire.
Second—Lower New York State and Long Island.
Third—Upper New York State and Northern Pennsylvania.
Fourth—Southern Pennsylvania.
Fifth—Virginia, Maryland, Delaware, New Jersey, and District of Columbia.
Sixth—Tennessee, North Carolina, and South Carolina.
Seventh—Alabama, Georgia, and Florida.
Eighth—Ohio and West Virginia.
Ninth—Indiana and Kentucky.
Tenth—Wisconsin and Michigan.
Eleventh—Illinois.
Twelfth—Arkansas, Mississippi, and Louisiana.
Thirteenth—North Dakota, South Dakota, Nebraska, Minnesota, and Iowa.
Fourteenth—Colorado, Kansas, and Missouri.
Fifteenth—Arizona, New Mexico, Texas, and Oklahoma.
Sixteenth—Washington, Oregon, Idaho, Montana, California, Nevada, and Utah.

Calls Out the Guard.

President Wilson also issued orders today for the mobilization of the entire National Guard of the country. Instructions were sent to the Adjutant General of the States to the effect that the National Guard not now in Federal service and enlisted men of the National Guard Reserve would be drafted into the Federal service on various dates, ranging from July 15 to Aug. 5. All National Guard coast artillery will be drafted on July 15. The organizations will be held at their rendezvous for about two weeks and will then be sent to concentration camps in the Southern, Southeastern, and Western Departments for training.

There are now 60,000 National Guardsmen in Federal service. There are more than 100,000 not yet in Federal service. These are to be called into Federal service under the orders issued today. New National Guard units will also be formed and all the guard units [illegible] expanded until 400,000 men [illegible] obtained. This will be desi[illegible] National Guard Army, [illegible]

Treasury Plans to Let the Banks Keep Funds Paid for Liberty Bonds

Institutions Subscribing $100,000 Favored—Subscriptions for the Bonds Increase Here—Bank of Commerce Takes $10,000,000 of the Issue.

Special to The New York Times.

WASHINGTON, May 18.—To avoid any disturbance of the money market in placing the Liberty Loan of 1917, the Treasury Department today, in behalf of Secretary McAdoo, who is out of town, issued a circular to banks and trust companies urging that they should buy Treasury certificates in as large amount as practicable, and at least to half their estimated subscriptions, for the new bonds. In the circular, to which his name was signed, Secretary McAdoo also suggested that banks having to make payments for $100,000 or more of bonds, and having qualified as depositaries, will be permitted to cover their payments, in excess of the amount of Treasury certificates taken by them, by placing credit on their books to the account of the Treasurer of the United States.

An indication of the extent to which employers of large forces of men and women are buying Liberty Loan bonds for their employes and permitting payments in small installments was given today when it was learned from one distributing firm in New York that fifty-two corporations either have adopted this plan of aiding their employes or were considering it. Of the fifty-two corporations, thirty-nine reported their number of employes as approximating 163,327. The other thirteen did not report the number of their workers.

California Takes $500,000.

The State of California set an example for other States today by subscribing to $500,000 of the Liberty Loan. Accompanying the application for the bonds was a statement to the effect that the State would take more later.

A subscription for $380,000 of Liberty Loan bonds was made by the Driggs-Seabury Ordnance Company of Utica, N. Y., and Sharon, Penn., makers of the Lewis machine gun, which has large contracts with the Government.

The Treasury circular, issued today, which was signed by Secretary McAdoo, was as follows:

"Banks and trust companies having payments to make on account of subscriptions, and which have qualified as depositaries, may make payment upon such subscriptions on June 28 as to any amounts not paid in Treasury certificates of indebtedness by credit on their books to the account of the Treasurer of the United States, of which credit notice will be given in duplicate to the Treasurer and to the Federal Reserve Bank of the district on or before June 28.

"The amounts so credited will be withdrawn from time to time as required. How long they may be permitted to remain will depend in large measure on the extent to which the privilege of prepayment for the bonds of the Liberty Loan on or before June 28 is availed of. It will be necessary that the early installments paid upon subscriptions to the loan be devoted largely to the payment of the short-term Treasury certificates of indebtedness, which have been and will be placed throughout the country chiefly for making loans to Governments engaged in making war against Germany, and in part to meet unusual war expenditures of our own Government.

Shifting of Credits.

"As practically all the proceeds of the Liberty Loan, whether advanced to foreign Governments or expended directly by departments of the United States, will be spent in this country in payment of indebtedness heretofore or hereafter incurred, the bank resources of the United States as a whole will not be diminished, and the operation involves only a shifting of credits.

"Because of the great amount of work involved in passing upon the qualifications and securities of the banks and trust companies, which will have payments to make, it is deemed necessary until after July 1 to limit to those banks and trust companies having payments to make on subscriptions for $100,000 or more bonds, the provision for making payment by credit, the object in providing for payment by credit being to avoid any disturbance in the money position which might result from large payments being made from June 28 to Monday, July 2, a period when there is customarily a heavy movement of funds due to corporate interest and other payments.

Proceeds to Be Redeposited.

"As soon after July 2 as practicable the qualifications and securities of other banks and trust companies desiring to participate in redeposits will be passed upon, and after provision has been made for the immediate disbursements which the United States will have to make, up to and including July 1, the proceeds of the loan received from time to time, in full or installment payments, will be redeposited with qualified banks and trust companies in a proportion, yet to be determined, based upon the amounts of bonds of the Liberty Loan for which

Continued on Page 11.

Bethmann and Czernin to Confer With the Kaiser

BERLIN, May 18, (via London.)—Chancellor von Bethmann Hollweg and Dr. Zimmermann, the Foreign Minister, left today for German Great Headquarters, where they will meet Count Czernin, the Austro-Hungarian Foreign Secretary. They will continue the conference begun at Vienna recently, when Dr. von Bethmann Hollweg visited there.

The Tageblatt says that it understands that the Polish question and details in connection with the proclamation issued on Nov. 5, 1916, concerning Poland will be discussed.

The Reichstag will reconvene on July 5 for a three days' session, which will comprise the Summer legislative period.

CAMERONIA SUNK; 140 ON BOARD LOST

10,000-Ton Anchor Liner Had Been Used as a Troopship by the British Admiralty.

STAYED AFLOAT 40 MINUTES

Troops Escaped by Jumping to Destroyers—Announcement of Loss Long Delayed.

LONDON, May 17, (Delayed by Censor.)—The British Admiralty announced today that the transport Cameronia has been sunk. The statement follows:

"The British transport Cameronia, with troops, was torpedoed by an enemy submarine in the Eastern Mediterranean on April 15. One hundred and forty men are missing and are presumed to have been drowned."

The survivors of the Cameronia say the vessel was torpedoed in fine, calm weather in the afternoon. The submarine was not seen.

A large number of casualties were due to the explosion of the torpedo, which struck where there happened to be many soldiers. There was some excitement and confusion at the outset after the torpedo had struck, but discipline soon prevailed. The boats were launched, but one of them was smashed, and many lives were lost.

The Cameronia was afloat for forty minutes after she was torpedoed, which enabled several destroyers to run alongside. Soldiers from the Cameronia jumped on these boats in disciplined succession. The destroyers ceased taking on men as soon as they had ob-

Continued on Page 3.

SEA-AND-AIR FIGHT IN THE ADRIATIC

Austrian Light Cruisers Raid Allied Drifter Line and Sink 14 British Minesweepers.

CHASED TO THEIR OWN PORT

Italian Airmen Aiding—British Cruiser Torpedoed and an Italian Destroyer Sunk.

LONDON, May 18.—The British Admiralty announced today that fourteen drifters had been sunk in a raid by Austrian light cruisers in the Adriatic Sea and that the British light cruiser Dartmouth was torpedoed in a subsequent engagement with the Austrian warships, but reached port safely.

The Admiralty said that the British warships Dartmouth and Bristol pursued the Austrian vessels to a point near Cattaro when, battleships coming to their assistance, the British vessels were compelled to withdraw. The text of the statement reads:

"The Admiralty announces that from reports received from the Rear Admiral commanding the Adriatic squadron, supplemented by the Italian official communication, it appears that cruisers, subsequently reinforced by destroyers, raided the allied drifter line and succeeded in sinking fourteen British drifters, from which, according to the Austrian communication, seventy-two prisoners were taken.

"His Majesty's ship Dartmouth, with the Italian Rear Admiral aboard, and H. M. S. Bristol immediately chased the

Continued on Page 3.

Committee Rejects McAdoo's Plan to Levy $445,000,000 More Taxes

Zone Postal Plan May Be Stricken from the Taxation Bill—House Approves Higher Excess Profits and Retroactive Income Imposts.

Special to The New York Times.

WASHINGTON, May 18.—Prior to the convening of the House today the Committee on Ways and Means decided that it would not attempt to raise, at this time, the additional $445,000,000 in indirect taxes requested yesterday in Secretary McAdoo's communication to Chairman Kitchin. Republican members of the committee, as well as some Democrats, rebelled against the proposal to revamp the War Taxation bill and greatly add to its total after the committee had spent weeks in preparing a measure to produce $1,800,000,000.

The House when it met showed a disposition to stand by the bill as presented by the committee. The retroactive income tax section was approved by a vote of 123 to 54, all proposed amendments being rejected. The House likewise approved the excess profits tax carried in the bill, defeating various amendments to reduce and to increase the tax.

That a majority of the members of the Ways and Means Committee have practically reached the conclusion that there should be a change in the second-class mail postage rates recommended in the bill was learned today. Before the bill is put on final passage the committee is to hold another meeting to consider a revision of these rates. The indications are that the "zone system" rates will be stricken from the bill, and the committee will offer an amendment carrying out the suggestion of Chairman Moon of the House Committee on Post Office, reading as follows:

Strike out the section (the zone system section) and insert: Upon all newspapers, magazines and other publications regularly admitted as matter of the second class, when mailed by the publisher and no other, 1 cent per pound. Provided, that parcel post rates shall be charged upon all that portion of such newspapers, magazines or other publications which is devoted to paid advertising matter when addressed to any Post Office in the third, fourth, fifth, sixth, seventh, or eighth zones.

Certain members of the committee believe that the Moon amendment will not only produce more revenue, but that it also has a better chance of approval in the House than the original committee proposal, which calls for a flat rate on all second class matter, fixed by zones, ranging from 2 to 6 cents a pound. In the general debate on the Revenue bill the argument was repeatedly made that the Government was carrying advertising matter at a great loss and the levy in postage should be against the advertising rather than the news sections of publications.

If the Moon amendment should be adopted the postal rate legislation will be less burdensome upon newspapers than magazines. Newspapers circulating within a comparatively limited field would not be materially affected. Periodicals and magazines with a country-wide circulation and a surplus of advertising matter would be hard hit by a levy of parcel post rates against the aggregate weight of all the advertising columns.

Excess Profits Tax Approved.

The House made fair progress today in its consideration of the tax measure. It approved the excess profits section and those portions of the bill levying additional taxes on beverages and tobaccos. The House reached but did not dispose of the sections imposing a 5 per cent. tax on various articles, including automobiles and musical instruments.

The Ways and Means Committee has agreed to consider the advisability of modifying the 5 per cent. levy on automobiles. This proposed tax has been strongly opposed by the automobile interests. No assurance has been given by the committee, however, that it will agree to a modification of the tax, but the question will be taken up in committee tomorrow, according to present plans.

Representative Madden of Illinois led an unsuccessful fight against the retroactive tax on incomes. This section provides that there shall be assessed against incomes for the calendar year 1916 an additional tax of one-third of the tax already paid. Under the section each person who has paid a tax on 1916 incomes would have to pay prior to Sept. 15 next, an amount equal to 33 1-3 per cent. of the original levy.

Nevertheless the House adopted the retroactive tax which the Ways and Means Committee estimates will produce $108,000,000.

Wet and Dry Forces Clash.

Wet and dry forces clashed for almost two hours today over an amendment by Representative Howard of Georgia, designed to eliminate the liquor tax increases. Representatives Howard, Cooper of Ohio, Hersey of Maine, and others maintained that the liquor interests were indorsing the proposed increases, hoping thus to strengthen their position against absolute prohibition. The amendment was overwhelmingly defeated. The section as it was approved increases the tax on whisky from $1.10 to $2.20 a gallon and that on beer from $1.25 to $2.50.

Only a perfunctory fight was made on the excess profits tax section. Its opponents will carry their objection to the Senate. Representative Good of Iowa made the chief opposition, offering an amendment patterned somewhat after the English law, but it was decisively beaten.

"All the News That's Fit to Print."

The New York Times.

THE WEATHER
Probably fair today; Friday thunder storms; moderate west winds.
For full weather report see Page 21.

VOL. LXVI...NO. 21,705. NEW YORK, THURSDAY, JUNE 28, 1917.—TWENTY-TWO PAGES. ONE CENT In Greater New York. | TWO CENTS Elsewhere N. Y. State, N. J., Conn. | THREE CENTS Other States.

FIRST AMERICAN TROOPS REACH FRANCE, SETTING RECORD FOR QUICK MOVEMENT; FRANTIC CROWDS CHEER THEIR LANDING

HUNT FOR REFUGE WHERE COCCHI HID AFTER THE MURDER

Prosecutor Finds Mysterious Entries in Records of an Immigrants' Home.

CLUE FROM MRS. COCCHI

Hurried Alteration of the Register Starts an Investigation by the District Attorney.

POLICE DELAYS ARE SHOWN

Many Hours Were Wasted in Cruger Case Before Machinery Was Set in Motion.

Acting on information furnished by Mrs. Marie Cocchi to the effect that she had learned from friends in Italy that her husband, Alfredo, had stayed in New York at least six days after the disappearance of Ruth Cruger on Feb. 13 last, Assistant District Attorney John T. Dooling sent Detective John Cunniff to examine the register at the home of the Society for Italian Immigrants, at 10 Water Street, where it had been suggested he might have hidden after his visit to Father Morretto of St. Raphael's Society. Cunniff reported yesterday that the register showed that one Francisco Ramella had entered the home on the afternoon of Feb. 15 and was registered as coming from Pensacola, Fla. He said that the same name was found on the record for Feb. 16 and every day thereafter until Feb. 20, when the register said the man had left for Europe on the Verdi.

The entry for Feb. 16, the detective reported, said that Ramella came from New York. The entry on the following day said that Ramella had purchased a ticket for $50 for Genoa.

When the register was brought to the District Attorney's office yesterday in response to a subpoena, an examination showed that the entry for Feb. 16 had been changed to read "from Philadelphia." The ink was plainly fresh, Mr. Dooling said, and the former entry was plainly distinguishable underneath it. Joseph Biondi, the bookkeeper of the home was sent for, and when questioned he asserted that he had been ordered to change the record by August V. Tozzi, the assistant manager of the institution. This was later denied by Tozzi, who was questioned by Mr. Dooling for an hour. Tozzi was unable to identify a picture of Cocchi. Subpoenas have been issued for several other officials and all of the employes of the home, who will be examined today.

Mrs. Cocchi Again a Witness.

At the request of Mrs. Cocchi, who was a witness again yesterday, Father Morretto came to the District Attorney's office and conversed privately with her for a half hour. Mr. Dooling was unable to say whether the visit was of a religious nature or not, as Mrs. Cocchi did not make any statement concerning what she wanted of Father Morretto. According to Aaron Marcus, Mrs. Cocchi's attorney, the priest would not discuss her husband's case with her. Mr. Marcus took issue with Father Morretto's statement that he had not seen or talked with Mrs. Cocchi in several years. He said that about six weeks ago Mrs. Cocchi telephoned to the priest and asked him to send her a mechanic to work in the motor cycle shop. Father Morretto at that time recalled who Mrs. Cocchi was, the lawyer said, and sent her a man, whom she employed.

District Attorney Swann said yesterday that Inspector Faurot and Detective Mahoney had held a conference with Assistant District Attorney Rorke in regard to the story told by Louise La Rue, now in the Polyclinic Hospital recovering from injuries she received in her jump from a window. Mr. Swann said that thus far nothing had been discovered which would throw any new light on the Cruger case. Mrs. La Rue had furnished the names of many prominent men who she said were among her acquaintances. Several of these men Mr. Swann said had been to see him in regard to preventing their names from being made public.

In a statement last night Mr. Swann charged that Detective Frank McGee had suggested to Mrs. Louisa Patterson, a friend of Mrs. Cocchi, that she get in touch with the City Club, which preferred charges against the District Attorney, and enlist its aid in keeping process servers away from Mrs. Cocchi's house. Mrs. Cocchi had complained to Mrs. Patterson that she was being annoyed by Mr. Swann's employes, who she said watched her day and night.

Acting on McGee's suggestion, Mrs. Patterson wrote to Nelson S. Spencer, President of the City Club, asking his help. In the reply which Mr. Swann made public Mr. Spencer said that Mrs. Patterson's complaint was "in line with other reports which have come to us."

Mr. Spencer referred the matter to Chase Mellen, counsel for the club.

Wallstein Presses Police Lieutenant.

The public examination of witnesses conducted yesterday by Leonard M. Wallstein, Commissioner of Accounts, in his office in the Municipal Building in the course of his investigation into the Police Department's management of the Cruger case had two sharp developments. First, according to testimony Police Lieutenant William Brown, who was in charge of the desk of the Fourth Branch Detective Bureau when the disappearance of Ruth Cruger was reported there by Mr. and Mrs.

Continued on Page 9.

Leather and Paper Fibre Used in Germans' Uniforms

Special Cable to THE NEW YORK TIMES.

LONDON, June 27.—Striking evidence of the growing straits of the German Army, a high official informed THE NEW YORK TIMES correspondent, was obtained recently from captured prisoners. Their clothing excited curiosity from its appearance, so it was analyzed. It was discovered that officers are now wearing woven cloth of leather fibre and enlisted men uniforms of paper fibre.

It is evident that such clothing is entirely unsuited to the rigors of a Winter campaign if the war lasts that long.

COAL OPERATORS FOR PRICE FIXING

Special Committee Approves Proposal for a Joint Governmental Board.

TRADE TO BE REPRESENTED

Secretary of the Interior and Federal Trade Commission to Join in Control.

WASHINGTON, June 27.—A proposal that coal prices during the war be fixed by a joint governmental commission, composed of the Secretary of the Interior, the Defense Council's Coal Production Committee, and the Federal Trade Commission, was approved tonight by a special committee of coal operators representing the trade in all sections of the country.

Tomorrow a resolution embodying this plan will be submitted to the convention of 400 operators meeting here for discussion of the problem, and indications are that it will be accepted. It then may be presented as a substitute for pending legislation proposing blanket authority for Government price fixing on the commodity, and backed by the operators as a compromise adjustment satisfactory both to producers and consumers.

The convention appointed the special committee after it had voted to reconsider a resolution adopted yesterday pledging the operators to insure proper prices through committees of their number working in conference with the coal production committee of the Defense Council. The reconsideration was decided on after speakers pointed out that such a procedure might make the operators liable to prosecution under the Sherman anti-monopoly law.

On the special committee was one operator from each coal State, Chairman Peabody of the Production Committee, and Commissioner Fort of the Federal Trade Commission. In support of the plan approved, it was argued that the proposed joint commission would not leave the trade without representation in the price-fixing, since a number of operators are members of the Production Committee.

The coal men, in appointing Commissioner Fort a member of the special committee, gave expression to an apparent feeling of reassurance as to the friendliness of the trade commission. In an address to the convention a short time before, the Commissioner had declared he and his colleagues were loath to fix prices at all and would not do so without giving the producers every opportunity to present their side of the case. He was loudly cheered.

Thirty per cent. of the embarrassment in the coal trade, the Commissioner said, was due to lack of transportation facilities. The commission, he assured the operators, had no intention of figuring coal costs down to a cent or five cents. It already was undertaking to determine coal production costs at the request of Secretary Daniels.

When the convention was in session the Senate Interstate Commerce Commission continued its hearing of operators and others on the bill giving blanket Government authority to fix the price of coal and railroad supplies. Most of the operators who appeared expressed a willingness to submit to reasonable Government regulation, but insisted that they were not responsible for high coal prices and should not be the objects of any punitive legislation.

William H. Mehlich of New York charged that in the city speculators controlled the coal output. It was impossible to get anthracite at all, he said, and the prices of other grades were high.

TILSON DESCRIBES GAS WARFARE TO HOUSE

Demonstrates Use of Gas Masks and Urges Large Grant for Aviation.

Special to The New York Times.

WASHINGTON, June 27.—Expressing the belief that "our road to victory is through the air" Representative John Q. Tilson of Connecticut, a member of the Military Affairs Committee, spoke for an hour in the House today on aviation and the use of gas in the European war. Mr. Tilson brought into the chamber three gas masks, such as are now being used by the Allies, and demonstrated their use.

The spending of a billion dollars or more, if necessary, for aviation was urged by Mr. Tilson, who said that the most vigorous sort of aerial warfare should be conducted against the Germans. Mr. Tilson was not an advocate of "frightfulness," but warned the House that desperate measures must be met by desperate measures.

Mr. Tilson, who served in the Spanish-American war and on the Mexican border, said the United States should put 100,000 airplanes over European battlefields "to blind the eyes of our enemy."

In a recent speech Mr. Tilson told of the invention by a young Pennsylvanian of a fragmentation bomb to be dropped from airplanes which would explode within a few feet of the ground. The final test of this was made a few days ago, and of it Mr. Tilson said:

"The results were highly satisfactory in every respect, and the officers having the matter in charge are quite enthusiastic. This bomb, in my opinion, is sure to be heard from before the war is over."

Mr. Tilson told the House that Pershing's troops would be equipped with gas masks.

"The type adopted by the United States Army for the protection of its troops in Europe," he said, "is of the box respiratory type in use in the English Army."

COMMITTEE VOTES WAR BAN ON BOTH BEER AND WHISKY

Compromise Rejected and Drastic Nation-Wide Prohibition Written Into Food Bill.

PERMITS MAKING OF WINES

But Only to Prevent Waste of Fruits and by Authorization of the President.

BILL OTHERWISE PERFECTED

Extends Control Over Industries—"Bone Dry" Fight Begins on Senate Floor Today.

Special to The New York Times.

WASHINGTON, June 27.—After tightening the liquor restriction so that wine alone might be manufactured in war time, the Senate Committee on Agriculture today reported the much-revised Food Administration bill to the Senate. Owing to prolonged consideration in committee, the bill was not ready until nearly 5 o'clock, and the Senate after receiving it adjourned until tomorrow noon, when debate on the measure will be begun.

The Committee on Agriculture rejected the compromise liquor amendment agreed upon by the sub-committee yesterday, which prohibited the manufacture of beer and wine, but authorized the President to permit their making and use if deemed in the public interest. Instead of giving discretionary power as to beer, the committee eliminated allusion to beer entirely, leaving wine as the only intoxicating drink that may be made for the remainder of the war.

New Prohibition Amendment.

Here are the liquor sections as amended by the committee:

Section 12. That from and after thirty days from the date of the approval of this act no person shall use any foods, food materials, or feeds in the production of alcohol, except for Governmental, industrial, scientific, medicinal, sacramental, or other nonbeverage purposes. Any person who willfully violates this section shall, upon conviction thereof, be punished by a fine not exceeding $5,000, or by imprisonment for not more than two years, or both.

Provided, That whenever the President shall find it necessary to conserve perishable fruits he is empowered to permit the use of such perishable fruits in the manufacture of vinous liquors; and when the question arises as to whether any particular fruit is perishable or nonperishable the President is authorized to determine that question, and his determination shall be conclusive for the purposes of this act.

Provided, further, That the Commissioner of Internal Revenue shall be charged with the administration of this section, and he is authorized, with the approval of the President, to require the taking out of such permits, the keeping of such records, the execution of such bonds, and the observance of such rules and regulations as may be necessary and proper for the execution of the same.

Section 13. That the President is authorized and directed to commandeer any or all distilled spirits in bond at the date of the approval of this act, for redistillation, in so far as such redistillation may be necessary to meet the requirements of the Government in the manufacture of munitions and other military and hospital supplies, or in so far as such redistillation would dispense with the necessity of utilizing products and materials suitable for foods and feeds in the future manufacture of distilled spirits for the purposes herein enumerated. The President shall determine and pay a just compensation for the distilled spirits so commandeered; and if the compensation so determined be not satisfactory to the person entitled to receive the same, such person shall be paid seventy-five per centum of the amount so determined by the President, and shall be entitled to sue the United States to recover such further sum as, added to said seventy-five per centum, will make up such amount as will be just compensation for such spirits, in the manner provided by Section Twenty-Four, Paragraph Twenty, and Section One Hundred and Forty-Five of the Judicial Code.

Wine as Nation's War Tipple.

If the Agricultural Committee amendment is enacted into law wine will be the nation's war drink, unless the President exercises the discretion given to him to prohibit that, too. The use of whisky in bond is not legislated against, but power is given to the President to commandeer all stocks of distilled spirits, and it is believed that if the Senate passes the drastic amendment against beer the President will take over the whisky. The argument has been advanced in the Senate lobby that to permit whisky to be sold and to prohibit beer would defeat the essential idea of prohibition.

The committee's action in eliminating beer was not expected. The impression in the Senate lobby was that the committee would adopt the compromise reached by the sub-committee. The committee used little time in accepting the revisions made in the bill as to food control, commandeering, purchasing, and licensing. These changes, it was considered, improved the measure so that opposition in the Senate probably would disappear.

But the liquor amendment met with no such sympathy. By a vote of 8 to 7 the committee rejected the compromise adopted by the sub-committee, and then, after much discussion, by a vote of 9 to 7 agreed upon the substitute putting the ban on beer.

Senator Gore, who is Chairman of the Agricultural Committee, said he thought the bill would be passed early next week. An effort is under way to hurry it to a vote by Saturday night, but Sen-

Continued on Page 2.

Two Saved from a Zeppelin After a Fall of 13,000 Feet

LONDON, June 27.—When the British recently brought down a Zeppelin on the East Anglian coast they captured two members of the crew, who in a miraculous manner escaped death as the airship plunged to earth. This fact was made known to the newspapers today by the Admiralty.

One of the prisoners is an officer and the other a private. The private sustained broken legs in the fall of the airship, but is recovering. His companion escaped virtually unscathed. The Zeppelin fell from a height of 13,000 feet and was in flames when it reached the ground. How the two Germans escaped death cannot be accounted for.

The above undoubtedly refers to the air raid on the east and southeast coasts of England Sunday morning, June 17, when a Zeppelin was brought down in flames.

HOLLAND STIRRED BY RATIONING PLAN

Still Hopes to Get Food from Us and Doubts if We Will Put On an Embargo.

WASHINGTON IS MOVING

First Recommendations of Exports Council Put in Wilson's Hands Yesterday.

Special Cable to THE NEW YORK TIMES.

THE HAGUE, June 27.—The announcement that rationing of neutrals is to come at last has caused some sensation, but not much surprise, in Holland, where there have been repeated rumors to the same effect for some time.

Today's pacifist Nieuws van den Dag says:

"It was to be expected that the falling away of the United States from the ranks of the neutrals would have unfavorable results for the latter. Before American intervention in the war the powerful North American republic was the champion of the neutrals against both sets of belligerents. Now this powerful nation has become a party to the struggle, and has itself interests conflicting with those of the neutrals, and speedily lets them know it.

"Scandinavia and the Netherlands will naturally be the first to feel the effects of the President's new rationing measures; but we must wait to see how far the United States is really in earnest in this restriction of free purchase. England naturally has every reason to press America along this course, but it is to be doubted whether America will really proceed to put these severe measures in force."

This attempt to throw the onus of all measures affecting Dutch food supplies upon one combatant is characteristic of the attitude of the Dutch press at the present moment. Still more characteristic and actually representing a widespread illusion in Holland is the hint that the American Government does not mean more than half it says.

NATION TO TAKE GRIP ON COAL

First Recommendation Made to Wilson by Exports Council.

Special to The New York Times.

WASHINGTON, June 27.—The first formal recommendation in regard to the control of exports, on which it is expected that President Wilson will base a proclamation, was signed today by the members of the new Exports Council and placed in the hands of the President. The President's sanction is expected quickly, as he called upon Secretary Redfield at the Department of Commerce soon afterward and discussed the operation of the control machinery.

No information was made public, but it can be said that coal and wheat have been placed on the list. One report said that attention had been given by the Council to bunker coal for cargo-carrying ships. By regulating the amount of this coal which can be taken out of the country the President can control shipping.

Control of shipping through operation of a licensing system for bunker coal was discussed by Secretary Redfield with Chairman Denman of the Shipping Board. The intention of the Government, it is said, is to force ships into necessary trades, and to draw from neutral and allied harbors shipping now held there because of fear of submarine attack.

The Exports Council is prepared to recommend drastic action on various lines as the situation develops. It is expected that among the exports which will be affected will be oil cake and oil cake meal, used for cattle fodder, which have been exported from this country to the neutrals in greatly increased quantities since the outbreak of the war.

The contention is made in some quarters that the heavy exports of this fodder are not only making necessary the use of corn and oats for cattle fodder here, but also driving American cattle to the slaughter house and causing undue increase in the price of milk and butter.

Figures obtained today showed that Sweden, which in the fiscal year ending June 30, 1914, imported but 5,514,051 pounds of oil cake and oil cake meal, imported 15,082,436 pounds during the first year of the war. Denmark's imports jumped from 347,584,172 pounds to 1,093,826,454 pounds. In the year ending June 30, 1914, Germany obtained from this country 275,000,000 pounds of this fodder, and obtained a great supply also from Argentina and other countries. This was cut off by the blockade of Great Britain.

FRANCE'S EXPENSES MOUNT.

Nearly Two Billion Dollars Needed for Third Quarter of 1917.

PARIS, June 27.—France will require for the third quarter's expenses $1,968,000,000, or about $43,000,000 more than for the second quarter of 1917, making total appropriations for thirty-eight months of $19,795,400,000.

These are the totals which will be submitted to the Senate tomorrow by M. Millies-Lacroix, General Reporter of the Appropriations Committee. He is authority for the statement that more than 20 per cent. of the appropriations already made have not been disbursed, although they have been allocated. Upward of $1,200,000,000 of the total has been advanced to France's allies.

U-BOAT SINKINGS SHOW FALLING OFF FROM LAST WEEK

Only 28 British Merchantmen Sunk, Against a Total of 32 in Previous Seven Days.

FEWER LARGER SHIPS LOST

American Sailing Ship Galena Is Destroyed by a Bomb Off the French Coast.

LINER IS SUNK OFF BOMBAY

P. & O. Steamer Mongolia Hits a Mine—Five Other Ships Are Reported Victims of U-Boats.

LONDON, June 27.—Twenty-one British vessels of more than 1,600 tons each and seven under 1,600 tons were sunk by mines or submarines last week, according to the weekly statement of losses issued by the Admiralty this evening. No fishing vessels met with disaster. The statement reads:

Arrivals, 2,875; sailings, 2,923.

British merchant ships over 1,600 tons, including one previously, sunk by mine or submarine, 21; under 1,600 tons, including one previously, seven.

British merchant ships unsuccessfully attacked, including seven previously, 22.

The above statement shows a falling off in the sinkings of British vessels from the announcement of last week, which recorded the loss of thirty-two vessels, twenty-seven of more than 1,600 tons, and five in the smaller division. The number of ships reported sunk in last night's announcement by the Admiralty is the smallest in the last three weekly bulletins.

BOMB SINKS THE GALENA.

American Sailer Was Refitted Since the War Began.

LONDON, June 27.—The American sailing ship Galena, of 1,048 tons, was sunk by a bomb on June 25 off Ushant Island, (off the coast of France, twenty-six miles northwest of Brest.) Fifteen survivors were taken to Brest. There were no casualties.

A Central News dispatch from Copenhagen says the Norwegian steamship Kong Haakon, of 2,231 tons, has been sunk by a German submarine and that only six of the crew were saved.

The Norwegian steamship Maggie, of 1,118 tons, has been sunk in the Atlantic. The crew was saved.

BOMBAY, India, June 27.—The Peninsular and Oriental Liner Mongolia struck a mine and sank off Bombay on June 23. Some of the passengers and crew have arrived here. The mails are believed to have been lost.

The Mongolia was bound from London. It is not known yet whether all the passengers and crew were saved.

The Mongolia, a vessel of 9,505 tons, was built in 1903 at Greenock. She was 520 feet long, had a 58-foot beam and a 24-foot depth of hold.

WASHINGTON, June 27.—Sinking of the Danish steamer Gunhild of 968 tons was reported to the State Department today. Survivors said the steamer was torpedoed without warning and sank before lifeboats could be lowered. Five of the crew were drowned. One was killed by the propeller. A British destroyer rescued the remainder of the crew and two passengers twenty minutes after the ship was struck. There were no Americans aboard.

The Greek steamship N. Hadzikyriakos was torpedoed and sunk by a German submarine about 300 miles off the English coast on May 31 with a loss of twenty-two lives, it was announced here yesterday by D. J. Theophilatos, agent here for the owners. The vessel, of 2,533 tons, was on her way from South America to England. Word of the destruction reached here in a cablegram from the chief engineer, one of the three survivors.

The submarine fired two torpedoes, according to the cablegram, the first missing the steamship and the second penetrating the engine room and causing an explosion. All but two men reached lifeboats successfully, but some were drowned or died from exposure during the next forty hours. The three survivors, picked up by an English ship, were rescued a second time when a submarine sank the vessel they were on. A British cruiser took them into an English port.

The American ship Galena, which has been sunk off the coast of France, was formerly the barkentine Fooling Suey. She left here March 22 with cargo for Rouen, France, and carried a crew of eighteen men. She was commanded by Captain F. V. Marshall. According to the records of the United States Commissioner of Shipping here there were eight American citizens aboard.

4 U-BOATS NEAR SILVERSHELL.

Wireless Operator Says the Only One Which Attacked Was Sunk.

Additional details of the sinking of a German submarine off the coast of Sardinia on May 30 by the American oil tanker Silvershell were told yesterday by H. T. Mapes, the senior wireless operator on the steamship, who arrived recently from a French port.

According to Mapes, the Silvershell sighted four submarines in all. The first U-boat was seen on the evening of May 29 and submerged before the after gun could be trained on her. The three others were sighted on the following afternoon. Two of these submerged, and the attack was made on the tanker by the fourth submarine shortly after 2 o'clock in the afternoon.

The Silvershell fired thirty-five shots against forty shrapnel shells that were fired at her by the enemy craft. One of the last shells from the tanker struck the U-boat amidships, Mapes said, and she was seen to keel over and go down stern first.

125 American Airplane Experts Reach England; Units of Lumbermen Also There to Begin War Work

Special to The New York Times.

WASHINGTON, June 27.—The Aircraft Production Board announced today the safe arrival at a British port of a group of nearly 125 experts, sent from this country to acquire and bring back to the United States all possible information regarding aircraft designing and the manufacture of both engines and planes. In the delegation are men representing legal, manufacturing, designing, engineering, military, and naval experience and training.

It will be the duty of this group to gather and bring to America as soon as possible the latest information regarding European aircraft development, which can then be easily made available for American manufacturers. Arrangements have been made through the allied Governments for placing expert American mechanics in the European aircraft plants in whose products the United States is interested.

The National Advisory Committee for Aeronautics and the Aircraft Production Board has made plans for a permanent exhibit of aircraft materials of all kinds, to be established in Washington for the benefit of army and navy engineers and American manufacturers. A building to house the exhibit is being constructed by the Government south of the Smithsonian Institute.

"The Aircraft Production Board has no illusions as to the size and character of the job before it," a statement issued by the board today, says, "but the whole task is one of industrial organization for quantity production, and in this we Americans are above all other nations fitted by experience and tradition to break records."

LONDON, June 27.—Ten units of American Woodmen sent over by New England States and organizations to turn various forests of the United Kingdom into lumber have arrived on English soil.

The complete equipment of the units caused much surprise and occasioned a great deal of favorable comment. The woodmen not only brought with them the necessary machinery, but were fully equipped in every way, even to lubricating oils. Their arrival found them ready to establish their sawmills and begin work at once. The only necessity for their maintenance is raw food, which their own cooks will prepare.

1,400 MORE ENLIST; STILL NEED 50,000

War Department Hopes for Greater Spurt in the Next Few Days to Fill Up Army Ranks.

NEW YORK AGAIN LEADS

Furnishes 245 Recruits of Total Obtained Tuesday—Governor Urges State to Co-operate.

WASHINGTON, June 27.—With recruiting week half gone, War Department officials estimated today that the regular army still is more than 50,000 men short of war strength, the goal it had been hoped to attain by Friday night. On the face of the returns so far, it is apparent that there has been no general response to President Wilson's call for 70,000 volunteers during the week.

Undoubtedly the remaining days of the week will see greater activity, and officials still hope great gains in recruiting totals will result. They believe many hundreds of men of the class called upon by the President are only beginning now to realize the urgency of the call and will not allow recruiting week to go by without offering themselves for their country's service.

Only nine States have completed their quota of war volunteers, and only eight others have their quota 75 per cent. complete. Twenty are below the 50 per cent. line and six are below 25 per cent. Nevada leads the honor roll with her total of war volunteers to date exceeding her quota by a ratio of almost 4 to 1. Vermont has obtained only 79 men in a quota of 710.

The percentages of all the States upon the returns up to Monday night follow: Nevada, 388; Oregon, 172; Utah, 172; Wyoming, 153; Montana, 137; Indiana, 129; Idaho, 109; Illinois, 108; Michigan, 105; Nebraska, 97; Pennsylvania, 96; California, 88; Missouri, 86; Kansas, 84; New Jersey, 79; Iowa, 79; Massachusetts, 76; Colorado, 74; New York, 72; Florida, 65; Washington, 64; Minnesota, 62; South Dakota, 61; Ohio, 59; Texas, 59; Georgia, 59; Kentucky, 50; West Virginia, 50; Oklahoma, 49; Delaware, 47; Connecticut, 45; Arizona, 45; Rhode Island, 43; District of Columbia, 42; Tennessee, 39; North Dakota, 39; Louisiana, 38; Maine, 37; New Hampshire, 35; New Mexico, 31; Wisconsin, 29; Maryland, 26; Virginia, 24; Arkansas, 24; Mississippi, 22; North Carolina, 22; South Carolina, 22, and Vermont, 11.

The returns for Tuesday's recruiting show that only 1,400 men were obtained throughout the country during the day. The daily statement issued by Adjt. Gen. McCain follows:

	Obt'ned June 26.	Total to June 26.		Obt'ned June 26.	Total to June 26.
Alabama	17	1,321	Nebraska	2	2,316
Arizona	..	187	*Nevada	2	622
Arkansas	12	779	N. Hamps.	..	302
California	55	4,236	New Jersey	85	4,106
Colorado	9	1,180	New Mex.	1	208
Conn.	16	1,673	New York	245	13,496
Delaware	7	198	North Car.	8	983
Dist. of C.	6	284	North Dak.	9	470
Florida	15	1,004	Ohio	93	5,721
Georgia	18	3,119	Oklahoma	22	1,674
*Idaho	4	712	*Oregon	16	2,231
*Illinois	104	12,326	Penn.	101	14,368
*Indiana	64	7,034	Rhode Isl.	4	409
Iowa	37	3,393	South Car.	2	748
Kansas	10	2,849	South Dak.	..	716
Kentucky	27	2,321	Tenn.	18	1,699
Louisiana	18	1,297	Texas	50	4,396
Maine	16	584	*Utah	9	1,288
Maryland	31	70[illegible]	Vermont	..	79
Mass.	102	5,223	Virginia	..	1,065
*Michigan	33	5,933	Washingt'n	17	1,484
Minnesota	28	2,611	West Va.	11	1,225
Mississippi	8	865	Wisconsin	61	1,326
Missouri	44	5,712	*Wyoming	1	445
*Montana	5	1,026			

*Quota obtained.
Total quota, 183,898.
Total obtained June 26, 1,400.
Total obtained since April 1, 127,800.

ALBANY, June 27.—The County Home Defense committees of New York were called upon by Governor Whitman today to co-operate in the work of recruiting for Federal and State military and naval organizations. Their attention was called to the fact that tabulation of returns of the recent State census is producing large numbers of

Continued on Page 2.

MOVES TO INSURE MEN SENT TO WAR

Secretary McAdoo Summons Representatives of Life Companies to a Conference.

WOULD SET A PRECEDENT

Federal Bureau May Undertake Task, or Government May Supplement Private Concerns.

Special to The New York Times.

WASHINGTON, D. C., June 27.—Government life insurance for the officers and men of the United States Army and Navy who serve in France will be discussed at a conference of life insurance experts to be held at the office of Secretary McAdoo here July 2.

The Secretary signed a call today on the leading life insurance companies doing business in the United States to send representatives to the meeting. This action was taken to overcome a condition about which there has been much complaint. It has been found practically impossible for men who expect to go to the firing line to get insurance. Old line companies decline to write such risks owing to the hazard due to submarines and the intensive trench fighting that marks the military operations in Europe.

Hitherto there has been only comparative difficulty in getting insurance for officers and men in the regular army or navy. Rates have not been considered unduly high, and but for the inconvenience of the rule that permits must be obtained for service in tropical countries army men have fared reasonably well at the hands of the insurance companies. In addition to the opportunity to take out insurance for the benefit of families of army and navy men there has been for the last ten years the further advantage of the benefit system maintained by the Government which officers and men are entitled, in case of death in the line of duty, to a payment to their designated beneficiaries of an amount equal to half their yearly pay at the time of death. It is not proposed to alter or repeal the benefit law, in arranging new insurance.

"The war risk insurance bureau of the Treasury Department," said Secretary McAdoo, "is insuring the lives of masters, officers, and seamen of the merchant marine of the United States, and the question has arisen as to how insurance on the lives of the officers and enlisted men of the army and navy can be effected most advantageously, through an extension of the powers of the war risk insurance bureau or through the combined agency or co-operation of the life insurance companies of the United States. It is expected that the discussion at the coming conference will prove of great value in determining the wisest policy to be adopted.

"This is a great problem, and it appeals immediately and instinctively to the highest thought and purpose of the country. Certainly everything possible should be done to give protection to those who are dependent upon the men who give their lives for their country, and to ameliorate the rigors and horrors of war. No organized effort has ever been made by any Government to provide this sort of protection and comforting assurance to its fighting men. Why should not America take the lead in this noble and humane action?

"I earnestly hope that as a result of the measures thus intimated a great system of insurance will be devised which will give to every officer, soldier, and sailor in the service of the United States the assurance that some provision is made for the loved ones he leaves behind if he is called upon to make the greatest sacrifice that a patriot can make for his country."

GEN. SIBERT IN COMMAND

Force, Arriving in Two Contingents, Moves to Its Camp.

SEAPORT DECKED IN FLAGS

All Troops in Excellent Shape and Enthusiastic Over the Successful Trip.

CONVOYED IN DANGER ZONE

Pershing Will Join Expedition Today—Its Place at the Front Not Known.

A FRENCH SEAPORT, June 27.—The second contingent of American troops arrived and disembarked this morning.

The troops landed amid the frantic cheers of the people, who had gathered for hours before in anticipation of duplicating yesterday's surprise.

Enthusiasm rose to fever pitch when it was learned that the transports and convoys had successfully passed the submarine zone. The port was speedily beflagged in honor of the occasion.

All the troops now arrived were transferred today to a camp not distant from this point, where Major Gen. William L. Sibert is installed. Thence they probably will go soon to a point near the front. All the troops are in excellent shape, enthusiastic over the successful trip and their reception, and eager for action.

Major Gen. Pershing, the American commander, is expected tomorrow.

The harbor is dotted with convoys. The streets are filled with soldiers in khaki and with bluejackets.

Great numbers of trucks are transporting immense supplies to the camp in which the troops are concentrating.

First of the Mighty Army.

WASHINGTON, June 27.—The advance guard of the mighty army the United States is preparing to send against Germany is on French soil tonight. In defiance of the German submarines, thousands of seasoned regulars and marines, trained fighting men with the tan of long service on the Mexican border, or in Haiti or Santo Domingo, still on their faces, have been hastened overseas to fight beside the French, the British, the Belgian, the Russian, the Portuguese, and the Italian troops on the western front.

News of the safe arrival of the troops sent a new thrill through Washington. No formal announcement was made at the War Department. None will be made, probably, until Major Gen. Pershing's official report has been received. Then there may be a statement as to the numbers and composition of the advance guard.

Press dispatches from France, presumably sent forward with the approval of General Pershing's staff, show that Maj. Gen. Sibert, one of the new Major Generals of the army, has been chosen to command the first force sent abroad, under General Pershing as commander in chief of the expedition.

One thing stands out sharply, despite the fact that the size of the task that has been accomplished is not fully revealed as yet. This is that American enterprise has set a new record for the transportation of troops.

Expedition Sets a Record.

Considering the distance to be covered and the fact that all preparations had to be made after the order came from the White House, the night of May 18, it is practically certain that never before has a military expedition of this size been assembled, conveyed, and landed without mishap in so short a time by any nation. It is a good augury of future achievements. The only rival in magnitude is the movement of British troops to South Africa in the Boer war, and that was made overseas that were unhampered by submarines, mines, or other obstacles.

The American forces will be a net gain to the Allies. It will throw no single burden of supply or equipment upon them. The troops will be fed, clothed, armed, and equipped by the United States. Around them at the camp on French soil tonight are being stored supplies that will keep them going for months.

General Pershing and his staff have been busy for days preparing for the arrival of the men. Despite the enormous difficulties of unpreparedness and submarine dangers that faced them, the plans of the Army General Staff have gone through with clocklike precision.

When the order came to prepare immediately an expeditionary force to go to France, virtually all of the men now across the seas were on the Mexican border. General Pershing himself was at his headquarters in San Antonio. There were no army transports available in the Atlantic. The vessels that carried the troops were scattered on their usual routes. Army reserve stores were still depleted from the border mobilization. Regiments were below war strength.

Organizing Pershing's Forces.

[illegible]

Mid-Week Pictorial

Americans of the Honor Guard at the training camp in France await General Pershing's arrival for a tour of inspection.

Daddy, what did YOU do in the Great War?

"All the News That's Fit to Print."

The New York Times.

THE WEATHER
Fair today and Sunday; warmer Sunday; moderate southwest winds.
For full weather report see Page 17.

VOL. LXVI...NO. 21,728. ... NEW YORK, SATURDAY, JULY 21, 1917.—EIGHTEEN PAGES. ONE CENT In Greater New York. | TWO CENTS Elsewhere N. Y. State, N. J., Conn. | THREE CENTS Other States.

DRAWING FOR NATION'S DRAFT ARMY ENDS AT 2:18 A. M. AFTER 16½ HOURS; MISSING CITY LISTS CAUSE WORRY

MICHAELIS CLAIMS GERMANY'S RIGHT TO VICTOR'S PEACE

Contemplates No New Offer, but Is Willing to Treat if the Allies Open Negotiations.

WILL CEDE NO TERRITORY

Ready to Fight America if U-Boats Do Not Shut Off Our Armies.

RESERVED AS TO REFORMS

Reichstag, by 214 to 116, Passes Peace Declaration and Votes New War Credit.

Special Cable to THE NEW YORK TIMES.

BERLIN, July 19, (via Copenhagen, July 20)—The Reichstag offered hearty greetings today to the new Chancellor, Dr. Georg Michaelis, who addressed a rather short speech to the House in which he could not cover the whole field of politics, which, he said, was impossible after only a few days in office. He appears rather slight of stature as seen from the press gallery, but impresses one at once with his quiet determination. His head and face seem larger in proportion than the rest of his body.

As he bowed to the House, crowded to its furthest corner, there came enthusiastic cheers from all sides. When he began to speak after the routine had been disposed of the House subsided into a silence which indicated the deepest interest.

The Chancellor speaks without the slightest affectation, his voice seldom varying in force, and he seems to have no use for gestures. Despite the fact that his utterances were not of an overwhelmingly original character and carried few surprises, the general opinion of the eager listeners was that Dr. Michaelis is an orator of great power. His clear voice, though restrained, penetrated the whole House. He spoke without haste but also without hesitation, like a man who knows exactly what he aims at and is not going to promise more.

Wants Germany's Future Secured.

After paying a high tribute to his predecessor, whose great work, he said, could only be appreciated by impartial history, Dr. Michaelis discussed the origin of the war. He spoke of Germany's different enemies and their responsibility, blaming especially England, whose Foreign Office, he said, never uttered one word to dissuade Russia from mobilizing while Chancellor von Bethmann Hollweg did his best up to the very last hour to prevent war. Several times the new Chancellor was interrupted in his praise of his predecessor by voices from the Right, but they were soon hushed and did not even make themselves heard again when the Chancellor reached in his speech the much-contested peace resolution, which is already known in America.

Every ear was strained when the Chancellor said: "We shall not continue this war one day longer to make conquest if we can make peace with honor." After emphasizing that such a peace must be lasting and must secure Germany's future and her frontiers on every side, he said that in that sense the Government found the resolution acceptable. There was loud applause from the Left and Centre, while the Right, where sat the Conservatives and National Liberals, who refused to sign the resolution, remained silent.

Then he continued and made it quite clear that Germany could not make another peace offer. The enemy had answered the Kaiser's first offer with derision and renewed efforts in the war, and there was nothing now for Germany but to fight until the enemy would tire. Here again enthusiastic cheers interrupted the Chancellor.

Prepared for American Armies.

Later, when the Chancellor spoke of America's entrance into the war, saying that Germany was prepared for the appearance of American armies on European battlefields if they should indeed manage to cross the ocean despite the vigilance of U-boats, he again had the whole House with him.

He then said that when he accepted his present office he intended to administer it with inflexible devotion. Since electoral reform was part of the Government's program, as decreed in the royal order of July 11, he was certainly going to make that his business. Here a restrained commotion was noticeable all over the House, and there were some cheers in the Centre, but the Right and Left remained silent. Dr. Michaelis said that, of course, whatever the Reichstag and the Empire's Government might do they must respect the rights of the Federated States as guaranteed.

The space behind the bench of the Ministers and the bench for Members of the Bundesrat was now densely crowded with high officials of all branches, and officers of the army and navy in shining uniforms, who strained their necks not to miss a single word which the new Chancellor had to say regarding this, to them, vital question. Just at this time several young Princes belonging to reigning houses of various German States appeared at the entrance behind the Chairman's cathedra, and modestly remained in the background.

Maintains Rights of Crown.

The Chancellor said he was very much in favor of closer co-operation of the Reichstag with the Government, and

Continued on Page 2.

Von Tirpitz Hopes to Return as Leader in Reichstag

LONDON, July 20.—A dispatch to the Exchange Telegraph Company from Amsterdam says German political circles expect the sensational entrance into political life of Admiral von Tirpitz, father of the submarine campaign.

It is believed that he will contest one of the vacant seats in the Reichstag as a National Liberal candidate, with a view to becoming a leader of the National Liberals jointly with Dr. Gustav Stresemann and Major Ernst Bassermann.

REPULSE GERMANS WITH HEAVY LOSS

French Mow Down Enemy in General Assault on Plateaux on the Aisne.

BEATEN AT ALL POINTS

Petain's Troops in a Counterattack Retake Part of Positions Lost Previously.

PARIS, July 20.—After their unsuccessful assaults yesterday afternoon on the Aisne front, in the region of Hurtebise and Craonne, the Germans renewed their attacks late last evening, hoping to catch the French off their guard. Everywhere on the front attacked, on the plateau before Craonne and Vauclerc, the enemy was repulsed after terrific hand-to-hand fighting, the French fighting with magnificent valor. The ground in front of their positions was covered with German dead.

Between the Californie Plateau and Casemates Plateau the enemy endeavored to extend the small success he gained early yesterday morning, but his efforts were unavailing. The French, by a counterattack, retook part of the positions they had lost there.

The text of the afternoon statement by the War Office follows:

In the region of Hurtebise and Craonne the artillery fighting continued with great violence. The Germans renewed their attacks until a late hour in the night. At about 3:30 o'clock, after a powerful bombardment with concentrated artillery, the enemy undertook a new general assault, with important forces, on the line along the plateau before Craonne and Vauclerc.

Hand-to-hand fighting occurred on the whole extent of this front, which our troops defended with magnificent valor. Their tenacious resistance broke up the furious assaults of the enemy. Everywhere our positions were maintained completely. In spite of the heavy sacrifices made by the enemy, he was not able to gain a footing on the Californie Plateau, on the Casemates Plateau, or in our positions further west. The ground in front of our lines, covered with the dead, bears witness to the violence of the battle and the sanguinary defeat of the enemy.

Between the Californie Plateau and the Casemates Plateau the efforts of the Germans to increase the advantage obtained yesterday were equally fruitless. An energetic counterattack enabled us to regain a position which the enemy had penetrated. We hold the crest of the plateau entirely. The enemy still holds a position about 600 meters long near the northern edge of the plateau, where one of our first-line positions was destroyed by the bombardment. We took a score of prisoners of the Guard.

In Champagne a surprise attack on our outposts between Navarin Farm and the St. Hilaire-St. Souplet road was broken up by our fire. On the left bank of the Meuse there was rather heavy artillery fighting in the region of Hill 304.

Tonight's statement says:

Southeast of St. Quentin there was activity by our own and our enemy's artillery. We have retaken a few elements of trenches in the region of the Moulin de Tout-vent.

There has been rather spirited artillery fighting to the north of the Aisne between Hurtebise and Craonne. The enemy, after his sanguinary failures of yesterday and last night, made no further attempts.

There were intermittent bombardments in Champagne to the south of Moronvilliers and on both banks of the Meuse. There was no infantry action. The remainder of the front was quiet.

French Trenches Won, Then Lost.

BERLIN, July 20, (via London.)—Artillery activity in Flanders increased yesterday to extreme violence, says the German War Office statement issued today. Part of the French positions on the Winterburg were captured by the Germans. Later some of these trenches were abandoned during a French attack.

The announcement follows:

Army Group of Prince Rupprecht—After a rainy morning which temporarily brought about an abatement of activity, the artillery battle in Flanders increased from the afternoon onward to extreme violence. Enemy advances at Lombaertzyde and east of Messines failed.

On the Artois front there was lively artillery activity between La Bassée Canal and Lens, especially southeast of Loos. At Gavrelle British battalions which attacked during the night were repulsed. The British also attacked again at Monchy after violent artillery preparation, without obtaining any further successes.

Southwest of St. Quentin the French three times made further fruitless attacks on the trenches we captured. They suffered sanguinary losses.

Army Group of the German Crown Prince—Northwest of Craonne Brandenburg and Guard troops, after short and violent artillery preparation, captured part of the French positions on Winterburg. The enemy offered stubborn resistance and suffered heavy losses. More than 375 men were taken prisoner and numerous trench weapons were captured.

The counterattacks of the French were not begun until evening. They led to heavy nocturnal engagements, in which some of the trenches we had captured were abandoned again. Elsewhere, apart from a few forefield

Continued on Page 4.

KERENSKY MADE RUSSIAN PREMIER AS LVOFF QUITS

New Chief Will Also Retain Posts as Minister of War and Marine.

SHOT FIRED AT KERENSKY

Attempt to Murder Him at Poltsk—Alleged German Agent Arrested.

TROOPS REFUSE TO FIGHT

Extremist Regiments Quit Trenches and Germans Make Large Gain.

PETROGRAD, July 20.—The Bourse Gazette announces that Premier Lvoff has resigned and that Alexander F. Kerensky has been appointed Premier, but will temporarily retain his portfolio of Minister of War and Marine.

M. Tseretelli has been appointed to the post of Minister of the Interior, which was held by M. Lvoff, but will retain his portfolio of Minister of Posts and Telegraphs.

M. Nekrasoff has been named provisionally as Minister of Justice, in place of M. Perevelzeff, who resigned Thursday.

An attempt to assassinate Kerensky was made today at the town of Polotsk. A shot fired at the Minister missed him. He has returned to Petrograd.

Koslovsky, an alleged agent of the German General Staff, has been arrested.

It is reported that Nikolai Lenine, leader of the recent outbreak here, has gone to Kronstadt disguised as a sailor.

A telegram of Kiev announces that the Ukraine radical Socialist organizations of soldiers, workmen, and students, as "representatives of the revolutionary democracy in the Ukraine," have telegraphed the Provisional Government assuring it of energetic support from this quarter in its struggle against the attempts to provoke civil war.

When detachments of the active army arrived at the capital last evening to reinforce the garrison for the restoration of order they were received with enthusiastic cheers by the crowds on the Nevsky Prospect. One after another the regiments which participated in the armed demonstration submitted to authority, expressing their regret for what had happened. They explained that they had been misled by irresponsible agitators.

The last remnant of a detachment of partisans of the Radical agitator Lenine were forced to evacuate the Modern Circus, where it had taken refuge.

The villa of Mlle. Kshesinska, long the headquarters of the Maximalists, who defied the authorities to dislodge them, capitulated after a slight brush. The occupants took refuge in the nearest Peter and Paul fortress. When the fortress was later surrounded by troops the Maximalists ran up a white flag and surrendered.

The troops received orders to clear out the Maximalists from the home of the celebrated dancer and take possession of the fortress. In the early hours of the morning a regiment of bicycle troops reached the capital and rode to the Field of Mars. A large body of newly arrived Cossacks also concentrated there. Meantime other troops approached from the rear of the fortress and dawn found the places surrounded.

The Maximalists fired a few shots from the Kshesinska house which were returned by the troops, after which the former began making their escape toward the fortress, held by a machine gun regiment and Kronstadt sailors. Emissaries from the Government later entered the fortress under truce flags and began a parley which lasted throughout the morning. Ready to surrender from the first if allowed to depart with arms, the Maximalists received until midday to quit unconditionally. Just before the expiration of the time limit the white flag was hoisted.

The casualties incident to the disorders here of the last three days are now given as 56 killed or dead from wounds and 650 wounded.

WASHINGTON, July 20.—Complete quiet has been restored in Petrograd, and plans for the reconstruction of the Cabinet on the same basis of party representation as before the crisis are now under way, according to semi-official dispatches today to the Russian Embassy here.

RUSSIANS MUTINY AS GERMANS ATTACK

Extremist Regiments Quit Trenches and Enemy Makes Sizeable Gain.

PETROGRAD, July 20.—The success of the German attacks yesterday in Galicia, both north and south of the Dniester River, is explained by the fact that some Russian regiments, influenced by extremist agitators, refused to obey orders and quitted the trenches in face of the enemy after debating whether or not they should fight. The retention of Halicz is endangered by these defections. Following is the official account of what happened:

In the direction of Vilna there was animated artillery fighting throughout

Continued on Page 2.

Germany's Latest U-Boats Able to Submerge 200 Feet

Special to The New York Times.

WASHINGTON, July 20.—Germany's latest submarines are capable of submerging 200 feet and of withstanding the pressure of the water at that depth, according to official reports received here. This achievement adds a new problem to those already confronting the Allies in combating the U-boats, as the latter are now said to be able to dive under any nets which the Allies have constructed.

Only a small number of these deep-diving submarines have been built, it is believed, although it is thought possible that Germany is turning toward them in anticipation of an effort by the Allies and America to "bottle up" her U-boats in the Baltic and at the mouths of the German rivers.

ERROR IN CABLING ON U-BOAT LOSSES

Company Admits Making Mistake in Times Dispatch—Correctly Written, Says Censor.

LONDON WEIGHS SITUATION

Lord Beresford Describes It as Crucial and Advises Rapid Building of Ships.

An error in the transmission of Charles H. Grasty's cable dispatch to THE TIMES, printed in Thursday morning's paper, in which Mr. Grasty called attention to the seriousness of the submarine situation, made the dispatch say the loss of ships by submarine "1,600,000 tons a month" instead of "600,000 tons a month," as Mr. Grasty wrote it.

The error came to light yesterday through a private dispatch from Mr. Grasty to THE TIMES, sent in reply to inquiries based on the startling figures received as coming from him. In reply to these inquiries he cabled:

"The figures sixteen hundred thousand did not appear in my dispatch as filed on Wednesday. The passage should read as follows: 'The loss of ships by submarine has totaled 600,000 tons per month, or from two to three times the total of new constructions.' I have instructed the Western Union to repeat this passage to you as filed."

Shortly after receipt of this message came one from the Western Union cable office in London where the original dispatch was filed, correcting the passage in question to read, "Six hundred thousand" instead of "sixteen hundred thousand" tons. Meantime, of course, the dispatch had been printed and circulated and had aroused widespread discussion.

No explanation of the error beyond the mere admission of it was obtainable from the Western Union company. The sole addition to the information on the subject from that source came in a dispatch to THE TIMES from the New York office of the company, giving the passage as erroneously received at this end of the cable as "sixteen hundred thousand."

A later dispatch yesterday from Mr. Grasty said: "My cable reads, 'Monthly loss six hundred thousand tons.' All the facts, figures, and conclusions in that dispatch came from an unimpeachable source, and were submitted to the Admiralty censor, who subjected it to critical supervision, cutting out portions."

In filing the original message every precaution had apparently been taken to avoid error. The total of shipping destroyed was sent not in figures, but was written out "six hundred thousand tons a month, or from two to three times the total of new construction." When this passage was received here erroneously as "sixteen hundred thousand tons a month," THE TIMES took the additional precaution of querying as far back as possible through the cable stations to find out if it had been correctly transmitted, and received a verification of the erroneous total.

Causes Commotion in London.

Special Cable to THE NEW YORK TIMES.

LONDON, July 20.—A commotion has been caused in various quarters here by the publication in The Daily Chronicle of a cable from New York quoting Charles H. Grasty as authority, in a dispatch to THE NEW YORK TIMES, for a statement that the monthly losses of ships by submarine warfare totaled 1,600,000 tons.

As the Government on various occasions has refused demands from both Members of Parliament and the press for the inclusion of tonnage figures in the weekly returns of submarine losses, and as even speculative figures on this point have been excluded from the English newspapers, the fact that the dispatch to an American paper had been allowed to pass by the censor attracted great attention.

Coupled with the astonishing figure cited, this departure became sensational. Readers of THE NEW YORK TIMES are already aware, from further figures cabled yesterday, that a mere trifle of a million tons had been added by an error in transmission to the figure mentioned by Mr. Grasty, and it is probable that some statement to that effect will be made here. Meanwhile Mr. Grasty has received the following from Captain Sir Douglas Brownrigg, Chief Censor at the Admiralty:

"This is to certify that I examined and passed your cable message of the 18th inst. concerning losses by submarines; that the message was in writing, and the figures you gave were written,

Continued on Page 4.

THOUSANDS LEFT IN DOUBT

Men Stand in Line All Night Here to Find Numbers.

A DAY WITHOUT DISORDER

At All Exemption Headquarters Quiet Patriotism Marked the Waiting Crowds.

CHOSEN MEN IN PARADE

Those Selected for First Army March Cheering Through Long Island City.

Hundreds of thousands of New Yorkers subject to military duty under the selective draft law waded through column after column of figures yesterday to discover what their position was as the numbers were drawn. Every edition of the afternoon newspapers was eagerly bought, and crowds about the news ticker machines listened eagerly as the man nearest the tape shouted out the numbers. Meanwhile every newspaper office in the city was a bureau of information to which anxious thousands telephoned to find out if some one young man was among the first few hundred numbers.

A more orderly day New York has never known. Not one unpleasant incident due to the momentous happenings in Washington was reported from any part of the city. The fact that many local exemption boards had failed to finish their alphabetically arranged lists with the serial red numbers caused much irritation, but in no instance did that lead to disorder.

Thousands of men in New York have been unable to find their serial number, and thus have no way of knowing their fate because those boards failed to post the lists yesterday. All day complaints from men who wanted to know why they could not find out what their numbers were reached the offices of the Mayor's Committee on National Defense. Roscoe Conkling, representing the State, and Philip J. McCook, representing the city, assured the complainants that they expected every board in the city to have its public list ready for inspection by noon today.

The thousands who gathered at the headquarters of the exemption boards took the situation seriously, and, in the great majority of cases, in a most patriotic spirit. Men studied the long columns of figures in a matter of fact way, but every now and then some young chap would strike his companion on the shoulder and say: "That's me," or "There's my number." If he found it among the first few hundreds one would sometimes hear: "Its France for me." The man who apparently did not relish fighting for his country kept very quiet. He found his number, looked glum, and went on his way.

Tampering Impossible.

In a few of the congested sections of the city, where the population, to a great extent, is foreign in origin, there was some excitement due to the efforts of men to get into the headquarters and find out their numbers. In a few of these districts the lists of eligibles was sent to the police stations, where Sergeants of Police read out the names and numbers to the waiting crowds.

Mr. Conkling, when asked if there was a chance that some person might tamper with the duplicate, or public, copies, of those lists which had not been completed when the drawing of the numbers began in Washington, laid special emphasis on the fact that all cards and lists of men who registered under the Selective Draft act have been protected against any tampering with the numbers since the beginning of the drawing in Washington and for several hours before it began.

"I know absolutely," Mr. Conkling said, "that persons representing this office were on the ground in every district where the duplicating and numbering of cards and the compilation of the serially numbered lists were delayed, and that the lists and cards in every one of these districts were protected. In one case, where the list required for use in the Provost Marshal General's office was not completed until a late hour last night, the list was taken at once to the nearest branch Post Office and deposited there in custody of the clerk in charge, while the corresponding cards were brought to our office.

"When a man's number is drawn today in Washington there is no chance of its being changed on the list. The cards are on their way to Albany and the lists are on their way through the mails to Washington, while copies of the lists are posted at headquarters and additional copies turned over to the press for publication. In order to change any number the change would have to be made on each of these several copies of the lists and on each of the different sets of cards. This precludes the possibility of any such change being made after the drawing started."

Serial No. 1 was drawn early last night, and is No. 1,983 in THE NEW YORK TIMES list this morning, while No. 4,000,

Continued on Page 5.

Congressman Kahn Recalls to Those Drafted The Words of Washington: "I Am Ready"

Special to The New York Times.

WASHINGTON, July 20.—Representative Julius Kahn of California, the ranking Republican member of the House Committee on Military Affairs, who led the Administration forces to victory when the Army Draft bill was under attack in the lower chamber, issued a ringing statement tonight incident to the drawing of numbers for the national army. Mr. Kahn was born in Germany. He came to this country when a child, and love of his adopted land has grown with the years.

Mr. Kahn today attended the drawing in the Government's great lottery in the Senate office building. He was blindfolded and drew the fifth number, which was 10,218. The importance of the event and the dramatic and patriotic incidents so impressed Mr. Kahn that he issued this statement tonight:

For the fourth time in our history we are ready to fight for the right of American citizens to sail the seas untrammeled. Our first difficulty after the Revolution was with France. In 1798 we broke off diplomatic relations with that Government. We ordered the immediate construction of a fleet of many vessels. Washington was appointed, by act of Congress, Commander of the American forces. France had interfered with our ships and our shipping. We were determined to fight rather than submit. France yielded our rights, and the incident was closed.

In 1812 we fought England for the rights of American citizens on the seas. Every schoolboy is familiar with the history of that war. In 1815 we threw down the gauge of battle for the third time and fought the Barbary corsairs who interfered with American ships in the Mediterranean. We brought them to terms and compelled them to recognize American rights on the seas without the payment of any tribute.

Now we are at war with Germany to again protect the rights of Americans on the seas. Today the national army of the United States was formed through the medium of the draft. Hundreds of thousands of our citizens between the ages of 21 and 31 years will give their lives, if need be, to the service of the country.

To those who were drawn today to bear the burdens of the Republic on the field of battle I would like to recall an incident in our national life. In 1798, when we broke off relations with France, the Congress appointed George Washington as commander of the American forces. He was in retirement at Mount Vernon. The Secretary of War himself brought the commission to General Washington and announced to him the action of Congress.

Washington was in the field at the time harvesting his crops. When the matter was stated to him by the Secretary of War, he said:

"I am ready for any service that I can give to my country."

In that spirit I am sure the young men of this day will accept their obligation to the Republic. In that spirit they will again show the world that American rights must be observed by all the world. In that spirit they will make it possible for future generations to still continue to enjoy the blessings of liberty which this country vouchsafed to its humblest citizens. In that spirit they will again carry the American colors to victory, and may God defend the right.

VOTE ON FOOD BILL IN SENATE TODAY

Bipartisan Agreement Opens Way for Its Passage, Probably by 51 to 24.

THEN TO GO TO CONFERENCE

President Said to be Dissatisfied with Three-Man Board and May Demand Change.

Special to The New York Times.

WASHINGTON, July 20.—The well-oiled machinery set up by the bipartisan legislative conference on the Food Administration bill early in the week, worked so smoothly today that little stood in the way, at the end of the day, of speedy passage of the measure tomorrow.

Whatever is to be done in recasting the bill after the Senate gets through with it tomorrow will have to come when it goes before the Conference Committee of the two houses. If President Wilson insists on adhering to the original idea of a single food administrator, instead of a board of three, as provided for yesterday, his only opportunity will be to bring pressure upon the House and Senate conferees.

That the President is dissatisfied with the Senate action in discarding his one-man food administration scheme is known to Senate leaders, but the Senate vote cannot be recalled. That Herbert C. Hoover will not serve upon the three-man board is asserted by those in his confidence. President Wilson furthermore is reported on reliable authority to have assured Mr. Hoover that he would not ask him to accept anything except full, unrestricted power as food administrator.

If the President's idea is to be carried out, it is conceded that the Food Administration bill will have to be operated on when it reaches the joint conference next week. If it has to go through the House and back to the Senate for revision to conform to the President's desire as to the food administrator, it is believed that it will delay its final passage for two weeks, if not longer.

Many Amendments Remain.

The bill in its entirety will be taken up tomorrow afternoon at 2:30 o'clock for final vote. By that hour, under the general consent agreement reached two weeks ago, all amendments must be disposed of. At least twenty-five amendments bearing upon various phases of the measure have been put in during the last few days, while the Senate has debated the broad amendments of the bipartisan conference and of the Agricultural Committee. Only one of the bipartisan amendments was passed today—that pro-

Continued on Page 3.

WILSON MOVES TO END SHIP ROW

Demands Action, but Hopes to Keep Both Goethals and Denman in Office.

FINAL CONFERENCE TODAY

Rumors of Resignations Denied and Goethals's Friends Think He Will Win on Most Points.

Special to The New York Times.

WASHINGTON, July 20.—Reports that President Wilson had again given personal attention to the shipbuilding row gave strength tonight to the belief that an adjustment might soon be expected which would permit speeding up the commandeering and construction program.

William Denman, Chairman of the Shipping Board, and Major Gen. Goethals will hold a final conference tomorrow morning, according to the present plan, to go over the matters on which they have differed. It is possible that they cannot agree, but there was a distinct feeling tonight that something of a definite nature would come of the meeting.

It was understood that General Goethals had been in touch with the President, and that Mr. Wilson had made it known to all concerned that further delay could not be countenanced. Later reports that General Goethals had resigned or intended to resign were denied on every hand.

Whatever may be the outcome of the personal row between General Goethals and Mr. Denman, the point that stood out today was that the Administration had come to a point where it was unwilling to permit personal feelings to delay ship construction. It is said to be the desire of the President to bring about that result without losing either General Goethals or Mr. Denman. Only the developments of the next few days can tell if that is possible.

It was understood here today that Mr. Denman and some of his followers on the Shipping Board were at work on a program which was in effect a modified form of that submitted by General Goethals in his letter of last Friday to Mr. Denman. Early in the afternoon it was reported that he never would agree to the Goethals program as first prepared, and that caused rumors that there was every likelihood of another clash within twenty-four hours. These were discouraged at the Shipping Board offices, where the statement was given out that satisfactory progress was being made. There was no statement of any kind from General Goethals. He did not attend any of the Shipping Board conferences either, but it is known he

Continued on Page 3.

BAKER OPENS CEREMONIES

Blindfolded, He Takes "258" as First Number; One Blank Found.

SOLEMN SCENE IN CAPITOL

Army Officers, Congressmen, and Other Officials Watch the Huge Glass Bowl.

RIGID PRECAUTIONS TAKEN

Triple-Check System Employed and Numbers on Blackboard Are Photographed.

Special to The New York Times.

WASHINGTON, July 21.—In a room in the Senate Office Building the Government yesterday began the greatest lottery in history to select the men who will be called first in the drafting of an army to go to France.

At 2:18 o'clock, sixteen and a half hours after the first number was drawn, the lottery was completed. The 9,000th number was called out at midnight, and thereafter the drawing proceeded rapidly. At 1 o'clock the tellers reached the last thousand capsules. Serial No. 2 was drawn at exactly 2 o'clock, and the last capsule was opened eighteen minutes later.

The final number was 5,217, and it was the 10,499th number drawn. There should have been 10,500, but one capsule, the 10,004th, when opened contained only a blank without any figure on it.

For a while it was undecided whether to mark the 10,004th place "Blank" or to proceed as if there had been no blank and make notes of the fact. The latter course was followed.

The next number drawn after the blank was 5,669, and this received the 10,004th place. The tellers were instructed to note on their tally sheets that a blank had been drawn at this point.

It was hoped that it would turn out that one extra capsule had dropped in containing a blank. But this hope did not materialize. As the drawing closed with the 10,500th place designated as a blank, it will now be necessary to check up the entire list of numbers carefully to locate the number that should have been on the blank.

There were 10,500 capsules in the glass container when Secretary of War Baker drew out the first at 9:49 o'clock yesterday morning. As the Secretary, following a brief address on the dignity and solemnity of the occasion, drew 258 as the first number in all the registration districts throughout the country, a scene of unusual dramatic appeal came to its climax. Mr. Baker was blindfolded and led to the large glass jar. He reached within deliberately, held a capsule in plain view of a distinguished audience and said:

"I have drawn the first number."

The First Number.

A clerk assigned by the War Department opened the capsule and announced "258." An officer seated at the long table upon which were spread the tally sheets repeated the number, and another clerk walked to a large blackboard at the rear and wrote upon it the figures.

Simultaneously there came the clicking of moving picture cameras and the noise of the shutters in the "still picture" cameras. Dozens of newspaper correspondents, stationed at a long table, rustled copy paper and messengers darted toward waiting telegraph instruments which flashed the first result of the lottery to the country.

Senator Chamberlain of Oregon, likewise blindfolded, drew the second number. He was plainly nervous. His hand was guided at the top of the jar, which was fourteen inches in diameter.

"The second number is 2,522," said the announcer, and again there came the click of cameras, the rustle of copy paper, and the murmur of excited men and women who thronged the committee room.

Members of Congress and high officials of the army attended the start of the drawing. Eight numbers were drawn by officials before the ceremony became routine, with students from various universities acting as the blindfolded withdrawers of the fateful capsules.

Officials Start Drawing.

Chairman Dent of the House Committee on Military Affairs drew the third gelatin capsule from the jar. The number within was 9,613. In turn Senator Warren, Representative Kahn, the ranking Republican of the House Committee on Military Affairs, Major Gen. Tasker H. Bliss, Acting Chief of Staff; Provost Marshal General Enoch H. Crowder, and Adjt. Gen. McCain were blindfolded and led to the glass bowl.

A round of applause greeted the appearance of General Crowder, who had worked tirelessly for days perfecting the details of the nation-wide lottery. Adjt. Gen. McCain, too, was applauded by the newspaper correspondents and the

Continued on Page 5.

"All the News That's Fit to Print."

The New York Times.

THE WEATHER
Fair today; fair, cooler tomorrow; light northwesterly winds.
For full weather report see Page 19.

VOL. LXVI...NO. 21,755. NEW YORK, FRIDAY, AUGUST 17, 1917.—TWENTY PAGES. ONE CENT In Greater New York. | TWO CENTS Elsewhere N. Y. State, N. J., Conn. | THREE CENTS Other States.

WILSON EXPECTED TO SOUND ALLIES AFTER STUDYING POPE'S PEACE NOTE; NO HOPE OF ACCEPTANCE IS SEEN

DEEP DISTRUST OF BERLIN

Allies Insist Germany Must Offer Redress For Wrongs Done.

U-BOAT QUESTION IGNORED

Comment on Failure to Mention Cause of America's Entrance Into the War.

EQUAL BLAME IS DENIED

Lansing Emphasizes That No Decision Has Been Reached—Asks Suspension of Judgment.

Special to The New York Times.

WASHINGTON, Aug. 16.—The receipt by this Government of the official text of Pope Benedict's peace note has not changed in any way the situation as it is understood to exist in this and other capitals of the nations engaged in fighting the Prussian autocracy.

Nobody is authorized to represent the views of President Wilson and Secretary Lansing, and nothing has been officially disclosed as to the attitude of the Entente Governments toward the Pope's move, but opinion in Washington official circles and among the diplomatic agents of the Entente is generally to the effect that the proposal of the Pope cannot be accepted in the absence of assurance from Germany of willingness to make redress for the wrongs she has committed and to furnish satisfactory guarantees for the future.

It was only today that the State Department received the official text of the Pope's communication, which had been transmitted by the Papal Secretary of State to King George and handed by the London Foreign Office to the American Ambassador to Great Britain, who cabled it to Washington.

To be Considered Maturely.

Secretary Lansing had said that no consideration of the terms of the note would be given by this Government until the official text had been delivered to him. He emphasized this statement today in denying, with considerable force, a published assertion that he had told three foreign representatives this morning that the Pope's views were unacceptable to the United States.

In making the denial Mr. Lansing said that he had not discussed the Pope's proposal with President Wilson or anybody else, and he repeated that it would be well for the public to suspend judgment and speculation on this new effort to bring the great war to a close. Mr. Lansing added that he had never expressed the views of either the Government or himself on the Pope's communication.

But Mr. Lansing's attitude has not succeeded in suppressing comment in diplomatic and Governmental quarters over the Pope's bid for peace. The subject is too big and important to permit those most concerned to hide their views. What Mr. Lansing has succeeded in doing is to show that the President does not intend to answer the Pope's suggestions without mature consideration.

It is accepted that the Pope would not have made the momentous decision to attempt a peace movement at this time without having given the most careful thought to all the issues involved. With this feeling the President and the Secretary of State are expected to study the Pope's communication and determine the course they think this Government should follow with respect to it.

Will Seek Allies' Views.

In the absence of authoritative information it is asumed that before responding to the Pontiff Secretary Lansing will seek to ascertain the views of the nations that are associated with the United States in the war against Germany. Perhaps he may not engage in direct formal exchanges with the Allies, but it is likely that he will have our envoys in the Entente capitals sound Ministers of Foreign Affairs with the intention of ascertaining the general view of the situation, from the allied point, created by the proposal of the Pope.

The President, of course, will be free to say what he pleases, but it is not believed that he will depart from the general course upon which the allied Governments will decide with reference to the peace move.

Among the Entente diplomats the Pope's note is criticised as having three defects that render his proposal unacceptable to the nations at war with Germany. These were stated to be the proposal that there should be a reciprocal restitution of occupied territory, the suggestion that territorial and political questions, such as Alsace-Lorraine, Trieste, the Trentino, the Balkans, Serbia, Armenia, and Poland, should be settled by negotiation, and the omission from the note of consideration of the German submarine campaign, which was the original cause of the entrance of the United States into the war.

Deny Equal Responsibility.

The allied nations, it is gathered, will never be willing to admit that they had an equal responsibility with Austria and Germany for starting the war. One im-

Continued on Page 2.

Assert Pope Has Conveyed German Terms; Text of Note Not Announced in Berlin

Special Cable to THE NEW YORK TIMES.

BERLIN, Aug. 15, (via The Hague, Aug. 16.) Although the Papal peace message has not yet been made public in full here, "a political personage" gives the Lokal-Anzeiger the following information regarding it:

"It is not merely incidental that the message is given to the world on the day on which the Catholic Church celebrates the Feast of the Assumption of the Blessed Virgin Mary. At this time last year the Holy Father declared Mary Queen of Peace, and, in singing a litany, interceded: 'Queen of Peace, pray for us.'

"The Pope is much too clever a diplomat to undertake such a step without first informing himself what reception it would get from the two groups of powers. I think I may say that Benedict XV. knows the German peace conditions, and surely has communicated his knowledge to the enemy group.

"It is absolutely wrong to characterize the Reichstag majority peace resolution as a prelude to the Pope's present action. The allegation that the Centrist Party was inspired by the Pope to play a pioneer part in his peace actions is just as far from the truth. There has grown, nevertheless, an association of events since the Reichstag resolution created a base which is now serving the Holy Father for his action.

"My conviction is that the peace work now furthered by the Holy Father will lead to a happy conclusion. Not a long time hence we shall hear of peace negotiations, and before the year is ended this war will have found its termination, so anxiously desired by the whole world."

The Lokal-Anzeiger adds: "We cannot believe the Pope has any real hope of reaching peace in this manner, but we must wait until we have seen the authentic publication."

The paper admonishes Germany to observe an attitude of cool reserve.

Berlin Press Divided on Proposal

AMSTERDAM, Aug. 16.—The Kreuz-Zeitung of Berlin, a copy of which has been received here, says sympathy with the Pope's wish for peace must disappear when it is seen that he has united himself with such conditions as restorations and no indemnities.

The Berlin Tägliche Rundschau considers that the nature of the peace outlined by the Pope must compel the Central Powers to refuse the offices of the Pontiff. This newspaper says it fears the affair will have an unhappy influence, not only in Austria, but among the Catholics in Germany.

The Kölnische Zeitung asserts that it is not aware of the German Government's attitude, but that it believes logic prescribes that the Government, in conformity with its previous attitude, should follow the path indicated by the Pontiff.

"The German people and Government have the will and courage for peace," says the Kölnische Zeitung. "The Entente people also earnestly desire peace, but the enemy Governments are dominated by the fear of peace, as is proved by their refusal to grant passports to their nationals to attend the Stockholm conference. The Pope's proposal will thus be another test of which side cherishes a sincere desire for peace."

The Cologne Volkszeitung expresses the hope that, despite all obstacles, the road to the reconciliation of the nations may be paved by the Pope's appeal.

BRITONS BITTER OVER POPE'S PLEA

See in Lloyd George's "Fight to a Finish" Talk Blow to Rome's Plan.

SAY KAISER IS BEHIND IT

Criticism Made That Benedict Has Stood Still Regardless of All That Urged Wilson On.

Special Cable to THE NEW YORK TIMES.

LONDON, Aug. 16.—While Lloyd George made no direct or specific reference to the Papal peace appeal in his speech in the Commons this afternoon, its tone showed not the slightest indication of any belief that the Vatican's intervention at this stage will bring about peace. The Premier, indeed, when speaking on the tonnage question referred to the requirements of 1918 and 1919 as if possibly war would still be continuing during those years.

It would, of course, be improper to construe Lloyd George's words into meaning that he believes the war will last another two or three years. He was merely making necessary calculations in regard to its prosecution in the event of its continuance for so long, or, in other words, in the event of Germany being still unbeaten or unwilling to make peace on terms that will make the world safe for democracy.

"This is a fight to a finish," declared the Prime Minister, and though, as already mentioned, his speech today cannot be regarded as a direct, specific reply to the Pope's message, the whole House vigorously applauded the phrase as reflecting the unfaltering determination of England to carry on the struggle till the ends, which Asquith later enunciated, unequivocally had been attained.

Say Pope Stands Still.

The complete text of the Papal appeal for peace furnishes no more ground for believing that peace can be made now than did the summaries telegraphed throughout the world yesterday. If anything, the Papal message in its entirety is more of a disappointment than encouragement to those who expected and hoped most from it. I have heard it compared today to President Wilson's peace message of December, 1916, and his league of nations speech, greatly to the disadvantage of the Pontifical essay.

Benedict X has stood still regardless of all that urged President Wilson to move forward. He talks of the substitution of the moral force of right for the material force of arms despite the significance of the fact that the United States has been forced to take up arms to defend her rights. He looks to general acceptance of arbitration which shall do away with armies while the world is still menaced by the greatest military organization in history. With that organization still dominant, how are the sanctions against States which would refuse to submit

Continued on Page 2.

SENATE WILL KILL PEACE RESOLUTION

Leaders Plan to Act on La Follette Measure After a Brief Debate.

HAVE WILSON'S APPROVAL

One Democrat and One Republican Will Answer Pacifists—Then End the Incident.

Special to The New York Times.

WASHINGTON, Aug. 16.—No peace resolution is to be adopted by the Senate calling upon President Wilson at this time to define the aims of the United States in the war or to suggest any policy for him to follow in dealing with Germany. That was definitely decided late today at a conference of Democratic and Republican leaders of the Senate after Senator King of Utah had conferred with the President at the White House.

The program of the Senate is to allow Senator La Follette of Wisconsin to bring up his peace resolution any time he wishes, and, after brief debate on it, to kill it by a decisive vote. Any effort in the meantime to get any other peace resolution through will be dealt with by consigning the resolution to the table, to stay there until the La Follette measure is brought up.

The Senate is determined to end by an overwhelming vote all efforts to embarrass the Administration by attempting to dictate a policy as to peace overtures. Senator La Follette and any other supporters of his resolution may talk as long as they wish. When they have exhausted themselves the scheme is to have some Democratic leader, who is likely to be Senator John Sharp Williams of Mississippi, and some Republican leader, probably Senator Lodge of Massachusetts, answer for both sides of the Chamber. After these two speeches have been made the leaders will insist upon a vote on the resolution.

Senate leaders say the La Follette resolution cannot have more than seven supporting votes—Gore, Norris, Vardaman, Stone, Gronna, Kirby, and La Follette himself. If all of these Senators insist upon being heard it is likely that the Senate will have at least a full day and possibly two or three of peace debate. And that will be the end of it.

Senator Stone is to have his own resolution ready for next week, but it will have to wait until Senator La Follette's comes up. After the defeat of La Follette's measure, Stone's, it is planned, will be quickly voted down.

Senator King conferred with the other Senate leaders for an hour after his talk with the President, and the program respecting the peace resolutions was evolved after Mr. King had urged that policy as being agreeable to the Executive.

Senator La Follette's resolution will lie on the table until after the War Revenue bill is voted upon, which is expected to be at the end of next week. The peace debate probably will not come up until a week from next Monday.

Officer of German Navy Arrested as a Spy With Alleged Accomplice at San Francisco

SAN FRANCISCO, Aug. 16.—Lieutenant Irving F. Schneider of the German Navy was arrested here on a Presidential warrant as a spy three days ago, Department of Justice officials announced today. Many maps and papers, declared to be of an incriminating nature, were found in his possession.

With Schneider was arrested Theodore Kasinger, a former department store employe, who is accused of aiding Schneider in obtaining maps and other military information. They are alleged to have occupied apartments with four Austrian officers, who are being sought. By the President's order the prisoners are being held incommunicado without bail and without the privilege of a hearing.

Among Schneider's effects was an iron cross, said to have been received by him for services rendered in the German Navy. He recently married a young woman of Oakland, Cal.

Federal authorities said Schneider tried to join an aviation corps and later another department of the military service here, but was prevented by circumstances not announced. He recently attempted to sail from this port on a Swedish vessel, it was said, but was balked by the Secret Service.

CROPSEY DECIDES TO STAY ON BENCH

Formally Announces That He Will Not Enter the Primaries Against Mayor Mitchel.

FUSION PICKS MORE MEN

Democrats Protest Vainly at Court Selections in Kings—Gannon to Run in Richmond.

Supreme Court Justice James C. Cropsey of Brooklyn issued a statement last night eliminating himself as a candidate for the Mayoralty nomination in the Republican primaries against Mayor Mitchel. Justice Cropsey, after thanking the citizens who signed petitions asking him to enter the race, made the point that even if nominated and elected he would have but three votes in the Board of Estimate, and therefore could not offset the votes of the other members who might not be in harmony with him. This is the statement:

The sentiment expressed by the many thousand voters who urged me to enter the primary as a candidate for Mayor is most gratifying. Their interest, support and good wishes are sincerely appreciated, and I cannot express adequately my heartfelt thanks. I have given the request most careful and conscientious consideration, and after much deliberation am convinced that I should not enter the primaries.

If I did and was nominated, the anti-Tammany ticket would not represent either the views of those who oppose the present administration or of those who favor it. The balance of the ticket would consist of the Fusion selections. If the people of the city want a continuance of the present administration they should re-elect all the officers. The city is governed by the Board of Estimate. The Mayor casts but three votes in the board out of a total of sixteen. The majority vote of that board must be in harmony on the fundamental propositions affecting the city, otherwise no constructive work can be accomplished. The Mayor's vote represents but a small minority unless the other members are in sympathy with him.

Were I to comply with the request and be nominated and elected, I would be in the position of one opposed both to the present administration and to Tammany, and could hardly expect the co-operation of the men selected either by the Fusion Committee or by Tammany.

Mr. Cropsey's statement was given out last night by Joseph Early, a close friend of the Justice. A statement of some kind setting forth the Justice's views had been expected ever since it was announced by Jacob A. Livingston, the Republican leader of Brooklyn, and chief Cropsey lieutenant, that Mr. Cropsey was seriously considering making the fight against Mayor Mitchel.

It was said last night by Brooklyn Republican leaders that Justice Cropsey, up to Monday night, practically had made up his mind to enter the Republican primary, but that the announcement of Controller Eugene M. Travis that he would support Mayor Mitchel and the Fusion ticket, took away the last support which the Justice had depended upon. Previous to that Senator Calder and F. J. H. Kracke, leader of the Mitchel forces in Brooklyn, as well as Governor Whitman, had said that they would not support a Cropsey movement.

Justice Cropsey's lieutenants hoped on Wednesday that they would be able to get several responsible Republicans in New York City and the other boroughs to accept places on his ticket as candidates for Board of Estimate offices, Mr. Cropsey feeling that he would have little show if he ran alone. It was said that efforts were made to have Borough President Marcus M. Marks go on the proposed ticket as candidate for Controller. President Marks refused to consider the proposal, however, and no candidates of importance could be found to run for the other offices.

Attitude of Fusionists.

The Cropsey situation has long been a thorn in the side of Fusion. The Fusion leaders feared that the movement would make a split in the Brooklyn Republican organization, and efforts were started last week to get Mr. Livingston to desert the Cropsey cause. An arrangement finally was made with Mr. Livingston whereby he was permitted to choose a candidate for Sheriff of Kings County if he would try to influence Justice Cropsey not to run. From that time the Cropsey cause began to fade and the Fusion leaders said that it did not matter much to them just what Mr. Cropsey did.

William Hamlin Childs, Chairman of the Executive Committee of the Fusion Committee, expressed satisfaction last night that the situation finally had been cleared up.

"I believe Mr. Cropsey's decision," he said, "will meet with the approval of all intelligent citizens of the city. Considering all the circumstances, it is a patriotic action and highly to be commended."

The Fusion leaders showed every disposition last night not to gloat over their triumph. They said they hoped that Justice Cropsey soon would see his way clear to come out in support of the entire fusion ticket.

The Fusion Committee of 250 wound up its preprimary work yesterday by selecting candidates for county offices in Richmond and candidates for the Supreme Court in the Kings and Queens district. For President of the Borough of Richmond Frank S. Gannon, Jr., was chosen. Thomas F. Banolf was selected

Continued on Page 5.

WOOD TO TRAIN A DRAFT DIVISION

Former Chief of Staff Placed in Command of 89th at Fort Riley, Kansas.

BELL GOES TO YAPHANK

His Division New York City Draft Troops—O'Ryan Commands New York Guards.

Special to The New York Times.

WASHINGTON, Aug. 16.—The division and brigade commanders of the main component parts of the army of 923,000 men composed of National Guardsmen and drafted men to be trained for service in France was announced by the War Department tonight.

The assignment of thirty-two Major Generals, one for each of the new national army divisions and one for each National Guard division, was announced in the list. In making the assignments the War Department necessarily utilized most of the new Major and Brigadier Generals whose nominations were sent to the Senate this week by President Wilson. But there were some notable exceptions, all six of the department commanders, Major Gens. Bell, Wood, Liggett, Edwards, Parker, and Barry, being assigned to take command of divisions.

Major Gen. J. Franklin Bell, Commander of the Department of the East, with headquarters at Governor's Island, will command the Seventy-seventh national army division, which is to be trained at Camp Upton, at Yaphank, L. I. This division will consist of the soldiers now being drafted from metropolitan New York.

Major Gen. Leonard Wood, former Commander at Governors Island, but now at Charleston, S. C., in command of the Southeastern Department, will command the Eighty-ninth national army division at Camp Funston, at Fort Riley, Kan. The division will be composed of men from Kansas, Missouri, and Colorado.

Major Gen. John F. O'Ryan of the New York National Guard will command the Twenty-seventh division at Camp Wadsworth, Spartanburg, S. C. This division will be made up of guardsmen from the Empire State.

Three Rank Pershing.

Three of the Major Generals who will command divisions—Wood, Bell, and Barry—in the order named, rank Major Gen. Pershing. They could not be sent to France in command of these divisions and serve under Pershing, unless he were promoted. For that reason Wood, Bell, and Barry have been placed in charge of the training of three of the new divisions of the national army. These will be formed of drafted men, who, in the natural order of events, would be the last to complete their training and the last to be ready to go to France. By the time these men are ready to go to the front it is expected that legislation will have been enacted permitting the promotion of Pershing to be a Lieutenant General or a full General. If Pershing should be made a full General, then Wood, Bell, and Barry would be in line for the rank of Lieutenant General and would be placed in command of army corps. The three Major Generals who do not rank Pershing and who are department commanders—Edwards, Parker, and Liggett—have been placed in command of divisions of the National Guard army, which, when trained, can be sent to France with these officers serving under Pershing as Major Generals.

Major Gen. Bell, who will command the drafted men from New York City, will have as his Chief of Staff Lieut. Col. Ewing E. Booth, a well known cavalry officer of the regular army. There will be two infantry brigades in this division. One of these, to be known as the 153d, will be commanded by Brig. Gen. Edmund Wittenmyer, an unassigned infantry officer, who was until this week a Colonel of regulars, but has just been nominated for Brigadier General in the National Army. The other infantry brigade of the Seventy-seventh Division will be commanded by Brig. Gen. Evan M. Johnson of the Fifth Infantry of the U. S. A. Johnson is 56 years old and Wittenmyer is 55. Brig. Gen. George W. Read, a cavalry officer, will have command of the 132d, or depot brigade, in General Bell's division, while Brig. Gen. John D. Barrette of the Coast Artillery will command the 152d Field Artillery Brigade in General Bell's division.

Major Gen. O'Ryan, in command of the Twenty-seventh Division, will have as his Chief of Staff Colonel Harry H. Bandholtz, who was until recently Major of the Thirtieth United States Infantry. Brig. Gen. James W. Lester is placed in command of the Seventy-second Depot Brigade of the Twenty-seventh Division. The officer chosen to command the

Continued on Page 11.

ALLIES SWEEP FORWARD IN FLANDERS; WIN LANGEMARCK, BEGIN NEW ADVANCE; 1,800 PRISONERS AND HEAVY GUNS TAKEN

Germany Is Now Not Able to Hold Her Own, Says Lloyd George, Telling of Haig's Success

LONDON, Aug. 16.—First announcement of the taking of Langemarck by the British troops in today's successful drive of the Allies in Flanders was made by Premier Lloyd George in the House of Commons. He stated that Field Marshal Haig had telegraphed that 1,200 prisoners and five guns had been captured by noon today.

The Premier added: "Germany now is barely able to hold her own—not even that."

The Premier then referred to Russia as "one claw of the nippers temporarily out of repair." Germany, he said, had been beaten in several great battles, with large losses, when Russia was practically out of the campaign. He asked what might be anticipated when Russia recovered and America was really in. America's troops had been seen marching through the streets, symbols of her resolute entry into the struggle. This was the hour, the Premier added, of Germany's difficulties.

Lloyd George Shows Britain U-Boat Campaign Has Failed

From 560,000 Tons in April Losses Have Dropped to Probable 175,000 Each for July and August, with Great Increase in Building—Food Situation Good.

LONDON, Aug. 16.—Giving for the first time actual totals of shipping tonnage lost from month to month through Germany's submarine campaign and estimates of the food supply, Premier Lloyd George, in the House of Commons today, proved to Parliament and the country that the Admiralty plans for dealing with the U-boats have been increasingly successful, and that "with reasonable economy" there is no chance of England being starved out. Enthusiastic cheering greeted his revelations.

The Premier said he agreed that the people of the country were all the better for being told even unpalatable truths. But they also must be told the truth even if it was palatable. They could not exercise reasonable judgment or come to decisions regarding facts unless both the cheery and discouraging sides were presented to them.

He purposed to deal with the food situation and submarines because special efforts were being made to create an impression not justified in the least by the facts. Earlier in the year he had called attention to the very anxious condition of the food supply. Since then, owing largely to the energetic efforts of Baron Devonport, the former Food Controller, and organization by the Shipping Controller, the situation had improved considerably.

Situation Last Year and This.

At this time last year, he said, the wheat in this country amounted to 6,480,000 quarters, and that now it was 8,500,000 quarters. (A quarter is equivalent to 480 pounds.) The stock of oats and barley also was higher.

There had been a considerable saving in bread consumption, and owing to closer milling and food economy there had been an addition to the wheat stock of 70,000 quarters per week. Moreover, there had been an increase in the sugar reserve.

Wheat under cultivation showed an increase of 1,000,000 acres. It was too early to give a prediction on this year's harvest because everything depended on the next two or three weeks. If the harvest was good—as it promised to be—and the weather not particularly capricious, the condition of the country regarding food supplies, taking everything into account, was very satisfactory. He still urged economy in view of the general wheat position. The more the country economized the less it would have to draw upon the reservoirs of the United States and Canada, from which Italy and France also had to draw.

The necessary labor for the harvest would be forthcoming, and by Spring there would be 8,000 tractors.

Dealing with the shipping situation, the Premier said that the Germans had been busy circulating figures regarding the destruction of shipping. They were doing it in Germany to cheer up their own people and were circulating a set of figures throughout Germany and Austria on the authority of the German Admiralty with the object of creating the impression that England could not last much longer.

The unrestricted submarine campaign began in February, and by April England had lost 560,000 tons of shipping in one month. The German official figures, he added, claimed that England was losing between 450,000 and 500,000 monthly after allowing for new construction. The figure of 560,000 tons for April was gross. In June the losses had fallen to 320,000 tons gross, and if the improvement were maintained those for July and August would be 175,000 each.

Steps had been taken for quickening shipbuilding, and a good many ships had been ordered abroad. In 1915 the new tonnage built was 688,000 tons. In 1916 it was 538,000 tons. For the first six months of this year it was 480,000 tons. The tonnage acquired during the last six months would be 1,420,000, of which 1,100,000 had been built in Great Britain. The total for the year would be 1,800,000 tons. A considerable addition also had been made in the program of naval construction.

The Shipping Controller so far had organized shipping by means of better loading and hiring of ships more quickly and by taking ships off longer voyages. Thus, although the tonnage was diminished, they were carrying more tons.

Premier Lloyd George said he believed the shipping losses would grow smaller. He was sure construction would increase if more ships were still needed. If the United States put forward her full capacity, as he had no doubt she was preparing to do in her own thorough way, there would be sufficient tonnage not only for the whole of 1918, but, if necessary, for 1919.

Outlook for Enemy Bad.

The Premier said he would not exchange the military situation with the enemy, adding: "Our difficulties will diminish and our powers will increase. The enemy's difficulties will increase and their power diminish."

"I do not think," he went on, "the time has come for a useful review of the military situation. The main facts are well known to the House and the country. I had anticipated this year a great converging movement against our foes. Russia was equipped for that part as she never before had been equipped. I venture to say that the nippers were beginning to grip, but, to be quite frank, one claw of the nippers is out of repair for the moment, and therefore we have not got the same converging pressure we had anticipated.

"But things are mending. The situation in Russia is a very difficult one, and I should be sorry to say anything which would make it more difficult, because it is quite obvious you cannot even state facts without embarrassing those who are trying to restore the situation in that country. But while they are doing it bravely, with great courage, and, I think, with great thoroughness, the brunt of the fighting must fall upon other countries. And considering all the difficulties with which we are confronted, our armies have won very conspicuous successes.

"It is difficult even to dwell on the difference which the temporary collapse of the Russian military power has made in the task with which our soldiers are confronted."

Mr. Lloyd George said that British divisions which have been fighting and temporarily are exhausted pass behind the lines until they are re-formed, but that the German divisions in the same condition go to Russia and hold a front which does not impose severe military obligation, while fresh divisions from Russia come to the western front. That increased the number of Germans on the western front.

Under those conditions what had been achieved was one of the most brilliant episodes in the history of the British army.

"The best that Germany can do now," Mr. Lloyd George continued, "when what practically was her most powerful opponent at the beginning of the war is paralyzed by internal difficulties, is to hold her own against the attacks of the British and French. And she isn't quite doing it. On the contrary, in this year she has been beaten in several great battles, with severe losses and with hundreds of her guns captured, which is not a bad test of winning or losing a battle.

"Russia recovered and America really in, with those fine troops of which we saw a specimen yesterday and which were a symbol of America coming into this world struggle with a virile swing—those are the things the Germans and their allies will have think about."

The Supreme Hour.

Mr. Lloyd George then read a message from Field Marshal Haig about the fighting in Flanders, and concluded.

"This is the supreme hour for patience, for courage, for endurance, for hope, for unity. Let us go through this hour with a temper that will enable us to destroy a great military despotism. Let us go through this hour with the old temper of our race, so that next year we shall begin, and then the world will begin, to reap the fruits of our valor."

Former Premier Asquith said that Great Britain could survey with satisfaction, if not with complacency—for who could survey complacently the scene now presented to the civilized world?—the results of her own effort. What had happened in Russia had frustrated one of the greatest military purposes of the Allies, and any criticism passed on this year's operations must bear in mind that important consideration. Mr. Asquith added:

"I hope that before long our Russian allies, whose work in the first two and a half years of the war furnished a glorious and inspiring chapter, will resume to the full their share of the great common task to which I believe the Russian nation still is devoted."

Mr. Asquith declared that the key to success today was not monetary expenditure but labor—labor on land and labor in shipping.

"We must be assured," he continued, "of the loyal co-operation of labor. We

Continued on Page 3.

STRIKE ON A 9-MILE FRONT

French On the Left and British Centre Win Much Ground.

RIGHT GAINS, THEN LOSES

After Capturing Langemarck, a Main Objective, British Troops Push On from the Town.

MORE FIGHTING NEAR LENS

Canadians Withstand Ten Furious Assaults—Nearly 900 Prisoners Taken There.

LONDON, Aug. 16.—Striking together on a nine-mile front east and northeast of Ypres in Flanders early this morning, British and French troops carried all their objectives except on the right flank, and tonight unofficial advices say that a new advance was ordered this afternoon.

The French, on the left, drove the Germans from the tongue of land between the Yser Canal and the Martjevaart and captured the bridgehead of Dreigrachten.

In the centre Haig's troops captured the village of Langemarck, which has been held strongly by the Germans ever since the allied attack of early this month, and pushed half a mile beyond. The Reuter correspondent at British headquarters reports tonight that fighting is proceeding well beyond the town.

On the right British troops attempted to seize the high ground almost directly east of Ypres, which lies north of the road to Menin. They swept up and gained the ground, but in the face of terrific losses the Germans attacked with great fury, and finally pressed the British back from the terrain they had won.

More than 1,800 prisoners, including thirty-eight officers, already have been counted by the Anglo-French forces. Some German guns have been taken.

In addition to the successes won in the Ypres sector the British have made further progress east of Loos and north of Lens. Severe fighting has been going on there ever since the Canadians won Hill 70 yesterday morning, but the repeated German assaults have been futile.

Official Account of Progress.

The night bulletin of the British War Office gives this account of the day's events:

The allied attacks, delivered early in the morning on a front of nine miles north of the Ypres-Menin road, have been continued during the day in the face of strong enemy resistance.

On the left the French troops, advancing on both sides of the Zuydschoote-Dixmude road, drove the enemy from the tongue of land between the Yser Canal and the Martjevaart and captured the bridgehead of Dreigrachten.

In the centre the British troops rapidly captured their first objectives, and, continuing their advance, carried the village of Langemarck after heavy fighting. They then forced their way forward a distance of half a mile beyond the village and established themselves in the German trench system, which constituted their final objective for the day.

On our right there has been fierce and continuous fighting since the early morning for the possession of the high ground north of the Menin Road. The enemy disputed our advance with determination, counterattacking with large forces. As the result of the counterattacks the enemy succeeded during the afternoon, at great cost, in pressing back our troops in this area from part of the ground won earlier in the day. This evening further enemy counterattacks in this neighborhood were broken up by our artillery fire.

The number of prisoners taken by the Allies in the course of this attack cannot yet be ascertained, but over 1,800, including 58 officers, already have been brought in. A few German guns also were captured.

Our troops made further progress this afternoon east of Loos. The number of troops we captured on this front since the opening of our attack yesterday has now reached a total of 806, including 22 officers.

Throughout yesterday's attack our airplanes co-operated successfully with the artillery and assisted effectively with machine gunfire in repelling the enemy's counterattacks. In the air fighting eleven German airplanes were brought down and four others were driven down out of control. Another was brought down by anti-aircraft fire. Three of our airplanes are missing. Today also our aircraft has done excellent work.

The early bulletin telling of the opening of the attack reads:

At 4:45 o'clock this morning the

Mid-Week Pictorial

German prisoners carrying their own disabled machine guns to the British lines in Flanders.

"All the News That's Fit to Print."

The New York Times.

THE WEATHER
Partly cloudy, cooler today; Thursday cloudy; light, variable winds.
For full weather report see Page 15.

VOL. LXVI...NO. 21,767. NEW YORK, WEDNESDAY, AUGUST 29, 1917.—TWENTY PAGES. ONE CENT In Greater New York. | TWO CENTS Elsewhere N. Y. State, N. J., Conn. | THREE CENTS Other States.

PRESIDENT REJECTS THE POPE'S PEACE PLAN; CANNOT TRUST GERMANY'S PRESENT RULERS; HER GREAT PEOPLE MUST FIND THE WAY OUT

SPEAKS FOR ALLIES

Entente May Merely Indorse President's Answer.

AIMED AT GERMAN PEOPLE

Washington Thinks His Declaration Marks the High-Water Mark of the War.

SHOWS INFLEXIBLE PURPOSE

Terminates All Efforts at Compromise Peace, According to the Capital View.

No Action by the Pope Pending Peace Replies

By The Associated Press.

PARIS, Aug. 28.—A dispatch to the Intransigeant from Rome says: "Vatican circles say that Pope Benedict does not intend to issue a second or explanatory note to clear up his peace proposals, as it had been reported he would do, but will wait until he has heard from the belligerents before offering any interpretation of his original communication."

By The Associated Press.

WASHINGTON, Aug. 28.—President Wilson's rejection of the Pope's peace proposals is regarded here as the high-water mark of the war. Furthermore, it is indicative of the virtual selection of the President by the Allies as their spokesman before the world.

The note comes as a climax to the remarkable series of State documents in which President Wilson has argued the cause of world democracy against autocracy in the high court of public opinion, and accepted more and more by the people of all the allied countries as expressing their ideals.

There appears to be no doubt that the United States was selected to make answer before the world, in advance of all the others. Whether the Entente nations will send extensive replies is not known here. It is regarded as probable that they will in large measure adopt the President's reasoning for their own and send notes of indorsement.

A high official is authority for the statement that the President's reply is "in line with the Allies' views."

The general tenor of the President's reply had been anticipated everywhere, but there was no inkling of the forceful terms he would employ to say that the world could have no faith in the autocratic Government of Germany. Students of diplomacy see in his denunciation of the military autocracy a fresh appeal to the war-ridden German people to throw off their military masters and join democracy with a Government fit to deal with the remainder of the world.

Although this appeal probably will not be permitted to become known in Germany, until the autocracy has attempted to mold the temper of the people for its reception by denunciation through a Government-controlled press of what has been characterized as interference in the internal affairs of Germany, the hope is that it will fall on fertile soil.

Considering the extraordinary character of the President's communication, its immense importance in definitely terminating for the present at least all efforts to reach a compromise, peace, and the assured fact that it represents the views of all of the Entente Allied Powers joined with America in the war against Germany, the time occupied in the preparation of the reply was remarkably short.

His Purpose Inflexible.

That the President's response to the Pope's overtures would be a courteous but firm declination had been generally believed, so that in this respect at least his communication will cause no surprise. The feature that is certain to fix public attention is the cold determination not even to permit the subject of peace negotiations to be broached so long as the evil and dominating forces of autocracy and militarism control the Central Powers. It is not even necessary to read between the lines of the President's response to see clearly apparent the inflexible purpose.

For this reason the President was not to be led into any discussion of the peace conditions detailed by Pope Benedict, though that field was made alluring by the Pontiff's adoption of some of the proposals laid down by President Wilson himself in early utterances. On the other hand, there was no effort to evade responsibility for an expression of view as to the bases of sound and enduring peace. For the President's response in its concluding paragraphs restates the purposes for which America entered the great war.

The radical difference that appears to exist between the Pope and the President touched/this very matter of a stable and

Continued on Page 2.

President Wilson's Reply to the Pope

WASHINGTON, D. C., Aug. 27, 1917.

To His Holiness Benedictus XV., Pope:

In acknowledgment of the communication of your Holiness to the belligerent peoples, dated Aug. 1, 1917, the President of the United States requests me to transmit the following reply:

Every heart that has not been blinded and hardened by this terrible war must be touched by this moving appeal of his Holiness the Pope, must feel the dignity and force of the humane and generous motives which prompted it, and must fervently wish that we might take the path of peace he so persuasively points out. But it would be folly to take it if it does not in fact lead to the goal he proposes. Our response must be based upon the stern facts, and upon nothing else. It is not a mere cessation of arms he desires; it is a stable and enduring peace. This agony must not be gone through with again, and it must be a matter of very sober judgment what will insure us against it.

His Holiness in substance proposes that we return to the status quo ante-bellum and that then there be a general condonation, disarmament, and a concert of nations based upon an acceptance of the principle of arbitration; that by a similar concert freedom of the seas be established; and that the territorial claims of France and Italy, the perplexing problems of the Balkan States, and the restitution of Poland be left to such conciliatory adjustments as may be possible in the new temper of such a peace, due regard being paid to the aspirations of the peoples whose political fortunes and affiliations will be involved.

It is manifest that no part of this program can be successfully carried out unless the restitution of the status quo ante furnishes a firm and satisfactory basis for it. The object of this war is to deliver the free peoples of the world from the menace and the actual power of a vast military establishment, controlled by an irresponsible Government, which, having secretly planned to dominate the world, proceeded to carry the plan out without regard either to the sacred obligations of treaty or the long-established practices and long-cherished principles of international action and honor; which chose its own time for the war; delivered its blow fiercely and suddenly; stopped at no barrier, either of law or of mercy; swept a whole continent within the tide of blood—not the blood of soldiers only, but the blood of innocent women and children also and of the helpless poor; and now stands balked, but not defeated, the enemy of four-fifths of the world.

This power is not the German people. It is the ruthless master of the German people. It is no business of ours how that great people came under its control or submitted with temporary zest to the domination of its purpose; but it is our business to see to it that the history of the rest of the world is no longer left to its handling.

To deal with such a power by way of peace upon the plan proposed by his Holiness the Pope would, so far as we can see, involve a recuperation of its strength and a renewal of its policy; would make it necessary to create a permanent hostile combination of nations against the German people, who are its instruments; and would result in abandoning the new-born Russia to the intrigue, the manifold subtle interference, and the certain counter-revolution which would be attempted by all the malign influences to which the German Government has of late accustomed the world.

Can peace be based upon a restitution of its power or upon any word of honor it could pledge in a treaty of settlement and accommodation?

Responsible statesmen must now everywhere see, if they never saw before, that no peace can rest securely upon political or economic restrictions meant to benefit some nations and cripple or embarrass others, upon vindictive action of any sort, or any kind of revenge or deliberate injury. The American people have suffered intolerable wrongs at the hands of the Imperial German Government, but they desire no reprisal upon the German people, who have themselves suffered all things in this war, which they did not choose. They believe that peace should rest upon the rights of peoples, not the rights of Governments—the rights of peoples, great or small, weak or powerful—their equal right to freedom and security and self-government and to a participation upon fair terms in the economic opportunities of the world, the German people, of course, included, if they will accept equality and not seek domination.

The test, therefore, of every plan of peace is this: Is it based upon the faith of all the peoples involved, or merely upon the word of an ambitious and intriguing Government, on the one hand, and of a group of free peoples, on the other? This is a test which goes to the root of the matter; and it is the test which must be applied.

The purposes of the United States in this war are known to the whole world—to every people to whom the truth has been permitted to come. They do not need to be stated again. We seek no material advantage of any kind. We believe that the intolerable wrongs done in this war by the furious and brutal power of the Imperial German Government ought to be repaired, but not at the expense of the sovereignty of any people—rather a vindication of the sovereignty both of those that are weak and of those that are strong. Punitive damages, the dismemberment of empires, the establishment of selfish and exclusive economic leagues, we deem inexpedient, and in the end worse than futile, no proper basis for a peace of any kind, least of all for an enduring peace. That must be based upon justice and fairness and the common rights of mankind.

We cannot take the word of the present rulers of Germany as a guarantee of anything that is to endure unless explicitly supported by such conclusive evidence of the will and purpose of the German people themselves as the other peoples of the world would be justified in accepting. Without such guarantees treaties of settlement, agreements for disarmament, covenants to set up arbitration in the place of force, territorial adjustments, reconstitutions of small nations, if made with the German Government, no man, no nation, could now depend on.

We must await some new evidence of the purposes of the great peoples of the Central Powers. God grant it may be given soon and in a way to restore the confidence of all peoples everywhere in the faith of nations and the possibility of a covenanted peace.

ROBERT LANSING,
Secretary of State of the United States of America.

AUTOCRACY A PERIL

Secretly Planned to Dominate World, Wilson Declares.

KNOW NO LAW OR MERCY

"Swept Whole Continent Within the Tide of Blood and Now Stands Balked."

CAN GIVE NO GUARANTEES

To Deal with Such a Power Now Would Abandon Russia to Certain Intrigue.

Special to The New York Times.

WASHINGTON, Aug. 28.—President Wilson's response to Pope Benedict's peace proposals is a courteous but firm refusal to have any dealings with the present German autocracy. The text of the President's answer, made public by the State Department tonight, contains a scathing, even bitter, indictment of the Imperial German Government for cruelty, injustice, dishonesty, a bloodthirsty disregard of human rights.

"This power," says the President, "is not the German people. It is the ruthless master of the German people." Until that power has changed, until guarantees from Berlin are "explicitly supported by such conclusive evidence of the will and purpose of the German people themselves as the other peoples of the world would be justified in accepting," the Government of the United States will enter into no negotiations for peace.

There is no mistaking the President's purpose. Peace at this time is impossible in his view. The President expresses appreciation of "the dignity and force of the humane and generous motives" that prompted the Pontiff's offer, but he views it as a suggestion that the nations at war return to the status quo ante bellum, with a settlement of many perplexing problems left to be based on the principle of arbitration, and he feels that no satisfactory basis for such a settlement can be afforded while it is dependent on the promises of "an irresponsible Government."

Sought World Domination.

That irresponsible Government, in the words of the President's indictment, "having secretly planned to dominate the world, proceeded to carry the plan out without regard either to the sacred obligations of treaty or the long-established practices and long-cherished principles of international action and honor, which chose its own time for the war; delivered its blow fiercely and suddenly; stopped at no barrier either of law or of mercy; swept a whole continent within the tide of blood—not the blood of soldiers only, but the blood of innocent women and children also and of the helpless poor; and now stands balked but not defeated, the enemy of four-fifths of the world."

Men who are in the President's confidence have been saying privately that he had set his teeth in the determination to go on with the war until the German autocracy had come to an end. His words confirm all that they have said.

The President's response fairly bristles with indignant denunciation of the German Government. He is careful to make a distinction between the German people and their rulers. He holds out the hope to the German people that they will not be made the subject of revenge on account of the crimes of those who have plunged them into the bloody struggle which has come from the ambition of these men. The object of the war, says the President, is to deliver the free peoples of the world from the menace and the actual power of a vast military establishment controlled by an irresponsible Government.

Contains Message to Russia.

To have peace on the Pope's terms would merely bring a repetition of the conditions that prevailed before the war, in the President's opinion. Germany would recuperate its strength and renew its policy, and it would be necessary for the other nations to form a hostile combination against the German people.

In this connection the President sends a message of hope and cheer to the Russians. A return to the ante-bellum conditions, he says, would result in abandoning the new-born Russia to the intrigues and all the malign influences "to which the German Government has of late accustomed the world."

In the form of a question, the President says, in effect, that peace based on a restitution of Germany's power, or on its word of honor to observe treaty obligations, would be impossible. To the German people he holds out the assurance that they will be included, "if they will accept equality and not seek domination," in the peace which he hopes for and in which the American people believe, resting upon the rights of peoples, not the rights of Governments.

The President consistently adheres to

KORNILOFF FEARS FOR RUSSIAN ARMY

Paints an Alarming Picture of Its Condition in Address to Moscow Council.

NEAR END OF ITS SUPPLIES

Kerensky Had Asked the General to Make No Statement, but He Went Ahead.

Moscow Council Cheers President Wilson's Message

LONDON, Aug. 28.—President Wilson's message promising the full support of the United States was read to the National Council at Moscow yesterday. A dispatch to the Exchange Telegraph Company says this was the first and only incident that brought complete agreement in the convention, all the delegates rising and cheering wildly.

MOSCOW, Monday, Aug. 27.—The second general sitting of the National Conference was held this afternoon. General Korniloff, the Commander in Chief, entered the hall in company with Premier Kerensky. His appearance was the signal for a prolonged and enthusiastic ovation. All the delegates cheered for Russia, the revolutionary Government and the army.

The Premier in introducing General Korniloff, said the Government had thought it necessary to invite the Commander in Chief to lay before the conference the situation at the front and in the army.

General Korniloff said the death penalty, restoration of which he had asked, together with other measures, constituted only a small part of what was necessary in an army stricken with the terrible evils of disorganization and insubordination. In the present mo... soldiers had killed four regimental commanders and other officers, and ceased these outrages only when they were threatened with being shot. Quite re-

Continued on Page 4.

GERMANY GIVES A NEW PLEDGE TO ARGENTINA

Will Pay Indemnity and Promises to Observe International Law Toward Shipping.

BUENOS AIRES, Aug. 28.—Germany's reply to Argentina's note embodying demands in connection with the submarine campaign as affecting Argentine shipping has been received.

The text of the note as handed to the Government by the German Minister is as follows:

The German Imperial Government desires to maintain cordial relations with Argentina, and, to prove with facts its friendly sentiment, has decided, after a new investigation of the Toro case, to indemnify the Argentine Government.

The Imperial German Government declares at the same time that the freedom of the seas, in which Argentine shipping would share, forms one of the objects of this war. As a consequence of the illegal acts of its enemies the liberty of action of the Imperial German Government is limited, but it willingly acknowledges the dictates of international law and will endeavor to observe them.

The naval forces of the German Empire have received orders and instructions in agreement with this viewpoint, and the Imperial German Government is convinced that after these declarations no incident will occur to disturb the friendly relations between Germany and Argentina.

The Foreign Office this evening issued a statement, saying that after the delivery of the second note to Berlin "Germany insisted on the condition that Argentina prevent her vessels from traversing the blockade." This was refused as "incompatible with the spirit of Argentina's demands." The statement concludes:

"Argentina's claims have been satisfied in all their terms and without any restrictions."

The Foreign Minister and the President are outspoken in their indignation that an intimation of the contents of the note was given to an afternoon newspaper by Count von Luxburg before it was made public by the Argentine Government, thus preventing secret consideration of the document before the gist of the reply was generally known.

Special to The New York Times.

WASHINGTON, Aug. 28.—The reported response of Germany to Argentina does not surprise observers here. Argentina has been a hotbed of German propaganda, it is to Germany's interest to prevent a break with the republic.

One feature of the report from Buenos Aires concerning the German answer to Argentina's demands is that it differs from the report that came from Zurich last week that Argentina's demand had been rejected. This suggests that the German Government has sent an answer to Argentina while seeking to create an impression at home that the Imperial Government had shown its usual contemptuous attitude toward a nation smaller than itself.

The German assurances to Argentina are regarded here as not worth the paper they are written on.

Trieste Civilians Evacuate City as the Armies of Italy Drive On

British Take a Mile Front Northeast of Ypres, Piercing Germans' Third Line—French Raid Champagne Trenches—Artillery Active Near Verdun.

Special to The New York Times.

WASHINGTON, Aug. 28.—That the fall of Trieste before the Italian advance is threatened is the encouraging news received by the Italian Embassy today from Rome.

The message states that news dispatches from Zurich to the Italian newspaper Corriere d'Italia bring confirmation from Austrian sources that on account of the dangers threatening Trieste the civilian population has been ordered by the military authorities to evacuate the city. The majority of the inhabitants, according to the Corriere's advices, has already departed, and everything of value has been transported to the interior.

ROME, Aug. 28, (British Admiralty, per Wireless Press.)—The Italians made further progress yesterday on the Bainsizza Plateau, on the front north of Gorizia, the War Office announces. The Austrians made violent counterattacks, but failed to recover positions taken by the Italians. The announcement follows:

On the whole battle front there were artillery actions principally yesterday. On the Bainsizza Plateau our troops, continuing their progress, have been in closer contact with the enemy. Vigorous local attacks assured for us some positions which the enemy failed to recapture, although he made violent counterattacks.

Unfavorable atmospheric conditions greatly impeded the activity of our airplanes.

LONDON, Aug. 28.—King George has telegraphed congratulations to King Victor Emmanuel on the achievements of the Italian Army, expressing the opinion that they will exercise a far-reaching effect on the war. The King said he was happy that British guns and monitors contributed to the success of the Italians.

VIENNA, Sunday, Aug. 26, (via London.)—Monte Santo, on the Isonzo front, was evacuated by the Austro-Hungarian forces on Friday night, without fighting, Army Headquarters announced today, the Italians occupying it. The text of the statement reads:

Italian War Theatre.—On the Carso there was no infantry engagement on a large scale yesterday. South of the Vippach Valley a night attack was repulsed. Near Bigglia minor Italian advances failed.

Fresh and heavy engagements developed in the Monte San Gabriele district, and thanks to the bravery of the defenders, among whom were Graz riflemen, Styrians and Hungarian territorials, the enemy, in spite of his heavy, sanguinary sacrifices, nowhere succeeded in piercing our front.

Monte Santo, which was evacuated by us without fighting on Friday night, has been occupied by the Italians.

There have been numerous engagements on the highlands of Bainsizza and Heiligegeist and also to the east of Auzza.

AUSTRIANS ADMIT PERIL.

Emperor, While at Front, Saw Victorious Italian Attack.

Special to The New York Times.

WASHINGTON, Aug. 28.—All the Austrian newspapers now admit that the Italian offensive is of exceptional importance, the daily communication from Rome to the Italian Embassy here announces.

"They speak of the difficult task of defense and do not appear to be confident of preventing the Italians from attaining General Cadorna's objectives," the communication goes on. "The clear sight and superiority of the Italian command are more evident daily. General Cadorna seems in these supreme hours to reincarnate the might and valor of the ancient Roman consuls leading the Latin legions to certain victory.

"The enemy, now in rout on the high plateau of Bainsizza, attacked and pushed back on the eastern side of the Carso, is vacillating under the continuous assaults and is trying to escape, leaving behind him great quantities of foodstuffs, guns and war materials of every description.

"The correspondent of the Tribune, describing the conquest of Monte Santo, says that this success crowns all the series of works and efforts since May on the Vodice, the ridge joining Monte Kuk, or Cucco, to Monte Santo, where the Italians for three months were subjected to an incessant fire. Before the offensive of May Monte Santo was a part of the Austrian defensive organization of the Bainsizza Plateau, which is situated between the Isonzo and Chiapovano Valleys. The enemy attempted to bar every possible access to the high plateau by establishing very formidable fortified lines resting on the strong natural fortresses such as Vodice, Monte Cucco, and Monte Santo, constituting a great defensive barrier of the Valley of Prohot.

"When Vodice fell to the Italians the Austrians withdrew the barrier on the line Monte Santo-Kroblilek. Today, after the capture of Monte Santo, the chief immediate advantages obtained by the Italians are the elimination of the barrier of the Prohot Valley on the way to the Bainsizza Plateau, the freeing of the Gorizia zone of Austrians, who theretofore had been able to fire upon the city, and the isolating of the Velik-

Continued on Page 3.

MINNESOTA GOVERNOR BARS PEACE COUNCIL

Prohibits Meeting in the State on the Ground That It Would Aid Nation's Enemies.

ST. PAUL, Aug. 28.—Governor Burnquist late today issued a proclamation prohibiting the People's Council of America for Democracy and Peace from holding its promised meeting in Minneapolis, or elsewhere in Minnesota.

The Governor's action followed a report from the Sheriff of Hennepin County in which the latter stated that after making a thorough investigation he believed the proposed meeting would result in bloodshed, rioting, and loss of life. In his proclamation the Governor added his conviction that the meeting could only aid enemies of the United States.

Every peace officer in the State is called upon to aid in the enforcement of the order.

URGE A NAVAL ATTACK ON SUBMARINE BASES

French Military Authorities Want the Anglo-American Fleet to Force Belgian Ports.

Special Cable to THE NEW YORK TIMES.

PARIS, Aug. 28.—Military authorities here strongly favor a more aggressive policy on the part of the British Navy in attacking German submarine bases.

It is argued that if such an objective is worth a military offensive from Verdun to Flanders, costing hundreds of thousands of casualties, both the British and American fleets should go in fearlessly and destroy the U-boat nests in Belgium.

GUARD MICHAELIS ON BELGIAN TRIP

Special Precautions Are Taken to Insure the Safety of the Chancellor in Brussels.

LONDON, Aug. 28. A dispatch to the Exchange Telegraph from Amsterdam says the Imperial German Chancellor left Berlin today for Belgium.

The dispatch adds that the Chancellor is expected to visit Brussels and that special measures have been taken for his safety.

LABORITES IN ROW OVER STOCKHOLM

French Attack Plan at Opening of London Session of Allied Council.

REFUSE TO CONFER ON IT

Henderson Pleads for Harmony—Commission Is Appointed to Consider Peace Terms.

LONDON, Aug. 28.—The inter-allied Socialist and Labor conference was opened in London this morning under the Presidency of Arthur Henderson, member of the House of Commons and former Minister without portfolio.

Mr. Henderson, according to the official report of the proceedings, said:

"The conference has met to consider and determine as impartially and justly as possible the future attitude of labor and Socialism in the allied countries toward war and peace. The main issues involved in the world conflict are so fundamental, far-reaching, and vital to the future of the human race as to demand dispassionate and faithful consideration both by the majority and minority sections of all the countries represented. No satisfactory results could be achieved by any attempts of the majority to outvote the minority.

"The better course is to begin by a clear recognition of their differences in an endeavor to reach by mutual agreement a basis of war aims calculated to provide a lasting, honorable, and democratic peace. Though none of the decisions of the conference will be binding upon the Government, they would be regarded throughout the world as the considered judgment of the organized proletariat of the countries represented."

It is understood that several speeches were delivered by French delegates, the tenor of which indicated wide differences of opinion on many essential points, and that these became more divergent when the conference considered the appointment of a commission to deal with the Stockholm conference and to submit recommendations concerning it. The French majority, which was opposed to the Stockholm conference, is reported to have declined practically to nominate any of its members to the commission.

A commission was appointed to deal generally with peace terms.

Seventy delegates, representing Great Britain, Belgium, Russia, France, Portugal, Greece, South Africa, and Italy, are present. More than half of

Continued on Page 5.

"All the News That's Fit to Print."

The New York Times.

THE WEATHER
Fair today and Tuesday; warmer Tuesday; moderate south winds.
For full weather report see Page 19.

VOL. LXVII...NO. 21,793. NEW YORK, MONDAY, SEPTEMBER 24, 1917.—TWENTY PAGES. ONE CENT In Greater New York. | TWO CENTS Within Commuting Distance. | THREE CENTS Elsewhere.

SAYS RELATIVES EXHUMED BODY OF MRS. BINGHAM

Husband's Counsel Reports Autopsy Performed and Vital Organs Taken.

DONE SECRETLY AT NIGHT

Detective William J. Burns and Several Physicians Said to Have Been Present.

ORGANS SENT TO NEW YORK

If Suspicion Becomes Audible Charge "It Will Be Met with Facts," Says Bingham's Counsel.

Special to The New York Times.

LOUISVILLE, Ky., Sept. 23.—Exhumation of the body of Mrs. Robert Worth Bingham, formerly Mrs. Henry M. Flagler, and the participation of William J. Burns in the case were announced here tonight in a statement issued by attorneys for former Judge Bingham after they had heard from the personal representative sent by them to Wilmington, N. C.

According to the statement, which says Mrs. Bingham's relatives were responsible, the body was exhumed at Wilmington Tuesday, in the presence of Burns and several physicians, an autopsy held, and the vital organs sent to New York for examination. It was not until after this had been done that a guard was placed on the grave, according to the attorneys. The statement concludes by saying that "when whispered suspicion becomes an audible charge, such charge will be met with facts."

Helm Bruce, counsel for heirs other than Judge Bingham, still maintains that he knows nothing of the exhumation.

The statement given out by Judge Bingham's attorneys reads:

"On Friday morning last (Sept. 21) the press was full of rumors to the effect that the body of the late Mrs. Robert Worth Bingham was to be disinterred. Her grave is in the cemetery at Wilmington, N. C.

"Neither Judge Bingham nor any of his friends knew anything whatever about the matter, and the same is true of Helm Bruce, counsel for the executors and legatees under Mrs. Bingham's will. The dispatches stated that the Health Officer of Wilmington would make no statement and would not even affirm or deny that he had granted any permit for disinterment.

"On Saturday a friend of Judge Bingham was in Wilmington to ascertain exactly the condition of affairs. It now appears that at 3 o'clock on last Tuesday morning, Sept. 18, the disinterment took place; that an autopsy was performed in the presence of William J. Burns and several physicians; that vital parts of the body were removed, and that these parts were turned over to some one and taken to New York. It is needless to say that all of this was surreptitious, and was a secret closely guarded until the object was accomplished.

"It is presumed that the disinterred body was reburied. It was then that with a blare of trumpets the supposed necessity arose of jealously protecting the grave from violation.

"It belongs to the public to form its own opinion of this ghastly drama.

"Mrs. Bingham was attended in her last illness by Dr. M. L. Ravitch, Dr. W. F. Boggess, and Dr. S. A. Steinberg. On Thursday, July 12, two weeks before her death, Mrs. Bingham had a severe attack. Her brother, William R. Kenan, was summoned by Judge Bingham, and came. He conferred fully with Dr. Ravitch concerning Mrs. Bingham's condition, and approved everything that was being done.

"On Sunday, July 22, Mrs. Bingham's condition was such that Judge Bingham wrote her sisters that he thought that they should come. Responsive to this, her sister, Mrs. Wise, came, arriving Wednesday evening, July 25. Mrs. Bingham was then fully conscious, and remained so until Thursday night. Mrs. Wise remained with her until the end came on Friday.

"There were two trained nurses. Their official charts and records are in the custody of Dr. Boggess. These records will be kept in a secure place and produced when a proper occasion arises.

"When, if ever, whispered suspicion shall become an audible charge, such charge will be met with facts."

WILMINGTON, N. C., Sept. 23.—When Judge Bingham's statement was shown to him tonight, Dr. C. T. Nesbitt, County Superintendent of Health, admitted that no court order had been presented to him directing the disinterment of Mrs. Bingham's body, but again declined to say whether a permit for such a proceeding had been issued.

Dr. Nesbitt declared he would not say that he did not issue the permit nor that he did, that permits of such nature were merely sanitary measures, did not constitute a public record, and were usually issued where public health was not endangered when requests came from relatives.

The Superintendent of the cemetery would make no statement whatever.

No statement will be made here now by the Kenan family.

Developments in the Case.

First reports that the body of Mrs. Bingham had been exhumed came from Wilmington on Thursday. On the following day Shepard Bryan of Atlanta, Ga., attorney for former Judge Bingham, started for Wilmington and arrived on Saturday to represent his client's interests. In the meantime the ex-Judge's attorneys in Louisville had issued a statement that they would seek to find if the body had been disinterred, and if so at whose instance, by what authority, and why without consulting her husband.

Meanwhile a report had been circu-

Continued on Page 8.

Germans Seize Males in Bruges Between Ages of 14 and 60

HAVRE, Sept. 23.—The German military authorities at Bruges, Belgium, are conscripting forcibly all the boys and men of that city between the ages of 14 and 60 to work in munition factories and shipyards. The rich and the poor, shopkeepers and workmen, all are being taken, only the school teachers, doctors, and priests escaping.

The Germans virtually conducted raids in the city, according to reports received here, seizing men in their homes, in the streets, and in all public places. The Provincial Committee has been ordered by the Germans to release 75 per cent. of its staff.

Bruges is the capital of the Province of West Flanders, lying fifty-five miles northwest of Brussels and fourteen miles east of Ostend. The population in 1914 was about 55,000.

HOOVER URGES ALL TO SAVE SUGAR

Appeals to the Nation to Cut Down the Normal Consumption by One-third.

MUST SUPPLY THE FRENCH

They Will Be Entirely Without It for Two Months if We Do Not Economize.

Special to The New York Times.

WASHINGTON, Sept. 23.—France needs 100,000 tons of sugar the coming month and Herbert C. Hoover, Food Administrator, has asked everyone to cut down the quantity used under normal conditions by one-third, so that the amount required for export may be spared without working a hardship in this country. In a statement today Mr. Hoover said:

"We have received a request from the French Government that we allow them to export from the United States 100,000 tons of sugar during the next month, and probably more at a later period. Our own situation is that we have just sufficient sugar to maintain our normal consumption until the first of January, when the new West Indian crop becomes available to all.

"Our consumption is at the rate of ninety pounds per person per year—a little under four ounces per day per person. The French people are on a ration of sugar equal to only twenty-one pounds per annum per person—or at the rate of less than one ounce per day per person—a little more than the weight of a silver dollar each day. The English and Italian rations are also not over one ounce per day.

"The French people will be entirely without sugar for over two months if we refuse to part with enough from our stocks to keep them supplied with even this small allowance, as it is not available from any other quarter.

"Sugar even to a greater amount than the French ration is a human necessity. If our people will reduce by one-third their purchases and consumption of candy and of sugar for other uses than preserving fruit, which we do not wish to interfere with, we can save the French situation.

"In the interest of the French people, and of the loyalty we owe them, we should divide our food for the maintenance of our common cause. I ask the American people to do this. It is unthinkable that we refuse their request.

"HERBERT HOOVER."

LA FOLLETTE ATTACKS WAR AND GOVERNMENT

Tells Ohio Socialists Declaration Against Germany Didn't Represent the People.

TOLEDO, Ohio, Sept. 23.—Denouncing war in general and the United States Democratic Government in particular, United States Senator Robert M. La Follette of Wisconsin addressed a large gathering in the Coliseum this afternoon, under the auspices of "The People's Church," made up of Socialists headed by Professor Scott Nearing.

Mr. La Follette attacked the American press, declaring that American newspapers are for the most part controlled by the "war party," the financial interests of the country.

He declared that his remarks in St. Paul last week were misconstrued, and that he was being deliberately misquoted throughout the country.

"I am one citizen of the United States who is ready to go against the wall to preserve democracy," said Senator La Follette.

Mr. La Follette declared that the President of the United States swayed Congress to such an extent that the declaration of war was not the representative opinion of a democratic Government. He advocated war in defense only, and in case of aggression to submit the question to the people of the nation in the form of a referendum.

In discussing the war tax feature in connection with the prosecution of the war, the Senator asserted that "wealth has won and the people lost."

Senator La Follette said that he hoped to be able to serve the people of this country from twenty-five to thirty years longer, and he prayed that his life, strength, and health be spared, so that he might fight for the principles of democracy and assure liberty and freedom to posterity.

U-BOAT SINKINGS CUT TO 62,000 TONS IN A WEEK

Record for Period Ending Sept. 16 Lowest Since "Frightfulness" Began.

CONVOYS THE CHIEF FACTOR

Credit Largely Due to American Destroyers, Although New "Dazzle" System Helps.

CHEERED BY HAIG'S VICTORY

British Optimism Increased by Evidence of Weakening in the Two Kaisers' Notes.

By CHARLES H. GRASTY.

Copyright, 1917, by The New York Times Company.

Special Cable to THE NEW YORK TIMES.

LONDON, Sept. 23.—This is the most cheerful week-end that England has had in a long time. Drooping spirits have had a sharp rebound, and there is every appearance that the recovery is on a solid basis. The German and Austrian notes, while not taken seriously as a peace move, are construed as a symptom of weakening and a measure to prepare the public of the Central Empires for altered war prospects. "They see the handwriting on the wall," is a comment often heard and expresses the prevailing view.

These notes must be construed in the light of military developments which are of the utmost significance. On land and sea Germany has suffered a serious check. After the first six months of the submarine campaign, averaging a weekly destruction, including sinkings by raiders, of almost 150,000 tons, July and August showed an average of slightly more than 116,000 tons a week.

As indicated in dispatches, the naval authorities were gratified, but not satisfied, with this reduction, recognizing the fact that, while destruction aggregating 450,000 tons a month was less bad than that of 600,000, it was still much greater than the situation would stand, as it was exceeding the building rate by approximately 300,000 tons a month.

The first week in September showed a further improvement, and then came the second week with a decrease of nearly 50 per cent. The figures, when translated into tons, show much the smallest loss in any week since the "frightfulness" began last February. The figures for the week ending Sept. 16 were 62,000 tons, as against a weekly average for August of 118,000 tons, for July of 115,000, and for the first six months of 135,000 tons, exclusive of losses by raiders.

A week, or even a month, is too short a period to make the basis of serious calculations, but the sustained reduction, together with the known facts in connection with the defensive campaign, justify a high degree of optimism. Berlin knows that the Allies are now countering effectively against the undersea attack upon which Germany has mainly built her hopes.

Convoys Largely Responsible.

The actual figures of recent losses have not been published here; therefore, the press has made much of the improvement and has erroneously attributed the bulk of it to smoke-boxes and other new devices. I can state positively that the improvement is due to the tightening and perfecting of the convoy system. In this work and its results America can take pardonable pride. We gave up the "eyes of our fleet" (the destroyers) to what appeared to be the paramount necessity of protecting Atlantic shipping. In this matter Secretary Daniels showed a bold initiative and is entitled to credit for his part in the strategy that halted the German attempt to cut the jugular of Allied Europe.

The U-boat was at the height of its prosperity when our destroyers, followed by innumerable other American craft, were sent to British waters. Meanwhile additional vessels have been dispatched as they could be got hold of, and experience pointed our needs. And we have

Continued on Page 6.

Germans Now Seeking to Buy Mineral Deposits in England

LONDON, Sept. 23.—Dr. Christopher Addison, Minister without Portfolio, in charge of reconstruction, speaking at Huddersfield last night, referred to the activity of the Germans, who, he said, were endeavoring to obtain supplies of materials for munitions and building from different parts of the world.

The Germans, he said, had been making, and still were making, efforts to acquire control of great mineral deposits, even attempting to purchase them in England during the war.

KORNILOFF PLOT LAID TO KERENSKY

Premier Accused of Planning March on Petrograd to Crush Bolsheviki Extremists.

MIXUP CAUSED BY LVOFF

Revelations Cause Great Sensation in Russia and Cabinet's Position Is in Peril.

PETROGRAD, Sept. 23.—The Korniloff mystery, arising out of the recent revolt, has developed dimensions which threaten the existence of the Cabinet, particularly the position of Premier Kerensky. The newspapers representing the Left and the Right parties demand an explanation from the Government, while the Bolshevik organs openly accuse the Premier, in the words of the Rabotchi Poot, of being in a conspiracy with Korniloff "to crush the Petrograd proletariat and the Workmen's and Soldiers' Delegates with the help of a cavalry corps sent against Petrograd." The newspaper asks why, if the published documents are forged, no denial has been issued.

Maxim Gorky's paper, Novaia Zhizn, which, being unfriendly toward Kerensky, must be taken with reserve, declares that the affair is causing a sensation in the ranks of the Government, and that M. Terestchenko, the Foreign Minister, yesterday conversed by telephone with M. Kerensky about this matter, whereupon Kerensky postponed his return to Petrograd. The newspaper adds that the members of the Government had decided that M. Kerensky ought to make a statement on the subject.

A more serious indication of trouble is that the Bolshevik group in the bureau of the Central Workmen's and Soldiers' Delegates has carried by an overwhelming majority a resolution demanding an explanation. The resolution refers to "revelations concerning the actions of members and agents of the Provisional Government in connection with the preparation in General Korniloff's headquarters of a conspiracy against the revolution," and continues:

Say Dictatorship Was Planned.

"The plan was to announce an individual or collective dictatorship, at the same time declaring Petrograd under martial law, then mercilessly to break up the Petrograd revolutionary and working class organizations, under the pretext of crushing an imaginary Bolshevik plot."

The signatories of the resolution demand that the members of the Workmen's and Soldiers' Delegates, who were then Cabinet Ministers, Skobeleff, (Labor); Avskentieff, (Interior,) and Tchernoff, (Agriculture,) make a statement of all the facts known to them.

General Savinkoff, ex-Director of the War Department and later Commander of the Petrograd troops sent against General Korniloff, declares that he was dispatched to General Korniloff by Premier Kerensky, who had resolved to proclaim martial law, with a mission to ask the Russian Commander in Chief to send to Petrograd a cavalry corps and the "Savage" Division under command of a General other than General Krymoff, who was in bad political repute. General Korniloff broke the agreement by sending both Krymoff and the "Savage" Division toward the capital.

The Rech says that General Korniloff drew up a plan for the salvation of the

Continued on Page 4.

Berlin Sends Message Repudiating Luxburg and Halts Argentine Deputies' Vote on Break

BUENOS AIRES, Argentina, Sept. 23.—Just as the Argentine Chamber of Deputies early this morning was preparing to vote on the question of breaking diplomatic relations with Germany an official communication was received from the Berlin Foreign Office.

The note disapproved of the ideas expressed by Count von Luxburg, the German Minister here, regarding Germany's "cruiser warfare." The word "cruiser" left some doubt in the minds of Government officials as to whether or not Germany intended to modify her submarine campaign.

A declaration of war by Argentina on Germany, however, was postponed by the receipt of the German note.

Foreign Minister Pueyrredon later gave out two notes which he had received from Dr. Luis B. Molina, the Argentine Minister at Berlin. The first reads:

"I confirm my telegram of Sept. 21, and am transmitting the exact text of the note from the German Government in reply to your communication. As you will see, the satisfaction cannot be more ample or definite. This note was delivered personally to me by the Imperial Chancellor, who has just returned from Munich and who repeats the sentiments of the note in a most expressive and definite manner. There is no doubt, therefore, that the German Empire condemns the conduct of Luxburg, whose opinions were purely personal, and it disapproves absolutely. You may be sure the German Government will faithfully keep its promises."

The second message received from the Argentine Minister says:

"I have to inform you of the untruth of the report sent out by the enemies of Germany that the Kaiser has sent Luxburg a message approving his conduct and has offered another diplomatic post to him. The Government has denied the report by wireless."

The Chamber of Deputies will meet tomorrow afternoon to take definite action on the messages from Minister Molina.

Deputies Veyga and Arce opposed each other in a duel with swords today as a result of words passed in Saturday's debate in the Chamber on the German situation. Veyga, whose remark caused the challenge, was wounded in the arm. Deputy Arce considers that his honor has been satisfied.

LONDON, Sept. 23.—A dispatch from Buenos Aires to Reuter's, Limited, says that Argentina has received a note from Germany which has given complete satisfaction to the Argentine Government.

TO OFFER BELGIUM FOR LOST COLONIES AND ALLIED PLEDGE

Michaelis to Make Proposal in Speech Thursday, According to Munich Journal.

GROUND FULLY PREPARED

Learned by Discreet Inquiries Peace Was Hopeless Without Giving Invaded Kingdom.

ALLIES MUST CUT DEMANDS

American Capital Barred from Devastated Region, Papal Nuncio Was Told.

COPENHAGEN, Sept. 23.—Dr. Michaelis, the German Imperial Chancellor, will discuss the Belgian question and German peace conditions in a speech Thursday, according to the Neuste Nachrichten of Munich.

The Chancellor will declare, the newspaper says, that Germany is ready to re-establish Belgian independence if the Entente Powers agree to restore the German colonies and to give up "their policy of territorial and economic conquest."

The correspondent at Vienna of the Berliner Tageblatt says:

"The replies of Turkey and Bulgaria will be forwarded to the Pope today. Turkey demands that her territory shall not be violated. Bulgaria demands that her frontiers shall be regulated in accordance with the principles of nationality."

Belgium as a German Pawn.

Special Cable to THE NEW YORK TIMES.

THE HAGUE, Sept. 23.—One feature of the German press comment on the Kaiser's reply to the Pope's peace proposal stands out prominently, namely, the unanimity with which the German papers draw a comparison between Germany's conciliatory tone and President Wilson's reply to the Pope. Thus, the Lokal-Anzeiger declares that Germany's reply will encourage the Pope to take further steps, whereas President Wilson's reply made further efforts appear hopeless. The same note is struck by all the annexationist papers, especially those, like the Cologne Volkszeitung, which, in other articles, violently attack the United States.

Thus one object of Germany's note is clear, namely, to encourage American pacifists, especially the Hearst group, in their belief that America alone, anyhow chiefly the American Government, stands in the way of peace. A second object also appears clearly, namely, to endeavor to persuade the French pacifists that England must be forced to disgorge what are termed ill-gotten gains, as the German colonies and Mesopotamia, in order that France may recover the districts now occupied by the Germans and Belgium be restored.

There is nowhere the faintest suggestion that Belgium will be restored as an unconditional preliminary to peace negotiations, although the Germans are perfectly well aware that this is indispensable. They have made the most elaborate attempts to obtain information on this point in Holland for the last two months, and THE NEW YORK TIMES correspondent has very good reason to believe that their neutral informants have left them no reasonable doubt regarding the opinion on this point of the whole civilized world.

Germany's actual proposals regarding Belgium as made known to the Papal Nuncio at Munich by Foreign Secretary von Kühlmann are nowhere detailed, although probably they are contained in various semi-official communications. One feature of these requirements is emphasized by the Cologne Volkszeitung, namely, that on the conclusion of hostilities Belgium shall not be restored by American capital. The paper argues at length that the uncompromising attitude recently adopted by the Belgian ex-Minister Derbrouqueville is mainly due to the certainty that American capital will be put into Belgium after the war. The paper says such a condition of affairs would be intolerable, as America, England, and France would control trade and industry.

Significantly, a similar point is made by the radical Georg Gothein, one of the three compilers of the Reichstag peace resolution. He declares that German trade via Antwerp must be facilitated immediately on the conclusion of fighting, and says cheap rates must be guaranteed for German goods via that route. The German idea of the restoration of Belgium thus involves the prevention either of economic or political rapprochement with Germany's present enemies and in particular the prevention of Belgium's obtaining capital for her restoration where it would probably be obtainable most readily and with the least selfish motive.

THE FRENCH CONDEMN REPLIES AS HOLLOW

Ignoring of Belgium, Alsace-Lorraine, and Poland Emphasized in Paris Press Comment.

Special Cable to THE NEW YORK TIMES.

PARIS, Sept. 23.—The French verdict on the Austro-German replies to the Pope may be summed up in the words, "Nothing new." All comment beyond that is little more than an attempt to indicate and explain the reason why the Central Powers, somewhat contrary to the general expectation here, have per-

Continued on Page 8.

DEADLY GERMS AND BOMBS WERE PLANTED BY GERMANS IN RUMANIAN LEGATION WHEN THEY LEFT IT IN AMERICAN HANDS

Directions in German Found in the Buried Box of Microbes Left in Legation Garden at Bucharest

Special to The New York Times.

WASHINGTON, Sept. 23.—When the Rumanian authorities, with William W. Andrews, the American Chargé in Bucharest, searched in the garden of the German Legation, already under the protection of the United States because war had begun between Rumania and the Central Powers, they found there boxes of explosives and microbes. On the box of disease germs, which bore the seal of the German Consulate at Kronstadt, were the following inscriptions:

Through messenger! Quite secret! Not to be roughly handled!
For M. Kostoff, Bucharest.
The Colonel and Military Attaché at the Imperial Bulgarian Legation at Bucharest, M. Semargieff.

Under this first envelope there was another envelope of white paper, and written on it in red pencil:

Quite secret! Through T. E. L. A.!!
To the Royal Colonel and Military Attaché, Herr von———

The name was scratched out with an ink eraser; but examination revealed the traces of the letters H-a-m—t-i-n. (Hammerstein?)

In the inside of this box, above a layer of cotton wool, this typewritten note in German was found:

Inclosed 4 small bottles for horses and 4 for cattle. Utilization as formerly stipulated. Each phial suffices for 200 head. If possible, to be administered directly into the animals' mouths, otherwise into their fodder. We ask for a small report about successes obtained there, and in case of good results the presence for one day of M. K— would be required.

BAKER REVIEWS RAINBOW DIVISION

Sees 27,000 Reorganized and Hardened Guardsmen Ready for Final Training.

MANY STATES REPRESENTED

Secretary Calls Them a Cross-Section of America and Proof of Our Unity.

Special to The New York Times.

CAMP MILLS, near Mineola, Sept 23.—America's already famous "Rainbow Division," drawn from twenty-six States and the District of Columbia, which, as Secretary of War Newton D. Baker expressed it this afternoon, is representative in the noblest sense of that word of the unity of the American people in the great struggle now before the country, passed in review before the Secretary, the Chief of the General Staff, and its own division commander this morning. More than 26,000 young men, every one of them a picked National Guardsman, swept with West Point-like precision past the head of the War Department, and when it was all over Secretary Baker turned to Major Gen. William A. Mann, commander of the Rainbow, and told him how proud he was of that splendid body of young American manhood. The picture presented as those thousands of khaki-clad fighters passed by he described as the most impressive and inspiring he had ever witnessed.

The number of men in line was greater than the total strength of the regular army at the beginning of the Spanish War in 1898. Then the regulars numbered just 25,000 men, or just 2,000 fewer than the maximum strength of the Rainbow Division. Likewise never before in the history of the United States have so many men from the South been seen in line north of the Potomac, and it was the first time New Yorkers have ever had an opportunity to view at close range the fighting men from the Pacific Coast, and the great agricultural regions of the Middle West.

It is a matter of common knowledge that the Rainbow Division will be among the first of the guard organizations to cross the Atlantic for service alongside its allied comrades in France, and so today's review may prove to be the Rainbow Division's farewell for months if not years, to the United States.

Gayety of Peace Parades Gone.

An air of solemnity pervaded the great throng which witnessed the review and there was not a civilian among those thousands who did not note the serious faces in that long line of American fighters. The happy, carefree smiles that mark the parades of peaceful times were missing. The men, officers and privates alike, marched with snap and vim and set faces. They looked straight ahead, save for the moment when at eyes right they passed the automobile from which Secretary Baker, Major Gen. Tasker H. Bliss, Chief of the General Staff; Major Gen. Mann, their own commander, and Colonel Douglas MacArthur, the Division Chief of Staff, reviewed them.

Secretary Baker and General Bliss, accompanied by their aids, arrived at Garden City a few minutes before 10 o'clock. At the station waited the escort, in this instance the Division Headquarters Troop, which was before the declaration of war the Second Troop of Louisiana Cavalry. Also in waiting was General Mann and his entire division staff. The route from Garden City to Division Headquarters, from in front of which Secretary Baker reviewed the troops, was lined with soldiers. Artillerymen, infantrymen, engineers, and signalmen stood single file and at atten-

Continued on Page 11.

SENATE UNLIKELY TO START INQUIRY

Members Believe It Would Shed No Light on Attempts to Influence Congress.

THINK SUSPICION BASELESS

Overman Will Consult Lansing, Who Is Expected to Oppose Investigation Now.

Special to The New York Times.

WASHINGTON, Sept. 23.—There is little chance of a Congressional investigation of German plots unless specific evidence is presented against members of the Senate or House. Several Senators who consented today to discuss the situation brought on by the recent remarks of Representative Heflin of Alabama, were all opposed to an inquiry being made at this time.

There was some resentment apparent against the intimation by the Congressman from Alabama that a dozen or more of the legislators probably had engaged in anti-war activities for self-advantage, but it was felt that an error would be made if an investigation were ordered because of this kind of suspicion.

It is probable that Senator Overman of North Carolina, Chairman of the Senate's Special Lobby Committee, will call on Secretary of State Lansing tomorrow to obtain the viewpoint of the State Department, and it is generally believed that Mr. Lansing will oppose an inquiry now. Several officials, it is said, feel that an investigating committee not only would find nothing worthy of discussion, but would provide Germany with an excuse for published statements that the Government was suspicious of its own legislators and had found it necessary to examine them.

As yet the special lobby committee has not been called together, and both branches of Congress are moving slowly in order, as far as possible, to avoid all bitterness and unfortunate discussion which might feature direct steps leading to an investigation.

Senator Reed of Missouri, a member of the Lobby Committee, discussed the veiled charges which have been made with a TIMES reporter today.

"It is inconceivable to me," said the Senator, "that any member of the American Congress has either before or since the opening of hostilities with Germany connived to defeat the best interests of his own Government in its relations with foreign countries, enemy or otherwise. I do not believe that an investigation should be even thought of until some one is prepared to present evidence which will justify a closer examination of the persons charged with sedition, treason or other crime of similar character.

"It must be realized that up to the time the United States entered the war there was a strong element in the United States opposed to war. The war came upon us suddenly. It was easier for some to accept the dictum that the hour for America to take hostile sides in the strife had struck than for others. The men who were slower than others to come to the opinion that America's place in the war had been defined by circumstances were not professional pacifists, of necessity; they were not even of necessity pro-German. Their conduct was a matter for their own judgment to approve.

"But we are in the war now. The Congress stands behind the executive branch of the Government as no legislative organization before has ever stood behind its Government. The people of the United States are in the war to win it. They are substantially a unit behind the American Government and more of a units, more stanchly and more sturdily behind every action, every

Continued on Page 2.

BUCHAREST PLOTTING BARED

Lansing Shows How Germans Exploited Our Protection There.

PLOT AIMED AT RUMANIA

Anthrax and Glanders Microbes Imported to Poison Cattle of Neutral Neighbor.

FOUND BURIED IN GARDEN

Explosives and Poison Sent from Berlin and Bore Official Seals and Directions.

Special to The New York Times.

WASHINGTON, Sept. 23.—Before the National capital had found time to recover from the amazing story of German intrigue disclosed in the Government's publication this morning of the activities of Count von Bernstorff and Wolf von Igel, a new chapter of German criminality was revealed tonight when Secretary Lansing made public documentary evidence of a plot of German military and diplomatic agents to use deadly microbes and powerful explosives against Rumania.

The evidence given out by the State Department shows that before Rumania had declared war against Austria-Hungary, and was observing strict neutrality, German official agents clandestinely introduced into Bucharest, the capital of Rumania, packages containing explosives powerful enough to wreck public works and vials containing deadly microbes destined to infect domestic animals and susceptible of provoking terrible epidemics among the human population of the country. The vials contained anthrax microbes and the bacilli of glanders.

The Rumanian Government is satisfied from its evidence that "in time of peace members of the German Legation, covered by their immunity, prepared in concert with the Bulgarian Legation the perpetration on the territory of a neutral and friendly State of plots directed against the safety of this State and against the lives of its subjects."

After its discovery of the plot the Rumanian Government called in William Whiting Andrews, the Chargé d'Affaires of the American Legation at Bucharest, who witnessed the digging up of the boxes of explosives and the packages containing the vials of microbes from the grounds of the German Legation, to which they had been secretly moved from the German Consulate in Bucharest on the eve of Rumania's declaration of war.

The explosives and microbes had been sent into Rumania secretly by German diplomatic couriers and hidden in the Consulate while Rumania was at peace.

Abused Our Protection.

Just before Rumania broke relations they were removed to the Legation. Some of the objects were even taken to the German Legation after the American Legation at Bucharest had taken over the protection of German interests.

Dr. Bernhardt, former confidential agent of the German Minister, and servants of the German Legation confessed that this had been done. In this respect the action of Germany's agent was a shameful abuse of the protection which the United States Government was giving to German interests in Bucharest. At the time the United States was at peace with Germany, and had agreed to take charge of Germany's legation in the Rumanian capital.

"The protection of the United States was in this manner shamefully abused and exploited," says the official report of Chargé d'Affaires Andrews to the State Department, made public tonight with the evidence; "in this instance, at least, the German Government cannot have recourse to its usual system of denial."

Some of the German diplomatic or military agents prominent in this plot against the safety of Rumania and the lives of its subjects were Werner von Rheinbaben, Counselor of the German Legation; Rudolph Kruger, Chancellor of the legation, and Colonel von Hammerstein, attached to the German Legation as Military Attaché.

They appear from the evidence to have been assisted by Constantin Kostoff, Delegate of the Bulgarian Railways in Rumania, and Colonel Samargieff, the Bulgarian Military Attaché. Kostoff, the man to whom the packages of explosives figuring in the plot were sent, under the seal of the German Consulate at Kronstadt by secret courier, to be delivered to Colonel von Hammerstein, was two days before Rumania's declaration of war suddenly presented to the Rumanian Ministry of Foreign Affairs in the quality of Attaché to the Bulgarian Legation at Bucharest.

The plot appears to have been frustrated by the extreme vigilance of the Rumanian Government and its action in severing relations with the allied powers of Austria-Hungary. This forced the various German and Bulgarian principals in the plot to leave Rumanian ter-

"All the News That's Fit to Print."

The New York Times.

THE WEATHER
Probably rain today; Thursday fair; fresh northeast winds.
For full weather report see Page 21.

VOL. LXVII...NO. 21,809. NEW YORK, WEDNESDAY, OCTOBER 10, 1917.—TWENTY-TWO PAGES. ONE CENT In Greater New York. | TWO CENTS Within Commuting Distance. | THREE CENTS Elsewhere.

BRITISH AND FRENCH SMASH THROUGH WIDE GERMAN FRONT NORTH OF YPRES; PLOT IN THE GERMAN NAVY FOR PEACE

BURLESON TELLS NEWSPAPERS WHAT THEY MAY NOT SAY

Forbids Impugning the Government's Motives or Improper Attacks on Our Allies.

BARS ANTI-DRAFT CAMPAIGN

Will Suppress Papers Asserting Wall Street or Munition Makers Control Government.

REGULATIONS ARE READY

Executive Order Prepared by President Under the Trading with the Enemy Act.

WASHINGTON, Oct. 9.—Restrictions on commerce and communication authorized by the Trading with the Enemy act will be put into effect within a few days under an executive order which President Wilson had virtually completed tonight after conferring with Cabinet members, Vance McCormick, Chairman of the Exports Administrative Board, and Acting Secretary Crosby of the Treasury.

Postmaster General Burleson announced after the Cabinet meeting that the provision authorizing the Post Office Department to license foreign language newspapers already was in operation, and that within ten days the department would begin to issue licenses. A number of papers already have filed applications and scores are expected within the next few days.

The Postmaster General said that publications need not fear suppression under the Trading with the Enemy act's censorship provision, unless they transgressed the bounds of legitimate criticism of the President, the Administra-

Exports Board Helps Allies to Get Supplies of Cotton

WASHINGTON, Oct. 9.—Stoppage of cotton shipments to northern European neutrals has resulted in such a surplus of the staple in this country that the Exports Administrative Board determined today to permit for an indefinite period the exportation of raw cotton to the Allies without licenses. When the licensing of exports became effective Sept. 7 last, the board permitted the exportation of cotton to the Allies without permits until Oct. 31 next.

It was explained that there is ample cotton in the United States to supply the nation's needs, including the increased quantity needed in the army and navy, and still have a great deal for shipment to the United Kingdom, France, Italy, Japan, and Russia.

TO SUE COLUMBIA, CATTELL'S THREAT

Quotes Dr. Seligman as Calling Trustees "Fools and Idiots" and Gets Prompt Denial.

UNIVERSITY COUNCIL TO ACT

Law Professor Draws the Line Between Seditious Propaganda and Free Speech.

A charge by Professor J. McKeen Cattell, expelled last week from the Chair of Psychology at Columbia University for disseminating disloyal doctrines in the war, that Professor Edwin R. A. Seligman, head of the Department of Economics at the university, had praised his views on the war and had called the Trustees "fools" and "idiots," added an unexpected complication last night to the incidents developed by the resignation of Charles A. Beard as Professor of Political Science at the university. Professor Cattell intimated that, following a suggestion from Professor Seligman, he would take his dismissal to the courts, adding that a "lawsuit will bring out facts concerning the Presi-

CONTROL OF FOOD BY GOVERNMENT TO BEGIN ON NOV. 1

President to Order Makers and Distributers to Operate Under Licenses.

TWENTY STAPLES ON LIST

Unreasonable Profits, Speculation, and Hoarding Among Evils Aimed At.

DEALERS' BOOKS TO BE OPEN

All Concerns with $100,000 Business a Year Affected—200 Conferences Held.

Special to The New York Times.

WASHINGTON, Oct. 9.—The Food Administration is on the trail of the food profiteer, and by an extensive licensing system which will reach even the retailer doing a gross annual business of $100,000 will endeavor to put an end to hoarding, speculation, and extortionate profits between producer and consumer. Co-operation is sought and expected in carrying through the program, but the big stick will be wielded, if necessary, to put virtually all the staple foods under Government control.

Announcement was made tonight that President Wilson, within a day or two, would issue a proclamation under the provisions of the food control law which will place the machinery in operation by Nov. 1. After that time licenses must be obtained and regular reports submitted by the individuals or firms included in the edict, which will cover dealings in all of the foods "forming the prime basis of life."

Eggs, poultry, milk, meats, vegetables, sugar, flour, bread, wheat and other

Germans Buy Argentine Hides in Anticipation of War's End

BUENOS AIRES, Oct. 9.—Coincident with the American demand for Argentine dry hides to meet military orders, and renewed British buying as a result of the lifting of the leather embargo, the Germans here are buying heavily, and their competition in the market is helping to increase prices.

German brokers say they are buying on German Government orders. They express confidence that the war will end in January or February. Prices of hides have risen 12 per cent. in the last ten days.

REGISTRATION AGAIN FALLS OFF

Total for Second Day Is 82,068, Against 122,833 Last Year.

FAR LESS THAN IN 1913

Two Days' Total Is 179,272—Last Year It Was 248,254—Mayor Disappointed.

The falling off in this year's registration continued yesterday. In every borough in the city except Queens the registration for the second day was lower than the registration on Monday. In Queens 2,187 more people registered yesterday evening than on Monday. In Manhattan, Brooklyn, Bronx, and Richmond, not only was there a large falling off in yesterday's figures as compared with the day before, but the result for the two days was far below the totals for previous years, including 1913, the last year a Mayoralty election was held, and last year, which was a Presidential year.

For the first two days in 1913 the total registration in New York City was 342,556. For the first two days this year it was 179,272, a falling off from four years ago of 163,284. Brooklyn fared as badly as Manhattan and the other boroughs, except Queens, showed no better results.

In Manhattan yesterday's registration was far below that of the total for the second day in other years. It fell 6,742

NAVY BUILDING 787 SHIPS; COST IS $1,150,400,000

Contracts Just Let to Five Companies for New Destroyers Calling for $350,000,000.

NUMBER A MILITARY SECRET

Will Be Largest, Fastest, and Most Formidable Afloat, Secretary Daniels Announces.

NEW PLANTS TO BE BUILT

Will Be Auxiliary to Private Shipyards and Be Owned by the Government.

Special to The New York Times.

WASHINGTON, Oct. 9.—Secretary Daniels today awarded contracts to five shipbuilding companies for the construction of $350,000,000 worth of destroyers. This is the biggest contract for vessels of this type ever awarded by any Government. When these destroyers have been completed it is expected that the United States will have the largest fleet of destroyers in the world.

With the award of these contracts the war construction program of the American Navy was brought to a total of 787 vessels, including all types, from superdreadnoughts to submarine chasers. Some vessels have been finished in the last few weeks and are now in service. The rest of the program is being pushed to completion as rapidly as possible. The total cost of the program is estimated at $1,150,400,000.

Commenting on the contracts awarded today, Secretary Daniels said:

Statement by Secretary Daniels.

"These destroyers will be built by five companies which have had experience in building this type—the Fore River

Move for New Peace Offer Reported in Berlin; Only Another Feeler, Washington Believes

AMSTERDAM, Oct. 9.—Germany and Austria-Hungary have agreed to make another peace offer to the Allies, the Deutsche Tageszeitung of Berlin says it learns on good authority.

The offer will have as its basis no territorial aggrandizement, the surrender of Belgium and French territory, the renunciation of positive territorial acquisitions for payments in money, and no indemnity on either side.

Special to The New York Times.

WASHINGTON, Oct. 9.—Only mild interest is taken in official quarters in the report from Amsterdam, credited to the Deutsche Tageszeitung, that the Central Powers have agreed to make another peace offer to the Allies. There is no confidence in German good faith in Washington. If this new peace offer is made, it will mean nothing, in the opinion of officials in a position to know the attitude of the Wilson Administration.

"The usual bait," was the way one authority characterized it. "Camouflage," said another.

German camouflage in regard to peace negotiations has excited amusement in the most authoritative quarters here—an amusement born of a conviction that German statesmanship and diplomacy are stupid. Surprise is expressed that the German people have not recognized this weakness on the part of their masters.

German statesmen, it is suggested in Washington, are deluding themselves with the belief that the people of the allied nations, or a large part of them, are being influenced gradually by the view that Germany is actuated by a real desire to have the war brought to an end. The truth of this appreciation of Germany's attitude is not denied in official circles here, where there is a thorough understanding of German and Austrian anxiety for peace, but officials are confident that the American people, at least, are well aware of the reason for Teutonic solicitude to have hostilities cease and are not deceived by it.

The Kaiser and the small group around him are supposed to have been led astray as to the sentiment of America by the speeches of Senator La Follette and others who follow his leadership. In some quarters the feeling prevails that their utterances are prolonging the war by encouraging Germany to fail to recognize the inevitable.

The terms of the reported German and Austrian offer are just as unsatisfactory to this Government, it is gathered, as those suggested by the Pope.

PLOT TO PARALYZE GERMAN FLEET

Reichstag Told of Plan to Compel the Government to End the War.

LAID TO RADICAL SOCIALISTS

Von Cappelle Makes Announcement of Plan to Which Michaelis Had Referred.

COPENHAGEN, Oct. 9.—Vice Admiral von Capelle, German Minister of Marine, announced in the Reichstag today that a plot had been discovered in the navy to for ma committee of delegates on the Russian model and to paralyze the fleet, so as to force the Government to make peace. The guilty parties have been arrested and have received their just deserts, the Minister added.

Admiral von Capelle attempted to link the Radical Socialists with the plot. He said the ringleader had discussed the plot with Deputies Haase and Vogtherr in the Radical Socialist conference room in the Reichstag Building. The Deputies had called attention to the dangerous nature of the plot and had advised the greatest caution, but had agreed to furnish propaganda material.

Socialist Deputies interrupted the speaker with cries of dissent. Deputy David of the Majority Socialists demanded the Government produce proof and that the Reichstag should suspend

PROMISES TO CURB PAN GERMAN PARTY

Abuses by Propagandists Will Be Stopped, Michaelis Tells Reichstag Committee.

FOE'S MAN POWER EBBING, FRENCH SAY

Officially Report "a Clear Decrease" in Germany's Total War Strength.

EXPECT DECISION IN 1918

British and French at Top Efficiency, with Our Troops Soon to Add Weight to Their Blows.

Special to The New York Times.

WASHINGTON, Oct. 9.—Proof that Germany has reached the zenith of her military man power was given to the public tonight when the French High Commission to the United States issued a highly important statement on the western front situation based on official data cabled to Washington by the French General Staff.

"Germany has made her supreme military effort," says the High Commissior's statement, after making a careful analysis of the extent to which Germany has been forced to send new divisions to the western front in the efforts of her General Staff to resist the incessant pounding of the British, French, and Belgian forces.

In another part of the statement, after showing that Germany has been forced to call out part of the class of 1919 and has been compelled to break up newly formed regiments to reinforce her fighting units, the French Commission asserts that for the first time during the war "a clear decrease in the total strength of the German forces is on record."

FRENCH GAIN 1¼ MILES

Advance on 1½-Mile Front, Occupying Mangelaere and Veldhoek.

BRITISH TAKE POELCAPELLE

All Haig's Objectives Gained in Operations Over Ground About 10 Miles in Extent.

FIGHTING IN A SEA OF MUD

Attack Launched at Dawn, with Allied Airplanes Co-operating Effectively in a Clear Sky.

LONDON, Oct. 9.—Attacking early this morning on a wide front, the British and French armies near Ypres made notable advances north and northwest of that city. The former drove the Germans from their last positions in the town of Poelcapelle and pushed on for nearly two miles to the northwest of that place. Field Marshal Sir Douglas Haig reports all his objectives gained and the capture of more than 1,000 prisoners. The French took more than 300 prisoners.

The French troops, operating on the left of the British line, north of Ypres, pierced the German positions to a depth of a mile and a quarter on a front of more than a mile and a half, capturing the villages of St. Jean de Mangelaere and Veldhoek, with numerous blockhouses, and reached the southern edge of Houthulst Wood, about seven miles north of Ypres.

To the south of the main British advance Haig's men pushed northeast from the Gravenstafel ridge to a point

Continued on Page 2.

Continued on Page 22.

Continued on Page 3.

Continued on Page 2.

Continued on Page 2.

Mid-Week Pictorial

During the British drive in France, many German guns were taken and fired by British artillerymen at German positions.

"All the News That's Fit to Print."

The New York Times.

THE WEATHER
Fair today and tomorrow; moderate northwest to north winds.
For full weather report see Page 21.

VOL. LXVII...NO. 21,839. NEW YORK, FRIDAY, NOVEMBER 9, 1917.—TWENTY-TWO PAGES. ONE CENT In Greater New York. | TWO CENTS Within Commuting Distance. | THREE CENTS Elsewhere.

REVOLUTIONISTS SEIZE PETROGRAD; KERENSKY FLEES; PLEDGE IS GIVEN TO SEEK "AN IMMEDIATE PEACE"; ITALIANS AGAIN DRIVEN BACK; LOSE 17,000 MORE MEN

WOODS MUST GO AS POLICE HEAD, HYLAN DECIDES

Mayor-Elect Will Ask Him to Retire if He Fails to Resign.

SUCCESSOR NOT YET FOUND

Murphy Will Refrain from Interference, Congressman Smith Declares.

HYLAN SHOCKS JOBHUNTERS

Announces Delay in Considering Appointments—Craig Against Pay-as-You-Go Plan.

Mayor-elect John F. Hylan, it was said yesterday, has no intention of retaining Arthur Woods at the head of the Police Department. Friends of the Mayor-elect said that he expected to find a man after his own liking, who measured up to the job, to succeed the Police Commissioner before Jan. 1, when the Mayor-elect assumes office. Unless Judge Hylan had received the resignation of Commissioner Woods by the time he was ready to appoint his successor, the Police Commissioner, it was said, would be asked to retire.

At the headquarters of Judge Hylan persons who enjoy the confidence of the Mayor-elect said last night that he regarded the administration of the Police Department under Commissioner Woods as having been one of the vital issues in the campaign, even though less attention was paid to it by Judge Hylan in his speeches than to some other branches of the Mitchel Administration. The wire-tapping episode, which aroused such a storm of protest in certain quarters at the time of the charities investigation, and in which the Police Department under Commissioner Woods was directly concerned, was condemned both by Tammany Hall and its organized allies, the Democratic Fusion Committee and the Business Men's Association, in their platforms. Judge Hylan, it was said, felt that he was bound by the terms of the platform on which he was elected.

Expect Woods to Resign.

It is the belief of Judge Hylan's friends that Commissioner Woods will follow the usual practice and submit his resignation when the change of administration occurs, even though a provision in the New York City Charter provides for a five-year term, which in the case of the present incumbent does not expire until April, 1919. But even should this belief not prove justified, the Charter provisions relating to the Police Commissionership are regarded by Judge Hylan's friends as sufficiently plastic to provide the Mayor-elect with the means of creating a vacancy at the head of the Police Department whenever he desires to do so.

It was said at Hylan headquarters last night that the Mayor-elect as yet had not given serious consideration to the task of finding a successor for Commissioner Woods. Reports indicating that the Police Commissionership would go to a "good Tammany man," of whom some have been named in the speculation over patronage, and that Charles F. Murphy, leader of Tammany Hall, was particularly anxious to have his wishes consulted in the filling of this office, it was said both at the headquarters of Judge Hylan and at Tammany Hall, might be discarded as without justification.

Judge Hylan, it was said last night by his friends, was keenly alive to the fact that Mayors stood or fell by the public verdict on the administration of the Police Department. Leader Murphy also, it was asserted, was not oblivious of the fact that, while Judge Hylan was Mayor, Tammany would be on trial, and that any attempt on the part of Tammany Hall to lay violent hands on the Police Department would arouse a storm of resentment at the very beginning of the new administration. Among the friends of Judge Hylan the prediction was made freely yesterday that the Mayor-elect would make clear to the political leaders that he did not need any help in picking a new Police Commissioner.

A statement made yesterday by County Clerk William F. Schneider, Chairman of the Democratic Fusion Committee, which body was largely instrumental in making Judge Hylan the nominee for Mayor, was regarded as not altogether void of significance.

Wants Hylan to be Foot Free.

"The appointment of a Police Commissioner should be left entirely to the Mayor," said Mr. Schneider. "The political organizations which were behind Judge Hylan's candidacy should scrupulously avoid any divided responsibility in the administration of the Police Department. Tammany's political foes have always made the Police Department an issue in city elections, and the course of Tammany in relation to police administration has been disastrous to that organization. The selection of a Police Commissioner should be undertaken by Judge Hylan solely on his own responsibility and without any interference or advice by politicians."

Leader Murphy did not appear at Tammany Hall yesterday. It was learned that the Tammany chief was preparing to go away for a rest, as is his practice after a hard-fought campaign. In his absence Congressman Thomas F. Smith, Secretary of Tammany Hall, did the talking.

"Mr. Murphy has been leader of Tammany Hall for sixteen years," said Congressman Smith. "In all that time he has neither recommended nor had anything to do with the selection of a Police Commissioner. There is every

Continued on Page 3.

Insists Emperor Charles Will Be Polish Ruler

Special Cable to THE NEW YORK TIMES.

THE HAGUE, Nov. 8.—In spite of recent denials, the Lokal-Anzeiger repeats that the Austrian Emperor is to be named King of Poland. It says this was decided on at a Crown Council on Monday.

Poland is to be joined to Austria, and Galicia is to belong to the future Kingdom of Poland. Lithuania and Courland will be separate States, such as Prussia, and be represented by Grand Dukes. The paper points out that in Austria even the Germanic parties appear to approve this, but that special emphasis is laid on and guarantees demanded for "the strengthening of Germanic-Austria."

The paper seems to question whether German interests have been sufficiently considered in this settlement.

THREAT OF DICTATOR IN GERMAN SNARL

Government Attempts to Force Dropping of Demand for Radical Vice Chancellor.

HERTLING DENIES PROMISES

Opposition to Attack Chancellor as Soon as Reichstag Meets Unless He Yields.

COPENHAGEN, Nov. 8.—The threat that a military dictatorship is inevitable unless insistence upon a radical Vice Chancellor is dropped and the Government of Count von Hertling as it now stands is accepted is held out over the progressive democratic elements in Germany.

Count von Hertling, through a semi-official note in the Norddeutsche Allgemeine Zeitung, announces that no promises whatever were made to give the radicals the two posts they desired. Representatives of the Reichstag majority have issued an equally authoritative announcement that they adhere to their old position.

The radical press indicates that the Chancellor's compromise proposal to appoint a radical Deputy to the newly created Ministry for occupied territories with a seat in the Prussian Cabinet is not acceptable because such a post would be merely temporary, and the occupant would be powerless in the face of the military authorities.

The situation is drifting rapidly toward the goal desired by the reactionaries, that is, a split in the present alignment in the Reichstag and the formation of a new coalition embracing the Conservatives and the National Liberals. Such a bloc, which would have a bare majority in the Reichstag, is by no means impossible, despite the apparent unity proclaimed by the majority caucus.

The Catholic Centrum is by no means adverse to following the Chancellor along a road marked with party advantages. The National Liberals, who for the most part are Conservatives and annexationists and whose hearts never were in the present majority bloc, intimate strongly in their formal announcement of Herr Friedberg's withdrawal of his acceptance of the Vice Presidency of the Prussian Cabinet their dissatisfaction with the attitude of the Radicals and the Socialists.

The Socialists apparently have abandoned the dictum expressed by Philipp Scheidemann on Sunday that the new von Hertling Government, which differs from that of Dr. Michaelis only in the person of its chief, provided all necessary guarantees of responsible popular Government as a pre-condition to peace.

The Tageblatt and other Radical newspapers say that if Chancellor von Hertling bows to the "hidden powers" and the influence of the Court clique, the opposition will introduce on Nov. 22, when the Reichstag reconvenes, a resolution of lack of confidence in the Government. Count von Hertling's position is much like that of Dr. Michaelis after his "as I interpret it" speech.

LONDON, Nov. 8.—The German political crisis is represented as being as acute as ever in special dispatches from Amsterdam. Some say that Count von Hertling's Chancellorship is in danger of immediate shipwreck.

The refusal of Herr Friedberg, leader of the National Liberty Party, to accept the Vice Presidency of the Prussian Ministry and the prospect that Dr. Helfferich is to be retained as Vice Chancellor are regarded as matters impossible of settlement. Count von Hertling is reported to have succumbed to military and junker influence.

The Cologne Gazette blames the Progressives and the Socialists for the reawakening of the crisis, and says that the prospect for a political truce has disappeared.

OTTO H. KAHN TALKS FINANCE WITH WILSON

New Yorker at the White House Discusses Economic Condition of the Country.

WASHINGTON, Nov. 8.—Otto H. Kahn, head of Kuhn, Loeb & Co., called today on President Wilson. He would not discuss his visit except to say that it was for the purpose of talking over the economic condition of the country.

Otto H. Kahn has given considerable attention to the question of war taxation, and has advocated methods that would lay as little strain as possible on business in general while taking heavy levies from profits or incomes which could afford it without danger of drying up the sources of revenue. In May, when the question of taxing profits was beginning to receive much consideration, he pointed out that a very heavy tax on excess profits would be more desirable than a moderate tax on general profits.

"It appears," he said at that time, "that a 40 per cent. tax on excess profits over and above the average earnings for the last three years would yield for the present year the amazing total of at least $800,000,000 in addition to the yield from the corporate income tax at the rate of 4 per cent."

In August he urged that undue burdens on incomes and business profits should be avoided, while the taxes should be laid as widely as possible in order not to lay so much burden on any one as to be crushing.

"All I am advocating," he said at that time, "is in effect that in the public interest not too much be exacted at once, but that by dividing the burden over a reasonable number of years, capital in no one year, and especially not during the first year of the war, should be so excessively taxed as to produce an unscientific and dangerous strain. If the great fund of capital is suddenly and too greatly reduced the effect upon commerce and industry is apt to be sudden and withering."

CADORNA IS OUTFLANKED

A General Among the Troops Cut Off on the Middle Tagliamento.

INVADERS CAPTURE 80 GUNS

Berlin Reckons Total at More Than 2,300; That of Prisoners Over 250,000.

ROME ADMITS WITHDRAWAL

Official Report Shows That Rearguard Actions Are Proceeding West of the Livenza.

BERLIN, Nov. 8, (via London.)—Austro-German forces in Northern Italy have crossed the Livenza River, and in outflanking operations on the middle Tagliamento have captured 17,000 Italian troops, among them a General. Eighty guns have been added to the booty, which now includes more than 2,300 guns. The total number of prisoners taken since the drive began now exceeds 250,000.

These developments of the campaign are announced in the afternoon report from Army Headquarters, the text of which follows:

Our detachments, advancing on the mountain roads, have broken the resistance of the enemy rear guard. By an outflanking movement our attacking columns cut off the retreat of the enemy troops still holding out on the middle Tagliamento between Tolmezzo and Gemona and on the permanent fortified works of Monte San Simeone.

Up to the present 17,000 Italians, among them a General, with 80 guns, have had to surrender.

In the plain, fighting has developed along the Livenza River. By a vigorous advance German and Austro-Hungarian divisions, in spite of destroyed bridges, have forced the crossing and have thrown the enemy back westward.

The total number of prisoners captured has now been increased to more than 250,000 and the booty in guns to more than 2,300.

Tonight's report says:

In Italy we are fighting our way forward in the mountains and on the plains.

Retreat Continues, Rome Reports.

ROME, Nov. 8.—The withdrawal of the Italian line was continued yesterday, the War Office announced today. The larger units retired unmolested.

Italian troops fought numerous rearguard actions, in the course of which they succeeded in holding up the Austro-German advance temporarily. Italian airplanes continued bombarding hostile forces along the Tagliamento and brought down five enemy machines.

The text of the statement follows:

During yesterday we continued the withdrawal of our line. The larger units have retired without being molested by the enemy.

Numerous engagements took place between the hills of Vittorio and the confluence of the Monticano and the Livenza, in the course of which our brave troops succeeded in detaining the enemy's advance.

In spite of strong resistance on the part of hostile machines, our aviators renewed their bombardments of enemy troops along the Tagliamento. Five enemy airplanes were brought down.

As the Vittorio hills and the Monticano River lie to the west of the Livenza, the statement of the Italian War Office is equivalent to an admission that the Austro-Germans have crossed the latter stream.

Final Stand Beyond the Livenza?

By The Associated Press.

ITALIAN ARMY HEADQUARTERS, Nov. 8.—The bulk of the Austro-German invading forces today presents a main frontage of about thirty-five miles along the Tagliamento River, with reconnoissance parties thrust forward eight or ten miles west of the river, for the purpose of feeling for the points of least resistance. This is producing detached engagements, but no battle in force has yet occurred.

The Livenza River, to which the Italian withdrawal is now in progress, is only one of a series of successive defense parallels. The Italian Army still has in reserve large bodies of troops, which, however, naturally feel the effects produced by the recent retirement of their main body. Heavy reinforcements at this moment, therefore, would render invaluable assistance, in the opinion of the military authorities.

The enemy territorial occupation in Eastern Friuli presents a sinister aspect far beyond its military purport. The Alps heretofore have been the traditional boundary between the Northern Teutonic and the Southern Latin races. The Austro-Germans recognize the Alpine boundary, except for Trent and Trieste.

Now for the first time the Teutonic forces are occupying territory in the Friuli plains, which are the easternmost part of Venetia and age-long possessions of the Latins. Such an invasion strikes at the very heart of the principle of nationality, and also thrusts a Teutonic wedge southward along the Adriatic. This brings up the grave question of whether Germany will finally secure territorial lodgment with ports and naval bases on the Adriatic, thus realizing her aim to

Continued on Page 4.

British Government Denies Lack of Concern for Italy

LONDON, Nov. 8.—The following official announcement was issued tonight:

"A statement from a correspondent of The Associated Press at Italian Headquarters appeared in the British press today. This statement set out to remind the Allies that something more than assurances were needed for getting reinforcements in men and munitions to the threatened Italian lines, and purported to reflect the feeling of Italians, who were represented as distrusting the allied efforts to help them. It was also stated that the enemy masses were so overwhelming that nothing but effective reinforcements would turn the tide.

"This alarmist statement is absolutely uncalled for and is calculated to do grave harm by suggesting that the seriousness of the military situation in Italy is not appreciated by her allies, and that the latter are not giving her the support she requires. There is no truth whatever in these assertions. The statement that the enemy masses are overwhelming is an absurd exaggeration."

The Associated Press issued this statement last night:

"The dispatch to which the foregoing British official statement refers was sent by The Associated Press correspondent at Italian Headquarters on Nov. 7. This correspondent is an American Staff man, who was present at the beginning of the Italian retreat and accompanied the Italian Army back to its present position.

"The dispatch in question was passed by the Italian military censors at General Cadorna's headquarters, and, as it was sent through France, also passed the French censorship."

LONDON HAILS OUR WAR MISSION

Comes at Critical Period of the War with New Assurance of Victory.

ENVOYS MAKE BRISK START

Begin Conferences on First Day—Benson Visits Jellicoe—Trip Was Uneventful.

Special Cable to THE NEW YORK TIMES.

LONDON, Nov. 8.—The American mission, headed by Colonel E. M. House, arrived in Europe at a crucial period of the world war. With Russia in the throes of a fresh revolution that may lead to anything, and with Italy engaged in a desperate struggle against both a foreign enemy and internal difficulties the landing of the American mission at a British port is an encouragement to the stalwart and a rebuke to the faint hearted.

To England in particular it possesses special significance. It is a concrete expression of the union of Anglo-Saxon races in the greatest war for liberty the world has ever seen, and also an augury of the victorious overthrow of despotic forces which make the world unsafe for democracy.

The statement which Colonel House gave to the British press tonight supplemented the announcement issued in America by the President. In all quarters it is hailed as a plain definition of the objects aimed at by America and a pledge of America's intention to fight on till those ends are attained.

Great Britain's confidence in the issue of the struggle has never been seriously undermined. There have been times of depression when the end seemed far distant but the country as a whole has set itself resolutely to travel the long and weary road. England never for one moment doubted its ability to win through itself.

There were those who questioned the possibility of a final decision being reached in this war. There still are a few of these, chiefly to be found among that clique which believes that a negotiated peace with an unregenerate and unrepentant Germany is an acceptable solution.

America's clear perception of the issue at stake and America's undivided purpose to fight, as Colonel House put it, until it becomes certain that no group of selfish men can again bring about disaster to the world, more than counterbalances all that history has written, or may yet write, on the wrong side of the allied ledger.

Colonel House explained today to the English newspaper representatives the circumstances under which the American mission had come to participate in the Allied War Council shortly to be held in Paris. He was asked if the United States was going to sign the pact of London and he quietly, but clearly, made it patent that the question did not arise.

Various phrases in President Wilson's announcement drew a query as to whether any criticism of the past conduct of the war by allied Governments was implied.

Colonel House decisively negatived any such suggestion. In this respect it may be stated emphatically that the American participation in the war council of the Allies is most heartily welcomed by those who most clearly see

Continued on Page 11.

AWAITS LIGHT FROM RUSSIA

Washington Reserves Judgment, Hoping Revolt Is Only Local.

EXPECTS A COUNTER-MOVE

Kerensky, with Conservatives and Perhaps the Army Behind Him, May Save the Country.

DARK DAYS SEEN AHEAD

And Allied War Conference Faces Another Huge Problem—Bigger Burden for Us.

Special to The New York Times.

WASHINGTON, Nov. 8.—Until accurate official reports are received, official and diplomatic Washington are reserving judgment on the new Russian crisis and all that it involves, including possibly civil war, and a still further weakening of Russia's position in the war against Germany.

Dark as the news dispatches make the situation in Petrograd appear, there is a strong hope among officials and diplomats that there may be a silver lining to the cloud. On every hand keen sympathy was expressed for Premier Kerensky and those who have been standing with him against terrific odds in opposing the extremist elements who, by their activities, have threatened to disorganize the Russian military machine, and have worked for separate peace, regardless of its effect on the future of Russia and her pledges to her allies.

The State Department has received no official confirmation of the Maximalist successes in Petrograd. In the last six days Secretary Lansing has received only two messages from Ambassador Francis, and neither dealt with the political situation. One bore date of Friday last and the other of Tuesday.

The Russian Embassy officials said they had no advices from Petrograd on the basis of which comment could be made. Jean Soukine, First Secretary, after a telephone conversation this afternoon with Ambassador Bakhmeteff, who is in Memphis, stated that in the absence of official intelligence the Embassy held that the action of the Maximalists in Petrograd, as told in the news dispatches, was local to the capital and by no means representative of the will or of the Russian nation.

This point was emphasized here today that the dispatches from Petrograd stated that the Maximalists had taken control of the telegraph offices and that this put them in a position to exaggerate reports of the situation in their own favor.

First Secretary Soukine stated that the Embassy was unable to present the views of the Government, being without instructions, but he pointed out that Petrograd was the centre of Bolsheviki activity. To this fact, he said, was due the present situation in Petrograd, which did not represent the conditions throughout Russia. Mr. Soukine stated that the local character of the disturbance was proved by the fact that the Central Executive Committee of the Petrograd Council of Soldiers' and Workmen's Delegates did not express the will of the Pan Russian Council's Executive Committee, which only a few days ago refused to approve the creation by the Petrograd Council's Executive Committee of a military revolutionary committee, and at the same time urged that measures be taken to prevent the consummation of the designs of the Bolsheviki.

The embassy officials suggested that "Petrograd is likely to be isolated." No interpretation of this statement was given, but it was believed to indicate a belief that the Bolsheviki would find themselves without national support and that the army might decline to accept orders from their Military Revolutionary Committee, which now, according to the announcement in Petrograd, is the sole Governmental authority.

Expect a New Government.

In many quarters it was thought that another Government will be formed for Russia, now that some members of the Provisional Government had been arrested. The new Government would probably be formed at Moscow, it was said, and be dominated by the conservative Socialist elements, although it might be a coalition, including members of the Constitutional Democratic Party as well as Socialists and Laborites, of which last-named party Premier Kerensky is a member.

No doubt was expressed in diplomatic circles that the Allied Powers would recognize any Government formed to oppose the Bolsheviki, even if the latter maintained their hold upon Petrograd. Moscow was regarded as the probable choice for the provisional capital, because all the elements there have been in sympathy with the Government as against the extremist Socialists. Moscow also is held to be a more purely Russian city, and, as compared with Petrograd, practically free from the elements that have made the life of the Government precarious.

It is believed that unless the army goes over en masse to the Bolsheviki, the temporary ascendency of the rad-

Continued on Page 2.

Reverses Cited as Showing Greater Need Than Ever For Unified Direction of Allied War Policy

By CHARLES H. GRASTY.

Copyright, 1917, by The New York Times Company.

Special Cable to THE NEW YORK TIMES.

ROME, Nov. 8.—My observations here confirm previous insistence upon the urgent need of centralized methods of managing the war. At bottom this war is the biggest business enterprise ever undertaken, and, while the Kaiser handles his end of it as such, each of the Allies is more or less playing its own separate game. With an infinity of resources, they have discussed and postponed critical decisions until the advantage has been lost.

To mention one recent instance: If the Korniloff movement had been handled by the Allies as the Kaiser would have handled such an opportunity, the Russian situation might have been stabilized and the Italian drive rendered impossible.

There has not been a single allied action, with the exception of the battle of the Marne, ranking as a great aggressive stroke. The Allies are not organized to initiate and execute big policies. Instead of looking ahead and planning on a big scale, they yield where pressure is applied, with the result that usually they trail along a few days or weeks behind Germany. Purely local and political matters divide and divert attention in the allied Chancelleries.

Coming on top of many previous heartbreaking lost opportunities, the present menace in Italy is quite serious enough to rally the Entente Powers at last into substituting for the town meeting some plan under which they can see the war situation as a whole and concentrate with foresight, originality, and driving power, as we understand those things in America.

In a word, after three years, it is time to quit playing amateur against professional. If America gives the lead, all the rest will follow, as there are directed against us none of the petty jealousies peculiar to Europe, and all the allied countries have complete confidence in our disinterestedness and sound leadership.

Plans for the conduct of the war on the basis of a unified western front extending from the North Sea to the Adriatic are now under consideration by Premiers Lloyd George and Painlevé and other high civil and military officials in conference in Rome.

STOCKS TUMBLE ON RUSSIAN NEWS

Flood of Liquidation Hits Exchange, Heightened by Action of Short Sellers.

NEWS CHECKS BROAD RISE

No Action Considered Yet in Regard to Publishing Proportion of Short Sales.

The stock market suffered one of the most drastic declines of the year yesterday, following the receipt of dispatches which told of the Kerensky Government's downfall. Owners of securities considered the Russian news more disturbing than developments on the Italian front, although in banking circles the new republic's reversion to a condition of political chaos did not seem to increase pessimism over the war outlook greatly. In a wild hour of trading the active speculative stocks dropped 4 to 11 points from their previous levels, thereafter recovering part of the distance under active bidding from investors and traders who covered short contracts and what looked like banking support.

The decline was made all the more emphatic because it occurred suddenly in the midst of a rather broad rise of prices. Starting slightly higher than Wednesday's closing quotations, the prominent railroad and industrial shares advanced in many cases more than a point before 11 o'clock, and were moving along normally when the first reports came from London of the changed conditions in Russia. There was a quick drop of a couple of points in the next quarter hour, and then a short period of steadiness, a lull before the storm.

Big Sales of Steel Common.

When brokerage houses with wire connections began to get in their orders after flashing out the Russian news, a flood of selling struck the Exchange, which was heightened by the operations of short sellers in the Street and out. Steel common was poured forth in blocks running as high as 5,000 shares, and International Mercantile Marine preferred dropped under heavy selling from 98 to 91½, frequently by quarters and half points, and without a period of recovery. Reading, Southern Pacific, New York Central, and Union Pacific were pressed for sale, and numerous high-grade railroad bonds lost more ground than in any preceding day since Jan. 1.

The movements of some of the more active stocks from their best to their lowest prices, with their net declines, are in the following table:

	Decline From Top.	Net Decline.	Last Price.
American Can	3½	2⅞	30⅜
American Smelting	5⅝	4	70⅜
American Sugar	6⅛	5½	90
Atchison	3½	2⅛	82⅝
Baldwin Locomotive	7½	3¾	51¼
Bethlehem Steel	9½	8¼	73
Brooklyn Rapid Transit	5⅞	2⅝	45¼
Canadian Pacific	4⅝	2⅞	133⅝
Crucible Steel	7	3½	52
General Motors	5⅝	3	80
Int. Mer. Marine pf	11	5	94
New York Central	3⅜	2⅝	65
Reading	6½	3⅞	63⅝
Republic Iron & Steel	6⅞	4⅜	68⅞
Union Pacific	5⅜	3	108⅝
United States Steel	7⅛	4⅝	90⅛

Russian Bonds Decline.

The Russian situation had a naturally adverse effect on the Russian bonds dealt in on the Curb. From Wednesday's last price of 56 the 5½s declined to 48, with sales of $30,000, and the 6½s dropped from 61 to 58 with transactions involving $25,000. Russian exchange fell away from 13.35 cents per ruble to 11.75 cents for transfers by check, approaching the previous minimum record of 11½ cents. At times the market was report-

Continued on Page 2.

HOPE STRONG MAN WILL RULE RUSSIA

Zemstvos' Agent Here and Herman Bernstein Agree That Kerensky Must Go.

GREAT REACTION EXPECTED

Salchnovsky Thinks Revolt May Lead to Constitutional Monarchy.

The elimination of Kerensky from the affairs of the Russian Government was declared to be the most probable as well as the most desirable result of the present Maximalist revolt by persons familiar with Russian affairs and in sympathy with the moderate parties there.

Alexander Sakhnovsky, head of the American offices of the Union of Zemstvos, predicted that the reaction toward a stronger form of government might go as far as the setting up of a constitutional monarchy under the Grand Duke Michael, who was named as the successor of Nicholas in the first announcements of the revolution last March, but was immediately pushed out of the way by the tide of radical sentiment.

"Russians who have landed in New York within the last few days," said Mr. Sakhnovsky, "bring reports that the whole nation outside of the radicals of Petrograd is disgusted with the violence, disorder, and uncertainty which have prevailed for months past. There is a strong tide setting toward a more compact and powerful government, and Moscow would undoubtedly be the natural centre of such a movement.

"In Moscow the Bolsheviki are not 1 per cent. of the total population, and all Russia outside of Petrograd would stand together, I believe, against the extreme policy of the Maximalists. This will be particularly true if, as is possible, Lenine and Trotzky call in the German fleet to their aid.

"In any event, it will take a stronger Government than that of Kerensky to bring about order. The excellence of Kerensky's motives and ideals is recognized, but he is too gentle a man for his position at the present time. It has been shown that the policy of mildness with the Bolsheviki does not pay. Moreover, he lacks the executive experience which is necessary to the head of the Government. A man like Prince Lvoff would be considerably more useful, and I believe, from the reports I receive, that sentiment in Russia is setting in that direction.

"As for the Grand Duke Michael, he has always been very popular, and the fact that he has married a woman not of royal blood, the divorced wife of a Moscow lawyer, has increased his popularity. I am confident that Russia as a whole will not yield to a faction of Petrograd."

Herman Bernstein, who was in Petrograd during the Maximalist riots of last July, said that he was confident that Trotzsky was only the agent of Lenine, who from his hiding had been directing this revolt, as he had done the rising of that period.

"It can't win," he said, "for Lenine and Trotzky are both extremely unpopular. They had a better chance last July, when, if they had only had well-laid plans, they would have been able to dominate Petrograd. As it was, they failed at the time, and the popular execration directed against Lenine after the bloodshed of July was such as to convince me that he will never be able to dominate the Russian people.

"But undoubtedly Kerensky cannot

Continued on Page 2.

MINISTERS UNDER ARREST

Winter Palace Is Taken After Fierce Defense by Women Soldiers.

FORT'S GUNS TURNED ON IT

Cruiser and Armored Cars Also Brought Into Battle Waged by Searchlight.

TROTZSKY HEADS REVOLT

Giving Land to the Peasants and Calling of Constituent Assembly Promised.

PETROGRAD, Nov. 8.—With the aid of the capital's garrison complete control of Petrograd has been seized by the Maximalists, or Bolsheviki, headed by Nikolai Lenine, the Radical Socialist leader, and Leon Trotzsky, President of the Central Executive Committee of the Petrograd Council of Workmen's and Soldiers' Delegates. Their action has been indorsed by the All-Russia Congress of Workmen's Councils.

A proclamation has been issued declaring that the Revolutionary Government purposes to negotiate an "immediate democratic peace," to turn the land over to the peasantry, and to convoke the Constituent Assembly.

Premier Kerensky has fled. He is variously said to be headed for Moscow and the northern front of the army, and orders for his arrest have been issued. Last night he was reported to be at Luga, eighty-five miles southwest of Petrograd. Several members of his Cabinet have been taken into custody.

The Preliminary Parliament is declared dissolved.

Little serious fighting has attended the revolt so far. The Provisional Government troops holding the bridges over the Neva and various other points yesterday were quickly overpowered, save at the Winter Palace, the chief guardians of which were the Women's Battalion. Here last night a battle royal took place for four hours, during which the Bolsheviki brought up armored cars and the cruiser Aurora and turned the guns of the Fort of St. Peter and St. Paul upon the palace before its defenders would surrender.

Prior to the attack the Workmen's and Soldiers' leaders sent the Provisional Government an ultimatum demanding their surrender and allowing twenty minutes' grace. The Government replied indirectly, refusing to recognize the Military Committee.

Vice President Kameneff of the Workmen's and Soldiers' Delegates told The Associated Press today that the object of taking possession of the posts and telegraphs was to thwart any effort the Government might make to call troops to the capital. The Russkia Volia and the Bourse Gazette have been commandeered.

The city today presented a normal aspect. Even the noonday band accompanying the guard of relief under the previous administration continued its function. There were the customary lines in front of the provision stores and children played in the parks and gardens. There was even a notable lessening of the patrols, only a few armed soldiers and sailors moving about the streets.

How the Revolt Developed.

The Maximalist movement toward seizing authority, rumors of which had been agitating the public mind ever since the formation of the last Coalition Cabinet, culminated Tuesday night, when, without disorder, Maximalist forces took possession of the Telegraph office and the Petrograd Telegraph Agency.

Orders issued by the Government for the opening of the spans of the bridges across the Neva later were overridden by the Military Committee of the Council of Workmen's and Soldiers' Delegates. Communication was restored after several hours of interruption. Nowhere did the Maximalists meet with serious opposition.

An effort by militiamen to disperse crowds gathered in the Nevski and Letainy Prospekts during the evening provoked a fight in which one man is reported to have been killed. Minor disturbances, some of them accompanied by shooting, occurred in various quarters of the city. A number of persons are reported to have been killed or wounded.

Yesterday morning found patrols of soldiers, sailors, and civilians in the streets maintaining order. Further than a continuation of suppressed excitement, the streets of the city presented no unusual aspects. The shops and banks which had opened for business began closing up about noon.

Shortly after noon a Soviet force occupied the telephone exchange, where a small guard had been stationed for weeks. An effort by Government forces to retake the exchange led to a brief fusillade, by which it is believed a number of casualties was caused. The Maximalists remained in possession of the building.

Toward 5 o'clock in the afternoon the Military Revolutionary Committee issued its proclamation stating that Petrograd was in its hands. It read:

To the Army Committees of the Active Army and to all Councils of Workmen's and Soldiers' Delegates and to the Garrison and Proletariat of Petrograd:

We have deposed the Government of Kerensky, which rose against the revolution and the people. The change which resulted in the deposition of the

Mid-Week Pictorial

Italian artillerymen in one of the valleys in the Trentino zone.

"All the News That's Fit to Print."

The New York Times.

THE WEATHER
Generally fair today and tomorrow; fresh northeast winds.
For full weather report see Page 21.

VOL. LXVII...NO. 21,843. NEW YORK, TUESDAY, NOVEMBER 13, 1917.—TWENTY-TWO PAGES. ONE CENT In Greater New York. | TWO CENTS Within Commuting Distance. | THREE CENTS Elsewhere.

LLOYD GEORGE SEES VICTORY IN UNITY, WITHOUT RUSSIA; WILSON TELLS LABOR VICTORY ALONE SPELLS PEACE; KERENSKY FIGHTING REBELS; ITALY FACING A GREAT BATTLE

GLYNN ORDERED G. O. P. BOSSES TO AID SUFFRAGE

Republican Help to Women a Move in Whitman's Fight for Presidency.

PLAYS FOR THEIR SUPPORT

County Leader Here Is Ready to Favor a Dual Organization.

WOMEN IN CONGRESS FIGHT

Democratic Club Formed in Brooklyn—City Suffrage Party for Nonpartisanship.

Many of the Old Guard Republican bosses up-State, it was learned yesterday, worked assiduously and against heavy odds to obtain a majority in favor of the woman suffrage amendment to the State Constitution at the recent election. To their activity more than to any other single factor is ascribed the heavy vote cast for its ratification in the Republican strongholds up-State. They are determined that the newly enfranchised women shall be pawns in their own political game.

Orders sent out on the eve of election by Chairman George A. Glynn of the Republican State Committee stirred the Republican leaders up-State into unwonted zeal for the measure they had fought bitterly when it was before the voters for ratification two years ago. Chairman Glynn sent out a letter on the Saturday prior to election urging every Republican County Chairman up-State to do all in his power to get out a big vote for the amendment. While it was not explicitly stated, the up-State Republican politicians were not slow to read between the lines the inverse meaning of Chairman Glynn's communication. The result was that in districts where there was strong opposition to woman suffrage the vote, and consequently the adverse majority, was comparatively light.

Whitman Wants Aid of Women.

Chairman Glynn in sending out these instructions acted merely as the mouthpiece of Governor Whitman, who expects to be a candidate for renomination in the State primaries next Fall, and has awakened to a realization of the fact that he will have a fight on his hands. The Governor places in the woman vote his chief reliance for the third-term victory he is doubly anxious to obtain, because without it he could scarcely figure conspicuously as a candidate for the Presidential nomination in 1920, the goal which the Governor, with the aid of his friends, hopes to attain.

Governor Whitman has been as active an advocate of woman suffrage as his office would permit him to be. He supported the woman suffrage amendment in 1915 when it was before the voters for ratification. He spoke warmly in support of woman suffrage at the convention of the Woman Suffrage Party in Saratoga last September. Mrs. Whitman has been actively interested for years in the fight for woman suffrage.

One of the Old Guard Republican leaders up-State who has been closely allied with Governor Whitman politically, rebelled against Chairman Glynn's instructions. The anti-suffrage insurgent was George W. Aldridge of Monroe. His district returned an adverse majority of approximately 3,500. In Albany, where Governor Whitman's political foe, William Barnes, rules, the vote was two to one against woman suffrage.

Governor Whitman will leave nothing undone to bring about the enactment of legislation to provide for a special enrollment so that women may vote in the State primaries next Fall. Recommendations for the passage of such a bill, it has already been announced in dispatches from Albany, will be embodied in the Governor's annual message to the Legislature. While some of the anti-Whitman Republicans, of whom there are more in the Senate than in the Assembly, may offer opposition in order to eliminate the woman voters as a factor in the primaries and lessen the Governor's chances of success in his fight for a third term, the present outlook is distinctly favorable to the women. The Senators will be compelled to go back and face their constituents next Fall, and it is not likely that many of those looking for re-election will be prepared to brave the wrath of women with ballots.

To Name Republican Conferrees.

Samuel S. Koenig, Chairman of the New York County Republican Committee, said last night, that at the regular meeting of the County Committee on Thursday, a special committee would be appointed to confer with leaders of the woman suffrage organization to devise ways to enable the enfranchised women to participate in the management of the Republican county organization, should they so desire. In the meantime the standing Committee on Legislation of the County Committee will be set to work to draft the necessary legislation for a special enrollment of the woman voters, so that they may participate in the primary fight next Fall.

"It is for the women to determine whether they will work together with us or form a separate organization of their own," Chairman Koenig said. "We are ready and willing to co-operate in any manner that will suit the women."

Chairman Koenig said that he was quite willing to have the bylaws of the County Committee amended so as to provide for associate leadership in each of the twenty-three Assembly districts in Manhattan, the associate leader to be a woman with her own staff of lieutenants and election district workers of her own sex. The women may also, should

Continued on Page 4.

Tirpitz Loses Faith in U-Boats; Fears Plan to Devour Germany

AMSTERDAM, Nov. 12.—At a meeting of the new Fatherland Party in Munich yesterday, Admiral von Tirpitz, former German Minister of Marine, made a speech saying that it was a mistake to believe that the submarine would prove sufficient protection against Great Britain, as some effective counterweapon was bound to be discovered.

He also delivered a violent utterance on annexation, asserting that the question whether Germany or Great Britain became the protector of Belgium would be the decisive issue of the war.

"A mistaken solution of the Belgian question would stunt our exports and the reserve capital of our industry, and degrade us to being the bond slave of Anglo-Americanism," said the Admiral. "Our military security lies in Belgium. It is the only way of obtaining compensation for our enormous economic losses."

The Admiral said that Germany must have Antwerp, that Austria must become the principal protecting power of the mouth of the Danube, and that Germany was interested in the settlement of the Adriatic question.

"Germany's struggle," he added, "is a terrific battle against the all-devouring tyranny of Anglo-Americanism."

PLAN STRICTER BAN ON MUNITION PLANTS

Waterfront Fire Here May Lead to Revision of Rules for Permits.

DEMAND GREATER CAUTION

Government to Insist That Its Own Interests Are Above Those of Employers.

Special to The New York Times.

WASHINGTON, Nov. 12.—The execution of the plan adopted by the Government almost from the beginning of the war to safeguard manufacturing plants engaged on war supplies is being questioned now by owners of warehouses and plants where fires and explosions have occurred under suspicious circumstances suggesting the activity of enemies. The permit system, it is urged, does not work, as plotters are still able to get employment where they can carry on their plans to the risk of large amounts of property and the hazard of human lives.

Government officials who are charged with the execution of the plan of granting permits complain that they have been made the target for blame by manufacturers on two counts. They have uniformly found the employers, they say, prone to plead for the retention of old enemy alien employes, and as an employer countersigns the permits obtained from the United States Marshal of the Judicial District where the plant is situated they say they have the right to retain such employes as they desire. For some reason, it was asserted, they have insisted that the special faithfulness of an employe should be considered, and have retained men who would otherwise have been kept out of war plants.

Many such enemy aliens have been in the employ of corporations or firms for years before the war in Europe. Employers cite such cases to back their contention that it would be a hardship to discharge such men, and they are usually emphatic in asking that they receive permits. When fires and explosions have occurred it was said manufacturers in several cases declared that the Government was lax in enforcing the permit plan and that had there been strict enforcement the trouble would not have occurred.

It is likely that in consequence of the New York waterfront fires there will be a more rigid inquiry into the antecedents and character of men vouched for by employers and that permits will not be so easily granted hereafter. The Government has proceeded, it was said, too much on the theory that the judgment of the employers in regard to their men could be relied on and that their own self-interest was sufficient to safeguard the industry. But officials now admit that this view is not conclusive of all contingencies and that a hard and fast exercise of caution is demanded. No new method of protecting munition plants will be employed, but there will be new regulations buttressing the administration of the existing method. The Government will insist on the view that its own interests are paramount and the necessity for the output of munition plants is so great that employers must bend to the rules to be laid down by the Government.

It was said to night that there has never been carried out in this country anything like the precautions taken in English and Canadian war plants. Their uniform practice has been to place barbed wire barriers around their works and employ large and competent forces of watchmen. All employes are subjected to the most rigid test of loyalty, and monitors are kept in the works during all working hours to note any suspicious conduct or any sign of defection that might give rise to trouble. The United States Government has no present intention of going as far as this, but the practical co-operation of employers will be expected, and there will be more thoroughly organized effort hereafter to protect munition manufacturing plants.

WANT WATER FRONT HERE MADE WAR ZONE

Suggestion Sent to Washington to Have 10,000 Soldiers on Guard—Washburn Blaze Unsolved.

A Federal official, one of the highest in authority so far as the enforcement of the enemy alien regulations in New York City is concerned, said yesterday that a suggestion had been submitted to the Government in Washington which, if adopted, would reduce to a minimum the danger of incendiary fires in munition works, the attempted bombing of

Continued on Page 4.

THE PRESIDENT TO WORKERS

Must Sink All Differences and Give Full Aid, He Says at Buffalo.

CONTEMPT FOR PACIFISTS

Asserts Germany Started War and Aims to Control Industry of World by Force.

AMAZED AT BOLSHEVIKI

Compounding with Germany Will Mean Russia's Destruction—No Opposition to Gompers.

Special to The New York Times.

BUFFALO, N. Y., Nov. 12.—Addressing the annual convention of the Ameracin Federation of Labor here today, President Wilson delivered a message to the American people as well as to American labor, and, many here believe, to the peoples of the warring nations of Europe, particularly Germany, Austria-Hungary, and Russia.

He made it clear that he was against any premature peace with Germany. He had contempt, he said, for the pacifists.

"I want peace," he said, "but I know how to get it, and they do not."

He sent Colonel House abroad, he explained, to take part in a conference as to how the war was to be won.

"And he knows, as I know," he said, "that that is the way to get peace if you want it for more than a few minutes."

Mr. Wilson appealed to American labor for full co-operation for the winning of the war. Incidentally, he paid tribute to the patriotism of Samuel Gompers, President of the Federation, and, referring to the aid Mr. Gompers had given the Administration in its war program, said:

"I like to lay my mind alongside a mind that knows how to pull in harness. The horses that kick over the traces will have to be put in a corral."

The President's references to Mr. Gompers were loudly applauded.

No Signs of Any Revolt.

The rumored revolt of pacifists and Socialists against President Gompers is not going to take place. That is the impression left by the opening day of the convention, although the election of officers does not come till the very end of the convention, two weeks hence, and it is possible that the insurgents, if there are any, are merely biding their time.

But from present indications Mr. Gompers and those who are associated with him in support of the war are going to remain in the saddle. Everything worked for them today, and notably the speech of President Wilson, who made a hurried trip from Washington to address the convention. When the President said that while his heart sympathized with the feeling of the pacifists, his mind had a contempt for them, because, while he, too, wanted peace he knew how to get it and they did not, the whole audience stood up and cheered wildly. They cheered also his vigorous praise of Mr. Gompers as a man of "patriotic courage, large vision, and a statesmanlike sense of what is to be done." They applauded when the President made appeals for the co-operation of all classes, employers and employes alike, as an essential to winning the war.

Naturally, the delegates were not a little pleased when the President said, not once, but twice, that the attitude of labor in industrial disputes was more often reasonable than that of capitalists, and they received with every token of agreement his declaration that "nobody has a right to stop the processes of labor until all the methods of conciliation and settlement have been exhausted."

The President's address was admirably balanced to forestall every conceivable objection that labor might have to aiding in the energetic prosecution of the war. Beginning with a portrayal of the menace of a militaristic Germany to peaceable industry, commerce and labor in other countries, he expressed amazement at the "ill-informed" Russian Bolsheviki, who thought that liberal reforms could flourish under the shadow of the German might, passed with rather amused contempt by the "stupidity" of American pacifists, and led on to the declaration that the only way to give freedom a chance to live was by utilizing every possible energy of America in loyal and complete co-operation.

Radicals were conciliated by his warning that certain practices still indulged in by employers must be corrected, and by his outspoken denunciation of mob law, even when employed against "organizations whose object is anarchy and the destruction of law."

But this disapproval of mob violence on the I. W. W. led directly to a warning, gentle but obvious, against "manifestations of the unwillingness to co-operate" between labor and capital, which come very near to mob law.

Temper of the German People.

The President in that part of his address devoted to the broader phases of the world conflict declared his belief that, were it not for the Pan Germans, the spirit of freedom would find "as fine a welcome in the hearts of Germans as it can find in any other heart. Power," he said, "cannot be used with concentrated force against free peoples, if it is to be used by a free people."

Speaking, probably of Austria, Mr. Wilson referred to the intimations of

Continued on Page 3.

Kaiser at Italian Front with Charles and Ferdinand

AMSTERDAM, Nov. 12.—The German Emperor arrived Sunday at the Italian front, where he met Emperor Charles and King Ferdinand of Bulgaria, according to a Gorizia dispatch. He congratulated Emperor Charles on his escape from drowning.

The Kaiser continued his journey along the front.

ITALIANS URGE US TO FIGHT AUSTRIA

Thus, They Say, America Can Render Them the Most Important Service.

COAL AND WHEAT NEXT

Need for Munitions Is Great, but Less Imperative Than for Food and Fuel.

Special Cable to THE NEW YORK TIMES.

PARIS, Nov. 12.—In a previous dispatch I set forth the necessity for American aid to Italy and the principal reasons of the internal weakness in Italy that rendered that aid so imperative. I will now try to indicate how in the opinion of the best informed Italians America's aid can be exercised most usefully.

To begin with, it is moral even more than material help that Italy requires at this juncture. It has been the misfortune of the Entente leaders to have but insufficiently recognized the importance of the moral factors in this war of peoples. It is only recently that they are beginning to understand the vital necessity of informing public opinion and directing it along right lines.

As I showed yesterday, the greater part at least of Italy's present troubles is due to the demoralization of the masses by anti-Italian elements. Obviously, then, the first thing to do is to recreate and strengthen a healthy morale in Italy, and in this America can aid enormously.

A moment's thought will show that the return to Italy of hundreds of thousands of Italian emigrants in the United States, who made what for them are fortunes, must have created an almost fabulous belief in the strength, richness, and importance of America. America's voice would carry weight in Italy superior even to that of the Roman Catholic Church.

What Italy Most Needs.

What, then, is America to say? First and most important, in the opinion of Italians, America must declare her solidarity with Italian aims by declaring war on Austria. No one who has not been recently in Italy can realize the harm done by crafty propaganda whose theme is America's abstention from war with Austria—which, say the propagandists, proves the justness of the Vatican's pacifism by showing that America also is not in sympathy with the war Italy is waging to complete her national unity.

How far that unity is in line with the Vatican's dream of temporal power may be judged by the fact that its heart and centre is Rome—the city which the Popes regard equally as the home pivot of their rule on earth. This question of Rome demarks immediately the vastness of the gulf between the Papal aspirations and those of Italy as a nation. For both parties Rome is a holy palladium whose possession guarantees and typifies everything they hold dear. Yet the Italian Government has in no way tried to hamper or interfere with the Vatican.

If the Vatican would confine its activities to spiritual affairs, no enlightened politician in Italy or France would have a word to say against it, but—and this is hard for American or Englishman to realize—the Roman Catholic Church in Continental Europe has always insisted and still insists on exerting political influence, which by the nature and traditions of the Vatican has always been absolutist and antidemocratic.

America's declaration of war on Austria and of complete solidarity with the Entente would take the strongest weapon from the hands of the anti-Italian elements in Italy. It is hard for Americans to realize the importance of this question.

To take a specific case: Cardinal Gasparri, at the time of the Pope's note and before the arrival of President Wilson's reply, gave an interview to a well known American journalist for publication in America. The whole tenor of the interview was an attempt to prove the exactitude with which the Papal views coincided with the statements and opinions of Wilson. The journalist in question was too well informed to be caught, and sacrificed a good "story" in the national interests.

When I add that the President's reply threw the Vatican literally into consternation it will be understood how fictitious was the parallel Gasparri tried to draw between the viewpoints of the Pope and our President.

This example may give an idea of what capital the Catholic Party can draw from America's failure to declare war on Austria.

Call for an American Mission.

The next most important aid, from the Italian standpoint, is that America should send to Italy an official mission, however small, of prominent men with the twofold obect of giving the Italian people concrete proof of American sympathy and of procuring for America a wider knowledge of the Italian situation. On similar lines the Italians ask that the press relations between the two countries should be strengthened, and that the leading American newspapers

Continued on Page 2.

RUSSIAN ARMIES CLASH

News of Fierce Encounter at Gatchina Reaches Minister Morris.

RESULT NOT YET KNOWN

Compromise at Moscow Reported After Battle There with 700 Casualties.

FIGHTING IN PETROGRAD

Military Cadets Attack Bolsheviki with Armored Cars, but Are Overpowered.

Seek Compromise Between Kerensky and Bolsheviki

PETROGRAD, Nov. 12, (12:30 P. M.)—Petrograd is still in the hands of the Bolsheviki after desperate street battles on Sunday in which a handful of military cadets was exterminated or captured by members of the Bolsheviki, upon whom they inflicted considerable losses.

The Committee of Public Safety agents have gone to Gatchina to try to arrange a compromise between the Kerensky forces and the Bolsheviki.

STOCKHOLM, Nov. 12.—A bloody encounter has taken place near Gatchina, thirty miles southwest of Petrograd, between soldiers from the front, headed by Premier Kerensky, and Bolsheviki forces from Petrograd, according to advices which have reached Ira Nelson Morris, the American Minister, from reliable sources.

The result of the battle was not reported to Mr. Morris.

It is reported that M. Kerensky is still issuing proclamations as Premier, and that strong forces are rallying against the Bolsheviki. General Kaledines, former Hetman of the Cossacks, has announced his refusal to recognize the Leninites, and Maxim Gorgy is issuing daily bulletins against them. The Committee of Public Safety, which was appointed by the Mayor and the City Duma, has obtained the support of the Mensheviki Social Revolutionists and the bourgeois parties generally, and is also receiving the support from the Railway Employes' Union and the Central Railway Committee.

Fleet Dissatisfied With Lenine.

The Committee of Public Safety sent an emissary to treat with the sailors of the fleet. He has reported that the sailors already are showing dissatisfaction with Lenine. The reports also say that the committee has issued an appeal to the city population and to the city militia to abstain from violence against the Bolsheviki, who have the support of the sailors and 50,000 [illegible] of the Petrograd garrison, and to await a peaceful solution of the situation.

All the Ministers of the provisional Government who were arrested at the commencement of the revolt have been released, except Foreign Minister Terestchenko and one other. The banks in Petrograd are still closed, but the shops are open.

The Bolsheviki's short day of triumph is rapidly nearing its close, in the opinion of M. Goulkevitch, the Russian Minister to Sweden, who bases his belief on information received from various sources during the last twenty-four hours. M. Goulkevitch, who was greatly depressed when The Associated Press correspondent first saw him immediately after Nikolai Lenine's coup, was beaming with optisim today.

"Everything is coming out all right," he said. "There no longer is any reason to worry over the situation. All the information that has reached me since Saturday shows that the crisis has virtually passed, and that it will be only a short time until the Bolsheviki will have played out their brief rôle.

"This thing had to come some time, and I believe it is well it came when it did. It was a state of sickness which could not be avoided, and convalescence will be rapid."

The correspondent referred to the fact that the Russian Ambassador to the United States had given formal notice of his refusal to recognize the Lenine Government, and asked M. Goulkevitch whether he had done the same.

"I have made it clear from the first day," the Minister replied, "that there could be no question of recognizing the Leninites, but I gave no formal notice to that effect. The whole thing is so absurd and even laughable that I considered it unnecessary formally to give notice of anything so obvious as my refusal to recognize the Bolsheviki."

LONDON, Tuesday, Nov. 13.—The Daily Mail's Petrograd correspondent, telegraphing at noon Monday, says reports from Moscow are contradictory, but that it seems probable order has been restored there, though conditions are uncertain. He adds that news from

Continued on Page 2.

War Will Be Shortened by Solidified Allied Action Insists British Premier; Confident of Final Triumph

From Lloyd George's Speech in Paris Yesterday.

I have spoken today with a frankness that is perhaps brutal, a the risk of being ill understood here and elsewhere, and not, perhaps, without risk of giving temporary encouragement to the enemy, because now that we have established this council it is for us to see that the unity it represents be a fact and not an appearance.

The war has been prolonged by particularism. It will be shortened by solidarity. If the effort to organize our united action becomes a reality, I have no doubt as to the issue of the war. The weight of men and material and of moral factors in every sense of the word is on our side. I say it, no matter what may happen to Russia or in Russia. A revolutionary Russia can never be anything but a menace to Hohenzollernism. But even if we are obliged to despair of Russia, my faith in the final triumph of the cause of the Allies remains unshakable.

TEUTONS CAPTURE 14,000 ITALIANS

Cut Off Retreating Forces in the Upper Piave and Cordevole Valleys.

ADVANCE DOWN THE PIAVE

Are Now Before Feltre, 17 Miles Below Belluno—Checked Elsewhere on River.

BERLIN, Nov. 12, (via London.)—The Austro-German forces in Northern Italy have cut off and captured 14,000 Italian troops—10,000 in the Upper Piave Valley and 4,000 in the Cordèvole Valley—according to War Office reports.

The German afternoon statement also says that the invading forces have advanced from Belluno down the Piave and are in front of Feltre.

The text of the afternoon report reads:

The energetic collaboration of Württemberg and Austro-Hungarian mountain troops, near Longarone, barred the way of the enemy retreating in the upper Piave Valley. Ten thousand Italians were compelled to surrender, and numerous guns, material, and war stores were captured.

Our troops, who pressed forward from Belluno down the Piave, are before Feltre.

On the lower Piave there was nothing new to report.

The supplementary report from General Headquarters issued tonight says:

In Cordèvole Valley, west of Belluno, 4,000 Italian prisoners were taken.

Italians Fighting on Northern Front.

ROME, Nov. 12.—The Italians have resisted the enemy everywhere on the northern front, along which the Austrians are attempting to outflank the Italian river line, the War Office reports. On the plain there is brisk firing across the Piave River.

An enemy action on the Asiago plateau, on the Trentino front, was a complete failure.

The text of the official statement follows:

From the Stelvio Pass to the Astico River there was no notable event yesterday. On the Asiago Plateau the enemy renewed yesterday afternoon his attack on our lines in the sector of Gallio, Monte Longara, Hill 1674 and Meletta di Gallio. The enemy actions failed completely under our artillery and rifle fire. On the extreme northern part of the front of the attack, where a bitter infantry struggle took place, our men counterattacked and succeeded in capturing some prisoners. On the remainder of the mountainous front, during contact engagements with the enemy vanguards, our advanced troops resisted everywhere.

On the plain across the Piave River brisk firing is reported.

Feltre is a town of about 4,600 inhabitants on a height near the Piave, seventeen miles southwest of Belluno. The town is situated about ten miles north of the Venetian plains. The military operations reported by the Germans in the mountainous region of Feltre have no direct bearing on the Italian line on the lower Piave.

Piave Defense Is Successful.

By The Associated Press.

ITALIAN HEADQUARTERS IN NORTHERN ITALY, Nov. 12.—The Italians are holding the Austro-German advance on the Piave line. Early reports from the front today were favorable.

Heavy shelling is in progress all along the new front.

The Italians are intrenched back of the west bank of the Piave River, and the Austro-German main force is now taking the place of the advanced guard on the east bank. The strip of water between the opposing lines is about half a mile, widening at some points to a mile.

An observer just back from a tour along the line told the correspondent that the cannonade had become continuous. The Austrians are using five-inch guns, not yet having brought up many of their heaviest pieces. The enemy is turning his fire against the high campanile (bell towers) of small villages fringing the western bank, to prevent

Continued on Page 2.

RUSH TO AID ITALY, EAGER FOR BATTLE

Heavy Allied Reinforcements Pouring In to Stiffen the Nation's Defense.

HOW FOES BROKE THROUGH

"Fraternizing" Austrians on Isonzo Secretly Replaced by German Shock Divisions.

By CHARLES H. GRASTY.

Special Cable to THE NEW YORK TIMES.

ROME, Nov. 11.—The greatest battle of history, with more men engaged, and possessing for the world large significance, is preparing in Italy. The Germans, on their side, are pressing the advantage gained by their successes, hoping to keep the Italians demoralized and prevent the recovery of equilibrium while the Italians, reinforced by the French and British, and aided by leaders accustomed to cope with Hun ingenuity and prowess, are seeking to organize resistance at a place and under conditions as favorable as possible.

In point of mere numbers the advantage lies with the Allies, but the Italian Army has suffered a rout which has momentarily destroyed its integrity. The immediate problem of the allied strategists seems to be to maintain an ordered rearguard action, reorganize the scattered units, and stop the contagion of panic that seized on parts of the army, and there are doubtless huge other problems known only to the higher command involving resistance to the Germans in the Trentino and the Cadore.

Reckoning numbers solely, Italy still has 4,000,000 enlisted men, conceding the German claim of half a million killed, wounded, captured, and missing or dispersed, and therefore should meet the invader on better than equal terms. As against the Italian deterioration, Mackensen must suffer the same exhaustion and difficulty from lengthened communication that made von Kluck's defeat possible at the Marne.

It is in guns that the Allies seem weakest. The German drive has already cost them 2,200. But here again comfort may be drawn from the Marne parallel. In that battle the French were vastly inferior to the Germans in artillery. The German advance to the Channel was checked. The French Army did it practically with rifle and bayonet against an enemy intrenched in commanding positions and well supplied with artillery and machine guns.

To carry the parallel further, the same man who struck the blow at the Marne and who was the master strategist at Lorette is helping and planning for the battle of the Venetian plain. He is General Foch, the coolest, most accomplished and audacious strategist of this war.

Arrival of Allied Aid.

Still another encouraging feature is the wholehearted and swift action of France and England. Men and machinery are pouring into Italy in quantities that seemed impossible. I have seen many of the troop trains and the sight stirs one's enthusiasm. Finer soldiers never wore boots. As one said of the Anzacs: "They're in the pink of condition and don't give a damn for anybody."

In train after train of French soldiers every man looks like an Alpine chasseur. The spirit among them is extraordinary. They treat the expedition as a big lark and when a stop is made at a station they are as lively as fox terriers.

The men seem delighted to leave the trenches and get into the open. As for Fritz and his gases and guns and propaganda and smart tricks generally, one bit afraid of him.

England and France appear to have put aside all narrow and petty considerations and to have given Italy of their very best. The handling of the transport has been a remarkable feat. Both French and Italians have perhaps they think they know him and are not formed miracles.

Work of the German Agents.

The German propagandists are working in harmony with Mackensen's ad-

Continued on Page 2.

PREMIER RECALLS ERRORS

Serbian and Rumanian Disasters Due to Lack of Joint War Direction.

ITALY ENFORCED THE NEED

He Was Ready to Quit if the Allies Had Not Taken This Forward Step Now.

AMERICA TO PARTICIPATE

Russia Also, He Believes—Bonar Law Suggests War Council Will Be Only Advisory.

PARIS, Nov. 12.—At a luncheon given today by Premier Painlevé in honor of David Lloyd George, the British Prime Minister, the latter discussed the plan for centralized direction of the Allies' military efforts. He said in part:

"Unfortunately we did not have time to consult the United States or Russia before creating this council. The Italian disaster necessitated action without delay to repair it. This made it indispensable to commence right now with the powers whose forces may be employed on the Italian front. But, in order to assure the complete success of this great experiment, which I believe is essential to the victory of our cause, it will be necessary that all our great allies be represented in the deliberations. I am persuaded that we shall obtain the consent of these two great countries and their co-operation in the work of the inter-allied council."

Mr. Lloyd George talked of the reasons for not taking the step earlier. He referred to "timidities and susceptibilities" when it came to treating questions on any front not commanded by Generals taking part in the inter-allied consultations. The Allies had committed a great fault, he said, in not assisting Serbia adequately in holding her line. The result was that the Central empires broke the blockade and procured men and supplies from the East, without which Germany would have been unable to maintain the force of her armies.

Reason for Balkan Disasters.

"Why was this unbelievable fault committed?" asked the Premier. "The reply is simple. It was because no one in particular was charged with guarding the Balkan gate. The united front had not become a reality. France and England were absorbed by other problems in other regions. Italy thought only of the Carso. Russia was mounting guard over a frontier of a thousand miles, and, even without that, she could not have passed through to have helped Serbia, because Rumania was neutral.

"It is true that we sent troops to Saloniki to succor Serbia, but, as always, they were sent too late. Half the men who fell in the vain effort to pierce the Western front in September that same year would have saved Serbia, saved the Balkans and completed the blockade of Germany.

"You may say this is an old story. I grant you that it was simply the first chapter of a series that has continued to the present hour; 1915 was the year of the Serbian tragedy; 1916 was the year of the Rumanian tragedy, which was a repetition of the Serbian story almost without change. This is unbelievable, when you think of the consequences to the Allies' cause of the Rumanian defeat. Opulent wheatfields and rich petroleum wells passed to the enemy and Germany was able to escape us.

"Through the harvest of 1917 the siege of the Central Powers was raised once more, and the horrible war was once more prolonged. That would not have happened, had there existed some central authority, charged with meditating upon the problem of the war for the entire theatre of the war."

Was Ready to Drop Responsibility.

After reviewing the Italian campaign the Premier said:

"As far as I am concerned, I had arrived at the conclusion that if nothing was changed I could no longer accept the responsibility for the direction of a war condemned to disaster from lack of unity. Italy's misfortune may still save the alliance, because without it I do not think that even today we would have created a veritable superior council.

"National and professional traditions, questions of prestige and susceptibilities all conspired to render our best decisions vain. No one in particular bore the blame. The guilt was in the natural difficulty of obtaining of so many nations, of so many independent organizations that they should amalgamate all their individual particularities to act together as if they were but one people."

Mr. Lloyd George said later:

"I have spoken today with a frankness that is perhaps brutal. At the risk of being ill understood here and elsewhere, and not, perhaps, without risk of giving a temporary encouragement to the enemy, because now that we have established this council it is

Mid-Week Pictorial

President Wilson (center) and members of the War Council of the American Red Cross.

Mid-Week Pictorial

Alvey Augustus Adee, Second Assistant Secretary of State.

Mid-Week Pictorial

Herbert C. Hoover, appointed by the President as Food Commissioner for the war.

"All the News That's Fit to Print."

The New York Times.

THE WEATHER
Fair today and Thursday; slight temperature change; west winds.
For full weather report see Page 23.

VOL. LXVII...NO. 21,865. NEW YORK, WEDNESDAY, DECEMBER 5, 1917.—TWENTY-FOUR PAGES. ONE CENT In Greater New York. | TWO CENTS Within Commuting Distance. | THREE CENTS Elsewhere.

PRESIDENT CALLS FOR IMMEDIATE WAR ON AUSTRIA; CONGRESS WOULD INCLUDE BULGARIA AND TURKEY; OUR WATCHWORDS ARE: JUSTICE, REPARATION, SECURITY

WILSON FOR VICTORY FIRST

"We Shall Not Slacken or Be Diverted Until It Is Won."

PACIFISTS TOUCH NO HEART

"May Be Left to Strut Their Uneasy Hour and Be Forgotten," Says President.

FIGHTING TO FREE GERMANY

Throng in the House Stands to Cheer Message—La Follette Remains Seated.

Special to The New York Times.

WASHINGTON, Dec. 4.—With dramatic suddenness, yet with no apparent effort at dramatic effect, President Wilson, addressing in person the Senate and the House of Representatives assembled in joint session today, recommended that "the Congress immediately declare the United States in a state of war with Austro-Hungary."

The legislators and the great crowd of spectators who filled floor and galleries were unprepared for the call for a declaration of war. On the contrary, some preceding parts of the President's address had tended to create the impression that the Vienna Government, although allied with Germany, was entitled to special consideration, to charitable treatment, in the realization that it was a mere tool of the military autocracy at Berlin. Then came the call for action against the Dual Monarchy.

The effect was electrical. Not for a moment was the President left in doubt as to the temper of Congress regarding this recommendation. A thrill went through that audience of men and women who had listened with increasing interest to every word that had come with clear-cut distinctness from the lips of the man, who, more than any other, controls the destinies of the nation at this critical time.

War Call Unexpected.

The assemblage had risen before to heights of patriotic enthusiasm over appealing passages of the President's address. But only a minute prior to the stirring declaration his auditors had heard expressions which brought the too ready interpretation that the hour was not at hand when the United States should undertake to deal in a hostile military way with Germany's chief partner in the war. He had named Austria specifically, along with Serbia and Poland, in mentioning the countries he had in mind when, last January, before America entered the great European conflict, he had declared that the nations of the world "were entitled not only to free pathways upon the sea but also to assured and unmolested access to those pathways."

The disappointment of those—and they were many—who had looked for a stirring denunciation of Austro-Hungarian intrigue and international criminality was short-lived. The temporary elation of the few pacifists who were there dropped like a dead weight in a vacuum.

Prior to the remarkable demonstration of patriotic fervor that followed the President's declaration, his auditors had had ample opportunity to find an outlet for their feelings, for the address was filled with statements that appealed in full measure to love of country and determination to see the sanguinary struggle on the battlefields of Europe to a finish.

An important feature of the address was the reiteration and amplification of the war aims of America: Belgium and Northern France must be delivered from Prussian conquest and Prussian menace, but the peoples of Austria-Hungary, the Balkans and Turkey, "alike in Europe and in Asia," must be freed also from Prussian domination; "we do not wish in any way to impair or rearrange the Austro-Hungarian Empire"; "our attitude and purpose with regard to Germany herself are of a like kind"; "we intend no wrong against the German Empire, no interference with her internal affairs."

Assailed Germans' Masters.

If the German people continued after the war to accept the Government of their present masters, the President said, "it might be impossible to admit them to the partnership of nations which must henceforth guarantee the world's peace," and "it might be impossible also to admit Germany to the free economic intercourse which must inevitably spring out of the other partnerships of a real peace"; "the wrongs, the very deep wrongs, committed in this war will have to be righted."

If the Marquis of Lansdowne can find comfort in the analogy between his own statement of war aims and those of President Wilson, he will be disappointed in the President's attitude toward the other proposal of the British statesman—that a reiteration of war aims shall be used as a basis for peace negotiations. President Wilson is not in sympathy with this program. He left no doubt on that score in his address when he declared that "the German power must be crushed," and empha-

Continued on Page 2.

The President's Address to Congress

WASHINGTON, Dec. 4.—Here is the full text of President Wilson's address to Congress today:

Gentlemen of the Congress:

Eight months have elapsed since I last had the honor of addressing you. They have been months crowded with events of immense and grave significance for us. I shall not undertake to detail or even to summarize those events. The practical particulars of the part we have played in them will be laid before you in the reports of the executive departments. I shall discuss only our present outlook upon these vast affairs, our present duties and the immediate means of accomplishing the objects we shall hold always in view.

I shall not go back to debate the causes of the war. The intolerable wrongs done and planned against us by the sinister masters of Germany have long since become too grossly obvious and odious to every true American to need to be rehearsed. But I shall ask you to consider again and with very grave scrutiny our objectives and the measures by which we mean to attain them; for the purpose of discussion here in this place is action and our action must move straight toward definite ends. Our object is, of course, to win the war, and we shall not slacken or suffer ourselves to be diverted until it is won. But it is worth while asking and answering the question, When shall we consider the war won?

From one point of view it is not necessary to broach this fundamental matter. I do not doubt that the American people know what the war is about and what sort of an outcome they will regard as a realization of their purpose in it. As a nation we are united in spirit and intention.

I pay little heed to those who tell me otherwise. I hear the voices of dissent—who does not? I hear the criticism and the clamor of the noisily thoughtless and troublesome. I also see men here and there fling themselves in impotent disloyalty against the calm, indomitable power of the nation. I hear men debate peace who understand neither its nature nor the way in which we may attain it, with uplifted eyes and unbroken spirits. But I know that none of these speaks for the nation. They do not touch the heart of anything. They may safely be left to strut about their uneasy hour and be forgotten.

What the War Is For.

But from another point of view I believe that it is necessary to say plainly what we here at the seat of action consider the war to be for and what part we mean to play in the settlement of its searching issues. We are the spokesmen of the American people and they have a right to know whether their purpose is ours. They desire peace by the overcoming of evil, but the defeat once and for all of the sinister forces that interrupt peace and render it impossible, and they wish to know how closely our thought runs with theirs and what action we propose. They are impatient with those who desire peace by any sort of compromise—deeply and indignantly impatient—but they will be equally impatient with us if we do not make it plain to them what our objectives are and what we are planning for in seeking to make conquest of peace by arms.

I believe that I speak for them when I say two things: First, that this intolerable Thing of which the masters of Germany have shown us the ugly face, this menace of combined intrigue and force, which we now see so clearly as the German power, a Thing without conscience or honor or capacity for covenated peace, must be crushed, and if it be not utterly brought to an end, at least shut out from the friendly intercourse of the nations; and, second, that when this Thing and its power are indeed defeated and the time comes that we can discuss peace—when the German people have spokesmen whose word we can believe, and when those spokesmen are ready in the name of their people to accept the common judgment of the nations as to what shall henceforth be the bases of law and of covenant for the life of the world—we shall be willing and glad to pay the full price for peace and pay it ungrudgingly. We know what that price will be. It will be full, impartial justice—justice done at every point and to every nation that the final settlement must affect, our enemies as well as our friends.

You catch, with me, the voices of humanity that are in the air. They grow daily more audible, more articulate, more persuasive, and they come from the hearts of men everywhere. They insist that the war shall not end in vindictive action of any kind; that no nation or people shall be robbed or punished because the irresponsible rulers of a single country have themselves done deep and abominable wrong. It is this thought that has been expressed in the formula, "No annexations, no contributions, no punitive indemnities."

Led People of Russia Astray.

Just because this crude formula expresses the instinctive judgment as to the right of plain men everywhere it has been made diligent use of by the masters of German intrigue to lead the people of Russia astray, and the people of every other country their agents could reach, in order that a premature peace might be brought about before autocracy has been taught its final and convincing lesson and the people of the world put in control of their own destinies.

But the fact that a wrong use has been made of a just idea is no reason why a right use should not be made of it. It ought to be brought under the patronage of its real friends. Let it be said again that autocracy must first be shown the utter futility of its claims to power or leadership in the modern world. It is impossible to apply any standard of justice so long as such forces are unchecked and undefeated as the present masters of Germany command. Not until that has been done can right be set up as arbiter and peacemaker among the nations. But when that has been done—as, God willing, it assuredly will be—we shall at last be free to do an unprecedented thing, and this is the time to avow our purpose to do it. We shall be free to base peace on generosity and justice, to the exclusion of all selfish claims to advantage even on the part of the victors.

Let there be no misunderstanding. Our present and immediate task is to win the war, and nothing shall turn us aside from it until it is accomplished. Every power and resource we possess, whether of men, of money, or of materials, is being devoted and will continue to be devoted to that purpose until it is achieved. Those who desire to bring peace about before that purpose is achieved, I counsel to carry their advice elsewhere. We will not entertain it.

Justice and Reparation.

We shall regard the war only as won when the German people say to us, through properly accredited representatives, that they are ready to agree to a settlement based upon justice and the reparation of the wrongs their rulers have done. They have done a wrong to Belgium, which must be repaired. They have established a power over other lands and peoples than their own—over the great empire of Austria-Hungary, over hitherto free Balkan States, over Turkey, and within Asia—which must be relinquished.

Germany's success by skill, by industry, by knowledge, by enterprise we did not grudge or oppose, but admired rather. She had built up for herself a real empire of trade and influence, secured by the peace of the world. We were content to abide the rivalries of manufacture, science, and commerce that were involved for us in her success and stand or fall as we had or did not have the brains and the initiative to surpass her. But at the moment when she had conspicuously won her triumphs of peace she threw them away to establish in their stead what the world will no longer permit to be established, military and political domination by arms, by which to oust where she could not excell the rivals she most feared and hated.

The peace we make must remedy that wrong. It must deliver the once fair lands and happy peoples of Belgium and northern France from the Prussian conquest and the Prussian menace, but it must also deliver the peoples of Austria-Hungary, the peoples of the Balkans, and the peoples of Turkey, alike in Europe and in Asia, from the impudent and alien domination of the Prussian military and commercial autocracy.

We owe it, however, to ourselves to say that we do not wish in any way to impair or to rearrange the Austro-Hungarian empire. It is no affair of ours what they do with their own life, either industrially or politically. We do not purpose nor desire to dictate to them in any way. We only desire to see that their affairs are left in their own hands, in all matters, great or small. We shall hope to secure for the peoples of the Balkan peninsula and for the people of the Turkish empire the right and opportunity to make their own lives safe, their own fortunes secure against oppression or injustice and from the dictation of foreign courts or parties, and our attitude and purpose with regard to Germany herself are of a like kind.

Our Attitude Toward Germany.

We intend no wrong against the German empire, no interference with her internal affairs. We should deem either the one or the other absolutely unjustifiable, absolutely contrary to the principles we have professed to live by and to hold most sacred throughout our life as a nation.

The people of Germany are being told by the men whom they now permit to deceive them and to act as their masters that they are fighting for the very life and existence of their empire, a war of desperate self-defense against deliberate aggression. Nothing could be more grossly or wantonly false, and we must seek by the utmost openness and candor as to our real aims to convince them of its falseness. We are in fact fighting for their emancipation from fear, along with our own, from the fear as well as from the fact of unjust attack by neighbors or rivals or schemers after world empire. No one is threatening the existence or the independence or the peaceful enterprise of the German empire.

The worst that can happen to the detriment of the German people is this, that if they should still, after the war is over, continue to be obliged to live under ambitious and intriguing masters interested to disturb the peace of the world, men or classes of men whom the other peoples of the world could not trust, it might be impossible to admit them to the partnership of nations which must henceforth guarantee the world's peace. That partnership must be a partnership of peoples, not a mere partnership of governments.

It might be impossible, also, in such untoward circumstances, to admit Germany to the free economic intercourse which must inevitably spring out of the other partnerships of a real peace. But there would be no aggression in that; and such a situation, inevitable because of distrust, would in the very nature of things sooner or later cure itself, by processes which would assuredly set in.

Rights of Central Powers.

The wrongs, the very deep wrongs, committed in this war will have to be righted. That of course. But they cannot and must not be righted by the commission of similar wrongs against Germany and her allies. The world will not permit the commission of similar wrongs as a means of reparation and settlement. Statesmen must by this time have learned that the opinion of the world is everywhere wide awake and fully comprehends the issues involved. No representative of any self-governed nation will dare disregard it by attempting any such covenants of selfishness and compromise as were entered into at the congress of Vienna.

The thought of the plain people here and everywhere throughout the world, the people who enjoy no privilege and have very simple and unsophisticated standards of right and wrong, is the air all governments must henceforth breathe if they would live. It is in the full disclosing light of that thought that all policies must be conceived and executed in this midday hour of the world's life.

German rulers have been able to upset the peace of the world only because the German people were not suffered under their tutelage to share the comradeship of the other peoples of the world either in thought or in purpose. They were allowed to have no opinion of their own which might be set up as a rule of conduct for those who exercised authority over them. But the congress that concludes this war will feel the full strength of the tides that run now in the hearts and consciences of free men everywhere. Its conclusions will run with those tides.

All these things have been true from the very beginning of this stupendous war; and I cannot help thinking that if they had been made plain at the very outset the sympathy and enthusiasm of the Russian people might have been once for all enlisted on the side of the Allies, suspicion and distrust swept away, and a real and lasting union of purpose effected. Had they believed these things at the very moment of their revolution and had they been confirmed in that belief since, the sad reverses which have recently marked the progress of their affairs toward an ordered and stable government of free men might have been avoided.

Truth as the Antidote.

The Russian people have been poisoned by the very same falsehoods that have kept the German people in the dark, and the poison has been administered by the very same hands. The only possible antidote is the truth. It cannot be uttered too plainly or too often.

From every point of view, therefore, it has seemed to be my duty to speak these declarations of purpose, to add these specific interpretations to what I took the liberty of saying to the Senate in January. Our entrance into the war has not altered our attitude toward the settlement that must come when it is over. When I said in January that the nations of the world were entitled not only to free pathways upon the sea but also to assured and unmolested access to those pathways I was thinking, and I am thinking now, not of the smaller and weaker nations alone, which need our countenance and support, but also of the great and powerful nations, and of our present enemies as well as our present associates in the war. I was thinking, and am thinking now, of Austria herself, among the rest, as well as of Serbia and of Poland. Justice and equality of rights can be had only at a great price. We are seeking permanent, not temporary, foundations for the peace of the world, and must seek them candidly and fearlessly. As always, the right will prove to be the expedient.

What shall we do, then, to push this great war of freedom and justice to its righteous conclusion? We must clear away with a thorough hand all impediments to success, and we must make every adjustment of law that will facilitate the full and free use of our whole capacity and force as a fighting unit.

War Against Austria.

One very embarrassing obstacle that stands in our way is that we are at war with Germany, but not with her allies. I therefore very earnestly recommend that the Congress immediately declare the United States in a state of war with Austria-Hungary. Does it seem strange to you that this should be the conclusion of the argument I have just addressed to you? It is not. It is in fact the inevitable logic of what I have said. Austria-Hungary is for the time being not her own mistress, but simply the vassal of the German Government. We must face the facts as they are and act upon them without sentiment in this stern business.

The Government of Austria-Hungary is not acting upon its own initiative or in response to the wishes and feelings of its own peoples, but as the instrument of another nation. We must meet its force with our own and regard the Central Powers as but one. The war can be successfully conducted in no other way. The same logic would lead also to a declaration of war against Turkey and Bulgaria. They also are the tools of Germany. But they are mere tools and do not yet stand in the direct path of our necessary action. We shall go wherever the necessities of this war carry us, but it seems to me that we should go only where immediate and practical considerations lead us and not heed any others.

Stricter Grip on Enemy Aliens.

The financial and military measures which must be adopted will suggest themselves as the war and its undertakings develop, but I will take the liberty of proposing to you certain other acts of legislation which seem to me to be needed for the support of the war and for the release of our whole force and energy.

It will be necessary to extend in certain particulars the legislation of the last session with regard to alien enemies; and also necessary, I believe, to create a very definite and particular control over the entrance and departure of all persons into and from the United States.

Legislation should be enacted defining as a criminal offense every willful violation of the Presidential proclamations relating to enemy aliens promulgated under Section 4,067 of the Revised Statutes and providing appropriate punishment; and women as well as men should be included under the terms of the acts placing restraints upon alien enemies. It is likely that as time goes on many alien enemies will be willing to be fed and housed at the expense of the Government in the detention camps, and it would be the purpose of the legislation I have suggested to confine offenders among them in penitentiaries and other similar institutions where they could be made to work as other criminals do.

Further Limiting of Prices.

Recent experience has convinced me that the Congress must go further in authorizing the Government to set limits to prices. The law of supply and demand, I am sorry to say, has been replaced by the law of unrestrained selfishness. While we have eliminated profiteering in several branches of industry it still runs impudently rampant in others. The farmers, for example, complain with a great deal of justice that, while the regulation of food prices restricts their incomes, no restraints are placed upon the prices of most of the things they must themselves purchase; and similar inequities obtain on all sides.

It is imperatively necessary that the consideration of the full use of the water power of the country and also the consideration of the systematic and yet economical development of such of the natural resources of the country as are still under the control of the Federal Government should be resumed and affirmatively and constructively dealt with at the earliest possible moment. The pressing need of such legislation is daily becoming more obvious.

The Legislation proposed at the last session with regard to regulated combinations among our exporters, in order to provide for our foreign trade a more effective organization and method of co-operation, ought by all means to be completed at this session.

And I beg that the members of the House of Representatives will permit me to express the opinion that it will be impossible to deal in any way but a very wasteful and extravagant fashion with the enormous appropriations of the public moneys which must continue to be made, if the war is to be properly sustained, unless the House will consent to return to its former practice of initiating and preparing all appropriation bills through a single committee, in order that responsibility may be centred, expenditures standardized and made uniform, and waste and duplication as much as possible avoided.

Additional legislation may also become necessary before the present Congress adjourns in order to effect the most efficient co-ordination and operation of the railway and other transportation systems of the country; but to that I shall, if circumstances should demand, call the attention of Congress upon another occasion.

Task of Winning Foremost.

If I have overlooked anything that ought to be done for the more effective conduct of the war, your own counsels will supply the omission. What I am perfectly clear about is that in the present session of the Congress our whole attention and energy should be concentrated on the vigorous and rapid and successful prosecution of the great task of winning the war.

We can do this with all the greater zeal and enthusiasm because we know that for us this is a war of high principle, debased by no selfish ambition of conquest or spoliation; because we know, and all the world knows, that we have been forced into it to save the very institutions we live under from corruption and destruction. The purposes of the Central Powers strike straight at the very heart of everything we believe in; their methods of warfare outrage every principle of humanity and of knightly honor; their intrigue has corrupted the very thought and spirit of many of our people; their sinister and secret diplomacy has sought to take our very territory away from us and disrupt the union of the States. Our safety would be at an end, our honor forever sullied and brought into contempt were we to permit their triumph. They are striking at the very existence of democracy and liberty.

It is because it is for us a war of high, disinterested purpose, in which all the free people of the world are banded together for the vindication of right, a war for the preservation of our nation and of all that it has held dear of principle and of purpose, that we feel ourselves doubly constrained to propose for its outcome only that which is righteous and of irreproachable intention, for our foes as well as for our friends.

The cause being just and holy, the settlement must be of like motive and quality. For this we can fight, but for nothing less noble or less worthy of our traditions. For this cause we entered the war and for this cause will we battle until the last gun is fired.

I have spoken plainly because this seems to me the time when it is most necessary to speak plainly, in order that all the world may know that even in the heat and ardor of the struggle and when our whole thought is of carrying the war through to its end we have not forgotten any ideal or principle for which the name of America has been held in honor among the nations and for which it has been our glory to contend in the great generations that went before us.

A supreme moment of history has come. The eyes of the people have been opened and they see. The hand of God is laid upon the nations. He will show them favor, I devoutly believe, only if they rise to the clear heights of His own justice and mercy.

WAR DECLARATION READY

Resolution Aligning Austria as Foe Likely to Pass This Week.

MANY WOULD GO FURTHER

Inclined to Declare War on Turkey and Bulgaria Unless Good Reason Is Given.

MESSAGE HIGHLY PRAISED

But Disappointment Keen at Failure to Urge War on All of Germany's Vassals.

Special to The New York Times.

WASHINGTON, Dec. 4.—Immediate action by Congress is to follow President Wilson's demand today for a declaration of war against Austria-Hungary. In both houses the sentiment is unwavering for such a declaration, and it is likely that the country will be arrayed as an enemy of Austria-Hungary by the end of this week.

The House Foreign Affairs Committee will tomorrow draft a resolution, which is likely to be offered before the day is over, declaring war on Austria-Hungary. The Senate Foreign Relations Committee will not meet until Thursday—the Senate having adjourned today until Friday—when a similar resolution will be prepared.

Representative Flood, Chairman of the House Foreign Affairs Committee, has called his committee to meet at 2 o'clock tomorrow afternoon. He is prepared to report a resolution declaring war against Austria-Hungary. There is no opposition to such a course, but action may be delayed by reason of a strong demand to include Turkey and Bulgaria in such a declaration. Indications are that the latter course will be pursued unless the President furnishes the committee with a compelling reason against the inclusion of Turkey and Bulgaria.

As to Austria-Hungary, nothing remains to be done but make the formal declaration, for only scant opposition is expected to spring up. Senators and Representatives who voted against the declaration of war against Germany were not talking today against the President's pronouncement for throwing down the gage of battle to Austria. An almost complete unanimity of sentiment prevailed as to the logic of putting Austria-Hungary in the enemy alignment.

Omission of Turkey and Bulgaria.

The talk at the Capitol after the President's message bore more upon the Executive's advice against a pronouncement against Turkey and Bulgaria than upon the demand for hostilities against Austria-Hungary. Leaders in both houses, Democrats and Republicans alike, expressed not only frank surprise, but regret that the President had not included Turkey and Bulgaria. They felt that Turkey, as one of the arch allies of Germany, ought to be embraced in any declaration of war, and that no obvious reason existed for leaving out Bulgaria.

Members of the Senate Committee on Foreign Relations and the House Committee on Foreign Affairs unhesitatingly expressed the belief that resolutions putting Turkey and Bulgaria along with Austria-Hungary as enemies of the United States would be offered in both houses and passed. For the United States to declare war against Austria-Hungary and not against Turkey, it was suggested by some, smacked of inconsistency. No disposition was manifest to quarrel with the President in having left Turkey and Bulgaria out of it. The opinion was ventured that the President must have had a sufficient reason for naming Austria-Hungary alone, depending, perhaps, upon Congress to take the initiative with the two other countries.

Senator Stone, Chairman of the Senate Committee on Foreign Relations, said that the committee would draft its resolution against Austria-Hungary on Thursday, and that it would be offered to the Senate the following day.

"All along, since the declaration of war against Germany, I have favored putting Austria-Hungary, Turkey, and Bulgaria in the list of America's enemies," said Senator Stone. "Congress will act quickly in declaring war on Austria-Hungary. I hope similar action will just as speedily be taken against Turkey and Bulgaria. If it develops that there is a diplomatic reason why we should not at this time include Turkey and Bulgaria, Congress naturally will withhold action. Such intimation would come, if there were occasion for it, from the White House. I believe I am safe in saying that, unless Congress hears that it would be unwise to act now, declarations will at once be made against Turkey and Bulgaria."

Senator Lodge, another of the Foreign Relations Committee, said he could not understand why the President did not ask for a declaration against Turkey and Bulgaria along with Austria-Hungary.

"I have always favored declaring war against all of Germany's allies," said Senator Lodge. "It seems to me

Assembly May Curb Bolshevist Power But Russia Cannot Continue War

Possible Terms of Peace Forecast—Plea for Friendship and Support of Old Ally to Save Her From Being Thrown Into Germany's Arms.

By HAROLD WILLIAMS.

Special Cable to THE NEW YORK TIMES.

PETROGRAD, Monday, Dec. 3.—Armistice negotiations began last night and will probably continue for several days. We are now faced with an exceedingly complicated situation which needs some unraveling.

First of all there is the internal political position. The Bolshevist movement is by no means simple. It is a curious jumble of conflicting elements ranging from the purest idealism to German intrigue and reactionary monarchism. These elements are temporarily agreed in a peace policy, and derive their authority from the strong pacifist tendencies of the soldiers and Socialists and the pacifist mood of the workmen.

The success or failure of the Bolsheviki depends on fulfillment or non-fulfillment of their promises. They have to deal not only with the fickleness of the mob that now supports them, but with the determined opposition of nearly all the intelligent section of the population and of whole territories, as Ukraine and the Cossack regions and Siberia.

The regular political and social machinery which is interfered with by the Bolsheviki is to a certain extent spoiled by them, but it persists in operating in spite of them. As regards the fickleness of the mob, those reactionaries who now work with the Bolsheviki are preparing to take advantage of a swing round of the popular mood when it does come. Internal rivalries, friction between incongruous and loosely co-ordinated factions, and personal jealousies must also be taken into account in estimating the stability of the Bolshevist power.

Another factor is daily increasing in importance. The elections to the Con-

Continued on Page 4.

Dukhonin Slain for Korniloff's Escape When Bolsheviki Take Headquarters

PETROGRAD, Dec. 4.—An official statement was issued today signed by Ensign Krylenko, the Bolshevist Commander in Chief, announcing the killing by infuriated members of the Bolsheviki of General Dukhonin, former Commander in Chief of the Russian Armies, who recently was deposed because of his refusal to request German army officials to enter into an armistice with the Bolsheviki.

General Dukhonin was killed by being thrown from a train after the Bolshevist forces had captured headquarters at Mohilev, where he had remained after his deposition. General Korniloff, also a former Russian Commander in Chief, and who some time ago started an unsuccessful revolt against the Kerensky Government, fled from Mohilev before the arrival of the Bolshevist forces.

The text of the communication of Krylenko follows:

Today I entered into Mohilev at the head of the revolutionary troops. The headquarters was entirely surrounded without fighting. The last obstacle to the cause of peace was fallen.

I cannot be silent on the sad act of lynch law practiced upon the former highest commander in chief, General Dukhonin. Popular hatred surpassed the limits of reason, and in spite of all attempts to save him he was thrown out of a railroad train at the Mohilev Station and killed. The flight of General Korniloff the day before the fall of headquarters was the cause of this excess.

I cannot allow the banner of the revolution to be stained, and it is necessary strongly to condemn such acts. A revolutionary people are fearful in a struggle, but they must be soft after victory.

An unofficial account says that General Dukhonin was dragged from a train in which it was intended to send him to Petrograd, and beaten to death.

A battle between detachments from the Petrograd garrison, commanded by Ensign Krylenko, and Cossacks is reported to be impending at Vitebsk. According to a telegram from Krylenko's Adjutant, the Cossacks have gathered on the flanks and in the rear of Krylenko's forces.

WASHINGTON, Dec. 4.—A cable from Rome today said the Russian Embassy in the Quirinal and the Russian Legation at the Vatican had given notice of their refusal to recognize the Lenine Government in Russia. They have stopped correspondence with the Lenine Ministry of Foreign Affairs.

Allies to Create Joint Naval Board; Framing Army Plan in Full Accord

Paris Council, It Is Announced, Concluded Agreements "Upon the Basis of a Complete Understanding and Close Solidarity" Regarding Economics, Finance, and Fighting Program.

PARIS, Dec. 4.—The Foreign Office officially announced today that at the recent Interallied Conference, in which the United States participated, agreements were concluded "upon the basis of a complete understanding and close solidarity among the Allies for the solution of the questions in which they have a common interest in the war."

It was also announced that the creation of a supreme interallied naval committee had been decided upon.

The Interallied General Staff, it was stated, was working upon a definite military program which was placing unity of military action in the way of certain realization.

The announcement regarding the results of the conference was made in the following official statement:

"The Minister of Foreign Affairs reported to the Cabinet today the results of the conference of the Allies. The reading of communications from the Presidents of each section of the Allied Conference, at which were present for the first time representatives of all the countries taking part with us in this war, has given felicitous results from every point of view. They give assurance of practical unity of action, economically, financially, and militarily.

"The agreements have been concluded upon the basis of a complete understanding and close solidarity among the Allies for the solution of the questions in which they have a common interest in the war. The financial needs of each of them, the requirements of their armament, their transport, their food, have been the subject of profound study which guarantees perfect satisfaction.

"The creation of a supreme interallied naval committee has been determined upon. Military unity of action has been placed upon the course of certain realization by the Interallied General Staff, which is at work upon an established program of all military questions.

"From a diplomatic point of view entire accord resulted from the discussions among the representatives of the powers upon all the business, which has been arranged together, to assure the common victory of their countries."

"All the News That's Fit to Print."

The New York Times.

THE WEATHER
Light snow today; cold; Tuesday fair and cold; northwest winds.
For full weather report see Page 19.

VOL. LXVII...NO. 21,877. NEW YORK, MONDAY, DECEMBER 17, 1917.—TWENTY PAGES. ONE CENT In Greater New York. | TWO CENTS Within Commuting Distance. | THREE CENTS Elsewhere.

COAL RECEIPTS HERE INCREASE; MORE ON WAY

Schley Says There Will Be 25,000 More Tons in the City Today.

WEATHER ONLY BARRIER

Some Difficulty in Delivery Is Feared Because of the Street Conditions.

SEES AMPLE SUPPLY SOON

Fuel Being Thawed Out and Rushed Here in Barges—Hotels Now Conserving Lights.

Unless weather conditions interfere with transportation, coal men here, who are interested in the movement of fuel, said yesterday that the situation has been mastered. Reeve Schley, Federal Fuel Administrator for Manhattan, declared that by working all night and day 20,000 tons of coal had been thawed out of the cars and carried on barges to New York yesterday.

"There are 75,000 tons of coal now at tidewater," said Mr. Schley yesterday, "and the movement is free to port. We will have 25,000 tons in New York by tomorrow morning. If the weather permits we will soon have enough here to supply all needs. Distribution of the coal depends largely upon the weather."

The coal coming in now is being used to supply emergency needs, keep hospitals and other institutions supplied, and to reach the poor as much as possible through the agency of the small distributer. The two great difficulties that have to be surmounted now, Cyrus Miller, Fuel Administrator for the Bronx, said yesterday, was the thawing out of the coal and its delivery.

Although the railroad men are confident that the situation will be met and the shortage soon relieved, thousands of families are unable to get more than a limited supply of coal. Hundreds of men, women, and children wait almost every day at the coal yards for a chance to get a bushel or two of fuel. It is said that users of coal do not share the feelings of the coal handlers. To the latter the situation is a pressing one and it is declared that those who have coal cannot look forward with any great assurance that they will be able to replenish their bins when empty. New York is conserving her coal supply through absolute necessity, and even the large users of fuel who are supplied by contract and who were stocked up in the Spring are "going slow."

Thawing Out the Coal.

In the Lehigh Valley yards at Perth Amboy 500 men are working night and day to thaw out and dump into barges the 47,000 odd tons that are on the rails there. The officials in charge of coal distribution for the railroads are using a special car as an office and they are directing their men personally. There is no shortage of coal barges and the Lehigh officials say that the coal is coming in in a satisfactory manner. Members of the wrecking crews have reinforced the regular workers and are assisting in steaming out the coal.

"I am fairly optimistic over the coal situation," said E. E. Loomis, President of the Lehigh Valley Railroad, yesterday. "With the closing of navigation on the Great Lakes, the anthracite operators are in a position to flood New York with coal. There is no reason for a panicky feeling."

Railroad men say the weather will be a determining factor in deciding whether New York gets enough coal within the next few days to relieve the shortage. At the Lackawanna, Erie, and other railroad yards handling coal there was the same scene of activity yesterday as at the Lehigh Valley yard and the same report of progress was made.

All day yesterday a force of clerks in the office of Burns Brothers, at 50 Church Street, was looking after the distribution of the coal. Burns Brothers, as well as some of the other large dealers, intend to devote their energy now to distributing coal in small quantities to those in the greatest need.

"If it does not snow again," said Frank Burns, "I believe the situation will take care of itself. It is improving right along and without another storm we will be able to supply enough to prevent any actual suffering."

Distribution in Brooklyn.

In Brooklyn the coal deliveries yesterday were estimated at 2,000 tons, and when this estimate was made another barge was reported near one of the distributing points.

In the Bronx five barges arrived early in the day, and others were expected. Men worked all night putting the loads into the coal pockets as fast as the barges arrived. Fuel Administrator Miller said that he expected, from reports received, that coal would continue to arrive in satisfactory volume during the next few days, and that his force was prepared to ship it to distributing points as quickly as it could be thawed out and reloaded.

"The Bronx today is in very good shape," he said. "We have more than 2,000 tons of coal now moving, and this will supply the emergency cases. The snow has hampered distribution, and in the outlying districts, where the drifts

Continued on Page Four.

American Troops Train For Capture of "Pill Boxes"

WITH THE AMERICAN ARMY IN FRANCE, Dec. 16.—(Associated Press.)—Intensive training in the science of attacking "Pill Boxes" has begun at one of the largest training grounds. Numerous concrete structures identical with those used by the Germans have been erected, and the troops are being taught how the British take them.

The system of attack involves automatic rifle fire from a number of points into the slots, a sufficient number of rifles being used from various points to assure a continuous stream of bullets entering every slot from each direction from which the pillbox is attacked. Under this fire bombers crawl to the pillbox and the firing ceases. The bombers then quickly hurl grenades inside the minute forts. This system, if faithfully carried out, seldom fails to bring about the capitulation of the largest of the pillboxes.

17 ENGINEERS LOST IN BATTLE

Americans Killed or Captured on Day They Voluntarily Helped the British.

'FIGHTING COP' AMONG THEM

Frank Upton Was a New York Policeman—Several Others from This City.

Special to The New York Times.

WASHINGTON, Dec. 16.—General Pershing today sent to the War Department a casualty list in which appeared the names of seventeen American army engineers recorded as missing as a result of the action of Nov. 30 last. The report did not say whether these men were killed or whether they had been taken prisoners by the Germans. Nor did it say where they were "missed," but in view of the known fact that it was on Nov. 30 that a large number of army engineers got into the action at Cambrai in the German counterattack on General Byng's army, it is reasonably certain that it was there these men were taken or killed.

Fifteen days having elapsed without any of the missing engineers reporting for duty, General Pershing has listed them as missing in action. Previously he had reported fifteen engineers of the same unit, mostly New York men, as having been severely wounded in the same action.

The casualty list, which also includes three deaths from natural causes, and one wounded, follows:

DEATHS.

WOLF, HERBERT J., bugler, headquarters troops, Dec. 11, scarlet fever septicaemia; emergency address, Morris Wolf, (father,) 77 Waumbeck Street, Roxbury, Mass.

MINKLER, CLARENCE M., private, first class, field hospital, Dec. 11, scarlet fever nephritis, acute; emergency address, Ira B. Minkler, South Street, Proctor, Vt.

SCHENKMAN, GEORGE, private, infantry, Dec. 14, tuberculosis chronic pulmonary; emergency address, Mrs. Yetta Schenkman, (mother,) 7 West 115th Street, New York.

MISSING.

IN ACTION.

UPTON, FRANK, Corporal, engineers, Nov. 30; emergency address, Mrs. Jane Upton, (wife,) 411 West Twenty-fourth Street, New York.

GOLDWETTER, SOLOMAN, private, engineers, Nov. 30; emergency address, Miss Rose Perlstein, (friend,) 62 119th Street, New York.

SEAMAN, GEORGE H. J., private, engineers, Nov. 30; emergency address, Mrs. Anna Seaman, (mother,) 1,032 Emerald Street, Woodhaven, L. I.

RANLET, DALTON, private, engineers, Nov. 30; emergency address, Daniel M. Ranlet, (father,) 115 Forty-fourth Street, Corona, N. Y.

GEOGHEHAN, CHARLES A., private, engineers, Nov. 30; emergency address, Mrs. Michael Geoghehan, (mother,) 511 West 185th Street, New York.

ANDREWS, HAROLD T., private, engineers, Nov. 30; emergency address, Frank Bradford, (uncle,) Union Montreal Building, Portland, Me.

McGRATH, ALPHONSO J., private, engineers, Nov. 30; emergency address, Timothy McGrath, 1,168 Boylston Street, Chestnut Hill, Mass.

VAN DE MARK, MYRON, private, engineers, Nov. 30; emergency address, Mrs. A. R. Van De Mark, (mother,) New Paltz, N. Y.

BROOKS, FRANK, private, engineers, Nov. 30; emergency address, Mrs. B. Warshopsky, (sister,) 949 Fox Street, New York.

MANEY, ULRICH N., private, engineers, Nov. 30; emergency address, John M. Maney, (father,) 1,792 Amsterdam Avenue, New York.

LALLY, JOHN, private, engineers, Nov. 30; emergency address, Michael Lally, (father,) Golden Bridge, Westchester County, N. Y.

LOVELY, LUKE A., private, engineers, Nov. 30; emergency address, Thomas Lovely, (father,) 101 North Stevens Avenue, South Amboy, N. J.

MASON, HARRY J., private, engineers, Nov. 30; emergency address, Mrs. C. Mason, (mother,) 357 Eighth Street, Jersey City, N. J.

SWENSON, PAUL M., Sergeant, engineers, Nov. 30; emergency address, Mrs. J. E. Swenson, (mother,) 366 Wadsworth Avenue, New York.

DINA, MICHAEL, private, engineers, Nov. 30; emergency address, James Dina, (father,) 147 East Fourth Street, New York.

TINGO, PETER J., private, engineers, Nov. 30; emergency address, Mrs. Anthony Tingo, (mother,) 2,419 Arthur Avenue, New York.

ULTZ, HERBERT F., private, engineers, Nov. 30; emergency address, Mrs. A. Karl, (mother,) 78 Union Street, Newark, N. J.

WOUNDED.

BOYLE, H. C., First Lieutenant, M. O. R. C., attached British forces, severely wounded, Dec. 7; emergency address, Mrs. Margaret Boyle, 200 Main Avenue, Luzerne, Penn.

Upton a New York Policeman.

Corporal Frank Upton mentioned in the list of missing is Francis Joseph Upton, one of New York's best known policemen, who immediately enlisted in the service after obtaining an indefinite leave of absence from Police Commissioner Woods when this country entered the war. His wife and three children

Continued on Page Three.

MEANS ACQUITTED OF KING MURDER; MAY BE TRIED HERE

Jury in Concord, N. C., Frees Agent of Wealthy Widow Who Was Shot.

DOOLING RETAINS EVIDENCE

Prosecutor Comes to New York with Documents Seized in Means's Rooms.

SWANN PLANS NEW MOVE

Says He Will Go Before the Grand Jury in Connection with Financial Affairs.

Special to The New York Times.

CONCORD, N. C., Dec. 16.—Gaston B. Means was acquitted here this morning of the murder of Mrs. Maude A. King, a wealthy widow who was shot at Blackwelder Spring, near Concord, on the night of Aug. 29. Means was Mrs. King's business agent, and had had charge of her affairs for the last few years.

The jury's verdict was returned at 10:22 o'clock to Judge E. B. Cline in the presence of the defendant, his wife, father and mother, and other relatives and friends. The case went to the jury at 7 o'clock Saturday night, when Judge Cline concluded his charge of two hours, marking the end of the third week of the trial. At 9:30 o'clock this morning, through Sheriff Caldwell, the jury sent a message asking that Judge Cline go to the Court House.

To the crowd that had assembled the Judge said that he did not know whether a verdict had been arrived at, but if it had there must be no demonstration when it was made known. He instructed Sheriff Caldwell to arrest any one violating this order. The Judge also warned that none of the jurors should be approached by any one after the verdict was announced until they had been discharged. His instructions had the desired effect, and there was no demonstration whatever when the decision was announced.

When the jurors filed into the courtroom Judge Cline said to them that in his charge Saturday afternoon he had inadvertently referred to the time of the tragedy at Blackwelder Spring as in the "evening," and asked whether any of the jurors had interpreted that as an expression of opinion on his part as to the fact of the time Mrs. King was shot. The jurors replied in unison that they had not. Clerk Stonestreet then asked the jury the formal questions and J. Frank Goodman, foreman, announced the verdict.

Means Regains Liberty.

Frank Osborne of counsel for the defense asked Solicitor Hayden Clement if he had any further charge against the defendant, who replied: "I have not." Mr. Osborne then made formal request for the release of the defendant, which Judge Cline granted.

Counsel and friends crowded about Means to extend congratulations. The smile he had worn almost constantly throughout the three weeks' ordeal broadened perceptibly. He threw his arm about his wife, and, surrounded by friends and relatives, they left the courtroom. Near the door they met a sister of Means, and she and Mrs. Means fell into each other's arms weeping.

For the first time since early in September, when he went to jail rather than attempt to get bail, Gaston Means walked upon the streets of his boyhood home a free man. Accompanied by his father-in-law, W. R. Patterson, who was associated with him in some of the financial transactions for Mrs. Means that were aired in the trial, he went about shaking hands with friends and receiving congratulations. To Mrs. Means, upon whom the possible fate of her husband rested heavily throughout the long trial, the verdict brought instant relief, and the sober look she had worn gave way to joy.

The verdict did not occasion much surprise in Concord, and to Means, his counsel, and friends was only the result they had predicted from the beginning. Means apparently never wavered in his conviction that he would be found innocent, although there was evident disappointment last night when the jury failed to bring in a prompt verdict of acquittal. Means expects to remain for a visit at his parents' home in Concord, but has given no intimation of what he intends to do later, although it is the general understanding that he will return to New York.

Assistant District Attorney Dooling, who left for New York last night, took with him the mass of papers and documents seized in Means's apartments in that city, and which were produced at the trial. Asked if there would be any action against Means by the New York authorities, Solicitor Clement said he did not expect any, but could not speak with authority.

Killing of Mrs. King.

Mrs. King was killed at Blackwelder Spring, a lonely spot in the country near here, Aug. 29 last, when, with Means and a party of his friends, she had stopped on an automobile drive to practice pistol shooting. Means and she were alone at the time, Captain W. S. Bingham and Afton Means, a brother of Gaston Means, having walked down the road to shoot at rabbits.

A Coroner's inquest accepted the

Continued on Page Five.

Kaiser Puts Submarines In Special Department

LONDON, Dec. 16.—An imperial decree prescribing for the duration of the war the formation of a new section in the German Imperial Navy Department to be called the U-Boat Department has just been published, according to an Amsterdam dispatch to Reuter's, Limited.

The new department deals solely with U-boat affairs, which heretofore have been handled by the dockyards section of the Navy Department.

CUT HARBOR NET TO SINK THE WIEN

Rizzo, with Two Launches, Torpedoed Austrian Battleship and Sister Craft.

SAWED CABLES IN DARK

Italians Braved Trieste Batteries and Mines and Escaped Without a Scratch.

By PERCEVAL GIBBON.

Copyright, 1917, by The New York Times Company.

Special Cable to THE NEW YORK TIMES.

VENICE, Dec. 13, (Delayed.)—There are men and deeds which shine athwart the fog of war, across its dreary routine and staleness, like a sunbeam through the clouds. Such men and such deeds came to light when two little ships and their crews gnawed their way through the bombs and nets which guard the inner harbor of Trieste and sank the battleship Wien where she lay moored to her buoy, with her sister ship, the Monarch, slumbering alongside of her, behind steel nets fringed with mines, and with sentries yawning by their guns on the mole and breakwater.

Italian sailors under Lieutenant Rizzo, of the Italian Navy, worked at the cables of the nets, within earshot of the forts and ships till they sawed them apart and could run in and do their work. It was more than a great feat of arms; it was a lark.

The Wien was one of three ships launched in 1895. Her sisters were the Monarch and Budapest. She carried four 10-inch guns and six 6-inch guns and a crew of 441 officers and men. The Italians almost got her a month ago when she was shelling the Lower Piave line and motor boats went for her with their torpedoes. She had other narrow escapes, too, and now she lies on the clean sandy bottom of Trieste harbor in about eleven fathoms of turquoise-blue water.

Feat Accomplished by Two Launches.

Lieutenant Rizzo and the crews of his two launches—craft not much bigger than a ship's lifeboat—are the men who put her there. Rizzo is one of those men in the Italian Navy who make a weird specialty of tickling the Austrian in his bed. He is 30 years of age, a Sicilian, with the strong, masculine good looks of his race. In charge of his second boat was a tough fire-eater of sixty-two years.

The thing had been well prepared, after careful study of the mined area. It seems that the Austrians had devised a system of combined nets and mines, so that Rizzo's chances were great, at best, of being blown to pieces. One of his chief problems was that of the huge steel cables attached to the nets; but he cut these handily asunder on the night of the 9th.

When the two little boats set out there was a mist on the sea. It was past midnight when they crawled in toward the coast, where lies the white city of Trieste, cascading in snowy traces down its radiant hillside to the piers and docks of its port. The two boats crawled in toward the harbor mouth.

Trieste harbor is an affair of three piers jutting seaward, making thus two channels, one on either hand of the central pier, which is also a breakwater. These channels were closed by booms and nets, with their mines all linked to the piers by great steel hawsers.

The boats glided alongside one pier and Rizzo climbed up its concrete side and reconnoitred the situation. There was nobody on that pier. On the middle pier, however, was a guardroom. There could be heard a confusion of voices and barkings of dogs, and from the railway station ashore the noise of an engine screaming vociferously, and between whiles the slapstep feet of the sentry patrolling the middle pier

Sawed Cables in Silence.

Lieutenant Rizzo crawled back and gave the order, and up came his men, crawling on hands and knees over the concrete, passing the big cutting tools from hand to hand, groping their way to the cables. Some set to work to cut them, while two men scouted inshore lest some sentry should arrive. I shouldn't have liked to be that sentry if that sentry had come, with those big, wet sailors lying armed behind the mooring bollards and waiting to silence that sentry.

The cutting instruments worked well. It needed only a strong jar to set the mines exploding, but the cutters bit their way through strand after strand of twisted steel wire. Three cables above water were severed without trouble; then five more below water were grappled and hauled to the surface and cut in their turn.

At last came the moment when the weight of the net and its attachments tore the last remaining steel strands asunder, the whole great cobweb of metal and explosives sank, and the harbor lay open. Rizzo and his men crawled back to their boats, and those boats moved like shadows into the Vaplone di Muggia, where the Wien and Monarch lay nosing their buoys. Near-

Continued on Page Two.

SHAKE-UP IN ARMY FORESEEN UNDER NEW WAR COUNCIL

Gives Baker a Chance to Shift General Crozier and Other Bureau Chiefs.

MOVED BY SENATE INQUIRY

War Secretary's Action Follows Ordnance Revelations and White House Conference.

CROZIER TO TESTIFY AGAIN

Committee to Hold Open Hearing Today Regarding Equipment of the Troops in France.

Special to The New York Times.

WASHINGTON, Dec. 16.—Washington began today to see additional significance in the announcement by Secretary Baker last night that he had issued an order forming a War Council within the War Department, with himself at the head and the Assistant Secretary of War and five general officers composing the additional personnel.

In some quarters the creation of the War Council is looked upon as a direct outgrowth of the revelations made to the Senate Committee on Military Affairs by the Chief of Ordnance concerning lack of guns and small arms, and the prospect that there will be additional revelations in regard to other delinquencies in military preparation as the inquiry proceeds. But interest was centred today in the significance of a sentence in Secretary Baker's statement, indicating that the general officers assigned to the War Council, all of whom are bureau chiefs of the War Department, would be freed from "administrative duties and responsibilities."

In addition to the Secretary and the Assistant Secretary of War, the members of the War Council are General Tasker H. Bliss, Chief of the General Staff; Major Gen. Henry G. Sharpe, Quartermaster General; Major Gen. Erasmus M. Weaver, Chief of Artillery; Major Gen. William Crozier, Chief of Ordnance, and Major Gen. Enoch H. Crowder, Judge Advocate General and Provost Marshal General.

It is known that the Secretary of War has a high opinion of the ability and capacity of several of these officers, but the idea is prevalent in Washington that the council was formed partly to permit the assignment of other officers to corps or bureaus in order to bring about a new deal in the administration of the military establishment.

Although Secretary Baker says in his statement that the plans for the creation of the War Council have been under consideration for some weeks, this has not served to dissipate the view that the announcement of its formation was directly the result of the developments before the Senate Military Committee. It is likely that before the committee's hearings have proceeded very far Senators will begin to ask what measures were taken to co-ordinate the work of the War Department or to provide for conferences between the Secretary of War and those high ranking officers in charge of war activities. The creation of the War Council would partly meet criticism arising from inquiry along that line.

General Bliss, who returned to this country yesterday with Colonel E. M. House, attended the Paris interallied war conference as the principal military adviser to Colonel House, the direct representative of President Wilson. He will reach the retiring age on Dec. 31, and it is generally understood that he will not be continued in active service as chief of the General Staff. Under the order issued yesterday the Chief of Staff will be a member of the War Council by virtue of his office. It is supposed here that Secretary Baker's notice that "while any officer is detailed to the council provision will be made to free him from administrative duties and responsibilities," means that the Chief of Staff will devote all his time to the business of the War Council. In fact, according to one sentence in Secretary Baker's statement, he will be the principal executive member of the council. "The council will act through the Chief of Staff," Mr. Baker says.

General Crowder has received much praise for his great work of carrying out the selective draft law. He has been a military observer in wars and has a high reputation as an administrator. His duties as Judge Advocate General of the Army could be transferred to another officer in order to give him the opportunity to devote his talents of organization and initiative to the work of the War Council. Other officers assigned to the new council have also earned much praise for their ability, and it is felt that they will be able to aid the Secretary of War greatly in determining military policies.

At the same time, the formation of the council will enable the Secretary of War to meet an embarrassing situation with reference to the demand for a reorganization of the Ordnance Department, sure to follow the current investigation by the Senate Military Committee, by relieving General Crozier from his administrative duties as Chief of Ordnance and directing him to devote all his time to the work of the War Council.

The announcement of the creation of

Continued on Page Four.

ARMISTICE IS SIGNED BY BOLSHEVIKI; PEACE NEGOTIATIONS TO BEGIN AT ONCE; TROTZKY THREATENS TO USE GUILLOTINE

Germans Now "Long for Conciliation"; Foes Urged to Avoid Victor's Heavy Hand

Special Cable to THE NEW YORK TIMES.

THE HAGUE, Dec. 16.—Commenting on Lloyd George's speech, the Lokal-Anzeiger says:

"The British Prime Minister is vying with Wilson in forceful language, and their ideas are so completely identical that it is difficult to tell one from the other. 'Victory first; negotiations afterward,' is their motto; they know no middle way. With us it is just the contrary. Some of us are longing for a middle way of conciliation, and they are anxious that the enemy should not feel the heavy hand of the victor.

"Even the prospect of prolonging the war for years does not frighten Lloyd George. We only ask how long the 'busy minorities' which he deplores so impressively will leave him a free hand in his peculiar bridge-building task. To bait Russia once more he will find very difficult, and Italy will feel her defeat no less intensely because the English Prime Minister has the kindness to call it only a passing misfortune.

"We, too, believe that the present hour is not a happy one for the Entente, and our leading Generals will take care it does not improve in 1918. Then England will probably reconsider the question of a premature peace, and perhaps look at it more closely than Lloyd George has been pleased to do until now."

Calls on Germany to Move Openly for Peace.

AMSTERDAM, Dec. 16.—The Berlin Socialist paper Vorwärts, commenting on the alleged attempt to open preliminary peace discussions between Great Britain and Germany, demands that the Government tell the German people what it intended to communicate to Great Britain.

Attacking secret diplomacy, the paper suggests that both Governments are afraid to take the initiative, lest it be considered a sign of hidden weakness.

"When will it be realized," the paper asks, "that it is a great honor, instead of a disgrace, to strive with the enemy for a means for reconciliation with freedom and self-respect to end this insane human slaughter?"

The Frankfurter Zeitung says:

"Balfour did not say whether Britain was still willing to discuss the question, but there is no apparent reason why there should be a change. It is worth something that Britain formally declares her readiness for such discussion."

GERMAN PRINCE WARNS OF FAILURE

Max of Baden Declares Empire's Sword Alone Will Never Bring Triumph.

TIRPITZ STILL HAS HOPE

Relies on U-Boats, but Admits That Up to the Present Britain Has Won.

Special Cable to THE NEW YORK TIMES.

THE HAGUE, Dec. 16.—Prince Max of Baden, President of the Baden Upper Chamber, in his address to the House yesterday, said:

"Wilson has no right to set himself up as judge of the world. Let us not, however, deceive ourselves. The American people does believe that the war must be continued in behalf of the ideal set up by Wilson.

"The democratic legend of our opponent has proved itself a colossal lie. In France and England influences are at work opposing a peace obtained by violence. Power alone can never secure our position, and our sword alone will never be able to tear down the opposition to us. The enemy must obtain the knowledge that behind our power stands an ecumenical conscience. This sign Germany must bear upon her standard, and in hoc signo vinces."

Prince Max of Baden, whose warning has created a sensation in Germany, has the reputation of being one of Germany's sanest and ablest democratic statesmen.

AMSTERDAM, Dec. 16.—The German papers contain lengthy accounts of the speech of Grand Admiral von Tirpitz before the Hamburg Branch of the Fatherland Party, in which the Admiral said:

"Up to the present in this war Great Britain has won, rather than lost. Peace based on the status quo ante or on renunciation, therefore, is out of the question for Germany."

With reference to the rumor that Germany would give up Zeebrugge and Ostend if the British evacuated Calais, von Tirpitz said:

"The evacuation of Calais would never be equivalent to the loss of such first-class security. Moreover, the Channel Tunnel will become a fact after the war. For real security, we should have, besides Flanders and Antwerp, Calais and Boulogne. The rumor in question is a screen behind which the question of Flanders might be permitted to disappear.

"The pretext that we cannot coerce Great Britain and America falls to the ground when we consider the growing scarcity of the cargo space of our ruthless arch-enemy. The time for final decision will come when real distress begins to take the place of merely threatening distress. That time will come. It is only a question of keeping cool."

ALLIES MAY TREAT WITH BOLSHEVIKI

United States Said to Have Counseled a More Tolerant Attitude.

MAY LONG RETAIN POWER

Entente's Aim Now to Furnish Relief to Russia From Economic Collapse.

LONDON, Dec. 16.—While the Russians were continuing to make progress in the ratification of an armistice arrangement with the Germans, the Entente Governments apparently were approaching an agreement for more sympathetic dealings with the Bolshevist Government. The adoption of a more tolerant attitude toward Russia is said to have been urged by the American delegates to the recent Paris conference, and this viewpoint now apparently has been adopted by all the members of the Entente. Lord Northcliffe's Weekly Dispatch says today:

"The belief here is that the Bolshevist Government is likely to remain in power for a long time. The principal aim of the Entente henceforth will be to try to assist in every effort to bring Russia relief from an economic collapse."

Dispatches during the last twenty-four hours from Petrograd tell of further efforts by the Bolsheviki to consolidate their Government in civil life and with the army, church and the courts and with regard to railway communication.

The railway men's union for the district around Petrograd has voted to and consented to transport Bolshevist and consented to transport Bolshevikist troops to the south to operate against General Kaledine. The union also has sent delegates to the front to arrange for the transportation of demobilized troops homeward. Two regiments, fresh from the front, paraded Petrograd Saturday, and the newspapers say the task of demobilization is proceeding rapidly, though in disordered fashion. In many cases companies have been reduced to the strength of 25 to 30 men by gradual departures of soldiers who demobilized themselves.

The railway situation, despite the brave front of the trade unions, is precarious everywhere. Many strikes are threatened, owing to the non-arrival of funds for the payment of wages.

The serious fuel question in Petrograd has now been complicated by strikes of employes in the Fuel Department, who refuse to work under the Bolshevist commissaries. A similar cause has been responsible for a strike of the employes in the Petrograd City Hall, who quit work on the appearance of the new Bolshevist Mayor, who formerly was a day laborer.

The Russian Church, which was one of the most powerful institutions under the old régime, now has received attention at the hands of the Bolsheviki, which has directed the confiscation of all church property, lands, money, gold, silver, and precious stones, and the abolition of religious instruction in the schools.

Little is heard from the Constituent Assembly in the day's dispatches. One

Continued on Page Two.

TRUCE "PROTECTS" ALLIES

Only Transfers of Troops That Had Begun Can Be Carried Out.

APPEAL MADE TO PEASANTS

With Workmen's Councils, Are Urged Not to Balk Success of Revolution.

WANT EX-CZAR IN CAPITAL

Soldiers Demand That Nicholas and Family Be Imprisoned There or at Kronstadt.

Trotzky Tells Opponents They May Expect Guillotine

PETROGRAD, Dec. 16.—The Executive Committee of the Workmen's and Soldiers' Delegates, by a vote of 150 to 104, today approved a decree declaring the Constitutional Democrats enemies of the people. The Peasants' Congress, by a vote of 360 to 321, denounced the arrest of members of the Constituent Assembly, and called upon the country and the army and navy to defend the Delegates with all their forces.

Leon Trotzky, the Bolshevist Foreign Minister, in an address to his opponents, said today:

"You are perturbed by the mild terror we are applying to our enemies.' But know that within a month this terror will take the terrible form of the French revolutionary terror—not the fortress, but the guillotine."

BERLIN, Dec. 16, (via London.)—An armistice agreement between the Bolshevist Government in Russia and the Teutonic allies was signed at Brest-Litovsk yesterday, according to an official communication issued today. The armistice becomes effective at noon Monday and is to remain in force until Jan. 14. A provision in the agreement is that peace negotiations are to begin immediately after the signing of the armistice. The text of the communication follows:

An armistice agreement was signed at Brest-Litovsk yesterday by plenipotentiary representatives of the Russian upper army administration on the one hand and those of the upper army administrations of Germany, Austria-Hungary, Bulgaria, and Turkey on the other hand.

The armistice begins at noon, Dec. 17, and remains in force until Jan. 14, 1918. Unless seven days' notice is given it continues in force automatically. It extends to all the land, air, and naval forces of the common fronts.

According to Clause 9 of the treaty, peace negotiations are to begin immediately after the signing of an armistice.

PETROGRAD, Dec. 16.—Announcement was made today by the Bolshevist official news agency that Russia and Germany had agreed upon the terms of an armistice. The Russian delegates constituting the Armistice Committee at Brest-Litovsk advised the Bolshevist authorities at the Smolny Institute that the agreement reached concerning the transfer of troops was to this effect:

"Both sides signing this agreement bind themselves until Dec. 30, 1917, (Jan. 12, 1918,) not to carry on operative military transfers on the front from the Baltic to the Black Sea, except such transfers as were already begun up to the moment of signing this agreement."

Leon Trotzky, the Bolshevist Foreign Minister, declared at a meeting of the Petrograd Council of Soldiers' and Workmen's Delegates last night that peace negotiations would be begun immediately after the armistice had been signed. The Foreign Minister announced that for a time a break in the negotiations seemed imminent because General Hoffmann, the German negotiator, insisted on the right to transfer troops in small units. The German commander finally accepted the Russian formula.

"We can't and won't aid militarism in any way," M. Trotzky said. "This question of transferring troops was most fundamental. I think our formula is considered by our allies to be satisfactory."

LONDON, Dec. 16.—A Russian Government wireless message received here says:

"Ensign Krylenko, Commander in Chief of the army, in a proclamation addressed to all the army commands on all the fronts and the Military Revolutionary Committee, announces that in consequence of the signing of the armistice, which begins Dec. 17, 'I propose, until receiving the full text of the treaty, to cease all military operations.'"

An official Russian statement received here by wireless from Petrograd says that the following proclamation signed by the Commissioners of Agriculture and War and the Bolshevist Premier

"All the News That's Fit to Print."

The New York Times.

THE WEATHER
Fair today; Thursday snow; diminishing northwest to north winds.
For full weather report see Page 23.

VOL. LXVII...NO. 21,900. NEW YORK, WEDNESDAY, JANUARY 9, 1918.—TWENTY-FOUR PAGES. ONE CENT In Greater New York. | TWO CENTS Within Commuting Distance. | THREE CENTS Elsewhere.

PRESIDENT SPECIFIES TERMS AS BASIS FOR WORLD PEACE; ASKS JUSTICE FOR ALSACE-LORRAINE, APPLAUDS RUSSIA, TELLS GERMANY SHE MAY BE AN EQUAL BUT NOT A MASTER

TROTZKY DISTRUSTS ALLIES

Thinks They Want Him to Give In to Berlin, and Make Peace.

THUS HELPING THEIR ENDS

Bolsheviki Will Fight, He Asserts, Unless Terms Desired Are Accepted by Teutons.

SAYS THEIR TROOPS REBEL

Jump from Trains When Sent West—Confirms Report of 25,000 Intrenched.

By ARTHUR RANSOME.

Special Cable to THE NEW YORK TIMES. Dispatch to The London Daily News.

PETROGRAD, Jan. 6.—I had a hurried talk with Leon Trotzky, the Bolsheviki Foreign Minister, at the Smolny Institute just as, after a final consultation with the Russian members of the peace delegation, he was starting for Brest-Litovsk.

He was leaving with the mistaken conviction that the Entente Governments wanted Germany to succeed in making an advantageous separate peace with Russia so that guarding herself in the east she might agree more willingly to surrender what the Allies want in the west. The Allies would then blame the Bolsheviki for the lost freedom of Poland, Lithuania, and Courland. He was under the impression that Lloyd George had made a statement that allowed such an interpretation.

I assured him that he was mistaken, but he was difficult to convince. He said: "That is the allied policy."

I asked his opinion of a possible international labor conference to decide the conditions of peace. He said: "It would do no harm."

I asked whether the Bolsheviki would fight in case the Central Powers refused to accept the decisions of that conference. He replied:

"The question is not fairly put, for it does not guarantee that the Entente Governments would accept the conference's rulings. In any case the Bolsheviki will fight independently of the rulings of such a conference unless they coincide with the democratic peace desired by Russia. The attitude of the Bolsheviki would not be influenced by the attitude of the allied Governments, but only by the attitude of the allied peoples."

I asked him what his own hopes were for a general and acceptable peace and whether he thought the Germans desired such a peace. He said:

"It is difficult to say, because Germany has not yet been offered a chance of a general acceptable peace. But they must need it. Today four German deserters came to me, a Lieutenant and three soldiers, and told me of the difficulty the Germans have moving troops from this front. They have given up trying to move large units. They take the men one at a time and the men, knowing where they are going to be sent, jump out of the train and escape. At this minute in the Kovno district, behind the German front, there are 25,000 German deserters concentrated together and armed with machine guns. The Germans have surrounded them, and being unable to get their own men to attack they are trying to reduce them by starvation."

I asked him what terms he actually hoped to get. He refused to be drawn and said laughing:

"If we were really logical we would declare war on England now for the sake of India, Egypt and Ireland. You have read our peace declaration."

I protested that Great Britain made nothing out of India. He replied:

"Then give up being so altruistic. You English are the most chauvinist nation on earth without knowing it."

He laughed, again shook hands, and was off.

RUSSIA SEEN ON VERGE OF UTTER COLLAPSE

Petrograd Faces Famine and Paralysis, While Anarchy Reigns in Provinces.

By HAROLD WILLIAMS.

Copyright, 1918, by The New York Times Company.

Special Cable to THE NEW YORK TIMES.

PETROGRAD, Jan. 6.—The Russian peace delegation, accompanied by Leon Trotzky, left last night for Brest-Litovsk to resume negotiations with the delegations of the Central Powers, who already have arrived there. Trotzky hopes to induce the Austro-Germans to transfer the conference to neutral territory—if not to Stockholm, then to Berne.

The negotiations with the German and Austrian commissions here in Petrograd have reached a deadlock. The Bolsheviki flatly refuse to agree to the German proposals for the resumption of trade or an exchange of prisoners until after peace is actually signed. At the

Continued on Page Three.

Germans Starve by Hundreds; Vorwaerts Sees Catastrophe

Special Cable to THE NEW YORK TIMES.

AMSTERDAM, Jan. 8. (Dispatch to The London Daily Express.)—"What was uncertain last year has now become a bitter reality. It can no longer be denied that people are starving by the hundreds in Germany."

This statement was made today by a Dutchman who has just spent five weeks traveling through Germany.

Leaflets are in circulation all over Germany, containing the following extract from a recently suppressed number of Vorwärts:

"Many people are dying of sheer hunger. Sixty million people are suffering. They will not always remain silent. Germany is on the verge of a catastrophe worse than Russia's, namely, a German defeat and loss of the whole war."

Any person found posessing a copy of the leaflet is liable to arrest and a heavy sentence of imprisonment.

HAIG SEES VICTORY VISIBLY NEARER

Says the Allies Have Discounted the Enemy's Gains Through Russia's Collapse.

WEATHER HIS CHIEF FOE

Only That Prevented Complete Victory in Flanders—Warm Welcome to Our Troops.

LONDON, Jan. 8.—"The additional strength which the enemy can obtain from the events in Russia and Italy already has been largely discounted, and the ultimate destruction of the enemy's field forces has been brought appreciably nearer," is the confident summing up by Field Marshal Haig, the British Commander in Chief in France and Belgium, of last year's work by the British Army on the western front. The statement is contained in an official report of General Haig's Spring and Summer campaigns, which occupies twenty-six pages in today's Official Gazette.

The report covers the period from the opening of the Arras offensive on April 9 to the conclusion of the Flanders defensive in November. Subsequent events of the year, including the battle of Cambrai, will be treated in a separate report, which is to be published soon.

Field Marshal Haig closes today's report with a brief tribute to the American troops.

"During the year," he says, "the United States has entered the war, and taken up their part with all the well-known energy and ability of that great nation. Already many thousands of American soldiers are in France. Warm as is the welcome they received from the French people, nowhere will they find a more genuine or friendlier greeting than among the ranks of the other great English-speaking armies."

At the outset of his report Sir Douglas explains how the general allied plan of campaign had to be modified on a wholesale scale from the very start, owing to a variety of unexpected developments, such as the Russian situation, the requirements of the Allies, and, particularly in later months, to adverse weather conditions.

He says that in the Flanders offensive the Germans "used up no less than seventy-eight divisions, of which eighteen were engaged a second or third time after being withdrawn to rest and refit," and that, "given a normally fine August, the capture of the whole ridge in a few weeks was well within the power of our men."

"Our captures in Flanders since the end of July," he continues, "amount to 24,000 prisoners, 74 guns, and 941 machine guns. It is certain that the enemy losses exceeded ours.

"The most important of all is that our new and hastily trained armies again have shown that they are capable of meeting and beating the enemy's best troops under conditions which favored his defense."

The report emphasies "the supreme importance" of training of troops "under officers who are to command them in the task which they are to be called upon to perform."

Among the causes for the miscarriage of the Allies' plans for 1917 Field Marshal Haig gives Russia's failure to "prevent the enemy from transferring forty fresh divisions from her front in exchange for tired ones, used up in the west, or from replacing his losses on the west by drafts of fresh men from the east."

Remarking that the British Spring offensive was launched before Italy was ready, and deploring the weakening of allied forces by the disaster to the arms of the latter, the Field Marshal continues:

"That under such circumstances we won the victories of Arras, Vimy, and Messines, and the French those at Moronvilliers, Verdun, and Malmaison constitutes a record of which the Allies have a right to be proud.

"In the operations at Arras, Messines, Lens, and Ypres, 131 German divisions were engaged and defeated by less than half that number of British.

"Without reckoning the possibilities opened up by our territorial gains in Flanders and without considering the effect which a less vigorous prosecution of the war by us might have had in the other theatres, we have every reason to be satisfied with the results achieved in the past year's fighting."

LONDON SEES NO PEACE

Fierce Fighting Ahead Despite the Lloyd George Statement.

NECESSITY PROMPTED IT

Solidification of Public Opinion by Removing Doubt Was Imperative.

TEUTON PRESS HOSTILE

Derisive Comment by German and Austrian Papers, Which Say Sword Will Force Peace.

Germany Announces Extension of the Submarine Barred Zone

LONDON, Jan. 8.—Further extension of the submarine barred zone is announced in a wireless statement sent out by the German Government. It becomes operative on Jan. 11.

The extensions which are particularized in the message affect the region around "enemy supporting points" on the Cape Verde Islands and the point of support of Dakar, French Senegal, with the adjoining coastal district.

The barred zone around the Azores is extended easterly over the Island of Madeira, which "serves our adversaries as a point of support."

Special Cable to THE NEW YORK TIMES.

LONDON, Jan. 8.—Dispatches from America indicate the existence of some measure of disquiet over Lloyd George's statement, based on an idea that its moderation implied belief in the possibility of approaches to peace being made now. Here in London this view finds acceptance only in circles where it may be said that the wish is father to the thought. Generally speaking, the pacifists and that other small section of opinion which believes in the miraculous regeneration of Germany are the only persons who think peace has been brought near at hand by the Prime Minister's statement.

The overwhelming preponderance of informed opinion is that the coming Spring and Summer will witness some of the bloodiest fighting of the war, and that Germany will exhaust every effort to inflict a crushing defeat on the European Allies before America can get fully in. Lloyd George's speech, though it has been described as a hold out to Germany of the olive branch in one hand and the sword in the other, was not determined upon by any considerations of the question whether the moment had arrived for extending the olive branch. The one great reason for the statement was domestic necessity. Solidification of British opinion by removing certain elements of doubt and suspicion was paramount.

Lloyd George, as already has been indicated in these dispatches, fully recognized that necessity. There were two questions in his mind. One was whether the present moment was the most opportune; the other was whether a statement should be made at once by the British Government alone, or should be issued as a joint declaration by the Allies, with America subscribing to it, or giving it a sort of imprimatur.

Upon these questions Lloyd George first of all consulted Asquith. Asquith gave it as his view that the moment was most opportune and that valuable time would be lost were the exchanges of views necessary to obtain a concerted statement by all the Allies entered upon. Also it was believed that clarity of statement might be more easily achieved were the British Government to issue a declaration on its own initiative. There was no likelihood of the British statement failing to meet with full approval of the Allies, seeing that there was a general agreement between the British and allied Governments on their war aims.

Lord Grey concurred, and it was arranged that the statement should be drafted and considered. The draft was drawn up by Lloyd George and was then studied by the War Cabinet. It was next referred to Asquith and Lord Grey, whose full approval was given just half an hour before Lloyd George read it at the trades union meeting in Central Hall, Westminster.

Its results upon British opinion came up to the highest expectations, and its approval by the Allies was equally satisfactory. "The statement solidified British opinion," said one authority today. "It will equally solidify German opinion. Alsace-Lorraine is the keystone of German patriotism."

Even if on all other points it were possible for the Entente Powers and Central Powers to arrive at a common ground admitting of compromise and negotiations, German acceptance of reconsideration of the Alsace-Lorraine question is only to be obtained from a militarily defeated Germany. This is the view taken by the best informed British opinion, and it is evident as a corollary that it is here believed that much fighting has yet to be done to obtain a satisfactory peace.

In other words there is little or no hope that Germany will come to terms until bowed down by the weight of America's millions, or at least till the tramp of America's armies sounds like a death knell in the ears of her helpless militarists.

Text of President Wilson's Speech

WASHINGTON, Jan. 8.—The President in his address to Congress today spoke as follows:

Gentlemen of the Congress:

Once more, as repeatedly before, the spokesmen of the Central Empires have indicated their desire to discuss the objects of the war and the possible basis of a general peace. Parleys have been in progress at Brest-Litovsk between Russian representatives and representatives of the Central Powers, to which the attention of all the belligerents has been invited, for the purpose of ascertaining whether it may be possible to extend these parleys into a general conference with regard to terms of peace and settlement. The Russian representatives presented not only a perfectly definite statement of the principles upon which they would be willing to conclude peace, but also an equally definite program for the concrete application of those principles. The representatives of the Central Powers, on their part, presented an outline of settlement which, if much less definite, seemed susceptible of liberal interpretation until their specific program of practical terms was added. That program proposed no concessions at all, either to the sovereignty of Russia or to the preferences of the population with whose fortunes it dealt, but meant, in a word, that the Central Empires were to keep every foot of territory their armed forces had occupied—every province, every city, every point of vantage—as a permanent addition to their territories and their power. It is a reasonable conjecture that the general principles of settlement which they at first suggested originated with the more liberal statesmen of Germany and Austria, the men who have begun to feel the force of their own peoples' thought and purpose, while the concrete terms of actual settlement came from the military leaders who have no thought but to keep what they have got. The negotiations have been broken off. The Russian representatives were sincere and in earnest. They cannot entertain such proposals of conquest and domination.

The whole incident is full of significance. It is also full of perplexity. With whom are the Russian representatives dealing? For whom are the representatives of the Central Empires speaking? Are they speaking for the majorities of their respective Parliaments or for the minority parties, that military and imperialistic minority which has so far dominated their whole policy and controlled the affairs of Turkey and of the Balkan States, which have felt obliged to become their associates in this war? The Russian representatives have insisted, very justly, very wisely, and in the true spirit of modern democracy, that the conferences they have been holding with the Teutonic and Turkish statesmen should be held with open, not closed, doors, and all the world has been audience, as was desired. To whom have we been listening, then? To those who speak the spirit and intention of the resolutions of the German Reichstag of the 9th of July last, the spirit and intention of the liberal leaders and parties of Germany, or to those who resist and defy that spirit and intention and insist upon conquest and subjugation? Or are we listening, in fact, to both, unreconciled and in open and hopeless contradiction? These are very serious and pregnant questions. Upon the answer to them depends the peace of the world.

But whatever the results of the parleys at Brest-Litovsk, whatever the confusions of counsel and of purpose in the utterances of the spokesmen of the Central Empires, they have again attempted to acquaint the world with their objects in the war and have again challenged their adversaries to say what their objects are and what sort of settlement they would deem just and satisfactory. There is no good reason why that challenge should not be responded to, and responded to with the utmost candor. We did not wait for it. Not once, but again and again we have laid our whole thought and purpose before the world, not in general terms only, but each time with sufficient definition to make it clear what sort of definite terms of settlement must necessarily spring out of them. Within the last week Mr. Lloyd George has spoken with admirable candor and in admirable spirit for the people and Government of Great Britain. There is no confusion of counsel among the adversaries of the Central Powers, no uncertainty of principle, no vaguenes of detail. The only secrecy of counsel, the only lack of fearless frankness, the only failure to make definite statement of the objects of the war, lies with Germany and her allies. The issues of life and death hang upon these definitions. No statesman who has the least conception of his responsibility ought for a moment to permit himself to continue this tragical and appalling outpouring of blood and treasure unless he is sure beyond a peradventure that the objects of the vital sacrifice are part and parcel of the very life of society and that the people for whom he speaks think them right and imperative as he does.

There is, moreover, a voice calling for these definitions of principle and of purpose which is, it seems to me, more thrilling and more compelling than any of the many moving voices with which the troubled air of the world is filled. It is the voice of the Russian people. They are prostrate and all but helpless, it would seem, before the grim power of Germany, which has hitherto known no relenting and no pity. Their power apparently is shattered. And yet their soul is not subservient. They will not yield either in principle or in action. Their conception of what is right, of what is humane and honorable for them to accept, has been stated with a frankness, a largeness of view, a generosity of spirit, and a universal human sympathy which must challenge the admiration of every friend of mankind; and they have refused to compound their ideals or desert others that they themselves may be safe. They call to us to say what it is that we desire, in what, if in anything, our purpose and our spirit differ from theirs; and I believe that the people of the United States would wish me to respond with utter simplicity and frankness. Whether their present leaders believe it or not, it is our heartfelt desire and hope that some way may be opened whereby we may be privileged to assist the people of Russia to attain their utmost hope of liberty and ordered peace.

It will be our wish and purpose that the processes of peace, when they are begun, shall be absolutely open, and that they shall involve and permit henceforth no secret understandings of any kind. The day of conquest and aggrandizement is gone by; so is also the day of secret covenants entered into in the interest of particular Governments and likely at some unlooked-for moment to upset the peace of the world. It is this happy fact, now clear to the view of every public man whose thoughts do not still linger in an age that is dead and gone, which makes it possible for every nation whose purposes are consistent with justice and the peace of the world to avow now or at any other time the objects it has in view.

We entered this war because violations of right had occurred which touched us to the quick and made the life of our own people impossible unless they were corrected and the world secured once for all against their recurrence. What we demand in this war, therefore, is nothing peculiar to ourselves. It is that the world be made fit and safe to live in; and particularly that it be made safe for every peace-loving nation which, like our own, wishes to live its own life, determine its own institutions, be assured of justice and fair dealings by the other peoples of the world, as against force and selfish aggression. All the peoples of the world are in effect partners in this interest and for our own part we see very clearly that unless justice be done to others it will not be done to us.

The program of the world's peace, therefore, is our program, and that program, the only possible program, as we see it, is this:

I.—Open covenants of peace, openly arrived at, after which there shall be no private international understandings of any kind, but diplomacy shall proceed always frankly and in the public view.

II.—Absolute freedom of navigation upon the seas, outside territorial waters, alike in peace and in war, except as the seas may be closed in whole or in part by international action for the enforcement of international covenants.

III.—The removal, so far as possible, of all economic barriers and the establishment of an equality of trade conditions among all the nations consenting to the peace and associating themselves for its maintenance.

IV.—Adequate guarantees given and taken that national armaments will reduce to the lowest point consistent with domestic safety.

V.—Free, open-minded, and absolutely impartial adjustment of all colonial claims, based upon a strict observance of the principle that in determining all such questions of sovereignty the interests of the population concerned must have equal weight with the equitable claims of the Government whose title is to be determined.

VI.—The evacuation of all Russian territory and such a settlement of all questions affecting Russia as will secure the best and freest co-operation of the other nations of the world in obtaining for her an unhampered and unembarrassed opportunity for the independent determination of her own political development and national policy, and assure her of a sincere welcome into the society of free nations under institutions of her own choosing; and, more than a welcome, assistance also of every kind that she may need and may herself desire. The treatment accorded Russia by her sister nations in the months to come will be the acid test of their good-will, of their comprehension of her needs as distinguished from their own interests, and of their intelligent and unselfish sympathy.

VII.—Belgium, the whole world will agree, must be evacuated and restored, without any attempt to limit the sovereignty which she enjoys in common with all other free nations. No other single act will serve as this will serve to restore confidence among the nations in the laws which they have themselves set and determined for the government of their relations with one another. Without this healing act the whole structure and validity of international law is forever impaired.

VIII.—All French territory should be freed and the invaded portions restored, and the wrong done to France by Prussia in 1871 in the matter of Alsace-Lorraine, which has unsettled the peace of the world for nearly fifty years, should be righted, in order that peace may once more be made secure in the interest of all.

IX.—A readjustment of the frontiers of Italy should be effected along clearly recognizable lines of nationality.

X.—The peoples of Austria-Hungary, whose place among the nations we wish to see safeguarded and assured, should be accorded the freest opportunity of autonomous development.

XI.—Rumania, Serbia, and Montenegro should be evacuated; occupied territories re[illegible] accorded free and secure access to the sea; and the relations of the several Balkan States to one another determined by friendly counsel along historically established lines of allegiance and nationality; and international guarantees of the political and economic independence and territorial integrity of the several Balkan States should be entered into.

XII.—The Turkish portions of the present Ottoman Empire should be assured a secure sovereignty, but the other nationalities which are now under Turkish rule should be assured an undoubted security of life and an absolutely unmolested opportunity of autonomous development, and the Dardanelles should be permanently opened as a free passage to the ships and commerce of all nations under international guarantees.

XIII.—An independent Polish State should be erected which should include the territories inhabited by indisputably Polish populations, which should be assured a free and secure access to the sea, and whose political and economic independence and territorial integrity should be guaranteed by international covenant.

XIV.—A general association of nations must be formed under specific covenants for the purpose of affording mutual guarantees of political independence and territorial integrity to great and small States alike.

In regard to these essential rectifications of wrong and assertions of right, we feel ourselves to be intimate partners of all the Governments and peoples associated together against the imperialists. We cannot be separated in interest or divided in purpose. We stand together until the end.

For such arrangements and covenants we are willing to fight and to continue to fight until they are achieved; but only because we wish the right to prevail and desire a just and stable peace, such as can be secured only be removing the chief provocations to war, which this program does remove. We have no jealousy of German greatness, and there is nothing in this program that impairs it. We grudge her no achievement or distinction of learning or of pacific enterprise such as have made her record very bright and very enviable. We do not wish to injure her or to block in any way her legitimate influence or power. We do not wish to fight her either with arms or with hostile arrangements of trade, if she is willing to associate herself with us and the other peace-loving nations of the world in covenants of justice and law and fair dealing. We wish her only to accept a place of equality among the peoples of the world—the new world in which we now live—instead of a place of mastery.

Neither do we presume to suggest to her any alteration or modification of her institutions. But it is necessary, we must frankly say, and necessary as a preliminary to any intelligent dealings with her on our part, that we should know whom her spokesmen speak for when they speak to us, whether for the Reichstag majority or for the military party and the men whose creed is imperial domination.

We have spoken now, surely in terms too concrete to admit of any further doubt or question. An evident principle runs through the whole program I have outlined. It is the principle of justice to all peoples and nationalities, and their right to live on equal terms of liberty and safety with one another, whether they be strong or weak. Unless this principle be made its foundation, no part of the structure of international justice can stand. The people of the United States could act upon no other principle, and to the vindication of this principle they are ready to devote their lives, their honor, and everything that they possess. The moral climax of this, the culminating and final war for human liberty, has come, and they are ready to put their own strength, their own highest purpose, their own integrity and devotion to the test.

APPEALS TO GERMAN PEOPLE

Wilson Declares We Must Know for Whom Their Rulers Speak.

READY TO FIGHT TO END

Insists That Principle of Justice to All Nations Is Only Basis for Peace.

DEMANDS FREEDOM OF SEAS

Congress Cheers Utterance as Momentous Declaration of Entente War Aims.

Special to The New York Times.

WASHINGTON, Jan. 8.—The terms upon which Germany may obtain peace were given to the American Congress for the benefit of the whole world by President Wilson today. With scant notice of his coming, notice barely sufficient to enable the Senate and the House to make the necessary arrangements for a joint session, the President appeared at the Capitol, and in an address, brief by comparison to the momentous issues discussed, enumerated the conditions for a cessation of hostilities, the rejection of which will place upon Germany the responsibility for the further bloodshed that must precede the final victory of the allied nations.

President Wilson's address bore a striking resemblance to the speech made last Saturday by Mr. Lloyd George, the British Prime Minister, before the Trade Union Conference on Man Power, in which he specified the war aims and peace conditions of the British Government. The diversions in the President's address from statements of the Prime Minister were for the most part more in the form than in the substance.

But in the opinion of many of those who compared Mr. Wilson's address with the utterances of Mr. Lloyd George the President was more definite in declaring that the wrong done to France through the annexation of Alsace-Lorraine must be righted and he differed from Mr. Lloyd George with regard to the Russian situation in that he held out to the Russian people an offer of assistance from America, and tendered sympathy for the aims that those now in control of the affairs of that perturbed country are seeking to achieve.

Leaves No Doubt of Unity.

By the President's official utterances he has pledged this Government to the achievement of ends that affect Europe more intimately and deeply than the United States. No doubt was left in the minds of those who listened to the President's words that this Government has entered heart and soul into the cause of the Entente Allies, to fight for the objects for which they are fighting, to free Europe from the menace of Prussianism, to take Alsace-Lorraine from German domination, to prevent Russia from becoming part of the German Empire, to see that Italy has restored to her those portions of the Austro-Hungarian Empire that are inhabited by a people who are Italian in heart and blood, to bring all the Polish peoples into a common Government, to restore Belgium, Serbia, and the small nations that have been devastated by Teuton hordes, to their own, to give the separate nationalities of Austria-Hungary, Turkey and the Balkan States the right to govern themselves as separate entities, to have Northern France restored to French control.

And, in addition to these aims, the allied nations, in order to find a peace acceptable to them, must be assured of freedom of the seas, the establishment of an equality of trade conditions among the nations of the world, the reduction of armaments, and an association of nations in a league to enforce peace. There must also be no secret agreements among nations that would threaten again the peace of the world.

Immediately following the delivery of the President's address, there was a disposition manifest to refer to his outline of the conditions which Germany must accept before the war could end as a definition of peace terms. But in the official quarters best qualified to interpret the meaning of the President, it was declared that his statement must be taken as a definition of war aims. The President left no doubt that, unless Germany consented to enter into peace exchanges on the basis of the conditions set forth in his address, the United States and the Allies would fight on until the Central Powers realized that there could be no peace in any other way. "It was an outline of war aims, not a peace address," declared one official.

Terms Clear and Definite.

Never before has President Wilson or any other spokesman for a nation at war with Germany made such a clear

GERMAN PRESS SAY 'NO' TO LLOYD GEORGE

Talks Like a Conqueror, They Say—Refuse to Take Speech as Peace Offer.

By GEORGE RENWICK.

Copyright, 1918, by The New York Times Company.

Special Cable to THE NEW YORK TIMES.

AMSTERDAM, Jan. 8.—The views in the German press regarding Lloyd George's speech are just what might have been expected from Germany in her present frame of mind.

The Düsseldorfer Nachrichten, which is the new name of the Düsseldorfer General Anzeiger now that it has passed into the Krupp sphere of influence, says England posing as the innocent victim of a German created war is now merely ridiculous. It continues:

"The main point is that England now has bound herself to fight to the last for Alsace-Lorraine. We do not believe the British people will carry the war to the uttermost for this aim. As far as we are concerned there is no Alsace-Lorraine question, and Kühlmann's 'No, never!' has been heard both in London and Paris. Lloyd George's speech, therefore, cannot serve the interests of peace. It is merely intended to bring the Brest-Litovsk negotiations into disrepute and whip up the failing spirits of the western powers. Let there be no more peace offers. Only swords can bring this enemy to reason."

The militarist Post says Lloyd George speaks like a conqueror, but "we will show him we are the victors, not the vanquished."

The Boersen Courier cannot see how the speech can be regarded as a peace offer.

The Boersen Zeitung looks upon it as an indication that the whole political and military situation has been changed and sees a complete forced alteration in England's war aims.

The Pan German Deutsche Zeitung believes that Lloyd George is endeavoring to drive a wedge between Germany and her allies by making a peace offer to the latter. Only victory over England can bring real peace, it adds.

The Cologne Volkszeitung wonders if a new Lloyd George is coming on the scene and it says that it will await with interest and see if he realy intends to improve his manners and follow in Lansdowne's footsteps. It lays no real importance, it says, on his statement regarding reconsideration of the great crime of 1871, with reference to Alsace-Lorraine, for the matter is one in which the main consideration is what France desires. On that point Germany harbors no illusions.

The Norddeutsche Allgemeine Zeitung, semi-official organ, says:

"Mr. Lloyd George knows today, as when he made his first war speech, that the territorial integrity of the Austro-Hungarian monarchy, as well as that of the other allies of Germany, must form the cornerstone in the building of a new peace. Nevertheless, he adheres to his imperialistic war aims, with their unmeasured demands, and only by a change in tone tries to give the impression that he takes into account the alteration of the military and political situation. It is characteristic of him and his allies."

A Vienna dispatch to the Pester Lloyd (Budapest) says that in political circles the peace conditions offered by the British Prime Minister are considered impossible of acceptance.

LONDON, Jan. 8.—A reply from the Central Powers to the statement of British war aims made by Premier Lloyd George Saturday is awaited here with the greatest interest. It is believed that Germany and her allies cannot decline to reply in some form.

While no German official or semi-official reply has yet been issued, much newspaper comment, however, has reached here by way of Amsterdam. Some of the German newspapers recognize the moderation of the speech, but, with the exception of the Socialist Vor-

Continued on Page Two.

"All the News That's Fit to Print."

The New York Times.

THE WEATHER
Rain early, then fair today; Friday fair; fresh northwest winds.
For full weather report see Page 21.

VOL. LXVII...NO. 21,929. NEW YORK, THURSDAY, FEBRUARY 7, 1918.—TWENTY-TWO PAGES. TWO CENTS In Greater New York and Within Commuting Distance. | THREE CENTS Elsewhere.

TUSCANIA, CARRYING 2,179 U. S. TROOPS, SUNK; 1,912 SURVIVORS LANDED AT IRISH PORTS; WASHINGTON FEARS 260 MEN ARE LOST

PRESIDENT SEEKS BLANKET POWERS FOR WAR PERIOD

Bill to Give Him Authority to Co-ordinate and Consolidate All Governmental Activities.

POWER OVER PUBLIC FUNDS

"We Might as Well Abdicate," Say Senators on Hearing Provisions of Bill.

CALLED ANSWER TO CRITICS

Simmons and Martin, Democrats, Would Not Introduce It—Overman Finally Did So.

Special to The New York Times.

WASHINGTON, Feb. 6.—Unrestricted power to the President to "co-ordinate and consolidate" all the governmental activities as a war emergency is contemplated in a bill offered in the Senate late today by Senator Overman of North Carolina, an Administration supporter.

The measure, which came from the President, caused the most profound sensation of the entire legislative session, in which sensations have been frequent. It was criticised tonight as intended to provide assumption of the entire power of Government by the Executive.

Leaders in the Senate, Democrats and Republicans alike, showed anger tonight over the proposal of the President to take over complete authority in the conduct of America's part in the world struggle.

"We might as well abdicate," said several Senators.

The bill was handed to Senator Overman by Postmaster General Burleson, the recognized intermediary between the White House and Congress, at the Capitol early in the afternoon. It r..., ...d the wishes of the President, Mr. Burleson said, in his effort to achieve the utmost efficiency in governmental war activity.

Far-Reaching in Scope.

In its scope the bill goes much beyond any other legislation attempted during the war. It outstrips in its delegation of power the authority contemplated in the War Cabinet bill and the measure for a Director of Munitions together.

In fact, Senate leaders said tonight, if the bill were enacted into law the President would be entirely independent of any further legislation in Congress except to ask—or insist—on measures carrying appropriations to conduct the war.

Frank amazement was expressed at the Capitol at the sweeping nature of the measure. Not only would it mean the abdication by Congress of its law-making power, Senators said, but it would carry in effect a wholesale repeal of laws by which Governmental departments or agencies have been established.

Under the measure the President might abolish all the war-making machinery of the Government, including the agencies created since the country entered the war. The bill would empower him to create any new bureaus, agencies, or offices he wanted in the place of those discarded.

Exactly the same bill, it was learned tonight, was given to Senator Martin, the Democratic floor leader, by Postmaster General Burleson or by the President himself a few days ago, with the request that the Virginia Senator offer it in the Senate. Although a staunch supporter of the President in his war policies, Senator Martin expressed the opinion that the bill went too far, and he declined to offer it.

Disapproved by Simmons.

Before making up his mind not to stand sponsor for the measure Senator Martin conferred with Senator Simmons, another firm Administration Democrat from North Carolina. Senator Simmons agreed with Senator Martin that the bill sought to delegate too much power to the President.

Postmaster General Burleson took the measure to Senator Overman during a lull in the war debate and urged him to put the bill in. The North Carolina Senator agreed to do so when told that the President wanted it.

Only a few Senators were in the Chamber when the bill was offered by Senator Overman. Without a word the measure was referred to the Judiciary Committee, which will decide whether it is to be reported out.

The measure gives the President power to "make any such re-distribution of functions among executive agencies as he may deem necessary, including any functions, duties and powers hitherto conferred upon any executive department, commission, bureau,

Continued on Page Five.

Teutons Bar Captives Released by Russians

Special Cable to THE NEW YORK TIMES.

PETROGRAD, Feb. 4, (delayed.)—The Germans and Austrians have established quasi quarantine conditions along the Russian front, and enemy prisoners are now finding it difficult to cross the trenches unless there is a reasonable certainty that they are not infected with revolutionary tenets. Incidentally, the escaping and released prisoners turned back by their compatriots naturally drift to the Petrograd district, where they are now said to number 40 000.

The enemy's measures to isolate himself an not allow news of internal disturbances to leak out have included the breaking off of direct telegraph and telephone communication between Brest-Litovsk and Petrograd, with the result that nothing has been heard of the Trotzky delegation for the last three days, which is ample time to allow the invention of the rumor now actively circulating that separate peace has already been signed.

TEUTONS TO TREAT WITH UKRAINIANS

Peace Negotiations with Bolsheviki Suspended After Argument Over Poland.

TROTZKY AGAINST ENVOYS

Petrograd, Isolated from Brest-Litovsk, Is Without News of Any Kind.

AMSTERDAM, Feb. 6.—Dr. von Kühlmann and Count Czernin, the German and Austro-Hungarian Foreign Ministers, left Berlin last night for Brest-Litovsk to continue the peace negotiations, a dispatch from the German capital says.

The Cologne Volkszeitung understands that the negotiations will be resumed Thursday in the direction of concluding peace with Ukraine.

General Hoffman, who took a prominent part in the negotiations during the early sessions, participated in the recent ministerial councils at Berlin, according to the Lokal-Anzeiger, and also had several interviews with Mathias Erzberger, one of the leaders of the Clerical Centre in the Reichstag. This paper understands that important decisions are impending regarding the eastern and Rumanian questions.

LONDON, Feb. 6.—The negotiations at Brest-Litovsk have been broken off, the correspondent at Petrograd of the Exchange Telegraph Company say he is informed.

German wireless dispatches bring the negotiations up to Feb. 3, when long discussions on the question of representatives of the Russian western border States and Poland joining in the negotiations failed to bring any result.

Leon Trotzky, the Bolshevist Foreign Minister, while declaring his readiness to recognize the independence and right of self-government of the Polish State, contended that the fact of foreign occupation prevented him from recognizing representatives of that State under existing conditions, and he argued that a State without either boundaries or King could be neither a State nor a kingdom.

Dr. von Kühlmann, the German Secretary of Foreign Affairs, observed that the negotiations would be facilitated if Trotzky would recognize the independence of the other border States.

Count Czernin, the Austro-Hungarian Foreign Minister, noted with satisfaction that by Trotzky's recognition of the existence and independence of the Polish State the standpoints of each side appeared to have been brought into greater unison. But he was unable to admit that the question whether the existing Polish Government was authorized to represent the Polish State could be submitted for arbitration to a third Government.

Both Count Czernin and Dr. von Kühlmann protested that they had not come to engage in an intellectual wrestling match, and, at the close, the German Secretary explained that he was obliged by unavoidable duties to depart for a short time, but said that during his absence the political and economic commissions could continue their negotiations.

An official Russian wireless dispatch contains a declaration by Lettish representatives from the Lettish Councils of Socialists and Soldiers protesting against the assertion of the Austro-German delegation at Brest-Litovsk that the Letts had expressed a desire for separation from Russia. The demand is expressed that the German and Russian forces be withdrawn from the Lettish territory so that the inhabitants can freely express their will for unconditional unity and undivided existence.

A declaration similar to that made by

Continued on Page Three.

BAKER HOPEFUL OF GETTING SHIPS FOR 1,500,000 MEN

Again Defends His Statement That Forces for France Depend on Transport.

BUT FIGURES ARE LACKING

Tells Senators He Is Unwilling to Disclose Plans Except in Secret Session.

ON STAND THREE HOURS

Inquiry Discloses That Some Officers Have Been Sent Home for Pro-German Leanings.

Special to The New York Times.

WASHINGTON, Feb. 6.—For three hours today Secretary Baker underwent interrogation before the Senate Military Affairs Committee, based upon his defense of last week that the Government's war machinery had not, as alleged, fallen down. The Secretary was led over a wide field of cross-questioning by Senators who wanted information about his handling of the War Department.

During the cross-examination a wrangle occurred among several of the Senators as to the propriety of asking the Secretary questions in public touching upon the number of men now in France and the means of sending more and keeping them supplied. Senator Reed thought some of these matters ought to be kept secret. The tilt between the Senators threatened, for a moment, to disrupt the hearing.

One controversial point in Secretary Baker's cross-examination arose over his statement, last week, that 1,500,000 men could be sent to France by the end of this year if adequate transportation facilities were available. Senators Weeks and Hitchcock wanted to know upon what the Secretary based this estimate. The Secretary, after the question had been put to him half a dozen times in different ways, exclaimed:

"If you want to know, just come with me to a committee room and I will tell you in three sentences."

Says Allies Aid Transport.

The Secretary later on told the committee that the War Department had not depended entirely upon American ships to transport its troops, but expected assistance from the Allies. But America, he said, would be able to supply a large proportion of the transport facilities.

The Secretary put himself on record as favoring legislation to give the President power to co-ordinate and reconstruct any department of Governmental activity so as to make for greater efficiency. This came when Senator Wadsworth asked him if he had in mind any measure that Congress might enact to "remove restrictions and do away with formalities that impede progress." This, Senator Wadsworth said, had been suggested by the President as advisable.

"I have a feeling that legislation which would simply free the President's hands and allow him to transfer functions and to consolidate and co-ordinate, as the developing needs of the several departments demonstrate, would be wise," said Secretary Baker.

The Secretary explained that all the departments were growing with the war pressure and that changes had to be made frequently. The President, he thought, ought to have unrestricted rein to create and distribute functions as occasion seemed to demand.

Senator Wadsworth wanted to know if the Secretary did not think that a Directorate of Munitions would serve a real purpose of co-ordination, but the Secretary thought it would only be cumbersome.

Defines Stettinius's Post.

Asked if he did not think legal authority was lacking in the War Industries Board and other agencies that have supervision over purchases, the Secretary of War replied that the President had general power over all of them. He defined the function of Edward R. Stettinius, Surveyor of Purchases, as doing "everything to help in the speedy procurement of supplies and co-ordination of industries."

Mr. Stettinius, he said, would develop the work over which he is placed according to the requirements.

Questions were asked regarding two army officers alleged to have been sent back from France for having expressed pro-German sympathies. The Secretary said they would be court-martialed if the facts warranted it. Senator Reed opposed evidence that tended to show, as he said, that the army "reeked with treason." He

Continued on Page Four.

Hindenburg and Ludendorff Now Established in Belgium

Special Cable to THE NEW YORK TIMES.

AMSTERDAM, Feb. 6.—Hindenburg and Ludendorff have moved their headquarters to Belgium. An interview with German army chiefs recently published in an Austrian journal indicated vaguely that their headquarters were somewhere in the Rhine region. The new locality where they are established is within easy reach of Brussels.

THREE BILLIONS ASKED OF BANKS

McAdoo Launches Sale of Treasury Certificates—Prelude to Third Liberty Loan.

HIS APPEAL NATION-WIDE

Wants 10 Per Cent. of Banking Resources—Bond Offer Probably in April.

Special to The New York Times.

WASHINGTON, Feb. 6.—In announcing today an offer of $500,000,000 Treasury certificates of indebtedness, Secretary McAdoo indicated somewhat the gigantic program of war financing that must be put through by July 1. There will be offers of Treasury certificates at intervals of two weeks, so that if the 25,000 banks of every character throughout the country respond to the appeal made that 1 per cent. of their gross resources be set aside each week at the disposal of the Government there may be raised $3,000,000,000 before the next bond issue.

Up to today there had been no intimation as to the time when the offer of the next bond issue would be made. It is now indicated, from the interval of time remaining to the end of the fiscal year, June 30, and the experience with the previous two issues of bonds, that the third will be announced in April.

The $500,000,000 of Treasury certificates of indebtedness offered today will mature May 9, and are offered at par at 4 per cent. interest, of date Feb. 8. With this announcement Secretary McAdoo sent to the 25,000 banks and trust companies of the country a telegram, appealing to them "as a matter of patriotic duty" to set aside each week about 1 per cent. of their gross resources and place that amount at the disposal of the Government by investing it in certificates of indebtedness as the Secretary shall offer them from time to time.

Ten Per Cent. of Gross Resources.

It is contemplated, if each bank will do its share, that as a maximum 10 per cent. of the gross resources of the banks, or approximately $3,000,000,000, will be raised between now and the next Liberty Loan, provided it is necessary to call upon the banks to that extent.

The Secretary's plan calls virtually for the loan by banks, big and little, of the $3,000,000,000 aggregate of certificate issues before the real Liberty Loan campaign starts. By this means, that sum would be guaranteed in the Liberty Loan drive, and the difference between that sum and the total of the Liberty Loan would have to come largely from individual private subscribers. Treasury officials also believe that the financial condition of the nation can be judged closely by the success met by the advance sale of certificates. About half of the first Liberty Loan was raised in advance by certificate sales, and about two-thirds of the second loan.

Already $400,000,000 worth of certificates of indebtedness have been sold in anticipation of the third loan, and about $1,145,000,000 certificates are outstanding to be received in payment of income and excess profits taxes by next June.

Certificate issues in the past have been absorbed largely by the bigger banks. Secretary McAdoo now hopes to distribute this burden more equally over the whole financial fabric of the country.

Secretary McAdoo's Appeal.

The telegram of Secretary McAdoo follows:

Feb. 6, 1918.

Between now and the time for making the next Liberty Loan I shall offer for subscription Treasury certificates for indebtedness in amounts of $500,000,000 or more every two weeks. I desire to postpone the next Liberty Loan issue until conditions will insure a wide distribution of the bonds throughout the country. In order successfully to carry through this program and to provide for the expenditures for the military operations of the United States and the Allies I must have the whole-hearted co-operation of the bankers of the United States, and to that end I request the Board of Directors or Trustees of each bank and trust company to reserve each week out of its loanable funds, for the use of the Government of the United States, about

Continued on Page Two.

The Torpedoed Transport Tuscania

Units That Were Aboard the Tuscania

Special to The New York Times.

WASHINGTON, Thursday, Feb. 7, 12:30 A. M.—The War Department now announces that the following units were on board the Tuscania:

Headquarters detachment and Companies D, E, and F of the 20th Engineers. (First Forestry Engineers, about 750 men, recruited from different parts of the country).

107th Engineer Train (one battalion of Michigan Engineers and one battalion of Wisconsin Engineers).

107th Military Police (parts of what were the Fourth and Sixth Regiments Wisconsin Infantry).

107th Supply Train (parts of what were the Fourth, Fifth, and Sixth Wisconsin Infantry).

Number 100 Aero Squadron.

158th Aero Squadron.

213th Aero Squadron.

Replacement detachments Nos. 1 and 2 of the 32d Division, composed of National Guard troops from Michigan and Wisconsin. This division trained at Camp MacArthur, Texas.

Fifty-one casual officers.

The War Department will not say that the above-named units composed all the troops on the Tuscania, but it knows that these units were on board.

CHARGE APATHY IN SHIPYARD DRIVE

Chairman of New York's Four-Minute Men Declares Recruits Were Turned Away.

OFFICIALS DENY REPORT

Head of Labor Reserve Says New York Has Sent 1,500 Men to Plants Near Here.

The campaign which has been carried on for more than a week by 800 volunteer speakers in moving picture theatres and elsewhere under the direction of the Four Minute Men for the purpose of enrolling skilled laborers for employment in shipyards has almost failed, so far, through lack of co-ordination, according to Joseph B. Thomas, the New York City chairman of the Four Minute Men.

Athough the Committee on Public Information sent out prepared speeches for the guidance of the Four Minute Men in every part of the country and Chairman Hurley of the United States Shipping Board wrote a confidential letter for circulation among the Four Minute Men to impress them with the importance of the campaign, no arrangements were made by any Government agency, Chairman Thomas said, to enroll or take care of the skilled workmen, whose patriotism had been excited by the speeches.

A report from Chairman Thomas to the Director of the Division of Four Minute Men in Washington quoted correspondence to show that Chairman Thomas had sought, beginning on Jan. 16, to learn where the workmen, who were begged to offer their services to the Government, should appear for enrollment.

According to the report, Mr. Thomas was referred from one organization to another through a long series of unsuccessful applications for information, which ended finally in the assurance that workmen should be sent to 22 East Twenty-second street, which is occupied by an office of the United States Employment Service.

Volunteers Turned Away.

After speakers at the moving picture theatres had been sending men to that address for several days Mr. Thomas said he began to get a flood of complaints from workmen seeking to enroll who had been turned away. He found upon investigation that this office had not been notified by the Shipping Board.

Continued on Page Five.

British Loss of Ships Held to 15 for the Week

LONDON, Feb. 6.—The Admiralty reports fifteen British merchantmen sunk by mine or submarine in the last week. Of these ten were 1,600 tons or over and five were under 1,600 tons. Four fishing vessels were also sunk.

A dispatch from Rome states that the Italian ship losses by mine or submarine in the week ending Feb. 2 were very light, only one steamer under 1,600 tons being sunk.

The French shipping losses, according to a dispatch from Paris, were two steamers of more than 1,600 tons, and one under that tonnage in the week ending Feb. 2.

The British losses by mine or submarine the last week are approximately the same as the previous week, when nine British merchantmen of more than 1,600 tons and six of lesser tonnage were destroyed.

OFFICER ARRESTED FOR SAILING TALK

Violated Rules by Telling Relative on What Ship He Was Going and When.

WASHINGTON, Feb. 6.—A young army officer who confided to a relative the name of the ship on which he was going overseas and the date of sailing is under arrest, pending an investigation of whether his superiors properly instructed him concerning the requirement of secrecy.

In announcing the arrest tonight the War Department said:

"The War Department authorizes the announcement that a young officer is held in arrest because he divulged to a relative the name of the vessel upon which he was about to start overseas and the schedule date of departure. As a result of this prohibited information, the relative of the young officer, a First Lieutenant, sent a telegram to him at the port of embarkation. This telegram, which was not in cipher, furnished information which, in the hands of the enemy, might have endangered the vessel and all aboard.

"The disclosure of such information by officers and men about to sail is strictly forbidden in General Orders No. 94, War Department, 1917, and warning is again issued that officers and men must not acquaint relatives or friends with details of arrangement for departure. Disciplinary action faces offenders.

"The case of the young officer in arrest in this instance is before the War Department for action, following an investigation at the port of embarkation.

"There is also to be further inquiry to ascertain whether the immediate superior of the officer held in arrest properly instructed this officer as to the requirement of secrecy concerning the names of vessels and sailing dates."

CAPITAL EXPECTED TRANSPORT ATTACK

Secretary Baker Had Information of German Plans on Jan. 27.

NOT LOOKED FOR SO SOON

Decoration of Commander Who Made Voyage to Cape Verde Island Recalled with Interest.

It was announced at Washington on Jan. 27 by Secretary of War Baker that the War Department had information of German plans for carrying on a more intense submarine warfare against American transports. In his official resume for last week Secretary Baker said:

"During the last fortnight enemy submarines have been recalled to home ports to be refitted, and the most powerful submarine offensive hitherto undertaken may be expected to be launched against our lines of communication with France, to interrupt the steady flow of men and munitions for our own armies and food supplies for the Allies.

"During the period under review renewed activity along the entire western front is noted. The region bordering the North Sea has once again become the scene of severe fighting."

The belief that Germany was going to undertake a more vigorous submarine war against American transports was widely held in Washington on information which had been received from Europe. A dispatch to THE NEW YORK TIMES from Washington on Jan. 27 said:

"There are naval officers in Washington who would not be surprised to find Germany this Spring ready to launch new and more powerful attacks against transatlantic routes."

Honor for U-Boat Commander.

Unofficial information came from Amsterdam on Jan. 7 that the German Emperor has conferred the order Pour le Merite on Commander Kophamel on his return from a cruise in a large German submarine to the Cape Verde Islands.

On Jan. 8 a German wireless statement was received in London, saying that Germany had established a new and broader submarine barred zone. It was then announced that the original submarine barred zone had been extended to include the Cape Verde Islands, the Island of Madeira, and part of French Senegal around Dakar. It was an-

Continued on Page Two.

SHIP WAS UNDER CONVOY

Anchor Liner Was in Use as an American Transport.

GOES DOWN IN WAR ZONE

War Department Announces Disaster, but Has No Names of the Saved.

NO BIG UNIT WAS ABOARD

Troops Included Scattering Detachments from All Parts of the Country.

Special to The New York Times.

WASHINGTON, Thursday, Feb. 7.—The British steamship Tuscania of the Anchor Line, under charter to the Cunard Line, serving as a transport for American troops, mostly National Guardsmen from Michigan and Wisconsin, has been torpedoed and sunk off the coast of Ireland with loss of life. How many American soldiers went to their deaths through this disaster, the first involving the sinking of a ship carrying American troops to France, is not known. At 1 o'clock this morning the official reports to the War Department and the State Department placed the number of missing at more than 200 out of a total of American troops on board of nearly 2,200. A list of the organizations on the ship appears in another column.

The survivors were landed on the north coast of Ireland at Buncranna, a point about ten miles north of Londonderry, and at Larne, about fifteen miles north of Belfast.

The War Department bulletin issued by the Committee on Public Information at 10.40 last night, was as follows:

The War Department has official advices of the sinking of the steamship Tuscania. The vessel was torpedoed and sunk, and survivors to the number of 1,100, so far as can be ascertained, have landed at Buncrana and Larne, Ireland. There was a total of 2,179 United States troops on this vessel. No names have been reported to the War Department, and no names of persons surviving have been reported. Additional particulars are promised as soon as received.

At 12:05 this morning the State Department issued the following more reassuring statement:

The latest advice received by the State Department from the Embassy at London in regard to the transport Tuscania is that at 11 P. M. Feb. 6, the latest information was that 1,912 officers and men on the Tuscania had been accounted for out of 2,173.

Taking the War Department figures of 2,179 soldiers on board, those lost number 267. Taking the State Department figures of 2,173 on board, the lost number 261.

It was 10:40 o'clock last night when the Committee on Public Information, in behalf of the War Department, made the announcement that the Tuscania, with 2,179 American soldiers on board, had been torpedoed and sunk. While the dispatch to the War Department did not say so, it was taken for granted that the sinking was done by a German submarine.

President Was at the Theatre.

President Wilson was at Keith's Theatre, enjoying the vaudeville performance at the time of the announcement. With him were Mrs. Wilson and her brother and sister-in-law, Mr. and Mrs. Joseph Bolling. The President did not reach the White House from the theatre, a block away, until 11:40 o'clock, and it was said that he received his first intimation of the disaster when he arrived there. Extra newspapers announcing the loss of the transport had just been issued, but the President did not hear the cry of the newsboys in his short journey in a motor car to the White House. Even the Secret Service men who were with the President at the theatre did not learn of the disaster until after they had seen the President safely within the White House doors.

Gives Names of Units.

After hours of consultation the War Department early this morning decided to make known to the press the identity of the military units on board the Tuscania. Prior to that time Secretary Baker had declined to give this information, being advised to withhold it b... Major Gen.

"All the News That's Fit to Print."

The New York Times.

THE WEATHER
Fair, warmer today; tomorrow fair, somewhat colder; westerly winds.
For full weather report see Page 21.

VOL. LXVII...NO. 21,962. NEW YORK, TUESDAY, MARCH 12, 1918.—TWENTY-TWO PAGES. TWO CENTS In Greater New York and Within Commuting Distance. | THREE CENTS Elsewhere.

WILSON PLEDGES OUR AID TO RUSSIA; EXPRESSES SYMPATHY, AND HOPES SHE MAY BE FREED OF GERMAN POWER

AMERICAN TROOPS, TAKING OFFENSIVE, MAKE 3 BIG RAIDS

Sweep Over Foe's First Line in Lorraine and Reach Second, 600 Yards Back.

GUNS CO-OPERATE FINELY

Germans Flee Before Shells, So Prisoners Are Few—French Aid in Two Operations.

SECRETARY BAKER IN PARIS

Met by Pershing, with Whom He Plans Conferences—Washington Expects Speedy Results.

WITH THE AMERICAN ARMY IN FRANCE, March 10, (Associated Press.)—American troops on the Lorraine sector carried out three raids last night and this morning. They swept past the German first line and penetrated to the enemy's second line, 600 yards back.

Two of the raids, made in co-operation with the French, were started simultaneously, one northwest and one northeast of —— (deleted,) after intense artillery preparation, lasting four hours, in which the German positions were leveled.

The two forces, each one of —— (deleted,) with small French forces on their flanks, moved upon the German objectives at midnight behind a creeping barrage, each on a front of 600 yards. When the Americans reached the German first lines the barrage was lifted so as to box in the enemy positions at both points.

The men dropped into the trenches, expecting a hand-to-hand fight, but found that the Germans had fled. Continuing the advance, they went forward 600 yards to the second German line. All the time American machine guns were firing on each flank of the two parties to prevent the enemy from undertaking flanking operations.

One French flanking party found two wounded Germans in a dugout and took them prisoner. The Americans found none.

The Americans remained forty-five minutes in the enemy's lines. They found excellent concrete dugouts, which they blew up, and brought back large quantities of material and valuable papers.

While they were in the German lines the enemy artillery began a vigorous counterbarrage, but it was quickly silenced by American heavy and light artillery, which hurled large quantities of gas shells on the batteries.

An American trench mortar battery, the homes of most of whose men are —— (deleted) participated in the artillery preparation preceding the raid, helping to level the enemy positions. The artillery, both light and heavy, was manned by soldiers mostly from —— (deleted).

Soon after these two raids had been completed, the Americans staged another at a point further along the line to the right. They went over the top after artillery preparation of forty-five minutes, in which the enemy's positions were obliterated for the most part.

At this place the dugouts were found to have been constructed principally of logs. Engineers accompanying the raiding party completed the artillery's work of destruction. The American infantrymen who took part in this raid are from —— (deleted) and the engineers from —— (deleted).

The raids were carried out skillfully, and but for the fact that the Germans fled more prisoners doubtless would have been taken.

The American gas shells are believed to have caused many casualties among the enemy. No Americans are unaccounted for.

A "Bold Raid," Says Paris.

PARIS, March 12.—Today's report of the War Office includes this statement: "American troops in Lorraine carried out a bold raid into the German lines."

CASUALTY LISTS MAY BE ISSUED WEEKLY

European Plan, It Is Held, Might Prove Means of Hiding Information from Enemy.

WASHINGTON, March 11.—In discussions today of the War Department's new policy of announcing names only in the casualty lists from France, it developed that the department officials were considering the adoption of the European custom of publishing casualties weekly or semi-monthly instead of daily.

This plan has been suggested on the ground that it would effectually conceal from the enemy the losses in particular engagements or series of engagements. Even if it is approved by the General Staff, however, final action on the suggestion is likely to await the return of Secretary Baker from Europe.

Lacking instructions to the contrary from President Wilson, the department will probably adhere to its decision to omit dates of deaths, designations of units, and home addresses of men from the daily lists. Major Gen. March, acting Chief of Staff, and his aids agree, it is understood, that General Pershing's judgment must be accepted on questions of this character. As the man on the ground, he is regarded as best fitted to gauge the results at the front.

As relatives of the men killed or

Continued on Page Three.

60 German Airplanes in Night Raid on Paris; Some Driven Back; Many Drop Bombs on City

LONDON, Tuesday, March 12.—German airplanes raided Paris Monday night. The first alarm was given at 9:10 o'clock, when seven squadrons of German airplanes were reported on their way to Paris. Bombs were dropped at 10:15 o'clock.

One of the raiders was brought down in flames and the crew taken prisoner.

The French official statement on the raid says that warning was given at 9:10 o'clock, and that "all clear" was sounded at midnight.

About sixty airplanes crossed the French line. Thanks to the artillery barrage which was maintained throughout the entire raid with great intensity, a certain number of machines were unable to reach their objective.

Nevertheless, the statement adds, numerous bombs were thrown on Paris and the suburbs. Several buildings were demolished or set on fire. The number of victims is not yet known.

Thirteen persons were killed and fifty wounded when German bombing airplanes raided Paris Friday night. Ten or twelve squadrons were reported to have taken part in the raid. One of the raiding machines was destroyed and its crew of four burned to death.

'DRYS' COMBINE ON RATIFICATION

All Alternative Measures Opposed as Obstructive at Senate Hearing in Albany.

"WETS" OUT IN FORCE, TOO

Committeemen Quick to Resent Allusions to Pro-German "Wet" Influence.

Special to The New York Times.

ALBANY, March 11.—"Wets" and "drys" had it out again this afternoon at a public hearing before the Senate Committee on Taxation and Retrenchment. The hearing was held on the Emerson bill for the prohibition of traffic in all intoxicants except wines and 3 per cent. beer, during the war, but the discussion covered practically the entire range of the prohibition measures now before the Legislature.

The liquor interests, aroused over the danger threatening from the present mood of the Legislature, put up a desperate fight, the last before the lawmakers act on ratification of the Federal Prohibition Amendment. In addition, spokesmen for banks and other business interests not directly related to the liquor traffic urged that immediate enactment of prohibition legislation in this State would amount to confiscation and cause upheaval and panic in the business world.

"If you are going to hurry the millennium ahead of the divine intent," said Arthur J. Westermayer, director of the National Investors' Protective League, "you should pay the incidental damages, and pay them in advance. You are more ruthless than the Prussians in Belgium in your treatment of other people's property."

"There should be no talk of compensation from the liquor interests until they have paid for the damage they have done to the public," said William H. Anderson, State Superintendent of the New York Anti-Saloon League, in hot retort.

Mr. Anderson and Mrs. Ella A. Boole, State Chairman of the Women's Christian Temperance Union, were the principal speakers for the prohibition cause. Mrs. Boole, referring to what another speaker had said about funds being supplied by German propagandists to defeat prohibition, aroused echoes of the rumors of a slush fund to beat ratification which it is said prominent advocates of that measure have set in circulation at the Capitol.

"The German money referred to by another speaker was raised by the German-American Alliance," said Mrs. Boole.

"Well, we never got a particle of it," said Elon R. Brown, President pro tem of the Senate, raising his voice to an angry pitch, but provoking only laughter. "The Germans are disposed to drink, but they have shown efficiency and an ability to fight, notwithstanding that weakness."

Rumors of "Dry" Defection.

The "wets" are anxiously awaiting the action of the Assembly tomorrow on

Continued on Page Five.

M'GOVERN OUT; TO BACK LENROOT

Quits Wisconsin Primary Race for Senator to Help Beat La Follette Man.

THINKS BERGER ELIMINATED

Indicted Socialist's Followers Will Flock to Thompson, Former Governor Says.

MILWAUKEE, Wis., March 11.—Former Governor Francis E. McGovern, candidate for the Republican nomination for United States Senator at the primary election March 19, filed late today with the Secretary of State notice of his withdrawal from the race and placed himself in the service of Congressman Irvine L. Lenroot, also a candidate for the nomination.

Mr. McGovern in a statement said his action was based on the indictment of Victor L. Berger, Socialist candidate, which "practically removes Berger from the list of candidates." Berger's followers, McGovern declared, were certain to go in a body to the support of James Thompson, the La Follette candidate, and make sure his nomination on the Republican ticket "should both Lenroot and I remain in the field to divide the patriotic vote of the party." The statement concludes:

"In the public interest, therefore, and so my party may not be disgraced and discredited for years to come, as now seems inevitable unless the choice of Republicans is narrowed down to one candidate on each side of the great, vital, and transcendent issue of loyal and patriotic Americanism, I now retire in Mr. Lenroot's favor and place my services at his disposal."

Berger, who was indicted in Chicago under the Espionage act, stated tonight that he had made all arrangements to furnish bond of $15,000, but so far no formal action had been instituted by Government officials. He said the indictment would in no way influence his campaign for United States Senator.

CHICAGO, March 11.—Bonds totaling $60,000, or $15,000 each, were filed with Federal Judge Landis late today by Seymour Stedman, attorney for J. Louis Engdahl, Irwin St. John Tucker, Adolphe Berger, and William F. Kruse, four Chicago Socialists, indicted on charges of violating the Espionage act. Bonds for Victor L. Berger, editor of The Milwaukee Leader, the fifth man indicted, were to have been arranged in Milwaukee, where he lives.

TWO NAVAL AIRMEN KILLED.

Skaggs and Harvie Victims of an Airplane Accident in France.

Special to The New York Times.

WASHINGTON, March 11.—Two additional fatalities in the American naval air service in France were announced today after the Navy Department had been notified of the deaths of Andrew Donnie Skaggs and Lee Shost Harvie as the result of an airplane accident while in the naval service in France.

Skaggs, a landsman, or quartermaster, in the navy, enlisted at Dallas March 29, 1917, and his mother lives at Newburn, Tenn. Harvie, a boatswain's mate of the first class, enlisted at New York Jan. 5, 1915. A sister lives at 1,324 Ray Street, Cincinnati.

T. Hitchcock, Jr., Lafayette Flier, Missing; Wallace Winter Killed in an Air Fight

Reports received here yesterday that Wallace Winter of the Lafayette Escadrille had been killed in an air fight, and that Corporal Thomas Hitchcock, Jr., was missing, aroused much regret among friends of the two boys and of their organization. Hitchcock was particularly well known, as only a month ago he received the French War Cross with two palms, as well as a money prize from the Lafayette Escadrille Committee and a special leave in Paris, as a reward for his bringing down two German airplanes in the same day. He had another to his credit before that.

Corporal Hitchcock is a son of Major Thomas Hitchcock of Westbury, L. I., well known as a horseman and polo player, and now in the Aviation Service himself. His mother was Miss Louise Eustis. When America came into the war he was a student at St. Paul's School at Concord, N. H., and, being only a little more than 17 years old, was ineligible for the American air service. Consequently he went to France last June and was admitted to the French service.

On Jan. 6 he brought down a German machine at a height of 20,000 feet, and on Feb. 13 he followed up this victory by attacking two German machines in succession. The first machine fell after the pilot had been killed; the second was forced down into an airdrome, and Corporal Hitchcock, following close upon it, killed both pilot and observer before they could leave the machine.

Wallace Winter was a son of Wallace C. Winter of Chicago and 375 Park Avenue, New York. He was a student at the Sheffield Scientific School in the class of 1918, and was a well-known football and golf player. He belonged to the Onwentsia and Lake Forest Clubs. When America declared war he was a member of the Naval Reserve at Southampton, and though he wanted to join the Lafayette Escadrille and had an application indorsed by Thomas Cochran, H. M. Farnum, and Lieutenant Raymond Noyes, who was one of the first American military aviators to go to France, he did not wish to leave the Naval Reserve unless he were sure of getting into the flying service. Five days' leave was required to give him a chance to pass the entrance tests, and he won this himself by personal appeal to Rear Admiral Nathaniel R. Usher, commandant of the Brooklyn Navy Yard and chief of the naval district which included the Southampton station. Admiral Usher gave him leave to try the tests, and, after his passage, recommended him for honorable discharge so that he might enroll in the Lafayette Escadrille.

AIKEN, S. C., March 11.—Thomas Hitchcock, Jr., of Aiken and Westbury, L. I., who enlisted in the French Aviation Service last June, has been captured by a German airman, according to unconfirmed information received here by the young man's father, Major Thomas Hitchcock. Major Hitchcock did not reveal the source of his information.

VOTE TO ROOT OUT FINANCIAL POWER OF GERMANY HERE

Senators Are Unanimous for Drastic Program in Seizure and Sale of Investments.

MAY NEVER BE RETURNED

Treaty of 1799 Is Held to be No Bar to the Action Now Contemplated.

SALE OF PIERS AUTHORIZED

Taking Over German Terminals at Hoboken Is Agreed to Without Debate.

Special to The New York Times.

WASHINGTON, March 11.—German financial influence in American affairs received a heavy blow in the Senate today when the amendment to the Urgent Deficiency bill, advocated by A. Mitchell Palmer, Alien Property Custodian, giving authority to seize and dispose of all German owned or controlled property in the United States, was adopted by a vote of 64 to 0. Just before that the Senate unanimously adopted without debate the amendment to the Trading with the Enemy act giving the President authority to take over and sell the Hamburg-American and North German Lloyd piers at Hoboken.

The passage of these two amendments—particularly that broadly affecting all German-owned property—was interpreted by Senators, in a two hours' debate, as aimed at exterminating every vestige of Prussian influence in American industrial life during the war. In its sweeping scope the amendment to the Urgent Deficiency bill was explained as giving power to the President to take over and sell all property in America that enables Germany to maintain an industrial foothold here. This German influence, it was pointed out, is directly wielded from Berlin through the widespread Junker interests in this country.

The Senate, before passing the amendment to the Urgent Deficiency bill, adopted a proviso put in by Senator Frelinghuysen of New Jersey that all sales of German property by the Government be made by public auction. This Senator Frelinghuysen advocated as a means of protecting minority stockholders in corporations whose plants might be taken over.

Affects a Billion Valuation.

Under the Senate action, if upheld by the House, the Alien Property Custodian would be empowered to seize all German-owned factories and other properties throughout the country, running considerably over $1,000,000,000 in value. These embrace munitions plants, factories in which clothing equipment for the United States forces is being made, breweries, and a great number of other industries. All of these, the amendment contemplates, could either be operated by the Government, through agents, or sold outright.

In the debate Senators Martin of Virginia, Underwood of Alabama, Poindexter of Washington, and others on both sides of the Chamber vehemently urged immediate action to enable the Government to wipe out Germanism from American commercial and industrial life. Senators Knox of Pennsylvania and Dillingham of Vermont raised the question of the right of the Government, under the treaty with Prussia of 1799, to seize the property of Germans. They merely wanted to make sure, they said, that no existing treaty was violated.

Senator Underwood, in reply, made the point that Germany had violated the treaty of 1799 by firing upon merchantmen flying the American flag. Germany's policy, he said, had been to seize all the property it could, regardless of international treaty obligations, and he urged that the United States was not in any sense bound by treaty in handling German property in this country.

"I'd rather fire one shot at the Junker clique in Berlin than a round of ammunition on the front that our American soldiers have taken over," said the Alabama Senator. "Let us down this Kaiser-governed Junker régime in Berlin and we'll deliver a staggering blow to Prussianism."

In offering the amendment to the Urgent Deficiency bill Senator Martin, as Chairman of the Appropriations Committee, told of Mr. Palmer advocating that legislation as necessary to put an end to German influence in American industries.

Wants Right to Sell Plants.

Senator Dillingham wanted to know how this amendment differed from the existing law under which the Alien Property Custodian has been taking over German property within the last few months.

"Under the present law the Custodian of Alien Enemy Property takes such property into his custody, but he has no right to sell it," replied Senator Martin. "The Custodian, appearing before the Senate committee, stated that he was conducting a great business in our country and in our island possessions with German property that he had taken over. He thought he ought not to be conducting this large business for the profit, possibly, of our enemies of the German Empire."

The Virginia Senator enumerated some of the industries which, he said, Mr. Palmer had alluded to as being owned or controlled by Germans in this country. Among them, besides munitions and clothing factories, were a huge chocolate factory in Connecticut.

Continued on Page Four.

CHINA TO ACT WITH JAPAN

Answers Favorably Inquiry by Tokio as to Her Intentions.

WILL SEEK AMERICAN LOAN

Two Army Divisions Going to Northern Manchuria to Safeguard Allied Interests.

CHINA ALREADY HAS ACTED

Her Troops Drove Bolsheviki from Harbin—Has Common Treaty Interests with Japan.

PEKING, March 11, (Associated Press.)—China, in response to an inquiry from Tokio, has signified her intention to co-operate with Japan in the protection of allied interests in the Far East.

The Chinese War Bureau has been requested to arrange for the sending of two divisions to Northern Manchuria. Japan will bear the expense pending the completion of a proposed American loan to China.

Even before the presence of ex-Premier Prince G. E. Lvoff was announced in Peking it was believed that he was somewhere in the Far East manoeuvring to out-general the Bolsheviki—if not to create a counter-revolution in Siberia, then, at least, to facilitate the protection of the American and Japanese supplies stored at Vladivostok, Harbin, and other places as far west as Irkutsk, where they had been left by the pro-German Minister of Transportation in the Fall of 1916. It was natural, too, that Lvoff should seek Chinese aid, for the Trans-Siberian Railway on its way westward to Irkutsk runs for 1,000 miles through Manchurian territory, which is Chinese. Moreover, since Aug. 14, 1917, China has been at war with Germany, and the embassies of the Allies have been the guiding influence at Peking.

Thus, as early as Jan. 26 officials at Harbin, Manchuria, closed the Trans-Siberian, and early in February Japan, as the first installment of arms promised Peking, shipped to Northern China a consignment of 648 machine guns, 324 field pieces, 50,000 rifles, and 5,000,000 rounds of ammunition. In early February, too, several hundred Chinese engineers went north into Manchuria.

Early in the present month came the news that the Bolsheviki were arming German and Austrian ex-prisoners along the Trans-Siberian Railway, between Irkutsk and the Manchurian frontier, and that for this reason Peking had found it necessary to increase the Manchurian garrisons. On the railway west of Irkutsk, General Semenoff, with his Cossacks, assembled in order to prevent the movement of the armed prisoners westward. Finally, on March 5, the Peking Government decided to send 20,000 Manchuli into Siberia itself to co-operate with Japan if the latter should deem it necessary to invade the country.

Meanwhile the first blood had been shed between the Bolsheviki and the Chinese. When the Chinese commander at Harbin closed the railway on Jan. 23 he was opposed by the Bolshevist Commissioner of Transportation and shot him.

The Bolshevist Government, like the Russian Imperial Government before it, claims the right of way over the Trans-Siberian in Manchuria on account of the treaty of Portsmouth of 1905; but by a subsequent treaty four months later China recognized Japan's right over the southern branches of the Trans-Siberian, and in 1912 a joint Japanese and Chinese enterprise began to extend these branches. It was Russia's penetration of Manchuria which was one of the chief causes of the Russo-Japanese war.

Aside from the Trans-Siberian and Manchurian railways the only way of communication between Irkutsk and Vladivostok is the Amoor River, which bounds Manchuria on the north. But this is not navigable until May.

Thus Manchuria, a dependency of China, of 363,610 square miles area and a population of 20,000,000, in which both Russia and Japan have certain commercial rights, but whose military administration is in the hands of the Chinese, forms a wedge between Southern Siberia and the Pacific Coast, penetrating as far north as the Amoor River, beyond which there are no lines of transportation.

RED GUARDS INVADE PERSIA.

Small Force of Russians Said to Plan Advance on Teheran.

WASHINGTON, March 11.—Invasion of Persia by small detachments of the Russian Red Guard was indicated to the State Department today in a telegram from Teheran.

According to the report there the force, which is not more than 400, is said to be planning an advance on Teheran.

Disbelief of a report that Ambassador Francis and the Japanese Ambassador are being detained at Vologda was expressed by State Department officials, although the last report from Mr. Francis was on March 6.

Text of President Wilson's Message of Sympathy to All-Russian Congress of Soviets at Moscow

WASHINGTON, March 11.—Following is the text of the message addressed to the people of Russia through the All-Russian Congress of Soviets which meets in Moscow tomorrow to indorse or reject the treaty made with the Central Powers by the Russian delegates to the recent peace conference at Brest-Litovsk:

May I not take advantage of the meeting of the Congress of the Soviets to express the sincere sympathy which the people of the United States feel for the Russian people at this moment when the German power has been thrust in to interrupt and turn back the whole struggle for freedom and substitute the wishes of Germany for the purpose of the people of Russia?

Although the Government of the United States is, unhappily, not now in a position to render the direct and effective aid it would wish to render, I beg to assure the people of Russia through the congress that it will avail itself of every opportunity to secure for Russia once more complete sovereignty and independence in her own affairs and full restoration to her great role in the life of Europe and the modern world.

The whole heart of the people of the United States is with the people of Russia in the attempt to free themselves forever from autocratic government and become the masters of their own life.

(Signed) WOODROW WILSON.

The message was telegraphed to the American Consul General at Moscow for delivery to the congress.

BOLSHEVIKI FEAR LVOFF'S REVOLT

Report That He Will Accompany Japanese Army Causes Talk of War.

LENINE DISMISSED TROTZKY

His Elimination Said to Have Followed Quarrel Over Treaty—Radek Denounces Terms.

Special Cable to THE NEW YORK TIMES.

PETROGRAD, March 9, (Delayed.)—A sensational dispatch has been received at the Smolny Institute from Irkutsk stating that Prince Lvoff, ex-President of the Council of Ministers of the Revolutionary Government, is in Peking, where he has constituted a new Russian Government and is awaiting the landing of a Japanese army at Vladivostok. This force, it is said, he will accompany in its invasion of Siberian territory.

Telegraphic communication between Vladivostok and Irkutsk is interrupted. Every effort is being made by the Government to arouse Siberia to resist the threatened invasion. The Bolshevist organ Pravda attaches great importance to the news, saying it means war with Japan, but Izvestia and other newspapers treat the dispatch as an ordinary item of news. In an editorial the Pravda says:

"The peace treaty between Rumania and the Central Powers stipulates that Rumania shall lend her assistance to transporting Teutonic troops to Odessa. Russia's former allies, it appears, have similar plans, and are agreed apparently on Japanese intervention—all except America, which is trying to modify the allies' policy of vengeance."

On some sectors of the northern front hostilities still continue, I hear.

The Bolshevist convention has adopted by thirty votes to twelve a resolution in favor of ratifying the treaty with the Central Powers. Trotzky, whose resignation as Minister of Foreign Affairs is confirmed by the Bolshevist organ the Communist, edited by Radek, will, it is understood, retain office until the meeting of the Moscow Congress of Soviets fixed for the 12th inst.

The Bolshevist party convention opened here Wednesday, but few delegates attended, owing to the disorganization of railway traffic. Lenine on the following day made an important speech stating that the Russian revolution had to collide with German Imperialism. It was useless, he said, to flourish a cardboard sword before Hindenburg, and without a respite Russia could not provide a new army. He would therefore sign any treaty which would enable them to prepare for a new struggle, and in this connection the reorganization of the railroads and reorganization of food supplies would be essential. A provisional peace now would facilitate the evacuation of Petrograd and save war material indispensable to the future struggle.

Arguments on the other side are set forth in Radek's article in the Communist, under the heading, "No Ratification of the Peace Treaty." Radek at the outset refers to the harsh economic conditions which have been forced by the Germans upon Russia and to the concessions made to the Ukrainian Rada for the sake of arriving at a perfidious peace with that authority.

Continued on Page Two.

KAISER IS ALSO AMONG PROFITEERS

Krupps, in Which His Holdings Are Great, Conceals Books from the Reichstag.

WIDE SCANDALS DISCLOSED

Daimler Company Makes $2,500 on a Single Motor, Sub-Committee Reports.

By GEORGE RENWICK.

Copyright, 1918, by The New York Times Company.

Special Cable to THE NEW YORK TIMES.

AMSTERDAM, March 11.—The reputation of Germany as a land of enviable organization receives many sharp knocks these days. Numerous cases of shameless profiteering are being tried throughout the country, and in the main committee of the Reichstag on Friday a scandal of vast proportions involving the famous Daimler Motor Company, which has just been placed under military supervision, was discussed and exposed.

Not long ago a Parliamentary subcommittee was appointed to inquire into the forcing up of prices, particularly in the automobile industry. Herr Lejsching, in presenting the report of the committee of inquiry to the main committee, unveiled the colossal profiteering of the Daimler Company. He said that a motor car which cost £250 in America cost £600 in Germany. At the head of this profiteering stood the Daimler Company.

He alleged that a Director had caused the books to be falsified in order to deceive the commission of inquiry. Higher wages, for instance, were said to have been paid than was actually the case.

The company now demanded a 50 per cent. rise in prices and threatened to stop night work were the increase not agreed to by the Government. That, said the speaker, was a strike threat.

Big Firms Conceal Profits.

Many big firms, he went on, refused to show their books to the Government officials.

In the sale of its particular motors, the speaker declared, the company had a monopoly, and for a motor which cost £250 to make it charged now £750 and threatened a strike if it did not obtain 50 per cent. more. Therefore it was urgently necessary for the Government to inquire closely into the whole war industry, "for this is not an isolated case."

Herr Noske, Socialist, said that among the firms refusing to show their books to the Government officials were the Krupps and the General Electricity Company. All they had done was to give incorrect information regarding the cost of production. He held that the Daimler Company's threat to cease night work and thereby reduce the number of motors of which the country had need was something like treason. Military authorities showed no such patience with workers as that which had been exercised in the case of this company.

It was absurd, he added, to believe that this was the sole case, for countless firms were taking the same unscrupulous advantage of the situation and the country was being robbed of milliards of marks.

The discussion was adjourned.

The Daimler Motor Company was founded in 1890 and has its main fac-

Continued on Page Two.

MESSAGE TO SOVIET CONGRESS

Consul General at Moscow Will Deliver It to Great Meeting Today.

HELP JUST NOW IMPOSSIBLE

But President Will Lose No Chance to Promote Aim of Complete Independence.

COUNTER-BLOW AT ENEMY

Message Will Offset Attempt to Rouse Fear of Japan's Action in Siberia.

Special to The New York Times.

WASHINGTON, March 11.—President Wilson took steps today to counteract any feeling that might have been aroused in Russia against the Allies. He sent a cable message to the people of Russia through the Soviet Congress, which meets in Moscow tomorrow, expressing the sympathy of the American people toward the Russian people over the manner of their treatment by the invading Germans. While regretting the inability of the United States Government to render direct aid at this time, the President gave assurance to the Russian people that it "will avail itself of every opportunity to secure for Russia once more complete sovereignty and independence in her own affairs and full restoration to her great rôle in the life of Europe and the modern world."

Through this cordial message President Wilson serves notice to the whole world that he still regards Russia as a party to the war against Germany and a co-belligerent of the United States and the other nations engaged in the effort to put an end to German autocratic methods. At the same time he brings to the minds of the Russian people that the allied purpose is remote from any desire to make a conquest of Russian territory.

Although no interpretation of the President's reasons for sending this message is offered in any authoritative quarter, it is obvious that it was the outcome, in part, at least, of a desire to counteract as far as possible the attempt to make it appear that the Japanese proposal to place armed forces in Siberia meant dismemberment of Russian territory at the hands of Japan. The representations made in response to Japan's invitation for a statement of the American view showed that the President was fearful that the presence of Japanese soldiers on Russian soil would lead to anti-Ally feeling among the Russian people. There has been evidence that the attempt to arouse this feeling is being made. Officials in Washington do not doubt that German agents in Russia will spread the report that Japan contemplates seizing Siberian territory and retaining it permanently.

President's Consistent Policy.

From the very beginning of the Russian collapse President Wilson has been insistent that it should be kept plainly before the Russian people that the United States Government was in sympathy with their democratic aims, and did not intend to permit the condition of chaos in which the country found itself to sway the firm friendship of America for Russia. He has voiced this policy before Congress, and to an extent consistent with the circumstances has emphasized it in the American communication to Japan concerning the suggestion of Japanese intervention in Siberia. He has taken occasion to show his lack of sympathy with the declaration of Mr. Lloyd George, the British Prime Minister, indicating that Great Britain expected nothing more from Russia. In these and other ways the President has made it manifest that the United States still has faith in the ability of Russia to "come back."

Today's message is the most pronounced example of the President's attitude toward demoralized and shattered Russia. In a measure it is a more important declaration than the "conversational" note to Japan in response to the invitation for a statement of American views as to the suggestion that Japanese troops should take possession of Eastern Siberia, for it is a public declaration delivered at a time when Russia is agitated over Japan's contemplated action.

It is quite evident to observers that the President wishes to keep before the world in the strongest possible light that he holds consistently to his view that nothing should be done by the allied powers that would seem to be at variance with the purposes of the Russian revolutionaries to gain complete freedom for themselves and recognition of their right of self-determination within the limits of what was once the Russian Empire.

His message to the Congress of the Soviets calls to mind that the danger in Russia results from the German invasion, which suggests that the people of Russia should concentrate their energies against the Teutonic conquerors and not against the Japanese. The President also promises that the United States Government will stand by the Russian people with the purpose of obtaining for

"All the News That's Fit to Print."

The New York Times.

THE WEATHER
Fair today; Sunday fair, warmer; northwest winds, becoming variable.
For full weather report see Page 21.

VOL. LXVII...NO. 21,966. ... NEW YORK, SATURDAY, MARCH 16, 1918.—TWENTY-TWO PAGES. TWO CENTS In Greater New York and Within Commuting Distance. | THREE CENTS Elsewhere.

ARMY GRATIFIED BY BAKER'S COMING; PROUD OF DEEDS

Eagerly Awaits Secretary's Inspection and Hopes for Cure of Small Deficiencies.

MAIL DELAY IS FOREMOST

Faster Service Needed, Officers Say, to Insure Maintenance of Morale.

SPRING SUN RENEWS VIGOR

Fighting Front and Training Camps See Increasing Zest Put Into All Work.

WITH THE AMERICAN ARMY IN FRANCE, March 12, (Associated Press.)—The troops on the front and in the training areas are on the tiptoe of expectation for the arrival of Secretary of War Baker, whose presence in France was announced in the Paris newspapers this morning and took the whole army by surprise.

Word of the Secretary's presence in France was spread rapidly by telephone from the bases to the furthermost outposts. Officers in villages at outlying points stopped the newspaper motors and asked for definite word when Mr. Baker would arrive. "The old man will find us ready to pass inspection," it was remarked.

In army circles there is general gratification over the coming of Mr. Baker in order that he may see close at hand what has been accomplished thus far in the face of the obstacles and the difficulties of distance, and especially may note the moral and physical condition of the troops, so that he may carry home a personal knowledge of easily remedied deficiencies and complaints.

The most serious of the deficiencies and complaints concern the mail service. Everywhere the rank and file complain of the absence or great delay in mail from home. Company officers generally say that the mail problem is one of the most serious they have to contend with because the men become lonely and anxious in the absence of word from their families. The ordinary mails are one month to six weeks ahead of the army mails, and the officers express the belief that there would be no better factor for the happiness of the men than the most expeditious mail service that it is possible to devise, even a faster service than through the ordinary civilian channels.

New Activity Comes With Sunshine.

After weeks of rain, snow, wind, and murky weather there came to the American front today its first bath of genial Spring sunshine. The skies were cloudless, and in the moderate temperature that prevailed sweaters were discarded by the men for the first time since last Summer while in the villages and cantonments.

In the training area the camps were decorated with rolls of bedding that were having an airing, while men and horses basked in the sunshine in the streets and on the hillsides—a grateful experience after the damp chill of Winter.

Everywhere one could see tent flaps and hut windows open and hospital patients breathing the Spring air. Meanwhile the transport work was being expedited by the rapidly drying roads.

In the training areas the fullest advantage was taken of the open weather, the officers crowding the men to willingly renewed efforts to make them fit for front-line service.

Under the sunshine and the still atmosphere airdromes all along the line sprouted flocks of planes, both on trial and on serious missions, and everywhere there was expectant readiness for an enemy offensive if it should develop.

Say Relatives Send Too Many Parcels.

WASHINGTON, March 15.—Unnecessary articles sent by relatives and friends to American soldiers overseas are taking up so much space, both in ships and on the congested French railroads, that drastic curtailment of the parcel post privilege to fighters in France will be necessary unless the public co-operates in decreasing the volume of this class of mail.

The Post Office Department, in making this statement tonight, said that a transport, reaching France this month, carried besides 715,980 letters, 335,840 pieces of parcel post and newspapers, the whole taking up 12,000 cubic feet of space, although weighing only 121¼ tons. The parcel post packages and newspapers filled nineteen French railroad cars. As cars are badly needed in France for war purposes, mail frequently has to wait at French ports for several days before means of transportation is available.

A twelve hours' inspection of the contents of parcel post packages for the soldiers, the statement said, showed that two-thirds of the articles were on General Pershing's canteen list and were sold to the soldiers at practically wholesale prices. Other articles found included a bouquet of flowers and a baby outfit, as well as a bottle of whisky as well as other unmailable matters, such as matches and cigar lighters.

"The question will have to be answered by the relatives of the soldiers," said the department's statement, "or it will of military necessity be answered drastically by the authorities in France charged with the responsibility for the success of the war."

The Postmaster General was requested, in a resolution adopted by the House today, to furnish information as

Continued on Page Two.

Demand on Finland for Release of American Seized by Germans and Taken to Dantzig

STOCKHOLM, March 15.—An Attaché of the American Legation left today for Finland carrying a formal protest from Minister Morris to General Mannerheim, Commander of the Government forces, against the arrest by Germans on the Aland Islands of Henry Crosby Emery. Demand is made that the Finnish Government obtain the release of Mr. Emery.

The American Attaché was accompanied by a member of the British Legation conveying a similar protest and demand regarding the arrest of sixteen Britishers in the same party with Mr. Emery, all of whom were taken aboard a German steamer and taken to Dantzig, Germany.

Minister Morris did not wait for instructions from Washington, but called a conference of Entente Ministers, which decided to take the matter straight to General Mannerheim, who will have a chance to show whether Finland is an independent State or a vassal of Germany.

Henry C. Emery, who was formerly Chairman of the United States Tariff Board by appointment of President Taft, and for nine years professor of political economy at Yale, sailed from New York in September, 1916, for Petrograd to represent the Guaranty Trust Company of this city in some special work in preparation for extension of American interests in Russia. He expected to visit all parts of the Empire.

7 MONTHS' SAVING OF DAYLIGHT VOTED

House Amends Bill to Extend Period for Setting Clocks Ahead an Hour.

SENATE TO ACCEPT CHANGE

New Time Will Begin at 2 A. M. Last Sunday in March—Economies Expected.

Special to The New York Times.

WASHINGTON, March 15.—The Daylight-Saving bill went through the last legislative stage when it passed the House today by a vote of 252 to 40. It is estimated by experts for the Government that millions of dollars will be saved in fuel in the seven months during which the standard time shall be advanced one hour. It would not be necessary, speakers said in the House today, to have lights burning in factories and places of employment during the period of the advanced time from March to October, and this would effect a large saving in coal used for illuminating purposes.

The bill provides that at 2 A. M. of the last Sunday of March of each year the standard time in each of the five zones in the United States shall be advanced one hour, and at 2 A. M. of the last Sunday in October the standard time of each zone shall be set back an hour.' The effect of this is to start and close all business activities an hour earlier than at present. This will give opportunity for recreation and outdoor work and activities long before sunset after the close of business.

While the strong argument advanced for the step was the saving of fuel consumed for illuminating purposes, agricultural experts and conservationists asserted that men employed in offices and factories would have plenty of time, through the earlier closing of places of employment, to work their gardens and thereby contribute to the food supply of the nation. The bill as it passed the Senate provided that daylight saving should start on the last Sunday of April and end on the last Sunday of September, a period of five months. On representations from Dr. Garfield and Mr. Hoover, who presented the saving of fuel and the conservation ideas, the House extended the time to seven months.

Senate Will Concur.

There will be no opposition in the Senate to the acceptance of the House's amendment. The bill will be concurred in by the Senate and go to the President next week, so that the plan can be carried into effect on March 31 next. The measure passed today reads:

"AN ACT

"*To Save Daylight and to Provide Standard Time for the United States:*

"Be it enacted by the Senate and House of Representatives of the United States of America in Congress assembled that, for the purpose of establishing the standard time of the United States, the territory of Continental United States shall be divided into five zones in the manner hereinafter provided. The standard time of the first zone shall be based on the mean astronomical time of the seventy-fifth degree of longitude west from Greenwich; that of the second zone on the ninetieth degree; that of the third zone on the 105th degree; that of the fourth zone on the 120th degree, and that of the fifth zone, which shall include only Alaska, on the 150th degree. That the limits of each zone shall be defined by an order of the Interstate Commerce Commission, having regard for the convenience of commerce and the existing junction points and division points of common carriers engaged in commerce between the several States and with foreign nations, and such order may be modified from time to time.

"SECTION 2. That within the respective zones created under the authority hereof the standard time of the zone shall govern the movement of all common carriers engaged in commerce between the several States or between a State and any of the territories of the United States or between a State or the territory of Alaska and any of the insular possessions of the United States or any foreign country. In all statutes, orders, rules, and regulations relating to the time of performance of any act by any officer or department of the United States, whether in the legislative, executive, or judicial branches of the Government, or relating to the time within which any rights shall accrue or determine, or within which any act shall or shall not be performed by any person subject to the jurisdiction of the United States, it shall be understood and intended that the time shall be the United States standard time of the zone within which the act is to be performed.

"SECTION 3. That at 2 o'clock antemeridian of the last Sunday in March of each year the standard time of each

Continued on Page Four.

TWO NEW SHIPS A DAY BY MAY

President Believes Year's Output Will Be Three to Four Million Tons.

AWAIT TEST OF CONCRETE

Wilson and Hurley Both Eager for a Report on Hull Just Finished in West.

WASHINGTON, March 15.—President Wilson today discussed the general shipbuilding situation with Senator Fletcher of Florida, Chairman of the Senate Commerce Committee, and Senator Ransdell of Louisiana, a member of the committee. The conference was understood to be the first of a series which the President plans to hold with members of the committee, which has been investigating the shipping situation for many weeks.

After listening to the results of the Senate committee's inquiry the President was said to have expressed satisfaction with the outlook at the present time and agreed with Senator Fletcher, that the nation should produce from 3,000,000 to 4,000,000 tons of shipping of all kinds this year. Mr. Wilson was understood to have expressed particular interest in the reinforced concrete ship launched yesterday on the Pacific coast and to desire that the vessel receive a thorough trial because of the short time in which this class of craft can be turned out.

Senator Fletcher told the President that a ship a day was being launched now, and that all indications pointed to two launchings a day by May. Some shipyards were handicapped, the Senator said, by slow movement of steel on the railroads, and the President promised to inquire into the advisability of greater priority in the movement of this material.

Chairman Hurley of the Shipping Board telegraphed the builders of the 5,000-ton concrete vessel which was launched successfully on the Pacific Coast yesterday, to report immediately what were the prospects for laying down additional hulls and what time would be required. An early test of the new ship was requested to settle remaining questions as to her strength and behavior in a heavy sea. A report on the launching said that the belief had been strengthened that concrete construction could be depended upon.

An important question remaining to be decided before concrete ships will be approved by Government officials, is what will be the effect of salt on concrete and on the iron reinforcing.

Four concrete ships of 3,500 tons each have been authorized by the Shipping Board as an experiment, and designs for them are being completed. One will be built at Brunswick, Ga.; one at San Francisco, and the others at yards to be selected later. If the 5,000-ton vessel, which was constructed for private owners, proves successful, the smaller size will be abandoned in the future by the Shipping Board and perhaps even a 7,500-ton craft constructed.

20,000 CASUALTIES IN TURKESTAN BATTLES

Adherents of Bolsheviki Waging War on Natives—Fighting in Ukraine.

LONDON, March 15.—Fierce battles between Soviet adherents and natives have occurred in Turkestan, according to an Exchange Telegraph dispatch from Petrograd under Wednesday's date. More than 20,000 casualties are reported to have resulted.

BERLIN, March 15, (British Admiralty Per Wireless Press.)—Military operations are continuing in Ukraine, where the town of Bachmach, about 100 miles northeast of Kiev, has been occupied, the War Office announces. The statement follows:

Enemy bands in Ukraine which threatened the railways from Gomel and Kieve to Bachmach were dispersed in several engagements. Bachmach was occupied.

Elsewhere there is nothing to report.

HERTLING RENEWS PLEDGE.

Will "Stand or Fall" with the Prussian Franchise Bill.

AMSTERDAM, March 15.—"I stand or fall with the bill for the equal franchise. I have pledged my word, and never in my life have I broken it."

Thus Count von Hertling, the Imperial German Chancellor, is quoted by a correspondent in Berlin as having replied to a question regarding the Chancellor's intentions in the event of the Prussian franchise bill being rejected.

JAMES STILLMAN, HEAD OF CITY BANK, DIES SUDDENLY

In Ill-Health for a Month, but His Condition Was Not Regarded as Alarming.

ACTIVE UP TO LAST WEEK

His Efforts Resulted in the National City Becoming the Most Powerful Bank in America.

BACKED BY ROCKEFELLERS

Banker's Wealth Estimated at $100,000,000—Gave Great Aid to French War Sufferers.

James Stillman, Chairman of the Board of Directors of the National City Bank, the Presidency of which he resigned in 1908, when he was succeeded by Frank A. Vanderlip, died suddenly yesterday afternoon at 5:30 o'clock at his home, 9 East Seventy-second Street. Mr. Stillman had not been in good health for a month, and during the last week he had been confined to his room.

At the Stillman home it was said last night that Mr. Stillman died suddenly of heart failure and that the family did not care to make public any further information as to the circumstances of his death at the time. No information as to the funeral arrangements could be had. Mr. Stillman was in his sixty-eighth year.

Urged Retirement of Financiers.

Before his retirement from the Presidency of the National City Bank in 1908, Mr. Stillman was reported to have suggested to the late E. H. Harriman, the late J. P. Morgan, and William Rockefeller that all four of them should wind up their financial and industrial careers and retire.

He was said to have held prolonged interviews with each of the three for the purpose of convincing them that their retirement would be a public service by putting an end to the campaign against Wall Street and the so-called "Money Trust," which campaign was, in the opinion of Mr. Stillman, undermining the confidence of the country in the financial world.

The panic of 1907 had just occurred. In every city of the country speakers from the street corners were charging that the wealth of the nation was controlled by half a dozen men, and the four men who took part in these conferences were among the conspicuous objects for this form of attack.

Mr. Stillman is said to have argued that the retirement of these four prominent leaders would show more clearly than anything else that the country was not held in the hollow of the hands of a small group of men of great wealth.

Mr. Stillman shortly after this retired voluntarily from the Presidency of the National City Bank. The three other men were not long to be active figures in big business. A little more than a year later E. H. Harriman died. J. P. Morgan gave less and less attention to finance, and was known more and more as a traveler and art collector. Because of ill-health, William Rockefeller was forced to give up the active management of most of his affairs. Mr. Stillman was in reality the last of the four to remain in harness, as he resumed an active place in finance after the war.

Mr. Stillman was one of the wealthiest men in the country, although his financial affairs were never the subject of public discussion as were those of other extremely wealthy men, and their details were known to only a very few of his closest associates. It was estimated by men familiar with the affairs of Wall Street, however, that his wealth was very probably more than $100,000,000.

Mr. Stillman was also Chairman of the Board of Directors of the American Red Cross, and advisory counsel. He had turned his Paris home into an auxiliary military hospital. In January, 1917, Mr. Stillman sent to Jules J. Jusserand, the French Ambassador at Washington, his draft for $200,000, payable to President Poincaré of France, to be used for the relief of children of members of the Legion of Honor whose fathers had lost their lives or may lose them "in the service of France."

Active to the Last.

Until his last illness Mr. Stillman was at the bank every day. Since Frank A. Vanderlip, the President of the bank, went to Washington for Government financial work, much of the business of the bank went over the desk of Mr. Stillman.

In its relation to finance Mr. Stillman's career formed an important part of the history of New York during the last generation. Few men had attained greater prominence in the financial affairs of this city. Mr. Stillman, though of Southern birth, was educated in the North. He was born in Brownsville, Texas, June 9, 1850, the son of a merchant, Charles Stillman. One of his remote ancestors, George Stillman, was born in London, England, in 1654, and while still a young man came to America and settled in Hadley, Mass.

On both his father's and the maternal side James Stillman was descended from patriots who fought in the American Revolution. His own father invested his money in the South, and it was while he was a resident of Texas that James Stillman was born. He moved to Hartford, Conn., where the son attended the public schools and later a private school in Ossining, N. Y.

Soon after he left school Mr. Stillman obtained employment in the New York cotton commission house of Smith &

Continued on Page Eleven.

MOSCOW CONGRESS RATIFIES PEACE; HAD RECEIVED PRESIDENT'S MESSAGE; WASHINGTON SPURS WAR EFFORTS

AMERICA'S TASK GRIMMER

Washington Officials Scout Rumors of an Early Peace.

NO ILLUSIONS ON GERMANY

Conquests in the East Destroy the Prospect of Teuton Concessions.

NEW SPIRIT IN WAR TASK

Co-operation with Congress a Sign of Determination to Fight to Victory.

Allies Will Make No Peace at Russia's Expense, Cecil Says

LONDON, March 15.—Replying to an inquiry as to whether there was any truth in the rumors that proposals had been received from Germany for a peace at the expense of Russia, Lord Robert Cecil, the Minister of Blockade, said in the House of Commons today:

"As far as I know, no such proposals are being considered or will be considered."

Special to The New York Times.

WASHINGTON, March 15.—In some curious way the impression has spread through the country that peace will come soon. Nobody seems able to formulate a reason for this impression, but many persons are satisfied in their own minds, judged by what is said and heard in Washington, to which opinion from all sections drifts naturally, that the end of the war is near.

An American soldier in France writes to his mother that the French are confident that hostilities will cease this year. A report comes to Washington that Wall Street knows that President Wilson is in frequent conference with certain bigwigs (unnamed) preparing the formulae for stopping the conflict. Others assert that they have this or that bit of information which points to an early peace. Most persons infected with the peace germ show their symptoms in some such expression as "I don't exactly know why, but I feel that the war won't go on much longer."

Sentiments and opinions of this character are exactly contrary to the Washington official view. A new spirit is noticeable here, a spirit of determination that carries with it the banishment of all illusions as to the task that confronts the United States and its cobelligerents.

The final collapse of Russia, the evidence that Germany is bent on conquest wherever it is possible, the knowledge that Austria-Hungary was using diplomatic camouflage in expressing sentiments that appeared to be at variance with Germany's desire to rule the world, the veiled threats of the Prussian autocracy to the Scandinavian nations, have brought to Washington a full realization that the future of democratic institutions depends upon the sword, and not on peace by understanding with Germany on the other side of the peace table.

New Motto Is "Live or Die."

"We have been going on the principle of 'Live and Let Live,'" said one of the foremost men of the Government. "From now on we are going on the principle of 'Live or Die.'"

The new spirit, or rather the forceful expression of the old spirit, is exemplified in the decision of Great Britain and the United States to commandeer Dutch ships. In this action, as in others of a similar character contemplated, the two English-speaking nations intend to live up to all the obligations of international law. But while they have satisfied themselves that the seizure is justified by international observance and precedent, including Prussia's seizure of British tonnage in the Franco-Prussian War, they contend that justification is emphasized on the moral ground that the Allies are fighting the battle of small neutral States which must stand their share of sacrifice in the struggle to aid them.

Under the new conditions that have arisen through the triumphal progress of Germany and Austria in Eastern Europe, the Washington Government feels that it is fighting more than ever for the basic principle of President Wilson's policy of protecting small States from the aggression of militaristic powers. "The League to Enforce Peace is now in operation" was the way the situation was expressed by one of those in a position to understand the President's point of view.

The Allies are banded together in the struggle to prevent Germany and her subservient partners from extending their domination over all the peoples who are unable to protect themselves. Russia, Serbia, Rumania, Montenegro, not to speak of Belgium, are feeling the effects of the conqueror's iron rule. It is realized that this condition arises out of the fortunes of war. But in the

Continued on Page Three.

Message of President Wilson to Soviets Delivered Two Days Before Congress Met

WASHINGTON, March 15.—The decision of All-Russian Congress of Soviets at Moscow to ratify the German peace terms, announced in press cables today, was reached after receipt of President Wilson's message to the Russian people assuring them that America would take the first opportunity to help them regain their complete sovereignty and independence.

A message received at the State Department today from American Consul Summers at Moscow said the President's message was delivered two days before the Soviets met.

LABOR REPUDIATES ALL TALK OF PEACE

Union Mass Meeting Roars Approval of Wilson's Plea for War Till Victory Is Won.

PLEDGED TO FULL EFFORT

British Delegates Assured by Resolution That American Unions Are Steadfast.

American labor in New York last night took a decided stand in favor of the "no peace without victory" policy enunciated by President Wilson. At a meeting of the New York Central Federated Union, in the Labor Temple, at 243 East Eighty-fourth Street, which had as its guests W. A. Appleton and Joshua Butterworth of the British Labor Mission visiting this country, a proposal to have trade unions in the United States get behind a movement to end the war by international conferences instead of fighting was howled down with a roar of protest.

"I want to tell you this," shouted Leon Rouse, delegate from "Big Six" Typographical Union, after it had been determined that American labor was not going into any conference which included Germans, "if you had adopted that proposal I would have walked out of this hall and asked my local to withdraw from this organization. The time to talk to German workers is when those fellows have done their bit to smash that autocracy which we are doing our best to down. We'll help them when they show the will and power to help themselves. I want to say, and I want you to tell England," he added, turning to the Englishmen, "that the American trade union movement throbs in unison with their British and French brothers for victory.

"If you show me a man with a thought of the failure of the allied force on the battlefield against the Kaiser, I'll show you a pro-German. You men must never forget that this is a war of determination or else it will be a war of extermination for us."

Mr. Rouse's words were applauded, and cries of "Good for you!" and "That's the way we feel!" greeted him as he walked to his seat.

British Labor Loyal.

The meeting was the weekly session of the Central Federated Union of New York, but it took on an added interest last night because of the presence of the two Britishers. Mr. Butterworth was the first speaker. He told of the experiences that the English Government had gone through trying to settle labor questions developed by the war. He told of how labor and capital had come together in an effort to solve any difficulties without embarrassing the Government. There was great applause when he said:

"In every question that has come up where the welfare of the individual organization or the man has come into opposition with the welfare of the Government in a vigorous prosecution of the war, the man and the organization have let their own interests go and have stood by the Government. Labor, for this reason, has the admiration and gratitude of the entire country."

Mr. Appleton followed Mr. Butterworth. He began with a résumé of the outbreak of hostilities, showing how Great Britain had tried to avoid the war forced on her by Germany.

He then passed on to the subject of international peace conferences.

"I have been traveling about your country for a couple of months," he said, "and many persons have asked me why we didn't make peace. They said that had British labor been willing, there could have been conferences with German labor, which would have settled the whole thing and saved millions of lives.

"I have said to those persons and I say to you that this is impossible. So far we have seen no disposition or power on the part of Germany to make peace on any terms that the world could stand. Russia is today a pitiful example of what comes of trusting Germany. You know now that all the time she was talking peace to the Russians she was preparing flying squadrons of troopers to advance on Russia whenever she got ready. She was taking, in absolute violation of her given word, strong and healthy soldiers from the eastern and transferring them to the western front. We may as well realize now that Germany is just as ready to exact the last pound of flesh today as she was in 1914, when she began her drive on Paris.

"I feel in my heart after seeing what

Continued on Page Two.

PEACE DEFEATS BOLSHEVIST AIMS

Terms Imposed by Germany Cannot Be Carried Out Under Present Regime.

ARE FATAL TO ABSOLUTISM

Yet Reds, if They Survive, May Form Nucleus of National Resistance to Enemy.

By HAROLD WILLIAMS.

Special Cable to THE NEW YORK TIMES.

PETROGRAD, March 11.—Premier Lenine and the other People's Commissaries left for Moscow last night. Petrograd is to be governed by a special committee headed by Zinoviev and nominated by the Petrograd Soviet. The work of this committee will be to maintain order and defend the approaches to Petrograd. The President of the military organization is Leon Trotzky, who had resigned his post as Commissary for Foreign Affairs, and will not attend the Moscow Congress.

The governing group is divided into a war and a peace party for immediate practical purposes.

The peace party headed by Lenine, now, obviously, has got the upper hand. Not, I imagine because any one, even among the most infatuated Bolsheviki, regards peace as tolerable or in the least degree final, but because a continuation of hostilities against the Germans at the present moment would be suicidal for the Bolshevist Government. They could not seriously fight. They would have to beat a precipitate retreat, with the certainty of being compelled ultimately to submit to a still more humiliating and destructive peace.

Lenine's Logic Convincing.

So far Lenine's logic is absolutely convincing. His argument from a contrast between the first and second Brest-Litovsk Conference is irrefutable, but then the position after peace is concluded will be hardly less difficult. Every clause of the peace treaty bristles with danger for the Bolsheviki. Lenine talks of a breathing space, and has outlined a program of further communist reforms to be put into execution when the war finally stops. But the execution of this program is incompatible with the practical fulfillment of the peace treaty. The financial and economic obligations imposed by Germany on Russia simply cannot be carried out under the present communal régime. Conflicts are inevitable as soon as the Germans come in and begin trading with Russia.

The peace terms will be enforced at the bayonet's point, and Socialist absolutism will no longer be possible.

The economic concessions to the Germans will make huge breaches in the Bolshevist system, but the Bolsheviki must be absolutist or nothing. Their power, their raison d'être, rests on the fact that they make continual efforts to destroy the capitalist system by decree and by direct action. Once their hands are tied by German intervention in the economic and social life of the country there remains no inherent reason why they should be a government at all, and this is why the war party, in spite of their defeat on the immediate issue, do not rest. They know that sooner or later a conflict with the Germans in some form is inevitable. For the sake of their Socialist aims they are driven into an attitude of bitter hostility to the Germans. I do not know whether they will be able ultimately to organize resistance, but it is clear that they now regard the Germans as the chief enemy, and that they are infusing into the masses a strong anti-German feeling.

Forced to Serve National Ends.

It is the strangest of paradoxes that those men who through their fanatical policy have put such tremendous advantages into the hands of Germany are now driven by their own policy to a point where they are compelled almost against their will to serve national ends and to organize national resistance. The whole internal situation is uncertain and incalculable, and the Bolsheviki may fall before they have time to reap the results of their peace policy and undertake the necessary measures of defense. They may be overturned by German influence. They are beset by German dangers from within and without. They stumble in economic pitfalls they themselves have done so much to create. They have aroused among the intelligent classes such hatred that many a short-sighted man in the street cries out for German rule as a relief from their despotism.

But as yet there is no alternative government in view, and if the Bolsheviki remain in power it is not at all im-

Continued on Page Two.

VOTE FOR PEACE 453 TO 30

Delegate of Professional Unions Quits Red Party After Ballot.

TEUTONS TO TAKE CONTROL

Commissioners with Veto Power Will Sit on the Russian Ministries.

RUSSIA-UKRAINE PARLEY

Joint Conference Opens at Kiev in Effort to End Hostilities, Vienna Hears.

PETROGRAD, March 14.—The All-Russian Congress of Soviets, meeting at Moscow today, by a vote of 453 to 30 decided to ratify the peace treaty with the Central Powers.

M. Ryazonov, a prominent Bolshevist theorist, representative of all the professional unions, resigned from the Bolshevist Party after the vote.

In view of the repeated violations by both the Germans and the Russians of the line of demarcation fixed for the Pskov front, the Germans have demanded the establishment of a new line ten versts east of the present Russian position. A German official explanation of this change in the line is that it is necessary to strengthen Germany's strategic position.

Germans to Oversee Ministries.

German authorities have announced that German commissions with the power of veto will be appointed to the Russian Ministries to control the fulfillment of the treaty of peace.

The Germans have occupied Razdielnaya, a station on the Odessa railway line, and the evacuation of Odessa and Nicholiev is proceeding.

The German Admiral, Siegert, has been appointed commander of Odessa. Before the occupation of Odessa by the Germans anti-Jewish riots occurred there.

Fresh disorders have occurred in the German fleet off the Aland Islands, according to the Russian military newspaper, Krasnaya Armia.

The Caucasus Government has issued a statement in which it refuses to indorse the Brest-Litovsk peace treaty, which cedes Kars, Batoum, and Ardahan to Turkey, and declares that peace with Turkey can only be signed by the Caucasus Government, which has sent its own delegation to Trebizond to discuss peace.

AMSTERDAM, March 13—(Delayed.)—The opening of peace negotiations at Kiev between Russia and Ukraine is reported in a Vienna dispatch to the Vossische Zeitung of Berlin.

The Ukrainian Rada, the dispatch says, will meet soon to ratify the peace treaty with the Central Powers.

Chaos Likely to Last a Long Time.

WASHINGTON, March 15.—Official expression here today indicated that America and the Allies expect the action of the Moscow Congress to have little direct bearing on the general Russian situation. It apparently was believed that chaotic conditions will continue in Russia for a long time to come, even though the Germans make every effort to re-establish order and to reorganize the country's industrial and agricultural life.

Officials here do not profess to know to what extent Germany plans to use her forces in policing the provinces Russia is compelled to relinquish or how much further German troops may penetrate Russia itself. They were deeply interested in a dispatch from Moscow which said that the Russian factions were declaring freely that peace would be temporary only and that Russia would gather herself together with a new socialistic army to resist the Germans. The fact that only slightly more than half of the delegates expected to attend the congress were reported as voting also caused comment.

The attitude of the American Government toward any German move for a general peace at the expense of Russia is directly in line with the expression of Lord Robert Cecil in the House of Commons today that even if such a proposal came from Germany it would not be considered.

LENINE'S MIGRATION A QUEER SCENE

Premier in Moscow, Capitalism's Stronghold, Serene Amid His Tattered Baggage.

By ARTHUR RANSOME.

Special Cable to THE NEW YORK TIMES.

MOSCOW, March 12.—Premier Lenine and his Government reached here last night, bringing back to Moscow its old rights of a capital city which Peter the Great took with him 215 years ago when he went north to build a new city on the swamps at the mouth of the Neva.

It was a strange homecoming. Never did any Government move with less pomp, unless it was the Government of Peter himself, who, like Lenine, had a

Section 1

"All the News That's Fit to Print."

The New York Times.

THE WEATHER
Fair, warmer Sunday; Monday fair; fresh southwest winds.
For full weather report see Page 23.

Section 1

VOL. LXVII...NO. 21,967. NEW YORK, SUNDAY, MARCH 17, 1918.—120 PAGES, In Nine Parts, Including Picture and Magazine Sections in Rotogravure. FIVE CENTS In Greater New York | Elsewhere SEVEN CENTS

FRENCH DEFY GERMAN OFFENSIVE WITH DEFENSES 20 MILES DEEP; SEE THE REAL PERIL IN U-BOATS

DEFENSIVE POWER DOUBLED

Multiplication of Trench Systems a Tremendous Factor of Safety.

WELCOMES AN ATTACK

"Let Us Pray for It," Says a General When Asked About the Prospects.

NEED OUR HELP AT SEA

Leaders in France Emphasize Importance of Ship Output to Offset Sinkings.

Tirpitz Again Predicts U-Boats Will Win Victory

LONDON, March 16.—"If we continue the U-boat war without flinching we can secure a peace with England which will insure for Germany's navy a base off the Flemish coast for all time," Admiral von Tirpitz is quoted as declaring in a recent telegram.

The Admiral's message, says the Exchange Telegraph correspondent at Amsterdam, was sent in reply to a telegram from the Director of the new von Tirpitz school at Swinemünde, Germany.

By G. H. PERRIS.

Special Cable to THE NEW YORK TIMES.

WITH THE FRENCH ARMIES, March 14 (Delayed).—The strange interval continues. We have had four months of unusually favorable weather, and yet the great German offensive constantly threatened and still discussed by the German press does not come to pass. This hesitation is significant and encouraging. Whatever we may think of the German Grand Staff, no one suggests that they are slackers, and all their traditions are against leaving their chief adversary in peace to accumulate new strength; and the growth of the Allies' power in the west goes on steadily. Its first purpose is of course defensive.

I spent yesterday in an important part of the front examining the new works that had been established in these quiet months. They cannot be described precisely, but it would not be too much to say that in this period the defensive power of the French armies has been doubled. At the beginning of the war the Allies had no time, and in the middle period they had little inclination, to multiply defense works. Any old ditch served before Ypres, and Verdun was saved not by any kind of fortification, ancient or modern, but by the unconquerable faithfulness of the poilu.

Those trials at least are things of the past. Never again will it be necessary to defend the front trenches to the death because there are no others ready behind them. Today the centre of France is plowed with trenches, bearded with wire. Fields, dotted with battery emplacements, all scientifically designed to give the most advantageous lines of fire. There is system behind system for a score of miles—I am not speaking figuratively—behind the present front.

I asked a very distinguished soldier the other day what he thought of the prospects of a great enemy attack.

"Let us pray for it," he replied. There was nothing lighthearted in his tone; the General knew what he was saying. His men would say with him: "Let us pray for it." No pacifist can teach him or them anything about hell or war, but they see a worse hell that it is in their power to refuse, and, having to fight, they know now the advantages of method of defense compared with which the Hindenburg line, so far as we know it, was but a student's essay. Even though the labor may have been in vain, it was their plain duty to take these precautions. Evidently they do not exhaust the program of the Allies.

The German press shows a nervous consciousness of this fact. It discusses with affected indifference the Versailles Council; it talks with a show of contempt of the Americans now holding sectors on the French front, and daily increasing in numbers and experience; but it does not seem to take any great satisfaction in the games its Governors are playing amid the chaos of Eastern Europe. It is, in fact, not the leaders of Germany only, but her people also, who have been schooled to face their principal adversary. In the hesitation of its chiefs we may plainly read the heart-sickness of the nation.

GERMAN CAPTIVES SHOW LOW MORALE

Those Taken by the British Near Ypres Complain of Underfeeding.

By PHILIP GIBBS.

Special Cable to THE NEW YORK TIMES.

WAR CORRESPONDENTS' HEADQUARTERS, March 14 (Delayed).—The

Continued on Page Two.

Allies See Victory Only in Defeat of U-Boats, And Look to America for Her Utmost Efforts

By CHARLES H. GRASTY.

Special Cable to THE NEW YORK TIMES.

PARIS, March 16.—I have received inside information calling renewed attention to the submarine situation. There has been too much optimistic generalizing on this subject. I am urged by expert authorities to point out to America constantly how useless will be all her strength and how utterly hopeless all her plans for defeating Germany unless the submarine is mastered. And it is not mastered yet. For eight months I have been digging out, and by hook or crook getting censors to pass to America, tonnage figures on submarine sinkings. Public appreciation there of the seriousness of this phase of the war has constituted a driving force to increase the effort in building destroyers and shipping. But twice as much tonnage was sunk in 1917 as was built. The year 1918 therefore opened with an accumulated deficit. It is safe to say that if we had twice the tonnage actually possessed by the Allies today we should still be far short of supplying Europe's needs and transporting the American army.

All estimates about the future are vitiated by the element of speculation. After a year of sinking twice the tonnage that was constructed we are still losing more than we are building. Optimists sharpen their pencils and figure on a certainty of construction overtaking the destruction by next June, and then unexpectedly British labor develops some strange distemper that slows down results in the shipyards. I am reliably informed that the hours necessary to produce a given unit have increased since the war in the proportion of eight to thirteen. There are so many possibilities in the submarine field that all estimates should have a liberal margin of safety. The Germans may upset the present naval balance by transferring their Baltic forces, released by the Russian collapse, to the North Sea and the Atlantic, thus crippling the convoy system and increasing the loss by submarines. Or they may make their U-boats larger and more of them. The field of invention is as open to them as it is to us.

The submarine situation should be opened up and dealt with frankly on both sides of the ocean. Much of the trouble now experienced in England with labor and war weariness is due to ill-advised concealment about the submarine. Democracies can fight best when they know the worst. Political coddling produces enfeeblement. For months London has been more concerned about stopping the air raids than beating the submarines. Remissness with the Government is a more potent force than righteous indignation against Germany or the firm resolve to win at all hazards. In a word, we deny in practice the very principle of publicity that we are fighting this war to vindicate and establish.

The leaders here who are bearing the burden of this war are anxious for America to understand and keep steadily in mind that, whatever may happen in any arena, the submarine remains the bull's-eye at which allied effort must be aimed. Assuming that the western front can be held for the time being, as asserted by General Foch and other authorities, Germany can be defeated militarily, despite her eastern conquests, by swift and effective measures against the submarine. Germany's strategy is conceived with a view to diverting popular interest to other and comparatively irrelevant matters, like air raiding, while the silent U-boats cut the allied jugular. With the western line holding intact, the problem chiefly is one of sustaining the life of the European Allies and transporting an American army strong enough to deal the deathblow to Prussia. The extent to which America is relied on for the extinction of the submarine may be judged from the expectation generally entertained that the United States from now on will contribute nearly three-fourths of the new construction. Until now, preliminary preparations have largely absorbed American effort, but henceforth shipping is expected in such quantity from the American yards as to restore normal conditions within six months, and assured transport thereafter.

SAYS GERMANY CAN DELAY HER BLOW

Tageblatt's Warning of Dangers of Haste Raises Doubts as to a Drive.

FAILURE EQUAL TO DISASTER

So Reasons "Inspired" Writer, While Professing Absolute Faith in German Generals.

Special Cable to THE NEW YORK TIMES.

THE HAGUE, March 15, (Delayed.)—Yesterday the Berlin Lokal-Anzeiger remarked that Germany could afford not to hurry with her offensive. Today the Tageblatt has an editorial entitled "The Ability to Wait," in which it asserts that the tension among the belligerents has never been so great as now, that decisive battles are approaching and that failure in this campaign would amount to disaster. Particular interest, the Tageblatt observes, attaches to the question, who will attack first, and it says that in Germany the army and the people are counting on a renewed offensive, confidence of success in which is founded in absolute faith in the high command.

"Our military leaders," it says, "will not be impelled by this confidence to hurry, but can quietly wait for the right moment to begin a big action. The ability to wait is one of the most important qualities of great Generals."

The Tageblatt writer closes by saying that the most important thing to note in the three and a half years of war on the west front, is the colossal military importance attached to Germany's march through Belgium.

"The views of our enemies," he says, "especially America, are strangely illustrated by certain articles published by THE NEW YORK TIMES relating to America's attitude toward Mexico after the war." Then he quotes the paragraph from the "American Jurist's" article relating to Mexico which has been already quoted by the majority of the German papers. "Comment," he says, "appears to be superfluous. The expression of THE NEW YORK TIMES, which represents public opinion in America, is inclined to take the mask from our enemy."

The Tageblatt article is evidently inspired, and in well-informed circles

Continued on Page Three.

BAKER IMPRESSED BY OUR NEW PORTS

Views Immensity of Terminal Work Done by Americans on the French Coast.

BERTHS FOR 40 BIG SHIPS

"I Only Wish Every American Could See the Work," Says Secretary, Enthusiastic.

ON BOARD SECRETARY BAKER'S SPECIAL TRAIN IN FRANCE, March 14, (Associated Press.)—Secretary Baker's first work after his conferences with the French statesmen and American Generals at the capital has been to begin his study of what the Americans are doing and ought to do in France by a survey of a great port department.

"I am still absorbing," said he, after a fourteen-hour day, yesterday. "I must say frankly that I did not know the immensity of the enterprise which we have undertaken in opening new ports, and when I see what we have accomplished here I am satisfied."

The American War Secretary at the particular port in question was attended by General Pershing, Major Gen. William M. Black, Brig. Gen. W. W. Atterbury, and the officers of the engineers who have been creating a vast new equipment for docking and unloading ships. He walked for three miles along the American Army's dock front, already constructed or in process of construction, as an extension to the berths for a number of ships placed at the disposition of the Americans by the French Government.

Two miles of this new sea frontage consisted of marshes on Oct. 1 last. The ground has been filled in from dredgings in deepening the waterfronts, and ships are already alongside some of these new berths. On other parts of the frontage concrete warehouses are going up and a great system of switches has been laid or is being laid.

"I like to come out here once a week," said a Colonel of the engineers to the correspondent, "and see how different things look from what they did the week before. I almost lose my way."

Dockage for Forty Large Ships.

This new dockage, with two other new frontages that are being developed in connection with it, will allow of forty

Continued on Page Two.

Dillon, as Party Leader, Demands Ireland's Freedom

ENNISKILLEN, Ireland, March 16.—John Dillon, who succeeded John Redmond as leader of the Irish Nationalists, replying to congratulatory addresses today, said his first task would be to tell England before the world that her statesmen must cease to talk of a league of nations or pretend to carry on this war in defense of small nationalities unless she first set her own house in order and set free a nation that had for 700 years groaned under her misgovernment.

WHITMAN IS OUT FOR THIRD TERM AGAINST HEARST

Expects Wilson's Support Because of His Co-operation in War Activities.

EXPECTS HEARST TO RUN

Meets with Republican Leaders Here and Will Make War the Issue.

POINTS TO RECENT LAWS

Work of State Officials Regarded as Aid to Government in Running Down Spies.

Governor Whitman said yesterday that he intended to run for a third term. He expects William Randolph Hearst to be his Democratic opponent. Friends of the Governor said yesterday that the Governor would make his campaign on his record as a war Governor, and that he would have the support of President Wilson, or at least, an expression from the Administration of recognition for his co-operation with the Government in the war measures taken in New York State.

Governor Whitman held a conference yesterday afternoon with many of the Republican Party leaders at the Hotel St. Regis. While no formal announcement of his candidacy for a third term was made, the Governor made no secret about his intention of running again, and intimated that he did not think the news of his decision would come as a surprise to any one.

Close friends of the Governor were elated yesterday over word they had received that the Federal Administration would openly express itself in favor of the Governor, and would give him cordial support, particularly if William Randolph Hearst received the Democratic nomination.

The Governor's political lieutenants hope to shape the campaign so as to make the war the main issue, the Governor asking for votes on a platform calling for a vigorous prosecution of the war.

While District Attorney Swann is said by some politicians to be carrying on his anti-gambling campaign for personal publicity, which might help his chances for the nomination for Governor, his chances are considered slender, and the Republican leaders are making their plans entirely upon the supposition that Mr. Hearst is to be the Democratic nominee.

The Republican leaders hope, by making the war the only campaign issue, to force the Democrats to make their State campaign on apologetic grounds, considering the position which Mr. Hearst has occupied as between the Allies and Germany and as a champion of an early peace.

Governor Whitman said yesterday that he understood that George T. Glynn, the Executive Auditor of the Governor, had resigned that position in order to devote his time exclusively to planning the campaign.

Two of Governor Whitman's claims to be considered as a strong war Governor will be the State military census, the value of which to the Federal Government has been acknowledged by the Shipping Board and other Federal officials, and the passage of the State "Spy act," which was backed by the Governor. This law is one which gives the State Attorney General powers which are possessed by no other State, County or Federal official in the nation and which led to the exposure of the Bolo Pacha conspiracy and the investigation of other cleverly hidden plots in this State.

Under this law the State Attorney General can serve a subpoena on a witness and he may be punished if he disregards it. The value of this law, which has forced confessions from many German propagandists, has been acknowledged by Government officials, who have handled some of their biggest spy cases through the State Attorney General's office.

BOLSHEVIKI ORDERED A MASSACRE AT ODESSA

General Muravieff Also Demanded 20,000,000 Rubles Payment by the City.

JASSY, Rumania, March 15.—After the Germans entered Odessa on Wednesday the Bolsheviki embarked on steamers for Sebastopol.

Before leaving, General Muravieff, the Bolshevist commander in chief, ordered the massacre of officers, capitalists and bourgeoise and demanded the payment of 20,000,000 rubles by the population of the city.

JAPAN SEEKS CHANCE TO AID RUSSIA; TOKIO PLANS SAFE AND SANE POLICY; WILSON WILL SPEAK SOON ON ISSUE

MAY MAKE ADDRESS MONDAY

Expected to Say Teutons' Course Shows They Are Not to be Trusted.

MAY REJECT PEACE TALK

Officials Agree That Czernin's Terms to Rumania Have Belied All His Professions.

JAPAN'S ACTION A PROBLEM

Tokio Has Shown Great Consideration for Our Views, Washington Admits.

Special to The New York Times.

WASHINGTON, March 16.—Conditions in Russia, complicated as they are by the subserviency of the Bolshevist authority to Germany, the civil conflicts in Russian territory, the agitation over the proposal that Japan take measures to protect allied interests in Eastern Russia, expected German aggression or propaganda, and the general state of chaos, economic, political, and military, prevailing in the territory formerly ruled by the Czar, are to be reviewed soon in public by President Wilson, according to an intimation given today.

In what manner the President will make known his position on the Russian situation is not made known, but it is accepted that he will follow the usual course of appearing before Congress in joint session and state the conclusions he has reached as to the attitude the United States should assume in the difficult problem that confronts the allied Governments as the result of the Russian collapse and the acceptance by the Congress of Soviets at Moscow of the harsh German conditions.

One suggestion heard today was that the President might present his views in a public statement, but this was mere surmise, and the more general opinion was that he would address Congress on the subject. It was reported that he was preparing a formal address.

Intimations of the character given today are usually followed quickly by the appearance of the President before the Senate and the House, and it would not be a surprise if he went to the Capitol on Monday.

There is an expectation that the President will take advantage of the opportunity to discuss the effect on peace prospects of the conditions resulting from the Russian collapse and the Teuton occupation of Russian territory. That he cannot avoid this subject in any consideration of the Russian situation is argued, and the hope is expressed that he will dissect the German and Austrian pretense of a desire for an ending of the war in accordance with the general principles enunciated by President Wilson.

Paralleling this hope is the strong feeling that the President will make his address an occasion for serving notice on the Central Powers that they have again shown that they are unworthy of trust among decent nations and that from now on the war must be waged by the Allies for the one purpose of overcoming the menace of militarism, which can be accomplished only by victory on the battlefield. What Germany and Austria have done to Russia makes Teutonic peace talk hereafter unworthy of the slightest consideration, according to the opinion that prevails generally in Washington.

The effect on the President's feelings of the Soviet's failure to answer in any effective manner his assurance of American sympathy and promise to help was not discussed today in connection with his reported purpose to make a public statement on the Russian situation.

The President has always shown sympathy with the democratic aims of those concerned in the revolution and insisted in an address to Congress that the Allies should not turn the perturbed former subjects of the Czar adrift to be the playthings of Germany and her allies. In this the President has gone contrary to sentiments expressed by Prime Minister Lloyd George, and there is no reason to believe that his policy has undergone any change.

Interest in Japanese Phase.

Much of the interest in the President's expected statement with respect to Russia centres in the Japanese phase of the problem. In this connection it was learned today that exchanges were still in progress between the Japanese and other allied Governments, and that Japan has not undertaken to put in operation her reported plan to invade Siberia with armed forces to maintain order, prevent the seizure of allied property sent to the Russian Government, protect foreigners, and check any attempt at German domination in that part of the Russian possessions.

It is now well recognized that Japan has shown a gratifying consideration for the doubts of the United States as to the wisdom of Japanese intervention in Siberia. Japan has emphasized this consideration through the fact that in her desire to enter Russian territory she has the support of Great Britain, France, and Italy. While it is accepted

Continued on Page Two.

Fears Wilson's Plans May Yet Win Russia; German Paper Warns of Danger in the East

Special Cable to THE NEW YORK TIMES.

THE HAGUE, March 15.—Discussing President Wilson's message to the Russian Soviets, the Berlin Vossische Zeitung says:

"The promises that Wilson has made to the Russian people are no guarantee that they will be kept, but are an indication that Wilson is in agreement with England and is pursuing a consistent Russian policy.

"We would remind our readers that through former Ambassador Gerard and by various other means Wilson has influenced Germany not to make annexations in the east."

The paper says he has kept to his purpose in order to bring Russia again under Anglo-Saxon influence. It goes on:

"Today when Germany through her buffer-State policy in the east has endangered Russian sympathy, Wilson sees the moment for the fulfillment of the second half of his program. He adopts an attitude fundamentally opposed to the German eastern policy and is likely to succeed by diplomacy in removing German influence from the border States. At any rate, he intervenes as a supporter of a reunion of all the old Russian territory."

The Zeitung remarks that in connection with this it must be remembered that the echoes in which the Anglo-American conception is audible are ever increasing, and the idea is that the eastern peace is not an accomplished fact but must be properly regulated at the general peace conference. The paper admits that it is evident that Russia under the influence of promises such as above will welcome any revision of the Brest-Litovsk peace and may even demand it. It goes on to say that this idea may be realized and that Germany may find that her gains are turned as a weapon against her and that England and America will restore the freedom of these States. It adds:

"Even more is it to be feared that this advantage for which the Entente is willing to sacrifice its whole political position in the world will be wholly or in great part gained, and without a world equivalent.

"It is not yet too late to point to this approaching danger that we have seen coming for a long time. A definite settlement of the border States to be separated from Russia has not yet been reached, and there still remains the possibility, when the decision is made, to allow freely, and even to advocate, a federation of these States with Russia.

"We are convinced now, as before, that a real majority of their people desire this federation and that from our own political viewpoint it is now a question whether they are to receive freedom from our hands or from Wilson's."

The Vossische Zeitung has disapproved of the eastern policy of Germany from the beginning.

CAN BREAK TREATY, LENINE ASSERTS

Soviets Vote to Raise Army of Both Sexes After Ratifying Agreement.

LEFT MEMBERS IN REVOLT

Resolution of "Appreciation" of Wilson Message Adopted—It Urges Class War.

MOSCOW, March 16.—Following the ratification of the peace agreement with Germany by a large majority in the Congress of Soviets, a Bolshevist resolution approving the acts of the Government of the Workmen's and Soldiers' Delegates and of the peace delegation, and calling for organization of the defense of the country by the creation of a national army of both sexes, was passed. This was the outcome of Lenine's restoration of peace among the warring factions and his statement that this action was the only way out, intimating that the treaty might be broken under changed circumstances.

The opposition, notably the social revolutionaries of the Left, made a valiant effort to prevent the acceptance of the treaty, which was characterized by the Minister of Justice as being "anti-revolutionary and anti-socialistic."

He stated that the Social Revolutionary Party repudiated responsibility for the acceptance of the peace treaty, would resign from the Government and devote all of its power and influence to the organization of armed resistance to German imperialism.

MOSCOW, March 14, (Associated Press.)—President Wilson's message of sympathy was received with marked applause when it was read at the opening session of the Congress. The Congress immediately adopted this resolution of appreciation:

The all-Russian Congress of Soviets expresses its appreciation to the American people and, first of all, the laboring and exploited classes in the United States for the message sent by President Wilson to the Congress of Soviets, in this time when the Russian Socialist Soviet Republic is living through most difficult trials.

The Russian Republic uses the occasion of the message from President Wilson to express to all peoples who are dying and suffering from the horrors of this imperialistic war its warm sympathy and firm conviction that the happy time is near when the laboring masses in all bourgeois countries will throw off the capitalist yoke and establish a Socialist state of society, which is the only one capable of assuring a permanent and just peace as well as the culture and well-being of all who toil.

The newspapers had eagerly awaited the publication of the message, and had generally commended the disposition of the United States to refrain from joining in any plan to dismember Russia.

The Congress is being held in the splendid banquet hall of the Nobility Club, where former Emperors were often entertained. Soldiers, sailors, and peas-

Continued on Page Two.

BIG PLANS CENTRE ABOUT BLACK SEA

Germans May Send Seized Russian Fleet Into Mediterranean to Harass the British.

ODESSA TO BE INDEPENDENT?

Submarines May Be Built Near—Loot in All Russia Likely to Total $2,000,000,000.

Special Cable to THE NEW YORK TIMES.

LONDON, March 15.—A correspondent writes in The Chronicle:

"True to their character of conscious or unconscious German agents, the Bolsheviki have concentrated the entire Black Sea fleet, (if my information is correct,) ready for delivery to the enemy. There is no doubt that it will be secured by the latter, and will constitute a new danger to the Allies. When to the Black Sea fleet have been added certain Turkish elements, now assembled in the Sea of Marmora, the whole naval force will be in a position to sally through the Dardanelles and embarrass the British operations in Palestine.

"With the aid of the Jewish inhabitants of Odessa, who number about 50 per cent., Germany hopes to erect Odessa into an independent republic and a free port. She will then use the port for shipping Ukrainian produce and raw materials as well as for her own goods destined for Persia through Batoum and Trebizond.

"In the vicinity of Odessa are large German settlements which have existed for 300 years. They number nearly a quarter of a million. Their influence is great. They publish their own newspaper, the Odessaer Zeitung, possess half a dozen clubs and two discreetly conducted branches of the German Navy League.

"The Odessa Jews are proverbially pro-German. They are anxious that this flourishing centre should be excluded from the Ukraine, whose treatment of them has been particularly rigorous. Indeed, the massacres which have occurred have all had their theatre within the new Ukrainian State.

"In the harbor at Odessa is now a collection of British, French, Italian, and Rumanian steamships, which have been stationary since Russia declared war on Turkey. Their approximate total tonnage is 100,000 tons, amply sufficient to maintain German trade on the Black Sea. This is the more necessary as Turkey needs great supplies of foodstuffs from the Ukraine.

"For the operations in the Black Sea the Germans have hitherto kept eight submarines at Constantinople. These will now be available for the Mediterranean.

"Again, at Nicolaieff, near Odessa, are large shipbuilding yards, capable of turning out dreadnoughts. The Germans will build submarines, for which coal and iron exist in the neighborhood.

"As to German plans in other parts, it is plain that it envisages the restoration of the monarchy in Great Russia after the Bolsheviki have completed their disintegration.

"Their loot already is enormous in war stores, machinery, foodstuffs and goods of all sorts. It may be estimated

Continued on Page Two.

WOULD LIKE OUR APPROVAL

Japanese Leaders See That Opposition Would Handicap Financially.

WANT TO BRING CHINA IN

Believe Siberian Crisis Offers Chance for Peking Government to Check Revolution.

LESS EXCITEMENT NOW

Japanese Much Upset at First by Prospect of Full Participation in the Great War.

TOKIO, Thursday, March 14, (Associated Press.)—When a week ago the possibility of Japanese intervention in Siberia became known and a flood of opinion from the Western press poured into Japan, there was considerable excitement, in the belief that speedy mobilization of the army and navy would be ordered.

Extremists pictured airplanes over Tokio and submarines from Vladivostok. The hysterical "Cutz" in the Diet heckled the Government, and the newspapers were filled with contrary views, according to the interests or the imagination of those responsible for the situation.

Presently, however, the tone became quieter, and it appears possible to see more clearly the true Japanese outlook, which is characterized in many quarters as "entirely safe, sane, and loyal."

Today practically the entire responsible press of the capital is advocating intervention in Siberia in co-operation with the Allies and China, not directed against Russia, but as an ally loyal to the Russians, wishing to save the country.

One of the most outspoken papers is the Kokumin Shimbun, owned and edited by Ichiro Tokutomi, who is a close personal friend of the Premier.

Japan realizes, it is authoritatively stated, that if the United States declines its support, the situation will be extremely delicate because financial and material assistance must come from America. Any feeling of distrust or unfriendliness seems to be lacking.

As a matter of fact, a large section of influential men in Japan favor the American viewpoint, while only a few chauvinists jeer at Premier Terauchi and Foreign Minister Motono as being under American influence.

Leading men, such as Baron Shibusawa, President of the American-Japanese Association, for the commercial section, and Yukio Ozaki, leader of the Constitutional Party, for the "outs," advocate extreme caution. Similarly, many strong supporters of the Administration point out that the hour for action has not yet struck.

They say that first it is absolutely necessary for all of Russia and the rest of the world to understand that Japan is engaged in no chauvinistic adventure, and desires nothing more than to safeguard the Far East, assist the Allies, and, if possible, save Russia from German domination, which means the mailed fist in the Far East.

The Chinese problem is one of the most serious features. It is recognized that this is China's great opportunity, and Japan is urging the leaders in the north and south to settle their differences by a sound compromise, form a capable national Government at Peking, and join Japan and the Allies in guarding the frontiers and helping Russia. Some indications are manifest that this effort may be successful.

Tang Shao-yi, who has held many posts in the Cabinet, was formerly Governor of Mukden Province, and is leader of the National Party of China, is on his way to Japan. Baron Hayashi, the Japanese Minister to China, has returned to Peking, and it is stated that there is reason to believe that by tactful diplomacy the obstacles to the effective co-operation between Japan and China in Siberia may be removed in time to enable both countries to share in the Far Easterners' real participation in the war.

Such an outcome of the present negotiations, resulting in agreement and co-operation between Japan and China, would mean, to the minds of Japanese statesmen, an alliance of vast importance.

CHINESE RIFT WORRIES TOKIO.

But Terauchi Says the Government Does Not Plan to Mediate.

LONDON, March 16.—In reply to a question in the Diet yesterday Count

Section 1

"All the News That's Fit to Print."

The New York Times.

THE WEATHER

Fair Sunday and Monday; slight temperature change.

For full weather report see Page 23.

Section 1

VOL. LXVII...NO. 21,974. ... NEW YORK, SUNDAY, MARCH 24, 1918.—108 PAGES, In Nine Parts, Including Picture and Magazine Sections in Rotogravure. FIVE CENTS In Greater New York | Elsewhere SEVEN CENTS

GERMANS SMASH BRITISH FRONT, DRIVE IN FOUR MILES; CLAIM 25,000 PRISONERS; HELD AT SOME POINTS, SAYS HAIG; GUN SAID TO BE 74½ MILES AWAY LANDS SHELLS IN PARIS

FRENCH CAPITAL UNDER FIRE

Ten Killed and Fifteen or More Wounded in Mysterious Bombardment.

62 MILES FROM THE FRONT

Projectiles of 9.5-Inch Calibre Show Rifle Marks and Evidently Came from a Gun.

PUZZLES ORDNANCE CHIEFS

No Cannon So Far Known to Ordnance Experts Can Cover Any Such Range.

PARIS, March 23.—Paris has been under bombardment of long-range guns today, beginning at 8 o'clock this morning. Shells of 240 millimeters (about 9.5 inches) have been reaching the capital and its suburbs at intervals of twenty minutes, killing about ten persons and wounding about fifteen. The shortest distance from Paris to the front is over 100 kilometers, (62 miles.)

The news of the bombardment was confirmed by an official announcement this afternoon. At that time it was stated that measures for counterattacking the enemy's cannon were under execution.

The city received its third warning of an air attack within twenty-four hours with unshaken nerves at 9 o'clock tonight. The "all clear" signal was given at 10:20 before the population could learn whether the warning was against an airplane raid or whether the long-distance German cannon had resumed operations. The people were crowding to music halls and theatres, fully confident nothing further would happen, only to be advised to seek the nearest shelter as quickly as possible.

The first daylight air raid on Paris also came today, which was one of perfect sunshine. The people refused to hide in cellars and other subterranean shelters, and, although the subway stations were crowded, the streets always had great crowds in them, watching for an aerial battle or some other stirring incident.

Await "All Clear" Signal.

As the day passed and the "all clear" signal was not given, the feeling grew that something new in the way of a raid was expected, and this was not explained until an official statement was issued saying that the delay was due to the bombardment by long-distance cannon.

The "all clear" was then sounded, and the normal life was resumed. The cable office reopened, to take up accumulated piles of dispatches.

Pieces of the shells on examination were found to bear rifling marks, which proved that they had not been dropped, but had been fired from a gun.

This apparently left a greater mystery than ever, as to where the gun in question was located, the nature of it, and by what method it was being operated.

Another thing which turned the thoughts of the officials at the municipal laboratory to the possibility that a cannon was being used was the regularity with which the bombs fell—one every twenty minutes.

People Venture Forth.

After the aerial battle most of those who had taken refuge in cellars, hearing no sound after half an hour's stay, came out and remained in the streets about their doors, wondering at the prolongation of the raid, which generally do not exceed three hours. School children were marched to shelters which had previously been allotted to them. Many restaurants were closed, but large stores, which had just finished arranging their windows lowered their shutters and sent their employes into the cellars.

Paris wore an aspect recalling the early days of the war in 1914. Telephone girls remained at their posts, very few taking advantage of the administration's permission to seek refuge if they wished. Tramways and auto buses stopped on the

Continued on Page Three.

Paris Reports That City Is Shelled From a Distance of 74½ Miles

PARIS, March 23.—According to the latest reports, the long-distance cannon which bombarded Paris this afternoon was firing from a distance of 120 kilometers (approximately 74½ miles) and was located about twelve kilometers beyond the French front.

London Distinctly Hears Big Guns

LONDON, March 23.—The guns in France are distinctly heard in London tonight. Particularly in high places there is a continuous throbbing. Many persons have gone to the housetops to listen.

CABLES PERSHING FOR NEWS OF DRIVE

War Department Has No Report —Rumors of Casualties Aggregating 250,000.

CONFIDENCE IS UNSHAKEN

But Officials Admit the Significance of Germany's Prodigal Sacrifice of Her Soldiers.

Special to The New York Times.

WASHINGTON, March 23.—Political Washington, which includes the executive, legislative, and diplomatic contingents, from those high in authority down to messengers in the Government departments, the Capitol and foreign establishments, was absorbed throughout this beautiful Spring day in the great events taking place in the theatre of war across the Atlantic. Newspaper bulletins were scanned carefully. Newspaper offices were importuned over the telephone for information. Officials left their desks to seek whatever could be learned from the adjoining press rooms.

Up to the time the War Department was officially closed for the day no word had come from General Pershing or any other authoritative source as to the progress of the great conflict between the British and German forces. Benedict Crowell, the Acting Secretary of War, said at the end of office hours that all that had been received from General Pershing today was a brief dispatch on another matter. Mr. Crowell declined to comment on the news of the battle.

Major Gen. Peyton C. March, Acting Chief of the Army General Staff, who recently returned to this country after service as Chief of Artillery of the American expeditionary forces, had no statement to make.

So intense was the interest, however, that the Acting Secretary directed that a message be cabled to General Pershing asking him for information as to the progress of the widespread engagement. General March went to the War Department tonight, and it was said there that he would remain until very late in the hope of receiving advices from General Pershing.

The big, white-domed building on Capitol Hill which shelters the Senate and the House of Representatives was full of rumors. A report that the casualties suffered by one side—which was meant was not clear—ran up to 250,000 soon had another 100,000 added to it before many minutes. The news that the German forces were making headway in their drive into the British lines came with too much emphasis to be doubted, and caused a gloom that increased as each rumor obtained its share of exaggeration, due in the main to careless repetition of the brief advices received by American newspapers through the grace of the censors.

Total Casualties Estimated at 250,000.

One of the Entente diplomatic establishments had a dispatch estimating the number of casualties on both sides as 5,000 per mile on the fifty-mile front which the Germans attacked. This would mean that the casualties—killed, wounded, and prisoners—would aggregate the staggering number of 250,000. Assuming that the estimate was fairly accurate, the only grain of comfort in the information came from the supposition that the heavier losses must have been suffered by the Germans as the attacking force, although there was disquietude among the officials over the statement from Berlin, which the British censors allowed to pass, that 25,000 prisoners had been taken by the Germans. This indicated that the Germans had managed to cut off a considerable portion of their opponents, for, even with such tremendous numbers engaged, it is not likely that as many as 25,000 prisoners would be taken in two days of hand-to-hand fighting.

That the Germans as the attackers, advancing in solid formation against well-protected artillery using high-explosive shells, must have suffered at least twice as many casualties as the de-

Continued on Page Two.

SAY GERMANS AIM AT CHANNEL PORTS

London Observers Think Hindenburg's Ultimate Purpose Is Made Plain.

ENGLAND FEELS CONFIDENT

Danger of the Drive at Anglo-French Junction Point Is Understood.

LONDON, March 23.—The attention of all England was centred today on the western front. There was no boastfulness, but the feeling was one of supreme confidence and pride in the army which stands on the first line of defense between democracy and autocracy.

While clouds of uncertainty obscure the details of the battle, some relief is felt that Germany has finally shown her hand.

The purpose and method of her long-talked-of blow are now thought to be plain. Hindenburg's objective is undoubtedly the Channel ports, but he purposes to take the first step toward them by breaking through the Allies' line near the junction of the French and British Armies.

The attack thus far has shown no new strategy, but appears to be simply a colossal blow with masses of guns and men, hitherto never used together on any battlefield.

No surprise is felt here that the British line has been forced back. Lines of defense have bent before all great offensives in this war. What the British people look to the army for is that it shall not break.

The newspapers warn against undue optimism, but they point out that the fighting instinct still lives in the British breast, notwithstandng the long years of peace and ignorance of military training, and that when that fighting instinct dies the world will see the death of the British nation.

Since it has developed that this is the heralded German offensive, the most colossal struggle in the world's history, the public and press are unanimously of the opinion that its failure will mean the end of the war. The Times says Germany is evidently resolved to stake all her chances on the western front, and adds:

"She has committed herself to the greatest gamble in history. We believe that she will fail, and it is precisely because the failure of the present attack must react disastrously upon Germany that we derive encouragement from the military position as it is disclosed today."

The Morning Post cautions the nation "to keep a cool head and allow no plausible argumentation upon scanty facts to persuade it to premature conclusions."

The Manchester Guardian says:

"If the Germans persist in attacks and lose they will have lost the war, and the only thing left doubtful will be the magnitude of their defeat."

This newspaper points out that at no point except one would a German victory be strategically decisive, adding:

"That point is south of St. Quentin, where a continuation of the present rate of advance would imperil the position of the French north of the Aisne. Here, then, south of St. Quentin, is the chief danger zone."

The Daily News says:

"Although the allied strength will reach its maximum only as the full force of America's contribution to the war is felt, the opening of the greatest battle the world has known is received with something like relief. * * * The salient fact about the offensive now in progress is that its authors cannot afford to fail. They cannot afford to face a country left, after another Summer of battle, to count its gains and find them no more than a myriad of nameless graves."

The newspapers dwell on the accuracy of the British Intelligence Service in divining the enemy's intentions and foreseeing the points and time of attack.

"Serious but not alarming" summed up the reception of today's news from the front. It is pointed out that in battles of such dimensions the attacking forces, by the employment of troops re-

Continued on Page Two.

SAYS BRITISH ARE BEATEN

Berlin Claims Victory Over "Considerable Part" of Foe's Army.

FIRST BATTLE STAGE ENDED

And German Forces Now Hold Line Northeast of Bapaume, Peronne, and Ham.

MANY TOWNS ARE CAPTURED

Third British Positions Reached or Penetrated at Some Points, It Is Stated.

BERLIN, March 23, (via London.)—"A considerable part of the English Army is beaten," says the official statement this evening from General Headquarters, which announces the end of the first stage of the great battle in France, with victories near Monchy, Cambrai, St. Quentin, and La Fère. It is further stated that the German forces are now on a line northeast of Bapaume, Péronne, and Ham.

The day announcement from headquarters told of successes along the battle front at many points, and stated that 25,000 prisoners, 400 guns, and 300 machine guns had been captured.

Between Fontaine-les-Croisilles and Mouevres German forces penetrated into the second enemy position and captured Vaulx-Vraucourt and Morches, (the former about 3⅛ miles and the latter about 2½ miles behind the former British front.)

The British evacuated their positions in the bend southwest of Cambrai, and were pursued by the Germans through Demicourt, Flesquières, and Ribecourt.

Between Gonnelieu and the Omignon stream the first two British positions were penetrated, and the heights west of Gouzeaucourt, Heudicourt, and Villers-Faucon were captured. The Germans now stand before the third British position.

Penetrated Third British Line.

Between the Omignon stream and the Somme, after the capture of the first British position, the Germans made their way through Holnon Wood and fought across the heights of Savy and Roupy, penetrating into the third hostile position.

South of the Somme the Germans broke through the hostile lines and in an uninterrupted forward movement drove the enemy over the Crozat Canal toward the west.

A crossing over the Oise west of La Fère was forced by Jaeger battalions, it is added.

Tonight's official statement reads as follows:

The first stage of the great battle in France is ended. We have won the engagements near Monchy, Cambrai, St. Quentin, and La Fère.

A considerable part of the English Army is beaten.

We are fighting approximately on a line northeast of Bapaume, Péronne, and Ham.

Tells of Towns Captured.

The day bulletin reads as follows:

Under the command of the Emperor and King, the battle of attack against the British front near Arras, Cambrai, and St. Quentin has been proceeding two days. Yesterday also good progress was made.

Divisions of Crown Prince Rupprecht stormed the heights north and northwest of Croisilles. Between Fontaine-les-Croisilles and Moeuvres they penetrated into the second enemy position and captured the villages, situated there, of Vaulx-Vraucourt and Morchies. Strong British counterattacks failed. Between Gonnelieu and the Omignon stream the first two enemy positions were penetrated. The heights west of Gouzeaucourt, Heudricourt, and Villers-Faucon were captured, and in the Valley of the Cologne stream Roisel and Marquaix were stormed.

The fighting around Epehy heights was bitter. These heights being encircled from the north and south, the enemy was compelled to leave them for our troops.

Between Epehy and Roisel the enemy vainly endeavored by means of strong counterattacks to bring our victoriously advancing troops to a standstill. He was driven back everywhere, with the heaviest losses.

The heights north of Vermand were stormed. We stand before the third enemy position.

Under the effect of this success the enemy evacuated his positions in the bend southwest of Cambrai. We pursued him through Demicourt, Flesquières, and Ribecourt.

Between the Omignon stream and the Somme, corps of the army group of the German Crown Prince, after the capture of the first enemy positions, made their way through Holnon Wood and fought across the heights of Savy and Roupy, penetrating into the third enemy position.

South of the Somme divisions broke through the enemy lines, and in an uninterrupted forward movement drove the enemy over the Crozat Canal toward the west.

Jaeger battalions forced a crossing of the Oise west of La Fère. In company with divisions following, they stormed the heights northwest of the town, which are crowned with the permanent works of La Fère.

The captures so far reported by the army group of Crown Prince Rupprecht are 15,000 prisoners and 250 guns; by the army group of the German Crown Prince, 10,000 prisoners, 150 guns, and 300 machine guns.

Artillery battles continue between the Lys and La Bassée Canal.

Americans Capture German In His Own Listening Post

WITH THE AMERICAN ARMY IN FRANCE, March 23, (Associated Press.)—A patrol of four Americans early this morning crawled nearly a mile, approached a German listening post from the rear, and jumped on the German there, throttling him before he had a chance to make an outcry. They returned to their lines as quietly as they went, bringing their prisoner with them. He was put through an examination by the intelligence officers.

VIENNA, March 23, (British Admiralty, per Wireless Press.)—The War Office announces that a great success has been won in the west.

Germany Sees Decisive Moment.

LONDON, March 23.—The German newspapers, says an Exchange Telegraph dispatch from Amsterdam, reflect a feeling of confidence concerning the present operations in the west, though the seriousness of the moment is recognized, according to the Dutch news agencies.

The German newspapers insist that the military and political leaders of the Central Powers have left nothing undone to spare their people "this terrible blood bath."

The Copenhagen correspondent of the Exchange Telegraph Company says that German press comment is to the effect that the present battles are the decisive exertion of strength on the part of the German people before peace comes. The newspapers say that Germany need hold on only a short time and that victory will be obtained.

Much attention is being paid, also, to the Italian front.

The Central News says that all sorts of details are being sent out by German war correspondents. One of them talks about 1,000,000 yards of piping behind the front.

Another says that the number of airplanes has been increased tenfold.

According to still another, tanks, batteries for projecting poison gas and flames, and other modern engines of war in great numbers are on the front.

BAKER NOW IN LONDON; VISITED KING ALBERT

Secretary Returns from Belgian Front Via Calais and Is Guest of Ambassador Page.

LONDON, March 23.—Secretary Baker arrived here from Calais at 5 o'clock this afternoon. He was accompanied by Major Frederick Palmer.

The Secretary was met by Ambassador Page, Generals Biddle and Bartlett, and by Colonel Lord Duncannon, representing the British War Office. He drove to the house of Ambassador Page, whose guest he will be during his stay in London.

Secretary Baker visited King Albert of Belgium and the Belgian front yesterday.

LINES HOLDING IN NORTH

But West of St. Quentin the British Are Swept Back by Massed Foe.

ASSAULTS ARE CONTINUING

Ninety German Divisions Now Reported Engaged—Kaiser's Cavalry Thrown In.

BIG STROKE NEAR LA FERE

Foe Seeks to Break Through Line There—British Take Up Prepared Positions.

LONDON, March 23.—Battle of the most intense character is proceeding along the entire front from the Scarpe River to La Fère, according to the report of Field Marshal Haig tonight.

The British commander says that despite the determined attacks of the Germans, regardless of their losses, the British have held their positions on the northern part of the line.

South and west of St. Quentin, however, Haig's forces have been forced to retire to new positions and are now meeting new assaults by the enemy.

The day report stated that the Germans, by massed attacks, backed by great weight of artillery, had broken through the "defensive system" in this area. Tonight's bulletin tells of the repulse of the foe near Jussy, (lying south of the Somme Canal and about four miles west of the British front previous to the present offensive.)

Heavy Engagements Continue.

Tonight's bulletin reads as follows:

The battle is continuing with the greatest intensity on the whole front south of the Scarpe River.

South and west of St. Quentin our troops have taken up their new positions and we are heavily engaged with the enemy.

During the night strong hostile attacks in the neighborhood of Jussy (south of St. Quentin) were repulsed with great loss to the enemy.

On the northern portion of the battle front the enemy's attacks have been pressed with the utmost determination and regardless of losses.

Our troops have maintained their positions on the greater part of this front after a fierce and prolonged struggle.

Great gallantry has been shown by the troops engaged in the fighting in this area and south thereof. The 19th and 9th Divisions distinguished themselves by the valor of their defense. In one sector alone six hostile attacks, in two of which German cavalry took part, were beaten off by one of our infantry brigades.

The enemy's attacks continue with great violence.

The day report from General Haig, telling of the break in the British defensive system west of St. Quentin, reads:

Heavy fighting continued until late hours last night on the whole battle front. During the afternoon powerful hostile attacks, delivered with great weight of infantry and artillery, broke through our defensive system west of St. Quentin.

Our troops on this part of the battle front are falling back in good order across the devastated area to prepared positions further west.

Our troops on the northern portion of the battle front are holding their positions.

Very heavy fighting with fresh hostile forces is in progress.

Fifty German Airplanes Downed.

An official statement of the aerial operations issued tonight says:

A thick morning mist on Friday prevented our airplanes from leaving the ground during the early part of the day. When the mist cleared, there was much activity in the air on one battlefront. The enemy's low-flying machines were particularly active, engaging our forward groups with machine guns.

The enemy's massed troops again

Continued on Page Two.

Emperor Commands and Directs the Drive in Person; Crown Prince and Hindenburg With Him in Belgium

LONDON, March 23.—Today's official announcement from Berlin states that Emperor William is in command on the western front.

This announcement is regarded as further evidence that the Emperor has staked his all on an offensive, hoping to win and to go down in history as the victor in this great and decisive world conflict.

Dispatches from Amsterdam picture the Emperor at Spa, Belgium, which is being kept isolated on a radius of fifteen kilometers.

The German Crown Prince, Field Marshal von Hindenburg, General von Ludendorff and other prominent Germans are also reported to be there with him.

Germans' Vast Superiority in Guns Is Backed By Fifty Divisions

One Cannon to Every Twelve Yards of Front—One British Division Fought Six Near St. Quentin—Massed Assailants Mowed Down at Point Blank Range.

By PHILIP GIBBS.

Copyright, 1918, by The New York Times Company.

Special Cable to THE NEW YORK TIMES.

The following are the first dispatches received in this country from any special correspondent at the scene of the battle:

WAR CORRESPONDENTS' HEADQUARTERS, March 22.—The enemy flung the full weight of his great army against the British yesterday. Nearly forty divisions are identified, and it is certain that as many as fifty must be engaged. In proportions of men, the British are much outnumbered, therefore the obstinacy of the resistance of the troops is wonderful.

Nine German divisions were hurled against three British at one part of the line, and eight against two at another.

All the storm troops, including the guards, were in brand-new uniforms. They advanced in dense masses, and never faltered until shattered by the machine-gun fire.

As far as I can find, the enemy introduced no new frightfulness, no tanks and no specially invented gas, but relied on the power of his artillery and the weight of the infantry assault.

The supporting waves advanced over the bodies of the dead and wounded. The German commanders were ruthless in the sacrifice of life, in the hope of overwhelming the defense by the sheer weight of numbers.

Long-range Guns on the Front.

They had exceeding power in guns. Opposite three of the British divisions they had a thousand, and at most parts of the line one to every twelve or fifteen yards. They had brought a number of long-range guns, probably naval, and their shellfire was scattered as far back as twenty-eight miles behind the lines. During the last hour of the bombardment they poured out gas shells, and continued to send concentrated gas about the British batteries and reserve trenches. The atmosphere was filled with poisonous clouds. With this they failed to achieve success. There were only six cases of gas poisoning this morning in one of the largest casualty clearing stations.

The main object of the enemy's attack on the left of the battle front probably was to bite off the Bullecourt salient and pierce through the three main lines of defense below Croisilles and St. Leger and turn the line, so that he could capture Spin Hill with his old Hindenburg tunnel trench.

The Germans never made ground on the extreme left by the old Hindenburg line. A very gallant division of men drove them back when they attempted to cross No Man's Land, and did not lose a foot of their ground.

A little to the right of them the Bullecourt salient was utterly smothered with fire. No men could hold such a position.

Pushed on in Face of Slaughter.

Fortunately, in all parts of the line such a state of things was foreseen, and the outpost lines had only to fall back upon the battle positions to the rear, where there was a stronger defensive system. When the enemy followed on, bringing forward light artillery with support lines of infantry, the British guns slashed down his ranks and left masses of dead on the field. The British armies all report that they have seen large numbers of German dead heaped amid the débris of the wire and in the open ground.

But still they came on, with most fanatical courage of sacrifice. When the first lines fell, their places were filled by others, and the British guns and machine-gun fire could not kill them fast enough.

At 5:30 in the afternoon the enemy made another attack in massed formation, crowding down the slopes of the Sensée Valley from Cherisy and Fontaine Wood, striking down to the north of Vaulx. The British gunners fired into them with open sights, cutting swaths in the ranks and checking their tide of assault.

When the darkness fell they had not gained anything like the objectives marked out for them, and during the night they made no further attempt.

This morning there was fierce fighting round St. Leger, and the British troops took some prisoners and four machine guns.

Intense Assault on Salient.

From Noreuil eastward from Lagnicourt, around the bend of the Cambrai salient, the fighting was of the same intensity and the bombardment was equally terrific, supported by the same numbers of men, advancing in deep formations.

The outpost lines became untenable under the bombardment, and the British were ordered to fall back to battle position behind.

The enemy, by great sacrifices of life, was able to penetrate the first British defensive system in the neighborhood of Lagnicourt, Bouries, and Hargicourt, after which they were held.

A number of tanks made a brilliant counterattack before dark last evening and recaptured some of the ground near Doignies.

The defense of the British everywhere was splendid. An especially heavy attack was made yesterday by six German divisions on one British division south of St. Quentin. In spite of this vast superiority of numbers they were stricken with losses and the attack was checked all day until night, when the enemy, being spent, could make no further effort.

The British line was withdrawn to a strong position behind the canal between St. Quentin and the Oise, where the enemy will be caught in a waste of waters and marshes if he tries to make any further advance.

How the Offensive Began.

Thursday, March 21.—A German offensive against the British front has begun.

At about 5 o'clock this morning the enemy began an intense bombardment of the lines and batteries on a very wide front—something like sixty miles, from the country south of the Scarpe and to the west of Bullecourt in the neighborhood of Croisilles, as far south as the positions between St. Quentin and the British right flank.

After several hours of this hurricane shelling, in which it is probable that a great deal of gas was used with the intention of creating a poison gas atmosphere around the British gunners and forward posts, the German infantry advanced and developed attacks against a number of strategical points on a front of about twenty-five miles between the Scarpe and Hargincourt, ten miles north of St. Quentin. Whether they have attacked still further south I do not yet know.

Among the places against which they seem to have directed their chief efforts are Bullecourt, Lagnecourt, and Noreuil, both west of Cambrai, where they once before penetrated the British lines and were slaughtered in great numbers; the St. Quentin Ridge, which was on the right of the Cambrai fighting, and the villages of Ronssoy and Hargicourt, south of the Cambrai salient.

It is impossible to say yet how far the enemy will endeavor to follow up the initial movement of his troops over any ground that he may gain in the first rush or with what strength he will press forward his supporting divisions and fling his storm troops into the struggle, but the attack already appears to be on a formidable scale, with a vast amount of artillery

"All the News That's Fit to Print."

The New York Times.

THE WEATHER
Fair today and Friday; moderate northwest to north winds.
For full weather report see Page 21.

VOL. LXVII...NO. 21,978. NEW YORK, THURSDAY, MARCH 28, 1918.—TWENTY-TWO PAGES. TWO CENTS In Greater New York and Within Commuting Distance. | THREE CENTS Elsewhere.

BRITISH, REINFORCED, BEAT GERMANS BACK; BERLIN ADMITS PROGRESS IS NOW SLOW; LLOYD GEORGE CALLS FOR AMERICA'S AID

MESSAGE TO LORD READING

Read by the Ambassador at Lotos Club Dinner Last Night.

SURE OUR AID WILL WIN

Envoy Tells Hosts Britain Is Heartened in Dark Days by American Promise.

FULL PLEDGES ARE GIVEN

American Speakers Promise Full Measure of Country's Power—Kind Words to Wilson.

Through the Earl of Reading, British High Commissioner in the United States, David Lloyd George, the British Premier, sent a message direct to the American people last night urging that reinforcements be rushed to France. The message was delivered by Lord Reading at a dinner given in his honor by the Lotos Club, and in reading it he made it clear that it was the Premier's desire that it should go out to all the nation.

That they might better voice the spirit which animated them as speaker after speaker brought home the crucial nature of the moment and the need for America to do her share and to hurry in the doing, the diners sent to President Wilson a message drafted by Frank R. Lawrence, President of the club, which read:

"Members of the Lotos Club, assembled to do honor to the British Ambassador, send you greetings. We congratulate you on your clear interpretation of the aims of the Allies, your words of sympathy and hope to distracted Russia, your message of inspiration to the peoples fighting to maintain not only the principles of democracy but democracy itself.

"We cheer you for your encouragement to the commander and soldiers now defending the lines of modern civilization in the greatest battle in history. May the Government at Washington, represented by yourself, spokesman for righteousness, justice, and humanity, lead our cause to speedy victory."

Mr. Lawrence, in introducing Lord Reading, described him as both Lord Chief Justice and his Britannic Majesty's own representative, and called the presence of such a distinguished gathering a pledge that our war work indeed is to be speeded up, pointing out that every man owing allegiance to this country now must prove himself a patriot or a traitor. Lord Reading rose in response to a standing toast drunk to him by the guests, and said;

Lord Reading's Address.

"Mr. President, your Excellency, and gentlemen: At the outset of my observations permit me to thank you with all my heart for the cordial welcome and reception which you have been good enough to give to the toast which has been proposed to you, and which I accept and recognize with supreme gratification as testifying your good-will to the country which I have the honor to represent.

"It is well, Mr. President, that we should face facts. I do not believe that either you in this country or we in ours are ever the worse off for knowing the facts, even though they may be unpalatable. We have had during the last few days conflicting currents of anxiety which have no doubt stirred you, as they have stirred our people, to the depths. We have had an enemy who has concentrated his attacks upon our forces with the object of driving us to a surrender of large bodies of our troops and to break our lines so as to compel on our part the acceptance of a peace at the dictation of Germany.

"The attacks have been heavy; we have been driven from positions which we held. The enemy has been enabled to do this by withdrawing masses of troops from Russia, assisted by the artillery which he has got, not only from there but also from Austria, all flung upon the part of the line which was held by the British troops. Deeds of valor have been done; acts of prodigious valor have been accomplished daily. Many of them, alas, must remain unsung; but in the end the epic will be written which will, I verily believe, prove the record of one of the glorious chapters of British arms. Our men have been compelled to give ground in consequence of sheer weight of numbers of men and guns. If you read the stories that are daily appearing in your press you will know some of the deeds which our people have been called upon to perform. I am not going to enumerate them, for the best of all reasons, that I know not the details; they have not yet been chronicled. But I do know this, and I have no hesitation in saying it to you, speaking, as I do, as an Englishman and as the representative of my nation, that we have withstood the attacks of the enemy; that we have held our line under circumstances which may well rebound to the credit of any nation which may be called upon to submit to like attacks. (Ap-

Continued on Page Three.

British Premier's Message Asking Us to Rush Help

Read by the Earl of Reading at the Lotos Club dinner last night:

We are at the crisis of the war. Attacked by an immense superiority of German troops, our army has been forced to retire. The retirement has been carried out methodically before the pressure of a steady succession of fresh German reserves, which are suffering enormous losses.

The situation is being faced with splendid courage and resolution. The dogged pluck of our troops has for the moment checked the ceaseless onrush of the enemy, and the French have now joined in the struggle. But this battle, the greatest and most momentous in the history of the world, is only just beginning. Throughout it the French and British are buoyed with the knowledge that the great Republic of the West will neglect no effort which can hasten its troops and its ships to Europe.

In war time is vital. It is impossible to exaggerate the importance of getting American reinforcements across the Atlantic in the shortest possible space of time.

PARIS EXPECTS US TO RUSH SUPPORT

Fate of the Defense, It Is Said, May Hinge on Action Within a Few Months or Weeks.

WOULD SHORTEN TRAINING

French Deputy Says That This Is Not So Important as Prompt Aid in Man Power.

By CHARLES H. GRASTY.

Copyright, 1918, by The New York Times Company.

Special Cable to THE NEW YORK TIMES.

PARIS, March 27.—One cannot overemphasize the importance of reserves in the great battle raging for Paris and world-conquest. Ultimately the side having the greatest strength left must win. While the Germans may not be able to break through with superiority of numbers, at the end they will be masters if their reserves are greater.

Allied Europe looks to America to rush hither the weight of numbers that will insure victory and save civilization. As stated by the military authorities quoted in THE NEW YORK TIMES, the western line can probably be held several months against the present assault; but only by America's rushing troops to the scene within the next few months, or even weeks, can a successful defense be assured.

It is hoped here that America understands, and that she will act with the promptitude, thoroughness, and resourcefulness characteristic of her.

"Third Phase of the Battle."

Special Cable to THE NEW YORK TIMES.

PARIS, March 26, (Delayed.)—"Now we are entering the third phase of the battle. The German masses, wearied by their prodigious efforts and weakened by their appalling losses, must face the first riposte in the shape of a counteroffensive of French troops." In these words Premier Clemenceau's paper sums up this morning the general French criticism of the battle to date, and expectation for the future. The military critics are practically unanimous in their judgment. The opening phase was the original drive which forced the British back to the Bapaume-Péronne-Ham line. Then came renewed attacks, directed first by a frontal drive along the Somme in the direction of Amiens, and, when this was checked, by flank movements on the north in the Bapaume-Combles region and southward toward Noyon.

The enemy had a measure of success in both operations; but the arrival of British reserves and counterattacks by Canadians from the north seem to have barred his advance on the banks of the River Ancre.

Southward he came into contact with the French troops, which, fighting furiously, gave back step by step toward the line of the Oise.

It is generally thought here that the main German objective is Amiens, but a writer in the Petit Journal suggests that the thrust toward the Oise Valley, the traditional route of a German advance against Paris, may be intended in the nature of a diversion.

French opinion holds that in the two phases of the battle now passed, the initiative has everywhere belonged to Germany, and that there is at hand a period of counteraggressiveness by the Allies, which it is hoped will produce stabilization, as was the case at Verdun when Pétain's reserves checked the enemy on the slopes around Douaumont.

Although Marcel Hutin expresses the

Continued on Page Two.

THE BATTLE FOR ALBERT

Amiens and Other Towns in Rear Bombed by Air Raiders.

FOE'S BIVOUACS SHELLED

Great Rain of Explosives Catches Masses of Men Lying Out in Moonlight.

NO GREAT ADVANCES MADE

Kaiser's Gray Legions Pause to Reorganize Their Line and Let Guns Come Up.

By PHILIP GIBBS.

Copyright, 1918, by The New York Times Company.

Special Cable to THE NEW YORK TIMES.

WAR CORRESPONDENTS' HEADQUARTERS, March 27.—Yesterday and today the enemy has not made further advances on a big scale between the Arras-Bapaume Road on the left of the battlefront and the village of Bray, on the Somme, but has paused in his massed attacks in order to reorganize his line and bring up artillery. He has made cautious movements forward over the old Somme battlefields which have led to sharp fighting at various points and renewed losses to his assault troops.

It has been marvelously clear weather since the first foggy morning on March 21, and though now much colder, with a strong easterly wind which is painful to the British troops at night in the open fields, the British air squadrons have reconnoitred, bombed, and machine-gunned his massed battalions with constant audacity.

They have reported heavy concentrations of German storm troops behind Maurepas, Ginchy, and Beugnatre, and the roads around Bapaume have been crowded with men and guns and transport passing down through Le Sars, with German cavalry along the Bapaume-Gudecourt Road and a steady drift downward to the town of Albert.

City the Centre of Fighting.

That poor, stricken city of the golden Virgin, head downward, with her babe in her outstretched arms, which I described so often in accounts of the battles of the Somme in 1916, when that falling statue was lit up by shellfire, was yesterday in the centre of the fighting north of the Somme. The night before their assault yesterday they bombed it heavily from the air, using the brilliant moonlight, which lay white over all the battlefields and these roofs, to fly low and pick their targets wherever they saw men moving or horses tethered.

In several cases it was not men they hit but women and children who, when the war seemed to have passed from this place a year ago, crept back to their homes and built little wooden booths in which they sold papers and picture postcards to the troops. Now suddenly the war has flamed over them again and they were caught, before they could escape, by thunderbolts out of the shining moonlight, terribly clear and revealing dead horses about the ruined streets.

When I passed through a morning ago British field guns were passing below the outstretched arms of the Virgin, and companies of those dusty men took up positions beyond the town below shell-pierced walls and sunken roads to await the enemy and make him pay a price of blood.

Some refugees were leaving their homes, lingering to pack up a few bundles on barrows. Some of the children and old people were weeping, but I noticed that the young girls held themselves bravely and smiled at the British soldiers as if to say, "We, also, are not afraid."

Yesterday afternoon the enemy, who had been working closer with his men and guns in face of heavy machine-gun and artillery fire, opened a fairly heavy bombardment on Albert and its neighborhood. From high ground this side of Albert the British observers could see an enemy column coming over the slopes south of the town by Meaulte. Batteries I saw about the red brick ruins of Albert caught the enemy in the open and tore gaps in his ranks and the British poured a rifle fire at his advancing waves as they came over the slopes.

During the night all the British heavy guns in position flung high explosives over those battlefields whose earth had been more mauled by gunfire than any ground in the world of war. The enemy's massed troops were here without shelter or cover of any kind. Stretched on the earth and sleeping if they could in the tearing cold wind, this bombardment must have kept them awake unless they were drunk with sleepiness, and many men must have been killed as they lay still under the high white moon.

Airmen Busy in the Night.

At the same time British air raiders went out and flew very low, so that their wings were loud above the heads of the German bivouacs and dropped bombs into their masses and spilt machine-gun fire over them, and knew by the turmoil and cries that they were hurting and demoralizing the enemy.

The Germans retaliated in their own way by bombing open towns full of civilians, and I was in one of them last night, not far from the lines now, when these night bombers came over and dropped their engines of death. I have never seen such moonlight in March. It was like a June night in Southern France. Every roof was sharply defined by a silver edge of light and the walls of the old houses were dazzling white and their shadows very black. There seemed something devilish and cruel in that white light.

Quite early in the evening the bombs began to fall and all about took cover under the shadows of old doorways. The raiders came over all through the night. This was in Amiens under the great shadow of that cathedral which in the moonlight looked as insubstantial as a dream, with all its pinnacles and buttresses white as snow.

The enemy's strength of attack does not seem so great for the time being as on the first three or four days, and there is no doubt of what the prisoners say, that his men are suffering under the strain and horror of their losses and fatigue. But the battles are by no means over, and this is only a pause before renewed assaults.

Baker Aids in the Emergency; Hurley Heartens the British

Special Cable to THE NEW YORK TIMES.

LONDON, March 27.—The heartiest appreciation is expressed in representative quarters here of immediate steps taken by the United States in the present emergency. Secretary Baker's visit here fortuitously but happily coincided with the necessity of energetic measures which, under other circumstances, might have entailed a lengthy discussion.

That America was all in the war was well recognized before, but after the arrangements now completed, British confidence that the Western Republic would spare nothing in the common cause of democracy is doubly assured.

Coming with Field Marshal Haig's night bulletin, read in conjunction with the German official statement that "our attack is slowly progressing," with its implied admission of the accuracy of the British Field Marshal's report, London is regarding tonight's news as of the happiest augury.

Considerable satisfaction is also expressed with Chairman Hurley's survey of American shipbuilding. The Daily Chronicle says that it is full of hope for the future, and that, in the record of the struggle against enormous difficulties, America's shipbuilding contribution to the war is in a sense the most important, since the possibility of her making good in the other difficulties depends upon it.

BRITISH SHIP LOSS LARGEST IN MONTHS

Total of Twenty-eight Vessels Sunk Includes Sixteen Over 1,600 Tons.

LONDON, March 27.—Submarines and mines have increased their weekly toll of British shipping. The Admiralty's report shows that in the last week twenty-eight merchantmen were sunk, sixteen of the vessels being of 1,600 tons or over and twelve under that tonnage. One fishing vessel was lost. Nineteen merchantmen were unsuccessfully attacked.

The arrivals at ports in the United Kingdom numbered 2,471; sailings, 2,488.

Losses of Italian shipping through submarine attacks during the week ended March 23 were three steamers of more than 1,500 tons, two sailing vessels of more than 100 tons, and three sailing vessels of less than that tonnage.

The French shipping losses for the week ended March 23 by mine or submarine were one merchantman of over 1,600 tons, and five merchantment under that tonnage.

The total of 28 British ships sunk in a week has not been equaled since the week of Sept. 16, 1917, when 8 vessels over 1,600 tons and 20 under that tonnage were sunk, with 6 unsuccessful attacks.

BERLIN REPORTS SLOW GAIN

Says the British Are Retreating on Both Sides of the Somme.

ALBERT IN GERMAN HANDS

Foe Say They Are Across the Ancre River North and South of the City.

TALE OF BOOTY GROWS

Increased Number of Prisoners Reported — Battling in Flanders and Lorraine.

BERLIN, March 27, (via London.)—"On both banks of the Somme our armies are engaged in a slowly progressing attack," says the German official communication issued this evening.

According to the announcement issued by Army Headquarters early in the day, the British began to retreat early this morning on a wide front on both sides of the Somme. The stubborn resistance of the hostile rearguard was overcome in the sharp pursuit, it was stated.

British and French divisions which were defeated on Monday endeavored again yesterday in the pathless crater fields of the Somme battle, the announcement added, to arrest the German advance, but the Germans broke through the enemy's lines.

To the north and south of Albert the Germans won crossings of the Ancre. Albert was captured last evening.

To the south of the Somme, after violent fighting, German forces drove the enemy back by way of Chaulnes and Lihons. Roye was taken by storm, and Noyon was cleared of hostile forces after bloody street fighting, the report said.

The day bulletin reads:

The British began a retreat this morning on a wide front on both sides of the Somme. The stubborn resistance of the hostile rearguard was overcome in the sharp pursuit.

British and French divisions which were defeated on March 25 tried again yesterday in the pathless crater fields of the Somme battle area to arrest our advance. Our attack broke through the enemy's lines.

To the north and south of Albert we won a passage across the Ancre. Albert fell in the evening.

To the south of the Somme after violent fighting we drove back the enemy by way of Chaulnes and Lihons. Roye was taken by storm and Noyon was cleared of the enemy after bloody street fighting.

At many points we have crossed our old positions, held before the Somme battle of 1916, toward the west. The number of prisoners grows and the booty increases.

There were artillery battles in Flanders, before Verdun, and in Lorraine.

Captain Baron von Richthofen has achieved his sixty-ninth and seventieth aerial victories.

In the other theatres there is nothing new.

KAISER GRIEVED BY RUIN.

Tells How Glad He Is That Germany Is Spared Such Things.

AMSTERDAM, March 27.—The Volkszeitung of Cologne says that, according to General von Ludendorff, Emperor William has been deeply impressed by the terrible devastation in the battle area, remarking:

"How glad we should be that our country has been spared such terrible things. Why did we succeed in keeping the fighting beyond our frontier? Because before the war we always urged the need of armaments. When mankind changes these things also will change, but first mankind must begin to change."

Long Trains of Wounded Stream Back To the Remotest Parts of Germany

AMSTERDAM, March 27.—Enormously long ambulance trains are passing through Liége and Namur, Belgium, on their way to Aix-la-Chappelle and other parts of Germany with wounded from the battle front, according to the Telegraaf frontier correspondent.

Many of the wounded have been detrained at Namur, says the correspondent, who adds that the hospitals in Northern France have not sufficient accommodations for the great stream of sufferers.

The Telegraaf's Zevenaar correspondent says that the first transports with wounded have arrived at frontier towns. Commenting on this fact, the Telegraaf says that, while the German communications speak of the slight German losses, it is significant that even in the most out of the way places in Germany wounded are arriving.

Estimate the German Losses at 300,000 Men

LONDON, Thursday, March 28.—According to a Daily Mail correspondent in France, observers at the front estimate the number of German casualties resulting from the present offensive at 300,000.

FRENCH FORCED TO GIVE GROUND

Heavy Attacks Compel Them to Fall Back East of Montdidier.

ARE HOLDING ELSEWHERE

Furious Assaults of the Foe Near Lassigny and Noyon Fail to Gain.

PARIS, March 27.—In furious attacks with fresh troops in superior numbers the Germans today forced the French to yield some ground to the east of Montdidier, (southwest of Roye.) Near Lassigny and Noyon, however, the French completely checked equally violent assaults.

Last evening and during the night the Germans showed the effect of their heavy losses by a retarding of their efforts.

The text of the night report follows:

The Germans, throwing into the battle fresh new troops, today attacked with redoubled violence our positions east of Montdidier. Our troops with praiseworthy tenacity checked the assaults of the enemy, who succeeded in advancing only by reason of a marked superiority in numbers.

In the regions of Lassigny and Noyon attacks not less powerful suffered a complete check, breaking down before the heroic resistance of our regiments.

Following is the afternoon statement:

Last evening and during the night the Germans, weakened by their heavy losses, were compelled to retard their efforts. The valor of the French troops, defending the ground foot by foot, is beyond all praise.

The French are holding a line running through l'Echelle, St. Aurin, and Beuvraignes, north of Lassigny, in front of the southern part of Noyon and along the left bank of the Oise. During the night the French repulsed strong reconnoitring parties which attempted to approach their positions northwest of Noyon.

On the remainder of the front there was an intermittent bombardment.

FOE'S WEDGE TACTICS A FAILURE THUS FAR

French and British, in Strong Positions, Defy His Attempts to Split Them.

WITH THE FRENCH ARMY IN FRANCE, March 26, (Associated Press.)—The German effort by a terrific rush to get between the French and British forces, with the object of defeating each separately, has failed up to the present and is likely to continue to fail. The fighting qualities of the allied soldiers have served to stay the impetuous advance, and today the Anglo-French line is on strong positions.

The next few days may change the situation entirely, as the Allies have had time to get their "manoeuvring reserve" to take the initiative. Noyon was evacuated late last night in good order, and the French took up a position near bq.

The correspondent passed today among troops who have borne a great share in the fighting of the last five days. Everywhere cheerfulness was to be found and perfect confidence in the future. Nowhere has the correspondent seen such splendid morale among troops after long, hard fighting, more especially when those troops had to fall back. Both officers and men, whether French or British, tell narratives of wonderful heroism on the part of individuals and units.

The gunners of a battery of French 75s in the neighborhood of Chauny were

Continued on Page Two.

NEW STROKE NEAR, SAYS CLEMENCEAU

Returns from Front and Tells Deputies He Was Never More Confident.

PREDICTS COUNTERTHRUST

And Believes the Foe Will Be Forced Back by the Reserve Armies.

PARIS, March 27.—Premier Clemenceau told the Army Committee of the Chamber of Deputies today that the moment was near when the reserves of the Allies would enter into action. The great battle now being waged in France would then take on a new phase, he said, and there was every reason to hope that the enemy would not retain the benefit of the gains made at such a bloody price.

There was a settling down along the British and French fronts, where the Germans were trying to break through, and even within the last few hours there had been noted a slackening in the enemy's effort, he declared.

The Premier was before the committee for more than an hour and a half. He dealt at length with the situation, and spoke with full confidence in the future. Strategical considerations, he said, did not belong to the domain of the Government, but he gave details of the military situation, with an explanation of the measures taken, in agreement between the high commands of the Franco-British armies to assure effective direction of the operations.

An official note issued today says:

"The Cabinet met this morning, President Poincaré presiding. Premier Clemenceau informed his colleagues of the military situation. The Premier has just returned from the front, where he passed the day Tuesday with President Poincaré and Louis Loucheur, the Minister of Munitions.

The Premier returned with a satisfactory impression.

In conversation with Deputies who surrounded him in the lobby before the Chamber assembled this morning, Premier Clemenceau declared that never was confidence more justified than now.

According to the latest news from the front, the force of the German attack seems to have been diminished by the deadly struggle of the last few days. Yesterday's onslaught was far from having the same violence as those which preceded it.

Deputies who took part in earlier campaigns express the opinion that, if the Germans can be held for forty-eight hours more, their offensive will prove to have been checked.

Few of the Deputies listened to the debate in the Chamber. Most of them remained in the lobbies, commenting on the latest official communication. Henry Franklin-Bouillon, President of the Foreign Affairs Committee, said that, although the situation was serious, it should be regarded with serenity. He pointed out that the French Army, whose valor the enemy recognizes, was intact.

"This is but a minute part of our army," he added. "Not even ten divisions have participated in the battle."

Edouard Ignace, Under Secretary for Military Justice, confirmed these words. Leon Abrami, Under Secretary for Pensions, summed up the situation thus:

"After hard combats with the British troops, the Germans are about to meet the shock of a powerful French Army, perfectly fresh, animated by a spirit of sacrifice, and protected by a curtain of artillery fire such as it is difficult to conceive of. This army has been taken to the scene of action by railroads and every other route. Most of these troops have not yet fired a bullet or a shell. Hitherto a few independent divisions have checked the enemy's progress.

"Furthermore, formidable British reserves of manoeuvre are arriving on the battlefield, so that the enemy's gains of ground can be but ephemeral."

HAIG HOLDS ON THE SOMME

Retakes Two Towns on the North Bank and One on the South.

NEW NORTHERN LINE INTACT

Unsuccessful German Attacks Result in Heavy Losses to the Assailants.

GERMANS TAKE ONE TOWN

Gain Footing in Ablainville, Near Albert—German Reserves Fill Roads.

British Cavalry in France Win a Brilliant Victory

OTTAWA, March 27.—British cavalry has been in action and has achieved a brilliant victory, according to a dispatch from the Reuter correspondent at British headquarters, received here tonight.

The message said that no details of the action had been given.

LONDON, March 27.—In a day of furious fighting all along the front of the German offensive the British troops have checked the enemy with heavy losses and by counterattacks have made several important gains.

The battle was renewed this morning with great violence north and south of the Somme. Near Rozières, south of the river, the Germans delivered a series of fierce attacks, all of which were beaten off with heavy casualties.

Further north the fortunes of battle fluctuated, the British, after a successful defense early in the day, falling back a short distance before a fresh German attack, but later counterattacking and regaining their original positions.

South of Albert, which, as the official report admits, is now held by German troops, the British retook a position and held it in the face of heavy German attacks.

Morlaincourt and Chipilly, villages a little to the north of the Somme, in the angle formed by that river and the Ancre, were recaptured from the Germans in British counterattacks; and immediately to the south of the river Haig's men advanced their lines to the village of Proyart.

Late in the day the Germans, attacking in great strength near Bucquoy and Ablainville, (villages north of Albert,) gained a footing in the latter. At all other points, says Field Marshal Sir Douglas Haig in a bulletin issued tonight, the enemy was beaten off with great loss.

The text of the night statement reads:

The battle was renewed this morning with great violence south and north of the Somme. Intense fighting has taken place during the day from south of Rosières to north of Ablainville (Ablainzevelle).

An unsuccessful attempt made by the enemy last night to drive in our line south of the Somme was followed this morning by a series of heavy attacks in the neighborhood of Rosières and to the south of that place. At Rosières all the enemy's assaults have been beaten off by our troops, who inflicted heavy casualties on the enemy.

Further north our line was maintained through the earlier part of the day in spite of great pressure from large hostile forces.

Later in the day a fresh German attack developed in this area, with the result that our line was taken back a short distance to the west. Later reports show that our counterattacks have again completely restored the situation.

During the day the enemy made a number of determined attacks against our positions between the Somme and the Ancre and north and south of Albert. Fierce fighting has taken place in this sector also.

Part of our position to the south of Albert, into which the enemy at one time forced his way, was re-

"All the News That's Fit to Print."

The New York Times.

THE WEATHER
Snow or rain, colder today; Thursday probably rain; northeast gales.
For full weather report see Page 23.

VOL. LXVII...NO. 21,991. NEW YORK, WEDNESDAY, APRIL 10, 1918.—TWENTY-FOUR PAGES. TWO CENTS In Greater New York and Within Commuting Distance. | THREE CENTS Elsewhere.

ANGRY PROTESTS ROUSED BY LLOYD GEORGE, AS HE ANNOUNCES CONSCRIPTION FOR IRELAND; GERMANS STRIKE HEAVY BLOW IN THE NORTH

SPEECH IN THE COMMONS

Premier Presents Bill for Drafting All Men 18 to 50.

BILL ADMITTED BY 299 TO 80

Irish Members Shouting Defiance and Vowing Never to Submit.

NEW LIGHT ON GREAT DRIVE

British Bravery Retrieved Initial Reverse—Dramatic Aid of Wilson Warmly Acknowledged.

Special Cable to THE NEW YORK TIMES.

LONDON, April 9.—Great Britain was asked this afternoon to place at the disposal of the Government the services of every able-bodied man up to 50 years old, and even in certain cases up to 55. The announcement was made that conscription was to be applied to Ireland.

Crowds gathered at the approaches to the Houses of Parliament, and the benches of the Commons were closely packed with members, who showed deep interest in the questions and the Premier's method of presenting the prime importance of the issues involved. There were no fireworks in his speech, but an earnest insistence on the peril of the moment and the necessity of taking every possible measure to meet it.

The House at question time had shown itself full of life. It rose to every controversial point, and it sent up a deep cheer of welcome as Captain Redmond took the oath on his reelection to his father's old seat. As Mr. Lloyd George began his speech it settled down to listen, and resented fiercely interruptions from pacifist members.

Premier Shows Gravity of Task.

The Premier seemed at first to be restrained by the gravity of the moment. "We have now entered the most critical phase of this terrible war," he began, and he spoke slowly and with constant consultation of his notes. For nearly an hour he reviewed the military situation, and though he expressed his entire confidence in the army and paid a high tribute to the courage, endurance, and skill of soldiers and Generals alike, it was clear that he was impressed by the vastness of the forces against the Allies and the reality of their danger.

Not until he spoke of General Carey and his "brilliant achievement" in stopping the German advance with a scratch corps of signalmen, engineers, and labor battalions did he arouse the enthusiasm of the House in a round of deep cheers.

As the Premier came to discuss the appointment of Foch as generalissimo it was clear that he felt himself to be on delicate ground. He spoke with something like his old animation, smote the box on the table, and looked the House squarely in the face. He was prepared for criticism and got applause, but it was not very cordial.

Replies to Saloniki Critics.

Once again, as Lloyd George replied to the critics of the subsidiary expeditions in Saloniki, Palestine, and Mesopotamia, he spoke with vigor, but the House was not inclined to show much interest in these matters when it was full of anxiety about the Government's man-power proposals.

At last Lloyd George reached these and in the main they did not create surprise. They had been forecast fairly accurately in the newspapers and the House received quietly the news that men up to 50 might be called up, that essential industries were to be combed out again, and that ministers of religion would be subject to noncombatant service.

Irish Create a Storm.

The real surprise came when the Premier announced shortly and decidedly:

"As to Ireland, it is not possible any longer to justify her exclusion from the act."

Like a field of wheat swept by gusts of wind, sharp interruptions burst out. Lloyd George appealed to the United States, more Irish than Ireland, he called it, where all were subject to conscription. "But not by the English," came back a retort by a member, shouted with a stentorian voice.

Cheers burst out in a great volume from all parts of the house except the Irish benches, and they answered with cries of protest. The Premier tried to continue his quiet, dispassionate speech, but Irish members were wound up to fierce excitement. Their quarter of the house was rocking with anger. Lines of members swayed to and fro.

"It is a declaration of war on Ireland," said one.

Quietly the Premier read out what Irish leaders like the late John Redmond had said of the justice of the war, and brought John Dillon, the new leader, to his feet in explanation of words he had used in 1914. But what especially roused the Irish to bitter anger was the Premier's insistence that this was a war in the interest of small nations. They flung back the words in his teeth, and stirred the rest of the House to angry reply, but the Premier, with only one protest that he be permitted to speak, went quietly on to his peroration.

Asquith Counsels Deliberation.

John Devlin wished to move an adjournment to permit the Government to consider the report of the Committee on Conscription of the Irish convention, but gave way to ex-Premier Asquith.

Mr. Asquith spoke calmly and coolly, dwelling on the reality of the crisis. He reserved the right to criticise the Government bill at a time when he had an opportunity to consider its details, and then obtained a sympathetic cheer from the House as he told of the heroism of the British soldiers, as he had just learned it from a letter from a "relative, in fact one of my own sons." As an old Parliamentarian, he advised the Premier not to rush the new bill, but to permit the House plenty of time to digest it.

Text of the Speech.

LONDON, April 9.—The full text of the Prime Minister's speech follows:

"We have now entered the most critical phase of this terrible war. There is a lull in the storm, but the hurricane is not over. Doubtless we must expect more fierce outbreaks, and ere it is finally exhausted there will be many more.

"The fate of the empire, the fate of Europe, and the fate of liberty throughout the world may depend on the success with which the very last of these attacks is resisted and countered.

"The Government, therefore, propose to submit to Parliament today certain recommendations, in order to assist this country and the Allies to weather the storm. They will involve, I regret, extreme sacrifices on the part of large classes of the population, and nothing would justify them but the most extreme necessity and the fact that we are fighting for all that is essential and most sacred in our national life.

"Before I come to the circumstances which led up to our submitting these proposals to Parliament, I ought to say one word as to why Parliament was not immediately summoned. Since the battle began the Government have been engaged almost every hour in concerting with the Allies the necessary measures to assist the armies to deal with the emergency.

Action "Far Removed" from Panic.

"The proposals which we intend submitting to Parliament required very close and careful examination, and I think there is this advantage in our meeting today, rather than immediately after the impact of the German attack, that we shall be considering these proposals under conditions which will be far removed from any suggestion of panic.

"I shall now come to the circumstances which have led to the present military position. It is very difficult at this time to present a clear, connected, and reliable narrative of what happened. There has been a great battle on a front of fifty miles—the greatest battle ever fought in the history of the world. Enormous forces have been engaged; there was a considerable retirement on the part of the British forces, and under these conditions it is not always easy for some time to ascertain what actually happened.

"The House will recollect the difficulty we experienced with regard to Cambrai. It was difficult to piece together the story of the event for some time, and Cambrai was a very trivial event compared with this gigantic battle.

"The Generals and their staffs are, naturally, engaged and have to concentrate their attention upon the operations of the enemy, and until the strain relaxes it would be very difficult to institute the necessary inquiries to find out exactly what happened, and to furnish an adequate explanation of the battle.

German Forces Slightly Smaller.

"However, there are two or three facts which stand out, and in stating them I should like to call attention to two things which I think above all must be avoided. The first is that nothing should be said which could give information to the enemy; nothing should be said which would give encouragement to the enemy, and nothing should be said which would give discouragement to our own troops, who are fighting so gallantly at this very hour.

"And the second question is that all recrimination at this hour must be shut out.

"What was the position at the beginning of the battle? Notwithstanding the heavy casualties in 1917 the army in France was considerably stronger on Jan. 1, 1918, than on Jan. 1, 1917. Up to the end of 1917—up to, say, about October or November—the German combatant strength in France was as two to the Allies' three. Then came the military collapse of Russia, and the Germans hurried up their released divisions from the eastern front and brought them to the west. They had a certain measure of Austrian support, which had been accorded to them.

"Owing to the growth of the strength of our armies in 1917, when this battle began the combatant strength of the whole of the German Army on the western front was only

Continued on Page Three.

Irish Coercion a Blunder and a Catastrophe, Says Daily Chronicle, Supporter of Lloyd George

Special Cable to THE NEW YORK TIMES.

LONDON, Wednesday, April 10.—The Daily Chronicle says editorially, in commenting on yesterday's proceedings in Parliament:

"The Irish proposal provoked immediate and stormy opposition from the Nationalist members. This was inevitable. We see no prospect of its being abated, and its result can hardly fail to be prejudicial both to the Irish question and the man-power question; to the former because it substitutes an atmosphere of coercion for that of reconciliation at a supremely inopportune moment, and to the latter because the controversy over this feature of the bill must tend to impede and obscure discussion over those more material features of it which affect Great Britain.

"Setting aside the views of the extreme Nationalist and Unionist partisans, one may doubt whether there is a single one of those more centrally minded Irishmen who have worked so hard for the triumph of the convention and the reunion of the Irish people who does not recognize that the attempt to enact Irish conscription at this juncture is a blunder and a catastrophe."

GREAT GAS ATTACK BY FOE

More Than 60,000 Poison Shells Rained on British During the Night.

SEVERAL TOWNS UNDER FIRE

Portuguese, Who Hold Part of Line, Sustain Fierce Onslaughts Gallantly.

BATTLE ON FAMOUS GROUND

Germans Hampered by Bad Weather and Bad Terrain for Their Offensive.

By PHILIP GIBBS.

Copyright, 1918, by The New York Times Company.

Special Cable to THE NEW YORK TIMES.

WAR CORRESPONDENTS' HEADQUARTERS IN FRANCE, April 9.—A heavy and determined attack was begun against us this morning a considerable distance north of our recent battles on about eleven miles of front between Armentières and La Bassée Canal. So far as the news comes to us up to this afternoon the enemy apparently has succeeded in driving in parts of the Allies' post lines, while the troops are holding him by Givenchy on the right and about Fleurbaix on the left.

This new attack was preceded by a long, concentrated bombardment, which had gradually been increasing during the last day or two, until it reached great heights of fury last night and early this morning. The enemy used poison gas in immense quantities, and it may be estimated that during the night he flung over 60,000 gas shells in order to create a wide zone of this evil vapor and stupefy the gunners, transport, and infantry if they were caught without their masks, which is improbable.

His gunfire reached out to many towns and villages behind the allied lines, like Bethune and Armentières, Vermelles and Philosophe, Merville and Estaires, and this did not cease around Armentières until 11:30 this morning, though further south from Fleurbaix his infantry attack was in progress at an early hour, certainly by 8 o'clock, and his barrage lifted in order to let his troops advance.

The strength of his attack is not yet known with any certainty, but three divisions are in that area, including the 44th Reserve and 81st and 11th Ersatz, and it is probable that he has other forces engaged.

Portuguese Troops in Line.

Part of the line was held by Portuguese troops, who for a long time have been between Laventie and Neuve Chapelle, holding positions which were subject to severe raids from time to time. They are now in the thick of this battle, most fiercely beset and fighting gallantly.

It is a battle over the old and famous ground where early in this war there was most deadly strife during the struggle around Neuve Chapelle in March of 1915 and at Festubert. It is ground where the Indian infantry attacked again and again with most gallant courage and where afterward the survivors held the lines through the Spring and Summer, so that the flat fields all around with fringes of willows along narrow canals that intersect all this moist land and the villages behind, like Estaires and Laventie, and places of ruin like La Gorgue and Richebourg and Quinque Rues, will be forever haunted with memories of those dark-dyed men, who to the French peasants seemed like fairy princes and figures out of the Arabian Nights tales. They disappeared long ago through the mists of these flats to other fighting fields in other countries.

Suddenly the enemy has struck, and the centre of strife for the moment has shifted. It is awkward ground for attack and bad weather for such ground, because the enemy has to advance across dead-flat marshes, cut

Continued on Page Two.

British Destroyer Sank in Collision; Whole Crew Lost

LONDON, April 9.—A British torpedo boat destroyer sank last Thursday as the result of a collision, and all hands on board are believed to have been drowned, according to an Admiralty statement issued tonight. The statement says:

"One of his Majesty's torpedo boat destroyers sank on the 4th instant as the result of a collision in the foggy weather. All hands are missing, and it is presumed they were drowned."

DEEDS OF DARING BY OUR ENGINEERS

Fought and Killed for Days Beside Canadians Retreating from St. Quentin.

PRAISED BY THE BRITISH

"Held On by Their Teeth Till the Last Moment," Says an Officer Who Saw Them.

WITH THE AMERICAN ARMY IN FRANCE, April 8, (Associated Press.)—The American railway engineers who helped stem the tide of the onrushing Germans during the opening days of the battle now in progress fought shoulder to shoulder with Canadian engineers in carrying out their task. They held their ground stubbornly, and only retired to previously prepared positions when forced to do so, and inflicted casualties by the thousand upon the Germans as they advanced in close formation—in one place in as many as seven waves, each wave 10 men deep and 100 yards from the next.

The Americans with the Canadians had all the ammunition they needed, and, although they were unsupported by the artillery and armed only with rifles and with a few machine guns, they poured streams of bullets into the enemy at several different times until their weapons were so hot as to be useless.

This handful of American soldiers, who were not hardened to such terrific slaughter, were sickened by the shambles they created, but fought furiously for several days, helping to hold the enemy all the way from near St. Quentin to the vicinity of Noyon. These were the Americans mentioned at the time in the official communiqués, but these details of their exploits it has only now been possible to obtain.

When the German attack began the Americans were working in the rear lines with the Canadians, under Canadian command. They quickly threw down their tools and seized the weapons with which they had been armed for some months, and formed themselves into a fighting unit. The Germans came on and finally reached the positions where the Americans were waiting.

The exact number of the engineers cannot be given, but they were comparatively small. They had no intention of retreating, however, and were bent upon killing all the Germans possible.

Tore Gaps in German "Waves."

As the first gray enemy wave advanced, the American forces let them come until they were within certain range; then opened fire, pouring in a storm of bullets. Gaps appeared in the advancing lines at many places, some of them large, where the machine guns had chewed through. Still the German waves came on, without firing a single shot—just advancing.

The Americans were unable to understand these tactics, but, nevertheless, were certain that it was a question of slaughtering the enemy or being themselves smothered under the advance. By this time their weapons were so hot that they could not be used effectively, and the enemy was close, so that the engineers retired, fighting, took up another position, then turned and began operations again. A British officer who witnessed the engagement is reported to have said:

"They held on by their teeth until the last moment, inflicting terrific casualties on the enemy. Then they moved back and waited for the Germans, and repeated the performance."

By the time the engineers reached a place somewhere near Noyon they were nearly exhausted and almost without equipment. There they had a chance to rest and re-equip. According to all reports, they were entitled to it, for certainly they gave the Germans a generous sample of what the enemy is to expect from the American Army.

A German Trick that Failed.

During a battle unusual stories always crop up, but the following is one which the correspondent heard from an unquestionable source, and it is said to have been verified:

In one of the periods when the Amer-

Continued on Page Six.

German Staff Fully Expected to Rout the Allies And Cause Withdrawal of Entire Western Front

WITH THE FRENCH ARMY IN FRANCE, April 9, (Associated Press.)—Prisoners captured on the Oise front say that the German staff fully expected to reach their objectives on the morning of April 6, counting on their superior numbers to overwhelm the French.

Other information from prisoners shows that the Germans expected immensely greater results from their surprise offensive. They not only hoped to push the Allies back from the Somme, but also looked for a general withdrawal all along the front, even far eastward of the line attacked.

German observers, both in the trenches and in sausage balloons, had orders to keep a sharp lookout for signs of a French retreat and report them to the staff. They were told to watch for burning villages and supply dumps, and were surprised when they saw nothing of the kind.

Still other prisoners, who have recently come from the Russian front, assert that the German authorities were profoundly disappointed concerning Russia. Much of the land there is uncultivated, while the greater part of the stocks of wheat has disappeared, through pillage or wastage. Reports regarding these conditions have reached the German people and caused considerable effervescence.

HAIG LINE PIERCED, BERLIN REPORTS

Germans Penetrated the English and Portuguese Positions, It Is Stated.

FRENCH LOSE THREE TOWNS

Further Gains Made by Hindenburg's Troops in Region South of Oise.

BERLIN, April 9, (via London.)—The War Office this evening issued the following communication:

North of La Bassée Canal we penetrated into English and Portuguese positions.

On both sides of the Somme there have been violent artillery duels.

On the southern bank of the Oise we threw back the enemy across the Oise-Aisne Canal between Coucy-le-Château and Brancourt.

The losses in March of enemy aerial fighting forces in the western theatre amount to twenty-three captive balloons and 348 airplanes. Of the latter 158 were brought down behind our lines. The others were observed to fall within the enemy's positions.

We lost eighty-one airplanes and eleven captive balloons.

The official communication issued earlier in the day said:

Lively artillery duels have frequently developed on the battlefront.

On the south bank of the Oise the troops of Generals von Schoeller and Wichisra again have attacked the enemy.

Between the Oise and Folembray they advanced across the Aillette as far as the Oise-Aisne Canal, and in a fierce battle captured the stubbornly defended wood east of Guny.

Attacking from the north and east, they climbed the steep slopes of the heights east of Coucy-le-Château and captured by storm strongly fortified enemy positions. Quency and Landricourt were taken, and Coucy-le-Château fell early this morning.

GERMANS ATTEMPT TO EXPLAIN DELAYS

Military Critics Seek to Allay Public Disappointment Over the Results of Drive.

By GEORGE RENWICK.

Copyright, 1918, by The New York Times Company.

Special Cable to THE NEW YORK TIMES.

AMSTERDAM, April 9.—The very slight German gains of the last few days have been reported in the German press with much the same wealth of headlines and resounding comment as greeted the first successes in March.

All the papers had frankly stated that the renewed fighting at the end of last week was the definite reopening of the offensive, and a good deal of effort has been expended by the critics in explaining away the wait, which certainly had not been expected in Germany before Amiens was reached. The Cologne Gazette says that the halt was occasioned by the need "on both sides" (the word "both" is interesting) to bring up the reserves, and it deals at length with the

Continued on Page Two.

AIRMEN BROKE UP GERMAN ATTACKS

Flew as Low as 68 Feet and Rained Bullets on Infantry Near Montdidier.

BAYLIES, DOWNED, ESCAPED

American Sergeant Fell Almost Into Enemy's Hands, but Got Back Amid Cheers.

From a Staff Correspondent.

Copyright, 1918, by The New York Times Company.

Special Cable to THE NEW YORK TIMES.

WITH THE FRENCH ARMIES, April 9.—Although the American infantry is not in action on the Picardy battlefield, the United States has been represented in the air from the outset of the German drive. Many American aviators serving under the French flag have been engaged in battle. A NEW YORK TIMES correspondent met today Sergeant Frank Baylies, from New Bedford, a member of the famous "Ace squadrilla" of storks to which Guynemer belonged.

Baylies joined the aviation service last June after two years in Macedonia with the French Red Cross, for which he was decorated with the War Cross with star, became a member of the Stork squadrilla Oct. 1, a few days after Guynemer's death, and has brought down two Germans for which he has been rewarded with two palms on the cross. Shortly after the opening of the German offensive the squadrilla went by air at an hour's notice to Montdidier and took active part in all subsequent operations.

When the town was captured by the enemy the airmen managed to remove all the machines and camions, but several fliers lost the greater part of their personal effects. Baylies was more fortunate.

Throughout the French retirement the airmen co-operated with the infantry and made three patrol flights—averaging from an hour and a half to two hours' duration—daily. As the German attacks were made almost without artillery or airplanes—for whole days no enemy planes were sighted—the fliers devoted themselves to harassing enemy infantry and convoys on the march.

Flew Low for Attacks.

Flying often as low as sixty-eight feet, airmen turned mitrailleuses pointblank on the enemy, who fled headlong or threw themselves flat to escape the stream of bullets. When convoys were attacked, horses plunging madly in death agony threw the whole line into confusion.

At such an altitude the aviator was greatly exposed to the fire of the German infantry, and injury to the motor forced an immediate landing, as the height was insufficient for a long volplane. On March 28 Baylies was thus downed near Mesnil-St. Georges. The young American—he is just 22—gave the following description of his experience:

"I had been annoying Fritz all morning and having a wonderful time when I spotted a body of infantry moving toward Tickish Wood just after luncheon. As I dived upon them over the trees, quickfirers concealed there riddled my machine with bullets. My impetus luckily carried me a little further into a grassy field, just between the two armies, where I landed not too abruptly.

"Unfortunately I was barely fifty feet from the boches and nearly a hundred yards from the French. At this point there were no trenches and both sides fought in the open, the Germans advancing in small groups from thicket to thicket and taking cover wherever possible. As they saw me falling the enemy began firing furiously and a party of five Germans ran out to intercept me. A French Alpine Chasseur

Continued on Page Six.

FOE GAINS NEAR LA BASSEE

Forces Back the British-Portuguese Centre on the River Lys.

BUT BRITISH FLANKS HOLD

Repulse Attacks at Givenchy and Fleurbaix, While Richebourg and Laventie Fall.

FOG AIDS THE ASSAILANTS

Battle, Which Began in the Morning, Still Rages on the 11-Mile Front.

LONDON, April 9.—Beginning with a bombardment of great intensity, German troops this morning delivered heavy attacks upon the British and Portuguese lines from the La Bassée Canal to the neighborhood of Armentières, (a distance of about eleven miles.)

The enemy forced back the Portuguese in the centre and the British on the flanks of the line of the River Lys between Estaires and Bac St. Maur.

Richeboucq-St. Vaast, (about a mile south of Neuve Chapelle,) and Laventie, (about two miles northeast of Neuve Chapelle,) were taken by the Germans in the assault.

The British withstood all attacks at Givenchy, (at the southern limit of the German assaults,) and Fleurbaix, at the north, about three miles southeast of Armentières.

The German attack was favored by the thick mist which shrouded the battlefield in the early morning.

Severe fighting continues on the whole of this front, according to Field Marshal Haig's night report.

South of Arras there were only minor engagements today on the British front.

Following is the text of the night bulletin:

This morning, after an intense bombardment of our positions from La Bassée Canal to the neighborhood of Armentières, strong hostile forces attacked the British and Portuguese troops holding this sector of our front. Favored by a thick mist, which made observation impossible, the enemy succeeded in forcing his way into the Allies' positions in the neighborhood of Neuve Chapelle, Fauquissart, and Cardonnerie Farm.

After heavy fighting, lasting throughout the day, the enemy succeeded in forcing back the Portuguese troops in the centre and the British troops on the flanks of the line of the River Lys, between Estaires and Bac St. Maur.

We held out positions on both banks [flanks?] about Givenchy and Fleurbaix. At both these latter places there was heavy fighting, but the enemy was repulsed.

Richebourg-St. Vaast and Laventie have been taken by the enemy.

Severe fighting is continuing on the whole of this front.

South of Arras only minor engagements, in which were secured a few prisoners, have taken place during the day on the British front.

The afternoon official statement reads:

Early this morning the enemy's artillery developed great activity on the front extending from La Bassée Canal to south of Armentières.

Elsewhere on the British front, except for heavy hostile shelling in the neighborhood of Villers-Bretonneux and Mericourt l'Abbé, there was nothing special to report.

Monday's Rain Checked Aviation.

The following official communication dealing with aviation was issued this evening:

With the exception of a few flights at low altitudes, there was [illegible]

"All the News That's Fit to Print."

The New York Times.

THE WEATHER
Fair until Sunday, warmer tonight; diminishing northwest winds.
For full weather report see Page 23.

VOL. LXVII...NO. 22,013. NEW YORK, THURSDAY, MAY 2, 1918.—TWENTY-FOUR PAGES. TWO CENTS In Greater New York and Within Commuting Distance. THREE CENTS Elsewhere.

AMERICANS WIN FIRST FIGHT ON AMIENS FRONT; REPEL FOE WITH LARGE LOSSES ON BOTH SIDES; VON ARNIM REORGANIZING HIS BROKEN FORCES

SAVANNAH LINER SUNK BY FRENCH WARSHIP, 67 LOST

City of Athens, Rammed in Dense Fog Near Delaware Coast, Sank Rapidly.

ONLY 68 COULD BE SAVED

Women Passengers, Roused from Sleep, Aided by American Marines and French Sailors.

LIFEBOATS WERE CAPSIZED

Complaints Made by Marines That Apparatus was Not in Proper Order—Searchlights Saved Swimmers.

AN ATLANTIC PORT, May 1.—The coastwise steamer City of Athens of the Savanah Line, bound for Savanah, Ga., was rammed by a French warship [name omitted at the request of the French Embassy] in a dense fog off Cape Romaine, near the Delaware coast, shortly after 1 o'clock this morning, sixty-seven lives being lost. The steel bow of the warship cut through the side of the steamer like paper, making a huge hole which began to fill up at once. The City of Athens was sinking rapidly before the warship could man boats for rescue, and within a few minutes after the shock the steamer shot down under the water bow foremost.

Three large lifeboats were put off from the sinking ship, one of which capsized as it hit the water and most of those on board were lost. Several life rafts followed, but the sinking took place so rapidly that several of the life-saving craft could not be launched. Many of those on the deck when the steamer went down were drowned almost immediately, while others remained afloat on wreckage and were either picked up by small boats from the cruiser or eventually lost. Because of the speed of the ship's sinking and the fog which impeded rescue, only sixty-eight of the passengers and crew were saved out of a total of 135.

Those Reported Drowned.

The following is the list of the passengers reported lost:

Bodziner, Richard....Mobile, Ala.
Cadron, Jean........New York City.
Clug, Edward........Savannah, Ga.
Dalzell, Isaac.......Paterson, N. J.
Denk, C. A..........Brooklyn.
Dixon, F. R.........U. S. Marine.
Graham, R. J........No address.
Ginsburg, S.........U. S. Marine.
Green, M............Astoria, N. Y.
Holthan, Mrs. F. D...Hyde Park, Mass.
Kahn, N.............No address.
Kastl, James J......Morristown, N. J.
Lillie, N. W........No address.
Mack, W. J..........U. S. Marine.
Reynolds, Rev. J. P...New York City.
Rosenfield, H.......U. S. Marine.
Stiles, Miss E. G....New York City.
Tynge, S. H.........U. S. Marine.
Van Hanegren, Peter..U. S. Marine.
Wetmore, H. E.......U. S. Marine.
Young, R. A.........Brooklyn.

The Known Survivors.

Among the known survivors are the following:

Bodziner, Mrs. Richard, Mobile, Ala.
Brooks, Dr. E. L., Atlanta, Ga.
Dixon, F. R., marine, Port Royal, S. C.
Gewehr, A. P., Brooklyn, N. Y.
Gewehr, Mrs. A. P., Brooklyn, N. Y.
Green, John, Paterson, N. J.
Harrison, Mrs. R., New York City.
Kemp, Dr. A. J., New York City.
Levy, Miss Etta, Bridgeport, Conn.
MacClaskie, Alden, New York City.
McMillan, D. H., marine, Port Royal, S. C.
O'Brien, J. F., Savannah, Ga.

French Sailors Reported Missing.

The following French sailors, who were among the passengers on the City of Athens, were reported missing:

Bouchard, H. — La Beste, J.
Carmes, E. — Le Nours, J.
Chevances, J. — Marzion, Y.
Coumereaux, H. — Michel, Y.
Droval, F. — Phillippe, J.
Giraud, F. — Pizieu, J.
Heraff, Y. — Quingard, Y.
Intervinow, F. — Rinquin, Y.
Itier, L. — Sauva, Y.
Jegow, A. — Seguillon, J.

Officers and Crew Saved.

The following officers and members of the crew were reported saved:

Forward, A. C., Captain.
Doersching, L. J., second officer.
Bevel, H. O., third officer.
Vollmer, C. W., wireless operator.
Connor, C. C., cadet, Naval Aux. Reserve.
Turner, R. H., cadet, Naval Aux. Reserve.
Sandbloom, F. G., cadet, Naval Aux. Reserve.
Stewart, H. W., chief engineer.
McGuire, J. D., first assistant engineer.
Kelly, H. A., second assistant engineer.
Falconer, J., chief steward.
Henderson, William J. R., seaman.
Nelson, M. R., seaman.
Ward, A., seaman.
Telbre, J. Y., seaman.
Armand, J. Y., water tender.
Besley, E., water tender.
Betshar, G., water tender.

Continued on Page Six.

1,000 "Match" the President As He Buys Bond at Theatre

WASHINGTON, May 1.—President Wilson went to a local theatre tonight and formally offered his "buy another bond" $50 subscription to a four-minute speaker. The audience rose and cheered justly. A landslide of subscriptions followed, more than half of the 2,000 persons present "matching the President," and the total ran over $300,000.

Some one speaking for Francis R. Mayer of New York offered to take $100,000 of bonds if 200 $50 subscriptions were forthcoming. Two hundred subscribers promptly responded, and the $100,000 sale was recorded.

PRESIDENT GIVES LOAN NEW VIM

Buys an Additional $50 Bond, and Clubs to "Match" Him Start Everywhere.

TOTAL LOAN $2.579,079,400

Tuesday's Subscriptions $121,-334,500. Leaving $420,920,-600 Yet to be Raised.

Special to The New York Times.

WASHINGTON, May 1.—The subscriptions to the Third Liberty Loan up to last night total $2,579,079,400. Today's returns are expected to make another record. This hope is based on the effect of President Wilson's example, set today, when he subscribed for a $50 bond on the monthly payment plan, and authorized the request that as many persons as possible match his final subscription. The President had previously made large subscriptions—nearly $20,000 and had gone as far as his present means would justify.

The Loan Publicity Bureau placed thousands of telegrams on the wires to every part of the country heralding the President's act and suggesting the formation everywhere of "Match the President" clubs. A telegram came to the White House from a little girl telling the President she had "matched him." The Philadelphia Committee wired that in one restaurant alone seventy-nine persons had matched the President's purchase during the lunch hour. Boston wired that the whole Loan Committee had promptly imitated the Chief Magistrate and thereby had started the entire city to doing the same.

At 20,000 meetings throughout the country four-minute speakers tonight invited their audiences to match the President. The invitation will be repeated at every public meeting in the United States until the close of the loan Saturday night.

Yesterday's total subscriptions were $121,334,500, as compared with $174,443,000 Monday, the red letter day of the campaign thus far. The amount to be raised in the last four days of the campaign is $420,920,600, a daily average of $105,230,150. The number of bond purchasers now exceeds 12,000,000.

Totals by Reserve Districts.

The totals by Federal Reserve districts follow:

District.	Quota.	Subscription.
Minneapolis	$105,000,000	$133,570,450
St. Louis	130,000,000	156,326,350
Kansas City	130,000,000	148,409,350
Chicago	425,000,000	406,947,000
San Francisco	210,000,000	194,938,900
Dallas	80,000,000	72,597,300
Boston	250,000,000	221,971,150
Cleveland	300,000,000	247,329,150
Philadelphia	250,000,000	207,805,000
Richmond	130,000,000	98,126,250
New York	900,000,000	633,956,800
Atlanta	90,000,000	57,101,700
Total	3,000,000,000	$2,579,079,400

Thus the New York district had yet to buy $266,043,200 of bonds to fill its quota, Chicago, $8,053,000; Dallas, $7,402,700; San Francisco, $15,061,100; Boston, $28,028,850; Cleveland, $52,670,850; Philadelphia, $42,195,000; Richmond, $31,873,750, and Atlanta, $32,898,300.

The percentages of quotas obtained by districts follow: Minneapolis, 127; St. Louis, 120; Kansas City, 114; Chicago, 95; San Francisco, 92; Dallas, 90; Boston, 88; Cleveland, 82; Philadelphia, 80; Richmond, 75; New York, 70, and Atlanta, 63.

The Minneapolis district reported that official figures showed that every State within its borders had oversubscribed, and that unofficial figures indicated that every county had made a similar record. A total of 2,468 communities in the district have gone over the top and been awarded honor flags.

"We believe this record beats anything in the United States," the report said. "If not, tell us what it is, and we will go out and beat that."

In so far as the records of the Treasury Department indicate, the Minneapolis claim is well founded. The St. Louis district, however, is pressing Min-

Continued on Page Four.

BRITISH GUARDS SAVED DAY

Fighting Back to Back They Held Line for 48 Hours, as Ordered.

THEN AUSTRALIANS CAME

First News That Famous Brigade Was in Battle Records Heroic Exploit.

FOE BUSY BURYING DEAD

Broken Divisions Being Replaced by Fresh Troops for Another Assault.

By PHILIP GIBBS.

Special Cable to THE NEW YORK TIMES.

WAR CORRESPONDENTS' HEADQUARTERS, Wednesday, May 1.—The Germans are very quiet in their lines since they were repulsed so utterly in their attacks against Scherpenberg and the British lines around Ypres. Even their guns were not very active last night, and today they are burying their dead and getting back their wounded, and taking the broken divisions out of the line to replace them with fresh troops for another battle.

I believe that will happen, because now that the enemy has Kemmel Hill his temptation to seize the three hills below is predominant, and there is no doubt that he will again risk the loss of many men to gain these positions. From the political point of view Ypres is also a lure to him, and there would be a great blowing of trumpets in Germany if their troops could capture that city of the salient, which as a name and a ruin is the great shrine of the British Army in this war.

Now that the French are with the British to strengthen the latter's defensive power, which has sustained such furious onslaughts by over 100 German divisions since six weeks ago, the next battle in Flanders may not give the enemy any further ground than the day before yesterday, which was nothing at all, and it is certain, anyhow, that not a yard of it will be yielded until the next waves of German soldiers have paid great sums of life.

Foe Used Two More Divisions.

In the last battle two additional divisions have now been identified as having been put in against the British front in Flanders, one being the 117th, near Voormezeele, and the other the 3d Guards Division, including the Maikaefer, or Cockchafers, whom the Welsh regiments shattered at Pilkem last year and who have fought against the British in the Cambrai salient.

Last night, when no doubt German reliefs were in progress, the British guns turned loose with shrapnel and high explosives upon the transport and troops crowding the track from Vierstraat to Wytschaete, and this morning the enemy had more dead to bury. So the slaughter goes on.

During a rare day without great news there is an opportunity of writing a few words about some of the British battalions who in the earlier fighting during these recent battles were wonderful in courage and endurance and self-sacrifice, but have not yet appeared in our narratives because for a time it was inadvisable to mention their presence in the battleline. They are battalions of Guards. There is no need for secrecy now, because the enemy met them at close quarters and knows how these men fought, sometimes in small bodies almost to the last man.

The recent history of the Guards begins with the battle of Arras on March 28, when the 56th London Division and 15th Scottish and the grand old 3d Division made their wonderful stand against one of the biggest efforts of the enemy.

Routed Foe With Bayonets.

On the 28th and 30th the Guards were heavily attacked and beat off the enemy's storm troops with exceedingly great losses to them, the Grenadiers making a counterattack near Boileaux St. Marc with fixed bayonets and flinging the enemy back from the ground they had gained.

But later than that battalions of Guards have been fighting in the north around the forest of Nieppe and between Lepinete and Vieux Berquin. That was from April 11 to 14, after the Germans had broken through the Portuguese line and with the full weight of their forces endeavored to widen the gap—did, indeed, widen the gap, pushing up between Armentières and Merville by gaining the crossings of the Lys.

The Grenadier, Irish, and Coldstream Guards were sent forward along the Hazebrouck-Estaires road when the situation was at its worst, when the men of the 15th Division and other units had fought themselves out in continual rearguard and holding actions, so that some of those still in the line could hardly walk or stand, and when it was utterly necessary to keep the Germans in check until a body of Australian troops had time to arrive. The Guards were asked to hold back the enemy until those Australians came and to fight at all costs for forty-eight hours against the German tide of men and guns which was attempting to flow around the other hard pressed men, and that is what the Guards did, fighting in separate bodies with the enemy pressing in on both flanks.

Fought Back to Back.

Greatly outnumbered, they beat back attack after attack and gained precious hours, vital hours, by the most noble self-sacrifice. A party of Grenadiers were so closely surrounded that their officer sent back a message saying:

"My men are standing back to back and shooting on all sides."

The Germans swung around them, circling them with machine guns and rifles and pouring a fire into them until only eighteen men were left. Those eighteen, standing among their wounded and their dead, did not surrender. The army wanted forty-eight hours. They fixed bayonets and went out against the enemy and drove through him. A wounded Corporal of Grenadiers, who afterward got back to the British lines, lay in a ditch, and the last he saw of his comrades was when fourteen men of them were still fighting in a swarm of Germans.

The Coldstream Guards were surrounded in the same way and fought in the same way. The army had asked for forty-eight hours until the Australians could come, and many of the Coldstreamers eked out the time with their lives. The enemy filtered in on their flanks, came crawling around them with machine guns, sniped them from short range and raked them from ditches and upheaved earth.

The Coldstream Guards had to fall back, but they fought back in small groups, facing all ways and making gaps in the enemy's ranks, not firing wildly, but using every round of small arms ammunition to keep a German back and gain a little more time. One private, an old timer, remained in an outpost until every-

Continued on Page Two.

Germans Leave "Souvenirs" To Kill Unwary Americans

WITH THE AMERICAN ARMY IN FRANCE, May 1, (Associated Press.)—Knowing that the Americans are persistent souvenir hunters, the Germans in the Toul sector have been strewing No Man's Land with all sorts of infernal devices.

These consist of electric wires attached to belts, helmets, rifles, and other paraphernalia connecting with concealed bombs.

In a number of instances American soldiers have tripped over these and escaped.

OUR MEN BEAT OFF ATTACK

Drive Back Three Assaulting Battalions Near Villers-Bretonneux.

FIERCE HAND-TO-HAND FIGHT

Germans Suffer Heavy Losses, Leaving Behind Many Dead and Five Prisoners.

OUR OWN LOSSES SEVERE

French Applaud the Bravery of Our Soldiers in the Violent Encounter.

WITH THE FRENCH ARMY, May 1, (Associated Press.) — A heavy German attack launched yesterday against the Americans in the vicinity of Villers-Bretonneux was repulsed with heavy losses for the enemy.

The German preliminary bombardment lasted two hours, and then the infantry rushed forward, only to be driven back, leaving large numbers of dead on the ground in front of the American lines.

The German bombardment opened at 5 o'clock in the afternoon and was directed especially against the Americans, who were supported on the north and south by the French. The fire was intense, and at the end of two hours the German commander sent forward three battalions of infantry.

There was hand-to-hand fighting all along the line, as a result of which the enemy was thrust back, his dead and wounded lying on the ground in all directions. Five prisoners remained in American hands.

The struggle, which lasted a considerable time, was extremely violent, and the Americans displayed marked bravery throughout.

It was the first occasion in which the Americans were engaged in the big battle which has been raging since March 21, and their French comrades are full of praise for the manner in which they conducted themselves under trying circumstances, especially in view of the fact that they are fighting at one of the most difficult points on the battlefront.

The American losses were rather severe.

Patrols' Clashes in Dark.

WITH AN AMERICAN ARMY ON A FRENCH BATTLEFRONT, April 30, (Associated Press.)—The situation along the American sector is gradually becoming stabilized.

There have been no infantry encounters in the last forty-eight hours, although small patrol parties or outposts have met in the darkness and mist.

Despite rain and poor visibility the American and French artillery have been most active in shelling enemy back areas. An American battery has been laying a heavy fire on enemy batteries and positions around a certain village which has been virtually wiped out.

The German artillery is less active than on the days immediately following the Americans' appearance on this sector. The Germans are throwing some gas shells.

Weather conditions prevent aerial activity on either side.

KAISER BOASTS IN FLANDERS.

Tells His Men They Will "Put the British Back on the Channel."

WITH THE BRITISH ARMY IN FLANDERS, May 1, (Associated Press.)—Emperor William appears to have been an interested and active visitor in the Flanders region yesterday. According to prisoners, he has been making his usual flamboyant speeches to the troops, and he told them the other day that the Germans were trying to separate the French and British armies, adding characteristically that the Germans were going to "put the British back on the English Channel, where they belonged."

All Allied Armies in France Now Fused Into One; Each Division Available for Service at Any Point

Special Cable to THE NEW YORK TIMES.
From a Staff Correspondent.

WITH THE FRENCH ARMIES, May 1.—THE NEW YORK TIMES correspondent is able to state on the best authority that the allied unity of command implies not only the sole direction of operations by General Foch and the utilization of reserves in common, but also the complete fusion of the American, British, and French Armies.

Henceforth divisions withdrawn from one battle sector, may be sent, (no matter what their nationality,) to any other sector along the whole line from the sea to Switzerland.

Hitherto there have been certain parts of the front set aside as British, French, or American. Unity of command changes all that.

In the battle sectors there will be fighting divisions of Americans, French, or English. In quiet localities there will be units of the three allied armies training for the big struggle, or recovering from the effects of having been engaged in it; but all distinctions will have vanished. The Allies now form one army in France, fighting for one purpose under one chief.

ALLIES NOW AHEAD IN FRESH FORCES

Number of Unused Divisions Available Much Exceed Foe's Total.

GERMAN LOSSES 350,000

Indicated by the Withdrawal of 186 Divisions—Capable of One More Big Drive.

Special Cable to THE NEW YORK TIMES.
From a Staff Correspondent.

WITH THE FRENCH ARMIES, May 1. The Allies now have a number of fresh divisions greatly superior to the Germans. In a battle such as this the wear and tear of the troops engaged is one of the most important factors. The French know that the enemy's losses have bens extremely heavy, and know, too, that their own and those of the British leave a big margin in favor of the Allies.

According to a conservative estimate the Germans have lost approximately 350,000 men in this battle to date. By a study of averages throughout the war 2,200 is shown to be the loss which a German division must suffer before it is withdrawn from the firing line. The Allies have already identified 186 German divisions that entered the battle and have been removed for reorganization and engaged or re-engaged, which permits an estimate of the enemy's losses. Of the total German forces on the western front only sixty-six divisions have not been thrown in at least once, of which it is known that at least ten Landsturm and the like are incapable of taking part in a battle of this character.

Allowing for refitted units, whose value is naturally greatly inferior both in morale and training to their predecessors, the enemy thus may be said to possess sufficient force for one more violent drive. When that fails, as the Allies are justified in believing it will, after having repelled the original onslaught, their turn will come.

The universal optimism which THE NEW YORK TIMES correspondent has remarked on the French front is evidenced in the extraordinary élan of the poilus, who are delighted to exchange the monotony of the trenches for what they term "real fighting." Those best qualified to know attribute French resistance against overwhelming odds largely to this factor. Its importance cannot be overestimated in view of the subsequent operations.

Sure Amiens Is German Objective.

It may have seemed astonishing to the American public that, despite the bitterness of the Flanders fighting and the heavy numbers engaged on both sides, French and British military critics have insisted that the Amiens front was the real centre of the German objective, and that against which the chief effort was always to be expected. The reasons are simple. Firstly, the concentration of German divisions is such that the great majority of the enemy forces are still aligned along the chord of the semicircle from Arras to Montdidier. Secondly, it is known to the French that the attack in Flanders was originally intended as a diversion only. The proof is that the Germans began the battle with the troops hold-

Continued on Page Two.

NEW GERMAN PEACE DRIVE IS FORESEEN

German Papers Announce Papal Mediation Offer at Whitsuntide—Berlin Welcomes It.

WASHINGTON IS SKEPTICAL

Allies Predict Teuton Concessions—Kaisers Soon to Meet—Sixtus Confers in Spain.

Special Cable to THE NEW YORK TIMES.

LONDON, May 1.—Many signs have been noted here which confirm Washington expectations of the probability of the Germans starting shortly a great peace offensive. THE NEW YORK TIMES correspondent learns that moves by enemy agents in Switzerland are under close observation and that the German policy is already foreseen.

In this connection Germany may try to take advantage of expected action by the Pope. A British Admiralty dispatch, per Wireless Press from The Hague, says that Cologne newspapers announce that the Pope intends to issue a new proposal for peace to all the belligerent nations at Whitsuntide. (May 19.) The document is to be of a more pressing nature than the former one from the Vatican and will contain concrete offers of mediation by the Holy See, with the possible co-opera- of the neutral sovereigns of Europe.

Similar information regarding the Pope's intention has reached Berlin, where it is stated to have been sympathetically received.

So far as Germany is concerned, it is not expected that the peace suggestions will be offered until the great attack in the Amiens-Arras region which Ludendorff is preparing has been launched. After that is over Berlin is expected to claim that it has won considerable advantages, but that it is ready, despite its victories, to offer peace on reasonable terms; that if they are rejected the responsibility must rest on the Allies, and that the Central Powers will pursue their irresistible course until they have driven their enemies into the sea.

The kind of terms that will probably be proposed include the restoration of Belgium, the cession of French Lorraine to France, no indemnities, and the return of the German colonies and other conquests from the Central Powers. The Germans have realized that their treatment of Russia is an absolute obstacle to any Government again putting faith in their promises, and they may even express a willingness to revise the treaties of Brest-Litovsk and Bucharest.

In well informed circles here, however, it is not believed that this peace offensive will produce any considerable reaction in its favor in this country. The German game is too easily seen through to win many converts, and the idea is laughed at that after the practical repudiation of the Reichstag's famous no annexation and no indemnities resolution of last Summer immediately the military situation looked rather brighter, and after the demonstration of Germany's powerlessness to win anything like a decisive victory on the western front any British leader of real authority will be found willing to swallow the new Hun bun.

Emperor Charles's Agents Active.

Already Emperor Karl has been talking peace to Italy. The expected Austrian attack in that quarter he has

Continued on Page Two.

ONLY GERMAN GUNS BUSY

Bethune Region Bombarded—Artillery Duels at Various Points.

FRENCH MAKE A LITTLE GAIN

They Improve Their Positions During the Night in the Critical Locre Area.

BRITISH CHECK A RAID

Rout Assailants Near St. Julien and Rush German Posts in the Meteren Sector.

LONDON, May 1.—Aside from heavy shelling by the Germans of French positions in the Locre sector and their bombardment of the back areas near Bethune there was little activity today on the Lys-Ypres front, the German High Command being evidently busy reorganizing the divisions shattered in the fighting of the last few days.

Field Marshal Haig reports that the French last night improved their lines in the neighborhood of Locre, and that his own troops yesterday repulsed a minor attack near St. Julien and rushed German posts in the Meteren sector, taking a few prisoners.

In the month of April, the British commander says, the English took 5,241 prisoners, including 136 officers.

Following is the text of the night bulletin:

> The enemy's artillery has been active today against the back areas in the neighborhood of Bethune and has heavily shelled French positions on the Locre sector.
>
> On the remainder of the front there is nothing to report beyond the usual artillery activity and local encounters on both sides.
>
> The number of German prisoners captured by the British armies in France during March was 1,061, including sixty-nine officers. In April a further 5,241 prisoners, including 136 officers, were captured. These figures are exclusive of the prisoners taken by the French.

The afternoon statement reads:

> A local attack made by the enemy yesterday upon one of our posts in the neighborhood of St. Julien was repulsed by machine-gun fire. Posts held by the enemy in the Meteren sector were rushed by our troops during the night and a few prisoners were secured by us.
>
> By a successful minor enterprise carried out last night French troops improved the positions held by them in the neighborhood of Locre.

The following communication dealing with aviation was issued tonight:

> Mist and rain again prevented flying Tuesday, except for a few low reconnoissances in the course of which bombs were dropped on the enemy's troops between Locre and Voormezeele.
>
> One hostile machine was forced to land behind our lines. One of ours is missing.

Germans Reorganizing for Attack.

WITH THE BRITISH ARMY IN FLANDERS, May 1, (Associated Press.) General von Arnim made no further move along the Flanders battlefront last night, nor had an attack been expected. The heavy defeat which the Germans suffered on Monday forced them to pause and bring up fresh troops before continuing their drive for the hill positions in the Kemmel region. A few more hours, however, will suffice for their reorganization, and another assault may be expected immediately.

The seriousness of the German intentions here has been evinced in numerous ways. On Monday, for example, they pushed at least one field gun forward to within 700 yards of the battleline, and other guns were brought close up.

Heavy artillery firing continued at various parts of the battleline during the night, and there were the usual outpost actions. The back areas

"All the News That's Fit to Print."

The New York Times.

THE WEATHER
Fair, warmer today; Sunday probably showers; wind south.
For full weather report see Page 23.

VOL. LXVII...NO. 22,029. NEW YORK, SATURDAY, MAY 18, 1918.—TWENTY-FOUR PAGES. TWO CENTS In Greater New York and Within Commuting Distance. | THREE CENTS Elsewhere.

FRENCH COMMAND EXPECTS IMMEDIATE GERMAN BLOW; AMERICAN TROOPS JOIN BRITISH ON LINES IN THE NORTH; GOVERNMENT DISCOVERS GERMAN PLOTTING IN IRELAND

MERCANTILE CO. TO SELL ITS 100 BRITISH SHIPS

Deal Involving 950,000 Tons and $125,000,000 Cash Practically Completed.

PART WITH FAMOUS SHIPS

Include Olympic, Adriatic, Baltic and Other Well-Known White Star Liners and 44 Freighters.

RETAIN 8 AMERICAN BOATS

Status of None of Craft Will Change Till After War—Price Ample to Meet Indebtedness.

Following a special meeting of the Directors of the International Mercantile Marine Company at noon yesterday it became known on good authority that the deal, long pending, whereby the company relinquishes control to British interests of its various British subsidiaries, and with them its entire fleet under the British flag, becoming a purely American concern, has been practically completed.

No official announcement to this effect was made, as there are still many details to be settled which, in a transaction of such magnitude, will necessarily take a long time to wind up. President Franklin who, on Thursday, following the regular Directors' meeting, had admitted for the first time that negotiations were in progress, yesterday would say only in very general terms that progress had been made with the affair, but that the complications were so numerous that no definite statement could be made.

The total number of ships involved in the transaction is approximately 100—the exact number has not recently been ascertainable because of the secrecy with which all maritime news and statistics are at present guarded—of a total tonnage of about 950,000 tons. The transfer of this number of ships is, so far as existing records go, without precedent for a single transaction, both as to number and tonnage. The ships to change hands include the Olympic, one of the largest and finest passenger liners afloat; the Adriatic, Baltic, and other well-known ships of the White Star Line, which have been plying regularly between New York and British ports for many years before the war, and the forty-four large freighters of the Leyland Line.

Six American Ships Retained.

The International Mercantile Marine Company after the completion of the sale will retain control of six ships of the American Line and two belonging to the Atlantic Transport Company of West Virginia, one of its American subsidiaries, and two belonging to the Société Anonyme de Navigation Belge-Americaine, the Red Star Line, which fly the Belgian flag. At the time the United States entered the war the company had fourteen vessels under construction, mostly in American shipyards, and had laid out an even more extensive program for increasing its fleet, including the construction in American yards of some of the largest passenger liners ever built.

All the ships under construction were commandeered on the ways last August by the United States Shipping Board. Every one of the British ships in its fleet has been under requisition charter to the British Ministry of Shipping since April, 1917; the Belgian ships are under requisition by the Belgian Government, and on Oct. 15 last such of its American ships as had not already been requisitioned for transport service were taken over by the Shipping Board.

The financial aspect of the transaction is the most immediately interesting, because the status of none of the ships will change until after the war, the British Ministry of Shipping retaining complete control over them. It is understood, however, that Sir Joseph Maclay, the British Shipping Controller, approved, if he did not actually assist, the arrangement of the transaction, with the intention of strengthening the position of British shipping after the war by putting an end to foreign, even though friendly, ownership and interest in British ships.

Price Not Remarkably High.

The total amount of the cash consideration in the transaction is said to be $125,000,000. Discussions over the amount and the manner of payment are supposed to have formed the chief obstacle to its completion in the six months which have passed since the proposal was first made, the British syndicate which made the offer wishing to pay £25,000,000 in London rather than $125,000,000 in New York. Another reported proposal was that part at least of the purchase price be transferred in the form of British Government war bonds. The price of around $125 a ton is not remarkably high, in comparison with some prices paid for tonnage since the shortage be[illegible] acute, but this was, it is believed, [illegible]itioned by the fact that actual con[illegible] the ships is not immediately [illegible] interesting possibilities and

[Co]ntinued on Page Six.

Soldiers to Lead in Remaking Empire After War, Says Kaiser

AMSTERDAM, May 17.—"I have rocklike confidence that my people will be equal to the great tasks of the future," the Cologne Volkszeitung quotes Emperor William as saying when inspecting the graves of soldiers during his recent visit to Aix-la-Chapelle.

"The soldier who has struggled through the iron time of the world war will be a teacher and leader of the growing youths at home in building up and consolidating the reborn empire.

"War's bloody sword will be reforged into plowshares in the work of peace and civilization, and in the new imperial forge we must, as united peoples of brothers, show ourselves worthy of comrades in eternity."

The Emperor is further reported as saying:

"Truly, it was not my will that the war has come."

PRESIDENT HERE TO AID RED CROSS

Tells Applauding Theatre Audience It Sees "a Tired Man Having a Good Time."

CITY GIVES WAR WELCOME

Every Appearance Stirs Great Throngs to Cheering and Cries of Approval.

President Wilson came to New York yesterday to start the drive for the city's share of the Red Cross $100,000,000 war fund. It was the first time the President had been here since last Fall, before American soldiers had gone into the trenches, and the city gave him a welcome that brought to his face, a bit lined since his last visit, a smile of pleasure.

Everywhere he went he got the same whole-hearted, cordial greeting, until it was evident that the city wanted the President to understand that it was with him to the last citizen's last breath.

At the Globe Theatre, where the President and Mrs. Wilson witnessed the performance of "Jack o' Lantern," the applause was so persistent that Mr. Wilson was compelled to make a speech. This is what he said:

"Ladies and gentlemen, you are laboring under a delusion. You think you see the President of the United States. You are mistaken. Really, you see a tired man having a good time."

The President and Mrs. Wilson arrived at the Pennsylvania Station shortly after 3 o'clock yesterday afternoon in a private car attached to a regular Pennsylvania train. In the party were the President's private secretary, Joseph P. Tumulty; Rear Admiral Cary P. Grayson, his personal physician; Charles Swem, the President's stenographer, and eight secret service men under Joseph Murphy, the White House guard.

Station Master Egan, who has met the President every time he came to New York, and Colonel E. M. House were at the station, together with a large guard of detectives and police under Inspectors Bolan and Faurot. They took the President up in the elevator and out of the south end of the concourse, where a space had been cleared.

Thousands Wait at Station.

Long before the train bearing the President came in a crowd numbering thousands waited about the Thirty-first Street entrance to the terminal. They knew President Wilson was expected, but did not know when he would arrive. When the President appeared a shout went up that almost shook the station. It rose and fell, as some strong voiced man would set the crowd going again each time it seemed about to stop cheering.

President Wilson seemed surprised at the enthusiasm displayed and wholly pleased. As he and Mrs. Wilson settled in an automobile he took off his hat and, rising, tried to smile at everybody. The crowd apparently thought it was going to hear a speech and became silent, but when the machine started it cheered again and again.

"We're with you, Woodrow," shouted a tall man, waving his hat wildly at the moving car. The President heard him and, half turning, smiled again.

From the station the party drove to the Waldorf, where a suite had been set apart for the President on the third floor on the Fifth Avenue side of the hotel. There was another crowd waiting at the hotel, and the enthusiasm again forced him to rise and acknowledge the cheering. After a half hour in the hotel the whole party went out for a motor ride.

Led by two motor cycle policemen, the President's car rolled up Fifth Avenue at the very height of the afternoon traffic on that thoroughfare. There was a car of plain clothes men and two more full of detectives on guard. The President and Mrs. Wilson rode with Colonel House, while Admiral

Continued on Page Eleven.

SINN FEIN LEADERS SEIZED

All Taken Into Custody in Dublin, Belfast and Elsewhere.

VICEROY'S PROCLAMATION

He Calls on All Loyalists to Join in Blocking the German Plans.

CALLS FOR ENLISTMENTS

Volunteers Asked for to Provide Ireland's Share of the Army.

Special Cable to THE NEW YORK TIMES.

DUBLIN, May 17.—All the Sinn Fein leaders, including De Valera, Darrell, Figgs, Griffiths, and the Countess Markievicz, were arrested in Dublin tonight. Similar arrests were made in Belfast and other places.

German Plot Proclaimed.

DUBLIN, May 17.—In a proclamation issued tonight the Lord Lieutenant says:

Whereas it has come to our knowledge that certain subjects of his Majesty, the King, domiciled in Ireland have conspired to enter, and have entered, into treasonable communication with the German enemy; and

Whereas such treachery is a menace to the fair name of Ireland and its glorious military record, a record which is a source of intense pride to a country whose sons always distinguished themselves and fought with valor; and

Whereas drastic measures must be taken to put down this German plot, which means will be solely directed against that plot; now, therefore, we, the Lord Lieutenant of Ireland and Governor General of Ireland, have thought fit to issue this proclamation as follows:

That it is the duty of all loyal subjects of his Majesty to assist in every way his Majesty's Government in Ireland to suppress this treasonable conspiracy and to defeat the treacherous attempt of Germany to defame the honor of Irishmen for their own ends.

That we hereby call upon all loyal subjects of his Majesty in Ireland to aid in crushing such conspiracy and so far as in them lies to assist in securing an effective prosecution of the war and the welfare and safety of the empire.

That as a means to this end we shall cause still further steps to be taken to facilitate and encourage voluntary enlistment in Ireland in his Majesty's forces, in the hope that, without resort to compulsion, the contribution of Ireland to these forces may be brought up to the proper strength and made to correspond to the contributions of other parts of the empire.

Many Arrests Are Made.

LONDON, Saturday, May 18.—Considerable number of arrests have been made in Dublin and throughout Ireland, according to a dispatch to The Times from Dublin, timed 2 o'clock Saturday morning.

News of the discovery of a German plot in Ireland reached London after midnight in brief telegrams from Dublin, and was followed some time later by the text of a proclamation concerning the plot issued by the Lord Lieutenant, Viscount French.

Communication between Dublin and London is slow, and at the moment of cabling, (4:17 A. M.) nothing is known beyond what is contained in the proclamation and a statement given to the press by Edward Shortt, Chief Secretary for Ireland.

That German intrigue has been in progress will cause little real surprise to th epublic. Hints had been given by several correspondents of London newspapers that something was going on between Sinn Fein agents and the enemy. The arrest of a man who landed in a collapsible boat from a German submarine, as cabled recently, is take nto confirm rumors.

Several other arrests in Ireland have been reported lately, though nothing has transpired which would necessarily connect them as treasonable doings. Indeed, in all cases the only information has been the mere fact of an arrest, as for instance, the arrest of ohn McKenna, Chairman of the Kerry County Council, on an unspecified charge under the Defense of the Realm act.

The reference in the proclamation to "steps to facilitate and encourage voluntary enlistment" seems to confirm recent predictions from various sources that the Government has abandoned, or at least postponed, enforcement of conscription in Ireland. The difficulties in carrying out conscription have seemed to increase ever since the first outburst by the Irish Nationalists and owing to Sinn Fein hostility to the proposal.

Opposition to conscription has come from some unexpected quarters. An instance is an article in the current number of The Church of Ireland Gazette, the leading organ of the Irish Protestant

Continued on Page Three.

France's 22-Inch Gun, Largest in the World

Mysterious Shots Fell in Dover; German Supergun Was Suspected

The Bombardment of April 26, When No German Airplanes Could Be Found by the British—Official Denial of the Supergun Theory—France Has a New 22-Inch Gun.

Special Cable to THE NEW YORK TIMES.

LONDON, May 17.—On inquiry at the Ministry of Information with reference to a report that a German supergun at or near Ostend had been firing shells into Dover, notably on April 26, THE NEW YORK TIMES was informed that the story was absolutely false. General Radcliffe, Director of Military Operations, also stated that the report was without foundation.

The story which reached New York is apparently an elaboration of speculations which were prevalent at the time when the Germans began the long-range shelling of Paris. Dover could not be shelled without London coming to know of it, and there have not been any reports of such a thing having happened, even in circles where Dame Rumor wags her tongue most busily.

The sand dunes of Ostend and the neighborhood do not present favorable situations for emplacing long-range guns, which, it is believed, would speedily be spotted and destroyed by British airmen.

The story that the port of Dover, situated on the southeast coast of England, was believed to have been shelled by a German supergun from Ostend, a distance of about sixty-five miles across the North Sea, was brought to New York by passengers recently arrived from England. It was told by one of these to THE TIMES as follows:

"Belgian spies in the employ of the British Intelligence Department reported on April 5 that a gun of about the same calibre as those set up near Laon and used in the bombardment of Paris had passed through Belgium from the Krupp Works at Essen on April 2, on its way to Ostend. This gun was said to be from 65 to 75 feet long and of 23 centimeters calibre.

"The supposed shelling of Dover occurred at 10 o'clock on Friday night, April 26, and was at first taken for an aerial attack. Fifty British fighting machines went up to drive back the boche aviators, but could not get any trace of them, and an alarm was sent to London that the Germans had dropped three bombs on Dover and proceeded toward the metropolis.

"The first missile fell short of the town of Dover and struck Shakespeare's Cliff, sending some hundreds of tons of chalk into the sea with a deafening report, which roused the people in their beds, and hundreds of them took to the cellars and caves for safety. The second and third missiles were better aimed, passed over the harbor and part of the town, and dropped in a residential street, demolishing two small houses. Those who were living near by said that the 'bomb,' they called it, made a great noise when it exploded, but did not have the destructive force of the bombs that had been previously dropped by airplanes.

Destroyer's Report Aroused Suspicion.

"The officers of the Flying Corps and the Naval Air Force stationed at Dover did not suspect that the missiles were shells fired by a German supergun until early next morning, when a report was received from the commander of a destroyer which had been out scouting during the night off the Belgian coast.

"The aviators on guard duty along the Kentish coast believed that they did not see the planes which were supposed to have attacked Dover, because they were flying at over 15,000 feet and the night was dark. When the alarm reached London the people were still in the theatres, but as it was nearly closing time they were not informed that German raiders had passed Dover. At 11 o'clock, as nothing more had been heard of the German planes at any of the air stations on the road from Dover to London, about seventy miles, the 'All clear' signal was given.

"The newspapers published next morning stated that the alarm had been given on account of the warning received from Dover, which had proved to be incorrect. They did not give any explanation regarding the three missiles dropped on the port, and there has been no mention of the big German gun being placed in position at Ostend.

"On April 14 it was reported in the Paris papers that the Germans had two of the seventy-mile-range guns in Ostend and that they were intended to be used on the English coast when the enemy had succeeded in breaking through to Boulogne or Calais.

"Belgian spies again got through the German lines into Holland at Maastricht on May 1, and said that they had seen the superguns at Ostend, with their shells lying on a concrete platform beside them. The weight of the shells was estimated to be about 200 to 225 pounds each. So far there has been no means of obtaining the weight of the shells fired from the German superguns into Paris, because they have all exploded when they fell and scattered into fragments.

"The British Admiralty declined to give out any particulars concerning the big guns at Ostend or the shelling of Dover on April 26, and the London newspapers were content with calling it the mysterious false alarm."

France Has Greatest Gun in the World.

Another person, who has just arrived from England, reports that the new 22-inch French gun, by far the greatest in the world, has been completed, and the first photograph of one of them is presented herewith. For obvious reasons it is not permitted to describe the gun in detail. It is conjectured that it is one of these guns that has succeeded in silencing the two German superguns located near Laon. Before the German superguns near Laon were put out of commission they are said to have killed in Paris 368 persons, wounded 300, and driven to places of refuge elsewhere in France many thousands of the population of Paris.

Fifteen experimental eighteen-inch rifles have been built by the United States Government for the protection of the Panama Canal. These were the largest hitherto known. It has been reported that the Krupps had made several seventeen-inch guns for the protection of Heligoland. It has been seriously questioned by ordnance experts whether the Germans possess a direct-fire rifle larger than sixteen-inch, although the existence of the seventeen-inch Skoda howitzer is no longer doubted. The long range guns which shelled Dunkirk were found to carry twelve-inch and fifteen-inch shells; those which have shelled Paris from near Laon, a distance of seventy-four miles, nine-inch. The maximum naval gun of the United States and British Navies is the sixteen-inch piece, firing from a floating emplacement a 2,100-pound shell twenty-two miles.

REICHSTAG SOCIALISTS DENOUNCE ARRESTS

Angry Altercations Over Imprisonments on Treason Charges at Dresden.

AMSTERDAM, May 17.—The German newspapers report strong Socialist speeches in the Reichstag recently, denouncing the arrest and imprisonment of Independent Socialists, and leading to stormy scenes.

According to the Socialist newspaper Vorwärts, Herr Hertzfeld, a Socialist Deputy, denounced the imprisonment of a number of young men at Dresden on treason charges. Amid the applause of fellow members of his party and stormy interruptions from other sections of the House, he said:

"By this sort of class justice the Supreme Court is doing everything it can to strengthen the power of the military dictatorship."

Angry altercations also took place between Socialist members and the Vice President of the Chamber.

Vorwärts reports several members of the Independent Socialist Party as having been arrested within the last few weeks at Cologne. The men sentenced at Dresden, with whose case Herr Hertzfeld dealt, were apparently Independent Socialists, as the Leipzig Volkszeitung states that twelve Independent Socialists have been sentenced by a Dresden court for high treason, [illegible] terms ranging from two to eight years in prison. They were charged with circulating pamphlets which were revolutionary in character.

TOMMIES CHEER OUR MEN

Promptly on Their Arrival in Flanders They Begin Training.

FIRST OF THE RUSH FORCES

They Are Commanded by an American General Who Has Been on the French Line.

DOUBLE PURPOSE SERVED

They Will Back Up Allies Where Needed and Be Fitted Quickly for Front Line.

By EDWIN L. JAMES.

Special Cable to THE NEW YORK TIMES.

WITH THE AMERICAN ARMY IN FRANCE, May 17.—American troops have taken their place in the British war zone in Northern France. Announcement to this effect was authorized by the American army authorities today.

The presence of American soldiers back of the British lines and of Americans fighting in co-operation with the French in Picardy, together with the Americans holding sectors northwest of Toul and in Lorraine, show that our men will have a chance to participate in heavy fighting whenever the next German drive may come.

There is no reason to doubt that as the American troops arrive, greater numbers will be found at other points on the western battle front.

The scattering of the American troops is not to be taken to cast the slightest doubt on the eventual unification of the American forces in France. Whenever the proper time comes in the opinion of the allied command, the United States troops will have their own organization and play their own rôle, and the glory of our army will be reflected upon the Stars and Stripes, as well as upon the general cause of the Allies.

Brigading Helps in Two Ways.

The assignment of American troops to the British and French armies at this time serves two purposes. Primarily it places fresh troops at points where they are needed, tending to lessen any chance that Germany might win the war this year. A secondary but no less important purpose is that the arrangement will give the American troops invaluable training which they could get in no other way.

There are indications that much of the warfare in future months may be open fighting. It is not easy for the Americans to get training in that kind of warfare except in this region.

Participation of the American units in warfare with the British and French units will also give our officers such training in modern warfare as they could get in no other way.

The great task of the Allies is to block the plans of the Germans to make further advances now. This is a task for America, no less than for England and France, especially since the Kaiser hoped to win the war before our growing weight could be thrown in serious strength against him. Therefore, the chance for Americans to help fight the foe on his chosen battlefield at this time is nothing less than an opportunity to make our rôle the more glorious.

There is something in the service of American fighters with the British and French that is in keeping with the spirit of our whole participation in the war—the spirit of unselfishness.

Grasp Opportunity to Fight.

While America's soldiers might prefer, if possible, to defeat the f[oe] under their own flag, this does not mean at all that they do not seize with the best spirit the opportunity to help defeat him somewhere else, until they can do it as it may suit them best.

Because of the uncertainties of war, it is impossible to say at this time how long the present arrangement will continue. It is safe to say that it will continue as long as there

Continued on Page Two.

Dutch to Send Ships Out Under Armed Convoy

THE HAGUE, May 17.—Jonkheer J. London, Minister of Foreign Affairs, announced in the Second Chamber today that it was intended to send several steamers to the Dutch East Indies under an armed convoy and accompanied by a collier. He said he could not say definitely that no international difficulty would arise out of convoying ships, but presumed that this act probably would not meet with interference.

The Entente allied Governments, he said, have been informed of this decision by the Netherlands Government.

RUSSIANS SELL OUT TO THE GERMANS

Turn Over Stock of Industrial and Financial Institutions at Panic Prices.

INTERVENTION UP AGAIN

London Newspapers Renew the Agitation for Action by the Allies Through Japan.

STOCKHOLM, May 16.—The chaotic economic conditions in Russia are being utilized to the full by Germany for increasing German influence and control over Russian industrial and financial institutions. Russian capitalists and corporations, threatened with ruin, see no escape except to sell their property to Germany.

Transactions of this nature are being carried out through M. Furstenberg, known also as M. Genetsky, foreign financial adviser of the Bolshevist Government, who is in Stockholm, with various associates. From Stockholm special messengers are sent into Russia under German protection in furtherance of this work. The messengers bring back the actual stock certificates and other securities.

The main object of the German effort is to obtain control of the Russian mines and metal industry, leather and banks. The Russians are selling out at panic prices.

LONDON, May 17.—The London press is urging the necessity of allied intervention of a prompt nature if what is alluded to as the rapid strengthening of the German grip on the country is to be successfully combatted. The newspapers refer to Lord Robert Cecil's House of Commons remarks and the accumulating indications of the inability or unwillingness of the Bolsheviki to resist the German penetration, and in some instances the advocates of intervention reiterate the earlier pleas for allowing Japan to act. The insistence upon Japan's disinterestedness is renewed, as is Japanese loyalty to the alliance.

The Daily Chronicle says that the more the Allies allow Russia to fall under German influence the harder it will be to extricate her eventually. It declares that Russia is now unable to recover herself without foreign military intervention, adding:

"The weight of our intervention would necessarily be Japanese, but it should be given a broadly allied and international character. For some time it has been said the obstacle has been Washington only, and now that—as we believe to be the case—the American Government's own agents are as much convinced as anybody else of the need for foreign troops, it is to be hoped that opposition will be withdrawn." The Daily Telegraph concludes its article with these lines:

"The statesmen at Tokio have made it quite clear that they have no covetous aims. In order to support the general policy of the Allies, and especially to protect Siberia from Teutonic rapacity, Japan, we are convinced, is ready to act in any way that promotes the ideals of the Entente Powers."

WASHINGTON, May 17.—How Germany is pursuing vigorously her policy of commercial penetration in Russia is further described in official dispatches today, which say all sorts of financial concerns, banks, corporations, and manufacturing enterprises were being bought up.

The dispatches add that many Russians frankly dislike to see German influence developing to such an extent, and would be glad if allied and American capital could be used to forestall the Prussian aggression.

BRITISH IN FINLAND BLEW UP SUBMARINES

Found They Could Not Dive Under Ice to Escape Germans—How They Got There.

LONDON, May 16.—An account of the destruction of the seven British submarines at Helsingfors was given to The

Continued on Page Two.

FOE'S DIVISIONS REGROUPED

Large Forces of Picked Troops Massed Behind the Battlefront.

ATTACK ON VIMY FORECAST

But General French Opinion Locates the Main Attempt Between La Bassee and Amiens.

FOCH'S TROOPS WELCOME IT

Say They Have the Germans' Measure and Will Soon Prove It.

By WALTER DURANTY.

Special Cable to THE NEW YORK TIMES.

WITH THE FRENCH ARMIES, Saturday, May 18, 12:30 A. M.—The blow may fall at any hour now. THE NEW YORK TIMES correspondent was told yesterday that in the last few days there was evidence that the Germans had finished regrouping their divisions with a view to a second great offensive, and, as before, had massed large forces of picked troops some distance behind the front, ready to be transferred by forced marches to a given point at the last possible moment. The present fine weather and moonlight nights favor such an operation, and there are other signs which indicate that the Germans may strike before these lines are in print.

It is still believed that the main attack will be made between La Bassée and the Amiens region. The allied line in Flanders is likely to be assaulted with almost equal force, and another drive may come between Amiens and Noyon, or elsewhere.

One officer, however, advances a slightly different theory.

"I shall not be surprised," he says, "if the boche makes his principal effort against the Vimy Ridge positions, which he regards as the key to the allied line between the sea and Amiens. It would be a terribly costly experiment, but success would hold out great opportunities."

Whenever and wherever the blow falls the Allies are more than ready, and the confidence and morale of the whole French army were never higher. I visited the front line trenches yesterday and talked with men who may be called on at any minute to bear the first brunt of the shock. All say the same thing:

"The sooner the boche comes the sooner it will all be finished. We know we have got his measure and when this attack has been checked we will prove it."

GERMAN GUNFIRE IS INCREASING

Lys Salient and the Hailles Region See Heaviest Shelling—Air Fights Are Numerous.

LONDON, May 17.—Increasing artillery activity by the Germans along the British front is noted by the War Office today in its official communication, but there has been no infantry action of consequence.

The centres of the German gunfire were along the Lys salient, notably near the Pacaut Wood, north of Hinges, (on the southern flank of the salient,) between Hinges and Locon, and from the forest of Nieppe to Meteren, (west of Bailleul.)

There was some raiding on both sides. The British rushed a German post north of Merris (southwest of Bailleul) and killed or drove out the men of the garrison. Another successful raid was carried out during the night near Beaumont-Hamel, (north of Albert.)

On the French front heavy fire was kept up last night in the region of Hailles, (southwest of Hangard.) A successful raid was made by the French southeast of Montdidier.

Field Marshal Haig's report from British Headquarters tonight says:

We carried out a successful raid last night in the neighborhood of Beaumont-Hamel and captured a few prisoners.

This morning a hostile post north of Merris was rushed by our troops. Its garrison was killed or driven out.

On the remainder of the front there

"All the News That's Fit to Print."

The New York Times.

THE WEATHER
Fair and warmer today; Tuesday, continued warmer; southwest winds
For full weather report see Page 21.

VOL. LXVII...NO. 22,059 .... NEW YORK, MONDAY, JUNE 17, 1918.—TWENTY-TWO PAGES. TWO CENTS In Greater New York and Within Commuting Distance. | THREE CENTS Elsewhere.

AUSTRIANS CROSS THE PIAVE AT TWO POINTS; CLAIM 16,000 PRISONERS, BUT ALLIES GET 3,000; AMERICANS DEFEAT THE GERMANS WITH GAS

RAIDING U-BOAT SINKS 2 NEUTRALS OFF VIRGINIA COAST

Norwegian Vessels Destroyed Near Scene of Previous Attacks.

WARSHIP RESCUES CREW

Bringing Krinsjaa's Survivors to Port—15 Saved from the Samoa.

U-BOAT HID FOR FOUR DAYS

Renewed Activity on Friday Morning, When She Shelled the Samoa.

Special to The New York Times.

WASHINGTON, June 16.—The Norwegian bark Krinsjaa and the Norwegian bark Samoa have been sunk by the German U-boat raiding on the Atlantic Coast, making twenty vessels which have been attacked. The announcement regarding the Krinsjaa was made by the Navy Department tonight at 11 o'clock, as follows:

"A United States man-of-war has picked up all of the survivors of the Norwegian bark Krinsjaa, which was sunk about ninety miles off the Virginia coast. They are being brought to an Atlantic port."

An earlier announcement by the Navy Department read:

"The Navy Department is informed that fifteen survivors of the Norwegian bark Samoa, which was sunk by gunfire about ninety miles off the Virginia coast at 8 A. M., on Friday, June 14, were picked up by a schooner and later transferred to another vessel, which is bringing them to an Atlantic port."

The last previously announced sinking was that of the Norwegian steamship Henrik Lund, 150 miles northeast of Hatteras, opposite the Virginia Capes, on the afternoon of June 10. Four days elapsed between the sinking of the Henrik Lund and of the Samoa.

When the Krinsjaa was sunk is not told in the announcement issued by the Government tonight, but the destruction of this vessel took place ninety miles off the Virginia coast in the same region where the Samoa was sunk on June 14 and both vessels may have been destroyed the same day. The Krinsjaa was a vessel of 1,500 tons, and the Samoa of 1,050 tons.

The announcement made today shows that German undersea craft were active along the coast as late as Friday morning last. The first reported sinking off the American coast in the present raid was that of the American schooner Edna on May 25. Twenty days later the Samoa was lost. This means that approximately three weeks had been covered by the span of German submarine activities along the coast up to last Friday morning.

Six of the twenty vessels officially reported as having been sunk or damaged were of Norwegian registry. The first was the Norwegian steamship Eidsvold, sunk on June 4. Then came the sinking of the Norwegian steamer Vinland on June 5. The Vendiggen and Henrik Lund, both Norwegian, were sunk on June 10. The Samoa and Krinsjaa were added to the list of Norwegian losses in today's announcement.

SURVIVORS AT NORFOLK.

Crew of Samoa Forced to Leave Ship Hurriedly.

Special to The New York Times.

NORFOLK, June 16.—The crew of the Norwegian bark Samoa, sunk by a submarine off this coast, fifteen officers and men, were landed at this port tonight. They were forced to leave their ship hurriedly, as was shown by the fact that several of the men were scantily clad.

The survivors were picked up by another sailing ship after being adrift at sea for several hours. Later they were transferred to a steamship and brought here.

The Samoa's crew, on being landed just after dark at Sewall's Point, were taken in charge by Naval Intelligence officials. The naval authorities said that the Norwegians had been instructed to give out no statement. When the men were taken to a hotel for supper they were guarded by sailors, who remained with them at the tables. It is believed that they have important information regarding the U-boat raider.

The details of the sinking of the Krinsjaa are yet to be received, but wireless reports are to the effect that

Continued on Page Six.

Japanese See Significance in Prince's Recall from Sea

TOKIO, June 13. (Associated Press.)—The press attaches significance to the fact that Prince Higashi-Fushimi has been relieved of the command of the Second Squadron and made a member of the Admiral's Council. The Prince was similarly relieved of an active command previous to the inauguration of the campaign at Tsing-tao.

French Naval Attaché Brylinski will leave at an early date for Washington for a consultation with the French Embassy there.

O'LEARY, ARRESTED, EXPECTED HANGING

Handcuffed, He Told Captors on Chicken Farm He Had Given Up Hope.

SHOTS FIRED AS SIGNAL

Secret Service Men and Posse Closed In on Propagandist While He Was Under Auto.

Special to The New York Times.

PORTLAND, Ore., June 16.—"I guess it is hanging for me," said Jeremiah A. O'Leary on Wednesday as he stood handcuffed in the centre of a group of Secret Service agents and a posse of six citizens of Clarke County on the three-acre chicken farm he had recently bought at Sara, Wash., fifteen miles north of here. A few hours later he was speeding toward New York with the detectives, and the party should reach that city tomorrow night.

Although, according to a man who worked on the farm, O'Leary knew the Secret Service men were on his trail, his capture was so sudden that he was dazed and unable to add to the words that indicated all hope was gone. Samuel F. Stein, his 70-year-old employe, says O'Leary was underneath a small automobile tinkering with it when three shots were fired. Before he could get on his feet there was a ring of men, called by this signal from the woods, about him and the handcuffs were on his wrists.

The chicken farm where the capture was made was formerly owned by T. L. Sagar of this city. The latter recently advertised it for sale, and it was bought by Thomas J. Corbett, who said he wanted it for his brother-in-law, who was ill and needed such a place to get well in.

Corbett, who said his brother-in-law's name was O'Leary, bought the farm for $900, paying $350 in cash and giving two notes to secure the mortgage. Corbett demanded immediate possession on May 16 and Sagar and his son left, Corbett telling them that he would bring all their belongings to Portland. Corbett then took possession of the ranch of 450 chickens and 50 rabbits.

Corbett had told Sagar that he was from Denver and was a "drummer" for a steel bridge concern. Corbett was about 30 years old, smooth shaven, clever, and a good talker.

O'Leary Looked Worried.

As Stein told his story in the office of Sheriff Beisecker, at Vancouver, Wash., on Friday, Corbett had hired him to help on the place. Stein had been taking care of chickens, he said, for many years, but he thought it queer that his papers and belongings were taken from him at the ranch and kept under lock and key.

Corbett told him one day that he expected to be called to Chicago at any time and that his brother-in-law, who was sick, would take charge of the farm for him. A couple of days later Corbett left and the same day O'Leary, the sick brother-in-law, appeared. Stein said O'Leary showed signs of illness and seemed greatly worried. He had the appearance of a man who had not slept comfortably for days.

O'Leary, Stein said, knew nothing about chickens, though he apparently took considerable interest in the ranch. His great desire was to have the chickens well housed and the rabbits watched. He insisted that they be moved away from in front of the house, so that he could see the roadway. He ordered a part of the place plowed and planted to potatoes. He also directed that strawberries be canned and much canned goods be purchased and a garden of beans and corn planted.

One day, said Stein, O'Leary drove to Ridgefield, and there he was identified as the man wanted in New York. From that time he was watched. The Secret Service men who had been notified gathered a posse of trusted civilians. All night Tuesday the posse lay in wait in the woods surrounding the ranch. It was expected that O'Leary would make another trip to Ridgefield or Vancouver, as he did almost daily, but the automobile wouldn't work, and

Continued on Page Four.

GOVERNMENT NEAR FULL AGREEMENT WITH RAILROADS

Plan for Protection of Roads During Control Is Nearly Completed.

LOOKS TO RETURN OF LINES

Document Emphasizes Fact That Congress Did Not Intend Government Ownership.

CLAIMS GO TO ARBITRATION

Provision Also Made for Repairs and Improvements at Government Expense.

Special to The New York Times.

WASHINGTON, June 16.—Government experts and railroad officials are expected soon to ratify formal agreements under which the Railroad Administration will operate the carriers at least for the period of the war.

Because of the many problems involved and the claims set forth by the Government and the private corporations concerning the burdens which each should bear, the task has proved an arduous one and has been the subject of long debate since the Government assumed control on Jan. 1. Details of the proposals made have been withheld.

THE TIMES is now able to present the more important points which have been incorporated in a proposed agreement, which it is stated on high authority will be the basis of the final decisions reached.

In it the railroad officials have insisted that every safeguard shall be thrown about their properties in anticipation of their return to private ownership. They have also held that emphasis should be laid on the fact that Congressional action indicated that the roads would not be held indefinitely under Government control.

The proposed agreement provides that the railroads shall receive rentals, as provided by Congressional action, in monthly installments. It also goes into detail concerning the liability of Government and private corporations for betterment and equipment.

War excess profits taxes are to be paid by the railroads out of their own funds and not by the Government from the current revenues received by the Federal operation of the roads. Other taxes, however, are to be borne by the Government and made chargeable against current revenue.

The Government is called upon to return the railroads to private ownership unimparied and the railroads are provided with a means of claiming exemption from payment for new equipment, such as motive power and extensions, which are chargeable now against capital account, if they wish later to claim that such equipment is not necessary to normal traffic after the war.

Arbitration Provided For.

Provision is made for a court of arbitration if the railroads or the Government are unable to agree upon the construction of the articles of agreement.

After reviewing the legislation under which the railroads were taken over by the Government the proposed agreement contains the statement that Congress, on the face of the act providing for Government control, declared it to be "emergency legislation enacted to meet conditions growing out of the war, and that nothing therein was to be construed as expressing or prejudicing the future policy of the Federal Government concerning the ownership, control, or regulation of carriers or the method or basis of the capitalization thereof."

The agreement sets forth that the properties of the carrier to be taken by the Government and the appurtenances thereof to be used upon or operated as part of its system of transportation shall embrace "all the properties of the said carrier, the operating revenues and expenses of which were used or which, if then in existence, would have been used under Section 1 of the said act of March 21, 1918, in computing the amount of its average annual railway operating income hereunder, but none of its properties not so used in its carrier operations, or the operating results of which were not or would not have been embraced in such income; the lines of such carrier so taken under Federal control being generally described as follows."

Another paragraph reads:

"It is expressly understood that no street or interurban electric railway, which has as its principal source of operating revenue urban, suburban, or interurban passenger traffic or sale of power, heat, and light, or both, is in-

Continued on Page Seven.

Germans Freed by Russia Will Be Used Against Allies

LONDON, June 16.—A dispatch to the Exchange Telegraph from Amsterdam says the Prussian War Minister has announced that all German prisoners of war repatriated from Russia will resume their military service after a short furlough.

It was officially stated in the Reichstag at the end of April that there were 157,000 German prisoners in Russia and Rumania.

NEXT LOAN LIKELY TO BE AT 4 1-2%

McAdoo Announces Plan to Sell $6,000,000,000 in Debt Certificates by October.

TO ANTICIPATE THE LOAN

Announced Rate Taken to Forecast a Similar Rate on the Coming Bond Issue.

Special to The New York Times.

WASHINGTON, June 16.—Secretary McAdoo, in a letter to the Presidents of banks and trust companies, made public tonight, outlines the financial need of the Government, which, he says, will require the sale of certificates of indebtedness in the next four months to the amount of $6,000,000,000. This will involve the issue every two weeks of about $750,000,000 of such certificates, the first issue of which will be dated June 25, and will mature on Oct. 25, with interest at 4½ per cent.

This policy of issuing certificates of indebtedness has been following in advance of the sale of every Liberty bond issue. Mr. McAdoo's letter is taken to mean that the next Liberty Loan will be floated in October, and will bear 4½ per cent. interest, as all previous loans have carried the same rate of interest as the certificates of indebtedness sold in advance of the bond sales.

There has been some talk in Congress that the next issue would be made more desirable to investors then those previously issued, by being made non-taxable up to an amount of holdings not exceeding $50,000. The position taken by Secretary McAdoo in his letter would appear to be against such a procedure and in favor of raising the interest rate on the next bond issue to 4½ per cent.

Mr. McAdoo's Letter.

Secretary McAdoo's letter to the banks is as follows:

"Following the same plan as that announced in my telegram of Feb. 6, 1918, I am writing to inform you of the program for the ensuing four months, so far as one can be made at this time, in order that every bank and trust company in the United States may have adequate notice and be able to prepare itself to meet patriotically the requirements of the Government.

"I am sending a similar letter to every bank and trust company in the United States. This policy, adopted in February last, was successful and, having fulfilled expectations in the sale of certificates of indebtedness prior to the Third Liberty Loan, demonstrated that the Government could rely upon the hearty support and co-operation of the banks when given opportunity in advance to make necessary preparations.

"The expenditures of the Government as nearly as can be estimated will require the sale of certificates of indebtedness up to Nov. 1, 1918, aggregating approximately $6,000,000,000.

"This would involve the issue every two weeks of about $750,000,000 of certificates substantially similar in character to those issued prior to the Third Liberty Loan, except that they will have various maturities not exceeding four months. For the months of July and August that program will be followed as nearly as possible.

"The first issue of certificates will be dated June 25, will mature October 25, with interest at 4½ per cent., and similar issues it is expected will be made on Tuesday of every other week following June 25.

"It is, however, contemplated that at a convenient and favorable period during the Summer an offering will be made to the general public directly and through the banks of an amount yet to be determined, perhaps $2,000,000,000, of certificates of suitable maturities for use by taxpayers in paying next year's taxes, viz: taxes payable June, 1919, levied under existing and pending legislation.

"To the extent that certificates of that character are sold substantially, an equivalent reduction in the amount of the regular fortnightly sale of certificates issued in anticipation of the next Liberty Loan will be effected. In giving this timely advice of the estimated re-

Continued on Page Seven.

OUR MEN WIN A GAS DUEL

Catch German Reserves with 7,000 Gas Shells After 48-Hour Attack

ON CHATEAU-THIERRY FRONT

Heavy Casualties in Kaiser's Favorite Divisions—Belleau Wood Attack Also Defeated.

TWO OTHER ATTACKS FAIL

One at Xivray and the Other in the New Alsatian Sector Beaten Off.

By EDWIN L. JAMES.

Special Cable to THE NEW YORK TIMES.

WITH THE AMERICAN ARMY ON THE MARNE, June 16, 4 P. M.—After forty-eight hours of continuous gassing of the American troops, northwest of Château-Thierry, the Germans today called off the attack. They called it off because the Americans had repaid them in their own coin.

On Friday the Germans started heavy gas shelling of our entire sector, and they kept it up all day Saturday. Yesterday the American artillery began to carry out the contemplated retaliation. One thousand gas shells were put down on the German lines, running from Bussiares to Belleau yesterday afternoon. Last night 5,000 gas shells from 75-calibre guns were hurled at the German positions in front of Bouresches and toward Château-Thierry, and this morning 1,000 heavy calibre lethal gas shells were put down on German reserve units in the vicinity of Epaux-Bezu.

Soon after this the German gas shelling stopped and there has been none since up to the time this was written. This experience shows that one way to meet gas attacks is with more gas.

We have evidence that the Germans believed the Amreicans were not equipped to fire gas shells, and therefore unable to retalatate in kind. They received a lesson they will not soon forget.

Our gas caught his reserves in a valley, which is an excellent place for shelling, and evidence is not lacking that we inflicted very heavy casualties, especially upon the Kaiser's favorite division, the well-known Twenty-eighth.

When America gets to producing gas shells in the quantity the army hopes she will our soldiers intend to give the enemy a large does of his own grim war weapon.

While the Germans have thus far always had the start in the gas farfare, Americans hope for the day when things will be the other way. Should a German clamor for mercy arise, the American gunners will remember some of their comrades who were gassed northwest of Château-Thierry.

Early this morning the Germans launched a strong attack on our positions at the northern end of the Bois de Belleau, and were repulsed with extra heavy losses.

The 1,500 assailants could not get within 500 yards of our positions.

The night was very dark, but by the light of flares after the attack the Americans could see the Germans dragging off their dead.

When daylight came many German bodies were seen still lying in the field across which the attack was made. Thirty-five were counted in one group.

Two Other Attacks Repulsed.

WITH THE AMERICAN ARMY IN FRANCE, June 16 (Associated Press.)—Two attacks were made on the American lines today, one in Alsace and another at Xivray, in the Toul sector. Both were repulsed.

About 600 German shock troops raided the American first line positions at the village of Xivray early this morning. Some of the enemy got

Continued on Page Three.

British on Italian Front Hold Line Intact Despite Foe's Desperate Efforts in Great Drive

By WARD PRICE.

Special Cable to THE NEW YORK TIMES.

ON THE ITALIAN FRONT, June 15.—The British sector formed the extreme right of the enemy's attacking front. Between British troops and the Brenta, which is the focus of one of the two main enemy efforts, there are sectors of a French and of an Italian army. It is on the front of the latter that the strongest concentration of Austrian troops had been gathered, but it seemed as if the enemy felt compelled to bring both the French and the British troops within the scope of his attack, so as to preclude any diversion that might otherwise be started in aid of the Italians.

The result of his offensive on the British positions, however, can hardly seem satisfactory to him. At the end of the day's fighting the line remains practically identical with what it was this morning, while the British have taken over 350 prisoners.

As elsewhere, the enemy bombardment opened at 3 A. M. He fired gas shells into the hollows of the pine woods behind the British line, and did his best to hinder traffic by bombarding the roads that feed the sector. Then at 7:30 the Austrians launched their infantry attack. It was an attack in depth and well organized, the first waves reaching the British line at what was found out later on from prisoners to be exactly on time.

The enemy came on in full view over the open ground that lies between the ruined village of Asiago and the foot of the black pine tree-covered hills where the British first lines are. On the right they were stopped completely with rifle and machine gun fire and had heavy losses. At the few points where the Austrian infantrymen reached the trenches they were at once thrust back.

On the front of the British left-hand division, where the Austrian objective was Monte Lemerle, they had an advantage in their advance under cover of the valley down which the railway from Asiago runs, and coming thus under comparative cover they managed to enter the front line on a breadth of about a mile.

The defense fell back on to two switch lines, inclosing the Austrians in a triangular pocket and enfilading them. The enemy's possession even of this fraction of line, however, was brief. A counterattack delivered by the British divisions of the left established the line as it had been before, taking most of the ground mentioned above. During their brief occupation the Austrians had had temporary possessions of four guns, which had been pushed far forward, but these guns were retaken by a counterattack at the end of the afternoon.

The result of the whole day for the Austrians, as regards the British front, has been that they dug themselves in somewhat further forward in what used to be No Man's Land, but their first day's objective, which was the line of heights consisting of Monte Pau and Cima di Fonte, commanding the plain, is as far off as it was this morning.

LOSS OF BELLEAU CRIPPLED GERMANS

Wood Taken by Americans Was an Important Base for Further Advance.

GERMANS UNDER PRESSURE

Franco-American Forces Give Them No Rest in the Clignon Valley Region.

By G. H. PERRIS.

Special Cable to THE NEW YORK TIMES.

WITH THE FRENCH ARMIES, June 16, (Morning.)—Looking from the high ground south of the Aronde Valley toward the long ridge that closes the horizon on the north under the rather chill sunshine of yesterday afternoon, it was strange, almost shocking, to remark the quiet beauty of the scene so filled with horror during the past week.

Green wheat fields slope gently down and away, broken by patches of olive woodland, and rise again more sharply to the purple line of the Mery and Belloy hills. Many French observation balloons floated overhead, and, like a series of German "sausages," helped to mark the irregular course of the front.

As usual, not a man of the hosts watching each other with murderous eyes was visible at a little distance, but the boom of guns and the crash of heavy shells, followed by spouts and hanging clouds of smoke and dust about Courcelles, Mery, St. Maur, and the hamlets of the Matz Valley, shouted the ugly truth against all the bright camouflage of Summertime.

This countryside, like so many others, has been deserted by most of its inhabitants. A few remain, however, and there are men and women bent at field work within the range of the enemy's guns, as though they could not tear themselves away from the land that is all to them, or could not believe that the tide of invasion would reach further. Perhaps they are too poor, too old, or too helpless to be able to face the search for new homes.

The battle is lost and won; the pressure on ambulance cars and hospital trains is relaxed; the processions of refugees have passed away to the south. In this interval, moving about behind the French lines, it comes home to me once more what a world of suffering an invasion makes apart from the direct wounds of battle. In the three weeks since this phase of the offensive began several large towns, especially Compiègne and Soissons, have been destroyed; others, like Château-Thierry and Villers-Cotteret, greatly damaged, and in wide stretches

Continued on Page Three.

BRITISH AVENGED LOUVAIN HORRORS

Saturday's Success Near Hinges Won Against the First Invaders of Belgium.

ZEEBRUGGE RAIDED NIGHTLY

Young British Aviator Describes Operations Which Have Done Immense Damage There.

By PHILIP GIBBS.

Special Cable to THE NEW YORK TIMES.

WAR CORRESPONDENTS' HEADQUARTERS, Sunday, June 16.—Late Friday night and in the small hours of Saturday morning some English and Scottish troops beyond the La Bassée Canal, in front of Hinges, made a very daring attack on the enemy's outpost lines on a front about two miles, and captured a long strip of ground, with 200 prisoners and about twenty-five machine guns.

The exact locality of this operation was between a place called La Pannerie, on the left, and Les Choquax, on the right, in the low flats of the mining country above Bethune, with black slag heaps high and conical among the miners' villages and the steel works, of pitheads, all broken now by years of shellfire, which became most violent last April, when the enemy drove across the Lys, came closer to Bethune, and flung shells about all this countryside, killing women and children behind the lines, wounding cattle in the fields, and completing the ruin of villages like Hinges.

Since that fighting on the Lys the German troops have not been living in nice places, but rather in a hell of their own making, and, as the British still held observation of their positions, they could not make a trench system without having it blown to bits, as prisoners have described very ruefully. In any case, however, the new German system of defense from outpost lines is based on linked shell craters and scattered machine gun posts, rather than on definite trench lines, which are targets for British guns, and this was how they defended the line parallel with La Bassée Canal.

The Germans in those pits and posts were of the Eighteenth Reserve Division, famous with their own people and infamous with the British as the first German division to enter Belgium at the beginning of the war and as the authors of the campaign of frightfulness at Louvain and Termonde. Since those days of shooting civilians they have pursued the ordi-

Continued on Page Three.

ITALIAN ARMY STRIKES BACK

Checks Massed Attacks by Austrians by Strong Counterattacks.

RECOVERS TWO MOUNTAINS

Enemy Detachments That Succeeded in Crossing Piave River Are Being Pressed Hard.

VIENNA CLAIMS WIDE GAINS

British Eject Invaders from Positions They Stormed at Beginning of the Drive.

ROME, June 16.—A battle of great violence, in which large masses of infantry are being used by the Austrians in an attempt to break through the Italian lines, particularly in the eastern sector of the Asiago Plateau, in the Brenta Valley, and on Monte Grappa, and during which they succeeded in crossing the Piave River at two places, is described in the official report from Italian Headquarters today.

Unofficial advices from the front say the objective of the drive across the Piave was Treviso, but that the enemy was pressed back.

The enemy's attacks in the mountains, which were met in the advanced defensive area, at first carried some of the Italian positions there, but later the line was re-established at most points.

The Italian forces are firmly holding the Asiago front. The War Office announcement says they have completely reoccupied their original positions on Asolone and Monte Solarola and are closely pressing the enemy who crossed the Piave.

During their wide offensive the Austrians, after a violent bombardment, attacked the French positions, (between Osteria di Monfenera and Maranzine,) but the very efficacious fire of the French broke down the thrusts. The enemy casualties were heavy, and in addition he left numerous prisoners in the hands of the French.

The battle is in progress along the whole of the front.

Official Version of the Battle.

The text of the official statement reads:

A great battle has been in progress on our front since yesterday.

After artillery preparation, which was exceptionally intense on account of the violence of the fire and the number of guns employed, the enemy has begun his expected offensive by launching large masses of infantry to attack our positions in the eastern sector of Asiago Plateau, at the end of the Brenta Valley and on Monte Grappa, by attempting at several points to force the Piave, and by carrying out heavy local demonstrative action on the remainder of the front.

Our infantry and that of the allied contingents fearlessly bore the tempest of the destructive fire, and, supported by a barrage of their own artillery, which had already prudently anticipated the enemy's preparation with a timely and deadly counter-preparation bombardment, bravely sustained the enemy's onslaught in the advanced defensive area.

On the 150-kilometre front more intensely attacked the powerful storming columns of the enemy occupied in their initial rush forward only a few front line positions in the Monte Di Val Bella region, in the Asolone area, and at the head of the Monte Solarola salient.

Some troops succeeded in passing to the right bank of the Piave River in the Nervesa area and in the Fagare-Musile region.

During the day our troops initiated along all the front, attacked energetic counterattacks, which succeeded in holding back the powerful pressure of the enemy and in regaining a good portion of the positions temporarily yielded, on some of which, however, isolated detachments had with great valor continued to remain at all costs.

The struggle did not diminish in violence during the night, and is continuing fiercely. But our troops are firmly holding the front along the Asiago Plateau, have completely reoccupied their original positions on Asolone and at the Monte Solarola salient, and are very closely pressing the enemy infantry which has passed to the right bank of the Piave.

The number of prisoners so far counted is more than 3,000, including 89 officers.

Our own and the allied airmen are taking a strong part in the battle by bombarding the crossing points on the Piave and by attacking the enemy's massed troops with machine gun fire.

Mid-Week Pictorial

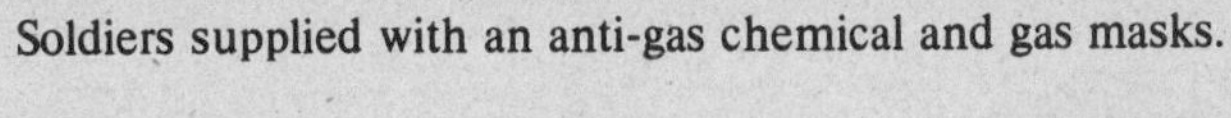

Soldiers supplied with an anti-gas chemical and gas masks.

Mid-Week Pictorial

A regiment experimenting with an anti-gas chemical.

"All the News That's Fit to Print."

The New York Times.

THE WEATHER
Showers today; Sunday probably fair; moderate winds, mostly west.
For full weather report see Page 17.

VOL. LXVII...NO. 22,078. NEW YORK, SATURDAY, JULY 6, 1918.—EIGHTEEN PAGES. TWO CENTS In Greater New York and Within Commuting Distance. | THREE CENTS Elsewhere.

CRYING 'LUSITANIA!' OUR MEN VICTORIOUSLY RUSH ON HAMEL; U. S. TRANSPORT COVINGTON SUNK; SIX OF THE CREW LOST; LLOYD GEORGE OFFERS PEACE TO GERMANY ON WILSON'S TERMS

HOUSE VOTES WIRE CONTROL; SENATE WAITS

Put Through Lower Body, 221 to 4, on White House Demand for Quick Action.

RECESS PLANNED TODAY

President Apparently Acquiesces in Senate Delay Until Five Weeks Hence.

STRIKE ON MONDAY ORDERED

Divergent Views of Executive Power to Take Lines Without Authority from Congress.

Special to The New York Times.

WASHINGTON, July 5.—After President Wilson had sent word to Democratic leaders of his desire for the immediate adoption of the resolution empowering him to take over the telegraph and telephone systems, the House today, under a rule limiting debate to two hours, passed the resolution by a vote of 221 to 4. Those voting negatively were Representatives Fordney and McLaughlin of Michigan; Woods of Iowa, and Sterling of Illinois, all Republicans.

After the House had passed the resolution, Majority Leader Kitchin surprised the members by announcing that the indications were that the President would not insist upon the Senate passing the resolution immediately, thereby permitting Congress to adjourn tomorrow night for a five weeks' recess. Mr. Kitchin said he based his conclusions upon a statement made to him by Senator Thomas B. Martin, Democratic leader of the Senate, who had told the President the Senate could not be expected to concur in the resolution at once. The President is reported to have made no objection to the Senate taking the long-planned recess without adopting the resolution. Mr. Kitchin said that tomorrow the House would adopt a resolution to take a recess from tomorrow night until Aug. 12.

Senator Martin, late tonight, said that if the House adopted the recess resolution tomorrow there would be no reason that he could see for the Senate refusing to agree to it. He said he had informed the President of the attitude of the Senate toward the telegraph-telephone resolution, and indicated that several weeks, at least, would be required by that body to consider the measure.

"I do not believe the President will insist upon the Senate passing the resolution before taking the proposed recess, and I think that Congress can adjourn by tomorrow night," added Senator Martin.

Hold Present Powers Ample.

Senate leaders have advised the President that eminent lawyers in the Senate are agreed that the legislation sought in the resolution is not necessary in case the strike order against the Western Union Telegraph Company by the Commercial Telegraphers Union for next Monday should become effective. Then, the President was told, he could take over the telegraphs and telephones, to protect the Government and the public. They say that the President, under the broad war provisions of the Constitution, has all the power required to deal with such a situation. Therefore, it is thought in the Senate, the President will not press for immediate adoption of the resolution, since it is apparent that it could not be passed and sent to him for his approval by next Monday, when the threatened strike may be on. Foreseeing his inability to get the power conferred in the resolution by next week, it is reported that the President, in conversation with Senator Martin, expressed himself as agreeable to Congress taking a recess.

Senator Knox is one of the lawyers, who gave the above opinion, and ex-Justice Charles E. Hughes is reported to have given a similar opinion. Postmaster General Burleson, in appearing before the House Committee on Interstate and Foreign Commerce this week, stated that the Department of Justice had advised the President that he had no authority to act in case a strike should tie up telegraphic communication. Mr. Burleson, however, said he did not believe the President's hands were tied, if such an emergency should arise, and he quoted Senator Knox, Mr. Hughes, and others as having said that the President had ample authority under the war powers of the Constitution.

Republican Opposition.

In the debate in the House today Republicans manifested opposition to passing the resolution hastily and without any message on the subject from the President. This opposition disappeared almost entirely when Representative E. W. Pou, Chairman of the Rules Com-

Continued on Page Seven.

Dutch Send Armed Convoy with Ships to East Indies

THE HAGUE, July 5.—Several Dutch steamers, under an armed convoy and accompanied by a collier, sailed today for the Dutch East Indies.

On May 17, Jonkheer J. Loudon, Dutch Minister of Foreign Affairs, announced that it was intended to send a fleet to the East Indies under an armed convoy. He said that he could not say definitely that no international difficulty would arise out of the fact that the ships were convoyed, but that he presumed there would be no interference.

It was indicated by the Foreign Minister that the Entente allied powers had been informed that such a fleet would sail.

FORCE REICHSTAG TO DISCUSS PEACE

Socialists, Led by Scheidemann, Open Active Agitation by Fight on Budget.

TELL OF ECONOMIC STRAIN

Leader Attacked in Berlin Press for Depicting German Misery Due to War.

Special Cable to THE NEW YORK TIMES.

LONDON, July 5.—A dispatch to The Daily Express from Amsterdam says:

"The attitude of the Socialists in the Reichstag naturally is the subject of much comment in Germany today and may have serious consequences, though not from a purely parliamentarian standpoint. The Socialists are 111 out of 397 members of the Reichstag, so their opposition could not block estimates or seriously interfere with the Government's prosecution of the war, but the effect of Scheidemann's official announcement that the Socialists will no longer vote for the budget until the peace question is cleared up is of far-reaching importance in view of the effect it is bound to produce in German and Austrian labor circles, and still more among the German and Austrian armies.

"It is said in Germany that Scheidemann's present attitude has been forced on him by an overwhelming majority of the German Socialists, who consider this is the only means of forcing the hands of the General Staff and the Government and compelling such a statement of terms as might bring an acceptable peace before Winter. There is the additional advantage that the German Socialists will be able to plead not guilty before the Socialists of the Entente countries when the question of reforming the International is discussed after the war. I hear from trustworthy sources that Scheidemann's recent conference with Troelstra at The Hague was chiefly devoted to explaining to the Dutch Socialist leader the intention of the German Socialists to cease supporting the Government until they have taken a reasonable step forward as regards peace. This is the message which Troelstra was to have brought to the London Socialist Conference. It remains to be seen what the immediate effect of Scheidemann's threat will have.

"It is not likely that the General Staff will allow the Socialists to dictate to them, so that a bitter conflict between Ludendorff and Scheidemann can be expected, unless, as many people believe in Germany, Scheidemann's move was made in agreement with headquarters in order to prepare public opinion for another German peace offer. As a matter of fact, peace talk in the German newspapers is growing in volume, if not in genuineness. One report has Cardinal Frushwirth, formerly Nuncio at Munich, actively engaged with the Pope over peace mediation possibilities.

"Great prominence is given to a Swiss report of a decidedly German origin to the effect that King Alfonso is secretly in Paris trying to induce the French Government to state their terms in view of his mediation. King Alfonso is also

Continued on Page Three.

NO TROOPS ON LOST VESSEL

Covington Attacked on Return Voyage Under American Convoy.

HIT AT NIGHT ON JULY 1

Engine Room Flooded After Torpedo Struck and Salvaging Operations Failed.

SUBMARINE WAS NOT SEEN

16,339-Ton Ship Was Formerly the Cincinnati—Fifth Big Transport Destroyed.

American Transport Afire; Reaches an Atlantic Port

WASHINGTON, July 5.—The United States Army transport Henderson has been afire at sea, but has made an Atlantic port in safety. There was no loss of life. Few details could be had at the Navy Department tonight, but it was said that the vessel was not badly damaged. It was not made known whether the Henderson was outbound or homeward bound, nor was there any information as to how the fire occurred.

Special to The New York Times.

WASHINGTON, July 5.—Delayed announcement was made by Secretary Daniels tonight of the loss of the army transport Covington, formerly the Hamburg-American liner Cincinnati, which was sunk the night of July 1 by a German submarine while en route from a French port to the United States without passengers or troops.

Every effort was made to save the Covington, but the engine and fire rooms filled with water rapidly and the vessel had to be abandoned to her fate. Those on board included only the officers and crew of the vessel. How many were on board is not disclosed, but the size of the crew was undoubtedly considerable, as the Covington was a vessel 608 feet long and of 16,339 gross tonnage, and when in the German merchant service caried a crew of 370 men.

All the officers and crew, except six, were saved and taken to a French port. The announcement tonight gives the names of the six members of the crew missing, and, as three of them were firemen, it is highly probable that they were killed when the torpedo struck just forward of the engine room bulkhead.

Official Report of Sinking.

The official announcement was issued at 9 o'clock tonight as follows:

"The Navy Department has received dispatches from Vice Admiral Sims stating that the United States steamer Covington was struck by a torpedo on the night of July 1 at 9:17 o'clock. The torpedo struck just forward of the engine room bulkhead, and the engine room and fire room were rapidly flooded.

"With its motor power gone, the vessel was helpless, and, facing the possibility of the torpedoing of another ship in the convoy, the Covington was temporarily abandoned. This was done in excellent order, and the officers and crew were taken on board a destroyer. The submarine was not seen.

"At daybreak the Captain, several officers, and a number of members of the crew returned to supervise salvaging operations. Another vessel and two tugs took the Covington in tow, in the effort to get her to port, but she was too badly damaged to keep afloat and sank.

"All the officers and crew, except six, were taken to a French port, none of those landed being seriously injured. The six men of the crew who, at last accounts, were still missing are:

"Ernest C. Anderson, fireman, third

Continued on Page Two.

Allied Council Takes Important Decisions in Secret Conference on War Situation

PARIS, July 5, (Havas Agency.)—The Supreme Allied War Council held its seventh session today. All the aspects of the present military situation were considered and important decisions were reached, according to an official statement issued at its close.

Among those present were Premiers Clemenceau, Lloyd George, and Orlando; Stephen Pichon, French Foreign Minister; A. J. Balfour, British Secretary of State for Foreign Affairs; Viscount Milner, British War Minister, Baron Sonnino, Italian Foreign Minister; Generalissimo Foch, Field Marshal Haig, and Major Gen. Sir Henry Wilson of the British Army; General John J. Pershing of the American Army, and General Guillain of the Belgian Army, as well as representatives of the other Allies at Versailles.

Sincere congratulations to the Italian Army and people for the victory over the Austro-Hungarian Army were expressed at the meeting. It was said it was thought that the victory won by the Italians, at a critical point of the war brought a valuable contribution to the Allies' efforts and pointed to the final success of their cause.

One of the features of the session was the presence of the Prime Ministers of Canada, Australia, and New Zealand, as well as several other Ministers of the British Dominions. On behalf of the Council Premiers Clemenceau and Orlando expressed to them the thanks of the Allies for the services rendered on the battlefield by the troops of the British colonies.

Transport Covington, Sunk by U-Boat.

200 GERMAN PLANES SENT TO OUR FRONT

But Our Air Fighters Face Them Boldly in the Chateau-Thierry Sector.

IN TWO COMBATS YESTERDAY

Four Defeat 8 of Foe—Eight Defeat 15 Others—Two Enemy Machines Downed.

By EDWIN L. JAMES.

Special Cable to THE NEW YORK TIMES.

WITH THE AMERICAN ARMY ON THE MARNE, July 5.—There are as yet no indications of a new German attack on the American lines northwest of Château-Thierry, but since the American aviators appeared on this sector German pursuit machines have been brought in opposite them in considerable number.

I learn that the enemy now has something more than 200 fighting airplanes on the front opposite the Americans.

Before the arrival of our airmen German observation machines sometimes made a hundred flights daily over this sector, going as far as twenty miles behind the lines.

Since Monday this has all been changed, and the enemy machines, both observation and pursuit, are challenged as they reach the line, and in many cases are met before they arrive there.

Despite the expectations that the Germans might be active on the night of July 4, the only infantry activity on the American front last night was patrolling by our soldiers, who brought in two prisoners.

There was an intermittent exchange of artillery fire, but this was in no wise equal to that of the two preceding nights.

Two German Planes Downed.

WITH THE AMERICAN ARMY IN FRANCE, July 5, (Associated Press.)—Two sharp air combats took place between American and German airmen over the front northwest of Château-Thierry today, and two of the German airplanes were brought down.

Lieutenants Carlisle Rhodes of Terre Haute, S. P. Thompson of Honeoye Falls, N. Y.; Waldo N. Heinrichs of Granville, Ohio, and John Mitchell of Manchester, Mass., engaged in a thrilling battle this morning. One German machine was downed during the combat. It is believed that Lieutenant Heinrichs was the American who sent the enemy airplane to earth.

The four Americans were patrolling five or six kilometers inside the German lines when they encountered six enemy machines. The battle began at an altitude of 4,200 meters, and continued twenty minutes, until the machines had dropped down to 2,200 meters from the earth.

An hour later eight American machines engaged in a battle with fifteen enemy airplanes at a height of 4,700 meters. The combat swayed backward and forward over the German and American lines near Château-Thierry. The German machines were higher than the Americans, but the latter manoeuvred their airplanes admirably.

Suddenly one of the enemy airplanes dived toward the earth and went spinning downward, being chased down by Lieutenants Ralph A. O'Neill of Nogales, Ariz., and J. C. Raible of New

Continued on Page Two.

FRENCH STROKES GETTING BOLDER

Foch at Little Loss Is Winning Lost Ground and Capturing Many Prisoners.

STRENGTHENING THE FRONT

Operations, Though Only Preparatory, May Develop an Important Offensive.

By G. H. PERRIS.

Special Cable to THE NEW YORK TIMES.

WITH THE FRENCH ARMIES, July 5.—Local actions conducted by the French armies become bolder and more extensive. Whether from weariness or from deliberate policy the enemy lies inert through the intervals between his major attacks, whereas the French, quickly recovering, harry him with pinpricks and take back the best part of his gains by the retail process.

The real aim of these local operations is, of course, preparatory. They are directed at observatories and other positions of particular value, and it is only in the future that their importance will be seen, but their immediate results are not to be despised.

When the offensive of June 9 was arrested, the German command claimed to have taken 15,000 prisoners. Well, since the same date the French and their American comrades have by these unostentatious assaults made about 10,000 prisoners and captured an extent of ground nearly equal to and as important as that previously captured by von Hutier.

Line Is Strengthened.

Four thousand German soldiers and a goodly number of their officers have been brought into the French lines during the last week. All the way across the Oise to the Marne at Château-Thierry the French front, which had the irregularity of a high-water mark after a storm, has been leveled and strengthened.

Most of the prisoners come from the sectors on either side of the forest of Villers-Cotterets, but more than a thousand have been taken in the last few days at very little cost on the side of the French in the neighborhood of Moulin-sous-Toutvent, the French salient between the Oise and the Aisne. Here the army of General von Boehn seems to be in a feeble condition.

On Wednesday morning two deep ravines north of Pulsieux Farm were occupied without serious difficulty by troops who have been engaged almost without rest since the middle of March. One of the German regiments attacked was practically wiped out, and 450 men with 7 officers and 84 noncoms were captured.

The same evening, a little to the southeast near Autreches, an advance of two-thirds of a mile was made on a front of a mile and a half, 600 prisoners being taken, including 14 officers. These included the whole of the bat-

Continued on Page Two.

'LUSITANIA' OUR BATTLE CRY

Americans with Anzacs Went Into Hamel Fight Seeking Vengeance.

NO TENDERNESS TO FOE

One Boy Corporal Slew Seven Germans, Although Thrice Wounded Himself.

ALLIES PRAISE OUR MEN

Some Had Never Been at the Front Nor Seen the Shellfire of Battle.

By PHILIP GIBBS.

Special Cable to THE NEW YORK TIMES.

WAR CORRESPONDENTS' HEADQUARTERS IN FRANCE, July 5.—After the Australian attack south of the Somme yesterday morning, the enemy, whose guns had been almost silenced during the battle by the intense counter-battery work, shelled some of the new allied positions rather heavily, and in the evening made three counterattacks. These seem to have been directed on the wings and centre of the Australian line, but were feeble and unsuccessful.

Groups of German machine gunners and infantry established themselves within fifty yards of the Australians, who were annoyed by this close approach and decided not to tolerate it. So last night a number of them went out, drove in the German outposts, and brought back another batch of prisoners to the number of something over fifty.

I was unable to mention yesterday one of the most interesting features of this action, and that was the share taken in the fighting by American troops. There were not many of them, compared with the strength of the Australian brigades, but these few companies were eager to go forward to meet the enemy face to face for the first time and prove their fighting quality. They have proved it up to the hilt of that sword, which is in their temper and spirit.

Australian officers with whom I spoke yesterday and today all told me the Americans attacked with astonishing ardor, discipline, and courage. If they had any fault at all, it was over-eagerness to advance, so that they could hardly be restrained from going too rapidly behind the wide belt of the British shellfire as the barrage rolled forward.

Our First Fight on British Front.

It was a historic day for them and for the British. It was the Fourth of July, the day of American independence, when, as I described yesterday, many French villages quite close to the fighting lines were all fluttering with the Tricolor and the Stars and Stripes in honor of their comradeship in arms and symbolizing the hope of peace in the united strength of the armies that now defend her soil.

And it was the first time the American soldiers had fought on the British front. They understood that on their few companies fighting as platoons among the Australians, rested the honor of the United States in this adventure. Their General and his officers addressed them before the battle and called on them to make good.

"You are going in with the Australians" they said, "and those lads always deliver the goods. We expect you to do the same. We shall be very disappointed if you do not fulfill the hopes and belief we have in you."

The American boys listened to these words with a light in their eyes. They were ready to take all the risks to prove their mettle. They were sure of themselves, and were tuned up to a high pitch of nervous intensity at the thought of going into battle for the first time and on the Fourth of July.

Thousands More Wanted to Go.

There were thousands of other American soldiers desperately eager to go with them, though a battle is not a pleasant pastime, but all their training, all their purpose in this war, and their pride in their own regiments lead up to the fighting line, and they wanted to pass the test of it and measure their spirit against its terrors and dangers. In the hearts of these men, new to war, the adventure of battle is greater than its chance of pain or death, and there is the call of the hunter's instinct in them, so they went gladly, strange as it may seem to people who, after four years of war, look only on the tragic side of it.

The Australians had many requests from American companies who were not allowed to share in the battle.

"Can't we lend you a hand?" they asked. "Can't we be of any use to you?"

In one case outside of the order of battle their offer was accepted. The Australians took so many prisoners that they found it difficult for the moment to provide a proper escort for them from the forward to the back inclosure.

"Some of your lads might help us to conduct prisoners," said an Australian officer in charge of this work.

They did help. No German prisoners had such a strong and proud escort as that provided by the Americans who had not the luck, as they thought it, to take part in the actual fighting with their comrades who had gone forward with the Australian infantry and the tanks into the smoke clouds and the light of shellfire.

Engulfed in Battle's Roar.

Up there these lads from America were engulfed in the frightful excitement of battle, and found it an easier and less fearful thing than they had thought, because of the utter surprise of the enemy, and the silencing of his guns. More formidable to them was the intensity of the British gunfire which swept the ground in front of them and close to them with a backward blast of shell splinters and an informal tumult of drumfire. They could not tell at first whether it was the British barrage or the enemy's. They seemed to be in the centre of its fury and were surprised to find themselves alive, still moving forward with their comrades and with the dark line of Australians on either side of them.

"The barrage passed like a storm," said an Australian officer, "leaving behind perfect peace." And it was in this peace of the battlefield like the peace of death that the Americans and Australians met groups of men who were the enemy, strange, uncanny creatures, many of them in gas masks and with hands up in submission, knowing that surrender was their only chance of life. Those who showed any fight, like some who used their machine guns to the last, had hardly a thread of a chance.

The Americans were not tender-hearted in that eighty minutes of the advance to the ultimate objective with any of the enemy who tried to bar their way. They went forward with fixed bayonets, shouting the word "Lusitania" as a battlecry.

Again and again the Australians heard that word on American lips, as if there was something in the sound of it strengthening to their souls and terrifying to the enemy. They might well have been terrified—any German who heard that name, for to the American soldiers it is a call for vengeance.

It is a curious fact that with less provocation than the French, who see their own towns destroyed before their eyes and a great belt of ruin across their country and a world of tragedy where their own families are separated from them by the German lines, the American soldiers have come over here with such a stern spirit and with no kind of forgiveness in their hearts for the men who caused all this misery.

Today the young American soldiers who come out of battle wounded tell their experiences, and through them all is the conviction that the Germans are "bad men," and that death is a just punishment for all that they have done.

A Corporal's Story of Combat.

One young Corporal with a most boyish look described in a simple way how before the battle he was placed in charge of twenty-four of his comrades because he had worked hard and done his best to become a good soldier, and how then they had gathered together the night before going into the line and had resolved to inflict as much loss upon the enemy as they could because that was their duty.

Not knowing that they would ever meet again in this life, they then shook hands with each other and the young Corporal placed himself at the head of the platoon and went with them up to the support line and afterward to the front line.

None of them had seen the front-line trench before, as their regiment had come to France only a few weeks ago, and for the first time they saw shellfire, and then, two minutes before the attack, a barrage. It astounded them so that they held their breath, but they kept their nerve.

"It was a real Fourth of July celebration," said one boy.

The line of country in front of them to Hamel Village and the trench system beyond was over a little ridge and then into a valley, and then over another small ridge of ground. In the valley they were held up for a few minutes by some barbed wire and machine gun fire, but got forward and did not meet much trouble in Hamel.

It was beyond that in the trench system that the Germans fought hard, though some surrendered without fighting. Two of them ran forward, shouting "Kamerad" to the young American Corporal, who did not understand their meaning and would have killed them but for an officer, who told him not to.

Then a little later he was wounded by a bullet, and as he stumbled to his knees two Germans ran at him with bayonets. He had his finger on the trigger of his rifle, and shot one dead as he came forward. But the other drew near with bayonet lowered.

"Then," said this Corporal, who is not more than a boy in looks, "I knew I had to get up and fight him like a man."

He stood up in spite of his wound, and with his fixed bayonet turned aside a lunge which the German made to kill him, and then swung up his rifle and cracked the man's skull.

One Boy Killed Seven Germans.

Another American Corporal, 21 years of age, was wounded three times, but killed seven Germans, which, as he reckons, is two boches for each wound and one over. He had an astonishing series of episodes in which it was his life or the enemy's. After going through the enemy's wire near Vair Wood, he found himself under fire from a machine gun hidden in a wheat field, and was wounded badly in the thigh with an armor-piercing bullet designed for tanks.

He fell at once, but staggering up again threw a bomb at the German gun crew and killed four of them. One ran and disappeared into a dugout. The American Corporal followed him down and the man turned to leap at him in the darkness, but he killed him with his bayonet.

He went up from the dugout again to the light of day above, and a German soldier wounded him again, but he paid a price for the blow with his own life.

Another German attacked him, wounded him for a third time, and was killed by this lad whose bayonet was so quick.

That made six Germans, and the seventh was a machine gunner whom he shot. By this time the American Corporal was weak and bleeding from his wounds, and while he lay, unable to go further, he hoisted a rag onto his rifle as a signal to the stretcher-bearers, who came and carried him back.

The American companies had very light casualties and are satisfied. They accounted for many of the enemy. They are glad of that in a simple, serious way, and the spirit shown by those American soldiers in action on the British front for the first time seems to me, in spite of their youth, like that of Cromwell's Ironsides, stern

Germany Can Have Peace on Terms Wilson Stated, Lloyd George Tells American Troops at Front

WITH THE AMERICAN ARMY IN FRANCE, July 5 (Associated Press).—Addressing American troops, after a review, Premier Lloyd George of Great Britain today said:

"Germany can have peace tomorrow with the United States, France, and Great Britain if she will accept the conditions voiced yesterday by President Wilson."

The Prime Minister paid high tribute to the Americans who fought at Chateau-Thierry, saying that they had shown the Kaiser that he had made another mistake in believing that the new American troops were not capable of meeting the trained Germans.

He then sketched the illusions of the German ruler regarding the United States getting into the war and her participation in the war, adding:

"Now that one million Americans have arrived, the Kaiser is beginning to realize that defeat, certain and inevitable, is staring him in the face."

U.S. Navy

U.S.S. Covington sinking off Brest, France, after being torpedoed by German submarine.

"All the News That's Fit to Print."

The New York Times.

THE WEATHER
Fair today and tomorrow; gentle northwest to north winds.
For full weather report see Page 23.

VOL. LXVII...NO. 22,081. NEW YORK, TUESDAY, JULY 9, 1918.—TWENTY-FOUR PAGES. TWO CENTS In Greater New York and Within Commuting Distance. | THREE CENTS Elsewhere.

GERMANS POISED FOR DOUBLE BLOW AT ALLIES; FRENCH GAIN SOUTH OF AISNE, CAPTURE 347; MOSCOW RISING IS CRUSHED WITH HEAVY LOSS

ARREST RUMELY; SAY GERMANY OWNS THE EVENING MAIL

Government Charges Perjury in Statement That Paper Is Under American Control.

$100,000 BAIL DEMANDED

Kaiser's Government Alleged to Have Invested $1,361,000 in the Paper.

PAID IT THROUGH DR. ALBERT

Whose Memorandum Shows the Cost Was Charged to His and Bernstorff's Joint Bank Account.

Edward A. Rumely, Vice President, Secretary and publisher of The New York Evening Mail, was arrested late yesterday afternoon by agents of the Government, charged with perjury. The charge grew out of a statement filed with A. Mitchell Palmer, the Alien Property Custodian, in which Rumely asserted that The Evening Mail was an American-owned newspaper. The Government is in possession of evidence which, it is held, shows that instead of being owned by Americans, the paper is in fact owned by the Imperial German Government, which on June 1, 1915, paid to Rumely, through Walter Lyon, of the former Wall Street house of Renskorf, Lyon & Co., the sum of $735,000, which transferred the control of the newspaper to the Kaiser.

Mr. Rumely was brought to the office of Attorney General Merton E. Lewis, at 51 Chambers Street, late yesterday afternoon. There he was questioned by Attorney General Lewis, Deputy Attorney General Alfred L. Becker, and by Assistant United States District Attorney Harold Harper, the last named representing the Federal Department of Justice. Following the announcement of Mr. Rumely's arrest the Attorney General said that the investigation which had culminated so sensationally just before dusk of yesterday, had been under way for several months, the Federal and State authorities working hand in hand and with the co-operation of A. Mitchell Palmer, the Alien Property Custodian.

Bail of $100,000 Is Demanded.

The charge upon which Mr. Rumely was committed to the Tombs, the papers in the case being signed by United States Commissioner Hitchcock, was sworn to by Deputy Attorney General Becker. No bail was fixed at the time of the commitment, but late last night it was announced that bail had been fixed in the sum of $100,000 and that friends of the accused publisher were trying to get bondsmen.

In many respects the financial features of the transactions which the Government charges transferred the control of The Evening Mail from American to German interests were similar to the plan followed by Bernstorff, Adolph Pavenstedt, and Hugo Schmidt in transferring the huge sum which was paid to Bolo Pacha, the executed French traitor, to debauch French public opinion in favor of a German-made peace. In the case of Bolo, the funds, which totaled about $1,700,000, passed through a number of banks before they reached Bolo.

In this case, according to the Government agents, there were also several transfers. Dr. Heinrich Albert, the former German paymaster in this country, drawing the money out of banks in the form of cashiers' checks, which went to Walter Lyon, who, in turn, indorsed them to the firm of Renskorf, Lyon & Co. Renskorf, Lyon & Co., it is alleged, subsequently paid the purchase amount in a single check to Lyon, who then, it is charged, paid it to Rumely. For this transaction, according to the Government, Lyon received a commission of $5,000. Fac similes of Dr. Albert's memorandum and the checks and other documents in the case are published in this issue of THE TIMES.

The banks which figured in the original transactions which involved the first payment of the purchase price of $735,000 were the Equitable Trust Company, the Manhattan Company, the Columbia Trust Company, and the Farmers' Loan and Trust Company.

But the $750,000 payment was only about one-half of the financial outlay expended by the Germans in their efforts to have their own public opinion-making New York daily. After The Evening Mail had passed into Rumely's control, the Attorney General said last night, it soon began to lose money. With its change from pro-Ally to pro-German sentiment its subscription lists began to dwindle and its income from other sources began to decline. The result was that, beginning in January, 1916, and up to the time that Bernstorff was dismissed from the United States The Evening Mail, according to the Government agents, cost the Kaiser an additional $626,000, or a total, including the purchase price, of $1,361,000.

In announcing the arrest of Mr. Rumely, and, subsequently, in making public some of the details of the international transaction, Attorney General Lewis, referring to the total sum of $1,361,000, added the comment that "this amount represents the total moneys paid so far as has been traced by the Federal and State officials up to the present time."

"The documents in the case," added the Attorney General, "indicate that Rumely purchased the stock of the

Continued on Page Four.

Dr. Edward A. Rumely,
Who Is Accused of Purchasing The Evening Mail with Money Supplied by the German Government and of Making False Statements About Its Ownership.

REJECTS REPORT ON WIRE CONTROL

Attempt to Put Problem Before Senate Without Investigation Meets Failure.

SENT BACK TO COMMITTEE

Point of Order by Penrose Sustained—Smoot and Reed Join in Criticism.

Special to The New York Times.

WASHINGTON, July 8.—Members of the Senate Interstate Commerce Committee who favor immediate action on the resolution empowering President Wilson to take over the telegraph and telephone systems were defeated today in their efforts to bring the question directly before the Senate without committee hearings or investigation. A report by Senator Smith of South Carolina, Chairman of the committee, was rejected on a point of order made against it by Senator Penrose to the effect that it was not a legal report under Senate rules.

This development returned the resolution to the committee for further action. Senator Smith, stung by the Senate's rejection of his report on what he regarded as a technicality, declared tonight he would take no further steps until the Senate had disposed of a resolution introduced early today by Senator Smith of Georgia discharging the Interstate Commerce Committee from further consideration of the telegraph question.

Senator Smith of Georgia offered this resolution before the Interstate Commerce Committee met to consider the telegraph resolution. Explaining it, Senator Smith said he did not plan to call it up immediately, and might never seek action upon it.

"I wish to have it before the Senate so that if it appears that the committee is likely unduly to delay reporting the telegraph resolution I can, with no delay, obtain action on my resolution of discharge," he said. But in view of the Senate's repudiation of the committee's report, Senator Smith is being urged to call up his resolution tomorrow for the purpose of getting from the Senate an expression of its will with respect to procedure on the telegraph resolution.

Seven Members Out of Seventeen.

Senator Penrose's point of order was based on the fact that of seventeen members of the Interstate Commerce Committee only seven attended today's meeting, which was hastily called by Senator Smith on his return from South Carolina, whither he had gone in the funeral party of the late Senator Tillman. Of these seven four voted to report the telegraph resolution back to the Senate immediately, with no recommendation as to what disposition the Senate should make of it, and three opposed this course. The four favoring a report were Smith of South Carolina, Saulsbury, Underwood and Lewis. Those opposing were Pomerene, Myers and Kellogg, the last named being the only Republican members of the committee at the meeting.

Under Senate rules, Senator Penrose pointed out, the favorable vote of four members of a committee of seventeen was not enough for a report. A rule requires a favorable vote of one-half of the majority of a committee to report a bill or resolution. The majority of a committee of seventeen would be nine, of which half would be five. Hence, as only four voted affirmatively, the point of order was sustained.

The sudden and unexpected report brought from Senator Penrose the query whether "the committee had not last week announced an intention of holding hearings on this resolution."

Senator Smith replied that, after due deliberation, the majority of the committee had thought otherwise.

"Were there not a number of requests for hearings?" asked Senator Penrose.

"I've received none," replied Senator Smith.

"I would like to be assured a quorum of the committee was present," continued Senator Penrose. Senator Smith answered that, "according to the rules of the committee," a quorum was present. Mr. Penrose asked what the rules of the committee were and was told that, with their consent, absentees are counted present.

"Was there a single minority member present?" asked Senator Smoot.

Senator Penrose said there was one, Senator Kellogg. Senator Poindexter,

Continued on Page Eleven.

DEMOCRATS TOLD HEARST WILL RUN

Up-State Consternation Not Abated by Later Repudiation of the Notification.

LEADERS IN CONFERENCE

Committee of Forty-two at Syracuse Today Will Recommend Candidates for Primaries.

Special to The New York Times.

SYRACUSE, N. Y., July 8.—Notice that William R. Hearst would enter the Democratic primaries and make a fight for the Gubernatorial nomination, was served today on the up-State Democratic leaders assembled here to consider party candidates and report to the Democratic State conference in Saratoga July 23.

Notwithstanding subsequent repudiation of this statement as unauthorized by Hearst representatives in New York City, there is not the slightest doubt that such a notification was communicated to the up-State leaders here by an up-State Democrat known to have been in recent consultation with the editor-politician.

Mr. Hearst will have his answer tomorrow. The Committee of Forty-two appointed at the conference of up-State Democrats here in April to canvass the State and find a candidate for Governor acceptable to Democrats outside of New York City will meet then to draft and adopt its final report. That report may recommend the designation of some man on whom all shall have agreed, although the outlook tonight is that as many as half a dozen names will be submitted to the Saratoga conference. In either event the name of Mr. Hearst will not appear.

Word that Mr. Hearst would be a candidate came this morning just as the "steering committee," a sub-committee of seven members selected by the Committee of Forty-two to feel out sentiment in different sections of the State regarding candidates in preparation for tomorrow's meeting, was preparing to go into session. The notification created more than a mild sensation, members of the sub-committee having about made up their minds that, in view of convincing evidence of his unpopularity with Democrats throughout the State that had accumulated during the last few weeks, Mr. Hearst would not become a candidate.

Circulating Hearst Petitions.

"Mr. Hearst has decided that his name should be presented to the Democratic voters in the primaries, his petitions are already being circulated, and there is nothing further to be said, except that Mr. Hearst is prepared to support the candidate selected in the Democratic primaries," was the word that came to the astounded leaders.

Following receipt of this notification the Steering Committee remained in practically continuous session behind closed doors all day. Tonight it was announced that the name of Mr. Hearst would not be included in the report to be made to the Committee of Forty-two tomorrow, and that if he should persist Democrats were prepared to make a fight against him in the primaries.

Mr. Hearst will not have a single vote in his favor in the Committee of Forty-two. The only up-State district in which the Democratic organization is credited with leanings toward Hearst, that of Albany, is not represented on the committee. Patrick McCabe, the veteran Democratic boss of Albany County, is regarded as being decidedly "off the reservation."

It was reported tonight that in all probability the following names of candidates for the Gubernatorial nomination regarded as available by the "Steering Committee" would be submitted to the full Committee of Forty-two:

Harry C. Walker, Mayor of Binghamton.

Alfred E. Smith, President of the New York Board of Aldermen.

James W. Gerard, ex-Ambassador to Germany.

William Church Osborn, ex-Chairman of the Democratic State Committee.

Charles B. Alexander, retired New York

Continued on Page Nine.

STREET BATTLE IN MOSCOW

Heavy Casualties in Quelling the Social Revolutionists.

ENVOY'S SLAYERS SHIELDED

Rebels Seized Part of City, but Were Ousted—Hundreds of Arrests Made.

GERMANS ACCUSE ALLIES

Rumors of March on Moscow as Teutons in Russia Are Heavily Reinforced.

LONDON, July 8.—A formidable counter-revolution was attempted in Moscow on Saturday at the time of the assassination of Count von Mirbach, the German Ambassador, according to dispatches received here today. These dispatches indicate that the outbreak was suppressed with much bloodshed.

The Russian wireless circulated the following, signed by M. Araloff, the chief Moscow Commissioner:

"The Social Revolutionists, by fraudulent means, captured for a few hours a small part of Moscow and the Government telegraph office, whence they issued false reports of the suppression of the Soviet in Moscow. I beg to announce that the mutiny was caused by a group of cheeky fools, and was suppressed without difficulty by the Moscow garrison. The mutineers have been arrested, and order has been restored.

"The counter-revolutionary rising in Moscow has been suppressed, and the Social Revolutionaries are making a most ignominious flight. Orders have been issued to arrest and to disarm all members of the Social Revolutionary detachments and to shoot on the spot all who resist.

"Several hundred participants in the rising have been arrested, among them Vice Chairman Alexandrovitch, while special orders have been issued to secure all members of the Executive Committee of the Social Revolutionary Party.

"The Red Guards must continue watchful. The mobilization of our forces must continue, and all Social Revolutionaries must disarm to the last man."

Fierce Fighting in Streets.

The Moscow outbreak was a "serious counter-revolution," according to a German semi-official Wolff Bureau telegram dated on Sunday from Moscow, and transmitted to London by the Exchange Telegraph Company's correspondent at Copenhagen. Fighting of great severity took place in the streets between the Bolshevist troops and Social Revolutionaries.

German newspapers are now pointing to General Savinkoff, who was War Minister in the Kerensky Cabinet, as the man behind the von Mirbach plot, which is being gradually developed by the Teuton press into a great anti-German movement backed by all those men whom Germany has found to be hindrances in her plans of aggression in Russia. A Moscow telegram circulated by the Wolff Bureau says:

"Savinkoff is considered to be responsible for the deed. He is, moreover, said to be closely connected with the Czechoslovak and Social Revolutionary movements. His whereabouts is unknown."

The German press is preparing the public for a radical move against Russia as punishment for the Mirbach affair. Exactly what this move will be is not as yet indicated, but Dutch and Scandinavian newspapers hint at a March on Moscow. Dispatches are printed showing that German forces are now about 300 miles west of that city and are being heavily reinforced.

German newspapers give many columns to developments in the Mirbach case, particularly long telegrams from Moscow praising the work that Count von Mirbach did there, and describing the alleged treacherous manner in which the assassins gained entrance to his office by posing as delegates of a commission for combating the social revolutionist movement. It is stated that they fired their revolvers, not only at Count von Mirbach, but also at German Councillor Kiezler and Lieutenant Müller, who were in the room. Immediately after the firing they jumped out of a window, hurling hand grenades back of them as they jumped. They leaped into a waiting automobile and escaped.

Trying to Put Blame on Allies.

Nikolai Lenine, the Bolshevist Premier, is endeavoring to placate the Germans by appointing an "extraordinary commission of investigation" to probe the death of Count von Mirbach. The commission is headed by "Comrade Peters." A German official account of the assassination concludes:

"The result of a preliminary inquiry permits the assumption that agents in the service of the Entente are implicated in the affair."

As soon as Emperor William heard of the assassination of Count von Mirbach, according to an Exchange Telegraph dispatch from Amsterdam, he ordered Foreign Secretary von Kühlmann to break off negotiations with the Russian delegates in Berlin. A strong guard has been placed before the house of the Bolshevist Ambassador in Berlin, as it is feared that the populace of the capital will inaugurate anti-Russian demonstrations.

The assassination of Count von Mirbach is seen as an event of great importance, which may have far-reaching results, by the newspapers here. The Daily Mail and The Daily Express agree that the assassination may have momentous consequences, and compare it to the murder of Archduke Francis Ferdinand at Sarajevo four years ago. The Express adds:

"German influence (in Russia) can

Continued on Page Two.

Japan to Double Its Army; Will Put 21 Corps in Field

LONDON, July 8.—Measures for perfecting the national defenses of Japan were decided upon and a plan for co-operation between the army and the navy was adopted by the council of Field Marshals and Admirals held recently in Japan.

The army, it is stated, will comprise twenty-one corps, with two divisions to the corps and three regiments to the division. The changes will not necessarily be effective immediately. The Times computes that the new measures will double the strength of the Japanese Army.

When Japan entered the war, on Aug. 23, 1914, her peace footing of 250,000 of all ranks was automatically expanded to 30,000 men in the regular army, 200,000 in the reserve, and 1,000,000 as reinforcements. Later the total was so reduced that the nation has had in active service about 600,000 officers and men, with the machinery for increasing in a few days the total to a body of 2,000,000 well-trained troops and officers.

Japan, having been on a nominal war footing for four years, will have no difficulty in bringing the 600,000 of the active army up to the 850,000 required by the twenty-one army corps.

NEAR AGREEMENT ON AIDING RUSSIA

Allies Consent to the Plan of Mixed Commission and Military Force.

FOCH TO ASSIGN TROOPS

Wilson Confers with Lord Reading on the Program—New Hope Seen in Russia.

Special to The New York Times.

WASHINGTON, July 8.—The details of the arrangement to be entered into by the Allied Governments for the help of Russia are now being worked out. Lord Reading, the British Ambassador, had a conference on the subject with President Wilson this afternoon. All that is being done is guarded with the greatest care, and while reports are in circulation that an official statement is to be forthcoming they have no definite sanction.

All signs point to a basic agreement among the Allies that is in the nature of a compromise between the two most extreme views as to what steps should be adopted to encourage the Russian people to re-establish their nationality. This Government, it is clear, wishes the allied action in Russia to be merely in the way of assistance, leaving to the Russian people to carry out the program of regeneration which the Allies will initiate and support until the Russians are able to become masters of the situation. The American plan is that of a civilian commission sent into Siberia with the backing of sufficient troops to enable it to carry out its work without interference from German forces and the native elements with which they are allied.

One of the most encouraging aspects of the situation is that the European Allies have abandoned adherence to the extreme view that the aid extended to Russia should be purely military. At the same time the United States Government is understood to have shown a conciliatory spirit in not insisting on its contention that only a very small force of troops should accompany the commission.

Mixed Comission Now Proposed.

It is now concluded that the conferences in progress contemplate sending with the commission into Siberia a force that will be able to give protection not merely to the personnel of the commission but to such local Governments as are established by the Russian people in the portions of Siberia into which the influence of the commission penetrates. The original plan of the United States was to send to Siberia a purely American commission. The policy now being arranged contemplates a commission in which all the Allies will be represented by distinguished citizens and backed by troops furnished by all the allied nations concerned.

Nothing has been disclosed as to the attitude of Japan on the new proposal, and, indeed, it is doubted that Japan has yet given expression to her views on the subject, except possibly in so far as her representative in the Supreme War Council at Versailles felt at liberty to speak.

Japan has adopted a waiting policy since the United States offered recommendations at variance with the proposal that came to this Government from Great Britain and France that Japan should send troops into Siberia to protect allied interests from the Germans and the Russian elements associated with them. At last accounts Japan was holding aloof from any action concerning Siberia until her Allies agreed as to the course that should be followed.

Foch May Fix America's Quota.

One of the most interesting features of the situation is found in the intimation today that the number of American troops which will participate in the proposed Allied military police force to be sent to Siberia with the Allied Civilian Commission wil be determined by General Foch.

The inference drawn from the intimation is that President Wilson intends to seek the judgment of General Foch as to the character and extent of military participation in the Siberian expedition, thus showing his

Continued on Page Two.

NEW BLOW BY PETAIN'S MEN

German Lines Southwest of Soissons Broken on a Two-Mile Front.

RIDGES WON BY VICTORS

Little Resistance Is Met in an Advance of Three-Fourths of a Mile.

MORE GAIN BY AUSTRALIANS

Forces Astride the Somme Push Ahead to Link Up with Lines to South.

PARIS, July 8.—French troops today delivered another stroke in the region southwest of Soissons.

This blow was delivered in the region of Longpont on the edge of the forest of Villers-Cotterets and about six and one-half miles southeast of Catry, the scene of another recent success by Petain's forces.

The German lines were broken on a front of 1.8 miles, the French troops advancing about three-fourths of a mile, occupying important ridges and taking 347 prisoners.

The night report of the War Office telling of this exploit, says:

> South of the Aisne our troops this morning attacked enemy positions in the outskirts of Retz forest, in the region northwest of Longpont.
>
> On a front of about three kilometers we advanced 1,200 meters, occupying Chavigny Farm and the ridges north and south of that farm.
>
> The unwounded prisoners counted up to the present number 347, including four officers.
>
> On July 6 and 7 fourteen enemy airplanes were brought down or put out of action, and two captive balloons were set afire. Our bombing machines dropped twenty-eight tons of projectiles in the course of their expeditions at night in the neighborhood of Fismes, Hirson, Fere-en-Tardennois, and Amagne Lucquy.

The day report of the War Office reads:

> The night was marked by artillery actions between the Forest of Villers-Cotterets and the Marne. There were no infantry actions.

Australians Make Another Stroke.

WITH THE BRITISH ARMY IN FRANCE, July 8 (Associated Press.)—Australian troops last night attacked and carried their line forward astride the Somme River to a depth of 600 yards on a front of 5,000 yards. The operation moved the defenses on the river ahead to correspond with the push made by the Australians and the Americans in their Fourth of July attack, just south of the river.

The Independence Day drive had left a triangular salient in the British line on the river west of Sailly-Laurette, and it was to remove this that the assault was undertaken.

The affair seems to have been a complete success. There was heavy retaliation from the German artillery between midnight and 4 o'clock this morning, but no counterattack has been reported.

The British gunners were exceedingly active during the night in maintaining a harassing fire along many sectors of the front.

LONDON, July 8.—The official report of the War Office today says:

> Last night Australian troops advanced their line slightly on a front of 3,000 yards astride the River Somme, capturing several prisoners.
>
> A successful raid carried out by Scottish troops south of La Bassée Canal resulted in the capture of a few prisoners.
>
> The enemy's trenches also were entered east of Hazebrouck by Australian troops, a few prisoners being brought back.
>
> Hostile artillery has been active astride the Somme, as the result of our operations, and also west of Beaumont-Hamel and in the neighborhood of Bethune.

Tonight's bulletin from Field Marshal Haig says that beyond local encounters, in which the British captured a few prisoners, there was nothing of interest to report.

The bulletin on aerial operations says:

> Hazy weather interfered with the work in the air on July 7, and observation was difficult. Seven enemy airplanes were destroyed during the day, and four were driven down out of control. Three of our machines are missing.
>
> We dropped sixteen tons of bombs during the day and the following night, the principal targets attacked being the Ostend docks and the railways at Tournai and Courtrai.

Germany Calls for 1,000,000; Takes Boys of 16 for Drive

Copyright, 1918, by The New York Times Co.
Special Cable to THE NEW YORK TIMES.

THE HAGUE, July 8.—Field Marshal von Hindenburg has just called for 1,000,000 more men. Recruits are being taken from the factories, and the vacancies are filled by prisoners and foreigners, as well as with exchanged prisoners of war, contrary to all agreements. Several crippled Germans recently repatriated from England are now working in the Krupp works, where conditions are comparatively good. The Krupp mansion near Bredney is strongly guarded against air attacks.

While every nerve is being strained to finish the war this year, there are already indications that Germany is preparing for the coming Winter. Recruits of 16, 17, and 18 are being called out for the coming drive on the west front. These go singing enthusiastically, but the older ones are less joyful.

There are posters everywhere picturing captured machine guns, cannon, and crowds of prisoners of war, and the statistics of victories are printed in large letters.

ENEMY AIR SCOUTS MUST FLY HIGH

Crack French Anti-Aircraft Batteries Spoil Their Chances of Observation.

CAN AIM IN A MINUTE

Yet Six Separate Operations Are Required to Get Range—Germans Take Few Chances.

By WALTER DURANTY.
Copyright, 1918, by The New York Times Company.
Special Cable to THE NEW YORK TIMES.

WITH THE FRENCH ARMIES, July 8.—A period like that of the present German preparation for an offensive lends added importance to the work of the anti-aircraft gunners, who force the enemy scouting and photographing planes to fly at a height from which observation is very difficult, and keep the German "sausages" at a respectful distance.

I visited one of the crack French batteries today the crew of which has reached such a pitch of skill that it can direct an accurate fire against an enemy flier at any but an exceptional height less than a minute after his presence is signaled. It is extraordinary to witness the rapidity with which calculations are made on complicated instruments, no less than six separate operations being necessary before the range is obtainable.

First the height, distance and speed of the airplane must be discovered, then the speed and direction of the wind, which varies greatly at different altitudes, and these calculations are followed by the actual work of aiming the cannon.

Just as the officer in charge of the batteries had finished explaining the methods employed one of the observers cried: "Two boches coming very high, about 10,000 yards away!" To an unaccustomed eye there was nothing visible in the sky, but almost immediately two little clouds of smoke to our right showed that a battery in that direction was already pursuing the enemy.

Instantly all was activity. Men sprang to each instrument, shouting rapid and incomprehensible figures. Before thirty seconds had elapsed the gun muzzle had swung up in a steep angle toward a cloud bank some 4,000 meters high, into which an airplane had disappeared. Eagerly we watched for it to emerge, but the boche was taking no chances. The distant hum of his motor grew fainter and finally faded away completely as he made off to a safer region.

"You see," cried the officer triumphantly, "that is the best proof of what the boche thinks of us. Our anti-aircraft guns have brought down so many recently that they are inclined to give us a wide berth."

We were in a neighborhood right on the Marne front, about three miles from the German lines, which were so quiet that it almost seemed suspicious. Half an hour before our automobile had run for a quarter of an hour along a road in full view of the enemy, only two miles away, on the heights across the river.

"It would be different if we were part of a convoy of trucks," said the Major who accompanied me. "The boche is behaving very nicely, but just the same we'd better return by a less exposed route. You can't trust him too far."

His words reminded me of a phrase used by one of the high aviation officers two days before the beginning of the Chemin des Dames battle: "The boche is so quiet that I cannot help thinking he is planning some surprise;" and I wondered whether, after all, these peaceful fields and woods of the Marne Valley might not soon be a hell of gas and high explosive.

Among the many guesses heard in the last three weeks as to where the enemy will launch his next attack, it seems safe to dismiss from consideration that of a frontal blow against the Marne. Yet the low, rolling hills, covered with patches of trees that stretch

Continued on Page Two.

NEW OFFENSIVE IS NEAR

Abbeville and Chalons, It Is Expected, Will Be Foe's Objectives.

DRIVE ON PARIS TO FOLLOW

660,000 Shock Troops Are Rejuvenated and Ready for Another Blow.

BUT ALLIES REMAIN CALM

Morale of Kaiser's Troops, Already Low, Has Been Shaken by Our Successes.

By EDWIN L. JAMES.
Copyright, 1918, by The New York Times Company.
Special Cable to THE NEW YORK TIMES.

WITH THE AMERICAN ARMY IN FRANCE, July 8.—The next German offensive is at hand. It is now a matter of a few days, or perhaps hours.

The German High Command apparently has the stage set in two places—for a drive against the British, with Abbéville as the grand objective, and for an attack in Champagne, with Chalons as the objective. They may make a stroke at both places at about the same time.

Somewhere back of the German lines are forty-four divisions (660,000 men) of the Kaiser's best troops, his army of manoeuvre, which he uses to make his drives [illegible] and well-trained [illegible] rejuvenated fro[m] [illegible] Aisne attacks a[illegible] effort.

It takes about forty days for the German High Command to prepare for a drive like that on the Somme. The Kaiser's storm troops who took part in this offensive, beginning on March 21, were withdrawn in detachments, beginning April 17.

The next drive, that on the Aisne, began on May 27, or just forty days afterward. The troops that pushed the advance as far as Château-Thierry were withdrawn, beginning June 6. Counting forty days from June 6 would give July 16. But the effort made on the Aisne was not so great as that on the Somme, and not so many shock troops were used, only three-fourths, it is estimated.

How Time Periods Work Out.

This might mean that a period of thirty days would be required to get ready, which would make the date July 6. If it took thirty-five days, this would mean July 11, or if it took the full forty days, it would mean July 16.

To understand how the Kaiser's army of manoeuvre works, it must be understood that in the German offensives not all the shock troops enter the battle at the outset. One wave which starts is replaced by a second, and so on. Therefore it is not necessary for all forty-four divisions to have completed their forty days' preparation when the drive begins. In the Aisne battle troops came into the line on the fifth day which were known to be in the training area on the first day of the assault on the Chemin des Dames.

These forty-four divisions of the army of manoeuvre are trained a considerable distance back of the line and rushed where the attack is to be made at the last moment after the stage is all set. That is why it is so difficult for the allied command to prevent German gains in the first few days. Many points must be protected, but the enemy makes his assault at one or at most two points. His supply of shock troops is drawn, as needed, on a scientific schedule, from the training area where the advance has been rehearsed.

Great Issues at Stake.

While it is true that the Germans have been good at beating the best allied forecasts, there is little sign of an attack now on the front between Montdidier and Château-Thierry. Beyond a doubt the greatest result for the Kaiser would be to reach Abbéville and cut the British Army off from the French, or to force the British lines to fall back on the Somme and give up the Channel ports. It is also true beyond any doubt that the cost of such an effort would be terrific for the Germans.

Perhaps the next best prize, always omitting Paris, would be Chalons. An offensive in Champagne, reaching Chalons, might force the Allies to fall back to a line from Château-Thierry through Chalons to St. Mihiel. This would give the enemy a new line of railroad communication from Metz through Chalons to Château-Thierry and greatly strengthen this portion of his front. Either of these drives would be easier than a drive at Paris.

It is not to be supposed that the offensive now about to begin will be the Germans' supreme effort. Evi-

"All the News That's Fit to Print."

The New York Times.

THE WEATHER
Fair today; Sunday fair, somewhat warmer; gentle shifting winds.
For full weather report see Page 17.

VOL. LXVII...NO. 22,092. NEW YORK, SATURDAY, JULY 20, 1918.—EIGHTEEN PAGES. TWO CENTS Metropolitan District 50 Mile Radius. | THREE CENTS Within 200 Miles. | FOUR CENTS Elsewhere.

ALLIED DRIVE NETS 17,000 PRISONERS, 360 GUNS; FRENCH AND AMERICANS GAIN BELOW SOISSONS; CRUISER SAN DIEGO SUNK NEAR FIRE ISLAND

100 OF THE SURVIVORS HERE

Sinking Variously Attributed to Mine, Submarine, and Internal Explosion.

SHOT AT SUPPOSED U-BOAT

Sailors at Point o' Woods Tell How Gunners Fired Until the Last.

DENY SUBMARINE DID IT

Survivors Arriving Here Say Explosion on Board Probably Wrecked Warship.

The San Diego, Sunk Off Long Island.

1,187 Officers and Men from the San Diego Saved

WASHINGTON, Saturday, July 20.—This announcement was made at 1 o'clock this morning by the Navy Department:

"The Navy Department early this morning received information that two steamships which are proceeding to port have aboard 1,156 officers and men of the U. S. S. San Diego. These are in addition to the one officer and thirty men previously reported landed. The men are said to be in good condition, and so far as known none was injured."

The United States armored cruiser San Diego, formerly the California, 13,680 tons, built in 1902, was blown up and sunk shortly after 11 o'clock yesterday morning ten miles south of Fire Island, and fifty miles from the entrance to New York Harbor by an explosion which, according to sailors who landed at Point o' Woods, L. I., was due to a torpedo from a submarine, although other survivors who arrived in this port last night said that she either struck a coast-defense mine or had an internal explosion.

Thirty-four sailors, who were the first survivors to be landed, said that a torpedo had struck the cruiser amidships on the port, following which two other explosions occurred.

One hundred survivors of the San Diego arrived in Quarantine late last night on a tanker and will be taken to the navy yard early today on the naval tug Narketta. No one was allowed to approach the tanker and talk with the men, but an officer who went on board from the guardship said there was no truth in the report that the warship had been sunk by a German submarine. The survivors told him that it was either a mine or an explosion of her boilers. In his opinion, from what he could learn, the latter was the cause of the disaster.

Two hundred more survivors will reach Quarantine, the officer said, on another steamship about 5 o'clock this morning. After the tanker anchored a number of naval motor launches circled round and prevented any boats from approaching near enough to converse with the survivors of the San Diego, who were all on deck waiting for the naval tug.

Said Submarine Was Seen.

Some of the sailors who were landed at Point o' Woods were sure that a submarine had been seen, and one was convinced that a shot had gone home and destroyed the undersea craft, but the officer and most of the other sailors were confident that no submarine had been seen.

Varying statements were made as to the loss of life. Some of the sailors said that many were killed and others hurt in the two explosions, but that all who escaped death or injuries by this cause had been rescued.

The Government report from Washington, however, placed the number of survivors at 1,187, which is seventy-three more than the official complement made public at the Navy Department.

One of the explosions was reported to be the bursting of the cruiser's boilers, while the second might have been due, according to the sailors, either to the explosion of the powder magazine or to a second torpedo.

Within a few seconds after the first explosion, the cruiser, according to the sailors, opened fire with several guns at objects, which were taken for periscopes, although it was reported that the gunners were not sure of the character of the marks at which they were aiming.

The cruiser sank rapidly and was reported to have gone out of sight within fifteen minutes after the first explosion. She went down so rapidly, according to survivors, that hundreds of the crew did not have time to get to boats and were forced at the last moment to plunge over the rail into the water, where they clung to the loaded lifeboats and liferafts until they were picked up by ships coming to the rescue.

Fired Guns Till the Last.

In order that no chance should be lost of scoring a possible lucky hit, the gunners, though reported as being more or less in the dark as to the whereabouts of the supposed U-boat, continued up to the last moment to fire in the direction from which the torpedo was believed to have come. Sailors said that the gunners kept at work until the list of the ship had brought the water almost up to the barrels of the guns, after which they saved themselves by diving directly from the guns' ports into the water.

The sinking of the San Diego came after the lookout of the cruiser had seen a barrel floating in the ocean on the port side, according to the men who landed at Point o' Woods. The barrel was moving so fast that it excited suspicion. The San Diego hove to and fired several shots at the barrel, but when nothing seemed to bear out the suspicions of the crew, the San Diego continued on her way. The barrel was sighted shortly after 10 o'clock in the morning. It disappeared after shots were fired at it.

The men who landed at Point o' Woods were taken away early in the evening on a patrol boat.

The men who arrived at Point o' Woods reported that the wireless apparatus of the cruiser had been demolished by the first explosion, so that it was impossible for the ship to signal for help. The sound of the explosion and of the firing which followed it, however, was heard by naval aircraft in the vicinity, and one naval airman was the first to see what had happened.

After catching sight of the sinking ship and seeing sailors and lifecraft in the water, he flew back to land and directed wireless operators to send S. O. S. calls. Naval ships from the station at Sayville, Coast Guard cutters, and other ships were soon on their way to the spot, and the survivors in small boats were rapidly picked up.

Attack at Night Reported.

After 7 o'clock last night heavy firing at sea was reported several miles out from the Point o' Woods, which was taken by navy people as indicating that possibly a submarine had been detected and was attacked by destroyers, which were said to have been sent out in numbers during the afternoon.

Residents at Summer hotels at the Point o' Woods, the nearest land to the scene of the disaster, told a TIMES reporter last night that the hour was 11:10 A. M. when they heard a powerful and vibrant, but dull, report some distance out at sea. This was followed, they said, by a great flash of fire, which was very white and distinct.

After the series of explosions which followed, persons on shore sought with glasses to make out what was happening at sea, but could discern nothing until the two lifeboats, No. 1 and No. 2, of the San Diego came ashore. All on board were sailors, with the exception of one officer, an Ensign. Many of the men were only partly dressed, and one had only one side of his face shaved.

Positive of Submarine.

A number of the residents went at once to get clothes for those who were partly undressed, and others provided hot drinks and food. According to those persons at Point o' Woods, who talked to the men, they were unanimous in their opinion that the sinking of the ship was due to a submarine attack. None believed that it could have been caused by a mine, all agreeing that the explosions had taken place almost amidships.

The wake of the torpedo had not been seen by any of the survivors either before or after the explosion. Some of the sailors said that they had seen the periscope as they were launching the boats, but the ensign said that by that time the smoke from the cruiser's own guns had made it impossible to distinguish objects from the deck of the ship.

Some sailors said they believed there had been considerable loss of life because of the explosions, and that some of the injured men had been rescued and taken into small boats. Later in the afternoon several ships were seen passing Point o' Woods on their way to the spot where the cruiser had disappeared, and later returning, evidently bound for New York. Persons with field glasses reported that they could make out that the decks of the returning ships were white, evidently with the uniforms of sailors who had been rescued.

A large number of airplanes were seen from Point o' Woods making for the sea, and one dirigible sailed past the island. They continued to circle about during the afternoon, some of them being engaged in sweeping the waters as if seeking sailors who might be on life rafts.

One of the sailors, who came ashore with the boat which landed at Point o' Woods, brought with him the flag of the ship, which had been carefully preserved. They all reported that the manning of the lifeboats and the leaving of the ships had been carried out with the smoothness of clockwork in spite of the explosions and the rapid sinking of the boat.

The first word that an attack on the cruiser San Diego had taken place or that the ship had been damaged by an internal explosion came to this city shortly before noon yesterday, when residents along the Babylon shore and on Fire Island reported a series of explosions at a point about ten miles off the south shore of Long Island and about fifty miles from the entrance to the harbor.

Got Warning of Submarines.

The belief that it was a submarine attack was strengthened by the fact that during the last few days masters of coastwise vessels have received orders to take a course that would keep them as close to the shore as safety would permit. Submarines were reported about a week ago considerably east of Cape Race on the northerly steamship route. The Navy Department had been expecting a repetition of the U-boat raids of last May.

Shortly after the sinking the naval authorities took charge of all the telephone and telegraph wires communicating with Fire Island and other points nearest the place where the explosions had been heard. It was stated that the communications were taken over by the Navy Department for official business. Attempts of civilians to use the wires were blocked, and information regarding the nature of the mishap to the vessel was prevented from being disclosed by the survivors. Inquirers who sought information at the naval stations and coast guard stations were referred to Washington, with the statement that peremptory orders on the subject had been received.

All of the boats of the Fire Island and Bay Island Coast Guard Stations went out at once about noon, after the first word of the sinking had been received. Up to 10:30 o'clock last night none of these had returned. It was reported that they had been engaged at first in landing men who had been picked up in the water and that later they had been engaged in transferring them from their places of landing to rescue ships and from one ship to another. No information was available to indicate the extent of the casualties or the manner in which the ship was damaged or sunk. It was reported that a considerable number of the survivors were being taken to this city.

Immediately after the accident great naval activity was observable, which seemed to strengthen the report that the San Diego had been the victim of an enemy attack, probably by one or more U-boats. Destroyers, patrol boats, and airplanes were reported to be taking part in what seemed to be a search for undersea craft.

One theory was that the cruiser might have been sunk by a cause which those on board could not identify positively as either a submarine attack or an internal explosion, but did not take into account the fact that persons on shore were sure that they had heard several reports, as if some kind of a naval engagement had taken place.

If the cruiser was hit by a torpedo, the submarine attack was one which took place much closer to shore than any of those during the raids of last May and June, a circumstance which might have been due to the fact that coastwise shipping has been hugging the shore under naval orders, while transatlantic craft have been better protected by measures worked out since the earlier raids.

Reports were in circulation that other ships had been attacked, but there was no verification for these rumors. Preparations were made yesterday at the base hospital at Fox Hills, S. I., which was recently opened, to receive wounded men, but the authorities there stated

Continued on Page Four.

FOE'S SURPRISE COMPLETE

Thought Foch's Reserves Had Been Exhausted, Captured Officer Says.

GUNS COVERED ADVANCE

Fire Curtain from Hundreds of Batteries Led the Infantry to Quick Victory.

FRENCH WADED A RIVER

With Water Up to Their Armpits, They Crossed Savieres and Rushed On.

By G. H. PERRIS.

Special Cable to THE NEW YORK TIMES.

WITH THE FRENCH ARMIES, July 19.—The French and American forces on either side of the Ourcq made 10,000 prisoners yesterday and took about 100 cannon.

German reserves today have been brought up in considerable number, and the struggle is more severe. Nevertheless, further progress has been made.

The splendid Franco-American advance between the Aisne and the Marne was above all a victory of surprise. This part of Boehm's army had recovered from a series of local reverses, but it supposed that the opening of the new offensive further east on Monday relieved it of all immediate anxiety. The armies of Generals Mangin and Dégoutte would, it was thought, have enough to do to hold the Crown Prince's onset without conceiving operations of their own.

"Did you not fear a flank attack?" a German officer taken prisoner was asked.

"Attack with what?" was the reply. "We thought Foch's reserves were exhausted."

The secret of the attack, which was very rapidly prepared, was perfectly kept. A violent storm helped our allies, and amid the continuous roll of thunder the noisy approach of large numbers of French tanks to their starting places was unnoticed. At 4:25 A. M. French and American infantry dashed forward behind a moving curtain of fire from hundreds of batteries great and small over a front thirty miles long, and enjoyed an advantage the thought of which must throw von Hutier himself into a rage of envy.

So hard was the attack pressed that in some parts of the field this element of surprise was preserved for several hours.

The best proof of the exceptional character of this success lies in the fact that for the first time for many a long day the French cavalry came into action, not as infantry but as mounted troops. At 11 A. M. some squadrons were reported to be in Vierzy village, four miles east of the much contested Chavignon Farm, on the old front. At 2 P. M. the more remarkable news came in that a body of dragoons was fighting in the streets of the village, which was fully six miles east of their starting point.

The most considerable advance of the allied line is on the north over the broad open plateau between the Reiz Valley, whence the attack started, and Soissons, and the centre, along the valley of the Ourcq. From Ambléný, Cettry, St. Pierre, Aigle, and Chavignon the battalions of assault rapidly broke through the lines they had faced for a month, crossed the Pernant and Saconin valleys and the Paris-Soissons highroad, and reached a line on either side of Chaudun, where they dominate the whole of the plateau and closely threaten Soissons. The ad-

Continued on Page Two.

Allied Raid Over Metz Proved to be Effective

LONDON, July 19, (British Wireless Service.)—Striking evidence of damage caused by the raids of British bombing squadrons upon the German railway system at Metz-Sablons is afforded by an official British photograph published today. This photograph, taken shortly after the double raid on July 6 and the night of July 6-7, from a height of over 10,000 feet, shows in minute detail the whole of the important railway junction at Metz, including the famous "railway triangle" at Metz-Sablons, where an immense number of lines converge from the Metz central station and the south toward the western front.

The effects of some exceptionally destructive bursts are visible in the photograph among the engine sheds and workshops in the centre of the triangle, and the remains of two trains, completely burned out, can be clearly seen. There also is evidence of great damage to the network of railway lines in the southern arm of the triangle.

Since the beginning of June at least twenty-one raids have been made upon Metz-Sablons.

METEREN RETAKEN IN BRITISH ATTACK

Over 400 Germans Bagged in This and Other Local Operations by Haig.

ENEMY TROOPS DEPRESSED

Have Visible Evidence of U-Boat Failure and Are Filled with Dire Foreboding.

By PHILIP GIBBS.

Special Cable to THE NEW YORK TIMES.

WAR CORRESPONDENTS' HEADQUARTERS, July 19.—"There is a lot of good news flying about this morning," said a young officer I met on a road, who had just heard of the capture of enemy ground at Meteren, and only vaguely then of the magnificent French success between the Marne and the Aisne. I was able to tell him the big number of prisoners and guns, and he said: "It makes one feel good."

Everywhere the victory of the French has cheered the spirits of the men, and the success at Meteren, though it is a small thing compared with the immense triumph of Foch and his troops, is a titbit which adds to the sense of the turning of the tide in our favor. Meteren was only a bit of a town, and now has been shot to a heap of ruin, but it is full of historical interest for the British. It was to Meteren that the German cavalry retreated in October, 1914, when they were chased off Mont des Cats after the death of Prince Max of Hesse in the old monastery up there, and out of Meteren they were driven back by the glorious old 3d Division to the line they held for years on Wytschaete Ridge.

All the British soldiers who fought in Flanders knew Meteren well, passing through it on their way to Bailleul or billeting there in its barns and red brick cottages and drinking thin beer in its old estaminet of "Le Véritable Cucou."

Useful as Observation Point.

From a military point of view today's advance there is useful, as it gave us some good observation of the enemy's ground. The Germans did not seem to expect an attack there, as their line was held by a small garrison, living wretchedly in cellars below the ruins, which they had organized as dugouts and machine-gun emplacements. The British heavy guns pounded above them continually, making the place hellish for them to get in or out, and they were not happy.

The attack this morning was at an unusually late hour and in broad daylight, at nearly 8 o'clock, with the sun streaming over the fields of tall grass, and of neglected crops all tinged with poppies and flowering weeds. The assault was made toward Meteren and south of it by British troops, including Scots, while further south Australians went out

Continued on Page Two.

AMERICANS DRIVE WEDGE

Gains to the South May Force the Evacuation of Soissons.

TAKE 52 GUNS IN ONE FIGHT

Eagerness of Troops Causes Waves of Attack to Overflow and Merge.

MANY WOUNDS ARE SLIGHT

Our Men Hailed as Deliverers by French Civilians Behind the Lines.

By EDWIN L. JAMES.

Special Cable to THE NEW YORK TIMES.

WITH THE AMERICAN ARMY, July 19.—The first thirty hours of the Franco-American offensive drove a deep point into the German lines south of Soissons and yielded a net gain of from five to fifteen kilometers on a forty-kilometer front.

Just before dark last night allied aviators saw French cavalry to the northeast of Soissons and scouting parties of Americans on the heights south of the city. French cavalry also penetrated far eastward, returning to make reports of conditions. Aviators reported that late yesterday the Germans began to draw back guns from the woods north of Château-Thierry.

While allied soldiers have been around Soissons, with the Americans holding Belleau, immediately to the south, there has been as yet no fighting direct for Soissons. If the Franco-American forces advance far enough south of the city, the Germans may evacuate it without a fight.

In gaining this terrain, the French and Americans took thousands of prisoners. Thirty-five hundred were credited to the Americans alone. It should be stated that the American forces compose a small proportion of the total allied forces involved in this operation. We have taken many guns and an immense quantity of ammunition.

The whole operation has shown how splendidly the French and Americans can co-operate in such an action. In no case have the Americans lagged behind. The only difficulties have come through their not stopping upon reaching their objectives.

There was a busy scene yesterday back of the battleline. I started out to a certain place to find one of our headquarters. When I got there, I found a lone doughboy, who said that headquarters had been moved ahead. I went there, and they had been moved again. Finally I found headquarters at a place which before the attack started had been in German hands.

As has been told, the attack started without artillery preparation. As the boys started, the artillery laid down a barrage of short duration, and then lifted it to the limit of the range. Our men reached that limit, and we had to stop firing until the horses could be hitched to the guns, which were carried further to the front.

The American attack schedule worked like this—a hundred yards in three minutes, a rest of five minutes, another 100 yards, and a rest of forty minutes. Because the boche was completely surprised and the going was found to be easy, many of our men disregarded the schedule and went on further. The waves which were supposed to overflow one another finally got going all together, and this proved to be not half bad when the Germans launched their counterattacks.

Our Men Take 52 Guns.

The most formidable German counterattack against the Americans was aimed at our troops near Soissons, but just as it started at noon the Americans started a fresh attack further south, which smashed the German counterattack and netted us a gain of three kilometers and several hundred prisoners. In this attack the Americans got fifty-two field guns.

A fleet of tanks did yeoman work, smashing their way through the German wire defenses. In several instances the Americans got ahead of the tanks and cut the wire with pliers.

The front on which our tanks were used was the only spot where the Germans were found to be the least

Continued on Page Two.

Official Reports of Operations

French

Paris, July 19.

Night Report—The battle begun yesterday between the Aisne and the Marne continued all day with extreme violence, the enemy reacting along the whole line with large reserves in an attempt to stay our progress. Despite his efforts we continued our advance over the greater part of the front.

On the left we maintained the plateau southwest of Soissons and in the region of Chaudun. In the centre our advance exceeded three kilometers at certain points along the line of Vaux-Castille, Villers-Helon, and Noroy-sur-Ourcq. On the right our troops occupied, after bitter fighting, the plateau northwest of Monnes and the height north of Courchamps and advanced beyond Torcy.

The number of prisoners counted up to the present exceeds 17,000, including two Colonels, with their Chiefs of Staff. We have captured more than 360 cannon, including one battery of 210's.

Day Report—Between the Aisne and the Marne our troops, surmounting the resistance of the enemy, which was increased by the arrival of new reserves, realized sensible progress at the close of yesterday. The number of prisoners counted is being augmented. The battle continues with violence along the whole front.

West of Rheims and south of the Marne our troops yesterday, by a vigorous attack, retook Montvoisin, and threw the enemy out of the outskirts of Oeuilly.

To the north of the Marne we have made progress in the Roi Wood and the Courton Wood and carried our line a kilometer to the westward. Further north the Italians have taken Moulin d'Ardre and conquered ground in the region of Bouilly.

In the course of these actions the French have captured four cannon, thirty machine guns, and 400 prisoners.

Between Montdidier and Noyon and also in the Woevre region, in raids against the German lines, we captured 100 prisoners.

German

Berlin, July 19, (via London.)

Night Report—On the battlefield between the Aisne and the Marne a fresh attempt by the French to break through our lines failed with heavy losses to the enemy.

Day Report—The battle has blazed up again between the Aisne and the Marne. There the French have begun their long-expected counteroffensive. By the employment of extremely strong squadrons of tanks they succeeded at first in penetrating by surprise into our front infantry and artillery lines at isolated points and in pressing back our line.

Afterwards our line divisions, together with reserves which had been held in readiness, frustrated the enemy from breaking through.

Toward midday French attacks on the line southwest from Soissons to Neuilly and northwest of Château-Thierry were defeated. In the afternoon very strong partial attacks of the enemy on the whole of the front of attack broke down against our new line. Enemy columns, which were endeavoring to reach the battlefield, were the objectives of our successful battleplanes.

Our chasing planes shot down thirty-two enemy airplanes.

On the front south of the Marne the French, since their failures of July 16-17, have only directed partial attacks southeast of Mareuil, which were repulsed.

Between the Marne and Rheims and east of Rheims the fighting activity has been confined to local operations. Enemy attacks in the Bois du Roi and on both sides of Pourcy broke down.

We have captured prisoners in successful attacks northwest of Troesnes, on the Suippes, and on both sides of Perthes. The number of prisoners brought in since the 15th exceeds 20,000.

BATTLE TO KEEP SOISSONS

Germans Rush Reserves from South to Win Back Vital Plateau.

FAIL AND ALLIES PRESS ON

Advance of Nearly Two Miles Is Made in the Centre of the Long Front.

IMPORTANT HEIGHTS WON

French South of the Marne and Italians North of River Also Make Progress.

LONDON, July 19.—In the face of heavy resistance by the enemy, who threw large reserves into the line, the French and American forces continued their advance today between the Aisne and the Marne.

Ground was gained along the greater part of the front, the progress amounting to about two miles at some points.

Seventeen thousand prisoners have already been taken by the allied troops, and 360 guns, according to the official bulletin of the French War Office tonight.

The stiffest fighting of the day was about the plateau southwest of Soissons, in the Crise River section, which was wrested from the Germans yesterday. The Paris communiqué says only that the allied position was maintained, but unofficial advices state that late this afternoon the Allies began to push ahead again.

Further south the Germans have been pushed back further from the line of Vau Castille-Villers-Helon-Noroy-sur-Ourcq.

Still further south, by dint of hard fighting, the Germans have been driven from the plateau northwest of Bonnes, and have been compelled to cede more ground to the north of Torcy.

French and Italians together have made advances southwest of Rheims. The Italians have made progress from Pourcy along the Ardre, and have also gained in the Bouilly region.

French troops just to the south have won some ground in the Courton Wood and Roi Wood.

South of the Marne the Germans have been driven from Montvoison and pushed back to Oeuilly.

Germans Hurried Troops North.

WITH THE AMERICAN ARMY BETWEEN THE AISNE AND THE MARNE, July 19, (Associated Press.)—The French and American troops made an advance late this afternoon on the Soissons-Château-Thierry front, averaging about two kilometers (about a mile and a quarter.)

Vicious German machine gun fire southwest of Soissons hampered the advance for only a short period.

In the same section the Germans attempted to use tanks against the Americans, but a hot fire soon compelled the tanks to retreat.

The advance began with a barrage, opening at 5:30 o'clock. Tanks were sent in by the Allies to assist the infantry and machine gunners, and the Germans endeavored to stem the tide with a heavy shellfire.

The advance was one of the best organized the Allies ever attempted, the system working wonderfully well from one end of the line to the other. The machine gun defense of the Germans was feeble and was quickly silenced, the Germans falling back upon their rear defenses.

Southwest of Soissons the Germans repeatedly attempted to reach the Allies' big guns. The German firing continued until long after dark, but the French and American guns responded in kind, and gave full protection to the allied forces

U. S. Signal Corps

Americans guard the Marne in Chateau Thierry, France.

Military policemen of the 1st Division march captured German soldiers through a deserted French village.

Section 1

"All the News That's Fit to Print."

The New York Times.

THE WEATHER
Fair Sunday and Monday; slight temperature change; shifting winds
☞For full weather report see Page 19.

Section

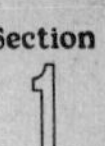

VOL. LXVII...NO. 22,093. NEW YORK, SUNDAY, JULY 21, 1918.—92 PAGES, In Nine Parts, Including Picture and Magazine Sections in Rotogravure. FIVE CENTS In Greater New York | Elsewhere SEVEN CENTS

ALL GERMANS PUSHED BACK OVER THE MARNE; ALLIES GAIN THREE MILES SOUTH OF SOISSONS; NOW HOLD 20,000 PRISONERS AND 400 GUNS

SAN DIEGO'S LOSS STILL UNEXPLAINED; 1,183 REACH PORT

Captain Christy, in Command, Believes She Was Victim of a U-Boat.

EVIDENCE AGAINST THEORY

Neither Wake of Torpedo Nor Periscope Was Seen—Facts Against Mine, Too.

FEW LIVES LOST WITH SHIP

Men Cheered Captain, Last to Jump from Ship, and Sang National Anthem as She Disappeared.

Special to The New York Times.

WASHINGTON, July 20.—In the opinion of Captain H. H. Christy, commanding the armored cruiser San Diego, formerly the California, which was sunk yesterday ten miles from Fire Island, his ship was torpedoed by a German submarine. He does not make this opinion positive, however, for reasons telegraphed to the Navy Department.

Five or six mines were found in the vicinity of the San Diego's sinking, and these may have been sown by a U-boat. But the cause of the San Diego's loss remains a mystery, which the naval authorities are seeking to solve. The Navy Department is, of course, taking appropriate measures to ascertain if a U-boat is in or near American coastal waters.

All the indications are that there was very little loss of life. The survivors were taken to various places, and it is difficult to get a record of all of them. The process of checking up on the saved is complicated also by the fact that only one muster roll of the San Diego is in existence, a duplicate having gone down in the vessel. The sole muster roll was at the navy yard at Portsmouth, N. H., and is now on its way to Washington. Lists of survivors have been coming to the Navy Department by telegraph all day, and as fast as these were received the Bureau of Navigation checked up on the names from its own records, and in order to relieve anxiety sent telegrams to the next of kin of all those reported rescued.

So far the Navy Department has received information that only three members of the crew of the armored cruiser are dead. All of them lost their lives through the explosion which sank the vessel. They are:

DAVIS, THOMAS E., Engineman, second class; father, Edwin Davis, 218 Twelfth Street, N. W., Canton, Ohio.

THOMAS, FRAZIER O., Machinist's Mate, second class; father, Lockard A. Thomas, Charleston, W. Va.

ROCHET, JAMES F., Engineman, third class, next of kin, Mrs. C. H. Dean, Blue Lake, Cal.

In giving out these names the Navy Department made this statement:

"Others have not been accounted for, and the exact number of the missing cannot be determined until all the survivors are checked up, which is being done as rapidly as possible, but reports indicate that the loss of life was small. The survivors were taken to port on different vessels, and one boatload was landed at a lighthouse on Long Island. The names of the survivors are being telegraphed to the Navy Department, and the next of kin are being notified as fast as the names are received."

Word was received from Canton, Ohio, late tonight that relatives of Thomas E. Davis, given as lost in the Navy Department's list, was safe in Pensacola, Fla.

Captain Christy's Reasons.

The Chief of Staff of the United States Naval Cruiser Force, whose headquarters are in New York, has telegraphed to the Navy Department Captain Christy's reasons for adopting the opinion that the San Diego was sunk by a torpedo. There was no evidence of a U-boat in the vicinity at the time, however, and this and other considerations have caused doubt to be expressed as to Captain Christy's theory. The theory that the vessel struck a mine is also discounted by the fact that the San Diego encountered the explosive abaft the beam. It is contended that if a mine had been the cause it would have been exploded at the very bow or forward of the ship. The report of the Chief of Staff in which Captain Christy's view is given is thus summarized in an official statement of the Navy Department:

The Captain of the San Diego reports that he is inclined to the belief that the ship was sunk by a torpedo. There are no conclusive factors, however, on which to base a definite opinion at present, in view of following circumstances:

1. Torpedo wake was not seen.

2. No convincing evidence that periscope was seen.

3. No submarine appeared, in spite of the fact that three unarmed rescue

Continued on Page Seven.

Moscow Now Attacked By Cholera Scourge

LONDON, July 20.—Cholera has spread to Moscow, according to a Russian wireless message received here today. Within the last twenty-four hous, the message says, there have been registered in Moscow 224 known cholera cases, 78 suspected cases, and 26 cases of stomach disease.

The dispatch says that so far as known 120 cases of cholera have occurred in the Province of Petrograd.

The message asserts that the Workmen's Commission of Moscow is combating the cholera and has proposed to the Regional Councils that all workrooms be taken over without delay and made freely available to investigation, so that the health of the persons employed in them can be supervised. The commission asks the council to order the compulsory expulsion of the workers from unhealthy rooms and their removal to more sanitary quarters.

OLDEST ROOSEVELT SON IS WOUNDED

News of Theodore's Injury Comes on Heels of Confirmation of Quentin's Death.

THIRD BLOW TO FAMILY

Capt. Archibald Not Yet Recovered from Wounds—President Sends Condolences.

Special to The New York Times.

OYSTER BAY, N. Y., July 20.—Hardly had Colonel Theodore Roosevelt received news today confirming the death of his son, Lieutenant Quentin Roosevelt, than he received a cablegram from his daughter-in-law, Mrs. Theodore Roosevelt, Jr., from Paris which stated that Major Theodore, Jr., had been wounded and was in Paris. The Colonel and his wife bore up bravely under the new trial.

The cable message read:

"Ted wounded. Not seriously. Here with me. Not any danger. No cause for anxiety."

The Colonel explained that Mrs. Theodore Roosevelt, Jr., was connected with a Red Cross hospital in Paris. It is thought that Major Roosevelt had been wounded at the front and removed to the hospital where his wife was.

No further communication has been received by the Roosevelt family and nothing has been heard from the War Department in Washington.

Major Theodore Roosevelt, Jr., went to France with the first American soldiers. About seven weeks ago he was gassed, He refused at that time to go to a hospital. Three weeks ago he was cited for gallantry.

Colonel and Mrs. Roosevelt received the news confirming the death of Quentin during the morning. With them were their two daughters, Mrs. Alice Longworth and Mrs. Richard Derby.

During the afternoon Colonel Roosevelt received the following message from President Wilson:

"The White House,
"Washington, D. C.

"Hon. Theodore Roosevelt:

"Am greatly distressed that the news of your son's death is confirmed. I had hoped for other news. He died serving his country and died with fine gallantry. I am deeply grieved that his service should have come to this tragic end. WOODROW WILSON."

Colonel Roosevelt replied as follows:

"President Woodrow Wilson, Washington, D. C.:

"I thank you for your courtesy and kindness in telegraphing me, and I deeply appreciate your expression of sympathy and of approval of my son's conduct.

THEODORE ROOSEVELT."

Hundreds of telegrams, cablegrams, and letters of sympathy were received at Sagamore Hill during the day.

Early in the evening the Japanese Red Cross Commission, the members of which are to be the guests of Henry Davison at Locust Valley, L. I., over Sunday, visited Colonel Roosevelt. The Japanese were headed by Prince Tokutawa, and with them were Mr. Davison and his son, Truby.

In addressing the commission the Colonel spoke of the great work the Red Cross was doing. He mentioned the peace at Portsmouth, for which he received the Nobel peace prize. The money, which was turned over to the Government, had been returned to him at his request, he said, and it will be given to war charities, the majority going to the Red Cross. A certain amount, he said, would be given to charities of the allied powers.

"There shall be only one peace," he said, "and that is the peace of right, and the only way to secure it is through a fighting force. No nation has been more efficient in this war than Japan, and no two nations in the world should work together better than Japan and the United States. Any man who works at this time against the interest

Continued on Page Six.

EX-CZAR OF RUSSIA KILLED BY ORDER OF URAL SOVIET

Nicholas Shot on July 16 When It Was Feared That Czechoslovaks Might Seize Him.

WIFE AND HEIR IN SECURITY

Bolshevist Government Approves Act, Alleging Plot for a Counter-Revolution.

PRISONER'S PAPERS SEIZED

Former Emperor's Diary and Letters from Rasputin Soon to be Made Public.

LONDON, July 20.—Nicholas Romanoff, ex-Czar of Russia, was shot July 16, according to a Russian announcement by wireless today.

The former Empress and Alexis Romanoff, the young heir, have been sent to a place of security.

The message announces that a counter-revolutionary conspiracy was discovered, with the object of wresting the ex-Emperor from the authority of the Soviet Council. In view of this fact and the approach of Czechoslovak bands, the President of the Ural Regional Council decided to execute the former ruler, and the decision was carried out on July 16.

The central executive body of the Bolshevist Government announces that it has important documents concerning the former Emperor's affairs, including his own diaries and letters from the monk Rasputin, who was killed shortly before the revolution. These will be published in the near future, the message declares.

The text of the Russian wireless message reads:

"At the first session of the Central Executive Committee, elected by the fifth Congress of the Councils, a message was made public that had been received by direct wire from the Ural Regional Council concerning the shooting of the ex-Czar Nicholas Romanoff.

"Recently Yekaterinburg, the capital of the Red Urals, was seriously threatened by the approach of Czechoslovak bands and a counter-revolutionary conspiracy was discovered which had as its object the wresting of the ex-Czar from the hands of the council's authority. In view of this fact, the President of the Ural Regional Council decided to shoot the ex-Czar, and the decision was carried out on July 16.

"The wife and the son of Nicholas Romanoff have been sent to a place of security.

"Documents concerning the conspiracy which was discovered have been forwarded to Moscow by a special messenger. It had been recently decided to bring the ex-Czar before a tribunal to be tried for his crimes against the people, and only later occurrences led to delay in adopting this course.

"The Presidency of the Central Executive Committee, having discussed the circumstances which compelled the Ural Regional Council to take its decision to shoot Nicholas Romanoff, decided as follows:

"'The Russian Central Executive Committee, in the person of its President, accepts the decision of the Ural Regional Council as being regular.'

"The Central Executive Committee has now at its disposal extremely important documents concerning the affairs of Nicholas Romanoff—his diaries, which he kept almost up to his last days, the diaries of his wife and his children, and his correspondence, among which are the letters of Gregory Rasputin to the Romanoff family. These materials will be examined and published in the near future."

Execution Foreshadowed.

There have been rumors since June 24 that ex-Czar Nicholas of Russia had been assassinated. The first of these stated that he had been killed at Yekaterinburg by Red Guards. This report was denied later, but this denial was closely followed by a Geneva dispatch saying that Nicholas had been executed by the Bolsheviki after a trial at Yekaterinburg. This report seemed to be confirmed by advices to Washington from Stockholm.

The next report was what purported to be an intercepted wireless message from M. Tchitcherin, the Bolshevist Foreign Minister, in which it was stated that Nicholas was dead. Still another report was to the effect that he had been bayonetted by a guard while being taken from Yekaterinburg to Perm. Of all these reports there was no direct confirmation

There seemingly is no question that

Continued on Page Eight.

Germans Try to Excuse Retreat Over the Marne

AMSTERDAM, July 20.—A semi-official statement received here from Berlin says the German Supreme Army Command had several aims in its attack on the southern bank of the Marne, the crossing of which river, it asserts, was unobserved by the Entente Allies. The statement goes so far as to claim that the German objectives have been fully attained.

The first aims of the Marne crossing, the semi-official statement says, were to broaden the basis of attack for a German blow on both sides of Rheims and to attack and to hold strong enemy forces. Furthermore, the attack on the southern bank of the Marne, which was so menacing for the Entente, the statement adds, finally unloosed the long-expected French counteroffensive.

After urging that the counteroffensive has miscarried because a break through has been prevented, the message naïvely adds:

"The task of the German troops fighting on the southern bank of the Marne was thereby entirely fulfilled and the further holding of the lines there was unnecessary. The German command could now withdraw the troops to the northern bank for fresh important tasks."

270,000 AMERICANS IN COUNTERBLOW

Also Rainbow Troops and Negro Regiment Are Fighting East of Rheims.

SEVEN DIVISIONS ENGAGED

General March Says 1,200,000 of Our Men Are Now in Europe or on the Atlantic.

Special to The New York Times.

WASHINGTON, July 20. — Seven divisions and one separate regiment of American troops participated, and are participating, in the great counteroffensive between Chateau-Thierry and Soissons and in the resistance to the German onslaught in the Champagne. The 42d, or Rainbow, Division, composed of National Guard troops from twenty-six States and the District of Columbia, including the New York 69th Infantry, now designated as the 165th Infantry, took part in the fighting in the Champagne east of Rheims.

The six other divisions were associated with the French in the counteroffensive between Château-Thierry and Soissons. These divisions are the 1st, 2d, 3d, and 4th of the regular army, the 26th National Guard Division, composed of troops from the six New England States, and the 28th, composed of the Pennsylvania National Guard. Marines are included in this number.

The separate regiment that has been fighting in the Champagne has not been identified at the War Department. It is a negro unit attached to the new 93d Division, which is composed entirely of negro troops. It may be the former 15th New York, now the 369th National Army Regiment, commanded by Colonel William Hayward, formerly Chairman of the New York City Public Service Commission.

1,200,000 Sent Abroad.

The identity of the divisions engaged in the great battle that has been raging west and east of Rheims was disclosed today by General Peyton C. March, Chief of the Army General Staff, in his weekly oral review to newspaper men of military operations in Europe. General March also imparted the information that more than 1,200,000 American troops were in Europe or on their way across the Atlantic. On July 8 President Wilson announced that up to June 30 we had sent overseas 1,019,000 men of all branches of the military service.

General March disclosed in answer to a question that the 77th National Army Division, composed mainly of troops from New York State and which was trained at Camp Upton, Yaphank, L. I., was "in the line near Luneville and is operating as a division, complete under its own commander." Luneville is in French Lorraine, far down to the southern end of the long battlefront and many miles from the scene of the present conflict around Rheims. The Rainbow Division was employed in this area before its recent transfer to the active sector east of Rheims. Announcement was made last Saturday by General March that the 77th Division was now commanded by Major Gen. George B. Duncan.

The approximate number of American troops engaged in the heavy fighting this week west and east of Rheims is easily ascertainable from an estimate furnished by General March as to the average strength of an American army division. If a division was complete in the current fighting, he said, its

Continued on Page Eight.

FIERCE FIGHTING YESTERDAY

Our Men in a Severe Struggle With the German Reserves.

SUCCESS AS SHOCK TROOPS

Americans, Previously Untried, More Than a Match for the Kaiser's Best.

OVER 6,000 PRISONERS NOW

German Machine Guns Firing Explosive Bullets at Our Men.

By EDWIN L. JAMES.

Copyright, 1918, by The New York Times Company. Special Cable to THE NEW YORK TIMES.

WITH THE AMERICAN ARMY, July 20.—On the bloody battlefield south of Soissons the American soldiers, along with their comrades of the allied arms, today were matching their strength with the best German warriors.

No one says yet how the battle goes because no one knows yet. We have gained and gained, but the struggle grows in fierceness as both sides throw fresh troops into the maelstrom of death and dust and flying shells out of which may come a result that will have much to do with the end of the war.

The German offensive of July 15 is now turned into a German defensive. Forced back by French and American troops at the start, it was to be expected that when the German high command hurled their shock troops against the French and Americans the progress after the first day would not be so rapid.

Our Men as Shock Troops.

Out of the storm where allied determination, leavened with the new spirit of Americanism, met the famed war machine of the German autocracy has already come one conclusion that augurs well for an allied victory. That is that the backbone of the United States fighting man is a stiff proposition for the Kaiser's warriors.

All the armies class as their best fighters their shock troops. This was a job of shock troops, performed by the Americans, and they have made good.

It was not the brilliant advance of the first day, good as it was, that told the story of the grit of Uncle Sam's fighting lads. It was not the furthest advance that told the real story. That came yesterday, when the new American attacks east of Vierzy and northeast of Chaudon met the German shock troops.

The fighting men were trained for more than a month by Ludendorff to take part in the offensive for Epernay and Châlons. Fresh and in the best of condition and on their tiptoes they were met by our men, who already had been fighting thirty hours.

Then the Germans tried to turn our attack into an advance for themselves. They failed.

Holding Their Gains.

Holding against a murderous machine gun fire, against bombs and bullets from hostile aircraft, against the unquestioned force of the German shock troops, the youthful Americans with their French comrades stood firm, and are so standing as this is written.

The full story of the fast and furious battle cannot yet be told. Word comes one minute that the Germans have a village, and ten minutes later another word comes that the Americans have that village.

Up the roads go trucks of ammunition and down the roads come the ambulances. German shells come groaning over, and in reply one hears a crescendo, oft repeated, which tells that bottled destruction is on its way from the American side.

Down the roads from the front come every now and then a big truckload of slightly wounded Americans, all angry to have been put out of the fight.

The truck halts. A stocky American lad, caked with dust, and with two bullet wounds through the shoulder, asks me for a cigarette, and I ask him what he thinks of it.

"I'll tell you," said he. "I was never in a battle before, and felt kind of squeamish a couple of hours before. I felt squeamish when I went over the top, but as soon as the real fighting started I forgot to be squeamish, and went on until the boche machine gunner got me. Honest to God, I had rather fight than eat now. I hope the 'doc' lets me back soon."

This lad was a coal miner eight months ago.

The Americans started their second attack at 5 o'clock yesterday morning. They had reached their objectives, a varying number of kilometers eastward, and were consolidating their positions when the shock troops struck them about noon.

Then began the battle, which is still going on with the fiercest struggles.

Against one American unit two German shock divisions were hurled. Against another came the famous Prussian Guards.

The Germans had machine guns mounted on wheels, and had rolled them to the edge of the woods. These guns shot explosive bullets, which are the latest piece of barbarity the German has invented.

One story was told by all the wounded whom I talked with, and that was the great number of machine guns the Germans have. This now appears, to be the favorite weapon of the Germans against Americans.

Our Huge Bag of Prisoners.

There is one feature of the battle which stands out—the number of prisoners taken by the Americans. The number placed to our credit south of Soissons is now something more than 6,000.

Two regiments have officially booked more than 2,800 German captives, including sixty-six officers.

Coming down the wooded hill I saw a sight that made me think I had run into the German Army, but when I came near I found only a corral of Germans taken by Americans. There were more than 3,000 in a barbed wire cage, and the dirtiest lot of humans I ever saw, with the exception of the Colonel and some of the officers. There they stood, sat, and squatted in the sunlight. The French officer told me they were the most unclean lot of men he had seen during the war.

These prisoners were mostly holding troops, caught in the French-American surprise, and not belonging to the crack German troops. Unshaven and unkempt in every way, they looked like beasts.

The officers captured were entirely different. The Colonel was of the most natty sort, glistening with many decorations. A Captain with whom I talked used to be a business man with an office in Manhattan and a home in New Jersey. He gave it as his opinion that the war would never end in a military victory, but in bankruptcy for one side or the other. He remarked:

"I am thinking of Germany. I am almost sure the Kaiser cannot win a complete military victory, but nothing is left now but to fight on in the hope of a favorable settlement by negotiation, for if we stop now the taxes will be so heavy for Germany that no one can live. We must fight on until the Allies pay us."

I noticed that all the German gas masks on the shock troops were equipped with a new attachment against the new allied gases.

This large number of captives gives reply to the lie that the American troops take no prisoners.

Clark Wililams a Worker.

This is the time to pay tribute to an American, Clark Williams, of New York, former Banking Commissioner. In the shade of a noble old château lay a yardful of American wounded, waiting for attention by the surgeons. There were slightly wounded and seriously wounded, happy wounded and discouraged wounded, and hungry wounded. There I found Mr. Williams representing the Red Cross. He had spent the night getting out from Paris five tons of food, and then sent the trucks back for surgical material. He was directing the helpers to feed the half-famished fighting lads, and was himself carrying cans of bouillon around. His pockets were filled with cigarettes and under his arms were packages of prunes. He was truly a working man.

The army surgeon in charge of the hospital asked that public thanks be given to the American Red Cross and Mr. Williams, whose aid had been invaluable.

I spent yesterday back of the fighting line, in territory that had been German the day before. I had seen some scenes of destruction in France, but these scenes were worse. On one road, for three miles, al the trees had been hit by shells and most of them were cut down.

Here is a village with not a building left standing. Here is another with an untouched church steeple, the only whole thing there. Here American and French shells fell when the attack started, and the German shells had hit as well. Caught between the millstones of war, this strip of country was ground to ruin. The shell holes are

Continued on Page Two.

Official Reports of the Day's Operations

French

PARIS, July 20.

Night Report.—We have not had long to wait for the result of our victorious counteroffensive. The Germans, violently attacked on their right flank and south of the Marne, have been compelled to retreat and recross the river.

We hold the whole south bank of the Marne.

Between the Aisne and the Marne Franco-American troops continue to progress and have driven back the enemy, who is resisting stubbornly

We have reached Ploisy and Parcy-Tigny and have passed beyond St. Remy-Blanzy and Rozet St. Albin.

Further south we hold the general line of the Priez Plateau, north east of Courchamps.

The number of prisoners we have taken since July 18 exceeds 20,000 Over 400 guns have been captured.

Between the Marne and Rheims violent combats continue. Franco-British troops, attacking vigorously, encountered large forces. Notwithstanding the enemy's desperate resistance, we gained ground in Courton Wood, the Ardre Valley, and in the direction of St. Euphraise.

Day Report.—Yesterday and last night French and American troops continued their advance over the greater part of the front between the Aisne and the Marne.

Vierzy has been reached and the troops have gone beyond Mauloy Wood, east of Villers-Helon, and conquered Neuilly-St. Front and Licy-Clignon.

South of the Marne our troops have driven back the Germans between Fossoy and Oeuilly and have gained ground toward the Marne.

German

BERLIN, July 20. (via London.)

Day Report.—The activity of the British increased in isolated sectors toward Meteren. They obtained a footing in Meteren, but otherwise their repulse left prisoners in our hands.

Between the Aisne and the Marne the battle continues. Again the enemy started an attack with a view to a breach on the whole front. Tanks penetrated early in the morning into parts of our foremost lines. After a desperate struggle the first enemy thrust had been defeated toward noon on the heights southwest of Soissons, west of Hartennes-St. Neuilly and northwest of Château-Thierry.

Between the Aisne and the Ourcq an attack broke down under our counterthrusts, and to the south of the Ourcq mostly by our fire. North of Hartennes we threw back the enemy beyond the original line. Our troops report the heaviest enemy losses. A large number of tanks were demolished before our front.

South of the Marne there was moderate firing activity during the day. Southeast of Mareuil enemy partial attacks were repulsed.

During the night our troops south of the Marne were withdrawn to the north bank of the river without being noticed by the enemy.

Northwest of Souain French advances were sanguinarily repulsed.

Yesterday again thirty enemy airplanes and seven captive balloons were shot down.

BERLIN ADMITS RETREAT

Says Troops Withdrew Without Being Noticed By the Enemy.

HAD TO RETIRE, SAYS PARIS

Violent Attacks Were Made South of River and Also North —British Aiding Here.

BIG THRUST ON THE OURCQ

French-American Forces Push Ahead Most in Centre—Command Soissons Bridges.

LONDON, July 20.—The German offensive has been broken and the Crown Prince's troops have been thrown back across the Marne River.

The Franco-Americans fighting on the Soissons-Château-Thierry front, up to noon today, had made an average gain of a mile, and an extreme advance, in the centre, of three miles.

The complete collapse of operations south of the Marne, which had previously witnessed a great and decisive defeat of the German invaders early in the war, was announced laconically by a Reuter correspondent at French Headquarters in a dispatch, timed this evening, which said:

"No Germans remain south of the Marne except prisoners and dead."

Official communications from the Paris and Berlin War Offices quickly confirmed the withdraway, the imminence of which had been indicated by earlier dispatches from correspondents at the front.

These told how the Germans south of the river had suffered a repulse at the hands of the Allies and were retreating toward the river, with French and American troops on their heels. Capture of the Bois de Misy and Port-à-Binsone (one and one-half miles west of Oeuilly) was announced early.

German Version of Retreat.

The day bulletin from the German headquarters, in announcing the retirement, says:

"South of the Marne there was moderate firing activity during the day. Southeast of Mareuil enemy partial attacks were repulsed.

During the night our troops south of the Marne were withdrawn to the north bank of the river without being noticed by the enemy."

The German communication insists that allied thrusts southwest of Soissons and southward along the Aisne-Marne front were repulsed, with heavy losses.

The French official bulletin says that the enemy was compelled to retire from below the Marne by the violent attacks of the allied forces. Its statement concerning the operations in that area reads:

"We have not had long to wait for the result of our victorious counteroffensive.

"The Germans, violently attacked on their right flank and south of the Marne, have been compelled to retreat and recross the river. We hold the whole south bank of the Marne."

The Paris bulletin also reveals that British troops are in action with the French on the front between the Marne and Rheims. Here vigorous attacks were made by the allied forces in co-operation with the drive south of the river, and important ground was gained in the region along the Ardre.

Continuation of the French and American advance between the Aisne and the Marne is chronicled.

Since and including Thursday the allied troops have captured more

"All the News That's Fit to Print."

The New York Times.

THE WEATHER
Showers, northwest wind today; Thursday fair; wind variable.
For full weather report see Page 19.

VOL. LXVII...NO. 22,103. NEW YORK, WEDNESDAY, JULY 31, 1918.—TWENTY PAGES. TWO CENTS Metropolitan District 50 Mile Radius. | THREE CENTS Within 200 Miles. | FOUR CENTS Elsewhere.

ALLIES AGAIN DRIVE FORWARD NEAR FERE; PRUSSIAN GUARDS PUSHED BACK TWO MILES; OUTWITTED AND OUTFOUGHT BY AMERICANS

ARCHANGEL OUSTS ALLIED ENVOYS; NOW IN LAPLAND

Local Soviet Refuses to Permit Embassies from Vologda to Stay There.

WOULDN'T GO TO MOSCOW

Tchitcherin, Who Invited Them, Said Vologda Was About to be Shelled.

WASHINGTON IS INDIGNANT

Belief There That Affront by Bolsheviki Will Not Be Overlooked by the Allies.

KANDALASKA, Russian Lapland, July 30, (Associated Press.)—The allied embassies, which recently left Vologda for Archangel, were not permitted to remain in Archangel and have arrived in Kandalaska.

The embassies left Vologda July 23 in response to a message of M. Tchitcherin, Bolshevist Foreign Minister, declaring that they were in great danger, and that a bombardment of Vologda was threatened for the next day. He urged the embassies to come to Moscow, but the Ambassadors decided to proceed to Archangel, where they expected to communicate with their Governments.

At Archangel, the Soviet, acting under orders from Moscow, refused to permit the foreign representatives to remain, but placed two small Russian ships at their disposal, and aboard these they left July 28, escorted by a Russian trawler, on an uneventful voyage across the White Sea.

On the night they were leaving Archangel it was reported that the Moscow Government had ordered that the sailing of the Ambassadors be prevented.

LONDON, July 30.—A Russian wireless communication received here tonight says that M. Tchitcherin, the Bolshevist Foreign Minister, has sent the following message to M. Joffe, Bolshevist Ambassador to Germany:

"The American Consul General, Mr. Poole, who is charged with the mission of maintaining diplomatic relations with the Council's Government at Moscow, visited the Commissary of Foreign Affairs and declared in the name of the British diplomatic representative and the Consul Generals of France, Italy, and Japan that they approved the declaration previously made by Mr. Poole to the Commissary, which essentially follows:

"'In conformity with the personal opinion of the allied Consuls there is no reason to believe the situation in general outlines is changed by the departure of the Ambassadors to Vologda. The representatives of the aforesaid powers expect to remain in Moscow as long as circumstances permit them to do so, and they are permitted to use the privileges attached to their functions, especially direct communication with their respective Governments, unless they receive other instructions.'"

Reds Dominated by Germany.

Special to The New York Times.

WASHINGTON, July 30.—Washington observers of events in Russia are being forced to the conclusion that the Bolshevist Government, acting in accordance with the wishes of Germany, is seeking to bring about war between the allied Governments and the so-called Government of Russia. Further evidence of this German-directed effort was afforded tonight by the news contained in a press dispatch from Kandalaska, Russian Lapland, that the allied embassies, which had been forced to leave Vologda by the Bolsheviki and had gone to Archangel, the White Sea port, were obliged by the Archangel Soviet to leave that place, and this accounted for their presence in Kandalaska.

The treatment accorded to the diplomatic representatives by the Bolshevist central authority is an affront that the allied Governments are not likely to overlook. No doubt is felt in some informed circles here that the Soviet Government is anxious to bring about a clash that will sever all relations between itself and the allied representatives.

Evidence has been accumulating that the Bolshevist Government at Moscow was completely subservient to the Germans. It is apparent to those who have followed the situation closely that the Bolshevist leaders, like Lenine and Trotzky, are willing to sacrifice Russia as long as they are retained in power by their German masters, to whom they sold out Russia through the treaty of Brest-Litovsk.

At this time the German Government, according to evidence furnished by the German press, is becoming concerned over the program that is being formulated by the allied Governments for the regeneration of Russia through sending

Continued on Page Five.

Flew from Front to England, Took Oath as M. P., Flew Back

Special Cable to THE NEW YORK TIMES.

LONDON, Wednesday, July 31.—According to The Morning Post, Major Gen. Davidson, who has been elected for the Fareham Division in place of Lord Lee, left general headquarters in France yesterday morning, came to England by airplane, motored from his landing place to Westminster, took the oath and sat in the House of Commons a while.

Then he went back as he had come and was probably on duty again, while the House was still talking about national shipyards.

He was anxious to take his seat before recess, could get only a few hours off, and there was no other way to come.

WANTS MINISTRY FOR WAR IN AIR

Senator Reed Urges One-Man Control to Spur Execution of America's Program.

CALL FOR DE HAVILANDS

Pershing Asks for More—Motors for Britain Delayed—Senate Inquiry On.

Special to The New York Times.

WASHINGTON, July 30.—Demand for an Air Ministry under which activities of both the army and navy would be co-ordinated, was made today by Senator James A. Reed of Missouri. Mr. Reed is a member of the Senate Military Affairs Subcommittee on Aviation which is now examining into aircraft production.

"Air service has come to be of such vast importance that it justifies the creation of a new Cabinet position," he said. "Some one man should have plenary powers, and should be surrounded by a staff of the most skilled aeronautical engineers, great practical fliers, and experts on manufacturing."

The need for central control of air activity and production has been emphasized before. Several bills to this effect were introduced last year. Senator Morris Sheppard of Texas was one of the prime movers for such a plan. Sentiment is increasing that instead of the army and navy having separate aeronautical departments they should be placed under one authority. It is felt that with responsibility for aircraft placed upon one man or one board there would be no difficulty or competition in obtaining necessary material, and many of the delays and criticisms which have developed heretofore would be obviated.

Pershing Calls for De Havilands.

The latest of these criticisms centres about the de Haviland airplane, which has been accused of "falling down." Secretary Baker was asked today about these charges, and replied:

"There are probably no perfect airplanes. Improvement in the best of them is constant and rapid, both as to types and succeeding numbers of the same type. This is true of the de Haviland and all others.

"The latest machines made of that type are better than the earlier ones, and this improvement we hope will be constant. General Pershing has requested a large shipment of de Haviland airplanes (de Haviland 4) of the present type on the priority schedule for August.

"The purpose of this is to set at rest the statement which was made from some quarter that General Pershing had directed that no more de Havilands be shipped, because he has asked for a very large shipment of the present type."

Senator Reed and Senator New of Indiana, of the Aviation Sub-Committee, heard officers testify today behind closed doors on the performance of the de Haviland at the Dayton Field. Captain Muhlenberg, Captain Schroeder, and Lieutenant Foote, all skilled fliers, told of the advantages and disadvantages of the machine. Committee members refused to comment on the testimony. It was said, by a man entirely conversant with the situation, that some of the newspaper statements regarding the de Haviland were "mere conjecture."

New Forecasts Full Inquiry.

All that Senator New would say, was:

"The committee is not talking about the testimony, and the fact that the officers have been called from Dayton Field suggests only one thing, and that is that the committee is making a thorough investigation into all rumors, from newspapers and other sources. We are trying to arrive at the exact facts on production, character, quality, and so on, with a view to changing conditions if conditions need changing."

It was learned that the sub-committee

Continued on Page Five.

CENTRAL POWERS FACE DEADLOCK OVER SPOILS

All Four Are Now Involved in Clashes for Which No Solution Is in Sight.

POLISH DISPUTE SHARPER

Austria Firm in Demand to Bring New Kingdom Under Hapsburg Rule.

TURKS REPROACH BULGARS

Ignore German Aims in Caucasus—Inspired Berlin Warning of Threatened Danger.

Special Cable to THE NEW YORK TIMES.

AMSTERDAM, July 30, (Dispatch to The London Daily Express.)—Trouble is admittedly brewing among the Central Powers, first between Germany and Austria over the Polish question, and also between Bulgaria and Turkey regarding the Dobrudja. Every possible solution of both questions has been repeatedly discussed by the four Governments, but no agreement is likely to be reached.

Germany will not hear of the Austrian annexation of Poland in any form whatever, whereas Austria considers the bringing of the "Kingdom" of Poland under the Hapsburg sceptre as a "vital necessity." It was hoped in Germany that once Czernin resigned no more would be heard of the "Austro-Polish" solution of the Polish question, and thus Austria was permitted to annex important Rumanian lands under the pretext of the "safety of her frontiers."

It appears from an inspired article by Emil Zimmermann in yesterday's Berlin Lokal-Anzeiger that Baron Burian is just as anxious as Czernin was about the Austro-Polish solution, over which Austria seems likely to remain most obdurate.

No peaceful solution is in sight regarding the Turkish-Bulgarian Dobrudja and Adrianople difficulties. The feeling is rising high in both Sofia and Constantinople. The Turks are accusing the Bulgarians as being "the Germans of the Balkans," while the Bulgarians are saying equally hasty things about the Turks.

Zimmermann urges the Central Powers not to fight among themselves during the war, for otherwise "what they have so far managed to gain will probably be lost."

Turks Take Free Rein in Caucasus.

AMSTERDAM, July 30.—Turkey is going to handle the situation in the Caucasus according to her own ideas. This is indicated in a telegram from Constantinople dated July 28, which quotes an article in the newspaper Nasfiri Ekfiar presenting the Turkish viewpoint.

"We have nothing to say against the principles laid down in the Brest-Litovsk treaty," says the article, "but when the Caucasus, newly reorganized, turned toward us and, master of its own destinies, refused to be bound by the treaty, what was more natural for us than to take into consideration the necessities of this new situation created on our important eastern front? Could we close our ears to the appeal of the Government of a people largely of the same race and same creed as ourselves?

"We are aware of the action, and its present progress, to place under German control Tiflis and Baku. That is a logical consequence of the application of the Brest-Litovsk treaty. How could this treaty be taken into consideration in the affairs of the Caucasus, seeing that the Bolshevist Government has not even been able to return to us, in accordance with the treaty, our eastern frontier, and that in the Caucasus influences entirely independent of the Bolshevist Government have arisen!"

This reported attitude on the part of Turkey may account in part for the report received through Copenhagen that Turkey and Germany had severed relations.

Early this month it was reported through Washington that Germany was becoming alarmed over the aggressive territorial tendencies of her allies, especially Turkey. Several weeks earlier it had been reported that Germany had ordered Turkey to stop her advance in the Eastern Caucasus.

Almost simultaneously announcement came from Berlin that German troops had been landed at Poti, on the Black Sea coast, an important point on the railroad running through Tiflis to Baku. On June 15 Turkey signed a peace treaty with the Transcaucasian Gov-

Continued on Page Five.

More American Troops Reach Italian Front

ITALIAN ARMY HEADQUARTERS IN NORTHERN ITALY, July 29, (Associated Press.)—American troops continue to arrive here. They are in excellent condition and splendid spirits, and are enthusiastic over the welcome that has been accorded them.

Nothing has been left undone by the Italians to show the Americans how much their presence in Italy is appreciated. The commanding General and his staff turned out to greet the men from overseas, while airplanes flew over them, dropping colored papers on which was printed "Viva Wilson."

The American Red Cross has established a small hospital at the American base.

GAIN 100,000 TONS A MONTH IN SHIPS

Geddes Tells House of Commons of Net Increase Against the U-Boats.

LOSS FALLS, BUILDING RISES

Britain and America Economize Skilled Labor in Newly Designed Vessels.

LONDON, July 30.—Sir Eric Geddes, First Lord of the British Admiralty, gave the House of Commons today a review of the naval situation.

The First Lord compared the situation today regarding tonnage with that of a year ago. Then the net loss in tonnage, he said, was 550,000 gross tons. Submarines then were not being destroyed as fast as the Germans were building them, while the merchant shipyards were short of men and material. Four hundred thousand tons net loss monthly was the British deficit. Every yard that could take naval work had been put on naval building.

Gradually during the last year, Sir Eric continued, the position had changed in many directions. Instead of losing tonnage, the world's net result in the last quarter had been a gain, roughly, of 100,000 tons a month. The allied and neutral world was as well off on June 30 as on Jan. 1, 1918. This result, he declared, had been obtained by reduced sinkings and increased buildings.

The reduced sinkings had been arrived at, said the First Lord of the Admiralty, by a greater productive effort devoted to warships and small craft of an anti-submarine character. Nothing commandeered or acquired tonnage was included in this result.

"The total increase in labor last year in shipbuilding yards," Sir Eric continued, "was 35,000 men. The original demand of a year ago was for 80,000 additional workers, part of them skilled. Owing to events on the western front and the great demands for technical men for the air force and the army, it was impossible to obtain the proper quota of skilled men by their withdrawal from the army. Unskilled men were offered freely, but they could not be absorbed because of the lack of skilled men."

The First Lord declared that skilled men still could not be obtained in sufficient numbers to man the existing yards. This situation had been feared, so the Government had decided to go ahead at once with a scheme for building a simple ship which could be constructed with a minimum of skilled labor. This ship was designed and originated in the Admiralty.

"It is interesting," added the First Lord, "that the very same problem confronted America, and America met it in practically the same way—the same class of yard and the same type of construction, and with excellent results."

Merchant ship repairs, said Sir Eric, were today engaging nearly two-thirds as many workmen as were engaged on new construction of merchantmen.

"But," he continued, "the submarines have found it too dangerous to work inshore, and are going far out. The number of ships damaged, as well as sunk, is decreasing, and the transfer of men from repairs to new construction is possible. The number of men employed on new construction of warships and auxiliaries is, roughly, 150,000, and on merchantmen 120,000."

"Britain has borne the preponderating burden to a preponderating extent of fighting the submarines. The new output of anti-submarine ships, mines, and implements has been preponderatingly ours, and the responsibility for combatting the menace has been ours. Even today the increased assistance brought about by the new construction of the Allies is small indeed, but times are changing.

"America's program is now beginning to come along. And I have had the pleasure of considering it with Mr. Roosevelt. My conferences with him have confirmed what I have relied upon, namely that when once the flow of destroyers and anti-submarine craft starts from the United States it will become a formidable torrent."

BAYONETS ROUTED GUARDS

Our Soldiers Whip the Kaiser's Shock Troops in Man-to-Man Fighting.

EPIC BATTLE FOR SERGY

Village Changed Hands Nine Times, but Is Now Back of American Line.

BROOKLYN BOY'S HEROIC ACT

Hyland Held Street with One Comrade After Rest of Platoon Was Shot Down.

By EDWIN L. JAMES.

Special Cable to THE NEW YORK TIMES.

WITH THE AMERICAN ARMY ON THE MARNE, July 30.—Sergy changed hands nine times in twenty-four hours. That tells the story of the bitter fighting when the German command threw two fresh Guard divisions against the Americans north of the Ourcq yesterday, in an endeavor to put them back across the stream.

The result may be best told by saying that the Americans are not only on the north side of the Ourcq this morning, but in positions further advanced than when the Crown Prince hurled his violent attacks against our line early yesterday. At least one German Guard division was rendered fightless for some time to come.

Had the Americans not held back these fighting Prussians the French would not have been able to make their advance north of Fère-en-Tardenois, and also on our right.

Germany's Best Shock Troops Beaten

The Prussians and Bavarians now trying to hold back the Americans were brought hurriedly from the rear, where they had been held to make an attack against the English, preparatory to the Crown Prince's grand drive in August.

It should be a source of the greatest pride to America that her youthful soldiers are able to hold their own against the Kaiser's best shock troops, for such the Prussian and Bavarian Guards are.

At Sergy was an American division which met the 4th Prussian Guard Division. The result speaks for itself.

As told in these dispatches yesterday, it was part of the German plan to stand on the north bank of Ourcq and hold the Americans while the withdrawal behind the lines was made more easily. The charge of the Americans across the river on Sunday, in which they took Seringes and Sergy and established themselves, broke up this part of the German plan.

Early yesterday morning the Americans in Sergy were attacked by the 4th Prussian Guard Division, which had arrived only a few hours before from the training area in Lorraine. Overwhelmed by vastly superior numbers, the Americans withdrew before a terrific small artillery and machine-gun fire.

But when the Prussians got into the town the German artillery could no longer shoot into it. That gave a chance for man to man in a hand-to-hand fight, and the Americans grasped the opportunity.

Machine Guns Under the Red Cross.

They rushed back into the village, up against a withering fire from machine guns placed practically in every building. When the charge was at its height, from a building bearing the Red Cross five machine guns spoke with telling effect. But soon the Americans got hand-to-hand with the Prussians. In repayment for the deadly machine-gun work our men got their bayonets into action, and no German has yet been known to stand before a bayonet with an American behind it. In half an hour we had possession of the town.

Down came the German artillery fire again, and we had to retire. Into the village came the Prussians, and when the artillery fire stopped, back went the Americans. Again we drove them out. No sooner had we got into the village, when back came the Prussians. The German airplanes rendered their men great aid, sweeping down close to the ground and raking our lines with machine guns. They also used bombs against us. Neither side would throw gas into Sergy, for fear of injuring their own troops.

The fighting went back and forth all morning. First we had the mauled village, and then the Prussians had it. Both sides made advances from edges of woods and retreated to that shelter. Finally, just after noon, when it was our turn in the village, the American artillery got down a heavy barrage, which caught the Prussian attackers and drove them back. By the time the enemy came again we were too strongly situated for them, and the result of the bloody battle was that we held Sergy.

Bitter Battle at Seringes.

Almost the same story tells the fighting yesterday for Seringes, only the battle was not so fierce and the village changed hands five times instead of nine.

To realize that this fighting was entirely different from the rear-guard actions of last week one has only to consider the hurrying of the Guard divisions, which are shock troops, into the line and the infantry counterattacks, whereas during the six previous days we had machine-gun opposition almost exclusively.

The truth of the matter is that the Germans wanted to hold their line on the north bank of the Ourcq for some days. Sergy and Seringes are strong villages on a series of hills running along the north side of the Ourcq, and evidence taken from prisoners showed that the Americans were supposed to have been held on the southern bank of the stream.

Evidence still points to the probability that the Germans intend to go back to the Vesle and hold there. The desire to hold the northern bank of the Ourcq is to be explained for the same reason.

Fighting to Save Supplies.

The Germans tried to hold the French and Americans in the southern part of the Forest de Ris. A trip through that forest today showed hundreds of tons of ammunition for big German guns, piled six feet high in rows a hundred yards long for some distances. This ammunition had been stored there to be used in the advance on Paris.

It is the belief that in Nesle Woods, north of the Ourcq, the Crown Prince has stored great supplies, and intends to get them out at any cost. Else why did he hurl against the Americans two divisions from the dwindling supply of his reserve divisions? This was done, of course, to stop the Americans, who could not be halted by ordinary German troops.

He succeeded in slowing down the Americans yesterday, but there are Americans in France who have not yet faced the Kaiser's fighters. The Germans have got to go further back, and they know it well. The throwing by the German command of fresh Guard divisions against the Americans is significant, when it is known definitely that it is planning another drive soon, perhaps against the British, for which it will need all available troops.

Lies Told to the Germans.

A captured officer said a regimental commander told his men two days ago that the Germans had hit the British and captured the Channel ports, but that the announcement had not yet been made by Ludendorff. He explained that Germany was still winning the war and that the withdrawal from the Soissons-Rheims sector was only for strategical reasons. The German command promised the German people to hit the British, and wants to make good.

Another significant factor in yesterday's counterattack against the Americans was that the Germans brought a large number of new airplanes, at least sixty, into the sector, and thus gained a temporary air supremacy which enabled the air fighters to do effective work against our troops. Undismayed by superior numbers, for the sixty were in addition to many chase machines the Hun already had, the American fliers went out to meet them, and there were many air fights all day long. British and French aviators also aided us. The Americans last night believed that they had brought down at least six airmen.

Grenades Under the White Flag.

The Germans are trying every art of their kind of warfare against our boys, but the Americans are learning fast. For instance, one squad advanced toward a platoon of Americans yesterday waving a white flag. The Americans let them come about a hundred yards and then cut loose and annihilated them. That they acted rightly was shown by the fact that the white flag had been tied to the handle of a live grenade, and while the Germans appeared at a distance to be weaponless, each was loaded down with deadly grenades.

Another favorite trick is that the German machine gunners, when seeing Americans approach, wait until our lads are close, when they cut loose with a final spurt of bullets, and then step out and cry "Kamerad!" Our men have adopted a rule that any German who shoots a ma-

Continued on Page Two.

German Masses Becoming Deeply Depressed; Realize Military Defeat; Food Stress Grows

Special Cable to THE NEW YORK TIMES.

GENEVA, Switzerland, July 30, (Dispatch to The London Daily Express.)—La Suisse states that a high neutral official who has just arrived at Basle from Berlin declares that, in spite of all German precautions to hide the defeat in the west, the truth has penetrated among the masses.

Such great moral depression has not been seen before during the war, which, it is now considered, is lost whenever Foch chooses his hour to strike.

The German people want the Government to make peace by ceding Alsace-Lorraine before it is too late.

The German losses during the last three months reached nearly a million. The losses during the last two offensives numbered 350,000, and these losses have completely disorganized the plans of the high command. Most of the wounded are greatly depressed and demoralized.

Munich Without Flour, Vegetables, or Fruit.

Special Cable to THE NEW YORK TIMES.

ZURICH, July 30.—The latest news and comments in all the German papers, especially the South German, show the food situation to be lamentable. The Munich Post writes:

"This year's fruit harvest is completely spoiled. The population is absolutely without fruits and vegetables, and it is impossible to obtain a pound of potatoes at any price. The potato harvest, despite official declarations, is less than two-thirds that of last year."

Terrible rumors are current in Bavaria that for days to come no flour will be available. Herr Dilly, President of the Vegetable Supply Department, declares it impossible to provide vegetables, and the population must submit to greater restrictions still in the near future.

A demonstration of women took place Friday in Munich, demanding bread and threatening the Town Hall and the Burgomaster. The deputation was received by the latter, who declared that everything was being done to deal with the misery of the population. Since July 26 the Munich municipality has been selling vegetables at reduced prices, to counteract monopolists, but the quantities are utterly insufficient and popular irritation increases daily.

OUR MEN DEFY BARRAGE

Rush Through Heaviest Fire; Now at Apex of Allied Advance.

STRUGGLE IS MERCILESS

Few Prisoners Taken After Americans Find Their Wounded in Sergy Were Bayonetted.

FRENCH ADVANCE ON WEST

Are Winning Plateau North of Grand Rozoy—Germans Gain Southwest of Rheims.

LONDON, July 30.—French and American troops in the region of Fère-en-Tardenois again thrust their lines forward, despite stiff resistance from the enemy.

The American troops have advanced from Sergy nearly two miles, again defeating the Prussian Guards and Bavarians. This followed a terrific German assault on the American lines, whereby the Germans won Cierges, [southeast of Sergy,] and apparently still hold it.

The French gains were made northeast of Fère and to the eastward of Sergy.

Heavy counterattacks were made by the Germans along almost the entire front to the east, but gained little ground except west of St. Euphraise [southwest of Rheims.]

In this same area the French troops have captured Romigny.

Some advance also has been effected by the Allies in the Ardre Valley, toward the village of Aubilly.

The main advance on the westerly side of the front seems to have been at Grand Rozoy, northwest of Fère-en-Tardenois. The French here are progressing north to the crest of the plateau between the Vesle and the Ourcq. The Germans drove the French out of Bengneux, but it was afterward retaken.

There has been heavy fighting near Buzancy, five miles south of Soissons, and also in Plessier Wood, about five miles further south.

There are now seventy-one German divisions in the Marne salient. Of these, ten belong to the northern army of Crown Prince Rupprecht of Bavaria. Five of these ten have been twice used in attacks.

Our Men Defy Barrage and Advance.

WITH THE AMERICAN ARMY ON THE AISNE-MARNE FRONT, July 30, (Associated Press.)—Through a barrage as deadly as any the Germans have laid down on any sector for months, the American soldiers, comprising men from the Middle West and Eastern States, pushed their line forward a little more today, and tonight it forms the apex of the long allied front between the Marne and the Vesle.

Their progress was somewhat less than two miles, but their operation is regarded as a brilliant one in view of the determined countering by the Germans.

On either side the French also moved forward, while steady pressure was maintained against the east and west flanks.

Information early in the day indicated the withdrawal of the 4th Division of Guards from this front, but it developed that that renowned organization and the Bavarians were still there, and the strong opposition they offered justified their reputation. But their sacrifice was in vain.

The Americans withstood two heavy attacks during the night, and at daylight began their operations, which left them tonight well to the north of Sergy, on the long slopes approaching the heavy woods beyond Nesles, a town directly east of Seringes-et-Nesles, for which the Germans fought bitterly.

The east end of the line swings northeasterly opposite this point, and then drops off sharply in the direction of Cierges and Ronchères. The Ourcq River has been left far be-

U. S. Navy

U. S. Naval railway battery.

Mid-Week Pictorial

German prisoners march through a French village.

Section 1

"All the News That's Fit to Print."

The New York Times.

THE WEATHER
Fair Sunday; Monday warmer; probably fair; east winds.
For full weather report see Page 17.

Section 1

VOL. LXVII...NO. 22,114. ... NEW YORK, SUNDAY, AUGUST 11, 1918—90 PAGES, In Nine Parts, Including Picture and Magazine Sections in Rotogravure. FIVE CENTS In Greater New York | Elsewhere SEVEN CENTS

SOMME SALIENT SMASHED, MONTDIDIER TAKEN; HUTIER'S ARMY FLEES AFTER FOCH'S NEW BLOW; 400 GUNS, MORE THAN 24,000 MEN CAPTURED

FALL OF THE REDS NOW IMMINENT, GERMANS LEARN

Rapidly Developing Events in Russia May Cause an Overthrow Any Day.

CZECHS CLOSE TO MOSCOW

Cut Off the City's Food Supply —Lenine and Trotzky Urge Resistance.

BRITISH MAKE REPRISAL

Emissary in London Placed Under Supervision Following Lockhart's Arrest.

LONDON, Aug. 10.—The German newspapers today admit that the situation in Russia is so critical that a change of Government may come any day, according to a Copenhagen dispatch to the Exchange Telegraph Company.

The Berlin Tägliche Rundschau says that events have developed rapidly in Russia in the last few weeks, and that Germany must be prepared for the overthrow of the Bolshevist Government in a few days. The paper says that the fact that Dr. Karl Helfferich, recently appointed German Ambassador to Russia in succession to the late Count von Mirbach, is in Berlin, indicates that Germany is prepared to meet any contingency.

The Frankfurter Zeitung says that the pressure against Moscow from the northeast and southeast is growing very serious, the Czecholovaks not only being within a short distance of the city, but having succeeded in cutting off the food supply. The paper adds that the opposition of the peasants to the Bolsheviki is growing stronger.

The headquarters staff of the Don Cossack Army announces that after three months' operations almost the whole of the Don region has been cleared of the Bolsheviki, according to dispatches from Kiev. The Don Cossack Army now consists of many thousands of excellently equipped soldiers, and a final decision is imminent, the dispatches add.

Lenine and Trotzky Exhort Reds.

AMSTERDAM, Aug. 10.—Hans Vorst, the Moscow correspondent of the Berlin Tageblatt, reporting the meeting of the Central Executive Committee of the Soviets on July 28, says that Nikolai Lenine, the Bolshevist Premier, was enthusiastically cheered. 'In the course of his speech Lenine referred to the dangers threatening the revolution and emphasized the necessity of combating war weariness, because the revolution, he said, was fighting for its existence. He instanced cases where the Red Army was withdrawing, although stronger than the opposing Czechoslovaks.

"The fatal plans of Anglo-French imperialism," said Lenine, "can only be frustrated if we succeed in crushing the Czechoslovaks and their counter-revolutionary partisans on the Volga, in the Urals, and in Siberia. This is the urgent task and all others must be relegated to the background. All our forces must be devoted to the war."

Leon Trotzky, the War Minister, said that enough Red Guards could be sent against the Czechoslovaks to outnumber them two or three times. He referred to the enthusiasm of the Czechoslovaks, which, apparently, was lacking among the Soviet troops, and added:

"We are now forced to send our best leaders among the workers to the front as agitators and organizers."

Complaining of the lack of officers, Trotzky said:

"The Russian officers are counter-revolutionaries, but the hour has come to master them. Concentration camps will be established for officers who do not loyally serve the Red Army. Several already serving have proved unreliable, and cases of treachery have occurred.

"Every officer in command must be watched on both sides by War Commissaries, with revolvers in their hands. No officer will be allowed to take a single step without supervision, and if he wavers he will be shot.

"Recruiting among the workmen will be extended. They must make a compact with death, for only then can they hope to make a compact also with victory."

General Semenoff, the anti-Bolshevist leader, with the help of Chinese artillery, has defeated the Russian Red Guards on the Chinese frontier and dispersed them, according to a Moscow telegram to the Rhenish Westphalian Gazette of Essen.

BRITISH REPRISAL FOR CONSUL'S ARREST

Reds' Emissary Is Placed Under Police Supervision — Lenine's Not a "Real Government."

LONDON, Aug. 10.—In reprisal for the arrest at Moscow of Robert H. B. Lockhart, British consular agent at Moscow, and other British officials by the Bolsheviki, M. Litvinoff, the Bolshevist emissary in London, has been placed

Continued on Page Five.

Lord Reading Is Proud of American Troops

By CHARLES H. GRASTY.

Special Cable to THE NEW YORK TIMES.

LONDON, Aug. 10.—I called on Lord Reading today, and in the course of a conversation on the war situation he said:

"I find here universal appreciation of what America has done. I can't help having a feeling of personal pleasure and delight at the way the American troops have acquitted themselves when called upon, and this feeling is shared by all our people.

"America appeared in force at the turn of the curve and their spirit and efficiency helped to restore the initiative, which has led to the splendid results we have seen in the great battle."

FLEW 621 MILES TO WARN VIENNA

D'Annunzio's Squadron Crossed the Alps at 10,000 Feet on Their Flight.

LOST ONLY ONE MACHINE

This Had to Land Because of Engine Trouble — Airmen Acclaimed on Return.

ROME, Aug. 10.—The feat of dropping manifestoes on Vienna Friday morning was accomplished by a patrol of eight Italian machines, and all returned safely except one. The squadron, commanded by Captain Gabriele d'Annunzio, comprised one biplane and seven monoplanes. The total flight was about 1,000 kilometers, (621 miles,) of which 800 were over enemy territory.

The airplanes left their base at 5:30 o'clock and, after surmounting fairly serious atmospheric difficulties, reached Vienna at 9:20. They dropped to a height of 800 meters and threw out several thousand manifestoes. Throngs in the streets could be seen plainly by the airmen.

The Italian machines returned by way of Vienna-Neustadt, Gratz, Laibach, and Triest. A semi-official note says that they were not attacked. The patrol kept close together throughout the journey and arrived at its base again at 12:40 P. M.

The missing machine appears to have been obliged to land near Vienna-Neustadt owing to engine trouble.

There were scenes of wild enthusiasm when Captain d'Annunzio and his comrades returned. The flight over the Alps was made in a great windstorm and through strong mountain currents at a height of about 10,000 feet.

The manifestoes dropped on Vienna contained a warning of what the Italians might do if they saw fit to return on a bombing expedition.

D'Annunzio Tells of Flight.

Captain d'Annunzio gave the following vivid description of the flight of his squadron:

"When we left at 6 o'clock in the morning the weather was splendid, but we soon were enveloped in a thick mist. We kept at a height varying from 8,000 to 11,000 feet.

"In crossing our former frontier I was deeply affected at looking down upon Cividale and the wide stretches of our country that have been held for the last nine months by the enemy.

"We reached Vienna about 9 o'clock in the morning, and descended to within 1,500 feet. The people in the streets were at first terrified and fled in panic until they saw that we were throwing out only manifestoes. Then crowds assembled and watched us with intense curiosity.

"I particularly wished to approach close to the museum that contains the authentic image of St. Catherine of Alexandria, and made a detour which permitted observation of this point.

"The weather became bad on our return trip, and we experienced dangerous air currents while crossing the Alps. We also were attacked by hostile artil-

Continued on Page Six.

GERMANS ON RUN, TIME TO HIT HARD, MARCH DECLARES

Moment for Utmost Effort to Prevent Their Recuperating, Says Chief of Staff.

WHY AMERICA HASTENS

Course of Battle Explains the Government's Eagerness to Extend Draft Ages.

FOE MUST DO THE GUESSING

British Prisoner Pens Full and All German Guns in New Salient Captured.

Special to The New York Times.

WASHINGTON, Aug. 10.—General Peyton C. March, Chief of Staff, said today in his weekly review of military operations that Marshal Foch had the enemy on the run. Marshal Foch, he said, was working on the sound principle "that when you get an enemy going you keep him going; never give him a chance to recuperate or think it over; keep on hitting him."

At the same time General March said that statements that indicated that the war was over should be discouraged. "This is the time for the greatest effort; keep the enemy running," said General March. He pointed out that this was the reason the United States was endeavoring to increase its man power through lowering and raising the draft age limits.

"It is no time to talk about the war being over," declared the Chief of Staff. "It is the time to hit him hard. The greatest advantage of this whole thing has been the change of the Allies from the defensive to the offensive, which is a great military asset. We have the enemy guessing now instead of guessing ourselves."

O'Ryan's Men May Be in Fight.

There is a bare possibility that the 27th Division, (New York National Guard,) commanded by Major Gen. John F. O'Ryan, is taking part in the latest offensive. General March revealed that the 27th when last reported was with the British on the Flanders front. No positive news has been received from any source, however, that the British in Flanders are engaging in anything more than local operations. The British official statement today mentions American troops as participating with the British in the present main drive in Picardy, the French province, which adjoins the Belgian Province of Flanders, but there is no mention in any statement, official or otherwise, that American troops are engaged in any Flanders offensive. In fact, the British official reports indicate that the Germans began to retire on the Flanders front.

General March said today that yesterday on the Flanders salient the Germans were withdrawing on the southern sector and the British occupied the abandoned territory. To a question as to whether the 27th was engaged, General March indicated that it might be a good guess. He said he could not identify the American commands with the British advance in Picardy east of Amiens, as no report concerning them had been received.

"As soon as it is indicated that American troops are in there I will give it to you," he added.

How splendidly allied troops have succeeded in their new offensive in Picardy was shown by a confidential cablegram which General March read to the newspaper men with permission to publish. The cablegram was as follows:

"Allied troops found little opposition and have captured more prisoners than is possible for them to handle, including a German General and his staff, showing elements of surprise of attack. British report their prison camps back of Amiens so full that it is impossible to hold any more. Allies have captured all the artillery in this sector."

Reviewing military operations in France and Belgium, General March said:

"Surveying the battle line broadly

Continued on Page Seven.

U-Boats Cannot Defeat the Allies, Says Munich Post, Admitting "Famine"

LONDON, Aug. 10.—Germany's unrestricted U-boat warfare could neither keep the army of the United States from taking part in the battles on the fields of France nor break the will of the Allies to continue the war, is the admission made by the Munich Post, a copy of which has been received here.

In a review of the situation at the beginning of the fifth year of the war, the Post says:

"Eighteen months of unrestricted submarine warfare could not break the enemy's will to war nor prevent America's putting a well equipped army of a million men on the western front. Hopes that after the conclusion of peace in the East the final struggle in the West would be decided in favor of Germany and bring a general peace have proved deceptive, and the Eastern peace itself is a disappointment, and not only politically."

The Post takes exception to the word "unfavorable" in describing the food situation in Germany, and says "chronic famine" would be nearer the truth.

Soldiers Blame Crown Prince for Reverses at the Marne

LONDON, Aug. 10.—The Reuter correspondent with the British Army in France sends the following dispatch concerning the German Crown Prince:

"According to the statements of prisoners, the German Crown Prince appears to be the most unpopular leader in the German Army. He is accused by them of being directly responsible for the Marne disaster.

"They say that the opinion is widely expressed by German soldiers that the Crown Prince's amateurish interference with the plans of their experienced Generals was the starting point for the present crushing misfortunes of the German armies."

PARIS EXPECTS WIDER TRIUMPH

Believes that Foch's Hammer Blows Will Be Rapid and Frequent from Now On.

ALLIES HAVE ALL TRUMPS

Wherever They Decide to Advance Germans Are Forced to Shift Reserves.

Special Cable to THE NEW YORK TIMES.

PARIS, Aug. 10.—Paris read the news of yesterday's brilliant British victory on the front of Amiens, (for everybody here generously thus describes it,) with a thrill of delight. This was not so much because another undoubted victory had been obtained, but because of the glowing prospects it opened up of another and even greater triumph even than that of the Aisne-Marne salient.

It is keenly realized here that yesterday's advance was but a prelude to what is almost certain to prove another great tactical success that will tear from the enemy's possession another great stretch of French territory alongside he broad area, redeemed as the result of Foch's slashing blow against the Crown Prince between Soissons and the Marne.

If the German people can be persuaded, when the present allied drive against Prince Rupprecht's armies comes to a natural end to measure Foch's new triumph by the map as their rules are fond of telling them to do in the case of Germany's own victories, there will be no more talk of Ludendorff's efforts to transform the allied success into "successful German strategical retreats." Von Hutier's forces, so far as it is humanly possible to predict, are doomed to a fate similar to that which recently befell their comrades in the Aisne-Marne salient.

The position this morning may be thus summed up: The German 2d Army and a small portion of the 18th Army were soundly beaten yesterday and started on the run. The greater part of the 18th Army, which is Hutier's occupies a country which forms the arc of a circle between Montdidier and the junction of the Matz and the Oise below Ribecourt.

Eleven to twelve miles from Soissons was the poin treached by the enemy in his drive on Compiegne.

The country here is hilly and filled with forests and badly supplied with roads. It is in sohrt the very worst kind of terrain in which a defeated and retreating army could find itself.

Between the Avre and the Oise are only three good roads which can be used by an army in retreat northward, and these all converge like sticks of a fan on Roye.

Beyond Roye there are only two roads, one leading toward Ham and the other through Nesle to the Somme.

The frightful confusion that must result from the efforts of von Hutier to withdraw his heavy artillery and innumerable convoys of all kinds along these few roads under the pressure of pursuit by victorious British and French can be imagined.

Whole Status Changed.

The revenge of the British confirms a prophecy I indulged in in my cable last Sunday, when I asserted that Foch's next blow would come much sooner than most people expected.

It is realized here that Foch's latest blow has been struck at a point which he himself had chosen after a careful

Continued on Page Two.

PRESS ENEMY ON THE VESLE

Americans Repulse Repeated Counterattacks and Make Gains.

PREPARED FOR NEXT TASK

That Will Depend on Outcome to North—Taking Vesle-Aisne Terrain Not Essential.

DISCOVER GERMAN TRAPS

Explosives Left Camouflaged in Many Ways and Food and Water Poisoned.

Five of Our Airmen Fight 12 Enemy Machines and Down 2

WITH THE AMERICAN ARMY ON THE VESLE FRONT, Aug. 10, (Associated Press.)—In a battle in the air between twelve German and five American airplanes, Lieutenant Walter Avery of Columbus, Ohio, and Harold Buckley of Agawam, Mass., each brought down a German.

There were no casualties among the Americans.

By EDWIN L. JAMES.

Special Cable to THE NEW YORK TIMES.

WITH THE AMERICAN ARMY, Aug. 10.—The American troops along the Vesle are keeping up a constant pressure against the enemy, making local but important gains. On the right and the left the French troops are pursuing the same policy.

In the last thirty-six hours the Germans have executed four counterattacks against the Americans between Bazoches and Fismes, using high explosive and gas preparation. All these attacks have been repulsed with losses, and our troops are holding along the Rheims-Soissons road and to the north of it in front of Fismes.

Lively artillery activity on both sides continues night and day.

From the body of a German officer who led one of yesterday's attacks was taken an order showing that the Germans are basing their operations on three lines—first, the line along the Vesle; second, the line along the heights between the Vesle and the Aisne, and third, the line behind the Aisne. The order directed the troops along the Vesle to hold at all costs for the present. Prisoners say they were ordered to hold along the Vesle until the Aisne defenses could be prepared.

Preparing for New Tasks.

Allied plans in this sector are in the making. It is not now essential to our plans to hold the region between the Vesle and the Aisne. Against determined German resistance it would not be worth taking at this stage. But affairs are going to shape themselves so that the Germans will go back of the Aisne when the proper time comes.

It is entirely probable the moves to be made on the Vesle line will be influenced by the outcome of the new allied drive in the region of Amiens. Meanwhile the Americans are steadily bettering their positions north of the Vesle, to be ready for whatever task may be given to them to do.

As our engineers clean up the territory from which the Germans have retreated they continue to find hundreds of infernal machines of all [illegible]orts. A favorite brand was to arrange the branches of trees to look [illegible] the camouflage of a door of a [illegible]ugout; when brushed aside they [illegible] set off mines.

Bombs of great strength have been found in foul rubbish piles, which would naturally be burned. Loose

Continued on Page Two.

Official Reports of the Day's Operations

British

LONDON, Aug. 10.

Night Report—The attack launched yesterday evening, in accordance with the allied plan of operations, on our right by the French First Army south of Montdidier was developed by our allies this morning with complete success. Enveloped from the north and from the southeast, Montdidier fell into the hands of the French before midday, together with many prisoners and great quantities of material.

During the remainder of the day the advance of the French First Army continued with the co-operation of the French army on its right and the right wing of the British Fourth Army. Pressing hard upon the retreating German troops south of Lihons, the British troops have overcome the enemy's resistance and made substantial progress.

The general line reached by the allied troops now runs virtually north and south from Lihons to Fresnoy-les-Roye, Lignières and Conchy-les-Pots.

The number of prisoners was increased.

Day Report—Yesterday afternoon and evening the advance of the allied armies continued on the whole front from south of Montdidier to the Ancre.

French troops, attacking south of Montdidier during the afternoon, captured Le Tronquoy, Le Fretoy, and Assainvillers, threatening Montdidier from the southeast. More than 2,000 prisoners were captured by our allies in this sector.

Canadian and Australian divisions have taken Bouchoir, Meharicourt, and Lihons, and have entered Rainecourt and Proyart.

In the evening English and American troops attacked in the angle between the Somme and the Ancre and met with immediate success. By nightfall all the objectives had been taken, including the village of Morlancourt and the high ground southeast of it. Counterattacks launched by the enemy in this sector were beaten off after sharp fighting.

The prisoners captured by the Allies since the morning of Aug. 8 exceed 24,000.

French

PARIS, Aug. 10.

Night Report.—On the Avre battlefront our attacks continued all day with increasing success. After the morning's operations Montdidier, outflanked on the east and the north, fell into our hands. Continuing our victorious advance on the right of the British forces, we carried our lines nearly seven miles to the east of Montdidier on a front running from Andechy to La Boissière and Fescamps.

Still enlarging our action southeast, we have attacked German positions on the right and left of the road from St. Just-en-Chaussée to Roye on a front of more than thirteen miles. We conquered Rollot, Orvillers-Sorel, Ressons-sur-Matz, Conchy-les-Pots, La Neuville-sur-Ressons and Elincourt, realizing at some points an advance of nearly seven miles.

In three days of battle French troops have progressed nearly fourteen miles along the Amiens-Roye road. The number of prisoners taken during the same period exceeds 8,000. Among the enormous material abandoned by the enemy we have counted up to the present 200 guns.

Day Report—The French troops, operating on the right of the British forces, continued their success throughout last evening and last night. Our troops made progress east of Arvillers and captured Davenescourt.

They attacked south of Montdidier, between Ayencourt and Le Fretoy, and occupied Rubescourt and Assainvillers and reached Faverolles.

German

BERLIN, Aug. 10, (via London.)

Night Report—In the centre of the battlefront the enemy has gained ground beyond Rosières and Hangest. Our counterattacks brought him to a standstill west of Lihons and east of the Rosières-Arvillers line.

During the night we withdrew our troops fighting on the Avre and on Dom Brook to the rear lines east of Montdidier. Southeast of Montdidier we repulsed strong partial attacks of the French.

We shot down thirty-two airplanes over the battlefield.

There has been lively activity on the part of the enemy between the Yser and the Ancre. At many points on this front the enemy launched thrusts and partial attacks which were repulsed before our lines in hand-to-hand fighting.

Yesterday the British and French, bringing strong reserves into action, continued their attacks on the whole battlefront between the Ancre and the Avre.

On both sides of the Somme and astride the Foucaucourt-Villers-Bretonneux Road we threw the enemy back by counterattacks. He suffered heavy losses here.

Americans in Picardy Battle Again Outfight the Germans

After Hard March They Run to Join British in Victory at Chipilly Spur—Teuton Lines Break Under Brilliant Attack and Our Losses Are Not Unduly Severe.

WITH THE BRITISH ARMY IN FRANCE, Aug. 10, (Associated Press.)—American troops have been thrown into the fighting in the great battle in the Amiens-Somme district. They succeeded in overcoming a stiff resistance, and helped the British capture important positions in an attack launched yesterday between the Ancre and the Somme.

The American machine gunners and infantry went into battle with their traditional enthusiasm. They met the Germans and defeated them here just as they did along the Marne. At places stiff resistance developed, but all along the line the Americans, British, and French smashed through the harassed enemy, who was trying to hold up their advance.

Details of the brilliant battle which the Americans and British fought for the spur are now available. In order to go over the top at the appointed time yesterday afternoon the Americans were forced to make a rapid march, in the last part of which they ran so as to be in the fight.

Hurried on their way by the advancing British, French, and American troops on the Amiens-Somme battlefield, the Germans throughout the day retired all along the line, attempting to save whatever they could as the French launched a new attack on Montdidier. The elements of the German divisions became badly confused in their operations through trying to hold up the Allies in their several attacks. It was a victorious day for the Allies, who smashed all the German resistance.

German Lines Broke.

In the American attack the German infantry held for a while and then broke, and the Americans kept going at some places without the assistance of the tanks. The ground, pitted with deep gullies, was unsuited for tank warfare.

There were no trenches, but a thin smoke screen blowing across the ground indicated where the enemy's positions lay. At the same time the German artillery became active and dropped shells in the direction of the American troops which inflicted a few casualties. The Americans, however, ran on and reached the smoke line just as it lifted. There they found themselves at grips with the enemy.

Meanwhile certain American units had reached positions in front of a wood when the Germans opened fire with machine guns. Many of these enemy machine gunners came up from deep dugouts after the American barrage had ceased and they placed their guns in prepared pits. The Americans faced a hail of bullets here.

The Americans and British have now advanced beyond their objectives north of the Somme. The whole of the Chipilly spur is now in their possession. Although the fighting was of the most desperate character, the casualties of the Americans were not more than was to be expected.

Capture of Chipilly Spur.

WASHINGTON, Aug. 10.—The British War Office official statement today on the drive in Picardy reveals for the first time the fact that American troops are taking part in this smashing blow there against the enemy. There had been no information here to show that men from this country were in the drive, and the identity of the unit or units is not known.

Large numbers of American soldiers are brigaded with the British for

Continued on Page Two.

DOUBLE STROKE TAKES CITY

French Plunge Forward Six Miles After Capturing Montdidier.

BRITISH GAIN IN THE NORTH

Capture Morlancourt and Chipilly Ridge and Drive Forward on Bray.

FOE THROWN IN CONFUSION

So Shaken by the Swift Allied Strokes That He Cannot Counterattack.

LONDON, Aug. 10.—Throwing his 1st. Army against the apex of the German salient southeast of Amiens, Marshal Foch today captured Montdidier, and followed up his success by smashing into the salient for an average depth of six miles on a thirteen-mile front, reaching a line extending from Andechy [seven miles northeast of Montdidier] to Elincourt [ten miles to the southeast.]

The attack on Montdidier, which was made from the north and southeast simultaneously, resulted in the capture of many prisoners and great quantities of material.

The whole allied line from Albert to the southern side of the Montdidier salient has been pushed eastward, reaching its maximum distance in that direction in the neighborhood of Chaulnes, at about the middle point of the fighting front of the last few days.

Between the Ancre and the Somme American troops have co-operated with British, and the two captured Morlancourt and held the village against heavy counterattacks.

The general line reached by the Allies in the Albert-Montdidier sector is described in Field Marshal Haig's night report as running from Lihons to Fresnoy-les-Roye, to Lignières, and Conchy-les-Pots.

The number of German prisoners was estimated in the British official day bulletin at 24,000, but this has been increased, according to the night report.

Allied Casualties Only 6,000.

LONDON, Aug. 10, (Associated Press.)—The advance of the allied armies on the Picardy battlefront continued today. Nowhere, it appears, have the Germans yet been able to orgánize for any severe counterstroke.

The guns captured by the Allies are now nearly 400 in number.

The total of prisoners is mounting rapidly because of the disorganization of the Germans.

Allied casualties, including all the killed, wounded, and missing, are less than 6,000, or not more than one-fourth of the number of prisoners counted. On the other hand, the German casualties have been very heavy.

The German communications have been so disorganized that thus far only two divisions of reserves have been identified, and these new troops have not been able to make any impression on the advancing Allies.

11 German Divisions Smashed.

Eleven German divisions have been defeated in the fighting of the last three days.

These eleven divisions are now in such condition that they can be of little use to the German command for a long time to come, and probably some can never be re-formed.

The two new divisions which appeared on the front were rushed down the two principal arteries of communication. It is along these arteries' however, that the Allies' forces are strongest, particularly in cavalry and tanks, and these reinforce-

U. S. Army

An American gun crew fires its 37mm gun during an advance against German positions in France.

U. S. Signal Corps

Sharpshooters take cover in the remains of a brick house in France.

"All the News That's Fit to Print."

The New York Times.

THE WEATHER
Fair today; Tuesday partly cloudy; moderate shifting winds.
For full weather report see Page 15.

VOL. LXVII...NO. 22,136. NEW YORK, MONDAY, SEPTEMBER 2, 1918.—SIXTEEN PAGES. TWO CENTS Metropolitan District 50 Mile Radius. | THREE CENTS Within 200 Miles. | FOUR CENTS Elsewhere.

LENINE REPORTED DEAD; WAS SHOT BY A GIRL; HAIG TAKES PERONNE AND 2,000 PRISONERS; PRESIDENT ASKS THE NATION'S UTMOST EFFORT

LENINE'S ASSASSIN CAUGHT

Official Bolshevist Paper Says She Is Girl of Intellectual Class.

ATTACK MADE IN FACTORY

Premier Had Been Addressing a Meeting of Laborers in Works at Moscow.

HELD UP BY TWO WOMEN

Both Shot at Him, Vienna Hears—Official Report Saturday Had Lenine Improving.

LONDON, Sept. 1.—Nikolai Lenine, the Bolshevist Premier, who was shot twice by an assassin last Friday night at Moscow, has died of his wounds, according to a telegram from Petrograd to the Exchange Telegraph Company by way of Copenhagen.

The latest official news concerning Lenine's condition is in the form of two bulletins by Russian wireless, timed 7:30 and 8:30 Saturday evening respectively. These bulletins described his general condition as good, with immediate danger past, and stated that no complications had arisen.

A medical bulletin issued at 11 o'clock Saturday morning at Petrograd, and received here by Russian wireless service, says that Lenine had a disturbed night. The bulletin adds:

"Pulse 112, temperature 37, Centigrade, (98.6 Fahrenheit, normal.) The effusion of blood in the pleura is not increasing.

Condition Serious, Stockholm Hears.

Copyright, 1918, by The New York Times Company.
Special Cable to THE NEW YORK TIMES.

STOCKHOLM, Sept. 1.—News has been received here of an attempt on the life of Nikolai Lenine. One of the bullets damaged his left lung, and, although Lenine is conscious and seemingly confident, it is feared his condition is more serious than at first supposed. There is internal hemorrhage and his pulse is very weak.

This is not the first attempt on Lenine's life and the fact that there have not been many more is not due to any efficient bodyguard. Rumors have been continually out about that Lenine never moved without guards. This is untrue, both concerning him and Trotzky. Both Trotzky and Lenine laughed at the efforts of their assistants to protect them. Trotzky, for example, more than once, impatiently waiting for a motor, set off on foot until pursued and captured by his secretary.

There is nothing easier than for one to go straight into the National Hotel and into Lenine's private room. Lenine is seldom accompanied by more than his own secretary or his wife, whereas Kerensky never moved, in Moscow conference or Democratic Assembly, unaccompanied by two armed adjutants. Lenine wanders about by himself, sits where he chooses, here or there, even in such conferences as that which ratified the Brest-Litovsk peace, where feeling ran very high, and some such attempt might easily have been expected.

AMSTERDAM, Sept. 1.—The condition of Nikolai Lenine against whose life an attempt was made Friday night, is reported by the Russian newspaper Pravda to be serious, owing to internal hemorrhages, according to a telegram from Moscow. The Pravda says the Premier was shot by a young girl belonging to the intellectual class. She was arrested.

The attack on Lenine was made Friday evening after a meeting of

Continued on Page Seven.

Coup d'Etat Is Threatened Over Chinese Presidency

Copyright, 1918, by The New York Times Co.
Special Cable to THE NEW YORK TIMES.

PEKING, Sept. 1.—Indications suggest that a coup d'état is impending over the Presidency. Several Northern Generals have telegraphed from the battlefront to the Government advocating a compromise with the South, also a postponement of the election for President.

Meanwhile the Canton Government announces the withdrawal of troops from Hunan and Kiang-si in order to concentrate at Fukien, suggesting that a compromise has been arranged by the Northern Generals and Southern leaders.

Reports from other sources indicate that President Feng Kuo-chang is endeavoring to obtain a postponement of the election, possibly also in the aim of compromising with the South.

SPAIN NOW SEIZES GERMAN SHIPPING

Cabinet Orders 90 Interned Vessels Taken Over in Compensation for U-Boat Loss.

SPURRED BY NEW SINKING

The Ataz-Mindi, Carrying Coal, Is Torpedoed Despite Madrid's Warning.

LONDON, Monday, Sept. 2.—The Spanish Government, after a Cabinet meeting Saturday night, seized one of the interned German steamers, according to a Madrid dispatch to The Daily Mail. This action was taken because of the torpedoing of the Ataz-Mendi.

MADRID, Aug. 31. (Associated Press.)—The Spanish Government tonight decided to take over all the German steamships interned in Spanish ports, in accordance with Spain's recent note to Berlin, because of the torpedoing of Spanish vessels by German submarines.

Foreign Minister Dato announced at the meeting of the Cabinet tonight that the Spanish steamship Ataz-Mendi, carrying a cargo of coal from England to Spain, had been torpedoed and sunk by a German submarine. The crew of the vessel was saved.

90 German Ships Interned in Spain.

Spain's decision to seize German shipping lying in Spanish harbors means an enemy loss of ninety vessels and marks another German diplomatic fiasco. Recent cable dispatches on the U-boat situation with regard to Spain have shown that the Dato Ministry, after displaying great reluctance, has been compelled to take action by a tremendous anti-German sentiment which has grown steadily in Spain.

On Aug. 8 Minister Dato briefly announced the dispatch of another note of protest to Germany, and three days later the question of retaliatory measures was again before the Council of Ministers presided over by King Alfonso. A long session occupied principally with discussion of the sinkings ended with a note to Berlin demanding satisfaction. Through London it was ascertained that Spain had threatened to seize all interned German ships, thus making the second note practically an ultimatum. The Dato Cabinet then gave out a résumé of German activities against Spanish shipping, reading in part:

"In the course of the recent meetings held at Madrid the Government considered the international question. As a consequence of the submarine campaign more than 20 per cent. of our merchant marine has been sunk, more than 100 Spanish sailors have perished, a considerable number of Spanish sailors have been wounded, and numbers have been shipwrecked and abandoned. Ships needed exclusively for Spanish use have been torpedoed without the slightest pretext, serious difficulties resulting to navigation."

The German Foreign Office then addressed several notes of "reassurance" to Spain, and followed these with what was in effect a diplomatically worded threat to break relations with Madrid if Spain carried out her intention of taking over German steamships.

A dispatch published in THE NEW YORK TIMES three days ago quoted the Havas Agency as recording a standstill in the German-Spanish exchanges, with Wilhelmstrasse temporizing and even promising a modification of the U-boat war.

President Wilson's Labor Day Message

Special to The New York Times.

WASHINGTON, Sept. 1.—President Wilson today issued the following appeal to organized labor and to the people of the nation generally to consecrate themselves anew to the task of winning the war against Germany:

My Fellow-Citizens:

Labor Day, 1918, is not like any Labor Day that we have known. Labor Day was always deeply significant with us. Now it is supremely significant. Keenly as we were aware a year ago of the enterprise of life and death upon which the nation had embarked, we did not perceive its meaning as clearly as we do now. We knew that we were all partners and must stand and strive together, but we did not realize, as we do now, that we are all enlisted men, members of a single army, of many parts and many tasks, but commanded by a single obligation, our faces set toward a single object. We now know that every tool in every essential industry is a weapon, and a weapon wielded for the same purpose that an army rifle is wielded—a weapon which if we were to lay down no rifle would be of any use.

And a weapon for what? What is the war for? Why are we enlisted? Why should we be ashamed if we were not enlisted? At first it seemed hardly more than a war of defense against the military aggression of Germany. Belgium had been violated, France invaded, and Germany was afield again, as in 1870 and 1866, to work out her ambitions in Europe, and it was necessary to meet her force with force. But it is clear now that it is much more than a war to alter the balance of power in Europe. Germany, it is now plain, was striking at what free men everywhere desire and must have—the right to determine their own fortunes, to insist upon justice, and to oblige Governments to act for them and not for the private and selfish interest of a governing class. It is a war to make the nations and peoples of the world secure against every such power as the German autocracy represents. It is war of emancipation. Not until it is won can men anywhere live free from constant fear or breathe freely while they go about their daily tasks and know that Governments are their servants, not their masters.

This is, therefore, the war of all wars, which labor should support and support with all its concentrated power. The world cannot be safe, men's lives cannot be secure, no man's rights can be confidently and successfully asserted against the rule and mastery of arbitrary groups and special interests so long as Governments like that which after long premeditation drew Austria and Germany into this war are permitted to control the destinies and the daily fortunes of men and nations, plotting while honest men work, laying the fires of which innocent men, women, and children are to be the fuel.

You know the nature of this war. It is a war which industry must sustain. The army of laborers at home is as important, as essential, as the army of fighting men in the far fields of actual battle. And the laborer is not only needed as much as the soldier. It is his war. The soldier is his champion and representative. To fail to win would be to imperil everything that the laborer has striven for and held dear since freedom first had its dawn and its struggle for justice began. The soldiers at the front know this. It steels their muscles to think of it. They are crusaders. They are fighting for no selfish advantage for their own nation. They would despise any one who fought for the selfish advantage of any nation. They are giving their lives that homes everywhere as well as the homes they love in America may be kept sacred and safe, and men, everywhere be free as they insist upon being free. They are fighting for the ideals of their own land—great ideals, immortal ideals, ideals which shall light the way for all men to the places where justice is done and men live with lifted heads and emancipated spirits. That is the reason they fight with solemn joy and are invincible.

Let us make this, therefore, a day of fresh comprehension, not only for what we are about and of renewed and clear-eyed resolution but a day of consecration also in which we devote ourselves without pause or limit to the great task of setting our own country and the whole world free to render justice to all and of making it impossible for small groups of political rulers anywhere to disturb our peace or the peace of the world or in any way to make tools and puppets of those upon whose consent and upon whose power their own authority and their own very existence depend.

We may count upon each other. The nation is of a single mind. It is taking counsel with no special class. It is serving no private or single interest. Its own mind has been cleared and fortified by these days, which burn the dross away. The light of a new conviction has penetrated to every class amongst us. We realize as we never realized before that we are comrades dependent upon one another, irresistible when united, powerless when divided. And so we join hands to lead the world to a new and better day.

WOODROW WILSON.

Cities of the East Obey the Rule To Keep Autos Idle on Sunday

Volunteer Committees Hold Up Recalcitrant Drivers Here—Riverside Drive and Fifth Avenue Show Startling Decreases in Automobile Traffic—Few Autos at Coney Island.

It required no coercive measure other than the pressure of patriotic public opinion to bring about a remarkable response from the people of this city to the request of the Fuel Administration that no gasoline be used on Sunday for pleasure auto riding. It meant that thousands and thousands of persons mindful of their duty to the Government in an hour of emergency had to stay at home, instead of utilizing the only free day of the week for the much cherished motor trip into the country, or to the park and seaside. But stay at home they did, not sulkily and not unwillingly, but with all that genuine readiness to sacrifice personal pleasures for a greater and common end, which has become characteristic of the people of this country ever since the winning of the war became the issue in American life.

Imagine standing at Fifty-ninth Street and Columbus Circle, regarded as one of the busiest traffic points in the world, and seeing not one passenger car gliding past in the space of an hour, with the exception of an occasional taxi. The traffic policeman all day long leaned on one foot and then the other, and many times almost yielded to the temptation of taking a seat in the park. Patriotism proved a far stronger force than force itself, and the policeman found his occupation gone. Best estimates indicate that the traffic at Columbus Circle, averaging about 2,500 automobiles an hour on an ordinary Sunday, produced not more than fifty or sixty automobiles from 8 A. M. to 1 P. M. yesterday.

That is a fairly good criterion of what took place at many of the other big traffic centres of the city, such as Fifth Avenue, Riverside Drive, Broadway, the Queensboro, Manhattan, and Brooklyn Bridges, and the various highways leading to and from Coney Island, New Jersey, and Long Island. Policemen were amazed at the readiness with which the city observed a rule that had no power of enforcement behind it and relied entirely for its effect upon the individual sense of obligation. All this, however, is not to say that there were no "slackers" in sight, who went forth on their joy rides as gaily as ever, measuring the public sense of duty by their own and believing that so long as the policeman could not stop them, "nobody would pay any attention to the rule anyway." They were sadly disappointed and often suffered censure much more coercive than a policeman's summons.

Volunteers Hold Up Slackers.

In many parts of the city, and especially in such districts as Flatbush, Borough Park, and Jamaica, which commanded the roads to Coney Island and other seaside resorts, they encountered volunteer vigilance committees, composed of citizens who were determined to see that no one went through their districts in an automobile without good cause. The work of these vigilance committees was one of the striking features of the day, for wherever they appeared they succeeded generally in stopping what few automobile "slackers" attempted to pass their way.

Thus in Flatbush a special committee, composed of residents and some soldiers and sailors, undertook to guard all the main highways to Coney Island. Any automobile attempting to pass would be stopped and citizens would challenge the passengers to tell where they were going and why they were going. If they declined to stop, some of the members of the committee would throw pieces of planking studded with nails in front of the wheels. When the drivers became belligerent the soldiers or sailors of the vigilance committee would call upon them to produce registration cards.

Under such conditions going to or coming from Coney Island by any of the Flatbush routes meant sure humiliation. At Ocean and Foster Avenues 470 cars appeared between 8 A. M. and 6 P. M., as compared to the many thousands of cars that pass that point on an ordinary Sunday. Of 470 cars only 70 were permitted to pass, the drivers proving that they had pressing errands. The others were turned back.

Similar occurrences, where citizens took in their own hands the enforcement of the no-gasoline rule were frequent on Long Island. In Queens the vigilance committees governed with a firm hand, and in many instances used their authority with such insistence that recalcitrant drivers would threaten to call the police. In every case, however, the committee would challenge the driver to call the policeman, and the policeman would come—not to interfere with the committee's ruling, but rather to support it with a severe admonishment to the driver and the occupants of the car.

With all the approaches to Coney Island so closely watched by vigilance committees, this resort had practically no automobile traffic. In the parkway space at Coney Island where normally hundreds of automobiles are to be found at any hour on Sunday, there were only four cars at 1 o'clock yesterday, and not more than eleven cars at 3 o'clock. The silent space was an eloquent tribute to patriotism.

Bridge Traffic at a Minimum.

Among the important traffic points which showed what the public was doing toward putting the gasoline saving rule into effect were the various bridge and ferry terminals through which traffic had to pass if engaged in the usual pleasure tours. On the Williamsburg Bridge, where there is usually a heavy traffic of pleasure cars bound to and from Long Island on Sunday mornings between the hours of 8 and 9 A. M., not one offender was seen yesterday during that time. The average there in that hour is from ten to twelve cars a minute, or more than 700 an hour. Yes-

Continued on Page Five.

Americans from New Positions See Spires of Churches in Laon

Captors of Juvigny Now Nearing the Soissons-St. Quentin Highroad—German Shell Bursts Among 200 Prisoners in a Cave—Shift of Wind Blows German Gas Back on German Lines.

By EDWIN L. JAMES.

Copyright, 1918, by The New York Times Company.
Special Cable to THE NEW YORK TIMES.

WITH THE AMERICAN ARMY, Sept. 1.—North of Soissons the Americans have pushed on beyond Juvigny, through the Bois d'Alsace, and are nearing the Soissons-St. Quentin highway. During the night, with the French on the right, we gained possession of the hills controlling the village of Leury, which is now in possession of our allies.

Before the Americans lie Terny and Seray on the Soissons-St. Quentin road, important positions controlling the western end of the long plateau running along north of the Aisne and constituting the strength of the Germans' Chemin des Dames position. To hold this plateau the Germans have made all their violent counterattacks of the last five days.

Following the capture of Juvigny the Germans massed a strong force. The Americans yesterday pushed uphill beyond the village and gained a footing on the plateau, from which repeated counterattacks by a division of young Germans were unable to budge them.

The Americans took Juvigny by storm. After being held up for three days, gaining foot by foot and then being driven back foot by foot, our troops, after getting a good flank footing and following strong artillery, rushed the village. When our troops went through, right after our artillery work, the Germans not killed were hiding in the cellars and numerous caves of the place. In mopping up the village our men took some 250 prisoners, belonging to the 223d Division. In the meanwhile the French on both sides had pushed forward.

The spires of the churches of Laon are visible from our front line where it climbs the face of the plateau. After capturing the stubbornly defended village the Americans took a breathing spell and again at 10 o'clock yesterday morning attacked in force way up the hill beyond Juvigny on to the plateau.

Map Revealed Trap for Our Men.

Just before starting one of our officers killed a German officer, and on the body found a map showing an elaborate and extensive machine gun trap which had been set for the Americans in the woods lying on the slope. We delayed our attack long enough to have the 75s wipe out those machine gun nests, and then went ahead.

With the German established positions out of commission the fight became one of stalking, scouting, and hand-to-hand combats, at which our men fear no Germans. After six hours of bloody fighting we gained a position on the plateau, and we not only hold it, but have pushed ahead toward the highway in front of us.

Last night the German artillery work was light, and what shells came over were of large calibre. This indicates that the enemy is busy moving back the lighter artillery, and that heavier guns in position further back are firing on us.

It is believed that much further movement of the allied forces eastward on the plateau will cause the Germans to withdraw from the Vesle to the Aisne or even further back to the Chemins des Dames position. There have been as yet no indications along the Vesle front that the enemy has begun a general withdrawal in that sector, where American troops are facing him with French on either side.

American headquarters north of Soissons were the scene yesterday of a dramatic war incident. In the mouth of a large cave some 200 German prisoners were lying about when a six-inch boche shell landed in the midst of them, killing eight and wounding thirty. Before the crash of the shell had died away some of the prisoners started running into the cave.

Another party of prisoners began to run in another direction when a surprised American Sergeant opened up on them with an automatic. In the excitement some one gave the gas alarm and in the scuffle for masks three Americans couldn't find theirs. When the excitement died down three Germans were found to be wearing American gas masks.

One of the Germans killed, a mere boy of 17, had just before shown an American officer a letter from his mother telling him as

Continued on Page Two.

Americans Fight in Belgium; Strongholds Taken by Them

WITH THE BRITISH ARMY IN FLANDERS, Sept. 1, (Associated Press.)—For the first time, American troops fought on Belgian soil today.

They captured Voormezeele and were engaged in the operations elsewhere in the same locality.

LONDON, Sept. 1.—Reuter's correspondent at British Headquarters says he hears the Americans, besides taking Voormezeele, have captured several strong positions between Voormezeele and Ypres.

AUSTRALIAN DASH DOOMED PERONNE

Number of Prisoners Taken by Antipodeans Exceeds Their Losses Ten Times.

TANKS ASSAILED REDOUBTS

Germans in Their Desperate Need of Reserves Use Cavalrymen as Infantry.

By PHILIP GIBBS.

Copyright, 1918, by The New York Times Company.
Special Cable to THE NEW YORK TIMES.

WITH THE BRITISH ARMY, Sept. 1.—Peronne has fallen today in consequence of the Australians' brilliant attack yesterday which resulted in the capture of Mont St. Quentin.

One of the fine features of the capture of Mont St. Quentin was the rapid way in which the Australians moved their guns forward over the Somme and fired at close range on the enemy. This was largely due to the work of their engineers at the river crossings. At one of these they discovered several land mines laid by the Germans with trip wires artfully concealed, but they routed them out and prevented their explosion.

Part of the secret of the light Australian losses in this attack was the quick way in which they dived into the German trenches before clearing them, getting shelter there after they had taken 150 prisoners so that the hail of machine gun bullets passed harmlessly over their heads.

In the fighting from Aug. 26 until yesterday morning they took fully ten times more prisoners than their own total casualties, which must be a record in this war.

The individual gallantry of the men reached the high summit of audacity, as when an Australian Corporal in a recent action one day heard his comrades debating how they could destroy an enemy post which was giving them great trouble and said to them:

"That's all right, I'll take it." He slipped one Mill's bomb in his pocket, crawled through tall corn, jumped into the German trench, felled the first man he saw, and by sheer force of spirit so cowed the garrison of the German post that one officer and thirteen men surrendered to him.

It is in the centre of our battlefront, by Bullecourt and Riencourt and Ecoust and Vraucourt, now recaptured by us today, that the enemy has been putting up the fiercest resistance, and that our men have had hard and bitter fighting.

I have narrated how our London lads captured Croiselles a few days ago and went on to Bullecourt, which they took also by grim assault. West Lancashire troops, on their left, had attacked and taken Hendecourt and some of their patrols had entered Riencourt, while on the right of this line of attack some Liverpool and other English troops had entered Ecoust, Dongatte, and Vraucourt.

That was the situation on Thursday and Friday, but under a fierce counterattack this part of our line was hard pressed and not all the ground we had made could be kept. It threatened the enemy's main line of defense in the Drouicart-Quéant line, which he must hold at all costs to safeguard the whole of his

Continued on Page Three.

AUSTRALIANS WIN PERONNE

English Carry Outlying Towns to the North of the City.

BULLECOURT IS NOW BRITISH

Germans Lose Another Hindenburg Line Post and Continue Their Lys Retreat.

ALLIED GAINS ON AILETTE

French Advance on Both Banks; Americans Forge Ahead Two Miles Beyond Juvigny.

LONDON, Sept. 1.—Péronne, the German stronghold at the great bend of the Somme, fell today before the assaults of the Australians, who took two suburbs of the town in the same operation.

Co-operating with the Australians, London troops captured Bouchavesnes [four miles north of Péronne] and Rancourt [five miles], both villages on the road to Bapaume.

More than 2,000 prisoners were taken in these operations.

Further north the British drove the Germans from several villages south of Bapaume.

The struggle astride the Hindenburg line northeast of Bapaume continued with success for the British, who, according to Field Marshal Haig's night report, now hold the bitterly contested ruins of Bullecourt and Hendecourt.

The Germans continue to retreat, and the British to advance, in the Lys salient. Haig's troops are in close pursuit of the enemy, and, having occupied in the last twenty-four hours several villages in a strip of territory about two miles wide, along a considerable part of a twenty-mile front, are fighting on the western borders of Neuve Eglise and Wulverghem. [The latter town is less than two miles west of the famous Messines Ridge.]

The British have reached the suburbs of Lens. Large fires are burning in the neighborhood of Lens and Armentières. These are regarded as an indication of a further German retirement.

It is officially announced that the British captured in the month of August 57,318 German prisoners, 657 guns, more than 5,790 machine guns and 1,000 trench mortars, besides immense quantities of war material of every description.

Fierce Fighting at Bullecourt.

BRITISH HEADQUARTERS IN FRANCE, Sept. 1, (Canadian Press.)—Yesterday saw fighting on the front of the British armies from north of Voormezeele to the south of Péronne. On both flanks the British troops advanced victoriously.

In the centre they bitterly contested the vast network of defenses guarding the Drocourt line. The battle around Bullecourt, although resulting in only slight territorial changes, has been particularly bitter. Saturday a formidable station redoubt that had been previously taken and lost was recaptured.

On the right another British division was fighting its way valiantly through the honeycombed defenses of Ecoust and Longatte. Long after the assaulting waves had gained their objectives "mopping-up" parties would unearth machine gun burrows, getting as many as ten machine guns. Small tanks captured many dismounted troopers who had been hurriedly thrown in to replace the infantry. This is considered an indication of a serious shortage of German reserves.

The British casualties have been amazingly small, working out at one-tenth the number taken prisoners.

FRENCH OCCUPY LEURY; ADVANCE ON AILETTE

Americans, Pushing Beyond Juvigny, Take 600 German Prisoners and Much Booty.

LONDON, Sept. 1.—French troops under General Mangin achieved successes north and south of the Ailette

"All the News That's Fit to Print."

The New York Times.

THE WEATHER
Showers early, fair late today; tomorrow fair, cool; wind northwest.
For full weather report see Page 23.

VOL. LXVII...NO. 22,140. NEW YORK, FRIDAY, SEPTEMBER 6, 1918.—TWENTY-FOUR PAGES. TWO CENTS Metropolitan District 50 Mile Radius. | THREE CENTS Within 300 Miles. | FOUR CENTS Elsewhere.

FRENCH WIN 30 TOWNS IN AILETTE ADVANCE; OUR MEN DRIVE GERMANS ACROSS THE AISNE; BERLIN IS DECLARED IN A STATE OF SIEGE

CONTRACT WITH RAILROADS MADE PUBLIC BY M'ADOO

Companies Can Accept It or Go Into Court of Claims for Compensation.

SECURITY HOLDERS OBJECT

Say Terms for Return of Roads Are Unfair and Threaten Untold Loss.

McADOO DEFENDS CONTRACT

Sees Federal Control as a Blessing to Roads—Text of Contract in Full.

Special to The New York Times.

WASHINGTON, Sept. 5.—Director General McAdoo today announced the form of contract which the Government is willing to make with the railroads covering Federal control and the compensation they are to receive. No company is compelled to accept the form of contract the Government offers. It is made plain by Mr. McAdoo that any road is free to go into the United States Court of Claims for compensation.

"I am convinced, however," said Mr. McAdoo, "that the contract offered by the Government is just and reasonable. The railroad owners have no right to assume more than that, and, if the Government offers less, they are fully protected by their right to reject the Government's offer and go into the Court of Claims."

There are provisions in the contract for operation and accounting during Federal control, for the maintenance of the railway properties, on substantially the same basis as the three-year test period which ended June 30, 1917, and for the return of the properties at the end of Federal control in substantially as good repair and as complete in equipment as on Jan. 1, 1918. There is also provision for the payment of taxes in accordance with the Federal Control act. The annual compensation, which is to be fixed in the case of each railroad in accordance with the Federal Control act, is to be paid to each company in equal installments on the last day of March, June, September, and December of each year; the first two installments are to be due as of March 31, 1918, and June 30, 1918, and "shall be paid on the execution of this agreement."

Meeting on Contract Here Today.

The form of agreement is not altogether satisfactory to all of the railroad interests concerned. It is understood that there will be a meeting of railway Presidents in New York City tomorrow to consider their attitude toward the proposals.

Secretary McAdoo in an accompanying statement deals with some of the objections raised by interests concerned, and asserts that "these objections are, in my opinion, without foundation."

It was insisted by some of the interests heard that the contract offered by the Government ought to leave open for litigation at the end of Federal control the question whether the railroad had been damaged by diversion of its business during Federal control.

"This claim is untenable," says Mr. McAdoo, "because the railroads have been taken over for war purposes, which necessitate diversion of traffic, hence there can be no escape from the view that Congress intended the compensation which it authorized to cover this element. This demand of certain interests is, in effect, for an opportunity to litigate and is a demand which need not be urged if the railroad company, instead of making the contract offered, should instead go to the Court of Claims to get its compensation. In this event the railroad company would get only a single compensation, covering its entire claim, including any damages for alleged diversion, and would not be allowed to litigate at the end of Federal control the question of diversion of business."

Mr. McAdoo not only regards this demand as "unreasonable," but says he is advised by the Solicitor General that he has "no lawful authority" to grant it.

Mr. McAdoo also refused to accede to the view that the contract ought not to require a railroad company to pay out of its compensation such additional money as may be necessary to bring a railroad which at the beginning of Federal control was in unsafe condition up to a condition of safe operation. He also regarded as unreasonable the contention that no part of a railroad company's compensation should be used to pay its debts to the Government except such part as might remain after the company's payment of its customary dividends.

Condition of the Railroads.

During the arguments that were made in opposition to certain features of the proposed contract form it was contend-

Continued on Page Ten.

German Capital Under Restraint to Check the Growing Unrest

AMSTERDAM, Sept. 5, (Received in New York, Friday, Sept. 6, 3:30 A. M.)—A decree signed by General von Linsingen, commandant of the Brandenburg Province, according to the Cologne Volks-Zeitung, places the city of Berlin and the Province of Brandenburg under "the law relating to a state of siege, which provides for a fine or imprisonment for persons inventing or circulating untrue rumors calculated to disquiet the populace."

A notice accompanying the decree calls attention to the circulation of frivolous and sometimes malevolent and traitorous gossip, exaggerating the transitory success of the enemy and casting doubt upon Germany's power for an economic resistance and depreciating the wonderful achievements of the German troops, who it declares are victoriously withstanding the enemy.

General von Linsingen expresses the hope that this admonition will suffice and that it will not be necessary to enforce the decree. The Volks-Zeitung adds that similar decrees have been issued in Breslau and other cities, all operative immediately.

Geneva Hears Hertling Has Resigned

LONDON, Sept. 6.—Count George F. von Hertling the Imperial German Chancellor, has resigned, giving bad health as the cause of his retirement, according to the Geneva correspondent of The Daily Express, quoting a dispatch received in Geneva from Munich, Bavaria.

DRAFT RAIDS HERE ANGER SENATORS

Arrests Denounced by Chamberlain, Calder, and Others, and Inquiry Is Demanded.

PRESIDENT ASKS FOR FACTS

Calls on Gregory for a Full Report—Bielaski Assumes Responsibility.

Special to The New York Times.

WASHINGTON, Sept. 5.—A vehement attack was launched in the Senate today against the "slacker raids" in New York and elsewhere. After various Senators had condemned the raids, Senator Smoot offered a resolution, which went over until tomorrow, calling upon the Military Affairs Committee to ascertain who was responsible for the roundup and the reasons for it. The resolution follows:

"Whereas, The daily papers have reported the seizure or arrest and temporary incarceration of many thousand citizens, particularly in the State of New York; and, whereas, such reports indicate that in the so-called 'roundup' sailors and soldiers in the uniform of the United States participated; therefore,

"Be it resolved, That the Committee on Military Affairs be directed immediately to investigate and report upon such alleged occurrences and as to who was or is responsible, if any one, for the presence of such sailors and soldiers, or either, in such so-called 'roundup' or arrest; and who, if any one, issued orders, if any, resulting in the presence of such soldiers and sailors and their participation in the said occurrences if they were so present and did so participate."

While Senators Calder of New York, Chamberlain, of Oregon, Johnson of California, and others were bitter in their denunciation of the raids, Senator Poindexter of Washington defended them as a legitimate effort of the authorities to single out slackers.

President Wilson today called on Attorney General Gregory for a full report on all the circumstances connected with the roundup.

It was announced tonight that the roundup was made by direction of the Department of Justice and that A. Bruce Bielaski, chief of the department's Bureau of Investigation, assumed full responsibility for the arrests. It was also said that an officer of the Provost Marshal's office had assisted in directing the raids and that the Military Intelligence Bureau and some navy officers participated in them. Nothing was said, however, as to who had authorized the use of soldiers and sailors in the work.

Chamberlain Brings It Up.

Senator Chamberlain, Chairman of the Military Affairs Committee, brought the matter before the Senate in referring to reports in New York papers of the arrest of 40,000 men, only some 200 of whom, after their detention, actually were found to be slackers.

"There is not a man in the Senate or in the country who despises a man who undertakes to evade his military duty as much as I do," said Senator Chamberlain, "but, notwithstanding that, these men who are slackers ought to be reached by due process of law. The whole Department of Justice, the Intelligence Bureaus of the War and Navy Departments, all the American Defense Societies, the United States Marshals, and all the officers of the law have means and instrumentalities for reaching the slackers. But here we have an instance where thousands and

Continued on Page Twenty-four.

LISTS 150 CHIEFS OF U-BOATS SUNK

British Announcement Backs Lloyd George's Figures on Loss of Submarines.

WORST OFFENDERS HUNTED

Men Who Destroyed Lusitania, Arabic, and Belgian Prince Among Those Run Down.

LONDON, Sept. 5.—Although the British Government does not intend to adopt the practice of giving proof of official utterances made by its Ministers, it has been thought desirable to print in tomorrow's newspapers the names of the commanding officers of 150 German submarines which have been disposed of in order to substantiate the statement of Premier Lloyd George in the House of Commons that "at least 150 of these ocean pests have been destroyed." The statement to be published tomorrow does not include the names of officers commanding Austrian submarines put out of action.

A majority of the 150 officers mentioned are dead. Some of them are prisoners of war, and a few are interned in neutral countries where they took refuge.

Among the officers named are:

Kapitan-Lieutenant Schweiger, who, while in command of the U-20, torpedoed the Lusitania in May, 1915. The U-20 was lost on the Danish coast in 1916, but Schweiger survived and was in command of the U-80, which was lost with all hands in September, 1917.

Kapitan-Lieutenant Paul Wagenfukr, who sank the steamer Belgian Prince July 31, 1917, and drowned forty of the crew whom he had ordered to line up on the submarine's deck when the U-Boat was about to submerge. His submarine, the U-44, was sunk with all hands about a fortnight later.

Kapitan-Lieutenant Rudolph Schmeidder, who torpedoed the steamer Arabic in August, 1915.

The statement says it is significant that the authors of particularly atrocious crimes have expiated them speedily after their commission. It says that the names of such men are carefully noted by the British Admiralty, and that special endeavors are made to bring their active careers swiftly to an end. Several commanders, it is added, have escaped retribution by finding refuge in shore appointments.

Prominent among those named as having escaped retribution, but whom the British Navy has on its list, are, according to the statement:

Korvetten-Kapitan Max Falentiener, who was responsible for many sinkings of vessels, among them the Norwegian steamer Magda, the Spanish steamer Pena Castillo, the Italian steamer Ancona, and the British steamer Persia.

Kapitan-Lieutenant Wilhelm Werner for the sinking of hospital ships.

Korvetten-Kapitan Freiherr von Forstner, who, when in command of the U-28, sank the British steamers Falaba and Aguila.

DUTCH DEMAND ON GERMANY

"Merciless Action" of U-Boat Rouses Holland to Vigorous Protest.

THE HAGUE, Sept. 5.—It is officially announced that the Dutch Minister in Berlin has been instructed to protest vigorously against "the merciless action" of a German submarine in shelling a Dutch trawler off Krommenie, North Holland, Aug. 7, in which fishermen were killed, and to demand compensation.

REDS AT MOSCOW RAID CONSULATE OF GREAT BRITAIN

All England Roused Over the Killing of Captain Cromie at Petrograd.

CABINET'S STAND APPROVED

London Press Denounces Outrage as Considered Act of the Bolshevist Leaders.

CZECHS CAPTURE CHITA

Surrender of Red-Teuton Army in Siberia Expected—Italian Troops Land at Archangel.

LONDON, Sept. 5.—The British Consulate at Moscow has been attacked, according to the Central News today.

While the report has not been confirmed, it is felt in diplomatic circles only too likely to be true, and anxiety exists over the fate of R. H. Lockhart, the Acting Consul General, and J. O. Wardrop, the Consul, who have been waiting at Moscow for safe conduct.

It appears that the Soviet Government insisted that M. Litvinoff, Bolshevist Ambassador to Great Britain, should be sent to Bergen before it would agree to issue permission for Mr. Lockhart and Mr. Wardrop to depart. The British Government declined to agree to such an arrangement. According to The Evening News, Litvinoff, his secretary and another member of the Bolshevist faction now in London, have been taken to Brixton Prison.

The attack on the British Embassy in Petrograd last Saturday, involving the sacking of the embassy and the killing of Captain Cromie, the British attaché, has aroused intense indignation here. The London morning newspapers in their editorials denounce the act in the strongest terms and indorse the British Government's action in the demand upon the Bolshevist Government for reparation and the threat of outlawry for the members of the Soviet Government should it fail to give complete satisfaction or should further acts of violence be committed against British subjects. They assure the Government that it will have the support of the nation in enforcing the punishment of the perpetrators.

The Times says that the account of the affair given by the Bolshevist newspaper Pravda shows that it was a considered act of the Bolshevist Government and not a mere outbreak of brigandage. It calls for the exemplary punishment of the murderers and their accomplices. It approves the British warning against further acts of violence, adding that there are about 100 British subjects yet in that part of Russia in which the Bolsheviki rule.

The Daily Telegraph interprets the meaning of the outrage thus:

"The Bolshevist leaders know that their course is nearly run, and having waded in blood to power they are resolved to shed still more before the fatal hour strikes for their own bloody end."

The Chronicle asks how much longer the Russian people will endure the corrupt and bloodstained tyranny which has ruined a once great country and made it a by-word of contempt.

According to the Foreign Office's advices, Captain Cromie opposed the Bolshevist troops and killed three soldiers with his own hands. Captain Cromie was killed and his corpse was mutilated. The documents at the embassy were destroyed.

It is feared that similar outrages will be committed against the French Embassy at Petrograd. Precautionary measures have been taken, the Foreign Office says, and some French soldiers already have arrived at Petrograd. The Bolsheviki are reported to be encouraging the populace to massacre the British and French.

Captain Francis Cromie, who had received the Distinguished Service Order, was one of the first officers to command a submarine. At the outbreak of the war he commanded the Hongkong submarine flotilla. In 1915 he commanded the E-19 in the Baltic, which torpedoed a German destroyer and the German cruiser Undine and sank or captured ten German steamers.

In November, 1915, Captain Cromie assumed command of the Baltic flotilla. The Distinguished Service Order was awarded him in May, 1916, and then came a succession of Russian honors. During the Russian revolution he handled the situation with with the greatest tact, and earned the respect of the Extremists for his fair dealing. He was responsible in April, 1918, for the destruction and evacuation of the British submarines in the Baltic after the Germans had obtained control over the Baltic coast. He was appointed to the staff of the British Embassy at Petrograd because of his knowledge of Russian and the prevailing conditions.

AMSTERDAM, Sept. 5.—Details of the "search" of the British Embassy in Petrograd last Saturday are given in a dispatch from Moscow, quoting the newspaper Pravda. Forty persons, for the most part British subjects, were arrested, the newspaper states. The reasons for the action were that the Moscow authorities had received a report regarding a connection between various

Continued on Page Six.

MASS GUNS AGAINST TANKS

Land Cruisers Source of Grave Worry to German High Command.

REAR GUARDS DIE IN VAIN

Haig Continues to Upset Schedule of Retreat of Enemy's Main Forces.

KAISER'S ARMY DEPRESSED

Victorious British Sweep Forward Exultingly to Music of Bagpipes and Bands.

By PHILIP GIBBS.

Copyright, 1918, by The New York Times Company. Special Cable to THE NEW YORK TIMES.

WITH THE BRITISH ARMIES, Sept. 5.—The enemy is still falling back under the close pressure of our troops and fighting bitter rearguard actions at machine-gun range, but is forced to give ground everywhere in advance of his program of retirement. The vital part of his line is still in the country south of the Sensée River below Douai and west of Cambrai, and it is here our men are following up their breach in the Drocourt line and driving spearheads into his positions eastward.

The German troops had been ordered to hold the line of the Tortille River and the crossings of the Canal du Nord, north of Péronne, at all costs in order to delay our advance, but in spite of holding the banks with fierce machine-gun fire, they were unable to prevent the passage of the English and Welsh battalions who attacked yesterday morning with the greatest gallantry, threw a bridge across under heavy fire and gained the other side of the canal.

Our troops then advanced before the retiring enemy and drove his rearguards out of the villages of Manancourt and Etricourt, and today are making further progress toward our old lines around Cambrai salient, which we took in a surprise attack last November.

Further north this movement is linked up with the still more important progress of the English troops around Moeuvres, which they entered yesterday, and north of the old Hindenburg line beyond Quéant and Inchy.

Garrisons Fight to Check Advance.

In all these villages northward from Péronne and westward of Cambrai the German garrisons are fighting desperately to gain time for the retreat of the main forces, who are burning their stores behind them, and their machine gunners are skilful and courageous, and as a rule do not escape or surrender until our men are close to them.

They have stronger support from the artillery, which is increasing along our front now that the German gunners withdrawn after the first panic caused by our break through of the Drocourt line have taken up new positions. Obeying the orders of the German command they are now disposing guns in great depth, with some very close to our lines, in order to destroy approaching tanks.

That menace is a cause of constant anxiety to the German command, as well it may be, and they are taking every means to check its demoralizing effect on their troops. "To present rumors about tanks alleged to have broken through," says a recent order, "denials will forthwith be communicated to all ranks."

The state of things behind the German lines undoubtedly is very distressing to them and full of grave weakness. One hesitates to emphasize the demoralization of the German infantry, which may be only a passing phase, due to the present disasters, but that it exists for the

Continued on Page Two.

Marne Anniversary Finds Foe Wearing Down; Losses Since March 21 Estimated at 1,200,000

By G. H. PERRIS.

Copyright, 1918, by The New York Times Company. Special Cable to THE NEW YORK TIMES.

WITH THE FRENCH ARMIES, Sept. 5.—Today is the fourth anniversary of the Battle of the Marne and of Joffre's memorable summons: "At the moment when a battle is joined on which depends the salvation of the country, every one must be reminded that the time has gone for looking backward. Troops who can no longer advance must at any cost hold the ground won and be slain rather than give way. In the present circumstances no failure can be tolerated."

The recollection of this famous victory at the moment when the Allies are again driving back the same enemy suggests thoughts, some of an encouraging and some of a sobering kind. The Central Powers, long prepared and greatly profiting by the Bolshevist pestilence, have been worn down, while the Grand Alliance is far from reaching its full strength, but the end is not yet.

Germany is still strong despite her defeats. Of her total of 245 divisions she has about 200 in the west. They are all much weakened. The reserve has fallen some fifty divisions since the beginning of the March offensive, that is to say, the equivalent of all the forces brought back from Russia has now been devoured.

A conservative estimate shows that the German losses since March 21 must total about 1,200,000 men, of whom, however, 60 per cent. would be capable of recuperating after an interval of from three to six months, leaving the permanent loss at about 500,000 men. The toll on the allied side has been nothing like so great.

The crisis of the enemy for effectives is certainly acute. The 1919 class is wholly engaged and has proved to be of inferior quality, doubtless because of the deprivation amid which it has grown up.

The 1920 class can hardly be better. The German Government has postponed its engagement as long as possible, drafting instead every man it can find capable of carrying a rifle. It has also cut down the battalion and company strength and is known to have dissolved at least forty regiments.

The Americans are now sending reinforcements every month equal to half of a year's German recruits.

These are grounds of confidence provided that the allied effort is sustained to the end. They provide no excuse for the view that the war is won or will run itself to a victorious conclusion. The German divisions still in reserve with the 1920 class in the field depots constitute a force not to be despised. The German Staff has scraped and saved in order to keep a mass of manoeuvre intact.

The enemy retreat in the last seven weeks has been for the most part compelled, but there has been in it also an element of choice. It procured a material shortening of the front on which it holds off the Allies. As long as the Allies can maintain unrelenting pressure they can keep the initiative, but if they let go Ludendorff will have a chance.

The allied effort of seven weeks is without a precedent. How long can it be continued? Distinguished soldiers ask this question not at all in anxiety or doubt of the army, but in fear lest exaggeration of the value of the present allied victories should lead to a slackening of the spirit that has sustained the alliance through four terrible years.

Germany is depressed and its army badly shaken, but its governing class still governs according to its own will, and still has powerful means in hand. Even now, when the Allies begin to see clearly it would be dangerous to underestimate such an enemy or take anything for granted in which he is concerned.

KAISER NOW TALKS OF DEFENSIVE WAR

Significance Also Seen in Crown Prince's Change from a Policy of Annihilation.

RULER HONORS KUEHLMANN

He Was Forced Out, Says Vorwaerts, for Smaller Offense Than the Crown Prince's.

By GEORGE RENWICK.

Copyright, 1918, by The New York Times Company. Special Cable to THE NEW YORK TIMES.

AMSTERDAM, Sept. 5.—Is it all beginning to tell at last, after weeks of extreme dullness, after many desperate efforts to hide the truth regarding the Fatherland's general situation? An important section of the German press today presented to the world a series of highly noteworthy items which illuminate the whole position in remarkable fashion.

The Kaiser in his latest utterance does not talk of victory by the sword and the annihilation of the enemy, but in a message which, according to the Lokal-Anzeiger, his Majesty has sent to the City of Dresden, he refers to the severity of the Fatherland's fight for its future and to the German people's determination to preserve their land and Kultur by "successful defense."

Then the official Reichsanzeiger states that his Majesty has been pleased to confer the Order of the Red Eagle of the First Class upon Herr von Kühlmann.

The Crown Prince, as Vorwärts rightly insists, has out-Kühlmanned the late Minister for Foreign Affairs, and, finally, the Cologne Gazette admits the serious economic situation of Germany and violently attacks the Wolff Bureau for its falsehoods. One could hardly expect a larger harvest in a day.

Compares Prince and Kuehlmann.

"Democracy is the necessity of our life," cries Vorwärts in a great headline across its front page, and it then deals with the Crown Prince in a high-

Continued on Page Two.

DYNASTY AT STAKE, HERTLING ASSERTS

Prussian Franchise Reform Fight Involves the German Crown, He Tells Lords.

REJECTS THE PRESENT BILL

Teutons Show Bitter Disappointment Over the Loss of Mount Kemmel.

AMSTERDAM, Sept. 5.—In appealing to the Constitution Committee of the Prussian Upper House to fulfill the Emperor's pledge for reform of the franchise, Chancellor von Hertling said that, in his honest conviction, "with this serious question the protection and the preservation of the crown and the dynasty are at stake."

Count von Hertling's address was delivered at the opening of the discussion by the committee on the Prussian franchise reform question.

"The Government," said the Chancellor, "considers that its task is to bring to fulfillment the royal pledge expressed in the July message. As all the sons of the Fatherland are defending the Fatherland, there is now no question of social discrimination at the next election.

"The object is one which I undertook to achieve when I accepted office and upon which I intend to stand or fall, but it is no question of Ministerial responsibility in the ordinary political sense. My honest conviction is that with this serious question the protection and the preservation of the crown and the dynasty are at stake.

"Therefore, endeavor to find a road that leads to an understanding. The Government sees no possibility of approving the bill in the form in which it came from the lower house.

"I fully appreciate the scruples regarding the introduction of general, equal suffrage but at the present time these scruples must give way to greater tasks, namely, the protection of the most precious treasures of our political life—the dynasty and the crown. The Government will exercise no pressure on you."

Apparently it has not been possible to hide from the German people the bitter disappointment among the German military authorities over the evacuation of Kemmel, one of the strategic strongholds southwest of Ypres. The Lokal-Anzeiger's military correspondent says that the evacuation was effected "with

Continued on Page Two.

COUCY IS IN FRENCH HANDS

Its Capture an Added Menace to the Chemin des Dames.

BIG GAINS NORTH OF VESLE

Allies Have Cleared Eight Miles of the Southern Bank of the Aisne.

BRITISH NEARER CAMBRAI

Continued Pressure Improves Their Positions North and South of Peronne.

Will Pursue Foe Implacably, Foch Tells Paris Council

PARIS, Sept. 5.—In a telegram replying to the congratulations of the Paris Municipal Council Marshal Foch, Commander in Chief of the Entente allied forces, thanked the council in his own name and on behalf of the French and allied armies, and added:

"The German rush which menaced Paris and Amiens has been broken. We will continue to pursue the enemy implacably."

LONDON, Sept. 5.—The French armies have today driven the Germans before them in Southern Picardy and, with the co-operation of the Americans, in the territory lying between the Vesle and Aisne Rivers.

In their advance along the whole Ailette front they have occupied more than thirty villages.

The Germans offered considerable resistance at certain points, but failed to check the advance, which in some parts of the line amounted to about seven miles.

Pushing eastward and southward from the Canal du Nord, [the waterway from Noyon to the neighborhood of Nesle, which should not be confused with the canal of the same name running north from Péronne,] the French crossed the Somme Canal at several points, approaching Ham, with its roads leading to St. Quentin and La Fère.

Further south, by their capture of Coucy-le-Château and several neighboring towns, they threaten the wooded defenses of the Chemin des Dames.

At Landricourt, near the edge of the Coucy forest, they are in possession of a part of their old front as it stood before the German offensive.

North of the Vesle, where Americans have taken part in the advance, the allied line has been pushed to the southern bank of the Aisne on a front of eight miles or more.

Germans North of the Aisne.

WITH THE AMERICAN ARMY ON THE AISNE FRONT, Sept. 5, (Associated Press.)—With the exception of a few machine gun detachments, left to sacrifice themselves in an effort to cover the retreat, the Germans were on the north side of the Aisne tonight.

The American and French troops, who have followed closely on the heels of the enemy since the evacuation of the Vesle Valley began, were still in contact, harassing the rearguard and hastening the movement of the whole force.

Long before nightfall the Americans had worked their way down into the lowlands toward the Aisne, off the plateau, from which they had been able to look over the next valley at the Cathedral towers in Laon, not fifteen miles away.

At that point is located the heart of the present German operations. Laon is a great communication center and must naturally be defended with the utmost determination if the allied forces are to be prevented from driving back to it the German lines from west and south.

The retirement of the Germans to positions north of the Aisne is regarded as only preliminary to their reoccupation of their old lines of defense along the Chemin des Dames. With their recrossing of the Aisne the second phase of the retreat from the Marne is ended.

The Present a Strategic Retreat.

In the first they were driven back mile by mile, and desperate fighting marked almost every bit of the terri-

Mid-Week Pictorial

French troops in a shell hole in southern France.

Mid-Week Pictorial

Kaiser Wilhelm, with his staff officers, tours the battlefield at Cambrai.

"All the News That's Fit to Print."

The New York Times.

THE WEATHER
Cloudy today; local showers; Tuesday fair; moderate south winds.
For full weather report see Page 19.

VOL. LXVII...NO. 22,150. ... NEW YORK, MONDAY, SEPTEMBER 16, 1918.—TWENTY PAGES. TWO CENTS Metropolitan District 50 Mile Radius. | THREE CENTS Within 200 Miles. | FOUR CENTS Elsewhere.

AUSTRIA APPEALS FOR A GENERAL PEACE, GERMANY FOLLOWS WITH OFFER TO BELGIUM; AMERICANS ADVANCE ON A 33-MILE FRONT

OUR AVERAGE GAIN 3 MILES

Guns of Metz Forts Now in Action Against Our Line.

PERSHING WINS ON MOSELLE

Captures Villages of Norroy and Vilcey—Total of Guns Taken Is 200.

GERMANS BEGIN DIGGING IN

Apparently Planning to Protect Railroads to Metz, Which Are Under Our Fire.

A "Magnificent Victory," Foch's Word to Pershing

By EDWIN L. JAMES.
Special Cable to THE NEW YORK TIMES.

WITH THE AMERICAN ARMY IN FRANCE, Sept. 15.—General Pershing has received from the allied Generalissimo the following message:

My Dear General:

The 1st American Army, under your command, on this first day won a magnificent victory by a manoeuvre as skillfully prepared as it was gallantly executed.

I extend to you, as well as to the officers and troops under your command, my warmest compliments.

MARSHAL FOCH.

LONDON, Sept. 15. — General Pershing's army is making fine progress. This afternoon it had advanced two to three miles on a thirty-three-mile front since yesterday afternoon, and the fortress guns of Metz have come into action against it.

American patrols are advancing at various points a couple of miles beyond the general advance.

The enemy appears to be withdrawing to some line which will protect the railway communications in the vicinity of Metz, which at present are under the long-range gunfire of the Americans.

The American line at noon today ran through Norroy, on the Moselle, Haumont, Doncourt and to Abaucourt [on the Verdun-Etain road] on the old line.

It has been discovered that there were six German divisions operating in the St. Mihiel salient. That would give a total strength of 60,000 men, or a rifle strength of 36,000. The Germans had broken up for them two more divisions in this action, thus reducing their strength in the west to 191 divisions, plus four Austrian divisions and some dismounted cavalry.

An unofficial report from the American front on the Moselle says that American patrols are approaching Pagny, on the west bank of that river.

German Defense Is Weak.

WITH THE AMERICAN ARMY IN LORRAINE, Sept. 15, (Associated Press.)—The advance of the victorious First Army continued today, but on a restricted front near the Moselle River. There was little opposition on the whole.

In the edge of a wood where the Germans had concentrated some smart machine-gun resistance was offered, but a smashing artillery fire silenced the enemy. A few additional prisoners were taken.

The Germans gave further evidence today that they intended to resist on that part of the Hindenburg line running through this sector. A detachment was digging in today about Dommartin [four and a half miles north of Thiaucourt], while between La Chaussée [two and a half

Continued on Page Six.

Austria's Statement and Her Note to the Powers

AMSTERDAM, Sept. 15, (by Associated Press.)— The official communication of the Austro-Hungarian Government and the text of its note to belligerent and neutral powers, suggesting a meeting for a preliminary and non-binding discussion of war aims, with a view to the possible calling of a peace conference, are as follows:

The Communication:

An objective and conscientious examination of the situation of all the belligerent States no longer leaves doubt that all peoples, on whatever side they may be fighting, long for a speedy end to the bloody struggle. Despite this natural and comprehensible desire for peace, it has not so far been possible to create those preliminary conditions calculated to bring the peace efforts nearer to realization and bridge the gap which at present still separates the belligerents from one another.

A more effective means must therefore be considered whereby the responsible factors of all the countries can be offered an opportunity to investigate the present possibilities of an understanding.

The first step which Austria-Hungary, in accord with her allies, undertook on Dec. 12, 1916, for the bringing about of peace did not lead to the end hoped for.

The grounds for this lay assuredly in the situation at that time. In order to maintain in their peoples the war spirit, which was steadily declining, the allied Governments had by the most severe means suppressed even any discussion of the peace idea. And so it came about that the ground for a peace understanding was not properly prepared. The natural transition from the wildest war agitation to a condition of conciliation was lacking.

It would, however, be wrong to believe that the peace step we then took was entirely without result. Its fruits consist of something which is not to be overlooked—that the peace question has not since vanished from the order of the day. The discussions which have been carried on before the tribunal of public opinion have disclosed proof of the not slight differences which today still separate the warring powers in their conception of peace conditions.

Nevertheless an atmosphere has been created which no longer excludes the discussion of the peace problem.

Without optimism, it at least assuredly may be deduced from the utterances of responsible statesmen that the desire to reach an understanding and not to decide the war exclusively by force of arms is also gradually beginning to penetrate into allied States save for some exceptions in the case of blinded war agitators, which are certainly not to be estimated lightly.

The Austro-Hungarian Government is aware that after the deep-reaching convulsions which have been caused in the life of the peoples by the devastating effects of the world war it will not be possible to re-establish order in the tottering world at a single stroke. The path that leads to the restoration of peaceful relations between the peoples is cut by hatred and embitterment. It is toilsome and wearisome, yet it is our duty to tread this path—the path of negotiation—and if there are still such responsible factors as desire to overcome the opponent by military means and to force the will to victory upon him, there can, nevertheless, no longer be doubt that this aim, even assuming that it is attainable, would first necessitate a further sanguinary and protracted struggle.

But even a later victorious peace will no longer be able to make good the consequences of such a policy—consequences which will be fatal to all the States and peoples of Europe. The only peace which could righteously adjust the still divergent conceptions of the opponents would be a peace desired by all the peoples. With this consciousness, and in its unswerving endeavor to work in the interests of peace, the Austro-Hungarian Government now again comes forward with a suggestion with the object of bringing about a direct discussion between the enemy powers.

The earnest will to peace of wide classes of the population of all the States who are jointly suffering through the war—the indisputable rapprochement in individual controversial questions—as well as the more conciliatory atmosphere that is general, seem to the Austro-Hungarian Government to give a certain guarantee that a fresh step in the interests of peace, which also takes account of past experiences in this domain, might at the present moment offer the possibility of success.

The Austro-Hungarian Government has therefore resolved to point out to all the belligerents, friend and foe, a path considered practicable by it, and to propose to them jointly to examine in a free exchange of views whether those prerequisites exist which would make the speedy inauguration of peace negotiations appear promising. To this end the Austro-Hungarian Government has today invited the Governments of all the belligerent States to a confidential and unbinding discussion at a neutral meeting place, and has addressed to them a note drawn up in this sense.

This step has been brought to the knowledge of the Holy See in a special note, and an appeal thereby made to the Pope's interest in peace. Furthermore, the Governments of the neutral States have been acquainted with the step taken.

The constant close accord which exists between the four allied powers warrants the assumption that the allies of Austria-Hungary, to whom the proposal is being sent in the same manner, share the views developed in the note.

[The official telegram proceeds to say that the note has been drawn up in French, and runs as follows:]

Text of the Note to the Powers:

The peace offer which the Powers of the Quadruple Alliance addressed to their opponents on Dec. 12, 1916, and the conciliatory basic ideas of which they have never given up, signifies, despite the rejection which it experienced, an important stage in the history of this war. In contrast to the first two and a half war years, the question of peace has from that moment been the centre of European, aye, of world discussion, and dominates it in ever increasing measure.

Almost all the belligerent States have in turn again and again expressed themselves on the question of peace, its prerequisites and conditions. The line of development of this discussion, however, has not been uniform and steady. The basic standpoint changed under the influence of the military and political position, and hitherto, at any rate, it has not led to a tangible general result that could be utilized.

It is true that, independent of all these oscillations, it can be stated that the distance between the conceptions of the two sides has, on the whole, grown somewhat less; that despite the indisputable continuance of decided and hitherto unbridged differences, a partial turning from many of the most extreme concrete war aims is visible and a certain agreement upon the relative general basic principles of a world peace manifests itself. In both camps there is undoubtedly observable in wide classes of the population a growth of the will to peace and understanding. Moreover, a comparison of the reception of the peace proposal of the Powers of the Quadruple Alliance on the part of their opponents with the later utterances of responsible statesmen of the latter, as well as of the non-responsible but, in a political respect, nowise uninfluential personalities, confirms this impression.

While, for example, the reply of the Allies to President Wilson made demands which amounted to the dismemberment of Austria-Hungary, to a diminution and a deep internal transformation of the German Empire, and the destruction of Turkish European ownership, these demands, the realization of which was based on the supposition of an overwhelming victory, were later modified in many declarations from official Entente quarters, or in part were dropped.

Thus, in a declaration made in the British House of Commons a year ago, Secretary Balfour expressly recognized that Austria-Hungary must itself solve its internal problems, and that none could impose a Constitution upon Germany from the outside. Premier Lloyd George declared at the beginning of this year that it was not one of the Allies' war aims to partition Austria-Hungary, to rob the Ottoman Empire of its Turkish provinces, or to reform Germany internally. It may also be considered symptomatic that in December, 1917, Mr. Balfour categorically repudiated the assumption that British policy had ever engaged itself for the creation of an independent State out of the territories on the left bank of the Rhine.

The Central Powers leave it in no doubt that they are only waging a war of defense for the integrity and the security of their territories.

Far more outspoken than in the domain of concrete war aims has the rapprochement of conceptions proceeded regarding those guiding lines upon the basis of which peace shall be concluded and the future order of Europe and the world built up. In this direction President Wilson in his speeches of Feb. 12 and July 4 of this year has formulated principles which have not encountered contradiction on the part of his allies, and the far-reaching application of which is likely to meet with no objection on the part of the Powers of the Quadruple Alliance also, presupposing that this application is general and reconcilable with the vital interests of the States concerned.

It is true it must be remembered that an agreement on general principles is insufficient, but that there remains the further matter of reaching an accord upon their interpretation and their application to individual concrete war and peace questions.

To an unprejudiced observer there can be no doubt that in all the belligerent States, without exception, the desire for a peace of understanding has been enormously strengthened; that the conviction is increasingly spreading that the further continuance of the bloody struggle must transform Europe into ruins and into a state of exhaustion that will mar its development for decades to come, and this without any guarantee of thereby bringing about that decision by arms which has been vainly striven after by both sides in four years filled with enormous sacrifices, sufferings, and exertions.

In what manner, however, can the way be paved for an understanding, and an understanding finally attained? Is there any serious prospect whatever of reaching this aim by continuing the discussion of the peace problem in the way hitherto followed?

We have not the courage to answer the latter question in the affirmative. The discussion from one public tribune to another, as has hitherto taken place between statesmen of the various countries, was really only a series of monologues. It lacked, above everything, directness. Speech and counterspeech did not fit into each other. The speakers spoke over one another's heads.

On the other hand, it was the publicity and the ground of these discussions which robbed them of the possibility of fruitful progress. In all public statements of this nature a form of eloquence is used which reckons with the effect at great distances and on the masses. Consciously or unconsciously, however, one thereby increases the distance of the opponents' conception, produces misunderstandings which take root and are not removed, and makes the frank exchange of ideas more difficult. Every pronouncement of leading statesmen is, directly after its delivery and before the authoritative quarters of the opposite side can reply to it, made the subject of passionate or exaggerated discussion of irresponsible elements.

But anxiety lest they should endanger the interests of their arms by unfavorably influencing feeling at home, and lest they prematurely betray their own ultimate intentions, also causes the responsible statesmen themselves to strike a higher tone and stubbornly to adhere to extreme standpoints.

If, therefore, an attempt is made to see whether the basis exists for an understanding calculated to deliver Europe from the catastrophe of the suicidal continuation of the struggle, then, in any case, another method should be chosen which renders possible a direct, verbal discussion between the representatives of the Governments, and only between them. The opposing conceptions of individual belligerent States would likewise have to form the subject of such a discussion, for mutual enlightenment, as well as the general principles that shall serve as the basis for peace and the future relations of the States to one another, and regarding which, in the first place, an accord can be sought with a prospect of success.

As soon as an agreement were reached on the fundamental principles, an attempt would have to be made in the course of the discussions concretely to apply them to individual peace questions, and thereby bring about their solution.

We venture to hope that there will be no objection on the part of any belligerents to such an exchange of views. The war activities would experience no interruption. The discussions, too, would only go so far as was considered by the participants to offer a prospect of success. No disadvantages would arise therefrom for the States represented. Far from harming, such an exchange of views could only be useful to the cause of peace.

What did not succeed the first time can be repeated, and perhaps it has already at least contributed to the clarification of views. Mountains of old misunderstandings might be removed and many new things perceived. Streams of pent-up human kindness would be released, in the warmth of which everything essential would remain, and, on the other hand, much that is antagonistic, to which excessive importance is still attributed, would disappear.

According to our conviction, all the belligerents jointly owe to humanity to examine whether now, after so many years of a costly but undecided struggle, the entire course of which points to an understanding, it is possible to make an end to the terrible grapple.

The Royal and Imperial Government would like, therefore, to propose to the Governments of all the belligerent States to send delegates to a confidential and unbinding discussion on the basic principles for the conclusion of peace, in a place in a neutral country and at a near date that would yet have to be agreed upon—delegates who were charged to make known to one another the conception of their Governments regarding those principles and to receive analogous communications, as well as to request and give frank and candid explanations on all those points which need to be precisely defined.

The Royal and Imperial Government has the honor to request the Government of ——, through the kind mediation of your Excellency, to bring this communication to the knowledge of the Government of ——.

[The names of the intermediary Government and of that addressed in the particular note dispatched are left blank.]

WASHINGTON IS HOSTILE

Feeling There that 'Force Without Stint' Should Answer Foe's Offer.

OFFICIALS AWAIT TEXT

White House Comment Withheld, but It Is Believed Overture Will Be Rejected.

FORMAL REPLY TO BE MADE

President Will Act After Full Consideration and Conference with Allies.

Special to The New York Times.

WASHINGTON, Sept. 15.—The feeling in Washington tonight is that "force without stint" until victory is achieved and a rejection of the overture will be the American Government's response to the Austro-Hungarian Government's invitation to all the belligerent powers to send delegates to some neutral meeting place to enter into nonbinding discussions with a view to peace.

Official comment on the Austrian communication was withheld tonight pending the official receipt of the message, which is probably being forwarded through the courtesy of the Swedish Government. But the unofficial text of the note reached Washington through news channels tonight, and after its contents had become known the most careful canvass of the situation failed to detect any disposition on the part of the Washington Government to accept the invitation to enter at this time such a conference as has been proposed by the Vienna Government.

Secretary Lansing declined to comment on the note, and, in the absence of the official text or of an exchange of views with our allies, no statement, naturally, was forthcoming for publication from the White House.

Note Will Be Answered.

There is no disposition to deal cavalierly with the communication from the Austrian Government. It will receive the same careful consideration that has been accorded by President Wilson and Secretary Lansing to the earlier peace overtures made by the German and Austrian Governments.

The communication is of a character that calls for a response, and there will be a reply. How that answer will be given remains to be determined after the Washington Government has had full opportunity to exchange views with its allies.

The substantially unanimous view of Congressional leaders, regardless of party affiliations, is that this is not the time to enter into peace discussions with the Central Powers. They feel that the tide of battle turned when the Germans were turned back from the Marne at Château-Thierry; that the initiative gained by the allied forces under the masterly leadership of Marshal Foch will be retained, and that the achievements of General Pershing's forces, as well as the victories of the British, French, and Italians, assure a victorious ending of the war on such terms as the Allies are disposed to grant.

The Administration attitude toward the continuation of the war toward a victorious end was voiced by General March in his talk with the Washington newspaper correspondents yesterday, by Secretary Tumulty the day before in his letter to Chairman Hays of the Republican National Committee, and ever since the President's milestone speech at Baltimore last Spring, in which he declared it to be the purpose to fight Germany with "force without stint." The President himself has emphasized and driven home the idea that this war is one of emancipation, and should be continued until it has been conclusively won.

No Inconclusive Peace.

"The President's war aims," said Mr. Tumulty in his letter to Chairman Hays on Sept. 12, a letter read by President Wilson before it was dispatched, "have been made the aims of all the nations fighting against the German Government. These aims have been stated unequivocally by the President upon a number of occasions since the war began. Not merely the American people, but all the world is familiar with these aims,

Teutonic Allies Agreed Austria Should Make a Bid for Peace

Kaiser Karl's Government Forced Germany to Consent at Recent Headquarters Conclave—Appeal to Catch Entente Pacifists and, Through Rejection, to Silence Cry at Home for Peace.

By GEORGE RENWICK.
Copyright, 1918, by The New York Times Company.
Special Cable to THE NEW YORK TIMES.

AMSTERDAM, Sept. 15.—The Austrian proposal for a peace conference, as I have good grounds for knowing, was first seriously considered at the recent imposing meeting at German headquarters. In fact, it is now quite clear that it was the only subject discussed at any length during the gathering.

So insistent was the Austrian demand that such a step should be taken that the German Government had to give rather unwilling consent. In doing so, according to my information, it acted in the hope that such a move might have a certain influence on Entente pacifists, whom the German Government persists in believing to be a very much stronger force than they really are.

It was thought, too, that the proposal might be not without effect in the event of a British general election, but, above all, that the German powers that be consented largely because of the renewed cry of peace. An offer mockingly rejected would be highly valuable at home.

Opposed by Military Men.

It is beyond all doubt that the German military authorities and the German Government do not want any such conference as Austria-Hungary suggests. I say the German Government without reservation because von Payer's speech clearly demonstrates that despite some advances there are no elements in the administration inclined or bold enough to break sufficiently away from Pan Germanism to make negotiations remotely posible for the Entente.

Much which I have recently reported regarding the state of affairs in

Continued on Page Two.

Germany Wants Belgium to Help Her Obtain the Return of Her Colonies

Proposes That Kingdom, Its Economic and Political Independence Restored, Shall Be Neutral—Germany Through Finland Also Offers Not to Invade Karelia if Allies Will Quit Murman Coast.

LONDON, Sept. 15.—Germany has made a definite peace offer to Belgium, according to information received here. The terms of this proposal are as follows:

That Belgium shall remain neutral until the end of the war.

That thereafter the entire economic and political independence of Belgium shall be reconstituted.

That the pre-war commercial treaties between Germany and Belgium shall again be put into operation after the war for an indefinite period.

That Belgium shall use her good offices to secure the return of the German colonies.

That the Flemish question shall be considered and the Flemish minority, which aided the German invaders, shall not be penalized.

The proposal contains no word respecting reparation or indemnities, no admission that Germany wronged Belgium.

It is understood that the Government has received the Austro-Hungarian peace note, and also a proposal that all the powers should withdraw their troops from the Murman territory.

Copyright, 1918, by The New York Times Company.
Special Cable to THE NEW YORK TIMES.

LONDON, Sept. 15.—It is not only toward Belgium that German secret diplomacy has been stretching out its tentacles in the hope of catching and breaking some of the strands of the Entente. Definite information of one other offer which will be made public in due time has reached THE NEW YORK TIMES.

These backstairs efforts, which in the main are chiefly concerned with exchanging "pawns" which Germany holds for colonial possessions whence Kaiserdom can draw raw material after the war, afford some indication of the uses to which Germany would put the confidential conference asked

Continued on Page Two.

London Regards the Proposals as Insincere Manoeuvers by Foe

Austrian Plea Will Be Considered, It Is Thought—If Reply Is Sent, Wilson May Be Spokesman—No Peace Requirements Met, It Is Held.

Copyright, 1918, by The New York Times Company.
Special Cable to THE NEW YORK TIMES.

LONDON, Sept. 15.—It is stated here that Austria's invitation to preliminary unbinding peace discussions will receive the full consideration of the allied Governments. This statement may be taken to mean nothing more than it literally says. Whatever form it may be decided by the allied Governments, who will act as one in accordance with the stipulations of the pact of London, to give to the reply, or whether any reply will be made by the Entente powers, individually or unitedly, cannot, of course, be yet stated, for there has been no time for consultation, but it is suggested that probabilities are that the Entente powers will simply notify the Austrian Government that they have taken notice of the proposals made and leave it at that.

Another suggestion is that President Wilson, whose expression of the Allies' policy has won universal admiration, will again act as spokesman of all the powers arrayed against Austria-Hungary and her confederates. In some quarters it is believed that Lloyd George had foreknowledge of the Austrian move, and that his speech at Manchester, in which he said victory was essential to a sound peace, sounded the note on which allied consideration of the Austrian note will be pitched.

The first impression today was that acceptance of Austria's invitation could have but one of two results, either it would prolong the war or it would lead toward an unsatisfactory peace, in which would be found the germs of future wars.

The Austrian proposals meet none of the requirements which British statesmen have laid down as essential preliminaries to peace discussions. It is also held here that they omit to take into consideration the vital point that President Wilson has laid down certain

Continued on Page Two.

"All the News That's Fit to Print."

The New York Times.

THE WEATHER
Partly cloudy today; Friday fair; moderate west winds.
For full weather report see Page 22.

VOL. LXVII...NO. 22,153. ••• NEW YORK, THURSDAY, SEPTEMBER 19, 1918.—TWENTY-FOUR PAGES. TWO CENTS Metropolitan District 50 Mile Radius. | THREE CENTS Within 200 Miles. | FOUR CENTS Elsewhere.

HAIG AND PETAIN PIERCE HINDENBURG LINE; TAKE 10 TOWNS, 6,000 MEN IN 22-MILE DRIVE; SERBS AND FRENCH DRIVE BULGARS 10 MILES

AUSTRIAN NOTE A DISTRESS CRY IS LONDON'S VIEW

Peace Move Believed to Have Been Prompted by Urgent Pressure of Conditions.

KAISER'S NERVES FAILING

British Capital Expecting Some Sensational Happening Behind German Scenes.

PEACE OPINION DIVIDED

Talk in Some British Quarters of Leaving an Open Door for Further Proposals.

Copyright, 1918, by The New York Times Company.
Special Cable to THE NEW YORK TIMES.

LONDON, Sept. 18.—The view that the Austrian peace note was issued under urgent pressure of conditions within the Central Empires is supported by all information that leaks across the frontiers. Responsible opinion in this country has always protested against any undue hopes being founded on the economical stress in Germany and Austria, and the British public has been urged to remember the extraordinary power of the human race to adapt themselves to a much lower scale of living, and the hopelessness of an attempt at revolution by old men, women, and children in these days of machine guns.

But in the last few days, rumors have taken on a new complexion. They are unconfirmed, but they point to some sensational happening behind the scenes in Germany. The Kaiser's recent speech to the Krupp workmen proves how overwrought he is, and certain passages in it, censored as they were, as the German press has complained, hardly read like the utterances of a sane man. There may consequently be some ground for the story that he is suffering from severe nervous breakdown.

Another rumor has it that the Kaiser, foreseeing the utter ruin of his house, is contemplating one of those dramatic moves so characteristic of his temperament. One of his most renowned predecessors, it is remembered, Charles V., in the sixteenth century, left the world for a monastery; and if he really may be thinking of some spectacular act of renunciation, it is remarked here, the Allies would easily provide a suitable place of retreat which the Lutheran Church might find it difficult to offer.

Setting aside these reports, however, another view of the Austrian note, widely accepted in London, is that it was issued to prepare the German people for a great retreat. That would make it out to be inspired by the military chiefs. They, it is contended, see that they must relinquish Belgium in order to shorten the line on account of their destroyed divisions; and they wish to prepare the German people for this practical acknowledgment of military failure.

Hope to Detach France.

Moreover, with characteristic misunderstanding of the psychology of their enemies, the Germans still believe they could detach France from her allies by the return of the occupied French territory and some concessions about Alsace-Lorraine; and for this reason they would like to see the Entente inveigled into informal secret conversations.

The proper reply to that, many here believe, would be a brief definite joint statement of the Entente's war aims. A year or two ago it might have been difficult to draft that; but now the Allies have reached quite a close enough agreement among themselves to make it simple to draw up such a pronouncement.

President Wilson's statement, issued through Secretary Lansing, of the attitude of the American Government is taken in conjunction with Balfour's skeptical analysis, to foreshadow the unmistakable ultimate rejection of the proposals for a conference embodied in the Austro-Hungarian note. One section of the British opinion, and that probably by far the numerically greatest and certainly most vociferous, hails the Sate Department's announcement as an example that should be followed by the Entente Powers in Europe. There is nothing in the Austrian note, they say, and it deserves only the briefest of answers. The Evening Standard says:

"The ordinary plain man's position is that of President Wilson. Such a man naturally argues that if it takes 4,000 words or so to reply to a proposition, there must be something to reply to. Therefore Balfour's brilliant impromptu effort was a mistake in tactics, and the honors are with Wilson's short and sharp rejection. Perhaps it would be less invidious to say that Balfour represents the old diplomacy, Wilson the

Continued on Page Five.

Full Text of Wilson's Note as Given Out by Lansing

Special to The New York Times.

WASHINGTON, Sept. 18.—Secretary Lansing today gave out the United States Government's reply to Austria in the form in which it was handed to the Swedish Minister, W. A. F. Ekengren. It reads:

Department of State,
Sept. 17, 1918.

Sir: I have the honor to acknowledge the receipt of your note, dated Sept. 16, communicating to me a note from the Imperial Government of Austria-Hungary, containing a proposal to the Governments of all the belligerent States to send delegates to a confidential and unbinding discussion on the basic principles for the conclusion of peace. Furthermore, it is proposed that the delegates would be charged to make known to one another the conception of their Governments regarding these principles and to receive analogous communications, as well as to request and give frank and candid explanations on all those points which need to be precisely defined.

In reply I beg to say that the substance of your communication has been submitted to the President, who now directs me to inform you that the Government of the United States feels that there is only one reply which it can make to the suggestion of the Imperial Austro-Hungarian Government. It has repeatedly and with entire candor stated the terms upon which the United States would consider peace, and can and will entertain no proposal for a conference upon a matter concerning which it has made its position and purpose so plain.

Accept, Sir, the renewed assurances of my highest consideration.

(Signed) ROBERT LANSING.

Mr. W. A. F. Ekengren, Minister of Sweden, in charge of Austro-Hungarian interests.

PRESIDENT'S REPLY CHEERS OUR ARMY

American Soldiers in France Are Enthusiastic for Continuing the War.

NOW COUNT AUSTRIA AS FOE

Placing of Kaiser Karl's Troops on Western Front Called a Fatal Teuton Mistake.

By EDWIN L. JAMES.
Copyright, 1918, by The New York Times Company.
Special Cable to THE NEW YORK TIMES.

WITH THE AMERICAN ARMY IN FRANCE, Sept. 18.—The news of President Wilson's rejection of the Austrian peace feeler has aroused the greatest enthusiasm in the American Army which has just begun to fight, and would keenly regret the calling off of the war before it can make further and larger efforts.

The army is beginning to realize its power, and nothing would cause greater dismay in the ranks of our fighting men than any steps which would be taken at this time to interfere with the materialization of its plans for next year. The American Army wants to make the German Army and the German nation deeply repentant and achieve America's purpose to end Prussianism. Every doughboy has this idea and hopes that diplomacy will not interfere with it.

I was at the front with a regiment which has been in the fighting when news first came that Austria would like to do something to call off the war. In American slang came from all sides the exclamation: "What a fat chance!"

If Austria hoped to make any impression on the American Army and if Germany, through Austria, hoped to affect our fighting men by peace dickers the Teutons made a fatal mistake by placing Austrian divisions against Americans. Before that was done the American doughboys were very sure that the Germans were their enemies, but were slightly hazy about the Austrians. Some of them actually did not realize that America was at war with Austria. But after they found themselves fighting the Austrians the situation became very clear cut and there is now no difference between the Germans and the Austrians. Therefore, our ranks are very barren soil for the Austrian proffer.

WITH THE AMERICAN ARMY IN FRANCE, Sept. 18, (Associated Press.)—From the manner in which the American Army received the news of Presi-

Continued on Page Three.

ARMY OF 4,800,000 IN 1919 AIMED AT IN MARCH'S PLANS

Chief of Staff Tells Congress 2,700,000 Will Be Called Under New Draft.

1,600,000 MORE FIGHTERS

Allowance Made for 1,100,000 "Wastage"—Total Under Arms Now 3,200,000.

CONGRESS MUST VOTE CASH

Committees Tackle Problem of Supplying $7,347,000,000 Required —Consumption Tax Proposed.

Special to The New York Times.

WASHINGTON, Sept. 18.—The demand of the War Department for an additional appropriation of $7,347,000,000 for this year caused a hurried conference today between members of the Senate Finance Committee and the House Appropriations Committee in an effort to find some way to meet the emergency. Unable to come to any agreement, it was decided that Senator Simmons, Chairman of the Finance Committee, and Representative Sherley, Chairman of the House Committee, should confer tomorrow with Secretary McAdoo.

General March, Chief of Staff, appearing before the House Appropriations Committee, said that the War Department must have the $7,347,000,000 in cash, instead of following the usual procedure of taking part of it in that way and the remainder in authorizations upon which payments in future might be based. The insistence of General March led to the conference of Senators and Representatives.

General March said that under the new draft it was proposed to call to arms 2,700,000 men. This number will include all those who may be deducted from actual service on account of exemptions, rejections, or other "wastage." Upon the basis of ninety-eight divisions, the maximum strength is placed at 4,800,000 men, and as there are now 3,200,000 in service, it will be necessary to have 1,600,000 fighting men out of the 2,700,000 to be called.

General Crowder, who also was a witness before the committee, explained that 50 per cent. of the men needed, or 1,350,000, could be obtained from the 19 to 20 and the 32 to 36 classes. This will make it possible to obtain the other 1,350,000 without going very deeply into the remaining classes.

If the War Department is to have the additional $7,347,000,000, it will mean an appropriation for this year for army purposes of approximately $24,000,000,000.

That part of the extra money asked for by the War Department be provided for in the War Revenue bill after it reaches the Senate was suggested to to the Senate Finance Committee today by House leaders. They advised that approximately $2,300,000,000 might be added to that measure. The Senate Committee, or the majority of it, did not look favorably upon the idea.

If $2,300,000,000 is added to the war revenue, it was pointed out, the established ratio of 33 1-3 per cent. of taxation to 66 2-3 per cent. of Government securities as a basis for revenue would have to be sacrificed.

Should the Senate decide to increase the War Revenue bill by the amount suggested by the House leaders, it would probably mean, one member said today, that a consumption tax would have to be resorted to. That tax would be applied to coffee, tea, sugar, condiments and like commodities, while essentials such as flour, meal, meats, fish, and vegetables would not be touched.

Senators for Consumption Tax.

Members of the Senate Committee favor a consumption tax, rather than one upon direct sales over the counter of articles of wearing apparel and other goods. The direct sales tax system, it is argued, might open the way for imposition by unscrupulous dealers.

The idea of raising any money by excess profits or war profits tax beyond that now contemplated in the War Revenue bill does not meet with the approval of the Finance Committee.

General March in his statement to the Appropriations Committee upset all calculations. The committee intended allowing only a relatively small part of the War Department appropriation in cash at this time. But General March told the committee that this would not do, that the money must be in cash, to be expended during the present fiscal year. He said that in no other way could the program of organizing ninety-eight divisions, of which eighty are to be dispatched to France, be handled. It is necessary, he explained, to provide at once for arming, clothing, equipping, and transporting this great army if success is to crown America's efforts during the coming Spring.

Allies Are Soon to Pool All Aviation Resources

By CHARLES H. GRASTY.
Copyright, 1918, by The New York Times Company.
Special Cable to THE NEW YORK TIMES.

PARIS, Sept. 18.—After spending several days at aviation headquarters on the American front John D. Ryan is back in Paris working with the British and French on aviation plans. He and Winston Churchill spent yesterday together and there is close co-ordination between them and the French.

Mr. Ryan's effort is in the direction of pooling resources and getting the greatest possible force to the front in the shortest possible time. Allied representatives are meeting him in the same spirit and they are getting results.

Mr. Ryan was much pleased with the showing made by our air service in the recent offensive, which he had an opportunity of observing.

SEA FORCES CALL FOR MEN IN DRAFT

Voluntary Induction Into Navy and Marine Corps, Involuntary if Necessary.

REOPEN ARMY AIR SERVICE

Men Wanted for Commissions, Also as Mechanics—Present Status of Air Program.

WASHINGTON, Sept. 18.—Provost Marshal General Crowder today announced orders to local draft boards which will permit the voluntary induction of draft registrants into the navy and Marine Corps and provide for drafts of men to be assigned to those services if voluntary inductions do not suffice to fill the demands.

Announcement was also made that the air service of the army had been reopened for candidates for commissions as pilots, bombers, observers, and balloonists, as well as for the induction of mechanics, irrespective of status in the draft, after having been closed, except for a few isolated classes, for the last six months.

Calls for men for the navy will go out before the end of this month, and Marine Corps contingents will be called within a few weeks. The order by General Crowder, quoting sections of the man-power law, which make the term military service include the navy and Marine Corps, announces that separate calls hereafter will be issued to secure men for all divisions of the service. State quotas will be allotted to fill the marine and naval requirements.

After a call has been issued, Marine Corps and navy recruiting officers may ask for the voluntary induction of men to fill the call. If the total is not secured by that method, the boards will order sufficient men forward to make up the quota. The men will be mobilized and transported in the same manner as are those of the National Army. Men responding either to the induction or call method will be counted upon the State's quota as having been furnished for the nation's military needs.

Physical qualifications are slightly higher for naval needs, and the order directs that local boards shall select no man for the navy who cannot use fully the English language and who has not a complete status as a citizen of the United States.

Special calls for men having technical or educational qualifications for the navy will also be issued from time to time. These will be filled by local boards in the same manner as army calls have been filled, with provision for voluntary induction.

Present Status of Air Service.

The War Department announcement regarding the Air Service reads:

"The fast-moving overseas of air squadrons, planes, motors, and material for American airdromes, fields, and assembly plants in France and England, together with the completion here of 29 flying fields, 1,200 de Haviland planes, 6,000 Liberty motors, the parts for the first heavy night bombers, 6,600 training planes, and 12,500 training engines has led to the necessity of increasing both the commissioned and the enlisted personnel in order to maintain full strength in this country and continue the necessary flow overseas. As a result the Air Service alone is now half as large again as the whole American Army at the outbreak of war.

"Civilians have not been given an opportunity to qualify as pilots since last March. During last Fall and early Winter a reservoir of over 6,600 prospective fliers accepted by the examining boards had been built up, and has since been gradually drawn off as room has been made for them in the aviation ground

Continued on Page Four.

BULGAR FRONT CRUMBLES

Four Thousand Prisoners and Fifty Guns Captured by Allies.

GERMANS ALSO IN ROUT

Troops Sent by Berlin to Aid Hard-Pressed Allies Are Forced to Give Way.

ALLIES CONTINUE ADVANCE

Enormous War Supplies Are Found Abandoned by the Fleeing Foe.

LONDON, Sept. 18, (Associated Press.)—Bulgarian resistence on the Macedonian front is weakening, and the allied troops have advanced an average of ten miles, according to the latest reports received from Saloniki. Fifty guns have been captured.

The Bulgarians fought well when the allied attack was launched, but their resistance has become less formidable, as the Allies have moved northward.

Germans Routed With Bulgars.

WASHINGTON, Sept. 18.—German troops sent to the Macedonian front to aid the hard-pressed Bulgarian forces have been put to flight along with the Bulgarians, says a Serbian official statement on today's operations received tonight at the Serbian Legation. The statement, which was sent from Saloniki by Colonel Peshitch, Assistant Chief of the Serbian General Staff, follows:

We have repulsed a number of violent counterattacks in the Koziak region. The German troops which were sent to the aid of the Bulgarians have been put to flight with the latter.

We continue to advance along the whole front. The village of Gradeschnitza is in our hands. The allied troops have taken the village of Starovina.

The number of prisoners exceeds 4,000. The number of captured guns exceeds fifty. The enemy has also abandoned enormous quantities of war material.

It has been hinted in military circles for some months that this Autumn would see a major operation on the Macedonian front, and from the news of the last few days it appears that that operation has begun. While it is not possible for military reasons to give the number of men intended to participate in this movement, its object is clear: to cut off Turkey from the other Central Powers, to crush Bulgaria, and to free Serbia, Rumania and the Jugoslavs of Southern Austria.

It is no surprise to the Allies to know that the Serbs are fighting gallantly, for they are at last near their homes and are fighting for the restoration of their native land. The Bulgarians already are having trouble among themselves and with Germany, Turkey and Austria. In some quarters it is believed that when they see the fortunes of war moving against them they may desert their allies and sue for separate peace, trying to save as much of their acquired territory as they can.

French Praise Gallantry of Serbs.

PARIS, Sept. 17.—Allied forces on the Macedonian front have penetrated to a depth of nearly four and a half miles on a front of fifteen and one-half miles, and have captured 4,000 prisoners, according to an official statement issued to-night by the War Office, and of which the following is the text:

Near East, Sept. 16.—Our operations undertaken on Sept. 15 on the Macedonian front were pursued today with every success. The breach made in the enemy's lines on Sept. 15 on the front of Sokol-Dobropolje-Vetrenik was widened to the west end and to the east for a distance of more than 25 kilometers and to a depth of 7 kilometers.

West of Sokol Serbian divisions captured the enemy fortified zone between Gradeshnitza and Sokol, crossing the Gradeshnitza River, drove the enemy back in disorder on to the Razim Bay ridge, where the enemy units were bombarded by allied airplanes.

East of Vetrenik the allied forces captured the Chlem and Golo Bilo massifs and the defenses of Zborsko.

A Jugoslav division, taking advantage of their initial success, today stormed the Koziak massif, the second enemy defensive position in this region.

The number of prisoners taken in the first two days of the operations totaled more than 4,000, including a Colonel with his staff, and more than 30 guns, numerous mine-throwers and machine guns, and a considerable quantity of material remained in our hands.

The offensive continues.

The Serbian troops are fighting with

Continued on Page Seven.

Germans Admit We Defeated Them at St. Mihiel; One Thousand Tanks Did It, They Assert

AMSTERDAM, Sept. 18.—The Frankfurter Zeitung's correspondent telegraphs the following from the west front under date of Monday:

"The Franco-American attack at St. Mihiel is now seen to have been a carefully planned undertaking of considerable magnitude.

"The number of attacking enemy divisions is not yet known for certain, but we know that our losses in prisoners were due to the extensive use by the enemy of tanks. More than 1,000 armored cars of all sizes participated.

"One of our divisions counted in its sector alone sixty large and forty small tanks. Troops who hold out stoutly in their positions are always liable to be surrounded by this mobile arm."

AMERICANS BUILD STRONG FRONT LINE

Germans Also Make Haste in Further Fortifying Hindenburg Positions.

WORRIED BY OUR GUNFIRE

American Aviators Perform Daring Acts—One Downs Nine German Balloons.

By EDWIN L. JAMES.
Copyright, 1918, by The New York Times Company.
Special Cable to THE NEW YORK TIMES.

WITH THE AMERICAN ARMY IN FRANCE, Sept. 18.—After five days of local actions the American First Army now has a new line built in the St. Mihiel sector running parallel with the Hindenburg line at an average distance of two and a half kilometers from the German positions.

A glance at our new line through Ronvaux, Manheulles, Pintheville, St. Hilaire, Doncourt, Woel, Haumont, Jaulny, Vandieres, and south to Chambley and Norroy, in comparison with the line on Friday, shows how we have pushed ahead in these local actions, in some places three kilometers. These actions have resulted in the capture of the important points of Fresnes and Haumont.

There was something of the burlesque in the German communiqué's statement of yesterday that they had repulsed attacks at Haumont and northeast of Thiaucourt. The Americans have held Haumont for three days, and they hold the terrain for a distance of seven kilometers northeast of Thiaucourt.

Americans Build Strong Defenses.

The Germans are constructing very strong works back of the Hindenburg line, evidently fearing another American effort in this sector, while the Americans have constructed strong defenses opposite that line.

The Germans last night were busy with artillery on the towns back of our line. Thiaucourt, Woinville, Haumont, and Combres were bombarded and St. Mihiel was bombed during the night. Gas was used on Haudimont and Saulx. Our artillery replied in force, reaching towns fifteen miles behind the German lines.

The last twenty-four hours have brought no important infantry action on either side, although there have been frequent contacts by patrols in No Man's Land between our St. Mihiel line and the Hindenburg front.

The last two days have been rainy, hindering aerial activity. However, our airplanes have been far more active than those of the Germans, who appear to have withdrawn some of the squadrons which were brought to this front Friday and Saturday.

Lieutenant Luke has brought down nine German balloons in three days.

Our aerial observers report a continuation of the heavy movement behind the German lines without a concentrated movement in any particular direction.

We continue to take prisoners every day from patrols which keep

Continued on Page Two.

BRITISH REGAIN OLD OUTPOST LINE

Drive Motley Crowd of Germans Out of Villages Lost in March Drive.

NOW FACE BIG GUN FIRE

Long-Range Weapons Sweep the Ground with Terrific Hail of High Velocities.

By PHILIP GIBBS.
Copyright, 1918, by The New York Times Company.
Special Cable to THE NEW YORK TIMES.

WITH THE BRITISH ARMIES, Sept. 18.—On a front of something like sixteen miles from below Gouzeaucort to Savy Wood, near St. Quentin, an attack was made by English, Scottish, Irish, and Australian troops this morning in co-operation with French battalions on the British right by Holnon Wood.

As I saw myself this morning, a considerable number of prisoners have been taken—about 3,000 were reckoned to be coming back—and the British by stubborn fighting against stiff opposition in some of the enemy's positions made good progress and scaled much of the high ground immediately west of the Hindenburg line.

On this southern part of our front several villages, including Peizières, Epehy, Templeux le Guérard, Leverguier, and Hargicourt have been the scene of fierce conflict, but these places are now in our hands, according to reports I have just received, and from one end of this line of attack to its other boundary the Germans have been forced to yield ground which they were ordered to hold at all costs in order to protect the forward positions of the Hindenburg line.

Our primary object this morning was to gain our old outpost line as it existed before last March, running along a ridge from which spurs strike down to St. Quentin Canal. The enemy had already withdrawn his artillery behind that canal and was relying mainly on long range high velocities to harass our positions and silence our batteries.

Many Long Range Guns Massed.

He is now strong in gun power for protection of the Hindenburg line, and from personal observation I can say he has a most unusual number of these long range guns, and he used them this morning to draw a line of fire across our country. He was, however, holding his outpost line, once ours as I have said, with many of the same troops who had borne the full brunt of our recent battles and suffered exceedingly, so that their spirit had been lowered to gloomy depths, while other divisions less mauled, though by no means unscathed, were being held by the German command to defend the Hindenburg line itself.

This has been the enemy's policy for some time owing to his increasing dearth of men after the allied attacks at so many parts of the line. He gives his troops no rest or support until they are thoroughly worn, when he stiffens them with material of better class. It is a merciless but, from the German point of view, necessary method. Since Aug. 8 our 4th Army, for instance, has engaged thirty-four divisions, twelve of which have been in battle for the

Continued on Page Two.

CLOSING IN ON ST. QUENTIN

British Four Miles from the City, French Are Only Three.

FAMOUS DEFENSES FALL

Outer Hindenburg Works Are Officially Reported Captured "in Wide Sectors."

FOE'S RESISTANCE STRONG

Victors' Advance of from 1¼ to 3 Miles Made Under Handicap of Rain.

LONDON, Sept. 18.—In co-ordinated operations on a twenty-two-mile front British and French troops have made notable advances upon the outlying defenses of St. Quentin.

The British attack was launched on a line sixteen miles in extent northwest of the city, and resulted in the capture of more than 6,000 prisoners and the occupation of ten villages and several other important enemy positions, including what Field Marshal Haig describes as "outer defenses of the Hindenburg line in wide sectors."

The advance of the British carried them across the Hindenburg line at two points—Villeret and Gouzeaucourt.

The maximum depth of the British thrust was about three miles. Fresnoy le Petit, the village which marks the nearest approach of the attack to St. Quentin, is only four miles northwest of that city.

The Germans offered a strong resistance, and the allied advance was also made under the handicap of a pouring rain.

Immediately to the right of the British, French troops attacked and pushed their lines forward a mile and a quarter on the six-mile front between Holnon and Essigny le Grand, reaching the western outskirts of Francilly-Selency [three miles west of St. Quentin] and the southern edge of Contescourt [four miles southwest of St. Quentin] in their nearest approaches to the German base.

Tonight's Paris bulletin announces the capture of a few hundred prisoners.

BERLIN, Sept. 18, (via London.)—The Germans are counterattacking against the British, who, they admit, have entered the German positions between Hargicourt and the Omignon Rivulet, according to the statement from Army Headquarters this evening.

HUGE NEW AIRPLANES SENT TO STOP BRITISH

German Machines Carry Eight Men and Drop Bombs Weighing a Ton Each.

WITH THE BRITISH ARMY IN FRANCE, Sept. 18, (Associated Press.)—The British troops made a powerful attack against the German lines to the west and northwest of St. Quentin today, and most important results were achieved. A deep advance into the enemy territory strengthened the already powerful grip the British have on St. Quentin, one of the most strongly fortified parts of the Hindenburg line.

To the south the French co-operated in what is likely to prove an operation of vast portent with respect to the Hindenburg defensive position.

The zone involved in the British movement lay, roughly, between Holnon, on the south, and Gouzeaucourt. Within a few hours Peizière, Templeux-le-Guérard, Epehy, Ronssoy, and Villeret were behind the advanced British forces, and bitter fighting was in progress at many other points in the forward zone.

The advance thus far recorded—in some places more than two miles—means that the British have at numerous points gained the crest of the ridge along which their old front line ran prior to the German offensive in March, and from their new positions are looking down on the Hindenburg line in the valley to the east.

Last night German airplanes were busy bombing the St. Quentin sector, and the enemy utilized a number of new

Mid-Week Pictorial

Bulgarians advancing under Serbian barrage fire.

Men of the 53rd and 54th Brigades collecting and preparing for burial some of the men killed in the last attack on the Hindenburg Line.

U. S. Signal Corps

U. S. Signal Corps

German prisoners being impressed as litter bearers to evacuate wounded after attack on the Hindenburg Line.

"All the News That's Fit to Print."

The New York Times.

THE WEATHER
Fair today; Tuesday, warmer; moderate southerly winds.
For full weather report see Page 17.

VOL. LXVIII...NO. 22,157. NEW YORK, MONDAY, SEPTEMBER 23, 1918.—EIGHTEEN PAGES. TWO CENTS Metropolitan District 50 Mile Radius. | THREE CENTS Within 200 Miles. | FOUR CENTS Elsewhere.

BRITISH WIPE OUT AN ENTIRE TURKISH ARMY; CAPTURE 18,000 IN 60-MILE DRIVE IN PALESTINE; HAIG STRIKES GERMAN LINE AT FOUR POINTS

PUTS RISE IN FOOD AT 3 1-2 PER CENT. SINCE LAST YEAR

Hoover Bureau Asserts That Increases Have Been Popularly Overestimated.

FARMERS' RECEIPTS SOARING

Prices Up 35 Per Cent., but Margin Narrowed Between Producer and Wholesaler.

BIG JUMP IN SOME FOODS

But General Cost Far Below That of Rent, Clothing, Transportation, and Other Items.

Special to The New York Times.

WASHINGTON, Sept. 22.—An analysis of the food situation and the increase in living costs was made today by the Food Administration, which holds that increases have been greatly overestimated by laying too much emphasis on special cases.

A table showing the relative increases and decreases in costs during 1917 and 1918 was made public to show that, according to wholesale quotations, the average increase in the national expenditure for foods grouped as breadstuffs, vegetables, meats, &c., for the second period of 1918, was only 3.5 per cent. over the same period in 1917. This is arrived at, however, by placing the decrease in the expenditure for vegetables at 83.1 per cent. Fruits jumped 50 per cent., oils and nuts 54 per cent., and poultry and eggs 16.5 per cent.

"The attached table," says the Food Administration, "is a computation of the national food bill for each three months, beginning with the second quarter of 1917, down to the second quarter of 1918. It is based on taking the total food consumed by the nation divided into the items of breadstuffs, vegetables, meat, dairy products, &c., at the average wholesale price for the quarter, and thus arriving at what the nation, as a whole, actually expended.

"The figures show that during the last twelve months there has been an increase in the national food bill per quarter from $2,563,600,904 to $2,693,751,871, or 3½ per cent. While this is the whole nation's expenditure at the wholesale prices and thus clearly indicates the national trend, it does not follow that there are no local variations.

"In those sections where there has been a great local increase in population there has been a disturbance of distribution and prices have increased to a larger per cent. On the other hand there are corresponding sections of the community where actual decreases or no increases have taken place.

"The cost of rent, clothing, transportation and other items of living has advanced several times as much as the aggregate increase in the cost of foodstuffs. There has been more than a 35 per cent. increase in prices paid to the farmer, but also a reduction of speculation and profiteering and narrowed margins between farmers and wholesale prices under food regulations."

Here is the Food Administration's analysis of the situation:

	Total Cost.	Cost Per Capita.
SECOND QUARTER 1917.		
Breadstuffs	$314,906,915	$3.0383
Vegetables	330,709,747	3.1905
Sugar	200,674,663	1.9363
Fruits	78,381,156	.7550
Oils and nuts	52,302,765	.5046
Fish	26,140,445	.2522
Meats	764,802,651	7.3804
Poultry and eggs	221,956,895	2.1417
Dairy products	573,665,667	5.5354
Total	$2,563,600,904	$24.7353
THIRD QUARTER 1917.		
Breadstuffs	$393,732,314	$3.7844
Vegetables	152,884,830	1.4694
Sugar	205,527,030	1.9754
Fruits	71,200,290	.6852
Oils and nuts	58,304,496	.5604
Fish	26,326,613	.2530
Meats	777,833,981	7.4705
Poultry and eggs	226,038,723	2.1726
Dairy products	564,068,678	5.6138
Total	$2,495,407,855	$23.9847
FOURTH QUARTER 1917.		
Breadstuffs	$348,554,753	$3.3372
Vegetables	136,899,969	1.3107
Sugar	210,439,897	2.0148
Fruits	70,506,614	.6750
Oils and nuts	68,495,813	.6558
Fish	33,133,947	.3172
Meats	878,708,620	8.4131
Poultry and eggs	266,590,892	2.5516
Dairy products	641,510,893	6.1421
Total	$2,654,751,258	$25.4175
FIRST QUARTER 1918.		
Breadstuffs	$351,952,618	$3.3567
Vegetables	143,179,060	1.3655
Sugar	190,016,407	1.8122
Fruits	75,057,007	.7158
Oils and nuts	72,652,456	.6929
Fish	40,631,802	.3875
Meats	858,387,693	7.9961
Poultry and eggs	304,216,881	2.9014
Dairy products	676,389,410	6.4510
Total	$2,692,483,304	$25.6791
SECOND QUARTER 1918.		
Breadstuffs	$[illegible]	$3.5216
Vegetables	[illegible]	1.1768
Sugar	[illegible]	1.7930
Fruits	103,881,529	.9868
Oils and nuts	81,964,541	.7786
Fish	24,702,191	.2349
Meats	958,789,269	5.8012
Poultry and eggs	262,577,561	2.4947
Dairy products	619,553,051	5.8863
Total	$2,693,751,871	$25.6919

Allies Have Taken 185,000 Prisoners in Two Months

PARIS, Sept. 22.—In a review of the battles in France during the last six months, the Havas Agency credits to the American troops the re-establishment of the balance on the western front, and points out the entire change that has taken place in the last two months. It goes on:

"In the last two months alone the Allies took 185,000 prisoners.

"The enemy losses in men who will never be able to return to the ranks are estimated at 600,000—a void which the 1920 class will not suffice to fill."

GERMANS RUSHING TO HELP BULGARS

Reinforcements Sent in Effort to Check the Allied Push.

ITALIANS JOIN IN THE DRIVE

Strike Enemy's Line East of Monastir—Serbs Advanced Twelve Miles on Friday.

WASHINGTON, Sept. 22.—Serbian troops pressing the Bulgarians and Germans in Central Macedonia advanced more than twenty kilometers Friday, and are now within four miles of the Uskub-Saloniki Railroad, the main artery for the supply of the Austro-German and Bulgarian forces opposing the British and French armies on the Serbian right.

The cutting of this railroad, it is said here officially, will force the retirement of the enemy left wing and cause a general readjustment of the enemy lines in this entire section.

Following is the text of the Serbian official statement:

We yesterday (Friday) advanced more than twenty kilometers toward the north. Our troops are several kilometers to the north of Kavarda. In addition to this town we have liberated another fifteen villages. Twelve guns have been taken by our cavalry.

Fresh Bulgarian and German troops are arriving continually to reinforce the enemy lines. During the retreat the Bulgarians set fire to the villages and plundered all that remained to the poverty stricken population, thus treating them as enemies, in spite of the claims of the Sofia Government that this population is not Serbian, but Bulgarian.

ROME, Sept. 22.—In conjunction with the general Entente allied offensive against the Teuton and Bulgarian forces in Macedonia, Italian troops yesterday began a vigorous advance in the bend of the River Cerna, to the east of Monastir. The official statement issued today by the Italian War Office says that the front enemy positions were captured.

PARIS, Sept. 22.—Concerning operations on the Macedonian front, Army Headquarters today made public the following:

Army of the East.—Bulgarian forces have been defeated and are being pursued between the Cerna and the Vardar, despite increasing rearguard resistance.

Serbian forces have advanced in the region of Cebren. On the right they captured high crests near Porta and Czena. Bulgarians burned villages which they had abandoned, and one complete battery of field pieces fell into our hands. Our aviators bombarded the retreating enemy with machine gun fire.

On both sides of the Vardar and north of Monastir there is great artillery activity.

VIENNA, Sept. 22, (via London.)—An official statement issued at the War Office today says:

"On the Albanian coast further Italian attacks were repulsed."

BUENA VENTURA SUNK; 64 OF CREW MISSING

American Steamer Returning from France Torpedoed—30 Survivors Land in Spain.

CORUNNA, Spain, Sept. 22.—Three officers and twenty-seven of the crew of the American steamer Buena Ventura have arrived here. The vessel was torpedoed last Monday. Three boats with sixty-four of the crew are missing.

The Buena Ventura was proceeding from Bordeaux, where she had unloaded a cargo of petroleum for Philadelphia.

The vessel was of 4,881 gross tons and belonged to the United States Steel Products Company.

AUSTRIANS IN MUTINY, HOIST THE RED FLAG

Regiment at Rovno Refuses to Go to France and Is Joined by Two Others.

BASLE, Sept. 22.—An Austrian regiment at Rovno, in the Russian province of Volhynia, is reported in a dispatch received here from Kiev to have refused to go to the battlefront in France.

The Austrians unfolded the red flag and are said to have been joined by two other regiments.

AMERICANS SLAIN BY RUSSIAN REDS, GERMAN REPORTS

Correspondent Says Vologda Leader Urged Murder of Allied Citizens.

FINLAND OFFERS REFUGE

But Asks Norway, Sweden, and Denmark to Help Share the Burden.

KAISER'S ORDER TO TEUTONS

Says All Germans and Austro-Hungarians in Russia Must Join Soviet Troops.

AMSTERDAM, Sept. 22.—The Russian People's Commissary at Vologda, according to the Petrograd correspondent of the Hamburg Nachrichten, has urged on the population of the entire Vologda Province south of Archangel Province the most ruthless persecution of British subjects and French and American citizens.

Rioting against Entente nationals has taken place in various towns, the correspondent says, and some Frenchmen and Americans are being murdered.

HELSINGFORS, Sept. 22, (via Copenhagen,) (Associated Press.)—"In view of the condition of anarchy and murder at Petrograd and the defenseless situation of a great part of the population," says an official statement issued here, "Finland's Government feels that on purely humanitarian grounds it cannot refuse to permit Russian, English, American, and Italian refugees to come to Finland."

The Finnish Government, however, the statement says, is compelled by the scarcity of provisions to beg the three Scandinavian countries—Norway, Sweden, and Denmark—to help in harboring a portion of the refugees.

LONDON, Sept. 22.—It is understood in official circles here that arrangements are progressing for the mutual repatriation of British subjects in Russia and Russians in Great Britain.

Information is said to have been received from M. Tchitcherin, the Russian Foreign Minister, which leads to the belief that British subjects will be got out of Russia safely.

PEKING, Sept. 22, (Associated Press.)—News has been received here that the German Emperor on Sept. 10 issued an order to all Austro-Hungarians and Germans in Russia, saying it was their first duty to join the Russian Soviet troops, and to oppose Japan and her allies, "who threaten to restore the Eastern front."

ARCHANGEL REVOLT WAS QUICKLY ENDED

Allied Diplomats and Military Chiefs Took Charge and Established a Protectorate.

ARCHANGEL, Sept. 11. (Associated Press.)—Colonel Tchaplin, leader of the recent attempt to overthrow the Provisional Government headed by M. Tschaikovsky, in Northwestern Russia, has resigned his post as Commander of the Russian Forces and has been succeeded by Colonel Ivanoff.

The labor disputes in Archangel are being rapidly settled. American soldiers who had been operating the street-car system have been transferred to other duties.

As a result of the attempt to overthrow the Government the Allied diplomatic and military chiefs assumed temporary direction and established a protectorate in the region in the rear of the Allied front pending the adjustment of political disputes. This decision followed the arrest of M. Tschaikovsky and all but two members of his Government early last Thursday by a party of conservative officers headed by Colonel Tchaplin, who sought to establish a new régime.

M. Tschaikovsky and his ministers were taken on a ship en route to the Solovetsk Monastery, whence they have been returned by order of the Allied Ambassadors with the approval of American Consul General Poole. Meanwhile the Allied forces, including the American troops, patrolled the city, assuring tranquillity and a just settlement of all disputes. Following is the text of the proclamation, which was signed by the American, French, British and Italian Ambassadors and Consul General Poole:

"To the People of the Northern Region: The undersigned representatives of the Allied nations and the commanders in chief of their forces seeing the confusion created in the minds of the people by proclamations by leaders of the oppos-

Continued on Page Three.

"German People, Be Hard," Hindenburg Tells Well-wishers

AMSTERDAM, Sept. 22.—Field Marshal von Hindenburg, replying to greetings sent to him from a patriotic meeting in Juterbog, said:

"The first replies from the enemy camp to the Austrian note reveal our enemies' state of mind. In the face of this there can be only one watchword, 'German people, be hard.'"

COPENHAGEN, Sept. 22.—America's answer to Austria-Hungary's recent peace note and the speech of Premier Clemenceau of France on the same subject should, according to the Lokal-Anzeiger of Berlin, be posted on billboards and be communicated to the German people by the distribution of millions of pamphlets.

"No German man or woman who knows the contents and significance of these declarations," the newspaper declares, "can doubt that peace is attainable only either through our victory or at the price of our utter destruction."

OUR MEN VICTORS IN ST. MIHIEL RAIDS

They Take 34 Prisoners and Gain Information of German Activities.

AMERICAN BARRAGE DEADLY

Germans Slow in Returning Our Fire, Which Killed Sixty at Haumont and Charey.

WITH THE AMERICAN FORCES IN LORRAINE, Sept. 22, (Associated Press.)—American troops made two successful raids on the German lines northeast of St. Mihiel early this morning, taking twenty-nine prisoners in the region of Haumont and five southeast of Charey. Both raids were preceded by barrages.

Patrols from the region of Haumont reported that at least forty Germans were killed or injured. Other patrols from the Charey region estimated that the barrage killed at least a score of Germans.

The prisoners taken southeast of Charey were machine gunners, the Americans capturing two heavy machine guns. At Haumont the Germans were captured in dugouts, where they had taken refuge from the stiff American barrage.

The Germans answered with their artillery along the American line. The first American barrage began soon after midnight. The other started at 2 o'clock. Both continued for two hours.

A unit of the American raiders entered Haumont, where the Germans had been using a church tower as an observation post. Sharp fighting took place in the streets of the village, the Americans getting the better of the Germans and obtaining the information desired. They then returned to their own lines.

A patrol found several new dugouts east of Haumont and indications that the Germans were continuing to dig in. Another patrol reported enemy trenches and numerous machine gun emplacements south of Dommartin.

When the American barrages started the Germans apparently believed that another offensive had opened, and filled the sky with rockets and signal shells. The heavy shelling apparently caused confusion on the enemy front, because it was more than twenty minutes after the first barrage before the Germans replied.

Sept. 21—German airplanes were active last night in the region between the Moselle River and St. Bénoit, northeast of St. Mihiel. The forward areas were bombed practically all night.

German artillery kept up a harassing fire on the Bois-le-Prêtre, Rappes Woods, and the village of Fey-en-Haye. The road to Thiaucourt is being shelled intermittently.

The Germans are reported to be working on dugouts to the west of Pagny and to the east of Haumont. Similar activity has been observed north of Dampvitou and south of Dommartin.

Operating a German Railroad.

WITH THE AMERICAN ARMY ON THE LORRAINE FRONT, Sept. 22, (Associated Press.)—The American engineers' detachment is now operating a complete German narrow-gauge railroad in the St. Mihiel salient, the Americans having captured thirty-eight one-man gasoline locomotives in the course of their offensive.

In Thiaucourt the Americans took

Continued on Page Two.

BRITISH IMPROVE POSITIONS

Take Prisoners in Night Attacks on Northern Hindenburg Outposts.

WIDE ADVANCE AT GAVRELLE

German Defenses All Carried on a Two-Mile Front North of the Scarpe.

NEW THRUST NEAR EPEHY

Germans Yield Several Points of Resistance—Artillery Is Active on French Front.

LONDON, Sept. 22.—British troops last night pushed their lines forward at four points on the front facing the northern part of the Hindenburg line.

The most extensive gain was made north of the Scarpe River, near Gavrelle, where they threw the Germans back on a two-mile front.

Further south, at Moeuvres, a German attack was repulsed yesterday afternoon, and Haig's men improved their positions.

To the right of this sector, south of Villers-Guislain, the Germans attacked last evening and were driven back after sharp fighting, the British following up their advantage and advancing their line.

East of Epehy the British attack of yesterday was renewed, and Little Priel Farm and other points of resistance were carried.

In each of these operations a number of Germans were captured.

Only local actions were fought today, but the British made slight gains south of Villers-Guislain and near Zillebeke, in the Ypres sector.

The French War Office reports some artillery activity north of the Aisne and in the St. Quentin region.

Haig's Important Gain Near Epehy.

WITH THE BRITISH ARMY IN FRANCE, Sept. 22, (Associated Press.)—A midnight advance of the London and English county troops resulted in the regaining of a large portion of the ground lost last Saturday after an attack along the fragments of the Hindenburg outpost line between Cambrai and St. Quentin.

During Saturday morning these battalions, with yeomanry and Australians on their right, stormed a series of redoubts and farms forming the backbone of the outpost system opposite Bellenglise and Vendhuille, a mile and a quarter west of the Scheldt Canal, between St. Quentin and Cambrai. They occupied the Guillemont, Quennemont, and Little Priel farms, the Tombois redoubts, and a chain of strong trenches, heavily banked with fire, connecting these positions.

Early Saturday afternoon counterattacks were delivered by Alpine Corps and the 38th Thuringian and 2d Guards Divisions, which were massed in the main Hindenburg system on the western bank of the canal. They drove in great strength down the trenches, but the British bombed them back slowly.

Four hundred prisoners had been taken by the British during Saturday morning, and half of those were released by the counterassault. The British retired about half way to their original positions west of Epehy and Ronssoy, maintaining a maximum advance of nearly a mile at some places, and stubbornly held their ground for the remainder of the day.

The result of the fighting of the last thirty-six hours has been the bringing of the British front within about three-quarters of a mile of the main Hindenburg system opposite Bellicourt on the canal and within a mile and a quarter of the Vendhuille bridgehead, eleven miles south of Cambrai.

Trench warfare, with constant bombing, is inevitable in the present phase of the British operations. The ground in front of the 3d and 4th Armies as far as the canal and for a half mile beyond is covered with ditches, redoubts, and fortified farms, making surprise attacks of great weight impossible.

The Germans are fighting stubbornly in the way they like best. While they are able to keep intrenched in the region of deep ravines and broad gullies they have less fear of the tanks or of being otherwise overwhelmed. Fresh German infantry has been put into the battle-line.

The weather is inclement, which has hampered the fighting troops.

Swiss Hear Bavarian Prince Shot at Hindenburg In Rage Over Differences, but Missed the Marshal

Special Cable to THE NEW YORK TIMES.

ZURICH, Sept. 22.—Many Swiss Socialist journals have heard from indirect sources that serious differences have arisen between South German politicians and the Prussian dictators.

The Central Schweiz Demokrat reports that a Bavarian commander attempted in an access of rage to attack Hindenburg, and German deserters are quoted as saying that a Bavarian Prince tried to shoot Hindenburg, but that the Field Marshal was not wounded.

These reports may be sensational versions of recent stories coming through neutral countries that Crown Prince Rupprecht was at odds with Hindenburg and was trying to dodge responsibility for the check of the July offensive. He is known to have left the Somme front for a time in August on a "vacation."

HAIG'S MEN FIGHT IN RAIN AND MUD

Soldiers Suffer from the Lack of Shelter After Their Rapid Advance.

SLOW ADVANCE NEAR EPEHY

Germans' Reinforcements Held Them Up Saturday, but Lost Ground Yesterday.

By PHILIP GIBBS.

Copyright, 1918, by The New York Times Company.
Special Cable to THE NEW YORK TIMES.

WAR CORRESPONDENTS' HEADQUARTERS, Sept. 22.—We have been having some wild weather here, with heavy rain, and the men in the fighting fields have been wet and muddy.

It is not pleasant in these fields, where even behind the lines twenty miles deep along all the front there is little shelter for the troops, except tents in swamps, a few groups of huts, slimy dugouts and tarpaulin sheets stopping up monstrous shell holes in broken houses.

The British armies are fighting, working, and sleeping in wet clothes, because when it rains so heavily as during the last few days waterproof capes are of slight avail against the storm, tents are leaky, and oozy mud and water squelch into marching boots.

There is something grimly picturesque about these rain pictures of the war. The steel helmets of a battalion marching up to the line are washed by the downpour and gleam with a blue light. Their rifles are tied about with rags to keep them dry. The rain pours down their shiny capes and beats into their mud-splashed faces. Great guns go by on caterpillar wheels, which grind up the soft tracks; field batteries move forward with the gunners hunched forward on mules which are flaked with mud up to the ears, and gun wheels splash through the young ponds.

Gangs Busy Repairing Roads.

The long roads through the battlefields, the Albert-Bapaume Road, the Arras Road, the Amiens-Péronne Road, those highways down which so much history of this war has passed with fire and fury, are golden tracks where the sun breaking through clouds shines on their puddles and on their rain-washed surface, and where gangs from labor battalions are at work filling up recent shell holes, smoothing out the bumps and gullies made by the heavy traffic of moving armies.

Storms break over the dead woods on either side of these highways, etched black against the gray of the sky or its white cloud-mountains, and out of the wet earth where countless trenches and shell craters are water-logged there rise the ruins of this world of ours—the high jagged walls of fallen houses, bits of churches, abbeys and monasteries with their stones washed white in the rain, masses of broken brick work from which the iron girders stick out, twisted fantastically, where once there were villages of France; and here and there a pile of rubbish which was a mill or sugar factory or wayside shrine.

The wind howls through these ruins and the rain beats down upon them, and British soldiers wander through them with steel helmets lowered to the storm or crouch in the scanty shelter they can give. Horses and mules are stabled there in roofless rooms, and gun limbers are stacked in gardens where flowers still grow in a wild chaos of sandbags and barbed wire, and away over the desolate fields of thistles which cover some of the litter of the infernal strife long trains are

Continued on Page Two.

TURKS OUTWITTED BY GEN. ALLENBY

Were Apparently Unprepared to Face Hostile Operations on So Large a Scale.

COUNTRY MOST DIFFICULT

British Fought Over Steep Hills and Masses of Boulders Till Foe Was Routed.

By W. T. MASSEY.

Special Cable to THE NEW YORK TIMES.

WITH THE BRITISH ARMY IN PALESTINE, Sept. 20.—It is impossible to estimate the vast quantity of captured machine guns, motors, ammunitions, stores, and rolling stock which the Turk will find it difficult to replace. On the low ground in the passes a great quantity of transport is immovable because the men had taken the horses to try to escape from the advancing troops, or they had been smashed by aircraft action.

Railway communications have been damaged everywhere, and Arab regulars and Bedouin levies have done invaluable service in cutting the Hedjaz Railway north and south of Derat and the line running westward thereof.

Though some of the enemy are putting up vigorous rearguard fights in the hills they cannot stop our progress, but large parties are bewildered at meeting our forces in unexpected places. We continually hear of Turks retiring on positions we occupied several hours previously.

Yesterday Londoners and Indians made a swift march from Wadi Falik across marshy ground to Tul Keram, where with the aid of a mounted brigade they rounded up much transport on the move. From Tul Keram the infantry moved to the north of the railway which the Australians destroyed yesterday, and deny this pass to Samaria to the Turks. Other infantry which carried the coastal defenses in one marvelous rush faced east.

The progress in the rough hilly country is rapid, considering the ease with which the mountain tracks could be defended by few machine guns. Some of the troops are approaching Samaria and Sudich.

Though they first stubbornly resisted, the rearguards of the Turks are now retreating hastily toward El Afule and Beisan, where our cavalry is waiting for them.

The attack near Nablus road, which began the operations, was brilliantly conducted. Welsh, Indian, and Cape Colony battalions all shared in the success. The mixed brigade commenced a most difficult night march on Wednesday over a mountainous country east of the road, getting over the watershed, then clambering down the steep faces of hills where they commence to fall toward the Jordan Valley.

The leading battalion passing over the rocks of the Wadi Samieh took the enemy posts and allowed the second battalion to pass through to the second objectives. These taken, the third battalion went on, driving the enemy from other strong points, then gave way to the fourth battalion, which faced west and carried the important feature El Mugheir with a rush and another hill westward. A Cape company battalion captured a hill northeast and took one gun.

Another brigade operation westward was equally meritorious. It attacked Forfar and Bidston Hills, about a mile and half apart, the southernmost hill being taken from the north, the north-

Continued on Page Two.

TURKS TRAPPED BY CAVALRY

Anglo-Indian Horsemen in Swift Dash Northward Bar Line of Retreat.

OCCUPY TOWN OF NAZARETH

While Hedjaz Arabs East of the Jordan Destroy Railroads and Bridges.

AIRMEN SLAUGHTER FOE

120 Cannon, Besides Airplanes and Vast Transport, Taken by Allenby's Fighters.

LONDON, Sept. 22.—The Turkish Army operating in Palestine between the Jordan and the Mediterranean has been virtually wiped out by the British under General Allenby.

In the rapid sweep forward of the British Army, following the overwhelming of the Turkish defense system north of Jerusalem, 18,000 prisoners have been rounded up so far, large numbers of the enemy have been killed or wounded, and in addition to the capture of 120 guns, booty including four airplanes and a large quantity of uncounted transport has fallen into the hands of the pursuing forces.

Cavalry units have advanced sixty miles from their original positions and occupied Nazareth, El Afule, and Beisan.

The British losses were surprisingly slight considering the importance of the advance.

Turks Cut Off from Escape.

The text of this evening's announcement follows:

By 9 o'clock on Saturday night on our left wing the infantry about Birafur had reached the line Beitdajan-Samaria-Birafur, shepherding the enemy on the west of the Jerusalem-Nabulus road into the arms of our cavalry operating southward from Jenin and Beisan.

Other enemy columns vainly attempted to escape into the Jordan Valley in the direction of Jisr-ed-Dameer, which still is held by us. These columns suffered severely from our aircraft, which constantly harassed them with bombs and machine-gun fire from low altitudes.

In the vicinity of Lake Tiberius our cavalry detachments hold Nazareth and the rail and road passages over the Jordan at Jisr-ed-Dameer.

Already 18,000 prisoners have been captured and 120 guns collected.

The appended statement was issued earlier in the day:

Palestine—By 8 P. M. on Sept. 20 the enemy resistance had collapsed everywhere save on the Turkish left in the Jordan Valley.

Our left wing, having swung around to the east, had reached the line of Bidieh, Baka, and Messudieh Junction, and was astride the rail and roads converging at Nabulus.

Our right wing, advancing through difficult country against considerable resistance had reached the line of Khan-Jibeit, one and one-fourth miles northeast of El-Mugheir and Es-Sawieh, and was facing north astride the Jerusalem-Nabulus road.

On the north our cavalry, traversing the Field of Armageddon, had occupied Nazareth, Afule, and Beisan, and were collecting the disorganized masses of enemy troops and transport as they arrived from the south. All avenues of escape open to the enemy, except the fords across the Jordan between Beisan and Jisr-ed-Dameer, were thus closed.

East of the Jordan Arab forces of the King of the Hedjaz had effected numerous demolitions on the railways radiating from Derat, several important bridges, including one in the Yurmak Valley, having been destroyed.

Several days must elapse before accurate figures of captures can be given, but already more than 8,000 prisoners, 100 guns, large quantities of both horse and mechanical transports, four airplanes, many locomotives, and much rolling stock have been counted.

Very severe losses have been inflicted on the masses of Turkish troops retreating over the difficult roads by our air services.

A German airplane, later ascertained to have been carrying mails, landed in the midst of our troops at Afule. The pilot, who believed the place still to be in Turkish hands, de-

"All the News That's Fit to Print."

The New York Times.

THE WEATHER
Fair today; tomorrow, fair, warmer; northeast winds.
For full weather report see Page 23.

VOL. LXVIII...NO. 22,172. NEW YORK, TUESDAY, OCTOBER 8, 1918.—TWENTY-FOUR PAGES. TWO CENTS

EXPECT WILSON TO REJECT TEUTON OFFERS; NOW CONFERRING WITH ALLIES ON REPLY; BRITISH ARE AGAIN DRIVING TOWARD LILLE; FRENCH GAIN ON AISNE, OUR MEN IN ARGONNE

PEACE DRIVE MUST NOT WEAKEN LOAN DRIVE, SAYS M'ADOO

Boys in the Trenches Won't Stop Fighting, He Declares, Because Foe Is on the Run.

TIME NOW TO FIGHT HARDER

Nation's Subscriptions Reported Up to Saturday Night Total $1,323,716,950.

ST. LOUIS LEADS WITH 47%

New York Ninth in Percentage of Quota Subscribed—Plea for More Energy Here.

Special to The New York Times.

WASHINGTON, Oct. 7.—Fear that the Austro-German peace drive might seriously interfere with the progress of the Fourth Liberty Loan drive, while the country is awaiting President Wilson's answer to the Central Powers, was reflected by Secretary McAdoo tonight when he issued an appeal to the nation to work harder than ever for the loan.

In his statement, the Secretary makes it plain that there is nothing in the present situation to warrant the slightest easing up in the campaign for subscriptions and that the loan should be carried "over the top" to insure accomplishment of the aims for which President Wilson and the Allies are fighting. Mr. McAdoo's statement follows:

"Our victories on the battlefield and peace overtures from our enemies serve only to emphasize the supreme importance of making the Fourth Liberty Loan a success in order to keep up the fighting pressure.

"Now is the time above all others not to relax but to intensify effort that the goal for which we are fighting and for which we have already made such great sacrifices inevitably shall be won.

"Our boys in the trenches are not going to stop fighting because the enemy is on the run. Now is the time to fight harder and to keep moving until the victory is clinched. There is more reasons than ever to put the Fourth Liberty Loan over the top."

The Treasury Department tonight gave out figures indicating that subscriptions to the loan now total $1,323,716,950, or about 22 per cent. of the total of $6,000,000,000 asked by Secretary McAdoo. With one-third of the campaign period over, slightly less than one-fourth of the total has been officially reported sold. But care was taken by Treasury officials to explain that the total subscriptions to the loan are somewhat larger than these figures indicated. It is believed that were all the facts known the total is easily more than $1,880,000,000, and probably close to $2,000,000,000.

The figures given out tonight are very incomplete and cover reports dealing with sales only up to Saturday night. They do not cover the sales of yesterday and today, nor do they include any new reports from the Chicago and St. Louis districts, which made no returns today. The Kansas City district, however, figures in the compilation for the first time tonight with a total of $24,740,100, which represents subscriptions which accumulated last week when there was no selling campaign in progress in that city. The campaign started officially in that district today and was reported to have opened with a rush.

Even on the face of the figures for sales to the close of business on Saturday the St. Louis district leads all others in the percentage race, having 47 per cent. of its quota subscribed. The Minneapolis district is second, with 40 per cent.; Boston third, with 36 per cent.; San Francisco fourth, with 30 per cent.; Dallas fifth, with 25 per cent.; Richmond sixth, with 22 per cent.; Chicago seventh, with 20 per cent.; Philadelphia eighth, with 17 per cent.; New York ninth, with 16 9-10 per cent.; Cleveland tenth, with 16 per cent.; Atlanta eleventh, with 12 per cent., and Kansas City last, with 9½ per cent.

Following are the subscriptions by districts:

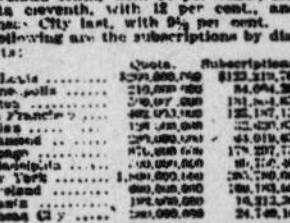

	Quota.	Subscriptions.
St. Louis	[illegible]	[illegible]
Minneapolis	[illegible]	[illegible]
Boston	[illegible]	[illegible]
San Francisco	[illegible]	[illegible]
Dallas	[illegible]	[illegible]
Richmond	[illegible]	[illegible]
Chicago	[illegible]	[illegible]
Philadelphia	[illegible]	[illegible]
New York	[illegible]	[illegible]
Cleveland	[illegible]	[illegible]
Atlanta	[illegible]	[illegible]
Kansas City	[illegible]	24,740,100
Total	$6,000,000,000	[illegible]

An unofficial report from St. Louis tonight said more than half the district's

Continued on Page Seventeen.

French Ships Seize Beirut; Joyfully Greeted by People

PARIS, Oct. 7.—A French naval division operating off the coast of Syria entered Beirut this morning. The enthusiasm of the populace is indescribable.

Beirut is the principal seaport on the Syrian coast. In October, 1915, it was the scene of those wholesale executions decreed by Djemal Pasha, then Military Governor of Syria, against the betrayed members of the famous Beirut Reform League.

The town is about ninety miles by rail northwest of Damascus and its modern growth has been more rapid industrially than any other town of the Levant. Before the war its imports were annually valued at $7,000,000; its exports at $3,000,000. Its harbor, although small and confined, is capable of being expanded. The population is about 150,000, of which only 60 per cent. is Moslem. When the war began the number of Europeans there was about 5,000.

NEW GOVERNMENT SET UP IN RUSSIA

Directorate of Five Created by State Convention at Ufa [illegible].

BACKED BY STRONG ARMY

Plans to Overthrow Red Rule and Act in Harmony with the Entente Allies.

Special to The New York Times.

WASHINGTON, Oct. 7.—Confidential information of a reliable official character has reached Washington indicating that the Russian people, as a nation, will swing back into line in steady and valuable support of the Entente Allies and the aims they seek to achieve in the great war.

President Wilson and the Allied Powers have committed themselves to the proposition of endeavoring to encourage the formation of a strong national government in Russia to assist in bringing about a complete restoration of law and order along with the ultimate obliteration of the Bolshevist reign of terror, to do everything possible toward removing the German menace that has cast its shadow athwart the path of Russian progress, and otherwise be of real service to the Russian people. Visible evidence of this commitment is seen in the progress being made by the allied military expedition now moving southward from Archangel and westward from Vladivostok.

The Russian Embassy was notified today by the newly formed Russian Provisional Government which was created by the State Convention at Ufa, that it had actually taken over the reins of power in succession to the Provisional Government of 1917. Russian diplomats throughout the world have been similarly notified and the facts are being communicated to the Entente Governments for their information.

The character of the Cabinet, or directorate, as it has been called, the representation in it of the various local Governments and other important national elements and information reaching Washington as to the character of the support it is receiving, all indicate that there is a strong trend in Russia toward a new era and that a really representative and constructive national Government appears to have been initiated at Ufa.

Second only in importance to the formation of the new Government is the fact that steps have been taken, with a remarkable degree of success, toward the recreation of a national army. This has been accomplished through the mobilization by the Omsk Government in Siberia of the two younger classes of youths, those of 1918 and 1919. This has resulted in the raising of more than 200,000 soldiers who are being trained along lines of strict discipline by more than 20,000 officers. The mobilization had not been expected to produce more than 140,000. The Academy of the General Staff is at Tomsk.

The text of the act signed by the representatives at the National Convention at Ufa, which is considered the most important Russian State paper that has been issued since the fall of the Keren[illegible]

Continued on Page Nine.

HAIG STRIKES IN FLANDERS

Advances on a 4-Mile Front North of the Scarpe.

MANY VILLAGES CAPTURED

German Rearguards on the Lens-Cambrai Front Are Cut to Pieces.

FRENCH TAKE BERRY-AU-BAC

Occupy Important Town on Left of Champagne Offensive, Holding Gains on Right.

LONDON, Oct. 7.—Resuming offensive operations north of the Scarpe River, the British today advanced on a four-mile front and captured the villages of Oppy and Biache-St. Vaast [the latter six miles southwest of Douai.]

Haig's troops last night established a post at the crossing of the Scheldt Canal north of Aubencheul-au-Bac [about five miles north of Cambrai] and pushed their lines slightly nearer Lille on the west and southwest. By the progress they have made north of Wez Macquart they are about five miles west of the city.

German rearguards who ventured to make a stand in opposing the British pursuit in Flanders were annihilated in every case.

Many explosions were observed today in the coal-mining region northeast of Lens, and fires are raging in Douai and many other towns of this district. Prisoners report that before the torch was applied to Douai the Germans indulged in an orgy of looting.

The French pressure in Champagne continues to yield results. Berry-au-Bac, at the junction of the River Aisne and the Aisne Canal and on the left wing of the general Champagne offensive, was taken today.

On the rest of the Champagne front the French have maintained their gains of yesterday and have even pushed further to the east and north of the Arnes River.

Heavy fighting continues between the French and Germans in the region north of St. Quentin. Repeated German counterattacks on Remaucourt and other positions captured by the French yesterday failed, with the exception of those against Tilloy farm, where the enemy recovered part of his lost ground.

Haig's Review of the Fighting.

Field Marshal Haig's summary of the British operations, as contained in his night bulletin, follows:

> In successful local operations this morning we advanced our line on a front of about four miles north of the Scarpe River, capturing the villages of Biache-St. Vaast and Oppy and more than 100 prisoners and a number of machine guns.
>
> Patrol fighting took place also northeast of Epinoy and north of Aubencheul-aux-Bois. We have progressed in both localities.

Following is the text of the British day report:

> In local fighting yesterday in the neighborhood of Aubencheul-aux-Bois we captured about 400 prisoners.
>
> Yesterday afternoon one of our patrols in the Oppy sector brought in thirty-four prisoners and four machine guns. During the night we established posts at the canal crossings north of Aubencheul-au-Bac, and also northeast and east of Oppy.
>
> A German post east of Berriau was captured by another of our patrols. We made slight progress north of Wez Macquart.

Many Flanders Towns Taken.

WITH THE BRITISH ARMY IN FRANCE, Oct. 8, (Associated Press.)—Many towns have been occupied by the British today in their advance after the retreating Germans along the sector of the front from Cambrai to Lens. In some cases the enemy's rearguards of-

Continued on Page Four.

Swiss Hear Kaiser Weeps and Talks of Abdicating

Copyright, 1918, by The New York Times Company.
Special Cable to THE NEW YORK TIMES.

PARIS, Oct. 7.—Circumstantial reports received here from good Swiss sources assert that the German Emperor is now suffering from insomnia and frequent crises of tears.

From time to time he suggests abdication, and then relinquishes the idea on the ground that the Kronprinz would be even less acceptable to the Allies than himself.

PERSHING CARRIES ARGONNE HEIGHTS

Drives Germans from Chatel-Chehery and Seizes Commanding Positions on Aire.

FOE FIGHTS DESPERATELY

His Tactics Indicate Determination to Force a Decisive Battle Here.

By EDWIN L. JAMES.
Copyright, 1918, by The New York Times Company.
Special Cable to THE NEW YORK TIMES.

WITH THE AMERICAN ARMY, Oct. 7, (9 P. M.)—A furious battle has been in progress all day for the possession of the north end forts of the Argonne. The Americans attacked from the east and south this morning. After a day of bitter fighting they have driven the Germans from the heights west of the Aire Valley and commanding the Argonne Forest from our line to the end of the jungle at Grand Pré. These heights include Hills 242, 244, and 269, on the crests of which our troops have dug in. This is the best advance we have made against the Argonne stronghold since the drive of the First American Army started on the morning of Sept. 26.

Our attack this morning was started by the troops on the line from Fleville, five kilometers southward, the troops moving due west. A short time after this attack started, at 6:30, the troops holding the line through the forest attacked northward. We used little artillery preparation, but put down heavy barrages ahead of our men.

This fire, while doing considerable damage to the Germans' communications, did not succeed in cutting the wire, because the thick woods deflected the shells to a great extent. The heavy wire entanglements had to be cut by the advancing infantry. Tanks, of course, could not be used to attack the forest.

Heavy Mist Aids the Attack.

Our attack was aided by a heavy mist, which enabled us to get upon the German positions before being seen. This precipitated a large amount of hand-to-hand fighting. The mist later developed into a cold rain, which still continues.

It is impossible to exaggerate the difficulties of the task of taking the Argonne Forest, so long regarded as impregnable. The Germans have thousands of steel and concrete positions bristling with machine guns, innumerable trenches running in all directions through the jungles, and many funnel-shaped traps commanded by nests of machine guns. They are fighting with desperation against the Americans, who are determined to wrest their highly prized stronghold from them.

The Germans gave up Châtel-Chéhéry without a strong fight, making their stand on the crest of the heights west of the Aire Valley. Using shellholes and tree stumps as shields, the Americans wormed their way up the hill and, leaping into the German trenches, routed the enemy with heavy losses to him.

Meanwhile, infantry elements had filtered through three ravines and caught the retreating Germans with machine gun fire. We organized our newly won positions on the Aire Heights and pushed down the western slopes of the hills, where we met with varying success. Our troops are being withdrawn tonight to organize the line.

In the fighting the Americans took prisoners and captured some artillery.

Continued on Page Three.

LONDON EXPECTS SWIFT 'NO'

Unanimous Press Opinion Here Taken as Forecast of Wilson's Action.

AN ARMISTICE IMPOSSIBLE

Request for It Should Have Been Addressed to Foch, Entente Leaders Hold.

PRESS CALL IT TRICKERY

Only Designed to Give the Beaten Foe a Breathing Spell, It Is Asserted.

Copyright, 1918, by The New York Times Company.
Special Cable to THE NEW YORK TIMES.

LONDON, Oct. 7.—The unanimous verdict of the American press on the Teuton peace proposals, as reflected in the editorials cabled here, that, in THE NEW YORK TIMES' phrase, "there can be no peace with the Hohenzollerns," was a feature of the afternoon's papers and is held to indicate clearly what will be the tenor of President Wilson's reply to Berlin.

Any idea that the proposal for an armistice could find favorable consideration for a moment in Washington is scouted. According to The Evening News, both Lloyd George and Clemenceau are of the opinion that the proposal to suspend military operations, which is regarded everywhere as impelled by military necessity, and a scheme by which Germany hoped to be able to extricate and regroup her armies, ought to have been addressed to Marshal Foch.

It was first thought in some quarters today that the German and Austrian notes to the President might have the effect of necessitating a united reply by the Entente Allies, supplementary to the response which President Wilson would make. That idea has today gone by the board. It is held that the unanimity of American opinion and the firm attitude of the President, which it foreshadows so unmistakably, mark the only outlines along which Germany can make any progress toward peace.

Germany and Austria, it is believed, will receive from the President so clear-cut a reply that the essentials of peace negotiation cannot be befogged by subsidiary questions, arising out of possible or problematical dissimilarities of view among the Allies. Such differences, it is held, can safely be left for settlement at the peace conference.

LONDON, Oct. 7, (Associated Press.)—In the view of authoritative quarters in London it seems certain that President Wilson, to whom the peace offer of the Central Powers was addressed, will take the initiative in replying. The official attitude to be adopted by the associated Governments can only be surmised, but it is safe to assume that they cannot entertain any proposal for an armistice.

According to foreign diplomats here, no armistice will be granted the Central Powers before the evacuation by them of allied territory and the cessation of the destruction and burning of allied cities. If the German propositions had been sincere, say these authorities, the German troops would already have ceased their wanton destruction.

One of the leading diplomats said the proposal for an armistice was put forward with the hope that the Allies would accept, and negotiations would be protracted for months in the hope that the offensive spirit of the allied armies would decline.

The fact that an armistice was requested indicated, according to this diplomat, that Germany knew she was defeated. Her collapse was only a question of time.

George Nicoll Barnes, member of the War Cabinet, in a speech at Derby last night, said that the latest peace offer showed no change of heart in Germany, but only indicated that the Germans realised the change in the military sit-

Continued on Page Two.

Say Hindenburg Resigned After Row With Kaiser; Told Ruler Retreat Was Necessary, War Was Lost

LONDON, Oct. 7.—Field Marshal von Hindenburg is reported to have resigned as Chief of the German General Staff after a heated interview with the Emperor in which the Field Marshal declared that a retreat on a large scale was impossible to avoid.

The statement comes in a dispatch from the Central News correspondent at Amsterdam, who states that his dispatch is based on reports from the frontier.

[Field Marshal von Hindenburg has been Chief of Staff since Aug. 30, 1916.]

By GEORGE RENWICK.
Copyright, 1918, by The New York Times Company.
Special Cable to THE NEW YORK TIMES.

AMSTERDAM, Oct. 6.—Events are following one another with the rapidity that characterized the fateful days at the end of July and beginning of August, 1914. At last the powerful alliance against the right has been forced to look the stern facts in the face.

My information, which I have every reason to believe is correct, is that the supreme army command in Germany had a great deal to do with the astonishing developments in the situation. Hindenburg and Ludendorff are said to have informed the Kaiser and the Government some time ago that they now recognized the military situation as hopeless. This view was impressed on the Chancellor by Hindenburg himself during his visit to Berlin.

Ever since the great German offensive began to stagger it has been amply demonstrated that it was Germany's last possible effort to impose her peace on the world.

The events since the Germans were hurled back over the Marne have emphatically shown that even the war of defense has become a hopeless and costly struggle, and nothing demonstrates that better than the latest communiqués from the west front.

PARIS DEMANDS FIRM PEACE FRONT

Wants Guarantees Before Moving to Accept Any Terms Which Foe Offers.

SEES TRICKERY ON ALSACE

Summary of French Opinion Shows No Prospect of Accepting Teuton Offer.

By CHARLES H. GRASTY.
Copyright, 1918, by The New York Times Company.
Special Cable to THE NEW YORK TIMES.

PARIS, Oct. 7.—Such French sentiment as was obtainable in Paris today, while accepting the proposal of the Central Empires seriously in the sense that they are in distress and that the démarche is the beginning of the end, seems inclined to the impression that there is no room for negotiation and that the causes which have produced the weakening should be allowed to operate until the work is finished.

In certain other quarters, where recently I found approval of President Wilson's speech of Sept. 27, the situation was viewed in a different sense. All are agreed on the main point that no negotiations shall be entered with Germany until she has accepted President Wilson's terms and given such guarantees as will make her acceptance binding.

No one is simple enough to take Germany on faith or to trust her mere word about anything. Before she can be treated with, she must, in the opinion of Europe, be deprived of all means of profiting by deceit or treachery. The crowd who have been running Germany have lost every shred of confidence, and while perhaps the establishment of parliamentary government in substitution for autocracy would bring the German people into a different relationship with other European peoples, some time must ensue before Germany can be regarded otherwise than as a militarist oligarchy.

Nobody here has the least nervousness lest President Wilson should be imposed upon by German scheming. He understands Berlin as thoroughly as any statesman in the world.

It would be a mistake to say that Europe accepts Wilson's leadership without some reserve, particularly since his speech of Sept. 27, but it is recognized that his leadership is dictated by the logic of events and is inevitable. Naturally, as in the past, he will act with considerate regard of the allied Governments, but his ideals and policy have been so consistent and have been so clearly stated as to leave little doubt regarding his aims.

Demand Guarantees for Peace.

It is reckoned in advance that there will be no premature negotiation with Berlin by Washington. There must be constitutional Government for the Central allies, which shall contain within itself guarantees for the future. There must be a cutting out, root and branch,

Continued on Page Two.

SENATE CONDEMNS NEW PEACE PLEAS

Unanimous Demand Made in Debate That War Go On Until Foe Is Helpless.

AN ARMISTICE NOW ABSURD

Would Mean Loss of War, Says Lodge, and Peace Should Be Dictated on German Soil.

Special to The New York Times.

WASHINGTON, Oct. 7.—Unequivocal rejection of the present peace overtures of Germany and Austria was urged today in vigorous speeches in the Senate. The unwavering sentiment was expressed that no proposals from the Central Powers could be regarded as sincere until all enemy troops had been withdrawn from conquered territory and the foe had displayed a willingness to accept the terms laid down by President Wilson, with indemnity for wanton war destruction as one of the basic conditions.

The Senate was in no receptive frame of mind over the overtures. Not one Senator who took the floor during the two hours the proposals were discussed advocated any other policy than to pursue the war until the Central Powers indicate a willingness to surrender unconditionally. The view was expressed that an armistice was issued merely to give the foe a breathing spell, during which he would apply himself to rehabilitating his weakened forces.

The sentiment of the Senate was voiced by Lodge of Massachusetts, Poindexter of Washington, Reed of Missouri, Hitchcock of Nebraska, Ashurst of Arizona, Nelson of Minnesota, McCumber of North Dakota, and others. Relentless prosecution of the war was advocated by every Senator who spoke and endorsed by those who did not participate. When peace terms are considered, it was urged, they ought to be taken up with actual representatives of the German people, and not the Hohenzollern military machine.

McCumber's Peace Resolution.

Senator McCumber of North Dakota, offered a resolution setting forth peace terms. The resolution, which was referred to the Foreign Relations Committee, follows:

> Be it resolved by the Senate of the United States, the House of Representatives concurring:
>
> That there shall be no cessation of hostilities and no armistice until the Imperial German Government shall disband its armies and surrender its arms and munitions, together with its navy, to the United States and her allies in this war;
>
> That before any armistice shall be considered the Imperial German Government shall unreservedly consent to the principles of reparation declared as terms of peace by our allies;
>
> That it will pay in damages the cost of rebuilding and reconstructing all the cities and villages destroyed by its armies, and restore to fertility the lands devastated by it;
>
> That it will repay every dollar and the

Continued on Page Eight.

REPLY MAY BE READY TO-DAY

Allies Expected to Unite Against Armistice or Bargaining.

NO CAPITAL FOR THE FOE

Answer to be in Terms That Cannot Be Turned to Account Against Us.

NATION'S ATTITUDE CLEAR

Senate Debate and Flood of Messages Show Stern Temper of the People.

Special to The New York Times.

WASHINGTON, Oct. 7.—The reply of President Wilson to the Austro-German peace proposals will be a rejection, in the convinced opinion of Washington.

When his answer is delivered the President will act as spokesman, not only for the United States Government, but also for all the nations allied in the fight against the Central Powers.

Exchanges have been in progress today between Washington, London, Paris, Rome, and Havre. The result of this comparison of views will be the presentation of a solid front in opposition to either an armistice or dickering with the Berlin and Vienna governments.

Speaking for himself and this Government alone, the President could have sent forward his reply to Germany early this evening. It is understood the President did not care to make such an answer, but preferred that it should have the augmented force of a combined reply from the Entente. For this reason, it is understood, he has indicated his views in advance to the allied Governments, and is obtaining their decisions before putting his answer in final form to be handed to the neutral diplomats in Washington, through whose Governments the note of rejection will be delivered.

When the President's answer will be forwarded and announced is dependent upon the time required for completing the interchange of views between the allied Governments. At the White House this evening it was thought that the consideration might reach a point where the President's decision can be announced tomorrow.

In any event, the reply will not be long delayed, and there is every incentive, on account of the Liberty Loan, and because of the official desire that the German peace offensive shall in no way act as a damper on American and Entente war activities, for a prompt speaking out of the decision of the President and his Allies in the great war.

Feels the Nation Is Behind Him.

The President is confident that his reply to the Austro-Germanic alliance will go forward with the unanimous support of the nation. Every evidence of this reached the White House from all parts of the nation today. Hundreds of telegrams were received. Regardless of party affiliation, the messages voiced the confident belief that the President would neither grant an armistice nor allow this nation to be drawn into any peace parley with the Central Powers. From all quarters the President was urged not to accept the German requests.

The President's position was further strengthened by the unequivocal stand taken by Senators Lodge, Hitchcock, Nelson, Poindexter, Reed, and others in debate in the United States Senate this afternoon, where the sentiment of the nation was patriotically and unmistakably reflected in every utterance. Not a single voice was raised in favor of yielding to the German manoeuvre, which was characterized as being intended as a trap for the Allies and evidence of a desire by the Central Powers to gain a breathing spell at the expense of the allied forces.

There was also encouragement for the President in summaries of [illegible]

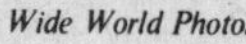

Wide World Photos

French troops prepare to fire a howitzer from the Meuse heights.

Site of the Meuse-Argonne offensive.

"All the News That's Fit to Print."

The New York Times.

THE WEATHER
Fair today; Friday cloudy; slight temperature change; wind south.
For weather report see next to last page.

VOL. LXVIII...NO. 22,189. NEW YORK, THURSDAY, OCTOBER 24, 1918. TWENTY-FOUR PAGES. TWO CENTS Within Greater New York and 50 Miles. | THREE CENTS Within 200 Miles | FOUR CENTS Elsewhere

WILSON HAS BUT ONE WORD—SURRENDER! FOR MILITARY AND AUTOCRATIC GERMANY; SENDS HER APPEALS TO ALLIES, BUT WARNS THAT TRUCE MUST LEAVE HER POWERLESS

Text of President Wilson's Reply to the German Government

FROM THE SECRETARY OF STATE TO THE CHARGE D'AFFAIRES OF SWITZERLAND, AD INTERIM IN CHARGE OF GERMAN INTERSTS IN THE UNITED STATES.

DEPARTMENT OF STATE, WASHINGTON, D. C., Oct. 23, 1918.

SIR: *I have the honor to acknowledge the receipt of your note of the 22d transmitting a communication under date of the 20th from the German Government and to advise you that the President has instructed me to reply thereto as follows:*

Having received the solemn and explicit assurance of the German Government that it unreservedly accepts the terms of peace laid down in his address to the Congress of the United States on the 8th of January, 1918, and the principles of settlement enunciated in his subsequent addresses, particularly the address of the 27th of September, and that it desires to discuss the details of their application, and that this wish and purpose emanate, not from those who have hitherto dictated German policy and conducted the present war on Germany's behalf, but from Ministers who speak for the majority of the Reichstag and for an overwhelming majority of the German people; and having received also the explicit promise of the present German Government that the humane rules of civilized warfare will be observed both on land and sea by the German armed forces, the President of the United States feels that he cannot decline to take up with the Governments with which the Government of the United States is associated the question of an armistice.

He deems it his duty to say again, however, that the only armistice he would feel justified in submitting for consideration would be one which should leave the United States and the Powers associated with her in a position to enforce any arrangements that may be entered into and to make a renewal of hostilities on the part of Germany impossible.

The President has, therefore, transmitted his correspondence with the present German authorities to the Governments with which the Government of the United States is associated as a belligerent, with the suggestion that, if those Governments are disposed to effect peace upon the terms and principles indicated, their military advisers and the military advisers of the United States be asked to submit to the Governments associated against Germany the necessary terms of such an armistice as will fully protect the interests of the peoples involved and insure to the associated Governments the unrestricted power to safeguard and enforce the details of the peace to which the German Government has agreed, provided they deem such an armistice possible from the military point of view. Should such terms of armistice be suggested, their acceptance by Germany will afford the best concrete evidence of her unequivocal acceptance of the terms and principles of peace from which the whole action proceeds.

The President would deem himself lacking in candor did he not point out in the frankest possible terms the reason why extraordinary safeguards must be demanded. Significant and important as the Constitutional changes seem to be which are spoken of by the German Foreign Secretary in his note of the 20th of October, it does not appear that the principle of a Government responsible to the German people has yet been fully worked out or that any guarantees either exist or are in contemplation that the alterations of principle and of practice now partially agreed upon will be permanent. Moreover, it does not appear that the heart of the present difficulty has been reached. It may be that future wars have been brought under the control of the German people, but the present war has not been; and it is with the present war that we are dealing. It is evident that the German people have no means of commanding the acquiescence of the military authorities of the Empire in the popular will; that the power of the King of Prussia to control the policy of the Empire is unimpaired; that the determining initiative still remains with those who have hitherto been the masters of Germany. Feeling that the whole peace of the world depends now on plain speaking and straightforward action, the President deems it his duty to say, without any attempt to soften what may seem harsh words, that the nations of the world do not and cannot trust the word of those who have hitherto been the masters of German policy, and to point out once more that in concluding peace and attempting to undo the infinite injuries and injustices of this war the Government of the United States cannot deal with any but veritable representatives of the German people who have been assured of a genuine Constitutional standing as the real rulers of Germany.

If it must deal with the military masters and the monarchical autocrats of Germany now, or if it is likely to have to deal with them later in regard to the international obligations of the German Empire, it must demand, not peace negotiations, but surrender. Nothing can be gained by leaving this essential thing unsaid.

Accept, Sir, the renewed assurances of my high consideration.

(Signed) ROBERT LANSING,

Mr. Frederick Oederlin, Chargé d'Affaires of Switzerland, ad interim in charge of German interests in the United States.

AMERICANS GAIN IN FIERCE BATTLE ALL ALONG FRONT

Occupy Brieulles and the Bois de Forêt, Where the Enemy Held Out a Week.

BANTHEVILLE TAKEN AGAIN

Changes Hands Several Times, but Hill 281, Dominating Cléry, Is Captured.

GRAND PRE BATTLE BITTER

Belle Joyeuse and Talma Farms Won by Our Men—Foe Gains and Then Is Hurled Back.

By EDWIN L. JAMES.

Copyright, 1918, by The New York Times Company. Special Cable to THE NEW YORK TIMES.

WITH THE AMERICAN ARMY IN FRANCE, Oct. 23.—The First American Army scored important successes today in severe fighting along the front north of Verdun.

On the left we again drove the Germans out of Grand Pré and advanced into the woods north of the town. In the centre we again took Bantheville and bettered our positions at several points in that vicinity. On the right we cleared the Germans from Brieulles.

The Germans held stubbornly to all these positions. We met very strong resistance in the region of Grand Pré and our attacks precipitated very heavy fighting in the region of Talma Farm and Bellejoyeuse Farm. In the Bois Trayes a bitter fight, with machine guns on both sides, took place.

Bantheville was again taken by virtue of our positions in the Bois Bantheville.

After our capture of Hills 297, 299, and 281 the enemy position in Brieulles was rendered untenable and our shellfire forced him to evacuate this morning. We sent in patrols in force, who in turn were shelled out by the Germans. Tonight we dominate the town.

Today's advances were the most important we have made in ten days, and our successes may indicate that the incessant night and day pressure by Pershing's men has somewhat worn down the German resistance in front of us.

Sky Full of Airplanes.

The day was marked by perhaps the most active aerial warfare we have seen. The sky was filled with machines all day. More than a hundred American bombing machines dropped several tons of bombs on German positions. The Germans retaliated with weak day bombing, but tonight were bombing the back areas of the American forces with vigor. Over one town American pursuit machines went into the air after German bombers.

There were many air battles along the front. Four of our Lieutenants—Wooley, Manning, Humes, and Colson—met four fokkers at a height of 3,800 metres. The Germans accepted the challenge, and in view of thousands of soldiers the four German machines were seen to come down. None of our airmen was hurt.

An idea of what our day bombers are doing may be gained by the statement that two tons of bombs were dropped on Buzancy today. Many fires were started in German depots.

Every foot of the infantry advance today was bitterly contested by the Germans with every tool of war they possessed. They are still fighting under orders to hold the Americans at all costs.

Line Swinging To and Fro.

WITH THE AMERICAN ARMY NORTHWEST OF VERDUN, Oct. 23, (Associated Press.)—The stiffest fighting of the American offensive west of the Meuse was under way today. The line is swaying back and forth.

Pershing's men captured the Belle Joyeuse and Talma farms and the

Continued on Page Five.

Haig's Armies Smash Foe's Lines; Gain 3 Miles, Take Many Prisoners

Several Villages Captured in Strong Advance on 17-Mile Front from Le Cateau to the Scheldt River—Enemy Reported to be Evacuating Ghent.

Belgians to Make Bruges Temporary Seat of Government

HAVRE, Oct. 23.—As the whole of the Province of Western Flanders, and part of Eastern Flanders, and Hainaut have been recovered from the Germans, the Belgian Government has decided to establish its administrative departments in Bruges.

WITH THE BRITISH ARMY IN FRANCE AND BELGIUM, Oct. 23, (Associated Press.)—The British Third and Fourth Armies smashed through strong German defensive positions by a new drive south of Valenciennes today. They gained ground to a depth of more than 5,000 yards (three miles) on an extended front, capturing many important villages and several thousand prisoners, together with numerous guns, and driving a wedge into the enemy positions at what probably is the most vital point of the lines the Germans are holding.

The fighting was of a desperate nature, the German machine gunners holding out to the last. Large numbers of the enemy were killed.

The advance continues and the menace to the Germans to the north and south of the front attacked is growing hourly. Further retreats are expected.

North of the Third and Fourth Armies the British First Army continued its attacks and reached positions well to the northeast of Valenciennes, which is gradually being squeezed out. It is probable that the Germans have already evacuated that town.

The British are approaching Le Quesnoy and were only about three miles from the gates of that place, according to late reports, and were still advancing.

The heaviest fighting seems to have been in L'Eveque Wood, which is still being cleared up, although the British have passed completely around it and are before the great Mormal Forest. On the edge of this the Germans were reported to be concentrating at Preux.

Catillon was taken early in the fighting by assault. Ors is in British hands. The Germans before retreating blew up all the bridges over the canal between Catillon and Ors.

Striking at a Vital Point.

WITH THE ALLIED ARMIES IN FRANCE AND BELGIUM, Oct. 23, (Associated Press.)—The attack of the British Third and Fourth Armies on a wide front south of Valenciennes today was of vital strategic importance.

The allied salient here menaces the German lines all the way to Holland, and if it is widened it will have a tremendous effect on the enemy front to the south also.

which the Germans have constructed.

Masses of British cannon, moved up during the comparative lull of the last few days, loosed tons of steel early today at the enemy, sprinkling front and rear areas freely. Later all the guns concentrated in a "crash barrage," behind which the infantry advanced in an early morning fog, storming the enemy defenses.

The Germans resisted strongly, especially the machine gunners. The enemy artillery fire was generally weak, indicating that his guns had been moved some miles east to the line known as the "Hermann Standing Place." This showed that the German command evidently did not have faith that the exhausted infantry would be able to hold the positions attacked today.

The town of Romeries was taken early in the attack, marking an advance of nearly two miles northeast of Solesmes.

British troops were fighting their way into the centre of Valenciennes early today. They were facing a strong enemy machine-gun fire from the east bank of the Scheldt Canal, which flows through the city.

The Germans on this front in the last few days have been following the tactics of retreating during the night. The British have not been able to establish contact with the enemy rearguards until noon the next day. The rearguards endeavor to hold the British in check until nightfall, when they again retreat.

Americans in Thick of Battle.

BRITISH HEADQUARTERS IN FRANCE AND BELGIUM, Oct. 23, (Reuter.)—The British forces are steadily linking up bridgeheads and footholds established along the west bank of the Scheldt.

Today's battle was difficult to follow, for, beginning along a connected front, it became a series of local struggles. Much of the ground is intersected by a network of little waterways, rendering it difficult for the troops to advance against a deliberate

Continued on Page Nine.

Allies in Full Agreement on Terms for Truce; Naval Terms Held to be of First Importance

LONDON, Oct. 23.—Reuter's Limited learns that the allied governments as a result of continual communications are perfectly acquainted with and agreed upon the terms under which it will be possible to enter into negotiations for an armistice. It should be observed that naval questions have never been dealt with in any negotiations between the United States and Germany, and they are of first importance from the Allies' viewpoint.

"The idea of the freedom of the seas as understood by Germany," says the Reuter dispatch, "is not a matter that any allied Government can accept at all. It would appear that the conditions precedent to an armistice must include the question of sea power, as well as of land power, but hitherto Germany has always limited her remarks to land power.

"America, Great Britain, France and Italy owe so much to sea power in carrying on the war and in national development that they cannot omit consideration of sea power from the discussions concerning the armistice.

"The President never assumed that his conditions would be limited to the evacuation of occupied territories, as the Germans always argued. He put a number of questions to Germany after receiving the first note, as a preliminary to placing the matter before the Allies."

More Than 2,000,000 of Our Men Abroad Or on the Way, Baker Reports to President

WASHINGTON, Oct. 23.—At the same time that the White House tonight made public the text of the reply to Germany's peace note there were given out letters exchanged between Secretary Baker and President Wilson, showing that since May 8, 1917, a total of 2,008,931 American soldiers had been embarked for overseas duty. Secretary Baker's letter read:

War Department,
Washington, Oct. 22, 1918.

My Dear Mr. President: More than two million American soldiers have sailed from the ports in this country to participate in the war overseas. In reporting this fact to you, I feel sure that you will be interested in the following data showing the progress of our military effort:

In my letter of July 1, 1918, I informed you that between May 8, 1917, and July 30, 1918, over a million men had either been landed in France or were en route thereto. Since July 1, 1918, embarkations by months have been as follows:

July	306,185
August	290,818
September	261,415
October 1 to 21	131,398
Total	989,816
Embarked to July 1, 1918	1,019,115
Grand total	2,008,931

In our overseas operations, I feel that we have good reason to be proud and thankful of the results obtained. Our losses have been exceedingly small, considering the size of the force transported and this is due to the efficient protection given American convoys by the naval forces. We also have been greatly assisted in the dispatch of troops abroad by the allocation of certain vessels from our allies, principally those of Great Britain.

Cordially yours,
NEWTON D. BAKER,
Secretary of War.
The President, the White House.

President Wilson sent this reply:

THE WHITE HOUSE, Washington, Oct. 22, 1918.

My Dear Mr. Secretary—I am very glad to have your letter of this morning, reporting that more than two million American soldiers have sailed from the ports of this country to participate in the war overseas. I am sure that this will be a matter of deep gratification and reassurance to the country and that every one will join me in congratulating the War and Navy Departments upon the steady accomplishment in this all-important application of force to the liberation of the world.

Cordially and sincerely yours,
WOODROW WILSON.

September Ship Losses Due to German U-Boats Were the Lowest in More Than Two Years

LONDON, Oct. 23.—The amount of merchant shipping sunk by enemy action, excluding marine risk, during September was lower than any month since August, 1916, according to an announcement by the Admiralty tonight.

The losses of British shipping due to enemy action and marine risk during the month totalled 151,593 gross tons, compared with 176,434 in August and 209,212 in September, 1917.

The losses for the quarter ending September were 510,551 gross tons, compared with 962,938 for the corresponding quarter of 1917.

Members of Congress Disagree In Views on President's Note

Will Produce Crisis in Germany, Says Hitchcock—Lodge Deplores Any Discussion with Enemy—Poindexter Fears That the President Would Make Terms with German People.

Special to The New York Times.

WASHINGTON, Oct. 23.—Members of Congress were interviewed for THE NEW YORK TIMES tonight on the President's note to Germany.

The Senate will meet tomorrow, and there will be full discussion of the note upon the floor.

Senator Lodge of Massachusetts, ranking Republican member of the Committee on Foreign Relations, said:

"The President says in his last sentence that, if we must deal with the military masters and autocrats of Germany, we must demand 'not peace negotiations, but surrender.' With this I am in full accord, as I was with the President's statement of Sept. 27.

"In the first paragraph the President says that, as the present German Government, which, as all the world knows, is controlled by the Kaiser and the military party, represents through its Ministers 'the majority of the Reichstag and an overwhelming majority of the German people,' he feels that he cannot decline to take up with the allied Governments the question of an armistice. With this I am not in accord, for the German Government described in the first paragraph and that described in the last sentence are one and the same.

"My own view is a very simple one. There is no German Government in existence with which I would discuss anything. I deplore at this stage, when we are advancing steadily to a complete victory, any discussion or exchange of notes with the German Government. The only thing now is to demand unconditional surrender. I would leave that to Marshal Foch and the Generals of the armies. When they report that the German Army has surrendered and ceased to exist as an army in being, then, and not until then, let the Allies and the United States meet and agree what terms they will impose on Germany to insure the safety of civilization and mankind."

Senator Hitchcock, Democrat, of Nebraska, Chairman of the Committee on Foreign Relations, said:

"I think the President has brought to a very logical climax the correspondence with Germany. However much difficulty we have had in understanding the German notes, the Germans can have no possible difficulty in understanding this note. The President practically tells them that they must democratize their Government in order to secure terms of peace and, as an alternative, that, if they persist in the retention of the old form of militaristic Government, he will consider nothing but unconditional surrender. It seems to me that it amounts to giving the German people their choice, and I believe it will produce a political crisis in Germany.

"I think the note will meet the approval of the American people, and I think it will receive the approving support of the Allies. I doubt there will be an armistice for some time, because it is almost certain that a crisis will follow in German internal affairs during which time nobody will have the power to make final arrangements."

A Diplomatic Triumph.

Senator King, Democrat of Utah, a member of the Foreign Relations Committee, said:

"The reply of the President is a diplomatic triumph and will result in the overthrow of Kaiserism and the military and junker class, and hasten a revolution, political in character, which will place the political power of the German people in representatives of their own selection. A casual perusal of the note may leave some disappointment, but when its meaning is understood, particularly in the light of the addresses made by the President and the notes submitted by the German Government, a genuine admiration for the manner in which the entire issues are treated must follow.

"It is perfectly obvious that the President recognizes the solidarity of the aims of the allied Governments and that in dealing with the war and all cognate questions the Central Powers must treat, not alone with the United States, but with her allies. While it is true the President has been the spokesman for the belligerent nations opposed to the Central Powers, his reply recognizes that, in dealing with the questions of armistice and peace negotiations and all matters relating to the war, the allies of the United States have a voice in their determination.

"The reply means there can be no armistice unless there is an unconditional surrender. While this is not stated in so many words, it is manifest that, when the entire question of armistice is remitted to the military authorities, they will require the same steps to be taken as were followed in the treatment of Bulgaria. Furthermore, it is clear that there cannot even be an armistice, so far as the United States is concerned, unless the great principles for which the President stands, and as they have been enunciated in his various addresses, are accepted by the German Government. So that, first, before there is an armistice, Germany must accept the democratic principles and all of the points stated by the President in his addresses, which would eventuate, of course, in a change in the form of the German Government and the absolute destruction of the military power of Germany.

"In my opinion, the reply will result

Continued on Page Two.

CALLS FOR DICTATED PEACE

No Truce Possible That Does Not Destroy Her Power to Renew War.

CLOSES DOOR ON KAISER

Notifies Germany That King of Prussia Still Rules Throughout the Empire.

FIRST CONSULTED ALLIES

Note Believed to Represent the Combined Views of All Our Cobelligerents.

Special to The New York Times.

WASHINGTON, Oct. 23.—"Not peace negotiations, but surrender."

This is the keynote of President Wilson's reply to the last German note as announced by Secretary of State Lansing at 9 o'clock tonight. It tells Germany that the power of the King of Prussia, who is also the German Kaiser, is still in unimpaired control of the empire, that the nations of the world do not trust even the word of those who have been masters of German policy, that the United States refuses to deal with any but veritable representatives of the German people, and that if our Government "must deal with the military masters and the monarchical autocrats of Germany now it must demand not peace negotiations but surrender."

With the idea of surrender and a dictated peace strictly in view, the President has decided to take up with the allied Governments the question of an armistice. The terms of this armistice are to be dictated by Marshal Foch, and by Generals Haig, Petain, Pershing, and Diaz and other military advisers of the allied Governments. These are the men who are to submit the terms of the armistice, and they are not to do so unless they consider an armistice possible from the military point of view.

Dealing on Military Basis.

Analysis of the note makes it plain that the President has brushed aside the matter of peace negotiations, and that he is dealing with the German overtures on a strictly military basis. Such an analysis will show that his action in taking up the question of an armistice with the allied Governments is strictly with the view of complete surrender by Germany to peace terms, and military guarantees and safeguards to be dictated and imposed by the Allied Powers.

The President's reply to Germany was announced so late tonight that it was difficult to round up the Congressional and diplomatic attitude toward his action. But it soon became apparent that the more the note was studied and analyzed by public men the more they regarded it as a strong and vigorous document and that his action would be fully justified by the rapid progress of events.

As opinion matured it became apparent that the President had dealt with all the German overtures, from the first note to the latest, in a most adroit, subtle, and vigorous fashion and that he had closed the door absolutely to negotiations with any German Government that remains under the control of the Kaiser and his clique.

What the President has done in taking up the question of an armistice with the Allies, and it must be borne always in mind that before this action was taken there were careful exchanges of views with the Allied Governments, has been to suggest to the Allies that the military advisers in the field be asked to fix the terms of the only kind of armistice they consider it possible to make from the military point of view. The President lays down specific rules for the guidance even of these military leaders in the making of this armistice, and there is ground for the statement that before he laid down these rules the Allied Governments were aware of their

U. S. Signal Corps

American machine gunners in France.

U. S. Signal Corps

Wounded Americans being carried to the rear by German prisoners.

"All the News That's Fit to Print."

The New York Times.

THE WEATHER
Fair today; tomorrow, fair, warmer; northeast winds.
For full weather report see Page 23.

VOL. LXVIII...NO. 22,172. NEW YORK, TUESDAY, OCTOBER 8, 1918.—TWENTY-FOUR PAGES. TWO CENTS Metropolitan District 50 Mile Radius | THREE CENTS Within 200 Miles | FOUR CENTS Elsewhere

EXPECT WILSON TO REJECT TEUTON OFFERS; NOW CONFERRING WITH ALLIES ON REPLY; BRITISH ARE AGAIN DRIVING TOWARD LILLE; FRENCH GAIN ON AISNE, OUR MEN IN ARGONNE

PEACE DRIVE MUST NOT WEAKEN LOAN DRIVE, SAYS M'ADOO

Boys in the Trenches Won't Stop Fighting, He Declares, Because Foe Is on the Run.

TIME NOW TO FIGHT HARDER

Nation's Subscriptions Reported Up to Saturday Night Total $1,323,716,950.

ST. LOUIS LEADS WITH 47%

New York Ninth in Percentage of Quota Subscribed—Plea for More Energy Here.

Special to The New York Times.

WASHINGTON, Oct. 7.—Fear that the Austro-German peace drive might seriously interfere with the progress of the Fourth Liberty Loan drive, while the country is awaiting President Wilson's answer to the Central Powers, was reflected by Secretary McAdoo tonight when he issued an appeal to the nation to work harder than ever for the loan.

In his statement, the Secretary makes it plain that there is nothing in the present situation to warrant the slightest easing up in the campaign for subscriptions and that the loan should be carried "over the top" to insure accomplishment of the aims for which President Wilson and the Allies are fighting. Mr. McAdoo's statement follows:

"Our victories on the battlefield and peace overtures from our enemies serve only to emphasize the supreme importance of making the Fourth Liberty Loan a success in order to keep up the fighting pressure.

"Now is the time above all others not to relax but to intensify effort that the goal for which we are fighting and for which we have already made such great sacrifices inevitably shall be won.

"Our boys in the trenches are not going to stop fighting because the enemy is on the run. Now is the time to fight harder and to keep moving until the victory is clinched. There is more reasons than ever to put the Fourth Liberty Loan over the top."

The Treasury Department tonight gave out figures indicating that subscriptions to the loan now total $1,323,716,950, or about 22 per cent. of the total of $6,000,000,000 asked by Secretary McAdoo. With one-third of the campaign period over, slightly less than one-fourth of the total has been officially reported sold. But care was taken by Treasury officials to explain that the total subscriptions to the loan are somewhat larger than those figures indicated. It is believed that were all the facts known the total is easily more than $1,500,000,000, and probably close to $2,000,000,000.

The figures given out tonight are very incomplete and cover reports dealing with sales only up to Saturday night. They do not cover the sales of yesterday and today, nor do they include any new reports from the Chicago and St. Louis districts, which made no returns today. The Kansas City district, however, figures in the compilation for the first time tonight with a total of $24,740,100, which represents subscriptions which accumulated last week when there was no selling campaign in progress in that city. The campaign started officially in that district today and was reported to have opened with a rush.

Even on the face of the figures for sales to the close of business on Saturday the St. Louis district leads all others in the percentage race, having 47 per cent. of its quota subscribed. The Minneapolis district is second, with 40 per cent.; Boston third, with 36 per cent.; San Francisco fourth, with 30 per cent.; Dallas fifth, with 25 per cent.; Richmond sixth, with 22 per cent.; Chicago seventh, with 20 per cent.; Philadelphia eighth, with 17 per cent.; New York ninth, with 16 9-10 per cent.; Cleveland tenth, with 16 per cent.; Atlanta eleventh, with 12 per cent., and Kansas City last, with 9½ per cent.

Following are the subscriptions by districts:

	Quota.	Subscriptions.
St. Louis	[illegible]	$123,219,700
Minneapolis	210,000,000	84,084,200
Boston	[illegible]	[illegible]
San Francisco	[illegible]	123,187,150
Dallas	[illegible]	[illegible]
Richmond	[illegible]	[illegible]
Chicago	[illegible]	[illegible]
Philadelphia	[illegible]	[illegible]
New York	1,800,000,000	[illegible]
Cleveland	[illegible]	[illegible]
Atlanta	[illegible]	[illegible]
Kansas City	[illegible]	24,740,100
Total	[illegible]	[illegible]

An unofficial report from St. Louis tonight said more than half the district's

Continued on Page Seventeen.

French Ships Seize Beirut; Joyfully Greeted by People

PARIS, Oct. 7.—A French naval division operating off the coast of Syria entered Beirut this morning. The enthusiasm of the populace is indescribable.

Beirut is the principal seaport on the Syrian coast. In October, 1915, it was the scene of those wholesale executions decreed by Djemal Pasha, then Military Governor of Syria, against the betrayed members of the famous Beirut Reform League.

The town is about ninety miles by rail northwest of Damascus and its modern growth has been more rapid industrially than any other town of the Levant. Before the war its imports were annually valued at $7,000,000; its exports at $3,600,000. Its harbor, although small and confined, is capable of being expanded. The population is about 120,000, of which only 30 per cent. is Moslem. When the war began the number of Europeans there was about 5,000.

NEW GOVERNMENT SET UP IN RUSSIA

Directorate of Five Created by State Convention at Ufa Takes Reins of Power.

BACKED BY STRONG ARMY

Plans to Overthrow Red Rule and Act in Harmony with the Entente Allies.

Special to The New York Times.

WASHINGTON, Oct. 7.—Confidential information of a reliable official character has reached Washington indicating that the Russian people, as a nation, will swing back into line in steady and valuable support of the Entente Allies and the aims they seek to achieve in the great war.

President Wilson and the Allied Powers have committed themselves to the proposition of endeavoring to encourage the formation of a strong national government in Russia to assist in bringing about a complete restoration of law and order along with the ultimate obliteration of the Bolshevist reign of terror, to do everything possible toward removing the German menace that has cast its shadow athwart the path of Russian progress, and otherwise be of real service to the Russian people. Visible evidence of this commitment is seen in the progress being made by the allied military expedition now moving southward from Archangel and westward from Vladivostok.

The Russian Embassy was notified today by the newly formed Russian Provisional Government which was created by the State Convention at Ufa, that it had actually taken over the reins of power in succession to the Provisional Government of 1917. Russian diplomats throughout the world have been similarly notified and the facts are being communicated to the Entente Governments for their information.

The character of the Cabinet, or directorate, as it has been called, the representation in it of the various local Governments and other important national elements and information reaching Washington as to the character of the support it is receiving, all indicate that there is a strong trend in Russia toward a new era and that a really representative and constructive national Government appears to have been initiated at Ufa.

Second only in importance to the formation of the new Government is the fact that steps have been taken, with a remarkable degree of success, toward the recreation of a national army. This has been accomplished through the mobilization by the Omsk Government in Siberia of the two younger classes of youths, those of 1918 and 1919. This has resulted in the raising of more than 200,000 soldiers who are being trained along lines of strict discipline by more than 20,000 officers. The mobilization had not been expected to produce more than 140,000. The Academy of the General Staff is at Tomsk.

The text of the act signed by the representatives at the National Convention at Ufa, which is considered the most important Russian State paper that has been issued since the fall of the Keren-

Continued on Page Nine.

HAIG STRIKES IN FLANDERS

Advances on a 4-Mile Front North of the Scarpe.

MANY VILLAGES CAPTURED

German Rearguards on the Lens-Cambrai Front Are Cut to Pieces.

FRENCH TAKE BERRY-AU-BAC

Occupy Important Town on Left of Champagne Offensive, Holding Gains on Right.

LONDON, Oct. 7.—Resuming offensive operations north of the Scarpe River, the British today advanced on a four-mile front and captured the villages of Oppy and Biache-St. Vaast [the latter six miles southwest of Douai.]

Haig's troops last night established a post at the crossing of the Scheldt Canal north of Aubencheul-au-Bac [about five miles northwest of Cambrai] and pushed their lines slightly nearer Lille on the west and southwest. By the progress they have made north of Wez Macquart they are about five miles west of the city.

German rearguards who ventured to make a stand in opposing the British pursuit in Flanders were annihilated in every case.

Many explosions were observed today in the coal-mining region northeast of Lens, and fires are raging in Douai and many other towns of this district. Prisoners report that before the torch was applied to Douai the Germans indulged in an orgy of looting.

The French pressure in Champagne continues to yield results. Berry-au-Bac, at the junction of the River Aisne and the Aisne Canal and on the left wing of the general Champagne offensive, was taken today.

On the rest of the Champagne front the French have maintained their gains of yesterday and have even pushed further to the east and north of the Arnes River.

Heavy fighting continues between the French and Germans in the region north of St. Quentin. Repeated German counterattacks on Remaucourt and other positions captured by the French yesterday failed, with the exception of those against Tilloy farm, where the enemy recovered part of his lost ground.

Haig's Review of the Fighting.

Field Marshal Haig's summary of the British operations, as contained in his night bulletin, follows:

In successful local operations this morning we advanced our line on a front of about four miles north of the Scarpe River, capturing the villages of Biache-St. Vaast and Oppy and more than 100 prisoners and a number of machine guns.

Patrol fighting took place also northeast of Epinoy and north of Aubencheul-aux-Bois. We have progressed in both localities.

Following is the text of the British day report:

In local fighting yesterday in the neighborhood of Aubencheul-aux-Bois we captured about 400 prisoners.

Yesterday afternoon one of our patrols in the Oppy sector brought in thirty-four prisoners and four machine guns. During the night we established posts at the canal crossings north of Aubencheul-au-Bac, and also northeast and east of Oppy.

A German post east of Beradau was captured by another of our patrols. We made slight progress north of Wez Macquart.

Many Flanders Towns Taken.

WITH THE BRITISH ARMY IN FRANCE, Oct. 7, (Associated Press.)—Many towns have been occupied by the British today in their advance after the retreating Germans along the sector of the front from Cambrai to Lens. In some cases the enemy's rearguards of-

Continued on Page Four.

Swiss Hear Kaiser Weeps and Talks of Abdicating

Copyright, 1918, by The New York Times Company. Special Cable to THE NEW YORK TIMES.

PARIS, Oct. 7.—Circumstantial reports received here from good Swiss sources assert that the German Emperor is now suffering from insomnia and frequent crises of tears.

From time to time he suggests abdication, and then relinquishes the idea on the ground that the Kronprinz would be even less acceptable to the Allies than himself.

PERSHING CARRIES ARGONNE HEIGHTS

Drives Germans from Chatel-Chehery and Seizes Commanding Positions on Aire.

FOE FIGHTS DESPERATELY

His Tactics Indicate Determination to Force a Decisive Battle Here.

By EDWIN L. JAMES.

Copyright, 1918, by The New York Times Company. Special Cable to THE NEW YORK TIMES.

WITH THE AMERICAN ARMY, Oct. 7, (9 P. M.)—A furious battle has been in progress all day for the possession of the north end forts of the Argonne. The Americans attacked from the east and south this morning. After a day of bitter fighting they have driven the Germans from the heights west of the Aire Valley and commanding the Argonne Forest from our line to the end of the jungle at Grand Pré. These heights include Hills 242, 244, and 263, on the crests of which our troops have dug in. This is the best advance we have made against the Argonne stronghold since the drive of the First American Army started on the morning of Sept. 26.

Our attack this morning was started by the troops on the line from Fleville, five kilometers southward, the troops moving due west. A short time after this attack started, at 6:30, the troops holding the line through the forest attacked northward. We used little artillery preparation, but put down heavy barrages ahead of our men.

This fire, while doing considerable damage to the Germans' communications, did not succeed in cutting the wire, because the thick woods deflected the shells to a great extent. The heavy wire entanglements had to be cut by the advancing infantry. Tanks, of course, could not be used to attack the forest.

Heavy Mist Aids the Attack.

Our attack was aided by a heavy mist, which enabled us to get upon the German positions before being seen. This precipitated a large amount of hand-to-hand fighting. The mist later developed into a cold rain, which still continues.

It is impossible to exaggerate the difficulties of the task of taking the Argonne Forest, so long regarded as impregnable. The Germans have thousands of steel and concrete positions bristling with machine guns, innumerable trenches running in all directions through the jungles, and many funnel-shaped traps commanded by nests of machine guns. They are fighting with desperation against the Americans, who are determined to wrest their highly prized stronghold from them.

The Germans gave up Châtel-Chéhéry without a strong fight, making their stand on the crest of the heights west of the Aire Valley. Using shell-holes and tree stumps as shields, the Americans wormed their way up the hill and, leaping into the German trenches, routed the enemy with heavy losses to him.

Meanwhile, infantry elements had filtered through three ravines and caught the retreating Germans with machine gun fire. We organized our newly won positions on the Aire Heights and pushed down the western slopes of the hills, where we met with varying success. Our troops are being withdrawn tonight to organize the line.

In the fighting the Americans took prisoners and captured some artillery.

Continued on Page Three.

LONDON EXPECTS SWIFT 'NO'

Unanimous Press Opinion Here Taken as Forecast of Wilson's Action.

AN ARMISTICE IMPOSSIBLE

Request for It Should Have Been Addressed to Foch, Entente Leaders Hold.

PRESS CALL IT TRICKERY

Only Designed to Give the Beaten Foe a Breathing Spell, It Is Asserted.

Copyright, 1918, by The New York Times Company. Special Cable to THE NEW YORK TIMES.

LONDON, Oct. 7.—The unanimous verdict of the American press on the Teuton peace proposals, as reflected in the editorials cabled here, that, in THE NEW YORK TIMES' phrase, "there can be no peace with the Hohenzollerns," was a feature of the afternoon's papers and is held to indicate clearly what will be the tenor of President Wilson's reply to Berlin.

Any idea that the proposal for an armistice could find favorable consideration for a moment in Washington is scouted. According to The Evening News, both Lloyd George and Clemenceau are of the opinion that the proposal to suspend military operations, which is regarded everywhere as impelled by military necessity, and a scheme by which Germany hoped to be able to extricate and regroup her armies, ought to have been addressed to Marshal Foch.

It was first thought in some quarters today that the German and Austrian notes to the President might have the effect of necessitating a united reply by the Entente Allies, supplementary to the response which President Wilson would make. That idea has today gone by the board. It is held that the unanimity of American opinion and the firm attitude of the President, which it foreshadows so unmistakably, mark the only outlines along which Germany can make any progress toward peace.

Germany and Austria, it is believed, will receive from the President so clear-cut a reply that the essentials of peace negotiation cannot be beclogged by subsidiary questions, arising out of possible or problematical dissimilarities of view among the Allies. Such differences, it is held, can safely be left for settlement at the peace conference.

LONDON, Oct. 7, (Associated Press.)—In the view of authoritative quarters in London it seems certain that President Wilson, to whom the peace offer of the Central Powers was addressed, will take the initiative in replying. The official attitude to be adopted by the associated Governments can only be surmised, but it is safe to assume that they cannot entertain any proposal for an armistice.

According to foreign diplomats here, no armistice will be granted the Central Powers before the evacuation by them of allied territory and the cessation of the destruction and burning of allied cities. If the German propositions had been sincere, say these authorities, the German troops would already have ceased their wanton destruction.

One of the leading diplomats said the proposal for an armistice was put forward with the hope that the Allies would accept, and negotiations would be protracted for months in the hope that the offensive spirit of the allied armies would decline.

The fact that an armistice was requested indicated, according to this diplomat, that Germany knew she was defeated. Her collapse was only a question of time.

George Nicoll Barnes, member of the War Cabinet, in a speech at Derby last night, said that the latest peace offer showed no change of heart in Germany, but only indicated that the Germans realized the change in the military sit-

Continued on Page Two.

Say Hindenburg Resigned After Row With Kaiser; Told Ruler Retreat Was Necessary, War Was Lost

LONDON, Oct. 7.—Field Marshal von Hindenburg is reported to have resigned as Chief of the German General Staff after a heated interview with the Emperor in which the Field Marshal declared that a retreat on a large scale was impossible to avoid.

The statement comes in a dispatch from the Central News correspondent at Amsterdam, who states that his dispatch is based on reports from the frontier.

[Field Marshal von Hindenburg has been Chief of Staff since Aug. 30, 1916.]

By GEORGE RENWICK.

Copyright, 1918, by The New York Times Company. Special Cable to THE NEW YORK TIMES.

AMSTERDAM, Oct. 6.—Events are following one another with the rapidity that characterized the fateful days at the end of July and beginning of August, 1914. At last the powerful alliance against the right has been forced to look the stern facts in the face.

My information, which I have every reason to believe is correct, is that the supreme army command in Germany had a great deal to do with the astonishing developments in the situation. Hindenburg and Ludendorff are said to have informed the Kaiser and the Government some time ago that they now recognized the military situation as hopeless. This view was impressed on the Chancellor by Hindenburg himself during his visit to Berlin.

Ever since the great German offensive began to stagger it has been amply demonstrated that it was Germany's last possible effort to impose her peace on the world.

The events since the Germans were hurled back over the Marne have emphatically shown that even the war of defense has become a hopeless and costly struggle, and nothing demonstrates that better than the latest communiqués from the west front.

PARIS DEMANDS FIRM PEACE FRONT

Wants Guarantees Before Moving to Accept Any Terms Which Foe Offers.

SEES TRICKERY ON ALSACE

Summary of French Opinion Shows No Prospect of Accepting Teuton Offer.

By CHARLES H. GRASTY.

Copyright, 1918, by The New York Times Company. Special Cable to THE NEW YORK TIMES.

PARIS, Oct. 7.—Such French sentiment as was obtainable in Paris today, while accepting the proposal of the Central Empires seriously in the sense that they are in distress and that the démarche is the beginning of the end, seems inclined to the impression that there is no room for negotiation and that the causes which have produced the weakening should be allowed to operate until the work is finished.

In certain other quarters, where recently I found approval of President Wilson's speech of Sept. 27, the situation was viewed in a different sense. All are agreed on the main point that no negotiations shall be entered with Germany until she has accepted President Wilson's terms and given such guarantees as will make her acceptance binding.

No one is simple enough to take Germany on faith or to trust her mere word about anything. Before she can be treated with, she must, in the opinion of Europe, be deprived of all means of profiting by deceit or treachery. The crowd who have been running Germany have lost every shred of confidence, and while perhaps the establishment of parliamentary government in substitution for autocracy would bring the German people into a different relationship with other European peoples, some time must ensue before Germany can be regarded otherwise than as a militarist oligarchy.

Nobody here has the least nervousness lest President Wilson should be imposed upon by German scheming. He understands Berlin as thoroughly as any statesman in the world.

It would be a mistake to say that Europe accepts Wilson's leadership without some reserve, particularly since his speech of Sept. 27, but it is recognized that his leadership is dictated by the logic of events and is inevitable. Naturally, as in the past, he will act with considerate regard of the allied Governments, but his ideals and policy have been so consistent and have been so clearly stated as to leave little doubt regarding his aims.

Demand Guarantees for Peace.

It is reckoned in advance that there will be no premature negotiation with Berlin by Washington. There must be constitutional Government for the Central allies, which shall contain within itself guarantees for the future. There must be a cutting out, root and branch,

Continued on Page Two.

SENATE CONDEMNS NEW PEACE PLEAS

Unanimous Demand Made in Debate That War Go On Until Foe Is Helpless.

AN ARMISTICE NOW ABSURD

Would Mean Loss of War, Says Lodge, and Peace Should Be Dictated on German Soil.

Special to The New York Times.

WASHINGTON, Oct. 7.—Unequivocal rejection of the present peace overtures of Germany and Austria was urged today in vigorous speeches in the Senate. The unwavering sentiment was expressed that no proposals from the Central Powers could be regarded as sincere until all enemy troops had been withdrawn from conquered territory and the foe had displayed a willingness to accept the terms laid down by President Wilson, with indemnity for wanton war destruction as one of the basic conditions.

The Senate was in no receptive frame of mind over the overtures. Not one Senator who took the floor during the two hours the proposals were discussed advocated any other policy than to pursue the war until the Central Powers indicate a willingness to surrender unconditionally. The view was expressed that an armistice was issued merely to give the foe a breathing spell, during which he would apply himself to rehabilitating his weakened forces.

The sentiment of the Senate was voiced by Lodge of Massachusetts, Poindexter of Washington, Reed of Missouri, Hitchcock of Nebraska, Ashurst of Arizona, Nelson of Minnesota, McCumber of North Dakota, and others. Relentless prosecution of the war was advocated by every Senator who spoke and endorsed by those who did not participate. When peace terms are considered, it was urged, they ought to be taken up with actual representatives of the German people, and not the Hohenzollern military machine.

McCumber's Peace Resolution.

Senator McCumber of North Dakota, offered a resolution setting forth peace terms. The resolution, which was referred to the Foreign Relations Committee, follows:

Be it resolved by the Senate of the United States, the House of Representatives concurring:

That there shall be no cessation of hostilities and no armistice until the Imperial German Government shall disband its armies and surrender its arms and munitions together with its navy, to the United States and her allies in this war;

That before any armistice shall be considered the Imperial German Government shall unreservedly consent to the principles of reparation declared as terms of peace by our allies;

That it will pay in damages the cost of rebuilding and reconstructing all the cities and villages destroyed by its armies, and restore to fertility the lands devastated by it;

That it will repay every dollar and the

Continued on Page Eight.

REPLY MAY BE READY TO-DAY

Allies Expected to Unite Against Armistice or Bargaining.

NO CAPITAL FOR THE FOE

Answer to be in Terms That Cannot Be Turned to Account Against Us.

NATION'S ATTITUDE CLEAR

Senate Debate and Flood of Messages Show Stern Temper of the People.

Special to The New York Times.

WASHINGTON, Oct. 7.—The reply of President Wilson to the Austro-German peace proposals will be a rejection, in the convinced opinion of Washington.

When his answer is delivered the President will act as spokesman, not only for the United States Government, but also for all the nations allied in the fight against the Central Powers.

Exchanges have been in progress today between Washington, London, Paris, Rome, and Havre. The result of this comparison of views will be the presentation of a solid front in opposition to either an armistice or dickering with the Berlin and Vienna governments.

Speaking for himself and this Government alone, the President could have sent forward his reply to Germany early this evening. It is understood the President did not care to make such an answer, but preferred that it should have the augmented force of a combined reply from the Entente. For this reason, it is understood, he has indicated his views in advance to the allied Governments, and is obtaining their decisions before putting his answer in final form to be handed to the neutral diplomats in Washington, through whose Governments the note of rejection will be delivered.

When the President's answer will be forwarded and announced is dependent upon the time required for completing the interchange of views between the allied Governments. At the White House this evening it was thought that the consideration might reach a point where the President's decision can be announced tomorrow.

In any event, the reply will not be long delayed, and there is every incentive, on account of the Liberty Loan, and because of the official desire that the German peace offensive shall in no way act as a damper on American and Entente war activities, for a prompt speaking out of the decision of the President and his Allies in the great war.

Feels the Nation Is Behind Him.

The President is confident that his reply to the Austro-Germanic alliance will go forward with the unanimous support of the nation. Every evidence of this reached the White House from all parts of the nation today. Hundreds of telegrams were received. Regardless of party affiliation, the messages voiced the confident belief that the President would neither grant an armistice nor allow this nation to be drawn into any peace parley with the Central Powers. From all quarters the President was urged not to accept the German requests.

The President's position was further strengthened by the unequivocal stand taken by Senators Lodge, Hitchcock, Nelson, Poindexter, Reed, and others in debate in the United States Senate this afternoon, where the sentiment of the nation was patriotically and unmistakably reflected in every utterance. Not a single voice was raised in favor of yielding to the German manoeuvre, which was characterized as being intended as a trap for the Allies and evidence of a desire by the Central Powers to gain a breathing spell at the expense of the allied forces.

There was also encouragement for the President in summaries of edi-

Continued on Page Eight.

"All the News That's Fit to Print."

The New York Times.

THE WEATHER
Fair, slightly cooler today; tomorrow, fair; moderate south winds.
For weather report see next to last page.

VOL. LXVIII...NO. 22,198. NEW YORK, TUESDAY, OCTOBER 29, 1918. TWENTY-TWO PAGES. TWO CENTS Metropolitan District 50 Mile Radius | THREE CENTS Within 200 Miles | FOUR CENTS Elsewhere

AUSTRIA 'ACCEPTS' ALL OF WILSON'S CONDITIONS, ASKS FOR IMMEDIATE AND SEPARATE PEACE; LONDON AND PARIS SAY GERMANY IS ISOLATED; ITALIANS AND BRITISH TAKE 9,000 AUSTRIANS

ROOSEVELT BITTER IN BEGINNING WAR ON THE PRESIDENT

Says President Puts Loyalty to Himself Before Loyalty to the Nation.

DENOUNCES WAR'S CONDUCT

"If We Had Prepared," He Declares, It Would Have Been Over in Ninety Days.

SEES NEED OF REPUBLICANS

Carnegie Hall Packed to Hear the Colonel's Speech at Rally for G. O. P. Candidates.

Speaking for more than two hours last night to a crowd that packed Carnegie Hall, Colonel Theodore Roosevelt bitterly assailed President Wilson and his conduct of the war. It was one of the longest speeches the Colonel ever made, and [illegible]

[illegible] rally in support of the Republican [illegible] ticket, given under the auspices of the Republican Club and the County Committee of New York, it was in reality a call to the Republicans of the nation to fight to the last ditch to offset the President's appeal and to return an overwhelming Republican Congress at the election. The Colonel referred to the State situation, but merely in passing.

Mr. Roosevelt in his address made this reference to Mr. Wilson:

"He does not ask for loyalty to the Nation. He asks only for support of himself. There is not the slightest suggestion that he disapproves of disloyalty to the Nation. I do not doubt that he feels some disapproval of such disloyalty; but apparently this feeling on his part is so tepid that it slips from his mind when he contemplates what he regards as the far greater sin of failure in adherence to himself."

Altogether the Colonel spoke nearly 20,000 words. He had prepared his speech early last week, and had, to add a long insert to deal specifically with the President's last Friday's appeal. There were other speakers, and all dealt largely with the President's appeal, but the Colonel was the main attraction. Besides the 5,000 or so within the hall, several thousand fought for admission and completely overwhelmed the police. Half a dozen speakers filled in the time till the Colonel arrived at 9:15 o'clock. His appearance on the stage was the signal for a great outburst of cheering. Fully one-half of the audience were women, and on the stage sat practically every Republican of prominence in the city and many from up-State.

Colonel Roosevelt's Speech.

After four minutes of cheering, yelling, and handclapping, the Colonel was allowed to start. In his speech he said:

"I come to this meeting as an American, and only as an American. In this crisis I do not consider politics at all whenever doing so conflicts in the slightest degree with the great cause of Americanism or with our immediate purpose of winning the war and of securing the peace of unconditional surrender by Germany. I make my appeal to all good Americans, in the name of Americanism, and I make it just as much to all independents and to all far-sighted, patriotic Democrats who are awake to the real needs of the situation as I do to Republicans.

"This meeting is held under peculiar circumstances. If the President of the United States is right in the appeal he has just made to the voters, then you and I, my hearers, have no right to vote at this election or to discuss public questions while the war lasts. If his appeal is justified, only that faction of the Democratic Party which accepts toward the President the rubber-stamp attitude of complete servility is entitled to control Congress; and no man who is a Republican, and no man whether a Republican or not who puts loyalty to the people ahead of loyalty to the servant of the people, is to have a voice in determining the greatest questions ever brought before this nation.

"In this election appeal which the President has issued to the voters of the country he states that he 'earnestly begs' the voters to return 'a Democratic majority to both the Senate and the House of Representatives,' and that although 'the leaders of the minority in the present Congress have unquestionably been pro-war they have been anti-Administration,' and that 'the return of a Republican majority to either house of Congress would certainly be interpreted on the other side of the water as a repudiation of my (President Wilson's) leadership.'

"This is an extraordinary document. It is an emphatic repudiation and reversal of the President's announcement of a few months back that 'poli-

Continued on Page Seven.

Senate Republicans Refuse to Take Recess at This Time

Special to The New York Times.

WASHINGTON, Oct. 28.—Republican leaders of the Senate today declined to agree to a resolution to adjourn Congress from tomorrow until Nov. 12. This disagreement was made in an informal talk which Senators Martin and Simmons had with Senators Lodge and Penrose. The latter held it was the duty of Congress to remain in session while peace overtures and other important matters were pending.

In expectation of an agreement by the Senate, the House passed a joint resolution, providing for adjournment. After the disagreement, Representative Kitchin asked for its reconsideration by the House and announced that Congress would remain in session unless the Senate should change its attitude Thursday, when the House meets again.

SENATE BATTLE OVER PRESIDENT

Wilson's Denial That His Peace Terms Look to Free Trade Read Into Record.

DEFENDED BY DEMOCRATS

[illegible] Attack Both His Terms for Peace and Political Appeal.

Special to The New York Times.

WASHINGTON, Oct. 28.—In a turbulent debate in the Senate today, inspired by President Wilson's call to the country for a return of a Democratic Congress, Republicans and Democrats hurled charges of partisanship at one another. Republican Senators bitterly attacked the President's appeal as an affront to loyal voters of their party.

President Wilson's allusion in his fourteen peace proposals to the "removal, as far as possible, of economic barriers and the establishment of trade conditions among all nations" after the war was attacked by Senators Brandegee of Connecticut and Penrose of Pennsylvania. They argued it would let down the bars to German commerce on an equality with that of the allied nations.

This assertion was denied by Senator Hitchcock of Nebraska, Chairman of the Foreign Relations Committee, who insisted that the President intended that the issue should be put up to the league of nations, so there would be no unjust discrimination against any signatory of the peace treaty.

Senator Hitchcock read into the record a letter he had received from President Wilson and one that Senator Simmons of North Carolina had received in response to letters of theirs in which the President had been informed of criticism by Republican leaders of his "economic barrier" proposal as tending to let down the barriers to Germany after the war.

The Senate debate, which raged for four hours, was precipitated by Senator Knox of Pennsylvania, who took up the President's appeal to the voters to elect a Democratic Congress. Senator Hitchcock replied to Mr. Knox and later Senator Pittman of Nevada vigorously attacked the Republican leaders in Congress, Colonel Roosevelt and Chairman Hays of the Republican National Committee, asserting that they were undermining the war policies of the President. Senator Poindexter of Washington wound up the debate for the Republicans with a vehement reply to Mr. Pittman, in which he insisted that the Republicans had supported the President, but that the President himself had been playing politics.

Prerogatives of Congress.

Mr. Knox insisted that the Senate's prerogative as the treaty-making body must not be usurped by the President.

"The excessive intermingling of the problem of a victorious ending of the war with a great variety of projects of world reconstruction renders our task most difficult," said Mr. Knox. "As a co-ordinate branch of this Government it is our duty, I believe, to make clear the Senate sense of the immediate necessity of clarification and simplification of any program that enters into the ending of the war or the building of the future, and the Senate's sense of the instant necessity of full counsel and accord upon all such programs between the Government of the United States and the Governments of our allies.

"And there is a necessity that underlies these needs. That is classification for the Senate itself of the policies to which it may be later called upon to consider giving its sanction. In this

Continued on Page Six.

NAMES CAILLAUX IN PLOT TO SPLIT ALLIES IN NEW WAR

Count James Minotto Confesses, Revealing Intrigue with Luxburg in Buenos Aires.

HE WAS THE GO-BETWEEN

Swift's Son-in law Says France, Italy, and Spain Were to Join the Teutons.

AGAINST BRITAIN AND RUSSIA

Confession Made Here to Deputy Attorney General Becker as Agent of French Republic.

Count James Minotto, the German nobleman who is a son-in-law of Louis F. Swift, the Chicago packer, and who, according to Secretary of the Navy Josephus Daniels, tried to get a place in the Naval Intelligence Service of this country, has made a startling [illegible] the former French Premier, [illegible] burg, former German Minister to the Argentine, and himself, to disrupt the Entente Alliance and to bring about a new war, in which the Teutonic powers, France, Italy, and Spain would be arrayed against Great Britain and Russia. The full report of the Minotto confession is now on the way to the French authorities in Paris.

Minotto, whose internment as an enemy alien was fought by his wife's family, who maintained that the Count was an Italian and an ally of the United States, was brought to New York last week from the internment prison near Fort Oglethorpe, Ga. He was taken before Deputy Attorney General Alfred L. Becker, who represented the French Government and the Federal authorities. At first, Minotto was not inclined to talk, but he finally told the story in all its details.

The Countess Minotto, mother of Count James, was, before her marriage, the famous German actress Agnes Sorma. Mme. Sorma will be remembered by old theatregoers as the star in Hauptmann's "Sunken Bell," which was played in German at the Irving Place Theatre some twenty years ago. The Countess and her husband are both in the United States at present. They went to Chicago last November to aid their son when he was fighting against the Government's order of internment.

Mr. Becker said last night that for the present he was not in a position to make public the full details of the confession made by Minotto. The story when told in full, he said, would be one of the most remarkable in the history of international intrigue and would show up Caillaux as a plotter compared to whom Bolo Pacha, was a mere novice. Bolo sought to corrupt French public opinion through the publication of a few newspapers. Caillaux on the other hand, sought to betray not only his own but two other nations as well, one of them Italy, an ally of France, and the other Spain, a friend of France. Had the plot succeeded, it was pointed

Continued on Last Page.

'Hold Fast' in This Grave Hour, Hindenburg Tells the Army

WITH THE AMERICAN ARMY NORTHWEST OF VERDUN, Oct. 28, (Associated Press.)—"Hold fast, an armistice has not yet been concluded," is the word sent to the German troops by Field Marshal von Hindenburg, Chief of the General Staff, according to a captured document now in the hands of the Americans. The German commander's appeal reads:

"German soldiers, be vigilant. The word 'armistice' is current in the trenches and camps, but we have not yet reached that point. To some the word represents a certainty, to others it is even a synonym of the peace so long desired. They believe that events no longer depend upon them. Their vigilance is relaxed, their courage and their endurance, as well as their spirit of defiance toward the enemy, are diminished.

"We have not yet reached our aim. The armistice has not been concluded. The war is still on—the same war as ever.

"Now, more than ever, you must be vigilant and hold fast. You are upon the enemy's soil, and on the soil of Alsace-Lorraine, the bulwark of our country. In this grave hour the Fatherland relies on you for its prosperity and for its safety."

FRENCH KEEP UP DRIVE BEYOND OISE

[illegible] on the Whole Front to the Serre.

GREATEST GAIN IS 2 MILES

They Have Crossed the Peron River, Capturing Many Villages in a Wide Area.

LONDON, Oct. 28.—While operations on the British front today have been limited to a slight advance of the lines south of Valenciennes, the French, continuing their pressure on the Germans between the Oise and the Serre, have thrown the enemy back about two miles at the apex of their attack, which was in the region of Bois-les-Pargny, east of the little River Peron, and have made substantial gains on either side.

French troops are in fresh contact with the enemy on the whole front between the Oise and Serre, and on the Aisne front, west of Château-Porcien, they have made an advance north of Herpy.

In Eastern Champagne American units in a brilliant local operation gained ground east of Attigny to a depth of about two-thirds of a mile.

French aviators on Sunday, flying over German back areas with 128 machines, effectively bombed enemy transport and troops. They reported many fires in the German-held parts of the Serre Valley and on the right bank of the Aisne.

The French operations of the day

Continued on Page Five.

Americans' Huge Guns Now Turned On Germans' Main Supply Railway

By EDWIN L. JAMES.

Special Cable to THE NEW YORK TIMES.

WITH THE AMERICAN ARMY NORTHWEST OF VERDUN, Oct. 28.—American guns of large calibre have begun firing on the Longuyon-Sedan-Mezières Railroad, the most important German line of communication, with the object of interrupting traffic and ultimately breaking the line.

Thus the offensive of the American First Army begun Sept. 26 begins to achieve its objective. Our advance of some eighteen kilometers now makes possible the shelling of the German communication line to defend which the German command has made such enormous efforts in past weeks. Of course, the nearer we get to the line the greater is the number of guns which can be used against it. It is not permitted to give details about the big guns, but it may be said that they are among the largest that have been used in the war.

Brisk local fighting continued today on both sides of the Meuse. East of the river there were heavy contacts in the Bois de la Grand Montagne and in the vicinity of Bois Belleu. We took Belleu Wood for the fifth time yesterday afternoon, only to be later driven out again. We have now retaken it again, despite terrific German artillery fire.

Just west of the Meuse our patrols pushing forward found that the Germans had deserted Clery le Grand.

North of Grand Pré the Germans also withdrew from Bellejoyeuse Farm, which has changed hands eleven times in the last ten days. We sent patrols into the farm to have the Germans open heavy machine gun fire from dominating woods. They had evidently set a trap, expecting a large force of Americans to rush into the place.

We have not occupied the farm, which is under constant fire from the hills of Bourgogne Woods. The farm in turn had firing command of the valley to the south, which we hold.

Two new German divisions have been identified north of Verdun.

Due to weather conditions the aerial activities today were slight.

DOOM OF GERMANY SEEN

With Austria Gone, She Cannot Hold Out Long, London Believes.

ALLIES CAN HIT FROM SOUTH

Likely to Harden Terms and Demand Complete Surrender by Deserted Berlin.

PARIS SEES END VERY NEAR

Whole Edifice of Central Alliance Crumbling and Peace Must Come Quickly.

Special Cable to THE NEW YORK TIMES.

LONDON, Oct. 28.—Suspicion, with which every German move, rightly or wrongly, is regarded here, is absent from the view taken of the Austrian position. While Germany wavers on the brink of surrender, it is said, Austria-Hungary has taken the [illegible]

The British Government has received a communication of Count Andrassy's unconditional acceptance of all the conditions upon which President Wilson made the entry into negotiations regarding armistice and peace dependent. Comparisons to the disadvantage of Germany and to the advantage of Austria-Hungary are made between the plain whole-heartedness of the Austro-Hungarian acceptance and the verbal trickeries which possibly exist in the guarded language of the German notes.

Austria-Hungary has followed Bulgaria in complete surrender, a fact which, it is pointed out, is very important, because it completes the isolation of Germany. Germany's reluctance to tread the same path is comprehensible, but that she will inevitably be forced to walk this Via Dolorosa is beyond doubt.

Although the terms of armistice to Austria-Hungary may not repeat in all respects the terms to Bulgaria, it is assumed that, in one case as in the other, provision will be made for the Allies to use the territory and railways of the surrendering country against any associate who continues the war.

Thus the Germans, if they decide on a war of defense, must be prepared to meet invasion of Germany from the Austrian side. They will find the whole Italian Army free to operate against them, while they themselves will lose the co-operation of the Austrian divisions on the west front. At the same time they will be cut in on from Rumania, and to a large extent from the Ukraine, and their supply problems will become insoluble. It is obvious that, without Austria-Hungary, Germany can only hold out for a strictly limited period, that all possibility of her improving her situation disappears, and that the only effect of further resistance on her part will be to render her still weaker after the war.

The action of Vienna in throwing up the sponge seems therefore the beginning of the end. The inevitable deduction is that Germany's claims to treat a purely military question, like the conditions of an armistice, on the basis of equality merit even less consideration than was the case when the President clearly indicated his view that an armistice must be determined on the basis of allied supremacy.

The news of the Austro-Hungarian surrender can only strengthen the determination of the military and naval chiefs of the Allies to exact adequate guarantees that Germany, if granted an armistice, will be in no position to renew hostilities in case the terms of peace ultimately to be put before her do not meet her views as to what constitutes a peace of justice.

While all the world waits on the decisions to be rendered in Paris, it is expected here that an essential feature of the reply which will be made

Continued on Page Two.

Text of the Austrian Note Replying to President Wilson

BASLE, Oct. 28.—The Austro-Hungarian Foreign Minister instructed the Austro-Hungarian Minister at Stockholm yesterday to ask the Swedish Government to send the following note to the Washington Government:

VIENNA, Oct. 28.

In reply to the note of President Wilson of the 19th of this month, addressed to the Austro-Hungarian Government and giving the decision of the President to speak directly with the Austro-Hungarian Government on the question of an armistice and of peace, the Austro-Hungarian Government has the honor to declare that equally with the preceding proclamations of the President, it adheres also to the same point of view contained in the last note upon the rights of the Austro-Hungarian peoples, especially those of the Czechoslovaks and the Jugoslavs.

Consequently, Austria-Hungary accepting all the conditions the President has laid down for the entry into negotiations for an armistice and peace, no obstacle exists, according to the judgment of the Austro-Hungarian Government, to the beginning of these negotiations.

The Austro-Hungarian Government declares itself ready, in consequence, without awaiting the result of other negotiations, to enter into negotiations upon peace between Austria-Hungary and the States in the opposing group and for an immediate armistice upon all Austro-Hungarian fronts.

It asks President Wilson to be so kind as to begin overtures [illegible]

ANDRASSY.

Text of President Wilson's Note to Austria-Hungary

Department of State.

WASHINGTON, Oct. [illegible]

From the Secretary of State to the Minister of Sweden.

SIR: *I have the honor to acknowledge the receipt of your note of the seventh instant in which you transmit a communication of the Imperial and Royal Government of Austria-Hungary to the President. I am now instructed by the President to request you to be good enough through your Government to convey to the Imperial and Royal Government the following reply:*

The President deems it his duty to say to the Austro-Hungarian Government that he cannot entertain the present suggestions of that Government because of certain events of utmost importance, which, occurring since the delivery of his address of the eighth of January last, have necessarily altered the attitude and responsibility of the Government of the United States. Among the fourteen terms of peace which the President formulated at that time, occurred the following:

X.—The peoples of Austria-Hungary, whose place among the nations we wish to see safeguarded and assured, should be accorded the freest opportunity of autonomous development.

Since that sentence was written and uttered to the Congress of the United States, the Government of the United States has recognised that a state of belligerency exists between the Czechoslovaks and the German and Austro-Hungarian Empires and that the Czechoslovak National Council is a de facto belligerent Government clothed with proper authority to direct the military and political affairs of the Czechoslovaks. It has also recognised in the fullest manner the justice of the nationalistic aspirations of the Jugoslavs for freedom.

The President is, therefore, no longer at liberty to accept the mere "autonomy" of these peoples as a basis of peace, but is obliged to insist that they, and not he, shall be the judges of what action on the part of the Austro-Hungarian Government will satisfy their aspirations and their conception of their rights and destiny as members of the family of nations.

Accept, Sir, the renewed assurance of my highest consideration.

(Signed) ROBERT LANSING.

MILITARY REGIME SEES ITS DOOM

Domestic Situation in Germany Serious as Feeling Against Old Regime Rises.

By GEORGE RENWICK.

Special Cable to THE NEW YORK TIMES.

AMSTERDAM, Oct. 27.—Germany has come to the end of an astounding and historic week and to the beginning probably of a more remarkable one.

The week, which concluded with the resignation of Ludendorff, was characterized throughout by extraordinary outspokenness in the Reichstag. It began with some hints that the reactionaries were in the ascendant. It ended with clear indications that their day is over.

It leaves behind the outstanding impression that Germany is in a parlous political condition. Now that Liebknecht is free, her "insurgent sons" have thrown to the winds all the restraint which autocracy so long imposed on them.

Ludendorff's resignation was a sensation in Berlin, and for it there were several causes. In the first place, his continuous interference in

Continued on Page Two.

9,000 AUSTRIANS, 51 GUNS CAPTURED

Italian and British Forces Advance Four Miles East of the Piave River.

ROME, Oct. 28.—More than 9,000 Austrians were taken prisoner in the operations on the Italian front yesterday, according to the War Office announcement today. Fifty-one guns were also captured. Subjoined is the text of the communication:

Our army, in conjunction with allied contingents, has crossed the Piave River by force of arms, engaging in bitter battles the enemy, who strove desperately to bar the way.

Between the slopes and heights of Valdobbiadene and the mouth of the Soligo Torrent our infantry assault troops passed, during the night, under violent fire to the left bank of the river, broke into the enemy's front lines, and carried them.

Supported by the fire of the artillery on the right bank they gained ground and repulsed enemy counter-attacks throughout the day.

To the south the Tenth Army, taking advantage of the successes of the British at Grave di Papadopoli, compelled the enemy to retire, and repulsed two counterattacks in the direction of Borgo Malanotte and Roncadelle. The prisoners taken yesterday aggregated more than 9,000. Fifty-one guns were captured.

Allied aircraft, with extreme daring,

Continued on Page Six.

VIENNA'S PLEA IS URGENT

Lays Stress on Desire for "Immediate" End of the Conflict.

LOOKS TO WILSON FOR AID

"Adheres to" President's Viewpoint Regarding the Czechoslovaks and Jugoslavs.

BELIEVED TO [illegible]

Washington Thinks Central Empires Are Seeking Peace in Full Accord.

WASHINGTON, Oct. 28.—While Germany's latest note to President Wilson was being delivered to the State Department today through the Swiss Legation, cable dispatches from Europe brought the information that the Austro-Hungarian Government had [illegible] another communication to be dispatched to the President, asking that immediate negotiations for peace and an armistice be entered into without awaiting the results of exchanges with Germany.

The Vienna Government asserted that it adhered to the same point of view expressed by the President in his last communication upon the rights of the Austro-Hungarian peoples, especially those of the Czechoslovaks and Jugoslavs, and requested that he begin overtures with the allied Governments, with a view to ending immediately the hostilities on all Austro-Hungarian fronts.

The official text of the German note did not differ materially from the unofficial version as received by cable. No official comment was forthcoming, but it is known that no response will be made at present to the communication, which is believed to have been dispatched with the primary purpose of satisfying the German public that their Government was not omitting any opportunity to forward the negotiations for an armistice and peace.

Armistice Question Separate.

Regarding the renewed assurance in the German note that the constitutional structure of the German Government has been and is being changed to democratic lines, it is pointed out that the truth of this statement and the scope of the changes already made or projected, after all, are matters to be dealt with in connection with peace and not in arranging an armistice. A strong indisposition seems evidenced officially to yield to the apparent intent of both the German and Austrian negotiators to combine these two essentially different functions in one phase of the negotiations.

In the case of the Austrian communication, now supposed to be on its way to Washington, through the medium of the Swedish Government, it also was noted that the effort was made to show that Austria had complied with the President's demand for the recognition of the rights of the Czechoslovaks, the Jugoslavs, and other oppressed nationalities in Austria. It does not appear that the complete independence of these people has been guaranteed, and probably sufficient assurance must be had on that point before the Austrian proposals will be transmitted to the Entente Powers for submission to the military experts.

Because of the wide extent of the disaffection in the Dual Empire, developments in that quarter are believed to be fraught with greater possibilities in the way of peace than in Germany. In some official quarters the opinion is freely expressed that Emperor Charles fully realizes that he must submit to any terms which the Entente Powers and America choose to impose, and that at present he is seeking simply to secure [illegible] onerous and humiliating.

He will be obliged to permit the Hungarians to shift for themselves in the peace settlement if they persist in the separatist movement already in full swing, but there are intimations in official quarters that by no such means can the Magyars escape the assumption of full responsibility for their share in the war and for th

United Press International

Marshal Foch as he leaves for Paris to turn over armistice documents to the French government.

"All the News That's Fit to Print."

The New York Times.

THE WEATHER
Fair, warmer today; tomorrow probably rain by night; wind south.
For weather report see next to last page.

VOL. LXVIII...NO. 22,208. NEW YORK, FRIDAY, NOVEMBER 8, 1918. TWENTY-FOUR PAGES. TWO CENTS In Greater New York and Metropolitan District | THREE CENTS Within 200 Miles | FOUR CENTS Elsewhere

GERMAN DELEGATES ON THE WAY TO MEET FOCH; FIRING STOPS ON ONE FRONT TO LET THEM PASS; GERMAN NAVY REBELS; OUR MEN TAKE SEDAN; FALSE PEACE REPORT ROUSES ALL AMERICA

CUT THROUGH SEDAN LINE

Americans Succeed in Drive Aimed to Bottle Up the German Forces.

PUT TWO ARMIES TO ROUT

Rainbows and First Division Made Whirlwind Drive Into Historic City.

RUSH ON EAST OF MEUSE

Enemy Abandons Vast Stores in Flight—100 Towns and 6,000 Civilians Liberated.

By EDWIN L. JAMES.

Copyright, 1918, by The New York Times Company. Special Cable to THE NEW YORK TIMES.

WITH THE AMERICAN ARMY IN FRANCE, Nov. 7.—When the German emissaries were dispatched to the front today to receive the armistice terms the German Army was all but bottled up, having only one avenue of escape, that through Liége. This bottling up was largely done by the First American Army, which is driving the last remaining Germans out of Sedan.

Thus the men fighting under the Stars and Stripes have achieved what is perhaps one of the most brilliant victories of the war and certainly the most important offensive victory.

Among the troops which reached Sedan was the 42d (Rainbow) Division, including the old 69th New York. Other divisions participating in our rush north are the 77th (New York), 78th (New Jersey and New York), 80th (Pennsylvania), 32d (Michigan and Wisconsin), 90th (Texas and Oklahoma), the 1st, 2d, 3d and 5th Regulars, 89th (Kansas and Nebraska), 26th (New England), and the 29th (New Jersey).

In the First Army's remarkable six days' advance of forty kilometers it not only liberated a hundred French villages and several thousand civilians, but also captured the city of Sedan, liberating 5,000 French folk. It also cut the main German railroad system of communication from the western front through Luxemburg. Moreover the Americans have driven the German Fifth and Third armies, which were holding the pivot of the whole front, in full retreat.

In the last twenty-four hours of our forward sweep we liberated these among other towns: Raucourt, Autrecourt, Haracourt, Angiecourt, Thelanne, Noyers, Wadlincourt, Frenois, Cheveuges, and Dignan.

Set Whirlwind Pace.

Our victorious troops set such a fast pace as to break all communication with the rear, and the weather made airplane observation impossible. That is why our commanders did not know until this morning that the doughboys had reached historic Sedan yesterday afternoon at 4 o'clock and had drawn their line along the river which cuts off a small portion of the city. Early this morning the work of putting across bridges started.

I have just returned from a vain attempt to get to Sedan. The roads are mined and torn and so filled with traffic that it was impossible to get to the city. But reports from there say that the Germans are getting back north of Sedan. The fires they started last night when they were quitting the city are still burning. There were no fires in the city on the other side, and the civilians could be seen in the streets cheering to the Americans. Our troops have been hailed as de-

Continued on Page Two.

Allied Fleets Will Reach Constantinople Tomorrow

LONDON, Nov. 7, (via Montreal.)—The allied fleets will anchor off St. Sophia, Constantinople, on Saturday, according to information received in London tonight.

BIG FRENCH GAINS ON 70-MILE FRONT

Troops East of Oise and North of Aisne Push Forward Ten Miles.

100 VILLAGES REDEEMED

Petain's Pursuit Is Incessant, While Haig Also Extends His Lines Eastward.

PARIS, Nov. 7.—French troops today advanced victoriously over the seventy-mile front east of the Oise and north of the Aisne. Their gains in a wide area were more than ten miles in depth.

A hundred villages, with a great number of civilians, were liberated in the course of the day.

French airplanes, acting in liaison with the infantry, have been bombing and machine gunning the retreating enemy.

The day's successes are thus summarized in the official communiqué issued tonight:

> Our troops continued without cessation their pursuit of the enemy during the day. On our left we crossed and went far beyond the road between Vervins and Avesnes, north of La Capelle. South of this locality we reached on the west the railway between La Capelle and Hirson on the general line of Effry and Origny-en-Thierache.
>
> Further east we are along the Thon River, an affluent of the Oise, as far as Leuze, 15 kilometers north of Rozoy-sur-Serre.
>
> On the Aisne front we hold the general line of the southern outskirts of the Signy Forest, Wagnon, Viel-St. Remy, Maseray, and La Hergne, realizing an advance of more than sixteen kilometers beyond the Aisne.
>
> On the right, in the valley of the Bar River, our advanced elements have gone beyond St. Aignan-sur-Bar, gaining a footing south of the Meuse on the heights which dominate Sedan.
>
> We have freed during the course of the day 100 villages and a great number of civilians.
>
> Aviation: Our airplanes, working in liaison with our infantry, attacked, bombed, and machine-gunned enemy columns in retreat, utilizing 15,500 kilos of bombs and 13,000 cartridges.

Following is the text of the day bulletin:

> The pursuit of the enemy was renewed this morning on the whole of the front. We are progressing east of the forests of Nouvion and Regnaval and north of the Serre and the Aisne. On the right, (where the French lines join the American,) French cavalry detachments are pushing in the direction of the Meuse.

French Pushing Toward Hirson.

WITH THE FRENCH ARMY IN FRANCE, Nov. 7, (Associated Press.)—The persistent rain and deepening mud, although making communications more difficult, do not appear to have checked the pursuit of the Germans retreating toward the Belgian frontier. Latest reports are that the French cavalry is moving toward the Meuse, while the infantry is advancing toward Mezières.

General Debeney's forces also were close upon the German rearguards, occupying numerous villages and carrying their advance toward Hirson. The capture of this important railway centre will bring about the final crumbling of the transportation organization of the German armies in France.

Subsequent operations may take on the character of a race between the armies in retreat and those in pursuit to Aix-la-Chapelle, as the American successes have made the line of the Meuse a most precarious refuge for the enemy.

HAIG'S ADVANCE CONTINUES.

Bavai, Eight Miles from Maubeuge, Taken in a Wide Sweep.

LONDON, Nov. 7.—The British troops today continued their steady advance along the whole front south

Continued on Page Five.

REDS SEIZE GERMAN NAVY

Workmen's and Soldiers' Council Now Rules Sea Bases.

U-BOAT MEN JOIN IN REVOLT

Great Part of Schleswig Taken and Move Spreads Along Baltic Coast.

BIG OUTBREAK AT HAMBURG

Army Command Sends Troops to Suppress Rising—Red Flag Over Warships.

Whole German Fleet Revolts; Mutineers Rule Heligoland

LONDON, Friday, Nov. 8, 12:45 A. M.—Virtually all the German fleet has revolted, according to a dispatch received from The Hague.

The men are complete masters at Kiel, Wilhelmshaven, Heligoland, Borkum and Cuxhaven.

At Kiel the workers have joined the navy men and declared a general strike, says the dispatch.

The greater part of the submarine crews in all the naval harbors have joined the revolt, according to an Exchange Telegraph dispatch from Copenhagen.

By GEORGE RENWICK.

Copyright, 1918, by The New York Times Company. Special Cable to THE NEW YORK TIMES.

AMSTERDAM, Nov. 7.—The important German naval base of Kiel is practically in the hands of a Soldiers' Council, formed on the approved Russian lines, by sailors, marines, and soldiers there. The governing authorities found themselves completely powerless before this newly constituted authority.

Trouble began Sunday, but discontent had been smoldering for some time, the main cause being the arrest of a number of sailors and marines for their refusal to obey orders, a reason similar to that which caused the naval mutiny a little more than a year ago. It was on the battleship Kaiser that matters first came to a head. On that battleship the sailors endeavored to haul down the war flag and hoist the red flag in its place. The officers defending the flag, with revolvers in their hands, were eventually overwhelmed by the men. The war flag was hauled down and the revolutionary flag run up.

Two officers, including the commander of the Kaiser, were killed and several were wounded. The men obtained complete control of the ship, and similar events took place on other vessels stationed there.

During the night four companies of infantry arrived in town with instructions to restore order. Three of them joined the mutineers, and the fourth was disarmed. The cavalry at Wansbeck was ordered to march on Kiel, but about a mile from the town they were held up by marines with machine guns and compelled to retire.

Soldiers' Council Takes Control.

Meanwhile the Soldiers' Council had been formed. It took control of the food supplies. Food has always been a source of trouble at Kiel for some reason or other.

Admiral Souchon, the Governor at Kiel, who had recently been appointed to that station—he will be re-

Continued on Page Seven.

Mackensen Army Must Disarm to Pass Through Hungary

BERNE, Nov. 7.—The German Field Marshal Mackensen, on requesting permission for his army to pass through Hungary from the Balkans to Germany, was informed by the Hungarian Government that the request would be granted on the condition that the troops lay down arms on entering Hungarian soil.

The arms are to be forwarded to Germany later.

CHAOS IN AUSTRIA AS ARMY RETURNS

Demoralized Troops Pillage Food Supplies in Villages Along Railroads from Italy.

AMAZING SCENES IN ALPS

Roads Blocked by Starving Hosts Who Wait Hours to Move a Few Yards.

BERNE, Nov. 7, (Associated Press.)—Complete chaos prevails in Austria, according to travelers returning here from that country. All the railroad villages in the Tyrol are flooded with the returning armies in full disorder. In the villages the demoralized troops, who are breadless, are plundering and requisitioning supplies. Food from the east has been completely cut off.

Artillerists are selling their horses for a trifle. Automobile drivers are going homeward as they please.

Many of the released Italian prisoners of war who are returning to Italy are trying to enter Switzerland.

WITH THE ITALIAN ARMY AT TRENT, Nov. 6, (Associated Press.)—Amid the rejoicings of this redeemed city scenes of destruction and starvation are common as one goes along the roads over which the Italians troops are trying to pass the thousands of Austrian prisoners who were cut off by the Italians southwest of Balzano. Every road leading up to this city is crowded with men, and on every hand there are evidences of the collapse of one of Europe's mightiest armies.

The horrors of Napoleon's retreat from Russia, it is said by military observers, were trifling compared with the suffering of the Austrian troops in this region. Great masses of men wait for long hours to move a few feet or a few hundred yards, to halt anew on a road littered with the carcasses of horses and with cannon, pieces of shields, pistols, rifles, broken-down auto trucks, and machine guns.

There is no swearing among these men. There are even moments of profoundest quiet, broken by snatches of song. Italian soldiers seem positively sorry that the end of the war is approaching. They say: "What's a few months more, now that we are sure of victory?"

Many Austrians are dying from sheer fatigue and starvation, and not wounds. The Italians are doing all they can to hurry up food supplies. This is difficult, and in the meantime dead horses are eaten, the flesh being cooked by the roadside by fires kindled by the soldiers.

Large bodies of Austrians are helpless. The correspondent passed between Rovereto and Trent, a distance of sixteen miles, an unending column of men, marching none knew whither. They

Continued on Page Eight.

CITY GOES WILD WITH JOY

Supposed Armistice Deliriously Celebrated Here and in Other Cities.

CROWDS PARADE STREETS

Jubilant Throngs Reject All Denials and Tear Up Newspapers Containing Them.

JUDGES CLOSE THE COURTS

Mayor Addresses Crowds at City Hall—Saloons Closed at Night to Check Disorder.

With the nervous tension of the years of war suddenly broken yesterday afternoon by the false report sent out by the United Press Association, a private coroprationn supplying news to many afternoon newspapers throughout the country, that Germany had signed an armistice with the Allies, all the joyful enthusiasm pent up by New Yorkers through the long ordeal of the business of war and the waiting for peace and victory was wasted on a fake. When the sirens, whistles and bells rose in a resounding clamor, about 1 o'clock in the afternoon, carrying the news of the supposed signing of the armistice and the cessation of hostilities, men and women of all ages, all stations, in every part of the city, with an unspoken accord, suddenly stopped their business and poured out into the streets to join through the afternoon in a delirious carnival of joy which was beyond comparison with anything ever seen in the history of New York.

New York was not the only victim of the deception; the United Press's false report of the end of the war had been carried throughout the country, and in country villages, small towns, and great cities—most notably, perhaps, in Chicago—there were celebrations as enthusiastic as that of New York.

The afternoon papers which carried the false rumor of peace were snatched off the stands and out of the hands of newsboys by the eager crowd and displayed everywhere, while no attention was paid to those which had stuck to less romantic realities and told only of the steady advance of the allied armies and of the outbreak of revolution in Germany. Not till late in the afternoon, when later editions told the city that the news was false, did the public at large learn that there was anything the matter with the good news, and many people were only angered by the offical denial, showing their wrath by tearing up the papers that printed the State Department's correction. Apparently millions of people never learned the truth at all last night. For after thousands of those who had danced in the streets and cheered themselves hoarse in the afternoon had gone home, thousands more—boys who welcomed the release from all inhibitions, hoodlums joyfully seizing any excuse for making a noise, and some who had drunk so much in the afternoon that they neither knew nor cared whether the peace story had any basis of foundation—stayed on the streets; and they were joined after nightfall by other thousands from the homes or from the outlying portions of the city who had seen no papers and still thought that the war was at an end. The crowd knew, anyhow, that the war was virtually over; they had seen

Continued on Page Three.

Route of the German Delegates Through Foch's Lines

The Germans have wirelessed the French command that they have had to bring road-builders to mend the roads for their journey.

Text of Messages Exchanged About Armistice; German Delegates Rebuilding Road to Get Through

PARIS, Nov. 7, (Associated Press.)—These documents relating to the armistice negotiations are published here tonight:

"There was received the 7th of November at 12:30 A. M. the following from the German high command, by order of the German Government, to Marshal Foch:

> The German Government, having been informed through the President of the United States that Marshal Foch had received powers to receive accredited representatives of the German Government and communicate to them conditions of an armistice, the following plenipotentiaries have been named by it:
>
> Mathias Erzberger, General H. K. A. von Winterfeld, Count Alfred von Oberndorff, General von Grünnel, and Naval Captain von Salow.
>
> The plenipotentiaries request that they be informed by wireless of the place where they can meet Marshal Foch. They will proceed by automobile, with subordinates of the staff, to the place thus appointed.

"A German wireless dispatch received Nov. 7 at 1 P. M. said:

> German General Headquarters to the Allies' General Headquarters; the German Commander in Chief to Marshal Foch: The German plenipotentiaries for an armistice leave Spa today. They will leave here at noon and reach at 5 o'clock this afternoon the French outposts by the Chimay-Fourmies-La Capelle-Guise road. They will be ten persons in all, headed by Secretary of State Erzberger.

"Orders were given to cease fire on the front at 3 o'clock P. M. until further orders.

"On Nov. 7 at 1:25 A. M. Marshal Foch sent the following to the German command:

> If the German plenipotentiaries desire to meet Marshal Foch and ask him for an armistice, they will present themselves to the French outposts by the Chimay-Fourmies-La Capelle-Guise road. Orders have been given to receive them and conduct them to the spot fixed for the meeting.

"The following wireless dispatch in German was received at 1:50 P. M.:

> German General Headquarters to the Allied General Headquarters: The Supreme German Command to Marshal Foch: From the German outposts to the French outposts our delegation will be accompanied by a road-mending company to enable automobiles to pass the La Capelle Road, which has been destroyed.

"The following wireless in German was received at 6 P. M.:

> The German Supreme Command to Marshal Foch: By reason of delay, the German delegation will not be able to cross the outpost line until between 8 and 10 o'clock tonight at Haudroy, two kilometres northwest [northeast?] of La Capelle.

UNITED PRESS MEN SENT FALSE CABLE

Armistice Message Signed by President Roy Howard and Simms, Paris Manager.

REACHED CITY AT 11:56 A. M.

News Association Will Not Admit Inaccuracy Despite Repudiation by Washington.

The United Press Association's false cable message announcing that an armistice had been signed by Marshal Foch, the allied Commander in Chief, and the German military and naval envoys was received in the office of the United Press, in the Pulitzer Building, 63 Park Row, at noon yesterday.

W. W. Hawkins, General Manager of the United Press service in this country, said last night that the message was received by the Western Union at 11:56 A. M., and immediately submitted to the censor, who returned it with his "O. K." at 11:59, or three minutes after the message arrived in New York. One minute later it was being flashed into the United Press offices in the Pulitzer Building, and a few minutes later the papers served by the United Press were on the streets with the startling news.

The message as received in the United Press office reads:

> Paris.
> Unipress, NY.
> Urgent. Armistice Allies Germany signed eleven smorning. Hostilities ceased two safternoon. Sedan taken by Americans.
> HOWARD.
> SIMMS.

The signers of the message are Roy W. Howard, the President of the United Press Association, and William Philip Simms, the manager of the Paris office of the service. The message was filed in Paris shortly after 11 A. M., New York time, which was about 4 P. M., French time, or nearly an hour before the time set for the first meeting of Marshal Foch and the German armistice emissaries. The word "urgent" in the message signifies that the highest rate was paid in order to expedite transmission.

The United Press Association is a private corporation selling news to afternoon newspapers. It has no connection with The Associated Press, which is a co-operative organization of the leading newspapers of the United States, oper-

Continued on Page Three.

LANSING IS SWIFT TO DENY TALE

False Story of Armistice Signing Causes Anger Among Officials at Washington.

BUT. CAPITAL CELEBRATES

Official Circles Do Not Expect Prompt Acceptance of the Allied Terms.

Special to The New York Times.

WASHINGTON, Nov. 7.—What is regarded in officialdom here as the most colossal news fake ever perpetrated upon the American people was the publication today through a dispatch from the United Press that Germany had signed the terms of armistice laid down by Marshal Foch and that the war was over.

This news dispatch, sent from Paris, was utterly without foundation of fact. Official denial of its authenticity was made by Secretary of State Lansing after he had taken the trouble to cable to Paris about it.

The news organization's dispatch on the ending of the war had the effect of startling the entire country. In every city the news spread "the war is over," and the country at large took it to be authentic.

This official denial of the accuracy of the United Press report was made by the Secretary of State this afternoon, immediately after having received a dispatch from Paris:

"The Secretary of State makes public the following:

"'The report that the armistice with Germany has been signed is untrue. When it reached the Department of State an inquiry was at once dispatched to Paris. At 2:20 o'clock this afternoon a telegram in reply to that of the department was received from Paris. It stated that the armistice had not yet been signed and that the German representatives would not meet Marshal Foch until 5 P. M., Paris time, or 12 noon Washington time.'"

Statement by Secretary Baker.

Later on Secretary of War Baker, pressed for information as to whether the War Department had any word as to the report that the armistice had been signed, dictated this statement:

"We have no confirmation. So far as the War Department is concerned, we

Continued on Page Two.

ROAD INDICATED TO ENVOYS

Armistice Delegates Due On the French Front Last Night

GERMANS ANNOUNCED TIME

Were to Arrive Between 8 and 10 O'Clock—Marshal Foch Fixed Their Route.

ERZBERGER IS THEIR CHIEF

Order to Cease Firing on That Part of Front Took Effect at 3 o'Clock in Afternoon.

PARIS, Nov. 7, 11 P. M., (Associated Press.)—German Grand Headquarters today requested Allied Grand Headquarters by wireless to permit the passage of the German delegation for armistice negotiations through the lines. The order was given to cease firing on this front at 3 o'clock in the afternoon until further orders.

The German wireless message, asking for an appointment to meet Marshal Foch, says:

"The German Government would congratulate itself in the interests of humanity if the arrival of the German delegation on the Allies' front might bring about a provisional suspension of hostilities."

The message announced that the German plenipotentiaries would arrive at the French outposts on the Chimay-Guise road on Thursday between 8 and 10 o'clock in the evening.

The mission is headed by Mathias Erzberger, Secretary of State and head of the War Press Department, and includes General H. K. A. von Winterfeld, former military attaché at Paris; Count Alfred von Oberndorff, former Minister at Sofia; General von Grunnel and Naval Captain von Salow.

Foch Prescribes Envoys' Route.

LONDON, Nov. 7, (Associated Press.)—Marshal Foch, the Allied Commander in Chief, has notified the German High Command that if the German armistice delegation wishes to meet him it shall advance to the French lines along the Chimay, Fourmies, La Capelle, and Guise roads.

From the French outposts the plenipotentiaries will be conducted to the place decided upon for the interview.

The British Foreign Office this evening stated, according to the Exchange Telegraph Company, that the rumor that an armistice with Germany had been signed was unfounded.

The British naval representative at the armistice negotiations will be Rosslyn Wemyss, First Sea Lord of the Admiralty, it is officially announced.

Earl Curzon, member of the British War Council, it is announced, has gone to the continent on official business.

French Awaited White Flags.

PARIS, Nov. 7, (Associated Press.)—Four German officers bearing white flags, it is officially announced, will probably arrive at the

U. S. Signal Corps

American flag being hoisted in Etrage Mense, France, after the last shot of the war had been fired.

National Archives

A German machine gunner dead only a week before the hostilities ended.

"All the News That's Fit to Print."

The New York Times.

THE WEATHER
Fair, slightly colder Sunday; Monday fair; fresh west winds.
For full weather report see Page 23.

Section 1

VOL. LXVIII...NO. 22,205. NEW YORK, SUNDAY, NOVEMBER 10, 1918.—84 PAGES, In Seven Parts, including Picture Section in Rotogravure and Book Section. FIVE CENTS In Greater New York | Elsewhere SEVEN CENTS

KAISER AND CROWN PRINCE ABDICATE; NATION TO CHOOSE NEW GOVERNMENT; MAX IS REGENT; ARMISTICE DELAYED; REVOLT SPREADS ON LAND AND SEA

FRENCH CROSS BELGIAN BORDER; CAPTURE HIRSON

Advance on a 30-Mile Front at Some Points Exceeds Nine Miles.

HAIG WINS ON WHOLE LINE

Germans in Hasty Retreat Before His Armies in Belgium and France.

IN TOURNAI AND MAUBEUGE

British Have Crossed Long Reaches of the Scheldt—Now Approaching Mons.

PARIS, Nov. 9.—French cavalry has crossed the Belgian border north and east of Hirson, the War Office announces tonight. Hirson itself, an important German position, has been occupied as well as several villages in its general neighborhood, and the French line has been carried forward more than nine miles at certain points.

Considerable gains have been made along the whole front of about thirty miles extending from the junction of the French and British armies to the Meuse east of Mezières.

The two water barriers of the Thon and Aure have been forced, and the plateaus to the north occupied.

Mezières has been more closely invested, and the Meuse has been crossed at a point three miles southeast of that town.

The night bulletin reads as follows:

Our troops continued their forward march, advancing fifteen kilometers at certain points during the course of the day.

On the left our cavalry crossed the Belgian frontier, overthrowing the enemy rearguards, taking prisoners, and capturing guns and considerable material, notably several railway trains.

Glageon, Formies, Hirson, Anor, and St. Michel were occupied by us. Our forces continued their pursuit beyond these localities on the general line of Momignies, the northern outskirts of the St. Michel Forest, Maquenoise, and Philippe Forge.

Further east, after having forced a passage of the Thon and Aure Rivers, we occupied the plateaus to the north, despite the enemy's spirited resistance. We took Signy-le-Petit, which was passed for considerable distance, and reached the Mezières-Hirson railway at the village of Wagny and south of Maubert-Fontaine.

On our right we are along the course of the Sormonne and have reached and surrounded Mezières and Mohon. We crossed the Meuse further east, opposite Lumes.

The text of the day statement follows:

There was artillery and machine-gun activity at several points on the front during the night. This morning the French resumed their march forward along the entire line.

Fires Behind the German Lines.

WITH THE FRENCH ARMIES IN FRANCE, Nov. 9. (Associated Press.)—The French forces today continued their push toward the Belgian frontier, with the Germans persisting in their delaying tactics of the last few days. The Germans used artillery and machine-gun fire at points where they needed more time to break contact with the French.

At other places on the front the progress of the French was maintained with undiminished speed.

HAIG ADVANCES RAPIDLY ON HIS WHOLE FRONT

British Capture Maubeuge and Tournai, Pass the Scheldt Over Wide Area.

LONDON, Nov. 9.—All the armies on the British front are advancing, according to the night bulletin from Field Marshal Haig.

The capture of Tournai has been

Continued on Page Seven.

Province of Poland Rebels and Germans Deport All Males

LONDON, Nov. 7.—The population of the Polish Province of Plock has risen against the Germans, and there have been conflicts in which a number of persons of both sides have been killed, according to a Zurich dispatch to the Exchange Telegraph Company.

The Germans have arrested and shot members of the Polish military organization, and the whole male population is being deported to Germany.

AMERICANS GAIN ALL ALONG FRONT

Clinch Control on Both Sides of Meuse and Take Ground East of River.

HEAR ABDICATION REPORT

Pershing's Men Think the War Virtually Over but Are Not Eager to Stop.

By EDWIN L. JAMES.

Copyright, 1918, by The New York Times Company. Special Cable to THE NEW YORK TIMES.

WITH THE AMERICAN ARMY IN FRANCE, Nov. 9, (9 P. M.)—The message that the Kaiser has decided to abdicate reached the American front this afternoon, being picked up by wireless and quickly spread among all ranks. This latest development in whirlwind world happenings increased the feeling of our fighters that so far as the Germans were considered, the war was "all over but the squealing." As for themselves, they are getting to like victories and would just as well have the war go on as end. They feel now, as they have always felt, that the war is going to end in but one way.

East of the Meuse Americans are pushing on in the direction of Montmedy. During the day two new crossings of the river were made at Mouzay and Villers-devant-Dun. This work was done under rather heavy shellfire, although the Germans abstained from infantry attacks. We have cleaned out Bois Remoiville.

Just east of Sedan there were the usual artillery and machine-gun duels during the day, while our engineers repaired ruined roads and needed supplies and ammunition were got up.

Our aviators report that Montmedy is a scene of great activity, with the Germans moving north. Therefore, we bombed and shelled Montmedy. All the roads in front of the Americans are crowded with boche trains carrying war material out of our reach. Heavy forces still hold the areas in front of us east of the Meuse, below Stenay, while above the enemy has an extra heavy aggregation of artillery and heavy infantry forces.

Unless the war ends our doughboys will be ready soon to tackle this job. News that the German emissaries have until Monday morning to accept or reject the armistice terms is known to soldiers of each side, and needless to say there is the keenest interest in the situation. American lads figure that they can keep the war going if the Germans choose.

Gains All Along the Line.

WITH THE AMERICAN ARMY ON THE SEDAN FRONT, Nov. 9, (Associated Press.)—The American troops fought their way forward today along virtually their entire line, despite the fact that the weather was about as bad as could be.

The resistance encountered was spirited on the whole, though consisting largely of machine-gun activity. The terrain crossed and captured was on par with the most difficult ground the Americans have taken thus far. It

Continued on Page Six.

GERMAN WARSHIPS CLASH

Loyalist Vessels Attack Fleet Seized by Reds—Kiel Is Under Fire.

MEANT TO ATTACK ENGLAND

Naval Officers Were Against Peace, but Men Rebelled Against Their Enterprise.

MANY CITIES JOIN REVOLT

Cologne, Hanover, Oldenburg, and Other Places Reported in Eruption.

Copyright, 1918, by The New York Times Company. Special Cable to THE NEW YORK TIMES.

COPENHAGEN, Nov. 9.—The Politiken states that the reason of the mutiny of the German fleet at Kiel was that the officers would not recognize the Government's peace policy, and had decided to attack England with the fleet.

The sailors then rebelled and forced the officers to leave the warships.

A special to the Koebenhaven from Vamdrup states that several hundred officers were killed at Kiel, and now the fleet, the depots, and the railway station are in the hands of the rioting mariners and soldiers.

Reports from Hamburg state that the railway connections from there are broken and trains to Denmark are starting from Neumunster.

Specials to both the Koebenhaven and the Politiken report the fleet firing at Kiel.

LONDON, Nov. 9.—German warships, manned by crews loyal to the monarchy, and others seized by Reds and now at Flensburg on the Schleswig coast are in battle, according to Copenhagen advices.

It is stated that six battleships anchored outside of Flensburg have directed their guns against the revolutionists. A bombardment was expected. The battleship Koenig, which refused to surrender, was taken after a hard fight.

Reports of growing disaffection and uprisings by the populace continue to pour in from the Continent.

An Associated Press dispatch from Copenhagen says:

"Rebellions have occurred in Hanover, Cologne, Brunswick, and Magdeburg, according to an official announcement at Berlin. These cities, however, are not wholly in the hands of the mutineers, the statement adds. At Magdeburg the garrison resisted."

A previous dispatch from The Associated Press correspondent at Copenhagen reads:

"The uprising in Northwestern Germany, according to the only direct news from Germany early today, is reported to have spread to Hanover, Oldenburg, and other cities. Generally the revolt is not attended by serious disturbances.

"Reports from the Danish border

Continued on Page Two.

Geddes Sure the German Fleet Was Ordered Out, But Men Rebelled Rather Than Fight British

LONDON, Nov. 9.—(British Wireless Service.)—At the banquet following the Lord Mayor's "Victory" show tonight, Sir Eric Geddes, First Lord of the Admiralty, made interesting disclosures. He said that those who were charged with responsibility had waited hourly for the possibility of a naval Armageddon. The whole stage was set for a great sea battle, but something was wrong. The arm that was going to try the last desperate gambling stroke was paralyzed.

"The German Navy, I am as convinced as I am standing here tonight," said the First Lord, "was ordered out, and the men would not come."

Half the German fleet, he declared, was flying the red flag—and the German fleet was flying the red flag because it realized that it was not engaged in a good cause.

BARRAGE DELAYS TRUCE COURIER

Paris Thinks German Government May Wireless Final Reply to Foch.

TERMS READ BY MARSHAL

Enemy Delegates Stunned by Realization of Extent of Nation's Defeat.

LONDON, Nov. 9, (British Wireless Service.) — The British Press Bureau issued the following announcement this afternoon:

"Owing to the heavy German barrage and machine gun fire on the battlefront the passage of the courier from Marshal Foch's headquarters to Spa was so delayed that he is not expected to reach German Headquarters until this afternoon. Consequently it is unlikely that any decision in regard to the armistice will be reached today."

AMSTERDAM, Nov. 9.—The German courier, bearing Marshal Foch's armistice terms, had some difficulty in crossing the German lines.

He was led to believe through the blowing up of an ammunition dump with a series of explosions that the Germans had not ceased firing, but he was informed of the cause of the explosions by wireless and instructed to pass the German lines without delay.

The terms are expected to reach Berlin momentarily.

PARIS, Nov. 9.—Germany's armistice delegates were received by Marshal Foch yesterday morning at 9 o'clock in a railroad car, in which the Commander in Chief of the allied force has his headquarters, according to the Petit Journal.

When the Germans' credentials had been opened and verified, Mathias Erzberger, leader of the enemy delegation, speaking in French, announced that the German Government had been advised by President Wilson that Marshal Foch was qualified to communicate to them the Allies' conditions and had oppointed them plenipotentiaries to take cognizance of the terms and eventually sign an armistice.

Marshal Foch then read the terms

Continued on Page Two.

MAY SIGN TRUCE IN TOWN OF SENLIS

Marshal Foch's Headquarters Scene of Atrocities by Germans Early in War.

PEOPLE AWAIT THE DAY

Remember When the Invaders Wantonly Shot Mayor and Fellow-Townsmen.

By WALTER DURANTY.

Copyright, 1918, by The New York Times Company. Special Cable to THE NEW YORK TIMES.

PARIS, Nov. 9.—The Temps says tonight:

"If the German answer is in the affirmative an armistice will be signed at Senlis, the headquarters of the allied Generalissimo."

It must be a strange experience for the inhabitants of the little French town, the whole main street of which was gutted by boche incendiaries in 1914, to see the French military automobiles containing the travel-worn German envoys flash by on their errand of humiliation. Doubtless they will remember that tragic day of September when their Mayor and fellow-townsmen were wantonly shot and nights far more recent when the earth shook, as I often experienced in that very spot, to the crash of bursting air bombs and the thunder of answering batteries.

With such memories in their hearts the people of Senlis salute the day of retribution.

"There is a striking change in the attitude of the German soldiers during the last few days," said a Lieutenant who arrived in Paris today on leave from Gouraud's army. "Until the beginning of the week the rearguards resisted strongly, but now the boches' chief anxiety seems to be to hurry backward, even if they must leave cannon or machine guns behind. The statement of a Saxon Feldwebel captured two days ago illustrates the general tone.

"'We would have been willing to fight to the end if there was anything to be gained thereby,' he said, 'but the people at home have lost their heads and the country is crumbling to pieces, so why sacrifice ourselves uselessly?'

"The Feldwebel, in charge of twelve men in a machine gun nest, surrendered without firing a shot when a patrol of French cavalry appeared on a hill crest—where they were an easy mark—to the right."

My informant thought the incident typical, adding:

"However one abominates the atrocities the boches committed, it

Continued on Page Two.

Irish Nationalists Appeal to Wilson to Support Demands Made on England

LONDON, Nov. 9.—The Irish Nationalist Party is sending to President Wilson a manifesto appealing for his assistance in settling the Irish question.

The document quotes at length from President Wilson's "great utterances on this war which we hold justify us to enforce the demand we have made for our nation on the British Government."

SOCIALIST AS CHANCELLOR

Prince Max Announces He Will Name Ebert Head of Cabinet.

PLAN NATIONAL ASSEMBLY

This Will Make Provision for the Future Form of German Government.

BRUNSWICK DUKE OUT

Head of House, Who Is Kaiser's Son-in-Law, Abdicates with His Heir.

Copyright, 1918, by The New York Times Company. Special Cable to THE NEW YORK TIMES.

LONDON, Nov. 9, 4:40 P. M.—Emperor William of Germany has abdicated.

PARIS, Nov. 9.—The abdication of Emperor William is officially announced from Berlin, according to a Havas dispatch from Basle.

LONDON, Nov. 9.—A Havas Agency dispatch from Amsterdam says that Prince Max of Baden has been appointed Regent of the Empire, according to the Berlin newspapers.

A Reuter dispatch, however, says he is yet to be named.

According to a German wireless message received here which announces the Kaiser's abdication, Friedrich Ebert, Vice President of the Social Democratic Party, is to be Imperial Chancellor under the regency, and wide reforms are planned, including the calling of a Constitutional German National Assembly to determine the future good of the nation.

The resignations of the German Ministers of the Interior, Instruction, Agriculture, and Finance are reported in a telegram from Berlin.

The Prussian Food Controller again requested to be relieved from office, and the resignation of the Prussian Minister of Public Works has been in the hands of the Cabinet some time.

Emperor William had not at a late hour [before his abdication] accepted the resignation of Prince Max of Baden, the Chancellor, according to a Berlin message to Copenhagen. The Emperor, who was kept thoroughly informed by the Chancellor regarding the general situation, the message adds, asked Prince Max to continue holding the office provisionally until the Emperor's final decision was reached.

The Socialists decided not to carry out at the time set their threat to withdraw from the Government if Emperor William had not abdicated by that hour, according to a Berlin dispatch. Instead they extended the time limit, it is stated, "in consideration of an eventual armistice."

Kaiser's Son-in-Law Abdicates.

LONDON, Nov. 9, (British Wireless Service.)—A telegram received at Copenhagen, from Brunswick by way of Berlin, asserts that Emperor William's son-in-law, the Duke of Brunswick, and his successor have abdicated.

The reigning Duke of Brunswick, Ernest Augustus, married the German Kaiser's only daughter, Princess Victoria Louisa, on May 24, 1913. He was then 26 years of age and she was five years younger. The Duke's heir is Prince Ernest Augustus, born on March 12, 1914. Two other sons came during the war—George William, born March 25, 1915, and Frederick, April 18, 1917.

The father of the Duke is the Duke of Cumberland, son of the late King George V. of Hanover and cousin of the late Queen Victoria. The kingdom of Hanover was absorbed by Prussia in 1866.

Text of Decree Announcing Kaiser's Abdication and the Plans for Other Changes in Germany

LONDON, Nov. 9.—A German wireless message received in London this afternoon states:

"The German Imperial Chancellor, Prince Max of Baden, has issued the following decree:

The Kaiser and King has decided to renounce the throne.

The Imperial Chancellor will remain in office until the questions connected with the abdication of the Kaiser, the renouncing by the Crown Prince of the throne of the German Empire and of Prussia, and the setting up of a regency have been settled.

For the regency he intends to appoint Deputy Ebert as Imperial Chancellor, and he proposes that a bill shall be brought in for the establishment of a law providing for the immediate promulgation of general suffrage and for a constitutional German National Assembly, which will settle finally the future form of government of the German nation and of those peoples which might be desirous of coming within the empire. THE IMPERIAL CHANCELLOR.

Berlin, Nov. 9, 1918.

Chancellor Sees All Hope Gone; Says Germany Is Forced to Yield.

LONDON, Nov. 9, (British Wireless Service.)—Just before Prince Maximilian of Baden offered his resignation as Imperial Chancellor he issued an appeal "To Germans abroad" in which he said:

"In the fifth year, (of hostilities,) abandoned by its allies, the German people could no longer wage war against the increasingly superior forces."

The text of the Chancellor's statement follows:

"In these difficult days the hearts of many among you, my fellow-countrymen, who outside the frontier of the German Fatherland are surrounded by manifestations of malicious joy and hatred, will be heavy. Do not despair of the German people.

"Our soldiers have fought to the last moment as heroically as any army has ever done. The homeland has shown unprecedented strength in suffering and endurance.

"In the fifth year, abandoned by its allies, the German people could no longer wage war against the increasingly superior forces.

"The victory for which many had hoped has not been granted to us. But the German people has won this still greater victory over itself and its belief in the right of might.

"From this victory we shall draw new strength for the hard time which faces us and on which you also can build."

AMSTERDAM, Nov. 7.—Absolute unity is necessary among the German people if they wish to avert unforeseen consequences, says Chancellor Maximilian in an appeal to the German people, which, according to an official dispatch from Berlin, reads as follows:

"For more than four years the German nation, united and calm, has endured the most severe sufferings and sacrifices. If at this decisive hour, when only absolute unity can avert from the entire German people great dangers for its future, internal strength gives way, then the consequences are unforeseeable.

"An indispensable demand in these decisive hours, which must be made by every people's Government, is the maintenance of the hitherto existing calm, under voluntary discipline. May every citizen be conscious of the high responsibility toward his people in the fulfillment of their duty!"

"Issue is Settled," Says Lloyd George, Who Announces Regency in Germany

LONDON, Nov. 9, (British Wireless Service.)—Premier Lloyd George spoke tonight at a banquet which followed the Lord Mayor's "Victory" Show.

"I have no news for you," said the Premier to the banqueters, who were expecting an announcement from him regarding the possible signing of an armistice with Germany.

"Owing to the rapid and triumphant advance of the allied troops and to their relentless pursuit, the German envoys have not been able to get through, and other means have had to be devised to enable them to cross the lines. Owing to these circumstances I have nothing to say to you this evening as to the result of the armistice negotiations. But for all that, it does not matter.

"The issue is settled. In the Spring we were being sorely pressed. The Channel ports were being threatened, and the steel of the enemy was pointed at our hearts.

"It is Autumn. The capital of Turkey is now almost within gunfire of our ships. Austria is shattered and broken. The Kaiser and the Crown Prince have abdicated. [Prince Max's decree said that the Kaiser had decided to abdicate.] A

"All the News That's Fit to Print."

The New York Times.

THE WEATHER
Fair today and Tuesday; diminishing northwest winds.
For weather report see next to last page.

VOL. LXVIII...NO. 22,206. NEW YORK, MONDAY, NOVEMBER 11, 1918. TWENTY-FOUR PAGES. TWO CENTS Metropolitan District 50 Mile Radius | THREE CENTS Within 200 Miles | FOUR CENTS Elsewhere

ARMISTICE SIGNED, END OF THE WAR! BERLIN SEIZED BY REVOLUTIONISTS; NEW CHANCELLOR BEGS FOR ORDER; OUSTED KAISER FLEES TO HOLLAND

SON FLEES WITH EX-KAISER

Hindenburg Also Believed to be Among Those in His Party.

ALL ARE HEAVILY ARMED

Automobiles Bristle with Rifles as Fugitives Arrive at Dutch Frontier.

ON THEIR WAY TO DE STEEG

Belgians Yell to Them, "Are You On Your Way to Paris?"

LONDON, Nov. 10.—Both the former German Emperor and his eldest son, Frederick William, crossed the Dutch frontier Sunday morning, according to advices from The Hague. His reported destination is De Steeg, near Utrecht.

The former German Emperor's party, which is believed to include Field Marshal von Hindenburg, arrived at Eysden, [midway between Liége and Maastricht,] on the Dutch frontier, at 7:30 o'clock Sunday morning, according to Daily Mail advices.

Practically the whole German General Staff accompanied the former Emperor, and ten automobiles carried the party. The automobiles were bristling with rifles, and all the fugitives were armed.

The ex-Kaiser was in uniform. He alighted at the Eysden station and paced the platform, smoking a cigarette.

Many photographs were taken by [of?] the members of the Imperial party. On the whole the people were very quiet, but Belgians among them yelled out "En voyage a Paris?" (Are you on your way to Paris?)

Chatting with the members of the staff, the former Emperor, the correspondent says, did not look in the least distressed. A few minutes later an imperial train, including restaurant and sleeping cars, ran into the station. Only servants were aboard.

The engine returned to Visé, Belgium, and brought back a second train, in which were a large number of staff officers and others, and also stores of food.

The preparations began for the departure at 10 o'clock this morning, but at 10:40 o'clock the train was still at Eysden. The blinds of the train were all drawn.

The Daily Mail remarks that, if the party arrived in Holland armed, all of them must be interned.

While other dispatches con-

Continued on Page Three.

Kaiser Fought Hindenburg's Call for Abdication; Failed to Get Army's Support in Keeping Throne

By GEORGE RENWICK.

Special Cable to THE NEW YORK TIMES.

AMSTERDAM, Nov. 10.—I learn on very good authority that the Kaiser made a determined effort to stave off abdication. He went to headquarters with the deliberate intention of bringing the army around to his side. In this he failed miserably.

His main support consisted of a number of officers, nearly all of Prussian regiments, who formed themselves into two regiments and placed themselves at his Majesty's disposal. To do anything with such support was seen, of course, to be Gilbertian.

During the night the Kaiser called the Crown Prince, Hindenburg, and General Gröner to him, and the consultation lasted a couple of hours. Both officers strongly pressed the Kaiser to bow to the inevitable, and Hindenburg informed him that any more delay in coming to a decision to abdicate would certainly have the most terrible consequences and lead to serious events in the army. For those consequences Hindenburg said he must refuse responsibility.

The Crown Prince, it is said, was the first to give way. General Gröner fully supported Hindenburg's view, but when the conference broke up the Kaiser remained unconvinced of the advisability of abdication. He is said to have come to his final decision an hour or so later, after several communications had reached him from Berlin and after another short and stormy talk with Hindenburg.

Meanwhile, his son-in-law, the Duke of Brunswick, for himself and his heir, had abdicated. "Brunswick's Fated Chieftain" was forced without fighting to abdicate. Reports have it that the republican movement in Brunswick, which long before the war was chafing under autocratic conditions, began to be noticed even before it was set in motion at Kiel.

Kaiser Shivered as He Signed Abdication

LONDON, Nov. 10.—Emperor William signed his letter of abdication on Saturday morning at the German Grand Headquarters in the presence of Crown Prince Frederick William and Field Marshal Hindenburg, according to a dispatch from Amsterdam to the Exchange Telegraph Company.

The Crown Prince signed his renunciation of the throne shortly afterward.

Before placing his signature to the document, an urgent message from Philipp Scheidemann, who was a Socialist member without portfolio in the Imperial Cabinet, was handed to the Emperor. He read it with a shiver. Then he signed the paper, saying:

"It may be for the good of Germany."

The Emperor was deeply moved. He consented to sign the document only when he got the news of the latest events in the empire.

The ex-Kaiser and former Crown Prince were expected to take leave of their troops on Saturday, but nothing had then been settled regarding their future movements.

GERMAN DYNASTIES BEING WIPED OUT

King of Wuerttemberg Abdicates—Sovereign of Saxony to Follow Suit.

PRINCES MAY BE EXILED

Socialists Are Demanding That Every Sovereign in the Empire Shall be Dethroned.

LONDON, Nov. 10.—A Havas dispatch from Basle says:

"Wilhelm II., the reigning King of the monarchy of Würtemberg, abdicated on Friday night."

A Wolff Bureau dispatch from Stuttgart, by way of Amsterdam, says that the King has issued a proclamation saying that his person would never serve to hinder the development of the wishes of the people.

According to a report received from Berne, the German Socialists are demanding that every dynasty in Germany be suppressed and all the Princes exiled. It is reported that the Kings of Bavaria and Saxony intend to abdicate soon.

Here is a list of the rules, until several days ago, of the various parts of the German Empire. Those who have abdicated and those reported to be on the point of abdication are marked by an asterisk.

ANHALT—Duke Edward, son of the late Duke Friedrich of Anhalt and of Princess Antoinette of Saxe-Altenberg. Succeeded his brother April 18, 1918.

BADEN—Friedrich II., succeeded to

Continued on Page Two.

MORE WARSHIPS JOIN THE REDS

Four Dreadnoughts in Kiel Harbor Espouse the Revolutionary Cause.

GUARDSHIPS ALSO GO OVER

Those Protecting Mines in the Great Belt and the Baltic Abandon Their Posts.

LONDON, Nov. 10.—The crews of the German dreadnoughts Posen, Ostfriesland, Nassau, and Oldenburg, in Kiel Harbor, have joined the revolution, says a Copenhagen dispatch. Marines occupied the lock gates at Ostmoor and fought down a coast artillery division which offered resistance.

According to the British Wireless Service three German destroyers have anchored outside of Stockholm. All the guardships in the Baltic, it is said, have joined the revolutionary movement.

Six more cruisers flying the red flag arrived at Hamburg last night, says a Wolff News Agency dispatch received in Copenhagen.

An Amsterdam dispatch states that the Berlin Vossische Zeitung and Vorwärts confirm the fact that the inception of the revolution at Kiel was mistaken for the idea that a cruise had been ordered and that it was intended to give battle to the British fleet.

Up to Friday night the number of persons killed at Kiel was twenty-eight, according to information re-

Continued on Page Three.

BERLIN TROOPS JOIN REVOLT

Reds Shell Building in Which Officers Vainly Resist.

THRONGS DEMAND REPUBLIC

Revolutionary Flag on Royal Palace—Crown Prince's Palace Also Seized.

GENERAL STRIKE IS BEGUN

Burgomaster and Police Submit—War Office Now Under Socialist Control.

LONDON, Nov. 10.—The greater part of Berlin is in control of revolutionists, the former Kaiser has fled to Holland, and Friedrich Ebert, the new Socialist Chancellor, has taken command of the situation. The revolt is spreading throughout Germany with great rapidity.

Dispatches received in London today announce these startling developments. The Workmen's and Soldiers' Council is now administering the municipal government of the German capital.

The War Ministry has submitted, and its acts are valid only when countersigned by a Socialist representative. The official Wolff telegraphic agency has been taken over by the Reds.

The red flag has been hoisted over the royal palace and the Brandenburg Gate. The former Crown Prince's palace is also in possession of the revolutionists.

There was severe fighting in Berlin between 8 and 10 o'clock last night and a violent cannonade was heard from the heart of the city.

Burgomaster and Police Join.

A Copenhagen dispatch states that Dr. Liebknecht, the famous Socialist, who spent many months in prison for antagonizing the German Imperial Government and who was recently released, has issued the following announcement in Berlin in behalf of the Workmen's and Soldiers' Council:

"The Presidency of the police, as well as the Chief Command, is in our hands. Our comrades will be released."

A dispatch from Berne states that the Burgomaster of Berlin has placed himself and his staff at the disposal of the new Government.

Some German newspapers describe the movement as Bolshevism. The people are shouting "Long live the Republic!" and singing the "Marseillaise."

Officers Shelled by Reds.

When revolutionary soldiers attempted to enter a building in Berlin in which they supposed that a number of officers were concealed shots were fired from the windows. The Reds then began shelling the building. Many persons were killed and wounded before the officers surrendered.

When the cannonade began the people thought the Reichsbank was being bombarded, and thousands rushed to the square in front of the Crown Prince's palace. It was later determined that other buildings were under fire. Among those killed in the fighting at the "Cockchafer" Barracks was one of the workmen's leaders known as "Comrade" Habersroth.

The Reds, at last reports, were maintaining order.

Berlin was occupied by forces of the Soldiers' and Workmen's Councils on Saturday afternoon, according to a Wolff Bureau report received in Copenhagen. News of Emperor William's abdication was received in the city on that afternoon with general rejoicing, which was tempered by the fear that it had come too late.

Russians Aid in Outbreak.

How far the example of the Russian Bolsheviki influenced the German upheaval is an interesting question. Red flags figured frequently in the various risings and Chancellor Ebert's motor car floats the international emblem.

The shoulder straps were torn from the uniforms of officers in a number of German cities and even the soldiers' insignia were stripped from them. Russian prisoners played a part in the demonstrations in two or three towns.

Delegates of the revolutionary German navy arrived in Berlin on Friday, according to a dispatch from Copenhagen. They conferred for several hours with the Minister of Marine and with members of the Reichstag majority parties.

It is stated that Hugo Haase, a Socialist leader in the Reichstag, has the situation at Hamburg in hand.

It is officially announced from Berlin, according to a Copenhagen dispatch, that the War Ministry has placed itself at the disposal of Chancellor Ebert. This action was for the purpose of assuring the provisioning of the army and assisting in the solution of demobilization problems.

Serious food difficulties are expected in Germany, owing to the stoppage of trains. The Council of the Regency will take the most drastic steps to re-establish order.

In the new German Government there will be only three representatives of the majority parties, namely, Erzberger, Gothein, and Richthofen, says a dispatch from Copenhagen. The other posts will be occupied by Socialists and independents.

Reds Announce Success.

BERLIN, Nov. 9, (German Wireless to London, Nov. 10)—(Associated Press.)—The German People's Government has been instituted in the greater part of Berlin. The garrison has gone over to the Government.

The Workmen's and Soldiers' Council has declared a general strike. Troops and machine guns have been placed at the disposal of the Council. Guards which had been stationed at the public offices and other buildings have been withdrawn.

Friedrich Ebert (Vice President of the Social Democratic Party) is carrying on the Chancellorship.

The text of a statement issued by the People's Government reads:

In the course of the forenoon of Saturday the formation of a new German People's Government was initiated. The greater part of the Berlin garrison, and other troops stationed there temporarily, went over to the new Government.

The leaders of the deputations of the Social Democratic Party declared that they would not shoot against the people. They said they would, in accordance with the People's Government, intercede in favor of the maintenance of order. Thereupon in the offices and public buildings the guards which had been stationed there were withdrawn.

The business of the Imperial Chancellor is being carried on by the Social Democratic Deputy, Herr Ebert.

It is presumed that, apart from the representatives of the recent majority group, three Independent Social Democrats will enter the future Government.

Scheidemann Exhorts Calm.

Deputy Scheidemann, (leader of the majority Socialists in the Reichstag,) in a speech today, said:

"The Kaiser and the Crown Prince have abdicated. The dynasty

Continued on Page Four.

Socialist Chancellor Appeals to All Germans To Help Him Save Fatherland from Anarchy

BERNE, Nov. 10, (Associated Press.)—In an address to the people, the new German Chancellor, Friedrich Ebert, says:

Citizens: The ex-Chancellor, Prince Max of Baden, in agreement with all the Secretaries of State, has handed over to me the task of liquidating his affairs as Chancellor. I am on the point of forming a new Government in accord with the various parties, and will keep public opinion freely informed of the course of events.

The new Government will be a Government of the people. It must make every effort to secure in the quickest possible time peace for the German people and consolidate the liberty which they have won.

The new Government has taken charge of the administration, to preserve the German people from civil war and famine and to accomplish their legitimate claim to autonomy. The Government can solve this problem only if all the officials in town and country will help.

I know it will be difficult for some to work with the new men who have taken charge of the empire, but I appeal to their love of the people. Lack of organization would in this heavy time mean anarchy in Germany and the surrender of the country to tremendous misery. Therefore, help your native country with fearless, indefatigable work for the future, every one at his post.

I demand every one's support in the hard task awaiting us. You know how seriously the war has menaced the provisioning of the people, which is the first condition of the people's existence. The political transformation should not trouble the people. The food supply is the first duty of all, whether in town or country, and they should not embarrass, but rather aid, the production of food supplies and their transport to the towns.

Food shortage signifies pillage and robbery, with great misery. The poorest will suffer the most, and the industrial worker will be affected hardest. All who illicitly lay hands on food supplies or other supplies of prime necessity or the means of transport necessary for their distribution will be guilty in the highest degree toward the community.

I ask you immediately to leave the streets and remain orderly and calm.

COPENHAGEN, Nov. 10.—The new Berlin Government, according to a Wolff Bureau dispatch, has issued the following proclamation:

Fellow-Citizens: This day the people's deliverance has been fulfilled. The Social Democratic Party has undertaken to form a Government. It has invited the Independent Socialist Party to enter the Government with equal rights.

WAR ENDS AT 6 O'CLOCK THIS MORNING

The State Department in Washington Made the Announcement at 2:45 o'Clock.

ARMISTICE WAS SIGNED IN FRANCE AT MIDNIGHT

Terms Include Withdrawal from Alsace-Lorraine, Disarming and Demobilization of Army and Navy, and Occupation of Strategic Naval and Military Points.

By The Associated Press.

WASHINGTON, Monday, Nov. 11, 2:48 A. M.—The armistice between Germany, on the one hand, and the allied Governments and the United States, on the other, has been signed.

The State Department announced at 2:45 o'clock this morning that Germany had signed.

The department's announcement simply said: "The armistice has been signed."

The world war will end this morning at 6 o'clock, Washington time, 11 o'clock Paris time.

The armistice was signed by the German representatives at midnight.

This announcement was made by the State Department at 2:50 o'clock this morning.

The announcement was made verbally by an officila of the State Department in this form:

"The armistice has been signed. It was signed at 5 o'clock A. M., Paris time, [midnight, New York time,] and hostilities will cease at 11 o'clock this morning, Paris time, [6 o'clock, New York time.]

The terms of the armistice, it was announced, will not be made public until later. Military men here, however, regard it as certain that they include:

Immediate retirement of the German military forces from France, Belgium, and Alsace-Lorraine.

Disarming and demobilization of the German armies.

Occupation by the allied and American forces of such strategic points in Germany as will make impossible a renewal of hostilities.

Delivery of part of the German High Seas Fleet and a certain number of submarines to the allied and American naval forces.

Disarmament of all other German warships

Wide World Photos

Armistice celebration on New York's Fifth Avenue.

Section 1 — "All the News That's Fit to Print."

The New York Times.

THE WEATHER — Fair and continued cool Sunday; fair Monday; moderate winds. [illegible] For full weather report see Page [illegible]. — Section 1

VOL. LXVIII...NO. 22,436. NEW YORK, SUNDAY, JUNE 29, 1919. 122 PAGES, In Nine Parts. [illegible] FIVE CENTS [illegible]

PEACE SIGNED, ENDS THE GREAT WAR; GERMANS DEPART STILL PROTESTING; PROHIBITION TILL TROOPS DISBAND

WILSON PROMISES TO ACT

Must Wait Until Complete Demobilization, His Word from Paris.

THIS WILL TAKE 7 WEEKS

President Calls Attention of Congress to His Request for Repeal.

LIQUOR MEN UNPREPARED

Had Hoped Until Announcement That Executive Would Intervene at the Eleventh Hour.

Special to The New York Times.

WASHINGTON, June 28.—President Wilson will not lift the ban which provides for war-time prohibition until the demobilization of the army has been terminated.

But when demobilization has been completed, the President will lift the ban. Formal announcement to this effect was made at the White House tonight. The President is in agreement with A. Mitchell Palmer, his Attorney General, that he cannot at this time lift the ban on wartime prohibition. He agrees with the Attorney General that the language of the law is such that he will be free to act on his own initiative, without Congressional action, not immediately after the signing of the treaty of peace, but when the army has been demobilized. As the army has not yet been demobilized, and there are yet a million men in the army, called into service under the emergency of war, the President, in the failure of Congress to vest him with power to call off wartime prohibition, takes the position that he cannot interfere with the putting of wartime prohibition into effect.

The responsibility for putting wartime prohibition into effect is put squarely up to Congress by the President. He takes the position that the law calling for wartime prohibition was an act of Congress, that its terms are clear, and that he had asked Congress to provide for the repeal of the legislation. Congress, having failed to act so far, has left the President's hands tied with legal strings so far as lifting the ban is concerned, and he makes this situation very plain in a cablegram sent to the White House just before he left Paris today.

President Wilson's cablegram was made public at the White House at 8 o'clock tonight by Joseph P. Tumulty, the Private Secretary to the President.

In his message the President said that he could not act until the army had been completely demobilized, and since there were still a million men in the service there was no chance of his taking immediate action. He called attention to the fact that the present difficulty could have been obviated if Congress had heeded his recommendation of several months ago.

The President in his message left no doubt as to what action he will take when demobilization is terminated.

"When demobilization is terminated," says the final sentence of his cablegram, "my power to act without Congressional action will be exercised."

When demobilization has been terminated will be determined by the President upon information to be supplied to him by Secretary Baker and by Attorney General Palmer. The prospects are that six, or perhaps seven, weeks will elapse before demobilization is terminated, which means that the President will probably not be in position, under his construction of the law, to act before the middle or latter part of August in lifting the ban.

It means that wartime prohibition will go into effect on July 1, even though there is no adequate provision legally made for its real enforcement, and that it will remain in effect until the termination of demobilization unless Congress meanwhile adopts the President's request for a repeal of the legislation which provided for the institution of wartime prohibition.

Congress is free at any time to enact the necessary legislation. So far all attempts to bring about repeal have failed on Capitol Hill and there is no present indication that Congress intends to change.

Not only has the President asked Congress to repeal the legislation standing in the way of lifting the ban, but in his cabled statement of today the President declares without equivocation that he will exercise his power to act when demobilization is terminated, and makes it clear he will then lift the ban unless Congress by repealing the act of Nov. 21, 1918, does away with wartime pro-

Continued on Page Eleven.

President Sends A Prohibition Message; Says He Will Act When Demobilization Ends

WASHINGTON, July 28.—The following message from President Wilson, stating his stand on the prohibition question, was made public at the White House tonight by Secretary Tumulty:

I am convinced that the Attorney General is right in advising me that I have no legal power at this time in the matter of this ban on liquor. Under the act of November, 1918, my power to take action is restricted. The act provides that after June 30, 1919, "until the conclusion of the present war and thereafter until the termination of demobilization, the date of which shall be determined and proclaimed by the President, it shall be unlawful, &c." This law does not specify that the ban shall be lifted with the signing of peace, but with the termination of the demobilization of the troops, and I cannot say that this has been accomplished. My information from the War Department is that there are still a million men in the army under the emergency call. It is clear, therefore, that the failure of Congress to act upon the suggestion contained in my message of the twentieth of May, 1919, asking for a repeal of the act of Nov. 21, 1918, so far as it applies to wines and beers, makes it impossible to act in this matter at this time. When demobilization is terminated, my power to act without Congressional action will be exercised.

WOODROW WILSON.

VIOLENCE GROWS IN BERLIN FERMENT

Bomb Hurled at Building in Which Officials Were Conferring on Strike.

SHOTS FIRED AT MINISTERS

Railway Strikers Ignore Orders from Noske and Union Chiefs to Resume Work.

Special Cable to THE NEW YORK TIMES.

BERLIN, June 28, (via Copenhagen.)—Vorwärts, even Die Freiheit and also Ledebour, in his first speech after his release from prison, earnestly warn the people against riots and political revolt which, in view of the enormous military strength gathered in Berlin, can only lead to awful bloodshed.

Doubtless the big leaders of the Independent Socialists do not wish any outbreaks at present. Nevertheless the air is charged with the spirit of rebellion, and nobody here would be surprised if tomorrow there were a repetition of the events of January and March on a much larger scale.

The minor leaders of the Independents, Communists and Sparticides desire to inflame this unrest, communicating it to ever-growing circles of the workers, and inciting the lawless elements to the most audacious and wholesale crimes. Unknown parties shortly after 2 o'clock this morning threw a bomb against the façade of the building of the Public Works Department. It exploded with a terrific noise, shattering about 200 windows. Nobody was hurt. Later, when the ministers and the railway employes' delegates left the building, after trying vainly all night to reach an agreement, unknown persons fired revolvers at the government members, without hitting any one.

Incite Lawlessness in Berlin.

Though ten or more members of the Executive Committee of the Berlin Soldiers' and Workers' Councils, after being arrested yesterday on suspicion of conniving with the Hamburg revolutionists for the overthrow of the Federal Government, have been released for lack of evidence nobody doubts for one moment that telephone congratulations were exchanged between them and the Hamburg revolutionists, as overheard by officials, but the identity of the man who answered the Hamburg announcement of the successful revolt with "Bravo!" and promised the Executive Committee's aid in starting a revolt against the Government in Berlin could not be established.

Members of that Executive Committee have never made any secret of their intention to overthrow the Government at the first opportunity, and doubtless the weaker heads among them yesterday believed that the time had come. The lawless element believe this, and it cannot be denied that they are quite right, if the absence of any effective policing of the capital is any justification.

Insecurity has reached an incredible degree. Lately men disguised as officers have been ascending street cars and, with pointed revolvers, collecting pocketbooks and jewels from the passengers in true Wild West fashion. This

Continued on Page Three.

DUTCH UNWILLING TO GIVE UP KAISER

Majority of the People Firmly Opposed to Yielding to Allies' Demand.

HOPEFUL AT AMERONGEN

Troelstra Says Chamber Would Surrender Ex-Ruler to Germany Only.

Special Cable to THE NEW YORK TIMES.

THE HAGUE, June 27.—The question of the delivery of the ex-Kaiser is again on the tapis here. There is no doubt that a majority of Netherlanders are already forgetting Germany's and the ex-monarch's record and violently oppose his surrender.

Appeals such as the recent one from the German Officers League and echoes from the German press only serve to strengthen these feelings. The officers' appeal stated that the German officers would be dishonored forever if Holland delivered the ex-Kaiser to the Allies, and ended with the statement: "It is even yet not certain whether a German can be found to sign the peace treaty."

The NEW YORK TIMES correspondent questioned Pieter Troelstra, the Socialist leader, the report emanating from Germany that the Dutch Social Democrats opposed the surrender of the ex-Kaiser. Troelstra replied:

"Our party has taken no official attitude. As we have not yet considered the question officially no resolution has been taken and no official correspondence carried on.

"It is true that we are against his surender on principle and would oppose it. I consider that we must wait until we receive the allied demand, so that the matter is not urgent.

"I can certainly say that as Socialists we believe in the right of asylum. English Socialists defend the right of asylum and London has always been a city for political refugees. Switzerland and the Netherlands have been free for centuries and it is a matter of tradition."

When asked if the question were put to a vote in the Dutch Chamber other parties would oppose the delivery of the ex-monarch, Troelstra replied in the affirmative.

"It is impossible," he said, "to deliver a refugee to an enemy. It is against all rights. If Germany should demand the Kaiser it would be another question. We should be in favor of that. I feel nothing but antipathy for his personality, but only his own Government has a right to demand him. I believe that all parties would vote in favor of a demand from the German Government."

Plead Ties with Dutch Queen.

Special Cable to THE NEW YORK TIMES.

BERLIN, June 28.—The League of Officers of the Former Prussian Army and German Navy has addressed a message to the Dutch Queen pleading that she had refused to extradite the "all highest war lord, our beloved unforgettable King, his Majesty Kaiser Wilhelm, who because of high treason in his own country, and not forced by the enemy's arms,

Continued on Page Three.

LEAGUE OPPONENTS UNITING

Republican Senators Now Seem Agreed on Policy of Reservations.

McCUMBER IS WON OVER

But North Dakota Senator Opposes Any Action Nullifying the Covenant.

SHANTUNG ACTION ASSAILED

Borah Calls It Indefensible—Norris Demands a Reservation Regarding It.

Special to The New York Times.

WASHINGTON, June 28.—With unexpected swiftness the Republican opposition in the Senate to the League of Nations covenant, as embraced in the Treaty of Peace, began to crystallize today, after the cables had brought word that Germany had signed the treaty, and that the President, in his message to the American people, had expressed the hope that the treaty would be "ratified and acted upon in full and sincere execution of its terms."

The President's message, coupled with his statement in interviews at Paris that he hoped the Senate woud ratify the treaty with the League of Nations covenant in it, without amendment, had the effect, it appeared, of bringing closer the elements of opposition among the opponents of the League. Instead of influencing wavering Senators toward an attitude favoring the ratification of the League of Nations covenant, the President's appeal appeared to have exactly the opposite effect.

While the opponents of the covenants, before Germany signed, were admittedly divided as to a policy to pursue in fighting the covenant when the treaty should come before the Senate, they seemed, for the first time since the League fight started, to have come to some general agreement.

Every Republican Senator to whom THE NEW YORK TIMES correspondent talked said decisively that he believed that, if the League covenant was to be accepted by the Senate some character of qualifying resolution would have to be passed, along with the treaty ratification, to express dissent from features objected to.

Even Senator McCumber of North Dakota, the one Republican member of the Foreign Relations Committee who has all along advocated adoption of the covenant, after the President's message had been read in the Senate, said that he believed it would be necessary for that body to adopt "explanatory reservations" in the ratification of the treaty, respecting features involved in the covenant. Mr. McCumber spoke of such reservations being necessary as to the Monroe Doctrine and the right of the United States to determine its purely domestic questions, like immigration, racial equality, and the tariff.

The North Dakota Senator made it clear that he would not favor any resolution of reservation that would have the effect of nullifying the covenant. He wanted the treaty of peace ratified, with the League of Nations included. But he insisted that the Senate should not hesitate to express its dissent from features that affected purely American affairs. If this were not done, he said, there might come some development in the future that might impel the Senate to take action which, in effect, would take America out of the League.

McNary for Interpretation.

Senator McNary, Republican, Oregon, who only a few days ago announced himself as favoring the League of Nations, declared today that he would not oppose a resolution that would enable opponents of the covenant to make clear their dissent from matters to which they objected. This, he said, might be done through a resolution of "interpretation," which was another way of saying one of "qualification."

At the same time Senator McNary agreed with Senator McCumber that no resolution ought to be adopted that would have the effect of rejecting the League of Nations covenant.

Talk of direct amendment of the covenant was not so insistent today among the more radical Senators. They appeared to be willing now to stand behind qualifying resolutions that would amply set forth the features subject to objection. They maintained, however, that Article X., guaranteeing the territorial integrity of members of the League, should come out. On this point

Continued on Page Five.

Wilson Says Treaty Will Furnish the Charter for a New Order of Affairs in the World

WASHINGTON, June 28.—The following address by President Wilson to the American people on the occasion of the signing of the Peace Treaty was given out here today by Secretary Tumulty:

My Fellow Countrymen: The treaty of peace has been signed. If it is ratified and acted upon in full and sincere execution of its terms it will furnish the charter for a new order of affairs in the world. It is a severe treaty in the duties and penalties it imposes upon Germany; but it is severe only because great wrongs done by Germany are to be righted and repaired; it imposes nothing that Germany cannot do; and she can regain her rightful standing in the world by the prompt and honorable fulfillment of its terms.

And it is much more than a treaty of peace with Germany. It liberates great peoples who have never before been able to find the way to liberty. It ends, once for all, an old and intolerable order under which small groups of selfish men could use the peoples of great empires to serve their ambition for power and dominion. It associates the free Governments of the world in a permanent League in which they are pledged to use their united power to maintain peace by maintaining right and justice.

It makes international law a reality supported by imperative sanctions. It does away with the right of conquest and rejects the policy of annexation and substitutes a new order under which backward nations—populations which have not yet come to political consciousness and peoples who are ready for independence but not yet quite prepared to dispense with protection and guidance—shall no more be subjected to the domination and exploitation of a stronger nation, but shall be put under the friendly direction and afforded the helpful assistance of governments which undertake to be responsible to the opinion of mankind in the execution of their task by accepting the direction of the League of Nations.

It recognizes the inalienable rights of nationality, the rights of minorities and the sanctity of religious belief and practice. It lays the basis for conventions which shall free the commercial intercourse of the world from unjust and vexatious restrictions and for every sort of international co-operation that will serve to cleanse the life of the world and facilitate its common action in beneficent service of every kind. It furnishes guarantees such as were never given or even contemplated for the fair treatment of all who labor at the daily tasks of the world.

It is for this reason that I have spoken of it as a great charter for a new order of affairs. There is ground here for deep satisfaction, universal reassurance, and confident hope.

WOODROW WILSON.

DEPORT THIRTY 'RED' AGITATORS

Fifteen Have Been Shipped Away in a Week—18 More Waiting at Ellis Island.

MOST OF THEM ANARCHISTS

Number Includes Some Suspected of Having a Hand in Plot Against Officials.

The deportation of alien agitators and conspirators who have abused their sojourn in America by preaching the overthrow of the United States Government, some of them coming under suspicion of the Secret Service for plots against President Wilson and other high public officials, has begun. Within the last seven days, fifteen of these disturbers, among them the editors of two anarchist newspapers, have been deported from New York, and eighteen others are now on Ellis Island awaiting the sailing of ships that will return them to the lands of their nativity.

The Secret Service agencies of the Government have been quietly, but thoroughly, at work for weeks, and every day or two a new batch of aliens who have urged the destruction of American institutions are rounded up and their records submitted to the proper authorities with a view to immediate deportation.

In the last four weeks thirty anarchist, I. W. W., and Bolshevist agitators have been deported by way of Ellis Island. This number does not include the Seattle and Spokane I. W. W. disturbers and other radicals who were sent East for deportation as a result of Bolshevist strikes in the Pacific Northwest several months ago. Some of those agitators also have been deported, and the cases of several others, recommended for the "homeward voyage," are soon to be decided by the courts.

Most of the deportations have taken place since bombs were set off at the homes of Attorney General Palmer and

Continued on Page Nine.

AMERICA GREETED BY KING GEORGE

"Brothers in Arms Will Continue Forever to be Brothers in Peace."

SENDS MESSAGE TO WILSON

"We Lay Down Our Arms in Proud Consciousness of Valiant Deeds Nobly Done."

LONDON, June 28, (Associated Press.)—King George has sent the following message to President Wilson:

"In this glorious hour when the long struggle of nations for right, justice and freedom is at last crowned by a triumphant peace, I greet you, Mr. President, and the great American people in the name of the British nation.

"At a time when fortune seemed to frown, and the issues of the war trembled in the balance, the American people stretched out the hand of fellowship to those, who on this side of the ocean were battling for a righteous cause. Light and hope at once shone brighter in our hearts, and a new day dawned.

Together we have fought to a happy end; together we lay down our arms in proud consciousness of valiant deeds nobly done.

Mr. President, it is on this day one of our happiest thoughts that the American and British people, brothers in arms, will continue forever to be brothers in peace. United before by language, traditions, kinship, and ideals, there has been set upon our fellowship the sacred seal of common sacrifice.

GEORGE, R. I.

After news of the signing of peace had been received here the following was issued over King George's signature:

The signing of the treaty of peace will be received with deep thankfulness throughout the British Empire. This formal act brings to its concluding stages the terrible war which has

Continued on Page Three.

ENEMY ENVOYS IN TRUCULENT SPIRIT

Say Afterward They Would Not Have Signed Had They Known They Were to Leave First by Different Way.

CHINA REFUSES TO SIGN, SMUTS MAKES PROTEST

These Events Somewhat Cloud the Great Occasion at Versailles—Wilson, Clemenceau, and Lloyd George Receive a Tremendous Ovation.

President Wilson Starts for Home

PARIS, June 28, (Associated Press.)—President Wilson left Paris on his homeward journey tonight. His train started from the Gare des Invalides for Brest at 9:45 P. M.

Mr. Wilson's party was accompanied to Brest by General Leorat and Colonel Lobez, the President's French aids, and also by Stephen Pichon, French Foreign Minister; Georges Leygues, French Minister of Marine, and Captain André Tardieu, a member of the French peace delegation. Ambassador Wallace, General Pershing, Premier Clemenceau, and Colonel House were at the station to say good-bye.

The crowd in the station, numbering upward of a thousand, wildly cheered the departure of the President, who raised his hat to cries of "Vive Wilson." Mrs. Wilson threw kisses to the crowd as the train departed.

The superdreadnought Oklahoma will accompany the George Washington to the United States.

VERSAILLES, June 28, (Associated Press.)—Germany and the allied and associated powers signed the peace terms here today in the same imperial hall where the Germans humbled the French so ignominiously forty-eight years ago.

This formally ended the world war, which lasted just thirty-seven days less than five years. Today, the day of peace, was the fifth anniversary of the murder of Archduke Francis Ferdinand by a Serbian student at Serajevo.

The peace was signed under circumstances which somewhat dimmed the expectations of those who had worked and fought during long years of war and months of negotiations for its achievement.

Absence of the Chinese delegates, who at the last moment were unable to reconcile themselves to the Shantung settlement, struck the first discordant note. A written protest which General Smuts lodged with his signature was another disappointment.

But bulking larger than these was the attitude of Germany and the German plenipotentiaries, which left them, as evident from the expression of M. Clemenceau, still outside of formal reconciliation and made the actual restoration to regular relations and intercourse with the allied nations dependent, not upon the signature of the "preliminaries of peace" today, but upon ratification by the National Assembly.

To M. Clemenceau's warning in his opening remarks that they would be expected, and held, to observe the treaty provisions loyally and completely the German delegates, through Dr. Haniel von Haimhausen, replied after returning to the hotel that had they known that they would be treated on a different status after signing than the allied representatives, as shown by their separate exit before the general body of the conference, they never would have signed.

Under the circumstances the general tone of sentiment in the historic sitting was one rather of relief at the uncontrovertible end of hostilities than of complete satisfaction.

The ceremony had been planned deliberately to be austere, befitting the sufferings of almost five years, and the lack of impressiveness and picturesque color, of which many spectators, who had expected a magnificent State pageant, complained, was a matter of design, not merely omission.

The actual ceremony was far shorter than had been expected, in view of the number of signatures which were to be appended to the treaty and the two accompanying conventions, ending a bare forty-nine minutes after the hour set for the opening.

Premier Clemenceau called the session to order in the Hall of Mirrors at 3:10 P. M.

The signing began when Dr. Hermann Müller and Johannes Bell, the German signatories, affixed their names. Herr Müller signed at 3:12 o'clock and Herr Bell 3:13 o'clock.

President Wilson, the first of the allied delegates, signed a minute later. At 3:49 o'clock the momentous session was over.

The most dramatic moment connected with the signing came unexpectedly and spontaneously at the conclusion of the ceremony, when Premier Clemenceau, President Wilson and Premier Lloyd George descended from the Hall of Mirrors to the terrace at the rear of the palace, where thousands of spectators were massed.

GREAT DEMONSTRATION FOR ALLIED LEADERS.

With the appearance of the three who had dominated the councils of the Allies there began a most remarkable demonstration. With cries of "Vive Clemenceau!" "Vive Wilson!" "Vive Lloyd George!" dense crowds swept forward from all parts of the spacious terrace. In an instant the three were surrounded by struggling, cheering masses of people, fighting among themselves for a chance to get near the statesmen.

It had been planned that all the allied delegates would walk across the terrace after signing, to see the great fountains play, but none of the other plenipotentiaries got further than the door.

President Wilson, M. Clemenceau and Mr. Lloyd George were caught in the living stream which [illegible] the great [illegible] became part of the crowd themselves. [illegible] and bodyguards struggled vainly t-

United Press International

The "Big Four" at the Versailles peace conference. From left: Vittorio Emmanuele Orlando of Italy; Lloyd Geroge of England; Georges Clemenceau of France; Woodrow Wilson of the U.S.

United Press International

President Woodrow Wilson leaving the peace conference.

Wide World Photos

The Palace of Versailles, site of the signing of the Peace Treaty, June 28, 1919

WORLD WAR TWO

Polish officer cadets in 1939 before their futile attempt to defend the Danzig "Corridor."

German troops ready for action in Poland

The German Army Infantry prepare to move up to the front.

"All the News That's Fit to Print."

The New York Times.

EXTRA

Partly cloudy and somewhat warmer today. Tomorrow generally fair with moderate temperatures.

Temperatures Yesterday—Max., 67; Min., 61

VOL. LXXXVIII...No. 29,805. Entered as Second-Class Matter, Postoffice, New York, N. Y. NEW YORK, FRIDAY, SEPTEMBER 1, 1939. THREE CENTS NEW YORK CITY and Vicinity | FOUR CENTS Elsewhere Except in 7th and 8th Postal Zones.

GERMAN ARMY ATTACKS POLAND; CITIES BOMBED, PORT BLOCKADED; DANZIG IS ACCEPTED INTO REICH

BRITISH MOBILIZING

Navy Raised to Its Full Strength, Army and Air Reserves Called Up

PARLIAMENT IS CONVOKED

Midnight Meeting Is Held by Ministers—Negotiations Admitted Failure

By The Associated Press.

LONDON, Friday, Sept. 1.—The British Parliament was summoned to meet today at 5 P. M. [12 noon in New York].

British Call Up Forces

By FERDINAND KUHN Jr.

Special Cable to THE NEW YORK TIMES.

LONDON, Friday, Sept. 1.—All attempts to bring about direct negotiations between Germany and Poland appeared to have broken down tonight as Great Britain mobilized her fleet to full strength, stretched her other defensive preparations close to the limit and began moving 3,000,000 school children and invalids from the crowded cities into the safety of the countryside.

Censorship was established over cables after London had been cut off for hours from communication with the Continent.

It was the peak of the crisis, but a day of rumors had not shifted the fundamental issue nor given a conclusive answer to the question of peace or war.

At midnight the British Government was not yet convinced that Germany really intended to attack Poland and provoke a world war.

Terms Called Smoke Screen

All that had happened during yesterday, including the sudden broadcasting of Chancellor Hitler's sixteen-point demands, was interpreted here as a smoke screen rather than as the flash of guns.

After hearing Herr Hitler's "terms" officials here quietly announced tonight that "the government primarily interested in the proposals is, of course, the Polish Government."

Until the Polish Government has had time to consider them, it was said in Whitehall that "it would be highly undesirable for any comment to be made."

It was fully expected that Poland would reject them later today; indeed, Polish circles here were describing them tonight as "utterly unacceptable," for they would involve dismemberment of Poland and loss of Poland's capacity to defend her independence. In any event, there was no sign of any intention here to put pressure on Warsaw to accept.

Much might have been said about the German "proposals" here tonight if the government had not been so anxious to leave the first decision to Warsaw without any prompting. That the British regarded them as artful went without saying, since they conveyed a first impression of reasonableness that was not borne out by the terms themselves.

Until the announcement on the German wireless tonight, the British Government had not been told about them officially, and the Polish Government was not informed until Josef Lipski, Polish Ambassador to Berlin, visited Foreign Minister Joachim von Ribbentrop a few minutes before the broadcast took place.

Shortly after midnight last night, Sir Nevile Henderson, the British Ambassador in Berlin, had heard the "points" read to him by Herr von Ribbentrop, but the reading was so fast that the Ambassador could not even take notes of them in detail. In any event, he was told Herr Hitler's "points" were not being given to him or his government officially, on the ground that it was already too late.

Time Limit Expired

On Tuesday Herr Hitler had asked that a Polish negotiator should arrive in Berlin within twenty-four hours; and as nobody had arrived from Warsaw when the time limit expired, Sir Nevile was told that the "points" could not even be communicated officially to London.

The German time table with the

Continued on Page Four

Bulletins on Europe's Conflict

London Hears of Warsaw Bombing

LONDON, Friday, Sept. 1 (AP).—Reuters British news agency said it had learned from Polish sources in Paris that Warsaw was bombed today.

French Confirm Beginning of War

PARIS, Friday, Sept. 1 (AP).—The Havas news agency said today that official French dispatches from Germany indicated that "the Reich began hostilities on Poland this morning."

The agency also reported that the Polish Embassy here had announced that "Germany violated the Polish frontier at four points."

"German reports of pretended violation of German territory by Poland are pure invention, as is the fable of 'attack' by Polish insurgents on Gleiwitz," the embassy announcement said.

Attack on Entire Front Reported

LONDON, Friday, Sept. 1 (AP).—A Reuters dispatch from Paris said:

"The following is given with all reserve: According to unconfirmed reports received here, the Germans have begun an offensive with extreme violence on the whole Polish front."

First Wounded Brought Into Gleiwitz

GLEIWITZ, Germany, Friday, Sept. 1 (AP).—An army ambulance carrying wounded soldiers arrived at the emergency hospital here today at 9:10 A. M.

The men, carried in a wagon, were on stretchers. One had on a first-aid field bandage. It could not be ascertained where the ambulance came from.

At about 9:30 a half-mile long truck train manned by the engineering corps drove through the heart of the city with pontoon bridge building material. In the train were caterpillar tread, twenty-passenger motor vans.

Obviously the train had been on the road for a considerable time. All equipment was thickly covered with gray mud.

A scouting plane of the air force was patrolling an area over Gleiwitz.

Early today Gleiwitz residents reported that artillery fire

Continued on Page Four

DALADIER SUMMONS CABINET TO CONFER

News of Attack on Poland Spurs Prompt Action—Military Move Thought Likely

By The Associated Press.

PARIS, Friday, Sept. 1.—Edouard Daladier, Premier and War Minister of France, informed that German troops crossed the Polish frontier today, summoned an urgent meeting of his Cabinet for 10:30 A. M.

It was probable that Parliament would be called tomorrow.

Reports of the German invasion came from Berlin and from the Polish Embassy here. The Ministers were called to the Elysee Palace to meet with President Albert Lebrun.

Upon receipt of word of the German operations M. Daladier rushed to the War Ministry and called General Marie Gustave Gamelin, supreme commander of land, sea and air forces, into consultation.

A little later Daladier summoned Foreign Minister Georges Bonnet.

The Polish Embassy said that Germans violated the Polish frontier at four points and at the same time it characterized German charges that Poles had crossed into Germany as "pure invention."

Havas, Frnch news agency, announced that "a German declaration of war against Poland probebly will lead France and Great Britain to take new military measures."

Britain and France are committed to aid Poland in any fight to save her independence.

Ministers Stand Firm

By P. J. PHILIP

Wireless to THE NEW YORK TIMES.

PARIS, Aug. 31.—The Cabinet met with President Albert Lebrun for more than two hours this evening at the Elysée Palace. At the close of the meeting Minister of the Interior Albert Sarraut handed the press the following communiqué:

"MM. Edouard Daladier, President of the Council, and Georges Bonnet, Minister of Foreign Affairs, laid before the Cabinet a detailed account of the international situation as a whole.

"The Cabinet was unanimous in formally maintaining the engagements taken by France."

Later M. Daladier had further conversations with M. Bonnet, Fi-

Continued on Page Four

BRITISH CHILDREN TAKEN FROM CITIES

3,000,000 Persons Are in First Evacuation Group, Which Is to Be Moved Today

By FREDERICK T. BIRCHALL

Special Cable to THE NEW YORK TIMES.

LONDON, Friday, Sept. 1.—The greatest mass movement of population at short notice in the history of Great Britain is under way. It is an evacuation, under government order, of little children, invalids, women and old men from congested areas.

From London, Birmingham, Manchester, Liverpool, Edinburgh, Glasgow and twenty-three other cities the great exodus is going on as this dispatch is being written. The numbers are stupendous. More than 3,000,000 of these helpless human beings are being taken out of danger of German bombs.

Nothing like it has ever been attempted anywhere; yet it is going on without mishap—so far, indeed, without serious confusion.

Scenes everywhere were much the same whether in the aristocratic West End or the proletarian East Side, but one that this correspon-

Continued on Page Three

HOSTILITIES BEGUN

Warsaw Reports German Offensive Moving on Three Objectives

ROOSEVELT WARNS NAVY

Also Notifies Army Leaders of Warfare—Envoys Tell of Bombing of 4 Cities

By JERZY SZAPIRO

Wireless to THE NEW YORK TIMES.

WARSAW, Poland, Friday, Sept. 1.—War began at 5 o'clock this morning with German planes attacking Gdynia, Cracow and Katowice.

At Gdynia three bombs exploded in the sea.

The regular German Army started an offensive in the direction of Dzialdowka—in Upper Silesia and Czestochowa. The German plan apparently is to cut off Western Poland along the line of Dzialdowka-Lodz-Czestochowa.

The offensive is developing, from East Prussia, toward Silesia and northwards from Slovakia.

At 9 o'clock an attempt was made to bombard Warsaw. The planes, however, did not reach even the suburbs.

A military attack on the garrison at Westerplatte in the Danzig area was repulsed.

The Foreign Office at 8:45 A. M. issued a communiqué saying that military action had begun in Westerplatte in the Danzig area as well as in Buschkowa near Gdynia, and in Dzialowka, Chojnice and Lowa.

Hostilities have begun and Poland has been attacked, said the communiqué.

Three cities in Upper Silesia suffered artillery bombardment, particulars of which are lacking, it was said.

While this dispatch was being telephoned, the air-raid sirens sounded in Warsaw.

Danzig Fighting Reported

WARSAW, Poland, Friday, Sept. 1 (AP).—It was reported today that Tczew and Czestochowa were bombed by German airplanes early this morning.

There was no official confirmation of the bombing.

Fighting was reported at Danzig.

It was reported officially that German troops had attacked Polish defenses near Mlawa, bordering the southern part of East Prussia. There was no announcement of the damage resulting from the bombing.

Mist and clouds were overhanging the city. A light drizzle apparently afforded momentary protection against air raids. Warsaw went to work as usual.

Roosevelt Warns Navy

WASHINGTON, Friday, Sept. 1 (AP).—President Roosevelt directed today that all naval ships and army commands be notified at once by radio of German-Polish hostilities.

The White House issued the following announcement:

"The President received word at 2:50 A. M. Eastern standard time

Continued on Page Five

FREE CITY IS SEIZED

Forster Notifies Hitler of Order Putting Danzig Into the Reich

ACCEPTED BY CHANCELLOR

Poles Ready, Made Their Preparations After Hostilities Appeared Inevitable

Special Cable to THE NEW YORK TIMES.

DANZIG, Friday, Sept. 1.—By a decree issued early this morning Albert Forster, Nazi Chief of State, proclaimed the annexation of the Free City to the Reich, thus settling by a fell stroke the original point of contention in the international crisis.

In a telegram to Chancellor Hitler Herr Forster explained his action as necessary to remove "the pressing necessity of our people and State." Herr Forster also issued a proclamation to the people of Danzig saying the hour awaited for twenty years had arrived because "our Fuehrer, Adolf Hitler, has freed us."

[A NEW YORK TIMES dispatch from Berlin this morning said Herr Hitler telegraphed Herr Forster today thanking him and all Danzigers, and stating:

"The law for reannexation is in effect immediately."

The Chancellor stated, furthermore, that Herr Forster was appointed head of the civil administration of the Danzig area.]

In a four-article decree Herr Forster declared the Constitution of Danzig no longer valid. He declared himself sole administrator of the Danzig part of the German Reich, and he declared that until the Reich's legal system had been introduced by command of Herr Hitler all laws except the Constitution remained in effect. Then Herr Forster immediately wired Herr Hitler of his action, begged the Chancellor to give his approval of the move and through Reich law complete the annexation.

The German flag is now flying everywhere over Danzig, Herr Forster said, and all church bells resound to the event. "We thank God," he declared, "that He gave the Fuehrer the strength and the possibility to free also us from the evil Versailles treaty."

Hitler Accepts Danzig

By The Associated Press.

BERLIN, Friday, Sept. 1.—The German official news agency, D. N. B., announced today that Albert Forster, Nazi Chief of State in Danzig, had proclaimed the reunion of the Free City with the Reich.

Herr Hitler today accepted the Free City of Danzig into the Reich.

"I acknowledge your proclamation of the return of the Free City of Danzig to the Reich," Herr Hitler's telegram said. "I thank you, Gauleiter Forster, and all Danzig men and women, for your loyalty which you have displayed for so many years.

"Greater Germany welcomes you with joy in her heart.

"The law of reunion will be enacted forthwith. I appoint you, Herr Forster, chief of the civil administration in the Danzig territory."

Forster's telegram to Herr Hitler read:

My Fuehrer.

I have just signed and then put into effect the following basic law, concerning the reunion of Danzig with the German Reich.

The basic State law of the Free State of Danzig and the reunion of Danzig with the German Reich is effective Sept. 1, 1939.

To lift the immediate distress of the people and State of the Free City of Danzig, I decree the following basic State law:

ARTICLE I

The Constitution of the Free City of Danzig has been suspended effective immediately.

ARTICLE II

All legal and administrative power will be executed exclusively by the head of State.

ARTICLE III

The Free City of Danzig with its territory and its peoples forms

Continued on Page Five

Soviet Ratifies Reich Non-Aggression Pact; Gibes at British and French Amuse Deputies

By G. E. R. GEDYE

Special Cable to THE NEW YORK TIMES.

MOSCOW, Aug. 31.—With Premier and Foreign Commissar Vyacheslaff M. Molotoff, working under high pressure—so suddenly applied without any previous indication and contrasting so sharply with earlier delaying tactics this week as to suggest German insistence that the matter be finally settled—the Supreme Soviet [Parliament] tonight unanimously ratified the Russo-German non-aggression pact.

Ratification, which was first foreshadowed at midday, was preceded by a speech by Mr. Molotoff so precise in its definition of Soviet obligations to refrain from participating on the side of Great Brit in and France in any war against Germany, so voluble in its defense against charges of inconsistency against Communist Russia for embracing Fascist Germany, and so insistent on the inevitability of friendship between "not merely the governments but also the peoples" of Germany and Russia as to extinguish the last faint hopes of the western democracies that Moscow might yet find loopholes or excuses for joining them at some subsequent date in resisting German aggression against Poland.

Mr. Molotoff's speech contained nothing to justify constantly repeated suspicions of the existence of a secret German-Soviet pact entitling the latter to participate in a partition of Poland.

The Premier's speech contained much trenchant and seemingly irrefutable evidence of blunders by the British and French Governments in handling the question of Soviet cooperation. It was not diffi-

Continued on Page Eight

Hitler Acts Against Poland

The port of Gdynia, north of Danzig (toward top of map), was blockaded this morning. At Gleiwitz (shown by cross) artillery fire was heard after a Polish-German skirmish had been reported there. Cracow, to the east, was among Polish cities said to have been bombed.

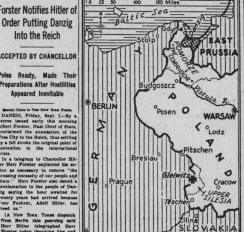

Hitler Tells the Reichstag 'Bomb Will Be Met by Bomb'

Chancellor Vows 'Fight Until Resolution' Against Poland—Gives Order of Succession As Goering, Hess, Then Senate to Choose

Chancellor Adolf Hitler of Germany, in a world broadcast this morning, opened "a fight until the resolution of the situation" against Poland, announcing that "from now on bomb will be met by bomb."

At the same time he announced, to face any eventuality, that if anything "happened" to him, Field Marshal Hermann Goering was to be in charge; if to Marshal Goering, Rudolph Hess; if to Herr Hess, the Senate, which he proposes to appoint, will select a successor.

The Chancellor, after attempting to narrow the conflict with Poland by assuring the Western powers that he had no designs on their frontiers, by assuring the neutrality of the sideline powers and by acknowledging the friendliness of Italy and the new relations with Russia, issued a defy to Poland's allies.

Says He Will Carry on

"I shall carry on this fight regardless of against whom I may come," he declared.

At the same time he held the door open for Poland to capitulate to his demands, declaring that he did not intend to make war against women and children. He said that if a solution did not come from the present Polish Government, it would come from a future Polish Government.

The Chancellor expressed confidence, toward the close of his address, that his decision, which was being broadcast over amplifiers hastily erected by electricians at the last moment in the streets of Berlin and the provincial capitals, would be accepted by the German people.

The scene enacted in the Kroll Opera House in Berlin was carried over sound waves to most of the nations of the world. From Berlin hook-ups had been arranged with the three major networks of the United States, and, according to the announcer for the German broadcasting system, over the Italian, Hungarian, Spanish, Norwegian, Swedish, Danish, Yugoslav, British and French national networks.

The summons to the Reichstag, ordered by Herr Hitler himself, had been sent out only a few hours before the meeting. Most of the members had been awaiting the signal, and when the opera house opened shortly before 10 o'clock [5 o'clock, New York time] this morning, they were dressed in the uniforms of their military formations.

After Herr Hitler finished speaking the deputies enacted a law incorporating Danzig into the Reich, declaring Danzig citizens were now Germans, voiding the Constitution of the Free City and extending to its territory the jurisdiction of German law.

At 5:10 A. M., Marshal Goering opened the meeting and turned the floor over to the Chancellor.

In the early part of his address, Herr Hitler electrified his audience with this declaration:

"We have all been suffering under the tortures that the Versailles treaty has been inflicting upon us."

Then, speaking with measured deliberateness of Germany's claims to the pre-war German areas, he announced, as he had on a previous occasion:

"The Treaty of Versailles is, for us Germans, and has been, for us Germans, not a law."

Anticipating what the announcement's reiteration would lead to, the Deputies roared applause. Then Herr Hitler, his indignation rising as he proceeded, set about building up the German case, asserting that his proposals for a peaceful solution of the problem of Danzig and the Polish Corridor had been rejected, and charging that the Poles had visited atrocities on Germans, especially women and children, "killing many of them."

SUMMARY OF SPEECH

A summary of Herr Hitler's speech was translated as follows:

"For months we have been suffering under the burdens of the Treaty of Versailles. Danzig was and is a German city. All these regions have only Germany to thank for their cultural development.

"Minorities in the Polish Corridor have been shamefully mistreated. Here, as in other respects, I have tried to solve the problems by peaceful means. In the fifteen years of National Socialism we have been

Continued on Page Three

HITLER GIVES WORD

In a Proclamation He Accuses Warsaw of Appeal to Arms

FOREIGNERS ARE WARNED

They Remain in Poland at Own Risk—Nazis to Shoot at Any Planes Flying Over Reich

By OTTO D. TOLISCHUS

Special Cable to THE NEW YORK TIMES.

BERLIN, Friday, Sept. 1.—Charging that Germany had been attacked, Chancellor Hitler at 5:11 o'clock this morning issued a proclamation to the army declaring that from now on force will be met with force and calling on the armed forces "to fulfill their duty to the end."

The text of the proclamation reads:

To the defense forces:

The Polish nation refused my efforts for a peaceful regulation of neighborly relations; instead it has appealed to weapons.

Germans in Poland are persecuted with a bloody terror and are driven from their homes. The series of border violations, which are unbearable to a great power, prove that the Poles no longer are willing to respect the German frontier. In order to put an end to this frantic activity no other means is left to me now than to meet force with force.

"Battle for Honor"

German defense forces will carry on the battle for the honor of the living rights of the reawakened German people with firm determination.

I expect every German soldier, in view of the great tradition of eternal German soldiery, to do his duty until the end.

Remember always in all situations you are the representatives of National Socialist Greater Germany!

Long live our people and our Reich!

Berlin, Sept. 1, 1939.

ADOLF HITLER.

The commander-in-chief of the air force issued a decree effective immediately prohibiting the passage of any airplanes over German territory excepting those of the Reich air force or the government.

This morning the naval authorities ordered all German mercantile ships in the Baltic Sea not to run to Danzig or Polish ports.

Anti-air raid defenses were mobilized throughout the country early this morning.

A formal declaration of war against Poland had not yet been declared up to 8 o'clock [3 A. M. New York time] this morning and the question of whether the two countries are in a state of active belligerency is still open.

Reichstag Will Meet Today

Foreign correspondents at an official conference at the Reich Press Ministry at 8:30 o'clock [3:30 A. M. New York time] were told that they would receive every opportunity to facilitate the transmission of dispatches. Wireless stations have been instructed to speed up communications and the Ministry is installing additional batteries of telephones.

The Reichstag has been summoned to meet at 10 o'clock [5 A. M. New York time] to receive a more formal declaration from Herr Hitler.

The Hitler army order is interpreted as providing, for the time being, armed defense of the German frontiers against aggression. The action is also surpected of forcing international diplomatic action.

The Germans announced that foreigners remain in Polish territory at their own risk.

Flying over Polish territory as well as the maritime areas is forbidden by the German authorities and any violators will be shot down.

When Herr Hitler made his an-

Continued on Page Three

"All the News That's Fit to Print."

NEWS INDEX, PAGE 21, THIS SECTION

The New York Times.

Copyright, 1939, by The New York Times Company.

EXTRA

Generally fair, little change in temperature today. Tomorrow cloudy, showers in afternoon or night.
Temperatures Yesterday—Max., 80; Min., 64

Section 1

VOL. LXXXVIII....No. 29,807 — Entered as Second-Class Matter, Postoffice, New York, N. Y. — NEW YORK, SUNDAY, SEPTEMBER 3, 1939. — P — Including Rotogravure Picture, Magazine and Book Review. — TEN CENTS | TWELVE CENTS Beyond 200 Miles Except in 7th and 8th Postal Zones.

BRITAIN AND FRANCE IN WAR AT 6 A. M.; HITLER WON'T HALT ATTACK ON POLES; CHAMBERLAIN CALLS EMPIRE TO FIGHT

SOVIET IN WARNING

British-French Action to Bring Western Border Revision, Berlin Hears

NAZIS GREET MISSION

Hitler to Receive New Russian Ambassador and General Today

By OTTO D. TOLISCHUS

Wireless to THE NEW YORK TIMES.

BERLIN, Sunday, Sept. 3.—According to well-informed quarters here Moscow is already supposed to have notified Paris and London that if France and Britain join in the present Reich-Polish conflict Russia will find herself compelled to revise her Western borders.

This is tantamount to the threat that any British and French help to Poland will merely hasten the partition of Poland between Germany and Russia. There are hints that Russia might also seek other "compensation" in regions even less convenient to Britain.

As an impressive demonstration of this new cooperation there arrived today by air from Stockholm a new Russian Ambassador, and a new embassy secretary, both of whom were said to be very close to Premier Vyacheslaff Molotoff, and a Russian military mission headed by a commanding general.

Officials Greet the Mission

The new Ambassador is Alexander Shkhartzeff, who, it is pointed out here, collaborated with Mr. Molotoff in the Commissariat of Foreign Affairs in Moscow. The new embassy secretary is Vladimir Perloff, up to now Mr. Molotoff's secretary and interpreter.

The military mission consists of General Maxim Purjakoff, designated as the Military Plenipotentiary of the U. S. S. R., and his staff; Brig. Gen. Michael Beljakoff, Colonel Nikolai Skornjakoff, Major Basanoff and Captain Alexander Seditch.

To show the importance of the occasion the members were met at Tempelhof Airfield by Dr. Ernst Woermann, Under-Secretary of State in the Foreign Office; Baron Alexander von Doernberg, Chief of Protocol, and other Foreign Office officials. Lieut. Gen. Seifert, commander of Berlin, headed the list of army officers greeting the Russians. A guard of honor presented arms.

The Russians received an ovation as their automobiles, flying the hammer-and-sickle flag of the Soviet Union, passed the Reich Chancellery. Those assembled along the street gave the Nazi salute.

Hitler to Receive Envoy

Adding importance to all this is the fact that it was announced at midnight that Herr Hitler would receive the new Ambassador, together with the Military Plenipotentiary, for the submission of credentials later today, which sets a precedent for diplomatic speed.

That such a formidable military mission was sent here to work out close collaboration with the German Army is taken for granted now. But German quarters still hold that the consultative clauses of the German-Russian pact are sufficient to cover all the collaboration necessary and a formal military alliance may be signed only as the last trump card to impress London and Paris.

Ambassador Joseph Lipski and his whole embassy staff left Berlin this morning under safe conduct en route to Sweden, which has also taken over the representation of Polish interests. The German Embassy staff was supposed to have left Warsaw at the same time. German interests in Poland are being represented by the Netherlands. Official quarters hold, however, that this merely represents a "cessation of direct diplomatic relations," not a formal break of relations, just as there is no declared state of war.

Meanwhile, since the German-Polish conflict is now being arbitrated by the roar of cannon the re-

Continued on Page Sixteen

Announcement of Final Ultimatum

By The Associated Press.

LONDON, Sunday, Sept. 3.—Following is the text of today's communique revealing the final ultimatum to Germany:

On Sept. 2 His Majesty's Ambassador in Berlin was instructed to inform the German Government that unless they were prepared to give His Majesty's Government in the United Kingdom satisfactory assurances that the German Government had suspended all aggressive action against Poland and were prepared promptly to withdraw their forces from Polish territory, His Majesty's Government in the United Kingdom would without hesitation fulfill their obligations to Poland.

At 9 A. M. this morning His Majesty's Ambassador in Berlin informed the German Government that unless not later than 11 A. M., British Summer time, today, Sept. 3, satisfactory assurances to the above effect had been given by the German Government and had reached His Majesty's Government in London a state of war would exist between the two countries as from that hour.

His Majesty's Government are now awaiting the receipt of any reply that may be made by the German Government.

The Prime Minister will broadcast to the nation at 11:15 A. M.

21 CIVILIANS KILLED IN RAID ON WARSAW

Women, Children Die as Bomb Hits Workers' Apartment—State of War Decreed

By The Associated Press.

WARSAW, Poland, Sept. 2.—Twenty-one dead and more than thirty wounded were counted tonight after German bombs had struck an apartment house in a Warsaw workingmen's quarter.

The bombs tore off the side of the apartment house as if it had been made of paper. Rescue workers still were clearing away the resultant pile of debris in a search for further casualties when this correspondent inspected it.

One of the bombs had dug a crater fully twenty feet in diameter, and the open ground was piled high with furniture and belongings.

In the center of a large park in the southern section of Warsaw, this writer also saw where a bomb had struck a simple wooden dwelling, killing two persons and wounding one. In an open field near the Vistula River, where ten light bombs apparently had been released simultaneously, they had dug craters in a 100-yard circle.

With the writer on this tour of inspection of damage done by the German air bombings were C. Burke Elbrick, secretary of the American Embassy; Clifford Norton, chargé d'affaires of the British Embassy, and officials of the Polish Foreign Office.

During the tour the party twice was forced to take refuge because of air-raid alarms, five of which in all sounded through the city today. Once the party took cover in a shallow dugout filled with working men, their wives and their crying children.

The worst scene of damage was at Kolo, the workingmen's quarter, where, in addition to wrecking one apartment building, the bombs had smashed windows in several others.

An old man gulped back tears as he said his wife and two children were dead. A woman, still staring blankly into space, said:

"My husband is gone."

An official news service communiqué stated that yesterday German raiders dropped 120 bombs on Warsaw and its vicinity, killing ten and wounding twenty-five in Warsaw proper, with the number of casualties in the suburbs still undetermined.

President Ignaz Moscicki declared that Poland was under a "state of war" today as official reports said that Polish forces were resisting German invasion on three fronts.

The "state of war" supersedes the

Continued on Page Fourteen

News dispatches from Europe are now virtually all subject to censorship

PARIS AUTHORIZED WAR DECLARATION

Chamber Voted Credits After Hearing Daladier—New Ultimatum Being Drawn

By The Associated Press.

PARIS, Sept. 2.—Premier Edouard Daladier today received implied authority from the Chamber of Deputies to declare war on Germany.

With that to support them, he and his Cabinet met at the War Ministry at 7:30 tonight to frame a demand that Chancellor Hitler reply to the British-French "last warning" of yesterday.

The power to declare war was vested in a war budget bill of 69,000,000,000 francs, which the sober Deputies, many wearing army uniforms, adopted unanimously by a show of hands after hearing M. Daladier say the government was still willing to negotiate if Germany would cease hostilities in Poland.

Whether the Premier uses the authority vested in him by adoption of the budget depends upon the possibility—frankly viewed as slight—that Herr Hitler would avail himself of a last-minute loophole for peace.

The Premier told the finance committee after the Chamber session that he planned to call the Chamber to approve an actual declaration of war if that became necessary, but he may simply ask for approval after, rather than before, the action is taken.

"The government will take the same chance as Parisians," M. Daladier told a Deputy who asked whether the government planned to leave Paris immediately.

The session was held in a tense atmosphere from 3 to 3:55 P. M.

Continued on Page Seventeen

ROME ASKED PEACE

Pressed Its Proposal for a 5-Power Parley on Britain and France

WAR MEASURES CUT

Press Expressed the Hope Germany Would Win in Poland

By The Associated Press.

ROME, Sept. 2.—Premier Mussolini tonight sought to prevent Polish-German hostilities from spreading into a general European war by arranging a negotiated settlement.

Conferences that the British and French Ambassadors had with Foreign Minister Count Ciano were believed to be connected directly with an Italian proposal of a five-power conference disclosed in London by Prime Minister Neville Chamberlain and Foreign Secretary Viscount Halifax.

The possibility of halting the German-Polish conflict and arranging a peaceable settlement was believed to have been discussed at the diplomatic conferences, but no official information was forthcoming.

Some foreign observers believed, however, that Signor Mussolini had been asked to use his influence on Adolf Hitler to halt fighting in Poland, call his army back and negotiate a settlement of his demands on the Poles.

For Wide Settlement

Here it was regarded as certain that any five-power conference proposed by Premier Mussolini would not be merely for settling the German-Polish conflict but would be aimed at complete revision of the Treaty of Versailles.

Under such a revision Italy and Germany would seek the political and economic concessions that they consider necessary to end European tension once and for all. This has long been Signor Mussolini's idea and Italian newspapers recently have been stressing it as the only real solution. [Italy has been demanding from France concessions concerning Tunisia, the Suez Canal and Jibuti, French Somaliland port.]

While the Ambassadors of France and Britain conferred with Foreign Minister Ciano Italy continued her policy of watchful waiting and avoidance of any military "initiative".

The important commentator, Virginio Gayda, in the Giornale d'Italia noted uneasily that French and British war preparations made it seem that only a miracle could prevent a "more general explosion." Italy, he said, rested on her arms, confident she had done everything possible to avoid war. He said she was following events

Continued on Page Fifteen

Fuller Breaks Own Bendix Race Records; Crosses Continent in 8 Hours 58 Minutes

Frank Fuller, San Francisco sportsman pilot, broke his own record in the Bendix Trophy Race from Burbank, Calif., to Cleveland yesterday and then kept on to Bendix, N. J., to break his own record for a transcontinental crossing in the event, opening feature of the National Air Races and the country's outstanding air derby.

Flying a stripped-down Seversky military plane equipped with the same twin Wasp engine he had in the 1937 race, when his earlier records were set, Fuller flew the 2,450 miles from Burbank to Bendix in an elapsed time of 8 hours 38 minutes 8.46 seconds. His average speed was 273.14 miles an hour. His elapsed time in 1937 was 9 hours 23 minutes.

The record for a transcontinental flight is 7 hours 28 minutes, established by Howard Hughes in a specially built plane about two years ago.

In crossing the finishing line at Bendix, Fuller, a wealthy paint manufacturer, won three prizes totaling $12,500. For being the first to reach Cleveland he received a prize of $9,000. As the first to fly over the line at Bendix he won another $1,000, and for breaking his 1937 record he won $2,500.

Fuller reached Bendix at 4:24:53 P. M., Eastern daylight time, and proceeded, without landing, to Floyd Bennett Field, where he brought his plane to earth at 4:35 P. M.

Max Constant of Burbank was the second racer to fly over Bendix, reaching there at 6:13:39 P. M. Arthur C. Bussy of Royersford, Pa., appeared at 7:08:15 P. M.

Although Constant arrived at Bendix ahead of Bussy, he took off from Burbank before him and Bussy was declared the second prize winner and received $5,000 for the flight to Cleveland and an additional $800 for continuing to Bendix and Floyd Bennett Field.

Mrs. Arline Davis of Cleveland landed at Newark Airport at 8 P. M., believing that she had crossed the official marker at Bendix and thereby won the $2,500 prize for the first woman to finish

Continued on Page Three

NAZIS REPORT GAINS

Hitler's Aims in Corridor Already Won, They Say, Telling of Big 'Trap'

RESISTANCE IS NOTED

But Armies Drive On and Navy Is in Command of Baltic, Germans Hold

Special Cable to THE NEW YORK TIMES.

BERLIN, Sunday, Sept. 3.—Defying the British and French ultimatums, the German armies reported continued advances into Poland yesterday.

By nightfall, it was asserted, not only had they attained the German war aims in the Polish Corridor as outlined in Chancellor Hitler's "sixteen points" but they were pushing forward in a concentric drive toward Warsaw. According to one report, the German forces stood less than fifty miles north of the Polish capital, and a big battle was believed developing along the Narew River.

According to the latest communiqués of the army command, which apparently have already been overtaken by developments, the German armies operating out of East Prussia and Pomerania had virtually cut the Corridor along the Netze and Vistula Rivers, so that all Polish troops remaining in the bottleneck north of it were hopelessly trapped.

Claim Capture of Teschen

In the South the Germans were reported to have taken the heavily fortified Jablunka Pass, the main strategic highway from Slovakia into Poland; to have captured Teschen and Pless [Pszczyna] and to be breaking through the Polish bunker line approaching Biala. This army group apparently has the task of capturing the Upper Silesian industrial section and the Teschen coal mines, taken by Poland from Czecho-Slovakia, and then of advancing along the Vistula toward Sandomierz, the new Polish armament and industrial center.

At the same time two other German Army groups, operating from the north out of East Prussia and from the southwest out of Silesia, apparently were conducting a pincers movement on Warsaw. The southwestern group was declared to have taken Wielun and to be advancing toward Radomsk and Sieradz.

The Northern army group, according to a communiqué, was advancing on Przasnysz, but, according to private reports, is already beyond that town and approaching a larger Polish army that is supposed to have taken a stand on the Narew, where the first real battle of the undeclared war may take place.

Reich Claims "Air" Domination

The communiqué asserted also that the German air force, after many bombing expeditions against air fields, railroads, military transports, retreating marching columns and other military objectives, in which many planes and the munition factory at Skarzysko-Kamienna were destroyed, now has "unchallenged air domination over the entire Polish territory and so is now free for other tasks in protection of the Reich."

In addition, the Germany Navy, which said it had bombed the fortifications and port of Hela and also Gdynia, reported the sinking of a Polish torpedo boat off Hela. It was said to command the Baltic so completely that the fishing embargo was lifted last night.

A communiqué issued by the high command early today, according to the official German News Bureau, declared:

"The German air force yesterday again proved its absolute superiority. The whole air area over the battle zone and the hinterland is completely controlled by the German air force. Attacks were confined exclusively to military objectives.

"After units of German armored cars had reached the Vistula, approximately at noon, the German

Continued on Page Twelve

Text of Chamberlain Address

The following is the text of the address by Prime Minister Chamberlain from 10 Downing Street this morning:

I am speaking to you from the Cabinet Room from 10 Downing Street. This morning the British Ambassador in Berlin handed the German Government the final note stating unless we heard from them by 11 o'clock [6 o'clock New York time] that they were prepared at once to withdraw their troops from Poland a state of war would exist between us. I have to tell you now that no such undertaking has been received and consequently this country is at war with Germany.

You can imagine what a bitter blow it is to me that all my long struggle to win peace has failed. Up to the very last it should have been quite possible to arrange a peaceful settlement between Germany and Poland.

Hitler has evidently made up his mind to attack Poland whatever may happen. Hitler claims that his proposals were shown to Poland and to us. That is not a true statement. The proposals never were shown to the Poles or to us.

The German Government prepared the proposals in German and the same night the German troops crossed the Polish frontier. Germany will never give up force and can only be stopped by force.

We are prepared to uphold our treaty with Poland and to protect them from the wicked and unprovoked attacks on the Polish people. France is joining Britain in fulfillment of her pledges. We have a clear conscience and the situation has become intolerable. Now that we have determined to finish it I know that you will all play your part.

When I have finished speaking several detailed announcements will be made on behalf of the government giving you plans under which it will be possible to carry on the work of the nation in these days of stress which may be ahead, but these plans need your help. You may be taking part in one of the fighting services or one of the other branches.

It is of vital importance that you carry on with your jobs. May God bless you all and may He defend the right for it is the evil things we shall be fighting against—brute force, broken promises, bad faith. But I am certain that right shall prevail.

Bulletins on European Conflict

Air Raid Warning in London

LONDON, Sept. 3 (Sunday).—Air raid sirens sounded an alarm in London today at 11:32 A. M. (5:32 A. M., E.S.T.).

The whole city was sent to shelters by the wail of the alarm but all clear signals were sounded seventeen minutes later.

Ribbentrop Gives Reply to British Envoy

BERLIN, Sunday, Sept. 3 (AP).—German Foreign Minister Joachim von Ribbentrop received British Ambassador Sir Nevile Henderson at 9 A. M. [4 A. M. in New York] today to hand him Germany's answer to the "final warnings" of Britain and France. Herr von Ribbentrop was expected to see the French Ambassador, Robert Coulondre, shortly before noon.

American Diplomats' Families Leave Reich

BERLIN, Sunday, Sept. 3 (AP).—About fifty women and children of the United States Embassy and consular staffs, as well as several other American families, left Berlin today at 8:50 A. M. [3:50 A. M. in New York] for Copenhagen in compartments reserved for them in a regular train.

They were due in Copenhagen at 5:35 P. M. [12:35 A. M. in New York].

War Announced in France

PARIS, Sunday, Sept. 3 (AP).—The radio announced to the French nation today that British Prime Minister Chamberlain had proclaimed Great Britain at war with Germany.

"No News" at the German Embassy

LONDON, Sunday, Sept. 3 (AP).—At the German Embassy in London at 9:30 A. M. today [5:30 A. M., New York], a half hour before the expiration of the British ultimatum, it was said, "There is no news." A spokesman said, "We are in constant communication with Berlin."

Denies Poles Got Five-Power Parley Offer

LONDON, Sunday, Sept. 3 (AP).—Exchange Telegraph Agency, British news agency, said today that Count Edward Raczynski, Polish Ambassador in London, informed it that "the Italian Government did not approach Poland" concerning a reported five-power conference to settle German-Polish issues.

"Apart from the declarations made yesterday in the British Parliament and apart from contradictory reports in the press," the agency quoted him, "the Polish Government has not knowledge of such a scheme."

Exchange Telegraph said the Ambassador declared that "any talk of such a conference" would be "ludicrous and fantastic" as long as "a single enemy soldier stands on Polish soil."

1,000 Americans Sail on French Liner

PARIS, Sunday, Sept. 3 (AP).—The French Line said today that the Ile de France had sailed from Havre with more than 1,000 Americans on board, bound for home.

Heavy Fighting Is Reported in Silesia

WARSAW, Sept. 2 (AP).—Although official information was lacking, it was reported tonight that severe fighting be-

Continued on Page Twelve

TO END OPPRESSION

Premier Calls It 'Bitter Blow' That Efforts for Peace Have Failed

WARNING UNHEEDED

Demand on Reich to Withdraw Army From Poland Ignored

Prime Minister Neville Chamberlain announced to the world at 6:10 o'clock this morning that Great Britain and France were at war with Germany. He made the announcement over the radio, with short waves carrying the measured tones of his voice throughout all continents, from 10 Downing Street in London.

Mr. Chamberlain disclosed that Great Britain and France had taken concurrent action, announcing that "we and France are, today, in fulfillment of our obligations, going to the aid of Poland."

France, however, had not made any announcement beyond stating that the French Ambassador to Berlin would make a final call upon Foreign Minister Joachim von Ribbentrop at 6 o'clock this morning, and it was assumed the French had proclaimed the existence of the state of war.

Speaks With Solemnity

With the greatest solemnity Mr. Chamberlain began his declaration by reporting that the British Ambassador to Berlin had handed in Great Britain's final ultimatum and that it had not been accepted. Without hesitation he announced Britain's decision and, after touching briefly on the background of the crisis, he expressed the highest confidence that "injustice, oppression and persecution" would be vanquished and that his cause would triumph.

Mr. Chamberlain appealed to his people, schooled during the last year as the crisis deepened in measures of defense and offense, to carry on with their jobs and begged a blessing upon them, warning that "we shall be fighting against brute force."

The declaration came after Great Britain had given Chancellor Adolf Hitler of Germany extended time in which to answer the British Government's final ultimatum of Friday. In the final ultimatum Herr Hitler had been told that unless German aggression in Poland ceased, Britain was prepared to fulfill her obligations to Poland.

Warning Was Sharp

Britain's last warning at 4 o'clock this morning, New York time, left no doubt of her stand, for the phrase, "fulfillment of Britain's obligations to Poland," was replaced by a flat statement that a state of war would exist between the two countries as of the hour of the deadline.

After Mr. Chamberlain had finished his statement, which had been introduced as "an announcement of national importance," the announcer warned the British people not to gather together, broadcast an order that all meeting places for entertainment be closed, and gave precautions to prepare the people against air bombings and poison gas attacks.

Mr. Chamberlain began his

Continued on Page Fifteen

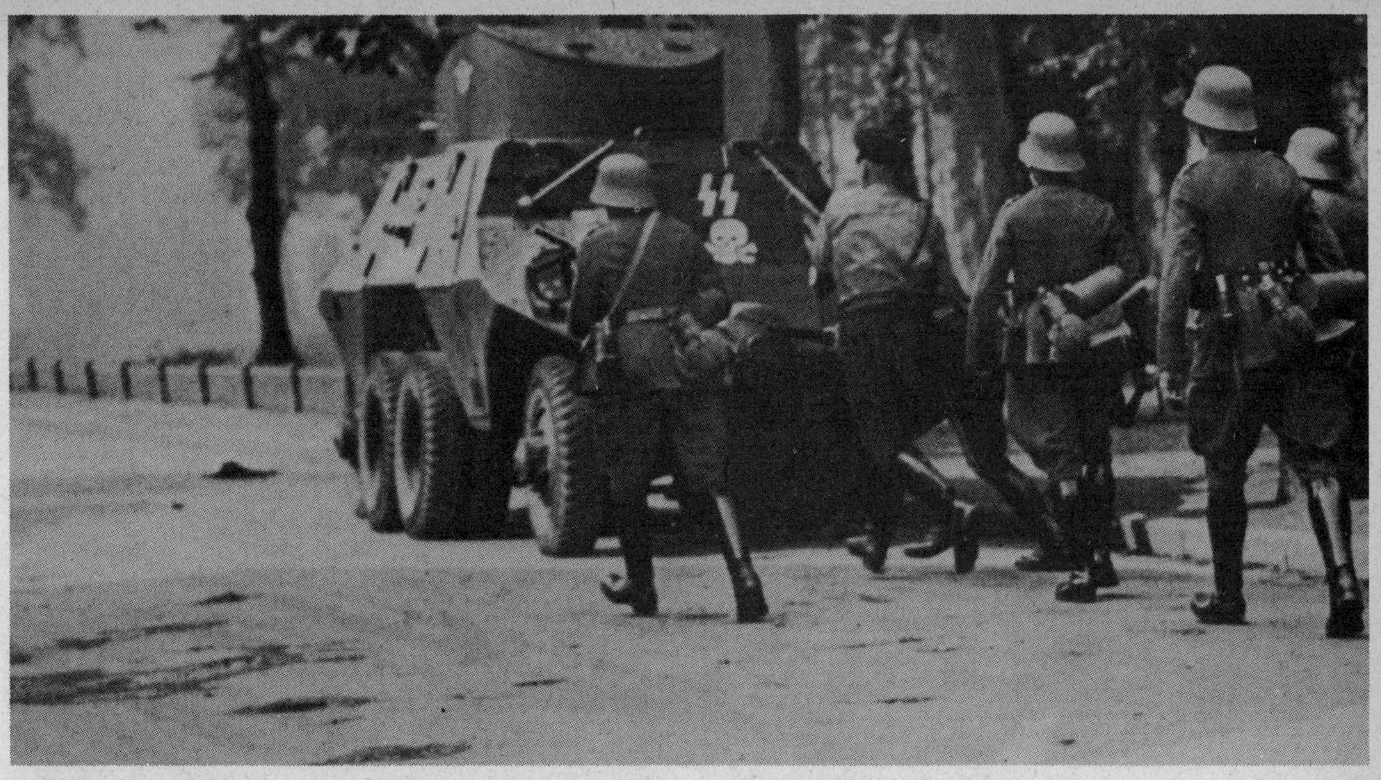

German troops advance into Danzig.

Germans pause on their way to Warsaw.

A smashed Polish supply coloumn.

"All the News That's Fit to Print."

The New York Times.

LATE CITY EDITION
Generally fair and warmer today. Tomorrow cloudy, continued warm, showers in afternoon or night.
Temperatures Yesterday—Max., 66; Min., 55

VOL. LXXXIX...No. 29,832. Entered as Second-Class Matter, Postoffice, New York, N. Y. NEW YORK, THURSDAY, SEPTEMBER 28, 1939. PP THREE CENTS NEW YORK CITY and Vicinity | FOUR CENTS Elsewhere Except in 7th and 8th Postal Zones.

ESTONIA REPORTED READY TO YIELD AS RUSSO-GERMAN PARLEYS BEGIN; WARSAW, A SHAMBLES, SURRENDERS

PITTMAN PREDICTS 'CASH-CARRY' LAW; SUPPORT GROWING

Senator Says on Radio Plan to Repeal Embargo Is Surer Way to Avoid War

SPEEDY ACTION IS CERTAIN

O'Mahoney Approves the New Neutrality Program—Foes Arrange for Mass Meeting

By TURNER CATLEDGE
Special to THE NEW YORK TIMES.

WASHINGTON, Sept. 27—A plea to the country to study closely the new neutrality resolution, to see if it is not in fact a stronger guarantee that America will not be involved in the European war than the present arms embargo, was broadcast tonight by Senator Pittman on the eve of the Foreign Relations Committee's formal consideration of the measure.

The Senator, who is chairman of the committee, coupled with his plea a prediction that the new resolution, repealing the embargo on arms and munitions and substituting a mandatory "cash-and-carry" system for all commerce between the United States and warring nations, would become law. He spoke over a network of the National Broadcasting Company.

Mr. Pittman's forecast as to the outcome was being adopted by more and more observers in Washington with each new addition to the "paper" majority which the Administration has claimed for embargo repeal from the start. The prediction was made on all sides tonight, even among opponents of repeal, that the resolution would be reported favorably by the Foreign Relations Committee tomorrow or Friday and that debate would start in the Senate early next week.

Opponents Keep On Fighting

In the face of appeals and predictions of the Administration forces, opponents of the resolution continued to insist that they would win in their efforts to retain the arms embargo, maintaining that the issue was at bottom one of peace or intervention by the United States.

Arrangements were completed tonight for a mass meeting of pro-embargo forces to be held Friday night at the Belasco Theatre, under the auspices of various peace and religious societies. Speakers scheduled for the meeting, described as "America's Town Meeting Against War," are Senators Capper of Kansas, Clark of Missouri and Nye of North Dakota; the Rev. Ernest Fremont Tittle of Chicago; Norman Thomas, former Socialist candidate for President; John T. Fly..n, economist, and Roland Hayes, Negro concert singer.

Among the sponsors of the meeting are the Women's International League for Peace and Freedom, the National Council for Prevention of War, the Fellowship of Reconciliation, the War Resisters League, the Keep America Out of War Congress, the Youth Committee Against War, World Peace Ways, the World Peace Commission of the Methodist Church and the Church of the Brethren.

Heavier Guard to Capitol

Meanwhile arrangements for a heavier guard at the Capitol were made today after a conference between Kenneth Romney, sergeant at arms of the House; Chesley Jurney, sergeant at arms of the Senate; J. Edgar Hoover, head of the Federal Bureau of Investigation, and Colonel E. W. Starling, head of the White House Secret Service detail.

This was another step in a movement growing quite general in Washington for extra precautions around government buildings. This already has meant the closing of the White House grounds to visitors. Special restrictions also will be invoked governing admissions to the galleries when the Senate starts debate on the neutrality resolution.

Senator Pittman contended in his radio address that many of the petitions and communications which had deluged members of the Senate against repeal of the embargo demonstrated that they were based upon ignorance of the intent of Congress or were the result of "vicious organized foreign propaganda."

Plans for Permanent Law

He emphasized that the proposed resolution did not repeal all neutrality legislation, but asserted that on the contrary it vitally strengthened the neutrality legislation.

The Senator took up each section of the resolution, asserting that it was broader, deeper and more definite than the provisions of present law. The major intent of the authors, he said was to leave as little as possible to the discretion of the President and write a law

Continued on Page Ten

Total of Idle in U. S. Lowest Since End of '37

A 4.3 per cent decline during August brought national unemployment to the lowest point since December, 1937, according to statistics made public yesterday by the National Industrial Conference Board. The number of jobless persons dropped from 9,852,000 in July to 9,424,000 last month, a reduction of 428,000.

Total employment in the United States rose from a July figure of 44,782,000 to 45,263,000 in August. Agriculture and manufacturing showed the greatest advances, with more than 200,000 additional employes recorded in each field.

The government's emergency labor force declined to 2,169,000 workers, a drop of 16.6 per cent from July. This was the sixth consecutive monthly cut in the emergency work force, and brought the total to the lowest point in twenty months.

BERGDOLL HID IN U. S. 7 YEARS, HE SWEARS

Returned Twice While Nation Thought He Was in Reich —Got 'Pot of Gold'

While the army, G-men and indignant patriots believed Grover Cleveland Bergdoll was a fugitive in Germany for nineteen years, the World War draft evader slipped back into this country twice and led a shadowy existence in his Philadelphia mansion for seven years, according to his story yesterday before a general court-martial.

The long, bizarre story of the Philadelphia millionaire, whose escapades stirred a storm of notoriety around his name and family and provoked a string of prosecutions and a Congressional investigation, was further enriched as Bergdoll told a variation of his pot-of-gold story.

Bergdoll was on his way to Maryland hills to dig up his pot of gold, with permission of the War Department, when he broke away from two sergeants and fled to Germany in 1920. But yesterday he said the $150,000 "pot" was sealed in concrete, right in his own home. He came back for it in the depression year, 1929, and stayed for four years. Then he returned again in 1935 and stayed until last October, he said.

The faces of the thirteen officers of the military court seemed to freeze as Bergdoll admitted passport irregularities, false statements to consular agents and fictitious names to dupe immigration officials.

Loses First Bout With Law

Bergdoll lost his first bout with military law when the court, with Brig. Gen. Irving J. Phillipson as president, refused to mitigate the first charge from "desertion in time of war" to "desertion in time of peace." This was important, inasmuch as the three-year statute of limitation applies to the peace-time offense. No time lapse in prosecution can invalidate a charge of wartime desertion.

It became apparent as the trial moved on, with Bergdoll's aged mother and other relatives as witnesses, that his testimony of clandestine sojourns in his native land was intended to pry Bergdoll loose from the military authorities by virtue of the time question.

Harry Weinberger, the prisoner's lawyer, asserted that a three-year limit applied to the desertion charge and two years to escape. When he was overruled he nevertheless pressed the question in the hope that a military reviewing authority might later decide otherwise. In that case Bergdoll's presence in this country, within reach of the authorities, would tend to make the statute of limitation applicable.

It was understood, however, that the military prosecutors will contend that even if Bergdoll returned he did so surreptitiously to outwit the authorities. Thus the charges would stand.

May Get Six Years More

Bergdoll is now serving the remainder of the five-year prison term imposed for desertion by a court-martial in 1920, three months before he escaped. For the new charge of desertion and escape in conspiracy he may get six years more.

Last evening, as the first session of the trial ended in the Y. M. C. A. gymnasium on Governors Island, a warrant was being prepared for the arrest of Bergdoll's brother, Erwin Bergdoll, who also is a convicted draft dodger. The warrant was to be based on his alleged evasion of subpoena servers seeking him as a witness.

Bergdoll, who returned to this country on May 25 finally to "face the music," took the stand at noon and within a few minutes told his first sensation—that he came back in June, 1929. The ship was the Duchess of Bedford out of Liverpool, and Bergdoll used the name and passport of Joseph Amann, porter of his hotel in Germany.

He landed in Montreal, said the

Continued on Page Eighteen

DEMOCRATS VOTE BENCH NOMINATION TO JUDGE LEHMAN

State Committee in Resolution Voices Hope for Nonpartisan Choice for Appeals Chief

LABOR TO ACT SATURDAY

Endorsement by Republicans Now Seen Likely—Jurist's Record Is Praised

Acting under authority delegated by the last State Convention of the party, the Democratic State Committee yesterday nominated Irving Lehman, senior Associate Judge of the Court of Appeals, for chief judge of that court. The meeting was held at the National Democratic Club.

Postmaster General James A. Farley, who presided as chairman of the committee, expressed the hope that the other major parties would endorse Judge Lehman.

The State Committee of the American Labor party will meet Saturday at the Hotel Commodore and endorse Judge Lehman. Whether the Republican State Committee at its meeting at the Hotel Ten Eyck in Albany next Tuesday will do so is uncertain.

Republican Action Awaited

A few days ago it seemed likely that the Republican committee would nominate a Republican and Supreme Court Justice Edmund H. Lewis of Syracuse was mentioned as a probability. Word has been received here that Justice Lewis does not wish the nomination, and the up-State pressure for the nomination of a Republican was said to have been reduced considerably.

The sentiment of up-State lawyers is reported to be for the endorsement of Judge Lehman by the Republican State Committee.

Judge Lehman's nomination for Chief Judge has been urged by the State Bar Association, the Association of the Bar of the City of New York, the New York County Lawyers Association and the Federation of Bar Associations of Western New York. Belief was expressed by Republican leaders here that the chances favored the endorsement of Judge Lehman by the Republican committee.

Nominating Resolution

Judge Lehman was placed in nomination by Howard Wilbur of Catskill, who offered the following resolution:

Whereas we note Judge Irving Lehman has served the people of the State of New York as a judge for thirty-one years since his first election to the Supreme Court in 1908.

Judge Lehman has long been recognized as one of the ablest, most conscientious and fairest judges in the history of our State judiciary. His high character and knowledge of the law, his broad vision, his independence and his unflagging devotion to duty have often been commended by bench and bar. He has received the un-

Continued on Page Nineteen

Report Thaelmann Freed To Attest Nazi-Soviet Tie

By The Associated Press.

BERLIN, Sept. 27—An unofficial but trustworthy source said tonight that Ernst Thaelmann, former Communist chieftain in Germany, and others associated with him had been released from prisons and concentration camps as a result of the new-found German-Soviet Russian cooperation.

Likewise, placards and books attacking communism have been removed from public view.

Herr Thaelmann, twice a candidate for President of Germany, was arrested March 3, 1933, slightly more than a month after Adolf Hitler, whom he bitterly opposed, became Chancellor.

No formal charges were ever placed against him. As the months passed without any formal accusation, Dr. Hans Frank, Reich Justice Commissioner, indicated it still would be a long time before "we can have the case fully ready for court."

In his first campaign for President in 1925 Herr Thaelmann, who boasted that he was once a hobo in the United States, placed fourth.

MEDIATION BY U. S. SUGGESTED IN CHINA

Basis for Peace Would Be the Return to 9-Power Treaty, Says Foreign Minister

Copyright, 1939, by United Press

CHUNGKING, China, Sept. 27—Chinese Foreign Minister Wang Chung-hui, in an interview today, said emphatically that the National Government would continue resistance against Japan until "final victory," but suggested that the United States, if that country were willing to act as mediator, was in a favorable position to bring the undeclared Chinese-Japanese war to an early end.

The Foreign Minister outlined the basis on which an honorable peace was possible. He said that China's foreign policy was not fettered by the events in Europe or elsewhere and added:

"Chinese policy is based on treaties, principally the Nine-Power Treaty. [That treaty is designed to protect the rights of foreign nations in China and China's territorial integrity.]

"The first point of our policy is the enforcement of these treaties for the preservation of our independence and integrity.

"Secondly, we favor economic co-operation with all friendly nations and this will apply to Japan as soon

Continued on Page Three

Pope Said to Seek Peace and a Free Poland, Protected Against Communism and Atheism

By Telephone to THE NEW YORK TIMES.

ROME, Sept. 27—Pope Pius has been working diplomatically through neutral States to get Britain and France to agree to a peace conference that would end with the creation of a Polish buffer State on ethnic lines, it is reported here.

This report has been current since last Friday but has not been confirmed. Your correspondent has received it from three different sources. Today an Italian correspondent repeats it from Berlin, so there seems to be something in it.

It is said the Pontiff feels that the great menace to Christian civilization comes from Russia and her recent eruption into Central Europe and that all States, including Germany, ought to get together to prevent the spread of communism and the atheism that accompanies it.

At the same time the Pope feels that anything is better than a continuation of the war, particularly as the worst effects of it are yet to be felt. Consequently, say these reports, he would be willing to accept, although not to condone, Germany's conquest of Poland if a settlement were arranged that would guarantee Europe a lasting peace and the Polish Catholics a State of their own which protected them from communism and the neo-paganism of Germany.

The diplomatic manoeuvre involved would be a delicate one since it presupposes the possibility of separating Germany and Russia. Otherwise, the Vatican would be ranged against Germany and Russia combined, which, in effect, would mean that it would be taking sides in the war. This is something the Pontiff has carefully avoided doing.

It should be noted that this supposed proposal by the Pope parallels Premier Mussolini's peace move. He has suggested a cessation of hostilities in acceptance of the German conquest and, indirectly, the formation of a purely Polish State.

It has not been suggested, however, that the Premier has been taking advice from the Vatican, for the Italian line of policy has been consistent in that regard ever since the war started and even before. Behind that openly declared policy there has been and still is intense diplomatic activity by the Italian Government to bring pressure on Britain and France, which is what the Pope is supposed to be doing.

If Premier Mussolini is really being backed by the Pontiff it would help to explain Rome's hopes that the British and French will yield. It also gives a clue to the extent of the pressure to which London and Paris are being subjected.

One thing does seem certain: that the Vatican is forming an organization to give religious aid to prisoners and probably to handle mail for them. Later there may be a supplementary organization to arrange for the exchange of prisoners.

This has been foreshadowed for several weeks. It is understood that the Vatican is almost ready to put the plan into operation. Similar work was done by the Vatican dur-

Continued on Page Five

20-DAY SIEGE ENDS

Polish Defenders Yield Last Stronghold to Nazi Invaders

3,000 SLAIN IN 24 HOURS

Blazing Capital Faced Famine and Pestilence—Occupation Is Set for Tomorrow

By The United Press.

BUDAPEST, Hungary, Sept. 27—The city of Warsaw surrendered unconditionally tonight, the German High Command announced, after twenty days of siege that saw the Polish capital bombed and burned "into an unspeakable inferno" with thousands of civilian dead.

Complete destruction of at least half of the once magnificent city on the Vistula, exhaustion of its defenders' ammunition, starvation and pestilence brought capitulation long after Polish resistance had been virtually wiped out in the rest of the nation.

For days the city had stood alone in defiance of the German conquest from the West and the Soviet Russian invasion from the East, fighting off German troops and tanks in the outskirts in hand-to-hand fighting while German long-range guns and bombing planes systematically wrecked the capital.

500 Fires Sweep City

In the last twenty-four hours of Warsaw's defense more than 3,000 persons, mostly women and children, were reported to have been killed. The Polish Transcontinental Press said 500 fires were sweeping what had been magnificent buildings, parks and homes.

The announcement of Warsaw's unconditional surrender was made by the German High Command in Berlin, but Polish radio dispatches confirmed the capitulation. The Berlin radio announced the surrender at 8:10 P. M. [2:10 P. M. New York time], then struck up "Deutschland ueber Alles" and the "Horst Wessel Lied."

The German High Command said actual surrender of the city to the German forces encircling it on all sides—in some places they have been within four miles of the center of the city for four days—probably would occur Friday.

The Germans estimated that 100,000 ragged and weary Polish troops of the Warsaw garrison would surrender and hand over their arms along with the civil administration headed by Mayor Stefan Starzynski, who has come to be known as "Stefan the Stubborn" because of his rejection of every German ultimatum during the twenty days of siege.

Formal Surrender Delayed

The German High Command's communiqué, announcing the end of what even the Germans admit was a heroic defense, said:

"The High Command announces that Warsaw has capitulated unconditionally. The formal surrender of the city to the German High Command is expected to occur on Sept. 29. The military garrison consists, according to present estimates, of more than 100,000 men."

Polish refugees here were fearful of the fate of Mayor Starzynski, assailed by the Nazis because he rallied men and women civilians to take up arms and beat off the Germans in the suburbs.

After agreeing to negotiate the city's surrender with the Germans, the Warsaw defenders designated their commander to negotiate with General Johannes Blaiskowitz of the German Army on the terms.

The German radio, describing the Nazi decision of last Friday to bomb and shell Warsaw into submission after rejection of repeated German ultimatums, insisted that Warsaw had been respected as an open city as long as possible.

Poles Proposed Surrender

"But Warsaw was transformed into a fortress by measures of the Polish commander, who restored the old forts and armed part of the civilian population," the Berlin radio said.

"Our attack yesterday brought into German hands the first line of defense north of the city and the second line in the south and as a result of these attacks the Polish commander today offered to surrender the city and garrison to the German Commander in Chief."

Although surrounded, Warsaw held out longer against the Ger-

Continued on Page Six

The International Situation

A Russian ship was torpedoed off the Estonian coast yesterday and with it, possibly, Estonia's hopes of escaping Soviet domination. With Moscow's ominous announcement of the sinking, pressure on the little Baltic country was increased to a point where it was believed ready to yield to Russian demands. This development coincided with the arrival of Estonian Foreign Minister Selter and German Foreign Minister von Ribbentrop in Moscow. Herr von Ribbentrop conferred with Joseph Stalin for several hours. [Page 1.]

Just what the Moscow discussions were all about was still a matter of speculation, but Berlin argued that not only Russia and Italy but also Turkey were now siding with the Reich, warned that a Russo-German military alliance was possible and told the Allies to end the war "while there is still time." [Page 4.]

In Bucharest it was generally believed that Turkey had been lost to the Allies and that Russia and Germany were laying out spheres of influence. In Rome the Russian intrusion into the Balkans was found disturbing. [Page 4.] Paris thought the Moscow conversations might prove a turning point in Chancellor Hitler's course, leading to sensational peace offers or a check on German expansion eastward. [Page 7.]

Warsaw's twenty days of heroic resistance ended in unconditional surrender, resulting from death, devastation, disease and a shortage of food and ammunition. [Page 1.] In the east of Poland the Red Army, harassed by guerrillas, continued its march and occupied the entire Galician oil fields, but found wells had been dynamited. [Page 5.]

Hopes that in the final disposition of Poland a buffer State would be set up were attributed to Pope Pius, who was understood to be working to get Britain and France to agree to a peace conference. [Page 1.]

Comparative peace seemed to have descended on the Western Front, where positions remained unchanged, but German guns were dropping shells in the French rear areas around Wissembourg. [Page 2.]

At sea Germany made her first attempt to break the British blockade with airplanes. Twenty of them attacked a British squadron in the North Sea. According to Berlin, an aircraft carrier was "destroyed," a battleship was hit and all the planes returned safely. According to London, no British ship was hit, no casualties were suffered, one German flying boat was shot down, another was damaged and a third came down on the sea, where its occupants were captured. [Page 1.]

This British report was made before a House of Commons session that voted without protest a schedule of drastic wartime taxes that include a basic income levy of 37½ per cent. [Page 1.]

A controversial note was injected into the Pan-American meeting at Panama by a Chilean proposal that the American nations refuse to recognize as contraband anything except actual articles of war. Argentina and Uruguay favored merely refusing to recognize as contraband foodstuffs and clothing. United States support for the latter idea was indicated. [Page 9.]

BRITISH TAXED 37½% OF INCOME FOR WAR

Levy on $10 Weekly Earnings and Surtaxes Up to 80% Voted Without Protest

By FERDINAND KUHN Jr.
Special Cable to THE NEW YORK TIMES.

LONDON, Sept. 27—The staggering cost of fighting this war was brought home to the British people today by imposition of the highest income tax in history and by new charges of all kinds that may leave their mark on British economy for generations to come.

Even in the darkest days of the World War and in the financial crisis of 1931 there never was anything like the tax program that Sir John Simon, Chancellor of the Exchequer, coolly announced in the House of Commons today.

The income tax was boosted mercilessly to a new record of seven shillings six pence in the pound, a basic rate of 37.5 per cent, more than six times what the British taxpayer had to bear at the end of 1914. To soften the blow slightly, a lower rate of seven shillings, or 35 per cent, will be charged for the remaining six months of this fiscal year, but after next April 1 the full rate will be in force, and there is no guarantee that it will not go higher as the war drags on.

Exemptions Are Slashed

Exemptions were slashed all along the line so that a single man earning the equivalent of $10 a week was brought into the income-tax-paying class. At the other end of the scale the surtax was raised so steeply that a capitalist earning £100,000 a year must surrender four-fifths of his entire income to the government.

No Labor Cabinet bent on equalizing distribution of wealth would have dared submit such a budget; but even the higher income tax was not the whole story. A universal excess profits tax of 60 per cent was substituted for the existing tax that applied only to armament firms. Nothing was said today about a capital levy, but the Chancellor of the Exchequer warned that at the end of the war the government might move toward "conscription of wealth" by tapping unearned war profits, such as those produced by increase in real estate values.

The estate duty was raised by 10 per cent at one stroke to help pay for Great Britain's colossal expenditure of £2,000,000,000 in a single year. Finally, a whole series of in

Continued on Page Eight

NAZI PLANES RAID THE BRITISH FLEET

One Shot Down, Says Churchill —Reich Claim of Hits on Warships Disputed

Wireless to THE NEW YORK TIMES.

LONDON, Sept. 27—Germany's first attempt to break the British blockade from the air has failed, Winston Churchill, First Lord of the Admiralty, told the House of Commons in a statement which indicated that a fast and well-armed battleship is still a match for a bomber.

[Berlin announced that a second British aircraft carrier had been "destroyed" and a British battleship crippled by a number of Nazi planes in what was described as "the first successful action of its kind in military history."]

Replying to the German claims that they had sunk a British aircraft carrier and successfully bombed several battleships in a North Sea battle, Mr. Churchill produced a radio message from Sir Charles Forbes, Commander-in-Chief of the Home Fleet, which read:

"Yesterday afternoon in the middle of the North Sea a squadron of British capital ships, together with an aircraft carrier, cruisers and destroyers, were attacked by about twenty German aircraft.

"No British ship was hit and no British casualties were incurred. One German flying boat was shot down and another is reported to be badly damaged."

House Cheers Statement

The First Lord of the Admiralty, who has been sweeping gloom out of the House with his eloquent and confident statements on naval warfare, read this radiogram with ill-concealed delight. When he had finished he looked up and smiled broadly. The House roared.

When they quieted down Mr. Churchill, who never fails to hold back a little information for a rebound, said:

"I might have added that another German aircraft came down in the North Sea. We sent a destroyer to collect her, and her crew of four have been brought in as prisoners."

Mr. Churchill also entered the dis-

Continued on Page Six

Dispatches from Europe and the Far East are subject to censorship.

SOVIET SHIP IS SUNK

Moscow Reports Vessel Torpedoed Off the Estonian Coast

SHARP DEMANDS EXPECTED

Ribbentrop Talks With Stalin on Questions Relating to Developments in Poland

By G. E. R. GEDYE
Wireless to THE NEW YORK TIMES.

MOSCOW, Thursday, Sept. 28—Ominous news of the sinking of a Soviet steamer was issued here last night. At 6 P. M. yesterday, it was stated officially, a submarine of unidentified nationality torpedoed and sank the Soviet steamer Metallist, 968 tons, in Narva Bay, off the coast of Estonia.

A Soviet naval patrol vessel in the neighborhood rescued nineteen members of the Metallist's crew; twenty-four others are missing, the statement said. This, following last night's hostile Soviet communiqué concerning Estonia, doubtless is a prelude to grave developments for the Baltic States.

The description "Narva Bay" may indicate Soviet territorial waters outside the town of Narva just south of the Gulf of Finland opposite the Estonian coastline.

Protests Soviet Flights

Later it was reported here that the Estonian Government had protested through its Foreign Minister, Karl Selter, who returned to Moscow yesterday, against the alleged violation of Estonian frontiers by Soviet airplanes and had denied all suggestions of connivance in the escape of a Polish submarine from Tallinn last week, but had nevertheless decided to yield to Soviet demands in view of the impossibility of obtaining any help in resisting any Soviet invasion.

While Lithuania was reported in the Soviet press to have decreased her military precautions, Latvian circles on the other hand were greatly alarmed by the hostile tone of Soviet references to Estonia. In view of the extremely short Estonian frontier any Soviet move against Estonia, the Latvians felt, would inevitably involve them.

It was thought possible yesterday that the Soviet demands on Estonia might not include actual occupation of Tallinn, but that the Soviets might content themselves with the installation of Soviet Army garrisons on certain Estonian islands commanding Tallinn, coupled with special privileges for the use of Tallinn as a port.

Joachim von Ribbentrop, German Foreign Minister, arrived in Moscow yesterday. The planes that brought him and his party were soon followed by another machine, from which Mr. Selter stepped. And during the day Premier and Foreign Minister Vyacheslaff Molotoff conferred with Shukru Saracoglu, Turkish Foreign Minister, also a guest here.

Von Ribbentrop Meets Stalin

In the small hours of this morning the Soviet Government issued a communiqué on Herr von Ribbentrop's visit—which was brief and unexpectedly noncommittal. Questions connected with developments in Poland, it stated, were discussed during a midnight interview. Count Friedrich Werner von der Schulenburg, German Ambassador to Moscow, and Alexander Shkhartzeff, Soviet Ambassador to Berlin, were present at the conversations, which took place in the presence of Joseph Stalin. The conversations lasted more than two hours, the communiqué said. [The talk lasted four and one-half hours, an Associated Press dispatch from Moscow said.]

Nothing was announced concerning new agreements or a date for renewal of the conversations. It is assumed, of course, that they will be resumed later today.

Shigenori Togo, Japanese Ambassador, upon his own urgent demand, saw Mr. Molotoff Tuesday night. Nothing was revealed concerning the purpose or result of the interview, but Japanese here do not conceal their alarmed feeling that the visit of Herr von Ribbentrop may result in a full Russo-German military alliance, so it is safe to assume that Mr. Togo requested full information for his government concerning the object of this visit, of which the Japanese learned in advance only through a Soviet radio broadcast.

One curious thing about this visit

Continued on Page Four

German troops parade through Warsaw, the capital of defeated Poland.

"All the News That's Fit to Print."

The New York Times.

LATE CITY EDITION
Cloudy and warmer today, showers tonight or tomorrow; cooler tomorrow afternoon and night.
Temperatures Yesterday—Max., 74; Min., 58

VOL. LXXXIX...No. 29,833. Entered as Second-Class Matter, Postoffice, New York, N. Y. NEW YORK, FRIDAY, SEPTEMBER 29, 1939. PPPP THREE CENTS NEW YORK CITY and Vicinity | FOUR CENTS Elsewhere Except in 7th and 8th Postal Zones.

REICH AND SOVIET JOIN FOR PEACE--OR WAR; NO BUFFER STATE; NEW PACT WARNS ALLIES; ESTONIA GIVES MOSCOW SEA AND AIR BASES

COMMITTEE VOTES 'CASH-CARRY' BILL TO END ARMS BAN

Eases Curbs on Air and Sea Lines Serving Americas and Tightens Credits

APPROVES PLAN BY 16 TO 7

Senate Starts Debate Monday—Pittman Predicts Decision in Three Weeks

By TURNER CATLEDGE
Special to THE NEW YORK TIMES.

WASHINGTON, Sept. 28—Administration forces won an opening skirmish today in the neutrality fight when the Foreign Relations Committee, by a vote of 16 to 7, approved and sent to the Senate the Pittman resolution repealing the arms embargo and substituting a strict "cash-and-carry" system for all American commerce with warring nations.

The committee adopted only two substantial changes in the resolution as drafted last week-end. One was designed to give some relief to American ships and airlines serving British and French possessions in the Western Hemisphere and to transpacific air lines flying between American ports and similar possessions in the Orient. The other aimed to tighten the provision for ninety-day short-term commercial credits to belligerent purchasers of goods in this country.

The committee's action, taken one week almost to the hour after President Roosevelt convened Congress in special session to buttress America's neutrality in the new European war, made it certain that the prospectively historic debate on foreign policy would begin next Monday. Despite the favorable committee report, the measure faces a "hell-to-breakfast" fight from the Senate isolationists who are intent upon retaining the arms embargo against all countries at war.

Committee to Meet Today

Senator Barkley of Kentucky, majority leader, obtained the Senate's consent at a brief session this noon for Senator Pittman, chairman, to file the committee's official report during the week-end recess. The committee has been called to meet again tomorrow to polish up the language of the resolution, which will go before the Senate as a substitute for the Bloom bill passed by the House at the last session.

Four of the committee majority which gave the favorable report reserved the right to seek amendment or vote against the resolution on the floor. Even with these exceptions the Administration gained a distinct advantage in avoiding further delay or an adverse recommendation in committee.

The isolationists did not make a stand in the committee room. They made no motions and offered no amendments. They hardly raised a voice in protest, preferring simply to record their votes and then wait for open battle on the Senate floor where they propose to make a last-ditch fight against repeal of the mandatory embargo. Except for the proposed embargo repeal, the isolationists look upon the Pittman resolution with great favor, particularly because of the mandates it puts upon the President and Executive departments to maintain this country's neutrality.

Line-up of the Committee

The vote on reporting the measure, which came after three hours' deliberation, was as follows:

For reporting—Pittman of Nevada, Harrison of Mississippi (by proxy), George of Georgia, Wagner of New York, Connally of Texas, Thomas of Utah, Van Nuys of Indiana, Pepper of Florida, Murray of Montana, Schwellenbach of Washington, Green of Rhode Island, Barkley of Kentucky, Reynolds of North Carolina, Guffey of Pennsylvania, Gillette of Iowa, Democrats; White of Maine, Republican.

Against reporting—Clark of Missouri, Democrat; La Follette of Wisconsin, Progressive; Shipstead of Minnesota, Farmer-Laborite; Borah of Idaho, Johnson of California, Vandenberg of

Continued on Page Eleven

The International Situation

Germany and Russia, in a pact announced early this morning, drew a line through Poland considerably to the east of Warsaw and said that was their frontier. Then, declaring that peace in Eastern Europe was thus settled, they warned Britain and France to make peace in the West, saying that otherwise they would "consult each other regarding necessary measures." The nature of such measures was forecast by a provision in the agreement that Russia would supply Germany with materials to be paid for "over a long time." [Page 1; text of the pact and supplementary documents begins on Page 1.]

Overshadowed by this development was the virtual disappearance last night of another European State. Estonia signed a mutual assistance pact with Russia; to be sure, it guaranteed the "sovereign rights" of both countries, but more significantly it granted Russia the right to sea and air bases on Estonian territory and the right to maintain armed forces—put by one source at 25,000 men—in the country. [Page 1; text of the pact, Page 8.]

Although the signing of this agreement coincided with the visit of the German Foreign Minister to Moscow, Berlin circles denied that the Russian move was part of the Nazi-Soviet understanding. [Page 4.]

As the last Polish fortress—that at Modlin—fell to the German Army, which advanced to its new "border" with Russia, Reich military circles were saying that their country must now be stronger than ever to be ready for an "inevitable dispute" with the Soviet some day. [Page 1.]

Berlin again claimed a success at sea, saying its planes had scored a hit on a British cruiser. The British again promptly disputed the claim; they said it probably arose from an unsuccessful attempt the day before to bomb a destroyer. [Page 1.] Nevertheless, the Germans did seem to be organizing a large-scale sea and air attack on British ships, bases and ports to break the blockade and impose one of their own. [Page 2.]

As part of this campaign, a German submarine sank another neutral freighter, a Swedish ship, whose captain was held aboard the U-boat for seven hours and whose crew was rescued. [Page 2.]

But Britain's success in countering the undersea menace was shown by news from Montreal that the convoy system was working. Fifteen freighters loaded with grain, constituting the first convoy of the war, reached Britain safely, and there have been others since that one. [Page 1.]

The Administration in Washington won the first round in the Neutrality Bill controversy when the Senate Foreign Relations Committee voted 16 to 7 to report out the Pittman resolution. Only two changes were made. [Page 1; text of the bill as approved by the committee, Page 10.]

HAMILTON OPPOSES 'PARTISANSHIP' BAN

Republican Chairman 'Resents' Plan to Make Party 'Rubber Stamp' in War Crisis

Expressing disagreement with President Roosevelt's suggestion for an "adjournment of partisanship" during the present European crisis, John D. M. Hamilton, chairman of the Republican National Committee, opposed last night such a move on the eve of the 1940 Presidential campaign.

Mr. Hamilton, who spoke at the organization meeting of the New York County Republican Committee at Manhattan Center, 311 West Thirty-fourth Street, declared that he resented any attempt in the name of emergency to stampede the Republican party into becoming a mere rubber stamp for Administration proposals. He said there had been an "adjournment of politics" in the name of emergency in 1933, with the result that millions of unemployed still walked the streets, and that the national debt had reached an all-time high.

"Should Not Be Diverted"

"Nothing would be more disastrous to this nation than an adjournment of politics which would permit a blackout of urgent domestic problems," Mr. Hamilton asserted. "As a party we would be faithless to our trust if we permitted what is happening in Europe to divert us from the task that is ours of correcting the errors of the last six and a half years and of redirecting our energies toward a useful and permanent recovery.

"We need to reorder our finances and we need to consider some of the ill-advised legislation that still remains on the statute books. There are many other vital domestic issues about which we need to think and to think deeply."

Mr. Hamilton asked what was the nature of the "limited emergency" proclaimed by the President, saying that no guns were leveled at the United States, that no threatening demands on the government had been made and that the nation was at peace and would remain at peace, if the will of the people was allowed to prevail.

With obvious reference to the differences of opinion regarding President Roosevelt's proposal for repeal of the embargo provision of the Neutrality Act, which cut across party lines, Mr. Hamilton said:

"There is no obligation or com-

Continued on Page Thirteen

CANADIAN CONVOYS ELUDE SUBMARINES

Cargoes of Vital Resources, Some From New York, Are Crossing Atlantic Unscathed

Special to THE NEW YORK TIMES.

MONTREAL, Sept. 28—The regulations of censorship heretofore have barred from the newspapers one of the greatest Canadian stories of the European war, the story of how the senior dominion of the British Commonwealth of Nations is supplying the motherland with resources with which to defeat nazism.

At regular intervals convoys are leaving the Atlantic coast escorting vessels laden with wheat, metal, manufactured goods and other products, and every ship is arriving safely in British ports.

The grain movement is perhaps the most important. During the first week or two of the war, wheat and corn from Great Lakes ports piled up in Montreal, jammed the elevators and made it necessary for laden lakers to anchor in the river to await unloading.

But Britain quickly organized her convoy system, and it was learned here today that the first successful convoy, comprising fifteen freighters with cargoes aggregating 500,000 bushels of grain, had reached England.

Since then other convoys have

Continued on Page Eight

NAVY RAIDED AGAIN

British Cruiser Bombed 'Successfully,' Berlin Version Declares

LONDON DENIES HITS

Plane Reported to Have Aimed at Destroyer but Missed

Conflicting claims on the results of a new battle between warship and plane were made by London and Berlin yesterday. Germans said they had "successfully attacked" a British heavy cruiser off the coast of Scotland. The British said a plane had aimed bombs at a destroyer in those waters but missed.

Wireless to THE NEW YORK TIMES.

BERLIN, Sept. 28—Following the success claimed yesterday in the German air attack on a squadron of the British fleet in the North Sea, the German High Command announced today that a heavy British cruiser of "the Washington type" was successfully attacked by airplanes near the Isle of May off the coast of Scotland not far from Edinburgh.

A German "fighting squadron" is alleged to have struck the fore portion of a 10,000-ton British cruiser with a 500-pound bomb. What happened to the ship after this is not reported.

[The "Washington-type" cruisers are the 10,000-ton vessels built after the Washington arms limitation treaty, which banned construction of larger ships of this type.]

Replying to the British denial of German success in the North Sea battle between British ships and German planes, a communiqué today repeats the assertion that a British airplane carrier and a battleship were hit by bombs. This attack was made by fourteen German land bombers, it is said. Fearing no resistance, such as would be anticipated in a land attack, the German planes are said to have been unaccompanied by pursuit planes.

A Foreign Office spokesman this afternoon suggested the British send neutral representatives of the foreign press stationed in Great Britain to see the squadron involved.

Chancellor Hitler meanwhile today unexpectedly went to Wilhelmshaven with Grand Admiral Erich Raeder, commander of the German Navy. He personally congratulated the commanders and crews of returned submarines on their "great successes."

Hint Ark Royal Was Hit

BERLIN, Sept. 28 (UP)—Still insisting that a British aircraft carrier was "reduced to a wreck" and that a British battleship was damaged when a fleet of planes attacked a large British naval squadron in the middle of the North Sea Tuesday, the German wireless broadcast a sarcastic statement to-

Continued on Page Two

British Flying Boat Escapes From Iceland; Danes Protest, Alleging Breach of Parole

Wireless to THE NEW YORK TIMES.

REYKJAVIK, Iceland, Sept. 28—Count Eduard Reventlow, Denmark's Minister to London, today protested to the British Government against the departure of a British naval plane from Iceland this morning.

The plane landed Tuesday evening at the lonely trading post of Raufarhofen in Northern Iceland, lost in the fog. The naval plane, with nine aboard, anchored in the harbor, and the commander was said to have given his word that he would submit to the government's orders.

It had been planned to fly the plane to Reykjavik at 8 o'clock this morning. The British plane, however, departed at 6 A. M. and disappeared at sea.

LONDON, Sept. 28 (UP)—The British Admiralty tonight ordered a service inquiry into charges by the Iceland Government that nine members of the crew of a Royal Air Force flying boat broke their parole after being interned by Iceland authorities.

It was announced earlier in the day that the nine fliers and the flying boat had returned to Britain after being forced down by fog near Raufarhofen in Northern Iceland. The fliers and the ship were interned by Icelandic authorities.

The Danish Minister in London, acting on behalf of the Reykjavik government, protested to the British Government tonight against the alleged action of the British fliers in breaking their parole and the inquiry was ordered.

If violation of parole is proved, "appropriate action" will be taken by the British Government, it was said.

TALLINN GIVES WAY

Capitulates to Demands as Russian Planes Fly Over the City

MUTUAL AID PROMISED

Trade Treaty Signed by Selter and Molotoff—Nazis Are Pleased

By G. E. R. GEDYE
Special Cable to THE NEW YORK TIMES.

MOSCOW, Friday, Sept. 29—Without its necessitating any immediate change in the uncertain map of Europe the Estonian Republic virtually ceased to exist in the early hours of today.

By the signature of two treaties, labeled "mutual assistance" and "trade agreement," the little Baltic republic passed under the full domination of the Soviet Union and yielded to Russia naval bases and airdromes and the right to maintain military forces in Estonian territory.

She fully accepted the implications of Soviet assertions about the operations of mysterious, unidentified submarines in Estonian waters and handed to Moscow the keys to her security and national existence, which she had held since the collapse of Russian Czarism and the formation of the Soviet Union.

The "mutual assistance" pact is to come into force upon the exchange of ratifications at Tallinn, the capital of Estonia, within six days. The pact is concluded for ten years. Unless it is denounced by either party within a year from the date of expiration, it is to continue for another five years.

It was signed by Premier and Foreign Commissar Vyacheslaff M. Molotoff of Russia and Foreign Minister Karl Selter of Estonia.

Negotiated in Kremlin

The final form of Estonia's political eclipse was "negotiated" within the walls of the Kremlin with the hapless Estonian Foreign Minister.

While Germany's Foreign Minister, Joachim von Ribbentrop, after a banquet at the Kremlin, sat watching the Russian Ballet in the Moscow Theatre, the little anti-communist state, which until now had been the playground of the Nazi forces, was handed over to the Russian colossus within a few months after her rejection of proposals to guarantee her frontiers against German aggression in the attempted Anglo-Franco-Russian peace front.

It was rumored that Estonia had made a vain appeal to Germany at the eleventh hour.

Estonia's "alliance" with Russia refers to the possible event of aggression by a "great power." Whether or not the Soviet Union's action is part of an agreement with Germany the fact remains that the only great power capable at the moment of adopting an aggressive attitude toward Estonia is Germany herself.

By secret agreement or by acceptance of a development she has been unable to hinder after having launched a new war, Germany has had to yield this northern zone of influence to the country against whom her influence was long exercised. Whether connivance or surrender flavored this dessert to Herr von Ribbentrop's banquet, it can hardly have been a particularly palatable dish.

The pact, the official communiqué says, was negotiated from Sept. 22 to 28 between Mr. Molotoff and Mr. Selter with the assistance of Joseph Stalin, Vice Premier A. I. Mikoyan, the Estonian Minister to Moscow, Alexandre Rey and others. The pact and the trade agreement were signed Sept. 28.

Terms of the Agreement

Article I of the Soviet-Estonian pact says the two contracting parties will give each other every assistance, including military, if direct aggression occurs on the part of any great European power against their respective frontiers in the Baltic Sea or their land frontiers or across the territory of the Latvian Republic, as well as against the bases in Estonia, that are granted to the Soviet Union,

Continued on Page Eight

Russo-German Agreements

By German Transocean Wireless.

MOSCOW, Friday, Sept. 29—The following are texts of the German-Soviet frontier and friendship agreement signed here early this morning and accompanying documents:

The German Reich Government and the Government of Soviet Russia, after the disintegration of the former Polish State, consider it their task to restore in this region law and order and to insure nationals living there an existence corresponding to their national character. With this aim in view they have agreed as follows:

Article I

The German Reich Government and the Government of the Soviet Republics lay down as the frontier of their respective spheres of interests in the region of the former Polish State the line which is drawn on the attached map and which will be described in detail in a supplementary protocol.

Article II

Both parties recognize the frontier laid down in Article I of the interest spheres of both States as definite and will decline interference of any kind by a third power with this settlement.

Article III

The necessary new political regulation is undertaken by the German Reich Government in districts west of the line laid down in Article I and by the Government of the Soviet Republic in districts east of this line.

Article IV

The German Reich Government and the Government of the Soviet Republic regard the before-mentioned settlement as a foundation for progressing development of friendly relations between their peoples.

Article V

This treaty will be ratified, and ratification documents will be exchanged in Berlin as soon as possible. The agreement comes into force on the day of its signature.

VON RIBBENTROP
MOLOTOFF

Protocol Statement

The following statement by the German Reich Government and the Government of the Soviet Russian Republic of Sept. 28, 1939, is attached to the protocol:

After the German Reich Government and the Government of the Soviet Russian Republic have definitely settled by the treaty signed today the question resulting from disintegration of the Polish State, thus creating a safe foundation for lasting peace in Eastern Europe, they unanimously express the opinion that it would correspond to the true interests of all peoples and make an end to the war existing between Germany on the one hand and England and France on the other hand. Therefore, both governments, if necessary in conjunction with one of the befriended nations, will direct their joint efforts toward searching this aim as soon as possible. But should the efforts of both governments fail, then the fact would be estab-

Continued on Page Four

LAST WARSAW FORT YIELDS TO GERMANS

Modlin Surrenders and Nazis Achieve War Aims in East—Distrust of Soviet Seen

By OTTO D. TOLISCHUS
Wireless to THE NEW YORK TIMES.

WITH THE GERMAN ARMY, Before Warsaw, Poland, Sept. 28—The German campaign in Poland came to an end today when the fortress of Modlin followed Warsaw in surrendering unconditionally at 7 o'clock this morning. At the same time the bulk of the German Army had returned to the western side of the German-Russian demarcation line, which army circles regard as the new Reich border.

With that surrender of the last fort defending the city, Germany has attained her war aims in the East, namely, the partition of Poland, in exactly four weeks. She is already at work organizing the newly won territory in order to enhance its agricultural and industrial resources.

Again Chancellor Hitler has proved himself the "Mehrer" or aggrandizer, of the Reich. To his political triumph he has added an unprecedented military triumph as well.

But German Army quarters are perfectly well aware that this new aggrandizement has been obtained at a high price that is not measured by German casualties, which are comparatively small, but by the fact that, in place of weak Poland, Germany has again put powerful Russia on her eastern flank. Army circles are so aware of this new situation that they frankly declare:

"Germany must now be stronger than ever, not only to win the conflict with France and Britain but also to prepare for the inevitable dispute with Soviet Russia that must come some day."

Consolation for the Conquered

In fact that is the consolation the German Army offers the conquered foe remaining on the German side of the demarcation line who still fear National Socialist Germany less than they do Bolshevist Russia.

The final dramatic scenes of Warsaw's and Modlin's surrender were witnessed by this writer together with a group of other foreign correspondents who arrived at the German front line on the edge of the capital yesterday afternoon to find Warsaw in flames and Modlin still being bombed and shelled to pieces.

We stood at the same spot on the Warsaw-Modlin road where General

Continued on Page Four

GERMAN ATTACKS IN WEST REPULSED

Heavy Guns Reported Active—Allied Air Forces Bring Down Nazi Planes

By G. H. ARCHAMBAULT
Wireless to THE NEW YORK TIMES.

PARIS, Sept. 28—The comparative lull continues on the West Front, with occasional raids. The French took a number of prisoners in a raid this afternoon in the sector nearest the Moselle River. There is also much firing of heavy guns. The weather now is becoming cold and it is very trying for men in the first lines, especially at night. But with the experience gained during the four Winters of the World War the Quartermaster Corps is ready to meet the emergency.

Today's General Headquarters communiqués follow:

"No. 49 [morning]. It was a quiet night on the whole.

"An enemy attack west of Saarbruecken failed.

"At sea commercial navigation returned to normal conditions, thanks to the organization of convoys and aerial patrols.

"Yesterday afternoon our air force, operating in conjunction with the British air force, brought down several enemy pursuit planes.

"During the night our reconnoissance planes were active."

"No. 50 [evening]. The local attack by our troops in the region immediately east of the Moselle River is proceeding favorably. Some prisoners were taken."

War Limited to One Front

With Warsaw fallen, the war has now become restricted to a single front where both sides can concentrate all their forces, for it is supposed here that the German High Command will leave in Poland only policing units—the partly trained Landwehr, Gestapo and detachments of Storm Troops. The Poles' gallant stand lasted only one month, but it has been invaluable.

It has enabled French mobilization and concentration to proceed unimpeded, as well as British concentration to begin in normal conditions. It has also enabled the allied High Command not only to enter German territory but to oc-

Continued on Page Five

Dispatches from Europe and the Far East are subject to censorship.

THREATEN 'STEPS'

Berlin and Moscow Will Act if Britain, France Reject Peace Move

FRONTIER IS FIXED

Russia Agrees to Give Germany Supplies on Extended Time

By The United Press.

LONDON, Friday, Sept. 29—The Moscow radio broadcast at 6:40 A. M. today made an official announcement that Russia and Germany had signed an agreement in Moscow fixing the German-Russian frontier and revealed that no Polish State would be formed.

The broadcast said that the Russian Premier and Foreign Commissar, Vyacheslaff M. Molotoff, and German Foreign Minister Joachim von Ribbentrop issued a joint statement that, after the liquidation of Poland, there was no necessity for a continuation of hostilities.

The joint statement added that if Britain and France, however, continued hostilities, then the responsibility rested with them, and Germany and Russia then would consult each other about "necessary steps."

The joint statement also said that the Soviet Government agreed to supply Germany with all necessary raw materials in exchange for German goods, which would be delivered over a longer period.

Reich Confirms Pact

BERLIN, Friday, Sept. 29 (UP)—The Foreign Office today announced the signing in Moscow during the night of a "frontier and friendship" treaty with Russia, liquidating Poland as a nation and creating a "secure foundation for permanent European peace."

"The German Reich Government and the Government of the U. S. S. R., by signing the treaty, finally regulated the question arising from the collapse of the Polish State and thus created a secure foundation for permanent European peace," the announcement said.

"They thus express agreement that it would be in the true interests of all peoples to put an end to the state of war between the Reich and Britain and France. The two governments will, therefore, make mutual efforts if necessary with other friendly powers to attain this end as soon as possible.

"Should, however, the two governments' efforts be unsuccessful, the fact would thus be established that France and Britain were responsible for continuation of the war, in which event the German and U. S. S. R. governments would consult regarding necessary measures."

Banquet for Ribbentrop

By G. E. R. GEDYE
Wireless to THE NEW YORK TIMES.

MOSCOW, Friday, Sept. 29—Following Wednesday night's Russo-German talks in the Kremlin—which, it was learned later, lasted not two hours, as the communiqué said, but five and a half hours—the conversations were resumed at 3 o'clock yesterday afternoon. For 7 P. M. a banquet was arranged at the Kremlin in honor of Joachim von Ribbentrop, German Foreign Minister; Count Friedrich Werner von der Schulenburg, German Ambassador here, and several members of Herr von Ribbentrop's suite.

In German circles the banquet was described as extremely cordial in tone. Herr von Ribbentrop sat down to the table not only with Joseph Stalin, Premier Vyacheslaff Molotoff and War Commissar Klementy Voroshiloff, but also with Lazar M. Kagonovitch, Commissar of Heavy Industry and Fuel, who happens to be Jewish, and with Vice Premier Anasthasius I. Mikoyan and Lorenti Beria, Commissar of Internal Affairs.

3 Vice Commissars Present

Three Soviet Vice Commissars of Foreign Affairs—Vladimir Potemkin, S. A. Lozovsky and V. G. Dekanozoff—the Soviet Ambassador to Berlin, Alexander Shkhartzeff; the Soviet Trade Commissioner to

Continued on Page Four

"All the News That's Fit to Print."

The New York Times.

LATE CITY EDITION
POSTSCRIPT
Cloudy, preceded by rain today, slightly colder tonight.
Temperatures Yesterday—Max., 51; Min., 44

VOL. LXXXIX...No. 30,026. Entered as Second-Class Matter, Postoffice, New York, N. Y. NEW YORK, TUESDAY, APRIL 9, 1940. P THREE CENTS NEW YORK CITY and Vicinity | FOUR CENTS Elsewhere Except in 7th and 8th Postal Zones.

GERMANS OCCUPY DENMARK, ATTACK OSLO; NORWAY THEN JOINS WAR AGAINST HITLER; CAPITAL IS REPORTED BOMBED FROM AIR

HOUSE TO CONSIDER WAGE ACT CHANGES EARLY NEXT WEEK

Leaders in Surprise Moves Also Slate Bill for Court Review of Agency Rulings

LABOR LAW ACTION LIKELY

Proponents of Amendments Expect Drive to Dispose of All Labor Legislation

House consideration next week was slated for the bill to amend the Wages and Hours Act and for the Logan-Walter bill to provide for a court review of decisions by governmental agencies. [Page 1.]

A refusal by the Supreme Court to review the Labor Board's order in the Republic Steel case sustained the reinstatement of 5,000 C. I. O. strikers with $5,000,000 back pay. [Page 20.]

The Socialist party convention, at Washington, stated in a resolution that "the interests of American working men and women will best be served by the making of an immediate peace between the C. I. O. and A. F. L." [Page 1.]

Colonel Harrington, WPA Administrator, will be questioned Thursday by the House Appropriations Subcommittee on evidence gathered by its investigators bearing on the 1941 relief outlay. [Page 20.]

The NLRB refused to relieve Mrs. Elinore M. Herrick of further responsibility in connection with the election of employes of the Consolidated Edison Company of New York after a charge of collusion with the company. [Page 20.]

Two Revision Bills Slated

By HENRY N. DORRIS

Special to THE NEW YORK TIMES.

WASHINGTON, April 8—House leaders decided today on consideration early next week of the Barden bill to amend the Wages and Hours Act, a decision which occasioned surprise in labor quarters since it had been assumed this measure would follow the Smith or Norton amendments to the National Labor Relations Act.

But this was not the only surprise, because the tentative calendar for next week also contained a place for the Logan-Walter bill providing court review of any decision of a governmental agency which has the force of law.

When these two measures are out of the way, proponents of amendments to the Wagner Act expect to win consideration of their measures. Just how they will manage this was not revealed, but it was said by one member that the procedure was for a "Bang! Bang! Bang!" program that would wipe the House calendar clean of labor legislation that has "plagued" it for more than a year.

The Barden bill has been pending since last August, when a rule was granted for its consideration. It was never considered, however, because of the "compromise" by which the lending-spending and United States Housing Authority bills—desired by the Administration—were taken up. Both of these failed to obtain consideration, but they served to crowd out the Barden bill, which primarily aims at a redefinition of the "area of production" provision of the Wages and Hours Act.

Would Remove "Ambiguities"

The amendment proposed by Representative Barden of North Carolina, a member of the House Labor Committee, proposes to remove the "ambiguities" of the "area of production" clause and the ruling subsequently made on it by the former Wages and Hours Administrator, Elmer F. Andrews.

Under that ruling processing plants located within ten miles of the area where agricultural products are grown or harvested are exempt from the provisions which require them to pay a minimum wage of thirty cents an hour or work their employes not to exceed forty-two hours per week without overtime pay of time and a half. The Barden amendment proposes

Continued on Page Twenty

The International Situation

War caught up two more countries in its clutches today as the Germans invaded Denmark and attacked Norway.

In the early morning Nazi troops crossed the southern border of Denmark, landed on Danish soil from warships and occupied the Danish capital, Copenhagen—all apparently without resistance. [Page 1.]

Almost at the same time a diplomatic dispatch to Washington announced that Norway was at war with Germany. [Page 1.] This development followed an attempt by German warships—more than 100 of which had been sighted last night moving northward in the Kattegat—to force an entry, with aerial support, into Oslo Fjord. At latest reports German troops were debarking on the Norwegian coast and had entered Navik, Bergen and Trondheim, while the Norwegians were said to have moved their capital, which was reported bombed.

Berlin explained it was taking Denmark and Norway under its "protection" to prevent any hostile attack upon them. [Page 4.]

There had been at least one suggestion yesterday of German troop movements in Scandinavia. A Nazi transport had been torpedoed off Southern Norway with a loss of 150 out of some 300 uniformed men aboard. In the same neighborhood a large German tanker was sent to the bottom. [Page 1.]

The mining of Norwegian waters had taken Norway completely by surprise and eight German freighters were apparently in the same predicament, as they were trapped in those waters and unable to get home. With British warships patrolling the mine fields the ore traffic at Narvik was halted and it seemed likely that Swedish iron shipments would be halved. [Page 3.] Norway protested to both Britain and France against the mining, terming it "an open breach of international law" and demanding that the mines be removed. [Page 1.] London had expected the protest and discounted it. But the British were believed to be ready to go to Norway's aid against the Germans. [Page 2.]

With a loophole in the blockade apparently plugged in Scandinavia the British gave some of their attention to the Balkans; their envoys to the countries of that region began their conferences. [Page 9.] At the same time Southeastern Europe was startled by Rumania's detention of a fleet of British barges carrying dynamite, which, according to the Germans, was to have been used for blocking the Danube. British quarters insisted the explosives were to have been used only for destroying river craft in the event of a German invasion of Rumania. [Page 1.]

ROOSEVELT EFFIGY 'FRONT' GUN TARGET

Healy Also Swears Cassidy Wanted 12 in Congress Shot in Capital as Gesture

Denis A. Healy, star prosecution witness in the trial of seventeen men indicted for conspiring to overthrow the United States Government, testified yesterday in the Brooklyn Federal Court that some of the defendants had used a likeness of President Roosevelt's head as a target during rifle practice.

He swore that John F. Cassidy, a defendant who was prominent in the Christian Front, had favored "going to Washington and shooting twelve Congressmen to show that the Christian Front means business," and he testified that William Gerald Bishop, another defendant, wanted to place Major General Van Horn Mosely, U. S. A. retired, at the head of a dictatorship after overthrowing the present government.

Telling of how members of the group practiced making crude bombs out of empty beer cans, Healy said that they had discussed committing acts of sabotage here if the United States entered the war. He declared that Bishop had boasted to him of knowing who was responsible for an explosion he said had occurred on an oil tanker in the lower bay a few days earlier.

Cross-Examination Begun

Healy finished his direct testimony at 2:30 P. M. yesterday after having been on the witness stand for five hours, beginning Friday afternoon. He began at once a hammering cross-examination at the hands of defense counsel, which they estimated would last for at least two full court days in their effort to discredit his story of having posed as one of the plotters, meanwhile keeping the Federal Bureau of Investigation informed of every development.

He was forced to admit that he had lied on numerous occasions, that he had pretended to be anti-Semitic in order to "carry out my role"; that he had once approached Bishop for aid in smuggling a relative into this country from Canada, and that he had once been convicted of street fighting, for which he received a suspended sentence.

Conceding that he had testified for the government in a previous case, Healy denied that he was a "professional witness," as was charged by former Magistrate Leo J. Healy, counsel for eleven of the defendants. He said the government had arranged a leave of absence for him from the New York Central Railroad, and was paying him the same salary while he was

Continued on Page Sixteen

BRITISH EXPLOSIVES HELD BY RUMANIANS

Fleet of Barges Detained at Danube Port—Nazis Charge Plot to Block River

By The Associated Press.

BUCHAREST, Rumania, April 8—Detention of a fleet of dynamite-laden British barges, said by Germans to be designed to blow up a narrow Danube gateway and block a German supply line, today electrified Southeastern Europe with the fear war soon might spread to this quarter of the world.

Rumanian police, acting on a tip said to have been supplied by the pro-Nazi Iron Guard, halted the fleet near Giurgiu, Danube River port whence Germany ships much-needed Rumanian oil supplies. Aboard were tons of dynamite.

Germans alleged the British planned to blockade the spot in the Danube known as the Iron Gate by sinking the barges and wrecking the narrow channel where the river cuts through the Carpathian barrier between high cliffs. The Iron Gate is 280 miles up river from Giurgiu.

Official British quarters, acknowledging the barges were loaded with explosives, insisted they were to be used only for destroying Allied river craft in case of a German invasion of Rumania.

The only official British statement on the matter was a communiqué saying merely that Rumanian authorities had seized two cases of firearms which a British barge captain had neglected to declare in passing customs.

Troops Guard Gateway

The British aim was reported in Germany to be the blocking of the Iron Gate with sunken barges and blasting of the narrow artificial channel through which all river shipping must pass.

Two hundred Rumanian and Yugoslav soldiers armed with machine guns tonight were guarding the gateway where the Danube forms the boundary between Rumania and Yugoslavia. Giurgiu was turned into a military zone by the Rumanian Army, which banned all entries without special permits.

The German version of the seizure, said to have taken place Saturday, reported more than 100 British Army, Navy and Air Force men, who were to have participated in the coup, had been arrested.

Both the Rumanian Foreign Office and British quarters, however, insisted there was no basis to the German reports that Britons had been seized aboard the barges, and official London sources declined to

Continued on Page Eight

REICH SHIP IS SUNK

150 Lost Off Transport Torpedoed by British Off South Norway

ALL MEN IN UNIFORM

Large Nazi Tanker Also Sunk by Allies, but Crew Is Rescued

Special Cable to THE NEW YORK TIMES.

OSLO, Norway, April 8—A British submarine torpedoed and sank the German troop ship Rio de Janeiro today off Lillesand, on the south coast of Norway. At least 150 German soldiers are believed to have perished.

It is reported here that the German transport, formerly a freighter on the South American run, had at least 300 men aboard and that fewer than 150 are accounted for. The ship, of 5,261 tons, was out of Hamburg and was classified here as a transport because all the men aboard were in uniform.

Another large German vessel, the tanker Posidonia, was also reported torpedoed today off the south Norwegian coast, but without loss of life.

[Lloyd's Register of Shipping does not list a German tanker Posidonia. The Associated Press, in recording the report of still a third sinking, that of the German tanker Kreta, indicated that there might be some confusion over the Posidonia's case, since the Kreta, apparently to conceal her identity, had sent out the call letters of the Posidonia. Other reports said that the Posidonia used the Kreta's signals.]

The report of the torpedoing of the Rio de Janiero received here states that the British submarine intercepted the transport off the Norwegian coast, hailed her and fired a warning shot across her bows. This was disregarded and the troopship altered her course, speeding toward land or territorial waters. The submarine then fired a torpedo.

Some Jump Overboard

With the explosion some of the Germans immediately jumped overboard. A Norwegian fishing vessel was near by and went to the rescue, taking these men out of the water.

As the transport appeared to be settling, the submarine fired a second torpedo, with terrific result. An iron bar from the ship was hurled 150 feet and struck the rescuing fishing vessel, killing three of the Germans who had been taken aboard.

The fishing vessel continued its work of rescue and was aided by other fishing craft that hurried out when an alarm was sounded along the coast. These ships took a total

Continued on Page Five

NAZIS IN NORWAY

Troops Debark at Ports—Government Leaves Oslo for Hamar

NARVIK IS OCCUPIED

Air Attacks on Capital Reported—Civilians Are to Be Evacuated

Sweden Is Mobilizing

By The United Press.

STOCKHOLM, Sweden, April 9—The Swedish radio announced today that the government had ordered general mobilization.

Wireless to THE NEW YORK TIMES.

LONDON, Tuesday, April 9—The Paris correspondent of Reuters, British news agency, reported this morning that the Oslo radio had announced that German troops had debarked in Norwegian ports at 3 A. M.

[Mrs. J. Borden Harriman, United States Minister to Norway, notified the State Department early this morning that she had been informed by the Foreign Minister that Norway considered herself at war with Germany.

[Mrs. Harriman also reported that at 5:30 A. M. Norwegian shore batteries were still engaged in battle with four invading German warships that were trying to force entry into Oslo Fjord.]

It was also announced that the Norwegian Government had left Oslo for Hamar, in Central Norway.

Reuters further reported that the Germans had occupied the cities of Bergen and Trondheim.

[The Oslo radio announced this morning that the Norwegian Government had ordered general mobilization after an all night session of the Cabinet, The Associated Press reported.]

Reuters also reported from Paris that the Oslo radio announced this morning that the Germans had occupied Narvik.

The Norwegian legation here issued the following communiqué this morning:

"The German Minister in Oslo saw the Norwegian Foreign Secretary at 4:30 o'clock this morning and demanded that Norway should be handed over to the German administration. If this was not done all resistance would be defeated. This demand was refused and hostilities have started."

LONDON, Tuesday, April 9 (AP)—A Reuters, British news agency,

Continued on Page Two

NEW THEATRE OF WAR IS OPENED

German troops invaded Denmark at 5 A. M. today. A few hours previously German warships attempted to force an entry into Oslo Fjord (cross). This action, which brought Norway into the war against the Reich, followed the sighting last night of a German armada steaming northward off Lassoe (3). Near Lillesand (1) a German troop transport was torpedoed by a British submarine and a U-boat was rumored to have been sunk. Off Faerder Light (2) one and perhaps two German tankers were sent down. The Allied mine fields off Norway are indicated by arrows.

NORWAY DECLARES WAR ON GERMANY

Washington Notified of Action by U. S. Minister at Oslo—Warships Sent There

Special to THE NEW YORK TIMES.

WASHINGTON, Tuesday, April 9—Norway is at war with Germany. This was the word received soon after 1 o'clock this morning by the State Department from Mrs. J. Borden Harriman, the American Minister at Oslo.

The startling information was received less than two hours after equally disturbing intelligence had been received of the German occupation of Denmark.

[President Roosevelt, at Hyde Park, kept in close touch with the State Department and his special train was held ready for a quick return to Washington, The United Press reported.]

The State Department announced the state of war in the following communique:

"The American Minister at Oslo, Mrs. J. Borden Harriman, telegraphed the Department tonight that the Foreign Minister had informed her that the Norwegians had fired on four German warships coming up Oslo Fjord and that Norway was at war with Germany. In response to a request by the British Minister to Norway the American Legation at Oslo has been authorized to take over British interests in Norway in case he is forced to leave."

Envoy's Request Explained

State Department officials, in answer to queries regarding the apparently ambiguous last paragraph of Mrs. Harriman's cable, said that there could be no doubt that Norway was at war against Germany. They pointed out that the Norwegians were firing on German warships and the British envoy was considering the possibility that he might have to evacuate, although he was not certain he would have to do so.

[The United Press said Mrs. Harriman reported that she had taken charge of the British and French Legations.]

It was reported on usually good authority that American warships in European waters had been ordered to proceed northward so they could take part in the evacuation of American citizens in Denmark,

Continued on Page Four

ALLIED MINES BRING A PROTEST BY OSLO

Breach of International Law Charged by Koht—Sweden Takes Defense Measures

By The Associated Press.

OSLO, Norway, April 8—Foreign Minister Halvdan Koht told Parliament today that Norway had protested to Paris and London against the mining of her waters at dawn, a sudden move by which the Allies hope to cut off Germany's Swedish ore shipments through Norway's western coastal waters.

In a public statement Mr. Koht charged the Allies with an "open breach of international law" and demanded that the mines "be removed at once and that the guard by foreign warships cease." Britain was patrolling Norway's waters near the new mine fields, stating such action would be for forty-eight hours to warn away neutral vessels.

In all Scandinavia statesmen, in realization that the dreaded day had arrived bringing the European war to the north, gathered to discuss the cloudy future and await a feared retaliation from Germany.

Leaders of the Norwegian Parliament, which was called into special session, said they were behind the government's action in the crisis. A Cabinet meeting was held in Oslo, which military and naval leaders attended.

Political Leaders Meet

Leaders of all of Denmark's political parties met in Copenhagen, and in Stockholm Swedish leaders watched gravely. The Swedish Foreign Office announced there had been no violation of Swedish waters, but officials admittedly were worried.

The Oslo newspaper Arbejdarbladet, a government organ, said that "the situation is particularly grave for our country, but in such times we must keep our heads cool."

"Any tendency toward nervousness or panic would only make it worse," the paper said. "Norway naturally will protest in a most emphatic way against any closing of her waters and demand respect for international laws. But it is a ques-

Continued on Page Four

Dispatches from Europe and the Far East are subject to censorship at the source.

Canadian Premier to See Roosevelt Soon, Stopping Off En Route South for a Vacation

By FREDERICK T. BIRCHALL

By Telephone to THE NEW YORK TIMES.

OTTAWA, April 8—Prime Minister W. L. Mackenzie King will leave Ottawa in a few days for a short holiday in the South of the United States. On his way through Washington he will pay a visit to President Roosevelt at the White House.

This will be Mr. Mackenzie King's first visit to Washington since war was declared. There are several questions he would like to take up with Mr. Roosevelt. There are doubtless also matters the President will be glad to discuss with the Canadian Prime Minister.

While there is no information here as to the precise subjects that may figure in the conversation, some of those ripe for discussion are well known. Among these are the progress of the St. Lawrence Waterway project, continuance of the trade agreements renewed last year and the extent to which the United States can aid Canada's war effort.

As to the St. Lawrence project, it is known that both administrations are anxious to have the treaty signed with as little delay as possible so that it may be submitted to Congress in time for consideration before adjournment. Since the project again came up opposition to it has developed in both countries. It will not have easy sailing.

Among matters even more pressing are the exemption of Americans resident in Canada from the conditions affecting the ownership of foreign currency and securities and the status of American fliers who desire to come here and enlist under the Air Training Plan and for overseas service.

It has been strongly urged that Canada modify for these the oath of allegiance now required from all who join her forces, which does not automatically give them Canadian citizenship, while causing them to lose their own.

Another point of interest is Canada's desire to obtain from the United States more airplanes for use in the initial stages of the commonwealth air training plan. The present prospect is that there will be a shortage of planes until Canadian plants, now in receipt of about $40,000,000 worth of orders, can reach the stage of advanced production.

Any or all of these topics may be profitably discussed between the

Continued on Page Five

COPENHAGEN TAKEN

Troops Cross Border as Ships Debark Others in Sudden Nazi Blow

DANES FALLING BACK

Germans Say They Act to Forestall Foe and Protect Neighbor

By SVEND CARSTENSEN

Wireless to THE NEW YORK TIMES.

COPENHAGEN, Denmark, Tuesday, April 9—German troops crossed the Danish frontier at 5 o'clock this morning.

Three German cruisers arrived at that same hour at Middelfart and troops immediately occupied streets of the town.

Copenhagen was also occupied by German troops this morning.

The invasion came without warning. For some hours before the crossing of the border reports had circulated here that the Germans of South Jutland were expecting German troop trains carrying 45,000 men to arrive at the town of Flensburg during the night. That German town on the border was characterized as a convenient port for shipping troops northward, and although Danish border guards had been put in the highest state of preparedness it was not thought that there would be any threat to Denmark.

This belief had been bolstered by the fact that the fleet of more than a hundred German warships that passed through the Great Belt into the Kattegat and Skagerrak yesterday and early today included troopships—and it was presumed that this fleet was on the way to Norway to retaliate against the British Navy.

More Centers Seized

Mr. Carstensen left Copenhagen after the entry of German forces and went to Kolding, where he filed the following dispatch:

Special Cable to THE NEW YORK TIMES.

KOLDING, Denmark, Tuesday, April 9—The German occupation continues here. It is reported that two ferry points on the Great Belt—Nyborg and Korsoer—have been occupied.

Troops have landed at Middelfart on a large scale. A Little Belt bridge has been reported seized and the city of Aalborg in North Jutland has been occupied.

Although there were no reports of clashes between Danish troops and the invaders today, military resistance was expected at Haderaleben, about thirty miles north of the German border. The placing of guns and erection of barricades were reported from that town.

After leaving Copenhagen I observed from my automobile swarms of fast German planes flying over towns dropping badly printed leaflets that laid responsibility for Germany's invading Denmark and Norway to what was termed a British intention to make Scandinavia a theatre of war.

The leaflets termed Winston Churchill, Britain's First Lord of the Admiralty, "the century's greatest warmonger," who planned to police Norwegian and Danish waters against the wills of the two countries.

The statement said that, since Norway and Denmark were unable to resist effectively, Germany had resolved to act in advance of a British attack and by her own forces take over "protection" of Danish and Norwegian neutrality and "guard" the countries during the war. It was asserted that Germany did not intend to obtain bases for her fight against Britain but solely aimed at preventing Scandinavia from being a battlefield for "British expansion of the war."

According to the statement, negotiations were going on between the German and Danish Governments to make Denmark "secure" and assure that her army and navy were maintained and the Danish people's freedom respected. The country's independence, it was said, is fully secured. The procla-

Continued on Page Two

"All the News That's Fit to Print."

The New York Times.

LATE CITY EDITION
POSTSCRIPT
Fair, not much change in temperature today. Tomorrow cloudy.

VOL. LXXXIX...No. 30,057. Entered as Second-Class Matter, Postoffice, New York, N. Y. NEW YORK, FRIDAY, MAY 10, 1940. THREE CENTS

NAZIS INVADE HOLLAND, BELGIUM, LUXEMBOURG BY LAND AND AIR; DIKES OPENED; ALLIES RUSH AID

U.S. FREEZES CREDIT

President Acts to Guard Funds Here of Three Invaded Nations

SHIP RULING TODAY

Envoy Reports to Hull on Germany's Attacks by Air and Land

Special to THE NEW YORK TIMES.

WASHINGTON, Friday, May 10—President Roosevelt early today ordered the freezing of all credits held by Belgium, the Netherlands and Luxembourg in this country.

He called a conference for 10:30 A. M. of heads of the State, War and Navy Departments to consider pressing problems of neutrality.

The President acted swiftly after news of Germany's invasion of the three European neutral countries reached Washington and galvanized high officials into action. His order with regard to the freezing of all the invaded countries' credits and cash balances here was a counterpart of the action taken after Germany invaded Norway and Denmark.

Congress this week completed action on legislation that specifically authorizes the President by decree to freeze all such cash and credits of any belligerent. The object is to prevent these resources from falling into the hands of the invading power.

Ships to Be Considered

The President's order directed Secretary of the Treasury Henry Morgenthau Jr. to freeze all Belgian, French and Luxembourg credits before the markets open this morning.

It was announced also that the conference to be held at 10:30 will consider the question of Belgian and Netherland ships that may be in United States ports. Attorney General Robert H. Jackson also will attend this conference.

The White House, meanwhile, indicated some skepticism of the official explanation of the invasion given by German Propaganda Minister Joseph Goebbels, who was reported to have said that the Germans moved because of information that Great Britain and France intended to invade the countries involved.

"Nevertheless," said Stephen T. Early, Presidential secretary, after he had quoted the Goebbels statement, "it remains to be seen who invaded who."

It was announced that the President would remain awake throughout the night, if necessary, to receive reports and consult with officials. Sumner Welles, Under-Secretary of State, at 1:45 A. M. joined the group of State Department officials who remained on duty at the department.

Report From Ambassador

A general invasion of the three neutrals by heavy German land and air forces was reported to the State Department and Mr. Roosevelt early today by Ambassador John J. Cudahy at Brussels.

After trying vainly to re-establish telephone connection with Secretary of State Cordell Hull, over which he had relayed a "blow-by-blow" description of developments several hours earlier, the Ambassador got through the following terse message:

"German planes continue to cross the border and are bombing the airport near Brussels. It seems to be a general attack on all three countries."

A State Department press liaison officer who was relaying latest diplomatic bulletins to reporters as they came in by transatlantic telephone, dropped the cryptic remark: "As the American Ambassador spoke from Brussels, an embassy military attaché stood at his elbow."

After relaying the information to the President that the Belgian Government had ordered all hands to stand by, Ambassador Cudahy again called Secretary Hull between 10 and 11 o'clock and said he had been informed by officials in Brussels that one German and

Continued on Page Two

The International Situation

In the midst of Britain's Cabinet crisis Germany struck another powerful blow early this morning by invading the Netherlands, Belgium and Luxembourg.

After swarms of planes had engaged in air fights over Amsterdam, parachute troops, some of them clad in Netherland uniforms, descended at strategic points while planes bombed air fields. The Netherlands resisted the incursion and promptly opened the dikes that are part of her water defense system. [Page 1.]

Parachute troops likewise made surprise landings in Belgium and bombs from 100 planes blasted the Brussels airport. [Page 1.]

Appeals for help were dispatched to the Allies by the invaded countries and it was understood that machinery of assistance was being set in motion. Queen Wilhelmina in a proclamation issued at The Hague declared, "I and my government will do our duty." [Page 1.]

As in the case of Norway, Berlin explained that the German action had been taken to forestall the Allies; an announcement said that an attack on Germany had been planned through the territory of the Low Countries. What the Reich was doing, it was declared, was safeguarding the neutrality of those countries. [Page 1.]

President Roosevelt lost no time in acting on the new situation. After night conferences he ordered the freezing of credits of the three invaded countries. Further measures are to be taken today. [Page 1.]

London, meanwhile, announced that British troops had occupied Iceland to prevent a possible German seizure of that former Danish possession. [Page 1.]

Before all these happenings Neville Chamberlain had appeared to be on his way out as Prime Minister, but today it was expected the new developments might save him.

Following upon his relatively narrow escape in the House of Commons vote on Wednesday night, Mr. Chamberlain set about yesterday to see what could be done to satisfy his critics. He offered Cabinet posts to two leaders of the Labor Opposition, but they refused to serve under him. As to whether they would serve under another Conservative, they delayed their reply. If Mr. Chamberlain steps out of office, it is thought probable his place will be taken by the present Foreign Secretary, Viscount Halifax, with Winston Churchill acting as government spokesman in the Commons, from the floor of which the peer would by tradition be barred. [Page 1.]

A new offset to the Norwegian reverses was a London announcement that British submarines had attacked three German convoys and scored eleven torpedo hits, in addition to destroying two ships sailing home. [Page 6.]

Moreover, the Allies' Narvik campaign seemed to be making progress. From that far northern area it was reported that two Allied columns closing in on the railway to the port were within ten miles of each other near the Swedish border; their intention apparently was to join and drive westward along the railroad to Narvik itself, which is held by the Nazis. The Germans, in their effort to thwart the besiegers, were said to be landing parachute troops and supplying them by air. [Page 4.]

In the aftermath of the campaign in the south of the country Foreign Minister Koht disclosed that four of Norway's six divisions had been lost—killed, wounded or captured by the Nazis or interned by Sweden. [Page 6.]

Bombs Drop on Swiss Soil

By The United Press.

BERNE, Switzerland, Friday, May 10—The army staff announced today that foreign airplanes had dropped bombs in the Berne Jura Alpine district between Delemont, near the frontier, and Mount Terr, damaging a railroad.

Traffic continued over the road, the army staff said. It added that other foreign planes were flying over Swiss territory near Basle but that no details had been received.

ALLIED HELP SPED

Netherland and Belgian Appeals Answered by British and French

TACTICS ARE WATCHED

London Thinks Move an Effort to Get Bases to Attack Britain

Italians Reported Massing

By The United Press.

BUENOS AIRES, Argentina, Friday, May 10—The Madrid radio was heard broadcasting today that the British had closed the Strait of Gibraltar and that Italy was massing troops on the French frontier.

Special Cable to THE NEW YORK TIMES.

LONDON, Friday, May 10—The British Government received appeals for help early today from both the Netherlands and Belgium.

The British and French reply to the Netherland-Belgian appeals was prompt. Representatives of the respective governments here were told by 8:30 A. M. (3:30 A. M. New York time) they could expect all the help Britain could give them.

The Netherland Legation here received assurance that its country and Belgium were now regarded as Allies of Britain and France.

Within a few minutes after receipt of official news of the invasion of the Low Countries, the British Cabinet was called to 10 Downing Street and was in session with Prime Minister Neville Chamberlain.

According to information here, the Belgian Cabinet was in Brussels and Premier Hubert Pierlot conferred with King Leopold.

The German invasion of the Low Countries had been expected in London, and it must be presumed the Allies were ready for it to some extent.

Allies Visible to Planes

The biggest handicap to the British and French was in the timing of the German thrust at dawn. This prevented the Allies moving troops under cover of darkness, and since hundreds of German planes already had flown over practically all of Netherland and Belgian territory for some hours, the disposition of Allied troops and their every movement must have been known to the German High Command.

While the Netherlanders and Belgians had taken every precaution

Continued on Page Four

BRUSSELS IS RAIDED

400 Reported Killed—Troops Cross Border at Four Points

PARACHUTE INVASION

Mobilization Is Ordered and Allied Aid Asked—Luxembourg Attacked

Wireless to THE NEW YORK TIMES.

BRUSSELS, Belgium, Friday, May 10—The invasion Belgium had feared since the outbreak of the European war came before dawn this morning. About a hundred German planes flew over this city and bombed the airport.

The airfield at Antwerp also was bombed. Parachute troops were landed at Hasselt in Eastern Belgium. Artillery fire was reported heard along the German and Luxembourg frontiers.

Anti-aircraft guns at the airport commenced firing with the appearance of the first invaders and kept up a steady barrage. Those in the center of the city went into action at 5:30 A. M.

Above the drone of airplane engines could be heard the staccato of machine guns. Bombs wrecked many houses in the vicinity of the airport and caused some loss of life. [Exchange Telegraph (British news agency) said 400 persons had been killed in the first raid.]

Reports from Antwerp and other parts of the country said German planes had flown constantly over since 4:30 A. M., keeping anti-aircraft batteries steadily in action.

Premier Hubert Pierlot and Foreign Minister Paul-Henri Spaak conferred with King Leopold and then called an emergency meeting of the Cabinet. The radio broadcast repeated summonses to all soldiers to join their units at once. A "state of alarm" was decreed throughout the country with the appearance of the first planes.

The Belgian radio also stated German parachute troops had fluttered down at Nivelles, less than twenty miles south of Brussels, and at Saint Trond, about thirty-five miles east of the capital.

The broadcast stated that Germany had made no demarche in Brussels before the invasion.

Wireless to THE NEW YORK TIMES.

LONDON, Friday, May 10—The Germans crossed the Belgian frontier at four points this morning, according to an announcement over

Continued on Page Two

NAZIS SWOOP ON THE LOW COUNTRIES

By land and air German troops descended this morning upon the Netherlands, Belgium and Luxembourg. The principal land incursion into the Netherlands was at Roermond.

AIR FIELDS BOMBED

Nazi Parachute Troops Land at Key Centers as Flooding Starts

RIVER MAAS CROSSED

Defenders Battle Foe in Sky, Claim 6 Planes as War Is Proclaimed

First Bombing in France

Special Cable to THE NEW YORK TIMES.

PARIS, Friday, May 10—The Bron airdrome, a big airport near Lyon, was bombed by German planes today. One German aircraft was shot down. The alarm was first given at 4:25 A. M. The all-clear signal was given at 6:45 A. M.

WASHINGTON, Friday, May 10 (AP)—United States Ambassador William C. Bullitt telephoned the State Department from Paris at 4 A. M. today that the Germans had bombed a number of fortified towns in France, "with [illegible]."

By The United Press.

AMSTERDAM, The Netherlands, Friday, May 10—Germany invaded the Netherlands early today, land troops being preceded by widespread air attacks on airdromes and by the landing of parachute troops.

The Netherlands resisted and announced she was at war with Germany. Anti-aircraft batteries and fighter planes engaged swarms of German aircraft when they appeared simultaneously over a score of Netherland cities.

An official proclamation said:

"Since 3 A. M. German troops have crossed the Netherland frontier and German planes have tried to attack airports. Inundations are effective according to plans. The army anti-aircraft batteries were found prepared. So far as is known six German planes have been shot down."

[French, Belgian and British planes were sighted over the Netherlands this morning, a Reuters (British news agency) dispatch said in quoting the Netherland radio station at Hilversum, near Amsterdam.]

German troops were first reported crossing the Netherland frontier near Roermond, eight miles north of the Belgian frontier. German planes landed troops by parachute at strategic points near Rotterdam, The Hague, Amsterdam and other large cities.

A large number of the German troops landed by parachute were said to be dressed in Netherland military uniforms.

Other Germans crossed the Maas River in rubber boats to Netherland territory. They were said to be reaching the Netherland side in "considerable numbers."

A fierce air battle raged over Amsterdam as Netherland fighter planes dived repeatedly on German bombers and troop transport planes with chattering machine guns.

Schiphol Airdrome outside Amsterdam, the nation's largest, was heavily bombed. Military authorities immediately threw a heavy guard around the airdrome in an effort to defend it against German parachute troops.

Planes identified as German Heinkels bombed Schiphol Airdrome repeatedly, loosing some thirty heavy caliber bombs on the landing field between 5:15 and 5:30 A. M.

Reports poured in of planes in great numbers over a score of Netherland cities. Netherland authorities, hurriedly organizing defense, flashed orders to the whole country to be on the alert against parachute troops.

Fifty planes were over Nijmegen, sixty miles southeast of Amsterdam on the German border.

A number of parachute troops reportedly landed at Sliedrecht, Delft and several other points. Delft is twelve and a half miles from The Hague. About 100 parachute troops

Continued on Page Three

MUSSOLINI TO LET 'ONLY FACTS' SPEAK

Press Assures Yugoslavia, but Reminds Her of Fate of Poland and Norway

By HERBERT L. MATTHEWS

By Telephone to THE NEW YORK TIMES.

ROME, May 9—The fourth anniversary of the founding of the new Italian Empire was celebrated today in an atmosphere of warlike preparation. The army was honored, Italian armed strength was glorified and the country was told by its leading commentators that the empire would soon earn that "freedom of the seas" which to Italians means domination of the Mediterranean.

Rome, like every other city in the empire, resounded today to martial music while thousands of soldiers paraded through streets from whose buildings hung innumerable flags. The great ceremony was at the Piazza Venezia this morning. Premier Mussolini awarded gold and silver medals to the kin of soldiers fallen in Fascismo's three wars in Ethiopia, Spain and Albania. Later, responding to the insistent appeal of the thousands of men massed below his balcony, he spoke very briefly, only to say that he was resuming his cloak of silence.

"May 9, 1936, was a great day in the history of the country, a day of solar victory," he said. "After my speeches, you must accustom yourself to my silence. Only facts will break it."

Small groups in the crowd thereupon began yelling "Tunisia!" and "Malta!" but the cries were not general.

At the same time this morning

Continued on Page Seven

ICELAND OCCUPIED BY BRITISH FORCE

Secret Expedition Is Justified as Thwarting Action There by Germany

By JAMES MacDONALD

Special Cable to THE NEW YORK TIMES.

LONDON, Friday, May 10—Forestalling a possible German swoop on the strategically valuable former Danish dominion of Iceland, the British have landed an expeditionary force there, it was announced this morning by the Foreign Office here.

Neither the size of the British contingent, which was sent out in the deepest secrecy, nor its place of landing was revealed in the official communiqué.

The landing of the expeditionary force was still going at an early hour this morning. Observers guessed that the landing place must be Reykjavik.

TEXT OF COMMUNIQUE

The official announcement read as follows:

Since the German seizure of Denmark it has become necessary to reckon with the possibility of a sudden German descent on Iceland.

It is clear that in the face of an attack on Iceland, even on a very small scale, the Icelandic Government would be unable to prevent their country from falling completely into German hands.

His Majesty's Government have accordingly decided to preclude this possibility which would de-

Continued on Page Three

Chamberlain Saved by Nazi Blow In Low Countries, London Thinks

By RAYMOND DANIELL

Special Cable to THE NEW YORK TIMES.

LONDON, Friday, May 10—The first effect of the German attack on the Low Countries is expected to be that Prime Minister Chamberlain will be saved just when it looked as if he was sure to fall.

It was believed that the Labor party, which so far has refused to serve under him in a truly national government, and only yesterday rejected a formal offer to do so, will now close ranks, forget political difficulties and take any Cabinet job offered to its leaders. Furthermore, the Labor party conference, which was supposed to start at Bournemouth on Monday, now will probably be called off.

There is just a possibility that Mr. Chamberlain may quit immediately and turn his seals of office over to First Lord of the Admiralty Winston Churchill. This was a strong but unconfirmed rumor as a Cabinet meeting held this morning came to an end.

In addition, it was said that under Mr. Churchill, Alfred Duff Cooper would receive the Admiralty post, Anthony Eden the War Office and that Viscount Halifax would remain at the Foreign Office.

Until the invasion of the Low Countries was known, the consensus of political observers here had been that the end of the Chamberlain Government could not be long delayed.

The two questions uppermost were how soon it would take place and who would succeed him at No. 10 Downing Street. The betting had been that it would be sooner rather than later and that Foreign Secretary Viscount Halifax would be the next Prime Minister, with Mr. Churchill serving as his spokesman in the House of Commons, from whose floor the present Foreign Secretary, as a peer, is barred by tradition.

The troubles of the 71-year-old Prime Minister, who struggled vainly to maintain Europe's peace by appeasement and who was accused in the House of Commons of bungling the business of war-making, increased rather than diminished during the day. However, the House, despite the gravity of the internal crisis and perils abroad, decided to take its usual twelve-day Whitsuntide holiday, subject to recall in the event of major developments, which followed promptly.

Mr. Chamberlain's efforts to broaden the base of his Cabinet by

Continued on Page Five

Ribbentrop Charges Allies Plotted With the Lowlands

By GEORGE AXELSSON

Wireless to THE NEW YORK TIMES.

BERLIN, Friday, May 10—Foreign Minister Joachim von Ribbentrop at 9 o'clock this morning announced that Reich forces had launched military operations against Holland, Belgium and Luxembourg to "protect their neutrality."

Earlier it was reported that German troops had occupied Maastricht, the Netherlands, and had "landed" contingents in Brussels, probably meaning parachute troops.

Herr von Ribbentrop said that Germany had received unimpeachable proof that the Allies were engineering an imminent attack through the Lowlands into the German Ruhr district wherefore the Germans felt compelled to take corresponding measures. He said the time had come for settling the final account with the "Franco-British leaders."

And thus the war to a decisive finish has at last started in the West. This was the assumption when Herr von Ribbentrop informed the world through newspaper men that the German action meant that she had decided to settle all accounts with the Allies.

"France and Britain dropped their mask," said Herr von Ribbentrop. "The alarm in the Mediterranean was a feint behind which the Allies were preparing an onslaught on German territory which the Reich could not tolerate."

The notes—handed to The Hague and Brussels simultaneously with a shorter note to the Grand Duchy of Luxembourg just prior to their invasion by Germany—accused the Lowlands with having been overwhelmingly partial toward the Allies, adding that the attitude of the press was objectionable to the Reich.

A memorandum similar in tone to that handed to Denmark and Norway last month stated:

"In the life-and-death struggle thrust upon the German people, the government does not intend to await an attack by Britain and France inactively allowing the war to be carried through Belgium and Holland onto German soil. The government, therefore, has issued orders to safeguard the neutrality of the two countries with all the military means of the Reich."

Ribbentrop Reads Statement

In eight points the memorandum outlines the German argument that Belgium and Holland had not observed the strictest neutrality upon which German respect for their territories was founded. The document accuses them with having even supported Germany's enemies in their hostile intentions. Belgium fortified exclusively her Eastern frontier against Germany, leaving the French frontier unfortified, one argument reads.

Berlin slept peacefully unaware

Continued on Page Four

HOLLAND'S QUEEN PROTESTS INVASION

Wilhelmina Vows She and the Government Will Do Duty—Bars Negotiation With Foe

By The United Press.

THE HAGUE, the Netherlands, Friday, May 10—Queen Wilhelmina said today in a statement on the German invasion of the country that "I and my government will do our duty."

The Queen, in a proclamation addressed to "my people," said:

"After our country, with scrupulous conscientiousness, had observed strict neutrality during all these months, and while Holland had no other plan than to maintain strictly this attitude, Germany last night made a sudden attack on our territory without any warning.

"This was done notwithstanding a solemn promise that the neutrality of our country would be respected so long as we ourselves maintained that neutrality.

"I herewith direct a flaming protest against this unprecedented violation of good faith and violation of all that is decent in relations between cultured States.

"I and my government now will do our duty.

"Do your duty everywhere and under all circumstances. And let every one go to the post to which he has been appointed and, with the utmost vigilance and with that inner calm and serenity which comes from a clear conscience, do his work."

The Netherland general military headquarters in a communiqué said:

"Never will the High Command or government enter into negotiations with the enemy."

Dispatches from Europe and the Far East are subject to censorship at the source.

Allied transport planes speed help to Netherlands.

Wide World Photos

A German field-artillery detachment passes under a destroyed bridge on its advance through Holland.

Winston Churchill, the new Prime Minister.

Neville Chamberlain, the former Prime Minister.

"All the News That's Fit to Print."

The New York Times.

LATE CITY EDITION
Partly cloudy, little change in temperature today. Tomorrow fair, temperature unchanged.
Temperatures Yesterday—Max., 79; Min., 49

VOL. LXXXIX...No. 30,058. Entered as Second-Class Matter, Postoffice, New York, N. Y. NEW YORK, SATURDAY, MAY 11, 1940. PPF THREE CENTS NEW YORK CITY and Vicinity | FOUR CENTS Elsewhere Except in 7th and 8th Postal Zones.

DUTCH AND BELGIANS RESIST NAZI DRIVE; ALLIED FORCES MARCH IN TO DO BATTLE; CHAMBERLAIN RESIGNS, CHURCHILL PREMIER

COALITION ASSURED

Labor Decides to Allow Leaders to Join New National Cabinet

OLD MINISTERS STAY

Churchill Asks Them to Remain Until They Can Be Replaced

The text of Chamberlain's statement is printed on Page 9.

By RAYMOND DANIELL
Special Cable to THE NEW YORK TIMES.

LONDON, May 10—In the gravest crisis Great Britain has faced since the World War, Winston Churchill became Prime Minister tonight as Allied armies raced across Belgium again for a death grapple with invading German armies.

Neville Chamberlain, who had headed the government since just after King George VI ascended the throne, resigned early in the evening after convincing himself that it was impossible to remain and give the country the truly national government that the people want.

A genuine coalition Cabinet was assured when the executive committee of the Labor party declared that it would accept a share in a government headed by a new Prime Minister who had the nation's confidence. This is expected also to result in the entry of Liberals into the government.

Invasion Fails to Save Cabinet

The German invasion of Belgium, the Netherlands and Luxembourg, which transformed the static conflict of the West into a total European if not yet World War, had been expected throughout the day to "freeze" Mr. Chamberlain in his job for a short time at least, despite the poor showing in Wednesday's division when the government's majority in the House of Commons was cut from 200 to eighty-one.

That Mr. Chamberlain would have to relinquish his high office became apparent last night when Clement R. Attlee and Arthur Greenwood, the Opposition Labor leaders, informed him to his face that they would not consent to serve in a Cabinet that he headed. Thus they provided the cue for the undecided Liberals and Conservatives who were critical of the government

Without these dissidents, it was felt it would be impossible for the man who brought back "peace in our time" from Munich to establish a government satisfactory to the disturbed Members of Parliament and their worried constituents. These were too angry at the let-down to their hopes of the Allied withdrawal from Norway after the optimistic build-up their press had given them about the success of operations across the North Sea.

Demand for Coalition

After the acrimonious debate that followed the Prime Minister's admission that the campaign in Central and Southern Norway was at an end, it was apparent that the country demanded a new administration in which the Opposition would share the responsibilities of leadership.

Early this evening Mr. Chamberlain drove to Buckingham Palace and told the King he thought the time had come for him to relinquish his seals of office. Soon afterward Mr. Churchill, who has been the nearest approach to a war leader this country has had since the conflict began, went to the Palace also and accepted an invitation to form a government.

This came as something of a surprise, for it was known that as late as last night, Mr. Chamberlain favored Foreign Secretary Viscount Halifax as his successor. A small crowd was waiting at Whitehall when the following announcement was issued from there:

"The Right Hon. Neville Chamberlain, M. P., resigned the office of Prime Minister and First Lord of the Treasury this evening, and the Right Hon. Winston Churchill, M. P., accepted His Majesty's invitation to fill the position.

"The Prime Minister desires that all Ministers should remain at their posts and discharge their functions with full freedom and responsibility while the necessary arrangements

Continued on Page Nine

The International Situation

The War in the Low Countries

The Netherlands—The defenders claimed to be holding the Germans along the lines of the Yssel and Maas Rivers. At Delfzijl, across the River Eems from the German stronghold of Emden, the Netherland troops appeared still to be in command, despite strong German attacks. [Page 1.] German troops, landed by air transports and parachute at Rotterdam, did not succeed in seizing the city; Rotterdam officials said the invaders there had been pressed into dangerous positions. [Page 6.] The Netherland Commander in Chief summed up: "The surprise attack is a failure." [Page 1.]

Belgium—Although dispatches agreed that in most places the Belgians had stopped the Germans at the frontier, it was reported that Limburg Province, in the northeast, had been overrun. Brussels, Antwerp and other important centers were bombed; in Greater Brussels forty-one persons were reported killed, eighty-two wounded. German troops were landed by parachutes extensively in the eastern part of the country, but no accounts of outstanding success at this kind of Blitzkrieg were received. The attitude in Belgium was that the army could hold out for a time, but help was needed quickly. King Leopold was at the front. [Page 1.]

Luxembourg—This small and armyless duchy was overrun by the Germans.

Allied Help—Paris emphasized that two hours after German troops had crossed neutral borders, meeting strong resistance, French and British troops had crossed into Belgium, receiving enthusiastic welcome.

Battle was engaged at many points. The French put the German attacking force at twenty-nine divisions. On both banks of the Moselle, which separates Luxembourg from Germany, a German operation was under way which, the French said, might be the beginning of a large-scale attack. French air fields, railways, coal mines and factories were attacked by air raiders. Generalissimo Gamelin said: "Germany has engaged us in a struggle to the death. The watchword is: 'For France and all her Allies: Courage, energy, confidence!'" [Page 1.]

Germany — Berlin made no great claims of immediate victory, aside from the general statement that enemy resistance in the border region had been broken. [Page 1.] In an Order of the Day to his troops, Chancellor Hitler said: "The fight beginning today decides the fate of the German nation for the next 1,000 years. Do your duty now!" [Page 4.]

The War Elsewhere

Britain changed pilots, Neville Chamberlain stepping down in response to popular demand, and Winston Churchill taking over. Mr. Churchill is expected to have full Labor and Liberal support; he asked all Ministers to carry on until he could form a new government. It was believed that Sir John Simon and Sir Samuel Hoare, Mr. Chamberlain's closest advisers, would lose their portfolios. [Page 1.]

In France political differences were composed under the pressure of the invasion. Louis Marin and Jean Ybarnegaray, who were leaders of the opposition to the inclusion of Socialists in the Cabinet, took portfolios as Ministers of State. [Page 10.]

At Rome, closely watched by Allied diplomats, there was no hint that Mussolini would enter the war. [Page 5.]

At Vatican City the Pope was reported deeply shocked at the German invasion. He is expected to issue a formal condemnation today. [Page 4.]

At Washington President Roosevelt, in a public address, said that the American people were "shocked and angered by the tragic news from Belgium and the Netherlands and Luxembourg." He added that it would be a "mistaken idea" to believe the Americas safe from would-be conquerers because of geographical distance. [Page 1.] The American Red Cross started a drive for a European war relief fund of at least $10,000,000. [Page 1.]

AMERICA ANGERED, SAYS ROOSEVELT

Citing 'Cruel Invasions' to Science Congress, He Warns of Danger to Americas

The President's address before Science Congress, Page 10.

By FELIX BELAIR Jr.
Special to THE NEW YORK TIMES.

WASHINGTON, May 10—President Roosevelt twice today condemned Germany's invasion of Belgium, Holland and Luxembourg as an unwarranted aggression on neutral countries and as threatening the cultural and scientific civilization of the world. Speaking indirectly but with obvious reference to developments of the past twenty-four hours, the Chief Executive pictured Nazi aggression as a definite threat to the security of the Americas.

On both occasions the President impressed his determination to keep America at peace and safeguard the nation's neutrality. But each time he raised a question whether the country could long stand idly by "if all the other continents embrace by preference or by compulsion a wholly different principle of life."

As a self-styled "pacifist," in common with citizens of the twenty-one American republics, President Roosevelt told the eighth American Scientific Congress in an internationally broadcast address that the time had come to apply common-sense principles to the situation now confronting the Americas. After emphasizing the pacific instincts of all Western Hemisphere republics, he said:

"But I believe that by overwhelming majorities in all the Americas, you and I, in the long run and if it

Continued on Page Ten

RED CROSS APPEAL SEEKS $10,000,000

President Says 'We Will Not Fail' Latest War Victims—$2,000,000 Quota Here

Special to THE NEW YORK TIMES.

WASHINGTON, May 10—The American Red Cross started a drive today for a European war relief fund of "at least" $10,000,000 to which "all sympathetic Americans" were urged to contribute generously and at once. The appeal was made by Norman H. Davis, National Chairman, under the authority voted by the Red Cross convention which ended a three-day session here Wednesday, and was supported in a special message issued from the White House by President Roosevelt this afternoon.

"I urge all Americans who have a feeling of deep sympathy for the peoples of those unfortunate countries who today have been added to the long list of those who are suffering the horrors of invasion and aerial bombardment to respond quickly and generously to this appeal," the President said.

"The American Red Cross, our official national volunteer relief agency, is efficiently organized to answer such emergency calls. It is, therefore, the logical agency through which our citizens can express their compassion for the innocent victims of the wars that rage overseas. I am confident we will not fail them."

In using the discretion conferred on him to call for war relief funds "if and when necessary," Mr. Davis said that "the invasion today of three small neutral nations and the spread of death and devastation among their innocent civilian populations" had created a situation requiring immediate action.

"The hour has struck, with a

Continued on Page Eight

AID IS SENT AT ONCE

French Enter Belgium—Britons Cross Sea to Netherlands

CONTACT SOON MADE

Allies Help Low Countries Meet First Thrust of 29 German Divisions

By G. H. ARCHAMBAULT
Wireless to THE NEW YORK TIMES.

PARIS, May 10—Two hours after the Germans invaded the Low Countries, French and British forces were crossing the border to help the Netherland and Belgian Armies withstand the shock of at least twenty-nine German divisions. Contact was made without delay, and by nightfall the battle had been engaged at many points.

[The landing of British troops by transport at Netherland ports was reported by The Associated Press from Amsterdam.]

On broad lines both the Netherlanders and the Belgians are resisting with determination on positions already prepared. Farther south, what may turn out to be an operation on a large scale, is in its preliminary phase on both banks of the Moselle River.

The Germans also made a demonstration in the extreme north at the mouth of the Ems River. Progress thence southward through the Netherlands would be impeded by marshes.

von Epp Plan Believed Used

The Germans apparently are putting into execution the von Epp plan, a modification of the famous Schlieffen plan. The French military authorities are very cautious in their commentaries, but it is pointed out that the von Epp plan foresaw disposing of the Netherlands in twenty-four hours.

This is France's battle. She has been waiting for it for eight months. Her army leaders have prepared for it in every detail. Every soldier knows what is at stake. It will be a fight to the finish.

General Maurice Gustave Gamelin gave the keynote when he sent the following general order to all troops:

"The attack which we have been anticipating since October was launched this morning.

"Germany has engaged against us in a struggle to the death.

"The watchword is 'For France and all her Allies: Courage, energy, confidence.'"

Although in their scrupulous regard for their duty as neutrals, the Netherlands and Belgium declined to hold conferences with the British and French general staffs before Germany showed her hand, and although King Lepold, like his father before him in 1914, has taken active command of the Belgian Army, it is understood that a general plan of action is being coordinated and that General Gamelin, virtually if not in name, becomes the supreme director of military operations. All information on military movements consequently is

Continued on Page Six

THE FIRES OF WAR LEAP ACROSS THE LOW COUNTRIES

Following upon Germany's lightning invasion there were no connected battle fronts yesterday, but many scattered points of major fighting. The main battle sectors in the Netherlands were at Delfzijl (1) and along the Yssel River (2) and the Maas River (4), while a struggle raged in the city of Rotterdam (3). In Belgium the Germans claimed to have advanced to the Albert Canal and taken Maastricht fortress (6), although there was stiff fighting along the canal. Brussels and Antwerp (5) were both attacked by Nazi bombers. Luxembourg (7) was overrun by the invaders, but the Allies were apparently engaging the Germans west of the Moselle River.

BELGIUM REPORTS NAZIS ARE HALTED

Leopold Is at Front as Active Commander—41 Killed, 82 Wounded in Brussels Raid

Wireless to THE NEW YORK TIMES.

BRUSSELS, Belgium, May 10—King Leopold today assumed command of the Belgian armies and is directing the resistance to the Nazi invasion as Allied forces are being rushed to their assistance. While Belgium was gathering her forces to resist this lightning attack, Brussels, Antwerp and numerous other points in the country had to withstand air raids.

Most of these attacks were directed against airports, but in most cases Belgian aviation had foreseen the attacks and the planes had been removed. The exception was the capital, which, according to an announcement by the government, contains no military centers.

This little country, twice invaded by German armies in the last twenty-five years, went methodically about insuring its defense and quickly became part of the Allied defense. The government issued an appeal to the population to preserve calm and assist in that way the military measures for defense. The people were asked to spot German sabotage and German troops in Belgian and Allied uniforms while mobilization is taking place.

Bridges and roads were being blown up to prevent the first German advance and the Belgian system of sluices for flooding were being put into service.

BRUSSELS, Belgium, May 10 (UP)—The Belgian Army, with King

Continued on Page Eight

Bulletins on European Conflict

Special Cable to THE NEW YORK TIMES.

AMSTERDAM, the Netherlands, Saturday, May 11—Amsterdam was bombed shortly after dawn today. The raid lasted twenty-five minutes, during which a number of heavy bombs fell. No casualties were immediately reported. Another wave of German bombers passed over the city a half hour later.

Widespread French Air Alarms

PARIS, Saturday, May 11 (AP)—Widespread air alarms sounded throughout France this morning. The alert in central-eastern France ended after thirty-two minutes.

Allies Recapture Airports

The British wireless said this morning in a broadcast received by the Columbia Broadcasting System that "with the exception of one," all airports in Belgium and the Netherlands occupied by the Germans "have now been recaptured by us."

Bomb Hits Argentine Legation

BUENOS AIRES, Argentina, May 10 (UP)—Foreign Minister José Marie Cantilo announced tonight that he had been informed by Carlos Brebbia, Argentine Minister to the Netherlands, that the Argentine Legation in The Hague had been struck directly by a powerful bomb.

Grounded Plane's Bombs Kill Many

PARIS, May 10 (UP)—A German bomber was brought down today in the town square of a Northern French village. The two German fliers, injured, attempted to flee but were caught by villagers. The entire village was gathered around the wrecked plane when its bomb cargo suddenly exploded, killing many.

Fair Will Open at 10 A. M. With Balmy Day Forecast

The New York World's Fair, 1940 edition, will open at 10 o'clock this morning, dedicated, in the words of its officials, to a good time for every one who comes.

The opening had the blessing of the United States Weather Bureau, which predicted partly cloudy skies, with little change from yesterday's balmy temperatures. This led to high hopes of a better "break" than the Fair received on the opening day on April 30, 1939. The forecast for tomorrow was "fair with little change in temperature."

In contrast with last year, when predictions of 1,000,000 visitors for the first day were freely made, estimates of probable attendance were lacking yesterday. Harvey D. Gibson, chairman of the board, declared he would be satisfied "if every one who comes to the Fair has a good time."

There were, however, many indications of keen public interest, including a 200,000 increase in advance ticket sales.

Mr. Gibson's brief statement was viewed by Fair planners as sounding the keynote of the entire 1940 exposition, which has been dedicated to fun and informality rather than to pomp and ceremony. Last year Grover A. Whalen, Fair president, enthusiastically predicted a crowd of 1,000,000 on opening day, and it was a post-mortem verdict that the idea of such a big crowd actually kept people away. This year Mr. Gibson, at the helm of the exposition, has refused firmly to talk of big crowds, but lays the emphasis rather on "lots of fun for little money."

"We feel," Mr. Gibson's statement said, "that we will have a happy, carefree crowd at the Fair on opening day. We are more in-

Continued on Page Twelve

EAST INDIES COLONY GETS MARTIAL LAW

Germans Interned and Ships Seized—Tokyo Announces Status Quo Policy

Special Cable to THE NEW YORK TIMES.

SINGAPORE, May 10—News of the German invasion of the Netherlands reached the Netherlands Indies by wireless. The Governor General issued a proclamation similar in terms to that of Queen Wilhelmina and announced that all Germans of military age, from 16 upward, would be interned immediately.

All the German merchant ships that have been lying in Netherlands Indies harbors since the outbreak of war were seized and other precautions were taken.

Within three hours it was announced that the majority of the Germans in Batavia, Sourabaya and other important towns were detained. Later in the evening the Governor General again went on the radio, reporting the latest developments and confirming the internment of the Germans.

According to the newspaper, The Straits Times, the Governor's resident authorities throughout the Netherlands Indies today received a telegram marked "Berlin" and acted according to previous instructions. They were required to report to the Governor General by noon tomorrow the situation regarding the internment of Germans.

While there is natural excitement among the Netherlanders through-

Continued on Page Ten

BORDER RESISTANCE BROKEN, NAZIS SAY

'Furious Attacks' Reported in Cooperation With Fliers Over a Broad Front

By GEORGE AXELSSON
Wireless to THE NEW YORK TIMES.

BERLIN, May 10—For the second time in little more than a quarter of a century the field gray columns of the German Army have been set marching "Nach Paris." Obviously aiming to flank the Maginot Line to stab the Allied armies from the rear the German troops crossed the frontiers into the Netherlands, Belgium and Luxembourg at 5:30 o'clock this morning establishing contact with the enemy along what the General Headquarters communiqué terms a broad front.

Even before this early hour, at the first gleam of dawn, Germany's mighty air armadas launched assaults upon enemy territory which now also include the Low Countries.

[Chancellor Hitler, in an order to his troops, declared that the "fate of the German nation for the next thousand years is at stake."]

German headquarters has chosen to reveal but little of what were the results of the first day of this "major war," upon the outcome of which hangs Europe's destiny. But from the scanty official information so far available observers feel justified in believing that the procedure successfully used in the Polish campaign is once more being

Continued on Page Four

HOLLANDERS FIRM

Report 100 Nazi Planes Shot Down as Troops Strike at Invaders

BOMBERS RANGE LAND

Air Attacks Continuous—Parachutists Land at Strategic Spots

By OSCAR MOHR
Wireless to THE NEW YORK TIMES.

AMSTERDAM, the Netherlands, May 10—The German invaders of the Netherlands are being held in check and the surprise element of their attack can be considered a failure, Lieut. Gen. Henri Gerard Winkelman, the Netherland supreme commander, declared tonight.

"In all parts of the country our forces stand firm in their positions as far as this is required by orders," General Winkelman said in an order to his troops, "and they even attack the enemy intrepidly and successfully where necessary for preventing execution of the enemy's plans."

General Winkelman's statement followed a High Command communiqué declaring that the Netherland forces were offering "serious resistance" along the Maas and Yssel Rivers and were maintaining their positions at Delfzijl "in spite of strong German attacks."

Heavy Toll of Planes Claimed

At least seventy German airplanes were shot down during the day as they attacked airdromes or attempted to land, the communiqué said. [A later communiqué raised the number to more than 100, The Associated Press and The United Press reported.] Four German armored trains were declared to have been blown up, one of them with the railway bridge at Venlo, along the German border.

The statement added that small German units that had landed in the interior were being "fiercely attacked" and it charged that Netherland prisoners of war were being used by the Germans as shields.

In declaring that "the strategic surprise attack can be regarded as a failure," General Winkelman expressed Queen Wilhelmina's "high satisfaction" over the quality of the resistance and said that "the firm attitude of our troops is reflected in the attitude of our people, who give proof of calm determination."

German bombers ranged over the country during the day.

In one of their earliest attacks they dropped more than 300 bombs on the Schiphol Airdrome outside Amsterdam and destroyed the landing field along with several buildings. The number of casualties in the first attack was reported to be surprisingly low—three persons wounded and two firemen shot dead by machine-gun fire.

Aerial Thrusts Combated

AMSTERDAM, the Netherlands, Saturday, May 11 (AP)—A Netherland communiqué early today said the number of German planes shot down over the Netherlands now exceeded 100, in addition to fourteen captured at reconquered airdromes.

With one exception, all the airports temporarily taken by the Germans now have been recaptured, the communiqué said.

Last night Germans bombed The Hague, governmental seat of the invaded nation, and one explosive fell close to the United States Minister, George A. Gordon. There were air alarms all evening at half-hourly intervals.

One German transport plane, carrying nineteen soldiers, plunged through the roof of a house in The Hague when it was shot down. The falling soldiers all wore Netherland uniforms.

The Germans succeeded in landing troops at two small fields near The Hague and gained control of them. They were at Okkenburg and Ypenburg. But the Germans were small units and were immediately surrounded.

Many small towns in the southern

Continued on Page Three

Dispatches from Europe and the Far East are subject to censorship at the source.

"All the News That's Fit to Print."

The New York Times.

LATE CITY EDITION
Cloudy with showers and little change in temperature today and tomorrow.
Temperatures Yesterday—Max., 65; Min., 57

VOL. LXXXIX..No. 30,089. Entered as Second-Class Matter, Postoffice, New York, N. Y.

NEW YORK, TUESDAY, JUNE 11, 1940.

THREE CENTS NEW YORK CITY and Vicinity | FOUR CENTS Elsewhere Except in 7th and 8th Postal Zones.

ITALY AT WAR, READY TO ATTACK; STAB IN BACK, SAYS ROOSEVELT; GOVERNMENT HAS LEFT PARIS

NAZIS NEAR PARIS

Units Reported to Have Broken Through Lines to West of Capital

SEINE RIVER CROSSED

3 Columns Branch Out From Soissons—Enemy Held, French State

By The Associated Press.

PARIS, June 10—Marauding German tanks were reported tonight to have reached the Paris region itself as the government left the capital.

While some German armored advance guards were said to have penetrated to the environs of Paris in isolated raids through the French lines, the main front was about thirty-five miles west and northeast of the capital. Although steadily approaching, the battle's roar still could not be heard here.

[The German High Command has no knowledge that Nazi tank units have reached the Paris region, The United Press reported.]

The battle, which had been waged heretofore on familiar World War territory for the most part, swung into virgin soil as the Germans advanced west of Paris.

In the triangle bounded by Amiens on the Somme, Rouen, seventy miles west of Paris on the Seine, and Vernon, forty miles west on the Seine, the Germans redoubled their attacks, crossing the river at several points. An armored column, which crossed the Bresle last week, led the assault.

The French took their main stand west of Paris all along the Seine in an effort to prevent the Germans from effecting further passages and taking the capital from the rear.

In the central sector of the Oise Valley, directly north of Paris where the Germans had suffered tremendous losses, they held back their infantry and sent out dive bombers in an effort to break down French resistance.

They broadened their salient, however, farther east, where they had crossed the Aisne. Three columns fanned out from Soissons through La Ferte Milon and Fere en Tardenois and toward Fismes.

Held Firm on East Flank

They were just north of Chateau-Thierry and the Marne, where they were stopped in their 1918 thrust by Americans fighting with the French.

On the east flank, where the French have been holding firm, fresh German infantry, tanks and planes battered the French lines, but with small gains.

But France, besieged on two sides by Germans driving on Paris from the north and the Italians entering the war on the south, proclaimed her grim determination to carry on the fight.

The main combats were centered in the Seine Valley to the west of Paris, with the High Command declaring that some German elements had crossed the Seine River at certain points, and in the Ourcq River Valley to the northeast of the capital.

The communiqué, however, said the "enemy is held everywhere by vigorous counter-attacks."

The French communiqué was filed from Paris, but was issued "Somewhere in France." The regular press conference of the War Office was not held this morning, as only a few attachés were in the office.

The High Command reported that the German break-through to the Seine resulted from increased pressure applied by the Nazis between the route from Amiens to Rouen and from Amiens to Vernon as far as the lower Seine.

In the other principal area of combat, east of the Oise River, German columns coming down from the region of Soissons have resumed their attack toward the Ourcq River.

The German offensive in the

Continued on Page Two

The International Situation

On the Battle Fronts

Italian guns will speak today in Europe. Italy's declaration of war against France and Britain became effective at 12:01 A. M., Rome time. Before 100,000 men and women, packed in the Piazza Venezia and near-by streets, Premier Mussolini yesterday announced his decision. It was war against "the plutocratic and reactionary democracies of the West." For the present that does not include the United States, but Rome reports that few Italians, from Signor Mussolini down, believe they will see the end of this war without having America against them.

The Italian Premier specifically excluded Turkey, Switzerland, Yugoslavia, Greece and Egypt from his military designs. Rome hoped Turkey would fail to keep her agreement to support the Allies in a Mediterranean war.

Demonstrators in Rome carried placards naming Italian objectives in the war—Tunisia, Jibuti, Corsica, Suez, Malta, Cyprus. There were reports that action against some of these places already had started. But Rome was convinced that nothing big would get under way until today. [All the foregoing, Page 1, Column 8.]

The sixth day of the Battle of France brought the German invaders still closer to Paris; at one point—south of Beauvais—they were said to be within twenty-five or thirty miles of their goal. On the French left wing the Germans crossed the Seine at several points in a dangerous advance that threatened to envelop the capital. In the center, they pushed through to the Ourcq Valley, a movement that similarly threatened to flank Reims. On the French right wing the German pressure was furiously increased; but the French said no great gains had resulted. Information from the French side was less complete than usual because the government press bureau was evacuated from Paris and had not yet established a stable headquarters. [Page 1, Column 1.]

The French Government moved, apparently to the neighborhood of Tours. An exodus of civilians from Paris got under way. [Page 1, Column 2.]

Berlin analyzed the front thus: A semicircle had been thrown around Paris, from which three wedges were being driven into the defense lines. The first, in the lower Seine Valley, succeeded in cutting off the extreme left of the French Army, which can now be pushed to the coast. The second was progressing toward the Marne from the Aisne below Soissons. The third, on the French right, had pierced the Aisne and was headed toward Reims. [Page 1, Column 5.]

London admitted the loss of the airplane carrier Glorious, two destroyers, a transport and an oil tanker—totaling 59,766 tons—in an engagement in the North Sea. King Haakon of Norway arrived in Britain with his government. Some Norwegian troops also were carried off and will continue the war on the Western Front. [Page 16, Column 3.]

Repercussions Elsewhere

President Roosevelt, in a broadcast speech, termed Italy's entry into the war a threat to the American way of life. "The hand that held the dagger has struck it into the back of its neighbor," he said. Declaring it an "obvious delusion that we of the United States can safely permit the United States to become a lone island in a world dominated by the philosophy of force," he advocated all possible material aid to the Allies. [Page 1, Column 4.]

The Canadian Parliament declared war against Italy; Prime Minister Mackenzie King denounced Premier Mussolini as "a carrion bird waiting for brave men to die." [Page 4, Column 5.]

Premier Reynaud, broadcasting to the French people after Italy's announcement, said France had won out over greater difficulties in the past. He asserted France always had been willing to negotiate Italian demands peaceably. [Page 12, Column 1.]

Berlin, jubilant over the entry of the Italians, expressed the belief that Premier Mussolini's military effort would be concentrated in the Mediterranean. It was said that no immediate Italian land attack on France was expected. [Page 5, Column 1.]

Switzerland reported much military activity, but no rumble of guns, in mountain passes between France and Italy. The Swiss were concerned about rumors that there were new German troop concentrations on the country's northern frontier. [Page 5, Column 5.]

Turkey stood ready to fulfill her engagements to the Allies under the mutual-assistance pact of last October. It was believed that the first step, once Italy made that pact operative by an aggressive move in the Mediterranean, would be the placing of Turkish ports and air fields at the disposal of the Allies. [Page 1, Column 7.]

Belgrade heard reports that the Italians had landed troops and much mechanized equipment at the Italian-owned port of Zara, which is on the Yugoslav coast, and on the Italian-owned island of Lagosta, near by. [Page 1, Column 6.]

FRENCH MINISTRIES MOVED SOUTHWARD

Tours Is Believed New Capital, but Reynaud Goes to Army —No Civilian Panic

By The Associated Press.

PARIS, June 10—The French Government left Paris tonight.

"Paul Reynaud, Premier, has gone with the armies," said a communiqué, which also declared:

"The High Command asked the Ministers to effect their withdrawal to the provinces in conformity with established dispositions. This withdrawal has been effected."

The announcement of the departure of the Ministers was made only after they were safely installed "somewhere in France" in the southern provinces.

The government transfer at General Maxime Weygand's request was approved last night at a Cabinet meeting.

Under cover of darkness the Ministers drove to their new offices

Continued on Page Ten

BRITISH NAVY GUNS HAMMER AT NAZIS

Shelling From Sea, Rushing of Troops and Planes Mark London's Share in Battle

By HAROLD DENNY
Special Cable to THE NEW YORK TIMES.

LONDON, June 10—Britain was rushing all available forces today into the battle in France, which was officially called here the "Battle of Paris and London" because of the Nazi threat to England. This reinforcement across the English Channel will continue, it was stated, "despite the imminent danger of German invasion of the United Kingdom."

The guns of British warships pounded the Germans to support Allied troops near the coast.

"Important contingents" of new troops have already gone to France, it was announced.

Even closer cooperation of the

Continued on Page Twelve

OUR HELP PLEDGED

President Offers Our Full Material Aid to Allies' Cause

AMERICA IN DANGER

Fate Hangs on Training and Arms, He Says at Charlottesville

The text of the President's speech will be found on Page 6.

By FELIX BELAIR Jr.
Special to THE NEW YORK TIMES.

CHARLOTTESVILLE, Va., June 10—"On this 10th day of June, 1940, the hand that held the dagger has struck it into the back of its neighbor." In these words tonight President Roosevelt condemned the decision of Premier Mussolini which took Italy into the war on the side of Germany.

The remark was interpolated by the President in an address at the graduation exercises of the University of Virginia here. There could be no missing the depth of his feeling, since he put into the words all the emphasis at his command.

Italy's intervention was denounced furthermore as a definite threat to the way of life and the trade and commerce of the Americas. This government, he said, would give all material aid to France and Great Britain as "opponents of force."

The Chief Executive of the United States spoke to the nation and to the world only a few hours after Premier Mussolini announced his decision to join hands with Chancellor Hitler and unleashed his fascist legions against France and Great Britain. More details were revealed by Mr. Roosevelt of his correspondence with the Italian dictator in an effort to keep Italy at peace and to prevent the spread of war to the Mediterranean basin.

"To the Regret of Humanity"

"Unfortunately—unfortunately, to the regret of all of us and to the regret of humanity—the chief of the Italian Government was unwilling to accept the procedure suggested, and he has made no counter proposal," the President said.

And a moment later:

"The Government of Italy has now chosen to preserve what it terms its freedom of action and to fulfill what it states are its promises to Germany. In so doing it has manifested disregard for the rights and security of other nations, disregard for the lives of the peoples of those nations which are directly threatened by the spread of this war, and has evidenced its unwillingness to find the means, through pacific negotiation, for the satisfaction of what it believes are its legitimate aspirations."

The President bespoke the prayers and hopes of this nation for those peoples beyond the seas who were battling for their freedom.

"In our American unity," he

Continued on Page Six

Nazi Tide Laps at Paris as Italy Joins War

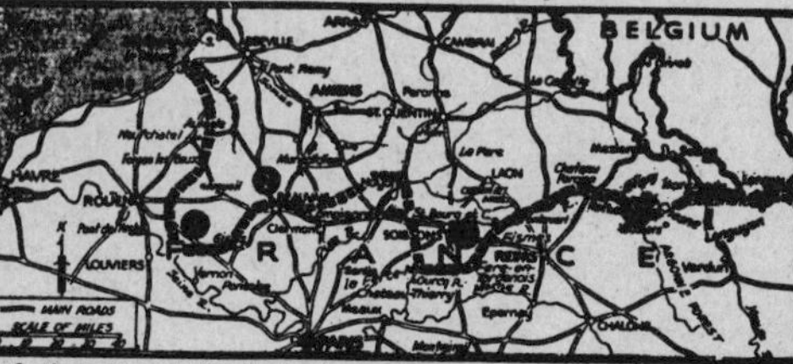

On the western end of the line the Germans pushed a wedge to the Seine southeast of Rouen (1) and struck mighty blows in the region of Beauvais (2). In the center they reached the Ourcq River below Soissons (3). To the east they crossed the Aisne at two points near Vouziers (4).

Italy's announcement of her entry into the war was accompanied by no attack anywhere. One report had Italian troops invading the French Riviera (1), but this was unsupported. Rome's troops landed at two Italian-owned points on the Yugoslav coast: Zara (2) and Lagosta (3). In Albania (4) Italian military preparations were accelerated.

NAZIS CLAIM BREAK IN SUPPLY ARTERY

Paris Cut Off From Havre by Thrust to Seine East of Rouen, Berlin Says

By C. BROOKS PETERS
Wireless to THE NEW YORK TIMES.

BERLIN, June 10—German forces in Northern France were fighting tonight to shorten the radius of a semicircle they are drawing about Paris, according to reports received here. Apparently they are attempting to drive three wedges into the remaining French territory north of the capital.

The first is on the Germans' extreme right wing, which is reported to have reached the lower Seine east of Rouen and therewith cuts off Paris from Havre. Mass tank formations, assisted by light motorized units, are claimed here to have made more than a sixty-mile ad-

Continued on Page Eleven

La Guardia Warns of Strict Neutrality Here; Consuls Told to 'Adhere to Consular Duties'

Mayor La Guardia went on the air over WNYC, the city broadcasting station, yesterday afternoon with a strong plea to the million persons of Italian blood in this city to preserve strict neutrality in the face of Italy's declaration of war.

Moving with characteristic rapidity, the Mayor telephoned the city broadcasting studio in the New York City Building at the World's Fair and said he would be on the air ten minutes later. He thought over the message he wanted to deliver while driving over from the World's Fair City Hall, and was prepared to speak immediately upon his arrival. Meantime, Morris S. Novik, director of the station, had made arrangements to rebroadcast the Mayor's talk over five commercial stations at intervals later in the day.

Speaking slowly and impressively, the Mayor stated his policy that the European war must be fought on the battlefields of Europe and not on the sidewalks of New York.

Recalling his war service as an ally of the Italian forces in Italy, the Mayor said he fully realized that the Italian entry into the war on the opposite side must be as painful to others of Italian blood as it was to him. Nevertheless, he insisted that the national policy of neutrality must be observed in the city. While he pledged full protection to consular officers of various European governments in the city, the Mayor made clear that these officials must stay within the bounds of their consular duties.

The Mayor's speech follows:

This is F. H. La Guardia, Mayor of the City of New York, talking.

On Sept. 3, 1939, when the Nazi

Continued on Page Eight

Three Italian Freighters Are Scuttled by Crews

By The Associated Press.

LA LINEA, Spain, Tuesday, June 11—Two Italian merchant ships, the 10,000-ton Chelina and the 3,000-ton Numbolia, were scuttled by their crews in Gibraltar waters late yesterday [Monday] when their crews heard the radio news that Italy had gone to war.

RIMOUSKI, Que., June 10 (UP)—The 3,921-ton Italian freighter Capo Noli was set afire by her crew tonight as she proceeded down the St. Lawrence, but the scuttling attempt failed.

The Marine Department said the Canadian pilot grounded the freighter near the Father Point pilot station. A naval control boat extinguished the flames.

The government salvage boat Lord Strathcona left Quebec tonight for the site with a large derrick in tow. The Capo Noli will be taken over by the Canadian Government and her crew probably will be interned.

ITALIANS REPORTED ON YUGOSLAV COAST

Said to Have Landed at Two Places Controlled by Rome—Mass on Greek Border

By The United Press.

BELGRADE, Yugoslavia, Tuesday, June 11—Large numbers of Italian troops were reported early today to have been landed along the Yugoslav coast at two Italian points as the Yugoslav Government prepared to fight in defense of its territory if necessary.

[It was reported from Berlin yesterday that Italian forces had invaded France through the Riviera, but this was denied in Rome, and German military quarters said later that they had no knowledge of any such movement.]

Reports from Split on the Adriatic coast said that large forces of Italian troops had been landed at

Continued on Page Four

TURKEY PREPARES UNDER ALLIED PACT

Partial Mobilization Expected Today—Troops Are on Move —Precautions in Balkans

By J. W. KERNICK
Special Cable to THE NEW YORK TIMES.

ISTANBUL, Turkey, June 10—Turkey, speeding her military preparations as a result of Italy's entry into the war, stood ready tonight to fulfill her obligations under her mutual-assistance agreement with Britain and France.

That accord, concluded last October, stipulates that Turkey will lend the Allies every assistance in her power in the event of hostilities in the Mediterranean as a result of aggressive action by a European power. Hence Turkish aid can be invoked as soon as the first shot is fired.

The Italian action has already resulted in the calling of several classes to the colors by the Turkish Government. It is believed that the next move will be to place ports and airfields at the disposal of the Allies.

[The Turkish Cabinet met last night to consider the question of war or peace, The Associated Press reported, but it was believed that Turkey's entrance into the war would be by gradual steps, not immediately.]

Italy's declaration of war caused neither surprise nor excitement in Turkey. The Turks had suspected for some time and lately became certain that Premier Mussolini could not forever remain an onlooker while Chancellor Hitler marched.

Premier Mussolini's assurances that he did not intend to attack Yugoslavia, Turkey, Greece, Switz-

Continued on Page Two

Dispatches from Europe and the Far East are subject to censorship at the source.

DUCE GIVES SIGNAL

Announces War on the 'Plutocratic' Nations of the West

ASSURES 5 NEUTRALS

Bid Is Made to Russia, But Rome Has No Pledge of Aid

'Hostilities' Are Reported

"Hostilities were started four hours ago, Central European time," Radio Roma, the official Italian short-wave radio, said last night at 11 o'clock Eastern daylight time in a broadcast recorded by Columbia Broadcasting System's short-wave listening station.

"The first Italian war bulletin is expected to be issued within a few hours."

At 2:15 A. M. today, however, the official British wireless said that "there have been no reports as yet of any engagements growing out of Italy's entrance into the war," Columbia's listening station reported.

By HERBERT L. MATTHEWS
By Telephone to THE NEW YORK TIMES.

ROME, Tuesday, June 11—Italy declared war on Great Britain and France yesterday afternoon, to take effect at one minute past midnight. The land, air and sea forces of the Italian Empire were already in motion.

It is a war, as Premier Benito Mussolini announced to the people from his balcony at the Palazzo Venezia at 6 in the evening, against the "plutocratic and reactionary democracies of the West." For the moment that does not include the United States, but few Italians believe that they will see the war to a finish without having the Americans against them.

Signor Mussolini expressly excluded Turkey, Switzerland, Yugoslavia, Greece and Egypt as enemies unless they attacked Italy or the Italian possessions.

Turkey provides the burning question of the day. Italians are absolutely convinced that the Turks will not move against them and will not honor their agreement with the Allies. It is hoped to confine Italian activity to France, Great Britain and the Mediterranean and to keep the Balkans tranquil. If that can be done, Italians think, the Turks will remain quiet.

Soviet Action Discounted

Russia has washed her hands of the struggle. The Italians know that any disturbance in the Balkans will immediately bring her in; but as long as the struggle is confined to the west and south the Soviet will do nothing either to hinder or help. This was told to your correspondent a few hours ago by a very authoritative source.

It was emphasized there were no agreements about furnishing material or anything else, nor any threats or promises.

The Italian Ambassador, Augusto Rosso, left in the morning for Moscow and Ivan Gorelkin, Soviet Ambassador, is coming back to Rome, thus ending a long period without such representation. The Italians were anxious to restore full diplomatic relations in this critical period, according to this writer's informant, and the Russians agreed, but without compromising themselves.

It thus appears that Premier Mussolini has embarked on this dangerous venture without really knowing what Soviet Russia will do in the long run.

President Roosevelt's speech clearly has come too late. There was nothing that the United States could do to halt this conflict, the Italians say. Whatever brake Mr. Roosevelt may have exercised was overcome by the momentum of the whole Fascist policy. Once it was set in motion, nothing could stop it.

The Italians do not believe that the United States can affect the issue, whatever it does. They are

Continued on Page Four

Italian colonial troops drilling.

"All the News That's Fit to Print."

The New York Times.

LATE CITY EDITION
Fair and warmer today and tomorrow.
Temperatures Yesterday—Max., 60; Min., 46

Copyright, 1940, by The New York Times Company.

VOL. XC...No. 30,198. Entered as Second-Class Matter, Postoffice, New York, N. Y. NEW YORK, SATURDAY, SEPTEMBER 28, 1940. THREE CENTS NEW YORK CITY and Vicinity | FOUR CENTS Elsewhere Except in 7th and 8th Postal Zones.

JAPAN JOINS AXIS ALLIANCE SEEN AIMED AT U. S.; ROOSEVELT ORDERS STUDY OF THE PACT'S EFFECT; BRITISH DOWN 130 RAIDERS, BLAST NAZI BASES

REPUBLICANS MAKE 3D TERM THE ISSUE; PICK STATE SLATE

BARTON IS CHOSEN

Leaders at Convention Turn Fire on the New Deal and Roosevelt

DEWEY SEES MENACE

Keynoter Assails 'One-Man Power'—Party Hears Willkie Tonight

Text of platform and Dewey and Barton addresses, Page 8.

By WARREN MOSCOW
Special to THE NEW YORK TIMES.

WHITE PLAINS, Sept. 27—The Republican campaign in New York State was started today at the Republican State Convention here, when the party organization nominated a strong slate headed by Bruce Barton for United States Senator, heard State and national leaders unite in a stinging castigation of the New Deal and adjourned until tomorrow evening to hear Wendell L. Willkie make his bid for New York support in a speech at the Empire City race track.

The delegates to the convention heard Thomas E. Dewey, National Chairman Joseph W. Martin Jr., State Senate Leader Joe R. Hanley and Mr. Barton unite in an onslaught on the New Deal's foreign and domestic policies as menacing our safety from within and from without. They spared neither the President nor his family as they tried to drive home the meaning of the violation of the anti-third term tradition.

Members of the Ticket

The ticket, nominated without opposition, is as follows:

For United States Senator: Bruce Barton of New York.

For Judges of the Court of Appeals: Benjamin B. Cunningham of Rochester, Edmund H. Lewis of Syracuse and Albert Conway of Brooklyn.

For Representatives at Large: Messmore Kendall of Westchester and Miss Mary Donlon of Oneida and New York.

Judges Lewis and Conway, Republican and Democrat respectively, are on the bench by appointment and will get an endorsement from the Democratic State Convention on Monday.

Justice Cunningham, now a member of the Appellate Division of the Fourth Department, was picked as a compromise nominee at a conference of party leaders during a convention recess and Judges James P. Hill of Norwich and Christopher J. Heffernan of Amsterdam, who had been deadlocked in a behind-the-scenes battle, both withdrew to make way for Justice Cunningham. The latter probably will get a Democratic endorsement, in view of the fact that he was appointed to the Appellate Division by Governor Lehman and won his last election to the Supreme Court with a bi-partisan endorsement. He is a Republican.

Starts on Fighting Key

The convention started on a fighting key with Mr. Dewey's speech, in the morning, as temporary chairman, and it came to a climax with an equally strong speech by Representative Barton, selected for the nomination yesterday at the insistence of Wendell L. Willkie.

"In the next six weeks the American people must decide whether to cast away the tradition which for 150 years has stood between them and the menace of one-man power; whether they will gamble with their liberties by electing a President for the third term," Mr. Barton told

Continued on Page Eight

Tonight Will Bring End Of Daylight Saving Time

With daylight saving time ending at 2 A. M. tomorrow, most New Yorkers were expected to turn their clocks back one hour tonight before retiring—thus regaining the hour of sleep lost when the Summer time became effective on April 28.

The New York Central Railroad is adding a new train to its Chicago-to-New York fleet. To be known as the Grand Central, the train will leave Chicago at 2:30 P. M., Central Standard time, and arrive in New York at 8:30 A. M., Eastern Standard time.

The Pennsylvania Railroad and the New York, New Haven & Hartford Railroad also are providing a new train from the Pennsylvania Station to Boston and New England points. It will be called the Bay State and, starting from Philadelphia, will depart from New York at 9:45 A. M. and arrive at Boston at 2:40 P. M.

WILLKIE DEMANDS OUR SYSTEM STAND

Change of Administration Is Needed to Save Democracy, He Says in Wisconsin

By JAMES A. HAGERTY
Special to THE NEW YORK TIMES.

MADISON, Wis., Sept. 27—Wendell L. Willkie ended his 6,000-mile Western trip tonight with a speech in the Field House of the University of Wisconsin to about 15,000 persons. He was introduced by Dean Christian Christiansen of the College of Agriculture.

Mr. Willkie criticized the President for trying to enlarge the Supreme Court on the ground that some of its members were too old.

"And yet," he continued, "the President recently appointed to a most important position, Secretary of War, a man older than the age he fixed as too old to render proper judicial decisions."

The candidate also recalled that President Roosevelt had tried to "purge" members of Congress of his own party who did not agree with him, offering another instance in which the Executive tried to infringe upon the powers of the other two departments of the Federal Government.

'Must Make System Work'

He declared that the present Administration had preserved the form but not the substance of democracy and had concentrated power in the Chief Executive.

"That is the road by which every ancient and every modern democracy has died," he added.

"Do you know that in Germany there is still a Reichstag and in Italy a parliament? There is still the form of democracy, but the substance is gone.

"You must take the American system of government and make it work, with its coordinate branches, as it is, or you must admit that it is a failure. I repudiate the latter notion with all the vigor of my being.

"This American system of government can be made, and will be made, if you put another Administration into power, the most effective and most pleasant way of life."

Mr. Willkie brought laughter by saying that Thomas Jefferson, sponsor after Washington of the no-third-term tradition, was the founder of the party which President Roosevelt, "in part," now leads.

He added that every attempt so far to violate the anti-third-term tradition had been defeated, and cited that in 1928 the United States Senate adopted a resolution against the third term. Although Madison is the home of Senator Robert M. La Follette, author of that resolution, Mr. Willkie did not mention him.

On his entrance to Wisconsin, the

Continued on Page Seven

LONDON BADLY HIT

Capital and Its Suburbs Bear Brunt of Heavy German Attacks

OTHER AREAS RAIDED

Coastal Towns Pounded —600 Planes Used in Daylight Assaults

By ROBERT P. POST
Special Cable to THE NEW YORK TIMES.

LONDON, Saturday, Sept. 28—The Germans changed their recent air-raid tactics yesterday and sent over by daylight wave on wave of bombers with fighter as chaperones above.

It is estimated that at least 600 Germans crossed the coast before dark, and of these the latest figures show 130 shot down for certain. The British loss at the time of writing is put at thirty-four fighters. Fifteen of the downed British pilots are safe.

This is a preliminary count. The figures may be higher when all precincts have reported. In any case it is probable that the number of German planes that will never fly again is considerably bigger than the British announce.

From all reports on the daylight raiding, it would appear that the Germans once again were testing the British fighter defenses and paying heavily for it. Some German planes flew "cloud hopping" over London, which had five air raids during the day. They dropped bombs that did some damage, but the worst destruction done in England before dark was on the outskirts of London and in certain coastal towns where the Germans, chased by Spitfires and Hurricanes, jettisoned their loads while trying to escape.

One of Worst Night Raids

At night the siren again wailed and the night raiders again came over to take advantage of a cloudy sky. And again the attack was directed mainly at the London area.

Several bombs crashed in the central area of London in the early morning as German planes continued to hum over the metropolis. A good many fires were started, but they were quickly extinguished.

[By early this morning, the attack had developed into one of the worst raids the capital has experienced in many nights, according to The Associated Press, with heavy bombs falling and anti-aircraft fire heaviest in the center of the city.]

But the rest of the country did not go free either by day or night. Two separate waves estimated at fifty each crossed the Dorset coast and went after the Bristol area. At night planes were reported over other towns. During the day, too, the countryside saw planes overhead. At Seven Oaks a big Junkers bomber dived to its death, narrowly missing the City Hall in High Street.

The raiders visited Northwest and Southeast England during the night, scattering explosives and incendiaries.

Big formations could be seen plainly over London during the day. In one police station a man

Continued on Page Four

New Air Defense Devices Reported Used in London

By The Associated Press.

LONDON, Sept. 27—New secret devices with which to combat night raiders were reported today in use in the London area, which last night had one of the lightest night raids in three weeks.

The devices were said to have been developed by British scientists, and observers declared there was a chance that, used together, two of the devices might make night bombing as hazardous as raiding by day.

In a gradual lifting of the curtain of censorship, British correspondents were permitted to comment upon new air-raid noises heard by Londoners in the last few nights. These were a heavy single explosion disintegrating into staccato cracks high up in the heavens, a flat roar that seems to strike a ceiling several miles up and bump its way clamorously along the top of the sky, and a muffled rattling like a "carpet slipper machine-gun."

"These queer noises are in fact caused by new types of weapons, or by well tried weapons adapted to new uses," said one observer.

R.A.F. RAKES NAZIS ON 500-MILE COAST

Pounds Invasion Fleet, Bombs Kiel Anew—Raids Gun Sites After Cross-Channel Duel

By JAMES B. RESTON
Special Cable to THE NEW YORK TIMES.

LONDON, Sept. 27—British bombers raided the German invasion fleet along 500 miles of European coast last night, bombed lines of communication deep in Nazi territory and penetrated the fortified naval base at Kiel, where the 26,000-ton German battleship Scharnhorst was said to be anchored, it was announced here today.

This afternoon, during a duel between German and British long-range guns, British bombers flew across the English Channel and attacked Nazi gun emplacements in France near Cap Gris Nez. In the artillery duel, which lasted an hour, shells fell in the Dover area, but there were no casualties and no serious damage was reported.

In the persistent night raids on Germany the British have three main objectives—to harass ships, men and supplies gathered along the coast for a possible invasion of this country, to cripple transportation and industrial production inside Germany and to carry the war to the German people. Last night's raid conformed to this general pattern, but whereas in the preceding few nights the Bomber Command centered its attention on communications and industrial plants, last night the British tried first of all to knock out the Scharnhorst.

When the first relays of bombers approached the naval basin at Kiel German guns immediately opened fire. Flying high, the raiders were able to stay out of range. They opened the attack by dropping incendiary bombs around the edge of the base and then, by the light of fires, hurled several sticks of high-explosive bombs into the basin, where two large ships were clearly seen.

An Air Ministry statement here

Continued on Page Five

HULL SEES NO SHIFT

Holds Accord Does Not Substantially Alter Recent Situation

DEFENSE AIDES MEET

Notables Ask President to Rush Increased Aid to Britain

By CHARLES HURD
Special to THE NEW YORK TIMES.

WASHINGTON, Sept. 27—President Roosevelt quickly directed today a sweeping search into the possibilities in the new German-Italian-Japanese alliance, but the Administration adopted an official attitude that the alliance momentarily creates little change in a situation that already existed.

Mr. Roosevelt declined to make any comment at the regular press conference in his office this morning. He merely told reporters that he had received no official notification of the conclusion of the accord.

However, while Secretary of State Cordell Hull gravely acknowledged the pact's existence at a State Department press conference, the President undertook studies involving every major branch of the government.

[A group of Americans prominent in business and political affairs called at the White House to urge that aid to Britain be increased and speeded in every form possible. They reported later that they were "enthusiastically encouraged" by the President's response, though they were unable to divulge what he said.]

Cabinet Studies Situation

A Cabinet meeting, regular scheduled for this afternoon, was devoted exclusively during a ninety-minute session to discussion of the latest developments in the foreign situation. It was preceded by a long conference in the President's office, to which were invited all the ranking officials of the War and Navy Departments.

These conferences were reported to have been concerned not only with political implications in the expanded Rome-Berlin Axis but also with economic possibilities, both from the standpoint of potential effects on American sources of commodities such as tin and rubber and a possible advancement from Oct. 16 of the effective date for the embargo on exports of scrap iron and steel, ordered yesterday

There also was informal discussion, without conclusive decision, of a possible extension of the embargo on scrap exports to exports of pig iron and steel which currently can be sent to Japan without restriction.

It was obvious that the government's attitude was based largely on the expectation that Britain would be able to hold her line against the German attack. A collapse of Britain would create an entirely new situation.

The President's refusal to comment at his press conference came about two hours after news services had first reported the new treaty. He declined smilingly but persistently to make any statement, saying all that he had heard thus far had been a rumor, that he had nothing official. When he was asked if the news was unexpected he replied, Well, yes and no, and referred inquirers to the State Department.

Hull Expresses Official View

At the State Department, where a press conference was held soon afterward, Secretary Hull did express the viewpoint of this government in phrases which he permitted to be quoted directly.

Speaking slowly and with care and marking his words by an unusually grave countenance, he summed up the official attitude as follows:

The reported agreement of alliance does not, in the view of the government of the United States, substantially alter a situation which has existed for several years. Announcement of the alliance merely makes clear to all a relationship which has long existed in effect and to which this government has repeatedly called attention.

That such an agreement has

Continued on Page Two

The International Situation

The German-Italian-Japanese Pact

Japan yesterday formally allied herself with Germany and Italy for the task of establishing a "new order" in Europe and East Asia by signing in Berlin a mutual assistance pact, by all indications aimed at the United States.

The three bound themselves for a period of ten years to come to the aid of any one of the others attacked by a power not at present involved in the European or Chinese-Japanese conflicts. Although political commitments of the three with Soviet Russia were specifically exempted by Article V of the six-article pact, a veiled threat to Moscow was seen.

By the terms of the pact, Japan recognized German-Italian hegemony in Europe. The two dictator nations in turn recognized Japanese hegemony in the Far East, apparently leaving to later determination of the fate of British, French and Netherland possessions there. [All the foregoing Page 1, Column 8.]

The official attitude of the United States, as stated by Secretary of State Hull, was that the announcement of the alliance merely publicly confirmed a relationship already existing. President Roosevelt began a study of the pact's possible effects by conferring with the Cabinet, War, Navy and Defense Commission officials but had no public comment. Possibility of quicker invocation of the embargo on scrap steel and iron to Japan, now scheduled to go into effect Oct. 16, and its possible extension to other war materials was reported discussed. [Page 1, Column 5.] The President was visited during the day by a group of prominent Americans asking more war aid for Britain.

The British Ambassador made a similar plea. [Page 2, Column 1.]

Yakichiro Suma, Japanese Foreign Office spokesman, said the alliance did not mean abandonment of Japan's attitude toward the United States and that hope still was held for a betterment of relations. Observers in Tokyo construed the formal junction with the Axis as a desperate gamble that Germany and Italy would defeat Britain before the United States was prepared to give effective aid. The benediction on the pact of Emperor Hirohito—spiritual as well as political leader of Japan—was broadcast to the nation. [Page 1, Column 7.]

Italians were surprised that Japan and not Spain proved the third party to the pact, but quickly recovered and immediately grasped its significance as a warning to the United States to keep out of the conflict. It also was accepted there as a challenge to Soviet Russia. [Page 3, Column 1.]

Information in Shanghai was that Germany was attempting to promote a rapprochement between Moscow and Tokyo, but that the Soviet had set a high price, including abrogation of most of the Portsmouth treaty, which ended the Russo-Japanese War in 1905. A Russian source in London said the pact placed the Soviet in a "dangerous and very grave" situation. [Page 1, Column 6.]

The London reaction was that the publicly announced alliance had served to clear the atmosphere, had brought Britain and the United States even closer together and had removed any brake on all possible aid to China. [Page 3, Column 8.]

The War in Europe and Africa

The Germans yesterday and last night launched the heaviest attacks in several days on London and other key cities in England. Heavy daylight raids on London and Bristol were reported turned back with a cost to the Germans by early evening of at least 130 planes against thirty-four British defenders, from which fifteen of the pilots jumped to safety. It was estimated at least 600 German planes engaged in the day raids. The day rounded out three weeks of aerial siege of the British capital. [Page 1, Column 3.]

The R. A. F. again Thursday night made devastating attacks on German invasion bases and canals, arterial highways, industrial plants and harbors in Germany proper, the Air Ministry said. The principal attack, a communiqué stated, was launched on the German naval base at Kiel, where the battle-scarred German battleship Scharnhorst is under repair. One raiding pilot said he had never seen such fires as he and his fellow fliers set there. A daylight bombing attack was made on German big gun emplacements at Cap Gris Nez after a short artillery duel with British batteries at Dover. [Page 1, Column 4.]

Both the British and Italians reported air attacks on the other's supply and military bases in Africa. Otherwise all was quiet on that front. [Page 5, Column 6.]

STALIN'S DEMANDS SAID TO BE LARGE

Reported Seeking to Cancel Many Tokyo Gains as Price of Accepting Axis Pact

By HALLETT ABEND
Wireless to THE NEW YORK TIMES.

SHANGHAI, China, Sept. 27—The immediate future of the international situation in the Far East now depends to a great extent upon what degree of understanding the Germans will be able to arrange between Japan and Russia.

It is understood that Max Stahmer, private emissary from Chancellor Hitler, having concluded the alliance satisfactorily, now is acting as go-between for Moscow and Tokyo.

[In Tokyo it was said Japan already had the assurances she required from Russia. Up to last evening, the Russian people had not been allowed to hear of the conclusion of the Axis-Japanese pact, according to The Associated Press.]

Joseph Stalin's terms as reported here, however, are extremely harsh from the Japanese viewpoint. He is said to demand first of all abrogation of the Portsmouth treaty, except that portion ceding the southern half of Sakhalin Island to Japan. This would cancel Japan's immensely valuable fishing concessions off the Siberian coast, which not only furnish an important por-

Continued on Page Four

WARNING TO U. S. IS SEEN IN TOKYO

Spokesman of Foreign Office Declines to Say Whether New Pact Affects Us Now

By HUGH BYAS
Wireless to THE NEW YORK TIMES.

TOKYO, Sept. 27—The forces driving Japan forward have finally decided to take all risks in pursuit of their Greater East Asia policy, formally allying Tokyo with Berlin and Rome. They gamble on Germany's winning the war before the United States is ready.

Any power not presently involved in the European War is menaced by their joint action if it attacks any of the contracting parties. Though no country is specified, the pact is an unmistakable warning to the United States.

The point of the document lies in Article III, which in the Foreign Office translation reads: "Japan, Germany and Italy undertake to assist one another with all political, economic and military means when one of the three contracting parties is attacked by a power not presently involved in the European War or the Sino-Japanese conflict."

Yakichiro Suma, Foreign office spokesman, declined to say whether United States assistance to Britain "short of war" would constitute an "attack" in the terms of the treaty.

Neither the word "attack" nor Greater East Asia are defined, he said. He added that Japan was not

Continued on Page Four

RUSSIA REASSURED

Accord Viewed as Threat to Soviet, in Spite of Safeguard Clause

WASHINGTON WARNED

Interference Barred With 'New Order' in Europe and Eastern Asia

Text of treaty and statements for three nations, Page 3.

By GUIDO ENDERIS
Wireless to THE NEW YORK TIMES.

BERLIN, Sept. 27—By another of those bold forays into the realm of "Blitz diplomacy" with which the world has now become familiar, the Reich's Chancellery at noon today became the birthplace of a tripartite military alliance linking Germany, Italy and Japan. Its implications seem designed to have a profound effect not only on the further course of Europe's war but more directly on the world situation in general.

It is expressly specified that the commitments assumed today shall not affect the political status existing between each of the three signatories and Soviet Russia.

Opinion in neutral diplomatic quarters tonight appears to concur on two points, one being by implication that the pact conjoins a veiled threat to Russia, while that to the United States is decidedly less obscure.

On the latter point advance press comment leaves no doubt, and opinions gathered in informed quarters also frankly suggest that the pact may be interpreted as being directed against "certain groups in the United States who are trying to disrupt relations between peoples and nations."

Ten-Year Pledge Given

In a highly ceremonial setting in the Chancellery's reception chamber, the German and Italian Foreign Ministers and the Japanese Ambassador pledged their respective countries for ten year to cooperation in the interest of lasting peace and to "the creation of the preconditions necessary to that new order that will promote the welfare and prosperity of their peoples."

The signing formalities occupied just about two minutes, after which Chancellor Hitler joined the scene, entering the chamber through a door opening from his private working apartments. It was the same chamber in which the German-Italian military pact was signed in 1939, but today's audience did not include the diplomatic corps. Those who witnessed the formalities comprised government officials, Nazi party leaders and representatives of the German and foreign press.

The pact negotiated today consists of a brief preamble and six articles. By its terms Japan recognizes Germany's and Italy's leadership in constituting "a new order in Europe." The Axis powers, for their part, recognize and respect Japan's priority rights in the establishment of "a new order in Eastern Asia." It was authoritatively stated that the Russian Government had been duly apprised of the impending conclusion of the three-power pact and informed that the signatory powers were in accord on this point.

Total Aid Promised

On the basis of these premises, the partners to the pact agree to support one another in fulfillment of their tasks and to throw their complete political, economic and military resources into the defense of any of the partners who may be attacked by any power not at present involved in the European war or in the Chinese-Japanese conflict.

In pronouncing his benediction on the pact after signing formalities were concluded, Foreign Minister Joachim von Ribbentrop declared: "Organized warmongers in the Jewish capitalistic democracies have succeeded in plunging Europe into a new war which was not wanted by Germany. Our fight is not directed against other peoples, but against the existence of international plotters who once before succeeded in plunging Europe into a sanguinary war."

The German Foreign Minister

Continued on Page Three

Jersey Poll Books Burned, Senators Hear; Charge of Move to Block Inquiry Renewed

Special to THE NEW YORK TIMES.

WASHINGTON, Sept. 27—Poll books in Hudson County, depended upon to show padded registry, have been destroyed, according to word received today by Senator Guy M. Gillette of Iowa, chairman of the Senate committee investigating election expenditures. Similar information was conveyed to Senator Charles W. Tobey of New Hampshire, one of the subcommittee authorized to inquire into the alleged election frauds.

Senator Tobey, who caused a sensation yesterday by asserting that pressure had been exerted to stop the hearing, planned in Jersey City, renewed his charges today in the Senate. He read into the record a dispatch printed in The Newark Evening News to the effect that Representatives Edward J. Hart and Mrs. Mary T. Norton of New Jersey had exerted pressure to delay or prevent the inquiry. Mrs. Norton said that she had never approached any Senator on the subject, while Representative Hart declined to discuss the question.

Senator Gillette later exonerated both New Jersey House members from any ulterior activities. He said that Mrs. Norton had never seen him about the situation in Hudson County, while Representative Hart had asked him when the hearing would begin, but had not suggested that it be delayed or stopped.

Renewing his charges of alleged pressure, Senator Tobey, speaking in the Senate, said:

"I charged in my statement yesterday that pressure had been applied on Senators to postpone in-

Continued on Page Seven

"All the News That's Fit to Print."

The New York Times.

LATE CITY EDITION
Occasional rain, little change in temperature today. Tomorrow partly cloudy, continued cool.
Temperatures Yesterday—Max., 47; Min., 40

NEWS INDEX, PAGE 51, THIS SECTION

VOL. XC No. 30,388. Entered as Second-Class Matter, Postoffice, New York, N. Y. NEW YORK, SUNDAY, APRIL 6, 1941. Including Rotogravure Picture, Magazine and Book Review. TEN CENTS New York City and Vicinity

GERMANS INVADE YUGOSLAVIA AND GREECE; HITLER ORDERS WAR, BLAMING THE BRITISH; MOSCOW SIGNS AMITY PACT WITH BELGRADE

U. S. STEEL STRIKE IS CALLED BY C. I. O., EFFECTIVE TUESDAY

Murray Says Wage Talks Failed and Plans Picketing in Tie-Up Involving 261,000 Men

ROOSEVELT MAY STEP IN

President Is Reported to Have Summoned C. I. O. Chief in Move to Bar Walkout

By The Associated Press.

PITTSBURGH, April 5 — The C. I. O. Steel Workers Organizing Committee tonight ordered its members in all steel mills of the giant United States Steel Corporation, employing about 261,000 wage-earners, to stop work at midnight next Tuesday.

The union said that negotiations for a wage increase and other benefits had collapsed.

Philip Murray, C. I. O. president and chairman of the Steel Workers Organizing Committee, telegraphed instructions to local union units of the corporation to establish continuous picket lines at all plant gates.

[The United Press reported from Pittsburgh last night it had learned authoritatively that President Roosevelt, concerned over the threatened stoppage, had invited Mr. Murray to a White House conference tomorrow or Tuesday.]

The company produces more than one-third of America's steel, an amount exceeding all of that made in England. It hold millions of dollars in defense contracts.

Mr. Murray termed the cessation of work a "lockout" rather than a strike, asserting that the company had rejected his suggestion to continue negotiations, which began March 20, another week, with any agreement to be retroactive to April 1. The company was said to be willing to make the agreement retroactive only to April 8.

The sudden development, threatening to spread the nation's strike area to the vital steel industry, came during an interim of wage negotiations, which still are scheduled to be resumed Monday at 10 A. M.

Mr. Murray called in 100 local union leaders today for conference. It was the third such meeting since the union made known its nine-point demands, which included a wage increase of 10 cents an hour, a closed shop, check-off of union dues by the company, liberalized vacations and establishment of seniority rights.

The company's minimum pay, established in 1937, is 62½ cents an hour, with the average pay of wage-earners about 87 cents an hour. This contract expired April 1 and was extended to April 8.

The company's original counter-offer of a 2½ cents an hour wage rise was rejected by Mr. Murray. Tonight it was learned this offer had been raised to five cents an hour but again was refused by the union. The company contended it made but $60,000,000 of its $102,000,000 profit last year in its steel plants. The other profits came from coal, cement shipping and other subsidiaries. The company has insisted it cannot increase wages without increasing the price of steel. The Government has firmly refused to sanction any such price advance.

In his instructions to local unions, Mr. Murray said:

"The Carnegie-Illinois Steel Company has either rejected entirely or submitted unsatisfactory counter proposals with respect to each of the points offered by the S. W. O. C. in its program.

"The S. W. O. C. will attempt to arrive at an agreement with the companies involved to provide for the continuance at work of the necessary maintenance men during the suspension of operations. Further instructions regarding this situation will be forwarded to you by wire.

"Peaceful picket lines shall be established at all plant gates and maintained at all times during the cessation of work. There should be no violence or other unlawful acts on the part of members or representatives of the S. W. O. C."

No comment was forthcoming from the company on the development.

Continued on Page Forty-one

The International Situation

SUNDAY, APRIL 6, 1941

Germany's armies this morning launched a vast attack upon Yugoslavia and Greece. The move was announced over the Berlin radio in an order of the day from Reichsfuehrer Hitler, read by Propoganda Minister Goebbels; it denounced "the Belgrade government of intrigue" and said German troops would not lay down their arms until "this band of ruffians" and every last Briton had been eliminated from Southeastern Europe. [Page 1, Column 8.]

As Belgrade's first air raid was reported, it was believed the principal Nazi attacks had been launched from Bulgaria, one across Southern Yugoslavia and another southward toward Salonika. Bulgaria's army was said to have an active role, but Hungary's was believed inactive for the present. The Yugoslavs were expected to fight a rear-guard delaying action until they reached their strong natural defense positions. The Belgrade Government had planned to evacuate the capital, going to some southern point. The United States Minister was reported remaining in Belgrade. [Page 1, Column 5.]

With dramatic suddenness Yugoslavia and Soviet Russia signed a five-year non-aggression and friendship pact providing that if either signatory became the victim of aggression by a third State the other would maintain a policy of "strictest friendship." The pact will take effect immediately and the articles of ratification will be exchanged in Belgrade "at the earliest possible moment." [Page 1, Column 4.]

On the African front, British Headquarters in Cairo reported that an Axis advance east of Bengazi, Libya, "has been successfully held and the situation is well in hand." Empire forces in Ethiopia crossed the Awash River, to a point only eighty miles from Addis Ababa, while other units driving down on the capital from Eritrea captured Adowa and Adigrat. [Page 1, Column 6; Map, Page 7.]

The British Air Ministry augmented early brief accounts of the R. A. F attack on Brest Friday night and early Saturday by stating that the 26,000-ton German battleships Gneisenau and Scharnhorst had been "very, very lucky" if they had escaped serious damage from new and powerful British bombs. R. A. F. aircraft, it was said, had dived to 1,000 feet to unleash their missiles on the Nazi raiders and had fired oil stores and warehouses near by, while other British planes dropped bombs on Rotterdam and the Ruhr. [Page 9, Column 1.]

The sharp British blow at the two German raiders coincided with a Berlin claim that 718,000 tons of British and Allied shipping had been sunk during March by German surface craft, U-boats, mines and airplanes. A German auxiliary cruiser operating "overseas" was said to have sunk the British auxiliary cruiser Voltaire of 13,255 tons. Moreover, Berlin said, U-boats in two days had sunk eighteen ships, totaling 106,000 tons, in a British convoy. [Page 13, Column 1.]

President Roosevelt's hint that he might soon lift combat-zone restrictions on the Red Sea to permit passage of American ships with war supplies for Britain aroused considerable interest in Washington. Senator George, chairman of the Senate Foreign Relations Committee, was said to feel that such action would necessitate Congressional amendment of the Neutrality Act; other members of Congress were believed to hold the President already had power to do this through provisions of the Lease-Lend Law. [Page 21, Column 1.]

Uruguay formally seized two Italian and two Danish ships in her harbors and placed the crews, comprising 119 men, under the direction of the Italian and Danish consuls, respectively. Many of the Danish seamen were reported to have expressed pleasure over the seizures and to have exhibited pro-British emblems. [Page 19, Column 1.]

COAL TIE-UP ENDED IN 65% OF THE MINES

Southern Operators Hold Out but Contract for Rest Will Be Signed Tomorrow

Yielding to pressure from the Federal Government, representatives of 65 per cent of the nation's soft-coal producers agreed yesterday to sign a new contract with the United Mine Workers tomorrow. At least 300,000 miners are expected to return to work Tuesday or Wednesday, ending a week's stoppage that threatened to cut off vital fuel supplies for defense industries.

Dr. John R. Steelman, director of the United States Conciliation Service, who succeeded in breaking the four-week deadlock between the C. I. O. union and the operators, predicted that virtually all the mines would be open within a week. Other government officials said they believed the settlement in the soft-coal fields would provide a key to peaceful adjustment of employer-union differences in steel and anthracite, thus removing two additional threats of delay in the defense program and insuring uninterrupted work for 1,000,000 men.

Thirteen associations of Southern bituminous operators were the sole holdouts against the tentative accord effected by Dr. Steelman, and there were indications that their ranks were beginning to crumble. Union officials said scattered companies in the Southern States had indicated their intention of signing with the John L. Lewis organization, whether or not their associations went along. The union relied on the pressure of competition to bring the others into line in a few days.

Under the terms of the proposed contract the United Mine Workers will win its full demand for a basic wage of $7 a day. This represents an increase of $1 over the rate previously in effect in the North and $1.40 over the Southern rate. The union's insistence on abolition of

Continued on Page Thirty-three

KNUDSEN ASSAILS RADICALS IN LABOR

Charges They Hamper Output for Defense—Cooperation by All Vital, He Warns

Text of Mr. Knudsen's address appears on Page 40.

Asserting that the most serious thing about the strike in the Allis-Chalmers plant in Milwaukee was not the time lost in the production of defense materials but the fact that it showed that "radical" labor leaders could tell the State and Federal Governments "where to get off," William S. Knudsen last night proposed a program for dealing with labor difficulties that he said would eliminate 90 per cent of the strikes.

The director-general of the Office of Production Management, who spoke at the Army Day dinner of the Military Order of the World War at the Hotel Waldorf-Astoria, said that the labor situation during the last month had grown worse and warned that the epidemic of strikes must be stopped or the effort for defense and aid to Great Britain, Greece and Yugoslavia would fail.

Interrupted by applause when he started to discuss the labor situation, Mr. Knudsen declared that time was the all-important element in America's defense program and declared that if the nation could put on a "little steam" in production during the eighty-nine days remaining before the Fourth of July "we might save a lot of blood later on."

"I do not believe that legislation against strikes is necessary or enforceable," Mr. Knudsen said, "but I do believe that during the emergency period a definite procedure should be followed in order that strikes may be held to a minimum.

"For instance, I believe that strike votes should be taken under the supervision of the Labor Department. I believe a certain mini-

Continued on Page Forty

TREATY NOW VALID

Moscow Discloses That Pledge of Friendship Was Made Yesterday

PEACE IS TERMED AIM

Strictest Neutrality Is Provided—Accord Is Hailed in London

By The Associated Press.

MOSCOW, Sunday, April 6—Soviet Russia and Yugoslavia have signed a treaty of friendship and non-aggression after several days of negotiation, Tass, Soviet official news agency, announced early today.

The agency said the pact had been signed yesterday by the Russian Premier and Foreign Commissar, Vyacheslaff M. Molotoff, and Milan Gavrilovitch, former Yugoslav Cabinet Minister and Yugoslavia's representative in Moscow.

The treaty declared that Russia and Yugoslavia were "inspired by the friendship existing between the countries and convinced that the preservation of peace forms their common interest" and hence had decided to conclude the pact.

The treaty was for five years.

Its first article provided neither country would attack the other and that each would respect the sovereign rights and territorial integrity of the other.

It provided that, in case of aggression against one of the countries by a third power, the other would observe a policy of friendly relations with the country attacked.

TEXT OF THE TREATY

MOSCOW, Sunday, April 6 (UP)—Tass News Agency gave out today the text of the treaty between the Soviets and Yugoslavia, as follows:

A treaty on friendship and non-aggression between the Union of Soviet Socialist Republics and the Kingdom of Yugoslavia.

The Presidium of the Supreme Soviet U. S. S. R. and His Majesty the King of Yugoslavia, inspired by friendship existing between the two countries and convinced that preservation of peace forms their common interest, decided to conclude a treaty on friendship and non-aggression and appointed for this purpose their representatives:

Presidium of the Supreme Soviet U. S. S. R.—Vyacheslaff M. Molotoff, chairman of the Council of Peoples Commissars and Peoples Commissar of Foreign Affairs; His Majesty the King of Yugoslavia — Milan Gavrilovitch, Envoy Extraordinary and Minister Plenipotentiary of Yugoslavia, Boshin Simich and Colonel Dragutin Savich, which representatives, after exchanging their credentials found in proper form and due order, agreed on the following:

ARTICLE I

The two contracting parties mutually undertake to desist from

Continued on Page Twenty-five

YUGOSLAVIA FIGHTS

Belgrade Has Air Raid as Armies Resist, Berne Hears

DRIVE FROM BULGARIA

Greeks Announce Nazi Attack—Stukas Clear Path, Germans Say

By RAY BROCK

Wireless to THE NEW YORK TIMES.

BELGRADE, Yugoslavia, Sunday, April 6—At 3:25 o'clock this morning the air-raid sirens in Belgrade sounded an alarm. For the Yugoslavs it was the first indication that the nation was at war.

An hour later, at 4:32, two Yugoslav fighter planes appeared over the city, flying in an easterly direction. They came from the Zemun airdrome. Two more fighter planes appeared a short time later.

[At this point wireless connections with Belgrade were cut.]

Greeks Announce Attack

The Greek High Command announced in a communiqué broadcast from Athens that since 5:15 A. M., Athens time, the German troops had been attacking Greek troops on the Bulgarian border, the Columbia Broadcasting System announced this morning. No further details were in the communiqué as it was received here.

The German Propaganda Ministry announced in a broadcast from Berlin, according to CBS, that swarms of German planes, including Stuka dive bombers, were "pouncing like hornets" on Greek and Yugoslav airdromes and railways in an effort to cripple the resistance to the invading German armies. The Nazi Propaganda Ministry also asserted that the planes were clearing a path for tanks and infantry, and that parachute troops were landing at strategic points within the Greek-Yugoslav defenses. There was no confirmation of these claims, however.

Belgrade Has Second Alarm

By Telephone to THE NEW YORK TIMES.

BERNE, Switzerland, Sunday, April 6—The Belgrade correspondent of THE NEW YORK TIMES reported at 5:30 o'clock this morning that naturally he had heard of the situation, but that "you wouldn't know the difference." Aside from two air-raid alarms in the capital early this morning, no incident had yet occurred. Reports as to the exact location of the fighting were very scant.

On the Greek frontier the invasion doubtlessly came from Bulgaria through the Struma Valley with a secondary attack down the Vardar Valley. This latter attack, however, would entail driving across the southeastern border of Yugoslavia—the Third Army region based on Skoplje under General Ilija Brasitch.

For some time before the Yugoslav crisis began to take on even faintly menacing tones, the Yugoslav High Command had been re-

Continued on Page Twenty-four

New Army Marches in Rain Here; Nation Joins in Military Tribute

By HANSON W. BALDWIN

The new Army of the United States paraded down the Fifth Avenues of many cities yesterday as the nation opened an unprecedented week-end celebration of Army Day.

Veterans of past wars marched with youngsters who may become veterans of a future war, as the muffled beats of drumheads dampened by the rain epitomized the somber attitude with which thousands of spectators in many cities viewed their marching men. Not since 1917 and another war has the nation so taken the Army—now truly a national army—to itself with quiet, restrained pride.

For the music of the bands was but a faint echo in people's minds of the growing thunder of Europe's guns, and the serious attitude of the onlookers was matched in New York, Washington and other Eastern cities by the weather. The skies were a sullen gray and the peaks of New York's skyscrapers were veiled in mist as the Army marched and drumheads burst and slickers poured off torrents of the rain.

The New York parade along upper Fifth Avenue, which had been expected to be the greatest Army Day event in the city's history, lost considerably in volume but gained in solemnity because of the weather. Not many more than half of the expected 30,000 marchers participated, and the sparse, umbrellaed crowd that watched could not have numbered at its peak more than 30,000 to 40,000. The crowd dwindled at times during the two-hour parade to less than half that number. The weather, too, turned the march-past into a real test of soldiering, particularly for 4,500 men of the Forty-fourth Division from Fort Dix, N. J., who had negotiated seventy-eight miles of roads slick with rain in motor convoys to participate in the parade.

Mayor La Guardia, huddled be-

Continued on Page Forty-two

Hitler's Order of the Day

Adolf Hitler's declaration that Germany was at war with Yugoslavia was read over the Berlin radio early today by Propaganda Minister Joseph Goebbels. As heard by the National Broadcasting Company's station in New York and translated from the German, it read:

In the name of the Fuehrer, Adolf Hitler, I am reading the following order of the day to the German Army of the East:

Berlin, April 6, 1941.

Soldiers of the Southeast Front:

Since early this morning the German people are at war with the Belgrade government of intrigue. We shall only lay down arms when this band of ruffians has been definitely and most emphatically eliminated, and the last Briton has left this part of the European Continent, and that these misled people realize that they must thank Britain for this situation, they must thank England, the greatest warmonger of all time.

The German people can enter into this new struggle with the inner satisfaction that its leaders have done everything to bring about a peaceful settlement.

We pray to God that He may lead our soldiers on the path and bless them as hitherto.

In accordance with the policy of letting others fight for her, as she did in the case of Poland, Britain again tried to involve Germany in the struggle in which Britain hoped that she would finish off the German people once and for all, to win the war, and if possible to destroy the entire German Army.

In a few weeks long ago the German soldiers on the Eastern Front, Poland, swept aside this instrument of British policy. On April 9, 1940, Britain again attempted to reach its goal by a thrust on the German north flank, the thrust at Norway.

In an unforgettable struggle the German soldiers in Norway eliminated the British within a period of a few weeks.

What the world did not deem possible the German people have achieved. Again, only a few weeks later, Churchill thought the moment right to make a renewed thrust through the British Allies, France and Belgium, into the German region of the Ruhr. The victorious hour of our soldiers on the West Front began.

It is already war history how the German Armies defeated the legions of capitalism and plutocracy. After forty-five days this campaign in the West was equally and emphatically terminated.

Then Churchill concentrated the strength of his Empire

Continued on Page Twenty-six

BRITISH HALT DRIVE IN LIBYA, GET ADOWA

Axis Checked East of Bengazi—South Africans Within 80 Miles of Addis Ababa

Wireless to THE NEW YORK TIMES.

CAIRO, Egypt, April 5—The British announced today that their forces in Libya had halted the advance of German and Italian armored units somewhere east of Bengazi. The situation here after the recapture of that port by the Axis was said to be "well in hand."

At the same time the swift progress of the British Imperial forces in East Africa resulted in the capture of Adowa [and of near-by Adigrat, according to The Associated Press] while South African troops in Ethiopia crossed the Awash River and struck to within eighty miles of Addis Ababa.

[Massawa, the Red Sea port toward which the British armies of East Africa are racing, was reported to have defied a British demand for surrender, according to an Associated Press dispatch from Khartum.]

South African Advance

After the British in the last two days took the two most easily defendable areas in East Africa, Italian resistance appeared to be crumbling fast. The South African troops, who have marched all the way from Italian Somaliland now are moving westward along the Jibuti railway. After a brisk but brief battle at the crossing of the Awash, this column is pushing through the African hill country toward the higher rolling grassland plateau around Addis Ababa.

It is said the South Africans averaged a twenty-five-mile advance every day in the last two months.

North of the capital, combined British and Indian forces are pursuing the fleeing Italians toward Dessye through difficult mountainous terrain. Between Asmara and Adowa they advanced with only slight skirmishing at many points that might have become other Cherens had Italian morale been good.

The occupation of Adowa again frees the battle site where in 1896 Ethiopia's Emperor Menelik routed the Italians, killing 6,000 and capturing 4,000, thus preserving his nation's independence until 1935. The town itself has a population of 6,000.

Despite the lightness of the fighting in this area, advancing British forces surprised and captured a battalion of Italian infantry. Italians are running southward, apparently almost wholly disorganized, throwing away their arms and surrendering on the slightest excuse.

Continued on Page Seven

NAZI UNITS CROWD YUGOSLAV BORDERS

Some Are Reported in Albania, Many in Southern Hungary—German Plane Downed

By C. L. SULZBERGER

By Telephone to THE NEW YORK TIMES.

BELGRADE, Yugoslavia, April 5—The German military encirclement of Yugoslavia was nearing completion tonight as eight new divisions reportedly jammed the Hungarian roads, a powerful armored unit concentrated at Bela Crkva, on the Rumanian frontier one and a half hours' drive from Belgrade, and the first Nazi troops entered Albania.

British information sources reported from Bucharest and Budapest that the invasion of Southeastern Yugoslavia by the German Army of the Struma was ready to begin at any moment.

It is only worth noting that most of the more pessimistic predictions emanate from German-controlled countries, such as Hungary, Rumania and Bulgaria, or from the Croat capital of Zagreb, which is the center of the small but active German-inspired Fascist movement.

The facts of the situation are clear. Once more the normal peasant life of Hungary has been thrown into turmoil by the huge disruption caused by the passage of German Armies, and eight separate divisions were said to have been sighted. The motorized units on three points of the Hungarian southern frontier—Mohacs, Szeged and Nagy Kanizsa—were increased, as were the concentration in the Rumanian Banat.

An absolutely reliable source said German soldiers were known to have arrived in Albania—the debarkation point coming as somewhat of a surprise and indicating the probability that airplane transport was employed. Four Tyrolean mountain divisions have entered Italy in the last four days.

The government ordered the closing of all frontiers this morning. Outerbridge Horsey, secretary of the United States Legation in Budapest, who is coming here by train for emergency work, was stopped at the Hungarian frontier and the legation here is trying to facilitate his transport now by automobile.

All Danube traffic on the Yugoslav stretch of the river has now been halted. A German Messerschmitt plane was shot down yesterday while cruising over Maribor and it crashed at Ptuj.

Circulation through the country save with special military permit has been halted. All cars are being stopped by the police and are being requisitioned unless they have special passes. A new War Press Bureau has been established. At the same time Yugoslav technical con-

Continued on Page Twenty-five

NAZI TROOPS MARCH

Goebbels Reads Order to Germans to Rid Europe of All Britons

QUICK BLOW PLEDGED

Greece Told She Invited It—U. S. Is Said to Share Blame

By DANIEL T. BRIGHAM

By Telephone to THE NEW YORK TIMES.

BERNE, Switzerland, Sunday, April 6—At 5 o'clock this morning German forces attacked Yugoslavia and Greece in the long-awaited culmination of the Balkan war of nerves.

The news broke on the world with startling suddenness when a German radio station announcer with a triumphant blast this morning introduced Dr. Joseph Goebbels, Minister of Propaganda, who then read Reichsfuehrer Hitler's order of the day to "my forces in Southeast Europe."

"Since dawn this morning," said Dr. Goebbels, "the German Reich has been at war with Yugoslavia and Greece."

It was indicated that the friendship pact signed between Yugoslavia and Russia yesterday was one of the factors of which Germany complained. This was another version of the Nazi charges of "aggressive encirclement of Germany," which have been used since Herr Hitler's advent to power.

Yugoslav Arming Held Cause

Another source of grievance, it would seem, was Belgrade's mobilization, a point that Herr Hitler mentioned in his order of the day as one of the chief reasons for the attack.

Immediately after Dr. Goebbels's broadcast, telephone communications to the eastward from this city—and south to Rome—were cut off.

[United States and British encouragement to the Yugoslavs in their resistance to German demands was also cited as grounds for Germany's attack, according to The Associated Press. Alleged American offers of material aid were also quoted.]

The German Army was told it would not lay down its arms until the "ruffians" and "plotters" in Belgrade had been deposed and the last Briton driven out of this territory.

Friendship for Greeks

German soldiers have been fighting in Greece since dawn today, the proclamation stated. It was indicated that the battle in Greece was not directed against the population but only against the "world enemy," Great Britain, who had dispatched troops there for an attack against the interests of the Reich.

Germany, Herr Hitler was quoted as saying, does not consider herself at war with Greece and will not molest any Greek who does not take up arms against the German Army, but any who lends his support to the British will be crushed.

"Soldiers of the Southeast Front," the Reichfuehrer proclaimed, "your hour has now come."

He then told these troops that they must emulate their comrades in Poland, Scandinavia, the Lowlands and France. He added that the general mobilization in Yugoslav'a was considered by the Reich as final proof that Britain had mixed into the internal affairs of Yugoslavia and would lead that country into hostile acts against Germany.

Yugoslav Provocation Charged

BERLIN, Sunday, April 6 (AP)—The German radio, in broadcasting Reichsfuehrer Hitler's order to the German Army, quoted him as saying Germany was unable longer to endure the Yugoslav attitude. The Reich was said to be reacting to the mistreatment, "attacks and murdering" of Germans in the Serb Kingdom.

The order said the greatest patience had been exercised by Germany respecting Yugoslavia and Greece, but that now the moment for action had arrived.

It was said that Herr Hitler had frequently called attention to the dangers in the Southeast.

Now, it was said, Germany was

Continued on Page Twenty-six

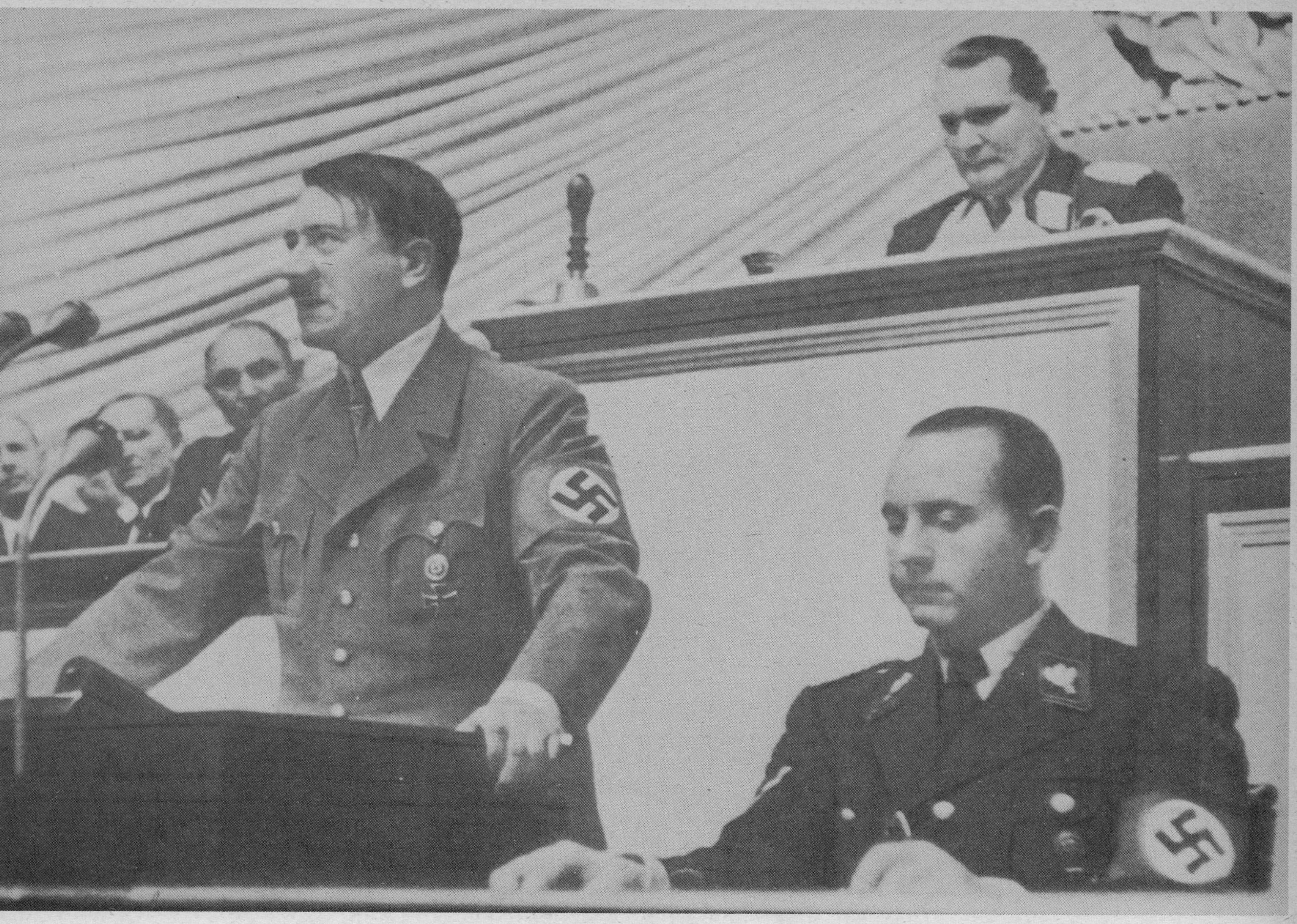

Hitler, during an impassioned speech in the Reichstag, in which he denounced Britain's anti-German policy.

"All the News That's Fit to Print."

The New York Times.

LATE CITY EDITION
Mostly cloudy and mild today. Tomorrow scattered showers and mild.
Temperatures Yesterday—Max., 58; Min., 37

VOL. XC...No. 30,396. Entered as Second-Class Matter, Postoffice, New York, N. Y. NEW YORK, MONDAY, APRIL 14, 1941. THREE CENTS NEW YORK CITY and Vicinity

RUSSIA AND JAPAN SIGN A NEUTRALITY TREATY; GERMANS CAPTURE BARDIA, PUSH INTO EGYPT; YUGOSLAVS COUNTERATTACK, GREEKS HOLD FIRM

WAR CASTS GLOOM OVER EASTER'S JOY IN MOST OF WORLD

Shocks of Conflict Mingle With Prayers for Peace in Much of Christendom

GREAT TURNOUT IN NATION

Churches and Fashion Parades Attract Throngs—Roosevelt at Service in Capital

While the civilized world alternately reeled under new shocks and grasped at glimmerings of hope on Easter yesterday—as black an Easter as mankind has known in modern times—all Christendom soberly celebrated the hallowed day of the resurrection of Jesus Christ.

It was Easter in New York, where thousands arose at dawn to worship at the cross and where 300,000 persons—the largest crowd in at least twenty years—overflowed from the broad sidewalks of Fifth Avenue to form a brilliant, moving carpet of fashion that could not be duplicated in any part of the world today.

It was Easter for desperately fighting British expeditionary forces, who hurled back panzer units in the shadow of Mount Olympus. It also was Easter in defeated France, where Marshal Henri Philippe Pétain and his people had foremost in their thoughts the hundreds of thousands of prisoners still held by the Nazis.

Perhaps the most sorrowful of all Easter notes came from the Vatican City, where Pope Pius XII, weighed down by emotion, broadcast his Easter message to the world. To the hushed crowds that gathered at the Vatican the Pope could bring no hope of any early attainment of a "just peace." Apparently fearful that poison gas may be brought into the conflict, he humbly begged that the belligerent nations refrain from using "still more homicidal instruments," and he pleaded for kindness for the prisoners of war and the dazed citizens of occupied countries.

No Peace in the Holy Land

In Jerusalem, profoundly impressive ceremonies took place on the ground made sacred by the tradition of Christ's resurrection nineteen centuries ago. "Christ is risen—He is risen, indeed!" the faithful told one another—and these words were echoed throughout Christendom. But there was no peace in the Holy Land, either, for everywhere there were khaki-clad British soldiers—constant reminders that even the land of the Prince of Peace is under threat today.

In Dublin, where twenty-five years ago Easter week saw the outbreak of the bloody Irish rebellion, Prime Minister Eamon De Valera somberly watched marching troops and warned his people that they must stand ever ready to resist attack.

In the capital of the United States President Roosevelt went to Easter services and heard his minister deliver a prayer that "peace with righteousness and justice may be established for the sake of all mankind." As the President listened with bowed head, the minister asked that the United States be led into doing "whatever is right" to re-establish righteousness in the world.

Vice President Wallace at Arlington Cemetery placed a cross of lilies on the Tomb of the Unknown Soldier—the Unknown Soldier of the first World War.

Cars Shunted from 5th Ave.

Yet, while elsewhere in the world husbands and fathers were herded into concentration camps, and wives, mothers and children knew the pinch of hunger, in America the people were not resigned to gloom. Throughout the breadth of the land the leaders and the plain citizens, the rich and the poor, momentarily forgetting the headlines, put on their finery in traditional American custom and paraded on the main streets of their cities and towns.

New York's Easter parade was spectacular. Shortly after noon, police were forced to rope off motor traffic between Fiftieth and Fifty-third Streets. Immediately, the huge crowds bubbled from the sidewalks and flowed into the street. Rich raiment of every hue and fa-

Continued on Page Twelve

300,000 Paraders Jam Fifth Ave.; Brilliant Pageant Ties Up Traffic

Mild Day Turns Street Into Huge Showcase of Styles—Cars Barred in One Area as Throngs Overflow Sidewalks

By KATHLEEN McLAUGHLIN

For New York, it was an epic Easter. Almost alone among the proudest boulevards of the world's greatest cities, Fifth Avenue marked as usual yesterday the surge and flow of multitudes celebrating the rebirth symbolized by the feast of the Resurrection.

Circumstances that produced this pageant were characteristic of 1941. Surface serenity was there, the deeply spiritual atmosphere, the seasonal blaze of color. But it had also disturbing undertones—implicit in the thin trickle of khaki and naval uniforms through the crowds; the frequent, crisp British phrases of pink-cheeked children; the spatter of French and less familiar foreign tongues; the officers' insignia, epaulets, and peaked caps, and the spread wings of the American eagle, each now a fashion motif.

Combined with the impetus of the war crisis, to which clergymen pointed for explanation of the densely packed pews in every midtown place of worship, was the moderate temperature, which, aided by a somewhat grudging sun, lured forth the teeming throngs to saunter much more leisurely than of recent years, when a brisk Easter promenade was not the exception but the rule. Fur coats and mittens, for years a badge of paraders, for once could be shed, and Spring suits stepped forth smartly, untroubled by a persistent breeze.

No such Easter morning jam has been experienced on the thoroughfare in the last twenty-two years, on the word of Deputy Inspector Valentine W. Corell, in charge of the special detachment of 225 police detailed to the upper Fifth Avenue sector. Inspector Corell took up his work as a rookie on guard at St. Patrick's Cathedral just twenty-seven years ago on Easter Sunday, and has not missed a survey of the annual traffic since.

At its peak, shortly after the noon hour, he estimated that there were 300,000 persons inching along the sidewalks and curbstones between Forty-sixth and Sixtieth Streets. This outpouring, especially from the pontifical high mass at St.

Continued on Page Thirteen

POPE PIUS ASKS BAN ON WORSE WEAPONS

Broadcast Believed to Have Referred to Gas—Calls for Imitation of Martyrs

The text of the Pope's Easter message appears on Page 3

By CAMILLE M. CIANFARRA

By Telephone to THE NEW YORK TIMES

ROME, April 13—In an Easter message broadcast to the Catholic world from his private library in the Vatican the Pope today appealed to all belligerents to abstain from using "still more homicidal instruments."

Although no one knows what type of arms he had in mind, the Pope made clear that the appeal sprang from his desire to alleviate the sufferings of the civilian population, which, he said, are often exposed to greater and more widespread perils of war than soldiers in the line of battle.

Vatican circles suggest that the Pope might have been referring to the use of poison gas. Except for this, nearly every other weapon that was used in the World War has already been tried. The Pope, they said, could not have meant large-scale bombings or mechanized warfare because both have been outstanding features of this war since its beginning. In support of this interpretation they pointed to the phrasing of the appeal which came soon after expressions of grave concern for the fate of noncombatants.

Asks Regard for Civilians

"May all the belligerents," said the Pope, "who also have human hearts molded by mothers' love, show the same feeling of charity for the sufferings of civilian populations, for defenseless women and children, for the sick and the aged, all of whom are often exposed to greater and more widespread perils of war than those faced by soldiers of the front!

"We beseech the belligerent powers to abstain until the very end from the use of still more homicidal instruments of warfare; for the introduction of such weapons inevitably results in their retaliatory use, often with greater violence and cruelty by the enemy.

"If already we must lament the fact that the limits of legitimate warfare have been repeatedly exceeded, would not a more widespread use of increasingly barbarous offensive weapons soon transform the war into an unspeakable horror?"

That the Pope felt it necessary to make this appeal was regarded as highly significant in Catholic quarters, since it is an established fact that the Vatican, because of its manifold sources, is always extremely well informed.

In the words that followed the Pope thanked the Catholics of the entire world for the fervent response to his invitation to prayer

Continued on Page Three

ALARMED CONGRESS TO RUSH SHIP BILL

No Opposition to Purchase of Immobilized Foreign Craft Is Apparent as Recess Ends

By JAMES B. RESTON

Special to THE NEW YORK TIMES.

WASHINGTON, April 13—Alarmed by Germany's success in Africa and the Balkans and apprehensive about the implications of the new Russo-Japanese nonaggression pact, members of Congress ended a ten day Easter recess tonight with predictions that a new effort will be made to rush all pending national defense legislation through both houses.

After a hurried roll-call tomorrow, when, despite the general apprehension about the war, the main event in the capital will still be the opening baseball game between the Washington Senators and the New York Yankees, both houses will get down to work Tuesday with special investigations of the national defense effort.

On Thursday President Roosevelt's request for authorization to purchase foreign ships immobilized in American ports will be studied in committee. Administration leaders expect this to be hurried to the floor of the House and probably passed early next week. There is a possibility that it will get to the floor of the House on Friday.

No Opposition in Sight

Even opposition Representatives showed no inclination to oppose the President's desire to supplement the United States merchant fleet with the foreign-owned vessels now in American ports. It is recognized in Republican quarters that unless new tonnage is added to the United States merchant fleet the Administration will not be able to import the 19,000,000 tons of raw materials needed for the 1941 national defense program. They also realize that by adding foreign-owned ships to the United States merchant marine the Administration is likely to delay the requisition of privately owned American ships.

Allied reverses in Libya and the Balkans have at the same time evidently induced members on all sides of the House to do everything possible to help the Administration increase production. There are still deep cleavages about what should be done with the war material once it 's produced but very little opposition to producing it as rapidly as possible.

Despite the improvement in both production and labor relations recently, some members of both houses are still dissatisfied with the defense program. The House Military Affairs Committee, which has been investigating this situation for weeks, will reopen its inquiry Tuesday, when either Donald Nelson, purchasing director for the Office of Production Management, or J. B. Matthews, chief investigator of the

Continued on Page Fourteen

SERBS SLOW NAZIS

Yugoslavs in Offensive at Five Points Report Gaining Territory

LONDON IS HEARTENED

More Germans Said to Be Needed to Avoid War of Position

By DANIEL T. BRIGHAM

By Telephone to THE NEW YORK TIMES.

BERNE, Switzerland, April 13—While little of a concrete nature developed in the Yugoslav situation during the last twenty-four hours, the Yugoslavs' resistance is stiffening and at several points they have taken the offensive.

Their tardiness in reacting to the undeclared war that commenced shortly after 5 o'clock in the morning one week ago has been largely due to the incompleteness of their preparations.

In the Morava Valley between Nish and Kragujevac, Yugoslav forces, supported by their own planes and the British air force, are successfully harassing German columns that have advanced so far that their lines are in danger of being cut. In this sector a medium Yugoslav force drove the Germans back from Kragujevac, which the Germans said they captured yesterday. About twenty miles farther south at Prokuplje the enemy was surrounded and many prisoners captured when the town fell.

Big Hungarian Losses Seen

Fighting rear guard actions against the Hungarian forces, the Yugoslavs are taking a heavy toll for every foot of ground the Hungarians are taking. Yugoslav losses in this area are reported to be very small in men and matériel, whereas the toll taken by repeated aerial bombardment of the Hungarian lines of communication is known from reconnaissance to be heavy.

As seen from here the German forces, after capitalizing on the fear value of their tremendous motorized columns for one whole week, are now forced to permit the Yugoslavs to open the second phase of the war. This phase, which may last another week, will consist mainly of guerrilla warfare, with German lines being menaced everywhere.

At the end of this second phase, unless Germany pours in much more man power and matériel than she appears to be prepared to do now, the German troops will be obliged to accept engagement on a fixed front. A war of position in the mountainous Drina region would be very costly for the attackers. Even if they succeed in forcing the issue the results cannot be considered conclusive. It is one thing to conquer the komitajis' territory; it is another to conquer the komitaji.

LONDON, April 13 (UP)—An authoritative British statement said the Yugoslavs, fighting in do-or-die units, had hurled the Germans back and recovered lost territory in five

Continued on Page Four

NILE ARMY RETIRES

Holds Fast in Tobruk, but Axis Forces Go Around Port

CLASH NEAR SOLUM

Reinforcements Rushed by the British—Nazi Losses Put High

Wireless to THE NEW YORK TIMES.

CAIRO, Egypt, April 13—Axis mechanized columns swept past British forces in the Tobruk area yesterday and have now occupied Bardia, seventy miles farther along the coast, it was announced here today. Following this news came reports that British reinforcements had been going steadily to the western desert for the last few days and that the situation in that respect was considerably better than last week.

It was said here that the British forces in the Tobruk area are not surrounded as Axis announcements claim and that it is still possible for British mechanized columns to establish contact across the desert. It is believed the German mechanized units are getting fuel supplies by air, but only in relatively small quantities.

Well-informed quarters here said the fighting was proceeding in the neighborhood of the Egyptian frontier port of Solum, but it was not established whether German forces had yet crossed the Egyptian border. In skirmishes at El Adem and El Gazala the Germans were reported repulsed.

[In Berlin it was assumed that the Axis forces were continuing their advance into Egypt. In Rome it was predicted that the swift offensive would push as far as possible toward Alexandria.]

Evacuation Not Explained

The British forces had previously evacuated Bardia, which is surrounded by Italian fortifications much like those at Tobruk. The reason for the evacuation was not revealed here. Although the German forward units are understood to be light, the movement of the present battle is so rapid it is difficult to ascertain the exact strength of the enemy.

The strength of the British garrison at Tobruk has not been revealed, but if it is large it would appear that the Germans are in considerable danger of having their communications cut.

The advancing Germans are said to have suffered fairly heavy casualties. According to information reaching here, all the British forces are still intact.

The patriot movement is reported to be growing rapidly in Ethiopia and the Italians in many cases are said to be asking protection from the natives. British forces are advancing northward from Addis Ababa, but the columns moving southward toward Gondar and

Continued on Page Two

The International Situation

MONDAY, APRIL 14, 1941

A new confusing element was added to the pattern of international affairs yesterday when Moscow announced the signing of a neutrality pact between Russia and Japan, guaranteeing each from attack in the rear should either be "the object of military activity on the part of one or several powers." The accord guaranteed as well the territorial integrity of Japanese-dominated Manchukuo and the Russian-dominated Mongolian People's Republic. [Page 1, Column 8; Map Page 8.]

Each of the major capitals interpreted the news of the treaty differently.

In Tokyo Premier Konoye said it would help "secure the peace of greater East Asia." [Page 10, Column 1.]

Washington officials declined to comment prior to official consultation, but it was generally believed that the pact had been signed by Moscow under German instigation. Though it will ostensibly free Japan's hands in the Far East, it was pointed out, it will also free Russia's hands for any eventuality in the Balkans or Near East, where Germany is advancing. [Page 1, Column 7.]

London emphasized that no mention of cessation of Russian aid to China had been included in the accord and responsible quarters held that the new treaty apparently nullified the Axis proviso of Japanese aid should Germany become involved in hostilities with Russia. [Page 18, Column 5.]

Berlin and Rome acclaimed the accord and termed it a direct menace to Anglo-American interests in the Pacific. [Page 8, Column 3.]

It became evident, meanwhile, that the German drive into Greece and Southern Yugoslavia was slowing, and in some sectors had stopped.

Scattered reports from Yugoslavia indicated that Yugoslav guerrilla tactics, and pressure in the Skoplje zone, had disrupted German supply lines and halted the drive down through Bitolj Pass against the Allied line in Greece. [Page 1, Column 4; Map, Page 4.]

Repeated German mechanized attacks against both flanks of the Allied line across Greece throughout the day were reported hurled back with losses to the attackers. The Royal Air Force and Allied aircraft were said to be doing heroic service in smashing and disrupting tenuous German supply lines. [Page 3, Column 1.]

The German Government announced the occupation of Belgrade by Reich forces one week after the opening of the invasion, bringing to thirteen the number of European capitals placed under Nazi domination since 1936. The capture of 12,000 Yugoslav troops, including twenty-two generals and 200 officers, in the Zagreb area was also reported. [Page 1, Column 6.]

The Axis armored divisions driving along the Mediterranean coast in Libya were said to have swept around a strong British garrison in Tobruk, to have taken undefended Bardia, seventy miles to the east, and to have reached Solum, eleven miles within Egypt, where, British circles in Cairo said, fierce fighting is in progress. Axis reports said the Tobruk garrison was "trapped." [Page 1, Column 5; Map, Page 2.]

Dispatches reaching Stockholm said forces from a British "torpedo boat" that had put into an unidentified port in Northern Norway had destroyed harbor works with the assistance of local anti-Nazi Norwegians. [Page 7, Column 3.]

Strong Royal Air Force night attacks on the Nazi-held bases of Brest and Lorient and on the airfield at Merignac were reported in London. German air activity over Britain was slight. [Page 7, Column 1.]

Pope Pius, in an Easter broadcast from the Vatican, appealed to the belligerents to refrain from the use of "still more deadly weapons." Observers familiar with the Vatican's wide sources of information feared that the Pope's message applied to an impending use of gas. [Page 1, Column 2.]

REICH NOW CLAIMS FALL OF BELGRADE

22 Yugoslav Generals and 100 Cannon Reported Taken in Fighting Near Zagreb

By C. BROOKS PETERS

By Telephone to THE NEW YORK TIMES.

BERLIN, April 13—German troops of the motorized group under the command of Col. Gen. Paul von Kleist began the occupation of Belgrade at 6:30 this morning, the High Command announced in a special communiqué.

There was not a single mention in today's communiqué of what, if any, military actions have been carried out by the German forces on the Greek front. The High Command reported merely that on the night of April 11 to 12 German bombers in an attack on the roads of Salamis sank an enemy vessel of 4,000 tons and hit four other "large" ships. Two storage tanks, one power plant and one mill in the harbor of Piraeus were "successfully" attacked, the German report continued, and one Hurricane was shot down.

On the same evening the German High Command declared other German bombers set fuel oil storage depots at the airport of Venezia on the island of Malta aflame.

Today, just one week after commencement of hostilities in the Balkans, the German armies operating in the Yugoslav Kingdom appeared from reports here to be rapidly completing the conquest of that country. Belgrade was captured early this morning by an attack from the south. Yesterday afternoon, however, the Germans declare, a small group of men under the command of Captain von Klingenberg, all from the "Reich" Division of the Elite Guards, forced their way across the Danube and into the city from the north and raised the German flag on the German Legation there.

In the process of cleaning up op-

Continued on Page Six

CAPITAL RESERVES JUDGMENT ON PACT

U. S. Relations With Soviet Are More Likely to Be Affected Now Than Those With Japan

By BERTRAM D. HULEN

Special to THE NEW YORK TIMES.

WASHINGTON, April 13—The announcement of the conclusion of the Soviet-Japanese pact today threw confusion into a situation that had already become black in consequence of the German military achievements in the Balkans last week, but some slight comfort was found in the fact that the pact did not go farther than it did.

Officials frankly declared that at first blush the agreement did not look pleasant. However, they did not regard it as a bombshell. They did interpret it as a diplomatic defeat for Moscow.

Undoubtedly, it was remarked, those who have been hoping that Russia might swing away from the Axis will be disappointed, but on its face the pact was considered important primarily as a political gesture and because of its psychological effects.

From the practical standpoint the most important feature was considered the Soviet recognition of Japan's suzerainty over Manchukuo. Not only is this the first time that such recognition has been accorded by other than an Axis power but the equivalent Japanese recognition of Russia's position in Outer Mongolia was interpreted as signifying that Moscow and Tokyo had agreed to partition North China for their own advantage.

From this standpoint, the pact was viewed as a blow to China. Whether it means that Japan will now feel free to move southward in the Pacific was considered far less certain.

The State Department received no official details or reports concerning the pact today and for that reason refrained from making any

Continued on Page Eight

ACCORD IN MOSCOW

Integrity of Manchukuo and Inner Mongolia Pledged by Both

PACT FOR FIVE YEARS

Matsuoka Rewarded on Second Visit—Stalin Sees Him Leave

Text of the Soviet-Japanese Pact and declaration, Page 8.

By The Associated Press.

MOSCOW, April 13—Soviet Russia and Japan, frequently opposed powers in the Far East, joined today in a neutrality pact.

In a four-point accord, each agreed to remain neutral throughout any period during which either of the signatories was the "object of military action on the part of one or several powers."

Each undertakes to respect the "territorial inviolability" of the other.

The pact, as it says, "guarantees peaceful and friendly relations" between the two powers.

The character of the pact was emphasized in an accompanying joint declaration pledging the Soviets to respect the territorial integrity of Japan's puppet State, Manchukuo, something to which the Soviet never before has agreed. Equally the subject of comment was Japan's parallel pledge to respect the status of the Moscow-dominated Outer Mongolian People's Republic.

Effective for Five Years

The pact is effective for five years and is renewable for an additional five-year term unless one side denounces it a year before expiration of the first period.

It is to be ratified as quickly as possible and the formal exchange of ratification documents is to take place in Tokyo.

The document was signed by Japan's touring Foreign Minister, Yosuke Matsuoka, and the Soviet Premier and Foreign Commissar, Vyacheslaff M. Molotoff, at the Kremlin at 2:30 P. M.

It was announced on the Moscow radio at 5 P. M., and Mr. Matsuoka, who had spent nearly a week in Moscow in secret negotiations, took the Trans-Siberian express for Tokyo fifty-five minutes later.

Joseph Stalin personally saw him off at the train, a high compliment to Mr. Matsuoka.

Mr. Matsuoka, for whom the pact was a signal triumph, arrived here March 23 for a one-day stay on his journey for Axis conferences in Berlin and Rome, where he saw Adolf Hitler and Benito Mussolini.

He saw Mr. Molotoff then in the presence of Mr. Stalin.

Conferences With Molotoff

Returning from Berlin and Rome last Monday, he saw Mr. Molotoff four more times, including one conference of three and a half hours, and another conference yesterday in which Mr. Stalin again engaged.

German Ambassador Count Friedrich Werner von der Schulenburg and Slovak Minister Franz Tiso left tonight for consultations with their governments in Berlin and Bratislava.

Slovakia is a part of the German-protected Czecho-Slovakia, of which Hungary also got a slice in Carpatho-Ukraine.

While Russia was putting the seals to her non aggression pact in the East, the official press gave prominent display to a Foreign Office communiqué reproving Hungary for invading a Slav nation, Yugoslavia.

"Considered especially significant" was the Foreign Office's reference to Hungary's own national minorities and the danger to Hungary should she become involved in trouble.

[Carpatho-Ukraine is largely inhabited by a people kindred to Russia's Ukrainians.]

The rebuke to Hungary was similar but more outspoken than the one administered to Bulgaria six weeks ago for permitting German troops to enter the country.

The papers also gave an extensive account of a broadcast by the Yugoslav Premier, General Dusan Simovitch, in which he was reported to

Continued on Page Eight

Danish Legation Backs Defiance Of Copenhagen by Minister Here

Special to THE NEW YORK TIMES.

WASHINGTON, April 13—Danish Minister Henrik de Kauffmann, although officially recalled by the German-controlled Copenhagen government, has the complete support of the staff of the legation in his defiance of the order, a spokesman at the legation said tonight.

All members of the legation and Danish consular officers throughout the United States will back Mr. de Kauffmann's agreement with the United States to permit this country to protect Greenland during the European war.

Einar Blechinberg, counselor of the legation, who was put in charge by the Danish Foreign Office in its message to Mr. de Kauffmann relieving him of his duties, supports the Minister's attitude completely, the spokesman said.

Mr. de Kauffmann, who is supported by the State Department, which will continue to recognise him as the Danish Minister, attempted today to see the Secretary of State but was unable to reach him. He expects to see Mr. Hull tomorrow.

The Minister said that he had prepared a report to submit to Mr. Hull. This report, he said, embodies the statements he gave to the press that the action of the Danish Foreign Office was taken under duress from the Nazis and that he has no intention of obeying the orders or of returning to Denmark.

"I came to this country to represent a free an democratic Denmark," Mr. de Kauffmann told reporters, "and I will continue to do so. I will not accept any orders emanating directly or indirectly from Germany."

The Danish Minister negotiated the agreement which allows this country to establish military bases in Greenland. He signed the agreement on behalf of King Christian X of Denmark, and before taking the step obtained the approval of the two royal governors of the island colony.

While both Berlin and Copenhagen have called the agreement illegal and contrary to international law, Mr. de Kauffmann and the United States recognize in it no deviation from the historic policy of

Continued on Page Fourteen

"All the News That's Fit to Print."

The New York Times.

LATE CITY EDITION
Fair and continued cool today and tomorrow.
Temperatures Yesterday—Max., 62; Min., 49

VOL. XC..No. 30,425. Entered as Second-Class Matter, Postoffice, New York, N. Y. NEW YORK, TUESDAY, MAY 13, 1941. THREE CENTS NEW YORK CITY and Vicinity

HESS, DESERTING HITLER, FLIES TO SCOTLAND; BERLIN REPORTED HIM MISSING AND INSANE; DARLAN MEETS HITLER; R. A. F. POUNDS PORTS

COAST SHIPYARDS SHUT BY PICKETS; RETURN REJECTED

Navy and Maritime Work Stops as Other Crafts Refuse to Pass Heavy Lines

POLICE STAY IN RESERVE

Union Leaders Declare Fight to Finish as Meeting Votes Against Lapsing Strike

By FOSTER HAILEY
Special to THE NEW YORK TIMES.

SAN FRANCISCO, May 12—A request from the Office of Production Management that striking machinists in eleven shipbuilding yards in the San Francisco Bay area return to work pending an attempt to settle their wage and hour demands in conference was unanimously rejected today by a mass meeting of those of the strikers affiliated with the American Federation of Labor.

Picket lines around the eleven plants, established by the 1,200 A. F. of L. machinists and the 700 who belong to the Congress of Industrial Organizations, brought a complete halt to operations as 15,000 to 18,000 other workers who are not on strike refused to pass through the machinists' picket lines.

The strike was called Friday midnight by Local 68 of the A. F. of L. and Lodge 1304 of the C. I. O. The latter is affiliated with the Steel Workers Organizing Committee, headed by Philip Murray, president of the C. I. O. The walkout is in protest against hourly wage and overtime provisions of a master contract for the whole coast signed April 22 in Seattle by representatives of labor, the OPM and the shipbuilders.

Reason for Refusal to Return

The request to go back to work pending a conference came from Joseph Keenan, A. F. of L. representative of the OPM. It was presented to a mass meeting of about 1,000 members of Local 68 by its business agents, E. F. Dillon and Harry Hook, who later said:

"Our members took the position, and passed a resolution to the effect, that inasmuch as we've never been able to get an agreement out of Bethlehem in the past twenty-two years, we don't feel any good purpose would be served by sending the men back to work before an agreement is reached now.

"We feel it would only prolong the controversy and probably result in a repetition of what we are going through now."

Although Bethlehem Shipbuilding, a division of Bethlehem Steel, is only one of the eleven plants involved in the strike, it is by far the largest, employing about 900 of the 1,200 A. F. of L. machinists who are on strike, and it is considered the bellwether of the group.

Out to Compel Settlement

"We intend to tell Mr. Keenan, if he telephones us from Chicago, the attitude of the strikers," Mr. Dillon said. "When he made the request yesterday he said he would call back today. (He had not called up to late tonight.)

"We would be glad to have a representative of the OPM on the ground here to go into a thorough analysis of the situation.

"As things stand now, the strike will continue in effect until we are able to make some agreement with Bethlehem and the rest."

No formal action was taken by the C. I. O. machinists, since the request was not directed to them, but pickets handed out leaflets signed by J. P. Smith, business agent of Lodge 1304, asserting that "hard-won conditions must be preserved and employers, under a smoke screen of national defense, are not going to destroy them." The C. I. O. was not represented in the negotiations for the master contract.

In a joint statement, Mr. Dillon and Mr. Hook said that the machinists, because of the "friendly attitude and fine spirit of the other metal trades organizations," intend to see to it "that all such metal trades men that respected our picket lines will be returned to their jobs without discrimination" and on a basis satisfactory to them.

Apprised of the strikers' position, Frank H. Fox, chairman of the Bay Area Shipbuilders Negotiating Committee and authorized spokesmen

Continued on Page Sixteen

'Peace' Pickets Routed At White House Gates

Special to THE NEW YORK TIMES.

WASHINGTON, May 12—One soldier and one Marine tonight broke up a line of eight pickets marching in front of the White House who represented the American Peace Mobilization. This organization has been charged with being a Communist Front group.

At the hour all Washington theatres were letting out, police emergency cars and motorcyclists roared through downtown Washington to the White House. The two assaulters were arrested and one picketeer was removed to Emergency Hospital where he was reported slightly injured. The picketing continued.

Tonight's fracas followed one at 3 A. M. when a larger group of soldiers and Marines attacked the pickets, tore up their placards and warned them they would be back if the picketing continued. In an earlier assault the policemen did not interfere. Tonight the assailants were seized and one was charged with simple assault. The police then closed and manned the White House gates for the night.

ROOSEVELT TO TALK TO NATION MAY 27

'Fireside Chat' Two Weeks From Today Is Substituted for Address Tomorrow

By FRANK L. KLUCKHOHN
Special to THE NEW YORK TIMES.

WASHINGTON, May 12—President Roosevelt will make a "fireside chat" to the nation May 27, but will not make his scheduled speech before the Pan American Union Wednesday night, it was announced at the White House today.

This change in plans was interpreted generally to mean that the President has in mind no important announcement on American foreign policy for two weeks and that, at least for this period, he does not contemplate any new type of aid for Britain.

The Executive seldom makes fireside chats except upon important matters, however, and his talk on the 27th is generally expected to present an outline of the current position of the United States as he sees it and the future steps that should be taken.

Mr. Roosevelt completed his seventh day in bed because of illness today, and his widely publicized speech was canceled to give him time to recover fully, according to official statements.

Stephen T. Early, White House Secretary, emphasized, however, that the President had never intended his talk before the Pan American Union to be of "world-shaking" importance.

Pressure on President

In informed circles it was understood that the Executive did not intend to be pushed into any important steps and that he considered the present time poor for any announcement of vital importance.

Speaking of the canceled Wednesday address, Mr. Early said:

"So, despite reports from abroad, there will be no world-shaking pronouncement from President Roosevelt Wednesday night, as this office has stated right along."

Three Cabinet officers, Secretaries Henry L. Stimson, Frank Knox and Claude Wickard, have urged use of the American Navy to protect shipment of war supplies to Great Britain, their speeches generally being interpreted as an appeal for escort of convoys by the American Navy. Other individuals or groups publicly have urged the Executive to go so far as ask for a declaration of war. Pressure has come from all sides on these controversial questions and others.

The decision to cancel Wednesday night's speech was revealed through White House announcement of a resolution adopted by the Board of Governors of the Pan American Union.

Diplomats Ask Postponement

"The Ambassadors, Ministers and chargés d'affaires of the republics of Latin America," the resolution said, "realizing that President Roosevelt has recently been indisposed and in view of the fact that the reception to be tendered him would involve strain upon him, take the liberty of suggesting that the reception be postponed until such time as President Roosevelt may

Continued on Page Eight

HAMBURG HIT HARD

Miles of Docks Fired in British Bombing a Second Night

BREMEN LIKE TARGET

U-Boat Yards and War Plants of Reich Bases Kept Under Attack

By DAVID ANDERSON
Special Cable to THE NEW YORK TIMES.

LONDON, Tuesday, May 13—Nine miles of docks along the River Elbe at Hamburg were laced with heavy British bombs and thousands of incendiaries over Sunday night when the Royal Air Force followed up its attack of the previous night with another vigorous raid on German war ports.

The Hamburg docks were "threaded and crossed with fire, continuing the destruction and disorganization of vital parts of this great seaport," the British Air Ministry reported.

Bremen, the Reich's second port in the size of its war activities, was attacked also with what R. A. F. officials moderately termed a "heavyweight of high-explosive and incendiary bombs."

Shipbuilding yards and especially the plants of the two ports where Germany has built most of her U-boat fleet were blasted.

Previous Havoc Extended

Explosives hammered down on industrial works in both cities, the Air Ministry stated, and vast fires were started to continue the havoc of previous attacks.

Last night "objectives" at the great German industrial center of Mannheim, also a frequent target for the British, were attacked by R. A. F. bombers, a brief official report early today said.

Sunday night attacks were made by the R. A. F. on a number of other targets in the Reich, including Emden again, and the docks of Rotterdam were also bombed.

Four aircraft of the Bomber Command were missing from all these operations, British officials said.

The Coastal Command carried out Sunday night attacks on docks at the Netherland port of Ijmuiden, and on the Nazi seaplane base on the island of Texel without loss.

The attacks seemed to mark a definite stepping-up of the R. A. F. offensive, as officials of the Bomber Command, in giving some detail of the operations, said the objective was to strike Hamburg again before that city could "recover from the impact of the attacks made Saturday night."

Weather Right for Bomb-Aimers

Fine weather and the brilliant moonlight enabled the British pilots to pick their spot with relative ease over "the vast expanse of docks which was the particular focus" of this raid, it was stated.

An R. A. F. flier's account of the Bremen attack said:

"It was not so cold as when we visited Bremen three nights before, but there was the same bright sky. All the way over there were patches of cloud which looked like stepping

Continued on Page Six

Russians See Advantage In R.A.F. Planes' Big Load

By The Canadian Press.

LONDON, May 12—Increased bomb loads carried by Royal Air Force bombers "partly offset" the German advantage of having air bases close to Britain, Red Star, organ of the Soviet Army, said in an article quoted today by the British Broadcasting Corporation.

The article commented on "the tremendous load of bombs that now can be carried by a single British machine."

In a review of war developments, the newspaper observed that "the hardest blows delivered by the German Air Force in recent weeks have been aimed at British ports and centers of shipbuilding" and also that "the experience of the last war proved that British and United States industry made up for sinkings by U-boats."

PAPEN SEES HITLER, RETURNS TO TURKEY

Envoy Is Expected to Reveal Nazi Plans for Near East—Soviet Move Studied

The following dispatch was received by direct voice broadcast through the Ankara wireless station last night. C. L. Sulzberger prefaced the broadcast in this way:

"The following direct broadcast from Ankara to THE NEW YORK TIMES, New York City, contains news dispatches for THE TIMES. These are exclusive property of the New York Times Company. Dispatches follow."

By C. L. SULZBERGER
Special Broadcast to THE NEW YORK TIMES.

ANKARA, Turkey, May 12—Franz von Papen, the German Ambassador to Ankara, came back to his post today aboard a large camouflaged Junkers troop transport plane, following a series of last-minute conferences with Reichsfuehrer Hitler at the latter's Obersalzburg retreat.

The Ambassador, who was accompanied by his wife and daughter, was met at the Ankara Airport by the diplomatic representatives of the countries that have signed the tripartite accord. He appeared in excellent spirits and conferred for several minutes with the Italian Ambassador.

Herr von Papen has been expected back almost daily for the better part of the last fortnight and the fact that he continually delayed his return and then at the last minute had a long personal conversation with Herr Hitler is regarded as significant.

Events are shaping up rapidly in the Middle East, and the only hand that now remains to be disclosed fully is that of Germany. Russia has abandoned her disinterest in this area by according full diplomatic recognition to the bellicose Rashid Ali Beg Gailani government of Iraq.

Britain, already engaged in extensive military operations in Iraq, has

Continued on Page Two

ADMIRAL HAS TALK

Berlin Says Ribbentrop Was Present—Place Is Not Disclosed

VICHY PRESS TENSE

U. S. Attitude Is Cause of Worry—Leahy May Protest Attacks

By The Associated Press.

BERLIN, Tuesday, May 13—Reichsfuehrer Hitler has received the French Vice Premier, Admiral François Darlan, in the presence of German Foreign Minister Joachim von Ribbentrop, it was officially announced early today.

The communiqué announcing the meeting did not say where or when it took place.

The announcement said:

"The Fuehrer, in the presence of the Reichsminister of Foreign Affairs, received the vice president of the French Ministerial Council, Admiral Darlan."

Hitler-Stalin Talk Forecast

VICHY, France, May 12 (AP)—Separate meetings of Reichsfuehrer Hitler with Premier Joseph Stalin and Premier Mussolini were considered in diplomatic circles here tonight as likely to result from the current political moves over Europe.

The object of the meetings, these circles said, probably would be complete economic if not military organization of the Axis-dominated Continent.

Observers listed the current shake-up of Spain's civil and military organization and Vice Premier Admiral François Darlan's negotiations with the Germans as indicators of forthcoming conferences of Herr Hitler and Mr. Stalin and Signor Mussolini.

U. S. Gives Press Concern

By G. H. ARCHAMBAULT
Wireless to THE NEW YORK TIMES.

VICHY, France, May 12—For the time being it is not possible to separate the two hemispheres in any discussion here of the world situation. That the situation is tense and is likely to remain so, at least until President Roosevelt has spoken, is admitted.

In every newspaper as well as in every conversation the United States and what it may or may not do is a recurrent topic.

There are some here who surmise that it may have been mentioned in Paris during the visit there of Vice Premier Admiral François Darlan, who is expected back in Vichy tomorrow to report to Marshal Henri Philippe Pétain, who himself returned this morning after a few days' rest in his Riviera estate.

A semi-official commentary declared today that the Marshal has expressed his satisfaction to the Admiral with the progress of his negotiations hitherto.

It is understood that another Admiral—William D. Leahy, the United States Ambassador—may also see Marshal Pétain in the near future for one of their periodical conversations on food supplies and cognate subjects.

To Stick to Collaboration

While there is complete official silence regarding the negotiations with Germany, as also regarding the United States, the Inter-France News Service, now situated in Vichy, which circulates editorials "for free reproduction by any newspaper," advanced the following arguments:

"Should war occur between the United States and Germany and should it be prolonged, the political reasons which led France to follow the road of collaboration would be reinforced by even more decisive practical reasons. For war between the United States and the Axis would immediately create a European solidarity that would be stronger than any sentimental factor.

"An American blockade, which would necessarily be extended to all our coasts, will develop the notion of a common interest among the peoples of old Europe, since from Brest to Koenigsberg and from Narvik [Norway] to Cadiz [Spain] we should be compelled to do without meat from Argentina and coffee from Brazil, to dispense with cotton from the United States and oil from Mexico. The French

Continued on Page Five

Nazis Allege 'Hallucinations'; Silent on Glasgow Arrival

Arrest of Hess's Aides Ordered Since Hitler Forbade Him to Fly—Letter He Left Said to Show Disordered Mind

By Telephone to THE NEW YORK TIMES.

BERLIN, May 12—Authoritative quarters in Berlin refused to comment late tonight on a British statement that Rudolf Hess, 47-year-old deputy leader of the National Socialist party and Reichsfuehrer Hitler's personal representative, had bailed out of a Messerschmitt plane near Glasgow, Scotland, and was in the hands of the British authorities. Earlier in the evening the Germans had officially reported Herr Hess to be missing.

The man who, on Sept. 1, 1939, was designated by Herr Hitler as his second choice, next to Reich Marshal Hermann Goering, in the line of succession for leadership of the German State, was last heard of in Augsburg, in Bavaria, on Saturday. He was reported to have taken an airplane there for an unknown destination in violation of Herr Hitler's orders prohibiting him from flying because of physical disability.

THE GERMAN STATEMENT

The news of the mysterious disappearance of Herr Hess was released, forty-eight hours after he had been reported missing, in the following communiqué:

Rudolf Hess has met with an accident.

Party Comrade Hess, who because of a disease that for a year has progressively worsened has been categorically forbidden by the Fuehrer to continue his flying activities, recently found means in violation of this command to come into possession of an airplane.

On Saturday, May 10, about 6 P. M., Party Comrade Hess took off from Augsburg for a flight from which until today he has not yet returned. A letter that he left behind unfortunately indicated, by its incoherence, symptoms of a mental derangement that permits the inference that Comrade Hess became the victim of hallucinations.

The Fuehrer immediately ordered the arrest of the adjutants of Party Comrade Hess, who alone knew of these flights and, knowing of their prohibition by the Fuehrer, did not prevent or immediately report them.

Under the circumstances, the National Socialist movement must regretfully assume that Comrade Hess has crashed or met with an accident somewhere on his flight.

Herr Hess last spoke in public in an official capacity on May 1 as the representative of Herr Hitler at the Labor Day demonstration of the party in Augsburg, where he addressed the congress of the Reich Labor Chamber.

Herr Hess, who also was a member of the German Cabinet as Minister Without Portfolio, was born in Alexandria, Egypt, on April 26, 1894. He became identified with the party in 1921, and in recognition of his services Herr Hitler appointed him as private secretary, a post that he held from 1925 until 1932, when he received more responsible positions in the party organization.

Despite his position as deputy

Continued on Page Four

The International Situation

TUESDAY, MAY 13, 1941

A laconic announcement from 10 Downing Street gave to an astounded world last night the news that Rudolf Hess, deputy leader of the Nazi party in Germany and the third most powerful figure in the Reich, had landed by parachute in Scotland and was in safe custody in a Glasgow hospital suffering from a broken ankle. The official statement gave no direct explanation for the dramatic development, but it was presumed that the man who was named at the outset of the war by Adolf Hitler as his second in succession had deliberately fled Germany.

Herr Hess flew to Scotland in a Messerschmitt 110, a plane incapable of carrying sufficient fuel for his return to Germany. The plane crashed Saturday night on the Duke of Hamilton's estate. The flier established his identity in the hospital, and the Foreign Office dispatched an attaché to interview him there. [All the foregoing, Page 1, Column 8.]

Berlin issued a communiqué earlier in the day stating that Herr Hess, apparently suffering from "hallucinations" induced by a long-standing ailment, had taken off by plane from Augsburg Saturday evening against the express orders of Herr Hitler and was "missing" and presumably had "met with an accident." It was announced that Herr Hess's adjutants had been ordered arrested. [Page 1, Column 6.]

Hundreds of German bombers flew over South England and the Midlands Sunday night, attacking airdromes and other objectives, and causing destruction over widespread areas. Nine Nazi planes were shot down. A Berlin statement that forty-five British airfields were attacked was contradicted by the British, who said the military damage was "not considerable." Few raiders were reported over Britain last night. [Page 6, Column 1.]

Over Sunday night the R. A. F. was sending wave after wave of bombers against German ports, particularly Hamburg and Bremen. Nine miles of docks and shipyards on the River Elbe were laced with fires from British incendiaries, and attacks were made on Emden, Rotterdam and Ijmuiden. Last night British planes again bombed Mannheim. [Page 1, Column 3.]

The return to Ankara of German Ambassador von Papen from an extended visit to Berlin gave rise to a belief that Germany would propose a far-reaching economic treaty to all but isolated Turkey. Ankara also looked for an early meeting between the Ambassador and the Iraqi Defense Minister, who has been visiting Ankara. [Page 1, Column 4.]

The situation in Iraq was described by the British as now "stabilized." R. A. F. planes harried remnants of Iraqi forces, and British mechanized forces completed the occupation of Rutbah, a vital point on the oil pipe line and site of an airplane base. [Page 2, Column 6.]

The British forces in Ethiopia tightened their pincer around Alagi, the last Italian stronghold on the Asmara-Dessye road. The Italian garrison at Gondar was said to be virtually isolated. In North Africa, the Admiralty announced, British warships bombarded Bengasi Saturday night, but Rome asserted the British vessels had been routed after having suffered direct hits. [Page 3, Column 4.]

Reichsfuehrer Hitler received Admiral Darlan, the French Vice Premier, in the presence of German Foreign Minister von Ribbentrop at an undisclosed place, it was announced in Berlin. The role that the United States might play in world events was believed in Vichy to loom large in any discussion of European affairs that might be going on. "Collaborationist" sources predicted a "European solidarity" in the event the United States engaged in war with Germany. [Page 1, Column 5.]

In Washington the ship-seizure bill sponsored by the Administration passed its first test in the Senate when the Commerce Committee reported it favorably by a vote of eleven to four, thus making it possible to bring the measure to the floor later this week. The committee defeated an attempt to prevent transfer to a belligerent of any of the ships that might be seized. [Page 7, Column 1.]

President Roosevelt's scheduled speech before the Pan-American Union tomorrow night has been canceled, but he will make a fireside chat to the nation on May 27, in which it is expected that he will deal with the position of the nation in the international situation and the future steps that should be taken. [Page 1, Column 2.]

BRITISH ASTOUNDED

Hitler's Deputy Is in Hospital After Bailing Out of War Plane

HAS A BROKEN ANKLE

London Believes Hess's Flight May Portend a New Purge in Reich

By ROBERT P. POST
Special Cable to THE NEW YORK TIMES.

LONDON, Tuesday, May 13—Rudolf Hess, deputy leader of the German Nazi party and the third-ranking personage in the German State, parachuted to earth in Scotland on Saturday night and is now a prisoner of war.

That may sound like something from a mystery thriller by Oppenheim. But in sober truth, 10 Downing Street issued a communiqué last night that is probably the strangest and most dramatic document ever to come from the official home of a British Prime Minister.

THE BRITISH STATEMENT

This statement said:

Rudolf Hess, the Deputy Fuehrer of Germany and party leader of the National Socialist party, has landed in Scotland in the following circumstances:

On the night of Saturday, the tenth, a Messerschmitt 110 was reported by our patrols to have crossed the coast of Scotland and to be flying in the direction of Glasgow. Since a Messerschmitt 110 would not have fuel to return to Germany, this report was at first disbelieved.

Later on a Messerschmitt 110 crashed near Glasgow with its guns unloaded. Shortly afterward a German officer who had bailed out was found with his parachute in the neighborhood, suffering from a broken ankle.

He was taken to a hospital in Glasgow, where he at first gave his name as Horn, but later on he declared that he was Rudolf Hess.

He brought with him various photographs of himself at different ages, apparently in order to establish his identity.

These photographs were deemed to be photographs of Hess by several people who knew him personally. Accordingly, an officer of the Foreign Office closely acquainted with Hess before the war has been sent up by airplane to see him in the hospital.

Identified by Official

Ivone A. Kirkpatrick, who used to be first secretary in the British Embassy in Berlin, was the official sent to Scotland, and the Ministry of Information announced early this morning that Herr Hess's identification had been definitely established.

Earlier the Germans had announced that Herr Hess, who was outranked only by Reichsfuehrer Hitler and Reich Marshal Hermann Goering in the Nazi hierarchy, had been suffering from hallucinations and had violated Herr Hitler's orders in taking the plane.

It was just before nightfall Saturday that Herr Hess was found by a Scottish farm worker; he was groaning in agony, with his parachute wrapped around him. He was taken first to a little two-roomed cottage and then was turned over to the military authorities. This morning he was in a military hospital somewhere near Glasgow.

That is the bare outline of the facts as they are known so far. What do they mean? The Germans have already announced that Herr Hess's "adjutants" have been arrested. The British are inclined to believe that there may be another purge in Germany—a purge similar to the one following the arrest of Captain Ernst Roehm, who was also one of Herr Hitler's closest collaborators, on June 30, 1934.

But from this distance it is almost impossible to say what this development means as far as Germany is concerned. One can record only what the British believe it means. One Briton told the writer that "this is the first 'break' we have had since the war started."

Alfred Duff Cooper, the Minister of Information, himself acted as messenger boy to take the British

Continued on Page Four

Bodies of Brewster and Wife Found In Plane Wreckage in Allegheines

The bodies of Benjamin Brewster, New York investment broker, and his wife, the former Leonie de Bary Lyon, who disappeared Friday on a projected flight from Roosevelt Field to Warren, Ohio, were found last night in the charred wreckage of their plane on a rugged mountain top forty miles north of Harrisburg.

The discovery was made after several pilots reported they had seen the badly damaged wreck nestled in tree branches on Shade Mountain near Beavertown.

The report that the bodies had been found was telephoned to Private Charles Hicklin of the Pennsylvania Motor Police by Private John Zeigler, one of a party sent out from the barracks at Selinsgrove.

The bodies were taken in charge by Dr. Charles W. Strand, coroner of Snyder County, who will remove them to Middleburg as soon as permission is received from members of the Brewster family.

Late last night positive identifica- [illegible]

vice president of the Stone & Webster Company, a brother-in-law of Mr. Brewster. In a telephone conversation with his sister, Mrs. Edward C. Brewster, Mr. Stone said the plane crashed against the side of a 1,500-foot mountain and then exploded. A reward of $1,000 had been offered by Mr. Stone to the person locating the plane.

The Brewsters' plane was a radio-equipped black and green Beechcraft with a Wright motor. Mr. Brewster was a prominent sportsman pilot and had more than 1,000 flying hours to his credit.

The tangled, charred wreckage was sighted at about 5 P. M. (daylight saving time) by two private pilots from Philadelphia, who were among more than seventy who searched the mountain area by air. They reported having circled the scene and sighted a twisted wing lying near by. The wing, they said, apparently had escaped the flames, and its black and green striping could be seen clearly. These fliers,

Continued on Page Nineteen

Rudolf Hess before his flight to Scotland.

Wide World Photos

German Army Infantry pushes toward the Eastern frontier shortly after Germany declared war on Russia.

"All the News That's Fit to Print."

NEWS INDEX, PAGE 35, THIS SECTION

The New York Times.

Copyright, 1941, by The New York Times Company.

LATE CITY EDITION

Partly cloudy and continued warm today and tomorrow.

Temperatures Yesterday—Max., 91; Min., 75.

Section 1

VOL. XC..No. 30,465. Entered as Second-Class Matter, Postoffice, New York, N. Y. NEW YORK, SUNDAY, JUNE 22, 1941. Including Rotogravure Picture, Magazine and Book Sections. TEN CENTS New York City and Vicinity

HITLER BEGINS WAR ON RUSSIA, WITH ARMIES ON MARCH FROM ARCTIC TO THE BLACK SEA; DAMASCUS FALLS; U.S. OUSTS ROME CONSULS

MUST GO BY JULY 15

Ban on Italians Like Order to German Representatives

U. S. DENIES SPYING

Envoys Told to Protest Axis Charges—Nazis Get 'Moor' Text

By BERTRAM D. HULEN

Special to THE NEW YORK TIMES.

WASHINGTON, June 21—The Italian Embassy was directed by the State Department in a note published today to close all its consular offices and other agencies in this country having connections with the Italian Government by July 15. This was the reply to the Italian demand for the closing of all American Consulates in Italy.

At the same time Sumner Welles, Under-Secretary of State, announced that he had sent to Dr. Hans Thomsen, the German Chargé d'Affaires, the text of President Roosevelt's message to Congress yesterday denouncing the sinking of the American freighter Robin Moor in the South Atlantic on May 21.

This message, which accused Germany of being an international outlaw, engaging in piracy and attempting to intimidate the United States by the sinking and to drive American commerce from the seas, contained notice that this country would not yield before such measures and stated that compensation would be sought for the sinking.

It was transmitted "for the information" of the German Government, but constituted in effect a note of protest. A further communication will be sent asking damages when a final determination has been reached of the extent of damages that should be sought.

Will Deny Improper Acts

In addition, the State Department instructed the American Embassies in Berlin and Rome to inform the respective governments that the United States objects to all allegations of improper acts by American consular officials in those countries and to complete arrangements for the withdrawal of the consular officials and their staffs by July 15, the limit set by the German and Italian Governments.

The Axis governments had charged that the American Consuls had spied for the British. No reply has been made by the State Department to the German protests against the order closing Nazi consulates in this country, but the protest will be rejected. The United States alleged subversive activities as the reason for the demand for them to be closed by July 10.

The notes to the German and Italian Embassies were sent by messenger last night. However, no direct charge of improper activities was made against the Italian consuls in the note Mr. Welles sent to Don Ascanio dei principi Colonna, the Italian Ambassador. He merely stated that the continued functioning of Italian consular establishments within United States territory "would serve no desirable purpose."

In addition, the closing of Italian agencies having connections with the Rome government was requested. The Italian Embassy, as in the earlier case of the German Embassy, was exempted, but the closing of the office of the Italian Commercial Counselor in New York was demanded, along with the consulates.

Welles Note to Colonna

The note from Mr. Welles to Prince Colonna follows:

June 20, 1941

His Excellency
Don Ascanio dei principi Colonna
Royal Italian Ambassador

Excellency:

I have the honor to inform Your Excellency that the President has directed me to request that the Italian Government promptly close all Italian consular establishments within United States territory and remove therefrom all Italian consular of-

Continued on Page Two

Hope Dims for Submarine; Diver Balked at 370 Feet

Knox Believes All 33 Are Dead on the O-9 and Expects Rites at Scene for Navy 'Heroes'—Pressure Halts Descent

By RUSSELL PORTER

Special to THE NEW YORK TIMES.

PORTSMOUTH, N. H., June 21—As hope faded rapidly for the crew of the Submarine O-9, which failed to rise after submerging yesterday morning twenty-four miles east of this city, it became known tonight that the Navy might be unable to complete its salvage operations, and might be compelled to leave the bodies entombed where they lie—440 feet below the surface of the Atlantic.

This theory was based upon the assumption that the two officers and thirty-one men must already be given up as lost, but that assumption has become stronger with every new development since the submarine was reported missing.

Last night cork insulation from the interior of the hull was picked up, showing that at least part of the submarine had collapsed, and early today, after fourteen hours of dragging, grapnels located an object believed to be the sunken craft. Since then no signals from the O-9 have been received on the sensitive sound-detection devices on the salvage ships in response to their repeated messages.

The view that the O-9's fate was sealed was strengthened this afternoon when reporters and photographers, visiting the scene in a Navy press boat, saw one of the Navy's most experienced divers fail in an attempt to reach the O-9 after descending 370 feet, or within seventy feet of where the Navy believes it has located the submarine with grapnel lines.

The diver, George Crocker, 30 years old, of Seattle, asked to be hauled up when he became convinced that he was not getting enough air pressure from his life lines of helium-oxygen mixture to overcome the increasing sea pressure as he went lower and lower.

A message from the Falcon said: "Diver descended 370 feet. Had difficulty in breathing. Brought to surface. Will continue attempts by varying diving techniques."

On the salvage ship the dive was called "the most dangerous in submarine history." It was pointed out that no one had ever made a successful "working" dive at 440 feet and that any diver who went down so far, where he would have to grope his way in complete darkness under terrific sea pressure, 196.8 pounds to the square inch, could do so only at extreme risk to his life.

Colonel Frank Knox, Secretary of the Navy, returning tonight on

Continued on Page Thirty

ARMY ASKS GUARD BE KEPT IN SERVICE

Recommends Congress Act to Hold State Troops, Reserve Officers Indefinitely

By HALLETT ABEND

Special to THE NEW YORK TIMES.

WASHINGTON, June 21—Members of the National Guard and Reserve Officers Corps will be kept in active service beyond the single year planned when they were called, if a recommendation made today by the War Department is approved by President Roosevelt and Congress.

Instead of a return to civilian life, starting Sept. 15, their terms of service in uniform may be extended indefinitely, or at least until the Army selectees have been sufficiently trained in ample numbers to permit the Guardsmen to be demobilized. The recommendation to the President does not specify any limit to the proposed extension of service.

At present there are 289,800 National Guardsmen, including their 21,800 officers, on active duty with the Federal Army. They were inducted into service in increments beginning Sept. 15 of last year. Some went into uniform as late as March of this year. Their terms of service, at time of induction, were limited to twelve months, which may not be extended except by act of Congress.

341,300 Would Be Affected

In addition to the National Guardsmen, who comprise eighteen divisions and one cavalry brigade now on active service, the government has called up 51,500 Reserve officers under the same terms, making collectively 341,300 officers and men who would be affected.

Today's War Department recommendation to the President that steps be taken to retain in the service these Guardsmen and Reserve officers was taken, according to the official announcement, because "the War Department has been flooded with queries from the field" as to whether or not the specified one-year limit of service would hold good or be changed.

"These queries are to be expected," continues the announcement, "because whatever the decision, there are many adjustments which the citizen-soldier must make in his affairs."

As yet no decision has been reached in the War Department whether or not to seek authority to retain selectees in the Army beyond the one-year training period specified in the Selective Service Act, but presumably such a step

Continued on Page Nineteen

NAVY MAY REPLACE SHIPYARD STRIKERS

Weighs Putting Own Machinists to Work to End Long Tie-Up in San Francisco

By The Associated Press.

SAN FRANCISCO, June 21—Striking A. F. L. machinists in a $500,000,000 defense program have come to a showdown with the United States Navy and their own international officers.

Reliable reports, not officially denied, indicated that the Navy might install its own machinists in the huge Bethlehem shipyards Monday if the local union did not heed the order of its international president to call off the strike by that time.

The same reports indicated that the Army also might be on hand

Continued on Page Twenty-eight

R. A. F. BLASTS FOE

Bags 26 Nazi Planes in Record Day Raids on Invasion Coast

GERMANY IS BOMBED

British on 11th Straight Night Offensive Into Western Reich

Special Cable to THE NEW YORK TIMES.

LONDON, Sunday, June 22—Twenty-six Nazi fighter planes were destroyed in daylight yesterday by Royal Air Force fliers on their fifth straight day of raiding the Germans' invasion coast and air bases in Northern France.

Twice before dark, waves of R. A. F. warcraft—reportedly numbering at least 150 planes each—swept over the Channel in offensive operations.

Bombers attacked the Nazi's airdromes on each occasion while strong forces of fighters blasted the way for the big planes through formations of German defense fighters. While the major raids were going on, other strong R. A. F. units patrolled over the French coast and battled Messerschmitts.

Attack Goes On; Big Bombs Used

Last night and early this morning the R. A. F. was still attacking the invasion coast, using some of the latest type of high-powered bombs.

Explosions rolled across the Channel like peals of thunder, shaking the ground and rocking buildings for miles along the Kentish coast, observers there reported.

A night curtain of fog hung over the Strait of Dover and little could be seen of the raids. The latest British attacks were apparently being made in the Boulogne area, where some of the heaviest daylight bombing was carried out.

Meanwhile R. A. F. bomber forces were again attacking Western Germany, officials here said briefly early today. The attacks marked the eleventh consecutive night in which the British have bombed industrial centers and war bases in the Reich.

Two Nazi bombers were shot down during the night in small scattered enemy raids on the east and southeast coasts of England. A few German bombs were reported dropped there; there were no accounts of casualties or damage.

The R. A. F. coastal patrol squadrons reported destroying at least two enemy planes and one Nazi

Continued on Page Eighteen

The International Situation

SUNDAY, JUNE 22, 1941

At 5:30 o'clock this morning, Berlin time, two statements were read over the German radio that constituted a declaration of war upon the Soviet Union by Germany. A proclamation of Adolf Hitler, read by Propaganda Minister Goebbels, said that Russia, with Britain and the United States, had sought to "throttle" Germany and that he had therefore decided to put the fate of the German people in the hands of the army. A statement by Foreign Minister von Ribbentrop contained the actual declaration of war. The Finns and the Rumanians were mentioned as allies. Berlin reported subsequently that troops were on the march in East Prussia. [Page 1, Column 8; with map.]

Yesterday was a good day for British arms.

In the Syrian campaign Damascus was occupied. The British announced its capture and Vichy reported its evacuation to avoid street fighting and destruction of the city. Another British force was pushing nearer Beirut, supported by the fleet and the air arm, while a third column was moving toward Tadmur. [Page 1, Column 5; Map on Page 12.]

No less encouraging to the British was a victory much closer to home in the largest British daylight air attack of the war. In a sweep two waves of 150 planes each pounded the French Channel coast, going particularly for airdromes, and engaged German air defenses. The British reported downing twenty-six Nazi planes in these attacks for a loss of five of their own. Late last night the British were continuing their attacks across the Channel. [Page 1, Column 4; Map, Page 18.]

The Libyan theatre was quiet, but British pressure in East Africa was indicated by a protest from Vichy against what was declared to be a virtual ultimatum from General Wavell to French Somaliland to join the Free French or suffer an intensified blockade. London confirmed the representations of General Wavell. [Page 14, Column 1.]

Washington continued the accelerated pace of its anti-Axis diplomatic offensive. The Italian Embassy was instructed to close the forty-nine Italian consulates and seven agencies in this country before July 15. President Roosevelt's message to Congress on the Robin Moor was handed to the German Embassy while the State Department instructed the United States embassies in Berlin and Rome to inform those governments that the United States objected categorically to any allegations of improper acts by United States consuls. [Page 1, Column 1.]

Italian consular circles here were silent concerning the Washington order, but Italian anti-Fascist quarters expressed jubilation. [Page 8, Column 1.]

SYRIAN CITY TAKEN

French Withdraw After a Hard Fight—British Closer to Beirut

TADMUR PUSH IS ON

Allied Planes Harassing Vichy Troops, Whose Defense Falters

By C. L. SULZBERGER

By Telephone to THE NEW YORK TIMES.

ANKARA, Turkey, June 21—French troops evacuated the city of Damascus today after a persistent bombardment by British artillery and withdrew to new positions outside the Syrian capital, according to official advices from Beirut. Early in the afternoon it was learned that the Allied vanguard was already beginning to enter the city. This evening the British reported complete occupation.

The Damascus airport at Mezze has been taken by Indian detachments of the Allied forces and one of the key points east of Damascus has been surrounded by Druz tribesmen fighting on the side of the British.

The Beirut radio announced tonight that a British motorized column pushing westward from Iraq was now heading toward Tadmur. The British column, it was said, has been bombed constantly by the French Air Force, which has just been reorganized and reinforced by French squadrons coming from North Africa. Some German planes also were said to have arrived in Syria.

Advance in High Gear

It is clear that the Allied advance is beginning to move into high gear. Unconfirmed reports that the British forces have reached Beirut indicate that it may also fall soon. Beirut's fate depends largely on whether the British will call in their superior naval forces to shell the city proper. So far this has been avoided in order to keep damage and casualties at a minimum.

[A dispatch from Cairo said that Australian forces had been progressing toward Beirut for two days and had passed Ras Damour.]

The Allies, convinced of the seriousness of the French resistance, evidently have begun to fight this undeclared war in earnest and intend to get it over with fast at any cost. The main center of French resistance in the east has been Damascus, and the capture of the city is of great importance.

The Allied counter-move to the French attack in the south, which developed earlier in the week, is now proceeding with dispatch in the Merdjayoun district. The fortress of Merdjayoun is in Allied hands and it is obvious that the region is being rapidly cleared, since the coastal advance is dependent to a large degree on a corollary advance in the center.

Considerable concentrations of French artillery had been brought up around Damascus. The French dug in and placed batteries in many of the villas and gardens in the outer sections of the city. These batteries were slowly picked off by British gunners with Royal Air Force support, but the principal British effort was artillery shelling. The British sought to avoid excess damage by aerial bombardment, which is less accurate than artillery fire.

Tadmur Believed in Peril

The French admission that a British column is pressing toward Tadmur would seem to indicate that perhaps the town is endangered. Several days ago reliable sources here reported the existence of the column, but this was steadfastly denied by Beirut.

While there have been new reports that the trouble for the British in Iraq is far from over, the fact that they are able to spare considerable forces from there would indicate that everything is under control. It is known that British forces also are working westward along the North Syrian frontier toward Aleppo, but the exact strength of these units is not known here.

British military circles admit that the Syrian adventure can no longer

Continued on Page Twelve

WHERE GERMAN ARMIES MARCH ON RUSSIA

Shown on the map is the western frontier of the Soviet Union, a battle line of more than 2,000 miles. Berlin indicated an attack from Norway to Rumania.

The Hitler Proclamation

The text of Adolf Hitler's proclamation, as recorded here by Columbia Broadcasting System, follows:

It was a difficult step for me to send my Minister to Moscow in order to attend to work against the policy of encirclement of Britain.

I hoped that at last it would be possible to put away tension.

Germany never intended to occupy Lithuania. The defeat of Poland induced me to again address a peace offer to the Allies. This was declined because Britain was still hoping to bring about European coalition.

That is why Cripps [Sir Stafford Cripps, British Ambassador] was sent to Moscow. He was commissioned under all circumstances to come to an agreement with Moscow. Russia always put out the lying statement that she was protecting these countries [evidently Lithuania, Estonia and Latvia, the Baltic States].

The penetration of Russia into Rumania and the Greek liaison with England threatened to place new, large areas into the war. Rumania, however, believed she was able to accede to Russia only if she received guarantees from Germany and Italy for the remainder of the country. With a heavy heart, I did this, for if Germany gives guarantees, she will fulfill them. We are neither Englishmen nor Jews.

I asked Molotoff [Soviet Foreign Commissar V. M. Molotoff] to come to Berlin, and he asked for a clarification of the situation. He asked, "Is the guarantee for Rumania directed also against Russia?"

I replied, "Against every one."

And Russia never informed us that she had even more far-reaching intentions against Rumania.

Molotoff asked further, "Is Germany prepared not to assist Finland, who was again threatening Russia?"

My reply was that Germany has no political interests in Finland, but another attack on Finland could not be tolerated, especially as we do not believe that Finland is threatening Russia.

Molotoff's third question was, "Is Germany agreeable that Russia give guarantees to Bulgaria?"

My reply was that Bulgaria is a sovereign State and I did not know that Bulgaria needed guarantees. Molotoff said Russia needed a passage through the Dardanelles and demanded bases in the Bosporus.

A few days later she [Russia] concluded the well known friendship agreement which was to incite the Serbs against Germany. Moscow demanded the mobilization of the Serbian Army.

When I still was silent, the men in the Kremlin went one step further. Russia offered to deliver war material against Germany. This was at the same time that I advised Matsuoka [Japanese Foreign Minister Yosuke Matsuoka] to bring about a lessening of the tension with Russia.

Serbian officers flew to Russia, where they were received as allies. Victory of the Axis in the Balkans at first foiled the plan to involve Germany in a long war and then, together with England and with the hope of American supplies, to throttle Germany.

Now the moment has come when I can no longer look at this development. Waiting would be a crime against Germany.

For weeks the Russians have been committing frontier violations. Russian planes have been crossing the frontier again and again to prove that they are the masters. On the night of June 17 and again on June 18 there was large patrol activity.

The march of the German Armies has no precedent. Together with the Finns we stand from Narvik to the Carpathians. At the Danube and on the shores of the Black Sea under Antonescu [Rumanian Dictator Ion Antonescu], German and Rumanian soldiers are united.

The task is to safeguard Europe and thus save all.

I have therefore today decided to give the fate of the German people and the Reich and of Europe again into the hands of our soldiers.

BAD FAITH CHARGED

Goebbels Reads Attack on Soviet—Ribbentrop Announces War

BALTIC MADE ISSUE

Finns and Rumanians Are Called Allies in Plan of Assault

Statement by von Ribbentrop is printed on Page 6.

By C. BROOKS PETERS

By Telephone to THE NEW YORK TIMES.

BERLIN, Sunday, June 22—As dawn broke over Europe today the legions of National Socialist Germany began their long-rumored invasion of Communist Soviet Russia. The non-aggression and amity pact between the two countries, signed in August, 1939, forgotten, the German attack began along a tremendous front, extending from the Arctic regions to the Black Sea. Marching with the forces of Germany are also the troops of Finland and Rumania.

Adolf Hitler, in a proclamation to the German people read over a national hook-up by Propaganda Minister Dr. Joseph Goebbels at 5:30 this morning, termed the military action begun this morning the largest in the history of the world. It was necessary, he added, because in spite of his unceasing efforts to preserve peace in this area it had definitely been proved that Russia was in a coalition with England to ruin Germany by prolonging the war.

Saw Stalemate in West

Herr Hitler, in his proclamation as reported here, made one vitally interesting statement, namely, that the supreme German military command did not feel itself able to force a decisive victory in the West—apparently on the British Isles—when large Russian troop concentrations were on the Reich's borders in the East.

The Russian troop concentrations in the East began in August, 1940, Herr Hitler asserted. "Thus, there occurred the effect intended by the Soviet-British cooperation," he added, "namely, the binding of such powerful German forces in the East that a radical conclusion of the war in the West, particularly as regards aircraft, could no longer be vouched for by the German High Command.

[The German radio announced early today that documentary proof would shortly be given of a secret British-Russian alliance, made behind Germany's back.]

Designed "to Save Reich"

The German action, Herr Hitler explained to his fellow-National Socialists, is designed to save the Reich and with it all Europe from the machinations of the Jewish-Anglo-Saxon warmongers.

The German Foreign Minister, Joachim von Ribbentrop, followed Dr. Goebbels on the air with a declaration of the Reich Government read before the foreign correspondents in the Foreign Office. Herr von Ribbentrop said he received V. G. Dekanosoff, the Russian Ambassador, this morning and informed him that in spite of the Russian-German non-aggression pact of Aug. 23, 1939, and an amity pact of Sept. 28, 1939, Russia had betrayed the trust that the Reich had placed in her.

"Contrary to all engagements which they had undertaken and in absolute contradition to their solemn declarations, the Soviet Union had turned against Germany," the Reich note asserted. "They have first not only continued, but even since the outbreak of war intensified their subversive activities against Germany in Europe. They have second, in a continually increasing measure, developed their foreign policy in a tendency hostile to Germany, and they have third massed their entire forces on the German frontier ready for action."

The Soviet Government, it was charged, had violated its treaties

Continued on Page Seven

Russian victims of a German attack.

U. S. Navy

The battleship U.S.S. Arizona burns furiously following the attack by Japanese aircraft on Pearl Harbor.

U. S. Navy

Pearl Harbor Naval Air Station taken by surprise during the Japanese aerial attack.

"All the News That's Fit to Print."

The New York Times.

LATE CITY EDITION
Increasing cloudiness with rising temperature today. Tomorrow cloudy, somewhat colder.
Temperatures Yesterday—Max., 34; Min., 25

VOL. XCI No. 30,634. Entered as Second-Class Matter, Postoffice, New York, N. Y. NEW YORK, MONDAY, DECEMBER 8, 1941. THREE CENTS NEW YORK CITY and Vicinity

JAPAN WARS ON U. S. AND BRITAIN; MAKES SUDDEN ATTACK ON HAWAII; HEAVY FIGHTING AT SEA REPORTED

CONGRESS DECIDED

Roosevelt Will Address It Today and Find It Ready to Vote War

CONFERENCE IS HELD

Legislative Leaders and Cabinet in Sober White House Talk

By C. P. TRUSSELL
Special to THE NEW YORK TIMES.

WASHINGTON, Dec. 7—President Roosevelt will address a joint session of Congress tomorrow and will find the membership in a mood to vote any steps he asks in connection with the developments in the Pacific.

The President will appear personally at 12:30 P. M. Whether he would call for a flat declaration of war again Japan was left unannounced tonight. But leaders of Congress, shocked and angered by the Japanese attacks, were talking of a declaration of war on not only Japan but on the entire Axis.

The plans for action tomorrow were made tonight in a White House conference at which the President, surrounded by his Cabinet and by Congressional leaders of both parties, went through reports, some official, some unconfirmed, of the continued assaults of the Japanese upon American Pacific outposts.

Meet Far Into Night

The conference lasted until after 11 o'clock and at its close an official statement was issued. This said that the President had reviewed for his conferees the latest advices from the Pacific and declared:

"It should be emphasized that the message to Congress has not yet been written and its tenor will, of course, depend on further information received between 11 o'clock tonight and noon tomorrow. Further news is coming in all the time."

Congressional leaders asserted as they left the White House that they did not know what the President would say tomorrow.

"Will the President ask for a declaration of war?" Speaker Rayburn was asked.

"He didn't say," answered the Speaker.

Asked whether Congress would support a declaration of war, Mr. Rayburn observed:

"I think that is one thing on which there would be unity."

Politics Declared Dropped

"There is no politics here," said Representative Joseph W. Martin Jr., Minority House Leader. "There is only one party when it comes to the integrity and honor of the country."

"The Republicans," said Senator Charles L. McNary of Oregon, the Senate minority leader, "will all go along, in my opinion, with whatever is done."

Unless international developments and plans changed overnight, it was indicated, the Presidential recommendations would be directed for the present, at least, at Japan only. This was asserted authoritatively in the face of widespread expectation that any

Continued on Page Six

TOKYO ACTS FIRST

Declaration Follows Air and Sea Attacks on U. S. and Britain

TOGO CALLS ENVOYS

After Fighting Is On, Grew Gets Japan's Reply to Hull Note of Nov. 26

By The Associated Press.

TOKYO, Monday, Dec. 8—Japan went to war against the United States and Britain today with air and sea attacks against Hawaii, followed by a formal declaration of hostilities.

Japanese Imperial headquarters announced at 6 A. M. [4 P. M. Sunday, Eastern standard time] that a state of war existed among these nations in the Western Pacific, as of dawn.

Soon afterward, Domei, the Japanese official news agency, announced that "naval operations are progressing off Hawaii, with at least one Japanese aircraft carrier in action against Pearl Harbor," the American naval base in the islands.

Japanese bombers were declared to have raided Honolulu at 7:35 A. M., Hawaii time [1:05 Sunday, Eastern standard time].

Premier-War Minister General Hideki Tojo held a twenty-minute Cabinet session at his official residence at 7 A. M.

Soon afterward it was announced that both the United States Ambassador, Joseph C. Grew, and the British Ambassador, Sir Robert Leslie Craigie, had been summoned by Foreign Minister Shigenori Togo.

The Foreign Minister, Domei said, handed to Mr. Grew the Japanese Government's formal reply to the note sent to Japan by United States Secretary of State Cordell Hull on Nov. 26.

[In the course of the diplomatic negotiations leading up to yesterday's events, the Domei agency had stated that Japan could not accept the premises of Mr. Hull's note.]

Sir Robert was summoned by

Continued on Page Five

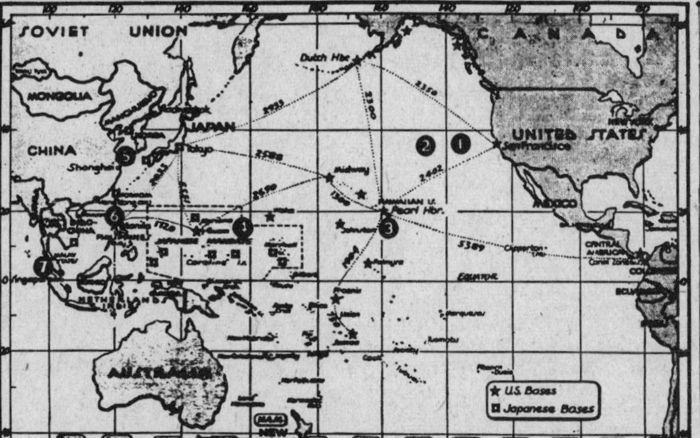

The International Situation

MONDAY, DEC. 8, 1941

Yesterday morning Japan attacked the United States at several points in the Pacific. President Roosevelt ordered United States forces into action and a declaration of war is expected this morning. [Page 1, Columns 7 and 8.] Tokyo made its declaration as of this morning against both the United States and Britain. [Page 1, Column 2.] The first Japanese assault was directed at Pearl Harbor Naval base in Hawaii. Many casualties and severe damage resulted. [Page 1, Columns 4 and 5; Map, Page 13.] United States Army aircraft took off from the Philippines this morning and some points in the Archipelago were bombed. [Page 8, Column 2.] Singapore and Hong Kong were bombed and a Japanese landing in Northern Malaya and a move on Thailand were reported. [Page 1, Column 3.] In Shanghai, Japanese marines occupied the waterfront; a British gunboat was sunk, a United States gunboat seized. [Page 9, Column 1.]

Factional lines dissolved as an angered Congress prepared to meet this morning. [Page 1, Column 1.] Secretary of State Hull accused Japan of having made a "treacherous and utterly unprovoked attack" after having been "infamously false and fraudulent" [Page 1, Column 6.] He released the text of diplomatic exchanges with Japan [Page 10], while the President gave out the text of his fruitless appeal to the Japanese Emperor. [Page 12.] The White House was the hub of Washington activity and news bulletins were released there. [Page 12, Column 3.]

The Federal Bureau of Investigation was ordered to begin a round-up of some Japanese in this country. [Page 6, Column 8.] As New York City went on a war footing and public precautions were taken; the FBI began the detention of Japanese nationals. [Page 1, Column 4.]

The unification of the country under the impact of the attack was swift. [Page 6, Column 6.] Formerly conspicuous isolationists indicated full support for the war effort. [Page 6, Column 4.]

Prime Minister Churchill notified Tokyo that a state of war existed. [Page 4, Column 1.] Declarations were made last night or early today by Australia, Canada [Page 14 Column 1], the Netherlands Indies [Page 7, Column 2] and Costa Rica. [Page 15, Column 1.]

Libya was the scene of a renewed tank battle and the Tobruk corridor was reported again clear of Axis forces. [Page 20, Column 2, with map.] On the Moscow front the German line was broken at two places, said Soviet sources. [Page 17, Column 2.]

PACIFIC OCEAN: THEATRE OF WAR INVOLVING UNITED STATES AND ITS ALLIES

Shortly after the outbreak of hostilities an American ship sent a distress call from (1) and a United States Army transport carrying lumber was torpedoed at (2). The most important action was at Hawaii (3), where Japanese planes bombed the great Pearl Harbor base. Also attacked was Guam (4). From Manila (6) United States bombers roared northward, while some parts of the Philippines were raided, as was Hong Kong, to the northwest. At Shanghai (5) a British gunboat was sunk and an American gunboat seized. To the south, in the Malaya area (7), the British bombed Japanese ships, Tokyo forces attempted landings on British territory and Singapore underwent an air raid. Distances between key Pacific points are shown on the map in statute miles.

JAPANESE FORCE LANDS IN MALAYA

First Attempt Is Repulsed—Singapore Is Bombed and Thailand Invaded

By The Associated Press.

SINGAPORE, Monday, Dec. 8—The Japanese landed in Northern Malaya, 300 miles north of Singapore, today and bombed this great British naval stronghold, causing small loss of life among civilians and property damage.

About 300 Japanese troops landed on the east coast of Malaya and began filtering through jungle-fringed swamps and rice fields toward Kota Bahru airdrome, which is ten miles from the northern terminus of a railroad leading to Singapore.

An official report from the

Continued on Page Two

Tokyo Bombers Strike Hard At Our Main Bases on Oahu

By The United Press.

HONOLULU, Dec. 7—War broke with lightning suddenness in the Pacific today when waves of Japanese bombers attacked Hawaii this morning and the United States Fleet struck back with a thunder of big naval rifles. Japanese bombers, including four-engined dive bombers and torpedo-carrying planes, blasted at Pearl Harbor, the great United States naval base, the city of Honolulu and several outlying American military bases on the Island of Oahu. There were casualties of unstated number.

[The United States battleship Oklahoma was set afire by the Japanese attackers, according to a National Broadcasting Company observer, who also reported in a broadcast yesterday that two other ships in Pearl Harbor were attacked.

[The Japanese news agency, Domei, reported that the battleship Oklahoma had been sunk at Pearl Harbor, according to a United Press dispatch from Shanghai.

[Governor Joseph B. Poindexter of Hawaii talked with President Roosevelt late yesterday afternoon, saying that a second wave of Japanese bombers was just coming over, and the Gov-

Continued on Page Thirteen

ENTIRE CITY PUT ON WAR FOOTING

Japanese Rounded Up by FBI, Sent to Ellis Island—Vital Services Are Guarded

The metropolitan district reacted swiftly yesterday to the Japanese attack in the Pacific. All large communities in the area, including New York City, Newark, Jersey City, Bayonne and Paterson, went on immediate war footing.

One of the first steps taken here last night was a round-up of Japanese nationals by special agents of the Federal Bureau of Investigation, reinforced by squads of city detectives acting under FBI supervision. More than 100 FBI men, fully armed, were assigned to the detail.

The prisoners were sent to Ellis Island, where they will be held pending action at Washington. It was indicated hundreds would be detained.

Earlier Mayor La Guardia had convened his Emergency Board and directed that Japanese nationals be confined to their homes pending decision as to their status and had their clubs and other meeting places closed and put under police guard.

A police sergeant and five policemen immediately went to the Japanese Consulate at 630 Fifth Avenue in Rockefeller Center where the Consul General, Morito Morishima, and his staff were preparing to leave, and posted a guard there. The Consul General and his staff were escorted to their homes when they left. They were not to move about the city without police in attendance.

Rear Admiral Adolphus Andrews, commander of the North Atlantic Squadron, told reporters at a conference in the Federal

Continued on Page Three

HULL DENOUNCES TOKYO 'INFAMY'

Brands Japan 'Fraudulent' in Preparing Attack While Carrying On Parleys

Texts of Secretary Hull's note and Japan's reply, Page 10.

By BERTRAM D. HULEN
Special to THE NEW YORK TIMES.

WASHINGTON, Dec. 7—Japan was accused by Secretary of State Cordell Hull today of making a "treacherous and utterly unprovoked attack" upon the United States and of having been "infamously false and fraudulent" by preparing for the attack while conducting diplomatic negotiations with the professed desire of maintaining peace.

But even before he knew of the attack, Mr. Hull had vehemently brought the diplomatic negotiations to a virtual end with an outburst against Admiral Kichisaburo Nomura, the Japanese Ambassador, and Saburo Kurusu, special envoy, because of the insulting character of the reply they deliv-

Continued on Page Eleven

Lewis Wins Captive Mine Fight; Arbitrators Grant Union Shop

The three-man arbitration board appointed by President Roosevelt to arbitrate the union shop dispute in the captive coal mines last night reversed the decision of the National Defense Mediation Board and ruled that all workers in the captive mines should be required to join John L. Lewis's United Mine Workers as a condition of employment.

The decision was made by a two to one vote, with Benjamin F. Fairless, president of the United States Steel Corporation, dissenting. Dr. John R. Steelman, who took a leave of absence from his post as director of the United States Conciliation Service to serve as chairman of the arbitration panel, and Mr. Lewis voted in favor of extension to the captive mines of the union shop provision of the standard Appalachian agreement.

Despite his dissent, Mr. Fairless promised that the coal mining subsidiaries of United States Steel would put the ruling into effect. All eight steel companies operating captive mines had given formal assurances before the decision was reached that they would accept it as binding.

The arbitration award ended a dispute in which Mr. Lewis had repeatedly defied the President by calling strikes that menaced the production of steel and that had had its repercussions in the enactment by the House of the Smith anti-strike bill.

In explaining his vote for the union shop, Dr. Steelman pointed out that 95 per cent of the 53,000 captive miners had voluntarily assumed membership in Mr. Lewis's C. I. O. union and that 99.5 per cent of all the miners in the nation were now members of the union.

Since the bulk of the industry, including many owners of captive mines, was already operating under the union shop, it could not be argued that the United Mine Workers was endeavoring to take

Continued on Page Forty-three

GUAM BOMBED; ARMY SHIP IS SUNK

U. S. Fliers Head North From Manila—Battleship Oklahoma Set Afire by Torpedo Planes at Honolulu

104 SOLDIERS KILLED AT FIELD IN HAWAII

President Fears 'Very Heavy Losses' on Oahu—Churchill Notifies Japan That a State of War Exists

By FRANK L. KLUCKHOHN
Special to THE NEW YORK TIMES.

WASHINGTON, Monday, Dec. 8—Sudden and unexpected attacks on Pearl Harbor, Honolulu, and other United States possessions in the Pacific early yesterday by the Japanese air force and navy plunged the United States and Japan into active war.

The initial attack in Hawaii, apparently launched by torpedo-carrying bombers and submarines, caused widespread damage and death. It was quickly followed by others. There were unconfirmed reports that German raiders participated in the attacks.

Guam also was assaulted from the air, as were Davao, on the island of Mindanao, and Camp John Hay, in Northern Luzon, both in the Philippines. Lieut. Gen. Douglas MacArthur, commanding the United States Army of the Far East, reported there was little damage, however.

[Japanese parachute troops had been landed in the Philippines and native Japanese had seized some communities, Royal Arch Gunnison said in a broadcast from Manila today to WOR-Mutual. He reported without detail that "in the naval war the ABCD fleets under American command appeared to be successful" against Japanese invasions.]

Japanese submarines, ranging out over the Pacific, sank an American transport carrying lumber 1,300 miles from San Francisco, and distress signals were heard from a freighter 700 miles from that city.

The War Department reported that 104 soldiers died and 300 were wounded as a result of the attack on Hickam Field, Hawaii. The National Broadcasting Company reported from Honolulu that the battleship Oklahoma was afire. [Domei, Japanese news agency, reported the Oklahoma sunk.]

Nation Placed on Full War Basis

The news of these surprise attacks fell like a bombshell on Washington. President Roosevelt immediately ordered the country and the Army and Navy onto a full war footing. He arranged at a White House conference last night to address a joint session of Congress at noon today, presumably to ask for declaration of a formal state of war.

This was disclosed after a long special Cabinet meeting, which was joined later by Congressional leaders. These leaders predicted "action" within a day.

After leaving the White House conference Attorney General Francis Biddle said that "a resolution" would be introduced in Congress tomorrow. He would not amplify or affirm that it would be for a declaration of war.

Congress probably will "act" within the day, and he will call the Senate Foreign Relations Committee for this purpose, Chairman Tom Connally announced.

[A United Press dispatch from London this morning said that Prime Minister Churchill had notified Japan that a state of war existed.]

As the reports of heavy fighting flashed into the White House, London reported semi-officially that the British Empire would carry out Prime Minister Winston Churchill's pledge to give the United States full support in case of hostilities with Japan. The President and Mr. Churchill talked by transatlantic telephone.

This was followed by a statement in London from the Netherland Government in Exile that it considered a state of war to exist between the Netherlands and Japan. Canada, Australia and Costa Rica took similar action.

Landing Made in Malaya

A Singapore communiqué disclosed that Japanese troops had landed in Northern Malaya and that Singapore had been bombed.

The President told those at last night's White House meeting that "doubtless very heavy losses" were sustained by the Navy and also by the Army on the island of Oahu [Honolulu]. It was impossible to obtain confirmation or denial of reports that the battleships Oklahoma and West Virginia had been damaged or sunk at Pearl Harbor, together with six or seven destroyers, and that 350 United States airplanes had been caught on the ground.

The White House took over control of the bulletins, and the Navy Department, therefore, said it could not discuss the matter or answer any questions how the Japanese were able to penetrate the Hawaiian defenses or appear without previous knowledge of their presence in those waters.

Administration circles forecast that the United States soon might be involved in a world-wide war, with Germany supporting Japan, an Axis partner. The German official radio tonight attacked the United States and supported Japan.

Axis diplomats here expressed complete surprise that the Japanese had attacked. But the impression gained from their attitude was that they believed it represented a victory for the Nazi attempt to divert lease-lend aid from Britain, which has been

Continued on Page Four

"All the News That's Fit to Print."

The New York Times.

LATE CITY EDITION
Cloudy followed by clearing and colder today. Tomorrow fair and moderately cold.
Temperatures Yesterday—Max., 44; Min., 25

VOL. XCI . No. 30,635. Entered as Second-Class Matter, Postoffice, New York, N. Y. NEW YORK, TUESDAY, DECEMBER 9, 1941. THREE CENTS NEW YORK CITY and Vicinity

U. S. DECLARES WAR, PACIFIC BATTLE WIDENS; MANILA AREA BOMBED; 1,500 DEAD IN HAWAII; HOSTILE PLANES SIGHTED AT SAN FRANCISCO

TURN BACK TO SEA

Two Formations Neared City on Radio Beams, Then Went Astray

ALARM IS WIDESPREAD

Whole Coast Has a Nervous Night—Many Cities Blacked Out

By LAWRENCE E. DAVIES
Special to The New York Times.

SAN FRANCISCO, Dec. 8—Two formations of "many planes," described as undoubtedly enemy aircraft, flew over the San Francisco Bay area tonight, it was announced officially by Brig. Gen. William O. Ryan, commander of the Fourth Interceptor Command, after a progressive blackout had blotted out naval and military establishments and whole cities along the Pacific Coast.

Conflicting reports spread, contributing to the "war of nerves," as the sirens wailed and broadcasting were silenced.

After another spokesman, through an error, had declared the blackout to be an air raid test, General Ryan said at the Presidio that it was no test but "the real thing."

The ships were detected first about 100 miles at sea, he said. In two formations they headed for the Monterey Peninsula, about eighty miles south of this city, and for San Francisco Bay itself.

Radio detectors plotted their course, bringing one formation in just north of the Golden Gate and the other to a point near Fort Barry, at the south end of the Golden Gate Bridge.

Planes Turn Back to Sea

After flying northward for some distance the planes turned south to a point thirty-five or forty miles down the peninsula section below San Francisco. Apparently trying to orient themselves, they flew about a while longer and then headed southwest to sea, General Ryan said.

The commanding officer, whose station is at Riverside and who said he just "happened" to be at the Presidio tonight, declared that the planes followed radio beams to these shores. When radio stations on the West Coast were silenced as part of the blackout the enemy craft apparently were not sure of their position.

No American planes were sent to the attack, he said, because "you don't send planes up unless you know what the enemy is doing and where he is going and you don't send planes up in the dark unless you know what you are doing."

Although there was no official explanation for the absence of anti-aircraft fire, it was indicated that the planes were hardly close enough for effective use of the guns.

Plane Carriers Rumored

Although General Ryan had no information, he said, as to the presence of enemy aircraft carriers hovering off the Pacific Coast, rumors of their presence had been broadcast during the day and this, it was acknowledged, would be the logical explanation for the appearance of the planes.

Lieut. Gen. John L. Dewitt,

Continued on Page Twenty-eight

NEWS BULLETINS

Please do not telephone The New York Times for war news. Every hour on the hour news bulletins are broadcast over Station WMCA—570 on the dial.

WEEKDAYS
8 a. m. through 11 p. m.
SUNDAYS
9 a.m., 1 p.m., 5 p.m., 11 p.m.

Philippines Pounded All Day As Raiders Strike at Troops

Air Base Near Capital Among Targets Hit by Japanese—Landing on Lubang With Aid of Fifth Columnists Reported

By H. FORD WILKINS
Wireless to The New York Times.

MANILA, Tuesday, Dec. 9—After a day of widespread aerial attacks throughout the Philippines, Japanese bombers swept in over Manila Bay early this morning and attacked Nichols Field, the United States Army air base on the outskirts of this capital, and simultaneously reports were received of a Japanese landing on Lubang Island, off the northwestern tip of Mindoro.

This morning's attack, which began shortly after 3 o'clock, was the first in the Manila area. The damage was believed to have been slight, but some casualties were reported. [A National Broadcasting Company correspondent reported that an official statement issued in Manila after the raid said: "In the raid on Nichols Field, which was conducted by approximately ten Japanese bombers, one hangar was damaged and one officers' quarters was burned. The casualty list consists of one soldier killed and twelve wounded—all Americans."]

The reported landing on Lubang, sixty miles southwest of Manila, was not officially confirmed, but the reports received credence here. [Other unconfirmed reports, relayed by the Columbia Broadcasting System, told of landings in the Davao region, on the southern island of Mindanao.]

The Manila area's first experience with bombs was a climax to a day and night of tension and activity. The explosions could be

Continued on Page Nine

PLANES GUARD CITY FROM AIR ATTACKS

Army Interceptors Join the Navy Patrols—Anti-Aircraft Apparatus Set Up Here

While long lines of men of fighting age waited impatiently outside of every Army, Navy and Marine Corps recruiting office in the city yesterday, representatives of the city, State and Federal Governments went ahead with the grim business of making New York City ready for war.

Beginning at dawn yesterday Army fighting planes took off at regular intervals from Mitchel Field to maintain, in conjunction with a Navy patrol, a constant fighting force in the air, so there could be no repetition here of the surprise in Hawaii. At the same time the First Interceptor Command called to active duty 40,000 volunteer civilian aircraft spotters at 1,300 posts scattered through thirteen eastern coastal States and the District of Columbia.

Anti-Aircraft Guns Set Up

The Sixty-second Coast Artillery of Fort Totten, Bayside, Queens, set up anti-aircraft apparatus at vantage points around the city. One base was in Prospect Park, Brooklyn.

Air raid wardens went on duty at midnight in every part of the city, as a result of a series of conferences among Police and Fire Department officers and representatives of the Board of Education and the Department of Housing, at which it was agreed that air raid warnings would be broadcast by the blowing of the sirens of all police radio cars and emergency trucks and all Fire Department apparatus.

Alternating long and short blasts of the sirens will be sounded from the moment the Army notifies the Police and Fire Departments of the approach of an enemy and will be continued throughout the duration of the raid. The all-clear signal will be given by a series of short blasts from the sirens, it was agreed.

Teachers to Be Warned

The Police and Fire Departments, with their network of communications reaching into every neighborhood in the city, also undertook to advise the 800 public schools of an impending raid when the alarm is sounded, so the teachers can shepherd their pupils to their homes in accordance with plans already made.

Precautions against sabotage of bridges, tunnels, railroads, reservoirs, dams, power plants and other points of key importance throughout the city also were discussed at conferences of high police officials with Commissioner

Continued on Page Twenty-six

MALAYA THWARTS PUSH BY JAPANESE

Thailand Capitulates and Is Seen Virtually in Axis—Two Raids on Singapore

By F. TILLMAN DURDIN
Wireless to The New York Times.

SINGAPORE, Dec. 8—The Japanese in the first eighteen hours of their attack on the Malaya peninsula have forced Thailand to capitulate, but do not now appear to have achieved any appreciable success in an invasion of British Malaya.

There was an air raid on Singapore this morning. Prai, on the mainland opposite Georgetown, more commonly known as Penang from the name of the island on which it is located, was also bombed, but damage was said to be slight.

[Bombs again started dropping on Singapore at 4 A. M. today, The Associated Press re-

Continued on Page Ten

1 BATTLESHIP LOST

Capsized in Pearl Harbor, Destroyer Is Blown Up, Other Ships Hurt

FLEET NOW IS FIGHTING

Aid Rushed to Hawaii—Some Congressmen Sharply Critical

By CHARLES HURD
Special to The New York Times.

WASHINGTON, Dec. 8—The Battle of the Pacific spread tonight over a 5,000-mile "front" from Hawaii to the Philippines while a badly battered United States Fleet fought back at Japanese sea and air forces that launched severe attacks yesterday afternoon.

Tonight the Japanese were reported to be launching their main attack at the Philippines, particularly at Palawan, the greatest natural harbor in the archipelago. That attack was preceded today, according to reports from Manila, by an onslaught against the United States military air fields there, which put these out of commission for the time being and set fire to storage tanks containing vital gasoline for air operations.

The Japanese Sunday attack on Hawaii was reported in informed quarters to have been launched from the mandated islands, rather than from Japan proper, and aircraft carriers apparently approached undetected within 250 or 300 miles of Pearl Harbor.

3,000 Casualties on Oahu

The White House announced officially that the attack on the Island of Oahu, site of Honolulu and the Pearl Harbor naval base, probably has cost about 1,500 lives and resulted in an equal number of wounded persons.

To the toll of lives announced for this region, and undisclosed casualties in the Philippines and at other points, was added official word that one "old battleship" had capsized in Pearl Harbor, a destroyer had exploded and that several other

Continued on Page Four

The International Situation

TUESDAY, DECEMBER 9, 1941

The United States yesterday made a formal declaration of war on Japan after President Roosevelt had addressed a joint session of Congress. [Page 1, Column 8.] The Senate approved by unanimous vote [Page 6, Column 1] while one woman in the House of Representatives dissented. [Page 6, Column 4.]

In the national effort the Supply, Priorities and Allocations Board mapped expanding production [Page 36, Column 1], leaders of organized labor pledged support [Page 38, Column 4], and Mayor La Guardia issued a proclamation giving air raid defense instructions [Page 34, Column 1.]

In San Francisco two formations of enemy aircraft were sighted over the city, which was blacked out. [Page 1, Column 1.]

White House announcements indicated that the battle of the Pacific was raging with the United States still on the defensive. [Page 1 Column 4; Map, Page 4.] There were extensive air attacks in the Philippines [Page 1, Columns 2 and 3; Map, Page 9], raids on Hong Kong [Page 11, Column 1] and a Tokyo report that both Guam and Wake had been put under the Japanese flag. [Page 12, Column 1; with map.] The British were mopping up on a Japanese landing party in Malaya, but Thailand had yielded. [Page 1, Column 3; Map, Page 10.]

The small detachment of United States Marines at Tientsin and Peiping was disarmed and detained by the Japanese and they closed the United States Consulate in Shanghai [Page 3, Column 1.] Imperial Headquarters in Tokyo made sweeping claims of victory in the battle of the Pacific, listing great damage to the United States forces. [Page 1, Column 5.]

In London, Prime Minister Churchill announced Britain's declaration of war to Parliament and made a stirring address to the world. [Page 14, Column 1.]

The American nations began to line up behind the United States. A conference will be held, but seven countries have already declared war on Japan, two have broken diplomatic relations and several others are preparing to act. [Page 22, Column 3.] China decided to declare war not merely on Japan but on Germany and Italy as well. [Page 9, Column 4.] The various European governments in exile also supported the United States. [Page 18, Column 1.] Russia's position is obscure. [Page 2, Column 2.]

The United States accused Germany of having egged Japan on; said lease-lend aid would continue. [Page 1, Column 6.]

Berlin gave out word that Winter had stopped the Germans short of Moscow and that the capture of the Russian capital had been put off until Spring. [Page 1, Column 7.]

In Libya, the Axis armored forces were attacked from three directions by the British and what was expected to be a major engagement was eventually merely a rearguard action. [Page 24, Column 3.]

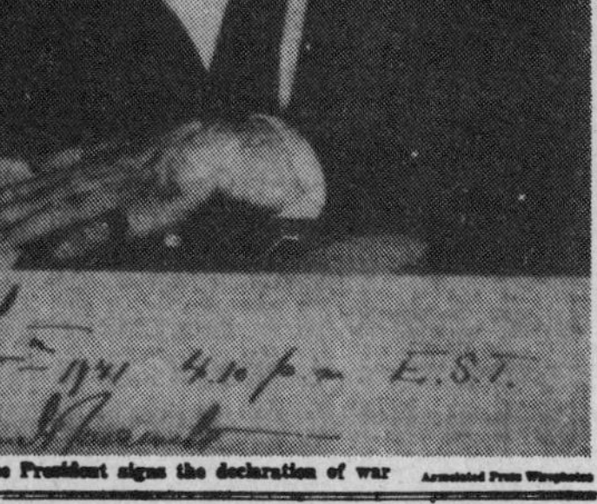

The President signs the declaration of war — Associated Press Wirephoto

LARGE U. S. LOSSES CLAIMED BY JAPAN

Tokyo Lists 2 Battleships, 1 Mine-Sweeper Sunk, 4 Capital Ships, 4 Cruisers Damaged

TOKYO, Tuesday, Dec. 9 (From Official Broadcasts, Distributed by The Associated Press)—Japanese Imperial Headquarters announced last night the sinking of two United States battleships and a mine-sweeper, severe damage to four other American capital ships and four cruisers and the destruction of about 100 American planes in Japan's surprise blows at Hawaii, the Philippines and Guam.

The official news agency, Domei, quickly interpreted "these magnificent early gains" as giving Japan naval mastery over the United States in the Pacific, and said that any force that the United States could muster now "would be regarded as utterly inadequate to accomplish any successful outcome in an encounter with the thus-far-intact Japanese fleet."

In addition, "many enemy merchant ships were captured" in the Pacific, it was announced, and the communiqué listed an unconfirmed report that a Japanese submarine had sunk an American aircraft carrier off Honolulu.

"No Japanese ships were lost during the fighting," it added.

Domei said today it was "understood that Japanese forces had destroyed more than 300 American planes, including 200 in dogfights and on the ground in Hawaii. The others, it said, were "believed" destroyed in the Philippines. Of the total, the news agency said, thirty were Fortress planes and thirty long-range bombers.

Japanese newspapers identified the two American battleships declared sunk Sunday at Pearl Harbor, Hawaii, as the 31,800-ton West Virginia, and the 29,000-ton Oklahoma. [An Italian broadcast, however, quoted Domei as listing the Oklahoma and the 33,100-ton Pennsylvania as lost. In Berlin, D. N. B. said in a Tokyo dispatch that an American transport ship carrying 350 men had been sunk off Manila.]

Japanese planes were reported to have again attacked the Philippines and British Hong Kong yesterday, inflicting "heavy damage" in a follow-up of the raids launched Sunday. "Twelve out of fourteen enemy planes on the ground were

Continued on Page Thirteen

The President's Message

Following is the text of President Roosevelt's war message to Congress, as recorded by The New York Times *from a broadcast:*

Mr. Vice President, Mr. Speaker, members of the Senate and the House of Representatives:

Yesterday, Dec. 7, 1941—a date which will live in infamy—the United States of America was suddenly and deliberately attacked by naval and air forces of the empire of Japan.

The United States was at peace with that nation, and, at the solicitation of Japan, was still in conversation with its government and its Emperor looking toward the maintenance of peace in the Pacific.

Indeed, one hour after Japanese air squadrons had commenced bombing in the American island of Oahu the Japanese Ambassador to the United States and his colleague delivered to our Secretary of State a formal reply to a recent American message. And, while this reply stated that it seemed useless to continue the existing diplomatic negotiations, it contained no threat or hint of war or of armed attack.

Attack Deliberately Planned

It will be recorded that the distance of Hawaii from Japan makes it obvious that the attack was deliberately planned many days or even weeks ago. During the intervening time the Japanese Government has deliberately sought to deceive the United States by false statements and expressions of hope for continued peace.

The attack yesterday on the Hawaiian Islands has caused severe damage to American naval and military forces. I regret to tell you that very many American lives have been lost. In

Continued on Page Six

U. S. TO CONTINUE AID TO BRITAIN

White House Charges Nazis Sought Pacific War, but Will Fail to Gain Ends

Special to The New York Times.

WASHINGTON, Dec. 8—A statement accusing Germany of having done everything in her power "to push Japan into the war" was issued this evening at the White House.

The statement declared that Germany's objective was "to put an end to the lease-lend program," which has aided the European enemies of Germany, including Britain and Russia and their allies and Turkey. It added that this program would continue "in full operation" and that the German attempt to end lease-lend shipments was "100 per cent" mistaken.

This statement took full cognizance of the belief in diplomatic circles here that Germany would carry out its pledges to Japan, its Axis ally, by declaring war on the United States and that Italy would

Continued on Page Seventeen

NAZIS GIVE UP IDEA OF MOSCOW IN 1941

Winter Forces Abandonment of Big Drives in North Till Spring, Berlin Says

By The Associated Press.

BERLIN, Dec. 8—Winter has stopped the Germans short of Moscow and the capture of the Soviet capital is not expected this year, a military spokesman declared tonight.

[A surprise Russian attack on Eastern Crimea from the Caucasus was revealed in a Moscow broadcast. A counter-attack from Sevastopol also was reported. The Soviet claimed important progress around Taganrog and on Moscow's defense lines.]

It seemed likely from the spokesman's statement that until Spring there could be no further major German offensive except along the extreme southern front. This word reduced the Russian campaign to secondary interest for the Germans for the first time, and attention focused instead on Ja-

Continued on Page Twenty-five

UNITY IN CONGRESS

Only One Negative Vote as President Calls to War and Victory

ROUNDS OF CHEERS

Miss Rankin's Is Sole 'No' as Both Houses Act in Quick Time

By FRANK L. KLUCKHOHN
Special to The New York Times.

WASHINGTON, Dec. 8—The United States today formally declared war on Japan. Congress, with only one dissenting vote, approved the resolution in the record time of 33 minutes after President Roosevelt denounced Japanese aggression in ringing tones. He personally delivered his message to a joint session of the Senate and House. At 4:10 P. M. he affixed his signature to the resolution.

There was no debate like that between April 2, 1917, when President Wilson requested war against Germany, and April 6, when a declaration of war was approved by Congress.

President Roosevelt spoke only 6 minutes and 30 seconds today compared with Woodrow Wilson's 29 minutes and 34 seconds.

The vote today against Japan was 82 to 0 in the Senate and 388 to 1 in the House. The lone vote against the resolution in the House was that of Miss Jeanette Rankin, Republican, of Montana. Her "No" was greeted with boos and hisses. In 1917 she voted against the resolution for war against Germany.

The President did not mention either Germany or Italy in his request. Early this evening a statement was issued at the White House, however, accusing Germany of doing everything possible to push Japan into the war. The objective, the official statement proclaimed, was to cut off American lend-lease aid to Germany's European enemies, and a pledge was made that this aid would continue "100 per cent."

A Sudden and Deliberate Attack

President Roosevelt's brief and decisive words were addressed to the assembled representatives of the basic organizations of American democracy—the Senate, the House, the Cabinet and the Supreme Court.

"America was suddenly and deliberately attacked by naval and air forces of the Empire of Japan," he said. "We will gain the inevitable triumph, so help us God."

Thunderous cheers greeted the Chief Executive and Commander in Chief throughout the address. This was particularly pronounced when he declared that Americans "will remember the character of the onslaught against us," a day, he remarked, which will live in infamy.

"This form of treachery shall never endanger us again," he declared amid cheers. "The American people in their righteous might will win through to absolute victory."

Then, to the accompaniment of a

Continued on Page Five

President to Talk On Radio Tonight

By The Associated Press.

WASHINGTON, Dec. 8—President Roosevelt will make a radio address to the nation tomorrow night at 10 P. M., Eastern standard time, at which time the White House said he would make "a more complete documentation" of the Japanese attack than has yet been possible.

Stephen Early, Presidential secretary, announced that the Chief Executive would speak for half an hour and that the address would be carried by all networks.

Mr. Roosevelt began dictating the speech tonight in his White House study.

U.S. Navy

The damaged and burning ships U.S.S. Arizona, U.S.S. Tennessee, and U.S.S. West Virginia after the Japanese attack on Pearl Harbor.

National Archives

Wrecked U.S.S. Downes and U.S.S. Cassin following the Pearl Harbor attack.

"All the News That's Fit to Print."

The New York Times.

LATE CITY EDITION
Fair, slowly rising temperature today. Tomorrow cloudy, moderately cold, occasional snow.
Temperatures Yesterday—Max., 34; Min., 24

VOL. XCI. No. 30,688. Entered as Second-Class Matter, Postoffice, New York, N. Y. NEW YORK, FRIDAY, DECEMBER 12, 1941. THREE CENTS NEW YORK CITY and Vicinity

U.S. NOW AT WAR WITH GERMANY AND ITALY; JAPANESE CHECKED IN ALL LAND FIGHTING; 3 OF THEIR SHIPS SUNK, 2D BATTLESHIP HIT

BLOCKED IN LUZON

But Japanese Put Small Force Ashore in South of Philippine Island

SABOTEURS ARE HELD

Some in Manila Seized for Spreading Rumor About City Water

By H. FORD WILKINS
Wireless to THE NEW YORK TIMES.

MANILA, Friday, Dec. 12—The United States Army Far East headquarters announced today that a small Japanese invasion force was reported to have pushed ashore at Legaspi, Southern Luzon, and "the enemy has improved his strength in Northern Luzon," where, however, the situation remains unchanged materially. The announcement added that the report of the Legaspi landing was still unconfirmed and there were no details.

[Small forces of Japanese apparently have been landed at Legaspi, it was said officially three hours after the morning communiqué had said merely that the Legaspi development had not yet been confirmed, a United Press dispatch from Manila said.]

There was no further indication of the progress of the sea war. The office of Admiral Thomas C. Hart, commander in chief of the United States Asiatic Fleet, remained silent.

One Japanese plane was shot down by an American fighter near Bancayan in the mountain mining district.

2,000 Families Are Moved

Manila took further emergency measures to evacuate portions of the old walled city. The Red Cross supervised the removal of 2,000 families, loading them into buses and trucks and taking them to safety zones considerably removed from the city. Identification cards were issued and checked as the evacuees lined up for removal

With Lieut. Gen. Douglas MacArthur's United States Far Eastern forces fully in control of the North Luzon invasion threat and his air force sufficiently active to disperse Japanese raiders headed for Manila, his intelligence service turned yesterday to mopping up fifth columnists.

Their latest trick was to circulate rumors that the city water supply had been poisoned. Army, city and government officials quickly scotched the rumors with assurances and proof that nothing whatever was wrong with the water supply. Several persons were arrested, including air-raid wardens, on a city-wide house-to-house campaign warning the people against "impure water."

Several persons entered hospitals asserting that they had been poisoned, but examination disclosed that nothing was wrong with them but upset stomachs and fear. Elaborate analysis proved that the water they drank was not contaminated.

The official communiqué asserting that mopping-up operations were progressing heightened the morale of the nation, suddenly plunged into total war and its first taste of conflict in forty years.

The sinking of a United States Army transport in Manila Bay, as announced by Tokyo, was denied officially here yesterday.

Interned Japanese, numbering around 2,000, were revealed to be extremely uncomfortable under the threat of bombs from Japanese planes, recognizing that bombs do not distinguish nationalities.

Legaspi Move Discounted

MANILA, Friday, Dec. 12 (UP)—The small Japanese landings at Legaspi, a port of about 36,000

Continued on Page Eight

Line-Up of World War II

THE ALLIES

Australia	Haiti
†Belgium	*Honduras
Canada	Netherlands Indies
China	New Zealand
Costa Rica	Nicaragua
Cuba	†Norway
†Czecho-Slovakia	*Panama
Dominican Republic	†Poland
*El Salvador	South Africa
Free France	†Soviet Union
Great Britain	United States
†Greece	†Yugoslavia
Guatemala	

THE AXIS

Finland	Japan
Germany	Manchukuo
Hungary	Rumania
Italy	Slovakia

*Have declared war on Japan only.

†At war only with Germany, Italy and their European allies.

CITY CALM AND GRIM AS THE WAR WIDENS

Loyalty and a Determination to Win Are Evident in Every Class and National Group

The people of New York City received the news that we are at war with Germany and Italy as well as Japan with profound calm and a quiet, stern determination to see it through, no matter how long it takes. Patriotism and loyalty were the spontaneous order of the day in every household, every business office, every factory, every school and every institution. The whole city rallied in support of the war.

All over the city the Stars and Stripes flew proudly from public and private buildings, and those in charge of Army, Navy, Coast Guard and civilian defense organizations swung promptly and forcefully into action to protect the city

Continued on Page Twenty-one

U. S. FLIERS SCORE

Bombs Send Battleship, Cruiser and Destroyer to the Bottom

MARINES KEEP WAKE

Small Force Fights Off Foe Despite Loss of Some of Planes

By CHARLES HURD
Special to THE NEW YORK TIMES

WASHINGTON, Dec. 11—A Japanese battleship, a cruiser and a destroyer have been sunk in the Pacific and a second battleship badly damaged by bomb hits, the United States forces announced in communiqués today recording their first major victories in the warfare that began last Sunday with surprise Japanese attacks.

Damage to the second battleship was revealed tonight in a Navy communiqué, which said a man-of-war of the Kongo class had been hit by Navy patrol planes off the coast of Luzon. This was "the second battleship to be bombed effectively by United States forces," the communiqué asserted.

The battleship sunk, also of the Kongo class, was believed to have been the 29,330-ton Haruna. She went down after having been set afire by aerial bombardment north of Luzon. She had been supporting an attack in which the Japanese effected a landing at Aparri, a remote village on the northern Philippine coast, separated from Manila by mountains and forests.

The cruiser, unidentified except that it was of the light class, and the destroyer were sunk also by fliers who took off from Wake

Continued on Page Six

The International Situation

FRIDAY, DECEMBER 12, 1941

The United States declared war yesterday on Germany and Italy. Congress acted swiftly without a dissenting vote. [Page 1, Column 8.] Then, without debate, it passed a bill to permit the use of all United States land forces anywhere in the world. [Page 1, Column 7.]

This action coincided with good news from the Pacific. Washington announced the sinking of a Japanese battleship, a cruiser and a destroyer and reported severe damage to a second battleship by bomb hits. [Page 1, Column 3, Map, Page 6.]

The American declaration came within a few hours after Germany and Italy had declared war on the United States. The Reich's declaration was made in a diplomatic note and in a Reichstag address by Adolf Hitler. [Page 4, Column 1.] Benito Mussolini proclaimed Italy's declaration. [Page 4, Column 5.]

In London, where news of America's full entry into the world war brought predictions of an Allied grand strategy [Page 13, Column 5], Prime Minister Churchill declared that the Allies would win ultimately at any cost. [Page 1, Column 4.] Mexico broke off relations with Germany and Italy, while ten other Latin-American nations declared war on those countries or prepared to take that step. [Page 9, Column 1.]

The Soviet radio asserted that any Axis hopes for a separate peace with Russia were in vain. The radio declared that Russia was determined to fight alongside the United States and Britain until the Allies won. [Page 19, Column 1.]

In all of yesterday's land fighting, Japan was checked. In the Philippines, attempts to win a firm foothold on Luzon appeared smashed, except for a landing of parachutists at an airport 180 miles northeast of Manila and another small landing on the southeastern coast of the island. [Page 1, Column 1; Map, Page 2.] The British reported a slow-down of Japanese attacks in Malaya. [Page 13, Column 1.] While British forces fought off new assaults on Hong Kong, a two-day Chinese offensive to relieve pressure there was reported to have inflicted 15,000 casualties. [Page 11, Column 1, with map.]

Tokyo claimed the destruction of an American destroyer, a submarine and eighty-one planes, in addition to the capture of 350 Americans on Guam. [Page 8, Column 5.] With the commander of Britain's Far Eastern Fleet among 595 men still missing in the sinking of the Prince of Wales and the Repulse, the British named a new commander. [Page 14, Column 3.]

Amid debate in Washington over a proposed investigation of what happened at Pearl Harbor Sunday [Page 10, Column 1], Secretary of the Navy Knox arrived in Honolulu, presumably to seek first-hand information on that attack. [Page 1, Columns 5 and 6.]

President Roosevelt called upon industrial and labor representatives to meet next week and reach a voluntary agreement to end labor disputes for the duration. [Page 29, Column 2.] It was revealed also that the Administration was considering the registration of all men between the ages of 18 and 65 for military and civilian service. [Page 34, Column 1.]

On the European fighting front the Russians reported further gains against German forces. [Page 18, Column 3.] The Berlin radio revealed that the Nazis had replaced their commander on the Moscow front. [Page 19, Column 3.] In Libya, the main Axis forces were still withdrawing westward, Cairo announced. [Page 17, Column 1.]

Left: The President set his signature to the act against Germany. Center: He checked the time with Senator Tom Connally. Right: After that he placed the United States officially at war with Italy.

Associated Press Wirephotos

AXIS TO GET LESSON, CHURCHILL WARNS

He Announces Replacement of Libyan General—Upholds Phillips's Judgment

Text of Mr. Churchill's speech will be found on Page 16.

By CRAIG THOMPSON
Special Cable to THE NEW YORK TIMES.

LONDON, Dec. 11—Prime Minister Winston Churchill delivered a review of the war in the Pacific, North Africa, Russia and the Atlantic today that contained a compound of gloom and of optimism, but he ended with this ringing declaration:

"Just handfuls and cliques of wicked men and their military or party organizations have been able to bring these hideous evils upon mankind. It would indeed bring shame upon our generation if we did not teach them a lesson which will not be forgotten in the records of a thousand years."

Precedes Declarations

He spoke to the House of Commons before the Axis war declarations and the United States' reply.

Mr. Churchill gave hitherto unpublished details about the sinkings of the Prince of Wales and the Repulse, which made plain that the British had lost the use of airdromes on the Malay Peninsula and that the ships had had to rely solely on their anti-aircraft guns for protection against the attacking planes. In so doing he stoutly defended the judgment whereby Vice Admiral Sir Tom S. V. Phillips, who appeared tonight to have been lost, undertook an attack on Japanese transports that resulted in the sinkings of the warships.

Mr. Churchill announced that Lieut. Gen. Sir Alan Gordon Cunningham had been replaced in Libya by Major Gen. Neil Methuen Ritchie, adding that General Cunningham "has been reported by medical authorities to be suffering from serious overstrain and was granted sick leave."

General Ritchie, the new commander of the Eighth Army, is 44 years old. His was one of three "young-men" appointments to the General Staff that were made last June. In the last war he was commissioned a second lieutenant in the Black Watch at the age of seventeen and was a captain when he was twenty. He fought in France, Mesopotamia and Palestine, and received the Distinguished Service Order and the Military Cross.

Mr. Churchill gave an indication of the size of British and Allied losses in merchantmen in the Battle of the Atlantic for November that would, from his statement, appear to have been no greater than 100,000 tons. This would be a

Continued on Page Seventeen

Our Declaration of War

Special to THE NEW YORK TIMES.

WASHINGTON, Dec. 11—Following are the texts of the documents wherein the President asked a war declaration against Germany and Italy, and Congress acted:

The President's Message

To the Congress of the United States:

On the morning of Dec. 11 the Government of Germany, pursuing its course of world conquest, declared war against the United States.

The long-known and the long-expected has thus taken place. The forces endeavoring to enslave the entire world now are moving toward this hemisphere.

Never before has there been a greater challenge to life, liberty and civilization.

Delay invites great danger. Rapid and united effort by all of the peoples of the world who are determined to remain free will insure a world victory of the forces of justice and of righteousness over the forces of savagery and of barbarism.

Italy also has declared war against the United States.

I therefore request the Congress to recognize a state of war between the United States and Germany, and between the United States and Italy.

FRANKLIN D. ROOSEVELT.

The War Resolution

Declaring that a state of war exists between the Government of Germany and the government and the people of the United States and making provision to prosecute the same.

Whereas the Government of Germany has formally declared war against the government and the people of the United States of America:

Therefore, be it

Resolved by the Senate and House of Representatives of the United States of America in Congress assembled, that the state of war between the United States and the Government of Germany which has thus been thrust upon the United States is hereby formally declared; and the President is hereby authorized and directed to employ the entire naval and military forces of the United States and the resources of the government to carry on war against the Government of Germany; and, to bring the conflict to a successful termination, all of the resources of the country are hereby pledged by the Congress of the United States.

(An identic resolution regarding Italy was adopted)

Secretary Knox Visits Honolulu; Bases There Were Raided 5 Times

Special to THE NEW YORK TIMES.

WASHINGTON, Dec. 11—The Navy Department announced tonight that Secretary Frank Knox had arrived in Honolulu this afternoon.

There was no previous announcement that he had left for Hawaii, nor was there any intimation of the specific purpose of his visit.

WASHINGTON, Dec. 11 (UP)—Delegate Samuel W. King of Hawaii disclosed tonight after a telephone conversation with Governor Joseph B. Poindexter that twenty Japanese planes were shot down during the Sunday raid on Pearl Harbor.

Mr. King said the information was authorized for release in Hawaii by Lieut. Gen. Walter C. Short and that Mr. Poindexter was permitted to make the disclosure by transpacific radio-telephone.

Mr. Poindexter told Mr. King that "civilian morale is 100 per cent throughout the territory.

"Civilian defense measures are working without a hitch," he added.

HONOLULU, Dec. 11 (UP)—In addition to two deadly attacks on the United States naval base at Pearl Harbor last Sunday, Japanese bombers followed with a third attack later that day and with a fourth Monday morning, it is possible to disclose today for the first time.

Censorship permits a cautious description of the attack. A few seconds after the first bombers came over, with the rising sun insignia of Japan on their wings, defending anti-aircraft batteries sent up a heavy barrage.

Within a few minutes heavy clouds of black smoke began rolling up from Pearl Harbor, fourteen miles from Honolulu.

Planes roared in over the harbor, dropping bombs on navy centers and ships. Torpedo planes splashed

Continued on Page Eleven

CONGRESS KILLS BAN ON AN A. E. F.

Swift Action Without Debate—Service Terms Are Extended to Six Months After War

Special to THE NEW YORK TIMES.

WASHINGTON, Dec. 11—Congress swiftly eliminated prohibitions against American expeditionary forces today and continued terms of enlistment or induction to a date six months after hostilities end. Acting without debate, the two houses dropped the A. E. F. ban by removing restrictions in the Selective Service Act on the use of troops outside the Western Hemisphere.

The Senate Appropriations Committee, meanwhile, added an undetermined sum to the $8,246,000,000 third supplemental national defense appropriation bill as passed by the House. This change was said to have raised the bill's total above $10,500,000,000.

A ranking member of the committee was unable to say tonight what the exact amount of the bill was, but he said he was "satisfied it is above $10,500,000,000." He added that the amendments approved by the committee were mostly for new items, regarded as emergency ones by the Army and the Navy and Coast Guard. If approved, the measure would set a record for the size of a single appropriation bill.

Fund for Army Pay Specified

Among the amendments approved by the committee was one setting at $314,000,000 the supplemental item for pay of the Army, but immediately following it was a proviso that this amount should not be taken to mean the limit if the Army inducted or enlisted thousands of new personnel. If this took place, under the amendment practical authority would be granted for pay of the personnel under Congressional promise to pass deficiency bills to whatever extent was necessary.

Some $390,000,000 was added to the bill for military air construction. The Signal Corps also received a sizable increase for construction and equipment, while to the Navy were granted increases of many millions for landing fields, yards and docks. The Coast Guard received $4,750,000 for extraordinary expenses and $8,743,000 for new equipment.

The Army Chief of Staff received $125,000,000 as an emergency fund, to be accounted for to Congress every three months, and various sums were voted for additions to forts and posts within the United States.

The measure changing the Selective Service Act regarding the tenure of service and the extent of service came on the heels of action by both houses in declaring war on Germany and Italy, follow-

Continued on Page Thirty-four

WAR OPENED ON US

Congress Acts Quickly as President Meets Hitler Challenge

A GRIM UNANIMITY

Message Warns Nation Foes Aim to Enslave This Hemisphere

By FRANK L. KLUCKHOHN
Special to THE NEW YORK TIMES.

WASHINGTON, Dec. 11—The United States declared war today on Germany and Italy, Japan's Axis partners. This nation acted swiftly after Germany formally declared war on us and Italy followed the German lead. Thus, President Roosevelt told Congress in his message, the long-known and the long-expected has taken place.

"The forces endeavoring to enslave the entire world now are moving toward this hemisphere," he said.

"Never before has there been a greater challenge to life, liberty and civilization."

Delay, the President said, invites great danger. But he added:

"Rapid and united effort by all of the peoples of the world who are determined to remain free will insure a world victory of the forces of justice and righteousness over the forces of savagery and barbarism."

For the first time in its history the United States finds itself at war against powers in both the Atlantic and the Pacific.

Quick and Unanimous Answer

Congress acted not only rapidly but without a dissenting vote to meet the Axis challenge. Within two and three-quarters hours after the reading of Mr. Roosevelt's message was started in the Senate and House at 12:26 P. M., the President had signed the declarations against Germany and Italy. Seventy-two hours previously the Japanese attack on Hawaii had brought about the declaration of war against the other Axis partner.

Congress also quickly completed legislation to allow selectees and National Guardsmen to serve outside the Western Hemisphere and set the term of service in the nation's forces until six months after the termination of the war.

In the Senate the vote was 88 to 0 for war against Germany and 90 to 0 for war against Italy. The vote in the House was 393 to 0 for war against Germany and 399 to 0 for war against Italy. The larger Congressional vote against Italy was attributable to the fact that some members reached the floor too late to vote on the declaration against Germany.

In the House, Miss Jeannette Rankin, Republican, of Montana, who cast the lone dissenting vote on Monday against declaring war on Japan, today voted a non-committal "present" with regard to Germany and Italy.

Ignoring Hitler's declarations before the Reichstag today regarding American policy, and Mussolini's to a crowd before the Palazzo di Venezia in Rome, Congress adopted identical resolutions against Germany and Italy. It merely noted that their governments had thrust war upon the United States.

Grim Mood in Congress

Congress acted in a grim mood, but without excitement. Not only on the floors of the Senate and House, but in the galleries the grim mood prevailed. President Roosevelt, busy at the White House directing the battle and production effort as Commander in Chief, did not appear to read his message, as he did when war was declared upon Japan.

There was a deeply solemn undernote as the members assembled at noon. Senator Walsh, chairman of the Senate Naval Affairs Committee, had announced that the

Continued on Page Five

"All the News That's Fit to Print."

The New York Times.

LATE CITY EDITION
Rain and warmer today.
Temperatures Yesterday—Max., 35; Min., 28

VOL. XCI..No. 30,703. Entered as Second-Class Matter, Postoffice, New York, N. Y. NEW YORK, MONDAY, FEBRUARY 16, 1942. THREE CENTS NEW YORK CITY and Vicinity

SINGAPORE SURRENDERS UNCONDITIONALLY; CHURCHILL ASKS UNITY IN HOUR OF DEFEAT; FOE POURS INTO SUMATRA, STRIKES IN BURMA

78% REGISTERED HERE ON FIRST DAY OF THE THIRD DRAFT

Estimates Place Those Enrolled at 468,000, With 7,020,000 Listed in the Nation

ROLLS TO CLOSE TONIGHT

20-44 Age Group Brings Out Many Middle-Aged Men Who Are Nationally Known

List of registration places will be found on Page 13.

The third registration under the Selective Service Act went into full swing yesterday, particularly in cities, and when the books closed for the day at 9 P. M., indications were that perhaps 7,020,000 men in the United States and 468,000 in New York City had been written into the record of the nation's manpower.

Exact figures, in accordance with an Army announcement ten days ago, will not be made public. But reasonably accurate estimates were made possible by the statement of Colonel Arthur V. McDermott, director of the New York City draft system, that about 78 per cent of those required to register this time had done so by closing time last night.

It has been generally believed that the current "T" or father-and-son draft would affect 9,000,000 men throughout the country and 600,000 within the five boroughs. The assumption that the local turnout would apply on a percentage basis from coast to coast seemed reasonable because of the sleety weather here; which some officials felt would mean that if the percentage differed elsewhere, it would be greater, but surely not less.

Every Class Is Tapped

Regardless of figures, the third draft, like the first two, tapped every stratum of American life. Applying to the 20-44-year age group, but not including those who signed up on either Oct. 16, 1940 or July 1, 1941, it dipped into the large group of men in early middle life that includes some of the nation's best known names in all fields of endeavor.

Many of them may not register until today — when registration centers will be open from 7 A. M. to 9 P. M. throughout the land. But today will be the last chance, and by tonight the roll of potential draftees will have been expanded to take in the following, including several who appeared yesterday:

Former Colonel Charles A. Lindbergh, 40 years old on Feb. 4; former District Attorney Thomas E. Dewey and his successor, Frank S. Hogan, both 39; Acting Governor Charles Poletti, 38; Council President Newbold Morris, 40; John Barbirolli, conductor, 42; Controller Joseph D. McGoldrick, 40; President R. M. Hutchins of the University of Chicago, 43, and Carl Hubbell, veteran baseball pitcher, 39.

Celebrated entertainers, writers, business men, educators and scientists also were on the list.

But the drama of the father-son draft lay not in the "big names" involved so much as in its bridging of two generations; and its reaching out to touch thousands of Americans whose national and racial backgrounds were as diffuse as their idiosyncrasies and their incomes.

Fathers literally appeared with sons, and in at least one case, a father was registrar while the son was registrant. Veterans who bore the scars of World War I appeared, ready to join the list of potential eligibles for World War II; a good example was Andrew W. Knebel of Addison, N. Y., State com-

Continued on Page Three

Australia Arrests Aliens Along Coast

By The Associated Press.

BRISBANE, Australia, Monday, Feb. 16—Hundreds of enemy aliens, mostly Italian sugar-field workers, were arrested in a wide-spread round-up Friday night and Saturday in North Queensland. The sugar belt lies along the coast where Japanese could land in an attempted invasion.

A special barred and guarded train is taking the aliens southward for internment at Townsville. The Italians had been boasting, according to newspapers, that "the Japanese won't touch us." Many had hidden firearms.

SYDNEY, Australia, Feb. 15 (From Australian broadcast recorded by The United Press in New York)—The government completed plans today for the registration of all male aliens tomorrow and Tuesday.

HEATING WITH GAS CURTAILED BY WPB

New York Is Among Seventeen States Named in Order to Supply War Industries

Special to The New York Times.

WASHINGTON, Feb. 15—Curtailment in the consumption of natural and mixed natural and manufactured gas was ordered by the War Production Board today to assure adequate supplies for war production activities.

Curtailment is necessary, the board said, because of increased gas requirements for both war purposes and civilian use, coupled with the scarcity of materials that would be required if existing systems were expanded.

One of increased war production uses of natural gas will be the program to manufacture 400,000 tons of synthetic rubber, the major part of which will be made from butadiene which is produced from natural gas.

Part of the WPB's order becomes effective on March 1 and applies to seventeen States, including New York and the District of Columbia "where the need for curtailment is greater." Other parts

Continued on Page Ten

PREMIER IS SOMBER

Calls Singapore Military Disaster, but He Warns Against Weakness

ACCLAIMS U. S. ENTRY

Lists It as Dream 'Come to Pass'—Gives Russia as Example in Peril

The text of Mr. Churchill's address is on Page 6.

By ROBERT P. POST

Wireless to The New York Times.

LONDON, Feb. 15—The entrance of the United States into the war is a fact that cannot be compared with anything else "in the whole world," Prime Minister Churchill said in a world broadcast tonight.

When he surveyed the power of the United States and its resources and felt that they were now in it "with the British Commonwealth of Nations, all together, however long it lasts, till death or victory," Mr. Churchill said that this was the first and greatest event he had to report to the British people.

"That is what I have dreamed of, aimed at and worked for and now it has come to pass," Mr. Churchill said.

But at the same time he balanced the good of the latest war developments—in which he included the efforts of Russia—against the heavy and grave events elsewhere. And frankly telling the people throughout the world that he spoke "under the shadow of a heavy and far-reaching military defeat," the loss of Singapore, Mr. Churchill went on to call for a spirit of unity and new exertions in this dark hour.

Adverse news "of many misfortunes and gnawing anxieties lie before us," Mr. Churchill said, but from that very fact he invoked a new spirit of toughness from the people who march against the Axis.

Perhaps with reference to the widespread spirit of uneasiness that has covered this country and

Continued on Page Six

SINGAPORE SURRENDERS: WHERE TERMS WERE SET AND 2 SIGNATORIES

The Ford Motor Company plant where commanding officers of British and Japanese armies conferred

Associated Press

Lieut. Gen. Tomoyuki Yamashita

Lieut. Gen. Arthur E. Percival

The War Summarized

MONDAY, FEBRUARY 16, 1942

Japan became the master of Singapore yesterday. At Rangoon, back door to China, civilian evacuation went on. Japanese troops were invading Southern Sumatra, stepping stone to Java. In London Winston Churchill warned the British people to remain united behind their government, but expressed no word of optimism regarding the immediate future in the Far Eastern war theatre.

Prime Minister Churchill announced the fall of Singapore a few hours after the Tokyo radio had announced that hostilities ceased. The British Army, according to the Tokyo report, surrendered unconditionally. The surrender came one week after the Japanese had started to storm the island. [1:8; map, p. 4.] Official Washington called the fall of Singapore the darkest moment of the war. [1:7.]

The British Prime Minister's broadcast drew Britain's attention to Russian firmness in supporting the government in the hour of peril and emphasized the great importance of American entry into the war. [1:3].

The invaders that landed in Southern Sumatra apparently intended to drive on the Palembang oil center. Netherland bombers attacked Japanese transports and scored hits. Fewer than 100 of 700 Japanese parachutists who had landed in the Palembang zone Saturday escaped, according to Batavia; the Tokyo radio claimed, however, that the parachutists had occupied several important positions. [1:5-6; map, p. 2.]

In Burma the Japanese were developing drives from two directions toward Thaton, on the Martaban - Rangoon Railway. Landing parties were moving inland from the seacoast above Martaban and the Japanese were moving out from their Salween River bridgehead up the river at Paan. Protected by American fighter planes, British bombers attacked enemy supply dumps at Paan and Martaban. [1:4; map, p. 2.]

General MacArthur's report from the Philippines indicated that the Japanese were advancing preparations for another full-fledged offensive against his Bataan positions. Enemy front-line forces, which had suffered heavy casualties, were being relieved by fresh troops. [1:5.]

Germany was reported to be drawing on her "Spring offensive" reserves for the campaign in Russia, but without, as yet, halting the Russian advance. Moscow said Soviet columns at one point were about seventy-five miles from the former Polish frontier. [9:2.]

British and Australian pilots flying planes made in the United States smashed a formation of thirty of the Axis' dive-bombers and fighters in Libya near El Gazala. Twenty of the enemy planes were shot down. In the Mediterranean, submarines sank two Axis supply ships and probably a third. A fourth ship was set afire by British bombers. On land the Germans seemed to be attempting to flank the British lines before Tobruk. [7:1]

2-WAY BURMA DRIVE AIMS AT RAIL TOWN

Japanese Strike for Thaton on Line to Rangoon—R. A. F. Bombs Supplies

By The Associated Press.

RANGOON, Burma, Feb. 15—Japanese forces struck from two directions tonight at Thaton, forty miles northwest of Martaban on the Rangoon railroad, and the battle for the east coast of the Gulf of Martaban neared its climax.

The invaders are attacking from seaside landing points above captured Martaban as well as from a deep salient thrust from their Salween River bridgehead at Paan, unofficial reports said.

The Army communiqué merely said:

"There were no further attacks on the Salween front but reports indicate the enemy is preparing for an attack in the area of Duyinzaik-Thaton."

British bombers, accompanied by American fighters, heavily bombed enemy supply dumps at Paan and Martaban and swept wide over enemy-occupied territory on reconnaissance flights. Canadians piloted two of the Blenheim bombers that blasted and machine-gunned a Japanese troop camp at Martaban and river craft and motor vehicles.

The Blenheims flew with a fighter screen of American and British fighters and pressed home two heavy attacks yesterday. Some defense fire was encountered but all Allied planes returned safely.

The Japanese have established bridgeheads over the Salween at Paan and Martaban and it was there that the British bombers concentrated.

The front flared into battle today; twenty-four hours after bombers had thinned the enemy lines so

Continued on Page Two

Ships Land Foe in Sumatra; Dutch Blow Up Oil Property

By F. TILLMAN DURDIN

By Telephone to The New York Times.

BATAVIA, Netherlands Indies, Monday, Feb. 16—The Japanese, having opened their drive on Sumatra with a parachute attack Saturday on the Palembang oil region, continued their campaign yesterday with a large-scale landing of troops from ships on the coast about sixty miles from Palembang. The landing was made in an area of marshes and mangrove swamps along the muddy banks of the Musi River, which leads to Palembang.

The Indies defense forces in the Palembang region have started the destruction of one of the world's greatest oil fields, together with refineries and other installations. The Japanese parachute-troop attack on Saturday, made in an attempt to forestall the destruction, has failed, and it was announced in Batavia yesterday that the wrecking of all "vital points" in the vicinity of Palembang began Saturday night.

The destruction of the Palembang oil fields, stores and machinery will represent a loss of properties worth more than $100,000,000. However, it is a move that will ultimately be a major contribution to the fight against the Japanese. It denies to the enemy more than 50 per cent of the oil production of the Netherlands Indies.

Enemy Aim Frustrated

Nearly all the other oil-producing areas of the Indies already have been destroyed and thus the main aim of the Japanese attack on Indonesia—to obtain oil quickly—has been frustrated.

The Netherlanders reported that nearly all the Japanese parachute troops who landed Saturday, in the vicinity of the refineries of the Socony-Vacuum and Netherland companies, had been accounted for. Of an estimated 700 soldiers

Continued on Page Two

M'ARTHUR EXPECTS BIG ENEMY ATTACK

Reports Japanese Regrouping on Bataan for a Resumption of Their Offensive

By C. BROOKS PETERS

Special to The New York Times.

WASHINGTON, Feb. 15—General Douglas MacArthur reported from his Philippine stronghold on the Island of Luzon today that enemy preparations for the long-anticipated all-out Japanese offensive against the American and Filipino positions in the Battle of Bataan were visibly under way. He suggested that the attack was imminent.

General MacArthur said that the enemy was regrouping his forces. The evident objective of such a regrouping, he added, would be "a resumption of the offensive."

Now that the mighty British bastion of the East, Singapore, has fallen, the Bataan front remains the only theatre of the war in which the Japanese have been unable to advance almost at will and achieve their objectives.

It may be that, regardless of the sacrifices in men and equipment that a devastating assault would cost, the enemy will consider an overpowering attack justified to

Continued on Page Four

Bataan 'One-Man Army' Kills 116 On Raids Behind Japanese Lines

By CLARK LEE

Associated Press Correspondent

ON THE BATAAN PENINSULA, Feb. 13 (Delayed)—Captain Arthur W. Wermuth of Chicago, who has killed 116 Japanese and captured many more, is America's No. 1 one-man army to his fellow-officers of the Fifty-seventh Filipino Scout Regiment.

He "absolutely accounted" for at least 116 Japanese with his 45-caliber tommy-gun and Garand rifle, his fighting companions said today. He has won the silver star for gallantry, the Distinguished Service Cross for extraordinary heroism, and the Purple Heart with two clasps.

Thrice wounded, he spent more than two weeks in January more behind the Japanese lines than in the American line. He has led so many scouting raids he has lost count. His actions have forestalled many enemy attacks and prepared the way for American counter-attacks.

I finally located him today, just out of the hospital and on his way to battle. At dinner, I got part of his story and other officers gave me the rest.

Captain Wermuth, who is from Chicago, fights the war as he played football for Northwestern Military Academy at Lake Geneva, Wis.—fearlessly and for keeps. This 190-pounder with a Van Dyke beard is at home in the Bataan Mountains, where he has spent many years. He knew life in the open before he saw Bataan. His

Continued on Page Four

WASHINGTON SEES DIRE BLOW IN EAST

Sumatra Is Expected to Fall, Cutting Off Allies' Main Oil Supply in the Indies

By JAMES B. RESTON

Special to The New York Times.

WASHINGTON, Feb. 15—The considered judgment of responsible officials in Washington is that the fall of Singapore marks the darkest moment of the war for the United Nations. Even the anticipation of the event and the rhetoric of Winston Churchill did not minimize the feeling that this blow may be decisive in the Southwest Pacific and may vitally affect the outcome of the conflict in China and the Middle East.

If there was any confidence in the fate of Sumatra, with its rich oil fields and coast line bordering the Malacca Strait, the feeling here would not be so pessimistic, but it is virtually conceded that Sumatra, too, must inevitably fall, cutting the United Nations off from their main supply of oil in the Southwest Pacific and leaving the Japanese free passage into the Indian Ocean, from where they can raid the Allied supply lines to China, Suez and the Persian Gulf.

The only bright spot in this dreary picture is some indication that more United States aircraft have arrived in Java, though deliveries to the Netherlands Indies from the United States are only about one-quarter of what the Dutch have ordered. The number of aircraft involved in these recent deliveries cannot be disclosed, but there is reason to believe that enough were landed to give the Dutch some chance of sending a few planes into the air against the invaders.

Also, there was confidence among United Nations' representatives here that the battle of production will bring the tools of war

Continued on Page Five

BRITISH CAPITULATE

Troops to Keep Order Until Foe Completes Occupation of Base

3 DRIVES HEM CITY

Tokyo Claims Toll of 32 Allied Vessels South of Singapore

By JAMES MacDONALD

Special Cable to The New York Times.

LONDON, Feb. 15—Singapore has fallen.

The long dreaded news that the key British base of the Pacific and Indian Oceans would be captured by the Japanese—a major reverse clearly foreseen many days ago—was announced tonight by Winston Churchill, a few hours after dispatches from Vichy and Tokyo reported that Lieut. Gen. Arthur E. Percival's forces had surrendered unconditionally at 3:30 P. M. today British daylight saving time [9:50 P. M. Sunday Singapore time and 10:30 A. M. Eastern war time].

London officials naturally declined to disclose what plans had been made or were perhaps in the making for establishing a naval base elsewhere to meet the grave emergency arising from the loss of Singapore. They could not or would not divulge how many Imperial troops were taken prisoner or how many got away.

Commanders Meet

According to the official Tokyo announcement, fighting ceased along the entire front three hours after a meeting between General Percival and the Japanese Commander in Chief, Lieut. Gen. Tomoyuki Yamashita, in the Ford motor plant at the foot of Timah Hill, where the documents of surrender were signed. The terms were not disclosed here, but a Japanese Domei Agency dispatch late tonight said that under the capitulation up to 1,000 armed British soldiers would remain in Singapore City to maintain order until the Japanese Army completed occupation.

Similar terms, it is recalled, were contained in the surrender of Hong Kong on Christmas Day.

The Tokyo radio said the Japanese had constantly kept pouring in fresh troops to make up for losses from the fierce resistance of British Imperial troops.

In the final battle, three Japanese columns were said to have advanced on the city. Yesterday the central column completed occupation of the water reservoirs and a part of this column reached the northern outskirts of the city on a six-mile front. Another column bypassed the reservoirs, crossed the Kalang River and cut the road from Singapore to the civil airport. The third column reached Alexandria Road in the western part of the city.

Some Resisting, Tokyo Says

[Japanese units left the main island in barges and seized Blakang Mati, the island opposite Keppel Harbor, thereby gaining control of the sea approach to Singapore from the south, according to a Tokyo broadcast recorded by The United Press.

[Japanese troops entered Singapore City today under the terms of the surrender by the British, but a Domei dispatch said some of the defending forces and "other hostile elements" still were resisting, another Tokyo broadcast heard by The United Press stated.]

The Berlin radio, quoting the Japanese newspaper Asahi, said the largest part of the British and Australian forces "obviously" left Singapore Friday for Sumatra.

Unofficial reports reached London late tonight that 2,000 persons

Continued on Page Four

"All the News That's Fit to Print."

The New York Times.

LATE CITY EDITION
Mild and windy today.
Temperatures Yesterday—Max., 40; Min., 37

Copyright, 1942, by The New York Times Company.

VOL. XCI—No. 30,734. Entered as Second-Class Matter, Postoffice, New York, N. Y. NEW YORK, WEDNESDAY, MARCH 18, 1942. THREE CENTS NEW YORK CITY and Vicinity

M'ARTHUR IN AUSTRALIA AS ALLIED COMMANDER; MOVE HAILED AS FORESHADOWING TURN OF TIDE; THIRD NATIONAL ARMY DRAFT BEGINS IN CAPITAL

PRESIDENT WARNS AGAINST RUSHING ANTI-STRIKES LAW

No Problem Exists at Present and Things Are Going Along Pretty Well, He Cautions

HE EXPLAINS 40-HOUR ACT

But Bill to Ban It Is Pushed to Hearings in House—Senate Also Swept by Debate

By W. H. LAWRENCE
Special to THE NEW YORK TIMES.

WASHINGTON, March 17 — President Roosevelt, at the moment when Congressional sentiment for anti-strike legislation became accentuated, stated today that there was no strike problem at the present moment and cautioned against rushing labor legislation to enactment when things were going along pretty well.

Congress, Mr. Roosevelt told his press conference this afternoon, could not pass a law that would make a man turn out more work. That, he observed, was up to the enthusiasm of the individual. More parades, band playing and flag waving, he suggested, would stir up enthusiasm more than restrictive law.

Organized labor, meanwhile, reported that the President was in agreement that the performance of labor was "exceptional, and, of course, satisfactory." It was agreed, spokesmen said, that voluntary action on the part of labor to yield its right to strike was a more satisfactory answer to the production problem than resort to legislation such as has been presented to the House in the last twenty-four hours.

Action Demanded in Congress

On Capitol Hill, however, steps toward legislative action persisted.

On the House side plans were made to go ahead with almost immediate hearings on a bill which would suspend the forty-hour week for the duration, would freeze open and closed shop conditions, and also clamp ceilings upon industry's profits on war contracts. Demands for Congressional action, which centered in the House yesterday, swept across the Capitol today to the Senate, where, for more than four hours, they displaced other thought and business.

Mr. Roosevelt told the press conference that he favors continuance of time-and-a-half pay for work over forty hours a week, but revealed that he had called upon the "combined Labor War Board," composed of six representatives of the American Federation of Labor and Congress of Industrial Organizations, to give up union contract rules which require double pay for work on Sundays. William Green, president of the A. F. of L., and Philip Murray, president of the C. I. O., and other representatives of both labor organizations visited the White House a few hours before the press conference.

Advocating continuous operation of plants to speed up the production of war materials, the President in his press conference remarks urged plant management to adopt a staggered shift system under which workers would receive double pay only if they worked seven consecutive days.

Says Law Is Misunderstood

Decrying "an amazing state of public misinformation," which he blamed in part upon the newspapers and irresponsible speeches in Congress, the President told of receiving a letter from a professional economist, who drew the conclusion that Japan would not have declared war and the United States would not have lost the Philippines or the Dutch East Indies if 30,000,000 man-days had not been lost by strikes in the first twenty-one months of the defense program.

The President said, with a smile,

Continued on Page Twenty

Gen. Homma Suicide Confirmed by Chilean

By The United Press.

SANTIAGO, Chile, March 17—The suicide of General Masaharu Homma, commander of the Japanese forces in the Philippines, as reported by General Douglas MacArthur, was confirmed today by Carlos Barry, a Chilean journalist stranded in Japan, in a report to his newspaper, the Chileno.

Señor Barry and five other Chilean newspaper men, guests of the Japanese Government on a visit to Japan and Manchuria, were on their way home on a Japanese steamer when the Japanese bombed Pearl Harbor. Their ship turned about and landed them again at Yokohama. They now await passage on a vessel returning exchanged Western Hemisphere diplomats.

50% AIRPLANE RISE REPORTED BY NELSON

He Warns Three-Month Gain Is Not Enough—K. T. Keller Asked to Head Output

Text of Mr. Nelson's address is printed on Page 18.

Special to THE NEW YORK TIMES.

WASHINGTON, March 17—Plane production has been stepped up 50 per cent since Pearl Harbor, Donald M. Nelson, chairman of the War Production Board, said tonight in a radio address. He warned, however, that there was no reason for complacency, because the country was nowhere near its goals.

"We need more and forever more of these weapons and we need them now," he said. "We have got to realize the value of time."

It was learned tonight that K. T. Keller, president of the Chrysler Corporation, had been strongly urged by the War Production Board to direct the agency's airplane production program and to effect "short cuts" which will make possible the production of a greater

Continued on Page Eighteen

3,485 FIRST NUMBER

All Night Is Required for Drawing That Affects 9,000,000 Men

USE IN NAVY IS URGED

Hershey Also Suggests Assigning Some Labor for War Projects

List of the draft numbers drawn is on Pages 12, 13 and 14.

Secretary of War Stimson drew the first number—3,485—from the famous goldfish bowl in Washington at 6:05 o'clock last night to begin America's third draft lottery in seventeen months, although its first in wartime since 1918.

The drawing continued throughout the night. By 6 A. M. 6,000 of the 7,000 numbers had been listed and it was expected that the lottery would be completed by 8 o'clock.

Green capsules containing the serial numbers of those who registered last month, drawn in this St. Patrick's Day lottery, gave to 9,000,000 men between 20 and 44 years of age the green light to go ahead in the tasks to which they may be assigned in total war against Hitler and the Japanese. Green cards will be used in Selective Service headquarters to record the order of their liability to military service.

In a brief introductory address Brig. Gen. Lewis B. Hershey, Director of Selective Service, urged conscription of men for the Navy as well as the Army and suggested that at least on some war projects labor also should be "selected."

The No. 1 boy of the draft in New York City, just as on the two previous occasions, was a Chinese—Chin Fong Ho, a 20-year-old waiter born in China, now living in New York's Chinatown and

Continued on Page Fifteen

The War Summarized

WEDNESDAY, MARCH 18, 1942

General Douglas MacArthur assumed command of the United Nations forces in Australia and the Southwest Pacific yesterday at a moment when both sides in the war were evidently devoting themselves principally to preparations for offensives later in the Spring. Only in Russia was there heavy action, with Soviet forces pounding furiously at the Staraya Russa sector and at Kharkov.

Washington announced that General MacArthur had already arrived in Australia by order of President Roosevelt. He has assumed command by request of the Australian Government. His command will include the Philippines, where he has been succeeded by Major Gen. Wainwright. Although the President announced that General MacArthur's withdrawal did not mean the Philippines were to be abandoned, the Japanese yesterday staged their first assault since March 8 on the Bataan defense line. They were sharply repulsed. [1:8.]

At the United States Army Headquarters in Australia it was disclosed that two Army planes had been used for General MacArthur's flight and that they had passed through areas of the most intense Japanese activity. The greatest secrecy was observed, and not even Premier Curtin of Australia was informed until the flight had been completed. [1:5-6.]

High officials of the government in Washington and Congressional leaders were unanimous in praising Mr. Roosevelt's decision to send General MacArthur to Australia. [4:4.]

In Britain General MacArthur's appointment was hailed as a demonstration of the coordination existing between the Empire and the United States. [4:1.]

Australians called the selection the best news since the outbreak of the war in the Far East. [1:7.]

In Burma Chinese troops on the Allied left flank routed Japanese-officered Thai troops. [8:1; with map.]

During a British parliamentary debate the assertion was made that the thirteen United Nations naval ships destroyed off Java had had to oppose a force of ninety-nine Japanese war vessels. [8:5.]

A possible new development in the European sphere was foreshadowed by a German order closing all Norway's ports from North Cape to Aalesund. The order suggested that German troop and naval movements of some importance were being screened. [1:4; map, P. 9.]

The Soviet reports indicated that the Germans were being forced back northwest and west of Kharkov in fierce hand-to-hand fighting. Advance units appeared to have broken through the surrounding fortifications at one point and to be engaged in a house-to-house battle. [7:1.]

Germany's increasing grip on French North Africa was demonstrated by a Vichy order for the internment of all Britons between the ages of 18 and 50 living on the coast of Morocco. [9:1.]

The sinking of three and possibly four vessels in our Atlantic waters was disclosed, including one Uruguayan ship. Uruguay promptly seized the German ship Tacoma, lying in Montevideo harbor. [1:5.] In Santiago, Chile, anti-Axis rioting broke out because of the sinking last Friday off New York of the Chilean ship Tolten. [17:1.]

M'ARTHURMEN: ON THE ALERT EN ROUTE TO AUSTRALIA

Gun crew manning a mobile anti-aircraft gun on one of the transports—the fighters and the gun are now on the island-continent
Additional photographs appear on Page 3.
The New York Times (official U. S. Navy)

NAZIS CLOSE PORTS OF NORTH NORWAY

Reported Adding to Forces—British Say Tirpitz Eluded Torpedo-Plane Attack

By The Associated Press.

LONDON, March 17—All Norway's ports from North Cape to Aalesund had been closed by the Germans today, presumably to screen stealthy marshaling of German military and naval forces that indicated that those far-northern waters were about to become a newly active major war theatre.

Speaking just after a disclosure that the mighty German battleship Tirpitz "appears to have avoided" a recent British torpedo-plane attack off Narvik, and thus even now is presumably loose upon the high seas, a responsible London informant speculated that the Germans were preparing attempts to isolate Russia's Arctic ports, cut her supply lines from her allies or even move against United States-garrisoned and British-garrisoned Iceland.

Another View Suggested

Another informant, who is in constant communication with the Norwegians, suggested a second possible interpretation—that the Germans were worried about the possibilities of United Nations response to Russian calls for the opening of a second front.

And in that connection he declared that Norway was seething against the Germans.

Among the day's accumulating incidents that pointed to major action in the north, the sharpest and most alarming in British eyes was the news that the Tirpitz had not been run to cover.

The British source who said that the Tirpitz "appears to have avoided" attacks in the vicinity of Narvik March 9 added that he had "no information" about her present whereabouts. After the torpedo-plane attack, he said, the Tirpitz retired to the coast under a smoke screen and was lost there among the fjords.

When the attack on the Tirpitz was made, he continued, she probably was within cover of fighter protection, but "the attacks were pressed home under rather difficult weather conditions."

He said that the Tirpitz and the German 10,000-ton cruiser Prinz Eugen had been located in a fjord near Trondheim before the Tirpitz had sailed, that the Prinz Eugen had been torpedoed on the passage to Trondheim, and that thus the three ships that made a dash recently through the English Channel—the Prinz Eugen and the Ger-

Continued on Page Nine

MacArthur Party in 2 Planes Soars Over Japanese Fronts

By BYRON DARNTON
Wireless to THE NEW YORK TIMES.

UNITED STATES ARMY HEADQUARTERS, in Australia, Wednesday, March 18—General Douglas MacArthur flew over some of the hottest fighting areas in the Southwestern Pacific on his journey of more than 2,000 miles from the Philippines to assume supreme command of the United Nations' forces in this area, it was revealed this morning when news of the general's arrival with his family and staff was made public.

Two United States Army planes were used for the journey. General MacArthur has not yet arrived at headquarters, although he is in Australia and has assumed command. Some of his officers are here, and they are in the best of health. It is understood that General MacArthur and his family are resting after their journey, but that he will arrive at headquarters soon. He is tired.

It was officially disclosed that the appointment of General MacArthur had been made with the "most enthusiastic" approval of Australia. American correspondents here have heard repeatedly from Australian civilians and soldiers the question, "Why don't you send us MacArthur?"

Details of the general's journey have not yet been fully revealed, but it was explained that the long flight had taken the party over the areas of the heaviest recent Japanese activity. Whether the planes used by the MacArthur party had been dispatched from Australia for that purpose or already were in the Philippines was not disclosed. But the feat demonstrates that communications exist between the

Continued on Page Five

URUGUAYAN VESSEL, TWO OTHERS SUNK

Nation Seizes German Ship in Retaliation—Fourth Craft Feared Lost in Bahamas

The sinking of at least three, and possibly four, ships by Axis submarines operating off our Atlantic coast was disclosed yesterday. The victims were a medium-sized merchant ship of United States registry, a 5,785-ton Uruguayan vessel, an unidentified vessel from which fifty-seven survivors were landed in Nassau, and possibly a large United States tanker reported sunk in the Bahamas.

Most important from the standpoint of international relations was the Uruguayan ship Montevideo, which was sent to the bottom with seventeen of her crew off Jeremie, Haiti. Her loss brought the number of South American republics that have suffered submarine sinkings to three. Four Brazilian ships have been torpedoed and on Monday the sinking of the Chilean freighter Tolten was announced.

In swift retaliation the Uruguayan Government seized the 8,268-ton German ship Tacoma, which had been interned in Uruguayan waters ever since the destruction of the pocket battleship Graf Spee in December, 1939.

Uruguay, which had already broken off relations with the Axis powers, ordered the suspension of further sailings of her ships until arrangements could be made to safeguard them. It was expected, according to The Associated Press, that the government would arm them. In view of the public indignation caused by the announcement of the sinking, the Uruguayan Government placed guards over the property of Axis nationals.

Previously 200 rioting students had stoned a toy shop operated by a Spaniard believed to be a member of the pro-Fascist Falangists and called for the imprisoning of a Uruguayan nationalist leader.

Foreign Minister Alberto Guani,

Continued on Page Seventeen

PLEASED AUSTRALIA GREETS A 'FIGHTER'

MacArthur Warmly Welcomed—British Expect That Policy of Defense Will End

By The Associated Press.

MELBOURNE, Australia, Wednesday, March 18 — General Douglas MacArthur's arrival to assume the United Nations command in the Southwestern Pacific was hailed jubilantly by the Australian press today as the most important and most welcome move thus far in the defense of this Commonwealth.

"It will be regarded as the best single piece of news since the outbreak of the Pacific war," said one editorial. "His gallant stand in the Philippines has fired the imagination of Australians, who love a fighter, and his command of Australians in addition to American troops will be an inspiration to the fighting forces."

[In London it was suggested that the appointment of General MacArthur, which was highly approved, meant that the United Nations intended to substitute offense for defense in the Far East.]

The selection of so high a United States officer for the important post, it was pointed out, gives emphasis to the statement by Secretary of War Henry L. Stimson that "considerable" American forces are here.

"It is also an indication," the newspaper added, "of President Roosevelt's realization of how important is the Southwest Pacific in this global war and of what aid the

Continued on Page Five

Bill for Women's Auxiliary Corps Of 150,000 Passed by the House

By NONA BALDWIN
Special to THE NEW YORK TIMES.

WASHINGTON, March 17—The House passed today a bill creating a volunteer Women's Army Auxiliary Corps, whose members, by taking over duties now performed behind the lines by enlisted men, would release many men for combat duty. The roll-call vote was 249 to 86.

The bill, sponsored by Representative Edith Nourse Rogers of Massachusetts, was passed with two amendments, the major one limiting the strength of the corps to 150,000. The other permits Army nurses to enroll in the corps.

The bulk of the four-hour discussion on the measure revolved around the extent to which Army discipline and military law would apply to members of the WAAC. Reading Section 2 of the Articles of War, Chairman May of the Committee on Military Affairs expressed the opinion that members of the WAAC would be subject to court-martial.

The issue was raised by Representative Nichols of Oklahoma in proposing an amendment to entitle members of the corps to the same compensation, pensions and disability claims that are extended to soldiers. The amendment was rejected by a standing vote of 70 to 30, but his contention that, under the

Continued on Page Twenty-one

GENERAL FLIES OUT

Wife, Child Accompany Him on Trip From Philippine Post

ORDER BY PRESIDENT

Roosevelt Asserts All Americans Back It—Expect Action Now

By CHARLES HURD
Special to THE NEW YORK TIMES.

WASHINGTON, March 17 — General Douglas MacArthur today became Supreme Commander of the United Nations forces in the Southwestern Pacific.

This dramatic shift of command and promotion for the dashing officer who has held the Japanese at bay on the Island of Luzon for three months and ten days was announced by the War Department simultaneously with his arrival in Australia. Traveling by plane, he arrived with his staff and his wife and child.

A few hours after announcement of the action, President Roosevelt told a press conference that he was "sure that every American" agreed with his decision to take General MacArthur out of the Philippines.

He recognized, he said, that Axis propaganda agents would see in this move abandonment of the Philippines, but this is not the case. General MacArthur will command everything, including sea and air forces, east of Singapore in the Southwestern Pacific, the President added, and will be more useful in Australia than on Bataan Peninsula.

President's Statement

Finally, the President authorized quotation of the following statement:

"I know that every man and woman in the United States admires with me General MacArthur's determination to fight to the finish with his men in the Philippines. But I also know that every man and woman is in agreement that all important decisions must be made with a view toward the successful termination of the war. Knowing this, I am sure that every American, if faced individually with the question as to where General MacArthur could best serve his country, could come to only one answer."

[Lieut. Gen. George H. Brett, United States Army, is Deputy Supreme Commander of the United Nations Forces in the Southwest Pacific and is in command of all the United Nations air forces in the region, according to a United Press dispatch from Melbourne, Australia.]

No move made by the United States Government since the war began has had a more vivid or optimistic reaction than this one. Officials in and out of Congress rushed to commend the action, and reports from New York indicated that the Stock Exchange immediately registered higher prices.

In the reaction manifested here were two indicated causes for optimism. One was the feeling that General MacArthur was equal to the task of stemming the Japanese advance southward, in view of his record in the Philippines, and of planning future offensive operations. The other was a belief that perhaps he had not been assigned to the High Command until United Nations intelligence officers felt that there was a good chance of changing the tide of battle.

On Washington's Birthday

In any event, he landed somewhere in Australia not long after the arrival of heavy United States air and ground forces, sent to augment the Australian troops. The action, in which Australia endorsed the choice of General MacArthur, has been a closely guarded secret since Feb. 22, when President Roosevelt ordered General

Continued on Page Three

"All the News That's Fit to Print."

The New York Times.

LATE CITY EDITION
Warmer with showers today.
Temperatures Yesterday—Max., 52; Min., 43

VOL. XCI. No. 30,776. Entered as Second-Class Matter, Postoffice, New York, N. Y. NEW YORK, WEDNESDAY, APRIL 29, 1942. THREE CENTS NEW YORK CITY and Vicinity

SALES PRICES, RENTS, SERVICE CHARGES FROZEN; ROOSEVELT SEES AXIS CRACKING, PLEDGES FIGHT TO VICTORY THROUGH 'WORK, SORROW AND BLOOD'

AURORA OF LIGHTS DIMS OUT IN CITY FOR THE DURATION

Skyscrapers Lost in Low Haze as Famed Display Here Is Darkened by Army

STREET BULBS GLOW DULLY

Great Signs in Times Square Found to Illuminate the Mist Lying Over the Area

New York City's neon aurora and skyscraper diadem were dimmed for the war's duration after sundown yesterday. Along with the rest of the Eastern seaboard the City of Light's nocturnal display was reduced by Army order to dispel sky glow that has brought our ships far at sea into sharp silhouette in Axis gunsights.

Skyscraper clocks—as in the Metropolitan, Paramount and other city towers—vanished from New York's evening skyline as dusk settled. Rockefeller Center, the Empire State Building, Wall Street's towers, the Chrysler Building and other great monoliths were lost in low haze even under the yellow moon.

Seen from the 102d floor of the Empire State Building after 8 o'clock the city's streets were squares of brooding shadow rimmed by sidewalk lamps and by red neon signs that bloomed like poppies. Red neon, incidentally, gave off the most glow. This was particularly noticeable over Times Square.

Commissioner Valentine was asked late yesterday afternoon whether Times Square's numerous spectacular signs would be dimmed. In a written answer he cited a passage from the Army's official orders: "Exterior illumination used for advertising * * * that cannot be shaded shall be extinguished." Most of the square's great signs are unshaded and last night they illuminated low-lying haze banks but kept burning just the same.

Charwomen Have to Learn

Toward the shank end of the evening skyscrapers that had been hidden in darkness began to show lights, high up, at different floors. It turned out, in most cases, that the offenders were charwomen come to do office floors. They were warned to pull the shades. In some hotels new guests who had not seen the newspapers also turned on lights without drawing shades, but were warned against repeating the offense.

Army observers stood out to sea to watch the effect of the dimming. Their report may not be ready until today. Major Gen.

Continued on Page Ten

President Included In Jersey Blackout

Special to THE NEW YORK TIMES.

MADISON, N. J., April 28—Plans for a practice blackout tonight in this Morris County community of 8,000 were so complete that even the President's radio speech was blacked out from 10 to 10:15 P. M.

When a practice darkening of Western and Southern New Jersey was ordered for tonight two weeks ago the Town Council decided to put it into effect by throwing a switch at the municipal power station, cutting off radios as well as electrical ice boxes. The town buys current from a power company and distributes it through one central station.

Frank Waters, superintendent of the distributing plant, was flooded with telephone calls today from residents who pointed out that the time for the blackout was the same as the time for the President's speech. Mr. Waters replied, however, that as the time for the President's speech was announced only yesterday it was too late to change the blackout plans.

Japanese Drive for Lashio With 5,000 Men; City Afire

Burma Road Terminus Blasted by Bombers —Chinese Fight Desperately to Turn the Tide in the Vicinity of Taunggyi

By DAVID ANDERSON
Wireless to THE NEW YORK TIMES.

LONDON, April 28—More than 5,000 Japanese have knifed through the northern Shan States in the direction of the Lashio terminus of the Burma Road. The invaders are reported to have re-entered Taunggyi, some 110 miles southeast of Mandalay, which was captured by the Chinese under United States Lieut. Gen. Joseph W. Stilwell with heavy losses four days ago.

The Chinese were making a desperate attempt to stem the tide by turning the Taunggyi force east toward Loilem to cut off the enemy from the rear. This is viewed here as a forlorn hope.

The main body of the invading force, slashing its way forward after what might prove to be a knockout blow to Burma, consists of 3,000 troops moving north toward Konghaiping, according to a Chungking report. Allied reconnaissance planes have sighted another enemy column of at least 2,000 men closing in on Kehsi Mansam, about seventy miles almost due south of Lashio. A third column of 2,000 is sweeping east toward Kunhing.

The two northbound columns are believed aiming to cut the Mandalay-Lashio railroad or to capture Mandalay. [A United Press dispatch from Chungking described the opposing forces as racing for Bhamo, about 100 miles north of Lashio, from which a good secondary road connects with the Burma Road. The German-controlled Paris radio broadcast a "Tokyo report" that the Japanese had taken Lashio, The Associated Press reported from London.]

The eastward Japanese advance presumably has the twofold objec-

Continued on Page Three

TAXI ARMY SPEEDS TO 'PROTECT' CITY

5,000 State Guardsmen Free Army's Mobile Units in First Cooperative Manoeuvre

Five thousand soldiers from the twelve metropolitan regiments of the New York Guard were mobilized at their armories last night and transported in a fleet of fifty buses and 200 taxicabs to 100 strategic points throughout the city in an emergency test of their readiness to deal with concerted city-wide sabotage by enemy agents and fifth columnists.

Railroad stations, airports, bridges, tunnels, ferry terminals and other "sensitive" spots in the life of the city were covered by the regiments of the First, Second and Fifth Brigades of the only military force authorized for the State of New York now that the National Guard has been incorporated into the Army.

The manoeuvres were staged as a joint Army and State Guard operation under secret orders issued

Continued on Page Eight

R. A. F. RAINS BOMBS ON TRONDHEIM BASE

Blasts Nazi Threat to Supply Line to Russia—Cologne and Norwich Also Suffer

By RAYMOND DANIELL
Wireless to THE NEW YORK TIMES.

LONDON, April 28—Norwich, with its vestiges of Roman and Norman culture, was selected last night by the Germans for their retaliation for British raids on German cities.

While the German bombers were trying to destroy that ancient city in East Anglia, 110 miles northeast of London, British bombers pounded Cologne, the third largest city in Germany, and carried out a heavy attack on Trondheim fjord in Norway, which the Germans have been building into a naval base for attacks on the Allied supply line to North Russia.

[German planes bombed two towns in Eastern England early today, The United Press reported, causing a number of casualties. The Berlin radio said one

Continued on Page Five

War News Summarized

WEDNESDAY, APRIL 29, 1942

President Roosevelt turned the thoughts of the people of the United States to the present need for uncompromising sacrifice and toward the future last night as the war picture in Burma became darker and the British stepped up their all-out air offensive over Europe.

The President in a broadcast to the nation pledged offensive war against the Axis in many parts of the world and suggested that Germany and Italy were beginning to crack. He warned that the United States would take measures to prevent Axis use of French territory for military purposes. He said the United States would use its air force in Europe and take the offensive from Australia and New Zealand and that aid would be sent to the Chinese even if Burma fell. [1:4.]

Japanese forces continued their advance through the Northern Shan States toward the Mandalay-Lashio railway and Lashio itself, gateway to the Burma Road. The columns driving through the mountains in Eastern Burma were said to have 2,000 to 3,000 men each. The Japanese also pushed on northward along the north-south railway. [1:2-3; map, P. 2.]

United Nations headquarters in Australia reported the Japanese had lost seven planes in a raid on Darwin and also announced raids on enemy shipping at New Ireland and in the Solomon Islands. A Japanese transport was sunk. [4:1.]

British air squadrons bombed Cologne, Trondheim Fjord, Norway, and points in Northern France. One observer reported a square mile of planes had gone over the Channel in a single raiding formation. The Germans bombed Norwich. The British acknowledged the loss of twenty-three planes. [1:3; map, p. 5.]

Russian reports suggested that a Soviet Spring offensive was starting in the Kharkov-Bryansk sector, threatening the Germans in the Northern Donets. It was asserted that two important positions had been taken. A Soviet advance had been made near Orel, but checked, according to German reports. [7:1.]

The British Admiralty announced the sinking of two heavily laden Axis supply ships and a minesweeper in the Mediterranean. [6-1.]

In France the Germans ordered the execution of five French hostages for the wounding of a German soldier at Rouen last Friday. [6:4.]

The Swiss heard that the famous General Giraud, who had escaped from a German prison camp, had been in France for some days and had seen Marshal Pétain. [6:2-3.]

BIG FORCES ABROAD

President Says 'Several Hundred Thousand' Are on Foreign Soil

A WARNING TO VICHY

Reveals Our Navy Is in Mediterranean and Indian Ocean

By FRANK L. KLUCKHOHN
Special to THE NEW YORK TIMES.

WASHINGTON, April 28—President Roosevelt gave a pledge tonight of offensive action by the United States in Europe and the Far East and called upon the American public to help win the war by sacrifices on the home front as its fighting men are beginning to turn the tide in battle.

In a nation-wide broadcast which was re-broadcast all over the world, he declared that our civilization would be saved and that we were willing to pay the cost in "hard work and sorrow and blood."

He interpolated that "several hundred thousands" of American Army and Navy forces already had been transported to "bases and battlefields thousands of miles from home." This was the first indication that such large operations had been effected. He also revealed American naval vessels were in the Mediterranean and Indian Ocean.

The President asserted that he would use his executive powers to the full to assure "total war," and attacked minority elements within the United States which are hampering the war effort.

Warning on French Territory

He indicated a belief that Germany and Italy were beginning to crack from within. He said emphatically that the United Nations would prevent the use of French territory by the Axis, that American flying fortresses soon would be in action over Europe and that Australia and New Zealand, where Japan's advance appeared to be checked, would be used as offensive bases.

Conceding that the situation in Burma appeared critical, he pledged that airplanes and munitions would be delivered to China by different routes. He paid high tribute to Russia's war effort.

He remarked that if "somebody" had dropped bombs on Tokyo, "it is the first time in history that Japan has suffered such indignities."

The President called for civilians at home, even those not engaged in defense industries, to look upon sacrifice as a privilege and pointed out that the "home front" civilian-soldier can play as great a part in winning the war as the heroes he cited for their extraordinary deeds on the battle lines.

He sharply attacked those Americans who approve self-denial for others but not for themselves; the "faint of heart" experts, "self-styled," in both the military and economic fields; "bogus patriots," using the freedom of the press to propagandize for Berlin and Tokyo, and, most energetically of all, the "handful of noisy traitors," themselves would-be dictators, who have yielded to Hitlerism in their hearts and would yield the republic also.

Fliers Active in All the World

"This great war effort must be carried through to its victorious conclusion by the indomitable will and determination of the people," the President declared.

It was to the war fronts that the Executive turned first, remarking that American troops had taken up positions all over the world and that "American planes, manned by Americans, are flying in actual combat over all the continents and oceans."

The President then hinted at offensive action in the Mediterranean area, remarking that, while surface aspects seemed the same,

Continued on Page Fourteen

ANNOUNCING REGULATIONS OF PRICE-CONTROL PROGRAM

Price Administrator Leon Henderson and Donald Gordon, chairman of the Canadian Wartime Prices and Trade Board, discussing phases of the new rules. Associated Press Wirephoto

The President's Broadcast

Following is the text of President Roosevelt's broadcast last night as recorded and transcribed by THE NEW YORK TIMES:

My Fellow Americans:

It is nearly five months since we were attacked at Pearl Harbor. For the two years prior to that attack this country had been gearing itself up to a high level of production of munitions. And yet our war efforts have done little to dislocate the normal lives of most of us.

Since then we have dispatched strong forces of our Army and Navy, several hundred thousand of them to bases and battle fronts thousands of miles from home. We have stepped up our war production on a scale that is testing our industrial power, our engineering genius and our economic structure to the utmost. We have had no illusions about the fact that this would be a tough job—and a long one.

American warships are now in combat in the North and South Atlantic, in the Arctic, in the Mediterranean, in the Indian Ocean and in the North and South Pacific. American troops have taken stations in South America, Greenland, Iceland, the British Isles, the Near East, the Middle East and the Far East, the continent of Australia and many islands of the Pacific. American war planes, manned by Americans, are flying in actual combat over all the continents and all the oceans.

On the European front the most important development of the past year has been, without question, the crushing counter-offensive on the part of the great armies of Russia against the powerful German Army. These Russian forces have destroyed and are destroying more armed power of our enemies—troops, planes, tanks and guns—than all the other United Nations put together.

In the Mediterranean area matters remain, on the surface, much as they were. But the situation there is receiving very careful attention.

Recently we have received news of a change in government in what we used to know as the Republic of France—a name dear to the hearts of all lovers of liberty—a name and an institution which we hope will soon be restored to full dignity.

Throughout the Nazi occupation of France we have hoped for the maintenance of a French Government which would strive to regain independence to re-establish the principles of "liberty, equality and fraternity," and to restore the historic culture of France. Our policy has been consistent from the very beginning. However, we are now greatly concerned lest those who have recently come to power may seek to force the brave French people to submission to Nazi despotism.

The United Nations will take measures, if necessary, to prevent

Continued on Page Fourteen

Price Order Will Ruin Grocers By Thousands, Protest Declares

Special to THE NEW YORK TIMES.

WASHINGTON, April 28 — Sharp protests against the Office of Price Administration's action in making March the governing period in fixing both retail and wholesale prices under today's universal price ceiling order will be registered this week by independent retail grocers, spokesmen indicated tonight. Grocers have contended that a time lag of at least sixty days should have been allowed for the proper adjustment of retail to wholesale prices.

Officials of the National Association of Retail Grocers will gather in Chicago tomorrow for a meeting to set a policy toward the price order.

Mrs. R. M. Kiefer, secretary, said that leaders of the association spent much time here last week trying to convince OPA officials that some provision for adjusting retail prices to replacement costs should be included in the order.

By telephone from Indianapolis she declared that unless the order is changed "thousands upon thousands of retail grocers who cooperated with the government in keeping prices at low levels will be ruined in the next few months."

The organization, she added, would call protest meetings in cities and towns through the country, with the grocers asked at these meetings to appeal to Congressional delegations to demand reconsideration of the order.

In another reaction to the order, the Retailers Advisory Committee called for rigid obedience to the order, asserting that adjustments

Continued on Page Seventeen

BUYING SUSPENDED BY RETAILERS HERE

Wholesalers Get No Orders as Storekeepers Lament Lag of 11% in Price Rise

Retailers, manufacturers and wholesalers began preparations yesterday to write a new page in American business history in the controlled economy to be established by the nation's first over-all price ceiling covering millions of merchandise items.

New orders at wholesale came virtually to a standstill yesterday as industry awaited details of the price regulations. Retail trade was reported to be fairly active, but volume in the last week or so has been showing smaller sales gains over a year ago as shoppers tapered off buying to gauge the effects of the impending price order.

Numerous "squeeze" adjustments involving many branches of production and distribution were foreseen as business moves to hold prices in retail and wholesale channels to the highest levels quoted by individual sellers in March. While most retailers did not base their prices in March or this month on wholesale replacement costs, some price advances did occur.

The result, when the order governing retailers goes into effect on May 18, will be to move these prices back to the levels in March. Retail quotations in that month, despite the lag between wholesale and retail price advances, were at their highest levels since the start of the war. They showed an average increase of 18.7 per cent over March, 1941, according to the Fairchild Index.

Retailers' Time Lag

Retailers were disappointed that the price-control order made no provision for a roll-back of manufacturers' or wholesalers' prices to take care of the retailers' time lag, estimated at about 11 per cent at the end of March.

In some quarters, however, attention was called to Section 4 of the price order, dealing with supplemental regulations, as "holding out the possibility of future adjustments for the retailer's time lag." This section, it was pointed out, provides that if the maximum prices established for any commodity fail equitably to distribute returns from the sale at retail among producers, manufacturers, wholesalers and retailers "the Price Administrator will by supplementary regulation establish such maximum prices for different classes of sellers, or fix such base periods for the determination of their maxi-

Continued on Page Eighteen

MARCH PRICES TOP

Practically Every Item in Cost of Living Put Under OPA Curb

LICENSING SYSTEM

Retailers Must Act May 18, Wholesalers and Factories May 11

The text of the order on price regulation, Pages 15, 16.

By CHARLES E. EGAN
Special to THE NEW YORK TIMES.

WASHINGTON, April 28—Prices of every major item affecting living costs were ordered frozen today by the Office of Price Administration.

Acting to halt inflationary spiralling which had carried the cost of living 15 per cent above pre-war levels, the OPA called upon retailers, wholesalers and manufacturers of all essential products to freeze their selling prices at March levels. In companion regulations the Federal agency fixed a ceiling on rents.

A licensing system under which retailers and wholesalers who violate terms of the orders can be deprived of the right to do business was set up to enforce compliance with the ceiling levels. Powers granted to the Price Administrator under the Emergency Price Control Act of 1942 were held sufficient to compel compliance with the rental order.

The price control measures, together with an expansion of rationing will assure families in the low and middle-income brackets of an equal opportunity with those of greater income to buy available goods, Leon Henderson, the Federal Price Administrator, said in announcing the orders.

Can't See All Ramifications

At a press conference where he outlined the inflationary influences which compelled aggressive action by the government, Mr. Henderson admitted that the orders are more comprehensive than many had expected.

"They are of such magnitude," he said, "that even we who have been busy framing them for the last few weeks, cannot fully visualize their ramifications."

Under the order on retail prices, stores are called upon, beginning May 18, to hold prices for goods they sell at the highest levels they charged during March. Beginning May 11, wholesalers and manufacturers prices likewise are frozen at the "highs" of last month.

Service industries, such as laundries, garages and so forth come within the scope of the order and go under price ceilings July 1, with

Continued on Page Fourteen

Limit on Delivery Of Papers Likely

By The Associated Press.

WASHINGTON, April 28—Deliveries of newspapers will be restricted to one edition a day at any one point beginning May 15, an Office of Defense Transportation official said today in an informal explanation of the ODT's April 20 order to eliminate special trips and reduce local trucking mileage.

Newspapers now deliver each edition to sales points or redistribution points, the number of such deliveries running as high as twenty-five a day in one instance, the official said.

The order to local delivery carriers applies to every type of commercial enterprise and to governmental agencies, including those of the Federal Government.

It was explained that some hardships of the order might be relieved by pooling arrangements or by special exemption upon application to the ODT.

Wide World Photos

The devastated city of Cologne.

"All the News That's Fit to Print."

The New York Times.

LATE CITY EDITION
Moderate temperature today.
Temperatures Yesterday—Max., 80; Min., 63

Copyright, 1942, by The New York Times Company.

VOL. XCI..No. 30,809. Entered as Second-Class Matter, Postoffice, New York, N. Y. NEW YORK, MONDAY, JUNE 1, 1942. THREE CENTS NEW YORK CITY and Vicinity

1,000 BRITISH BOMBERS SET COLOGNE ON FIRE; USE 3,000 TONS OF EXPLOSIVES IN RECORD RAID; GERMANS ARE HURLED BACK IN BID FOR TOBRUK

NEAR 'MIRACULOUS,' IS MAYOR'S RETORT TO ARMY ON DIMOUT

'Good Job Is Being Done,' He Insists, Taking Issue With Report of Air Survey

HE INVITES AN INSPECTION

Westchester, Other Sections Say They Are Observing Regulations Strictly

Great progress has been made in dimming out the lights of New York City, Mayor La Guardia declared yesterday in his weekly radio broadcast over WNYC, the municipal radio station. He maintained that considering the extent and population of the city and its normal illumination the success of the dimout "borders on the miraculous."

Mayor La Guardia took issue with the report released Saturday by Major Gen. T. A. Terry, commanding the Second Corps Area, which characterized the observance of dimout regulations throughout the metropolitan area as "in general disappointing." He stoutly maintained that the dimout "has been very successful" and he invited an inspection of Broadway or any other thoroughfare of the city.

"Oh yes, I read the papers this morning," the Mayor said. "I read the report and I am quite certain that Major Gen. Terry regrets the characterization and the description in that report as much as I do. I say I am sure that Major Gen. Terry regrets it, because he told me so this morning."

Says "Good Job Is Being Done"

Mayor La Guardia contended that "if you will strip the report of its characterizations and descriptions, using diamonds very profusely, it will be seen that a good job is being done."

The Mayor announced that arrangements had been made to dim-out the Lewisohn Stadium at City College for the usual Summer season of symphony concerts and that the series would start this year on June 17.

When General Terry was informed of the Mayor's remarks about the Army report, he merely said:

"The city, so far as I know, is cooperating splendidly in the dim-out effort, but it is a big job and it has quite a way to go."

Persons familiar with General Terry's struggle to reduce the sky glow over the metropolitan area explained that the report was meant to be helpful and not to be critical, and that the difference between the general and the Mayor was simply a difference of opinion as to literary style. The Mayor did not like the way the report was written, they said, but the general did. They denied that the general had expressed regret at the language of the report; they said he had merely expressed regret that the Mayor didn't like it.

Colonel Frederick L. Devereux, chief director of civilian protection of Westchester County, made a personal inspection yesterday to make sure that Westchester communities obeyed the blackout regu-

Continued on Page Eight

If in Doubt, Put It Out

Army officials are still perturbed over many "flagrant" instances of non-compliance with the dimout regulations and are continuing their efforts to educate citizens to the vital importance of extinguishing all unnecessary lights and shielding all those that are necessary.

Pointing out that the massed effect of countless thousands of lights in New York City and its surrounding area is to create a sky glow that silhouettes ships for enemy submarines far at sea, they are endeavoring to drive home to the public the slogan of the Second Corps Area: "If in doubt, put it out."

Swedish Ship Brings 908 From War Zone

The Swedish-American liner Drottningholm, bringing 908 citizens of the United States and other American republics from the war zones in Europe, arrived in the Narrows at 7 o'clock last evening and anchored to wait until this morning. According to the Navy Department, she will dock at 8 A. M. today at Pier F, Jersey City.

Her passenger list includes many diplomats and consular officials with their families, war correspondents from Africa, Egypt, Italy and other countries in Europe and the East.

G. Hilmer Lundbeck, managing director of the Swedish-American Line, who will meet the Drottningholm at the pier, said the ship would leave again on June 3 or 4 for Lisbon and make a return trip to New York bringing back more American citizens.

DECEPTION IS LAID TO STANDARD OIL

Arnold in New Complaint Says Firm Misled Senators on Buna Rubber and Plane Gasoline

By C. P. TRUSSELL
Special to THE NEW YORK TIMES.

WASHINGTON, May 31—The Standard Oil Company of New Jersey "covered up" and "distorted facts" in its rebuttal to charges that the company's cartel arrangement with I. G. Farbenindustrie of Germany had hampered the development of synthetic rubber in the United States, Thurman Arnold, assistant attorney general, asserted today.

The head of the Anti-Trust Division of the Department of Justice accused the company of similar misrepresentations about the effect of the cartel on aviation gasoline for the United States and about the company's sale of gasoline to Axis airlines and negotiations with Matsui, a Japanese firm, before the war.

Mr. Arnold will present tomor-

Continued on Page Seven

NAZIS HELD IN LIBYA

British Hammer Enemy by Land and Air With Hint at Offensive

R. A. F. RAIDS FURIOUS

Rommel Force Reported in Trap Facing Flight or Annihilation

By JOSEPH M. LEVY
Wireless to THE NEW YORK TIMES.

WITH BRITISH FORCES in the Western Desert, May 31—After four days of miscalculated Blitzkrieg, Field Marshal Erwin Rommel and his Axis armored forces, together with reinforcements that he had rushed through gaps forced in mine fields in a vain effort to solve his supply problem, were making a last attempt today to achieve their original objective—Tobruk.

As the British Eighth Army continued to batter the enemy in the fighting in Eastern Libya, it seemed most probable that the British commander, Lieut. Gen. Neil Methuen Ritchie, would turn from the defensive to the offensive.

Credit for the decisive turn in the battle goes jointly to the Royal Air Force, which cut the German supply columns to pieces, and to the British armored forces, which, with the help of United States-built tanks, attacked the Axis armored elements.

Enemy Gets Panicky

Although the German moves, in the main, were orderly, around Harmat, about eighteen miles northeast of Bir Hacheim, the Nazis were so bewildered that they destroyed or abandoned thirty-five of their own tanks, while at a few other points they showed similar signs of nervousness.

Magnificent fighting by the British and the Free French, coupled with the ceaseless attacks by the R. A. F. that previously had blocked the German bid for Tobruk, turned the enemy westward. Thus, for all their efforts the Ger-

Continued on Page Seven

War News Summarized

MONDAY, JUNE 1, 1942

Britain's Air Force subjected Cologne, Germany's third city, early yesterday to the heaviest single air raid ever undertaken, while the situation on the world battle fronts changed little, though there was heavy fighting in Libya.

A thousand or more bombers participated in the great raid on Cologne and in all 1,250 planes took part in the operation. Some 3,000 tons of bombs were dropped on the city in ninety minutes, according to the British, and returning pilots said they had seen a cloud of smoke 15,000 feet high rising above Cologne. The smoke remained visible as far as the Netherland coast, 135 miles away. Forty-four British planes failed to return. [1:8; map, P. 2.]

Pilots who gave a more detailed picture of the raid said that they had left Cologne a sea of flame. One of the returning pilots said that seven-eighths of Cologne had been set afire. [1:7.]

The great assault involved elaborate planning. At least thirteen different types of planes were used. They took off from sixty different airfields and had to go in over the objective at six-second intervals. [1:6.]

The German High Command granted that the British had done "great damage" to Cologne in the "terror raid," but alleged that it was mostly in residential sections. German broadcasts also claimed that only seventy British planes had taken part and that the figure given by the British was fantastic. [3:1.]

The Prague radio announced that eighteen more Czechs had been executed, raising to eighty-one the total since the attack on Reinhard Heydrich, the notorious deputy chief of the Gestapo. Herr Heydrich was believed to be near death. [4:1.]

Vichy reported that two policemen had been killed and three others wounded in a food riot in Paris. [1:5.]

British forces in Libya were battering at the Axis troops making a last attempt to get at their objective, Tobruk. The battle appeared to have taken a decisive turn in favor of the British. [1:3; map, P. 7.]

The Russians claimed to have taken important enemy lines on the Kalinin front northwest of Moscow. Only local encounters were reported from the Kharkov front. [1:4.]

United Nations Headquarters, Australia, announced that three Japanese midget submarines probably had been destroyed during a wholly unsuccessful Japanese mass submarine attack on Sydney harbor. [1:5-6.]

Chungking announced attacks on eight Japanese positions in Anhwei Province some 200 miles west of Shanghai. The Japanese were making a new landing on the coast of Chekiang Province and pressing their attack in that region. [6:3-4.] The Chinese military attaché at Washington urged the United Nations to strike quickly at Japan from air bases in the Chinese coastal region now threatened by the Japanese. [6:2.]

The United States Navy released the news of the sinking of three United States merchant vessels in the Caribbean and one Norwegian vessel in the Gulf of Mexico. [6:7.]

TEA AFTER THE GREATEST AIR RAID IN HISTORY

A warming cup from an American-donated canteen is welcomed by Canadian bombers

Associated Press Rad-ophoto, passed yesterday by British censor

NAZIS' LINES SEIZED IN KALININ FIGHTING

Red Army Takes the Initiative After Repelling Heavy Blows —Izyum Barrier Holds

By RALPH PARKER
Wireless to THE NEW YORK TIMES.

MOSCOW, May 31—While fighting on the Kharkov front subsides, action on other fronts is characterized by reconnaissance in considerable force by both sides. This reconnaissance, when challenged by one side or the other, leads to sharp and bitter fighting.

Action of this sort has developed on the largest scale on what the Russians still call the Kalinin front, although Red Army troops are fighting far from the city of Kalinin itself. Kalinin Province is large, stretching from the Latvian border to a point east of Moscow.

The army newspaper Red Star reports that several days ago the Germans showed considerable activity in several sectors of this front, starting frequent attacks after having accumulated heavy forces. The failure of these local attacks seems to have discouraged them from persisting and their activities have decreased. But in several areas the Russians now have taken the initiative and have captured lines described as highly favorable for future action.

[A Russian communiqué said, according to The Associated Press, that Soviet forces had seized important lines after three days spent in repulsing German counter-attacks. The Germans left 1,100 dead or wounded on the field, it was added.]

Von Leeb Forces Routed

It also is reported that two battalions of the German 254th Division, which is part of General Field Marshal Wilhelm Ritter von Leeb's army on the Leningrad front, were routed in an attempt to advance through swampy country. Russian artillery checked German tanks using a road, but German flanking movements through swamps made some progress until the enemy forces were trapped. The Germans fled after severe hand-to-hand fighting with Russian grenadiers. The Russians are constantly improving their positions on this front, Red Star says.

On the Kharkov front the Russian river barrier in the Izyum-Barvenkova sector, southeast of Kharkov, was firmly held against new German attempts to cross it. Reports reaching Moscow from the

Continued on Page Five

3 Midget Submarines Raid Sydney; All Believed Sunk

By The United Press.

MELBOURNE, Australia, Monday, June 1—Three Japanese midget submarines penetrated the great harbor at Sydney, Australia's largest city, last night, but they were believed to have been destroyed after they had damaged one small vessel, it was announced today.

The raid, first threat to this part of Australia, was thought to indicate the presence of at least a small Japanese naval force off the southeastern—and most populous—section of the country. Midget submarines, which have only a short range, operate from a mother ship and it was felt that such a vessel hardly would travel unescorted.

The first submarine was sighted moving slowly along the main harbor channel, its periscope and upper conning tower exposed. It passed close to a harbor ferry loaded with passengers. Depth charges, released by naval vessels soon afterward, rocked waterfront buildings, and gunfire echoed across the harbor.

Announcement of the raid by the two-man submarines—of the type used in the attack on Pearl Harbor last Dec. 7—was made in a special communiqué issued by General Douglas MacArthur's headquarters.

"The enemy's attack was completely unsuccessful," the communiqué said. "Damage was confined to one small harbor vessel of no military value."

One of the submarines was believed to have been destroyed by

Continued on Page Six

2 POLICEMEN SLAIN IN PARIS FOOD RIOT

More Wounded in Bitter Clash —Gang Raids Shop, Throws Goods to Waiting Queue

By LANSING WARREN
By Telephone to THE NEW YORK TIMES.

VICHY, France, May 31—Crowds mobbed a food store in Paris today and in the clash that followed two policemen were killed and three wounded. A considerable number of other persons were injured.

The trouble started when persons inside the store began looting supplies and throwing foodstuffs and canned goods from the windows to those who were waiting in the food lines outside. The police were called and met with armed resistance from the rioters.

Arrests were made after the riot, showing, according to the police, that the incident had been organized by "Communist agitators." Those accused will be brought before the special court-martial.

The store where the clash took place is located on the left bank of the river, on the Rue de Seine.

In another quarter of Paris youths of a political organization during the night overturned the statue of Edward VII. The statue to the founder of the Entente Cordiale was located in the small

Continued on Page Four

FINE TIMING USED IN R. A. F. ASSAULT

Coordination at Home Fields Sends a Plane Over Reich City Every 6 Seconds

Wireless to THE NEW YORK TIMES.

LONDON, May 31—A vast amount of intricate planning and preparation preceded last night's attack on Cologne by more than 1,000 bombers. The operation, the first in which all Royal Air Force commands were concerned in one night's activity, called for perfect timing and perfect coordination. At least thirteen different types of aircraft were used—the greatest assortment ever engaged together.

More than 1,000 bombers had to be got into the air from scores of fields in a very short space of time at exactly regulated intervals. Each plane had to have a bomb load appropriate to its type and suitable for the part it was to play in the great raid.

The nicest timing was required of the "intruder" squadrons, whose task it was to keep German fighters busy while the bombers slipped through the defenses and attacked the objectives. Another bit of fine timing was required to arrange the bombers' arrival so that they would be coming in from all direc-

Continued on Page Three

COLOGNE 'INFERNO' ASTONISHES PILOTS

Defenses Overwhelmed, British Fliers Say—Germans on Air Describe Horrors

By The United Press.

LONDON, May 31—Seven-eighths of Cologne, a city the size of Boston, was in flames, an inferno "almost too gigantic to be real," when the history-making raid was over last night, pilots who took part in it said tonight.

"When we got there, I almost felt like leaving and trying to find another target. It didn't seem possible to do more damage than had already been done," Wing Commander Johnny Fauquier, Canadian pilot officer, related.

"Cologne was just a sea of flames," said Squadron Leader Len Frazer of Winnipeg, one of the more than 1,000 Canadien airmen who had a hand in the epic raid.

"I saw London burning during the Battle of Britain, and it was nothing compared with Cologne," Pilot Officer H. J. M. Lacelle of Toronto, gunner in the tail of a Canadian bomber, contributed.

Their reports were typical of the thousands being sifted tonight and compiled into a record of the mightiest piece of destruction ever devised by man.

Defenses Overwhelmed

The lurid sky over Cologne for ninety minutes was as busy as Piccadilly Circus as the great Lancasters and Halifaxes, Stirlings and Manchesters, streaked in at the rate of one every six seconds to unload their total cargo of steel-cased death.

Before the overwhelmed and bewildered German defenses could focus on one plane, it was zooming away and another was on its tail. The Royal Air Force plan of supersaturating the enemy's target field was described as an absolute success. German fighter planes were there, but not enough to interfere seriously with the attack.

"It was almost too gigantic to be real," said the pilot of one Halifax. "But it was real enough when we got there. Below us in every part of the city buildings were ablaze. Here and there you could see their outlines, but mostly it was just one long stretch of fire.

"It was strange to see the flames reflected on our aircraft. It looked at times as if we were on fire ourselves, with the red glow dancing up and down our wings."

"I could identify every type of

Continued on Page Three

A 90-MINUTE RAID

R. A. F. Causes Havoc in the Rhine City—Nazis Admit 'Great Damage'

COST IS 44 PLANES

250 Extra Aircraft Hit Foe's Bases—Attack a Start, Says Churchill

By RAYMOND DANIELL
Wireless to THE NEW YORK TIMES.

LONDON, Monday, June 1—More than 1,000 British bombers dumped 3,000 tons of high explosive bombs Saturday night on Cologne and elsewhere in the Rhineland and in the Ruhr.

"Cologne was the main objective," the Air Ministry said, and British officials asserted the raid was the biggest air attack in the history of warfare.

Prime Minister Winston Churchill, congratulating Air Marshal A. T. Harris, chief of the Bomber Command of the Royal Air Force, who planned and directed the devastating attack on one of Germany's largest and industrially most important cities, described it as "a herald of what Germany will receive city by city from now on."

Losses Relatively Slight

It was indeed the heaviest blow the R. A. F. has delivered yet in its promised air offensive against the Nazis, and it will not be long now before the American Air Force joins the British. The shadow that two years ago was no bigger than a man's hand has grown to a huge cloud threatening the whole Reich.

Forty-four British planes failed to return to their bases from the Saturday night operations, which included heavy attacks on Nazi coastal bases and airfields and fighter action against enemy interception.

This was the largest number of planes the British have ever lost in one raid, but it was still little more than 4 per cent of all the planes that were used.

That the losses for an assault upon a German city defended, as Cologne was, by 120 searchlights and at least 500 anti-aircraft guns and big Nazi night fighter forces, were not heavier was due largely to new tactics used by the R. A. F.

Tactics Counter Nazi Defenses

The bombers went in over their target at the rate of one every six seconds to distract and confuse the searchlight operators and the German gun crews and prevent their concentrating long on any single plane.

At the same time at least 250 other planes were drawn from every command of the R. A. F. and swarmed over the Nazi airports, from which enemy fighters might have been drawn to intercept the Cologne attackers.

[The Germans claimed to have shot down forty-seven British planes, thirty-six over Cologne and eleven near the coast. Berlin, while reporting "great damage" at Cologne, tried to discount the size of the raid by saying only seventy R. A. F. bombers were over the city. At the same time, Nazi officials talked of "reprisals."

[British bombers were over Western Germany again last night, according to a Berlin broadcast recorded by The Associated Press early today.]

Offensive Goes on During Day

Saturday night's supreme effort by no means exhausted the R. A. F. In daylight yesterday British fighters made several sweeps over Nazi-occupied France and Belgium. They shot down four Nazi fighters and lost eight of their own planes.

Off the Netherland coast British planes set afire and sunk a German armed trawler and two other vessels were driven aground, ac-

Continued on Page Two

"All the News That's Fit to Print."

The New York Times.

LATE CITY EDITION

Warmer with gentle winds today.

Temperatures Yesterday—Max., 80; Min., 67

Copyright, 1942, by The New York Times Company.

VOL. XCI..No. 30,812. Entered as Second-Class Matter, Postoffice, New York, N. Y. NEW YORK, THURSDAY, JUNE 4, 1942. THREE CENTS NEW YORK CITY and Vicinity

JAPANESE BOMB DUTCH HARBOR, ALASKA, TWICE; R. A. F. HAMMERS RUHR AND NORTHERN FRANCE; ROMMEL DRIVES WIDE WEDGE IN LIBYAN LINE

HOUSE BODY VOTES TO ELIMINATE CCC, SAVING $75,818,000

Appropriations Committee Cuts Item From Labor-Security Bill and Leaves $1,058,451,660

DIVIDES 15 TO 12 ON CAMPS

Scarcity of Farm Labor Cited, but Foes of Abolition Move to Take Fight to Floor

Special to THE NEW YORK TIMES.

WASHINGTON, June 3—Abolition of the Civilian Conservation Corps was voted by the House Committee on Appropriations today when it struck from the Labor Department-Federal Security Agency supply bill for the coming fiscal year the entire $75,818,000 with which the Administration sought to continue the CCC at 350-camp strength. The committee sent to the House a bill totaling $1,058,451,660.

This year the corps has been operating under a $246,960,000 fund, appropriated by Congress without contest.

The 15-12 vote for abolition came suddenly today, just before the committee reported the measure, with thirteen of its forty members absent. A fight for restoration of the much-reduced operating fund was begun immediately and will be carried to the House floor, probably tomorrow.

Committee action followed a tie vote of 3 to 3 in the subcommittee which handled the Labor-Security measure, when the issue of continuing or shutting down the nine-year-old project was taken to its first test.

Several factors entered into the voting of the committee members today.

Boys Needed Badly on Farms

The CCC, it was found, was drawing enrollees heavily from areas where farm labor was so scarce that warnings had been sounded that the "food-for-freedom" program was endangered.

In 1940, committeemen were told in executive session, recruitment from farm areas constituted about 19 per cent of the corps' strength. Last year, it was asserted, 43 per cent of the enrollees came direct from farms, and an additional 20 per cent from small towns in agricultural districts.

Meanwhile, from a peak of about 1,500 camps and 300,000 enrollees, the CCC had been reduced to 400 camps with 80,000 members and dropped further, as of the day before yesterday, to the 350 camps which, it was decided, were to be continued.

About 200 of the remaining camps are on military reservations and 150 on forest-protection projects, including forty-eight in national park areas.

Congressional approval of the Appropriations Committee's action, it was learned, would wipe out a personnel of 40,000 enrollees working on military reservations

Continued on Page Twelve

West Coast Radios Off in 'Precaution'

Special to THE NEW YORK TIMES.

SAN FRANCISCO, Calif., June 3—Radios were silenced along the West Coast from the Canadian frontier to the Mexican border tonight at the direction of the Fourth Fighter Command.

The action was described as "merely a precautionary measure in view of the situation earlier today"—a reference, presumably, to the Japanese raid on Dutch Harbor, Alaska.

While radios were off the air a "blue" alert signal was sounded at 10:28 P. M., but the "all clear" came nine minutes later. There was no actual blackout, but the radios continued silent even after the alert period ended.

Headquarters of the Western Defense Command and Fourth Army announced afterward that an "unidentified target" that was "later identified" led to the alert. The statement did not say whether or not the "target" had been identified as "friendly."

A.F.L. UNION STRIKES AT BENNETT FIELD

Jurisdictional Dispute Over $3,000 Cables Hampers Navy $8,120,000 Program

A strike of 250 electricians, growing out of a jurisdictional conflict affecting $3,000 worth of work installing telephone cables, has tied up all electrical work on the Navy's $8,120,000 program for the expansion of Floyd Bennett Field since last Friday, it became known yesterday.

Because of the interdependence of the various construction crafts, the electrical tie-up has impeded other phases of construction on the Brooklyn naval air base, a vital link in the nation's coast defense, but officials were hopeful that operations would be resumed in time to prevent a full shutdown.

The strike was called by Local 3 of the International Brotherhood of Electrical Workers, A. F. of L.,

Continued on Page Fourteen

500 FIGHTING SHIPS TO COST 8 BILLIONS ASKED IN NEW BILL

Huge Aircraft Carrier Program Dominates, and Not a Single Battleship Is Called For

1,000 WARSHIPS NAVY'S AIM

As Vinson Presents New Measure, House Votes 3 Billion Bill—It Adds 100 Submarines

By C. P. TRUSSELL

Special to THE NEW YORK TIMES.

WASHINGTON, June 3—The greatest of the nation's new naval building programs, to add 500 fighting ships and 800 patrol, mine-laying and tending craft to the fleet and double its striking power as a completed two-ocean Navy in twenty-four months, was presented to the House today. It was sponsored by the chairman of the Naval Affairs Committee, Representative Vinson, after consultations with the Navy High Command.

The estimated expenditure of $8,300,000,000 would carry the defense and war commitments of the last three years past $170,000,000,000.

Even as the record-setting measure was introduced, the House, by a separate bill, voted $2,797,080,740 to the Navy in direct supplemental appropriations and contract powers, largely for the high-speed construction of more than 100 submarines and 500,000 more tons of auxiliary vessels to operate "in connection with the submarine program."

Though explanations were guarded as the latter appropriations measure was called up, it was indicated that the $1,115,000,000 of new auxiliary craft to be constructed, purchased or converted, might be used to service long-range operations of our submarines in the Pacific and other far-flung waters.

To avoid any delay, the House waived the rules by unanimous consent and voted the money even

Continued on Page Eleven

War News Summarized

THURSDAY, JUNE 4, 1942

Japanese planes raided the United States base at Dutch Harbor in Alaskan waters yesterday, the Axis somewhat strengthened its position in Libya, and Essen, Germany, was bombed again. There was some sharp but indecisive fighting on the Russian and Chinese fronts.

Dutch Harbor was raided twice, the second raid coming six hours after the first, in which four Japanese bombers and about fifteen fighters took part. In the first attack little damage was done. [1:8.]

Japanese forces in Chekiang Province continued to push toward Chuhsien, site of an important air base on the Hangchow-Nanchang railway, according to Chungking reports. There was also heavy fighting in Kiangsi Province south of Nanchang, where the Japanese had started southward in the general direction of the Hankow-Canton railway. [6:3, with map.]

From the European front the British reported that Tuesday night R. A. F. bombers returned to Essen to follow up the preceding night's raid. A few hundred aircraft took part in the latest raid on the Ruhr region, but the affair was described in London as a routine attack. [1:5.]

Stockholm heard from Berlin that several first-aid trains and strong Gestapo detachments had been sent to bombed Cologne and the Ruhr. [1:5-6.]

In Libya Marshal Rommel succeeded in making a larger breach in the British-mined and semi-fortified Bir Hacheim line and securing a better connection with his forces to the west of that line and then turned to strike back at the British. Meanwhile the British seized a position well to the west, from which they can harass German communications. [1:6-7; map, P. 4.]

Moscow announced that Russian shock troops in a surprise attack on the Kalinin front had created a strategically important salient. The Germans claimed to have crushed an encircled Russian force on the central front. [8:2.]

Twenty-five more Czechs have been executed, according to the Prague radio, bringing the total to 133 since the attempt to assassinate the notorious Gestapo leader, Reinhard Heydrich. [9:3.]

Vichy accused Britain and Russia of attempting to provoke civil war in France. The statement was read to the press by Pierre Laval's chief of press and propaganda, Paul Marion. [4:1.]

In Washington the House of Representatives adopted three resolutions declaring war on Bulgaria, Hungary and Rumania without a dissenting vote. Little interest was displayed in the routine proceedings since the three States are merely minor instruments of Berlin. [9:1.]

Legislation was introduced in the House for construction of 500 new warships to cost a total of $8,300,000,000. [1:3.]

The Navy announced three new sinkings of United Nations merchant vessels. [11:1.] The sinking of eighteen United Nations cargo ships in the Bay of Bengal last April 6 was also disclosed. Among them was one United States vessel. [6:4.]

Commandos in Raid On Boulogne Area

By The United Press.

LONDON, Thursday, June 4—Special Service troops landed on the coast of Northern France early today and made a "reconnaissance raid" on the Boulogne-Le Touquet area, a special communiqué announced today. The troops obtained valuable information, the communiqué said.

The British Navy escorted and re-embarked the raiding force, while the Royal Air Force Fighter Command provided a protective "umbrella" for the operations.

Boulogne lies directly across Dover Strait from the southeast coast of England and is about thirty-two miles from Folkestone. Le Touquet is twelve miles south of Boulogne and also on the coast.

FASCIST PRESSURE ON VATICAN FAILS

Mussolini Unable to Bring Pope to Take a Stand on Axis Side in the War

The following article is by a former Rome correspondent of THE NEW YORK TIMES who has just arrived in this country.

By CAMILLE M. CIANFARRA

Since Italy's intervention in the war the relations between the Vatican and the Fascist Government have become increasingly strained as a result of Premier Benito Mussolini's policy of curbing the temporal activity of the Pope.

It would be an exaggeration to say that the Pope today is a prisoner in the Vatican, as was Pope Benedict XV during the first World War. Yet the fact remains that many important clauses of the 1929 Lateran Treaty between the Holy See and Italy that were drawn with the specific aim of safeguarding the temporal independence of the Pontiff were systematically violated when they did not fit in with Signor Mussolini's plans.

The geographical position of the Vatican State, in the heart of Italian territory, makes this policy easy to pursue. Signor Mussolini has many means with which to disturb the temporal life of the tiny State and is taking full advantage of them to apply pressure to the Pontiff in an effort to win the moral support of the Catholic Church for the Axis.

Yugoslav Minister Ousted

When Italy and Germany invaded Yugoslavia in April, 1941, the Yugoslav Minister to the Holy See was ordered to leave Italy. He protested that he intended to take up residence in the Vatican, where quarters were already being prepared for him. He pointed out that an article of the Concordat clearly specified that members of the diplomatic corps accredited to the Holy See might reside within the Vatican grounds. In reply, the Italian Government ordered him to leave Italy within twenty-four hours. A strong protest by the papal secretariat of State failed to alter this decision.

Another example of Fascist tactics occurred soon after Italy's intervention in the war. The Vatican newspaper Osservatore Romano was limited by Signor Mussolini almost exclusively to religious news. The fault of that newspaper, in the eyes of Fascisti, was the printing of impartial dispatches which, by their very fairness, contradicted those appearing in the Italian press.

For a few days the Osservatore Romano continued its editorial policy of absolute impartiality. As a result every issue was seized as soon as it came out, and Italians who asked for it at news stands found waiting Blackshirts who clubbed them on the charge of being traitors.

The church has been humiliated in Italy, its clergy having the

Continued on Page Ten

BRITISH RAIDS GO ON

Ruhr Area Again Is Hit, Though Scale of Blow Is Not So Large

ATTACK IN DAYLIGHT

Fighters Sweep Coastal Areas—Nazis Claim 58 British Planes

By RAYMOND DANIELL

Wireless to THE NEW YORK TIMES.

LONDON, Thursday, June 4—Essen, home of the Krupps, and the industrial region around it with homes and factories still smoldering after the raid by 1,036 heavy and medium bombers Monday night, was attacked again Tuesday night by "strong" forces of the Royal Air Force, it was announced yesterday.

While the German Propaganda Ministry sought desperately to minimize the British raids on Cologne and Essen and to magnify their own reprisal attacks on British cathedral cities, including Canterbury, the British made no attempt to present Tuesday night's operations as anything more than they were—a routine assault by a few hundred aircraft.

That it was on a large scale, however, was indicated by the fact that the British revealed the loss of fourteen planes. British bombers shot down two enemy fighters that tried to destroy them in the Ruhr raid. It was not certain that the full strength of the British raiding force was directed against Essen again, but on the contrary it was indicated that the attacks were spread out over the Ruhr and German-occupied France.

[Royal Air Force bombers again struck at Germany during the night, it was authoritatively learned today, an Associated Press dispatch from London said.]

[The Berlin radio reported this morning that British planes attacked several towns in the Northwest German coastal area, damaging business and residential quarters. German night-fighter planes and anti-aircraft batteries shot down ten of the raiders, the broadcast said, an indication that the British forces may have been numerous.]

Dampens Expectations

A Royal Air Force commentator yesterday took up the same line as Prime Minister Winston Churchill when he warned in the House of Commons against the expectation that the great feat of the Bomber Command in concentrating more than 1,000 aircraft over a single objective in a short space of time could or would be duplicated every night.

The Air Ministry's commentator said that, now the practicability and advantage of sending huge air armadas over targets to the point at which sheer numbers "saturate" defenses had been demonstrated, there was every intention of repeating and increasing the "dose."

Continued on Page Four

Havoc in Essen Bad as in Cologne; Rescue Trains Off to Bombed Cities

By GEORGE AXELSSON

By Telephone to THE NEW YORK TIMES.

STOCKHOLM, Sweden, June 3—Several first-aid trains of the N. S. V., the Nazi party social welfare organization, have left for Cologne and the Ruhr, according to news from Berlin today. Strong Gestapo detachments have also been dispatched to West Germany, as there appears to be much looting in the bombed area. As the seat of the organized Catholic opposition, the Ruhr district has never been on the party's good books, anyway.

Essen, Duisburg and Oberhausen have been badly hit by the Royal Air Force raids. The damage done is every bit as considerable as that inflicted Sunday morning on Cologne, according to fragments of news received here from Berlin permitting this deduction.

Essen newspapers have now been added to the list of publications "missing" on the Berlin newsstands. Cologne newspapers were missing following the first R. A. F. mammoth raid. This does not necessarily mean that the newspapers have stopped publishing, but it proves conclusively that at least the damage caused by the raids was widespread.

The Berlin news agency, Dienst aus Deutschland, said tonight that the Royal Air Force raids constituted a new problem for the Reich,

Continued on Page Four

ENEMY BOMBS FALL IN ALEUTIAN ISLANDS

Four Japanese bombers escorted by fifteen fighters conducted a fifteen-minute raid on Dutch Harbor (cross on upper map) yesterday. Six hours later a second raid was made. The position of Dutch Harbor on Unalaska Island is shown on the lower map.

Battle in Desert Is Centered On Axis Salient in Mine Field

By JOSEPH M. LEVY

Special Cable to THE NEW YORK TIMES.

CAIRO, Egypt, June 3—With a wedge driven into the British mine fields that extend from El Gazala to Bir Hacheim, and with guns placed to protect their flanks, Axis forces in Libya engaged today in a threefold task—fighting off British attempts to isolate that part of the German armored corps that was operating well east of the mine-field gap, protecting communications in the Axis rear areas from British advances and making preparations for another effort of their own.

The first phase of the Axis offensive now seems to be definitely over. Its results for the Axis appear to be that the Germans and Italians failed in every aim, although they did stave off disaster and greatly improve their situation by forcing two small gaps about nine miles apart in the British mined area and then squeezing out those British forces that were between the gaps—forces that endeavored in vain to prevent the Axis units from consolidating those avenues for supplies into a single, rather broad thoroughfare.

The Germans have not had a single moment of real rest, however. And the second phase of this campaign opens with all observers—and, perhaps, even participants—in doubt regarding who is on the defensive and who is on the offensive.

The Germans undoubtedly expect and hope to make another bid

Continued on Page Four

ROMMEL LECTURED BRITONS ON TACTICS

Writer, Captured in Libya, Tells How the German General Twitted Prisoners

The following is the second of a series of articles by a correspondent of THE NEW YORK TIMES who was captured in Libya six months ago and has just returned to this country:

By HAROLD DENNY

When something occurs as drastic as capture in battle, one cannot quite grasp it at first. It is one of those things that can happen to other persons, but never to oneself.

We correspondents had all accepted the possibility of being killed or wounded, though the mathematical chance of being hit really was small. But we had hardly thought of being captured.

"I don't believe it," said Edward Ward, the B. B. C. correspondent, as we trotted along, our upraised arms flopping ridiculously. "These things just don't happen. This is a dream."

We half expected to be disposed of with machine guns, for a large group of prisoners is a hindrance to a flying column in the desert. But we were not. To give the devil his due, the German troops behaved honorably in that battle. There was no unnecessary shooting. Once the Germans had conquered British resistance the killing ceased.

But before we got off that battlefield there was another flurry of firing from somewhere. A few shells burst fairly close and some machine gun bullets whistled by us. But we had been through so much that day that they hardly registered on our minds.

Groups of prisoners, flushed from their various coverts, were gradu-

Continued on Page Five

U. S. BASE IS TARGET

Both Raids on Navy and Air Establishments Made by Daylight

FIRST ATTACK IS LIGHT

Four Bombers, Fifteen Fighters Set Fire to 'a Few Warehouses'

Special to THE NEW YORK TIMES.

WASHINGTON, June 3—The Japanese air force today made two daylight raids on the important American Naval and Air Base at Dutch Harbor, Alaska.

The first attack occurred at 6 A. M., Alaskan time [noon, E. W. T.]. The second attack took place six hours later, at noon Alaska time [6 P. M., E. W. T.].

The Naval communiqué announcing the second raid was released here at 9 P. M. It stated merely that "a brief report just received in the Navy Department" told of the attack "but no further details are available at this time."

The Navy released three communiqués in all this afternoon and evening recounting the enemy activity over Alaska. The first announced merely that a raid on Dutch Harbor had occurred. The second said that "there were but few casualties" and that "a few warehouses were set on fire but no serious damage was suffered."

None of Foe Reported Downed

The Navy made no mention of the effect of the second aerial assault. None of the Navy's communiqués recorded that any of the enemy planes was shot down in either attack.

Only a small Japanese force took part in the first raid. The Navy said there were only four enemy bombers and approximately fifteen fighter planes. On the basis of this early information it was not thought in local naval circles that the Dutch Harbor base could have been greatly injured by an attack on this scale.

The first attack was said to have lasted for fifteen minutes. The duration of the second attack was not announced.

Both attacks carried new significance in that they opened a new battle zone, removed by 2,000 miles from any other place where Japanese and American forces have clashed. They also marked the first occasion enemy bombs have been dropped on the North American Continent.

On the basis of the first advices to reach Washington of the initial assault on Dutch Harbor, it was not felt that this attack alone could be construed as representing the Japanese response to the American attack of April 18 on Tokyo and other Japanese cities. To regain face, in the words of Secretary of War Henry L. Stimson, it was thought the enemy would have to embark on a more important project than attacks on a distant outpost of the continental United States.

Dutch Harbor is on Unalaska, one of the Aleutian Islands, about 2,000 miles northwest of San Francisco and 2,835 miles northeast of Tokyo. It is just about due north of Hawaii, where the Japanese began the war with their devastating surprise raid on Dec. 7.

What forces and equipment are based at Dutch Harbor is a military secret, but they are probably large. Great efforts are known to have been made to fortify this area since the beginning of the "emergency" that preceded entry of the United States into the war.

For many years the Dutch Harbor establishment represented the northern end of a naval patrol line that extended roughly southward to the Hawaiian Islands and southwestward to the Panama Canal. More recently, however, it has become also a vital air link along the northern route to Asia.

In considering the extension of

Continued on Page Three

If in Doubt, Put It Out

The Army is trying to discourage the use of blue electric lamps in such places as theatre marquees, open lobbies, and amusement places because scientific measurements have shown they are not effective in reducing the amount of light contributed to the glow over the metropolitan area, it was learned yesterday at the headquarters of the Second Corps Area.

As a substitute Army experts recommend the use of red bulbs of low wattage, which contribute little if any light to the city's sky glow. In its campaign to reduce land horizon brightness to a point where it will no longer silhouette ships at sea for Axis submarines, the Army urges the public to remember the slogan of the Second Corps Area: "If in doubt, put it out."

Wide World Photos

Field Marshal General Erwin Rommel (center), accompanied by Field Marshal Kesselring (left), walk through a desert village at the Libyan front.

Wide World Photos

Rommel confering with members of his staff at the Libyan front.

Russian workers' battalion defending themselves against Nazi attack.

"All the News That's Fit to Print."

The New York Times.

LATE CITY EDITION
Continued warm today and probably scattered showers or thunderstorms in the afternoon.
Temperatures Yesterday—Max., 83; Min., 66

Copyright, 1942, by The New York Times Company.

VOL. XCI...No. 30,820. Entered as Second-Class Matter, Postoffice, New York, N. Y. NEW YORK, FRIDAY, JUNE 12, 1942. THREE CENTS NEW YORK CITY and Vicinity

SOVIET AND BRITAIN SIGN WAR AND PEACE PACT; MOLOTOFF AND ROOSEVELT PLAN FOR 2D FRONT; ARMY FLIERS BLASTED TWO FLEETS OFF MIDWAY

BIG BOMBERS WON

Routing Japanese Task Force June 4 Vital in Pacific Victory

CARRIERS TARGETS

Enemy's Invasion Ships Met and Pounded First Far West of Island

By ROBERT TRUMBULL
By Telephone to THE NEW YORK TIMES.

WITH UNITED STATES ARMY AIR FORCES, Hawaii, June 11—Officers of the United States Army Air Forces disclosed today some of the carnage spread by their high altitude bombers in conjunction with the Navy among the Japanese invasion fleet that massed off Midway last week in futile effort to take this vital island in the American Pacific defense chain.

The Army fliers who actually dropped the bombs reported personally that they made hits on three Japanese carriers, one cruiser and one other large vessel that may have been either a cruiser or a battleship, one destroyer and one large transport. The Air Forces' reports on the battle are still incomplete.

American gunners aboard the planes shot down an undetermined number of Japanese Zero fighters. Two United States Army planes were lost out of a large force in the operations.

Army airmen interviewed here emphasized that their operations against the enemy fleet were just one phase of a well-coordinated attack involving the Army, Navy and Marines. Their stories revealed the accuracy of Japanese anti-aircraft fire, which they said heretofore had been underestimated, and they spoke highly of the Japanese Zero fighters, which are manned by expert pilots.

Flying Fortresses Did Job

Another emphasis was on the power of the American B-17 bomber, the Flying Fortress. It was clear in several accounts of the action that the Japanese fighter planes were not anxious to tangle with these aerial dreadnoughts.

The introduction to the story was given by Brig. Gen. Willis H. Hale of Colorado Springs, Col., who is in charge of all the Army bombers in the Hawaiian area. Every squadron under General Hale's command participated in the action, which stretched over the two days of June 3 and 4.

General Hale expressed the belief that the Battle of Midway was primarily won in the blasting by the Flying Fortresses of a Japanese naval task force, including carriers, off the island on the morning of June 4.

Midway was pounded by Japanese planes from the carriers the previous afternoon and again that morning while the Flying Fortresses were away. Later all the American planes were gathered

Continued on Page Nine

If in Doubt, Put It Out

The advent of warm weather had brought a new problem to complicate the observance of the Army's dimout regulations, it was said yesterday by civilian lighting experts who have been working with the Army on the matter. They said many persons, particularly small shopkeepers, who have carefully shielded their windows in the prescribed manner are now thoughtlessly leaving outside doors open.

Pointing out that light streaming through these openings helps to build up the loom over the city that aids enemy submarines at sea to spot shipping of the United Nations, the experts said that when doors are left open for ventilation a screen should be placed where it can cut off direct rays of light from the interior. The general rule for lights should remain: "If in doubt, put it out."

'Gas' Ration Unit Is Doubled To Tide Over 2 Weeks More

Emergency Period Is Extended From June 30 to July 15—OPA Says Time Is Needed to Train for Permanent Plan

Special to THE NEW YORK TIMES.

WASHINGTON, June 11—The gasoline ration unit of "A" and "B" cards in the seventeen East Coast rationed States was increased by the Office of Price Administration today from three to six gallons, effective after midnight Sunday, to tide drivers over a two-week extension of the temporary rationing plan which was originally set to expire June 30. The present ration cards, with whatever units are left on them, must last through to July 15.

The two, weeks extension is needed, the OPA said, to train registrars and members of rationing boards in handling the permanent rationing system scheduled now to go into effect July 15 instead of July 1.

Card holders who have exhausted their card units by Monday may apply to local rationing boards for additional ration cards, but these will be effective only for the

Continued on Page Fifteen

Jones Beach Buses Not Curbed by ODT

Special to THE NEW YORK TIMES.

WASHINGTON, June 11—A recent order of the Office of Defense Transportation calling for elimination of unnecessary intercity bus transportation, particularly to "places conducted primarily for purposes of amusement and entertainment" has "no direct application" to transport of recreation seekers to Jones Beach on Long Island, the ODT announced today.

The policy was set forth in a telegram from Joseph B. Eastman, ODT director, to Robert Moses, president of the Long Island State Park Commission and the Jones Beach State Parkway Authority.

The order, Mr. Eastman said, does not apply to Jones Beach inasmuch as it is less than fifteen air miles from New York's boundaries. His telegram, however, added rather cryptically:

"Because of the rubber situation we believe that parks such as Jones Beach should be served by rail to the fullest extent possible."

HOUSE COMMITTEE RAISES TRAVEL TAX

Doubles Transport Impost, Adds to Cigarette and Cigar Levies—125 Million Gained

Special to THE NEW YORK TIMES.

WASHINGTON, June 11—The Ways and Means Committee voted today to double the present 5 per cent transportation tax, voted increases in cigar, tobacco and cigarette levies and postponed until tomorrow final action on other excise tax changes recommended by the Treasury.

The net additions to present revenue were estimated at $125,800,000. The transportation tax increase was estimated to yield an additional $35,000,000. It would provide for a flat 10 per cent tax

Continued on Page Twenty-eight

YOUNG DECK CREW DESTROYS U-BOAT

Freighter Gets 3d, Perhaps 5th, Raider Sunk in Caribbean—2 Allied Vessels Lost

By The United Press.

HAVANA, June 11—The gun crew of an American merchant ship, most of them youths of 20 or less, has sunk an Axis submarine after a brief running gun fight, thus raising the total of enemy U-boats sunk in recent weeks in waters of the Greater Antilles to three—and possibly five—authoritative but unofficial sources said tonight.

Braving withering bursts of machine-gun fire that swept the decks of their vessel, the gunners fired at the submarine until it was

Continued on Page Twelve

War News Summarized

FRIDAY, JUNE 12, 1942

The United States, Soviet Russia and Great Britain stood last night in full agreement on the question of opening a second front in Europe this year and on the fundamental problems of building a post-war era of peace and security.

Russia and Britain had entered a close war alliance and a twenty-year pact of mutual assistance and cooperation. The historic document, whose wording guarded the Soviet Union from any commitment against Japan, banned a separate peace with Germany and her European satellites and pledged common action to preserve peace and resist aggression in the future. Both countries agreed not to seek "territorial aggrandizement" nor to interfere in the "internal affairs" of other nations. [1:8.]

The Soviet Union reached an unwritten agreement with the United States on the "urgent" matter of a second front, on measures for increasing war shipments to Russia and on post-war cooperation. In addition, the Russians signed a master lease-lend agreement providing for mutual defense aid. The decision on the second-front question was not disclosed. [1:4.]

The three-power understanding, announced in London and Washington, evolved from secret flying visits to those capitals by Russia's Foreign Commissar, Vyacheslaff M. Molotoff. [1:6:7.] The Soviet-British treaty evoked cheers in Moscow, where hope rose for a continental invasion in the West. [2:2.] Diplomats from the Baltic States pinned their faith on the Atlantic Charter for the restoration of their governments—a question skirted by the pact. [4:5.]

On the Russian war front, German tanks and infantry advanced in the Kharkov area against fierce resistance. Their immediate aim, Berlin conceded, was to straighten their dented lines. Sevastopol's defenders reported they had killed 15,000 Germans in three days. [1:5.]

In Libya, a battered Free French-British garrison withdrew from Bir Hacheim, southern anchor of the defense line, after a sixteen-day siege. The withdrawal eased the Axis supply problem and presaged a drive on Tobruk. [1:5-6; map, P. 2.]

In China's Kiangsi Province three Japanese columns moved swiftly eastward, threatening to outflank Chinese defenders along the Nanchang-Hangchow railroad and to make a juncture with westbound Japanese forces around Chuhsien. [7:1.]

The American victory at Midway Island loomed even larger as Army fliers turned in reports—still incomplete—of their blows to two Japanese invasion armadas—a battle fleet and a group of transports. [1:1.] A Japanese naval expert confirmed the loss of two aircraft carriers, rather than one, as Tokyo had announced Wednesday. [8:3.]

U. S., SOVIET AGREE

Russian, Here Secretly, Maps War Action in 1942 With President

LEASE PACT SIGNED

Provides Reciprocal Aid and Plans for a 'Better World'

Text of White House statement will be found on Page 6.

By W. H. LAWRENCE
Special to THE NEW YORK TIMES.

WASHINGTON, Friday, June 12—The United States and Russia have reached a full understanding on the "urgent tasks of creating a second front in Europe in 1942," and have signed a master lease-lend agreement providing reciprocal defense aid and designed to create "a new and better world" after victory is won, it was announced officially yesterday.

A White House announcement at midday was the first public revelation that Vyacheslaff M. Molotoff, Soviet Foreign Commissar, had flown secretly to the United States and in several conferences with President Roosevelt and other political and military leaders of the United States Government between May 29 and June 4 had achieved unity on these three main propositions:

1. The urgent tasks of creating a second front in Europe in 1942.
2. Measures for increasing and speeding up the supplies of planes, tanks and other kinds of war materials from the United States to the Soviet Union.
3. Fundamental problems of cooperation of the Soviet Union and the United States in safeguarding peace and security to the freedom-loving peoples after the war.

"Link in Solidarity Chain"

At midnight the State Department announced that Secretary of State Cordell Hull and Maxim Litvinoff, the Soviet Ambassador, had signed a master lease-lend pact, which was described as "an additional link in the chain of solidarity being forged by the United Nations in their twofold task of prosecuting the war against aggression to a successful conclusion and of creating a new and better world."

"The agreement reaffirms this country's determination to continue to supply in ever-increasing amounts aid to the Soviet Union in the war against the common enemy," the State Department announcement said. "The agreement also provides for such reciprocal aid as the Soviet Union may be in a position to supply. But no matter how great this aid may prove to be, it will be small in comparison with the magnificent contribution of the Soviet Union's armed forces to the defeat of the common enemy."

Washington's two agreements with the Soviet Union were disclosed shortly after similar pacts between the Russians and the British had been announced to the House of Commons by Anthony Eden, British Foreign Secretary, with whom Mr. Molotoff had negotiated secretly before visiting the United States. The Anglo-Soviet agreements included an identical reference to the establishment of a second front and a twenty-year mutual assistance pact against "Hitlerite Germany."

Japan Not Mentioned

Neither announcement in Washington mentioned discussions of Russian cooperation in the war of the United States and Great Britain against Japan, with whom Soviet Russia remains at peace, but it was pointed out that no announcement would have been likely under the circumstances even if

Continued on Page Six

THE SOVIET FOREIGN COMMISSAR AT THE WHITE HOUSE

Vyacheslaff M. Molotoff with President Roosevelt at the recent historic conference.
Associated Press Wirephoto

STRONG NAZI DRIVE FOUGHT IN UKRAINE

Russians Report Fierce Battle at Kharkov—Sevastopol Siege Gains Little

By The Associated Press.

MOSCOW, Friday, June 12—The Germans have thrown strong tank and infantry forces against Russian defense positions on the Kharkov front, and fierce battles have developed, the government announced today.

Stubborn fighting continued in the Crimea, where the Germans were smashing against the Soviet naval fortress of Sevastopol. The Red Army was reported inflicting heavy losses on the Nazis in repulsing their attacks.

In three days of fighting there alone, the midnight Soviet communiqué declared nearly 15,000 German officers and men were killed. The Nazis lost more than fifty tanks and sixty planes in the same period.

[The German High Command reported that Soviet counter-attacks at Sevastopol had been unsuccessful. Semi-official sources described the Sevastopol and Kharkov actions as preliminary to "the coming great offensive."

The communiqué said there were no significant changes in other sectors, although earlier bulletins had reported action over a wide front that, combined with the great land battles of the Crimea and the Ukraine, brought the war on the Russian front to the highest pitch of the year.

There was mass aerial combat

Continued on Page Nine

Molotoff's London-U. S. Trip Was Best-Kept War Secret

Special Cable to THE NEW YORK TIMES.

LONDON, June 11—The secrecy surrounding the visit here of Soviet Foreign Commissar Vyacheslaff M. Molotoff, which was imposed at the request of the Russians on the grounds of security, was lifted today and the general public was at last told the details. Though diplomatic circles and many other persons in London knew he was here, it was not a matter of general knowledge even after he was accompanied by Anthony Eden and Ivan M. Maisky to call on the King at Buckingham Palace.

Mr. Molotoff's first visit lasted one week and was supplemented on his return from the United States by another stay of two days, during which military matters were discussed.

The usual formalities of signing an important treaty were adhered to, but nothing was allowed to be published about it until today.

Mr. Molotoff made all trips between here, Russia and the United States in a big Russian plane with an all-Russian crew. All members of the crew have been decorated in this war.

Mr. Molotoff arrived somewhere in Britain on May 20. With him were Arkady Soboleff of the Soviet Foreign Office, General Shelovski, and General Feodor Issayeff, who has already been wounded in this war. There was also his interpreter and party assistants, including two women typists.

The British Government gave the Russian party a special train to London, which stopped at a suburban station. There were few people on the platform and practi-

Continued on Page Four

Special to THE NEW YORK TIMES.

WASHINGTON, June 11—The flying visit of Vyacheslaff M. Molotoff from Moscow to London, then to Washington and back to London and Moscow, was one of the best kept secrets of the war.

Only a few high government officials, diplomats and newspaper men pledged to secrecy knew that Mr. Molotoff, after signing a twenty-year pact with Britain, had flown to Washington in a Soviet bomber, accompanied by Arkady Soboleff, Secretary General of the Foreign Office; V. Lapshoff, Chief of Chancellery for the Deputy Prime Minister; S. P. Kozyreff, Chief of Chancellery of the Foreign Office, and a group of technical advisers.

The Russian party arrived here late Friday afternoon and was taken immediately to the White House, where Mr. Molotoff was the guest of President Roosevelt. The discussions continued through Mon-

Continued on Page Four

Bir Hacheim Falls to Axis in Libya; Free French Retire After 16 Days

By JOSEPH M. LEVY
Special Cable to THE NEW YORK TIMES.

CAIRO, Egypt, June 11—Although the gallant Free French defenders of Bir Hacheim had repulsed for sixteen days constant attacks by German tanks, guns, infantry and dive-bombers, they were finally forced to withdraw from that outpost in the Libyan defense line last night, it was announced today. The French troops inflicted heavy losses on the Axis attackers and made it necessary for them to use a heavy concentration of their best armor to obtain final success.

Despite the effectiveness of their own arms, the French had not been left alone, for British armored and motorized forces had been doing their best to relieve the garrison by attacking the rear and flank of the Axis forces. The defenders also had extensive air support, which seems to have caused the German Air Force and ground units considerable trouble. Captured German prisoners, some of whom saw service in Russia, complained that it was the weakness of the German air support that had made them unable to overrun the Bir Hacheim positions sooner.

The fall of Bir Hacheim is a step for the Nazis in securing their southern flank. They will be in a slightly better position to thrust northeast toward Tobruk, fifty miles away, or toward El Gazala, on the Mediterranean coast fifty miles to the northwest, but there is no guarantee that their communications will be safe in any event. British mobile columns can continue to swing around the Axis southern positions to attack German supply routes.

The occupation of Bir Hacheim will absorb infantry that the Axis needs elsewhere. Moreover, if the

Continued on Page Two

NO SECRET IN PACT, BRITISH ARE TOLD

Commons Cheers the News of Open Treaty—Agreement Is Hailed as Peace Safeguard

By ROBERT P. POST
Special Cable to THE NEW YORK TIMES.

LONDON, June 11—The loudest cheers—or rather a loud but gentlemanly "Hear, hear!"—greeted Secretary Anthony Eden's announcement in the House of Commons today that there were no secrets in the British-Russian treaty and no commitments not made public. The cheers were an indication of the Members' relief on learning that Britain was not going to be drawn into any possible Continental demands on the part of Russia.

The second loudest response came when Mr. Eden announced that there had been complete agreement on a second European front in 1942.

The immediate Parliamentary reaction came from Arthur Greenwood, official leader of the Labor Party outside the Government, who said the House had received the statement with the most profound satisfaction "that we are working together as comrades in the war, and would be working together in times of peace."

Then came a little surprise as David Lloyd George rose amid another Parliamentary chorus.

"As one who has labored over twenty years to establish good understanding between Soviet Russia and this country," he said, "I

Continued on Page Two

A 20-YEAR TREATY

Mutual Aid Agreement Bars Separate Peace and Annexations

JAPAN NOT COVERED

Pact Based on Atlantic Charter Is Hailed by King and Kalinin

Text of White Paper, treaty and Eden's speech, Page 3.

By RAYMOND DANIELL
Wireless to THE NEW YORK TIMES.

LONDON, June 11—A treaty has been signed binding Russia and Great Britain in close alliance in the war against Nazi Germany and the countries "associated with her in acts of aggression in Europe" and pledging cooperation and mutual assistance for twenty years on the principles of the Atlantic Charter.

This momentous announcement was made by Foreign Secretary Anthony Eden in the House of Commons late this afternoon. He introduced the White Paper containing the text of the treaty and the speeches made by him and by Soviet Foreign Commissar Vyacheslaff M. Molotoff when they affixed their signatures to the historic document May 26 at the Foreign Office.

The White Paper also included the texts of the messages exchanged between King George VI and President Mikhail I. Kalinin, in which the alliance between this democratic nation and the world's first Communist State was hailed as the foundation on which the post-war world would be built.

Prime Minister Winston Churchill, in a message to Premier Joseph V. Stalin, said he thought the treaty would go far toward "overcoming barriers" between the two countries and expressed "the conviction that victory will be ours."

Mr. Stalin in reply said he hoped the treaty would strengthen relations not only between the Soviet Union and Britain but also with the United States, whose close collaboration is sought "after the victorious conclusion of the war."

Accord on Second Front

A Foreign Office communiqué issued at the same time as the White Paper was presented said that during the visit of Mr. Molotoff, which was kept a closely guarded secret until he had returned safely to Moscow after visiting President Roosevelt in Washington, "a full understanding was reached between the two parties with regard to the urgent task of creating a second front in Europe in 1942." Mr. Molotoff, Soviet Ambassador Ivan M. Maisky, Major Gen. Issayeff, Rear Admiral Kharlamoff, Mr. Churchill, Deputy Prime Minister Clement R. Attlee, Mr. Eden and the British Chiefs of Staff all took part in the discussions of this subject, the communiqué disclosed, although naturally it did not reveal what decisions were taken. Obviously it is just as possible to agree not to do things as to do them.

By inserting the words "in Europe," Russia limited her commitment so that she is not bound to lift a finger against the other enemy of Britain and the United States, Japan, except in the unlikely event that her armies or navy should enter this war-torn Continent. This limitation is cheerfully accepted here, for it is felt that the Russians have their hands full already.

There was considerable relief in parliamentary and diplomatic circles that the treaty contained no reference to post-war boundaries. One section of the treaty that Mr. Eden read to the Commons pledged both countries not to seek "territorial aggrandizement" and held a promise not to interfere in "the

Continued on Page Three

"All the News That's Fit to Print."

The New York Times.

LATE CITY EDITION
Warm today.
Temperatures Yesterday—Max., [illegible]; Min., [illegible]

Copyright, 1942, by The New York Times Company.

VOL. XCI...No. 30,827. Entered as Second-Class Matter, Postoffice, New York, N. Y. NEW YORK, FRIDAY, JUNE 19, 1942. THREE CENTS NEW YORK CITY and Vicinity

CHURCHILL HERE FOR TALKS ON SECOND FRONT; BRITISH RETIRE IN LIBYA, TOBRUK AGAIN IN PERIL; SEVASTOPOL THROWS BACK NEW NAZI ATTACKS

TRUMAN CHARGES WPB AIDES CAUSED WAR WORK DELAYS

Attack on 'Dollar-a-Year' Men as Slowing Conversion Spurs Defense of Nelson

CONNALLY, LUCAS HAIL HIM

Report Urges Posts for Labor, Small Business—Nelson Asked It Be Held Up

By JAMES B. RESTON
Special to THE NEW YORK TIMES.

WASHINGTON, June 18—In a special report which Donald M. Nelson regarded as a reflection on his policy and which some Senators declared should not be published, the Truman committee charged today that the War Production Board had not fully measured up to its responsibility of converting the nation's industry to war production, and called on Mr. Nelson to demote some dollar-a-year men and promote labor and small business in the battle of production.

The report, which Mr. Nelson urged the special committee investigating the national defense program to withhold, was sharply criticized in the Senate on the ground that it tended to obscure and distort recent production progress which Senator Truman himself admitted had been made.

The Truman committee, voting 9—1 to publish the document, conceded that a satisfactory program of curtailing civilian production was "at last under way," but asserted that there was still no satisfactory program for attaining maximum war production.

Group Sets Responsibility

Responsibility for this failure was blamed in part on some dollar-a-year men whose integrity was said to be unquestioned but who were accused of being "unable to divorce themselves from their subconscious gravitation to their own industries."

Senator Lucas of Illinois, Senator Connally of Texas and Senator Burton of Ohio, all members of the committee, sought in the debate to distinguish between the situation which existed several months ago and the situation now existing. Senator Lucas said the WPB was doing "a magnificent job." Senator Connally stated that mistakes had been made but noted that conversion of the country's industry to war production was a little harder than pressing a button for a Senate page. Mr. Burton stressed that the committee wanted to commend Mr. Nelson for increasing national production and merely hoped that by pointing out mistakes production could be increased even more. Mr. Truman agreed with Mr. Burton's observation.

Speaking to Senator Truman, Mr. Lucas said:

"I doubt if a man could be found

Continued on Page Twelve

Queen Wilhelmina Flies to Canada; Visits Daughter and Grandchildren

Netherland Sovereign to Stay With Juliana at Her Summer Home in Lee, Mass.—Will Pay Visit to the Roosevelts

Special to THE NEW YORK TIMES.

OTTAWA, June 18—Queen Wilhelmina of the Netherlands arrived in Ottawa today by plane from Great Britain. She will remain only a few days before going to Lee, Mass., where her daughter, Princess Juliana, has rented a home for the Summer.

During her stay in Ottawa Queen Wilhelmina will be a guest at Government House with the members of her party.

It is stated that she will visit Washington as a guest of President and Mrs. Roosevelt. No other announcement has yet been made with regard to her itinerary, however.

Princess Juliana and her two children, accompanied by Canadian Prime Minister W. L. Mackenzie King and by representatives of the

Continued on Page Four

ROYAL VISITOR

Queen Wilhelmina
Monkmeyer

WILLKIE CAUTIONS HIS PARTY ON HASTE

Advises Careful Weighing of Candidates' Records on War and World Affairs

Wendell L. Willkie urged the Republican party in New York State yesterday to maintain an open mind in its selection of a State ticket in the Fall elections and to study the records of all available candidates to choose the strongest possible slate.

Holding that any Republican ticket, if it is to be successful, must, of necessity, be one that would attract support from a "large number" of supporters of the war and post-war programs throughout the State as well as gain the confidence of labor, Mr. Willkie, in a press interview at his office at 15 Broad Street, demanded that all candidates for State-wide office in the Republican ranks make "clear and unequivocal statements" as to how they stand "toward the interests of American labor and toward the international situation."

He declared that he "earnestly" hoped that the Republicans would be victorious in the State elections and expressed the conviction that such a victory would strengthen greatly "our democratic two-party system and give an enormous impetus to the war effort of the United Nations." But he declared that the hopes for such a Republican sweep would be harmed if the party attempted to push through any slate without thoroughly considering the potentialities of all candidates.

He revealed that in the last few

Continued on Page Twenty-four

COURT RULE SAVES 3,000 TEACHER JOBS

Right of Board of Education to Hire Out-of-License Instructors Is Upheld

Special to THE NEW YORK TIMES.

ALBANY, June 18—Modifying an order of the Appellate Division, first department, the Court of Appeals ruled today that the New York City Board of Education had the right to assign out-of-license teachers to conduct junior high school classes. The effect of the court's decision is that some 3,000 teachers in the New York City school system are assured of their positions.

The board was challenged by Nathan Davis of the Bronx, who stood fifth on an eligible list for appointment to a position as a teacher of mathematics. He contended that the board had no right to appoint an out-of-license teacher, but the modification order of the court pointed out that the board may do so until July 1, 1943.

Mr. Davis, who argued his own case before the court, contended there were twenty-one vacancies in the mathematics teaching force. The board insisted there were no vacancies and that there was a plentiful supply of teachers, who, although not licensed to teach mathematics, could be assigned to teach that subject and thus fill the mathematics needs of the school system.

The court's opinion stated that Mr. Davis was entitled to the relief which the appellate division accorded him when it reversed an order of the Bronx County special term dismissing the complaint.

"After that order was made the

Continued on Page Eighteen

CRIMEA CITY HOLDS

People Vow Not to Yield as Red Army Keeps Besiegers Off

UKRAINE LINE IS FIRM

Nazis Halted at River—Berlin Claims Bastion Near Naval Base

By The United Press.

MOSCOW, Friday, June 19—Russian armies fighting from recaptured trenches repulsed fresh attacks at Sevastopol and inflicted new heavy losses in German ranks yesterday, it was announced today as the city's besieged people flashed word to the outside world that they would "die to the last soul" before surrendering.

The midnight Soviet communiqué had little to report beyond the assertion that new attacks were hurled back at the Crimean naval base and that no material changes had taken place in other sectors.

Reports from the front said the Russians also had thwarted mass German attempts to cross a strategic Ukraine river—evidently the Donets—near Kharkov, killing 3,000 more Germans there and at Sevastopol. "Huge" forces of German infantry, tanks and artillery tried repeatedly to storm across the river, only to be beaten back from the bank, Pravda reported.

Siege Fails, Russians Say

The German offensive against Sevastopol has failed, the Moscow News asserted. It said the Germans had lost so many planes in the fourteen-day assault that air attacks on the beleaguered Black Sea base had been reduced sevenfold.

[The German High Command said German and Rumanian troops, in fierce hand-to-hand fighting, stormed into Sevastopol's main northern fortifications, captured the Maxim Gorki Fort, "the most modern and strongest bastion of the whole fortress," and carried the attack to within less than two miles of the harbor. Air attacks destroyed matériel depots and supply transports in the harbor area, the communiqué said.]

A unanimous resolution from the people of Sevastopol was sent by Fedor Menshikoff, secretary of the Crimean Communist party, saying that despite the attacks of hundreds of dive-bombers, artillery and ten divisions of infantry numbering some 150,000 troops, the city would never yield.

"Hundreds of thousands of bombs and shells only serve to inspire heroic efforts of soldiers and civilians alike," the resolution said. Mr. Menshikoff also reported that hundreds of girls were enlisting for army training, learning how to fight under actual fire, against the day when they might be called into battle.

Russians in Counter-Blows

Pravda's correspondent reported from Sevastopol that hordes of German tanks and motorized infantry repeatedly charged the northern and southern approaches to the city, but were beaten back in mangled disorder at a cost of another 1,500 killed.

Vicious Soviet counter-attacks in one Sevastopol sector drove the Germans from an outer line of trenches that they had managed to seize but were unable to consolidate, the army newspaper Red Star reported.

At the same time Red Fleet marines, equipped with hand grenades and combustible bottles, hurled themselves at German tanks that had punched into the Soviet positions and destroyed them.

Sevastopol anti-aircraft gunners and fighter pilots downed seven German planes and damaged three Wednesday, Pravda reported. It

Continued on Page Six

DESERT UNITS SPLIT

British Fall Back Toward Egypt, but Some Take Up Posts in Tobruk

NAZIS AMID DEFENSES

Drive Into Rezegh and El Adem, in Outer Rim—Coast Road Still Open

By JOSEPH M. LEVY
Wireless to THE NEW YORK TIMES.

CAIRO, Egypt, June 18—Onslaughts by Axis armored forces in the battle in Libya have forced the British to evacuate Rezegh and El Adem, strong points in the perimeter defenses of Tobruk, it was announced today. This retirement allowed the Axis forces to get within a few miles of the sea and made the isolation of Tobruk a possibility that had to be faced, although the British still clung to the coastal road to the east.

British mobile forces were still fighting south and west of Tobruk, giving the Germans some trouble to their flank and rear, but it appeared that the Nazis had succeeded in establishing a salient through the British defensive area south of Tobruk. Rezegh is twenty miles southeast of Tobruk and El Adem is eighteen miles south of the port. The position today was thus roughly analogous to that of a few days ago, when the Germans developed the so-called Cauldron salient through the British defenses south of El Gazala.

Can Withstand Siege

Tobruk now occupies a position relative to the German thrust similar to that of El Gazala a few days before its evacuation this week—with two important differences. Tobruk has a far better harbor, which keeps it in close touch with the sea, and its defenses and living quarters are permanent, permitting it to stand a much longer siege than El Gazala could have stood. Whether the British will find it necessary or advisable to hold out there for a long period remains to be seen.

The present German position is not regarded here as unduly strong, despite the apparent success of the Axis armored forces, for their salient is threatened from north and south by strong British positions. Thus if the Nazis have any hope of reaching Egypt they must first surround or storm Tobruk and the British strong points to the south.

A storming of Tobruk still appears a most unpromising procedure for any army, but the Nazis might try to repeat their success at Bir Hacheim by similar tactics on British fortifications still standing south of the new Axis salient. Further progress by the Germans depends not only on their ability to push on against determined resistance by British forces of tanks

Continued on Page Three

War News Summarized

FRIDAY, JUNE 19, 1942

For the second time since the United States entered the war, Prime Minister Winston Churchill arrived in this country yesterday for conferences with President Roosevelt which, it was hinted, are to deal in part with the opening of a second front in Europe. Military aides accompanied the Prime Minister, and the official announcement of his presence said his meetings with the President would concern "the war, the conduct of the war and the winning of the war." [1:8.]

In Moscow, Foreign Commissar Molotoff, also a recent visitor to Washington, announced that plans worked out during his stay there called for the dispatch of $3,000,000,000 worth of fighting material from the United States to the Soviet Union. The Supreme Council of Soviets ratified the Anglo-Soviet agreement and approved the government's foreign policy. [1:2-3.]

On the Soviet fighting front, the Russians reported the recapture of outer trenches before beleaguered Sevastopol and the repulse of a German attempt to cross a strategic river in the Ukraine, evidently the Donets. The German High Command, however, claimed the capture of Maxim Gorki Fort, Sevastopol's "strongest bastion," within two miles of the harbor entrance. [1:4; map, P. 6.]

In Libya, the British evacuated El Adem and Rezegh, making the isolation of Tobruk a possibility, although they still clung to the coastal road east of the stronghold. [1:5; map, P. 3.]

The American heavy bombers that attacked the Italian fleet in the Mediterranean last Monday scored repeated direct hits on the battleships Littorio and Conte di Cavour, Washington announced. [1:7.]

The Nazi-controlled Prague radio in a communiqué announced the capture and execution of "the assassins" of Reinhard Heydrich, Gestapo Protector of Bohemia-Moravia. Captured in hiding in a Prague church, the men proved to be Czechs "dropped over the Protectorate by British planes" to make the attack, the communiqué said. [1:5-6.]

Secretary of War Stimson declared that the Japanese threat to the Pacific Coast was "temporarily much less" as a result of the naval battles in the Pacific. [8:3.]

In China Chungking revealed the existence of a United States Army bomber command, announcing the appointment of Colonel Caleb V. Haynes as its commander. [9:3.]

HERE AGAIN

Winston Churchill
The New York Times, 1941

British Link Churchill Trip To Shifts in War Situation

By RAYMOND DANIELL
Special Cable to THE NEW YORK TIMES.

LONDON, Friday, June 19—Strategic problems of the greatest possible import were believed here to lie behind Prime Minister Winston Churchill's second visit to the United States since the country entered the war. That much seemed indicated by the fact, as officially announced here early today, that he was accompanied by General Sir Alan Brooke, Chief of the British Imperial General Staff, and Major Gen. Sir Hastings Ismay, chief of Mr. Churchill's personal staff as Defense Minister.

And it is perhaps significant that the Prime Minister's transatlantic trip came at a time when apparently events in the Middle East have taken a turn for the worse.

News of Mr. Churchill's safe arrival in the United States was released here long after early editions of the London morning papers had gone to press, so there was little opportunity given the newspapers for comment or speculation.

The general line that was indi-

Continued on Page Three

U. S. NAMES 2 SHIPS HIT IN ITALY'S FLEET

Battleships Littorio and Conte di Cavour Struck by Our Fliers, Army Reveals

By CHARLES HURD
Special to THE NEW YORK TIMES.

WASHINGTON, June 18—The American heavy bombers that attacked the Italian fleet in the Mediterranean on June 15 in cooperation with Royal Air Force units scored repeated direct hits on the Italian battleships Littorio and Conte di Cavour, the War Department reported here tonight.

The American four-engined bombers, of the Consolidated B-24 type, weathered a "considerable amount of anti-aircraft fire," which did no serious damage to them.

This was the gist of a communiqué based upon preliminary reports from Colonel Harry A. Halverson, commander of one bombing force that flew to the attack from a base in North Africa. Damage to the two battleships, coincident with extensive damage done by R. A. F. bombers to cruisers and destroyers in the Italian fleet, caused it to turn back from its apparent object of attacking an important British convoy.

The American bombers went out with R. A. F. planes early on Monday morning and found their target at 6 A. M., local time, the communiqué stated.

The ineffective anti-aircraft fire of the Italians apparently left them a clear field for bombing oper-

Continued on Page Four

PREMIER'S 2D VISIT

Visitor to See President on 'Winning the War,' Says Early

SECRECY IS IMPOSED

Arrival First Hint of Trip—No Further Statement Expected This Week

By FRANK L. KLUCKHOHN
Special to THE NEW YORK TIMES.

WASHINGTON, June 18—Prime Minister Winston Churchill of Great Britain arrived in the United States today for conferences with President Roosevelt on "the war, the conduct of the war and the winning of the war," the White House announced shortly after 8 o'clock tonight.

Speculation that the talks would cover the task of opening a second front in Europe would be "perfectly justified," a spokesman affirmed.

Mr. Churchill was scheduled to begin his conferences with President Roosevelt "immediately." It was said at the White House that no further statements on his visit should be expected this week.

The Prime Minister was accompanied by ranking British staff officers and two personal aides. It was apparent that considerable secrecy would be maintained until the talks were completed. No information was vouchsafed as to how Mr. Churchill reached here for his unannounced visit.

Follows Molotoff Visit

The arrival of the British Prime Minister, who had spent late December and early January in this country soon after its entry into the war, followed by only a few days the visit of Vyacheslaff M. Molotoff, Soviet Foreign Commissar. The latter led to a full understanding between the United States and Soviet Russia on "the urgent tasks of creating a second front in Europe in 1942."

It was thought natural here that the Roosevelt-Molotoff conferences would be followed by others between the President and Mr. Churchill. It was noted that the talks between the American and British leaders followed visits of ranking United States Army, Navy and Air officers to London and of British military and supply leaders here. It was thought in diplomatic circles that final policy might be determined in the talks that began today.

Although it had been known since early afternoon that Mr. Churchill was arriving, it was only about fifteen minutes before the announcement that reporters were called to the White House. Stephen Early, Presidential secretary, dictated the following informal statement to reporters in his office without referring to notes:

"Mr. Winston Churchill, Prime Minister of Great Britain, is again in the United States. The Prime Minister will confer while here with the President.

"The conferences will begin immediately. The subject of the conferences will be, very naturally, the war—the conduct of the war and the winning of the war.

"With the Prime Minister when he arrived were General Sir Alan Brooke [Chief of the British Imperial General Staff]; Major General Sir Hastings Ismay [Secretary of the Imperial Defense Council]; Brig. Gen. G. M. Stewart [Director of Plans of the War Office]; Sir Charles Wilson [Mr. Churchill's personal physician]; Commander C. V. R. Thompson, secretary and aide, and Mr. John Martin, private secretary to the Prime Minister.

"I do not anticipate any further statements by the President or Prime Minister this week."

A reporter asked Mr. Early whether the discussions would deal with the opening of a second front. The Presidential aide replied, "I

Continued on Page Two

If in Doubt, Put It Out

Among the enemies of the dimout are reflections from polished surfaces, civilian lighting experts who have been cooperating with the Army pointed out yesterday. Even though a street light or parking lot light is properly shaded to throw its rays downward, an automobile thoughtlessly parked underneath it may reflect them toward the sky and thus defeat the precautions that have been taken.

Untiring vigilance is necessary in the campaign to reduce the amount of light above the metropolitan area, which has been so helpful to U-boat captains in spotting our shipping along our coast. Full compliance with the dimout regulations from an hour after sundown, which is at 8:31 o'clock tonight, is a distinct help to the war effort. The Army continues to exhort all citizens to bear in mind the slogan: "If in doubt, put it out."

Soviet Ratifies Pact With Britain; Molotoff Pledges 'Mighty' Blows

By RALPH PARKER
Wireless to THE NEW YORK TIMES.

MOSCOW, June 18—The Supreme Soviet, Russia's Parliament, at its first meeting since the war began, tonight formalized the people's acceptance of the treaty with Britain and, linked with it, the agreements documented in the Washington and London pronouncements.

In the presence of Premier Joseph Stalin, the agreements negotiated by Foreign Commissar Vyacheslaff M. Molotoff with Britain and the United States were rubber-stamped in the name of the workers, peasants and fighting men of the entire Soviet Union. In factories and farms, dugouts and barracks, these momentous understandings already had received the seal of popular approval.

There were few vacant seats in the great hall of the Kremlin when the people's representatives assembled. Each constituent republic of the Soviet Union, including those that adhered to it in 1939 and 1940, was represented. Thousands of spectators were massed in the gallery. Sir Archibald Clark Kerr, the British Ambassador, was one of the few foreign diplomats present.

The deputies, representing 180,000,00 persons, of whom a considerable proportion are under Adolf Hitler's yoke, presented a somewhat somber sight in the brilliantly lighted hall as they sat with head-phones clamped over their heads. A surprising number wore the little skullcaps of the mid-Asian republics. Some were women, and many of these had

Continued on Page Six

Heydrich Killers Slain, Say Nazis, As Ultimatum to Czechs Expires

By DANIEL T. BRIGHAM
By Telephone to THE NEW YORK TIMES.

BERNE, Switzerland, June 18—The German Gestapo vigilantes announced tonight that they had succeeded "in the early hours of this morning" in capturing and killing the authors of the fatal attack upon Deputy Reich Protector Reinhard Heydrich. Their principal accomplices were captured, it was said.

The actual "arrest" was carried out in a Prague church by the "Prague section of the State Police," according to the German communiqué.

This announcement came just after the expiration of the "last chance" accorded the Czech populace to deliver the guilty parties at 8 o'clock this evening, failing which the reprisals were definitely going to take a serious turn, according to official German announcements. The communiqué issued before 10 o'clock tonight and read over the Prague radio, follows:

"The murderers of the Deputy Reich Protector of Bohemia-Moravia, S. S. [Elite Guard] Obergruppenfuehrer and General of Police Heydrich, were discovered in a church of Prague in which they had taken refuge for some time, during the early hours of the morning of June 18. They were shot immediately on arrest.

"Their delivery was due to the vast searches undertaken to this end by the direction of the State Police of Prague. On the same occasion the principal accomplices were also discovered. All the criminals were of Czech nationality and had been dropped over the Protec-

Continued on Page Seven

United Press International

German paratroopers attack a Russian strong point with mortars.

"All the News That's Fit to Print."

The New York Times.

LATE CITY EDITION
Little change in temperature today.
Temperatures Yesterday—Max., 85; Min., 60

Copyright, 1942, by The New York Times Company.

VOL. XCI. No. 30,830. Entered as Second-Class Matter, Postoffice, New York, N. Y. NEW YORK, MONDAY, JUNE 22, 1942. THREE CENTS NEW YORK CITY and Vicinity

TOBRUK FALLS, AXIS CLAIMS 25,000 PRISONERS; GERMANS DRIVE WEDGE INTO SEVASTOPOL LINES; JAPANESE ASHORE ON KISKA IN THE ALEUTIANS

'GAS' DROUGHT CUTS HOLIDAY PLEASURE AS CITY SWELTERS

New Yorkers Stay at Home or Drive Only to Suburbs—Many Avoid Main Roads

CROWDS AT SOME RESORTS

Others Are Hard Hit as Travel Is Spotty—Humidity Soars and Mercury Reaches 84°

New Yorkers, afflicted with the first sweltering Sunday of the season under the gasoline shortage, stayed at home yesterday, sitting on the sidewalks or in penthouse or roof gardens, or went to near-by parks and beaches. Pleasure driving was only half of normal, by and large, and the resorts, particularly the distant ones, bore the brunt of the decline. Relatives and friends in the suburbs apparently had many visitors.

The heat was not record-breaking. Temperatures rose from a low of 60 degrees at 8:45 A. M. to a high of 84 degrees at 5:30 P. M. The humidity, however, remained at 75 per cent, which the Weather Bureau said was extremely high for such high temperatures. In the morning two-tenths of an inch of rain fell and skies were overcast long after, accounting for many of the stay-at-homes in the city.

Brooklyn's first heat prostration of the season was reported last night when John Chambers, 45 years old, of 244 West End Avenue, Coney Island, collapsed as he was walking in Flatbush Avenue near East Twenty-sixth Street, Brooklyn. He was removed to Coney Island Hospital, where his condition was described as fair.

Motoring Is Spotty

The drop in pleasure driving, although marked as far as resorts were concerned, and severe if parkway use was an accurate indication, did not fully reflect the gasoline supply situation.. With many stations dry, traffic on the George Washington Bridge was reported normal for a Sunday, through the Holland Tunnel a third off, and over other bridge and tunnel exits the reduction was not significant.

Yet on the Westchester parkways motor traffic was 30 per cent of normal and on the Long Island parkways about 60 per cent of normal. Police traffic experts believed that this reflected the spotty character of the gasoline shortage, which was acute in Westchester and near-by Long Island and some sections of New Jersey, but not serious in others.

Those who had gasoline in their tanks apparently went pleasure driving in spite of the appeals to save gasoline, but avoided the parkways and resorts, where they would be conspicuous. Many, the traffic experts thought, must have gone to visit friends and relatives

Continued on Page Nine

If in Doubt, Put It Out

Carelessness remains the greatest enemy of the Army's dimout regulations, it was said yesterday by civilian lighting experts who have been working with the Army on ways of cutting down the nightly illumination over the city that is used by enemy submarines in spotting shipping off our coast.

Windows and doors thoughtlessly opened for relief from the heat continue to loose light rays that help build up the sky glow over the metropolitan area, these experts said. They urged that whenever a window or door is opened for this purpose, it should be properly shaded or screened to prevent direct rays of light from emerging. These and other precautions should be placed in effect by one hour after sundown, which is at 8:31 P. M. tonight.

Meanwhile, the Army adjures all citizens: "If in doubt, put it out."

Peter of Yugoslavia Reaches Washington

Special to THE NEW YORK TIMES.

WASHINGTON, June 21—King Peter of Yugoslavia arrived here by airplane today. He was accompanied by M. Nincitch, the Yugoslav Foreign Minister.

They will discuss with President Roosevelt and other officials their country's continued opposition to the Axis. One of their objectives, it is understood, will be to obtain lease-lend aid for the guerrilla forces resisting the Nazis in Yugoslavia.

The King and his entourage will spend tonight at Blair House and will leave tomorrow to spend a few days in the country. He is traveling incognito until Wednesday, when he will return to Washington to begin the official program of his visit to the United States.

DIMOUT 'FAILURE' IS LAID TO MAYOR

Defense Council Members Say He Has Not Ordered Police to Enforce Army Rules

Charges that Mayor La Guardia has failed to give the Police Department orders to enforce the Army's dimout regulations, but has endeavored unsuccessfully to get the Army to modify its specifications, were advanced yesterday by two members of the executive board of the Lower West Side Defense Council, acting as a special committee in behalf of the council.

Howard Mulligan, a lawyer, of 103 Waverly Place, and J. B. C. Woods of 38 Perry Street, made public copies of a letter they had sent to the Mayor charging that conditions in their area were "deplorable." Mr. Mulligan explained that he and Mr. Woods had been authorized to take this action at a meeting at the council's headquarters, 27 Barrow Street, last Tuesday evening.

"Nightly, men are dying and ships are being sunk by the enemy off our coast because you, sir, prefer not to carry out the Army's orders," the letter charged.

In his weekly radio broadcast on June 7 Mayor La Guardia an-

Continued on Page Thirteen

RED ARMY RETIRES

Paris Radio Says Nazi Troops Have Reached Town of Sevastopol

AXIS LOSSES SEVERE

Placed at 7 Divisions—Germans Repelled on Kharkov Front

By RALPH PARKER
Wireless to THE NEW YORK TIMES.

MOSCOW, Monday, June 22—The Russian High Command acknowledges in its communiqué this morning that the Germans have succeeded, at a high cost in lives lost, in driving a wedge into the defenses of Sevastopol. But the bulletin also reports the repulse of numerous severe German assaults on the Sevastopol front.

[The German-controlled Paris radio said today that German troops had reached the town of Sevastopol after breaking through the Russian inner defense lines, The United Press reported from London. German sappers smashed their way through the final defense line outside the town with flame throwers, the Paris broadcast claimed.]

[The Germans reported the Red Army forces on the Kharkov front, where fighting on any considerable scale appears to be confined to one narrow sector, are said to have achieved an important success. After two enemy regiments had crossed a river barrier and advanced on the eastern bank, the Russians struck back, driving the Germans into and across the river. The Russians themselves then crossed the river and captured points on the western bank.

Press reports yesterday indicated that the Germans were continuing to pour troops into the Sevastopol fighting and that the situation there was grave. These reports said that waves of German and Rumanian infantry, attacking Russian lines in the southern sector of the Crimean base's defenses while planes dive-bombed Soviet artillery positions, had

Continued on Page Five

NEW LANDING MADE

Japanese Cruiser Is Hit in Army Air Blow at Kiska's Harbor

TRANSPORT IS SUNK

U. S. Fliers See Enemy's Temporary Buildings on Aleutian Isle

By C. BROOKS PETERS
Special to THE NEW YORK TIMES.

WASHINGTON, June 21—The Japanese forces that have been operating in the western Aleutian Islands since June 3 have succeeded in occupying Kiska, 650 miles west of Dutch Harbor, strategic American operations base, the Navy Department announced today.

Enemy occupation of Attu, westernmost island of the American chain and some 275 miles northwest of Kiska, was acknowledged in a Navy announcement on June 12.

Flying conditions in the Aleutian region—in which "foul weather and fog" are the general rule, the Navy reported recently—were sufficiently satisfactory in the last few days to permit "some restricted air operations against Kiska," today's Navy communiqué asserted.

Long-range Army aircraft attacked a small force of Japanese ships in Kiska's harbor and reported hits on a cruiser, the Navy announced. An enemy transport was sunk.

Tents of Japanese Seen

The American planes that finally were able to penetrate to the remote island of Kiska, where until the Japanese occupation the United States Navy maintained a weather station, observed that the enemy had set up tents and "minor temporary structures on land."

The communiqué added that operations in that area continued to be restricted "by considerations of weather and great distances."

Last Monday the Navy Department reported that Army and Navy planes were continuing air assaults "against the Japanese forces which recently were reported to have landed on western islands of the Aleutian group." At that time the Navy asserted that at least three Japanese cruisers, one destroyer, one gunboat and one transport had been damaged, "some of them severely," by air attacks.

Since the announcement on June 12 of the occupation of Attu naval circles in Washington have minimized the seriousness of Japanese landings in the western Aleutians, characterizing them as having been inspired primarily by a desire "to save face" after the defeat administered by American Army and Navy forces in the Coral Sea and off Midway Island.

Supply Problem Difficult

Military experts here have stated that supply would be a major problem for any enemy forces that endeavored to establish themselves in the Aleutians. The distance from bases in Japanese territory to the Aleutian Islands is so great, these circles have contended, that aerial transport is not feasible, particularly in view of the uncertain weather conditions. Therefore, supplies must be transported by surface craft, which are constantly exposed to attack by American submarines.

There is, however, a possibility that in the Rat Island group, of which Kiska is one island, the Japanese could conceal submarine mother ships and perhaps even small aircraft carriers, the experts here said. Submarines from such bases might prove effective should Japan attack Russia, they added.

But for the most part, according to the opinion conveyed to reporters in Washington by military circles, the enemy will have to be

Continued on Page Four

War News Summarized

MONDAY, JUNE 22, 1942

Tobruk fell yesterday, and the resultant threat to Egypt and the British position in the Eastern Mediterranean changed the war picture drastically, while the Russians acknowledged a significant German advance at Sevastopol, though at the cost of heavy enemy losses.

Tobruk fell to a smashing blow delivered by waves of German tanks according to London reports. The Germans claimed that 25,000 prisoners had been taken. In London the opinion prevailed that there had not been time to lay minefields around Tobruk before the Axis attack. [1:8.]

Military observers in London referred to the fall of Tobruk as an "incontestable disaster." The Germans were believed to have obtained a large quantity of stores. General Rommel was expected to drive on Suez. [2:2.]

British bombers attacked Emden, German submarine base, for the second successive night, airfields in the Netherlands and enemy shipping off the Netherland coast. Heavy air attacks were also made on the French and Belgian coasts. [1:5.]

Moscow granted that the defenders of Sevastopol had been forced to fall back as the enemy forced a wedge in their lines, but declared that the action had crippled five German and two Rumanian divisions. Sharp activity was reported in the Kharkov and Leningrad sectors. [1:3.]

President Kalinin of the Soviet Union, in a review of a year of war, stated that the Germans no longer were capable of a general offensive. [5:5; map, P. 5.]

Lord Beaverbrook, addressing a "Salute to Russia" meeting in Britain, again urged the United Nations to open a second front. He asserted that the British Army was now sufficiently prepared. [3:1.]

Chungking reported that the Japanese had been halted in Kiangsi and had lost 1,300 troops in Honan. The Minister of War asserted that the Japanese soon would be so bogged down in China that they would not be able to attack Russia with full strength. [4:1.]

The United States Navy announced that Japanese forces in the Aleutians had succeeded in occupying the island of Kiska, 650 miles west of Dutch Harbor. Bomb hits were made on a Japanese cruiser and a Japanese transport was sunk. [1:4; map, P. 4.]

Colonel J. L. Ralston, Canadian Defense Minister, disclosed that a government telegraph station at Estevan Point, Vancouver Island, had been shelled by a submarine Saturday night, but no damage was done. [1:5-6.]

As President Roosevelt and Prime Minister Churchill continued their conversations yesterday Washington reported that the fall of Tobruk and Russian withdrawals at Sevastopol had checked "second front speculation." Concern was being shown over the necessity for holding the present front in Egypt. [1:7.]

ROMMEL'S FORCES TAKE IMPORTANT PORT IN LIBYA

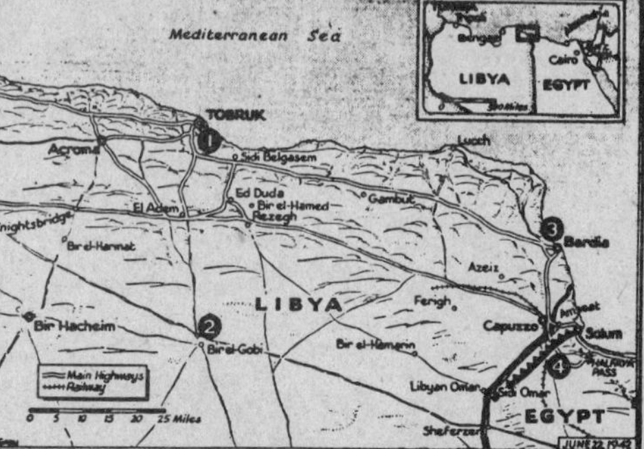

Tobruk (1) has been overwhelmed and captured with its garrison by the Axis, which also claimed the capture of Bir el-Gobi (2) and the minor port of Bardia (3). There were indications that the Germans were working their way from Bardia southward to Capuzzo for an assault across the border into Egypt. Here they will find defenses between Solum and Sidi Omar (4).

Vancouver Island Shelled; Northwest Coast Dims Out

By P. J. PHILIP
Special to THE NEW YORK TIMES.

OTTAWA, June 21—Estevan Point on Vancouver Island was shelled by an enemy submarine at 10:35 o'clock, Pacific time, last night (1:35 A. M., Sunday, Eastern war time), Colonel J. L. Ralston, the Defense Minister, announced here today. The submarine was presumed to be Japanese.

The enemy's objective was the government wireless and telegraph station there. No damage was done, said a report from Lieut. Gen. Kenneth Stuart, Canadian Chief of Staff and acting Commander in Chief of the West Corps defenses.

[Coastal dimouts in the States of Washington and Oregon were put into effect last night, following the shelling of Estevan Point, which is about 125 miles north of the United States border.]

There is an airfield near Estevan Point, but no report has come through as to whether action was taken against the attacking submarine.

The attack was the first against Canadian soil in the history of Canada as a Dominion. Last month two ships were torpedoed and sunk in the Gulf of St. Lawrence.

The Defense Minister's announcement said:

"The Commander in Chief, West Coast defenses, reported that the Dominion Government telegraph station at Estevan Point, Vancouver Island, was shelled by a submarine at 10:35 P. M. (Pacific time) on Saturday night. No damage resulted."

Estevan Point lies halfway along the western shore of Vancouver Island, about 150 miles northwest of Victoria. Its only importance seems to be the estab-

Continued on Page Four

R. A. F. PAYS EMDEN 2D VISIT IN 2 NIGHTS

Also Hammers Other Targets in Northwest Reich—Hits Ship Off Dutch Coast

By JAMES MacDONALD
Wireless to THE NEW YORK TIMES.

LONDON, June 21—A large number of British bombers hammered Emden, Germany, last night for the second night in succession and also other objectives in Northwest Germany and air bases in the Netherlands.

At the same time American-built Hudson planes of the Coastal Command, ever on the lookout for enemy shipping, searched waters off the Netherland coast, where a Canadian flying crew dropped two bombs on a medium-sized cargo vessel.

The communiqué announcing these operations did not divulge the number of planes engaged, but said the raids cost the Royal Air Force six bombers and one Coastal Command plane. The R. A. F. losses were increased today when one fighter plane failed to return home from a daylight attack on Dunkerque.

[The Berlin radio went off the air at 1:50 A. M. today, a possible sign that British bombers were again over Germany, The United Press reported from London.

[German planes dropped bombs early today in a sharp attack on the south coast of England, The Associated Press reported. Two of the raiders were shot down and two more Nazi planes destroyed over Europe.]

As in the case of the R. A. F. raids on Emden late Friday night and early yesterday morning, the Air Ministry did not go into details about the targets for the night or indicate the extent of damage.

While patrolling along the Netherland coast during the night Coastal Command fliers caught up with an enemy convoy of three ships. The rear gunner on a Canadian-manned plane said on his return to his base that he saw two bombs hit one vessel amidship, hurling debris high in the air in the resulting explosions. Whether the vessel sank was not determined. What became of her two companion ships was not learned here.

Although the sky was clear, there was less daylight activity to-

Continued on Page Five

NEWS PUTS DAMPER ON CHURCHILL VISIT

But Washington Sees Mid-East Crisis as Incidental in His Planning With Roosevelt

By JAMES B. RESTON
Special to THE NEW YORK TIMES.

WASHINGTON, June 21—Washington was in a sober and realistic mood tonight. The fall of Tobruk and the situation of the Russians at Sevastopol have put a damper on the unrestrained second-front speculation that has surrounded the Roosevelt-Churchill talks. The chief immediate concern was viewed as the holding of the second front the United Nations now have in Egypt, rather than opening up new fronts on the European Continent.

The President and Mr. Churchill continued their talks during the day, and the chiefs of staff of the United States and Britain, General George C. Marshall and General Sir Alan Brooke, who came to the United States with Mr. Churchill, continued their exchange of information and their planning for the future.

The plain and simple truth about these important discussions is that only a few persons know what has gone on since Mr. Churchill arrived, and they are not telling what they know.

The purpose of the conversations is much less complicated, dramatic and urgent than one would tend to deduce from the secrecy with which they have been surrounded.

It is undoubtedly true, as Stephen Early, White House secretary, has said, that they are dealing with the future plans of the

Continued on Page Eight

'Never a Dull Moment' at Midway, Reporter Watching Battle Found

The following account of the Battle of Midway is by a correspondent of THE NEW YORK TIMES who was aboard one of the United States warships.

By FOSTER HAILEY
Special to THE NEW YORK TIMES.

WITH THE PACIFIC FLEET, at Sea, June 4 (Delayed)—Today is the day. Mark it on your calendar in red ink, Thursday, June 4. It may be the one on which the tide definitely turned in the battle of the Pacific.

This morning at dawn the Japanese launched planes from a strong striking force northwest of Midway. We are in a position to strike them on the flank. If our planes can only get to their carriers before the Japanese planes attacking Midway can return, the result may be a naval disaster for the Japanese.

White water is curling away from the clipper bows of the cruisers and the big carriers, whose escort we are, as we drive on at high speed with the destroyers ahead and on the flanks. It is a relief for the nerves when the first alarm is sounded. It turns out to be false, but the activity has eased the tension.

There is another spurt of activity as another air contact is reported, but it turns out to be a big patrol plane from Midway that joins the force to act as an anti-submarine guard.

"Midway was attacked at 8:48 A. M.," our Admiral and Chief of Staff says crisply when an inquiry on the situation is made.

"We should be in launching distance soon."

The dawn was a gloomy one, but now the clouds are breaking up.

Continued on Page Four

NAZIS NEAR EGYPT

British Are on Border as Rommel Presses On After Victory

PORT'S LOSS SERIOUS

Plan for a Second Front Seen Upset by Need to Hold New Line

By DAVID ANDERSON
Special Cable to THE NEW YORK TIMES.

LONDON, June 21—A smashing blow delivered yesterday by waves of German tanks, heavily supported from the air, crushed the defenses of Tobruk in Libya. The War Office tonight confirmed the loss of the town, already claimed by the enemy, who said 25,000 prisoners, including "several generals" had been captured.

The story of what happened, as given by both German and Italian sources, appears to cover the battle fairly fully, but the accuracy of these reports cannot be checked at present. Briefly, it can be said Field Marshal Erwin Rommel's armored units that had passed Tobruk in pursuit of the British Eighth Army did so to make certain whether the British showed any signs of preparing a counter-attack.

When the German Marshal was satisfied this was not the case he reversed his forces, bringing back tanks against Tobruk from the south, driving from the vicinity of Ed Duda, and did this fiercely with every ounce of power at his command. At the same time the Luftwaffe began intensive bombing of Tobruk's defenses. Within a matter of hours the battle was over.

Tobruk Long in Battle

Tobruk must have been softer in its last moments than during the many other attacks it beat off during the last seventeen months since it was captured from the Italians on Jan 22, 1941. It has been on the fringe of the Libyan battlefield for some weeks with inevitable strain as strategy wavered between one of concentration of strength there and one of evacuation.

Despite the presence of a large garrison when Tobruk fell it is believed there was not time to lay minefields on its perimeter or otherwise strengthen its defenses to face an immediate storming.

A Cairo communiqué, released here at noon today, paved the way for the worst. It read:

"Yesterday the enemy attacked the perimeter of Tobruk in great strength. In spite of most determined resistance by our forces the enemy succeeded in penetrating the defenses and in occupying a considerable area inside them."

Twelve strong points in the defenses were taken by the first wave of enemy tanks, according to Berlin. This made a wedge two and a half miles wide, and German sources state the British defenders then realized that further resistance was useless.

Bombers Blast Defenses

But they had other reasons for weighing most seriously the advantages of carrying on the fight. The Germans said today that "numerous bombers' ceaseless attack wrought great destruction in the fortifications and other military works of the port and town."

It was not long after noon yesterday when large formations of German bombers swooped down on a group of four anti-aircraft batteries, all of which were silenced, it was reported by Berlin. Still more of the Luftwaffe's heavy aircraft, laden with high explosives, cruised over a column of twenty tanks, setting many of them ablaze.

Finally, the German radio said, "About 2 P. M. another great attack was made on Tobruk, which lasted three hours without interruption and caused numerous fires.

Continued on Page Two

"All the News That's Fit to Print."

The New York Times.

LATE CITY EDITION
Somewhat warmer today.
Temperatures Yesterday—Max., 70; Min., 61

Section 1

NEWS INDEX, PAGE 35, THIS SECTION

Copyright, 1942, by The New York Times Company.

VOL. XCI—No. 30,836. Entered as Second-Class Matter, Postoffice, New York, N. Y. NEW YORK, SUNDAY, JUNE 28, 1942. Including Magazine and Book Sections. TEN CENTS New York City and Vicinity

FBI SEIZES 8 SABOTEURS LANDED BY U-BOATS HERE AND IN FLORIDA TO BLOW UP WAR PLANTS; ALLIES PLEDGE MOVES TO RELIEVE RUSSIANS

PRICE OF GASOLINE GOES UP 2½ CENTS IN EAST TOMORROW

OPA Also Orders Increase of 2 Cents on Oils, Including Four of the Fuel Types

LACK OF SUBSIDY DECRIED

Henderson Calls Higher Costs Unfair to Public—Wider Ration Area Expected

Special to THE NEW YORK TIMES.

WASHINGTON, June 27—Gasoline will cost Eastern motorists 2½ cents a gallon more beginning Monday.

Increases of 2 cents a gallon, effective at the same time, also were ordered by the Office of Price Administration today for range oil, kerosene, tractor fuel, distillate Diesel fuel oils, gashouse oils and Nos. 1, 2, 3 and 4 fuel oils. Residual fuel oils are not affected.

The increases, third allowed by the OPA on gasoline and other oils since the beginning of the year, were made necessary, Leon Henderson, Price Administrator, said, by increased costs of moving petroleum to the East Coast by means other than tanker.

Word came also that when permanent gasoline rationing goes into effect in the East July 22 the boundaries of the affected area will in all probability be extended to include the ninety-three counties in Western New York, Pennsylvania, West Virginia, Maryland and Virginia which have been exempt to date.

OPC Approval Reported

According to reports here tonight, the Office of Petroleum Coordinator favors such an extension, and it is said to have gained favor with the Office of Price Administration because of a view that the problem of rationing administration would be greatly simplified by having the area bounded by State lines.

The plan would carry rationing to Buffalo and other important cities which have been exempt.

The ninety-three counties were exempted when emergency rationing became effective May 15, because the Office of Petroleum Coordination found that they had sufficient supplies of gasoline to take care of demand. Officials warned at that time, however, that the exemption might be only temporary.

In a special statement accompanying his announcement of the price increases on gasoline and other oils, Mr. Henderson declared that it was unfair to make Eastern consumers shoulder the expense of moving gasoline by means other than by tanker, but that for the time there was nothing that could be done about it in the absence of arrangements for subsidies.

"The Office of Price Administration," he said, "is keenly aware of the inequity of making consumers of petroleum products bear the entire cost of the submarine warfare

Continued on Page Twenty-eight

If in Doubt, Put It Out

The outdoor weenie roast and the beach fire are out for the duration, civilian defense offficials said yesterday as a reminder for picnickers. Sings, story-telling and hayrides are among the outdoor pastimes in which groups of people can join after dark without adding to the sky glow that helps enemy submarines find our ships. Vacationists are learning that a darkened circle is just as conducive to sociability as a blazing fire that shoots sparks into the skies.

All dimout regulations go into effect one hour after sunset. Tonight the sun sets at 8:32 o'clock. Don't take a chance with any outdoor light. Play safe and remember the Army's admonition: "If in doubt, put it out."

Major Sports Results

RACING

Whirlaway won the Brooklyn Handicap by two lengths from Swing and Sway on Aqueduct's closing day, which netted a minimum of $100,000 for Army-Navy relief. Warren Wright's thoroughbred thereby boosted his earnings to $404,486, only $33,244 less than Seabiscuit's all-time record.

BASEBALL

The Reds upset the Dodgers, 3—1, on Pinch-hitter Ray Lamanno's three-run homer with two out in the ninth. The Giants defeated the Pirates, 5—2, behind Bob Carpenter. At Chicago, Joe DiMaggio and Buddy Hassett led the Yankees to a 7-3 triumph over the White Sox.

GOLF

Frank Tatum Jr. of Stanford captured the N. C. A. A. golf title by downing Manuel De La Torre of Northwestern, 5 and 4, at South Bend. Vincent Raskopf vanquished Olin P. Boone, 2 up, in Long Island junior final at Cherry Valley. Miss Betty Jameson of San Antonio won the women's Western open at Chicago.

(*Complete Details in Section 5.*)

WILLKIE DEMANDS 'MEN OF FORESIGHT'

Backing Baldwin for Post in Connecticut, He Says Party Must Have Such Leaders

By JAMES C. HAGERTY
Special to THE NEW YORK TIMES.

WESTPORT, Conn., June 27—Wendell L. Willkie, speaking here this afternoon at a luncheon meeting sponsored by the Fairfield County Republican Women's Association, threw the full weight of his position as titular leader of the Republican party behind the candidacy of Raymond E. Baldwin as the party's nominee for Governor of Connecticut.

In supporting Mr. Baldwin, who served as Governor from 1938 to 1940 and who acted as one of the Willkie floor managers at the 1940 Republican National Convention, the former Republican Presidential candidate declared that he favored Mr. Baldwin because he represented the type of leadership so urgently needed in the Republican party. He said that his action was

Continued on Page Thirty-one

ROMMEL PUSHES ON

Enemy Units in Egypt Slow Down 15 Miles From Matruh

BRITISH HARRY FOE

Two-Week Halt in Axis Supplies to Bengazi Reported Forced

By DAVID ANDERSON
Special Cable to THE NEW YORK TIMES.

LONDON, June 27—General Field Marshal Erwin Rommel's Axis war machine was reported tonight to be slowly rolling toward a standstill in front of the British line that extends from Matruh, Egypt, to a point some forty miles inland.

Cairo gives little sign of knowing when or where the enemy will strike, but has issued reports of heavy aerial activity against advancing German supply columns and of delaying actions fought by British mechanized units.

The latest definite information from Cairo is that Marshal Rommel's forces are about fifteen miles from Matruh and apparently are tending to bear somewhat in the direction of the seacoast.

Opinion in London

Prudent observers here believed tonight that it would be safer to assume that the pace of the invasion of Egypt had slowed down of its own accord than to indulge in wishful thinking that the enemy had been checked.

[The Associated Press reported from Cairo that the British Eighth Army stood reinforced at full strength against a powerful Axis striking force, and, in a dispatch from Alexandria, said it had been learned unofficially that, with British submarines blasting away at Axis supply vessels, not a single enemy convoy had reached Bengazi, Libya, in the past fortnight.]

Speculation concerning the anticipated battle has not yet entirely ruled out the possibility that Marshal Rommel may risk the great gamble of attempting to swing southward of the Qattara Depression.

Fierce running fights have been going on along the tracks of the

Continued on Page Six

REPORT ON PARLEYS

Roosevelt and Churchill Say Germans Will Be Diverted by Push

STATEMENT HOPEFUL

Cuts in Shipping Losses, Blows at Japan, Help for China Projected

By W. H. LAWRENCE
Special to THE NEW YORK TIMES.

WASHINGTON, June 27—Coming operations by the military forces of the United Nations "will divert German strength from the attack on Russia," it was announced today by President Roosevelt and Prime Minister Churchill in a final communiqué on their week-long series of conferences in which the offensive strategy of the war was mapped.

For obvious reasons, the two leaders offered no more enlightenment on the methods they had agreed upon to carry out a previous British-Soviet-American understanding on the "urgent tasks of creating a second front in Europe in 1942."

They left the leaders of Germany and Italy with only a guess as to when, where and how the operations would be begun that would require the diversion of Axis man power now pressing against the Soviet armies on the eastern front.

Churchill Left Thursday

The second-front declaration, purposely vague, was the high point of the joint statement issued simultaneously at 11:30 A. M. here and in London after Prime Minister Churchill had arrived safely home by airplane from the United States, which he left secretly Thursday night.

Other major strategy decisions indicated by the joint statement were:

New plans for using the naval forces of the United Nations to reduce the toll of merchant shipping were made. In recent months losses have outstripped ship building.

Measures against Japan have been prepared.

New methods to relieve sorely pressed China will be undertaken.

Statement Is Optimistic

The Roosevelt-Churchill statement was optimistic. They reviewed the circumstances of their meeting in August, 1941, when the Atlantic Charter was drawn at sea before the United States entered the war, and again in late December, 1941, after the attack on Pearl Harbor. They declared their belief that "the over-all picture is more favorable to victory than it was either in August or December of last year."

But they warned against complacency. The task ahead, they said, must not be underrated and the conferences here have been conducted "with the full knowledge of the power and resourcefulness of the enemy."

Nowhere in the statement did the two leaders mention the sharp British reverses in the North African campaign, which took place while Mr. Churchill was en route here and during his stay in this country. These have aroused considerable criticism of the Prime Minister in Britain, but Mr. Churchill assured a Congressional delegation on Thursday that Egypt would be held and he minimized the advances of the Axis armies led by General Field Marshal Erwin Rommel.

Big Production Stressed

Mr. Roosevelt and Mr. Churchill said that their survey of the production of munitions of all kinds disclosed "an optimistic picture" on the whole, and that the arsenals of the two countries were approaching maximum production "on schedule." This was borne out by the President's special production report yesterday, which dis-

Continued on Page Two

War News Summarized

SUNDAY, JUNE 28, 1942

In New York last night J. Edgar Hoover announced the arrest of eight Nazi saboteurs, who were landed from submarines on Long Island and the Florida coast with TNT, maps, $150,000 in cash and instructions for blowing up such objectives as Hell Gate Bridge, the Aluminum Company of America, vital rail terminals and major war plants. [1:8.]

President Roosevelt and Prime Minister Churchill issued yesterday a joint statement asserting that the military forces of the United Nations would engage in operations that would divert German strength from the attack on Russia. The statement indicated decisions had been reached calculated to lower the submarine toll of shipping and to expedite aid to China. It was issued after the safe arrival of Prime Minister Churchill in Britain. [1:4.]

The Prime Minister returned to face political difficulties arising from the defeat in Libya, but it was still indicated that there was no serious challenge to his leadership. [2:2.]

A large vanguard of the United States Army Air Forces has been established in the British Isles and is making preparations to engage soon in mass attacks on Germany, coordinated with those of the Royal Air Force, according to London reports. Friday night there were a number of British attacks on German-occupied regions, and the Germans attacked fairly severely the city of Norwich. [1:7.]

Moscow granted that Soviet troops were being slowly pushed back in portions of the Kharkov front but said that the Germans were making no rapid advances and had gained no immediate military advantage except the capture of Kupyansk. The Sevastopol front was holding under the same sort of heavy German pressure. [1:5.]

Cairo announced that the main Axis forces were only fifteen miles west of Matruh, major British base on the Egyptian coast. A big battle seemed imminent and may have begun. [1:3; map, P. 6.]

British submarines were reported to have attacked many Axis supply vessels in the Mediterranean, and it was said in Alexandria that not an enemy convoy had reached Bengazi in the past two weeks. [6:5.]

The Chinese admitted the loss of Lishui, last of three major air bases in the Eastern Kiangsi-Chekiang area from which Japan could be bombed. The Japanese recapture of Kweiki on the Hangchow-Nanchang railway also was acknowledged. [12:3, with map.]

At Atlanta, Ga., it was disclosed that the first major expeditionary force of the United States Marine Corps had landed at a South Pacific base with a formidable arsenal of modern equipment. [1:5-6.]

EXPLOSIVES HIDDEN BY NAZI SABOTEURS ON FLORIDA BEACH

Four boxes containing TNT which was to have been used to destroy war plants
The New York Times (FBI)

First Major Marine A. E. F. Reaches South Pacific Port

By The Associated Press.

ATLANTA, June 27—This war's first major expeditionary force of United States marines has landed at a South Pacific port apparently equipped for offensive landing in that theatre of war. The far-off arrival of "transports swarming with marines" was revealed here today by Major Meigs O. Frost, Southern public relations chief for the Marine Corps.

Accompanying the announcement that the convoy carried the Marines' biggest overseas contingent of the war was the first story to be released as written by one of the Marines' own war correspondents assigned to combat forces.

The story told merely of the human side of life aboard the transports during the voyage from an unrevealed American port to the undisclosed destination, but contained clear implications of the job ahead of the task force.

With a number of Southern leathernecks known to have been included, first official advice regarding the force was relayed here from Washington by Brig. Gen. Robert L. Denig, Marine Headquarters Public Relations Director, in line with an effort to bring Marine news close to home.

The anonymous sergeant correspondent related how some of the Marines enjoyed the tropical nights by sleeping in Higgins landing boats aboard their ships.

The sergeant's story recorded no attacks on the convoy.

Recalling blacked-out nights, band concerts and swing sessions, the sergeant decided that the trip was far from dull and "living conditions aboard ship weren't as bad as anticipated."

"Most popular place aboard ship was the soda fountain, where Marines and sailors relaxed on cokes and ice cream.

"The chaplain's library was pop-

Continued on Page Eleven

RED ARMY CHECKING NAZI UKRAINE PUSH

Axis 'Fist' Kept From Spreading Out Beyond Kupyansk—Sevastopol Gain Slow

By RALPH PARKER
Wireless to THE NEW YORK TIMES.

MOSCOW, June 27—Though yielding ground slowly in fierce rear-guard fighting, Marshal Semyon Timoshenko has prevented the Germans from taking immediate or spectacular advantage of the capture of Kupyansk.

Russian dispatches from the southwestern front describe the fighting as of exceptional fierceness, but though it is apparent that General Field Marshal Fedor von Bock is trying to widen the battle front, the stubbornness of the Russian defense in depth has prevented his powerful armored force, attacking in a narrow sector, from ripping open the Russian lines and causing confusion.

The "fist" that struck is, as it were, still clenched, with its tanks and motorized infantry bunched together, though after the capture of Kupyansk it probably was the German plan to thrust probing fingers into various sectors of the Russian resistance.

[The midnight Soviet communiqué said Sevastopol's defenders had repulsed more attacks that cost the Axis heavily, while on the other fronts there were no significant changes. Berlin reported that a new Russian attempt to land at Kerch had been frustrated and said additional positions had been captured at Sevastopol.]

At Sevastopol yesterday a dangerous German wedge was driven into the northeastern sector. Though the pressure now is heavy on all fronts as new German regiments hastily brought from other fronts come into line, Col. Gen. Fritz Erich von Mannstein's gains are measured in yards. Small groups of shock troops succeeded in skirting through in the southern sector, where three enemy divisions now are believed to be operating, but these in no way represent any general advance and are vigorously engaged in hand-to-hand combat.

Much of the fighting now is described as a close-quarter struggle in trenches and gun emplacements, and here the Red Army men and

Continued on Page Nineteen

U. S. AIR ACTIVITIES IN BRITAIN RUSHED

Increasing Forces Arrive to Join From Own Bases in Offensive Against Nazis

Special Cable to THE NEW YORK TIMES.

LONDON, June 27—With preparations of the British Royal Air Force about complete for continuing—or rather, doubling in power—its attacks against Germany, such as that on Thursday night, which left still-smoking ruins at Bremen, authoritative sources here directed attention today to the important part predicted for the United States Army Air Forces in the offensive over Europe.

A great deal has been said about the arrival of tens of thousands of American soldiers in the British Isles; but little or nothing has been permitted to be published hitherto about the large number of United States Air Forces personnel now reaching here.

These American airmen have been taking over flying fields in the United Kingdom, studying the operational systems of the R. A. F. and working on plans for close coordination with the British.

The preparations indicated the establishment of United States air bases in Britain from which American units would bomb Germany in joint operations with the R. A. F.

[The R. A. F. bombed Germany again last night and a Berlin broadcast heard at London said Bremen had been attacked once more, according to a United Press dispatch.]

The time is rapidly approaching when the Liberators, Flying Fortresses and other giant United States bombers will be augmenting the R. A. F.'s Stirlings, Halifaxes,

Continued on Page Fifteen

Japan Bombed With 20-Cent Sight; Arnold Gives D. F. C. to 23 Raiders

By C. BROOKS PETERS
Special to THE NEW YORK TIMES.

WASHINGTON, June 27—The American B-25 bombers that carried out the daring surprise attack on Tokyo and other Japanese objectives last April 18 were equipped with improvised bombsights that cost about 20 cents each.

This and other interesting details of the aerial assault carried out by a force under the command of Brig. Gen. James H. Doolittle were revealed by the War Department today as the Distinguished Flying Cross was pinned on twenty-three members of the Army Air Forces who participated in the raid.

Because the raid on Japan was planned as a low-altitude operation, "with the planes' wings barely skimming the treetops as they flew toward their objective," it seemed inevitable that some of the planes might fall into Japanese hands (not one did, however), which would have given the enemy an opportunity to become familiar with the Norden bombsight.

But low-altitude bombing does not, in the Army's opinion, require the extreme accuracy of the Norden bombsights and they were not used in the planes participating in the attack. Major Charles R. Greening, armament officer of the squadron and one of the officers decorated today, improvised the 20-cent bombsights.

Five Japanese cities were marked for bombing in the April 18 raid: Tokyo, Yokohama, Nagoya, Kobe and Osaka. Objectives were tank, armament and aircraft

Continued on Page Eighteen

INVADERS CONFESS

Had TNT to Blast Key Factories, Railroads and City Water System

USED RUBBER BOATS

Carried $150,000 Cash—All Had Lived in U. S.—Face Death Penalty

By WILL LISSNER

Two groups of saboteurs, highly trained by direction of the German High Command at a special school for sabotage near Berlin, carrying cases of powerful explosives and nearly $150,000 in cash, were landed on the Long Island and the Florida coasts from submarines in the last fortnight with orders to blow up certain key plants and to cause panics in large cities, it was disclosed last night.

Despite their training the two gangs of four men each fell afoul of special agents of the Federal Bureau of Investigation almost immediately and the arrest of all eight was announced last evening by J. Edgar Hoover, director of the Bureau. They were in custody within a month after they had shipped on their expedition out of a submarine base on the French coast.

Mr. Hoover reported the arrests to President Roosevelt and released full biographies of the men, which showed that they were former waiters, machinists and German-American Bund agitators, long resident here and fluent in English, who were repatriated by the German Embassies in the United States and Mexico to be recruited for the sabotage school.

Carried List of Objectives

In the possession of the men was a list of special assignments of industrial plants they were to sabotage and department stores in which they were to create panics. The plants were the following:

Aluminum Corporation of America, Alcoa, Tenn.

Aluminum Corporation of America, Massena, N. Y.

Aluminum Corporation of America, East St. Louis, Ill.

Aluminum Corporation of America, Cryolite (aluminum base) plant, Philadelphia.

Chesapeake & Ohio Railroad (around industrial areas.)

Pennsylvania Railroad (at Newark, N. J.)

Hell Gate Bridge (railroad bridge from Astoria, Queens, to the Bronx.)

Canals and locks of the Ohio River from Cincinnati to St. Louis. (St. Louis, contrary to German geography, is not connected with the Ohio River.)

Specified department stores and

Continued on Page Thirty

Spy Crew Escaped From a Coast Guard

A story was told in Amagansett, L. I., last night that purported to give details of the landing of the sabotage crew there. According to this version, when the gang had finished burying its cases of equipment on the beach, the saboteurs were discovered by a young Coast Guardsman on shore patrol. He challenged them and the spies attempted to bribe him with some of their large store of money. He spurned the bribe and they fled.

Unable to round the men up single-handed, the Coast Guardsman ran back to his station, gave the alarm and called out patrols. The Army sent a detail to the scene and, together with the Coast Guard, the Army men searched the area, but the saboteurs had made good their escape, temporarily.

"All the News That's Fit to Print."

The New York Times.

LATE CITY EDITION
Continued warm and humid, probably scattered showers and thunderstorms today.
Temperatures Yesterday—Max., 78; Min., 72

Copyright, 1942, by The New York Times Company.

VOL. XCI..No. 30,866. Entered as Second-Class Matter, Postoffice, New York, N. Y. NEW YORK, TUESDAY, JULY 28, 1942. THREE CENTS NEW YORK CITY and Vicinity

RUSSIANS EVACUATE ROSTOV, WITHDRAW SOUTH OF THE DON; RAID LEAVES HAMBURG AFIRE

SOVIET CITIES FALL

Novocherkassk Is Lost—Nazis Push Across Don Farther East

RUSSIANS EXACT BIG TOLL

Germans Claim a Town South of Rostov on Oil Pipeline—Gain Near Stalingrad

By The Associated Press.

MOSCOW, Tuesday, July 28—Red Army troops have withdrawn from Rostov and from Novocherkassk, twenty miles to the northeast, before the steady German drive into the Caucasus, the Soviet High Command announced today. After fighting grimly in the streets of the shell-wrecked cities, which are north of the Don River, the Russians retreated to positions south of the river.

[The German High Command, which had claimed the two cities last week, reported yesterday the capture of Bataisk, five miles south of Rostov on the railway and oil pipeline from Baku. The Germans also reported southward advances east of Rostov and said that Axis troops in the Don bend had reached the river on a broad front in a push toward Stalingrad.]

The Russians also were imperiled all along the lower Don River, as far east as Tsimlyansk, 120 miles from Rostov. In that sector the Germans continued to throw pontoon bridges across the Don faster than the Russians could smash them.

Russians Counter-Attack

This morning's bulletin described the Tsimlyansk action as follows:

"The enemy repeatedly attempted to cross the river. Fighting is going on with fluctuating successes. In one sector the Germans succeeded in pushing forward, but were stemmed by a counter-attack by Soviet troops and lost during this engagement 350 officers and men killed."

The phrase "fluctuating successes" bore out press dispatches that acknowledged that the Germans were flowing across the Don despite the wrecking of numerous pontoon spans by Soviet airmen and artillery.

According to the dispatches, the Don was crossed between Rostov and Tsimlyansk only at terrific cost to the Germans. Thousands of dead Germans littered the banks of the river or slipped downstream along with smashed pontoons, the dispatches said. But long lines of German reserves always were ready to take the place of the fallen.

Last November a civilian army of men, women and children at Rostov joined hands with the Red Army to repulse huge German forces that had entered the city. The German withdrawal from Rostov was the turning point in Ger-

Continued on Page Three

600 R. A. F. Planes Strike Searing Blow at Reich Port

175,000 Incendiaries and Many 2-Ton Bombs Loosed in 50-Minute Attack—London's Guns Active as Nazis Hit Back in Britain

By RAYMOND DANIELL
Wireless to THE NEW YORK TIMES.

LONDON, Tuesday, July 28—For fifty minutes Sunday night British bombers to the number of about 600 dumped fire and explosives on Hamburg, Germany's largest port and most heavily defended submarine building center.

For the first thirty-five minutes of the concentrated attack two waves of the big Royal Air Force planes unloaded about 175,000 incendiary bombs and regular high explosives upon Hamburg's yards and industries.

Then a third wave of bombers followed up entirely with high explosives, including many of the 4,000-pound missiles that have a terrific blasting power.

Yesterday afternoon, the Air Ministry reported, many of the R. A. F.'s Wellington bombers struck again in Northwestern Germany.

London's anti aircraft guns went into action early today and the city had a raid alarm as Nazi planes, hitting back apparently in more force than on recent enemy raids, went overhead. Some German bombs were reported to have fallen in the Home Counties outside London, but none in the city itself. The all-clear sounded after an hour or so of intermittent gunfire.

The heaviest German attack was on a town in the West Midlands. Nazi planes were reported over Northern Ireland, where United States troops are stationed, but no bombing there was indicated. Eight Nazi planes were downed in Britain during the night, officials said.

Air Marshal Sir Arthur T. Harris, chief of the Bomber Command, declared the Sunday-night raid on Hamburg "one of the outstandingly successful attacks" of the war.

British officials reported the loss of twenty-nine big planes in the night's operations, including bomb-

Continued on Page Four

A.L.P. RIGHT WING IS OUT FOR MEAD; 3D PARTY SHELVED

But It Retains Right to Run Own Man if Bennett Is Named for Governor

KELLY CENTER OF INTEREST

Brooklyn Chief May Be Called to White House in Move to Get Him to Back Senator

The right wing of the American Labor party last night endorsed the candidacy of Senator James M. Mead for Governor and withdrew in his favor its threat of a third-party ticket. This wing controls the party's State Committee, has controlled all State conventions in the past, and represents to a larger degree than the left wing the last-ditch New Deal vote in the State.

The threat, made a week ago, was conditioned on the then expected nomination by the Democrats of Attorney General John J. Bennett Jr., who is not acceptable to the American Labor party. The action last night was taken by the State Executive Committee, meeting at the Hotel Claridge. The full State Committee will meet next Monday and will set Saturday, Aug. 22, as the date of the party's State convention, two days after the end of the Democratic session.

The action by the executive committee does not bind it to support the nominee of the Democratic convention should it turn out to be Mr. Bennett, who still maintained yesterday his pledged majority to the Democratic convention, despite the continuance of the New Deal drive for Mr. Mead.

If Mr. Bennett is nominated, the A. L. P. still plans to run its third-party candidate on the theory that it will be the Old Guard of the Democratic party, rather than the New Deal, that will meet consequent defeat in the November elections. On the other hand, there is no bar to the support by the A. L. P. of some New Deal candidate other than Mr. Mead, should some such candidate emerge as the eventual nominee of the Democratic convention.

Text of the Resolution

The resolution adopted unanimously by the Labor party committee follows:

"The State Executive Committee of the A. L. P. has gone on record repeatedly as urging the Democratic party of the State of New York to nominate for Governor a candidate who would unite behind him all the New Deal and labor forces of New York State.

"The candidacy of United States Senator James M. Mead—declared in response to public appeal—presents both the Democratic party and the A. L. P. with just such a candidate. In Senator Mead we have an outstanding candidate

Continued on Page Eighteen

SENATORS REJECT TAX EXEMPTS LEVY AND JOINT RETURNS

Committee Cuts 400 Millions From Treasury's Request for $2,400,000,000 Rise in Bill

10% ON ALL INCOME ASKED

M. L. Seidman of Board of Trade Denounces Bill—Ruml Urges Current Tax Collection

By THOMAS J. HAMILTON
Special to THE NEW YORK TIMES.

WASHINGTON, July 27—Disregarding Secretary Morgenthau's plea for action against two "special privileges, the Senate Finance Committee today rejected his recommendations for mandatory joint income returns and the taxation of income from outstanding issues of State and municipal securities.

The committee's vote, which, according to Senator George, the chairman, was taken earlier in order to "confine our hearings to subjects that possibly will be included in the tax bill," eliminated $400,000,000 of the $2,400,000,000 additional revenue which Secretary Morgenthau asked for last week.

Senator George emphasized that the question of taxing income from future issues of State and municipal securities had been "left open," but remarked that if this plan were adopted it would bring virtually no money into the Treasury during the current year.

Also left open was the question of abolishing percentage depletion allowances on mines and oil wells, the third of the "special privileges" which Mr. Morgenthau asked to be abolished. Each of these, the Treasury says, costs it $200,000,000 a year.

George Says Action Is Final

The House had already disregarded Mr. Morgenthau's recommendations with regard to these three types of exemption, and Senator George said that the committee's action meant there was no chance of including in the bill mandatory joint returns or taxation of income from existing State and municipal securities.

He explained, however, that the committee had left undecided the question of taxing income of families in the "community property" States on the same basis as those in the rest of the country. If this plan were adopted, he said, it would yield between $85,000,000 and $87,000,000 more. Mr. George recalled that a similar provision was voted by his committee last year, but was rejected in the Senate.

In the community property States husband and wife share their income equally, and by submitting individual returns they have been able to avoid the higher rates in the upper brackets.

Mandatory joint returns, which were intended primarily to stop this practice, would have yielded $420,-

Continued on Page Eight

SUPREME COURT IS CALLED IN UNPRECEDENTED SESSION TO HEAR PLEA OF NAZI SPIES

RECALLED FROM ARMY TO JUDICIAL DUTY

Supreme Court Justice Murphy, now a lieutenant colonel in the Army, was reached at Dilworth, N. C., over a field telephone for tomorrow's special session to consider Nazi saboteur case.

The New York Times (U. S. Army)

TO SIT TOMORROW

Full Bench to Decide if It Will Hear Saboteurs' Habeas Corpus Petition

CIVIL TRIAL SEEMS AIM

Military Proceedings Halted Until Thursday—Justices Are Hastily Summoned

By LEWIS WOOD
Special to THE NEW YORK TIMES.

WASHINGTON, July 27—A history-making special session of the Supreme Court will be held on Wednesday to consider whether the highest tribunal shall receive petitions to file writs of habeas corpus from the eight Nazi saboteurs now on trial before a military commission.

In a startling move Chief Justice Stone called the special session with the approval of his eight colleagues. All will be here, even Associate Justice Douglas, now speeding east from Oregon, and Associate Justice Murphy, now a lieutenant colonel in the Army on manoeuvres in North Carolina.

Possibly the court will decide that same day whether to reject or receive the petition to file the writs; possibly it will take the motions under consideration. At any rate, Attorney General Francis Biddle and Major Gen. Myron C. Cramer, judge advocate general, the prosecutors of the Nazis, will resist the proposal in every way possible.

Move Entirely Unexpected

The astonishing announcement that the court would meet in special session came without the slightest advance indication. Shortly after the Army colonels named by President Roosevelt to represent the saboteurs closed their case newspaper men received word to be at the Supreme Court Building at 5:45 P. M. There, Charles Elmore Cropley, clerk of the court, handed this statement to them:

"The Chief Justice directs that it be announced that the Supreme Court will convene a special term of the court on Wednesday, July 29, at noon, in order that petitions for writs of habeas corpus, on behalf of certain persons now being tried by a military commission appointed by the President, may be submitted to it.

"The petitions will be presented by counsel on July 29, and the prisoners will not be present at the bar of the Supreme Court on that day."

Neither Mr. Cropley, any of the defending Army colonels, nor, in fact, any one connected with the case, would speculate upon the moves of the defense. Nevertheless, it was believed their arguments would attack perhaps the Presidential order creating the military commission, and, most of all, the accompanying petition spe-

Continued on Page Ten

PATROLS MEET FOE IN NEW GUINEA PUSH

Contact Shows Enemy Gain of 55 Miles From His New Landing Point in Papua

By The United Press.

AT UNITED NATIONS HEADQUARTERS, Australia, Tuesday, July 28—Allied patrols have made contact with Japanese forces near Oivi, fifty-five miles inland from Japanese-held Gona Mission on the northeast coast of New Guinea, where Allied bombers have blown up an ammunition dump in a new raid, a United Nations communiqué disclosed today.

Oivi is east of Kokoda, half-way point on the 110-mile overland road from Gona Mission to the Allied base of Port Moresby on the south coast. The Japanese had thus penetrated fifteen miles farther inland from the Awala area, where they were reported yesterday to be in contact with United Nations patrols.

The communiqué said a lone Japanese flying boat raided Townsville, on the northeast coast of Australia, which also was attacked ineffectively early last Sunday, but caused no damage.

[The Australian radio, heard by The United Press in San Francisco, yesterday said Allied dive bombers are continuing their attacks against Japanese forces in New Guinea and carried out two strong night assaults on the Timor Island stronghold of Kupang, where hits were scored on the airdrome and nearby barracks, according to the United Nations headquarters communiqué. A small Japanese raiding force of about five planes twice raided Port Darwin, but there were no casualties or damage, the communiqué added.]

Australia Warns of Spies

Wireless to THE NEW YORK TIMES.

CANBERRA, Australia, July 27—"Almost positive evidence" of activities of enemy agents is causing anxiety in governmental circles today.

The possibility of landings of spies for the Japanese from submarines at infrequented spots along Australia's long and lonely coastline is not discounted in view of recent revelations in the United States. It is also considered possible that the enemy governments may have planted agents in Australia before the war who have succeeded in disarming suspicion and making Australian friends, from whom they obtain information.

The existence of illegal radios in the Commonwealth has long been

Continued on Page Three

U. S. AIRMEN ROUT RAID ON CHUNGKING

Only 4 of 50 Enemy Planes Reach Chinese Capital for First Attack in 11 Months

By The United Press.

CHUNGKING, China, July 27—United States Army fighter planes, battling beneath a full moon, routed fifty Japanese bombers that took off from Hankow to make their first raid of the year on Chungking tonight, letting only four of them get through to attack the outskirts of this Chinese capital.

Pilots of the American Twenty-third Pursuit Group roared into the sky from a West China base as soon as advance observation posts flashed the alarm that the Japanese were on the way from Hankow, 460 miles to the northeast, at 6:30 P. M.

An air defense headquarters communiqué announced that the Americans intercepted the raiding party and blazed into combat over Eastern Szechwan Province, some 120 miles from Chungking. Except for the few American Volunteer Group veterans, these Americans were having their first big crack at the enemy since their arrival in China.

Only Four Reach Capital

Observers said that twenty-seven Japanese planes got as far as Kiangpei, across the Kialing River just north of Chungking, but only four actually flew over the capital at 8:30 P. M.

The raiders left Hankow for the first attack on Chungking in eleven months with the advantage of bright moonlight, but low clouds had gathered by the time the four bombers reached their objective. They dumped their bombs far from any important target at a point well outside the city. The communiqué said the raid was a complete failure.

The defense authorities, remembering how large numbers of enemy planes had bombed the city in daylight throughout the Summers of 1939, 1940 and 1941, could hardly believe that the disappearance of the four bombers was the end of the raid. The all-clear signal was delayed another hour until 9:30 P. M.

The communiqué said that "the extreme calmness and best order maintained in dugouts by the citizens of this city were admirable, indeed." One reason for the calmness was the confidence manifested when word spread that the Americans were out to intercept the Japanese.

It was virtually a three-hour tea party for the people gathered in the bomb-proof dugouts, which had

Continued on Page Six

War News Summarized

TUESDAY, JULY 28, 1942

The Germans appeared yesterday to be on the verge of establishing strong positions south of the lower Don, but suffered a heavy British aerial attack on the important city of Hamburg.

Moscow acknowledged that Rostov and neighboring Novocherkassk had been evacuated and that the Soviet forces in the sector had withdrawn south of the Don. The Germans were said to be seeking to mutiply their bridgeheads, notably in the Tsimlyansk sector, some 120 miles up-river from Rostov. Soviet gains near Voronezh and near Bryansk were claimed again. [1:1; map, P. 2.]

Berlin claimed that Bataisk, five miles south of Rostov on the railway to Baku, had been captured. Farther east on the lower Don front the Germans were also advancing southward, according to Berlin. German troops were said to have reached the river on a broad front in the great Don bend west of Stalingrad. [3:1.]

British troops in Egypt resumed their attacks and some Axis prisoners were taken. Royal Air Force planes again bombed Tobruk successfully Sunday night after an attack by United States and R. A. F. bomber crews Saturday night that caused large fires. [4:1.]

London announced that about 600 R. A. F. bombers had dropped many two-ton bombs and 175,000 incendiaries on Hamburg Sunday night. Air Marshal Harris called the raid one of the most successful of the war. London had an air raid alarm early today as Nazi planes, attacking in the Midlands, went overhead. [1:2-3.]

Allied patrols made contact with Japanese forces near Oivi, in Papua, fifty-five miles inland from Gona and half-way point on the road toward Port Moresby, United Nations base on the south coast of Papua, on the Island of New Guinea. [1:2.]

Witnesses who have reached London reported the destruction of the Norwegian village of Televaag near Bergen in revenge for the killing of two Gestapo agents. According to the report, eighteen hostages were killed and the rest of the male population was sent to work in Germany. [3:2.]

United States fighter planes routed forty-six of fifty Japanese bombers bound for a raid on Chungking. The four raiders that got through to the outskirts of the Chinese capital were unable to hit any important target. [1:3.]

The German Transocean News Agency broadcast a report asserting that Premier Tojo of Japan had told an audience of 20,000 at Osaka that "Japan is determined to destroy the United States and Great Britain." [6:7.]

Downpour Halts Railroads; Two Die in Storm in City

A series of violent rainstorms that began early yesterday morning and continued in various parts of the city and suburbs most of the day disrupted commuter service between Westchester and Manhattan in the early rush hour and led to two deaths in the metropolitan area.

Thousands of residents of Southern and Central Westchester got to their jobs late, while others did not get to work at all. Those who remained at home found their county flooded in many sectors, with hundreds of small boats waterlogged along the shore, cellars and everything in them ruined and, in Bronxville, the high school isolated by a temporary lake.

The storm also produced several lightning scares, although tumbling bricks and one slight fire were the worst effects. It turned main highways into quagmires, spread a coating of mud on the Bronx's Webster Avenue, marooned automobiles, turned the meandering little Bronx River into a miniature Mississippi on a rampage and led to some unprecedented commuter routes to New York.

Shunted Onto Freight Line

One of the most unusual of these which became one of the most common during the worst of the morning, began with the harassed passengers on the New York, New Haven & Hartford shore line being shunted just below New Rochelle into the Harlem River Branch, which takes freight into New York via Hell Gate Bridge.

Had the trains been able to proceed to the bridge and into the city via Queens and Pennsylvania Station, the rain-weary passengers would have been relatively lucky, though late. As it turned out, they were taken only to the vicinity of the Westchester Avenue station, in a section of the East Bronx of which many of them had barely heard. It was a long, muddy trek in most cases to the nearest subway, bus or cab connection to Manhattan.

The freakish weather, while helping the city's water supply and coming when most needed by Suffolk County vegetable growers, also caused emergency scheduling and delay on the Bronx division of the Eighth Avenue-Independent subway—and turned into a dreary morass the thriving eight-acre farm of Mrs. Rose Falasca at Morris Park Avenue and Eastchester Road. Her chickens and a German

Continued on Page Eleven

WLB REFUSES RISE, CITES PAY FORMULA

Reasoning as in Steel Case, It Finds 1,200 Rand Workers Already Have Increase

By LOUIS STARK
Special to THE NEW YORK TIMES.

WASHINGTON, July 27—The National War Labor Board refused today to give a general wage increase to 1,200 employes of the Remington-Rand Company and in doing so applied the wage stabilization formula used in the recent "little steel" case.

The United Radio, Electrical and Machine Workers, C. I. O., representing the employes in the plants at Tonawanda and North Tonawanda, N. Y., had requested an increase of 10 cents an hour.

The vote of the board was 4 to 2, the public and industry members joining together, while the labor representatives dissented. The board, however, made one adjustment by adding 2½ cents an hour to the wage of female employes on an incentive basis in order to iron out an inequality resulting from a growing disparity between wages paid to men and women working in the company's plants.

The board asserted that the "little steel" formula has already served as a decelerator and stabilizer of the wage movement.

Previous Rises Are Noted

Wayne Lyman Morse, dean of the University of Oregon Law School, who wrote the board's opinion, said that the Remington-Rand employes had received two wage increases since Jan. 1, 1941, totaling 18 cents an hour for men and 11 cents for women.

Since these increases exceeded the 15 per cent rise in the cost of living during the Jan. 1, 1941-May, 1942, period, he concluded that "the employes are not entitled to a further wage increase at this time on the basis of any change in the cost of living since Jan. 1, 1941, in view of the wage stabilization formula laid down by the board in

Continued on Page Nine

Credit Rules Eased On Heating Change

By The Associated Press.

WASHINGTON, July 27—To facilitate the conversion of oil-burning heating equipment on the East Coast to coal because of the expected oil shortage this Winter, the Federal Reserve Board liberalized credit restrictions today.

The board will no longer require down payments or repayments within a limited term of months in connection with the conversion of heaters, installation of weatherstripping or insulation or other devices to conserve fuel. Dealers and contractors will be at liberty to establish whatever requirements they choose.

Under previous Federal Reserve regulations, if conversion were financed on the installment plan it would have to be paid for one-third down and the balance in twelve months.

The board also removed credit restrictions on the repair or replacement of property damaged or lost in a flood.

Last Extra Session Was Held in 1920

Special to THE NEW YORK TIMES.

WASHINGTON, July 27—Only once before in contemporary times has a special session of the Supreme Court been called, but ample authority exists in Section 338 of the Judicial Code, which says:

"The Supreme Court shall hold at the seat of government one term annually commencing on the first Monday in October and such adjourned or special terms as it may find necessary for the dispatch of business."

The only other instance of modern annals when the court met suddenly in a special term was on April 13, 1920, in connection with a dispute over oil flowing wildly from the famous Burk-Burnett properties in the Southwest. The court had appointed Jacob G. Dickinson as receiver in a title controversy between Oklahoma and Texas over the oil. He refused to serve, and the court, then in a three-week recess, was hurriedly summoned to name Frederic A. Delano, the uncle of President Roosevelt.

United Press International

Destruction at Stalingrad.

"All the News That's Fit to Print."

The New York Times.

LATE CITY EDITION
Scattered showers today; moderate temperatures.
Temperatures Yesterday—Max., 74; Min., 59
Sunrise, 6:[illegible] A. M.; Sunset, 7:19 P. M.

Copyright, 1942, by The New York Times Company.

VOL. XCI..No. 30,908. Entered as Second-Class Matter, Postoffice, New York, N. Y. NEW YORK, TUESDAY, SEPTEMBER 8, 1942. THREE CENTS IN NEW YORK CITY

PRESIDENT TO CONGRESS: CURB PRICES OR I WILL; WILL TAKE WAR TO GERMANY, HE TELLS NATION; NAZIS GAIN IN FRONTAL ATTACK ON STALINGRAD

BATTLE IS WIDENED

Red Army Retires West of Volga City—Line to Southwest Holds

FOE HIT IN CAUCASUS

Defenders of Road to Oil Wells of Grozny Put Nazis to Flight

By RALPH PARKER
Wireless to THE NEW YORK TIMES.

MOSCOW, Tuesday, Sept. 8—General Field Marshal Fedor von Bock attacked Stalingrad yesterday on a new line, west of the city, and made some progress against stiff Red Army resistance. A Soviet communiqué issued today says, in announcing the shift in the battle, that Soviet troops in one western sector withdrew to new positions after they had repelled four German attacks.

Russian forces southwest of Stalingrad are reported to have hurled back several violent German attacks of great strength. The Germans suffered heavy losses, it is said, and in close-range fighting in one sector Red Army men destroyed eight of thirty German tanks that were carrying out an assault.

This Russian bulletin also reports hard fighting in the Novorossiisk region of the Black Sea coast, where the Russians again lost ground, and on the southern bank of a river near Mozdok, where the German invaders of the Caucasus are attempting to advance to the Grozny oil fields. In the Mozdok area, the communiqué states, the Germans were counter-attacked successfully.

[The Germans, who claimed Novorossiisk on Sunday, said nothing more yesterday about the fighting in the Caucasus, but they reported an advance at Stalingrad. The city's defenders were said to have lost 108 tanks in futile counter-attacks.]

Nazi Wedge Pushed Out

Enemy attacks southwest of Stalingrad were increasing in fury. According to reports received yesterday, German tanks managed to advance into the Russian lines Sunday night. Russian machine-gunners and mortar detachments made a flank attack on the intruders and the salient was forced out.

The Russians were reported yesterday to have regained ground northwest of Stalingrad, and the situation there appears today to be unchanged. The enemy's northern flank is somewhat exposed as a result of his failure to take Voronezh and of the initiative shown by the Russians in the Kletskaya sectors.

The German Air Force continues to play an important part in the operations near Stalingrad, and although the Soviet Stormovik assault planes—whose designer received a high decoration yesterday—are giving valuable support to Red Army troops, the German dive-bombers appear to have the ascendancy. A new type of Messerschmitt fighter plane, with an

Continued on Page Two

U. S. Fliers Smash Japanese Returning to Solomon Isles

Enemy Suffers Severe Losses in Troops and Boats—Small Units Believed Ashore—Raid on Guadalcanal Is Ineffective

Special to THE NEW YORK TIMES.

WASHINGTON, Sept. 7—Several small Japanese detachments attempting landings on the swampy western reaches of Guadalcanal Island, in the Solomons have suffered heavy losses in attacks by United States planes, it was announced by the Navy tonight.

The Navy's communiqué did not say whether all the enemy landing forces had been repulsed, and it was assumed that small parties had made their way to shore in an attempt to reinforce the isolated Japanese patrols that had withdrawn to the mountains and jungles of the island when United States forces first occupied the Guadalcanal-Tulagi area. United States Marine forces are hunting down the scattered Japanese units.

This latest report on the efforts of the Japanese to regain a foothold on what had been their southernmost base was released a few hours after a Navy announcement that American fighter planes had shot down two Japanese bombers and one fighter out of a group of forty-six planes that raided Guadalcanal shortly after noon on Saturday (Solomon Islands time). The raiders—twenty-six bombers with an escort of twenty Zero fighters—inflicted only minor damage.

On the same day the Japanese

Continued on Page Five

United States planes have attacked enemy landing operations off San Jorge Island (1) and near the western end of the island of Guadalcanal (2).

PRESIDENT SPEAKS

Vital Decisions Made on Taking the Offensive, He Says on Radio

'RUSSIA WILL HOLD'

New Japanese Blows Are Predicted—Hopeful on the Near East

The text of the President's speech will be found on Page 17.

Special to THE NEW YORK TIMES.

WASHINGTON, Sept. 7—The United States and Great Britain, confident that Soviet Russia will hold out despite serious setbacks, have made vital military decisions designed to put their armies on the offensive against Germany at one or more of a dozen different points in Europe, President Roosevelt told the country and the world by radio tonight.

"The power of Germany must be broken on the battlefields of Europe," he said.

The Chief Executive, after explaining why he had called upon Congress again for legislation to hold down living costs, reviewed the progress of the war to date. He was cautiously optimistic in his appraisal of the future for the United Nations as he warned again that great sacrifices of blood, treasure and convenience must be expected before victory over the Axis powers can be assured.

Situation on Four Fronts

He gave the world this sketch of the developments to date on the four major battle fronts:

The Russian Front: A smashing victory still eludes Hitler and, though he has captured important territory, he still has been unable to accomplish his major objective—the destruction of a single Russian army. Millions of Germans seem doomed to spend another cruel and bitter Winter on the Russian Front, while Soviet forces continue to kill more Nazis and destroy more airplanes and tanks than are being smashed on any other front. In spite of any setbacks, Russia "will hold out and, with the help of her Allies, will ultimately drive every Nazi from her soil."

The Pacific Ocean Area: One major Japanese offensive was stopped at Midway, with heavy losses to the Japanese fleet, but the enemy still possesses great strength and "will undoubtedly

Continued on Page Seventeen

REPORTS ON HOME AND OVERSEAS FRONTS

The President addressing the nation last night

Associated Press Wirephoto

TIME ULTIMATUM

President Sets Limit of Oct. 1 to End 110% Farm Parity Law

HE TO CURB WAGES

Quick Tax Bill Action Is Asked in Message—For $25,000 Income Top

Text of the message to Congress is printed on Page 14.

By W. H. LAWRENCE
Special to THE NEW YORK TIMES.

WASHINGTON, Sept. 7—President Roosevelt sent to Congress today an ultimatum on anti-inflation controls, calling for enactment by Oct. 1 of legislation authorizing the stabilization of farm prices at parity or present levels. He warned that if the Congress fails to act in the next twenty-three days he will put the program into effect, along with wage stabilization, under his wartime powers as Commander in Chief despite the restrictions of the present Price Control Act.

Having laid his demands before Congress, the President spoke to the country by radio tonight. He told the people that two legislative steps which he had called for in his original anti-inflation program were vital if the perilous [illegible] spiral already noted was to be checked. These two legislative actions were, one, the grant of power to control farm prices now restricted by the 110 per cent farm-parity law and, two, increased taxation. At the same time the President reviewed the progress of the war.

In his bristling message to Congress, reminiscent of the [illegible] action he asked for and received in the "first 100 days" of his first term, the President said that he was determined to check the rising cost of living with or without Congressional sanction because "a vicious spiral of inflation" would stagger the whole economic system and make it more difficult to win the war.

He took the unprecedented step of establishing a definite deadline for the independent legislative branch, with the explanation that "we cannot hold the actual cost of food and clothing down to approximately the present level beyond Oct. 1."

No Word on Super-Board or 'Czar'

Contrary to expectations in some official quarters, the President took no steps to set up an economic "czar" or to create a super-board which would coordinate Federal policy on prices, wages, taxes, credits and savings. He asked nothing of Congress which had not been requested in his seven-point anti-inflation program of April 27, but he demanded speed in carrying out his proposals for removing restrictions on farm price control and for increasing taxes.

The message, sent to the Capitol at noon, brought mixed reactions from the few members of Congress who stayed in Washington during the semi-recess of Congress.

Administration leaders, calling the membership back to begin consideration of the message next Monday, were confident that it would be approved by Congress, since many who opposed the President's tactics in threatening to act independently were, themselves, in favor of removing Price Control Act restrictions which forbid the setting up of farm commodity ceilings no lower than 110 per cent of parity, below the highest price from 1919 to 1929, or below the prices prevailing on Oct. 15 or Dec. 15, last year.

Aim Favored, Method Criticized

Among those who favored the President's objectives, but criticized his methods, were the Republican floor leader, Senator McNary, who was the Republican

Continued on Page Fourteen

War Spurring Discoveries 20 Years Ahead of Peace

By WILLIAM L. LAURENCE
Special to THE NEW YORK TIMES.

BUFFALO, Sept. 7—In a thousand and one chemical laboratories throughout America chemists are discovering new continents of matter at such a rapid pace under the pressure of war that "the world of 1940 has already become an antiquity," Dr. Charles M. A. Stine said tonight at the opening general session of the American Chemical Society's meeting.

Dr. Stine is a vice president of E. I. du Pont de Nemours & Co., Inc., and its adviser on research and development.

"The inconceivables of only two years ago are today's realities," he said. "The war is compressing into the space of months developments which might have taken us half a century to realize if necessity had not forced the pace.

"These pressures are unprecedented. The developments are unprecedented. Give us a victorious peace and the freedom of enterprise it should guarantee, and our progress will be unprecedented. Let our swords be mighty and mighty indeed will be our plowshares."

When the war is won, he said, we will have at our command ten to a hundred times what we had before in new materials. These new materials are not mere predictions, but are actually on the way, he added.

The newest models of our motor cars, frozen in dealers' storehouses, have aged two decades since their creation, and developments which would not have come until 1960 could be incorporated in the automobile of today, were production to be resumed.

Dr. Stine enumerated many sci-

Continued on Page Twenty-one

AXIS IS REINFORCING ITS FRONT IN EGYPT

Rommel Is Preparing Stand Under Harrying Attacks—British Hit 12 Enemy Ships

By A. C. SEDGWICK
Wireless to THE NEW YORK TIMES.

WITH THE BRITISH EIGHTH ARMY, in Egypt, Sept. 7—The enemy force that fought a delaying, rearguard action in the southern sector while the main body of the German Africa Corps was withdrawing under British pressure appears to have "thickened" during the last twenty-four hours. The bringing up of reinforcements no doubt made this process possible.

Although the British light armored units are harrying the enemy flanks, he has now taken up positions in the Qaret el Himeimat area as well as an area about seven miles to the north. The high ground of the former area is particularly well worth his while to hold. For this purpose he has some tanks, although not many,

Continued on Page Nine

NEW FORTRESS RAID AVENGES U. S. LOSS

Rotterdam, Utrecht Bombed, 12 Nazis Downed—R. A. F. Hits Duisburg and Ports

By FRANK L. KLUCKHOHN
Special Cable to THE NEW YORK TIMES.

LONDON, Tuesday, Sept. 8—The United States Flying Fortresses yesterday bombed shipyards at Rotterdam and rail yards at Utrecht in the Netherlands and more than paid back the Nazis for the enemy's destruction of two Fortress planes Sunday by shooting down, with the aid of Allied fighter escorts, at least twelve Nazi planes at the cost of one Allied fighter.

The four-motored American bombers, with the swarms of Allied fighters around them, were seen going out by watchers on British beaches.

A few moments later they were over Rotterdam and Utrecht. There, taking advantage of clear visibility, they pounded the Schiedam shipyards at Rotterdam and the Utrecht rail objectives.

Amid air fighting in which Reich Marshal Hermann Goering's fliers tried vainly to repeat their first

Continued on Page Eight

Roosevelt Stirs Congress By Threat to Act on Prices

By FREDERICK R. BARKLEY
Special to THE NEW YORK TIMES.

WASHINGTON, Sept. 7—The few members of Congress who were in Washington today received President Roosevelt's anti-inflation message and demand for new farm ceiling legislation with pretty general agreement that inflation must be prevented, with less general agreement that farm prices must be kept from going up and with several vigorous expressions of alarm over the President's assertion that, if Congress did not act by Oct. 1 to block the inflationary threat, he had the power to do so and intended to use that power.

Senator Taft asserted that if the President could take such action, Congressional elections might as well be suspended, because Congress would become "a shell of a legislative body."

Senator La Follette declared that the President virtually "placed a pistol at the head of Congress." Both he and Senator McNary, the minority leader, voiced doubt that the President had the constitutional power he threatened to use.

The general view, however, was that Congress would buckle down to the task of revising farm legislation to permit the placing of price ceilings no higher than parity instead of the 110 per cent of parity to which farm prices may go under existing law before controls can be imposed.

The office of Speaker Rayburn announced that he would leave his Texas home for Washington tonight and that he wanted all members of the House back by next

Continued on Page Fifteen

RAID ALARM CAUSED BY A U. S. BOMBER

Army Admits Lag in Explaining the Alert—Protective Units' Turnout Gratifies Mayor

An unidentified plane sighted off the coast caused the sounding of an air raid alarm in New York City and parts of Westchester, Long Island and New Jersey early yesterday morning. Later it was identified as an Army bomber. At 2:22 A. M., nine minutes after the first preliminary signal and only one minute after the sirens actually began to wail, the Army ordered the all-clear sounded because the plane had been recognized as a friendly one.

In that brief space of time, however, two persons died from the alarm—one of a heart attack and the other of a fall in the dark—a third was probably fatally injured; millions of slumberers were roused from their sleep by the eerie sound of the sirens; radio stations went

Continued on Page Eighteen

U. S. Troops at Bases In Ecuador and Isles

By The United Press.

QUITO, Ecuador, Sept. 7—United States troops have taken over bases on the Santa Elena Peninsula, westernmost area of Ecuador, and in Ecuador's Galapagos Islands, 650 miles to the west, Defense Minister Colonel Carlos Guerrero disclosed at a secret session of Congress tonight.

Colonel Guerrero said the action was taken with the full approval of the Defense Ministry as a step in continental defense.

Ecuador has broken off diplomatic relations with the Axis countries, but has not declared war.

174 Ships Launched in One Day And Keels Are Laid for 49 More

Labor in the nation's shipyards spent its traditional holiday at work yesterday, setting a record of 223 ships launched or begun. The metropolitan area about New York contributed its share, while in a lunch-hour speech to the workers in the busy Navy Yard in Brooklyn Rear Admiral E. J. Marquart, congratulating the men, described the achievements since Pearl Harbor as a "staggering total almost beyond the belief of one's own eyes."

The launchings totaled 174—consisting of naval craft of many types, as well as a number of 10,500-ton Liberty ships—while keels were laid for forty-nine more.

For the New York area Admiral Marquart sounded the note that echoed through all the shipyards everywhere in the nation. Speaking into a microphone on his desk, knowing that his words were carried to the ears of every one of thousands of men in the yard, his and their observance of Labor Day was without ceremony. Work was too urgent for display; they listened as they munched their lunches.

"As we in the Navy look back on the past nine months," he said, "we—you and I—can take pride in our recovery from the treacherous blow we received at Pearl Harbor.

"The battles at Midway Island and in the Coral Sea; at Alaska and at the Solomon Islands just one month ago today; the clashes with enemy undersea fighters right here in our own watery front yard, the Atlantic, all testify that you have worked thoroughly and well. Ship for ship, just as man for man, we are faster and tougher than the enemy. If our foes still harbor any doubts on that score we of the Navy still invite battle; we seek out the chance to convince

Continued on Page Three

War News Summarized

TUESDAY, SEPTEMBER 8, 1942

German troops, checked northwest and southwest of Stalingrad, have begun a direct frontal assault from the west, according to Moscow, and have made some progress. The Russians acknowledged that the Germans had penetrated their lines near Novorossiisk, Black Sea Caucasus port, but did not concede that it had fallen, as claimed by Berlin. [1:1.]

United States Flying Fortresses with fighter escort attacked successfully Rotterdam's shipyard area and Utrecht in the Netherlands, shooting down twelve German planes and losing none of their own. This followed a heavy night attack by the Royal Air Force on Duisburg and the Ruhr region. Single R. A. F. bombers attacked Emden and Bremerhaven in daylight. [1:5.]

In Egypt Marshal Rommel's defeated force was braced by reinforcements after it had been pressed back, in some areas, beyond the starting point of its recent offensive, according to Cairo reports. British naval headquarters at Alexandria announced that British submarines had sunk five large and two medium-sized Axis ships recently on the Italy-to-Libya supply route. [1:2.]

After sending a message to Congress with an ultimatum on the matter of inflation control, President Roosevelt reviewed the war in a broadcast in which he said that the United States and Britain were preparing offensive action at one or more of a dozen points in the European area. He expressed confidence that Russia would hold out despite setbacks. [1:4.]

A Navy Department communiqué suggested that small parties of Japanese had landed on United States-held Guadalcanal Island in Solomons after suffering heavy casualties. A force of twenty-six Japanese bombers and twenty Zero fighters also attacked positions on Guadalcanal, but with little effect. Two enemy bombers and one fighting plane were shot down. [1:2-3.]

A United Nations Headquarters communiqué from Australia disclosed that Japanese forces had advanced in the Kokoda-Myola sector in New Guinea but with estimated casualties of 1,000. [5:1.]

Nation Travels Without Its Cars And Saves Lives on Labor Day

The railroads, buses and the subways bore the brunt yesterday of transporting what was pretty strictly a pedestrian throng of Labor Day holidaymakers. By contrast, the bridges and tunnels leading into the city carried a flow of vehicular traffic that was less than that of a normal weekday.

Acting Police Commissioner Louis F. Costuma put 4,000 extra men on duty, 2,000 of them detailed to handle traffic at tunnels and bridges. They were almost idle, but the men stationed at the rail and bus terminals had plenty of work. Through most of the day, and particularly in early evening, the sidewalks of New York were jammed from building line to curb in the midtown amusement area, while the streets were comparatively empty.

In New York and throughout the nation the day proved one fact—a sure way to reduce traffic fatalities is to take the automobiles off the highways. A compilation by The Associated Press of fatal highway accidents in the nation from Friday at 6 P. M. until mid-afternoon yesterday showed 164, as compared to 423 for the same period last year. Adding the violent deaths from other causes, the week-end total was brought to 255, as compared to 626 in 1941. The rationing of rubber and gasoline was credited with this result.

With the largest population, New York was in third place in the number of traffic fatalities by States with twelve. California recorded the largest number with 18, Michigan had fourteen and Illinois had eleven. Gasoline rationing applies only to the Eastern States.

In the big rail terminals here, Pennsylvania Station and Grand Central, it was said that peak travel loads were handled smooth-

Continued on Page Thirteen

"All the News That's Fit to Print."

The New York Times.

LATE CITY EDITION
Somewhat cooler today.

Copyright, 1942, by The New York Times Company.

VOL. XCII...No. 30,943. Entered as Second-Class Matter, Postoffice, New York, N. Y. NEW YORK, TUESDAY, OCTOBER 13, 1942. THREE CENTS IN NEW YORK CITY

PRESIDENT FOR DRAFTING YOUTHS AT 18 YEARS; SAYS OUR OFFENSIVES WILL AID RUSSIA, CHINA; 3 U. S. CRUISERS SUNK IN EARLY SOLOMONS FIGHT

JEFFERS HITS BACK AT SENATE CRITICS; HE'LL RUN OWN JOB

Cotton Group Is Defied to Stop Him If Army Wants to Use Rayon in Heavy-Duty Tires

'GAMBLING TOO LONG' NOW

Let's Win War First, He Says, and Denounces Interference by Pressure Groups

Special to THE NEW YORK TIMES.

WASHINGTON, Oct. 12—William M. Jeffers, rubber administrator, told the Senate Agriculture Committee today that if the Army wanted to substitute rayon for cotton as a base for its heavy duty rubber tires the Army would get rayon regardless of the protests of any Congressional group or any one else.

His response to cotton State Senators who had asked him to appear in order to quiz him on the rayon substitution report was blunt.

"We have been gambling with this war too damned long," he said. "I don't intend to be influenced by anybody, any time or anywhere."

In rapid exchanges with his questioners, Mr. Jeffers said that the War Production Board had approved expansion of the rayon manufacturing industry to help provide fabric for the Army's tire needs. The questions came so fast that the witness at times had three or more before him almost simultaneously.

Agreeing with Senator Stewart of Tennessee that the Army had not yet completed its tests of rayon as a tire fabric, Mr. Jeffers said that nevertheless these tests already had proved that rayon-base tires for big Army trucks had higher tensile strength and a greater resistance to deterioration from heat.

Bombarded With Questions

"But why should we embark on an untried scheme in the middle of the war?" Senator McKellar of Tennessee demanded.

"Didn't representatives of the big rayon companies on the WPB have a voice in reaching this decision to use rayon?" asked Senator Stewart.

"What about the charge that seven of the nine WPB officials who recommended this change have financial interests either in rayon companies or big tire companies?" asked Senator ("Cotton Ed") Smith, the committee chairman.

Mr. Jeffers finally managed to interpose that he understood that

Continued on Page Fourteen

1917 Shell Casing To Go to War Again

The casing of the first shell fired into Germany by United States forces in the last war is going back at Hitler's legions. Max Weinstein, president of Russeks Fifth Avenue, said yesterday that it would be turned into Manhattan's scrap drive on Thursday. In the last war he obtained it from Arthur Guy Empey, Canadian author of "Over the Top," by buying a $50,000 Liberty Bond. It has been on his desk since. Mr. Weinstein is also going to throw into the heap a pair of bronze doors designed by Stanford White, originally valued at $5,000.

In the Hunter College contribution, two tons in all, to be given today to Borough President Edgar J. Nathan Jr., will be two stoves from the homes of President Roosevelt and his mother, Sara Delano Roosevelt, at 47 and 49 East Sixty-fifth Street. The houses have been bought for the college for extra-curricular activities and named the Sara Delano Roosevelt Memorial House.

Declares Picketing Intolerable in War

By The United Press.

DETROIT, Oct. 12—Lieut. Gen. William S. Knudsen told the Economic Club today that Detroit would not long tolerate picket lines at its war plants.

"We cannot afford to lose an hour for any reason whatever," he said.

"I can't for the life of me think of a picket line with banners on a battle front in Europe or the Solomon Islands. The boys who are there have only one thing to fight with. That is what Detroit's brains, hands and man-hours can give them."

MAYOR IN CAPITAL TO FIGHT JUNK MEN

Will Try to Break Bottleneck in Scrap Movement—Bronx Collection Is On Today

The collection of scrap metal for the great and growing war machine of the United States will begin in the Bronx this morning at 7 A. M. while Mayor La Guardia, in Washington, will seek to break the bottleneck that is threatened by the attitude of junk dealers.

Borough President James J. Lyons of the Bronx predicted yesterday that the Bronx would yield more than 50,000 tons of scrap metal. With 72,175 tons already collected, this figure would push the city total well above its quota of 100,000 tons.

Six hundred trucks, 570 of them from the Department of Sanitation and 30 from the office of the Borough President, will begin rolling this morning. Already the citizens of the Bronx have piled their offerings on the sidewalks for the collectors. Five dump plots have been designated: at Goulden Avenue and 200th Street, 150th Street and Exterior Street, Zarega and Lafayette Avenues, the Baychester land fill at Bartow Avenue and a lot at Metcalf Avenue and Eastern Boulevard.

Lyons to Lead the Way

Ahead of the trucks, Mr. Lyons will leave the Goulden Avenue dumping ground at 6:30 A. M. to lead in the gathering of the first truckload. Each of the trucks will have a woman member of the Bronx Civilian Defense Volunteer Office or other civic organization to guide the drivers to collections.

To preserve the piles for the collectors—against the possible depredations of unauthorized junkmen—the police had instructions to maintain special watch through last night and to prohibit junkmen from entering areas where scrap had been piled on the streets.

Although it was believed that the Mayor looked somewhat favorably upon the plan offered by Samuel Bassow, head of Bassow

Continued on Page Fifteen

U. S. ITALIANS AIDED

Biddle Announces Lifting of the 'Alien Enemy' Stigma on Monday

PRESIDENT APPROVES

Loyalty of 600,000 in Nation Said to Have Been Demonstrated

The text of Mr. Biddle's address is on Page 12.

Six hundred thousand unnaturalized Italians living in the United States will be freed from the stigma of being alien enemies of this country, beginning next Monday, it was announced last night by Attorney General Francis Biddle in a speech at a Columbus Day celebration at Carnegie Hall. His address was carried over a nation-wide radio hook-up of the Mutual Broadcasting System.

This action, which Mr. Biddle said was taken with the approval of President Roosevelt, will free these Italians from many restrictions that have hampered them until now. It will permit them to travel freely, to possess cameras and firearms except where local regulations forbid, to remain out after the curfew now prescribed for alien enemies on the West Coast, and will free them from the necessity of carrying identification cards.

Mr. Biddle declared that this exoneration of Italians living in this country has been well earned by their loyalty to the United States.

Only 228 Italians Interned

In ten months of unprecedented wartime vigilance, he said, during which the government has acted on a policy of taking no chances with any one who might be dangerous, it has been necessary to intern only 228 Italians, or fewer than one-twentieth of 1 per cent.

The Attorney General also declared he had asked Congress to change the naturalization laws in a way that would make it possible for 200,000 of the older Italians living in this country to become citizens. This would be done by eliminating the necessity for taking a literacy test in the case of persons who are 50 years old or more, and have lived in this country continuously since before July 1, 1924.

Because of the obvious value to this country to be derived from spreading the news of the government's action through Axis Europe, Mr. Biddle's speech was carried last night on virtually all the short-wave radio stations now under government control. It was understood also that the British Broadcasting Corporation and the

Continued on Page Twelve

SEA BATTLE IN DARK

Quincy, Vincennes and Astoria Lost While Shielding Marines

FLARES GUIDED FOE

Guns, Torpedoes Fired at Close Range—Most of Crews Saved

By CHARLES HURD

Special to THE NEW YORK TIMES.

WASHINGTON, Oct. 12—The American Navy paid three heavy American cruisers—the Quincy, Vincennes and Astoria—as part of the price for successful occupation of the Japanese air field on Guadalcanal Island in the Solomons, the Navy revealed tonight.

The Quincy and the Vincennes were sunk in action and the Astoria succumbed to fire a few hours after a large Allied naval force had engaged in an old-fashioned gun and torpedo clash at close range with a Japanese battle force as searchlights and star shells lit the early morning darkness of Aug. 9.

"The enemy fire was heavy and accurate," said a communiqué announcing the loss of these vessels.

The Navy previously had announced the loss of two destroyers and four transports in the Solomons, while stating that one unidentified American cruiser had been sunk and two others damaged. The actual announcement of the loss of the 10,000-ton fighting ships was withheld until replacements could be sent into the Southwestern Pacific for them and for the Canberra, an Australian cruiser sunk in the same engagement and earlier announced as lost.

The "majority" of the personnel of the three American cruisers was saved, the Navy stated, but many men were lost. Among those definitely known to have died in action was Captain Samuel N. Moore of the Quincy. There was no word of the fate of Captain F. L. Riefkahl of the Vincennes or of Captain William G. Greenman of the Astoria.

Almost 3,000 men were known to have been aboard the cruisers when they were destroyed. There were

Continued on Page Four

Chicago Court Backs Petrillo; Dismisses U. S. Injunction Suit

Special to THE NEW YORK TIMES.

CHICAGO, Oct. 12—The government lost its anti-trust suit against James C. Petrillo and his American Federation of Musicians today when Judge John P. Barnes of the Federal District Court dismissed the Department of Justice petition for an injunction to end the union's ban on the recording of music for radio, juke boxes, and other public reproductions. Judge Barnes held that the dispute was essentially a labor dispute and did not come under the anti-trust laws.

Immediately afterward Mr. Petrillo, in triumphant vein, announced that his ban on canned music "still stands."

Thurman Arnold, head of the anti-trust division of the Department of Justice, who had come to Chicago from Washington to argue for the injunction, said merely, "The government will appeal the case."

The suit was based on Mr. Petrillo's order, effective Aug. 1, barring union musicians from making "canned music" not for home use.

In the nation-wide controversy which followed, union spokesmen argued that their action was a case of self-preservation that the "canned music" which musicians made actually tended to destroy their own livelihood as live musicians.

Against this, radio spokesmen and others, including the government, contended that the ban had the earmarks of a monopoly, and threatened to put many small radio stations and other businesses out of existence. These points were argued today in the hearing before Judge Barnes.

Last week both the government and Joseph Padway, attorney for

Continued on Page Seventeen

SCENE OF ACTION IN WHICH ALLIED CRUISERS WERE LOST

When the foothold on Guadalcanal and Tulagi was being strengthened Aug. 9 Allied screening forces of cruisers and destroyers were placed on both sides of Savo Island (A and B) and an additional screening force (C) was placed near the transports and supply ships (D). By the dark of early morning Japanese cruisers and destroyers sped past Savo (1) and, on sighting covering unit A, opened fire, hitting the Australian cruiser Canberra, which later sank. The enemy then swung to the northeast of Savo and a close-range battle was fought at (2) with covering unit B. There the American cruisers Quincy and Vincennes were sunk and the Astoria was set afire; she later sank, too. The enemy withdrew northwest. Inset shows the surrounding region.

CHURCHILL TALLIES NEW ALLIED GAINS

Stresses Increases in Ships, Bombing of Germany, U. S. Arrivals and Air Power

The text of Mr. Churchill's speech is on Page 8.

By RAYMOND DANIELL

Special Cable to THE NEW YORK TIMES.

LONDON, Oct. 12—Reviewing the progress of the war when he received the freedom of the city of Edinburgh today, Prime Minister Churchill declared that the last two months were the "least bad" since January in the battle of the Atlantic.

"The months of August and September have been—I will not say the best but the least bad months since January," he said. "They have seen new building of merchant ships that substantially out-

Continued on Page Eight

War News Summarized

TUESDAY, OCTOBER 13, 1942

The United States Navy disclosed the loss of three heavy cruisers on Aug. 9 in the opening phase of the battle for the Southern Solomons. All three were sunk by the fire of Japanese war vessels during a night engagement in which the enemy was forced to withdraw without attacking United States transports landing troops and equipment. The previously announced sinking of the Australian cruiser Canberra occurred in the same battle. Japanese losses in the engagement were not known. [1:4.]

From Russia came the news that the Germans had resumed heavy fighting inside Stalingrad and that one regiment had gained slightly in one block with the aid of fifty tanks. In the Caucasus the Russians advanced in a number of sectors, according to Moscow. The Germans also claimed gains in the Caucasus. [1:7; map, P. 3.]

Malta announced that the Axis air forces had resumed heavy raiding and had suffered the loss of at least thirty-seven planes without accomplishing much in the way of damage. It was noted that such heavy assaults on Malta had generally accompanied the movement of important Axis convoys toward Africa. United Nations bombers were reported to have scored hits on two freighters, a destroyer and a schooner in the Eastern Mediterranean. [3:1.]

Prime Minister Churchill, speaking in Edinburgh, said that the last two months had shown less relative loss than any since January in the battle of the Atlantic and stressed the series of effective raids on Germany recently. [1:5.]

In Washington it was explained that Under-Secretary of State Sumner Welles's Boston speech on Axis activity in Argentina and Chile was meant to show that Chilean President Rios's contemplated visit to the United States did not involve United States acceptance of the Chilean policy of neutrality. [1:6-7.]

At the Columbus Day celebration in New York commemorating the four hundred and fiftieth anniversary of the discovery of America Attorney General Biddle announced that the 600,000 Italian citizens living in the United States would no longer be regarded as enemy aliens or treated as such. [1:3.]

From Washington President Roosevelt broadcast a recommendation that 18 and 19-year-old youths be drafted for military service and indicated that a general labor draft might become necessary to keep up production. [1:8.]

Wendell Willkie, returning from his world tour of United Nations battle fronts, reached Canada by plane via Siberia from Chungking. [1:6-7.]

U. S. Rebuke to Chile Based On Proof of Nazi Spy Haven

By HAROLD CALLENDER

Special to THE NEW YORK TIMES.

WASHINGTON, Oct. 12—It was learned authoritatively here today that the references to Axis influence and espionage in Chile and Argentina, embodied in the speech that Sumner Welles, as acting Secretary of State, delivered at Boston last Thursday were made because this government had proof that Axis agents in those countries had transmitted information that has led to the sinkings of ships in American waters.

The reason Mr. Welles spoke out at that moment, it was explained, was that this government desired to remove the impression that the then projected visit to Washington of the President of Chile, Juan Antonio Rios, would signify that the United States was satisfied with Chile's policies—the facts being precisely the contrary.

In consequence of Mr. Welles's speech, the Chilean Ambassador, Rodolfo Michels, notified Mr. Welles today of the "postponement" of President Rios's visit.

In its protest Saturday against Mr. Welles's charges, the Chilean Government, quoted Admiral Julio Allard, commander of the Chilean Fleet, as saying that no ships had been sunk in the Pacific south of Panama and that information originating in Chile could not be responsible for sinking of ships "several thousand miles from Chile."

To this the reply made here today was that an Axis agent whom the Chilean authorities themselves had arrested in Sep-

Continued on Page Ten

NAZIS AGAIN STRIKE INSIDE STALINGRAD

But Make Only Slight Gain—Russians in Mozdok Region of Caucasus Advance

By The United Press.

MOSCOW, Tuesday, Oct. 13—German armored and infantry forces resumed attacks in the Stalingrad area yesterday after a short lull, and in one sector of the city the Russian defenders were pressed back slightly, the Soviet High Command announced today.

The Russian communiqué, bearing out earlier front reports that the Red Army was taking the initiative in the Caucasus, also said that Russian troops had advanced in some sectors of the Mozdok area and had counter-attacked successfully southeast of Novorossiisk, in the Black Sea coastal region.

In its report on Stalingrad, the Soviet bulletin said that a regiment of German troops, led by

Continued on Page Three

Willkie in Canada, Starting East; Explains Second Front Stand

By The Associated Press.

EDMONTON, Alberta, Oct. 12—Wendell Willkie, arriving here tonight from Fairbanks, Alaska, on his globe-girdling flight, said he thought it inappropriate while abroad to reply to "flippant statements made by certain public officials concerning the expression of my opinion in Russia on the question of a second front."

Mr. Willkie arrived here about 7:30 P. M., mountain daylight time, and will leave by plane tomorrow morning for Minneapolis.

In a prepared statement he said:

"The last lap of the flight around the world, from China through the republic of Mongolia, Siberia and Alaska, was among the most fascinating experiences of the whole trip. All members of the party and the crew performed marvelously in this undertaking, which involved flying over some wide areas never before traveled by civilians and by few, if any, military air men.

"Some several months ago I decided I could be helpful to the war effort if I visited various fighting fronts, some of our Allied countries and some of the countries in the Middle East which have not yet decided officially on their course of action in this war.

"My objectives were several—to give encouragement to our Allies, to give an impetus to action by the undecided countries and to report to the American people on the facts I found and the conclusions I reached.

"I asked the President for the necessary consent now required to travel abroad. After we had discussed the subject on several occasions he said it would be satisfactory for me to go, provided in addition I did some specific jobs

Continued on Page Six

MAY DRAFT LABOR

President in Radio Talk Warns That Legislation May Be Necessary

SHIPS OUTPACE FOE

He Found People in High State of Morale on His War Plants Tour

The text of the President's address is on Page 5.

By W. H. LAWRENCE

Special to THE NEW YORK TIMES.

WASHINGTON, Oct. 12—President Roosevelt recommended tonight the drafting of 18 and 19 year old youths for military service as an essential measure to speed victory, and indicated that it may become necessary to draft labor for mine, mill, factory and farm to meet the country's huge war production commitments.

In a confident 30-minute multi-topic speech to the nation and the world by radio, the President renewed his pledge of offensive action by the United States to relieve the pressure on Russia and China, but, of course, refrained from giving any indication as to when, where and how these new fronts would be opened.

We are getting ahead of our enemies in "the bitter battle of transportation," and in "the battle of production," he declared. The United Nations are going to win the war "and do not let any one tell you anything different."

The Axis leaders, Mr. Roosevelt continued, know their defeat is inevitable.

Tells of His War Plant Tour

Reporting on his recent two-week tour of war production and armed forces' establishments from coast to coast, the President praised the spirit of the people, rebuked the critics of the censorship he ordered and of the limited press coverage permitted, and announced that he would make other trips for similar purposes in the same way.

He had a good word for Congress, declaring that its "prompt and effective" action against inflation "was a splendid example of the operation of democratic processes in wartime."

He was scornful of the "typewriter strategists" for newspapers and radio stations who furnish military commentaries. Their trouble, he said, is that, "while they may be full of bright ideas, they are not in the possession of much information about the facts or problems of military operations."

Faith was affirmed in the war planning by the military leadership. The President mentioned Admiral William D. Leahy, his own Chief of Staff; General George C. Marshall, Army Chief of Staff; Admiral Ernest J. King, Chief of Naval Operations and Commander in Chief of the United States Fleet, and Lieut. Gen. H. H. Arnold, Chief of the Army Air Forces.

These officers, he said, have con-

Continued on Page Five

U. S. Discloses Bases In Fijis and Hebrides

Special to THE NEW YORK TIMES.

WASHINGTON, Oct. 12—The existence of American bases in the New Hebrides and the Fiji Islands became officially known tonight with mention of these island groups in a Navy communiqué on the sinking of the cruisers Quincy, Vincennes and Astoria near Guadalcanal Island on Aug. 9.

There was no information about the size or type of these bases, but the communiqué named them as among the points that would have been threatened by the enemy if development of Japanese bases on the Solomons had not been checked.

U.S. Air Force

North American B-25 "Mitchell" flies over North African desert enroute to target.

U.S. Air Force

A German fighter plane crashed into this B-17 while it was bombing German supply lines in North Africa.

"All the News That's Fit to Print."

NEWS INDEX, PAGE 47, THIS SECTION

The New York Times.

LATE CITY EDITION
Cold this morning.
Temperatures Yesterday—Max., 63; Min., 50
Sunrise, 7:17 A. M.; Sunset, 6:08 P. M.

Section 1

VOL. XCII..No. 30,955. Entered as Second-Class Matter, Postoffice, New York, N. Y. NEW YORK, SUNDAY, OCTOBER 25, 1942. Including Magazine and Book Sections. TEN CENTS New York City and Vicinity

ALLIES GAIN IN BIG NORTH AFRICAN OFFENSIVE; BRITISH BOMBERS BATTER MILAN, TURIN, GENOA; HALSEY REPLACES GHORMLEY IN THE SOLOMONS

YEAR OF TRAINING OF 18, 19-YEAR-OLDS IS VOTED BY SENATE

Bill Is Then Passed After Final Plea by Army's Chief Fails to Avert the Restriction

HELP FOR FARMS ORDERED

Amendment, Adopted by 62 to 6, Provides for Deferring Workers Now Employed

By C. P. TRUSSELL
Special to THE NEW YORK TIMES.

WASHINGTON, Oct. 24—By a vote of 58 to 5 the Senate passed tonight, after eight hours of controversy and clashes with the Administration and Army command, its own bill to lower the Selective Service minimum age to 18 years, but provided especially that no inductee under 20 years of age should be sent into actual combat overseas without a full year of training.

In the face of renewed protest and warning from General Marshall, Chief of Staff, with President Roosevelt entering his personal appeal against restrictions, the Senate, by 39 to 31, wrote into its measure this provision:

"No person under 20 years of age inducted under this act shall be placed in actual combat duty beyond the territorial boundaries of continental United States until after he has had at least one year's training following his induction."

This amendment, sponsored by Senator O'Daniel of Texas, shunted aside another proposal offered previously by Senator Norris which would have prohibited the sending of inductees under 19 years of age into combat zones unless the same training had been received. Two hours after the O'Daniel provision was adopted, Senator Lucas, who had voted for it, urged the Senate to provide that any inductee under 20 who volunteered for foreign combat service might do so, provided he had received "adequate" training. The Senate voted this down, 32—33.

The Senators who voted against final passage of the bill were Bulow and Clark of Idaho, Democrats; Johnson of California, Nye and Shipstead, Republicans.

Induction After 45 Banned

Just before the bill was passed this evening, the Senate, with a voice vote, adopted the Ellender amendment under which no Selective Service registrant would be inducted for training or service after he had attained the age of 45.

It provided, too, by a 62-to-6 record vote, for the holding of labor on the farms. Under the amendment, sponsored by Senator Tydings, a bona fide farm worker, so engaged regularly, would be deferred from training or service in the land or naval forces so long as he remained on his job, or until replaced. The amendment, Mr. Tydings, said, had been prepared at his request by the Selective Service System, which entered no objections to it.

For months, farm State Senators and Representatives had warned against the depletion of farm labor by enlistment, the draft and the lure of wartime industrial wages, and had worked for such a provision of law as the Senate accepted late today.

With a voice vote, the Senate later rejected a second O'Daniel amendment which would have barred the payment of overtime to workers in industry for the duration of the war, existing law to the contrary notwithstanding. In effect, it would have suspended the 40-hour week.

As to the educational status of the new inductees, the Senate stood by the original form of its own bill, which would permit students in high schools or similar institutions to complete their academic year before induction, pro-

Continued on Page Thirty

Pacific Command Shake-Up Is Laid to Guadalcanal Crisis

Shift to Offensive Is Seen in Washington in Selection of 'Fighting' Admiral Halsey as Commander in the South Pacific

By CHARLES HURD
Special to THE NEW YORK TIMES.

WASHINGTON, Oct. 24—The Navy has relieved Vice Admiral Robert L. Ghormley of command of the Solomon Islands action and replaced him with Vice Admiral William F. Halsey Jr., it was announced here today. Admiral Halsey distinguished himself last Spring in conducting the notable hit-and-run air and sea raid on Japanese installations in the Gilbert and Marshall Islands in the Japanese-controlled region southwest of Hawaii.

The change in command was made public without other official comment by the Navy, but surprise that might have been occasioned by a shift in the midst of battle was somewhat tempered by reports in recent weeks indicating that the occupation of key points in the Solomon Islands had become a stalemate if not a critical defensive situation.

Admiral Chester W. Nimitz, Commander in Chief of the Pacific Fleet, continues in supreme command of naval operations in the Pacific area, except for Australia and New Guinea, where General Douglas MacArthur controls, but Admiral Halsey, as the new commander of naval forces in the South Pacific area, now inherits direct responsibility for pursuing the Solomons attack.

The view expressed in informed quarters here was to the effect that the new Solomons commander would be expected to turn that venture from a currently defensive operation into an aggressive fight such as first characterized the occupation.

Admiral Ghormley's future was left in doubt, the Navy announcement stating only that his "new duties will be announced at a later date."

Coincident with this major change the Navy also announced relief of Vice Admiral William S. Pye as commander of a Pacific

Continued on Page Forty-one

FRICTION MARRING PACIFIC TEAM-WORK

Times Writer Finds It Behind Lines, Though the Services Cooperate Well at Front

Following is the third of a series of articles by the military editor of THE NEW YORK TIMES, who has just returned from a Pacific tour.

By HANSON W. BALDWIN

Army, Navy and Marine ground and air forces are working together in close harmony in combat areas in the Pacific, but behind the lines there is some friction and considerable mutual criticism.

In the Solomons area, where elements of all three services have been in action, the cooperation appeared to this correspondent to be close and successful. There was good-natured joshing between the services, but little criticism. Each expressed an admiration for the other's commander; most personnel submerged their differences in the common good.

From one important air strip in the New Hebrides, carved out of the jungle at record speed, great four-motored B-17's and Army and Navy and Marine Corps fighters were operating; there was no bick-

Continued on Page Thirty-nine

SEAPLANE TENDER BOMBED AT RABAUL

Heavy Allied Planes May Have Sunk 17,600-Ton Vessel in New Attack on Harbor

By The Associated Press.

AT UNITED NATIONS HEADQUARTERS, Australia, Sunday, Oct. 25—A large Japanese seaplane tender was believed destroyed at Rabaul, New Britain, by Allied bombers, the High Command announced today.

The tender was one of the targets picked out by heavy bombers that struck again at the harbor of Rabaul, where Japanese ships have been concentrated, presumably for an impending assault on American-held Guadalcanal in the Solomon Islands to the southeast. An assault the day before resulted in the sinking or damaging of ten Japanese ships, including a cruiser and a destroyer.

[An American naval force raided the Gilbert and Ellice Islands, sank two small patrol boats and damaged a destroyer and a merchantman, Washington reported yesterday.]

Today's communiqué said that the second assault, made at night, had resulted in a hit with a 500-pound bomb amidships of a sea-

Continued on Page Forty

Major Sports Yesterday

FOOTBALL

Paced by two freshman backs, Yale achieved its first major victory since 1940 at the expense of Dartmouth. Notre Dame, though trailing at half-time, stopped previously undefeated Illinois. Penn and Army flashed powerful running attacks to down Columbia and Harvard, respectively. Manhattan toppled Duquesne on a field goal. Princeton crushed Brown and unbeaten Georgia Tech routed Navy. Scores of leading games:

Alabama	14	Kentucky	0
Amherst	27	Wesleyan	0
Army	14	Harvard	0
Baylor	6	Texas A.&M.	0
Boston Coll.	27	Wake Forest	0
Brooklyn	38	N. Y. Aggies	0
California	19	Washington	6
Detroit	6	Georgetown	0
Duke	28	Pittsburgh	0
Georgia	35	Cincinnati	13
Ga. Tech	21	Navy	0
Holy Cross	28	N. C. State	0
Iowa	14	Indiana	13
Lehigh	28	Rutgers	10
Manhattan	10	Duquesne	7
Mich. State	14	Great Lakes	0
Minnesota	16	Michigan	14
Miss. State	26	Florida	12
Missouri	45	Iowa State	6
Nebraska	7	Oklahoma	0
Notre Dame	21	Illinois	14
Ohio State	20	Northwest'n	6
Penn	42	Columbia	12
Penn State	13	Colgate	10
Princeton	32	Brown	13
S. M. U.	21	Corp. Christi	6
Stanford	14	So. Calif	6
Susquehanna	6	C. C. N. Y.	0
Syracuse	12	Cornell	7
Tennessee	52	Furman	7
Texas	12	Rice	7
T. C. U.	21	Pensacola N'l	0
Tulane	29	No. Carolina	14
U. C. L. A.	14	Santa Clara	6
Wash. State	26	Oregon St.	13
Williams	47	Tufts	6
Wisconsin	13	Purdue	0
Yale	17	Dartmouth	7

HORSE RACING

Boysy won the Scarsdale Handicap by a neck from Spiral Pass at Empire City, where 27,126 racegoers wagered $1,661,293, a record for the track. At Laurel, Md., Whirlaway took the Washington Handicap and Askmenow captured the Selima Stakes.

(Complete Details of These and Other Sports Events in Section 5.)

ITALY UNDER RAIDS

R. A. F.'s Lancasters Hit Milan in Low-Level Daylight Attack

NIGHT BLOWS GO ON

Genoa Fires Rekindled, Other Ports Pounded—Fighters Harry Nazis

By RAYMOND DANIELL
Special Cable to THE NEW YORK TIMES.

LONDON, Sunday, Oct. 25—The Royal Air Force's biggest bombers from Britain are giving Northern Italy a severe pounding by day and night.

A large force of the powerful four-motored Lancasters attacked Milan by daylight yesterday.

Three bombers were lost in the Milan attack, the Air Ministry said. Preliminary reports showed the raid was successful; the attack was pressed home at a low level as the Lancasters went under clouds to loose their bombs.

[A Vichy report, transmitted by The Associated Press via London last night, said fifty four-motored British bombers flew over unoccupied France in daylight and that one of them machine-gunned a barracks and railway station at Montluçon, west of Vichy.]

Last night, indicating that the R. A. F. was at it again, air raid alarms sounded at Berne, Switzerland, at 9:05 o'clock, according to a Reuter report from the Swiss capital.

Genoa Raids Cut Rommel's Supply

Genoa was raided Friday night for the second night in a row by "another strong force" of British bombers, and other squadrons of the big planes bombed the Italian industrial center of Turin and the port of Savona, twenty miles west of Genoa.

In the Friday night operation, almost at the hour when the British Eighth Army in Egypt, supported by the British Navy and Allied air forces, was beginning its offensive for Allied mastery of North Africa and the Mediterranean, Lancaster, Stirling and Halifax bombers and two-motored Wellingtons roared over the Alps and unloaded hundreds of tons of incendiary and demolition missiles on blazing and battered Genoa, major port from which Field Marshal Erwin Rommel has drawn a large part of his Axis reinforcements and supplies.

By daylight yesterday also the R. A. F.'s Spitfires and Mustang fighters of the Army Cooperation Command went on with their offensive against the Nazis over the French and Netherland coasts—without losing a plane.

The fighters shot up enemy military buildings, ships and trains, rounding off one of the most intensive weeks of daylight air blows at the Germans that saw R. A. F. bombers make thrusts over the Reich on four successive days.

Milan a Center of Axis Industry

The Milan raid was carried out before dusk presumably on lines similar to those used in the R. A. F. attack at Le Creusot in occupied France on Saturday, Oct. 17, when ninety-four Lancasters blasted the Schneider armament plants there.

Milan is about seventy-five miles northwest of Genoa and is an important industrial city. The Caproni bomber plants are located there.

The weather for Friday night's raid on Genoa was not as good as on Thursday night, when the whole "strong force"—usually meaning many more than 100 planes—of R. A. F. bombers that made the attack then returned safely. In the Friday night attack, the Air Ministry reported, three bombers were lost.

Men of the crews that participated in the new blasting of Genoa

Continued on Page Four

NEW YORK OBSERVES WARTIME NAVY DAY

Sailors passing the reviewing stand on Fifth Avenue — The New York Times

300,000 ACCLAIM NAVY DAY PARADE

10,000 March Down 5th Ave. in 2-Hour Demonstration—British Seamen in Line

The Navy took over on Fifth Avenue between Eighty-seventh and Sixty-second Streets for nearly two hours yesterday and a throng estimated by the police at 300,000 obviously had a fine time watching and cheering the 10,000 marchers.

It was the city's first Navy Day parade since the attack on Pearl Harbor and accordingly was replete with unprecedented features. There were nearly as many uniformed women as swung down the avenue in the all-women's parade of April 11. There were British seamen and marines. And there was the weather itself, more like an early April day than one on the rim of November.

The demonstration was unusual even in its lacks. Mayor La Guardia, usually a fixture in the reviewing stand at Sixty-seventh Street, was out of town. The scheduled grand marshal, Rear Admiral Edward J. Marquart, was prevented from appearing by illness and his place was taken by Rear Admiral Lamar R. Leahy.

And there was a noticeable absence of one naval group whose nonparticipation provoked this exchange between two women spectators just south of the reviewing stand:

"Say, I wonder what happened

Continued on Page Thirty-eight

U. S. Soldiers' Gifts Are Sunk in Atlantic

By The Associated Press.

WASHINGTON, Oct. 24—The Army Postal Service said today that 4,986 sacks of United States mail bound for American armed forces in the British Isles had been lost in the sinking of a United Nations cargo ship.

Much of the shipment was parcel post and represented one of the first parcel shipments of Christmas mail.

The War Department said that the lost mail was deposited in the United States during the latter part of September. Mails reaching the New York Port of Debarkation Army Postoffice later than Oct. 3 were not included in this shipment.

FLIERS STILL HUNT FOR RICKENBACKER

Long-Range Patrol Craft of Navy Find No Trace of Lost Army Plane in Pacific

Special to THE NEW YORK TIMES.

WASHINGTON, Oct. 24—Long-range naval patrol planes that are considered ideally suited for searches at sea have joined in the hunt for the United States Army plane in which Captain E. V. Rickenbacker was a passenger, the Navy Department announced today. They are operating from an island base southwest of Honolulu.

No word of the missing craft

Continued on Page Forty-one

War News Summarized

SUNDAY, OCTOBER 25, 1942

Britain's Eighth Army, strongly supported by both British and United States air units, struck yesterday before dawn to open the third British North African offensive and cracked through the Axis positions. United Nations airmen had clear-cut superiority. The land attack was frontal on the German line between the sea and the Qattara Depression. Axis airfields and bases behind the lines were bombed incessantly. [1:8; map, P. 3.]

American-built light naval vessels of unusual speed shelled the Axis supply port of Matruh on the Egyptian coast during the night and got away safely without loss of a ship, despite a three-hour Axis air counter-attack. [5:1.]

London announced that Genoa and Turin had been attacked for the second successive night and Milan also bombed by day in a third raid. Rome acknowledged notable damage at Savona, a shipbuilding center twenty-five miles west of Genoa. [1:4.]

Moscow stated that reinforced German troops had been thrown back inside Stalingrad after hard fighting. The Germans had made a slight advance toward Tuapse, on the Black Sea coast, from their inland positions in the Caucasus. [1:7.]

United Nations Headquarters, Australia, reported that bombers attacking Japanese vessels in the harbor of Rabaul, New Britain Island, were believed to have destroyed a seaplane tender of 17,600 tons. [1:3.] No action was reported in the Solomon Islands. Washington disclosed that a naval expedition to the Gilbert and Ellice Islands, between Hawaii and the Solomons, had sunk two small Japanese patrol boats and damaged a destroyer and a merchant ship. [40:1; map, P. 40.]

The Navy Department announced that Vice Admiral Robert L. Ghormley had been relieved of command of the Solomon Islands action, being replaced by Vice Admiral William F. Halsey Jr., who conducted the successful hit-and-run raid in the Gilbert and Marshall Islands last Spring. [1:2-3.]

MORE NAZI THRUSTS FAIL IN STALINGRAD

German Losses Mount Rapidly in Several Volga Sectors—Berlin Claims Gains

By The Associated Press.

MOSCOW, Sunday, Oct. 25—The Germans threw two freshly reinforced infantry divisions, eighty tanks and "large" air forces against Russian positions in Stalingrad yesterday, a Soviet communiqué said today, but after bitter hand-to-hand fighting the Nazis were thrown back with heavy losses.

The new attack, launched after fresh troops were brought in to replace nearly 10,000 that the Russians said they had killed in two days, was directed at the factory district in the northern part of the battle-torn city. In this area alone, the communiqué said, more than 1,500 Germans were killed yesterday and seventeen tanks destroyed.

[The Germans reported new gains in Stalingrad's Red October factory and for the third time officially claimed to have reached the Volga. A dominating mountain northeast of Tuapse in the Caucasus was captured in a hard battle, Berlin said.]

The heaviest German losses were in a southern sector of the Stalingrad front, where one Soviet formation was said to have killed 7,000 men, destroyed fifty-seven tanks, 100 guns and twenty-six planes. The Russians also captured 150 German tanks that had been disabled in previous engagements and were being used as firing positions.

Heavy fighting was continuing both northwest of Stalingrad and south of the city. In one sector northwest of the city, the Russian communiqué said, Soviet troops "made a slight advance, overcame enemy minefields and barbed-wire entanglements and broke into enemy positions." The Germans launched four counter-attacks, but were forced to fall back after losing about 250 men.

Farther south in the Caucasus the Russians were on the defensive both in the Mozdok area and along the Black Sea. The communiqué said, however, that all attacks were repulsed and that the positions remained unchanged.

Strong Nazi Attacks Fail

By RALPH PARKER
Wireless to THE NEW YORK TIMES.

MOSCOW, Oct. 24—The German Air Force resumed its activity at Stalingrad yesterday, operating in force to support ground forces numbering 7,000 to 8,000 men, which with tanks maintained their attacks in the northern part of the city. It is estimated that 1,500 bombs were dropped on the Russian lines and behind them. Coordinated with this, heavy artillery and

Continued on Page Eighteen

AXIS LINES DENTED

Allied Troops Reported Pouring Through Gap Ripped From the Air

TANKS ARE CLOSING IN

British General's Order to the Troops Is to 'Destroy Rommel'

Special Cable to THE NEW YORK TIMES.

LONDON, Oct. 24—In an offensive against the enemy in the Alamein sector of the Egyptian Western Desert battlefront, Britain's Eighth Army has smashed through Axis defenses at several points, according to latest press reports reaching London tonight from Cairo. Security reasons make it impossible to specify the objectives reached.

That the attack is important was emphasized by Lieut. Gen. Bernard L. Montgomery's order of the day, issued on the eve of the attack, calling on the British forces to "destroy Rommel and his army" and adding:

"Victory should swing our way."

General Montgomery is field commander of the Eighth Army.

The land fighting that has so far developed is described as fierce because of the narrow nature of the present front, which measures only forty miles, from El Alamein to the Qattara Depression, although the lines themselves twist and wind over a greater length. The attack, which was preceded by the heaviest air offensive yet seen in Egypt, indicates that the Allies won the battle that had been going on over the last eight weeks for effective building up of supplies.

Rommel Held Worried

There are indications that General Field Marshal Erwin Rommel is having worries over his supply lines—worries largely created by Allied airmen, who over the last fortnight have been playing havoc not only with Axis supplies going to the front but to Marshal Rommel's ports as well. It is believed that he has two German armored divisions, two Italian armored divisions, one German motorized division; the 164th German Infantry Division, which is partly motorized, and about a half-dozen Italian infantry divisions that are probably not up to half strength.

Failure to get sufficient arms and ammunition for these forces may lose Marshal Rommel the battle. But for weeks the enemy has been strengthening his lines and extending their defense in depth, and it is remarked that no sensationally rapid advance can be expected on the part of the Allied forces.

Italian newspaper comment this week-end showed how worried the Italians were getting over the arrival of American troops in Africa and the growing strength of the Allied air forces in the Middle East. These newspapers paint a gloomy picture for their readers. They hint

Continued on Page Three

King Christian X In Serious Relapse

By The Associated Press.

STOCKHOLM, Sweden, Sunday, Oct. 25—A special bulletin issued in Copenhagen early today said King Christian X, who was injured last week when he fell from a horse, had taken a sudden change for the worse and was in a serious condition.

The 72-year-old monarch had been reported improving rapidly since the accident, but about 7 P. M. Saturday night his heart developed an abnormal action.

His physician administered a stimulating treatment which resulted in a slight recovery.

Queen Alexandrine, Crown Prince Frederik and Prince Knud were summoned to the hospital last evening and spent the night there.

"All the News That's Fit to Print."

The New York Times.

LATE CITY EDITION
Colder today.
Temperatures Yesterday—Max., 61; Min., 43
Sunrise, 7:19 A. M.; Sunset, 5:06 P. M.

VOL. XCII..No. 30,957. Entered as Second-Class Matter, Postoffice, New York, N. Y. NEW YORK, TUESDAY, OCTOBER 27, 1942. THREE CENTS IN NEW YORK CITY

JAPANESE OPEN MAJOR ATTACK ON GUADALCANAL; HIT CARRIER, SINK DESTROYER; WASP LOST SEPT. 15; WILLKIE DEMANDS SECOND FRONT, BURMA DRIVE

COFFEE RATIONING ON CUP-A-DAY BASIS ORDERED ON NOV. 29

Limitation Applies to Every Person in the Country, With None for Those Under 15

SUGAR BOOK TO BE USED

WPB Tells OPA to Act as Stock Dwindles—Retailers to Stop Selling Nov. 22 for Week

Special to THE NEW YORK TIMES.

WASHINGTON, Oct. 26—The OPA announced today that it will start rationing coffee to civilians starting at midnight Nov. 28, and will grant an allowance of one pound every five weeks to every individual in the country 15 years old or over. As worked out unofficially by government men and those in the coffee trade here, the ration will provide slightly more than one cup a day to each individual.

In giving warning of the impending rationing, the OPA departed from the policy of secrecy it has followed heretofore in dealing with any product capable of being hoarded. Leon Henderson, Federal Price Administrator, cautioned, however, that "there is no reason for any one to run to the corner grocer, put the 'squeeze' on him and try to force him to help a hoarder. There is absolutely no excuse for hoarding coffee at this time."

Consumers will get their coffee ration by surrendering the last stamp of War Ration Book No. 1, the book now used only for sugar rations. The stamps which will be used for coffee rationing are those numbered from 28 down to and including 19, but because of the make-up of the book the first stamp to be detached for the coffee allowance will be Stamp No. 27, followed by No. 28, No. 25, No. 26, etc.

None for Those 14 Years Old

No book on which the age of the holder is stated at 14 years or younger will be valid for the coffee ration. Use of the book for sugar will continue exactly as in the past. Those who did not obtain the sugar ration books, it was added, may do so now by applying to their War Price and Ration Boards.

Estimates of the number of cups of coffee to be obtained from a pound varied from thirty-five to forty-five among OPA officials, but on the basis of forty cups the new ration will work out to slightly more than a cup a day for consumers.

"We're announcing the forthcoming rationing now because we're going to have to talk to a lot of people in the coffee industry and elsewhere about the administration of the rationing program," Mr. Henderson said.

"Naturally stories and rumors will be creeping around about what we propose to do. Most of them will be entirely garbled and thus create more confusion and hysteria than even now exists on the subject of coffee. We are therefore stating what we plan to do so that the public can get the story straight and from an official source.

"The coffee story is this: For ten years before 1941 we consumed about thirteen pounds of coffee per capita per year. Last year, due to abnormal demands, this figure jumped to about sixteen pounds. Thus far in 1942 we have consumed coffee at the rate of about 12.5 pounds annually. Therefore, a ration of one pound each five weeks a person over 15 certainly is not a drastic reduction."

Retailers' Supplies Dwindled

OPA was directed to undertake the rationing program by the War Production Board after it became apparent that the available coffee supply in retail stores—65 per cent of normal—was not sufficient to meet current demand. This, the

Continued on Page Eighteen

Chilean Fisticuffs Debate Axis Break

By Reuter.

SANTIAGO, Chile, Oct. 26—Two groups of about 400 persons, some demonstrating for a break with the Axis and some against it, came to blows here today. The police intervened immediately and arrested ten persons. Several were injured.

SANTIAGO, Oct. 26 (AP)—Joaquin Fernandez y Fernandez took up his duties as Chile's new Foreign Minister today amid a clamor throughout the country for breaking relations with the Axis.

Mass meetings sponsored by the democratic parties and organized labor were held throughout the nation calling for rupture of diplomatic ties with Germany, Italy and Japan.

VALPARAISO, Chile, Oct. 26 (UP)—Eight persons, including two women, were arrested by police today on suspicion of Axis espionage activities and authorities said they believed that a German shipping agency, fully staffed although it has handled no shipping for the past three years, is the center of a local spy ring.

ACTION ON DRAFT SNAGGED IN HOUSE

Move to Accept Year's Training Imposes Delay Past Election —Hershey Urges Wider Call

By FREDERICK R. BARKLEY
Special to THE NEW YORK TIMES.

WASHINGTON, Oct. 26—Postponement of final action on the teen-age draft bill until after the election a week from tomorrow appeared almost certain today as the House ran into a snag in attempting to send the differing House and Senate versions to conference.

Representative Rankin of Mississippi moved to instruct the House conferees to approve a Senate amendment requiring that these youths receive a full year's training in the United States before being sent to combat duty abroad.

This proposal, adopted by the Senate, 39 to 31, despite opposition of Administration and Army leaders, is believed to have considerable support in the House.

Mr. Rankin's motion came after Representative Thomason, ranking Democrat on the Military Affairs Committee, said that he could not pledge that his conferee group would assure a separate vote on the training plan.

Speaker Rayburn then directed withdrawal of Mr. Thomason's motion to send the bills to conference by unanimous consent, pointing out that the House was acting under an informal agreement not to handle any controversial questions until after the election, and that with many members absent for the final week of the campaign a quorum for a vote would not be available.

However, the House will meet

Continued on Page Nineteen

QUICK AID IS URGED

Republican Leader Would Relieve Pressure on Russia and China

FOR PACIFIC CHARTER

Millions Said to Look to U. S. for Liberty Now and After the War

The text of Mr. Willkie's report is on Page 8.

In his promised report to the American people on his recently completed trip to the Middle East, Russia and China, Wendell L. Willkie renewed last night his demand for the establishment of a second fighting front in Europe, and added to it an expression of hope that our forces in India could soon begin an all-out attack on Burma.

"Thus we will relieve the pressure of our enemies on China and Russia, those two superb fighting allies," Mr. Willkie declared.

Declaring that the era of imperialism had ended, Mr. Willkie said that our Allies in the East expected us "now—not after the war—to use the enormous power of our giving to promote liberty and justice." The peoples of the East, he said, want the United States to join them in "creating a new society, global in scope, free alike of the economic injustices of the West and the political malpractices of the East."

The 1940 Republican Presidential nominee spoke to the nation over the combined networks of the Columbia Broadcasting System, the National Broadcasting Company, the Mutual Broadcasting System and the Blue Network, from 10:30 to 11:07 P. M. He made his address from the CBS studio at 49 East Fifty-second Street.

Believed Heard by 36,320,000

Broadcasting officials, on the basis of one of the commercial surveys used to check the response to programs, estimated last night that 36,320,000 persons had tuned in on Mr. Willkie's broadcast. This figure, it was said, represented about twice the normal listener response to a topnotch commercial broadcast, and compared with the record of 62,100,000 auditors reached by President Roosevelt's address on Dec. 9, 1941, just after Pearl Harbor.

Although we are on the road to winning the war, Mr. Willkie said, we are running a grave risk of spending far more in men and materials than is necessary. We are also in danger of losing the friendship of half of our allies before the war is over, and then of losing the peace, he warned, unless we recognize that "in many important respects we are not doing a good job," and correct our errors.

He hotly assailed the contention that private citizens, particularly those not expert in military affairs

Continued on Page Eight

DESERT ARMY FIRM

Allies Consolidate Their Successes—Tanks in Minor Clashes

1,450 OF FOE SEIZED

Our Air Forces Deliver More Heavy Blows at Front and at Sea

By DAVID ANDERSON
Special Cable to THE NEW YORK TIMES.

LONDON, Oct. 26—Striving to gain elbow room in which to fight on the scale and in the fashion that the occasion demands, the British Eighth Army in Egypt spent the third day of battle in consolidating its initial successes and in inching forward wherever possible. Tanks at last made their appearance in minor clashes.

Laconic reports from Cairo reaching here indicate the wish to save comment until later, when there should be something substantial to put in the communiqués.

Today it was announced that 1,450 Axis troops had been captured up to last evening. There were no important advances by British troops, although the Allied air forces kept up their all-out offensive.

No Dislodging by Axis

The statement that the Eighth Army is holding on to its new positions is not as defensive as it sounds, for the enemy is expected to achieve local success from time to time. But lately there have been no counter-attacks with sufficient weight to dislodge the advancing Allied troops.

The job of pushing General Field Marshal Erwin Rommel's defenses aside is bound to be a long one, especially as the attackers have for their plan the paving of avenues over which British tanks can roll. Days of tedious fighting are seen to be ahead before sappers and infantry can hack their way into the open.

Indeed, there is some support here for the belief that the Eighth Army may have to resort to dull pounding tactics, with a column of supplies lying in the rear and the soundness of supply lines being the final margin for British victory. That could go on for weeks.

Nothing coming in from the battlefront suggests that the main German defenses have been breached, or, for that matter, even

Continued on Page Five

THE WASP AFIRE AFTER BEING STRUCK BY TORPEDOES

Smoke rises from U. S. aircraft carrier following a Japanese submarine attack in South Pacific
Associated Press Wirephoto (U. S. Navy)

RED ARMY HOLDING IN SEESAW COMBAT

Germans in Stalingrad Drive in Wedge but Are Thrust Back by Counter-Blow

By The Associated Press.

MOSCOW, Tuesday, Oct. 27—The Red Army maintained its lines in Stalingrad yesterday in a seesaw battle in which the Germans drove a wedge into Russian positions in one sector and then were forced to withdraw, the Soviet High Command announced today.

The main fighting took place in a factory area in the northern part of the city—presumably around the Red October foundry works—where attacking German tank and infantry forces lost three tanks and 750 men killed in a five-hour combat.

"The Germans succeeded in driving a wedge into the Soviet defenses," the Soviet communiqué said, "but were attacked from the

Continued on Page Three

Japanese Bomb East India; Say Allies Plan Burma Push

By HERBERT L. MATTHEWS
Wireless to THE NEW YORK TIMES.

NEW DELHI, India, Oct. 26—The long-expected Japanese air attacks on our bases in East India began yesterday, it was announced in today's British General Headquarters communiqué. "Chittagong and some airdromes in Northeast Assam" were involved. Chittagong is in Bengal on the Bay of Bengal, not far from the Burma border, while Assam is a province in Northeast British India, adjacent to Burma.

More detailed information is expected later, but preliminary reports, according to the communiqué, indicate that civilian and military casualties "were extremely light and damage was small."

"Civilian labor employed in the areas attacked," the communiqué said, "displayed extremely high morale and their devotion to routine duties was most marked."

[Domei stated yesterday that the Japanese air attack on air bases in East India on Sunday was a preventive measure against a contemplated major-scale United Nations offensive against Burma, according to Tokyo broadcasts recorded by The Associated Press. The Associated Press reported that the Japanese raids were renewed yesterday on the Assam objectives.]

The reference to civilians in the British communiqué was an important one, for much depends on the Bengalis holding firm.

The reference to Northeastern Assam—as a glance at the map will show—also is most significant. That means the Japanese are aiming at bases of British Army forces

Continued on Page Nine

FIRES IN HONG KONG GUIDE A NEW RAID

Americans Also Blast Enemy's Airfield Near Canton—23 Japanese Planes Downed

By HARRISON FORMAN
Wireless to THE NEW YORK TIMES.

CHUNGKING, China, Oct. 26—All Chungking was electrified by the news that American bombers with fighter escorts Sunday afternoon and again early this morning dumped twenty tons of bombs on Hong Kong's docks, shipping and warehouses, blowing up the power station and shooting down ten and probably five more of eighteen Zeros and I-45's.

The Japanese planes attempted to intercept the returning American formation, which suffered one bomber lost. One American fighter plane was forced down, but the pilot was reported safe.

A terrific scare was thrown into the Japanese throughout North China, Manchuria, Korea and Japan proper only four days ago by the blasting by American bombers

Continued on Page Nine

ALL-OUT PUSH IS ON

Naval Shelling Supports Japanese Attack on U. S. Flank on Isle

ENEMY CRUISERS HIT

2 of Foe's Carriers Hurt in Naval Clash—Wasp Victim of Torpedoes

By CHARLES HURD
Special to THE NEW YORK TIMES.

WASHINGTON, Oct. 26—The Japanese have launched a massive air, land and sea attack against the American forces on Guadalcanal, in the Solomon Islands, the Navy announced in a communiqué issued tonight.

Word of this long-expected attack came a few hours after the Navy had announced that the aircraft carrier Wasp had been sunk on Sept. 15, as the result of a Japanese submarine attack, while engaged in covering the movement of reinforcements and supplies to Guadalcanal. About 90 per cent of the Wasp's personnel were saved.

In the current fighting, the later Navy announcement said, the Navy has suffered "severe damage" to another carrier and has lost the destroyer Porter. In addition, "other United States vessels have reported lesser damage."

The shock of the announcement of the loss of the Wasp, quickly manifested in official circles here, was overshadowed by the later announcement of news that had been expected here for almost a month, but that none the less came as a dramatic climax to the venture that began on Aug. 7, when American forces smashed their way onto Guadalcanal.

A Decisive Engagement

No one in authority would hazard a guess as to the outcome of the current engagement, but there was a general agreement in informed circles that the engagement probably would be fought to a decisive finish. On it, most authorities agreed, probably will depend the course of the war in the southwestern Pacific for the next year.

The Japanese are believed to have thrown into the fight the bulk of their sea power, as well as air power, which has continued to function despite the enemy's loss of about 400 planes in the Solomons. What forces the United States Navy carried into the fight to support the Marine and Army troops on land necessarily was not announced.

The Navy's communiqué on the new Japanese attack was unequivocal in picturing the seriousness of the enemy's effort to wrest from American hands the small airfield hewn out of the jungle on

Continued on Page Six

Roosevelt Confers With Naval Chiefs

By The Associated Press.

WASHINGTON, Oct. 26—President Roosevelt called the Naval High Command into conference late today as the defenders of Guadalcanal, in the Solomons, apparently faced one of the most terrific ordeals in American history.

With reinforced Japanese obviously bent on throwing everything they have into the drive to overwhelm the Marines and Army men, an atmosphere of tense expectation was apparent in some Washington quarters.

Conferring with the President were Admiral Ernest J. King, Commander in Chief of the Fleet, and Mr. Roosevelt's personal Chief of Staff, Admiral William D. Leahy. The conferees said nothing to newspaper men, but it was considered probable that the conference dealt with strategic and combat problems in the Southwest Pacific, particularly the Solomon Islands.

Byrnes Turns Down Farm Bloc; Roosevelt Ceiling Basis Stands

By W. H. LAWRENCE
Special to THE NEW YORK TIMES.

WASHINGTON, Oct. 26—An angry Senate farm bloc, demanding revisions in Federal price policies which would permit prices paid to farmers for their products to go higher, was turned down today by James F. Byrnes, Economic Stabilization Director; Leon Henderson, Federal Price Administrator, and Secretary Wickard.

Mr. Henderson, denouncing an attempt to "gun" him out of his job and to "sabotage" the Office of Price Administration, estimated that granting of farm bloc demands would add $100,000,000 annually to the price of bread alone. He offered no estimates of the over-all increase in living costs which would result from the proposed revision.

The basic issue debated before the Senate Agriculture and Forestry Committee was whether President Roosevelt had authority of Congress to direct Messrs. Byrnes, Henderson and Wickard to "consider present governmental payments to agricultural producers, and subsidy payments, in arriving at the minimum ceiling prices."

The farm bloc contended that he did not have such authority, and Senator Reed of Kansas charged flatly that the President's execu-

Continued on Page Nineteen

War News Summarized

TUESDAY, OCTOBER 27, 1942

The United States Navy Department disclosed that a major land, sea and air battle was under way in the Solomon Islands, with both United States and Japanese warships suffering. The action started with a coordinated Japanese attack on Guadalcanal Island positions Sunday morning. In a sortie carried out by the United States planes from the carriers of a task force two Japanese carriers were damaged. The United States destroyer Porter was sunk and a carrier damaged. [1:8; map, P. 6.] Loss of the carrier Wasp Sept. 15 by submarine torpedoes was disclosed. [6:1.]

In Eastern India Japanese planes bombed British air bases. Chittagong and points in Eastern Assam were attacked. Casualties and damage were reported to have been light. Domei, Japanese news agency, claimed that three planes were shot down and thirty-nine destroyed on the ground and called the attacks a preventive action to check a move on Burma. [1:6-7; map, P. 9.]

United States fliers again bombed Hong Kong, destroying a power station. At Canton an airfield was bombed successfully. Ten Japanese planes were shot down. One United States bomber was lost during the operations in the sector yesterday and the day preceding. [1:7.]

On the Egyptian battlefront United Nations troops were swarming through widening gaps in the Axis defensive line and 1,450 prisoners had been taken. Four Junkers troop-carrying planes were shot down and a munitions ship was blown up in the harbor of Tobruk. [1:4.]

A German spokesman placed the United Nations force in Egypt at 1,000,000 men and 1,000 tanks. Berlin claimed that all attacks on the Axis line had been repulsed. [4:5.]

An Italian communiqué stated that 354 persons had been killed and more than 3,000 injured during the week-end bombings of Genoa. Most of the deaths were understood to have occurred when the crowd in a large air raid shelter broke in panic. [5:1.]

Wendell L. Willkie, reporting in a national broadcast on his recent tour, renewed his demand for a second front in Europe and expressed hope that an offensive would be undertaken in Burma. He warned that the United States stood to lose half its friends abroad if it did not start making a better job of the war. [1:3.]

Wasp Crew's Battle With Fires To Save Carrier Told by Skipper

By FOSTER HAILEY
By Telephone to THE NEW YORK TIMES.

HONOLULU, Oct. 26—The last hours of the aircraft carrier Wasp as her heroic officers and crew fought to save her and then, hopes of that gone, swam to each other in the water and gave life belts to those who could not swim, were described today by her skipper, Captain Forrest P. Sherman.

Already back in an active post as Chief of Staff to Vice Admiral John H. Towers, commander of Naval Air Forces in the Pacific, Captain Sherman laid aside his work for a few minutes to tell newspaper men of the loss of his ship.

Time and again in his recital of the desperate hours after 2:44 P. M., Sept. 15, when three Japanese torpedoes hit the Wasp, he returned to the heroism shown by his officers and men in fighting the fires that finally ravaged her and led to the decision to abandon ship and sink her.

"I can't say too much for the spirit of the men of the Wasp from the time we first went down there until I saw them last," Captain Sherman said. "I visited every injured man on the hospital ship before I left and there wasn't a one that didn't want to get out of there and back on a ship after the Japs. That was the only request I got—to go with me on another carrier."

Captain Sherman singled out for

Continued on Page Six

"All the News That's Fit to Print."

The New York Times.

LATE CITY EDITION
Much colder today with diminishing winds.
Temperatures Yesterday—Max., 65; Min., 50
Sunrise, 7:30 A. M.; Sunset, 5:48 P. M.

Copyright, 1942, by The New York Times Company.

VOL. XCII..No. 30,972. Entered as Second-Class Matter, Postoffice, New York, N. Y. NEW YORK, WEDNESDAY, NOVEMBER 11, 1942. THREE CENTS IN NEW YORK CITY

HITLER TO TAKE OVER ALL FRANCE AND CORSICA; OUR TROOPS IN ORAN, SPEEDING TOWARD LIBYA, TANKS IN CASABLANCA; ROOSEVELT TELLS PLANS

ALLIES IN ACCORD

President Reveals Stalin Was Informed of Plan by Churchill

'NOW IT CAN BE TOLD'

How Decision on Second Front Move Was Made Is Described

By W. H. LAWRENCE
Special to THE NEW YORK TIMES.

WASHINGTON, Nov. 10—Declaring that a second front has to be tailor-made and custom-built and cannot be purchased ready made in a department store, President Roosevelt gave his press conference today a detailed account of the months of planning that preceded the French North African expedition and the limiting factors that made impossible a large-scale Allied offensive across the English Channel before the middle of 1943.

In excellent humor, Mr. Roosevelt leaned back in his chair, puffing at a cigarette and described tersely how Prime Minister Winston Churchill and he had decided on the African offensive as early as the end of June, but had to take it on the chin in silence when ignorant outsiders, who could not have been cognizant of the fact, were demanding something—a second front—that had already been decided upon by the two governments after consultation with their principal fighting allies.

Chronology of Planning

The President's chronology of offensive planning, with the first decision to attack across the English Channel being changed to an expedition into French North Africa, cleared up a major change in language relating to a second front from the June 12 joint communiqué issued by Mr. Roosevelt and Vyacheslaff M. Molotoff, Soviet Foreign Commissar, and the June 27 joint statement of the President and Prime Minister Churchill.

On June 12, when the President and Commissar Molotoff said that the United States and Russia had reached a full understanding on the "urgent tasks of creating a second front in Europe in 1942," a final decision to abandon the Channel offensive in favor of the North African attack had not yet been made, it appeared from the President's recital.

But on June 27, when the President and Prime Minister said simply that coming operations by the military forces of the United Nations would "divert German strength from the attack on Russia," this government and Great Britain already were in agreement on shifting the offensive to North Africa.

The final decisions on the North African move, including the points of attack, the number of men to be employed and the problems of transport and naval protection, were settled toward the end of July at the London conferences of the Prime Minister and British military and naval leaders with General George C. Marshall, Army Chief of Staff; Admiral Ernest J. King, Commander in Chief of the United States Fleet and Chief of Naval Operations, and Harry L. Hopkins, personal representative of the President. The actual date of attack was decided by the end of August, he said.

As the President explained it, in response to a request for a "now it can be told story," the inception of the offensive action in which the American and British armies are engaged in North Africa goes back to about two weeks after Pearl Harbor, when the President invited Prime Minister Churchill and his joint staff to come to Washington just before Christmas. The time had come, he said,

Continued on Page Seven

Thanksgiving Feast Is Set for Army

Here is the menu, announced yesterday by the War Department, for the Thanksgiving dinner on Nov. 26 to be served to American soldiers in all parts of the world as well as in the United States:

Fruit Cup
Roast Turkey — Dressing and Cranberry Sauce — Giblet Gravy
Mashed Potatoes
Corn — Peas
Stuffed Celery — Tomato Salad
Assorted Pickles
Bread — Butter
Pumpkin Pie
Apples — Grapes
Coffee
Candies — Nuts

MANPOWER DRAFT OPPOSED IN REPORT

Management and Labor in WMC Policy Group Join in Backing Voluntary Plan

The war manpower report is printed on Page 21.

Special to THE NEW YORK TIMES.

WASHINGTON, Nov. 10—A Management-Labor Policy Committee, unanimously opposing enactment of a national war service act for the conscription of labor at this time, has submitted a broad-scale voluntary program designed to eliminate serious manpower problems which now threaten successful prosecution of the war, it was announced today.

After the White House had made public the report submitted Friday, President Roosevelt told his press conference that, while he had been giving considerable study to the recommendations, he had not yet decided whether to put any of them in effect. He said there was no immediate emergency which would require executive action or a request for legislation at once, but added that the problem would grow increasingly serious in the months ahead and that something would be done in a few weeks.

In response to a question, the President said he had not yet decided whether to shift the Selective Service system, which handles the drafting of men for the Army, from its present independent status to the War Manpower Commission, which was one of the recommendations of the Management-Labor Policy Committee.

Major Policy Changes Proposed

Warning that "major weaknesses exist in the present approach to the over-all manpower situation, weaknesses that require immediate attention and correction, and which, if not corrected, will seriously impede the war effort," the committee suggested these major changes in governmental policy if an industrial and military force of 62,500,000 men

Continued on Page Twenty-one

ORAN BATTLE BRIEF

500 Miles of Africa's Coastline Now in Hands of Allies

PLANES, SHIPS HELP

New Assault Southeast of Algiers Reported by Paris Radio

By The Associated Press.

LONDON, Nov. 10 — United States expeditionary armies wiped out effective resistance along 500 miles of Africa's Western Mediterranean coast today with the conquest of Oran, Algeria's second city, and a German report said that the Bey of Tunis had granted President Roosevelt's request for the passage of American troops to Libya.

[In Washington, President Roosevelt said yesterday that he had received no reply to his message to the Bey of Tunis.]

On the Atlantic coast, the resistance of Casablanca, the chief city of Morocco, was fast crumbling under all-out naval and air assault by United States Rear Admiral Henry K. Hewitt's heavy warships and dive-bombers as American armored columns infiltrated the city's eastern suburbs with tanks.

Rabat, the normal seat of French power in Morocco, on the coast above Casablanca, evidently was isolated and evacuated by the Vichy commander, General Charles Nogues.

Broad Victory Seen Near

Hence it appeared that in a matter of hours the United States armies commanded by Lieut. Gen. Dwight D. Eisenhower would be in effective control of all French North Africa, save for Eastern Algeria and Tunisia.

[Yves Chatel, Governor General of Algeria, has moved his headquarters to Constantine, in the east, and reassumed his administration there, the Vichy radio announced last night, according to The Associated Press in New York.

[In London The United Press recorded a Paris broadcast saying that American forces were advancing from Algiers in the direction of Bou Saada, 120 miles southeast.]

American contingents evidently were well on their way to Libya, either through Tunisia or around it. The report of the Bey's acquiescence was received with some reserve here lest it be merely an attempt to justify the movement of Axis troops into Tunisia.

Time and time again today Vichy's radio insisted that "all is calm" in Eastern and Central Algeria and Tunisia. Some broadcasts, however, reported fighting at Blida, twenty-five miles inland from Algiers.

Official Allied Headquarters as-

Continued on Page Four

AMERICAN OPERATIONS IN AFRICA PROCEED SMOOTHLY

Tangier reports had United States troops still going ashore at Agadir and Mogador (1). The principal, almost the only, center of resistance was at Casablanca (2), where the United States Navy largely subdued Vichy naval opposition and three American tank columns were said to have smashed into the outskirts. Oran (3) fell to an American pincers manoeuvre and one occupying force moved east to deal with a Vichy counter-attack near Orleansville. Land operations had ceased at captured Algiers (4), but there was some resistance at Blida, to the south. From Algiers the Americans were reported to have struck southeastward toward Bou Saada (5), and from Philippeville (6) they were said to be moving eastward in the direction of the frontier of Tunisia.

CHURCHILL CREDITS PLAN TO PRESIDENT

His Own Role That of 'Active and Ardent Lieutenant' in African 'Second Front'

The text of Mr. Churchill's address is on Page 4.

By RAYMOND DANIELL
Wireless to THE NEW YORK TIMES.

LONDON, Nov. 10—The first public utterance by Prime Minister Winston Churchill since General Sir Bernard L. Montgomery's victory in Egypt and the landing of Lieut. Gen. Dwight D. Eisenhower's American Army in French Colonial Africa was made today at Mansion House. It was a renunciation of any Allied territorial aims, a pledge that France should rise again, and a flat declaration that the sole purpose of the Allied landings in Morocco and Algeria was

Continued on Page Four

Tanks Batter Casablanca; Battleship Afire in Harbor

By The United Press.

LONDON, Nov. 10—Vichy broadcasts recorded here reported today that three United States tank columns had crashed into Casablanca, Morocco, and that the city was under heavy attack by superior American forces and was being bombarded violently. Governor General Charles Nogues of Morocco has fled from Rabat to the interior, the radio added.

The broadcasts said that "our troops still are holding out east of Casablanca," while coastal artillery and field guns were resisting vigorously.

Three tank columns closed in on Casablanca, the French said, and swarmed into its outskirts.

A Tangiers dispatch revealed that Fighting French forces were in action at Casablanca against the Vichy troops. It said the Fighting French were battling in the old part of the city, where they were encircled. Americans held the Casablanca reservoir, enabling them to cut off the city's water

Continued on Page Eight

NEW ALLIED FLEET REPORTED MASSING

Concentration of Warships and Transports Noted in Gibraltar Harbor

By The Associated Press.

LONDON, Nov. 10 — Reports from France tonight said another powerful fleet of United Nations warships and a great number of merchantmen were gathering at Gibraltar, while throughout European waters and in the Atlantic naval activities were reported on a vast scale.

Reports from the Continent said some of the vessels of that portion of the French fleet stationed at Toulon had slipped off into the Mediterranean. There was speculation as to whether they were heading for the vicinity of Bizerte, Tunisia, through which American land forces proposed to advance on what is left of General Field Marshal Erwin Rommel's force in Libya.

The German High Command made an unsupported announce-

Continued on Page Six

HITLER, MUSSOLINI, LAVAL IN A PARLEY

Rome Reported Scene of Talks —Duce Said to Ask Nazis for Aid in Crisis

By DANIEL T. BRIGHAM
By Telephone to THE NEW YORK TIMES.

BERNE, Switzerland, Nov. 10—Negotiations for an alliance of Germany, France and Italy against the United Nations were reported under way "somewhere in Europe" tonight.

Most indications pointed to the scene as Rome, although Balkan speculation suggested Munich and other sources hinted at Salzburg. The Brenner Pass, in view of the reported presence of Adolf Hitler and Pierre Laval, Vichy Chief of Government, with their suites at the conferences, is not regarded as sufficiently equipped to house such a parley.

The negotiations and discussions of the future agreement are understood to be in the hands of Herr Hitler, who is accompanied by Reich Marshal Hermann Goering and General Field Marshal Wilhelm Keitel, for the Germans. M. Laval is attended only by his envoy to the Vatican, Leon Berard, and Premier Mussolini is being advised by General Ugo Cavallero, on the military side, and Count Ciano, Italian Foreign Minister.

Asked at his usual press conference for foreign newspaper men today for confirmation on denials of the reports of such a gathering

Continued on Page Ten

War News Summarized

WEDNESDAY, NOVEMBER 11, 1942

The Paris radio reported early today that Adolf Hitler had ordered his army to march into unoccupied France "to repel a possible American or British landing." In a letter to Marshal Pétain, Hitler said that he wished "as far as possible, in collaboration with the French Army, to protect the African possessions of European powers." [1:8.]

United States forces eliminated major resistance along the greater part of the Mediterranean coast of French North Africa yesterday with the fall of Oran. [1:3.]

General Eisenhower, Allied commander in North Africa, told correspondents that he expected the fall of Oran would be the signal for the cessation of organized resistance in the French colonies. [7:1.]

United States troops supported by tanks were reported to have entered the outskirts of Casablanca, Morocco, and a British broadcast said that all resistance of the Vichy naval forces at Casablanca had ceased. An Allied headquarters communiqué disclosed that the new French battleship, Jean Bart, was out of action and burning in the harbor. [1:5-6.]

There were reports that a United States column had struck out eastward in Algeria in the direction of Tunisia. President Roosevelt said that no reply had been received to his notification to the Bey of Tunis that United States troops would be sent through the protectorate. [2:2.]

Vichy reported that another powerful Allied convoy had reached Gibraltar. Berlin announced destruction of two Allied cruisers and a transport by Axis submarines and planes. London told of the torpedoing of an Italian cruiser off the north coast of Sicily. [1:6.]

Berne heard that Adolf Hitler, Benito Mussolini and Pierre Laval were in conference "somewhere in Europe." [1:7.]

President Roosevelt disclosed that the decision to open a North African front this year had been made last Summer after it had been decided that it would be impossible to open an effective second front in the northern portion of the European continent this year. [1:1.]

Prime Minister Churchill said that the landings in Africa were the prelude to a new front against Hitler and declared that the plan had been devised by President Roosevelt. [1:4.]

Action on the Egyptian-Libyan front was limited to minor rearguard activity at Sidi Barrani and Solum. The enemy's position was apparently becoming increasingly catastrophic. [3:2.]

Soviet troops registered some small successes at Stalingrad and near Tuapse on the Black Sea. German assaults were repulsed. [13:1.]

East Faces Gasoline Ration Slash And Possible 5% Fuel Oil Cut

By CHARLES E. EGAN
Special to THE NEW YORK TIMES.

WASHINGTON, Nov. 10—Faced with increasing difficulties in maintaining petroleum supplies on the East Coast, the government plans a further slash in the amount of gasoline to be allowed civilian motorists in this area.

Suggestions to cut the fuel-oil allowance to householders have been studied but, according to reports, there is strong opposition to any substantial cut, on the ground that the health hazards created by reducing allowable home temperatures below 65 degrees are too great to justify more than a slight decrease.

A formal announcement on both these proposals is expected later in the week from the War Production Board.

Official concern over the difficulties in transporting petroleum to the Atlantic Coast area, where gasoline rationing is in effect, was evident in many quarters here today. Shipments by railroad tank car, which have exceeded 800,000 barrels a day in some weeks, declined to 753,504 barrels a day last week, and averaged 759,233 the week before. This fact was called to the attention of the WPB at its regular weekly meeting today, along with a request that it authorize a reduction in gasoline rations.

Although no official announcement of the WPB's action was made, one report was that the board had actually approved a proposed slash of one-fourth in the gasoline allowance to be given "A" card holders in the seventeen Eastern States.

In addition, it was stated, the

Continued on Page Eleven

Darlan in U. S. Hands at Algiers; Petain 'Commands' Vichy's Forces

By DAVID ANDERSON
Wireless to THE NEW YORK TIMES.

LONDON, Nov. 10—Admiral François Darlan, chief of Vichy's armed forces, is now in Allied hands at Algiers "being entertained by one of our American generals with the respect and dignity due an officer of his rank," London headquarters of the Allied force announced tonight. No detail was given as to how and when Admiral Darlan got into his present situation.

Ever since his presence in French North Africa was confirmed soon after American operations began—he had gone ostensibly for a check-up on Vichy's defenses—it was suspected here that Admiral Darlan might permit himself to be caught or might voluntarily walk into General Dwight D. Eisenhower's camp.

Admiral Darlan has never been one to carry resistance to extremes, especially when there is something to gain by following the opposite course. He has long been known for his marked dislike of the British, however, and that has been given as an explanation of many of his actions at Vichy.

Many observers here feel that Admiral Darlan would not be able to re-establish his fortunes just by joining the United Nations, as did General Henri Giraud. The admiral is considered too unreliable.

LONDON, Nov. 10 (AP)—With Admiral Darlan definitely a prisoner of General Eisenhower at Algiers, old Marshal Henri Philippe Pétain, stubbornly repeating his order for resistance, took over the disorganized and melancholy defense of all

Continued on Page Four

LETTER TO PETAIN

Hitler Says Occupation of Whole Country Is Made Necessary

HE SOLICITS ACCORD

Versailles to Be Seat of Puppet Regime Under Nazi Soldiery

By The United Press.

LONDON, Wednesday, Nov. 11—Adolf Hitler has ordered German troops to occupy the remainder of France and the Mediterranean island of Corsica, 200 miles north of the coast of Africa, to counter the United States invasion of French possessions in Northern Africa, the Paris radio announced today.

The Paris radio said Hitler announced his decision was to "prevent further British-American aggression against French territory."

[A wireless dispatch to THE NEW YORK TIMES this morning from Berne, Switzerland, said five German divisions entered the Northern Rhone Valley as the Nazis began the occupation of all of France.]

A letter from Hitler to Marshal Henri Philippe Pétain, read by an official German [illegible] spokesman over the Paris station, announced that Hitler had decided to lift armistice restrictions forcing the French Government to be located in the previously-unoccupied zone of France.

[The French Government will be moved from Vichy to Versailles, said a Paris broadcast recorded by The Associated Press.]

"I have given orders to the German Army to advance through the unoccupied zone to take up positions in order to safeguard the zone against Anglo-American attack," said Hitler's announcement to the French people.

The United States and Britain, after various attempts to carry the war into Europe, "now have proceeded to attack the territories of the French Empire, thereby threatening Corsica as well as the south coast of France," Hitler said.

HITLER LETTER TO PETAIN

LONDON, Nov. 11 (AP)—German troops were reported speeding through unoccupied France today toward a Mediterranean area at which Adolf Hitler said American and British troops proposed landings as a sequel to the American coup in North Africa.

A Paris broadcast quoted Hitler as saying "we have known for twenty-four hours" that Allied attacks were planned upon the French fleet, Corsica and the French mainland coast. He said British and American strategists had "regard to the weakness of the French forces in these parts."

"In these circumstances," Hitler said, "I felt compelled to order the German Army immediately to march through the unoccupied zone—and this is now being done—and to march to the point aimed at by the Anglo-American landing troops."

The letter from Hitler to Marshal Pétain said:

"We have known for twenty-four hours that it is the intention of our enemies to direct the next attack against Corsica, which island they will occupy, and against the south of France."

"I have given this (order) with one single aim, and that is to repel an American and British landing."

"I have given the order to the troops to look after the interests of France," Hitler's letter went on. "The German Government desires as far as possible in collaboration with the French army to prevent

Continued on Page Six

"All the News That's Fit to Print."

The New York Times.

Copyright, 1942, by The New York Times Company.

LATE CITY EDITION

Rain and moderately cool today

Temperatures Yesterday—Max., 50; Min., 40

Sunrise, 7:04 A. M.; Sunset, 5:30 P. M.

VOL. XCII...No. 30,986. Entered as Second-Class Matter, Postoffice, New York, N. Y. NEW YORK, WEDNESDAY, NOVEMBER 25, 1942. THREE CENTS IN NEW YORK CITY

NAZIS' GRIP ON STALINGRAD BROKEN; 15,000 SLAIN AS SOVIET PUSH GAINS; BRISK FIGHTING SPREADS IN TUNISIA

EXTORTION CHARGED BY MAYOR IN ROW OVER STIRRUP PUMPS

Herlands Says Effort Was Made to 'Shake Down' a Dealer by Promise to 'Fix' Council

REPORT HELD 'RECKLESS'

Solomon, Ex-Deputy Controller, Modell, La Guardia Critic, Deny the Accusations

Mayor La Guardia and William B. Herlands, Commissioner of Investigation, charged yesterday that an attempt had been made to "shake down" a stirrup-pump distributor on the claim that a proposed local law could be killed by the City Council as the result of "influence."

The Mayor said that he learned of the "crude and brazen attempt of a shakedown" from Commissioner Herlands on Saturday and that it was for this reason that he announced on Sunday his plans to have the city sell stirrup pumps directly to consumers.

Copies of Mr. Herlands' official report supplying details of the alleged extortion attempt were given yesterday afternoon to District Attorney Frank S. Hogan and to the grievance committee of the Association of the Bar of the City of New York.

Modell Called "Contact Man"

Named as principals in the Herlands' report were:

Henry Modell, president of Modell's, a sporting goods and uniform store at 198 Broadway, described as "the contact man."

Milton Solomon, an attorney with offices at 165 Broadway, former Deputy City Controller and one-time Democratic candidate for President of the Board of Aldermen, listed as the "alleged fixer."

Maurice Holt, owner of the Triangle Appliance Corporation of 11 West Forty-second Street, which is said to have a stirrup pump distribution monopoly. Although he appeared cast in the role of victim, the report indicated he went through with the deal on the advice of the Department of Investigation.

"Stated baldly, this is the case of a lawyer trying to obtain a large sum of money from a business man by assuring him that he, the lawyer, had the 'influence' to 'kill' certain legislation which was objectionable to said businessman," Commissioner Herlands' report said.

"Outrageous," Says Solomon

Mr. Solomon described the charges as "outrageous" and "reckless" when informed of the contents of the report at his home, 9 Prospect Park West, Brooklyn, last night.

Mr. Modell declared that the accusations were "a dastardly lie" and a "red herring," and declared that he would not allow the Mayor "to get away with it." On Sunday Mr. Modell had assailed the Mayor for putting the city into the pump-selling business, declaring this municipal venture to be unfair competition with business men who were selling the equipment at retail at a small profit.

Councilman Walter R. Hart, chairman of the City Council Defense Committee, declared that he was surprised and astounded by the charges. The report quoted Mr. Solomon as boasting to Mr. Holt that Mr. Hart was his "man" and could kill the pending bill.

According to Commissioner Herlands's report, Mr. Holt was disturbed over the prospect of enactment of a local law sponsored by Councilman Hugh Quinn, Queens Democrat. This measure, still pending before the Council, eliminates stirrup pumps from the list of fire fighting weapons that building owners or tenants must have under the Air Raid Law. As the law now stands they may be used as an alternative to rubber hose under certain conditions.

Mayor Charges Shakedown

"When I made my statement Sunday announcing my decision to give the consumers the benefit of direct sale of stirrup pumps as provided by the Office of Civilian Defense, I did so because it was the only way to put an end to the crude and brazen attempt at a shakedown," the Mayor told reporters yesterday afternoon after he had conferred with Commissioner Herlands.

"I received Saturday a report from the Commissioner of Investigation. That report was given to District Attorney Hogan this after-

Continued on Page Thirty

Two Thanksgivings For Pacific Troops

Wireless to THE NEW YORK TIMES.

WELLINGTON, N. Z., Nov. 24—There will be two Thanksgiving Days this year—one on the western side of the International Date Line as well as that on the American side.

For the first time, Thanksgiving Day will be nationally celebrated in the Antipodes wherever United States troops are now stationed. In the Fiji and Samoan Islands it may cause a headache. The date line bisects these islands and forces in American Samoa will mark the continental American day, but in Fiji it will be a day earlier if Americans are there.

WAR POWERS BILL STRIKES NEW SNAG

House Group Considers Repeal of Income Curb, Calling It Invasion of Rights

Special to THE NEW YORK TIMES.

WASHINGTON, Nov. 24—New manifestations against "government by bureaucracy" became plain in Congress today, leaving the future of the Third War Powers Bill in doubt and suggesting that moves were afoot for application of brakes to administrative authorities when the new session begins in January.

Only a technicality prevented what was viewed as an almost certain insertion into the powers-granting measure by the Ways and Means Committee of a provision which would nullify by statute President Roosevelt's recent executive order limiting annual salaries to $25,000 net.

Sponsors of the proposed "repealer" said they had sufficient committee votes in sight to write it into the bill, if Representative Doughton, the chairman, had not ruled it not germane, and thus out of order. Further attempts will be made, it was asserted, when and if the legislation reaches the Senate, if not before.

During two executive sessions, lasting most of the day, the Ways and Means body dealt with protests by members against Executive Department interpretations of limitations written into previously enacted power-giving legislation by the Congress, it was reported later.

No Decision as to Hearings

The salary limiting order, it was brought out, was only one of many administrative actions drawing the fire of members as allegedly having gone beyond the intent of Congress in the carrying out of its directives.

The Ways and Means Committee refused to write the $25,000 limitation into the tax bill when the proposal was made specifically. Mr. Roosevelt acted under a clause in the anti-inflation pri[illegible] and wage control bill.

At the end of the day no decision had been reached even as to the holding of hearings on the modified draft of the powers program, which was approved unanimously by a subcommittee Saturday after the committee had rejected the Administration's sweeping draft. Doubt was expressed by members that the legislation could get through both the House and Senate before Congress adjourned.

Committee members insisted, however, that further hearings should be held before any bill was reported, and a decision on this phase may be made tomorrow. They maintained further, that

Continued on Page Thirteen

PRESIDENT WARNS PRODUCTION CHIEFS TO RECONCILE AIMS

If They Can't Agree He Will Put Them in Foodless Room Until They Reach Solution

NEW CONTROL PLAN DENIED

WPB-Armed Services Dispute on Aircraft Brushed Aside at Press Conference

By W. H. LAWRENCE

Special to THE NEW YORK TIMES.

WASHINGTON, Nov. 24—With reports current in the capital of a growing crisis within the Administration on the issue of civilian versus military control of the country's economy, President Roosevelt today brushed aside questions as to whether the War Production Board or the armed forces have the final authority on war production problems.

While Washington speculated about a possible Presidential move to break the stalemate between the civilian and military leaders, now manifested in a quarrel over a new master production set-up, the Chief Executive, at his press conference, said that WPB, Army and Navy officials are supposed to agree, and, when they do not, he will lock them in a room and tell them they will get no food until they come out with an agreement.

Denying reports that he was working on plans for a new one-man control of production, supply, manpower and related wartime problems, the President said that, on the whole, the present system is working very well.

WPB Circles Apprehensive

The President's optimism was not shared in well informed WPB circles, which apprehensively heard reports that the Army was attempting to take control of manpower and looked upon the aircraft stalemate as the first challenge to Donald M. Nelson's authority to take back powers over production which he himself delegated to the Army and Navy last March. The WPB official said, half seriously and half jokingly, that he feared "quasi-martial law" was ahead for the country.

Persons familiar with the views of the armed services denied, however, that there was any challenge to Mr. Nelson in the dispute revolving around the creation of a new aircraft production committee, representing the Army and Navy and headed by Charles E. Wilson, former president of the General Electric Corporation. These persons, expressing the highest admiration for Mr. Wilson's production abilities, were confident of a compromise solution which would give influence in aircraft matters to Lieut. Gen. William S. Knudsen, former OPM head and now War Department Production Director, and would eliminate Harold E. Talbott of WPB from the committee.

While the aircraft production fight may be settled amicably without a definite test of authority, there was no doubt in informed quarters, where production authorities have been discussed with the civilian and military leaders, that there is a conflict between the services and Mr. Nelson over how much authority he should exercise over such matters as production scheduling.

The armed services feel that WPB should give its major atten-

Continued on Page Twelve

Valtin Arrested for Deportation; Board Cites 'Wavering Loyalties'

Special to THE NEW YORK TIMES.

WASHINGTON, Nov. 24—Jan Valtin, author of "Out of the Night," was arrested today in Bethel, Conn., on a warrant issued by the Immigration and Naturalization Service and held for deportation to Germany. The arrest was announced here soon afterward by Attorney General Biddle.

Valtin, who is 37 years old and whose real name is Richard Julius Herman Krebs, had been the subject of extended hearings before the Board of Immigration Appeals. The deportation order is not expected to be carried out until after the war, and Valtin probably will be interned meanwhile.

The board found that Krebs entered this country illegally after once having been arrested and deported and after committing a crime involving moral turpitude, in this case perjury. Technically, the board unanimously voted to order the deportation after first denying an application for suspension of deportation proceedings on the ground that Krebs had not been "a person of good moral character for the past five years, as required by law, and that he was otherwise deportable."

Within the last five years, the board asserted, Krebs "has been considered an agent of Nazi Germany."

The board minced no words in ordering the deportation. Unanimously, said Thomas G. Finucane, chairman, the members found the author's life "so marked with violence, intrigue and treachery that it would be difficult, if not wholly unwarranted, to conclude

Continued on Page Fifteen

ALLIES' GAIN SLOW

Attack of Axis Armored Unit Broken Up by Chutist Forces

MORE CLASHES IN SOUTH

New Landings Reported at Sfax and Gabes as U. S. Planes Shoot Up Troop Train

By RAYMOND DANIELL

Special Cable to THE NEW YORK TIMES.

LONDON, Nov. 24—Sharp fighting took place today in several sectors of Tunisia, where the Allied forces are advancing on Axis-held Tunis, the capital, and Bizerte, the vital naval base. There has been no major clash yet, however, although air activity is increasing as the opposing forces manoeuvre for positions.

The official Allied communiqués continued to be as uninformative as the Axis radios were misleading. However, the communiqués contained enough information to indicate that the Allies were advancing on a broad front while the Axis continued its hasty preparations to make the Tunis-Bizerte corner a sort of Tobruk.

Tonight's communiqué from headquarters, mentioning "local engagements" of Allied forward units, gave few details. Continued activity was reported from the southern sector, where French patrols are operating. A unit of Allied paratroopers repulsed an enemy mechanized column, taking prisoners, according to the communiqué. Unofficial sources reported that British troops advancing eastward along the coastal road had engaged in several minor brushes with enemy patrols.

Four enemy aircraft were shot down by British and American fighters, which also attacked an enemy troop train near Gabès, while heavy bombers raided Bizerte and Tunis. All the bombers and fighters returned safely to their bases, the communiqué said.

[The Vichy radio said that the Axis had landed large troop formations on the Tunisian east coast at Sfax and Gabès, far below Bizerte and Tunis, The Associated Press reported from London. Another Associated Press dispatch, from Allied Headquarters in North Africa, said that British troops had driven back a German advance screen in Northern Tunisia while the

Continued on Page Six

U. S. BOMBERS SCORE BULL'S-EYE IN TRIPOLI HARBOR

Smoke (arrow) marks direct blast on the Spanish Mole during a raid on the Libyan port

Associated Press Radiophoto (U. S. Army Air Forces)

BRITISH PUSH FOE TOWARD AGHEILA

Take Oasis Far to Southeast as Axis Forces Continue Retreat Across Libya

Special Cable to THE NEW YORK TIMES.

CAIRO, Egypt, Nov. 24—If there is to be a battle at El Agheila it is likely to begin soon, for the German rear guard is moving southwestward from Agedabia toward there, putting up only enough of a fight to keep from being overrun.

Agedabia is now in British hands. The need for consolidation and building of supply services is undoubtedly a greater factor in determining the British rate of advance in that area now than are any efforts of the weak rear guard screens.

The Germans have few tanks left and not too many guns. But they must cast the die one way or the other soon. They must either rush back to Tripoli or fight desperately at El Agheila.

It is regarded as a question whether the present members of the German Africa Corps will be anxious to fight a hopeless battle

Continued on Page Six

War News Summarized

WEDNESDAY, NOVEMBER 25, 1942

Adolf Hitler's forces in the Stalingrad salient of the eastern front appeared to be on the verge of total disaster yesterday. The situation on the African fronts was little changed and activity in the Pacific war theatre was limited.

West of Stalingrad the Russian Army was reported to be advancing on a 200-mile front and to have penetrated as deep as twenty-five miles into enemy-held territory, while other Soviet troops drove down into the city from the north through the encircling German lines. Another 15,000 German soldiers were reported killed and 12,000 more taken prisoner. [1:8.]

Berlin acknowledged that the Russians had penetrated the German defensive line in the Don bend region. [8:2.]

Rumanian troops, fighting with the Germans in the region, were said to be surrendering in masses and apparently the Germans were retreating and leaving them to their fate. [1:6-7.]

It still seemed doubtful that Marshal Rommel's forces in Libya would give battle at El Agheila. The Axis rear guard was approaching El Agheila rapidly and was offering little opposition. [1:5.]

Sharp clashes took place in Tunisia between Axis forces and Allied troops advancing out of Algeria, but battle had not yet been joined and the Germans and Italians continued to strengthen their positions around Bizerte and Tunis. [1:4; map, P. 6.]

In London a Labor member of Parliament asserted that Prime Minister Churchill had suppressed a broadcast scheduled by the chief of the Fighting French, General de Gaulle, after Foreign Secretary Anthony Eden had approved it. A charge that "reactionary tendencies" were gaining the upper hand was raised in connection with the incident. [6:1.]

The Polish Government in Exile announced that the German Gestapo Chief, Heinrich Himmler, had ordered half the Jews in Poland killed by the end of this year in preparation for the eventual slaughter of all Jews in the country. [10:1.]

Secretary of the Navy Knox told reporters that Japanese reinforcements had not been landed recently on Guadalcanal and that the island could probably be kept isolated from further Japanese infiltration. United States troops advanced farther west of Henderson Field. [1:7.] The situation of the Japanese defending Buna in Northeastern New Guinea remained desperate. [3:1.]

United States bombers based on India raided the railway installations at Mandalay, Burma, again Sunday and reported that the previous raid last Friday had been very effective. [4:1.]

Nazis Retreat, Some in Panic, Leaving Rumanians in Lurch

By RALPH PARKER

Wireless to THE NEW YORK TIMES.

MOSCOW, Nov. 24—While the Red Army's two-barbed thrust was plunging deeper into the enemy's flanks, Stalingrad's defenders grasped the initiative and, exactly three months after the city was first assaulted, began to clear the Germans systematically from fortresses and cellars.

Continuing their gradual advance last night, the Russians took blockhouses by storm and broke resistance in both the northern factory and southern regions of the impregnable city.

On the Don steppes, on the western slopes of the Ergeni Hills and southwestward along the main highway and railroad toward the Kuban, the counter-offensive is maintaining its tempo and proceeding according to a careful strategic plan to undermine the entire position of the German armies in the south. This is a reward, the newspaper Izvestia asserts, for the heroic resistance of the Red Army, the skillful training of its commanders and other tireless work in the rear.

Russia's allies, too, had a share in it, the paper adds, for the Germans' strategic difficulties were aggravated by the Allies' operations in Africa and the threatening prospect of a continental invasion. It is understood that British and American-built tanks are being used in the present offensive.

No attempt is made to minimize the stern tasks ahead of the Red Army on the Don-Volga front. The Germans' resilience and power in defensive fighting are known from bitter experience, reserves are being accumulated hastily to meet the Red Army's advance and time is reducing the advantages gained by the element of surprise—prisoners' testimony agree that the

Continued on Page Eight

GUADALCANAL FOES CUT OFF, KNOX SAYS

Secretary Asserts Enemy Can Not Send In Aid—Nimitz Denies Naval Battle

By CHARLES HURD

Special to THE NEW YORK TIMES.

WASHINGTON, Nov. 24—The Navy believes it has closed the routes by which the Japanese may reinforce their garrisons on Guadalcanal Island, Secretary of the Navy Frank Knox said today. This result was credited to the naval victory recently won by American sea forces against "seemingly hopeless odds" in the waters around the Solomon Islands.

[Admiral Chester W. Nimitz, Commander in Chief of the Pacific Fleet, said yesterday that, so far as he knew, there was no naval action going on in the Solomons area such as had been reported by the Japanese radio Monday night.]

Secretary Knox expressed the belief that our own soldiers and marines now face a straitened enemy, while further dispatches from Guadalcanal reported that the Americans there were extending

Continued on Page Four

Chicago Trio Get Death Penalty For Treason, Wives Prison Terms

Special to THE NEW YORK TIMES.

CHICAGO, Nov. 24—Three German-Americans who aided and sheltered Herbert Hans Haupt, executed Nazi saboteur and spy, were sentenced to death for treason today by Federal Judge William J. Campbell "as a timely and solemn warning to all who would attempt the smallest act of sabotage." Their wives, who were convicted of the same crimes, were ordered to prison for twenty-five years and fined $10,000 each.

"The sentence must serve notice upon the enemy that the cunningly devised scheme for the use of American citizens of German birth as pawns in the game of sabotage and espionage in this country is doomed to failure," the judge asserted.

The men are Hans Max Haupt, father of Herbert, who was captured with seven other saboteurs after they had landed in June from German submarines on the Long Island and Florida coasts; Walter Wilhelm Froehling, uncle of Herbert, and Otto Walter Wergin, close friend of the Haupts and Froehlings. Their wives are Erna Emma Haupt, Lucille Froehling and Kate Martha Wergin. All had been convicted by a jury of eight women and four men on Nov. 14.

Judge Campbell set Jan. 22 as the execution day, but the defense filed an appeal this afternoon, and Paul A. F. Warnholtz, chief counsel, said he would fight the sentences to the Supreme Court.

If the death sentences are sustained the three men will be executed at either the Cook County jail in Chicago or at the State-

Continued on Page Fifteen

12,000 MORE TAKEN

Russians Smash Ahead, Capture Many Places in Multiple Drive

HELP REACHES VOLGA CITY

Column Arrives From North—Three Divisions With Generals Among Forces Encircled

By The Associated Press.

MOSCOW, Wednesday, Nov. 25—The three-month-old Nazi grip on Stalingrad was weakening today after a swiftly advancing Red Army had killed 15,000 more Germans yesterday and captured 12,000, including three divisional generals, in a great Winter offensive rolling so fast that some Nazi units were cut down from behind in panicky retreat.

Russian official announcements raised the toll of Nazis to 77,000 dead or captured, not counting huge numbers of wounded who apparently are freezing to death on the frozen steppes, as did other German units last Winter in the rout from Moscow.

The Red Army's effort to encircle the entire Nazi army stalemated before Stalingrad, estimated at 300,000, clearly was gaining in power. Two communiqués told of vast stocks of war equipment falling to the Soviet tide, of at least one enemy airdrome being seized so swiftly that scores of German planes were unable to take to the air.

Stalingrad Defenders Gain

Inside Stalingrad the Russians in frontal assaults also were gaining against Nazi detachments whose rear communications had been slashed by Russian flanking armies sweeping across the Don River far to the west.

[The German High Command admitted the gravity of the situation by acknowledging the penetration of Nazi defenses southwest of Stalingrad. But it said "countermeasures" were under way and reported "savage battles" in the Don bend region. The London Express quoted a Stockholm report that the Germans had "begun to pull out of Stalingrad."]

The midnight Soviet communiqué said 900 Germans were killed and dozens of enemy blockhouses occupied in a slow but steady advance inside Stalingrad, while in the Caucasus Red Army units cut down additional hundreds of Nazis in successful stands in the Nalchik and Tuapse sectors.

This bulletin added some details to the striking Russian successes above and below Stalingrad and inside the Don River bend, as announced in a special communiqué. One Red Army unit captured a Nazi airdrome so swiftly, it said, that forty-two enemy planes did not have time to take to the air. Twenty-five of these planes were destroyed and the seventeen others were captured intact.

In some sectors there was evident Axis demoralization, because hundreds of fleeing Germans were being struck down from behind as

Continued on Page Eight

Daladier and Others Seen in Nazi Hands

Wireless to THE NEW YORK TIMES.

ON THE SPANISH FRONTIER, Nov. 24—France's former leaders who had been held at the Pourtalet prison in the Pyrenees, including former Premiers Paul Reynaud, Edouard Daladier and Léon Blum and General Maurice Gustav Gamelin, are reported to have been moved to Bordeaux in the last forty-eight hours to be sent to Germany, according to a statement here today by a Frenchman who has just crossed the frontier.

The informant said the dossiers for the Riom war-guilt trials had been demanded by the German Ministry of Justice for study and that Vichy officials had surrendered them to the Germans.

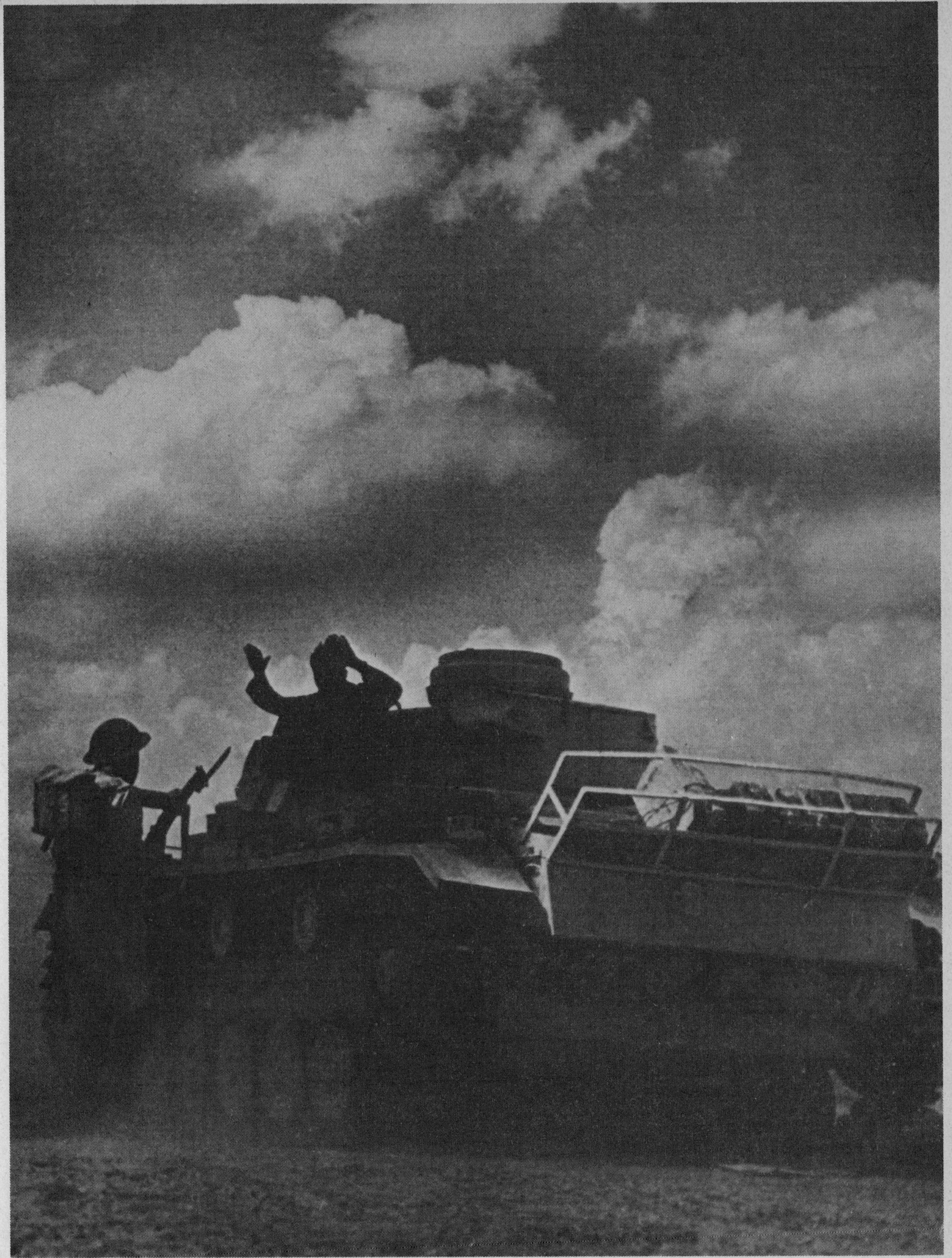

Imperial War Museum

German tank commander surrenders to a British Infantryman during one of many battles for North Africa.

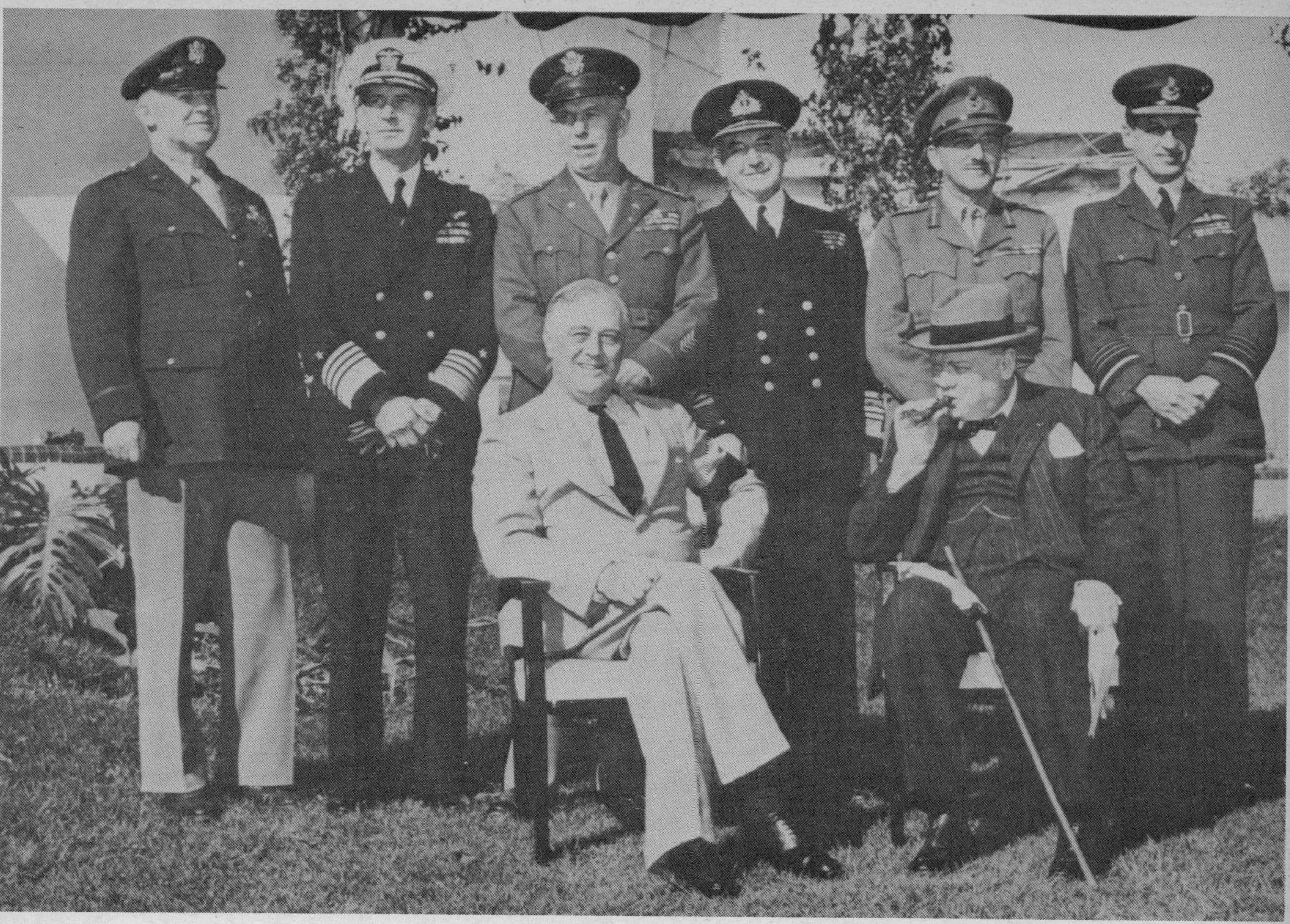

U.S. Air Force

President Franklin Delano Roosevelt with Prime Minister Winston Churchill at the Casablanca Conference.

"All the News That's Fit to Print."

The New York Times.

LATE CITY EDITION
Continued moderately cold and windy today.
Temperatures Yesterday—Max., 48; Min., 30
Sunrise, 8:13 A. M.; Sunset, 6:06 P. M.

VOL. XCII..No. 31,049. Entered as Second-Class Matter. Postoffice, New York, N. Y. NEW YORK, WEDNESDAY, JANUARY 27, 1943. THREE CENTS IN NEW YORK CITY

ROOSEVELT, CHURCHILL MAP 1943 WAR STRATEGY AT TEN-DAY CONFERENCE HELD IN CASABLANCA; GIRAUD AND DE GAULLE, PRESENT, AGREE ON AIMS

15,000 QUIT WORK IN DRESS PAY ROW; PEACE MOVES START

85,000 in 2,000 Shops Here Due to Be Out This Week Unless U. S. Calls Halt

STEELMAN AIDE ARRIVES

But Need for WLB Action Is Seen—Mayor Asks OPA to Modify Price Order

Between 15,000 and 20,000 dressmakers, members of the International Ladies Garment Workers Union, quit their jobs yesterday in what the union called a "spontaneous" stoppage to enforce demands for wage readjustments after the breakdown of negotiations with employers on Monday. No war production is involved.

Both employers and union spokesmen predicted that all 85,000 workers in the industry, affecting 2,000 shops in New York City and vicinity, would be tied up by the end of the week if the stoppage was not arrested. Spokesmen for five employer associations charged the stoppage was in violation of the current agreement in the industry, which does not expire until Jan. 31, 1944.

While David Dubinsky, president of the I. L. G. W. U., reaffirmed the union's willingness to abide by arbitration or to call off the stoppage if the War Labor Board assumes jurisdiction in the controversy, efforts to settle the dispute were begun by the United States Conciliation Service and Mayor La Guardia.

Complaint Filed Against Union

Upon complaint filed with Harry Uviller, impartial chairman of the dress industry, charging violation of contract by the union, Mr. Uviller will confer with employer and union representatives in his office at 1440 Broadway this morning. He, too, however, expressed the belief that the dispute could be settled through action by the War Labor Board.

Involved in the controversy is the declaration by Mr. Dubinsky that the union would oppose the application of the War Labor Board's Little Steel formula in the dress stoppage on the ground that it had been voided by the rise in the cost of living. Acceptance of the union's position would invalidate for all industries subject to President Roosevelt's wage stabilization order the board's criterion of measuring the justification of wage increases on the basis of living costs as they stood in May, 1942.

The position taken by the employers in the dress industry is that while they are cognizant of the justice of the union's demand for a wage equalization because of the rise in living costs, they are unable to grant it as long as prices remain frozen under OPA order.

Mayor Seeks OPA Order Change

Efforts to bring about modification of the OPA order were being pressed by Mayor La Guardia yesterday, as Bernard J. Forman, Federal conciliator, acting on instructions of Dr. John R. Steelman, director of the United States Conciliation Service, arrived in the city and met representatives of the employers and the union. Both employers and union officials were of the opinion that Mr. Forman's intervention was not likely to succeed and that Dr. Steelman would have to ask Frances Perkins, Secretary of Labor, to certify the dispute to the War Labor Board.

After conferring yesterday afternoon at City Hall with George A. Sloan, city Commissioner of Commerce, Mr. La Guardia disclosed that he had recommended to Prentiss Brown, OPA administrator in Washington, that OPA order 287, which fixes maximum prices for the dress industry, be modified. In

Continued on Page Eighteen

Rationalizing of Industry Undertaken in War Drive

WPB Officials Outline Steps Purposing to Make Entire Lines of Enterprise Act as a Single Manufacturer

By The Associated Press.

WASHINGTON, Jan. 26—A far-reaching plan to "rationalize" a vast segment of American industry—to end duplication of effort and other practices described as wasteful—is in the final stages of consideration in the War Production Board, high officials disclosed tonight.

The aim, the officials said, was to increase war production, but they predicted that in peace years the plan would mean more goods for consumers at cheaper prices.

These officials, who prefer to remain unidentified at this time, said the immediate objective was to solve the crucial problem of "components"—the valves, engines, heat exchangers, instruments and other bottleneck items for which many of the "must" war production programs are competing.

The net result, if carried through as contemplated, would be to make an entire industry function as a single manufacturer, ending what is termed the "wasteful" use of critical machines, equipment, manpower and transportation.

Inefficiency results when each of several companies in an industry is making a score of different objects, it was explained. The WPB idea is that total output can be increased if each company is concentrated on a few products. Similarly, the effort will be made to get rid of the waste motion involved when several companies are making several versions of the same product.

WPB intends to attack the problem, it was disclosed, by going direct to industry, bringing leaders from each industry to Washington—probably as WPB employes on a "without compensation" basis—

Continued on Page Fifteen

E. J. FLYNN QUITS PARTY COMMITTEE

Move Apparently Spells Favorable Vote by Senate Group on His Nomination

By W. H. LAWRENCE
Special to The New York Times.

WASHINGTON, Jan. 26—Edward J. Flynn resigned today as a Democratic National Committeeman from New York and this step apparently cleared the way for a close but favorable vote by the Senate Foreign Relations Committee on his nomination to be Minister to Australia.

The resignation was announced by Frank C. Walker, who succeeded Mr. Flynn as chairman of the national committee.

The Senate Foreign Relations Committee will meet in executive session tomorrow morning to vote on recommending Mr. Flynn's nomination. While most observers believed that he would win approval by a very slender margin, opponents were still hopeful that they could deadlock the committee by a tie vote in the absence of favorable proxy from Senator Glass of Virginia, who is ill at his Lynchburg home.

Senate to Vote Monday

The Senate itself will consider the nomination on Monday and a vigorous floor fight is expected.

Mr. Flynn's resignation of all party political positions assured him the vote of Senator Clark of Missouri, who had made this action the price of his support and who had told Democratic leaders that if it were not forthcoming he and Senator Hatch of New Mexico would wage an intensive campaign among Senate Democrats to block Mr. Flynn's confirmation.

Although Mr. Flynn had said when he quit as national chairman that he would retain his committee membership, administration leaders felt that they needed the support of Senators Clark and Hatch and persuaded the New Yorker to reconsider this decision, although it meant, in all probability, that the New York place on the national committee would go to James A. Farley, who now is counted among the anti-New Dealers and an opponent of any effort to win a fourth term for the President.

If Mr. Farley doesn't take the job himself, he is expected to dictate the selection of Mr. Flynn's successor by the New York Democratic Committee.

"With full appreciation of his great services both as chairman and New York National Committeeman, I feel the exercise of his duties in the post to which the President has appointed him and the implied absence from the

Continued on Page Forty-two

250 SLAIN RESISTING NAZIS IN MARSEILLE

Seventy Women Victims of the Fighting as 40,000 Are Ousted From Port Area

By MILTON BRACKER
Special Cable to The New York Times.

LONDON, Jan. 26—One hundred and eighty men and seventy women have been shot in connection with the round-up of what the Germans term "subversive elements" and evacuation of the Old Harbor area of Marseille, according to Swiss reports.

The occupation authorities have reiterated their warning that whoever enters the forbidden area, now under a state of siege, will be executed.

Although naturally more concerned with the return of General Charles de Gaulle from his conference, Fighting French circles in London have closely followed reports from France's greatest seaport, hitherto not regarded as a

Continued on Page Ten

NAZI RING IS CUT UP

Only 12,000 of Foe Left in Stalingrad Force—'Liquidation' Near

RAIL LINES CLEARED

Red Army's Offensives Increase in Violence, Berlin Reports

By The Associated Press.

LONDON, Jan. 26—Russian troops have killed or captured all but 12,000 German troops of the huge forces trapped at Stalingrad and have freed the three main railways radiating westward for the continuing offensive that has carried the Red Army forward 245 miles, Moscow announced tonight in a special communiqué recorded by the Soviet monitor here.

[Soviet troops have entered Stalingrad from the west through the former Nazi seige lines, said a Moscow broadcast recorded by The United Press at London early today.]

Since Jan. 10, the Russians said, they have killed more than 40,000 Germans and captured 28,000, leaving 12,000 split there in two pockets yet to be liquidated.

Two Groups Isolated

"We have not yet liquidated two small enemy groups, separated and isolated from each other, totaling in all no more than 12,000 men, one to the north of Stalingrad and the other nearer to the central part of the town," the communiqué continued. "Both these groups are doomed and their liquidation is only a question of two or three days."

[The Germans said their remaining troops in Stalingrad were concentrated in a narrow space and were continuing their "heroic resistance" under the command of their generals. The Soviet onslaught on large parts of the front were said to have increased in violence.]

Twenty-two Nazi divisions of some 220,000 men had been reported encircled in the Don-Volga pocket before Stalingrad after the Russians began their November offensives above and below the Volga River city.

The Russians threw a cordon

Continued on Page Twelve

War News Summarized

WEDNESDAY, JANUARY 27, 1943

President Roosevelt and Prime Minister Churchill, together with their joint chiefs of staff and other military and civil officials, have concluded a ten-day conference at Casablanca, Morocco, in which a general program of military strategy for 1943 was worked out. The President disclosed that the United Nations would be satisfied with nothing short of the enemy's unconditional surrender. He said the objectives for the year would be to maintain and extend the initiative won late in 1942, to dispatch all possible aid to Russia and to give assistance to the Chinese armies. General Giraud and General de Gaulle met during the conference and reached an agreement to cooperate in the prosecution of the war. [1:8.]

Washington believed that the conference would result in a continuing planned offensive on all fronts and observers were struck by the fact that the aim to win an unconditional surrender of the enemy excluded the possibility of a negotiated peace. [1:5.]

Other dispatches concerning the conference appear on Pages 1 to 6.

United States troops supported by other units broke through a pass northwest of Kairouan in Tunisia and recaptured considerable territory seized by the Germans in a recent clash. Britain's Eighth Army captured Ez Zauia, thirty miles west of Tripoli. [9:1, with map.]

A report was heard in London that the Germans had killed 250 French inhabitants of Marseille, including seventy women, during resistance to their effort to clear the Old Harbor district. Some 40,000 persons were moved out of the area, according to the Vichy radio. [1:3.]

A Soviet special communiqué announced that the Russians had killed or captured all but 12,000 of the Axis soldiers trapped at Stalingrad. Three main railway lines leading out of the city were reported freed. [1:4.] Reports from Berlin reaching Switzerland indicated that the force trapped at Stalingrad had been written off. [12:1.]

President Ryti of Finland, in closing the session of Parliament, expressed the hope that friendly relations would be restored with the United States. [12:4.]

From Australia came a protest by Prime Minister Curtin in an Australia Day broadcast. He said that the Pacific area was too important to be left to a force of "caretakers." [13:2.]

A large force of Japanese planes approaching Guadalcanal was driven off by United States planes and four Zeros were shot down without loss to the Americans. United States ground forces consolidated their position at Kokumbona village. [13:4.]

CAPITAL SEES PLAN

Offensive With Common Strategy Is Viewed by Washington as Key

FRENCH UNION A GAIN

Bar Upon a 'Negotiated Peace' Cited as Blow to Hopes of Axis

By HAROLD CALLENDER
Special to The New York Times.

WASHINGTON, Jan. 26—The meeting at Casablanca of President Franklin D. Roosevelt and Prime Minister Winston Churchill was regarded in official circles here as a council of war designed to clear the way for Allied unity and a common strategy on all fronts, and to plan a continuing offensive whose object is, not the negotiated peace for which the Axis has at times angled and may angle again, but "unconditional surrender" of the enemy. It was the first time this phrase had been used in an official definition of the war aims of the United Nations.

As an expression of the common strategy that is being worked out, it was expected by many that a war council of the "big four"—Britain, Russia, China and the United States—would emerge, and that the mutual aid and coordinated purposes of the United Nations would receive increasing emphasis in the form of more inclusive consultations on all major aspects of the war and on the distribution of the sinews of war in the future.

This was the interpretation placed by observers here tonight upon those words of the official announcement concerning efforts to include Premier Joseph Stalin and Generalissimo Chiang Kai-shek in the dramatic meeting on the coast of Morocco, which symbolized the growing offensive power of the Allies on the southern margin of the European war theatre and the alignment of the bulk of the French Empire on the side of the United Nations.

Parley Essentially Military

It was emphasized in official circles here that the gathering at Casablanca was essentially military, as indicated by the presence there of the highest American and British strategists of the navies, armies and air forces, including the commanders of the North African operations, and that the major preoccupation was the winning of the war rather than political issues, save as they directly affected the grand strategy of the Allied coalition.

Tonight's announcement from Casablanca cleared up some of the mystery that has surrounded the proceedings since Jan. 9, when the press was informed by the Office of Censorship that President Roosevelt was going on a trip and the attention of correspondents was drawn to the code of voluntary censorship, which forbids publication of any hints or speculation about the President's movements.

In the seventeen-day interval of silence that followed, private guesses had placed the President at numerous widely separated spots all the way from Alaska to Moscow. One rumor was that he had gone to London; others had him at intervening points; but most guesses were warm in that they pointed to the coast of Africa as the probable place of his rendezvous with Mr. Churchill and the leaders of the Allied fighting services.

Rumor About Stalin

Some expected that Mr. Stalin and the Chinese Generalissimo would turn up at the appointed meeting place to personify, with the American and British leaders, the over-all unity lately discussed.

It was generally assumed that, wherever the meeting, the question of union of the French forces on a military rather than a political basis and the formulation of

Continued on Page Two

President Pays Surprise Visit To U. S. Troops in Morocco

Roosevelt Reviews Soldiers at Base Outside Casablanca—Visits Graves of Americans Who Fell During Landings

By WALTER LOGAN
United Press Correspondent

CASABLANCA, French Morocco, Jan. 21 (Delayed)—President Roosevelt inspected American troops in French Morocco today, surprising them by his presence and leaving their faces wreathed in smiles.

The President reviewed the troops from a jeep driven by Staff Sergeant Oran Lass of Kansas City, Mo., who was the proudest soldier in the United States Army but maintained an air of impeccable dignity throughout.

In the jeep with the President were Lieut. Gen. Mark Clark, Commander of the United States Fifth Army; Charles Fredericks, the President's personal bodyguard, and the general officer

Continued on Page Five

HONORED BY PRESIDENT

Brig. Gen. William H. Wilbur, who received from Mr. Roosevelt in Africa the Congressional Medal of Honor. Associated Press Wirephoto

[Story on Page 5]

The Official Communique

By The Associated Press.

CASABLANCA, French Morocco, Jan. 26—Following is the text of the official communiqué on the conference of President Roosevelt and Prime Minister Churchill:

The President of the United States and the Prime Minister of Great Britain have been in conference near Casablanca since Jan. 14.

They were accompanied by the combined Chiefs of Staff of the two countries; namely,

FOR THE UNITED STATES:

General George C. Marshall, Chief of Staff of the United States Army; Admiral Ernest J. King, Commander in Chief of the United States Navy; Lieut. Gen. H. H. Arnold, commanding the United States Army Air Forces, and

FOR GREAT BRITAIN:

Admiral of the Fleet Sir Dudley Pound, First Sea Lord; General Sir Alan Brooke, Chief of the Imperial General Staff, and Air Chief Marshal Sir Charles Portal, Chief of the Air Staff.

These were assisted by:

Lieut. Gen. B. B. Somervell, Commanding General of the Services of Supply, United States Army; Field Marshal Sir John Dill, head of the British Joint Staff Mission in Washington; Vice Admiral Lord Louis Mountbatten, Chief of Combined Operations; Lieut. Gen. Sir Hastings Ismay, Chief of Staff to the Office of the Minister of Defense, together with a number of staff officers of both countries.

They have received visits from Mr. Murphy [Robert Murphy, United States Minister in French North Africa] and Mr. Macmillan [Harold Macmillan, British Resident Minister for Allied Headquarters in North Africa]; from Lieut. Gen. Dwight D. Eisenhower, Commander in Chief of the Allied Expeditionary Force in North Africa; from Admiral of the Fleet Sir Andrew Cunningham, naval commander of the Allied Expeditionary Force in North Africa; from Major Gen. Carl Spaatz, air commander of the Allied Expeditionary Force in North Africa; from Lieut. Gen. Mark W. Clark, United States Army [commander of the United States Fifth Army in Tunisia], and, from Middle East Headquarters, from General Sir Harold Alexander, Air Chief Marshal Sir Arthur Tedder and Lieut. Gen. F. M. Andrews, United States Army.

The President was accompanied by Harry Hopkins [chairman of the British-American Munitions Assignment Board] and was joined by W. Averell Harriman [United States defense expediter in England].

With the Prime Minister was Lord Leathers, British Minister of War Transport.

For ten days the combined staffs have been in constant session, meeting two or three times a day and recording progress at intervals to the President and Prime Minister.

The entire field of the war was surveyed theatre by theatre throughout the world, and all resources were marshaled for a more intense prosecution of the war by sea, land, and air.

Nothing like this prolonged discussion between two allies has ever taken place before. Complete agreement was reached between the leaders of the two countries and their respective staffs upon war plans and enterprises to be undertaken during the campaigns of 1943 against Germany, Italy and Japan with a view to drawing the utmost advantage from the markedly favorable turn of events at the close of 1942.

Premier Stalin was cordially invited to meet the President and Prime Minister, in which case the meeting would have been held very much farther to the east. He was unable to leave Russia at this time on account of the great offensive which he himself, as Commander in Chief, is directing.

The President and Prime Minister realized up to the full the enormous weight of the war which Russia is successfully bearing along her whole land front, and their prime object has been to draw as much weight as possible off the Russian armies by engaging the enemy as heavily as possible at the best selected points.

Premier Stalin has been fully informed of the military proposals.

The President and Prime Minister have been in communication with Generalissimo Chiang Kai-shek. They have apprised him of the measures which they are undertaking to assist him in China's magnificent and unrelaxing struggle for the common cause.

The occasion of the meeting between the President and Prime Minister made it opportune to invite General Giraud [General Henri Honoré Giraud, High Commissioner of French Africa] to confer with the Combined Chiefs of Staff and to arrange for a meeting between him and General de Gaulle [General Charles de Gaulle, Fighting French Commander]. The two generals have been in close consultation.

The President and Prime Minister and their combined staffs, having completed their plans for the offensive campaigns of 1943, have now separated in order to put them into active and concerted execution.

LEADERS GO BY AIR

Aim at 'Unconditional Surrender' by Axis, President Says

MILITARY AIDES TALK

French Chiefs Declare Groups Will Unite to Liberate Nation

By DREW MIDDLETON
Special Cable to The New York Times.

CASABLANCA, French Morocco, Jan. 24 (Delayed)—President Roosevelt and Prime Minister Churchill today concluded a momentous ten-day conference in which they planned Allied offensives of 1943 aimed at what the President called the "unconditional surrender" of the Axis powers.

The President flew 5,000 miles across the Atlantic with his Chiefs of Staff to confer with Mr. Churchill and British military, naval and air chieftains in a sun-splashed villa within sound of Atlantic breakers. Every phase of the global war was discussed in conferences lasting from morning until midnight. Both war leaders emphasized that the conference was wholly successful and that complete agreement had been reached on great military enterprises to be undertaken by the United Nations this year.

General Henri Honoré Giraud, High Commissioner for French North Africa, and General Charles de Gaulle, leader of Fighting France, met at the conference and found themselves in accord on the primary task of liberating France from German domination. President Roosevelt predicted that French soldiers, sailors and airmen would fight beside the Allied armies in the liberation of France.

Stalin Kept Informed

The President and Mr. Churchill expressed regret for Premier Joseph Stalin's inability to leave the Russian offensive, which he is directing personally, but emphasized that all results of the conferences had been reported to the Soviet leader. [Generalissimo Chiang Kai-shek was similarly advised, The Associated Press reported.]

Assurance of future world peace will come only as a result of the total elimination of German and Japanese war power, the President declared. He borrowed a phrase from General Grant's famous letter to the Confederate commander at Forts Donelson and Henry—"unconditional surrender"—to describe the only terms on which the United Nations would accept the conclusion of the war.

He emphasized, however, that

Continued on Page Six

Trondheim Blasts Heard in Sweden

By The United Press.

STOCKHOLM, Sweden, Jan. 26—Residents of the Swedish frontier area tonight reported having heard thunderous explosions throughout the day from the direction of Trondheim on the Norwegian coast.

[Trondheim Fjord, reputed still the berth of important German warships, including the battleship Tirpitz, extends inland from Trondheim to within thirty miles of the Swedish border.]

The explosions were described as of an intensity comparable with those of last Spring when British planes bombed the Trondheim area.

Border district residents at first thought the explosions were from gunfire, but later thought it more likely an air raid was under way, advices reaching here said.

However, no planes were visible and the explosions resounded steadily from 10:30 A. M. to 5 P. M. except for brief intervals—an unusually long period for an air attack.

"All the News That's Fit to Print."

The New York Times.

LATE CITY EDITION
Slightly warmer today with moderate winds.
Temperatures Yesterday—Max., 41; Min., 27
Sunrise, 7:57 A. M.; Sunset, 6:34 P. M.

Copyright, 1943, by The New York Times Company.

VOL. XCII..No. 31,063. Entered as Second-Class Matter, Postoffice, New York, N. Y. NEW YORK, WEDNESDAY, FEBRUARY 10, 1943. THREE CENTS IN NEW YORK CITY

PRESIDENT ORDERS 48-HOUR WEEK IN WAR EFFORT; GREAT 'INVASION OF EUROPE' IN 1943 THE GOAL; GUADALCANAL IS OURS; RUSSIANS TAKE BELGOROD

FOE QUITS ISLAND

Japan Abandons Few Troops Remaining on Guadalcanal

SETS NEW STRATEGY

Enemy Hopes to Hold Isles to North—Knox Weighs Moves

By CHARLES HURD
Special to THE NEW YORK TIMES.

WASHINGTON, Feb. 9—The long and hard-fought battle for the island of Guadalcanal in the Solomons apparently has ended, Secretary of the Navy Frank Knox said here today. His declaration, made at a press conference, was the first authoritative statement of a United States victory that has been indicated by the Navy communiqués for the past two or three weeks.

The conquest of this island, or specifically a few square miles of territory around Henderson Airfield on its northern shore, gives American forces undisputed possession both of the airfield and an excellent harbor near by, which becomes a threat to Japan's major bases in the South Pacific. This conclusion was voiced by Secretary Knox.

The Secretary's comment was inspired by a broadcast Japanese communiqué, which announced that units of troops had been withdrawn from Guadalcanal. Mr. Knox said this appeared to be correct. He added the speculative statement that possibly the sea action that was announced as occurring last week and the previous week in the Solomons, with some loss for our Navy, might have been precipitated by the Japanese to cover withdrawal of troops rather than as an attack on our forces.

Question on Resistance

"Has all enemy resistance on the island ceased?" a reporter asked Mr. Knox.

"It has apparently ceased," the Secretary replied, noting that some isolated groups of Japanese still remained there.

The Japanese announcement stated that certain units had been transferred from Guadalcanal and New Guinea early in February.

Secretary Knox told those present at his conference that when he returned from a recent tour of the South Pacific, including a visit to Guadalcanal, he had then stated the opinion that significant Japanese opposition on Guadalcanal had collapsed. He quoted Major Gen. Alexander D. Patch, Army commander on Guadalcanal, as having estimated at the time of his visit (Jan. 21-22) that there were 4,000 to 6,000 enemy troops still on Guadalcanal.

Small Groups Surrounded

"We are satisfied by our air and ground reconnaissance," Mr. Knox said, "that there is no large number of Japanese in one group. Several small groups have been surrounded and cut off from supplies and reinforcements."

When he gave the opinion today that perhaps the recent Japanese naval action, as yet not reported in any detail, may have covered withdrawal efforts, he emphasized that this was only speculative and "we will have to await confirmation."

The isolated groups still on the island, Mr. Knox went on, now face "either death or surrender as their only alternative." The Navy Secretary, speaking in response to questions, said that the conquest of the tiny battlefield has "both positive and negative value."

"The negative value," he explained, "is that it denies to the Japanese an opportunity for raids on our communications. Affirmatively, it has brought us up to where we are in striking distance of some of their most important bases."

His statement obviously referred

Continued on Page Four

RADIATION CENTER OF AMERICAN POWER IN THE PACIFIC

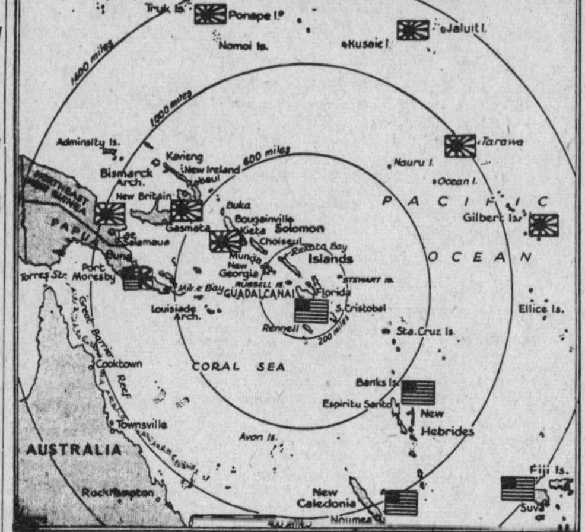

Conquest of Guadalcanal and abandonment of the island by the Japanese have put our forces "in striking distance of some of their most important bases," according to Secretary Knox. Japanese flags on the map show enemy bases in this region and circles indicate distances from Guadalcanal.

PEYROUTON SETS UP ECONOMIC COUNCIL

Group Including Arabs Will Be Elected by Leaders of Various Elements Involved

Wireless to THE NEW YORK TIMES.

ALLIED HEADQUARTERS IN NORTH AFRICA, Feb. 9—Marcel Peyrouton, Governor General of Algeria, created a Permanent Council of War Economy today to tackle the complex Algerian economic situation.

The creation of the council also marks the first step toward a rebirth of representative government here, for its members will be elected by various economic groups. This carries out the prediction of the American Minister, Robert Murphy, that General Henri Honoré Giraud, the French civil and military commander in chief, would move "slowly but surely" toward

Continued on Page Seven

Tunisia Air Offensive Grows, Raises Losses of Axis to 625

By DREW MIDDLETON
Wireless to THE NEW YORK TIMES.

ALLIED HEADQUARTERS IN NORTH AFRICA, Feb. 9—American air power struck heavily at vital Axis air bases, shipping and docks in widespread and successful air assaults over Tunisia yesterday. Eighteen enemy fighters were shot down, increasing the Axis losses since the opening of the North African campaign to 625 aircraft.

At the same time, the astounding story of the one-day toll of the British submarine P-211, revealed today, vividly demonstrated the Royal Navy's part in the offensive against Field Marshal General Erwin Rommel's communications with Italy and Sicily, an offensive that is gaining in weight with each passing week. The P-211 sank three ships and destroyed another in one day of patrol in the Tyrrhenian Sea.

[American Liberator raids on Sicily, reported from Cairo, gave rise to the belief in London that the augmented air warfare

Continued on Page Six

War News Summarized

WEDNESDAY, FEBRUARY 10, 1943

Major news from the battlefronts yesterday concerned the continued rapid Soviet advance and the final defeat of the Japanese land forces on Guadalcanal Island.

Moscow announced the capture of Belgorod, fifty miles northeast of Kharkov, one of the important strong points on the German defense line in Russia, and of Shebekino, forty miles northeast of Kharkov. Russian armies were advancing on Kharkov from three directions. They were also pounding at the outer defenses of Rostov and from Kramatorsk in the Ukraine they continued to thrust southward in an effort to trap the Germans in the Rostov and Taganrog regions. [1:5; map, P. 9.]

Secretary of the Navy Knox announced that serious enemy land resistance had ceased on Guadalcanal. [1:1.] Japanese Imperial Headquarters broadcast an announcement that Japanese forces on Guadalcanal had been evacuated to other points. [4:1.]

Before the House Foreign Affairs Committee the Secretary of the Navy suggested that in connection with lend-lease arrangements the United States should negotiate to acquire after the war a string of naval and air bases reaching across the Pacific into Asiatic waters. [3:1.]

Chungking announced that a major battle was under way on the Yunnan-Burma frontier. The largest number of United States bombers sent against Rangoon in a single day to date heavily bombed the docks and railway facilities. [4:6.]

United States bombers struck heavily at various points in Tunisia and attacked Messina, Sicily. [1:3-4.]

In Algeria Governor General Peyrouton established an economic war council that is to be elected by various economic groups. [1:2.]

General de Gaulle, chief of the Fighting French, told correspondents in London that an agreement with General Giraud's regime in North Africa was impossible until the laws of the French Republic had been reestablished there. [7:1.]

German planes killed two children and two teachers when they bombed schools in Southeastern England. There was a certain amount of air activity on both sides of the Channel. [3:2.]

Prime Minister Churchill, appearing in Parliament after his trip, said that Britain was dipping into her food reserves, but the situation was not crucial. [3:5.]

CLOTHING IN PLENTY, NEEDS NO RATIONING

WPB and OPA Assure Country There Is No Shortage as Shoes Order Starts Buying

By CHARLES E. EGAN.
Special to THE NEW YORK TIMES.

WASHINGTON, Feb. 9 — As a step to halt any rush of consumers to buy clothing on the theory that it would follow shoes in the list of rationed articles, Donald M. Nelson, chairman of the War Production Board, and Prentiss M. Brown, Federal Price Administrator, asserted in a joint statement today that there was no shortage of clothing and therefore no need of rationing.

The statement read as follows:

"Announcement of shoe rationing appears to have stimulated scare buying in some parts of the country. Such buying is unnecessary.

"Supplies of wool in the United States are larger by several hundred million pounds than they were when the Japs struck at Pearl Harbor.

"The War Production Board has not directed the Office of Price Administration to undertake the rationing of clothing.

"The Office of Price Administration has set up no machinery for rationing clothing.

"A continuance of overbuying can create temporary maldistribution of clothing stocks, and its only effect is to handicap persons with a legitimate need for new clothing. It is contrary to the best interest of the war program, and is totally unnecessary for the protection of the individual."

Washington merchants who sold four times the normal amount of apparel items and had to contend with clamoring throngs who sought to stock up on topcoats, suits and accessories were caustic in criticism of the manner in which the government had handled the announcement of the shoe rationing order Sunday. Merchants insisted

Continued on Page Nineteen

NAZI LINE TOTTERS

Kharkov's Peril Grows as Rail Junction Falls in Three-Way Drive

ROSTOV FIGHT RAGES

Counter-Attacks Holding Russians Below Don, Berlin Claims

By The Associated Press.

LONDON, Feb. 9—The entire German line in Southern Russia appeared to be caving in tonight as the Russians, in a special communiqué recorded here by the Soviet monitor, announced the capture of Belgorod with a smashing Red Army blow that further imperiled Kharkov, chief Nazi base east of the Dnieper River.

Belgorod was the second huge German base and railway center, held tenaciously through all the Russian counter-offensives of the Winter of 1941-42 and the Spring of 1942, to fall to the Red Army in forty-eight hours. The city is only fifty miles northeast of Kharkov, industrial center of the Ukraine, and is seventy-eight miles southeast of Kursk, the big defense center that fell only yesterday.

Along with Belgorod, the Russians took Shebekino, only forty miles northeast of Kharkov's city limits and twenty miles southeast of Belgorod. Belgorod is at the junction of the Kursk-Kharkov line and a handy railway that runs northwest to Gomel and the central front. One of Kharkov's strongest outer defenses, it was a nut that Russian armies tried in vain to crack a year ago.

Nazi Supply Lines Tangled

The speed with which the Russian forces were toppling strong German defense centers one after another apparently had tied German communications and transportation into knots, and everywhere along a 500-mile snowy front, from Novorossiisk in the Caucasus to north of Orel, the Red Army was reporting mounting successes.

[The German communiqué reported heavy defensive battles "against enemy attempts to break though and outflank German positions, conducted with large forces." German counter-attacks in defense of Rostov were reported. On the lower Don, in the entire Donets area and west of the Oskol River, Soviet attacks on a broad front were said to have been repulsed in fierce fighting or checked by counter-attacks.]

Orel, at the top of the line, 200 miles south of Moscow, appeared to be left dangerously suspended by the fall of Kursk to the south and a massive thrust past that former German bastion toward Lgov

Continued on Page Eight

WLB Denies Pay Increase In 'Big Four' Packers Case

Industry and Public Members Outvote Labor Group on Cost-of-Living Plea and Hold to the 'Little Steel' Formula

By LOUIS STARK
Special to THE NEW YORK TIMES.

WASHINGTON, Feb. 9—Refusing to modify its "Little Steel" formula, the War Labor Board denied a wage increase to 180,000 employes of the "Big Four" meat packing companies today and thus presaged a showtown between the Administration and John L. Lewis.

Wage demands of the packing house employes and those of the 450,000 bituminous coal miners are parallel inasmuch as both groups of employes have received wage increases above the 15 per cent rise in living costs between January, 1941, and May, 1942.

The WLB's 7-to-4 decision, concurred in by public and employer members while labor members dissented, stood squarely behind the anti-inflation act of Congress of Oct. 2, 1942, and President Roosevelt's executive order the next day naming James F. Byrnes as Director of Economic Stabilization.

The board granted to the unions maintenance of membership and the check-off. The industry members dissented on these provisions and also on those providing retroactive overtime pay, termination of the contract date and premium for night work.

In a concurring opinion on the wage question, the industry members urged that extension of the present forty-hour work week to forty-eight hours would permit many workers, including packing-house employes, to increase their "take home" earnings while, at the same time the longer work week would ease pressure on the board for wage increases to influence the flow of manpower.

The dissent of labor members will not be made public for a day or two.

Among the wage cases, besides that of the miners, which will be affected by the packing house decision are the recommendations for

Continued on Page Seventeen

VOTE PAY INQUIRY ON SUBVERSIVES

Members of House Adopt Cannon Resolution for Hearings on Charges

By HENRY N. DORRIS
Special to THE NEW YORK TIMES.

WASHINGTON, Feb. 9—By an overwhelming voice vote House Democrats and Republicans joined today in adopting the Cannon resolution to investigate charges of radicalism in the Federal Government personnel.

A five-man subcommittee of the Appropriations Committee, to be appointed tomorrow by its chairman, Representative Cannon, was instructed under the resolution to accord hearings to all government employes accused by the Dies committee or other groups of communistic affiliations. Mr. Cannon promised that these hearings would be conducted promptly, so that the House could determine whether to strike at "convicted" radicals by cutting them off the Federal payroll through riders to appropriation bills as they come up.

After adopting the resolution the House agreed by a roll-call vote of 267 to 136 to strike out of the Treasury - Postoffice supply bill an amendment by Representative Hendricks, previously adopted, denying further pay to William

Continued on Page Seventeen

48-HR. WORK AREAS LIMITED AT FIRST

WMC Aide Doubts It Will Ever Be Applied Here Unless Situation Gets 'Tighter'

By The Associated Press.

WASHINGTON, Feb. 9—Paul V. McNutt, War Manpower Commissioner, said tonight that "until further notice" the executive order establishing the 48-hour week would apply only to thirty-two "labor shortage" areas listed by him.

In those areas, it will apply to all employment, covering retail stores, newspapers and even domestic servants, Deputy Commissioner Fowler V. Harper said, and will be mandatory rather than be merely a statement of policy which they may follow or disregard.

While the order is to take effect immediately in these areas, employers will receive time to attain a 48-hour week gradually over a period of several weeks.

Mr. McNutt, in a statement, made this comment on the President's order.

"The purpose of the executive order is to make more manpower available as needed and to increase production. It is imperative that this be done in an orderly manner.

"Those establishments in which the minimum work week is less than forty-eight hours are to stop recruiting (labor) at once unless they can go to a forty-eight-hour week without need for releasing workers or due to expansion or production schedules still need more workers.

"They will go on a forty-eight-hour week in such a manner as will assure orderly absorption of surplus workers by absorption or transfer within the employers' operations.

"No employer should prior to March 31 release workers for the purpose of attaining the forty-eight-hour week. If by March 31, 1943, an employer has not attained a forty-eight-hour week without the need for releasing workers for other employment, he will advise the area representative of the War Manpower Commission of what number need be released to attain a forty-eight-hour week. The employer will at that time present a proposed schedule for release of workers for further absorption within his own plant in order to attain the forty-eight-hour week. The area director will then authorize a proper schedule of release or

Continued on Page Eighteen

Labor Party Bill in State Senate Is Backed by Democratic Leader

Special to THE NEW YORK TIMES.

ALBANY, Feb. 9—Senator John J. Dunnigan, Democratic minority leader, appeared today as the sponsor of the first program bill submitted by the American Labor party. The bill, sent up by the State Committee of the Labor party, would make the State and all its agencies the enforcement officers for Federal price-fixing regulations for protection of the consumer.

The political significance of Senator Dunnigan's sponsorship of the measure lies in the fact that never before, in the six sessions that the American Labor party has existed as a recognized political group, has any Democratic leader appeared as sponsor for any of its measures.

Senator Dunnigan made his move with the background of the last election in mind. He is convinced, it was learned, that the Democratic party in the city and the State must work with the Labor party, if it is to win the Mayoralty or the Governorship the next time either is at stake.

Senator Dunnigan, it was learned, made the move on his own responsibility, after consultation with leaders of the American Labor party. The Assembly sponsor of the measure was Assemblyman Crews, Brooklyn Republican, who has already introduced some of the Labor party's measures.

Governor Dewey has conferred with Labor party leaders over the telephone and presumably would not be adverse to winning the group to his support. He has had under consideration for some time the appointment of a man from that party to his Cabinet.

There were two other signs in the Legislature today of activity and alertness on the Democratic side, which up to now had been quiescent to the point of arousing comment.

Senator Gutman of Brooklyn

Continued on Page Forty-six

SHARP RISE IN PAY

Overtime Rates Stand for Those Now on 40-Hour Basis

NOT EFFECTIVE HERE

Order Applies at Start to 32 Areas—Plan Detailed by Byrnes

Byrnes's speech and the 48-hour week order appear on Page 18.

Special to THE NEW YORK TIMES.

WASHINGTON, Feb. 9—A minimum wartime work week of forty-eight hours was decreed tonight by President Roosevelt. Paul V. McNutt, War Manpower Commission chairman, announced that it would apply immediately to thirty-two labor shortage areas, not including New York City.

Making public the Presidential order in a nation-wide broadcast, James F. Byrnes, Director of Economic Stabilization, pictured it as one step in general preparations for an Allied invasion of Europe "within a measurable period of time," presumably in 1943.

To prepare the way, prices and wages must be kept down, Mr. Byrnes said, asserting that the Administration would stand pat on the "Little Steel" wage formula and other wage and price control measures

His position on wages was supported by a War Labor Board decision denying employes of the "Big Four" packing companies an increase in pay, holding it would be a violation of that formula.

Weekly Wage Earnings to Rise

For workers who heretofore have been on a forty-hour week, the President's executive order ultimately will result in a 30-per-cent increase in pay at time and one-half for the additional eight hours under the Forty-Hour Week Act, which was not affected by the order.

For the 15,434,000 workers in manufacturing industries who put in an average of forty-four hours a week in November, the order will eventually mean an average increase of 13.6 per cent in weekly wages.

The President's order and Mr. Byrnes's speech marked the opening of a government campaign to win support from the people in anticipation of a showdown fight with John L. Lewis, president of the United Mine Workers of America, who has demanded a $2 per day wage increase for 450,000 soft-coal miners.

Under the "Little Steel" formula, which limits general pay increases to a total of 15 per cent since Jan. 1, 1941, in order to compensate for increased living costs up to May, 1942, the bituminous miners would not be entitled to any further increase.

The 48-hour order, which applies to all war and non-war

Continued on Page Eighteen

Churchill on Radio Soon About His Trip

By The Associated Press.

LONDON, Wednesday, Feb. 10—London's morning newspapers said today that Prime Minister Winston Churchill would discuss his recent travels in a broadcast to the nation, scheduled tentatively for next Sunday or the following Sunday, Feb. 21.

"He will deal at length with his recent travels and talks with President Roosevelt and warn the country that in spite of our successes there are hard days ahead," said The Daily Mail.

The Prime Minister, who returned Sunday from his trip to North Africa and the Middle East, told the House of Commons yesterday that he would make a statement soon on the war situation.

U.S. Marine Corps

The bodies of two Japanese jungle fighters are half buried on the beach at Guadalcanal in the Solomons.

"All the News That's Fit to Print."

The New York Times.

LATE CITY EDITION
Continued cold and windy today.
Temperatures Yesterday—Max., 34; Min., 22
Sunrise, 7:56 A. M.; Sunset, 6:26 P. M.

VOL. XCII..No. 31,065. Entered as Second-Class Matter, Postoffice, New York, N. Y. NEW YORK, FRIDAY, FEBRUARY 12, 1943. THREE CENTS IN NEW YORK CITY

CHURCHILL PLEDGES INVASION WITHIN 9 MONTHS; SEES GAINS AT SEA; SAYS 500,000 ARE IN AFRICA; EISENHOWER, PROMOTED, IN SUPREME COMMAND

50 CITY BUILDINGS NOW FACE CLOSING IN FUEL SHORTAGE

Court in Brooklyn Must Shut Down and Others Are Said to Be 'in a Bad Way'

GOVERNOR CONFERS HERE

Seeks to Build Up Reserves in State—Fire Houses, Police Stations Are Affected

The Pennsylvania Avenue Court House in Brooklyn, which houses both Magistrate's and Municipal Courts, will definitely have to shut down and about ten other courts will have to curtail their activities because they have burned their fuel oil rations too fast, City Fuel Oil Administrator Edwin A. Salmon declared yesterday.

The restaurant in the Bronx Terminal Market must close "immediately" for the same reason, according to Mr. Salmon, who said that about fifty of the 650 public buildings in this city which burn oil were "in a bad way." Most of the fifty buildings, Mr. Salmon said, would have to operate at lower temperatures.

It was in Pennsylvania Avenue Court that the leaders of the Brooklyn murder syndicate were first brought to book and held on vagrancy charges, while Kings County District Attorney William O'Dwyer built up the murder cases which later led to smashing of the racket ring.

Although the city will not appeal to the Office of Price Administration for extra rations for any of the buildings that have been unable to budget their three-month allowance so that it will reach to March 31, when the next period begins, an appeal has been made to the Petroleum Administrator for War in behalf of the municipal fireboats, Mr. Salmon said.

Listing Called "Oversight"

The appeal, said Mr. Salmon, was made necessary by "an oversight" through which PAW failed to list fireboats among the essential users exempt from the 40 per cent cut in fuel oil rations for purposes other than heating.

"It is impossible to cut the rations of fireboats," he said. "They must keep steam up at all times. The city's appeal has been made for restoration of that cut, and it will be granted."

Four fire houses which have been burning fuel oil faster than their rations warrant will, however, have to get along until March 31 on what is left of their current allotment, Mr. Salmon said. The houses are in the Bronx, Brooklyn and Queens.

While the municipal administration wrestled with its own heating problem, Governor Dewey, in the city for a short visit, conferred yesterday at the Hotel Roosevelt with PAW officials and petroleum industry representatives on steps that might be taken during the warm months to build up fuel oil reserves throughout the State.

Transportation and storage and the possibility of making greater use of the State Barge Canal for bringing in petroleum supplies were discussed.

Distribution Gains Seen

The petroleum experts and the Governor also took up the recent critical distribution situation that led Mr Dewey to order an investigation by Attorney General Nathaniel L. Goldstein. Mr. Dewey was told that while the fuel oil shortage was still serious, the distribution problem had been greatly improved and that holders of ration coupons could, in most cases, redeem them for fuel oil without difficulty.

Among those at the conference with Mr. Dewey were Walter P. Heddon, director of port development of the Port of New York Authority; William C. Eberle, director of the district PAW transpor-

Continued on Page Thirty-eight

Victory Bond Drive in April Will Seek $12,906,000,000

Morgenthau Hopes New Appeal Will Yield at Least as Much as the Sum Obtained in December and Hails Small Investors

By FREDERICK BARKLEY
Special to THE NEW YORK TIMES.

WASHINGTON, Feb. 11—Secretary Morgenthau disclosed today that the next large financing operation of the Treasury Department would come in April and that it would seek to get "at least as much as and probably more than" the record-breaking $12,906,000,000 obtained from individual and corporate investors in the December Victory Loan drive.

The Secretary, just returned from a vacation in Cuba, told his first press conference since December that he expected to spend most of his time between now and April working on plans for the second Victory Loan campaign planned for that month.

Although he voiced hope for larger returns to the Treasury than were yielded in the first drive, he said that the amount which would be asked from investors had not yet been decided. In the first drive the goal was set at $9,000,000,000 and this objective was exceeded by more than 35 per cent. This permitted postponement of the second drive until April, whereas the Treasury's original plan was to hold one either in late February or early March.

At the same time Mr. Morgenthau released statistics which he said showed that voluntary war-bond investments in the present war exceeded any previous government financing in world history, both as to dollar volume and the number of people participating therein.

From the inception of the war-bond program in May, 1941, through December, 1942, the statement said, nearly 50,000,000 Americans bought the $25 maturity value war-savings bonds at a cost price of more than $7,000,000,000.

Continued on Page Thirty-two

ARNOLD NOMINATED FOR CIRCUIT COURT

President Names 'Trust Buster' to Succeed Rutledge on Washington Bench

Special to THE NEW YORK TIMES.

WASHINGTON, Feb. 11—Thurman Arnold, familiarly known as the "trust buster" of the Department of Justice, was named by President Roosevelt today as an associate justice of the Circuit Court for the District of Columbia, to take the place of Wiley B. Rutledge, recently confirmed by the Senate for a Supreme Court seat.

The Arnold nomination came as no surprise, for when President Roosevelt chose Mr. Rutledge for the highest court, on Jan. 11, it was indicated that the assistant attorney general could have the appellate court vacancy if he desired.

Washington has been filled with stories of Mr. Arnold's being "kicked upstairs" in order to call

Continued on Page Thirty-eight

HOUSE TAKES STEPS TO RECLAIM POWERS

Adopts, 294 to 50, Move to Set Up Executive Agencies Study —Funds Inquiry Voted

By HENRY N. DORRIS
Special to THE NEW YORK TIMES.

WASHINGTON, Feb. 11—The House moved in two new directions today toward reclaiming some of the power it delegated to the executive department, and halting alleged abuses of the powers, by adopting resolutions to set up a new investigating committee and giving subpoena powers to the Appropriations Committee.

The first resolution, adopted by a roll-call vote of 294 to 50, was offered by Representative Smith of Virginia. It would set up a seven-man committee to investigate government agencies and bureaus to determine whether they have exceeded delegated authority.

The second resolution, giving

Continued on Page Thirty-eight

War News Summarized

FRIDAY, FEBRUARY 12, 1943

Prime Minister Churchill delivered yesterday his anticipated report on the Casablanca conference to the House of Commons. He declared that the meeting had laid out United Nations offensive plans for the next nine months and that there were almost 500,000 Allied troops in Africa now. He was optimistic about the war against the U-boats, disclosing that sinkings of them had reached a new peak and that Allied ship losses caused by them during the last two months had been the lowest in a year. [1:8.]

Another repercussion of the Casablanca conference came with the announcement of a unified command in North Africa. General Eisenhower will be the commander in chief. Next under him will be General Sir Harold Alexander, Air Marshal Sir Arthur Tedder and Admiral of the Fleet Sir Andrew Cunningham. The North African commander was promoted by President Roosevelt to the temporary rank of full general. [1:6-7.]

It was also announced that Lieut. Gen. Arnold, chief of the United States Army Air Forces, and Field Marshal Dill had visited India and China to discuss war plans with Field Marshal Wavell and Generalissimo Chiang Kai-shek. [1:7.]

The British Eighth Army had its first clash of any importance with Marshal Rommel's troops in Tunisia when the enemy threw tanks into an engagement east of Ben Gardane. In Northern Tunisia Allied forces were said to have passed to the attack in the Mateur area, about fifteen miles south of Bizerte, but the report was not confirmed. According to the dispatch, the Allied troops advanced eight miles and gained their primary objectives. [1:5.]

General Juin, French commander in North Africa, in an order of the day to his troops announced that some of his forces were being withdrawn from action to be re-equipped and trained by the Allies under his supervision. [6:3.]

Meanwhile, in a smashing thirty-five-mile advance from Barvenkova, Russian forces seized the town of Lozovaya in the Ukraine, cutting the main railroad from Kharkov to the Crimea. This push put the Red Army only sixty-five miles east of Dniepropetrovsk and the Dnieper River. Before Rostov the Russians continued to advance. [1:4, Map, P. 8.]

General MacArthur's headquarters reported that the Japanese had been decisively defeated in the Wau region of New Guinea and were retiring toward Mubo, twelve miles from the big enemy base at Salamaua. Two hundred more enemy dead were said to have been counted following recent fighting. [1:5-6.]

RUSSIANS SWEEP ON

Cut Key Kharkov Line at Lozovaya in Drive Toward Dnieper

ROSTOV RING TIGHTER

Red Army Takes Towns North of City, Widens Grip on Black Sea

By The Associated Press.

LONDON, Feb. 11—The Red Army, in its smashing semi-encirclement of Kharkov, has cut the Ukraine bastion's main railway to the south and the Crimea by capturing the key rail junction of Lozovaya, the Moscow radio announced tonight in a special communiqué recorded here by the Soviet monitor.

The capture of Lozovaya apparently represented a thirty-five-mile advance westward from Barvenkova by a force that, threatening at any moment to turn southward toward the Sea of Azov, is menacing from the rear hundreds of thousands of German troops in the area of Rostov.

Kharkov, which has been the Germans' strongest position in all Russia east of the Dnieper, already has had the main railway from the north cut and is engulfed by Red Army troops on a fifty-mile arc reaching as close as twenty-two miles.

Thrust Aimed for Dnieper

The Red Army's westward push to Lozovaya brings it within sixty-five miles of the great Dnieper River, along which many observers believe the Germans are planning to make a stand in retreat. From Lozovaya, which is seventy-five miles south of Kharkov, the nearest point on the Dnieper is the city of Dniepropetrovsk, site of the great hydroelectric dam that the Russians destroyed in their retreat more than a year ago.

[The Germans intend to withdraw their line to the Dnieper and Dvina Rivers if their present positions prove untenable, The United Press reported from Stockholm on "good authority." Such a withdrawal would mean abandonment of Estonia and half of Latvia. The German communiqué reported "considerable defensive successes" with increasing counter-attacks.]

By knifing through to the Kharkov-Crimean railway at Lozovaya the Russians have cut off the German armies at Kharkov from direct communication with those in the Donets Basin. Lozovaya was taken by the Germans in their initial push through this area in the Fall of 1941, was recaptured by the Russians on Jan. 30, 1942, in the Red Army's first Winter offensive, and then was won back by the Germans in their Summer offensive of 1942.

Rostov Ring Contracts

While General Kulagin's forces in this action further increased the threat to the German forces at Rostov, other Russian forces in the immediate vicinity of the Caucasus gateway drove in still closer. The official German agency D. N. B. acknowledged a Red Army flank attack across the ice of the Sea of Azov in the area of the Don estuary, but said it collapsed under Nazi artillery fire.

The Germans also told of Russian pressure on the Nazi Caucasus forces surrounded in the vicinity of the Black Sea naval base of Novorossiisk, reporting that Soviet reinforcements had landed during the night near the base.

[The London radio reported that Novorossiisk was "to a great extent in the hands of the Russians," according to the Office of War Information.]

A Moscow broadcast, also re-

Continued on Page Eight

FIGHT BY ROMMEL

German Tanks and Guns Battle 8th Army Units—Ben Gardane the Prize

GAIN BY ALLIES CITED

British-French Thrust of Eight Miles in Mateur Area Is Reported

By Reuter.

WITH THE BRITISH EIGHTH ARMY in Tunisia, Feb. 11—Field Marshal General Erwin Rommel is showing fight at last. In the biggest action since his belated stand at El Agheila, Libya, he has thrown tanks, infantry and artillery against forward forces of the British Eighth Army in the marshy frontier area of Tunisia.

The fight has developed into a battle for the mud tracks that lead directly to the northwest—to the important center of Ben Gardane. Both sides are deploying light mobile forces.

Use of tanks usually foreshadows withdrawal by Marshal Rommel, but on this occasion it is prompted not only by anxiety for his forces on the coast, which are likely to be cut off, but also by the threat to Ben Gardane with its promise of easier movements on better tracks.

Tanks also have been put in to counterbalance the growing grip by units of the British Seventh Armored Division, which have thrust across the frontier south of the great marshes of Marset El Briga.

This move apparently took the Germans by surprise. They never believed that the British could move so quickly in heavy going after rains.

Eight-Mile Drive Reported

LONDON, Feb. 11 (AP)—British and French troops were reported tonight by a field correspondent in the Mateur area to have set the long-dormant northern front in Tunisia into action with a continuing attack that had advanced them about eight miles.

The report came from a Reuter correspondent in the Mateur sector—fifteen to twenty miles south of Bizerte—who declared that Allied forces, including British and French Commando troops, had attacked the Italian-held line in the northern area at dawn yesterday.

The smash carried eight miles deep over an area of about 100 square miles, he said, adding:

"By evening the men reached their primary objectives.

"According to information so far available, the operation has gone well, but full results will not be known until the second sweep now in progress has been completed."

There was no word of the attack immediately from any other source.

Wireless to THE NEW YORK TIMES.

ALLIED HEADQUARTERS IN NORTH AFRICA, Feb. 11—The

Continued on Page Two

THE NEW UNITED NATIONS SET-UP IN AFRICA

The map shows General Eisenhower's command, stretching from the west coast of Africa to the Egyptian border. The chart depicts the organization of his staff. How French General Giraud fits into this picture was not disclosed in yesterday's announcements.

British Land, Air, Sea Chiefs To Serve Under Eisenhower

By DREW MIDDLETON
Wireless to THE NEW YORK TIMES.

ALLIED HEADQUARTERS IN NORTH AFRICA, Feb. 11—The strongest possible team of Allied commanders, including what General Dwight D. Eisenhower called "the three stars of the British Empire," has been formed under the direct command of General Eisenhower for the final drive against the Axis forces in Tunisia. The Britons are General Sir Harold R. L. G. Alexander, Admiral Sir Andrew Browne Cunningham and Air Marshal Sir Arthur Tedder.

This group, serving under its American commander, will probably also be the directing body of the first great Allied attack into Europe, for which the clearing of Tunisia is prerequisite. The British Eighth and First Armies and their American comrades of the Fifth Army and other forces probably provide the spearhead for that attack.

[The advancement of the American commander to the temporary rank of full general was announced by President Roosevelt yesterday.]

Command Area Defined

The Allied North African theatre, of which General Eisenhower is Commander in Chief, extends in theory from Casablanca, French Morocco, east to the Tripolitanian frontier as a result of the command changes announced today. For practical purposes, however, it extends farther east to the British Army's supply bases in Tripolitania and Libya.

General Alexander, a hard-bitten veteran of Dunkerque and Burma, is to have command under General Eisenhower of all British, American and French ground forces east of Algiers. General Sir Bernard L. Montgomery's veteran British Eighth Army and Lieut. Gen. Kenneth A. N. Anderson's British First Army come under General Alexander's immediate di-

Continued on Page Three

Japanese Smashed in Wau Area; Flee Toward Base Near Salamaua

By The United Press.

AT UNITED NATIONS HEADQUARTERS, Australia, Friday, Feb. 12—The Japanese have been "decisively defeated" in the Wau sector of New Guinea on the approaches to enemy-held Salamaua in a twelve-day encounter that cost them nearly 1,000 dead and many more wounded, the Allied command announced today.

The Japanese, whose main lines were pushed back six miles on Wednesday by Australian jungle fighters, are retreating toward the village of Mubo, only twelve miles southwest of the port of Salamaua, which the Japanese have held since March, 1942. The Wednesday fighting was outside the former gold-mining town of Wau, which is thirty-five miles southwest of Salamaua.

The communiqué announced that an additional 200 Japanese dead had been counted in the area, most of which were counted yesterday after the ferocious Australian attack cracked the enemy lines on Wednesday after they began their drive on Tuesday.

The estimated 1,000 killed since Jan. 30 ran the total Japanese dead in the Wau Mubo area for this year to about 1,500. A total of 416 was reported killed during January, according to Allied communiqués which recorded two Allied raids lasting three days each, the last of which ended on Jan. 29.

A headquarters spokesman added

Continued on Page Ten

ALLIED GENERALS SEE CHIANG, WAVELL

Gen. Arnold and Marshal Dill Visit China and India to Press War on Japan

By The Associated Press.

NEW DELHI, India, Feb. 11—American and British generals have concluded ten days of conferences in India and in China, where they consulted Generalissimo Chiang Kai-shek on ways to press home the battle to Japan.

A joint war communiqué today said "a complete accord was reached in coordination of offensive plans and signifying the united determination of the powers concerned to insure full cooperation and mutual assistance against the Japanese."

The presence of the war leaders in India and China gave rise to the belief that the Oriental theatre would blaze with new Allied offensive action. One immediate result is expected to be an increase in supplies to China.

Confer With Wavell

Field Marshal Sir John Dill, British joint staff mission member, and Lieut. Gen. Henry H. Arnold, United States Army Air Chief, reached India with their staffs about ten days ago from the unconditional surrender conference at Casablanca. Representing Prime Minister Churchill and President Roosevelt, they conferred with Field Marshal Sir Archibald P. Wavell. After inspecting military installations in Eastern India, Marshal Dill and General Arnold flew over the Himalayas for discussions with General Chiang.

Brig. Gen. A. C. Weddemeyer, representing the United States Chief of Staff General George C. Marshall, accompanied them.

In Chungking the conference was joined by Lieut. Gen. Joseph W. Stillwell, General Chiang's American chief of staff, and General Ho Ying-ching, Chinese Minister of War. After leaving Chungking, the Dill-Arnold party returned to India for final conferences with Marshal Wavell.

The communiqué said that subsequent conferences would be held between Marshal Wavell and General Douglas MacArthur, United

Continued on Page Two

TO BLEED GERMANY

Prime Minister in Talk to Commons Declares Aim to Smash Nazis

TALKS OF LANDINGS

Says Fight on U-Boats Shows Steady Gain Since Start of War

The text of Mr. Churchill's address in Commons, Page 4.

By The Associated Press.

LONDON, Friday, Feb. 12—Prime Minister Winston Churchill, disclosing that nearly half a million Allied troops were now in Africa at the great bridgehead to Europe and that the Casablanca parleys had produced an immense and detailed Allied offensive pattern for the next nine months, solemnly proclaimed yesterday the Allied resolve to make the Nazis "burn and bleed" on other fronts as they had already over the length of Russia.

In an exuberant appearance before the House of Commons, where, as he looked out upon the grand vista of the war, he found obvious difficulty in adhering to what he called "the strictest standards of anti-complacency opinions," the Prime Minister made these disclosures:

First—"We have now a complete plan of action which comprises apportionment of forces as well as their direction, and this plan we are going to carry out according to our policy during the next nine months, before the end of which we [Mr. Churchill and President Roosevelt] will make efforts to meet again. * * * Everything in human power is being done and will be done to bring British and American forces into action against the enemy with the utmost speed and energy and on the largest scale."

Battle Against U-Boat Vital

Second, that the Allies were drawing steadily ahead toward winning the greatest of all battles of this war, a battle that stood at the forefront of every other discussion at Casablanca—the battle against the submarine.

Third, that the supreme commander of the Allied armies of North Africa was General Dwight D. Eisenhower, U. S. A. ("one of the finest men I ever knew," Mr. Churchill observed) and that Britain would gladly and loyally go forward as subordinates to this essentially American enterprise.

"Great Britain and the United States," the Prime Minister told the House proudly, "are now warrior nations, walking in fear of the Lord, very heavily armed and

Continued on Page Five

President Reports On Africa Tonight

Special to THE NEW YORK TIMES.

WASHINGTON, Feb. 11—President Roosevelt will report to the country by radio at 9:30 o'clock, E. W. T. tomorrow night on his Casablanca war conferences with Prime Minister Churchill, the White House stated.

The President's speech, which is to be broadcast by all radio networks, probably will deal also with problems of the home front, including the fight against inflation and the effort to keep both wages and prices stabilized, it was indicated.

The speech will take up about twenty minutes, according to Stephen T. Early, White House press secretary.

Mr. Early said also that the President would make a speech on Feb. 22 to the country and celebrants at Washington Day birthday dinners sponsored by the Democratic National Committee as a means of raising funds for party activities.

Three leading figures in the American high command. From left:,Lieutenant General Omar Bradley, Supreme Commander Dwight D. Eisenhower, and the Third Army's General George Patton.

United Press International

Germans lie dead where Russian artillery and machine gun fire mowed them down.

"All the News That's Fit to Print."

The New York Times.

LATE CITY EDITION
Slightly warmer today with gentle to moderate winds.
Temperatures Yesterday—Max., 32; Min., 21
Sunrise, 7:54 A. M.; Sunset, 6:27 P. M.

VOL. XCII..No. 31,066. Entered as Second-Class Matter, Postoffice, New York, N. Y. NEW YORK, SATURDAY, FEBRUARY 13, 1943. THREE CENTS IN NEW YORK CITY

PRESIDENT PLEDGES MANY INVASIONS IN EUROPE, OUSTING FOE FROM CHINA AND ATTACK ON JAPAN; RUSSIANS TIGHTEN TWO TRAPS, TAKE KRASNODAR

RULING HITS SPORTS IN COLLEGES PICKED FOR ARMY TRAINING

Chief of Special Courses Says Soldiers Will Have No Time for Varsity Teams

PROGRAM BEGINS MARCH 1

Athletic Officials, Surprised by Ban, Hope to Carry On for Those Not in Service

By The United Press.

WASHINGTON, Feb. 12—The Army today struck a heavy blow at football and other major college sports when it ruled that students under its new specialized training program at colleges and universities could not participate in intercollegiate athletics.

Colonel Herman Beukema, director of the program, said at a press conference that the intensity of the Army's heavy training schedule would preclude participation in such activities.

He said the schools would decide whether they could maintain a normal athletic program with civilian students only, but the ruling appeared to presage difficult sledding for football particularly, inasmuch as selective service "rejects" and youths under 18 soon will comprise the greater part of the civilian student body.

The Navy, a joint participant with the Army in the college training program, has not disclosed whether it will follow the Army's lead.

Several hundred colleges and universities will feel the impact of the decision. The War Manpower Commission already has announced 271 schools at which certain advanced Army and Navy courses will be given under the program, and another long list of institutions eligible to give more elementary courses will be issued shortly.

Beukema said the first courses under the Army phase of the program would begin March 1 and that the program would be in full swing by April 1. No contracts with institutions have been signed by the Army or Navy, but they will be shortly.

50,000 Graduates This Year

Apart from aviation cadets, the Army program will turn out approximately 50,000 students this year and in 1944 probably about 150,000.

Officer candidate schools generally will have first claim on college youths on completion of their basic training at Army camps, Beukema said. Youths of sufficient maturity and qualifications will go directly to such schools.

Those who need further development and others with special technical qualifications who require additional specialized training will be assigned to colleges and universities under the plan.

Selection of candidates for the first courses—advanced engineering in at least one university in each service command—will begin in a few days at Army camps, Beukema said. Initial candidates all will be chosen from men already on active duty or about to finish basic training. The entire list of eligibles is more than ample to fill the first contingents.

Beukema said the training program would include twenty-four or twenty-five hours a week in classroom and laboratory, additional outside studies, five hours a week of military training and an hour daily for physical training. Competitive intramural sports will be part of this schedule.

Approximately 29,000 enlisted Army reservists now in college who are not in certain special categories are subject to call for active duty at the end of the first college term ending after Dec. 31, 1942. For some, this will mean the end of the Fall semester and for others the end of the Winter quarter. Many of these will be returned to schools under the new

Continued on Page Sixteen

Eisenhower Is Told By Wife of New Rank

Wireless to THE NEW YORK TIMES.

ALLIED HEADQUARTERS IN NORTH AFRICA, Feb. 12—A cablegram from his wife last night made the promotion to full general "official" for General Dwight D. Eisenhower, Allied Commander in Chief in North Africa.

The first news of his promotion—he is the youngest American full general—came from a naval officer who heard it on the ship's radio.

The official notice came through this morning just as an enterprising French jeweler appeared at headquarters bearing twelve hand-made silver stars for the general.

PETRILLO PROPOSES FEES FOR RECORDS

Levy to Go to a Union Fund Not to Musician Asked as Basis of Peace Plan

A new type of union demand, under which the employe would not receive a wage increase, but the employer would pay a fixed amount directly to the union itself, was announced yesterday by James C. Petrillo, president of the American Federation of Musicians, as a proposed basis for settlement of the controversy over recordings.

Mr. Petrillo said that the money received from the record manufacturers and "juke-box" operators, in the form of a fee on each disk sold and on each phonograph in operation, would go into a special fund administered by the union's national headquarters and would be spent as follows:

"For the purpose of reducing unemployment which has been created in the main by the use of mechanical devices, and for fostering and maintaining musical talent and culture and musical appreciation, and for furnishing free, live music to the public by means of symphony orchestras, bands and other musical combinations."

While the plan would improve the economic position of the musicians as a group, Mr. Petrillo said that he had been advised by his lawyers that it did not conflict with the wage stabilization act as administered by the War Labor Board. His chief attorney is Joseph A. Padway, general counsel for the American Federation of Labor.

"It is no wage increase," Mr. Petrillo said. "We discussed it with our attorneys, and they say we're all right. There's no precedent for it. This is something absolutely new."

Beyond stating specifically that the individual musician who made a record would not benefit financially from the plan, Mr. Petrillo declined to discuss details of administering the special fund.

"First, we've got to get the fund," he remarked.

Mr. Petrillo said that he had in-

Continued on Page Twenty-four

DEWEY PROMISES MOVE TO END CRISIS ON FARMS OF STATE

Will Summon Thousands of Volunteers to Work as a Patriotic Duty

STUDENTS ARE SINGLED OUT

Governor at Lincoln Dinner Says the People Need No Directive to Win War

Warning that there was a critical shortage of farm labor in New York, Governor Dewey declared last night that the State had a plan to meet the emergency and keep up food production.

The Governor, who spoke at the fifty-seventh annual Lincoln dinner of the National Republican Club at the Waldorf-Astoria Hotel, disclosed that this plan contemplated the use of students in the high schools and women's colleges and the aid of persons in business who ordinarily work in other occupations in community efforts throughout the State in harvesting and processing the crops.

"Within ten days," Governor Dewey said, "I expect to be able to go on the radio to talk to all the people of the State—the farmers, the men and women of the cities and the small towns, the high school boys and college girls, and tell them in detail what they can do to meet the food crisis. I am confident that when they know what they can do they will need no orders or directives from any one. They will rally to the job and do it."

Other speakers were Mgr. Fulton J. Sheen of the Catholic University, Washington, who said that the young men in the armed services on their return from the war would want jobs and would be entitled to them, whether they were members of a union or not, and United States Senator Albert W. Hawkes of New Jersey, who asserted that the United States was headed straight for "state socialism" and that only vigorous action could change this course.

Bishop William T. Manning offered the invocation and Rabbi Jonah B. Wise of the Central Synagogue pronounced benediction. Secretary of State Thomas J. Curran, president of the club, presided. Charles H. Tuttle, chairman of the dinner committee, was toastmaster. The attendance was more than a thousand.

Recalling that during his campaign for election he had urged action to meet the impending food shortage, Governor Dewey said there was no use in complaining that something should have been done a year ago.

"We are in a war and we cannot stop to argue about the failures and the lack of foresight of others," he said. "We have to save the situation as far as possible.

"Whatever the difficulty, we

Continued on Page Seven

NAZIS' PERIL GROWS

Encircling of 500,000 Threatened in Fall of Donets Rail Key

KUBAN UNITS PENNED

Loss of Caucasus Base Drives Them to Sea—Rostov Pressed

By The Associated Press.

LONDON, Feb. 12—The Red Army of the Ukraine was reported officially tonight to have captured Krasnoarmeisk, a main rail junction twenty-five miles northwest of Stalino, thus threatening to trap some 500,000 Axis troops already hard pressed by other Russian units attacking in the Donets Basin and Rostov areas to the east.

A special Russian communiqué, recorded by the Soviet monitor here, told of the cutting of the main Dniepropetrovsk-Stalino railway at Krasnoarmeisk.

Other important developments included the capture of Krasnodar, Kuban Cossack capital in the Western Caucasus; Shakhty, a railroad town forty-five miles above Rostov, and Voroshilovsk, twenty-five miles southwest of Voroshilovgrad, Donets Basin industrial center.

Nazis Penned in Caucasus

The capture of Krasnodar left other sizable German forces based at Novorossiisk, on the Black Sea coast, stranded. Their best hope appeared to be an attempted flight by sea to the Crimea. But Moscow has reported that the Soviet Black Sea Fleet's big guns already are in action off Novorossiisk and the Germans have told for days of fighting Red marines landing along the coast to prevent a Nazi evacuation by boat.

German announcements, indicating that the Nazis were in trouble at Novorossiisk, said the Black Sea Fleet had tried to batter its way into the port and that a German tank division had frustrated Russian outflanking efforts on land. The Nazi communiqué appeared to be contradictory or at least confused. After saying Russian attacks had abated, it added that "mobile defense battles are, however, continuing with undiminished force."

Shakhty fell to the Russians striking southward toward Rostov, where, unofficial estimates say,

Continued on Page Six

RUSSIAN STEAMROLLERS CONTINUE TO CRUSH RESISTANCE

Soviet forces took more places south of Kursk (1) and closed in on Kharkov (2). They captured the railway junction of Krasnoarmeisk (3), threatening to trap 500,000 Axis troops, and also gained Voroshilovsk (4). Shakhty (5) was seized, but the German defenders of Rostov stiffened. In the Caucasus, Timoshevsk (6) and Krasnodar (7) fell to the Russians. The Nazis claimed to have driven off Soviet warships trying to penetrate the harbor of Novorossiisk (8).

TERRITORY CLAIMS LISTED BY RUSSIAN

Pravda Editor Says Estonia, Latvia, Lithuania, Bessarabia Are Part of Soviet Union

By BERTRAM D. HULEN

Special to THE NEW YORK TIMES.

WASHINGTON, Feb. 12—The latest and most emphatic assertion of the claim of the Soviet Union to Bessarabia, Estonia, Latvia and Lithuania on the ground that they are legally a part of Russia is contained in an editorial in Pravda, which was circulated in English translation today by the Soviet Embassy in its information bulletin.

It aroused deep interest in diplomatic circles because the claim has heretofore been asserted only by implication.

The editorial was written by David Zaslavsky, one of the editors of the newspaper, and appeared on

Continued on Page Six

Wilhelmshaven Raided Hard By R. A. F. in War on U-Boats

By JAMES MacDONALD

Special Cable to THE NEW YORK TIMES.

LONDON, Feb. 12—Resuming its around-the-clock offensive, the Royal Air Force bombed the German naval base of Wilhelmshaven last night and carried out many attacks during daylight today over Northwestern Germany, the Netherlands, Belgium and Northern France. The night and day attacks across the North Sea struck new blows in the anti-submarine warfare.

British aerial activity seemingly continued tonight because Nazi broadcasting stations that usually shut down during R. A. F. raids went off the air just after 5:30 o'clock and remained dead for some time. The Hilversum station in the Netherlands was silent for three and a half hours and the Friesland and Bremen stations, also on the North Sea coast, were off the air for ninety minutes.

Many R. A. F. heavy bombers dropped two and four-ton missiles on Wilhelmshaven in a raid concentrated into twenty minutes of attack that cost three British planes.

Fast Mosquito bombers were over the same area in the daylight offensive and returned without loss. One R. A. F. fighter was missing from the hundreds of sorties over German-occupied territory.

Airmen in the night raid reported a terrific explosion set off by their missiles at Wilhelmshaven, an important U-boat building center that was pounded by Flying Fortresses and Liberators on Jan. 27 in the first raid made by the United States Army Air Forces on Germany proper. The R. A. F. at-

Continued on Page Two

JAPANESE CONTINUE NEW GUINEA FLIGHT

Seek Refuge Near Salamaua—135 More Killed in Papua—Allies Batter Rabaul

By The United Press.

AT UNITED NATIONS HEADQUARTERS, Australia, Saturday, Feb. 13—The Japanese retreat is continuing northeast of Wau on the approaches to the New Guinea port of Salamaua, the Allied command announced today in a communiqué which also said that 225 more enemy troops had been killed or found dead in Papua.

"The enemy continues his withdrawal," the bulletin said in reference to the situation at Wau, thirty-five miles southwest of Salamaua, where the Japanese have been defeated decisively after a twelve-day encounter that cost them nearly 1,000 killed and many more wounded.

The Japanese were reported retreating toward the village of

Continued on Page Four

HARD BLOWS IN '43

Roosevelt Promises 'Bad News' for Nazis, Italians and the Japanese

AIR-LAND AID TO CHINA

Executive, on Radio, Tells World Quislings and Lavals Must Go

The Text of the President's address appears on Page 8.

By W. H. LAWRENCE

Special to THE NEW YORK TIMES.

WASHINGTON, Feb. 12—President Roosevelt declared tonight that great Allied operations designed to drive the enemy into the Mediterranean Sea were imminent in Tunisia and would be followed by "actual invasions of the Continent of Europe."

The Commander in Chief not only pledged more than one invasion of Europe but also promised that "great and decisive action against the Japanese will be taken to drive the invader from the soil of China." In addition to great land and air actions in China, he said, there would be air action against Japan itself.

Speaking to 700 members and guests at the annual dinner of the White House Correspondents Association here, and by radio over all networks to the entire country, Mr. Roosevelt expressed confidence in the success of military operations planned at the Casablanca war conferences with Prime Minister Churchill and looked ahead to complete victory over all the Axis nations—"to the day when United Nations forces march in triumph through the streets of Berlin, Rome and Tokyo."

He pictured a post-war world in which nations, while free to determine their own form of government as assured by the Atlantic Charter, would in no instance be permitted to choose "the fascist form of government or the Nazi form of government or the Japanese war-lord form of government." His warning appeared directed at those in France who remained loyal to the Vichy regime and was in part a reply to critics here of collaboration with former Vichy men. He said he was sure that France would never select any totalitarian form of government by free will.

Although he declared that "we do not expect to spend the time it would take to bring Japan to final

Continued on Page Three

Spellman Reported Arriving at Madrid

By Reuter.

LONDON, Feb. 12—A German news agency report says that the Catholic Archbishop of New York today arrived at Madrid airdrome from Lisbon, Portugal. He was met by the United States Ambassador in Madrid, and the Papal Nuncio to Spain. It is supposed that the Archbishop will shortly proceed to Rome by air.

Special to THE NEW YORK TIMES.

WASHINGTON, Feb. 12—It was learned from official sources here tonight that Archbishop Spellman of New York recently was planning a trip to the "Iberian Peninsula." These sources believed it to be purely a church matter.

Mgr. John J. Casey, secretary of the Archdiocese of New York, said last night that Archbishop Francis J. Spellman was making a tour of Army camps and visiting Catholic chaplains in his capacity of Military Vicar for the Armed Forces of the United States. Mgr. Casey said he did not know whether or not the Archbishop was at present outside the continental United States.

Landon Assails 'Nazi New Dealers'; Likens Wallace Aims to Hitler's

By The Associated Press.

OMAHA, Feb. 12—Former Governor Alfred M. Landon of Kansas urged tonight "a coalition of real Democrats and the Republican party" as a guarantee that Vice President Wallace "and his fellow-travelers will not lead us down the same disastrous primrose path in which Hitler has led his people."

In a speech at a Republican Lincoln Day banquet the former Presidential nominee asserted that "at last the practical progressives and the real liberals of the Democratic party are awake to the fact that by use of Trojan horse methods a small but dominant group of Nazi New Dealers who seek to establish here what Hitler described in his early days as the National Socialistic state have seized control of their party."

"The tangle of domestic policies and managing bureaucracy which prevented our return to prosperity under the Roosevelt Administration," he went on, "is preventing an efficient prosecution of the war.

"We are being compelled to fight on two fronts—one a global war, the other a Nazi bureaucratic war. Instead of leadership uniting us with 'an eye single to the task' on the war front we have a bureaucratic leadership in Washington thirsting for power and just as obviously determined to establish a permanent control of our lives, thus creating a second front at home."

Referring to President Roose-

Continued on Page Seven

War News Summarized

SATURDAY, FEBRUARY 13, 1943

President Roosevelt, in a broadcast speech last night, announced that operations to "drive our enemies into the sea" in Tunisia would not be long delayed. He said the Allies would gain control of the strait across the Mediterranean, and would invade Europe at more than one point. He warned the nation that the battles to come would be costly and appealed for calm courage on the home front. He promised action to drive the Japanese from China. Speaking of the post-war world, he said that every nation would be completely free but no Fascist governments would be permitted. [1:8.]

The Russians continued to advance unchecked in the Ukraine and the Caucasus. Krasnoarmeisk, a rail junction between Stalino and Dniepropetrovsk, fell to the Soviet forces, as well as Voroshilovsk, twenty-five miles southwest of Voroshilovgrad. In the Caucasus the rail center of Krasnodar was retaken. [1:4.]

The Soviet Embassy in Washington gave wide circulation to a Pravda editorial that was interpreted in diplomatic circles as a Russian claim on Bessarabia and the Baltic States. [1:5.]

In Tunisia, as ground activity was restricted by snow and the main air action was an attack on Sened, details were revealed of a successful Allied Commando raid on the Bizerte area Tuesday night. [3:1.]

On the political scene in North Africa it was announced that Charles Brunel, an ardent de Gaullist, had been put in charge of the important new Algerian Council of War Economy. [2:2.]

Britain's Air Force resumed its aerial offensive in Europe Thursday night with a raid on the naval base of Wilhelmshaven. Yesterday raids were made on targets in Northwestern Germany, the Netherlands, Belgium and Northern France. [1:6-7.]

General MacArthur's headquarters reported that the retreat of the Japanese from the Wau region of New Guinea was continuing. [1:7.]

Heavier fighting was reported from Burma, where the Japanese launched a series of sharp counter-attacks above Akyab. A British communiqué said that the assaults had been repelled with heavy enemy losses. [5:1, with map.]

Premier Mussolini made more changes in the Italian Cabinet. Six Under-Secretaries and three Ministers were replaced by men believed to be more loyal to Il Duce. [4:1.]

Canterbury Rebuked by Manning For Note Favoring Church Union

Bishop William T. Manning, head of the Protestant Episcopal Diocese of New York, made public last night a letter to the church press protesting against the "ecclesiastical intrusion" of the Archbishop of Canterbury (William Temple) in the controversy now going on in the Episcopal Church in this country over a proposed organic union with the Presbyterian Church.

In church circles here it was said it was unprecedented for an American Episcopal Bishop to administer a public rebuke to an Archbishop of the Church of England. The action with which Bishop Manning took issue was the writing of a letter by the Archbishop last October to Bishop Edward L. Parsons, retired, of California, chairman of the Commission of Approaches to Unity of the Episcopal Church, saying that success of the union movement would be "a very great contribution to the cause we all have at heart."

The Archbishop gave Bishop Parsons permission to publish his letter, and it was published recently in the Episcopal Church press, together with a statement by Bishop Parsons noting the interest shown by Americans in the Archbishop's utterances.

Bishop Manning's letter follows:

Bishop Parsons, the retired Bishop of California and chairman of our commission, a majority of which proposes to unite the Episcopal Church with one

Continued on Page Fourteen

"All the News That's Fit to Print."

The New York Times.

LATE CITY EDITION
Warmer today with moderate winds.
Temperatures Yesterday—Max., 46; Min., 26
Sunrise, 6:46 A. M.; Sunset, 7:17 P. M.

VOL. XCII—No. 31,111. Entered as Second-Class Matter, Postoffice, New York, N. Y. NEW YORK, TUESDAY, MARCH 30, 1943. THREE CENTS IN NEW YORK CITY

ROMMEL FLEES AS BRITISH BREAK MARETH LINE; WARSHIPS SHELL GABES, WITH FOE RACING THERE; R. A. F. AGAIN HITS BERLIN, RUHR AND ST. NAZAIRE

MEAT STOCK FREED BY ARMY AND NAVY TO HELP CIVILIANS

Lend-Lease Also Cooperating With OPA to Give Temporary Relief in Shortage Areas

TO REPLACE SUPPLY LATER

Clamor for Meat Dies Down Here—Coupons Treasured as Rationing Starts

The Army, Navy and Lend-Lease Administration agreed yesterday to cooperate with the Office of Price Administration to provide meat supplies for relieving acute shortages which may develop in any district in the first few days of coupon rationing. Slaughterers were permitted for two weeks to cease setting aside specified percentages of their output for war purposes. [1:1.]

New York City received its first emergency supplies of meat, but there was almost no retail buying on the first day of meat rationing. [12:1.]

Most of the nation's cities had little demand for meat. Supplies were in most cases adequate, but Detroit, Birmingham and some others had acute shortages. The OPA released large emergency stocks for Chicago. Poultry wholesalers in Cleveland and Detroit closed to enforce a demand on the OPA for a chance to make a profit. [14:1.]

Chester C. Davis appointed Jesse W. Tapp, another banker, as his assistant in the War Food Production Office. He conferred with Secretary Wickard and indicated they were in agreement that there should be no delay. [13:3.]

Action in Washington

By CHARLES E. EGAN

Special to The New York Times.

WASHINGTON, March 29—Cooperation has been promised by the Army, Navy and Lend-Lease Administration to relieve any unusually acute meat shortages which may develop during the next few days, the Office of Price Administration stated today.

According to government officials the meat earmarked for other uses will be made available to civilians on a temporary basis, insuring that it will be replaced as rapidly as improvement in shipments into a given area permits.

The arrangement was only one phase of a general move to ease the meat shortage as point-rationing went into effect today. It was a companion piece to the announcement by the Department of Agriculture that the order requiring livestock slaughterers to set aside certain percentages of their production for direct war purposes has been suspended for two weks.

This action was taken, department officials said, to enable wholesalers and retailers to build up their inventories after last week's unprecedented rush, so that meat will be available to retailers to meet consumer demand under the rationing program.

Says Several Days Are Needed

Prentiss M. Brown, OPA Administrator, in announcing the cooperative agreement his office has reached, said that the buying policies of the Army, Navy and Lend-Lease Administration were being adjusted temporarily to help meet the initial civilian demands as housewives began buying meat under rationing.

"Supplies throughout the nation are believed adequate to meet the civilian demand under rationing, but several days may be needed to get meat in sufficient varieties and quantities into all areas," Mr. Brown said.

"Therefore, it behooves every housewife to bear with her local butcher and the government in this initial period.

"I am particularly gratified at

Continued on Page Twelve

Soft Coal Strike Is Averted By New Presidential Move

White House Sends Dr. Steelman Here as 'Personal Representative' and Southern Operators Agree to Continue Talks

By JOSEPH SHAPLEN

President Roosevelt intervened again in the soft coal wage dispute yesterday and averted the threatened strike in the Southern area of the Appalachian region.

As a consequence of the President's new action the Southern Coal Producers Association, employing 135,000 men and representing a third of the nation's bituminous output, agreed to a thirty-day extension of the current agreement with the United Mine Workers, expiring at midnight Wednesday, with continuance of collective bargaining.

The operators of the Northern Appalachian region, employing 172,000 of the nation's 450,000 bituminous coal diggers, had signed an agreement with the union last week providing for extension of the old contract until May 1. Extension of the agreement for thirty days in both the Southern and Northern sections as proposed by the union assures uninterrupted operation of the mines after April 1.

The principal points at issue in the wage negotiations are the demands of the union for a basic increase of $2 a day, computation of a day's work from portal to portal, and unionization of some 50,000 minor bosses. The Northern operators have rejected these demands as unacceptable for financial and managerial reasons, but have expressed willingness to discuss them. By their action yesterday the Southern operators have followed suit.

The President's renewed intervention came in the form of the arrival here yesterday morning of Dr. John R. Steelman, director of the United States Conciliation Service of the Department of La-

Continued on Page Ten

MME. CHIANG PUTS WAR TO WORKERS

2,000 on Coast Cheer Clenched-Fist Demand for Ceaseless Production to End Conflict

By LAWRENCE E. DAVIES

Special to The New York Times.

SAN FRANCISCO, Calif., March 29—With clenched fists which she pounded on a table to give emphasis to fighting words, Mme. Chiang Kai-shek exhorted workers of America tonight to increase industrial production to end the war "at the earliest moment possible."

At an unscheduled meeting which was unprecedented on her transcontinental tour, Mme. Chiang spoke in the C. I. O. hall to 2,500 union members, chiefly longshoremen, with leaders of American Federation of Labor, Congress of Industrial Organizations and Railroad Brotherhoods on the platform. She told them that what she was going to say was "meant for all workers in America."

"Your cause is China's cause," she said. "Because my own people have suffered and bled for six long years I have a message I'd like to bring to you.

"That is: Unity is strength.

"I've often said we must not only win the war, we must also win the peace. But in order to win the peace we must first win the war and that at the earliest moment possible.

"Your task is not one whit less important than that of the fighting forces at the front. You must

Continued on Page Fourteen

WLB EXTENDS RULE OVER LABOR FIELD

Morse Opinion Asserts Power Covers Disputes Regardless of Direct War Tie-Up

By LOUIS STARK

Special to The New York Times.

WASHINGTON, March 29—The National War Labor Board claimed today jurisdiction over all labor disputes, large and small, whether in war industries or not, whether they are disputes affecting intrastate commerce or interstate commerce, whether they involve strikes or threats of strikes in hotel barbershops, in laundries or cleaning and dyeing establishments or elsewhere.

Wayne Lyman Morse, public member, who wrote the board's opinion in a case affecting 100 salesmen who solicit advertising for classified telephone directories published in New York by the Reuben H. Donnelley Corporation, said:

"After more than a year's experience in finally determining a large number of wartime labor disputes involving all sorts of issues and almost every conceivable type of dispute, the WLB takes judicial notice of the fact that any labor dispute of whatever nature which threatens to result in a strike or lockout does, in fact, affect the prosecution of the war on the home front."

The WLB had taken formal jurisdiction of the Donnelley case on Jan. 23 unanimously and had designated Mr. Morse, dean of the University of Oregon Law School, to write the opinion. The case af-

Continued on Page Ten

Mayor to Join Protest Tonight Against 2 Executions by Russia

Mayor La Guardia entered yesterday the battle between rights and lefts in the labor movement over the execution by the Soviet Government of Henryk Ehrlich and Victor Alter, when it was announced that he would be a speaker at the memorial protest meeting for the two Polish labor leaders at Mecca Temple tonight.

The announcement was made by the Committee of 250, headed by David Dubinsky, president of the International Ladies Garment Workers Union. Mr. Dubinsky will preside at the meeting, which will be addressed, among others, by William Green, president of the American Federation of Labor; James B. Carey, secretary-treasurer of the Congress of Industrial Organizations; Senator James M. Mead of New York and Representative Jerry Voorhis of California.

Speaking as president of the New York State Federation of Labor, with a membership of 1,500,000, Thomas J. Lyons addressed the following message to Mr. Dubinsky:

"The American people are in the midst of a great struggle for self-preservation, for the survival on this continent and everywhere in this world of the undying principles of humanity without which life is worthless.

"We in America do not intend to dictate domestic policies to any of our friends or allies, but we cannot fail in our duty to protest from the depth of our hearts when we see the principles of humanity for which we are fighting trampled under foot by those with whom we are engaged in a struggle against a common enemy.

"That is why I join with you in

Continued on Page Eight

AIR BLOWS 'HEAVY'

British Bomb German Capital for Second Time in 3 Nights

U-BOAT BASE FIRED

Day Raiding Pressed on Nazis in North France and Netherlands

By The Associated Press.

LONDON, Tuesday, March 30—The Royal Air Force bombed Berlin last night for the second time in three nights and also attacked targets in the Ruhr Valley, British officials announced today.

The raid on the German capital, which was subjected Saturday night to an assault more devastating than any it had undergone before, followed a series of daylight attacks by squadrons of the British Bomber Command on targets in France and the Netherlands.

Sunday night, in the interlude between the raids on Berlin, heavy British bombers blasted the great German submarine base at St. Nazaire, leaving fires from which smoke still was coiling 15,000 feet into the air yesterday afternoon.

The Air Ministry, in describing Sunday night's forty-sixth raid on St. Nazaire as "heavy and concentrated," indicated that the attack probably was as destructive as that of Feb. 28, when 1,000 tons of Britain's heaviest bombs shattered and burned the same target.

Visibility for the all-out bombing assault on the big U-boat nest was excellent, and R. A. F. crewmen said their bombs struck squarely on the docks and left large fires raging which were visible long after they left the target.

"There were seven large fires merging together," one pilot related. "They seemed to be bubbling and seething. The whole attack was remarkably concentrated."

Many crews described a huge explosion at the southern end of the docks, accompanied by a burst of orange flame and clouds of black smoke, indicating that a bomb had found its mark on a torpedo depot or ammunition dump.

The fifth bombing attack there this month fell on the first anni-

Continued on Page Eight

RETREAT IN TUNISIA: ROMMEL STARTS ON HIS WAY

Britain's Eighth Army captured the Mareth Line defenses and the strong points of Mareth (1), Toujane and Matmata (2) after the flanking column's seizure of El Hamma (3) had made the Axis position to the south untenable. The enemy started falling back on Gabès (4), which was bombarded from the sea. If Marshal Rommel seeks to escape northward along the coast he must run an Allied gantlet: Americans are pressing forward east and southeast of El Guettar (5), east of Maknassy (6) and east of Fondouk (C on inset); French forces are holding a salient near Ousseltia (B) and British and French troops are pushing out east of Djebel Abiod (A).

U. S. STRATEGY SET FOR PACIFIC 'ACTION'

Joint Staff Chiefs and Top Aides of MacArthur, Nimitz and Halsey Map Offensive

By SIDNEY SHALETT

Special to The New York Times.

WASHINGTON, March 29—Future fighting plans for every area of the Pacific Ocean were outlined in Washington at a series of "post-Casablanca" conferences just concluded between the Joint Chiefs of Staff and fifteen top-ranking representatives of Admiral Chester W. Nimitz, General Douglas MacArthur and Admiral William F. Halsey Jr., the War Department revealed today.

The War Department itself described the meetings as "important," and said that the plans discussed concerned "future actions" in the various Pacific theatres.

Among the conferees who came

Continued on Page Five

'Impossible' Waste Crossed By British Flanking Column

By DON WHITEHEAD

Associated Press Correspondent

WITH THE BRITISH EIGHTH ARMY, West of Gabès, March 28 (Delayed)—In his biggest gamble of the entire African campaign General Sir Bernard L. Montgomery has outfoxed the "Fox of the Desert" by one of the boldest and most daring manoeuvres accomplished by the British Eighth Army in its campaign to drive Field Marshal Erwin Rommel out of North Africa.

Strong elements of British troops outflanked the Mareth Line through a wild, sandy, dust-blown fringe of the Sahara across country that seemed impossible for an army to move over. I have just come across this waterless wasteland, which Marshal Rommel apparently thought could never be crossed by armor. Never in the almost 2,000 miles of advance from El Alamein, Egypt, have I seen country that punishes men and machines more than this land does. But the Eighth Army accomplished the final phase of the move in a spectacular dash at almost unbelievable speed.

It was not a case of playing safe and taking no chances—not this move. It was the greatest gamble that General Montgomery had taken—a cool, calculated gamble that forced Marshal Rommel to divide his army into two parts in Southern Tunisia.

Three weeks ago a force went around the Matmata hills and then toward Gabès, pioneering the wasteland. When the Germans repulsed the break-through in the

Continued on Page Four

YANKS SCALE PEAK UNDER GERMAN FIRE

Djebel el Mcheltat, in Central Tunisia, Is Captured After Day-Long Hammering

By The United Press.

BEYOND EL GUETTAR, Tunisia, March 29—American infantry, hammering ahead through fierce mortar and artillery fire, captured the German stronghold of Djebel el Mcheltat, a 1,500-foot hill, during the night after attacking it throughout yesterday.

The enemy is now entrenched on Djebel Chemsi, twelve miles east of El Guettar. Another American column on the right of the Gabès road is still attacking the east slopes of Djebel Berda, in the low hills overlooking the road.

All day yesterday our boys crept forward over hills and through ravines, slowly gaining ground in a tough, slugging battle that de

Continued on Page Three

War News Summarized

TUESDAY, MARCH 30, 1943

The British won one of the war's major battles when, after eight days of relentless struggle, General Montgomery's Eighth Army brought about the collapse of the Mareth Line in Tunisia.

A combined frontal and flanking attack overwhelmed the key points of Mareth, Toujane and Matmata. Marshal Rommel was retreating yesterday over low country toward Gabès through an ever-narrowing gap and under attack from the air. Gabès itself was bombarded from the sea. The Americans pushed ahead east of El Guettar over difficult terrain and against strongly entrenched German positions in Central Tunisia, while in the north the British First Army advanced near Djebel Abiod. [1:8.]

A correspondent with the Eighth Army said that General Montgomery took the greatest military gamble of his career in moving the armor of his flanking column across the fringe of the Sahara and in doing so outfoxed Marshal Rommel, who apparently thought such a feat was impossible. [1:6-7.]

The Axis also suffered in Europe. The R. A. F. bombed Berlin again last night and hit in the Ruhr Valley, after a heavy, concentrated raid Sunday night on the U-boat base at St. Nazaire that left a fourth of the French port afire. In daylight yesterday British bombers were over the Netherlands and France. [1:4.]

Action in Russia was limited, with Soviet troops advancing slowly toward Smolensk and holding the Germans on the Donets. [1:6-7.]

Japan received her share of attention at Washington, where a three weeks' conference ended after having outlined Allied fighting plans in the Pacific. The United Nations Joint Chiefs of Staff and fifteen ranking officers from the Pacific theatre participated in the sessions. [1:5.]

Accord between pro-Allied French forces is believed near, reports from Algiers said. General Catroux, who as General de Gaulle's representative has been conferring with General Giraud, will hold a press conference today. [4:1.]

Post-war problems were other subjects of discussion in Washington as well as in London. A United States Treasury spokesman said a full-dress international conference on post-war monetary stabilization would be held soon to clear up Anglo-American differences. [6:3.]

An Allied high commissioner for education in Germany was suggested at a conference of educators in London, to undo the domestic effects of Nazi propaganda. [6:4.]

Russians Gain Toward Smolensk; Tanks and Infantry Hit Defenses

By The United Press.

LONDON, Tuesday, March 30—Russian tanks and infantry shock troops, fighting their way into the main German defense system before Smolensk, have smashed a series of enemy pill boxes and captured three inhabited places, the Soviet Monday midnight communiqué said today.

Moscow dispatches said that the Russians had been slowed by the mud as well as by the formidable defenses of one of the largest fortification systems on the entire Eastern Front, and Axis broadcasts said that the Red Army had opened a new and heavy attack in the north, trying to free the main communications of Leningrad before the ice melted on Lake Ladoga, across which they had moved supplies all Winter.

The midnight Red Army communiqué, recorded here from the Moscow radio, reported that on the Smolensk and Donets River fronts the Russians were fighting in territory dotted by German pill boxes, blockhouses and dugouts.

In their two-pronged drive on Smolensk the Russians yesterday engaged in fighting largely of local importance, the midnight bulletin said. But announcement that pill-boxes as well as fortified villages had started to fall meant that the Red Army had begun its task of driving into thick defense belts, preparing for a Spring drive after the thaw.

In one Smolensk sector the Russians stormed a German strong point, killing 160 Germans, and Red Army tanks smashed three German tanks and a trench mortar battery. One of the tank crews de-

Continued on Page Seven

MAIN FORTS TAKEN

Attackers Pour Through Breaches—Gain on Flank Reported

ALLIES PERIL ROAD

Strong Forces in Center and North Drive for Coastal Highway

By C. L. SULZBERGER

Wireless to The New York Times.

ALLIED HEADQUARTERS IN NORTH AFRICA, March 29—The British Eighth Army under General Sir Bernard L. Montgomery has outflanked and occupied the main positions of the Mareth Line after a brilliant enveloping move across the fringe of the Sahara, it was officially announced today. Bearing down hard on the enemy's right wing after having encountered difficulties in his smashing frontal attack, General Montgomery has scored a decisive strategic victory.

The strong-points of Mareth, Toujane and Matmata have been overwhelmed and Field Marshal General Erwin Rommel's Africa Corps is now withdrawing across the low-lying plains toward the Gabès gap under fiercely incessant Allied air attacks. The Gabès area is under heavy naval bombardment.

[The Axis-controlled "Voice of the Arab World" said in an Arabic broadcast heard by The United Press in London, that "we have received news that the English have occupied Gabès."]

Spitfires and Airacobras swept over the Gabès-Mezzouna communications lines while Kittyhawk bombers shattered the Gabès-El Hamma road.

British Pour Through Breaches

After days of battle in which the veteran British and German armies had been standing almost toe to toe along the stark ridges bordering the gates to Central Tunisia, the British desert fighters are now pouring through the breaches in the best prepared positions on the Southern Mediterranean shore. The Western Desert Air Force, despite high winds screaming out of the south with swirling dust-clouds, is hammering the withdrawing enemy formations as they approach the sixteen-mile Gabès-El Hamma region through which they are being herded. [This gap has been narrowed to fourteen miles by a British advance beyond El Hamma, according to an Algiers broadcast recorded by Reuter.]

The British have won one of the decisive battles of the war by sheer staying power, excellence and quantity of equipment, supreme cooperation between ground and air units and generalship of the first order. There is no indication where Marshal Rommel's battered forces may again seek to make a stand. By sound strategic and tactical concepts, General Montgomery has again succeeded in smashing a skilled opponent by a combination of frontal and flanking attacks. Every success has been fuller than that initially achieved at El Alamein, Egypt. Not only has Marshal Rommel been forced to withdraw in the Mareth Line area but the formidable triangular range of mountains between Zeltene, Toujane and Matmata has been entirely abandoned.

[The Algiers radio, according to Reuter, said tonight that it was generally believed in military circles that Marshal Rommel would retreat to a line north of Sousse, since the positions in the plains bounded by Chott Djérid, Kairouan, Sousse and Gabès are untenable.

[Reports from Algiers to Madrid said that Marshal Rommel had established headquarters in the region of El Djem, forty-two miles north of Gabès, The United Press reported. He was arranging Axis withdrawals and counter-attacks along his flanks to

Continued on Page Four

Wide World Photos

Field Marshal Erwin Rommel

"All the News That's Fit to Print."

The New York Times.

LATE CITY EDITION
Rain today with little change in temperature; fresh winds.
Temperatures Yesterday—Max., 56; Min., 50
Sunrise, 5:43 A. M.; Sunset, 8:00 P. M.

Copyright, 1943, by The New York Times Company.

VOL. XCII..No. 31,154. Entered as Second-Class Matter, Postoffice, New York, N. Y. NEW YORK, WEDNESDAY, MAY 12, 1943. THREE CENTS NEW YORK CITY

CHURCHILL ARRIVES FOR TALK WITH ROOSEVELT; FOE CUT OFF ON CAP BON PENINSULA COLLAPSING; GERMANS IN SOUTH SURRENDER TO THE FRENCH

ANTI-STRIKE BILL RECAST, TIGHTENED BY HOUSE GROUP

Connally Measure Shifted to Punishment for Leaders and Union Members

SMITH'S IDEAS ARE PUT IN

Word That WLB Members Felt Satisfied Fails to Stop Committee's Action

By C. P. TRUSSELL
Special to THE NEW YORK TIMES.

WASHINGTON, May 11—Brushing aside the protests of organized labor and holding that the Senate-adopted Connally bill was inadequate for strike control in time of war, the House Military Affairs Committee, in executive session, completely rewrote that legislation today, converting it into a measure directed more at punishment for strikers, their leaders and their unions than at government seizures of property.

By a vote of 21 to 0, the committee left only basic provisions of the Connally plant-seizure legislation, avoided giving the President new, specific powers for taking over strike-bound factories and mines, and substituted virtually all the stringent provisions of a bill, sponsored by Representative Smith of Virginia, which the House passed a few days before Pearl Harbor but which died in the Senate. The legislation will be reported formally to the House as soon as the official draft can be made ready.

WLB Message of No Avail

The committee's action was taken in the face of a unanimous agreement by the National War Labor Board, to which the pending legislation would give more authority to settle management-labor disputes and enforce its decisions, that the Connally bill met with its general approval. This decision was communicated to the House committee in the midst of its deliberations.

When it had completed its revisions and substitutions, the committee sought to make it unlawful, under penalties of loss of union status under the National Labor Relations Act, for workers to strike in a war production plant until the expiration of the thirty days from the date on which written notice of intent was given the Secretary of Labor. It would be unlawful also for management to effect a lockout within such a period.

Those inducing and leading strikes in plants held by the government would face the severe penalties of the Connally bill, including fines and imprisonment.

It would be unlawful, under terms of the legislation, for employes in a war plant to strike until after the Secretary of Labor had directed the United States Conciliation Service to take a secret ballot of the workers and the results of this voting had been published.

No person who refused to strike, the bill provides, could be deprived of his union benefits.

No Outsiders as Pickets

Further, it would be unlawful for any one, by force or violence, to prevent another from accepting employment or continuing employment under any war contractor, whether or not the plant involved had been seized by the government. Permission for picketing would be restricted to those who had been bona fide employes of a strike-bound plant when the management-labor dispute developed.

Also, it would be unlawful for any person or group to stage a strike in a plant, whether it was on war production or not, in order to induce or attempt to induce or require a war contractor to recognize, deal with, or employ members of any labor union.

As in the Connally bill, the

Continued on Page Sixteen

Pact in Hard Coal Likely; Lewis Promises a Statement

Optimism Grows as Talks Continue Here and Chairman of WLB Panel Suspends Hearings on Dispute in Washington

By JOSEPH SHAPLEN

Prospect of an agreement between the United Mine Workers and anthracite operators before expiration of the fifteen-day truce under which the entire coal industry is now operating appeared yesterday, together with a possibility that the threatened resumption of the recent coal stoppage upon expiration of the truce may be averted in both the anthracite and bituminous fields.

The situation looked brighter in the anthracite than in the bituminous dispute, however. The truce now in effect in the industry expires at midnight next Tuesday.

John L. Lewis, president of the United Mine Workers, may cast light on the situation when he makes a statement at 4 o'clock this afternoon at the union's headquarters in the Hotel Roosevelt, breaking a silence of more than a week.

Mr. Lewis announced that he would make such a statement as another session of anthracite operators and miners ended at the Waldorf-Astoria yesterday.

Hope of a direct agreement for the anthracite industry was seen in the unexpected announcement in Washington yesterday by Morris L. Cooke, chairman of the War Labor Board's panel considering the coal crisis, that the anthracite hearings of the panel have been indefinitely postponed because negotiations between hard coal operators and miners were proceeding in New York.

Mr. Cooke's statement was fol-

Continued on Page Fifteen

250 POULTRY SHOPS IN CITY ON STRIKE

Dealers Suspend Business to Break 'Black Market'—Fish Wasted Off Jersey

By JEFFERSON G. BELL

Hundreds of New York City food merchants are refusing to handle poultry and fish under conditions established by Office of Price Administration regulations, it was learned yesterday.

As the revolt of food purveyors gained momentum 250 poultry dealers, organized as Chicken Dealers of the Lower East Side, closed their doors and went on "strike," to the dismay of thousands of customers. Along the New Jersey seacoast fishermen began dumping hundreds of thousands of pounds of fresh whiting back into the sea from their nets because Manhattan dealers will not handle whiting under the OPA ceiling of 4 cents a pound.

The strike of the East Side poultry dealers has unusual features because it is aimed at what some of the strikers call the black market and because it has left three local unions of the Amalgamated Meat Cutters, American Federation of Labor, virtually helpless to act even in self-defense. The unions do not know whether it would do any good to establish a picket line, because their members are not on the payrolls of the employers on strike.

The strike of the poultry dealers began on Monday and continued yesterday. The three unions of poultry workers dressing the poultry normally supplied to the striking shopkeepers anxiously are

Continued on Page Thirty-three

BUCK'S RE-ELECTION DEFIES THE MAYOR

Unanimously Returned, School Board Head Scores 'Attacks' and 'Unwarranted Slander'

By unanimous vote the Board of Education re-elected Ellsworth B. Buck, Staten Island member, as its president yesterday, thus ignoring the recent warning of Mayor La Guardia that he would "fire" Mr. Buck the first chance he got.

In accepting the nomination Mr. Buck assailed those who attack the schools and warned that freedom from political control was essential. Without mentioning the Mayor by name, he asserted that while the board and the city must operate harmoniously, they must remain separate entities. Mr. Buck told his colleagues he would not accept a third term as board president.

The board's action was in direct defiance of the Mayor, who declared on April 12, after the vote against Mark Starr, that he had "lost confidence" in Mr. Buck. No other candidate was nominated for president yesterday, and the members joined in praising Mr. Buck for his "integrity" and his "independence and sound judgment."

Fackenthal Is Vice President

Joseph D. Fackenthal, Brooklyn member, was elected vice president, succeeding Dr. Alberto C. Bonaschi of the Bronx. A hold-over member since May, 1942, Dr. Bonaschi was renominated for the post of vice president but declined, explaining that he did not expect to remain on the board much longer, and that his health did not permit him to take on additional responsibilities. Mayor

Continued on Page Forty-eight

President Says Our Plane Output Exceeds That of Rest of World

Special to THE NEW YORK TIMES.

WASHINGTON, May 11—President Roosevelt announced today that production of airplanes by the United States now exceeded that of all other nations combined, with emphasis being placed on the four-engined bomber to carry out plans for greater offensives against the Axis.

Converting airplane production statistics into the weight of planes instead of their number as a better test of output, the President told his press conference that United States factories turned out 87,000,000 pounds of airplanes in 1941, 291,000,000 pounds in 1942 and were expected to produce 911,000,000 pounds in 1943 and 1,417,000,000 pounds in 1944.

Declaring that our war plans called for this country and its allies to go more and more on the offensive, the President said that the four-engined bomber, a prime attack weapon, now was being produced at a rate six months ahead of the schedule set in December. The modern four-engined bomber, he said, weighed ten times as much as a single-engined fighter plane.

Not only had the number of airplanes produced in this country greatly increased since 1941, he continued, but the type of plane had changed radically. In the beginning, he said, we concentrated on defense airplanes, including fighters, light bombers and dive-bombers. Now, he said, our emphasis was on four-engined bombers, two-engined heavy bombers, long-range fighters and cargo planes.

'LAST TANK BATTLE'

Armor Clashes at Base of Peninsula—British Race Up Coasts

100,000 PRISONERS

Enemy in Zaghouan Area Told to 'Surrender Unconditionally'

By FRANK L. KLUCKHOHN
Wireless to THE NEW YORK TIMES.

ALLIED HEADQUARTERS IN NORTH AFRICA, May 11—British armored forces and troops were advancing far up the coast roads on either side of the Cap Bon Peninsula today after having closed its mouth. Thus far they have taken about 20,000 new prisoners, who are being concentrated near Beni Alchoun, on the south coast.

Organized enemy resistance has collapsed and there will be no Axis "Bataan" on this peninsula. Elements of the British Sixth Armored Division are destroying the remaining tanks of the German Tenth Armored Division near Grombalia, at the peninsula's base, in what it is hoped will be the last tank battle of the campaign. The war in Africa now seems to be within hours of its close.

Already almost 100,000 Germans and a few Italians have been captured. When the remaining pocket of resistance inland collapses, as it must, the complete destruction of Germany's and Italy's African armies is expected to result in a total of about 150,000 prisoners.

Germans Yield to French

In the inland bulge of about 650 square miles opposite the Cap Bon Peninsula, where large enemy forces are trapped in a hopeless position, the Germans east of Zaghouan and on Djebel Zaghouan, southwest of the town, asked the French for an armistice. The French replied with a demand for unconditional surrender and the turning over of all matériel intact.

[The Germans accepted the French ultimatum, The Associated Press reported.]

Earlier French reports had said that large numbers of German

Continued on Page Two

MR. CHURCHILL BACK IN WASHINGTON FOR WAR TALKS

The British Prime Minister driving to the White House with President Roosevelt last night
Associated Press Wirephoto

FLOW OF CAPTIVES TAXES FIRST ARMY

Prisoners of Cap Bon Action Pour In Too Fast for Questioning—Many Shed Uniforms

By DREW MIDDLETON
Wireless to THE NEW YORK TIMES.

BRITISH FIRST ARMY HEADQUARTERS, Tunisia, May 10 (Delayed)—Strong tank and infantry formations of the British First Army cut down behind the Axis forces facing the British Eighth Army and continued to mop up the enemy positions at the base of the Cap Bon Peninsula today as the campaign in Tunisia moved rapidly toward its close.

West of Tunis all the enemy forces have been "bagged." The First and Thirty-fourth Divisions of the Second United States Corps and the British forces are working in the closest cooperation.

Continued on Page Three

War News Summarized

WEDNESDAY, MAY 12, 1943

Prime Minister Winston Churchill arrived in Washington last evening for his fifth war conference with President Roosevelt. He was accompanied by a staff of military and naval experts and was preceded by Lord Beaverbrook.

It was believed in Washington that Mr. Churchill and Mr. Roosevelt would discuss world-wide strategy of the United Nations and closer cooperation with the Soviet Union. The opening of a second front in Europe and shipment of increased supplies were considered the best aid to Russia. [All the foregoing, 1:8.]

London interpreted the presence of Lord Beaverbrook in Washington as evidence that a serious move would be made to heal the breach between Russia and Poland. He was said to have a plan to bring the two nations together. If it meets with President Roosevelt's approval, he may proceed to Moscow to present it to Joseph Stalin. [3:1.]

Organized Axis resistance in the Tunisian fighting was said to have crumbled. Prisoners were surrendering in droves. East of Zaghouan a French commander had the distinction of imposing terms of unconditional surrender on a German general for the first time in this war. Mopping up operations were proceeding on most fronts, and the British were advancing up both sides of the Cap Bon Peninsula after having closed its mouth. [1:4; map, P. 2]

Nearly 200 American bombers escorted by more than 100 fighters raided Marsala in what appeared part of a campaign to destroy the airfields, harbors and other military installations of Sicily. In the North African campaign the Allies had destroyed 3,000 Axis planes and lost 679. [1:6-7; map, P. 4.]

Italy was reported to have decreed a "state of emergency" in the Calabrian Peninsula as part of the defense against anticipated Allied invasion. Civilians throughout Italy were said to be fleeing for safety to the center of the country. [1:7]

A German High Command communiqué asserted Marshal Rommel had been ill in Germany for two months. [4:2.] But a report from the Near East said the erstwhile "Desert Fox" had paid a visit to Crete as part of his new job of strengthening Axis defenses in the Balkans. [4:6.]

On the Russian front the Red Army announced capture of a strong point near Novorossiisk and destruction of fifty-six Nazi planes. German railroad communications behind the lines were heavily raided. [6:5.]

British troops were reported arriving in Dominica from Barbados "in connection with the Martinique situation." There was no comment from Washington. [1:6-7; map, P. 3.]

300 Planes Bomb Marsala; Pantelleria Attacked Twice

Special Broadcast to THE NEW YORK TIMES.

ALLIED HEADQUARTERS IN NORTH AFRICA, May 11—The United States Army Air Force continued the destruction of Sicily's airfields, harbors and installations today by attacking Marsala on the west coast, leaving fires the smoke of which was visible over the African coast. Almost 200 bombers and more than 100 fighters took part in this all-American raid.

The harbor, railroad, yard and warehouses at Marsala were special objectives. Flying Fortresses, Mitchells and Marauders went in in waves, with Lightnings darting about to give them protection. The smoke of numerous fires rose to a height of 10,000 feet, casting a pall over the whole area.

Two Airfields Bombed

Yesterday Flying Fortresses dealt further punishing blows to the Axis air force by bombing the Sicilian airfields of Milo and Borizzo. Strings of bombs fell on a line of thirty to forty aircraft at Milo, leaving half of them aflame. Two other large fires were started.

Four large fires threw smoke 5,000 feet high after the Borizzo raid. The Fortresses and their Lightning escorts were attacked over the latter target by German and Italian fighters. Two Messerschmitts were shot down.

It was also announced that Wellingtons had dropped two-ton bombs on the docks, industrial areas and power stations at Palermo, Sicily, the night of May 9-10, after the big daylight Fortress raid of May 9.

[Malta-based planes bombed airfields, railway stations and power plants at Biscari, Marsala and Porto Empedocle in Sicily,

Continued on Page Four

'TOE' OF ITALY PUT IN STATE OF ALERT

Many Families Said to Flee From Calabria and Even Rome—Fortifications Lacking

By DANIEL T. BRIGHAM
By Telephone to THE NEW YORK TIMES.

BERNE, Switzerland, May 11—Dropping secrecy regarding the seriousness of the situation following the latest developments in North Africa, the Italian Government tonight decreed a "state of emergency" for the Calabrian Peninsula—the southern tip of Italy, forming the toe of the boot.

This measure, it is learned, was decided upon following an alleged British broadcast early yesterday morning warning Sicilians "to make their choice," according to Italian sources. Long since this choice appears to have been made for them, for all of the port material that could be spared had been transferred to the mainland "for other uses." For days past arms and munitions sent to the island in preparation for reshipment to Tunisia have been in the process

Continued on Page Four

British Send Troops to Dominica, Cite U. S.-Martinique 'Situation'

The British radio announced last night that a British West Indian detachment had embarked for little Dominica Island, a British possession that lies between Martinique and Guadeloupe in the French West Indies.

About the same time, according to The United Press, Germany reported that United States naval forces were moving against Martinique and Guadeloupe.

Officials at both Washington and London declined all comment on the reports.

Early today a United Press dispatch from San Juan, P. R., a United States naval base, said a high-placed source there characterized the German radio report that United States vessels were moving to the occupation of Martinique as "pure baloney." Informed sources at San Juan, the dispatch went on, said the next move in the Caribbean area probably would be directed against Guadeloupe.

The German report was broadcast by the German Transocean agency. It said that it was "reported" that American naval forces were on the way to Martinique and Guadeloupe, intending to "capture" both islands.

The strength of the United States forces was not reported. Transocean said, but the enemy agency "assumed" that they would be supported by the American warships "at present blockading Martinique."

"The French islands will hardly

Continued on Page Three

INVASION ONE TOPIC

Prime Minister's Party Includes High Army and Navy Experts

COMMAND AN ISSUE

White House Talks May Cover Leadership of Armies in Europe

By W. H. LAWRENCE
Special to THE NEW YORK TIMES.

WASHINGTON, May 11—Prime Minister Winston Churchill arrived in Washington late today for conferences with President Roosevelt relative to preparations for a second front in Europe and other offensive actions against the Axis around the world.

The official announcement that Mr. Churchill, accompanied by a staff of military and naval experts, had reached Washington and had been met by the President was released by the White House at 6:48 P. M., E.W.T.

The White House statement was confined to the bare announcement of his arrival and the fact that he would be the guest of the President for the duration of his stay. But the timing of the visit, coming as it did just at the climax of the Allied operations in North Africa, and the military character of Mr. Churchill's traveling companions made it obvious that the two leaders were ready to talk about the next moves necessary to achieve the "unconditional surrender" goal they set at their last meeting in Casablanca in January.

Broad Survey Indicated

It was expected that the President and Prime Minister would survey the war situation in every world theatre and make plans for Anglo-American operations in each of them in cooperation with the other United Nations.

It was considered certain that high on the agenda was a series of steps to aid the Russian armies battling against the Germans in Eastern Europe, including a second front or series of fronts in Western and Southern Europe, as well as measures to speed up the movement of supplies.

Secretary of the Navy Frank Knox said today that the liquidation of the Axis armies in Africa would reopen the Mediterranean to

Continued on Page Three

Hitler Tours West, Ousts Paris Chief

By The Associated Press.

LONDON, May 11—A German broadcast recorded by Reuter tonight said that Adolf Hitler, whose headquarters had been long described as on the Eastern Front, now is at an unspecified point in the West. There was no immediate elaboration.

Wireless to THE NEW YORK TIMES.

BERNE, Switzerland, Wednesday, May 12—Back in Paris after a two-day inspection tour of his "Atlantic wall" defenses, Adolf Hitler late yesterday ousted Col. Gen. Ernst von Schaumburg as commander of the occupation forces in the Paris region and appointed 52-year-old General von Beulenburg-Wehrfeldt as commander of all forces in the "northwestern region," according to a Berlin announcement received here early today.

The move followed long conversations with his military advisers, during which the Reichsfuehrer "acted on the latest reports from Tunisia." A usually well-informed Berlin source reported that Herr Hitler intends to extend his shake-up of the Western command to all ranks. Col. Gen. Dietloff von Arnim has been mentioned as a possible appointee, though it is still doubted here whether he escaped the Allied ring in Tunisia.

"All the News That's Fit to Print."

The New York Times.

LATE CITY EDITION
Moderate temperatures and moderate winds today.
Temperatures Yesterday—Max., 81; Min., 61
Sunrise, 5:24 A. M.; Sunset, 8:27 P. M.

Copyright, 1943, by The New York Times Company.

VOL. XCII..No. 31,185. Entered as Second-Class Matter, Postoffice, New York, N. Y. NEW YORK, SATURDAY, JUNE 12, 1943. THREE CENTS IN NEW YORK CITY

PANTELLERIA YIELDS, CONQUERED BY AIR MIGHT; ROOSEVELT INVITES ITALY TO OUST MUSSOLINI; 200 U. S. PLANES HAMMER REICH U-BOAT YARDS

ODT RULE CAUSES POTATOES TO ROT EN ROUTE TO CITY

Refrigeration Barred on Cars From South, Huge Quantities Arrive Badly Spoiled

LOSSES 10 TO 80 PER CENT

California Shipments, Iced at Start and Twice in Transit, Reach Here Undamaged

By JEFFERSON G. BELL

Huge quantities of new potatoes shipped here from the South to relieve New York City's recent potato famine have rotted in transit, it was learned yesterday, because they were shipped without refrigeration in accordance with orders of the Office of Defense Transportation.

The loss of precious potatoes while the nation's food situation daily becomes more alarming is the subject of adverse comment in the food trade. Spokesmen for the food industry conceded it was logical to expect a shortage of refrigerator cars, but some of them would not agree that it was necessary to eliminate refrigeration altogether.

The first indication of a shocking loss of potatoes was found in "Miscellaneous Fruit and Vegetable Report No. 103," issued as of Thursday by the local office of the Food Distribution Administration of the United States Department of Agriculture. The report on shipments from Florida and other parts of the South cited "many showing considerable decay."

Large Quantities Rot

Inquiries made to F. H. Vahlsing, wholesale produce, 127 Warren Street, one of the largest potato dealers in the city, revealed that new potatoes shipped here from the South were rotting in large quantities, while potatoes from California were arriving in good condition.

California potatoes are iced before shipment and twice in transit. Shipments from the South come through without refrigeration. According to a Vahlsing spokesman, the percentage of rotten potatoes runs as high as 75 to 80 per cent in some cars and from 10 to 20 per cent in others. The Atlantic Commission Company, 102 Warren Street, buying for the A. & P. chain, reported that it had been compelled to reject "many carloads" of potatoes because of decay.

H. P. Schwarzman, director of purchases for the non-profit Joint Purchasing Corporation, which buys for many of New York City's voluntary hospitals and other charitable institutions, likewise reported that new potatoes arriving here were in badly rotted condition.

Employes of the fruit and vegetables division of the Food Distribution Administration of the United States Department of Agriculture reported that fifty-nine carloads of new potatoes had arrived yesterday, that eighty-five carloads had been unloaded and that sixty-nine cars remained on track.

Decayed Stock "Dull and Weak"

The fruit and vegetable report for June 10, citing new potatoes, declared that the market for the best quality was "unsettled with weaker feeling," and that stock showing decay was "dull and weak." Florida, 100-pound sacks, Katahdins, Sebagos, U. S. No. 1, were quoted at $4.75 to $5, while the "slightly decayed" were quoted at $4 to $4.50.

The report added that "many showing considerable decay, including some Bliss Triumphs, B size, and commercials," had been sold at $1.50 to $3.75.

Out of this situation have developed the so-called "victory grades," according to the report, which showed that prices ranged from $3.75 to $4, while prices ranging as low as 75 cents to $3.50 were paid for "many showing considerable decay, including some Sebagos and Bliss Triumphs."

Fund to Aid Schools Urged by Senators

By The Associated Press.

WASHINGTON, June 11—Legislation to authorize $300,000,000 of Federal aid to education annually was approved today by a Senate Labor subcommittee.

Offered by Senators Lister Hill, Democrat, of Alabama, and Elbert D. Thomas, Democrat, of Utah, the bill would authorize allocation of $200,000,000 a year to the States on a school-attendance basis during the war for payment of increased teachers' salaries and other unusual expenses.

In addition, it proposes the setting up of a permanent annual fund of $100,000,000 for allocation to States on the basis of financial need to equalize teachers' salaries and strengthen the school systems of the poorer States.

ROOSEVELT DENIES SHIFT ON SAVINGS

He Says He Does Not Endorse Compulsory Plan to Help Close Inflationary Gap

By JOHN H. CRIDER

Special to THE NEW YORK TIMES.

WASHINGTON, June 11—President Roosevelt denied today that he endorsed compulsory savings at his Tuesday press conference. He explained that if he gave that impression it was because he was discussing the theory of taxation.

The President's apparent change in position was of great importance because the technical staffs of the Treasury and the Budget Bureau and the Director of Economic Stabilization are at work on a fiscal program against inflation which the Chief Executive may convey to Congress in a message soon.

The President said on Tuesday in a general discussion of the tax situation that the inflationary gap could be closed in one way or another. One way, he said, was compulsory savings and the other was taxes—probably a combination of the two.

President Explains Views

He added that this was just as necessary now as when he asked Congress in January to legislate an additional $16,000,000,000 of revenue by taxes, savings or both, to be effective during the fiscal year 1944, which starts July 1.

After the President explained that he did not mean on Tuesday to endorse compulsory savings, a reporter asked him a question which ended with Mr. Roosevelt making the statement that it was possible to legislate what the reporter called "voluntarism."

Recalling that in his budget message the President had asked Congress for $16,000,000,000 more in taxes, savings or both, the reporter asked:

"Now what kind of legislation could there be, sir, on savings,

Continued on Page Six

GERMANY HIT AGAIN

American Big Bombers Pound Wilhelmshaven and Cuxhaven

EIGHT ARE MISSING

'Large Number' of Nazi Fighters Bagged—RAF Makes Night Attack

By The Associated Press.

LONDON, Saturday, June 12—A formation of more than 200 American heavy bombers renewed the Allied aerial offensive against Western Europe yesterday by smashing at German shipyards and port installations at Wilhelmshaven and Cuxhaven.

The big four-motored bombers flew a round trip of more than 600 miles without a fighter escort. A United States Eighth Air Force communiqué said eight of them failed to return.

One large section of the American sky fleet smashed through swarms of Nazi fighters to blast the submarine yards at Wilhelmshaven. The communiqué said the bombers shot down a "large number" of challenging enemy planes.

U-boat yards and harbor installations were the objectives at Cuxhaven. Bomb bursts were seen on the targets at both Reich ports, the communiqué said.

Royal Air Force heavy bombers kept up the renewed offensive with an attack in Germany last night, British officials announced today.

First U. S. Raid on Cuxhaven

The Wilhelmshaven - Cuxhaven raid was the first concentrated attack on Hitler's European fortress by heavy bombers from British bases since May 29, when American Flying Fortresses and Liberators struck a triple daylight blow at St. Nazaire, La Pallice and Rennes in France and the Royal Air Force followed up with a devastating night assault on Wuppertal in Germany.

Yesterday's raid was the fifth by American heavy bombers on Wilhelmshaven but their first on Cuxhaven, thirty miles away to the northeast. It was the sixty-second air attack of the war for American bombers.

It was the seventy-ninth Allied attack on Wilhelmshaven, which last was raided May 21, also by American heavy bombers. Wilhelmshaven was the first target in Germany to be hit by the American airmen last Jan. 27.

Cuxhaven, formerly Hamburg's pleasure resort and a nest for submarines, has been attacked seventeen times by the R. A. F., the last time on Nov. 9, 1941.

The R. A. F. added to the renewal of Allied aerial blows with daylight sweeps in which fighters attacked enemy targets in France and the Netherlands and Ventura bombers battered the coke ovens

Continued on Page Three

ALLIES PLANT FLAG ON FIRST MEDITERRANEAN STEPPING-STONE

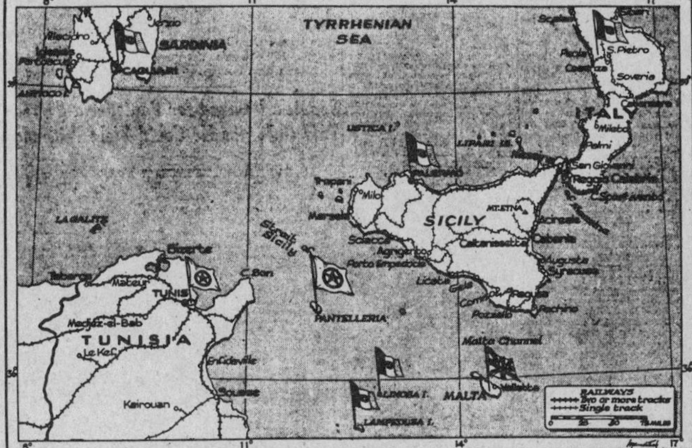

Pantelleria surrendered yesterday and with its occupation other Italian territory was placed in greater jeopardy. (United Nations holdings are indicated by the arbitrary star-in-circle flags.) Lampedusa (bottom of map) is now virtually isolated by the Allied arc of Tunisia-Pantelleria-Malta. An unconfirmed report told of another Commando sortie on the island. Sicily, where new raids were made on Gela and Pozzallo, on the southeastern coast, is now brought within easier fighter-plane range through possession of the airfield on the Italian "Gibraltar." A detailed map of the island of Pantelleria will be found on Page 2.

ISLAND IS OCCUPIED

The Italian 'Gibraltar' Is Knocked Out by Record Avalanche of Bombs

ALL GUNS SILENCED

Troops Take Over in 22 Minutes as New Design in Warfare Emerges

By DREW MIDDLETON

By Wireless to THE NEW YORK TIMES.

ALLIED HEADQUARTERS IN NORTH AFRICA, June 11—Blasted into ruins by hundreds of tons of bombs, the Italian island of Pantelleria, the last Axis stronghold in the Sicilian Strait, surrendered to overwhelming Allied air power this morning rather than endure another day of death and destruction under the most concentrated aerial attack in the history of warfare.

Allied assault craft darted ashore at noon soon after air crews had sighted a white cross of surrender on the airfield and cruisers and destroyers that supported the landing had spied a white flag flying from Semaforo Hill, 2,000 yards from the Harbor of Pantelleria. There was slight resistance from Axis troops, dazed by thirteen days of continuous bombing, and all primary objectives were reached by 12:22 P. M. [London estimates placed the garrison at 8,000 Italians, The Associated Press said.]

It was evident that the island was so disorganized by the bombing and frequent shelling by British cruisers and destroyers that news of the surrender had failed to reach all the enemy troops on the island although the commander had surrendered by displaying the white flag and white cross.

German Dive-Bombers Routed

British troops scrambled up the rocky beaches past wrecked gun batteries—the last enemy gun was silenced by dusk yesterday—and the people of the island crept from shelters to watch with eyes dulled by fear.

[Within an hour after the surrender of Pantelleria, fifty to sixty German dive-bombers attempted to break up the landing forces, but Americans in Lightning fighters routed the Germans, forcing them to jettison their bombs haphazardly in flight, The Associated Press reported. An Algiers broadcast said that naval and infantry casualties in the occupation were negligible.]

The major share of credit for opening the first breach in Italy's chain of island strongholds goes to air power, such air power as never before had been concentrated on a target of similar size.

The climax came yesterday when more bombs were dropped on the island than were dropped in the entire month of April on all targets in Tunisia, Sicily, Sardinia and Italy.

As great a weight of bombs was unloaded on the island in the intensified aerial offensive from May 29 to June 10 as was dropped on all targets in the African theatre in the month of May. And this round-the-clock assault was preceded by six days of heavy intermittent attacks.

Yielded After Third Demand

The capitulation in the form of the white cross on the airfield came as formations of Flying Fortresses, Mitchells and Marauders were over the island. Two previous requests to surrender were ignored by the commander of the Axis garrison. Once emblems of surrender were sighted by the Allied air and naval forces [at 11:40 A. M., according to The Associated Press], the Allied military commander started occupation of the island.

[The surrender also was made known by Admiral Pavesi, senior Italian officer on the island, in a message to an American air base, saying, "Beg sur-

Continued on Page Two

STRIKE BILL VOTED BY HOUSE, 219-129

Conference Compromise Wins Bipartisan Backing—Vote in Senate Due Today

Special to THE NEW YORK TIMES.

WASHINGTON, June 11—The House, by a bipartisan vote of 219 to 129, adopted today a compromise version of the Strike and Labor Control Bill, but Senate efforts to complete legislative action went over until tomorrow when the debate turned to the terms of the compromise, which was developed in conference.

House action came early in the day after an hour's debate. The Senate took up the compromise at 5 P. M. after disposing of the Agriculture Department Appropriation Bill, but abandoned efforts to act on it just before 6 o'clock despite the hope voiced yesterday by Senator Tom Connally, Democrat, of Texas, author of the Senate version, that the measure could be

Continued on Page Seven

President Warns Italians After Pantelleria Victory

By W. H. LAWRENCE

Special to THE NEW YORK TIMES.

WASHINGTON, June 11—Hailing the surrender to Allied forces of the Mediterranean island of Pantelleria as a portent of things to come, President Roosevelt openly invited the Italian people today to overthrow Premier Benito Mussolini and the Fascist party and to expel the Germans so that they could be restored to a respected position in the European family of nations.

As long as Premier Mussolini ruled and the Germans dominated Italian life, the President said, the United Nations had no alternative but to prosecute the war against Italy to a complete victory.

Mr. Roosevelt's bid for an Italian revolt was predicated on his declaration that the Italian people were, by and large, a peace-loving people, who would not be subjected to the horrors of war had they not been betrayed by Premier Mussolini.

The present effects of the British-American campaign against Italy, he continued, were the perfectly logical and inevitable result of the ruthless course that had

Continued on Page Three

AIR WAR LANDMARK SEEN BY DOOLITTLE

He Links First Conquest Due to Aviation Alone to Events Facing Germany and Japan

By The Associated Press.

STRATEGIC AIR FORCE HEADQUARTERS IN NORTH AFRICA, June 11—Major Gen. James H. Doolittle, in a statement tonight, declared that the conquest of Pantelleria by air power "is definitely a landmark in the history of military aviation."

General Doolittle's statement follows:

"This is no surprise to us whatsoever. If the Italians had not capitulated it would have surprised us and we would have to be thinking up a lot of alibis. But the way it worked out was only what we planned and expected. That's the way any airman would look at it.

"This is the first time in the history of warfare that territory has been conquered, as far as I know, by air power alone without occupation. Crete was subdued by air power, but occupied by accompanying forces landed by parachute, gliders and crash-landed transports.

"It was merely a proposition of steadily increasing the Pantelleria bombardment to a point at which it was physically impossible for them to stand up under it.

"At that point they capitulated.

"This was brought about by Royal Air Force night bombers

Continued on Page Two

SOVIET EXTOLS U. S. AS POST-WAR ALLY

Lavish Praise of Our War Role Predicts 'Protracted Peace' Based on Firm Accord

By C. L. SULZBERGER

By Wireless to THE NEW YORK TIMES.

MOSCOW, June 11—To the accompaniment of the most lavish and enthusiastic praise of the United States ever promulgated in the Soviet Union, the Russian people were informed today that British-Russian-American cooperation, cemented in blood, would lead to the complete smashing of the European Axis, abetted by a direct Allied assault on the Continent. They were also told that increased understanding and collaboration between the three great powers would facilitate the establishment of a "just and protracted peace" in which the free nations of the world could live in an atmosphere "of creative labor for the good of humanity."

The occasion for these pronouncements was the first anni-

Continued on Page Four

Senate 'Holds Line' on Prices, Balking Plan to Bar Roll-Backs

By C. P. TRUSSELL

Special to THE NEW YORK TIMES.

WASHINGTON, June 11—The Senate shunned today the responsibility for a possible "breaking of the price line," and declined, by a vote of 36—37, to suspend its rules and adopt legislation concededly designed to prevent roll-backs of food costs. A two-thirds vote was required.

By its action the upper house appeared to follow the advice of Senator Bennett C. Clark, Democrat, of Missouri, who urged that a "club" be kept "in the closet" while the legislative branch waited to see what the Administration did to hold the line on the coal-strike front.

Mr. Clark predicted that if the Administration yielded to John L. Lewis, this "club," in the form of the vetoed Bankhead bill to prohibit the deduction of any farm benefits in the fixing of price ceilings, would be wielded promptly to override the President's veto.

The Bankhead bill was recommitted to the Agricultural Committee in April, after Mr. Roosevelt had returned it to Congress, pronouncing it a measure that would give farmers "an unwarranted bonus at the expense of the consumers" and set off "an inflationary tornado."

Although the Senate had passed it originally by a vote of 78—2, it then lacked the votes to pass it over the veto, so it was left in a state of suspended animation until "a more propitious time."

The issue was brought to a new

Continued on Page Six

War News Summarized

SATURDAY, JUNE 12, 1943

The white flag of surrender rose over Pantelleria shortly before noon yesterday, ending the fiercest aerial blitz in history. Within twenty-two minutes Allied landing parties completed occupation of the Italian "Gibraltar." They found an estimated 8,000 fear-stunned, thirsty soldiers huddled in the ruins of the island on which Allied planes had cascaded a greater tonnage of bombs from May 29 to June 10 than had been unloaded in the entire remainder of the Mediterranean theatre in May. [1:8; maps, pages 1 and 2.]

Some details of the assault that overwhelmed Pantelleria came from jubilant, air-minded officers in Washington, who hailed it as the first example of conquest of territory primarily by air attack. They said that since the beginning of June 3,500 tons of bombs had blanketed the island, with 1,000 planes joining in throwing the "Sunday punch." Our plane losses during the entire operation were less than one-half of 1 per cent. [3:1.]

President Roosevelt utilized the Allied victory to call upon the Italian people to oust their German-dominated government. The President urged Italians to depose Premier Mussolini and make peace with Allies. [1:5-6.]

More than 200 bombers of the United States Air Force in Britain swept over Northwestern Germany to strike at the submarine bases of Wilhelmshaven and Cuxhaven. It was the first large-scale attack by British-based planes since May 9. The RAF struck in Germany last night. [1:3.]

Aerial warfare got top billing on the Russian front, too. Seven hundred Soviet planes attacked enemy airports, destroying or damaging more than 150 enemy aircraft on the ground, and shooting down ten others. [4:1.]

A significant chorus of editorial praise was accorded the United States and Great Britain by the Russian press on the first anniversary of the Russian-American agreement. This unanimous outburst was believed to have been approved if not inspired by the Kremlin and was said to mark the beginning of a new Russian policy of fuller collaboration with Britain and the United States. [1:6.]

Among the French factions in North Africa, Generals de Gaulle and Giraud were still at loggerheads. General de Gaulle was insisting on the immediate removal of high French officers who had opposed the Fighting French, but his letter of resignation was rejected. [3:5.]

Daily Gasoline for 1,000 Bombers Cut Off by Texas Refinery Strike

Special to THE NEW YORK TIMES.

WASHINGTON, June 11 — Advised by the War Department of an unauthorized strike closing a Shell Oil Company refinery near Houston, Texas, where high-octane aviation gasoline sufficient to fuel a bomber mission of 1,000 planes a day over Europe is produced every twenty-four hours, Secretary Harold L. Ickes, Solid Fuels Administrator for War, said today he would take all possible steps to bring the walkout to an end.

Efforts were made by Federal officials to reach Philip Murray, president of the Congress of Industrial Organizations. The strike was called by a local of that organization's Oil and Refinery Workers International Union.

Robert P. Patterson, Under-Secretary of War, was understood to be deeply disturbed by the strike, which was caused by a dispute between a supervisor at the Deer Park Refinery and an employe who had been discharged for intoxication.

Dr. R. H. Waser, manager of the plant, said that the employe assaulted the supervisor. The local union version was that the employe had been assaulted by the supervisor before his dismissal. Thus the union demanded that the supervisor also be dismissed. The company refused, offering to suspend the supervisor until the dispute was settled, but this was rejected by the union.

War Department officials felt that at this stage of the war the no-strike pledge made by labor leaders following Pearl Harbor

Continued on Page Seven

U.S. Marine Corps

U. S. Marines moving through muddy terrain on their way to the front lines on Bougainville.

"All the News That's Fit to Print."

The New York Times.

LATE CITY EDITION
Continued cool with moderate winds today.
Temperatures Yesterday—Max., 82; Min., 60
Sunrise, 5:27 A. M.; Sunset, 8:32 P. M.

Copyright, 1943, by The New York Times Company.

VOL. XCII—No. 31,204. Entered as Second-Class Matter, Postoffice, New York, N. Y. NEW YORK, THURSDAY, JULY 1, 1943. THREE CENTS IN NEW YORK CITY

M'ARTHUR STARTS ALLIED OFFENSIVE IN PACIFIC; NEW GUINEA ISLES WON, LANDINGS IN SOLOMONS; CHURCHILL PROMISES BLOWS IN EUROPE BY FALL

MAYOR FACES FIGHT WITH OPA ON PLAN FOR HANDLING MEAT

Gives Approval for Sales by Slaughterers to Retailers on Consignment Basis

FEDERAL ACTION LOOMS

Price Agency Director Here Promises Move Should Violation Be Found

A direct conflict between Mayor Fiorello H. La Guardia and the Office of Price Administration appeared inevitable last night, after the Mayor had announced that he had approved, on his own responsibility, a plan for independent slaughterers to sell meat to the public at consumer ceiling prices through consignments to retailers, despite the OPA's objections to the plan.

"If they go ahead with a plan that is in violation of the regulations, OPA will be forced to take action," Frank C. Russell, district OPA director, retorted when informed of the Mayor's decision. "Apparently, the Mayor has given his permission for something which the OPA legal department has turned down."

Former Municipal Court Justice Nathan Sweedler of 225 Broadway, who, as counsel for the Eastern States Independent Meat Packers and Slaughterers, proposed the plan approved by the Mayor after the OPA had turned it down, announced that his organization hoped to have meat on sale in some retail shops today and expected to have a large quantity available by Saturday.

Sees Quick Meat Supply

Mr. Sweedler has estimated that his group could provide 25,000 pounds of beef within twenty-four hours after the Mayor gave his approval to the plan and eventually could gear its output to 1,000,000 pounds a week, but the Mayor was even more optimistic. He said that the plan might provide the city with 1,000,000 pounds a week "and it may be 5,000,000 pounds."

Under the plan the meat would be sold on consignment, the retailer keeping 21 per cent of the selling price. According to Mr. Sweedler, the remaining 79 per cent would pay for the cost of livestock, freight and slaughtering. He contends that under his plan meat could be sold at the consumer ceiling prices, and any butcher violating the ceiling would be deprived of meat through a voluntary policing system.

The Mayor announced his approval of the plan to reporters at City Hall and then released a letter to Commissioner of Markets Daniel P. Woolley in which he argued that the plan did not conflict with any existing regulations and that it should be accepted as a temporary measure.

Holds Plan Feasible

"I have carefully studied the report you submitted to me with plan for direct consignment of food from the original processor to retailer direct, and selling by such retailer to consumer at ceiling prices or lower," the Mayor said in his letter. "I do not see how any such plan could conflict with any existing rules or regulations of any Federal agency, provided the producer, farmer or livestock man is paid the market price and the retailer sells at ceiling prices or lower.

"The whole purpose of food control is to make food available and fix ceiling prices. There is nothing in the rules that prevents anyone from selling below ceiling prices. Surely, in the protection of the consumer, we could not or would not prosecute a retailer for selling below ceiling prices provided his food is wholesome and complies with all health requirements and government inspection.

"In fact, if an original processor or retailer wanted to give food

Continued on Page Seventeen

OWI Closes Twelve Regional Branches

By The Associated Press.

WASHINGTON, June 30 — Twelve regional and thirty-six branch offices of the Office of War Information throughout the country began closing at midnight tonight as the fiscal year ended.

The OWI said an official would remain in each of the twelve regional offices for a few days to liquidate the affairs of both the regional and branch offices.

The shutdown was made necessary, the OWI said, because the Senate voted to appropriate only $3,000,000 for the domestic branch of the organization and earmarked the amount, allowing none for maintaining the regional and branch offices. The House had voted to abolish the domestic service entirely.

"It isn't likely that the Congressional conference committee, which has yet to act finally, would go above the Senate's $3,000,000, so we are closing down the offices," an agency spokesman said.

CONGRESS CRUSHES SUBSIDY PROGRAM

Ban on Payments to Cut Prices Stays in CCC Bill Passed by Overwhelming Majorities

By The Associated Press.

WASHINGTON, June 30—Congress, handing the Roosevelt Administration another legislative setback, today forbade use of subsidies to push down retail food prices and ordered the meat-butter price "roll back" ended by Aug. 1.

The ban was incorporated in legislation extending the life of the Commodity Credit Corporation for two more years from midnight tonight and adding $750,000,000 to its present $2,650,000,000 lending powers. Both Senate and House approved the measure by far more than the two-thirds majority which would be necessary to override a veto. The House vote was 160 to 32, and the Senate vote, 62 to 13.

Less restrictive than the original House measure, the bill permits continued use of subsidies, up to $150,000,000 to meet increased transportation costs such as are now being paid on the movement of oil to the East Coast and on coffee imports, and to promote production of critical metals and war-essential foods. It also allows incentive payments on canning and specialty crops, price support for domestic vegetable oils and fats, and payments for sale of wheat for feeding purposes. However, no subsidies could be paid simply to reduce prices.

Before final passage, a provision prohibiting Government agencies from deducting farm benefit payments in calculating agricultural price ceilings was stricken out.

Speaking for final Congressional action, Lou R. Maxon, deputy administrator of the Office of Price

Continued on Page Seventeen

WALLACE AND JONES RENEW THEIR ROW AFTER 2-HOUR TALK

Conference Called by Byrnes Fails 'to Resolve and Determine' Controversy

SHARP STATEMENTS ISSUED

Secretary Says Charge of Delay by RFC in War Effort Is 'Dastardly' and 'Untrue'

By JOHN H. CRIDER

Special to THE NEW YORK TIMES.

WASHINGTON, June 30—An attempt by the War Mobilization Director, James F. Byrnes, to harmonize the differences between Vice President Henry A. Wallace and Secretary of Commerce Jesse H. Jones, failed today after he had summoned them to his office for a two-hour discussion this afternoon.

Tonight the Vice President issued a statement which somewhat tempered his bitter accusations against Mr. Jones made yesterday but said the fundamental differences remained.

To this the Secretary replied:

"Mr. Wallace in his statement tonight repeats that delays of the RFC have retarded the war effort. This dastardly charge is as untrue as when he first made it. As for the rest of his statement, Mr. Wallace was not authorized to speak for me. I will continue to speak for myself, and, as previously stated, I shall insist upon a Congressional investigation."

The Vice President's statement made it clear that the basic differences between himself and Mr. Jones had been altered only to the extent that "Mr. Jones did not object" to Mr. Wallace's plan to ask Congress after its recess for funds for foreign procurement which would make it independent of the Reconstruction Finance Corporation, headed by the Secretary of Commerce.

There was no mention of Mr. Byrnes in the Vice President's statement, although it was the fruit of the War Mobilization Director's efforts to play the role of peacemaker for the Federal Bureaucracy cast for him by President Roosevelt's Executive Order of May 28 calling upon him to "resolve and determine controversies between such agencies or departments."

Meanwhile, the Senate, showing little indication at this point of being in a mood to grant the broad authority over foreign procurement expenditures sought by Mr. Wallace, inserted in the War Agencies Appropriation Bill an amendment by Senator Kenneth McKellar, Democrat, of Tennessee, providing that BEW could not use for foreign purchases any of the $36,000,000 appropriated without approval of a majority of the

Continued on Page Eleven

Cattle Grower Says 'Policymakers' Are to Blame in Meat Shortage

By JAY G. HAYDEN

North American Newspaper Alliance.

WASHINGTON, June 30—Joseph G. Montague, general counsel for the Texas and Southwestern Cattle Raisers Association, put the blame for the meat shortage today on "the unofficial policymakers close to the President," thereby bringing into the open a charge which figured behind the scenes in the Congressional rejection of food subsidies and the retirement of Chester C. Davis as Food Administrator.

Speaking before the Senate Agricultural Committee, Mr. Montague said:

"Surrounding the President are a group of people who have no responsibility, yet determine policy and cause confusion in the meat situation. They are entrenched in power and determined to change the economic and social order."

Mr. Davis is believed to have had substantially this same thought in mind when he gave as his first reason for resignation that "I find I have assumed a public responsibility while the authority, not only over broad food policy, but day-to-day actions, is being exercised elsewhere."

Mr. Davis, according to his close friends, became convinced that the real policy-makers were the same old New Deal inner cabinet, including particularly Harry L. Hopkins, Associate Justice Felix Frankfurter and Judge Samuel Rosenman, which has functioned prominently throughout the Roosevelt Administration. Whether he was speaking of his own knowledge or merely

Continued on Page Seventeen

UNITED NATIONS FORCES MOVE FORWARD IN THE SOUTHWEST PACIFIC

American troops landed on Rendova and New Georgia Islands (1), in the vicinity of the enemy air base at Munda, and engaged the Japanese. The inset shows this area in detail. To the west the Allies occupied Woodlark Island (2) and the Trobriand Islands (3) without opposition. In New Guinea they occupied Nassau Bay (4), just below Salamaua; the landing craft encountered only slight resistance. Apparently these widespread operations have as their ultimate goal the reduction of Rabaul (5), which was bombed.

76 BILLIONS SPENT IN U.S. FISCAL YEAR

71 of the Total Were for War —Public Debt Up to 140 Billions, Deficit to 55

Special to THE NEW YORK TIMES.

WASHINGTON, June 30 — The United States ended its fiscal year tonight with a record of expenditures of more than $76,000,000,000, receipts of more than $21,000,000,000, a gross public debt of more than $140,000,000,000 and a deficit of more than $55,000,000,000.

The latest figures available at the Treasury were for June 28, four days before the actual end of the fiscal year. On that date total war expenditures for the year were $71,014,000,000, as against $25,515,000,000 on the same date in 1942.

Spending for civilian purposes was $5,375,000,000, as compared with $5,800,000,000 on the same day a year earlier. The War Department spent $41,690,000,000 and the Navy $20,513,000,000. War expenditures of the Agriculture Department totaled $2,005,000,000. The Maritime Commission spent $2,733,000,000.

In one year the public debt increased from $76,560,000,000 to $140,028,000,000 and the deficit advanced from $19,152,000,000 to $55,242,000,000.

Receipts of $21,625,000,000 up to

Continued on Page Twelve

Prime Minister Warns Axis Allied Attacks Are Imminent

By RAYMOND DANIELL

By Cable to THE NEW YORK TIMES.

LONDON, June 30—Prime Minister Churchill warned the Axis today that the Allies were preparing heavier blows on land and sea and by air from east, south and west to bring about the unconditional surrender that he and President Roosevelt declared at Casablanca was the price of peace.

The text of Mr. Churchill's address is printed on Page 4.

In the Mediterranean and "elsewhere," he said, heavy fighting probably would develop "before the leaves of autumn fall," but he added that large-scale amphibious operations take months to prepare.

Significantly, he dwelt at length and in considerable detail upon the growing scale and intensity of the British-American air offensive against Germany from this island, and indicated that Russian air power, long tied down to the battle lines, would soon be able to join in the attack on Nazi industry from the east.

A Major Victory at Sea

Reviewing the Battle of the Atlantic, he said a victory had been won at sea against the submarines two months ago comparable with the Allied conquest of Africa with the capture of 350,000 German and Italian prisoners and vast quantities of war material. He likened the victory in Tunisia to the Russian triumph at Stalingrad.

The Prime Minister was speaking in the ancient Guildhall, where he received freedom of the City of London, that square mile of the British capital that still bears the

Continued on Page Four

BERLIN EVACUATION REPORTED PLANNED

Swedes Hear Exodus Is to Start in Fall—Wuppertal Held Beyond Rebuilding

By GEORGE AXELSSON

By Telephone to THE NEW YORK TIMES.

STOCKHOLM, Sweden, June 30—Berlin will evacuate in the Fall women and children not engaged in the war industries, according to reliable information received here today through private channels.

Fear of heavier and more frequent Allied air raids with the coming of longer nights has prompted this decision, and authorities have already begun the preliminary arrangements, it is stated.

The extent to which the Ruhr has been hit by the RAF raids is indicated by a statement by Adolf Hitler's chief city planning consultant, Armaments Minister Albert Speer, just back from a tour of inspection of the devastated area.

He said it was not worth while to try to rebuild Wuppertal.

Continued on Page Three

MARTINIQUE YIELDS, ASKS TERMS OF U. S.

Robert, 'to Avoid Bloodshed,' Ready to Accept Change of French Authority

The Martinique radio broadcast a statement last night by Admiral Georges Robert, Vichy's High Commissioner on the island, asserting that he had asked the United States Government to dispatch a "plenipotentiary to fix the terms for a change of French authority."

The broadcast said that Admiral Robert had taken the action "to avoid bloodshed." It was recorded by Federal Communications Commission monitors, The United Press said.

The admiral has, since the fall of France, stood firm in his determination to hold Martinique and nearby French islands in the Caribbean under his own rule, loyal to Marshal Henri-Philippe Pétain, French Chief of State.

The reception of the broadcast was marred by technical difficulties, but those portions of the broadcast that could be heard said:

"Communiqué to the population:

"In order to avoid bloodshed between the French and * * * I have asked the Government of the United States, under the double condition of its renewing the guarantee to maintain French sovereignty in these islands and of the nonintervention of American forces, to send a plenipotentiary to fix the terms for a change of French authority. "* * * my duty to the people and the Marshal * * *

"Admiral Robert."

Recently there have been unconfirmed reports of clashes between the Admiral's troops and elements favoring the rule of the islands by

Continued on Page Eight

2-PRONGED DRIVE

Americans Battle Enemy on New Georgia and Rendova Islands

SALAMAUA IN PERIL

Allies Seize Trobriand and Woodlark Isles—Rabaul Pounded

By SIDNEY SHALETT

Special to THE NEW YORK TIMES.

WASHINGTON, Thursday, July 1—Combined Army and Navy forces under General Douglas MacArthur have opened the long expected offensive against the Japanese in the south and southwest Pacific.

Fighting was in progress on Rendova and New Georgia islands, which were hit by ground, naval and air forces in "closest synchronization," a communiqué from General MacArthur's headquarters in Australia reported today. Nassau Bay, ten miles south of the big Japanese base of Salamaua in New Guinea, fell to the Allies after a slight skirmish, and the Trobriand and Woodlark island groups, 300 to 400 miles west of the New Georgia group, were occupied without opposition.

The Allied push—aimed, observers here believe, at the major Japanese base of Rabaul, on New Britain Island—got under way yesterday, Solomons time, which was Tuesday here.

Nutcracker Move Seen

It was believed here, on the basis of early reports, that the fighting and occupations reported so far were preliminary to major actions to come. If bases in the New Georgias are consolidated, a two-way push against Rabaul might be developing, with one arm advancing northwestward from the Central Solomons and the other swinging across eastward from new bases in New Guinea.

United States heavy bombers carried out an attack on Rabaul during the night, dropping nearly twenty-three tons of high-explosive, fragmentation and incendiary bombs throughout the dispersal areas at the Vunakanau and Lakunai airdromes, the communiqué from Australian headquarters reported. "Several explosions" and "numerous fires" were observed, one of which was visible for 100 miles, the announcement said.

The big bombers, which have punished Rabaul extensively in recent weeks, ran into heavy Japanese anti-aircraft fire and interference from some enemy night fighters. One American bomber was missing after the raid.

The Trobriand and Woodlark islands will be valuable as steppingstones in a chain of fighter-plane bases from the Allied stronghold of Milne Bay, on the tip of New Guinea. Japanese-held Gasmata and Rabaul may be raided with comparative ease with the aid of these bays.

Navy Gives First News

The first report of landing actions came early yesterday when the Navy announced here in a communiqué that combined United States forces had landed June 30 (Solomons time) on Rendova Island, in the New Georgia group, which is only five miles from the important Japanese air base of Munda, on New Georgia Island, but that communiqué said, "No details have been received."

A hint that the fighting had extended came later from Secretary of the Navy Frank Knox in Los Angeles, where he is inspecting Pacific Coast installations. The Secretary declared that the Rendova attack was the beginning of "an offensive against the Japanese base at Munda and surrounding bases." Navy officials in Washington yesterday declined, however, to con-

Continued on Page Three

War News Summarized

THURSDAY, JULY 1, 1943

The Allied Southwest Pacific and South Pacific Commands have started a broad offensive against Japanese positions. The first results of the combined naval, air and land operations are:

Landings on Rendova and New Georgia Islands in the Central Solomons, where fighting is going on.

Occupation, without opposition, of the Trobriand Islands and Woodlark Island off the southeastern tip of New Guinea at the north end of the Coral Sea.

A landing at Nassau Bay, ten miles south of Salamaua in New Guinea.

Heavy aerial bombardment of the big Japanese base at Rabaul, New Britain.

Gen. Douglas MacArthur is in general command of the combined operations, with Admiral William F. Halsey Jr. directing the offensive of the South Pacific forces. The battle area extends 500 miles north of Guadalcanal to Rabaul and 750 miles northwest to Salamaua [All the foregoing, 1:8.]

In London, Prime Minister Churchill pledged that after Hitler's defeat "every man, every ship and every airplane in the King's service that can be moved to the Pacific will be sent and there maintained in action * * * for as many years as are needed to make the Japanese, in their turn, submit or bite the dust."

Mr. Churchill then announced that "very probably there will be heavy fighting in the Mediterranean and elsewhere before the leaves of autumn fall." He characterized Tunisia and the campaign against the U-boat as the two greatest Allied victories of the war, and promised that every corner of Germany would be bombed as thoroughly as the Ruhr had been. [All the foregoing, 1:5-6.]

On the other war fronts, Flying Fortresses raided Le Mans in France and the RAF hit targets in western Europe [5:2-3], Reggio Calabria and Messina were bombed in the Mediterranean [6:2], and Russian troops captured a strong position on the Velikiye Luki front. [7:1.]

Admiral Robert, Vichy's High Commissioner in Martinique, asked the United States for terms under which the West Indies islands could be transferred to other French authority. [1:7.]

Laundry Workers Held Essential But the WMC Restricts Services

Special to THE NEW YORK TIMES.

WASHINGTON, June 30 — The War Manpower Commission extended to the country's laundries today the same preferential treatment in the allocation of manpower as is given to essential war industries.

Laundries classified as "locally needed" by regional directors of the WMC will be supplied with workers by the United States Employment Service, will be protected from labor piracy and will have their existing labor force stabilized, except that there will be no occupational deferment under the Selective Service Act. They will receive this aid only if they discontinue luxury services to their patrons.

To be classified as "locally needed" they must meet standards agreed upon by the War Labor Board's Office of Civilian Requirements and the WMC. These standards are designed to enable the laundries to give adequate essential service to more people than they are now doing with their available labor force and to put maintenance services on a "rock-bottom, first-things-first basis."

Under the new ruling hand ironing, the retouching of all flat work and the retouching of wearing apparel by hand after pressing, except for a bare minimum required to make it presentable; fancy packaging and unnecessary folding are eliminated, and customers will be limited to one grade of starching of their shirts and other wearing apparel.

Laundries are expected to cooperate in inducing hotels, boarding houses and tourist homes to change bed linen only once a week for any one patron; limit each patron to one face towel and one bath towel

Continued on Page Ten

"All the News That's Fit to Print."

The New York Times.

LATE CITY EDITION
Showers, warm and humid today; moderate winds.
Temperatures Yesterday—Max., 79; Min., 66
Sunrise, 5:36 A. M.; Sunset, 8:30 P. M.

VOL. XCII. No. 31,213. Entered as Second-Class Matter, Postoffice, New York, N. Y. NEW YORK, SATURDAY, JULY 10, 1943. THREE CENTS IN NEW YORK CITY

ALLIED TROOPS START INVASION OF SICILY; NAVAL ESCORTS BOMBARD SHORE DEFENSES; LANDINGS PRECEDED BY SEVERE AIR ATTACK

ROOSEVELT VOICES DOUBT ON MAKING LEWIS OBEY WLB

He Asks at Press Conference How to Force Someone to Sign Against His Will

ORDER TO WARD IS CITED

He Declares He Could Take Property but Probably Could Not Seize Union

By SAMUEL B. BLEDSOE
Special to THE NEW YORK TIMES.

WASHINGTON, July 9—President Roosevelt indicated today that he had no intention of taking action to force John L. Lewis, head of the United Mine Workers, to obey the War Labor Board's directive that he sign an agreement with the bituminous mine operators.

Asked at his press conference whether he intended to reaffirm the board's order in the mine union case, the President said that, after all, the order was that of a quasi-judicial body and spoke for itself. He asked what action he could take —send a little polite note on pink paper and say, "Dear Mr. Lewis, I hope you will sign the contract"?

Pressed to say what he would do if Mr. Lewis did not sign, the President inquired in turn what the reporter would do and got the reply, "I don't know. I'm not President." The President then commented upon the difficulty of forcing some one to sign something against his will.

Montgomery Ward Case Cited

A reporter reminded that Sewell Avery, head of Montgomery Ward & Co., had been directed by the President to sign a wage agreement which provided for a maintenance of membership clause and check-off of union dues after the company had defied a WLB order.

President Roosevelt said that, although he did not want to take over Montgomery Ward, he had authority to do so, but doubted that he had similar authority to take over the mine union.

Asked if he felt he needed some sanction of law to deal with recalcitrant miners, Mr. Roosevelt replied that there was Section 8 of the Smith-Connally Anti-Strike Act and the first seven sections of the bill. He suggested that these sections be examined.

War Labor Board officials refused to be quoted on Mr. Roosevelt's statements. They said they still were hoping that the President intended to crack down on Mr. Lewis, but they also disclosed that they feared the board had been left high and dry.

Interpretation of WLB Order

They said that while the directive of June 18 did not specifically order Mr. Lewis to sign an agreement with the operators, such action clearly was implied by the directive. Although the matter had been put up to President Roosevelt, there was no indication, they stated, that the President had asked Mr. Lewis to obey the directive and no indication that he intended to do so.

One official declared that the real issue in the Lewis case was whether an individual, or pressure group, could continue in wartime to defy a Government directive intended to further prosecution of the war.

If President Roosevelt does not intend to take further action in the Lewis case, but continues to operate the mines under the direction of Secretary Ickes, some officials here declared, a good deal will be heard about the differences in handling a situation when an employer defies the WLB and when a union defies it.

Obedience by Ward Forced

Acting as "Commander in Chief in time of war," the President issued the order to Montgomery Ward & Co. last December. The company had objected strenuously to the maintenance-of-membership

Continued on Page Seven

Cripps Bids Workers Back New Air Phase

By Wireless to THE NEW YORK TIMES.

LONDON, July 9—Appealing for maximum production and the cessation of absenteeism and strikes among aircraft workers, Sir Stafford Cripps, Minister of Aircraft Production, declared in a radio broadcast tonight that this country has entered a new and more intensive phase of the war "and almost at any moment there may be a great intensification" of the present offensive.

He asked the workers to support this offensive to their utmost.

"An assault upon the Axis powers in Europe and the Far East," Sir Stafford said, "entails dislodging them from occupied territories. That will be a costly task. Our casualties will inevitably be heavy but we can help to keep down those losses."

PRESIDENT BARS DATA FOR INQUIRY

On His Order Army, Navy, Budget Bureau Deny Radio Committee's Request

By WINIFRED MALLON
Special to THE NEW YORK TIMES.

WASHINGTON, July 9—Acting on the order of President Roosevelt, the War and Navy Departments refused today to transmit information requested by the House committee investigating the Federal Communications Commission.

Their reply stated that production of documents and testimony of witnesses relative to the proposed executive order transferring to the War and Navy Departments the radio intelligence activities of the commission had been forbidden by the President as "contrary to the public interest."

In a letter to the committee, James V. Forrestal, Under-Secretary of the Navy, wrote:

"The President of the United States authorized me to inform the committee that he, the President, refuses to allow the documents described in your letter to be delivered to the committee, as such delivery would be incompatible with the public interest.

"I must decline to permit the appearance of naval officers, active or inactive, before your committee, as such appearance would be incompatible with the public interest."

A letter to the same effect was received from Robert P. Patterson, Under-Secretary of War.

On similar ground Harold D. Smith, Director of the Budget, declined to testify at today's hearing of the committee and refused to deliver Budget Bureau data.

James Lawrence Fly, chairman of the FCC, appearing as chairman of the Board of War Communications, also declined to answer questions, declaring himself bound

Continued on Page Seven

RUSSIANS STIFFEN

Red Army Repels Heavy Attacks in Orel and Kursk Sectors

AXIS LOSSES SOAR

Both Sides State Fight Grows in Intensity—Nazis Win 'Inches'

By The Associated Press.

LONDON, Saturday, July 10—The Russian armies of the center bloodily beat off savage German attacks all along the Orel and Kursk fronts yesterday, held their own in the Belgorod sector to the south, and destroyed 193 Nazi tanks and 94 planes in the great battle of attrition, the Soviet command announced early today.

The German dead, in two battle areas specifically mentioned, were nearly 5,000 for the day, Moscow declared in the regular midnight communiqué recorded here by the Soviet monitor, thus bringing to about 40,000 the total German casualties for five days of violent action.

German losses in matériel also were rising to tremendous proportions:

Yesterday's destruction raised to 2,036 the number of enemy tanks thus far listed as knocked out, and to 904 the number of Nazi planes smashed since the beginning of the offensive.

In the Orel-Kursk sector, said the bulletin, the Nazis after four days of heavy losses had "gained no success" and had been forced to shift the weight of attack to other areas, reinforcing their "battered troops" by nine infantry divisions and one tank division.

Twenty Attacks Beaten Back

A score or more of German attacks were beaten off—thirteen of them in a single area of action—and fighting at times was hand-to-hand.

Fifteen hundred Nazis were wiped out in these actions, said the Soviet command, as was most of a German battalion in a near-by action.

About Belgorod—scene of four previous German penetrations against which the Russians had battered all day—no further Nazi progress was reported, although it was declared the invaders were "bringing into battle all their reserves, striving at any cost to achieve success."

In the Belgorod sector 2,000 Germans were killed during the day; in a near-by action 1,000 more fell. But it was in the Kursk-Orel sector where the supreme Nazi efforts were being made.

The Germans themselves, in a long broadcast propaganda report, spoke of "ferocious fighting" south of Orel, where Nazi troops "could gain ground only inch by inch."

Further German advances—

Continued on Page Four

MUNDA HAMMERED

Planes, Warships, Guns Batter Japanese at New Georgia Base

GROUND PUSH GAINS

Enemy's Counter-Blows to Ward Off Assault Are Declared Weak

By TILLMAN DURDIN
By Wireless to THE NEW YORK TIMES.

ALLIED HEADQUARTERS FOR THE SOUTHWEST PACIFIC, Saturday, July 10—American planes unloosed the most terrific aerial attack yet made on Japanese positions on New Georgia Island yesterday. More than a hundred bombers escorted by fighters pounded Munda and the Bairoko Harbor areas early in the morning. At the same time United States destroyers shelled Munda.

Seventy tons of bombs, including two thousand-pounders, were used to blast the camp areas, supply dumps and anti-aircraft positions. The biggest group of bombers concentrated on the area between Munda Point and the Lamberti coconut plantation, where part of the main Japanese defenses around the Munda airdrome are located.

While dive bombers and level bombers were circling and hurling their bombs in this area American artillery from across Blanche Channel on Rendova shelled Japanese anti-aircraft sites. Other groups of bombers pounded the Japanese at Bairoko harbor, port across the peninsula from Munda and Enogai inlet, three miles north of Bairoko Harbor.

Heavy Damage Done

There is every reason to believe that the combined aerial, naval and land artillery bombardment of yesterday morning heavily damaged the Japanese defenses. It was one of the most devastating artillery and air attacks ever made in the Pacific on a land target. The destroyers shelled the base before dawn.

Forty-five Japanese fighters attempted to intervene in the battle for Munda early yesterday afternoon. They appeared over Rendova Island, where they were intercepted by patrolling American fighters. Four were shot down in the

Continued on Page Five

ISLAND OF SICILY IS INVADED BY ALLIED FORCES

General Eisenhower announced that his troops had debarked at various points on Sicily early today. The landings were preceded by furious air assaults and warships accompanying the transports shelled the coastal defenses. Troops got ashore at the western tip of the island (cross), according to the Algiers radio. Strong forces of tanks were reported being used. The invasion had been preceded by heavy bombings of a variety of targets (bomb devices).

PRESIDENT PARRIES FRENCH BIAS QUERY

There Is No France Now, He Explains—Giraud Wins Arms for 300,000

By HAROLD CALLENDER
Special to THE NEW YORK TIMES.

WASHINGTON, July 9—Commenting upon the accusation that the United States was interfering in French affairs, President Roosevelt at his press conference today said that 95 per cent of the French people were still under the German heel and that there was no France now.

When a correspondent remarked that, at any rate, there was a French committee, and asked whether this Government would recognize it, the President said that question had not arisen.

Regarding the visit here of General Giraud, who is also Commander in Chief of the French forces in North and West Africa, Mr. Roosevelt said merely that at lunch yes-

Continued on Page Four

RAF Pounds Cologne Again In 1,000-Ton 'Repeat' Attack

By FREDERICK GRAHAM
By Cable to THE NEW YORK TIMES.

LONDON, July 9—Cologne, which was the first city to feel the weight of a 1,000-plane raid in the British attack of May 30, 1942, was plastered again last night by the Royal Air Force with more than 1,000 tons of bombs. The raid was the 119th of the war on the Rhine city, and it was described by officials here as effecting "a crushing setback to the German attempts to revive the skeletonized industrial life of the town."

Despite an intense Nazi anti-aircraft barrage and severe icing conditions and electrical storms, the heavy British and Canadian bombers pressed home an "affectively concentrated" attack at a cost of only eight planes, the Air Ministry reported.

[British heavy bombers raided Germany again last night, said a brief London announcement early today, reported by The Associated Press.

[RAF fighters and light bombers raided northern France in force by daylight yesterday and attacked German shipping along the coast. The St. Omer airfield was bombed and Mustang fighters punished Nazi traffic.

[Nazi raiders attacked the London area yesterday afternoon, two of the about ten attackers being shot down. Bombs caused casualties in the suburbs. In a southeast English town an enemy raider landed a bomb in a movie theatre filled with children and at least twelve persons were reported killed and injured.]

Authoritative comment on the

Continued on Page Three

BOMBS TORE SICILY BEFORE INVASION

Allied Fliers Ripped Airfields, Communications and Plants in Week-Long Blitz

By Wireless to THE NEW YORK TIMES.

ALLIED HEADQUARTERS IN NORTH AFRICA, July 9—Swarms of Allied bombers maintained their round-the-clock pounding of Axis air bases in Sicily, and formations of fighter bombers, including new A-36's, which are also fitted as dive-bombers, hammered transport, communications and industrial plants on the besieged island yesterday as the great Allied aerial offensive centered on Sicily for the sixth straight day.

The new A-36 fighter-bomber, which was developed from North American's P-51 Mustang fighter, is the newest "plane of all work." It is used as both a dive and glide bomber and takes part in strafing missions as well. The Mustang is supposed to be the world's most effective fighter under 15,000 feet,

Continued on Page Two

SEVERAL LANDINGS

American, British and Canadian Troops Carry Out the Attack

A 'LIBERATION' START

But Eisenhower Urges French Be Calm Till Their Hour Strikes

By DREW MIDDLETON
By Wireless to THE NEW YORK TIMES.

ALLIED HEADQUARTERS IN NORTH AFRICA, Saturday, July 10—Allied infantry landed at a number of places on the rocky Sicilian coast under a canopy of naval gunfire early this morning as the long-awaited invasion began.

Gen. Dwight D. Eisenhowed, Allied Commander in Chief, speaking to the people of metropolitan France, called the attack "the first page in the liberation of the European Continent," and promised "there will be others."

Allied headquarters announced the invasion in the following communiqué:

Allied forces under command of General Eisenhower began landing operations on Sicily early this morning.

The landings were preceded by Allied air attack.

Allied naval forces escorted the assault forces and bombarded the coast defenses during the assault.

[The Algiers radio, in an English-language broadcast to North America at 12:40 A. M. today, said that Allied forces had landed on the rocky western tip of Sicily, 260 miles from Rome. The broadcast was recorded by United States Government monitors.

[The broadcast said the landings were made in good weather, with German and Italian air forces providing "fierce" opposition. In anticipation of the assault, the island's Italian-German defenders blew up harbor installations, the broadcast said.]

"Softened Up" By Air Attack

A heavy attack was carried on by planes of the Northwest Africa Air Force and the Middle East Air Command for nearly two weeks, reaching blitz proportions in the last week, when a round-the-clock assault blasted Axis air bases and communication centers with hundreds of tons of bombs. This came to a furious climax yesterday and last night.

The Allied naval force that escorted the invading troops pounded the formidable defenses of Sicily with salvos of shells while infantrymen, their bayonets twinkling in the starlight raced ashore from landing crafts. Many tanks were landed.

Sicily, largest island in the Mediterranean, has a population of just under 4,000,000 persons and has been strongly fortified, specially along the southern coast, since 1939. The coasts are heavily mined and beaches are covered by batteries of artillery that fire from hills.

French Urged to Be Calm

General Eisenhower's announcement to the French people, which was sent by radio, asked them to remain calm and not to expose themselves to reprisals through "present rash actions."

Many of the troops involved in the invasion of Sicily are veterans of the Tunisian campaign.

Military men here expect very heavy fighting. The Germans are known to have reinforced the island comparatively recently, and despite the prolonged aerial bombardment strong fortifications remain to be overcome.

Many military objectives were hit by American and British bombers during the two weeks' attack on the island. The main weight of the bombing at night was directed against the airfields, particularly

Continued on Page Two

War News Summarized

SATURDAY, JULY 10, 1943

American, British and Canadian troops landed early this morning on Sicily, the last-stepping stone to Italy. While the size of the invasion force was not known, the War Department said naval forces had escorted the invasion troops and bombarded Sicilian coast defenses. The enemy is believed to have between eleven and thirteen divisions on the rugged island, of which nine or ten are Italian and the rest German.

As the Allies struck, General Eisenhower broadcast an appeal to the French people warning them against rash actions that would bring upon them reprisals from the Nazis. He urged them to listen to Allied broadcasts. "When the hour of action strikes," he declared, "we will let you know." [All the foregoing, 1:8.]

The invasion came on the heels of six consecutive days of powerful Allied air assaults on Sicily, during which air bases, communications centers and industrial plants had been pounded almost incessantly. During the last day twenty-one enemy planes had been destroyed and a quarter of a million pounds of bombs had been dropped on Catania alone. [1:7.]

The German offensive along the Orel-Kursk-Belgorod front increased in fury yesterday as the Nazis threw ten more divisions against the Russians near Belgorod. But the Russians said their forces were holding at all points and had destroyed another 193 tanks and ninety-four planes and had slain 5,000 men. In the four days since the Germans opened their drive the Russians claim to have killed 40,000 men and knocked out 2,036 tanks and 904 planes. [1:3.]

Germany, too, was blasted as the RAF inflicted another powerful blow on Cologne. Making their 119th raid on the Ruhr city, the fliers lost only eight bombers as they dropped more than a thousand tons of bombs in what was termed "a crushing setback to German attempts to revive the skeletonized industrial life" of Cologne. [1:6-7.]

More than 100 Allied bombers joined warships and artillery in launching the strongest barrage to date against the Japanese base of Munda. The Japanese sent forty-five Zeros over Rendova Island, but they were dispersed and four were destroyed. The enemy also tried, with small success, a dive-bombing attack on our base at Nassau Bay, New Guinea. [1:4; map, P. 5.]

A joint American-British announcement said that Allied and neutral shipping losses from U-boat attacks during June were the smallest since the United States entered the war. [1:6-7.]

June Losses to U-Boats Lowest Since We Entered the Conflict

Special to THE NEW YORK TIMES.

WASHINGTON, July 9—Intimations that the United Nations have been winning the war against the submarine were confirmed by a joint statement issued today by the British and United States Governments.

June losses of Allied and neutral ships by submarine attack, said the report, were the lowest since this country entered the war, sinkings of Axis submarines were substantial, and the main transatlantic convoys were now proceeding practically unmolested.

The statement was as follows:

1. In June the losses of Allied and neutral merchant ships from submarine attacks were the lowest since the United States entered the war. The losses from all forms of enemy action were the second lowest recorded since the war between Britain and Germany began.

2. The number of targets offered to the anti-submarine vessels and aircraft of the United Nations was not as great in June as previously, but the sinkings of Axis submarines were substantial and satisfactory.

3. The heavy toll taken of the U-boats in May showed its effect in June in that the main transatlantic convoys were practically unmolested, and the U-boat attacks on our shipping were in widely separated areas. However, every opportunity was taken of attacking U-boats leaving and returning to their bases on the west coast of France.

4. The merchant shipping ton-

Continued on Page Three

Son-in-Law Held in Oakes' Murder; Bahaman Police Cite Fingerprints

By The United Press.

NASSAU, Bahamas, July 9—Alfred de Marigny, 36, was booked at the police station here tonight on a charge of killing his father-in-law, the multimillionaire British baronet, Sir Harry Oakes.

A formal charge of murder was placed against the bearded accused, who denied any connection with the slaying.

Sir Harry was known to have been unhappy over the marriage of his eldest daughter, Nancy, then 17 years old, to M. de Marigny at New York in May, 1942. It was the second marriage for the Count, who had been divorced in Miami, Fla., in 1937.

He was arrested at 6 o'clock tonight by Lieut. Col. R. A. Lindop and Major Embert Pemberton of the Nassau constabulary.

Capt. E. W. Melchen of the Miami Police Department, summoned by airplane to aid in the investigation after Sir Harry's body was found on a bed that had been set afire Thursday morning, said the arrest and charge were based on "hair analysis, fingerprints and interrogation."

Attorney General Eric Hallinan reported that Sir Harry had been bludgeoned to death. There were four severe head wounds, he said, as well as burns on the body.

Officers believed an electric fan had blown out the flames before they had destroyed the bed.

The charge against Count de Marigny came as a sensational climax to the death of Sir Harry, one of the world's richest men, with a fortune unofficially estimated to be as great as $200,000,000.

Until the announcement came, details of the slaying had been

Continued on Page Twenty-six

United Press International

The first day of the Sicilian invasion.

"All the News That's Fit to Print."

The New York Times.

LATE CITY EDITION
Moderately warm today with moderate winds.
Temperatures Yesterday—Max., 83; Min., 70
Sunrise, 5:44 A. M.; Sunset, 8:25 P. M.

VOL. XCII..No. 31,223. Entered as Second-Class Matter Postoffice, New York, N. Y. NEW YORK, TUESDAY, JULY 20, 1943. THREE CENTS IN NEW YORK CITY

ALLIED BOMBS BLAST ROME MILITARY AREAS; TIMES MAN FROM AIR SEES SHRINES SPARED; AXIS FORCES STEADILY FALL BACK IN SICILY

REPUBLICAN GROUP WARNS ISOLATION MEANS '44 DEFEAT

Post-War Conference Holds Such a Stand Would Force Voters to Favor 4th Term

PLATFORM ADOPTED HERE

Conference Calls on Spangler to Have His Appointees Adopt Its Proposals

The most determined drive yet seen to force the Republican party into a vigorous policy of internationalism manifested itself yesterday at the Hotel Commodore, as 300 delegates attended the eastern regional conference of the unofficial Republican Post-War Policy Association.

With supporters of Wendell L. Willkie dominating the proceedings, the kid gloves of diplomacy were taken off, and notice was served that unless the Republican party drops "narrow nationalism," the voters will have to choose a fourth term for Roosevelt in preference to what the Republicans will be offering.

While prominent speakers stressed the need for Republican leadership in international affairs, and argued that Republican traditions called for this leadership, the real keynote was sounded by Mayo Shattuck, president of the Massachusetts Bar Association and chairman of the conference's committee on resolutions.

Warns Party on Isolationism

Mr. Shattuck, in presenting the platform, unanimously adopted a few minutes later, said:

"We believe that the Republican party is about to be given its chance again for leadership and for power in the United States. But our people are not fools. Just as they are intelligent enough to have decided long ago that the so-called New Deal is nothing but a hopeless mess, from the standpoint of domestic policy, so they have sense enough to believe that another return to normalcy—and, incidentally, to smug isolationism—would be worse yet. If they have to make that choice, they will make what I believe to be the intelligent choice, as between them. They will continue to take the New Deal.

"I, for one, without warning that I would be standing here, am so glad that some of the intelligent, hard-hitting members of my party have sensed this problem and intend to do something about it, that I hardly know how to express my joy.

"Gentlemen, Mr. Chairman, if you will show the people of the United States that the election of a Republican administration does not mean another gang of inward-turning, narrow-minded isolationist stuffed shirts—if you will present to the people a big and broad-gauge man who will undertake to define and to pursue a problem for the participation by our fraction of the human race in such affairs as affect all of the human race, you will be given power just as surely as you are in this room, and what an opportunity and what a world stand before us! We are on the threshold of magnificent plenty and great, enlightened human cooperation, and we are just fumbling with the key to the lock.

"So, Mr. Chairman, don't falter in any respect. The failure, if it is a failure, may be the end of our party, and, what is more important, it could mean the end of our Republic in anything like the form which we have come so to love."

Action by Party Group Demanded

His remarks, because of their bluntness, overshadowed a drive at the conference to take over the official Republican post-war policy committee named by the Republican national chairman, Harrison Spangler.

At the request of Deneen Watson, chairman of the unofficial group, Mr. Watson was authorized to call on Mr. Spangler and demand action by the Spangler group on the platform adopted by the conference. Mr. Spangler was in New York yesterday, but had no comment to make on the demand. Since political leaders believe that the Spangler group was appointed to head off the Willkie group, a showdown in the near future seems likely.

Those attending the conference included organization Republicans from Connecticut and Vermont in force and a generous leavening of leading Republican figures from

Continued on Page Nine

'Dud' Enemy Bombs Make China's Dyes

So many of the Japanese bombs dropped in China's northwest territories have failed to explode that the picric acid taken from them has been found sufficient to dye this year's entire Chinese blanket supply, the New York Committee of the National War Fund revealed yesterday.

"Word to this effect reached the committee yesterday through United China Relief," the committee spokesman said. "In addition, the committee learned, the Japanese bomb canisters are being melted down and recast into farm implements.

"The blankets for which the Japanese are supplying the dye in this unintentional way are produced locally by the Chinese spinning and weaving cooperatives, which, with similar industrial cooperatives throughout free China, have proved a mainstay in China's fight."

PRICES ARE FROZEN IN EATING PLACES

April 4 to 10 Base Period for Fixing Charges in 250,000 Hotels and Restaurants

Restaurant and hotel prices of food and beverages were ordered frozen yesterday by the Office of Price Administration at the levels prevailing April 4 to 10, inclusive. The order was signed by Sylvan L. Joseph, regional administrator, and becomes effective next Monday. Two hundred and fifty thousand eating places from New York to Washington, D. C., are said to be affected.

Promulgation of the freeze order yesterday morning represented an abandonment of the attempt to hold restaurant and hotel food prices at the April scale entirely through voluntary cooperation by the trade. In a "statement of considerations" issued simultaneously with the order, Mr. Joseph said that "since April 10, 1943, restaurant prices have continued to rise and are threatening to rise further."

Area Reductions Coming

The statement said also that the OPA soon would begin the issuance of supplemental orders directing reductions in restaurant prices in special areas and by specified operators.

"Records of many operators showed wider gross operating margins in February, March and April, 1943, than in the corresponding period of 1942, together with very substantial increases in net operating costs," Mr. Joseph said.

The order applies to Region II of the OPA, which covers New York, New Jersey, Pennsylvania, Delaware, Maryland and the District of Columbia.

"In some areas within the region and for some operators there is every indication that the April 4-10 prices are excessive and should be rolled back," Mr. Joseph said. "As soon as further data are collected on these areas and operators, the necessary corrective action will be taken."

At the regional OPA offices it was indicated that restaurant prices in the New York City area were not as far out of line as in other sections. Washington and Baltimore were specifically cited by Mr. Joseph as areas in which there should be substantial rollbacks in eating place prices when

Continued on Page Thirteen

SOVIET SWEEPS ON

Red Army Captures 130 Populated Places in Advance on Orel

RUSSIANS 12 MILES AWAY

3 Prongs Closing on Nazi Base Despite Stubborn Fight—Axis Loses Rail City

By The Associated Press.

LONDON, Tuesday, July 20—Russian armies pounding on a semi-circle around Orel captured 130 villages and populated places in advances from four to six miles yesterday to the north, east and south of the great German base 200 miles south of Moscow, the Soviet command announced today.

Earlier reports from Moscow had placed the Red Army within twelve miles of Orel and said the Russians were wheeling up artillery within range of the city. Berlin reported the whole Russian front ablaze with Red Army attacks all the way from Leningrad to Novorossiisk in the western Caucasus.

Among the towns captured was Malo Arkhangelsk, twenty-five miles south of Orel, on the railway running to Russian-held Kursk.

Another seventy-two German tanks and ninety-six planes were destroyed, running the toll of attrition exacted from the Germans since their attack of July 5 to 3,516 tanks and 2,094 planes. These latest reported German losses were suffered Sunday.

The midnight communiqué, recorded by the Soviet monitor from the Moscow radio, said the Germans were fighting back stubbornly, mounting a dozen counter-attacks during Monday. All were declared repulsed with heavy losses.

Troops pounding down from the north achieved the greatest successes, scooping up seventy populated places, the communiqué said. Troops pressing up from the south toward a junction with the column atop and behind Orel were said to have captured twenty populated places. A junction of these columns would pinch off the Orel salient and trap large German forces in the base.

Other troops moving in frontally from the east were credited with seizing forty places.

Front Is "S"-Shaped

The 255-mile front from Belgorod to Sukhinichi is formed like an "S," with a German bulge in the Russian lines around Orel and with a Russian bulge pointing out from Kursk. It was in the Kursk area that the battle was joined July 5, when the Nazis opened their offensive.

The communiqué said only patrol activities had been reported from the Belgorod area at the extreme southern end of the front. It was near Belgorod that the Germans achieved some penetration early in the month, but were unable to exploit it.

[The Germans have brought

Continued on Page Five

RAID IS EXPLAINED

Axis Troops Were Using Rome Railways to Rush Aid to Sicily

BOMBERS ARE ACCURATE

Press Observers in the Planes See No Damage to Sacred Centers in the City

By HERBERT L. MATTHEWS
By Wireless to THE NEW YORK TIMES.

ALLIED HEADQUARTERS IN NORTH AFRICA, July 19—The last of the capitals of the warring powers in Europe to remain untouched today shook under the impact of one of the heaviest bombing raids yet launched in the Mediterranean theatre. Hitherto inviolate because it was the sacred city of Catholicism and all Christendom, it could no longer be ignored in the military strategy of the war, for it is the chief bottleneck for supplies from Germany and northern Italy.

It had to be bombed, but Catholics everywhere may rest assured that most extraordinary precautions were taken to avoid hitting Vatican City, any of the four ancient basilicas with which Christian history is linked or any other sacred targets. St. John Lateran was a mile and a half away. With precision bombing there was no possibility of coming anywhere near that "mother church" of the Catholic world.

The Vatican and St. Peter's were four miles away and their windows probably did not even rattle. In Pantellaria our planes dropped bombs within 1,000 yards of Allied troops quite safely, and any good bombardier can guarantee to leave unscathed anything half that distance from his target.

Three Military Targets Hit

Three highly important military targets, the San Lorenzo freight yards just outside the main railway station in the southeastern part of Rome, the Littorio freight yards on the northern edge and the Ciampino airfield four miles southeast of the city, received tremendous punishment in daylight today. No other parts of Rome were damaged.

I know because I was over Rome

Continued on Page Four

CIVILIANS IN SICILY SURRENDER THEIR ARMS

Turning in their weapons after our men captured Comiso
The New York Times Radiophoto, passed yesterday by censor

U. S. TROOPS PRESS MUNDA FROM EAST

Kill 179 Japanese in Advance—Salamaua Gain Made as Planes Aid Both Attacks

By TILLMAN DURDIN
By Wireless to THE NEW YORK TIMES.

ALLIED HEADQUARTERS IN THE SOUTHWEST PACIFIC, Tuesday, July 20—Allied ground forces made gains on both the Munda and Salamaua fronts yesterday against sharp fighting by the Japanese, Gen. Douglas MacArthur's communiqué today reported.

In the battle for Munda airdrome on New Georgia Island of the Central Solomons American troops enlarged a beachhead recently established at Lilio, about two and a half miles east of the enemy's airfield after a fierce engagement. One hundred and seventy-nine Japanese dead were counted in the sector the United States soldiers took over after the battle.

Punching into the Japanese defenses around Munda the Ameri-

Continued on Page Six

Americans Close In on Enna; Axis Center Is Breaking Up

By Wireless to THE NEW YORK TIMES.

ALLIED HEADQUARTERS IN NORTH AFRICA, July 19—Bronzed veterans of the British Eighth Army have hammered their way to within three miles of Catania, key to the defense of eastern Sicily, while in the center of the Allied advance American and Canadian forces have dashed through feeble Italian resistance to points ten miles from Enna, center of the island's road and railroad system.

The Americans stormed and captured Caltanissetta yesterday while to the southeast the Canadians drove the Italians out of Piazza-Armerina on the main road from the coast to Enna. Each of these towns is thirteen miles from Enna, whose possession will give the Allies control of transportation in central Sicily.

[American and British troops have reached Enna, the Moroccan radio reported. The Algiers radio said that aerial reconnaissance had noted the enemy's "general movement of retreat" toward Messina in northeastern Sicily. "By road and rail enemy forces are falling back on Messina with heavy and light equipment," it stated. The broadcasts were reported by the United States Foreign Broadcast Intelligence Service.

[The Algiers radio also broadcast a report that Axis headquarters in Sicily had been moved to Reggio Calabria in Italy. The Associated Press said.]

The Axis situation resembles a rout in the central sector, where Italians are surrendering by companies to the onrushing tide of khaki. The Allies have now captured 35,000 prisoners. The Americans have taken 23,000 of these, while the Eighth Army and Canadians have sent 12,000 back to their cages.

Only in the extreme east, in front of Catania, has resistance been stiff. The Germans have

Continued on Page Three

NOTED CHURCH HIT, ITALIANS REPORT

Stefani and Vatican Radio Say Pope Visited the Damaged San Lorenzo Basilica

By DANIEL T. BRIGHAM
By Telephone to THE NEW YORK TIMES

BERNE, Switzerland, July 19—Casualties in the bombing of Rome, according to Italian semi-official sources, were heavy. No official statement has been made.

The greatest damage was inflicted in the Prenestena workers' suburb, where, according to the Stefani news agency, civilian residences were pulverized. Stefani said damaged places included the Basilica of San Lorenzo fuori le Mura, property of the Vatican less than 500 yards from the San Lorenzo freight yards; the cemetery of Campo Verano, University City, the Polyclinic and the working-class quarters of San Lorenzo and Tiburtino.

The air-raid alarm lasted three hours, during most of which the bombers were overhead.

To counteract the effect of the Allied leaflets, warning of the bombing, fascist militiamen throughout the afternoon handed out leaflets reading:

"Italians! Allied planes have dropped leaflets over Italy calling on you to accept a dishonorable peace. While they drop these leaflets, however, those same Allied

Continued on Page Two

RAIL CENTERS HIT

San Lorenzo, Littorio Yards and Ciampino Airfield Targets

NO U. S. PLANES LOST

Religious Edifices Marked in Red on Fliers' Maps to Be Avoided at All Cost

By DREW MIDDLETON
By Wireless to THE NEW YORK TIMES.

ALLIED HEADQUARTERS IN NORTH AFRICA, July 19—Waves of Allied bombers pounded sprawling freight yards and other industrial military objectives at Rome this morning in the first air assault ever made on the capital of crumbling Italy.

[Most of the planes were American, manned by Americans. Cairo reports to The United Press said that British planes of the Middle East Command took part in the raid and John Thompson, representing the combined United States press, said British fighters aided in escorting the medium bombers. No American planes were missing, although some landed on emergency fields, according to The Associated Press. About 500 planes took part, according to the London radio.]

Weeks of special training prepared the Allied airmen for attacks only on military targets. The chief of these were freight yards, through which pass thousands of tons of military matériel each day and thousands of German reinforcements intended for Axis fighters in Sardinia and Sicily, or on their way south to hold the wavering Italian people in bondage.

Extensive war industries have been built up by Premier Mussolini in and around Rome in the belief that they would never be bombed by Allied air power. Many of these were built close to churches and shrines. In some holy places the vibration of high powered generating plants that run war factories can be felt.

Leaflets Warn Population

Allied bombardiers also attacked these war industries as they flew high over the city, whose population of about 1,200,000 had been warned of the raid by leaflets dropped before the bombs were dropped. These leaflets said that Italians or Germans might bomb the center of Rome or even Vatican City in an effort to rouse Catholic opinion throughout the world against the Allies.

[The basilica of San Lorenzo fuori le Mura was "seriously damaged" and was visited by Pope Pius, according to the Vatican radio.]

The attack on Rome was the climax of months of careful planning. Once it was decided that railroad yards and industrial objectives in and around Italy's capital had to be bombed to check the flow of troops and matériel southward special bomber crews were selected for training.

A huge map of the target areas was studied by each crew. Pilots, navigators and bombardiers memorized it so well that before the start of the mission they had a clear picture not only of their targets but also of the exact location of Vatican City, holy places, architectural treasures and museums that were to be left untouched.

The briefing was done by intelligence officers who had lived in Rome before the war and who knew the locations of factories and railroad junctions, which the Italians believed were immune from bombing because of their location.

Rome a Railway Center

The Italian capital is one of five great junctions that control the Italian railroads. The others are Naples, Foggia, Milan and Bologna. Naples and Foggia have been hammered by bombers flying from this theatre.

Two main railroads from Genoa and Bologna enter Rome from the north. There is a spur line to the

Continued on Page Three

War News Summarized

TUESDAY, JULY 20, 1943

Rome, the only European capital of the great warring countries to have been spared the horrors of war, was heavily bombed by Allied airmen yesterday. Fliers of the Mediterranean Air Command from North Africa and Libya concentrated upon military targets after earlier planes had dropped leaflets warning the people of the impending attack and promising to avoid all cultural and religious centers. After the attack Rome, the military center, was devastated, but Rome, "the Eternal City" was untouched.

The three principal targets were the San Lorenzo railroad yards in southeast Rome, the Littorio yards at the northern edge of the city and the Ciampino airfield, four miles southeast of the city. Liberators of the Ninth United States Air Force were over the Littorio yards for more than an hour and dropped 350 tons of bombs. In its warning leaflets the Allied command said the yards were "of the greatest importance to the Axis war effort and in particular to the movement of German troops." [1:8; map, P. 3.]

How well the Allies respected their pledge not to harm Vatican City and other shrines was attested by a correspondent of THE NEW YORK TIMES, who was one of seven newspaper men in a Flying Fortress that was part of the last wave to attack Rome. The pilots and bombardiers had been specially trained for weeks before the raid and the sacred places were marked on their maps "must on no account be damaged." [1:4.]

The Axis immediately condemned the attack upon the center of Catholicism. Rome said the Pope planned a protest to President Roosevelt and Prime Minister Churchill. [1:7.] London accepted the raid as a military necessity [1:6-7] and Washington observers voiced general approval mixed with regret that the bombing finally had to take place. [3:1.]

In Sicily, Allied troops continued their advances. Americans captured Caltinesetta, the Canadians took Piazza Armerina, and both closed in on Enna. The British were overcoming fierce opposition on the outskirts of Catania. [1:6-7; map P. 2.] A formation of Lightning P-38s annihilated a force of fifteen Junkers-52 transport planes rushing reinforcements from Sardinia. [3:5.]

In Russia, the Red Army advanced another five miles to within twelve miles of Orel, capturing 130 inhabited places during the advance. [1:3.]

Allied forces in the South Pacific edged closer to the Japanese airfield at Munda on New Georgia Island and the enemy base at Salamaua, New Guinea. [1:5.]

More than 300 Republicans, including party leaders and office holders from northeastern States, met in this city yesterday, and served notice that unless the party dropped its "narrow isolationism" the voters would have no other choice than to vote for a fourth term. [1:1.]

Green Warns of Wage Demands Unless Food Prices Are Reduced

Special to THE NEW YORK TIMES.

DETROIT, July 19—Charging that the Government had failed to hold the line against inflation and that labor and consumers were being discriminated against by Congress, William Green, president of the American Federation of Labor, declared in an address here today that "unless prices of food are brought down to a reasonable level" organized labor will have "no other recourse but to demand wage increases."

He spoke before 700 delegates to the national convention of the Brotherhood of Maintenance of Way Employes and his speech was applauded.

Delivering what was in effect an ultimatum to Government agencies having to do with wage and price controls, he asserted that "drastic action must be taken at once to avert a breakdown of our wartime economy."

"Our domestic war economy," he said, "has not been geared to the need of protecting the workers against the hazards of inflation and its concomitant evils. This situation is becoming more and more serious each day. Profiteers and speculators are sapping the strength of the nation's army of workers."

He declared that AFL surveys showed that food prices had increased from 50 to 200 per cent since the beginning of the war and demanded "intelligent and orderly action to assure workers and their families of a decent place to live in and enough nourishing food to

Continued on Page Ten

British Press Is Solid in Support Of Bombing War Targets in Rome

By JAMES MacDONALD
By Cable to THE NEW YORK TIMES.

LONDON, Tuesday, July 20—If the British press is any guide to public opinion then that opinion is unanimous in its endorsement of yesterday's air raid against military objectives in Rome.

It is universally recognized that Rome is unique in that it embraces Vatican City and has many cultural monuments. At the same time it is emphasized that Rome also has important objectives such as freight yards and key railroad lines that are liable to legitimate attack.

The Times of London says that much unnecessary and irrelevant controversy over the Rome bombing will be averted if people bear in mind that the raid was a "military operation, pure and simple." The editorial reminds its readers that it was clearly intimated months ago by the United States and British Governments that they regarded Rome as containing objectives subject to legitimate attack.

It says terrorization by promiscuous bombing is not and never has been a factor in Allied strategy and adds:

"No Allied commander in his senses would send young airmen to risk their lives in destruction of 'cultural monuments.' The war will be won by unconditional concentration upon the ruin of the armed forces and war potential of the enemy. To that purpose our bombing policy has conformed and will continue to conform and from

Continued on Page Four

"All the News That's Fit to Print."

The New York Times.

LATE CITY EDITION
Moderately warm today, with gentle winds.
Temperatures Yesterday—Max., 85; Min., 70
Sunrise, 5:46 A. M.; Sunset, 8:19 P. M.

Copyright, 1943, by The New York Times Company.

VOL. XCII..No. 31,229. Entered as Second-Class Matter, Postoffice, New York, N. Y. NEW YORK, MONDAY, JULY 26, 1943. THREE CENTS IN NEW YORK CITY

MUSSOLINI OUSTED WITH FASCIST CABINET; BADOGLIO, HIS FOE, MADE PREMIER BY KING; SHIFT BELIEVED FIRST STEP TOWARD PEACE

PEACE INITIATIVE URGED BY WALLACE ON AMERICA NOW

For 'Common Man' He Asks Full Production, Employment and Security

WITH DEMOCRACY FOR ALL

Vice President, at Detroit, Accuses 'Fascists' of Trying to Undermine Roosevelt

The text of Mr. Wallace's address is on Page 10.

By The United Press.

DETROIT, July 25—Vice President Henry A. Wallace called upon America today to take the initiative now and plan a war-proof post-war world pledged to enlightenment of all peoples, "full production and full employment" and cooperation with other nations to enforce international justice and security.

Urging America to heed a destiny "that calls us to world leadership," he assailed "small but powerful groups which put money and power first and people last" and declared that "nothing will prevail against the common man's peace in a common man's world."

A crowd of 20,000, composed predominantly of workers, filled the center grandstand at the State fairgrounds track to hear Mr. Wallace's thirty-minute address, "America tomorrow," which was also broadcast by radio.

"Defeatists" for "Good Old Days"

The Vice President deviated from his prepared address to voice indirectly the charge he made yesterday that "certain American Fascists" had turned against the present Administration because President Roosevelt "stopped Washington from being a way station on the way to Wall Street."

He asserted that "defeatists who talk about going back to the good old days of Americanism (after the war) mean the time when there was plenty for the few and scarcity for the many."

Then, departing from his text, he raised his right arm and said:

"Or the days when Washington was only a way station in the suburbs of Wall Street."

Mr. Wallace was introduced by R. J. Thomas, president of the United Automobile Workers, CIO, as "the architect and crusader for a new world."

It was Mr. Wallace's first address since President Roosevelt abolished the Board of Economic Warfare, which Mr. Wallace had headed, to end a public quarrel between the Vice President and Secretary of Commerce Jesse Jones over war buying policies.

Roosevelt Foes Denounced

Indicating no rift in his relations with the President, Wallace assailed persons sniping at the Chief Executive while he is engaged in prosecuting the war.

He charged that powerful money-minded groups—"some call them isolationists, some reactionaries and others American Fascists"—seek to destroy Mr. Roosevelt's domestic achievements of the past ten years by capitalizing on his preoccupation with the war.

"I have known the President intimately for ten years and in the final showdown he has always put human rights first," he said. "Sooner or later the machinations of these small but powerful groups which put money and power first and people last will inevitably be exposed to the public eye."

He inveighed against those who oppose post-war planning now to hold to the realities of the past or cling to the present without thought of the future.

"Both opinions," he said, "are fighting delaying actions against our destiny in the peace—a destiny

Continued on Page Ten

Cheers Halt Games As Duce Strikes Out

The thousands of baseball spectators at parks where the Mussolini incident was announced yesterday roared and jumped up from their seats. Games were halted as happy men and women thronged the aisles and shouted the news to each other.

At the Yankee Stadium, where 36,779 had suffered with the Yankees as the New Yorkers lost the first game of a double-header to the White Sox, baseball momentarily ceased to exist when the news of the resignation came through the loudspeakers in the sixth inning of the second contest. The rest of the announcement, to the effect that King Victor Emmanuel had taken over, was lost in the tumultuous reaction.

A similar circumstance was reported in Pittsburgh, where 30,309 onlookers saw the Pirates sweep a double-header from the Brooklyn Dodgers.

NORTH JERSEY OPA DROPS DRIVING BAN

Maze of Rulings, Plus Vacation Permits, Is Too Confusing—Inspectors Tired of Abuse

Enforcement of the "pleasure driving" ban in northern New Jersey broke down completely yesterday with Office of Price Administration officials in that area frankly admitting that they were making no effort to enforce the restriction. New Jersey highways leading from bridge and tunnel exits that had been more or less deserted since initiation of the "pleasure ban" were heavily burdened yesterday with motorists blandly disregarding the ban and inspectors conspicuous by their absence.

OPA inspectors indicated that they were "throwing up the sponge" because they found themselves entangled in a maze of conflicting rulings from Washington and by local ration boards. In addition they are tired of being sneeringly referred to as "Gestapo agents, sneaks and snoopers" by drivers they stop for questioning.

No Inspectors on Roads

"It is true there were no inspectors on the highways today," Nathan L. Jacobs, chief OPA enforcement attorney in the northern New Jersey area, said. "We have discovered that ration boards have issued so many vacation permits that it is a waste of time to stop cars."

While other OPA officials refused to be quoted it was generally conceded that no effort was being made to enforce the "pleasure ban."

"We are continuing to the best of our ability to enforce the law," an inspector declared. "However, the maze of conflicting rulings

Continued on Page Thirty-two

RUSSIANS PUSH ON

Drive 2½ Miles Closer to Orel and Take 30 More Villages

NAZI STAND STIFFER

Enemy Counter-Attacks Desperately to Hold Escape Corridor

By The Associated Press.

LONDON, Monday, July 26—The great Russian counter-offensive battering upon Orel from three directions engulfed thirty more populated places and swept forward two and a half to five and a half miles yesterday, Moscow announced in a special communiqué. Complete encirclement of the great Nazi base appeared only a matter of time.

Red Army columns driving down behind Orel have cut to within seven miles or so of the Bryansk railway feeding supplies and reinforcements into the stronghold.

The Russians are steadily narrowing the fifty-mile escape corridor held open by the half-encircled Germans, for another Soviet column is pushing up from the south to the west of the city.

Beating down severe German counter-attacks, the Red Army slogged on to capture the important railroad station of Glazunovka and the populated places of Poponov, Chizhovka and Narykovo on the western bank of the Oka River northeast of Orel, said the communiqué, broadcast by Moscow and recorded by the Soviet monitor.

Other villages included among the thirty reported captured yesterday were Rybnitsa, Gremyache, Zakharovka, Lebedikha, Voronets, Verkhneye Sagino and Nizhneye Sagino.

South, in the Belgorod area, there were scouting engagements and "fighting of local importance," while scouts increased their activities in the battle areas on the Donets front still farther south, it added.

Advance on Three Sides

The regular midnight communiqué said the Red Army had advanced on the north, east and south sides of Orel, knocking out twenty-eight tanks, killing 2,840 Germans, taking prisoners and capturing an important height on the south side of the city.

Several populated places were captured east and south of Orel, the announcement added. In several places the Germans mounted strong counter-attacks.

In other sectors, the communiqué said, twenty-one more German tanks were destroyed and over 800 Germans killed.

A previous special announcement of the Soviet command had declared that the German wedge, nine by twenty-two miles, that had been driven into Russian lines at

Continued on Page Eight

LONDON IS CAUTIOUS

Evidence of Crack in the Rome-Berlin Axis Is Viewed With Joy

BADOGLIO 'WAR HERO'

Britons See Possibility of His Being 'Front' for Fascist Deal

By RAYMOND DANIELL
By Cable to The New York Times.

LONDON, Monday, July 26—London's first reaction to the news that Benito Mussolini had stepped down as head of the Fascist Government of Italy was that it left the military situation unchanged.

It was seen as the first tangible evidence of a crack in the Rome-Berlin Axis. But emphasis was put on the point that, whatever internal troubles led Signor Mussolini to get out in favor of Marshal Pietro Badoglio on the eve of his sixtieth birthday after twenty years of dictatorship over Italy, King Victor Emmanuel's proclamation made it clear that for the moment at least Italy intended to carry on the fight.

The possibility that the dramatic shift in leadership by Italy might be the forerunner of an attempt to sue for a separate peace was not overlooked, however.

For a long time it has been suspected here that, when things got too tough for the Fascists or the Nazis in the Reich, they would try to save their necks by elevating someone they believed acceptable to the United Nations as front man to arrange a soft armistice.

Not Trusted by Britain

Marshal Badoglio, 73-year-old Italian Army Chief, who has been regarded as a critic of Mussolini and as a bogus friend of Britain, is one of those men. Count Dino Grandi, a former Ambassador to London, is another.

But the fact that Victor Emmanuel chose his old friend, Marshal Badoglio, who rallied Italy in World War I after the Caporetto disaster, instead of Count Grandi, is susceptible to two interpretations.

The first, taking the proclamations of the Italian King and his new Premier at their face value, is

Continued on Page Five

ONE IS OUT, THE OTHER IN

Benito Mussolini and his successor as Premier, Marshal Pietro Badoglio. Associated Press

British Eighth Army Opens New Drive to Take Catania

By DREW MIDDLETON
By Wireless to The New York Times.

ALLIED HEADQUARTERS IN NORTH AFRICA, July 25—Routed in the west by the hard-hitting American Seventh Army, the battered Axis forces are retreating across the north central sector of Sicily today to the sanctuary of the Germans' new "Etna line." The southern and southwestern faces of this line are already being hammered by the British Eighth Army, which is inflicting dreadful casualties on the stubborn German defenders of the position. The Canadian forces, striking northward and northeastward on the Eighth Army's left flank, are making good progress. [The Canadians have driven a wedge well into the enemy's lines, the United Press said.]

After two weeks of smashing success unequaled by any other American Army in this war, the Seventh Army is wheeling east-

Continued on Page Three

BERLIN RADIO SEES MUSSOLINI AS 'ILL'

First Nazi Comment Arrives Five Hours Late—Official Statement Lacking

LONDON, Monday, July 26 (AP)—The Berlin radio in its first comment on the Mussolini resignation—made almost five hours after Rome's first announcement—quoted the Italian-Stefani news agency as saying that the change of Italian Government was believed to have been owing to the Premier's health. Premier Mussolini "has been ill for some time," Berlin said.

Official Comment Lacking

By Telephone to The New York Times

BERNE, Switzerland, Monday, July 26—Official quarters in Berlin were still out of telephonic touch with Berne at an early hour Monday morning, and authoritative reaction to the resignation of Signor Mussolini and his Cabinet

Continued on Page Two

ITALY SEEN MAKING FIRST PEACE STEP

Observers in Washington Look for Similar Action by Axis Satellites in Balkans

By HAROLD CALLENDER
Special to The New York Times.

WASHINGTON, July 25—The transfer of power in Italy from Premier Mussolini to Marshal Pietro Badoglio was interpreted by military and diplomatic observers tonight as a first step toward an Italian appeal for peace. They thought that this would be quickly followed by similar appeals from Hungary, Rumania and Bulgaria, which might seek favorable terms by acting swiftly.

The immediate consequences, military men thought, would be an Allied occupation of Italy, especially the air bases in the north near the German border, and the surrender of the Italian Army, Navy and air fleet.

In diplomatic circles it was predicted that Marshal Badoglio would seek a negotiated peace, but it was assumed that the unconditional surrender doctrine would be applied in the qualified form given to it by the recent statement to Italians by President Roosevelt and Prime Minister Churchill. This implied generous treatment for Italy once the fascist regime had disappeared.

It has been authoritatively indicated here that the Allied Govern-

Continued on Page Six

ARRESTS REPORTED

Berne Hears the Fascist Leaders Are Being Held in Homes

'PEACE' CRY IN ROME

Nazis in Milan Said to Have Fired on Mob of Demonstrators

By DANIEL T. BRIGHAM
By Telephone to The New York Times.

BERNE, Switzerland, July 25—King Victor Emmanuel announced to Italy tonight that he had accepted the "resignations" of Premier Benito Mussolini and his entire Cabinet. He ordered Marshal Pietro Badoglio to form a military government "to continue the conduct of the war."

The announcement was made in a proclamation that was broadcast to the people of Italy from Rome at 11 P. M. Rome time. The Rome radio then signed off for twenty minutes, resuming its broadcast at 11:20 to carry a proclamation by Marshal Badoglio. Before giving this, however, the announcer said:

"With the fall of Mussolini and his band, Italy has taken the first step toward peace. Finished is the shame of fascism! Long live peace! Long live the King!"

Badoglio Says He'll Fight

Marshal Badoglio's proclamation was then read. It appealed to the nation for "calm" in this hour of trial, saying:

"Italians! On the demand of His Majesty the King-Emperor, I have assumed the military government of the country with full powers. The war will continue. Italy, bruised, her provinces invaded, and her cities ruined, will retain her faith in her given word, jealous of her ancient traditions.

"We must tighten our ranks behind the King-Emperor, the living image of the country, who stands as an example for all today. The task I have been charged with is clear and precise. It will be executed scrupulously, and whoever believes he can interrupt the normal progress of events or whoever seeks to disturb internal order will be struck down without mercy.

"Long live Italy! Long live the King! PIETRO BADOGLIO."

For the first time in twenty-one years the Italian radio signed off a nation-wide program by playing only the royal march. "Giovinezza," the fascist anthem, like fascism, is dead.

[Field Marshal General Albert Kesselring, German Commander in Chief in Italy, and Hans-Georg Viktor von Mackensen, the Ger-

Continued on Page Three

Mayor Expects Italy To Surrender Soon

Mayor Fiorello H. La Guardia declared yesterday afternoon that in view of the dismissal of Premier Benito Mussolini he expected the complete capitulation of Italy within a few days.

His statement follows:

"I anticipate the complete capitulation of Italy within the next few days. Of course to me it's a source of great satisfaction that Mussolini has been finally discovered. He will go down in history as the betrayer of Italy.

"If there is one amusing sidelight to this whole thing, that is the cheap, gutter politicians in this country who catered to Mussolini when they thought he was going strong. I had to fight that very tendency in 1929 and 1933.

"In so far as Italy is concerned, she is out of the war.

"We must now prepare to meet the situation, as the Nazis will consolidate their lines. The Office of War Information is now free to release the appeal that I made to the King several months ago."

Mayor Sees Slight Hope for Meat; Warns City Will Boycott $1 Eggs

Although the meat supply for New York City looks better for the coming week, there is no assurance that the civilian population will get it, Mayor Fiorello H. La Guardia warned yesterday in his weekly radio broadcast. He said the black market would continue until there was proper identification of meat, tracing it from the slaughterhouse to the retailer.

The outlook is serious on eggs, the Mayor said, with prices at present as high as 66 cents a dozen for jumbos, 62 cents for extra large and 60 cents for large. He said the news that the price ceilings of eggs would go up about a cent a week was "disturbing" and that some persons were predicting egg prices would reach $1 a dozen before winter.

"I hope not," he declared. "Now I just want to serve notice on everybody that if eggs continue to increase in price much higher and before it arrives at the dollar a dozen, we in New York will adjust ourselves to substitutes for eggs. I hope that will not be necessary, but I am not in a position now to say that New York City will take a-dollar-a-dozen eggs without protest."

Mayor La Guardia expressed disappointment that the Office of Price Administration and the Food Distribution Administration had not yet taken final action on his proposal to cut the ration point values of pork products and eliminate some of them from rationing entirely, which, he said, would have relieved the meat situation.

"Our Government is paying millions of dollars in subsidies to

Continued on Page Thirty-two

War News Summarized

MONDAY, JULY 26, 1943

The Fascists surrendered their control over Italy yesterday when Premier Mussolini quit. He presented his own resignation and those of his Cabinet to King Victor Emmanuel, who immediately accepted them and named Marshal Badoglio as Prime Minister. Thus, after twenty years of complete power, Mussolini became the first Axis dictator to have run his course.

The King gave the news to the world when a proclamation signed by him was broadcast to the Italian people, saying that Marshal Badoglio would form a military government to continue the conduct of the war. The Rome radio announcer declared the development was the first step toward peace, but the Marshal said the war would go on.

The Italian people immediately demonstrated in the streets, looking for Blackshirts. A report from Milan said German troops had fired on demonstrators. [All the foregoing 1:8.]

While London welcomed the first sign of a crack in the Rome-Berlin Axis, observers were not too greatly impressed. They saw in it an effort to make the best peace terms by putting an anti-Fascist at the head of the Italian Government. They also saw an attempt by the Italian King to save his crown. [1:4.]

The Italian political upheaval served to overshadow what was one of the most active days on the military fronts. Allied troops in Sicily were pressing the Axis defenders into a small triangle, with Messina as the apex. [1:5-6; map P. 2.] Flying Fortresses flew 1,500 miles without meeting any opposition to blast the north Italian rail junction at Bologna, while other planes concentrated on southern Italian communications. [3:1.]

British and American air forces struck their heaviest blows against Germany. The RAF rocked Hamburg Saturday night with 2,500 tons of bombs. Yesterday Flying Fortresses hit that port again and pounded Kiel and other centers. The RAF's big bombers raided Germany again last night. [1:6-7.]

The Red Army captured another thirty villages, halted incessant German counter-attacks and virtually encircled the enemy base at Orel. [1:3.]

The Fourteenth United States Air Force in China beat off four waves of more than 100 planes when the Japanese attacked advanced American bases in Hunan Province. Forty-four enemy planes were destroyed or damaged; damage to the air bases was slight. [9:4.]

More than 200 Allied planes gave the beleagured Japanese base at Munda, in the Solomons, its heaviest bombing of the South Pacific war. [9:1.]

Biggest RAF-U. S. Raids on Reich Blast Hamburg, Hit Baltic Cities

By The United Press

LONDON, Monday, July 26—United States heavy bombers struck deep and hard into Germany by daylight yesterday, hammering aircraft factories at the Baltic port of Warnemuende and showering hundreds of high explosives into the smoking ruins of Hamburg, gutted by the British Royal Air Force's night bombers twelve hours earlier in the greatest bombing assault of the war.

At the same time, other American heavies struck in force at the great German shipyards in Kiel and raided the Baltic industrial center of Wustrow, twenty-five miles west of Rostock.

The attack marked the biggest around-the-clock aerial assaults yet made by the American-British bombing teams. The raid on Warnemuende, seaport for the big manufacturing center of Rostock, was the deepest penetration of Germany yet made by the United States Eighth Air Force.

The RAF's night bombers in fifty blazing minutes blasted Hamburg with 2,300 tons of explosive and incendiary bombs, a far greater weight of bombs than ever before had been dropped in a single operation. [The British Air Ministry gives its figures in tons of 2,240 pounds; at 2,000 pounds to the ton, the RAF blasted Hamburg with 2,576 tons of bombs.]

RAF heavy bombers returned to the assault on Germany during last night. British officials reported early today. Channel coast watchers reported that a ninety-minute procession of heavy bombers flew

Continued on Page Seven

"All the News That's Fit to Print."

The New York Times.

LATE CITY EDITION
Warm and humid today; light winds.
Temperatures Yesterday—Max., 85; Min., 72
Sunrise, 5:46 A. M.; Sunset, 8:15 P. M.

Copyright, 1943, by The New York Times Company.

VOL. XCII..No. 31,230. Entered as Second-Class Matter, Postoffice, New York, N. Y. NEW YORK, TUESDAY, JULY 27, 1943. THREE CENTS IN NEW YORK CITY

ITALY PUT UNDER MARTIAL LAW BY BADOGLIO TO PREVENT CIVIL WAR; FASCIST RULE ENDED; HAMBURG BLASTED AGAIN; RUSSIANS DRIVE ON

30 MINERS INDICTED AS KEY PROMOTERS OF WILDCAT STRIKE

Grand Jury at Pittsburgh First to Act Under New Federal War Labor Disputes Law

STIFF PENALTIES LOOM

Government Charges Coal Pits It Was Operating Were Tied Up by Leaders of Walkout

By LOUIS STARK
Special to THE NEW YORK TIMES.

WASHINGTON, July 26—Thirty leaders of the recent strike by insurgent coal miners in southwestern Pennsylvania were named in indictments returned today by a Federal grand jury at Pittsburgh, the first to be handed down on charges of violating the new Smith-Connally War Labor Disputes Law. Under the law the maximum penalty is a fine of $5,000 or imprisonment for one year, or both, on each count.

The defendants are charged with having directed strikes and to have otherwise interrupted the operations of twenty-four coal mines which were in the possession of the Government.

The indictments, which were disclosed here by Attorney General Francis Biddle, charge violations of the law beginning June 26 and continuing up to the present time. All the defendants are officers or members of local unions of the United Mine Workers of America.

The May grand jury reconvened July 14 after Charles F. Uhl, Federal attorney, had petitioned Federal Judge F. P. Schoonmaker for the grand jury's consideration of "matters of great importance to the United States."

FBI Investigates Strike

After a refusal by the insurgent leaders to obey the orders of their union officials to return to work, the grand jury investigation was begun. Agents of the Federal Bureau of Investigation spent several weeks in the coal region gathering evidence.

Large numbers of miners had refused to return to work at the end of the third coal strike called since May 1 by John L. Lewis and the United Mine Workers. Their refusal was based on the fact that their leaders had not succeeded in arranging a contract with the bituminous coal operators.

Interruption of production by the insurgents caused a temporary shutdown of steel furnaces and by-product coke plants in the California-Brownsville district of Pennsylvania.

The cases were presented to the grand jury by Henry Schweinhaut and Irving Hill, special assistants to the Attorney General, assisted by the Federal attorney, Mr. Uhl.

In one indictment against twenty-one defendants there is one count charging them with conspiring to interfere by strike and by other interruptions with production in all the Government-operated coal mines in Fayette, Greene and Washington Counties, and thus to bring about a complete work stoppage.

The other nineteen counts in this indictment charge the defendants with specific acts of interference, such as recruiting, securing, transporting and leading pickets; picketing, inducing and encouraging mine employes to strike, and the calling of local union meetings at which they endorsed, urged and counseled strikes.

21 Named in One Indictment

Defendants under this indictment include the following:

Alphonse Congelio, Tower Hill, Pa.—Employed at the Isabella mine and president of the Isabella Local, UMW.

Amidee Barnes, Allison, Pa.—Employed at the Isabella mine and a member of the Isabella Local, UMW.

Alvin Biddle, Brownsville, Pa.—Employed at the Bridgeport mine and check-weighman for Bridgeport Local, UMW.

Williard Biddle, Brownsville—Em-

Continued on Page Twenty-one

Wake Isle Bombed, Axis Radio Reports

A Tokyo dispatch broadcast by the Berlin radio yesterday said that eight Liberator bombers had attacked Japanese-held Wake Island early Sunday, The Associated Press reported.

Two of the raiders were declared to have been brought down, against a loss of two Japanese fighter planes, one of which was credited with purposely crashing into one of the bombers to carry it to earth. The broadcast did not touch on the damage aground.

Presumably the planes were American-manned, although the report of the raid was not confirmed in United States announcements.

8 FROM U. S. INDICTED AS AIDING THE AXIS

Ezra Pound, Jane Anderson and Other Expatriates Face Trials for Treason

Special to THE NEW YORK TIMES.

WASHINGTON, July 26—Eight American citizens, including two women, who have been broadcasting Axis propaganda from Germany and Italy, were indicted for treason today by a District of Columbia grand jury. Whenever possible, they will be tried and on conviction can be punished by penalties ranging from death down to five years and a $1,000 fine.

Seven have been sending out their venom by radio short-wave from Germany. The eighth broadcasts from Rome. The grand jury named them as these:

Ezra Pound, 57, Idaho-born poet, at one time of New York.

Frederick Wilhelm Kaltenbach, 48, formerly of Dubuque, Iowa.

Robert Henry Best, 47, formerly of Sumter, S. C.

Douglas Chandler, 54, formerly of Baltimore.

Edward Leo Delaney, 57, formerly of Olney, Ill.

Constance Drexel, 48, a native of Germany, once employed in Philadelphia.

Jane Anderson, 50, formerly of Atlanta.

Max Oscar Otto Koischwitz, 41, formerly of New York.

Pound has been broadcasting from Rome. The others are hired by the Nazis and transmit from Berlin and other Reich points.

The action of the grand jury proves, said Attorney General Francis Biddle, that this country will not tolerate traitors at home or abroad.

"It is our intention when we can," he added, "to apprehend these defendants and to bring them to trial before a jury of their fellow-citizens, whom they are charged with betraying.

"It should be clearly understood that these indictments are based not only on the content of the propaganda statements, the lies and falsifications which were uttered, but also on the simple fact

Continued on Page Six

FORTRESSES STRIKE

Hit Hamburg 4th Blow in Two Days—Pound Other Reich Ports

RAF BATTERS ESSEN

2,000-Ton Bombing of Ruhr City a Part of Vast Air Offensive

By The United Press.

LONDON, Tuesday, July 27—Guided by a 20,000-foot column of smoke rising from the burning city, American Flying Fortresses blasted Hamburg yesterday for the fourth pounding of the big enemy port in forty-eight hours and also hit Wilhelmshaven and Wesermuende to lay out a flaming path of destruction across Germany's northwest coast.

Still another Fortress formation swept far inland and wrecked one of Germany's biggest synthetic rubber plants at Hanover, 112 miles west of Berlin, as the Allied air offensive rose to a new pitch that saw more than 2,000 heavy bombers and many hundreds of smaller aircraft loosing their fury.

The unescorted Fortresses encountered strong enemy fighter opposition and shot down more than fifty German planes.

Since midday Saturday there has been hardly an hour of the day or night without the crash of Allied bombs on Germany and Nazi-occupied territory. Of all the targets, Hamburg had taken the worst beating.

Essen Blow Is Concentrated

Yesterday's daylight attacks followed the heaviest raid of the war on Essen in the Ruhr by Royal Air Force heavy bombers over Sunday night. British and Canadian planes dropped 2,000 tons of explosive and incendiary bombs on the No. 1 Nazi arms center and home of the great Krupp Works. Fires of gigantic proportions sent smoke four miles into the air, pilots said.

The blasting of Essen was "concentrated and effective," carried out within fifty minutes beginning at 12:25 A. M., the British Air Ministry said.

In addition, on Sunday night the RAF sent out fast Mosquito bombers that made an attack on Hamburg and raided Cologne. The Bomber Command planes shot down two Nazi fighters during the night.

Mosquito planes of the British Fighter Command flew on intruder patrol over Nazi bases in northwest Germany, the Low Countries and France, destroying three Nazi planes.

By daylight, medium bombers of the United States Eighth Air Force struck at the St. Omer airfield in north France and "good bombing results were reported on all targets," said a joint American-British communiqué.

Many squadrons of RAF and Allied Spitfire fighters and Ty-

Continued on Page Five

Mussolini's Arrest In Flight Reported

By The Associated Press.

LONDON, July 26—Stockholm and Berne dispatches reported the broken Benito Mussolini had been arrested while trying to flee to German sanctuary from the nation he brought to the brink of disaster after twenty-one years of dictatorship.

Mussolini was said in a dispatch from Berne, Switzerland, to be under heavy guard at a villa near Rome, but this was not confirmed directly from Italy.

LONDON, July 26 (U.P.)—The extraordinarily stern martial law regime in Italy, suspending every normal means of travel, might indicate determination by the new government that Benito Mussolini must not escape.

AMERICANS DRIVE FOR EASTERN SICILY

Seventh Army Races to Join Big Offensive on Enemy's Last Major Defenses

By DREW MIDDLETON
By Wireless to THE NEW YORK TIMES.

ALLIED HEADQUARTERS IN NORTH AFRICA, July 26—The victorious American Seventh Army smashed eastward today to join in the general assault on the "Etna line," taking 7,000 more prisoners including six generals and an admiral. More than 70,000 prisoners are already in the Allies' hands.

The Germans rushed the Twenty-ninth Motorized Infantry Division into the Messina bridgehead, increasing the number of Axis combat troops in northeastern Sicily to about 97,000. Of these, about 52,000 are Germans.

Planes Attack Northern Port

While the ground forces concentrated for what may be the final struggle of the campaign, Allied planes attacked the north coast port of Milazzo, through which the Germans have been moving supplies and troops since Messina was made virtually useless by Allied bombs. The port was heavily bombed by Royal Air Force Bostons and Mitchells of the United

Continued on Page Two

OUR TERMS STAND

Hull Cites 'Surrender,' Calls Italy's Status a Military Question

PRESIDENT CHEERFUL

Recent U.S. Contact With Badoglio or House of Savoy Is Denied

By HAROLD CALLENDER
Special to THE NEW YORK TIMES.

WASHINGTON, July 26—That the exit of Italy from the war was for the present a military question and that the Allies' "unconditional surrender" terms were unlikely to be modified was indicated by Secretary of State Cordell Hull and other officials here today.

President Roosevelt made no comment, but visitors reported him in a cheerful mood that they associated with the news from Rome.

Mr. Hull denied reports that this Government had been in contact with Marshal Pietro Badoglio recently. To a question regarding similar contacts with the Vatican in connection with Italy's future, he replied he had heard nothing to that effect.

As to negotiations with Italy's royal house of Savoy, Mr. Hull said he had not discussed that with the President and so far as th State Department was concerned the question had not arisen.

Fighting Is Our Present Task

While remarking that fascism carried within it the seeds of its own destruction and that the timely and appropriate end of Benito Mussolini's power seemed to him the first major step in the early and complete destruction and eradication of every vestige of fascism, nationally and internationally, Mr. Hull insisted that everything waited upon military developments.

When asked what this Government was doing meanwhile, he replied that we were fighting like the devil.

To a question whether unconditional surrender applied to Hungary, Rumania and Bulgaria as well as the major Axis countries,

Continued on Page Three

Badoglio's Cabinet Is Seen As Step to Avoid Surrender

Berne Diplomats Expect Negotiations for an 'Honorable Capitulation' While German Forces Get Time to Flee

By Telephone to THE NEW YORK TIMES.

BERNE, Switzerland, July 26—With a celerity indicative of definite ideas of what his task would be, Premier Pietro Badoglio announced tonight the members of his "transitory military government which will operate with full powers from the King."

It contains not one new member who might not belong to an "armistice cabinet." Several might have belonged to a new "conservative fascist" government, but none belongs to the rabidly "anarchistic" group hitherto in the saddle, which was prepared to sacrifice all for survival.

The new government is expected in diplomatic quarters here to present a "solid national front" to the Allies while Premier Badoglio negotiates an "honorable capitulation" rather than an "unconditional surrender."

While peace negotiations may already be under way—such a report was semi-officially denied in Italian diplomatic circles tonight—his next greatest task will then be to present a sop to Germany, which still has strong forces in Italy, by giving German commanders more time for "preliminary" evacuation. This point, it is believed, is what caused the marshal to say last night that the war would continue.

Having successfully negotiated these first two hurdles, he would then face the problem of an "orderly and peaceful reconstruction" without revolution fomented by the long-suppressed parties with socialist leanings. His tasks are so huge that diplomatic circles reserved estimates as to the probable duration of his new cabinet.

The new chief of government's consultations were few. A bidding from him to join the cabinet appears to have been received as an order from the King. With one exception, understood to be that of

Continued on Page Five

Russians Take 70 Villages, Gain 6 Miles in Orel Drive

By The Associated Press.

LONDON, Tuesday, July 27—Russian troops captured seventy villages, gained six miles and killed 5,000 enemy soldiers yesterday in their steady semi-encirclement of the big German base at Orel, where thousands of Axis troops risk entrapment, it was announced early today in Moscow.

With the Russian troops within eight miles of the city's northeastern and eastern gates, a special communiqué said, other units have swept across the Oka River directly above the base in a wide wheeling movement threatening to cut the last supply line into Orel—the railway running northwest to Bryansk.

[The Russians have cut the Orel-Bryansk Railroad and crossed the Oka at new points in wild fighting that cost the Germans almost 9,000 men killed, The United Press reported.]

Village after village on the west bank of the Oka River fell to the Russians. One column also took Berestna, forty-five miles northwest of Orel. The vastness of the Russian drive indicated that Bryansk, as well as Orel, was an objective. Both are the keystones to the entire German south-central front in Russia.

Two thousand Germans were killed northwest of the city in a desperate effort to halt the first successful Red Army summer offensive of the war.

South of Orel, Russian troops, pushing up the railway from Kursk captured Kurakina and Yeropkino, which is only seventeen miles below Orel. The Germans lost 2,100 men before retreating in furious counter-attacks along the railway, including one stiff engagement at Glazunovskaya. The

Continued on Page Nine

GERMAN COMMENT IS STILL WITHHELD

Foreign Office Insists Ouster of Mussolini Is 'Internal' Affair of Italy Alone

By GUIDO ENDERIS
By Telephone to THE NEW YORK TIMES.

BERNE, Switzerland, July 26—Responsible German quarters made no comment tonight on the resignation of Premier Mussolini.

The Foreign Office disposed of inquiries today with the remark that Mussolini's disappearance after twenty-one years' rule concerned Italian internal policy alone. The earlier explanation that his retirement had been caused by ill health was abandoned during the day.

Up to a late hour serious comment on the effect of Mussolini's ouster on the tri-partite pact, Axis relations with Japan and particularly Axis collaboration in the Balkans was still lacking. Marshal Pietro Badoglio's slogan, "The war goes on," was the one dream of hope from which official circles professed to extract comfort. It was put to the fore in all comment.

Berlin and the rest of Germany got the first news of the Roman

Continued on Page Five

ITALIANS REJOICING

Crowds in Streets Call for Peace—Mussolini's Paper Plant Burned

LEFTISTS ISSUE CALL

Five Parties Urge That Fascists Be Punished for Causing War

The text of the manifesto by Marshal Badoglio on Page 4.

By DANIEL T. BRIGHAM
By Telephone to THE NEW YORK TIMES.

BERNE, Switzerland, July 26—Manifestations of popular approval of the departure of Benito Mussolini began in Rome late last night and continued in all the largest cities of Italy throughout the day. Late this afternoon in Milan a mob stormed the offices of Mussolini's newspaper, Popolo d'Italia, in which fascism was created after World War I. According to a report from the Corriere della Sera of Milan, the office was destroyed.

While the spontaneity of this and other demonstrations is beyond doubt, and their widespread recurrence would appear to point to a coordinated direction, no reports received from Italy indicated the country was passing through a revolution. Aside from a free-for-all fist fight in Bologna early this afternoon, no bloodshed was reported.

Martial Law Is Proclaimed

Marshal Pietro Badoglio, the Premier, proclaimed martial law. He ordered that all armed police and militia be put under his orders and that their commanders report to local army commanders for instructions.

A dusk-to-dawn curfew was ordered, with only priests, doctors and midwives permitted on the streets. Civilians using night trains were ordered to carry identification papers.

Public places, including theatres, movies and sports halls, were ordered closed during curfew hours. Gatherings of more than three persons, including any behind locked doors, were forbidden.

Though long dormant political parties were lifting cautious heads in various political centers, Italy appeared to be waiting developments, patiently, but ready to make trouble. An indication of this came from Turin late tonight in a proclamation to the Italian workers, signed by five leftist political parties. It left no doubt as to the fate of the fascist leaders if the workers get power.

Five Parties Proclamation

As printed in the Stampa Sera of Turin, the proclamation read:

"Italians!

"The painful nightmare that has dominated our political life for the past twenty years is now ended.

Continued on Page Four

Armistice Talks In Vatican Reported

By The Associated Press.

LONDON, Tuesday, July 27—A Reuter dispatch from Stockholm today said preliminary negotiations for an armistice between Italy and the Allies were begun in Vatican City last night. The Berne correspondent of Svenska Dagbladet was the source of the report. There was no confirmation whatever.

While negotiations were going on in the Vatican, it was said, the German Ambassador to Rome, Hans Georg Viktor von Mackensen, was holding a series of talks with Marshal Badoglio.

An Italian and German communiqué on the von Mackensen-Badoglio talks was expected shortly, the dispatch said.

ALGIERS, July 26 (Reuter)—Declaration of Rome as an open city is considered here as a likely step toward ultimate surrender of Italy.

Beer Shortage Develops in City; Brewers Are Rationing Supply

A beer shortage has developed because of the inability of brewers to get corn and other grains, spokesmen for the industry agreed yesterday. It is expected to get worse as the summer wears on and reserves that were brewed a month or six weeks ago are used up, but a measure of relief is possible in the fall when the new grain crop becomes available, according to one authority.

Intensifying the shortage of beer are equipment and transportation difficulties. Some brewers are short of bottles, others of barrels, and all brewers in the Eastern gasoline shortage area are feeling the effects of delivery restrictions imposed by the Office of Defense Transportation.

As yet no industry-wide program for apportioning available supplies among retail outlets has been adopted, but each brewer is using a form of rationing of his own devising. Some are pro-rating available supplies among regular customers, others are curtailing their delivery areas, still others are concentrating on the output of either draft or bottled beer, according to an official of the United States Brewers Association.

One of the first effects of the shortage has been a marked curtailment in the flow of beer from one production area to another; brewers are apparently delivering a major part of their production to the markets in the immediate vicinity of their plants, making their biggest cuts on shipments to distant points.

In Washington, receipts of out-

Continued on Page Thirteen

War News Summarized

TUESDAY, JULY 27, 1943

General rejoicing and celebration marked Italy's first day in more than twenty years free from the yoke of fascist rule. The fact that the Italian Empire had disappeared and that most of Sicily had been conquered did not seem to impress the people as much as the fact that Mussolini had gone.

Marshal Badoglio formed his Cabinet and immediately proclaimed martial law. He mustered the fascist militia into the King's service, imposed a dusk-to-dawn curfew and forbade the gathering of three or more persons. [All the foregoing 1:8.]

The new Italian Cabinet was considered a potential "armistice Cabinet" that would demand of the Allies "honorable capitulation" rather than "unconditional surrender." [1:6-7.]

The downfall of Mussolini was characterized by the German Foreign Office as an internal matter having no relation to the war. [1:7.] In London, the British War Cabinet met and every indication was that the peace terms remained unchanged—unconditional surrender and free use of Italy as a base against Germany. [3:6.] Although the White House withheld comment, Secretary of State Hull hailed the disappearance of Mussolini as the first step in the eradication of fascism throughout the world. He said the State Department had had no contact with Marshal Badoglio. [1:5.]

In Algiers the French Committee of National Liberation made it clear that, as Italy's closest neighbor and victim, France must be represented in any settlement with Italy. [3:1.]

Across the narrow Strait of Messina, Italy was still at war with the Allied invaders in Sicily. Canadian troops in the center of the Catania front were meeting fierce resistance, while the Americans were smashing eastward to join the assault on the Etna line. [1:4; map, P. 2.]

Combined Allied air forces continued their smashing attacks on Germany. The RAF and RCAF heavily bombed Essen, Hamburg and Cologne on Sunday night. Yesterday Flying Fortresses hit Hamburg again, as well as Hanover, Wilhelmshaven and Wesermuende, and destroyed more than fifty enemy fighters. Airfields in France and Belgium were also battered. Forty-six bombers were lost in all the attacks. [1:3, map P. 5.]

In Russia the Red Army cut the vital Bryansk-Orel railway, crossed the Oka River and captured more than seventy additional villages. More than 9,000 Germans died in yesterday's fighting around Orel. [1:6-7.]

Allied ground forces made a general advance in front of the Japanese base at Munda in the Solomons, aided by bombardment from the air and shelling from naval forces. Other enemy strongholds in the South Pacific were also heavily attacked by Allied fliers. [8:1.]

OWI Broadcast to Italy Calls Ruler 'Fascist' and 'Moronic Little King'

The Office of War Information, in transmissions beamed to Italy and the rest of Europe, broadcast yesterday statements characterizing King Victor Emmanuel as "the moronic little King" and "the Fascist King." The OWI short-wave stations, which are known collectively as "The Voice of America," also assailed Marshal Pietro Badoglio as "a high-ranking Fascist."

Immediately after Premier Benito Mussolini's "resignation" was made known Sunday, the overseas division of the OWI merely broadcast that there was "no essential change" in the government of Italy. Yesterday, however, the government propaganda agency directed its fire against the two new Italian leaders personally.

In presenting "typical unofficial reaction" to the events in Italy, the OWI employed the device of quoting an imaginary "American political commentator," "John Durfee." According to "Mr. Durfee," it was announced, the United States will continue the war irrespective of whether Signor Mussolini, Marshal Badoglio or "the Fascist King himself" rules Italy.

The OWI also quoted extensively from a Sunday-night radio speech by Samuel Grafton, columnist for The New York Post. It was Mr. Grafton who described King Victor Emmanuel as "the moronic little King."

This reference was carried in the hourly English-language transmission at 2 P. M., as broadcast over the 16, 19 and 23 megacycle bands.

Continued on Page Three

"All the News That's Fit to Print."

The New York Times.

LATE CITY EDITION
Moderate temperatures today with moderate to fresh winds.
Temperatures Yesterday—Max., 76; Min., 62
Sunrise, 6:09 A. M.; Sunset, 7:50 P. M.

Copyright, 1943, by The New York Times Company.

VOL. XCII.. No. 31,253. Entered as Second-Class Matter, Postoffice, New York, N. Y. NEW YORK, THURSDAY, AUGUST 19, 1943. THREE CENTS IN NEW YORK CITY

RAF BLASTS SECRET NAZI RESEARCH AREA; ARMIES READY TO GO, SAYS EISENHOWER; ALLIES BID PEOPLES OF EUROPE PREPARE

SANCTIONS FIXED AGAINST STRIKERS IN WAR INDUSTRIES

President Orders Withdrawing of Union Funds or Contract by WLB Under New Law

DRAFT DEFERMENT TO END

Stoppage of Materials, Fuel or Transportation Authorized if Employers Defy the Board

Text of the President's letter and order appears on Page 40.

Special to The New York Times.

WASHINGTON, Aug. 18—New powers by which the National War Labor Board may proceed against war industry employe as well as employer refusing to comply with its orders were bestowed by President Roosevelt in action disclosed today.

The Selective Service System was authorized to cancel draft deferments of recalcitrant individual union employes. Power was granted to withhold in escrow union dues collected under union agreements by employers in plants which have been seized by the Government because of strikes.

The law gives the Government power to seize plants of an employer refusing to comply with WLB orders. "Less drastic sanctions" were authorized, however, such as "control of war contracts, of essential materials and of transportation and fuel," if these steps could be taken without impeding the war effort. Fred M. Vinson, director of the Office of Economic Stabilization, was directed to follow this policy hereafter.

Executive Order Issued

In a letter to William H. Davis, chairman of the WLB, released by the President's office, Mr. Roosevelt revealed that an executive order had been issued under the War Labor Disputes Law (the Smith-Connally act). It appeared necessary, he said, "for bringing about compliance in the relatively few cases in which executive action may become necessary."

The order was described by a WLB official as "putting a lower set of teeth" in the powers of that agency.

This official noted that there had been widespread criticism of the fact that the only penalties heretofore imposed for strikes in war industries had been seizure of the employer's plant, even though the employer was innocent.

"This gives the board teeth with which to bite the employes as well as the employers in case of noncompliance with board directives," he said.

The directive was seen here as strengthening the hand of the WLB in the still unsettled coal mine dispute. Under it miners' dues now going to John L. Lewis' United Mine Workers could be withheld if the union refused to sign a new contract with the operators.

Action Up to Union Leaders

The essential effect of the order regarding unions was described by Mr. Roosevelt as follows in his letter:

"When a local union refuses to comply, by directing or advising workers not to work under the terms and conditions prescribed by the board, action by the responsible national or international officers has thus far, in all but one or two cases, sufficed to bring about compliance.

"If such action should prove ineffective, or if a national or international union should itself be the offender, the plant will be taken over under the War Labor Disputes Act and operated by the Government, if this is necessary to prevent interference with production and to protect the workers who wish to work."

The letter said that when the Government had to take over plants or industries because of labor noncompliance, "Government operation will be conducted with the least possible interference with existing management."

The letter also noted that as to "certain types of interference with production by individuals, the law provides penalties enforceable by the Attorney General."

The board was praised for its "remarkable record" in the last eighteen months of disposing of more than 1,000 disputes and of having had to refer only seven to the President "because of persistent non-compliance."

The industry, labor and public members of the board had each played an effective part in making

Continued on Page Forty

Eisenhower Praises Land, Sea, Air Aides

By The Associated Press.

ALLIED HEADQUARTERS IN NORTH AFRICA, Aug. 18—Gen. Dwight D. Eisenhower, commander of Allied Forces in North Africa, sent congratulations today to his land, air and naval chiefs—Gen. Sir Harold Alexander, Air Chief Marshal Sir Arthur Tedder and Admiral Sir Andrew Browne Cunningham—asking each to extend appreciation to the officers and men for the successes they have achieved.

The message to General Alexander said:

"With the Sicilian campaign at an end, I have the happy opportunity once again to express to you my appreciation of the outstanding services you continue to render the Allied cause and assure you of my personal thanks for always making my own task easier.

"I hope you extend to Generals Montgomery and Patton and to the magnificent troops serving under them my commendations and congratulations for their energy, determination and aggressiveness in driving the enemy out of Sicily. With such soldiers as these we can look forward with confidence to the future."

COAL PAY CASE GOES TO THE WLB AGAIN

Operators Get Board to Take It After They and Union Fail to Agree on Wage

Special to The New York Times.

WASHINGTON, Aug. 18—At the request of the Anthracite Coal Operators Association, the National War Labor Board announced today that it would resume jurisdiction over the four-and-one-half-month-old wage dispute between the operators and the United Mine Workers of America and set a public hearing on the issue here for Monday morning.

The WLB announcement said the action was taken after counsel for the operators sent word that they had not been able to reach an agreement with the union despite long negotiations.

The board sent telegrams to Walter Gordon Merritt, operators' counsel, and John L. Lewis and Thomas Kennedy, respectively president and secretary treasurer of the UMW, stating that "you and your associates are invited to attend" the hearing.

May Await Private Custody

"Unless an application under the provisions of Section 5 of the War Labor Disputes Act is made for a change in wages and other terms and conditions of employment in the manner specified in said section," the telegram stated, "any order which the board might make changing the wages or other terms and conditions of employment existing in any particular mine would become effective together with any retroactive provisions upon return of such mine to private operation and not during the period of Government operation."

Section 5 of this act (the Smith-Connally law) provides that the WLB may order changes in wages and working conditions of a seized war facility if either party applies for such a change.

The anthracite wage negotiations, affecting about 80,000 miners, began on March 31, when the miners' union presented twenty-one demands which the operators said would necessitate an increase

Continued on Page Seventeen

GENERAL HAILS MEN

Solid Victory Won in Real Combined Operation, Eisenhower Says

FOE'S CASUALTIES 167,000

1,691 Enemy Planes Destroyed or Taken—25,000 of Our Troops, 274 Aircraft Lost

By MILTON BRACKER

By Wireless to The New York Times.

ALLIED HEADQUARTERS IN NORTH AFRICA, Aug. 18—With the battle of Sicily over ahead of schedule, although an artillery combat raged across the Strait of Messina, Gen. Dwight D. Eisenhower sat down in a map-walled room today and hailed the American soldiers for having achieved a solid victory that was a combined operation in the most literal sense.

"It was a real victory and our troops have done everything that the best troops in the world could have done—and that includes the three services," the Allied Commander in Chief in this theatre declared. The cooperation between the American Seventh Army and the British Eighth Army, he added, could be described as a "one-two punch" that Gen. Sir Harold R. L. G. Alexander could bring into action whenever he desired.

Losses 167,000 to 25,000

General Eisenhower's staff issued a statistical summary of the campaign showing that, up to Aug. 10, German and Italian prisoners taken had exceeded 135,000, while the enemy's losses in killed and wounded were not fewer than 32,000. It was estimated that the total of prisoners alone might eventually reach 200,000. General Eisenhower indicated that the total Allied casualties, on the basis of incomplete figures, stood at about 25,000. The casualties suffered by the Seventh Army were known to have been relatively severe in the fighting around Troina.

The first month of the thirty-eight-day struggle cost the Axis 260 tanks and 502 guns. Through Aug. 17, 1,691 enemy aircraft were shot down or captured, against the Allies' loss of 274.

The great majority of the planes lost by the enemy were captured on deserted airfields. Many of them have already been reconditioned and put to use. Moreover, many thousands of military vehicles of all types fell into our hands and quantities of stores are still being collected all over the island.

General Glad It's Over

General Eisenhower sat at the head of a table, surrounded, at both chair and floor level, by correspondents. He wore ribbons symbolizing only two decorations—the Knight Commander of the Bath, recently awarded by King George VI, and a French medal presented by Gen. Henri-Honoré Giraud.

General Eisenhower made it plain that he was glad that the job had been done and that he was particularly satisfied at new evidence of coordination among the Allies and

Continued on Page Four

AT QUEBEC: THE MEN WHO WILL DETERMINE NEXT PHASES OF THE WAR

Principals at the conference: With President Roosevelt in the front row are Prime Ministers Churchill (right) and King; in the rear row, left to right, are Gen. Henry H. Arnold, Air Marshal Sir Charles Portal, Gen. Sir Alan Brooke, Admiral Ernest J. King, Field Marshal Sir John Dill, Gen. George C. Marshall, Admiral Sir Dudley Pound and Admiral William D. Leahy.

Associated Press Wirephoto

GERMANS QUITTING CALABRIA FOOTHOLD

Flee by Land and Sea Under Bombardment by Allies' Artillery and Planes

By The United Press.

ALLIED HEADQUARTERS IN NORTH AFRICA, Aug. 18—The Germans have begun evacuating the Reggio Calabria area of southern Italy opposite Messina, it was reported today.

As their overland escape route by southern Italy continued to suffer heavy aerial bombardment, the Germans were reported to be taking to boats to run through the Strait of Messina around to the port of Palmi, twenty miles north of Reggio Calabria on the Gulf of Gioia. The battle of Italy had apparently begun.

Allied planes roared back and forth across the strait, battering railroads and highways and pouncing on Axis escape boats sailing along under the protection of anti-aircraft guns but with virtually no air cover.

Allied and Axis artillery traded

Continued on Page Three

Eden Joins Quebec Parley; Political Phase Is Reached

By JOHN H. CRIDER

Special to The New York Times.

QUEBEC, Aug. 18—The momentous conference at which President Roosevelt and Prime Minister Churchill are planning the military strategy to end the war took a definitely political turn today with the arrival of Anthony Eden, Britain's much-traveled Foreign Secretary.

Joining the conferees any day now, perhaps tomorrow, will be Cordell Hull, Secretary of State, to round out the foursome who will decide such pressing problems as how to deal with Italy and Germany on their surrender, recognition of the French Committee of National Liberation, greater political and military collaboration with Soviet Russia, and the parts that the military forces of each United Nation, including the exiled governments, will have in the impending invasion of continental Europe.

It was significant that no observers from any of the United Nations other than the United States, Great Britain and Canada were in attendance here, according to an authorized spokesman.

Meanwhile, as President Roosevelt proceeded speedily into conferences with Mr. Churchill and military advisers after his arrival

Continued on Page Five

RUSSIANS RESUME KHARKOV ADVANCE

Capture Key Town in Smash Across Donets—New Gains Deepen Other Fronts

By The United Press.

LONDON, Thursday, Aug. 19—The Russian Army, resuming a general advance after crushing counter-attacks into which the German command had thrown its reserves, made important gains yesterday in all three areas of the Kharkov front—southeast, northwest and west of the city.

Zmiyev, a key town twenty-one miles southeast of Kharkov, was captured after a new break across the Donets River. Three towns nine miles south and southeast of the big German base of Sumy were taken northwest of Kharkov. On the west, the Red Army captured Oposhnya, twenty-four miles north of the rail and agricultural center of Poltava and seventy miles west of Kharkov, on the way to the Dnieper River.

In all, more than fifty towns and villages were taken on the Kharkov front in gains of more than six miles, made in the face of continued counter-attacks.

The Russian midnight communi-

Continued on Page Nine

ALLIES' RADIO HINTS AT EARLY INVASION

Occupied Countries Told to Get Ready—Signal for Blow to Come at Last Minute

By The Associated Press.

LONDON, Aug. 18—The United Nations radio in Algiers told the people of occupied Europe tonight to perfect their preparations "for the day when you will hear the call of the Allied High Command" on the eve of the invasion of the Continent.

The broadcast said that, although "we are obviously not going to reveal where the next blow will fall," the people of "the occupied country that is to be the first to welcome the armies of liberation will be notified at the last minute." It added that the time might be near at hand.

Although the broadcast especially mentioned metropolitan France, in effect all those awaiting freedom from Greece to Norway were told to make their preparations for "the new phase, the liberation of the occupied countries," which, it said, has already begun. The announcer concluded the broadcast by saying that the message was from the "Allied High Command."

[The heavy American assaults on French airfields are viewed by the Germans as the prelude to the invasion of France, The Associated Press said on the basis of German dispatches to Stockholm.]

Gen. Dwight D. Eisenhower broadcast the first warning to occupied countries to prepare for the battle of Europe on July 10, when the invasion of Sicily began. Speak-

Continued on Page Five

RECORD DAY IN AIR

3,000 Planes Smash 16 Targets in Non-Stop Attrition Drive

BERLIN RAIDED 71ST TIME

Other Blows Range From Baltic to France—New Night Raids in Europe Indicated

By The United Press.

LONDON, Thursday, Aug. 19—Royal Air Force and Canadian bombers attacked targets in Germany Tuesday night, singling out a secret German research and development plant on the Baltic coast for a 1,500-ton attack, and coast observers reported new streams of bombers beating steadily toward Europe last night on routes usually taken to Germany.

Mosquito bombers gave Berlin its seventy-first raid of the war Tuesday night, topping off a twenty-four-hour non-stop attack that probably set a record in air war history.

The German mystery plant, hidden in a four-and-a-half-square-mile patch of woods at Peenemuende, in northeastern Germany, was ripped open by more than 1,500 tons of high explosives and incendiaries showered down by the RAF and RCAF bombers from a low level.

Nearly 3,000 British, American and Canadian planes carried out sixteen separate operations, closely coordinated, in the twenty-four-hour period at a price of thirty-six American and forty-one RAF heavy bombers in two major operations alone.

Northern Airdromes Attacked

Today American Marauder medium bombers, under an escort of British, Canadian and other Allied Spitfire fighters, maintained the attack by raiding German airdromes at Woensdrecht, the Netherlands, and Lille, France.

The raids were a complex pattern in Allied plans to cripple German industry from the first manufacturing processes to the finished products, to soften the path for the opening of a new front in western Europe and to drain the blood from the German fighter air force.

[Government monitors reported that the Allouis and Paris radio stations shut down last night, indicating that Allied bombers might be raiding the Continent for the fifth straight night. An air alert in Switzerland indicated raids in the Lake Constance area of Germany, according to a Rome broadcast heard by the Columbia Broadcasting System. A large force of Allied bombers passed over Hungary from south to west, evidently bound for Austria, Reuter reported.]

The great four-motored bombers of the RAF, in their night raid, attacked heavily in bright moonlight the research factory at Peenemuende, sixty miles northwest of Stettin on the Bay of Pomerania at the estuary of the Peene River. The town, never before attacked, is the site of the biggest German research and development station, specializing in scientific work on aircraft radio-location and armament.

Loss of Bombers Heavy

Enemy fighters battled the raiders along a great part of their 1,200-mile round trip flight, and the forty-one bombers reported missing represented the greatest RAF loss since the heavy raid on Krefeld on June 21, when forty-four planes were lost.

An undisclosed number of German night fighters were shot down by the raiding force and RAF quarters indicated that the importance of the targets at Peenemuende justified the heavy losses sustained.

Supporting the main attack, speedy Mosquito bombers raided Berlin for the fourth time in the last five nights and RAF intruder planes stabbed at airfields and railway targets in France, the Low

Continued on Page Ten

U. S. Ruling on Austria's Status Asked by Court on Alien's Plea

The State Department will be asked to take a definite stand on the question of the incorporation of Austria into the German Reich under one of three decisions bearing on the status of aliens of Austrian origin, handed down yesterday by the United States Circuit Court of Appeals.

The court held, in one case that Frederic Walker D'Esquiva was not a "citizen" of Germany, whether or not this country recognizes the disappearance of Austria into Germany. But if the State Department has recognized the factual absorption of D'Esquiva's native land, he may be considered a "native" of Germany. D'Esquiva is in custody as a "dangerous alien enemy." The Department will be asked to settle the question of recognition, before his status under the Alien Enemy Law is settled.

The court also ruled that, regardless of the attitude of the State Department, Germany had no right to force German citizenship upon Austrians not living in their own country, without either their tacit or express consent.

With this ruling it reversed a District Court decision that Dr. Paul Schwarzkopf was a citizen of Germany. The lower court was directed to sustain a writ of habeas corpus obtained by Dr. Schwarzkopf and discharge him from custody. This procedure would usually take about two weeks, unless the Government should win a stay pending appeal of the decision to the Supreme Court.

The third case was that of Ivan

Continued on Page Six

War News Summarized

THURSDAY, AUGUST 19, 1943

British, American and Canadian bombers yesterday ripped Germany in widespread night and day raids in a record twenty-four-hour assault by nearly 3,000 planes. The chief target was Peenemuende, site of a secret Nazi research and development factory on the Baltic coast. Forty-one British heavy bombers were lost. [1:8, map, P. 10.]

The people of occupied Europe were told by the Allied-controlled radio in Algiers to "perfect preparations" for their part in the imminent invasion of the Continent. "The new phase, the liberation of occupied countries, has begun," the message declared. [1:7.]

In preparation for the assault on Hitler's fortress, President Roosevelt and Prime Minister Churchill worked with military leaders in Quebec over a detailed master plan for forcing and taking the Nazi bastion. British Foreign Secretary Anthony Eden arrived in the Canadian city. At the close of the conference President Roosevelt is to visit Ottawa, where he may address a special session of the Canadian Parliament. [1:5-6.]

On the Russian front the titanic struggle continued, with the Red Army surging ahead in a general advance on the Kharkov line after encountering bitter counter-attacks into which the Germans had thrown huge reserves. The Russians captured Zmiyev, twenty miles south of Kharkov, and more than fifty smaller places. On the Bryansk front the Soviet forces took forty villages in an advance of four to six miles. [1:6; map, P. 9.]

With the Sicilian campaign over, Allied forces gave the enemy no rest as beaches, roads and communications in southern Italy came under air and artillery attack. Every effort was being made to disrupt Axis efforts to reorganize the forces that had fled across the Strait of Messina. [1:4; map, P. 2.]

General Eisenhower disclosed at a press conference at Allied Headquarters in North Africa that Axis losses in the thirty-eight-day battle for Sicily were 135,000 captured and 32,000 killed and wounded against our 25,000 casualties, with tremendous losses to the enemy in matériel yet to be estimated. [1:3.]

Marshal Badoglio and former Premier Orlando addressed the Italian nation by radio and bemoaned the loss of Sicily. [4:2.]

Allied planes in the southwest Pacific returned to blasted Wewak in New Guinea to finish off all but ten of 225 enemy planes there. An Allied sea victory was reported in Vella Gulf in the Solomons. [12:2.]

Americans' Way Lit by Full Moon On Last Night of Battle for Messina

By HERBERT L. MATTHEWS

By Wireless to The New York Times.

MESSINA, Sicily, Aug. 17 (Delayed)—The Sicilian campaign ended at dawn today when patrols of the American Third Division entered Messina, to find it deserted by the Germans.

Only a few snipers remained. Three hours later the British patrols, followed by tanks that had been held back by demolitions, entered Messina from the south.

The Germans deserve credit for having fought skillfully and tenaciously throughout. They left a minimum of material and men to be captured. However, their divisions had been severely mauled, particularly at Troina, so it is doubtful whether they got away with most of their strength.

The end came suddenly and almost tamely. It had been foreseen, but it was always possible for the Germans to make a final delaying stand.

Contact with them had been lost at dusk last night and units of our Third Division began pressing up the road that goes across the ridge straight to Messina, as well as the coastal road that makes a great loop. Meanwhile, Rangers had reached a secondary road running north and south along the ridge.

Such good progress had been made before midnight that it was obvious that Messina would fall very soon. The all but full moon was an extraordinary blessing for everybody but the Germans. It gave a character of unreality to

Continued on Page Three

"All the News That's Fit to Print."

The New York Times.

LATE CITY EDITION
Little change in temperature; showers and cooler in evening.
Temperatures Yesterday—Max., 89; Min., 71
Sunrise, 6:16 A. M.; Sunset, 7:40 P. M.

VOL. XCII ... No. 31,260. Entered as Second-Class Matter, Postoffice, New York, N. Y. NEW YORK, THURSDAY, AUGUST 26, 1943. THREE CENTS IN NEW YORK CITY

ROOSEVELT WARNS HITLER TO SURRENDER NOW; SAYS ALLIES WILL END 'GANGSTERISM' IN WORLD; MOUNTBATTEN TO COMMAND IN SOUTHEAST ASIA

VAST WAR EXPORTS DELAYED BY LACK OF RAIL LABOR HERE

Scarcity of Freight Handlers Holds Up Thousands of Cars Along Seaboard

URGENT PLEA TO WORKERS

Roads Combing Inland Points to Recruit Own Employes to Help Meet Crisis

An acute railroad manpower shortage is threatening the movement of huge quantities of military and lend-lease exports in the New York area and elsewhere along the Atlantic seaboard, it was disclosed yesterday.

With insufficient labor to unload freight cars as they come in to the yards along the New Jersey shore, thousands of cars have been delayed in recent weeks, and it was reported that 8,000 cars were waiting for freight handlers yesterday. At a more acute period within the last few weeks there were 10,000 cars in the backlog.

An appeal for the mobilization of hundreds of workers has been made to the Railroad Retirement Board at its regional headquarters in New York, and the railroad companies themselves are conducting enlistment campaigns among their own employes at inland points, where trackmen, office employes and others who can be spared are being recruited and sent to seaboard points.

According to spokesmen for the board and the railroads, at least 3,200 men are needed at once in the New York area alone, and Robert Ware, Retirement Board official at the 58 Hudson Street office, said the various railroad lines involved in the shortage had reported 7,000 vacancies among their staffs in New York and the immediate New Jersey shore area.

New Task Is Taken On

The Retirement Board, charged by law with the administration of the Railroad Unemployment Insurance Act, promotes employment stabilization within the industry. During the war it has taken on the task of keeping the roads supplied with sufficient men for adequate operation.

In the last seven weeks the board has furnished 3,000 workers in the New York district alone, and 10,000 in the entire region extending from Manhattan to and including Maryland and the District of Columbia.

Appeals for men are constantly made through advertisements in newspapers, through public appeals in municipalities and with the aid of civic and veterans' groups. The urgency of getting war materials unloaded for arriving convoys is stressed.

A spokesman for the affected railroads, which include the New York Central, Baltimore & Ohio, Jersey Central, Lackawanna, Lehigh Valley, Erie, Pennsylvania and the West Shore Division of the New York Central, said that while a very acute tie-up some days ago had been relieved through the joint efforts, the situation was still critical and will continue to develop.

Port Itself Is Threatened

"It not only menaces the war effort and the movement of supplies but it is threatening the position of the Port of New York," he said. "We ought to have another 1,600 men every day at the very minimum. We have had such heavy business in recent weeks that there simply hasn't been enough men to handle the cargo. The number of freight cars entering the area with goods is greater by far than at any time in the history of the port."

The shortage was attributed to the "raiding" of railroad manpower by other industries that pay higher wages, to the draft and to the failure of rail workers to obtain a wage increase.

The local War Manpower Commission offices in Newark communicated the appeal for men to the regional Railroad Retirement

Continued on Page Thirteen

SUPREME COMMANDER IN SOUTHEAST ASIA

Lord Louis Mountbatten
Associated Press, 1943

Jersey OPA Secretly Allots 'Gas' to Party Fishing Boats

While some of the Long Island gasoline stations reserved for use of war workers because of the Eastern petroleum drought ran dry yesterday before noon, it developed that the Office of Price Administration had secretly granted special gasoline allotments for party fishing boats in Atlantic City and other New Jersey coastal resorts.

A spokesman for the Atlantic City rationing board said that the special allotments—which enabled several boatloads of amateur fishermen to put out last Saturday and Sunday—had been authorized by the OPA district office at Camden. He said the Camden OPA had instructed local boards to "keep quiet" about the grants lest "hordes of fishermen" descend on the piers and quays.

The plan of secrecy went awry when Atlantic City's municipal press agent, not bound by any promises to OPA, let the cat out of the fishbag with a rosy announcement of the catches in store for anglers who took advantage of the rationing board's liberality.

"Coast Guard regulations still bar the boats from going to sea, but big schools of weakfish, kingfish, croakers and flounders are back in the bays, waiting to be caught," read the blurb that Mall Dodson, the municipal barker, sent to the fish-and-game editors of newspapers.

OPA Here Taken by Surprise

The situation took OPA officials in New York by surprise. At the district office, which has jurisdiction over Sheepshead Bay and the Long Island resorts whose party fishing boats have been idle since the ban against pleasure-driving was held to include such craft, it was said that no rations had been issued here for such boating and

Continued on Page Twenty-five

KELLAND DEMANDS 'IMPREGNABLE' U. S.

Defense System From Dakar to Far Pacific Suggested to Supplement Alliances

A program of American imperialism in the post-war world, as opposed to American participation in any "Utopian super-state," will be presented to the Republican Post-War Policy Committee meeting to be held at the call of Republican National Chairman Harrison Spangler at Mackinac Island in early September.

Its author, Clarence Budington Kelland, a member of the Spangler committee, National Committeeman from Arizona and former executive director of the Republican National Committee, outlined the plan here yesterday and asserted that it had considerable support within the Spangler group, which was set up to counteract the unofficial Republican Post-War Policy Association, inspired by Wendell Willkie.

Mr. Kelland advocated a "five-ocean" navy, making the Pacific an American lake by holding all necessary islands; the taking "by treaty or by occupation" of bases in Iceland, Greenland, Dakar and

Continued on Page Thirty-eight

WLB Voids Lewis' Illinois Deal, Calling It Hidden Mine Pay Rise

By LOUIS STARK
Special to THE NEW YORK TIMES.

WASHINGTON, Aug. 25—The War Labor Board, by a vote of eight to four, with the labor members dissenting, has rejected the agreement negotiated by John L. Lewis, president of the United Mine Workers, with the Illinois Coal Operators Association, providing for the payment of $1.25 a day to cover travel time from portal to portal, according to an announcement today by William H. Davis, chairman of the WLB.

Mr. Davis, who is preparing the majority opinion and the formal directive, said that the public and industry majority of the board had been unable to approve the settlement made on behalf of 3,500 Illinois miners because it was not related to what the union might have recovered under the Fair Labor Standards Act and did not constitute a "genuine settlement of claims arising under the act" as directed by the board on May 25.

In effect, the board held that the $1.25 a day was a hidden wage increase.

Matthew Woll, vice president of the American Federation of Labor, fought all day yesterday to win the board's acceptance of the Illinois agreement, which was made public on July 21 by the miners' union and the operators and submitted to the board for approval.

A labor member of the WLB, Mr. Woll read correspondence between himself and Mr. Lewis covering various objections previously raised by board members. It is

Continued on Page Thirteen

BURMA DRIVE SEEN

Lord Louis Is Named at Ottawa as Result of Allied Parleys

LIKELY TO ACT SOON

As Head of Combined Operations Admiral Led Commandos

By JOHN H. CRIDER
Special to THE NEW YORK TIMES.

OTTAWA, Aug. 25—The creation of a separate Allied Southeast Asia Command and the appointment of Lord Louis Mountbatten, an acting vice admiral, as its commander were announced today from the Citadel in Quebec, where President Roosevelt and Prime Minister Churchill mapped their war strategy in the historic conference that ended yesterday. The announcement was made by British spokesmen who accompanied the President here.

Thus, within a day of the conclusion of the sixth war conference of the President and Mr. Churchill, the pattern of new events in the Pacific began to unfold. In their statement at the conclusion of their conference the leaders emphasized that the greater part of their Quebec talks were devoted to Pacific strategy.

Of equal importance to the appointment of the colorful Chief of Combined Operations, which includes the Commandos, to head the new Southeast Asia Command, was the fact that such a command has now been created. Lord Louis is a second cousin of King George.

Announcement of Shift

"It has been decided," the brief announcement said, "to set up a separate Southeast Asia Command for the conduct of operations based on India and Ceylon against Japan. It will be an Allied command similar to that set up in North Africa.

"The King has been pleased to approve the appointment of Acting Vice Admiral the Lord Louis Mountbatten, G. C. V. O., D. S. O., A. D. C., to be Supreme Allied Commander, Southeast Asia."

The announcement carried three important implications:

1. That President Roosevelt and Mr. Churchill meant not only ac-

Continued on Page Four

RAF GOES OUT AGAIN

New Blows in Germany Indicated—French Air Bases Pounded

BERLIN BOMBED ANEW

Mosquitos Add to Havoc—Big Plants Wrecked, Human Toll Heavy

By The United Press.

LONDON, Thursday, Aug. 26—Powerful forces of British heavy bombers swarmed last night toward the Continent, where large areas of Berlin have been devastated in two nights of "Hamburg pattern" bombing.

The four-motored bombers thundered across the Channel in an hour-long procession that coastal observers said was as great as the armada that blasted the German capital Monday night.

As they streamed out in a southeasterly direction Axis radio stations in Germany and the occupied countries fell silent one by one, from Paris to Munich. British radio monitors reported that the radio silence blanketing the Continent was more complete than at any time in their memory.

In the midst of the unprecedented radio blackout a radio "ghost voice" crashed in powerfully on continental wave lengths with an ominous warning to the German people that Adolf Hitler "is sending you to your deaths."

Mosquitos Return to Berlin

Tuesday night the RAF's fast Mosquito bombers, following the pattern that virtually destroyed Hamburg last month, opened the second round of the Battle of Berlin by heaping their bombs on the fires still blazing in the battered German capital from Monday's record raid.

American and British medium bombers swarmed over France, striking hard at the enemy's network of coastal airfields without loss.

B-26 Marauders of the Eighth United States Air Force attacked the airdrome at Tricqueville, northeast of Caen, and blasted a power station near Rouen. RAF Mitchells bombed the St. Martin airfield at

Continued on Page Nine

War News Summarized

THURSDAY, AUGUST 26, 1943

Speaking to 30,000 Canadians, on Parliament Hill in Ottawa yesterday, President Roosevelt gave the Nazis stern warning that "surrender would pay them better now than later." He added that at the Quebec Conference he, Prime Minister Churchill and their military leaders had "talked constructively of our common purpose in this war." That purpose is "a determination to achieve victory in the shortest possible time." Revealing no actual decisions of the historic meeting, Mr. Roosevelt said: "We are going to be rid of outlaws this time." [1:8.]

The people of Canada's capital city gave Mr. Roosevelt, first United States President to visit Ottawa, an ovation on his arrival. [3:2-3.]

From the Citadel in Quebec came the announcement that Lord Louis Mountbatten, cousin of King George VI and British Chief of Combined Operations, has been named Supreme Allied Commander in Southeast Asia. In a post similar to the North African Command of General Eisenhower and the Southwest Pacific Command of General MacArthur, Lord Louis will direct the attack against Japan from India and Ceylon. [1:4, map P. 4.] In London the announcement was interpreted as presaging the near completion of plans for an all-out offensive against Japan. [4:2.] Visiting the Allied Headquarters in the Southwest Pacific, Under-Secretary of War Patterson predicted blows of increasing strength against Japan. [5:1.]

In the European theatre, Berliners found no rest from the continuing air assaults on their city. British Mosquito bombers knifed through the smoke of fires set in Monday night's 700-plane raid to wreak fresh destruction. Last night a strong force of Allied heavy bombers was reported sweeping out across the English Channel. [1:5.]

Maj. Gen. Harold L. George, Chief of the United States Transport Command, predicted economic collapse for Germany by the end of the year if the air offensive could be continued with a reasonable rise in tempo. [9:1].

Allied raids on Italian communications and transport facilities continued. Rail lines south of Naples were torn by British Wellington bombers, and a lone American fighter-bomber blew the stern off an Italian cruiser, leaving the vessel sinking. Enemy air opposition was nonexistent [6:4.]

The Russian Army continued to plunge deep into the Ukraine, capturing Zenkov, eighty-five miles northwest of Kharkov, and sixty other places. In the Donets Basin far to the southeast other units captured several towns and considerably improved their positions. The Nazis resisted feverishly the enveloping Soviet drives. [1:7; map, P. 10.]

PRESIDENT ADDRESSING CANADIANS

Franklin D. Roosevelt at Ottawa yesterday
Associated Press Wirephoto

President Says Surrender Will Free Axis Peoples

Special to THE NEW YORK TIMES.

WASHINGTON, Aug. 25—Except for the "responsible fascist leaders," the peoples of the Axis need not fear unconditional surrender to the United Nations, President Roosevelt declared today in a letter transmitting to Congress a report which showed that lend-lease assistance to our Allies had reached the total of $13,973,339,000 on July 31.

For the first time, the report showed, monthly lend-lease aid exceeded a billion dollars in June. The total in July exceeded the June figure by $20,000,000. Aid to Russia reached a peak in April, but dropped off sharply in May and June, while aid to Great Britain continued a steady rise.

Mr. Roosevelt, in his letter of transmittal, assured the Axis peoples that the unconditional-surrender proclamation of his Casablanca conference with Prime Minister Winston Churchill did not mean they must trade "Axis despotism for ruin under the United Nations," but that the Allies' goal was "to permit liberated peoples to create a free political life of their own choosing and to attain economic security."

He also brought out that the might of the United States and its Allies was being felt in the Axis satellite nations of the Balkans and middle Europe as well as in Nazi Germany.

"Crushing Force" Widespread

"From Hamburg on the North Sea to Ploesti in Rumania," the President declared, "the people know from first-hand experience with what crushing force the United Nations can strike."

The subjugated peoples of Nazi Europe are now aware that the European fortress is not impregnable, he stated.

"The great offensives of the So-

Continued on Page Eleven

RED ARMY EXTENDS WEDGE IN UKRAINE

Zenkov and 60 Other Places Fall in Renewed Drive—Donbas Threat Grows

By The United Press.

LONDON, Thursday, Aug. 26—Driving ahead after smashing strong German resistance, the Russian Army yesterday captured more than sixty towns and villages northwest of Kharkov, including the flour milling center of Zenkov, to reach a new farthest west point in their offensive.

Zenkov, a town of 11,000 persons, is eighty-five miles northwest of Kharkov and 101 miles southwest of Belgorod, where the Red Army started its great summer attack.

Desperate fighting raged over the whole Kharkov and Donets Basin fronts and a Russian operational bulletin revealed that the big base of Akhtyrka, twenty-three miles northeast of Zenkov, had changed hands several times since its capture Aug. 11, until it was finally won by storm. The Germans had claimed that they had surrounded the Russians at Akhtyrka.

West and south of Kharkov the Russians continued their advance.

Continued on Page Ten

Coordinator of Post-War Planning Is Reported Chosen by Roosevelt

By JOHN MacCORMAC
Special to THE NEW YORK TIMES.

WASHINGTON, Aug. 25—Appointment of a coordinator of the plans which are being made by over a dozen different Government departments and agencies for the reconversion of American agriculture and industry to peace will be announced early next week by President Roosevelt, it is understood. It will be a corollary to the plans made at Quebec.

Who is to be the President's choice for the post, which is likely to prove as difficult as it is important, is not yet known. The names of Secretary of Commerce Jesse H. Jones, Chairman Donald M. Nelson of the War Production Board and Leo T. Crowley, Alien Property Custodian and head of the Office of Economic Warfare, were being mentioned today, but all three were said to have denied to friends that they were seeking or would get the appointment. Lewis W. Douglas, deputy administrator of war shipping, was believed to be another possibility.

Whoever proves to be the appointee, the heads of four of the Government branches which would have to participate in the making of post-war plans admitted that they thought the time ripe for an announcement by the Government that arrangements were being made to allow industry, when the time comes, to be reconverted without dislocation or undue delay to the manufacture of civilian goods.

They said this would have a salutary effect on war production.

Continued on Page Thirteen

PRESIDENT IS GRIM

Only Long Peace Could Justify Sacrifices, He Declares in Ottawa

POST-WAR AIMS SET

Chief Executive Shows Scope at Quebec Was Wider Than Reported

The text of the President's address is printed on Page 2.

By P. J. PHILIP
Special to THE NEW YORK TIMES.

OTTAWA, Aug. 25—As a sequel to the Quebec conference President Roosevelt in Ottawa today summoned Adolf Hitler and his generals to surrender now before it is too late.

Standing in the Gothic archway of the great Peace Tower that forms the principal entrance to the Canadian Parliament, he gave Hitler this warning:

"If he and his generals had known our plans they would have realized that discretion is still the better part of valor and that surrender would pay them better now than later."

What these plans are, he added, would be communicated in due time to Germany, Italy and Japan "in the only language their twisted minds seem capable of understanding."

Thirty thousand persons had gathered on the lawns in front of the building to welcome the President and to hear him speak and their cheers rolled up in a storm when he uttered that warning.

They cheered again with hope when he declared that "during the past few days in Quebec we have talked constructively of our common purposes in this war—of our determination to achieve victory in the shortest possible time—of our essential cooperation with our great and brave fighting Allies. And we have arrived harmoniously at certain definite conclusions. * * * We are making sure—absolutely, irrevocably sure—that this time the lesson is driven home to them once and for all. Yes, we are going to be rid of outlaws this time."

Much Post-War Discussion

But the Quebec conference, he said, was not concerned only with winning the war. There was much talk, he said, of the post-war world—a discussion doubtless duplicated simultaneously in dozens of nations in hundreds of cities and among millions of people.

"There is a longing in the air," he said and the road to its realization lies first in absolute victory, which will prove what concerted action can accomplish. He said that by such concerted action greater freedom from want could be assured than the world had ever known while "by unanimous action in driving out the outlaws and keeping them under heel forever we can attain freedom from fear of violence."

The President's visit to Ottawa was a fitting culmination to the Quebec conference. It gave the capital and the Canadian people a long-awaited opportunity of expressing the depth of their feeling toward the people of the United States and their personal regard for the President.

To the enthusiasm of their cheering the recent successes in Sicily and Kiska gave a joyous note. A gust of laughter swept the great crowd when the President, referring to the Japanese withdrawal from the Aleutians, said:

"We have been told that Japs never surrender; their headlong retreat satisfies us just as well."

Flays Band of Gangsters

But there was also fierce approval in the handclapping that broke out after such a sentence as this:

"We spend our energies and our resources and the very lives of our sons and daughters because a band

Continued on Page Three

"All the News That's Fit to Print."

The New York Times.

LATE CITY EDITION
Moderately cool with gentle winds today.
Temperatures Yesterday—Max., 80; Min., 73
Sunrise, 6:28 A. M.; Sunset, 7:21 P. M.

Copyright, 1943, by The New York Times Company.

VOL. XCII..No. 31,268. Entered as Second-Class Matter, Postoffice, New York, N. Y. NEW YORK, FRIDAY, SEPTEMBER 3, 1943. THREE CENTS NEW YORK CITY

ALLIES LAND IN ITALY OPPOSITE MESSINA; 8TH ARMY LEADS, WITH AIR-NAVAL COVER; RUSSIANS DRIVE AHEAD, CAPTURING SUMY

HULL TO TAKE REINS OVER ALL AGENCIES IN ECONOMIC FIELD

Coordination of OEW, OFRRO and Lend-Lease Under State Department Is Due Soon

NOT ALL FRICTION ENDED

WFA and OEW at Odds—Capital Speculates on What Course Lehman Will Pursue

By JOHN MacCORMAC
Special to THE NEW YORK TIMES.

WASHINGTON, Sept. 2—The coordination of the Office of Economic Warfare, the Office of Lend-Lease Administration and the Office of Foreign Relief and Rehabilitation Operations by the State Department in a way which will give the department complete control over their activities and leave them as instruments executing its policies has been planned and will shortly be put in effect, it was learned today.

Part of the plan is the formulation of a definite and coordinated policy with regard to the international economic activities of the Government. Hitherto there has been a general understanding in theory, but in practice some of the agencies which were supposed to execute economic policy have worked at cross-purposes.

The conflict between the foreign activities of some of the Reconstruction Finance Corporation subsidiaries and those of the Board of Economic Warfare exploded recently in the row between Vice President Wallace and Secretary Jones, which led to the coordination of these activities by the OEW under Leo T. Crowley as its new head.

Some Friction Still Exists

But there is still uncertainty regarding the representative spheres of OEW, Lend-Lease and OFRRO and, for that matter, friction between OEW and the War Food Administration as regards foreign food purchases. The plan, therefore, is to have the State Department effect a final coordination of their efforts, and there is a possibility that some or all of them might be absorbed in the process.

This is not only believed to be the policy of the President and Secretary Hull, but it is understood to be approved by Mr. Crowley and Edward Stettinius Jr., lend-lease administrator. There is some doubt, however, whether ex-Gov. Herbert H. Lehman is willing to subordinate OFRRO to the State Department to the extent desired.

From a spokesman for Mr. Crowley it was learned that close collaboration with the State Department has from the first been one of his objectives. Mr. Crowley has indicated that as soon as the coordination is made and the administrative facilities have been set up, the time will have arrived for a substantial simplification of the Government's foreign economic set-up.

OEW Changes Held Temporary

It was because of these views that the reorganization of OEW announced Tuesday was regarded as of a transitory rather than permanent character.

For instance, James L. McCamy, who was appointed assistant to the director, will soon leave again to join the Bureau of the Budget. Hugh B. Cox, who will act as general counsel, will work only part time with OEW, and the rest of the time as assistant attorney general of the United States. No executive director was named, and Lauchlin Currie, who will act as executive officer, is on "loan" from the President's office.

Before OEW and lend-lease are placed under the State Department, however, the details of foreign economic policy will have been worked out and men of the requisite business ability will have been added

Continued on Page Seven

Meat Ration Points Are Cut But Butter Will Need More

Thirty-five Meat Items Are Reduced 1 to 2 Points on Report of Larger Supplies—Changes Take Effect Sunday

Special to THE NEW YORK TIMES.

WASHINGTON, Sept. 2—Point values of most meats were lowered today by the Office of Price Administration, effective Sunday through September. An exception to the increased purchasing power of red stamps was creamery butter. It will call for twelve instead of ten points a pound. The buying power of blue stamps was reduced by an increase in the point values of many processed fruits and vegetables.

The changes in red stamp values were based on the belief that more meat would be available to civilians for the rest of this month. The ration costs of most lamb and bacon cuts were reduced one to two points a pound. Lower values were fixed for sirloin steak, roasts of beef and several variety meats.

The increase in the point value of creamery butter is not likely to be noticed in most urban areas, where dealers, because of acute shortages, have been restricting customers to a quarter pound at a time and getting three points for the quarter pound, or twelve points a pound.

Farm or country butter was listed separately for the first time in the new point value schedules. To it a point value of six points a pound was assigned. Previously country butter had the same point value as creamery butter. The reduction was intended to spur the movement of farm-churned butter to urban markets to relieve the shortage of creamery butter.

"The further increase in the point value of creamery butter is necessary because purchases near butter-producing areas have been so large at a ten-point value that shortages developed in other parts of the country," the OPA said. "In addition butter production during

Continued on Page Eight

CONGRESS TAX MOVE IRKS MORGENTHAU

Joint Committee Plans to Subpoena Data Direct From Internal Revenue Body

Special to THE NEW YORK TIMES.

WASHINGTON, Sept. 2—A conflict has arisen between the joint committee of Congress on internal revenue taxation and the Treasury over the committee's power to obtain tax data direct from officials of any Government department or agency and this may lead to a test in the courts of the committee's authority.

The 1942 revenue act empowered the committee to obtain such data from officials of the Bureau of Internal Revenue or any other department without sending its requests through departmental heads.

The committee, jointly set up by the Senate Finance and House Ways and Means Committees, has seldom agreed with the Treasury on tax matters in recent years. Of late it has been paying less and less attention to the Treasury's views and insisting on writing its own tax bills.

It was to give Colin F. Stam, the committee's chief of tax experts, opportunity to make use of the fiscal and economic experience to be found in Government departments and particularly in the Internal Revenue Bureau that Congress was asked to authorize it to go over the head of Secretary Morgenthau to his subordinates and to deal similarly with other divisions.

Although neither the Treasury nor Mr. Stam would comment on

Continued on Page Ten

1,330 JAPANESE SAIL ON EXCHANGE LINER

Gripsholm Leaves on Second Trip—Teia Maru to Bring Americans Back Home

The exchange liner Gripsholm, painted white and carrying in huge letters on her side the word "Diplomat," sailed from her anchorage in New York Harbor early yesterday on her second mission to exchange Japanese civilians for Americans who have been interned in the Orient since December, 1941.

Gaily painted like the cruise ship she was before the United States Government chartered her in the spring of 1942 from the Swedish-American Line, the big vessel carried the gold and blue marks of Sweden, painted flags and brilliant lighting arrangements to identify her through submarine-infested waters.

In her cabins there were, according to announcements of the War and State Departments in Washington, 1,330 Japanese civilians who will be exchanged for Americans and nationals of other Western Hemisphere nations in the port of Mormugao, Portuguese India, on or about Oct. 15.

The Americans and their fellow internees—1,500 of them, including 1,250 citizens of the United States—are to travel from the Orient on the Japanese-flag liner Teia Maru.

The Washington announcements said that the Teia Maru was scheduled to leave Japan on Sept. 15, touching at ports in China, the Philippines and Indo-China to take on additional passengers, and calling at Singapore for fuel and wa-

Continued on Page Five

Browder Charges 'Bad Faith' Delays Opening a Second Front

Earl Browder, general secretary of the Communist party of the United States, asserted at a party meeting last night in Manhattan Center, 311 West Thirty-fourth Street, that Anglo-American relations with Soviet Russia would "deteriorate sharply" unless a second front in Western Europe was opened before the end of summer.

The meeting was a special one called to hear Mr. Browder discuss the present situation. About 3,000 persons were in the hall.

Mr. Browder argued that we should not wait until next spring in the hope that victory can then be "bought much more cheaply," but should land in full force now in an effort to win a quick victory and take some of the burden of land fighting off the Red Army. He held that military occupation by "fighting armies" was the only way nazism could be ended.

Mr. Browder, who is not a military expert, vigorously expressed the opinion that our troops were overwhelmingly able to open a second front whenever their leaders gave the word. But the British and American general staffs, he charged, have acted in the role of "politicians subject to reactionary influence," and have overruled themselves as military leaders, in which capacity, he said, they realize the need for a second front. Counting out "weakness" as a reason for not opening a second front, he said the only alternative was "bad faith."

Mr. Browder charged that "dark and sinister forces" in this country were accusing the Soviet Union of

Continued on Page Four

AIR BLOWS PRESSED

French Fields Pounded as Fortresses Join British in Sweeps

POWER PLANT IS HIT

Canal Locks Smashed on Key Dutch Route Serving Antwerp

New, Heavy Air Raids As Allies Land in Italy

By The United Press.

LONDON, Friday, Sept. 3—Powerful forces of Allied bombers ranged over the northern flank of the European continent early today, almost simultaneously with the invasion of Italy.

A long procession of bombers streamed out over the British coast, flying so high they could not be seen from the ground, although the roar of their motors was audible.

By The United Press.

LONDON, Friday, Sept. 3—American Flying Fortresses, culminating an evening of widespread activity that saw Royal Air Force Fighter Command planes in their biggest operation of the year, blasted enemy airfields at Mardyck and Denain in northern France late yesterday, a joint British-American communiqué reported today.

Squadrons of British Spitfires and Typhoons escorted medium B-26 Marauder bombers of the Eighth United States Air Force and RAF Boston, Mitchell and Ventura bombers in attacks on targets in Pas de Calais Department.

Fast and deadly P-49 Thunderbolts covered the Fortresses in their hard-hitting foray against the northern French airfields. "Good bombing results were observed on all targets," the joint communiqué said, adding that four enemy aircraft were destroyed—one by the Fortresses and three by Spitfires. One medium and one light bomber and two fighters were lost in the heavy operation.

The B-26 Marauder medium bombers of the Eighth United States Air Force attacked the power station at Mazingarbe, near Bethune, France, "with good results," the fighter pilots reported.

Continued on Page Six

RED ARMY ROLLING

Storms Ukraine Citadel and Seizes Towns on Kiev Rail Line

DONBAS KEYS TAKEN

Nazis Retreat Toward Dnieper—550 Places Fall in Two Days

By The Associated Press.

LONDON, Friday, Sept. 3—Moscow announced early today that five Red armies plunging westward had cut the Bryansk-Kiev railway 150 miles from Kiev, smashed German reinforcements in a six-mile gain on Smolensk and rolled up Axis lines in a new forty-five-mile-wide spurt in the Donets Basin.

Premier Joseph Stalin, in an order of the day, announced late yesterday that the Ukraine citadel of Sumy, ninety miles northwest of Kharkov, had fallen to Gen. Nikolai Vatutin's army, and a communiqué announced the capture of Krolevets and Yampol, two points on the vital Bryansk-Kiev railway linking the enemy's central and southern fronts.

Lisichansk, Voroshilovsk, Slavyanoserbsk and other cities were seized in the Donets Basin, while Budennovka, twenty miles from Mariupol, was taken in the push along the rim of the Sea of Azov, said the communiqué, recorded by the Soviet monitor.

250 More Places Overrun

The swiftness of the Russian advances and the tone of the communiqué indicated that the Germans were engaged in a large-scale retreat toward the Dnieper River, particularly in the huge Donets Basin. The bulletin, however, emphasized that the Germans were fighting stubbornly all along the 600-mile front.

More than 9,000 Germans were killed yesterday as the Red Armies overran nearly 250 cities and villages, many of them strategic prizes, for a two-day bag of nearly 550 localities.

Germany's 1941 invasion lines now have been cracked by the Russians in a 1943 offensive that has carried the Red Army more than half way along the comeback trail

Continued on Page Four

War News Summarized

FRIDAY, SEPTEMBER 3, 1943

Allied forces crossed the Strait of Messina from Sicily and landed in southern Italy early this morning to start the long-awaited invasion of Europe, according to a communiqué issued by the Allied Headquarters in North Africa. The landing was the culmination of a series of devastating air blows. [1:8, maps pages 1, 2 and 3.]

The Russian war machine rolled relentlessly on yesterday. The important Ukrainian town of Sumy was captured, the Bryansk-Kiev railway was severed and a wide advance was made in the Donets Basin, with every indication that a German retreat to the Dnieper River was in full swing. [1:5, map P. 4.]

Continuing the softening-up process on the Continent, Allied fighters and bombers hit airfields in Northern France shortly after RAF fighters had returned from the Netherlands, where they struck at some of the most vital water communications controlled by the Germans. The bomb racks were unloaded on the strategic Hansweert Canal, where three locks were hit. The RAF reported that 107,520 American tons of bombs had been dropped on Germany in the first eight months of 1943. [1:4, map p. 6.]

The Navy Department in Washington still withheld details of Tuesday's raid on the Marcus Islands, but some of the mystery was dispelled by the Japanese, who acknowledged damage to the strategic air and observation base and estimated the American task force at 160 fighter and bomber planes from two carriers. Military observers at Pearl Harbor believe that the Marcus raid was just a feint and that a major blow against Japan's outer defenses is near. [5:1.]

Allied bombers dropped a record of 206 tons of bombs on the Japanese bases at Madang, New Guinea, General MacArthur reported. Ground troops also were strafed at Salamaua. [5:5, with map.]

The Pacific phase of the war is believed to be one of the principal subjects being discussed by Prime Minister Churchill and President Roosevelt in Washington. They have been holding day and night sessions. The Prime Minister also has conferred with high military and supply mission heads. [4:4.]

Another indication of the stepped-up pace to launch a second or a third front was the report from Washington of an August output of 7,700 planes as against 7,373 for July and indications that the figure might top 8,000 in September. [1:7.]

ACROSS NARROW WATERS TO EUROPE

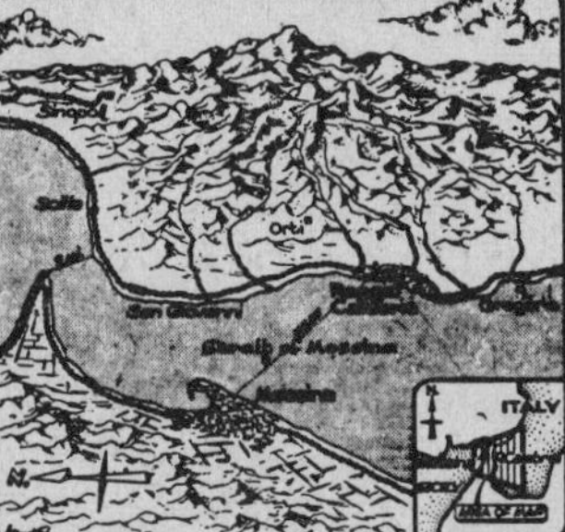

Allied forces spanned the Strait of Messina this morning to land on the toe of Italy. This map, a perspective view looking eastward, gives an idea how the mainland appeared to the invaders.

Other Invasions This Year Anticipated in Washington

By ROBERT F. WHITNEY
Special to THE NEW YORK TIMES.

WASHINGTON, Friday, Sept. 3—While Washington slept, its somnolent thousands secure in the knowledge that plans laid at Quebec last week would be efficiently carried out, the word was flashed to the capital that the invasion of the Italian mainland had begun. It was the first penetration by the Allies of Fortress Europe and thus a historic event which defied the pledge of Adolf Hitler that his Reich, by its aggressions, would secure its future for a "thousand years."

Unlike the invasion of North Africa by American troops nearly a year ago and the opening of the Sicilian campaign about two months ago, the invasion was not announced in Washington. The first news to the public came in flashes from North Africa.

The announcement, as received here, told of Allied troops swarming across the Strait of Messina. Only on Tuesday Prime Minister Churchill, in his Canadian speech, had stated that the Germans had augmented their forces in Italy and intended to make a battleground of that country.

The Allied invasion was seen here as an answer both to that challenge by the Germans and to the demands that a second front be opened in Europe this year.

When the news came, it is probable that the President and Mr. Churchill, the pair who are directing the strategy of the two English-speaking nations of the United Nations, were awaiting the news of a successful landing together in the White House study, as it is known that when they meet neither one retires early.

It was hoped here in semi-official quarters that the invasion of Italy would answer the prayers of Russia that her Allies in the west would lift some of the load off her shoulders by an attack on the European Continent.

While it was confidently expected that the invasion of Italy

Continued on Page Three

PLANE OUTPUT 7,700 FOR AUGUST, A JUMP

Production This Month May Reach 8,000, WPB Says—Rise Despite New Designs

Special to THE NEW YORK TIMES.

WASHINGTON, Sept. 2—Aircraft production last month totaled 7,700 planes, compared with 7,373 in July, the WPB reported today in tones of elation.

On the basis of the August figure, airplane production in September will top 8,000, it was said.

The rise in output last month as compared with July was at the rate called for in the production schedule. Both July and August production were below the original schedule, WPB officials said. But they maintain that the schedules are "unrealistic" in that they do not take into consideration the shifts in production occasioned by design changes and by many other factors.

Schedules have been adjusted three times so far this year, one official said, and are likely to be changed again. He added that "I'd rather make 6,500 planes of the type we needed than to meet the schedules which include many of the types we don't need and would rather not have."

He contended that "we got the planes we wanted. Those we didn't want we didn't get."

The discrepancy between the

Continued on Page Seven

Portugal Weighs Idea of Fighting; Premier Tells People to Prepare

Neutral diplomatic quarters in London reported yesterday that Portugal was contemplating a declaration of war against Japan and might follow it with declarations against other Axis powers, according to The United Press.

The Portuguese action is said to arise from the fact that the Japanese established military control over Macao, in China near Hong Kong, as well as from Japanese occupation of Timor, in the southwest Pacific north of Australia.

Portuguese naval reservists have been called up during the past ten days. It was understood reliably that 10,000 reservists were being called to the Army. It was suggested that Portugal was now prepared to send expeditionary forces to free Macao and Timor.

The Government of Portugal on Wednesday night issued a formal statement "following fantastic rumors" and this statement gave the impression Portugal was on the eve of some important action.

LISBON, Sept. 2 (AP)—Premier Antonio de Oliveira Salazar stated today that Portugal's stepped-up military preparations were defensive but "in the unfortunate times in which we are living may have to be used against foreign enemies as much as against internal elements of national disintegration."

Clamping a tight censorship on speculation regarding the military preparations, Dr. Salazar cautioned against expecting any change in the country's foreign policy.

[The London Evening Standard interpreted the "mobiliza-

Continued on Page Five

DAWN IS ZERO HOUR

British and Canadians Storm Over Narrow Strait of Messina

ROME SAYS NOTHING

Allies Invade on Fourth Anniversary of Their War Declaration

By MILTON BRACKER
By Wireless to THE NEW YORK TIMES.

ALLIED HEADQUARTERS IN NORTH AFRICA, Friday, Sept. 3—The Allies have breached the "Fortress of Europe." On the fourth anniversary of the British and French declaration of war against Germany, Allied troops are striving to establish a bridgehead on the Italian side of the Strait of Messina.

Under the thunderous support of Allied sea and air power, British and Canadian forces of the British Eighth Army crossed the narrow strip of water to bring the war at long last to the mainland of the Continent that Germany has enslaved.

Preceded by a pounding artillery barrage across the strait and by a number of reconnaissance landings, the main party set foot on the tip of the Calabrian Peninsula, opposite Messina, at 4:30 A. M. today [10:30 P. M. Thursday, Eastern War Time].

No details were available on either this morning's historic assault or the previous reconnaissance missions. The latter were, plainly, those referred to in German broadcasts as landing attempts beginning on Aug. 29, which the Germans said had been repulsed with heavy losses.

[A Mutual Broadcasting System commentator, speaking from Algiers, quoted an official Allied spokesman today as saying that the Allies were "apparently engaged in heavy fighting," The Associated Press reported from London.]

A special communiqué issued here at 7:30 A. M. said merely: "Allied forces under General Eisenhower continued their advance. British and Canadian troops of the Eighth Army, supported by Allied sea and air power, attacked across the Strait of Messina early today and landed on the mainland of Italy."

Field Guns Pave Way

ALLIED HEAQUARTERS IN NORTH AFRICA, Sept. 2 (UP)—British, Canadian and other troops of the British Eighth Army spearheaded the invasion armies, swarming across the Strait of Messina from Sicily under cover of Allied aircraft and the big guns of British and American warships. The Eighth Army's field guns helped to pave the way for the invasion troops with a thunderous barrage that silenced several of the

Continued on Page Two

Arnold in Britain To Meet Air Chiefs

By The Associated Press.

LONDON, Sept. 2—Lieut. Gen. Henry H. Arnold, chief of the United States Army Air Forces, and Maj. Gen. William C. Lee, commander of an air-borne division, who is known as the father of American parachute troops, arrived in Britain today from the United States. They plunged immediately into a study of the military set-up and recent operations by the Eighth United States Air Force.

General Arnold is here for conferences with Air Chief Marshal Sir Charles Portal, Lieut. Gen. Jacob L. Devers, commanding all United States forces in the European theatre; Maj. Gen. Ira C. Eaker, commander of the Eighth Air Force, and other British and American officers.

"All the News That's Fit to Print."

The New York Times.

LATE CITY EDITION
Continued moderately cool today; moderate winds.
Temperatures Yesterday—Max., 74; Min., 67
Sunrise, 6:29 A. M.; Sunset, 7:11 P. M.

VOL. XCII..No. 31,274. Entered as Second-Class Matter, Postoffice, New York, N. Y. NEW YORK, THURSDAY, SEPTEMBER 9, 1943. THREE CENTS IN NEW YORK CITY

ITALY SURRENDERS, WILL RESIST GERMANS; ALLIED FORCES LAND IN THE NAPLES AREA; RUSSIANS IN STALINO, CLEAR DONETS BASIN

SOVIET TIDE RISES

Swift Red Army Blows Capture Key City, Free Rich Region

DRIVE NEARS DNIEPER

More Rail Hubs Fall—Thrust Toward Kiev Also Extended

By The United Press.

LONDON, Thursday, Sept. 9—The Red Army recaptured Stalino, Russia's twelfth city, yesterday and freed the Donets Basin, which before the war produced more steel than Japan and Italy combined, in a great surge that took it to Grishino, ninety miles east of Dniepropetrovsk on the lower Dnieper River.

While the armies of Gen. Rodion Y. Malinovsky and Gen. Fedor Tolbukhin drove the enemy from the rich Donets Basin, crowded with coal mines and factories, the army of Gen. Konstantin Rokossovsky drove to a point ninety-six miles northeast of Kiev by capturing Borzna, twenty-three miles west of Bakhmach.

Bakhmach and Romni, forty-two miles to the southeast, were surrounded on three sides, a Moscow radio bulletin reported, and thus the Bakhmach-Kremenchug railroad was cut. The roads leading from Bakhmach to Kursk and Gomel had been cut previously and only the lines to Kiev and Odessa remained open.

Picked Troops Take Stalino

Red Army shock troops, picked from the sixteen infantry divisions that had driven the Germans through city after city in six days of tireless fighting, took Stalino by storm.

The Russian communiqué said the Red Army troops drove in on Stalino throughout Tuesday night and yesterday morning. They fought through the suburbs and then stormed the city from north and south, routing the enemy in a street-by-street fight and capturing a great store of spoils.

Twenty-five miles northwest of Stalino the Russians took Krasnoarmeiskoye, a big railroad junction controlling two of four rail roads leading west from the basin.

In all the Russians took, in addition to Stalino, a city of 462,000 persons, more than 150 towns in the Donbas alone, twenty of them important, in gains of up to twelve and a half miles. During their Donbas offensive the Russians took twelve towns of more than 50,000 persons each.

The Germans at Krasnoarmeiskoye were so swiftly beaten that the Russians took nineteen planes and several loaded railroad trains.

March on Kiev Gains

On the Kiev front, the Russians took more than sixty towns in advances of up to twelve and a half miles. Their capture of Borzna in that area meant that the battle for the Dnieper River line had started. An advance of twenty-three miles to Nezhin would cut the only remaining German supply line east of the river. The Russians had already advanced 101 miles in nine days from Rylsk, half the distance to Kiev.

More than 1,000 Germans were killed at Borzna, and 1,000 were killed in another sector.

South of Bryansk the Russians advanced up to six miles to take several villages. They were reported only twenty miles south of Bryansk. The Soviet communiqué, recorded from the Moscow radio, reported that the Russians were advancing west of the Navlya railroad junction in this area, driving the Germans through dense forests.

West and southwest of Kharkov nearly four miles were gained in some sectors and about 1,200 Germans were killed.

The Germans were first to ad

Continued on Page Twenty-two

New Fascist Regime Set Up, Nazis Report

By Cable to The New York Times.

LONDON, Thursday, Sept. 9—The German radio announced early today that a "National Fascist government has been set up in Italy and functions in the name of Benito Mussolini."

The announcement, called a "proclamation by the National Fascist Government of Italy," said "this Badoglio betrayal will not be perpetrated. The National Fascist Government will punish traitors pitilessly."

The broadcast, in Italian, said nothing about the whereabouts of Mussolini, who has been reported under arrest. It was preceded by the playing of "Giovinezza," the Fascist anthem.

FOE'S MARCUS LOSS 80%, NIMITZ SAYS

U. S. Carrier Planes Alone Hit at Japanese Isle—Hell Cat Fighter Excels in Test

By ROBERT TRUMBULL

By Telephone to The New York Times.

PEARL HARBOR, Sept. 8—Admiral Chester W. Nimitz, Commander in Chief of the Pacific Fleet, issued today a communiqué that gave the first details of the raid on Marcus Island Sept. 1. Coincidentally three naval air officers who participated in the action gave an interview covering all phases of the raid, which they said destroyed a surprisingly well-fortified Japanese air base.

Action Consisted of Bombing

Admiral Nimitz's communiqué said that a United States Pacific Fleet task force under command of Rear Admiral Charles A. Pownall attacked the little island, 1,185 miles southeast of Tokyo, at dawn Sept. 1. The air officers revealed that the action consisted entirely of bombing and strafing by carrier-borne aircraft.

They said that the new Grumman F6F Hellcat fighter was employed in combat for the first time in the

Continued on Page Twenty-two

IN HEART OF ITALY

American 7th Army Is Reported in Van of Naples Operation

MORE POINTS NAMED

Landings Rumored at Genoa, Pizzo, Gaeta and Leghorn

By Wireless to The New York Times.

ALLIED HEADQUARTERS IN NORTH AFRICA, Thursday, Sept. 9—The Allies have carried the land campaign against the Nazis in Italy to the vicinity of Naples in new operations announced within twelve hours of the disclosure by Gen. Dwight D. Eisenhower that the Italian armed forces had unconditionally surrendered.

The news was announced here a few minutes past 6:30 A. M. in the following thirteen words:

"Further operations have started on the Italian mainland in the vicinity of Naples."

In the absence of the slightest expansion of the communiqué, no details are available as to the forces participating. The single fact remained that the attack had been pressed near Italy's southern metropolis and port, second only to Genoa, in what obviously was a major amphibious thrust.

Naples is a city of more than 700,900 population—nearer 1,000,000 if the suburbs are included. The assault was launched eighty-three years and two days after Garibaldi entered the city alone in a dramatic liberation gesture, which culminated in the unification of the country ten years later.

Although there is no indication just how near the city itself the landing or landings were carried out, it is plain that Naples is the objective of the sea-borne invaders.

[This dispatch did not indicate the make-up of the landing parties. A Tunis radio broadcast

Continued on Page Four

U. S. SOLDIERS IN LONDON CHEER THE NEWS

Americans in front of the Red Cross Washington Club in the British capital when the news of Italy's surrender was announced.

Associated Press Radiophoto, passed yesterday by censor

Announcements of the Surrender

By Broadcast to The New York Times.

ALLIED HEADQUARTERS IN NORTH AFRICA, Sept. 8—The texts of the proclamations by Gen. Dwight D. Eisenhower and Premier Pietro Badoglio follow:

By GENERAL EISENHOWER

This is Gen. Dwight D. Eisenhower, Commander in Chief of the Allied Forces.

The Italian Government has surrendered its armed forces unconditionally. As Allied Commander in Chief, I have granted a military armistice, the terms of which have been approved by the Governments of the United Kingdom, the United States and the Union of Soviet Socialist Republics. Thus I am acting in the interest of the United Nations.

The Italian Government has bound itself to abide by these terms without reservation. The armistice was signed by my representative and the representative of Marshal Badoglio and it becomes effective this instant.

Hostilities between the armed forces of the United Nations and those of Italy terminate at once. All Italians who now act to help eject the German aggressor from Italian soil will have the assistance and the support of the United Nations.

By PREMIER BADOGLIO

The Italian Government, recognizing the impossibility of continuing the unequal struggle against the overwhelming power of the enemy, with the object of avoiding further and more grievous harm to the nation, has requested an armistice from General Eisenhower, Commander in Chief of the Anglo-American Allied forces. This request has been granted. The Italian forces will therefore cease all acts of hostility against the Anglo-American forces wherever they may be met. They will, however, oppose attack from any other quarter.

War News Summarized

THURSDAY, SEPTEMBER 9, 1943

Italy has surrendered unconditionally, and all hostilities between that country and the United Nations ceased yesterday. An armistice was signed last Friday, the same day that Italy was invaded, but the victors reserved the right to withhold announcement until the most favorable moment for the Allies. The armistice terms had been approved by the United States, Britain and Russia.

General Eisenhower, announcing the surrender, promised support to all Italians who helped fight the Germans. Marshal Badoglio issued a proclamation ordering all fighting against the "Anglo-American forces" to cease and commanding resistance to "attacks from any other quarter."

Allied radios and planes carried messages urging the Italians to take vengeance on their "German oppressors" and to prevent trains, ships and trucks from carrying German troops or supplies. [All the foregoing, 1:8; map, P.3.]

Landings in the Naples area followed only a few hours after the surrender announcement and it was believed the Allies were attempting to cut off German troops in southern Italy. The American Seventh Army was reported among the invading forces. [1:3; map, P. 4.] Earlier, the Italian Navy and merchant marine had been urged to take their ships to designated points and to scuttle the vessels as a last resort to keep them from the Germans. [7:5.]

Wild demonstrations of joy were reported from all over Italy, but in the north they gave way to sober realization of continued danger when the Germans occupied Milan and other cities and imposed martial law. [3:1.] No official comment came from Berlin, but the German radio, after withholding the news for hours, was furious at the "treachery." [1:5-6.]

Germany's Balkan satellites were so shaken by the Italian surrender that Bulgaria, Rumania and Hungary were reported ready to follow Italy out of the war. [10:3.]

President Roosevelt, in a radio address last night, termed the surrender a great victory for the Italian people as well as for the United Nations. But he warned: "The time for celebration is not yet. Our ultimate objectives in this war continue to be Berlin and Tokyo." [1:5-6.]

The actual fighting in Italy was of a minor nature. Land forces advanced on both coasts. [3:6.] Airfields were hit by Allied bombers and the Rome radio reported heavy raids on suburbs of the city. [4:1.]

With one Axis partner out of the war, the two others continued to be hit hard. The Red Army captured Stalino and cleared the Germans out of the Donets Basin. [1:1; map, P. 22.] Allied bombers from Britain struck enemy airfields in France and Belgium [23:2], while down in New Guinea Japanese troops were providing weak opposition as the Allies closed in on Lae. [22:1.]

The naval task force that raided Marcus Island Sept. 1 destroyed 80 per cent of the Japanese military installations. We lost three planes. [1:2.]

CITY 'JUMPS GUN' IN WAR BOND DRIVE

Rallies, Sales Begin on Vast Scale—State Savings Banks Will Invest $600.000.000

As President Roosevelt and Secretary of the Treasury Henry J. Morgenthau Jr. opened the Third War Loan Drive for $15,000,000,000 last night over the radio, it was announced here that in the campaign to raise the State's quota of $4,709,000,000 the mutual savings banks in the State would buy $600,000,000 in Government bonds. The United States Steel Corporation and its subsidiaries will buy $100,000,000 in Government securities, with parts of the total allocated to districts where the corporation operates.

Restive to get its drive under way, New York City held preliminary rallies yesterday as Army convoys took into the five boroughs Navy gunners who had been rescued at sea. The largest meetings were held in Times Square and on the steps of the Sub-Treasury Building at Wall and Broad Streets.

Burgess Hails Italy's Surrender

The thousands assembled in the streets for these two gatherings cheered wildly as speakers announced the capitulation of Italy. Ticker tape, confetti and torn paper were thrown from the windows of buildings where workers in the financial community were listening to the rally.

The unconditional surrender of Italy is "bullish news" and will be a great help in the bond drive, W. Randolph Burgess, chairman of the War Finance Committee for New York State, said later in the

Continued on Page Sixteen

President Hails Victory But Warns of Real Foes

By JOHN H. CRIDER

Special to The New York Times.

WASHINGTON, Sept. 8—President Roosevelt hailed the surrender of Italy tonight as "a great victory for the United Nations" and also "a great victory for the Italian people" against "their real enemies, the Nazis," but cautioned against over-optimism. Addressing the nation on the opening of the Third War Bond drive, the President said "the time for celebration is not yet" and added that "our ultimate objectives in this war continue to be Berlin and Tokyo."

Toward the middle of his speech the President interpolated three words which gave basis to reports that Allied armies already were on the move again in the Mediterranean when he spoke of troops in landing barges moving up to enemy coasts "at this moment."

"This war does not and must not stop for one single instant," he declared. "Your fighting men know that. Those of them who are moving forward through jungles against lurking Japs—those who are landing at this moment in barges moving through the dawn up the strange enemy coasts—those who are diving their bombs down on the target at roof-top level at this moment—every one of these men knows that this war is a full-time job and that it will

Continued on Page Seventeen

Germans Charge Betrayal by Italy In Plot With Russian Government

By GEORGE AXELSSON

By Wireless to The New York Times.

STOCKHOLM, Sweden, Sept. 8—Berlin's newspapers branded Italy's capitulation as cowardly treachery last night. The German press abounds in scatching denunciation of Premier Pietro Badoglio and King Victor Emmanuel, as well as the Italian people.

"Mussolini was too great a person for a nation like that," a German official said. This is the second time that Victor Emmanuel has broken his word, the newspapers say, because the King "left Germany in the lurch" in 1915 when he joined the Allies.

Forgetting its praise of the Italians during the heyday of their pact, Berlin now condemns the Italians as third-rate individuals. "The cowardly perfidy of Badoglio cape the crime," one paper said, "by being committed in collusion with the Soviet Government, which is treason not only against Italy and Germany but also against all Europe."

Berlin added that the Germans had no intention of giving up their entrenchments in Italy, where they hoped to offer efficient resistance. Italy, since last night, is German-occupied territory to the extent that the Germans have been able to gain a firm footing there. In the Italian provinces occupied by the Germans, Berlin boasts fascism will be revived even if "we leave it to the Italians in those provinces to organize themselves along fascist lines."

Official circles are reviving accusations of broken words of honor

Continued on Page Nine

GEN. EISENHOWER ANNOUNCES ARMISTICE

Capitulation Acceptable to U. S., Britain and Russia Is Confirmed in Speech by Badoglio

TERMS SIGNED ON DAY OF INVASION

Disclosure Withheld by Both Sides Until Moment Most Favorable for the Allies—Italians Exhorted to Aid United Nations

By MILTON BRACKER

By Wireless to The New York Times.

ALLIED HEADQUARTERS IN NORTH AFRICA, Sept. 8—Italy has surrendered her armed forces unconditionally and all hostilities between the soldiers of the United Nations and those of the weakest of the three Axis partners ceased as of 16:30 Greenwich Mean Time today [12:30 P. M., Eastern War Time].

At that time, Gen. Dwight D. Eisenhower announced here over the United Nations radio that a secret military armistice had been signed in Sicily on the afternoon of Friday, Sept. 3, by his representative and one sent by Premier Pietro Badoglio. That was the day when, at 4:50 A. M., British and Canadian troops crossed the Strait of Messina and landed on the Italian mainland to open a campaign in which, up to yesterday, they had occupied about sixty miles of the Calabrian coast from the Petrace River in the north to Bova Marina in the south.

The complete collapse of Italian military resistance in no way suggested that the Germans would not defend Italy with all the strength at their command. But the capitulation, in undisclosed terms that were acceptable to the United States, the United Kingdom and the Union of Soviet Socialist Republics, came exactly forty days after the downfall of Benito Mussolini, the dictator who, by playing jackal to Adolf Hitler, led his country to the catastrophic mistake of declaring war on France three years and three months ago this Friday.

Negotiations Begun Several Weeks Ago

The negotiations leading to the armistice were opened by the war-weary and bomb-battered nation a few weeks ago, it was revealed today, and a preliminary meeting was arranged and held in an unnamed neutral country.

The Italians who had approached the British and American authorities were bluntly told that the terms remained what they had been: unconditional surrender. They agreed, and the document was signed five days ago. But it was agreed to hold back the announcement and its effective date until the moment most favorable to the Allies.

That moment came today, when the Allied Commander in Chief, in a historic broadcast, announced the armistice. He concluded with the reminder that all Italians who aided in the ejection of the Germans from Italy would have the support and assistance of the United Nations.

One hour and fifteen minutes after the General's voice had gone out over the air, Marshal Badoglio faced a microphone in Rome and confirmed the armistice. He concluded with the promise that the Italian forces would oppose attacks "from any other quarter," although they were laying down the arms that they had taken up against the Anglo-American armies.

Military Aspect Emphasized

Although it was emphasized that the armistice was a strictly military instrument, "signed by soldiers," it was disclosed that it contained a clause binding Italy to comply with political, economic and financial conditions to be imposed at the Allies' discretion.

[It was believed that the armistice conditions were substantially the same as those imposed on France in 1940, which allowed the Germans to use all strategic French ports and military bases to wage war against Britain, The United Press reported.]

Immediately after the announcement of the armistice, the Allies made two appeals—one to the Italian people and one to the Italian Fleet—urging them to rally to a cause that was, in effect, the liberation of their own country. The appeal to the people was disseminated by radio and air-borne leaflet, while that to the Navy was broadcast by Admiral Sir Andrew Browne Cunningham, the Allies' Mediterranean naval commander.

The Italian people, particularly transport, railroad and dock workers, were asked not to give the slightest aid to the Germans. The men who man Italian ships received specific instructions how to bring their vessels into the protection of the United Nations.

Although the fear was proved unjustified by Marshal Badoglio's broadcast, the Allies had taken no chances of a German move to forestall his giving the news to the people. As a safeguard, they had obtained from the Italians an agreement to leave one senior military representative behind when the others returned to Rome. This man is now in Sicily and presumably, had Marshal Badoglio not gone on the air, his representative would have broadcast the decision to the Italian public.

As a further earnest of good faith, Marshal Badoglio had arranged to send the text of the proclamation that he made this evening to Allied Headquarters here. He kept his word.

1,181 Days at War and Losses

Italy quit the war after 1,181 days, during which she steadily lost territory and prestige. Last May 7, with the fall of Tunis and Bizerte, the last Italian soldier in North Africa was doomed. Since then, Sicily, part of Metropolitan Italy, was occupied in thirty-eight days.

The Italians endured two raids on military targets in Rome

Continued on Page Three

"All the News That's Fit to Print."

The New York Times.

LATE CITY EDITION
Slightly warmer today with moderate to fresh winds.
Temperatures Yesterday—Max., 60; Min., 46
Sunrise, 7:04 A. M., Sunset, 6:30 P. M.

VOL. XCIII..No. 31,308. Entered as Second-Class Matter, Postoffice, New York, N. Y. NEW YORK, WEDNESDAY, OCTOBER 13, 1943. THREE CENTS IN NEW YORK CITY

ITALY WILL DECLARE WAR ON GERMANY TODAY; 3 POWERS TO GIVE HER COBELLIGERENT STATUS; PORTUGAL GRANTS ALLIES USE OF AZORES BASES

PRESIDENT REPLIES TO SENATE CRITICS OF WAR AND ALLIES

Does Not Know if Russia Is Ready to Tackle Japan Too, He Remarks on Lodge

THEN HE CITES SOME FACTS

Senate Debates Reports in an Open Session as Ellender Is Denounced by Hatch

By JOHN H. CRIDER
Special to THE NEW YORK TIMES.

WASHINGTON, Oct. 12—President Roosevelt, commenting on the report of Senator Henry Cabot Lodge Jr. that a million American lives could be saved if Russia would make Pacific bases available to the United States, declared this afternoon that he did not know enough about the facts to say whether Russia was ready to declare war on Japan.

Certainly, the President said, Russia is busy on her western front, and, having knocked down the Nazis several times, maybe they'll stay down next time.

This was one of several contentions of the five Senators recently returned from battlefronts, which President Roosevelt contradicted at his press conference this afternoon; but although he admitted that the performance of the Senators had, on the one hand, caused some embitterment abroad—he referred specifically to England—on the other hand the debate which followed their statements did lead to a more sound public opinion. He was, he said, of two minds on the question whether the whole thing was good or bad.

Senate Debates the Reports

The President was not alone in commenting on the situation created by the reports of the committee members, for the Senate itself spent most of the day in a public debate on the question which rivaled in intensity the meetings held behind closed doors last week at which the five "fellow-travelers," as the President called them, made their secret reports.

The President was told of "a serious article" in THE NEW YORK TIMES reporting from London the feeling in Britain that the Senate development was an unfortunate thing, and he was asked if he felt that way.

You've always got to remember, the President said, that when members of a legislature get up on their feet and say things, the effect of which is not well thought out, it may create bitterness. He then pointed to some quotations on his desk from the British press, commenting that editorials in the British press certainly showed that this incident had created some bitterness.

But, he added, The Daily Telegraph of London declared that the so-called "secrets" were "childish nonsense" and perhaps it would be a good thing for Anglo-American relations if the whole thing was subjected to public debate.

That's why he was of two minds on the question, Mr. Roosevelt continued. It takes a certain amount of time to dig up this stuff like he had been talking about today (the factual denials of some of the Senators' reports) and last week (a reference to the facts he gave the press last week on arrangements with Britain on the use of petroleum resources).

One Effect of the Discussion

Getting the information to rebut such contentions is time consuming, President Roosevelt said, but it does lead to a more sound public opinion. It gets the public interested, teaches geography, teaches problems of supply and of moving men overseas, the need for more ships, the need for more planes—more than everything else.

So in one sense, he declared, it's a damned nuisance, and in the other sense probably it's a good thing.

Mr. Roosevelt added that it made for publicity and discussion, and he had never deliberately dodged that.

The President was asked if

Continued on Page Nine

Motorists' Requests For Ration Books Lag

The New York District Office of Price Administration, Empire State Building, disclosed yesterday that local rationing boards and automobile dealers throughout the city had reported that only a handful of gasoline ration book holders had asked for their application renewal blanks.

Oct. 21 is the deadline for motorists to present their ration renewal blanks, according to a warning by William H. McKenna, chief District OPA Rationing Officer. Those failing to do so face a three-week delay between Nov. 8, when the present books expire, and Dec. 1, when they may apply again.

OPA representatives cautioned also that motorists should fill out their applications before they go to public schools next Tuesday, Wednesday and Thursday afternoons, Oct. 19, 20 and 21, from 3 to 7 o'clock, to obtain their new A books.

POPE SAID TO SPURN 'HAVEN' IN GERMANY

Pontiff Refuses Request to Seek Safety in Liechtenstein or Reich, Neutrals Say

By The United Press.

LONDON, Oct. 12—The Germans have advised Pope Pius XII to leave Rome because they cannot guarantee the Vatican's safety if the city becomes a battleground, and they have "offered" to move him to the neutral Principality of Liechtenstein or to Germany, dispatches from neutral capitals said today.

The Pope refused the "offer" and said that he would not leave the Vatican while he was alive, the dispatches said.

[A German broadcast, apparently designed deliberately to give the impression that the Vatican anticipated military action or at least demolitions in the Rome area, said that Vatican City had "started building some great water reservoirs" as a "precautionary measure in connection with war circumstances," according to the Federal Communications Commission].

An Algiers dispatch to the Stockholm Social Demokraten said that the German envoy in Rome had advised the Pope to seek refuge in Liechtenstein, a predominantly Catholic State nestled along the eastern border of Switzerland.

These reports were not verified in any official quarters.

Germany announced on Sept. 10 that her troops had assumed the "protection" of the Vatican, policing St. Peter's Square in place of Italian carabinieri formerly posted there to protect the Vatican against "irresponsible elements." Since that time German broadcasts have maintained that relations with the Vatican were "normal."

Not long after German troops had moved into Rome, however, the Berlin radio broadcast a statement by Benito Mussolini's National Fascist Republican Government assailing the Vatican for alleged anti-fascist attitudes.

1373 PACT INVOKED

British Land Troops—Blow to U-Boats and Aid to Invasion Seen

REPRISALS DOUBTED

Churchill Gives Lisbon Assurance, However, of Aid in 'Emergency'

The text of Mr. Churchill's statement is on Page 8.

By JAMES B. RESTON
By Cable to THE NEW YORK TIMES.

LONDON, Oct. 12—Portugal has agreed, at the request of the British Government, to permit the United Nations to use the Azores, her watchtower archipelago in the mid-Atlantic for the protection of the great convoys that must in the next few months bring the invasion armies of the United States to Britain and North Africa.

This was announced today by Dr. Antonio de Oliveira Salazar, Portuguese Premier, and by Prime Minister Churchill, who emphasized that this concession was in accord with an Anglo-Portuguese treaty of 1373 and did not alter the desire of both countries to keep Portugal out of the war.

British forces have already landed on the nine islands of the Azores, which lie along main Atlantic shipping lanes 1,000 miles from Lisbon, 900 from Africa and 1,400 from Newfoundland. So far as can be discovered, no United States troops took part in the operation; but United States warships and aircraft will use the naval and air bases in the islands whenever they like.

The arrangement is for the duration of the war and includes provision for British assistance in furnishing material and supplies to Portuguese armed forces. It does not, Mr. Churchill told the House of Commons, prejudice Portuguese sovereignty in any way, and in the British view it is not incompatible with Portugal's neutrality.

Nazi Reprisal Doubted

At a late hour blacked-out Lisbon was peaceful and the general feeling in London was that the Nazis are too busy in Russia and Italy and on the home front to risk any punitive expedition across the Pyrenees.

The acquisition of bases in the Azores must be considered in relation to the invasion of the Continent, which President Roosevelt and Prime Minister Churchill have promised will come "at the right moment."

The Azores lie alongside not only the southern route from the United States to Britain but directly on the route between Venezuela, where Britain gets a lot of her oil, and the United Kingdom.

They will also serve as a supply base for planes and ships protecting convoys into the Mediterranean and be of great assistance as a center of meteorological information.

Considerable engineering works

Continued on Page Eight

OPENING OF NEW BASE TO THE ALLIES BRIDGES GAP IN THE ATLANTIC

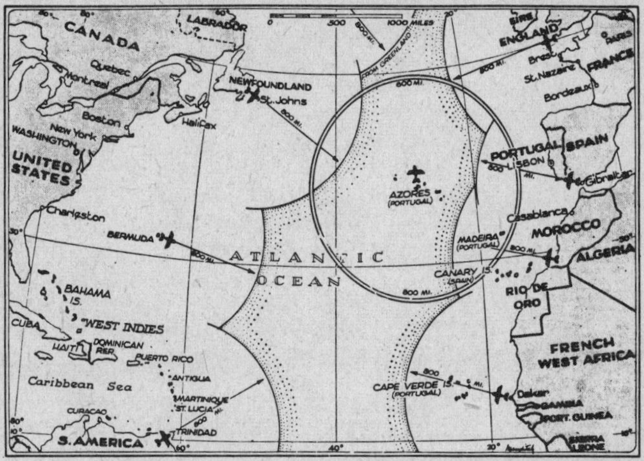

Oct. 13, 1943

Portugal has agreed to allow Britain and the United States to use the Azores in the war against U-boats, and the British have already landed there. The mid-Atlantic area bounded by the arcs on the map is the zone that it has not been possible to patrol with land-based planes. With the Azores as a base the area within the large circle will be brought within bomber range and so a substantial and important section of the "open" area will be removed. Thus the routes from the United States to the British Isles and the Mediterranean, as well as from South America to Britain, will now be better protected against submarine attacks.

U.S. TO USE AZORES, PRESIDENT AFFIRMS

He Stresses Joint Action With British to Guard American Lives and Shipping

By BERTRAM D. HULEN
Special to THE NEW YORK TIMES.

WASHINGTON, Oct. 12—President Roosevelt indicated definitely at his press conference today that the United States would use the Azores along with the British.

What could be said at present, he explained, was that the British and we are allies, that we are trying to win the war, and that we conduct joint operations. While we have no agreement with Portugal,

Continued on Page Five

Russians Deepen Thrusts Over Dnieper, Flank Kiev

By The Associated Press.

LONDON, Wednesday, Oct. 13—Soviet forces widened their areas of penetration on the west bank of the Dnieper in close-quarter fighting yesterday after battering down German counter-attacks, and the Berlin radio said the Red Army had opened a new drive "north of Kiev." The Russian operational bulletin and midnight supplement, broadcast from Moscow and recorded by the Soviet monitor, disclosed today that Red Army troops had edged closer to the White Russian citadel of Vitebsk in the north in the face of stern enemy opposition.

[Moscow heard reports that German demolition squads had begun a systematic destruction of Kiev preparatory to evacuat-

Continued on Page Ten

U. S. ASKS ITALIANS TO BACK BADOGLIO

Berle Brings Roosevelt Pledge to Labor Group Here That No Regime Will Be 'Imposed'

Quoting an authorized statement by President Roosevelt to give point to his utterances, Adolf A. Berle Jr., Assistant Secretary of State, asked Italian-American anti-Fascists in a Columbus Day address here last night to halt present criticism of the government of Marshal Pietro Badoglio and to cooperate with it for the reconquest of Italy.

Revealing also, in what amounted to an official statement, that the State Department will support an immediate move by organized labor to re-establish free trade unions in Italy, Mr. Berle spoke before 1,200 persons at a dinner held in the Hotel Roosevelt under the auspices of the Italian-American Labor Council.

Mr. Berle also declared that the

Continued on Page Four

INVADERS OF ITALY CONSOLIDATE GAINS

Artillery Takes Larger Role as Battle Northwest of Capua Is Reported by Cairo

By Wireless to THE NEW YORK TIMES.

ALGIERS, Oct. 12—Both Allied armies in Italy have come to a virtual standstill, it was officially announced yesterday. Aside from continued artillery exchanges on the central front and patrol activity up and down the line, the campaign has reached its greatest lull since Lieut. Gen. Mark W. Clark's Fifth Army landed below Salerno on Sept. 9.

[A thundering artillery exchange blazed across the Volturno Valley as Allied troops prepared to storm the river barrier, The United Press reported. It quoted a Cairo radio report that a heavy battle was in progress northwest of Capua, on the far side of the Volturno.

[German broadcasts admitted that British and Canadian troops in the middle of the line had thrust to the area of Jelsi in a new ten-mile advance putting them twenty-three miles north of Benevento and only eight miles southeast of Campobasso.]

Both the Fifth and the British Eighth Armies had plenty to do in bringing up supplies and consolidating positions. But their distance from Rome remained the

Continued on Page Three

War News Summarized

WEDNESDAY, OCTOBER 13, 1943

Important developments have been quick to follow Allied successes in the Mediterranean. Private advices reaching THE NEW YORK TIMES said that Italy, with the consent of the United States, Great Britain and Russia, would declare war on Germany today and become a cobelligerent. [1:8.]

Portugal effectively threw in her lot with the United Nations by granting Great Britain's request for the use of the Azores as an Allied naval and air base. The islands, which lie at the apex of a triangle approximately 1,000 miles from Newfoundland and England, will provide added protection for the large convoys for the invasion of Europe. The British, who were already on the new bases, assured Portugal that her sovereignty was unaffected and that all forces would be withdrawn after the war. [1:3.]

The United States will also use the base, President Roosevelt indicated. He also indicated that the Cape Verde Islands, between Africa and South America, would become available. [1:4.]

In Lisbon Premier Salazar declared that Portugal had not altered her determination to remain neutral [8:1.], and Spain saw nothing in the developments to change her attitude. [6:1.] The Axis was apparently caught by surprise. Berlin had no official comment. [7:1.]

Another diplomatic setback for the Axis was seen in the report that Brazil's Foreign Minister Aranha had indicated the likelihood of an Argentine break with Germany and Japan. [1:6-7.]

In the fighting in Russia the Red Army widened its bridgeheads across the Dnieper in moves to flank Kiev. Moscow heard the Germans were preparing to abandon that city. [1:5-6.]

Bad weather over the Italian front continued to hold up ground action, which was limited to patrol activity and artillery exchanges. [1:7; map P. 2.] Yugoslav Partisans reported additional gains. [3:1-2.]

Four Thunderbolts fought it out with thirty-two Japanese planes over Wewak, New Guinea, and shot down eight and probably ten of the enemy without loss. [15:1.] President Roosevelt told his press conference that our Navy, mainly with submarines, in the last six months had sunk Japanese ships at the rate of 130,000 tons a month. He said that 855 United States planes had participated in last Friday's raid on Bremen. [13:1.]

Mr. Roosevelt took issue with many of the criticisms voiced by Senators recently returned from a world tour. He said Russia was too busy knocking down Hitler to protect any Siberian bases she might let us use if Japan should declare war against her. [1:1.]

Navy Secretary Knox said the British midget submarines that damaged the Tirpitz were two-man craft, and added that our Navy was taking over a British airfield as a bomber base. [10:3.]

In an effort to halt coal strikes and assure fuel for all purposes Great Britain plans to conscript coal miners on the same basis as soldiers. [16:2.]

Argentine Break With Axis Near, Brazil Report to Hull Indicates

By The United Press.

RIO DE JANEIRO, Brazil, Oct. 12—Preliminary moves for an Argentine break with the Axis have been completed and an announcement is expected within two weeks, an unimpeachable diplomatic source said tonight.

The return to Buenos Aires of Norman Armour, United States Ambassador to Argentina, and the appointment of Adrian Escobar as Argentine envoy to Washington were direct consequences of the moves preliminary to a break, the informant said.

Secretary of State Cordell Hull, at Natal on his way by plane to attend the American-British-Russian diplomatic conference, conferred there with Brazilian Foreign Minister Oswaldo Aranha and Jefferson Caffery, our Ambassador to Brazil. Dr. Aranha and Mr. Caffery gave Mr. Hull first-hand information on the prospective Argentina-Axis break, it was believed.

[Reuter reported from Montevideo, Uruguay, last night a Cabinet shake-up in Argentina in which the Ministers of Finance, Public Works and Justice and Public Instruction had resigned.]

One consequence of the expected break, the informant said, probably would be United States financial aid to Argentina in some form.

The informant understood that Argentina's basis for a break would be simply compliance with the terms of the Pan-American agreements, to which Argentina is a signatory.

Brazil was understood to be playing a leading role in negotiations

Continued on Page Six

Ickes Turns Back Last Coal Mines, Terminates Government Operation

Special to THE NEW YORK TIMES.

WASHINGTON, Oct. 12—Government possession of coal mines ended today when Secretary Ickes, as Coal Administrator, turned back to private owners the 1,700 coal mines remaining under Government control.

With the announcement that "we are now out of the coal mining business," Mr. Ickes said the Coal Mines Administration will be liquidated immediately. The agency was established last July to operate the 3,300 mines taken over by the Government on May 1, when failure of miners and operators to agree on a new wage contract had stopped production.

About 1,600 mines had been turned back to private ownership previously, the first group having been restored to the control of their owners on Aug. 20. Most of the miners still have no contract.

"We are grateful that sufficient progress has been made in restoring the mines as nearly as possible to normal productive efficiency, all things considered, thus allowing us to terminate this emergency function and wind up the affairs of the Coal Mines Administration," Mr. Ickes said.

The Administrator praised the work of Carl E. Newton, deputy coal administrator, and members of his staff who are resigning.

"I want to express my thanks to Mr. Newton for having left his important post as president of the Chesapeake & Ohio Railroad in Cleveland to come here in this emergency to share an extremely heavy load," Mr. Ickes said. "To him and to his hard-working staff, who are resigning with him, I say,

Continued on Page Sixteen

TO JOIN THE ALLIES

Badoglio Regime's Move to Have Backing of the U. S., Britain, Russia

FLEET ACTION IS SEEN

Operation of Warships by Italians Is Hinted At by Churchill

Italy formally will declare war on Germany today and will be recognized as a cobelligerent against her former Axis partner, according to private advices reaching THE NEW YORK TIMES last night.

The action, it was understood, will be taken with the approval of the United States, Britain and Russia, which have agreed to grant Italy cobelligerent status, according to the report. Such recognition would not include Italy among the United Nations, although presumably the Allies would be compelled to equip with lend-lease material any large Italian forces put into the field.

The declaration of war, to be made, apparently, by the Badoglio Government as at present constituted, would, however, regularize the position in which Italy has found herself since the fall of Mussolini last July 25 and the surrender negotiated by King Victor Emmanuel and Marshal Pietro Badoglio.

Already Acts With Allies

For although technically in a condition of occupation by victorious armies, Italy through her military leaders has already been acting with British and American commanders on Italian soil in regard to "military operations of mutual interest." That was the phrase used in the official communiqué to describe the topics discussed Sept. 30, when Marshal Badoglio and his military aides met Gen. Dwight D. Eisenhower, Admiral Sir Andrew Browne Cunningham and other Allied leaders aboard a warship at Malta.

Also, it was recalled, Marshal Badoglio, although the head of a surrendered and therefore presumably nonbelligerent government, early called on all Italians to consider the Germans as enemies. Meanwhile, at least skeleton Italian forces have remained in being behind the Allied lines in Italy, and Italian regular troops have been reported carrying on guerrilla war against the Germans in the north.

The report of Italy's forthcoming action and her recognition as a cobelligerent by the three large Allied nations came at a time when representatives of those powers already were setting up a joint military-political commission for the Mediterranean area at Algiers. One of the principal aims of the body, named the Politico-Military Commission, is cooperative action in establishing the broad plan of operations in the Italian sphere.

The recognition of Italy as a cobelligerent by the three great powers fighting the Axis in Europe may serve as a counter to whatever Italian strength has been mustered behind the puppet government set up by the Germans in the north under the purported leadership of Mussolini.

Suggest Hint by Churchill

What forces a cobelligerent Italy might be able to send to war against Germany currently probably is obscure to all except the Allied High Command, but some saw a hint last night in a statement of Prime Minister Winston Churchill that the Italian Fleet might fight under its own commanders on the United Nations side.

The British Prime Minister in a reply to a House of Commons questioner yesterday revealed not only that more than 100 Italian warships were in Allied hands but that their employment still was under advisement. He added, according to The Associated Press, that the

Continued on Page Four

"All the News That's Fit to Print."

The New York Times.

LATE CITY EDITION
Showers and cooler this afternoon; partly cloudy tonight.
Temperatures Yesterday—Max., 56; Min., 43
Sunrise, 7:31 A. M.; Sunset, 5:48 P. M.

VOL. XCIII. No. 31,332. Entered as Second-Class Matter, Postoffice, New York, N. Y. NEW YORK, SATURDAY, NOVEMBER 6, 1943. THREE CENTS IN NEW YORK CITY

SENATE VOTES 85 TO 5 TO COOPERATE IN PEACE; ALLIES GAIN IN ITALY, RUSSIANS DRIVE ON KIEV; 500 U. S. BOMBERS SMASH AT TWO BIG NAZI CITIES

MINE PAY INCREASE APPROVED BY WLB IN VOTE OF 11 TO 1

Board Sanctions Lewis-Ickes Pact With Some Qualifications as Morse Dissents

HE HITS 'ECONOMIC FORCE'

Davis Upholds the Award as Meeting Stabilization Policy—Union Speeds Return

By LOUIS STARK
Special to THE NEW YORK TIMES.

WASHINGTON, Nov. 5—The National War Labor Board, by a vote of 11 to 1, approved tonight the contract arranged between Secretary Ickes and the United Mine Workers of America, subject to clarification and resubmission of some details to the board. Wayne Lyman Morse, public member, filed a sharp dissent.

The vote was taken at 10:45 o'clock tonight at the conclusion of the second day's discussion, during which the board considered the contract submitted to it forty-eight hours ago.

Following the board's announcement, John L. Lewis and members of the union's policy committee met and decided to seek clarification from Secretary Ickes of the questions raised in the decision, such as that over piecework. Mr. Lewis then sent the members to the coal fields to press for the early return of all of the 530,000 miners. It was estimated that 15 to 20 per cent were back at work today and that production would be fully resumed Monday.

The WLB chairman, William H. Davis, in a separate statement, pointed out that the Ickes-Lewis contract would pay the day-rate men $1.50 an hour for an extra full hour of work.

Increases totaling 70 cents a day, in addition to allowances for tools and vacation payments, were approved for the anthracite field.

Statement by Davis

The text of the statement by Mr. Davis follows:

"The contract signed by Secretary Ickes and the president of the United Mine Workers pays the day-rate mine workers one dollar and a half for an extra full hour of work each day. This is what they would get under the present contract. When corrected for tonnage workers it will be within the limits of the national wage stabilization policy, because the increased daily earnings will then all be in payment for increased production of coal.

"Four stoppages of work have occurred in this basic industry since the president of the UMW announced to the country that he was going to obtain for no more work a $2-a-day wage increase, no more, no less, regardless of the wage stabilization policies of this board. Under the contract with the Government the extra pay is for extra work paid for at the old rate or for overtime pay required by the Fair Labor Standards Act."

Morse Assails the Action

In his dissenting opinion Mr. Morse, dean of the University of Oregon Law School, opposed approval on the ground that the contract was "the product of the use of economic action against the Government and the nation and, therefore, should be disapproved as being against sound policy."

Charging that the acceptance of the agreement by the board violated the Government's policy that strikers must first return to work, Mr. Morse declared that the example set by the procedure in this case "is likely to cause serious interruption of production in any other industry in which there may be irresponsible union officials who are not loyal to their no-strike pledge."

In a letter to Secretary Ickes Chairman Davis said that while the proposed contract applied to employes working on a day-wage basis who were paid for portal-to-portal time under the Fair Labor Standards Act for time worked after forty hours weekly, "the provisions as to tonnage workers do

Continued on Page Nine

President Names 5 of WLB For Cost of Living Inquiry

Order to Report in 60 Days Is Interpreted as 'a Delaying Action' to Counter Move to Scrap Wage Formula

By ROBERT F. WHITNEY
Special to THE NEW YORK TIMES.

WASHINGTON, Nov. 5—President Roosevelt named a five-man committee of War Labor Board members today to investigate the cost of living and to report within sixty days. This move, coinciding with the decision of the Congress of Industrial Organizations to scrap the "Little Steel" formula, was interpreted as "a delaying action," which insured retention of that wage program for at least two months.

At the same time WLB personnel, in unofficial comment on the CIO decision, expressed the opinion that scrapping the "Little Steel" formula would open the door to inflation, as it would require an all-round wage adjustment for the country's wage-earning classes as well as for revision of farm costs.

Just how much of a revision in the "Little Steel" formula and in the present wages in the steel industry would satisfy the CIO was not indicated today. In labor circles it was believed that while the American Federation of Labor and CIO might come out for a 10 per cent upward adjustment, a compromise of 6 or 7 per cent would be acceptable.

Applied to a national wage bill of at least seventy-five billion dollars, it was estimated that such an adjustment would add between $4,500,000,000 and $5,000,000,000 to the annual income of the 54,000,000 employed.

Coming on the heels of the agreement made by Secretary Ickes and John L. Lewis in the coal crisis, the CIO abandonment

Continued on Page Nine

CIO TO OPEN FIGHT ON PAY RISE CURB

Wage Demand for 900,000 Steel Workers to Begin Drive —Murray Is Re-elected

By WALTER W. RUCH
Special to THE NEW YORK TIMES.

PHILADELPHIA, Nov. 5—A flat increase of at least 15 cents an hour for 900,000 steel workers will be the opening demand in the campaign of the Congress of Industrial Organizations for wage increases greater than those allowed by the "Little Steel" formula, it was learned tonight.

The demand, having the effect of increasing the basic hourly wage rate for common labor in the steel industry from 78 cents to 93 cents, will presage many similar requests from thousands of CIO locals throughout the country, it can be stated.

The CIO views the agreement between John L. Lewis and Secretary Harold L. Ickes, as Solid Fuels Administrator, to give to soft and hard coal miners a wage increase of $1.50 a day not as the cause for their action but as the coup de grace to a series of blows violating the "Little Steel" formula, it was said.

The CIO campaign will begin on Monday when the executive board of the United Steel Workers of America, whose president, Philip Murray, also is president of the CIO, meets here to lay the groundwork for a drive to raise wages for 900,000 in that industry, covered by 1,300 individual contracts.

Other unions in the CIO, which embraces 5,285,000 members, will take their cue from the action by the steel workers, it was learned. More than 9,000 contracts cover CIO war workers.

These things were learned tonight as the CIO national conven-

Continued on Page Nine

U. S. COLLEGES SET OWN 'LEND-LEASE'

Plan to Train Large Number of Foreign Students to Rebuild Occupied Lands

By BENJAMIN FINE

Plans for the immediate training in American colleges, universities and technical schools of a considerable number of persons from the occupied countries, to prepare them to work in specific fields of reconstruction and rehabilitation in their own lands, have been approved by educational leaders of the United States and representatives of foreign nations, it was revealed yesterday.

A sixteen-point program of action, setting up standards for the most extensive system of scholarships ever attempted in this country, has been adopted. This action is the culmination of nearly two years of conferences and discussions between educators here and abroad. Final details still are to be worked out, but the broad outlines of the project have been determined.

Greece, Poland, Czechoslovakia and Norway already have agreed in principle to the program of scholarship exchange, Dr. Stephen Duggan, director of the Institute of International Education, who has just returned from London, where he studied the problem, reported. Other nations are expected to become part of the general program soon.

Educators from this country and representatives of many of the occupied nations of Europe attended an Institute on International Exchanges and Scholarships at New York University yesterday afternoon under the auspices of the United States Committee on Educational Reconstruction. Dr.

Continued on Page Eight

Curran in 2A on Hershey Order; Future Induction Is Not Likely

Joseph Curran, 37-year-old president of the National Maritime Union, once again had his draft classification changed yesterday from 1-A to 2-A—and this time his deferment as an essential union leader, by order of Maj. Gen. Lewis B. Hershey, national director of Selective Service, should finally and safely remove any possibility of his induction into the armed forces because he will reach his thirty-eighth birthday before this reclassification for six months expires.

Mr. Curran was placed in 1-A on Sept. 17 by Selective Service Appeal Board No. 4 of this city, which held that he was "not necessary" in either the operation of his union or American ships and therefore not entitled to deferment in Class 2-A, which is reserved for civilian activity. Col. Arthur V. McDermott, New York City Director of Selective Service, had appealed Mr. Curran's 2-A classification by Local Board 18 at 1133 Broadway.

Announcement of the reclassification order from General Hershey, contradictorily designating Mr. Curran, who is married but has no children, as "essential to civilian activity," was made by the Rev. Francis K. Shepherd, chairman of Local Board 18 and also pastor of the North Baptist Church at 232 West Eleventh Street. The reversal of Appeal Board No. 4 here, Mr. Shepherd said, resulted from an appeal to the President by officials of the National Maritime Union.

The President has authority to delegate his rights and prerogatives in Selective Service matters

Continued on Page Nine

5TH ARMY STRIDES

Reaches the Garigliano River, a Little Over 75 Miles From Rome

8TH WINS SAN SALVO

Drives On Toward Nazis' Adriatic Anchor as Foe Yields Along Line

By MILTON BRACKER
By Wireless to THE NEW YORK TIMES.

ALGIERS, Nov. 5—With the German line snapped in two at Isernia and the retreating Nazis flooding some western coastal sectors in the path of the advancing Allies, both the Fifth and Eighth Armies in Italy drove ahead faster yesterday.

Gen. Sir Bernard L. Montgomery's British and Canadians finally wrested San Salvo on the Adriatic front from the enemy while Lieut. Gen. Mark W. Clark's Americans and British swept up the Tyrrhenian coast to the south bank of the Garigliano River just over seventy-five miles from Rome.

The Germans were expected to repeat their tactics of digging in on high ground across the Garigliano in the hope of slowing the Allied advance, once the two armies, and the Fifth in particular, complete the literally downhill battle made possible by the cracking of the Massico-Isernia line.

Eighth Army Nears Vasto

On the Eighth Army front the capture of San Salvo along with the establishment of several more bridgeheads around Montemitro despite stubborn counter-blows powered by German tanks, put General Montgomery's veterans within four miles of Vasto, which is the northern anchor of the enemy's transpeninsular front. The capture of Vasto will mean that the first stage of the battle for Rome has definitely ended.

The fall of Isernia brought swift Allied envelopment of a number of other towns, as has been foreshadowed in the past few days. The Eighth Army took Carpinone, five miles east of Isernia on a secondary road loop, while the Fifth seized San Agapito, four miles south of Isernia and two miles behind the new Isernia-Vallecupa line.

Vallecupa, also on the American

Continued on Page Five

ALLIES CONTINUE TO ADVANCE SWIFTLY IN ITALY

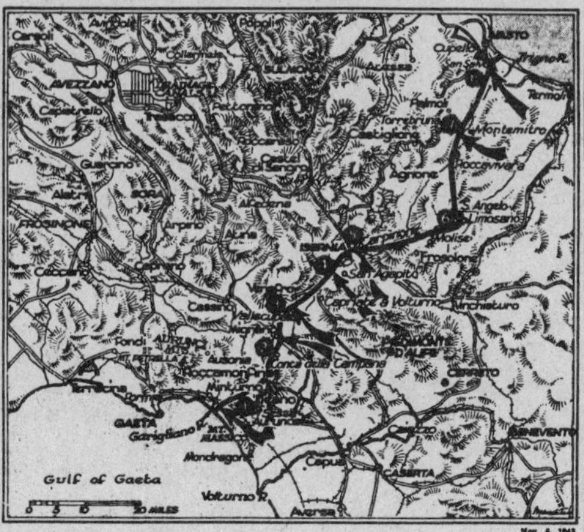

Nov. 6, 1943

The Fifth Army, reaching the south bank of the Garigliano, overran a score of villages between the coast and Roccamonfina (1). It pushed ahead to within a mile of Mignano (2), captured Vallecupa (3) and reached the outskirts of Venafro. San Agapito (4) and Carpinone (5) also fell to General Clark's men. A rectification of the Eighth Army's line showed it holding San Angelo and Limosano (6) rather than advance points previously claimed. It gained more bridgeheads near Montemitro (7) and seized San Salvo (8) despite counter-attacks.

GELSENKIRCHEN HIT IN DAYLIGHT BLOWS

Big Planes With Fighter Cover All Way Batter Ruhr City, Muenster—Bag 38 Nazis

By DREW MIDDLETON
By Cable to THE NEW YORK TIMES.

LONDON, Saturday, Nov. 6—In the heaviest American daylight attack on the Reich, close to 500 Flying Fortresses and Liberators flew through an unprecedented barrage of Nazi anti-aircraft fire yesterday to blow the heart out of the great oil manufacturing center of Gelsenkirchen in the Ruhr and shatter the railroad yards at Muenster to the northeast.

The assault by the United States Eighth Air Force's heavies was the most telling strike in a day of widespread operations. American

Continued on Page Six

Red Army in Kiev Suburbs; Dnieper Delta Freed of Nazis

By The Associated Press.

LONDON, Saturday, Nov. 6—Soviet forces swarmed down from the north into the northern and western suburbs of Kiev to outflank that historic cathedral city and surround it on three sides in a major new Russian drive that broke through two German defense lines, Moscow announced today.

Entrenched for more than a month on a Dnieper River island a few hundred yards from the eastern cliffs of Kiev, the Russians suddenly pounced down on the city from their bridgehead in the north and in a sixteen-mile advance in twenty-four hours broke the German defense lines one after the other.

A number of strongly fortified settlements fell to the victorious Russians as large German forces fled, a midnight bulletin said.

The Russians captured Priorka, three miles north of Kiev, and then smashed into Svyatoshino, four miles to the west, cutting first the railway to Korosten, eighty-two miles to the northwest, then the highway to Zhitomir, eighty miles to the west.

"Large enemy forces were routed," said the Moscow midnight communiqué supplement recorded by the Soviet monitor.

"The enemy is desperately trying to halt the advance of the Soviet troops. He is hastily bringing up reserves of infantry and tanks and throwing them into the battle from the march.

"Eleven Hitlerite counter-attacks were repulsed with heavy losses to them. About 3,000 German officers and men were wiped out."

The Russians said their troops

Continued on Page Three

JAPAN'S WARSHIPS RUSHING TO RABAUL

Convoys With Cruisers and Destroyers on Way From Truk—One Attacked

By The Associated Press.

ALLIED HEADQUARTERS IN THE SOUTHWEST PACIFIC, Saturday, Nov. 6—Presaging heavy naval and air battles to come, Japan is ruhsing both heavy and light cruisers and destroyers down from Truk to Rabaul in a frantic effort to halt the Allied drive up the Solomons, headquarters disclosed today.

It appeared likely that at least five such convoys now are southbound over the 800 miles from Truk toward Kavieng, New Ireland, and Rabaul, New Britain.

The largest convoy spotted by Allied reconnaissance planes included five heavy cruisers, three light cruisers, five destroyers, two corvettes, a whaling ship and three freighters, of which one probably is a transport.

General MacArthur said the Japanese were trying to "retrieve the

Continued on Page Six

War News Summarized

SATURDAY, NOVEMBER 6, 1943

Having smashed through the center of the German line in Italy at Isernia, the Allied armies struck yesterday toward both anchors, taking San Salvo on the Adriatic front and moving ahead to the Garigliano River on the Tyrrhenian end. The Germans flooded the coastal area in the path of the Fifth Army advance. [1:4.]

Making the second record daylight assault in three days, 500 United States bombers blasted war industries at Gelsenkirchen and railway yards at Muenster in western Germany while American and British medium bombers attacked targets in northern France. [1:5.]

Kiev, third largest city in Russia, was flanked on the west by Russian forces that plunged sixteen miles south and cut the main Zhitomir highway. The city is now hemmed in on three sides. In the south thirty places were captured between the Dnieper and the Black Sea. [1:6-7, map P. 2.]

Washington reported that Russia and Czechoslovakia would sign a twenty-year defensive alliance against Germany [3:2.], while in Stockholm it was indicated that Finland and Russia would get together on peace talks within the next few days. [3:8.] Despite the success of the Moscow conference, which some observers thought would obviate the much-heralded Roosevelt - Churchill - Stalin meeting, President Roosevelt said in Washington that he was very anxious to meet Premier Stalin. [3:6.]

Although conceding that the Moscow conference was a step along the right road toward Axis defeat, the French Committee of National Liberation was outspokenly piqued for having been excluded from the talks. It announced in Algiers that France would not be bound by decisions in which she had not participated. [3:1.]

In the Balkans, Tito's Partisans reported victories over the Germans in Montenegro and claimed that the important Spalato-Sinj railway in Dalmatia had been "destroyed." [4:1.]

General MacArthur announced that the Japanese were heavily reinforcing Rabaul, New Britain, their principal remaining base in that area, and probably would fight hard to keep it. He said five convoys with warships were on their way to replace losses inflicted by United States bombers there. [1:7.]

Complete agreement on the prosecution of the continental campaign in the Far East has been reached after a five-day conference between Generalissimo Chiang Kai-shek and British-American military leaders in Chungking, President Roosevelt announced. [1:6-7.]

Reversing a position taken twenty-four years ago when the League of Nations was snubbed, the Senate voted, 85 to 5, to approve United States participation in a general international organization to keep the peace. [1:8.]

Roosevelt Says Land Offensive Against Japan Is All Mapped Now

By JOHN H. CRIDER
Special to THE NEW YORK TIMES.

WASHINGTON, Nov. 5—President Roosevelt announced today the successful conclusion of a five-day British and American military conference with Generalissimo Chiang Kai-shek on plans for a continental offensive against Japan. It means bad news for the Japanese, he said.

The conference was seen as bringing nearer the stepped-up Pacific war program agreed upon by the President and Prime Minister Churchill at the Quebec conference, which was immediately followed by the appointment of Admiral the Lord Louis Mountbatten as supreme commander for Southeast Asia.

Admiral Mountbatten, the President said, was one of the participants in the Chungking conference. Others were Lieut. Gen. Joseph W. Stilwell, American commander of operations in China; Maj. Gen. Claire L. Chennault, our air commander in that theatre, and Lieut. Gen. Brehon B. Somervell, chief of the Services of Supply.

Shortly after the President's press conference General Somervell called on the Chief Executive to report on the Chungking conference, carrying with him as souvenirs a stone battle axe of New Guinea tribesmen and a bow and cluster of arrows used by the head-hunting natives of the Naga Naga Hills, in Burma.

[The President declared General Somervell's presence in China obviously was concerned

Continued on Page Seven

WORLD STAND MADE

Moscow Pact Is Backed in Adopting Post-War Organization Policy

ALL CHANGES LOSE

President Expresses His Satisfaction—Johnson Again in Minority

By C. P. TRUSSELL
Special to THE NEW YORK TIMES.

WASHINGTON, Nov. 5—The Senate, by a record vote of 85 to 5 with announced positions of absentees carrying the margin to 90 to 6 to represent its entire membership, declared late today for post-war collaboration to secure and maintain peace for the world and for the establishment of a general international organization that might become a new League of Nations.

Voting against the recently revised Connally resolution containing the declaration were two Democrats, Senators Burton K. Wheeler of Montana and Robert R. Reynolds of North Carolina, chairman of the Committee on Military Affairs, and three Republicans, Senators Hiram Johnson of California, William Langer of North Dakota and Henrik Shipstead of Minnesota.

Senator Johnson voted against the Treaty of Versailles of World War I. Senator Robert M. La Follette Jr., Progressive of Wisconsin, whose father joined Mr. Johnson in opposing that treaty, was announced, in his absence, as desiring to vote against the resolution adopted today.

Voting for the resolution were fifty-one Democrats and thirty-four Republicans. Four absent Democrats, Senators Carter Glass of Virginia, Josiah W. Bailey of North Carolina, Homer T. Bone of Washington and Pat McCarran of Nevada, and one Republican, Senator Styles Bridges of New Hampshire, were announced as desiring to vote for the measure.

Copy Sent to White House

Before making its decision, which was hailed promptly by participants as a great stride toward establishing the international policy of the United States, the nation's treaty-ratifying body voted down, viva voce and in rapid succession, five amendments or substitutes for the draft upon which the Senate divided for a time following the American-British-Russian-Chinese declaration of Moscow.

As adopted, the measure remained unchanged.

Although the resolution does not require White House approval or disapproval, the Senate decided unanimously to send an engrossed copy of it to President Roosevelt as an expression of its sentiment on post-war policy.

Senator Alben W. Barkley, majority leader, who proposed this action, at first suggested that the copy be sent to the Chief Executive "for his advice." He withdrew this when Senator Robert A. Taft, Republican, of Ohio, objected, asserting that advice to the President in the constitutional sense could be forwarded only by a two-thirds vote of the Senate.

President Voices Satisfaction

The resolution is one which apparently will please Mr. Roosevelt.

At his press-radio conference this morning he viewed as a grand idea the incorporation in the Connally resolution of Article 4 of the Moscow Agreement, in which recognition is given to a necessity for a general international organization open to all peace-loving nations, for maintenance of future world security.

At the same time the President gave his answer to apprehension which had arisen in some Senate quarters that the Moscow declaration might have by-passed the requirement for Senate ratification of any treaty affecting American participation in the proposed international organization or to carry out other phases of the declaration

Continued on Page Two

"All the News That's Fit to Print."

The New York Times.

LATE CITY EDITION
Fair and cold today; not so windy.
Temperatures Yesterday—Max., 39; Min., 29
Sunrise, 7:[illegible] A. M.; Sunset, 5:[illegible] P. M.

VOL. XCIII. No. 31,350. Entered as Second-Class Matter, Postoffice, New York, N. Y. NEW YORK, WEDNESDAY, NOVEMBER 24, 1943. THREE CENTS IN NEW YORK CITY

RAF BOMBERS RETURN TO DEVASTATED BERLIN AFTER 2,300-TON ATTACK, GREATEST IN HISTORY; U. S. FORCES CAPTURE MAKIN, GAIN ON TARAWA

SUBSIDIES BEATEN IN HOUSE, 278 TO 117; SENATE ACTS NEXT

Vote Against Administration on Food Prices Great Enough to Override a Veto

COMPROMISE MOWED DOWN

98 Democrats, 178 Republicans Join in Final Roll-Call on Adopting Measure

By SAMUEL B. BLEDSOE
Special to THE NEW YORK TIMES.

WASHINGTON, Nov. 23—The House late today adopted and sent to the Senate the Commodity Credit Corporation Bill, which would end food subsidies after Dec. 31. The vote was 278 to 117.

The majority for the anti-subsidy measure was more than the two-thirds necessary to override a Presidential veto, but the issue was not clear-cut on final passage, since some subsidy supporters, including Representative Wright Patman of Texas, voted for the bill. In addition to the ban on the use of food subsidies to hold down the cost of living, the measure would extend the life of the Commodity Credit Corporation, the $3,000,000,000 agency which finances many agricultural programs, from Dec. 31 until July 1, 1945.

A coalition of Republicans and Democrats defeated the Administration on the highly controversial issue, as on a similar occasion last summer during the consideration of a Commodity Credit Corporation bill. This measure reached the White House, was vetoed and the House sustained the President. During debate today Representative John W. McCormack of Massachusetts, the House majority leader, predicted another veto if the pending bill reaches the White House. Subsidy opponents said tonight that they were confident that the Senate would vote against the Administration.

How the Parties Lined Up

On the vote on final passage 178 Republicans, 98 Democrats and two minor party members voted for the measure and 100 Democrats, 15 Republicans and two minor party members against it.

The result had been a foregone conclusion, since the House, by a teller vote, rejected, 154 to 120, an amendment by Representative A. S. Mike Monroney, Democrat, of Oklahoma, which would have provided $750,000,000 for a continuation of the food subsidy program until Oct. 1, 1944, but would have tied the continuation of subsidies to the "Little Steel" wage formula.

In the event of a general wage increase, the subsidy program would have been discontinued under Mr. Monroney's amendment.

Continued on Page Twelve

Says Army Will Run Bay State Plants

By The United Press.

BOSTON, Nov. 23—State Labor Commissioner James T. Moriarty said tonight that the Army would take over thirty-two Salem and Peabody leather plants now tied up by a strike of 2,500 workers.

Picketing around the plants continued today, despite orders by the regional and National War Labor Boards and President Roosevelt that the strikers return to work. The three-week-old strike is the result of a jurisdictional dispute between the International Fur and Leather Workers (CIO) and the Independent National Leather Workers Association.

Special to THE NEW YORK TIMES.

WASHINGTON, Nov. 23—The only word available at the War Department tonight concerning the leather strike in Massachusetts was that it had as yet received no directive to take over operation of plants there.

The WLB recently referred the matter to the White House, and it was said that since then Army officers had been on the scene looking over the situation.

Up-State Snow Cuts City's Milk Supply

A warning that New York City's supply of milk would be "exceedingly short" today as a result of the heavy snowstorm in Eastern New York and New England was released from Mayor La Guardia's office last night.

"Consumers not having children in the family are requested not to buy milk in order that it will be available for children first," the announcement added. "This particularly applies to restaurants and places of public eating. The supply will be normal as soon as weather conditions permit."

Spokesmen for the major milk distributors explained that the storm had "played havoc" with truck and rail transportation, particularly in the Champlain Valley, where the snowfall was twenty inches. Describing the snowfall as "the toughest first storm of the season in years," the milk company representatives estimated that supplies here today would be cut at least 20 per cent.

LIMIT ON SLAUGHTER OF CATTLE IS LIFTED

Quotas for Civilian Supplies Dropped Until Further Notice —Point Values May Be Cut

In an effort to move the nation's record surplus of 17,000,000 head of cattle, the War Food Administration announced yesterday suspension of quota limitations on slaughter of livestock. The new order permits packers and butchers holding Government slaughter licenses to kill livestock for civilians without quota limitations until further notice.

"This action was taken to facilitate the marketing and slaughter of record numbers of livestock produced by the nation's farmers in answer to the call for more food," according to a WFA statement released here by the local offices of the Food Distribution Administration, 150 Broadway.

"The original suspension order lifted limitations of slaughter for civilian consumption through September and October. This period was subsequently extended to Dec. 1."

Ration-Point Revision Seen

At the same time word came from Washington that heavy current slaughtering might bring an early reduction in the number of ration points required for meats next month. Formal announcement of the new point values is expected on Dec. 3, and reports in the capital indicate that OPA is giving serious consideration to lower point values because supplies of meats for civilians have improved in recent weeks.

Meanwhile, over the telephone from Washington, former Judge Joe C. Montague, counsel for the Texas and Southwestern Cattle Raisers Association, declared that the suspension of quota limitations on slaughter for civilians would not help the civilians until meat-

Continued on Page Twelve

SUCCESS IN PACIFIC

Our Troops Mop Up Foe on Makin, Dig In on Tarawa, Gain on Betio

ABEMAMA IS IN HAND

Army and Navy Planes Blast Nauru—Tokyo Forecasts Fleet Fight

By GEORGE F. HORNE
By Telephone to THE NEW YORK TIMES.

PEARL HARBOR, Nov. 23—Makin atoll in the northern Gilbert Islands has been captured and our invasion of other islands is progressing well.

Admiral Chester W. Nimitz, Commander in Chief of the Pacific Fleet, announced today the capture of Makin. He said that on Tarawa the United States Marines were consolidating their positions and that they were making progress against enemy concentrations on the eastern end of Betio Island, an important isle in Tarawa atoll and the one on which desirable air strips are our main objectives.

On Abemama, which we invaded in a second attack following the initial assault on Tarawa and Makin, the situation is "well in hand," the admiral's communiqué reported. Everywhere in the central Pacific offensive, which is initiating a new and brilliant phase of this important year's operations against the Eastern enemy, we are surging ahead, and details made available today make it clear that the surging was against considerable resistance, at least on Betio, where the Japanese garrison put up a terrific fight to hold their land air base.

Our Men Shove Foe Back

It has been in vain, for the Second Marines, including veterans of Guadalcanal and other fighting in the Pacific, have pushed the enemy back to Betio's eastern end, indicating that we landed on the western approaches when the action began last Saturday morning.

Today's communiqué, issued at 11:30 A. M. Hawaiian time, reads as follows:

"Our forces have captured Makin. On Tarawa the marines have consolidated their positions and are making good progress against enemy concentrations on the eastern end of Betio Island, with capture assured. The situation on Abemama is well in hand.

"Raids are being continued against the Marshalls by carrier aircraft and Army Seventh Air Force Liberators."

Spokesmen revealed that the Marshall carrier plane blow was on Mili atoll and that it took place yesterday. Enemy air activity was limited. The bases attacked by Maj. Gen. Willis H. Hale's Seventh United States Army Air Force were not identified.

As to the mopping up phase of Makin, it was stressed that the Makin atoll was entirely in our hands and that the mopping up consisted of cleaning out snipers. The mopping up, it is said, is now being completed and the termina-

Continued on Page Three

SCENE OF WORLD'S MOST DESTRUCTIVE AERIAL BOMBARDMENT

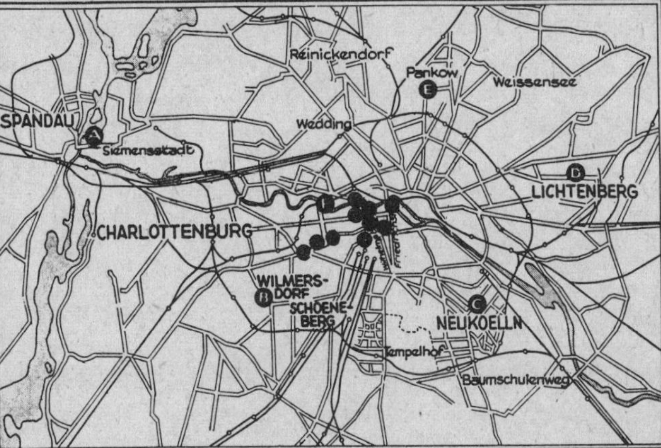

Royal Air Force planes showered 2,300 tons of bombs on Berlin and its industrial suburbs Monday night. The suburbs hit included Spandau and Siemensstadt (A), Wilmersdorf (B), Neukoelln (C), Lichtenberg (D) and Pankow (E). In the heart of the city (F) the Kaiser Wilhelm Gedaechtniskirche (1) was reported damaged, as were the Hungarian Legation (2) and the Swedish Legation (3). The Potsdam railroad station (4) was said to have been destroyed and the British Embassy (5) and the French Embassy (6) were declared to have been razed. Other places reported damaged were the Finnish Legation (7), the Danish Legation (8), the State University (9) and the Foreign Office (10). Vast fires were set and casualties were estimated at 10,000 killed and wounded.

NIMITZ SEES CHINA AS JAPAN'S NEMESIS

Says Final Defeat of Foe Will Come From Chungking's Area —Cites Men, Airfields

By Telephone to THE NEW YORK TIMES.

PEARL HARBOR, Nov. 23—The final defeat of Japan will come from China, in the opinion of Admiral Chester W. Nimitz, Commander in Chief of the United States Pacific Fleet.

In a press conference this afternoon, his first in nearly a year, he said that "my opinion is that Japan will be defeated from China." "China, with her reservoir of personnel and the possibility of airfields in easy striking distance of Japan, is one of the steps along the road," he remarked.

Seated behind his table with his schnauzer puppy at his feet and more than a score of reporters and

Continued on Page Four

Patton Struck Ailing Soldier, Apologized to Him and Army

By MILTON BRACKER
By Wireless to THE NEW YORK TIMES.

ALGIERS, Nov. 23—Lieut. Gen. George S. Patton Jr. struck and insulted a shell-shocked American soldier in an evacuation hospital in Sicily last August and ordered the patient to return to the front lines, it was officially revealed today. Gen. Dwight D. Eisenhower denounced the conduct of the commander of the American Seventh Army as "despicable" and threatened to break him unless he made amends at once. General Patton thereupon apologized to the soldier, to the officers and patients who had witnessed the incident and to the Seventh Army.

Although there were at least fifteen witnesses to the incident, none was a professional reporter. The first two reporters to check on the episode arrived at the hospital about twenty-four hours later. One of them was Merrill Mueller of the National Broadcasting Company, who gave his version today in the

Continued on Page Six

RUSSIANS RETREAT TOWARD KIEV AGAIN

Germans Win Several Towns at High Cost, but Red Army Gains on Other Fronts

By The United Press.

LONDON, Wednesday, Nov. 24—German forces, driving back toward Kiev and the Dnieper line without regard for prodigious losses, yesterday reached the vicinity of Brusilov, less than fifty miles from the Ukraine capital, Moscow acknowledged today.

The Soviet operational and supplementary communiqués reported that the Red Army had abandoned several towns and villages north of Zhitomir, in the area of Chernyakhov, and east of the rail junction recaptured Saturday by the Nazis, around Brusilov.

On other fronts the bitter and long-continued battle for the Dnieper favored the Russians.

At the northern end of the active front Moscow reported slow prog-

Continued on Page Eight

'DOOMSDAY' SCENE IN BERLIN PAINTED

Swedish Traveler Reports Fires Created Almost a Summer Temperature

By GEORGE AXELSSON
By Cable to THE NEW YORK TIMES.

STOCKHOLM, Sweden, Nov. 23—An eyewitness from Berlin of the British bombing attack last night told the writer here today that the French Embassy on the Pariser Platz and the British Embassy on Wilhelmstrasse were razed by explosives and incendiaries.

Reich Foreign Minister Joachim von Ribbentrop's official residence on Wilhelmstrasse was destroyed. The top stories of the Foreign Office building and of Adolf Hitler's Wilhelmstrasse residence were burned out. Dr. Joseph Goebbels' Propaganda Ministry building across the street from Hitler's residence was undamaged. [Other persons reaching Stockholm said the Hitler residence was destroyed, Reuter reported.]

The big Potsdam railroad station was wiped out, as were the Haus Vaterland and the Potsdamer Platz restaurant near by.

At the Anhalter station the tracks were torn up and no trains were able to arrive or leave there today. The Stettin station was badly damaged and tracks at the Lehrter station were torn up. The Friedrickstrasse station was not hit, but the district immediately north of it was battered.

On the north side of the Pariser

Continued on Page Five

BIG BLOWS PRESSED

Reich Capital Set Afire, City's Heart Blasted by 775 Planes

CLOUDS PROVE AN AID

British Lose 26 Craft—Nazis Claim a Greater Toll in New Assault

Heavy bombers of the Royal Air Force rained fresh destruction on Berlin last night as the German capital lay smoking and devastated from a record British assault twenty-four hours earlier, London officials stated early today, according to The Associated Press.

The new attack apparently was carried out in great force.

The preliminary British announcement gave no details, but it confirmed the fact of the new blow, of which first word came in a German broadcast reported by the Federal Communications Commission.

New Blow Expected, Nazis Say

"The attack was expected and special defense precautions were taken," the German broadcast said, asserting that "a considerable number" of attacking planes were shot down.

"The weather favored the defense more than the previous night," the German-language broadcast added.

It characterized the attack with the customary Nazi propaganda designation for a heavy assault—"terror raid."

A later Nazi broadcast early today, reported by The Associated Press from London, said that new devastation had been wrought by the attackers in several sections of the smoldering capital.

This broadcast said that the British planes had been attacked by Nazi fighters before they reached the coast of Europe.

Aim Is End of Berlin

By DREW MIDDLETON
By Cable to THE NEW YORK TIMES.

LONDON, Wednesday, Nov. 24—A great armada of British bombers won one of the war's most significant victories Monday night when in the heaviest air assault of history it blew the heart out of Berlin with more than 2,300 long tons of high explosive and incendiary bombs and repaid the debt of London.

The force, which this writer estimates at about 775 four-motored bombers, dropped its missiles at a rate of seventy-seven tons a minute in a half hour's time. It left the German capital ablaze with scores of huge fires and shattered by explosions.

All accounts by the returning airmen and reports from the Continent agreed that Berlin suffered its severest blow as Air Chief Marshal Sir Arthur T. Harris and his Royal Air Force Bomber Command continued the Allies' inexorable campaign to knock the city and Germany out of the war.

Soon after dark last night more strong forces of British heavy bombers streamed out toward Europe. For about three-quarters of an hour an unbroken procession of planes swept across the Strait of Dover.

Victory at a Low Price

The destruction of the center of Berlin and of part of the city's important industrial suburbs was only a portion of the RAF's signal triumph Monday night.

The attack was made through heavy clouds that kept the Nazi night fighter interference at a minimum and enemy anti-aircraft fire, although heavy, was wild.

The British lost twenty-two heavy bombers and the Royal Canadian Air Force reported four missing.

For this proportionately low price of twenty-six planes the RAF bought victory. The cascade of bombs, which included hundreds of two and four ton block busters, wrecked the center of Berlin.

The reports from the Continent spoke of widespread devastation

Continued on Page Five

U. S. Cracks Down on Bootleg Ring; 44 Seized in 36 Liquor Raids Here

Fanning out in a three-pronged drive, Federal agents swept yesterday through Manhattan, Brooklyn and the Bronx and, in a smashing blow against the revived bootleg industry in New York City, conducted thirty-six liquor raids in which forty-four persons, including an alleged ringleader, were arrested.

Reinforced by thirty city policemen, seventy Federal men under W. E. Dunigan, assistant district supervisor of the Alcohol Tax Unit of the Treasury Department, seized vast quantities of illicit liquor in simultaneous descents upon taverns, grocery stores, a wholesale butcher, a newsstand dealer, and other places on the calling list of the bootleg mob.

Jacob Kessler, described by Mr. Dunigan as the head of the ring operating here, was arrested in his office at 1123 Broadway with three other alleged members of the ring. These three were identified as Jack Schiff, Isadore Schimmel and Isadore Jaffe. According to Mr. Dunigan, Kessler, who lives at the Windermere Hotel, 666 West End Avenue, is a familiar figure in bootlegging circles, having been head of a gang in prohibition days, maintaining offices then as now in the same Broadway building where he was seized yesterday.

What was termed by the agents as the "cutting" plant of the ring was found in the home of Vincent and Jennie Luciano at 1458 West Eightieth Street, Brooklyn, where Mrs. Luciano was arrested. Agents said they found sixty-five five-gallon cans of alcohol, a number of

Continued on Page Thirteen

War News Summarized

WEDNESDAY, NOVEMBER 24, 1943

The RAF returned to Berlin last night to carry on the work of destruction begun Monday, when 775 bombers gave the German capital the worst pounding ever administered to any city from the air. In that attack more than 2,300 tons of explosives fell on the target at the rate of seventy-seven tons a minute. The center of the city and the suburbs were left a "sea of flames." Twenty-six planes, four Canadian, were lost. [1:8.]

A Swedish traveler who returned to Stockholm yesterday reported that Berlin had suffered an "all-time major catastrophe." When he left in the afternoon the city was still ablaze and the acrid smoke was so thick in places one could not see at arm's length. Embassies and Government buildings were razed, he said, and he estimated the dead and homeless in tens of thousands. [1:7.]

The Pacific end of Hitler's Axis also suffered severe blows. Makin atoll in the Gilberts was captured by American troops and neighboring Tarawa was about to fall to the marines, who had herded the Japanese into the eastern end of Betio Island. [1:3; map, P. 2.] In the South Pacific, Allied planes heavily bombed Gasmata on New Britain for the third consecutive day. [3:3-4.]

Admiral Nimitz told reporters at Pearl Harbor that the Gilberts were securely in our hands but that the final defeat of Japan would come from China. Sooner or later the enemy fleet must join battle with us, he said. [1:4.] In Washington, Navy Secretary Knox said the attack on the Gilberts was the beginning of a new campaign "on a much more direct route to Japan." [3:1.]

In the European land fighting the Russian armies scored important advances on most fronts, but admitted withdrawing from several more inhabited places in the Chernyakhov-Brusilov area, indicating that the Germans had pushed part way back to Kiev from Zhitomir. [1:6; map, P. 8.]

Mud virtually halted ground activities in Italy. Allied fliers were busy, particularly in the area from Pescara to Ancona on the Adriatic coast and inland to Foligno. [4:3.] The British announced the evacuation of the Aegean Island of Samos. [4:7.]

General Eisenhower disclosed that Major General Patton had slapped and cursed a shell-shocked soldier in Sicily last August and had ordered the private out of the hospital. General Patton was told to apologize to all concerned and he did so, even apologizing to as many soldiers as could be assembled at all Seventh Army divisional headquarters. [1:5-6.]

Washington Censorship Blocks Carol's Radio Talk From Mexico

The radio address that was to have been delivered last night from Mexico City by former King Carol of Rumania over the Columbia Broadcasting System was canceled a few hours before the exiled monarch was to have gone on the air. An order of the Office of Censorship in Washington rescinded its previous approval of the broadcast.

The Office of Censorship issued the following statement to CBS, which was made public from the CBS offices here:

"Owing to considerations that we are not at liberty to disclose, we find it necessary to cancel the previously authorized use of the lines from Mexico City for the scheduled broadcast tonight by former King Carol of Rumania."

Copies of the scheduled address had been given out by Russell Birdwell of 30 Rockefeller Plaza, the former King's press representative in this country, before news of cancellation of the broadcast arrived.

In disclosing the order of the Office of Censorship forbidding the broadcast, Columbia made public the following statement:

"The text of Carol's proposed broadcast was submitted to censorship by CBS last Saturday. It was cleared, and leaders of anti-Carol movements in the United States were asked to nominate a spokesman to speak on the same program after Carol had finished reading his statement from Mexico City

"The former King of Rumania had frequently been quoted in the press, but since his exile he has never before been scheduled to talk

Continued on Page Seven

U. S. Navy

Sprawled bodies on beach of Tarawa testify to the ferocity of the struggle for this stretch of sand.

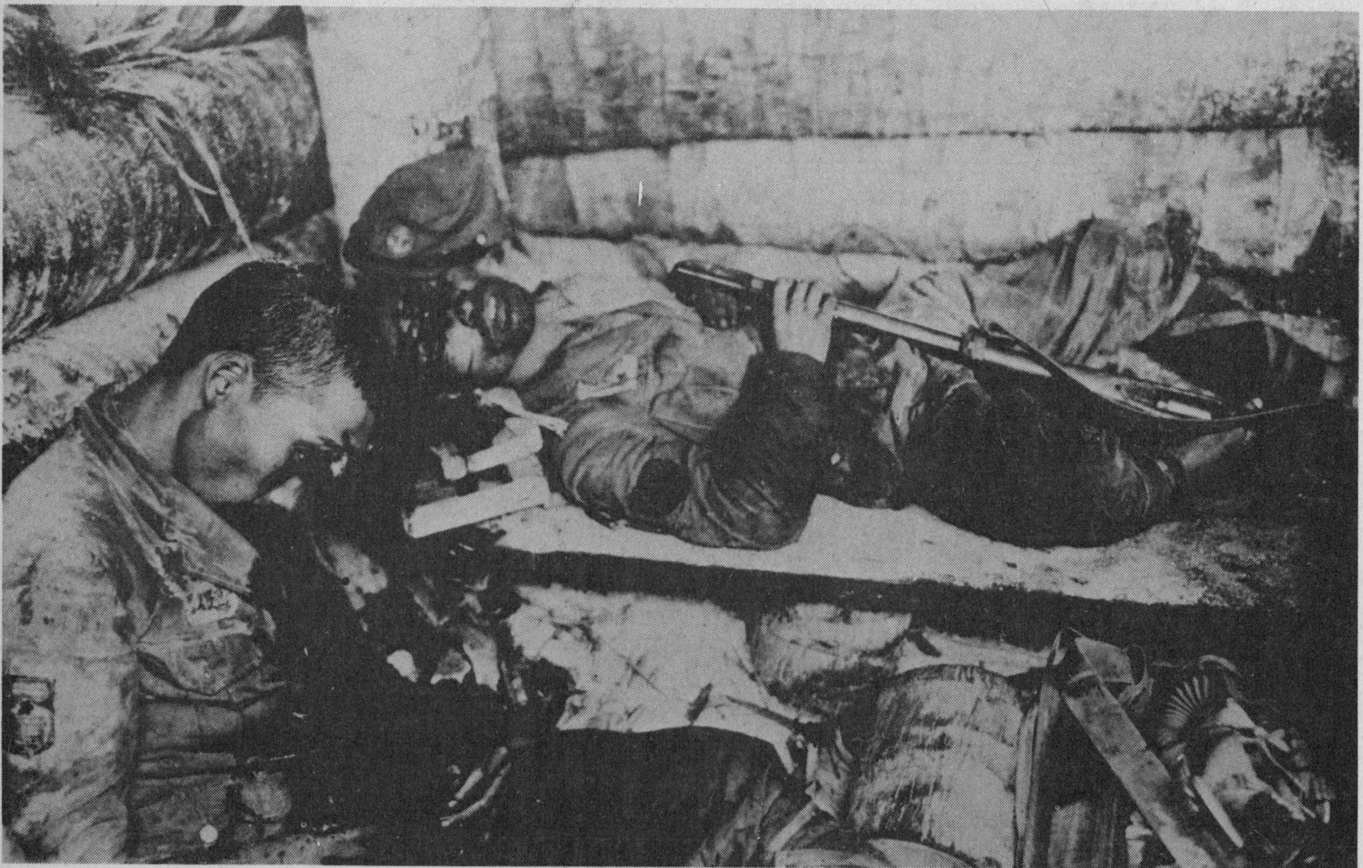

U. S. Marine Corps

Bodies of Japanese troops lie in their bunker on Tarawa.

"All the News That's Fit to Print."

The New York Times.

LATE CITY EDITION
Fair, not quite so cold in morning; cloudy, warmer later.
Temperatures Yesterday—Max., 46; Min., 36
Sunrise, 8:01 A. M.; Sunset, 5:30 P. M.

Copyright, 1943, by The New York Times Company.

VOL. XCIII..No. 31,358. Entered as Second-Class Matter, Postoffice, New York, N. Y. NEW YORK, THURSDAY, DECEMBER 2, 1943. THREE CENTS IN NEW YORK CITY

CRUSHING OF JAPAN MAPPED AT CAIRO PARLEY; EMPIRE WILL BE STRIPPED TO PRE-1895 STATUS; 8TH ARMY DRIVES ON; U. S. FLIERS AGAIN HIT REICH

1,440 ON GRIPSHOLM WILDLY HAPPY HERE; RETICENT ON TRIALS

Civilians Freed by Japanese Burst Into Song at Sight of Statue of Liberty

FBI CHECKS ON ARRIVALS

Overcrowding and Poor Food in Camps Described but Most Are Healthy After Voyage

Sun-tanned, healthy and ecstatically happy, but exceedingly reticent about many of their experiences, more than 1,000 of the 1,440 passengers—1,222 Americans and 217 Canadians—aboard the diplomatic exchange liner Gripsholm debarked yesterday after the 18,353-ton Swedish ship docked at Pier F, Jersey City.

Two hundred of the passengers were still on the ship late last night, awaiting the same exhaustive examination that agents of the Federal Bureau of Investigation and officers of Army and Navy Intelligence already had given their companions. Navy press relations officers expressed hope they would all be cleared by midnight, but said that many of the passengers, including some already cleared, would voluntarily remain on the Gripsholm until this morning.

An undisclosed number of those aboard were removed by the FBI to Ellis Island for further investigation. The officials in charge of the search were reluctant to discuss this aspect of the arrival, but it was recalled that when the exchange ship Drottningholm docked last June they found among the expatriates a man named Herbert Karl Friedrich Barr, who subsequently was convicted of espionage.

Canadians Take Sealed Train

The Canadians on the Gripsholm were among the first to land. By an agreement between the Canadian and the United States Governments they were escorted to buses which took them to a special train, which was sealed and guarded en route to prevent anyone from having access to them as they were speeding north to Montreal.

Joy at their safe arrival in this country and concern lest some careless remark might be carried back to their former jailers and infuriate the Japanese against the 6,800 Americans still remaining in the internment camps seemed to be the emotions most strongly felt by the hundreds who passed the gantlet of questioning and were permitted to land.

Their delight at their return, which prompted those on deck when the big liner passed the Statue of Liberty to burst spontaneously into "God Bless America," was visible in every countenance, from those of children of 3 or 4 to those of gray-haired missionaries who were back home after thirty, forty or more years in the East.

Others Remain Prisoners

But even though they were bubbling over with the sheer happiness born of freedom, it was evident that not for a minute did they forget their unfortunate former companions who are still at the mercy of the Japanese. As 9-year-old Suzanne Hazard of San Francisco put it when reporters and photographers clustered about her and her 6-year-old sister Joan:

"We can't tell you all of the things about the camp."

Before they were permitted to leave at least one of the internment camps, it was learned, some of those who arrived yesterday were sternly warned by Japanese officials not to criticize conditions upon their arrival here. This warning was reinforced by the injunctions of State Department officials on the Gripsholm, who are even now hoping to arrange another exchange and wish to avoid antagonizing Japanese officialdom.

Those who would tell about the camps at all gave almost unanimous testimony to the terrific overcrowding and the entire lack

Continued on Page Eighteen

Colombians Urged To Give Their Blood

By Cable to THE NEW YORK TIMES.

BOGOTA, Colombia, Dec. 1—Colombia is not likely to send troops to battle fronts, but Colombian blood will be shed for the United Nations here as the result of a decree, issued today, calling for blood plasma.

Following unanimous approval by the House of Representatives of a state of belligerency against Germany it is expected the Conservatives will support the Government despite the vote of thirteen Conservative Senators against the belligerency resolution and the charge by Conservative Senator Guillermor Leon Valencia that American submarines sank the Colombian schooner Ruby. The sinking caused the action against Germany.

BEEF AND 15 FOODS GET CUT IN POINTS

Citrus Fruit Juices and Most Soup on Ration-Free List—Higher Values on Cheese

By CHARLES E. EGAN
Special to THE NEW YORK TIMES.

WASHINGTON, Dec. 1—Ration point values on meats and on fifteen types of processed foods were reduced by the Office of Price Administration today in establishing a scale which will apply beginning Sunday through December. The reductions reflected a seasonally easier supply situation in meats, and improvement in available stocks of a variety of processed foods, OPA officials said.

The average point value of all meats was brought to slightly less than five a pound, lowest since rationing began. Changes were confined almost entirely to beef cuts, where point slashes averaged two to three points.

Veal steaks and chops were lowered two points and veal leg roasts were lowered one point, but other veal cuts, as well as all lamb and mutton, which were reduced substantially for November, were not changed.

Reductions made on many pork cuts in mid-November, when point values were brought down an average of more than 25 per cent, were left in force except on all hams and most bacon cuts, which were increased one point.

Grapefruit juice and other citrus juices, ready-to-serve soups (except tomato), and canned sauerkraut were made ration-free for this month. Reductions of one to ten points were made on fifteen items of processed food, the largest number of slashes made at any one time since rationing began.

Tomato Products Raised

Other reductions in point values included green and wax beans, soy beans, all varieties of canned dry beans, including pork and beans, carrots, spinach and dry frozen beans and some other frozen fruits and vegetables.

Three items, tomato soup and two varieties of tomato sauces, were raised one to three points.

The adjustments on processed

Continued on Page Twenty-three

GERMANS HOLD ON

Fiercest Air Support of Mediterranean War Resisted in Italy

COUNTER-BLOW SEEN

Capture of Three More Towns Is Reported—Fifth Army Gains

By MILTON BRACKER
By Wireless to THE NEW YORK TIMES.

ALGIERS, Dec. 1—The smashing British Eighth Army offensive that has now brought the Allies complete control of the ridge dominating the Sangro Valley in the coastal sector surged ahead yesterday against fiercely resisting Germans.

The enemy suffered the heaviest tactical strafing and bombing ever provided by any air force in the entire Mediterranean campaign. But even wave after wave of bombers and fighter-bombers could not rout the Germans, who, it is believed, still cling to the immediately threatened points of Lanciano and Castelfrentano and have yet to throw in a major counter-attack.

The capture of Lanciano, Castelfrentano and Casoli was announced tonight by the Algiers radio, but the broadcast could not be confirmed through regular channels. If true, this would mean that the Eighth Army had surged over at least two-thirds of the inland road loop from San Vito Chietino, on the coast, to Casoli and that, at Castelfrentano, it was within fifteen miles of Chieti, the capital of Abruzzi, just below the Pescara-Rome transverse road.

Germans' Losses Heavy

The Germans have suffered heavy losses in violent hand-to-hand infantry fighting since the British, Indian and New Zealand troops crossed the flood-swollen Sangro River. The enemy has lost killed, wounded and prisoners in a series of stubborn but futile counter-jabs. But, despite the unbalancing of the entire Adriatic defense line by the loss of the ridge below Foccacesia, the Germans show every tendency to keep fighting and there is no indication of an untroubled Allied procession northward to the Pescara-Rome road.

On the Fifth Army's front the situation remains largely unchanged, but Gen. Mark W. Clark's forces made slight gains north of Venafro and generally straightened and consolidated their positions.

The Fifth Army encountered large quantities of barbed wire, which had not been used in this campaign before. It has added to the more modern hazards of mines, demolitions and booby traps.

Artillery exchanges continued all along the front. Our positions at Galluccio, behind the line between Calabritto and Mignano, suffered particularly from violent shelling.

The height of the day's action occurred just before the broad Sangro bridgehead, where nine separate waves of light bombers,

Continued on Page Thirteen

Only 197 of 3,000 Quit in Schools; No Disturbance as AFL Fills Jobs

The strike called yesterday by John L. Lewis' School Custodial Workers Union, Local 112, an affiliate of the United Construction Workers of the United Mine Workers of America, was an almost complete failure.

An official tabulation made public last night by the Bureau of Operations at Police Headquarters showed that only 197 of the 3,000 workers at forty-three of the city's 767 elementary and high schools responded to the strike call issued by Leon Zwicker, regional director of the United Construction Workers, and officials of Local 112. The strikers' places were filled by AFL unions holding jurisdiction over the school custodians and their employes. Not a single school was closed and not a classroom suffered any inconvenience. Mr. Zwicker's boast that at least 2,300 of the 3,000 employes would join the walkout proved to be unfounded.

The police tabulation showed the effects of the strike by boroughs as follows: Manhattan, six schools affected, thirty-four employes absent; Bronx, twenty-one schools, seventy-two absent; Brooklyn, seven schools, forty-three absent; Queens, eight schools, forty-seven absent; Richmond, one school, one absent.

Although Mr. Zwicker had promised that there would be no picketing, a group of pickets appeared at 3 o'clock at the Thomas Jefferson High School in Brooklyn as classes were being dismissed. The pickets did not molest anyone. The police, who kept close watch on the situation, reported no picketing

Continued on Page Twenty-two

PRINCIPALS IN THE WAR CONFERENCE HELD AT CAIRO

Generalissimo Chiang Kai-shek, President Roosevelt, Prime Minister Churchill and Mme. Chiang Kai-shek.
The New York Times (OWI Radiophoto)

FORTRESSES STRIKE AT SOLINGEN AGAIN

Deal Second Heavy Blow in 24 Hours at Cost of 27 Planes—Coast Airdromes Strafed

By DREW MIDDLETON
By Cable to THE NEW YORK TIMES

LONDON, Dec. 1—Strong formations of Flying Fortresses and Liberators battled their way through clouds of German fighters to hammer the important industrial city of Solingen, north of Cologne, in the Rhineland, today, in a most important series of punishing attacks by Allied bombers on German targets in northern Europe. It was the second attack on Solingen in two days.

Bombs cascaded onto Solingen through heavy overcast in another United States Eighth Air Force

Continued on Page Fourteen

Bid to Soviet Is Discerned In Some of 'Stripping' Terms

By JOHN H. CRIDER
Special to THE NEW YORK TIMES.

WASHINGTON, Dec. 1—The dramatic meeting of the Pacific Big Three was hailed in Washington today as a turning point in the war which timed intensification of the drive against Japan with the faster ticking of Germany's clock of doom.

Aside from the tremendous importance to the conduct of the war and to post-war international collaboration attached to President Roosevelt's first meeting with Generalissimo Chiang Kai-shek and his seventh war conference with Prime Minister Churchill, the following points were noted here as of special significance rising out of their joint communiqué:

1. Agreement to strip Japan's empire down to its original basis before the Sino-Japanese War of 1895, is a statement of war aims in the Pacific going beyond "unconditional surrender"—it is unconditional surrender, plus.

2. This stripping of the Japa-

Continued on Page Four

War News Summarized

THURSDAY, DECEMBER 2, 1943

Japan's "East Asia Co-Prosperity" dream has been shattered in Cairo, where President Roosevelt, Prime Minister Churchill and Generalissimo Chiang Kai-shek drew up a Pacific Charter stripping Japan of all her possessions gained since 1895. The highest military leaders of the three United Nations simultaneously perfected plans to make the declaration effective.

The conferences lasted five days, from Nov. 22 to 26. A communiqué issued yesterday declared that the "three great Allies" sought no gain or territory but were pledged to "punish the aggression of Japan" by:

1. Stripping Japan of all her Pacific islands;

2. Returning to China all territory wrested from her, including Manchuria;

3. Granting independence to Korea, and

4. Expelling Japan from all other territory acquired "by violence and greed."

Among the military chiefs in the Cairo talks were Generals Marshall, Eisenhower and Stilwell, and General MacArthur's Chief of Staff, Admirals King and Leahy, Admiral Mountbatten, Air Marshal Tedder and Generals Dill and Alexander. [All the foregoing, 1:8; map P. 5.]

Washington observers believed that the Cairo decision, since it might result in restoring to Russia territory she lost in the Russo-Japanese War, could be viewed as a bid for Soviet military action against Japan. [1:5-6.] London authorities considered Cairo an excellent prelude to a conference with Premier Stalin [3:1], while Axis propagandists sought to belittle the sessions as a sign of Allied weakness. [5:3-4.]

Yesterday saw the return of nearly 1,500 Americans and Canadians from Japanese prison camps. They reached New York on the Gripsholm, but would not talk for fear of reprisals against those still held prisoner. [1:1.]

In the war against Japan Allied warships shelled Madang on New Guinea and Gasmata on New Britain. [1:6-7; map, P. 7.] The Chinese regained full possession of Changteh and recaptured several other cities [11:2], and in Burma Allied fliers battered enemy positions in wide attacks. [8:1.] The Navy announced that our losses on Tarawa were 1,026 killed and 2,557 wounded; on Makin and Abemama sixty-six killed, 123 wounded. [19:1.]

The Eighth Army in Italy pushed ahead against bitter German resistance [1:3] and in Russia Hitler's generals launched numerous counter-attacks in an effort to bring the Red Army advance to a halt. [1:6.] Flying Fortresses attacked Solingen in the Ruhr for the second consecutive day, meeting strong fighter and rocket opposition. We lost twenty-seven bombers. [1:4.]

Sweden lodged a "most urgent request" with Germany, "in the interest of future Swedish-German relations," to cancel the arrest and deportation of 1,200 Norwegian students and professors seized at Oslo. [17:3.]

RED ARMY SLOWED BY GERMAN BLOWS

Only Minor Gains Made as Foe Throws Fresh Forces Into Fierce, Spreading Battles

By The Associated Press.

LONDON, Thursday, Dec. 2—The Germans have struck out with new vigor in every sector of the Russian front in a major bid to stem the Russian offensive, counter-attacking yesterday as many as fifteen times in one area and slowing the Red Army to minor gains along the 600-mile front.

The intensity of the fighting was undiminished, equal perhaps to the heaviest of the war, but Moscow reported only a dozen populated places taken—a slowdown after four months of steady progress. All of them were in three areas—north of Gomel, along the Pripet River and in the Dnieper River bend.

There was fighting in other sectors but it won no mention in either the operational bulletin or the midnight supplement recorded

Continued on Page Twelve

SCENE OF PARLEY LIKE ARMED CAMP

Each Delegate's Villa and Hotel Where Sessions Were Held Under Heavy Guard

By Cable to THE NEW YORK TIMES.

CAIRO, Egypt, Dec. 1—Not since the days of the Ptolemys has Egypt been such a cynosure of attention from the civilized world.

The fact that something big was about to happen was a wide-open secret in the rumor-ridden cities of the African periphery for weeks. Finally, after a flood of rumors, it was blandly announced on the morning of Nov. 22 that Prime Minister Churchill, President Roosevelt and Generalissimo Chiang Kai-shek, accompanied by their principal military advisers, had arrived here.

Chiang Flies in American Plane

Dr. Hollington Tong, the Chinese Vice Minister of Information, then told about the Generalissimo's first visit thus far west except for his trip to Moscow several years ago. The Chinese party came in two four-engined American planes with American crews. General Chiang's plane arrived at 7 P. M. on Nov. 21. Mme. Chiang was not in good health but felt that her presence was needed. Only two long stops were made on the four-day journey, General Chiang's first from China since his trip to India in 1942.

Major George Durno, a former White House correspondent who is handling Mr. Roosevelt's press relations, then spoke of the Presi-

Continued on Page Four

Warships Push Into New Areas To Shell Foe in Southwest Pacific

By The Associated Press.

ALLIED HEADQUARTERS IN THE SOUTHWEST PACIFIC, Thursday, Dec. 2—American light naval craft shelled Gasmata, New Britain, and Madang, New Guinea, during the night and dawn hours of Nov. 29 and 30. It was the first sea bombardment of these enemy strongholds.

The naval vessels—probably destroyers—sought to blast out Japanese shore installations at Gasmata, and aerial spotters, a headquarters spokesman said, termed their marksmanship "effective."

The attack on Madang, strong enemy aerial and barge point on Astrolabe Harbor, northeast New Guinea, was a foray deep into Japanese territory. Shells were hurled into shore installations, and a small, unidentified enemy vessel was sunk in Dallman Passage.

These bold naval strokes not only accelerated the action against the enemy in the New Guinea-New Britain area, which has been pounded heavily by Allied aircraft of late, but also gave some indication of the policies of Vice Admiral Thomas C. Kinkaid, who recently was made chief of naval forces in the Southwest Pacific. It was Admiral Kinkaid who commanded naval forces in the Aleutians when Americans won back Attu and reoccupied Kiska.

In another phase of the concentrated attacks on the enemy's bases in the Southwest Pacific, Allied bombers again hit the Japanese air strips at Cape Gloucester, on the western tip of New Britain,

Continued on Page Seven

ALL-OUT WAR SET

Allies Plan to Retake Manchuria, Formosa and Seized Islands

PLEDGE FREE KOREA

Will Relinquish Own Claims and Help Rebuild China

By C. L. SULZBERGER
By Cable to THE NEW YORK TIMES.

CAIRO, Egypt, Dec. 1—What might be termed a Pacific Charter, outlining a specific program for obtaining the unconditional surrender of Japan and her reduction to her frontiers before 1895 with the ensuing liberation of her vast Asiatic mainland and Pacific island empire, was published tonight following a sensational five-day series of conferences among President Roosevelt, Prime Minister Churchill and Generalissimo Chiang Kai-shek and their principal military and political staffs.

The meetings took place somewhere in Africa from Nov. 22 through Nov. 26. All Allied principals departed for unannounced destinations before the disclosure of a historic communiqué outlining crystallized Allied pledges, dated Cairo, Dec. 1.

In brief this document promised full agreement on the strategy of future military operations against Japan that the three great powers discussed.

It resolved:

1. To press unrelentingly the war against their brutal enemies by sea, land and air and stated that pressure is already rising.
2. To renounce all territorial gains for themselves and to strip the Japanese of all Pacific islands seized since 1914.
3. To restore to China the lost lands of Manchuria, Formosa and the Pescadores.
4. To expel Japan from all other territories she has taken by violence and greed.
5. To guarantee the future independence of enslaved Korea.
6. To persevere in the serious and prolonged operations necessary to procure the unconditional surrender of Japan.

Confer Day and Night

These grimly determined pledges to reduce the Japanese Empire to the non-menacing status of those days prior to the date when, by seizing Formosa in 1895, later expanding at the expense of Russia, Korea and China and finally climbing on the Allied bandwagon in the last war, she seized strategic German island positions and has never ceased expanding, were formulated at a series of day and night staff talks in which virtually every military luminary of the three powers except Gen. Douglas MacArthur as well as numerous political leaders participated. General MacArthur was represented by his Chief of Staff, Major Gen. Richard K. Sutherland.

It is obvious both from the type of strategic talks held, whose specific results obviously are the most secret, and the political pledges from the chiefs of state that any criticism to the effect that the Asiatic war will be considered a "second class" affray must now be ended.

China's position as a great power ally, already boosted as a result of the Moscow conference, now unquestionably is established on terms of full equality, and it is equally certain that the Anglo-American delegates considered the war in Europe now advanced far enough toward victory so that increased attention could be directed toward Asia.

It was the first face-to-face meeting for Generalissimo Chiang with either President Roosevelt or Prime Minister Churchill. The chiefs of state were in constant consultation throughout the parleys, which were held in their residences with the Generalissimo's wife, who accompanied Generalissimo Chiang's delegation as an interpreter. The purely strategic

Continued on Page Three

"All the News That's Fit to Print."

The New York Times.

LATE CITY EDITION
Cloudy, little change in temperature today; moderate winds.
Temperatures Yesterday—Max., 52; Min., 46
Sunrise, 6:?6 A. M.; Sunset, 5:29 P. M.

Copyright, 1943, by The New York Times Company.

VOL. XCIII..No. 31,360. Entered as Second-Class Matter, Postoffice, New York, N. Y. NEW YORK, SATURDAY, DECEMBER 4, 1943. THREE CENTS IN NEW YORK CITY

ROOSEVELT, STALIN, CHURCHILL AGREE ON PLANS FOR WAR ON GERMANY IN TALKS AT TEHERAN; 1,500 MORE TONS OF BOMBS DROPPED ON BERLIN

SOLDIER-VOTE BILL SHIFTED BY SENATE TO LET STATES RULE

Republicans Join With Southern Democrats in Scrapping the Plan for Federal Control

CONGRESS ONLY TO ADVISE

Opponents Charge Substitute Will Make Balloting Impossible for Forces Abroad

By C. P. TRUSSELL
Special to THE NEW YORK TIMES.

WASHINGTON, Dec. 3—After spending six days in rewriting the Green-Lucas Service Men's Absentee Voting Bill, the Senate threw that measure aside today and passed instead, by a vote of 42 to 37, a substitute sponsored by three Southern Democrats which would put the balloting program for the armed forces back into the hands of State election officials and under State laws.

The substitute now goes to the House, where key men predicted tonight that it would be adopted there in principle if not with the same text.

The Senate's shift from its extensive patchwork on the program of the coalition which chose the substitute measure came quickly. Senators who had been successful in getting amendments into the original measure, seeing what was coming, moved to transfer their proposals to the State law program before it was brought to its showdown vote.

Sponsored by Senators James O. Eastland of Mississippi, John I. McClellan of Arkansas and Kenneth McKellar of Tennessee, the substitute won the votes of twenty-four Democrats, including all thirteen representatives of poll tax States who were present (Alabama, Arkansas, Georgia, Mississippi, South Carolina, Tennessee, Texas and Virginia) and of eighteen Republicans. Twenty-five Democrats and twelve Republicans opposed it. The much amended Green-Lucas bill, brought in by the Committee on Privileges and Elections was thus not permitted to come to a vote.

Some Easterners for Change

Among the Democratic Senators voting for the substitute were Gerry of Rhode Island, Walsh of Massachusetts and Walsh of New Jersey. The Republican group favoring the substitute included Buck of Delaware, Danaher of Connecticut, Hawkes of New Jersey, Tobey of New Hampshire and White of Maine.

Senator Scott W. Lucas, Democrat, of Illinois, co-author of the Green-Lucas bill, declared today's action "the hardest blow that was ever struck at the political rights of a soldier in time of war."

"Those who favored the passage of this amendment will have to accept the responsibility to the soldiers, their fathers, mothers, wives and friends," he said.

Supporters of the Green-Lucas bill, who insisted that the measure would permit service men and women throughout the world to take part by millions in the election of the President, Vice President and Seventy-ninth Congress next year, contended that the Eastland-McClellan-McKellar substitute would make it "impossible," because of restrictions in State election laws, for those serving overseas to vote.

Those supporting the substitute contended that it would "make the service absentee voting program constitutional" and put the responsibility for getting out the vote of their citizens upon the States themselves. They said that they did not share the disbelief expressed by supporters of the Green-Lucas bill that Legislatures would get busy and amend their election laws so as to make possible absentee voting by those in the armed forces from their States, here and abroad.

Power Only to Recommend

By the terms of the substitute, Congress instead of setting up a Federal War Ballot Commission to administer the absentee-voting program and prescribing the system of balloting, would express itself as favoring and recommending to the States that they enact legis-

Continued on Page Eight

British Reveal Cost of Fields Lent to Us

By Cable to THE NEW YORK TIMES.

LONDON, Dec. 3—Britain is spending more than the equivalent of $4,000,000 for each airfield being used by the United States Air Forces in this country, the Committee of Public Accounts made known today. This is written down as reciprocal aid.

The question of reconverting the land to its original use will be one for Parliament to settle, since the cost of ripping up the concrete runways and removing buildings will be high, far more than the cost of buying the land.

OLIVE OIL IMPORTS ARE BANNED BY U. S.

Importers Here Say Bumper Crop in Mediterranean Area May Go Begging

By JEFFERSON G. BELL

New York importers disclosed yesterday that the Mediterranean area's bumper crop of olive oil this year may go begging. They revealed that to date they had failed to win the State Department's permission to bring in some 3,000,000 gallons to ease the domestic shortage.

As the nation's relief program contemplates the shipment of some 2,000,000,000 pounds of fats and oils abroad, the olive oil importers were not impressed by the State Department's reasons for not issuing a permit for importation.

Nine European occupied countries exclusive of Soviet Russia have reported to the United Nations Relief and Rehabilitation Administration that in the first six months following the cessation of hostilities their aggregate needs of oilseeds, oils and fats requiring shipping space will be approximately 1,076,000 metric tons.

The Olive Oil Association of America, Inc., 52 Stone Street, disclosed that its usual sources had reported that not only Spain and Portugal but even war-torn Tunisia were harvesting a record-breaking crop of olive oil.

Members said that there was virtually no demand for the surplus among southern Europeans. They added that Norway, which normally used substantial quantities for its sardine packing, had been entirely cut off from the market since German occupation.

Bumper Crop in Spain Seen

"Reliable reports indicate that Spain will have a bumper crop of olive oil this year," declared the Olive Oil Association of America, Inc. "The figure is said to exceed 425,000 tons—about 123,250,000 gallons. This constitutes one of the best productions of olive oil in the history of Spain and, for the first time in many years, leaves a sizable export surplus. The domestic consumption in Spain is about 300,000 tons, thus, there should be available for export and stockpiling 125,000 tons.

"Due, no doubt, to the insistence of the olive oil importers and packers in the United States, under leadership of the Olive Oil Association of America, Inc., an associa-

Continued on Page Fourteen

1,000 BIG BOMBERS, 7,789 OTHER PLANES BUILT IN NOVEMBER

Record Productions Achieved at Pace of One Every Five Minutes Around Clock

NEW PEAKS IN NAVY YARDS

250,000-Ton Output Is Largely of Combat Ships, Among Them Many Aircraft Carriers

Special to THE NEW YORK TIMES.

WASHINGTON, Dec. 3—More than 1,000 four-engined bombers were among 8,789 planes turned out by aircraft factories in November, and about a dozen aircraft carriers were included in more than 250,000 standard displacement tons of naval craft completed in shipyards during the month, which set new records in war production.

Announcements of the production achievements were made today by Donald M. Nelson, chairman of the War Production Board; Frank Knox, Secretary of the Navy, and James Forrestal, Under-Secretary in charge of the Navy's program.

November airplane production was 97 per cent of the month's goal and brought the total of planes produced this year to 76,000. A plane goal for 1943 of 125,000 was announced by President Roosevelt on Jan. 6, 1942, but this figure was revised downward as average plane weights were revised upward.

Airplanes rolled off the production lines continuously day and night at a rate faster than one every five minutes, exceeded the October output by 427 planes, notwithstanding the shorter month, and exceeded the total weight of October's output by 7 per cent, Mr. Nelson reported.

2,000 Planes for the Navy

The Navy's war contractors turned out well over 2,000 planes, of which nearly 2,000 were fighters and bombers, Mr. Knox said. He declared he was particularly gratified by the excellent fighter plane production record, since the Navy had set "extremely steep" schedules to make up for delays caused by the introduction of two new types, the Corsair and the Hellcat.

"By far the largest percentage" of the more than 250,000 tons of ships produced were combat vessels, but the Secretary said he was unable to reveal the exact number of carriers completed. Eight were escort carriers, however. The Wasp, of 27,000 tons, was completed Nov. 24, it had been previously announced.

Under-Secretary Forrestal said that the Navy should be able to turn out at least eight aircraft carriers each month now, including the converted merchantman "Baby Flat-top" type. Several admirals in charge of war output bureaus reported that, for the most part, production bottlenecks had been "licked."

This week-end President Roosevelt's 1943 goal of 260 destroyer

Continued on Page Four

Heavy 'Retaliation' Threatened by Nazis

By The Associated Press.

LONDON, Dec. 3 — Again threatening retaliation for the air war upon Germany, the Berlin radio said today that the German High Command "intends by one fell, drastic stroke to end the unbridled mass murder," and added that "mankind is not far from the point where it can at will blow up half the globe."

The broadcast quoted the periodical Reich as saying that "the commencement of retaliation no longer depends on technical matters, but solely on the object which is to be attained by it."

"The retaliation," it continues, "will be so powerful and will be started at such a psychologically opportune moment as to influence the development of the war. It would be superfluous to retaliate for ruins with ruins. The sense of retaliation will find quite a different and surprising expression spiritually as well as politically."

WALKER OPPOSES POSTAL RATE RISES

Tells Senators Department Is Studying Issue — Swope Fights Racing Levy

Special to THE NEW YORK TIMES.

WASHINGTON, Dec. 3—Postmaster General Frank C. Walker opposed before the Senate Finance Committee today the increase in postal rates carried in the $2,140,000,000 tax bill passed by the House.

Other witnesses opposed the increase in the fur tax carried in the House bill; the proposed 5 per cent pari-mutuel tax and a proposal to place a graduated tax on distilled spirits held in a bonded warehouse longer than four years. The witnesses who appeared in opposition to the liquor and pari-mutuel increases were questioned by Senator Alben W. Barkley of Kentucky, majority leader, apparently indicating sympathy with their position.

Drew Pearson, newspaper columnist, was scheduled to appear for questioning regarding published statements made by him that Ellsworth C. Alvord, Wash-

Continued on Page Eight

AIR BATTLES SHARP

Nazi Fighters and Guns Down 41 of RAF's Attacking Planes

SOUTH BERLIN HIT

New Factory Area the Target in Fifth Heavy Blow in 15 Nights

By DREW MIDDLETON
By Cable to THE NEW YORK TIMES.

LONDON, Dec. 3—More than 500 Lancaster and Halifax bombers of the Royal Air Force cracked the strongest defense the Germans had yet been able to organize and hammered Berlin last night with more than 1,500 long tons of bombs in a signal victory.

Great fires raging in the south and southeastern sections of the Reich capital were visible 200 miles from the target as the British and Canadian formations flew homeward.

What was believed to be the largest night engagement of the air war was fought along the approaches to Berlin and over the city during the fifth major assault on Berlin in fifteen nights. More than 500 Nazi fighters, favored by every advantage the weather could give, hacked at the RAF planes.

Forty-one bombers, one of them a Canadian craft, were missing as a result of the enemy's interception and very heavy anti-aircraft fire.

[London officials said early today that British bombers during the night again attacked Germany. The announcement followed reports that RAF formations had flown out toward the Continent after midnight, a change in timing from the evening operations of previous big blows in the current aerial offensive.]

Despite the well-planned defense, including an "avenue of flares" starting fifty miles from Berlin, returning British fliers said, the big bombers penetrated to the areas marked out by pathfinder planes and bombed their targets heavily. They shot down three Nazi fighters during the attack, which began just after 8 o'clock

Continued on Page Four

8th Army Drives 6 Miles Up Coast Toward San Vito

Town 15 Miles From Key to Road to Rome Is Reported Taken — Inland, Montgomery Wins Castelfrentano—5th Army Gains

By MILTON BRACKER
By Wireless to THE NEW YORK TIMES.

ALGIERS, Dec. 3—The Eighth Army has captured Castelfrentano and moved up the coastal road from Fossacesia toward San Vito. [The coastal advance covered six miles, The Associated Press said.]

The Allied air offensive continued with increasing violence in front of the Fifth Army, notably at points around Cassino, and Royal Air Force Spitfire pilots reported fierce fighting between the Germans and Lieut. Gen. Mark W. Clark's American and British forces.

The progress of Gen. Sir Bernard L. Montgomery's British, New Zealand and Indian troops on the Adriatic front was somewhat slower than the day before. The enemy repeatedly counter-attacked at Castelfrentano after the Allies had seized the town and a furious battle was going on for Lanciano, three miles nearer the coast than Castelfrentano along the inland road loop. Mines and demolitions continued to impede the advance.

[The Algiers radio reported that the Eighth Army had captured San Vito, which is fifteen miles from its objective, Pescara, and a DNB broadcast from Berlin said that the Germans had evacuated Lanciano.]

No details were available here regarding the bitter fighting on the Fifth Army front observed by British airmen, but it was officially announced that General Clark's men had managed to make short

Continued on Page Five

Red Army Tightens Noose On Rail Junction of Zhlobin

By The Associated Press.

LONDON, Saturday, Dec. 4—Mud-spattered Red Army troops bit into the important German railway network northwest of Gomel in two directions yesterday, stood firm against repeated Nazi counter-attacks in the hotly contested Cherkassy area and expanded their Dnieper River bridgehead below Kremenchug to twenty miles west of the city through powerfully defended territory, Moscow announced early today.

German troops recoiling before the Russian attacks northwest of Gomel suffered heavy losses, the Soviet midnight bulletin said, as the Russians swept up more than 100 villages and hamlets. Key points taken in this drive—carried out through blizzards, howling winds and rain—were Sverzhin and Dovsk, twelve miles and eighteen miles east of Rogachev, respectively, and Soltanovka, twelve miles southeast of Zhlobin on the Gomel railroad.

[An additional thrust beyond Soltanovka carried the Red Army to the village of Staraya Rudnya, nine miles southeast of Zhlobin.]

The towns captured yesterday screen the approaches to the hubs of the German rail network in that region — Zhlobin and Rogachev. Seven hundred Germans were killed alone in one sector of the fighting in that area.

Determined Soviet troops, blasting their way forward through complex German trench systems and dug-outs protected by mine fields and barbed wire entanglements, took Novogeorgiyevsk, a district center of the Kirovograd region, and killed hundreds of Germans, the communiqué said.

[The Russians also announced the capture of Klochkovo, twenty miles west of Kremenchug along the right bank of the Dnieper.]

With their westward thrust into the Dnieper sack below Kremenchug the Russians moved to relieve the pressure on their com-

Continued on Page Six

AUSTRALIANS PERIL ANOTHER HUON BASE

Close In on Wareo, Japanese Stronghold in New Guinea—New Britain Is Battered

By The Associated Press.

ALLIED HEADQUARTERS IN THE SOUTHWEST PACIFIC, Saturday, Dec. 4—Australian jungle troops, supported by artillery, are closing in on Wareo, a Japanese stronghold on the Huon Peninsula of northeastern New Guinea.

Wareo is inland about eleven miles northwest of coastal Finschhafen, the base which the Allies captured Oct. 2.

Gen. Douglas MacArthur's headquarters, announcing the latest progress today, said that the Australians were mopping up on enemy strong points along the track that leads from Allied-won Bonga on the coast north of Finschhafen westward to Wareo.

To the east, just across narrow waters from the peninsula, General MacArthur's bombers continued to hit at targets on New Britain in an area of that important enemy island that is most vulnerable to invasion.

For the second straight day Borgen Bay's dumps and supply barges were the targets. Sixty-three tons of explosives were dropped by Mitchell medium bomb-

Continued on Page Three

DECISIONS VARIED

Moscow Radio Asserts Political Problems Were Settled

PARLEY NOW IS OVER

Axis Reports Predict an Appeal to Germans to Quit Hitler

By JAMES B. RESTON
By Cable to THE NEW YORK TIMES.

LONDON, Saturday, Dec. 4—The Moscow radio announced early this morning that President Roosevelt, Prime Minister Churchill and Premier Stalin had met in Teheran, Iran, "a few days ago" to discuss questions relating to the war and the post-war period.

"A few days ago," the Moscow radio said shortly after midnight, "a conference of the leaders of the three Allied nations — President Roosevelt, Prime Minister Churchill and Premier Stalin—took place at Teheran.

"Military and diplomatic representatives also took part. The questions discussed at the conference related to the war against Germany and also to a range of political questions. Decisions were taken which will be published later."

[An Associated Press dispatch from London quoted the Soviet monitor as saying that full details of the conference might be announced between noon and 2 P. M., Eastern war time today, basing this prediction on the usual routine of the Moscow radio when announcing future broadcasts.]

The radio announcement, which came as a surprise to official quarters in London, said nothing about the present location of Mr. Roosevelt and Mr. Churchill, who held a five-day meeting with Generalissimo Chiang Kai-shek last week and made plans for the defeat of the Japanese and the dismemberment of their empire.

Details Are Awaited

Early this morning the Moscow radio had not indicated the nature of political and military discussions that took place in the Iranian capital, but it was generally assumed they dealt with the coordination of military plans for the final assault on Hitlerite Germany and with the unification of political plans for making peace with Germany on the basis of "unconditional surrender."

Official information that has come back to London since the Prime Minister left the capital has been extremely limited and indeed until the Moscow radio made its announcement the German radio was the main source of reports on the movements of the three leaders. It was, however, generally expected in London that the three leaders would in the course of their discussions decide to appeal to the German people over the heads of their Government to surrender or take the consequences of the air war in the west and an invasion of Russian armies from the east.

Stalin Crosses Own Border

While Mr. Churchill and Mr. Roosevelt had had seven previous conferences on the war, this was the first among the three leaders, and so far as is known it marked the first time that Mr. Stalin had left the Soviet Union since the revolution in 1917. The meeting was foreshadowed after the Quebec conference when Mr. Churchill told the House of Commons he "hoped" to meet with Mr. Roosevelt and Mr. Stalin before the first of the year.

The Prime Minister had met Premier Stalin once before in the autumn of 1942, when he journeyed to Moscow to explain to him why it was impossible for the United States and Britain to invade the continent of Europe from the west that year.

Previous to that conference the United States and Britain had undertaken to concern themselves with the "urgent tasks" of creating a second front in 1942, and it is now known that the first Stalin-

Continued on Page Two

Longo, Hague Foe, Is Imprisoned; Edison Joins U. S. Inquiry Plea

Special to THE NEW YORK TIMES.

JERSEY CITY, N. J., Dec. 3—John R. Longo, former deputy Hudson County clerk and long a political foe of Mayor Frank Hague of this city, was sentenced today by Judge Thomas H. Brown to a prison term of eighteen months to three years on a charge of "fraudulently altering" his voting record.

The sentencing of Longo came only a few hours after Gov. Charles Edison declared it was "not only the right but the imperative duty" of the Department of Justice to investigate alleged suppression of civil rights in Hudson County. The investigation was demanded in a petition filed yesterday by the City Affairs Committee of Jersey City with United States Attorney General Francis J. Biddle. The Longo case was one of several cited as emphasizing a need for the inquiry.

Governor Edison said that under the "ineffective 99-year-old State Constitution few powers are granted to a Governor of New Jersey and among the powers he lacks is that of protecting the civil liberties of the people of his State." The Governor added that he "deeply regretted the existence of the situation complained of in Jersey City."

Longo, convicted Nov. 15 by a jury before Judge Brown, was denied a certificate of reasonable doubt by Judge Brown today after Raymond Chasan, his counsel, presented a writ of error, issued by the New Jersey Supreme Court, to the judge. In denying the certifi-

Continued on Page Twenty-six

War News Summarized

SATURDAY, DECEMBER 4, 1943

The Moscow radio announced last night that the historic conference of President Roosevelt, Prime Minister Churchill and Marshal Stalin was held "a few days ago" in Teheran, Iran, and that plans were laid to knock Germany out of the war. Political as well as military questions were discussed by diplomatic and military representatives, with the decisions to be given to the public later. [1:8.]

Meeting the stiffest resistance to date, 500 Lancaster and Halifax bombers dropped more than 1,500 tons of bombs on Berlin in Thursday night's attack, the fifth heavy blow there in fifteen nights. Huge fires in Berlin's southern and southeastern industrial sections were visible 200 miles away, but the RAF lost forty-one bombers at the hands of 500 German night fighters. [1:5.] In November more than 13,000 tons of British bombs hit Germany in ten major attacks. [1:6-7.]

In the Mediterranean area, the assault on the Marseille submarine pens also unleashed fierce air fighting, twenty-five German pursuit planes attacking the American Fortresses. All the bombers returned and eleven Germans were downed. Three Lightnings and four enemy fighters were lost yesterday in renewed attacks on Bolzano. [5:1.]

Throwing back repeated counter-attacks in Italy the Eighth Army captured Castelfrentano and moved north along the Adriatic coastal road toward San Vito. The Fifth Army, under increasing air cover, advanced locally near Calabritto. [1:6-7; map, P. 5.] General Clark himself was under fire, but was unhurt. [5:2-3.]

Soviet armies, moving south along the Dnieper River to outflank the railroad junction of Zhlobin, took the highway center of Dovsk, while other troops occupied Soltanovka, twelve miles southeast of the town. The Russians fought off attacks on their Cherkassy bridgehead and took Novogeorgiyevsk, four miles west of Kremenchug. [1:6-7; map, P. 6.]

Evidently fearing a Balkan invasion following the Teheran conference, the Germans were reported sending thousands of reinforcements to Yugoslavia. Troops were massing at Metkovic, in northern Dalmatia, Partisan reports said. [6:2.]

Washington believed President Benes of Czechoslovakia attended the Allied conference, acting as mediator in the Russo-Polish dispute. [2:8.]

Answering critics of heavy marine losses at Tarawa, Secretary of the Navy Knox told a press conference the island was struck by 2,900 tons of bombs and shells before the landing—more than fell on Berlin in the heaviest air attack. [3:1.]

In the southwest Pacific, Australian troops with artillery support closed in on the Japanese stronghold of Wareo, eleven miles from Finschhafen on New Guinea's Huon peninsula. Bombers hit Borgen Bay, New Britain, and the Kara and Ballale airdromes in the Bougainville sector. [1:7.]

RAF's Twin-Target Tactics Show Power in Month's Blows at Reich

By Cable to THE NEW YORK TIMES.

LONDON, Dec. 3—The British Air Ministry, outlining today the triumphs of the Anglo-American bombers in this theatre during November, when the Allies dropped 22,170 tons of bombs on Germany and Nazi-occupied territory — a figure that is believed to represent a record—stressed the importance of the twin-target type of attack in the winter air war tactics.

Three of the four heaviest Royal Air Force assaults on Germany last month were of this type, with two high-priority targets bombed simultaneously, thus splitting the Luftwaffe's interceptor forces and preventing the concentration of Nazi mobile anti-aircraft artillery around one target, such as Berlin.

The three twin-target assaults that featured the RAF's November operations were in "very great strength" — the Air Ministry's highest category of attacks. Others are in "great strength," such as last night's assault on Berlin, and "medium" and "moderate" attacks.

The writer estimates that "very great strength" means 750 to 1,000 bombers employed and "great strength" represents the use of 500 to 750 planes.

The twin-target attacks were the nights of Nov. 3, on Duesseldorf and Cologne; Nov. 18, Berlin and Ludwigshafen, and Nov. 26, Berlin and Stuttgart.

These blows and the concentrated attack on Berlin the night of Nov. 22 were the heaviest in a month in which 13,000 tons of British bombs fell on Germany and another 1,500 tons on occupied ter-

Continued on Page Four

"All the News That's Fit to Print."

The New York Times.

LATE CITY EDITION
Showers in forenoon; clear in afternoon; fair at night.
Temperatures Yesterday—Max., 50; Min., 35
Sunrise, 8:06 A. M.; Sunset, 5:29 P. M.

VOL. XCIII...No. 31,363. Entered as Second-Class Matter, Postoffice, New York, N. Y. NEW YORK, TUESDAY, DECEMBER 7, 1943. THREE CENTS IN NEW YORK CITY

'BIG 3' CHARTS TRIPLE BLOWS TO HUMBLE REICH AND AGREES ON A PEACE TO ELIMINATE TYRANNY; CARRIERS ATTACK MARSHALLS; 5TH ARMY GAINS

MAYOR PORTRAYED AS SCHOOL RULER BY OUSTED OFFICIAL

Kuper, Former Law Adviser to Board, Tells NEA Inquiry Appointments Were Blocked

SEES MORALE IMPAIRED

Fear of Having Funds Held Up Kept the Members From Asserting Rights, He Says

Charges that Mayor La Guardia has interfered with the city school system, causing educational officials to bow to his will and robbing the Board of Education of its independence by threatening to withhold funds, were made at the National Education Association school inquiry, which began public hearings here yesterday.

A behind-the-scenes version of how the board operates, and of the role of the Mayor in deciding matters of school policy, was presented by Theodore Fred Kuper, law secretary of the board for eleven years until he was dismissed recently by order of the Mayor. Mr. Kuper took the witness stand at 10 A. M. and did not complete his testimony until the hearing adjourned late in the afternoon.

Hearing in Bar Building

Held in the trial room of the Bar Association Building, 42 West Forty-fourth Street, the open sessions are the culmination of three months of investigation and study by the National Education Association's panel of educators appointed to determine the charges of City Hall interference with school issues.

Dr. Ernest E. Cole, former New York State Commissioner of Education, who is acting as counsel for the inquiry, is conducting the hearings. Members of the panel include Dr. Orville C. Pratt, past president of the NEA and superintendent emeritus of schools at Spokane, Wash.; Dr. Ernest O. Melby, chancellor of the University of Montana; Miss Mabel Studebaker, president of the NEA's department of classroom teachers, and Dr. Donald DuShane, past president of the NEA and secretary of its commission for the defense of democracy through education.

Representatives of various school, civic and parents' groups appeared at the opening session. The investigation was requested by the New York High School Teachers Association and the Kindergarten-6B Teachers Association, two of the city's largest educational bodies. Mrs. Johanna M. Lindlof, president of the kindergarten group and former Board of Education member, sat through the entire session; she is to take the stand this morning.

Testimony by Kuper

Mr. Kuper marshaled a parade of statements and figures to support his contention that Mayor La Guardia interfered with local school independence and "frightened" board officials into submission. He cited incidents to illustrate the many points he raised. Members of the panel or Dr. Cole interrupted frequently to ask questions.

As a result of the Mayor's control over the school board 100 appointments to clerical and administrative positions, for which funds were provided in the budget, have been blocked, Mr. Kuper declared. This has resulted in decreased efficiency as well as a lowering of morale among the employes, he testified.

Important administrative positions, which the board sought to fill and for which money was present in the budget, remain vacant because the city Budget Director does not give the necessary certificates, it was brought out. One instance was cited in which the Superintendent of Plant Operation and Maintenance requested a supervising custodian; the position was approved by the Board of Education, but it took 404 days before the Mayor gave his consent.

"Bear in mind that the Board of Education has the inherent legal power and, in my opinion, the duty to fill these positions," Mr. Kuper

Continued on Page Twenty

Stalin Says U. S. Aid Saved the Allies

By Cable to The New York Times.

CAIRO, Egypt, Dec. 6—The greatest tribute possibly ever paid American industrial production came from Premier Stalin during the Teheran talks.

In a toast at a dinner party the Soviet Premier said:

"Without American machines the United Nations never could have won the war."

He should know.

It is understood Premier Stalin said Russia was manufacturing 3,000 planes monthly against 3,500 British and 10,000 American.

FROZEN FOOD SPACE IS TO BE EXPANDED

Warehouses Here Are to Add Million Cubic Feet—Row Brews Over U. S. Hoards

By JEFFERSON G. BELL

Major warehouse interests of New York City disclosed yesterday that they already had taken steps to expand freezer capacity at least 1,000,000 cubic feet. This move is part of a program to ease storage, transportation and other problems caused by the Federal Government's vast hoard of food.

The Government stockpiles have so taxed the capacity of warehouses, notably freezer space, that the Office of Defense Transportation last week appealed for help to the War Food Administration and the Office of Price Administration.

The refrigeration expansion program was revealed by local WFA and warehouse spokesmen as chilly relations between national WFA and OPA on one side and ODT on the other threatened to develop into an interdepartmental row over charges that foods needed by civilians are being allowed to deteriorate or spoil because of improper warehousing.

Release of Supplies Suggested

In view of the explanation by warehouse interests here that they could not increase their freezer capacity sooner than sixty to ninety days, food-trade circles were unable to see what would be the solution of warehouse congestion unless supplies were released.

When Joseph B. Eastman, director of the Office of Defense Transportation, confirmed last week reports that he had asked WFA and OPA to take steps to ease the congestion of freezer facilities, he disclosed that he had received a letter promising "immediate" action. Neither Mr. Eastman nor any member of the ODT staff was reached yesterday for comment on the disclosure that plans for freezer expansion here held no promise of relief for another two or three months.

The local office of the Food Distribution Administration, WFA, 150 Broadway, disclosed that a survey of storage facilities here had showed that New York City warehouses are operating at 89 per cent of capacity.

"When we are operating at 90 to 95 per cent of capacity," explained

Continued on Page Twenty-three

BATTLING IN ITALY

3 More Camino Peaks Are Taken Despite Fierce Resistance

COUNTER-BLOW FAILS

Germans Beaten Back at Venafro—Eighth Army at Moro River

By MILTON BRACKER
By Wireless to The New York Times.

ALGIERS, Dec. 6—The battle of the mountains continued yesterday in Italy as Lieut. Gen. Mark W. Clark's Fifth Army wrested three more peaks of the Mount Camino group from the Germans, who are putting up a fanatic battle for every inch of the rocky ground.

The slow and tortuous envelopment of the numberless ridges and peaks proceeded in an epic of difficult fighting in which the individual soldier had to combine the technique of the jungle fighter with that of the mountain goat. More rain tended to retard the four-day-old offensive as German gunfire swept the slopes and crevices from deeply dug-in positions. But the British and American infantry ground steadily forward and mopped up the isolated resistance strong points by-passed by the Allies' spearheads.

There is at least one ridge that our forces have pressed beyond and flanked without being able to silence the German fire from its crest. The entire tone of the struggle is one of a fierce will to resist. Despite severe losses, the German Tenth Army is setting a standard of savage defensive fighting that its opponents will never forget.

[American artillery has begun shelling Cassino, The United Press reported.]

Counter-Attack Repulsed

In the Venafro sector of the Fifth Army's front, above the Via Casilina, the Germans flung in another sharp counter-attack against American units. As they have done several times before, the Americans hurled back the attack, leaving the positions in this sector about the same.

On the British Eighth Army's front, too, the weather was bad. The Germans poured in reinforcements as the battles for Orsogna and Guardiagrele raged unabated. Both points remained in the enemy's hands.

The Eighth Army has, in general, pressed nearer to the Moro River from San Vito Chietino, however, and, at Casone, some four miles inland, three miles above Lanciano and 1,000 yards from the Moro's south bank, the Allies' infantry and tanks crushed several advanced German machine-gun posts in their drive to the bank.

The Eighth Army captured at least one German tank that proved to be without question a flame-thrower. This settled the dispute that began here on Nov. 29, when a flame-throwing tank was first

Continued on Page Sixteen

THE LEADERS OF THE 'BIG THREE' MEET IN TEHERAN

Marshal Stalin, President Roosevelt and Prime Minister Churchill on the porch of the Russian Embassy

The New York Times (U. S. Twelfth Air Force)

HEAVY TASK FORCES STRIKE IN PACIFIC

Blow at the Marshall Islands Comes as Allies Step Up Air Drive Against New Britain

By GEORGE F. HORNE
By Telephone to The New York Times.

PEARL HARBOR, Dec. 6—Strong carrier task forces and heavy Navy bombers have attacked a number of bases in the Japanese-held Marshall Islands in the last few days, indicating a new development in the central Pacific offensive, which was touched off by our invasion of the Gilbert Islands.

[In the southwest Pacific, Allied fliers struck with increasing violence against invasion-menaced New Britain Island, on which lies Rabaul, main Japanese base in that war theatre. Our airmen poured 155

Continued on Page Seventeen

New Cairo Talks Reported To Get Turkey to Join War

By JAMES B. RESTON
By Wireless to The New York Times.

LONDON, Dec. 6—The conversations that Prime Minister Churchill and, presumably, President Roosevelt had with President Ismet Inonu of Turkey in Cairo after the Teheran parleys have led to considerable speculation about the possibility of Turkey's entering the war. The background of these conversations would seem to justify this speculation. The question for Turkey, as an ally of Britain, now seems to be not whether but when and how she will help the Allies. This, it is presumed, is the question being discussed by Messrs. Churchill and Inonu.

[Reports that Messrs. Churchill, Roosevelt and Inonu were conferring in Africa have come from enemy and neutral sources.]

The basis of these conversations is the Anglo-French-Turkish treaty of alliance of Oct. 19, 1939. Article II stated: "In the event of an act of aggression by a European power

Continued on Page Seven

UKRAINE RAILWAY IS CUT BY RUSSIANS

Huge German Forces Are Split—Red Army Is Only 23 Miles From Kirovograd

By The Associated Press.

LONDON, Tuesday, Dec. 7—Russian troops smashed the enemy's Smela-Znamenka line in the central Ukraine yesterday, splitting huge German forces guarding those vital junctions on railways leading to Rumania and putting the Red Army within twenty-three miles of the Axis bastion of Kirovograd.

A Moscow communiqué and a midnight supplement announced the capture of Tsybulevo, eight miles northwest of Znamenka on the double-track railway leading to Smela, and the fall of Alexandriya, twenty miles east of Znamenka. Twenty other towns and villages were swept up, said the bulletin, recorded by the Soviet monitor from a Moscow broadcast.

[The crossing of the Znamenka-Smela line probably took place in the Krasnoselye-Tsybulevo sector. Each village is two miles from the railroad line and represents the farthest penetration in yesterday's advance.

Continued on Page Twelve

WASHINGTON HAILS UNITY AT TEHERAN

Hull Stresses 'Concerting' of Plans to Crush Axis Forces—Congress Leaders Pleased

By BERTRAM D. HULEN
Special to The New York Times.

WASHINGTON, Dec. 6—Opinion in the executive branch of the Government concerning both the Teheran and the Cairo conferences was set forth by Secretary of State Cordell Hull today in a statement declaring that the concerted plans adopted "will undoubtedly result in making effective to the fullest extent the fighting strength of all of the United Nations."

Opinion in general in the capital was that the communiqué issued on the Teheran conference showed that the three Chiefs of Government, President Roosevelt, Prime Minister Churchill and Premier Stalin, had had a meeting of minds and had reached detailed decisions for destroying the German Army, even though the declaration, perhaps significantly, did not use the phrase "unconditional surrender."

All in all, the announcement gave grounds for encouragement at a time when America is entering the third year of the war.

Way Open for Small Nations

It was of first importance that the three leaders had met, it was felt. And in meeting they had agreed to cooperate in the war and in the peace, and to invite the collaboration of small nations.

There were conjectures as to whether this collaboration might include the German people, if they sought it as a chastened people free of nazism and militarism.

Military details, obviously, could not be revealed, it was realized, but

Continued on Page Eleven

War News Summarized

TUESDAY, DECEMBER 7, 1943

President Roosevelt, Premier Stalin and Prime Minister Churchill announced to the world yesterday that "no power on earth can prevent our destroying the German armies by land, their U-boats by sea and their war plants from the air."

The three leaders, in a declaration dated Teheran, Dec. 1, said they had "reached complete agreement as to the scope and timing of operations which will be undertaken from the east, west and south."

"We came here with hope and determination," the three men said. "We leave here friends in fact, in spirit and in purpose." One of the purposes is to "work together in the peace" that will follow the war. All countries, large and small, were invited into "a world family of democratic nations" pledged to eliminate tyranny, oppression and intolerance and to "banish the scourge and terror of war for many generations."

In a second declaration the conferees pledged the independence and territorial integrity of Iran as a token of their determination to protect small nations. [All the foregoing 1:8; map P. 5.]

The meetings were held in the Soviet Embassy at Teheran about a round table ten feet in diameter. It was the first time Mr. Roosevelt had ever met Premier Stalin and the first time the latter had left his country since 1909. [3:1.]

A third international meeting was reported to have followed in North Africa, where, it was said, Mr. Roosevelt and Mr. Churchill conferred with President Inonu of Turkey regarding his country's entrance into the war. [1:5-6.]

The military plans laid at Teheran were expected to be in full effect by March or April of next year, when invasion from Britain would follow the Russian winter drive and an all-out aerial offensive against Germany. [1:6-7.]

Secretary of State Hull declared that the fighting strength of the United Nations could now become fully effective [1:7] and London opinion held that the Teheran announcement was designed to conceal more than was revealed. [9:2.] The people of Moscow were delighted that agreement on timing all blows against Germany had ended the "second-front" issue. [10:1.]

Allied troops continued to make progress on all fronts. Both the Eighth and Fifth Armies in Italy pushed forward against bitter opposition, reaching the Moro River and bringing Cassino under artillery fire. [1:3; map, P. 16.] The Red Army, smashing southwest of Kremenchug, was only four miles from Znamenka as it cut the Smela-Znamenka rail line. [1:6; map, P. 12.]

In the Pacific 155 tons of bombs were showered on Cape Gloucester as the assault on the western end of New Britain was maintained. [17:2-3.] A strong American carrier force attacked Japanese positions in the Marshall Islands [1:4] and United States submarines sent eleven more enemy ships to the bottom. [16:6.]

First Quarter of 1944 Likely to See Fruition of the Teheran Strategy

By DREW MIDDLETON
By Cable to The New York Times.

LONDON, Dec. 6—Military plans for the defeat of the Wehrmacht drawn at Teheran, Iran, by President Roosevelt, Prime Minister Churchill and Premier Stalin, will probably be fully activated in the first three months of 1944.

During that period the strategic aerial offensive against Germany will assume its maximum proportions, the winter offensive of the Red Army should have brought it to the Dniester in the south and into Poland in the north and the Anglo-American invasion of northern Europe from Britain will be ready to start, with the tactical air forces already operating against the defenses in Western Europe and the lateral communications on which those defenses rely.

One of the first tangible results of the Teheran conference should be the arrival of Gen. George C. Marshall, United States Army Chief of Staff, in Britain to take up his position as Commander in Chief of all Allied invasion forces.

Once the invasion leader is settled into his job it is considered likely that the long-awaited announcement of the formation of an Allied Tactical Air Force and the names of its commanders and the appointment of American and British commanders to lead Allied Army groups involved in the invasion, will follow.

It may well be that the southern Europe front now represented by a slow, painful advance in Italy may

Continued on Page Five

2d Brooklyn Jury Scores Mayor For Failing to Hire Enough Police

Already under censure by the August grand jury in Kings County for alleged failure to suppress crime in the Bedford-Stuyvesant section of Brooklyn, the administration of Mayor La Guardia was accused yesterday by the holdover July grand jury of inadequately policing the entire borough.

"We charge," the July panel declared in a presentment to County Judge Franklin Taylor, "that the present administration over a long period of years has utterly failed to take adequate measures to promptly fill the vacancies regularly occurring in the department, and also to provide additional patrolmen during this time."

At the same time County Judge Nathan R. Sobel was charging the December grand jury and pointing out, for the guidance of the August panel, that its presentment was faulty in that it had the effect of "indicting" an entire people for the crimes of a very few and "stirring up resentment, hatred and fear."

The August panel reconvened yesterday, continuing its inquiry into what it declares to be widespread and unchecked lawlessness in Brooklyn's "Little Harlem." It heard the testimony of several witnesses, then adjourned without disclosing when it would meet again.

In its presentment the July grand jury, whose term had been extended to permit it to investigate police protection in the city's most populous borough, attributed the critical police situation to the "short-sighted, improvident policies of this administration," which it said "have in large part contributed to the development of a situ-

Continued on Page Twenty

ATTACK PLANS SET

Dates Fixed for Land Drives From the East, West and South

IRAN TO BE FREED

Allied Leaders Say 'No Power on Earth' Can Balk Our Victory

The texts of the three-power declarations appear on Page 4.

By C. L. SULZBERGER
By Cable to The New York Times.

CAIRO, Egypt, Dec. 6—Final concord on a campaign to destroy the German military power by land, sea and air and to erect an enduring peace in which all nations, both great and small, shall participate, was agreed upon in the momentous Teheran meeting between President Roosevelt, Premier Stalin and Prime Minister Churchill.

Simultaneously, the three leaders, as a sign of their faith in each other and as proof of the validity of their intentions toward little nations, guaranteed the post-war independence, sovereignty and territorial integrity of Iran.

These Allied agreements were announced to the world today in two joint declarations signed in order by President Roosevelt [the only titular Chief of State among the three], Premier Stalin and Prime Minister Churchill. They were issued in Teheran Dec. 1 after a long final sitting of the leaders and their innermost circles of advisers in the magnificent Soviet Embassy where President Roosevelt lived as a guest.

3-Pronged Attack Pledged

Their military promises can be summed up accordingly: the three powers will work together throughout the war; their military staffs have concerted plans for the destruction of German forces; these staffs have reached a "complete agreement as to the scope and timing of operations which will be undertaken from the east, west and south."

Guarantees satisfactory to the three chiefs now exist that the final victory will rest with the United Nations. "No power on earth can prevent our destroying the German armies by land, their U-boats by sea and their war plants from the air," says one of the joint declarations. "Our attacks will be relentless and increasing."

Seal Doom of Hitler

Thus in four days of deliberation in the romantic Iranian capital the "Big Three" laid the second half of the plans for ending the global war and establishing lasting peace for the benefit of all in its ruins. The Asiatic talks in North Africa between Mr. Roosevelt, Mr. Churchill and Generalissimo Chiang Kai-shek already had laid the program for accelerating the defeat of Japan and for building up a new Asia.

Now European talks of exactly the same length have rounded off the final plans for smashing Hitler which obviously must precede the destruction of Japan in the over-all scheme of the Allied grand strategy planners. Britain and America have clearly coordinated their ultimate schedule for the invasion of Europe from several points from the west and south with a program for new Russian offensives against the Reich.

It may be assumed that once the fulfillment of these plans comes about and Moscow's long pleas for a second front are entirely answered that the Soviet Union might conceivably alter its present neutral attitude toward Japan. This certainly was discussed at Teheran but the outcome of these discussions is not known.

It would seem a fair assumption from a complete survey of both the present wartime and future post-war problems indicated in the latest declarations that the three powers must now have agreed on

Continued on Page Four

"All the News That's Fit to Print."

The New York Times.

LATE CITY EDITION
Cloudy and warmer today; fresh winds.
Temperatures Yesterday—Max., 30; Min., 9
Sunrise, 8:18 A. M.; Sunset, 6:34 P. M.

VOL. XCIII. No. 31,381. Entered as Second-Class Matter, Postoffice, New York, N. Y. NEW YORK, SATURDAY, DECEMBER 25, 1943. THREE CENTS IN NEW YORK CITY

EISENHOWER NAMED COMMANDER FOR INVASION; 3,000 PLANES SMASH FRENCH COAST; BERLIN HIT; ROOSEVELT PROMISES NATION A DURABLE PEACE

STRIKE CALLED OFF BY 230,000 IN TRAIN AND ENGINE UNIONS

But Non-Operating Men Meet Carriers and Reject Offer Made for Overtime Pay

GIVE BYRNES NO ANSWER

He Says Agreement Must Meet Requirements Set Forth in the Stabilization Program

By LOUIS STARK

Special to THE NEW YORK TIMES.

WASHINGTON, Dec. 24—The Brotherhood of Locomotive Engineers and the Brotherhood of Railroad Trainmen today canceled notices for a strike of their 230,000 members on Dec. 30 in view of President Roosevelt's offer and their acceptance of arbitration by the Chief Executive.

The conductors, firemen and switchmen's unions, also members of the "Big Five" operating and transportation brotherhoods, representing more than 120,000 employes, have rejected arbitration by the President and have not called off the strike of their members set for Dec. 30.

The other major development today in the railroad wage situation was a three-hour conference in the office of James F. Byrnes, chief of the Office of War Mobilization, participated in by committees of the railroads and of spokesmen for the fifteen non-operating unions, whose 1,100,000 members are scheduled to strike on Dec. 30.

At this meeting it was reported that the non-operating unions asked for a wage increase of 6 cents an hour as compensation for overtime after forty hours. These employes receive overtime after forty-eight hours of service. The carriers are reported to have offered 4 cents an hour for overtime, but it is understood that this was rejected by the unions.

Insists on Negotiations

B. M. Jewell, chief negotiator for the unions, is said to have been pressed by Mr. Byrnes for a reply to the President's demand that the non-operating employes permit him to act as sole and final arbiter in their dispute with the carriers.

The union leader is said to have replied with some asperity that the President last night gave the unions until Monday to reply to the arbitration proposal, and that in the meantime they had obtained from the President authority to proceed and seek an agreement with the carriers, whose committees were headed by Jacob Aronson, vice president of the New York Central Railroad.

The offer of 4 cents an hour for overtime was understood to be above the 4 to 10 cents an hour sliding scale wage increase recommended in the non-operating unions' case by an emergency board, convened after Frank M. Vinson, the Economic Stabilization Director, had rejected the 8 cents an hour proposal of a previous emergency board.

Byrnes' Statement

The conference in Mr. Byrnes' office, which was attended for a short time by Mr. Vinson, ended at 5:30 P. M. and the following statement was issued on Mr. Byrnes' behalf:

"The representatives of the carriers and the non-operating brotherhoods met in the conference room of the Office of War Mobilization.

"The representatives of the carriers were not present at the conference the President held with the representatives of the brotherhoods yesterday afternoon. Justice Byrnes advised the carriers' representatives that the President desired to know whether they would object to his arbitrating the differences between the carriers and the non-operating brotherhoods.

"The representatives of the carriers stated that they were entirely willing to agree that the President should arbitrate the differences just as they had agreed in

Continued on Page Twenty-six

17 Perish as Fire Sweeps 42d Street Lodging House

Scores Hurt in 'Bowery-Type' Building Disaster, Worst of Its Kind Here in Years—Many Trapped Asleep

Sixteen bodies had been removed last night from a five-story brick structure at 437-439 West Forty-second Street, between Ninth and Tenth Avenues, the four upper floors of which were occupied by a "Bowery-type" lodging house, after one of the city's worst fires in years virtually had consumed the entire interior.

A seventeenth victim died at 7:15 P. M. in Roosevelt Hospital, to which most of the score of injured were removed.

The actual loss of life probably never will be known. With most of the victims burned beyond recognition and in many cases nothing remaining but bones, the task of counting the dead and identifying them was proving almost impossible. Authorities, after checking for hours, could not even determine how many persons were in the building at the time of the fire. They were faced with the fact that the lodging house had beds in three-foot by six cubicles, separated by flimsy plywood partitions, and in hall-like dormitories "accommodating" 248 persons. It was said the beds were well filled with restaurant and other night workers.

The fire, believed to have smoldered for three hours, started at 2 P. M. as if set by a hundred torches. Trapped in their sleep many were burned to death in their "cells," rooms so tiny that a lodger had literally to crawl into bed through a special door on a central vertical hinge that folded to permit entry.

The victims groped through con-

Continued on Page Twenty-six

WLB PEACE OFFER WIRED STEEL UNION

Davis Tells Murray Retroactivity Can Be Reconsidered Within Wage Formula

Special to THE NEW YORK TIMES.

WASHINGTON, Dec. 24—William H. Davis, chairman of the War Labor Board, telegraphed today to Philip Murray, president of the CIO United Steel Workers, that if labor members of the board desired to reconsider their vote on the retroactive pay issue "the public members will favor such reconsideration."

But, while he indicated that a retroactive basis might be approved within the framework of the present ("Little Steel") wage stabilization formula, Mr. Davis stated in his message that the public members could not now determine "any question of retroactivity that might come up in any future change in the wage stabilization policy."

Presuming that any such future change would be applied to "all wage-earners," he wrote that retroactivity in general or in particular ought to be decided when and if the change is made.

[A production stoppage was reported early this morning by The Associated Press with the expiration of contracts at midnight covering 35,000 employes at the Republic Steel Corporation and Youngstown Sheet and Tube Company. At these plants in Youngstown and in Cleveland picketing began.]

"Misunderstanding" Deplored

Mr. Davis' telegram said:

"You are quoted as saying that the proposal of the public members of the War Labor Board as to retroactivity in the steel negotiations violates principles enunciated by the board in the recent cases affecting hundreds of thousands of workers, that the proposal of the

Continued on Page Twenty-six

CITY AN OPEN HOUSE FOR WARTIME YULE

Heart-Warming Parties for Service Men and Women Are Chief Among Festivities

New York was far from a big, cold, gray city as it ushered in its third wartime Christmas last night with heart-warming church services, gay parties, gifts for the ill and unfortunate, and messages of good-will that brought cheer to its teeming millions and to the men and women visitors in the services.

It will not be a white Christmas, according to the weather man, but it will be cold.

Tens of thousands of visitors, many of them members of the families of service men, were in the city for the week-end. Railroads, doing a peak business, were handicapped by the bitter cold in the surrounding country. Virtually every train to and from the city was loaded to capacity, with standees in the aisles. Because of the cold, many trains were late.

Grand Central Terminal and the Pennsylvania Station were packed. Policemen kept the crowds moving. Buses and bus terminals throughout the city did a land-office business, too.

Stores Experience Let-Up

Only in the stores did Christmas Eve bring a let-up. While business was brisk, the real crush had subsided and only last-minute shoppers were on hand.

The churches of all faiths welcomed the Holy Day with midnight services, offering prayers for a victorious peace. There were many men in uniform at masses, carol services and communion.

Virtually every Roman Catholic church celebrated a midnight mass by permission of Archbishop Francis J. Spellman. Episcopal churches celebrated communion, while many churches of other faiths held can-

Continued on Page Nine

Biggest of War Plants Will Make Army Bomber Engines at Chicago

By The United Press.

CHICAGO, Dec. 24—The country's largest war plant, a series of structures sprawling over 500 acres of land, was ready today to turn out an unending stream of engines for Army bombing planes.

The giant inland plant on Chicago's South Side was built by the Dodge division of the Chrysler Corporation. Willow Run could be set down in the main building with enough room left to lay out twenty baseball diamonds.

There are nineteen buildings in the plant, all ready for production. The main building, the machining-assembly unit, covers eighty-two acres.

The plant has fourteen cafeterias and kitchens, butcher shops and bakeries to feed employes.

A parking lot a mile and a quarter long will accommodate 14,000 automobiles. The interplant communication system has 500 miles of telephone lines. Utility services are sufficient for a city of 75,000 population.

Officials revealed that the machine shops had been turning out parts for 2,200-horsepower, eighteen-cylinder Wright engines.

The plant, already called "Hitler's headache," will employ more than 25,000 persons when it enters mass production.

Prior to the completion of the Chicago plant, the bomber factory owned by the Government and operated by Henry Ford at Willow Run, twenty-five miles from Detroit, was called the largest war production unit in the world. It covers two square miles.

RECORD AIR BLOW

'Forts,' Liberators and Medium Bombers Rock 'Special' Targets

ALL CRAFT RETURN

RAF Pounds the German Capital With 1,120 Tons Before Dawn

By DAVID ANDERSON

By Cable to THE NEW YORK TIMES.

LONDON, Dec. 24—The greatest number of American heavy bombers ever to take off from Britain attacked "special military installations" of the Germans along the coast of northern France today as part of record operations of probably 3,000 Allied warplanes across the Channel.

Before dawn hundreds of the most powerful bombers of the Royal Air Force struck Berlin again with more than 1,120 tons of high explosives and fire missiles.

Several features of this two-fisted battering by the Allied air forces on the eve of Christmas made the day a memorable one for the enemy, even taking into account the Anglo-American achievements of recent weeks.

Headquarters of the United States Eighth Air Force announced that 1,300 planes handled by American crews took part in the daylight missions.

An even greater number of RAF, Dominion and Allied planes were out. Every one of the bombers and fighters of the joint forces returned to its base, according to a communiqué issued by headquarters of the United States Army here and the British Air Ministry.

Included in the American force were the largest formations of Flying Fortresses and Liberators ever sent into the air. Since an estimated 750 United States "heavies" at one time have attacked targets in western Germany within the past month, the day's operations entailed the use of close to, if not exceeding, 800 four-motored bombers.

The most concentrated attacks were carried out in the Pas-de-Ca-

Continued on Page Three

TO KEEP IT BY ARMS

President Says 4 Nations Agree on This for as Long as Necessary

'COST MAY BE HIGH'

German Might Must End, He Says on Air, Warning 'Japs' of Bad News

The text of the President's address appears on Page 8.

By JOHN H. CRIDER

Special to THE NEW YORK TIMES.

HYDE PARK, N. Y., Dec. 24—President Roosevelt promised the country and the world this Christmas Eve that they could look for insured peace with "certainty," even though "the cost may be high and the time long," and said that the United States, Great Britain, Soviet Russia and China were agreed to use force to maintain that peace "for as long as it may be necessary."

Speaking from the study in the Franklin D. Roosevelt Library, one of his favorite rendezvous, with his family gathered informally around him, the President gave his first comprehensive report on his recent conferences in the Middle East over the most extensive broadcast facilities ever set up in this country.

For the first time the President tempered his "unconditional surrender" ultimatum of Casablanca by stating that the United Nations did not want to enslave the German people but wanted them to have "a normal chance to develop in peace as useful and respectable members of the European family."

Here appeared to be one of the great achievements of the conference at Teheran—a united view by the Allies in Europe on what kind of a post-war Germany they would look for, which closes the gulf which appeared to exist between the Anglo-American "unconditional surrender" demand, and the more hopeful outlook for the future which the Russians have been

Continued on Page Eight

War News Summarized

SATURDAY, DECEMBER 25, 1943

President Roosevelt proudly announced to the world yesterday the appointment of General Dwight D. Eisenhower as supreme commander of the Anglo-American invasion forces—a selection, he said, that was made at the Teheran conference, where every point concerning the impending east-west-south attack on Germany had been decided.

It was announced from London that General Wilson would succeed General Eisenhower as commander of the Allied forces in the Mediterranean theatre; that General Montgomery would be chief of British Army units under General Eisenhower; that General Alexander would head the Allied forces in Italy, and that General Spaatz would be American Air Force commander against Germany. [All the foregoing, 1:8.]

Peace is certain, but the cost of bringing it about will be high and the realization may be distant, President Roosevelt declared during the Christmas Eve broadcast from his Hyde Park home. He said the United Nations had no desire to enslave the German people but wanted them to develop as respectable members of the European family. As for Japan, he said that empire is being enveloped in a band of steel and there is plenty of bad news for the Japanese in the offing. [1:5.]

Speaking from the German-surrounded Vatican, Pope Pius XII made a plea for a just peace and declared that a normal measure of power and the employment of force were needed to achieve it, but he decried any harsh imposition supported by arms alone. [1:6-7.]

An estimated 3,000 American and British planes of virtually all types—the greatest concentration in air history—bombed the Pas-de-Calais area of France, where, it is believed, the Germans have implanted rocket guns. In this, the fifth straight assault on these targets, the American Eighth Air Force sent 1,300 planes, a record number for any single operation. All Allied planes returned. The attack followed a Royal Air Force blow at Berlin, reportedly hitting the southeast industrial area near Tempelhof. [1:4, map P. 3.]

The fortified town of Gorodok, seventeen miles from Vitebsk and on the Vitebsk-Nevel railroad, was successfully stormed by the Russian Army, which drove ahead to capture sixty other places. Southwest of Zhlobin, in southern White Russia, large German tank and infantry attacks were beaten back. [1:7, map, P. 5.]

The British Eighth Army captured Vezzani, three miles southwest of the Adriatic port of Ortona, where fighting continued in the streets. There was little activity except for patrol thrusts on the Fifth Army front, because of deep mud. Medium Allied bombers struck at the Riviera coast, hitting bridges, railroads and viaducts. [1:6-7.]

Cape Gloucester, which seems to be shaping up as another possible invasion point on New Britain Island, was hit by 300 more tons of Allied aerial bombs, bringing the total tonnage dropped since Dec. 1 to 2,500. [6:1.]

The Navy announced that the United States submarine Grayling was presumably lost with her complement of sixty-five men. [6:2.]

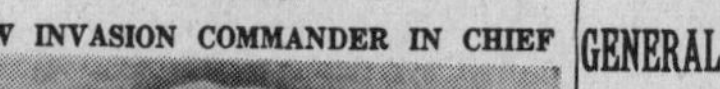

NEW INVASION COMMANDER IN CHIEF

Gen. Dwight D. Eisenhower

The New York Times, 1943

Pope Prays for Just Peace Kept by Wise Use of Force

By The Associated Press.

LONDON, Dec. 24—Praying that this may be the last war Christmas and that a truly Christian peace may be celebrated in the coming year, Pope Pius XII today called for the world's responsible leaders to check the instincts of hate and vengeance and give rise to "the resplendent dawn of a new spirit of world union."

The text of the Pope's address appears on Page 10.

Raising his voice to a vibrant ring in outlining "the principles for a peace program," the Pontiff called for a "normal measure of power," sanctions and "the employment of force" to achieve and maintain peace, but warned that true peace "can never be a harsh imposition supported by arms" alone.

"An hour like the present—so full of possibilities for vast beneficent progress no less than for fatal defects and blunders—has perhaps never been seen in the history of mankind," said the Holy Father, who spoke on Christmas Eve from the bayonet-circled Vatican, where he has been isolated except by radio since the Germans occupied Rome in September.

The 35-minute address was delivered on the radio in Italian, but an official English language translation later was made available.

Juridical Basis for Peace

"A true peace is not the mathematical result of a proportion of forces, but in its last and deepest meaning is a moral and juridical process," said the Pope, speaking from what he called the "abysmal ruins of this terrible war."

"It (peace) is not, in fact, achieved without the employment of force, and its very existence

Continued on Page Ten

RED ARMY TAKES KEY TO VITEBSK

Gorodok, 17 Miles From Goal, Falls After Russian Feint Outwits Nazi Defense

By The Associated Press.

LONDON, Saturday, Dec. 25—The Russian Baltic Army cracked a model German defense-in-depth line and captured the heavily fortified lake town of Gorodok, seventeen miles north of Vitebsk yesterday, sweeping on over 2,000 German dead in a continuing offensive to take sixty more towns and hamlets, Moscow announced early today.

Resuming their drive after a two-day slow-down, the Russians swept to within fifteen miles of the Vitebsk-Polotsk rail line, an important east-west supply artery for the Germans, as they advanced southward along the Nevel-Vitebsk railroad.

In another fighting area to the south—southwest of Zhlobin—the

Continued on Page Five

8th Army Wins Town Near Ortona; Americans Take a Hill, Lose One

By MILTON BRACKER

By Wireless to THE NEW YORK TIMES.

ALGIERS, Dec. 24—The Allied armies in Italy kept up pressure all along the line yesterday despite the imminence of Christmas, but were unable quite to complete the capture of Ortona or accomplish substantial gains on the Tyrrhenian half of the front.

Although Canadian units of Gen. Sir Bernard L. Montgomery's Eighth Army had driven back the last German defenders of Ortona to the northwest corner of the shell-blasted and tank-razed town, the defenders kept returning fire and apparently intended to deprive the Allies of the full use of the most important port immediately below Pescara as long as possible.

Evidence of the toll the Germans have been paying for their desperate defense of the area was the discovery of a new cemetery at the crossroads just southwest of Ortona with at least 100 German graves.

The Eighth Army did manage to wrest from the enemy another village three miles southwest of Ortona and a mile beyond the Ortona-Orsogna road. It was Vezzani, which is three and a half miles from the coast and, like Ortona, just about twelve from Pescara. Other units of General Montgomery's veteran army have also penetrated to the outskirts of Villa Grande, a mile northeast of Vezzani on a secondary road paralleling the coast.

On the Fifth Army front the

Continued on Page Three

GENERAL IS SHIFTED

Choice of 'Big 3' Parley, He Has Montgomery as British Field Leader

WILSON IS SUCCESSOR

Mid-East Head Honored —Spaatz to Direct U. S. Air Strategy

Special to THE NEW YORK TIMES.

HYDE PARK, N. Y., Dec. 24—President Roosevelt announced today the appointment of Gen. Dwight D. Eisenhower to lead the invasion of Europe from the north and west, and from London came word that Gen. Sir Bernard L. Montgomery of North African fame would head the British troops under General Eisenhower to form a proved and hard-hitting team to lead the assault on Adolf Hitler's "Fortress Europe."

The President's announcement of General Eisenhower's selection at the recent Teheran conference to lead the main attack against Germany also set to rest the old rumors regarding the probable appointment of Gen. George C. Marshall, Army Chief of Staff, to that post.

The President, in his radio report today on the recent conferences at Teheran and Cairo, also named Lieut. Gen. Carl A. Spaatz as commander of "the entire American strategic bombing force operating against Germany."

This was taken to mean that while General Eisenhower will confine his command to the mass attack on Europe from the north and west, General Spaatz' command over all American strategic bombardment of Germany extends to operations against Germany from all neighboring bases.

Quashes Marshall Rumors

The President gave a vivid picture in his radio report of complete agreement between Prime Minister Churchill, Premier Stalin and himself regarding a detailed program for the annihilation of Germany by land and air from all directions.

He also paid high tribute to General Marshall, presumably to set old rumors at rest. Some persons have argued that the position to be occupied by General Eisenhower is of greatest importance, but the official decision now revealed seems to give credence to the opinion that the most important position in the Army is that of Chief of Staff, just as Washington is the only place from which the whole global operation can be commanded.

"To the members of our armed forces, to their wives, mothers and fathers, I want to affirm the great faith and confidence that we have in General Marshall and Admiral King (Chief of Naval Operations), who direct all of our armed might throughout the world," the President declared.

Their Military Genius Stressed

"Upon them," he said, "falls the responsibility of planning the strategy; of determining where and when to fight. Both of these men have already gained high places in American history: places which will record in that history many evidences of their military genius that cannot be published today."

The announcement from London told not only of General Montgomery's appointment to head the British invasion forces under General Eisenhower but also of Gen. Sir Henry Maitland Wilson's appointment to replace General Eisenhower as commander of the Mediterranean Theatre and Gen. Sir Harold R. L. G. Alexander's appointment to command all Allied forces in Italy.

The Teheran military decision announced by the President proved as much as anything else that the American handling of the invasion of North Africa and of Italy had deeply impressed the United States allies. Those invasions may now be regarded as the testing phase of the main European invasion, since the American officers identi-

Continued on Page Two

U.S. Army

General Dwight D. Eisenhower with paratroopers.

U.S. Marine Corps

Marine artillerymen load their 75mm. howitzer as they blast Japanese positions on Cape Gloucester.

U.S. Marine Corps

Marine machine gunners fire on Japanese troops in the jungles of Cape Gloucester.

"All the News That's Fit to Print."

The New York Times.

LATE CITY EDITION
Cloudy, moderate temperature; partly cloudy and warmer tonight.
Temperatures Yesterday—Max., 35; Min., 16
Sunrise, [illegible] A. M.; Sunset, [illegible] P. M.

Copyright, 1943, by The New York Times Company.

VOL. XCIII..No. 31,387. Entered as Second-Class Matter, Postoffice, New York, N. Y. NEW YORK, FRIDAY, DECEMBER 31, 1943. THREE CENTS IN NEW YORK CITY

RUSSIANS BREACH LINE, ROUT 22 DIVISIONS; BIGGEST U. S. AIR ARMADA SMASHES REICH; MARINES WIN CAPE GLOUCESTER AIRFIELD

ICKES BARS WEST FROM ANTHRACITE TO AID EAST COAST

Puts 3-Month Embargo on All Shipments to West of Ohio-Pennsylvania Line

100,000 TONS A MONTH GAIN

New York to Get 4,000 More Tons of Bituminous a Day—8,000 of Anthracite 'Frozen'

By WINIFRED MALLON
Special to THE NEW YORK TIMES.

WASHINGTON, Dec. 30—To make up the coal shortages which are assuming crisis proportions along the Eastern seaboard, Secretary Ickes said today that from New Year's Day until April 1 shipments of anthracite to points west of the Pennsylvania-Ohio line will be prohibited.

These supplies, amounting to 100,000 tons a month, will be diverted to the East Coast region. By this means, Mr. Ickes said, it is hoped that allocations already made may be filled, despite the falling off in anthracite production.

Meanwhile, to meet the present and prospective shortage in the New York metropolitan area, additional daily supplies of 4,000 tons of the run, low volatile (smokeless) bituminous coal will be made available.

To provide for householders who cannot under any circumstances use even the best soft coal, an order has been issued "freezing" for distribution to such consumers only, 8,000 tons of anthracite now on hand or in transit to New York.

The "freeze" order, Mr. Ickes said, refers only to anthracite within the limits already allocated to New York, the total amount of which cannot be increased, and must be used in full recognition of that fact.

Says Those Who Can Must Use It

"There just isn't anthracite enough to go around, and anyone who can use bituminous must do so," Mr. Ickes said.

"Much of the trouble in New York, Jersey City and Atlantic City has been due to the refusal of dealers to accept bituminous coal, of which there is plenty. They wait for anthracite shipments that will not and cannot be forthcoming.

"People will have to be realistic about these things and know that whether they have ever used soft coal before or not, they will have to do it now, as nearly all of them can, and as we intend to see they have an opportunity to do. If the dealers will not accept it, we will ship it in anyhow, and see that it is made available to those who need and will be glad to use it."

Says Some Soft Coal Is Rejected

One company in New York, for instance, Mr. Ickes said, refused last week to take 6,500 tons of bituminous coal which it might have had. Dealers in Atlantic City also were refusing coal available to them, he added, and were insisting on specifically better grades.

"They want to know even what mines the coal is from," Mr. Ickes said. "And still other dealers, who have been supplying only anthracite, are refusing to take any bituminous of whatever grade.

"Such an attitude, in times like these, is unreasonable and inexcusable, and cannot be allowed to keep from consumers coal they need and could have."

According to officials here, there is very little difference between the low volatile bituminous coal and the hard coal which many consumers have been using. Smokeless bituminous can be substituted for anthracite in many home furnaces, Mr. Ickes said, and for those who cannot by any possibility use it, allocations will be made from the 8,000 tons of anthracite reserved for their special needs.

"But I am not God," Mr. Ickes said. "I can't make anthracite available if there just isn't any to be had."

Says Miners Are Drawn Away

All coal production fell off last week, the Secretary went on, but production of anthracite has been decreasing steadily for the last five weeks, largely because miners were taking jobs in near-by war plants.

To "a considerable extent, and increasingly so," he declared, the coal shortage was a manpower crisis. He took issue here with the view expressed yesterday by Lawrence A. Appley, executive director of the War Manpower Commission, who attributed the coal shortage to miners' strikes and de-

Continued on Page Thirty

Traffic Lights Go On Throughout the City

Announcing that the traffic lights would go on again all over the city on New Year's Day, Chief Magistrate Henry H. Curran said yesterday that uniform fines would be imposed for passing red lights. The night fine, he said, would be reduced from $10 to $5, and the day fine increased from $2 to $5.

The disks that have covered traffic lights will have been removed from all signals by tomorrow, he said, and "they will be as they were before the war, the old friendly green and the forbidding red shining out again."

ARMY SAYS UNIONS BALK RAIL RETURN

Two of Them Only 'Postpone' Strike, It States—Case Mishandled, Say 3 Chiefs

By LOUIS STARK
Special to THE NEW YORK TIMES.

WASHINGTON, Dec. 30—Government operation of the railroads for an indefinite period seemed likely tonight as President Roosevelt and eighteen railway unions prepared for a show-down fight on wages.

The War Department announced that so long as the wage issues were not settled it would be unable to return the roads to their owners. In a statement the War Department virtually accused two of the three operating unions which called off the strike last night as having acted in bad faith, since the department had been led to understand that the strike order would be canceled rather than that it would be postponed.

The War Department's statement, issued by its Bureau of Public Relations, said:

"The War Department made public today that the orders issued by certain of the railway brotherhoods do not cancel the strike order, as it had been given to understand, but merely postpone it. Mr. [D. B.] Robertson's order to the Brotherhood of Locomotive Firemen and Engine men reads: 'Due to Federal control of railroads strike postponed.'

"A general chairman of Mr. [H. W.] Fraser's organization of the Order of Railway Conductors, issued orders reading: 'Due to Federal control of railroads, strike by members of the O. R. C. and others of our craft, which has been called for 6 A. M., Dec. 30, has been postponed. Please consider this bulletin not to leave the service Dec. 30.'

"The wording of the order issued to the Switchmen is not known to the War Department.

"However, as long as this condition persists the War Department will not be able to gratify its desire to return the railroads to private ownership, as the orders merely relate to the temporay situation during Government control."

In reply to this statement, spokesmen for the firemen, conductors and switchmen's brotherhoods declared that, under their laws, once a strike vote were taken it remained "alive" until the issues which called it forth were settled. The unions, as observers see it, thus have reserved the right to strike at any time, not against the Government but against the owners, when and if the roads are returned to private hands, provided the dispute is still unsettled.

Later tonight, the chiefs of the firemen, conductors and switchmen, in a joint statement, charged the Administration with delays and accused it of mishandling the wage dispute.

One major aspect of the dispute which has led the Administration into serious conflict with the rail-

Continued on Page Eight

JAPANESE CRUSHED

Americans Capture Key New Britain Airdrome After 4-Day Battle

MANY OF ENEMY KILLED

Marines Take Strong Points With Flame Throwers—Our Casualties Are Light

By FRANK L. KLUCKHOHN
By Wireless to THE NEW YORK TIMES.

ADVANCED ALLIED HEADQUARTERS IN NEW GUINEA, Friday, Dec. 31—United States marines have captured the Cape Gloucester airdrome, their objective, just four days after their landing on the northwestern tip of New Britain.

One of the airdrome's two strips was won late Wednesday night after a severe aerial bombing and artillery pounding. Then, on Thursday, following a devastating air attack and artillery preparation, the final land assault was begun on the second strip, the more easterly of the two. By noon it was taken, completing the conquest of the airdrome.

The speed with which the Cape Gloucester air base was captured contrasted with the period of more than a month taken last summer to reduce the Munda airfield on New Georgia Island in the Solomons. Possession of the newly won airdrome increases the threat to Rabaul, main southwest Pacific bastion of the Japanese, and brings Kavieng, New Ireland, and the Admiralty Islands within easy range of Allied bombers. Domination of the Dampier and Vitiaz Straits, enemy supply routes to New Guinea, is also insured.

Snipers Cleaned Out

The Marines advanced four to six miles from their landing points through a tangle of trees and undergrowth to reach the Cape Gloucester airdrome. "Alligators" played a major role, their six-man crews driving them straight into deep-rooted trees while enemy snipers were cleaned out by Americans who knew more tricks than the Japanese in this type of fighting.

Meanwhile heavy attacks from the Borgen Bay area, where the marines set up their main bridgehead, were repulsed with heavy enemy losses. The marines cut down the attackers in large numbers from entrenched positions that the Japanese were unable to dent.

Fighters based on the airfield in the American Bougainville bridgehead made another attack on Rabaul. They shot down eighteen enemy fighters and probably seven more for a loss of three fighters. Fifty Japanese Zeros and a smaller number of American planes took part in the battle.

United States Army troops at Empress Augusta Bay on Bougainville Island smashed an enemy strong point east of the Torokina River's mouth on Tuesday.

Softened by Air Assaults

ADVANCED ALLIED HEADQUARTERS IN NEW GUINEA, Friday, Dec. 31 (AP)—Details of the final hours of the battle for the

Continued on Page Two

1,300 CRAFT STRIKE

Hit Southwest Targets—34 Machines Lost to Enemy's 23

2,240 TONS ROCK BERLIN

20 of 750 Bombers Missing in Night Attack—24-Hour Offensive Sets Record

By DREW MIDDLETON
By Cable to THE NEW YORK TIMES.

LONDON, Friday, Dec. 31—More than thirteen hundred American heavy bombers and fighters, the largest force ever dispatched by the United States Army Air Forces in any theatre, blasted targets in southwest Germany yesterday to bring to a climax an offensive that involved more than 2,000 Allied planes, including strong formations of American and British medium bombers and hundreds of fighters.

[The American targets in southwestern Germany were not immediately identified by the United States Eighth Air Force, but British press reports from Switzerland said the main target had been the I. G. Farbenindustrie's poison gas plant at Ludwigshafen, 450 miles from Britain and one of the Reich's biggest chemical centers, The United Press reported.]

This great onslaught followed the smashing British victory in the Berlin offensive Wednesday night in which between 750 and 1,000 four-engined bombers, piloted by Britons, Canadians and Australians, pounded the German capital with more than 2,240 tons of bombs, starting vast fires that were visible for 200 miles and raising a funeral plume of smoke 16,000 feet high over the stricken city.

The RAF Bomber Command apparently continued the offensive last night. Bombers roared out over one southeast coast district toward France for half an hour just after nightfall. Two hours later a number of bombers were heard returning from the Continent.

Allied Losses Light

It was considered likely that 3,000 aircraft were employed by the Allies in the twenty-four hour period in a demonstration of overwhelming Allied air power in this theatre. This power, dwarfing any exerted heretofore, is being employed to paralyze industrial Germany and to disrupt and weaken the outer defenses of Festung Europa for the Allied invasion.

Twenty-three enemy fighters

Continued on Page Two

GERMAN ARMIES ARE SENT REELING WESTWARD

Moscow reported continued gains in the Vitebsk area (1), where the Soviet drives threaten to unhinge the entire German line northward. In the sectors west of Kiev, according to Moscow, twenty-two enemy divisions have been routed and deep gains made along a 186-mile front (shaded area) in six days of the offensive there. The Russians have reached Luginy (2), forty-two miles from the pre-war Polish border, and Chervonnoarmeisk (3), forty-six miles from it. In addition they have captured the junction of Kazatin (4) in their menacing southwestward slant. Near Zaporozhye the Red Army occupied Tomakovka and Belenkoye (5).

WORLD EDGE IN AIR IS WON BY ALLIES

RAF Reports More U-Boats Sunk by Planes in 1943 Than in 3 Prior Years Combined

By The Associated Press.

LONDON, Dec. 30—The Allies have achieved air superiority in every theatre of the war and sent planes on the offensive all around the world, the Royal Air Force announced today.

In a triumphant review of the aerial war of 1943 Britain's air arm said the year's fighting produced these victories and accomplishments in various fields of operation:

1. Nine of Germany's twenty-one industrial cities with populations of more than 250,000 each have been "so seriously devastated that in all probability they have been forced for some time to consume more than they produce."

2. Many more U-boats have been

Continued on Page Three

Admiral King Plans to Hit Japan Before Nazi Defeat

By The Associated Press.

WASHINGTON, Dec. 30—A tremendous offensive against Japan in 1944 is planned, it was made clear today by Admiral Ernest J. King, who said the United Nations would begin shifting their power from the Atlantic to the Pacific theatre before the final defeat of Germany. The naval Commander in Chief stood before a chart in his office, using a cigarette holder as a pointer, to give in an interview the frankest discussion of the Pacific war by a high naval figure. These were his main points:

1. He agrees with Gen. Dwight D. Eisenhower that defeat of Germany next year may be expected and, meantime, "unremitting pressure on Japan will be continued and increased."

2. Strategy for the defeat of Japan and the "main lines of attack" have been determined. The means for carrying out this strategy will be available with the transfer of power from the European theatre. "Studies have been under way for several months," he said, "looking to a shift of power from the European theatre to the Pacific theatre not only when Germany is defeated but as her defeat seems near at hand."

3. He discounted the possibility that the Japanese can, as they have threatened, launch offensive operations in 1944. "I don't quite see how they are going on the offensive where they are in contact in the Pacific," he said. "What they may do in China, Manchuria or even Burma is something else." A restraining factor against a Japanese offensive is the enemy's shortage of shipping, he said, add-

Continued on Page Four

8TH ARMY PUSHES TOWARD PESCARA

Fifth Army Storms Mountain—DNB Tells of Allied Landing Above Garigliano's Mouth

By MILTON BRACKER
By Wireless to THE NEW YORK TIMES.

ALGIERS, Dec. 30—The British Eighth Army has pushed a mile beyond Ortona along the direct coastal route to Pescara and is now barely eleven miles from the Adriatic terminus of the trans-peninsular road to Rome.

Farther inland Gen. Sir Bernard L. Montgomery's troops occupied a dominating position a half mile north of Villa Grande. Eighth Army troops are just over nine miles from Chieti, capital of Abruzzi, eight miles inland from Pescara.

The Canadian captors of Ortona found the area seeded with booby traps and time-bombs that hampered their progress out of the town toward Francavilla and Pescara. The weather was cloudy and cold.

[The German news agency

Continued on Page Four

NAZI ARMIES FLEE

6-Day Russian Push Rips 186-Mile Gap Through Zhitomir Defenses

KAZATIN JUNCTION FALLS

Germans in Dnieper Bend Face Loss of Supply Route—Vitebsk Front Aflame

By RALPH PARKER
By Wireless to THE NEW YORK TIMES.

MOSCOW, Friday, Dec. 31—Premier Joseph Stalin revealed yesterday in an order of the day that the seven-day-old counter-offensive of Gen. Nikolai F. Vatutin had sent twenty-two of Hitler's divisions reeling in flight along a 186-mile front north, west and south of Zhitomir. In the first six days of the Red Army offensive more than 1,000 towns and villages have been recaptured from the Germans.

The Zhitomir-front offensive has restored most of the original gains made in the Russian drive last month, and has added much additional territory to the south that Soviet forces had not yet overrun before beginning their retreat under Field Marshal Gen. Fritz von Mannstein's abortive campaign to recapture Kiev.

Conspicuous among the new positions gained during the new week-long Soviet offensive was the capture of Kazatin, important railway junction seventeen miles southeast of Berdichev.

General Vatutin's offensive is striking southwestward at a pace that threatens the enemy with a disaster as overwhelming as that which overtook the armies of Field Marshal Gen. Friedrich von Paulus at Stalingrad almost a year ago. Inexorably, the powerful German forces in the Dnieper bend are having their escape route narrowed to lines that lead toward the Balkans and away from the Polish frontier. At their closest point, Luginy, the Russians are now forty-two miles from the old Polish border.

Premier Stalin announced that in the six days for which he gave an accounting eight German tank divisions and fourteen infantry divisions had been routed. Advances of from thirty to sixty-two miles had been made, he said.

Zaporozhye Drive Gains

LONDON, Friday, Dec. 31 (UP)—The tremendous break-through along a 186-mile front found the Germans throwing away their arms in their haste to escape as General Vatutin's First Ukranian Army swept into Kazatin, one of the two key junctions on the Nazi's last double-tracked railroad leading out of the Dnieper bend.

Important gains also were scored west of Zaporozhye, where Gen. Rodion Y. Malinovsky's Third Ukrainian Army drove nineteen miles and captured Chumaki, twenty-eight miles beyond the Dnieper dam city in the second day of a new offensive. The entire Ger-

Continued on Page Two

Higher Rank Is Seen For Marshall, King

By The Associated Press.

WASHINGTON, Dec. 30—The Army and Navy Journal expressed belief today that President Roosevelt intends some new and special rank for Gen. George C. Marshall, Army Chief of Staff, and Admiral Ernest J. King, Commander in Chief of the Navy.

The unofficial service publication said there had been sentiment in the past for making General Marshall a field marshal and designating Admiral King as admiral of the fleet.

It recalled President Roosevelt's praise of the two men in his recent radio address and said, "there is likelihood the President may reinstate the movement to give them higher rank."

The publication also said:

"There is some talk that General Marshall may visit England for inspections and conferences prior to the invasion, but it is not believed that he would stay there long."

'Emergency' in Fire Department Gives Men 8 Extra Payless Hours

A "state of emergency" for the Fire Department of this city was declared last night by Fire Commissioner Patrick Walsh after a brief conference with Mayor La Guardia at 4:30 P. M.

In the emergency, Mr. Walsh said, the 6,590 firemen and officers would be required to work one extra eight-hour tour of duty a week without the $420 bonus that was canceled by the Mayor after the men rejected it.

"I don't know how long it's going to last. I might have to change it, but I have to have men to man the apparatus," the Commissioner declared as he left the Mayor's office at City Hall.

Commissioner Walsh said the special departmental order would be read to all tours of duty today and tomorrow. Effective at 12:01 A. M., Saturday, every man in his department is to serve three eight-hour tours of extra duty during the cycle of three six-day tours. The extra duty will occur at the end of the tour of the third working day in the fireman's work week.

Shortly after Mr. Walsh's announcement Vincent J. Kane, president of the Uniformed Firemen's Association, said this plan was virtually the same as that submitted by the membership of his organization a little more than a week ago. The plan was rejected.

Mr. Kane said the next meeting of the U. F. A. was scheduled for Jan. 18, but that a special meeting would be held if the members petitioned for it.

A meeting of representatives of the four line organizations of the Fire Department—chiefs, captains,

Continued on Page Eight

War News Summarized

FRIDAY, DECEMBER 31, 1943

The Nazi defense wall west of Kiev has cracked wide open on a 186-mile front. Russian troops surged through the breaks yesterday and advanced up to sixty-two miles, capturing 300 places, including Kazatin, on the vital Kiev-Vinnitsa railway. This junction is fifteen miles southeast of Berdichev, which, with Zhitomir, is one of the immediate Soviet objectives. The fall of Kazatin put the Russians within 100 miles of Rumania and forty-two miles from the old Polish border. It was estimated that twenty-two Nazi divisions of about 300,000 men were in the reported rout. [1:8.]

Targets in southwest Germany were blasted by the largest American bomber and fighter force ever sent into enemy territory after Berlin had received a terrific pounding by 2,240 tons of explosives dropped by the Royal Air Force Wednesday night. The operations involved more than 2,000 planes, of which 1,300 were American. Fires left in the Reich capital sent plumes of smoke 16,000 feet into the air and could be seen for 200 miles. The "rocket-gun coast" of France also was hit heavily by the Eighth Air Force. [1:4.]

As the year neared its end the Royal Air Force reviewed Allied achievements and was able to announce air superiority in every theatre of war. [1:5.]

The British Eighth Army advanced one mile beyond Ortona—bomb-shattered and full of booby traps—to within eleven miles of the Adriatic port of Pescara, from where one of Italy's main arteries leads westward to Rome. Heights just north of Villa Grande also were taken. A German report said there had been an Allied landing at the western end of the line. [1:7.]

In Washington Admiral King disclosed that, in preparation for a great offensive against Japan in the coming year, the Allies would start shifting their weight from the Atlantic to the Pacific even before the defeat of Germany, which he forecast for 1944. [1:6-7.]

Speaking in London, General Devers pictured 1944 as the year of deliverance with significance unparalleled in history. [4:1.]

Reich Propaganda Minister Goebbels wrote that 1944 would be "a dangerous year," but insisted that German morale was strong and victory certain. [4:5.]

Using flame-throwers and artillery against Japanese pillboxes, the United States Marines have captured the important airdrome on Cape Gloucester, New Britain, four days after their landing. Eighteen enemy fighters were downed while challenging a bombing of Rabaul, air and supply base on the northeast tip of the island. [1:3; map, P. 2.]

Mail Rights Denied to Esquire; Magazine to Fight Order in Court

By The Associated Press.

WASHINGTON, Dec. 30—Esquire Magazine, in which the Varga girl drawings and other material offended the Postoffice Department's sense of modesty, was ordered deprived of its second-class mailing privileges tonight.

Without ruling directly on the question whether the magazine was obscene, a question much debated during long hearings, Postmaster General Frank C. Walker ordered the mail privileges revoked effective Feb. 28.

The action was taken on the ground that the magazine failed to meet the requirements of being "originated and published for the dissemination of information of a public character or devoted to literature, the sciences, arts, or some special industry."

During the long hearings Postoffice Department lawyers sought to show that the magazine was not only obscene but lewd and lascivious. In turn the publication marshaled a long list of witnesses, including Henry L. Mencken, who defended the use of such words as "backside" and "bawdy house"; and a neuropsychologist who called the lightly clad Varga girls' "good, clean pictures, a tribute to American womanhood."

Describing the language of the second-class mailing act as "plain and specific," Postmaster General Walker said:

"Whatever the featured and dominant pictures, prose and verse of this publication may be, they are not 'information of a public character' or 'literature, the sciences, arts or some special industry,' contributing to the public wel-

Continued on Page Thirteen

"All the News That's Fit to Print."

The New York Times.

LATE CITY EDITION
Fair and continued cold today; winds slowly diminishing.
Temperatures Yesterday—Max., 37; Min., 17
Sunrise, 7:07 A. M.; Sunset, 6:13 P. M.

Copyright, 1944, by The New York Times Company.

VOL. XCIII..No. 31,420. Entered as Second-Class Matter. Postoffice, New York, N. Y. NEW YORK, WEDNESDAY, FEBRUARY 2, 1944. THREE CENTS IN NEW YORK CITY

U. S. FORCE WINS BEACHES ON MARSHALLS ATOLL; BATTLES RAGE ON FIRST JAPANESE SOIL INVADED; ALLIES ATTACK BELOW ROME; RUSSIANS ADVANCE

ROLL-CALL RECORD ON SOLDIERS' VOTE REFUSED BY HOUSE

180 Republicans, 52 Democrats Opposed — 146 Democrats, 11 Republicans for It

A 'STATE RIGHTS' VICTORY

President Says People Need to Know How Members Stand—Senate Test Likely Today

By C. P. TRUSSELL
Special to THE NEW YORK TIMES.

WASHINGTON, Feb. 1 — The House by a vote of 233 to 160 refused today to subject itself to the "stand-up-and-be-counted" showdown between Federal and State ballot plans for the armed forces as President Roosevelt urged in his recent message to Congress.

On the question of forcing a roll-call test on the Worley Federal ballot bill, endorsed by the Administration, in direct competition with the "States' rights" (Eastland-Rankin) measure, the House divided as follows:

For a roll-call test: 146 Democrats, 11 Republicans, 2 Progressives and 1 American-Laborite.

Against a roll-call test: 180 Republicans, 52 Democrats and 1 Farmer-Laborite.

Vote Is on Committee Rule

While the vote was construed as an expression of attitude on the Worley bill, as against the Eastland-Rankin bill, the question upon which the issue was joined was a parliamentary one.

The Eastland-Rankin bill had been taken to the floor under a rule of the Rules Committee which did not assure a record vote on the Worley bill. To amend this rule the House was required to defeat a motion to close consideration and debate at the end of an hour's debate. Instead the motion carried and the rule was adopted. Thus the roll-call was blocked.

Fifty of the fifty-two Democrats who helped block the roll-call were from Southern States. Five were from Alabama, three from Arkansas, nine from Georgia, one from Kentucky, six from Louisiana, seven from Mississippi, the solid vote of the delegation; two from North Carolina, one from Oklahoma, three from South Carolina, one from Tennessee, eight from Texas and four from Virginia. The others were Representatives Slaughter of Missouri and Jellicott of California.

The eleven Republicans voting to assure the roll-call vote were Representatives Andrews, Kearney, Mruk and Taylor of New York; Anderson and Welsh of California, Bender of Ohio, Burdick of North Dakota, Gale of Minnesota, La Follette of Indiana and Wolverton of New Jersey.

President's Remark on Test

President Roosevelt, when told of the House's action at his press conference soon after the vote was taken, observed that roll-calls were a part of representative government, and said that he could not cast an intelligent vote in an election without knowing how his Congressman voted.

The House having made the first voting decision in the controversy, the Senate, after six hours of heated debate over constitutional phases of the issue and the President's charge that the "States' rights" bill passed by the Senate was a "fraud," as well as the delay in test voting in Congress, agreed to vote not later than noon tomorrow on the Overton amendment to the Green-Lucas Federal ballot bill.

This amendment would prescribe that while the Federal ballot might be used, State and local election officials would determine the validity of the votes cast in accordance with State law. The principal effect would be to repeal provisions of the existing soldier voting law which suspend requirements for personal registration and payment of poll taxes and, to an undetermined extent, invalidate the Federal ballot.

Members of the "States' rights"

Continued on Page Twelve

Public Told to Delay '44 Tax Estimates

Taxpayers are being advised not to file their estimates of 1944 income with their tax returns for 1943, because Washington legislation is expected to affect the rates on 1944 income. Internal revenue officials in New York City believe Congress will authorize a delay of at least thirty days for the declarations.

"We are trying to discourage taxpayers from filing their declarations of estimated 1944 income until we get the new forms," one internal revenue official said. He indicated that the new legislation could not be made effective before March 1 and that April 15 was regarded as a logical date for the necessary extension.

RISE IN CITY RENTS FOUGHT BY MAYOR

He Urges OPA 'Unqualifiedly' to Reject Landlords' Plea for 10% Blanket Increase

By LEE E. COOPER

Mayor La Guardia has asked the Office of Price Administration to reject "unqualifiedly" the petition of New York City landlords for a blanket increase of at least 10 per cent in housing rents, it became known last night.

In a 10,000-word memorandum filed with the OPA "as Mayor and on behalf of the tenants residing in the City of New York," Mr. La Guardia replied in detail to each of the objections to the rent ceiling regulations voiced by property owners in their plea for an increase, and called an upward adjustment of charges for living quarters here "unjustified and unwarranted."

He charged that the petitioners had "only one real aim—to impair the successful administration of rent control in New York."

The Mayor's brief challenges as "false and fantastic" the estimates of the petitioning groups that there were upward of 79,000 habitable apartment units available for rent in the five boroughs on Oct. 8, 1943.

He cited figures and surveys, including many by the Real Estate Board of New York, to support his contention that New York owners have been enjoying the "best rental market in almost two decades," disputed the argument that there had been a general increase in realty taxes and in scathing tone answered the statistics regarding foreclosures and depressed conditions in the realty market.

The Mayor's memorandum was tinged with sarcasm also in his answer to the plea that higher operating costs of buildings justified a rent rise. He expressed the view that the increase in apartment occupancy alone had "entirely or at least substantially offset any increase in building maintenance costs," while many building owners at the same time, he charged, were employing fewer workers and curtailing service. Although there has been a rise in fuel costs, he added, "thousands of tenants have

Continued on Page Fifteen

TWIN GAINS IN ITALY

British 16 Miles Below Rome After Cutting Coastal Railway

CISTERNA IS MENACED

Americans Half Mile From Town—Allies on Lower Front Gain

By MILTON BRACKER
By Wireless to THE NEW YORK TIMES.

ALGIERS, Feb. 1—Smashing ahead against furious resistance, American troops have driven into the suburbs of Cisterna, the most vital choke-point in the German supply system below Rome.

There the Appian Way and the main coastal railway intersect. Through the town enormous quantities of supplies have passed to the German forces on the lower front.

[The Americans were only a half-mile from Cisterna proper, according to The United Press.]

British units farther west have eased the Americans' task by driving three miles beyond Aprilia along the road from Anzio, cutting the railroad at the Campoleone station ten miles above Cisterna and hammering into the outskirts of Campoleone proper, one mile beyond.

But, while the Allies appear to be about to sever the electrified trackage at two points and the historic highway at one, the Germans have finally brought down reinforcements from north of Rome. Thus, although the British and American penetrations threaten the flank of the German defense line along five miles of the railway between the Campoleone station and Cisterna, the Allies must be prepared to meet a thrust from the north on their own exposed left flank.

No Factor of Surprise

The probability of new German pressure from the north has long been expected and in no way gives the Germans the advantage of surprise. But how large a force the enemy has been able to divert to the south and whether he can build it up to constitute a grave menace are not known.

Offsetting factors are the continuing Allied air offensive against all the supply routes leading to Rome, which militates against further troop movement, and the fine weather around the beachheads, which is permitting the Allies to expand on an even more solid foundation.

The battlefield is still wedge-shaped. Its point is at the Anzio-Nettuno area and its rim extends between Campoleone and Cisterna. At the outskirts of the former village the British are barely sixteen miles from Rome, while the Americans clamping down on Cisterna are twenty-six miles from the capital. The ten-mile stretch between, along which the Germans have built their defenses, is within easy range of light artillery. Continued naval bombardments between the beachhead and Formia throttled

Continued on Page Eight

$103,889,600 in War Bonds Sold At Rally on Stock Exchange Floor

After being "told" by the marines—specifically Lieut. Gen. Alexander A. Vandegrift, commandant of the Marine Corps—Wall Street yesterday "told" it to Hitler and Hirohito by subscribing for $103,889,600 in bonds of the Fourth War Loan.

General Vandegrift, addressing 2,000 brokers and employes at a rally on the floor of the New York Stock Exchange, Wall and Broad Streets, declared the quick success of the drive would be "equal to a major victory on the battlefield—and it will not cost a single drop of blood."

Emil Schram, president of the Exchange, announced the day's total, which brought the aggregate of both purchases and sales made by members of the Exchange in 322 cities and forty-six States to $501,000,000 in the current drive.

Another large subscription announced yesterday was $55,000,000 by the Mutual Life Insurance Company of New York. Lewis W. Douglas, president, said it was the company's way of celebrating its 101st birthday. The Mutual Life's Government bond holdings have increased by $310,344,000 since Pearl Harbor, he said.

Huge sales were recorded in city, State and nation yesterday, the first day on which the books were opened in the drive for corporate subscriptions. At the same time sales of E-bonds, the type favored by the small investor, continued to soar as they have since

Continued on Page Fourteen

MARSHALL ISLANDS BASE WHERE WE HAVE ESTABLISHED BEACHHEADS

The Japanese airfield on Roi (left). Coral strip connects it with Namur (right), on which the enemy has a roadway.
Associated Press Wirephoto (U. S. Navy)

BERLIN'S BLOT-OUT PUT NEARER BY RAF

10,000 Tons of Bombs Loosed in January on City—Sunday's Blow Fired Plant Areas

By DREW MIDDLETON
By Cable to THE NEW YORK TIMES.

LONDON, Feb. 1—The city of Berlin, until lately the heart of Hitler's great military empire, is dying under the British bombing assault, which in January devoted about 10,000 tons of missiles to the destruction of the Reich capital in six great assaults.

[During daylight RAF Coastal Command planes attacked German shipping off Norway, sinking a mine-sweeper, setting a cargo ship afire and shooting up an escort vessel.

[Telephone contact between Stockholm and Berlin was broken early Tuesday night, but was re-established at 11:45 P. M. and Swedish correspondents in the Reich capital gave no indication that there had been a new at-

Continued on Page Seven

Soviet Republics Get Right To Own Armies and Envoys

By W. H. LAWRENCE
By Wireless to THE NEW YORK TIMES.

MOSCOW, Feb. 1—The Supreme Soviet late tonight unanimously approved a proposal by Foreign Commissar Vyacheslaff M. Molotoff for major changes in the Soviet constitutional system under which each of the sixteen constituent republics will form its own army formations and have separate diplomatic representation abroad.

[The text of Mr. Molotoff's statement appears on page 10.]

In less than four hours of debate, including the forty-three-minute opening address by Mr. Molotoff, both chambers approved the constitutional changes by a show of hands without having the full text read to them. They had copies of the proposal in their desks but they waived the reading of it.

On the motion of President Mikhail I. Kalinin, the Supreme Soviet also elected Nikolai Shevrnik as first Vice President of the Presidium of the U.S.S.R. and then adjourned sine die.

While Premier Joseph Stalin looked on from a back-row seat on the platform, Mr. Molotoff gave a general outline of the Government's new plan which, he said, resulted

Continued on Page Ten

KINGISEPP IS TAKEN IN RED ARMY SWEEP

Entry of Estonia Is Indicated as Three-Way Drive Squeezes the Germans in Pocket

By The United Press.

LONDON, Wednesday, Feb. 2—Gen. Leonid A. Govoroff's Leningrad army captured the German stronghold of Kingisepp yesterday after brief street battles, while his advanced spearheads pushed on toward Estonia along a ten-mile front, reaching to within less than a mile of the border at the town of Keikino. [The western edge of Keikino is only 300 yards from the border.]

The Red Army was nearing the border on a front northwest of Kingisepp and it was probable that some units might have crossed into the Baltic State.

More than fifty towns and settlements were captured yesterday—the eve of the first anniversary of the German defeat at Stalingrad — by General Govoroff's army, which concentrated its over-all offensive in three directions along a sixty-five-mile front curving down from the Gulf of Finland to within thirty-three miles north-

Continued on Page Eleven

FLEET CONFIDENT ON WAY TO ATOLL

Fight Tougher Than Tarawa Seen but Men Were Sure Marshalls Would Fall

By ROBERT TRUMBULL
By Wireless to THE NEW YORK TIMES.

ABOARD A FLAGSHIP APPROACHING KWAJALEIN ATOLL, Jan. 30 (Delayed)—A large part of the American Navy, constituting the most powerful sea force ever assembled, is converging from north and south today on Kwajalein Atoll in the Japanese mandated Marshall Islands. We have already attacked with planes and naval gunfire, and tomorrow we land our troops.

Today a number of battleships, including our newest and largest, opened fire on Kwajalein's principal shore installations.

For the first time we are invading a part of the Japanese empire and in so doing we are exposing ourselves to possible strong aerial and submarine opposition and natural hazards of which we have little knowledge. We are in waters now that have been the cruising area of the Japanese fleet exclusively for many years. We would like very much to meet that fleet here and now.

Tomorrow the Fourth Marine Division and the Seventh Army Division comprising an amphibious force under command of Rear Admiral Richmond Kelly Turner will make the most audacious attack attempted by the United States in this war.

We expect Kwajalein to be tougher than Tarawa. We know we will lose many men on the beaches. We expect Japanese dive bombers and submarines to sink

Continued on Page Four

War News Summarized

WEDNESDAY, FEBRUARY 2, 1944

American marines and soldiers set foot for the first time in this war on Japanese territory and established beachheads near Roi and Kwajalein Islands in the Marshalls. Under the cover of hundreds of planes and the guns of battleships, cruisers and smaller craft, the American forces were beating down strong opposition with apparently moderate casualties.

The Seventh Infantry Division landed near Kwajalein and the Fourth Marine Division near Roi, both in the Kwajalein Atoll. The combined air forces pounded Maloelap, Wotje, Mili, Jaluit and Eniwotek and Wake Island in addition to Kwajalein. [All the foregoing 1:8, map P. 2.]

A large part of our Navy sailed confidently into a ring of Japanese air and submarine bases to hammer the Marshalls and protect the landing forces. [1:7.] Tokyo papers said an American victory there would be a "regrettable loss." [3:5.]

In the Southwest Pacific and in Burma the Japanese were also under heavy attack. At Rabaul, New Britain, they lost at least twenty-three planes and it was revealed that an Allied post had been established within Netherland New Guinea. [3:1, with map.] American-trained Chinese troops advanced five miles in two days in the Hukawng Valley in Burma. [7:5.]

President Roosevelt answered Japanese propaganda by saying our troops were in India not for political but for military purposes—"to assure the defeat of Japan." [4:2.] He repeated assurance that the individuals responsible for atrocities against prisoners would be tracked down and brought to justice. [5:5.]

The Fifth Army fighting on the beachhead below Rome had reached the outskirts of Campoleone and Cisterna, threatening to close a pincers around the Germans, who were said to be rushing reinforcements from northern Italy. [1:3; map P. 8.] American fliers hit the enemy's refueling airfields at Klagenfurt, Austria, and Aviano and Udine; the RAF struck Trieste. [8:1.]

Russian troops captured Kingisepp and moved to within a few hundred yards of the Estonian border. More than ninety places were recaptured in gains on many fronts. [1:6; map P. 11.]

Moscow presented a sudden, new development when the Supreme Soviet unanimously approved proposals of Foreign Commissar Molotoff changing the constitutional system whereby the sixteen constituent republics would have their own army formations and their own diplomatic corps. This would tend to give Russia sixteen votes at the peace conference. [1:5-6.] A writer in the Soviet newspaper Izvestia said the Vatican's policy was "pro-fascist in character." [1:6-7.]

Izvestia Calls Pope Pro-Fascist; Says Catholics Are Disillusioned

By The United Press.

MOSCOW, Feb. 1—The Government newspaper Izvestia asserted today that Vatican foreign policy had disillusioned Catholics throughout the world and "earned the hatred and contempt of the Italian masses for supporting fascism."

Endorsing a report issued on Jan. 15 by the Foreign Policy Association, New York, which said that a rising tide of anti-clericalism might be expected in Italy, the Soviet organ said the Vatican pledged its support to Italian fascism following conclusion of the Lateran treaty in February, 1929, "but the Vatican's support for fascism wasn't limited solely to Italy. It approved many acts of aggression by fascism although the true meaning of these aggressions was no secret.

"The Vatican is now suffering the consequences of its endorsement of the Italian conquest of Abyssinia and is now reaping the fruits of the débâcle of the Italian African empire."

Reviewing Vatican foreign policy before and during the present war, Izvestia said "the disgraceful role the Vatican played in Hitler's and Mussolini's Spanish adventure is widely known. The Vatican emerged in the role of a supporter of armed intervention."

It said Generalissimo Francisco Franco of totalitarian Spain was a "Vatican pet" and that Generalissimo Franco's Spain was the "image of the clerical States of post-war Europe" which the Vati-

Continued on Page Eleven

GRIP ON KWAJALEIN

Marine and Infantry Units Strike, Shielded by Record Armada

LOSSES ARE MODERATE

Our Forces as Close to Japan as Foe Was to U. S. at Pearl Harbor

By GEORGE F. HORNE
By Telephone to THE NEW YORK TIMES.

PEARL HARBOR, Feb. 1—Tremendous American amphibious forces have invaded the Marshall Islands and established beachheads in bitter fighting on islands of the Kwajalein Atoll.

Admiral Chester W. Nimitz, Commander in Chief of the Pacific Fleet and of the Pacific Ocean Areas, announced this morning what most of the world had surmised: that United States fighting strength was being pitted on Japanese soil for the first time in what must be considered a decisive battle in the war of the Pacific.

Protected by fire power overshadowing anything we had concentrated against the fierce warriors who dreamt of dictating peace terms in the White House, well-trained forces, both marines and Army infantrymen now skilled in amphibious operations, stormed ashore yesterday morning in daylight.

As they went in at fighting pitch and armed with the best weapons ingenuity can provide, carrier aircraft and surface forces bombarded and raked near-by atolls to blanket the enemy.

The assault forces landed on unidentified islands in the vicinity of Roi and Kwajalein, both in the Kwajalein Atoll.

Strong opposition has been encountered, but first reports from the area, necessarily meager, are in an optimistic tone. The first stages of the operation appear to have opened successfully.

[Besides Kwajalein and Roi, the landing forces had as an objective a third Japanese base, Namur Island.

[A Japanese Imperial Headquarters announcement recorded from the Tokyo radio by CBS said Army and Navy garrisons had counter-attacked and that "furious fighting is now in progress."]

Admiral Nimitz's communiqué stated that "initial information indicates that our casualties are moderate."

Spruance Again in Command

Vice Admiral Raymond A. Spruance, who directed the successful Gilberts invasion only ten weeks ago, again is in command.

Roi Island is in the northern

Continued on Page Three

We Lose 22 Planes, Save All but 6 Men

By The United Press.

WASHINGTON, Feb. 1—The Navy revealed tonight that twenty-two Corsair fighter planes from a twenty-three-plane marine squadron were lost in a severe storm last Friday while on a "routine flight" between the American-held Gilbert and Ellice Islands.

All but six of the pilots have been rescued. The body of one was also recovered.

One of the twenty-two planes made a crash landing in the Ellice Islands, but the other twenty-one, so far as is known, were forced down at sea.

The Navy said search operations were started immediately after the one plane had arrived safely at the Ellice Island base.

The next of kin of the dead pilot and the five still missing have been notified.

Loss of the planes was revealed in a Pacific Fleet headquarters announcement released here and at Pearl Harbor.

U. S. Marine Corps

Marines advancing on Majuro in the Marshall Islands.

Two Japanese soldiers surrender to Marines during the battle of the Marshalls.

U. S. Marine Corps

"All the News That's Fit to Print."

The New York Times.

LATE CITY EDITION
Cloudy and windy with showers this afternoon; colder tonight.
Temperatures Yesterday—Max., 45; Min., 28
Sunrise, [illegible] A. M.; Sunset, [illegible] P. M.

Section 1

NEWS INDEX, PAGE 43, THIS SECTION

Copyright, 1944, by The New York Times Company.

VOL. XCIII..No. 31,424. Entered as Second-Class Matter, Postoffice, New York, N. Y. NEW YORK, SUNDAY, FEBRUARY 6, 1944. Including Magazine and Book Sections. TEN CENTS New York City and Suburban Area (15c Elsewhere)

BRITISH REPEL NAZI TANK ATTACKS; RUSSIANS TAKE LUTSK AND ROVNO; KWAJALEIN ISLAND IS CAPTURED

FEDERAL VOTE FOES BALKED IN SENATE ON POINT OF QUORUM

Barkley Brings Quick End to Saturday Sitting as His Side Is Outnumbered

MEMBERS STILL ARRIVING

Only 44 on Hand When Count Is Made, With at Least 24 Listed for State Plan

By C. P. TRUSSELL

Special to THE NEW YORK TIMES.

WASHINGTON, Feb. 5—Quick action by Administration forces brought an extraordinary Saturday session of the Senate to an abrupt halt without the transaction of any business today when it appeared that the Green-Lucas bill for the service men's ballot under Federal auspices was heading into new difficulties.

Senator Alben W. Barkley, the majority leader, moved for adjournment after only forty-four members had responded to the quorum calls. He acted so unexpectedly that opponents of the Green-Lucas measure were caught off guard. Senators arriving in the chamber a little later were surprised to find the session ended.

Twenty-six of those present when the adjournment motion came had supported the motion of Senator John H. Overton of Louisiana yesterday to lay aside the Green-Lucas bill and take up amendments to the House-adopted Eastland-Rankin "States' Rights" bill, a motion which lost by a tie vote of 42 to 42. Only seventeen of those who had opposed the Overton motion, which was scheduled to be renewed today, had made their appearance.

Alignment of Absentees

Among the absentees were twenty-four who were opposed to taking up the House amendments before completing action on the Green-Lucas bill and only sixteen who voted yesterday for adoption of the Overton motion.

A checking of the quorum roll call showed further that twenty-four supporters of the Senate "States' Rights" substitute for the Green-Lucas bill, which was defeated yesterday by a vote of 46 to 42, but provisions of which are scheduled for further tests, were present, while only twenty Green-Lucas bill backers were on hand.

The absentees included twenty-six Senators who had helped defeat the "States' Rights" substitute yesterday and eighteen of its supporters.

The Overton motion had the status of being not only renewable, but privileged, and could have taken preference over the issue now pending before the Senate. This issue is an amendment by Senator John A. Danaher, Republican, of Connecticut, to provide that the proposed Federal ballot, which would be issued in blank form automatically to all eligible voters in the armed forces, would be valid only if received by the appropriate election officials of the district, county or other voting unit of the State of residence of the voter not later than 12 o'clock noon on the date of the election.

1942 Arrest Motion Cited

Some States permit the counting of absentee ballots which arrive nearly a week after election day, while some require that they arrive twenty-four hours before the election.

In the light of Senator Barkley's maneuver today it was recalled that during the Saturday session of Nov. 14, 1942, he offered a motion for the arrest of absentee Senators. That was when the poll tax bill filibuster was on.

Whereas forty-three Senators were reported to be out of town on that day, Senator Barkley spoke of only three as being out of town today and one ill. All four opposed both the Overton motion and the "States' Rights" substitute yesterday. Their absence, Senator Barkley said, was a factor in his decision to move adjournment.

Postponement of further action in the Senate until Monday brought with it an indication that the soldier voting issue will remain on the floor well into next week, despite the asserted urgency of action on the legislation providing for continuance of the Commodity Credit Corporation, which is handling much of the consumer price subsidy program, beyond Feb. 17, to which it was extended when

Continued on Page Thirty-four

£20,000 to Churchill By Strakosch Will

By Cable to THE NEW YORK TIMES.

LONDON, Feb. 5—Winston Churchill, Field Marshal Jan Christiaan Smuts, Viscount Simon, Minister of Information Brendan Bracken and Sir Otto Niemeyer and Sir Findlater Stewart, financial experts, are included among a number of prominent people mentioned as legatees in the will of Sir Henry Strakosch, banker and economist, which was made public today.

Sir Henry, who died last Oct. 30, bequeathed £20,000 to Mr. Churchill "as a token of friendship and gratitude for his and his wife's great kindness and hospitality." Marshal Smuts, with whom Sir Henry had a long association, receives £10,000, Lord Simon £5,000 and Mr. Bracken, Sir Otto and Sir Findlater £2,500 each.

Sir Henry left more than £2,454,500 gross in the largest individual fortune to be probated since that of Walter Melville Wills, British tobacco magnate, who died in January, 1941, leaving a fortune of more than £4,371,300.

E-BOND BUYERS SET CITY RECORD IN DAY

Individuals' Purchases Now 53% of Quota—Over-All Total Here at 86%

New York City's growing army of small investors rang up their biggest single day in the Fourth War Loan drive on Friday when they bought $8,772,000 worth of E bonds, according to figures released yesterday by the War Finance Committee of New York. Manhattan accounted for $5,357,600 worth.

For the entire city total sales of all issues to individual investors have reached $373,408,800, or 53.5 per cent of the city's quota for individuals. Subscriptions by all classifications of buyers are now within 14 per cent of the over-all drive quota of $3,683,311,000. This is made up largely of "big money" purchases of the market issues.

In Washington, the Treasury reported that sales in the fourth war loan drive totaled $10,752,000,000 through today, or 77 per cent of the $14,000,000,000 goal, according to The Associated Press. Sales to individuals totaled $2,637,000,000 and to corporations $8,115,000,000.

In a nation-wide radio program yesterday afternoon Under-Secretary of the Treasury Daniel W. Bell accredited 1,500,000 Boy Scouts as war bond aides for Boy Scout Week, which begins Tuesday. They will make a door-to-door canvass throughout the country.

Addressing 400 Scouts at the National Broadcasting Company studio here, Capt. Eddie Rickenbacker, a member of the national executive board of the Boy Scouts of America, emphasized the need for greater effort on the home front. He reminded the Scouts that they were now "tackling the biggest, the most important, mission in Scout history." He said that if each Scout sold ten bonds it "might help tip the balance and bring victory closer."

Dr. Elbert K. Fretwell, Chief Scout Executive, recalled that in the last war the Scouts, with a membership of less than 400,000, sold $2,300,000 worth of Liberty Bonds, or more than five bonds apiece. With a present membership of four times that of World War I, he suggested, the Scouts

Continued on Page Seventeen

HOSPITALS TO GET 100% MORE BUTTER FROM U. S. STOCKS

Prices Tumble in Black Market as Many Consumers Shift to Use of Oleomargarine

STORES' SUPPLIES RISING

But Government Sounds Note of Caution—City Patients Due to Get Chicken

By JEFFERSON G. BELL

The Federal Government is doubling the allotment of butter recently made to hospitals from its huge hoard of 130,000,000 pounds. At the same time the black market is offering stocks at reductions of as much as 11 cents a pound.

Those and other surprises in a rapid succession yesterday found the trade agog along the butter front. Not the least speculation centered around another big shipment of butter reported en route from Argentina.

Stocks of butter in the hands of local retailers gradually are increasing. Improved supplies are attributed not only to increased national production but to larger production in the New York milkshed as handlers find they must churn large quantities of heavy cream that cannot compete with Western cream, about $5 a tin cheaper, in the manufacture of ice cream and sour cream.

Butter Consumption Lower

Moreover, the trade reports a huge drop in butter consumption may be attributed in part to butterless luncheons begun by restaurants and hotels in response to proclamations by Mayor La Guardia.

Cottage cheese, marmalade and, above all, oleomargarine have taken the place of butter on luncheon menus. There is much speculation on the extent to which these substitutes permanently may supplant butter. This speculation is based in part on Government statistics showing that the nation's production of oleomargarine jumped to 610,131,000 pounds in 1943, from 423,277,000 in 1942 and 365,209,000 in 1941. As production of margarine goes up production of butter goes down.

The nation's production of creamery butter totaled 1,685,825,000 pounds in 1943, representing a drop of 4 per cent in 1942 production and 3 per cent in the ten-year average from 1931 to 1942.

The improvement in local supplies of butter in retailers' hands was estimated last week at 30 per cent above the preceding week by City Markets Commissioner Henry M. Brundage. The increase was sufficient to restore confidence among some shopkeepers who began to paste signs in their windows, reading:

"Yes, we have butter; come in and get it."

A Note of Caution Sounded

Government representatives are prompt to sound a note of caution against overoptimism based on what they characterize as only a very slight improvement in butter supplies. They point out that huge quantities still are required for the armed forces, lend-lease and other priority groups. They explain that the release of additional supplies to hospitals has been made possible by a number of other factors than by increased January production.

Last November the War Food Administration released some 5,000,000 pounds of butter from excess stocks to hospitals throughout the country. Stocks were sufficient to allow each patient three-

Continued on Page Thirty-six

50 Shells From Freighter's Gun Fall in 2 Staten Island Villages

The quiet of the old residential villages of Grymes Hill and Ward Hill on Staten Island was shattered early yesterday afternoon by exploding shells, accidentally fired from a 20-millimeter rapid-fire anti-aircraft gun mounted on a freighter anchored in Upper New York Bay, between Tompkinsville and Stapleton.

Within two minutes more than fifty shells, unexploded and exploded, crashed into streets and yards, shattering a garage door, blasting a tree and wrecking the rear of a parked automobile. There was great excitement among the 800 residents of the villages, but the police reported that no one had been injured.

Residents said that the whine of the shells in flight and the resultant explosions resembled a miniature battle. The ship is anchored about two miles from the two villages, which are on high elevations. It was reported that fifty-six shell cases, automatically ejected after firing from the gun's mechanism, were found on the deck of the vessel. The police said they had been informed that a gunner on the vessel was removing a canvas storm cover from the gun when it was inadvertently set into action.

Several shells landed in the street near the home of Mr. and Mrs. Louis Marchi, who were at home with their two sons, Ensign John Marchi, 22 years old, and Ferdinand Marchi, 19, who soon will enter the armed forces. Mr. Marchi was ill.

"The shells as they came over

Continued on Page Twenty-seven

Nazis Say Norway Fears Russian Blow

DNB broadcast a report from Oslo yesterday saying that Norwegians feared a Russian attempt to launch an invasion on the northern tip of Norway. The broadcast, recorded by The United Press, quoted the newspaper Aftenposten as saying:

"The fact that Soviet landing barges were sailing in a convoy that was recently attacked by U-boats off Murmansk has caused wide anxiety in Norway. What do the Soviets intend to do with these landing barges? It is evident that they could be used only against Norway."

NEW ALLIED POLICY ON FRENCH IS SEEN

Algiers Committee Now Viewed as an Asset—Dropping of Italian King Held Likely

By JOHN MacCORMAC

Special to THE NEW YORK TIMES.

WASHINGTON, Feb. 5—A reorientation of Anglo-American foreign policies that will entail closer cooperation with the French Committee of National Liberation, recognition of the hopeless unpopularity of King Victor Emmanuel of Italy and his son, Crown Prince Humbert, and continued pressure on Spain to drop all connection with the Axis is believed to be imminent.

The lack of definiteness in Anglo-American policy in regard to political situations in Europe, for which Washington and London have been criticized, has been largely caused, it is said, by military exigency. In French North Africa, in Italy and in Spain military considerations were recognized as paramount and, as a result, political action has been subject to the continuing vetos of the Combined Chiefs of Staff and the military commanders in the field.

In Italy, for instance, all political activity was prohibited until a few weeks ago by a Combined Staff directive. Since then, another directive has been issued giving the commanding general discretion to allow political meetings.

Relations with Spain have also

Continued on Page Seven

3 MORE ISLES WON

Southern Tip of Giant Kwajalein Atoll Taken After 4-Day Battle

WAKE ISLAND IS HIT AGAIN

U. S. Bombers Also Strike at Eniwetok, Jaluit and Mili in Marshalls Campaign

By GEORGE F. HORNE

By Telephone to THE NEW YORK TIMES.

PEARL HARBOR, Feb. 5—Seventh Division Army troops have captured Kwajalein Island and two other important isles of the Kwajalein Atoll, Pacific Fleet headquarters announced today, and the most successful naval and military operation in the central Pacific campaign is nearing its final phase.

Kwajalein's defenses collapsed under the unrelenting pressure of the veterans of Attu, the amphibious troops of Maj. Gen. Charles H. Corlett's infantry division. It was struck by our fighting men last Tuesday and they have fought their way doggedly across the reef-fringed island, about two and one-half miles long, against bitter resistance.

In the first stages of the battle the enemy dead reached more than 1,000, and as the garrison was estimated to have numbered only 2,000 men, the extension of the battle through four days is a clear indication that the enemy still fights to the end when cornered.

Our Losses Are Light

Our losses continued to be moderate, it was indicated.

Ebeye and Loi were the two other islands that fell to the Americans, Admiral Chester W. Nimitz said.

[An attack by landing troops on strongly fortified Gugegwe Island, four and one-half miles north of Loi, was under way and its fall was expected soon.

[Ebeye Island is a seaplane base equipped with hangars, shops and a radio station.]

The speed with which the invasion was accomplished has surprised everyone, including the enemy, and the moderate American losses in both the Seventh Infantry

Continued on Page Twenty

GERMANS PUNCH AT OUR LINE IN ITALY

Feb. 6, 1944

The enemy lunged fiercely at British forces on the Anzio-Nettuno beachhead, possibly between Aprilia and Campoleone or south of the German defense line between Campoleone and Cisterna. The Germans continued to say they had trapped Allied "battalions" north of Aprilia and beaten off relief tank attacks.

Russians Take 200 Places In 50-Mile Thrust in Poland

By RALPH PARKER

By Wireless to THE NEW YORK TIMES.

MOSCOW, Sunday, Feb. 6—The Russians last night announced the capture of Rovno, Lutsk and Zdolbunovo, as well as 200 other places deep in Poland. At the same time, it was announced that 2,000 prisoners had been taken so far in the resumed offensive of Gen. Nikolai F. Vatutin and that remnants of the Eighteenth and Nineteenth Hungarian Divisions had been routed in battle.

[The Russians are now eighty-five miles inside Poland on an east-west line, The Associated Press announced. A fifty-mile gain from the last reported positions held by the First Ukrainian Front armies was thereby indicated.]

The Soviet announcement also stated that strong German tank attacks launched south of Shpola and west of Zvenigorod in an attempt to break out of the middle Dnieper trap had failed. It was reported that, instead, the ring had tightened on the enemy.

[Two Russian columns, following the Dnieper River and advancing toward each other from the Kanev and Cherkassy areas, effected a junction near Kreshchatik, at the northeastern section of the ring containing the trapped Nazis. The Germans hugging the Dnieper thereby lost their last foothold on the river.]

On the Leningrad front Soviet forces were clearing the eastern bank of the Narva River and advancing along Lake Peipus. Further advances on Luga from the north also were announced.

Earlier last evening Premier Joseph Stalin had announced the spectacular Red Army gains in Poland. In an order of the day the fall of Rovno, Lutsk and Zdolbunovo Junction were announced, and

Continued on Page Twelve

BIG U. S. PLANES HIT FRENCH AIRFIELDS

1,800-Ton Blow at Nazi Bases Beyond Paris Paces Attack by 2,000 Allied Craft

By JAMES MacDONALD

By Cable to THE NEW YORK TIMES.

LONDON, Feb. 5—Powerful formations of American Flying Fortresses and Liberators escorted by large numbers of fighters—an estimated 1,200 Allied warplanes were on the mission—penetrated deep into France today. The "heavies" blasted six Nazi air bases around and beyond Paris.

The attack was one of the deadliest air onslaughts of the war, designed to weaken the Germans' waning power to attack.

United States Army headquarters here said among the targets hit were three bomber fields, on which were based the Heinkel 177's that launch the robot glider-bombs used recently in Nazi forays on Allied convoys. Others were fighter training bases and the big Luftwaffe repair depot at Villacoublay.

Tonight indications were that the Royal Air Force was attacking Germany—perhaps Berlin again.

Continued on Page Eleven

NEW BLOW AWAITED

Heavy Losses Inflicted on Germans Striking Back Near Rome

FOE CLINGS TO CASSINO

Americans Flank Stronghold on South—Berlin Reports Half of Town Lost

By MILTON BRACKER

By Wireless to THE NEW YORK TIMES.

ALGIERS, Feb. 5—Like louder rumbles before the storm, the Germans continued their counter-attacks in the Allies' wedge below Rome yesterday while, sixty miles to the south, other German troops clung to Cassino despite a see-saw battle in the northeast corner, where streets and buildings changed hands many times.

[Each side holds half the town, according to a Berlin broadcast recorded by The Associated Press.

[American troops slashed southward through the mountains behind Cassino on Saturday, leaving the town three-fourths encircled, The United Press reported from the front.]

The latest German blows on the upper front were aided by tanks. But this was not believed to be the main counter-offensive, which is expected at any time and is regarded as having serious possibilities. But the British and Americans have so far proved equal to the situation.

Yesterday British troops threw back the defenders, with heavy losses. Ninety more German prisoners were taken, to raise the total in this sector since the landing to 1,500 and the grand total for the campaign to more than 10,000.

Blow Struck Near Aprilia

The latest German punch was put in north of Aprilia, ten miles due north of Anzio on the main road connecting with the Appian Way. As in the previous counter-attacks north of Padiglione and near Cisterna, the exact site of the battlefield was not specified.

This was particularly puzzling today because it was known that several days ago, British spearheads had thrust four miles beyond Aprilia to cross the coastal railway at the Campoleone station and push on to Campoleone proper. The possibility was noted, therefore, that the latest German assault had been made across the road between Aprilia and Campoleone and had thus threatened to cut off the northernmost British forces.

It seemed more likely that the attack had been made somewhat east of the road and had been based on the known German defense line along the coastal electrified trackage linking the Campoleone station and Cisterna, ten miles below. This would also be northwest of Padiglione, and the theory would tend to confirm yesterday's suggestion that the present German striking forces were somewhere between the railway defenses and Padiglione.

Some of the latest prisoners in this area were identified as belonging to the German Twenty-sixth Armored Division. This made at least the third German division identified on this front. It indicates how, despite the ceaseless Allied air and naval support, the Germans have been able to provide reinforcements for the region. The Allies' air offensive, which was greatly curtailed yesterday by the weather, has recently hammered at Popoli and Avezzano, on the Pescara-Rome road along which, conceivably, the Germans would travel from the Adriatic to the Rome area.

Cassino Position Unchanged

The general picture around Cassino yesterday duplicated that of the previous day. The Americans, who have tortuously hooked their way to the back door of the town via the Gustav Line and the mountains to the north, drove ceaselessly downhill from Mount Majola to the northeastern rim of their objective.

Tanks were brought up with

Continued on Page Four

War News Summarized

SUNDAY, FEBRUARY 6, 1944

The German Twenty-sixth Armored Division continued to probe the perimeter of the Allied bridgehead below Rome yesterday in what Algiers believed was only the preliminary to a full-scale assault. Allied headquarters said British elements had contained the German attacks. [1:8.]

Moscow announced with a full salute of guns the capture of Rovno and Lutsk in Poland. Berlin had announced "evacuation" of the two centers two days before. The Russians said the advance was on a sixty-five-mile front and that they had liberated 200 towns and captured 2,000 Hungarian soldiers during the drive. The expanding salient put the Red armies eighty miles inside Poland and within 290 miles of the pre-war German border. To the southeast other Soviet forces continued to attack the ten German divisions caught in the middle Dnieper River pocket. The Red Air Force shot down twenty-two more Junkers transport planes, bringing the two-day bag to 106 planes. [1:6-7; map, P. 12.]

American heavy bombers based on Britain shifted their target for the day from German factories to German airfields and heavily attacked six airdromes in the vicinity of Paris. The Luftwaffe declined the issue. Only two bombers were lost. Headquarters said that three of the airfields hit were those from which German glider-launching bombers had been taking off for raids on Atlantic convoys. At least 700 of our bombers and 500 fighters were believed to have participated. While the "heavies" were hitting the Paris airfields medium bombers were ranging fighter strips and other enemy defenses along the Channel coast. [1:7.]

Other American heavy bombers, based in the Mediterranean, attacked the former French naval base at Toulon for the first time since Nov. 24. The Vichy radio said they had hit and left burning the 26,500-ton battleship Dunkerque, which the French Navy scuttled and which the Germans were reported attempting to salvage [8:1.]

Halfway around the world, in the Marshall Islands of the central Pacific, United States combined operations cleaned out remaining Japanese resistance on three islands of Kwajalein Atoll, putting all but eleven of the thirty coral spits in full American control. Admiral Nimitz announced at the same time that during the last three days Army and Navy planes had raided Jaluit, Mili, Eniwetok and Wake to keep immobilized any possible air retaliation from those Japanese bases against the Kwajalein operation. [1:5; map, P. 20.]

That the Japanese were becoming daily more concerned was indicated in a broadcast by Premier Tojo. He told his people the war was "increasing in ferocity" and that the nation must be even more completely mobilized than it is now "to win the decisive victory." [19:3.]

On the diplomatic front, Washington observers saw in the offing a reorientation of British-American foreign policies involving closer cooperation with the French Committee of National Liberation, a recognition of the unpopularity of the throne in Italian political circles and continued pressure on Spain to sever all Axis ties. [1:4.]

U. S. to Lay Oil Line in Near East; 1,200-Mile Pipe to Aid Our Forces

By JOHN H. CRIDER

Special to THE NEW YORK TIMES.

WASHINGTON, Feb. 5—By building a pipeline about 1,200 miles across Saudi Arabia from Persian Gulf refineries to the Mediterranean at a cost of $130,000,000 to $165,000,000 the United States is going to obtain a minimum reserve of 1,000,000,000 barrels of petroleum to meet military and naval needs.

Announcement of the pipeline project was made tonight by Secretary Ickes in his capacity of President of the Petroleum Reserves Corporation.

The announcement marked the end of long negotiations between Mr. Ickes and three American oil companies which have interests in the Persian Gulf region, in which the Secretary lost out on proposals which oil company sources indicated would have carried the Government's participation in development of Arabian oil resources into the area of part ownership or control.

Under the agreement announced by Secretary Ickes between the Government and the Arabian-American Oil Company (owned by Standard Oil of California and the Texas Company) and Gulf Exploration Company (owned by the Gulf Oil Corporation), the Government undertakes to construct the pipeline.

More than the fact that this is

Continued on Page Seventeen

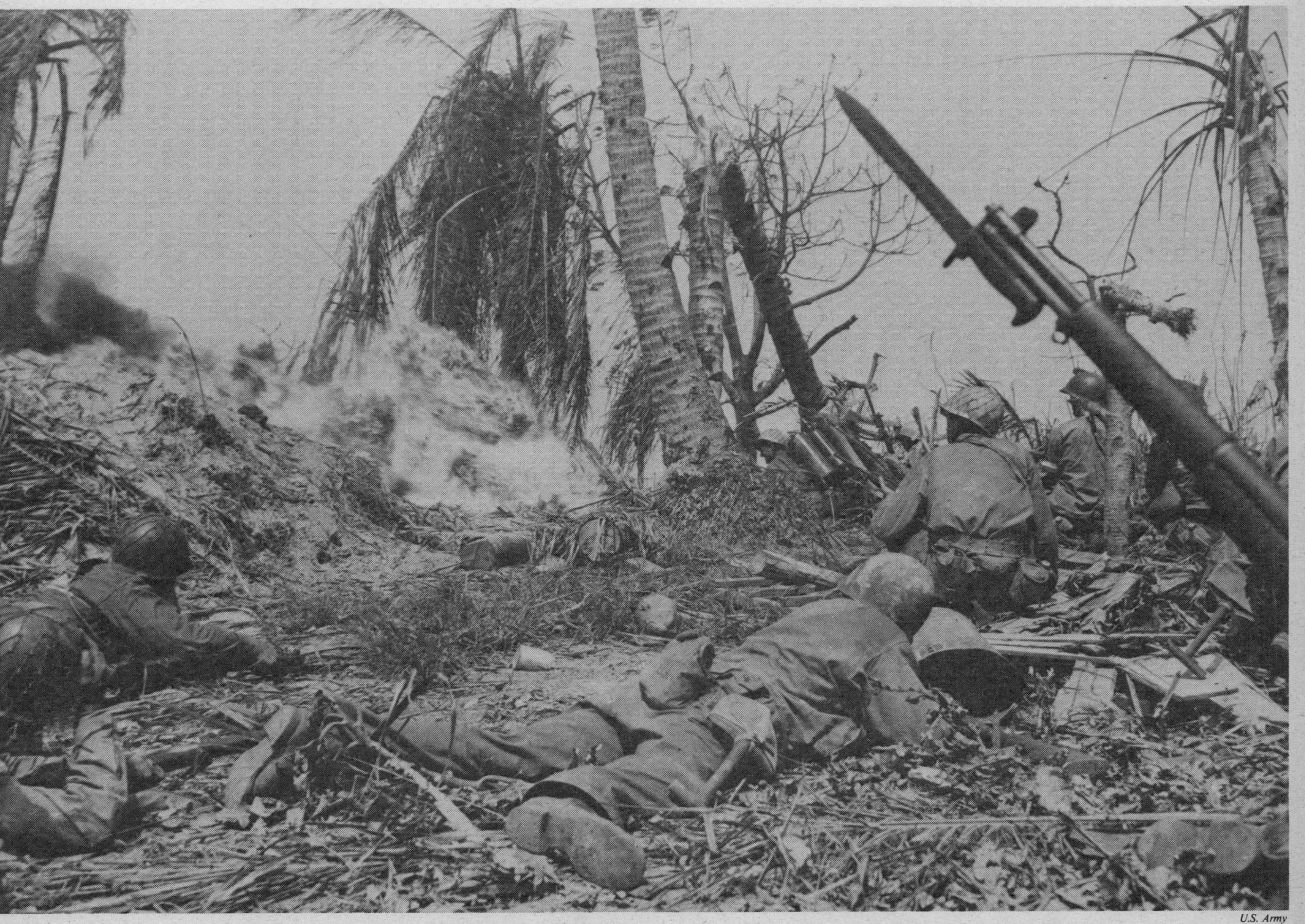

U.S. Army

U.S. Army 7th Division using flamethrowers on a Japanese blockhouse as troops invade Kwajalein Island.

Wide World Photos

View of Berlin street destroyed by allied air raids.

"All the News That's Fit to Print."

The New York Times.

LATE CITY EDITION
Rain and warmer, with fresh to strong winds.
Temperatures Yesterday—Max., 46; Min., 22
Sunrise, 7:21 A. M.; Sunset, 6:34 P. M.

Copyright, 1944, by The New York Times Company

VOL. XCIII..No. 31,454. Entered as Second-Class Matter. Postoffice, New York, N. Y. NEW YORK, TUESDAY, MARCH 7, 1944. THREE CENTS IN NEW YORK CITY

800 U. S. BOMBERS SMASH AT BERLIN BY DAY; 68 LOST IN BATTLES, 123 OF FOE SHOT DOWN; SOVIET DRIVE SLASHES ODESSA-LWOW LINE

ROOSEVELT CALLS ON AFL TO ALLOW CIO A VOICE IN ILO

Green Is Told That Rival Group Must Have Delegate at Philadelphia April 20

MURRAY'S DEMAND HEEDED

President Said to Have Asked for Solution by a Method to Share Representation

By LOUIS STARK
Special to THE NEW YORK TIMES.

WASHINGTON, March 6—President Roosevelt is reported to have informed William Green, president of the American Federation of Labor, today that the Congress of Industrial Organizations will have to be represented in the top delegation at the meeting of the International Labor Office in Philadelphia on April 20.

The President took a hand to settle a question that has been a thorny one for the Administration since 1936 when the CIO, through John L. Lewis, first made a demand that it have an official workers-delegate representative at the ILO rather than be limited to a certain number of labor advisers.

The AFL view has been that the constitution of the ILO provides that the workers-delegate and the industry-delegate shall be chosen from nominations made by the "most representative" labor and industry organizations. Thus far it has been held that these organizations in the United States are respectively the AFL and the Chamber of Commerce of the United States.

AFL Asked to Change Position

Mr. Green is said to have informed Mr. Roosevelt of the federation's objection to sharing the top workers' delegation with the CIO, which it regards as a "rival, rebel organization."

In the presence of Secretary of Labor Perkins who has usually been the Administration's go-between in matters dealing with delegates to the ILO, the President is understood to have indicated to Mr. Green that a way would have to be worked out to give the CIO adequate top recognition at the ILO conference.

How definite a reply Mr. Green made to the President was not ascertained. But it was later reported that Mr. Green would probably canvass opinions of members of the federation's executive council.

In this situation the Administration is reported to be between two fires because the CIO has become strong enough to challenge the position of the AFL and to threaten retaliation by a policy of "non-cooperation" in certain labor projects of the Administration.

Demand for 'Realistic' Policy

Several months ago a State Department committee on labor standards and social security, on which the AFL and CIO were represented, drew up a report which bore upon the work of the ILO.

Philip Murray, president of the CIO, refused to sign the report, contending that if the ILO was to handle such problems in "realistic" fashion it should be sufficiently "realistic" to include a CIO delegate in its top labor group at next month's meeting.

A memorandum to that effect was formulated by J. Raymond Walsh, CIO research chief, and served on Secretary Perkins. Since then the matter of a CIO delegate had been held in abeyance.

A Western Hemisphere meeting, fostered by the ILO in Havana in 1939, had two workers-delegates from the United States, George M. Harrison of the AFL Railway Clerks and James B. Carey of the CIO.

The AFL at that time asserted that Mr. Carey's appointment had not been made in consonance with an agreement which the federation had with Secretary Perkins. She is understood to have promised that "it will not happen again."

This incident was put in the "unofficial" category, since the Havana meeting was termed an "unofficial" and not "regular" meeting of the ILO.

However, now that President Roosevelt insists on CIO recognition, the AFL may have to decide on its formula for such representation. At Havana Mr. Harrison and Mr. Carey each had a half vote. Some such method may be the present solution.

The workers-delegate from the United States on the governing body of ILO since 1936 has been Robert J. Watt. He has also been the workers-delegate to the regular ILO meetings.

May 21 Designated As New Citizens Day

Special to THE NEW YORK TIMES.

WASHINGTON, March 6—President Roosevelt, acting under authority of a Congressional resolution, issued today a proclamation designating Sunday, May 21, as "I Am an American Day," a public occasion for giving "special recognition to all of our citizens who have attained their majority or have been naturalized during the past year."

The proclamation urged that exercises be held throughout the nation "to assist our citizens, both native-born and naturalized, to understand more fully the great privileges and responsibilities of citizenship in our democracy."

"Our nation," it said, "has been enriched, both spiritually and materially, by the naturalization of many thousands of foreign-born men and women and by the coming of age of great numbers of our youth, who have thereby achieved the full stature of citizenship, and these citizens have strengthened our country by their services at home and on the battlefield."

SOLDIER VOTE BILL IS REVAMPED AGAIN

Conferees' Move to Allow Some Use of Federal Ballot Here Stirs Mixed Opposition

By C. P. TRUSSELL
Special to THE NEW YORK TIMES.

WASHINGTON, March 6—The long contested service men's voting legislation ran into new troubles today when Senate and House conferees, meeting to give final approval to the "States' Rights" course adopted last week, decided instead to permit use of the Administration-endorsed Federal short) ballot in the United States under some circumstances.

By an undisclosed vote, the conferees adopted a provision under which service personnel from States having no absentee balloting laws, whether stationed in this country or overseas, could use the short ballot, provided the Governors of the States made two certifications by July 15.

First, the Governors would be required to certify that their States had made no provision for absentee balloting, and then that the use of the Federal ballot had been authorized by State law.

Previously the conferees had voted to prohibit the use of the short ballot by service personnel stationed in continental United States. Today's action was taken in the interest of citizens of Kentucky and New Mexico, and of South Carolina if its Legislature, now in session, fails to provide an absentee voting measure.

Mixed Opposition Encountered

The proposed relaxation of Federal ballot bans, the first since the conferees began tightening up the legislation, provoked adverse reactions, not only among the conferees themselves, but in the House, where the Eastland-Rankin bill, providing only for the use of State ballots, was adopted last month by the "stand-up-and-be-counted" vote for which President Roosevelt had asked.

Complaints were registered by backers of the Federal ballot as well as by those who wanted no relaxation at all. Representative Eugene Worley of Texas, head of the House conferees and himself the author of a Federal ballot plan, joined the dissenters.

Contending that the move on behalf of Kentucky and New Mexico was discriminatory, Mr. Worley in-

Continued on Page Thirty-four

Rebuilt U. S. Tanker Yugoslav Flagship

By The Associated Press.

MALTA, March 6—The American tanker Ohio was taken over today by the Yugoslav Navy as headquarters ship after a thorough overhauling.

The Ohio's battered hulk arrived in Malta in August, 1942, her cargo of oil intact, after being heavily attacked while crossing the Mediterranean in a convoy.

[The Ohio was built in 1940 at Chester, Pa., for the Texas Oil Company. The 9,624-ton vessel is 488 feet long and carried a crew of forty-three.]

CAIRO, Egypt, March 6 (Reuter)—Two Ministers of the Royal Yugoslav Government have been sent to London. This is regarded in the Middle East as the first move in important developments with regard to the Yugoslav émigré Government.

CAPITAL HOPEFUL OF AMERICAS' UNITY

Resolution Opposing Recognition of Argentine Regime Voted by Uruguay Chamber

Special to THE NEW YORK TIMES.

WASHINGTON, March 6—Hopes are held here that Uruguay and Paraguay will withhold recognition from the Farrell government in Argentina and that Chile will be found to have been the only Government to break the inter-American bloc by extending recognition in the present status of affairs.

Both countries were still watched closely today for signs indicating the course they would follow. Eyes also were focused on Brazil, not because of any special reports but apparently in the feeling that, if she extended recognition in the face of the refusal of the United States to do so, American solidarity would definitely be cracked.

[The Uruguayan Chamber of Deputies on Monday approved a motion suggesting that Uruguay not recognize the present Argentine Government, The United Press reported from Montevideo. The resolution termed the Farrell regime pro-fascist.]

Chile's Ties Understood

There is understanding here why Chile took her step, in view of her close relations with Argentina. But if the movement spread to other countries the diplomatic situation in this hemisphere would be altered. There were informal predictions that in this event the efficacy of the good-neighbor policy might be called into question.

There were hopes not only that Chile would be the only American Government, apart from the revolutionary junta in Bolivia, to recognize Argentina as matters stand but that the effect of her action might be softened by her using her influence in Buenos Aires to have Argentina carry out the measures urged by the United States.

It was apparent that hopes were being maintained that Argentina would straighten affairs satisfactorily to us. It was felt the Government might do so voluntarily. If it is not disposed to do so, there are elements in Argentina that

Continued on Page Eleven

ENEMY IS ISOLATED

20-Mile Breach Severs Foe's Direct Supply Route to Ukraine

TARNOPOL HUB MENACED

Red Army 11 Miles From Goal —Additional Soviet Attack Reported Farther East

By W. H. LAWRENCE
By Wireless to THE NEW YORK TIMES.

MOSCOW, Tuesday, March 7—The Soviet High Command announced last night that Marshal Gregory K. Zhukoff's troops of the First Ukrainian Front had smashed across the vital Odessa-Lwow railway and occupied a twenty-mile stretch of it between Proskurov and Tarnopol. The Russian communiqué said that preliminary reports of the first two days of this offensive had resulted in the death of more than 15,000 German officers and soldiers and the destruction or capture of large amounts of enemy material.

The most important news contained in the communiqué was that of the Red Army's severance of the Nazis double-track supply line by the capture of Volochisk. Volovtsy, fifteen miles east of Volochisk, and Narkevichi, eighteen miles west of Proskurov, also were captured.

The loss of this railroad on such a wide front presents a grave danger for the German troops remaining in the southern and western Ukraine, for it was the main line connecting them directly with Poland and Germany—and it was on that railroad that they had relied in large part for their supplies.

Because of their disaster they must fall back on lesser and indirect railroads that lead across the southern Ukraine into Bessarabia. They could, of course, be supplied or leave Russia by highway, but by any military standard such a method is inferior to the use of a good main-line railroad.

Red Army men moving on Tarnopol, well inside the western Ukraine and seventy-five miles east of Lwow, were doing their part to dismember the German communications system. The capture of Zbarazh, eleven miles northeast of Tarnopol, reveals that they have cleared the Shepetovka-

Continued on Page Eight

BACK FROM OUR FIRST ATTACK ON BERLIN

Pilots of Mustang fighters discussing their experiences after returning to their base in England on Saturday. Left to right: Lieuts. Carl G. Bickel, Alhambra, Calif.; Charles Koenig, Oakland, Calif.; Felix W. Rogers, West Newton, Mass., and James P. Keane, Penllyn, Pa.

The New York Times (U. S. Signal Corps Radiotelephoto)

ITALIAN CAMPAIGN SAPS FOE IN WEST

Germans Forced to Use Crack Anti-Invasion Troops and Drain Reserve Pool

By C. L. SULZBERGER
By Wireless to THE NEW YORK TIMES.

WITH THE FIFTH ARMY, in Italy, March 6—Although the Allies' campaign in Italy has clearly been disappointing and negative in its results, from the short-range viewpoint, in the effort to expand the Anzio beachhead, and simultaneously to penetrate the Liri Valley, effecting an eventual junction, it is necessary to view certain positive accomplishments in terms of the broad strategic picture.

This secondary front is indubitably aiding both the Russian advances and the western invasion potentialities by forcing the Germans to commit some of their best divisions and drain their shrunken reserves on the virtual eve of a climactic spring. Thus, as the Germans are devoting perhaps 50 per cent of their war production toward defense of the Continent and have left only perhaps 18 per

Continued on Page Six

U. S. Troops Go Into Action In Burma, Trap 2,000 of Foe

By The Associated Press.

NEW DELHI, India, March 6—American infantry units, in action for the first time on the Asiatic continent, have opened an attack in northern Burma under the direction of Lieut. Gen. Joseph W. Stilwell, who swore he would get even with the Japanese for the "hell of a beating" they gave him two years ago.

Veterans of the jungles of Guadalcanal and the southwest Pacific, scoring their first success in the drive to open a short-cut to China's Burma Road, have marched 200 miles behind the thick bush and struck the enemy a surprise blow from the rear, a communiqué from General Stilwell's headquarters announced.

Using an American adaptation of the roadblock—a tactic used by the Japanese in Burma two years ago and a trick that General Stilwell never forgot—the Americans planted themselves squarely across the Japanese line of retreat from Maingkwan, chief village of the Hukawng Valley.

Chinese Press From North

About 2,000 of the enemy were believed cut off by the American column that marched 117 miles from their railhead in northeast India, then struck eastward, then southward and eastward again and came out on the Walawbum Trail.

General Stilwell's Chinese troops, who have been pushing the Japanese back steadily for nearly two months in the Hukawng Valley, pressed in from the north, taking Maingkwan, while the Americans took Walawbum, ten miles southeast of Maingkwan.

Another strong force of Chinese moved to within ten miles of closing the encirclement by capturing a point to the northeast of Maingkwan, completing mopping-up operations at Wagahtawng, surrounding an enemy force at Lashu Ga and advancing southward.

The Americans were about seventy miles northwest of Myitkyina, the northern end of the railroad from Mandalay and 110 miles west of the Salween River, which in good

Continued on Page Two

AMERICANS JUMP NEARER TO MADANG

Amphibious Force Lands 30 Miles Above Saidor—Our Troops Gain in Admiralties

By FRANK L. KLUCKHOHN
By Wireless to THE NEW YORK TIMES.

ALLIED HEADQUARTERS IN THE SOUTHWEST PACIFIC, Tuesday, March 7—Troops of the dismounted First Cavalry Division pushed northward on the narrow peninsula of Los Negros Island in the Admiralties under Japanese artillery fire, and a small American amphibious force landed behind the enemy lines at Yaula Plantation, thirty miles northwest of Saidor on the New Guinea coast, Gen. Douglas MacArthur stated today.

Motor torpedo boats, instead of destroyers, along with bombers paved the way for the United States forces that leap-frogged the Japanese above Saidor in the Allied drive toward Madang. American patrols had already reached Herwarth Point, twenty miles above Saidor.

The landing at Yaula Plantation was a replica of the preceding larger landings in every sense. Royal Australian Air Force Kittyhawks and Bostons unloaded their explosives, while the PT boats kept up a constant fire as the infantrymen hit the beaches, following a preliminary shelling of enemy shore artillery. The Americans stormed ashore Sunday morning.

On Los Negros, in the Admiral-

Continued on Page Two

AIR WAR AT PEAK

Fortresses, Liberators Loose 2,000 Tons on German Capital

FIGHTERS SWARM ON NAZIS

Three-Hour Combat Over the Reich Gives Major Victory Against Luftwaffe

By DREW MIDDLETON
By Cable to THE NEW YORK TIMES.

LONDON, Tuesday, March 7—The war in the air reached a new and perhaps decisive phase yesterday when about 800 American heavy bombers fought their way through the massed strength of the Germans' metropolitan air force to blast factories, airfields and other military installations in the Berlin area.

The air battles that raged around and within the tight, wedge-shaped formations of Flying Fortresses and Liberators were the greatest in history, with American fighters, hundreds of which accompanied the bombers, and the "heavies" engaged throughout the mission.

Preliminary reports on the American victories said that eighty-three Nazi fighters were knocked down by the Mustangs, Thunderbolts and Lightnings of the United States Eighth and Ninth Air Forces and Royal Air Force that escorted and supported the big bombers.

The total of enemy fighters destroyed by the bombers had not yet been tabulated, but the gunners of one division alone of our "heavies" destroyed at least forty Nazi planes, boosting the minimum number of enemy aircraft shot down to 123.

Bombing Is Effective

In addition to these heavy losses to the Nazi fighter force, already suffering from the effects of two weeks of the Allies' heavy day and night attacks over the Reich, returning pilots reported "first rate" bombing results in the Berlin district.

[Probably more than 2,000 tons of bombs were dropped on Berlin's vital industrial and military targets, The Associated Press reported.]

American losses in the big blow at the Nazi capital were serious. Sixty-eight heavy bombers and eleven fighters were missing—representing a loss of nearly 700 trained airmen—Lieut. Gen. Carl A. Spaatz's Strategic Air Forces headquarters here reported.

The German radio claimed that 129 American planes had been shot down.

Last night RAF bombers continued the offensive. The British Air Ministry said in a first report only that the planes, which flew out soon after dusk, had struck in enemy-occupied territory.

The Nazi radio station at Frankfort on the Main, carrying out the new German warning system, said during the evening that "enemy planes are circling over our town." About the same time Hanover was heard saying that "enemy aircraft are on their flight back."

Stockholm reported telephone service to and through Berlin cut off, possibly by a direct American bomb hit on the Berlin exchange.

Berlin Vulnerable Day and Night

Talks with high American officers here last night made it clear that the air war had entered a new stage, one in which Berlin is vulnerable to day as well as night attacks and in which those German factories that the RAF's mass bombing by night has missed will be attacked repeatedly by daylight precision bombing until they too are eliminated from the enemy's war industry.

The attack, which was not the biggest daylight air operation of the war, was by far the heaviest daylight attack on Berlin. The hundreds of tons of bombs loosed by the United States planes started pillars of smoke climbing skyward.

"Bombs were seen to fall on assigned targets," said General Spaatz's communiqué; but many of the missiles were loosed through a heavy overcast.

The air battles began as soon as

Continued on Page Four

War News Summarized

TUESDAY, MARCH 7, 1944

The United States Army Air Forces went all out against Berlin for the first time yesterday. Some 800 Flying Fortresses and Liberators, escorted by hundreds of fighters, fought their way through massed enemy air defenses to the Reich's capital for the heaviest daylight attack Berlin had ever suffered. First-rate results were reported by the bombardiers who had aimed at factories and other military targets.

The bombing attack involved fighting the greatest air battle in history almost from the coastline to Berlin and back. The enemy charged into our tight formations, losing eighty-three planes verified, at least thirty-five probably destroyed and seventeen damaged. These losses were inflicted by our fighters alone. The bombers' score was not completed, but one division reported having knocked out at least forty enemy fighters. Sixty-eight of our bombers and eleven fighters failed to return. [All the foregoing 1:8.]

Yesterday's attack was believed to mark the start of literal round-the-clock bombing of Berlin and the rest of the Reich. The Allies have set out to destroy the German Air Force in the shortest possible time, shooting down planes already built and blasting factories to prevent their replacement. [4:1.] Strategic bombing, having now reached its height, can be expected to demonstrate in the near future whether air power alone is more effective than when used in tactical cooperation with ground forces. [4:4.]

The Nazis continued to take a terrific beating on the Russian front also. The Odessa-Lwow railroad was cut along a twenty-mile stretch, imperiling a vast German force in the lower Ukraine now dependent upon inadequate communications for supplies and for retreat. More than 200 places were captured by the Russians. [1:5; maps, P. 8.]

Finland was warned by the Communist newspaper Pravda that if she mistook the "generosity" of Moscow's peace proposal for weakness she would be "bitterly disillusioned." Delay in replying to the offer was creating doubt of Finland's good faith, Pravda said. [8:1.]

The slow pace of Allied progress in Italy was reported compensated by the long-range gain in tying up so many of Hitler's best divisions. [1:5.] Rain put a virtual halt to military operations, but it was revealed that it had cost the Germans 24,000 casualties to try vainly to crack the Anzio beachhead. [7:1.]

The United States Army went into action for the first time on the Continent of Asia when it captured Walawbum, southeast of Maingkwan, in an encircling movement in Burma's Hukawng Valley. With American-trained Chinese troops they were closing a trap around 2,000 Japanese in that area. [1:6-7; map P. 2.]

General MacArthur "leap-frogged" a small force up the New Guinea coast to seize Yaula Plantation, behind the Japanese lines near Madang. Progress was being made in the Admiralties against shelling from 12-inch naval guns on six neighboring islands. [1:7.]

County Chiefs Shun Transit Issue; Windels Makes Pleas for Action

The proposed 10-cent fare on the city-owned transit lines remained a political orphan yesterday, despite Mayor La Guardia's best efforts in his Sunday broadcast to have it adopted by the four county leaders, who, he said, "control the two major parties."

Edward J. Flynn, Democratic leader in the Bronx, commenting on the Mayor's assertion that the Legislature in Albany and the City Council would "take the nod" from the four leaders, would say only:

"As far as I know, I'm neither a member of the Legislature nor of the City Council."

Thomas J. Curran, Republican leader of Manhattan, said tersely: "I have no comment."

John E. Crews, Republican leader of Brooklyn, recalled that he had voted against higher-fare legislation back in 1921 and indicated he intended to be consistent.

Frank V. Kelly, Democratic leader of Brooklyn, the fourth named by the Mayor, is on his way home from the South.

But an appeal was made to the four leaders to declare a political armistice and meet the controversial issue on its merits. In making this plea in an open letter to the leaders, Paul Windels, chairman of the newly created Citizens Transit Committee pictured the Mayor as being unwilling to take a forthright stand on the higher fare without the support of the other political leaders. Mr. Windels also heads the Committee of Fifteen that sponsored the bill now pending in the Legislature for a Transit Authority in the city under mandate to collect a self-sustaining fare not to exceed ten cents. His letter follows:

"I am writing to you as the

Continued on Page Thirty-four

U. S. Sent 28,000 Planes to Allies And Kept 122,000 in Three Years

Special to THE NEW YORK TIMES.

WASHINGTON, March 6—The United States has sent almost 28,000 airplanes to the growing air forces of its Allies, together with $1,600,000,000 worth of aircraft engines and parts, since lend-lease began three years ago, Leo T. Crowley, Foreign Economic Administrator, disclosed today.

The country has done this, he said, while creating the greatest army and naval air forces for itself. Since March, 1941, the United States has produced 150,000 aircraft, of which 122,000 have been retained for its own use. This is a production achievement, Mr. Crowley commented, that will not "be of any aid or comfort to our enemies."

The administrator explained that $1,000 of the planes shipped or ferried abroad were sent under lend-lease provisions. The other 7,000 were paid for in cash, principally by the British.

A total of 7,800 planes went to the Soviet Union, 4,000 to Allied forces in the Pacific and Far East theatres, and more than 16,000 to all other combat and training areas abroad.

Three-fourths of the planes have been combat types, and one-fourth trainer and transport planes. There have been 9,800 four-engine, two-engine and single-engine bombers sent across, and 10,700 single-engine and two-engine fighter planes. Four thousand of the aircraft have been naval planes.

"The British and the Russians produce, themselves, most of the planes they are using in this war," said Mr. Crowley. "But American lend-lease planes, with British,

Continued on Page Five

"All the News That's Fit to Print."

The New York Times.

LATE CITY EDITION
Fair and warmer; cloudy late in day.
Temperatures Yesterday—Max., 33; Min., 20
Sunrise, 7:15 A. M.; Sunset, 6:55 P. M.

VOL. XCIII. No. 31,458. Entered as Second-Class Matter, Postoffice, New York, N. Y. NEW YORK, SATURDAY, MARCH 11, 1944. THREE CENTS IN NEW YORK CITY

IRISH REFUSE TO OUST AXIS ENVOYS, DENYING THEY SPY ON OUR TROOPS; RUSSIANS BREAK 110-MILE FRONT

PROGRESSIVE GROUP IN EDUCATION TAKES NEW NAME, POLICY

Now the American Education Fellowship, It Will Center on Community, Not Child

SEEKS WIDER MEMBERSHIP

Opposition Leader Describes Shift as 'Surrender' to Traditional Teaching

By BENJAMIN FINE

By a membership vote of nearly ten to one, the Progressive Education Association, for the last twenty-five years the spearhead for the progressive movement in the American school field, has adopted a new program and changed its name to the American Education Fellowship, it was learned yesterday.

At the same time, the association has dropped its monthly publication, Frontiers of Democracy, edited by Dr. Harold Rugg of Teachers College, and is now considering a substitute name for its official journal, the magazine Progressive Education. Later this month the board of directors of the fellowship will meet to decide on a substitute name for this publication, although it is known that some members wish to retain the present title.

In a statement of policy sent to all members, the association outlined "a new program for new times." The base of the organization has now been broadened, and parents, interested lay citizens and youths from 17 to 22 will be admitted to membership.

Board to Be Reconstituted

Under the plan of reorganization, the association will pay greater attention to the community and less to the child itself. The board of directors is to be reconstituted and at least four vacancies are to be filled at once by representative leaders of the community—such as a parent, business man, farmer and a member of organized labor. The aim will be to build a board "as cross-sectional of American interests as possible," but with teachers and other educators strongly represented.

"Whereas the earlier period of progressive education was marked by strong concern for the interests and capacities of the individual child, and with group activities largely within the school itself," the new program explained, "the period which we are now entering should be marked by a more intimate and fruitful relationship with parents, interested groups, adult education—in short, with all aspects of the community which surround the child and curriculum, and which largely determine whether the schools are or are not to function as people's schools."

Credited With Strong Influence

Founded in 1919, the Progressive Education Association, through its regional and national conferences, its publications and studies, has been in the forefront in trying to get "progressive" principles adopted in the classrooms of this country. Its journal has served as a sounding board for many ideas and deliberations in this area. The organization, in a sense, built its philosophy around the doctrines of John Dewey, its honorary president.

Frequently attacked, the association has been credited with exerting a strong influence on American schools despite its rather small roll of active members. It has numbered around 10,000, although since the war began the membership has dropped to 7,000.

Continued on Page Sixteen

Tax Form Baffles Even Prof. Einstein

By The Associated Press.

PRINCETON, N. J., March 10—Prof. Albert Einstein, world famous mathematician and wizard of the fourth dimension, said tonight that he, like millions of ordinary Americans who are mulling through complex income tax forms, had to call in a tax expert to help him prepare for the March 15 deadline.

Asked what his reaction was to the maze of income tax questions, Professor Einstein, whose theory of relativity is supposedly understood by only seven persons in the world, replied:

"This is a question too difficult for a mathematician. It should be asked of a philosopher."

WPB STEMS INFLOW OF CANE BEVERAGES

Issues Quota Order to Obtain More Molasses for War Alcohol—Protests Arise

Special to The New York Times.

WASHINGTON, March 10—All imports of alcoholic beverages derived from cane sugar will be reduced by an order issued today by the War Production Board putting them under strict quotas beginning March 15.

The order, designed to "prevent further excessive diversion to beverages of molasses vital to war-essential alcohol production," affects imports from Mexico, Cuba and other Latin countries as well as from Puerto Rico and the Virgin Islands.

After obtaining data from the trade on imports for each calendar quarter from 1940 to date, the WPB will assign the quotas under the order which, it said, "follows directly upon the recently concluded negotiations with Cuba." It added:

"However, the Cuban agreement permits the island's exports of beverage liquor to the United States to equal the high record figure of 14,300,000 proof gallons exported to the United States in 1943 and it is anticipated that quotas assigned to other foreign countries will be worked out on much the same basis."

Hearing Set by House Group

With this basis indicated by an expected reduction of cane beverage imports from Cuba exceeding 50 per cent, the order had immediate repercussions in the trade and in Congress.

Importers asserted that the WPB had exceeded its authority by interfering with treaties and talked of a court test. In reply, spokesmen for the WPB maintained that it had ample authority and disclosed that before acting it had consulted the State Department and the Foreign Economic Administration.

An insular affairs subcommittee of the House set Monday to hear representatives of the WPB, the Foreign Economic Administration and the State Department on the matter.

The committee was said to be particularly interested in the molasses and industrial alcohol agreement with Cuba recently negotiated by a committee headed by Sidney Scheuer, representing the FEA.

Mr. Scheuer was understood to have told the Cubans that in exchange for limiting Cuba beverage alcohol imports into the United States to 14,300,000 proof gallons for 1944, this Government would undertake to limit shipments from Puerto Rico, the Virgin Islands and Mexico to 1943 levels this year.

Producers in Puerto Rico have complained to the committee that the order of the WPB was issued to make good on Mr. Scheuer's promises to the Cubans. They

Continued on Page Twenty-eight

M'ARTHUR, STASSEN CAN BE NOMINATED UNDER NEW RULING

But a Regular Officer Must Not Himself Seek to Be Picked by a Party, Army and Navy Say

ROOSEVELT TELLS OF PACT

Reserves Can File as Candidates but All in Service Are Barred From Campaigning

By CHARLES HURD

Special to The New York Times.

WASHINGTON, March 10—Regular officers of the armed services can accept such nominations for political office as come to them without solicitation by themselves, according to an interpretation of regulations announced today by President Roosevelt. This means that Gen. Douglas MacArthur would be eligible to run for the Presidency if selected by a convention, but would not be able to authorize the use of his name on primary ballots or in any pre-convention activity.

In contrast to this ruling on regular officers, reserve officers will be permitted to file as candidates in the pre-convention period. Lieut. Comdr. Harold Stassen, former Governor of Minnesota and also prominently mentioned for a Presidential nomination, is General MacArthur's counterpart in this category.

The interpretations were made public by the President in a statement embodying a joint Army and Navy agreement signed by Secretary Stimson and Secretary Knox.

In actual practice political observers here believe that the distinction between regular and reserve officers is without much importance.

Restrictions on Campaigning

General MacArthur's sponsors have been championing his candidacy without public word from the general and Commander Stassen has consistently refused to take an active part on his own behalf.

Otherwise these two possible candidates for the Presidency, and any other officers who might be named for similar or subsidiary positions, are under the same restrictions. None may take time out from military duties to devote to politics and none may perform duties to which he may be elected while he remains on active service. Neither can the officers make speeches or conduct election campaigns while on active duty.

If elected to office, national or State, any officer will be retired or honorably discharged, according to the type and length of his service.

The position of regular officers is set by a law which specifically prohibits any such officer from holding any type of elective or appointive public office in civilian life while performing military duties. The Army-Navy agreement added:

"A member of the regular components of the land or naval forces, while on active duty, may accept a nomination for public office, provided such nomination is tendered without direct or indirect activity or solicitation on his part. He may then file such evidence of his candidacy as is required by local law."

This was taken to mean that if the Republican National Convention should nominate General MacArthur he could then comply with formalities necessary to put his name on State ballots.

Since reserve officers have essentially a civilian status, it was ruled that these, "while on active duty may become candidates for

Continued on Page Nine

THIRD DRIVE OPENS

Red Army Wins Major Stronghold of Uman in 44-Mile Advance

HUGE NAZI FORCE ROUTED

20,000 Germans Die and 300 Villages Fall—Two Other Ukraine Pushes Gain

By W. H. LAWRENCE

By Wireless to The New York Times.

MOSCOW, Saturday, March 11—The Soviet High Command last night announced a smashing new offensive on the Second Ukranian front, where Marshal Ivan S. Koneff's men in a five-day battle were reported to have inflicted a heavy defeat on fourteen German divisions, killing 20,000 Germans, capturing 2,500 prisoners and seizing large amounts of material while advancing twenty-five to forty-four miles on a 110-mile front.

Marshal Koneff's army, which had paused only briefly to regroup forces after completing the liquidation of the ten encircled German divisions in the Dnieper bend, drew a salute of twenty salvos from 244 Moscow guns tonight in celebrating its capture of the important towns of Uman and Khristinovka, as well as more than 300 inhabited points.

With the Second Army again on the move, the Germans' hard-pressed forces remaining in the southern Ukraine are being smashed back toward the Black Sea and Rumania by three Russian separate armies, all of which are reported to be making remarkable progress despite an early spring thaw that is producing deep mud on the flat steppes.

Tarnopol Fighting Continues

Marshal Gregory Zhukoff's First Ukrainian Army was reported last night to be continuing its street fighting in Tarnopol, as well as moving on Proskorov and smashing German communications centers north of Vinnitsa.

Gen. Rodion Y. Malinovsky's Third Ukrainian Army, whose offensive was announced Thursday night, continued to advance today, taking Novgorodka and Bashtanka, as well as more than 150 other inhabited points, inflicting large losses of men and material upon the retreating Germans.

The biggest news, of course, was the resumption of Marshal Koneff's

Continued on Page Five

A NEW RUSSIAN BREAK-THROUGH IN THE SOUTH

The Red Army advanced nine miles closer to Nikolayev by capturing Dobroye (1) and also took Baratovka (2). In a smashing new drive along a 110-mile front extending from Kapustino (3) to Monastyrishche (5) it overran an area (shown by striping) reaching as far south as Kamenechye and Kocherzhintsy (4) and captured the important bases of Uman and Khristinovka. In the drive toward Vinnitsa the Russians seized Yanov and Khmelnik (6). In the Proskurov area Gorbasov and Krasilov (7) were taken. Street fighting continued inside Tarnopol (8).

FOE REPORTS ALLIES ON DALMATIAN ISLE

1,500 British, U. S. Commandos Under 'Gen. Churchill' Struck at Lissa, Berlin Says

By The Associated Press.

LONDON, March 10—The Berlin radio said today that 1,500 British and American "commandos"—"under the command of General Churchill"—had landed on the tiny Adriatic island of Lissa and that other raids on the Dalmatian coast and near-by islands might be expected.

The German reference to a "British general with the name of Churchill" suggested it might be Capt. Randolph Churchill, 32-year-old son of Prime Minister Churchill, who was recently reported to have parachuted into Yugoslavia to confer with Marshal Tito (Josip Broz).

British sources said they had no information about the reported landing or whether the raiders were led by Captain Churchill. There has been no official an-

Continued on Page Seven

War News Summarized

SATURDAY, MARCH 11, 1944

The New York-born Prime Minister of Eire, Eamon de Valera, has categorically refused the United States Government's request that he close the German and Japanese Ministries in Dublin, it was announced in Washington yesterday. In a written confirmation of a verbal "no" given when the request was made on Feb. 21, Mr. de Valera denied Axis officials were successfully transmitting military intelligence on Allied ship and troop movements, and declared the Eire Government was well able to keep espionage under control and was determined to maintain its present neutral status. [1:8.]

When the American note was received, it was reported in London, the Irish interpreted it as an ultimatum and took military steps to contest any violation of their sovereignty by United States or British forces, increasing the border guard and placing special details at all airports and seaports. [1:7.]

Against this diplomatic setback, the day brought news of a new Russian drive in the Ukraine that portended a climactic battle in the Russian-German war. The new drive of the Red armies, under way for five days, Moscow announced, is in the center of what now is a 500-mile-long battleline. To the northwest the troops of Marshal Zhukoff were still fighting in the streets of Tarnopol. To the southeast the armies of General Malinovsky were pressing on in the Dnieper Bend toward the Black Sea ports of Nikolayev and Kherson. The action in the center, under Marshal Koneff, had for its first major prize the Nazi stronghold of Uman. [1:4.]

With the United States Air Force in Britain earthbound and a night attack by RAF heavy bombers on an airplane plant near Marseille the only major air activity of the last twenty-four hours [6:1], the Mediterranean arm of Allied air might swung into action with another attack on the railroad yards of Rome. On land, in Italy, two sharp but small-scale attacks on the Anzio beachhead were hurled back. [1:6-7.]

On the eastern side of the Adriatic, the sea separating Italy from the Balkans, a combined British-American force landed on the island of Lissa, twenty-five miles below the Yugoslav port of Spalato, the Berlin radio announced. The Germans said the troops were under the command of "General Churchill." [1:5, map, P. 7.]

The marines who landed Monday on the Willaumez Peninsula of New Britain took the Talasea airport Wednesday and the town Thursday, General MacArthur announced, giving the Allied forces in the southwest Pacific a second air base within 150 miles of the Japanese base of Rabaul. [1:6-7; map, P. 3.]

Lieut. Gen. Joseph Stilwell's Chinese - American forces in Burma continued to make progress in their campaign to oust the Japanese from the Hukawng Valley on the flank of the Ledo Road to China. [3:1.]

Talasea Airfield Captured By Marines in New Britain

By The Associated Press.

ALLIED HEADQUARTERS IN THE SOUTHWEST PACIFIC, Saturday, March 11—United States marines captured Talasea airdrome Wednesday and then wheeled north to occupy the township the following day, thus cutting in two the Willaumez Peninsula of north New Britain, which they invaded only last Monday.

Headquarters reported the victories today. The successes firmly implanted Gen. Douglas MacArthur's forces more than 100 miles east of their Cape Gloucester holdings and within 170 miles of bomb-ravaged Rabaul.

No details were available concerning the final fight for the airstrip and town, but a spokesman said enemy reaction, which had developed several hours after units of the First Marine Division gained its beachhead Monday, reached its peak of intensity Tuesday.

The leathernecks, who landed on the peninsula's west coast opposite Talasea, cleared a path through land mines and pushed across the five-mile-wide peninsula.

Trap Set Up on Peninsula

The occupation of Talasea trapped any Japanese caught on the northern tip of the narrow land strip, which sticks up like a thumb from the northern coast.

[Japanese troops broke through American barbed-wire entanglements on the northern perimeter of our positions on Bougainville and captured several pillboxes. Their artillery shelled two American air strips, but the air strips were still in use, according to word from the area.]

In the invaded Admiralty Islands to the north of the New Britain action, troops of the dismounted First Cavalry Division have pushed their steadily expanding lines three and a half miles northwest of captured Momote airdrome on Los Negros. Japanese planes strafed the sector without effect.

In still another action on the borders of the Bismarck Sea, Amer-

Continued on Page Three

DUBLIN MOBILIZES, SEEING ULTIMATUM

Border, Ports, Airfields Are Guarded—Politics Suspected in de Valera's Reaction

By JAMES B. RESTON

By Cable to The New York Times.

LONDON, March 10—The Irish Government not only rejected the United States request that German and Japanese diplomatic missions be closed but chose to interpret the State Department's note as an ultimatum and immediately took military precautions against an Anglo-American invasion of southern Ireland.

All leaves in the Irish Army were canceled immediately after David Gray, United States Minister in Dublin, presented the State Department's protest, special guards were placed over airfields, ports and other strategic positions; bridges leading from Ulster into southern Ireland were mined and the Irish local defense volunteers were mobilized and armed.

It is understood that despite Mr. Gray's statements the State Department's note meant just what it said and did not imply a threat to take over the Irish ports or to "invade" the country. Mr. de Valera took all precautions and cabled immediately to his Minister in Washington for reassurances that the note was not an

Continued on Page Four

Our Bombs Rip Rome Rail Yards, Blow Up Warehouses and Cars

By The Associated Press.

ALLIED HEADQUARTERS, Naples, March 10—Fighter-escorted American medium bombers attacked railroad yards in Rome again today, and heavy damage was reported. On the Anzio beachhead the Germans made two localized attacks yesterday.

[The Nazi-controlled Rome radio, telling of Friday's bombing, said "a large number of houses were hit, and it is feared casualties are high." The broadcast made the claim, unsupported in Allied announcements, that two of the raiders crashed in flames near the outskirts of the city. The Swiss radio, meanwhile, quoted the German commander of Rome as saying that Rome was considered an open city and had no anti-aircraft guns.

[Thursday night Royal Air Force bombers based in Britain bombed a factory at Marignane, near Marseille, that has been constructing six-engined flying boats and converting French planes into troop carriers.]

The Tiburtina yards in Rome's eastern suburbs were hit by Marauders escorted by American-piloted Spitfires, and rolling stock and warehouses were declared blown up.

Thunderbolt-escorted Mitchells struck the Littorio yards on the northern limits of the city, which were bombed last Tuesday.

Photographs indicated that the main rail line from Rome to Florence, down which the Germans have been sending supplies to

Continued on Page Seven

U. S. DEMANDS BAN

Charges Eire Is a Base for Espionage That Imperils Our Army

NOTE BACKED BY BRITAIN

De Valera Replies That Close Watch Is Kept—Use of Nazi Radio Denied

Our note and the Irish Government's reply are on Page 4.

By BERTRAM D. HULEN

Special to The New York Times.

WASHINGTON, March 10—An appeal by the United States for the Irish Government to remove German and Japanese consular and diplomatic representatives from the country because of their espionage activities, coupled with a hope that this would be followed by Ireland's severing diplomatic relations with the Axis, has been rejected by Prime Minister Eamon de Valera.

The American request was based on the contention that there were espionage activities that constituted a danger to the lives of American soldiers and to the success of the Allied military operations.

Mr. de Valera replied at once orally and later formally that it was "impossible" to comply with the request. To do so, he declared, would mean the first step toward war and a betrayal of Ireland and her neutrality. There was no basis to the charges, he declared.

Britain Supports Our Action

Britain supported the American action which was in the form of a note delivered by David Gray, the American Minister in Dublin, on Feb. 21. We stressed that the Axis representatives through their official position had been able to gather important military information and transmit it by radio to Germany.

The note was made public by the State Department tonight, and the Irish Legation then gave out the reply of Prime Minister de Valera, which was dated March 7.

Mr. de Valera contended that the American charges were "out of harmony" with the facts and that his Government was doing everything possible to prevent espionage.

[An official spokesman in Dublin said early Saturday morning that neither the German nor Japanese envoys here has a diplomatic mail pouch and that neither has a way of communicating with his country except by cable, which passes through London.]

"Should American lives be lost," he said, "it will not be through any indifference or neglect of its duty on the part of this State."

He promised that Ireland would continue to safeguard the interests of the United States.

Objects to "Grave" Note

Pleading for friendship, he nevertheless considered our note of "so grave" a character that it should never have been sent.

What action the United States and Britain will now consider taking to impress upon Eire the seriousness of the situation was not indicated here.

President Roosevelt was asked at his press conference what could be done by Ireland to help the United Nations.

"What an if question!" he exclaimed, and dismissed the subject.

However, Mr. de Valera in his note referred to a personal message he had received from Mr. Roosevelt on Feb. 26, 1942, to the effect that we would never invade Ireland and said Mr. Gray had now repeated it to him. This was reinforced by renewed assurances on Feb. 29 that no military or other measures were being contemplated because of his refusal to comply with our request.

Axis Spying Is Stressed

The note delivered by Mr. Gray declared flatly that it had been demonstrated "over and over again" that Axis representatives in neutral countries had used their

Continued on Page Four

First Lady Guessing On Fourth Term, Too

By Wireless to The New York Times.

SAN JUAN, P. R., March 10—Asked at a press conference today whether the President would run for a fourth term, Mrs. Franklin D. Roosevelt said:

"It's something I know nothing about, although no one ever believes it. I've never asked the President. I believe a man's family has no right to influence such a decision. Circumstances at the time control the decision, and probably the President himself does not know what he is going to do."

She held the press conference after a day in which she visited Army and Navy bases and inspected several stations for the distribution of milk for children.

20 School Annexes to Be Closed By La Guardia to Save $1,345,000

Mayor La Guardia announced yesterday that he would close the twenty annexes in the academic high schools termed "unnecessary" in a survey earlier this week prepared by Manhattan Councilman Stanley M. Isaacs and Theodore Fred Kuper, former law secretary of the Board of Education. By closing the annexes, the Mayor said, the city would need 431 fewer teachers at a saving of $1,345,000.

In discussing the Legislature's failure to take a definite stand thus far on restoring the cut in State aid, amounting to $4,500,000 for this city, the Mayor declared that closing of the annexes would go a "long way" toward making up the deficiency in school funds. He also indicated that some of the vocational annexes would be closed, but did not know the number until the board's report on the subject was completed.

The question of whether the twenty academic and twenty-four vocational annexes could be closed was raised in the Isaacs-Kuper study. Figures were cited showing that most of the annexes, especially in the academic division, could be discontinued with a saving in maintenance costs and an improvement in facilities.

"Have you anything to say on the Legislature's apparent decision not to increase State aid to schools?" Mayor La Guardia was asked.

"The problem is solved for us," the Mayor answered. "We don't have to worry about this any more. I'm taking the recommendation of the National Education Associa-

Continued on Page Twenty-eight

"All the News That's Fit to Print."

The New York Times.

LATE CITY EDITION
Increasing cloudiness, and somewhat warmer.
Temperatures Yesterday—Max., 43; Min., 25
Sunrise, 6:57 A. M.; Sunset, 7:10 P. M.

Copyright. 1944, by The New York Times Company.

VOL. XCIII...No. 31,469. Entered as Second-Class Matter, Postoffice, New York, N. Y. NEW YORK, WEDNESDAY, MARCH 22, 1944. THREE CENTS NEW YORK CITY

MARINES ON ISLE 600 MILES FROM TRUK; RUSSIANS 28 MILES FROM THE PRUT RIVER; NAZIS SHIFT TROOPS TO DOMINATE HUNGARY

SAYS WHITE HOUSE SILENCED REDMAN ON FCC 'BUNGLING'

Rep. L. E. Miller Asserts Rear Admiral Drew Fire for His Data to House Group

PERIL TO NAVY FORCE TOLD

Missourian Declares Threat of Demotion Was Used—Fly Charges 'Innuendoes'

Special to THE NEW YORK TIMES.

WASHINGTON, March 21—Representative Louis E. Miller, Republican, of Missouri, declared today that because of "bungling" by the Federal Communications Commission a Navy task force in Alaskan waters was ordered out on a fruitless mission, in the course of which a man was disabled, and that for disclosing the fact to the Special House Committee investigating the FCC demotion was recommended of Rear Admiral Joseph R. Redman, director of naval communications, and representative of the Navy Department on the Board of War Communications.

Mr. Miller's statement, made at today's hearing by the committee, identified, for the first time, Admiral Redman as one of the naval officers upon whom, together with Rear Admiral Stanford C. Hooper, now retired, T. A. M. Craven, FCC Commissioner, testified last December that "reprisals" were visited for opposition to the policies of James Fly, chairman of the commission, and of the War Communications Board.

That Admiral Hooper was one of the two officers referred to by Commissioner Craven, who gave the names to the committee in executive session, was revealed last Dec. 10 by Representative Clinton Anderson, Democrat, of New Mexico.

"Disciplinary Action" Was Urged

It was reported at the time, but not officially confirmed, that "disciplinary action" had been recommended but not taken, in the case of Admiral Redman for supplying information to the committee, as had Admiral Hooper, before the Presidential order forbidding cooperation with it by officers of the Army and Navy.

The matter was brought up at today's hearing of Charles Denny, FCC counsel, when the witness was asked by Representative Miller to "furnish a copy of the letter written by an Under-Secretary of the Navy in reference to the demotion of Admiral Redman."

Mr. Denny said that he had no knowledge of such a letter, and Mr. Miller outlined its "factual background" as follows:

"Admiral Redman had testified before the staff of this committee. He had given certain testimony regarding Pearl Harbor and regarding an accident that had occurred to the task force operating in Alaskan waters. After this testimony was given by Admiral Redman, a copy of his statement was requested by the White House. After the contents had been learned, Mr. Fly read, in the presence of Commissioner Craven, a letter presumably from the White House in which it was stated that certain things might happen to Commissioner Craven and others who testified in secret before the committee investigating the FCC. A copy of this alleged letter or note from the White House was shown to Commissioner Craven."

Would Produce a Letter

Mr. Miller added that if the Navy Department would relax its rules and permit him to do so he would produce the letter, and Mr. Denny replied that he wished he would, because he would "love to know the date when this task force is supposed to have gotten into difficulties because of information given by the FCC."

Mr. Miller suggested that he get in touch with Admiral Hooper, who could tell him "what task force it was, where it was, and what happened as a result of the bungling of the FCC."

Mr. Denny protested that the charge was a "terribly serious" one, of which there "is no evidence whatever," to which Representative Miller retorted sharply:

"Of course there is no evidence, because Admiral Hooper has been silenced by executive order. You know that and I know that and everybody here knows that."

Mr. Denny entered a "categorical denial" of the incident, declaring that when he was informed as to "when it is supposed to have happened" it would be "affirmatively disproved."

"You mean you propose to af-

Continued on Page Thirteen

President Kept In By Another Cold

Special to THE NEW YORK TIMES.

WASHINGTON, March 21—President Roosevelt was confined to his quarters today with a head cold, but was reported to have no fever.

The President was sneezing and restless during the night, according to Stephen T. Early, his press secretary. Mr. Early said that Vice Admiral Ross T. McIntire, the President's physician, treated him for a head cold and ordered all appointments canceled for the day. Thus the usual Tuesday press conference was not held. Admiral McIntire later described Mr. Roosevelt's condition as definitely improved.

The President earlier this year had grippe, from which he was reported slow to recover. He lost ten pounds from that illness, it was said.

WILLKIE CONDEMNS ISOLATIONIST VIEWS

He Tells Wisconsin Voters That if Republicans Campaign on Them Roosevelt Will Win

By JAMES A. HAGERTY
Special to THE NEW YORK TIMES.

GREEN BAY, Wis., March 21—With more vehemence than he had previously shown in his Wisconsin campaign, Wendell L. Willkie hit today at his rivals for the Republican Presidential nomination. He charged avoiding discussion of issues, denounced a campaign of defamation against him, stuck firmly to his position for cooperation of the United States with other nations to maintain peace after the war, and declared that, if isolationists of the school of thought represented by The Chicago Tribune prevailed at the national convention and adopted a platform and named the candidate, Franklin D. Roosevelt would continue to be President for at least another four years.

Emphasizing the importance of the election of delegates pledged to him in the Wisconsin primary, Mr. Willkie struck directly at his rivals in this primary, Governor Thomas E. Dewey of New York, Lieut. Comdr. Harold E. Stassen of Minnesota, and Gen. Douglas MacArthur. Informed of Commander Stassen's message to Secretary Knox, that he was not an active candidate for the Presidential nomination but would accept if nominated, Mr. Willkie said:

"It is difficult to know from the announcement whether Governor Stassen is a candidate or not. As I have emphasized in this campaign in Wisconsin, the only way our system can function is through public discussion. The primary in Wisconsin is for the purpose of providing the people of Wisconsin with a method of making a choice after they have heard a discussion of the issues.

Discussion or Withdrawal

"Obviously those who seek the preference of the voters of Wisconsin should discuss the issues with them or, if they have rendered themselves unable to do so, then it occurs to me that they should decisively, not ambiguously, withdraw from the contest.

"All the men for whom delegates are running in Wisconsin can say in very simple and unambiguous language that they do or do not desire the voters of Wisconsin to vote for the delegates pledged to their respective candidacies."

Before his comment on the Stassen message, which in effect called upon Messrs. Dewey, Stassen and MacArthur to tell the Wisconsin voters how they stood on issues or withdraw, Mr. Willkie in a speech to the students and Navy trainees of Lawrence College in the college

Continued on Page Thirty-six

BALKAN UNITS MOVE

3 Divisions From Serbia Sent to Crush Forces Resisting in Hungary

SOUTH GRIPPED BY CHAOS

Liberation Units Seen Merging—March on Rumania and Action in Sofia Reported

By DANIEL T. BRIGHAM
By Telephone to THE NEW YORK TIMES.

BERNE, Switzerland, March 21—Overwhelmed by developments for thirty-six hours in which German forces seized most of the key objectives in the occupation of Hungary, internal resistance in that country since early this morning has coalesced into what may develop into an "Army of Liberation," information from the Balkans indicated tonight.

[German troops were reported Wednesday to have taken over vital communication facilities in Sofia and Nazi armored columns were said to be moving swiftly on Bucharest, indicating that both Bulgaria and Rumania might soon share the fate of Hungary, The Associated Press said.

[The United Nations radio in Algiers said Tuesday that the Budapest radio had gone off the air after announcing an air raid.

[Broadcasting from the Hungarian capital was interrupted a second time some time later, United States Government monitors reported.]

Bucharest Lines Restored

With Budapest communications still severed, most of the information received in Berne tonight came via Bucharest, with which communications were re-established this morning.

Eyewitnesses who had eluded German patrols along the Transylvanian frontier told of "complete chaos" throughout southern Hungary, where isolated forces appear to have refused to accept orders from the regime supposedly set up by the pro-Nazi Bela Imredy, and in at least two large garrison towns they have successfully resisted all German efforts to disarm them.

So serious does the potential military reaction appear that this afternoon the command of all German occupation operations was given to Field Marshal Baron Maximilian von Weichs, who is reported proceeding toward Budapest with at least three Elite divisions of Balkan fighters from northeastern Serbia, where they had been re-formed after a fierce encounter with the forces of Marshal Tito [Josip Broz] about a fortnight ago.

Their progress is expected to be slow, since railway communications have been attacked by sapper units of the regular Hungarian Army.

Field Marshal Franz Szombathelyi, Hungarian Chief of Staff, erroneously reported as arrested by the Germans, is now known to have accepted responsibility for the defense of the Carpathian region, whither he had proceeded as early as March 13 to take charge of what is believed to be nearly an

Continued on Page Twelve

NAZI RAIL LINK CUT

Red Army Drives Wedge Into Retreat Route Near Rumania

HOLD ON DNIESTER GROWS

310 Places Fall in 6 Sectors—Two More Strong Points Imperiled by Advance

By W. H. LAWRENCE
By Wireless to THE NEW YORK TIMES.

MOSCOW, Wednesday, March 22—The Red Army, capturing more than 310 inhabited points in its sustained advance in six sectors on the southern Soviet-German front, was reported last night to have cut the Beltsy-Cernauti railway, fifteen miles beyond the Dniester at its Mogilev-Poolski crossing and the only rail line leading directly to Germany from central Bessarabia.

[The point at which the rail line was cut, in the vicinity of Drokiya, is only twenty-eight miles from the Prut River border of Rumania, where German and Rumanian forces launched the southern wing of the invasion of Russia in June, 1941.]

While the western thrust for Lwow and parallel drives for the Black Sea ports from Novoukrainka and Bobrinets continued to make progress, the most important news was that Soviet forces had made another successful crossing of the Dniester in the region of Mogilev-Podolski, which was taken two days ago, and had widened their bridgehead on the right bank until the forces cut across the railway.

Germans Forced to Detour

Loss of this railway severely hampers the Germans. It forces an important detour for railmoved supplies and reinforcements from Germany and the satellite states destined for the southern Ukrainian troops. They now must be diverted through Jassy, which is inside Rumania.

In the Bessarabian area, despite increasing German resistance, including greater use of the Luftwaffe, the Russians said, their troops took the district center of Ataki and more than forty other inhabited points.

The drive for Lwow southwestward from Dubno netted fifty pop-

Continued on Page Eleven

ALLIED RING FORGED IN BISMARCK ARCHIPELAGO

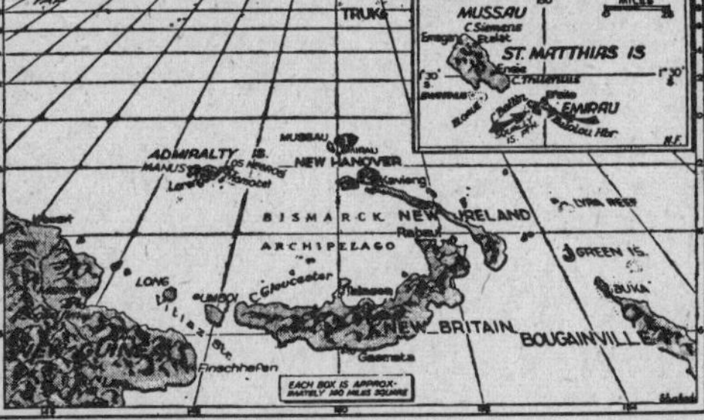

March 22, 1944

United States marines have landed on Emirau Island (1), a favorable site for air and naval bases, and have thus effectively cut off Japanese troops to the south and placed our forces within 600 miles of Truk (top of map). The marines went ashore at the east end of the island and over reefs at the southwestern corner (inset). At the same time the enemy base at Kavieng (2) was in part leveled by a three-and-a-half-hour bombardment by our battleships.

Finland Rejects Armistice; Russia Warns of Dire Fate

By The Associated Press.

LONDON, March 21—Finland announced the rejection of the Russian armistice terms today and a few hours later an official Soviet statement broadcast from Moscow declared that the refusal placed full responsibility for the consequences on the Finnish Government. Together the two declarations indicated a complete and final breakdown in peace negotiations.

[The texts of the Finnish and Russian statements are on Page 10.]

The Moscow statement was brief, outlining tersely the order and substance of the notes exchanged by the two Governments leading up to Finland's rejection of Russia's six-point proposal.

"By this action it [the regime of Premier Edwin Linkomies] has taken upon itself full responsibility for what will follow," said the statement, recorded by the Soviet monitor.

The statement was signed by the Information Bureau of the People's Commissariat for Foreign Affairs of the U.S.S.R.

It pointed out that Finland's first answer to the offer of peace, made public March 1, had been a reply that the Soviet terms were difficult to accept.

The Soviet Government informed

Continued on Page Ten

ALLIES' BIG ATTACK IN CASSINO BOGGED

Momentum of Assault Cracks as Germans Reoccupy Wreckage of Hotel

By C. L. SULZBERGER
By Wireless to THE NEW YORK TIMES.

WITH THE FIFTH ARMY AT CASSINO, March 21—The Allies' third major attack on Cassino appeared today to have bogged down temporarily after seven days of sharp and continuous fighting.

The initial momentum gained by New Zealand and Indian troops after the unprecedented aerial bombing and the terrific artillery barrage of March 15 that enabled them to occupy virtually all the leveled town has ground to an apparent standstill for the moment. New German reserves, including armored grenadiers, have moved into the line supporting the First Parachute Division and the Germans probably have about nine combat battalions well dug in in strong points around the town and south of it, as well as on the rugged hill topped by the battered Abbey of Mount Cassino.

During the past forty-eight hours the positions have been relatively static. There has been reshuffling on both sides, although a considerable exchange of fire by all arms continues by night and day.

Last night and today the initiative appeared to have been fairly evenly distributed. It is evident that the Allies will have to put their shoulders to the wheel once again and dislodge the enemy from

Continued on Page Thirteen

WORLD UNITY URGED BY HULL AS OUR AIM

He Says Our Foreign Policy Requires Cooperation of All Under Atlantic Charter

The text of Secretary Hull's statement is on Page 12.

By BERTRAM D. HULEN
Special to THE NEW YORK TIMES.

WASHINGTON, March 21—The foreign policy of the United States was defined by Secretary of State Cordell Hull tonight in terms of our fundamental national interests and our responsibility for cooperating with other nations in a statement issued through the State Department.

The announcement was in the form of a summarization of basic points of the policy as defined by Mr. Hull in public addresses and pronouncements over the past two years. It amounted to a restatement of policy.

It was preliminary to a radio address further developing the subject, which Mr. Hull said he was now preparing with the view of delivering it soon. He was not able, however, as yet to set the date for his radio address.

In all this he explained that he was taking notice of the growing interest in foreign policy manifested in the United States and an increasing number of requests for information on the subject.

Congress' Interest Increases

That interest has also been manifested in a growing demand in Congress for a more definite exposition of our foreign policy by the Administration, including requests for enlightenment from Republican members who have supported the Administration's foreign policy in the past.

Mr. Hull indicated that he would deal with the Atlantic Charter in his address. Asked at his press conference whether the principles of the charter still prevailed and whether they could be reconciled with the realities of a world or

Continued on Page Twelve

BY-PASS KAVIENG

U. S. Forces Meet Feeble Opposition in Moving on Emirau Isle

BATTLESHIPS IN ACTION

Pour 1,000 Tons of Shells Into Kavieng, Japanese Base on New Ireland

By FRANK L. KLUCKHOHN
By Wireless to THE NEW YORK TIMES.

ALLIED HEADQUARTERS IN THE SOUTHWEST PACIFIC, Wednesday, March 22—With planes strafing the beaches before them, United States Marines landed on Emirau Island, potential air and sea base less than 600 miles from Truk, and quickly overran the Japanese scattered, ineffective opposition. Elomusao, an islet half mile offshore, was also occupied.

Coincidentally, American battleships leveled parts of the enemy's New Ireland stronghold at Kavieng, seventy-five miles to the southeast, with a terrific three-and-one-half-hour bombardment. The battleships hurled 1,000 tons of shells into Kavieng in perhaps the heaviest shelling of the war on a point at which we did not intend to land. The enemy's shore batteries started to bark as the "battlewagons" moved close inshore, but our big guns quickly silenced them.

The twofold operation was carried out early Monday under Gen. Douglas MacArthur's strategic direction by Admiral William F. Halsey Jr. with important elements of the United States Fleet, including cruisers and destroyers as well as battleships.

Entrapment of Japanese forces remaining in the Bismarcks and the Solomons is now complete. We hold the Admiralties to the east of the blockaded enemy on New Guinea and northwest of New Britain, the Solomons to the south, the Green Islands to the southeast and the seizure of Emirau puts a stopper in the northern end.

Marines Land Easily

This correspondent watched the mighty armada from the air as it stretched out over the sea on its way to deal the Japanese another heavy blow. Once again our forces landed where the Japanese were not present in force, the marines going in easily on the beach at the eastern end of the eight-miles-by-five island and in amphibious tracked landing craft over the reef at the southwest end of Emirau.

Kavieng, where the enemy has a considerable force, as well as Rabaul, even farther south, were by-passed, a result of their virtual isolation even before this move by General MacArthur's surprise capture of the Admiralties. However, the sixteen-inch guns of the big gray battleships, pounding hour after hour, eliminated the so-called "Chinese quarter" of Kavieng and further advanced the destruction of gun emplacements, ammunition dumps and other installations already severely punished by the South Pacific Air Force. Our ships suffered no losses.

When the marines dashed through the surf surrounding the green, dagger-shaped island housing a Japanese radio station they knew they were closer to the enemy's central Pacific base of Truk than any other Americans. While Emirau is probably too far from Truk for bombers to hit with fighter escort, its seizure tightens the net around the bastion and permits two-way bombing as we already hold Eniwetok to the east.

Solomons Heroes Participate

Among the landing troops were raider battalions which had already made history in retaking the Solomons. They were commanded by Brig. Gen. Alfred H. Noble of the Marine Corps. Commodore Lawrence F. Reifsneider commanded the amphibious task force.

Just north of Emirau lies Mussau Island, the largest of the St. Matthias group. Schadel Bay there has been consistently used by Japanese float planes and was employed by German South Seas raiders in the last war.

In the landing party were picked

Continued on Page Two

War News Summarized

WEDNESDAY, MARCH 22, 1944

United States Marines landed early Monday (Australian time) on Emirau Island in the St. Matthias group, eighty-four miles northwest of the major Japanese base of Kavieng, on New Ireland, and less than 600 miles from Truk, General MacArthur's headquarters announced. Little opposition was met. In a diversionary action, battleships of the Pacific Fleet pounded Kavieng with 1,000 tons of shells. [1:8.]

One of the explanations for the American advances in the Pacific was given in an announcement in Washington that United States submarines had sunk fifteen more Japanese vessels, one of them a large transport, and a communiqué from London that British submarines had sunk seven more. [3:1.]

In Burma the Japanese still were advancing "in force" toward the Indian frontier through the Kabaw Valley. Part of the enemy force was the so-called Indian National Army recruited by the Indian renegade Subhas Chandra Bose. [2:2; map, P. 2.]

The Russian armies drove on across Bessarabia to cut the last north-south railway in German hands. They stood yesterday, Moscow said, within twenty-eight miles of the Prut River, pre-war boundary of Rumania. "The battle of the south has been won," declared the official army organ, Red Star. [1:4; map, 11.]

The news from Hungary was still somewhat confused and came via Rumania and other sources. What was certain was that the Germans had marched in, perhaps as many as 100,000 of them. The Hungarian Commander in Chief, Marshal Szombathelyi, was said to have taken a stand in the mountains with loyal troops and to be resisting, or preparing to resist. [1:3.]

The developments in Hungary were said to have created a great impression in Finland, but they did not change the position of the Government, which officially announced it had rejected the Russian armistice terms. A Moscow statement warned the Finns they now must take the consequences. [1:5-6.]

The Battle of Cassino settled down to a stalemate with the Germans infiltrating back around the town and still firmly holding the approaches to the Liri Valley gateway to Rome. [1:6.]

Germany had a respite from air attack during the day, but her army did not as Liberators bombed the Pas-de-Calais area and Mustang fighters made a 450-mile sweep across Nazi airdromes in France. Seven fighters but no bombers were lost. [6:1.]

Secretary Hull announced in Washington that he was working on a speech that would clarify the United States foreign policy which, he said in his statement, basically, was a protection of national interests and international cooperation. [1:7.]

The Army announced that General Patton, who had slapped a shell-shocked soldier during the Sicilian campaign, had been replaced as head of the Seventh Army by Maj. Gen. A. M. Patch, from the South Pacific, but had received another command. [1:6-7.]

Eric Johnston Accepts Stalin Bid To Visit and Study Soviet Russia

By JOHN H. CRIDER
Special to THE NEW YORK TIMES.

WASHINGTON, March 21—Eric A. Johnston, president of the Chamber of Commerce of the United States, has accepted an invitation from Premier Stalin to visit Soviet Russia. Tentative plans call for his leaving about May 12 and returning to the United States June 20.

Mr. Johnston, an outspoken proponent of the American free enterprise system, accepted the invitation so he could have a look at how the Soviet system operates from the point of view of an American business man.

It can be taken for granted, according to persons close to the chamber president, that he will be as blunt in his statements to the Soviet people as he was in talking to the British when he visited England last summer.

Mr. Johnston's view regarding Soviet Russia has been that Americans must recognize that it has a different economic system but American business men welcome the competition of any other systems and are confident theirs can out-produce them. He also has stated that while we underestimated Russia's economic and military strength before the war, we must not underestimate it after the war.

Characteristic of Mr. Johnston's outspoken approach to the prob-

Continued on Page Ten

Patton Shifted to New Command As Patch Heads the Seventh Army

By The Associated Press.

NAPLES, March 21—Lieut. Gen. George S. Patton Jr., known in the field as "Old Blood and Guts," has been replaced by Maj. Gen. Alexander M. Patch, a veteran of the Pacific fighting, as commander of the American Seventh Army, headquarters announced today.

[In Washington the War Department announced that General Patton had been put in command of "another army," but Army officials declined to identify the unit or reveal his present whereabouts. It was assumed that his new assignment was connected with plans for the invasion of western Europe.]

While several units formerly with the Seventh Army have been assigned to the Fifth Army in Italy, the whereabouts of the Seventh Army has not been disclosed. It has been the subject of considerable guesswork by the Germans, who at one time reported that it had gone to sea.

General Patton led the Seventh Army to victory in Sicily. His forces took Messina, the last Sicilian city captured. Later he received wide publicity over an incident involving the slapping of an American soldier in a field hospital near Palermo.

He was rebuked by Gen. Dwight D. Eisenhower, and he apologized to the officers and men of the Seventh Army. His nickname is derived from his explosive temperament, which finds him contemptuous of his personal safety in the heat of battle. He is also known

Continued on Page Thirteen

"All the News That's Fit to Print."

The New York Times.

LATE CITY EDITION
Partly cloudy and warmer today; gentle to moderate winds.
Temperatures Yesterday—Max., 56; Min., 41
Sunrise, 6:53 A. M.; Sunset, 7:18 P. M.

Copyright, 1944, by The New York Times Company.

VOL. XCIII..No. 31,472. | Entered as Second-Class Matter. Postoffice, New York, N. Y. | NEW YORK, SATURDAY, MARCH 25, 1944. | THREE CENTS IN NEW YORK CITY

RUSSIANS REACH BUKOVINA BORDER; REICH CITIES AND LONDON BOMBED; CHURCHILL PLEDGES INVASION SOON

NEWS SUPPRESSION BY ADMINISTRATION CHARGED BY DEWEY

Governor Says Capital Seems Embarked on a 'Deliberate and Dangerous' Policy

PARATROOP LOSS IS CITED

Effort to 'Discredit' Congress Seen in Attacks on Its Attitude Toward Peace

The text of Governor Dewey's address is on Page 10.

Asserting that much important news from abroad has been released only after it leaked out and became the subject of widespread gossip, Governor Dewey charged last night that the Roosevelt Administration seemed to have embarked on "a deliberate and dangerous policy of suppression of news at home."

Citing the loss of twenty-three transport planes and 410 American paratroopers in Sicily, which became known eight months after it occurred, and the limited extent to which the public was informed of what happened at Teheran, the Governor declared:

"One such incident might be charged to blunder; two such incidents begin to lay the unpleasant suspicion of Administration policy."

Governor Dewey, widely mentioned for the Republican Presidential nomination, though he disavows such ambition, delivered his sharpest thrust at Administration policy in weeks as he awarded prizes at the ninth annual exhibit of the Press Photographers Association of New York at the Museum of Science and Industry in Rockefeller Center.

Signs of Curbs on News

In the speech, which ran for fifteen minutes and was broadcast over a nation-wide hook-up from Station WEAF, the Governor declared a free press had kept Americans "the best informed people in the world," but he said there have been "increasing signs of late that our newspapers are being denied the right to print all the news."

"Only now do we learn, because it leaked out," he said, "of the shooting down of twenty-three transport planes and the killing of 410 American paratroopers in Sicily eight months ago. Even after a Presidential broadcast we still know precisely nothing of what really happened at the much-heralded conference in Teheran. We only know of the disquieting evidences of disunity which have since occurred, in the Pravda attacks on the British and the Vatican, followed by the startling repercussions brought out by the President's announcement of the three-way division of the Italian fleet."

Admitting the need for military censorship to keep such news as troop movements from the enemy, Governor Dewey said the events of which he spoke "have not been suppressed to keep information from the enemy so much as to keep them from our own people."

"When we find the State Department requesting the British censor to suppress political news sent to American papers by American correspondents abroad, it begins to amount to a deliberate policy of suppression of the news at home," he said.

"Being Constantly Surprised"

"Despite millions of dollars spent on War Information Service, we are constantly being surprised. Often we learn of important events through the pronouncements of foreign statesmen or by reading dispatches cabled back to this country from foreign papers. After making all due allowances for wartime conditions, it still remains that we know far too little about our own foreign policies and practically nothing about our diplomatic commitments."

Hailing the cooperation of the American press in accepting "voluntary censorship," Governor Dewey asserted that the "stakes in this war are too high for it to be fought in the dark."

"There seems to be too little recognition," he said, "of the fact that free people cannot fight a war with blinders on their eyes. Knowing the present dangers and the hardships ahead, they will brace themselves to any task. They will sacrifice as deeply as the welfare of the nation demands. They can do neither if they are not told where they are going and why. Our people can take the bad news with the good, but they have a right to know the facts. We need a free,

Continued on Page Ten

Soldier Vote Action Is Set for Midweek

Special to THE NEW YORK TIMES.

WASHINGTON, March 24—President Roosevelt said today that he would wait until the middle of next week to act on the Soldier Vote Bill.* He has until midnight of next Friday to approve it, veto it or let it become law without his signature.

When he said that there would probably be something on the bill by midweek, a reporter asked whether it would be a message. The President replied, hesitating, that perhaps it ought to be called a statement.

Some observers construed this to mean that he might let the bill become law with an explanatory statement, because if it were to be vetoed there would be a message.

Only a veto message would be expected just before the deadline for action. In any event, the President's remark at his press conference appeared to be offhand.

RULING BY WALLACE ANGERS SENATORS

McKellar Denounces 'Legislative Trick' Phrase—TVA Curbed, Agencies Doomed

By C. P. TRUSSELL
Special to THE NEW YORK TIMES.

WASHINGTON, March 24—The Senate, after a week's controversy, passed the $8,000,000,000 Independent Offices Appropriations bill this evening and sent it back to the House loaded with provisions forced into it in one of this year's bitterest political floor fights.

The clashes over the bill reached a climax this afternoon with a row centering about Vice President Wallace's ruling against a proposal from the floor which he suggested would amount to "a legislative trick."

His phrase angered Senator Kenneth McKellar of Tennessee, who denounced the statement as "damnable," it being made during consideration of the admissibility of Mr. McKellar's amendment to put the Tennessee Valley Authority under tight Congressional control.

Senator Bennett C. Clark of Missouri backed the Tennessean, asking whether the Vice President could "flagrantly and brazenly" disregard the rules of the Senate by so ruling.

Ruling Is Overridden

The Vice President, asserting that he meant no reflection on the Tennessee Senator, said that he would be "happy" to withdraw his statement. Then, by a vote of 46 to 17, the Senate overrode Mr. Wallace's ruling.

With attention focused on the President's Fair Employment Practices Committee, the Senate voted for the abolition of all Presidentially created agencies which have functioned for a year unless Congress makes specific appropriations to maintain them.

This was done after a Republican-sponsored amendment, exempting the FEPC from the restrictions of the amendment offered by Senator Richard B. Russell of Georgia had been adopted, reconsidered and then killed.

Victories for McKellar

Without debate, the Senate approved the amendment of Senator McKellar under which all officials and employes of the Government in executive departments and agencies who receive $4,500 or more a year would have to be confirmed by the Senate.

A Republican-sponsored motion to reconsider this action was voted down, 31 to 23.

By a vote of 39 to 26, the Senate

Continued on Page Nine

NEW DRAFT ORDERS SPEED CALL TO MEN WHO ARE NOT YET 26

Status of Older Registrants Will Not Be Changed Until the Younger Are Screened

WMC ACTS ON VITAL SKILLS

War Agency Committee Headed by McNutt to Apportion All Deferments of Experts

By CHARLES E. EGAN
Special to THE NEW YORK TIMES.

WASHINGTON, March 24—Five major rules which must be followed by State Directors of Selective Service in inducting men in the age group under 26 were sent out tonight by Gen. Lewis B. Hershey, Director of Selective Service.

The regulations, which followed conferences among war agency heads, the Army, Navy and Selective Service, represent their solution of the difficult problem presented by the necessity of filling the forces' needs for young men without disrupting war activities. The services intend to build their strength to 11,300,000 by July 1. The total now is at 10,600,000.

Earlier in the day the War Manpower Commission set up a special committee under the chairmanship of Paul V. McNutt, chairman of the WMC, which will screen and submit to Selective Service recommendations for special deferments of irreplaceable men in approved war activities and plants.

The "claimant agencies" which will be represented on the new committee include the production executive committee of the War Production Board, spokesman for war-production activities; the Petroleum Administrator for War, Solid Fuels Administration, the Rubber Director, Office of Defense Transportation, the War Food Administration, Maritime Commission, the War Shipping Administration and the armed services.

Agencies Will Submit Requests

The requests of these agencies for deferments must be in the committee's hands by Monday and, after screening by the committee, will be sent to Selective Service directors in the various States in the form of quotas. Decisions on deferments for individuals are to be made in the States within the quotas assigned.

The five provisions outlined by General Hershey included instructions to give first attention to those up to 26 in reviews and reconsideration of draft deferments before taking up cases of registrants in the age group of 26 to 37 years.

The detailed instructions were as follows:

(1) The War Department, Navy Department, the Maritime Commission, War Production Board, Office of Defense Transportation, War Food Administration, War Shipping Administration, Petroleum Administrator for War, Solid Fuels Administration, and the Office of the Rubber Director are authorized to designate representatives in each State to endorse special requests for deferment of key registrants under the age of 26 in war activities other than agriculture, and employed in establishments coming within their jurisdiction.

(2) State Directors of Selective Service are directed to issue orders to report for pre-induction physical examination by the armed forces to all registrants under the age of 26 who are occupationally deferred in Class 2-A, that is, those deferred for work in support of the war effort; and in 2-B those

Continued on Page Eight

Drinks Go Up 2 to 4 Cents April 1; Tax Adds Cent for Glass of Beer

Special to THE NEW YORK TIMES.

WASHINGTON, March 24—Higher excise taxes effective April 1 will add 2 to 4 cents to the by-the-drink price of liquor or sparkling wine and 1 cent to the cost of an eight-ounce glass of beer, ale, porter or stout, the Office of Price Administration stated today.

Allowable increases for straight or mixed drinks as made public by the OPA are:

Drinks containing not less than half an ounce and not more than an ounce of distilled spirits of 80 proof or more, 2 cents; more than an ounce but less than 1¾ ounces, 3 cents; 1¾ ounces or more, 4 cents.

Drinks containing one ounce or more of distilled spirits of less than 80 proof, 2 cents.

Drinks of 2½ ounces or more of still wines containing more than 14 per cent but not over 21 per cent of alcohol, 1 cent.

Drinks of 3 ounces or more of champagne, sparkling wine, carbonated wines or wine-based cordials, 3 cents.

The new excise rates increase the tax on distilled spirits from $6 to $9 a gallon while the tax on beer jumps from $7 to $8 a barrel.

Wine with less than 14 per cent of alcohol will be taxed 15 cents per gallon under the new law, compared to 10 cents now. Wine containing from 14 to 21 per cent of alcohol is to be taxed 60 cents per gallon as against the old rate of 40 cents.

Sparkling wine, now taxed at 10 cents a half pint, will be taxed at 15 cents a half pint and all other wines at 10 cents a half pint, double the prevailing scale.

BERLIN IS HIT AGAIN

RAF Blow Follows U. S. Attack on Frankfort and Schweinfurt

FRENCH AIRFIELDS BOMBED

Few Enemy Fighters Are Seen on Day After Americans Felled 61 Nazi Planes

By GENE CURRIVAN
By Wireless to THE NEW YORK TIMES.

LONDON, Saturday, March 25—Establishing a new United States Air Force record for attacks against Hitler's Continental fortress, Flying Fortresses and Liberators blasted away yesterday at the Reich and other European points for the nineteenth time this month.

The Royal Air Force followed up the American attack with a heavy blow on Berlin last night, a British communiqué announced. A force that required an hour to pass an East Coast town went over the Reich, with the capital as the principal objective.

[A broadcast of the German news agency DNB said Leipzig, transport and heavy industry center, ninety-three miles south-southwest of Berlin, and Weimar, 145 miles southwest of Berlin, also had been bombed, The United Press reported.]

[Describing the attack on the Reich capital, the Berlin radio said high explosives and fire bombs blanketed all Berlin.]

While the RAF was over Berlin, a sizable number of German bombers rained high explosives and incendiary bombs on London for more than an hour.

A number of fires were burning in the British capital long after the "all-clear" signal.

American targets in Germany yesterday were Schweinfurt, where the much-damaged ball bearing plant was pounded again and Frankfort on the Main aircraft and distribution center, still burning after Wednesday's 3,360-ton bombardment.

German Air Base Hit

At the same time the Liberators swept through heavy flak but little other opposition to bomb fighter bases at Nancy and St. Dizier in northeast France. In another branch of this general operation 100 Thunderbolts strafed and attacked the airfield at Bernay St. Martin thirty-five miles from Havre. Machine-gun fire and

Continued on Page Five

ALLIED LEADERS INSPECT U. S. SOLDIERS IN ENGLAND

Prime Minister Churchill and General Dwight D. Eisenhower reviewing paratroopers
Associated Press Radiophoto, passed yesterday by censor

ROOSEVELT WARNS GERMANS ON JEWS

Says All Guilty Must Pay for Atrocities and Asks People to Assist Refugees

The President's statement on aid to refugees, Page 4.

By JOHN H. CRIDER
Special to THE NEW YORK TIMES.

WASHINGTON, March 24—President Roosevelt took the unusual step today of appealing to the German people, as well as the peoples of all subjugated Europe, to do all in their power to assist the escape of Jews and other victims of Nazi persecution. With particular reference to the Jews who escaped to Hungary and the Balkans from Germany, he declared it would be a "major tragedy" if they should "perish on the very eve of triumph over the barbarism which their persecution symbolizes."

[Secretary of State Cordell Hull, on Friday, called upon Hungary to rise against the Nazis. He declared that resistance to the German invader was the only way for the Hungarians to regain the respect and friendship of the free nations of the world.]

The President said his statement

Continued on Page Four

War News Summarized

SATURDAY, MARCH 25, 1944

A new catastrophe appeared to be in the making for the German Armies in the Tarnopol-Proskurov region at the northwestern end of the Ukrainian front yesterday as the Red Armies that had broken through the Nazi lines above and below Tarnopol drove on to the Dniester on the south and across the Sereth River to the north to sever most of the escape routes. Far to the south and east other Russian forces took the Bug River strong point of Voznesensk. [1:8; map, P. 2.]

Hitler continued to pour reserves into the Balkans in an apparent effort to set up a defense line at the Carpathians. Nazi troops marched into Slovakia and probably also into Rumania. The status of the latter country was somewhat clouded. The Rumanian legation in Turkey was reported as saying the Germans had "occupied" the country, but this was contradicted from sources in Switzerland. [4:1.]

President Roosevelt issued an appeal to those Germans who do not approve Hitler's campaign of terror against the Jews and to all men of good-will everywhere in Europe to hide refugees and help them escape. He said it would be a tragedy if the Jews who had fled to the Balkans should be caught now so near the hour of deliverance. [1:5.]

The American air force carried the round-the-clock attack on the Germans through its third day with virtually unopposed assaults on the industrial cities of Frankfort and Schweinfurt and fighter fields at Nancy and St. Dizier. Three bombers and five fighters were lost. It was the nineteenth American operation in March for a new record and followed RAF night attacks on the Lyon area and the railway yards at Laon. The RAF attacked Berlin last night. [1:4; map, P. 5.] The Germans struck back at London in what was reported as an unusually heavy fire raid. It was the fourth straight night the sirens had sounded. [5:4.]

Two statements by British leaders were interpreted as indicating preparations for invasion were near an end. Prime Minister Churchill told American troops Thursday they "soon will have the opportunity" to strike a blow for freedom. General Montgomery, addressing a London luncheon, gave the invasion watchword as "Let God arise and let His enemies be scattered." [1:6-7.]

As the New Zealanders in Cassino started a drive from the east toward Abbey Hill, the stubbornly fighting Germans were reported to have continued their infiltration of the ruins and to hold now several new strong points embracing at least a quarter of the town. [1:7.]

Allied headquarters in India reported that the Japanese columns converging on Imphal were being heavily engaged and that successes had been scored at several points. [1:6-7.]

Fight for a Better World, Premier Tells U. S. Troops

By DREW MIDDLETON
By Cable to THE NEW YORK TIMES.

LONDON, March 24—Prime Minister Churchill has reviewed thousands of American air-borne troops and told them yesterday of the great part they will play "soon" in the invasion of Europe. Mr. Churchill, with Gen. Dwight D. Eisenhower, Allied Commander in Chief, and Lieut. Gen. Omar N. Bradley, senior United States ground commander in Britain, inspected what the Prime Minister called "the most modern expression of war"—air-borne soldiers. His review helped heighten the impression here that the invasion force was now completing its training for the great operation.

[The text of Mr. Churchill's remarks is on page 3.]

It seems clear that organization has progressed so swiftly that the opening of Anglo-American operations now depends on other factors, such as the Russian advance and the conclusion of the campaign to break the Luftwaffe, rather than on the readiness of the vast number of troops concentrated in these islands.

Gen. Sir Bernard L. Montgomery, who will command some of the finest divisions ever raised in the British Army, outfits schooled on the battlefields from Belgium to the Nile, gave his countrymen the invasion watchword in a speech at a "Salute the Soldier" luncheon at the Mansion House today.

It was "Let God arise and let His enemies be scattered," a war cry that reflects the grim Cromwellian character of the commander of the British group of armies.

[Terming the approaching test the "biggest tug-of-war the world has ever seen," General Montgomery said it might last a year or longer, The United Press reported. "It will be a magnificent party and we shall win," he added.]

General Montgomery also appealed for a national reawakening to the tasks that face the invasion troops and asked the nation to help

Continued on Page Three

GERMANS RETAKE FOURTH OF CASSINO

Using Underground Passages, They Infiltrate Allied Lines—Hold 6 Strong Points

By The United Press.

NAPLES, March 24—Stubbornly fighting Germans, infiltrating the ruins of Cassino by subterranean passages and hidden gullies, have recaptured one-fourth of the town after winning possession of six strong points, front dispatches disclosed tonight.

The Germans now hold a belt of territory along the western side of the town running from the southern extremities of Cassino past Highway Six into the northern section.

The Germans' northern toe-hold in the ruin of the town is anchored within 250 yards of the most advanced point reached by the Allies before the deluge of bombs that preceded the present battle, James E. Roper, United Press correspondent with the Fifth Army forces fighting for the town, reported.

Three Enemy Tanks in Hotel

German "Green Devil" parachutists seized this belt of ruined buildings in fierce street fighting, Roper's dispatch said.

Three German tanks have been sneaked into the Hotel Continental, one of the six key positions in the embattled city, where their cannon fire now is added to the German

Continued on Page Three

British Drive the Japanese Back On One Invasion Route to India

By The United Press.

NEW DELHI, India, March 24—British Imperial troops have driven the Japanese from three positions covering the Tiddim-Imphal invasion road into India and smashed enemy attacks in the Kabaw Valley border sector, inflicting heavy casualties, Admiral Lord Louis Mountbatten's headquarters announced today.

Japanese columns were scattered over a 180-mile "front," from the Chin Hills, south of Manipur State, to the Somra Hills tract, and some enemy units still were within twenty-five miles of Imphal, but a spokesman said none of the invaders had reached the Imphal Valley.

Superior British forces were closing in from the north and south on a Japanese road block seventeen miles north of Tiddim after inflicting considerable losses on the counter-attacking enemy. The Japanese also suffered heavy casualties when they were thrown out of a newly occupied vantage point in the Chin Hills.

On the central sector of the border front the Japanese advanced into the hills north of Tamu, seventy miles northeast of Tiddim, but failed in attempts to gain a foothold on the Tamu-Palel road, which links Imphal with the Kabaw Valley. One enemy detachment approaching the important link was dispersed Tuesday, the communiqué said, and another was thrown back when it attacked a British administrative unit on the road.

Imperial troops ambushed a

Continued on Page Six

VITAL RAIL LINE CUT

Red Army in Outskirts of Beltsy as Other Unit Chokes Off Supplies

VOZNESENSK IS CAPTURED

Zhukoff's Offensive Plunges 30 Miles in 24 Hours to Gateway of the Balkan States

By RALPH PARKER
By Wireless to THE NEW YORK TIMES.

MOSCOW, Saturday, March 25—Spearing southward between Tarnopol and Proskurov, the Red Army yesterday made a spectacular thirty-mile gain to reach the Dniester River at the town of Zaleshchiki, twenty-five miles from Cernauti. In taking Zaleshchiki, the troops of Marshal Gregory K. Zhukoff took possession of the "gateway to the Balkans," situated on the border of Bukovina, former northern frontier province of Rumania.

The Second Ukrainian Army, led by Marshal Ivan S. Koneff, continued its race across Bessarabia by pushing to the outskirts of the large railroad junction city of Beltsy. By capturing Floreshty, eighteen miles east of Beltsy, the Russians severed the Beltsy-Slobodka railroad, the next to last east-west rail route supplying the Germans in the Nikolayev-Odessa section of the lower Ukraine. Reports indicated that Red Army troops already were fighting in the outskirts of Beltsy. Peleniya Station, three miles northwest of the junction, was among the fifty localities taken in the Bessarabian drive.

Bug River Citadel Falls

Gen. Rodion Y. Malinovsky's Third Ukrainian Army, meanwhile, captured the lower Bug River citadel of Voznesensk, giving the Russians control of the river as far as the outer defenses of Nikolayev, which itself is about two-thirds encircled.

[While the Russians were scoring their victories in the Ukraine, the Germans reportedly staged a coup in the far north. According to London diplomatic sources Friday, the Nazis have landed troops on the Finnish Aaland Islands, commanding the entrance to the Gulf of Bothnia. Dispatches from Stockholm on Saturday, however, quoted competent sources in Helsinki as denying the truth of the report.]

The advance of Marshal Zhukoff to the junction of Zaleschiki, which is about sixty miles from the boundary of pre-war Czechoslovakia, places the Red Army within a like distance of Jasina Pass in the Carpathians. The Jasina Pass route was followed by the Imperial Russian Army ninety-five years ago when it moved into Hungary.

Drive Is Four Days Old

Premier Stalin's order of the day to Marshal Zhukoff announced the news yesterday of the swift advance to Bukovina. The order also named the important towns of Chortkov and Gusyatin as among the 400 places captured in the drive southward. Marshal Zhukoff's renewed offensive, opened four days ago with a surprise attack, has covered some sixty-five miles and drawn an iron screen across the westward retreat route of all German forces north of the Dniester and west of Marshal Koneff's salient.

The German forces, believed to be substantial, are now confined to the railway running southward to Kamenets-Podolsk, beyond which, according to official British maps, the line does not go. A rough road runs from there across the Dniester to Cernauti and other Bukovina towns.

The fact that many of Marshal Zhukoff's most celebrated generals were listed in Premier Stalin's order means that very powerful forces are involved in the new offensive toward the Carpathians.

Besides capturing 400 places in the four-day drive, Marshal Zhukoff's armies killed more than 20,000 Germans and captured 3,500. In addition, large quantities of war

Continued on Page Two

National Archives

London street after biggest German night raid of the war.

"All the News That's Fit to Print"

The New York Times.

LATE CITY EDITION
Cloudy; rain tonight. Cloudy, showers and colder tomorrow.
Temperatures Yesterday—Max., 57; Min., 48
Sunrise today, 5:53 A. M.; Sunset, 7:54 P. M.

VOL. XCIV..No. 31,876. Entered as Second-Class Matter. Postoffice, New York, N. Y. NEW YORK, THURSDAY, MAY 3, 1945. THREE CENTS IN NEW YORK CITY

BERLIN FALLS TO RUSSIANS, 70,000 GIVE UP; 1,000,000 SURRENDER IN ITALY AND AUSTRIA; DENMARK IS CUT OFF; HAMBURG GIVES UP

$7,445,000,000 CUT IN COMING BUDGET ASKED BY TRUMAN

He Tells Congress Most of It Can Be Sliced From Program for 1946 Shipping

CUTS AGENCIES $80,000,000

Studies Leading to Additional Economies Are Continuing, President Assures Press

President Truman's statement on cuts in war costs, Page 38.

By BERTRAM D. HULEN
Special to THE NEW YORK TIMES.

WASHINGTON, May 2—President Truman started an economy program today with proposals looking to the saving of more than $7,445,000,000.

The biggest cut was applied to the Maritime Commission through a recommendation in a letter to Congress for reduction of funds for ship construction of more than $7,000,000,000 in current appropriations and contract authorizations.

In another recommendation the President called for a reduction of more than $80,000,000 in the budgets of eight agencies for the fiscal year beginning July 1.

Mr. Truman also informed Congress that he was terminating the Office of Civilian Defense by June 30 and withdrawing its proposed budget of $369,000 for the next fiscal year.

The Joint Congressional Committee on Internal Revenue has been continuing tax studies for months and the leaders in Congress are hopeful that the question can be taken up actively after V-E Day.

Details at Press Conference

So far as the Maritime Commission is concerned, Vice Admiral Emory S. Land, the chairman, assured ship contractors that there would be funds for the completion of the construction program under which 12,000,000 deadweight tons of new ships are being built this year.

In addition he expects that reserves of many millions of dollars can be set up for Government agencies for the current fiscal year.

Furthermore, the President said at his press conference, the second he has held since entering the White House, that other cuts were under consideration. Studies are now being made of possible reductions in employe personnel.

Indications were that the President was hopeful that tax revision would be possible, once substantial reductions in expenditures had been accomplished and hostilities had ceased in Europe. He said he was discussing tax matters with Secretary Morgenthau.

In Line With Congress Policy

The approaching end of the European war and the favorable progress of the war in the Pacific have made the savings possible. Moreover, the President's action is in line with the policy set by Congress last year in the second Deficiency Bill requiring a continuous study of appropriations and contract authorizations and their review by the President.

It is regarded as certain that Congress will adopt the recommendations. They are taken as meaning not only immediate economies, but also as signifying that President Truman is bent upon having the Executive Branch conducted primarily through the Cabinet departments rather than through agencies and boards, many of which have been set up in recent years for emergency purposes.

The agencies affected by the recommendations today are the Office of War Information, War Production Board, Office of Censorship, Office of Defense Transportation, Petroleum Administration for War, Federal Security

Continued on Page 38, Column 2

De Valera Proffers Sympathy to Reich

By The United Press.

DUBLIN, May 2—Prime Minister Eamon de Valera made a personal call at the German Legation today to express condolances for Adolf Hitler's death.

He was accompanied by Joseph Walsh, Secretary of the Department of External Affairs, and was received by the German Minister, Dr. Eduard Hempel.

Hitler's death was widely discussed throughout neutral Eire and received wide play in newspapers.

The Portuguese Government ordered two days of mourning for Hitler and flags will be flown at half-staff on "all public buildings," the American Broadcasting Station in Europe said yesterday, according to the Office of War Information.

BRITISH GO ASHORE SOUTH OF RANGOON

Force Moves to Join the 14th Army Troops North of City in Attack—Isles Shelled

By The United Press.

CALCUTTA, India, May 2—In a daring amphibious thrust, British troops landed today on the southern tip of Burma, twenty miles south of Rangoon, and stormed northward in order to join forces with Fourteenth Army troops twenty-eight miles north of Rangoon for a two-way assault on the Japanese-held capital.

The landings were made on both sides of the wide mouth of the Rangoon River where it empties into the Gulf of Martaban. They followed a drop yesterday by parachute troops from low-flying transport planes to clear the landing beaches for the amphibious forces.

Before the landings warships of the British East Indies fleet swept the Gulf of Martaban and destroyed ten Japanese craft filled to the gunwales with enemy troops fleeing Rangoon. A Southeast Asia Command communiqué announced that the British ships suffered no damage or casualties.

Andaman Sea Isles Shelled

It was not disclosed what type of warships participated in the operations in the Gulf of Martaban, but it was officially announced that other powerful British units, including aircraft carriers and the French battleship Richelieu, had carried out a two-day strike at Japanese airfields and installations in the Nicobar and Andaman Islands, far to the southwest in the Andaman Sea.

Battleships, cruisers and destroyers, the communiqué said, bombarded airfields on Car Nicobar Island, 675 miles southwest of Rangoon, and steamed northward to shell port installations at Port Blair, 425 miles southwest of Rangoon. Carrier planes followed up both operations.

[A BBC dispatch asserted that

Continued on Page 13, Column 3

WAR IN ITALY ENDS

Last Enemy Force Gives Up Just 20 Months After Landings

DEFEAT IS COMPLETE

Unconditional Surrender Opens 'Back Door' to German Bastion

By VIRGINIA LEE WARREN
By Wireless to THE NEW YORK TIMES.

ADVANCED ALLIED HEADQUARTERS, Italy, May 2—Twenty months after the Allies' troops first set foot on Italian soil the war for Italy ended at noon today, when hostilities ceased under the unconditional surrender signed by the Germans last Sunday afternoon at Allied Headquarters in Caserta.

The terms, revealed only today, cover all land, sea and air forces, estimated at almost 1,000,000 men. They apply to all northern Italy to the Isonzo River in the northeast and to the Austrian provinces of Vorarlberg, Tyrol and Salzburg and portions of Carinthia and Styria.

The surrender of the Austrian provinces swept away most of the area that the Germans had claimed that they would use for a redoubt. It also greatly lessened the chances for any last-ditch stand on the Continent. The portion of Italy not included in the surrender lies along the Yugoslav border and takes in the Istrian Peninsula, already in the hands of Yugoslav Partisans.

Germans Must Disarm

Soon after noon today the German command's radio ordered its forces still trying frenziedly to flee into the Alps before the Fifth and Eighth Armies to lay down their arms. The unconditional-surrender terms call for the "immediate immobilization and disarmament of the enemy's ground, sea and air forces."

The Germans gave up just twenty-one days after the Eighth Army and fourteen days after the Fifth Army had begun the spring offensive that swept over every important city in northern Italy, brought in more than 160,000 prisoners and sealed off all the major Alpine passes. The surrender of Col. Gen. Heinrich von Vietinghoff-Scheel, the German Commander in Chief in the southwest and Commander in Chief of Army Group C, marked the first time in this war that Germany had formally acknowledged the loss of a country that she had dominated. Even Field Marshal Sir Harold R. L. G. Alexander, the Allies' commander in this theatre, had said that Italy might well be the last battlefield.

The instrument of surrender was signed in the former summer palace of the Neapolitan Kings in Caserta by one German represent-

Continued on Page 3, Column 1

Spain Detains Laval for Allies After His Flight to Barcelona

By PAUL P. KENNEDY
By Cable to THE NEW YORK TIMES.

BARCELONA, Spain, May 2—Pierre Laval, former French Premier, who arrived at the Barcelona airport this afternoon seeking refuge, tonight was in the Montjuich fortress outside Barcelona, interned for disposition by the Allied Governments.

With him in custody are fellow-passengers and the crew of an armed Junkers military plane which arrived at the airport at 12:30 P. M. The passengers included Abel Bonnard, former Vichy Minister of Education; Maurice Gabolde, former Vichy Minister of Justice; Mme. Laval, Paul Neraud, Laval's private secretary, and Eugene Bonnard, son of the former Minister.

David Key, United States Consul General here, said Laval had the choice of leaving Spain immediately or internment pending disposal of his case by the Allied powers. After two hours of debate among the party, during which the plane was refueled and made ready to depart, Laval informed the authorities they chose internment.

Laval said he did not desire to be sent to France, because he feared he would not receive a fair trial there.

The Spanish Government apparently was surprised by the plane's arrival. Barcelona's Civil Governor, Antonio Correa Verglis-

Continued on Page 7, Column 1

GERMANS AND ALLIES SIGNING UNCONDITIONAL SURRENDER IN ITALY

Left: Representative of Col. Gen. Heinrich von Vietinghoff-Scheel affixing signature to the document in royal palace at Caserta as his aide looks on. Right: Lieut. Gen. W. D. Morgan, British Army, placing his name on the articles. Standing behind him are (left to right) Air Vice Marshal George Baker, Chief of Staff to the Allied Mediterranean Air Forces; Maj. Gen. A. P. Kislenko and Lieut. M. Vraevsky, both representing Russia, and Maj. Gen. Lyman L. Lemnitzer, American deputy chief of staff in the Mediterranean.

The New York Times (British Official via U. S. Signal Corps Radiotelephoto)

BIG THREE WRESTLE AGAIN OVER POLAND

Russian Arguments Persist but Hope Remains—Changes in Dumbarton Plan Weighed

By JAMES B. RESTON
Special to THE NEW YORK TIMES.

SAN FRANCISCO, May 2—The United States, Great Britain and Soviet Russia made another attempt to solve the Polish Government controversy today and, while they did not succeed, the negotiations are active again and not entirely without hope.

Two major conferences were held during the day. This morning, Vyacheslaff M. Molotoff, Foreign Commissar, went to the headquarters of the American delegation and met with W. Averell Harriman and Sir Archibald Clark-

Continued on Page 16, Column 3

Goebbels and Fuehrer Died By Own Hands, Aide Says

By Cable to THE NEW YORK TIMES.

LONDON, Thursday, May 3—A deposition by Joseph Goebbels' chief assistant that both the German propaganda chief and Adolf Hitler had committed suicide in Berlin was given to the world early today by Red Army forces after they had occupied the capital of the crumbling Reich.

Hans Fritsche, Goebbels' deputy, was quoted in the Soviet communiqué as having reported also the suicide of General Krebs, who was disclosed to have been appointed Chief of the German General Staff in place of Field Marshal Gen. Wilhelm Keitel, lately believed to have been backing Heinrich Himmler's peace bid to the Western Powers.

The statement of Fritsche, who was captured in Berlin with a large assortment of defense chiefs, added another version of the Fuehrer's demise to two already given —that he had died in battle and

Continued on Page 10, Column 1

War News Summarized

THURSDAY, MAY 3, 1945

Berlin fell to the Russians yesterday and more than 70,000 prisoners were taken. The German pocket southeast of the capital was liquidated. The Baltic ports of Rostock and Warnemuende were won. [1:8; map P. 6.]

Unconditional surrender was accepted by Col. Gen. von Vietinghoff, commanding German forces in northern Italy and western Austria. The terms, signed Sunday, became effective yesterday; thus another enemy pocket vanished. [1:3; map P. 2.]

The end was near on the Western Front, according to front-line dispatches that told of rapidly disappearing resistance. The British seized Hamburg, Luebeck and Wismar—only thirty miles from the Russians at Rostock. The United States Ninth Army linked up with the Russians northwest of Berlin, and in the south the Bavarian pocket was being reduced. [1:6, map P. 6.]

Moscow declared that Hitler and Goebbels had committed suicide in Berlin. [1:5-6.] General Eisenhower denied that Hitler had died a hero's death, indicating he had succumbed to a cerebral hemorrhage. [10:5.]

Acting Secretary of State Grew made public a chronology of the dealings with Himmler, during which President Truman told the Germans to surrender to Allied local commanders. [12:1.]

Despite reports of capitulation in Scandinavia the German commanders in Norway and Denmark ordered their men to fight on, probably in anticipation of a final U-boat thrust by Admiral Doenitz. [1:6-7.] The new Fuehrer dismissed von Ribbentrop as Foreign Minister and appointed Count Lutz Schwerin von Krosigk his successor. [4:6.]

Pierre Laval, attempting to escape from Germany, landed in Spain. When he refused to leave he was interned. [1:2.3.]

Invasion of Tarakan Island, east of Borneo, by Australians was confirmed by General MacArthur. Americans on Mindanao reached the western edge of Davao. [14:2, with map.]

British paratroops and invasion forces landed on both banks of the Rangoon River below Rangoon in Burma. [1:2; map P. 13.] Americans gained 1,400 yards on Okinawa and were a mile from Yonabaru. [13:4, with map.] United States submarines have sunk twenty-one more Japanese ships. [13:1.]

Another attempt was made at San Francisco by Great Britain, the United States and Russia to settle the Polish question. While no progress was reported the atmosphere was said to have been improved and discussions will continue. [1:4.]

DENMARK CUT OFF; HAMBURG YIELDS

Luebeck Also Occupied, With the Surrender of Holland Believed Imminent

By The Associated Press.

LONDON, Thursday, May 3—British forces have occupied Hamburg, a broadcast by the Hamburg radio declared today.

The broadcast announcing the fall of the big North German port was in the German language but evidently it was made by the British.

It decreed a curfew for the entire population and declared that restrictions on civilian movements depended upon "the behavior of the population."

Hamburg is Germany's second largest city. It had a pre-war population of 1,682,220.

Hamburg had earlier been declared an open city, the Hamburg

Continued on Page 6, Column 1

Copenhagen Certain Foe Must Go, But Nazis Deny Norse, Danish Exit

By SVEND CARSTENSEN
By Telephone to THE NEW YORK TIMES.

COPENHAGEN, Denmark, May 2—The Germans are still staying in Copenhagen, but it looks as if they are on the way out. Optimism here about their immediate departure from Denmark subsided considerably today, but it was reasoned here that if the Danes have waited five years they can afford to wait another two weeks.

Therefore the Danes are lying low in the expectation that events will force the Nazis to evacuate Denmark in the shortest order whether they mean to or not.

[Upsetting reports that the Nazis were negotiating to vacate Denmark and Norway, the German High Commands in both countries announced a fight to the death, The United Press reported. This action was linked to the possibility of a final, desperate U-boat campaign from Norway.

[At the same time Grand Admiral Karl Doenitz announced the ousting of Joachim von Ribbentrop as German Foreign Minister and his replacement by Count Lutz Schwerin von Krosigk.]

King Christian and former Premier Vilhelm Buhl conferred repeatedly today and it was generally thought that Mr. Buhl's visits to the royal castle concerned the formation of a constitutional

Continued on Page 5, Column 1

MOSCOW JOY MAD AS BERLIN IS WON

Stalin Announcement Starts Unprecedented Celebration in Honor of Victory

By CYRUS L. SULZBERGER
By Wireless to THE NEW YORK TIMES.

MOSCOW, Thursday, May 3—News of the fall of Berlin was received here with wild acclaim although it had been expected hourly for several days.

It was Marshal Stalin's order of the day officially announcing the capture of the Nazi capital which really set things off.

It is poetic justice that among the Soviet officers specially singled out in Marshal Stalin's order for participating in the conquest of Berlin was his son, Col. Vassily Stalin, who took part as a Red Air Force pilot in the aerial destruction of the city.

While the news electrified the already jubilant capital of the Soviet Union, which was concluding the two-day May Day holiday, it is noteworthy that no more than the usual salute given for the conquest of an enemy or the liberation of a friendly capital was ordered in the case of Berlin—324 guns firing twenty-four salvos each.

But never has this largest Soviet salute been received with more acclaim. Shouting Muscovites, usually quite restrained even with the

Continued on Page 6, Column 6

EPIC SIEGE IS OVER

Shell of German Capital Yielded to Red Army by Beaten Nazis

343,000 LOST BY FOE

Baltic Link With British Is Near as Rostock and Warnemuende Fall

By The Associated Press.

LONDON, Thursday, May 3—Berlin, greatest city of the European Continent, fell yesterday afternoon to the Russians as 70,000 German troops laid down their arms in the surrender that Adolf Hitler had said never would come.

The Soviet triumph, after twelve days of history's deadliest street fighting, was announced last night by Premier Stalin in an Order of the Day and in the Soviet communiqué broadcast from Moscow this morning.

Marshal Stalin first issued an Order of the Day announcing destruction of the German Ninth Army trapped southeast of Berlin, with the capture of 120,000 of its men and the slaughter of at least 60,000.

Rostock and Warnemuende Fall

A second Order announced the capture of Germany's big Baltic ports of Rostock and Warnemuende in a forty-four-mile drive by the Second White Russian Army.

Then Marshal Stalin proclaimed the fall of Berlin. It capitulated at 3 P. M., Moscow time, and by 9 P. M. 70,000 of its staggering defenders had been rounded up and counted by the Russians.

[The defense of Berlin cost the Germans 343,000 men killed or captured, according to Soviet casualty figures, The United Press reported.]

For the conquest of Berlin his proclamation called for the top Moscow victory salute of twenty-four salvos from 324 cannon in tribute to the armies that took Berlin, the First White Russian and the First Ukrainian.

Those armies, commanded by Marshals Gregory K. Zhukoff and Ivan S. Koneff, had jumped across the Oder River sixteen days previously and on April 21 had fought into Berlin. They encircled the sprawling city, which already had been wrecked by American and British bombers, and tore the remains to bits in some of the bitterest big-scale street fighting of all time.

End of Six-Year Empire

Thus fell the once mighty capital, which Marshal Stalin described as "the center of German imperialism and heart of German aggression" and Hitler had proclaimed as the seat of his "thousand-year Reich" empire—the empire that in less than six years died as it had been born, in blood and suffering.

The greatest city ever to fall in battle, Berlin lay a 341-square-mile monument to the death of millions and to the diseased ambition of one man, Adolf Hitler.

How many persons died there will never be known with accuracy but before the war that greatest of continental cities had a population of 4,335,000, and only Monday night the Russians announced that the fanatical Nazi defenders were killing many of the civilians with their fire.

The fury of that defense was everything that Hitler had said it would be, and even Wednesday afternoon his dwindling cohorts had contended over the Hamburg radio that resistance in Berlin was "not yet broken," even while admitting that the garrison had been ripped into isolated pockets.

The finale came in the innermost heart of the city, in the govern-

Continued on Page 5, Column 5

"All the News That's Fit to Print"

The New York Times.

LATE CITY EDITION
Cloudy and warmer with showers; probably thunderstorms today.
Temperatures Yesterday—Max., 65; Min., 41
Sunrise, 6:04 A. M.; Sunset, 7:44 P. M.

VOL. XCIII..No. 31,502. Entered as Second-Class Matter, Postoffice, New York, N. Y. NEW YORK, MONDAY, APRIL 24, 1944. THREE CENTS NEW YORK CITY

AMERICANS LAND ON NORTH NEW GUINEA COAST; ADMIRAL KING SEES PACIFIC VICTORY ROAD OPEN; 2-WAY BLOWS MARK 7TH DAY OF AIR OFFENSIVE

ROOSEVELT ORDERS WARD STRIKE END PENDING NLRB POLL

Deadline Set at Tomorrow Noon, With Company Under Command to Obey WLB

NEW ACTION THREATENED

Any Defiance to Be Met With Step in Nation's 'Interests'—Union Wires Compliance

By WALTER H. WAGGONER

Special to THE NEW YORK TIMES.

WASHINGTON, April 23—President Roosevelt today set Tuesday noon as the deadline by which Montgomery Ward & Co., which has refused to comply with an order by the National War Labor Board, and the company's union employes, who are on strike, must take initial steps which he laid down for the settlement of their dispute.

He directed the union to end its strike, which has been in progress since April 12, and the company, to obey the WLB order, both to take these actions "forthwith," and warned:

"Unless, before noon Tuesday, April 25, I am informed by each of you that the steps to be taken by the company and the union, as herein outlined, have been initiated, I shall take such further action as the interests of the nation require."

Duplicate Telegram Sent

The orders were contained in a telegram sent simultaneously to Sewell Avery, president of the mail-order house, and Samuel Wolchok, national head of the United Retail, Wholesale and Department Store Employes of America, a CIO union.

[Mr. Wolchok wired from New York yesterday, according to The Associated Press, that he would order the strikers to return to work in compliance with President Roosevelt's order.]

In the telegram the Chief Executive sternly ordered both parties also to cooperate in a National Labor Relations Board election to determine whether the union should be the bargaining agent for the company's employes.

A union contract with the company expired in December and Mr. Avery, questioning whether the union still represented a majority of the employes, refused to continue it.

By inference, the President's message refuted the contention in arguments by the company that the mail-order house was not engaged in war work and was therefore immune from Government seizure.

The President said that he was "informed" that the dispute involved several thousand workers and was holding up delivery of farm equipment and machinery, repair parts, electrical appliances, automobile tires "and other goods essential for the economy in wartime."

"Danger" of Strike Spread

He asserted that he had also been told that the strike was being supported by other unions and that there was "grave danger" it would spread to other industries.

"These conditions cannot be permitted to continue in a nation at war," he declared.

More than half of the telegram consisted of a summary of the background of the deadlock which the President has been asked, by all members of the WLB, to adjudicate.

Extensive speculation during the past week over the action the Government might take brought the report that Jesse Jones, Secretary of Commerce and Director of the Reconstruction Finance Corporation, might take over for the Government, an action which would be without precedent.

This possibility was not ruled out by the President's wire. The phrase "further action" was generally interpreted to mean seizure of the company. Seizure has been a solution, in most cases temporary, for

Continued on Page 12

Western Union Asks To Send Greetings

By The Associated Press.

WASHINGTON, April 23—The American Communications Association (CIO), union of telegraph workers, today made public a protest to the Board of War Communications against a request of the Western Union Telegraph Company for permission to resume transmission of congratulatory telegrams.

The protest was echoed in a letter by Representative Marcantonio of New York to James L. Fly, board chairman.

Joseph P. Selly, president of the union, said the telegraph company's wartime service would be impeded if the request, pending before the Federal Commission, was granted.

Western Union, with the permission of the FCC, on Sept. 18, 1942, eliminated singing telegrams and fixed-text holiday and social greetings, and three months later stopped accepting congratulatory and holiday messages except to soldiers and sailors in expeditionary forces.

PUBLISHERS REPORT UNITY FOR VICTORY

Gathering Here for Meetings Starting Today, They See War Overshadowing Politics

By FRANK S. ADAMS

Americans in all sections of the country are grimly intent on winning the war, and are determined to let nothing stand in the way of attaining victory as speedily as possible, according to publishers who are in New York for the annual meeting of The Associated Press today and the fifty-eighth annual convention of the American Newspaper Publishers Association on the three succeeding days.

Although some concern was expressed over the slow progress of Allied armies in Italy, the consensus of those interviewed was that on the whole the military situation was developing favorably. They reported that the coming invasion of western Europe by the American and British forces under Gen. Dwight D. Eisenhower was of course being tensely awaited by residents of every part of the United States.

Manpower Still a Problem

Manpower shortages are still causing pinches in many areas, but nevertheless production records in both the agricultural and the industrial fields are being maintained at astonishingly high records, the publishers declared. They expressed less concern over problems of re-conversion than spokesmen for some other business groups who have gathered here recently.

Several of those interviewed expressed their belief that Governor Dewey would be the Republican nominee for the Presidency. On the whole the feeling seemed to be, however, that the political situa-

Continued on Page 17

NAVY IS CONFIDENT

Chief Says in Report We Are Ready to 'Travel Far and Fast'

CITES RISING MIGHT

Japan Muffed Chance Off Savo, He States—Lauds Team-Work

By SIDNEY SHALETT

Special to THE NEW YORK TIMES.

WASHINGTON, April 23—Emphasizing the enormous strategic and material gains made by the United States Navy since the beginning of the war, when, he frankly admitted, it was powerless to launch an offensive, Admiral Ernest J. King declared in an unprecedented report, made public tonight, that the future is "as dark and threatening to Japan as it is full of promise to us" and that "the encirclement of Germany is in sight."

Admiral King, Commander in Chief of the United States Fleet and Chief of Naval Operations, said that Japan's position was even worse than the war maps indicated, for her losses at sea and her dwindling recuperative powers, countered by our growing might, represented strategic defeats that must be added to the actual territory she has lost.

In the first report of its type he has submitted to Secretary of the Navy Frank Knox, Admiral King gave a sweeping and revealing picture of progress in combat, production and training, and held forth extremely confident hopes for the future. He did not hesitate to give some of the unfavorable aspects of naval operations, revealing, for instance, with perhaps more frankness than any high Navy official previously has shown, what a severe defeat we suffered through inexperience and bad planning at Savo Island in August, 1942.

High Points of Report

The high points of the admiral's 50,000-word report were:

1. Though long roads still lie ahead both in Europe and in the Pacific, we now are prepared to "travel far and fast to victory."
2. Even without the losses sustained at Pearl Harbor, the Navy could not have carried the war to the enemy, as neither the Army nor the Navy was sufficiently expanded. Nor could our fleet have saved Manila, even if the Pearl Harbor disaster had not occurred.
3. The Japanese muffed an opportunity to strike a disastrous blow against our weakened Pacific Fleet after our Savo Island defeat and subsequent loss of two carriers, just as the Germans made a serious mistake by delaying for more than a month in fully opening their U-boat campaign after the declaration of war.
4. Nazi submarines in the Atlantic

Continued on Page 10

NAZI BASES RIPPED

Bombers, Fighters From Britain Hit All Day in France, Belgium

RAF HAMMERS REICH

Duesseldorf a Target—U. S. Planes From Italy Rock Austrian Plants

By GENE CURRIVAN

By Cable to THE NEW YORK TIMES.

LONDON, Monday, April 24—On the seventh day of the greatest sustained air offensive the world has even known, seemingly unending streams of Allied planes shuttled back and forth yesterday between Britain and the Continent, blasting the military installations and traffic centers of western Europe that are the backbone of Hitler's defenses against impending invasion.

Daylight attacks on Nazi airfields and other vital enemy objectives in northern France and Belgium followed with little respite a four-pronged assault by the Royal Air Force over Saturday night on three Reich cities and a locomotive depot at Laon, France.

More than 1,000 British and Canadian planes participated in the night bombings of Duesseldorf, Brunswick and Mannheim, Germany, and Laon. An estimate of 1,500 would be conservative for the number of American, British and Allied aircraft out by day.

Last night great formations of RAF bombers flew out again over the familiar sky lanes toward the Continent.

[From Italy on Sunday about 500 American heavy bombers attacked Nazi plane production centers at Wiener Neustadt and two other places in Austria.

[Sunday night, according to Axis radio reports, Budapest and Békés, a rail town in eastern Hungary, were attacked by Allied planes. Berlin said Allied aircraft were over Germany.

[German raiders caused alerts along the south coast of England early Monday and bombs were dropped at several points, The Associated Press reported.]

All day observers on the south-

Continued on Page 3

AMERICANS LEAP-FROG UP THE NEW GUINEA COAST

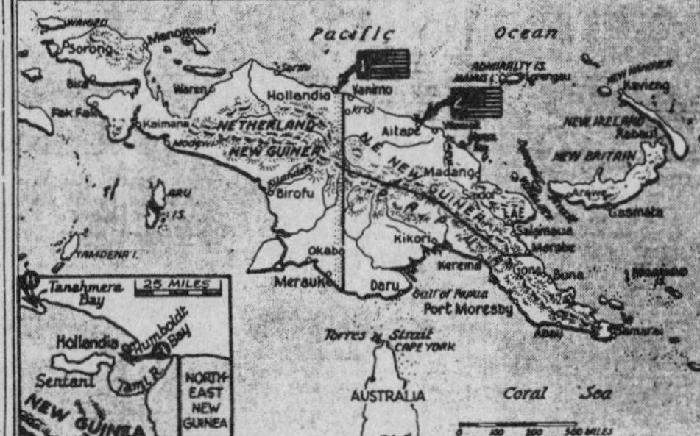

April 24, 1944

In the greatest amphibious operation of the southwest Pacific, American troops, covered by strong naval forces, landed at Hollandia (1) and Aitape (2), isolating 60,000 Japanese to the east. At Aitape the airdrome is already in our hands. Around Hollandia the landings were made at Humboldt Bay (A on inset) and Tanahmera Bay (B). The troops' objectives there are three airfields: two of them west of Hollandia and the third at Lake Sentani. General map on Page 9.

Allies Assert Death Blow For Luftwaffe Is in Sight

By HAROLD DENNY

By Cable to THE NEW YORK TIMES.

LONDON, April 23—American and British air forces have at last turned the corner of their long and desperate battle to knock the Luftwaffe out of the skies and are within sight of victory. The Germans, who converted their aircraft construction from bombers to fighters in a confidence bred of their own defeat in the Battle of Britain that fighters were the answer to the Allied bombing, are losing another gamble. They have not stopped the Allied bombing nor prevented it from growing in intensity and effectiveness. And now for the first time the Luftwaffe is losing more fighter planes than the Reich can produce.

The authorities for these happy conclusions are the British Air Ministry and the United States Strategic Air Forces in Europe.

[The text of their statement appears on Page 4.]

These authorities recently have been exercising unusual conservatism in estimating the effects of Allied air activity. Appropriately they chose today—St. George's Day devoted to England's patron saint who slew the dragon—to is-

Continued on Page 4

REVOLT ON 3 SHIPS CRUSHED BY GREEKS

Clash Bares Demand, Laid to Officers and Leftists, for Ouster of Late Regime

By C. L. SULZBERGER

By Wireless to THE NEW YORK TIMES.

CAIRO, Egypt, April 23—A mutiny in the Greek fleet which, according to an official British naval communiqué, had lasted three weeks, was partly quelled last night when Greek officers and men, acting under orders from their Commander in Chief, Vice Admiral Petros Voulgaris, boarded three warships and, after some fighting, assumed control.

[An Associated Press dispatch from Alexandria ascribed the revolt to the arrest of Army, Navy and Air Force officers who had demanded the ouster of the Cabinet of Emmanuel Tsouderos, who later resigned as Premier. The United Press in a Cairo dispatch said left-wing elements had mutinied.]

Machine-gun and rifle shots inflicted casualties. There was no official mention of any use of heavier weapons.

The vessels stormed were the destroyer Ierax and the corvettes Apostolis and Sachtouris of the

Continued on Page 5

JADE CENTER WON BY BURMA ALLIES

Air-Borne Chindits in Lonkin—Japanese Fall Back From Besieged Kohima

By The United Press.

SOUTHEAST ASIA HEADQUARTERS, Kandy, Ceylon, April 23—Air-borne troops have captured the jade center of Lonkin in the course of their attacks on Japanese communications in North Burma while in eastern India the defeated besiegers of Kohima have fallen back to regroup, it was disclosed tonight.

The air-borne troops, known as Chindits, were trained in behind-the-line warfare by the late Maj. Gen. Orde Charles Wingate and are now commanded by Maj. Gen. W. D. A. Lentaigne. They took Lonkin at an unspecified date. Lonkin is forty miles northwest of the rail town of Mogaung, which is being approached from the north by Chinese under Lieut. Gen. Joseph W. Stilwell.

The Lonkin mines produce the finest jade in the world and before Burma fell all exports were bought by China for the extensive jade-carving trade.

Allies Firm in Kohima

British Imperial troops are consolidating their successes in and around Kohima, the greater part of which was in Japanese hands for twelve days while a Home Counties regiment stood off attacks until relieved.

The British are consolidating gains northeast of Imphal but eighteen miles southwest of that Manipur capital hard fighting is under way in the area of Bishenpur, terminus of a secondary road leading to the Assam-Bengal railroad, where "the enemy advance is

Continued on Page 11

GREAT PACIFIC LEAP

MacArthur and Nimitz Join in 500-Mile Jump to Hollandia Base

AITAPE ALSO INVADED

General Directs Attack as Troops Pour Ashore and Win First Goals

By FRANK L. KLUCKHOHN

By Wireless to THE NEW YORK TIMES.

ALLIED HEADQUARTERS IN NEW GUINEA, Monday, April 24—With many warships of the mighty United States Fleet protecting the landing by pouring shells on the beaches, Gen. Douglas MacArthur hurled large forces ashore along a 150-mile stretch of northern New Guinea early on Saturday, cutting off the Japanese Eighteenth Army, estimated to number 60,000 men.

General MacArthur, personally directing his troops from a cruiser, again surprised the enemy, who concentrated his forces farther east. The American forces poured ashore virtually unopposed at Hollandia and Tanahmera Bay, Netherland New Guinea, and at Aitape, within Australian New Guinea, and quickly attained initial objectives against light enemy opposition.

With the support of a large part of the Pacific Fleet operating under Admiral Chester W. Nimitz, the American forces thus jumped about 500 statute miles up the coast from Saidor on the route to the Philippines and Japan. This is perhaps the Pacific equivalent of the opening of the "second front," since the major United States Navy, Army and Air Forces in the Pacific have joined in an offensive.

Good Harbor Is Captured

Excellent harborage in Humboldt Bay has already been won. Important Japanese air fields near Hollandia are expected soon to be in our hands for further advances toward the heart of the Japanese empire. These are only 1,100 miles southeast of Davao in the Philippines. It is the first Netherland territory recaptured so far in the war.

Three big forces of cruisers and destroyers raked each landing beach for an hour with roaring, smothering fire. When the dizzy crisscross of their streaking tracers and the throaty boom of exploding shells ceased, dive-bombers and trim fighters from many carriers screamed down to bomb and strafe gun positions, installations and finally the beach itself, making the shore a mass of billowing black smoke. Then, with rocket boats making the immediate objective a hell of red fire, every type of landing craft gathered from the entire Pacific carried the first waves of infantry ashore from transports, dock slips and destroyer transports.

Japanese Are Tricked

One reason for the surprise was that vessels making up the three task forces involved steamed in the direction of Palau from a rendezvous point north of the Admiralties. Destroyers and heavy light cruisers swept the seas ahead, while escort carriers were providing protection astern. The carrier force, with its own screen, and other units, acted as separate forces.

At the last moment the giant convoy, which traveled about 900 miles from the embarkation point, swung south. This was on Friday at 7 P. M. At 5 A. M. Saturday the three task forces stood off the various landing beaches. So great was the surprise that abandoned Japanese breakfasts were found on one beach.

The first troops ashore hit the easternmost beach at Aitape at 6:45 A. M. after Japanese positions on two offshore islands had been bombarded. Following scattered fighting in swamps in which at least fifteen Japanese were killed

Continued on Page 9

65 Feared Lost as Liberty Ship Breaks in Half on Alaskan Run

By The Associated Press.

SEATTLE, April 23—The Liberty ship John Straub, laden with explosives for the Alaska war theatre, broke its back and sank with a presumed loss of sixty-five of the eighty men aboard, E. M. Murphy, superintendent of the Alaska Steamship Company, announced today.

Master of the Straub, a new vessel making its third voyage, was Capt. A. W. Westerholm of Seattle, a veteran of twenty-six years with the Alaska Steamship Company.

All ship's officers, forty merchant seamen, fourteen Navy men and the cargo security officer were reported lost.

The wreck occurred twenty-one miles off Sanak Island, a small island south of the pass between Unimak Island and the Alaska Peninsula, which extends westward to the beginning of the Aleutian chain.

First reports mentioned a fire and explosions, but a party of Coast Guardsmen which boarded the after part of the wreck found no evidence of fire, Mr. Murphy said.

All but one of the lifeboats on the Straub had been accounted for, Mr. Murphy said, leaving but scant hope that more survivors of the wreck would be found.

The accident occurred at 5:30 A. M. Wednesday. The Straub, north bound, was reported by the boarding party to have parted aft the engine bulkhead. The forward section sank immediately.

The Coast Guardsmen reported no evidence of life on the after part, which sank fourteen hours after the break.

The fifteen survivors were taken to the Army Hospital at Cold Bay, Alaska, where only the names of

Continued on Page 22

War News Summarized

MONDAY, APRIL 24, 1944

The greatest American offensive in the Southwest Pacific fell suddenly upon surprised Japanese along a 150-mile front on New Guinea Saturday morning and made good two landings: at Hollandia and at Aitape. Some 60,000 enemy troops were encircled by the latest move and, in the words of General MacArthur's communiqué issued last night: "Their situation reverses Bataan."

Great bodies of American soldiers poured ashore after a terrific air and sea bombardment. Tadji airfield at Aitape was promptly seized, and after beachheads had been made secure on Humboldt Bay forces were rushed inland to capture Hollandia's cluster of three airfields. At Hollandia the Allies recovered the first Netherland territory from the Japanese.

General MacArthur watched the operations from a cruiser—operations that brought the Philippines within range of land-based bombers. American losses were slight. [All the foregoing 1:8; maps Pages 1 and 9.]

The news from the Southwest Pacific served to emphasize the assertion of Admiral Ernest J. King, Commander in Chief of the United States Fleet, that the future for Japan is "as dark and threatening as it is full of promise for us." In a frank "Report of Progress" Admiral King traced the growth of our naval might from its weak defensive Pearl Harbor days to its offensive strength today. In the Atlantic, he said, U-boats have been "reduced from a menace to a problem." [1:3; related stories and charts P.10.]

The air war against Germany continued without pause. An estimated 1,500 American and British planes battered at least seven widely separated enemy air bases in northern France and Belgium yesterday. Saturday night the RAF heavily attacked Duesseldorf, Brunswick, Mannheim and the French railroad center of Laon. [1:4; map P. 2.] The British and American Air Forces, in a joint statement, said Germany was losing more fighters than she could produce. As the air battle neared a climax enemy plane reserves were called a "mere trickle in the pipeline between factory and operating units." [1:5-6.]

American bombers from Italy added their weight to the destruction of German fighter production with a heavy assault on the main Messerschmitt plant at Wiener Neustadt and other targets in Vienna's suburbs. [3:1.]

Fighting on the European land fronts was desultory. American troops at Cisterna, on the Anzio beachhead, made some slight gains [8:2.] while Moscow reported that "no important changes took place on the fronts." [5:1.]

Chinese troops in Burma captured Lonkin, threatening Mogaung and the Burma railroad. The situation at Imphal and Kohima was reported well in hand. [1:7.] The Japanese were making progress in heavy fighting around Chengchow in China. [9:1.]

British Rehearse for Air Invasion; Enemy Threatens Surprise Blow

By The United Press.

LONDON, April 23—Thousands of British glider and parachute troops have completed one of the biggest and most dramatic maneuvers yet held in cooperation with the Royal Air Force and the American troops, who, like them, are poised for the invasion of western Europe, it was disclosed tonight.

Air Chief Marshal Sir Arthur Tedder, deputy to Gen. Dwight D. Eisenhower, the Allies' Commander in Chief, and other high British and American officers watched the operation, held yesterday somewhere in England while the Germans nervously speculated on the time set for D-Day. Gliders, towed by twin-motored Albemarle bombers, and special twin-motored planes of other types were used in the exercise, a grimly realistic simulation of a landing in the heart of enemy territory to seize high ground near a canal so that a British infantry division could attack the enemy in the flank.

From the landing area to the horizon, the lines of gliders and their towing planes dotted the sky. One thousand men or more landed from each wave of planes. It took twenty minutes for the gliders, swooping down at intervals of only a few seconds, to land their men.

The parachutists wearing American-style steel helmets, were dropped at a near-by airdrome, along with doctors, stretcher-bearers, a chaplain and, attached to special parachutes, an arsenal of weapons in addition to folding bicycles, radio sets and rations. So accurate was the timing that only a few parachutists failed to land on the airdrome itself. Within a few minutes, all the parachutists had collected their arms and taken cover. As they did so, a

Continued on Page 3

"All the News That's Fit to Print"

The New York Times.

LATE CITY EDITION
Cloudy with scattered showers today; somewhat warmer.
Temperatures Yesterday—Max., 60; Min., 53
Sunrise, 5:30 A. M.; Sunset, 8:16 P. M.

VOL. XCIII. No. 31,534. Entered as Second-Class Matter, Postoffice, New York, N. Y. NEW YORK, FRIDAY, MAY 26, 1944. THREE CENTS IN NEW YORK CITY

AMERICANS LINK THE ANZIO AND MAIN FRONTS; NAZIS FLEE PONTINE MARSHES TOWARD ROME; 5 ALLIED AIR COMMANDS BLAST INVASION AREAS

HOUSE GROUP HEARS INSPECTORS CHARGE SHIP YARD FRAUDS

WSA Men Facing 'Lopping Off' by Tuesday Tell of Payroll Padding and Overloading

FOUND GAMBLING 'CASINO'

100 'Workers' Busy at Cards and Dice—One Says Reports Brought Threats on Life

Employes of the Field Service Division of the War Shipping Administration, scheduled for "lopping off" by next Tuesday, unfolded yesterday stories of payroll padding, labor overloading and general loafing in ship repair yards here and at Boston. They testified before Subcommittee No. 6 of the House Merchant Marine and Fisheries Committee at a hearing in the Federal Court Building in Foley Square.

The men appeared before the group of which Representative Louis J. Capozzoli, Democrat, of New York City is chairman, in defense of their work which has, to date, saved the Government an estimated $10,000,000 in ship repairs.

A story of the value of the service was given by John Donovan, a field service inspector and instructor temporarily attached to the Boston area, who was one of the last witnesses to testify. He maintained that there was no justification for any decrease in the force, and that leaving a busy ship repair area such as Boston with only nine inspectors was ridiculous.

6,000-Hour Claim Disallowed

To back up his assertion of the value of the work of the field service men, he said that in the first two weeks of work on the Cunard-White Star liner Aquitania, undergoing repair and overhaul in Boston, 6,000 man-hours had been disallowed the Bethlehem-Simpson yard. He added that this report had been approved by the WSA port office of maintenance and repair and by the port auditor. At current shipyard wage scales, this represented a saving to the public of approximately $10,000, he said.

At this point, Representative Capozzoli interrupted, saying that the Navy employs between 16,000 and 19,000 men to do much the same work that the Field Service performs for the WSA on merchant ships, and added that if the Navy thought this type of inspection valuable enough to hire that many men on less repair work than is done on merchant ships, there ought to be good reason not only to maintain the service at its present personnel level of 430, but to expand it to fit the 1943 Congressional appropriation for 1,500 inspectors.

Found Gambling Casino on Ship

Earlier, Robert M. Lennon, an inspector with a background of service in the Seabees and in two shipbuilding companies, testified that he and two other men had searched one of the superliners for almost two weeks, through some twenty-four miles of passageways and alleys, before they located a gambling casino.

Mr. Lennon declared that more than 100 men were crowded into one section of the vessel and that several card and dice games were going on. He told of reporting this to the prime contractor, Bethlehem Steel's Hoboken Division, and how the game had then moved to quarters he couldn't locate.

The witness asserted that with twelve sub-contractors also working on the job it was next to impossible to check properly for overloading of labor. He cited one incident in which a foreman claimed twenty hours a day work for seven straight days and was paid $246 for his "labors," which Mr. Lennon declared were definitely not what he claimed.

Representative Henry M. Jackson, Democrat, of Washington, interrupted to ask if authorities had

Continued on Page 10

Tainted Drug Distribution Laid to Chemical Company

U. S. Charges One Patient Treated With Medicine Made by Winthrop Concern Died—Others Developed Symptoms of Fever

The wide distribution of contaminated medicinal supplies was charged yesterday to the Winthrop Chemical Company, Inc., in a criminal information filed in Federal court here by United States Attorney James B. M. McNally. The prosecutor said that, as the result of quick action by the Federal Food and Drug Administration, the Winthrop concern had called in 73,600 ampules of dextrose solution and about 22,000 combination packages containing distilled water and either atabrine, neoarsphenamine or phenarsine.

The criminal information, which has much the same force as an indictment except that it is not the result of grand jury action, was drawn up by Richard J. Burke, chief of the criminal division of Mr. McNally's office.

Mr. Burke said the allegedly tainted products had been shipped during May, June, July and August of last year—each of the twelve counts of the charge related to a shipment of one or another of the four products, made during that period. The prosecutor indicated that the sub-standard supplies had been taken out of circulation, and said the damage had been caused apparently by failure of the concern's plant at Rensselaer, N. Y., to cleanse its distilling apparatus as often as it should. The plant, he said, was turning out its pharmaceutical products at high, wartime speed.

The Food and Drug Administration got wind of the situation, Mr. Burke said, when seven persons—one of whom died—showed unusual symptoms after receiving

Continued on Page 7

HUGE RATION RING FOILED BY RAIDERS

Secret Service Agents Seize Counterfeiting Equipment and Operators in Two Plants

Simultaneous raids by Secret Service agents on two downtown printing plants were credited by United States Attorney James B. M. McNally yesterday with the frustration of "one of the largest black market counterfeiting syndicates in the country."

At the Bellemir Press, Mr. McNally reported, the agents seized zinc plates for printing shoe ration stamps and arrested Harry H. Du Bitsky, operator of the shop. At the Hermine Press, the agents arrested Max Spiegel, proprietor, and took possession of memoranda containing plans for the printing of 1,560,000 shoe stamps of the airplane, No. 2 type, as well as 5,120,000 gasoline ration A coupons, each good for three gallons.

Plants Watched a Week

The shops—the Bellemir is at 270 Lafayette Street and the other at 188 West Fourth Street—were entered just before midnight on Wednesday by investigators who had been watching the premises and their occupants for a week, according to Thomas F. Murphy, assistant to Mr. McNally. The inquiry is proceeding, with a special interest in persons indicated by the seized memoranda to have contracted to buy the spurious stamps that were to be produced. Among those sought is the artist who drew a large group of sketches of the great seal of the United States, from which was made a zinc printing plate for the production of the faint background included in all ration stamps.

The records found at the Hermine plant, Mr. McNally said, dis-

Continued on Page 13

SAY CORRIGAN FIRM GOT $300,000 FEES

Truman Committeemen Report Officer's Company Received This From 6 Contractors

Special to The New York Times.

WASHINGTON, May 25—Six important Navy contractors have paid more than $300,000 in consultant fees to a private engineering and managing corporation of which Comdr. John D. Corrigan, a Navy officer charged with expediting war production, is half owner, the Senate Truman Defense Investigating Committee said today.

Commander Corrigan received a substantial share of the fees paid his firm by the war contractors, who hired it in each instance, it is alleged, almost simultaneously with his inspection visits to their plants and his reported criticism of their production accomplishments.

The Navy officer, who was on the stand most of the day, held that there was no sinister connection between his firm's retention and his visits to the plants of the hiring companies in his official capacity. Every instance in which the firm was retained was approved by his superior officer, he asserted, and in no case would the fees paid come out of Government payments to the contractors. The committee challenged the latter statement.

Navy Suspends the Officer

Following the committee statements, it was learned that the Navy Department had suspended Commander Corrigan from duty.

A naval spokesman told the press:

"The Navy was informed of this situation by the Truman Committee and has itself begun an investigation. Pending the outcome of these investigations, Commander

Continued on Page 10

CIO Assails Work-or-Fight Bill, Says Army, Navy Worry Needlessly

By C. P. TRUSSELL

Special to The New York Times.

WASHINGTON, May 25—The Congress of Industrial Organizations, through Philip Murray, president; Lee Pressman, general counsel, and a battery of other spokesmen, attacked the Bailey-Brewster "work or be drafted" bill before the Senate Military Affairs Committee today as a measure built upon a foundation of labor crises such as could and had been solved without resort to legal sanctions.

High officials of the War and Navy departments and other war agencies, as well as industry management, were the targets of sharp criticism during the three hours of CIO testimony.

"We don't know of any manpower shortage brought to the attention of the War Manpower Commission that has not been solved where the CIO has been involved," Mr. Pressman told the committee.

Labor itself, he implied in further testimony, had done more to meet labor shortage crises than had the Government agencies and departments which were supporting the Bailey-Brewster bill as a second choice to the Austin-Wadsworth National Service Act.

Mr. Pressman contended that the Brewster-Bailey bill would, in effect, transfer the Manpower Commission to Selective Service.

"The Director of Selective Service," he said, "would be a mighty

Continued on Page 10

BOMBS TEAR RAILS

Airfields, River Traffic and Bridges Bombed in Record Attack

TOULON AND LYON HIT

RAF Blasts Aachen and Antwerp Areas With Heavy Loads

By Cable to The New York Times.

LONDON, Friday, May 26—The full weight of the five Anglo-American air commands, the greatest concentration of air power yet assembled for a single offensive, blasted and scourged the foundations of German resistance to an invasion in the west in the twenty-four hours ended at midnight last night. The Eighth, Ninth and Fifteenth American Air Forces and the Bomber Command and the Second Tactical Air Force of the Royal Air Force united to attack those targets in France, the Low Countries and Western Germany whose destruction would vitally affect the Wehrmacht's ability to resist an invasion.

Eighth Hits 13 Targets

The heaviest blow was struck by the Eighth Air Force, which sent between 750 and 1,000 Fortresses and Liberators out to bomb nine freight yards and four airdromes in France and Belgium under a cover of hundreds of fighters. Meanwhile strong forces of heavy bombers of the Fifteenth Air Force delivered a smashing assault on railway yards in the areas of Toulon and Lyon, the latter attack representing the deepest penetration into France yet made by bombers based in Italy.

These operations were accompanied by a series of heavy blows by the two tactical air forces stationed in Britain, the United States Ninth Air Force and the RAF's Second Tactical Air Force. Railway yards, bridges, river traffic, trains, airfields and coastal shipping positions on the Atlantic wall all were pounded by many hundreds of American and British medium, light and fighter bombers.

Yesterday's great assault followed another extensive operation

Continued on Page 6

War News Summarized

FRIDAY, MAY 26, 1944

The Fifth Army's beachhead was merged with the main Italian front yesterday following a brilliant sixty-mile advance in fourteen days over what was officially described as the "most difficult terrain of the whole Italian campaign." Great tank forces and overpowering air blows compelled the Germans to evacuate the Pontine Marshes and ground forces cut two of the four roads leading to Rome.

On what had been the main front Pontecorvo was cleared of the enemy and Sonnino and Roccasecca dei Volsci, beyond Terracina, were captured. The Germans, still clinging to Piedimonte and Aquino, tried vainly to start counter-attacks. [All the foregoing 1:8; map, P. 2.]

Advance units of engineers met at a small bridge near Borga Grappa, south of Littoria, to effect the union of Allied forces. [1:6-7.] Secretary of War Stimson, identifying the men who had made the sixty-mile march as new divisions of the Second Corps of the Fifth Army, said their "inspiring" performance had been the result of a new system of immediate replacements of battle-worn troops. [3:1].

The full weight of five Allied air commands in Britain and Italy fell upon tactical objectives yesterday. More than 2,500 heavy and 1,200 medium bombers, together with hundreds of fighters, attacked France, the Low Countries and Germany. Eighth Air Force Fortresses and Liberators struck nine rail yards and four airfields in France and Belgium; the American Ninth and British Second Tactical Air Forces pounded the usual targets and coastal shipping; the Fifteenth, from Italy, made its deepest penetration into France to strike Lyon and also battered Toulon. On Wednesday night the RAF hit Berlin, Aachen, Antwerp and targets in France. [1:4; map, P. 6.]

Reports from Turkey indicated that Germany had taken over Bulgaria as she had Hungary. Five Nazi divisions were said to be stationed at strategic points and other units to have manned Black Sea coastal defenses. [3:6.]

Naval task forces over last week-end attacked Marcus Island, it was confirmed at Pearl Harbor. Wake was also attacked. Only two Japanese planes were seen and the only one to take to the air was shot down. We lost four aircraft and three men. [5:1.] General MacArthur's troops reached the Maffin Bay airfield in the Wakde area of New Guinea after bitter fighting. [5:5.]

Japanese counter-attacks in Burma were driven off in every sector in which the enemy tried to strike back. Chinese troops wiped out 1,000 of the foe at Tatangtzu on the Salween front and gained important ground toward Lashio. [6:1.] Tokyo claimed to have captured Loyang in Honan Province, but Chungking insisted the city had not fallen. [6:5.]

It was learned in Washington that the Administration had drafted a peace plan, called the "Hull Plan," similar to the post-war organization outlined by Prime Minister Churchill yesterday. [1:5.]

FIFTH ARMY EFFECTS A HISTORIC JUNCTION

Its commander, Lieut. Gen. Mark W. Clark, witnesses the meeting, surrounded by cheering American troops in the Pontine Marshes.

The New York Times (OWI radiophoto from British Army)

WORLD PEACE PLAN FOSTERED BY HULL

Program Outlined by Churchill for Control by Powers Is Studied by Senators

By JAMES B. RESTON

Special to The New York Times.

WASHINGTON, May 25—The Administration has drafted a peace plan similar to the world order outlined by Prime Minister Churchill in the House of Commons yesterday and will make it public in the near future, it was learned today.

The plan, though it is understood to be as vague as the political realities of an election-year demand, is said to foresee in its present state the creation of a world council of the great powers, which would provide the necessary power to enforce peace, and a

Continued on Page 8

Fifth Army Unites Forces At a Small Rustic Bridge

By A. C. SEDGWICK

By Wireless to The New York Times.

ANZIO, May 25—The Fifth Army's beachhead no longer exists, for it is now fused with the rest of the Allied front in Italy. The strategic tactical advantages gained thereby are of far-reaching importance. The daring venture, carried out at great risk just over four months ago when the Allied forces landed and fought their way to the possession of ninety square miles, is now vindicated.

The junction between the main Allied forces and those on the beachhead was effected early this morning on a stretch of flat, smiling farmland with poppies growing among the wheat over which a skylark sang. Another sound was the whirring of a Piper Cub reconnaissance plane, while in the distance were occasional detonations.

The blasts were the last huffy expressions of the beaten foe blowing up the road in a vain attempt to prevent the merging of the two forces. In the vicinity we came upon one machine gun so placed as to sweep the road from Anzio, but no one was manning it.

Damage Quickly Repaired

The damage that the enemy did the road was repaired in such short order in every case that a forced march from Terracina via the coastal route was delayed not much more than an hour and a half.

The contingent advancing from the beachhead passed through some exploded mine craters. A few hours before this territory nominally belonged to the enemy.

A small bridge near the village of Borga Grappa, which arches over a dried water course a few miles from the now non-existent beachhead perimeter was the meeting place. This, like many bridges

Continued on Page 3

STAND ABOVE ROME BY FOE IS EXPECTED

Nazi Retreat to Line Beyond Capital May Be Kesselring's Only Hope of Escaping Trap

By DREW MIDDLETON

By Cable to The New York Times.

LONDON, May 25—The speed of the Allied advance in Italy in the last forty-eight hours, plus indications that Field Marshal Gen. Albert Kesselring lacks reserves to bolster his shattered divisions, has led some well-informed sources to predict that that German field marshal will withdraw the German Tenth and Fourteenth Armies beyond Rome to form a new defensive line before his weakened units are trapped on their present positions by the severance of the Via Casilina as well as the Appian Way.

An extremely well-informed source said to this correspondent:

"The push up the Liri Valley and drive northeastward from the Anzio beachhead jeopardize German troops from Roccasecca to Sezze, and even if the Alban Hills prove a more formidable barrier than is now thought we believe the enemy will be forced to make a wholesale retreat to positions north of Rome."

There has been talk of a Ger-

Continued on Page 3

Britons Forego Holiday Travel; Nazis Bolster Defenses in France

By The Associated Press.

LONDON, May 25—Thousands of British families have canceled plans for the traditional Whitsun holiday week-end travel under the stern warning that train service is subject to stoppage without notice as the hour for the invasion of Europe nears.

Germans tried to probe the secrets of the gathering Allied storm by E-boat patrol dashes across the English Channel today and by spy-plane coastal raids.

A Tass dispatch from Moscow said it was rumored in Berlin that Heinrich Himmler, German Gestapo chief, had left suddenly for France. Virtually the entire Nazi hierarchy, with the exception of Hitler, have been reported in France during the last month, checking the defense system and tightening control over the restive population.

One explanation of Himmler's reported eleventh-hour trip was that it was an attempt to counteract the purposeful broadcast of Gen. Dwight D. Eisenhower's invasion instructions to the European underground.

Meanwhile other German propaganda sought to ease the shocks of continued Nazi retreats in Italy by proclaiming the imminence of invasion from the west. Hitler's newspaper, the Volkischer Beobachter, said:

"The battle is very hard and it is a prelude to the severe large-

Continued on Page 4

APPIAN WAY CLEAR

Allies Take Pontecorvo as They Surge Ahead in All Sectors

CISTERNA TOTTERING

Aquino Reported Given Up by Germans, Who Rush Men From North

By MILTON BRACKER

By Wireless to The New York Times.

NAPLES, May 25—Forward elements of the onrushing main Fifth Army forces established contact with beachhead patrols on the coastal highway between Anzio and Terracina early this morning as the Italian offensive neared the end of its second week. And a battered Wehrmacht now faces a concerted all-out drive by the full power of Gen. Sir Harold R. L. G. Alexander's armies, pledged to liberate Rome.

The junction of Lieut. Gen. Mark W. Clark's Americans took place in the vicinity of Borgo Grappa, which is some six miles southeast of Bargo Sabotino or "Gusville," the long stalemated corner of the beachhead.

The patrols met after another day of sweeping success in which the Allies captured Pontecorvo, Sonnino and Roccasecca dei Volsci, and smashed across both the Appian Way and main coastal railroad near tottering Cisterna, thus severing two of the four main arteries between Rome and the south.

The beachhead forces, with tremendous tank power and overwhelming air superiority concentrated around Valmontone, also took the village of La Villa, one mile west of Cisterna. Cisterna, a town of 3,000, is itself under thunderous attack from three sides.

Pontine Marsh Area Evacuated

In the face of the surge of the Allies in the coastal sector, Field Marshal Gen. Albert Kesselring's forces have evacuated the entire Pontine Marsh area. This afternoon correspondents drove all the way from Cassino to Anzio and back by way of the Appian Way—turning off a few miles below embattled Cisterna.

Thus the fear that the flooding of the marshes would inundate the highway and deprive the Allies of its use as a major supply route to the north apparently was baseless. The splendid macadamized road runs along an embankment fully ten feet above the marsh surface and ought soon to be in service of the beachhead, along with feeder

Continued on Page 2

Pacific Submarines Add 15 Ships to Toll

Special to The New York Times

WASHINGTON, May 25—Fifteen more enemy vessels, including a destroyer, have been sunk in Pacific and Far Eastern waters by the growing United States submarine fleet, which since the first of the year has maintained an average of better than one ship sunk a day, the Navy announced today.

The latest bag of enemy vessels, the sinking of which further increased the serious strain on Japanese shipping, included, in addition to the destroyer, a large cargo transport, a large tanker, two medium-size cargo transports, seven medium-size cargo vessels, a small transport, a medium tanker and a small tanker, the communiqué detailed.

The total of Japanese ships reported sunk by American submarines since the war began now stands at 573. In addition, thirty-six "probable" sinkings and the damaging of 115 other ships have been reported, but since the first of the year the Navy has stopped reporting its gains in these categories and has listed only ships definitely sunk.

U. S. Navy

A Nazi shell explodes on the beach at Anzio narrowly missing an amphibious duck streaking in with supplies from cargo ships anchored off shore.

U. S. Air Force

Consolidated B-24 Liberator drops its bombs on marshalling yards at Forli, Italy.

U. S. Air Force

Bomb damage at Cisterna, Italy.

"All the News That's Fit to Print"

The New York Times.

LATE CITY EDITION

Partly cloudy, slightly warmer today; gentle to moderate winds.
Temperatures Yesterday—Max., 63; Min., 55
Sunrise, 5:26 A. M.; Sunset, 8:23 P. M.

VOL. XCIII..No. 31,544. Entered as Second-Class Matter, Postoffice, New York, N. Y. NEW YORK, MONDAY, JUNE 5, 1944. THREE CENTS NEW YORK CITY

ROME CAPTURED INTACT BY THE 5TH ARMY AFTER FIERCE BATTLE THROUGH SUBURBS; NAZIS MOVE NORTHWEST; AIR WAR RAGES ON

TRANSIT MEN BALK AT MAYOR'S INQUIRY INTO OUTSIDE JOBS

Demand for Sworn Statements Covering Family Earnings Evokes Union Protest

RESENTMENT WIDESPREAD

Many Department Heads Cold Toward Policy and Some Authorize Dual Work

By PAUL CROWELL

Widespread resentment among city employes against Mayor La Guardia's crusade to keep them from holding outside jobs on their own time was intensified yesterday. It became known that Investigation Commissioner Edgar Bromberger, by direction of the Mayor, had asked the 35,000 employes of the unified transit system to make sworn answers to forty questions concerning their own employment and that of all working members of their families.

The Transport Workers Union and other organizations representing city transit workers already have registered informal protests and are considering formal action. It was reported that the TWU was prepared to ask its members receiving such questionnaires from Commissioner Bromberger's office to turn them over to the union.

The questionnaire, of a type said to have been sent to employes of other city agencies, asks the transit worker to give full details about his own job, any job his wife may have outside, any job his children may be filling. Full details concerning pay rates on all such jobs are demanded. The workers are asked also how they obtained outside jobs, whether they paid anyone to get them and whether they are making payments to anyone in connection with outside jobs.

Board Members Dislike Policy

The regulations of the Board of Transportation do not forbid the holding of outside jobs and individual members of the board were known to feel that so long as employes were punctual and efficient in their tasks their outside activities were their own affair. Despite this feeling, however, the board is prepared to carry out the policy laid down by the Mayor. An informal survey of other city agencies conducted last week indicated that most of their heads held about the same attitude, but felt that the Mayor's policy must be carried out if he insisted upon it.

The Mayor's insistence that city employes, regardless of departmental rules forego such activities, led him recently to demand that charges be brought against an electrical engineer employed by the Board of Transportation who was teaching one night a week at City College, receiving $12 for each night's work. An exchange of views between the Mayor and the Board of Transportation resulted in a decision to let the employe continue teaching until the end of the current term, with the understanding that he would not resume teaching in the fall.

The electrical engineer, who is a graduate of one of the country's leading technical schools, was certified by the Board of Transportation, after investigation, to be efficient, painstaking and punctual, and the Mayor was told that his outside work made him a better city servant, while the small additional income was a welcome addition to his modest salary. It was also pointed out to the Mayor that there was nothing in the board's rules or the law to bar the outside work. The Mayor is reported to have replied that the man must keep one job or the other, but could not hold both.

Outside work by employes is a live issue in the Board of Transportation, where it is estimated that at least 10 per cent of the 35,000 transit workers have extra work to increase family income.

Resentment against the Mayor's

Continued on Page 11

Laval Tries to Shift Funds to Argentina

Pierre Laval, chief of the Vichy government, recently tried to transfer $50,000 from Spain to Argentina, the Brazzaville radio said yesterday in a broadcast recorded at the Columbia Broadcasting System's short-wave listening station.

"A Madrid bank revealed to the Spanish authorities that a deposit of $50,000 had been made with them for transfer to an Argentinian bank," the French radio said. "An inquiry was opened, and the person behind the depositor was discovered: He is Pierre Laval."

The same broadcast reported: "Germans in France have been buying gold at very high prices. Among the German agents arrested by French police for illegal traffic in gold was one who identified himself in order to be freed. He told the police commissioner that he was the director of a bank in a small German town. Because of his age, he had not been drafted into active military service, but his competence in financial matters made possible his being used in this work, in which he had been engaged since 1940."

JOHNSTON IN RUSSIA SCOFFS AT U. S. REDS

Business Leader Also Praises Soviet 'Capitalism'—Calls Ideologies Bridgeable

By The United Press.

MOSCOW, June 4—With straight-from-the-shoulder frankness, Eric Johnston, president of the United States Chamber of Commerce, told 100 Soviet trade leaders yesterday that a gulf separated the economies of the United States and Russia, but that bridges of practical cooperation could be thrown across that gulf.

Mr. Johnston advocated extensive post-war trade and visits between American business and "Soviet capitalists" as one bridge, but said that "each of our countries should be allowed to pursue its own unique economic experiment unimpeded by the other."

Bluntly, he told the Russians that Americans "were most private-minded and most individual-minded and, make no mistake, we are determined to remain so and even become more so."

Mr. Johnston, who arrived in Russia last week, was luncheon guest of A. I. Mikoyan, Soviet Foreign Trade Commissar, at Spiridonovka House. At the table sat Soviet trade experts, members of the Soviet Foreign Office, United States Ambassador W. Averell Harriman and Soviet military men.

At first the Russians appeared nonplussed by Mr. Johnston's bluntness, but later they burst into gales of mirth at his sallies at American Communists and Marxians.

"I shall try to show you my admiration for your heroic deeds and

Continued on Page 6

FOE 'EXPLAINS' STEP

Hitler Ordered Troops Out to Save Rome, Germans Assert

ENEMY PLEA BARED

Kesselring Made Last-Minute Renewal of Open-City Offer

By The Associated Press.

LONDON, June 4—The Germans announced tonight in a special communiqué—broadcast after the Allies had liberated Rome—the withdrawal of German troops to the northwest of the city and said that the Allies had received a plan whereby Rome would have been regarded as an "open city."

The open-city proposals were said to have been advanced at 11 P. M. on Saturday, less than twenty-four hours before Rome changed hands. The first word from Adolf Hitler's headquarters in several days asserted that the fight in Italy would continue and that measures were being taken "to force final victory for Germany and her allies." The communiqué said:

"As the front line, in the course of the present fighting in Italy, was gradually approaching nearer and nearer to the city of Rome, there was danger that Rome, one of the oldest cultural centers of the world, would be directly involved in the present fighting. Hitler has ordered the withdrawal of German troops to the northwest of Rome to prevent the destruction of Rome.

"The struggle in Italy will be continued with unshakable determination to break the enemy attacks and to force final victory for Germany and her allies. The necessary measures for an eventual German victory are being taken in close collaboration with fascist Italy and other allied powers.

"The year of invasion will bring Germany's enemies an annihilating defeat at the most decisive moment."

Kesselring's Proposals Listed

Field Marshal Gen. Albert Kesselring, the German commander in Italy, sent the Allies proposals that Rome be regarded as an open city, a special announcement from Hitler's headquarters said. The statement was broadcast by the German radio and was received only after a dispatch filed from Rome had announced the crushing of the last German resistance units within the city. The broadcast said:

"The German High Command announced that the supreme commander of German troops in Italy, Field Marshal Kesselring, had submitted proposals to the Vatican with the request that they should be conveyed to the Anglo-American High Command. The proposals confirmed the recognition of Rome

Continued on Page 4

THE FIRST OF EUROPE'S WAR CAPITALS TO FALL TO THE ALLIES

The sign tells the troops they have entered Rome. The New York Times (U. S. Signal Corps Radiotelephoto)

U. S. 'HEAVIES' BOMB IN FRANCE ALL DAY

Attack Boulogne Area Twice, Rip Rail, Air Targets Near Paris—Genoa Blasted

By JAMES MacDONALD

By Cable to The New York Times.

LONDON, Monday, June 5—Continuing to pave the way for the Allied invasion of the Continent hundreds of Allied bombers and fighters from Britain scorched a 200-mile stretch of the French coast yesterday and penetrated inland.

Three separate missions were carried out by the Flying Fortresses and Liberators of the United States Eighth Air Force with fighter escort over northwestern France. They met little Luftwaffe opposition; the enemy flak ranged from moderate to heavy.

In the morning and again in the afternoon strong formations of the

Continued on Page 5

Road to Rome Hard Fought, Yet Crowded With Civilians

By MILTON BRACKER

By Wireless to The New York Times.

IN THE OUTSKIRTS OF ROME, June 4—The Fifth Army's entry into the suburbs of Rome was made along Highway 6—the Via Casilina—which runs into Rome at Centocelle, a suburb best known for its airport. But the advance did not mean a simple triumphal procession into the heart of Rome. It meant going in in careful infantry columns along the sides of the road. Most of the men had their bayonets fixed and they wore deadly earnest expressions because two wrecked Sherman tanks along the approaches told what had happened to other Americans earlier today.

Just before 4 P. M., a huge column of smoke billowed up from the southwest corner of the city, indicating a demolition. At the same time, a mine went off with a terrible burst beyond the farthest of the two tanks, and it tore an Italian woman to pieces. As the afternoon wore on, the sniping

Continued on Page 4

CONQUERORS' GOAL REACHED BY ALLIES

Fifth and Eighth Armies Drive Up From South on Rome in a Historic Campaign

By HERBERT L. MATTHEWS

By Wireless to The New York Times.

ROME, June 4—The Allies' troops fought their way into Rome this morning and at nightfall they were still fighting on the outer edges, which the Germans were defending despite all their protestations about considering Rome an open city. Other large German units faced entrapment south of Highway 6 unless they could be pulled back across the Tiber or through Rome.

But Rome has been reached—the goal of conquerors throughout the ages, though none was ever before able to make the almost impossible south-north campaign. What Hannibal did not dare to do, the Allies' generals accomplished, but at such a cost in blood, matériel and time that it will probably never again be attempted.

All roads from all over the world led to Rome today as a United

Continued on Page 3

CITY'S FALL FOCUSES POLITICAL CHANGES

Victor Emmanuel's Promise to Retire Recalled—Badoglio Cabinet May Step Down

Special to The New York Times.

WASHINGTON, June 4—Pending receipt of final details of the fall of Rome, most Government leaders tonight refrained from direct comment. It was felt that the first official reaction to the Allied victory would come from President Roosevelt in the radio address that the White House announced he would make tomorrow night.

Interest in the news of the capture of the Italian capital centered not so much in the military victory as in the probable political consequences, particularly those stemming from King Victor Emmanuel's recent statement that he planned to retire as Italy's ruler as soon as Rome fell to the Allies.

The King announced April 12 that he intended to turn Italy's affairs over to Crown Prince Humbert, and said the transfer of power would take place "on the day on which the Allied troops entered Rome."

Even more important than this move are the effects the change may have on the future of the Italian Government now headed by Marshal Pietro Badoglio. Developments, it was said, will be watched closely not only as to other high appointments to be made after Prince Humbert takes over control but also as to any alterations in the structure of the Italian Government.

While the diplomatic and politi-

Continued on Page 4

AMERICANS IN FIRST

U. S. Armor Spearheads Thrust Through Last Defenses of Rome

FINAL BATTLE BITTER

Fifth and Eighth Armies Rush On Beyond City in Pursuit of Foe

By The United Press.

NAPLES, June 4—The Fifth Army captured Rome tonight, liberating for the first time a German-enslaved European capital. German rear guards were fleeing in disorganized retreat to the northwest.

Except for the railway yards, smashed by the Allies' bombs, the city is 95 per cent intact United Press correspondents reported, after their arrival in the city.

Late tonight, the British Eighth Army, rushing into Rome from the southeast along the Via Casilina, was reported to be joining the Fifth Army in close pursuit of the hard-pressed enemy remnants, under orders to destroy them to a man if possible. Only enough troops to maintain order and ferret out any German snipers or suicide nests were to be left in Rome as the Allies' main armies pounded on without pausing to celebrate their greatest triumph, coming 270 days after the start of the Italian campaign.

[The Allies battled German rear guards to the edge of the ancient Forum, The Associated Press reported. A force from the old Anzio beachhead completed the mopping up of German forces at 9:15 P. M. by knocking out an enemy scout car in front of the Bank of Italy, almost within the shadow of Trajan's Column.]

Final Stand at Rome's Gates

At the very gates of Rome, the Germans had made a final stand but Lieut. Gen. Mark W. Clark, after having waited three hours for the enemy troops to withdraw in accordance with their own declaration of Rome as an open city, ordered a violent anti-tank barrage. Then masses of Fifth Army men and weapons crashed into the city and began mopping up enemy snipers and a few tanks and mobile guns trying to cover the retreat.

More of the enemy survivors of the Allies' whirlwind offensive were streaming in congested retreat to the northwest at the mercy of the Allies' planes, which, during the day, destroyed or damaged 600 enemy trucks and other vehicles. The Germans' jammed traffic columns stretched fifty-five miles to Lake Bolsena.

Direct radio contact with American correspondents in Rome was established tonight. A United Press reporter said that the main entry into the city had been made along the Via Casilina, which passes through the Porta Maggiore at the southeastern edge of the city. Other Allied troops were reported to have fought their way through the Ostiense freight yards, just south of St. Paul Gate, the main entrance to the city from due south and only one and one-quarter miles from the Venice Palace.

The entry into Rome came with dramatic suddenness after the Al-

Continued on Page 3

War News Summarized

MONDAY, JUNE 5, 1944

Rome was liberated from the Nazi-Fascist aggressors last night. The first European capital to be wrested from the enemy came under full Allied control when a force that had fought its way up from the old Anzio beachhead knocked out a German scout car in the center of the city. There was fierce fighting with enemy rear-guard detachments at the outskirts of Rome before the city was liberated.

Fifth Army units and the vanguard of the Eighth Army, which entered the Eternal City later, were sent in hot pursuit of the fleeing Germans. Rome was found to be 95 per cent intact, with destruction centered in the railroad yards. [All the foregoing 1:8; maps P. 2.]

German artillery and snipers held off the Allied advance between the airport at Centocelle and the city limits. Civilians, obviously happy over the departure of the Nazis, remained calm as United Nations troops moved in. [1:5-6.]

Hitler's headquarters announced after the Fifth Army had entered the city that the Germans had withdrawn to new lines northwest of Rome. Shortly before the city fell they dispatched a proposal that Rome be declared an open city. [1:3.]

Capture of Rome, according to military observers in London, made it much more likely that the main objective of the offensive—destruction of the German Tenth and Fourteenth armies—would be accomplished, with possible enemy losses reaching up to 100,000. [3:1.]

The AMG, following closely upon the victorious Allied forces, was fully prepared to undertake the gigantic task of feeding some 2,000,000 civilians. Vast stocks of food have been accumulated for distribution. [1:6-7.]

Washington withheld official comment until President Roosevelt's radio address tonight, but the capital was interested in how soon King Victor Emmanuel would fulfill his promise to retire when Rome had fallen to the Allies. [1:7.]

American heavy bombers from Britain smashed three times at enemy installations in France yesterday as the air invasion continued unabated against little enemy opposition. Italian-based aircraft struck rail lines on the French-Italian border. [1:4.]

United States troops resumed the offensive against the three airfields on Biak Island, off New Guinea. Thirty Japanese planes were shot down in widespread fights from Biak to Truk. [8:2.] Continued improvement in Allied positions was reported from Burma [8:3] although in China the Japanese made some gains toward Changsha while losing ground in other sectors. [8:4-5.]

Eric Johnston, president of the United States Chamber of Commerce, told 100 Soviet trade leaders at a Moscow luncheon that a gulf separating American and Russian economies lay in closer knowledge and greater mutual respect. [1:2.]

Enraged Bull Kills 2 Brothers, Gores Neighbor on Long Island

Special to The New York Times.

BABYLON, L. I., June 4—Two dairy farmers, brothers, were found this morning gored and trampled to death on the Ames Farm in North Babylon, victims of their Guernsey bull, which had run wild and scattered their herd of thirty cows over near-by roads. A neighbor, trying to round up the scattered herd, was gored in the groin by the infuriated animal.

State troopers were forced to shoot and kill the belligerent bull.

The victims were George W. Ames, 41 years old, and his brother, James Hawley Ames, 35, who operated the Ames Farm on Phelps Lane, North Babylon. So far as is known no one saw the unequal encounter that cost them their lives. Their bodies were discovered, lying about 100 feet apart, several hundred yards from the cow barn.

The first intimation that anything was amiss came with complaints to the State Police in North Babylon that the Ames cows were wandering off the pasture and on the near-by Phelps Lane and Belmont Road. Two State troopers were sent to the farm and succeeded in getting most of the cows back into the pasture along with the bull. They put in a call for two additional troopers to round up the remainder of the herd.

Their suspicions aroused by the fact that the milk delivery truck, fully loaded, was standing in its place although it usually left on its rural route at 8 A. M., the troopers made their way to the farmhouse. There they found Mrs. Kathleen Ames, mother of the two men, and her daughter, Jane L. Ames, a school teacher.

A search of the farm was begun and Trooper Anthony Cherry came

Continued on Page 20

AMG Will Rush Food for Rome, Teeming With 750,000 Refugees

By HAROLD CALLENDER

By Wireless to The New York Times.

ALGIERS, June 4—The fall of Rome will add about 2,000,000 persons to those whom the Allies have assumed responsibility of feeding, Allied authorities estimated today. But the Allied Military Government, now operating under the Allied Control Commission, has long prepared for the task and is believed to be ready.

The normal population of the Italian capital is estimated to have been swollen by 750,000 refugees from Naples and other places.

Allied authorities have stocks of wheat, canned milk and dehydrated vegetables ready to send to Rome quickly with the cooperation of the Fifth and Eighth Armies regarding transport by trucks.

At Anzio landing facilities have been built since the establishment of the bridgehead, and ships can be unloaded at Gaeta.

In the plans already made Rome has been divided into regions for the distribution of foodstuffs by Italian and Allied personnel under the authority of the commission. An emergency system has been prepared to provide strict control over the black market, which otherwise might absorb the local produce destined to go into the Allied pool for distribution on a ration basis to the masses who cannot afford the black market.

Capt. Matthias F. Correa, former United States Attorney for the Southern District of New York, has a staff of investigators, including 150 Guardia di Finanza, ready to combat the black market

Continued on Page 4

President to Talk On Rome Tonight

By The United Press.

WASHINGTON, June 4—A fifteen-minute radio address will be made by President Roosevelt to the nation tomorrow night on the liberation of Rome, the White House announced tonight.

Mr. Roosevelt will speak from 8:30 to 8:45 P. M.

The President's message will be broadcast over all major networks.

United Press International

Civilians cheering the allied 5th Army in Rome.

U. S. Army

American assault troops land on a beachhead on the Northern Coast of France.

Imperial War Museum

Royal Air Force planes assembled for the Normandy invasion.

U. S. Air Force

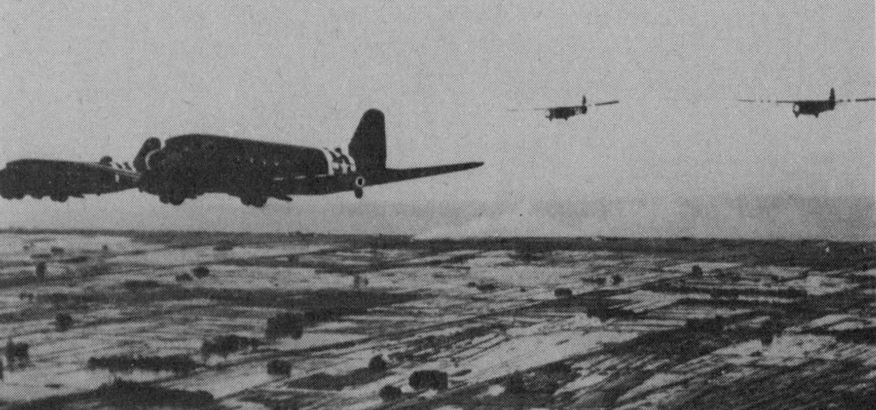

Douglas C-47s towing gliders to Normandy coast in Invasion Day.

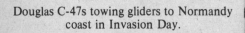

"All the News That's Fit to Print"

The New York Times.

6 A. M. EXTRA
Partly cloudy and warmer today; moderate to fresh winds.
Temperatures Yesterday—Max., 67; Min., 51
Sunrise, 5:25 A. M.; Sunset, 8:24 P. M.

Copyright, 1944, by The New York Times Company.

VOL. XCIII. No. 31,545. Entered as Second-Class Matter, Postoffice, New York, N. Y. NEW YORK, TUESDAY, JUNE 6, 1944. THREE CENTS IN NEW YORK CITY

ALLIED ARMIES LAND IN FRANCE IN THE HAVRE-CHERBOURG AREA; GREAT INVASION IS UNDER WAY

ROOSEVELT SPEAKS

Says Rome's Fall Marks 'One Up and Two to Go' Among Axis Capitals

WARNS WAY IS HARD

Asks World to Give the Italians a Chance for Recovery

The text of President Roosevelt's address is on Page 5.

By CHARLES HURD
Special to THE NEW YORK TIMES.

WASHINGTON, June 5—President Roosevelt hailed tonight the capture of Rome, first of the three major Axis capitals to fall, as a great achievement on the road toward total conquest of the Axis. Rome, he said, marked "one up and two to go."

The President spoke for a quarter-hour on the radio, as had been announced yesterday, but his speech was notable for its lack of heroics. It was in no sense a speech of triumph, but rather a tribute to the United Nations forces and leadership that drove the Germans from Rome.

With this tribute he combined a solemn warning that much greater fighting lies ahead before the Axis is defeated, as well as high tributes to the Italian people, whom he again welcomed as a people into the family of nations opposed to the Axis.

"Italy should go on," Mr. Roosevelt said, "as a great mother nation, contributing to the culture and the progress and the good-will of mankind, developing her special talents in the arts, crafts, and sciences, and preserving her historic and cultural heritage for the benefit of all peoples.

"We want and expect the help of the future Italy toward lasting peace. All the other nations opposed to fascism and nazism ought to help to give Italy a chance."

Shrines Should Live, He Says

President Roosevelt saw considerable significance in the fact that Rome should be the first Axis capital to fall. He remarked its shrines, "visible symbols of the faith and determination of the early saints and martyrs that Christianity should live and become universal," and added that "it will be a source of deep satisfaction that the freedom of the Pope and of Vatican City is assured by the armies of the United Nations."

There is significance, too, he added, in the fact that Rome was liberated by a composite force of soldiers from many nations.

Reviewing the military picture, the President pointed out that "it would be unwise to inflate in our own minds the military importance of the capture of Rome." He cautioned his auditors that while the Germans have retreated "thousands of miles" across Africa and back through Italy "they have suffered heavy losses, but not great enough yet to cause collapse."

"Therefore," he added, "the victory still lies some distance ahead. That distance will be covered in due time—have no fear of that. But it will be tough and it will be costly."

Turning to the relief problem in the newly liberated portion of Italy, Mr. Roosevelt noted that some persons thought of the financial cost, but he maintained that the work would pay dividends "by eliminating fascism" and any future desire by Italians to "start another war of aggression." Relief has been planned, he added, but transport demands are so great that "improvement must be gradual."

He warned Italy that it "cannot grow in stature by seeking to build up a great militaristic empire,"

Continued on Page 5

Conferees Accept Cabaret Tax Cut

By The Associated Press.

WASHINGTON, June 5—A House-Senate conference committee agreed today to cut back the cabaret tax from 30 to 20 per cent, but eliminated a provision exempting service men and women from the levy.

The group decided to put the national debt limit at $260,000,000,000 as originally requested by the Administration.

The action is subject to House and Senate votes. The conferees met informally today, but members said that the decisions probably would stand as their final recommendation.

The House, at the insistence of a group of Republicans, passed a bill raising the debt ceiling only from $210,000,000,000 to $240,000,000,000. The Senate then put the figure at $260,000,000,000 and attached a rider reducing the cabaret tax from 30 to 20 per cent and exempting men and women in uniform from paying the tax on their checks.

Some tax experts argued that this exemption would make administration of the excise on night clubs impossible.

FEDERAL LAW HELD RULING INSURANCE

Supreme Court, 4-3, Decides Business Is Interstate and Subject to Trust Act

Special to THE NEW YORK TIMES.

WASHINGTON, June 5—The Supreme Court, by a four-to-three decision today, held that the insurance companies of the country, with assets of $37,000,000,000 and annual premium collections in excess of $6,000,000,000, are in interstate commerce and thus subject to the Sherman Anti-Trust Law.

The decision upset precedents which began with a contrary decision by the court more than seventy-five years ago and have been reaffirmed repeatedly since the adoption of the anti-trust law in 1890.

The majority decision, written

Continued on Page 13

PURSUIT ON IN ITALY

Allies Pass Rome, Cross Tiber as Foe Quits Bank Below City

PLANES JOIN IN CHASE

1,200 Vehicles Wrecked —Eighth Army Battles Into More Towns

By The Associated Press.

ROME, June 5—The Allies' armor and motorized infantry roared through Rome today without pausing, crossed the Tiber River and proceeded with the grim task of destroying two battered German armies fleeing to the north.

Fighter-bombers spearheaded the pursuit, jamming the escape highways with burning enemy transport and littering the fields with dead and wounded Germans. The enemy was tired, disorganized and bewildered by the slashing assault, which in twenty-five days had inflicted a major catastrophe on the Germans and liberated Rome almost without damage.

Railway Yards Bombed

Five hundred American heavy bombers blasted railway yards at five points in northern Italy between Venice and Rimini along which the Germas might attempt to move reinforcements and equipment to bolster their beaten armies. Hour after hour, the Allies' planes swept down on highways leading northward and tore the fleeing enemy apart. Twelve hundred combat vehicles were destroyed from dawn to dark yesterday, and hundreds more today. Farther north, medium bombers smashed bridges and rail facilities.

[The Germans have abandoned the entire left bank of the Tiber from Ostia, at its mouth, to Rome, according to a Vichy broadcast quoted by The Associated Press.

[The Germans are already entrenched in mountain positions

Continued on Page 2

FIRST ALLIED LANDING MADE ON SHORES OF WESTERN EUROPE

June 6, 1944

General Eisenhower's armies invaded northern France this morning. While the landing points were not specified, the Germans said that troops had gone ashore near Havre and that fighting raged at Caen (1). The enemy also said that parachutists had descended at the northern tip of the Normandy Peninsula (2) and heavy bombing had been visited on Calais and Dunkerque (3).

EISENHOWER ACTS

U. S., British, Canadian Troops Backed by Sea, Air Forces

MONTGOMERY LEADS

Nazis Say Their Shock Units Are Battling Our Parachutists

Communique No. 1 On Allied Invasion

By Broadcast to THE NEW YORK TIMES.

LONDON, Tuesday, June 6—The Supreme Headquarters of the Allied Expeditionary Force issued this communiqué this morning:

"Under the command of General Eisenhower, Allied naval forces, supported by strong air forces, began landing Allied armies this morning on the northern coast of France."

By RAYMOND DANIELL
By Cable to THE NEW YORK TIMES.

SUPREME HEADQUARTERS ALLIED EXPEDITIONARY FORCES, Tuesday, June 6—The invasion of Europe from the west has begun.

In the gray light of a summer dawn Gen. Dwight D. Eisenhower threw his great Anglo-American force into action today for the liberation of the Continent. The spearhead of attack was an Army group commanded by Gen. Sir Bernard L. Montgomery and comprising troops of the United States, Britain and Canada.

General Eisenhower's first communiqué was terse and calculated to give little information to the enemy. It said merely that "Allied naval forces supported by strong air forces began landing Allied armies this morning on the northern coast of France."

After the first communiqué was released it was announced that the Allied landing was in Normandy.

Caen Battle Reported

German broadcasts, beginning at 6:30 A. M., London time, [12:30 A. M. Eastern war time] gave first word of the assault. [The Associated Press said General Eisenhower, for the sake of surprise, deliberately let the Germans have the "first word."]

The German DNB agency said the Allied invasion operations began with the landing of airborne troops in the area of the mouth of the Seine River.

[Berlin said the "center of gravity" of the fierce fighting was at Caen, thirty miles southwest of Havre and sixty-five miles southeast of Cherbourg, The Associated Press reported. Caen is ten miles inland from the sea, at the base of the seventy-five-mile-wide Normandy Peninsula, and fighting there might indicate the Allies' seizing of a beachhead.

[DNB said in a broadcast just before 10 A. M. (4 A. M. Eastern war time) that the Anglo-American troops had been reinforced at dawn at the mouth of the Seine River in the Havre area.]

[An Allied correspondent broadcasting from Supreme Headquarters, according to the Columbia Broadcasting System, said this morning that "German tanks are moving up

Continued on Page A Following Page 3

War News Summarized

TUESDAY, JUNE 6, 1944

The invasion of western Europe began this morning.

General Eisenhower, in his first communiqué from Supreme Headquarters, Allied Expeditionary Force, issued at 3:30 A. M., said that "Allied naval forces supported by strong air forces began landing Allied armies this morning on the northern coast of France."

The assault was made by British, American and Canadian troops who, under command of Gen. Sir Bernard L. Montgomery, landed in Normandy. London gave no further details but earlier Berlin had broadcast that parachute troops had landed on the Normandy Peninsula near Cherbourg and that invasion forces were pouring from landing craft under cover of warships near Havre. Dunkerque and Calais were being heavily bombed, the Germans said.

Later announcements from Berlin said that there was fighting between Caen and Trouville and that shock troops had swung into action to halt the invasion. [All the foregoing, 1:8.]

General Eisenhower, in an order of the day to each member of the "great crusade," told his men the enemy would fight savagely and added: "We will accept nothing less than full victory. Good luck." In a broadcast to the "Peoples of Western Europe," he said the day would come when he would need their full help. A special word to France added that Frenchmen would rule the country. [1:6-7.] Almost simultaneously it was announced that General de Gaulle had arrived in London. [6:2.]

The liberation of Rome in no way slowed the Allied pursuit of the tired and disorganized German armies in Italy yesterday. Armored and motorized units sped across the Tiber River to press hard upon the retreating enemy's heels. Five hundred heavy bombers joined with lighter aircraft to smash rail and road routes leading to northern Italy and to add to the foe's demoralization. The Eighth Army, despite heavy opposition, especially northeast of Valmontone, captured a number of strategic towns. [1:3; map P. 2.]

General Clark said that parts of the two German armies had been smashed. He doubted the ability of the German Fourteenth to put up effective opposition and declared that the Tenth had taken a bad beating. [3:1.]

King Victor Emmanuel fulfilled his promise and turned over all authority to his son, Crown Prince Humbert. [1:5-6.]

President Roosevelt warned the people of the United States in a radio talk last night not to over-emphasize the military significance of the liberation of Rome. "Germany has not yet been driven to surrender," he said. "Victory still lies some distance ahead. * * * It will be tough and it will be costly." The President appealed to the world to give Italy a chance to contribute her share to a lasting peace. [1:1.]

In the Pacific theatre Americans were converging on the Biak airfields. Allied planes sank one and damaged two Japanese destroyers and shot down at least eighteen aircraft. [8:1.]

POPE GIVES THANKS ROME WAS SPARED

Voices Appreciation to Both Belligerents in Message to Throng at St. Peter's

By Wireless to THE NEW YORK TIMES.

VATICAN CITY, June 5—Pope Pius XII appeared on the balcony of St. Peter's at 6 P. M. today to thank God that Rome had been spared from the ravages of war while before him in the densely packed square of St. Peter's and the new broad Via Della Conciliazione tens of thousands of Romans cheered themselves hoarse.

It was the third time today that the Pontiff had showed himself to cheering crowds, as he had appeared twice at a window of his office this morning. But this was a solemn, sacred occasion and no one knowing anything about Pius XII can doubt the fervor of his thankfulness that Rome had been saved.

The Pontiff seemed strong and well and his voice carried far, though it was difficult to hear every word he said because of the crowd.

"We must give thanks to God for the favors we have received," said the Pope. "Rome has been spared. This day will go down in the annals of Rome."

He went on to say he hoped that Italians would be worthy of the grace shown them and put aside hatred and all personal vendettas. He then thanked both belligerents—the Allies and Germany—for having left Rome intact.

After a prayer of thankfulness to the Blessed Virgin and Saints Peter and Paul, guardians of Rome, the Pontiff gave his blessing, "urbe et orbis," as the immense crowd knelt before him.

[The Associated Press estimated the crowd was between 250,000 and 500,000.]

The world has changed for Rome but the Vatican goes on imperturbably as it has through so many other conquests in centuries gone by. It is neutral in fact and spirit. The Pope and all high officials went about their daily routine today as in the past. Except for the tanks and armored cars running along the street in front of St. Peter's one could never know what had happened today.

Continued on Page 5

Italy's Monarch Yields Rule To Son, but Retains Throne

By The Associated Press.

NAPLES, June 5—Victor Emmanuel III stepped aside as King of Italy today, as he previously had said he would do upon the liberation of Rome, and handed to his 39-year-old son, Crown Prince Humbert, all "royal prerogatives." Italian political pressure had been brought to bear against him since the occupation of Naples.

In a decree signed by himself and countersigned by Premier Pietro Badoglio, head of the Italian Liberation Government, the King named his son Lieutenant General of the Realm. The monarch, however, retained his title as head of the House of Savoy and remains as King without power.

[The first act of the Council of Ministers after the transfer of royal powers was a formal denunciation of the 1940 armistice treaty inflicted on France, The United Press said.]

Victor Emmanuel, who became King July 29, 1900, had announced last April 12 his "irrevocable" decision to withdraw from public life "on the day on which Allied troops enter Rome."

Little more than a figurehead since Benito Mussolini assumed the dictatorship of Italy, Victor Emmanuel had won a reputation in the first years of his reign as a sympathetic monarch, interested in his people and their problems.

Prince Humbert, tall and erect, opposed fascism in Italy at the start, but later made a truce with Mussolini. In effect, Humbert becomes the King's regent.

TEXT OF ROYAL DECREE

The King's withdrawal decree:

I, Victor Emmanuel III, by the grace of God and by the will of the nation King of Italy, in collaboration with the President of the Council of Ministers and with the agreement of the Council, have ordered and order as follows:

My beloved son, Humbert of Savoy, Prince of Piedmont, is nominated our Lieutenant General. In collaboration with responsible Ministers he will in our name superintend all matters of administration and exercise all royal prerogatives without exception, signing royal decrees which will be countersigned and authenticated in the usual way.

We order all concerned to observe this decree and to see that it is observed as the law of the State.

Given at Ravello June 5, 1944.

VICTOR EMMANUEL.
(Countersigned) PIETRO BADOGLIO.

The withdrawal was presented to

Continued on Page 4

ALLIED WARNING FLASHED TO COAST

People Told to Clear Area 22 Miles Inland as Soon as Instructions Are Given

By Cable to THE NEW YORK TIMES.

LONDON, Tuesday, June 6—The British Broadcasting Corporation began its 8 A. M. news bulletin this morning with quotations from a Supreme Headquarters' "urgent warning" to inhabitants of the enemy-occupied countries living near the coast.

Gen. Dwight D. Eisenhower has directed that whenever possible in France a warning shall be given to towns in which certain targets will be intensively bombed.

This warning, the broadcast said,

Continued on Page B

PARADE OF PLANES CARRIES INVADERS

Witness Says First 'Chutists Met Only Light Fire When They Landed in France

The first eyewitness account of the Allies' invasion of Europe was given in a pool broadcast from London this morning by Wright Bryan of the National Broadcasting Company, who accompanied the airborne troops in their landings.

His account said the first spearhead of Allied forces landed by parachute in northern France in the first hour of D-day.

"In the navigator's dome in the flight deck of a C-47, I rode across the English Channel with the first group of planes from the United States Ninth Air Force Troop Carrier Command to take our fighting men into Europe," Mr. Bryan said.

He added that just before he left French soil for the return trip he saw seventeen American paratroopers, led by a lieutenant colonel, jump with their arms, ammunition and equipment into German-occupied France."

He declared that his group at the head of the leading wing was met with "only scattering small

Continued on Page B

Eisenhower Instructs Europeans; Gives Battle Order to His Armies

Following are the texts of a statement by Gen. Dwight D. Eisenhower broadcast to the people of western Europe and his Order of the Day to the Allied Expeditionary Force as recorded by The New York Times and the Columbia Broadcasting System:

People of western Europe! A landing was made this morning on the coast of France by troops of the Allied Expeditionary Force. This landing is part of the concerted United Nations plan for the liberation of Europe, made in conjunction with our great Russian Allies. I have this message for all of you. Although the initial assault may not have been made in your own country, the hour of your liberation is approaching.

All patriots, men and women, young and old, have a part to play in the achievement of final victory. To members of resistance movements, whether led by national or outside leaders, I say: "Follow the instructions you have received." To patriots who are not members of organized resistance groups I say, "continue your passive resistance, but do not needlessly endanger your lives until I give you the signal to rise and strike the enemy. The day will come when I shall need your united strength. Until that day, I call on you for the hard task of discipline and restraint."

Citizens of France! I am proud to have again under my command the gallant forces of France. Fighting beside their Allies, they will play a worthy part in the liberation of their

Continued on Page 3

"All the News That's Fit to Print"

The New York Times.

LATE CITY EDITION
POSTSCRIPT
Partly cloudy; cooler tonight.
Temperatures Yesterday—Max.,83; Min.,65

Copyright, 1944, by The New York Times Company.

VOL. XCIII..No. 31,552. Entered as Second-Class Matter, Postoffice, New York, N. Y. NEW YORK, TUESDAY, JUNE 13, 1944. THREE CENTS IN NEW YORK CITY

AMERICANS WIN CARENTAN, A KEY TO CHERBOURG; CAPTURE FOREST 7 MILES FROM ST. LO JUNCTION; PRESIDENT SAYS INVASION SPEEDS PACIFIC WAR

HIS TONE CONFIDENT

Roosevelt Says Our Men Are Ready to Defeat Nazi Counter-Attack

OPENS BOND DRIVE

Nation Urged Over Radio to Continue to Forge Weapons of Victory

Roosevelt's address opening Fifth War Loan drive, Page 14.

By CHARLES W. HURD
Special to THE NEW YORK TIMES.

WASHINGTON, June 12—Reporting that "we have firm footholds in France with losses lower than expected, " President Roosevelt asserted tonight that our policy of smashing Germany first would make it possible to "force the Japanese to unconditional surrender or to national suicide much more rapidly than has been thought possible.' Our invasion forces, he added, "are now ready to meet the inevitable counter-attack of the Germans with power and confidence."

The President spoke over a national radio program starting the Fifth War Loan with a goal of $16,000,000,000, and in addition to giving firm assurance of initial success on the Normandy beachhead he took this opportunity to give an up-to-the-minute report on the war, which he said now is marked by Allied offensives around the world.

There is much more war being fought, Mr. Roosevelt remarked, than the contest on the English Channel that currently engages the greatest attention.

As for Germany, "our enemy first on the list," the President said that country has its back against "three walls at once." These he listed as Italy, where the Germans are retreating from the center of the peninsula, the Russian front and the Western front.

"On the East," he said, "our gallant Soviet allies have driven the enemy back from the lands which were invaded three years ago. Great Soviet armies are now initiating crushing blows."

Says Impossible Was Achieved

In France, he went on, "millions of tons of weapons and supplies, and hundreds of thousands of men assembled in England are now being poured into the great battle in Europe."

"From the standpoint of the enemy," Mr. Roosevelt said, "we have achieved the impossible. We have broken through their supposedly impregnable wall in Northern France. The assault has been costly in men and materials. Some of our landings were desperate adventures, but from the advices received so far, the losses were lower than our commanders had estimated would occur.

"We have established a firm foot-hold; and are now prepared to meet the inevitable counter-attacks of the Germans—with power and confidence. We all pray that we will have far more than a firm foot-hold."

While detailing these gains, the President voiced the cautioning note that "no one front can be considered alone without its proper relation to all."

Gains Over Japan Reviewed

In the Pacific, he said, "we have deprived the Japs of the power to check the momentum of our ever-growing and ever-advancing military forces."

"We have reduced their shipping," President Roosevelt reported, "by more than 3,000,000 tons. We have overcome their original advantage in the air. We have cut off from a return to the homeland tens of thousands of beleaguered Japanese troops, who now face starvation or surrender. We have cut down their naval strength so that for many months they have avoided all risk of encounter with our naval forces.

"True, we still have a long way to Tokyo. But, carrying out our

Continued on Page 14

Americans Escort Japanese to Vatican

By The United Press.

VATICAN CITY, June 12—American soldiers in two jeeps and on six motorcycles escorted Ken Harada, Japanese Ambassador to the Vatican, from Rome into Vatican City today to see Vatican authorities, and shepherded him back into Rome where he and other Axis diplomats are living under Allied protection.

During his two-hour visit Mr. Harada arranged to move into neutral Vatican City.

It is expected that the Japanese, German, Hungarian, Rumanian and Slovak delegations to the Vatican will move into the Vatican City apartments vacated by Harold Tittman, President Roosevelt's Vatican representative, and the British, French, Belgian and other Allied envoys, who can now live in Rome.

16 POST-WAR STEPS URGED ON CONGRESS

Senate Committee and Byrnes Call for Immediate Action to Assure Employment

By C. P. TRUSSELL
Special to THE NEW YORK TIMES.

WASHINGTON, June 12—The Senate received from its special Post-War Economic Policy and Planning Committee today a budget of sixteen legislative obligations for Congress to meet without delay in preparing for the impacts of unemployment and readjustment when war production ceases. No extended Congressional recess, the committee contended, should even be considered pending action on the problems.

Referring to Bernard M. Baruch's recommendations, the committee, which is headed by Senator Walter F. George of Georgia, said that if Congress discharges its obligations, "we can well have what Mr. Baruch called an adventure in prosperity."

"If it does not survey these fields and reach wise decisions in them," the committee said, "we can have economic chaos."

As the report awaited formal presentation to the Senate, James F. Byrnes, Director of War Mobilization, appeared before the Senate Military Affairs War Contracts Subcommittee on behalf of the George-Murray bill, which is being drafted around the Baruch-Hancock post-war readjustment report issued last February.

Says Cut-Backs Are Likely

Mr. Byrnes urged a general speeding up of Congressional action on post-war legislation, and warned that the program for termination of war contracts "can only limp along" until the House passes the legislation adopted by the Senate providing for a uniform system of such operations. He presented eight specific recommendations.

"Assuming that Germany is still at war with us when we reach the fourth quarter of this year," Mr.

Continued on Page 26

ALL-OUT AIR COVER

1,400 U. S. 'Heavies' in Record Strike Bomb 16 Luftwaffe Fields

NAZI PLANES FIGHT

Allies in 10,000 Sorties Down 53 of the Foe—RAF Hits Rail Points

By E. C. DANIEL
By Cable to THE NEW YORK TIMES.

LONDON, Tuesday, June 13—The first really good flying weather since the Allied invasion of western Europe began a week ago released 1,400 United States heavy bombers—the largest number ever dispatched on a single mission—for attack yesterday on sixteen Nazi air bases and other targets in France, all within a few minutes' flying time of our Normandy beachhead.

The Nazi Air Force took up the mighty Allied challenge to its dwindling strength in greater force than at any time since D-day.

"If anybody asks you where the Luftwaffe is, we saw 'em this morning," said First Lieut. William J. Weaver of Webster, N. D., a fighter-bomber pilot.

But not one of the Eighth Air Force's Flying Fortresses and Liberators, which also attacked six vital bridges, fell to enemy fighters, although seven failed to return as a result of flak or other damage. The strong escorting forces of Mustangs, Lightnings and Thunderbolts diverted the enemy from our big bombers, losing fourteen fighters to seventeen of the Luftwaffe they shot down.

RAF Again Out in Strength

The clearing skies also meant resumption of around-the-clock bombing on a grand scale. The Royal Air Force's "heavies," which blasted four more of the enemy's key rail points in France Sunday night, were out again last night in greater numbers than usual. Some headed southward from the English coast before dark.

Targets in the new night bombings were in both France and Germany, said a brief British announcement early today. A Nazi DNB broadcast about 1:30 A. M. said Cologne, a major Rhineland rail point for the movement of enemy reserves, had been hit by British bombers.

Latest reports on yesterday's vast Allied air operations over France gave fifty-three Luftwaffe planes shot down, plus seventeen destroyed on the ground.

The Allies' total losses for the day were thirty-nine planes, including the seven American heavy bombers, thirty-one fighters and one medium bomber.

[At least 10,000 Allied sorties were flown Monday, probably 7,000 up to noon, The Associated Press estimated.]

One whole sky train of American carrier planes that delivered 23,000 pounds of supplies to American units on the Cherbourg Penin-

Continued on Page 4

CONGRATULATIONS ARE IN ORDER ON THE INVASION BEACHHEAD

Lieut. Gen. Omar N. Bradley (left), commander of our ground forces in France, is greeted by Gen. George C. Marshall, Chief of Staff of the United States Army. Looking on is Gen. H. H. Arnold, chief of the United States Army Air Forces.

The New York Times (U. S. Signal Corps Radiotelephoto)

RUSSIANS ADVANCE, BUT FINNS STIFFEN

Red Army Batters Out Gains of 4 to 6 Miles as Foe Pours In Strong Reserves

By W. H. LAWRENCE
By Cable to THE NEW YORK TIMES.

MOSCOW, Tuesday, June 13—The Red Army drove forward yesterday along the tortuous forest roads between lakes and swamps in the face of strong defensive fortifications to capture the rail station of Raivola, forty miles below Viborg, as well as thirty other inhabited points on the Karelian Isthmus, the Soviet High Command announced last night. Gains of four to six miles were punched through the Finnish lines in the day's fighting.

The Soviet communiqué, which contained few details, indicated that a strong force of infantry,

Continued on Page 4

Periled Americans Saved Beach, Says Montgomery

By The Associated Press.

WITH ALLIED TROOPS IN FRANCE, June 11 (Delayed)—High praise was given by Gen. Sir Bernard L. Montgomery to American troops at a press conference tonight, when he revealed that prisoners had included some Japanese and that snipers in action in France included women who had been killed while shooting at Allied soldiers.

"A great many of the enemy have been killed," General Montgomery said.

The Japanese—regular soldiers, not merely observers—were fighting alongside their Axis partners, General Montgomery said, and small numbers of them have already been taken prisoners and others killed.

Outspokenly pleased with the feats of American troops, General Montgomery said:

"The beach where the landing of the Americans took place east of the Carentan estuary was found being defended by a German division which was not a coastal divi-

Continued on Page 5

GERMAN 14TH ARMY DISPERSED IN ITALY

10th Army Fleeing in Broken Units—Allies Pound Ahead Across Peninsula

By The Associated Press.

ROME, June 12—The German Fourteenth Army has been "dispersed to the four winds," Allied headquarters declared today as the Fifth Army, pursuing the disorganized Germans up the Italian west coast, approached Orbetello, seventy-one miles northwest of Rome.

As depleted enemy units fell back toward the Florence area with the greater part of their equipment lost, the German High Command faced the immediate necessity of sending heavy reinforcements from France or elsewhere in Europe if any real attempt were to be made to hold northern Italy.

"It is now quite clear," the Allies' announcement said, "that the original Fourteenth Army * * * has been dispersed to the four winds. All that remains is a few scattered remnants who mainly are engaged in stealing one an-

Continued on Page 7

VICHY'S AUTHORITY VANISHING RAPIDLY

Germans Take Over in Capital as Petainists Gather in Madrid Around Envoy

By JOHN MacCORMAC
By Wireless to THE NEW YORK TIMES.

LONDON, June 12—So strong is French patriots' resistance that the extension of German control over a large part of central France, including Vichy, was announced today by the Vichy radio.

Armed uprisings by patriots have reached such proportions that it has apparently been found necessary to supplant or reinforce Chief of Government Pierre Laval's authority in a territory within which he had sought so long and faithfully to serve German interests. That this did not mean the end of collaboration, however, was indicated by the Paris radio announcement that the mobilization of the militia would be hastened to cope with the situation.

Other measures demonstrating that French resistance was beginning to complicate German defense plans included the extension of the 9 P. M. -7 A. M. curfew to all inhabitants of Limoges, said to be one of the chief centers of revolt, and the suspension of all motor traffic except movements of doctors and food trucks in the Allier, Haute-Loire and Puy-de-Dôme departments.

[The Brazzaville radio, heard by The United Press, said that, while France might be considered to be in a state of latent insurrection, the underground, in com-

Continued on Page 6

War News Summarized

TUESDAY, JUNE 13, 1944

Carentan has fallen to the Allied forces, who now hold a sixty-mile strip along the French coast. The day's advances carried American troops to within fourteen miles of Cherbourg and seven miles of St. Lô. The Forest of Cerisy was cleared of Germans. Marshal Rommel has thrown three motorized divisions into the battle at Caen, and the enemy was estimated to have 240,000 men along the fighting front. More than 10,000 prisoners have been taken. [1:8; map P. 2.]

Among the prisoners were some Japanese troops fighting alongside their Axis partner, General Montgomery said. The Germans were also using women snipers, he added. The Allied ground leader gave high praise to United States troops who were compelled to beat down a German field division before gaining 100 yards on the beach. [1:5-6.]

Every type of Allied plane struck every kind of military target along a 400-mile arc from St. Nazaire to Lille in the best flying weather since the invasion. The Eighth Air Force sent out more than 1,400 bombers in its greatest single operation of the war to hit sixteen airfields and six bridges. The Luftwaffe put up its heaviest opposition, and at the end of the day seventy enemy planes had been destroyed; thirty-nine Allied aircraft were missing. [1:3.]

Prime Minister Churchill and General Eisenhower led two separate groups of high ranking leaders on a five-hour visit to the battlefields. [1:6.7.]

Vichy authorities in southern France was reported to be disintegrating in the face of patriot sabotage. [1:7.] The German radio estimated Allied troops in the beachhead at 500,000 as the Reich propaganda tone shifted from boastful to cautious. [4:1.]

Allied troops continued to sweep forward along the entire Italian line, and Allied Headquarters declared that the German Fourteenth Army had been dispersed as a fighting unit. [1:6; map P 7.] The Red Army, smashing through Finnish defenses, captured more than thirty towns on the Karelian Isthmus, including Raivola on the main railroad to Viborg. [1:4; map P. 4.]

A United States carrier task force struck at the Marianas Sunday for the second day in a row, hitting Guam, Tinian, Saipan and Rota. [12:2.] Fourteenth Air Force fliers were raising havoc with Japanese troops in the Changsha area of China, one mission killing or drowning 1,000 of the enemy. [12:7.] In Burma the Chinese captured the jade center of Lonkin. [12:3.]

President Roosevelt, opening the Fifth War Loan drive last night, said "we can force the Japanese to unconditional surrender or to national suicide much more rapidly than had been thought possible" as a result of the strategy of concentrating first upon Hitler. The Allied beachhead in France is now strong enough to meet the inevitable German counter-attacks, he declared. [1:1.]

President Predicts Murder Orgy By Nazis to Wipe Out Minorities

Special to THE NEW YORK TIMES.

WASHINGTON, June 12—President Roosevelt, notifying Congress formally today of his action last week in setting up a camp for 1,000 war refugees at Fort Ontario, Oswego, N. Y., declared that the Nazis, with defeat in the war approaching, were determined to complete their plans to exterminate minorities in Europe.

"As the hour of the final defeat of the Hitlerite forces draws closer," he said in a special message to Congress, "the fury of their insane desire to wipe out the Jewish race in Europe continues undiminished. This is but one example; many Christian groups also are being murdered. Knowing that they have lost the war, the Nazis are determined to complete their program of mass extermination. This program is but one manifestation of Hitler's aim to salvage from military defeat victory for Nazi principles—the very principles which this war must destroy unless we have fought in vain."

Recalling that in January he had established the War Refugee Board, the President said that the board "was entrusted with the solemn duty of translating this Government's humanitarian policy into prompt action."

Such action, he asserted, "has brought new hope to the oppressed peoples of Europe."

"From various sources," he went on, "I have received word that thousands of people, wearied by their years of resistance to Hitler and by their sufferings to the point

Continued on Page 8

Text of President's message on refugees, Page 8.

Churchill Inspects the Beachhead; Our Top Military Men Also There

By The Associated Press.

SUPREME HEADQUARTERS, Allied Expeditionary Force, June 12—Prime Minister Churchill set foot on French soil today for the first time since 1940, while General Eisenhower, commander of the Allied invasion forces, led a party of top United States military and naval commanders on a tour of the American-held section of the Normandy battlefront.

Great Britain's Prime Minister was accompanied by Field Marshal Jan Christiaan Smuts, Premier of South Africa, and Gen. Sir Alan Brooke, Chief of the Imperial General Staff.

In General Eisenhower's party were Gen. George C. Marshall, United States Army Chief of Staff; Gen. Henry H. Arnold, American Air Chief; Admiral Ernest King, Commander in Chief of the United States Fleet; Lieut. Gen. Omar N. Bradley, commander of American ground forces in France, and Rear Admirals Alan G. Kirk and John Leslie Hall, commanders of naval task forces in the invasion.

Mr. Churchill and his companions crossed the Channel today on the British destroyer Kelvin, and while they were aboard the ship it took part in bombarding a German position on the northeastern Normandy flank.

Arriving on the beaches shortly before noon, they spent three hours ashore; lunched with Gen. Sir Bernard L. Montgomery, commander of Allied ground forces in France; visited Army Headquarters; watched the landing of troops and supplies, and then steamed through the battle fleet that was bombarding the shore.

During the day Mr. Churchill

Continued on Page 5

NAZIS FIGHT HARD

U. S. Battleships Forced to Batter Carentan to Aid Infantry

PATROLS NEAR PORT

British Battle Fiercely for Caen—Captives Rise to 10,000

5 A. M. Communique

By The United Press.

SUPREME HEADQUARTERS, Allied Expeditionary Force, Tuesday, June 13—Steady progress has been made on sectors of the Allied front in France but no marked advances have been recorded, the Allied communiqué said today.

Strong enemy resistance continues in the Tilly-sur-Seulles sector west of Caen.

The capture of Carentan "materially strengthens the link established between our two major bridgeheads," the communiqué said, and the build-up of positions "is progressing satisfactorily."

Allied planes attacked enemy troops, railroad targets and vehicles in great strength throughout Monday afternoon and evening, and bombed French railway junctions during the night. Our planes also bombed a tank concentration in the Grimbosq Forest, southwest of Caen, and blew up an enemy ammunition dump.

By DREW MIDDLETON
By Cable to THE NEW YORK TIMES.

SUPREME HEADQUARTERS, Allied Expeditionary Force, Tuesday, June 13 — Allied forces extended their hold yesterday on that slender strip of Europe reclaimed from the Nazis after four years of blood and sweat and toil and tears.

Almost four years since he made his bootless appeal to France to carry on as Britain's ally Prime Minister Churchill returned to France to see for himself how the fighting was going.

It was going well when the Prime Minister and an assortment of political and military big-wigs toured beachheads, indicating by their presence that the ground so hardly won was held securely.

Carentan had fallen to the American infantry. Elsewhere on the perimeter of that sixty-mile front, patrols had penetrated to within fourteen miles of Cherbourg's defenses and had fought their way to a point seven miles from St. Lô.

Drive to Cut Off Peninsula

Lieut. Gen. Omar N. Bradley's forces on the right wing of Gen. Sir Bernard L. Montgomery's Twenty-first Army Group rolled forward in a drive to isolate the Cherbourg peninsula.

North and northwest of Carenta the Americans fanned out, crossing

Continued on Page 3

London Has 2 Alerts, First Since April 27

By The Associated Press.

LONDON, Tuesday, June 13—The Luftwaffe sent a small number of raiders over Britain early today, apparently in an effort to divert attention at home from the weakness of Nazi air support in the battle for Normandy, giving London its first alert since April 27.

A few casualties were caused when some persons were trapped in a building hit by a high explosive bomb.

Downtown London had two alerts within an hour, and outlying sections heard three warnings. At least one enemy plane was shot down, crashing into East London houses.

Raiders were also over East Anglia and southern England.

Mortars being fired on German positions at St. Lo.

The destruction at St. Lo.

U. S. Marine Corps

Marines crawling to their assigned positions under enemy fire on the beach at Saipan.

U. S. Marine Corps

A Navy Corpsman administers blood plasma to a wounded Marine on the front lines on Saipan.

"All the News That's Fit to Print"

The New York Times.

LATE CITY EDITION
POSTSCRIPT
Partly cloudy and warmer today
Temperatures Yesterday—Max., 67; Min., 57
Sunrise, 5:23 A. M.; Sunset, 8:29 P. M.

VOL. XCIII—No. 31,555. Entered as Second-Class Matter, Postoffice, New York, N. Y. NEW YORK, FRIDAY, JUNE 16, 1944. THREE CENTS IN NEW YORK CITY

OUR SUPERFORTS BOMB CITIES IN JAPAN; AMERICAN FORCES LANDING IN MARIANAS; ALLIES GAIN ON CHERBOURG PENINSULA

NAZI ROADS IN PERIL

Americans Are Nearing Two Vital Points on Cherbourg Neck

GERMAN TANKS LOSE

British Gain in Caen Sector—Battleship Shells Le Havre

5 A. M. Communique

By The United Press.

SUPREME HEADQUARTERS, Allied Expeditionary Force, Friday, June 16—Allied forces on the Cherbourg peninsula have made further progress west of Pont l'Abbé, seventeen miles from the west coast, a communiqué said today.

No major change has been made in any sector, the communiqué 21 said.

All attempts by the Germans to seize the initiative have been frustrated and their counter-attacks have been repelled.

At midnight Thursday, it was learned American troops were six miles from La Haye du Puits, where western communications along the peninsula narrow to a junction before running on southward.

By DREW MIDDLETON

By Cable to The New York Times.

SUPREME HEADQUARTERS, Allied Expeditionary Force, Friday, June 16—Americans, supported by tanks, are advancing on a front of ten miles across the neck of the Cherbourg Peninsula, threatening La Haye du Puits and St. Sauveur-Le Vicomte, two of the most important links in the enemy's chain of communications with Cherbourg.

Late yesterday Allied patrols were reported fighting in Pretot, four miles northeast of La Haye, and at Reigneville, only three miles northeast of St. Sauveur-Le Vicomte, after the occupation of Baupte, nine and a half miles east of La Haye and five miles west of Carentan. Baupte was occupied yesterday morning as the Allied American offensive to cut off the great Norman port developed swiftly.

The Allied line in this area is now only about seven miles from the main enemy supply network on the western side of the peninsula.

Quinéville, on the east coast of the peninsula, four and a half miles northeast of Montebourg, has also been captured and the American right now is firmly anchored on the sea.

No Major Fight in Quadrilateral

Although there were still a number of sharp skirmishes in the quadrilateral of Balleroy, Tilly-sur-Seulles, Villers-Bocage and Caumont, neither side launched a major attack yesterday. German armored divisions suffered "substantial" tank casualties in Wednesday's fighting, which culminated in a "very heavy" assault in the Villers-Bocage area in which eight Panther and nine Tiger tanks were destroyed by British tanks and anti-tank guns. British veterans, including men of a once famous division in the Troarn area, were slowly pushing forward southwest of Troarn in the face of bitter enemy resistance.

Hundreds of airplane engines sounded reveille over the front at dawn yesterday as the United States Ninth Air Force and the British Second Tactical Air Force launched large-scale operations in support of the ground forces. Fighter-bombers and fighters skimmed over Allied tanks and troops to harry German troop concentrations, tanks, convoys and supply dumps in the battle area.

The flow of enemy reinforcements to the fighting zone was seriously hampered by Marauders and Havocs, which bombed bridges at Conde-sur-Noireau, St. Lô, Lessay, Chartres, Coltainville and a road junction at Argentan.

The Navy's part in the cam-

Continued on Page 6

President Outlines U. S. Plan For World Security Union

Four Major Powers Would Have Permanent Place in Elected Council—All Would Keep Forces to Halt War

By CHARLES HURD

Special to The New York Times.

WASHINGTON, June 15—President Roosevelt advanced a plan today for post-war international security calling for the formation of "a fully representative organization" of peace-loving countries. It would elect a smaller council on which the four major United Nations would be constantly represented with a "suitable" number of smaller countries. An international court of justice would be set up.

"The purpose of the organization," the President's statement said, "would be to maintain peace and security and to assist the creation, through international co-operations of conditions of stability and well-being necessary for peaceful and friendly relations among nations."

Of course, he said, the plan will become possible only when our present enemies are defeated "and effective arrangements are made to prevent them from making war again."

Mr. Roosevelt suggested no formal name for the proposed organization and made no recommendations as to the details of establishing it. He said, however, that "we are not thinking" of a super-state with its own armies and police forces. Instead "we are seeking" effective arrangements through which the nations would maintain adequate forces to prevent war and make impossible deliberate preparations for war and, when necessary, to have such forces available for joint action.

At first glance the plan, in the skeleton outline by the President, rested on about the same basis as the League of Nations; that is, an

Continued on Page 12

DE GAULLE NAMES NORMANDY AGENT

Appointing of Commissioner While on Beachhead Visit Presents Poser to Allies

By E. C. DANIEL

By Wireless to The New York Times.

LONDON, June 15—Without waiting for an agreement with the United States and Great Britain on the civil administration of France, Gen. Charles de Gaulle has already installed a Commissioner for Civil Affairs in Normandy.

This action, which became known today upon the general's return from his visit to France, apparently was taken without consulting Allied military or political authorities.

At first glance the functions of this Commissioner would seem to duplicate those of the civil affairs section which the Allied Supreme Command has organized to administer liberated areas in the rear of the advancing armies.

However, if the United States and Britain do not take umbrage at General de Gaulle's haste in in-

Continued on Page 7

ALLIED TIDE IN ITALY ENGULFS ORVIETO

8th and 5th Armies Break New German Line, Win Narni, Aquila, Many Other Places

By The Associated Press.

ROME, June 15 — Bursting through another line of defenses hastily thrown up by the retreating Germans beyond Rome, Allied forces have captured the large Italian towns of Orvieto, Aquila and Narni in a general advance and were fighting tonight in the outskirts of the important industrial and communications center of Terni, forty-five miles north of the capital.

American troops shoving up the Tyrrhenian coast captured Magliano and threatened Bengodi, only fourteen miles from Grosseto, after having seized vast quantities of Nazi food supplies at Orbetello. They had entirely cleared lateral highway 74, running inland from the coast past the northern shore of Lake Bolsena.

Eighth Army columns, now carrying the brunt of the inland advance, fought their way into Orvi-

Continued on Page 9

SAIPAN IS STORMED

Americans Fight Way Inland on Base Vital to Japan's Defense

BATTLING IN TOWN

Navy's Fire Covers Leap to Marianas, 1,465 Miles From Tokyo

By GEORGE F. HORNE

By Telephone to The New York Times.

PACIFIC FLEET HEADQUARTERS, June 15—American troops who fought their way ashore on Saipan Island in the Marianas Islands on Wednesday have firmly established their beachheads and are making good progress in an advance inland against heavy opposition, Admiral Chester W. Nimitz said in a communiqué tonight.

The enemy is fighting bitterly and has attempted several counter-attacks with tanks, but they have been broken up by our troops with the support of aircraft and warships lying offshore. Thus the most important battle fought so far in the Pacific offensive, now reaching to within 1,465 statute miles of Tokyo and a threat to the Japanese homeland itself, was going well for the invaders.

Tonight's communiqué was the second of the day issued by Admiral Nimitz. The first confirmed previous Japanese reports that Saipan was being invaded.

Defenses Well Organized

Tonight the Commander in Chief of the Pacific Fleet told of the advance inland. He said that in general the fighting was heavy and the defenses well organized.

We have captured Agingan Point, on the southwestern extremity of the big island, he said, and troops have forced their way into the town of Charan-Kanoa, where brisk fighting was still going on. Charan-Kanoa is the center of Saipan's big sugar refining industry and has a number of mills.

Between Charan-Kanoa, the first Japanese community to witness an engagement between land forces of the United States and Japan, and Agingan Point, a distance of about two miles, stretches a flat beachland and trees. Outside is a reef.

Our control of the air over Saipan and possibly over other Mari-

Continued on Page 3

STUNNING BLOWS STRIKE FOE IN PACIFIC ARENA

Introducing a new weapon for this global war, the United States sent Superfortresses from Asiatic bases to rain explosives on Japan (1). Tokyo said several cities on the island of Kyushu had been hit (detailed map Page 2). Earlier, American amphibious forces stormed ashore on Saipan Island (2) in the Marianas group, outpost of Japan itself (detailed map Page 3). From General MacArthur's command long-range planes struck at the bases of Yap (3) and Truk (4).

B-29'S MAKE DEBUT

Tokyo Reports Assaults on Industrial Heart of Kyushu Island

20TH AAF CREATED

New Command Will Be the Air Equivalent of a Naval Task Force

Details of new Superfortress bomber plane are on Page 4.

By SIDNEY SHALETT

Special to The New York Times.

WASHINGTON, June 15—The air war against the heart of the Japanese Empire has begun, the War Department announced this afternoon. B-29 Superfortresses of the new Twentieth Air Force, which is part of a new "super-air force" under the personal command of Gen. H. H. Arnold, bombed Japan today, a special communiqué revealed.

There are three epochal factors in the announcement:

First, that the monster B-29, half again as big as the Flying Fortress, is in operation.

Second, that the type of aerial attrition that reduced Germany to the stage where an invasion of Europe could be launched has commenced against Japan proper.

Third, that, in creating the Twentieth Air Force, a special organization that is not subject to the jurisdiction of any theatre commander, the Joint Chiefs of Staff have set up what virtually amounts to a separate air force.

Tokyo Road Shortened

The importance of this new phase of the Pacific war was emphasized by statements from Gen. George C. Marshall, Chief of Staff, who termed it the beginning of "a new type of offensive against our enemy"; from General Arnold, commanding general of the AAF, who declared it was "the fruition of years of planning for truly global warfare," and Secretary of War Henry L. Stimson, who asserted that the action had "shortened our road to Tokyo."

The history-making communiqué was confined to the following bare statement, personally handed out by Maj. Gen. Alexander D. Surles, War Department Director of Public Relations, at 1:39 o'clock this afternoon:

"B-29 Superfortresses of the United States Army Air Forces Twentieth Bomber Command bombed Japan today."

No details of where we struck the enemy, or how hard we hit, were revealed, although it was understood that the War Department would release this information as quickly as it felt the story might be told without imperiling security.

Representative Joe Starnes of Alabama, member of the Military Subcommittee of the Appropriations Committee, told the House that Tokyo was the target, and that a "heavy task force" of B-29's had "successfully" bombed

Continued on Page 4

PETRILLO IS ORDERED TO END RECORDS BAN

WLB Tells Union, Companies to Agree on Royalty Plan—Musicians' Head Defiant

By LOUIS STARK

Special to The New York Times.

WASHINGTON, June 15—The War Labor Board ordered the American Federation of Musicians today to end the ban which it put on production of phonograph recordings on Aug. 1, 1942.

In its directive, the board also provided that the transcription companies should set up machinery for the payment of royalties on records, reversing a panel recommendation which opposed payments.

Although the board did not specifically order the payment of royalties into the union unemployment fund, as had been requested, it provided that the money be held in escrow. The board did not fix the amount of these payments but proposed that the parties agree on this detail by direct conference. Failure to agree, the board stated, would result in arbitration by the board itself.

The industry members who, with the public members, made up the eight-man majority, favored the seven-point program proposed by the public spokesmen reluctantly lest a worse compromise be the alternative, it was stated.

The four labor members dissented. They did not state their reasons but it was reported that they sided with Mr. Petrillo, who had asserted that the ban was not really a strike, that the WLB had no jurisdiction of the case and that the dispute did not affect war production.

The companies involved in the case were the National Broadcasting Company, radio recording division; the Columbia Recording Corporation, and the RCA Victor division of the Radio Corporation of America.

The board held that contracts for royalty payments to the union made by a group of companies led by Decca Recordings did not require board approval since the funds set up did not involve a wage increase and thus did not require board approval under the wage stabilization program.

The union announced that it had signed agreements with more than eighty companies and it withdrew

Continued on Page 20

Tokyo Tries to Belittle Raid; Claims Two Superfortresses

By The United Press.

SAN FRANCISCO, June 15—The official Japanese radio announced today that American warplanes, including B-29 Superfortresses, had bombed Yawata, home of the great Imperial Steel Works; Moji, a communications center, and Kokura in northern Kyushu Island of the Japanese homeland Friday morning, June 16 (Japanese time).

The broadcast, recorded by United Press, admitted the attacking planes had started "two or three fires," but claimed they were "extinguished immediately."

Late news broadcasts from Tokyo continued to minimize the effects of the raid, claiming that damage was "limited" to "two or three light industrial shops."

The attacking force took off from a China air base and flew "by way of Antung, situated on the Manchukuo-Chosen border," Tokyo claimed, adding that the presence of the B-29's "came as no surprise."

The Japanese claimed their intercepting planes had shot down six of the attacking American aircraft. Two of these, said the Japanese announcement, were B-29 Superfortresses.

The Tokyo radio also reported that the railway line between Orio and Hasaka had been "slightly damaged" in the raid. The Japanese broadcast said the rail line "was repaired at once * * * and traffic service has been resumed without any hitch."

Moji is the site of the Mitsui

Continued on Page 2

RED ARMY EXPANDS WEDGE IN FINLAND

Breach Widened to 46 Miles With Spearhead Thrusting Closer to Viborg

By The United Press.

LONDON, Friday, June 16—Red Army forces have widened their breach in the Finnish lines across the Karelian Isthmus to more than forty-six miles and have pushed to within thirty-three miles of Viborg by capturing the heavily fortified town of Kanneljaervi, near the Leningrad-Helsinki Railroad, Moscow announced last night.

The Moscow bulletin announced that Gen. Leonid A. Govoroff's Leningrad Army, in the six days it has been on the offensive, had smashed through two powerful Finnish defense belts, advanced a total of almost twenty-five miles and widened its break-through to

Continued on Page 8

Bond Purchases by Armed Forces Help City to Raise 8.7% of E Quota

New York City fighting men purchased war bonds aggregating $4,641,751 in value between June 1 and June 10, it was announced yesterday by Nevil Ford, chairman of the War Finance Committee for New York, who said that their action has helped to lift the city's total sale of E bonds in the Fifth War Loan drive to $19,785,345, or 8.7 per cent of its E bond quota of $227,526,600.

"This striking evidence of double-action patriotism by our men and women in the armed forces should give every citizen something to think about," Mr. Ford declared. "Not only are they offering their lives—something that we are not asked to do—but they are also allotting large sums from their service pay to help speed the day of victory.

"If anyone, after reading today's headlines, still needs to be prodded in order to do his full share in raising the largest War Loan quotas ever asked of our city and State, let him think this over."

Sales of all types of issues to individual purchasers in New York City soared to a total of $48,964,276 through the close of business on Wednesday, according to Mr. Ford. Single day sales totaling $15,400,000 on Wednesday to individual purchases in New York State brought the Fifth War Loan total for the State to $69,000,000.

The State-wide total sales of E bonds have risen to $33,500,000, or 9.1 per cent of the State's quota of $367,000,000 in this category. It was explained that the daily totals of E bond sales for both the city and State are one day behind those of the sales of other types to individual investors, because of the amount of work involved in processing sales from the great num-

Continued on Page 10

Air Attack on Korea Reported by Tokyo

By The Associated Press.

The Japanese Domei agency said early today in a broadcast reported by Federal Communications Commission monitors that several "enemy" planes had raided Korea, Asiatic mainland area immediately opposite Japan.

The broadcast, transmitted to occupied East Asia areas, said the planes had hit in southern Korea. It quoted an announcement issued by the Japanese Army in Keijo (Seoul) that "we suffered no losses."

A Tokyo broadcast said later an "enemy task force" had attacked the Bonin Islands southeast of the Japanese mainland Thursday afternoon. This group stands midway between Japan and the Marianas, where American forces have effected a landing.

Invasion and Other War News Summarized

FRIDAY, JUNE 16, 1944

Japan felt the force of two mighty American blows, while her Axis partner was being steadily pushed back on the fields of Normandy.

The new B-29 Superfortresses made their initial major bow with a sudden heavy assault on the island of Kyushu, part of the Japanese home territory. It was the first time bombs had fallen on Japan itself since General Doolittle's Shangri-la sweep more than two years ago. The only details disclosed by Washington were that the B-29's had "probably" operated from bases in China and were from a new Twentieth Air Force.

This force, under direct command of General Arnold and supervision of the Joint Chiefs of Staffs, will be used as an aerial battle fleet, or major task force, in future operations. [All the foregoing 1:8.]

Tokyo's version of the attack said that Yawata, site of the Imperial Steel Works, the communications center of Moji and the suburbs of Kokura, all near Shimonoseki, had been hit. The Japanese asserted two Superfortresses and five other American planes had been shot down. [1:6-7; map P. 2.]

The B-29 flies so high and so fast that it appears to ground defenders as a small gnat with a vapor trail. It carries the heaviest bomb load of any plane in the world. [4:2-8.]

While Japan was bearing this blow at home it was announced that American amphibious forces had stormed ashore on the strategic island of Saipan in the Marianas. A four-day battering by ships and planes preceded the first assault on Wednesday. Strong forces have landed and are battling fierce enemy opposition. A late communiqué said beachheads had been secured and our troops were advancing inland. [1:4; map P. 3.]

Tokyo reported early today that an American task force had attacked the Bonin Islands, midway between Japan and Saipan, and that hostile planes had attacked Korea. [Box 1:8.]

Southwest Pacific planes kept the enemy occupied by dumping 180 tons of bombs on Truk in the heaviest attack yet made on that island by General MacArthur's fliers. Yap and other neighboring places were also hit. [3:8.]

In Burma airborne Chindits launched a sudden attack on Mogaung, supporting base for Myitkyina, but along the Shweli River the Japanese recaptured Hsiangta and threatened to win back Lungling. [4:1.]

The invasion of Normandy showed steady progress yesterday. Americans advancing on a ten-mile front across the neck of the Cherbourg Peninsula menaced La Haye. Baupte and Quineville were captured and the Germans suffered heavy tank losses in strong counter-attacks in the Caumont-Tilly sector. Battleships and cruisers poured shells into enemy positions and Le Havre. [1:1; map P. 6.]

More than 7,000 Allied aircraft gave close support to the ground troops. The E-boat base at Le Havre was heavily bombed, and on Wednesday night the RAF struck again at the German synthetic oil center of Gelsenkirchen in the Ruhr. [5:1.]

General de Gaulle, described by his headquarters as "President of the Provisional Government of the French Republic," before returning from the beachhead installed a Commissioner for Civil Affairs without consulting Allied military or political leaders. [1:2.]

In Italy, too, the Germans were being pushed back. The Allies smashed through another defense line to take Orvieto, Aquila and Narni, and to come within eighty miles of Florence. [1:3; map P. 9.] The Red Army continued to beat down strong Finnish resistance and was only thirty-three miles from Viborg and twenty-six from Koivisto. [1:7; map P 8.]

President Roosevelt made public an outline of his plan for post-war security. He suggested an organization of all peace-loving countries, a smaller council on which the four major powers and small nations would be represented and an international court of justice. "We are not thinking of a super-state with its own police forces," he said, but of peace by agreement. [1:2-3.]

"All the News That's Fit to Print"

The New York Times.

LATE CITY EDITION
POSTSCRIPT
Cloudy and cooler today.
Temperatures Yesterday—Max., 80; Min., 63
Sunrise, 5:24 A. M.; Sunset, 8:31 P. M.

VOL. XCIII..No. 31,559. Entered as Second-Class Matter, Postoffice, New York, N. Y. NEW YORK, TUESDAY, JUNE 20, 1944. THREE CENTS IN NEW YORK CITY

JAPANESE LOSE 300 PLANES IN SAIPAN BATTLE, BIGGEST SINCE MIDWAY; ISLAND AIRFIELD TAKEN; U. S. UNITS 8 MILES FROM CHERBOURG; ELBA WON

DEWEY WILL VISIT CHICAGO TO ACCEPT, SPRAGUE DECLARES

Otherwise 'Do You Think We Would Be Here to Draft Him?' Asks Campaign Chief

POINTS TO POPULAR POLLS

Convention Headquarters to Be Opened Today—Warren Pushed for the Ticket

By JAMES A. HAGERTY
Special to THE NEW YORK TIMES.

CHICAGO, June 19—J. Russel Sprague, national committeeman from New York, announced at a press conference today that he, Edwin F. Jaeckle, State chairman, and Herbert Brownell Jr., chairman of the law committee of the Republican State Committee, representing the Republican voters and the Republican organization of New York State, had come to Chicago to get the Republican National Convention to draft Gov. Thomas E. Dewey for the nomination for President.

Mr. Sprague added that in his opinion Governor Dewey would come to Chicago to accept the nomination and would be elected in November.

He also announced that headquarters of the New York Republican organization to work for the nomination of Governor Dewey would be opened tomorrow on the twenty-fifth floor of the Hotel Stevens.

He predicted Governor Dewey's nomination without qualification, but would not say that it would be on the first ballot.

Despite the recent statement of Gov. Earl Warren that he was not a candidate for the Vice Presidential nomination and knowledge that he does not want it, the California Governor continued to be the first choice of the Dewey supporters for second place on the ticket.

"Double Draft" Is Pressed

Although there is ample precedent for refusing to run for Vice President—Senator Hiram Johnson missed a chance for the Presidency by declining to consider a second place nomination in 1920 and Frank O. Lowden refused such a nomination after it had been made in 1924—supporters of Governor Dewey still hope to have Governor Warren as Governor Dewey's running mate in a "double-draft" movement.

Although Mr. Sprague would give no detailed figures on the number of delegates counted as certain to vote for the nomination of Governor Dewey, except to declare the support of ninety-two of the ninety-three delegates from New York, in other sources the Dewey strength in the convention was estimated at 750 to 800 votes, or 200 to 250 more than the number needed to nominate.

About thirty reporters were at Mr. Sprague's press conference in Room 1205-A of the Stevens Hotel. Mr. Sprague apologized for the smallness of the room and said that tomorrow the State committee would have adequate headquarters.

"To identify myself, I will say that I am Republican National Committeeman and delegate-at-large from New York," Mr. Sprague said. "With me are Ed Jaeckle, State chairman, and Herbert Brownell, chairman of our law committee. We are here representing the Republicans of New York State and its Republican organization.

Cites Votes of 1942 and 1943

"There will be ninety-three delegates from New York State and ninety-two of them are unanimous for drafting Governor Dewey for the nomination for President. Governor Dewey carried New York in 1942 by a plurality of 647,000 and is the one Republican to be elected Governor of New York in more than twenty years. A Republican Lieutenant-Governor was elected in New York last year by

Continued on Page 12

Asks Senate Seats For Ex-Presidents

By The Associated Press.

WASHINGTON, June 19—Representative Gordon Canfield, Republican, of New Jersey, introduced a bill today to make former Presidents voteless members-at-large of the Senate for life.

Their pay and allowances would be the same as for an elected member.

Presidents are "outstanding leaders of public opinion," Mr. Canfield said. "They rate high in their ability to voice with force and accuracy the views and aspirations of a great number of their fellow-citizens. Congress is itself the nation's sounding board of public opinion.

"Except for William H. Harrison, Polk, Taylor, Lincoln, Garfield, Arthur, McKinley, Wilson and Harding, every President has survived his term long enough to have to face the problem of 'and now what?'—and without help from the people."

Governor Dewey had expressed himself as favorable to the idea, Mr. Canfield said.

BOND SALES IN U. S. TOTAL $854,000,000

14% of Individual Quota of $6,000,000,000 Raised—City Figure $85,631,918

War bond sales to individuals in the Fifth War Loan drive totaled $854,000,000 at the close of the first week of the campaign, which began June 12 and is scheduled to continue through July 8, it was announced yesterday by the Treasury Department in Washington. This represents 14 per cent of the $6,000,000,000 quota for individuals in the over-all drive for $16,000,000,000.

Sales to individual investors in New York City stood at $85,631,918 as of the close of business Saturday night, it was announced here by Nevil Ford, State chairman of the War Finance Committee of New York, while in New York State sales of all issues to individuals aggregated $117,600,000 at the close of the first week of the drive.

New York City, with total E bond purchases of $27,900,765, has attained 12.3 per cent of its goal in this category, according to Mr. Ford. The city's E bond sales objective in the drive is $227,526,600. Friday's sales of this issue, which the Treasury is particularly anxious to place in the hands of investors of small and moderate means, were 49 per cent higher than those of Thursday.

Bronx Retains Its Lead

The Bronx retained its leadership among the five boroughs, with 18.3 per cent of its E bond quota attained. Queens, with 15.8 per cent, passed Richmond and moved into second place by the narrow margin of 0.5 per cent.

A table showing the sales of E bonds, and of all other issues, to

Continued on Page 17

Auto Use Tax Assailed as Unfair To 'A' Driver in Plea for Repeal

Immediate Congressional repeal or revision of the $5 Federal automobile "use tax" on the ground that it is unfair to auto owners who are limited to A gasoline rations, was urged yesterday by the Automobile Club of New York. The new stamps must be pasted on car windshields by July 1.

In telegrams to Senator Walter F. George, chairman of the Senate Finance Committee; Representative Robert L. Doughton, chairman of the House Ways and Means Committee, and to Senators and Representatives from the metropolitan area, it was asserted that the tax was both "unsound in theory and inequitable in practice."

William A. Gottlieb, president of the Automobile Club, contended in the telegram that it was unfair to collect the same sum from the A card driver, who at best gets gasoline for 1,440 miles annually, as is asked of the C card holder, with no maximum mileage, and the taxi man, whose cab may operate 49,200 miles.

He compared the 1,440 miles with the 3,900 miles allowed to B ration holders in the East; the 4,800 miles for B card drivers in the West and the 5,700 miles allowed on B cards in the Midwest, pointing out further that trucks and buses with TT rations running up "huge mileages" are taxed no more than the A driver.

"Gross inequities in the present method of taxing are apparent, with all classes of users paying the same amount of tax though legal use permitted shows tremendous differences," Mr. Gottlieb said. "A rationed users are obviously taxed way out of proportion when based on the Government's established measures of use. B rationed

Continued on Page 17

U. S. NOT TO BE BOUND BY MONEY PARLEY, MORGENTHAU SAYS

Any Compact on World Bank or Stabilizing of Currency Would Be Up to Congress

TAX REVISION IS UNLIKELY

Early Change Doubtful in View of Public Debt, He Says—Bond Drive Not Aided by War

Special to THE NEW YORK TIMES.

CHICAGO, June 19—Secretary of the Treasury Henry Morgenthau Jr. said today that no commitments binding on the United States could be made at the world monetary conference which would meet July 1 at Bretton Woods, N. H.

Whatever agreements are made for stabilizing currencies and establishing a world bank will be subject to Congressional approval as far as this country is concerned, he said.

"The results of the conference will be referred to President Roosevelt, who in turn will submit the matter to Congress," the Secretary said.

American Delegates Chosen

The personnel of the American delegation has been completed and will be announced in a day or so, Mr. Morgenthau disclosed.

Mr. Morgenthau spent the day in Chicago in connection with the promotion of the Treasury's Fifth War Loan drive. He touched on a number of subjects during a forty-minute press interview.

In reply to questions, Mr. Morgenthau said that he foresaw little likelihood of a major revision in the Federal tax system in the early post-war years. Specifically he was doubtful that the present dual taxation of corporation profits, which are levied when earned and again later when paid out in dividends, would be eliminated.

"After all, we have a big public debt that must be paid off and the quicker we do that the better," he said. "It is sound fiscal policy to retire the war debt as rapidly as possible. As long as I remain in the Treasury I will stand by that policy, but of course I cannot forecast with certainty what future tax policies will be."

Denies Stifling of Incentive

Mr. Morgenthau said that business had no reason to fear that the post-war tax structure would stifle the incentive to take ventures in an attempt to make money.

"This reasoning is not sound, because if business and, in turn, workers, failed to make money, the Government would be unable to retire the national debt," he said.

One reporter asked if taxes would continue to climb between now and the end of the war. The Secretary smiled and said:

"Thank you, gentlemen, for coming. I'm afraid I'll have to be moving along now."

Mr. Morgenthau referred to the Congressional action raising the

Continued on Page 34

KEY PORT SHELLED

American Forces Drive Close to the Last Hills Outside Nazi Bastion

BY-PASS VALOGNES

British Fight Their Way Into Tilly—Allies Put New Troops in Lines

5 A. M. Communique

By The Associated Press.

SUPREME HEADQUARTERS, Allied Expeditionary Force, Tuesday, June 20—American forces making coordinated attacks northward toward the port of Cherbourg have made further advances, Supreme Headquarters announced today.

One of the advances was made east of Valognes, ten miles southeast of the port, communiqué No. 29 said. This drive carried to within two miles of this town. Westward the road from Valognes to captured Bricquebec was cut.

Lieut. Gen. Bradley's troops in their drive for Cherbourg penetrated to the outskirts of Rauville-La Bigot, eight miles southwest of the port on the road from Bricquebec.

The British recaptured Tilly-sur-Suelles on their sector of the beachhead front toward the east.

By DREW MIDDLETON
By Cable to THE NEW YORK TIMES.

SUPREME HEADQUARTERS, Allied Expeditionary Force, Tuesday, June 20—The American assault on Cherbourg has started with remarkable speed and success.

Advancing more than ten miles in twenty-four hours, Lieut. Gen. Omar N. Bradley's veteran divisions have smashed their way to a point within eight miles of the port and are shelling it.

Bricquebec, eleven and a half miles south of Cherbourg, fell yesterday and it is probable that

Continued on Page 3

War News Summarized

TUESDAY, JUNE 20, 1944

More than 300 Japanese planes were shot down in a furious battle off the Marianas when the enemy attacked the Pacific Fleet task force covering the landings on Saipan. It was the biggest carrier engagement since the Battle of Midway. Our air losses had not been tabulated when Admiral Nimitz announced the fight, but only one of our ships was hit and damage was minor.

American soldiers and marines on Saipan captured the Aslito airstrip, and Seabees immediately set to work to repair it. The drive carried to Magicienne Bay, the west shore of which is in our possession. A large body of enemy troops was cut off and nearly one-third of the island had been captured. [All the foregoing 1:8; maps P. 10.]

The Chinese driving on Burma evacuated Lungling to avoid encirclement, but farther north pushed their gains along the Shweli River. [8:1, with map.] The Japanese were only fifty miles from the Chinese railroad city of Hengyang, south of Changsha, and civilian evacuation was said to have been ordered. Changsha still fought off the invaders. [10:2.]

The United States Ninth Division in Normandy pushed ahead ten miles in twenty-four hours to bring the port of Cherbourg within artillery range, and shells from "Long Toms" began to fall on that German stronghold yesterday. Bricquebec was captured as the Americans by-passed Montebourg and Valognes. At the other end of the line the British beat off furious enemy counter-attacks and fought their way into Tilly-sur-Seulles, recapturing the town. Allied warships continued to pour shells into German tank groups near Caen. [1:4; map P. 2.]

The Ninth Division, despite rain and fatigue, pursued the beaten Germans so relentlessly that the enemy never had a chance to regain his balance. Advance elements were eight miles from Cherbourg. [1:5-6.]

The British disclosed that Hitler's latest weapon, the robot bomber, was a jet-propelled machine launched from a ramp and controlled by a gyroscope. It has a 150-mile range, a speed of 350 miles an hour and carries a ton of explosives. [4:5.] A NEW YORK TIMES correspondent on a ship in the English Channel saw a "super-robot" streak by at an estimated speed of 600 miles an hour. [1:7.]

The Germans on Elba surrendered when the French invasion forces captured Porto Longone. More than 1,800 prisoners and vast stores of matériel were taken. [1:6; map, P. 5.] The Allied advance in Italy continued with the capture of Assisi. Fighting was reported in the outskirts of Perugia. [5:5.] The Allies recognized the Bonomi Government and it was expected Marshal Badoglio would find a place in the Cabinet. [6:5.]

The Russian Army widened the breach in the Mannerheim Line to about thirty miles between Muolaa and the Gulf of Finland and was ten miles from Viborg. [7:4-5, with map.]

Prime Minister Churchill said that Allied victories this summer might lead to "full success" and relieve the world "of the curse which has been laid upon us by the Germans." He looked forward to international cooperation, in which "the rights of small nations will be upheld and protected." [1:6-7.]

THE SIGN POINTS TO THEIR OBJECTIVE

Americans rest beside a marker showing the way to Cherbourg and telling that the speed limit is thirty kilometers an hour.

Associated Press Wirephoto (U. S. Signal Corps Radiophoto)

Americans Rush On in Rain As Speed Bewilders Nazis

By HAROLD DENNY
By Wireless to THE NEW YORK TIMES.

WITH THE AMERICAN FORCES IN FRANCE, June 19—United States troops, advancing with unexpected rapidity, got to a point eight miles from Cherbourg today. Artillery followed in close behind the infantry and this afternoon 155-mm. rifles—'Long Toms'—began to shell that important port.

Today a cold slanting rain drenched our men and turned the roads into quagmires. Nevertheless, for all the weariness of many days of constant fighting and unbelievably rapid advances, our troops lunged at the Germans again with as much spirit as ever.

This morning's main attack was northward and met little opposition, indicating the Germans had been thrown off balance by our recent swift progress. We took Bricquebec, an important road junction, almost unopposed. Montebourg, which had been taken and lost and had caused us much trouble, was by-passed. It is held by German troops, but they will be mopped up in due course.

We also by-passed Valognes, an

Continued on Page 4

ELBA SURRENDERS TO FRENCH TROOPS

German Resistance Ends With Loss of Porto Longone—1,800 Prisoners Taken

By A. C. SEDGWICK
By Wireless to THE NEW YORK TIMES.

ELBA, June 19—The white flag was hoisted this morning at Porto Longone to signify the German surrender of this island to French Colonial troops.

French artillery had been pounding this site of the enemy's last stand throughout the night. It was a powerful bombardment, made possible by a mass of artillery lodged in gullies.

[In Italy the British Eighth Army took Assisi and drove within three miles of Perugia, which, according to the German radio, has been evacuated. The Fifth Army gained against increasing resistance north of Grosseto.]

Constant patrols by the Allies' fighters and fighter-bombers had destroyed almost all the enemy's transport on the island. The air force and naval vessels had destroyed almost every craft from rowboats to calques that the enemy might have used to escape. It is believed unlikely that any of the enemy attempted to get away and the check of prisoners now going on may uncover several high German officers.

All the enemy's equipment has

Continued on Page 5

NEW ROBOT SPEEDS 600 MILES AN HOUR

Spitfires Fade Like Gliders in Pursuit of Latest German Missile Passing Over Ship

By GENE CURRIVAN
By Cable to THE NEW YORK TIMES.

ABOARD THE JOHN E. WARD, Off England, June 19—Adolf Hitler's newest terrifying weapon, a jet-propelled bomb larger and faster than anything heretofore revealed, passed over this ship last night among twenty-seven similar but smaller pilotless planes that streaked through the skies toward the English coast. Its speed is such as to make pursuing Spitfires appear as gliders.

It was the first of a procession of robot planes that started at 6:30 P. M. and continued until 4 o'clock this morning. The last, which appeared as a ball of fire directly over this ship, was less than 1,000 feet over the stack.

[The flying torpedoes hurtled over England early Tuesday for the sixth consecutive day, The United Press reported. It was disclosed that a United States anti-aircraft battery shot down the first enemy projectile the night of June 15.]

The "super-robot" came in at 1,000 to 2,000 feet. It shot on a straight line, apparently from the Calais area toward a port on the southeast coast not far from our position. At a distance the robot bomb's sound is like that of an approaching E-boat or motor torpedo boat.

The missile suddenly appeared off the ship's bow, cutting in front of four Spitfires headed for France. As it shot by them, slightly below their line of flight, the pilots realized it was an enemy craft, and one by one they peeled off and darted after it. As it passed our

Continued on Page 4

Churchill Sees Victory in Summer As Possible Fruit of Teheran Plan

By JOHN MacCORMAC
By Wireless to THE NEW YORK TIMES.

LONDON, June 19—The plan of campaign adopted in the accord with Russia at Teheran is being steadily unrolled and may bring victory this summer, Prime Minister Churchill said Thursday in a speech to diplomats, the text of which was released today.

In his address, delivered at a luncheon given by the Mexican Ambassador, the Prime Minister said that the longer the struggle continued, the more terrible would it be in the end for Germany.

"It may be," he said, "that events will occur in the next few months which will show us whether we are soon to be relieved of the curse which was laid upon us by the Germans. Whether it be this year or next, the British and American peoples will never falter or withdraw their hands from the task they have undertaken."

[Perhaps a million men are now embroiled in the fighting in France, the Prime Minister said, according to The Associated Press.]

Mr. Churchill regretted the inconvenience suffered by the diplomatic corps through the pre-invasion curb on communications but justified it by noting that though many thousands knew the secrets of the invasion, they had been well kept. He continued:

"Of course, we have not embarked on this great adventure without being in full accord with our Russian allies and the decisions taken in Teheran, and although the execution of the plans

FLEET IS ATTACKED

Our Carrier Task Force Beats Off Swarms of Japanese for Hours

ONE U. S. SHIP IS HIT

But Damage Is Minor—We Cut Enemy Forces in Two on Saipan

By GEORGE F. HORNE
By Telephone to THE NEW YORK TIMES.

PACIFIC FLEET HEADQUARTERS, Pearl Harbor, June 19—The greatest air-sea battle since Midway was fought off the Marianas yesterday, when the American carrier task force supporting the ground attack on Saipan shot down more than 300 out of swarms of Japanese planes, a number of which apparently came from Japanese carriers.

American fliers and ship gunners so successfully fought off the severe attack, lasting for hours, that, according to present information, only one of our ships was damaged, and this damage was minor. Our plane losses were not yet determined.

Meanwhile, on Saipan American marines and Army troops captured the Aslito airdrome, 1,465 miles from Tokyo and 1,470 from Davao in the Philippines, and Seabees are already putting the airfield's excellent 3,600-foot strips in condition.

Garrison Cut in Two

Coupled with this, our ground forces have cut off a number of enemy troops by fighting across the island to Magicienne Bay. We hold the western shore of the bay now and are gradually moving up the island although the enemy continues to counter-attack fiercely.

There is no indication that we have found the Japanese carriers that sent planes in support of embattled Saipan and there is no information here on the strength of their force.

Admiral Chester W. Nimitz's communiqué does not state that the enemy planes came from carriers but that "it is believed a portion of the enemy planes were carrier based and used near-by shore bases as shuttle points."

Somewhere north or west of Saipan the enemy carrier force may have come within range of land and sent off the planes to land staging points.

"However," the communiqué said, "the effectiveness of this procedure was sharply limited by our systematic bombing and strafing of the airfields at Guam and Rota."

It is altogether possible for the enemy to stage planes from the Philippines via Palau and Yap or from Truk to the southeast. It is 516 nautical miles from Davao to Palau, 830 from Palau to Saipan. From Truk to Guam it is 559 and another 111 to Saipan. It is 474 miles from Woleai to Saipan.

Ninth Day in the Marianas

All the bases have air facilities but they are being closely watched by our forces and are kept busy with bombings and strafings.

For some gun crews the battle with the Japanese planes was the first major action in which they had participated and it was something for which they had been intensively trained.

Yesterday was the ninth day of action in the Marianas. It began on June 10 when our carrier forces opened a two-day assault on Saipan and other Marianas Islands, followed by surface craft bombardment and the landing of troops on June 14.

The Seabees were working feverishly on the Aslito airfield. This is work to which they are accustomed and it should not take long. Our own airfield on Saipan will make it possible to give closer support to ground troops and keep watch over other enemy islands.

We now hold between one-fourth and one-third of Saipan with the exception of enemy pockets.

There are two pockets of enemy

Continued on Page 10

U.S. Marine Corps

These Marines have just tossed a charge of TNT into a Japanese dug-out position on Saipan.

U.S. Marine Corps

Marine Infantrymen run to take new positions in Garapan, principal city of Saipan.

"All the News That's Fit to Print"

The New York Times.

LATE CITY EDITION
POSTSCRIPT
Partly cloudy and warm today
Temperatures Yesterday—Max., 84; Min., 64
Sunrise, 5:26 A. M.; Sunset, 8:32 P. M.

VOL. XCIII. No. 31,566. Entered as Second-Class Matter, Postoffice, New York, N. Y. NEW YORK, TUESDAY, JUNE 27, 1944. THREE CENTS IN NEW YORK CITY

CHERBOURG FALLS TO AMERICAN TROOPS; ENEMY LEADERS AMONG 30,000 PRISONERS; RUSSIANS CAPTURE VITEBSK AND ZHLOBIN

REPUBLICANS MAKE QUICK END TO WAR THEIR BATTLE CRY

Warren, Keynoter, Says Party Will Bring Victorious Boys Home With All Speed

DISPUTES OVER PLATFORM

Dewey Avalanche Piles Up, With Californian Unchallenged as His Running Mate

Governor Warren's keynote address is printed on Page 10.

By TURNER CATLEDGE
Special to THE NEW YORK TIMES.

CHICAGO, Tuesday, June 27—A triple pledge to bring the boys back home quickly and "victorious," to reopen the doors of opportunity to "all Americans," and to guard the peace in the future, was sounded yesterday as the Republican battle-cry at the opening of the party's twenty-third national convention.

While it was being uttered by Gov. Earl Warren of California, temporary chairman, in his keynote address to a cheering throng in the Chicago Stadium, THE NEW YORK TIMES gained access to a plank which policy writers had evolved Saturday, pledging the party to a post-war cooperative organization "among sovereign nations," to prevent military aggression and attain permanent peace in the future.

Word had come meanwhile from Wendell L. Willkie, the nominee of 1940, that he considered the foreign policy plank, as he understood it, ambiguous, and therefore was disappointed in it.

Willkie's Backers Upset

This note of controversy came as a distinct shock to a group of former backers of Mr. Willkie who have been attempting these last few days to bring him in line with the platform, and with a ticket of Thomas E. Dewey of New York for President and Governor Warren for Vice President, which is considered certain of nomination by tomorrow night.

Meanwhile, another complication appeared in the hitherto placid convention picture when the seventeen Governors who are delegates demanded opportunity to examine and possibly suggest changes in the platform before it is submitted to the convention, probably tonight, for ratification.

The Governors did not protest any particular item in the platform as it was agreed to in principle last night. They did protest the fact, however, that, as one of them put it, an "oligarchy" of Senators, members of the House and other party leaders, had assumed the prerogative of speaking for the party

The Governors feel, as Governor Warren reflected in his keynote address, that they have been the spearhead, more than members of Congress, for the resurgence of Republicanism during the last three years. What happened here when the Governors demanded and obtained permission to appear before the resolutions committee was another chapter in a protest which first came to light at the Mackinac Island conference in September.

Led by New Englanders

The action was led, as was the move at Mackinac, largely by a New England group, in which Gov. Raymond E. Baldwin of Connecticut and Gov. Sumner Sewall of Maine were active.

These new possibilities of trouble ahead did not divert the main line of appeal upon which the party was centering—an appeal to the soldier vote, to those Americans who are weary of the New Deal, and, above all, to those wanting to avoid the tragedy of war in the future.

It was the note on which Gov. Dwight Green of Illinois opened the meeting with a welcoming ad-

Continued on Page 9

Convention Events Listed for Today

Special to THE NEW YORK TIMES.

CHICAGO, June 26—The official program for tomorrow's sessions of the Republican National Convention is as follows:

Tuesday, June 27, 10:15 A. M.
(Central War Time)

Convention called to order by the temporary chairman.

National Anthem: Miss Mildred Maule of East St. Louis, Ill.

Prayer: The Rev. Joseph Simonson, pastor of Christ Lutheran Church, St. Paul.

Report of Committee on Credentials.

Report of Committee on Permanent Organization.

Election of permanent chairman and permanent officers.

Address by permanent chairman.

Report of Committee on Rules and Order of Business.

Election of National Committee.

Report of Resolutions Committee.

Recess until 8:15 P. M.

Tuesday, June 27, 8:15 P. M.

Convention called to order by the permanent chairman, Representative Joseph W. Martin Jr.

National Anthem: Miss Mona Bradford of the Chicago Civic Opera Company.

Prayer: Rabbi Abba Hillel Silver of The Temple, Cleveland.

Music.

Address: Herbert Hoover.

Address: Representative Clare Boothe Luce of Connecticut.

Adjourn until Wednesday.

WILLKIE CONDEMNS PEACE-POLICY PLAN

Republican Draft on Foreign Relations Could Be Used to Balk Cooperation, He Says

A few hours after Wendell Willkie had received the text of the proposed Republican foreign-policy plank, the 1940 Presidential candidate issued a statement denouncing the plan as ambiguous, subject to opposing interpretations and capable of being used to throttle effective collaboration by the United States with other countries to maintain peace.

Mr. Willkie's views on the platform committee's suggestions were presented to reporters who had been invited to visit his offices at 15 Broad Street. He explained that he chose this form of making them public because he was not a delegate to the convention.

Likening the language proposed for this year's platform to that employed in 1920, Mr. Willkie recalled that thirty-one leading Republicans had assured the country that the 1920 formula "was the surest road to an effective international organization," but that President Harding, immediately after the election, "announced that the League of Nations was dead."

"A Republican President elected under the proposed platform of

Continued on Page 13

ACCORD OF NATIONS FAVORED IN PLANK ON FOREIGN POLICY

'Participation in Cooperative Organization' Provided 'to Attain Permanent Peace'

TAFT PREDICTS ADOPTION

Declaration Calls for Seeking 'Economic Stability,' Pledges Constitutional Procedure

By JAMES B. RESTON
Special to THE NEW YORK TIMES.

CHICAGO, Tuesday, June 27—The Republican party platform will favor "participation by the United States in post-war cooperative organization among sovereign nations to prevent military aggression and to attain permanent peace."

The party's Foreign Affairs Committee, headed by Senator Warren Austin of Vermont, has approved unanimously a plank which calls on the future world peace organization to "develop effective cooperative means to direct peace forces to prevent or repel military aggression."

Pending the formation of this world peace organization, the plank recommends that the United States should "pledge continuing collaboration with the United Nations."

Senator Robert A. Taft, chairman of the party's Resolutions Committee, to which the platform will be submitted later this morning, said he was certain that the foreign affairs plank as recommended by Senator Austin's committee would be adopted.

Objectives of Peace Treaties

After stating that the party favored "prosecution of the war to total victory against all our enemies in full cooperation with the United Nations and the speedy return of our armed forces," the plank emphasized that justice in the writing of the peace was the essence of realism.

"We believe that peace and security do not depend upon the sanction of force alone, but should prevail by virtue of reciprocal interests and spiritual values recognized in these security agreements," the Foreign Affairs Committee said.

"The treaties of peace should be just; the nations which are the victims of Axis aggression should be restored to sovereignty and self-government, and the organized cooperation of the nations should concern itself with basic causes of world disorder."

Elaborating on "cooperation," the committee continued:

"We shall seek, in our relations with other nations, conditions calculated to promote world-wide economic stability, not only for the sake of the world, but also the end that our own people may enjoy a high level of employment in an increasingly prosperous world. We

Continued on Page 14

3-Cornered Baseball Game Yields $56,500,000 in Fifth Bond Drive

A crowd of 50,000 baseball fans, all of whom paid their way into the park by buying war bonds, turned out last night at the Polo Grounds to witness a bizarre contest in which the Yankees, Giants and Dodgers participated in a nine-inning contest. The Brooklyn nine won the game, tallying five runs; the Yankees scored one and the Giants nothing.

The program, as arranged by the Fifth War Loan Sports Committee, helped to swell New York's quota in the current bond drive by $56,500,000. Fifty million dollars of this sum came, according to an announcement by Mayor La Guardia, from the coffers of the City of New York. The remainder was contributed by the crowd as "admission fee," plus a one-million-dollar bond purchase of an autographed score card by the Bond Clothing Stores.

During the day the drive moved into high gear with the announcement of many large subscriptions here totalling around $1,000,000,000 and the disclosure that purchases throughout the nation had reached $4,591,000,000, or 29 per cent of the quota for the campaign.

Devised and conceived by Stanley Oshan of the War Finance Committee, the baseball game was followed closely by the huge throng that was seeing three major league teams tangle with each other on the same field for the first time. While Mr. Oshan was the originator of the idea it required a Columbia University professor of mathematics, Paul A. Smith, to produce a method of scoring it.

Professor Smith's assistance proved helpful, indeed, for the

Continued on Page 20

ALLIED WARSHIPS SHELLING GERMAN POSITIONS IN CHERBOURG

The U. S. S. Quincy (left) and H. M. S. Glasgow bombarding the port
The New York Times (British Admiralty via U. S. Signal Corps Radiotelephoto)

U. S. TROOPS SCALE LOFTY SAIPAN PEAK

Tapotchau, Dominating Island, Is Reported Won — Carrier Planes Batter Guam and Rota

By GEORGE F. HORNE
By Telephone to THE NEW YORK TIMES.

PACIFIC FLEET HEADQUARTERS, Pearl Harbor, June 26—Mount Tapotchau on Saipan Island has been scaled by United States Marines who are now established in positions near the summit. Marines and Army troops have made substantial gains on both the eastern and western shores of the island.

[A front dispatch said that Tapotchau which dominated the island and has been the goal of our men ever since they landed on Saipan, had been captured by troops who held it against a before-dawn Japanese counter-attack Sunday.]

Admiral Chester W. Nimitz stated that the Kagman Peninsula, forming the upper arm of Magicienne Bay, was now entirely in our hands and that troops had

Continued on Page 7

Russians Begin Encircling Mogilev and Orsha Citadels

By The United Press.

LONDON, Tuesday, June 27—The Red Army, tearing out the northern and southern anchors of the German defense line in White Russia, captured the fortress cities of Vitebsk and Zhlobin yesterday and seized more than 1,700 towns and settlements, while the vanguard of their victorious forces advanced more than twenty-two miles toward Minsk for a great pincer assault on that city.

Striking with unprecedented power and speed, four Soviet armies sprinting along a 285-mile front raced to within eighty-four miles of Minsk, approached to within thirty-five miles of the Polish border, outflanked Orsha and drove to within six miles of Mogilev.

Vitebsk, the most powerful Nazi stronghold on the route to East Prussia, and Zhlobin, 157 miles to the south, fell on the fourth day of the Red Army's summer offensive—four days in which Russian troops advanced as much as fifty-six miles, seized 3,040 towns and settlements and killed more than 31,500 Germans.

More than 6,000 of the German garrison of five infantry divisions

Continued on Page 6

VIENNA WAR PLANTS GET HEAVY BOMBING

Italy-Based Planes Pound Oil, Aircraft Works—Weather Cuts Invasion Support

By The Associated Press.

SUPREME HEADQUARTERS, Allied Expeditionary Force, Tuesday, June 27—United States Flying Fortresses and Liberators 500 to 750 strong roared from Italian bases to the Vienna area yesterday through the heaviest Luftwaffe opposition in recent weeks and attacked oil refineries, rail yards and a Nazi aircraft plant.

Poor weather over western Europe halted for the day the pounding from Allied air bases in Britain and Normandy of German supply and communication lines behind the French front.

Indications of renewed Allied aerial activity came last night as the German radio interrupted programs to say an alert had been sounded in all parts of southwestern Germany. In Hungary, where British bombers of the Mediterranean Allied Air Forces attacked oil works Sunday night, the Budapest radio went off the air again at 10 P. M.

The Flying Fortresses and Liberators and their escorting Mustangs, Lightnings and Thunderbolts of the United States Fifteenth Air Force shot down large numbers of enemy planes on the route to the Vienna area, headquarters announced.

They struck refineries at Schwechat, ten miles southeast of

Continued on Page 5

War News Summarized

TUESDAY, JUNE 27, 1944

Cherbourg fell to the Americans this morning after General Bradley's troops had fought the desperate German defenders from dock to dock along the ruined waterfront. The enemy held out in four or five strong points, principally around the naval base, until each fortified nucleus had been overrun. Lieut. Gen. von Schleiben, Cherbourg garrison commander, and Admiral Hennecke, head of the German sea force off Normandy, were captured. The total of prisoners may reach 30,000.

At the eastern end of the Normandy line the British opened a new drive from Tilly-sur-Seulles and gained as much as four miles, threatening to cut the Caen-Avranches highway at the base of the Cotentin Peninsula. Since the initial landings three weeks ago the Allies have liberated more than 1,000 square miles of France, have taken more than 50,000 prisoners and have destroyed four German divisions. [All the foregoing 1:8; map, P. 2.]

Three United States battleships headed a force of fourteen Allied vessels that pounded Cherbourg's main fortifications into rubble shortly after noon Sunday. The massed naval rifles poured shells into the targets for more than three hours, clearing the way for the troops. [1:7.]

A British naval intelligence officer said in this city that the Germans had been so skillfully outmaneuvered that they massed their air defenses to counter a feint invasion aimed at Calais and Boulogne, leaving Normandy without protection. [5:1.]

Dense fog halted air operations from Britain, but a heavy force of American bombers from Italy smashed oil refineries, rail yards and an airplane plant in the Vienna area. The Luftwaffe offered the heaviest opposition in weeks. [1:6.]

Another vaunted German line crumbled when the Red Army captured Vitebsk and Zhlobin, anchors of the "Fatherland Line." More than 45,000 enemy troops were trapped at Vitebsk, and at one point the Russians were thirty-four miles from the old Polish frontier. A record number of 1,700 places was liberated in the general advance. Gains were also reported from the Karelian Isthmus on the Finnish front. [1:5-6; map P. 6]

The Fifth Army in Italy entered the port of Piombino without a fight and, inland, advanced to within fifteen miles of Siena and forty-five of Florence. The Eighth Army crossed the Chienti River northeast of Foligno in hard fighting. [6:1.]

Marines on Saipan, in the Marianas, have scaled Mount Tapotchau and dug in at the summit. The southern part of Garapan, on the west, was in American hands, and the Japanese have been cleared from Kagman Peninsula on the east. Carrier planes did widespread damage to shipping, installations and grounded enemy aircraft at enemy bases on Guam and Rota. [1:4; maps P. 7.]

Allied forces have captured Mogaung in Burma and gained on all fronts from the Indian border to China, where Hsiangta was recaptured. [7:5.] The Japanese, after seizing Hengshan and Yuhsien, were unable to push closer to Hengyang in China's Hunan Province. [7:4.]

14 WARSHIPS SHELL CHERBOURG AT ONCE

British Newsman Describes Destruction of Batteries Defending Harbor

By DESMOND TIGHE
Reuter Correspondent

ABOARD H.M.S. GLASGOW, off Cherbourg Harbor, June 25 (Delayed)—American battleships and heavy cruisers, supported by two British cruisers and seven destroyers, are firing broadside after broadside into German shore batteries at vital key points on the fringes of Cherbourg harbor in support of the Army.

The bombardment started at exactly eleven minutes past 12 this morning and has lasted for more than three hours with German long-range 450-mm. shore batteries returning the fire vigorously.

As I watched this bombardment from the bridge of H.M.S. Glasgow, victor of the recent Bay of Biscay battle, we are steaming steadily some 15,000 yards off the breakwater of Cherbourg harbor.

Air Resounds With Crashes

Our six-inch guns are blazing away as shells scream into a German fort. The air resounds with the crash of broadsides from the battleships, cruisers and destroyers. The Channel sea is whipped with wicked looking grey-black splashes as we are straddled time and time by German shore batteries.

The German gunnery is good and although we are plastering their concrete gun emplacements with tons of high explosives some of them keep on firing.

The United States bombardment task force is commanded by Rear Admiral Morton L. Deyo, United States Navy. Admiral Deyo is flying his flag in the heavy cruiser Tuscaloosa. Among the warships in his battle squadron are the battleships Texas, Nevada, Arkansas; the American cruiser Quincy, and the two British cruisers, Glasgow and Enterprise. We are escorted by a

Continued on Page 4

Pockets of Nazis Kept on Sniping As Americans Overran Cherbourg

By HAROLD DENNY
By Wireless to THE NEW YORK TIMES.

WITH THE AMERICAN FORCES at Cherbourg, June 26—The Germans fought a last-ditch defense in Cherbourg this evening, though the outcome was inescapable. Substantial elements of the American forces got into the city from the south only after a piece-by-piece conquest of succeeding strong points and the Germans were still firing on them in the city and from two pillboxes remaining on Fort du Roule with 88-mm. field-pieces and machine guns. The city has been considerably damaged but less than one would have thought. As a whole it is intact, though many individual buildings have been smashed.

Dominating all was the arsenal, where the last important holdout group was still firing rifles while large portions of the structure were burning with a red glow and towering black smoke.

Holding out about equally with the arsenal was one last desperate little group of cannoniers at Fort du Roule.

It stands like Gibraltar and should have been impregnable. Its fortifications of reinforced concrete, several stories deep and tunneled into solid rock, remind one of the Maginot Line fortresses, which I visited the first winter of this war. They include an electric light plant, underground barracks, an underground hospital and abundant stores of everything conceiv-

Continued on Page 4

VICTORY IN FRANCE

Capture of Port Seals First Phase of Allied Liberation of Europe

FIGHT SHARP TO END

British Reported Near Main Enemy Highway at Base of Peninsula

5 A. M. Communique

By The Associated Press.

SUPREME HEADQUARTERS, Allied Expeditionary Force, Tuesday, June 27—The capture of Lieut. Gen. Carl Wilhelm von Schleiben, commander of the Cherbourg garrison, and Rear Admiral Hennecke, Nazi sea defense commander of Normandy, was announced today in Allied communiqué No. 43 confirming the fall of Cherbourg.

"Cherbourg's liberation came after a final day of fierce fighting in the northwestern part of the city," the communiqué said.

"In the battle the enemy has lost the greater part of four infantry divisions, numerous naval and marine units and line of communication troops."

Of the British gains on the east side of the beachhead, it said:

"A strong attack toward the Villers-Bocage-Caen main road has secured Cheux and Fontenay, and has advanced several miles in the face of heavy German armor and infantry. Progress continues."

By DREW MIDDLETON
By Cable to THE NEW YORK TIMES.

SUPREME HEADQUARTERS, Allied Expeditionary Force, Tuesday, June 27—Cherbourg, France's third greatest port, has fallen to the American troops in the first outstanding victory of the Allied campaign to liberate France.

The fall of Cherbourg, after a siege that lasted a week from the moment the first shells from American field guns began to pound its defenses, was officially announced here this morning just after 7 o'clock double British summer time [1 A. M. in New York.]

With the taking of the city the first phase of the campaign in which the Allies were forced to build up their armies without the use of a large port came to an end. It was estimated here recently that supplies for two divisions could be moved through Cherbourg within forty-eight hours after its fall.

Captives May Total 30,000

Last night American patrols mopped up the remaining German resistance in the vicinity of the naval base and arsenal and cleaned out snipers from buildings along the waterfront, where individual Germans held out until the last.

Although there has been no official estimate of the number of prisoners yet, it is probable the city's fall will bring more than 30,000 German soldiers and sailors into the Allied cages.

Cherbourg was the second French port and naval base to fall to Lieut. Gen. Omar N. Bradley. Bizerte in Tunisia was taken by the United States Second Army Corps under his command on May 7, 1943.

The struggle for Cherbourg drew to its victorious close yesterday when in the rain and chill wind doughboys mopped up the port. By nightfall more than one-third of the port had been occupied and by midnight two-thirds of the city was in Allied hands.

At dawn Monday 3,400 German prisoners had been taken and it is probable that twice that number was captured in the mopping up operations yesterday.

The Germans were driven from five remaining strongholds during the early evening by grenade, bay-

Continued on Page 3

U.S. Signal Corps

Cherbourg's General von Schlieben and Admiral Hennecke were among the first top Nazis captured.

"All the News That's Fit to Print"

The New York Times.

LATE CITY EDITION
POSTSCRIPT
Partly cloudy and warm today.
Temperatures Yesterday—Max., 80; Min., 66
Sunrise, 5:29 A. M.; Sunset, 8:31 P. M.

VOL. XCIII...No. 31,573. Entered as Second-Class Matter, Postoffice, New York, N. Y. NEW YORK, TUESDAY, JULY 4, 1944. THREE CENTS IN NEW YORK CITY

RUSSIANS CAPTURE MINSK ON 11TH DAY OF PUSH; AMERICANS OPEN NEW OFFENSIVE IN NORMANDY; NEW U. S. LANDING MADE IN SOUTHWEST PACIFIC

COMMUTERS DEFY MAYOR TO TAX THEM FOR SUBWAY COSTS

Westchester, Jersey City and Nassau Ready to Fight Levy on Those Who Work Here

LEGALITY IS QUESTIONED

Councilman Cohen Warns of Retaliation—City Leaders Still Studying Rent Tax Plan

Mayor La Guardia's proposal to tax commuters forty cents a week, as part of a transportation tax to cover the cost of subway deficits and transit improvements, met instant opposition in suburban areas yesterday. In the city, leaders of business, taxpayer, civic and real estate organizations refrained from comment on the Mayor's tax plan until they could study it further.

The Mayor, in his Sunday broadcast, offered the transportation tax, comprising six different levies, to raise $51,700,000, to be submitted with an alternative proposal of a 10-cent fare to the voters at a special referendum election before July 1, 1945. The defeat of both would retain the 5-cent fare, with the mounting subway deficit—now $41,118,808—carried by the real estate tax as at present.

Mayor's Estimates of Revenue

The tax on commuters working in the city but not living here was estimated by the Mayor to yield $5,200,000. A total of $44 500,000 would be raised through a 2 per cent tax on rents of residential properties, to be paid by tenants, a 2 per cent tax on charges for rooms in hotels and lodging houses, and a 2½ per cent tax on rents of non-residential properties. In addition there would be a 1 per cent tax on interest on mortgages, to yield $2,000,000, to be paid by the person or institution receiving the interest. The Mayor's alternative proposal of a 10-cent fare would raise an estimated $125,000,000.

In Mineola, L. I., County Executive J. Russel Sprague announced that "Nassau County would oppose any attempt of New York City to tax Nassau County commuters for the support of New York City's subway system." As a Republican national committeeman and a leader of the State Republican party, Mr. Sprague's influence would be felt in the Legislature, from which the city would have to get authorization for the new tax and its component parts. Marcus G. Christ, county attorney, concurring in Mr. Sprague's opposition, said he would study the Mayor's plan closely.

Westchester Starts Inquiry

In White Plains the Westchester County Board of Supervisors directed County Attorney William A. Davidson and its committee on miscellaneous affairs to investigate the commuter tax proposal after Supervisor Francis T. Leonard of New Rochelle had characterized the proposed tax as "unfair to residents of suburban areas such as Westchester County." Mr. Leonard, a lawyer who commutes daily to New York, said thousands of Westchester commuters would be affected. He also doubted the legality of the commuter tax.

Gustavus T. Kirby, chairman of the Westchester County Planning Commission, called the tax "asinine and ruinous." He said that increasing the subway fare would be far better, "but the whole thing is that La Guardia is afraid an increase would kill him politically."

County Executive Herbert C. Gerlach said the tax was too controversial for him to comment on at this time. Mayor Stanley W. Church of New Rochelle said that "offhand" he was opposed to it, but wanted to study it before reaching a final conclusion.

In Jersey City Mayor Frank Hague announced through a spokesman that he would fight the proposed levy on salaries of workers who commute to New York. The spokesman said:

"Mayor Hague will offer vigorous opposition to this or any new

Continued on Page 33

Flag of U. S. Capitol Flies in Rome Today

By The United Press.

ROME, July 3—The American flag that flew over the Capitol in Washington on Dec. 8, 1941, when Congress declared the existence of a state of war with Japan, and three days later, when war was declared on Italy and Germany, will be flown from the first captured enemy capital on July 4, it was announced today.

President Roosevelt originally suggested that the Stars and Stripes be unfurled over Rome on Independence Day. It will be flown from a special flagpole now being erected on the Piazza Venezia, the scene of many of Benito Mussolini's bombastic speeches.

Reveille and retreat ceremonies will be arranged by the Rome area Allied command. American military bands and the Fifth Army color guard of honor will take part.

WORLD BANK URGED BY KEYNES AS VITAL

He Says It Would Cut U. S. Risks on Loans, Promote 'Expansion,' Not 'Inflation'

By RUSSELL PORTER

Special to The New York Times.

BRETTON WOODS, N. H., July 3—Lord Keynes, chairman of the British delegation to the United Nations Monetary and Financial Conference, described for the first time today the broad outlines of the plan for setting up of a $10,000,000,000 international bank for reconstruction and development to "guarantee" international loans somewhat after the fashion of the Reconstruction Finance Corporation in domestic loans.

Speaking at an afternoon meeting of the bank commission, which will draw up proposals for approval by the conference as a whole, Lord Keynes, who is economic adviser to the British Treasury, said that the plan originated in the United States Treasury.

He called it a sound, fundamental contribution to the post-war task of rebuilding the world for a new age of peace and progress and declared that it would promote "expansion" and not "inflation."

Asks Speeding of Bank Work

The World Bank program is entirely separate from the currency stabilization goals of the proposals for an international monetary fund, also being considered here, but both plans are closely related, not only to one another, but also to the whole broad United Nations program of international cooperation to lay the economic foundation for the post-war world. The bank and the fund are intended to be permanent institutions.

Lord Keynes urged the delegates and their technical advisers, who had not given as much attention to the bank as to the fund, since they have considered the fund to be the more urgent problem, to speed their consideration of the bank proposals.

He asserted that the bank should be ready by the end of the war,

Continued on Page 15

DRIVE ON LA HAYE

Bradley's Troops Seize Hills North of Town and Village to East

GUNS POMMEL FOE

British Widen Salient Again—Attack by U. S. Surprises Germans

5 A. M. Communique

By The Associated Press.

SUPREME HEADQUARTERS, Allied Expeditionary Force, Tuesday, July 4—Allied troops in the neck of the Cherbourg Peninsula made gains up to two and one-half miles yesterday despite heavy rain that restricted air support, communiqué No. 57 announced today.

American troops pressed their offensive toward La Haye du Puits and at their most advanced point stood within about two and one-half miles of this key road junction.

The Germans made more counter-attacks against the British in the Odon River bridgehead in the Caen sector, but all were beaten off.

"The weather improved somewhat yesterday evening and defended localities, gun positions and a fuel dump in the Lessay area were effectively attacked by fighter bombers," the communiqué said.

By DREW MIDDLETON

By Cable to The New York Times.

SUPREME HEADQUARTERS, Allied Expeditionary Force, Tuesday, July 4—The American First Army has launched an offensive southward from the base of the Cherbourg peninsula toward La Haye du Puits. The assault, which smashed forward on a thirty-mile front in a driving rain, began yesterday morning at 5:30 o'clock after days of hammering at German positions by massed artillery, and by late last night it had swept forward from a mile to three miles along the entire front.

While the American line sprang forward in the First Army's second large-scale attack of the campaign, the British Second Army to the east, after four days of beating off savage counter-attacks by Field Marshal Gen. Erwin Rommel's armored divisions, captured the village of Brettevillette on the west of the salient and broke up a small enemy counter-blow early in the morning.

Rain Soaks British Sector

Operations were slowed down throughout the British sector by torrential rains that turned roads into swamps, hindering artillery as well as aerial bombardment.

Four weeks after the opening of the invasion the Allies are driving forward to the west and have retained their grip of the salient southwest of Caen to the east. Most of this has been accomplished

Continued on Page 3

DANISH PATRIOTS IN DEMONSTRATION AGAINST NAZI RULE

The caption for this picture, received here yesterday from Stockholm, says it shows citizens around a street barricade in a workers' district of Copenhagen.

Associated Press Radiophoto

ARNOLD SAYS REICH RATIONS AIR FUEL

Doubts Luftwaffe Will Fight Effectively Again—Predicts Similar Blows at Japan

By SIDNEY SHALETT

Special to The New York Times.

WASHINGTON, July 3—The United States Army Air Forces have definite information that, because of its blows against German oil centers, which have reduced the enemy's fuel supply to an estimated 30 per cent of normal, the Luftwaffe and the rest of Germany's mechanized forces are being "rationed," Gen. H. H. Arnold revealed today. It is at least a possibility, he indicated, that the

Continued on Page 6

Doughboys Land on Numfor, Swiftly Win Main Airfield

By FRANK L. KLUCKHOHN

By Wireless to The New York Times.

ALLIED HEADQUARTERS, in New Guinea, Tuesday, July 4—American troops have landed on Numfor Island, roughly 100 miles west of Biak Island and 800 miles southeast of the Philippines, as Gen. Douglas MacArthur resumed his advance toward his announced goal.

General MacArthur again fooled the Japanese, throwing his infantry ashore at an unexpected point on the west side of the island near the key Kamiri airdrome at 8 o'clock Sunday morning without opposition except from scattered shore guns, which American and Australian cruisers, destroyers and bombers quickly silenced. Less than two hours later at 9:51 A. M. the Kamiri airdrome, best of Numfor's three airfields, was captured.

Moving southward, our troops

Continued on Page 12

War News Summarized

TUESDAY, JULY 4, 1944

The First and Third White Russian Armies swung suddenly together from two sides of Minsk yesterday and captured the German-held citadel in a climax of their present offensive. Elsewhere along the battle line the Red Army carried the fighting into the streets of Polotsk and the outskirts of Molodechno and also drove closer to Baranovichi. More than 1,000 towns were liberated and almost 75,000 Germans, including two divisional commanders, were captured. The campaign in Finland also progressed. [1:8; map, P. 5.]

The United States First Army launched a new offensive south toward La Haye du Puits in an evident attempt to isolate the Cotentin Peninsula from the rest of France. A day-long artillery barrage preceded the assault, which was carried forward from one to three miles along a thirty-mile front. Heavy rains did not halt the American troops, who routed German machine-gun nests while wading chest-deep across flooded mine fields. Although the mud held down the use of tanks, British forces in the Caen sector scored several gains. [1:3; map, P. 2.]

On the third European front, the Fifth Army in Italy captured Siena, thirty-one miles below Florence, and on the western coast was only fifteen miles from Leghorn. German delaying positions around Lake Trasimeno in the center were broken and the Eighth Army moved to within fifteen miles of Arezzo. Ancona, on the Adriatic coast, lay less than nine miles from the Allies' positions. [1:6; map, P. 8.]

Throughout German-occupied Europe the enemy was also in trouble, disorders on a mounting scale being reported from many countries. [7:1.] The threat of starvation, instead of halting the Copenhagen general strike, was reported to have resulted in spreading resistance. [1:7.]

Some 750 Fortresses and Liberators from Italy smashed enemy oil facilities in the Balkan countries for the second consecutive day. [4:1.]

The Allies' bombing of Germany's oil resources has resulted in rationing for the Luftwaffe and motorized divisions, General Arnold said. The enemy's fuel supply has been cut to 30 per cent of normal and aircraft production has been reduced by 70 per cent, he declared, adding that the same fate was in store for Japan. [1:4.]

General MacArthur launched his Philippine-bound forces 100 miles nearer their goal in a swift amphibious operation against Numfor Island, west of Biak. Opposition was slight and Kamiri airfield was seized within two hours. [1:5-6, map, P. 12.] On Saipan, in the Marianas, Americans were advancing through the ruins of Garapan, the capital city, and a final battle was expected in the narrow northern end of the island. [12:1.]

The Japanese, slowed down at Hengyang in China, were reported using poison gas again. They by-passed the city and cut in from Anjen to below Leiyang, nearly fifty miles south of Hengyang and that much closer to Canton. [12:4.]

Ambassador Armour, recalled from Argentina, is expected in Washington today. [1:6-7.] He probably will clarify the assertion of the Argentine War Minister that the State Department's summary of his "expansionist" speech was so altered and mutilated as to change its meaning completely. [13:1.]

ALLIES TAKE SIENA, ART TREASURE CITY

Americans and French Find It Undamaged—5th, 8th Armies Drive Toward Gothic Line

By The Associated Press.

ROME, July 3—American and French forces occupied the medieval city of Siena, thirty-one airline miles from Florence, early today without damage to its famous art and architectural treasures, while American troops on the west coast who had evicted the Germans from Cecina in bitter house-to-house fighting thrust on within fifteen miles of the prize port of Leghorn.

The quick and virtually uncontested capture of Siena by French infantry and American artillery and tank units followed weeks of hard fighting on its mountainous approaches. A special announcement of the city's fall came immediately after a communiqué said the French had fought to within two miles of its ancient walls.

[Monday's German High Command communiqué said Nazi troops were withdrawn north of Siena without pressure to spare

Continued on Page 8

DANES PUSH STRIKE, DEFY BOMB THREAT

Copenhagen Halt Spreads to Provinces—Nazis Said to Agree to Oust Quislings

By The United Press.

STOCKHOLM, Sweden, July 3—Copenhagen remained under a state of siege today and a general strike spread to the Danish mainland despite appeals of municipal authorities and labor leaders for an end of demonstrations which had caused the Germans to threaten to starve the capital and, if necessary, to bomb it.

The situation was not clear, but reports that the strike had ended were premature. There were new clashes during the night in Copenhagen, according to advices. Many failed to return to work today and the strike spread to about twenty provincial towns, including Aarhus on the mainland. Many dairy farms were idle.

[Declaring that the "Copenhagen clique" had "run riot," the German Foreign Office's NPD agency said in a dispatch monitored by the Federal Communications Commission that the Danish capital would "remain cut off from all provisions" until the general strike was ended and order restored.]

Though water, gas and electric services had been restored by the Germans in Copenhagen, most factories remained closed. It was reported that the Germans resumed essential services in fear that passive resistance would become active. The Danish patriot press service here said that a German economic delegate in Copenhagen had insisted, in an angry dispute

Continued on Page 7

Increased Pressure on Argentina Is Possible After Hull Sees Armour

By BERTRAM D. HULEN

Special to The New York Times.

WASHINGTON, July 3 — The Argentine situation will be taken up for intensive study upon the arrival here tomorrow of Norman Armour, who was recalled from his post as United States Ambassador in Buenos Aires, for consultation.

If Mr. Armour holds views similar to those said to be held by a number of our diplomatic staffs in the field and of some Latin-American diplomats here, there may be no further rupture in the situation.

Until he arrives, however, and outlines his views at some length, nothing can be taken for granted in this respect.

It was said today that the State Department would not confront Mr. Armour with a set program and that the conversations would be fluid. At the same time there were indications that Secretary of State Cordell Hull might make a statement on the situation in a few days. This might lead to economic sanctions or only to continuing the present avoidance of ambassadorial relations and the diplomatic isolation that that entails.

On the other hand, some constructive measures can be envisaged; the present breach may be subjected to a healing process.

If economic sanctions should be applied, it is assumed that some measures would have to be devised to find substitute sources for essential war products now obtained from Argentina. She supplies meat to Great Britain and through that channel to our soldiers serving in

Continued on Page 13

Nation's E Bond Total Lags at 60% With 92% of Over-All Quota Sold

Sales of Series E bonds—the issue of lower denominations designed for purchase by the man in the street—lagged sadly last night as the city, State and nation rapidly approached over-all quotas in the Fifth War Loan Drive ending Saturday.

The nation, with $14,685,000,000 of a $16,000,000,000 quota already in hand, had attained 92 per cent of its goal. The State had raised 84.7 per cent of its $4,801,000,000 quota, with sales totaling $4,067,600,000. New York City's sales, totaling $3,632,140,972 was 87.2 per cent of its $4,167,028,000 goal.

These were over-all sales, however, including issues designed for large individual investors, banks, corporations and other groups not eligible for the Series E bond. In the E bond category the nation had reached only 60 per cent of its quota, the State 36.2 per cent and the city 35.6 per cent.

In point of actual sales in bonds of this category, the national figure was $3,607,000,000, as against a $6,000,000,000 goal; the State figure $133,000,000, as against $367,000,000; and the city figure $81,075,131, as against $227,526,600.

A heartening note, because of the stress that has been placed on E bond sales in this drive, was the fact that all the figures on E sales were forty-eight hours old. Because of the volume of business, the Treasury Department was unable to tabulate Sunday and Monday sales. It was hoped that such a tabulation would reveal a sizable

Continued on Page 32

BASTION TOPPLES

Fate of Minsk Garrison in Doubt as Nazis Flee on Bottleneck Roads

FIGHTING IN POLOTSK

Street Battles Rage in Junction—Drive for the Baltic States Looms

By The United Press.

LONDON, Tuesday, July 4—Red Army forces yesterday captured the ancient White Russian capital of Minsk, last major enemy bastion in pre-war Russia on the road to Warsaw, while troops of the Soviet northern wing moving toward Latvia and Lithuania pushed into the streets of Polotsk, where vicious fighting was reported.

Minsk was captured on the eleventh day of a whirlwind Soviet offensive that has driven the Nazis 165 miles back across White Russia and Poland and cost them more than 213,000 men killed or captured.

The city of 238,000 was captured by the combined forces of Gen. Ivan D. Chernyakhovsky's Third White Russian Army and Marshal Konstantin K. Rokossovsky's First White Russian Army, which outflanked Minsk and then took it by storm, Premier Stalin announced in an order of the day.

While Minsk was falling, other Soviet forces smashed through powerful defense belts to open a street battle with the Germans in Polotsk, five-point rail junction 122 miles northeast of Minsk.

Red Army Near Molodechno

Forty miles northwest of Minsk the Russians smashed into the outskirts of Molodechno rail junction in what appeared to be the beginning of a drive against Vilna, sixty-five miles to the northwest on the Minsk-Molodechno-Koenigsberg railroad. On the southern end of the 400-mile front the Russians cleared a thirty-mile stretch of the Sluch River, pre-1939 frontier of Poland and Russia.

A dispatch from Moscow, filed after 324 Moscow guns had fired twenty-four salvos to salute the triumph, said:

"The fall of Minsk marked the collapse of the entire German position in White Russia and is regarded here as one of the decisive battles of the war. The Germans are now retreating in disorder under the threat of encirclement."

The Germans still had open a fifty-six-mile-wide escape gap leading westward from Minsk across country devoid of first-class roads.

The Germans now hold only about 8,000 square miles of pre-war Soviet territory — approxi-

Continued on Page 5

Stimson in Italy To Inspect Front

By Wireless to The New York Times.

ROME, July 3—Henry L. Stimson, United States Secretary of War, arrived today at an airfield in Italy for a brief tour of this theatre of war. He plans to visit the front line and inspect troops and hospitals as well as to hold conferences with important figures.

Mr. Stimson was accompanied on the trip from the United States by Harvey H. Bundy, special assistant to the Secretary; Maj. Gen. Alexander D. Surles, director of public relations for the War Department; Maj. Gen. Norman T. Kirk, War Department Surgeon General; Lieut. Col. William H. Kyle, aide to Mr. Stimson; Col. T. E. Kreps, the Secretary's pilot; Capt. William T. Hodge and an enlisted stenographer.

Somewhere in Africa the Secretary's party was joined by Maj. Gen. I. H. Edwards and Lieut. Col. E. Shumaker, aide to Lieut. Gen. Jacob L. Devers, deputy supreme commander of the Mediterranean theatre.

"All the News That's Fit to Print"

The New York Times.

LATE CITY EDITION
Partly cloudy with moderate winds today.
Temperatures Yesterday—Max.,80; Min.,66
Sunrise, 5:43 A. M.; Sunset, 8:22 P. M.

Copyright, 1944, by The New York Times Company.

VOL. XCIII..No. 31,590. Entered as Second-Class Matter, Postoffice, New York, N. Y. NEW YORK, FRIDAY, JULY 21, 1944. THREE CENTS NEW YORK CITY

ROOSEVELT NOMINATED FOR FOURTH TERM; HITLER ESCAPES BOMB, PURGES GENERALS; CAEN DRIVE GAINS; RUSSIA OPENS NEW PUSH

FUEHRER 'BRUISED'

Bomb Wounds 13 Staff Officers, One Fatally—Assassin Is Dead

'USURPERS' BLAMED

Hitler Names New Chief of Staff—Himmler to Rule Home Front

Texts of Hitler, Doenitz and Goering speeches, Page 3.

By JOSEPH SHAPLEN

Adolf Hitler had a narrow escape from death by assassination at his secret headquarters, the Berlin radio reported yesterday, and a few hours later in a radio broadcast to the German people he blamed an "officers' clique" for the attempt to kill him. His address disclosed a movement in the armed forces to overthrow him and his regime. He announced that a purge of the conspirators was under way.

Thirteen members of his military staff were injured, one fatally and two seriously, by a bomb set off at an undisclosed place while many of his highest advisers were assembled around him. The man who played the role of assassin, Hitler said, was Colonel Count von Stauffenberg, one of his collaborators, who stood only six feet away from him as he hurled the bomb. Von Stauffenberg is dead, Hitler announced.

Waiting to see Hitler before the assassination attempt was Benito Mussolini. Reich Marshal Hermann Goering, who rushed to Hitler's side, was in the immediate vicinity. Hitler escaped with singes and bruises.

Army Clique Blamed

While Dr. Joseph Goebbels and Nazi radio propagandists at first tried to put the blame for the attempt to kill the Fuehrer upon the Allies, Hitler himself exploded the bombshell by announcing that the culprits were a group of German Army officers. He thus confirmed reports of a serious rift between the Nazi High Command and German military elements.

In his broadcast, recorded by the Federal Communications Commission, Hitler told the German people: "If I address you today I am doing so for two reasons: first, so that you shall hear my voice and know that I personally am unhurt and well, and, second, so that you shall hear the details about a crime that has no equal in German history.

"An extremely small clique of ambitious unscrupulous and at the same time foolish, criminally stupid officers hatched a plot to re-

Continued on Page 3

Nazi-Army Rift Is Revealed In Gravest Reich War Crisis

'Usurpers' Who Hatched Plot Not Named—Accused of Being Officer Group Wanting to Repeat the 1918 'Stab in the Back'

By RAYMOND DANIELL
By Cable to The New York Times.

LONDON, July 20—Broadcasting so that the German people could hear his voice and know that he was unhurt after the attempt to assassinate him, Chancellor Adolf Hitler confirmed tonight all rumors and suspicions of disaffection and unrest in the Reich.

Heinrich Himmler, the Fuehrer said, has been made commander in chief of the home army to "create order once and for all." Hitler also ordered that no "military authority, no leader of any unit, no private in the field" was to obey any orders emanating from "usurpers" who were seeking peace.

He left the identity of those usurpers something of a mystery, for he referred to them as "a small group that emerged in Germany, just as in Italy, in the belief that they could repeat the 1918 stab in the back." Later he said they had "no bond with or nothing in common with the Wehrmacht, and, above all, none with the German people."

It is clear that a real crisis has arisen in the Reich and it remains to be seen whether the Nazis have chosen the wisest way to deal with it. A purge is as likely to widen the schism as not, and the German people, with their traditional respect for their officer class, may feel that if the Nazis choose war, and the old officers favor peace, the time may have come to question the infallibility of the Fuehrer.

The announcement left open to speculation the question of not only who was behind the assassination attempt but, even more interesting, the question of who in Germany was in position to make the attempt.

That Germany is going through

Continued on Page 3

Admiral and General Told To Form New Tokyo Regime

Gen. Kuniaki Koiso, a member of the same Kwantung Army group to which former Premier Gen. Hideki Tojo belongs, arrived in Tokyo from Korea yesterday to participate with Admiral Mitsumasa Yonai in the formation of a new "critical decisive wartime" Cabinet by "command" of Emperor Hirohito, it was disclosed in Japanese broadcasts and press dispatches reported to the Office of War Information by the Federal Communications Commission.

General Koiso, Governor General of Korea, and Admiral Yonai, a former Premier and member of the Supreme War Council, were summoned as "senior leaders of the army and navy," the Japanese Domei agency said. Each is 64 years old.

Meanwhile, the Domei agency, in a wireless dispatch to the controlled East Asia press, warned its bureaus to be "on the alert" for new developments, presumably regarding an announcement of the new Cabinet's membership.

"Competent political observers expect that the new Cabinet will be formed swiftly," Domei said. Another Japanese account predicted that the new Government would be formed by "Friday morning at the latest."

Co-Premiership Doubted

Koiso and Yonai were designated to form a new Government after Emperor Hirohito had called in Marquis Koichi Kido, Lord Keeper of the Privy Seal, to sound out Japan's "elder statesmen" for candidates to serve as the nucleus for what Domei termed a "more powerful Cabinet."

In a continuation of the "elder statesman" system of choosing Cabinet leaders, Kido then called a caucus of former Premiers. After this meeting, the following an-

Continued on Page 3

ALLIES STORM ARNO ON A 25-MILE FRONT

Americans, in Hot Pursuit of Bewildered Germans, Plunge to Town 12 Miles From Pisa

By The Associated Press.

ROME, July 20—American troops battered their way across the Arno River Valley on a 25-mile front between Pisa and Florence today as German forces, bewildered by the sudden breakthrough, retreated to escape across the Arno into the mountain defenses of their Gothic Line.

Lieut. Gen. Mark W. Clark's doughboys held complete control of hill masses overlooking the Arno from the south, and American artillery raked the entire valley in search of German rear-guard units protecting the withdrawal of the main body of enemy forces to the north of the stream.

German resistance was confined almost entirely to these small groups armed with automatic weapons—tactics similar to those that delayed the entry of General Clark's troops into Rome an entire day. One American column was firmly established on the south bank of the Arno at Pontedera, twelve miles inland from Pisa.

An Allied spokesman said Ger-

Continued on Page 5

Nazi Party Clashes With Army Reported

BERNE, Switzerland, July 20 (UP)—Skirmishes took place in various parts of Germany today between Nazi party members, led by SS [Elite Guard] Troopers, and groups of the regular army, according to unconfirmed reports reaching here tonight.

Conferences of the Nazi party organization were held in all principal cities of the Reich this evening, and members were asked to reaffirm their loyalty to the party and to Adolf Hitler, according to reliable information. Zurich reported that responsible quarters there had information that a subversive movement was under way in various parts of the Reich.

By Wireless to The New York Times.

BERNE, Friday, July 21—There were unconfirmed reports at the Swiss-German frontier shortly after 1 o'clock this morning that some shooting had occurred on the other side of the line, but whether or not it indicated mutiny could not yet be ascertained.

Allies Report Belgian Uprising Comparable to French Sabotage

By Wireless to The New York Times.

SUPREME HEADQUARTERS, Allied Expeditionary Force, July 20—Belgium's extensive and complicated network of rail and road communications was reported in a special Allied communiqué today to have been "largely disrupted" as the result of the "highly satisfactory" operations of the Belgian underground. The communiqué was the first from Supreme Headquarters to mention the Belgian resistance movement that has been declared by Belgian authorities to be a formal military organization the same as the French Forces of the Interior.

Reporting that Belgian operations "throughout the entire country" had "contributed substantially to the delaying movement of enemy reinforcements to the battle area," the communiqué also said that French forces had detained a Panzer division moving toward Normandy for thirty hours and had wrecked twenty-six strategic bridges between June 24 and July 6.

Eighty Germans were killed and 300 wounded in the attack on the Panzer division, said the communiqué, which also confirmed an earlier French report that patriots had destroyed a train carrying flying bombs in eastern France.

From July 4 to 15, the communiqué said, the French forces continued operations "in face of violent German attacks," defeating or eluding the Germans in every case.

In addition, the French slowed traffic on the "whole railway sys-

Continued on Page 4

BRITISH PUSH SOUTH

Take Troarn Rail Depot While Second Column Captures Bourguebus

ENEMY SLOWS DRIVE

Strong Anti-Tank Belt Checks Smash Toward Plains Before Paris

By DREW MIDDLETON
By Cable to The New York Times.

SUPREME HEADQUARTERS, Allied Expeditionary Force, Friday, July 21—Tanks and infantry of the British Second Army, battling stubborn German rearguards at Troarn and St. André-sur-Orne, yesterday, widened the eleven-mile front south and east of Caen that Lieut. Gen. Miles C. Dempsey's troops have punched out in three days of audacious and arduous fighting.

Strong German anti-tank positions northwest of Vimont slowed down the advance to the southeast toward Vimont, momentarily at least. However, British artillery and infantry were assaulting these positions last night as the second stage of the great trial of strength with the Seventh German Army opened.

British Positions Solid

Bourguebus, five and a quarter miles southeast of Caen, was the most important of a dozen towns and villages taken by the British in the twenty-four hours ended at midnight last night. It is almost in the center of an arc extending from the Orne west of St. André to the railroad station at Caen, which marks the area in which the Second Army is solidly established.

Farther to the south, southeast and east, in front of the main positions, British tanks were operating against the German lines, seek-

Continued on Page 4

LWOW IS MENACED

Red Army Near Polish City—New Wedge Is Driven From Kovel

GRIP ON BUG WIDENS

Foe's Supply Lines Cut—Dvinsk Rail Link Slashed on West

By W. H. LAWRENCE
By Wireless to The New York Times.

MOSCOW, Friday, July 21—Revealing another terrific Red Army offensive, Marshal Joseph Stalin announced last night that forces led by Marshal Konstantin K. Rokossovsky, after three days' fighting in the Kovel sector, had driven a wedge thirty-one miles deep on a 123-mile front, pushing the Germans back to the western Bug River.

He disclosed, also, that Marshal Ivan S. Koneff's First Ukrainian Army had captured Rawa Ruska, an important rail junction, severing the most direct supply and retreat route for the Germans' outflanked Lwow garrison.

These new triumphs over the battered, reeling German Army at the southern end of the eastern front were celebrated in Moscow at 10 and 11 P. M. by two salutes of twenty salvos each from 224 guns—demonstrations that brought hundreds of thousands of Muscovites into the streets.

The first salute was directed to Marshal Rokossovsky in tribute to the drive of his forces from Kovel through the strongly fortified German defense line, which culminated in reaching the western Bug at Opalin and in the capture of more than 400 inhabited points. Opalin, on the eastern side of the Bug, is less than fifteen miles from Chelm on the road to Lublin.

Other forces under Marshal Kon-

Continued on Page 6

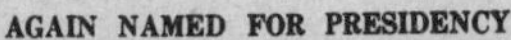
AGAIN NAMED FOR PRESIDENCY

Franklin Delano Roosevelt
Associated Press, 1944

Roosevelt's Acceptance

Following is the text of President Roosevelt's acceptance speech from a Pacific Coast naval base, as recorded and transcribed by THE NEW YORK TIMES:

Mr. Chairman, ladies and gentlemen of the convention, my friends:

I have already indicated to you why I accept the nomination that you have offered me, in spite of my desire to retire to the quiet of private life.

You in this convention are aware of what I have sought to gain for the nation, and you have asked me to continue.

It seems wholly likely that within the next four years our armed forces, and those of our Allies, will have gained a complete victory over Germany and Japan, sooner or later, and that the world once more will be at peace, under a system, we hope, that will prevent a new world war. In any event, whenever that time comes new hands will then have full opportunity to realize the ideals which we seek.

In the last three elections the people of the United States have transcended party affiliation. Not only Democrats but also forward-looking Republicans and millions of

Continued on Page 3

War News Summarized

FRIDAY, JULY 21, 1944

An almost successful attempt on Hitler's life and Emperor Hirohito's command to two jingo war lords to form a new Japanese Cabinet pushed actual battlefield developments into the background yesterday.

Hitler was conferring at his secret headquarters with the staff of the German High Command, Berlin said, when Col. Count von Stauffenberg, one of his collaborators, threw a bomb at the Fuehrer. Although the assassin was only six feet away Hitler escaped with bruises and burns. One of the thirteen staff officers was killed and two others were seriously injured.

Shortly after the explosion Hitler informed the German people of what had happened, blaming an "officers' clique" that wished to bring about a revolt. He immediately placed Gestapo Chief Himmler in absolute command within the Reich, said the "criminal elements" would be ruthlessly exterminated and indicated grave concern by warning all soldiers and civilians not to obey orders unless they had been confirmed. He also named Col. Gen. Guderian Chief of Staff, replacing Field Marshal Gen. Keitel. [All the foregoing 1:1.]

In Japan, Admiral Mitsumasa Yonai, Premier during the tense days of early 1940, and his then Overseas Minister and later Governor General of Korea, Gen. Kuniaki Koiso, were commissioned to form a "critical decisive wartime" Cabinet. Both men are militarists and expansionists of the Tojo type. [1:2-3.]

Allied statesmen saw in both developments evidence of crisis in the enemy camps. London observers believed that Hitler's order for a new purge indicated clearly that unrest within Germany was general [1:2-3], while former Ambassador Grew and Secretary of State Hull in Washington expressed the prevalent opinion that Tokyo had at last admitted the gravity of the military situation. They warned, however, against expecting a Japanese collapse. [3:6.]

On the actual war fronts Allied gains were reported everywhere. The British Second Army in France was widening its eleven-mile bulge south and east of Caen and trying to force Field Marshal Rommel into a decisive tank battle. Americans advanced in the St. Lô area and crossed the River Ay to a depth of 300 yards in the Lessay sector. [1:4, map P. 2.] The resistance movement that has proved so effective in France has spread into Belgium. [1:2-3.]

Although torrential rains slowed Allied progress in Italy the Fifth Army reached the Arno River along a twenty-five-mile front above Leghorn and was close to Pisa. [1:3.]

Overhead some 2,000 planes from Britain and nearly 1,000 from Italy teamed in a coordinated attack on aircraft plants, ball-bearing factories, airfields and other targets in southeast Germany. It was one of the war's most concentrated blows. [5:1.]

The Russians scored the most impressive gains in a new offensive in the Kovel area. The Red Army reached the western Bug River on a wide front after driving as deep as thirty-one miles on a 123-mile line in three days. Another advance brought Soviet troops to within five miles of Lwow and a flanking thrust cut the main German supply and escape railroad. [1:5; map P. 6.]

Action in the Pacific was on a lesser scale. American planes blasted Guam with 721 tons of bombs in two days. [7:5.] Chinese troops were attacking the Japanese from within Hengyang and from outside the Hunan city [7:1] while along the Burma front other Chinese routed an enemy relief force trying to reach Pingka. [6:6.]

PRESIDENT FAVORS TRUMAN, DOUGLAS

Would Take Either as Running Mate, Letter to Hannegan Says—Battle Gets Hotter

By JAMES A. HAGERTY
Special to The New York Times.

CHICAGO, July 20—In an attempt to bolster the waning strength of Senator Harry S. Truman of Missouri for the nomination for Vice President, Robert E. Hannegan, Democratic national chairman, made public tonight the letter written to him by President Roosevelt, saying that either Senator Truman or William O. Douglas, justice of the United States Supreme Court, would be satisfactory to him as a running mate and would add strength to the ticket.

Mr. Hannegan said he had not made the letter public earlier because he considered it necessary to obtain the consent of the sender before releasing a personal letter for publication. He said he had talked today with President Roosevelt by telephone and had received such consent.

The letter, which was written on White House stationery and dated July 19, 1944, was as follows:

"Dear Bob:

"You have written me about Harry Truman and Bill Douglas. I should, of course, be very glad to run with either of them and believe that either one of them would bring real strength to the ticket.

"Always sincerely,
"FRANKLIN D. ROOSEVELT."

The letter was addressed to

Continued on Page 10

ARMS USE TO KEEP PEACE IS PLEDGED

Platform Backs World Role on Sovereignty Basis—Opposes Racial Vote Ban

Text of the Democratic platform is on Page 12.

By CHARLES E. EGAN
Special to The New York Times.

CHICAGO, July 20—A platform calling for the participation of this country with the United Nations in a world organization, empowered to use armed force when necessary to preserve international peace, was adopted by the Democratic convention tonight.

It committed the party to support a program to have the United States join in "the establishment of an international organization based on the principle of the sovereign equality of all peace-loving states, open to membership by all such states, large and small, for the prevention of aggression and the maintenance of international peace and security."

Embodied also in the platform was a plank stating that racial and religious minorities "have the right to live, develop and vote equally with all citizens and share the rights that are guaranteed by our Constitution."

The platform, of 1,500 words, carried expressions in favor of the opening of Palestine to unrestricted Jewish immigration and

Continued on Page 12

VOTE IS 1,086 TO 90

Byrd Gets 89, Farley One—President on Radio Accepts

STANDS ON RECORD

Says 'Experience,' Not 'Immaturity,' Will Win War, Peace and Jobs

Wallace and Barkley texts, Page 10; Jackson's, Page 11.

By TURNER CATLEDGE
Special to The New York Times.

CHICAGO, July 20—Franklin Delano Roosevelt of New York was nominated today for a fourth term as President of the United States by a noisy, irritable Democratic convention, meeting in the same hall where he was chosen for his first term in 1932 and for a third in 1940.

A few hours later, speaking to the convention directly by radio from his train at a Pacific Coast naval base, he accepted the nomination and opened his re-election bid on the note of "experience" versus "immaturity."

Mr. Roosevelt asserted that he considered the convention's action as a call upon him to serve. He said it was up to the American people in the November election to decide whether plans already made and men already serving to achieve victory and make America and the world a better place in which to live were to be continued or supplanted by an administration with no program but to oppose.

His Three-Point Program

He presented a three-point program—to win the war, to secure the peace with force if necessary, and to build an economy with full employment and a high standard of living—as a promise of himself and the party which had called him again to lead.

In this election, he said, the people would not consider "glowing words or platform pledges," but would decide on the record made in the war and in "domestic achievements."

The President said he was too busy, and the emergency too serious, to permit him to engage in an active campaign for re-election.

But he added that he should "feel free" to report to the American people from time to time on the progress of their efforts and to "correct misstatements of fact" which might be made by the Republican opposition.

He disclosed that he was on the West Coast now in pursuance of his "constitutional duties" in connection with the war.

Roar of Cheering for Speech

The President's words came strong and magic-like through the loud speaker system—just as it did in his acceptance speech at his third-term nomination in this hall four years ago.

At the end the crowd in the arena and galleries broke into uproarious cheering. People were still shouting in a deafening roar when adjournment was moved. They attempted to shout down the motion.

The motion was carried, however, and the convention recessed at 10:55 o'clock until 11:30 tomorrow morning when it will reassemble to settle the Vice Presidential nomination.

The renomination of the President went through swiftly.

Mr. Roosevelt received 1,086 votes on the first roll call. Senator Harry F. Byrd, who was not a candidate, received 89, and James A. Farley, former chairman of the Democratic National Committee, who would not let his name go before the convention, received one from the Byrd block of New York.

A telegram notifying the President of his nomination was dispatched to him immediately by Senator Samuel D. Jackson, Per-

Continued on Page 9

U.S. Marine Corps

Marines place the first U.S. flag on Guam.

U.S. Marine Corps

Marines with flame thrower on Guam.

"All the News That's Fit to Print"

The New York Times.

LATE CITY EDITION
Clear with light to moderate winds today.
Temperatures Yesterday—Max., 76; Min., 66
Sunrise, 5:43 A. M.; Sunset, 8:21 P. M.

VOL. XCIII..No. 31,591. Entered as Second-Class Matter, Postoffice, New York, N. Y. NEW YORK, SATURDAY, JULY 22, 1944. THREE CENTS IN NEW YORK CITY

NAZIS BLOCK PLOT TO SEIZE GOVERNMENT; AMERICANS LAND ON GUAM, PUSH INLAND; TRUMAN NOMINATED FOR VICE PRESIDENCY

2D BALLOT DECIDES

Wallace, Leading 429½ to 319½ on First, Is Crushed 1,100 to 66

BREAK BY MARYLAND

Real Fight Ends With Big Shift by Illinois—Ready, Says Senator

By TURNER CATLEDGE
Special to THE NEW YORK TIMES.

CHICAGO, July 21—Senator Harry S. Truman of Missouri was nominated tonight as the Democratic candidate for Vice President in the fifth and final session of the twenty-eighth national convention of the party.

He appeared immediately before the cheering delegates massed in the arena of the great hall to accept his "responsibility" as a running mate in President Roosevelt's bid for a fourth term in the White House.

Directly following the nomination, support of the ticket was pledged by Vice President Henry A. Wallace, James A. Farley, former National Chairman, and Sidney Hillman, head of the CIO Political Action Committee, which had supported Mr. Wallace.

Mr. Truman's victory, which was also an overwhelming defeat for the renomination hopes of Vice President Wallace, came on the second ballot. The official announcement of the tally clerks gave the Missouri Senator 1,100 votes to 66 for Mr. Wallace and 4 for Associate Justice William O. Douglas.

[A tabulation of this ballot by The Associated Press from official records of the convention gave: Truman 1,031, Wallace 105. Other votes in the compilation were: Governor Cooper of Tennessee, 26; Senator Barkley of Kentucky, 6; Justice Douglas, 4 and Paul V. McNutt, 1.]

Truman Speaks to Throng

Mr. Truman, who rose from comparative political obscurity in Kansas City to win the second highest honor of his party, was sitting on the platform eating a sandwich when the result was announced.

Pulled up to the microphone by Senator Samuel D. Jackson of Indiana, permanent chairman of the convention, Senator Truman responded to the demands from the crowd for a word.

"You don't know how very much I appreciate the very great honor which has come to the State of Missouri," he said in a halting, shy manner. "It is also a great responsibility which I am perfectly willing to assume.

"Nine years and five months ago I came to the Senate. I expect to continue the efforts I have made there to help shorten the war and to win the peace under the great leader, Franklin D. Roosevelt.

"I don't know what else I can say, except that I accept this great honor with all humility. I thank you."

It was the shortest speech of the day and was appreciatively applauded by a crowd that literally had become surfeited with oratory. A moment later the convention passed into history on a motion by Governor Herbert O'Conor of Maryland to adjourn sine die.

"This convention has completed the business for which it was assembled, to nominate the next President and Vice President of the United States," he said.

Swing Led by Maryland

Senator Truman, President Roosevelt's second choice for place, ran through to win the nomination after having trailed Vice President Wallace on the first ballot by 110 votes.

On the opening roll-call Mr. Wallace received 429½ ballots and Mr. Truman 319½, with the remainder scattered among fourteen other candidates who had been named in nominating speeches or

Continued on Page 8

ROOSEVELT'S RUNNING MATE

Harry S. Truman — Blackstone, 1944

Monetary Parley Agrees On Terms of World Bank

By RUSSELL PORTER
Special to THE NEW YORK TIMES.

BRETTON WOODS, N. H., July 21—The United Nations Monetary and Financial Conference reached an agreement today on a plan for an $8,800,000,000 International Bank of Reconstruction and Development to guarantee post-war international investments. The total capital of the world bank is the same as the aggregate of the international monetary fund to stabilize currencies which was accepted last week. Thus two vital parts of the post-war program to try to insure world peace and prosperity have been accepted, with some reservations, by all the forty-four United and Associated Nations participating in the conference, subject to the approval of the Congress of the United States and the executive and legislative branches of other Governments.

In order to reach an agreement, the United States delegation had to abandon its position that the subscriptions to the bank, which represent each country's risks in guaranteeing international loans, should be the same as the quotas in the fund, which represent a country's rights to acquire foreign exchange with which to buy goods in the world market.

However, it is the opinion of the United States delegation, after receiving the advice of its four members of Congress, two Republicans and two Democrats, and its one banker member, Edward E. Brown, president of the First National Bank of Chicago, that the fund and bank agreements have been

Continued on Page 28

BIG CITY BOSSES WON OVER HILLMAN

Two Presidential Letters Had Important Influence on Convention Strategy

By JAMES A. HAGERTY
Special to THE NEW YORK TIMES.

CHICAGO, July 21—Somewhat belatedly, leaders of the Democratic organizations in a score and a half of States, headed by big city bosses, Edward J. Flynn and Frank V. Kelly of New York, Mayor Edward J. Kelly of Chicago, Mayor Frank Hague of Jersey City and Robert E. Hannegan, national chairman, of St. Louis, brought about the nomination of Senator Harry S. Truman of Missouri for Vice President by the Democratic National Convention.

By the nomination the Democratic politicians won a victory over Sidney Hillman, chairman of the Congress of Industrial Organizations Political Action Committee, who stuck to Vice President Henry A. Wallace to the last and whose influence had been suffi-

Continued on Page 10

Farley Pledges Roosevelt Backing, Accepting Decision of Convention

Special to THE NEW YORK TIMES.

CHICAGO, July 21—James A. Farley, former Democratic national chairman and former Postmaster General, announced tonight that he would support President Roosevelt for re-election despite his opposition to a fourth term.

"I have been opposed on principle to a third or fourth Presidential term," Mr. Farley said in a statement, which he released just after the nomination of Senator Truman for Vice President. "For that reason, I voted for the nomination of Senator Harry F. Byrd of Virginia for President.

"Having participated in the proceedings of the convention, I accept its decision and will support the party nominees."

Mr. Farley declined to amplify his statement. He resigned recently as chairman of the New York State Democratic Committee and is not expected to take an active part in the campaign.

Mr. Farley, who was of great help to Mr. Roosevelt in the latter's first nomination for President and in his first and second campaigns for election, broke with the Chief Executive during the latter part of Mr. Roosevelt's second term.

Secretary of the New York State Democratic Committee in 1928, when Mr. Roosevelt was first elected Governor of New York, Mr. Farley was promoted to State chairman and managed Mr. Roosevelt's campaign for re-election as Governor in 1930. Mr. Roosevelt's plurality of 730,000 at that elec-

Continued on Page 9

RUSSIANS RACE ON

Bug River Is Crossed Again on Wide Front Due East of Lublin

LWOW BATTLE BEGUN

Brest-Litovsk Railway to Chelm Cut—Ostrov Is Captured in North

By W. H. LAWRENCE
By Cable to THE NEW YORK TIMES.

MOSCOW, Saturday, July 22—The Soviet battle for the liberation of Poland began in earnest yesterday as the Red Army smashed across the Bug River from Lyuboml on a thirty-seven-mile front and advanced up to nine miles beyond the west bank. In that operation the railroad between Chelm and Brest-Litovsk was severed.

Other Red Army forces moved closer to Lwow and to Brest-Litovsk, and the Soviet High Command announced that Soviet troops had captured 570 inhabited points on both the northernmost and the southernmost sections of the front.

At the northern end of the front, troops of the Third Baltic Front executed an outflanking maneuver and captured the important enemy stronghold and communications hub of Ostrov—a victory that Moscow celebrated with a salute of twelve salvos from 124 guns.

Although the capture of Ostrov won the salute, from a military and strategic point of view the biggest news was the crossing of the Bug west of Lyuboml by Marshal Konstantin K. Rokossovsky's First White Russian Army and the nine-mile advance beyond it, which sent his troops streaming toward Lublin and Warsaw.

In the sector southwest of Brody, where four or five German divisions are encircled, Marshal Ivan S. Koneff's First Ukrainian Army continued the process of extermination, capturing 2,000 more prisoners and 100 artillery pieces. The

Continued on Page 5

BEACHHEADS SET UP

Americans Invade Guam After Mighty U.S. Blow From Sea and Air

OPPOSITION IS LIGHT

Resistance Increases as Japanese Are Pushed Toward Inland Hills

By GEORGE F. HORNE
By Telephone to THE NEW YORK TIMES.

PEARL HARBOR, July 21—United States assault troops and sea forces began yesterday the long awaited invasion of the big island of Guam and have established good beachheads against light opposition, although resistance increased in some sectors as the Americans drove inland.

[Front dispatches reported that the landings were made on either side of Port Apra, The Associated Press said. From the shore areas, where Japanese defenses had been blown to pieces, the invaders drove swiftly toward a range of hills in the interior.]

They stormed ashore after enemy defenses received their seventeenth straight day of heavy attack from the air. All this week, up to the time of the landings, surface units of the Fifth Fleet had battered the island with tons of steel. They continued yesterday, covering the marines and Army assault troops making the invasion. A terrific rain of 627 tons of bombs and 147 rockets was unloosed by our planes in the day preceding the landings.

Admiral Chester W. Nimitz, Commander in Chief of the Pacific Fleet and Pacific Ocean areas, announced the landings at 1:30 o'clock this morning.

Japanese Are Weakened

With Saipan securely in our hands, the tremendous Pacific forces have turned, as was expected, to carry retribution to the Japanese where their strongly armed and confident forces poured ashore

Continued on Page 7

War News Summarized

SATURDAY, JULY 22, 1944

The few facts seeping through the tight German censorship yesterday indicated that the anti-Hitler revolt was still alive and that a purge of anti-Nazi leaders was still under way. German army officers who attempted to take Hitler's life simultaneously tried to take over the government offices in Berlin, the German radio said. The same source declared the revolt had been mercilessly suppressed and that Propaganda Minister Goebbels had frustrated the attempt to seize the Government offices. A Stockholm report said two German divisions had revolted Wednesday in East Prussia, while another dispatch from Switzerland relayed unconfirmed reports of a revolt among German naval units at Kiel and Stettin. [1:8.]

Secretary of State Hull attributed the unrest in Germany and the attack on Hitler to a spreading realization in the Reich of impending defeat. He cautioned, however, against overoptimism on an early end of the war in Europe. [3:2-3.]

Red Army forces blasted a thirty-seven-mile-wide hole in Hitler's much-publicized "East Wall" defenses along the Bug River and are threatening to crumble the whole German defense structure guarding Warsaw, now only eighty-two miles away. Other Russian troops seized Ostrov, the last Nazi fortress before the Latvian border on the direct route to Riga. The Red Army was increasing its threat to the imperiled strongholds of Lwow, Brest-Litovsk, Kaunas and Dvinsk by the hour, as beaten German armies fell back everywhere along an almost continuous 800-mile front from Finland to the Carpathian foothills. [1:4; map P. 5.]

Allied troops in Normandy slugged through rain and mud to cement positions below Caen to a depth of five miles. Canadians seized St. André-sur-Orne and St. Martin-de-Fontenay near Caen as the enemy gave ground slowly. American forces increased their pressure on Périers after winning a foothold on the road from St. Lô to Périers. [1:6-7; map P. 3.]

The two-way aerial offensive from Britain and Italy continued for the fourth consecutive day as nearly 3,000 American bombers and fighters pounded a dozen German targets. [4:1.] Ground troops in Italy pierced strong German Arno River defenses, forcing the water barrier into the mountain fringes of the "Gothic Line" in at least one place. [1:7.]

Striking at Japan's inner defense zone, American assault troops landed on Guam Island, first American territory seized by the Japanese, early Thursday and have established good beachheads. Admiral Nimitz reported that additional troops were landing against light initial Japanese resistance, and that casualties were moderate. A terrific naval and aerial bombardment of the strategic island, 1,565 miles southeast of Tokyo, softened up the enemy defense before our landings. As our troops moved inland the Japanese put up stiffened resistance in some sectors. [1:5; map P. 7.]

In China fierce fighting raged around Hengyang for the twenty-sixth day as relief forces attacking Japanese troops who have besieged that major junction on the Canton-Hankow railroad drove deeper into the enemy lines. [6:1.]

Drive South of Caen Stalls As Rain Floods Battle Area

British Forced to Withdraw Armored Units—Canadians Beat Off Fierce German Counter-Attacks in Mud and Mists

By DREW MIDDLETON
By Cable to THE NEW YORK TIMES.

SUPREME HEADQUARTERS, Allied Expeditionary Force, Saturday, July 22—British and Canadian infantrymen, their uniforms muddy and sodden after thirty-six hours of heavy rains, were fighting a grim, bloody battle for Verriers and St. Martin-de-Fontenay on the British Second Army sector south of Caen last night, but the remainder of the Allied front in Normandy was quiet save for the measured pounding of cannon and mortars.

The offensive launched by the Second Army Tuesday morning with such high hopes had stalled, frustrated as much by the thick dough-like mud that covered the roads and fields as by the lethal fire of German anti-tank positions around Vimont. These positions now must be rooted out by infantry and artillery, under adverse conditions for the attackers, while British armored divisions follow the example of German Panzer units and retire from the battlefield until the stage has been set for a great armored battle for the road to Paris.

The gains registered yesterday were all on the western flank of the Second Army's salient along the east bank of the Orne River. Canadians were fighting German infantrymen for Etavaux and St. André-sur-Orne in conditions reminiscent of World War I.

At St. Martin-de Fontenay, half a mile south of St. André-sur-Orne, the Canadians took the village and then stood off a heavy German counter-attack supported by tanks. When the counter-attack was over the Canadians went forward to find German dead lying thick on the muddy ground. The enemy casualties were "satisfactory," a report from the front said.

There was mud and mist everywhere and little knots of men were fighting silently with bayonets in a dank, dripping world where gun flashes were the only light.

The weather, which has favored the enemy since D-day, has imposed a stalemate on the operations in this sector, although farther west British infantrymen

Continued on Page 3

British Label Hitler Attack Rivals' Bid for False Peace

By Cable to THE NEW YORK TIMES.

LONDON, July 21—Although the news from Germany is taken as an indication of a grave crisis within the Reich, there is no disposition here to regard it as a ground for hoping for an early termination of hostilities. As The Times of London will say tomorrow, when the enemy "wavers," that is the time for throwing in reserves, not for relaxing.

It is strongly felt here that Adolf Hitler's rivals, far from being converts to the Allied cause, are merely another brand of champions of militarism who merely believe themselves better able to rescue the Reich from disaster than the present Nazi leaders.

Their game, it was said, is to supplant Hitler so as to try to make peace on terms that would preserve the Wehrmacht for another war under more favorable conditions. Therefore, it is recognized by the people as well as officials that even had the officers' coup succeeded, peace would still be a long way off.

Generals Reach Conclusion

"Unconditional surrender" is still an Allied condition of an armistice, and there is little conviction here that even the generals who would like to rid their country of Hitler would accept that without continuing the struggle in the hope of getting better terms later.

However, this evidence of a rift in the façade of German unity is recognized as important evidence that at least some German military leaders have reached the conclusion that the Nazi direction of the war has brought Germany to a

Continued on Page 3

U. S. PATROLS STAB ACROSS ARNO RIVER

Pierce Mountain Fringes of Gothic Line While British Thrust Nearer Florence

By The United Press.

ROME, July 21—American Fifth Army combat patrols pierced strong German Arno River defenses today, forcing the river into the mountain fringes of the Gothic Line in at least one point, while artillery blasted German installations north of the river from captured high points on the south bank.

The Americans took advantage of improved weather to roll up scattered German resistance groups south of the river, while on the coast German guns of all calibers hammered the battered port of Leghorn from advantageous positions on Mount Pisano, northeast of Pisa.

This height, on which the Germans have installed many field guns, anti-aircraft batteries, machine guns and pillboxes, affords

Continued on Page 5

Invaders Find Defenses of Guam Blown to Shreds by Our Attacks

By JOHN R. HENRY
Of International News Service
For the Combined Allied Press

ABOARD A FLAGSHIP AT GUAM, July 21 (Guam Time)—A liberation force of Third Amphibious Corps marines and Army troops thundered ashore at Guam today with the destructive blast of a Pacific typhoon.

The Leathernecks spearheaded two separate beachhead assaults, storming across coral-studded shorelines in the wake of a 17-day sea and air bombardment that reached a stupefying crescendo as landing craft churned into remnants of the Japanese coast defenses.

Casualties were described as "light" for United States forces. The Japanese dead were uncounted.

At nightfall Maj. Gen. Roy Geiger's Third Amphibious Corps troops dug in on perimeters between Adlup and Asan, a point north of Orote Peninsula, and from the shattered town of Agat to Bangi Point, south of the rocky finger of land.

The northern beachhead, where the terrain was most rugged, stretched in an arc several thousand yards. The southern force shoved inland and established its own substantial beachhead. General Geiger is a marine aviator and veteran South Pacific commander.

So effective had been the preparatory barrages that troops flowed ashore with negligible initial resistance and in record time.

Despite sprinkling enemy fire

Continued on Page 7

HITLER HUNTS FOES

Thousands of Officers Reported Arrested in Purge of Army

MUTINY IS RUMORED

Sailors at Kiel, Stettin and Troops in East Said to Revolt

By RAYMOND DANIELL
By Cable to THE NEW YORK TIMES.

LONDON, Saturday, July 22—Although reports from Berlin insist that the plot of army officers to overthrow the Nazi regime and seize power themselves has been suppressed and its instigators liquidated, the isolation of the Reich from the rest of the world continues and it is apparent that counter-measures are being pressed.

[A Swiss report to The United Press said it was understood that German naval units had revolted at Kiel and Stettin. Stockholm dispatches said 5,500 German officers had been arrested throughout Germany and that there had been disorders in eastern Germany and East Prussia.]

Everything suggests that the plot that had its climax in the attempt to assassinate Adolf Hitler was deep and well laid, with far-reaching ramifications. On evidence supplied by the highest Nazi authorities it is known that the plotters, who included Col. Gen. Ludwig Beck, who was dismissed as Chief of Staff by Hitler in November, 1938, attempted to kill Hitler and bring off a coup d'état.

The scheme apparently succeeded to the point where the conspirators were able to issue orders in conflict with the plans of Hitler and other Nazi leaders.

Leaders Revealed Troubles

The extent of the disaffection seemingly caused such consternation in the Nazi camp that Hitler, Reichmarshal Hermann Goering and Grand Admiral Karl Doenitz felt impelled in the small hours yesterday morning to try to set things straight by urgent appeals, even though their action involved disclosure to a hostile world that a rift had developed between some high army officers and the Nazi party on the best way to save Germany from destruction.

There is no evidence to show that the challenge to Hitler's leadership and domination of the Nazi party has spread to the civilian population but Transocean, German news agency, revealed that certain "precautionary measures" had been taken in the center of Berlin.

Alfred Rosenberg, Nazi party "philosopher," writing in a special edition of the Voelkischer Beobachter yesterday morning, called the attempt on Hitler's life the opening of hostilities on a "fifth front."

Some additional light on what happened in the Reich in those crucial hours preceding Hitler's broadcast was provided last night from Berlin. According to the official story, provided for soldiers in the field, a clique that was connected with "an enemy power" had obtained control of "certain means of communications" through a subordinate officer.

Major Informed Goebbels

Through these channels, it was said, orders were sent to Major Remer, commandant of a battalion of the Berlin guard, telling him Hitler was dead, that disorders had been reported in the Reich and that the Wehrmacht had taken over the government. Major Remer was directed to occupy with his force the administrative headquarters at Berlin, which he did.

But then, according to this account, Major Remer immediately communicated with Propaganda Minister Joseph Goebbels, head of the Berlin municipal administration, who convinced him that he had been obeying faked orders. The fact that "traitors" had laid hands on certain communications systems brought about yesterday

Continued on Page 2

"All the News That's Fit to Print"

The New York Times.

LATE CITY EDITION
Fair and continued warm today but less humid.
Temperatures Yesterday—Max., 88; Min., 75
Sunrise, 5:57 A. M.; Sunset, 8:06 P. M.

VOL. XCIII—No. 31,607. Entered as Second-Class Matter, Postoffice, New York, N. Y. NEW YORK, MONDAY, AUGUST 7, 1944. THREE CENTS NEW YORK CITY

FOUR U. S. COLUMNS ARE DRIVING TOWARD PARIS; ALLIES TURN WHOLE GERMAN LINE BELOW CAEN; 46 JAPANESE SHIPS SUNK OR DAMAGED IN BONINS

STRIKERS GO BACK IN PHILADELPHIA; SOLDIERS ON CARS

Six-Day Transit Tie-Up Ends in Rush to Comply With Army's Work Deadline

LEADERS ARE OUT ON BAIL

Grand Jury to Start Inquiry Wednesday Into Possible Plot to Cause Walkout

By WALTER W. RUCH
Special to The New York Times.

PHILADELPHIA, Monday, Aug. 7—Virtually complete service was restored to the lines of the Philadelphia Transportation Company early today as hundreds of striking workers, returning to their posts in a steadily increasing stream, broke the back of the six-day, unauthorized walkout.

Officials of the company, making a survey under supervision of Army officers, said that at midnight service over the various subway, elevated, bus and trolley lines was about 90 per cent of normal for a Sunday night. They reported, too, that 95 per cent of all the striking employes had signed cards indicating their intention of being on the job today.

The strike was broken as steel-helmeted soldiers in full battle dress rode each vehicle throughout yesterday and last night to protect the driver and passengers.

Discrimination Disproved

There was no violence. The only untoward incident reported came last evening when a Negro, mistaking a soldier's command to move to the rear of a bus as an attempt to enforce a Jim Crow custom prevailing in the South, left the bus at the next intersection to spread word through the Negro neighborhood that the soldiers were discriminating against Negroes.

Investigation disclosed that the soldiers, to keep bus aisles clear, were directing everyone, white and Negro alike, to the rear when seats were available there.

Additional police protection was sent into the area of the incident and police cars began to escort buses on the line.

No statement was issued from the headquarters of Maj. Gen. Philip Hayes, War Department representative handling the operation of the transit system, but the Army made no secret of its satisfaction with developments.

The strike, which began at 4 A. M. Tuesday in protest against the employment of Negroes as operators of passenger-carrying equipment, ended with the same conditions prevailing as provoked the walkout. By Army order, all employes are to go back to their same positions and this would mean that the eight Negroes who on Tuesday were undergoing training to operate vehicles would take it up again this morning if they desired.

Some Yield Grumblingly

The back-to-work movement began early yesterday in response to the swift series of developments Saturday night when, in rapid succession, General Hayes issued his uncompromising ultimatum to the strikers, four of the strike leaders were arrested on Federal warrants charging violation of the Smith-Connally anti-strike law, more than 5,000 fully armed troops poured into the city and a Federal grand jury investigation of the strike was ordered.

In his ultimatum General Hayes said that strikers who disobeyed his deadline would lose their jobs, be barred from other work during the war and, if between the ages of 17 and 37, be sent into the armed services.

Counseled by their leaders not to remain out any longer, the strikers started to yield, some grumblingly, before dawn yesterday. At every car barn the spirit of resistance began rapidly to melt away.

With the back-to-work movement under way, scores of agents

Continued on Page 24

Term Black Widow Deadliest Plane

By The Associated Press.

HAWTHORNE, Calif., Aug. 6—The Northrop Aircraft, Inc., announced today that the War Department had approved the release of heretofore carefully guarded details of the P-61 Black Widow night fighter, termed the world's largest and most powerful pursuit plane.

The company gave this picture:

Black Widow crews and ammunition boxes are protected from .30 and .50 caliber enemy machine gun fire by specially designed armor plate, bullet resistant glass and deflector plates.

Incorporated into the ship is the first full-span landing flap, for low landing speed, combined with a new-type aileron which retracts into the upper section of the wing, giving the Black Widow unusual maneuverability.

OIL TERMS REACHED BY U. S. AND BRITAIN

Creation of an International Commission Is Expected to Be Announced This Week

By JAMES B. RESTON
Special to The New York Times.

WASHINGTON, Aug. 6—The United States and Great Britain will createa, probably this week, an International Oil Commission designed to regulate the development and distribution of world petroleum supplies.

This commission, which was arranged during the negotiations between Richard Law, British Minister of State; Lord Beaverbrook, British Lord Privy Seal; Secretary of State Cordell Hull and Secretary of the Interior Harold Ickes, will be opened to all the other oil countries of the world and both British and American officials will seek to have other nations join the commission and do their business through it.

The agreement, negotiated in Washington during the last fortnight, takes note of Great Britain's need to acquire dollars from the sale of oil in the Middle East, and the right of Great Britain to raise the difficult question of her dwindling dollar reserves has been protected in the agreement.

Some Progress Toward Peace

The oil agreement is regarded as evidence that the Administration is making some progress from war to peace, but in the international as in the national field most observers here believe that military events are running ahead of the Government's plans.

As a result of past international conferences certain agreements have been made with the other United Nations on policies to govern the control of relief and rehabilitation, food, international currency and civil affairs in the countries now in the process of liberation.

In other fields at least tentative

Continued on Page 7

FLEET HITS CONVOY

Task Force Sinks 17 Ships, Including Five Japanese Warships

CRUISER LEFT AFIRE

U. S. Surface and Air Forces Strike Bonin, Volcano Islands

By GEORGE HORNE
By Telephone to The New York Times.

PEARL HARBOR, Aug. 6—Forty-six Japanese ships and small craft were sunk or damaged on Thursday and Friday when a fast United States carrier task force caught a large convoy in the Bonin and Volcano Islands area, and slashed away at it in a continuing action for the two full days, Admiral Chester W. Nimitz announced today.

Along with these successes Admiral Nimitz told of a widespread attack by the task force the same two days on the Bonin and Volcano Islands, near Japan's front door.

Of the convoy craft at least five warships of destroyer or destroyer-escort class were sunk and several others damaged. Seventeen ships are listed as definitely sunk, six possibly sunk and more than twenty-three craft were damaged, including a number of barges, two of which were carrying troops. The convoy included cargo vessels, oilers and landing craft.

Convoy Virtually Destroyed

Admiral Nimitz said that the convoy was virtually wiped out by air and surface units of the task group. On Thursday, the 3d, planes sank four cargo ships of about 4,000 tons each, three escorting destroyers or destroyer-escorts and four barges. One cargo vessel and the balance of the escorting war craft, not identified as to type, were damaged.

That day another large destroyer, a cargo ship, one small oiler and several barges were sunk by our surface vessels. One damaged escort vessel escaped.

The next day the American sea force "continued the sweep," the admiral said. Carrier planes sank one escort vessel and two other small craft and damaged five barges including the two troop carriers, a landing craft and three smaller vessels.

One light cruiser and five small vessels were left burning and listed as possibly sunk. In addition damage was inflicted on ten small craft and a destroyer escort. A large cargo vessel which had been hit in one of the earlier attacks was struck again and two landing ships were damaged.

The carrier task force attacked enemy bases throughout the Bonin and Volcano Islands, shelling shipping and shore installations at Chichi Island and destroying Omura, a town on that island. On

Continued on Page 8

High of 88° Is Recorded for Day; Millions Seek Relief at Beaches

The current heat wave tapered off slightly yesterday, with temperatures in the city ranging from one to twelve degrees below those of the previous forty-eight hours, when three local Weather Bureau records were established.

In addition light breezes and low-hanging, moisture-laden clouds that hid the sun throughout most of the day made pedestrians a bit more comfortable. The high for the day was reached at 2 P. M., when the official reading atop the Whitehall Building at 17 Battery Place was 88 degrees. At that time the reading at La Guardia Field was 85.2, the day's high there.

The Weather Bureau said that there was little likelihood that the heat wave would break in the next seventy-two hours, the extent of publishable predictions, but announced that today would continue warm and there would be a sharp drop in the amount of humidity.

The five city-operated beaches reported near-capacity crowds, but parks were virtually empty except for the lake areas of Central and Prospect Parks, where hundreds braved the heat to wait in line for boats. The Rockaways reported 1,325,000 visitors and Coney Island more than a million. Jones Beach was host to 55,000 persons, one of its largest assemblages since the war.

Although the normal for Aug. 6 is 76 degrees and the record high is 93.3, set in 1918, the mercury stood at 79 at midnight, dropped to a low of 75 at 5 A. M. and then moved slowly upward. At noon it had climbed to 85. The day's high was seven degrees less than the top for Saturday.

After 2 P. M. the temperature dropped steadily and at 10 o'clock last night was a fairly livable 77. However, the humidity, which was only 49 per cent when the high

Continued on Page 24

THE AMERICAN FORCES MOVE INTO THE KEY CITY OF RENNES

Vehicles passing through a narrow path left in a street by cheering citizens of the Brittany capital
Associated Press Wirephoto (U. S. Signal Corps Radiophoto)

8TH ARMY FIGHTING INSIDE OF FLORENCE

Troops Surge Over Arno Span as German Guns Shell South Part of City, Periling Art

By The United Press.

ROME, Aug. 6—Eighth Army troops crossed the Arno River on debris-littered Ponte Vecchio into the heart of Florence today and engaged enemy troops in sharp street fighting as the Germans, despite repeated assurance that Florence would be an open city, opened fire with 170-mm. guns—largest German guns in Italy—against Allied-held sectors of the great cultural center south of the river.

[The London radio, reported by the Columbia Broadcasting System, said Sunday that "Florence is virtually in our hands," but cautioned that a British Broadcasting Corporation reporter described it as "still something of a No Man's Land."

[The BBC reporter said that South African troops had thrown pontoon bridges across the river

Continued on Page 6

Urge Lend-Lease to Britain Continue After Reich Falls

By LANSING WARREN
Special to The New York Times.

WASHINGTON, Aug. 6—Continuation of lend-lease aid to Britain after Germany's defeat and at least until Japan surrenders is under discussion in high Administration circles, according to a statement in The NAM News, weekly publication of the National Association of Manufacturers, appearing today.

British officials, the statement says, have told our leaders that such action is absolutely necessary to stave off a serious economic situation in England and is essential if Britain is to play the part expected of her in the Pacific war.

The proposal, it was said, would cost the United States $2,500,000,000 and up a year above war costs, and would be a wide departure from the present lend-lease program, which is primarily devoted to prosecution of the war.

What worries those in favor of the project most is how to obtain the support of Congress and also how to avoid similar claims from Russia, France, Belgium, Holland and other countries.

United States officials supporting the proposal, according to the manufacturers' publication, have

Continued on Page 16

RUSSIANS CAPTURE HUGE OIL REFINERY

Drogobych in Galicia Yields 700,000 Tons a Year—Fight Is Severe at Warsaw

By The United Press.

LONDON, Monday, Aug. 7—Russian troops yesterday captured the great Polish oil center of Drogobych, wiping out the next to last major source of fuel for Hitler's war machine, while other Soviet forces extended their control of the Vistula River's east bank to more than 200 miles.

Drogobych, a city of 32,600 population in the Carpathian foothills forty-four miles southeast of Przemysl, was seized by troops of the Fourth Ukrainian Army, apparently under a new commander, Col. Gen. I. Y. Petroff, a hero of Novorossiisk and the Kuban bridgehead.

Its capture was announced in an order of the day issued by Premier Stalin, and it was the first time that the Fourth Ukrainian Army, last reported commanded by Gen. Feodor N. Tolbúkhin, had been re-

Continued on Page 6

FIGHT TO A FINISH PLEDGED BY HITLER

Nazi Party Leaders Informed at Meeting Germany Needs Man Who Won't Capitulate

Adolf Hitler told his party leaders in a meeting at his headquarters that the "criminal clique" that made the bombing attempt on his life on July 20 was "limited in numbers but important in influence," DNB, German news agency, said yesterday.

Quoting the National Socialist party organ, the Nationalsozialistische Parteikorrespondenz, DNB said Hitler told the assembled officials that "one day they would realize that this deed, which at the moment was so shameful, had perhaps been most beneficial for the whole German future," since it had made it possible to eliminate the "criminal clique" which up to then had not been uncovered.

Hitler said that since July 20 he had "gained a confidence" he had never had before and that he was now able to "carry on the struggle" better than anyone else who might lead the German people.

"Necessary to the Nation"

"I believe that I am necessary to the nation, that it needs a man who will under no circumstances capitulate," Hitler was quoted.

The meeting with the Nazi party leaders was held Friday at Hitler's headquarters, said the DNB dispatch, which was reported by the Federal Communications Commission.

Reichsleiter General Ritter von

Continued on Page 7

War News Summarized

MONDAY, AUGUST 7, 1944

Paris was the objective of four American armored spearheads that had passed a point fifty-three miles northeast of Rennes and were within 140 miles of the French capital at the nearest point after roaring through the towns of Mayenne, Laval and Chateau-Gontier yesterday. Other American troops, having overrun Brittany, were fighting in Brest and near Lorient, St. Nazaire and Nantes, all prize ports. [1:8, map P. 3.] All seven ships of a convoy thought to be evacuating German troops from St. Nazaire were sunk; another convoy was shelled back into port. [1:6-7.]

Almost 2,000 planes took off in continuing good weather from Britain and Italy to smash military installations in Germany and in the Rhône valley of France. Berlin, Hamburg and Kiel inside Germany and the submarine base at Toulon in southern France were among the targets. [4:1.]

In Italy Allied troops stormed across the Arno River into the heart of historic Florence and were engaged in street fighting with the enemy, who was bombarding Allied-held sectors of the great cultural center. [1:4.]

The Red Army seized Drogobych, a large oil refinery center in southern Poland. Other Soviet forces were battling fiercely resisting Germans east of the curving Vistula River near Warsaw. Before East Prussia the Red Army continued to move forward, but its pace was slowed by fresh German reinforcements. Berlin reports told of a German withdrawal on a wide front around Lake Peipus in Estonia. [1:6; map P. 6.]

The leaders of the Polish government in exile and the new Polish Committee of National Liberation met in Moscow for the first time to try to work out a solution for their differences over Poland's internal problems and her relations with Soviet Russia. [6:2.]

Adolf Hitler told a meeting of Nazi party leaders last Friday that Germany needed a leader who would "under no circumstances capitulate" and that he was that man. [1:7.]

The American Navy scored one of its greatest triumphs in a daring two-day assault on the Bonin and Volcano Islands on Thursday and Friday during which our planes and warships sank or damaged forty-six Japanese vessels. An entire enemy convoy was "virtually wiped out" and shore installations on the islands, which are less than 600 miles from Tokyo, were also blasted. [1:3.]

In China, Japanese forces smashed into the heart of Hengyang. In southwestern Kwangtung Province, the invaders are threatening Limkong at the base of the Hoihong Peninsula. [8:6.] The Japanese base of Tamu, forty-seven miles southeast of Imphal, fell to the Allied offensive in Burma. [8:1; map P. 8.]

Seven Fleeing German Ships Sunk, Others Turn Back to St. Nazaire

By The United Press.

LONDON, Aug. 6—An entire German convoy of seven ships, possibly evacuating German troops from Brittany, was sent to the bottom early today off the Breton Peninsula by a British and Canadian cruiser and destroyer flotilla, the Admiralty announced tonight.

The convoy was steaming south from St. Nazaire, menaced by flying American armored columns, when it was surprised and brought under the guns of the British cruiser Bellona and the destroyers HMS Tartar, HMS Ashanti, HMCS Iroquois and HMCS Maida. In the ensuing action all German vessels, including the escort craft, were destroyed.

Later today another German convoy was spotted off St. Nazaire, but it hurried back into port. It was believed that the British and Canadian ships that stalked the second convoy had caused some damage the extent of which was not known.

A broadcast by DNB, German news agency, apparently referring to the first engagement, claimed that Allied bombers supported the British warships in the attack, which occurred between 3 A. M. and 5 A. M. Although the German report claimed the German vessels suffered little damage, it admitted that a number were "killed and wounded" aboard the ships.

The German broadcast said that several hits were scored on the attacking British destroyers, and the Admiralty acknowledged that "we suffered a small number of casualties."

In still another sea and air action off the French coast DNB claimed that a Nazi torpedo plane formation sank three Anglo-American destroyers in the Seine Bay, damaged two light cruisers or destroyers and scored a hit on a 14,000-ton transport.

LE MANS NOW GOAL

One Spearhead Near Key Rail and Road Center on Way to Paris

ROUTE IS WIDE OPEN

Little Opposition Met—13 German Divisions Declared Eliminated

By E. C. DANIEL
By Cable to The New York Times.

SUPREME HEADQUARTERS, Allied Expeditionary Force, Monday, Aug. 7—The American Army that overran the length and breadth of Brittany in four days has whipped its left flank eastward on two main roads directly toward Paris, shoving out one armored spearhead toward Le Mans, which dominates the rail network southwest of the French capital.

Without waiting for the completion of the conquest of Brittany, which has set a 1944 style in blitzkrieg for western Europe, Lieut. Gen. Omar N. Bradley has driven four spearheads to points as near Paris as is Caen at the northern end of the Allied battle line. The advance is being made on a forty-mile front, extending from Ambrieres la Grande, fifty-three miles northeast of Rennes, and southward through Mayenne, Laval and Château-Gontier, all of which have been occupied.

[A United Press report from the front said the Germans were retreating before the advancing American columns in "complete and utter confusion."]

Fighting in Brest

Meanwhile other American units were fighting in Brest, at and near St. Malo, had captured Vannes, between Lorient and St. Nazaire, and were pressing forward toward both those ports.

A report from the field said one American column had pressed twenty miles beyond Mayenne, while a second from Château-Gontier was said to be advancing on Le Mans, forty-two miles to the east and 110 miles from Paris. Roads from all these places converge on Le Mans, the hub of five main line railways, three of which lead to Paris.

Ahead of this drive no coordinated German defense line has yet taken shape. Behind it enough Allied infantry already has been poured into the Breton Peninsula from Normandy to hold all positions overrun by the armored columns. And the Americans are fanning out everywhere from St. Pois, in Normandy, to the mouth of the Loire River, on the southern side of Brittany, to build a firm base for their unflagging offensive.

German Position Critical

Alarmed Germans reported yesterday that Americans had driven up to Laval with "several" tank and infantry divisions "and were being constantly reinforced." In this area the Germans, faced with two evils—whether to concentrate on the Caen sector nearer Paris or on the more remote American threat in the west—apparently had been hoodwinked into making the wrong choice. A different choice might still have produced the same result in the end.

The Germans even began to inch back yesterday from those costly and assiduously dug-in positions south of Caen that they valued so highly. The Canadians, who have skillfully kept the Germans occupied southeast of Caen while the Americans were rampaging out to the west and the British were cleaning up the central sector, seized three villages yesterday.

The quick American hook toward Paris threatens to make all these positions around Caen useless to the Germans.

There seemed to be an air of expectancy here last night.

There was no doubt General Bradley was playing a fancy game for high stakes—stakes much higher than the conquest of Brittany. Every one is keeping his fingers crossed.

"My view," said a high British staff officer in Normandy last

Continued on Page 3

The British liberated Caen after one of the most bitter and destructive battles of the entire war.

U. S. Signal Corps

A soldier and Cherbourger toast to the liberation of Paris.

"All the News That's Fit to Print"

The New York Times.

LATE CITY EDITION
Showers, ending before noon; clearing, cooler later today.
Temperatures Yesterday—Max., 86; Min., 69
Sunrise, 6:14 A. M.; Sunset, 7:41 P. M.

VOL. XCIII. No. 31,624. Entered as Second-Class Matter, Postoffice, New York, N. Y. NEW YORK, THURSDAY, AUGUST 24, 1944. THREE CENTS IN NEW YORK CITY

PARIS IS FREED; RUMANIA QUITS; MARSEILLE AND GRENOBLE WON; GERMAN FLIGHT NEARS A ROUT

BREAK IN BALKANS

King Proclaims Nation's Surrender and Wish to Help Allies

NAZIS IN AREA FIGHT

New Bucharest Regime Asks United Nations Aid Against Hungary

By DANIEL T. BRIGHAM
By Telephone to The New York Times.

BERNE, Switzerland, Aug. 23—In a brief proclamation to the Rumanian people broadcast from Bucharest at 9:25 o'clock this evening, King Michael of Rumania ordered his armed forces to cease fire against the forces of the Allies, saying he had accepted their terms of unconditional surrender in the name of the nation.

The youthful King called on the nation to take up the fight immediately by the side of the Soviet forces on Rumanian soil against their common enemy, Germany.

Dramatic and apparently sudden as was the entire announcement the Germans were obviously forewarned, for when the home broadcast service at Bucharest interrupted its regular transmission at 9:24 P. M., within thirty seconds the two powerful Bucharest transmitters were shrouded by interference from a battery of German jammers of all varieties.

[Moscow, which broadcast the Rumanian surrender—beaming it especially to Germany—soon after the Bucharest announcement, reported later in the night that German troops were fighting Rumanian forces that were withdrawing from the Red Army front.

Bulgaria Expected to Quit

[Bulgaria's withdrawal from the war was believed to be imminent, according to reports from Cairo, which said the Allies were insisting on the return of territory seized in the war.]

King Michael, who had until recently been virtually a prisoner of the Gestapo, has overthrown the pro-Nazi dictatorship, ousting the Premier and Commander in Chief, Marshal Ion Antonescu. [The Berne radio, heard by Columbia Broadcasting System, said early Thursday that Antonescu had fled to Germany.]

He named as Chief of Government and Marshal of Rumania the master of his military household, Gen. Constantin Sanatescu. He announced a new Cabinet that constituted a Government of national union.

The new Cabinet includes Peasant party leader Juliu Maniu, as Minister of State Without Portfolio, and the leader of the Liberal party, Dinu Bratianu, in a similar post.

[Lucretiu Patrascanu, a Rumanian Communist party leader, and Constantin Petrescu, a Socialist leader, were also named Ministers of State, said a Bucharest broadcast recorded by the Federal Communications Commission.]

War With Hungary Evident

The new Rumanian Government is made up of a wide grouping of forces from the liberal, independent center to the extreme left.

King Michael's proclamation announced the denunciation by Rumania of the Treaty of Vienna of Aug. 30, 1940, by which the Nazis gave Transylvania to Hungary. It made it plain that Rumania is now at war with Hungary to recover Transylvania and seeks Allied backing in that effort.

A new Rumanian General Staff, as well as the country's political leaders, met at the King's palace,

Continued on Page 11

President Tells Delegates 'Four of Us' Can Keep Peace

Staying Friends and Meeting Often May Mean Generations Without War, He Says —Washington Studies U. S. Plan

By JAMES B. RESTON
Special to The New York Times.

WASHINGTON, Aug. 23—President Roosevelt told delegates to the Washington Conversations on International Organization today that if the United States, Soviet Russia and Great Britain could maintain their new and close friendship and spread that friendship around the world "we may have a peaceful period for our grandchildren to grow up in."

Speaking informally to the delegates at the White House during a recess in their labors to draft an effective security league, Mr. Roosevelt seemed to emphasize the special responsibility of the great powers in maintaining peace, by the use of force if necessary.

"We have got to make not merely a peace but a peace that will last," the President said, "and a peace in which the larger nations will work absolutely in unison in preventing war by force. But the four of us have to be friends, conferring all the time on the basis of getting to know each other."

Although no representative of China was present, the President's reference to "the four of us" was interpreted as an indication that when Mr. Roosevelt thinks of "the great powers" he counts China as one of those nations.

It was a remarkable fact, Mr. Roosevelt said, that the great powers had attained such unanimity during the war, and he added that the hope of the future lay in the ability of the nations to perpetuate that unity for a long time to come.

"The prisoners of 17, 18, 20 that

Continued on Page 13

The text of the President's remarks is on Page 13.

RED ARMY SPEEDS DEEP INTO RUMANIA

Bendery and Akkerman Taken —Polish Plane Center Falls —Russians Near Tartu

By The Associated Press.

LONDON, Thursday, Aug. 24—The two-fisted Soviet offensive that knocked Rumania out of the war roared through its fourth day yesterday, capturing Vaslui, 140 miles northeast of the Ploesti oil center, and toppling the two big Bessarabian bastions of Bendery and Akkerman on the west bank of the Dniester, besides more than 400 other towns.

Disregarding developments on the political front, at least for the present, the Second and Third Ukrainian Armies deepened to as much as sixty miles the holes they have ripped in the German-Rumanian defenses and advanced within 167 miles of the capital city of Bucharest.

Rumania still was garrisoned with thousands of German troops, and the Russians were likely to continue their lightning campaign to drive the Nazis entirely out of the country, regardless of what the Rumanian troops chose to do.

While this campaign was bearing its first great fruitz in Rumanian surrender, the First Ukrainian Army of Marshal Ivan S. Koneff in southern Poland lashed out westward and seized the city of Debica, a large aircraft industry center and communications point sixty-four miles east of Cracow and nineteen miles east of Tarnow, next

Continued on Page 10

47 RAILROADS SUED AS WESTERN TRUST

J. P. Morgan & Co., Kuhn-Loeb and Two Associations Accused of Conspiracy

By LEWIS WOOD
Special to The New York Times.

WASHINGTON, Aug. 23—In a civil suit filed at Lincoln, Neb., today major railroad interests of the United States were accused by the Federal Government of violating the Sherman Anti-Trust Act by collusive rate-fixing and discouraging improvements in service and equipment in the western part of the country.

The Department of Justice made these charges against the American Association of Railroads, its officers and directors; the Western Association of Railway Executives; J. P. Morgan & Co., Inc.; Kuhn, Loeb & Co.; forty-seven railroads and their chief executives, and thirty-one other individuals.

Attorney General Francis Biddle, now on the Pacific Coast, announced the action here through Wendell Berge, assistant Attorney General, in charge of anti-trust prosecutions.

In a forty-page complaint, the Government charged that a "combination of private financial, industrial and railroad interests have acted collusively to maintain non-competitive rates for transportation and to prevent and retard improvements in the services and facilities of railroads for the western part of the United States. (They) have retarded and suppressed the development and growth of the

Continued on Page 20

Willkie Would Empower President To Use U. S. Forces to Keep Peace

By LEO EGAN

In a series of talks in the last week and a half with Republican Senators and Representatives who have sought his views with respect to the international conference at Dumbarton Oaks, Wendell L. Willkie, it was learned yesterday, has been urging Republican support for the proposal to give the President power to use the military forces of the United States, without the prior approval of Congress, in fulfillment of American obligations to any international organization set up to preserve peace.

Mr. Willkie's advice on this score has been coupled with two other suggestions as to Republican policy: 1. That the party insist that the organic structure of an international security organization be established and American participation therein approved at once, without waiting for the treaties formally ending the present conflict; and, 2, that it insist upon the fullest possible information and discussion of all proposals considered at the Dumbarton Oaks Conference and that it take the lead in developing a body of public opinion within the United States favorable to American participation in international peace machinery.

As to the form that an international security organization should take, Mr. Willkie's views, as con-

Continued on Page 13

FRENCH TAKE PORT

Pockets of Resistance Are Being Cleared Up in Marseille

ARMY JUNCTION SEEN

American Dash Inland Said to Have Carried to Annecy, Near Border

By The Associated Press.

ROME, Aug. 23—Marseille, France's second city and greatest seaport, fell to the swift onslaught of French infantry and armor today as American forces swept 140 miles inland from the Mediterranean and were within less than 240 miles of a junction with Gen. Dwight D. Eisenhower's legions below liberated Paris.

Only eight days after the landings in southern France the inspired Poilus battered their way into the heart of Marseille against slight resistance and tonight were cleaning out pockets of last-ditch defenders.

The unexpectedly easy capture of the great port assures the Seventh Army an adequate flow of supplies and reinforcements for speedy continuation of the thrust toward northern France. Prior to the city's fall, other French troops had cut the last escape route for the German garrison along the coast to the west.

Toulon Still Holding Out

The encircled and doomed German force in Toulon, big naval base twenty-seven miles east of Marseille, still was holding out tonight, but French troops had fought their way within a few hundred yards of the docks.

[Confirmed reports in Berne said American troops had entered Annecy, less than eighteen miles from the Swiss frontier. Radio France at Algiers said Allied patrols had reached Avig-

Continued on Page 6

HAILING THE LIBERATION OF PARIS

Lily Pons leads the gathering in Rockefeller Plaza in singing "The Marseillaise"
The New York Times

GRIMNESS TINGES JOY OF FRENCH HERE

Concern for Kin and Thoughts of Tasks Ahead Mingle With Jubilation Over Paris

By MEYER BERGER

The French in New York City celebrated the liberation of Paris yesterday with impressive restraint. They sang "La Marseillaise" while ticker tape and handmade confetti danced above them in the sun, but hearts were still weighed down by worry over kin from whom they have not heard for years.

A few left the streets for quiet French churches to thank God for

Continued on Page 5

French Armored Division Sent Into Paris by Bradley

The following dispatch by a representative of the Columbia Broadcasting System, the first American correspondent to enter Paris, was cabled to London and broadcast from there.

By CHARLES COLLINGWOOD

PARIS, Aug. 23—The French Second Armored Division entered Paris today after the Parisians had risen as one man to beat down the German troops who had garrisoned the city.

It was the people of Paris who really won back their city. It all happened with fantastic suddenness.

The American Army was occupied with the drive through Evreux to the mouth of the Seine, after which it planned to invest Paris. But yesterday a Frenchman burst into Lieut. Gen. Omar N. Bradley's headquarters. He was the chief of the French Forces of the Interior in Paris and he had a staggering, incredible story to tell.

He said that he had concluded an armistice with the German forces in Paris. The people of Paris had risen and had so hounded the Germans that the German commander had requested an armistice. He wanted to withdraw troops from the road blocks west and south of Paris, where they had been facing the Americans, and pass them through the city.

The armistice was to expire at noon today.

This news caused a sensation in General Bradley's headquarters because, although we had known that rioting had been going on in Paris since Saturday, we had not known that things had gone so far that obviously the French had given the Germans a terrific beating.

The whole operation was geared to the complete encirclement of the

Continued on Page 5

ENEMY FLEES 'KILL' BY ALLIES AT SEINE

Americans Drive North, British Near Le Havre—3d Army Rolls Toward Troyes

By DREW MIDDLETON
By Cable to The New York Times.

SUPREME HEADQUARTERS, Allied Expeditionary Force, Thursday, Aug. 24—The last German army south of the Seine River and west of Paris is being destroyed.

The American forces thrusting along the south bank of the Seine have taken Evreux and smashed on more than seven miles, while the British and Canadian troops on the left and center of the Allies' line are hammering the Germans back into a pocket south of Le Havre and Rouen. Two hundred miles to the east, the American column at the nose of the Third Army's salient is rolling eastward toward Troyes, on the road to Germany, in a bold operation that threatens to cut off all southern France from reinforcement from Germany.

It is estimated that almost 90,-

Continued on Page 4

War News Summarized

THURSDAY, AUGUST 24, 1944

Germany sustained a double blow yesterday when the citizens of Paris threw out the invaders and Rumania deserted the Axis to join with the United Nations.

The liberation of the French capital came after four days of hard fighting. Some 50,000 French resistance troops, supported by large bodies of unarmed civilians, had risen on signal from underground leaders. The Paris police, who had previously gone on strike, seized strategic centers. Generals Eisenhower and Patton kept their men from entering the city while the French people went about the job of creating another Bastille Day. [1:8; map, P. 2.]

King Michael proclaimed the immediate end of the war for Rumania as an Axis satellite and the joining of his country with the Allies against Germany. He ousted the Antonescu dictatorship, said armistice terms had been accepted and formed a new Government to conclude peace with the United Nations immediately. [1:1.]

Bulgaria was expected soon to follow Rumania out of the war. The Allies were reported to have demanded Bulgaria's evacuation of all territory seized in Yugoslavia and Greece and withdrawal to pre-war boundaries. [10:1.] Prime Minister Churchill planned with officials of the Greek Government in Exile that country's future military activities. [10:5.] Nothing was heard from Hungary or Finland.

Meanwhile Allied armies continued to roll through France. Marseille and Grenoble were liberated, most of Toulon had been taken, Lyon was threatened and American troops were reported in Annecy, less than twenty miles from the Swiss frontier. [1:4; map P. 6.] In northern France the Germans south of the Seine were being rapidly destroyed and herded into a pocket south of Le Havre and Rouen. The American Third Army was nearing Troyes. [1:7; map P. 4.]

Italian-based Allied planes smashed the Vienna area for the second straight day, meeting heavy opposition. Medium bombers flew deep into France to attack targets around Lyon. [8:4.]

Russian successes were reported from all fronts. The Red Army was only four miles from Tartu and eight miles from Lomzha. In the Rumanian sector they brought both points of a great pincers to within thirty-five miles of closing. [1:2, map P. 10.]

The only victory Berlin could announce was the heaviest dawn barrage of flying bombs yet to strike England. [9:1.]

Allied bombers in the Pacific virtually wiped out a Japanese convoy off the Bonins and struck Davao, in the Philippines. [1:6-7.] The Japanese Premier warned his people that the United States was planning an invasion of the home islands. [11:1.]

President Roosevelt told delegates to the Dumbarton Oaks conference that "we have got to make a peace that will last" so that "we may have a peaceful period for our grandchildren to grow up in." [1:2-3.] Wendell Willkie has urged Republicans to support the State Department's proposal to permit the use of American military forces without prior approval of Congress and to approve a security organization at once, apart from the peace treaties. [1:2-3.]

U. S. Bombers Set Davao Aflame In Stepped-Up Philippines Blow

By The Associated Press.

GENERAL HEADQUARTERS, Southwest Pacific, Thursday, Aug. 24—Striking into the southern Philippines for the tenth time in two weeks United States Navy Liberators touched off towering fires at Davao and sank a small Japanese freighter northeast of Mindanao, headquarters reported today.

Five other enemy vessels, one a destroyer tender, were hit in raids ranging from Celebes, south of Mindanao, to Palau in the Caroline Islands north of New Guinea.

[On Wednesday Pearl Harbor reported the sinking of two Japanese cargo ships caught in a convoy by Navy bombers near Chichi, in the Bonin Islands.]

Air patrols bombed Palau Monday night, setting fires and explosions, and returned Tuesday to attack the destroyer tender and leave it dead in the water. Two enemy fighters ineffectively attempted interception, the only aerial interference reported in the raids listed today.

Near Celebes, patrol planes sank or badly damaged a small freighter and three coastal vessels on Tuesday.

In the ten raids in the southern Philippines announced since Aug. 7, the planes have bombed Davao airdromes and waterfront four times and have sunk three ships and damaged five.

Continuing aerial assaults

Continued on Page 11

PARISIANS ROUT FOE

50,000 FFI Troops With Civilians' Aid Battle Germans 4 Days

POLICE HELP REBELS

Turn Ile de la Cite Into Fortress—Casualties Among People High

By RAYMOND DANIELL
By Cable to The New York Times.

LONDON, Aug. 23—Paris is free again and, because of that, the rest of the world can breathe a little more freely. In a manner befitting a capital with the history and tradition of Paris, its own citizens rose and threw off the tyrant's yoke as soon as their own troops and the Allies' armies of liberation had given them the opportunity to challenge their conquerors on equal terms.

In leaving it to the French themselves to announce that the swastika had been lowered and the Tricolor had been raised over their own gracious and lovely capital, the Allies were following a policy that was both strategically and politically sound.

Gen. Dwight D. Eisenhower's columns were able to continue their eastward sweep unimpeded by the need for pausing to mop up, and France, which was knocked out of the war more than four years ago, was able to stand before the world on her own feet again.

Armored Division Enters

The French Second Armored Division, which fought its way across the African desert under Maj. Gen. Jacques LeClerc, seems to have been the first Allied force to enter Paris. It went in after the local leader of the FFI had concluded an armistice with the Germans, it was said here.

But before many more hours have passed, the Arc de Triomphe at the head of Champs-Elysées will be the scene of yet another pageant in the panoply of history, when the tread of victorious armies will mark the close of more than four years in which the City of Light had been the outpost of the jack-booted forces of darkness.

Paris, which began to weep but not to cringe on June 14, 1940, when the German heel first echoed in the boulevards, will laugh and sing again to welcome an army of repatriates and of aliens who come not to conquer but to insure the newly won freedom.

Koenig Announces Liberation

Maj. Gen. Joseph Pierre Koenig, commander of the French Forces of the Interior, informed the world that the French people had at last chased the Germans out of their beloved capital. He gave some of the details. But the full story of what happened in Paris between Aug. 19 and today is a saga that will have to be written by many men over a long period before the whole story is told.

Tonight, however—seventy-seven days after D-day—the world can rejoice without asking the whys and wherefores, for Paris is free again. "The Marseillaise" again is sung there, the Tricolor flies there again and the German tide is on the ebb in western Europe.

Until the newspaper correspondents now in Paris or waiting on the outskirts to get there can write their stories and transmit them, General Koenig's terse official statement will have to suffice.

A general insurrection, he said, began four days ago, when, in response to the orders of the underground leaders and the self-styled Provisional Government of France for a general uprising against the Germans, 50,000 members of the FFI armed and supported by "several hundred thousand unarmed

Continued on Page 3

"All the News That's Fit to Print"

NEWS INDEX, PAGE 43, THIS SECTION

The New York Times.

LATE CITY EDITION
Clear in morning, becoming partly cloudy and rather warm later.
Temperatures Yesterday—Max., 80; Min., 67
Sunrise, 6:38 A. M.; Sunset, 7:07 P. M.

Section 1

VOL. XCIII...No. 31,648. Entered as Second-Class Matter, Postoffice, New York, N. Y. NEW YORK, SUNDAY, SEPTEMBER 17, 1944. Including Magazine and Book Sections. TEN CENTS New York City and Suburban Area (15c Elsewhere)

ROOSEVELT AND CHURCHILL PLEDGE QUICK SHIFT OF FORCES TO CRUSH 'BARBARIANS OF PACIFIC'; AMERICANS WIDEN BREACH IN THE SIEGFRIED LINE

U. S. BUILDING CURBS EASED TO RELIEVE HOUSING SHORTAGE

New WPB Order Permits Wide Apartment Remodeling in All Areas Lacking Homes

CITY TO BE SO CLASSIFIED

Thousands of New Suites in a Few Months Seen as Builders Prepare to Rush Work

By LEE E. COOPER

Federal officials opened the way yesterday for widespread remodeling of large apartments and outmoded tenements under a liberalized wartime program that is expected to help materially in relieving the critical housing shortage in New York.

The New York Regional Office of the War Production Board reported that it had received word from Washington of a joint announcement by the WPB and the National Housing Agency designed to provide housing relief in congested areas.

Under this revised plan the WPB will cooperate by granting priorities for conversion work in communities where the NHA decrees that "an extreme housing shortage" exists. For this purpose the H-3 program has been amended to permit an almost unlimited amount of housing conversions and remodeling, and without any cost limitation on an individual project. H-3 authorizations heretofore have been limited strictly to extreme hardship or emergency cases, such as where a man's house was badly damaged by fire or storm.

Order Expected Today

No work can be carried out under the amended policy unless a district is specified as a critical area. It was learned from an authoritative source that Charles S. Ascher, head of the NHA for the New York region, would act at once to put New York in this category. He is known to have favored the revised procedure to provide additional housing units quickly in this city, and an order to that effect is expected from him today.

A wave of housing improvements here is predicted by builders and realty men as a result of the liberalized program. Realty boards, the Building Trades Employers Association, building trades unions and other groups have joined in pleas to the WPB, the NHA and the Federal Housing Administration for permission to carry out remodeling work to meet the need for additional living quarters here. The petitions have declared that thousands of new suites would be created within a matter of months if the wartime restrictions were relaxed.

Most of these groups had suggested liberalization of the L-41 order, which limits structural changes in an apartment building to $1,000 annually, or in a private home to $200, unless an authorization for additional work is given by the Federal agencies. Virtually no such authorizations were being issued here and civilian residential construction activity has been at a standstill while a considerable amount of work in store and loft buildings has been going forward under a separate category with "industrial" authorizations.

Must Provide More Homes

The WPB made it clear that these limits on residential building changes still apply through L-41, as do former provisions for maintenance and repairs. The change involves only the H-3 order under which conversion work and renovations to provide additional home units are permitted. FHA approval is mandatory for this type of construction and applications must be filed with that agency, which is a unit of the

Continued on Page 34

Priorities Offered For Storm Repairs

Special to The New York Times.

WASHINGTON, Sept. 16—Every effort to make available lumber and all other building materials needed to repair damage caused by this week's hurricane will be made by War Production Board officials, it was stated here today.

The Facilities Bureau of WPB, which passes on applications for materials made by the Federal Housing Administration and by the War Food Administration (which handles applications from farmers) is prepared to give special priorities to those Atlantic Coast residents whose homes or farm buildings were wrecked or damaged by the high winds.

Jesse Jones, Secretary of Commerce, today announced that the Reconstruction Finance Corporation loan agencies at Charlotte, Richmond, Philadelphia, New York and Boston, have been instructed to give particular attention to disaster loans in those areas.

DEWEY CABINET JOB PLEDGED FAR WEST

Governor Says New Deal Has Neglected Area and That His Party Will Aid Vast Growth

By WARREN MOSCOW
Special to The New York Times.

SPOKANE, Wash., Sept. 16—Governor Dewey came to the Pacific Northwest today, to promise its people special consideration of its problems and a post in the national Cabinet, and to express his own faith in the frontiers of the country which he asserts the New Deal has disowned.

At the same time, in a press conference on his arrival here, he discussed the power distribution problem of the Pacific Northwest in such a way as to indicate that he was against straight Federal distribution of power produced at the great dams of Bonneville, Grand Coulee and their future rivals, but favored local option on the subject.

"I have always believed," said Mr. Dewey, "that the great natural resources must be developed by the Federal Government for the benefit of the people. I have always felt that way about the Niagara and the St. Lawrence, and have been enthusiastic about Bonneville."

He was asked his views on power distribution, the big political problem of the area. Mr. Dewey's answer was:

"That is a matter up to the local community. The Federal Government should distribute it at the bus bar in accordance with the wishes of the local community, so that the greatest advantage would be obtained from it in accordance with the desires of the people."

"You mean no Federal distribution?" he was asked.

"My answer speaks for itself," said the candidate.

The press conference was the

Continued on Page 40

FOE IS NEAR PANIC

German Civilians Flee, With First Army 28 Miles From Cologne

PATTON SMASHES ON

British, Canadians Also Drive Forward—Patch Pushes Near Belfort

By DREW MIDDLETON
By Cable to The New York Times.

SUPREME HEADQUARTERS, Allied Expeditionary Force, Sunday, Sept. 17—German civilians were streaming eastward across the Rhine yesterday as the American breach in the Siegfried Line was widened and extended by veteran armored divisions of Lieut. Gen. Courtney H. Hodges' American First Army. The whole Allied front from the North Sea to Switzerland was rolling forward. Lieut. Gen. George S. Patton's Third Army was smashing toward Germany east of Metz and Nancy after having won half a dozen grim battles, and the Canadian First and British Second Armies were pushing northward over the Netherland border, driving stubborn German rear guards before them.

Defenses Breaking Up

The German organization for the defense of the Siegfried Line was breaking under the test imposed upon it by Lieut. Gen. Omar N. Bradley. Confused by American attacks in a half dozen places the enemy has not been able to husband enough men to check the main drive east of Aachen. The elastic defense that depends on extreme mobility for defenders is impossible to the numerically inferior German units fighting gamely but vainly in the outmoded fortifications of the Siegfried Line.

Two new forces arrived on the German frontier yesterday and are probably across it by now. The Germans reported that an American armored column had crossed to the eastern bank of the Sauer River on the Luxembourg-German frontier north of Echternacht, which is approximately seven and a half miles northwest of Trier in Germany, where another American column was already operating.

Latest reports from the front said these troops were only 500 yards from the German frontier and were driving through trenches dug only five days ago. The last village west of the German frontier in this area was stormed by the onrushing Americans.

North of the main penetration east of Aachen front line reports said a First Army column had crossed the river north of Mechelen and was approaching the Roer River.

Shells Pummel Aachen

There was heavy fighting in Aachen, where German soldiers were fighting a desperate rearguard action from house to house,

Continued on Page 12

AFTER REACHING DECISIONS ON THE WAR IN EUROPE AND THE PACIFIC

Allied leaders in Quebec yesterday at the conclusion of their talks. Front, left to right: Gen. George C. Marshall, Chief of Staff of the United States Army; Admiral William D. Leahy, Chief of Staff to the President; President Roosevelt; Prime Minister Churchill; British Field Marshal Sir Alan Brooke and British Field Marshal Sir John Dill. Rear, left to right: British Maj. Gen. Hollis, British Lieut. Gen. Sir Hastings Ismay, Admiral Ernest J. King, Commander in Chief, United States Fleet; British Air Marshal Sir Charles Portal, Gen. H. H. Arnold, Chief of the United States Army Air Forces, and British Admiral Sir Andrew B. Cunningham.

Associated Press Wirephoto

MAGINOT LINE GUNS FIRED AT GERMANS

Americans Solve Technical Problems and Then Batter Enemy Across Moselle

By FREDERICK GRAHAM
By Wireless to The New York Times.

ALONG THE MOSELLE RIVER, in France, Sept. 16—Fed up with taking shelling by German artillery, a cannon company of a famous infantry division manned German guns installed in a Maginot Line fort on the west bank of the Moselle facing Thionville today and gave both the German gun positions and the dug-in soldiers

Continued on Page 14

Red Army in Bulgar Capital, Widens Gains Near Warsaw

By The Associated Press.

LONDON, Sunday, Sept. 17—Red Army troops yesterday pushed through the capitulated Bulgarian capital of Sofia in their drive toward Yugoslavia, only thirty miles beyond, while other Soviet forces shelled burning Warsaw and began laying pontoon assault bridges across the Vistula River from the captured suburban area of Praga.

Berlin broadcasts reported without Soviet confirmation that three Soviet armies, using upward of 400,000 men in a big new offensive in the north, had begun a drive on Riga and that one spearhead in an eighteen-mile advance was twenty miles south of the Latvian capital on the Baltic Sea.

A late dispatch said the Russians had begun stringing pontoons

Continued on Page 38

MARINES CAPTURE PELELIU AIRDROME

Kill 1,400 Japanese Seizing Prized Field — Tokyo Says Davao Has Been Evacuated

By ROBERT TRUMBULL
By Telephone to The New York Times.

PEARL HARBOR, Sept. 16—The Peleliu airfield, primary objective in the assault on that small island in the Palau group, was captured by the First Marine Division yesterday, with American artillery, tanks, naval gunfire and carrier-based bombers supporting the marines' determined drive through well-organized Japanese defenses.

Today's communiqué from the headquarters of Admiral Chester W. Nimitz, Commander in Chief of the Pacific Fleet, made it plain that the fighting on Peleliu had been of the severest intensity and said that it was continuing.

Fourteen hundred Japanese dead were counted by our troops by nightfall yesterday, about thirty hours after the landing. There was no mention of the marine casualties, although yesterday's communiqué said our losses on the first day were light.

[On Morotai Island, 300 miles from Mindanao in the Philippines, army troops pushed the rebuilding of the Pitu airdrome and consolidated positions with-

Continued on Page 5

GERMANS DEFIANT ON OUSTER BY FINNS

Profess Difficulty of Moving Troops—Clashes Reported as War Declaration Looms

By The Associated Press.

LONDON, Sept. 16—Finnish troops tonight were waging an undeclared war against their former German allies. Vehicles began streaming across the northern borders as war-weary Finns tried to escape to Sweden in view of an open declaration of hostilities this week-end.

The German Army in Russia will henceforth be guided "by the viewpoint of its own security against any aggressors," a German High Command statement said.

Trying to explain why several German divisions remained in Finland, a communiqué broadcast from Berlin said:

"German divisions that so far

Continued on Page 39

War News Summarized

SUNDAY, SEPTEMBER 17, 1944

President Roosevelt and Prime Minister Churchill brought their war talks in Quebec to a close yesterday with a pledge to launch a devastating assault on Japan with all the resources of the British Empire and the United States as soon as Europe is freed from "the corroding heel of Nazism." The two leaders said they had reached quick and complete unanimity on plans for prosecuting the war against "the barbarians of the Pacific." [1:8.]

Seasoned marines who conquered Guadalcanal appeared to be well on their way toward hitting the Japanese with the same sort of lightning again. A little more than a day after their invasion of Peleliu island in the Palau group, 610 miles east of Davao in the Philippines, the battle-scarred veterans had fought through strong enemy tank and artillery fire and had conquered the island's airfield. Meanwhile, General MacArthur's Army troops, fashioning the southern claw of a pincers aimed at the Philippines, were putting the captured airfield on Morotai into shape. Alarmed Tokyo had no doubt as to the why of the two American invasions and ordered evacuation of Davao in the southern Philippines. [1:7.]

Allied forces all along the western front from the North Sea to Switzerland moved forward. The spotlight continued to blaze on the American First Army, which was widening and extending its breach of the Siegfried Line east of Aachen. This drive toward the Rhine continued unchecked, and German organization for defense of the Siegfried Line was breaking down under the impact of American hammer blows at half a dozen places at the same time. General Patton's Third Army was winning the battle of the Moselle River and was reaching for the German frontier east of the great fortress city of Metz. Canadian and British troops rolled northward over the Dutch border after overcoming stubborn German resistance. [1:3; map, P. 12.]

The Red Army entered Sofia, capital of Bulgaria, which capitulated shortly after the Russians crossed the frontier on Sept. 8, and were within sixty miles of the main German escape route from Greece. Soviet patrols were crossing the Vistula River to scout enemy positions in Warsaw, which was under terrific artillery bombardment. Berlin reports said a massive new Russian offensive in the Baltics had put the Russians within twenty miles of Riga, capital of Latvia. [1:5-6; map, P. 28.]

Finns and Germans continued to fight each other as Hitler maintained that German troops had been unable to leave Finland by Sept. 15 and would continue "to protect their security" against any attackers. Finland, which has not yet formally concluded peace with Soviet Russia, was reported moving toward a declaration of war on Germany. [1:6.]

In Italy, a great tank battle was raging within three miles of Rimini. [26:4.]

Harlem Gets Big New Playground Reclaimed From 6½ Acres of Slum

On a six-and-a-half-acre site that seven months ago was cluttered with dilapidated garages, small commercial buildings and tenements, one of the largest playgrounds in the city was opened yesterday in Harlem at Lenox Avenue between 143d and 145th Streets, with only coal bunkers between it and the Harlem River.

Two thousand fathers, mothers, youths and children from the congested neighborhood came for the opening, watched with sparkling eyes a parade, applauded when city officials and Negro leaders spoke of other improvements to come and the social importance of the playground, and remained to play ball on its new asphalt surface, to use its swings, chutes and teeter boards and to toss basketballs.

The playground, named in honor of Col. Charles Young, a Negro officer who was graduated from West Point, served in the Spanish-American War, the Philippine Insurrection and the World War and was buried in Arlington National Cemetery, was built now because Mayor La Guardia and Park Commissioner Robert Moses were able to obtain priorities for sufficient materials. Fencing is lacking for the large playfield within the playground and construction of a recreation house with bandstand will have to wait until after the war. But meanwhile there is a large area for supervised and safe play where none existed before in a heavily populated district.

Commissioner Moses, as chairman of the ceremonies, said the

Continued on Page 40

Henry Ford Will Increase Wages 'As Soon as Government Permits'

Special to The New York Times.

WASHINGTON, Sept. 16—Henry Ford, in a statement released today by his representatives, said:

"I have been thinking about raising wages for some time and I am going to do it as soon as the Government will permit me."

The statement marked the third time in the forty-year history of the Ford Motor Company that Mr. Ford has announced a decision to raise wages above the general standard of the country.

In 1914 Mr. Ford set a $5-a-day minimum wage when the average daily wage was much lower and in 1929 he increased the Ford minimum to $7 a day.

"I would like to raise the pay of all Ford workers despite the fact that their wages are already higher than those of the rest of the industry," he declared in today's statement.

"As long as I live I want to pay the highest wages in the automobile business. If the men in our plants will give a full day's work for a full day's pay, there is no reason why we can't always do it.

"Every man should make enough money to own a home, a piece of land and a car."

The statement came soon after indications here that the National War Labor Board's Little Steel formula limiting wage increases to

Continued on Page 35

UNITY IS STRESSED

Churchill Asserts Britain Asked a Bigger Part in War on Japan

NAZIS SEEN NEAR END

Roosevelt Says Pacific Is Too Big to Have One Commander

By JOHN H. CRIDER
By Telephone to The New York Times.

QUEBEC, Sept. 16—President Roosevelt and Prime Minister Churchill promised today the earliest possible shift of the full weight of British and American arms from Europe for the "destruction of the barbarians of the Pacific," but were unprepared to specify when the war in Europe would end.

Addressing correspondents as they did thirteen months ago on the deck of the Citadel's historic ramparts 300 feet above the broad St. Lawrence, the leaders of the two countries commanding the greatest combined military and naval strength in the world pledged that the doom of Japan would be written in the months to come, just as Germany's collapse is "now approaching its final stages" as the result of similar decisions reached here last year. They spoke as prophets with a record of fulfillment.

Their Joint Statement

The main points of their half-hour press conference, which concluded the second Quebec conference, were summarized in a joint statement as follows:

"The President and the Prime Minister and the Combined Chiefs of Staff held a series of meetings, during which they discussed all aspects of the war against Germany and Japan. In a very short space of time they reached decisions on all points both with regard to the completion of the war in Europe, now approaching its final stages, and the destruction of the barbarians of the Pacific.

"The most serious difficulty with which the Quebec conference has been confronted has been to find room and opportunity for marshaling against Japan the massive forces which each and all of the nations concerned are ardent to engage against the enemy."

The two great men of the Anglo-American nations faced 160 correspondents and photographers, looking just as grim and determined as they did a year ago, but they had aged perceptibly. The Prime Minister, with his big cigar, was less florid of complexion as he

Continued on Page 4

German Peace Plea To Russia Reported

By Reuter.

STOCKHOLM, Sweden, Sept. 16—The Berne correspondent of the Swedish newspaper Morgentidningen, citing a "reliable German source," said today that Adolf Hitler had asked an intermediary to ask Russia for peace.

Germany offered to evacuate Finland and the Balkans, retaining her economic connections with the latter, and to accept the Polish demarcation line fixed by Germany and Russia in 1939, the report said. The same German source, the correspondent added, heard strong rumors that the Japanese at the same time had asked Russia to make contact with the Americans and British for peace terms.

The intermediary used by Hitler is said to be Hiroshi Oshima, Japanese Ambassador in Berlin.

U.S. Marine Corps

Marines pinned down under heavy enemy fire on Pelelieu, September, 1944.

U.S. Marine Corps

U. S. Marines aboard landing craft prepare for invasion of Palau on September 15, 1944.

"All the News That's Fit to Print"

The New York Times.

LATE CITY EDITION
Cloudy with fresh to strong winds; rain tonight.
Temperatures Yesterday—Max., 67; Min., 53
Sunrise, 7:19 A. M.; Sunset, 6:09 P. M.

VOL. XCIV..No. 31,681. Entered as Second-Class Matter, Postoffice, New York, N. Y. NEW YORK, FRIDAY, OCTOBER 20, 1944. THREE CENTS IN NEW YORK CITY

M'ARTHUR INVADES CENTRAL PHILIPPINES; FOOTHOLD TO SPLIT ISLANDS FIRMLY HELD; ROOSEVELT PROMISES JAPAN A LESSON NOW

10,000 POLICE READY TO GUARD ITINERARY OF PRESIDENT HERE

He Will Arrive in Brooklyn, Then in an Open Car Tour Three Other Boroughs

TO ATTEND WAGNER RALLY

Trip Will Be Made Tomorrow Preceding Foreign Policy Talk, Rain or Shine

Police Commissioner Lewis J. Valentine yesterday canceled all police leaves for Saturday and recalled all officers of the rank of captain or higher from vacations for that day to provide a police guard for President Roosevelt's campaign tour of the city that will be adequate for all emergencies. It was estimated that the Commissioner's actions will make a force of 10,000 policemen, including detectives, available for the President's protection during his stay in the city.

Robert E. Hannegan, Democratic National Chairman, released yesterday the itinerary for the President's trip and said that the tour will be made rain or shine. The President is planning to make the tour in an open car, he added.

Laughing aside a question as to whether Mayor La Guardia was taking over direction of the campaign, that had been prompted by the Mayor's supervision of the arrangements for the President's tour, Mr. Hannegan said that Mr. La Guardia "has been cooperating with us in arranging plans for visits here to this city of which he is the Mayor."

Not Solely a Health Tour

The Democratic chairman denied that the tour was arranged to prove that the President's health was good, but he conceded that it might serve that purpose.

"After the people have seen him they can make up their own minds as to his vigor and health," he explained. "The people will have a chance to see him as the correspondents do twice a week."

The President's itinerary, as released by Mr. Hannegan, provides for his arrival at the Brooklyn Army Base Terminal in the Bay Ridge section of Brooklyn. From there the President will go to the New York Navy Yard in Brooklyn via Fifty-eighth Street, Fourth Avenue, Ashland Place, Navy Street and Flushing Avenue, entering the yard through the Cumberland Street gate.

Upon leaving the Navy Yard the White House party will drive along Cumberland Street, Park Avenue, Tillary Street, Washington Street, Fulton Street and Bedford Avenue to Ebbets Field, where the President is scheduled to greet Senator Robert F. Wagner at about 10:30 A. M. This is the only time announced for a stop on the entire tour.

Wagner to Join Party

Senator Wagner is joining the Presidential party at Ebbets Field and will ride with the President for the rest of the trip. Leaving the ball park, the President will go to the United States Naval Training School, Women's Reserve (Hunter College), the Bronx, via Bedford Avenue, Empire Boulevard, Washington Avenue, Classon Avenue, Eastern Parkway, Pitkin Avenue, Pennsylvania Avenue and Interboro Parkway to Queens.

Leaving the Interboro Parkway at Metropolitan Avenue, the President and his group will cross Queens by way of Union Turnpike, Queens Boulevard, Thirty-ninth Street, Steinway Street and Astoria Boulevard north to the Triborough Bridge.

Arriving in the Bronx on the Triborough Bridge, the President will follow Bruckner Boulevard, 138th Street, St. Ann's Avenue, 149th Street, Prospect Avenue, Boston Road, Southern Boulevard, East Tremont Avenue, Washington Avenue, Fordham Road, University Avenue, Kingsbridge Road, Reservoir Avenue and Goulden Avenue

Continued on Page 12, Column 5

Moscow Is Paying For Petsamo Mines

Special to THE NEW YORK TIMES.

OTTAWA, Oct. 19—The Government of the Soviet Union has agreed to pay 20,000,000 United States dollars to the Government of Canada for the interests in the nickel mines in the Petsamo district of Finland, owned by the International Nickel Company of Canada and its subsidiary, the Mond Nickel Company of the United Kingdom.

Announcement of the agreement, which was signed in Moscow by the British and Canadian Ambassadors, was made this evening by Prime Minister W. L. Mackenzie King. The Petsamo district was ceded to the Soviet Union by Finland under the armistice agreement of Sept. 19.

Payment will be made during six years in equal installments.

HURRICANE LASHES CAROLINA COASTS

Charleston Is Dark as Storm Roars Northward—Florida Citrus Growers Lose Millions

By The United Press.

CHARLESTON, S. C., Oct. 19—A tropical hurricane which caused damage to Florida's rich citrus crop estimated in the millions, and at least twenty-five deaths since boiling up in the Caribbean more than a week ago, lashed at this shipbuilding and naval center tonight, plunging the city into darkness through power failure.

At 8:30 P. M., the Weather Bureau said the center of the disturbance was in the Atlantic off Parris Island, site of the big marine boot training camp, but already gale winds of 55 to 60 miles an hour were sweeping this city.

Waves were pounding over the seawall at the Battery, and low parts of the old city were expected to be flooded.

[Little damage and no casualties were reported by The Associated Press from the hurricane's progress over the Carolines. Power was restored at Charleston at 1 A. M. High water caused slight damage at the Battery. Florence, S. C., and Southport, N. C., had forty to sixty-five-mile winds.]

Because of the power failure, The News and Courier was unable to publish tomorrow's editions.

Florida Citrus Crop Is Hard Hit

JACKSONVILLE, Fla., Oct. 19 (AP)—The hurricane swept northward tonight along the South Atlantic Coast after crossing Florida, causing two deaths in Miami and estimated damage of $20,000,000 to the citrus crop.

The Weather Bureau said the storm probably would reach a point off Cape Hatteras, N. C., early Friday and pass out to sea.

Relatively little damage occurred at Jacksonville, which had its worst blow since 1928, but nearly fifty beach houses were destroyed by wind and tides at Fer-

Continued on Page 32, Column 2

ALLIES NEAR VENLO

British Troops, Our Tanks Push Foe Back Upon Meuse in Holland

AACHEN MOSTLY WON

Canadians Speed Drive to Chase the Germans From Antwerp Area

By CLIFTON DANIEL
By Wireless to THE NEW YORK TIMES.

SUPREME HEADQUARTERS, Allied Expeditionary Force, Oct. 19—Parallel columns of British and American tanks, driving through incessant rain and soggy Netherland fields, closed in today toward Venlo, on the great bend of the Meuse River thirty miles east of Eindhoven, and major junction of the main railway from the Ruhr and Rhineland industrial areas to Eindhoven. At the nearest point the Allied forces fighting under Lieut. Gen. Sir Miles C. Dempsey's command were within eleven miles of Venlo in a drive south and east of Venray.

The gains here, as elsewhere on the Western Front, were limited by persistently unfavorable weather. Canadian Army troops, pressing west against the shrinking perimeter of the German pocket on the south shore of the Scheldt estuary, approached to within 2,000 yards today of the center of the pocket at Oostburg [near Waterlandkerkje, The Canadian Press reported]. British tactical aircraft gave close support to the advance.

American First Army troops were working in the streets of Aachen. Outside Aachen today the Germans were thrown out of pillboxes that they had occupied during the night in the Haaren area, northeast of the city. A German counter-attack there gained ground this afternoon, but Americans struck back and recaptured the lost yardage.

German Armor Attacked

Generally bad weather curtailed air operations, but American Thunderbolts, operating beyond Lieut. Gen. George S. Patton's Third Army front, hit railway rolling stock at Kaiserslautern and made an accurate attack on a concentration of German tanks east of Luneville, fifteen miles southeast of Nancy.

A German counter-blow against the British Second Army advance toward the Meuse was made today from the vicinity of the village of Overbroek, just southeast of Venray. It was contained, and the Allied forces now hold a line roughly along a secondary road from Overbroek to the southwest. The American part of this Allied force was working through swamp lands south of Venray along the railway from Eindhoven and Deurne to Venlo. About 750 prisoners were taken in this area yesterday, 150 of them by the Americans.

Fighting against the French

Continued on Page 3, Column 3

EAST PRUSSIA IS HIT

Huge Red Army Blow Takes German Town, Berlin Reports

DANZIG SECOND GOAL

Soviet Pincers Feared—Debrecen's Defenses Crack in Hungary

By The United Press.

LONDON, Friday, Oct. 20—The Red Army has invaded East Prussia, capturing at least one German town in "one of the war's bloodiest struggles," Berlin said last night, while Moscow reported that other Soviet forces had cracked the German defense line south of Debrecen, Hungary's third city, and seized more than 11,000 prisoners.

Using more than 500 tanks to spearhead single thrusts, Russian troops captured the German frontier station of Eydtkau, half a mile inside the eastern border of the Junkers stronghold, and pushed across German soil toward the great East Prussian rail hub of Insterburg, thirty-eight miles to the west, Berlin said.

German broadcasts, stressing the gravity of the "mammoth" Russian offensive and speaking of a "grand assault" by "monstrous" Soviet forces, said the deepest penetration of German soil was made west of Eydtkau as the Russians drove past the town to within striking distance of the strategic rail junction of Stallupoenen.

Moscow Remains Silent

While the German radio gave a day-long picture of German troops fighting desperately against an avalanche of men and material and yielding only blood-stained ground, Moscow remained silent on the battle that reportedly has been raging for three days.

At the same time German commentators told of a grandiose Soviet plan apparently aimed at throwing a steel ring around East Prussia's 14,000 square miles. While Red Army forces attacked East Prussia's eastern borders on a fifty-mile front between the frontier station of Schirwindt and the former Polish city of Suwalki, annexed to Adolf Hitler's Greater Reich, Berlin said Soviet forces

Continued on Page 6, Column 4

GENERAL M'ARTHUR FULFILLS A GALLANT VOW

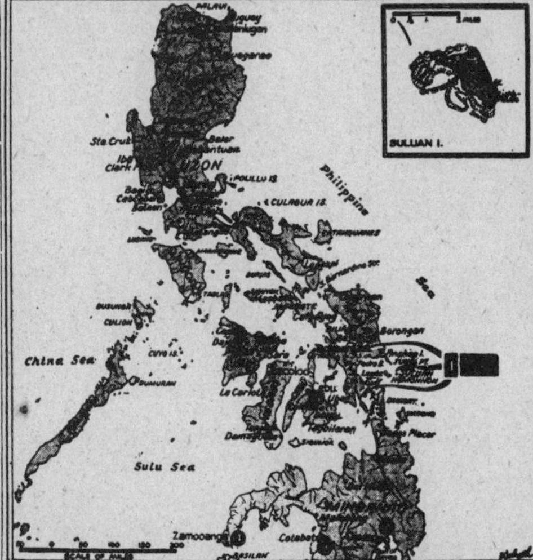

Oct. 20, 1944

The return to the Philippines began at Leyte Gulf (1). Tokyo said the Americans had first invaded Suluan Island (shown in detail on inset). General MacArthur announced the capture of Tacloban in northern Leyte Island, a landing near Cabalian at the southern tip and occupation of the whole eastern side of the island. Bombings were reported at Davao (2), Cotabato (3), Zamboanga (4), Cebu (5), the much-bombed area of Clark Field and Manila (6) and Aparri (7).

2 POLISH FACTIONS NEARER TO ACCORD

Parley Suspends Temporarily, but London Spokesman Is Frankly Optimistic

By The Associated Press.

MOSCOW, Oct. 19—Leaders of the Soviet-sponsored Polish Committee of National Liberation have reached a tentative understanding with Premier Stanislaw Mikolajczyk of the London Government in Exile, and a spokesman for M. Mikolajczyk's delegation said:

"We expect it will be only a matter of weeks before both Polish

Continued on Page 6, Column 2

'We'll Strangle' War Lords, Roosevelt Statement Says

Special to THE NEW YORK TIMES.

WASHINGTON, Friday, Oct. 20—The White House declared in a statement early today that American troops had landed in the Philippines to redeem the pledge made for our return on the surrender of Corregidor and that we would press on to bring about the utter defeat of Japan. Coincident with this announcement President Roosevelt sent a message of congratulations to Gen. Douglas MacArthur, telling him that the whole American nation exulted that the day had come when he had returned to the Philippines and said:

"You have the nation's gratitude and the nation's prayers for success as you and your men fight your way back to Bataan."

[The texts of the President's statement and messages are on Page 11.]

In another message to Admiral Chester W. Nimitz and Admiral William F. Halsey, the President told of the pride with which "the magnificent sweep" of the fleet into enemy waters had been observed and praised them for their "fine cooperation" with General MacArthur.

In still another message President Roosevelt informed President Osmena of the Philippine Government that when the Japanese had

Continued on Page 11, Column 5

OUR PACIFIC FORCES KEYED FOR BIG TASK

Marvels of Land-Sea Warfare Performed by Hard-Hitting Precision Machine

By LINDESAY PARROTT
By Wireless to THE NEW YORK TIMES.

ADVANCED HEADQUARTERS IN THE SOUTHWEST PACIFIC, Oct. 19—What has at last become one of the most elaborate and best trained military precision machines in the world and one that is perhaps unique in the history of warfare was built up for the long, hard push into the Philippines under the leadership of Gen. Douglas MacArthur.

Veterans of the early fighting

Continued on Page 10, Column 5

BEACHHEADS WON

Americans Seize East Coast of Leyte Isle, Are Widening Hold

TACLOBAN CAPTURED

Casualties Are Reported Small in Mighty Blow by Air and Sea

By The Associated Press.

GENERAL MACARTHUR'S HEADQUARTERS in the Philippines, Friday, Oct. 20 (Army radio pool broadcast)—American invasion of the Philippines was officially proclaimed today by Gen. Douglas MacArthur.

Two years and six months after he took sad leave of the islands and relinquished them to Japanese invaders, vowing "I shall return," he announced that his Navy and air-covered ground forces had landed in the archipelago.

[Japanese broadcasts, beginning some twenty-four hours previously, had listed at least three landings, all in the central sector where the invaders would be in position to split the archipelago's 150,000 defenders in half.]

General MacArthur, aboard a warship, went along with the huge convoy from New Guinea, and within four hours after his forces landed began making plans to go ashore.

East Coast Seized

The special communiqué text, in part, follows:

"In a major amphibious operation we have seized the eastern coast of Leyte Island in the Philippines, 600 miles north of Morotai and 2,500 miles from Milne Bay from whence our offensive started nearly sixteen months ago.

"The landing in the Visayas is midway between Luzon and Mindanao and at one stroke splits into two Japanese forces in the Philippines. The enemy expected the attack on Mindanao.

"Tacloban was secured with small casualties. The landing was preceded by heavy air and naval bombardment which was devastating in effect. Our grounds troops are already extending their hold."

General MacArthur said supplies were rolling ashore.

225,000 of Foe in Isles

Among participants in the action were the Sixth United States Army, Navy forces of the Seventh United States Fleet, the Third United States Fleet and the Far Eastern Air Force.

The landings pitted the invaders against Japanese Philippine defenders, estimated at 225,000 under command of Field Marshal Juichi Terauchi.

[The Japanese exulted exactly four days ago that their alleged naval-air victories off Formosa had set back "the impending invasion of the Philippines by at least two months." It turned out that they didn't score any naval-air victories either.]

Eyewitness accounts from the scene reported the American Navy and airforce were on hand in such mammoth strength that the Japanese Navy was nowhere in sight and the Japanese air force, knocked out at all airfields in the Philip-

Continued on Page 10, Column 1

Dewey Backs State Department In Warning Nazis Over Murder

By WARREN MOSCOW
Special to THE NEW YORK TIMES.

ALBANY, Oct. 19—Before leaving tonight for a major address in Pittsburgh tomorrow, Governor Dewey issued a statement approving the State Department's warning to Germany against acts of terrorism and extermination of victims of Nazi aggression still held in German concentration camps.

Mr. Dewey declared that the information that the Nazis were making threats to exterminate victims still alive in occupied countries came to this country "from unquestionably reliable sources."

His statement read:

"Information comes to this country from unquestionably reliable sources that the Nazis, trapped and knowing that they are faced with inevitable defeat, are now resorting to the known gangster terror device of threatening to exterminate their very victims—Poles, Jews and other non-German nationals—now imprisoned by them in their horrible concentration camps in parts of Poland and other countries still occupied by the Nazis.

"The civilized world is now in a position in unmistakable terms to warn the Nazis—military commanders, members of the German Government, their aiders, abettors and supporters—that certain and inevitable justice awaits them for these brutal and wanton murders if their schemes should be carried out.

"I am happy to note that our State Department has issued a

Continued on Page 13, Column 4

War News Summarized

FRIDAY, OCTOBER 20, 1944

General MacArthur, at the head of the United States Sixth Army and Australian units, has landed in the Philippines.

The east shore of Leyte Island has been seized and supplies and heavy equipment are pouring onto the beachheads, he reported today. The landings were made under the guns of the United States Third and Fifth Fleets, an Australian squadron and an umbrella of carrier planes, the RAF and the Far Eastern Air Forces.

The Leyte area is the hardest part of the Philippines to defend; guerrillas there have continually harassed the Japanese occupation troops. It is about 450 miles from Manila, but represents an advance of 600 miles from Morotai and 2,500 miles from Milne Bay, from which General MacArthur started the drive back up the Pacific sixteen months ago.

Meanwhile, Admiral Halsey sent some of his carrier planes over the Manila area to pin down the enemy and wreck more than 100 aircraft. [All the foregoing 1:8; maps, Pages 1 and 10.]

President Roosevelt, calling the landing just a stepping-stone to Japan, radioed General MacArthur: "The whole American nation today exults at the news that the gallant men under your command have landed on Philippine soil." [1:6-7.]

During the past year a task force of unprecedented power has been built up in the Pacific for the reconquest of the Philippines. [1:7.]

Far to the west Allied carrier planes and naval guns battered the Nicobar Islands in the Indian Ocean, Tokyo said [9:5.] and in Burma Tiddim was recaptured by the British. [11:1.]

Foul weather hampered activity on Europe's Western Front. Nevertheless, British and American armor closed in on Venlo, rail junction for the Ruhr and Rhineland, and the Netherland town of Breskens on the Scheldt estuary seemed about to fall to the Canadians. [1:3; map, P. 2.] The battle for Aachen was rapidly drawing to a close against diminishing resistance. [3:1.]

In Italy the Eighth Army bridged the Pisciatello River and captured two towns near Cesena. The Fifth Army took important heights near Bologna and on the west coast. [5:2-3.]

The Red Army, according to Berlin, has invaded East Prussia, capturing the frontier station of Eidtkau and pushing on six miles to threaten Stallupoenen. Moscow was silent on this front, reporting successes only in Latvia, Transylvania and near Debrecen, Hungary, now nearly encircled. [1:4; map, P. 6.]

A tentative understanding was reported reached in Moscow between the contending Polish factions. Premier Mikolajczyk will return to London to obtain his Cabinet's approval. The Lublin Committee was optimistic. [1:3.]

Kaiser Presents to the President 'Specific Pattern' for Reconversion

By C. P. TRUSSELL
Special to THE NEW YORK TIMES.

WASHINGTON, Oct. 19—Henry J. Kaiser, industrialist, put before President Roosevelt today "an immediate specific pattern" for industrial reconversion to peacetime production which he and other manufacturers could begin to carry into operation "right away."

On leaving the White House, Mr. Kaiser reported that the President was "tremendously impressed," adding: "I am convinced that he believes that this pattern of aiding industry is an important step to assure now the transition to full employment in peacetime."

Under the pattern, Mr. Kaiser and other manufacturers, whom he declined to identify, would begin at once to take over war plants which have completed their contracts and are going out of business. The Kaiser group would then transfer to these plants the contracts and machine tools which are preventing reconversion to civilian production in other plants by using floor space required for peacetime production machinery.

Some manufacturers, Mr. Kaiser said, are willing to remain in war production and to take over the partly completed contracts and the machinery which handicaps the transition sought by those desiring to return to civilian manufacture as soon as possible without interfering with the war program.

To insure full-scale production for war, Mr. Kaiser emphasized, the projected reconversion pattern would have to operate gradually. However, he added, the important

Continued on Page 27, Column 1

Fleeing Toward Foe, Halsey Tells Nimitz

By The United Press.

PEARL HARBOR, Oct. 19—Admiral Chester W. Nimitz, Commander in Chief of the Pacific Fleet, said today:

"I have received from Admiral Halsey the comforting assurance that he is now retiring toward the enemy following the salvage of all the Third Fleet ships recently reported sunk by radio Tokyo."

"All the News That's Fit to Print"

The New York Times.

LATE CITY EDITION
Sunny, cool and windy; fair and becoming cooler tonight.
Temperatures Yesterday—Max., 69; Min., 51
Sunrise, 7:19 A. M.; Sunset, 6:01 P. M.

VOL. XCIV..No. 31,687. Entered as Second-Class Matter, Postoffice, New York, N. Y. NEW YORK, THURSDAY, OCTOBER 26, 1944. THREE CENTS IN NEW YORK CITY

U. S. DEFEATS JAPANESE NAVY; ALL FOE'S SHIPS IN ONE FLEET HIT; MANY SUNK; BATTLE CONTINUES

SPECIAL PRIVILEGE SOLD BY NEW DEAL, DEWEY CHARGES

Says Roosevelt Backs Plan for 1,000 to Put '$1,000 on the Line' to Aid Campaign

PARTY LETTER IS QUOTED

Governor Declares in Chicago Administration Lacks 'Honesty' to Solve Post-War Problems

The text of Mr. Dewey's speech will be found on Page 13.

By ALEXANDER FEINBERG
Special to THE NEW YORK TIMES.

CHICAGO, Oct. 25—Governor Dewey declared tonight that "for $1,000 laid on the line to finance the fourth-term drive, this Administration boldly offers for sale 'special privilege.'" which includes the "assisting in the formulation of Administration policies."

Attacking the "rudimentary honesty" of the New Deal, Mr. Dewey, in a major campaign address preceding the appearance of President Roosevelt here Saturday, charged that the Chief Executive himself was the sponsor of the fund raising idea.

The Chicago Stadium, which accommodates 25,000 persons, was packed to capacity, with several thousand others clamoring to obtain admittance. Gov. Dwight H. Green of Illinois presented Mr. Dewey, who was received with tumultuous acclaim. He kept pointing to the microphone to still the demonstration, but it was just short of five minutes before he could begin his speech.

Governor Dewey said that the fund raising plan was disclosed in a letter signed by H. L. McAlister and Sam J. Watkins, State finance chairman, and written on the letterhead of the National Democratic Campaign Headquarters, Little Rock, Ark.

Dewey Quotes Letter

Mr. Dewey quoted the letter as follows:

"This is an invitation to you to join the One Thousand Club.

"The idea of such a club originated at a recent conference at the White House between the President, Robert E. Hannegan, chairman of the Democratic National Committee, and Edwin W. Pauley, treasurer of the committee. At this meeting the President commented:

"'I think it would be a good idea to have a list of one thousand persons banded together from all over the United States to act as a liaison to see that facts relating to the public interest are presented factually to the President and members of Congress.'

"Members of this organization undoubtedly will be granted special privilege by party leaders. These members will be called into conference from time to time to discuss matters of national importance and to assist in the formulation of Administration policies.

"To be eligible for membership in the One Thousand Club will require a contribution of $1,000 to the National Democratic campaign fund."

Mr. Dewey declared that "there in crude, unblushing words is the ultimate expression of New Deal policies," adding:

"And the sponsor of this idea is frankly stated in that letter to be the President himself. The man who holds the highest office within the gift of the American people at a conference in the White House sponsors an idea to sell 'special privilege' and a voice 'in the formulation of Administration policies' for one thousand dollars on the barrelhead."

The Governor said that New

Continued on Page 13, Column 1

No Extra Gasoline For Trip to Polls

By The Associated Press.

WASHINGTON, Oct. 25—Chester Bowles, OPA head, in a letter to Senator Davis, Republican, of Pennsylvania today stated that the OPA could not allow extra gasoline rations for private automobiles to take voters to the polls if other means of transportation are available.

Pennsylvania has no absentee voting law and Senator Davis contended that many persons from his State working elsewhere would be unable to return to cast their ballots unless they received extra gas rations.

"A special ration may be granted to carry persons to and from the polls for the purpose of voting in public elections (including primary elections), provided reasonably adequate alternative means of transportation are not available," Mr. Bowles wrote.

Where no other form of transportation is available those wishing to use cars for voting may apply to their local ration boards on special forms which the boards have available.

WAGNER ACCLAIMS PARTY FARM POLICY

He Says That Dewey Is Vague on Agriculture—Calls His Platform 'Double Talk'

By CLAYTON P. KNOWLES
Special to THE NEW YORK TIMES.

SYRACUSE, N. Y., Oct. 25—The farm plank in the Republican platform offers nothing but "double talk" and Governor Dewey, rather than clarifying the issue, puts forward proposals "as vague and airy as a wisp of smoke," Senator Robert F. Wagner declared tonight as he carried his campaign for re-election into this city in the heart of the farm area.

"Mr. Dewey ridicules the so-called aphabetical agencies," he declared. "But how could low-interest loans have been provided without the Farm Mortgage Corporation? How could farm prices have been supported without the Agricultural Adjustment Administration? How could the number of farms with central electric service have been multiplied three times without the Rural Electrification Administration?

"These programs are not perfect. They need to be improved, but they are solid, they can be seen, they can be felt. When Mr. Dewey talks about the farmer, what he proposes is as vague and airy as a wisp of smoke."

His address, broadcast over a State-wide hook-up by the Columbia Broadcasting System, said that Governor Dewey's Commissioner of Agriculture last spring set minimum milk prices "far above

Continued on Page 12, Column 4

PRESIDENT ELATED

Gives News From Halsey That Foe Is 'Defeated, Damaged, Routed'

TEST IS ON, KING SAYS

Practically All Japanese Fleet in the Battle, Admiral Believes

By LEWIS WOOD
Special to THE NEW YORK TIMES.

WASHINGTON, Oct. 25—President Roosevelt exultantly announced late today the receipt of a report from Admiral William F. Halsey saying that the Japanese Navy in the Philippine area had been "defeated, seriously damaged and routed" by our forces.

Two hours earlier Admiral Ernest J. King, Commander in Chief of the United States Fleet and Chief of Naval Operations, had disclosed that virtually all of the long elusive Japanese Fleet had been engaged at last in the furious sea battle of the Philippines.

These two startling revelations, exciting Washington as nothing has done since the European invasions, were taken here to mean that the vaunted Japanese naval power had been seriously crippled and the road to Tokyo made much easier. At last, it was presumed, the principal part of Japanese naval strength had been nettled out of hiding and then decisively beaten.

Announcement Is Dramatic

The circumstances of the President's statement were thrilling. When only a half dozen newsmen remained in the White House press room at 5:20 P. M., Press Secretary Stephen T. Early appeared at the door.

"Come quick," he cried, slapping his palms together for emphasis.

Rushing to the President's oval-shaped office, the reporters found him seated at his desk, smiling broadly. Obviously he had been interrupted in his late afternoon dictation. Before him lay scattered papers, but directly in front of him was a single sheet of paper, inscribed apparently with his own handwriting.

He had, said the President beamingly, a "real flash," just telephoned to him by Admiral William D. Leahy, Chief of Staff to the President as Commander in Chief of the Army and Navy. Picking up the paper, Mr. Roosevelt slowly and distinctly read:

"The President received today a report from Admiral Halsey that the Japanese Navy in the Philippine area has been defeated, seriously damaged and routed by the United States Navy in that area."

For a moment there was a pause. No one said a word. Then

Continued on Page 3, Column 3

U. S. and Britain Recognize Italy; Action Is First With an Ex-Enemy

By BERTRAM D. HULEN
Special to THE NEW YORK TIMES.

WASHINGTON, Oct. 25—Diplomatic relations with Italy were resumed by the Allies tonight.

Recognition is being accorded by the United States, the other American republics in the United Nations and Britain. The Soviet Union had previously extended recognition to the Government of Premier Ivanoe Bonomi.

Our action was announced by Edward R. Stettinius Jr., acting Secretary of State, who said that Alexander C. Kirk, who has been serving as our diplomatic representative in Rome with the personal rank of Ambassador, would now be accredited to the Italian Government with the rank of Ambassador.

It is expected that Italy will now send an Ambassador here. The appointment of Count Carlos Sforza, long a friend of the United States, to the post, has been forecast since it became evident that recognition would not long be delayed.

Announcement of the recognition has been made at London and is expected at the Latin-American capitals, except for Buenos Aires. Argentina never severed relations with Italy, although she did with Germany and Japan.

The announcement by Mr. Stettinius follows:

"After consultation with the other American republics, as provided in the Resolutions of Rio de

Continued on Page 10, Column 5

SEA POWER OF LAND OF THE RISING SUN SHATTERED IN BATTLE

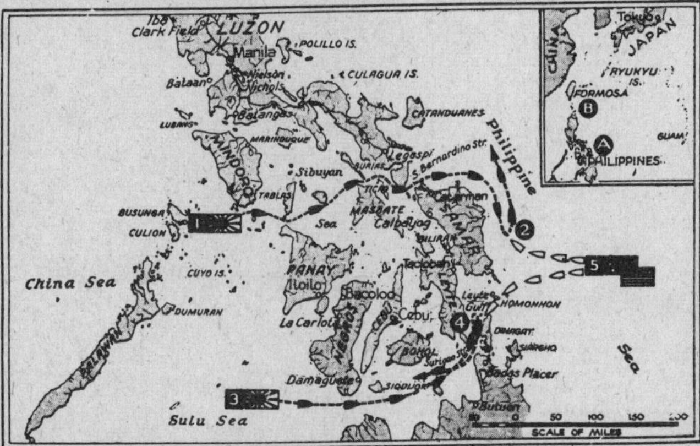

Oct. 26, 1944

Piecing together the statements of Admiral Nimitz and General MacArthur gives this picture of the battle around the Philippines: One Japanese force, including four battleships, ten cruisers and thirteen destroyers, first sighted south of Mindoro (1) steamed east, across the Sibuyan Sea, through San Bernardino Strait and down the coast of Samar (2), where Admiral Kinkaid's combined force (5) attacked it and forced it to retire northward with perhaps ten ships damaged. It was apparently in this action that the American light carrier Princeton was sunk. A second enemy force, first sighted southwest of Negros (3), included two battleships, one or two cruisers and four destroyers. It moved east across the Sulu Sea and through Surigao Strait (4). Admiral Kinkaid attacked this group and it lost one battleship and several cruisers and destroyers; the rest of the force retreated west through the strait. This whole battle scene is at (A) on the inset. A third Japanese force was engaged southeast of Formosa (B).

ALLIES CUT UP FOE IN WEST HOLLAND

British Hammer Germans in One Area of 's Hertogenbosch—Canadians Tighten Traps

By CLIFTON DANIEL
By Wireless to THE NEW YORK TIMES.

SUPREME HEADQUARTERS, Allied Expeditionary Force, Oct. 25—The Germans were rapidly losing their grip tonight on their strongholds between the North Sea and the British Second Army's salient in the Netherlands.

British forces converging from three sides drove them out of all

Continued on Page 7, Column 3

'17 Hours of Hell' Raised In Sea Battle Off Leyte

By RALPH TEATSORTH
United Press Correspondent

ABOARD ADMIRAL KINKAID'S FLAGSHIP, off the Philippines, Thursday, Oct. 26—The Tokyo Express rammed into the American Navy Limited today. The pride of Japan was wrecked so badly it may never make another long run. It was the day our Navy had dreamed about for considerably more than a year.

It was seventeen hours of concentrated hell and the most amazing thing about the battle was that our Pacific Flight Carrier Force—which nobody thought could deliver such a terrific punch—held off the bulk of the Japanese fleet all day and had it on the run all afternoon.

When evening came and most of

Continued on Page 4, Column 7

AIR PLANT IN JAPAN SMASHED BY B-29'S

Omura Target Is 'Perfectly Patterned,' Pilots Say—Foe Lists 100 Planes in Attack

Special to THE NEW YORK TIMES.

WASHINGTON, Oct. 25—While the remnants of the demoralized Japanese Fleet were fleeing from Admiral William F. Halsey's forces in Philippine waters, United States Army Superfortresses today were carrying the war another step closer to the heart of Japan by carrying out a successful mission against the key aircraft assembly plant at Omura on the island of Kyushu.

Twentieth Air Force Headquarters here announced that a medium-sized task force of the mammoth bombers, operating from Twen-

Continued on Page 4, Column 4

AMERICANS MAKE BIG LEYTE JUMPS

Troops Push Westward on Isle—Southern Coast of Samar to the North Now Held

By The United Press.

ADVANCED HEADQUARTERS ON LEYTE, Thursday, Oct. 26—American dismounted cavalry troops have invaded Samar, third largest of the Philippines and last island barrier on the road to Luzon and Manila, while forces fighting on Leyte have punched nine miles inland to seize the key road junction of Burauen.

Gen. Douglas MacArthur also announced in a special communiqué that Field Marshal Count Juichi Terauchi's Japanese defenders of the northern Leyte front were "disintegrating" under the American hammer blows.

The three-mile American advance that occupied Burauen, southern terminus of an inland highway, split the Japanese lines in northern Leyte and threw the enemy back toward the hills, where Filipino guerrillas were reported in action.

The new American triumphs pushed our lines nine miles inland and raised to thirty-one the number of towns and villages captured. Six airfields also have been seized.

The invasion of Samar, with an

Continued on Page 4, Column 5

War News Summarized

THURSDAY, OCTOBER 26, 1944

The Japanese Navy came out to fight in the waters off the Philippines and was severely mauled. One force of four battleships, ten cruisers and thirteen destroyers moved up south of Mindoro into the Sibuyan Sea. Every battleship and at least one cruiser was hit. This flotilla rounded Samar and fled north. We lost an escort carrier.

A second force of two battleships, two cruisers and four destroyers came into the Sulu Sea from southwest of Negros Island. After all the ships had been hit it turned tail and retreated.

A third force, this one with carriers, came down from home waters and the battle was still going on. Most of the engagements were fought from the air and the enemy suffered heavily in plane losses. Our light carrier Princeton was hit and its magazine subsequently exploded. Most of the crew were saved. The Third Pacific Fleet took on the enemy carrier force and the Seventh turned back the two others. [All the foregoing 1:8.]

President Roosevelt, in an impromptu press conference, said that Admiral Halsey, commanding the Third Fleet, had just reported that the Japanese Navy had been "defeated, seriously damaged and routed." Earlier Admiral King had said that almost the entire enemy naval strength was involved in the Philippines battle. Fighting covered an area 600 miles north and south and 250 east and west. Navy officials were elated and felt the whole course of the war might be speeded. [1:3.]

On Leyte American troops had pushed twenty miles north of Tacloban and nine miles inland from Dulag. Additional landings on the northern part of Leyte and the southern part of Samar won control of San Juanico Strait, which separates them. [1:7; map P. 2.]

Superfortresses delivered a smashing assault on Japan's key aircraft plant at Omura on the island of Kyushu. One B-29 was missing. [1:6.]

German positions in the Belgium-Netherland pocket were becoming increasingly untenable as Canadian and British troops drew closer and menaced the enemy retreat line. [1:4; map P. 7.] More than 2,200 American and British bombers lashed rail and oil targets in the Reich. Six bombers and one of a great fighter escort were missing. [9:1.]

Russian forces captured the German port and U-boat base of Kirkenes in Norway and thirty other Norwegian villages. [1:6-7; map P. 11.] To the south the Red Army renewed its drive on Warsaw, gained more ground in East Prussia and liberated all of Transylvania by capturing Satu-Mare and Carei. [12:1, with map.]

Mount Belmonte, guarding the southern approaches to Bologna, was captured by Americans of the Fifth Army in Italy. The British Eighth Army gained three miles in the Adriatic sector. A German withdrawal was indicated. [10:7.]

The United Nations have resumed diplomatic relations with Italy, the first former enemy state to receive recognition. [1:2-3.]

Russians Invade North Norway; Take Kirkenes in Wide Advance

By W. H. LAWRENCE
By Wireless to THE NEW YORK TIMES.

MOSCOW, Oct. 25—Entering their ninth country in less than seven months, Red Army forces smashed across the Norwegian frontier today and liberated the Barents Sea port of Kirkenes and thirty other Norwegian villages just fifty-four months and twenty-one days after the beginning of Adolf Hitler's treacherous invasion of the Scandinavian country.

This new expedition of Russian troops outside the Soviet Union was announced by Premier Joseph Stalin in a special order of the day and was saluted by Moscow's massed guns and highlighted in tonight's communiqué.

The Soviet Union's Norwegian campaign brings Allied armies back on the soil of that restless country for the first time since June 15, 1941, when the British had to withdraw their poorly equipped forces in the face of numerically superior German forces.

[On its European front the Red Army reopened the battle for Warsaw by outflanking the Polish capital on the north, drove farther into East Prussia against desperate resistance and completed the liberation of Transylvania.]

It would be wrong to assume from this dash across the Norwegian frontier at its northernmost point that the liberation of

Continued on Page 11, Column 4

BATTLESHIP IS SUNK

Seventh Fleet Smashes Two Japanese Forces Converging on Leyte

REMNANTS IN FLIGHT

They Are Hotly Pursued—Third Enemy Force Is Hit Off Formosa

The Imperial Japanese Fleet has been brought to battle. It is suffering a crushing defeat. Two of its divisions have been routed. One has been almost destroyed. Contact has been made with the main force southeast of Formosa by Admiral William F. Halsey's Third Fleet. That engagement is continuing, said the last communiqué.

Two strong Japanese naval forces converged on Leyte Gulf through the San Bernardino Strait in the Philippines to the north and the Surigao Strait to the south. Vice Admiral Thomas C. Kinkaid's Seventh Fleet smashed these two forces and put the remnants to flight after sinking or heavily damaging every ship in the southern enemy force.

One big Japanese carrier has been sunk. Two more have been heavily damaged and undoubtedly are out of action. One Japanese battleship of the Yamasiro class has been sunk. At least four others have been heavily damaged. Several enemy cruisers and destroyers have been sunk. Many others have been hit, both by bombs and torpedoes.

Enemy Defeated and Routed

The only announced American loss is the converted cruiser-carrier Princeton sunk. Other escort carriers were damaged by fire from one of the enemy battleship forces.

Gen. Douglas MacArthur reported triumphantly that "the Japanese Navy has suffered its most crushing defeat of the war." Admiral Ernest J. King, in Washington, said that "practically all" of the Japanese fleet was engaged and that he was confident of the outcome. President Roosevelt called a special press conference to announce receipt of a message from Admiral William F. Halsey reporting that the enemy has been "defeated, seriously damaged and routed."

Pending official word from Pearl Harbor, it appeared the greatest surface and naval air action in the history of naval warfare was being fought and won by the Pacific Fleet, the greatest naval force that ever went down to the sea.

Fate of Leyte Decided

SEVENTH FLEET HEADQUARTERS, Philippines, Thursday, Oct. 26 (UP)—Japan lost the first, and possibly the decisive, round in an all-out battle to halt on the Philippines line the American advance toward her home islands.

This occurred early yesterday morning when Admiral Kinkaid's outnumbered fleet battered and put to rout Japanese battle forces converging on Leyte Gulf.

Complete results are lacking as the action is continuing, with planes from Admiral Kinkaid's hurt but still fighting carrier force hitting the surviving enemy warships as they are retiring. [General MacArthur said the Japanese force that came through Surigao Strait fled back through it to the west and the other was in flight in a northerly direction.]

[Gordon Walker in a Mutual broadcast from the Philippines said "a Navy spokesman here claimed that practically every

Continued on Page 3, Column 2

"All the News That's Fit to Print"

The New York Times.

LATE CITY EDITION
Cloudy and colder today. Cloudy, cold with snow or rain tomorrow.
Temperatures Yesterday—Max., 35; Min., 12
Sunrise, 8:30 A. M.; Sunset, 8:48 P. M.

VOL. XCIV...No. 31,757. Entered as Second-Class Matter, Postoffice, New York, N. Y. NEW YORK, THURSDAY, JANUARY 4, 1945. THREE CENTS IN NEW YORK CITY

1ST ARMY OPENS DRIVE AT TOP OF BELGIAN BULGE; 3D GAINS BEYOND BASTOGNE, 7TH FORCED BACK; U. S. FLIERS BOMB LUZON, FORMOSA AND JAPAN

DEWEY ASKS STATE TO SPEND BILLION IN POST-WAR AIDS

Urges More Social Welfare, $6,500,000 Pay Rise in Reading Message to Legislature

FOR NEW SURPLUS FREEZE

Advises Present Commercial Rents, More Housing Here and Present Tax Rate

The text of the Governor's message appears on Page 12.

By LEO EGAN
Special to The New York Times.

ALBANY, Jan. 3—Addressing the opening session of the State Legislature of 1945 today, Governor Dewey outlined a huge program of State public works, to be undertaken in the post-war period at a cost that might exceed $1,000,000,000. He recommended an immediate start toward expanding the State's social welfare laws and advocated "locking up" an expected Treasury surplus of $150,000,000 with the $163,000,000 put aside from last year.

Delivering his message in person at a joint meeting of the Senate and the Assembly and speaking for an hour, the Governor also advised a program of pay increases for State employes, including members of the Legislature, that will increase payrolls by about $6,500,000 a year; reforms to meet the problems of juvenile delinquency and the rehabilitation of criminals; changes in the methods of selecting judges and more State aid for education.

High Points Broadcast

A condensed version of the message was delivered by the Governor in a State-wide broadcast from 6:15 to 6:40 o'clock in the evening. In the broadcast, as in the message, he declared that the overriding task for all in the country was still the winning of the war, and so far as that job was concerned, the most trying months were still ahead.

But, as a result of measures that had been adopted in New York, the State was today better able to meet the demands of the future than at any time in its history. As the result of the establishment of a post-war reconstruction fund the State would be able to plan a construction program as a unit. This would serve the twofold purpose of taking up the slack in employment caused by the cessation of war industries and meet the needs of the people of the State.

Political Angle Seen

It was the Governor's first major public appearance since his defeat for the Presidency and there were some among his listeners who saw political significance in his suggestions for expanding social welfare laws. The expansions, in general, aim to put into effect for the State the change he advocated on a national scale in his San Francisco and Los Angeles speeches in the Presidential campaign.

Without specifically endorsing the adoption of a merit rating system for levying unemployment insurance taxes, the Governor presented the major arguments in favor of such a change and recommended that a decision on the subject be reached at the current session.

Of particular interest to New York City were recommendations that the Legislature approve measures for freezing commercial rents within the city; enact laws designed to curb and eliminate racial and religious discrimination, and allocate an additional $35,000,000 of the State Housing bond issue of $300,000,000 for low cost housing for New York City.

At the outset of his address, the Governor disclosed that the State's budgetary surplus this year would be about $150,000,000, roughly $20,000,000 higher than unofficial estimates made as recently as a week ago. He recommended that this surplus be locked up in a post-war reconstruction fund as was the

Continued on Page 13, Column 6

Mayor Forecasts Increase In Realty Valuations Here

Says No One Can Tell Tax Rate for Next Year — Wants Sales and Other Emergency Levies Made 'Permanent'

By PAUL CROWELL

Whether the basic real estate tax rate for 1945-46 is higher or lower than the current rate of $2.74 for each hundred dollars of assessed valuation, there will be substantial increases in realty valuations for the coming fiscal year, Mayor La Guardia indicated yesterday in his annual message to the City Council.

At the same time, in a review of the city's wartime fiscal problems, he gave notice that the Legislature would be asked to make "permanent" the existing emergency taxes, chief of which is the 1 per cent sales tax, and also restore to the city the public utility and stock transfer taxes collected in the city.

The Mayor's remarks on taxes and valuations gave point to a ninety-five-minute talk to the Council, in which he painted the city as a solvent organization and described its huge post-war capital outlay program and the need for funds to maintain essential city services.

The message, delivered by the Mayor in person, told the Council that the 1945-46 real estate rate was unpredictable at this time, but that he wanted to say "with all its significance" that property values throughout the city had increased during the past year. As he was leaving City Hall the Mayor was asked whether the quoted words indicated that increased valuations were in the offing.

"Atta boy! You've guessed it!" he replied.

"At this moment," the Mayor declared, in his message to the Council, "I do not believe there is anyone in the City of New York who can predict whether we will have a higher or a lower tax rate. It all depends on local, State and national conditions. We have a

Continued on Page 20, Column 2

18-25 Farm Labor in Draft; Hershey Acts on Byrnes Plea

By JOHN H. CRIDER
Special to The New York Times.

WASHINGTON, Jan. 3—Maj. Gen. Lewis B. Hershey, Director of Selective Service, telegraphed to State directors this afternoon directions to re-examine all deferred farm workers of 18 through 25 years of age for possible induction. His action followed receipt of a letter from James F. Byrnes, Director of War Mobilization and Reconversion, asking him in behalf of President Roosevelt and himself to look into the draft status of the 364,000 men in the 18-25 group deferred in agricultural employment.

Only two days ago, in his report to Congress, Mr. Byrnes urged legislation to permit the Government to compel men classified as 4-F to work in war jobs or join the armed services.

Both actions reflected the critical manpower situation resulting from demands of the War and Navy Departments for more young fighting men which, Mr. Byrnes said in a letter to General Hershey, will exhaust "the eligibles in the 18 through 25 year age group at an early date."

General Hershey's telegrams to State directors contained the text of the Byrnes letter and requested them to forward the letter to local and appeal boards and to direct local boards to review promptly "the cases of all registrants ages 18 through 25 deferred in Class II-C, excluding those identified by the letters 'F' or 'L.'"

The letters "F" and "L," Selective Service officials explained, apply to some 800,000 men either rejected or approved for limited service last spring, who were permitted to retain their occupational deferments if they continued working at their essential jobs.

The telegrams also asked directors to direct local boards "to issue orders for pre-induction physical examination" to all of the same category of registrants "in accord-

Continued on Page 11, Column 3

WALLACE IS ASKING FOR COMMERCE POST

Preference for Secretaryship Is Said to Have Been Stated in Letter to President

By LEWIS WOOD
Special to The New York Times.

WASHINGTON, Jan. 3 — Vice President Henry Wallace has written to President Roosevelt, expressing his preference to become Secretary of Commerce, if that post should be open, it was stated in Administration circles today. The President, it was added, has not replied unless he did so recently.

It has been variously reported that Mr. Wallace would like to head the Commerce establishment, but this, it is said, is the first disclosure that he conveyed his desire to the President in a letter rather than in person. On the other hand, it was said that Mr. Wallace had scrupulously refrained from any conversation with Mr. Roosevelt on the subject, holding that this might embarrass his chief. The Vice President has also refused at least one offer of personal intervention.

From the same source it was ascertained that Mr. Wallace's ambition to become Secretary of Commerce is based on a belief that he might be able to use some Government funds for the benefit of the small business man, instead of

Continued on Page 36, Column 2

96,369 Planes Produced in 1944, Frame Weight Is 50% Above 1943

Special to The New York Times.

WASHINGTON, Jan. 3—In a production effort corresponding to the record-breaking achievements of other war industries last year, the country's aircraft plants turned out 96,369 planes of all types in 1944, with a total air-frame weight of 1,112,000,000 pounds, J. A. Krug, chairman of the War Production Board, announced in a year-end report today.

Even with planned reductions in aircraft production undertaken as early as last summer, when the first cutbacks were announced, the output in 1944 was substantially greater than the previous record of 85,946 planes delivered in 1943. First-of-the-year plans, however, called for 109,000 planes in 1944.

Nevertheless, in air-frame weight, the achievement was even more impressive, since total weight of all planes last year exceeded by about 50 per cent their total air-frame weight in 1943. This rise indicated the degree by which war planners were shifting from the light planes, such as trainers, to the heavy combat bomber.

Production in December alone, Mr Krug said, was "a good accomplishment" only when the short month and Christmas holidays were taken into consideration. Overall output of 6,697 planes fell

Continued on Page 23, Column 4

DIES GROUP IS PUT ON PERMANENT BASIS BY HOUSE, 207 TO 186

70 Democrats Join in Surprise Move as Congress Meets on Note of Win the War Quickly

RAYBURN CALLS FOR UNITY

Warns Against Over-Optimism and Urges 'Total Duty'— 600 Bills Are Offered

By C. P. TRUSSELL
Special to The New York Times.

WASHINGTON, Jan. 3—The Seventy-ninth Congress convened today in an atmosphere denoting determination to see the war through as quickly as possible, but marked by expressions of uncertainty as to the courses its legislative programs will take. Caution on war and peace plans was the watchword, while the members awaited President Roosevelt's message on the state of the Union, which will be read Saturday.

The House, however, departed unexpectedly from routine business to vote, 207 to 186, to make permanent the special Committee on Un-American Activities, a group which the Administration has opposed since its creation in 1938.

This action was viewed on Capitol Hill as a confirmation of predictions that, despite the Democratic gains in November, the President would still have to deal with coalitions in Congress, on home-front issues at least. Seventy Democrats, sixty-three of them from Southern States, voted in favor of the committee.

Senate Accepts Bust of Hull

The Senate, meanwhile, barred legislative business, inducted its newly elected and re-elected members, departed from its routine only to permit the presentation of a bust of former Secretary of State Hull and adjourned until Saturday.

In cloakroom and corridors, members viewed seriously the news of setbacks on the Western Front and spoke apprehensively, though with frank admission that first-hand knowledge was lacking, of political and other developments abroad. Some legislators reported that their constituents were press-

Continued on Page 28, Column 4

ENEMY HIT HARD THROUGHOUT FAR EAST THEATRE

Jan. 4, 1945

As neutralizing attacks against Japanese bases on Iwo and Haha Islands (1) were pressed by Army bombers, B-29's, directed from a new headquarters on Guam, hammered Nagoya, on Honshu (2). Carrier-based planes struck at Okinawa in the Ryukyu Islands (3) and at Formosa (4). These carrier blows were probably preparatory to important future operations focusing on Luzon (5). The southeastern tail of that island was raked by Allied planes, which also sank or fired twenty-five enemy ships off the west coast. In Burma the Chinese captured Wanting (6) and with a column below Bhamo (7) clamped a pincers on Namhkam. The British took Ye-u (8).

25 Ships Sunk or Set Afire Off Luzon; Carriers Strike Formosa and Okinawa

MacArthur's Fliers Cause Much Luzon Damage—New Landings Made on Mindoro—Leyte Casualties Go Up to 121,064

By The Associated Press.

ADVANCED HEADQUARTERS, on Leyte, Thursday, Jan. 4—American forces, putting increasing pressure on the northern Philippines, sank or set afire twenty-five Japanese ships along the west coast of Luzon New Year's Day while American troops made two additional unopposed landings on the east and west coasts of Mindoro.

The heavy blows against enemy shipping ranged virtually the full

Continued on Page 10, Column 4

Japanese Record Sounds Made by Superfortresses

Domei said yesterday that the Japanese Broadcasting Association had recorded the sound of the engines of the Superfortresses and that the recordings would be broadcast "to familiarize the public with the sound." The dispatch was reported by the Federal Communications Commission.

Navy Fliers Attack Foe's Base Only 310 Miles From Japan—Iwo Gets Its 26th Bombing—Army Planes Bomb in Bonins

By ROBERT TRUMBULL
By Telephone to The New York Times.

PEARL HARBOR, Jan. 3—Pacific Fleet carrier planes made simultaneous strikes yesterday at Formosa and Okinawa. The latter base is in the Ryukyu Islands, only 310 nautical miles from the southern tip of Japan proper.

The attacks, announced by Fleet Admiral Chester W. Nimitz this morning, were the second seaborne operation of the war against both of these extremely important air bases, deep within the enemy's inner defensive zone.

No details of the strikes were available here today. The ships participating, believed to be composed of fast carrier task forces from Admiral William F. Halsey's Third Fleet, under immediate command of Vice Admiral J. S. McCain, presumably are not yet in a position to break radio silence. It is possible that the attacks are continuing, although the communiqué gave no such indication.

The blow at Formosa followed the first Philippine base air attack of the war on this island Sunday by Navy Liberators, presumably from Mindoro. Formosa had previously been hit by B-29's from airdromes in Asia.

Fleet Admiral Nimitz also announced today the twenty-sixth consecutive bombing of Iwo in the Volcano Islands and an attack on the town of Okimura on Haha in

Continued on Page 9, Column 5

War News Summarized

THURSDAY, JANUARY 4, 1945

The United States First Army went over to the offensive on the northern flank of the German salient in Belgium, complementing the Third Army's smash in the south fanning out from Bastogne. No details were available on the progress of the new American assault, but General Patton's men were punching out small gains against heavy resistance.

In the Saar the enemy was attacking along a thirty-nine-mile front in an effort to drive the Americans in that area from Reich soil. The Seventh Army, although holding or slowing the Germans, was reported to have withdrawn to a line behind the Lauter River, in the east. [All the foregoing 1:8; maps P. 4.]

The Eighth Air Force established a new winter record of twelve consecutive days of bombing yesterday when it showered 3,000 tons on more than a dozen communications centers in western Germany. The RAF again struck benzol plants, this time near Dortmund. [3:1.]

Germans trying to relieve their trapped garrison in Budapest drove through Russian lines southeast of Komarno, thirty miles from the Hungarian capital. In Czechoslovakia the Red Army drew closer to Lucenec. [1:6-7; map P. 2.] Fifth Army patrols in Italy pushed toward Massa, the strongest German position on the Tyrrhenian. [5:7.]

General Plastiras has formed a new Greek Government described as liberal but not radical. In addition to the Premiership he took over the War, Navy, Air and Merchant Marine posts. [8:3.]

Japan was hit heavy blows from several directions in coordinated attacks participated in by Superfortresses, carrier planes and land-based aircraft.

Pacific Fleet bombers struck Formosa and Okinawa, largest of the Ryukyu Islands, 310 miles southwest of Japan. Installations on the Bonin Islands were hit by other planes and Iwo Island, in the Volcanos, was smashed for the twenty-sixth straight day. [1:7.]

B-29's carried the war to industrial targets on the main home island of Honshu. Tokyo said ninety Superfortresses had bombed Nagoya, Osaka and Hamamatsu. One big bomber was lost. [10:1.]

General MacArthur sent his aircraft against Luzon, sinking or setting afire twenty-five ships on a sweep of the island's west coast, smashing installations and barracks from Legaspi to Batangas in the south and destroying at least eleven planes in an attack on Manila's Clark Field. American troops made new unopposed landings on both the east and west coasts of Mindoro. [1:5.]

Wanting, on the Burma Road, was captured by Chinese troops who pushed on to Kiuko, leaving only fifteen miles of the Ledo-Burma supply route to be cleared. In central Burma the British occupied Ye-u. [1:6.]

Turkey, in response to American and British requests, will break diplomatic and economic relations with Japan on Saturday. [9:1.]

BURMA ROAD POINT IS WON BY CHINESE

Wanting Is Regained—British Occupy Ye-u in the Drive Toward Mandalay

By The Associated Press.

CHUNGKING, China, Thursday, Jan. 4—The Chinese High Command announced today the recapture of Wanting, Burma Road town on the Chinese-Burma border, in a smashing climax to China's first real offensive of the war.

A communiqué said that the town, which was captured by the Japanese in May, 1942, fell at 4 P. M. yesterday and that "enemy dead and war trophies were being counted, while enemy remnants were fleeing southward, with our troops in pursuit."

[The Chinese at Wanting also

Continued on Page 10, Column 4

Nazis Push Back Toward Budapest; Take Danube Towns From Russians

By The Associated Press.

LONDON, Thursday, Jan. 4—Strong German counter-attacks northwest of Budapest, which the Russians said were aimed at relieving the trapped Nazi garrison in the embattled Hungarian capital, have overrun several towns on the south bank of the Danube, Moscow announced last night.

The broadcast Soviet communiqué declared enemy blows southeast of Komarno, on the Danube, almost forty-five miles northwest of Budapest, had been repulsed, then added:

"At the cost of heavy losses in men and matériel, the enemy was able to capture several populated places on the southern bank of the Danube."

The names and locations were not reported, but the communiqué referred to "large enemy forces of infantry and tanks." An early morning report from Moscow said more than forty German tanks were destroyed and "several thousand" Germans killed in that area.

The Soviet communiqué also announced that troops of Marshal Rodion Y. Malinovsky, driving on Lucenec, communications center in southern Slovakia near the Hungarian border northeast of Budapest, had captured Sacher, a town

Continued on Page 2, Column 3

U. S. MOVE IS VEILED

Point of Drive Against Salient Not Disclosed—Patton Widens Breach

SNOW CURBS FLIERS

7th Army Burns Bridges in Withdrawal—Foe Still Seeks Weak Spot

By DREW MIDDLETON
By Wireless to The New York Times.

SUPREME HEADQUARTERS, Allied Expeditionary Force, Jan. 3—Gen. Dwight D. Eisenhower dealt the shrewdest blow of his counter-offensive today, when, with Lieut. Gen. George S. Patton's tanks and infantry fanning out east, west and north of Bastogne on the south, he launched the American First Army against the northern flank of the German salient in Belgium.

The attack opened at a grave moment for the Allies. The Germans are pressing their southern attacks along the thirty-nine-mile front from Shaffhausen, in the Saar, to Phillipsbourg in the Eastern Vosges, and, although the American resistance in that area is stiffening, the Germans are still on the move, threatening to drive the Allies out of the Saar on the west and menacing control of the Alsace plain on the east.

From the area south of Liége, on the north, to Wissembourg gap on the south Allied and German armies were locked in a great battle. The American Third and First Armies were assaulting the flanks of Field Marshal von Runstedt's offensive in the north, but to the south the initiative lies with the enemy, who is hammering boldly and successfully at American positions.

Little Tactical Air Support

For the first time in nine days American armies fought without extensive support from tactical air forces. With fighter-bombers and medium bombers of the Ninth Air Force pinned on their airfields by weather and the Second Tactical Air Command restricted to a few sorties by Mitchells and Bostons against Houffalize, north of Bastogne, it was once again left to the Eighth Air Force to deliver the heaviest Allied attacks.

More than 1,100 Flying Fortresses and Liberators hammered rail and road centers northwest of Karlsruhe in the area behind the German attacks in northern Alsace and near the Belgian-German frontier, among other targets.

The First Army's assault in the north has placed von Rundstedt in a defensive position for the first time since he opened his offensive Dec. 16. With eight divisions in line, four of them armored, he has managed to hold the attack by General Patton's Third Army on the southern flank in check so long as there has been no important Allied attack against the northern flank of his position.

Halts German Offensive

Little is known here of the assault from the north save that it has begun. However, since Lieut. Gen. Courtney H. Hodges — who, according to last reports here, is still in command of the First Army —has had more than two weeks to collect his forces, the attack is believed to be on a considerable scale. Its start certainly relieves the Allies of any concern about serious continuation of the German offensive westward in this area.

Moreover, it is now clear that von Rundstedt has committed a considerable proportion of his Panzer and Panzer Grenadier divisions to the defense of the Ardennes salient. It may prove impossible to cut off these divisions, but with the start of the First Army's attack it is clear that they will be brought to battle and perhaps destroyed.

The movement that the American First Army began today is not part of a pincers operation. It is the opening on the north of an Allied counter-offensive against a

Continued on Page 4, Column 5

U.S. Army

American foot soldiers trudge down a snow-covered Belgian road to link up with other units advancing against enemy forces.

U.S. Marine Corps

A Marine flame-throwing tank goes into action, along with Marine snipers, as the battle for the possession of Iwo Jima rages on.

U.S. Navy

Fourth Marine Division moving up the beach of Iwo Jima

"All the News That's Fit to Print"

The New York Times.

LATE CITY EDITION
Sunny with moderate winds.
Temperatures Yesterday—Max., 44; Min., 34
Sunrise today, 7:30 A. M.; Sunset, 6:41 P. M.

Section 1
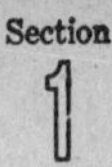

NEWS INDEX, PAGE 39, THIS SECTION

Copyright, 1945, by The New York Times Company.

VOL. XCIV..No. 31,809. Entered as Second-Class Matter, Postoffice, New York, N. Y. NEW YORK, SUNDAY, FEBRUARY 25, 1945. Including Magazine and Book Sections. TEN CENTS New York City and Suburban Area (15c Elsewhere)

AMERICANS DRIVE FOUR MILES BEYOND THE ROER; OUR CARRIER AIRCRAFT SLASH AT TOKYO AGAIN; MARINES WIN HALF OF IWO'S CENTRAL AIRFIELD

WMC DASHES HOPES OF EASED CURFEW; MAYOR ACTS TODAY

He Is Expected to Announce Order to Guide Cafes—Latter to Drop 25,000

LICENSE REFUND PLEA SET

Clubs Packed by Many Having Last Fling and Big Crowds Are Due Tonight

Hopes fostered by operators of night clubs and other amusement places that tomorrow night's midnight "curfew" might be eased to 1 A. M. received a jolt yesterday when the War Manpower Commission, in Washington, decreed that the "request" for midnight closing as originally announced by War Mobilization Director James F. Byrnes would not be altered.

Meanwhile, as night spots were packed and prepared for larger crowds tonight for last-minute flings, Mayor La Guardia stood his ground on the position he took Friday that the closing time for New York City places would remain the same until he had an opportunity to study the WMC edict.

The Mayor will confer with Mrs. Anna M. Rosenberg, regional director of the WMC, at 11 o'clock this morning in City Hall and is expected to make some definite announcement in his weekly broadcast over WNYC, city-owned station.

A survey of midtown night clubs, both in the Broadway area and on the East Side, showed they were doing a capacity business, but the managers were unanimous in declaring that capacity business had been the rule on Saturday night for some time past. All said, however, that reservations and telephone queries indicated larger crowds than usual tonight.

Tavern Owners Accuse Drys

Tavern owners throughout the city lined up with Billy Rose, owner of the Diamond Horseshoe, who had charged that the "curfew" was an "insidious move on the part of the drys to force prohibition back on the country."

Joseph Maguire, president of the United Liquor Dealers of Manhattan, tavern owners' group, said last night that at least 25,000 persons employed in the city's 7,500 taverns will get "pink slips" tonight.

After a meeting of his organization and the Bronx Tavern Owners Association, headed by John Kyle, at 2b7 Broadway, Mr. Maguire said a resolution was adopted characterizing the Byrnes order as "discriminatory" and declaring that "no increased war effort will be justifiably accomplished through its operation."

Tavern owners in New York City, he said, will send a committee to call upon the New York State Liquor Authority tomorrow morning to "demand a refund" on the $1,200 license fee they pay for operating until 4 A. M. six days a week and 3 A. M. on Sundays.

Says Men Can't Do War Work

"The men who will be thrown out of work as a result of this order are definitely unsuitable for any important part in the war effort," Mr. Maguire said. "Our industry has been gone over with a fine toothcomb by the Army and those now employed would be of little use in any war plant.

"Speaking for the tavern owners in this city and throughout the country, we cannot make too emphatic our feeling that this is just another move on the part of the million-dollar dry lobby in Washington to use the war as an instrument for forcing prohibition back on us."

Mr. Maguire said that his organization was sending a letter to Governor Dewey demanding that he "declare himself in keeping State rights intact." The Byrnes order, he asserted, is a direct violation of State rights in that it

Continued on Page 36, Column 2

Germans Are Gloomy About U.S. Offensive

By The Associated Press.

LONDON, Feb. 24—Amid unconfirmed reports that the Russians were crossing the final German defense lines before Berlin, German commentators said today that the "greatest mass of men and material ever assembled since the Normandy invasion" was forcing open the historic gate between the Maas [Meuse] River and the Eifel Mountains.

The German commentator, Capt. Ludwig Sertorius, declared that the Allies had hurled at least forty divisions at the Maas-Eifel sector alone and he predicted still greater blows to the south. Cologne was reported to be aflame after an aerial hammering and Berlin admitted that "many" bridgeheads had been merged across the Roer River between Linnich and Dueren in the past twenty-four hours as the Americans wedged deeper into the German defenses.

JOINT ARMS BOARD SHAPED IN MEXICO

Inter-American Parley Likely to Set Up Defense Council—U. S. Backs Proposal

By CAMILLE M. CIANFARRA
Special to The New York Times.

MEXICO CITY, Feb. 24—The Inter-American Conference on Problems of War and Peace is expected to create a permanent military board to draft and develop joint plans for the defense of this hemisphere, it was learned today.

This step, which is supported on the whole by the United States, is proposed in a resolution that Mexico will submit next week. It will call for the creation of a body composed of representatives of the general staffs of all the American nations represented at the Chapultepec conference.

Its aim is to build machinery for unified military action against any power outside or on this continent that attacks an American nation. One objective will be the standardization of military equipment and training methods throughout the hemisphere.

Latin-American delegates said that, if approved, Mexico's suggestion would represent a highly important development in the evolution of inter-American collaboration. Fundamentally it is designed to implement and strengthen the plans submitted by many nations here, including the United States, Colombia and Uruguay, for a regional security system within the framework of the Dumbarton Oaks proposals.

Some of these plans advocate the use of force in the event of aggression against an American nation, and the Mexican resolution would provide for machinery to implement that principle. The view of the Mexican delegation is that its suggestion would be not only in harmony with the Dumbarton Oaks plan for dealing with threats to the peace or acts of aggression, but also a valuable addi-

Continued on Page 17, Column 4

BIG FORCE STRIKES

Tokyo Indicates 1,600 Planes Hit in Waves—Sky Fights Swirl

5TH FLEET OFF COAST

Military, Naval and Air Bases Are Targets, Nimitz Announces

By Wireless to The New York Times.

ADVANCED HEADQUARTERS, Guam, Sunday, Feb. 25—Our fleet is at it again. A great force of carriers and battleships is steaming along close to Japan's shore while hundreds of carrier aircraft, perhaps as big a force as that which hit the same territory nine days ago, are striking again at the same target, the industrial center of Tokyo.

[Tokyo broadcasts estimated that the attacking force numbered as many as 1,600 planes, about 400 more than were believed to have taken part in the previous smash at the Japanese capital on Feb. 16 and 17.]

Remnants of the Japanese air force, which lost 500 planes positively destroyed and 150 damaged in the previous American attack on the Japanese capital, were presumed to be rising to the defense of its homeland as our Hellcats strafed military objectives, airfields and naval installations.

[Enemy broadcasts recorded by the Federal Communications System said Japanese planes were battling the attackers over the Tokyo area.]

Spruance in Command

The attack was announced briefly in a communiqué from Admiral Chester W. Nimitz reading as follows:

"Carrier aircraft of the Fifth Fleet are attacking military, naval and air installations in and around Tokyo. Admiral Raymond A. Spruance is present in command of the Fifth Fleet and Vice Admiral Marc A. Mitscher is in tactical command of the fast carrier task force making the attack."

Admiral Mitscher's force, the famous Task Force 58, is presumed to include fifteen to twenty of the fastest carriers and swiftest battleships, protected by a screen of destroyers, cruisers and minesweepers.

When the force struck on Feb. 16 and 17 we escaped without a single Japanese plane's having hit the floating bases from which the Hellcats had come, despite the fact that the attack lasted two days. In that strike the Hellcats bore the burden the first day, hitting the airfields. Helldivers and Grumman Avengers struck aircraft factories, engine, power and electronic plants the second day. This attack may be following the same pattern, although no information on this is available here.

The Tokyo radio was off the air most of the morning. The enemy

Continued on Page 25, Column 5

JAPANESE OVERRUN

Marines Smash Through Maze of Defenses in Bloody Iwo Battle

REACH PLATEAU'S TOP

Drive to Strip's Center, Widen Beachhead, Mop Up on Volcano

By WARREN MOSCOW
By Wireless to The New York Times.

ADVANCED HEADQUARTERS, Guam, Sunday, Feb. 25—Despite bazooka-type weapons and new 1,100-pound rocket bombs used by fiercely fighting Japanese in a mass of powerful interlocking defenses, the marines on Iwo Island pushed northward 300 to 500 yards to overrun half of the fighter airstrip in the center of the island on Saturday.

In a general push they widened the beachhead on the eastern coast by 600 yards, overcoming a maze of connecting pillboxes, blockhouses and fortified caves. They passed through heavily mined areas to make the advances, the greatest in one day since the landing on Monday.

[Secretary of the Navy James V. Forrestal is at Guam for conferences with Admiral Nimitz after having gone ashore at Iwo, The Associated Press reported.]

In a single area of 400 by 600 yards on the east coast, the marines had to neutralize about 100 caves, thirty to forty feet deep, indicating clearly why the seventy-four-day aerial bombardment of the island and the three-day ship shelling prior to our landing failed to decimate the garrison or its supplies.

Supplies Pouring Ashore

The marines are benefiting from the capture of Mount Suribachi, volcano at the southern end of the island, and the advance northward. Enemy artillery fire no longer is dominating the ..terior area under American control. The mortar fire on the marines' landing places has been reduced and supplies are pouring ashore.

Apparently the Japanese on Iwo are using new techniques developed from lessons of previous American

Continued on Page 28, Column 4

OLD GLORY GOES UP OVER IWO

Marines of the Fifth Division hoist the American flag atop Mount Suribachi

Associated Press Wirephoto (Navy radio from Guam)

EGYPTIAN PREMIER SLAIN IN CHAMBER

Extremist Lawyer Shoots Him After Reading of Decree Putting Nation in War

By SAM POPE BREWER
By Wireless to The New York Times.

CAIRO, Egypt, Feb. 24—Premier Ahmed Maher Pasha was shot and killed in Parliament tonight after he had read a royal decree declaring war against Germany and Japan.

Critically wounded by four revolver shots, the Premier was carried to a first-aid room in the

Continued on Page 10, Column 2

Eisenhower Points New Push At Knockout Blow in West

By Wireless to The New York Times.

SUPREME HEADQUARTERS, Allied Expeditionary Force, Feb. 24—Gen. Dwight D. Eisenhower asserted today that the offensive on the western front was expected "to destroy every German" in its path west of the Rhine and that, if necessary to quell German resistance, the Allied armies would drive on into the center of the Reich to meet the Russian armies.

"Our liaison with the Russians has always been as close and as intimate as was necessary to meet the situation at a particular moment," he told a press conference here. "The Russians have furnished me with all the information I have needed to know and they have done it willingly and cheerfully."

The Supreme Commander seemed entirely satisfied with the progress so far made in the resumed advance toward the Rhine and indicated that he expected that the offensive would be carried through without unusual losses. However, he held out no hopes for a quick and final victory over Germany and, with a laugh at the sourness of his own previous prediction, declined to forecast the date of the end of the war.

For the first time, officially, he disclosed that the American Ninth Army, one of the two that attacked across the Roer River yesterday, had remained under the control of Field Marshal Sir Bernard L. Montgomery, after it had been trans-

Continued on Page 4, Column 2

SOVIET FORCES GAIN IN 'POLISH CORRIDOR'

Red Army Stabs Up to 3 Miles on Wide Front—15 Blocks Captured in Breslau

By The United Press.

LONDON, Sunday, Feb. 25—Red Army troops, advancing up to three miles on a sixty-five-mile front up the "Polish Corridor" and across eastern Pomerania, yesterday hacked to within thirty-three miles south of Danzig and sixty-four miles of the Pomeranian coast in a drive to seal off the former free city and its twin Baltic port of Gdynia.

Troops of Marshal Konstantin K. Rokossovsky's Second White Russian Army threatened the German stronghold of Preussisch Friedland in Pomerania, and in the "Polish Corridor" drove to a point nine

Continued on Page 21, Column 1

War News Summarized

SUNDAY, FEBRUARY 25, 1945

The American drive toward the Rhine smashed four miles beyond the Roer River, its first major obstacle, and engulfed at least twenty-one towns as it achieved its preliminary objectives on schedule and with light casualties. The American Ninth Army, under Marshal Montgomery, was crashing through a string of villages beyond Juelich and Linnich, while the First, under General Bradley, was fighting through Dueren, main bastion of the Germans' Roer defenses. All enemy counter-attacks were beaten off, and it was believed the American drive had yet to reach its peak. [1:8; maps P. 3.]

First Army troops battering their way through Dueren already had occupied half of that industrial town in house-to-house fighting and reinforcements and supplies were reaching them over several bridges flung across the swollen river by engineers. [5:1.] Enemy resistance along the Ninth Army front was described as moderate and some Germans captured were youths of 15, but opposition was expected to become more intense as we penetrate deeper. [4:1.]

General Eisenhower spurred on his men by telling them the goal of the offensive was the destruction of every German west of the Rhine. He termed the progress of the First and Ninth Armies "certainly satisfactory" and said the Allied forces, if necessary, would drive into central Germany to meet the Russians moving in from the east for the kill. [1:8-7.]

The most devastating aerial offensive of the war continued in its twelfth day with fleets of heavy bombers blasting submarine yards and oil refineries in northwestern Germany. [3:1.]

The Red Army rolled toward the Baltic on a sixty-five-mile front, reaching within thirty-three miles of Danzig and sixty-four of the Pomeranian coast. [1:7.]

Hitler called on the German people to fight to the bitter end, warning them that "whoever is weak must perish." [13:1.]

Admiral Mitscher's naval task force again moved into the waters off Tokyo and its carrier planes renewed their attack on the Japanese capital. [1:3.]

The marines on Iwo captured half of the island's central airfield in the face of fierce resistance. [1:4; map P. 28.]

Manila's liberation was completed after a three-week battle as the last remnant of the Japanese garrison was destroyed. [1:6-7.] American troops in the Philippines achieved another signal success when they seized the Japanese internment camp at Los Banos, thirty-five miles southeast of Manila, freeing 2,146 prisoners. [26:3, with map.]

Just after he had read a decree declaring war on the Axis, Egypt's Prime Minister was shot and killed in the Chamber of Deputies in Cairo. [1:5.]

A permanent military board to plan for the defense of this hemisphere is expected to be set up at the Inter-American conference in Mexico City. [1:2.]

Foe's Manila Garrison Wiped Out; 2,146 Civilians Freed in Camp Raid

By The Associated Press.

MANILA, Sunday, Feb. 25—The three-week-old fight for Manila ended Saturday with the complete destruction of the Japanese garrison. Already more than 12,000 enemy dead have been counted.

Skyborne troops, infantrymen and Filipino guerrillas rescued 2,146 civilians from the Japanese internment camp at Los Banos, thirty-five miles south of Manila, at dawn Friday after killing the entire Japanese guard contingent of 243.

The internees, mostly Americans, were evacuated from the camp in amphibious tractors across Laguna de Bay before an estimated 8,000 enemy troops in the district could interfere with more than patrol fire. Two internees were hurt, and two rescuers were killed and two wounded.

Gen. Douglas MacArthur announced the conclusion of the slow, bloody street-by-street fight in Manila brought to a climax by overwhelming of enemy troops in Intramuros, the old walled city. Three thousand civilians of many nationalities were liberated in the final onslaught.

"Troops of the Thirty-seventh Infantry and First Cavalry Divisions of the Fourteenth Corps overwhelmed the enemy's final positions in South Manila and completed the destruction of the trapped garrison," General MacArthur announced. "More than 12,000 enemy bodies have already

Continued on Page 23, Column 2

More Men, 30 to 34, to Be Drafted Unless Necessary to Industry

By JOSEPH A. LOFTUS
Special to The New York Times.

WASHINGTON, Feb. 24—Men up to the age of 34 will have to meet more rigid specifications to be eligible for occupational deferments under new regulations announced today by Selective Service headquarters.

Asserting that demands for the armed forces are rapidly depleting the younger age groups, a memorandum to local boards told them to dig deeper into the age brackets of 30 through 33. Registrants of those ages to be eligible for deferment must be "necessary to and regularly engaged in" an activity in war production or in support of the national health, safety or interest.

Previously the only requirement was that registrants in this age group, to be eligible for deferment, must be "regularly engaged in" an activity in support of the national health, safety and interest or in an activity in war production.

The memorandum also states that "if all other factors are equal, a father should be given greater consideration for occupational deferment than a non-father in this age group."

Concerning registrants of the ages thirty-four through thirty-seven, the memorandum states that "merely the determination is required that the registrant is

Continued on Page 31, Column 2

21 TOWNS ENTERED

1st Army Captures Half of Dueren as 9th Drives On East of Juelich

4,000 CAPTIVES TAKEN

Third Army Clears 21 More Places in 5-Mile Gain Along Saar

By CLIFTON DANIEL
By Wireless to The New York Times.

SUPREME HEADQUARTERS, Allied Expeditionary Force, Feb. 24—The all-out American offensive to reach the Rhine and destroy the German forces west of it has rolled four miles beyond the Roer River in its first two days, overrunning twenty-one German towns and villages, penetrating four more and bringing in more than 4,000 prisoners.

Battling the racing flood of the Roer, the American First and Ninth Armies established a bridge and ferry system last night to move a steady flow of troops across the stream and now have a series of firm and well-manned lodgments on the east side of the Roer along a twenty-two-mile front. From the river, Lieut. Gen. William H. Simpson's and Lieut. Gen. Courtney H. Hodges' troops were fanning out onto the Cologne Plain "according to schedule," which means the Allies' Supreme Command is thoroughly satisfied.

Patton Gains Five Miles

Both the Canadian First and the American Third Armies took advantage of the German fluster over the powerful Roer assault to step up gains north and south of the new attack.

British infantry and armor swept through the Scottish troops south of Goch to resume the attack on Gen. H. D. G. Crerar's front. Along the line General Crerar's forces were thrusting toward Weeze and closing in around Uedem and Calcar. In the Uedem district there was slight evidence of a German withdrawal.

With advances up to five miles today, Lieut. Gen. George S. Patton's Third Army captured twenty-one towns and squeezed the tip of the German salient along the Luxembourg border down to a space three miles long and two miles wide. The tip is expected to be sliced off momentarily. Up to this morning the Third Army had dragged more than 1,000 prisoners out of the area. Resistance was becoming disorganized.

First Wins Half of Dueren

While the Ninth Army was ripping through a series of villages around and beyond Juelich and Linnich, the American First Army, only twenty miles from Cologne, drove the enemy out of half of Dueren, the largest of the Roer River towns and the main hinge of the German line. The First Army also swept out villages on both sides of Dueren, and the Ninth Army was reported from the front to have pushed on four miles beyond the Roer in the maximum advance. Together, the armies already are well established beyond the main road paralleling the east bank of the Roer and are approaching the edges of the thick forest lands east of Juelich, which are the first great natural obstacles in their path.

The two armies—the Ninth under the operational command of Field Marshal Sir Bernard L. Montgomery's Twenty-first Army Group and the First under Lieut. Gen. Omar N. Bradley's Twelfth Army Group—were disclosed by Supreme Commander Dwight D. Eisenhower to have crossed the Roer in strength—that is, on a major scale and with the intention of a strong, steady advance. Berlin reports said that the full force of the offensive had yet to be reached and that Generals Simpson and Hodges had massed twenty divisions, in-

Continued on Page 3, Column 5

"All the News That's Fit to Print"

The New York Times.

LATE CITY EDITION
POSTSCRIPT
Partly cloudy today. Fair tomorrow
Temperatures Yesterday—Max., 49; Min., 32

Copyright, 1945, by The New York Times Company.

VOL. XCIV—No. 31,822. Entered as Second-Class Matter, Postoffice, New York, N. Y. NEW YORK, SATURDAY, MARCH 10, 1945. THREE CENTS NEW YORK CITY

1ST AND 3D ARMIES TRAP 5 NAZI DIVISIONS; RHINE BRIDGEHEAD GROWS, FOE REPELLED; 300 B-29'S FIRE 15 SQUARE MILES OF TOKYO

PRODUCTION LAGS CHARGED TO UAW; THOMAS HITS BACK

Romney Tells Senators That Stoppages and Strikes Mark Union Usurpation Plan

1,266,000 MAN-DAYS 'LOST'

Union Leader Says Industry Is Clearing Way for 'Aggression' Against Labor

DETROIT, March 9—Conflicting views on the reasons for the decline in war production by automobile plants were given today before a Senate sub-committee in testimony from leaders of the industry and of labor.

George Romney, as spokesman for the auto industry, called the CIO, of which the United Automobile Workers Union is an affiliate, "the most powerful private organization in the history of our country" and alleged that labor was reducing its production efficiency in auto plants by 25 to 50 per cent despite war needs.

On the other hand, R. J. Thomas, international president of the United Automobile Workers, told the subcommittee that automotive executives were "sacrificing war requirements to preparations for a quick grab at post-war civilian sales."

Mr. Romney charged that through the fostering by the union of disputes, stoppages and strikes, all designed as an attempt at usurpation of the functions of management, 1,266,000 man-days were lost in the industry in the first eleven months of 1944. This, he declared, was the equivalent of 4,200 regular workers.

Mr. Romney, managing director of the Automotive Council for War Production, testified at the opening hearing conducted by the Mead War Investigating Committee studying manpower needs in the Detroit area. He spoke as the representative of the entire automotive industry and of other employers throughout Michigan.

"Organized Anarchy" Charged

He cited "documented" instances of alleged interference in purely plant management affairs by the UAW union in an effort to show that "organized anarchy" existed in the industry. Most strikes and stoppages now, he charged, were being called to prevent management from discharging its functions, as contrasted with disputes over union recognition and wages and hours before the war. Forty-three per cent of 1,045 strikes and work stoppages in 1944 were of this character, he declared.

Asserting that he based his figures on the Government's own Bureau of Labor Statistics, Mr. Romney said that there were five times as many strikes in automotive plants in 1943 as there were in 1940.

"It is a deplorable fact," he stated, "that during the first eleven months of 1944 there were more strikes and work stoppages in the automotive industry than there were in 1937, the year of the infamous sitdown strikes."

The post-war aim of the CIO, Mr. Romney charged, was to "divide and rule" through union-management Government boards. To thwart this and to correct existing abuses he urged legislation now to end the privileged status of unions and at the same time set forth a detailed "modern national labor policy."

Attacking as the "heart of the problem" the question whether union leaders were to be backed by the Government "in further usurpation of the functions, authority and responsibility of management," Mr. Romney said:

"The question in the minds of production men who built this great industry and its efficient production record is whether the

Continued on Page 12, Column 4

12 Japanese Ships Sunk by Submarines

Special to The New York Times.

WASHINGTON, March 9—Another Japanese escort aircraft carrier, a destroyer and ten merchant vessels have been sunk by United States submarines operating in Far Eastern waters, raising the total of announced sinkings by our submarines to 1,057, the Navy announced tonight.

American submarines now have definitely sunk three Japanese carriers, including one of a large type, probably sunk two others and damaged another two. Forty-seven destroyers, seventeen cruisers, three tenders and forty-two other naval vessels have been sunk.

The merchant ships reported sunk in the latest communiqué include a large cargo transport, a large tanker, two medium-sized cargo transports, five medium cargo vessels and a small cargo transport. Non-combatant ship sinkings total 945.

In addition, several hundred other ships have been probably sunk or damaged.

DAKOTA FARMER NAMED TO SENATE

M. R. Young, Republican, Will Back Roosevelt's Foreign Policy as Did Moses

By Telephone to The New York Times.

BISMARCK, N. D., March 9—State Senator Milton R. Young, a farmer and a member of the conservative wing of the Republican party who has pledged support of President Roosevelt's international policies, was named United States Senator from North Dakota today to succeed John R. Moses, Democrat, who died Saturday after a long illness.

The appointment by Gov. Fred G. Aandahl, a Republican, set at rest reports that Gerald P. Nye, former isolationist Senator from this State, who was unseated by Mr. Moses last November, might regain his place in the Senate.

Active in politics since 1933, Mr. Young, who will serve until the 1946 election, is 47 years old and operates a large farm near Berlin in LaMoure County, in the populous eastern part of the State.

Factors in the Selection

His appointment is a combination of political reward for his efforts in managing the conservative Republican faction campaigns since 1942 and also is based on "geographical" reasons.

The eastern part of the State had been without representation in the Senate for some years. Mr. Moses was from Bismarck and so is Governor Aandahl.

A towering six-footer, Mr. Young was born of farmer parents in Berlin. He is married and has three children. He entered politics in 1933 with his election to the State House of Representatives and four years later was elected to the State Senate.

He often has been referred to as

Continued on Page 11, Column 4

RECORD AIR ATTACK

B-29's Pour Over 1,000 Tons of Incendiaries on Japanese Capital

BOMBS RAIN 1½ HOURS

Tremendous Fires Leap Up in Thickly Populated Center of Big City

By BRUCE RAE
By Wireless to The New York Times.

GUAM, Saturday, March 10—A blanket of fire was thrown over an area of fifteen square miles in the heart of Tokyo early today by a fleet of 300 B-29's in the largest and most intensified raid on that city to date.

This announcement by headquarters was made after the force of Superfortresses returned to their three operating bases in the Marianas with ranks virtually intact. The raid was designed to attack an area of ten square miles, but clear weather and the fact that the bombing was visual widened the territory that could be set ablaze by 50 per cent. The airmen reported the flames so high and so bright that they read watch dials at an altitude of 20,000 feet while smoke arose 18,000 feet.

Enemy Is Surprised

More than 1,000 tons of incendiary bombs fell on the city's center in this all-out incendiary attack, and these rushed down on a section where the density of population is 100,000 to the square mile and where heavy industrial sections, residential neighborhoods and wholesale and retail districts adjoin.

[A Tokyo broadcast Saturday recorded by The United Press said, "the enemy is now attempting to make a landing on Japan proper," but the context made it doubtful that that is what the announcer intended to imply.]

At one point the fringe of the bombed area is only two miles from the Imperial Palace. The home of Emperor Hirohito was not touched, however, although block after block of buildings flamed close by.

The raiding planes operated from Guam, Saipan and Tinian. The Superfortresses, which can carry as much as ten tons of the incendiaries, took along on this attack the largest bomb load ever transported to Japan.

The B-29's sowed their loads well, the 300 ships riding in a designed pattern over Tokyo from 2 A. M. until 3:30 A. M.

"There was every indication that the Japanese were caught flat-footed," said an officer. "Although the anti-aircraft fire was heavy and concentrated, the fighter opposition, at least half-way through the raid, was meager."

The record flight was directed from headquarters here by Maj. Gen. Curtis E. LeMay, who remained at his post throughout last

Continued on Page 6, Column 2

Brooklyn Bridge Car Runs Wild; 54 Are Injured as It Hits Pole

A forty-year-old wooden BMT trolley car, its air brakes "gone," careened wildly down the steep grade of Brooklyn Bridge and crashed into a steel power pole at the loop leading to the Manhattan terminal at 6:05 o'clock last night.

The impact sheared the trolley's body from its undercarriage and it landed on its side across the tracks. Fifty-four of the 100 passengers, most of them workers at the Navy Yard in Brooklyn, were injured, two critically and six seriously. It was believed unlikely that trolley service over the bridge would be resumed before morning.

Herman Mann of 637 East 175th Street, the Bronx, the motorman, discovered the air-brake failure as the trolley started down the 1,000-foot grade from the center of the span, quickly realized the danger and shouted to the passengers to huddle in the rear. Many were in front of the turnstile and they frantically hurdled the barrier and climbed over one another in their haste to obey.

Mann stayed by his controls, trying to get the brake system working. When he realized it was futile, he appealed to men near him to help turn the crank-driven hand-brake, a slow process. Before it could be wound up, the trolley, gathering speed, rounded the turn, 200 feet from Park Row, and smashed into the supporting power pole.

The wooden framework sprawled grotesquely across the tracks, its turnstiles ripped from the floor, every pane of glass broken and seats torn from the bolts. Even the roof was shattered. The metal undercarriage stood firm.

The motorman's chant of "get

Continued on Page 13, Column 3

WHERE THE HISTORIC CROSSING WAS MADE OVER THE RHINE

The Ludendorff Bridge at Remagen that was captured intact by the Ninth Armored Division of the First Army. This picture was taken from the east bank of the river on Thursday, the day after the span was seized. The New York Times (U. S. Signal Corps Radiotelephoto)

REINS IN INDO-CHINA WRESTED BY JAPAN

French Disarmed, Key Points Seized—U. S. Operates Air Base There, Tokyo Says

By The Associated Press.

LONDON, Saturday, March 10—The Japanese wiped out the last vestige of French control over the puppet state of Indo-China early today, taking over full administration of the land after charging that French officers had tried secretly to join hands with the Allies.

Moving swiftly, the Japanese Army seized all key installations and facilities from the "resisting" French and announced that they

Continued on Page 6, Column 6

Bridge Over Rhine Seized With 10 Minutes to Spare

By GLADWIN HILL
By Wireless to The New York Times.

AT THE RHINE BRIDGEHEAD, March 9—Details of the American capture of the Ludendorff railroad bridge across the Rhine at Remagen revealed today that the Americans had seized the bridge just before the Germans had planned to blow it up. [The Associated Press said they had just ten minutes to spare.]

As the Americans reached Remagen Wednesday afternoon German prisoners told them that the Germans had ordered the bridge destroyed at 4 P. M. They raced for the structure.

As the Americans approached, a German demolition worker in a tower at the west end of the bridge pulled a switch and ran across to the east bank. Some damage was caused, but before the remainder of the charges could be set off the

Continued on Page 2, Column 5

RUSSIANS 10 MILES FROM DANZIG PORT

Foe Intimates Soviet Force Has Entered Kuestrin—Stettin Outposts on Oder Fall

By The United Press.

LONDON, Saturday, March 10—Red Army troops have driven to the outskirts of both Stettin and Danzig, Moscow dispatches said last night, and a German report implied that the key Oder fortress of Kuestrin, thirty-eight miles east of Berlin, had fallen.

Advancing as much as eighteen miles, the Russians pushed the eastern flank of their 165-mile long Baltic front to within ten miles west of Danzig, capturing Przyjazd, and to the west compressed a siege arc on Stettin and its harbor.

Three armored columns, followed by motorized infantry, were converging in Danzig's suburbs from west, east and south, unofficial Moscow reports said. A Soviet army of twenty-five rifle divisions, four tank corps and a cavalry

Continued on Page 5, Column 4

GERMAN COLLAPSE IN BONN AREA SEEN

Divisional Chief and 3,200 Men Among Prisoners Captured in Third Army's Sweep

By GENE CURRIVAN
By Wireless to The New York Times.

WITH THE UNITED STATES THIRD ARMY in Germany, March 9—The United States Third and First Armies joined forces on the Rhine tonight, giving the Americans virtually a forty-six-mile front on the last great natural barrier between them and Berlin. There are still pockets of resistance along this line, especially in the area just above Coblenz, but for all practical purposes the west side of the river from Cologne to the area just above Coblenz is in American hands.

The junction was made in the vicinity of Andernach and Brohl, two Rhine cities captured by the Eleventh Armored Division of the Third Army after it had paralleled the Fourth Armored Division spearhead across Germany on the north. Meanwhile, Third Army infantry fanned out below them, cleaning out pockets and consolidating the advances.

These multi-direction thrusts have made imminent the military collapse of the enemy north of the Moselle.

In the area above the Moselle, in a seventy-mile stretch between Trier and Coblenz, a narrow, unhealthy corridor has been formed and it is from here that the Germans are now withdrawing back

Continued on Page 3, Column 2

War News Summarized

SATURDAY, MARCH 10, 1945

Both banks of the Rhine quivered under the impact of Allied blows yesterday as our forces sought to pry open the door to the interior of Germany.

The American First and Third Armies trapped five or six German divisions as they joined forces west of the river barrier between Coblenz and Remagen, while other American forces threw back a German counter-attack against their bridgehead on the east bank opposite Remagen. Meanwhile, reinforcements and supplies were pouring across the 1,300-foot Remagen bridge, captured intact in a daring maneuver, to strengthen and expand the bridgehead, which reports indicated was ten miles wide and five deep.

Capture of the university city of Bonn was completed and at the northern end of the front enemy troops still holding out on the Rhine's west bank near Wesel were being pushed slowly toward the river in hard fighting. [All the foregoing, 1:8; maps Pages 2 and 3.]

The capture of the Remagen Bridge, one of the war's great exploits, was made only ten minutes before it was to have been blown up. [1:5-6.]

A new American Army, the Fifteenth, commanded by Lieut. Gen. Leonard T. Gerow, has been added to General Bradley's forces, which means that more than 1,000,000 Americans under that veteran leader are now ready to add to the Germans' woes. [4:6-7.]

More than 1,000 American heavy bombers backed up the ground forces in smashing attacks on German industrial and communication centers, particularly facilities through which the Germans must transport vital raw materials from the Ruhr. [4:1.]

The Red Army punched out new gains as it drew closer to both Stettin and Danzig, after rolling up huge areas of Pomerania and former Polish territory. Moscow maintained silence on operations before Berlin, but enemy reports intimated that the Oder fortress of Kuestrin, thirty-eight miles east of the German capital had fallen. [1:6; map P. 5.]

In the war against Japan more than 300 Superfortresses carried out the greatest attack against Tokyo by dropping more than 1,000 tons of bombs on a ten-square-mile area near the center of the enemy capital, starting huge fires in the world's third largest city. [1:3; map P. 6.]

The bitter battle on Iwo continued, with the American marines grimly advancing yard by yard against the small northern end of the battle-scarred island still remaining in enemy hands. [7:1.] General MacArthur announced that our troops in the Philippines had broken into the enemy Shimbu defense line east of Manila, but he said nothing about a Japanese report that we handed Thursday on Mindanao. [8:2.]

In Burma, Indian troops pushed deeper into Mandalay after seizing a strategic hill in that storied metropolis. [7:5.]

Japan announced that she had imposed complete military control over Indo-China. [1:4.]

V-E Day Will Bring the Return Of Troops for Redeployment

Special to The New York Times.

WASHINGTON, March 9—A "big load" of soldiers, now fighting in Europe, will return to this country after V-E day before redeployment to the Far East, while others will be shipped directly to the Orient, Lieut. Gen. Brehon Somervell stated tonight.

"The redeployment problem is by all odds the most difficult the War Department has had to face," the commander of the Army service forces asserted in a nationwide radio speech marking the third anniversary of the service and supply branch of the Army.

He stated that ASF had closed about one-fourth of the capacity of Army posts in the United States and was holding them in readiness for troops who would return from Europe, either for discharge or redeployment to the Pacific.

Addressing himself to the men and women of the organization, he said:

"Our job will be larger, not smaller, after V-E day. We will rejoice when Hitler is defeated, but it will be too early for celebration or relaxation."

Emphasizing some of the other difficulties, he pointed out that occupation troops in Germany must be supplied; that "millions of tons" of supplies and equipment must be divided between needs of the occupation troops and needs of the Pacific war; that new staging areas and port facilities must be provided, and that camps must be reopened and equipped for training of men for the Far Eastern war.

The war itself "will be hard and it may be long," General Somer-

Continued on Page 8, Column 4

U. S. COLUMNS JOIN

Clear Rhine West Bank From Cologne South to Coblenz Area

FOE SHELLS BRIDGE

9th Army Guns Pound Essen Area—15th Army Now on West Front

By DREW MIDDLETON
By Wireless to The New York Times.

PARIS, March 9—A series of lightning moves by the United States First and Third Armies of Lieut. Gen. Omar N. Bradley's Twelfth Army Group insured the destruction of five or six divisions of the German Seventh Army west of the Rhine while other units of the First Army extended and expanded their bridgeheads over the river.

Forces from the two American armies linked up on the Rhine between Remagen and Coblenz, trapping the German divisions to the west.

Today was one of unbroken success all along the Allies' long front. The First Infantry Division of the United States First Army completed the capture of Bonn, twelve and a quarter miles north of the First Army's bridgehead across the Rhine at Remagen.

German Attack Smashed

The Ninth Armored Division, which made the original crossing of the Rhine, repulsed a German armored counter-attack against the bridgehead today, sending the enemy reeling back with heavy losses. Reinforcements and supplies were pouring across the 1,300-foot, three-span Ludendorff bridge at Remagen as the bridgehead was being steadily expanded and strengthened.

[An Associated Press dispatch from that front early Saturday said the Germans were shelling the bridge while German columns were converging on the area. The United Press said jet-planes also were attacking the bridge.

[An earlier dispatch from the front Friday said German columns had been sighted by fliers moving toward the bridgehead area.]

According to a dispatch from the front, Erpel, near the eastern end of the Remagen Bridge, has been captured by First Army forces. One report said the bridgehead had been expanded to a depth of five miles and a width of ten miles. The German radio said tonight that Amer-

Continued on Page 2, Column 3

Young Ohio Butcher First Across Rhine

By The Associated Press.

ON THE RHINE BRIDGEHEAD, March 9—A gangling, embarrassed young butcher from Holland, Ohio, received the praise today of his commanding general for having led the heroic charge across Remagen Bridge and completed the capture of the span that gave the United States First Army the first Allied bridgehead across the Rhine.

A careful check disclosed that Sgt. Alexander A. Drabik actually was the first American to step on the east bank of the Rhine. And behind him came ten riflemen, shooting as they ran, in a wild dash that surprised the Germans before they could blow up this vital link, which right now is perhaps the most valuable bridge in the world.

This takes none of the glory from Lieut. Emmet Burrows, Jersey City officer, whose platoon was in the fight also and helped capture Remagen Bridge.

Maj. Gen. William M. Hoge of Lexington, Mo., praised Drabik's heroism as the greatest single factor in establishing the bridgehead and singled him out as the man who deserved the most individual credit.

U.S. Signal Corps

Men of the Third Army's 89th Infantry Division cross the Rhine at Oberwesel, Germany.

"All the News That's Fit to Print"

NEWS INDEX, PAGE 37, THIS SECTION

The New York Times.

Copyright, 1945, by The New York Times Company.

LATE CITY EDITION
Fair and warmer today. Partly cloudy, continued mild tomorrow.
Temperatures Yesterday—Max., 57; Min., 41
Sunrise today, 6:30 A. M.; Sunset, 7:36 P. M.

Section 1

VOL. XCIV. No. 31,851. Entered as Second-Class Matter, Postoffice, New York, N. Y. NEW YORK, SUNDAY, APRIL 8, 1945. Including Magazine and Book Sections. TEN CENTS New York City and Suburban Areas (15c Elsewhere)

U. S. FLIERS SINK JAPAN'S BIGGEST WARSHIP; BRITISH NEAR BREMEN; HANOVER FLANKED; PATTON SEIZES NAZI HOARD OF GOLD AND ART

FOUR STABILIZERS ASK FIRM CONTROL BEYOND END OF WAR

Policy 'With Boldness' Is Vital to Prevent Any Runaway Inflation, They Assert

SAY 'LINE IS HELD' TO DATE

Davis, Bowles, Jones, Taylor Summarize Their Work in Report to Roosevelt

The report on price and wage control is on Page 34.

Special to THE NEW YORK TIMES.

WASHINGTON, April 7—A call for continuance of price and wage controls during the transitional period after the war to provide stabilization and guard against inflation was made to President Roosevelt today by the four officials who exercise primary responsibility in those fields. Their report told the Chief Executive that, to date, "essential stabilization has been achieved."

The report was made in a letter on the second anniversary of the President's "hold-the-line" order by William H. Davis, director of the Office of Economic Stabilization; Chester Bowles, administrator of the Office of Price Administration; Marvin Jones, administrator of the War Food Administration, and George W. Taylor, chairman of the National War Labor Board. It was given out for publication by the White House without comment.

Post-War Tasks Stressed

The joint communication stressed the difficulty of the tasks ahead, while expressing confidence that the American people "will be wary of those who will call for an abrupt ending of controls" and "insist that the problems of transition be attacked with boldness."

"There is still the gravest danger of a runaway price rise which would undo all that we have accomplished thus far, delay victory and cause untold personal suffering," the report warned. "But at the same time that we exert ourselves to prevent such a development we must prepare to deal with the deflationary tendencies which may appear in the transition period. To maintain stability in the face of the dangers ahead will require the full support of yourself, Mr. President; the Congress and the American people."

The report recalled that a year ago "we reported that the line had been held," and in stating that the line was still being held it said that the nation's cost-of-living index now stands "little more than 2 per cent above its level of two years ago."

A large number of items has been held absolutely steady, while some items, chiefly in the food group, have declined, the report pointed out. Although clothing prices have had a gradual unbroken rise during the past two years, it promised that new programs will stop the rise and added that "plans are under way to roll back prices on essential clothing items."

Wage Costs Called Stable

Average straight - time hourly earnings were estimated, in the report, to be 10 per cent above the level of two years ago, "largely as a result of promotions and increased production," but wage costs were pictured as having been kept relatively stable and not to have contributed to "any significant rises in the cost of living through pressures on production costs."

Stabilization too, was said also to have been effective for farm and industrial levels, with prices having increased only about 2 per cent in a period of record industrial and farm production.

The "slight increases" in the

Continued on Page 34, Column 3

309,258 Germans Seized in 2 Weeks

By The Associated Press.

PARIS, April 7—In one of the most dramatic fortnights of the war—since the Allies carried their offensive across the Rhine—the Germans have lost more than 309,258 troops in prisoners alone and roughly 18,000 square miles of territory east of that river.

The number of Germans captured since the Rhine crossing already exceeds the 250,000 captured in the three-week March mop-up west of the Rhine, which Gen. Dwight D. Eisenhower declared "one of the greatest victories of this or any other war."

The figure of 309,258 does not include the thousands catch of Army Group B pinned in the Ruhr or the other thousands of Army Group H caught in the western Netherlands.

PRESIDENT PRAISES RECONVERSION PLAN

Letter Hails Gardner for Idea of OWM Board to Stress Peacetime Abundance

Correspondence on post-war reconversion is on Page 30.

Special to THE NEW YORK TIMES.

WASHINGTON, April 7—President Roosevelt made public today an exchange of correspondence with O. Max Gardner, chairman of the War Mobilization and Reconversion Advisory Board, in which he applauded Mr. Gardner's demand for post-war full employment to be obtained "under our system of competitive free enterprise" and without "any compromise with traditional American institutions."

"America is fortunate to have such a reaffirmation of the uninterrupted tradition of an advancing America enunciated by men who represent great organizations of labor, industry and agriculture working together with others who represent the public," the President declared.

The President virtually reiterated the words of Mr. Gardner when he called for "a peacetime economy far more abundant and productive than we have ever had before." But, he added:

"Victory without the use of abundance of the powers we have developed in production for war would be, indeed, a hollow victory. We must plan security and abundance together. Such a strong American economy will be essential to carry out the responsibilities that lie in plans made at Bretton Woods, Hot Springs and Dumbarton Oaks. Similarly, abundance at home depends upon organization for order and security in the world."

In view of the board's recently expressed desire to be consulted, the following passage of Mr. Gardner's letter suggested that he might have taken this occasion to express the board's hope that the

Continued on Page 30, Column 3

VIENNA ARC WIDENS

Capital Is Three-fourths Ringed—Russians at Danube to North

ESCAPE GAP SHRINKS

Munich-Linz Trunkline Slashed—Red Army 12 Miles From Teschen

By The Associated Press.

LONDON, Sunday, April 8—Red Army tank columns, in a fourteen-mile sweep around western Vienna, three-fourths encircled the Austrian capital yesterday, leaving to the enemy garrison a twenty-four-and-a-half-mile escape gap, as other shock troops gained in a frontal assault through the city's streets.

By reaching the Danube River northwest of the city, Russian troops sliced across six of Vienna's escape routes and left the imperiled capital with only seven of an original twenty-two major railroads and highways.

Berlin reports said that the escape gap to the north already had been narrowed. Soviet cavalrymen were said to have forded the Morava River northeast of Vienna and to have established bridgeheads that threatened to close the enemy's last retreat roads.

At the same time, Berlin reported that Soviet tank spearheads had broken twenty-three miles through the Vienna Woods west of the capital.

While Moscow officially confirmed that Soviet forces had broken across Vienna's southern city limits and were battling toward its heart, Soviet troops elsewhere on the Eastern Front carved out new gains.

12 Miles from Teschen

Cleaning out southwestern Poland, the Russians moved within twelve miles of Teschen [Cieszyn], and in Czechoslovakia gained up to ten miles on an eighty-mile front. In Yugoslavia, other Russian units battered to within 100 miles of Italy at a point forty-two miles northeast of the Croatian capital of Zagreb.

As the Germans proclaimed that Vienna "will be defended to the last sewer," two Soviet armies extended the siege arc around Vienna to 112 miles on the west, south and east. Moscow reports said high German officials already were fleeing over the last crowded roads out of the city.

The greater part of the city was encircled when Marshal Fedor I. Tolbukhin's Third Ukrainian Army tankmen battered fourteen miles through the Vienna Woods in a two-day advance, sweeping through the town of Pressbaum, seven miles west of the city, to reach the Danube at Klosterneuburg, one mile from Vienna's northwestern limits.

The swift surge that isolated

Continued on Page 25, Column 1

ALLIES RACE AHEAD

British 13 Miles From Bremen While Ninth Heads for Brunswick

1ST CROSSES WESER

Third Smashes Strong German Attack—7th Gains 36 Miles

By DREW MIDDLETON
By Wireless to THE NEW YORK TIMES.

PARIS, April 7—American and British armored forces broke out from their bridgeheads east of the Weser River today and raced across the province of Hanover, while on the left flank of the advance the British Seventh Armored Division struck northward to positions that field reports say were only thirteen miles from Bremen early this afternoon.

Battered by the sledge-hammer blows of the armored columns and harried by clouds of fighter-bombers, Germany is failing apart in the north. Pilots of the Royal Air Force, flying over the front of the British Second Army today, reported no coherent resistance anywhere in the British sector.

The United States First and Third Armies in the center of the Allies' battleline were relatively inactive today according to the scanty reports available here. [Press service reports from the front, however, said the Third Army had smashed a heavy German counter-attack northwest of Muelhausen and had destroyed forty German tanks.]

[Other press service reports said the First Army had crossed the Weser River at numerous points and was now engaged in a raging battle with German troops held in their battle positions by officers with pistols.

[A United Press dispatch from the Seventh Army front late Saturday declared that the Tenth Armored Division had broken through for a thirty-six-mile gain and had captured the town of Crailsheim, ninety-four miles northwest of Munich and forty-

Continued on Page 12, Column 1

JAPANESE FLEET REMNANTS BATTERED ANEW

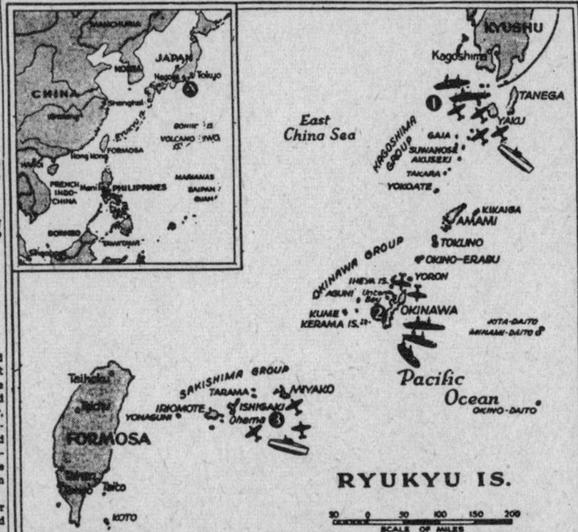

April 8, 1945

An enemy flotilla that had steamed around the southern tip of Kyushu into the East China Sea was caught fifty miles southwest of that Japanese home island (1) by our carrier planes, which sank the foe's most powerful battleship, two cruisers and three destroyers. Previously 116 enemy aircraft had been downed in an attack on our invasion flotilla off Okinawa (2). A British carrier force smashed airfields and other targets on Miyako and Ishigaki in the Sakishima group (3). It was disclosed that plane plants in Tokyo and Nagoya (A on inset) had been hit by more than 300 Superfortresses escorted by Mustang fighters from our new airfields on Iwo Island.

100 Tons of Gold and Cash Found in German Salt Mine

By The United Press.

WITH THE NINETIETH INFANTRY DIVISION, Merkers, Germany, April 7—American soldiers found a vast treasure trove, said to include the entire German gold reserve, in a salt mine today. Dr. Fritz Vieck, a Reichsbank official, was on guard. He said that the subterranean vaults contained approximately 100 tons of gold bullion; $2,000,000 in American currency, 1,000,000 francs in French currency, £110,000 in British currency, 4,000,000 Norwegian crowns and lesser amounts in other currencies. The salt mine also sheltered

Continued on Page 16, Column 3

ALLIES ERASE ARMY OF 50,000 IN BURMA

Enemy in Mandalay-Meiktila Pocket Crushed—5,000 of Foe Killed in China Battle

By The Associated Press.

CALCUTTA, India, April 7—The shattered Japanese Fifteenth Army in central Burma, officially estimated three weeks ago at 50,000 men, "no longer exists as an effective fighting force," a Southeast Asia communiqué announced today. A headquarters spokesman said that two other enemy armies, the Thirty-third and Twenty-eighth, had been badly mauled in attempts to rush relief.

"There are no organized Japanese forces" left inside the Mandalay-Meiktila pocket, the announcement said.

The communiqué, stating that

Continued on Page 9, Column 1

TWIN B-29 ATTACKS BLAST 173 PLANES

'Superforts' Have Their Biggest Fight in Escorted Blow at Tokyo and Nagoya Plants

By Wireless to THE NEW YORK TIMES.

GUAM, Sunday, April 8—The deadly Superfortresses have written another bad chapter for the Japanese—this time with the aid of Mustang escorting fighters, it was made known today by the Twenty-First Bomber Command. It was the first time the B-29's had fighter protection on the long jaunt to Japan.

[On Sunday, Japanese time, a "substantial force" of B-29's from the Marianas hit Japan again, bombing military targets in the Kanoya area on the southern tip of Kyushu Island, Twentieth Air Force headquarters reported.]

The twin attack yesterday was directed at the Mitsubishi engine plant at Nagoya and at the Musashino-Nakajima factory in the suburbs of Tokyo. Both targets were hit squarely by 500-pound demolition bombs. The Superfortresses shot down or damaged 136 Japanese planes, while the Mustangs accounted for thirty-seven, for a total of 173.

Another "first" on the double attack was the fact that it led to

Continued on Page 5, Column 5

VICTORY IN PACIFIC

Carrier Planes Sink the Battleship Yamato and 5 Other Warships

BATTLE OFF KYUSHU

Foe Loses 417 Planes, Bulk of Them in Blow at Fleet Off Okinawa

By BRUCE RAE
By Wireless to THE NEW YORK TIMES.

GUAM, Sunday, April 8—The United States Fifth Fleet, after shattering an all-out Japanese aerial attack off Okinawa, on Friday (East Longitude time) launched a counter-offensive in the sky Saturday and delivered a smashing blow to the remnants of the Imperial Navy—sinking six warships, including the most powerful remaining unit, the battleship Yamato. The sinkings were in the East China Sea about fifty miles southwest of Kyushu, southernmost island of the Japanese homeland.

[In Washington an official Navy spokesman said "a good 25 per cent of the remaining Japanese major combat force" was lost or put out of action in the engagement.]

Admiral Chester W. Nimitz announced the victories last night as the Navy clocks neared midnight and this morning he supplemented his statement.

Four hundred and seventeen Japanese planes were shot down, most of them in the Okinawa area of the Ryukyus during the Japanese aerial assault, which was resumed in a minor way Saturday and again crushed.

Score of Two-Day Battle

The score:

Japanese ship losses—ships sunk, one battleship, the Yamato, 45,000 tonner; one light cruiser of the Agano class, about 5,000 tons; one smaller light cruiser or large destroyer and three destroyers. In addition, three Japanese destroyers were left burning. About three enemy destroyers escaped. Further, four small cargo ships and many smaller craft were sunk off the Ryukyus.

United States ship losses—three destroyers sunk in the Japanese air attack. One heavy unit and several destroyers and smaller craft were damaged by the Japanese planes. The heavy unit, presumably a battleship or carrier, remained in operation. Seven United States aircraft were lost in the carrier plane attack on the Yamato and other enemy warships.

Early Saturday morning search aircraft of Fleet Air Wing One cruising on the watch for enemy planes or ships sighted a large group of Japanese ships. The enemy fleet was moving southward from Kyushu, presumably making an effort to reach sorely pressed Okinawa. The enemy ships had steamed out of the quiet, sunlit waters of the Inland Sea and had turned into the reaches of the East China Sea.

Task Force Gets the Word

The search planes flashed the discovery over the intervening miles back to the fast task force of Vice Admiral Marc A. Mitscher. The task force, as usual, was prowling around hopefully, hoping that an honest-to-goodness Japanese warship or two would turn up. The word that went to the delighted vice admiral, his staff and his boat loads of eager fliers was that the Yamato, the Agano class cruiser and the other warships were within reach.

Admiral Mitscher's men and his ships went into high gear. The sea foamed from the bows of the fast carriers, and the engine rooms hummed. At high speed the task force went for the enemy, and as noon drew near put the enemy under air attack.

Plane after plane from carrier

Continued on Page 3, Column 2

Army Day Parade Minus the Army Is Cheered by 200,000 in 5th Ave.

Under perfect spring skies, New York paid a colorful and dramatic tribute yesterday to the nation's Army, as 18,000 men, women and children marched down Fifth Avenue in the eighteenth annual observance of Army Day.

From the green-brown uniform of close-stepping marines to the gay colors of drum majors and youth organizations in gold, yellow, blue and red, the marchers presented a pageant of tribute to the men and women of the Army, a tribute which took on added dramatic quality by the absence of regular Army units in the line of march. Police estimated that between 200,000 and 250,000 spectators lined the city's traditional parade avenue from Ninetieth Street to Sixty-fourth.

Lieut. Gen. George Grunert, commanding general of the Eastern Defense Command, who reviewed the marchers at the official stand at Sixty-seventh Street, agreed with other notable guests that it was the most successful Army Day parade since the observance became official in 1928. This year, as in the past, the occasion was sponsored by the Military Order of the World Wars.

It took the long line of paraders nearly two hours to pass the reviewing stand. They came in two divisions, with the youth organizations in first place, followed by the older units, including contingents of the Navy, Marine Corps, Waves, American Legion posts, the Red Cross and many women's volun-

Continued on Page 37, Column 4

War News Summarized

SUNDAY, APRIL 8, 1945

An important segment of the Japanese Fleet ventured out of hiding and quickly regretted its boldness. The American Fifth Fleet, waiting for just such a move, sent carrier planes against the enemy force, sinking six Japanese warships, including the 45,000-ton battleship Yamato, two light cruisers and three destroyers, in an action fifty miles southwest of Kyushu. We lost seven planes. Three of our destroyers were sunk by enemy planes off Okinawa but we destroyed 417 Japanese aircraft.

In the ground fighting on Okinawa our Marines continued to push forward to the north with little resistance to reach the vicinity of Nago on the west coast and Ora Bay on the east coast. The drive to the south toward Naha, the capital, faced stubborn opposition from the enemy entrenched in strongly prepared positions. [All the foregoing, 1:8, maps P. 1 and 4.]

A Navy spokesman in Washington said the sea action had put one-fourth of the Japanese Navy's remaining major combat force out of action, leaving only such enemy strength as "could be handled easily." [3:1.]

A shake-up of the military and air commands accompanied the formation of a new Japanese Cabinet headed by Baron Suzuki. The 77-year-old Premier, who took office in the presence of Emperor Hirohito, told his countrymen that the war had reached a "crucial state" and that "the very basis of our Empire's existence" was threatened. [6:1.]

At least 173 Japanese planes were destroyed or damaged by 300 Superfortresses and Iwo-based fighter escorts that attacked plane plants in Tokyo and Nagoya. B-29's bombed Japan again today. [1:7.]

In Burma, too, the Japanese were suffering reverses. The Japanese Fifteenth Army, estimated to number 50,000, has been destroyed. [1:6.]

American troops in the Philippines made new gains. Netherlands Indies fliers struck a Japanese cruiser. [7:3.]

German armies on the northern end of the Western Front were disintegrating as Allied forces smashed from bridgeheads east of the Weser toward Hanover. British troops were only thirteen miles from Bremen. However, the enemy force of 100,000 or more encircled in the Ruhr pocket offered bitter resistance. [1:4; map P. 12.]

The United States Third Army seized a gold cache valued at more than $100,000,000 in a hidden salt mine 140 miles southeast of Berlin. [1:5-6.]

At least eighty-seven of a fleet of German planes that sought to intercept a force of 1,300 American heavy bombers and 850 fighters, which hit in the Kiel-Hamburg-Bremen area, were shot down in a big air battle. Our losses were twenty-two bombers and three fighters. [15:1.]

The Red Army swept around western Vienna and had more than two-thirds of the Austrian capital encircled. Soviet shock troops drew closer to the heart of the city. [1:3; map P. 25.]

In Italy, the American Fifth Army captured Mount Fragolito in its drive along the west coast toward La Spezia. [27:5.]

Patton's Contempt of German Army Deals Hard Blow to Enemy Morale

By GENE CURRIVAN
By Wireless to THE NEW YORK TIMES.

WITH THE UNITED STATES THIRD ARMY, in Germany, April 7—Most German commanders would rather fight almost anywhere than in front of Lieut. Gen. George S. Patton Jr. He not only worries them to death with his unorthodox moves but has now added a contemptuousness that must reduce to a minimum any remaining German morale.

When General Patton's armored columns take off in the morning on one of their now-familiar spearheading drives they seldom slow up before sundown. When cities or towns in their path become too rough they merely by-pass them and leave the enemy garrison wondering what is coming next. General Patton's armor moves out in two columns, flanking the city and keeps going while infantry following in its wake takes over the task of capturing the city. Tanks and narrow crowded streets are not militarily compatible anyway and this type of battle against a dug-in garrison is infantry work, although armored units have often tackled it successfully. This by-passing procedure is sound tactically but the added element of contempt gives that little discouraging feature that doesn't exactly bolster the enemy's spirit.

The same applies in the bridging operations, where, after the first few days of hell, the military supply train runs bumper to bumper

Continued on Page 13, Column 6

U.S. Marine Corps

Battleship U.S.S. Idaho firing off Okinawa.

U.S. Marine Corps

A Marine Corsair fires eight five-inch rockets while flying over Japanese positions on Okinawa.

"All the News That's Fit to Print"

The New York Times.

LATE CITY EDITION
Clearing and warm today.
Fair, continued warm tomorrow.
Temperatures Yesterday—Max., 74; Min., 54

Copyright, 1945, by The New York Times Company.

VOL. XCIV...No. 31,856. Entered as Second-Class Matter, Postoffice, New York, N. Y. NEW YORK, FRIDAY, APRIL 13, 1945. THREE CENTS IN NEW YORK CITY

PRESIDENT ROOSEVELT IS DEAD; TRUMAN TO CONTINUE POLICIES; 9TH CROSSES ELBE, NEARS BERLIN

U. S. AND RED ARMIES DRIVE TO MEET

Americans Across the Elbe in Strength Race Toward Russians Who Have Opened Offensive From Oder

WEIMAR TAKEN, RUHR POCKET SLASHED

Third Army Reported 19 Miles From Czechoslovak Border—British Drive Deeper in the North, Seizing Celle—Canadians Freeing Holland

By DREW MIDDLETON
By Wireless to The New York Times.

PARIS, April 12—Thousands of tanks and a half million doughboys of the United States First, Third and Ninth Armies are racing through the heart of the Reich on a front of 150 miles, threatening Berlin, Leipzig and the last citadels of the Nazi power.

The Second Armored Division of the Ninth Army has crossed the Elbe River in force and is striking eastward toward Berlin, whose outskirts lie less than sixty miles to the east, according to reports from the front. [A report quoted by The United Press placed the Americans less than fifty miles from the capital.] Beyond Berlin the First White Russian Army has crossed the Oder on a wide front and a junction between the western and eastern Allies is not far off.

[The Moscow radio reported that heavy battles were raging west of the Oder before Berlin, indicating that Marshal Gregory K. Zhukoff had launched his drive toward the Reich's capital. The Soviet communiqué announced further progress by the Red Army forces in and around Vienna.]

Paris is wild with excitement tonight. A special edition of the newspaper France-Soir carries a report by the radio station "Voice of America" that places American forces fifteen and five-eighths miles from Berlin after an airborne landing that had linked up with Lieut. Gen. William H. Simpson's forces advancing eastward from the Elbe. This would put American forces only seventy-five miles from the Red Army vanguard.

No Confirmation at Headquarters

There was no confirmation of this report at Allied Supreme Headquarters, which by its own admission was thirty-six hours behind developments on some sectors of the front.

Resistance was continuing only on the northern and southern flanks. The center had burst wide open. Weimar fell to Lieut. Gen. George S. Patton's infantry, and reports from the front said Erfurt also had been cleared. Schweinfurt and Heilbronn, two German bastions on the south, had fallen to United States Seventh Army forces, who were driving on Bamberg, while farther north Third Army forces were about thirty-five miles from the Czechoslovak frontier in the area east of Coburg.

[The German radio reported American Third Army forces at Lichtenberg, nineteen miles from the Czechoslovak border, The United Press said.]

The offensives to liberate the Netherlands and reduce the Ruhr

Continued on Page 12, Column 2

OUR OKINAWA GUNS DOWN 118 PLANES

Japanese Fliers Start 'Suicide' Attacks on Fleet, Sink a Destroyer, Hit Other Ships

By W. H. LAWRENCE
By Wireless to The New York Times.

GUAM, Friday, April 13—Japanese attempting to halt the American march to Tokyo, have started "desperate, suicidal" aerial attacks upon our ships and men in the Okinawa area, losing 118 planes on Thursday alone, Fleet Admiral Chester W. Nimitz announced today.

The Japanese succeeded in sinking a destroyer and damaging several other surface units, the communiqué said. All of the damaged vessels remained in action.

It was the first time that the Navy had revealed the suicidal nature of the Japanese air missions against our ships and men. The Japanese radio has been saying that this type of assault was being carried on by a "special attack corps" known in Japanese as "kamakazi," which, translated literally, means "divine wind."

Attack at Low Levels

The Japanese fliers launched their attacks upon our ships and men at a high speed and from low levels, diving directly into a ship or troop concentration to explode their bombs as they crashed.

There was no official estimate of the total number of enemy aircraft engaged in the Okinawa area attack other than the report of the 118 enemy planes destroyed.

Admiral Nimitz reported that the attacks began early on April 12 (Eastern Longitude time) with seven enemy planes shot down during the morning in the vicinity of the Hagushi beaches.

The tempo of the attack was stepped up in the afternoon as the Japanese bore in on our ships in wave after wave. Admiral Nimitz said that ships' guns, carrier aircraft and shore-based anti-aircraft shot down 111 of the attackers.

The revelation of the suicidal Japanese air attacks was the highlight of Admiral Nimitz' regular morning communiqué, which also disclosed the identity of two Marine and two Army divisions that have gone into action on Okinawa. These included the Twenty-seventh Army Division, formed from New York National Guard units, which are seeing action for the first time since the Saipan campaign and previously had engaged in the Gilbert Islands assault. It is com-

Continued on Page 12, Column 3

Army Leaders See Reich End at Hand

By The Associated Press.

WASHINGTON, April 12—High Army officials told Senators today that the end of organized fighting in Germany probably would come within a few days.

Describing the pell-mell dash of American Armies across Germany, General Staff officers expressed the opinion to members of the Senate Military Committee that a collapse of German arms was imminent.

Those who attended said the army chiefs declared that they were so sure of the results that orders had been drawn for a drastic reduction in shipments of durable equipment to Europe.

Franklin Delano Roosevelt
1882-1945

SECURITY PARLEY WON'T BE DELAYED

State Department Urges That World Be Shown We Plan No Changes in Policy

By JAMES B. RESTON
Special to The New York Times.

WASHINGTON, April 12—The United Nations Security Conference will open in San Francisco on April 25, despite the death of President Roosevelt, Secretary of State Edward R. Stettinius Jr. announced tonight.

Mr. Stettinius said that he had been authorized by President Harry Truman to make this announcement after a meeting of the Cabinet at the White House.

Most of the overseas delegations to the San Francisco conference have either arrived in this country or are now on their way, but while this was said to have been a factor in the decision to proceed with the conference, State Department officials urged that every attempt be made to give immediate evidence to the world that President Roosevelt's foreign policy would be sustained by the new Administration.

President Roosevelt had planned to address the San Francisco conference. His interest in an international organization of nations to maintain peace and security had gone back to his service in the Wilson Administration, when he sat in the gallery of the Senate and listened to the debate that resulted in the rejection of the League of Nations Covenant. He had expressed to friends his desire to participate in the San Francisco conference and to see the United States enter the new league during his term in office.

The sudden elevation of Presi-

Continued on Page 2, Column 1

War News Summarized

FRIDAY, APRIL 13, 1945

President Roosevelt died yesterday afternoon, suddenly and unexpectedly. He was stricken with a massive cerebral hemorrhage at Warm Springs, Ga., on the eve of his greatest military and diplomatic successes—the impending fall of Berlin and the opening of the San Francisco Conference to set up a World Security Organization that would make the world free from martial and economic strife [1:7-8.]

Mr. Roosevelt had been sitting in front of the fireplace of his Little White House, having gone to Warm Springs on March 30 for a three-week rest. About 2:15 Eastern war time he said, "I have a terrific headache," lost consciousness in a few moments and died at 4:35. He was 63 years old. [1:6.]

The tragic word spread quickly around the world. Expressions of sorrow poured in from all sections. [4:5.] American soldiers and sailors refused to believe the reports until there was no longer doubt that their Commander in Chief had gone. [4:2-3.]

Harry S. Truman was sworn in as President at 7:09 o'clock last night, and a few minutes later Mrs. Roosevelt left for Warm Springs. [1:7.] The new President immediately called a Cabinet meeting and declared that Mr. Roosevelt's policies would be continued, that the war would be carried on until Germany and Japan surrendered unconditionally and that the San Francisco Conference would open April 25 as scheduled. [1:3.]

Some 500,000 American soldiers of the Third and Ninth Armies, and thousands of tanks, sped along a 150-mile front toward Berlin and Leipzig. The Ninth, surging across the Elbe, according to delayed reports was less than fifty miles from the German capital and 115 from the Russians along the Oder. The Third Army captured Weimar, home of the late German Republic, and was twenty-three miles below Leipzig, with the First closing a pincers from the north. [1:1-2; map P. 2.]

The Moscow radio reported that the Red Army was waging fierce battles east of Berlin, indicating resumption of the drive on that city. Elsewhere Russian troops scored wide gains and cut the last escape railroad from Vienna. [13:1.]

Open cities were ruled out and every German was ordered by Himmler to fight to the death, although Goebbels said "the war cannot last much longer." [12:6-7.]

The Ninth Air Force destroyed at least 117 more German planes yesterday. [11:8.]

In Italy the Eighth Army advanced along a thirty-mile front toward Bologna and the Po Valley; the Fifth Army also made good gains and was eleven miles from La Spezia. [13:8, with map.]

Japanese planes resumed their suicide attacks on American ships off Okinawa, sinking a destroyer and damaging several other vessels. One hundred and eighteen enemy planes were shot down. [1:2.] The Americal Division invaded Bohol, last of the enemy-held central Philippines. [18:6.] The B-29 attack on Koriyama, 110 miles north of Tokyo, set a new Superfortress distance record. [18:2.]

Secretary of State Stettinius and Secretary of War Stimson, denouncing Germany's "steadily increasing" mistreatment of American prisoners, said those responsible would be brought to justice. [13:6-7.]

Clashes between Right and Left wing elements in Iran were reported from Moscow. [12:2.]

LAST WORDS: 'I HAVE TERRIFIC HEADACHE'

Roosevelt Was Posing for Artist When Hemorrhage Struck —He Died in Bedroom

By The Associated Press.

WARM SPRINGS, Ga., April 12—President Franklin D. Roosevelt's last words were:

"I have a terrific headache."

He spoke them to Comdr. Howard G. Bruenn, naval physician.

Mr. Roosevelt was sitting in front of a fireplace in the Little White House here atop Pine Mountain when what was described as a massive cerebral hemorrhage struck him.

The President's Negro valet, Arthur Prettyman, and a Filipino messboy carried him to his bedroom. He was unconscious at the end. It came without pain.

Dr. Bruenn said that he saw the President this morning and he was in excellent spirits at 9:30 A. M.

"At 1 o'clock," Dr. Bruenn added, "he was sitting in a chair while sketches were being made of him by an artist. He suddenly complained of a very severe occipital headache (back of the head).

"Within a very few minutes he lost consciousness. He was seen by me at 1:30 P. M., fifteen minutes after the episode had started.

"He did not regain consciousness, and he died at 3:35 P. M. (Georgia time)."

The artist sketching Mr. Roosevelt was N. Robbins of 530 West 129th Street, New York.

Only others present in the cottage were Comdr. George Fox, White House pharmacist and long an attendant on the President; William D. Hassett, Presidential secretary; Miss Grace Tully, con-

Continued on Page 4, Column 2

END COMES SUDDENLY AT WARM SPRINGS

Even His Family Unaware of Condition as Cerebral Stroke Brings Death to Nation's Leader at 63

ALL CABINET MEMBERS TO KEEP POSTS

Funeral to Be at White House Tomorrow, With Burial at Hyde Park Home—Impact of News Tremendous

By ARTHUR KROCK
Special to The New York Times.

WASHINGTON, April 12—Franklin Delano Roosevelt, War President of the United States and the only Chief Executive in history who was chosen for more than two terms, died suddenly and unexpectedly at 4:35 P. M. today at Warm Springs, Ga., and the White House announced his death at 5:48 o'clock. He was 63.

The President, stricken by a cerebral hemorrhage, passed from unconsciousness to death on the eighty-third day of his fourth term and in an hour of high triumph. The armies and fleets under his direction as Commander in Chief were at the gates of Berlin and the shores of Japan's home islands as Mr. Roosevelt died, and the cause he represented and led was nearing the conclusive phase of success.

Less than two hours after the official announcement, Harry S. Truman of Missouri, the Vice President, took the oath as the thirty-second President. The oath was administered by the Chief Justice of the United States, Harlan F. Stone, in a one-minute ceremony at the White House. Mr. Truman immediately let it be known that Mr. Roosevelt's Cabinet is remaining in office at his request, and that he had authorized Secretary of State Edward R. Stettinius Jr. to proceed with plans for the United Nations Conference on international organization at San Francisco, scheduled to begin April 25. A report was circulated that he leans somewhat to the idea of a coalition Cabinet, but this is unsubstantiated.

Funeral Tomorrow Afternoon

It was disclosed by the White House that funeral services for Mr. Roosevelt would take place at 4 P. M. (E. W. T.) Saturday in the East Room of the Executive Mansion. The Rev. Angus Dun, Episcopal Bishop of Washington; the Rev. Howard S. Wilkinson of St. Thomas's Church in Washington and the Rev. John G. McGee of St. John's in Washington will conduct the services.

The body will be interred at Hyde Park, N. Y., Sunday, with the Rev. George W. Anthony of St. James Church officiating. The time has not yet been fixed.

Jonathan Daniels, White House secretary, said Mr. Roosevelt's body would not lie in state. He added that, in view of the limited size of the East Room, which holds only about 200 persons, the list of those attending the funeral services would be limited to high Government officials, representatives of the membership of both

Continued on Page 3, Column 5

TRUMAN IS SWORN IN THE WHITE HOUSE

Members of Cabinet on Hand as Chief Justice Stone Administers the Oath

By C. P. TRUSSELL
Special to The New York Times.

WASHINGTON, April 12—Vice President Harry S. Truman of Missouri, standing erect, with his sharp features taut and looking straight ahead through his large, round glasses, became the thirty-second President of the United States in a ceremony lasting not more than a minute in the Cabinet Room of the White House at 7:09 o'clock tonight.

The oath was administered by Chief Justice Harlan F. Stone two hours and thirty-four minutes after the sudden death of President Roosevelt at Warm Springs. Mr. Truman had picked up a Bible from the end of the big Cabinet conference table, held it with his left hand and placed his right hand upon the upper cover. After repeating the oath, he bowed his head, lifted the Bible to his lips and kissed it.

Even before he had taken the oath Mr. Truman had asked President Roosevelt's Cabinet to continue in service. He also authorized Edward R. Stettinius Jr., Secretary of State, to announce that the United Nations Conference for International Organization would go on as scheduled.

To the newsmen at the White House he sent this word, through Stephen Early, press secretary:

"For the time being I prefer not to hold a press conference. It will be my effort to carry on as I believe the President would have done, and to that end I have asked the Cabinet to stay on with me."

Soon after he became President, Mr. Truman left the White House for the five-room Connecticut Avenue apartment where he has resided with Mrs. Truman and their 20-year-old daughter, Mary Margaret, for four years. He said he was "going home, to bed."

It was shortly after he had finished presiding over the Senate debate on the United States-Mexican Water Treaty late this afternoon that Mr. Truman received word from the White House of President Roosevelt's death. This was at about 5:15 P. M., a half hour before the news was made public. Reaching for his hat, he dashed out of the office, calling back to his staff that he was going to the White House.

Arriving at the White House, he

Continued on Page 3, Column 6

Byrnes May Take Post With Truman

Special to The New York Times.

WASHINGTON, April 12—James F. Byrnes, recently resigned as Director of War Mobilization and Reconversion, known to be one of President Truman's warmest friends in official Washington, is expected to be called to the White House for consultation, and possibly to take an important post in the Cabinet, in the immediate future.

President Truman's admiration of former Justice Byrnes is well known here. He undoubtedly would have been Mr. Truman's choice as a successor to Cordell Hull as Secretary of State.

"All the News That's Fit to Print"

The New York Times.

LATE CITY EDITION
Showers, cloudy and warmer today.
Partly cloudy and warm tomorrow.
Temperatures Yesterday—Max., 51; Min., 47
Sunrise today, 6:18 A. M.; Sunset, 7:37 P. M.

VOL. XCIV . No. 31,860.

Entered as Second-Class Matter, Postoffice, New York, N. Y.

NEW YORK, TUESDAY, APRIL 17, 1945.

THREE CENTS IN NEW YORK CITY

TRUMAN ASKS WORLD UNITY TO KEEP PEACE; 7TH IN NUREMBERG; SOVIET PUSH REPORTED; NAZIS LOSE 905 PLANES, MOSTLY AGROUND

NAZI BASE ENTERED

Hitler's Shrine Stormed After Full-Scale Drive by Patch's Forces

FIRST FLANKS LEIPZIG

9th Deepens Bridgehead Over Elbe—Canadians Clear North Holland

By The Associated Press.

PARIS, Tuesday, April 17—Three American armies battled possibly seventy-five to eighty-five miles from Russian lines today, hammering five miles beyond the Elbe River, outflanking the great fortress of Leipzig and driving a steel wedge thirty miles from the enemy's eastern front base of Dresden.

The Paris radio reported without official confirmation early today that American and Russian spearheads had met in th' Elbe River Valley south of Dresden.

The broadcast did not give the source of the report, which said the alleged meeting had taken place between Pirna and Tetschen.

[Tetschen is a Czechosolvak customs station, five miles inside the Czechoslovak border on the Prague-Dresden railroad, The United Press said.]

Another United States Army, the Seventh, broke into the Nazi shrine city of Nuremberg, ninety miles north of Munich.

New Elbe Crossing Reported

The United States Ninth Army was fifty-two miles southwest of Berlin, after having hacked out a foothold five miles beyond the Elbe, and unconfirmed German reports said the Americans had forced a new crossing farther north at Havelberg, forty-five miles northwest of Berlin and some eighty-five miles from Russian lines.

The United States First Army cut loose with a fourteen-mile tank dash that swept into Wurzen, twelve miles east of Leipzig, where an estimated 1,000,000 civilians faced an ordeal of fire and steel because 30,000 German troops are bent on making a Stalingrad of that refugee-swollen fifth city of the Reich. Infantry battled up four miles south of the city and artillery began to shell it.

The United States Third and First Armies were slashing into the rear area of German forces on the Eastern Front. Both were up to, if not across, the western boundary of German territory marked for Russian occupation.

Third Besieges Chemnitz

The Third Army laid siege to Chemnitz, was seven miles from the border of Czechoslovakia and pushed out a steel fist northeast of Chemnitz thirty miles from the Elbe and Dresden.

The First Army at Wurzen was eighteen miles from the Elbe—along which the Germans may make their final stand in central Germany—and was less than two miles from the river farther north as it opened an attack at the approaches to Dessau, fifty-two miles southwest of Berlin.

With the British and Canadians threatening the north German ports of Bremen, Emden and Hamburg in resumed offensives, and with the Allies squeezing enemy pockets in the western Netherlands, the Ruhr and on France's Atlantic coast, German soldiers were giving up by the thousands.

A total of 66,191 prisoners was counted Sunday, most of them from the Ruhr, where a German Panzer Lehr Division that had fought in North Africa and Normandy surrendered. Equally surprising was the abrupt capitulation of tough German marines to the Canadians at Groningen, the Netherlands' fifth largest city.

For all that, Gen. Dwight D. Eisenhower dampened any optimism that the end of the war in Europe was imminent.

He told visiting radio corre-

Continued on Page 3, Column 2

218,000 Prisoners Taken in 72 Hours

By The United Press.

WITH THE AMERICAN FIRST ARMY, in Germany, April 16—The American First, Third and Ninth Armies have taken more than 218,000 German prisoners in the past seventy-two hours in a mass round-up that at many points has lost all resemblance to war.

LONDON, April 16 (Reuter)—Gen. Dwight D. Eisenhower today announced the greatest daily haul of prisoners in this war.

His communiqué said the Allies in the west took 87,779 prisoners on Saturday alone. This is four times greater than the highest prisoner total for one day in the previous greatest Axis collapse of the war—in Tunisia two years ago.

AIRBORNE RUSSIANS SAID TO LEAP RING

Red Army Paratroops Within 18 Miles of Berlin as Drive Opens, Germans Say

By The Associated Press.

LONDON, Tuesday, April 17—The Germans reported today that Soviet parachutists had landed behind German lines in Berlin's defense ring somewhere between the city's eastern limits and heights won by the Red Army twenty-three miles to the east. German reports indicated that four Russian armies, totaling perhaps 2,000,000 men, were on the move.

The long-expected offensive burst upon the Germans at 3:50 A. M. yesterday, the German High Command announced, and drove forward along a 120-mile front at two points eighty-five miles from the American Third and Ninth Armies. Berlin conceded that a rapid link-up was possible.

The thunder of 1,000 Russian guns was heard throughout the day in Berlin, the enemy acknowledged, as Soviet assault units battled into massive reinforced fortifications under cover of hundreds of planes bombing and machine-gunning German positions on Berlin's eastern approaches.

New Footholds Reported

All along the front, Red Army engineers were speeding amphibious tanks and armored units into bridgeheads across the Oder and Neisse Rivers that were being built up hourly, according to German reports. At least two new footholds across the Oder were reported—the latest at the river's elbow east of Eberswalde, some eighteen airline miles northeast of Berlin's city limits.

Overshadowed by the reported operation, not yet officially confirmed by the Soviet High Command, were Red Army drives in Austria, Czechoslovakia and East Prussia.

In the Austrian Alps, Marshal Fedor I. Tolbukhin's Third Ukrai-

Continued on Page 4, Column 2

LUFTWAFFE IS 'OUT'

U. S. Fighters Spearhead 6,000-Sortie Assault Over All Germany

8TH HITS 40 AIRFIELDS

Big Bombers Rip Rails—Strategic Forces' Job Done, Spaatz Says

By The Associated Press.

LONDON, Tuesday, April 17—At least 845 German planes were destroyed yesterday by Allied fighters in a cataclysmic blow against the Nazi Air Force, and last night an observer commented, "The Luftwaffe has been knocked out."

[The figure for the "kill" of German planes Monday rose with additional reports from Allied air units. A United Press dispatch gave it as 905.]

Gen. Carl A. Spaatz, commander of the United States Strategic Air Forces in Europe, issued a special order of the day saying the strategic air war against Germany had ended victoriously and that hereafter United States heavy bombers would be used for tactical operations.

More than 6,000 Allied planes joined in the mighty daylight assault on the enemy. Some 2,000 fighter pilots smashed 812 Nazi planes on the ground and shot thirty-three from the skies.

RAF "Heavies" Strike by Night

Last night a big armada of Royal Air Force heavy bombers battered railway targets on both sides of the German-Czech frontier, where United States and Red Army troops are near a meeting. Other planes hit Berlin again, the British Air Ministry reported.

The United States Eighth Air Force, which sent nearly 2,100 warplanes from bases in Britain during the day, reported early today that eight of its heavy bombers and thirty-four fighters were missing.

More than forty Nazi airfields in the Pilsen-Prague area of Czechoslovakia were punished by the Eighth Air Force fighters that escorted the Eighth's heavy bombers on a mission against enemy communications targets in Bavaria. The Allies' tactical air forces based on the Continent fanned out in a series of attacks against enemy airdromes and targets over a wide area.

The Eighth's Mustangs and Thunderbolts, whose services as escorts for our heavy bombers were scarcely needed, dropped down for gunning runs and destroyed at least 647 planes on the ground. They shot down three others in combat during the Nazis' only effort at interception.

Some 1,000 Ninth Air Force fighters and fighter-bombers, at a loss of two planes, wrecked 159

Continued on Page 4, Column 5

THE THIRTY-SECOND PRESIDENT MAKING HIS FIRST SPEECH TO CONGRESS

President Truman addressing the joint session in the House chamber yesterday

Associated Press Wirephoto

ALLIES' ITALY PUSH CAPTURES VERGATO

5th Army Topples Apennine Barrier—British Eighth 1 Mile From Argenta

By MILTON BRACKER

By Wireless to THE NEW YORK TIMES.

FIFTEENTH ARMY GROUP HEADQUARTERS, Italy, April 16—Heralded by the greatest use of air power in the history of the Mediterranean theatre, the long-awaited all-out offensive in Italy began this morning, with the American Fifth Army hammering forward through the last Apennine barriers before Bologna.

Exhorted by their commanders to strike the blows that will mean final victory, both the Fifth and the Eighth Armies scored important gains along a fiery fifty-mile

Continued on Page 6, Column 2

B-29'S WIPE OUT 50% OF TOKYO INDUSTRY

Gutted Area Tops 27.5 Square Miles—368 Japanese Craft Destroyed in Five Days

By GEORGE E. JONES

By Wireless to THE NEW YORK TIMES.

GUAM, Tuesday, April 17—Fire-blackened and burning Tokyo is emerging today from a week-end of misery and horror visited on that crowded, inflammable metropolis by incendiary-laden Superfortresses and swarms of long-range land-based fighters. [This was the first mention of fighter planes in the latest attacks.]

[United States fliers and land and ship gunners destroyed 368 Japanese planes in five days of air warfare ranging from Oki-

Continued on Page 8, Column 4

Soviet Will Insist Lublin Act for Poland at Parley

By The United Press.

LONDON, Tuesday, April 17—The Moscow radio reported today that the Soviet Government had decided to insist on the admission of the Provisional Polish Government—the former Lublin regime—to the San Francisco Conference despite negative replies by the American and British Governments to a previous proposal.

Radio Moscow, in its 4 A. M. news broadcast, devoted its entire time to an account of President Truman's address before Congress yesterday and a reading of the Moscow communiqué on the Russian war fronts.

The Moscow radio, recalling the Soviet approach to the American, British and Chinese Governments regarding the admission of the Warsaw representatives to the United Nations' Conference, said:

"The answer of the British and American Governments has been negative. The Chinese Government answered that it so far had taken no decision on the subject, pointing out that since the Anglo-Americans had turned down the proposal, the Chinese Government's agreement or disagreement has no practical importance.

"It is reported the Soviet Government has decided to insist on its proposal to admit representatives of the Provisional Polish Warsaw Government to the San Francisco Conference."

London Poles Dissatisfied

By Wireless to THE NEW YORK TIMES.

LONDON, April 16—Reports that Polish underground leaders are conferring with Soviet authorities on the creation of a new Polish Government have been so persistent that even the exiled Polish

Continued on Page 15, Column 4

TRUMAN SEES EDEN, AWAITS MOLOTOFF

President Gets Churchill Messages—Talks by Radio to Armed Forces Tonight

By BERTRAM D. HULEN

Special to THE NEW YORK TIMES.

WASHINGTON, April 16—President Truman conferred today with Anthony Eden, the British Foreign Secretary, who brought to him messages from Prime Minister Churchill.

Mr. Eden arrived at the White House at 10 A. M., accompanied by the Earl of Halifax, the British Ambassador. Secretary of State Edward R. Stettinius Jr. was present during the conference, which lasted twenty minutes.

On leaving, Mr. Eden said:

"I was very pleased to have the privilege of calling on the President and very grateful that he found time to see me on this day when he has his first important speech to deliver.

"Naturally I brought him some messages from the Prime Minister telling him how gratified we are

Continued on Page 14, Column 1

STATES HIS POLICY

President Pledges U. S. to Work for World Security League

TO PUSH WAR TO END

Congress Told Roosevelt Drive for Common Man Will Be Continued

The text of the President's address is printed on Page 12.

By FRANK L. KLUCKHOHN

Special to THE NEW YORK TIMES.

WASHINGTON, April 16—President Truman pledged himself today to carry out the war and peace policies of Franklin D. Roosevelt.

The pledge was given in a speech before a joint session of Congress, attended by the Cabinet, Supreme Court justices and representatives of foreign nations, including Anthony Eden, British Foreign Secretary.

Mr. Truman appealed for united public support of a program for unconditional surrender of the enemy, as already determined by the United Nations, and to establish "a strong and lasting United Nations Organization" for world peace.

He received an ovation both when he entered the House chamber and when he departed after his appeal for national support, which was broadcast throughout the country and the world. He was applauded frequently during his address.

"I call upon all Americans to help me keep our nation united in defense of those ideals which have been so eloquently proclaimed by Franklin Roosevelt," the new President said.

Will Keep Military "Team"

He disclosed that he intended to maintain the present American High Command for waging "the fight for freedom until no vestige of resistance remains," adding:

"I appeal to every American, regardless of party, race, creed, or color, to support our efforts to build a strong and lasting United Nations Organization."

On the domestic front, he pledged that the drive begun by Mr. Roosevelt to improve the lot of the common people would be continued, but the bulk of his speech was devoted to the war and approaching peace problems.

Regretting the death of Mr. Roosevelt and remarking that "no man could possibly fill the tremendous void left by the passing of that noble soul," Mr. Truman asserted that the world was looking to America for "enlightened leadership" and emphasized that this could be offered only by a country which was itself united.

War Will Be Pushed

Germany and Japan, he continued, could both rest assured that our fight would be pressed against them until all resistance ended, adding that, although we knew "much hard fighting" lay ahead, we already had paid a high price, and "America will never become a party to any plan for partial victory."

To do otherwise, he said, would mean only a temporary breathing space, concurrently putting in jeopardy future world security.

"Our demand has been, and it remains—unconditional surrender!" Mr. Truman asserted, pounding the table before him in one of the two gestures he made during his speech.

The victors, he asserted, must be responsible for the making of the peace and, although unnecessary and unjustified suffering must be avoided, war criminals must be

Continued on Page 12, Column 1

War News Summarized

TUESDAY, APRIL 17, 1945

Allied Armies continued to whittle down the area of Germany still in enemy hands, with Berlin reports placing the United States Ninth Army forty-five miles from the capital. Leipzig was outflanked by the First Army. The Seventh broke into Nuremberg, and the Third laid siege to Chemnitz, while in the north the British Second Army resumed its assault on Bremen and the Canadian First Army captured Groningen in the Netherlands. [1:1; maps Pages 2 and 4.]

Despite the disintegration of German lines General Eisenhower said he did not expect the war to end until all of Germany had been occupied and that there would be no announcement of V-E Day until every important enemy pocket on the Western Front had been wiped out. [5:4.]

French troops captured Royan, at the mouth of the Gironde River, in the battle to reopen the port of Bordeaux. [4:3-4.]

There was little left of the Luftwaffe after Allied fliers swept German airfields to destroy the record number of 905 enemy planes, most of them on the ground. Strategic bombing is over for the Germans, as there are no more targets, said General Spaatz. [1:3.]

Although Moscow maintained silence on any move toward Berlin from the east, the German radio said that Russian parachutists had landed less than twenty-three miles from the city and that four Soviet armies, totaling 2,000,000 men, were on the move. [1:2.] Hitler issued an order of the day asking the Germans to drown the Russians in a sea of blood and hold Berlin at all costs. [6:5.]

The Allies have opened their spring offensive in Italy, striking along a fifty-mile arc in a determined effort to end the war. Two days of unprecedented air blows in the Mediterranean area heralded the drive. [1:4; map, P 6.]

Vast fires and explosions visible more than 100 miles away were left by B-29's in their latest attack on Tokyo. At least half the city's industry has been destroyed and the burned out area is not less than 27.5 square miles. [1:5.] Pacific Fleet planes destroyed 368 Japanese planes in raids over Kyushu, the Ryukyus, and the Okinawa area. There was little change in position on Okinawa, although Ie Island, off the west coast, was invaded. [8:1.]

Taungup, last Japanese coastal supply base in the Arakan area of Burma, was captured by British and Indian troops. [10:3, with map.]

President Truman, addressing Congress for the first time, pleaded for united public support to help him "defend those ideals which have been so eloquently proclaimed by Franklin Roosevelt." Unconditional surrender remains our war aim, he said, and there will be no change in military leadership. He pledged himself to fight for a "strong and lasting United Nations organization." [1:8.]

The Moscow radio said Russia insisted upon the presence of the Polish Provisional (Lublin) Government at the San Francisco Conference despite British and American opposition. [1:6-7.]

18,000 Vote Phone Strike Here; Delay Likely to Let Truman Act

A strike that might cripple local and long line telephone service in New York, and spread to other sections, was voted last night by an overwhelming majority of 18,000 workers affiliated with two independent unions in protest against a War Labor Board order of a $3 a week increase in pay.

There were 14,471 valid ballots cast, the National Labor Relations Board announced, and of these 94 per cent were marked in favor of a strike.

Unless a Presidential seizure order is issued, the unions involved—the Traffic Employes Association, representing 12,000 operators, and the Federation of Long Lines Telephone Workers—may possibly walk out soon after their executive boards meet in joint session at 2 P. M. today at the office of the latter union, 260 West Broadway. The local operators are employed by the New York Telephone Company and the others by the American Telephone and Telegraph Company.

Only 540 of the traffic workers voted against a strike while 9,999 were in favor, according to a representative of the NLRB who supervised the balloting that started at 7 A. M. yesterday and ended at 10 P. M.

The long distance workers did not complete their vote until after 11 P. M and it followed the same pattern, 3,814 voting to strike while only 118 voted "no."

Both unions originally had demanded a $5 weekly pay rise. Telephone company officials had offered them $4, and had given the WLB data in support of the increase. On Saturday the board refused to reconsider the matter and

Continued on Page 24, Column 3

Roosevelt Estate Is Left in Trust To Widow and Then to 5 Children

Special to THE NEW YORK TIMES.

POUGHKEEPSIE, N. Y., April 16—The will of Franklin D. Roosevelt, leaving his estate, after certain minor bequests, to his wife and children, was filed at 4:30 o'clock this afternoon before Frederick S. Quinterro, Surrogate of Dutchess County, by Henry T. Hackett, a Poughkeepsie attorney and personal friend of the President.

[The text of Mr. Roosevelt's will appears on Page 18.]

There was nothing in the document to indicate the value of the estate. Under the will of his mother, Mrs. Sara Delano Roosevelt, Mr. Roosevelt inherited nine-tenths of her estate. It was appraised at $1,069,872, according to a New York State transfer tax appraisal filed on April 23, 1942.

The late President directed that his residuary estate should be held in trust for Mrs. Roosevelt for her lifetime. At her death half of the principal is to be divided equally among their five children, Mrs. Anna Roosevelt Boettiger and James, Elliott, Franklin Jr. and John Roosevelt. The remaining half of the principal is to be divided into separate trusts for their benefit.

He directed that his wife should have the right to select any personal property that she desired to utilize during her lifetime and that each of the five children should have the right to select one-fifth of the rest of the personal property.

Any personal property not chosen by them is to be offered by the executors to the United States Government as a gift for

Continued on Page 18, Column 3

U.S. Army

Battle-weary German soldiers surrender to men of the 94th Infantry Division during the Twentieth Corps' advance in Germany.

"All the News That's Fit to Print"

The New York Times.

LATE CITY EDITION
Sunny and cool today. Increasing cloudiness, warmer tomorrow.
Temperatures Yesterday—Max., 52; Min., 47
Sunrise today, 5:00 A. M.; Sunset, 7:46 P. M.

VOL. XCIV..No. 31,871. Entered as Second-Class Matter, Postoffice, New York, N. Y. NEW YORK, SATURDAY, APRIL 28, 1945. THREE CENTS IN NEW YORK CITY

U. S. AND RED ARMIES JOIN, SPLIT GERMANY; 3D ARMY IN AUSTRIA; RUSSIANS IN POTSDAM; PARLEY BARS LUBLIN, SOVIET GETS 3 VOTES

RUSSIAN ISSUES OUT

Plea for 4 Chairmen Won but Stettinius Will Head Vital Committees

EQUALITY CALLED AIM

Heads of 14 Delegations Are Nâmed as Members of Executive Group

By JAMES B. RESTON
Special to The New York Times.

SAN FRANCISCO, April 27—The United Nations Conference on International Organization today accepted two of the three requests put before it by Soviet Russia, and rejected the third.

First, the delegates of the forty-six nations gathered here to establish an international security organization accepted Russia's request that there should be four presidents of the conference, Edward R. Stettinius Jr., American Secretary of State; Vyacheslaff M. Molotoff, Russian Foreign Commissar; Anthony Eden, British Secretary of State for Foreign Affairs, and T. V. Soong, Chinese Foreign Minister.

They agreed, however, that while the four presidents would preside in turn over the plenary sessions of the conference, the four presidents would delegate to Mr. Stettinius the chairmanship of the Executive and Steering Committees of the conference, and allow him to preside over the meetings of the four presidents whenever they conferred.

Second, they accepted Marshal Stalin's proposal that two of the sixteen Soviet Republics, White Russia and the Ukraine, should become initial voting members of the new world security organization, after President H[illegible] S. Truman had instructed th[illegible] States delegation to fulf[illegible] n D. Roosevelt's promise [illegible] t this action.

Third, they rejected Russia's request, made publicly in Moscow, and brought up privately but not pressed here, that the present Polish Provisional Government of Warsaw (classed as the Lublin regime) be allowed to attend the conference. Instead, the conference passed a resolution expressing the hope that Poland would be represented at the conference as soon as the present difficulties over the "broadening" of the Polish Government were resolved.

Reply on Poland Drafted

On this latter point there was one important development. Marshal Stalin's reply to the report he received on the conversations which took place with President Truman and the Foreign Ministers of "the Big Three" in Washington several days ago has been received and studied here. It does not, in the opinion of those members of the American and British delegations who have seen it, change the basic issue over the expansion of the Warsaw Government to include "democratic elements" from inside and outside Poland.

A reply to Marshal Stalin's note has been drafted here and has been approved by Washington and sent to London for Prime Minister Churchill's observations. It will be sent to Moscow, probably this week-end. In the meanwhile, the deadlock continues.

It is generally admitted here that Mr. Molotoff received approval on the two issues on which he insisted. He wished to establish two principles and made this clear to the heads of the delegations:

First, he wanted to establish the principle of equality among the four sponsor powers running the conference; second, he desired to establish the principle that the Soviet Republics were independent entities with the right to sit and vote at international conferences. These two principles were accepted in this afternoon's plenary session

Continued on Page 10, Column 2

Parley Sessions Opened to Press

By The Associated Press.

SAN FRANCISCO, April 27—A United States proposal to apply the principle of free information to the United Nations Conference was adopted today by the steering committee of forty-six chiefs of delegations.

Secretary Stettinius told a news conference that plenary sessions of the conference and meetings of the four principal commissions would be held in public, open to complete reporting.

He also said that principal officers of the conference would hold regular meetings with accredited press, radio and photography representatives.

The commissions, however, were authorized to hold some closed meetings, at their own direction, and sessions of technical committees and subcommittees were made secret.

The Dumbarton Oaks Conference, at which the original proposals for a world security conference were drafted, was entirely closed.

DRAFT EXTENSION SENT TO PRESIDENT

House Adopts Senate Training Amendment After Hearing 'Declaration of Intent'

By C. P. TRUSSELL
Special to The New York Times.

WASHINGTON, April 27—The House accepted unanimously today the Senate amendment to the Draft Extension Bill which bars the Army from ordering 18-year-old inductees into combat until they have had at least six months of military training.

In sending the measure to President Truman, the House went on record with an interpretation of the amendment whereby 18-year-old soldiers already on battle fronts will not be withdrawn and marines will be classified with soldiers in training requirements.

The amendment provides:

"That no man under 19 years of age who is inducted into the land or naval forces under the provisions of this (Selective Service) act shall be ordered into actual combat service until after he has been given at least six months of military training of such character and to the extent necessary to prepare such inductee for combat duty.

"This proviso shall not be construed as preventing the assignment of enlisted men of the Navy or Coast Guard and the reserve components thereof to duty for training on combat vessels of the Navy or Coast Guard and at naval bases beyond the continental limits of the United States."

Before taking the question to the floor, the House Military Affairs Committee had decided that the measure, which extends the draft for a year from May 15, should not be sent to conference because of

Continued on Page 9, Column 7

BERLIN NEAR FINISH

Spandau Arsenal and Potsdam Fall—Koneff Wins Big Airfield

¾ OF CAPITAL SEIZED

Two Columns Strike West—Russians Drive to Seal Baltic Ports

By C. L. SULZBERGER
By Wireless to The New York Times.

MOSCOW, Saturday, April 28—Russian assault groups overwhelmed the southern half of Berlin yesterday, capturing four city districts, including the famous Tempelhof airdrome, and advancing to within one mile of Unter den Linden. [Three-fourths of the capital was in the Red Army's hands, The Associated Press reported.]

At the same time the Russians ground their way into martial Potsdam, where lie the remains of Frederick the Great, and seized Spandau, where since that monarch's reign the best German small-arms weapon had been manufactured in old ordnance plants.

On the western outskirts of the city it was Marshal Gregory K. Zhukoff's First White Russian Army group that battered its way through Potsdam and Spandau, last two strongly held outer bastions of Berlin's crumbling defense. In the south Marshal Ivan S. Koneff's well-schooled street fighters plunged through the rubble of Neukoelln, Steglitz, Schmargendorf and central Tempelhof, on whose airdrome Adolf Hitler's lackeys landed and from which perhaps they had hoped to fly to doubtful and impermanent havens.

[The United Press reported from Moscow that small Soviet bombers were able to land on captured Tempelhof airdrome.

[Lieut. Gen. Kurt Dittmar, German strategist, whose surrender this week to the American Ninth Army was announced Friday, added his voice to the Germans' insistence that Hitler was in the capital. He said that the war was over and that the great redoubt was largely a myth.]

Ring Being Closed Anew

Only two smoking districts separate the southwestern segment of the iron ring around Berlin from Charlottenburg and Unter den Linden—Wilmersdorf and Schoenberg.

Marshal Zhukoff's forces took 8,500 prisoners around Berlin.

It seemed early today as if the Russians had penetrated the Grunewald Forest, south of Charlottenburg. Bitter fighting continued in the northern and northeastern areas under ever-growing smoke layers.

Marshal Koneff made a sensational advance all the way from the western suburbs of Berlin to the Elbe River, capturing Wittenberg and making imminent a new

Continued on Page 5, Column 2

State Leads in Care of Veterans, Dewey Says in 'Report to People'

Special to The New York Times.

ALBANY, April 27—Governor Dewey, in a radio report tonight to the people of the State, hailed "the tremendous news of the final juncture of the Allied and Russian armies in Nazi Germany" and said New York has led all other States in providing for its returning war veterans.

[The text of the Governor's address will be found on Page 9.]

The Governor, before discussing the accomplishments of the 1945 Legislature and of his administration, said the news from Europe offers occasion for reaffirmance of our determination to bring about complete defeat of our remaining enemies in Germany and Japan and rigorous punishment of war criminals. He added:

"At the same time the United Nations work earnestly at San Francisco to make the peace to come secure and lasting."

Governor Dewey's talk covered a wide range of subjects, from aid for veterans to experience rating in unemployment insurance. He asserted:

"Of one thing you may be sure. Your State Administration has given progressive and financially sound administration. The rights of our workers have been advanced and the opportunities in business and employment have been increased."

Governor Dewey will give another radio report to the people next Friday night. It was explained that the large number of new laws and administrative changes made it impossible for him to cover the entire field in a single

Continued on Page 9, Column 1

HANDS ACROSS THE ELBE: AMERICANS AND RUSSIANS MEET IN REICH

United States First Army infantrymen and Soviet troops on a broken bridge over the river at Torgau
Associated Press Wirephoto (U. S. Signal Corps Radiophoto)

GENOA IS ENTERED BY 5TH ARMY MEN

Partisans Seize Large Part of Italy's Greatest Port—Allies Dash Toward Milan

By VIRGINIA LEE WARREN
By Wireless to The New York Times.

ADVANCED ALLIED FIELD HEADQUARTERS, Italy, April 27—Genoa, Italy's largest port, with nearly 1,000,000 inhabitants, was entered by a Fifth Army task force this morning after Italian Partisans had gained control of a large part of the city. Commanded by Maj. Gen. Edward M. Almond and operating directly under the Fifteenth Army Group, the task force was made up of the

Continued on Page 6, Column 5

First Link Made Wednesday By Four Americans on Patrol

By HAROLD DENNY
By Wireless to The New York Times.

AT A RED ARMY OUTPOST, on the Elbe, April 27—The United States and Russian armies have met on the Elbe. The Western and Eastern fronts are at last linked up and Germany is cut in two. First contact was made two days ago—at 4:40 P. M., April 25, by a four-man patrol of the 273d Infantry Regiment of the Sixty-ninth Infantry Division and a Russian outpost at the sizable town of Torgau, twenty miles west of our then most advanced forces.

On the American side the honor of making this historic junction goes to Gen. Courtney H. Hodges' United States First Army, which forced the Normandy beaches last June and has advanced 700 miles through France, Belgium and Ger-

Continued on Page 4, Column 5

SURRENDER OFFERS BY NAZIS REPORTED

Group Said to By-Pass Hitler in Bid to Western Allies, Who Stand on Role by Russia

By SIDNEY SHALETT
Special to The New York Times.

WASHINGTON, April 27—Reports current in Washington—reports more numerous and more authoritative than any of the sort previously heard in this capital—indicated tonight that Nazi Germany had made known a willingness to surrender unconditionally to the United States and Britain, but not to the Soviet Union, and that the Western Allies have told the enemy negotiators that they will accept "only for all."

The reports stirred belief here that a formal admission of defeat from Germany was imminent.

This information is not made

Continued on Page 2, Column 2

MEETING OF ARMIES HAILED BY TRUMAN

Says Last Hope of 'Hitler and His Gangster Government Has Been Extinguished'

Text of President's announcement of junction, Page 3.

By BERTRAM D. HULEN
Special to The New York Times.

WASHINGTON, April 27—President Truman announced today that the Anglo-American armies and the Soviet forces have made their long-expected junction "where they intended to meet—in the heart of Nazi Germany."

The junction was made, the White House said, at Torgau, a town on the Elbe River, seventy-five miles south of Berlin. According to the War Department the forces met yesterday at 10 A. M., E. W. T. Patrols had made contact on Wednesday at 10:30 A. M., E. W. T.

Simultaneous announcements were made in London and Moscow.

In making the announcement, President Truman's statement declared that "the enemy has been cut in two." However, he warned that this was not the final victory in Europe, although, he said, the hour for which all "have toiled and prayed so long" was drawing near.

It means, he asserted, that "the

Continued on Page 3, Column 2

War News Summarized

SATURDAY, APRIL 28, 1945

The eagerly awaited announcement that the Allied armies that entered Europe via the beachheads of Normandy and the Red Army that turned back the Nazi tide at Stalingrad had met in the heart of Germany came simultaneously yesterday from Washington, London and Moscow. The epochal linking of the western and eastern fronts took place on Wednesday afternoon at Torgau, on the Elbe River, twenty-eight miles northeast of Leipzig. [1:8; map P. 2.]

The armies' first contact was between patrols of the Sixty-ninth Division of General Hodges' American First Army and the Fifty-eighth Guards Division of Marshal Koneff's First Ukrainian Army. The meeting was accidental and the Russians mistook the Americans at first for Germans. [1:5-6.] The splitting of the German forces is expected to speed the destruction of the enemy, for Allied armies now can turn their might toward either side, with the reduction of the redoubts in the north and south having top priority. [5:6]

With three-fourths of Berlin in Russian hands, the Red Army struck westward for a new junction with Allied forces, this time with the American Ninth Army west of the rubbled German capital. A thirteen-mile gap separated the two army forces. German resistance within Berlin was crumbling. The Russians seized Tempelhof airport and Potsdam and it appeared that few, if any, of the Nazi leaders in the capital would be able to escape. [1:3.]

Hitler is still in Berlin and intends to die there, according to General Dittmar, who surrendered to American troops. The Nazi officer, who was the radio voice of the German High Command, predicted that the war would end in a few days with the fall of Berlin. [4:1.]

In Italy, the American Fifth Army slashed into Genoa, the last German naval base on the Mediteranean, and swept closer to Turin and Milan through weak and disorganized resistance. [1:4; map P. 6.] Benito Mussolini was captured by Italian Partisans as he tried to cross the Swiss border, according to information at the frontier. [6:6.]

In the Pacific, American forces hammered through Japanese defenses on southern Okinawa to the area of Machinato, two miles from Naha, the island's capital. [1:6.] Our troops on Mindanao, in the Philippines, were within sight of Digos, on Davao Gulf, after a ten-mile eastward push. [5:6.]

The United Nations conference in San Francisco agreed to give White Russia and the Ukraine a vote each in the proposed Assembly of the new world security organization, but refused to invite the provisional Polish regime in Warsaw. The delegates accepted the Soviet request for four presidents at the conference. [1:1.]

General Gain Made on Okinawa; 27th Division Nears Key Airfield

By ROBERT TRUMBULL
By Wireless to The New York Times.

GUAM, Saturday, April 28—In a day of general advances by Army troops on Okinawa, elements of the Twenty-seventh Infantry Division [former New York National Guard organization] were approaching the Machinato airstrip on the western side of the island Thursday, Fleet Admiral Chester W. Nimitz reported in a communiqué this morning.

Twenty-seventh Division troops were in the vicinity of the airfield by 6 o'clock Thursday evening. Attacks in this and other sectors on a front bisecting the narrow island were resumed yesterday morning.

American aircraft were operating from airfields previously taken.

The situation continued to be quiet in the northern section of Okinawa, held by marines of the Third Amphibious Corps under Maj. Gen. Roy S. Geiger. Activity was restricted to patrolling Thursday and Friday.

A minesweeper shot down three Japanese planes early yesterday, a great feat for such a small vessel. Very few enemy aircraft appeared over the American forces.

In the southern Ryukyus, carrier aircraft of the United States Pacific Fleet carried attacks on the Sakishima Islands into the third successive day. This group has five major airstrips on the islands of Miyako and Ishigaki, which have been pounded incessantly by American and British carrier planes throughout the past month.

Routine air operations elsewhere in the Pacific included attacks on harbor installations on Chichi Island in the Bonins by Marine

Continued on Page 5, Column 7

FIRM LINK FORMED

Junction of Two Armies Splits Rest of Reich Into Huge Pockets

PATTON RACES SOUTH

Crosses Austrian Border Without Opposition—New Linkup Impends

By DREW MIDDLETON
By Wireless to The New York Times.

PARIS, April 27—Two armies of plain men who had marched and fought from the blood-splashed beaches of Normandy and the shattered streets of Stalingrad have met on the Elbe River in the heart of Germany, splitting the Third Reich and sealing the doom of the German Army, whose tread shook the world only three short years ago.

The junction on the Elbe River of Gen. Courtney H. Hodges' United States First Army and Marshal Ivan S. Koneff's First Ukrainian Army transcends all other developments on the Western Front, even a thrust across the Austrian border by an armored column of Gen. George S. Patton's United States Third Army, which is driving eastward toward Marshal Fedor I. Tolbukhin's Soviet forces smashing westward eighty miles away.

Junction Made Wednesday

The first official contact between the Red Army and the Allies' Expeditionary Forces was made at 4:40 P. M. on Wednesday, when a second lieutenant and three men of an intelligence and reconnaissance platoon of the 273d Regiment of the Sixty-ninth Infantry Division of the First Army met elements of the 173d Regiment of the Fifty-eighth Guards Division of the First Ukrainian Army on the girders of a demolished bridge at Torgau on the Elbe, twenty-eight miles northeast of Leipzig. Yesterday afternoon at 4 o'clock Maj. Gen. Emil F. Reinhardt, commanding the Sixty-ninth Division, conferred with the commander of the Soviet Guards Division at Torgau on the mutual exchange of liberated prisoners of war.

Tonight the meeting of the East and West is sealed and details of both armies are guarding the roads between the two fronts while senior officers of both sides pay their respects to their comrades in arms.

The German front was split after a junction that ended a drive of 1,400 miles to the west by the Red Armies starting from Stalingrad and 700 miles to the east by the First Army, whose first elements came ashore in Normandy last June.

Mop-Up Work Remains

From now on pockets and redoubts of varying sizes and strengths are the main tactical objectives of the Anglo-American and Red Armies and the advances will be to the north and south rather than to the east and west, as so long has been the case.

With the American and Red Armies now in firm contact to the north, the United States Third Army and Marshal Tolbukhin's Third Ukrainian Army are moving swiftly toward each other and another junction in Austria which would isolate the Bohemian redoubt in western Czechoslovakia. At the same time the United States Seventh Army and the French First Army have broken German defenses in the western part of the Bavarian foreland and are rolling down on the northern boundary of Hitler's Alpine redoubt.

At last reports tonight columns of both the United States Seventh and Third Armies were less than forty miles from Munich, key to the outer defenses of the redoubt, and tanks of the Tenth Armored Division on the Seventh Army's right flank were only twenty-seven miles north of the Austrian frontier at the western end of the redoubt.

The swift advances of the last

Continued on Page 3, Column 6

"All the News That's Fit to Print"

NEWS INDEX, PAGE 39, THIS SECTION

The New York Times.

Copyright, 1945, by The New York Times Company.

LATE CITY EDITION

Cloudy and cool; showers tonight. Clearing and warmer tomorrow.

Temperatures Yesterday—Max., 54; Min., 41
Sunrise today, 5:36 A. M.; Sunset, 7:48 P. M.

Section

VOL. XCIV. No. 31,872.

Entered as Second-Class Matter, Postoffice, New York, N. Y.

NEW YORK, SUNDAY, APRIL 29, 1945.

Including Magazine and Book Sections.

TEN CENTS
New York City and Suburban Areas (15c Elsewhere)

ALLIES BAR PEACE PLEA THAT OMITS RUSSIA; SURRENDER REPORT UNTRUE, TRUMAN SAYS; MUNICH REVOLTS; HITLER SAID TO BE DYING

RUSSIANS DEMAND IMMEDIATE SEATING OF TWO REPUBLICS

Latin-Americans Then Insist That Argentina Be Admitted —Settlement Is Likely

PEACE TALK STIRS PARLEY

Small Countries Find the Big 4 Striving to Speed Actions Before V-E Day Comes

By JAMES B. RESTON
Special to THE NEW YORK TIMES.

SAN FRANCISCO, April 28—The phase of political maneuvering at the San Francisco Conference is drawing to a close, but it is not quite finished.

A new controversy among the United States, Britain and Soviet Russia developed today over the insistence of the Soviet Foreign Commissar, Vyacheslaff M. Molotoff, that the representatives of White Russia and the Ukraine be seated in the conference before the working committees of the conference start their deliberations.

This controversy, referred to the Executive Committee of the conference, is further complicated by the fact that some of the Latin-American countries are insisting that, if the two Soviet republics are seated, Argentina should be invited to join the United Nations and attend.

Every effort is being made by the American and British delegations to keep these two questions from being involved with each other, while it is becoming increasingly evident that the Russians are sensitive to the voting power of the countries of the Western Hemisphere. There is, however, reason for saying that the basis for a private agreement has already been reached under which all three will be seated in the conference next week.

Small Powers Give Views

While this question was being discussed behind the scenes, the delegates gathered in the Opera House this morning and again this afternoon for two plenary sessions at which the representatives of the smaller countries expressed a general willingness to accept the Dumbarton Oaks security formula.

Reports of the German surrender, which were circulated in newspaper headlines on the floor of the opera house during this afternoon's plenary session, led to demonstrations of exultation.

The demonstrations took place while the official translator was reading an English translation of the Uruguayan Foreign Minister's address before a plenary session of the conference.

The head of the Honduran delegation, Julian R. Caceres, walked into the opera house with a copy of a San Francisco paper in his hand. It was an extra edition with a headline reading: "Nazis Quit." Mr. Caceres walked down the aisle holding the paper above his head, circled in front of the audience and held the newspaper aloft.

Delegates all over the chamber stood up and broke into applause. It was several minutes before order was restored.

It was increasingly evident today that the possibility of an imminent peace in Europe was beginning to play an important part in the deliberations of the four powers sponsoring the conference.

Russian Question Speeded

That is why the question of seating the Russian delegates was being dealt with at once.

Mr. Molotoff, it is now learned, told the Steering Committee yesterday that he wanted the two Soviet republics brought into the conference immediately. There was a tendency on the part of some members of the committee to accede to this request at once, but

Continued on Page 28, Column 1

Berlin's 'Fleet' Sails To Elbe to Surrender

By The Associated Press.

WITH THE UNITED STATES NINTH ARMY, on the Elbe River, April 28—American doughboys on this topsy-turvy front have now seen everything. The ultimate was reached last night when a German "fleet" sailed up the Elbe and surrendered. It had come from Berlin through inland waterways.

The fleet consisted of six tugboats, ten river barges, three houseboats and eleven assorted escorts loaded with wounded and marked with red crosses. The entire fleet surrendered to Lieut. Andrew Gadek of 43 Fremont Street, Woodbridge, N. J.

A German major in charge said they feared the approach of the Russians because of their "inhumanity." Gadek replied there were a few scenes of "inhumanity" near there, where the Germans had burned 1,100 prisoners to death in a barn.

An English-speaking nurse replied: "Oh, that's different."

ANTHRACITE MINES FACING SHUT-DOWN

Union Withholds Approval of Contract Extension—Lewis Sees New Pact Possible

A shut-down of Pennsylvania anthracite production Tuesday was threatened yesterday when the United Mine Workers withheld approval of the request of Secretary of the Interior Harold L. Ickes for a thirty-day extension of the coal contract, which expires at midnight tomorrow.

While anthracite operators, meeting at the Waldorf-Astoria Hotel, telegraphed Mr. Ickes of their agreement to his request, the union announced it was "continuing to give the subject consideration."

John L. Lewis, president of the UMW, insisted that an extension would lead to "prolongation of uncertainty and is in every way undesirable." He said that "we think the [anthracite coal] conference is in a position to complete the execution of a new contract before Monday night."

"We see no reason for procrastination," he asserted. "We are deferring any decision on the request for a thirty-day extension until we can determine whether or not this conference is going to finish its work."

Lewis Stand Not Challenged

Although there have been no announced compromises on the miners' demands, none of the operators challenged Mr. Lewis' statement that "the issues of the conference are boiled down and concentrated to certain specific items on which decision can easily be made by Monday night." In addition he said that "we think every moral, economic and national consideration calls for completion of

Continued on Page 31, Column 2

REICH ARMY REBELS

Uprisings Led by Revolt in the Cradle of Nazism Sweep South Germany

TROOPS DROP ARMS

Bloody Disorders Follow Abortive Coup Tuesday in City of Salzburg

By DANIEL T. BRIGHAM
By Telephone to THE NEW YORK TIMES.

BERNE, Switzerland, April 28—Led off by the city of Munich, home of the National Socialist movement, which rose to throw off the yoke of nazism at 3 o'clock this morning, the civilian population of southwestern Germany, joined by increasing numbers of German Army garrisons that are deserting en masse right up to the Swiss frontier tonight, is in the throes of one of the bloodiest revolutions in German history.

[Allied Headquarters in Paris said more than 80,000 Germans had been captured on the western front on Friday while Soviet reports declared taht 27,000 Germans had given up the fight in the Berlin area.]

Everywhere from the outskirts of the Alpine redoubt back up railway and road lines of communications to the foremost spearheads of the Allied armies marching southward come reports from neutral automobile and truck drivers, from refugees and even the military telling of pitched battles between the German Army and Nazi party with most of the engagements turning entirely in favor of the former.

From semi-official sources it also was learned tonight that a second "freedom movement" had sprung up Tuesday in Salzburg where a dissident government headed by Reichsbank President Walther Funk called on Austrians inside the redoubt to rise and "throw off your oppressors." The move is said to have failed.

Rebels Hold Half of Munich

At Munich itself the uprising, according to the latest information pieced together from official and clandestine German sources as well as neutral Swiss reports, shows that after an initial success of some nine hours the revolt turned briefly against the rebels, permitting the Nazis to recapture the Munich radio station, which at midnight tonight was still in party hands. But broadcast orders on army radios of the German Army show that the situation is rapidly turning back in favor of the insurgents, who now hold more than half of the city of Munich, from the Isar River to its northwestern outskirts at Rothkirchen.

First news of the outbreak came at 7:30 this morning, when the Munich radio station suddenly announced its program was being

Continued on Page 10, Column 1

Philippines' Summer Capital Falls To Americans After Long Battle

By The Associated Press.

MANILA, Sunday, April 29—Baguio, mile-high Philippine summer capital and one-time Japanese military headquarters on northern Luzon, fell to the Thirty-third and Thirty-seventh United States Infantry Divisions on Friday, after one of the longest and bitterest fights of the Philippine campaign.

Gen. Douglas MacArthur's announcement today said the important city, one of the greatest gold-mining centers of the entire archipelago, was taken by the Thirty-third Division under Maj. Gen. Percy W. Clarkson, newly augmented by the Thirty-seventh under Maj. Gen. Robert S. Beightler. The Thirty-seventh helped conquer Manila in February.

Mountainous Baguio, a prime objective of General MacArthur's men since their Jan. 9 invasion of Luzon island at Lingayen Gulf, was taken in a gradual encircling move with artillery and aircraft strongly supporting the foot soldiers.

The Japanese garrison was destroyed, General MacArthur said. American casualties were termed "amazingly light."

Twenty-fourth Division troops, meantime, completed their crossing of southern Mindanao from Moro Gulf to Davao Gulf by reaching Digos, twenty-five road miles south of Davao City, a principal port of the Philippines.

General MacArthur announced that the Thirty-first Army Division had joined the Twenty-fourth for the push to Davao, where the

Continued on Page 25, Column 3

BERLIN TOTTERING

Germans Squeezed Into 25 Square Miles of Shattered Heart

27,000 TROOPS YIELD

Soviet Forces North of Capital Strike Out for Hamburg Pocket

By C. L. SULZBERGER
By Wireless to THE NEW YORK TIMES.

MOSCOW, Sunday, April 29—The defenses of inner Berlin were cracked wide open yesterday as two giant Soviet armies captured 27,000 prisoners in wholesale surrenders and as Russian assault groups plunged deep into the shattered capital from all points of the compass.

Marshal Ivan S. Koneff's troops smashed into three more city districts in the western part of the metropolis, occupying Friedenau, Grunewald and Ruhleben, while in the woods to the southeast his First Ukrainian Army joined forces with Marshal Gregory K. Zhukoff's First White Russian Army to surround a large pocket of Germans.

In the northwestern part of the flaming citadel, meanwhile, Marshal Zhukoff thundered through Charlottenburg as far as Bismarckstrasse and occupied completely the western section of the Moabit district, which had already been largely overrun, and the eastern part of Schoenberg. Thus, Marshal Zhukoff's forces have almost entirely surrounded Berlin by themselves, except for the southwestern and part of the southern segment of the steel ring compressing Berlin.

Two army groups have effected a new junction below Siemens-

Continued on Page 5, Column 7

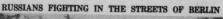

RUSSIANS FIGHTING IN THE STREETS OF BERLIN

Red Army tanks and infantrymen advancing along Berlinerstrasse

The New York Times (Sovfoto Radiophoto)

7TH ARMY CROSSES AUSTRIAN FRONTIER

Enters at Two Points Near Innsbrueck as Gen. Patton Speeds Salzburg Drive

By DREW MIDDLETON
By Wireless to THE NEW YORK TIMES.

PARIS, April 28—Tanks and doughboys of Lieut. Gen. Alexander M. Patch's United States Seventh Army have smashed the last German defenses in the Bavarian foreland and have swept over the Austrian frontier at two points to hammer the northern gates of Hitler's Alpine redoubt after an advance that has covered 130 miles from Nuremberg in nine days.

The United States Third Army's thrust down the Danube toward

Continued on Page 7, Column 1

War News Summarized

SUNDAY, APRIL 29, 1945

President Truman denied last night that there was any foundation for widely circulated reports, emanating from San Francisco, that Germany had surrendered unconditionally. General Eisenhower, reached by the White House, said there was no basis for the rumors.

The denials came in the wake of widely circulated reports throughout the day that the final collapse of Germany was an hourly possibility and that the Allies had given her an ultimatum to accept their terms before Tuesday. Heinrich Himmler was said to have declared that Hitler was dying and that he, as second in command, wanted to surrender to the United States and Britain. This offer was rejected with the emphatic statement that nothing less than unconditional surrender to all three big powers would be acceptable. [1:8.]

Munich, where nazism was born and nourished into a hydra-headed menace to the world, and other areas in southwestern Germany were swept by revolts. Die-hard Nazis were reported in bloody combat with German troops. [1:3.]

Berlin was tottering, with almost all the German capital, except a twenty-five square-mile pocket in the shattered city's center, in Soviet hands. While enemy resistance was fanatical in some places, thousands were surrendering to the Russians. Meanwhile the Red Army north of Berlin gained another twenty-two miles as it slashed across the Mecklenburg plains on an expanding front toward Rostock and Hamburg. [1:4; map P. 5.]

The American Seventh Army lanced across the Austrian border at two places, after advancing 130 miles from Nuremberg in nine days, to batter at the northern gates of Hitler's mountain redoubt. The Third Army took Augsburg and was within twenty-seven miles of Munich. In the center of what had been the Western Front, held by the First Army, there was little fighting, but thousands of Germans, seeking escape from the Soviet tide around Berlin, were moving into our lines to surrender. [1:5.]

Allied troops in Italy seized Bergamo, thirty miles from the Swiss border and 125 from the Brenner Pass, and Brescia, thirty miles southeast of Bergamo, as they continued their swift dash northward. [1:7; map P. 12.] Marshal Graziani, former commander of Italian armies in north Africa, and several lesser Fascists were captured. Swiss reports said Benito Mussolini had been taken to Milan after his capture near Lake Como. [13:1.]

In the Pacific, Japanese aircraft attacked American warships off Okinawa, sinking an auxiliary surface vessel. Fifty-seven enemy planes were shot down in this and related actions. Our troops on the island increased their pressure toward Naha, the capital. [25:1.] American troops in the Philippines captured Baguio, on Luzon Island, the summer capital. [1:2-3.]

In Burma the peril to Rangoon mounted hourly as the British raced sixty-four miles toward the big port against light Japanese resistance and at last reports were fifty-four miles from the city. [24:1; with map.]

The New York Times regrets that it is obliged to omit large quantities of advertising from today's issue in order to make available adequate space for the present heavy flow of news. In doing this The New York Times is following the policy it has pursued from the beginning of newsprint rationing. This policy is based on the premise that news must be given the right of way.

15th Army to Occupy Reich, With No Pampering of Foe

By The Associated Press.

PARIS, April 28—Lieut. Gen. Leonard T. Gerow's United States Fifteenth Army will take over the occupation of the United States section of Germany—and see to it that there is no pampering of the vanquished—headquarters indicated today. Its field of occupation is expected to embrace much of southern Germany.

The general's headquarters said German civilians would be allowed a maximum diet of 1,150 calories a day—only about a third as bountiful as that of American soldiers in the German theatre, and slightly more than half as great as the average for civilians in liberated countries.

How well the Germans eat will depend largely on how willing they are to help themselves by producing the foodstuffs, it was made clear, because the plans call for importation of food into Germany only if necessary to avert famine and disease.

The Germans will be expected to produce enough to feed themselves and displaced Russians, French, Belgian, Polish and other nationals awaiting transportation home, a spokesman said.

Food to Be Third of Ours

At the office of Col. Thomas J. Moroney of Dallas, Tex., assistant chief of staff of G-5 under General Gerow, an officer said the maximum diet of 1,150 calories meant lean meals, but that not all Germans received that much now.

The average American soldier in the theatre to be occupied receives 4,000 calories a day and the average civilian in liberated countries receives 2,000.

Control of the German diet by the occupying forces will be exercised through civilian provincial and local officials, it was said. Fewer than one-fourth of the 2,210,000 German prisoners taken on the western front have put to work, but in these final weeks of the war the Allies are considering a plan to make them work and

Continued on Page 9, Column 1

ESCAPE ROUTES CUT BY ALLIES IN ITALY

Fifth Army Takes Bergamo and Brescia at Foot of Alps as German Debacle Develops

By VIRGINIA LEE WARREN
By Wireless to THE NEW YORK TIMES.

ROME, April 28—Fifth Army forces, which burst out of the Apennines just nineteen days ago to sweep the Po Valley clean of the bulk of the Wehrmacht, have almost cut off the remaining German troops in northwest Italy by capturing Bergamo at the foot of the Alps thirty miles from the Swiss border, and Brescia, about thirty miles east of Bergamo.

[The Swiss radio said Saturday night that the Germans had agreed to surrender in Lombardy and Piedmont and that all fighting had ceased in those two north Italian provinces, which border on Switzerland, The Associated Press reported. The broadcast, which was unconfirmed, said that a German general and colonel had made the surrender to Gen. Rafaele Cardona, commander of Italian forces in northern Italy, and to an American and a British officer.

[Milan and Turin were freed of German troops except for isolated pockets, according to Italian Partisan radio stations, which also broadcast a report "from a non-official source" that

Continued on Page 12, Column 1

Stuttgart Row Reported Settled; French Troops Will Stay in City

By GLADWIN HILL
By Wireless to THE NEW YORK TIMES.

PARIS, April 28—The French announced semi-officially tonight that "a satisfactory solution" had been reached in the question of the replacement of French troops by Americans in Stuttgart.

The settlement, which was attributed to "a high degree of understanding by General Eisenhower" was understood from an authoritative source to constitute a revocation, at least in principle, of the Sixth Army Group's order to the French to leave the city and authorization for the French military government to remain there in line with the French Cabinet declaration yesterday.

[The French have handed Stuttgart over to the Americans, according to a Brussels broadcast that said the information was obtained from official sources. The Exchange Telegraph Agency recorded the broadcast, according to The United Press.]

Supreme Headquarters said today the French First Army had been ordered out of Stuttgart—the first big German city occupied by the French—by the Sixth Army Group, of which it is a part, because the city's "important rail communications and supply center" had been "selected to serve the military requirements of the Seventh United States Army." The statement said that, in the absence of the Stuttgart facilities, inferior ones would have to be developed.

The immediate French reaction, however, was that they were be-

Continued on Page 8, Column 1

NAZIS' END NEAR

But President on Word From Eisenhower Corrects Rumor

HIMMLER IN CHARGE

He Must Capitulate for Beaten German Army to Big 3 Powers

Special to THE NEW YORK TIMES.

WASHINGTON, April 28—President Truman announced at 9:36 o'clock tonight that there was no foundation for a report that Nazi Germany had surrendered unconditionally.

The report was circulated from San Francisco, after information had been received that Heinrich Himmler had offered a German surrender to the United States and Britain. The Western Allies stood on the terms that Germany must surrender unconditionally to the three great powers, including the Soviet Union.

The fact that there was no foundation for the full-surrender rumor was established by Fleet Admiral William D. Leahy, the President's Chief of Staff, through a telephone call to General Dwight D. Eisenhower.

Truman's Direct Statement

President Truman summoned reporters to his office in the White House and stated that he had heard the rumor while working in his office this evening.

The White House permitted direct quotation of President Truman's announcement. This is it:

"Well, I was over here as you can see doing a little work, and this rumor got started.

"I had a call from San Francisco and the State Department called me.

"I just got in touch with Admiral Leahy and had him call our headquarters Commander in Chief in Europe, and there is no foundation for the rumor. That is all I have to say."

Earlier in the evening the report had been generally accredited in White House circles, and members of the secretariat and other officials returned to the Executive Offices.

Plans Made for Broadcast

In case the rumor should have been verified, President Truman started preparation of a proclamation to be read to the American people over all the radio networks to announce the fall of Germany.

[The Moscow radio said it had been "confirmed by responsible Soviet circles" that Himmler had made an offer to surrender Germany unconditionally to the United States and Britain and that the Western Allies had rejected the proposal.

[Himmler, who transmitted his offer through Sweden, is understood to have told London and Washington Adolf Hitler was dying and that he was acting as next in command, The Associated Press reported.

[A United Press dispatch from San Francisco said Allied diplomatic quarters there suggested that Himmler had put Hitler to death to give cynical evidence to the Allies of his "good faith" in offering to surrender Germany unconditionally.

[These quarters said Himmler had advised the Allies through Stockholm that Hitler "may not live another twenty-four hours." The timing of the Himmler message was such, it was believed, that Hitler may already be dead at the hands of the man who was his lieutenant in terrorism, The United Press added.]

The President told White House reporters that he had returned to his office after dinner from Blair House, his temporary residence, and it was about that time, 7:35

Continued on Page 3, Column 2

"All the News That's Fit to Print"

The New York Times.

LATE CITY EDITION
Partly cloudy today. Mostly clear and warmer tomorrow.
Temperatures Yesterday—Max., 63; Min., 41
Sunrise today, 5:37 A. M.; Sunset, 7:59 P. M.

Copyright, 1945, by The New York Times Company.

VOL. XCIV..No. 31,873. Entered as Second-Class Matter, Postoffice, New York, N. Y. NEW YORK, MONDAY, APRIL 30, 1945. THREE CENTS IN NEW YORK CITY

U. S. 7TH IN MUNICH, BRITISH PUSH ON BALTIC; RUSSIANS TIGHTEN RING ON BERLIN'S HEART; MILAN AND VENICE WON; MUSSOLINI KILLED

BIG POWERS SCAN 4 OAKS CHANGES PROPOSED BY U. S.

Revising of Charter by Later Parley and Wider Scope for Assembly Are Emphasized

LEAGUE FUNCTIONS KEPT

Soviet-Latin Trade on Bids to Argentina and Lublin Reported Sought

By JAMES B. RESTON
Special to The New York Times.

SAN FRANCISCO, April 29—Delegates of the big four nations at the San Francisco Conference began exchanging views on amending of the Dumbarton Oaks proposals this weekend, but the question of bringing Argentina and Poland into the United Nations Conference on International Organization continued to hamper progress on this important subject.

There were several private meetings among various members of the sponsor nations yesterday and today. In one of these it was apparently decided that White Russia and the Ukraine should be brought into the conference this week, but when the question of inviting Argentina was raised the Russian Foreign Commissar, Vyacheslaff M. Molotoff, again proposed inviting representatives of the Polish government in Warsaw.

This suggestion, which had been defeated in the steering committee, was again opposed in the firmest manner by the American Secretary of State and the British Foreign Secretary, and it now is likely that the Russians will not insist on forcing the Polish issue to a vote, although they are clearly not yet happy about inviting Argentina.

Four Changes Offered

The United States suggested to the other sponsor powers that four changes be made in the Dumbarton Oaks proposals. These changes would provide:

First, that the charter to be written at this conference be subject to revision in a United Nations constitutional convention at a future date. The principle of writing a temporary rather than a permanent charter has been accepted by all members of the American delegation and is supported by the British, but the amendment as it now stands does not stipulate when the constitutional convention would be held and some members of the delegation think that it should. This will be discussed when the conference commissions are set up this week and the subject will be followed up in the commissions by Comdr. Harold E. Stassen.

Second, that all members obligate themselves to settle disputes in accordance with justice and fundamental human rights, and specifically to adhere to the principles of the Atlantic Charter.

Third, that the assembly have the right to recommend the revision of treaties and the removal of conditions that might lead to a breach of international peace and security.

Fourth, that the charter make provision for taking over responsibility of the functions of the old League of Nations, including responsibility for the League mandates, and also provde for a system of trusteeship over colonial areas.

Some Vandenberg Points Fail

In the final meetings here among members of the American delegation on the Dumbarton Oaks proposals, several specific proposals by various members of the delegation were rejected. Although Senator Arthur H. Vandenberg, Republican, of Michigan, put in several amendments that were accepted in the points listed above, two of his proposals dealing with the rights of the General Assembly were rejected.

One of these was that the General Assembly should—contrary to the Dumbarton Oaks proposals—be authorized to make recom-

Continued on Page 10, Column 4

Moscow Blackout Ends for May Day

By Wireless to The New York Times.

MOSCOW, April 29—Moscow's stifling blackout ends tomorrow after almost four years of war. For some weeks now, increasing numbers of street lamps have been turned on, but the obscuring of lights in homes remained rigidly enforced.

The removal of this confounded nuisance will add to the general festivities accompanying the May Day holiday and the imminent fall of Berlin and the end of the European conflict. Workmen on scaffolds have been putting light bulbs back into the huge stars on the Kremlin's towers.

CARRIER ROOSEVELT IS CHRISTENED HERE

Widow Speaks at Floating of $90,000,000 Ship—Forrestal Reveals Navy's Strength

As gray sea water lapped at her keel in building dock 5 of the New York Navy Yard in Brooklyn, a gigantic new aircraft carrier was christened the Franklin D. Roosevelt in impressive ceremonies yesterday morning. The 45,000-ton vessel, built at a cost of $90,000,000, is one of a class of three ships described by the Navy as the largest warships afloat and the biggest ships of any type ever built in this country.

At the ceremony Mrs. Franklin D. Roosevelt, clad in deepest mourning, made her first public appearance since her husband's funeral. In a brief, unscheduled address she expressed her gratitude that the Navy had given her husband's name to the new carrier, previously scheduled to be called the U. S. S. Coral Sea, and voiced a prayer that the ship would bring her officers and men home safe and victorious.

James V. Forrestal, Secretary of the Navy, who made the principal address, revealed some hitherto secret figures about the present size of the United States Fleet. He said that it now consisted of twenty-three battleships, twenty-six combat aircraft carriers, sixty-five escort carriers, sixty-seven cruisers, 386 destroyers, 368 destroyer escorts, and 240 submarines.

For Strong Naval Force

Secretary Forrestal warned those at the ceremony that the United States must retain the military ability "for swift and effective application of force" if peace is to be maintained in future years. He said that the retention of force b the United States would not conflict with her aspirations at the San Francisco Conference, but was essential for realizing the aims sought there.

Unlike the previous 45,000-ton ships built at the New York Navy Yard, the battleships Iowa and Missouri, the Franklin D. Roosevelt was not launched in the traditional fashion down greased building ways into the East River.

Continued on Page 32, Column 2

SLAIN BY PARTISANS

Italy's Former Dictator Shot After Trial—Other Fascists Executed

SEIZED AS HE FLED

Onetime Premier Begged for Life—Bodies on Display in Milan

By MILTON BRACKER
By Wireless to The New York Times.

MILAN, April 29—Benito Mussolini came back last night to the city where his fascism was born. He came back on the floor of a closed moving van, his dead body flung on the bodies of his mistress and twelve men shot with him. All were executed yesterday by Italian Partisans. The story of his final downfall, his flight, his capture and his execution is not pretty, and its epilogue in the Piazza Loretto here this morning was its ugliest part. It will go down in history as a finish to tyranny as horrible as any ever visited on a tyrant.

At 9:30 A. M. today, Mussolini's body lay on the rim of the mass of corpses, while all around surged a growing mob wild with the desire to have a last look at the man who once was a Socialist editor in this same city. The throng pushed and yelled. Partisans strove to keep them back but largely in vain. Even a series of shots in the air did not dissuade them.

Bullet Hole in Head

Mussolini had changed in death, but not enough to be any one else. His closely shaved head and his bull neck were unmistakable. His body seemed small and a little shrunken, but he was never a tall man. At least one bullet had passed through his head. It had emerged some three inches behind his right ear. There was another small hole nearer his forehead where another bullet seemed to have gone in.

As if he were not dead or dishonored enough, at least two young men in the crowd broke through and aimed kicks at his skull. One glanced off. But the other landed full on his right jaw and there was a hideous crunch that wholly disfigured the once-proud face.

Mussolini wore the uniform of a squadrist militiaman. It comprised a gray-brown jacket and gray trousers with red and black stripes down the sides. He wore black boots, badly soiled, and the left one hung half off as if his foot were broken. His small eyes were open and it was perhaps a final irony that this man who had thrust his chin forward for so many official photographs had to have his yellowing face propped up with a rifle-butt to turn it into the sun for the only two Allied cameramen on the scene:

When the butt was removed the face flopped back over to the left. Meanwhile I crouched over the body to the left in order not to

Continued on Page 7, Column 1

THE INGLORIOUS END OF A DICTATOR

Benito Mussolini in Milan's Piazza Loretto after his execution by Italian Partisans. Also seen is the body of Clara Petacci

The New York Times Radiophoto

5TH SEIZES MILAN, FASCISM'S CRADLE

Americans Surge On to Como—8th Army Takes Venice and Cuts Adige Line

By VIRGINIA LEE WARREN
By Wireless to The New York Times.

ADVANCED ALLIED FIELD HEADQUARTERS, Italy, April 29—United States Fifth Army troops today entered Milan, Italy's largest, wealthiest and most politically conscious city, where the history of

Continued on Page 2, Column 4

Nazis in Berlin Compressed Into 18-Square-Mile Pocket

By C. L. SULZBERGER
By Wireless to The New York Times.

MOSCOW, Monday, April 30—Determined Russian troops drove deeper into the heart of Berlin's wreckage yesterday, nearing the hastily fortified Tiergarten from two sides and edging to within a mile of the Reichstag as division after division gave itself up to the Red Army. Within the past forty-eight hours the First White Russian Army and the First Ukrainian Army have captured more than 50,000 prisoners in and around the burning capital.

Southeast of the city, in the

Continued on Page 4, Column 5

War News Summarized

MONDAY, APRIL 30, 1945

Munich, birthplace of nazism, and Milan, cradle of fascism, were entered by American troops yesterday while the world waited for further word on what Himmler was going to do about the Allied demand that Germany surrender unconditionally to Great Britain, the United States and the Soviet Union. Count Bernadotte, who carried the Nazi's proposal to give up to the western Allies only, was returning from seeing Himmler again, presumably with a reply to the Allied ultimatum. [1:7.]

It was the United States Seventh Army that smashed into Munich after a twenty-mile advance. Opposition was light, and the Americans were soon in occupation of that beer cellar from which Hitler launched his ill-fated revolt in 1923. Front reports said Munich had been captured. The Third Army was advancing on Berchtesgaden and Salzburg, while in the center the Ninth burst from its Elbe River bridgehead toward the Russians in the Wittenberg area. To the north the British Second Army crossed the Elbe southeast of Hamburg, and the Canadians progressed along the coast. The French First Army was twelve miles from Austria in the Alps. [1:8; map P. 3.]

Milan was taken by the United States Fifth Army, which also reached Como and the north end of Lake Garda. The British Eighth Army captured Venice and seized Mestre, eighty-five miles from Trieste. The Brazilian Expeditionary Force compelled a German division to surrender. The captured Marshal Graziani was arranging for the surrender of his Fascist Ligurian army. [1:4; map, P. 3.]

Mussolini's body was dumped from a moving van into a Milan square, where it received the scornful attention of the residents. He, his mistress and more than a dozen other Fascists had been executed by Partisans near Como. [1:3.]

Berlin's last-ditch defenders were squeezed into an eighteen square mile area in the center of the city, and Russian troops were within half a mile of Hitler's ruined chancellery. A German pocket southeast of the city was liquidated, while in the north two Soviet armies joined forces and swept toward Rostock and Swinemuende. [1:5-6, maps P. 4.] A wave of suicides was said to be sweeping Berlin. [4:1.]

Washington and London learned from Moscow that a provisional anti-fascist government had been set up in Austria headed by Dr. Karl Renner, former Chancellor and last president of the free Assembly. [1:6.]

A marked trend toward the Left was shown in early returns from France's first elections since 1937. Communists jumped into the lead in Paris. [1:6-7.]

A clearly marked Navy hospital ship was attacked off Okinawa by a Japanese plane, which killed twenty-nine and injured thirty-three; one man was missing. Some 200 other enemy planes kept the Pacific Fleet under prolonged attack, damaging some light units; 104 of the enemy aircraft were destroyed. On shore, troops captured the northern half of Machinato airfield in a general advance. [1:2-3.]

Americans on Mindanao seized the Padada airfield along Davao Gulf and advanced up to seventeen miles in the center. [8:5.] Japanese resistance slowed the British drive on Rangoon, in Burma. [8:7.]

AUSTRIA CREATES INTERIM REGIME

Moscow Announces Renner Is Premier—Britain and U. S. Not Consulted

By Wireless to The New York Times.

MOSCOW, April 29—An Austrian Provisional Government, the first independent authority in that German-speaking country since the Nazi annexation of more than seven years ago, has been created in Vienna under the leadership of Dr. Karl Renner, 74, a Social Democrat.

His Cabinet of thirteen men includes three non-party representatives, three Social Democrats, four Christian Socialists and three Communists. The Communists hold the key posts of the Interior and Education Ministries as well as one of the three seats on the political

Continued on Page 4, Column 7

NEW NAZI PROFFER ON PEACE AWAITED

Stalin Note to Truman and Churchill Said to Spurn Himmler's Proposals

By CLIFTON DANIEL
By Wireless to The New York Times.

LONDON, Monday, April 30—London took Saturday night's "peace scare" calmly and yesterday confidently marked time in anticipation of an actual capitulation by Germany and peace in Europe within a matter of days. Amid reports about negotiations with Heinrich Himmler and a variety of rumors of the death of Adolf Hitler, official quarters here quietly awaited a Nazi reply to the British and American Governments' statement that unconditional surrender could be accepted only by all three major Allies.

Opinion was strong that Himmler's offer of surrender would be extended to the Russians—an opinion based on the belief that the Gestapo chief, now evidently ruler of the Reich, would never have made his proposal if Germany's situation had not been so desperate as to preclude further resistance.

[Reuter reported that Premier Stalin in a note to President Truman and Prime Minister Churchill has urged rejection of Himmler's proposals. Mr. Church-

Continued on Page 3, Column 2

Communists Take Lead in Paris As France Holds First Elections

By The Associated Press.

PARIS, April 29—Communist candidates for municipal office in Paris held a commanding lead on the basis of almost complete returns today.

Election returns from other metropolitan centers indicated that their voters, too, had supported candidates of the leftist parties in contests for municipal offices, the only ones at stake in today's voting. Only a few returns had been received from traditionally conservative country districts.

In Paris and other principal cities the Communists' lead seemed to be safe, while Socialists and Radicals ran well ahead of center parties and rightists. Political observers speculated that eleventh-hour Communist demands for the quick trial and conviction of Marshal Henri-Philippe Pétain had drawn support to the party candidates, including many voters unaffiliated with any party.

André Mornet, Attorney General, who will conduct the case against Pétain, was returned to office with a heavy plurality. Edouard Herriot, former President of the Chamber of Deputies, who has just reached Switzerland from a German prison camp, was elected to the Municipal Council of Lyon by a 4-to-1 margin. Six members of the Cabinet who ran for city offices were also elected.

Joseph Paul-Boncour, a member of the French delegation to the San Francisco Conference, was also elected by a big margin.

Not only was this the first election that France had held since her fall to the Germans but it was the first time that women were al-

Continued on Page 5, Column 6

Enemy Suicide Pilot Dives Plane On U. S. Hospital Ship Off Okinawa

By W. H. LAWRENCE
By Wireless to The New York Times.

ABOARD AMPHIBIOUS FLAGSHIP, off Okinawa, April 28 (Delayed)—A Japanese "suicide" pilot machine-gunned and then crashed his bomb-laden plane squarely into the well-lighted, unarmed United States naval hospital ship Comfort fully loaded with casualties from Okinawa in clear weather about sixty miles southeast of here at 8:58 o'clock tonight.

Twenty-nine were killed by the exploding airplane, which apparently struck the surgery section of the hospital ship as she was bearing wounded toward rear area hospitals.

Although first reports from the ship indicated that it would be necessary to abandon ship, it later was found that the damage was not as heavy as it seemed, and the vessel was able to continue under her own power.

Tempers ran high in naval circles at this premeditated and cold-blooded attack upon the hospital ship, which was proceeding alone with full illumination, including powerful searchlights that lighted up huge red crosses painted on the sides, superstructure and stack.

It was the first time that the Japanese had been known to attack an American hospital ship deliberately, although two other hospital ships were menaced during the Okinawa operation. Until tonight's incident, naval men had been inclined charitably to attribute these attacks to mistakes.

But there was no possibility of mistake about tonight's attack. There was a full moon and the sky was clear. The Japanese plane, one of several in the area, swept in

Continued on Page 8, Column 3

3 DIVISIONS ENTER

Americans Roll Into Nazi Birthplace Without Meeting Opposition

ITS FALL IS REPORTED

British Cross the Elbe and Drive Northeast to Cut Off Denmark

By DREW MIDDLETON
By Wireless to The New York Times.

PARIS, April 29—American and British Armies dealt shattering blows to waning German hopes of holding out in the southern and northern redoubts today.

Troops of the United States Seventh Army crashed into Munich, birthplace of the Nazi party and the principal enemy stronghold barring the roads to the redoubt in the Austrian Tyrol while Tommies of the British Second Army smashed over the Elbe southeast of Hamburg.

Elements of the Twelfth Armored and Forty-second Infantry Divisions entered Munich at 4 o'clock this afternoon, meeting only light resistance, according to reports from the front. Later the Twentieth Armored Division rolled in.

Beer Cellar Occupied

Reports from the front line tonight said that Munich had fallen. There was no confirmation of these reports, either at Supreme Headquarters or at any Army group, but in view of the slackening resistance all over Germany and the failure of the enemy to attack the first troops entering the city, it is entirely possible that Munich has been taken.

Munich was reached after a twenty-mile advance by Seventh Army columns. According to reports from the front the Americans hold the beer cellar where Hitler planned his premature putsch of 1923 and where he addressed Nazi leaders yearly. The cellar was partly destroyed by a bomb in the autumn of 1939.

The infamous concentration camp at Dachau is believed to have been overrun in the advance to the city.

Push on Redoubt Gains

The thrust into Munich was accompanied by a general advance to the south and southeast toward the northern face of the redoubt by the United States Third and Seventh Armies, while on the right flank of the Seventh Army infantry felt its way southeastward into the redoubt, pushing toward Innsbruck and the valley of the Inn River, the most important, indeed the only communications system within the redoubt.

The thrust over the Elbe by the Fifteenth Scottish Division and the British First Commando Brigade to the north followed a bombardment in typical Montgomery fashion in which more than 400 guns were employed. It was accompanied by heavy blows on the German line west and east of the Weser and the flattening of an enemy salient northeast of Bremen.

The Ninth Army front, long dormant, awoke today when Lieut. Gen. William H. Simpson's troops suddenly attacked out of their bridgehead over the Elbe, capturing the towns of Zerbst, Jutrichau and Bias and advancing northeast and southeast of the towns. This attack was described here as a "local attack."

Four divisions, the Twelfth and Twentieth Armored and the Third and Forty-second Infantry Divisions, moved on Munich this morning. The Twentieth is a new division, fed into the battle yesterday by Lieut. Gen. Alexander M. Patch.

Between Munich and the Austrian frontier around Fuessen, other armored, cavalry and infantry units of the Seventh Army drove on toward the southeast, crossing the Lech River in force.

The Forty-fourth Infantry Division, which is moving methodically

Continued on Page 3, Column 6

"All the News That's Fit to Print"

The New York Times.

LATE CITY EDITION
Clearing and warmer today. Cloudy with moderate winds tomorrow.
Temperatures Yesterday—Max., 51; Min., 44

VOL. XCIV. No. 31,875. Entered as Second-Class Matter, Postoffice, New York, N. Y. NEW YORK, WEDNESDAY, MAY 2, 1945. THREE CENTS IN NEW YORK CITY

HITLER DEAD IN CHANCELLERY, NAZIS SAY; DOENITZ, SUCCESSOR, ORDERS WAR TO GO ON; BERLIN ALMOST WON; U. S. ARMIES ADVANCE

MOLOTOFF EASES PARLEY TENSION; NEW MOVES BEGUN

Russian Says Country Will Cooperate in World Plan Despite Argentine Issue

4 COMMISSIONS SET UP

They Will Deal With Council, Assembly, Court and Some General Problems

By JAMES B. RESTON
Special to THE NEW YORK TIMES.

SAN FRANCISCO, May 1—The United Nations Conference on International Organization has survived its first basic crisis and after six days of political maneuvering on secondary issues, it began to move at rapid tempo today toward its primary task—the creation of a world organization which would stop what Field Marshal Jan Christiaan Smuts called "this pilgrimage of death."

The test came last night. Rebuffed by the conference on his attempts to keep Argentina out of the conference and bring the Warsaw Poles in, Soviet Foreign Commissar Vyacheslaff M. Molotoff went late last night to Secretary Stettinius' penthouse at the Fairmont Hotel. He immediately made his position clear.

He still disapproved the conference actions on the Poles and the Argentine, but he wanted the conference to succeed; he would cooperate in its labors, and while he was under urgent pressure by the events in Europe to return to Moscow, he would remain at least for a few days until the major issues on the charter were thrashed out among the four sponsor powers. Then, he said, he would have to leave, probably at the week-end or early next week.

"Friendly Meeting" Is Held

Immediately, in what the Foreign Ministers of the United States, Great Britain and China described to their colleagues as "the most friendly meeting of the conference," the big four approved the formation of the working commissions and committees of the conference, and other committees began discussing, not the personalities or procedures of the conference, but the basic questions of creating an organization which would win the support, with the power, of the great nations without violating the rights and principles of all nations.

The three main developments of the day were as follows:

First, the conference approved four commissions to deal with the security council of the proposed organization, the general assembly, the judicial agency and general problems, and established twelve committees to study specific problems under these four commissions.

The heads of the four commissions were: Trygve Lie of Norway, Security Council; Field Marshal Smuts, General Assembly; Carraciolo Parra Rez of Venezuela, judicial organization; and Paul Henri Spaak of Belgium, general provisions.

Second, Field Marshal Smuts called on the four major powers to accept the special responsibilities which flow from the special authority given them under the Dumbarton Oaks proposals and urged all the nations here to pay more attention to the spiritual and economic aspects of the new charter than they had in the past.

Third, the Russians began studying in some detail the sixteen amendments to the Dumbarton Oaks proposals which were submitted by the United States. The other delegations started circulating amendments and exchanging views on proposals already circulated.

The facts on the crisis among the Big Three over Poland, Argentina, White Russia and the Ukraine can now be put down with assur-

Continued on Page 15, Column 6

Allies Invade North Borneo; Fighting Fierce, Tokyo Says

Australia Informed of Landing by Treasury Minister—MacArthur Reports Only Air Attacks and New Gains on Luzon

By The United Press.

MANILA, Wednesday, May 2—An official Australian announcement said yesterday that Allied troops had invaded Borneo, the world's third largest island, but Gen. Douglas MacArthur's communiqué early today reported only that heavy bombers were neutralizing enemy bases and airdromes on the oil-rich island.

Tokyo also reported the landings and said they had been made on the ten-square-mile island of Tarakan on the northeast coast, a region rich in oil wells, which the Netherlanders destroyed before the Japanese captured them in 1942. The enemy broadcast said "fierce fighting" was in progress.

[A later Japanese broadcast, picked up in San Francisco, reported that Allied units had landed on Tarakan Island at 6:30 A. M., Tuesday, Tokyo time. The broadcast said "the enemy had been bombarding the island since April 27, and on Monday morning began approaching the island in their landing attempts." It reported the landing force consisted of "about 5,000 soldiers" and said Japanese forces on the island "are holding secure their positions, obstructing the enemy's advance."]

General MacArthur announced that heavy bombers in attacks on Borneo had struck Kuching, Macassar and Kendari, while medium units and fighters had attacked Japanese gun positions on Tarakan.

General MacArthur announced that on Mindano Island the Twenty-fourth Division, in another swift drive, had advanced eleven miles

Continued on Page 16, Column 2

NEW CIGARETTES FACE PRICE INQUIRY

OPA Calls on Manufacturers of 21-Cent Brands to Prove Quality Merits Charge

By JAMES E. POWERS

Manufacturers of hitherto unheard of brands of cigarettes that have appeared on the market in recent weeks and are being retailed at four or more cents a package higher than ceiling prices for scarce popular brands will be called upon by the Office of Price Administration to show that the new products are of a quality rating the prices charged, it became known yesterday.

Daniel P. Woolley, regional OPA administrator, said an investigation was in progress as a result of complaints by smokers who said they had paid 21 cents a package for cigarettes "they had previously never heard of."

The United Wholesale Tobacco and Cigarette Distributors Association, a sub-jobbers' group, in a telegram to Senator William Langer of North Dakota, who recently introduced a resolution to set up a committee to look into the "black market" in cigarettes, demanded an immediate investigation of the entire cigarette shortage.

Mr. Woolley declared that as a result of OPA prosecution of violators of price ceilings, the black-market condition largely had been corrected here. He said he was centering on the pricing of the new cigarette brands.

Mr. Woolley added that studies were being made to determine

Continued on Page 40, Column 4

HARD COAL 'HOLIDAY' BRINGS WLB BAN

New Order by Board Asserts Output Is Urgent—Seizure Action Is Postponed

By JOSEPH A. LOFTUS
Special to THE NEW YORK TIMES.

WASHINGTON, May 1—The War Labor Board issued a new order tonight to the United Mine Workers and the operators to resume the production of hard coal. To give the UMW leaders an opportunity to act on the order it decided to defer for twenty-four to forty-eight hours a recommendation to President Truman for Government seizure of the mines.

The miners went on a holiday today after expiration of their contract at midnight.

Dr. George W. Taylor, WLB chairman, in a telegram to both parties took cognizance of the miners' traditional "no contract, no work" policy.

"The board's order provides for a continuing contract," he said. "It is urgent that production should be immediately resumed."

As in acting on the soft coal dispute a month ago, the WLB provided in the new order that any legal wage adjustment agreed upon or finally ordered be retroactive to the expiration date of the old contract.

Union spokesmen told the WLB at a brief hearing that the Tri-District Scale Committee had voted to advise the miners to return to work when the operators accepted the settlement proposal made by Secretary of Labor Perkins.

Dr. Taylor, in questioning John Owens of the UMW, noted that

Continued on Page 40, Column 3

Eisenhower Halted Forces at Elbe; Ninth Had Hoped to Storm Berlin

By The Associated Press.

WITH THE UNITED STATES NINTH ARMY, in Germany, April 26 (Delayed by Censorship)—A direct order from Supreme Allied Headquarters halted the United States Ninth Army's drive to Berlin at the Elbe River at a time when the most pessimistic officers were predicting that Lieut. Gen. William H. Simpson's forces could reduce the German capital in ten days, "even if the Germans fought hard."

General Eisenhower's order said the Ninth would halt on the Elbe and await the arrival of Russian forces from the east, thereby leaving the capture of the capital to the Red Army. It also was understood that the American First and Third and British and Canadian armies received similar orders to halt at the Elbe.

It was not clear whether General Eisenhower's order was dictated by political policy agreed upon by the Great Powers or in a belief that it was a military necessity.

It was felt by high staff offficers in the field, however, that the Ninth and other American forces could push on to the capital without great difficulty. While the order disappointed some staff officers, it was not altogether unexpected. It was known that the Ninth Army had pushed past the eventual British-American occupation area when it crossed the Weser River.

While the staff officers were disappointed, the American doughboys and tankmen who had to do the fighting and dying to get to Berlin expressed no regret. Almost to a man, they felt they could do with-

Continued on Page 4, Column 4

REDOUBTS ASSAILED

U. S. 3d, 7th and French 1st Armies Charging Into Alpine Hideout

NEAR BRENNER PASS

British in North Close About Hamburg—Poles Gain in Emden Area

Von Rundstedt Caught

By The Associated Press.

WITH UNITED STATES SEVENTH ARMY, Wednesday, May 2—Field Marshal Karl von Rundstedt has been captured by United States Seventh Army troops.

The Seventh Army caught the former German commander in the west in its drive into the Nazis' southeastern redoubt area.

By DREW MIDDLETON
By Wireless to THE NEW YORK TIMES.

PARIS, May 1—The last defenses of the Third Reich were crumbling as Allied tanks and infantry swept almost unopposed into the northern and southern redoubts.

Gen. George S. Patton's United States Third Army has resumed its offensive into Austria, crashing to within twenty miles of Linz, and is only fifty-four miles from Amstetten, where Marshal Fedor I. Tolbukhin's Third Ukrainian Army was last reported. According to reports from the front, radio contact has been established between tanks of the United States Eleventh Armored Division and the vanguard of the Soviet armies.

Other armored columns of the

Continued on Page 14, Column 1

NAZI CORE STORMED

Russians Drive Toward Chancellery Fortress, Narrowing Noose

BRANDENBURG TAKEN

Stralsund Port Swept Up in New Baltic Gains—Vah Valley Cleared

By C. L. SULZBERGER
By Wireless to THE NEW YORK TIMES.

MOSCOW, Wednesday, May 2—Street battles within smoldering Berlin today entered their twelfth day since the Russians first broke into the city, with Nazi die-hards still holding grimly to the central part of the town, whittled down by yesterday's fighting, in which Marshal Gregory K. Zhukoff's First White Russian Army group completely occupied Charlottenburg and Schoeneberg and more than 100 blocks in the capital's central region.

Some 14,000 prisoners were taken within the city on Monday, the Russians announced. At the same time, the remnants of a hold-out group south of Berlin, part of which had been annihilated at Wendisch Buchholtz, was split in two and the survivors are being ground to death by Marshal Zhukoff's men.

Curiously enough, the midnight communiqué does not mention Marshal Ivan S. Koneff's First Ukrainian Army group, which has been working from the southwestern sector of the city toward the desperately defended Tiergarten.

Marshal Zhukoff's forward spearheads meanwhile struck deep into Brandenburg Province, capturing the city of Brandenburg, halfway to Magdeburg from Berlin.

While Gen. Andrei I. Yeremenko proceeded apace in his lightning

Continued on Page 3, Column 2

War News Summarized

WEDNESDAY, MAY 2, 1945

Hitler is dead, according to the Hamburg radio, and on Monday, the day before he allegedly fell at his command post in the Chancellery in Berlin, he appointed Admiral Karl Doenitz to be the new Fuehrer. The head of the German Navy, who had made his mark directing the enemy's U-boats campaign, pledged continuance of the war. [1:8.]

Washington received the news, as did London, with some skepticism and a desire to see the body. Selection of Admiral Doenitz was considered logical in view of his strong Nazi feelings. [1:7.]

The new development was interpreted in London as a move to counteract Himmler's reported peace bids, but Prime Minister Churchill broadly intimated in the Commons that he might have "information of exceptional importance" to impart before Saturday. Peace will probably come before all enemy forces have surrendered, he said. [1:6-7.] Germany was reported to have begun evacuation of Denmark and to be ready to leave Norway. Count Bernadotte said in Sweden he had no new Himmler proposals, and the Nazis' Scandinavian withdrawals were related there to a prospective general capitulation. [11:1.]

Meanwhile, general Allied progress on the battlefields against slight resistance continued. The United States Third Army, on the day Hitler was declared to have died, captured Braunau, his birthplace. The drive into Austria was resumed and had reached to within twenty miles of Linz and fifty-four of the last known Russian position. The Seventh Army smashed through the Tyrol on a broad front and cleared Munich. The British Second Army, by-passing Hamburg, raced to within eighteen miles of the Baltic port of Luebeck. [1:4; map P. 14.]

General Eisenhower, it was revealed, personally ordered the halt of the Allied drive on Berlin from the west to permit the Russians to take the capital. [1:2-3.]

The Russians greatly cut down the German holding in Berlin, capturing the districts of Charlottenburg and Schoeneberg. West of the city they occupied Brandenburg and along the Baltic they seized Stralsund. [1:5; maps Pages 2 and 14.]

New Zealand troops in Italy made contact with Yugoslav Partisans at Monfalcone near Trieste and the British entered Udine. While the Eighth Army was closing a trap along the Swiss border, the Fifth neared France. [1:6-7; map P. 14.]

Mussolini and his mistress were buried in unmarked paupers' graves in Milan. [13:1.] Admiral Horthy, former Regent of Hungary, was captured. [4:3.]

Invasion of Borneo was officially disclosed in Australia, although no word of the break into the Japanese-held Netherlands East Indies had come from General MacArthur. On Mindanao in the Philippines, Americans were within six miles of the city of Davao. [1:2-3; map P. 16.]

Seventh Division troops on Okinawa resumed their southward advance, entering the village of Kuhazu. [15:1.] More than 400 starved, naked Allied prisoners of war were liberated by the British as they drove on Rangoon in Burma. [15:3.]

Good progress was made at the San Francisco Conference. Foreign Commissar Molotoff, after assuring Secretary of State Stettinius of his desire that the conference succeed, announced that pressure of events would compel his return to Moscow within a few days. [1:1.]

ADOLF HITLER — The New York Times, 1939

Clark's Troops Meet Tito's In General Advance in Italy

By VIRGINIA LEE WARREN
By Wireless to THE NEW YORK TIMES.

AT ADVANCED ALLIED HEADQUARTERS, in Italy, May 1—After advancing fifty-five miles in less than a day along the coastal road rimming the Gulf of Venice, units of one division of the Fifteenth Army Group made contact this afternoon with Marshal Tito's forces at Monfalcone while other troops under Gen. Mark W. Clark continued to sweep German remnants from the valleys of north Italy and to seal off the few remaining escape routes through the Alps.

No details of the meeting at the small seaport northwest of Trieste between Marshal Tito's men, who had driven fourteen miles from Trieste, and leading elements of the Eighth Army's Second New Zealand Division were given in tonight's communiqué.

On the other side of Italy another historic meeting was imminent as Fifth Army troops, continuing their drive along the Gulf of Genoa, advanced on the Aurelian Way to within sixty miles of the French border, which has already been crossed by French troops headed this way.

General Clark announced yesterday that the military power of Germany had virtually collapsed, but there still are drives for his two armies to make and engagements still to be won. The Germans, trying to regroup for their flight across the Alps, were deprived of two key road junctions leading to mountain passes west of Brenner when Belluno and Udine were occupied this afternoon by units of the Eighth Army.

Udine, which was taken by the British Sixth Armored Division, is twenty-eight miles southwest of Caporetto, the scene of the Italian disaster in World War I. The forces that entered Belluno went on five miles to Ponte nell 'Alpi, guardian of the approach to Italy's

Continued on Page 13, Column 5

DOENITZ' ACCESSION VIEWED AS A BLIND

Capital Lays His Designation to General Ignorance of His Allegiance to Party

By The Associated Press.

WASHINGTON, May 1—If Adolf Hitler really designated Grand Admiral Karl Doenitz his successor, military men here believe, he did so for the following reasons:

1. Doenitz is a Nazi supporter who could be counted on to keep German resistance going if possible.

2. But he is not associated in the Allies' minds with German atrocities and the extreme policies of the Nazi party. Therefore, Hitler probably figured that he might be able to get better treatment from the Allies when the hour of surrender came.

3. He is immensely popular with the German people.

There was a disposition here tonight to look for continued organized resistance whose core would now be centered in the Baltic and North Sea port areas. Those places are the homes of the German Navy and especially of the U-boat fleet that Doenitz commanded from 1936 until he succeeded Grand Admiral Erich

Continued on Page 5, Column 1

Churchill Hints Peace This Week; 2-Day Celebration Is Authorized

By CLIFTON DANIEL
By Wireless to THE NEW YORK TIMES.

LONDON, May 1—The general belief that peace with Germany will be announced this week persisted in Britain today, encouraged by Prime Minister Churchill himself and by Grand Admiral Karl Doenitz's announcement of the death of Adolf Hitler.

The War Cabinet again held a session tonight but so far as was known did not have any concrete proposal to consider. The chances that Heinrich Himmler ultimately will deliver an acceptable peace are now held in some official quarters to be only "fifty-fifty."

Nevertheless the buoyant Prime Minister told the House of Commons today that he might have "information of importance" to announce before Saturday.

The public's hopes were raised still further by a long Home Office circular giving the Government's views on how Britain should observe V-E Day, which the British, it appears, will be expected to celebrate strictly according to form.

[Stockholm reported, with the return there of Count Bernadotte, the "imminent liberation" of Denmark and Norway—already taking effect locally in Denmark—as a phase of a prospective general German capitulation that must be acceptable to the Allies' military commands.]

The hurrahing will begin with the announcement of the cessation of hostilities by Mr. Churchill over a nation-wide radio network. The King will speak at 9 o'clock that evening. And throughout that day

Continued on Page 16, Column 4

ADMIRAL IN CHARGE

Proclaims Designation to Rule—Appeals to People and Army

RAISES 'RED MENACE

Britain to Insist Germans Show Hitler's Body When War Ends

By SYDNEY GRUSON
By Cable to THE NEW YORK TIMES.

LONDON, May 1—Adolf Hitler died this afternoon, the Hamburg radio announced tonight, and Grand Admiral Karl Doenitz, proclaiming himself the new Fuehrer by Hitler's appointment, said that the war would continue.

Crowning days of rumors about Hitler's health and whereabouts, the Hamburg radio said that he had fallen in the battle of Berlin at his command post in the Chancellery just three days after Benito Mussolini, the first of the dictators, had been killed by Italian Partisans. Doenitz, a 53-year-old U-boat specialist, broadcast an address to the German people and the surviving armed forces immediately after the announcer had given the news of Hitler's death.

[The British Foreign Office said that it would demand the production of Hitler's body after the end of hostilities, The Associated Press reported.]

First addressing the German people, Doenitz said that they would continue to fight only to save themselves from the Russians but that they would oppose the western Allies as long as they helped the Russians. In an order of the day to the German forces he repeated his thinly veiled attempt to split the Allies.

Radio Prepares Germans

Early this evening the Germans were told that an important announcement would be broadcast tonight. There was no hint of what was coming. The stand-by announcement was repeated at 9:40 P. M., followed by the playing of excerpts from Wagner's "Goetterdaemmerung."

A few minutes later the announcer said: "Achtung! Achtung! In a few moments you will hear a

Continued on Page 5, Column 4

Copenhagen Writer Again Phones Story

By Cable to THE NEW YORK TIMES.

STOCKHOLM, Sweden, May 1—For the first time in more than five years THE NEW YORK TIMES correspondent in Copenhagen, Svend Carstensen, tonight telephoned a story from the Danish capital. The Nazi-imposed censorship there has been lifted. Mr. Carstensen said:

"The Danes are overjoyed at their imminent liberation, but it is not noticeable on the Copenhagen streets.

"Anxious to avoid trouble on May Day, Copenhageners have been staying indoors. The black-out is still enforced and it is pitch dark in Copenhagen tonight. All Copenhageners are glued to radios listening to broadcasts on Hitler's death.

"We expect King Christian will resume his functions and name a new Cabinet any day now. In the meantime the strictest discipline is being observed so as not to give the Germans any excuses for starting more trouble."

On April 9, 1940, Mr. Carstensen was the first to give the world the news of the German invasion of Denmark in a wireless dispatch to THE NEW YORK TIMES. His dispatch was cleared less than an hour before the Nazis seized the radio station and was the last to be sent.

A defeated German officer.

German evacuees leaving Rheindahlen meet defeat—hungry, homeless, hopeless.

U.S. Army

Infantrymen on the alert for snipers in the battered city of Zweibrucken, Germany.

"All the News That's Fit to Print"

The New York Times.

LATE CITY EDITION
Fair and continued cool today; moderate winds.
Temperatures Yesterday—Max., 54; Min., 38
Sunrise, 6:13 A. M.; Sunset, 7:38 P. M.

VOL. XCIII..No. 31,496. Entered as Second-Class Matter, Postoffice, New York, N. Y. NEW YORK, TUESDAY, APRIL 18, 1944. THREE CENTS IN NEW YORK CITY

BRITISH BAN ENVOYS' TRAVEL AND CODE USE IN MOVE TO PROTECT INVASION SECRETS; RED ARMY HEMS IN BATTERED SEVASTOPOL

AIRLINER CROSSES COUNTRY IN 7 HOURS, SETTING A RECORD

TWA-Lockheed Transport Clips 30 Minutes Off Time From Coast to Coast

SPEED 355 MILES AN HOUR

Howard Hughes at Controls of Giant Plane Capable of Carrying 100 Troops

By The Associated Press.

WASHINGTON, April 17—A new giant of the air paths, the Lockheed Constellation, crossed the continent today in 6 hours 58 minutes, an average speed of about 355 miles an hour, a speed well beyond anything flown previously for a similar distance.

The big triple-ruddered ship with a shark's body contour flew east from Burbank, Calif., in the colors of Transcontinental & Western Air, Inc., which sponsored its development, but it is being turned over to the Army for use in war transport work.

Compared with the Constellation's time for the non-stop flight is the previous fastest cross-country trip of 7 hours 28 minutes flown in a specially designed plane by Howard Hughes on Jan. 19, 1937. Hughes flew from Burbank to Newark, N. J., on a 2,445-mile route at an average speed of 327 miles an hour.

In contrast with his lone trip, however, the Constellation carried seventeen persons, and there was room in its cabin for forty more passengers with luxury accommodations. As a troop transport it could carry 100 soldiers with full equipment.

The fastest transport crossing previously flown was 10 hours 22 minutes by Leland S. Andrews and H. B. Snead in a two-engine Vultee from Los Angeles to Washington on Feb. 20, 1935, at an average speed of 221.6 miles an hour.

Hughes at the Controls

Hughes, an outstanding figure in aviation as well as a motion-picture producer, shared the controls of the Constellation with Jack Frye, president of the TWA. They flew between 15,000 and 19,000 feet, with some help from tail-winds. Despite the record, it was understood that the plane was slightly behind schedule.

Army officers declined to permit publication of any official figures on the flight, but did permit Frye and Hughes to say that the flight was a record.

"It is a perfectly marvelous ship," Mr Frye said. "It is simply great. It flies and handles like a pursuit [meaning a fighter plane]. I guess the thing to say is that it flies like a dream."

Greeting Guy W. Vaughan, president of Wright Aeronautical Corporation, which builds the 2,200-horsepower Whirlwind engines used in the Constellation, Mr. Frye said the power plants "purred like kittens all the way."

The plane left Burbank at 3:56 A. M. Pacific War Time and was over the Washington National Airport at 1:54 P. M. Eastern War Time. It made a perfect landing four minutes later after circling once. The time is figured from the moment the wheels begin rolling at the take-off until the finish line is crossed in flight.

Payload of 14 Tons

The Constellation has a gross weight of around forty tons and a payload of more than fourteen tons. Its wingspread is 123 feet, slightly longer than the flight of the Wright brothers at Kittyhawk and thirteen feet longer than the span of a B-24 Liberator.

The airline distance between Los Angeles and Washington is 2,663 miles. The great circle distance which the Constellation probably attempted, is 2,292 miles. Its actual distance probably was somewhere between the two figures.

In addition to Hughes and Frye as pilots, the crew comprised Howard Bolton, navigator; R. I. Proctor, flight engineer, and C. E. Glover, radio operator.

The passengers were L. J. Chiappino, Leo Baron, Robert L. Loomis, E. J. Minser, Orville R. Olson, Lee Spruill and Richard De Compo of TWA; Richard Stanton, R. L. Thoren and Thomas Watkins of Lockheed; S. J. Solomon, chairman of the airlines' committee on post-war aviation policy, and Lieut. Col. ~ A. Shoop of the Army Air Forces.

CHICAGO, April 17 (U.P.)—Designed for civilian "super luxury" but drafted into wartime duty, that's the story told today by the men behind the Constellation.

Built for TWA by Lockheed, the

Continued on Page 8

Hull to Put Policy Before 6 Senators

By The Associated Press.

WASHINGTON, April 17—Secretary Hull is scheduled to begin discussions this week with a bi-partisan Senate committee in an apparent effort to keep the main lines of American foreign policy out of the channels of political controversy.

Mr. Hull's expressed hope is to obtain from the committee, which consists of three Republicans and three Democrats, such advice and guidance on post-war issues, including a world organization to maintain peace, that it will be possible eventually to go to foreign governments with American plans which are assured of national and Congressional support.

The proposition was discussed by the Secretary and Chairman Connally of the Senate Foreign Relations Committee at Mr. Hull's office today.

The Secretary then told a press conference that the coming meeting was a result of his invitation expressed in a recent speech.

35 YEARS TO LIFE GIVEN TO LONERGAN

Wife Slayer Rushed to Prison After One Minute in Court—Broderick Plans Appeal

With the same apparent indifference that characterized his conduct during both his trials, Wayne Thomas Lonergan heard General Sessions Judge James G. Wallace sentence him yesterday to "thirty-five years to imprisonment for the rest of your natural life" for the slaying of his wife, Patricia.

The proceedings before Judge Wallace took less than a minute, one of the briefest in a murder sentence, and included denial of a motion by Edward V. Broderick, Lonergan's lawyer, to set aside the verdict of the blue-ribbon panel that convicted the former Royal Canadian Air Force aircraftman on March 31 of second-degree murder. Mr. Broderick said he would appeal.

Soon after 2 P. M. Lonergan arrived at Sing Sing prison and gave Mr. Broderick as his "only friend." When asked if he had any money or other valuables, he said. "I have nothing."

After the brief court session Mr. Broderick announced his intention to appeal, saying: "Last week District Attorney Frank S. Hogan received a major setback when the Court of Appeals reversed another murder conviction obtained by his office. I expect my appeal will add to the list of Mr. Hogan's setbacks." Court attachés said the cases had little in common.

Contempt Case Up Friday

Mr. Broderick and Mr. Hogan will be adversaries again Friday when the defense lawyer must answer a contempt of court citation issued by General Sessions Judge John J. Freschi as an outgrowth of Mr. Broderick's conduct in the abortive attempt last February to obtain a jury in the first Lonergan trial. After four days of turmoil a mistrial was declared without a juror having been chosen. Mr. Hogan will represent the State at the contempt hearing.

Evidently surprised at the severity of the sentence, since any term of twenty years or more is discretionary with the court, Lonergan, after a startled glance at Mr. Broderick, promptly and quietly accompanied court attendants to his Tombs prison cell to await transfer to Sing Sing Prison. He is eligible to ask for parole after twenty-three years and four months.

Soon after 1 P. M. Lonergan was

Continued on Page 13

RAIL HUBS BOMBED

U. S. Planes Rock Sofia and Belgrade—Hit Air Plants and Field

RAF STRIKES AT BUDAPEST

Russian and American Fliers Attack Rumania—Blow at Pas-de-Calais in West

By Wireless to The New York Times.

NAPLES, April 17—The Allied aerial offensive against rail centers and Nazi aircraft production centers in the Balkan-Danubian region continued in full swing today, with the heavy bombers of the United States Fifteenth Air Force attacking the Sofia and Belgrade rail yards and two plane plants at Belgrade in full strength.

British Wellingtons and Liberators made a new smashing attack on the Budapest rail yards last night.

Our Flying Fortresses and Liberators paid their first visit of the war to the enemy-held Yugoslav capital, although yesterday's program of the Mediterranean Allied Air Forces included blows by the "heavies" at the Zemun airfield and an adjacent factory on the outskirts of Belgrade, which the Luftwaffe ravaged three years ago this month.

Double Blows at Rumanian Town

During a 1,800-sortie day yesterday American four-motored giants also bombed the rail yards at Brasov, Rumania, on the northern slope of the Transylvanian Alps,* and at Turnu Severin in western Rumania.

[Soviet bombers Sunday night attacked the Rumanian port of Galati on the lower Danube, key point behind the southeastern end of the Nazi line facing the Red Army.

[Britain-based American Liberators on Monday resumed the air assault on western Europe with a 250-plane bombing of the German anti-invasion targets in the Pas-de-Calais area of France. German radio warnings Monday night reported Allied planes over the Reich.]

Turnu Severin had undergone bombardment Saturday night by the Royal Air Force's Wellingtons from Italy, roaring over the historic Iron Gate of the Danube.

Thus the offensive against sources of the strength and the movement of German troops facing the Russians in southeastern Europe has become literally a day-and-night affair, with the Fifteenth Air Force's "Forts" and Liberators and the RAF's Liberators and two-motored Wellingtons virtually overlapping in assaults on targets, most of which had not been hit prior to this month.

The Bulgarian capital of Sofia, which was last bombed for the eighth time, March 30, is the virtual hub of all Balkan rail lines. Belgrade, where early reports indicated today's bombing was successful, is also on the Zagreb-Bucharest line, which is the major Nazi feeder route to the Eastern Front from Austria and Yugoslavia.

Besides the rail yards the targets at the Yugoslav capital, which

Continued on Page 2

FOE FIGHTS HARDER

Russians Force Siege Lines Closer to Port From South and East

KEY TO BALAKLAVA TAKEN

Varnutka Junction Falls—Nazis Herded Into Corner—Kishinev Battle Raging

By The United Press.

LONDON, Tuesday, April 18—A Red Army flanking column swept twelve miles down the southern Crimean coast yesterday to capture the key highway junction of Varnutka, eleven miles southeast of Sevastopol, while other Soviet forces driving in from the north and east were meeting stiffened resistance from enemy troops fighting in fortifications built by the Russians during the 1941-42 siege.

The Moscow midnight war communiqué announced that troops of Gen. Andrei I. Yeremenko's Independent Maritime Army advancing toward Sevastopol from the southeast through the Baidary Valley were in hot pursuit of the enemy, who were abandoning arms and equipment in retreat.

Gen. Feodor I. Tolbukhin's Fourth Ukrainian Army, however, was meeting "strong resistance" as it reached the approaches of a powerful ring of German fortifications anchored on the heights east and northeast of the city. In yesterday's fighting the Fourth Army captured Mekenziyev, four miles northeast of Sevastopol across Sevastopol Bay, and Cherkez-Kermen, eight miles east of the city.

Kishinev Fighting Is Severe

The Moscow communiqués told of fighting on only one other sector of the long southern front, that in the Kishinev area of Bessarabia, where troops of Gen. Rodion Y. Malinovsky's Third Ukrainian Army captured bridgeheads on the west bank of the Dniester River Monday. Moscow said the Russians had fought yesterday to widen the bridgehead, and that one Soviet mobile detachment broke into the enemy's rear and wiped out nearly a battalion of 1,000 men.

Moscow dispatches said furious fighting was in progress east of Kishinev, where the Germans were holding strong positions anchored in the marshy terrain. The Berlin communiqué reported strong Soviet attacks in that area. It also told of

Continued on Page 2

ODESSA HAILS ITS LIBERATORS

Residents cheering Russian soldiers as they entered the city
The New York Times (Sovfoto Radiophoto)

U.S., SOVIET EXEMPT

Sealed Mail Pouches of Diplomats Also Are Prohibited

ACTION IS UNPRECEDENTED

Britain Will Send Messages for Others in Own Diplomatic Code if Necessary

By RAYMOND DANIELL
By Wireless to The New York Times.

LONDON, April 17—Britain took an action, unprecedented in international law, tonight to safeguard the lives of Allied troops who will soon be hurled against the battlements of Adolf Hitler's Festung Europa.

Without prior warning an edict was handed down by the Government that wrote a wartime finis to anything resembling diplomatic immunity both for Allied and neutral envoys with those of Russia and the United States as the sole exceptions.

Henceforth the rule is that no foreign diplomats or members of their staffs can go home. Nor can they send or receive telegrams in code. They are forbidden even uncensored use of diplomatic pouches, a privilege accorded to foreign legations in every capital under the sun for generations.

Other Measures Taken

This trail-blazing diplomatic precedent was undertaken by the British Government in the interest of security as part of a general campaign to isolate the happenings on this island until it is too late for the enemy to profit by the knowledge of what forces are being gathered here, what kind of arms they bear and where they are planning to strike. It is but one of many measures that have been taken and that are contemplated to safeguard secrets of military importance and thus give the Anglo-American assault force that essential element of strategic surprise when "D-day" comes.

Some steps in this direction have been taken already. Telephone and telegraph communication with Eire has been cut off and travel has been made difficult between this country and that part of the British Commonwealth of Nations that chose to remain neutral. Ships of the Royal Navy are doubtless guarding Ireland's coast not only against incursions by the Germans, but to make certain that there will be no surreptitious landings of submarines there to circumvent Britain's interest in strict neutrality.

Britain's unprecedented act in ending diplomatic privileges for all missions resident in London, whether neutral or Allied, was part and parcel of the present attempt to make this island impregnable to espionage. There has been some reason to suspect that indirectly at least the Germans have had several spyglasses focused from London on the invasion front.

British Inform Diplomats

Some neutrals have made it perfectly plain that their sympathies lay with the enemy. Others, who have enjoyed the privileges of diplomatic immunity in London, have been a fence for Hitler. With military operations of decisive nature impending it would be foolhardy under the circumstances for the British to maintain the pretense of observing the Marquess of Queensberry rules in a fight that long since has become a knock down and drag out affair in which Hitler himself has said that only one side can survive.

And so tonight the heads of all diplomatic missions here were informed that from midnight on they would have no privileges of communication with their governments and no facilities of travel other than any other foreign resident or subject of the King enjoyed. As one diplomat phrased it, Britain has taken steps that are sure to bring criticism even from her friends, but it is "nothing to what would be said of her if she had overlooked a leak that would have enabled the enemy to concentrate a sufficient force to beat off an invasion at any given time or place; Britain is

Continued on Page 5

ALLIES CUT BLOCK ISOLATING KOHIMA

Vital Gain Against Burma Foe Insures Dimapur Supply Link—Imphal Front Improves

By The Associated Press.

NEW DELHI, India, April 17—Tanks and infantry have cleared Japanese road blocks four miles north of Kohima on the road to Dimapur in heavy fighting in which Rajputs, Punjabis and British were involved, a front-line account from an Indian eyewitness said today.

Enemy artillery in the area was outgunned five to one, it was said.

"Everyone in Dimapur"—important operating center or the Bengal-Assam supply railroad—"now has an operational role" in patrolling and guarding the vital line of communications and making reconnaissances in the hills, it was said. Important installations were reported under guard.

The Dimapur personnel includes many American soldiers who as transport troops took over operation of the railway several months ago.

Enemy Losses Heavy

KANDY, Ceylon, April 17 (AP)—Japanese invasion forces that cut the important Allied supply road between Kohima and Dimapur in eastern India last week have been thrown from important positions and have suffered "very heavy"

Continued on Page 12

Badoglio Cabinet Resigns; Coalition to Govern Italy

By MILTON BRACKER
By Wireless to The New York Times.

NAPLES, Italy, April 17—The short-lived government of Premier Pietro Badoglio fell today. But it fell easily; and, as expected, King Victor Emmanuel accepted the resignation with the request that the marshal, who gave the Allies the armistice last September, form a new Cabinet on "a broad foundation" taking account of the wishes of "all the parties."

Thus the first post-armistice phase of Italian politics ended along lines that had been plainly marked since the King announced his willingness to retire in favor of Crown Prince Humbert when Rome is liberated.

A statement of less than fifty words, at first issued unofficially, but subsequently labeled "official," wound up the government. It read:

> Today Marshal Badoglio presented to the King the resignation of the Ministry presided over by him.
>
> The King took note of the resignation and has asked Marshal Badoglio to form a new Ministry with a broad foundation taking account of the wishes expressed by all the parties.

A series of conferences began today between Marshal Badoglio and representatives of the six parties that make up the executive junta of the opposition. It was interesting, if not significant, that the first to call at the seat of government was Palmiro Togliatti [M. Ercoli], Communist leader. Tomorrow the Socialists will present a list of potential Cabinet members, and so on until each of the groups that on Saturday agreed in lukewarm fashion to share in a new Government has had a chance to bid for places.

A source high in Allied political circles expressed the belief tonight that it would be a matter of only a few days before a new Cabinet was established. In no informed quarter was there a suggestion that Marshal Badoglio might be unable to form a Cabinet.

The question thus came down to who would make up the new Cabinet, which will be entrusted with the job of putting Italy more fully and efficiently behind the work of driving the Nazis out. Some of the former Cabinet members will

Continued on Page 6

5,000 NEW PLANES LOST BY GERMANS

Result of 6 Months of USAAF Blows at Luftwaffe Supply Centers an Invasion Factor

By DREW MIDDLETON
By Cable to The New York Times.

LONDON, April 17—The Luftwaffe has suffered its most serious defeat of the war in the past six months, according to a reliable source here today.

The United States Army Air Forces have drawn the fangs of the German Fighter Command, according to figures supplied by this source, and that command, although it will undoubtedly be a factor in the enemy's anti-invasion effort, will be far below its planned strength for that operation.

Here are the latest figures of Nazi air losses, figures that, according to the source, are the product of the most exhaustive research and careful checking.

Nearly 5,000 single and twin-engined fighters have been denied the Luftwaffe since early last November by damage done to its basic factories, assembly plants and replacement areas by the heavy bombers of the United States Eighth Air Force from Britain and the Fifteenth Air Force from Italy. That is, German production was cut by this amount as a result of our bombings.

In actual combat since the first of this year, 3,560 German fighters have been destroyed by the heavy bombers of the Eighth Air Force and their fighter escorts and by the medium bombers and fighters of the Ninth Air Force, all flying from Britain.

Probably 1,700 more Nazi inter-

Continued on Page 3

New Chemical Magic Transmutes Soft Woods Into Best of Timber

By WILLIAM L. LAURENCE

A new chemical process that transmutes all types of soft wood into wood of any desired hardness, thus providing a chemical magic wand with which hundreds of millions of acres of American forests of pine and other soft woods can be transformed into woodlands yielding the best of timber, was announced yesterday by E. I. du Pont de Nemours & Co.

With the new process, it was announced, "poplar becomes harder than hard maple, which in turn can be made harder than ebony." The compressive strength of wood is so increased and other properties imparted by the process to such an extent, it was added, "that the result is actually no longer natural wood, but a new material that may be termed transmuted wood."

The chemicals used in the process are derived from coal, air and water. The first step is to use these three for synthesizing ammonia, carbon dioxide and methanol (synthetic wood alcohol). The carbon dioxide and ammonia react to form urea, a substance widely used as a fertilizer. The methanol yields formaldehyde, which condenses with urea to form a substance named di-methyl-urea. When the latter is mixed, in water, with urea, compounds are formed that are known as methylol-urea. These chemicals are the magic wands that can transform soft woods in a few hours into hard woods that take nature a hundred years to grow.

Both urea and di-methylol-urea, it was explained, are commercially

Continued on Page 38

War News Summarized

TUESDAY, APRIL 18, 1944

Great Britain last night stripped all foreign diplomats, except those from the United States and Soviet Russia, of privileges hitherto customary in international relations. The unprecedented move, designed to seal every possible leak in connection with invasion plans, forbade any foreign representative, neutral or Allied, to leave Great Britain, to send or receive code messages, or to use the sacrosanct "diplomatic pouch." It is believed that the new embargo, by safeguarding the element of strategic surprise, will save many lives during the invasion of Western Europe. [1:8.]

Germany, giving every indication of her conviction that the Allies would strike sooner than had been expected, was reported to have laid a mine belt three miles wide off Jutland in Denmark. Increased protection for defending troops against air blows was being rushed. [1:6-7.].

The power of the Luftwaffe to counter the invasion has been drastically reduced by the air war waged from Britain and Italy, an American authority reported. He said Germany had lost at least 5,000 fighter planes through damage to aircraft factories in the past six months and that since Jan. 1 United States fliers from Britain had shot down in combat 3,560 enemy interceptors, while fliers from Italy had shot down 1,700 more. [1:7.]

The Allied aerial pincers were closing as tightly around the Balkans as around Germany. Russian bombers blasted the rail junction and Danube inland port of Galati, Rumania, setting great fires and many explosions. Galati is only 115 miles from Brasov, Rumania, hit Sunday by American planes from Italy. Yesterday Sofia, capital of Bulgaria, and Belgrade, capital of Yugoslavia, were daylight targets following a Sunday night attack on the Hungarian capital of Budapest. British-based American planes struck the Pas-de-Calais area of France. [1:3; map, P. 2.]

The Red Army was battling its way through artificial barriers and the Crimean mountains toward the outskirts of Sevastopol, the Germans' last remaining foothold. Other Russian forces were exploiting their bridgeheads over the Dniester in the Kishinev area. [1:4; map P. 2.]

For the second day in a row an American patrol made a raid two miles deep into German lines behind the Anzio beachhead in Italy, blowing up an ammunition dump. [3:1.] Marshal Badoglio and his Ministers resigned yesterday. King Victor Emmanuel immediately asked the marshal to form a new Ministry "with a broad foundation taking into account the wishes expressed by all parties." [1:6-7.]

Allied forces in India and Burma continued to improve their positions. [1:5.] In the Pacific American fliers ranged over wide areas from Kavieng, New Ireland, to Timor, with the heaviest blows struck at Wakde Island, off New Guinea, and also at Truk and the Marshall Islands. [12:5.]

German Invasion Alarm Growing; Jutland Coast Is Reported Mined

By Cable to The New York Times.

LONDON, April 17—The Germans have completed a mine belt three miles wide along the west coast of Jutland in Denmark as part of their invasion defenses, and preparations to meet the Anglo-American onslaught from the west have been reviewed in Berlin where Adolf Hitler and Field Marshal Gen. Wilhelm Keitel, chief of staff to the Supreme Command, met Field Marshal Gen. Karl von Rundstedt, commander of the Wehrmacht in France.

These developments, reported from Stockholm today, appear to be part of a general program forced on the enemy by recent events. The extension of Allied fighter range through introduction of long-range fighters such as the Mustang and Thunderbolt has made it necessary to prepare defenses for coasts that two years ago would have been considered "safe" from invasion because they were outside fighter range.

Lately, also, German newspaper and radio reports have indicated that the High Command now believes the invasion will come much earlier than originally expected. According to the Berlin correspondent of the Swedish newspaper Aftonbladet, the second half of May is judged in Berlin as the period that will be "most critical."

Through all reports that are relayed from Germany by Stockholm and other neutral news centers runs a thin vein of truth or at least a plausible supposition.

It is not probable that the enemy is blasting "huge caves in the cliffs of the Channel coast," as

Continued on Page 5

"All the News That's Fit to Print"

The New York Times.

LATE CITY EDITION
Cloudy with showers today. Partly cloudy and cooler tomorrow.
Temperatures Yesterday—Max., 64; Min., 47
Sunrise today, 5:40 A. M.; Sunset, 7:59 P. M.

VOL. XCIV..No. 31,881. Entered as Second-Class Matter, Postoffice, New York, N. Y. NEW YORK, TUESDAY, MAY 8, 1945. THREE CENTS IN NEW YORK CITY

THE WAR IN EUROPE IS ENDED! SURRENDER IS UNCONDITIONAL; V-E WILL BE PROCLAIMED TODAY; OUR TROOPS ON OKINAWA GAIN

ISLAND-WIDE DRIVE

Marines Reach Village a Mile From Naha and Army Lines Advance

7 MORE SHIPS SUNK

Search Planes Again Hit Japan's Life Line—Kyushu Bombed

By WARREN MOSCOW
By Wireless to THE NEW YORK TIMES

GUAM, Tuesday, May 8—In an island-wide American advance on Okinawa yesterday the First Marine Division drove south to the edge of Dakeshi Village, about a mile from Naha, the capital, straightening out the line on our right flank. In the center the Seventy-seventh Army Division used flame-throwing tanks for considerable advances, while the Seventh Army Division moved forward on the left flank.

[Airfields on Kyushu, southern Japan, were bombed Monday and Tuesday by Superfortresses, two of which were lost in heavy air opposition.

[Allied fliers started operating from the Tarakan airfield although fighting continued on that island off Borneo, and in the Philippines American troops made advances on Mindanao and Luzon.]

Japanese Dead at 36,535

As the United States forces on Okinawa resumed their drive, Fleet Admiral Chester W. Nimitz revealed that Japanese killed on the island had mounted to 36,535 on Monday, showing that the Americans were maintaining their rate of 1,000 a day.

The Americans have not yet taken the main Japanese artillery emplacements on Okinawa, which were the principal targets of the fleet off the island. The fleet's guns continued yesterday, along with carrier aircraft, to support the ground movements.

Meanwhile search bombers of Fleet Air Wing 1 continued to give an impressive demonstration of what the tightening air blockade of Japan will mean. Attacking at mast-head height with bombs and machine guns, these long-range aircraft, based in the Okinawa area, sank four more ships in waters off Korea and damaged five others.

The ships sunk were a large cargo ship, a medium cargo ship, a medium oiler and a large fleet tanker. Two small freighters were

Continued on Page 12, Column 2

Leopold Rescued By 7th Army Troops

By The Associated Press.

WITH THE UNITED STATES SEVENTH ARMY, Tuesday, May 8—Léopold III, King of Belgium, and his wife, Princess Rethy, have been liberated by the Seventh Army, it was announced today.

They were found near Strobl, eight miles east of Salzburg. The Americans had been told of their whereabouts by civilians.

With the King and his wife were eighteen members of their staff and four children. All were in good health.

Elements of the American 106th Cavalry Group had to overpower German Elite Guards to make the rescue. Seventh Army troops are now closely guarding the royal party.

The Pulitzer Awards For 1944 Announced

The Pulitzer Prize awards announced yesterday by the trustees of Columbia University included: For a distinguished novel, to "A Bell for Adano," by John Hersey; for an original American play of the current season, to "Harvey," by Mary Chase.

Among the newspaper awards were those to Hal Boyle, Associated Press war reporter, for distinguished correspondence; to James B. Reston of THE NEW YORK TIMES for his reporting of the Dumbarton Oaks Security Conference; to Joe Rosenthal, Associated Press photographer, for his photograph of marines raising the American flag at Iwo and to The Detroit Free Press for "distinguished and meritorious public service" in its investigation of legislative corruption at Lansing, Mich.

Further details of the awards will be found on Page 16.

MOLOTOFF HAILS BASIC 'UNANIMITY'

He Stresses Five Points In World Charter, but His View on One Is Questioned

By JAMES B. RESTON
Special to THE NEW YORK TIMES.

SAN FRANCISCO, May 7—The major allies who forced Germany's unconditional surrender have reached "unanimity" on the kind of world security organization which should be created at the United Nations conference to protect their newly won victory, Vyacheslaff M. Molotoff, Russian Foreign Commissar, said today.

While the delegates at the conference celebrated the end of the European war, and three Foreign Ministers, T. V. Soong of China, Paul Henri Spaak of Belgium and Trygve Lie of Norway left the conference to deal with urgent official business elsewhere, Mr. Molotoff told the press that the Soviet Union attached the "greatest importance" to five agreements reached by the heads of the Big Four delegations.

First, he said, these leaders agreed to support the principles of justice, international law, human rights and fundamental freedom for all.

Second, he added, the Big Four agreed not to make provision in the security charter for the revision of treaties.

His statement on this point was ambiguous and led to some speculation as to the unanimity of all four on the question.

Revision Power Called Danger

A reference in the United Nations charter to the necessity of revising treaties, Mr. Molotoff stated, "would play into the hands of enemy countries, which would certainly like to undermine and emasculate these treaties." Furthermore, he declared, to give the new League of Nations authority to consider revision of treaties would be a violation of national sovereign rights, which are guaranteed in the Dumbarton Oaks Charter.

For these reasons, he concluded, "the idea of revising treaties was rejected as untenable."

Third, Mr. Molotoff said, it was agreed among the Big Four that treaties directed against Germany, such as Russia's twenty-year alliances with Britain, France, Czechoslovakia, Yugoslavia and the Warsaw Poles, "should remain in force until such time as the Government concerned felt that the international security organization was really in a position to undertake the accomplishment of the tasks of

Continued on Page 15, Column 2

GERMANY SURRENDERS: NEW YORKERS MASSED UNDER SYMBOL OF LIBERTY

Thousands filling Times Square in spontaneous celebration yesterday. The New York Times

PRAGUE SAYS FOES ACCEPT SURRENDER

Czechoslovak Radio Reports All Fighting in Bohemia Will Be Ended Today

By The Associated Press.

LONDON, Tuesday, May 8—The Czechoslovak-controlled Prague radio announced today that the Germans in Prague and throughout Bohemia, a last major holdout pocket of German resistance, had accepted unconditional surrender.

The announcement came as the United States Third Army was reported to have advanced to the outskirts of the Czechoslovak capital, and three Russian armies hammered toward the same goal from the east and north.

"The German military plenipotentiary is negotiating with the Czechoslovak National Council on the modalities of unconditional surrender," said the broadcast, detailing what purported to be the

Continued on Page 11, Column 2

Wild Crowds Greet News In City While Others Pray

By FRANK S. ADAMS

New York City's millions reacted in two sharply contrasting ways yesterday to the news of the unconditional surrender of the German armies. A large and noisy minority greeted it with the turbulent enthusiasm of New Year's Eve and Election Night rolled into one. However, the great bulk of the city's population responded with quiet thanksgiving that the war in Europe was won, tempered by the realization that a grim and bitter struggle still was ahead in the Pacific and the fact that the nation is still in mourning for its fallen President and Commander in Chief.

Times Square, the financial section and the garment district were thronged from mid-morning on with wildly jubilant celebrators who tooted horns, staged impromptu parades and filled the canyons between the skyscrapers with fluttering scraps of paper. Elsewhere in the metropolitan area, however, war plants continued to hum, schools, offices and factories carried on their normal activities, and residential areas were calmly joyful.

One factor that helped to dampen the celebration was the bewilderment of large segments of the population at the absence of an official proclamation to back up the news contained in flaring headlines and radio bulletins. With the premature rumor of ten days ago fresh in everyone's mind, and millions still mindful of the false armistice of 1918, there was widespread skepticism over the authenticity of the news.

By mid-afternoon loudspeakers were blaring into the ears of the exulting thousands in the amusement district the news that President Truman's proclamation was being held up by the necessity of coordinating it with the announcements from London and Moscow, and that the formal celebration of the long-awaited V-E Day would be delayed until today.

This sobering note gradually

Continued on Page 7, Column 6

SHAEF BAN ON AP LIFTED IN 6 HOURS

Action Comes After Protests From Newspapers and Public—Writer Still Barred

Suspension of filing facilities of The Associated Press in the European theatre was clamped on by Supreme Headquarters, Allied Expeditionary Forces (SHAEF), yesterday in an unprecedented action and was lifted six hours and twenty minutes later.

The ban was continued, however, on all copy submitted for clearance by Edward Kennedy, chief of the press association's staff on the Western Front, who sent the momentous story announcing Germany's final surrender in a dispatch from Reims, France, which was received in New York over the AP wires at 9:35 A. M. (EWT).

It was not until seven hours and fifty-five minutes had elapsed aft-

Continued on Page 4, Column 2

GERMANS CAPITULATE ON ALL FRONTS

American, Russian and French Generals Accept Surrender in Eisenhower Headquarters, a Reims School

REICH CHIEF OF STAFF ASKS FOR MERCY

Doenitz Orders All Military Forces of Germany To Drop Arms—Troops in Norway Give Up—Churchill and Truman on Radio Today

By EDWARD KENNEDY
Associated Press Correspondent

REIMS, France, May 7—Germany surrendered unconditionally to the Western Allies and the Soviet Union at 2:41 A. M. French time today. [This was at 8:41 P. M. Eastern Wartime Sunday.]

The surrender took place at a little red schoolhouse that is the headquarters of Gen. Dwight D. Eisenhower.

The surrender, which brought the war in Europe to a formal end after five years, eight months and six days of bloodshed and destruction, was signed for Germany by Col. Gen. Gustav Jodl. General Jodl is the new Chief of Staff of the German Army.

The surrender was signed for the Supreme Allied Command by Lieut. Gen. Walter Bedell Smith, Chief of Staff for General Eisenhower.

It was also signed by Gen. Ivan Susloparoff for the Soviet Union and by Gen. Francois Sevez for France.

[The official Allied announcement will be made at 9 o'clock Tuesday morning when President Truman will broadcast a statement and Prime Minister Churchill will issue a V-E Day proclamation. Gen. Charles de Gaulle also will address the French at the same time.]

General Eisenhower was not present at the signing, but immediately afterward General Jodl and his fellow delegate, Gen. Admiral Hans Georg Friedeburg, were received by the Supreme Commander.

Germans Say They Understand Terms

They were asked sternly if they understood the surrender terms imposed upon Germany and if they would be carried out by Germany.

They answered Yes.

Germany, which began the war with a ruthless attack upon Poland, followed by successive aggressions and brutality in internment camps, surrendered with an appeal to the victors for mercy toward the German people and armed forces.

After having signed the full surrender, General Jodl said he wanted to speak and received leave to do so.

"With this signature," he said in soft-spoken German, "the German people and armed forces are for better or worse delivered into the victors' hands.

"In this war, which has lasted more than five years, both have achieved and suffered more than perhaps any other people in the world."

LONDON, May 7 (AP)—Complete victory in

Continued on Page 3, Columns 2 and 3

Summary of News of the War and German Surrender

TUESDAY, MAY 8, 1945

The war ended in Europe yesterday after five years, eight months and six days of the bloodiest conflict in history. Grand Admiral Karl Doenitz surrendered unconditonally to the Allies in a little red schoolhouse at Reims, France. At 8:41 P. M. Sunday, New York time, Col. Gen. Gustav Jodl signed for the enemy and Lieut. Gen. Walter Bedell Smith, General Eisenhower's Chief of Staff, for the Allies. In the absence of any official announcement there was some confusion as to the compliance with the surrender. Fighting had been going on in Czechoslovakia and nothing had been heard from German pockets along the French coast. [1:7-8.]

President Truman planned a broadcast from the White House at 9 o'clock this morning. Washington, gratified that the war in Europe was over, was confused by lack of confirmation. [2:2.]

Prime Minister Churchill will also broadcast at 9 A. M. from London and Premier Stalin is expected to make a simultaneous announcement in Moscow. King George will talk over the radio six hours later. [2:8.] London will celebrate V-E Day today, but, unable to restrain its joy, staged many impromptu celebrations yesterday. [2:7.]

Most New Yorkers took the news calmly and thankfully, sobered by realization that the war in the Pacific was far from over. There were, however, noisy outbursts in such centers as Times Square and Wall Street. Scrap paper showers fluttered from roofs and windows. [1:4-5.]

German Foreign Minister Lutz Schwerin von Krosigk broke the news to his people. The future will be difficult, he warned, and then added: "We must make right the basis of our nation. In our nation justice shall be the supreme law and the guiding principle. We must also recognize law as the basis of all relations between the nations." This sudden, complete reversal in German policy was received with skepticism by the Allies. [3:1.]

Perhaps one reason for this was the announcement from Moscow that 4,000,000 men, women and children had been done to death by gas, shooting, famine, poisoning and torture in the German extermination camp at Oswiecim, Poland. [12:5.]

The actual situation in Czechoslovakia was obscure. Late last night a Patriot broadcast said the Germans were negotiating with the Czechoslovak National Council details of surrender in Prague and Bohemia. Fighting had continued throughout yesterday and German planes had bombed public buildings and hospitals. [1:3; map P. 11.].

The United States Third Army continued its general advance into Czechoslovakia and the Fifth and Seventh Armies joined again in the Alps. The British Second Army moved to Denmark and Poles entered the shattered port of Wilhelmshaven. [11:1.] Breslau fell to the Red Army after an eighty-four-day siege; 40,000 Germans were captured. [11:5.]

Japan accepted the surrender of her Axis partner with a statement that she never had expected German aid and would go on to victory without the Reich. [13:1.]

Infantry and marines on Okinawa scored another general advance after naval bombardment had pulverized Japanese strong points. Pacific Fleet planes sank or damaged thirteen more ships off Korea and Japan. [1:1; map, P. 12.] B-29's maintained their assault on Kyushu airfields. Two of the big planes were shot down. [14:3-4.]

On Tarakan Allied troops were within a mile and a half of the eastern shore. Americans gained on Mindanao and Luzon in the Philippines. [12:3-4.]

Foreign Commissar Molotoff said in San Francisco that unanimity on amendments to Dumbarton Oaks assured success of the conference. He declared that the Big Four consultations had ended. [1:2.]

U.S. Marine Corps

A Japanese soldier reaching for his rifle on Okinawa.

U.S. Marine Corps

Marines advance on Okinawa.

U.S. Marine Corps

Marines breaking up a Japanese sniper nest at Okinawan church.

U.S. Marine Corps

Japanese soldier flushed from a cave by a smoke grenade surrenders to Marines.

"All the News That's Fit to Print"

The New York Times.

LATE CITY EDITION
Sunny and warm today. Tomorrow fair and warm.
Temperatures Yesterday—Max., 82; Min., 62
Sunrise today, 5:24 A. M.; Sunset, 8:31 P. M.

VOL. XCIV..No. 31,926.
Entered as Second-Class Matter, Postoffice, New York, N. Y.
NEW YORK, FRIDAY, JUNE 22, 1945.
THREE CENTS IN NEW YORK CITY

OKINAWA IS OURS AFTER 82 DAYS; 45,029 U. S. CASUALTIES, FOE'S 94,401; GEN. STILWELL HEADS 10TH ARMY

HOUSE REPUBLICANS SEEK TO STRIP OPA OF FOOD CONTROLS

Leaders Act on Hoover Plan to Give Real Authority to the Secretary of Agriculture

'BUNGLING' IS CHARGED

Limitation to Six Months and Cost-Plus for Farms Are Expected to Fail

Special to The New York Times.

WASHINGTON, June 21—Republican support for a reorganization of the price control structure along the lines suggested by former President Hoover developed today as the House ended two days of general debate on the Administration bill to extend the present price control act without change.

The Democratic and Republican leaders planned, with doubtful prospects of success, to seek a final vote tomorrow.

The "Hoover Plan," made public by the former President in a letter to Representative Jenkins of Ohio, was embodied by Mr. Jenkins in an amendment which would give the Secretary of Agriculture control over production, processing, distribution and pricing of food, and leaving to the Office of Price Administration only the routine mechanism of rationing.

There was a prospect that the Republicans in general would make their greatest effort to push through this amendment, hoping to recruit Democratic dissenters, particularly because the new Secretary of Agriculture, Representative Clinton P. Anderson of New Mexico, is an Administration Democrat popular with his colleagues.

Attacks Likely to Fail

It was indicated that the two other major attacks on continued price control as the Administration wants it would not succeed. These controls include the Wherry Senate amendment to guarantee farmers and stockmen a "cost-plus" price formula, and another amendment to limit the extension of the OPA to six months rather than a year.

The Democrats were especially anxious to reach a vote tomorrow. They fear that a postponement of the decision until Saturday might weaken their position by reducing their numbers on that customarily inactive day.

The day's debate found Administration speakers attacking the Wherry "cost-plus" amendment and the effort to limit OPA's extension to six months. Republican speakers, led by Representative Martin, the minority leader, attacked the administration of the Price Control Act.

Mr. Martin, asserting that "bungling and inefficiency" in OPA had been confirmed by the Democrats themselves, insisted that OPA, "right from the beginning has been run by crackpot theorists."

"And I am not referring," he added, "to the head man."

He continued:

"I will say," without publicly mentioning just what amendments he proposed to support, "that the situation has gone far enough. Congress has permitted this agency a free hand in the adoption of its regulations. We have given it every opportunity to order its affairs and to create a stable and sane method of operation which would guarantee to our people at least a minimum of the necessities of life."

Opposes Limited Extension

Representative Monroney of Oklahoma, a member of the House Banking Committee and a leader for the Administration in the fight over the bill, protested that an extension of OPA for only six months would "demoralize" the agency.

As to Republican claims of "unfairness" and poor administration in OPA, he declared the administration had in fact been "sensible" on the whole, adding:

"The umpire can't always call the plays in favor of your team."

Of the Wherry amendment, Mr. Monroney argued that it would be impossible to reach any agreed determination as to what was the legitimate "cost of production" of the farmers of the country, and that it would actually operate against the farmer's best interests by causing him to be blamed for "the devastating rise in prices" that would result.

He submitted a statement by Chester Bowles, head of OPA, declaring that the present act had ample provisions "to afford protection to farm producers."

Round-World Flight For Civilians Is Set

The round-the-world flight on commercial passenger planes of Pan American Airways in eighty-eight hours flying time on the resumption of post-war travel was announced yesterday by the Atlantic division of that organization, with headquarters at La Guardia Field. The cost of the flight was listed as $700, or less than the present round-trip rate to Europe.

Reservations have been made by eleven passengers, including several who have become nationally known as "pioneers" on first flights to new destinations.

The route from New York will cover Lisbon, Marseille, Rome, Athens, Cairo, Basra and Karachi to Calcutta of the Atlantic division, and then return via Bangkok, Canton, Tokyo, Paramushiru, Anchorage, Seattle and San Francisco to New York.

MEAT BETTERMENT PLEDGED BY TRUMAN

President Forecasts Single Control Over Prices, Food—Praises Trade Bill Passage

By The Associated Press.

OLYMPIA, Wash., June 21—President Truman promised improvement in the meat situation and forecast a single control over prices and food at a press conference today, his first outside the White House. After the conferences he went on a salmon fishing trip.

The President wore a wool pull-over sweater borrowed from Gov. Mon C. Wallgren, who, with Senator Magnuson, Democrat, of Washington, sat in on the meeting. It was knitted by the Indians over on Vancouver Island, Mr. Truman explained.

The President also told reporters that he had expected the United Nations Conference to be a success; expressed confidence that Congress would pass the Bretton Woods monetary agreements as it had done with the reciprocal trade program, and called General Eisenhower a grand gentleman who is entitled to anything he wanted, adding that the President would see that he received it.

Mr. Truman spoke reassuringly of the food situation and added that the Administration was at work on a plan for single control over prices and food, but did not disclose how it would function.

Sees Meat Shortage Easing

He said that the meat shortage would automatically be straightened out as soon as Representative Anderson, Democrat, of New Mexico, took office as his new Secretary of Agriculture and War Food Administrator. The President asserted that it would have been straightened out under the contemplated program under Marvin Jones, retiring Food Administrator, as well.

He told a questioner he had not seen a statement of former President Hoover that food controls over meat distribution had broken down. He added that Mr. Hoover had been very helpful in his recent White House talk on the subject.

Saying that the San Francisco Conference seemed to have accomplished its purpose, the President pointed out that the delays were technical, involving translations into many languages which consumed time.

He said he would address the closing session Tuesday, leaving here Monday by plane, stopping over in Portland for a brief tour of the city, and flying on to San Francisco.

"The action of the Senate in ap-

Continued on Page 22, Column 5

7TH LOAN OVER TOP AT $15,982,000,000; E-BOND SALES LAG

On 39th Day of Drive Nation Passes Its Over-All Quota by Nearly 2 Billions

INDIVIDUAL GOAL IS NEAR

Both City and State Achieve Objectives in This Class—Further Effort Stressed

With the aid of heavy corporation investments, the Seventh War Loan drive surged yesterday past its $14,000,000,000 over-all national goal by almost $2,000,000,000, but the anti-inflationary E Bond Series scored up only two-thirds of quota, The Associated Press reported in Washington. Secretary of the Treasury Henry Morgenthau Jr. warned the nation that complete success would not be achieved until the total set for individuals had been reached.

Both New York State and City surpassed their quotas for individual sales, but local War Finance Committee officials feared they might fail to meet their separate goals in E Bonds by the campaign deadline June 30.

On the thirty-ninth day since the drive opened May 14, total sales throughout the country climbed to $15,982,000,000. Of that sum corporation sales accounted for $9,782,000,000 and individual sales for $6,200,000,000. Each category had a quota of $7,000,000,000.

In contrast to that, sales of E Bonds, the popular securities for small investors, had reached a total of only $2,779,000,000 of the $4,000,000,000 goal.

Morgenthau Hails Achievement

Commenting on the progress of the drive, Secretary Morgenthau said it was "most gratifying to the Treasury" but that it meant corporations had passed their quota. A large job remained to be done, he noted, before the final accounting period ends July 7.

"Reports reaching me give me every confidence that our $7,000,000,000 goal for individuals will be met by that date," he added.

Frederick W. Gehle, New York chairman of the War Finance Committee, announced that the State had exceeded its goal of $1,124,000,000 for sales to individuals. The total—$1,139,200,000—constituted a new record in war financing for New York, he said.

But, with E Bond sales continuing in a "slump," New Yorkers faced the possibility that their purchases of that series would be insufficient to meet the city and State drive quotas, he pointed out.

"This fact," he commented, "increasingly evident during the past week, means that unless subscribers put forth greater effort than at any time during the war, the current campaign, in so far as the vitally important, anti-inflationary E Bonds are concerned, will fall short of full success. The factor that counts most is represented in E Bonds and not enough people are buying them."

67.1 Per Cent of E Bonds Sold Here

To date $192,707,215 in E Bonds has been sold in the city, which is 67.1 per cent of the $287,300,000 quota. All sales to individuals amounted to $12,695,613 on Wednesday, bringing the drive total in this group to $892,986,250, or 105.4 per cent, of the local goal of $847,430,000.

All investors purchases — including corporate and financial institutions—totaled cumulatively $2,535,049,837, or 74.2 per cent of the

Continued on Page 22, Column 7

Okinawa Costliest Of Pacific Battles

By The Associated Press.

GUAM, Friday, June 22—The conquest of Okinawa was the longest and costliest of all the campaigns in the central and western Pacific.

With casualty figures still incomplete, the toll of enemy and American killed, captured and wounded all but equals the grand total of casualties in six major campaigns which led up to Okinawa.

The eighty-two days it took to break all organized resistance dwarfs the twenty-six days of Iwo Island. The latter, however, is less than eight square miles in area, and Okinawa is roughly 485 square miles.

The figures for Okinawa, which include Japanese casualties through June 20 and American casualties only through June 19, compared with those of six other campaigns follow:

	Japanese		American	
	Killed	Captured	Killed	Wounded
Okinawa	90,401	4,000	11,260	33,769
Iwo	23,244	1,038	4,630	15,308
Saipan	27,586	2,161	3,426	13,099
Guam	17,442	524	1,437	5,648
Palau	13,354	435	1,302	6,115
Tarawa	5,000	150	913	2,037
Tinian	6,939	523	314	1,515

Note: Figures for Americans killed include missing.

LONDON IS PICKED AS INTERIM SEAT

Connally and Vandenberg Will Speak in Senate Two Days After Conference Adjourns

By JOHN H. CRIDER

Special to The New York Times.

SAN FRANCISCO, June 21—The United Nations Conference selected London, the "nursery" of the League of Nations, as the site for meetings of the committee which will do the planning to put life into the new world organization, as it became known today that the effort in the Senate for ratification of the new charter would start two days after the conference adjourns on Tuesday.

Senator Tom Connally of Texas, chairman of the Foreign Relations Committee, and Senator Arthur H. Vandenberg of Michigan, the two Senate representatives of the United States delegation, will make speeches Thursday, the day after they arrive by air in Washington from this conference.

Persons close to Senator Vandenberg said they were convinced

Continued on Page 5, Column 2

OKINAWA CONQUEST EXPANDS OUR ATTACKING RADIUS

June 22, 1945

With the end of the campaign on the chief island of the Ryukyu group (1), southern Japan is brought within reach of our fighter-bombers and virtually the entire enemy empire within reach of our long-range aircraft. Already apprehensive over the next American step, the enemy reported that planes had scouted Kyushu (2) and southern Honshu (3). B-29's attacked the latter island. On the Asiatic mainland the Chinese advanced thirty-one miles beyond Wenchow(4).

AUSTRALIANS SEIZE BORNEO OIL PLANT

Make New Surprise Landing in Lutong Area, 80 Miles South of Brunei Bay

By The United Press.

MANILA, Friday, June 22—Australian Ninth Division troops have landed unopposed in Borneo's Lutong oil refinery area, eighty miles down the west coast from Brunei Bay, and dispatches from the front today said that the Australians already had captured the important refinery there—potentially the most productive in the British Empire.

Gen. Douglas MacArthur announced the new amphibious operation—this one aimed at the heart of northern Borneo's rich oil industry. A dispatch from the front said the Australians sent pa-

Continued on Page 2, Column 6

'Vinegar Joe' in Command Of Okinawa's Conquerors

By The United Press.

MANILA, Friday, June 22—Gen. Joseph W. Stilwell has been named to lead the triumphant United States Tenth Army, conquerors of Okinawa, to new battles against the Japanese, it was announced today. The disclosure was made on the very day that Fleet Admiral Chester W. Nimitz announced the complete victory on Okinawa.

General Stilwell was appointed by Army Gen. Douglas MacArthur, acting in his capacity of commander of all United States Army forces in the Pacific. He succeeds the late Lieut. Gen. Simon Bolivar Buckner, who was killed last Monday on Okinawa by a Japanese shell. The new command lifts General Stilwell out of his post as Commander of Army Ground Forces in the United States and gives him an active combat command in the field, which virtually guarantees that he will be one of the leading figures in the final destruction of Japan.

General Stilwell already is in the Pacific and has been inspecting battle conditions on northern Luzon.

The Tenth Army comprises veteran units of the Pacific fighting, including the First, Second and Sixth Marine Divisions, and the Ninety-sixth, Seventy-seventh, Twenty-seventh and Seventh Infantry Divisions.

General Stilwell is a veteran of the Burma and China fighting. He speaks several Chinese dialects. Up until last Oct. 28 he was commander of United States forces in the China-Burma-India theatre, Chief of Staff to Generalissimo Chiang Kai-shek and deputy to British Ad-

Continued on Page 2, Column 2

450 B-29'S SMASH TARGETS IN HONSHU

Kure Arsenal Is Main Site of 3,000-Ton Explosive Blow—Foe Sees Invasion Move

By Wireless to The New York Times.

GUAM, Friday, June 22—Six important industrial targets in Japan, headed by the Kure naval arsenal, one of the two most important naval arsenals in Japan, were hit today in a daylight strike by a large force of approximately 450 American "Superforts," operating from bases in the Marianas.

Earlier the Tokyo radio had linked recent air strikes to preliminary operations for an invasion of Japan.

The Kure arsenal, plus the Hiro arsenal, which was virtually destroyed in a B-29 strike on May 5, furnished the weapons and the powder for the Japanese.

There is not much of a Japanese fleet left, but what there is, we are out to deprive of supplies.

The "bombs away" signal over the six separate targets came in

Continued on Page 3, Column 3

ISLE DECLARED WON

1,700 Japanese Troops Surrender Last Day of Bitter Battle

OTHERS JUMP INTO SEA

Great Base That Opens All of Japan to U.S. Attack Already in Operation

By WARREN MOSCOW

By Wireless to The New York Times.

GUAM, Friday, June 22—The battle of Okinawa is officially at an end. In a special communiqué issued at 10 o'clock last night, Fleet Admiral Chester W. Nimitz reported the end of organized resistance, and in a second one this morning he told of mopping-up operations.

Today's communiqué revealed how costly has been the price for the island for which we battled for eighty-two days. United States casualties so far disclosed amount to 45,029, and they are sufficiently far behind to indicate that the island bastion, four hundred statute miles from Japan, will have cost nearly 50,000 men in dead, missing and wounded from United States Army, Navy and Marine forces.

The cost of the Okinawa campaign was twice the toll of bloody Iwo, up to Okinawa the most costly of all our Pacific campaigns.

90,401 Japanese Killed

Through June 19 we had lost 6,990 men killed or missing in the land operations from the Army and marines and had 29,598 wounded for a total of 36,588.

The fleet losses, far higher than in any other campaign, have not been announced past May 23, almost a month ago. At that time 4,270 sailors had been killed or were missing and 4,171 wounded. This brings the Okinawa casualties to 45,029. It is likely that a month's fleet losses and the last two days of organized resistance plus what comes from mopping up will carry the total to the 50,000 mark.

The Okinawa campaign cost the Japanese around 94,401. Of these, 90,401 had been killed on Okinawa or in the Kerama Islands or on Ie Island, the three major battle-grounds of the Ryukyus campaign. About 4,000 Japanese had been captured up to last night, with the number growing rapidly. About 1,700 gave up yesterday alone.

The communiqué that announced the end of Okinawa resistance was brief and to the point. Issued at 10 P. M., Guam time, last night, it read:

"After eighty-two days of fighting, the battle of Okinawa has been won. Organized resistance ceased on June 21. Remnants of the enemy garrison in two small pockets in the southern portion of the island are being mopped up."

"Well Done," Says Nimitz

The communiqué was No. 400, issued from Pacific Fleet Headquarters. Ironically, the first communiqué, issued on June 4, 1942, told of the beginning of the Battle of Midway in the form of an announcement of a Japanese air attack on that island. Previously communiqués had been issued from Washington. That battle was the high watermark of the Japanese advance in the Pacific.

Shortly after telling of the end, Admiral Nimitz sent a "well done" to the officers and men under his command. It read as follows:

"To officers and men of all United States armed forces of the Pacific Ocean areas and of the British Pacific Fleet who have had their part in achieving this important victory, well done."

Communiqué No. 401, issued this morning at 10 o'clock, revealed that Japanese resistance ceased first in the Marine Corps sector of the island at 10:27 yesterday morning, Okinawa time. Two small pockets were still being cleaned up in the Army sector last night. All over the island's southern tip our troop movements were being hampered by the Okinawan civilians, who had been living underground

Continued on Page 3, Column 3

Queen Mary Never Saw a Torpedo As She Roamed Seven Seas Alone

By GEORGE HORNE

The role of the Atlantic liner Queen Mary at war is a story of high adventure—the tale of a ship with a charmed life.

It is one that should be spun from the rich memory of Sir James Gordon Partridge Bisset, K.B.E., commodore of the Cunard White Star Line, who stood on the bridge of the towering sea giant for more than three years, coursing the seven seas across the Atlantic, and from the Clyde to Sydney, from Halifax to the storm-wracked Cape, to Singapore, Bombay and Trincomalee.

And spun it was yesterday by Sir James himself, a stocky man with a bit of a roll to his gait and a rich mingling in his speech of the original Scottish burr with the salty sea jargon that knows no nationality.

"I was born in Liverpool of a Scot family," he said, stating first things first.

"I'm half Scotch and half soda," he went on, and then quickly corrected himself, "English, I mean."

Sir James loves the Queen Mary, and well he might. She has traveled 600,000 miles in the war, delivering 500,000 American soldiers where their generals wanted them to be, and another 100,000 British troops in addition. She has carried a heavy armament of fifty or sixty guns, some of them manned by

Continued on Page 6, Column 2

War News Summarized

FRIDAY, JUNE 22, 1945

Okinawa has been conquered by infantrymen and marines of the United States Tenth Army, backed by the guns and planes of the Pacific Fleet. Fighting, except for two small pockets around Medeera and Mabuni, ended yesterday on the eighty-second day of the invasion. Through Wednesday 90,401 Japanese had been killed and 4,000 taken prisoner. Tenth Army casualties to the day before were 6,990 killed and missing, 29,598 wounded. Pacific Fleet casualties to May 24 were 4,270 killed and missing, 4,171 wounded. [1:8.]

There was no final "banzai" charge by fanatical Japanese; to the contrary, the enemy at the end surrendered in unprecedented numbers. The campaign, started on Easter Sunday, April 1, was the most bitterly fought and costliest in the Pacific war. Rapid progress has been made in converting the island into a major base for future operations. [3:1.]

General MacArthur has appointed General Stilwell to succeed the late Lieutenant General Buckner in command of the Tenth Army. General Stilwell, who was in the Pacific on an inspection tour as Commander of Ground Forces, may lead an invasion of China or head an Army group against Japan. [1:6-7.]

In China Japanese troops were chased thirty-one miles up the coast from Wenchow, with indications that the enemy was abandoning the entire coast between Canton and Ningpo. Three Chinese columns were closing in on Liuchow. [2:1.]

Australians hopped eighty miles down the Borneo coast to land unopposed at Lutong in the heart of the Seria-Miri oil refining center. [1:5; map P. 2.] Filipino guerrillas captured Tuguegarao, capital of Cagayan Province, fifty miles south of Aparri, thus splitting the enemy forces. [3:6-7.]

B-29's switched to heavy explosives yesterday; great numbers dropped heavy loads on military and industrial targets on Honshu, Japan's main island. Tokyo continued to forecast an early American invasion. [1:7.]

Senator Kilgore declared that secret documents had revealed detailed plans by German industrialists to rearm the Reich for another attempt at world conquest, and the intention to finance an underground Nazi movement. Field Marshal Montgomery, from his headquarters in Germany, said members of the German General Staff would be kept in isolated prisons outside the country until militarism was broken up and that SS troops would be imprisoned for twenty years. [1:6-7.]

Yugoslavia, submitting a detailed report on 10,000 Fascist crimes, asked for the surrender of General Mikhailovitch and protested against the lenient treatment of Italian war criminals. [4:4-5.] Crowds in Milan demonstrated for a severe purge of Fascists and demanded more food and jobs. [4:3.]

German Staff to Be Kept in Exile; Kilgore Reports Third War Plot

By The United Press.

TWENTY-FIRST ARMY GROUP HEADQUARTERS, Germany, June 21—The Allies plan to stamp out German militarism by imprisoning the German General Staff in isolated camps outside Germany and holding all SS troops in North German camps for the next twenty years, Field Marshal Sir Bernard L. Montgomery announced today.

He did not state how long the officers of the German General Staff would be held, but he left no doubt of the Allies' determination to make sure that there was an end to Germany's ceaseless planning of wars and world conquest. The General Staff, which remained

Continued on Page 6, Column 4

Special to The New York Times.

WASHINGTON, June 21—Secret documents not presently identifiable as to source show that German industrialists last August laid plans for re-industrialization and rearming of Germany after the expected defeat, Senator Harley M. Kilgore of West Virginia asserted today.

Mr. Kilgore, who recently returned from a trip to Europe in his capacity as chairman of the war mobilization subcommittee of the Senate Military Affairs Committee, released an analysis of the documents to the press.

"Masquerading as 'neutral' business men without political allegiance," he asserted, "they [the Ger-

Continued on Page 6, Column 6

"All the News That's Fit to Print"

The New York Times.

LATE CITY EDITION
Sunny and warm today. Showers and warmer tomorrow.
Temperatures Yesterday—Max., 74; Min., 67
Sunrise today, 5:26 A. M.; Sunset, 8:31 P. M.

VOL. XCIV..No. 31,931. Entered as Second-Class Matter, Postoffice, New York, N. Y. NEW YORK, WEDNESDAY, JUNE 27, 1945. THREE CENTS IN NEW YORK CITY

TRUMAN CLOSES UNITED NATIONS CONFERENCE WITH PLEA TO TRANSLATE CHARTER INTO DEEDS; B-29'S KEEP UP ASSAULT ON HONSHU PLANTS

TWO BLOWS IN DAY

50 'Superforts' Batter Oil Works Few Hours After Strike by 500

TOP REFINERY IS HIT

Five Bombers Lost, 70 Reach Iwo From the Earlier Japan Mission

By The Associated Press.

GUAM, Wednesday, June 27 — Nearly fifty B-29's struck the Utsube River oil refinery on Honshu, Japan's principal producer of aviation gasoline, in a precision demolition attack before midnight last night.

The attack followed by half a day the greatest Superfortress demolition assault to date, a pinpointing of Honshu industries in which nearly 500 of the sky giants blasted ten enemy war factories with 3,000 tons of bombs.

[Twentieth Air Force headquarters in Washington reported five B-29's missing after the earlier Tuesday assault, which it said hit "the largest number of individual military and industrial targets yet attacked on a single Superfortress mission."

[Twenty-first Bomber Command crews reported "good to excellent" results in the multiple attack. They met slight Japanese fighter opposition and meager anti-aircraft fire.]

Refinery Damaged Previously

The Utsube refinery is located near Yokkaichi, eighteen miles southwest of Nagoya on Ise Bay. Since the destruction of Japanese fuel centers at Tokuyama and Otake by B-29's on May 10, the Utsube plant was the enemy's largest remaining producer of aviation gasoline.

The city of Yokkaichi was heavily damaged in an incendiary assault June 18. Some fire bombs fell into the Utsube refinery area in that attack, causing slight damage to the plant, but last night's strike was the first with the Utsube plant and storage area as the primary objective.

Ice-coated, as the result of soupy weather on their great demolition strike, more than seventy B-29's of the huge fleet in the early Tuesday attack made emergency landings on Iwo Island, the Twenty-first Bomber Command reported.

At one time Superfortresses were stacked in circles above our

Continued on Page 2, Column 6

Generalissimo Rank For Stalin Indicated

By The Associated Press.

LONDON, June 26—The Presidium of the Supreme Soviet conferred its four highest awards today on Premier Joseph Stalin and created a new rank of generalissimo to be given "for particularly outstanding services to the motherland in the task of commanding all armed forces of the state during war," Moscow said tonight.

The broadcast did not say who would be named generalissimo, but the requirement given for this highest possible military rank seemed to indicate that Marshal Stalin might receive it.

The principal decoration conferred upon the Russian leader was the Order of Victory "for exceptional services in the organization of all the armed forces of the Soviet Union and for skillful leadership of these forces in the great patriotic war, which ended in full victory over Hitlerite Germany."

He received the Hero of the Soviet Union medal as the Marshal "who headed the Red Army in defense of our motherland and its capital, Moscow, and with exceptional courage directed the struggle against Hitlerite Germany." He also received the Order of Lenin and the Gold Star.

New Invasion Attack Near South of Japan, Tokyo Says

Enemy Reports Our Convoys Moving North From Okinawa and Speculates That Upper Ryukyus May Be Goal

By The United Press.

WASHINGTON, June 26—Tokyo hinted tonight that a new United States invasion blow was impending against the northern Ryukyus, 180 miles south of Kyushu. An invasion fleet of some 200 transports, cruisers, destroyers and a battleship was moving northward along both coasts of Okinawa, Japanese broadcasts said, as recorded by the Federal Communications Commission.

[The Tokyo radio reported Tuesday night that Allied troops had landed on Kume Island, fifty miles west of Okinawa, according to The Associated Press. Later, a Japanese Domei agency broadcast said "the Japanese garrison intercepted the enemy and heavy fighting is now in progress." The broadcast, recorded by the Federal Communications Commission, referred to the Kume invasion as a "fresh landing."]

At the same time it was speculated that the Americans needed still more "stepping-stone" bases before carrying out their "certain" invasion of the home islands.

A Yomiuri Hochi newspaper dispatch quoted by Tokyo asserted that Amami and Kikai Islands, 180 miles south of Kyushu, had been chosen as the objectives of the next landing attempts. The two islands lie side by side 110 miles north of Okinawa, at the end of the Ryukyu chain.

"Apparently the enemy intends to make Okinawa the main base for the invasion of the Japanese homeland," the correspondent wrote. "Large amounts of war material are being poured into Okinawa from the Philippines and the Marianas."

However, he added, the Americans will need 500,000 to 1,000,000 men to carry out an invasion of the home islands and auxiliary bases will be needed to debark and quarter them, as well as to move

Continued on Page 3, Column 2

INDIANS IN ACCORD ON WAVELL BASIS

Viceroy's Plan for a Regime Almost Entirely Native Is Accepted by Conferees

By TILLMAN DURDIN

By Wireless to The New York Times.

SIMLA, India, June 26—Today's conference between the Viceroy, Field Marshal Viscount Wavell, and Indian political leaders is authoritatively understood to have agreed to the overall acceptance of the Wavell plan for the formation of a new central government for India almost entirely Indian in composition.

This acceptance of the main principle of the Wavell proposals represents a big stride toward a successful outcome for the "little round table" sessions here and hopes are high that full accord will be reached. Difficult problems remain to be settled, however, and these may still wreck the conference.

Probably the main unsolved problem is the allocation of posts in the new government among the various political and religious groups. In accepting the Wavell proposals, the conference members agreed on parity between caste Hindus and Moslems in the new government, but it is still to be decided whether all the Moslems will be members of Mohammed Ali Jinnah's Moslem League or whether all caste Hindus will be representatives of the Congress party.

Other Problems Canvassed

After assembling at 11 o'clock this morning, the conference adjourned at 12:30 and issued a brief statement saying provisional agreement had been reached on certain main principles and that the conference had adjourned to enable the delegates to consider the remaining problems in private discussions outside the conference chamber.

It was decided to meet again tomorrow morning. This afternoon the Congress party delegates conferred with Mohandas K. Gandhi and Moslem League leaders held separate talks. Later Pandit Govind Vallabh Pant, one of the Congress party delegates, visited Mr. Jinnah in the latter's hotel room, where it is assumed the problem of apportioning posts in the new government was discussed.

In addition to accepting the Wavell plan providing for equal numbers of caste Hindus and Moslems among the Ministers of the proposed new Government, it was learned, the conference agreed on other important points, all stated outright or implied in Viscount Wavell's recent broadcast of his proposals.

It was decided that the new Government's Cabinet or Executive Council, as it is called, would

Continued on Page 4, Column 4

2 JAPANESE CHIEFS OKINAWA SUICIDES

Generals Stabbed Themselves in Formal Ceremony on Cliff —Aides Hastened Deaths

By The United Press.

OKINAWA, June 26—The bodies of Lieut. Gen. Mitsuru Ushijima, Japanese commander in chief on Okinawa, and his chief of staff, Lieut. Gen. Isama Cho, were found yesterday in shallow graves on the southern sea cliff where they had been taken after a dramatic harakiri ceremony.

The two generals had decided to kill themselves June 21 when their last stronghold, an elaborate system of inter-connecting caves on Mabuni ridge, had been surrendered, according to a prisoner of war.

The prisoner, who had been

Continued on Page 4, Column 3

GOLDSTEIN, O'DWYER TO BE UNOPPOSED IN THE PRIMARIES

Surpless Withdraws Despite Having More Than Enough Backing to Enter Race

MANY DEMOCRATIC FIGHTS

Six Candidacies for Public Office and 10 Leaderships in Tammany Involved

General Sessions Judge Jonah J. Goldstein of Manhattan and District Attorney William O'Dwyer of Brooklyn were assured uncontested nominations for Mayor yesterday as the deadline for filing designations was reached at 5 P. M. without the appearance of any opposition petitions. There still remained a remote possibility that opposition petitions might be placed in the mails before midnight.

The last threat of primary opposition to Judge Goldstein was removed earlier in the day when George H. Ittleman announced that Magistrate Abner C. Surpless of Brooklyn would not make a contest for the Republican nomination despite the fact that more than enough signatures had been collected to enter him in the race. Mr. Ittleman had been serving as chairman of the Surpless campaign committee.

O'Dwyer's Mates in Clear

Mr. O'Dwyer was without opposition from the start for the Democratic and American Labor nominations, and there were no last minute surprises in this respect yesterday.

An appearance of opposition to Mr. O'Dwyer's running mates on the Democratic and Labor party tickets, Vincent R. Impellitteri for President of the Council and State Senator Lazarus Joseph for Controller, was created through the filing of the Queens Democratic designating petitions bearing the names of other candidates for these offices. But the Queens candidates have already signed declinations that will be filed before the Friday deadline and Mr. Im-

Continued on Page 8, Column 2

War News Summarized

WEDNESDAY, JUNE 27, 1945

The United Nations Conference in San Francisco ended its work at 8:39 last night, completing a historic nine weeks of deliberations designed to give nations security, peoples liberty and the world peace. Adjournment came at the close of President Truman's speech, which followed signing by the fifty nations present of the Charter of the United Nations. [1:6-7.]

"You have won a victory against war itself," Mr. Truman told the conferees, and have just created "a solid structure upon which we can build a better world." But this is only a first step, he emphasized, adding: "If we fail to use it we shall betray all those who have died in order that we might meet here in freedom and safety to create it."

No nation or group can expect special privileges and all must make sacrifices for the Charter to work, Mr. Truman said. He pointed out that powerful nations have "no right to dominate the world" but must "assume the responsibility for leadership toward a world of peace," resolved that "power and strength shall be used not to wage war, but to keep the world at peace and free from the fear of war."

Fascism did not die with Mussolini nor nazism with Hitler, the President declared, and the forces of tyranny are even now trying to undermine the Allied unity that made the Charter possible. [All the foregoing 1:8.]

President Truman will personally present the Charter to the Senate on Monday and urge prompt ratification. Opposition strength was estimated at twelve to fifteen votes [1:7.]

Allied forces in the Pacific stuck to their job of defeating Japan. B-29's hit the main enemy home island of Honshu again. The city of Yokkaichi, near Nagoya, was bombed during the night only a few hours after a massive attack upon ten key factories, the largest number of such targets hit on a single B-29 mission. [1:1; map, P. 2.]

Two American columns in Luzon's Cagayan Valley were less than twenty miles from closing a trap on the Japanese between Tuguegarao and the north. [2:6.] Capture of Miri by Australians completed the reconquest of west Borneo oilfields. Allied planes concentrated on Macassar Strait targets. [4:2, with map.] Chinese forces were within 165 miles of Shanghai. [2:8, with map.]

Tokyo, still fearing invasion, declared Allied landings were imminent on Amami and Kikai, between Okinawa and the home islands. Twelve Japanese planes were shot down in a futile attack on Okinawa. [1:2-3.]

In Europe it appeared that the American plan for mass trial of war criminals by an international military tribunal would be approved by the four-power conference. [6:4.] The Big Three may discuss Russia's proposal to ease restrictions on use of the Dardanelles. [7:5-6.] The London Poles will refuse to cede authority until a new Government is chosen at free elections. [6:1.]

All factions in India were reported to have accepted in principle the new British proposals for a revised central Government, including parity of caste Hindus and Moslems. [1:2.]

PRESIDENT WITNESSES SIGNING OF SECURITY PACT

Mr. Truman looking on as Secretary of State Stettinius affixes his name to the document

100,000 HOMES HERE FACE HIGHER RENTS

U. S. Court Order on Luxury Apartments Scored by Mayor —OPA Weighs Next Step

By LEE E. COOPER

One hundred thousand families in the New York area who pay $100 or more a month in rent are subject to higher charges under the decision handed down on Monday by the United States Emergency Court of Appeals, holding rent for the so-called luxury type of living quarters to be "inadequate" under present ceilings, a study of rental records showed last night. Nearly 50,000 of these higher-rent suites are in Manhattan, and about 8 per cent of the apartments there are affected by the order.

While officials of the Office of Price Administration were considering whether they should grant an increase without further ado or try a court appeal, it was reported in authoritative circles that if the former course of action were followed the OPA order probably would not call for much more than a 5 per cent rise in the higher-priced suites.

Rentals of $99 or less are not affected by the order, and even for the "luxury" apartments and hotel suites present rentals will apply until the OPA acts. The appeals court gave the rent officials thirty days, or until July 25, to comply with its decision.

Reactions to the Decision

Mixed reactions and some uncertainty followed announcement of the decision, which applies to all of New York City, Nassau and Suffolk Counties.

Mayor La Guardia, who had opposed the appeal by the Metropolitan Fair Rent Committee and other representatives of landlords for a blanket rise of 10 per cent on rent for housing here, expressed disappointment over the court's position.

"I don't like it," he commented. "From the facts submitted, I do not believe the finding is warranted. Here we broke our backs to reduce realty taxes, and immediately the rents are raised. The court is wrong!"

Spokesmen for several realty organizations expressed gratification, but contended that the decision did not go far enough and that increases were in order also for apartments renting for less than $100, on the ground that operating costs and other charges had risen for all types of buildings. OPA executives expressed the view that the ruling was a victory for rent control because present ceilings and the general purposes of control were upheld and the order for a rise affected "only a small per-

Continued on Page 36, Column 3

Nation After Nation Sees Era Of Peace in Signing Charter

By LAWRENCE E. DAVIES

Special to The New York Times.

SAN FRANCISCO, June 26—A Charter drawn to give the world a new start on the way to lasting peace was signed today by the men and women from fifty nations who had fashioned it during nine weeks of laborious effort. They sat, one at a time, at a huge round table, autographing their handiwork while newsreel and newspaper camera men recorded the event for millions, now and later, to see and hear. Great spotlights, focused on the signers and their surroundings, made the scene in the Veterans Building look like a Hollywood movie set.

To China, first of the United Nations to suffer attack by a member of the Axis, went the honor of signing first. Dr. V. K. Wellington Koo, Chungking's Ambassador to the Court of St. James, using his country's writing brush, inscribed his name at noon in two freshly printed and freshly bound volumes, one containing the text of the Charter and the statute of the New International Court of Justice and the other authority for a preparatory commission to begin at once the enormous task of getting the new league functioning.

Signing Schedule Changed

The Big Powers began the day's work, with the United States, as the host nation, listed in the official advance order as the last signer. As things worked out, however, Russia, led by Ambassador Andrei A. Gromyko, followed China, with the United Kingdom third and Argentina slipping in ahead of France.

And the delegates of the United States, instead of waiting for the

Continued on Page 11, Column 6

TRUMAN WILL HAND CHARTER TO SENATE

President Will Speak Before Chamber Monday — Plans for Ratification Pushed

By C. P. TRUSSELL

Special to The New York Times.

WASHINGTON, June 26—President Truman will personally present the Charter, signed today at the United Nations Conference, to the Senate on Monday in one of the rare appearances of a Chief Executive before a single chamber of Congress.

As he presents the pledge of international collaboration to secure the peace and block future aggressions, the President will make a statement to the Senate, whose function it will be to ratify its provisions.

These plans came to light at the Capitol today as the Senate and the House, while grappling with war and administrative appropriations, followed as closely as they could the concluding proceedings at San Francisco and looked to the first-hand reports which are to be made to the Senate by its own rep-

Continued on Page 10, Column 2

Storm Skirts City and Goes to Sea, Giving Relief From the Heat Wave

After two days of mild apprehension over a tropical storm that was swinging erratically northward along the Atlantic Coast, New York City unexpectedly enjoyed its most agreeable recent weather yesterday, as the storm veered out to sea. Only cooling winds and storm warnings for small craft marked its passing in this area.

Temperatures, as a result, touched a high of only 74 degrees in midafternoon, compared with 90 on Monday. The mean temperature was 72—one degree above the normal of 71 for the date—but the humidity was in the 80's most of the day.

Benjamin Parry, meteorologist in charge of the Weather Bureau here, announced in the forenoon that the storm would skirt the city. At that time it appeared likely, however, that New York would have stiff winds and rain most of the day.

Instead, the storm center plowed steadily northeastward at about twenty miles an hour, passing some seventy miles east of Nantucket last evening. The winds here did not reach their expected maximum velocity of thirty miles an hour until just before 6 P. M. The steady rain mentioned in earlier forecasts did not materialize.

Sunny, warm weather, with the highest temperature near 80 and with moderate northerly winds was the forecast for today. For tomorrow the Weather Bureau foresaw showers and warmer weather.

NEW WORLD HOPE

President Hails 'Great Instrument of Peace,' Insists It Be Used

HISTORIC LANDMARK

Meeting Gives Standing Ovation as Executive Pictures Peace Gain

President's address, Page 10; other texts, Pages 12, 13 and 14.

By JOHN H. CRIDER

Special to The New York Times.

SAN FRANCISCO, June 26—The United Nations Conference ended at 5:28 this afternoon with a demand by President Truman to translate the lofty words of the new world Charter into worthy deeds ringing in the ears of the delegates from fifty nations.

The conference had presented to the world for the second time in three decades the outlines of machinery for the maintenance of world peace — better machinery, all of the speakers at the closing session agreed, than it had ever had before. But, as President Truman admonished in his address closing the conference, "the world must now use it."

"If we fail to use it," he declared to the solemn final meeting of the delegates, "we shall betray all those who have died in order that we might meet here in freedom and safety to create it.

"If we seek to use it selfishly—for the advantage of any one nation or any small group of nations—we shall be equally guilty of that betrayal."

Fervent Interpolation

The President, speaking in the auditorium of the War Memorial Opera House, built in memory of sons of the Golden Gate city who gave their lives in the first World War, in which he himself had served, seemed to give unconscious expression to the solemn feeling of the occasion when, at the outset of his speech, he interpolated the words, half a hope, half a prayer:

"Oh, what a great day this can be in history!"

Just before the plenary session the President accompanied the eight United States delegates to the auditorium of the Veterans' Memorial Building to witness their signing of the new world security Charter.

The signing had not been completed by the time of the closing session and, for the President to witness the United States signatures, the American delegates were permitted to sign out of turn, after Nicaragua, at about 3:15. The United States was the thirty-eighth nation to sign, leaving twelve to sign. Signing was completed at 7:20.

The plenary session began at 3:50 with three bangs of the gavel by Secretary Stettinius, presiding. The President, while waiting to make the closing speech, sat, tight-lipped, reading the English versions of speeches given in seven languages which preceded his in the two-hour final session.

The President's voice had been heard once before, when he opened the conference nine weeks ago with an address delivered by wire from Washington.

Points Stressed in Speech

Points he emphasized most strongly today were:

That this Charter is only a beginning—"our thinking and all our actions must be based on the realization that it is in fact only a first step."

That the Charter is no more perfect than was our own Constitution, it must be made to live.

That the fact there is a charter, in view of the diversity of interests, "is a great wonder" for which we should give "profound thanksgiving to Almighty God."

The differences which developed at this conference, he said, were resolved in the democratic way,

Continued on Page 11, Column 2

"All the News That's Fit to Print"

The New York Times.

LATE CITY EDITION
Fair, warm and less humid today and tomorrow.
Temperatures Yesterday—Max., 85; Min., 68
Sunrise today, 5:47 A. M.; Sunset, 8:17 P. M.

VOL. XCIV..No. 31,961. Entered as Second-Class Matter, Postoffice, New York, N. Y. NEW YORK, FRIDAY, JULY 27, 1945. THREE CENTS IN NEW YORK CITY

CHURCHILL IS DEFEATED IN LABOR LANDSLIDE; ATTLEE PROMISES PROSECUTION OF PACIFIC WAR; ALLIES ORDER JAPAN TO QUIT OR BE DESTROYED

SUSPENDED OPA MAN ACCUSES WOOLLEY OF INTERFERENCE

Ross Alleges Chief Hampered Enforcement in the Milk and Cigarette Drives

DEMANDS PUBLIC HEARING

Makes His Counter-Charges at Last Minute in 25,000-Word Reply in Dismissal Action

By CHARLES GRUTZNER Jr.

The twice-deferred showdown over maladministration of price control in this five-State area was made public yesterday when Paul L. Ross, suspended regional enforcement executive of the Office of Price Administration, filed his defense and counter-allegations to the charges lodged against him last month by Daniel P. Woolley, regional OPA head.

Mr. Ross' reply, loaded with accusations of interference by Mr. Woolley with his own enforcement division in the carrying out of national policies, and mentioning companies said to have benefited by Mr. Woolley's action, was brought to regional OPA headquarters in the Empire State Building by a messenger from the office of Paul O'Dwyer, counsel to the suspended official, at 4:59 P. M., sixteen minutes before the deadline for making answer.

The 25,000-word reply was accompanied by a demand for a public hearing of Mr. Woolley's charges and the counter-charges by Mr. Ross before an impartial board.

Woolley Has No Comment

Mr. Woolley had left the office before the messenger arrived with the bulky document, which was accepted for Mr. Woolley by Charles Staff, regional personnel officer. A spokesman for Mr. Woolley said later that the Regional Administrator had "no comment to make at this time on the contents of the answer." He said the document had been turned over to the regional legal and civil service staffs for study and that Mr. Woolley's ouster action against Mr. Ross would be carried out in compliance with civil service procedure, which permits but does not require a public hearing in such a case.

Besides accusing Mr. Woolley of hampering the effectiveness of price control by going counter to national enforcement policy—in some cases to serve his own political ambitions, according to Mr. Ross—the reply defended Mr. Ross' record of enforcement. It said that in May court proceedings were brought in this region in some 975 price cases, 30 per cent of the national total, and that OPA "was successful in 99.4 per cent of the cases." This region covers New York, New Jersey, Delaware, Maryland, Virginia and the District of Columbia. The only region with a higher percentage of success was the New England region, with a perfect score, but that was based on only 130 cases, 4 per cent of the national total, Mr. Ross pointed out.

Charges Early Interference

The cases cited by Mr. Ross in support of his contention that Mr. Woolley had hampered enforcement ranged from one involving the Continental Food Company in December, 1943, less than a month after Mr. Woolley joined the OPA, to a cigarette drive last winter that Mr. Ross said had been engineered by Mr. Woolley, to the detriment of more important food price control work, because Mr. Woolley believed the resultant publicity would strengthen his political chances.

There were allegations also of "unwarranted interference" by the regional administrator in cases involving the Dairymen's League and the price of milk; Fan & Bill's, a well-known restaurant in Washington, and Dinty Moore's restaurant in this city. The roll of alleged interference extends to April

Continued on Page 10, Column 1

Truman Pledges Free World As He Reviews U. S. Troops

Tells Them They Fought So 'We Can Live, Think and Act as We Like'—He Says He Will Follow Roosevelt Ideas

By DREW MIDDLETON
By Wireless to The New York Times.

FRANKFORT ON THE MAIN, Germany, July 26—The United States Commander in Chief saw his countrymen in arms today and they, lean young men who had fought halfway across the Continent of Europe, looked back and liked what they saw.

On a day so hot and so bright that it was like those "dog" days of the great Missouri region from which he comes, President Truman, accompanied by Secretary of State James F. Byrnes and Gen. Dwight D. Eisenhower, drove fifty miles through rigid lines of soldiers, saw the United States Army now settled into its job of occupation and told them simply how much he would have liked to have been in uniform and how soldierly they looked.

"You fought so the United States and the nations of the world can live and act and do as they like," he said. I want to implement that in following the footsteps of my predecessor, Franklin Delano Roosevelt.

At the end of the tour the President stood on an airfield outside Frankfort on the Main and pinned Distinguished Service Medals on the tunics of four officers, three British and one Canadian.

They were Gen. H. D. G. Crerar, Commander in Chief of the Canadian First Army; Maj. Gen. Sir Frederick W. De Guingand, chief of staff of the Twenty-first Army Group; Air Marshal Sir Arthur Conningham, commander of the British Second Tactical Air Force, and Air Marshal Sir James M. Robb, former Deputy Chief of Staff for Air at Supreme Allied Headquarters.

It was the first time that an American President had decorated the soldiers of an allied nation on

Continued on Page 5, Column 2

Supporters Set the Stage For Implementing Charter

By JAMES B. RESTON
Special to The New York Times.

WASHINGTON, July 26—The Administration has not only assured during the present Senate debate the almost unanimous ratification of the United Nations Security Charter, according to general agreement, but has also greatly improved its chances of implementing the Charter effectively.

When the debate started on Monday there was some doubt about the way in which the Administration would assure that effective force could be put at the disposal of the League and used by it without reference in each case to Congress.

In the last four days, however, the supporters of the Charter, its opponents admit, have succeeded in establishing these two important points:

Once the treaty is ratified by the Senate on Saturday or early next week, the President, as Commander in Chief of the armed forces and particularly as the officer charged with carrying out treaty obligations, will be authorized to use the American quota of troops to "maintain international peace and security" through the World Security Council.

Cannot Bind Senate

Instead of being bound to decide on the size and type of the league forces by a treaty, as it seemed obligated to do at the beginning of the debate, the administration will be free to decide this question through the device of a joint resolution of both houses of Congress, which requires a majority of both houses of Congress.

There is, of course, no way in which the administration can bind a future Senate to agree to the record which has been established in the debate, but the record now emphasizes the following three things:

The treaty obligates this country

Continued on Page 9, Column 2

MEAT RISE OF 11% IS DUE IN AUGUST

Public Will Also Gain by Cuts in Point Values—Sugar for East Increased

Special to The New York Times.

WASHINGTON, July 26—About 11 per cent more meat, a little more sugar for the East and fewer canned goods appeared today to be in prospect for civilians during August.

With more meat available to civilian consumers as a result of reductions in military demand, the Office of Price Administration lowered by one and two points a pound, and in one instance by three points, the ration values of nearly all cuts of beef, lamb and veal for the rationing period beginning Sunday, July 29.

As much as 80,000,000 more pounds of sugar will be directed into the East by September as a result of a reshuffling of sugar quotas throughout the country. This resulted from an amendment to War Food Order 131.1, which allocates sugar among various consumers and refiners for the period of April through September.

The ruling, while not increasing the total amount of sugar available to civilians, is understood to

Continued on Page 20, Column 5

Federal Jobs Up 126,130 in June; Byrd Asks Reduction of 300,000

Special to The New York Times.

WASHINGTON, July 26—The number of Federal civilian employes increased by 126,130 in June, and of that total 110,049 were hired by the War Department outside the United States, Senator Byrd, chairman of the Joint Committee on Reduction of Non-Essential Federal Expenditures, said today. The number of Army employes within the United States was reduced by 3,378 in the same month.

Reporting that the civilian payroll of the Government in this country had passed the three-million mark without reference to the more than a half-million War Department employes abroad, Senator Byrd said that it was his firm conviction "that at least 300,000 Federal employes could be immediately eliminated without interference with the prosecution of the war."

After the war ended, he said, "we should return to a total Federal employment of certainly less than a million employes," adding that even this figure was in excess of the Federal employment of normal times.

The increase during June, Senator Byrd stated, meant that 100 civilian employes were added to

Continued on Page 11, Column 3

TERMS LAID DOWN

U. S., Britain and China Plan Disarmament and Occupation

DOOM THE WAR LORDS

Offer Japanese People Opportunity to Gain Democratic Rule

Text of Allies' ultimatum to Japan to end war, Page 4.

By RAYMOND DANIELL
By Wireless to The New York Times.

BERLIN, July 26—Against the background of the Three-Power conference in the heart of shattered Germany, President Truman and retiring Prime Minister Churchill, with the concurrence of Generalissimo Chiang Kai-shek, called on the Japanese Government and people tonight to surrender unconditionally or face "prompt and utter destruction" at the hands of the Allied land, sea and air forces "poised to strike the final blows."

The joint declaration, it was said, was drawn by Messrs. Churchill and Truman after their arrival here. Its text was transmitted to Generalissimo Chiang and released here as soon as his concurrence had been received in a personal message to Mr. Truman. At 9:30 P. M., after the President's return from Frankfort, the text of the proclamation was issued here and orders were cabled to the Office of War Information in Washington to get the message to the Japanese people by every means possible.

The joint proclamation was in the nature of an ultimatum. While it reiterated the demands for unconditional surrender, it repeated the Cairo declaration that Japan's sovereignty would be limited to her home islands, stripped of the power to wage war. It promised that the Japanese people would be neither "enslaved as a race nor destroyed as a nation."

The Japanese militarists will have to go to make way for a

Continued on Page 4, Column 2

WINNER AND LOSER IN BRITISH ELECTIONS

Clement R. Attlee — Associated Press

Winston Churchill — © British Combine

3 JAPANESE CITIES FIRED BY 350 B-29'S

Omuta, Chemical Center, Is Hit in 2,200-Ton Triple Blow—Shanghai Ripped Again

By W. H. LAWRENCE
By Wireless to The New York Times.

GUAM, Friday, July 27—More than 2,200 tons of petroleum jelly incendiary bombs were dumped early today by a Mariannas-based force of more than 350 Superfortresses on the Japanese cities of Omuta, Matsuyama and Tokuyama.

The three urban targets had a combined population of 377,000, most of it engaged in war production.

[Meanwhile Gen. George C. Kenney's Far East Air Forces, returning to Shanghai in strength, blasted five major airdromes and

Continued on Page 6, Column 3

War News Summarized

FRIDAY, JULY 27, 1945

Great Britain swung to the left so completely in the recent elections that the Labor party and the Conservative party almost exactly changed their positions. Labor won 390 out of 640 seats in the Commons, compared with 163 in the outgoing Parliament, while Prime Minister Churchill's party, which had had 358, won only 195. Labor received nearly half of the popular vote. Mr. Churchill and his Foreign Secretary, Anthony Eden, were about the only survivors among Conservative Cabinet members. The Liberal and Communist parties also fared badly.

"I regret that I have not been permitted to finish the work against Japan," Mr. Churchill said after relinquishing the post he had held since May, 1940. "For this, however, all plans and preparations have been made and the results may come quicker than we have hitherto been entitled to expect." [All the foregoing 1:8.]

"We have first of all to finish the war with Japan," Clement Richard Attlee, who was advanced by the election from Deputy Prime Minister to Prime Minister, told a Labor meeting. "We want the fullest cooperation of all nations,' he added. "We want a security that will banish war forever. We want a widespread prosperity among all the peoples and nations of the world." [1:6-7.]

The Big-Three conference was in recess and President Truman visited American troops along the Rhine. He told them he wanted to follow in President Roosevelt's footsteps. [1:2-3.]

Japan was ordered to surrender unconditionally quickly or face "utter devastation." Mr. Truman, Mr. Churchill and Generalissimo Chiang Kai-shek gave their answer to the enemy's pleas for softer terms in a proclamation that reaffirmed the principles of the Cairo Declaration: the end of militarism, punishment of war criminals, establishment of democracy and limitation of Japanese territory to the home islands. [1:4.]

General Devers said United States troops were being trained in "radical" new methods of warfare for a single gigantic blow against Japan. [1:6-7.]

Planes continued to carry the war to Japan and her occupied territory. B-29's set three industrial cities on Honshu, Shikoku and Kyushu afire; Iwo-based Privateers hit shipping in the Gulf of Sagami south of Tokyo; Okinawa-based planes struck Korean waters and airfields on Honshu, and 300 bombers smashed five airfields at Shanghai. [1:5; map P. 6.]

British and American carrier planes of the Third Fleet beat off the first enemy air attack since the warships went into action off Japan on July 10. Four out of ten enemy aircraft were shot down. [5:6.]

Chinese troops recaptured the seventh of eleven former American air bases lost to the Japanese when they seized Namyung, 150 miles northeast of Canton. Inconclusive fighting was raging on other fronts. [5:1, with map.]

A member of the de Gaulle Government sustained the legality of the Vichy regime in testifying against Marshal Pétain on trial for treason in Paris. The defendant was again accused of betraying France. [8:3-4.]

Attlee in First Talk Backs Harmony With U.S., Russia

By SYDNEY GRUSON
By Cable to The New York Times.

LONDON, July 26—Maj. Clement R. Attlee, in his first speech as Britain's Prime Minister, pledged anew tonight this nation's determination "to finish the war with Japan" and expressed the belief that the result of the British election would give heart throughout the world to those "who believe in freedom, democracy and social justice."

Coming directly from Buckingham Palace after accepting King George VI's commission to form a new Government, Mr. Attlee addressed a wildly enthusiastic Labor party victory rally in Westminster Central Hall, not more than 100 yards from the House of Commons his party now dominates.

Seeming just the slightest bit dazed by the tumultuous day, Mr. Attlee outlined his new Government's job in a few sentences.

"We have, first of all, to finish the war against Japan," he declared. "We shall see to it that our men in the East get all the support they need.

"We want the fullest cooperation with all nations.

"We want a security that will banish war forever.

"We want a widespread prosperity among all the peoples and nations of the world.

The Tasks at Home

"Here at home we have our own great tasks. We have to bind up the wounds of war. We have to reconstruct our ruined homes—a great task in itself. We have to bring back in due course the workers who have been working on the war to be workers for peace. We have a job to build up in this country the highest standard of life that we can achieve for all."

Flanked by his chief lieutenants, Herbert Morrison and Ernest Bevin, and with the wives of all three beaming beside them, Mr. Attlee called on the crowd of 2,000

Continued on Page 3, Column 6

BRITISH BUSINESS IN GENERAL IS CALM

Coal, Power Industries Shaken by Nationalization Prospect, Rest Expect Little Change

By CHARLES E. EGAN
By Wireless to The New York Times.

LONDON, July 26—Britain's business circles reacted calmly to Labor's election sweep today. Coal and power interests were shaken because the victorious party is deeply committed to nationalization in both those fields, but other industries, including cotton, iron and steel and manufacturing generally saw little immediate change in prospect.

"Leaders of the Labor party are all men with Cabinet experience accustomed to the responsibilities of government," a leading industrialist said today. "There is little danger of ill-considered radical policies sweeping the country.

"Members of my organization feel it is improbable that the party will vote to take over any of the enterprises mentioned except fuel and power. They are so deeply committed on the coal and electric power industries that it is impossible to see how they can avoid nationalizing them."

The Financial Times in its leading editorial tomorrow will say that both business and financial

Continued on Page 2, Column 4

7,000,000 Troops for Single Blow At Japan Planned, Says Devers

By SIDNEY SHALETT
Special to The New York Times.

WASHINGTON, July 26—The United States Army will train and deploy its European veterans and its new troops so that, in conjunction with divisions already in the Pacific, it can hurl 7,000,000 men in a coordinated "single blow" against Japan, instead of attempting to do the job 'piecemeal,' Gen. Jacob L. Devers, new Commanding General of Army Ground Forces, declared today.

At his first news conference since he succeeded Gen. Joseph W. Stilwell, now in the Pacific, as head of the Ground Forces, General Devers, who commanded the Sixth Army Group in southern France, hinted at the plans for a massive blow against the enemy's homeland, and also asserted that our forces being prepared for the Pacific would be trained in "radical" new methods of warfare.

General Devers explained that he should not be taken "too literally" in his description of a 7,000,000-man blow against Japan. Obviously, he pointed out, an Army does not land that many men overnight on an enemy beachhead.

But the Army Ground Forces does intend, he asserted, to have the 7,000,000 men who will consti-

Continued on Page 7, Column 2

BRITISH TURN LEFT

War Regime Swept Out as Laborites Win 390 of 640 Seats

CHURCHILL BIDS ADIEU

Hints at Early Peace—He Stays in House, but Many Ex-Aides Lose

By HERBERT L. MATTHEWS
By Cable to The New York Times.

LONDON, July 26—In one of the most stunning election surprises in the history of democracy, Great Britain swung to the Left today in a landslide that smothered the Conservatives and put Labor into power with a great majority.

Winston Churchill has resigned as Prime Minister and Clement R. Attlee has accepted the King's invitation to form a Laborite Government. The Liberals went down to an equally surprising defeat. The world, which looked to Britain for a guiding trend, has had its tremendous answer. Today and tomorrow and for months or years to come, the Left is the dominating power in global politics.

When the final result came in from the constituency of Hornchurch at 10:30 P. M., Labor had a staggering total of 390 seats out of a Parliament of 640, of which the holders of thirteen seats will not be known until early in August. In the last Parliament, Labor had only 163 and in its greatest previous triumph, in 1929, it had 288.

Conservatives Cut to 195 Seats

The Conservatives had fallen from 358 seats to 195. The Liberals, too, lost seven seats and now have only eleven members in Parliament.

Adding fourteen Liberal Nationals and one National, the former Government is down to 210 seats, whereas if the Liberals, Independent Labor with three seats, the Commonwealth with one, the Communists with two and the Independents with ten are added to Labor, one gets a total of 417.

Such a tremendous majority means that the Labor party can confidently count on a full five-year tenure of office, for it cannot be beaten on any vote of confidence. Out of nearly 25,000,000 votes, Labor alone won nearly 12,000,000. The Conservatives got a little more than 9,000,000 votes. The Labor party did not lose a single seat to the Conservatives, although it gained 130 from that party.

[The vote, according to the press services, was: Labor, 11,962,678; Conservative, 9,018,235; Liberal, 2,280,135; Independent, 545,862.]

The results were a personal, decisive repudiation of Mr. Churchill as a peacetime leader. He himself

Continued on Page 3, Column 2

Churchill Reported Ending Berlin Role

By Cable to The New York Times.

LONDON, July 26—The News Chronicle will say tomorrow that Winston Churchill will not return to the Berlin conference, although the first thing Prime Minister Attlee did was to ask him to do so.

Anthony Eden, former Foreign Secretary, who has been re-elected to the Parliament, said today: "I am anxious still to do my best to help our nation hold its head high in the world as it has the right and pride to do."

Asked whether he would return to Berlin, Mr. Eden said that his services were at the country's disposal and, if he were asked to return tomorrow, as had been previously arranged, he would continue to do his best to help.

LONDON, July 26 (UP)—When Prime Minister Attlee was asked whether Mr. Churchill would return to Berlin with him, he smiled and remained silent.

"All the News That's Fit to Print"

The New York Times.

LATE CITY EDITION
Fair and less humid today. Partly cloudy and warm tomorrow.

Copyright, 1945, by The New York Times Company.

VOL. XCIV..No. 31,968. | Entered as Second-Class Matter, Postoffice, New York, N. Y. | NEW YORK, FRIDAY, AUGUST 3, 1945. | THREE CENTS IN NEW YORK CITY

GERMANY STRIPPED OF INDUSTRY BY BIG 3; 5 POWERS TO PLAN PEACE; FRANCO BARRED; BOMBERS FIRE GREAT NAGASAKI SHIPYARDS

ENEMY PORT RUINED

14 Vessels Are Smashed and 6 Planes Downed by 250 Okinawa Planes

DAY'S BAG 26 SHIPS

Kenney Fliers Wreck 12 in Coast Sweep—Toll of Carrier Blow Soars

By FRANK L. KLUCKHOHN
By Wireless to THE NEW YORK TIMES.

MANILA, Friday, Aug. 3—Nagasaki, one of the three major shipbuilding centers of Japan and ninth port of the empire, was left aflame yesterday, its dockyards smashed and its harbor littered with sunken ships by over 250 planes of Gen. George C. Kenney's Far East Air Force.

Mitchells, Liberators, Mustangs and Thunderbolts, concentrating upon this western Kyushu port, hit the Mitsubishi, Tategami and Koyagishima shipyards, plus the largest marine engine works in Japan. They left flames that were visible for twenty-five miles.

tanker and nine freighters were sunk and a submarine and three other ships were damaged.

[At least twelve other ships of varying size were sunk or damaged in widespread attacks on enemy-controlled waters from Korea southward to Borneo and the Celebes, Gen. Douglas MacArthur's communiqué said today, according to The Associated Press.]

[About one hundred American P-51 Mustang fighter planes, led by a "small number" of B-29's attacked "military targets at scattered points" in the Kanto district of central Honshu, which includes the metropolitan district of Tokyo, for one and a half hours Friday morning (Japanese time), the Japanese Domei agency reported, as recorded by the Federal Communications Commission.

[Fleet Admiral Chester W. Nimitz reported additional damage in Monday's carrier plane attacks on Japan, raising the total of enemy vessels sunk or damaged to 116, of which forty-five were warships, and of planes destroyed to 124.]

Attack at Low Level

Twenty Japanese fighters rising from the inferno of burning and exploding ships and large oil tanks at Nagasaki, were dived on by the Mustangs. Six of them were shot down, each of our fighters getting at least one Japanese plane, the rest fleeing.

Thunderbolts, flying at mast-head height and carrying 1,000-pound bombs, initiated the attack that lasted for hours by sinking the tanker with seven direct hits. More Thunderbolts, arriving twenty-five minutes later, found only debris to hit among oil storage tanks and warehouses.

Penetrating the blinding weather the speedy Mustangs thereupon dive-bombed with 500-pounders, leaving a 5,000-ton freighter burning and rocked by internal explosions.

Taking the ball, a group of Mitchells hit other shipping. Heavies — Liberators — came in next, turning a 6,000-ton freighter on its side with sticks of bombs.

Before the Japanese could recover a second group of Liberators roared in, hitting a transport in the drydock and blasting storage areas.

A lone American reconnaissance plane reported that after this wave the Japanese began to creep from their shelters to fight the raging fires and attempt to rescue personnel from the flaming ships.

At that moment more Thunderbolts and Mitchells came in flat off the water, hitting oil stores, and warehouses and throwing débris, according to eye-witnesses, half a mile over the water. The

Continued on Page 2, Column 3

Army, Navy Deaths Rise to 249,264

By The Associated Press.

WASHINGTON, Aug. 2—Almost a quarter million American soldiers and sailors have died in the war—a total 249,264.

Army figures announced today by Secretary Stimson show 197,676 dead. The latest Navy count of its killed is 51,588. A week ago the dead were 196,918 for the Army and 51,219 for the Navy.

Total casualties from all causes for both services are 1,060,727, or 1,885 more than the 1,058,842 announced a week earlier.

Army wounded are 570,766, missing 34,734 and prisoners of war 117,741. Navy wounded are 72,855, missing 11,611 and prisoners 3,756.

STIMSON REFUSES SPEEDIER RELEASES

Rate to Stand for Present With Point Revisions Later, He Says —War Needs Put 'First'

Special to THE NEW YORK TIMES.

WASHINGTON, Aug. 2—Secretary Stimson declared today that the Army discharge system of eighty-five points would be revised, but not until next year, and that for the present the War Department would not increase its present rate of discharges.

Replying apparently to pressure from members of Congress and other sources for speed-ups in the release of soldiers, Mr. Stimson said:

"We shall not let any man go whose going jeopardizes the life of the men who remain to fight. The operations of the point system must be subordinate to the fighting needs of General MacArthur.

He further declared that many men with more than the required eighty-five points would not be released until replacements with similar skills had been obtained.

Since May 12, when demobilization for "high-point" men began, 235,000 have been released, the Secretary said. At present 565,000 others with eighty-five points or more were eligible for release. He reiterated the Army's pledge that 1,500,000 men would be released under the point system by June 1, 1946.

MacArthur's Needs Emphasized

In referring to General MacArthur's needs, Secretary Stimson inferentially criticized Harold L. Ickes, Secretary of the Interior, who declared recently that unless the Army released men for the coal mines civilians would be short of fuel this winter.

Stating that "our first duty is to give General MacArthur the men he needs to win the war with the least loss of men and time," Mr. Stimson interjected:

"And that's a point you want to remember when somebody says you're going to be in need of coal next winter—or some other special reasons."

The Secretary declined, however, to reply to the attack by Sen-

Continued on Page 13, Column 2

ECONOMY MAPPED

Drain on German State Called Relatively Mild —War Curbs Severe

SOVIET NEEDS FACED

Big Powers to Supervise Small Nations' Share in the Indemnity

By JOHN H. CRIDER
Special to THE NEW YORK TIMES.

WASHINGTON, Aug. 2—The Big Three agreement on reparations was believed by officials here to reflect the view of American experts that German reparations should be of a nature and amount to provide neither the excuse for rebuilding the German industrial war potential nor a need for Allied assistance in providing for the reindustrialization that would be necessary if she were to make high cash reparation payments.

The principles laid down in the reparations section of the Potsdam agreement appeared to be mild in comparison with the exactions made of Germany after the last war, but in terms of transfer from Germany of the industrial basis for her great war-making power and the stripping of her economy down to a level merely sufficient to sustain her "peaceful needs" it was regarded as much more severe.

The reparations accord of the Big Three not only sanctioned the removal of vast amounts of Germany's industrial potential across her borders but also employed language that approves such removals as Russia has already made and will make in the immediate future.

General Principles Stated

Except for exposition of the basic "deal" between Russia, on one hand, and the United States and Britain, on the other, the Big Three confined themselves to a statement of reparation principles that will be spelled out in detail by the Allied Commission on Reparations and the Allied Control Council.

Regarded as of extreme importance was the inclusion of France as a party to the basic determination, deferred by the Big Three, which will be to decide the precise level of economic activity that should be permitted in post-war Germany and how much capital equipment she will need to sustain herself on that basis.

The Potsdam agreement continued, however, the principle that reparations shall be handled in the first instance by the great powers, with the smaller Allied nations presumably applying through them for their share of reparations and indemnity.

Specific provision is made that the Soviet Union undertakes to settle the reparation claims of Poland from its own share of reparations.

Reference to the basic determination in relation to the whole

Continued on Page 9, Column 4

THE EUROPEAN COUNTRIES AFFECTED BY BIG THREE DECISIONS

Aug. 3, 1945

The conference agreed on the principles of a coordinated policy for Germany (1) involving complete demilitarization, territorial losses and severe economic control. For Austria (2), extension of the authority of the Russian-sponsored provisional government to the whole country will be considered. Arrangement of peace treaties first with Italy (3) and then with Bulgaria (4), Rumania (5), Hungary (6) and Finland (10) was made the business of a five-power Council of Foreign Ministers, which is to meet regularly in London (11). Revision of procedure of the Allied Control Commission on reportorial freedom in southeastern Europe was furthered. The "orderly, humane" transfer of Germans from Hungary, Czechoslovakia (7) and Poland (8) was backed. Russian proposals for Poland's western boundary and Soviet acquisition of the Koenigsberg area (9, with detailed map on Page 8) were supported. The Big Three banned application for United Nations membership by the Franco Government of Spain (12).

NO WORD ON JAPAN

Russia Gets Majority of Reparations, Sharing in Western Zones

FRONTIERS PUT OFF

Poland Interim Ruler of Part of Reich—United Nations Bar Spain

The text of the communiqué by the Big Three is on Page 8.

By FELIX BELAIR JR.
Special to THE NEW YORK TIMES.

WASHINGTON, Aug. 2 — The broad outlines of a post-war Germany reduced to a third-rate industrial power with all its economy operating at subsistence levels, incapable of waging war and stripped of East Prussia and a large area along the Oder River were laid down in a joint communiqué today by the Big Three, reporting on the meeting in Berlin.

Bearing the signatures of J. V. Stalin, Harry S. Truman and C. R. Attlee, the document, released simultaneously at 5:30 P. M. in Washington, London and Moscow, ended any further debate whether Germany was to have a "hard" or "soft" peace. That peace, in the language of the communiqué, will be designed "to convince the German people that they have suffered a total military defeat and that they cannot escape responsibility for what they have brought upon themselves since their own ruthless warfare and the fanatical Nazi resistance have destroyed German economy and made chaos and suffering inevitable."

The document did not mention Russia's intentions on the Pacific war but it ended on the significant note that "during the conference there were meetings between the Chifs of Staff of the three Governments on military matters of common interest." If these "matters" went beyond European zones of occupation, the communiqué did not explain.

The conference warned the present Government of Spain that it need not apply for admission to the United Nations' organization. That Government, according to the communiqué, "having been founded with the support of the Axis powers, does not, in view of its orogin, its nature, its record and its close association with the aggressor states, possess the qualifications necessary to justify such

Continued on Page 8, Column 2

CONFERENCE SCENE REVEALS DILEMMAS

Problem of Keeping Equality of Delegations Complicated by Layout of Palace

By TANIA LONG
By Wireless to THE NEW YORK TIMES.

BERLIN, Aug. 2—A little of the drama of the Big Three conference just ended and much of the flavor and atmosphere in which the historic meeting took place were revealed today when correspondents were allowed into the hitherto closed areas where the delegations

Continued on Page 10, Column 2

Communique Highlights

By The United Press.

WASHINGTON, Aug. 2—Highlights of the Big Three communique from Potsdam:

No mention was made of the Pacific war, nor of Russia's connection with it. But the communiqué said that the Chiefs of Staff held meetings on "military matters of common interest."

Agreement was reached on reparations from Germany. Each of the three nations will fill its own claims, largely by taking goods and equipment from its own occupation zone. In addition, Russia will get 10 per cent of removable industrial capital equipment from the western zones as a flat payment, and an additional 15 per cent for which she will pay in goods. The Western Allies retain sole claim to captured gold.

Russia will get Koenigsberg and adjacent territory in East Prussia. Poland will get a slice of Germany, including the rest of East Prussia, and the former free city of Danzig.

Germans in Poland, Czechoslovakia and Hungary shall be transferred to Germany "in an orderly and humane manner." Agreement was reached on a detailed program for the control of Germany, to strip the Reich of war-making capacity, smash huge cartels, drive out nazism and "convince the German people that they have suffered a total military defeat."

Under disarmament, all German land, naval and air forces, and all Nazi militaristic organizations will be "completely and finally abolished."

War criminal trials will begin soon. The first list of defendants will be published before Sept. 1. A Council of Foreign Ministers of the Big Five, includ-

Continued on Page 8, Column 2

PRESIDENT SAILS AFTER SEEING KING

Monarch and Truman Confer at Luncheon and Exchange Visits at Plymouth

By CHARLES E. EGAN
By Wireless to THE NEW YORK TIMES.

PLYMOUTH, England, Aug. 2—President Truman was en route home tonight aboard the cruiser Augusta after a six-hour stop-over in Britain during which he had luncheon with King George and discussed with him the results of the Big Three conference.

The informal visit took the President considerably out of his way, but it was made at his insistence as a tribute to the fighting spirit of the British people. Mr. Truman expressed regret to the King that his stay could not be longer, but explained that it was imperative that he get home and report on the conference to the American people.

Today's trip gave the President his first glimpse of Britain. As an officer in World War I, he went directly to France and returned to the United States directly from there. It also was the first time in twenty-six years that a President of the United States had visited Britain. President Wilson paid a state visit at the time of the peace conference after the last war. The

Continued on Page 10, Column 6

War News Summarized

FRIDAY, AUGUST 3, 1945

Detailed plans for the extermination of nazism and militarism in Germany were drawn up at the Berlin Conference in terms sufficiently clear "to convince the German people that they have suffered a total military defeat and that they cannot escape responsibility for what they have brought upon themselves." Just what was accomplished by the Big Three was made public in Washington, London and Moscow yesterday.

Germany will be decentralized politically and economically at the earliest possible date.

A Council of Foreign Ministers, including those of China and France, was created to prepare tentative peace treaties for all European Axis countries other than Germany. The first task will be a treaty with Italy.

Boundaries were generally left for the peace conference, except that Russia's request for the Baltic port of Koenigsberg was recognized and Poland's claims to a frontier along the Oder and the Neisse were tentatively approved. Full freedom in Poland and in the Balkans was promised to Allied correspondents.

So long as Spain is ruled by Franco she will not be invited to join the United Nations.

Japan was referred to only obliquely—through the inclusion of China in the Council of Foreign Secretaries; as one of the reasons for expediting peace with Italy, which has gone to war with Japan; and through the statement that "military matters of common interest" had been discussed by the American, British and Russian Chiefs of Staff. [All the foregoing 1:8; maps Pages 1 and 8.]

A large measure of agreement was reached on problems of German reparations. [1:3.]

President Truman is on his way home after having had luncheon with King George VI. He will report to the American people upon his return. [1:7.]

Pierre Laval, who wept during interrogation in Fresnes Prison, will testify at the Pétain trial today. [1:6-7.]

In the Pacific, 250 Far East Air Force planes left the port and railway terminal of Nagasaki, on Kyushu, in flames. Ten ships were sunk; three others and a submarine were damaged. One B-29 out of the 820 that dropped the record load of 6,632 tons on Honshu targets was lost. Waters between Korea and Japan were heavily mined. [1:1; map P. 2.]

Additional reports raised the havoc wrought by Third Fleet carrier planes on the Tokyo, Nagoya and Maizuru areas last Monday. Tokyo said O Island, at the mouth of Tokyo Bay, had been shelled. [2:1.]

Japanese troops pushed their floating pocket in China closer to Nanchang. Ifeng was recaptured by the Chinese and a bitter battle was reported on the outskirts of Kian. [2:8.]

Vandenberg Proposes Government Call Industry-Labor Peace Parley

By LOUIS STARK
Special to THE NEW YORK TIMES.

WASHINGTON, Aug. 2—Senator Vandenberg, Republican, of Michigan, in a letter suggested today that Secretary of Labor Schwellenbach sponsor a labor-industry-Government conference so that all groups interested in industrial peace "frankly face the need for a better, a surer and wiser code for their mutual advancement in the desperately uncertain times that lie ahead in an otherwise chaotic post-war world."

Mr. Schwellenbach immediately endorsed the idea, which had originated from Mr. Vandenberg's observations at the United Nations Conference in San Francisco. The Secretary plunged at once into a series of meetings which will serve as the ground work for a plan to be submitted to President Truman on the latter's return from Europe.

In his reply to the Vandenberg letter, Mr. Schwellenbach said that he had "been thinking more and more during these last few weeks about the desirability of calling a conference of industry and labor," and he pointed to his views on the subject as set forth in an address at Superior, Wis., on July 21.

Spokesmen for labor and indus-

Continued on page 15, Column 2

Laval Summoned to Testify Today; Petain's Counsel Protests Strongly

By G. H. ARCHAMBAULT
By Wireless to THE NEW YORK TIMES.

PARIS, Aug. 2—Pierre Laval must testify tomorrow in Marshal Henri-Philippe Pétain's treason trial, Judge Pierre Mongibeaux ruled today.

The decision was taken on the initiative of the jurors, who conferred for more than one hour with the three judges. As soon as the decision had been announced, Fernand Payen, the leading defense counsel, raised a point of law. He argued that, under the rules of evidence, there should be a preliminary hearing before an examining magistrate, after which Laval's testimony would be communicated to both the prosecution and the defense. He added that Laval might introduce the names of many political leaders and army commanders who would insist on being heard and thus bring the trial back to the controversial phase that the court declared yesterday to be positively ended. The court overruled the objection.

Léon Noel, Ambassador in Warsaw when the war broke out and later one of the French armistice delegates, was called by the de-

Continued on Page 6, Column 4

Big Three Prescribe Freedom of Press

By The United Press.

WASHINGTON, Aug. 2—The Big Three conference communiqué had this to say about freedom of the press in Europe:

In Poland—"The three powers note that the Polish Provisional Government * * * has agreed to the holding of free and unfettered elections * * * and that representatives of the Allied press shall enjoy full freedom to report to the world upon developments in Poland before and during the elections."

In other former Axis countries—"The three Governments have no doubt that, in view of the changed conditions resulting from the termination of the war in Europe, representatives of the Allied press will enjoy full freedom to report to the world upon developments in Rumania, Bulgaria, Hungary and Finland."

Yugoslavia was not mentioned.

In Germany—"Subject to the necessity for maintaining military security, freedom of * * * [the] press * * * shall be permitted."

"All the News That's Fit to Print"

The New York Times.

LATE CITY EDITION
Partly cloudy, less humid today. Cloudy and warm tomorrow.
Temperatures Yesterday—Max., 72; Min., 66
Sunrise today, 5:07 A. M.; Sunset, 8:06 P. M.

VOL. XCIV..No. 31,972. Entered as Second-Class Matter, Postoffice, New York, N. Y. NEW YORK, TUESDAY, AUGUST 7, 1945. THREE CENTS IN NEW YORK CITY

FIRST ATOMIC BOMB DROPPED ON JAPAN; MISSILE IS EQUAL TO 20,000 TONS OF TNT; TRUMAN WARNS FOE OF A 'RAIN OF RUIN'

HIRAM W. JOHNSON, REPUBLICAN DEAN IN THE SENATE, DIES

Isolationist Helped Prevent U. S. Entry Into League—Opposed World Charter

CALIFORNIA EX-GOVERNOR

Ran for Vice President With Theodore Roosevelt in '12—In Washington Since '17

Special to The New York Times.

WASHINGTON, Aug. 6—Senator Hiram Warren Johnson of California lifelong isolationist who helped prevent this country's entry into the League of Nations and fought all "foreign entanglements" through a second World War, died in his sleep this morning at Bethesda Naval Hospital, nine days after, ill but consistent, he had paired his vote against ratification of the United Nations Charter. Death was caused by a thrombosis of a cerebral artery. Mrs. Johnson was with him when the end came.

When word reached the Capitol of the passing of the oldest member of the Senate in point of service, save Senator Kenneth McKellar, the President pro tempore, the mourning was deep. With great personal affection colleagues paid humble tribute to his integrity of character, his liberalism and his steadfastness to his ideals and convictions. They joined in declaring that the country had lost a great statesman.

Senator Johnson, who was serving the fourth year of his fifth term in the Senate, would have been 79 years old on Sept. 2. Although his health had been failing during the last two years and though the thundering voice which had conveyed his eloquence through innumerable stirring debates had become little more than a whisper, friends believed he planned to seek a sixth term in 1947.

He went to the hospital July 18. Five days before that he had cast the lone vote in the Foreign Relations Committee, of which he was the ranking minority member, against reporting the new World Charter to the Senate without change. He did not participate in the floor debate on this document, which won Senate approval by a vote of 82—2. However, he clashed spiritedly with colleagues while the hearings were in progress.

Funeral arrangements awaited the arrival of the Senator's son, Lieut. Col. Hiram W. Johnson Jr., who was flying here from California.

Capper Becomes the Dean

The death of Senator Johnson made Senator Arthur Capper of Kansas, who last month marked his eightieth birthday, the Republican dean of the Senate. It also elevated him to the ranking minority membership on the Foreign Relations Committee, with which Senator Johnson had been so conspicuously identified through the many years of his unshaken position on foreign policy. Mr. Capper, too, with Senators McKellar, Carter Glass of Virginia, David I. Walsh of Massachusetts and Peter G. Gerry, was in the League fight of 1919 and 1920. He supported it, with reservations.

The career of Senator Johnson, from his entrance into the Senate from the Governorship of California in March of 1917, was one distinctly lacking in compromise or reservation. In 1912 he had bolted his party with Theodore Roosevelt and had become his running mate on the Bull Moose ticket. In 1932 he again bolted to support Franklin D. Roosevelt for the Presidency but broke bitterly with the President when he ran for his third term.

In 1919 Mr. Johnson joined with Senators Lodge, Borah, Reed,

Continued on Page 23, Column 4

Jet Plane Explosion Kills Major Bong, Top U. S. Ace

Flier Who Downed 40 Japanese Craft, Sent Home to Be 'Safe,' Was Flying New 'Shooting Star' as a Test Pilot

By The United Press.

BURBANK, Calif., Aug. 6—Maj. Richard Bong, America's greatest air ace, died today in the flaming wreckage of a jet propelled fighter plane which crashed while he was testing it.

Only 24 years old, he wore twenty-six decorations including the nation's highest award, the Congressional Medal of Honor. He had survived countless air battles and shot down forty Japanese planes without a scratch.

The knowledge he gained in those battles was too valuable to risk, so he was brought home to "safe" duty. He was on that "safe" duty today when his P-80, the Shooting Star, hurtled over a clump of trees and burst like a bomb in a field.

Witnesses did not agree on the cause of the crash. One Army flier said that Major Bong overshot the Lockheed airport. Another witness, John McKinney of North Hollywood reported that he saw something fall out of the plane's tail.

"The plane started to wobble up and down, then went into a left bank and hit the ground," he stated. "It exploded and burned and scattered wreckage over about a block square."

Major Bong was trying to get out of the ship when it crashed. He had released the escape hatch and was partly clear. He had pulled the ripcord to his parachute, and the silken folds lay about the body as the flames swept over it.

With a roaring sigh, the plane, like a giant blowtorch, shot over the airport just before 3 P. M. and then lurched over the trees and nosed down into the field, a mile away.

Smoke and flame surged up and crowds rushed from the airport. By the time anyone could reach the scene the ship had been almost consumed.

The crash scene was near the intersection of Cahuenga and Oxnard Boulevards and barely out-

Continued on page 15, Column 2

MORRIS IS ACCUSED OF 'TAKING A WALK'

Fusion Official 'Sad to Part Company'—McGoldrick Sees Only Tammany Aided

The No Deal ticket, headed by Council President Newbold Morris, "can only serve the interests of Tammany Hall," Controller Joseph D. McGoldrick, candidate for re-election on the Republican-Liberal-Fusion party slate, declared yesterday in a fresh attack on the third-party ticket injected over the week-end into the city Mayoralty campaign.

A short while later Gabriel A. Wechsler, general secretary of the City Fusion party, which supported Mayor La Guardia and Mr. Morris in previous city campaigns, accused Mr. Morris of "taking a walk away from the good government forces."

To both charges Mr. Morris declared he would stand on his statement of Sunday that he was not interested in "just taking votes" away from Judge Jonah J. Goldstein, Republican-Liberal-Fusion candidate for Mayor, or from William O'Dwyer, his Democratic-American Labor party opponent.

"I have no comment," he said, "since I stand on my statement of Sunday. We are waging an affirmative campaign."

Informed that Hyman Blumberg,

Continued on Page 19, Column 6

CHINESE WIN MORE OF 'INVASION COAST'

Smash Into Port 121 Miles Southwest of Canton—Big Area Open for Landing

By The Associated Press.

CHUNGKING, China, Aug. 6—Chinese troops have broken into the South China port of Yeungkong and cleared a fifty-mile stretch of the Chinese "invasion coast" west of Hong Kong, Generalissimo Chiang Kai-shek's headquarters said today.

Swaying block-by-block street fighting is raging in the strategic coastal highway town, 121 miles southwest of Canton, a communiqué said.

By breaking into Yeungkong Chinese forces won control of a fifty-mile coastal stretch leading west to Tinpak, which lies east of Luichow Peninsula on the South China Sea. The coastal area now is open to a virtually unopposed landing should American forces choose it for a staging point for supplies to the armies of South China.

West of Luichow Peninsula another 145-mile coastal stretch extending to the Indo-China frontier is under Chinese control and observers believe the Chinese soon may launch a concerted drive from the west and east that would seal off the Japanese on the Luichow

Continued on Page 2, Column 7

Turks Talk War if Russia Presses; Prefer Vain Battle to Surrender

By SAM POPE BREWER

By Wireless to The New York Times.

ANKARA, Turkey, Aug. 6—Russo-Turkish relations weigh heavy on Turkish minds these days. All leading editors commented today on various aspects of the Russian claims against Turkey.

The Potsdam conference leaves the situation virtually unchanged so far as the Turks can see, but they seem to agree that they would go to war, however hopeless such a war might be, rather than yield before the threat of force. Suggestions from London and Washington that the Russians have been asked to moderate their demands give little reassurance here.

The Potsdam communiqué created more confusion than confidence and the Turks are still trying to decide whether the fact that the conference did not deal with certain specific questions means that it was a failure.

Many point out that all the really thorny questions still are unsettled. The Turks probably do not see a relative importance among world problems of Russian demands on Turkey, but point out that the important question of principle is involved. The general and apparently official argument is that the status of the Straits cannot be modified by a bilateral agreement but must be discussed at a conference of the signatories of the Montreux Convention, with America replacing Japan. The signatories were Great Britain, France, Russia, Japan, Turkey, Greece, Rumania, Yugoslavia and Bulgaria.

The grounds for the Russian claims to Kars and Ardahan are not clear, but throughout the Near and Mideast in recent months

Continued on Page 12, Column 1

KYUSHU CITY RAZED

Kenney's Planes Blast Tarumizu in Record Blow From Okinawa

ROCKET SITE IS SEEN

125 B-29's Hit Japan's Toyokawa Naval Arsenal in Demolition Strike

By FRANK L. KLUCKHOHN

By Wireless to The New York Times.

MANILA, Tuesday, Aug. 7—More than 400 fighters and bombers, speeding at chimney-top level for two hours Sunday over Tarumizu in southern Kyushu in the largest single attack launched by Gen. George C. Kenney's Far East Air Forces to date, leveled that city's munitions factories and aircraft and munitions storage depots and waterfront installations.

Rockets and demolition bombs were poured by waves of B-26 Invaders, B-25 Mitchells and Mustangs and Thunderbolts of the Fifth and Seventh Air Forces from Okinawa, supported by a few B-24 Liberators carrying big bombs.

[Tarumizu, about 350 miles from Okinawa, appeared to be a site at which the Japanese might be preparing a rocket campaign against the American base, said a United Press dispatch. FEAF pilots reported seeing in the area, which has extensive cave construction, what seemed to be Japanese robot planes and also a huge catapult-like machine, extending over the water, that might be a rocket launcher.

[About 125 B-29's hit the Toyokawa naval arsenal of Japan in a demolition bombing Tuesday noon, Strategic Air Forces headquarters at Guam reported.]

The planes over Tarumizu met scant resistance, as our fliers took their time to assure the highest

Continued on Page 11, Column 2

War News Summarized

TUESDAY, AUGUST 7, 1945

One bomb hit Japan on Sunday night, but it struck with the force of 20,000 tons of TNT. Where it landed had been the city of Hiroshima; what is there now has not yet been learned.

The attack, dramatically announced by President Truman sixteen hours after the missile had struck, was with an atomic bomb, a "harnessing of the basic power of the universe," he said. "The force from which the sun draws its power has been loosed against those who brought war to the Far East. And the end is not yet."

Details of the missile are closely guarded, but the 125,000 workers who saw materials pour into their factories never saw anything go out. The bomb is the result of pooling British-American scientific knowledge begun in 1940. "We have spent two billion dollars on the greatest scientific gamble in history—and won," Mr. Truman said, and warned:

"We are now prepared to obliterate more rapidly and completely every productive enterprise the Japanese have above ground in any city. It was to spare the Japanese public from utter destruction that the ultimatum of July 26 was issued at Potsdam. If they do not now accept our terms they may expect a rain of ruin from the air."

Secretary of War Stimson detailed the story of research and production and forecast improvements to increase the effectiveness of the "atomic bomb" several times. Congress will be asked to establish a committee to control peacetime use.

Hiroshima was a major military target, a city of 318,000 persons thickly settled around a quartermaster's depot, an embarkation port, armament and airplane parts plants. [All the foregoing 1:8.]

All production was in the United States at two plants at Oak Ridge, near Knoxville, Tenn., and one at Richland, Wash. A scientific laboratory was maintained in Sante Fe, N. M. [1:6.]

Former Prime Minister Churchill told of Britain's part, including costly attacks on German "heavy water" plants and the race to outstrip the Nazis. He praised American scientific achievement and gave full credit to President Roosevelt and his advisers. [1:5.]

Tokyo made no mention of what had happened to Hiroshima but rail service in that area was canceled. [1:7.]

Okinawa sent out 400 planes that left Tarumizu, on Kyushu's Kagoshima Bay, in flaming wreckage. About 125 "Superforts" bombed Toyokawa naval arsenal by daylight. [1:4; map p. 11.]

Chinese troops have broken into the port of Yeungkong and have cleared a large stretch of the south China coast west of Hong Kong and east of the Luichow Peninsula. [1:3; map P. 2.]

Moscow, moving to implement Potsdam decisions, has resumed diplomatic relations with Finland and Rumania. [11:4.]

The Germans received an opportunity to develop democratic talents when the United States and Great Britain authorized local trade unions and political parties in their zones of occupation. [12:2.]

France is expected to ratify the United Nations Charter and then the Bretton Woods monetary plan in the near future. [13:6.] Marshal Pétain was accused of having asked Hitler for help in regaining France's colonies. [13:1.]

Argentina has lifted the state of siege in effect since Pearl Harbor. [14:6.]

REPORT BY BRITAIN

'By God's Mercy' We Beat Nazis to Bomb, Churchill Says

ROOSEVELT AID CITED

Raiders Wrecked Norse Laboratory in Race for Key to Victory

The text of Mr. Churchill's statement is on Page 8.

By CLIFTON DANIEL

By Wireless to The New York Times.

LONDON, Aug. 6—The hitherto secret details of the grisly race between Germany and the Allies to find a weapon so destructive that it would insure absolute victory—a race not only between scientists but also between under-cover agents—were recounted in London tonight after it had been disclosed that the first atomic bomb had been dropped on Japan.

"By God's mercy British and American science outpaced all German efforts," said a statement by former Prime Minister Churchill written before he left office and issued from 10 Downing Street by his successor, Clement R. Attlee.

"The possession of these powers by the Germans at any time might have altered the result of the war," Mr. Churchill said, "and profound anxiety was felt by those who were informed."

The British Isles, which endured the terrors of flying bombs and rockets, did hear repeated rumors that Adolf Hitler's V-3 weapon was to be an atomic bomb, but they never knew until tonight how close they came to being the first victims of its destructive power. Much less did they suspect what

Continued on Page 9, Column 1

Steel Tower 'Vaporized' In Trial of Mighty Bomb

Scientists Awe-Struck as Blinding Flash Lighted New Mexico Desert and Great Cloud Bore 40,000 Feet Into Sky

By LEWIS WOOD

Special to The New York Times.

WASHINGTON, Aug. 6—A blinding flash many times as brilliant as the midday sun and a massive, multi-colored cloud boiling up 40,000 feet into the air accompanied the first test firing of an atomic bomb on July 16, three weeks ago today. Set in the remote desert-lands of New Mexico, the experiment was seen against a wild background where rain poured in torrents, and lightning pierced the sky up to the zero hour of the explosion at 5:30 A. M.

A steel tower from which the atomic weapon hung was vaporized. In its place was only a huge, sloping crater. At the moment of the explosion a mountain range three miles distant stood out sharply in brilliant light.

"Then," said the War Department in a description, "came a tremendous, sustained roar and a heavy pressure wave which knocked down two men outside the control tower (10,000 yards, or more than five miles, away.)"

Before the detonation scientists waited in tense expectancy. Minutes lengthened seemingly to hours. Lying face downward, with their feet toward the steel tower, the watchers waited, nearly breathless. They were "reaching into the unknown" and did not know what would happen.

On the instant that all was over these men leaped to their feet. The terrible tension ended, they shook hands, embraced each other and shouted in glee. Behind their triumph was sober consciousness of possessing the means to "insure the speedy conclusion of the war and save thousands of American lives."

The scene of the great drama was the Alamogordo Air Base, 120 miles southeast of Albuquerque. Here the scientists strove to unlock the secret upon which $2,000,000,000 had been spent.

Graphic word pictures of the

Continued on Page 5, Column 1

ATOM BOMBS MADE IN 3 HIDDEN 'CITIES'

Secrecy on Weapon So Great That Not Even Workers Knew of Their Product

By JAY WALZ

Special to The New York Times.

WASHINGTON, Aug. 6—The War Department revealed today how three "hidden cities" with a total population of 100,000 inhabitants sprang into being as a result of the $2,000,000,000 atomic bomb project, how they did their work without knowing what it was all about, and how they kept the biggest secret of the war.

One of these, Oak Ridge, situated where only oak and pine trees had dotted small farms before, is today the fifth largest city in Tennessee. Its population of 75,000 persons has thirteen supermarkets, nine drug stores and seven theatres.

A second town of 7,000 was built for reasons of isolation and security on a New Mexico mesa. The third, named Richland Village, houses 17,000 men, women and children on remote banks of the Columbia River in the State of Washington.

None of the people, who came to these developments from homes all the way from Maine to California, had the slightest idea of what they were making in the gigantic Gov-

Continued on Page 3, Column 2

TRAINS CANCELED IN STRICKEN AREA

Traffic Around Hiroshima Is Disrupted — Japanese Still Sift Havoc by Split Atoms

By The United Press.

WASHINGTON, Aug. 6—The Osaka radio, without referring to the atomic bomb dropped on Hiroshima, hinted tonight at the terrific damage it must have caused by announcing that train service in the Hiroshima and other areas had been canceled.

First mention of the bomb came in a Japanese Domei agency dispatch announcing that President Truman and Prime Minister Attlee had disclosed that the new missile had been dropped on Hiroshima.

The Office of War Information began telling the Japanese today what hit them. OWI branch transmitters in San Francisco, Hawaii and Saipan beamed President Truman's statement on the atomic bomb to Japan.

Edward Barrett, director of the OWI's overseas branch, said that the President's announcement and related information on the atomic bomb will dominate the OWI's normal Japanese transmissions for the next several days.

LONDON, Tuesday, Aug. 7 (UP)—The Japanese Domei news agency, in a dispatch recorded by the British radio, said today that

Continued on Page 7, Column 3

Reich Exile Emerges as Heroine In Denial to Nazis of Atom's Secret

Special to The New York Times.

WASHINGTON, Aug. 6—How Germany twice narrowly missed the secret of harnessing atomic energy by splitting uranium atoms and releasing the most powerful destructive force on earth was recalled today in War Department reports on the atomic bomb.

Development of the bomb after more than ten years of experimentation and research marks the first time that Prof. Albert Einstein's theory of relativity has been put to practical use outside the laboratory: the equation by which he showed the existence of a definite relationship of matter, energy and the velocity of light.

That the new bomb may be far from its maximum devastating potential was indicated by the War Department's statement that said:

"The energy we are now able to utilize in the atomic bombs, at 100 per cent efficiency, constitutes only one-tenth of 1 per cent of the total energy present in the material. But even one-hundredth of 1 per cent is still the most destructive force by far on this earth."

The principal character in the dramatic story of the long search for a method of releasing atomic energy is Dr. Lise Meitner, a woman physicist whom the Nazis expelled from Germany as a "non-Aryan." With her associates, Dr. Otto Hahn and Dr. F. Strassmann, both chemists, she had been working in the Kaiser Wilhelm Institute in Berlin, bombarding uranium atoms with neutrons and then submitting the uranium to chemical analysis.

As the War Department tells the story:

To their amazement, they found the element barium in the debris of the smashed uranium atoms.

Continued on Page 7, Column 1

NEW AGE USHERED

Day of Atomic Energy Hailed by President, Revealing Weapon

HIROSHIMA IS TARGET

'Impenetrable' Cloud of Dust Hides City After Single Bomb Strikes

Truman, Stimson statements on atomic bomb, Page 4.

By SIDNEY SHALETT

Special to The New York Times.

WASHINGTON, Aug. 6—The White House and War Department announced today that an atomic bomb, possessing more power than 20,000 tons of TNT, a destructive force equal to the load of 2,000 B-29's and more than 2,000 times the blast power of what previously was the world's most devastating bomb, had been dropped on Japan.

The announcement, first given to the world in utmost solemnity by President Truman, made it plain that one of the scientific landmarks of the century had been passed, and that the "age of atomic energy," which can be a tremendous force for the advancement of civilization as well as for destruction, was at hand.

At 10:45 o'clock this morning, a statement by the President was issued at the White House that sixteen hours earlier—about the time that citizens on the Eastern seaboard were sitting down to their Sunday suppers—an American plane had dropped the single atomic bomb on the Japanese city of Hiroshima, an important army center.

Japanese Solemnly Warned

What happened at Hiroshima is not yet known. The War Department said it "as yet was unable to make an accurate report" because "an impenetrable cloud of dust and smoke" masked the target area from reconnaissance planes. The Secretary of War will release the story "as soon as accurate details of the results of the bombing become available."

But in a statement vividly describing the results of the first test of the atomic bomb in New Mexico, the War Department told how an immense steel tower had been "vaporized" by the tremendous explosion, how a 40,000-foot cloud rushed into the sky, and two observers were knocked down at a point 10,000 yards away. And President Truman solemnly warned:

"It was to spare the Japanese people from utter destruction that the ultimatum of July 26 was issued at Potsdam. Their leaders promptly rejected that ultimatum. If they do not now accept our terms, they may expect a rain of ruin from the air the like of which has never been seen on this earth."

Most Closely Guarded Secret

The President referred to the joint statement issued by the heads of the American, British and Chinese Governments, in which terms of surrender were outlined to the Japanese and warning given that rejection would mean complete destruction of Japan's power to make war.

[The atomic bomb weighs about 400 pounds and is capable of utterly destroying a town, a representative of the British Ministry of Aircraft Production said in London, the United Press reported.]

What is this terrible new weapon, which the War Department also calls the "Cosmic Bomb"? It is the harnessing of the energy of the atom, which is the basic power of the universe. As President Truman said, "The force from which the sun draws its power has been loosed against those who brought war to the Far East."

"Atomic fission"—in other

Continued on Page 2, Column 2

U.S. Air Force

Mushroom cloud forms over Nagasaki, Japan, after atomic bomb attack on 9 August 1945.

"All the News That's Fit to Print"

The New York Times.

LATE CITY EDITION
Sunny with low humidity today. Partly cloudy, warmer tomorrow.
Temperatures Yesterday—Max., 77; Min., 66
Sunrise today, 5:59 A. M.; Sunset, 8:06 P. M.

VOL. XCIV. No. 31,974. Entered as Second-Class Matter, Postoffice, New York, N. Y. NEW YORK, THURSDAY, AUGUST 9, 1945. THREE CENTS IN NEW YORK CITY

SOVIET DECLARES WAR ON JAPAN; ATTACKS MANCHURIA, TOKYO SAYS; ATOM BOMB LOOSED ON NAGASAKI

TRUMAN TO REPORT TO PEOPLE TONIGHT ON BIG 3 AND WAR

Half-Hour Speech by Radio to Cover a Wide Range of Problems Facing the World

HE SIGNS PEACE CHARTER

And Thus Makes This Country the First to Complete All Ratification Requirements

By The Associated Press.

WASHINGTON, Aug. 8—President Truman will report to the country on the Potsdam conference over all radio networks at 10 P. M., Eastern war time, tomorrow in a thirty-minute speech.

The Presidential secretary, Charles G. Ross, said today that the speech, which probably would also be short-waved abroad, would go into greater detail than the communiqué issued by the Big Three at the close of the meeting July 26.

Mr. Truman worked on the speech today as well as on a mass of other paper work which accumulated during his month-long absence, and signed into full ratification the United Nations Charter.

He held his calling list to a minimum, including brief conferences with Senators Hatch of New Mexico and Kilgore of West Virginia, and Henry L. Stimson, Secretary of War.

The Stimson conference was devoted to further discussion of the atomic bomb.

Associates of the President indicated that his report on the Potsdam conference would probably mention the new and revolutionary bomb used for the first time against Japan.

Full Appraisal May Be Given

A full appraisal of revised conditions, including Russia's declaration of war against Japan, may come in Mr. Truman's broadcast.

Originally the speech was expected to be primarily a report on the Soviet-British-American agreements announced at the end of the Potsdam conference. These dealt mainly with Europe, keeping Germany under strict surveillance, and the writing of peace treaties.

It became known today that Mr. Truman had four or five names under consideration for the vacancy on the Supreme Court, and the decision appeared imminent.

One of the names is that of Senator Austin, Republican, of Vermont, who has been endorsed by his Democratic colleague, Senator Hatch. It was to renew his suggestion that Mr. Austin be appointed to succeed Justice Owen Roberts, who retired, that brought Mr. Hatch to the White House today.

"Of course the President made no commitments," Mr. Hatch told reporters later, "but he definitely is considering both the appointment of a Republican and Senator Austin. Of course that is only a possibility."

Justice Roberts, appointed by President Hoover in 1930, was one of two Republicans in the present makeup of the high court. Chief Justice Harlan F. Stone is the remaining member of that party.

Charter Goes to Archives

Special to The New York Times.

WASHINGTON, Aug. 8—When President Truman signed today the document by which he ratified the Charter of the United Nations, the United States thereby became the first country to complete its action for bringing the Charter into force.

Several other countries have ratified or taken action with a view to ratification, but no instrument of ratification has yet been received from any of them by the State Department, which is the

Continued on Page 3, Column 5

Foreigners Asked To Stay at Home

Special to The New York Times.

WASHINGTON, Aug. 8—Discouragement of unessential travel by foreigners to the United States was ordered by the Government today through the State Department.

"The Department of State has always traditionally done everything in its power to promote the travel of citizens of other countries of the Western Hemisphere to the United States," said the announcement. "However, the United States Government is now engaged in a gigantic military operation in deploying forces and supplies from the European theatre to the Pacific area. This tremendous task places an unprecedented burden on the transportation system."

The citizens of other countries should realize the situation, the statement said, and postpone trips to the United States unless they were directly connected with the war.

TAMMANY OUSTS LAST OF REBELS

County Committee Ratifies Executive Group's Action—Meeting Picketed

Without the slightest opposition, the New York County Democratic Committee, popularly known as Tammany, last night ratified the selection of an executive committee on which there remained no opposition to the leadership of Edward V. Loughlin or to the influence in the organization repeatedly exercised by Bert Stand, secretary, and Clarence H. Neal Jr., chairman of its elections committee.

In Brooklyn the Kings County Democratic Committee nominated United States Attorney Miles F. McDonald for District Attorney of Kings County to run for the vacancy caused by the resignation of William O'Dwyer, Democratic and American Labor party candidate for Mayor. Mr. McDonald, a graduate of Holy Cross College and Fordham Law School, in accepting the nomination, told the members of the committee that he would resign as United States Attorney.

Nearly 2,000 members, the largest number in recent years, attended the Tammany meeting in the Central Commercial High School, 214 East Forty-second Street. All resolutions presented were adopted unanimously by voice vote.

The committee ratified action taken by the executive committee in seating Robert B. Blaikie as leader of the Seventh Assembly District in place of Joseph H. Broderick and Assemblyman Patrick H. Sullivan, in spite of the claim of Mr. Broderick that he had elected a majority of county com-

Continued on Page 17, Column 2

2D BIG AERIAL BLOW

Japanese Port Is Target in Devastating New Midday Assault

RESULT CALLED GOOD

Foe Asserts Hiroshima Toll Is 'Uncountable' —Assails 'Atrocity'

By W. H. LAWRENCE

By Wireless to The New York Times.

GUAM, Thursday, Aug. 9—Gen. Carl A. Spaatz announced today that a second atomic bomb had been dropped, this time on the city of Nagasaki, and that crew members reported "good results."

The second use of the new and terrifying secret weapon which wiped out more than 60 per cent of the city of Hiroshima and, according to the Japanese radio, killed nearly every resident of that town, occurred at noon today, Japanese time. The target today was an important industrial and shipping area with a population of about 258,000.

The great bomb, which harnesses the power of the universe to destroy the enemy by concussion, blast and fire, was dropped on the second enemy city about seven hours after the Japanese had received a political "roundhouse punch" in the form of a declaration of war by the Soviet Union.

Vital Transshipment Point

GUAM, Thursday, Aug. 9 (AP)—Nagasaki is vitally important as a port for transshipment of military supplies and the embarkation of troops in support of Japan's operations in China, Formosa, Southeast Asia and the Southwest Pacific. It was highly important as a major shipbuilding and repair center for both naval and merchantmen.

The city also included industrial surburbs of Inase and Akunoura on the western side of the harbor, and Urakami. The combined area is nearly double Hiroshima's.

Nagasaki, although only two-thirds as large as Hiroshima in population, is considered more important industrially. With a population now estimated at 253,000, its twelve square miles are jam-packed with the eave-to-eave buildings that won it the name of "sea of roofs."

General Spaatz' communiqué reporting the bombing did not say whether one or more than one "mighty atom" was dropped.

Hiroshima a 'City of Dead'

The Tokyo radio yesterday described Hiroshima as a city of ruins and dead "too numerous to be counted," and put forth the claim that the use of the atomic

Continued on Page 6, Column 3

RED ARMY STRIKES

Foe Reports First Blow by Soviet Forces on Asian Frontier

KEY POINTS BOMBED

Action Believed Aimed to Free Vladivostok Area of Threat

By The United Press.

SAN FRANCISCO, Aug. 8—Russia's mighty Far Eastern Army began hostilities against Japan at 12:10 A. M. Thursday [Russian time], launching a sudden attack along the eastern Soviet-Manchuria border only nine minutes after Moscow's declaration of war became effective, the enemy reported today.

A Kwantung Army headquarters communiqué issued at Changchun [Hsinking] and recorded here reported the attack and also announced that the Red Air Force already was bombing strategic points in Manchurian territory be- [illegible]

No details of the attack were given, but presumably the Russians would drive west from the Vladivostok area into Japanese-held territory north of the tip of Korea. Vladivostok is only about twenty miles east of the border, separated from the Japanese by fortified positions along the rugged, mountainous terrain.

The communiqué made it clear that ground forces had opened the attack—part of the Soviet Union's Far Eastern Army of more than 1,000,000 well-equipped troops, who never were called into action against Germany, but remained along the border, a constant threat to Japan.

Although the communiqué did not locate the fighting, it was believed the Russians would strike out as quickly as possible from the Vladivostok region, which is highly

Continued on Page 4, Column 6

CIRCLE OF SPEARHEADS AROUND JAPAN IS COMPLETED

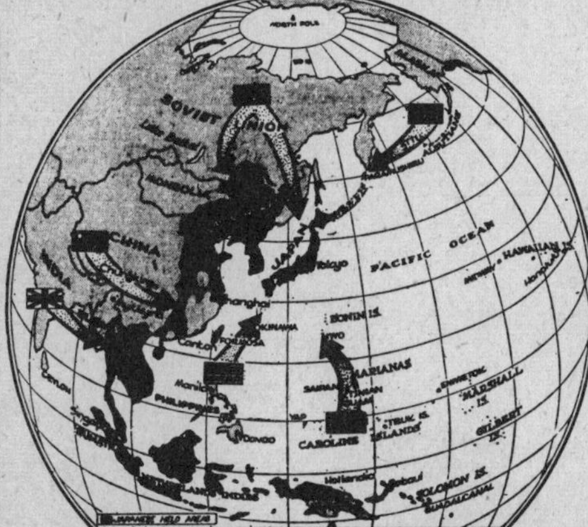

Aug. 9, 1945

With the entry of the Soviet Union into the war against Japan, the enemy is confronted with armed might from new directions—the north and northeast. Japan was already being battered by American power pressing in from the northeast and the south and by Chinese and British power from the west and southwest. The Russians are reported attacking Manchuria.

385 B-29'S SMASH 4 TARGETS IN JAPAN

Tokyo Arsenal and Aircraft Plant Are Seared—Fukuyama and Yawata Cities Ripped

By Wireless to The New York Times.

GUAM, Thursday, Aug. 9—Gen. Carl A. Spaatz, armed with the confirmed knowledge that his Strategic Air Force possesses in the atomic bomb the most powerful destructive agent devised by man since gunpowder was discovered, sent four separate forces

Continued on Page 2, Column 1

U. S. Third Fleet Attacking Targets in Northern Honshu

By ROBERT TRUMBULL

By Wireless to The New York Times.

GUAM, Thursday, Aug. 9—Admiral William F. Halsey's mighty Third Fleet, including British carriers, is now throwing strong air attacks at northern Honshu in the Japanese home islands, where the enemy has twenty to twenty-five airfields, Fleet Admiral Chester W. Nimitz announced this morning.

Although no specific targets were designated, the communiqué said shipping, air installations and "other military targets" were hit by strong air attacks beginning at dawn.

Today's communiqué broke nine days of silence by the Third Fleet after strikes in the Tokyo area July 30. It is possible that persistent fogs, caused by the warm Japanese Current at this time of year, forced Admiral Halsey to desist during that time from the sea-borne attacks carried out in conjunction with land-based air activity over the empire.

Northern Honshu, an area of 30,669 square miles, a little smaller than Maine and populated by 9,500,000 persons, has twenty to twenty-five airfields that are considered operational although some are small, poorly developed bases and probably are used only for the dispersal of the Japanese air force hiding out in that area.

While the northern Honshu district as geographically defined is outside the main military and industrial area of the island there is

Continued on Page 2, Column 8

TRUMAN REVEALS MOVE OF MOSCOW

Announces War Declaration Soon After Russian Action —Capital Is Startled

By FELIX BELAIR JR.

Special to The New York Times.

WASHINGTON, Aug. 8—President Truman announced a few minutes after 3 P. M. today that Russia had just declared war on Japan. The dramatic statement, issued with all the casualness of a routine proclamation, came during the shortest White House press conference on record.

Flanked by Secretary of State James M. Byrnes and Admiral William D. Leahy, his Chief of Staff, the President stood before hastily summoned reporters and in steady, matter-of-fact tones declared: "I have only a simple an-

Continued on Page 3, Column 1

RUSSIA AIDS ALLIES

Joins Pacific Struggle After Spurning Foe's Mediation Plea

SEEKS EARLY PEACE

Molotoff Reveals Move Three Months After Victory in Europe

By BROOKS ATKINSON

By Wireless to The New York Times.

MOSCOW, Aug. 8—Russia declared war on Japan tonight. In a dramatic press conference held at 8:30 P. M., Foreign Commissar Vyacheslaff M. Molotoff read the declaration, which was announced to the public at 10 P. M., Moscow time [3 P. M. New York time].

In view of Japan's refusal of the Allies' demand for unconditional surrender, Mr. Molotoff said, the Allies proposed that the Soviet Union "join the war against Japanese aggression and thus shorten the duration of the war, reduce the number of victims and facilitate the speedy restoration of universal peace.

"Loyal to its Allied duty," the Foreign Commissar continued, "the Soviet Government has accepted the proposal of the Allies and has joined in the declaration of the Allied Powers of July 26. The Soviet Government considers that this policy is the only means able to bring peace nearer, free the people from further sacrifice and suffering and give the Japanese people the possibility of avoiding the dangers and destruction suffered by Germany after her refusal to capitulate unconditionally."

Closing his concise statement, Mr. Molotoff declared:

"In view of the above, the Soviet Government declares that from tomorrow, that is Aug. 9, the Soviet Union will consider itself to be at war with Japan."

The Soviet Government's declaration comes three months after the victory over Germany, supporting rumors that some months ago the Soviet Government intimated it would join in the war against Japan three months after victory was won in Europe.

For the first time Mr. Molotoff revealed that the Japanese Government had asked the Soviet Union to mediate for a cessation of hostilities about the middle of June. Japanese Ambassador Naotaka Sato delivered the message, and also a special message from

Continued on Page 5, Column 2

Tokyo 'Flashes' News 3 Hours After Event

By The Associated Press.

SAN FRANCISCO, Aug. 8—Japan's first recorded wireless reaction to Russia's war declaration was a brief factual announcement of that action by the Domei agency in an English-language transmission to Europe.

The Domei account, broadcast five hours and fifty-five minutes after the Moscow announcement, reported:

"Flash! Flash! Tokyo, Aug. 9—Tass News Agency announced late last night that Foreign Commissar Vyacheslaff M. Molotoff communicated to Naotake Sato, Japanese Ambassador to Russia, that the Soviet Union will consider itself in a state of war with Japan from Thursday, Aug. 9, according to the Moscow radio recorded here this morning."

By the time the "flash" was read, the state of war already had existed for several hours.

War News Summarized

THURSDAY, AUGUST 9, 1945

Russia has declared war against Japan because that country is the only great power standing in the way of peace. Foreign Commissar Molotoff so informed Ambassador Sato in Moscow yesterday. He said it was in the interests of shortening the war and bringing peace to the world that Moscow acceded to the Allied request to join the war in the Far East and subscribed to the Potsdam ultimatum of July 26. Mr. Molotoff revealed that Japan had asked the Soviet Union to mediate for peace, but that proposal "lost all foundation" when Tokyo rejected the Potsdam demands. [1:8.]

Hostilities were begun nine minutes after the war declaration went into effect at 12:01 this morning, according to Tokyo, when Soviet troops struck along Manchuria's eastern frontier with Siberia. Air attacks, it was said, quickly followed. [1:4.]

President Truman broke the news when he told a hastily called press conference: "Russia has declared war against Japan—that is all." [1:7.] Secretary of State Byrnes declared there was "still time—but little time—for the Japanese to save themselves from the destruction which threatens them." Mr. Byrnes said the President had convinced Premier Stalin that Russia must enter the war if she was to be responsible for peace. [4:2.]

Congress, jubilant and confident that Russia's aid and the atomic bomb would shorten the war materially, expected to be called back soon. [4:1.]

Japan received another blow when the second atomic bomb to fall struck Nagasaki on Kyushu. Crew members reported good results. "Practically all living things" in Hiroshima were destroyed beyond recognition by heat and pressure from the first atomic bomb, Tokyo reported. [1:3.] Fires leaped seven rivers. [6:3, with map.]

The Third Fleet, after nine days of silence, sent its carrier planes in a strong attack, still continuing at last reports, against northern Honshu and its score of airfields. [1:6-7.] B-29's hit four Japanese cities in twenty-four hours and mined home waters. [1:5; map P. 2.]

Wuhu Island, at the mouth of the Min River east of Foochow, was captured by the Chinese. [8:2, with map.]

Russia, Britain, France and the United States have signed an agreement for the occupation and administration of Austria similar to that in effect in Germany. Complete separation from Germany, restoration of the 1937 frontiers and return of democratic government were set as Allied goals. [1:2-3; maps P. 11.]

A new code of international law was adopted by the Big Four listing wars of aggression as a crime against peace. [1:6-7.]

General de Gaulle and his Cabinet, contrary to the wishes of the Consultative Assembly, will submit the questions of a new constitution and government responsibility to a referendum on Oct. 21. [13:5.]

President Truman signed the United Nations Charter yesterday. He will discuss the Potsdam Conference and the military situation in a broadcast at 10 o'clock tonight. [1:1.]

Allies Cut Austria Into Four Zones With Vienna Under Joint Control

By LANSING WARREN

Special to The New York Times.

WASHINGTON, Aug. 8—A four-power control machinery, including France with the Big Three, has been established in Austria in accordance with an agreement between the Soviet Union, the United States, the United Kingdom and France, it was announced today.

The system resembles the military control arrangement for Germany. It divides Austria into four zones of occupation and provides that Vienna, the capital city, shall also be occupied by the forces of the four controlling powers. It creates an Allied Council, consisting of the four military commissioners, who will govern Austria as a whole. The commissioners will make the decisions for all Austria and will insure a uniformity of action in the different zones.

[The text of the statement on Austria is on Page 11.]

Under the direction of this combined Allied council each military commander will have full authority in his zone. The council will act through the commanders and through an executive committee, which will advise the council and carry out its decisions.

By this means the agreement seeks to prevent a situation that would separate too rigidly the

Continued on Page 11, Column 5

4 Powers Call Aggression Crime In Accord Covering War Trials

By CHARLES E. EGAN

By Wireless to The New York Times.

LONDON, Aug. 8—A new code of international law, defining aggressive warfare as a crime against the world and providing punishment for those who provoke such wars, was announced here today.

By agreement among representatives of the United States, Great Britain, the Soviet Union and France, the legal framework necessary for the trial of the key German and Italian leaders held by the Allies was promulgated this afternoon. The document sets precedents in international law and, in the words of United States Supreme Court Justice Robert H. Jackson, the American representative, "ought to make clear to the world that those who lead their nations into aggressive war face individual accountability for such acts."

"If we can cultivate in the world the idea that aggressive war making is the way to a prisoners' dock rather than the way to honors," he said "we will have accomplished something toward making peace more secure."

[The texts of the War Crimes Committee report and Mr. Jackson's statement are on Page 10.]

The agreement, upon which the international committee has been laboring since June 26, represents

Continued on Page 11, Column 6

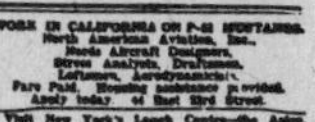

"All the News That's Fit to Print"

The New York Times.

LATE CITY EDITION
Sunny and warm today. Warm tomorrow, cloudy in afternoon.
Temperatures Yesterday—Max., 86; Min., 65
Sunrise today, 6:01 A. M.; Sunset, 8:01 P. M.

VOL. XCIV. No. 31,976. Entered as Second-Class Matter, Postoffice, New York, N. Y. NEW YORK, SATURDAY, AUGUST 11, 1945. THREE CENTS IN NEW YORK CITY

JAPAN OFFERS TO SURRENDER; U. S. MAY LET EMPEROR REMAIN; MASTER RECONVERSION PLAN SET

WPB READY TO ACT

Snyder Said to Sanction Wide Program to Start as Soon as War Ends

RATION SHIFTS LOOM

Agencies Rush to Map Future Work as Many Face Liquidation

By WILLIAM S. WHITE
Special to THE NEW YORK TIMES.

WASHINGTON, Aug. 10—In the midst of a redoubling of a study by the multitude of war agencies today to speed a transformation of the country's economy from a war to a peace-time basis, it was reported that John W. Snyder, Director of the Office of War Mobilization and Reconversion, had approved a master reconversion plan to be put into effect immediately upon the end of the war with Japan.

The plan, it was declared, had been prepared by the War Production Board, which received on Thursday from President Truman the chief role in the task of switching over the country's industry to peace-time requirements.

Details of the program approved by Mr. Snyder, it was understood, would be made public Monday or sooner if the Japanese capitulation details were agreed upon before then.

Plan Classed as "Sound"

According to WPB officials who commented, the plan was "sound, simple and clear," with the purpose of "preventing a mad scramble for materials and facilities."

It is understood to include the five spurs and controls asked by Mr. Truman in his letter to J. A. Krug, WPB chairman, Thursday.

Meanwhile, in the belief that hostilities with Japan were about to end, the war agencies in Washington began working hard on plans for changing their individual programs, running from outright liquidation on the one hand to more intensive labors on the other. Staff meetings were held all over the capital.

A general survey indicated that plans for reconversion in some fields were far advanced.

In matters affecting the home, these are the prospects:

Gasoline

Rationing will end soon, probably almost immediately after Japan is out of the conflict.

Food

Some easing of the civilian supply is likely soon, although the Department of Agriculture took a restrained view, a spokesman stressing that the future demands of the Army were yet to be made known and that in a few commodities, notably sugar, fats and oils, the shortages were so pronounced and world-wide that not even universal peace would give early hope of an easing in those items. Nevertheless, it was stated that the department had long been planning for "V-J Day plus X"—that is, the time when post-victory military demands are made known—and that it would not find the department "unprepared."

Manpower Controls

The future of these was tied in with reconversion in general, which is to be carried on largely through the War Production Board, the one major civilian war agency which is likely to have a job as big as it had before in maintaining controls, especially since President Truman's order of yesterday.

Price Controls

These are certain to be carried on indefinitely if the Administration has its way, although some members of the Administration

Continued on Page 18, Column 4

Foe Curbs 'Traitors' In Kwantung Area

By The United Press.

SAN FRANCISCO, Aug. 10—The Japanese imposed martial law on the Kwantung area west of Korea Saturday afternoon, Tokyo time, for the "prevention of traitorous acts," the Tokyo radio reported tonight in a broadcast recorded here.

The Kwantung area consists of the southern tip of Liaotung Peninsula, extending southward from Manchuria. It was ceded to Japan from Russia under terms of the 1905 Treaty of Portsmouth.

Tokyo said a state of siege had been ordered at Dairen, major Japanese-held port on the peninsula, twenty miles east of Port Arthur, by the Japanese defense committee for Dairen and Port Arthur.

The enemy broadcast did not amplify the reference to "traitorous acts."

'PARTY POLITICS' LOOMS WITH PEACE

End of War Will Bring Return of Old Government System, the Capital Thinks

By CHARLES HURD
Special to THE NEW YORK TIMES.

WASHINGTON, Aug. 10—The indication of an early peace prompted questions in the capital today about the political changes that might be expected. There were signs that the wartime coalition would crumble almost as soon as Japan formally surrenders.

Some observers recognized that there would be some regrets at this reversion to "party politics," but others reflected that the democracy of the United States required this conflict, just as the British parliamentary system hinges on the existence of what is known as His Majesty's Loyal Opposition.

It may be expected that President Truman will combine his inherited role of national leader with that of leader of the Democratic party, as well as probable candidate for re-election in 1948.

These political factors involve a speed-up in Cabinet changes expected since President Truman took office and a re-shaping of Government operations to fit the pattern of political responsibility, rather than of expediency for emergencies.

This possibility is considered particularly strong in view of the cordial association between President Truman and the Democratic leaders on Capitol Hill.

It is fully expected that the President will accept soon the resignation of Secretary Stimson, head of the War Department, and replace the veteran Republican with a Democrat. No one criticizes the operations of Secretary Stimson. In fact the President has paid spe-

Continued on Page 8, Column 7

CABINET BACKS BID

Domei Says Ministers Unanimously Voted to Sue for Peace

ASKS QUICK ANSWER

Reports Emperor Issued Orders After Appeal to Soviet Failed

The text of the Tokyo Broadcast is on Page 3.

The Japanese Government's decision to sue for peace was voted unanimously by the full Cabinet, including the War and Navy Ministers, at a meeting that lasted from Thursday until dawn Friday, Domei, the Japanese news agency, reported last night.

Domei said earlier that the Japanese Government had addressed a message to the Swiss and Swedish Governments for transmission to the United States, Great Britain, China and the Soviet Union accepting the Potsdam ultimatum on the understanding that Emperor Hirohito's sovereignty was not questioned, the Federal Communications Commission reported.

Domei, quoting the message, said at 7:35 A. M. [EWT]:

"In obedience to the gracious command of His Majesty the Emperor, who, ever anxious to enhance the cause of world peace, desires earnestly to bring about an early termination of hostilities with a view of saving mankind from the calamities to be imposed upon them by further continuation of the war, the Japanese Government asked several weeks ago the Soviet Government, with which neutral relations then prevailed, to render good offices in restoring peace vis-a-vis the enemy powers.

Claims Peace Move Failed

"Unfortunately, these efforts in the interest of peace having failed, the Japanese Government, in conformity with the august wish of His Majesty to restore the general peace and desiring to put an end to the untold sufferings engendered by the war as quickly as possible, have decided upon the following:

"The Japanese Government are ready to accept the terms enumerated in the joint declaration which was issued at Potsdam on July 26, 1945, by the heads of the Governments of the United States, Great Britain and China and later subscribed to by the Soviet Government with the understanding that the said declaration does not comprise any demand which prejudices the prerogatives of His Majesty as a sovereign ruler.

"The Japanese Government hope sincerely that this * * *"

At this point the transmission

Continued on Page 3, Column 5

GI's in Pacific Go Wild With Joy; 'Let 'Em Keep Emperor,' They Say

By W. H. LAWRENCE
By Wireless to THE NEW YORK TIMES.

GUAM, Saturday, Aug. 11—There was nothing conditional today about the jubilant all-night celebration by American fighting men in the Pacific that the Japanese were willing to surrender.

In offices, barracks and tents the shouting discussion of the almost unbelievable news went on for hours and few believed that the Allies would decline the Japanese condition that the position of the Emperor must not be impaired.

Most of the men out here had known about and accepted an earlier high policy decision that the Emperor should not be bombed because he was the one single force that could be counted upon to control all Japanese troops if he decided to surrender. Only yesterday Superfortresses had dropped 3,000,000 leaflets to the Japanese people designating the Emperor as the person to whom the people should appeal to end the war so it would not be necessary for us to employ the deadly atomic bomb again against Japanese cities and people.

Men shouted and pounded each other on the backs when the first news of the Japanese surrender offer reached here by radio. Wacs cried with joy. Marines ran from tent to tent spreading the news. Bottles of whisky long hoarded suddenly appeared and were rapidly consumed.

There was no comment from any of the high officials, but most of them were smiling broadly as they

Continued on Page 4, Column 5

NEW YORK CROWDS THRILLED BY THE GREAT NEWS

Happy civilians and service men in Times Square yesterday — The New York Times

SOBER CITY AWAITS OFFICIAL V-J WORD

New York's Joy Pent Up in Contrast to Celebration in Other Countries

London, so recently delivered from V-bomb and fire, went wild in celebration yesterday over Japan's surrender offer. Chungking, remembering that China's children grew to manhood in the flames kindled by the Japanese, was beside itself for joy. Liberated Manila was hysterical. In virtually every Allied capital the world over, there were scenes of wild celebration.

In New York yesterday—and this was true of the nation as a whole—there was, except for a little release of emotional steam, only discussion, speculation, sober

Continued on Page 9, Column 2

U. S. Has List of Foe's Isles For Our Occupation at Once

By JAMES B. RESTON
Special to THE NEW YORK TIMES.

WASHINGTON, Aug. 10—The detailed terms of surrender for Japan will demand that the Suzuki Government hand over all strategic islands in the Pacific to the United Nations, but the United States will insist on the sole occupation of all Pacific islands considered essential to our future security until we agree to their final disposition at the Pacific Peace Conference.

The Administration has carefully defined what islands it wants. This list, for various reasons, cannot be disclosed at present, but it is known to include the main Japanese mandated islands from which the Japanese attacks originally were launched against the United States and also such other important strategic islands as Okinawa, which were not given to Japan by the League of Nations.

In the preliminary negotiations

Continued on Page 6, Column 6

War News Summarized

SATURDAY, AUGUST 11, 1945

The Japanese Government has offered to surrender under an interpretation of the Potsdam ultimatum that would leave the Emperor's sovereignty unimpaired. The White House disclosed it was in communication with Britain, Russia and China, and it was reported to be willing to leave the question of the Emperor's prerogatives out of the armistice terms without, however, accepting the Japanese interpretation of the Potsdam ultimatum. [1:8.]

The Japanese peace bid was voted unanimously by the full Cabinet, including the War and Navy Ministers, after an all-night meeting, Domei reported. [1:3.]

The British Government announced that it was in communication with the Big Four powers but could make no further statement. [5:2-3.] It was believed to be prepared to follow whatever lead the United States proposes on the question of Emperor Hirohito, although British military leaders were said to feel he should be treated as a war criminal. [4:1.]

At the great American Pacific base on Guam the troops celebrated jubilantly all night. The opinion was expressed generally that the Japanese proposal that the position of the Emperor should not be impaired should be accepted. [1:2-3.]

In Chungking there was great rejoicing and enthusiasm for the Americans. [3:1.] American soldiers surged through the streets of Paris yelling. [5:1.]

Russian troops in Manchuria advanced 105 miles in a day in the Trans-Baikal sector and took Hailar on the Chinese Eastern Railway. [1:6; map, p. 2.]

Strategic Air Forces headquarters on Guam announced that no Superfortress attack would be made against Japan today. General MacArthur's forces did not halt. [1:7.]

The Third Fleet also said it would conduct no offensive operations today. It disclosed that its planes had left a trail of wreckage at northern Honshu bases Thursday and yesterday. [4:8.]

Preliminary assessment of atom-bomb damage at Nagasaki showed 30 per cent of the built-up area had been destroyed. [1:6-7.]

The Navy announced that thirteen more vessels, including a light cruiser, had been sunk by United States submarines in the Far East. A delayed dispatch disclosed that a submarine pack had made heavy inroads on shipping in the Japan Sea. [7:1.]

Chinese forces moved up to besiege Tsangwu, West River port, on the way to Canton. Three columns pushed toward Lingling. [2:8.]

The final day of the trial of Marshal Pétain went strongly in his favor with two former members of the Resistance offering testimony for him. [10:5.]

RUSSIANS ADVANCE 105 MILES IN DAY

Speed Past Hailar From West as Four Siberian Forces Converge on Harbin

By The Associated Press.

LONDON, Aug. 10—Russian mobile columns ripped 105 miles into Japan's stolen Manchurian empire today in a spectacular sweep from the west along the Chinese Eastern Railroad, the Soviet High Command said tonight.

Four mighty Soviet forces were pouring in growing masses across the 2,000-mile Russo-Manchurian frontier from Outer Mongolia to the border area seventy-five miles northwest of the Russian port of Vladivostok, Moscow's second Japanese war communiqué said.

Tokyo said the Russians also had invaded the Japanese-conquered land of Korea and had smashed into the southern half of Sakhalin Island

Continued on Page 2, Column 3

B-29'S, NAVY HALT ATTACKS ON JAPAN

Spaatz Calls Off 'Superforts' for Day, Fleet Schedule Bare —MacArthur Presses Fight

By Wireless to THE NEW YORK TIMES.

GUAM, Saturday, Aug. 11—The United States Army Strategic Air Forces and the United States Navy announced here today they would conduct no offensive operations against the Japanese home islands during the day.

The announcements did not mean for a certainty that the war with Japan was over. Both announcements that there would be no offensive actions were confined to "today."

Gen. Carl A. Spaatz, commanding general of the USASAF, made the statement in midmorning that the Superfortresses would fly no bombing missions against Japan for the day. It was believed previously that B-29 strikes had been planned.

[Gen. Douglas MacArthur's headquarters announced Saturday that the war still is on for the forces under his command and that Far East Air Forces bombers are carrying out their scheduled missions against Japan, said an Associated Press dispatch from Manila.

[The Tokyo radio reported today a Japanese air attack on our Okinawa base at 9 P. M. Friday, Japanese time (10 A. M., EWT).

Continued on Page 4, Column 6

Atom Bomb Razed 1/3 of Nagasaki; Japan Protests to U. S. on Missile

By Wireless to THE NEW YORK TIMES.

GUAM, Saturday, Aug. 11—Gen. Carl A. Spaatz announced today that the atomic bombing of Nagasaki on Thursday destroyed 30 per cent of that city's sprawling industrial area, including the big Mitsubishi steel and arms works, the Mitsubishi-Urakami ordnance plant and other heavy industries that played a major role in the Japanese war.

[The Japanese Government was reported by the Domei agency to have filed a protest with the United States Government Friday "against its attack on Hiroshima with an atomic bomb" and to have sent a message through the Swiss Government, protecting power for Japanese interest, "requesting it immediately to discontinue the use of such an inhuman weapon."

[The dispatch, recorded by the Federal Communications Commission, said that news of the request was "officially revealed" in Tokyo.

[The Japanese Government also asked the Swiss Minister to explain the "objectives of the Japanese Government's protest" to the International Red Cross.]

Reconnaissance photographs taken yesterday showed that the destruction in Nagasaki was centered along both sides of the Urakami River, the most important industrial section of this city of 250,000. Nagasaki had a total built-up area of 3.3 square miles, of which .98 of a square mile was in ruins after the new and terribly destructive weapon went off Thursday.

The damage covered two miles

Continued on Page 5, Column 5

ALLIES MAP REPLY

Truman Is Said to Favor Retention of Hirohito as Spiritual Leader

END BELIEVED NEAR

Pleas Based on Potsdam and 'Understanding' Emperor Will Stay

Special to THE NEW YORK TIMES.

WASHINGTON, Aug. 10—The war with Japan was rapidly drawing to a close tonight. An offer from Japan today to accept the Potsdam surrender ultimatum and her request for clarification on the status of Emperor Hirohito was being studied by the United States, Great Britain, the Soviet Union and China.

Discussions at the White House between President Truman and his Cabinet had reached a point tonight where it can be said that this Government will not insist as an armistice condition that the Japanese rid themselves of Hirohito or that he be brought immediately to trial as a war criminal.

Armistice Terms Studied

An agreement between the four powers regarding the exact status of the Emperor in the future remained the chief obstacle to the drafting of an armistice formula after a day of continuous communication between Washington and the Allied capitals of London, Moscow and Chungking.

The only official word on the surrender offer, which came to the State Department in the middle of last night, was issued in a White House statement by President Truman's secretary, Charles G. Ross, as follows:

"Our Government, through its regular diplomatic channels, is in communication with Great Britain, Russia and China regarding the Japanese surrender offer. That is all that can be announced at this time and no further White House statement will be forthcoming today or tonight."

How long it would take the Allied powers to formulate their separate armistice terms and then draw them up in shape for presentation to the Japanese as a joint reply was a matter of conjecture, but if the feverish activity that marked the business day at the White House and the State, War and Navy Departments was any criterion, it should not take very long.

Truman Calls Cabinet

From his desk in the White House executive wing President Truman sent out hurry calls for Secretary of State James F. Byrnes, Secretary of War Henry L. Stimson and Secretary of the Navy James V. Forrestal a few minutes after he arrived at the White House at 8:30 A. M. and the three Cabinet members were on hand before 9 o'clock.

Emerging from the President's office nearly half an hour later, Mr. Byrnes said this Government had not received any official surrender offer from the Japanese Government, but it was learned that a communication containing the proposal was then on its way to his office.

Beyond this negative reply to questions, Mr. Byrnes would say only that this Government would take no action on the Japanese offer to capitulate, if and when one were received, without consultation with the other Allied Governments.

So it went throughout the day. The regular Friday Cabinet session convened and adjourned after lengthy discussion of the problems arising out of the Japanese surrender offer, but the members departed in silence. It had been

Continued on Page 3, Column 1

"All the News That's Fit to Print"

The New York Times.

LATE CITY EDITION
Cloudy, warm; showers this afternoon or evening. Showers tomorrow.
Temperatures Yesterday—Max., 88; Min., 67
Sunrise today, 6:02 A. M.; Sunset, 7:59 P. M.

Section 1

NEWS INDEX, PAGE 41, THIS SECTION

Copyright, 1945, by The New York Times Company.

VOL. XCIV No. 31,977. Entered as Second-Class Matter, Postoffice, New York, N. Y. NEW YORK, SUNDAY, AUGUST 12, 1945. Including Magazine and Book Review. TEN CENTS New York City and Suburban Areas (15c Elsewhere)

ALLIES TO LET HIROHITO REMAIN SUBJECT TO OCCUPATION CHIEF; M'ARTHUR IS SLATED FOR POST

EMPLOYERS, LABOR ASKED TO FIND JOBS MID NEW CUTBACKS

$12,000,000,000 Slash in War Contracts Is Reported—Navy Reduction Is $1,200,000,000

AGENCIES DRIVE SWIFTLY

Snyder Calls on Management and Workers for Unity to Expand Civil Industries

By JOHN H. CRIDER
Special to The New York Times.

WASHINGTON, Aug. 11—Facing the gigantic task of reconversion much earlier than had been expected, the Administration called today for cooperation of management and labor to keep the problem under control, while the War and Navy Departments were ordering the first of the expected flood of contract terminations. The new terminations were estimated as approaching $4,000,000,000 in value.

[More than $12,000,000,000 in war material cutbacks, coincident with the Japanese movement toward surrender, were reported officially and unofficially today through The Associated Press. Heads of Government agencies received instructions from the White House to keep their post-war programs under wraps until President Truman gives the signal. The purpose of this, it was explained, was to allow coordination of plans of agencies and prevent disclosure before peace was an accomplished fact.]

The Navy Department announced specifically the cancellation of $1,200,000,000 of shipbuilding contracts, stopping work on ninety-five ships, including the carrier Reprisal, under construction at the New York Navy Yard, but John W. Snyder, War Mobilization and Reconversion Director, declared these Navy cutbacks were not the result of the Japanese surrender offer.

While stating that the Army would make "immediately" a sharp reduction in its buying program, Mr. Snyder stressed that the cutbacks resulted "from reviews of procurement programs held over the last few weeks."

It was evident all over the capital city that officials were working feverishly to meet the problem which came to them so much earlier than had been expected and were striving to prove untrue the prediction made ten days ago by the Senate's Mead War Investigating Committee that "should the war with Japan end at an early date we will be in a sorry state economically."

Aim to Avoid Undue Idleness

The problem was to cut down war production gradually so as not to cause undue unemployment, yet rapidly enough to speed the reconversion of the war plants which can shift into civilian production and hire those workers displaced from war jobs. The national economy is now running at an annual production rate of about $200,000,000,000, of which almost half is accounted for by Government war purchases.

A Budget Bureau official estimated that an early surrender by Japan would require a $30,000,000,000 slash in the budget for the current fiscal year.

Mr. Snyder, in a statement, called upon industry and management to "cooperate in this difficult reconversion period." He asked for cooperation in the following ways:

1. Workers displaced by contract cancellations should register themselves immediately with the nearest office of the United States Employment Service.

2. Employers having job oppor-

Continued on Page 38, Column 3

Congress to Return Sept. 4; Recess Cut on Truman Plea

Barkley, After 90-Minute White House Visit, Tells Plan for Call—Lists Five Measures for Preparatory Committee Action

Special to The New York Times.

WASHINGTON, Aug. 11 — At the request of President Truman, Congress will be called back Sept. 4, about a month earlier than the scheduled Oct. 8 end of the recess. Senator Barkley, majority leader, made this announcement on leaving the White House today after a ninety-minute visit with the President.

In preparation for the reconvening committees will work to make ready for floor action legislation which is regarded as urgent.

Most House members have been away since about July 21, but the Senate did not finish its business until July 28.

The House would be called back into session by its majority leader, Representative McCormack of Massachusetts, Senator Barkley stated.

"The President feels that Congress should reconvene as soon as possible," he declared, "but he realizes there would be no point in bringing the members back if there is no legislation ready to be handled.

"So I am going out now to talk with the committees of the Senate to see what can be done about getting this emergency legislation ready. I think it can be ready by Sept. 4, but I am not prepared to say that definitely."

He listed five measures which he regarded as "emergency legislation" in view of the imminent end of the war with Japan:

1. Amendment of the Social Security laws to raise the unemployment compensation payment to $25 a week for twenty-six weeks. Recommended by President Roosevelt, this is regarded as an essential relief measure for the tem-

Continued on Page 27, Column 4

5,000,000 EXPECTED TO LOSE ARMS JOBS

U. S. Officials Predict Great Unemployment 60 Days After Japanese Surrender

By The Associated Press.

WASHINGTON, Aug. 11—Government officials estimated today that perhaps 5,000,000 munitions workers will lose their jobs within sixty days after Japan surrenders.

This news as peace negotiations continued was in sharp contrast with another home-front prospect—the end of gasoline rationing two or three weeks after V-J Day and elimination of travel restrictions a few months later.

The estimate of the cut in munitions employment, made by qualified officials who asked anonymity, would trim by about 63 per cent the total of around 8,000,000 workers now engaged in war production.

Of the 5,000,000 slated for release, it was said that a great number — perhaps half — would leave the labor market and would not be classed as jobless.

The others would be added to the current unemployment roll to swell the total to around 4,000,000 persons.

How long it will take for the majority of these to be absorbed in civilian production is anybody's guess, the officials said, although they look for openings quickly in peacetime industries.

They said also that no doubt the War Manpower Commission would be called upon for a vigorous pro-

Continued on Page 14, Column 1

RESIST COMMUNISM, HOOVER DEMANDS

In Speech on 71st Birthday He Asks America to Voice Faith in System of Freedom

Special to The New York Times.

LONG BEACH, Calif., Aug. 11—Asserting that communism was sweeping over Europe and that a form of collectivism was already in evidence here, Herbert Hoover declared today that the time had come for America to reaffirm the heritage of its system of freedom.

"America should again proclaim our faith," he said. "We should proclaim our resolution to hold it. We should cease to apologize for it. Our first post-war purpose should be to restore it."

The former President spoke at the annual picnic of the Iowa Association of Southern California, which honored the seventy-first anniversary of his birth in Iowa, where he lived until he was 10 years old.

Mr. Hoover discussed "a great decision" confronting the people of the Western Hemisphere, "which is fast becoming the last hope of free men."

"Today communism or creeping socialism are sweeping over Europe," he said. "They are beginning in Asia. The causes lie deep in the holocaust of misery from the war, from power politics, from the impulse for any change from the bitter years which have passed, and from the years of propaganda of a new Utopia.

"A score of fascist nations have

Continued on Page 34, Column 5

Study of Baseball 'Color Line' To Be Made by Mayor's Group

Mayor La Guardia announced yesterday that he had mailed letters to ten prominent citizens, including Larry S. MacPhail, president of the New York Yankees, and Branch Rickey, president of the Brooklyn Dodgers, asking them to serve as a committee to make a thorough study of the question of racial discrimination or, as he termed it, "color line" in organized baseball and submit specific recommendations directly to the proper officials of the National and American Baseball Leagues.

In making public the text of his letter to Mr. MacPhail, the Mayor disclosed he was appointing the committee at the request of the Mayor's Committee on Unity, of which Charles E. Hughes Jr. is chairman. This committee was named by the Mayor several years ago as a means of promoting better inter-racial relations.

Others invited by the Mayor to serve on the committee are former Supreme Court Justice Jeremiah T. Mahoney, Daniel E. Higgins of the Board of Education, Edward Lazansky, former presiding justice of the Appellate Division in Brooklyn; Dr. John H. Johnson of the advisory board of the Department of Welfare, Arthur Daley, sports columnist of THE NEW YORK TIMES; Supreme Court Justice Charles S. Colden of Queens, Prof.

Continued on Page 41, Column 1

RUSSIANS DRIVE ON

Add 50 Miles to Gains as Spearheads Smash Closer to Harbin

VASILEVSKY AT HEAD

Veterans Lead 3 Armies in Sweep, Ignoring Surrender Talk

By The Associated Press.

LONDON, Aug. 11—Russian armored spearheads, in lightning fifty-mile advances, burst across the Great Hingan Mountain range in western Manchuria today and broke into the river-cut valleys leading down to the Japanese war arsenal city of Harbin, Moscow announced.

The pile-driving Soviet smashes, which have covered 155 miles in two days, tore through natural Japanese defenses in western Manchuria in disregard of the exchange of peace notes between Japan and the Allied nations.

Moscow's third Japanese war bulletin revealed that three Soviet Far Eastern armies had been thrown into the battle for Manchuria. Veteran commanders of the European Eastern Front led the assault under supreme command of Marshal Alexander M. Vasilevsky, former Red Army Chief of Staff.

Three Armies Bore Deeper

The three tank-tipped armies, breaking into Manchuria at least at five points along the mountainous 2,000-mile frontier, were converging on Harbin from the west, north and east in drives that threatened to cut off Japanese armies in northern Manchuria.

The Soviet advances brought hope of quick liberation to many American prisoner-of-war camps in Manchuria. The Khabarovsk radio called on Red Army men to fight with determination, demanding the "merciless destruction of the enemy."

Japanese resistance varied. In the west, Russian armored columns tore through the Japanese lines without much opposition, but in the heavily wooded, hilly terrain 100 miles northwest of Vladivostok fanatic enemy defenders of the Kwangtung Army held the Rus-

Continued on Page 13, Column 1

JAPANESE GET HINT

Press Points to Gravity of Situation—Bars National Suicide

NEED OF UNITY CITED

Papers and Broadcasts Still Fail to Mention Peace Bid, However

As if to prepare the Japanese people for surrender, the Tokyo newspaper, The Yomiuri Hochi, printed an editorial yesterday saying that "a nation does not have the right to commit suicide" and that "the highest duty of a nation is to continue her existence."

The Tokyo newspaper, the Asahi, also called on all Japanese in an article in its Sunday edition "to do his or her part as His Majesty's subjects in fullest obedience of the august wish of His Majesty" and to maintain national unity "if worst comes to worst," Domei, the Japanese news agency, reported in a broadcast recorded by the Federal Communications Commission.

The Yomiuri Hochi editorial, also quoted by Domei, added:

"There is an ebb and a flow in the tides of the affairs of every nation. Statesmen require the greatest courage when they think not of themselves but of the nation. Individuals must have the courage of self-immolation, but it may be said that a nation does not have the right to commit suicide. Therefore there are times when statesmen must have the courage to save the nation at the cost of their own lives. However, in such cases, political and military farsightedness are necessary."

Japanese Quote Confucius

The editorial recalled the story of the war between the ancient States of Wu and Yueh 2,500 years ago, in which the leader of Yueh, after having suffered a humiliating defeat, lived a life of hardship and self-deprivation for twenty years and then came back to win a great victory.

The editorial then added: "Confucius said that it is the maintaining of victory and not the winning of it which is difficult."

All Japanese metropolitan newspapers joined editorially in "admit-

Continued on Page 9, Column 1

REPORTED CHOSEN SUPREME COMMANDER

General of the Army Douglas MacArthur

Allied Commander Choice Recognizes U.S. Leadership

By WILLIAM S. WHITE
Special to The New York Times.

WASHINGTON, Aug. 11—General of the Army Douglas MacArthur, Commander in Chief of United States Army forces in the Pacific, has been designated the Allied Supreme Commander to accept Japan's capitulation when it comes, it was authoritatively indicated today.

The White House announced simply that the representative of the United States and her Allies in this assignment of historic triumph would be "an American" but in other quarters this was expanded with the addition of the general's name.

General MacArthur, it was pointed out, is the senior officer in the Orient, both as to American and Allied forces; he has the longest acquaintance with the Orient among the top commanders and of them all has been engaging the Japanese enemy the longest.

His appointment to act for all the Allies in the surrender as the Supreme Commander suggested that command of the occupying forces probably would be offered to him. He thus would hold in the post-war cleanup period the highest exclusive responsibility granted to an American officer overseas.

The War Department declared itself without official knowledge of the arrangement, which underscored the unquestioned leader-

Continued on Page 4, Column 1

FLEET IS PREPARED TO AID SURRENDER

On War Basis Pending Notice—Heavy Attack on Kyushu Made Friday by FEAF

By ROBERT TRUMBULL
By Wireless to The New York Times.

GUAM, Sunday, Aug. 12 — In what may have been the final great naval blow at Japan in this war, struck on Thursday and Friday, American and British carrier task forces destroyed or damaged 711 planes on fields of northern Honshu and sank or damaged ninety-four ships.

Fleet Admiral Chester W. Nimitz, giving revised figures on the two-day strike in his communiqué this morning, made no mention of further action by Admiral William F. Halsey's Third Fleet, which in-

Continued on Page 11, Column 1

U. S. STATES TERMS

Insists on Free Election in Japan as Provided in Atlantic Charter

REPLY IS DUE TODAY

Truman's Answer Calls for Enemy Guarantee of Captives' Safety

Tokyo Communique Reports War Actions

A Japanese Imperial Headquarters communiqué, issued in a Domei agency broadcast at 3:30 P. M. Sunday, Japanese time, 2:30 A. M. Sunday, EWT, gave indication that enemy headquarters then considered the war still in progress.

The broadcast communiqué, recorded by the Federal Communications Commission, said a Japanese submarine unit had attacked an Allied convoy off Okinawa Saturday afternoon, sinking three craft.

The enemy also reported Red Army gains against "fierce fighting" by the Japanese in Manchuria.

By FELIX BELAIR Jr.
Special to The New York Times.

WASHINGTON, Aug. 11—President Truman, in replying today on behalf of the United States, Great Britain, Soviet Russia and China to Japan's offer of surrender and her request for a clarification of the status of the Emperor, said the ruler would be permitted to remain on the throne for the time being subject to the commander of the Allied occupation forces.

On behalf of the Big Four the President further insisted that the future of the "Son of Heaven" be determined in a popular election "by the freely expressed will of the Japanese people," in accordance with provisions of the Atlantic Charter and the Potsdam ultimatum and that occupation forces remain in Japan until the democratic purposes of the ultimatum had been achieved.

Reply Made at 10:30 A. M.

The position of the Allied powers was set forth in a note by Secretary of State James F. Byrnes, which was delivered at 10:30 A. M. today to Max Grassli, Chargé d'Affaires of the Swiss Legation.

[The notes on the Japanese surrender offer appear on Page 3.]

No return communication had been received by this Government through the Swiss when the Federal establishment shut down for the night and none was expected before tomorrow.

But for all practical political purposes and except for the working out of occupation and formal surrender arrangements, the war with Japan that began the day after her sneak attack on Pearl Harbor on Dec. 7, 1941, was considered at an end.

There was no question of Japan's final answer to President Truman's final statement of the Allied position and not a great deal of interest in it either.

Says Japan Will Accept

As Senator Alben W. Barkley, majority leader, said as he left the White House, it did not make much difference what the Japanese thought of the discredited position of their Emperor nor what they had to say in reply to the President's note.

Senator Tom Connally made the flat prediction that "Japan will

Continued on Page 3, Column 4

War News Summarized

SUNDAY, AUGUST 12, 1945

The Allied powers have agreed to the Japanese proposal to surrender on the basis of the Potsdam ultimatum, but on the condition that the Japanese Emperor come under the authority of the Allied Commander in Chief to act as his agent to assure the full accomplishment of the armistice terms. President Truman, in the name of the Allied powers, informed the Japanese that the Emperor's future status must be determined in a free election and that Allied troops would remain in Japan long enough to see that the democratic purposes of the Potsdam ultimatum were accomplished. [1:8.]

General MacArthur was reported designated the Allied Supreme Commander to accept the surrender of Japan. [1:6-7.]

Tokyo newspapers were preparing the people for capitulation, emphasizing the theme that it was the duty of a nation not to commit suicide. [1:5.]

Moscow reported sweeping gains all along the Manchurian front and revealed that Marshal Vasilevsky was in supreme command of the Far Eastern theatre. On the Trans-Baikal front an advance of 155 miles has been made in two days. [1:4; map P. 13.]

Generalissimo Chiang Kai-shek ordered his armies to keep on fighting until the order to cease fire is received. Chinese troops occupied Tsangwu on the road to Canton. [10:3.]

Admiral Nimitz in a communiqué issued Sunday morning Guam time made no mention of further attacks on Japan. He had previously issued orders to all forces under his command to continue attacking the enemy. Five hundred Far East Air Force planes on Friday smashed at the city of Kumamoto on Kyushu, a military supply center. [1:7.]

It was officially revealed that the atomic bomb that erased a third of Nagasaki had a revised destructive function that made the first one, which was used on Hiroshima, obsolete. [28:1.]

The record to date shows that Japanese Kamikaze fliers have sunk twenty United States warships and damaged at least thirty more. [1:6-7.]

General de Gaulle and Foreign Minister Bidault are to come to the United States the last week of this month on invitation from the White House, it was disclosed in Paris. [21:1.]

Prosecutor André Mornet, summing up the State's case against Marshal Pétain, demanded the death penalty. [20:1.]

50 Ships Smashed by Kamikazes; Craft Once Glutted Repair Yards

By HANSON W. BALDWIN

Japanese suicide weapons in the last months of the war sank at least twenty naval vessels and damaged at least thirty and possibly scores of others. The Kamikazes caused more loss, damage and personnel casualties to the American Navy in the period between the Leyte invasion last October and the present than in any previous period in its history.

During the Okinawa campaign, when our ship damages were at their peak, West Coast shipyards were glutted with ship repairs and some of the worst-damaged vessels were sent to East Coast yards.

Japanese suicide attacks probably were experienced by some ships one or two years ago. But they were not undertaken on a large scale and were unimportant in results achieved until the Leyte invasion. The Japanese Naval Air Force then commenced what it called "body-ramming" tactics with the "special attack" units of the Kamikaze, or "Divine Wind" squadrons, so named for the "divine wind" (typhoon) which, according to Japanese legend, broke up the fleet of Kublai Khan in 1281. The Japanese Army Air Force then undertook the organization of suicide squadrons, and the semi-fanatical, though care-

Continued on Page 32, Column 1

"All the News That's Fit to Print"

The New York Times.

LATE CITY EDITION
Warm and humid; thunder showers this afternoon and tomorrow.
Temperatures Yesterday—Max., 85; Min., 69
Sunrise today, 6:03 A. M.; Sunset, 7:57 P. M.

VOL. XCIV..No. 31,978. Entered as Second-Class Matter, Postoffice, New York, N. Y. NEW YORK, MONDAY, AUGUST 13, 1945. THREE CENTS IN NEW YORK CITY

ALLIES TO LOOSE MIGHTY BLOWS ON JAPAN IF SURRENDER IS NOT MADE BY NOON TODAY; CARRIER PLANES RENEW TOKYO ATTACKS

ATTLEE ASSURES U.S. OF COOPERATION ON ATOMIC CONTROL

Pledges That Britain Will Help Guard Bomb's Secret Until It Can Be Fully Regulated

TO AVERT WORLD HAVOC

A Power for Peace Is Seen—Industrial Use of Force Within Decade Predicted

By The Associated Press.

LONDON, Aug. 12—Prime Minister Clement R. Attlee tonight pledged British cooperation with President Truman's proposal that the secret of the atomic bomb be guarded until complete control of the devastating weapon was assured.

The Prime Minister, back at 10 Downing Street after spending Saturday night at his Chequers country place, made this announcement:

"Since I issued the statement on the day of the release of the first atomic bomb a week ago, the vast and terrible effects of this new invention have made themselves felt.

"The last of our enemies has offered to surrender.

"The events of these tremendous days reinforce the words in that statement to the effect that we must pray that the discovery which led to the production of the atomic bomb will be made to conduce to peace among the nations, and that instead of wreaking measureless havoc upon the entire globe, it may become a perennial fountain of world prosperity.

Influence for Peace

"President Truman in his broadcast of Aug. 9 has spoken of the preparation of plans for the future control of this bomb, and of a request to the Congress to cooperate to the end that its production and use may be controlled and that its power may be made an overwhelming influence toward world peace.

"It is the intention of His Majesty's Government to put all their efforts into the promotion of the objects thus foreshadowed and they will lend their full cooperation to that end."

In Bangor, Wales, the National Council of the Independent Labor party, which is not affiliated with the Labor party Government, adopted a resolution declaring that the discovery of the use of atomic energy "could be of the greatest benefit ever vouchsafed to man" in a socialist world.

The resolution said the human race "must go forward to a new order of world socialism if it is to survive." The Independent Labor party has three seats in the new House of Commons.

Industrial Use in Decade Seen

WASHINGTON, Aug. 12 (UP)—Sir James Chadwick, chief British scientist in the atomic bomb project, said today there was a possibility that within about ten years atomic energy could be used for industrial purposes.

The Nobel Prize winner in physics in 1935 also declared that the atomic bomb was not strictly a British-American secret, asserting that any nation could learn the secret in about five years of experimentation, assuming it had access to the necessary raw materials.

"I think this is a very serious point," he said.

Sir James was chief scientific adviser to the British members of the American - British - Canadian policy committee that developed the bomb that wrecked Hiroshima and Nagasaki in Japan.

The work of this committee, he told a press conference, was confined to developing atomic energy for purely military purposes and very little attention was paid to the industrial possibilities. However, he said it would be "nearer

Continued on Page 10, Column 3

Expect Early End Of Clock War Time

By The United Press.

WASHINGTON, Aug. 12—War time is expected to be an early casualty of peace.

The clocks may go back one hour soon after Congress reconvenes and has time to pass a resolution.

The stepped-up schedule has not been popular with the legislators. Chairman Cannon, of Missouri, of the House Appropriations Committee, said recently that he intended to end it as soon as conditions permitted.

POLICE KILLING LAID TO 3 YOUNG GUNMEN

Gang Rounded Up After Series of Hold-Ups—Two Others Held as Confederates

Three young two-gun hoodlums, one a Navy deserter, who, according to the police, ran riot in a score of hold-ups and burglaries in one of which a policeman was killed, were rounded up early yesterday by Queens detectives. Seized also were two other members of the gang, their alleged driver and a fence who disposed of their loot.

Between July 15 and Aug. 9 the three thugs stole $8,000 in cash and $1,000 worth of jewelry. Specializing in robberies at dining places in Queens, they included forays also in the Bronx and Greenwich, Conn. Living riotously, they went through their money almost as quickly as they stole it. When their women friends, horse-race betting and liquor had taken their toll, they had hardly a dime left.

The three gunmen charged with homicide in the shooting of Patrolman Howard H. Hegerich on the morning of July 30 were: Victor (Vicki) Gelson, 25 years old, of 35-11 103d Street, Corona; Louis A. Boyce, called "Louis the Lip," 23, of 23-10 Steinway Street, Astoria, and Robert Fish, dubbed "Big Fish," 23, of Jamestown, N. Y.

Other Members of Gang

Gelson served a term in Elmira for a hold-up; Boyce was wanted for violating his parole from Sing Sing where he was sent in 1941 to serve four to eight years for assault and robbery, and Fish, a seaman first class, had been picked up in Flushing and was seized by police in the Navy brig at Harts Island.

The two other members of the band were Raffaele Pellegrino, 23, of 103-92 Fifty-second Avenue, Corona, a chauffeur charged with acting in concert, and Joseph Mancuso, 41, of 95-01 Roosevelt Avenue, Corona, charged with receiving stolen goods.

The importance police attached to their quarry was evident when the five were brought to Police Headquarters in Manhattan later in the day. They were placed under continuous guards, powerful lights were focused on their cells so their movements were under observation every minute, and they were stripped of every article that

Continued on Page 32, Column 3

WASHINGTON FACES WAR-END EXODUS OF ITS MIGRANTS

Many on the Swollen Staffs of Bureaus and in Services Are Glad to Return Home

GLAMOR ATTRACTS OTHERS

Emergency Agencies Will Not Expire for Some Time—Their Rules Continue in Effect

By The Associated Press.

WASHINGTON, Aug. 12—"Where do we go from here?"

This question was on the lips of thousands of Federal workers today as they concluded that the end of the war was at hand.

They were not alone with this question. Service men stationed in and around Washington, wives of service men marking time until their return and thousands of others who fall into no particular category were framing the same question.

For many the answer is: "I'm going home."

Home for many in Washington is any city, town or hamlet in any far corner of the country, but not Washington.

The war, which began almost four years ago for this country, has drawn thousands into the nation's capital, where there was a job to be done, but in few cases do these migrants consider Washington as their permanent home.

Reconversion at the Capital

Though thousands will be needed for many months to come to keep the wheels of the most complicated Government in the world rolling, others know that with the end of the war many agencies will die. And with them will go the jobs which brought so many people here.

Washington's reconversion program is unique. The city has no large factories, no shipyards, no aircraft plants. Reconversion here means the probable elimination of some wartime agencies, the trimming down of others and the return of numerous non-war bureaus crowded out of the capital and dispersed over the country.

The bustling city will never approach the position of becoming a ghost town, but such things as housing shortages, transportation jams and other discomforts brought on by overcrowding will diminish.

Mixed Feelings on Departure

Before the war, in 1940, Washington had a population of about 663,000. Now about a million persons make their home here. Many more commuting thousands live in near-by Virginia and Maryland.

Not all persons who plan to leave are unhappy about it. A certain Senator's secretary, whose job lasts only for the duration, had this to say:

"Washington is a funny town. It is a place where a person has to

Continued on Page 32, Column 6

DAWN STRIKE MADE

Fleet Goes Into Action While Our Land Planes Hit Kyushu Heavily

ENEMY GETS IN BLOW

Aerial Torpedo Damages Major U. S. Warship in Bay at Okinawa

By ROBERT TRUMBULL

By Wireless to The New York Times.

GUAM, Monday, Aug. 13—Admiral William F. Halsey's carriers are attacking the Tokyo area today (Monday, Japanese time), Fleet Admiral Chester W. Nimitz announced in his communiqué this morning. The attack started at dawn.

[Japanese planes were hitting back at Admiral Halsey's ships off Tokyo more strongly than before, a United Press correspondent with the fleet reported. At least one enemy torpedo plane was shot down early.

[Planes of our Far East Air Forces struck heavily at Kyushu cities on Saturday and continued attacks Sunday and Monday.]

Admiral Nimitz reported that a "major unit" of the Pacific Fleet was torpedoed Sunday night in Buckner Bay off Okinawa, with undetermined damage. The torpedo was dropped by a single low-flying plane.

A major unit would be either a battleship, heavy cruiser, large carrier or converted cruiser-type carrier.

After a respite while Admiral Halsey's Third Fleet with an attached British carrier task force moved southward after a two-day strike Thursday and Friday against northern Honshu, the war is on again for the Navy, as much as it ever was.

There were few details available this morning of the attack on the United States ship off Okinawa Sunday night. The attack occurred at about 10:45, Okinawa time,

Continued on Page 4, Column 3

THE WHOLE NATION JOINED IN THEIR VIGIL

Waiting outside the gates of the White House for news from Japan

Associated Press Wirephoto

Russians Swarm Ashore To Win Korean Naval Base

By The Associated Press.

LONDON, Aug. 12—Russian marines, invading Korea under the protecting guns of the Soviet Pacific Fleet, captured the big Japanese naval base of Rashin and the near-by port of Yuki today after having stormed ashore ninety miles southwest of Vladivostok, the Soviet High Command announced. [This was the first Soviet announcement of the invasion of Korea, which Japan reported several days ago.]

The ports fell as Tokyo reported a massive new Russian drive in Manchuria that threatened to trap perhaps 500,000 Japanese troops in China, cutting them off from Manchuria and the Japanese homeland.

The Red Army drive, if substantiated, would threaten to split an estimated 1,500,000 Japanese troops on the Asiatic mainland into two huge pockets.

Headquarters of the Japanese Kwantung Army in Manchuria said that the drive was launched by Soviet troops striking from Outer Mongolia across Inner Mongolia toward the Yellow Sea northeast of Peiping, ancient capital of China.

The Russians were hammering across barren, mountainous terrain toward the road and air-base center of Linsi in southwestern Manchuria, lunging over an old caravan route from Wuchumutsin in Inner Mongolia 150 miles to the north, the enemy said.

Linsi is 240 miles northwest of the Yellow Sea coast. A drive to the coast would isolate the enemy in China. The town, 197 miles from the Chinese frontier, is only seventy miles north of the northernmost rail line linking central China with the Manchurian city of Mukden.

There was no confirmation of the Japanese report from the Soviet High Command, but Moscow's fourth Japanese war bulletin told

Continued on Page 2, Column 2

CHIANG TELLS REDS TO OBEY HIS ORDERS

Reasserts Control Over Yenan Armies, Instructed by Own Chiefs to Disarm Japanese

By The United Press.

CHUNGKING, China, Aug. 12—Chinese Communist leaders, who issued instructions to their troops to disarm Japanese forces and occupy areas hitherto held by the enemy, were told by Generalissimo Chiang Kai-shek today to "remain in their posts and wait for further directions."

General Chiang ordered Gen. Chu Teh, commander of the Eighteenth Group Army, and his deputy, Peng Teh-huai, "never again to take independent action."

[Though nominally under com-

Continued on Page 5, Column 2

TOKYO NEWSPAPERS AGAIN URGE UNITY

Call Upon People to Obey Every Command of Emperor in Nation's 'Worst' Crisis

For the second day the Tokyo radio broadcast yesterday excerpts from editorials in the leading Tokyo newspapers stressing the need for national unity and obedience to the commands of the Emperor in what some of the newspapers described as the gravest crisis in Japan's history.

Before the editorials appeared Domei, the official Japanese news agency, broadcast and then retracted an "imperial" communiqué announcing that the Japanese "Army and Navy had begun an offensive along all fronts against enemy Allied armies."

One of the editorials quoted, that in the Yomiuri Hochi, warned the Japanese people that the "gravity of the situation is undoubtedly more than words signify" and called on them to "face the stark reality of the present crisis with the utmost calmness and composure."

"What we should do at this critical moment is to wait for the

Continued on Page 2, Column 4

U. S. IRKED AT DELAY

Truman Stays at Office All Day Vainly Waiting for Japanese Reply

REJECTION IS DOUBTED

Secretary to President Says V-J Day Will Not Come With Acceptance

By LANSING WARREN

Special to The New York Times.

WASHINGTON, Aug. 12—Unless a Japanese surrender, awaited fruitlessly today, has been received in Washington by tomorrow noon there was every prospect that all the pent-up fury of the overwhelming Allied strength, including more atomic bombs, would burst again with inconceivable violence on Japan.

The Allies set no time limit for a reply to their note to Japan but they have checked their assault to allow the enemy to consider the terms, even though fighting has not ceased. Russian forces were reported advancing through Manchuria, and our Third Fleet carrier aircraft attacked military targets around Tokyo today. But no atomic bomb has fallen in the Pacific since the second terrible missile dropped on Nagasaki, and the Allies have reduced the tempo of their blows.

U. S. Patience Running Out

In Washington tonight there was evidence that patience was beginning to run out, and it is understood that without warning the attack may be renewed with such an avalanche of power as the world has never seen.

From Saturday through Sunday Washington and other capitals waited in vain for Japan's reply to the note of Secretary of State James F. Byrnes that had been transmitted with all speed to Tokyo. In it the Allies gave the Japanese Emperor permission to remain, which was the only point the Japanese had raised. Prompt acceptance now is needed to avert the destruction that is poised and may perhaps make the surrender come too late.

At 10:30 P. M. Charles G. Ross, press secretary to the President, called in correspondents to deny formally a report that Japan had surrendered.

Calls Peace Report False

"The President has not announced that Japan has accepted surrender terms from the Allies," said Mr. Ross. "There has been nothing received by the State, War or Navy Departments, the President, or anyone else."

Mr. Ross also told the reporters that President Truman had retired shortly after 10 P. M., with the request that he be called should any word from Japan be received before midnight.

Shortly before midnight Mr. Ross told reporters that the White House was shutting down for the night, and that no news regarding Japanese acceptance of the Allies' surrender terms would be issued from there before 9 A. M. tomorrow.

[At 1:40 A. M. Monday [EWT], the Tokyo radio said that Emperor Hirohito had received Foreign Minister Shigenori Togo for the second time in two days, the Federal Communications Commission reported.

[Soon after FCC engineers heard a Tokyo wireless code station calling a similar post in Switzerland, through which any Tokyo reply would be forwarded.]

When the surrender is received President Truman does not expect to proclaim V-J Day at once, it was officially announced. This must await the formal signature of the armistice conditions that will be presented at once to the Japanese,

Continued on Page 3, Column 2

War News Summarized

MONDAY, AUGUST 13, 1945

A tense world waited in vain yesterday for Japan's expected surrender. As Tokyo delayed its answer to the note by the four Allied Governments, in which it was agreed to permit Emperor Hirohito to retain his throne for the time being provided his authority was subject to that of a supreme Allied commander, the patience of the Allies grew thin. Unless the enemy's surrender is received by noon today, there was every expectation that the full might of the Allies would be unleashed against the harassed enemy. [1:8.]

A false "flash" that Japan had surrendered led to many premature celebrations throughout the United States and Canada last night. [1:6-7.]

A plea for national unity under "the great command from the throne" was the universal theme of gloomy Tokyo broadcasts that emphasized anew that the Japanese were confronted with the gravest crisis in their history. [1:7.] The Emperor's brother, Prince Takamatsu, was lavishly praised. [3:2-4.]

Hostilities continued. Admiral Halsey's powerful Third Fleet sent carrier planes to assault the Tokyo area at dawn Monday, Japanese Time, in the first offensive action against Japan since the Third Fleet broke off a two-day attack on northern Honshu on Friday. The Japanese succeeded in hitting a major American warship at Okinawa with an aerial torpedo. [1:4; map P. 4.]

More than 400 American Army planes under the command of General MacArthur struck targets on the Japanese homeland. The main objective was the Kurume supply and distribution center on Kyushu. [5:1.]

The Red Army also disregarded the apparent imminence of the end of World War II by initiating a new offensive as it sent amphibious forces into Korea. In the first official Russian announcement of the invasion of that Japanese-held territory, Moscow reported that Soviet troops had captured the ports of Yuki and Rashin, twelve and nineteen miles south of the Korean-Siberian border. Meanwhile other Russian armies far to the west smashed completely through the Great Hingan Mountains in their drive toward the major Japanese stronghold of Harbin. [1:6-7; map, P. 2.]

Chinese troops menaced the enemy's escape route up the Kwangsi-Hunan railway by reaching within five miles of the railway city of Tungan. [5:6.]

Generalissimo Chiang Kai-shek ordered Chinese Communist leaders who had issued instructions to their men to disarm Japanese troops and to occupy areas held by the enemy to "remain in their posts and wait for further directions." The Generalissimo condemned "independent action" by the Communist commanders. [1:5.]

Prime Minister Attlee pledged Britain's cooperation to guard the secret of the atomic bomb until complete control and use of it for the maintenance of peace had been assured. [1:1.]

General Eisenhower was the guest of Premier Stalin as the two men, together with high Russian Government dignitaries, stood atop Lenin's tomb in Moscow to watch a spectacular parade of 40,000 men and women athletes in the first mass civilian festival since the start of the war. [1:2-3.]

Eisenhower and Stalin Review Parade of 40,000 in Red Square

By BROOKS ATKINSON

By Wireless to The New York Times.

MOSCOW, Aug. 12—Forty thousand young people representing the entire Soviet Union participated today in a superbly designed and executed spectacle in honor of Premier Stalin and the nation's physical prowess.

It was the first sports day parade since the war against Germany broke out. It demonstrated the untapped human resources behind the Red Army. As the deep-toned bell of the Kremlin clock struck noon, Generalissimo Stalin, in a white uniform with red trim and gold braid, mounted a platform above Lenin's tomb in Red Square with members of the Politburo.

After they had been acclaimed by the crowd, Premier Stalin sent the Red Army's Chief of Staff, Gen. A. E. Antonoff, to invite Gen. Dwight D. Eisenhower; the American Ambassador, W. Averell Harriman, and Maj. Gen. John R. Deans, head of the American military mission, to join him on the reviewing platform. It is believed that they are the first foreigners to have shared with Premier Stalin the honor of reviewing a national spectacle from Russia's national shrine against the Kremlin wall.

They saw a stupendous parade and carnival. Red Square, one of

Continued on Page 6, Column 6

Erroneous 'Flash' of Surrender Starts Many Wild Celebrations

An erroneous news flash, carried to the public by radio, that Japan had accepted the surrender terms touched off wild celebrations in the United States, Canada and elsewhere last night although the report, transmitted over the leased wires of The United Press at 9:34 P. M., was "killed" two minutes later.

Hinting that someone had tampered with its circuits, The United Press announced that, although the message bore a Washington dateline, it had not been transmitted by its bureau there. It said that it had asked the Federal Bureau of Investigation and the Federal Communications Commission to "ascertain who could have cut into the UP's wire system with the intent to disseminate false information."

In addition, Hugh Baillie, president of The United Press, offered a reward of $5,000 for "information leading to the identification and conviction of the person who transmitted the mysterious flash over The UP circuit."

Long after last midnight crowds were still milling about major cities in the United States. They were no longer celebrating, but merely waiting near newsstands for morning papers, to find a full explanation of the erroneous radio report. This was the third major news event related to the war that was marred by a false radio report. The others were the first accounts of D-Day and V-E Day.

In New York and throughout the

Continued on Page 3, Column 6

"All the News That's Fit to Print"

The New York Times.

EXTRA
Sunny, continued warm and humid today and tomorrow.
Temperatures Yesterday—Max., 82; Min., 70
Sunrise today, 6:05 A. M.; Sunset, 7:56 P. M.

VOL. XCIV—No. 31,979. Entered as Second-Class Matter, Postoffice, New York, N. Y. NEW YORK, TUESDAY, AUGUST 14, 1945. THREE CENTS IN NEW YORK CITY

JAPAN DECIDES TO SURRENDER, THE TOKYO RADIO ANNOUNCES AS WE RESUME HEAVY ATTACKS

WPB ACTS TO SPUR BUILDING OF PLANTS FOR CIVILIAN OUTPUT

Krug Reveals Plan to Aid Industrial Expansion and 'Create' Millions of Jobs

BASED ON PRIORITIES HELP

Army Urges Use of Broadcast to Halt War Production on V-J Day and Speed Shifts

Special to The New York Times.

WASHINGTON, Aug. 13—A program to speed the expansion of manufacturing capacity and the construction of new facilities for the production of civilian goods was made known today by the War Production Board. The plan is being furthered through the relaxation of its regulation, L-41, which has sharply limited construction and building for all except the most critical war purposes.

J. A. Krug, WPB chairman, described the move as "a major step toward clearing the way for industrial expansion that will create employment for millions."

Without predicting when the full effect of the relaxation would be felt, he asserted that industry knew we were "nearing the point when we can give the full green light."

"Emphasis is being placed," he declared, "on industrial expansion that will give employment to workers as fast as they are released from war production."

Scope of Priorities Aid

Priorities assistance for materials will be extended to builders of the following three general categories of construction:

1, additions to or alterations of existing facilities for making civilian goods; 2, facilities for production of certain "bottlenecks" materials or components holding up other aspects of production, war or civilian; and 3, facilities needed for essential civilian production.

Industry divisions of the WPB would "give every assistance" in locating supplies of scarce materials and parts, Mr. Krug said.

Other major developments in the task of swinging industry from a total war to a total peace economy were awaiting the official proclamation of Japanese surrender by President Truman.

The WPB "master plan" of reconversion, embodying five points laid down by the President in a letter to Mr. Krug last week, was still a highly secret document, understood to be prefaced by the warning that premature publication of its contents in detail would be subject to terms of the Espionage Act.

Early Releases Expected

This document, however, and another omnibus report by the Office of War Mobilization and Reconversion, "From War to Peace; a Challenge," are expected to be made public immediately upon the official announcement of V-J Day.

With War Department procurement machinery set for a quick halt as soon as the Japanese surrender, Army sources have proposed to the WPB a plan whereby much red tape can be eliminated in reconversion.

The plan, reported to have come from the Army Ordnance Department, is this:

Let the WPB issue preliminary instructions to war contractors advising them that formal notices will not be necessary for the cessation of war production. Then, as soon as V-J Day is proclaimed let Mr. Krug go on the air and broadcast the word for war production to stop.

The flow of raw materials into war production could immediately

Continued on Page 32, Column 5

THE GENERAL AND THE MARSHAL MEET AGAIN

Gen. Dwight D. Eisenhower (right) with Marshal Gregory K. Zhukoff (left) after the commander of American forces in Europe arrived in Moscow. The New York Times (Sovfoto Radiophoto)

ACHESON LEAVING STATE DEPARTMENT

Byrnes Accepts Resignation of His Assistant Secretary on the Latter's Request

By JAMES B. RESTON
Special to The New York Times.

WASHINGTON, Aug. 13—The expected reorganization of the Department of State started today. Dean Acheson, assistant secretary of state, has resigned and his resignation has been accepted by Secretary Byrnes.

The initiative was taken by Mr. Acheson, who had indicated even before the death of President Roosevelt that he wished to leave the department and was said to have rejected an appointment as Solicitor General. Other resignations are expected to be taken up before or soon after the first meeting in London on Sept. 1 of the Foreign Ministers Council of the Big Five.

Mr. Byrnes has in his hands the resignations of all other appointive officials in the department, including those of Under-Secretary and the other five assistant secretaries. These have been at his disposal ever since he took office, but he has been at the Potsdam Conference most of the time since then and he has had pressing tasks since he returned.

Consequently officials who have inquired, since Mr. Byrnes returned, where they stood, have been advised by his aides that the Secretary has not had an opportunity to complete reorganization of his department.

Other Changes Expected

Meanwhile Mr. Acheson sought an interview with Secretary Byrnes and is said to have expressed a desire to be relieved of his responsibilities so that he could return to private law practice. Mr. Byrnes granted the request.

Mr. Acheson has been in charge of the State Department's relations with Congress since the last reorganization of the department several months ago. He held this responsibility throughout the period when revision of reciprocal trade agreements, the Bretton Woods agreement and the United Nations' Charter were under consideration.

As to other and forthcoming changes in the State Department, all that is known at the moment is that Secretary Byrnes has a commission from the President to reorganize the department as he pleases; that Mr. Byrnes intends to reorganize the department at the assistant secretary level and elsewhere and that he has a detailed report which is critical of

Continued on Page 22, Column 2

Japanese Militarist Urged The Destruction of Allies

Before the Tokyo radio announced Japanese acceptance of the Allies' Potsdam terms Field Marshal Prince Norimasa Nashimoto, honorary president of the Japanese Imperial Reservists Association and Chief Priest of the Grand Shrines of Ise, called on the empire's reservists yesterday "ultimately to destroy completely the strong enemy" and "consummate the purpose of this holy war," in a special message beamed to Japanese-occupied territories by Domei, the official Japanese news agency and recorded by the Federal Communications Commission.

A short time later Domei broadcast excerpts from an editorial in the newspaper Tokyo, warning against a "fatal internal split"

Continued on Page 2, Column 8

RED ARMY DEEPENS MANCHURIAN BULGE

Races Toward Harbin, Cuts Rail Line—Russians Land in South Sakhalin, Tokyo Says

By The Associated Press.

LONDON, Aug. 13—Russian armies, lunging toward the arsenal city of Harbin, tore out gains up to twenty-eight miles in Manchuria today and cut a vital Japanese communication line. Tokyo reported a Soviet invasion of Sakhalin Island, which lies twenty-six miles north of the Japanese homeland.

Swift, tank-tipped Soviet thrusts threatened to disrupt the entire Japanese communication system in Manchuria, playing havoc with the enemy's supply and leaving pockets of enemy troops open to encirclement and annihilation.

Japanese broadcasts said that Russian marines had swarmed ashore on Karafuto, Japanese territory on the southern half of Sakhalin Island, and established two beachheads on the west coast in a swift follow-up of the seaborne invasion of Korea. There was no Soviet confirmation.

Moscow's broadcast communiqué announced that Marshal Alexander M. Vasilevsky's five-pronged drive toward Harbin had seized at least twenty-two strong points in converging sweeps into central Manchuria from the west, northwest, north, northeast and east.

The Russians ripped across one of Manchuria's three vital north-south rail lines and threatened another, the 950-mile line linking Dairen and Mukden with extreme northern Manchuria, Moscow's war bulletin disclosed.

The easternmost of Manchuria's north-south lines, running from the Korean port of Seishin to Kiamusze on the Sungari River, was severed when Marshal Kirill A. Meretskoff's First Far Eastern Army captured the rail junction of Linkow, 170 miles northwest of Vladivostok.

Capture of the three-way junction put the Russians 177 miles east of Harbin, great war-produc-

Continued on Page 5, Column 1

B-29'S BOMB AGAIN

Superforts' by Hundreds Attack Honshu—Rail Center First Target

ARSENALS BATTERED

Japanese Suicide Planes Jab at Third Fleet—Kenney Fliers Busy

By The Associated Press.

GUAM, Tuesday, Aug. 14—Superfortresses, already more than 400 strong and growing in numbers steadily, resumed the assault on Japan at noon today in a maximum effort that is still continuing. Fighters from our forward bases escorted some of the strikes.

It could be the greatest onslaught of the war, and gave sharp notice to the procrastinating enemy to make up his mind on his tentative surrender proposals. Three major attacks had been made by mid-afternoon.

After laying off since last Friday, the B-29's lashed out at southern Honshu, ending a period of watchful waiting induced by a conditional peace offer of the enemy—who had not halted his suicide-plane blows.

[Admiral William F. Halsey's American and British carrier planes of our Third Fleet smashed 117 Japanese planes on airfields in the Tokyo area Monday and twenty-one enemy planes that tried to attack the fleet were shot down. Kamikaze planes were striking at the Third Fleet on Tuesday, Japanese broadcasts said.

[Kyushu ports and airfields and ships off southern Japan were battered Sunday in a 600-plane attack by Gen. George C. Kenney's Far East Air Forces.]

The new B-29 attacks, warning

Continued on Page 4, Column 4

Guam Demand Rises For Occupation Map

By Wireless to The New York Times.

GUAM, Aug. 13—Army engineers of a topographic battalion attached to Fleet Admiral Chester W. Nimitz's staff here are being swamped with demands for maps to be used by occupation troops in Japan.

Maps had already been completed for new bombardments of Japan by Admiral William F. Halsey's Third Fleet, it was revealed by the topographic battalion's commander, Lieut. Col. M. C. Shetler of Clinton, Iowa.

TRUMAN MESSAGE DUE AFTER 9 A. M.

President Retires With No Official Word From Japan —No Hint on V-J Day

By The United Press.

WASHINGTON, Tuesday, Aug. 14—Although Tokyo broadcasts reported early today that Japan had accepted the Allied unconditional surrender demand, no Allied confirmation was likely before 9 A. M.

If the enemy reports were true, World War II was over except for the formal signing of surrender documents by the defeated Japanese.

It meant that the Japanese had given up 3 years 8 months and 1 week to the day after their infamy at Pearl Harbor plunged the United States into a two-front war that cost scores of thousands of lives and billions of dollars.

It meant that Japan could retain Emperor Hirohito but that he had to take orders from the Allied Supreme Commander to be named to administer Japan. Gen. Douglas MacArthur was expected by most quarters to be chosen for that role.

President Retired Early

President Truman, who retired early last night when no word had been received from Tokyo, planned to announce Japan's surrender to a nation-wide radio audience when the official word was received.

He will not proclaim V-J Day, however, until after the official surrender papers are signed.

The "lid was on" at the White House until 9 A. M. This meant that nothing was expected from that quarter until later in the morning. Reporters rushed to the White House, however, when the Tokyo broadcasts were received, to be prepared for any eventuality.

There was a possibility that no announcement would be made at 9 A. M. even if the Tokyo reports were true. It was presumed that the Japanese reply was on its way, but it normally requires twelve hours to transmit messages through neutral nations.

The Tokyo reports came as patience with the enemy's long delay in replying was growing thin and as Allied might strove to force Tokyo to a quick decision by unleashing devastating new blows against the already battered and broken enemy homeland.

Attlee at Work Early

LONDON, Aug. 13 (AP)—Prime Minister Attlee arrived at 10 Downing Street early today and a crowd gathered outside in hopes of hearing news of a Japanese surrender.

His only early caller was the Lord President of the Council, Herbert Morrison.

At the Foreign Office, Foreign Minister Ernest Bevin conferred with Alfred Duff Cooper, British Ambassador to Paris.

King George VI will broadcast to the British Empire on the evening of V-J Day, it was officially announced.

In Whitehall it was comparatively quiet. There was no Cabinet meeting.

War News Summarized

TUESDAY, AUGUST 14, 1945

At 2:49 P. M. today Tokyo time (1:49 A. M., EWT), Domei announced that Japan had decided to accept the Allies' surrender terms in the war that she had entered three years eight months and seven days earlier with the sneak attack on Pearl Harbor. Japan's announcement came more than sixty-three hours after the dispatch of the Allies' note setting forth their terms.

The disclosure that meant the end of the Second World War almost six years after it had been begun by Japan's Axis partner, Germany, followed growing American suspicions that the enemy was "stalling." Earlier, Tokyo had declared that the Allies' reply to its surrender offer had been delivered only yesterday morning but this was branded a lie by a Swiss Government spokesman. [All the foregoing, 1:8.]

Official Washington remained silent, however. President Truman will have no statement until at least 9 A. M. [1:6.]

Domei's promise of imminent peace followed by only a few hours its broadcast of a message from Field Marshal Prince Norimasa Nashimoto, held up since Saturday, urging enemy reservists "ultimately to destroy completely the strong enemy." This appeal had lent credence to some observers' belief that there was a serious rift among Japanese factions on the surrender issue. [1:3-4.]

The Allies were continuing their military action even as Domei announced the Government's decision. By mid-afternoon hundreds of B-29's with fighter escort had struck a rail yards, an army arsenal and a naval arsenal on Honshu. More than 600 other planes blasted enemy shipping and rail facilities at Kyushu and a heavy cruiser in Tsushima Strait. [1:4; map, P. 4.]

At dawn on Monday, Japanese time, carrier planes of the United States Third Fleet had smashed at airfields and military installations in the Tokyo area and destroyed or damaged 138 planes. [4:3.]

The Red Army sent five armor-tipped columns thundering through Manchuria on their way to the major Japanese stronghold of Harbin, and gains ranged to twenty-eight miles. The Russians seized at least twenty-two Japanese strong points, including Linkow, 177 miles east of Harbin. Tokyo said that Soviet marines had invaded Karafuto, Japanese-held southern half of Sakhalin Island. [1:3; map P. 5.]

Some time before Domei's announcement, it was reported, Japanese troops in Chekiang Province, south of Shanghai, had ceased firing after the first disclosure of their Government's surrender offer and had begun negotiating their capitulation. [8:3.]

Chungking is believed to be making plans to outwit the Communists by a rapid reoccupation of Japanese-held China, possibly with airborne troops, when Japan surrenders. Meanwhile Chinese Communist leaders hit back at Generalissimo Chiang Kai-shek and charged that his order to Communist General Chu Teh, condemning "independent action" by the Communists in accepting Japanese surrenders, indicated that he was plotting a civil war in china. [10:6.]

POTSDAM TERMS ACCEPTED, DOMEI SAYS

'An Imperial Message Is Forthcoming Soon,' Official News Agency Reports in Broadcast at 1:49 A. M.

DISCLOSES LONG SESSION BY CABINET

FCC Monitors Hear Code Dispatch Being Sent by Japanese to Switzerland—Washington Began to Suspect 'Stalling'

The Japanese Government has accepted the Allies' surrender formula embodied in the note dispatched to Tokyo by the United States, Domei, the Japanese news agency, said today [Tuesday] in a wireless dispatch recorded by the Federal Communications Commission.

"It is learned that an Imperial message accepting the Potsdam proclamation is forthcoming soon," the English-language wireless dispatch said, as directed to the American zone.

The Domei wireless dispatch was transmitted at 1:49 A. M., Eastern War Time, today.

Although the dispatch did not flatly say that Japan had surrendered and that the action was final, the fact that Domei put out such a statement indicated that that was in fact the case. Domei is controlled by the Japanese Government.

The statement was repeated a few moments later.

No other information was forthcoming from the Japanese immediately.

The Domei dispatch announcing that an Imperial message accepting surrender terms was expected soon followed by thirty-eight minutes another Domei dispatch reporting that the Japanese Government was deliberating on Allied surrender terms and that its reply probably would be available as soon as "legal procedures" had been completed.

Message to Switzerland Heard

The earlier Domei broadcast said:

"Immediately upon receipt of the Allied reply yesterday, Monday, the Japanese Government started deliberations upon its terms, which as a Reuter diplomatic correspondent pointed out 'created a very serious problem' for the Japanese people. The Cabinet has been in continuous session until late Monday night. It is understood the Japanese Government's reply probably will be available any time as soon as legal procedure is completed."

FCC engineers reported about the same time that a Tokyo code station had been sending long code messages to Switzerland since 12:48 A. M., Eastern war time, today.

Japanese press and radio transmissions did not elaborate immediately on the one-sentence Domei report. FCC monitors reported that the Tokyo radio in a Japanese-language broadcast to occupied Asia at 2 A. M. [EWT] had made no mention of surrender, indicating that the Japanese people in occupied territory were still being kept in the dark on the negotiations.

They also reported that there was no indication that the Japanese people in the home islands had been told of the surrender offer and the Allies' reply.

At the White House it was said that President Truman was asleep and that there was no intention of waking him up to inform him of the report from the Tokyo radio.

Cheering Greets Report in Guam

GUAM, Tuesday, Aug. 14 (AP)—The communications room of United States Pacific Fleet headquarters flashed word over the Guam radio today that the Tokyo radio had reported Japan had accepted the Potsdam ultimatum to surrender. There was no announcement as to where the broadcast was picked up.

Waves of cheering were heard as the Guam radio broke into a regular broadcast to make the announcement at 3:58 P. M. Guam time [1:58 A. M., EWT].

The news came as the United States Third Fleet—most powerful naval force in the world—was patroling just off Japan. It was believed that the fleet would head for Japanese ports shortly.

Capital Awaited Reply All Day

By FELIX BELAIR Jr.
Special to The New York Times.

WASHINGTON, Aug. 13—President Truman, as spokesman for the Allied powers, waited all day for Japan's acceptance of his surrender terms.

Some officials versed in the exactions of international law were beginning to suspect bad faith by the enemy in first requesting a clarification of the status of the Emperor in the note accepting the terms of the Potsdam Declaration.

In the long absence of word from the Japanese Government, therefore, they could only speculate that the delay was being caused by a Cabinet crisis or other machinations calculated to save face, probably through the

Continued on Page 3, Column 2

"All the News That's Fit to Print"

The New York Times.

LATE CITY EDITION
Thunderstorms, warm, humid; clear and cooler tonight. Fair tomorrow.
Temperatures Yesterday—Max., 84; Min., 71
Sunrise today, 6:16 A. M.; Sunset, 7:56 P. M.

VOL. XCIV..No. 31,980. Entered as Second-Class Matter, Postoffice, New York, N. Y. NEW YORK, WEDNESDAY, AUGUST 15, 1945. THREE CENTS IN NEW YORK CITY

JAPAN SURRENDERS, END OF WAR!
EMPEROR ACCEPTS ALLIED RULE;
M'ARTHUR SUPREME COMMANDER;
OUR MANPOWER CURBS VOIDED

HIRING MADE LOCAL

Communities, Labor and Management Will Unite Efforts

6,000,000 AFFECTED

Draft Quotas Cut, Services to Drop 5,500,000 in 18 Months

By LEWIS WOOD
Special to THE NEW YORK TIMES.

WASHINGTON, Aug. 14—All manpower controls over employers and workers were abolished tonight, the War Manpower Commission announced, enabling employers to hire men where and when they pleased.

The end of the war threw on the Government the difficult task of trying to readjust perhaps 8,000,000 war workers into new employment. Nevertheless, the WMC said, all its facilities would be used to help workers find new places, with preference going to veterans, displaced migratory war workers and other preferentials.

At the same time President Truman announced that monthly inductions into the Army would be immediately slashed from 80,000 to 50,000, and said 5,000,00 to 5,500,000 men probably would be released from the service within the next year or eighteen months.

The induction rate of 50,000 monthly, the President said, would be sufficient to maintain the occupation forces and allow men of long service overseas to return to their homes.

Under the WMC program, the manpower controls are to be lifted at once and voluntary community action to hurry reconversion will be substituted. In every community, the number of displaced workers and returning veterans will be ascertained in cooperation with local management-labor groups. Full facilities of the United States Employment Service offices will be made available to all employers. Service for veterans will be enlarged.

The WMC program embraced these seven points:

1. All manpower controls are to be lifted at once and in their place voluntary community action to

Continued on Page 13, Column 3

Third Fleet Fells 5 Planes Since End

By The Associated Press.

GUAM, Wednesday, Aug. 15—Japanese aircraft are approaching the Pacific Fleet off Tokyo and are being shot down, Admiral Chester W. Nimitz announced today.

Five enemy planes have been destroyed since noon today, Japanese time, or 11 P. M. EWT.

Gen. Douglas MacArthur has been requested to tell the Japanese that American defense measures require the Third Fleet to destroy any Japanese planes approaching United States warships.

GUAM, Wednesday, Aug. 15 (U.P.)—When Admiral Halsey received word of Japan's capiculation today ,he sent this message to his fliers:

"It looks like the war is over, but if any enemy planes appear shoot them down in friendly fashion."

SECRETS OF RADAR GIVEN TO WORLD

Its Role in War and Uses for Peacetime Revealed in Washington and London

By WILLIAM S. WHITE
Special to THE NEW YORK TIMES.

WASHINGTON, Aug. 14—The great drama of radar, the war's most powerful "secret weapon" until the atomic bomb was devised, was displayed before a world audience today.

The Joint Board on Scientific Information Policy permitted the Office of Scientific Research and Development, the War Department and the Navy Department to tell the story of a device of which millions had known vaguely for two years, a device which at least three times stood between survival or defeat by the Axis powers for the United States and Great Britain.

It was radar, short for "radio detection and range," that helped the small surviving British air squadrons to beat the German blitz of 1940, thus not only saving the home islands but preserving them as the essential Anglo-American base from which the continental invasion went forward on June 6, 1944.

It was radar, which "sees through the heaviest fog and the blackest night," that more than any other factor broke in 1942 the German submarine attack in the Atlantic which was threatening to starve and strangle the British homeland.

And it was radar that permitted the remnants of the blasted United States Pacific Fleet to stay alive

Continued on Page 14, Column 3

ALL CITY 'LETS GO'

Hundreds of Thousands Roar Joy After Victory Flash Is Received

TIMES SQ. IS JAMMED

Police Estimate Crowd in Area at 2,000,000—Din Overwhelming

By ALEXANDER FEINBERG

Five days of waiting, of rumor, intimation, fact, distortion—five agonizing days following the first indication of a Japanese surrender, days of alternately rising hopes and fears—came to an end for New York, as for the nation and the world, a moment or two after seven o'clock last night. And the metropolis exploded its emotions, harnessed for the most part during the day, with atomic force.

"Official — Truman announces Japanese surrender."

These were the magic words, flashed on the moving electric sign of the Times Tower, at 7:03 P. M. that touched off an unparalleled demonstration in Times Square, packed with half a million persons.

The victory roar that greeted the announcement beat upon the eardrums until it numbed the senses. For twenty minutes wave after wave of that joyous roar surged forth.

Restraint was thrown to the winds. Those in the crowds in the streets tossed hats, boxes and flags into the air. From those leaning perilously out of the windows of office buildings and hotels came a shower of paper, confetti, streamers. Men and women embraced—there were no strangers in New York yesterday. Some were hilarious, others cried softly.

By 7:30 P. M. the crowd in the Square had risen to 750,000 persons; by 8:45 it had swelled to 800,000 and the number continued to rise. People were packed solidly between Forty-third Street and Forty-fifth Street. Individual movement was virtually impossible; one moved not in the crowd but with it.

At 10 P. M. Chief Inspector John J. O'Connell estimated that 2,000,000 persons were in the Times Square area from Fortieth to Fifty-second Street, between Sixth and Eighth Avenues. This constitutes an all-time record, police officials said. At that hour people were still pouring into the Square from subways, buses and on foot.

Those at the north end of the

Continued on Page 5, Column 1

PRESIDENT ANNOUNCING SURRENDER OF JAPAN

Mr. Truman reading the message in the White House. Seated are Admiral William D. Leahy, Secretary of State James F. Byrnes and former Secretary of State Cordell Hull. Standing (left to right) are Maj. Gen. Philip Fleming, head of the Federal Works Administration; William H. Davis, Economic Stabilizer; John W. Snyder, Reconversion Director; James Forrestal, Secretary of the Navy; Fred Vinson, Secretary of the Treasury; Tom Clark, Attorney General, and Lewis Schwellenbach, Secretary of Labor.

Associated Press Wirephoto

PETAIN CONVICTED, SENTENCED TO DIE

Jurors Recommend Clemency Because of His Age—Long Indictment Upheld

By G. H. ARCHAMBAULT
By Wireless to THE NEW YORK TIMES.

PARIS, Wednesday, Aug. 15—Marshal Henri-Philippe Pétain was convicted at 4:15 A. M. today of intelligence with the enemy and sentenced to death. Because of his age—the former head of the Vichy regime is 89—the jury expressed the hope that the death sentence might not be carried out.

Guards had to arouse Pétain in

Continued on Page 15, Column 5

Terms Will Reduce Japan To Kingdom Perry Visited

By JAMES B. RESTON
Special to THE NEW YORK TIMES.

WASHINGTON, Aug. 14—The Allied terms of surrender will not only demobilize and demilitarize Japan but also deprive her of 80 per cent of the territory and nearly one-third of the population she held when she attacked Pearl Harbor. Thus these terms, already approved by President Truman and our major Allies, will not only destroy the vast empire she conquered in the first eighteen months of this war but also reduce her to little more than the territory she occupied when Commodore Perry introduced her to the western world in 1853.

The main terms of surrender, as

Continued on Page 11, Column 2

TREATY WITH CHINA SIGNED IN MOSCOW

Complete Agreement Reached With Chungking on All Points at Issue, Russians Say

By Cable to THE NEW YORK TIMES.

LONDON, Aug. 14—The Soviet Union and China have signed a treaty of friendship and alliance, the Moscow radio announced tonight, and have reached "full agreement on all other questions of common interest."

The broadcast said the treaty and "other agreements" would be published shortly after they had been ratified by the two countries.

These are the first fruits of the talks that have been proceeding in

Continued on Page 6, Column 3

World News Summarized

WEDNESDAY, AUGUST 15, 1945

World War II became a page in history last night.

President Truman announced at 7 P. M. that he had received the Japanese reply to the Allied note of last Saturday and that he deemed it full acceptance of the Potsdam declaration of July 26. The Chief Executive said that the Japanese surrender would be made to Gen. Douglas MacArthur in his capacity as Supreme Allied Commander in Chief. Allied military commanders were ordered to stop fighting, but the proclamation of V-J Day will await the signing of the peace treaties. [1:7-8.]

Simultaneously with the President's announcement, Admiral Nimitz flashed "cease fire" orders to all units under his command. [8:3-4.]

The official announcement that the Japanese sneak attack on Pearl Harbor had resulted three years and 250 days later in the inglorious end of the Japanese Empire touched off unrestrained celebrations throughout the Allied world. Here in New York the flash on the moving electric sign on the Times Tower, "Official—Truman announces Japanese surrender," signaled a wild demonstration. [1:3.]

Emperor Hirohito announced the Japanese surrender to his people in his first broadcast to the nation. Weeping Japanese gathered outside the Emperor's palace to bow to the ground in their shame because their "efforts were not enough." [3:2.]

The fury of Allied military might continued to strike the Japanese up to the very last. Even as the Tokyo radio announced that the Japanese reply to the Allied note of Saturday was on its way, our Superfortresses were winging from the Marianas to the Japanese homeland. More than 1,000 planes struck Honshu with 6,000 tons of bombs in a fourteen-hour assault ending early yesterday. [8:1.]

In the midst of rejoicing it was disclosed that the heavy cruiser Indianapolis had been sunk, presumably by an enemy submarine, shortly after she had delivered an atomic bomb cargo to Guam. All men aboard were casualties. [1:6-7.]

The Red Army unleashed fierce new attacks. Russian armored forces raced ninety-three miles unchecked across western Manchuria toward Harbin and other Soviet columns scored new gains all along the 2,300-mile front. [8:6; Pacific area map P. 8.]

The Soviet Union signed "a treaty of friendship and alliance" with China after an agreement had been reached between the two nations on all questions of common interest. [1:6.]

Chinese Communists informed the Generalissimo that they refused to accept his command to remain at their posts. [6:1.]

A French jury sentenced Marshal Pétain to death. [1:4.]

YIELDING UNQUALIFIED, TRUMAN SAYS

Japan Is Told to Order End of Hostilities, Notify Allied Supreme Commander and Send Emissaries to Him

MACARTHUR TO RECEIVE SURRENDER

Formal Proclamation of V-J Day Awaits Signing of Those Articles—Cease-Fire Order Given to the Allied Forces

By ARTHUR KROCK
Special to THE NEW YORK TIMES.

WASHINGTON, Aug. 14—Japan today unconditionally surrendered the hemispheric empire taken by force and held almost intact for more than two years against the rising power of the United States and its Allies in the Pacific war.

The bloody dream of the Japanese military caste vanished in the text of a note to the Four Powers accepting the terms of the Potsdam Declaration of July 26, 1945, which amplified the Cairo Declaration of 1943.

Like the previous items in the surrender correspondence, today's Japanese document was forwarded through the Swiss Foreign Office at Berne and the Swiss Legation in Washington. The note of total capitulation was delivered to the State Department by the Legation Charge d'Affaires at 6:10 P. M., after the third and most anxious day of waiting on Tokyo, the anxiety intensified by several premature or false reports of the finale of World War II.

Orders Given to the Japanese

The Department responded with a note to Tokyo through the same channel, ordering the immediate end of hostilities by the Japanese, requiring that the Supreme Allied Commander—who, the President announced, will be Gen. Douglas MacArthur—be notified of the date and hour of the order, and instructing that emissaries of Japan be sent to him at once—at the time and place selected by him—"with full information of the disposition of the Japanese forces and commanders."

President Truman summoned a special press conference in the Executive offices at 7 P. M. He handed to the reporters three texts.

The first—the only one he read aloud—was that he had received the Japanese note and deemed it full acceptance of the Potsdam Declaration, containing no qualification whatsoever; that arrangements for the formal signing of the peace would be made for the "earliest possible moment;" that the Japanese surrender would be made to General MacArthur in his capacity as Supreme Allied Commander in Chief; that Allied military commanders had been instructed to cease hostilities, but that the formal proclamation of V-J Day must await the formal signing.

The text ended with the Japanese note, in which the Four Powers (the United States, Great Britain, China and Russia) were officially informed that the Emperor of Japan had issued an imperial rescript of surrender, was prepared to guarantee the necessary signatures to the terms as prescribed by the Allies, and had instructed all his commanders to cease active operations, to surrender all

Continued on Page 2, Column 3

Hirohito on Radio; Minister Ends Life

The Japanese Domei agency said at 11 o'clock last night that Emperor Hirohito had been "graciously pleased to personally read an imperial rescript accepting the Potsdam declaration."

The Domei English-language wireless dispatch, directed to the United States and recorded by the Federal Communications Commission, said that the Emperor had read the rescript over a nation-wide broadcast at noon Wednesday, Tokyo time.

Previously Domei had reported that weeping people had gathered before the Imperial Palace and "bowed to the very ground" in shame.

Japanese War Minister Korechika Anami committed suicide Domei reported this morning. The wireless dispatch, directed to the American zone, said Anami had taken his life at his "official residence" to "atone for his failure in accomplishing his duties as His Majesty's Minister."

A complete story appears on Page 3.

Two-Day Holiday Is Proclaimed; Stores, Banks Close Here Today

By The Associated Press.

WASHINGTON, Aug. 14—Tomorrow and Thursday are days off for Government workers and holidays for pay purposes for workers in general.

And V-J Day, when it comes, will be a premium pay day, too.

President Truman announced both rulings tonight.

He directed agency heads throughout the Government to cut their forces down to a bare skeleton staff Aug. 15 and 16 and not to charge the two days against the employes' annual leave. He said it was in "inadequate" recognition of the four-year efforts on "one of the hardest working groups of war workers."

For other workers under wage control, Wednesday and Thursday count like Christmas and the few other accepted holidays for purposes of overtime pay and in figuring the number of days worked in a week. Many employers already have obtained approval for regular time pay to workers who take the day off.

Postal service for the next two days will "approximate holiday service," the Postoffice Department said.

Local postmasters will have wide discretion in carrying out the President's wishes, it was indicated, and those postal employes required to work tomorrow and next day will have compensating time off at a later date.

It was presumed, but not specifically stated, that Government workers generally will be off on V-J Day, too.

The White House said that the next two days are to be regarded as legal holidays.

Preston Delano, Controller of the

Continued on Page 6, Column 7

Cruiser Sunk, 1,196 Casualties; Took Atom Bomb Cargo to Guam

Special to THE NEW YORK TIMES.

WASHINGTON, Aug. 14—The American heavy cruiser Indianapolis was sunk by enemy action in the Philippine Sea with 1,196 casualties, every man aboard, the Navy announced today.

The 9,950-ton ship left San Francisco on July 16 on a special, high-speed run to deliver essential atomic bomb materials to Guam. The cargo was delivered. The cruiser was lost after having left Guam.

The sinking, which took one of the Navy's heaviest tolls of lives since Pearl Harbor, was disclosed a few minutes before President Truman announced Japan's surrender.

Casualties included five Navy dead, including one officer; 845 Navy missing, including sixty-three officers; 307 Navy wounded, including fifteen officers; thirty Marine missing, including two officers, and nine enlisted Marine wounded. Next of kin have been notified.

The skipper, Capt. Charles B. McVay 3d, 47, of Washington, was wounded.

The Navy Department also reported for the first time that in a previous action on March 31 the Indianapolis, flagship of the Fifth Fleet, was damaged by a suicide plane off Okinawa. She had been at the Mare Island, Calif., Navy

Continued on Page 10, Column 6

MacArthur Begins Orders to Hirohito

By Wireless to THE NEW YORK TIMES.

MANILA, Wednesday, Aug. 15—Gen. Douglas MacArthur in his first action as Allied Supreme Commander today directed Emperor Hirohito and the Japanese Government to furnish a radio station in the Tokyo area for "continuous use in handling radio communications between this headquarters and your headquarters." The message, sent in the clear, called for "the earliest practicable" arrangements to end hostilities.

"All the News That's Fit to Print"

The New York Times.

LATE CITY EDITION
Clearing early today; cooler.
Clear and cool tomorrow.
Temperatures Yesterday—Max., 88; Min., 72
Sunrise today, 6:23 A. M.; Sunset, 7:28 P. M.

Section 1

NEWS INDEX, PAGE 33, THIS SECTION

VOL. XCIV. No. 31,998. Entered as Second-Class Matter, Postoffice, New York, N. Y. NEW YORK, SUNDAY, SEPTEMBER 2, 1945. Including Magazine and Book Review. TEN CENTS New York City and Suburban Areas (15c Elsewhere)

JAPAN SURRENDERS TO ALLIES, SIGNS RIGID TERMS ON WARSHIP; TRUMAN SETS TODAY AS V-J DAY

HOLIDAY TRAFFIC NEAR 1941 LEVEL; 'GAS' IS PLENTIFUL

Exodus From City Is Greatest Since Pre-War Days but Congestion Is Avoided

GOOD WEATHER PROMISED

Near-by Resorts Do Capacity Business—3 Persons Die in Queens Accidents

America's millions, deprived since 1941 of the chance to cruise the highways of their nation, hit the road in traditional Labor Day week-end style yesterday.

There was a plentiful supply of gasoline, the sun shone warm out of blue skies, and everyone felt free from war worries. This combined to roll up traffic that continued heavy all day.

New York City's heat-ridden population took to car, train, bus and plane. The exodus to near-by mountain and seashore resorts was the greatest since that of 1941.

The weather formed a perfect lure. Not even the thunder showers predicted by the Weather Bureau for late afternoon took place. Today's prediction is for clearing weather early, followed by cooler, with the highest temperature around 80 degrees, and with fresh to strong northwest winds. A clear and cool Monday is forecast by the bureau. The temperature yesterday reached 88 degrees at 3:30 P. M. with the humidity at 52 per cent. The all-time high for the date was set in 1924 with 92.5 degrees and the low in 1872 with 51.

Many Cars Come Into City

Travel in the city was two-way. As cars streamed out of the city over bridges, on ferries and through tunnels, out-of-towners poured in. The main idea for Labor Day seemed to be change of scenery.

Thousands of automobiles, many of them looking as though they had just been taken off the jacks for the first time in years, formed a continuous procession along the main highways leading up-State, out on Long Island and to the South Jersey shore.

The Port of New York Authority reported that 69,400 automobiles had crossed the George Washington Bridge into New Jersey. Forty-five thousand cars passed through the Holland Tunnel during the sixteen hours preceding 6 o'clock last night. Lincoln Tunnel police said traffic was heavier than usual.

Few serious accidents were reported. "Maybe it's because the cars just don't have the pep," remarked a Westchester County parkway policeman.

Sights along the parkways bore out his contention. Many cars became pathetically silent as their drivers resignedly hauled them over to the side of the road to patch up tires or to fume over engine repairs.

Gasoline Supplies Abundant

Assured of as much gasoline as they wanted, motorists traveled leisurely and did not cause congestion. Filling station pumps received their heaviest workout in years. Station operators estimated that demands for gasoline ranged from 10 to 30 per cent over last week-end, but they reported there was no difficulty in obtaining supplies.

The Cities Service Oil Company said it was having difficulty in meeting orders for premium gasoline, ordinarily accounting for 25 per cent of sales, as the supply was limited, but no company reported shortages of non-premium gasoline. No motorist was forced to stay in town because of lack of fuel.

Trains, buses and airlines were crowded, as they have been all through the war. The airlines re-

Continued on Page 30, Column 2

Times Sq. Takes V-J News Quietly

Times Square throngs, which had greeted Japanese capitulation explosively last month, took the formal signing of terms in much calmer fashion last night.

Two hundred policemen, including twenty-five mounted patrolmen, who had been assigned to the area in case of another outburst of feeling, reported that the street crowds took the flashing of the bulletin from Times Tower at 10:04 P. M. with a few cheers and good-natured remarks, and did not attempt to start a celebration.

In numbers the crowd was no larger than an average Saturday night, and of the persons present perhaps half or more were out-of-town visitors here for the Labor Day week-end, the police estimated. Other parts of the city were similarly quiet.

Mayor La Guardia had said earlier that the people "have had their big time and are satisfied." He decided not to hold a celebration in Central Park today as had been planned.

PRESIDENT STRESSES LABOR DAY OF PEACE

But He Warns That After Six Holidays of Hostilities Great New Problems Lie Ahead

Special to THE NEW YORK TIMES.

WASHINGTON, Sept. 1—President Truman hailed the first Labor Day of peace in six years today and declared a grateful world would always remember the workers of all free nations for their contribution to victory.

Secretary Forrestal and J. A. Krug, chairman of the War Production Board, also lauded the men and women of labor, and Philip Murray, chairman of the Congress of Industrial Organizations, told a radio audience that America's vast war plant must be put to work on peacetime products which would give prosperity unlimited to this country.

Mr. Truman's statement said that six years ago today the workers of the United States, and of the world, awoke to a Labor Day in a world at war, and added:

"We in the United States had two years of grace, but the issue was squarely joined at that hour, as we now know. There was to be no peace until tyranny had beer outlawed.

"Today we stand on the threshold of a new world. We must do our part in making this world what it should be, a world in which the bigotries of race and class and creed shall not be permitted to warp the souls of men.

"We enter upon an era of great problems, but to live is to face problems. Our men and women did not falter in the task of saving freedom. They will not falter now in the task of making freedom

Continued on Page 24, Column 3

HAILS ERA OF PEACE

President Calls On U.S. to Stride On Toward a World of Good-Will

SALUTES HEROIC DEAD

Cautions Jubilant Nation Hard Jobs Ahead Need Same Zeal as War

Text of the President's address proclaiming V-J Day, P. 4.

By WILLIAM S. WHITE
Special to THE NEW YORK TIMES.

WASHINGTON, Sept. 1—President Truman, in remembrance of all who have fallen and in an appeal to all Americans to go forward now in hope and fraternity toward "a new and better world of peace and international good-will," tonight solemnly proclaimed tomorrow to be V-J Day.

The moment that he began to speak was, in the official and historical sense, the first moment of peace this country had known since a December day nearly four years ago, when, at a sudden, a harsh and an incredible blow the whole of the Pacific world went into flames.

Into the human calendar of great American holidays, like the Fourth of July and the Eleventh of November, the President thus entered another date, the Second of September, although it does not technically signify the end of the "duration" and will have no basis as a legal end of the war. The termination of hostilities, for purposes of computing military service, for setting the limit to war agencies and for all other like formalities, will be set only by final decision of Congress.

Japanese Surrender Signaled

But Mr. Truman's speech was a speech to the heart of a country that had had the skill to make the atomic bomb and could now "use the same skill and energy and determination to overcome all the difficulties ahead," rather than to the keepers of its books of law.

It was notice from the White House, so long awaited, that nearly four years of war, a struggle of sacrificial grandeur such as the United States had never known, had at last come to an end, and that the terrible ledger opened at Pearl Harbor had now been balanced and closed.

The President spoke in this mood, a mood of valedictory and of dedication, as he proclaimed "this . . . victory of more than arms alone . . . this . . . victory of liberty over tyranny." He had just received the signal from across the world that the Japanese had signed, aboard the great battleship Missouri, the last, humiliat-

Continued on Page 4, Column 1

JAPANESE FOREIGN MINISTER SIGNING SURRENDER ARTICLES

Mamoru Shigemitsu (right, seated), on behalf of Emperor Hirohito, affixes his signature to document as Gen. Douglas MacArthur (left) and Lieut. Gen. Richard K. Sutherland (center) look on during ceremony aboard the Missouri in Tokyo Bay.

Associated Press Wirephoto (via Navy Radio from U. S. S. Iowa)

BYRNES FORESEES A PEACEFUL JAPAN

Says People Are Expected to Force Development—World Amity Vital, Hull Warns

Special to THE NEW YORK TIMES.

WASHINGTON, Sept. 1—Secretary of State James F. Byrnes declared tonight that with Japan's surrender we have entered the second phase of our war—"what might be called the spiritual disarmament of that nation, to make them want peace instead of wanting war."

The intention of this Govern-

Continued on Page 5, Column 1

Japan's Surrender Ordered Over Militarist Opposition

By FRANK L. KLUCKHOHN
By Wireless to THE NEW YORK TIMES.

TOKYO, Sept. 1—In the rubble of this once-proud imperial capital the story of how the Japanese Army opposed the surrender and how the Emperor made the final decision to capitulate after having heard the opinions of all his advisers, and how War Minister Korechika Anami had committed suicide was unfolded today by one of a handful of those in a position to know without bias what occurred.

It was also learned how the Japanese reacted step by step to wartime developments and how propaganda that Japan could win had been continued to the last moment, thus leaving the industrious long-

Continued on Page 7, Column 1

U. S. CHIEFS DIVIDED ON ITALY'S COLONIES

State Department Split Over Russia and Influence Zones Is Projected by Issue

By JAMES B. RESTON
Special to THE NEW YORK TIMES.

WASHINGTON, Sept. 1—A fundamental issue has developed in the Department of State over the future of the Italian colonies, particularly Eritrea, Libya and Italian Somaliland.

The issue is whether these colonies should go back to Italy as part of her sovereign territory, be taken from her and administered by the United States, Britain, France and the Soviet Union under the United Nations Organization or be administered by a neutral international commission under the United Nations.

The major powers that defeated Germany are soon to start draft-

Continued on Page 15, Column 1

TOKYO AIDES WEEP AS GENERAL SIGNS

Imperial Staff Chief Hastily Scrawls His Signature—Shigemitsu Is Anxious

By The Associated Press.

ABOARD U. S. S. MISSOURI in Tokyo Bay, Sunday, Sept. 2—The solemn surrender ceremony, on this battleship today, marking the first defeat in Japan's 2,600-year-old semi-legendary history, required only a few minutes as twelve signatures were affixed to the articles.

Surrounded by the might of the United States Navy and Army, and under the eyes of the American and British commanders they so ruthlessly defeated in the Philippines and Malaya, the Japanese representatives quietly made the marks on paper that ended the bloody Pacific conflict.

The Japanese delegation came aboard at 8:55 A. M., 7:55 P. M. Saturday, E. W. T., as scheduled. They reached the Missouri in personnel speed boats flying the American flag.

Foreign Minister Mamoru Shigemitsu led the delegation. He climbed stiffly up the ladder and limped forward on his right leg, which is artificial. He was wounded by a bomb tossed by a Korean terrorist in Shanghai many years ago.

On behalf of Emperor Hirohito, Mr. Shigemitsu signed first for

Continued on Page 9, Column 1

WAR COMES TO END

Articles of Capitulation Endorsed by Countries in Pacific Conflict

M'ARTHUR SEES PEACE

Emperor Orders Subjects to Obey All Commands Issued by General

The texts of the surrender documents and statements, P. 3.

By The Associated Press.

ABOARD THE U. S. S. MISSOURI in Tokyo Bay, Sunday, Sept. 2—Japan surrendered formally and unconditionally to the Allies today in a twenty-minute ceremony which ended just as the sun burst through low-hanging clouds as a shining symbol to a ravaged world now done with war.

[A United Press dispatch said the leading Japanese delegate signed the articles at 9:03 A. M. Sunday, Tokyo time, and that General MacArthur signed them at 9:07 A. M.]

Twelve signatures, requiring only a few minutes to inscribe on the articles of surrender, ended the bloody Pacific conflict.

On behalf of Emperor Hirohito, Foreign Minister Mamoru Shigemitsu signed for the Government and Gen. Yoshijiro Umezu for the Imperial General Staff.

MacArthur Voices Peace Hope

Gen. Douglas MacArthur then accepted in behalf of the United Nations, declaring:

"It is my earnest hope and indeed the hope of all mankind that from this solemn occasion a better world shall emerge out of the blood and carnage of the past."

One by one the Allied representatives stepped forward and signed the document that blighted Japan's dream of empire built on bloodshed and tyranny.

First was Admiral Chester W. Nimitz for the United States, then the representatives of China, the United Kingdom, the Soviet, Australia, Canada, France, the Netherlands and New Zealand.

The flags of the United States, Britain, the Soviet and China fluttered from the veranda deck of the famed superdreadnaught, polished and scrubbed as never before. More than 100 high-ranking military and naval officers watched.

Pledges Justice and Tolerance

"As Supreme Commander for the Allied powers," General MacArthur told the Japanese, "I announce it my firm purpose, in the tradition of the countries I represent, to proceed in the discharge of my responsibilities with justice and tolerance, while taking all necessary dispositions to insure that the terms of surrender are fully, promptly and faithfully complied with."

All through this dramatic half hour, only those aboard the battleship knew of what was taking place, because the Missouri has no broadcasting facilities.

But recordings were rushed to the near-by communications ship Ancon, and the solemn words of General MacArthur beginning the ceremony—"We are gathered here, representatives of the major warring powers"—were flashed around the world.

The Japanese representatives were present at the command of Emperor Hirohito contained in a proclamation issued by order of the Supreme Allied Commander.

The Emperor further commanded his officials "to issue general orders to the military and naval forces in accordance with the direction of the Supreme Commander

Continued on Page 2, Column 3

Public Gets Big Army Food Stocks; Whipping Cream Is Freed of Bans

Special to THE NEW YORK TIMES.

WASHINGTON, Sept. 1—The national food situation continued its steady improvement today as the Department of Agriculture, with four orders, increased the supplies of butter, canned salmon and ice cream and signalled the return of whipping cream.

This action was a direct consequence of the sharp reduction of military requirements of these foods. With the discontinuance of butter purchases by the armed forces, the Department explained, it is now possible to revoke the limitations on the sale of heavy cream and the use of butter fat in the production of all frozen desserts. Both these rulings will make whipping cream and ice cream of a higher butter fat content readily available.

In a simultaneous direction, the agency ordered released for civilian use all butter currently held by creameries and receivers for the armed forces and other Government buyers. Although as much as 20,000,000 pounds of butter may be returned to civilian consumers under this ruling, ration values will not be changed, it was indicated.

"At the time ration point values were established for September, the Office of Price Administration recognized the possibility of these

Continued on Page 33, Column 1

World News Summarized

SUNDAY, SEPTEMBER 2, 1945

The rulers of Japan, who set the Pacific ablaze nearly four years ago with their surprise attack on Pearl Harbor and hoped to culminate that assault with a peace dictated in the White House, formally signed their unconditional surrender to the Allied powers in Tokyo Bay. Foreign Minister Shigemitsu signed the historic document for his country in the shadow of the sixteen-inch gun muzzles of the battleship Missouri. General MacArthur, who signed in behalf of the Allies, said mankind hoped a better world would result from the solemn occasion. [1:8; map P. 12.]

President Truman proclaimed today as V-J Day. He urged the nation to observe the day of victory over Japan in a spirit of dedication and as a symbol of "victory of liberty over tyranny." He also asked his countrymen to remember "our departed gallant leader, Franklin D. Roosevelt." [1:3.]

Japan's decision to surrender was dictated by Emperor Hirohito after he had overruled a strong faction within the Cabinet and the army that wanted to keep on with the war in the belief that the Japanese could defeat an invasion of the homeland, according to well-informed observers in Tokyo. [1:5-6.]

Medical "experiments" recalling medieval sadism were carried out on dying American prisoners of war by young Japanese Army doctors, two American physicians interned with their compatriots said aboard a United States hospital ship. [1:6-7.]

With the Foreign Ministers' Council scheduled to meet in London next week to begin consideration of peace terms, it was learned that a serious division of opinion over the disposition of the Italian colonies had developed in the State Department. [1:6.]

Former Secretary of State Stettinius said in London that the development of the atomic bomb emphasized the need for "the speedy creation of the United Nations Organization to keep the peace of the world" and predicted that as soon as the organization began functioning it would appoint a military staff to deal with the use of atomic bombs, as well as all other types of force in preserving peace. [18:2.]

"ALL THE NEWS THAT'S FIT TO PRINT"

In the first eight months of this year, The Times published 6,092 more columns of news than any other newspaper. With World Peace still to be won, and reconversion a topic of daily import, The New York Times continues to print the complete news.

Enemy Tortured Dying Americans With Sadist Medical 'Experiments'

By ROBERT TRUMBULL
By Wireless to THE NEW YORK TIMES.

ABOARD THE HOSPITAL SHIP BENEVOLENCE, in Tokyo Bay, Sept. 1 — Seriously ailing American prisoners at Shinagawa, the only hospital serving 8,000 prisoners of war held in the Tokyo area, were guinea pigs for fantastic experiments recalling the sorcery and sadism of the middle ages, Drs. Mack L. Gottlieb and Harold W. Keschner, both of New York, told this correspondent today.

Both doctors are recuperating aboard this ship after their rescue from Shinagawa on Wednesday by a special Navy evacuation mission headed by Comdr. Harold A. Stassen, former Governor of Minnesota and now Assistant Chief of Staff and Flag Secretary to Admiral William F. Halsey, commander of the Third Fleet.

[In an interview in Tokyo the Japanese Army doctor to whom some of these practices were charged confirmed the cruel treatment of American prisoners.]

Dr. Gottlieb, who had his home and office at 307 East Forty-fourth Street, was a Naval officer captured at Guam. Dr. Keschner, of 451 West End Avenue, was taken with an Army force in the Philippines. Both are in good physical

Continued on Page 14, Column 1

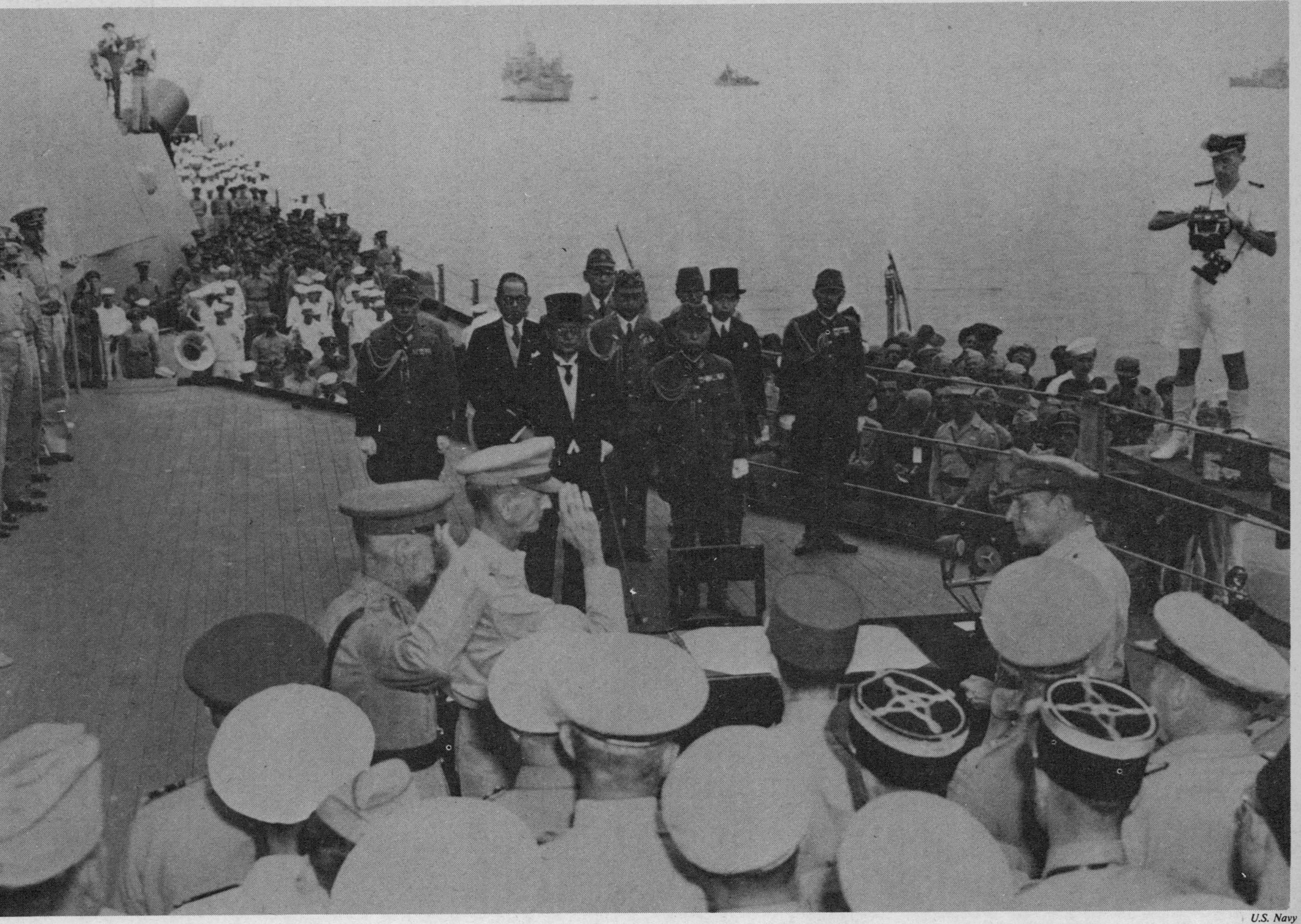
U.S. Navy

General Douglas MacArthur (right) at the signing of the Japanese surrender document aboard the battleship Missouri on September 2, 1945.